Collins

SCRABBLE™
BRAND Crossword Game
DICTIONARY

Published by Collins
An imprint of HarperCollins Publishers
Westerhill Road
Bishopbriggs
Glasgow G64 2QT

Fourth Edition 2015

10 9 8 7 6 5 4 3 2

© HarperCollins Publishers 2006,
2010, 2011, 2013, 2015

ISBN 978-0-00-758913-5
ISBN 978-0-00-822979-5

www.collinsdictionary.com
www.harpercollins.co.uk/scrabble

Typeset by
Davidson Publishing Solutions

Printed and bound by
CPI Group (UK) Ltd, Croydon, CR0 4YY

A catalogue record for this book is
available from the British Library.

If you would like to comment on any
aspect of this book, please contact us
at the given address or online.
E-mail: puzzles@harpercollins.co.uk
 facebook.com/collinsdictionary
 @collinsdict ·

Contents

v–vi

Introduction

vii–viii

Using the Scrabble Dictionary

1–902

Scrabble Dictionary

Introduction

Collins Scrabble Dictionary is an invaluable tool for any competitive or club player, as well as for those who play with their friends and family. This is the fourth edition of the dictionary in paperback. It contains over 4,000 new words recently added to the official Scrabble wordlist, reflecting how the English language continues to grow and change, as well as the enduring popularity of the game itself.

This dictionary contains every word of between two and nine letters, with either a definition or a cross-reference to a defined root word.

It allows every Scrabble player, whether a beginner or veteran, access to the definitions of all the most useful words in Scrabble, enabling them to learn words by meaning rather than simply as combinations of letters. For many players, definitions are the key to remembering words, and to using them in Scrabble, and the ability to check meanings, inflections, and variant spellings will add interest to most social games.

The definitions are succinct and practical. In many cases, only a single definition is given, and in general only those parts of speech necessary for existing inflections are included. Cross-referred words include noun plurals, verb inflections, the comparative and superlative forms of adjectives, and variant spellings. Adjectives formed with obvious suffixes, such as *-like* and *-less*, are also cross-referred to the root word when the meaning is easily deduced.

Some of the exciting new additions from the realms of computing and electronic communication are FACETIME, WEBAPP, and PWN (as well as HASHTAG and TWEEP from the world of social media); new borrowings from other languages include BARFI and SHEHNAI from India, DHIKR from the Middle East, and BUTOH and KAWAII from Japan; while slang and informal English have given us OBVS, RIDIC, and DENCH.

However, of greatest strategic importance to the game are the five new words featuring Q without U: CINQ, meaning five; KAMOTIQ or QAMUTIK, an Inuit sled with wooden runners; NIQAAB, a type of veil; and QAJAQ, a variant spelling of kayak.

In any Scrabble game, most words will be between two and nine letters in length. Therefore, this book contains only those words, and does not include words between 10 and 15 letters in length. This accounts for the omission of some plurals and inflected forms of words that are themselves in the dictionary.

Unlike a conventional dictionary, every word in each section is listed in strict alphabetical order, regardless of the relationship between words. Thus there may be many words between the singular form of a noun and its plural. This strict alphabetization allows rapid checking of words – which is particularly important during Scrabble tournaments.

Collins would like to give warm thanks to Darryl Francis, Allan Simmons, and David Sutton for their enormous contribution to the wordlist in this dictionary. They worked tirelessly with the editorial team to get this right. Any errors – and all the definitions in this book – are the responsibility of the publisher.

Disclaimer
This dictionary includes all playable Scrabble words, and no word is excluded on the grounds of religion, gender, race, or for any reason other than that it is an invalid word form for the game of Scrabble. The presence or exclusion of any word does not in any way represent the views of the Publisher, HarperCollins.

Using the Scrabble Dictionary

This book includes all playable words of two to nine letters in length, in one straight alphabetical list. These words are either defined or cross-referred. Cross-referred words include noun plurals, verb inflections, the comparative and superlative forms of adjectives, and variant spellings. Adjectives formed with obvious suffixes such as -like and -less are usually also cross-referred to the root word.

In *Collins Scrabble Dictionary*, only a single definition is given for each part of speech, and in general only those parts of speech necessary for existing inflections are included. Definitions are based on those of the *Collins English Dictionary*, complete and unabridged, but have been shortened to make them more concise. Some definitions have been specifically written for this dictionary.

Word order	*Collins Scrabble Dictionary* is in strict alphabetical order.
Accents	as English language Scrabble tiles are not accented, no accents are shown in *Collins Scrabble Dictionary*.
Main entry words	printed in bold capitals, eg:

        AA

        all entry words, in one alphabetical sequence, eg:

            AA
            AAH
            AAHED
            AAHING
            AAHS
            AAL
            AALI

Parts of speech	shown in italics as an abbreviation, eg: **AA** *n* when more than one part of speech is given, the change of part of speech is shown after an arrow, eg: **ABANDON** *vb* desert or leave ▷ *n* lack of inhibition
Cross-references	noun plurals, verb inflections, comparatives and superlatives, and derivatives are cross-referred to their root form, eg: **ABASH** *vb* cause to feel ill at ease ... **ABASHES >** ABASH **ABASHING >** ABASH **ABASHLESS >** ABASH **ABASHMENT >** ABASH
Variant forms	variant forms and synonyms are cross-referred to the most commonly used form of a word, eg: **CAFTAN** *same as* **>** KAFTAN noun plurals, verb inflections, comparatives, superlatives, and derivatives of the variant form are all cross-referred to the root form of that particular variant, eg: **CAFTAN** *same as* **>** KAFTAN ... **CAFTANS >** CAFTAN
Phrases	when a word is most comonly used in a phrase, the phrase is given in italics and defined, eg: **BANGALORE** as in *bangalore torpedo* explosive device in a long metal tube, used to blow gaps in barbed-wire barriers
Offensive terms	*Collins Scrabble Dictionary* includes words which may be deemed rude or offensive.

Aa

AA *n* volcanic rock
AAH *vb* exclaim in pleasure
AAHED > AAH
AAHING > AAH
AAHS > AAH
AAL *n* Asian shrub or tree
AALII *n* bushy shrub
AALIIS > AALII
AALS > AAL
AARDVARK *n* S African anteater with long ears and snout
AARDVARKS > AARDVARK
AARDWOLF *n* nocturnal mammal
AARGH *same as* > ARGH
AARRGH *same as* > ARGH
AARRGHH *same as* > ARGH
AARTI *n* Hindu ceremony
AARTIS > AARTI
AAS > AA
AASVOGEL *n* South African bird of prey
AASVOGELS > AASVOGEL
AB *n* abdominal muscle
ABA *n* type of Syrian cloth
ABAC *n* mathematical diagram
ABACA *n* species of banana
ABACAS > ABACA
ABACI > ABACUS
ABACK *adv* towards the back; backwards
ABACS > ABAC
ABACTINAL *adj* situated away from the mouth
ABACTOR *n* cattle thief
ABACTORS > ABACTOR
ABACUS *n* mathematical instrument
ABACUSES > ABACUS
ABAFT *adv* by the rear of (a ship) ▷ *adj* closer to the stern
ABAKA *n* abaca
ABAKAS > ABAKA
ABALONE *n* edible sea creature
ABALONES > ABALONE
ABAMP *same as* > ABAMPERE
ABAMPERE *n* cgs unit of current
ABAMPERES > ABAMPERE
ABAMPS > ABAMP
ABAND *vb* abandon
ABANDED > ABAND
ABANDING > ABAND

ABANDON *vb* desert or leave ▷ *n* lack of inhibition
ABANDONED *adj* deserted
ABANDONEE *n* person to whom something is relinquished
ABANDONER > ABANDON
ABANDONS > ABANDON
ABANDS > ABAND
ABAPICAL *adj* away from or opposite the apex
ABAS > ABA
ABASE *vb* humiliate or degrade (oneself)
ABASED > ABASE
ABASEDLY > ABASE
ABASEMENT > ABASE
ABASER > ABASE
ABASERS > ABASE
ABASES > ABASE
ABASH *vb* cause to feel ill at ease
ABASHED *adj* embarrassed and ashamed
ABASHEDLY > ABASHED
ABASHES > ABASH
ABASHING > ABASH
ABASHLESS > ABASH
ABASHMENT > ABASH
ABASIA *n* disorder affecting ability to walk
ABASIAS > ABASIA
ABASING > ABASE
ABASK *adv* in pleasant warmth
ABATABLE > ABATE
ABATE *vb* make or become less strong
ABATED > ABATE
ABATEMENT *n* diminution or alleviation
ABATER > ABATE
ABATERS > ABATE
ABATES > ABATE
ABATING > ABATE
ABATIS *n* rampart of felled trees
ABATISES > ABATIS
ABATOR *n* person who effects an abatement
ABATORS > ABATOR
ABATTIS *same as* > ABATIS
ABATTISES > ABATTIS
ABATTOIR *n* where animals are killed for food
ABATTOIRS > ABATTOIR
ABATTU *adj* dejected
ABATURE *n* trail left by hunted stag

ABATURES > ABATURE
ABAXIAL *adj* facing away from the axis
ABAXILE *adj* away from the axis
ABAYA *n* Arab outer garment
ABAYAS > ABAYA
ABB *n* yarn used in weaving
ABBA *n* Coptic bishop
ABBACIES > ABBACY
ABBACY *n* office of abbot or abbess
ABBAS > ABBA
ABBATIAL *adj* relating to abbot, abbess, or abbey
ABBE *n* French abbot
ABBED *adj* displaying strong abdominal muscles
ABBES > ABBE
ABBESS *n* nun in charge of a convent
ABBESSES > ABBESS
ABBEY *n* dwelling place of monks or nuns
ABBEYS > ABBEY
ABBOT *n* head of an abbey of monks
ABBOTCIES > ABBOT
ABBOTCY > ABBOT
ABBOTS > ABBOT
ABBOTSHIP > ABBOT
ABBS > ABB
ABCEE *n* alphabet
ABCEES > ABCEE
ABCOULOMB *n* unit of electric charge
ABDABS *n* highly nervous state
ABDICABLE > ABDICATE
ABDICANT > ABDICATE
ABDICATE *vb* give up a responsibility
ABDICATED > ABDICATE
ABDICATES > ABDICATE
ABDICATOR > ABDICATE
ABDOMEN *n* part of the body
ABDOMENS > ABDOMEN
ABDOMINA > ABDOMEN
ABDOMINAL > ABDOMEN
ABDUCE *vb* abduct
ABDUCED > ABDUCE
ABDUCENS *n* as in *abducens nerve* cranial nerve
ABDUCENT *adj* (of a muscle) abducting
ABDUCES > ABDUCE
ABDUCING > ABDUCE

ABDUCT *vb* carry off, kidnap
ABDUCTED > ABDUCT
ABDUCTEE > ABDUCT
ABDUCTEES > ABDUCT
ABDUCTING > ABDUCT
ABDUCTION *n* act of taking someone away
ABDUCTOR > ABDUCT
ABDUCTORS > ABDUCT
ABDUCTS > ABDUCT
ABEAM *adj* at right angles to a ship
ABEAR *vb* bear or behave
ABEARING > ABEAR
ABEARS > ABEAR
ABED *adv* in bed
ABEGGING *adj* in the act of begging
ABEIGH *adv* aloof
ABELE *n* white poplar tree
ABELES > ABELE
ABELIA *n* garden plant with pink or white flowers
ABELIAN > ABELIA
ABELIAS > ABELIA
ABELMOSK *n* tropical plant
ABELMOSKS > ABELMOSK
ABER *n* estuary
ABERNETHY *n* crisp unleavened biscuit
ABERRANCE > ABERRANT
ABERRANCY > ABERRANT
ABERRANT *adj* showing aberration ▷ *n* person whose behaviour is aberrant
ABERRANTS > ABERRANT
ABERRATE *vb* deviate from what is normal
ABERRATED > ABERRATE
ABERRATES > ABERRATE
ABERS > ABER
ABESSIVE *n* grammatical case indicating absence
ABESSIVES > ABESSIVE
ABET *vb* help in wrongdoing
ABETMENT > ABET
ABETMENTS > ABET
ABETS > ABET
ABETTAL > ABET
ABETTALS > ABET
ABETTED > ABET
ABETTER > ABET
ABETTERS > ABET
ABETTING > ABET
ABETTOR > ABET

ABETTORS > ABET
ABEYANCE n state of being suspended
ABEYANCES > ABEYANCE
ABEYANCY n abeyance
ABEYANT > ABEYANCE
ABFARAD n unit of capacitance
ABFARADS > ABFARAD
ABHENRIES > ABHENRY
ABHENRY n unit of inductance
ABHENRYS > ABHENRY
ABHOR vb detest utterly
ABHORRED > ABHOR
ABHORRENT adj hateful, loathsome
ABHORRER > ABHOR
ABHORRERS > ABHOR
ABHORRING > ABHOR
ABHORS > ABHOR
ABID > ABIDE
ABIDANCE > ABIDE
ABIDANCES > ABIDE
ABIDDEN > ABIDE
ABIDE vb endure, put up with
ABIDED > ABIDE
ABIDER > ABIDE
ABIDERS > ABIDE
ABIDES > ABIDE
ABIDING adj lasting ▷ n action of one who abides
ABIDINGLY > ABIDING
ABIDINGS > ABIDING
ABIES n fir tree
ABIETIC adj as in abietic acid yellowish powder
ABIGAIL n maid for a lady
ABIGAILS > ABIGAIL
ABILITIES > ABILITY
ABILITY n competence, power
ABIOGENIC adj abiogenetic
ABIOSES > ABIOSIS
ABIOSIS n absence of life
ABIOTIC > ABIOSIS
ABITUR n German examination
ABITURS > ABITUR
ABJECT adj utterly miserable ▷ vb throw down
ABJECTED > ABJECT
ABJECTING > ABJECT
ABJECTION > ABJECT
ABJECTLY > ABJECT
ABJECTS > ABJECT
ABJOINT vb cut off
ABJOINTED > ABJOINT
ABJOINTS > ABJOINT
ABJURE vb deny or renounce on oath
ABJURED > ABJURE
ABJURER > ABJURE
ABJURERS > ABJURE
ABJURES > ABJURE
ABJURING > ABJURE
ABLATE vb remove by ablation
ABLATED > ABLATE

ABLATES > ABLATE
ABLATING > ABLATE
ABLATION n removal of an organ
ABLATIONS > ABLATION
ABLATIVAL > ABLATIVE
ABLATIVE n case of nouns ▷ adj relating to the ablative case
ABLATIVES > ABLATIVE
ABLATOR n heat shield of a space craft
ABLATORS > ABLATOR
ABLAUT n vowel gradation
ABLAUTS > ABLAUT
ABLAZE adj burning fiercely ▷ adv on fire
ABLE adj capable, competent ▷ vb enable
ABLED adj having physical powers
ABLEGATE n papal envoy
ABLEGATES > ABLEGATE
ABLEISM n discrimination against disabled people
ABLEISMS > ABLEISM
ABLEIST > ABLEISM
ABLEISTS > ABLEISM
ABLER > ABLE
ABLES > ABLE
ABLEST > ABLE
ABLET n freshwater fish
ABLETS > ABLET
ABLING > ABLE
ABLINGS adv possibly
ABLINS adv Scots word meaning perhaps
ABLOOM adj in flower
ABLOW adj blooming
ABLUENT n substance used for cleansing
ABLUENTS > ABLUENT
ABLUSH adj blushing
ABLUTED adj washed thoroughly
ABLUTION n ritual washing of a priest's hands
ABLUTIONS > ABLUTION
ABLY adv competently or skilfully
ABMHO n unit of electrical conductance
ABMHOS > ABMHO
ABNEGATE vb deny to oneself
ABNEGATED > ABNEGATE
ABNEGATES > ABNEGATE
ABNEGATOR > ABNEGATE
ABNORMAL adj not normal or usual ▷ n abnormal person or thing
ABNORMALS > ABNORMAL
ABNORMITY > ABNORMAL
ABNORMOUS > ABNORMAL
ABO n offensive word for an Aborigine
ABOARD adv onto a vehicle ▷ adj onto a vehicle
ABODE n home, dwelling ▷ vb forebode
ABODED > ABODE
ABODEMENT > ABODE
ABODES > ABODE

ABODING > ABODE
ABOHM n unit of resistance
ABOHMS > ABOHM
ABOIDEAU n dyke with sluicegate
ABOIDEAUS > ABOIDEAU
ABOIDEAUX > ABOIDEAU
ABOIL adj boiling
ABOITEAU same as > ABOIDEAU
ABOITEAUS > ABOITEAU
ABOITEAUX > ABOITEAU
ABOLISH vb do away with
ABOLISHED > ABOLISH
ABOLISHER > ABOLISH
ABOLISHES > ABOLISH
ABOLITION n act of abolishing
ABOLLA n Roman cloak
ABOLLAE > ABOLLA
ABOLLAS > ABOLLA
ABOMA n South American snake
ABOMAS > ABOMA
ABOMASA > ABOMASUM
ABOMASAL > ABOMASUM
ABOMASI > ABOMASUS
ABOMASUM n compartment of a stomach
ABOMASUS n abomasum
ABOMINATE vb dislike intensely
ABONDANCE same as > ABUNDANCE
ABOON Scots word for > ABOVE
ABORAL adj away from the mouth
ABORALLY > ABORAL
ABORD vb accost
ABORDED > ABORD
ABORDING > ABORD
ABORDS > ABORD
ABORE > ABEAR
ABORIGEN n aborigine
ABORIGENS > ABORIGEN
ABORIGIN n aborigine
ABORIGINE n original inhabitant
ABORIGINS > ABORIGIN
ABORNE adj Shakespearean form of auburn
ABORNING > ABEAR
ABORT vb terminate ▷ n termination or failure
ABORTED > ABORT
ABORTEE n woman having an abortion
ABORTEES > ABORTEE
ABORTER > ABORT
ABORTERS > ABORT
ABORTING > ABORT
ABORTION n operation to end a pregnancy
ABORTIONS > ABORTION
ABORTIVE adj unsuccessful
ABORTS > ABORT
ABORTUARY n place where abortions are performed

ABORTUS n aborted fetus
ABORTUSES > ABORTUS
ABOS > ABO
ABOUGHT > ABY
ABOULIA same as > ABULIA
ABOULIAS > ABOULIA
ABOULIC > ABOULIA
ABOUND vb be plentiful
ABOUNDED > ABOUND
ABOUNDING > ABOUND
ABOUNDS > ABOUND
ABOUT adv nearly, approximately
ABOUTS prep about
ABOVE adv higher (than) ▷ n something that is above
ABOVES > ABOVE
ABRACHIA n condition of having no arms
ABRACHIAS > ABRACHIA
ABRADABLE > ABRADE
ABRADANT > ABRADE
ABRADANTS > ABRADE
ABRADE vb wear down by friction
ABRADED > ABRADE
ABRADER > ABRADE
ABRADERS > ABRADE
ABRADES > ABRADE
ABRADING > ABRADE
ABRAID vb awake
ABRAIDED > ABRAID
ABRAIDING > ABRAID
ABRAIDS > ABRAID
ABRAM adj auburn
ABRASAX same as > ABRAXAS
ABRASAXES > ABRASAX
ABRASION n scraped area on the skin
ABRASIONS > ABRASION
ABRASIVE adj harsh and unpleasant ▷ n substance for cleaning
ABRASIVES > ABRASIVE
ABRAXAS n ancient charm composed of Greek letters
ABRAXASES > ABRAXAS
ABRAY vb awake
ABRAYED > ABRAY
ABRAYING > ABRAY
ABRAYS > ABRAY
ABRAZO n embrace
ABRAZOS > ABRAZO
ABREACT vb alleviate through abreaction
ABREACTED > ABREACT
ABREACTS > ABREACT
ABREAST adj side by side
ABREGE n abridgment
ABREGES > ABREGE
ABRI n shelter or place of refuge, esp in wartime
ABRICOCK n apricot
ABRICOCKS > ABRICOCK
ABRIDGE vb shorten by using fewer words
ABRIDGED > ABRIDGE
ABRIDGER > ABRIDGE
ABRIDGERS > ABRIDGE
ABRIDGES > ABRIDGE

ABRIDGING > ABRIDGE
ABRIM adj full to the brim
ABRIN n poisonous compound
ABRINS > ABRIN
ABRIS > ABRI
ABROACH adj (of a cask, barrel, etc) tapped
ABROAD adv in a foreign country ▷ adj in general circulation ▷ n foreign place
ABROADS > ABROAD
ABROGABLE adj able to be abrogated
ABROGATE vb cancel (a law or agreement) formally
ABROGATED > ABROGATE
ABROGATES > ABROGATE
ABROGATOR > ABROGATE
ABROOKE vb bear or tolerate
ABROOKED > ABROOKE
ABROOKES > ABROOKE
ABROOKING > ABROOKE
ABROSIA n condition involving refusal to eat
ABROSIAS > ABROSIA
ABRUPT adj sudden, unexpected ▷ n abyss
ABRUPTER > ABRUPT
ABRUPTEST > ABRUPT
ABRUPTION n breaking off of a part
ABRUPTLY > ABRUPT
ABRUPTS > ABRUPT
ABS > AB
ABSCESS n inflamed swelling ▷ vb form a swelling
ABSCESSED > ABSCESS
ABSCESSES > ABSCESS
ABSCIND vb cut off
ABSCINDED > ABSCIND
ABSCINDS > ABSCIND
ABSCISE vb separate or be separated by abscission
ABSCISED > ABSCISE
ABSCISES > ABSCISE
ABSCISIC adj as in abscisic acid a type of acid
ABSCISIN n plant hormone
ABSCISING > ABSCISE
ABSCISINS > ABSCISIN
ABSCISS same as > ABSCISSA
ABSCISSA n cutting off
ABSCISSAE > ABSCISSA
ABSCISSAS > ABSCISSA
ABSCISSE same as > ABSCISSA
ABSCISSES > ABSCISSE
ABSCISSIN n plant hormone
ABSCOND vb leave secretly
ABSCONDED > ABSCOND
ABSCONDER > ABSCOND
ABSCONDS > ABSCOND
ABSEIL vb go down by a rope ▷ n instance of abseiling

ABSEILED > ABSEIL
ABSEILER n person who abseils
ABSEILERS > ABSEILER
ABSEILING > ABSEIL
ABSEILS > ABSEIL
ABSENCE n being away
ABSENCES > ABSENCE
ABSENT adj not present ▷ vb stay away
ABSENTED > ABSENT
ABSENTEE n person who is not present
ABSENTEES > ABSENTEE
ABSENTER > ABSENT
ABSENTERS > ABSENT
ABSENTING > ABSENT
ABSENTLY adv in an absent-minded manner
ABSENTS > ABSENT
ABSEY n alphabet
ABSEYS > ABSEY
ABSINTH same as > ABSINTHE
ABSINTHE n liqueur
ABSINTHES > ABSINTHE
ABSINTHS > ABSINTH
ABSIT n leave from college
ABSITS > ABSIT
ABSOLUTE adj complete, perfect ▷ n something absolute
ABSOLUTER > ABSOLUTE
ABSOLUTES > ABSOLUTE
ABSOLVE vb declare to be free from sin
ABSOLVED > ABSOLVE
ABSOLVENT n something that absolves
ABSOLVER > ABSOLVE
ABSOLVERS > ABSOLVE
ABSOLVING > ABSOLVE
ABSONANT adj unnatural and unreasonable
ABSORB vb soak up (a liquid)
ABSORBANT n absorbent substance
ABSORBATE n absorbed substance
ABSORBED adj engrossed
ABSORBENT adj able to absorb liquid ▷ n substance that absorbs
ABSORBER n thing that absorbs
ABSORBERS > ABSORBER
ABSORBING adj occupying one's attention
ABSORBS > ABSORB
ABSTAIN vb choose not to do something
ABSTAINED > ABSTAIN
ABSTAINER > ABSTAIN
ABSTAINS > ABSTAIN
ABSTERGE vb cleanse
ABSTERGED > ABSTERGE
ABSTERGES > ABSTERGE
ABSTINENT adj refraining from a certain activity

ABSTRACT adj existing as an idea ▷ n summary ▷ vb summarize
ABSTRACTS > ABSTRACT
ABSTRICT vb release
ABSTRICTS > ABSTRICT
ABSTRUSE adj not easy to understand
ABSTRUSER > ABSTRUSE
ABSURD adj incongruous or ridiculous ▷ n conception of the world
ABSURDER > ABSURD
ABSURDEST > ABSURD
ABSURDISM n belief that life is meaningless
**ABSURDIST > ** ABSURDIST
ABSURDITY > ABSURD
ABSURDLY > ABSURD
ABSURDS > ABSURD
ABTHANE n ancient Scottish church territory
ABTHANES > ABTHANE
ABUBBLE adj bubbling
ABUILDING adj being built
ABULIA n pathological inability to take decisions
ABULIAS > ABULIA
ABULIC > ABULIA
ABUNA n male head of Ethiopian family
ABUNAS > ABUNA
ABUNDANCE n copious supply
ABUNDANCY n abundance
ABUNDANT adj plentiful
ABUNE Scots word for > ABOVE
ABURST adj bursting
ABUSABLE > ABUSE
ABUSAGE n wrong use
ABUSAGES > ABUSAGE
ABUSE vb use wrongly ▷ n prolonged ill-treatment
ABUSED > ABUSE
ABUSER > ABUSE
ABUSERS > ABUSE
ABUSES > ABUSE
ABUSING > ABUSE
ABUSION n wrong use or deception
ABUSIONS > ABUSION
ABUSIVE adj rude or insulting
ABUSIVELY > ABUSIVE
ABUT vb be next to or touching
ABUTILON n shrub
ABUTILONS > ABUTILON
ABUTMENT n construction supporting the end of a bridge
ABUTMENTS > ABUTMENT
ABUTS > ABUT
ABUTTAL same as > ABUTMENT
ABUTTALS > ABUTTAL
ABUTTED > ABUT
ABUTTER n owner of adjoining property

ABUTTERS > ABUTTER
ABUTTING > ABUT
ABUZZ adj noisy, busy with activity etc
ABVOLT n unit of potential difference in the electromagnetic system
ABVOLTS > ABVOLT
ABWATT n unit of power
ABWATTS > ABWATT
ABY vb pay the penalty for
ABYE same as > ABY
ABYEING > ABYE
ABYES > ABYE
ABYING > ABY
ABYS > ABY
ABYSM archaic word for > ABYSS
ABYSMAL adj extremely bad, awful
ABYSMALLY > ABYSMAL
ABYSMS > ABYSM
ABYSS n very deep hole or chasm
ABYSSAL adj of the ocean depths
ABYSSES > ABYSS
ACACIA n tree or shrub
ACACIAS > ACACIA
ACADEME n place of learning
ACADEMES > ACADEME
ACADEMIA n academic world
ACADEMIAS > ACADEMIA
ACADEMIC adj of a university ▷ n lecturer at a university
ACADEMICS > ACADEMIC
ACADEMIES > ACADEMY
ACADEMISM n adherence to rules
ACADEMIST > ACADEMY
ACADEMY n society for arts or sciences
ACAI n berry
ACAIS > ACAI
ACAJOU n type of mahogany
ACAJOUS > ACAJOU
ACALCULIA n inability to make calculations
ACALEPH n invertebrate
ACALEPHAE > ACALEPH
ACALEPHAN > ACALEPH
ACALEPHE n acaleph
ACALEPHES > ACALEPHE
ACALEPHS > ACALEPH
ACANTH n acanthus
ACANTHA n thorn or prickle
ACANTHAE > ACANTHA
ACANTHAS > ACANTHA
ACANTHI > ACANTHUS
ACANTHIN n organic chemical
ACANTHINE adj of or resembling an acanthus
ACANTHINS > ACANTHIN
ACANTHOID adj resembling a spine
ACANTHOUS adj of an acanthus

ACANTHS > ACANTH
ACANTHUS n prickly plant
ACAPNIA n lack of carbon dioxide
ACAPNIAS > ACAPNIA
ACARBOSE n diabetes medicine
ACARBOSES > ACARBOSE
ACARI > ACARUS
ACARIAN > ACARUS
ACARIASES
> ACARIASIS
ACARIASIS n infestation of hair
ACARICIDE n any drug for killing acarids
ACARID n small arachnids ▷ adj of these arachnids
ACARIDAN same as
> ACARID
ACARIDANS > ACARIDAN
ACARIDEAN > ACARID
ACARIDIAN > ACARID
ACARIDS > ACARID
ACARINE n acarid
ACARINES > ACARINE
ACAROID adj resembling a mite
ACAROLOGY n study of mites and ticks
ACARPOUS adj producing no fruit
ACARUS n type of mite
ACATER n buyer of provisions
ACATERS > ACATER
ACATES n provisions
ACATHISIA same as
> AKATHISIA
ACATOUR n buyer of provisions
ACATOURS > ACATOUR
ACAUDAL adj having no tail
ACAUDATE same as
> ACAUDAL
ACAULINE adj having no stem
ACAULOSE same as
> ACAULINE
ACAULOUS adj having a short stem
ACCA n academic
ACCABLE adj dejected or beaten
ACCAS > ACCA
ACCEDE vb consent or agree (to)
ACCEDED > ACCEDE
ACCEDENCE > ACCEDE
ACCEDER > ACCEDE
ACCEDERS > ACCEDE
ACCEDES > ACCEDE
ACCEDING > ACCEDE
ACCENDS > ACCEND
ACCENSION > ACCEND
ACCENT n style of pronunciation ▷ vb place emphasis on
ACCENTED > ACCENT

ACCENTING > ACCENT
ACCENTOR n songbird
ACCENTORS > ACCENTOR
ACCENTS > ACCENT
ACCENTUAL adj of accents
ACCEPT vb receive willingly
ACCEPTANT adj receiving willingly
ACCEPTED adj generally approved
ACCEPTEE n person who has been accepted
ACCEPTEES > ACCEPTEE
ACCEPTER > ACCEPT
ACCEPTERS > ACCEPT
ACCEPTING > ACCEPT
ACCEPTIVE adj ready to accept
ACCEPTOR n person signing a bill of exchange
ACCEPTORS > ACCEPTOR
ACCEPTS > ACCEPT
ACCESS n right to approach ▷ vb obtain data
ACCESSARY same as
> ACCESSORY
ACCESSED > ACCESS
ACCESSES > ACCESS
ACCESSING > ACCESS
ACCESSION n taking up a position ▷ vb make a record
ACCESSORY n supplementary part ▷ adj supplementary
ACCIDENCE n inflectional morphology
ACCIDENT n mishap, often causing injury
ACCIDENTS > ACCIDENT
ACCIDIA same as
> ACCIDIE
ACCIDIAS > ACCIDIA
ACCIDIE n spiritual sloth
ACCIDIES > ACCIDIE
ACCINGE vb put a belt around
ACCINGED > ACCINGE
ACCINGES > ACCINGE
ACCINGING > ACCINGE
ACCIPITER n hawk
ACCITE vb summon
ACCITED > ACCITE
ACCITES > ACCITE
ACCITING > ACCITE
ACCLAIM vb applaud, praise ▷ n enthusiastic approval
ACCLAIMED > ACCLAIM
ACCLAIMER > ACCLAIM
ACCLAIMS > ACCLAIM
ACCLIMATE vb adapt to a new climate
ACCLIVITY n upward slope
ACCLIVOUS
> ACCLIVITY
ACCLOY vb choke or clog
ACCLOYED > ACCLOY
ACCLOYING > ACCLOY
ACCLOYS > ACCLOY

ACCOAST vb accost
ACCOASTED > ACCOAST
ACCOASTS > ACCOAST
ACCOIED > ACCOY
ACCOIL n welcome ▷ vb gather together
ACCOILS > ACCOIL
ACCOLADE n award ▷ vb give an award
ACCOLADED > ACCOLADE
ACCOLADES > ACCOLADE
ACCOMPANY vb go along with
ACCOMPT vb account
ACCOMPTED > ACCOMPT
ACCOMPTS > ACCOMPT
ACCORAGE vb encourage
ACCORAGED > ACCORAGE
ACCORAGES > ACCORAGE
ACCORD n agreement, harmony ▷ vb fit in with
ACCORDANT adj in conformity or harmony
ACCORDED > ACCORD
ACCORDER > ACCORD
ACCORDERS > ACCORD
ACCORDING adj in proportion
ACCORDION n portable instrument
ACCORDS > ACCORD
ACCOST vb approach and speak to ▷ n greeting
ACCOSTED > ACCOST
ACCOSTING > ACCOST
ACCOSTS > ACCOST
ACCOUNT n report, description ▷ vb judge to be
ACCOUNTED > ACCOUNT
ACCOUNTS > ACCOUNT
ACCOURAGE vb encourage
ACCOURT vb entertain
ACCOURTED > ACCOURT
ACCOURTS > ACCOURT
ACCOUTER same as
> ACCOUTRE
ACCOUTERS > ACCOUTER
ACCOUTRE vb provide with equipment
ACCOUTRED > ACCOUTRE
ACCOUTRES > ACCOUTRE
ACCOY vb soothe
ACCOYED > ACCOY
ACCOYING > ACCOY
ACCOYLD > ACCOIL
ACCOYS > ACCOY
ACCREDIT vb give official recognition to
ACCREDITS > ACCREDIT
ACCRETE vb grow together
ACCRETED > ACCRETE
ACCRETES > ACCRETE
ACCRETING > ACCRETE
ACCRETION n gradual growth
ACCRETIVE
> ACCRETION
ACCREW vb accrue
ACCREWED > ACCREW
ACCREWING > ACCREW
ACCREWS > ACCREW

ACCROIDES n red alcohol-soluble resin
ACCRUABLE > ACCRUE
ACCRUAL n act of accruing
ACCRUALS > ACCRUAL
ACCRUE vb increase gradually
ACCRUED > ACCRUE
ACCRUES > ACCRUE
ACCRUING > ACCRUE
ACCUMBENT adj lying against
ACCURACY n representation of truth
ACCURATE adj exact, correct
ACCURSE vb curse
ACCURSED adj under a curse
ACCURSES > ACCURSE
ACCURSING > ACCURSE
ACCURST same as
> ACCURSED
ACCUSABLE > ACCUSE
ACCUSABLY > ACCUSE
ACCUSAL n accusation
ACCUSALS > ACCUSAL
ACCUSANT n person who accuses
ACCUSANTS > ACCUSANT
ACCUSE vb charge with wrongdoing
ACCUSED n person accused of a crime
ACCUSER > ACCUSE
ACCUSERS > ACCUSE
ACCUSES > ACCUSE
ACCUSING > ACCUSE
ACCUSTOM vb make used to
ACCUSTOMS > ACCUSTOM
ACE n playing card with one symbol on it ▷ adj excellent ▷ vb serve an ace in racquet sports
ACED > ACE
ACEDIA same as
> ACCIDIE
ACEDIAS > ACEDIA
ACELDAMA n place with ill feeling
ACELDAMAS > ACELDAMA
ACELLULAR adj not made up of or containing cells
ACENTRIC adj without a centre ▷ n acentric chromosome or fragment
ACENTRICS > ACENTRIC
ACEPHALIC adj having no head or one that is reduced and indistinct, as certain insect larvae
ACEQUIA n irrigation ditch
ACEQUIAS > ACEQUIA
ACER n type of tree
ACERATE same as
> ACERATED
ACERATED adj having sharp points
ACERB adj bitter
ACERBATE vb embitter or exasperate
ACERBATED > ACERBATE

ACERBATES > ACERBATE
ACERBER > ACERB
ACERBEST > ACERB
ACERBIC adj harsh or bitter
ACERBITY n bitter speech or temper
ACEROLA n cherry-like fruit
ACEROLAS > ACEROLA
ACEROSE adj shaped like a needle
ACEROUS same as
> ACEROSE
ACERS > ACER
ACERVATE adj growing in heaps or clusters
ACERVULI > ACERVULUS
ACERVULUS n spore-producing part of plant
ACES > ACE
ACESCENCE > ACESCENT
ACESCENCY > ACESCENT
ACESCENT adj slightly sour or turning sour
▷ n something that is turning sour
ACESCENTS > ACESCENT
ACETA > ACETUM
ACETABULA n deep cuplike cavities on the side of the hipbones that receive the head of the thighbone
ACETAL n colourless liquid
ACETALS > ACETAL
ACETAMID same as
> ACETAMIDE
ACETAMIDE n white or colourless soluble deliquescent crystalline compound
ACETAMIDS > ACETAMID
ACETATE n salt or ester of acetic acid
ACETATED adj combined with acetic acid
ACETATES > ACETATE
ACETIC adj of or involving vinegar
ACETIFIED > ACETIFY
ACETIFIER > ACETIFY
ACETIFIES > ACETIFY
ACETIFY vb become vinegar
ACETIN n type of acetate
ACETINS > ACETIN
ACETONE n colourless liquid used as a solvent
ACETONES > ACETONE
ACETONIC > ACETONE
ACETOSE same as
> ACETOUS
ACETOUS adj containing acetic acid
ACETOXYL n medicine used to treat acne
ACETOXYLS > ACETOXYL
ACETUM n solution that has dilute acetic acid as solvent
ACETYL n containing the monovalent group CH_3CO-

ACETYLATE vb introduce an acetyl group into (a chemical compound)
ACETYLENE n colourless flammable gas used in welding metals
ACETYLIC > ACETYL
ACETYLIDE n any of a class of carbides in which the carbon is present as a diatomic divalent ion ($C_2{}^{2-}$). They are formally derivatives of acetylene
ACETYLS > ACETYL
ACH interj Scots expression of surprise
ACHAENIA > ACHAENIUM
ACHAENIUM n achene
ACHAGE n pain
ACHAGES > ACHAGE
ACHALASIA n failure of the cardiac sphincter of the oesophagus to relax, resulting in difficulty in swallowing
ACHAR n spicy pickle made from mango
ACHARNE adj furiously violent
ACHARS > ACHAR
ACHARYA n religious teacher and spiritual guide
ACHARYAS > ACHARYA
ACHATES same as
> ACATES
ACHE n dull continuous pain ▷ vb be in or cause continuous dull pain
ACHED > ACHE
ACHENE n type of fruit
ACHENES > ACHENE
ACHENIA > ACHENIUM
ACHENIAL > ACHENE
ACHENIUM n achene
ACHENIUMS > ACHENIUM
ACHES > ACHE
ACHIER > ACHY
ACHIEST > ACHY
ACHIEVE vb gain by hard work or ability
ACHIEVED > ACHIEVE
ACHIEVER > ACHIEVE
ACHIEVERS > ACHIEVE
ACHIEVES > ACHIEVE
ACHIEVING > ACHIEVE
ACHILLEA n type of plant with white, yellow, or purple flowers, often grown in gardens
ACHILLEAS > ACHILLEA
ACHIMENES n tropical plant of the S America with showy red, blue, or white tubular flowers
ACHINESS > ACHY
ACHING > ACHE
ACHINGLY > ACHE
ACHINGS > ACHE
ACHIOTE n annatto
ACHIOTES > ACHIOTE
ACHIRAL adj of a tuber producing arrowroot
ACHKAN n man's coat in India

ACHKANS > ACHKAN
ACHOLIA n bile condition
ACHOLIAS > ACHOLIA
ACHOO interj, n (sound of) a sneeze
ACHOOS > ACHOO
ACHROMAT n lens designed to bring light of two chosen wavelengths to the same focal point, thus reducing chromatic aberration
ACHROMATS > ACHROMAT
ACHROMIC adj colourless
ACHROMOUS same as
> ACHROMIC
ACHY adj affected by a continuous dull pain
ACICLOVIR same as
> ACYCLOVIR
ACICULA n needle-shaped part
ACICULAE > ACICULA
ACICULAR > ACICULA
ACICULAS > ACICULA
ACICULATE adj having aciculae
ACICULUM n needle-like bristle that provides internal support for the appendages (chaetae) of some polychaete worms
ACICULUMS > ACICULUM
ACID n one of a class of compounds, corrosive and sour when dissolved in water, that combine with a base to form a salt ▷ adj containing acid
ACIDEMIA n abnormally high level of acid in blood
ACIDEMIAS > ACIDEMIA
ACIDER > ACID
ACIDEST > ACID
ACIDHEAD n person who uses LSD
ACIDHEADS > ACIDHEAD
ACIDIC adj containing acid
ACIDIER > ACIDY
ACIDIEST > ACIDY
ACIDIFIED > ACIDIFY
ACIDIFIER > ACIDIFY
ACIDIFIES > ACIDIFY
ACIDIFY vb convert into acid
ACIDITIES > ACIDITY
ACIDITY n quality of being acid
ACIDLY > ACID
ACIDNESS > ACID
ACIDOPHIL adj (of cells or cell contents) easily stained by acid dyes ▷ n acidophil organism
ACIDOSES > ACIDOSIS
ACIDOSIS n condition characterized by an abnormal increase in the acidity of the blood and extracellular fluids
ACIDOTIC > ACIDOSIS
ACIDS > ACID

ACIDULATE vb make slightly acid or sour
ACIDULENT same as
> ACIDULOUS
ACIDULOUS adj rather sour
ACIDURIA n abnormally high level of acid in urine
ACIDURIAS > ACIDURIA
ACIDY adj resembling or containing acid
ACIERAGE n iron-plating of metal
ACIERAGES > ACIERAGE
ACIERATE vb change (iron) into steel
ACIERATED > ACIERATE
ACIERATES > ACIERATE
ACIFORM adj shaped like a needle
ACINAR adj of small sacs
ACING > ACE
ACINI > ACINUS
ACINIC > ACINUS
ACINIFORM adj shaped like a bunch of grapes
ACINOSE > ACINUS
ACINOUS > ACINUS
ACINUS n parts of a gland
ACKEE n tropical tree
ACKEES > ACKEE
ACKER same as **>** ACCA
ACKERS > ACKER
ACKNEW > ACKNOW
ACKNOW vb recognize
ACKNOWING > ACKNOW
ACKNOWN > ACKNOW
ACKNOWNE adj aware
ACKNOWS > ACKNOW
ACLINIC adj unbending
ACMATIC adj highest or ultimate
ACME n highest point of achievement or excellence
ACMES > ACME
ACMIC same as **>** ACMATIC
ACMITE n chemical with pyramid-shaped crystals
ACMITES > ACMITE
ACNE n pimply skin disease
ACNED adj marked by acne
ACNES > ACNE
ACNODAL > ACNODE
ACNODE n mathematical term
ACNODES > ACNODE
ACOCK adv cocked
ACOELOUS adj not having a stomach
ACOEMETI n order of monks
ACOLD adj feeling cold
ACOLUTHIC adj of an afterimage
ACOLYTE n follower or attendant
ACOLYTES > ACOLYTE
ACOLYTH n acolyte
ACOLYTHS > ACOLYTH
ACONITE n poisonous plant with hoodlike flowers
ACONITES > ACONITE

ACONITIC > ACONITE
ACONITINE n poison made from aconite
ACONITUM same as > ACONITE
ACONITUMS > ACONITUM
ACORN n nut of the oak tree
ACORNED adj covered with acorns
ACORNS > ACORN
ACOSMISM n belief that no world exists outside the mind
ACOSMISMS > ACOSMISM
ACOSMIST > ACOSMISM
ACOSMISTS > ACOSMISM
ACOUCHI n South American rodent with a white-tipped tail
ACOUCHIES > ACOUCHY
ACOUCHIS > ACOUCHI
ACOUCHY same as > ACOUCHI
ACOUSTIC adj of sound and hearing
ACOUSTICS n science of sounds
ACQUAINT vb make familiar, inform
ACQUAINTS > ACQUAINT
ACQUEST n something acquired
ACQUESTS > ACQUEST
ACQUIESCE vb agree to what someone wants
ACQUIGHT vb acquit
ACQUIGHTS > ACQUIGHT
ACQUIRAL > ACQUIRE
ACQUIRALS > ACQUIRE
ACQUIRE vb gain, get
ACQUIRED > ACQUIRE
ACQUIREE n one who acquires
ACQUIREES > ACQUIREE
ACQUIRER > ACQUIRE
ACQUTRERS > ACQUIRE
ACQUIRES > ACQUIRE
ACQUIRING > ACQUIRE
ACQUIS n as in acquis communautaire European Union laws
ACQUIST n acquisition
ACQUISTS > ACQUIST
ACQUIT vb pronounce (someone) innocent
ACQUITE vb acquit
ACQUITES > ACQUIT
ACQUITING > ACQUIT
ACQUITS > ACQUIT
ACQUITTAL n deliverance and release of a person appearing before a court on a charge of crime, as by a finding of not guilty
ACQUITTED > ACQUIT
ACQUITTER > ACQUIT
ACRASIA n lack of willpower
ACRASIAS > ACRASIA
ACRASIN n chemical
ACRASINS > ACRASIN
ACRATIC > ACRASIA

ACRAWL adv crawling
ACRE n measure of land, 4840 square yards (4046.86 square metres)
ACREAGE n land area in acres ▷ adj of or relating to a large allotment of land, esp in a rural area
ACREAGES > ACREAGE
ACRED adj having acres of land
ACRES > ACRE
ACRID adj pungent, bitter
ACRIDER > ACRID
ACRIDEST > ACRID
ACRIDIN n acridine
ACRIDINE n colourless crystalline solid
ACRIDINES > ACRIDINE
ACRIDINS > ACRIDIN
ACRIDITY > ACRID
ACRIDLY > ACRID
ACRIDNESS > ACRID
ACRIMONY n bitterness and resentment felt about something
ACRITARCH n type of fossil
ACRITICAL adj not critical
ACRO n event where acrobatic skiing moves are performed to music
ACROBAT n person skilled in gymnastic feats requiring agility and balance
ACROBATIC > ACROBAT
ACROBATS > ACROBAT
ACRODONT adj (of the teeth of some reptiles) having no roots and being fused at the base to the margin of the jawbones ▷ n acrodont reptile
ACRODONTS > ACRODONT
ACRODROME adj (of the veins of a leaf) running parallel to the edges of the leaf and fusing at the tip
ACROGEN n flowerless plant
ACROGENIC > ACROGEN
ACROGENS > ACROGEN
ACROLECT n most correct form of language
ACROLECTS > ACROLECT
ACROLEIN n colourless or yellowish flammable poisonous pungent liquid
ACROLEINS > ACROLEIN
ACROLITH n (esp in ancient Greek sculpture) a wooden, often draped figure with only the head, hands, and feet in stone
ACROLITHS > ACROLITH
ACROMIA > ACROMION
ACROMIAL > ACROMION
ACROMION n outermost edge of the spine of the shoulder blade
ACRONIC adj acronical

ACRONICAL adj occurring at sunset
ACRONYCAL same as > ACRONICAL
ACRONYM n word formed from the initial letters of other words, such as NASA
ACRONYMIC > ACRONYM
ACRONYMS > ACRONYM
ACROPETAL adj (of leaves and flowers) produced in order from the base upwards so that the youngest are at the apex
ACROPHOBE n person afraid of heights
ACROPHONY n use of symbols to represent sounds
ACROPOLIS n citadel of an ancient Greek city
ACROS > ACRO
ACROSOMAL > ACROSOME
ACROSOME n structure at the tip of a sperm cell
ACROSOMES > ACROSOME
ACROSPIRE n first shoot developing from the plumule of a germinating grain seed
ACROSS adv from side to side (of)
ACROSTIC n lines of writing in which the first or last letters of each line spell a word or saying
ACROSTICS > ACROSTIC
ACROTER n plinth
ACROTERIA n acroters
ACROTERS > ACROTER
ACROTIC adj of a surface
ACROTISM n absence of pulse
ACROTISMS > ACROTISM
ACRYLATE n chemical compound in plastics and resins
ACRYLATES > ACRYLATE
ACRYLIC adj (synthetic fibre, paint, etc) made from acrylic acid ▷ n man-made fibre used for clothes and blankets
ACRYLICS > ACRYLIC
ACRYLYL n type of monovalent group
ACRYLYLS > ACRYLYL
ACT n thing done ▷ vb do something
ACTA pl n minutes of meeting
ACTABLE > ACT
ACTANT n grammatical term
ACTANTS > ACTANT
ACTED > ACT
ACTIN n protein
ACTINAL adj part of a jellyfish
ACTINALLY > ACTINAL
ACTING n art of an actor ▷ adj temporarily performing the duties of
ACTINGS > ACTING

ACTINIA n type of sea anemone
ACTINIAE > ACTINIA
ACTINIAN n sea anemone
ACTINIANS > ACTINIAN
ACTINIAS > ACTINIA
ACTINIC adj (of radiation) producing a photochemical effect
ACTINIDE n member of the actinide series
ACTINIDES > ACTINIDE
ACTINISM > ACTINIC
ACTINISMS > ACTINIC
ACTINIUM n radioactive chemical element
ACTINIUMS > ACTINIUM
ACTINOID adj having a radiate form, as a sea anemone or starfish ▷ n member of the actinide series
ACTINOIDS > ACTINOID
ACTINON same as > ACTINIDE
ACTINONS > ACTINON
ACTINOPOD n type of single-celled invertebrate
ACTINS > ACTIN
ACTION n process of doing something ▷ vb put into effect
ACTIONED > ACTION
ACTIONER n film with a fast-moving plot, usually containing scenes of violence
ACTIONERS > ACTIONER
ACTIONING > ACTION
ACTIONIST n activist
ACTIONS > ACTION
ACTIVATE vb make active
ACTIVATED > ACTIVATE
ACTIVATES > ACTIVATE
ACTIVATOR > ACTIVATE
ACTIVE adj moving, working ▷ n active form of a verb
ACTIVELY > ACTIVE
ACTIVES > ACTIVE
ACTIVISE same as > ACTIVIZE
ACTIVISED > ACTIVISE
ACTIVISES > ACTIVISE
ACTIVISM n policy of taking direct and often militant action to achieve an end, esp a political or social one
ACTIVISMS > ACTIVISM
ACTIVIST > ACTIVISM
ACTIVISTS > ACTIVISM
ACTIVITY n state of being active
ACTIVIZE vb make active
ACTIVIZED > ACTIVIZE
ACTIVIZES > ACTIVIZE
ACTON n jacket
ACTONS > ACTON
ACTOR n person who acts in a play, film, etc
ACTORISH > ACTOR
ACTORLY adj of or relating to an actor

ACTORS > ACTOR

ACTRESS n woman who acts in a play, film, broadcast, etc

ACTRESSES > ACTRESS

ACTRESSY adj exaggerated and affected in manner

ACTS > ACT

ACTUAL adj existing in reality

ACTUALISE same as **>** ACTUALIZE

ACTUALIST n person dealing in hard fact

ACTUALITE n humorous word for truth

ACTUALITY n reality

ACTUALIZE vb make actual or real

ACTUALLY adv really, indeed

ACTUALS pl n commercial commodities that can be bought and used

ACTUARIAL > ACTUARY

ACTUARIES > ACTUARY

ACTUARY n statistician who calculates insurance risks

ACTUATE vb start up (a device)

ACTUATED > ACTUATE

ACTUATES > ACTUATE

ACTUATING > ACTUATE

ACTUATION > ACTUATE

ACTUATOR > ACTUATE

ACTUATORS > ACTUATE

ACTURE n action

ACTURES > ACTURE

ACUATE adj sharply pointed ▷ vb put into action

ACUATED > ACUATE

ACUATES > ACUATE

ACUATING > ACUATE

ACUITIES > ACUITY

ACUITY n keenness of vision or thought

ACULEATE adj cutting ▷ n insect, such as a bee, with a sting

ACULEATED same as **>** ACULEATE

ACULEATES > ACULEATE

ACULEI > ACULEUS

ACULEUS n prickle or spine, such as the thorn of a rose

ACUMEN n ability to make good judgments

ACUMENS > ACUMEN

ACUMINATE adj narrowing to a sharp point, as some types of leaf ▷ vb make pointed or sharp

ACUMINOUS > ACUMEN

ACUPOINT n any of the specific points on the body where a needle is inserted in acupuncture or pressure is applied in acupressure

ACUPOINTS > ACUPOINT

ACUSHLA n Irish endearment

ACUSHLAS > ACUSHLA

ACUTANCE n physical rather than subjective measure of the sharpness of a photographic image

ACUTANCES > ACUTANCE

ACUTE adj severe ▷ n accent (´) over a letter to indicate the quality or length of its sound, as in café

ACUTELY > ACUTE

ACUTENESS > ACUTE

ACUTER > ACUTE

ACUTES > ACUTE

ACUTEST > ACUTE

ACYCLIC adj not cyclic

ACYCLOVIR n drug used against herpes

ACYL n member of the monovalent group of atoms RCO-

ACYLATE vb chemical

ACYLATED > ACYLATE

ACYLATES > ACYLATE

ACYLATING > ACYLATE

ACYLATION n introduction into a chemical compound of an acyl group

ACYLOIN n organic chemical compound

ACYLOINS > ACYLOIN

ACYLS > ACYL

AD n advertisement

ADAGE n wise saying, proverb

ADAGES > ADAGE

ADAGIAL > ADAGE

ADAGIO adv (piece to be played) slowly and gracefully ▷ n movement or piece to be performed slowly

ADAGIOS > ADAGIO

ADAMANCE n being adamant

ADAMANCES > ADAMANCE

ADAMANCY n being adamant

ADAMANT adj unshakable in determination or purpose ▷ n any extremely hard or apparently unbreakable substance

ADAMANTLY > ADAMANT

ADAMANTS > ADAMANT

ADAMSITE n yellow poisonous crystalline solid that readily sublimes

ADAMSITES > ADAMSITE

ADAPT vb alter for new use or new conditions

ADAPTABLE > ADAPT

ADAPTED > ADAPT

ADAPTER same as **>** ADAPTOR

ADAPTERS > ADAPTER

ADAPTING > ADAPT

ADAPTION n adaptation

ADAPTIONS > ADAPTION

ADAPTIVE > ADAPT

ADAPTOGEN n any of various natural substances used in herbal medicine to normalize and regulate the systems of the body

ADAPTOR n device for connecting several electrical appliances to a single socket

ADAPTORS > ADAPTOR

ADAPTS > ADAPT

ADAW vb subdue

ADAWED > ADAW

ADAWING > ADAW

ADAWS > ADAW

ADAXIAL adj facing the axis

ADAYS adv daily

ADBOT n form of spyware that collects information about a person's online behaviour in order to display targeted adverts in their browser

ADBOTS > ADBOT

ADD vb combine (numbers or quantities)

ADDABLE > ADD

ADDAX n antelope

ADDAXES > ADDAX

ADDEBTED adj indebted

ADDED > ADD

ADDEDLY > ADD

ADDEEM vb adjudge

ADDEEMED > ADDEEM

ADDEEMING > ADDEEM

ADDEEMS > ADDEEM

ADDEND n any of a set of numbers that is to be added

ADDENDA > ADDENDUM

ADDENDS > ADDEND

ADDENDUM n addition

ADDENDUMS > ADDENDUM

ADDER n small poisonous snake

ADDERBEAD n type of prehistoric ornamental bead

ADDERS > ADDER

ADDERWORT n plant of the dock family

ADDIBLE adj addable

ADDICT n person who is unable to stop taking drugs ▷ vb cause (someone or oneself) to become dependent (on something, esp a narcotic drug)

ADDICTED > ADDICT

ADDICTING > ADDICT

ADDICTION n condition of being abnormally dependent on some habit, esp compulsive dependency on narcotic drugs

ADDICTIVE adj causing addiction

ADDICTS > ADDICT

ADDIES > ADDY

ADDING n act or instance of addition ▷ adj of, for, or relating to addition

ADDINGS > ADDING

ADDIO interj farewell ▷ n cry of addio

ADDIOS > ADDIO

ADDITION n adding

ADDITIONS > ADDITION

ADDITIVE n something added, esp to a foodstuff, to improve it or prevent deterioration ▷ adj characterized by or produced by addition

ADDITIVES > ADDITIVE

ADDITORY adj adding to something

ADDLE vb become muddled ▷ adj indicating a muddled state

ADDLED > ADDLE

ADDLEMENT > ADDLE

ADDLES > ADDLE

ADDLING > ADDLE

ADDOOM vb adjudge

ADDOOMED > ADDOOM

ADDOOMING > ADDOOM

ADDOOMS > ADDOOM

ADDORSED adj back to back

ADDRESS n place where a person lives ▷ vb mark the destination, as on an envelope

ADDRESSED > ADDRESS

ADDRESSEE n person addressed

ADDRESSER > ADDRESS

ADDRESSES > ADDRESS

ADDRESSOR > ADDRESS

ADDREST > ADDRESS

ADDS > ADD

ADDUCE vb mention something as evidence or proof

ADDUCED > ADDUCE

ADDUCENT > ADDUCE

ADDUCER > ADDUCE

ADDUCERS > ADDUCE

ADDUCES > ADDUCE

ADDUCIBLE > ADDUCE

ADDUCING > ADDUCE

ADDUCT vb draw towards medial axis ▷ n compound

ADDUCTED > ADDUCT

ADDUCTING > ADDUCT

ADDUCTION > ADDUCT

ADDUCTIVE > ADDUCE

ADDUCTOR n muscle that adducts

ADDUCTORS > ADDUCTOR

ADDUCTS > ADDUCT

ADDY n e-mail address

ADEEM vb cancel

ADEEMED > ADEEM

ADEEMING > ADEEM

ADEEMS > ADEEM

ADELGID n type of small sap-feeding insect

ADELGIDS > ADELGID

ADEMPTION n failure of a specific legacy, as by a

a

testator disposing of the subject matter in his lifetime
ADENINE n chemical
ADENINES > ADENINE
ADENITIS n inflammation of a gland or lymph node
ADENOID adj of or resembling a gland
ADENOIDAL adj having a nasal voice caused by swollen adenoids
ADENOIDS pl n tissue at the back of the throat
ADENOMA n tumour occurring in glandular tissue
ADENOMAS > ADENOMA
ADENOMATA > ADENOMA
ADENOSES > ADENOSIS
ADENOSINE n nucleoside formed by the condensation of adenine and ribose
ADENOSIS n disease of glands
ADENYL n enzyme
ADENYLIC adj as in adenylic acid nucleotide consisting of adenine, ribose or deoxyribose, and a phosphate group
ADENYLS > ADENYL
ADEPT n very skilful (person) ▷ adj proficient in something requiring skill
ADEPTER > ADEPT
ADEPTEST > ADEPT
ADEPTLY > ADEPT
ADEPTNESS > ADEPT
ADEPTS > ADEPT
ADEQUACY > ADEQUATE
ADEQUATE adj sufficient, enough
ADERMIN n vitamin
ADERMINS > ADERMIN
ADESPOTA n anonymous writings
ADESSIVE n grammatical case denoting place
ADESSIVES > ADESSIVE
ADHAN n call to prayer
ADHANS > ADHAN
ADHARMA n wickedness
ADHARMAS > ADHARMA
ADHERABLE > ADHERE
ADHERE vb stick (to)
ADHERED > ADHERE
ADHERENCE > ADHERE
ADHEREND n something attached by adhesive
ADHERENDS > ADHEREND
ADHERENT n devotee, follower ▷ adj sticking or attached
ADHERENTS > ADHERENT
ADHERER > ADHERE
ADHERERS > ADHERE
ADHERES > ADHERE
ADHERING > ADHERE
ADHESION n sticking (to)
ADHESIONS > ADHESION

ADHESIVE n substance used to stick things together ▷ adj able to stick to things
ADHESIVES > ADHESIVE
ADHIBIT vb administer or apply
ADHIBITED > ADHIBIT
ADHIBITS > ADHIBIT
ADHOCRACY n management that responds to urgent problems rather than planning to avoid them
ADIABATIC adj (of a thermodynamic process) taking place without loss or gain of heat ▷ n curve or surface on a graph representing the changes in two or more characteristics (such as pressure and volume) of a system undergoing an adiabatic process
ADIAPHORA n matters of indifference
ADIEU n goodbye
ADIEUS > ADIEU
ADIEUX > ADIEU
ADIOS sentence substitute Spanish for goodbye ▷ n goodbye
ADIOSES > ADIOS
ADIPIC adj as in adipic acid crystalline solid used in the preparation of nylon
ADIPOCERE n waxlike fatty substance formed during the decomposition of corpses
ADIPOCYTE n fat cell that accumulates and stores fats
ADIPOSE adj of or containing fat ▷ n animal fat
ADIPOSES > ADIPOSIS
ADIPOSIS n obesity
ADIPOSITY > ADIPOSE
ADIPOUS adj made of fat
ADIPSIA n complete lack of thirst
ADIPSIAS > ADIPSIA
ADIT n shaft into a mine, for access or drainage
ADITS > ADIT
ADJACENCE > ADJACENT
ADJACENCY > ADJACENT
ADJACENT adj near or next (to) ▷ n side lying between a specified angle and a right angle in a right-angled triangle
ADJACENTS > ADJACENT
ADJECTIVE n word that adds information about a noun or pronoun ▷ adj additional or dependent
ADJIGO n SW Australian yam plant with edible tubers
ADJIGOS > ADJIGO
ADJOIN vb be next to

ADJOINED > ADJOIN
ADJOINING adj being in contact
ADJOINS > ADJOIN
ADJOINT n type of mathematical matrix
ADJOINTS > ADJOINT
ADJOURN vb close (a court) at the end of a session
ADJOURNED > ADJOURN
ADJOURNS > ADJOURN
ADJUDGE vb declare (to be)
ADJUDGED > ADJUDGE
ADJUDGES > ADJUDGE
ADJUDGING > ADJUDGE
ADJUNCT n something incidental added to something else
ADJUNCTLY > ADJUNCT
ADJUNCTS > ADJUNCT
ADJURE vb command (to do)
ADJURED > ADJURE
ADJURER > ADJURE
ADJURERS > ADJURE
ADJURES > ADJURE
ADJURING > ADJURE
ADJUROR > ADJURE
ADJURORS > ADJURE
ADJUST vb adapt to new conditions
ADJUSTED > ADJUST
ADJUSTER > ADJUST
ADJUSTERS > ADJUST
ADJUSTING > ADJUST
ADJUSTIVE > ADJUST
ADJUSTOR > ADJUST
ADJUSTORS > ADJUST
ADJUSTS > ADJUST
ADJUTAGE n nozzle
ADJUTAGES > ADJUTAGE
ADJUTANCY > ADJUTANT
ADJUTANT n army officer in charge of routine administration
ADJUTANTS > ADJUTANT
ADJUVANCY > ADJUVANT
ADJUVANT adj aiding or assisting ▷ n something that aids or assists
ADJUVANTS > ADJUVANT
ADLAND n advertising industry and the people who work in it
ADLANDS > ADLAND
ADMAN n man who works in advertising
ADMASS n mass advertising
ADMASSES > ADMASS
ADMEASURE vb measure out (land, etc) as a share
ADMEN > ADMAN
ADMIN n administration
ADMINICLE n something contributing to prove a point without itself being complete proof
ADMINS > ADMIN
ADMIRABLE adj deserving or inspiring admiration

ADMIRABLY > ADMIRABLE
ADMIRAL n highest naval rank
ADMIRALS > ADMIRAL
ADMIRALTY n office or jurisdiction of an admiral
ADMIRANCE n admiration
ADMIRE vb regard with esteem and approval
ADMIRED > ADMIRE
ADMIRER > ADMIRE
ADMIRERS > ADMIRE
ADMIRES > ADMIRE
ADMIRING > ADMIRE
ADMISSION n permission to enter
ADMISSIVE > ADMISSION
ADMIT vb confess, acknowledge
ADMITS > ADMIT
ADMITTED > ADMIT
ADMITTEE n one who admits
ADMITTEES > ADMITTEE
ADMITTER > ADMIT
ADMITTERS > ADMIT
ADMITTING > ADMIT
ADMIX vb mix or blend
ADMIXED > ADMIX
ADMIXES > ADMIX
ADMIXING > ADMIX
ADMIXT > ADMIX
ADMIXTURE n mixture
ADMONISH vb reprove sternly
ADMONITOR > ADMONISH
ADNASCENT adj growing with something else
ADNATE adj growing closely attached to an adjacent part or organ
ADNATION > ADNATE
ADNATIONS > ADNATE
ADNEXA pl n organs adjoining the uterus
ADNEXAL > ADNEXA
ADNOMINAL n word modifying a noun ▷ adj of or relating to an adnoun
ADNOUN n adjective used as a noun
ADNOUNS > ADNOUN
ADO n fuss, trouble
ADOBE n sun-dried brick
ADOBELIKE > ADOBE
ADOBES > ADOBE
ADOBO n Philippine dish
ADOBOS > ADOBO
ADONIS n beautiful young man
ADONISE vb adorn
ADONISED > ADONISE
ADONISES > ADONISE
ADONISING > ADONISE
ADONIZE vb adorn
ADONIZED > ADONIZE
ADONIZES > ADONIZE
ADONIZING > ADONIZE
ADOORS adv at the door
ADOPT vb take (someone else's child) as one's own

ADOPTABLE > ADOPT
ADOPTED adj having been adopted
ADOPTEE n one who has been adopted
ADOPTEES > ADOPTEE
ADOPTER n person who adopts
ADOPTERS > ADOPTER
ADOPTING > ADOPT
ADOPTION n ADOPT
ADOPTIONS > ADOPT
ADOPTIOUS adj adopted
ADOPTIVE adj related by adoption
ADOPTS > ADOPT
ADORABLE adj very attractive
ADORABLY > ADORABLE
ADORATION n deep love or esteem
ADORE vb love intensely
ADORED > ADORE
ADORER > ADORE
ADORERS > ADORE
ADORES > ADORE
ADORING > ADORE
ADORINGLY > ADORE
ADORKABLE adj charmingly unfashionable
ADORN vb decorate, embellish
ADORNED > ADORN
ADORNER > ADORN
ADORNERS > ADORN
ADORNING > ADORN
ADORNMENT > ADORN
ADORNS > ADORN
ADOS > ADO
ADOWN adv down
ADOZE adv asleep
ADPRESS vb press together
ADPRESSED > ADPRESS
ADPRESSES > ADPRESS
ADRAD adj afraid
ADRATE n price or tariff that businesses pay to advertise
ADRATES > ADRATE
ADREAD vb dread
ADREADED > ADREAD
ADREADING > ADREAD
ADREADS > ADREAD
ADRED adj filled with dread
ADRENAL adj near the kidneys ▷ n adrenal gland
ADRENALIN n hormone secreted by the adrenal glands in response to stress
ADRENALLY > ADRENAL
ADRENALS > ADRENAL
ADRIFT adv drifting
ADROIT adj quick and skilful
ADROITER > ADROIT
ADROITEST > ADROIT
ADROITLY > ADROIT
ADRY adj dry
ADS > AD
ADSCRIPT n serf
ADSCRIPTS > ADSCRIPT

ADSORB vb condense to form a thin film
ADSORBATE n substance that has been or is to be adsorbed on a surface
ADSORBED > ADSORB
ADSORBENT adj capable of adsorption ▷ n material, such as activated charcoal, on which adsorption can occur
ADSORBER > ADSORB
ADSORBERS > ADSORB
ADSORBING > ADSORB
ADSORBS > ADSORB
ADSPEAK n kind of language or jargon used in advertising or in advertisements
ADSPEAKS > ADSPEAK
ADSUKI same as > ADZUKI
ADSUKIS > ADSUKI
ADSUM sentence substitute I am present
ADUKI same as > ADZUKI
ADUKIS > ADUKI
ADULARIA n white or colourless glassy variety of orthoclase
ADULARIAS > ADULARIA
ADULATE vb flatter or praise obsequiously
ADULATED > ADULATE
ADULATES > ADULATE
ADULATING > ADULATE
ADULATION n uncritical admiration
ADULATOR > ADULATE
ADULATORS > ADULATE
ADULATORY adj expressing praise, esp obsequiously
ADULT adj fully grown, mature ▷ n adult person or animal
ADULTERER n person who has committed adultery
ADULTERY n sexual unfaithfulness of a husband or wife
ADULTHOOD > ADULT
ADULTLIKE > ADULT
ADULTLY > ADULT
ADULTNESS > ADULT
ADULTRESS n US word for a female adulterer
ADULTS > ADULT
ADUMBRAL adj shadowy
ADUMBRATE vb outline
ADUNC adj hooked
ADUNCATE adj hooked
ADUNCATED adj hooked
ADUNCITY n quality of being hooked
ADUNCOUS adj hooked
ADUST vb dry up or darken by heat
ADUSTED > ADUST
ADUSTING > ADUST
ADUSTS > ADUST
ADVANCE vb go or bring forward ▷ n forward

movement ▷ adj done or happening before an event
ADVANCED adj at a late stage in development
ADVANCER > ADVANCE
ADVANCERS > ADVANCE
ADVANCES > ADVANCE
ADVANCING > ADVANCE
ADVANTAGE n more favourable position or state
ADVECT vb move horizontally in air
ADVECTED > ADVECT
ADVECTING > ADVECT
ADVECTION n transferring of heat in a horizontal stream of gas
**ADVECTIVE > ** ADVECTION
ADVECTS > ADVECT
ADVENE vb add as extra
ADVENED > ADVENE
ADVENES > ADVENE
ADVENING > ADVENE
ADVENT n arrival
ADVENTIVE adj (of a species) introduced to a new area and not yet established there ▷ n such a plant or animal
ADVENTS > ADVENT
ADVENTURE n exciting and risky undertaking or exploit ▷ vb take a risk or put at risk
ADVERB n word that adds information about a verb, adjective, or other adverb
ADVERBIAL n word or group of words with the grammatical role of an adverb ▷ adj of or relating to an adverb
ADVERBS > ADVERB
ADVERSARY n opponent or enemy
ADVERSE adj unfavourable
ADVERSELY > ADVERSE
ADVERSER > ADVERSE
ADVERSEST > ADVERSE
ADVERSITY n very difficult or hard circumstances
ADVERT n advertisement ▷ vb draw attention (to)
ADVERTED > ADVERT
ADVERTENT adj heedful
ADVERTING > ADVERT
ADVERTISE vb present or praise (goods or services) to the public in order to encourage sales
ADVERTIZE same as > ADVERTISE
ADVERTS > ADVERT
ADVEW vb look at
ADVEWED > ADVEW
ADVEWING > ADVEW
ADVEWS > ADVEW
ADVICE n recommendation as to what to do

ADVICEFUL > ADVICE
ADVICES > ADVICE
ADVISABLE adj prudent, sensible
**ADVISABLY > ** ADVISABLE
ADVISE vb offer advice to
ADVISED adj considered, thought-out
ADVISEDLY > ADVISED
ADVISEE n person receiving advice
ADVISEES > ADVISEE
ADVISER n person who offers advice, eg on careers to students or school pupils
ADVISERS > ADVISER
ADVISES > ADVISE
ADVISING > ADVISE
ADVISINGS > ADVISE
ADVISOR same as > ADVISER
ADVISORS > ADVISOR
ADVISORY adj giving advice ▷ n statement giving advice or a warning
ADVOCAAT n liqueur with a raw egg base
ADVOCAATS > ADVOCAAT
ADVOCACY n active support of a cause or course of action
ADVOCATE vb propose or recommend ▷ n person who publicly supports a cause
ADVOCATED > ADVOCATE
ADVOCATES > ADVOCATE
ADVOCATOR n person who advocates
ADVOUTRER n adulterer
ADVOUTRY n adultery
ADVOWSON n right of presentation to a vacant benefice
ADVOWSONS > ADVOWSON
ADWARD vb award
ADWARDED > ADWARD
ADWARDING > ADWARD
ADWARDS > ADWARD
ADWARE n computer software
ADWARES > ADWARE
ADWOMAN n woman working in advertising
ADWOMEN > ADWOMAN
ADYNAMIA n loss of vital power or strength, esp as the result of illness
ADYNAMIAS > ADYNAMIA
ADYNAMIC > ADYNAMIA
ADYTA > ADYTUM
ADYTUM n sacred place in ancient temples
ADZ same as > ADZE
ADZE n woodworking tool ▷ vb use an adze
ADZED > ADZE
ADZES > ADZE
ADZING > ADZE
ADZUKI n type of plant
ADZUKIS > ADZUKI

AE *determiner* one

AECIA > AECIUM

AECIAL > AECIUM

AECIDIA > AECIDIUM

AECIDIAL > AECIDIUM

AECIDIUM *same as* > AECIUM

AECIUM *n* area of some fungi

AEDES *n* type of mosquito which transmits yellow fever and dengue

AEDICULE *n* opening such as a door or a window, framed by columns on either side, and a pediment above

AEDICULES > AEDICULE

AEDILE *n* magistrate of ancient Rome

AEDILES > AEDILE

AEDINE *adj* of a species of mosquito

AEFALD *adj* single

AEFAULD *adj* single

AEGIRINE *n* green mineral

AEGIRINES > AEGIRINE

AEGIRITE *n* green mineral

AEGIRITES > AEGIRITE

AEGIS *n* sponsorship, protection

AEGISES > AEGIS

AEGLOGUE *n* eclogue

AEGLOGUES > AEGLOGUE

AEGROTAT *n* (in British and certain other universities, and, sometimes, schools) a certificate allowing a candidate to pass an examination although he has missed all or part of it through illness

AEGROTATS > AEGROTAT

AEMULE *vb* emulate

AEMULED > AEMULE

AEMULES > AEMULE

AEMULING > AEMULE

AENEOUS *adj* brass-coloured or greenish-gold

AENEUS *n* aquarium fish

AENEUSES > AENEUS

AEOLIAN *adj* of or relating to the wind

AEOLIPILE *n* device illustrating the reactive forces of a gas jet: usually a spherical vessel mounted so as to rotate and equipped with angled exit pipes from which steam within it escapes

AEOLIPYLE *same as* > AEOLIPILE

AEON *n* immeasurably long period of time

AEONIAN *adj* everlasting

AEONIC > AEON

AEONS > AEON

AEPYORNIS *n* type of large extinct flightless bird whose remains have been found in Madagascar

AEQUORIN *n* type of protein

AEQUORINS > AEQUORIN

AERADIO *n* radio system for pilots

AERADIOS > AERADIO

AERATE *vb* put gas into (a liquid), as when making a fizzy drink

AERATED > AERATE

AERATES > AERATE

AERATING > AERATE

AERATION > AERATE

AERATIONS > AERATE

AERATOR > AERATE

AERATORS > AERATE

AERIAL *adj* in, from, or operating in the air ▷ *n* metal pole, wire, etc, for receiving or transmitting radio or TV signals

AERIALIST *n* trapeze artist or tightrope walker

AERIALITY > AERIAL

AERIALLY > AERIAL

AERIALS > AERIAL

AERIE *a variant spelling (esp US) of* > EYRIE

AERIED *adj* in a very high place

AERIER > AERY

AERIES > AERIE

AERIEST > AERY

AERIFIED > AERIFY

AERIFIES > AERIFY

AERIFORM *adj* having the form of air

AERIFY *vb* change or cause to change into a gas

AERIFYING > AERIFY

AERILY > AERY

AERO *n* of or relating to aircraft or aeronautics

AEROBAT *n* person who does stunt flying

AEROBATIC *adj* pertaining to stunt flying

AEROBATS > AEROBAT

AEROBE *n* organism that requires oxygen to survive

AEROBES > AEROBE

AEROBIA > AEROBIUM

AEROBIC *adj* designed for or relating to aerobics

AEROBICS *n* exercises designed to increase the amount of oxygen in the blood

AEROBIONT *n* organism needing oxygen to live

AEROBIUM *same as* > AEROBE

AEROBOMB *n* bomb dropped from aircraft

AEROBOMBS > AEROBOMB

AEROBOT *n* unmanned aircraft used esp in space exploration

AEROBOTS > AEROBOT

AEROBRAKE *vb* use airbrakes to slow aircraft

AEROBUS *n* monorail suspended by an overhead cable

AEROBUSES > AEROBUS

AERODART *n* metal arrow dropped from an aircraft as a weapon

AERODARTS > AERODART

AERODROME *n* small airport

AERODUCT *n* air duct

AERODUCTS > AERODUCT

AERODYNE *n* any heavier-than-air machine, such as an aircraft, that derives the greater part of its lift from aerodynamic forces

AERODYNES > AERODYNE

AEROFOIL *n* part of an aircraft, such as the wing, designed to give lift

AEROFOILS > AEROFOIL

AEROGEL *n* colloid

AEROGELS > AEROGEL

AEROGRAM *n* airmail letter on a single sheet of paper that seals to form an envelope

AEROGRAMS > AEROGRAM

AEROGRAPH *n* airborne instrument recording meteorological conditions

AEROLITE *n* stony meteorite consisting of silicate minerals

AEROLITES > AEROLITE

AEROLITH *n* meteorite

AEROLITHS > AEROLITH

AEROLITIC > AEROLITE

AEROLOGIC > AEROLOGY

AEROLOGY *n* study of the atmosphere, particularly its upper layers

AEROMANCY *n* using weather observation to foretell the future

AEROMETER *n* instrument for determining the mass or density of a gas, esp air

AEROMETRY *n* branch of physics concerned with the mechanical properties of gases, esp air

AEROMOTOR *n* aircraft engine

AERONAUT *n* person who flies in a lighter-than-air craft, esp the pilot or navigator

AERONAUTS > AERONAUT

AERONOMER *n* scientist studying atmosphere

AERONOMIC > AERONOMY

AERONOMY *n* science of the earth's upper atmosphere

AEROPAUSE *n* region of the upper atmosphere above which aircraft cannot fly

AEROPHAGY *n* spasmodic swallowing of air

AEROPHOBE *n* person suffering from aerophobia

AEROPHONE *n* wind instrument

AEROPHORE *n* device for playing a wind instrument

AEROPHYTE *another name for* > EPIPHYTE

AEROPLANE *n* powered flying vehicle with fixed wings

AEROPULSE *n* type of jet engine

AEROS > AERO

AEROSAT *n* communications satellite

AEROSATS > AEROSAT

AEROSCOPE *n* device for observing the atmosphere

AEROSHELL *n* parachute used to slow spacecraft

AEROSOL *n* pressurized can from which a substance can be dispensed as a fine spray

AEROSOLS > AEROSOL

AEROSPACE *n* earth's atmosphere and space beyond ▷ *adj* of rockets or space vehicles

AEROSPIKE *n* type of rocket engine

AEROSTAT *n* lighter-than-air craft, such as a balloon

AEROSTATS > AEROSTAT

AEROTAXES > AEROTAXIS

AEROTAXIS *n* movement away from or towards oxygen

AEROTONE *n* bath incorporating air jets for massage

AEROTONES > AEROTONE

AEROTRAIN *n* train driven by a jet engine

AERUGO *(esp of old bronze) another name for* > VERDIGRIS

AERUGOS > AERUGO

AERY *adj* lofty, insubstantial, or visionary

AESC *n* rune

AESCES > AESC

AESCULIN *n* chemical in horse-chestnut bark

AESCULINS > AESCULIN

AESIR *n* chief of the Norse gods

AESTHESES > AESTHESIS

AESTHESIA *n* normal ability to experience sensation, perception, or sensitivity

AESTHESIS *variant of* > ESTHESIS

AESTHETE *n* person who has or affects an extravagant love of art

AESTHETES > AESTHETE

AESTHETIC *adj* relating to the appreciation of art

and beauty ▷ *n* principle or set of principles relating to the appreciation of art and beauty

AESTIVAL *adj* of or occurring in summer

AESTIVATE *vb* pass the summer

AETATIS *adj* at the age of

AETHER *same as* ▷ ETHER

AETHEREAL *a variant spelling of* ▷ ETHEREAL

AETHERIC > AETHER

AETHERS > AETHER

AETIOLOGY *n* philosophy or study of causation

AFALD *adj* single

AFAR *adv* at, from, or to a great distance ▷ *n* great distance

AFARA *n* African tree

AFARAS > AFARA

AFARS > AFAR

AFAWLD *adj* single

AFEAR *vb* frighten

AFEARD *an archaic or dialect word for* > AFRAID

AFEARED *same as* > AFEARD

AFEARING > AFEAR

AFEARS > AFEAR

AFEBRILE *adj* without fever

AFF *adv* off

AFFABLE *adj* friendly and easy to talk to

AFFABLY > AFFABLE

AFFAIR *n* event or happening

AFFAIRE *n* love affair

AFFAIRES > AFFAIRE

AFFAIRS *pl n* personal or business interests

AFFEAR *vb* frighten

AFFEARD > AFFEAR

AFFEARE *vb* frighten

AFFEARED > AFFEAR

AFFEARES > AFFEARE

AFFEARING > AFFEAR

AFFEARS > AFFEAR

AFFECT *vb* act on, influence ▷ *n* emotion associated with an idea or set of ideas

AFFECTED *adj* displaying affectation

AFFECTER > AFFECT

AFFECTERS > AFFECT

AFFECTING *adj* arousing feelings of pity

AFFECTION *n* fondness or love

AFFECTIVE *adj* relating to affects

AFFECTS > AFFECT

AFFEER *vb* assess

AFFEERED > AFFEER

AFFEERING > AFFEER

AFFEERS > AFFEER

AFFERENT *adj* bringing or directing inwards to a part or an organ of the body, esp towards the brain or spinal cord ▷ *n* nerve that

conveys impulses towards an organ of the body

AFFERENTS > AFFERENT

AFFIANCE *vb* bind (a person or oneself) in a promise of marriage ▷ *n* solemn pledge, esp a marriage contract

AFFIANCED > AFFIANCE

AFFIANCES > AFFIANCE

AFFIANT *n* person who makes an affidavit

AFFIANTS > AFFIANT

AFFICHE *n* poster

AFFICHES > AFFICHE

AFFIDAVIT *n* written statement made on oath

AFFIED > AFFY

AFFIES > AFFY

AFFILIATE *vb* (of a group) link up with a larger group ▷ *n* person or organization that is affiliated with another

AFFINAL > AFFINE

AFFINE *adj* involving transformations which preserve collinearity ▷ *n* relation by marriage

AFFINED *adj* closely related

AFFINELY > AFFINE

AFFINES > AFFINE

AFFINITY *n* close connection or liking

AFFIRM *vb* declare to be true

AFFIRMANT > AFFIRM

AFFIRMED > AFFIRM

AFFIRMER > AFFIRM

AFFIRMERS > AFFIRM

AFFIRMING > AFFIRM

AFFIRMS > AFFIRM

AFFIX *vb* attach or fasten ▷ *n* word or syllable added to a word to change its meaning

AFFIXABLE > AFFIX

AFFIXAL > AFFIX

AFFIXED > AFFIX

AFFIXER > AFFIX

AFFIXERS > AFFIX

AFFIXES > AFFIX

AFFIXIAL > AFFIX

AFFIXING > AFFIX

AFFIXMENT > AFFIX

AFFIXTURE > AFFIX

AFFLATED *adj* inspired

AFFLATION *n* inspiration

AFFLATUS *n* impulse of creative power or inspiration, esp in poetry, considered to be of divine origin

AFFLICT *vb* give pain or grief to

AFFLICTED > AFFLICT

AFFLICTER *n* one who afflicts

AFFLICTS > AFFLICT

AFFLUENCE *n* wealth

AFFLUENCY *n* affluence

AFFLUENT *adj* having plenty of money ▷ *n* tributary stream

AFFLUENTS > AFFLUENT

AFFLUENZA *n* guilt or lack of motivation experienced by people who have made or inherited large amounts of money

AFFLUX *n* flowing towards a point

AFFLUXES > AFFLUX

AFFLUXION *n* flow towards something

AFFOGATO *n* drink made by pouring espresso over ice cream

AFFOGATOS > AFFOGATO

AFFOORD *vb* consent

AFFOORDED > AFFOORD

AFFOORDS > AFFOORD

AFFORCE *vb* strengthen

AFFORCED > AFFORCE

AFFORCES > AFFORCE

AFFORCING > AFFORCE

AFFORD *vb* have enough money to buy

AFFORDED > AFFORD

AFFORDING > AFFORD

AFFORDS > AFFORD

AFFOREST *vb* plant trees on

AFFORESTS > AFFOREST

AFFRAP *vb* strike

AFFRAPPED > AFFRAP

AFFRAPS > AFFRAP

AFFRAY *n* noisy fight, brawl ▷ *vb* frighten

AFFRAYED > AFFRAY

AFFRAYER > AFFRAY

AFFRAYERS > AFFRAY

AFFRAYING > AFFRAY

AFFRAYS > AFFRAY

AFFRENDED *adj* brought back into friendship

AFFRET *n* furious attack

AFFRETS > AFFRET

AFFRICATE *n* composite speech sound consisting of a stop and a fricative articulated at the same point

AFFRIGHT *vb* frighten ▷ *n* sudden terror

AFFRIGHTS > AFFRIGHT

AFFRONT *n* insult ▷ *vb* hurt someone's pride or dignity

AFFRONTE *adj* facing

AFFRONTED > AFFRONT

AFFRONTEE *adj* facing

AFFRONTS > AFFRONT

AFFUSION *n* baptizing of a person by pouring water onto his head

AFFUSIONS > AFFUSION

AFFY *vb* trust

AFFYDE > AFFY

AFFYING > AFFY

AFGHAN *n* type of biscuit

AFGHANI *n* monetary unit of Afghanistan

AFGHANIS > AFGHANI

AFGHANS > AFGHAN

AFIELD *adj* away from one's usual surroundings or home

AFIRE *adj* on fire

AFLAJ > FALAJ

AFLAME *adj* burning

AFLATOXIN *n* toxin produced by a fungus growing on peanuts, maize, etc, which causes liver disease (esp cancer) in humans

AFLOAT *adj* floating ▷ *adv* floating

AFLUTTER *adv* in or into a nervous or excited state

AFOCAL *adj* relating to a method for transferring an image without bringing it into focus

AFOOT *adj* happening, in operation ▷ *adv* happening

AFORE *adv* before

AFOREHAND *adv* beforehand

AFORESAID *adj* referred to previously

AFORETIME *adv* formerly

AFOUL *adj* in or into a state of difficulty, confusion, or conflict (with)

AFRAID *adj* frightened

AFREET *n* powerful evil demon or giant monster

AFREETS > AFREET

AFRESH *adv* again, anew

AFRIT *same as* > AFREET

AFRITS > AFRIT

AFRO *n* bush-like frizzy hairstyle

AFRONT *adv* in front

AFROS > AFRO

AFT *adv* at or towards the rear of a ship or aircraft ▷ *adj* at or towards the rear of a ship or aircraft

AFTER *adv* at a later time

AFTERBODY *n* any discarded part that continues to trail a satellite, rocket, etc, in orbit

AFTERCARE *n* support given to a person discharged from a hospital or prison

AFTERCLAP *n* unexpected consequence

AFTERDAMP *n* poisonous gas formed after the explosion of firedamp in a coal mine

AFTERDECK *n* unprotected deck behind the bridge of a ship

AFTEREYE *vb* gaze at someone or something that has passed

AFTEREYED > AFTEREYE

AFTEREYES > AFTEREYE

AFTERGAME *n* second game that follows another

AFTERGLOW n glow left after a source of light has gone

AFTERHEAT n heat generated in a nuclear reactor after it has been shut down, produced by residual radioactivity in the fuel elements

AFTERINGS n last of the milk drawn in milking

AFTERLIFE n life after death

AFTERMATH n results of an event considered together

AFTERMOST adj closer or closest to the rear or (in a vessel) the stern

AFTERNOON n time between noon and evening

AFTERPAIN n pain that comes after a while

AFTERPEAK n space behind the aftermost bulkhead, often used for storage

AFTERS n sweet course of a meal

AFTERSHOW n party held after a public performance of a play or film

AFTERSUN n moisturizing lotion applied to the skin to soothe sunburn and avoid peeling

AFTERSUNS > AFTERSUN

AFTERTAX adj after tax has been paid

AFTERTIME n later period

AFTERWARD adv after an earlier event or time

AFTERWORD n epilogue or postscript in a book, etc

AFTMOST adj furthest towards rear

AFTOSA n foot-and-mouth disease

AFTOSAS > AFTOSA

AG n agriculture

AGA n title of respect

AGACANT adj irritating

AGACANTE adj irritating

AGACERIE n coquetry

AGACERIES > AGACERIE

AGAIN adv once more

AGAINST prep in opposition or contrast to

AGALACTIA n absence or failure of secretion of milk

AGALLOCH another name for > EAGLEWOOD

AGALLOCHS > AGALLOCH

AGALWOOD n eaglewood

AGALWOODS > AGALWOOD

AGAMA n small lizard

AGAMAS > AGAMA

AGAMETE n reproductive cell

AGAMETES > AGAMETE

AGAMI n South American bird

AGAMIC adj asexual

AGAMID same as > AGAMA

AGAMIDS > AGAMID

AGAMIS > AGAMI

AGAMOGONY n asexual reproduction in protozoans that is characterized by multiple fission

AGAMOID n lizard of the agamid type

AGAMOIDS > AGAMOID

AGAMONT another name for > SCHIZONT

AGAMONTS > AGAMONT

AGAMOUS adj without sex

AGAPAE > AGAPE

AGAPAI > AGAPE

AGAPE adj (of the mouth) wide open ▷ n love feast among the early Christians

AGAPEIC > AGAPE

AGAPES > AGAPE

AGAR n jelly-like substance obtained from seaweed and used as a thickener in food

AGARIC n type of fungus

AGARICS > AGARIC

AGAROSE n gel used in chemistry

AGAROSES > AGAROSE

AGARS > AGAR

AGARWOOD n aromatic wood of an Asian tree

AGARWOODS > AGARWOOD

AGAS > AGA

AGAST adj aghast ▷ vb terrify or be terrified

AGASTED > AGAST

AGASTING > AGAST

AGASTS > AGAST

AGATE n semiprecious form of quartz with striped colouring ▷ adv on the way

AGATES > AGATE

AGATEWARE n ceramic ware made to resemble agate or marble

AGATISE same as > AGATIZE

AGATISED > AGATISE

AGATISES > AGATISE

AGATISING > AGATISE

AGATIZE vb turn into agate

AGATIZED > AGATIZE

AGATIZES > AGATIZE

AGATIZING > AGATIZE

AGATOID adj like agate

AGAVE n tropical plant

AGAVES > AGAVE

AGAZE adj gazing at something

AGAZED adj amazed

AGE n length of time a person or thing has existed ▷ vb make or grow old

AGED adj old

AGEDLY > AGED

AGEDNESS > AGED

AGEE adj awry, crooked, or ajar ▷ adv awry

AGEING n fact or process of growing old ▷ adj becoming or appearing older

AGEINGS > AGEING

AGEISM n discrimination against people on the grounds of age

AGEISMS > AGEISM

AGEIST > AGEISM

AGEISTS > AGEISM

AGELAST n someone who never laughs

AGELASTIC > AGELAST

AGELASTS > AGELAST

AGELESS adj apparently never growing old

AGELESSLY > AGELESS

AGELONG adj lasting for a very long time

AGEMATE n person the same age as another person

AGEMATES > AGEMATE

AGEN archaic form of > AGAIN

AGENCIES > AGENCY

AGENCY n organization providing a service

AGENDA n list of things to be dealt with, esp at a meeting

AGENDAS same as > AGENDA

AGENDUM same as > AGENDA

AGENDUMS same as > AGENDA

AGENE n chemical used to whiten flour

AGENES > AGENE

AGENESES > AGENESIS

AGENESIA n imperfect development

AGENESIAS > AGENESIA

AGENESIS n (of an animal or plant) imperfect development

AGENETIC > AGENESIS

AGENISE same as > AGENIZE

AGENISED > AGENISE

AGENISES > AGENISE

AGENISING > AGENISE

AGENIZE vb whiten using agene

AGENIZED > AGENIZE

AGENIZES > AGENIZE

AGENIZING > AGENIZE

AGENT n person acting on behalf of another ▷ vb act as an agent

AGENTED > AGENT

AGENTIAL > AGENT

AGENTING > AGENT

AGENTINGS > AGENT

AGENTIVAL adj of the performer of an action

AGENTIVE adj (in some inflected languages) denoting a case of nouns, etc, indicating the agent described by the verb ▷ n agentive case

AGENTIVES > AGENTIVE

AGENTRIES > AGENTRY

AGENTRY n acting as agent

AGENTS > AGENT

AGER n something that ages

AGERATUM n tropical American plant with thick clusters of purplish-blue flowers

AGERATUMS > AGERATUM

AGERS > AGER

AGES > AGE

AGEUSIA n lack of the sense of taste

AGEUSIAS > AGEUSIA

AGFLATION n inflation due to a rise in the demand for and price of agricultural products

AGGADA n explanation in Jewish literature

AGGADAH same as > AGGADA

AGGADAHS > AGGADAH

AGGADAS > AGGADA

AGGADIC adj of aggada

AGGADOT > AGGADA

AGGADOTH > AGGADA

AGGER n rampart

AGGERS adj aggressive

AGGIE n American agricultural student

AGGIES > AGGIE

AGGRACE vb add grace to

AGGRACED > AGGRACE

AGGRACES > AGGRACE

AGGRACING > AGGRACE

AGGRADE vb build up by the deposition of sediment

AGGRADED > AGGRADE

AGGRADES > AGGRADE

AGGRADING > AGGRADE

AGGRATE vb gratify

AGGRATED > AGGRATE

AGGRATES > AGGRATE

AGGRATING > AGGRATE

AGGRAVATE vb make worse

AGGREGATE n total ▷ adj gathered into a mass ▷ vb combine into a whole

AGGRESS vb attack first or begin a quarrel

AGGRESSED > AGGRESS

AGGRESSES > AGGRESS

AGGRESSOR n person or body that engages in aggressive behaviour

AGGRI adj of African beads

AGGRIEVE vb grieve

AGGRIEVED adj upset and angry

AGGRIEVES > AGGRIEVE

AGGRO n aggressive behaviour

AGGROS > AGGRO

AGGRY adj of African beads

AGHA same as > AGA

AGHAS > AGHA

AGHAST adj overcome with amazement or horror

AGILA n eaglewood
AGILAS > AGILA
AGILE adj nimble, quick-moving
AGILELY > AGILE
AGILENESS > AGILE
AGILER > AGILE
AGILEST > AGILE
AGILITIES > AGILE
AGILITY > AGILE
AGIN prep against, opposed to
AGING same as > AGEING
AGINGS > AGING
AGINNER n someone who is against something
AGINNERS > AGINNER
AGIO n difference between the nominal and actual values of a currency
AGIOS > AGIO
AGIOTAGE n business of exchanging currencies
AGIOTAGES > AGIOTAGE
AGISM same as > AGEISM
AGISMS > AGISM
AGIST vb care for and feed (cattle or horses) for payment
AGISTED > AGIST
AGISTER n person who grazes cattle for money
AGISTERS > AGISTER
AGISTING > AGIST
AGISTMENT > AGEISM
AGISTOR n person who grazes cattle for money
AGISTORS > AGISTOR
AGISTS > AGIST
AGITA n acid indigestion
AGITABLE > AGITATE
AGITANS adj as in paralysis agitans Parkinson's disease
AGITAS > AGITA
AGITATE vb disturb or excite
AGITATED > AGITATE
AGITATES > AGITATE
AGITATING > AGITATE
AGITATION n state of excitement, disturbance, or worry
AGITATIVE > AGITATE
AGITATO adv (to be performed) in an agitated manner
AGITATOR n person who agitates for or against a cause, etc
AGITATORS > AGITATOR
AGITPOP n use of pop music to promote political propaganda
AGITPOPS > AGITPOP
AGITPROP n political agitation and propaganda
AGITPROPS > AGITPROP
AGLARE adj glaring
AGLEAM adj glowing
AGLEE same as > AGLEY
AGLET n metal tag
AGLETS > AGLET
AGLEY adj awry

AGLIMMER adj glimmering
AGLITTER adj sparkling, glittering
AGLOO same as > AGLU
AGLOOS > AGLOO
AGLOSSAL > AGLOSSIA
AGLOSSATE > AGLOSSIA
AGLOSSIA n congenital absence of the tongue
AGLOSSIAS > AGLOSSIA
AGLOW adj glowing
AGLU n breathing hole made in ice by a seal
AGLUS > AGLU
AGLY Scots word for > WRONG
AGLYCON n chemical compound
AGLYCONE same as > AGLYCON
AGLYCONES > AGLYCONE
AGLYCONS > AGLYCON
AGMA n symbol used to represent a velar nasal consonant
AGMAS > AGMA
AGMINATE adj gathered or clustered together
AGNAIL another name for > HANGNAIL
AGNAILS > AGNAIL
AGNAME n name additional to first name and surname
AGNAMED adj having an agname
AGNAMES > AGNAME
AGNATE adj related through a common male ancestor ▷ n descendant by male links from a common male ancestor
AGNATES > AGNATE
AGNATHAN n type of jawless eel-like aquatic vertebrate
AGNATHANS > AGNATHAN
AGNATHOUS adj (esp of lampreys and hagfishes) lacking jaws
AGNATIC > AGNATE
AGNATICAL > AGNATE
AGNATION > AGNATE
AGNATIONS > AGNATE
AGNISE vb acknowledge
AGNISED > AGNISE
AGNISES > AGNISE
AGNISING > AGNISE
AGNIZE vb acknowledge
AGNIZED > AGNIZE
AGNIZES > AGNIZE
AGNIZING > AGNIZE
AGNOLOTTI n small pasta shapes stuffed with fillings
AGNOMEN n name used by ancient Romans
AGNOMENS > AGNOMEN
AGNOMINA > AGNOMEN
AGNOMINAL > AGNOMEN
AGNOSIA n loss of power to recognize familiar objects
AGNOSIAS > AGNOSIA

AGNOSIC > AGNOSIA
AGNOSTIC n person who believes that it is impossible to know whether God exists ▷ adj of agnostics
AGNOSTICS > AGNOSTIC
AGO adv in the past
AGOG adj eager or curious
AGOGE n ancient Greek tempo
AGOGES > AGOGE
AGOGIC n musical accent
AGOGICS > AGOGIC
AGOING adj moving
AGON n ancient Greek festival
AGONAL adj of agony
AGONE an archaic word for > AGO
AGONES > AGON
AGONIC adj forming no angle
AGONIES > AGONY
AGONISE same as > AGONIZE
AGONISED > AGONISE
AGONISES > AGONISE
AGONISING > AGONISE
AGONISM n struggle between opposing forces
AGONISMS > AGONISM
AGONIST n any muscle that is opposed in action by another muscle
AGONISTES n person suffering inner struggle
AGONISTIC adj striving for effect
AGONISTS > AGONIST
AGONIZE vb worry greatly
AGONIZED > AGONIZE
AGONIZES > AGONIZE
AGONIZING > AGONIZE
AGONS > AGON
AGONY n extreme physical or mental pain
AGOOD adv seriously or earnestly
AGORA n place of assembly in ancient Greece
AGORAE > AGORA
AGORAS > AGORA
AGOROT > AGORA
AGOROTH n agorot
AGOUTA n Haitian rodent
AGOUTAS > AGOUTA
AGOUTI n rodent
AGOUTIES > AGOUTI
AGOUTIS > AGOUTI
AGOUTY n agouti
AGRAFE same as > AGRAFFE
AGRAFES > AGRAFE
AGRAFFE n loop and hook fastening
AGRAFFES > AGRAFFE
AGRAPHA same as > AGRAPHON
AGRAPHIA n loss of the ability to write, resulting from a brain lesion
AGRAPHIAS > AGRAPHIA

AGRAPHIC > AGRAPHIA
AGRAPHON n saying of Jesus not in Gospels
AGRARIAN adj of land or agriculture ▷ n person who favours the redistribution of landed property
AGRARIANS > AGRARIAN
AGRASTE > AGGRACE
AGRAVIC adj of zero gravity
AGREE vb be of the same opinion
AGREEABLE adj pleasant and enjoyable
AGREEABLY > AGREEABLE
AGREED adj determined by common consent
AGREEING > AGREE
AGREEMENT n agreeing
AGREES > AGREE
AGREGE n winner in examination for university teaching post
AGREGES > AGREGE
AGREMENS n amenities
AGREMENT n diplomatic approval of a country
AGREMENTS n amenities
AGRESTAL adj (of uncultivated plants such as weeds) growing on cultivated land
AGRESTIAL adj agrestal
AGRESTIC adj rural
AGRIA n appearance of pustules
AGRIAS > AGRIA
AGRIMONY n yellow-flowered plant with bitter-tasting fruits
AGRIN adv grinning ▷ n type of protein
AGRINS > AGRIN
AGRIOLOGY n study of primitive peoples
AGRISE vb fill with fear
AGRISED > AGRISE
AGRISES > AGRISE
AGRISING > AGRISE
AGRIZE vb fill with fear
AGRIZED > AGRIZE
AGRIZES > AGRIZE
AGRIZING > AGRIZE
AGRO n student of agriculture
AGRODOLCE n Italian sweet-and-sour sauce
AGROLOGIC > AGROLOGY
AGROLOGY n scientific study of soils and their potential productivity
AGRONOMIC > AGRONOMY
AGRONOMY n science of soil management and crop production
AGROS > AGRO
AGROUND adv onto the bottom of shallow water ▷ adj on the ground or bottom, as in shallow water

AGRYPNIA n inability to sleep
AGRYPNIAS > AGRYPNIA
AGRYZE vb fill with fear
AGRYZED > AGRYZE
AGRYZES > AGRYZE
AGRYZING > AGRYZE
AGS > AG
AGTERSKOT n final payment to a farmer for crops
AGUACATE n avocado
AGUACATES > AGUACATE
AGUE n periodic fever with shivering
AGUED adj suffering from fever
AGUELIKE > AGUE
AGUES > AGUE
AGUEWEED n N American plant with clusters of pale blue-violet or white flowers
AGUEWEEDS > AGUEWEED
AGUISE vb dress
AGUISED > AGUISE
AGUISES > AGUISE
AGUISH > AGUE
AGUISHLY > AGUE
AGUISING > AGUISE
AGUIZE vb dress
AGUIZED > AGUIZE
AGUIZES > AGUIZE
AGUIZING > AGUIZE
AGUNA n (in Jewish law) woman whose husband will not grant her a divorce
AGUNAH same as **>** AGUNA
AGUNOT > AGUNA
AGUNOTH > AGUNA
AGUTI n agouti
AGUTIS > AGUTI
AH interj exclamation expressing surprise, joy etc ▷ vb say ah
AHA interj exclamation
AHCHOO interj sound made by someone sneezing
AHEAD adv in front
AHEAP adv in a heap
AHED > AH
AHEIGHT adv at height
AHEM interj clearing of the throat in order to attract attention
AHEMERAL adj not constituting a full 24-hour day
AHENT adv behind
AHI n yellowfin tuna
AHIGH adv at height
AHIMSA n the law of reverence for every form of life
AHIMSAS > AHIMSA
AHIND adv behind
AHING > AH
AHINT adv behind
AHIS > AH
AHISTORIC adj not related to history; not historical
AHOLD n holding

AHOLDS > AHOLD
AHORSE adv on horseback
AHOY interj hail used to call a ship
AHS > AH
AHULL adv with sails furled
AHUNGERED adj very hungry
AHUNGRY adj very hungry
AHURU n type of small pink cod of SW Pacific waters
AHURUHURU same as **>** AHURU
AHURUS > AHURU
AI n shaggy-coated slow-moving animal of South America
AIA n female servant in East
AIAS > AIA
AIBLINS Scots word for **>** PERHAPS
AID n (give) assistance or support ▷ vb help financially or in other ways
AIDA n cotton fabric with a natural mesh
AIDANCE n help
AIDANCES > AIDANCE
AIDANT adj helping ▷ n helper
AIDANTS > AIDANT
AIDAS > AIDA
AIDE n assistant
AIDED > AID
AIDER > AID
AIDERS > AID
AIDES > AIDE
AIDFUL adj helpful
AIDING > AID
AIDLESS adj without help
AIDMAN n military medical assistant
AIDMEN > AIDMAN
AIDOI adj of the genitals
AIDOS Greek word for **>** SHAME
AIDS > AID
AIERIES > AIERY
AIERY n eyrie
AIGA n Māori word for family
AIGAS > AIGA
AIGHT adv all right
AIGLET same as **>** AGLET
AIGLETS > AIGLET
AIGRET same as **>** AIGRETTE
AIGRETS > AIGRET
AIGRETTE n long plume worn on hats or as a headdress, esp one of long egret feathers
AIGRETTES > AIGRETTE
AIGUILLE n rock mass or mountain peak shaped like a needle
AIGUILLES > AIGUILLE
AIKIDO n Japanese self-defence
AIKIDOS > AIKIDO
AIKONA interj South African expression meaning no

AIL vb trouble, afflict
AILANTHIC **>** AILANTHUS
AILANTHUS n type of deciduous tree with small greenish flowers and winged fruits, planted in Europe and N America
AILANTO n Asian tree
AILANTOS > AILANTO
AILED > AIL
AILERON n movable flap on an aircraft wing which controls rolling
AILERONS > AILERON
AILETTE n shoulder armour
AILETTES > AILETTE
AILING adj sickly
AILMENT n illness
AILMENTS > AILMENT
AILS > AIL
AIM vb point (a weapon or missile) or direct (a blow or remark) at a target ▷ n aiming
AIMED > AIM
AIMER > AIM
AIMERS > AIM
AIMFUL adj with purpose or intention
AIMFULLY > AIMFUL
AIMING > AIM
AIMLESS adj having no purpose
AIMLESSLY > AIMLESS
AIMS > AIM
AIN variant of **>** AYIN
AINE adj French word for elder (male)
AINEE adj French word for elder (female)
AINGA n Māori word for village
AINGAS > AINGA
AINS > AIN
AINSELL n Scots word meaning own self
AINSELLS > AINSELL
AIOLI n garlic mayonnaise
AIOLIS > AIOLI
AIR n mixture of gases forming the earth's atmosphere ▷ vb make known publicly
AIRBAG n safety device in a car
AIRBAGS > AIRBAG
AIRBALL n missed shot that fails to touch the rim of the basket
AIRBALLS > AIRBALL
AIRBASE n centre from which military aircraft operate
AIRBASES > AIRBASE
AIRBOARD n inflatable body board
AIRBOARDS > AIRBOARD
AIRBOAT n boat
AIRBOATS > AIRBOAT
AIRBORNE adj carried by air

AIRBOUND adj heading into the air
AIRBRICK n brick with holes in it, put into the wall of a building for ventilation
AIRBRICKS > AIRBRICK
AIRBRUSH n atomizer that sprays paint by compressed air ▷ vb paint using an airbrush
AIRBURST n explosion of a bomb, shell, etc, in the air ▷ vb (of a bomb, shell, etc) to explode in the air
AIRBURSTS > AIRBURST
AIRBUS n commercial passenger aircraft
AIRBUSES > AIRBUS
AIRBUSSES > AIRBUS
AIRCHECK n recording of a radio broadcast
AIRCHECKS > AIRCHECK
AIRCOACH n bus travelling to and from an airport
AIRCON n air conditioner
AIRCONS > AIRCON
AIRCRAFT n any machine that flies, such as an aeroplane
AIRCREW n crew of an aircraft
AIRCREWS > AIRCREW
AIRDATE n date of a programme broadcast
AIRDATES > AIRDATE
AIRDRAWN adj imaginary
AIRDROME same as **>** AERODROME
AIRDROMES > AIRDROME
AIRDROP n delivery of supplies by parachute ▷ vb deliver (supplies, etc) by an airdrop
AIRDROPS > AIRDROP
AIRED > AIR
AIRER n device on which clothes are hung to dry
AIRERS > AIRER
AIREST > AIR
AIRFARE n money for an aircraft ticket
AIRFARES > AIRFARE
AIRFIELD n place where aircraft can land and take off
AIRFIELDS > AIRFIELD
AIRFLOW n flow of air past a moving object
AIRFLOWS > AIRFLOW
AIRFOIL same as **>** AEROFOIL
AIRFOILS > AIRFOIL
AIRFRAME n body of an aircraft, excluding its engines
AIRFRAMES > AIRFRAME
AIRGAP n gap between parts in an electrical machine
AIRGAPS > AIRGAP
AIRGLOW n faint light in the night sky

AIRGLOWS > AIRGLOW
AIRGRAPH n
photographic reduction
of a letter for sending
airmail
AIRGRAPHS > AIRGRAPH
AIRGUN n gun fired by
compressed air
AIRGUNS > AIRGUN
AIRHEAD n stupid person
AIRHEADED > AIRHEAD
AIRHEADS > AIRHEAD
AIRHOLE n hole that
allows the passage of air
AIRHOLES > AIRHOLE
AIRIER > AIRY
AIRIEST > AIRY
AIRILY adv in a
light-hearted and casual
manner
AIRINESS n quality or
condition of being fresh,
light, or breezy
AIRING n exposure to air
for drying or ventilation
AIRINGS > AIRING
AIRLESS adj stuffy
AIRLIFT n transport of
troops or cargo by aircraft
when other routes are
blocked ▷ vb transport by
airlift
AIRLIFTED > AIRLIFT
AIRLIFTS > AIRLIFT
AIRLIKE > AIR
AIRLINE n company
providing scheduled
flights for passengers and
cargo
AIRLINER n large
passenger aircraft
AIRLINERS > AIRLINER
AIRLINES > AIRLINE
AIRLOCK n air bubble
blocking the flow of liquid
in a pipe
AIRLOCKS > AIRLOCK
AIRMAIL n system of
sending mail by aircraft
▷ adj of, used for, or
concerned with airmail
▷ vb send by airmail
AIRMAILED > AIRMAIL
AIRMAILS > AIRMAIL
AIRMAN n member of the
air force
AIRMEN > AIRMAN
AIRMOBILE adj using
aircraft as transport
AIRN Scots word for ▷ IRON
AIRNED > AIRN
AIRNING > AIRN
AIRNS > AIRN
AIRPARK n car park at
airport
AIRPARKS > AIRPARK
AIRPLANE same as
▷ AEROPLANE
AIRPLANES > AIRPLANE
AIRPLAY n broadcast
performances of a record
on radio
AIRPLAYS > AIRPLAY
AIRPORT n airfield for

civilian aircraft, with
facilities for aircraft
maintenance and
passengers
AIRPORTS > AIRPORT
AIRPOST n system of
delivering mail by air
AIRPOSTS > AIRPOST
AIRPOWER n strength of a
nation's air force
AIRPOWERS > AIRPOWER
AIRPROOF vb make
something airtight
AIRPROOFS > AIRPROOF
AIRPROX n near collision
involving aircraft
AIRPROXES > AIRPROX
AIRS pl n manners put on
to impress people
AIRSCAPE n picture or
view of sky
AIRSCAPES > AIRSCAPE
AIRSCREW n aircraft
propeller
AIRSCREWS > AIRSCREW
AIRSHAFT n shaft for
ventilation
AIRSHAFTS > AIRSHAFT
AIRSHED n air over a
particular geographical
area
AIRSHEDS > AIRSHED
AIRSHIP n lighter-than-
air self-propelled aircraft
AIRSHIPS > AIRSHIP
AIRSHOT n shot that
misses the ball completely
AIRSHOTS > AIRSHOT
AIRSHOW n occasion
when an air base is open to
the public
AIRSHOWS > AIRSHOW
AIRSICK adj nauseated
from travelling in an
aircraft
AIRSIDE n part of an
airport nearest the aircraft
AIRSIDES > AIRSIDE
AIRSOME adj cold
AIRSPACE n atmosphere
above a country, regarded
as its territory
AIRSPACES > AIRSPACE
AIRSPEED n speed of an
aircraft relative to the air
in which it moves
AIRSPEEDS > AIRSPEED
AIRSTOP n helicopter
landing-place
AIRSTOPS > AIRSTOP
AIRSTREAM n wind, esp
at a high altitude
AIRSTRIKE n attack by
military aircraft
AIRSTRIP n cleared area
where aircraft can take off
and land
AIRSTRIPS > AIRSTRIP
AIRT n point of the
compass ▷ vb direct
AIRTED > AIRT
AIRTH same as ▷ AIRT
AIRTHED > AIRTH
AIRTHING > AIRTH

AIRTHS > AIRTH
AIRTIGHT adj sealed so
that air cannot enter
AIRTIME n time divisions
on radio and TV
AIRTIMES > AIRTIME
AIRTING > AIRT
AIRTRAM n cable car
AIRTRAMS > AIRTRAM
AIRTS > AIRT
AIRVAC n evacuation by
air ambulance
AIRVACS > AIRVAC
AIRWARD adj into air
AIRWARDS adv into air
AIRWAVE n radio wave
used in radio and
television broadcasting
AIRWAVES > AIRWAVE
AIRWAY n air route used
regularly by aircraft
AIRWAYS > AIRWAY
AIRWISE adv towards
the air
AIRWOMAN > AIRMAN
AIRWOMEN > AIRMAN
AIRWORTHY adj (of
aircraft) fit to fly
AIRY adj well-ventilated
AIS > AI
AISLE n passageway
separating seating areas
in a church, theatre, etc, or
row of shelves in a
supermarket
AISLED > AISLE
AISLELESS > AISLE
AISLES > AISLE
AISLEWAY n aisle
AISLEWAYS > AISLEWAY
AISLING Irish word for
▷ DREAM
AISLINGS > AISLING
AIT n islet, esp in a river
AITCH n letter h or the
sound represented by it
AITCHBONE n cut of beef
from the rump bone
AITCHES > AITCH
AITS > AIT
AITU n half-human
half-divine being
AITUS > AITU
AIVER n working horse
AIVERS > AIVER
AIYEE interj expressing
alarm
AIZLE n Scots word for
hot ashes
AIZLES > AIZLE
AJAR adv (of a door) partly
open ▷ adj not in harmony
AJEE same as ▷ AGEE
AJI n type of spicy pepper
AJIS > AJI
AJIVA n Jainist term for
non-living thing
AJIVAS > AJIVA
AJOWAN n plant related to
caraway
AJOWANS > AJOWAN
AJUGA n garden plant
AJUGAS > AJUGA

AJUTAGE n nozzle
AJUTAGES > AJUTAGE
AJWAN n plant related to
caraway
AJWANS > AJWAN
AKA n type of New Zealand
vine
AKARYOTE n cell without
a nucleus
AKARYOTES > AKARYOTE
AKARYOTIC > AKARYOTE
AKAS > AKA
AKATEA n New Zealand
vine with white flowers
AKATEAS > AKATEA
AKATHISIA n inability to
sit still because of
uncontrollable movement
caused by reaction to
drugs
AKE vb old spelling of ache
AKEAKE n New Zealand
tree
AKEAKES > AKEAKE
AKEBIA n E Asian climbing
plant
AKEBIAS > AKEBIA
AKED > AKE
AKEDAH n binding of Isaac
in Bible
AKEDAHS > AKEDAH
AKEE same as ▷ ACKEE
AKEES > AKEE
AKELA n adult leader of a
pack of Cub Scouts
AKELAS > AKELA
AKENE same as ▷ ACHENE
AKENES > AKENE
AKENIAL > ACHENE
AKES > AKE
AKHARA n (in India)
gymnasium
AKHARAS > AKHARA
AKIMBO adj as in with arms
akimbo with hands on hips
and elbows projecting
outwards
AKIN adj related by blood
AKINESES > AKINESIS
AKINESIA n loss of power
to move
AKINESIAS > AKINESIA
AKINESIS same as
▷ AKINESIA
AKINETIC > AKINESIA
AKING > AKE
AKIRAHO n small New
Zealand shrub with white
flowers
AKIRAHOS > AKIRAHO
AKITA n large dog
AKITAS > AKITA
AKKAS slang word for
▷ MONEY
AKOLUTHOS n leader of
Byzantine Varangian
Guard
AKRASIA n weakness of
will
AKRASIAS > AKRASIA
AKRATIC > AKRASIA
AKVAVIT same as
▷ AQUAVIT

a

a

AKVAVITS > AKVAVIT
AL same as > AAL
ALA n winglike structure
ALAAP n part of raga in Indian music
ALAAPS > ALAAP
ALABAMINE old name for > ASTATINE
ALABASTER n soft white translucent stone ▷ adj of or resembling alabaster
ALACHLOR n type of herbicide
ALACHLORS > ALACHLOR
ALACK archaic or poetic word for > ALAS
ALACKADAY same as > ALACK
ALACRITY n speed, eagerness
ALAE > ALA
ALAIMENT old spelling of > ALLAYMENT
ALAIMENTS > ALAIMENT
ALALAGMOI > ALALAGMOS
ALALAGMOS n ancient Greek war cry
ALALIA n complete inability to speak
ALALIAS > ALALIA
ALAMEDA n public walk lined with trees
ALAMEDAS > ALAMEDA
ALAMO n poplar tree
ALAMODE n soft light silk used for shawls and dresses, esp in the 19th century
ALAMODES > ALAMODE
ALAMORT adj exhausted and downcast
ALAMOS > ALAMO
ALAN n member of ancient European nomadic people
ALAND vb come onto land
ALANDS > ALAND
ALANE Scots word for > ALONE
ALANG n type of grass in Malaysia
ALANGS > ALANG
ALANIN n alanine
ALANINE n chemical
ALANINES > ALANINE
ALANINS > ALANIN
ALANNAH interj term of endearment ▷ n cry of alannah
ALANNAHS > ALANNAH
ALANS > ALAN
ALANT n flowering plant used in herbal medicine
ALANTS > ALANT
ALANYL n chemical found in proteins
ALANYLS > ALANYL
ALAP n Indian vocal music without words
ALAPA n part of raga in Indian music
ALAPAS > ALAPA
ALAPS > ALAP

ALAR adj relating to, resembling, or having wings or alae
ALARM n sudden fear caused by awareness of danger ▷ vb fill with fear
ALARMABLE > ALARM
ALARMED > ALARM
ALARMEDLY > ALARM
ALARMING > ALARM
ALARMISM > ALARMIST
ALARMIST n person who alarms others needlessly ▷ adj causing needless alarm
ALARMISTS > ALARMIST
ALARMS > ALARM
ALARUM n alarm, esp a call to arms ▷ vb raise the alarm
ALARUMED > ALARUM
ALARUMING > ALARUM
ALARUMS > ALARUM
ALARY adj of, relating to, or shaped like wings
ALAS adv unfortunately, regrettably
ALASKA n dessert made of cake and ice cream
ALASKAS > ALASKA
ALASTOR n avenging demon
ALASTORS > ALASTOR
ALASTRIM n form of smallpox
ALASTRIMS > ALASTRIM
ALATE adj having wings or winglike extensions ▷ n winged insect
ALATED adj having wings
ALATES > ALATE
ALATION n state of having wings
ALATIONS > ALATION
ALAY vb allay
ALAYED > ALAY
ALAYING > ALAY
ALAYS > ALAY
ALB n long white robe worn by a Christian priest
ALBA n song of lament
ALBACORE n tuna found in warm seas, eaten for food
ALBACORES > ALBACORE
ALBARELLI > ALBARELLO
ALBARELLO n jar for drugs
ALBAS > ALBA
ALBATA n variety of German silver consisting of nickel, copper, and zinc
ALBATAS > ALBATA
ALBATROSS n large sea bird with very long wings
ALBE old word for > ALBEIT
ALBEDO n ratio of the intensity of light
ALBEDOES > ALBEDO
ALBEDOS > ALBEDO
ALBEE archaic form of > ALBEIT

ALBEIT conj even though
ALBERGHI > ALBERGO
ALBERGO n Italian word for inn
ALBERT n watch chain
ALBERTITE n black solid variety of bitumen that has a conchoidal fracture and occurs in veins in oil-bearing strata
ALBERTS > ALBERT
ALBESCENT adj shading into, growing, or becoming white
ALBESPINE old name for > HAWTHORN
ALBESPYNE old name for > HAWTHORN
ALBICORE n species of tunny
ALBICORES > ALBICORE
ALBINAL > ALBINO
ALBINESS n female albino
ALBINIC > ALBINO
ALBINISM > ALBINO
ALBINISMS > ALBINO
ALBINO n person or animal with white skin and hair and pink eyes
ALBINOISM > ALBINO
ALBINOS > ALBINO
ALBINOTIC > ALBINO
ALBITE n type of mineral
ALBITES > ALBITE
ALBITIC > ALBITE
ALBITICAL > ALBITE
ALBITISE same as > ALBITIZE
ALBITISED > ALBITISE
ALBITISES > ALBITISE
ALBITIZE vb turn into albite
ALBITIZED > ALBITIZE
ALBITIZES > ALBITIZE
ALBIZIA n mimosa
ALBIZIAS > ALBIZIA
ALBIZZIA n mimosa
ALBIZZIAS > ALBIZZIA
ALBRICIAS interj expression of joy
ALBS > ALB
ALBUGO n opacity of the cornea
ALBUGOS > ALBUGO
ALBUM n book with blank pages for keeping photographs or stamps in
ALBUMEN same as > ALBUMIN
ALBUMENS > ALBUMEN
ALBUMIN n protein found in blood plasma, egg white, milk, and muscle
ALBUMINS > ALBUMIN
ALBUMOSE the US name for > PROTEOSE
ALBUMOSES > ALBUMOSE
ALBUMS > ALBUM
ALBURNOUS > ALBURNUM
ALBURNUM former name for > SAPWOOD
ALBURNUMS > ALBURNUM

ALBUTEROL n drug used to treat lung diseases
ALCADE same as > ALCALDE
ALCADES > ALCADE
ALCAHEST same as > ALKAHEST
ALCAHESTS > ALCAHEST
ALCAIC n verse consisting of strophes with four tetrametric lines
ALCAICS > ALCAIC
ALCAIDE n commander of a fortress or castle
ALCAIDES > ALCAIDE
ALCALDE n (in Spain and Spanish America) the mayor or chief magistrate in a town
ALCALDES > ALCALDE
ALCARRAZA n Spanish water container
ALCATRAS n pelican
ALCAYDE n alcaide
ALCAYDES > ALCAYDE
ALCAZAR n Moorish palaces or fortresses
ALCAZARS > ALCAZAR
ALCHEMIC > ALCHEMY
ALCHEMIES > ALCHEMY
ALCHEMISE same as > ALCHEMIZE
ALCHEMIST n person who practises alchemy
ALCHEMIZE vb alter (an element, metal, etc) by alchemy
ALCHEMY n medieval form of chemistry concerned with trying to turn base metals into gold and to find the elixir of life
ALCHERA n mythical Golden Age
ALCHERAS > ALCHERA
ALCHYMIES > ALCHYMY
ALCHYMY old spelling of > ALCHEMY
ALCID n bird of the auk family
ALCIDINE adj relating to a family of sea birds including the auks, guillemots, and puffins
ALCIDS > ALCID
ALCO same as > ALKO
ALCOHOL n colourless flammable liquid present in intoxicating drinks
ALCOHOLIC adj of alcohol ▷ n person addicted to alcohol
ALCOHOLS > ALCOHOL
ALCOLOCK n breath-alcohol ignition-interlock device
ALCOLOCKS > ALCOLOCK
ALCOOL n form of pure grain spirit distilled in Quebec
ALCOOLS > ALCOOL
ALCOPOP n alcoholic drink that tastes like a soft drink
ALCOPOPS > ALCOPOP

ALCORZA n Spanish sweet

ALCORZAS > ALCORZA

ALCOS > ALCO

ALCOVE n recess in the wall of a room

ALCOVED adj with or in an alcove

ALCOVES > ALCOVE

ALDEA n Spanish village

ALDEAS > ALDEA

ALDEHYDE n one of a group of chemical compounds derived from alcohol by oxidation

ALDEHYDES > ALDEHYDE

ALDEHYDIC > ALDEHYDE

ALDER n tree related to the birch

ALDERFLY n insect with large broad-based hind wings, which produces aquatic larvae

ALDERMAN n formerly, senior member of a local council

ALDERMEN > ALDERMAN

ALDERN adj made of alder wood

ALDERS > ALDER

ALDICARB n crystalline compound used as a pesticide

ALDICARBS > ALDICARB

ALDOL n colourless or yellowish oily liquid

ALDOLASE n enzyme present in the body

ALDOLASES > ALDOLASE

ALDOLS > ALDOL

ALDOSE n type of sugar

ALDOSES > ALDOSE

ALDOXIME n oxime formed by reaction between hydroxylamine and an aldehyde

ALDOXIMES > ALDOXIME

ALDRIN n brown to white poisonous crystalline solid

ALDRINS > ALDRIN

ALE n kind of beer

ALEATORIC same as > ALEATORY

ALEATORY adj dependent on chance

ALEBENCH n bench at alehouse

ALEC same as > ALECK

ALECITHAL adj (of an ovum) having little or no yolk

ALECK n irritatingly oversmart person

ALECKS > ALECK

ALECOST another name for > COSTMARY

ALECOSTS > ALECOST

ALECS > ALEC

ALECTRYON n type of tree found in Australasia, SE Asia, and Micronesia

ALEE adj on or towards the lee

ALEF n first letter of Hebrew alphabet

ALEFS > ALEF

ALEFT adv at or to left

ALEGAR n malt vinegar

ALEGARS > ALEGAR

ALEGGE vb alleviate

ALEGGED > ALEGGE

ALEGGES > ALEGGE

ALEGGING > ALEGGE

ALEHOUSE n public house

ALEHOUSES > ALEHOUSE

ALEMBIC n anything that distils

ALEMBICS > ALEMBIC

ALEMBROTH n mercury compound in alchemy

ALENCON n elaborate lace worked on a hexagonal mesh

ALENCONS > ALENCON

ALENGTH adv at length

ALEPH n first letter in the Hebrew alphabet

ALEPHS > ALEPH

ALEPINE n type of cloth

ALEPINES > ALEPINE

ALERCE n wood of the sandarac tree

ALERCES > ALERCE

ALERION n eagle in heraldry

ALERIONS > ALERION

ALERT adj watchful, attentive ▷ n warning of danger ▷ vb warn of danger

ALERTED > ALERT

ALERTER > ALERT

ALERTEST > ALERT

ALERTING > ALERT

ALERTLY > ALERT

ALERTNESS > ALERT

ALERTS > ALERT

ALES > ALE

ALETHIC adj of philosophical concepts

ALEURON n outer layer of seeds

ALEURONE same as > ALEURON

ALEURONES > ALEURONE

ALEURONIC > ALEURON

ALEURONS > ALEURON

ALEVIN n young fish, esp a young salmon or trout

ALEVINS > ALEVIN

ALEW n cry to call hunting hounds

ALEWASHED adj showing effects of beer drinking

ALEWIFE n North American fish

ALEWIVES > ALEWIFE

ALEWS > ALEW

ALEXANDER n cocktail made with creme de cacao

ALEXIA n disorder of the central nervous system

ALEXIAS > ALEXIA

ALEXIC > ALEXIA

ALEXIN n complement

ALEXINE same as > ALEXIN

ALEXINES > ALEXINE

ALEXINIC > ALEXIN

ALEXINS > ALEXIN

ALEYE vb allay

ALEYED > ALEYE

ALEYES > ALEYE

ALEYING > ALEYE

ALF n uncultivated Australian

ALFA n type of grass

ALFAKI same as > ALFAQUI

ALFAKIS > ALFAKI

ALFALFA n kind of plant used to feed livestock

ALFALFAS > ALFALFA

ALFAQUI n expert in Muslim law

ALFAQUIN same as > ALFAQUI

ALFAQUINS > ALFAQUIN

ALFAQUIS > ALFAQUI

ALFAS > ALFA

ALFERECES > ALFEREZ

ALFEREZ n Spanish standard-bearer

ALFILARIA n plant with finely divided leaves and small pink or purplish flowers

ALFILERIA same as > ALFILARIA

ALFORJA n saddlebag made of leather or canvas

ALFORJAS > ALFORJA

ALFREDO adj cooked with a cheese and egg sauce

ALFRESCO adj in the open air ▷ adv in the open air

ALFS > ALF

ALGA n multicellular organism

ALGAE > ALGA

ALGAECIDE n substance for killing algae

ALGAL > ALGA

ALGAROBA same as > ALGARROBA

ALGAROBAS > ALGAROBA

ALGARROBA n edible pod of these trees

ALGARROBO n carob

ALGAS > ALGA

ALGATE adv anyway

ALGATES adv anyway

ALGEBRA n branch of mathematics using symbols to represent numbers

ALGEBRAIC adj of or relating to algebra

ALGEBRAS > ALGEBRA

ALGERINE n soft striped woollen cloth

ALGERINES > ALGERINE

ALGESES > ALGESIS

ALGESIA n capacity to feel pain

ALGESIAS > ALGESIA

ALGESIC > ALGESIA

ALGESIS n feeling of pain

ALGETIC > ALGESIA

ALGICIDAL > ALGICIDE

ALGICIDE n any substance that kills algae

ALGICIDES > ALGICIDE

ALGID adj chilly or cold

ALGIDITY > ALGID

ALGIDNESS > ALGID

ALGIN n seaweed solution

ALGINATE n salt or ester of alginic acid

ALGINATES > ALGINATE

ALGINIC adj as in alginic acid powdery substance extracted from kelp

ALGINS > ALGIN

ALGOID adj resembling or relating to algae

ALGOLOGY n branch of biology concerned with the study of algae

ALGOMETER n instrument for measuring sensitivity to pressure or to pain

ALGOMETRY > ALGOMETER

ALGOR n chill

ALGORISM n Arabic or decimal system of counting

ALGORISMS > ALGORISM

ALGORITHM n logical arithmetical or computational procedure for solving a problem

ALGORS > ALGOR

ALGUACIL n Spanish law officer

ALGUACILS > ALGUACIL

ALGUAZIL n Spanish law officer

ALGUAZILS > ALGUAZIL

ALGUM n type of wood mentioned in Bible

ALGUMS > ALGUM

ALIAS adv also known as ▷ n false name ▷ vb give or assume an alias

ALIASED > ALIAS

ALIASES > ALIAS

ALIASING n error in a vision or sound signal arising from limitations in the system that generates or processes the signal

ALIASINGS > ALIASING

ALIBI n plea of being somewhere else when a crime was committed ▷ vb provide someone with an alibi

ALIBIED > ALIBI

ALIBIES > ALIBI

ALIBIING > ALIBI

ALIBIS > ALIBI

ALIBLE adj nourishing

ALICANT n wine from Alicante in Spain

ALICANTS > ALICANT

ALICYCLIC adj (of an organic compound) having aliphatic properties, in spite of the presence of a ring of carbon atoms

ALIDAD same as > ALIDADE

ALIDADE *n* surveying instrument
ALIDADES > ALIDADE
ALIDADS > ALIDAD
ALIEN *adj* foreign ▷ *n* foreigner ▷ *vb* transfer (property, etc) to another
ALIENABLE *adj* able to be transferred to another owner
ALIENAGE > ALIEN
ALIENAGES > ALIEN
ALIENATE *vb* cause to become hostile
ALIENATED > ALIENATE
ALIENATES > ALIENATE
ALIENATOR > ALIENATE
ALIENED > ALIEN
ALIENEE *n* person to whom a transfer of property is made
ALIENEES > ALIENEE
ALIENER > ALIEN
ALIENERS > ALIEN
ALIENING > ALIEN
ALIENISM *n* study and treatment of mental illness
ALIENISMS > ALIENISM
ALIENIST *n* psychiatrist who specializes in the legal aspects of mental illness
ALIENISTS > ALIENIST
ALIENLY > ALIEN
ALIENNESS > ALIEN
ALIENOR *n* person who transfers property to another
ALIENORS > ALIENOR
ALIENS > ALIEN
ALIF *n* first letter of Arabic alphabet
ALIFORM *adj* wing-shaped
ALIFS > ALIF
ALIGARTA *n* alligator
ALIGARTAS > ALIGARTA
ALIGHT *vb* step out of (a vehicle) ▷ *adj* on fire ▷ *adv* on fire
ALIGHTED > ALIGHT
ALIGHTING > ALIGHT
ALIGHTS > ALIGHT
ALIGN *vb* bring (a person or group) into agreement with the policy of another
ALIGNED > ALIGN
ALIGNER > ALIGN
ALIGNERS > ALIGN
ALIGNING > ALIGN
ALIGNMENT *n* arrangement in a straight line
ALIGNS > ALIGN
ALIKE *adj* like, similar ▷ *adv* in the same way
ALIKENESS > ALIKE
ALIMENT *n* something that nourishes the body ▷ *vb* support or sustain
ALIMENTAL > ALIMENT
ALIMENTED > ALIMENT
ALIMENTS > ALIMENT

ALIMONIED *adj* provided with alimony
ALIMONIES > ALIMONY
ALIMONY *n* allowance paid under a court order to a separated or divorced spouse
ALINE *a rare spelling of* > ALIGN
ALINED > ALINE
ALINEMENT > ALINE
ALINER > ALINE
ALINERS > ALINE
ALINES > ALINE
ALINING > ALINE
ALIPED *n* bat-like creatures ▷ *adj* having digits connected by a membrane
ALIPEDS > ALIPED
ALIPHATIC *adj* (of an organic compound) having an open chain structure
ALIQUANT *adj* denoting or belonging to a number that is not an exact divisor of a given number
ALIQUOT *adj* of or denoting an exact divisor of a number ▷ *n* exact divisor
ALIQUOTS > ALIQUOT
ALISMA *n* marsh plant
ALISMAS > ALISMA
ALISON *same as* > ALYSSUM
ALISONS > ALISON
ALIST *adj* leaning over
ALIT *rare past tense and past participle of* > ALIGHT
ALITERACY > ALITERATE
ALITERATE *n* person who is able to read but disinclined to do so ▷ *adj* of or relating to aliterates
ALIUNDE *adj* from a source under consideration
ALIVE *adj* living, in existence
ALIVENESS > ALIVE
ALIYA *same as* > ALIYAH
ALIYAH *n* immigration to the Holy Land
ALIYAHS > ALIYAH
ALIYAS > ALIYA
ALIYOS *n* remission of sin in Jewish faith
ALIYOT > ALIYAH
ALIYOTH > ALIYAH
ALIZARI *n* madder from Middle East
ALIZARIN *n* brownish-yellow powder or orange-red crystalline solid
ALIZARINE *n* alizarin
ALIZARINS > ALIZARIN
ALIZARIS > ALIZARI
ALKAHEST *n* hypothetical universal solvent sought by alchemists

ALKAHESTS > ALKAHEST
ALKALI *n* substance which combines with acid and neutralizes it to form a salt
ALKALIC *adj* geological term
ALKALIES > ALKALI
ALKALIFY *vb* make or become alkaline
ALKALIN *adj* leaning over
ALKALINE *adj* having the properties of or containing an alkali
ALKALIS > ALKALI
ALKALISE *same as* > ALKALIZE
ALKALISED > ALKALISE
ALKALISER > ALKALISE
ALKALISES > ALKALISE
ALKALIZE *vb* make alkaline
ALKALIZED > ALKALIZE
ALKALIZER > ALKALIZE
ALKALIZES > ALKALIZE
ALKALOID *n* any of a group of organic compounds containing nitrogen
ALKALOIDS > ALKALOID
ALKALOSES > ALKALOSIS
ALKALOSIS *n* abnormal increase in the alkalinity of the blood and extracellular fluids
ALKALOTIC > ALKALOSIS
ALKANE *n* saturated hydrocarbon
ALKANES > ALKANE
ALKANET *n* European plant whose roots yield a red dye
ALKANETS > ALKANET
ALKANNIN *same as* > ALKANET
ALKANNINS > ALKANNIN
ALKENE *n* unsaturated hydrocarbon
ALKENES > ALKENE
ALKIE *same as* > ALKY
ALKIES > ALKY
ALKINE *n* alkyne
ALKINES > ALKINE
ALKO *n* heavy drinker or alcoholic
ALKOS > ALKO
ALKOXIDE *n* chemical compound containing oxygen
ALKOXIDES > ALKOXIDE
ALKOXY *adj* of type of chemical compound containing oxygen
ALKY *n* heavy drinker or alcoholic
ALKYD *n* synthetic resin
ALKYDS > ALKYD
ALKYL *n* of or containing the monovalent group C_nH_{2n+1}
ALKYLATE *vb* add alkyl group to a compound

ALKYLATED > ALKYLATE
ALKYLATES > ALKYLATE
ALKYLIC > ALKYL
ALKYLS > ALKYL
ALKYNE *n* any unsaturated aliphatic hydrocarbon
ALKYNES > ALKYNE
ALL *adj* whole quantity or number (of) ▷ *adv* wholly, entirely ▷ *n* entire being, effort, or property
ALLANITE *n* rare black or brown mineral
ALLANITES > ALLANITE
ALLANTOIC > ALLANTOIS
ALLANTOID *adj* relating to or resembling the allantois
ALLANTOIN *n* chemical used in cosmetics
ALLANTOIS *n* membranous sac growing out of the ventral surface of the hind gut of embryonic reptiles, birds, and mammals. It combines with the chorion to form the mammalian placenta
ALLATIVE *n* word in grammatical case denoting movement towards
ALLATIVES > ALLATIVE
ALLAY *vb* reduce (fear or anger)
ALLAYED > ALLAY
ALLAYER > ALLAY
ALLAYERS > ALLAY
ALLAYING > ALLAY
ALLAYINGS > ALLAY
ALLAYMENT *n* mitigation
ALLAYS > ALLAY
ALLCOMERS *n* everyone who comes
ALLEDGE *vb* allege
ALLEDGED > ALLEDGE
ALLEDGES > ALLEDGE
ALLEDGING > ALLEDGE
ALLEE *n* avenue
ALLEES > ALLEE
ALLEGE *vb* state without proof
ALLEGED *adj* stated but not proved
ALLEGEDLY *adv* reportedly
ALLEGER > ALLEGE
ALLEGERS > ALLEGE
ALLEGES > ALLEGE
ALLEGGE *vb* alleviate
ALLEGGED > ALLEGGE
ALLEGGES > ALLEGGE
ALLEGGING > ALLEGGE
ALLEGIANT *n* loyalty
ALLEGING > ALLEGE
ALLEGORIC *adj* used in, containing, or characteristic of allegory
ALLEGORY *n* story with an underlying meaning as well as the literal one

ALLEGRO *adv* (piece to be played) in a brisk lively manner ▷ *n* piece or passage to be performed in a brisk lively manner
ALLEGROS > ALLEGRO
ALLEL *n* form of gene
ALLELE *n* genes with alternative characteristics
ALLELES > ALLELE
ALLELIC > ALLELE
ALLELISM > ALLELE
ALLELISMS > ALLELE
ALLELS > ALLEL
ALLELUIA *n* song of praise to God
ALLELUIAH *interj* alleluia
ALLELUIAS > ALLELUIA
ALLEMANDE *n* first movement of the classical suite, composed in a moderate tempo in a time signature of four-four
ALLENARLY *adv* solely
ALLERGEN *n* substance capable of causing an allergic reaction
ALLERGENS > ALLERGEN
ALLERGIC *adj* having or caused by an allergy ▷ *n* person suffering from an allergy
ALLERGICS > ALLERGIC
ALLERGIES > ALLERGY
ALLERGIN *n* allergen
ALLERGINS > ALLERGIN
ALLERGIST *n* physician skilled in the diagnosis and treatment of diseases or conditions caused by allergy
ALLERGY *n* extreme sensitivity to a substance, which causes the body to react to it
ALLERION *n* eagle in heraldry
ALLERIONS > ALLERION
ALLETHRIN *n* clear viscous amber-coloured liquid
ALLEVIANT *n* medical treatment that reduces pain but does not cure the underlying problem
ALLEVIATE *vb* lessen (pain or suffering)
ALLEY *n* narrow street or path
ALLEYCAT *n* homeless cat that roams in back streets
ALLEYCATS > ALLEYCAT
ALLEYED *adj* having alleys
ALLEYS > ALLEY
ALLEYWAY *n* narrow passage with buildings or walls on both sides
ALLEYWAYS > ALLEYWAY
ALLHEAL *n* plants with reputed healing powers
ALLHEALS > ALLHEAL
ALLIABLE *adj* able to form an alliance
ALLIAK *n* Inuit sledge

ALLIAKS > ALLIAK
ALLIANCE *n* state of being allied
ALLIANCES > ALLIANCE
ALLICE *n* species of fish
ALLICES > ALLICE
ALLICHOLY *n* melancholy
ALLICIN *n* chemical found in garlic
ALLICINS > ALLICIN
ALLIED *adj* joined, as by treaty, agreement, or marriage
ALLIES > ALLY
ALLIGARTA *n* alligator
ALLIGATE *vb* join together
ALLIGATED > ALLIGATE
ALLIGATES > ALLIGATE
ALLIGATOR *n* reptile of the crocodile family, found in the southern US and China
ALLIS *n* species of fish
ALLISES > ALLIS
ALLIUM *n* type of plant
ALLIUMS > ALLIUM
ALLNESS *n* being all
ALLNESSES > ALLNESS
ALLNIGHT *adj* lasting all night
ALLOBAR *n* form of element
ALLOBARS > ALLOBAR
ALLOCABLE > ALLOCATE
ALLOCARPY *n* production of fruit through cross-fertilization
ALLOCATE *vb* assign to someone or for a particular purpose
ALLOCATED > ALLOCATE
ALLOCATES > ALLOCATE
ALLOCATOR > ALLOCATE
ALLOD same as > ALLODIUM
ALLODIA > ALLODIUM
ALLODIAL *adj* (of land) held as an allodium
ALLODIUM *n* lands held in absolute ownership, free from such obligations as rent or services due to an overlord
ALLODIUMS > ALLODIUM
ALLODS > ALLOD
ALLODYNIA *n* pain caused by a normally painless stimulus
ALLOGAMY *n* cross-fertilization in flowering plants
ALLOGENIC *adj* having different genes
ALLOGRAFT *n* tissue graft from a donor genetically unrelated to the recipient
ALLOGRAPH *n* document written by a person who is not a party to it
ALLOMERIC *adj* of similar crystalline structure
ALLOMETRY *n* study of the growth of part of an

organism in relation to the growth of the entire organism
ALLOMONE *n* chemical substance secreted externally by certain animals, such as insects, affecting the behaviour or physiology of another species detrimentally
ALLOMONES > ALLOMONE
ALLOMORPH *n* any of the phonological representations of a single morpheme
ALLONGE *n* paper extension to bill of exchange ▷ *vb* (in fencing) lunge
ALLONGED > ALLONGE
ALLONGES > ALLONGE
ALLONGING > ALLONGE
ALLONS *interj* French word meaning let's go
ALLONYM *n* name assumed by a person
ALLONYMS > ALLONYM
ALLOPATH *n* person who practises or is skilled in allopathy
ALLOPATHS > ALLOPATH
ALLOPATHY *n* orthodox method of treating disease, by using drugs that produce an effect opposite to the effect of the disease being treated
ALLOPATRY *n* condition of taking place or existing in areas that are geographically separated from one another
ALLOPHANE *n* variously coloured amorphous mineral consisting of hydrated aluminium silicate and occurring in cracks in some sedimentary rocks
ALLOPHONE *n* any of several speech sounds that are regarded as contextual or environmental variants of the same phoneme
ALLOPLASM *n* part of the cytoplasm that is specialized to form cilia, flagella, and similar structures
ALLOSAUR *n* any large carnivorous bipedal dinosaur common in North America in late Jurassic times
ALLOSAURS > ALLOSAUR
ALLOSTERY *n* condition of an enzyme in which the structure and activity of the enzyme are modified by the binding of a metabolic molecule
ALLOT *vb* assign as a share or for a particular purpose

ALLOTMENT *n* distribution
ALLOTROPE *n* any of two or more physical forms in which an element can exist
ALLOTROPY *n* existence of an element in two or more physical forms
ALLOTS > ALLOT
ALLOTTED > ALLOT
ALLOTTEE *n* person to whom something is allotted
ALLOTTEES > ALLOTTEE
ALLOTTER *n* person who allots
ALLOTTERS > ALLOTTER
ALLOTTERY *n* something allotted
ALLOTTING > ALLOT
ALLOTYPE *n* additional type specimen selected because of differences from the original type specimen, such as opposite sex or morphological details
ALLOTYPES > ALLOTYPE
ALLOTYPIC > ALLOTYPE
ALLOTYPY *n* existence of allotypes
ALLOVER *n* fabric completely covered with a pattern
ALLOVERS > ALLOVER
ALLOW *vb* permit
ALLOWABLE *adj* permissible
ALLOWABLY > ALLOWABLE
ALLOWANCE *n* amount of money given at regular intervals
ALLOWED > ALLOW
ALLOWEDLY *adv* by general admission or agreement
ALLOWING > ALLOW
ALLOWS > ALLOW
ALLOXAN *n* chemical found in uric acid
ALLOXANS > ALLOXAN
ALLOY *n* mixture of two or more metals ▷ *vb* mix (metals)
ALLOYED > ALLOY
ALLOYING > ALLOY
ALLOYS > ALLOY
ALLOZYME *n* any one of a number of different structural forms of the same enzyme encoded by a different allele
ALLOZYMES > ALLOZYME
ALLS > ALL
ALLSEED *n* type of plant
ALLSEEDS > ALLSEED
ALLSORTS *n* assorted sweets
ALLSPICE *n* spice made from the berries of a tropical American tree
ALLSPICES > ALLSPICE

ALLUDE vb refer indirectly to
ALLUDED > ALLUDE
ALLUDES > ALLUDE
ALLUDING > ALLUDE
ALLURE n attractiveness ▷ vb entice or attract
ALLURED > ALLURE
ALLURER > ALLURE
ALLURERS > ALLURE
ALLURES > ALLURE
ALLURING adj extremely attractive
ALLUSION n indirect reference
ALLUSIONS > ALLUSION
ALLUSIVE adj containing or full of allusions
ALLUVIA > ALLUVIUM
ALLUVIAL adj of or relating to alluvium ▷ n soil consisting of alluvium
ALLUVIALS > ALLUVIAL
ALLUVION n wash of the sea or of a river
ALLUVIONS > ALLUVION
ALLUVIUM n fertile soil deposited by flowing water
ALLUVIUMS > ALLUVIUM
ALLY vb unite or be united, esp formally, as by treaty, confederation, or marriage ▷ n country, person, or group allied with another
ALLYING > ALLY
ALLYL n containing the monovalent group CH_2:$CHCH_2$
ALLYLIC > ALLYL
ALLYLS > ALLYL
ALLYOU pron all of you
ALMA same as > AKMAH
ALMAGEST n medieval treatise concerning alchemy or astrology
ALMAGESTS > ALMAGEST
ALMAH n Egyptian dancing girl
ALMAHS > ALMAH
ALMAIN n German dance
ALMAINS > ALMAIN
ALMANAC n yearly calendar with detailed information on anniversaries, phases of the moon, etc
ALMANACK same as > ALMANAC
ALMANACKS > ALMANACK
ALMANACS > ALMANAC
ALMANDINE n deep violet-red garnet
ALMANDITE n form of garnet
ALMAS > ALMA
ALME same as > ALMEH
ALMEH n Egyptian dancing girl
ALMEHS > ALMEH
ALMEMAR n area in a synagogue

ALMEMARS > ALMEMAR
ALMERIES > ALMERY
ALMERY n cupboard for church vessels
ALMES > ALME
ALMIGHTY adj all-powerful ▷ adv extremely
ALMIRAH n cupboard
ALMIRAHS > ALMIRAH
ALMNER n almoner
ALMNERS > ALMONER
ALMOND n edible oval-shaped nut which grows on a small tree
ALMONDIER > ALMONDY
ALMONDITE n violet-red garnet
ALMONDS > ALMOND
ALMONDY adj containing or resembling almond
ALMONER n formerly, a hospital social worker
ALMONERS > ALMONER
ALMONRIES > ALMONRY
ALMONRY n house of an almoner, usually the place where alms were given
ALMOST adv very nearly
ALMOUS Scots word for > ALMS
ALMS pl n gifts to the poor
ALMSGIVER n one who gives alms
ALMSHOUSE n (formerly) a house, financed by charity, which offered accommodation to the poor
ALMSMAN n person who gives or receives alms
ALMSMEN > ALMSMAN
ALMSWOMAN n woman who gives or receives alms
ALMSWOMEN > ALMSWOMAN
ALMUCE n fur-lined hood or cape
ALMUCES > ALMUCE
ALMUD n Spanish unit of measure
ALMUDE same as > ALMUD
ALMUDES > ALMUDE
ALMUDS > ALMUD
ALMUG n type of wood mentioned in Bible
ALMUGS > ALMUG
ALNAGE n measurement in ells
ALNAGER n inspector of cloth
ALNAGERS > ALNAGER
ALNAGES > ALNAGE
ALNICO n alloy including iron, nickel, and cobalt
ALNICOS > ALNICO
ALOCASIA n type of tropical plant
ALOCASIAS > ALOCASIA
ALOD n feudal estate with no superior
ALODIA > ALODIUM
ALODIAL > ALODIUM
ALODIUM same as > ALLODIUM

ALODIUMS > ALODIUM
ALODS > ALOD
ALOE n plant with fleshy spiny leaves
ALOED adj containing aloes
ALOES another name for > EAGLEWOOD
ALOESWOOD n aromatic wood of an Asian tree
ALOETIC > ALOE
ALOETICS > ALOE
ALOFT adv in the air ▷ adj in or into a high or higher place
ALOGIA n inability to speak
ALOGIAS > ALOGIA
ALOGICAL adj without logic
ALOHA a Hawaiian word for > HELLO
ALOHAS > ALOHA
ALOIN n crystalline compound
ALOINS > ALOIN
ALONE adv without anyone or anything else
ALONELY > ALONE
ALONENESS > ALONE
ALONG adv forward
ALONGSIDE adv beside (something)
ALONGST adv along
ALOO n (in Indian cookery) potato
ALOOF adj distant or haughty in manner
ALOOFLY > ALOOF
ALOOFNESS > ALOOF
ALOOS > ALOO
ALOPECIA n loss of hair
ALOPECIAS > ALOPECIA
ALOPECIC > ALOPECIA
ALOPECOID > ALOPECIA
ALOUD adv in an audible voice ▷ adj in a normal voice
ALOW adj in or into the lower rigging of a vessel, near the deck
ALOWE Scots word for > ABLAZE
ALP n high mountain
ALPACA n Peruvian llama
ALPACAS > ALPACA
ALPACCA same as > ALPACA
ALPACCAS > ALPACCA
ALPARGATA n Spanish sandal
ALPEEN n Irish cudgel
ALPEENS > ALPEEN
ALPENGLOW n reddish light on the summits of snow-covered mountain peaks at sunset or sunrise
ALPENHORN same as > ALPHORN
ALPHA n first letter in the Greek alphabet
ALPHABET n set of letters used in writing a language
ALPHABETS > ALPHABET

ALPHAS > ALPHA
ALPHASORT vb arrange in alphabetical order
ALPHATEST vb subject (an experimental product such as computer software) to an initial test
ALPHORN n wind instrument
ALPHORNS > ALPHORN
ALPHOSIS n absence of skin pigmentation, as in albinism
ALPHYL n univalent radical
ALPHYLS > ALPHYL
ALPINE adj of high mountains ▷ n mountain plant
ALPINELY > ALPINE
ALPINES > ALPINE
ALPINISM > ALPINIST
ALPINISMS > ALPINIST
ALPINIST n mountain climber
ALPINISTS > ALPINIST
ALPS > ALP
ALREADY adv before the present time
ALRIGHT adj all right
ALS > AL
ALSIKE n clover native to Europe and Asia
ALSIKES > ALSIKE
ALSO adv in addition, too
ALSOON same as > ALSOONE
ALSOONE adv as soon
ALT n octave directly above the treble staff
ALTAR n table used for Communion in Christian churches
ALTARAGE n donations placed on altar for priest
ALTARAGES > ALTARAGE
ALTARS > ALTAR
ALTARWISE adv in the position of an altar
ALTER vb make or become different
ALTERABLE > ALTER
ALTERABLY > ALTER
ALTERANT n alternative
ALTERANTS > ALTERANT
ALTERCATE vb argue, esp heatedly
ALTERED > ALTER
ALTERER > ALTER
ALTERERS > ALTER
ALTERING > ALTER
ALTERITY n quality of being different
ALTERN adj alternate
ALTERNANT adj alternating
ALTERNAT n practice of deciding precedence by lot
ALTERNATE vb (cause to) occur by turns ▷ adj occurring by turns ▷ n person who substitutes for another in his absence

ALTERNATS > ALTERNAT
ALTERNE n neighbouring but different plant group
ALTERNES > ALTERNE
ALTERS > ALTER
ALTESSE n French word for highness
ALTESSES > ALTESSE
ALTEZA n Spanish word for highness
ALTEZAS > ALTEZA
ALTEZZA n Italian word for highness
ALTEZZAS > ALTEZZA
ALTHAEA n type of plant
ALTHAEAS > ALTHAEA
ALTHEA same as > ALTHAEA
ALTHEAS > ALTHEA
ALTHO conj short form of although
ALTHORN n valved brass musical instrument
ALTHORNS > ALTHORN
ALTHOUGH conj despite the fact that; even though
ALTIGRAPH n instrument that measures altitude
ALTIMETER n instrument that measures altitude
ALTIMETRY n science of measuring altitudes, as with an altimeter
ALTIPLANO n high plateau
ALTISSIMO adj (of music) very high in pitch ▷ n as in in altissimo the octave commencing an octave above the treble clef
ALTITUDE n height above sea level
ALTITUDES > ALTITUDE
ALTO n (singer with) the highest adult male voice ▷ adj denoting such an instrument, singer, or voice
ALTOIST n person who plays the alto saxophone
ALTOISTS > ALTOIST
ALTOS > ALTO
ALTRICES pl n altricial birds
ALTRICIAL adj (of the young of some species of birds after hatching) naked, blind, and dependent on the parents for food ▷ n altricial bird, such as a pigeon
ALTRUISM n unselfish concern for the welfare of others
ALTRUISMS > ALTRUISM
ALTRUIST > ALTRUISM
ALTRUISTS > ALTRUISM
ALTS > ALT
ALU same as > ALOO
ALUDEL n pear-shaped vessel
ALUDELS > ALUDEL
ALULA n tuft of feathers
ALULAE > ALULA

ALULAR > ALULA
ALULAS > ALULA
ALUM n double sulphate of aluminium and potassium
ALUMIN same as > ALUMINA
ALUMINA n aluminium oxide
ALUMINAS > ALUMINA
ALUMINATE n salt of the ortho or meta acid forms of aluminium hydroxide
ALUMINE n French word for alumina
ALUMINES > ALUMINE
ALUMINIC adj of aluminium
ALUMINISE same as > ALUMINIZE
ALUMINIUM n light silvery-white metal that does not rust
ALUMINIZE vb cover with aluminium
ALUMINOUS adj resembling aluminium
ALUMINS > ALUMIN
ALUMINUM same as > ALUMINIUM
ALUMINUMS > ALUMINUM
ALUMISH adj like alum
ALUMIUM old name for > ALUMINIUM
ALUMIUMS > ALUMIUM
ALUMNA n female graduate of a school, college, etc
ALUMNAE > ALUMNA
ALUMNI > ALUMNUS
ALUMNUS n graduate of a college
ALUMROOT n North American plants having small white, reddish, or green bell-shaped flowers and astringent roots
ALUMROOTS > ALUMROOT
ALUMS > ALUM
ALUMSTONE same as > ALUNITE
ALUNITE n white, grey, or reddish mineral
ALUNITES > ALUNITE
ALURE n area behind battlements
ALURES > ALURE
ALUS > ALU
ALVAR n area of exposed limestone
ALVARS > ALVAR
ALVEARIES > ALVEARY
ALVEARY n beehive
ALVEATED adj with vaults like beehive
ALVEOLAR adj of, relating to, or resembling an alveolus ▷ n alveolar consonant, such as the speech sounds written t, d, and s in English
ALVEOLARS > ALVEOLAR
ALVEOLATE adj having many alveoli
ALVEOLE n alveolus
ALVEOLES > ALVEOLE

ALVEOLI > ALVEOLUS
ALVEOLUS n any small pit, cavity, or saclike dilation, such as a honeycomb cell, a tooth socket, or the tiny air sacs in the lungs
ALVINE adj of or relating to the intestines or belly
ALWAY same as > ALWAYS
ALWAYS adv at all times
ALYSSUM n garden plant with small yellow or white flowers
ALYSSUMS > ALYSSUM
AM see > BE
AMA n vessel for water
AMABILE adj sweet
AMADAVAT same as > AVADAVAT
AMADAVATS > AMADAVAT
AMADODA pl n grown men
AMADOU n spongy substance made from fungi
AMADOUS > AMADOU
AMAH n (in the East, formerly) a nurse or maidservant
AMAHS > AMAH
AMAIN adv with great strength, speed, or haste
AMAKOSI > INKHOSI
AMALGAM n blend or combination
AMALGAMS > AMALGAM
AMANDINE n protein found in almonds
AMANDINES > AMANDINE
AMANDLA n political slogan calling for power to the Black population
AMANDLAS > AMANDLA
AMANITA n type of fungus
AMANITAS > AMANITA
AMANITIN n poison from amanita
AMANITINS > AMANITIN
AMARACUS n marjoram
AMARANT n amaranth
AMARANTH n imaginary flower that never fades
AMARANTHS > AMARANTH
AMARANTIN n protein
AMARANTS > AMARANT
AMARELLE n variety of sour cherry that has pale red fruit and colourless juice
AMARELLES > AMARELLE
AMARETTI > AMARETTO
AMARETTO n Italian liqueur with a flavour of almonds
AMARETTOS > AMARETTO
AMARNA adj pertaining to the reign of the Pharaoh Akhenaton
AMARONE n strong dry red Italian wine
AMARONES > AMARONE
AMARYLLID n plant of the amaryllis family
AMARYLLIS n lily-like plant with large red, pink,

or white flowers
AMAS > AMA
AMASS vb collect or accumulate
AMASSABLE > AMASS
AMASSED > AMASS
AMASSER > AMASS
AMASSERS > AMASS
AMASSES > AMASS
AMASSING > AMASS
AMASSMENT > AMASS
AMATE vb match
AMATED > AMATE
AMATES > AMATE
AMATEUR n person who engages in a sport or activity as a pastime rather than as a profession ▷ adj not professional
AMATEURS > AMATEUR
AMATING > AMATE
AMATION n lovemaking
AMATIONS > AMATION
AMATIVE a rare word for > AMOROUS
AMATIVELY > AMATIVE
AMATOL n explosive mixture
AMATOLS > AMATOL
AMATORIAL same as > AMATORY
AMATORIAN > AMATORY
AMATORY adj relating to romantic or sexual love
AMAUROSES > AMAUROSIS
AMAUROSIS n blindness, esp when occurring without observable damage to the eye
AMAUROTIC > AMAUROSIS
AMAUT n hooded coat worn by Inuit women
AMAUTI same as > AMAUT
AMAUTIK same as > AMAUT
AMAUTIKS > AMAUTIK
AMAUTIS > AMAUT
AMAUTS > AMAUT
AMAZE vb surprise greatly, astound
AMAZED > AMAZE
AMAZEDLY > AMAZE
AMAZEMENT n incredulity or great astonishment
AMAZES > AMAZE
AMAZING adj causing wonder or astonishment
AMAZINGLY > AMAZING
AMAZON n any tall, strong, or aggressive woman
AMAZONIAN > AMAZON
AMAZONITE n green variety of microcline used as a gemstone
AMAZONS > AMAZON
AMBACH same as > AMBATCH
AMBACHES > AMBACH
AMBAGE n ambiguity
AMBAGES > AMBAGE
AMBAGIOUS > AMBAGE
AMBAN n Chinese official

AMBANS > AMBAN

AMBARI same as **>** AMBARY

AMBARIES > AMBARY

AMBARIS > AMBARI

AMBARY n tropical Asian plant that yields a fibre similar to jute

AMBASSAGE n embassy

AMBASSIES > AMBASSY

AMBASSY n embassy

AMBATCH n tree or shrub

AMBATCHES > AMBATCH

AMBEER n saliva coloured by tobacco juice

AMBEERS > AMBEER

AMBER n clear yellowish fossil resin ⊳ adj brownish-yellow

AMBERED adj fixed in amber

AMBERGRIS n waxy substance secreted by the sperm whale, used in making perfumes

AMBERIES > AMBERY

AMBERINA n type of glassware

AMBERINAS > AMBERINA

AMBERITE n powder like amber

AMBERITES > AMBERITE

AMBERJACK n type of large fish with golden markings when young, found in Atlantic waters

AMBEROID n synthetic amber made by compressing pieces of amber and other resins together at a high temperature

AMBEROIDS > AMBEROID

AMBEROUS adj like amber

AMBERS > AMBER

AMBERY adj like amber

AMBIANCE same as **>** AMBIENCE

AMBIANCES > AMBIANCE

AMBIENCE n atmosphere of a place

AMBIENCES > AMBIENCE

AMBIENT adj surrounding ⊳ n ambient music

AMBIENTS > AMBIENT

AMBIGUITY n possibility of interpreting an expression in more than one way

AMBIGUOUS adj having more than one possible meaning

AMBIPOLAR adj (of plasmas and semiconductors) involving both positive and negative charge carriers

AMBIT n limits or boundary

AMBITION n desire for success

AMBITIONS > AMBITION

AMBITIOUS adj having a strong desire for success

AMBITS > AMBIT

AMBITTY adj crystalline and brittle

AMBIVERT n person who is intermediate between an extrovert and an introvert

AMBIVERTS > AMBIVERT

AMBLE vb walk at a leisurely pace ⊳ n leisurely walk or pace

AMBLED > AMBLE

AMBLER > AMBLE

AMBLERS > AMBLE

AMBLES > AMBLE

AMBLING n walking at a leisurely pace

AMBLINGS > AMBLING

AMBLYOPIA n impaired vision with no discernible damage to the eye or optic nerve

AMBLYOPIC > AMBLYOPIA

AMBO n early Christian pulpit

AMBOINA same as **>** AMBOYNA

AMBOINAS > AMBOINA

AMBONES > AMBO

AMBOS > AMBO

AMBOYNA n mottled curly-grained wood

AMBOYNAS > AMBOYNA

AMBRIES > AMBRY

AMBROID same as **>** AMBEROID

AMBROIDS > AMBROID

AMBROSIA n anything delightful to taste or smell

AMBROSIAL > AMBROSIA

AMBROSIAN > AMBROSIA

AMBROSIAS > AMBROSIA

AMBROTYPE n early type of glass negative that could be made to appear as a positive by backing it with black varnish or paper

AMBRY n cupboard in the wall of a church

AMBSACE n double ace, the lowest throw at dice

AMBSACES > AMBSACE

AMBULACRA n radial bands on the ventral surface of echinoderms, such as the starfish and sea urchin, on which the tube feet are situated

AMBULANCE n motor vehicle designed to carry sick or injured people

AMBULANT adj moving about from place to place

AMBULANTS > AMBULANT

AMBULATE vb wander about or move from one place to another

AMBULATED > AMBULATE

AMBULATES > AMBULATE

AMBULATOR n person who walks

AMBULETTE n motor vehicle designed for transporting ill or handicapped people

AMBUSCADE n ambush ⊳ vb ambush or lie in ambush

AMBUSCADO n ambuscade

AMBUSH n act of waiting in a concealed position to make a surprise attack ⊳ vb attack from a concealed position

AMBUSHED > AMBUSH

AMBUSHER > AMBUSH

AMBUSHERS > AMBUSH

AMBUSHES > AMBUSH

AMBUSHING > AMBUSH

AME n soul

AMEARST old form of **>** AMERCE

AMEBA same as **>** AMOEBA

AMEBAE > AMEBA

AMEBAN > AMEBA

AMEBAS > AMEBA

AMEBEAN same as **>** AMOEBEAN

AMEBIASES > AMEBIASIS

AMEBIASIS n disease caused by amoeba

AMEBIC > AMEBA

AMEBOCYTE n any cell having properties similar to an amoeba, such as shape, mobility, and ability to engulf particles

AMEBOID same as **>** AMOEBOID

AMEER n (formerly) the ruler of Afghanistan

AMEERATE n country ruled by an ameer

AMEERATES > AMEERATE

AMEERS > AMEER

AMEIOSES > AMEIOSIS

AMEIOSIS n absence of pairing of chromosomes during meiosis

AMELCORN n variety of wheat

AMELCORNS > AMELCORN

AMELIA n congenital absence of arms or legs

AMELIAS > AMELIA

AMEN n term used at the end of a prayer or religious statement ⊳ vb say amen

AMENABLE adj likely or willing to cooperate

AMENABLY > AMENABLE

AMENAGE vb tame

AMENAGED > AMENAGE

AMENAGES > AMENAGE

AMENAGING > AMENAGE

AMENAUNCE n person's bearing

AMEND vb make small changes

AMENDABLE > AMEND

AMENDE n public apology

AMENDED > AMEND

AMENDER > AMEND

AMENDERS > AMEND

AMENDES > AMENDE

AMENDING > AMEND

AMENDMENT n improvement or correction

AMENDS n recompense for injury, insult, etc

AMENE adj pleasant

AMENED > AMEN

AMENING > AMEN

AMENITIES > AMENITY

AMENITY n useful or enjoyable feature

AMENS > AMEN

AMENT n mentally deficient person

AMENTA > AMENTUM

AMENTAL > AMENTUM

AMENTIA n severe mental deficiency, usually congenital

AMENTIAS > AMENTIA

AMENTS > AMENT

AMENTUM same as **>** AMENT

AMERCE vb punish by a fine

AMERCED > AMERCE

AMERCER > AMERCE

AMERCERS > AMERCE

AMERCES > AMERCE

AMERCING > AMERCE

AMERICIUM n white metallic element artificially produced from plutonium

AMES > AME

AMESACE same as **>** AMBSACE

AMESACES > AMESACE

AMETHYST n bluish-violet variety of quartz used as a gemstone ⊳ adj purple or violet

AMETHYSTS > AMETHYST

AMETROPIA n loss of ability to focus images on the retina, caused by an imperfection in the refractive function of the eye

AMETROPIC > AMETROPIA

AMI n male friend

AMIA n species of fish

AMIABLE adj friendly, pleasant-natured

AMIABLY > AMIABLE

AMIANTHUS n any of the fine silky varieties of asbestos

AMIANTUS n amianthus

AMIAS > AMIA

AMICABLE adj friendly

AMICABLY > AMICABLE

AMICE n item of clothing

AMICES > AMICE

AMICI > AMICUS

AMICUS n Latin for friend

AMID prep in the middle of, among ⊳ n amide

AMIDASE n enzyme

AMIDASES > AMIDASE

AMIDE n any organic compound containing the group —CONH$_2$

AMIDES > AMIDE

AMIDIC > AMIDE

AMIDIN n form of starch
AMIDINE n crystalline compound
AMIDINES > AMIDINE
AMIDINS > AMIDIN
AMIDMOST adv in the middle
AMIDO adj containing amide
AMIDOGEN n chemical compound derived from ammonia
AMIDOGENS > AMIDOGEN
AMIDOL n chemical used in developing photographs
AMIDOLS > AMIDOL
AMIDONE n pain-killing drug
AMIDONES > AMIDONE
AMIDS same as > AMID
AMIDSHIP adj in the middle of a ship
AMIDSHIPS adv at or towards the middle of a ship ▷ adj at, near, or towards the centre of a vessel
AMIDST same as > AMID
AMIE n female friend
AMIES > AMIE
AMIGA n Spanish female friend
AMIGAS > AMIGA
AMIGO n friend
AMIGOS > AMIGO
AMILDAR n manager in India
AMILDARS > AMILDAR
AMIN same as > AMINE
AMINE n chemical
AMINES > AMINE
AMINIC > AMINE
AMINITIES > AMINITY
AMINITY n amenity
AMINO n as in amino acid type of organic compound which is an essential component of proteins
AMINOS > AMINO
AMINS > AMIN
AMIR n (formerly) the ruler of Afghanistan
AMIRATE > AMIR
AMIRATES > AMIR
AMIRS > AMIR
AMIS > AMI
AMISES > AMI
AMISS adv wrongly, badly ▷ adj wrong, faulty ▷ n evil deed
AMISSES > AMISS
AMISSIBLE adj likely to be lost
AMISSING adj missing
AMITIES > AMITY
AMITOSES > AMITOSIS
AMITOSIS n unusual form of cell division in which the nucleus and cytoplasm divide by constriction without the formation of chromosomes

AMITOTIC > AMITOSIS
AMITROLE n pesticide
AMITROLES > AMITROLE
AMITY n friendship
AMLA n a species of Indian tree
AMLAS > AMLA
AMMAN same as > AMTMAN
AMMANS > AMMAN
AMMETER n instrument for measuring electric current
AMMETERS > AMMETER
AMMINE n chemical compound
AMMINES > AMMINE
AMMINO adj containing ammonia molecules
AMMIRAL old word for > ADMIRAL
AMMIRALS > AMMIRAL
AMMO n ammunition
AMMOCETE n ammocoete
AMMOCETES > AMMOCETE
AMMOCOETE n larva of primitive jawless vertebrates, such as the lamprey, that lives buried in mud and feeds on microorganisms
AMMOLITE n fossilized ammonite shell
AMMOLITES > AMMOLITE
AMMON n Asian wild sheep
AMMONAL n explosive
AMMONALS > AMMONAL
AMMONATE same as > AMMINE
AMMONATES > AMMONATE
AMMONIA n strong-smelling alkaline gas containing hydrogen and nitrogen
AMMONIAC n strong-smelling gum resin obtained from the stems of a N Asian plant
AMMONIACS > AMMONIAC
AMMONIAS > AMMONIA
AMMONIATE vb unite or treat with ammonia
AMMONIC adj of ammonia
AMMONICAL > AMMONIC
AMMONIFY vb treat or impregnate with ammonia or a compound of ammonia
AMMONITE n fossilized spiral shell of an extinct sea creature
AMMONITES > AMMONITE
AMMONITIC > AMMONITE
AMMONIUM n type of monovalent chemical group
AMMONIUMS > AMMONIUM
AMMONO adj using ammonia
AMMONOID n type of fossil
AMMONOIDS > AMMONOID
AMMONS > AMMON
AMMOS > AMMO
AMNESIA n loss of memory
AMNESIAC > AMNESIA

AMNESIACS > AMNESIA
AMNESIAS > AMNESIA
AMNESIC > AMNESIA
AMNESICS > AMNESIA
AMNESTIC adj relating to amnesia
AMNESTIED > AMNESTY
AMNESTIES > AMNESTY
AMNESTY n general pardon for offences against a government ▷ vb overlook or forget (an offence)
AMNIA > AMNION
AMNIC adj relating to amnion
AMNIO n amniocentesis
AMNION n innermost of two membranes enclosing an embryo
AMNIONIC > AMNION
AMNIONS > AMNION
AMNIOS > AMNIO
AMNIOTE n group of animals
AMNIOTES > AMNIOTE
AMNIOTIC adj of or relating to the amnion
AMNIOTOMY n breaking of the membrane surrounding a fetus to induce labour
AMOEBA n microscopic single-celled animal able to change its shape
AMOEBAE > AMOEBA
AMOEBAEAN adj of or relating to lines of verse dialogue that answer each other alternately
AMOEBAN > AMOEBA
AMOEBAS > AMOEBA
AMOEBEAN same as > AMOEBAEAN
AMOEBIC > AMOEBA
AMOEBOID adj of, related to, or resembling amoebae
AMOK n state of murderous frenzy, originally observed among Malays
AMOKS > AMOK
AMOKURA n type of sea bird
AMOKURAS > AMOKURA
AMOLE n American plant
AMOLES > AMOLE
AMOMUM n plant of ginger family
AMOMUMS > AMOMUM
AMONG prep in the midst of
AMONGST same as > AMONG
AMOOVE vb stir someone's emotions
AMOOVED > AMOOVE
AMOOVES > AMOOVE
AMOOVING > AMOOVE
AMORAL adj without moral standards
AMORALISM > AMORAL
AMORALIST > AMORAL
AMORALITY > AMORAL
AMORALLY > AMORAL
AMORANCE n condition of being in love
AMORANCES > AMORANCE

AMORANT > AMORANCE
AMORCE n small percussion cap
AMORCES > AMORCE
AMORET n sweetheart
AMORETS > AMORET
AMORETTI > AMORETTO
AMORETTO n (esp in painting) a small chubby naked boy representing a cupid
AMORETTOS > AMORETTO
AMORINI > AMORINO
AMORINO same as > AMORETTO
AMORISM > AMORIST
AMORISMS > AMORIST
AMORIST n lover or a writer about love
AMORISTIC > AMORIST
AMORISTS > AMORIST
AMORNINGS adv each morning
AMOROSA n lover
AMOROSAS > AMOROSA
AMOROSITY n quality of being amorous
AMOROSO adv (to be played) lovingly ▷ n sherry
AMOROSOS > AMOROSO
AMOROUS adj feeling, showing, or relating to sexual love
AMOROUSLY > AMOROUS
AMORPHISM > AMORPHOUS
AMORPHOUS adj without distinct shape
AMORT adj in low spirits
AMORTISE same as > AMORTIZE
AMORTISED > AMORTISE
AMORTISES > AMORTISE
AMORTIZE vb pay off (a debt) gradually by periodic transfers to a sinking fund
AMORTIZED > AMORTIZE
AMORTIZES > AMORTIZE
AMOSITE n form of asbestos
AMOSITES > AMOSITE
AMOTION n act of removing
AMOTIONS > AMOTION
AMOUNT n extent or quantity ▷ vb be equal or add up to
AMOUNTED > AMOUNT
AMOUNTING > AMOUNT
AMOUNTS > AMOUNT
AMOUR n (secret) love affair
AMOURETTE n minor love affair
AMOURS > AMOUR
AMOVE vb stir someone's emotions
AMOVED > AMOVE
AMOVES > AMOVE
AMOVING > AMOVE
AMOWT same as > AMAUT
AMOWTS > AMOWT
AMP n ampere ▷ vb excite or become excited

AMPASSIES > AMPASSY

AMPASSY n ampersand

AMPED > AMP

AMPERAGE n strength of an electric current measured in amperes

AMPERAGES > AMPERAGE

AMPERE n basic unit of electric current

AMPERES > AMPERE

AMPERSAND n character (&), meaning and

AMPERZAND n ampersand

AMPHIBIA n class of amphibians

AMPHIBIAN n type of animal that lives on land but breeds in water

AMPHIBOLE n any of a large group of minerals consisting of the silicates of calcium, iron, magnesium, sodium, and aluminium

AMPHIBOLY n ambiguity of expression, esp where due to a grammatical construction

AMPHIGORY n piece of nonsensical writing in verse or, less commonly, prose

AMPHIOXI > AMPHIOXUS

AMPHIOXUS another name for the **>** LANCELET

AMPHIPATH adj of or relating to a molecule that possesses both hydrophobic and hydrophilic elements

AMPHIPOD n type of marine or freshwater crustacean with a flat body

AMPHIPODS > AMPHIPOD

AMPHOLYTE n electrolyte that can be acid or base

AMPHORA n two-handled ancient Greek or Roman jar

AMPHORAE > AMPHORA

AMPHORAL > AMPHORA

AMPHORAS > AMPHORA

AMPHORIC adj resembling the sound produced by blowing into a bottle. Amphoric breath sounds are heard through a stethoscope placed over a cavity in the lung

AMPING > AMP

AMPLE adj more than sufficient

AMPLENESS > AMPLE

AMPLER > AMPLE

AMPLEST > AMPLE

AMPLEXUS n mating in amphibians

AMPLIDYNE n magnetic amplifier

AMPLIFIED > AMPLIFY

AMPLIFIER n device used to amplify a current or sound signal

AMPLIFIES > AMPLIFY

AMPLIFY vb increase the strength of (a current or sound signal)

AMPLITUDE n greatness of extent

AMPLOSOME n stocky body type

AMPLY adv fully or generously

AMPOULE n small sealed glass vessel

AMPOULES > AMPOULE

AMPS > AMP

AMPUL n ampoule

AMPULE same as **>** AMPOULE

AMPULES > AMPULE

AMPULLA n dilated end part of certain tubes in the body

AMPULLAE > AMPULLA

AMPULLAR > AMPULLA

AMPULLARY > AMPULLA

AMPULS > AMPUL

AMPUTATE vb cut off (a limb or part of a limb) for medical reasons

AMPUTATED > AMPUTATE

AMPUTATES > AMPUTATE

AMPUTATOR > AMPUTATE

AMPUTEE n person who has had a limb amputated

AMPUTEES > AMPUTEE

AMREETA same as **>** AMRITA

AMREETAS > AMREETA

AMRIT n liquid used in the Amrit Ceremony

AMRITA n ambrosia of the gods that bestows immortality

AMRITAS > AMRITA

AMRITS > AMRIT

AMSINCKIA n Californian herb

AMTMAN n magistrate in parts of Europe

AMTMANS > AMTMAN

AMTRAC n amphibious tracked vehicle

AMTRACK same as **>** AMTRAC

AMTRACKS > AMTRACK

AMTRACS > AMTRAC

AMTRAK same as **>** AMTRAC

AMTRAKS > AMTRAK

AMU n unit of mass

AMUCK same as **>** AMOK

AMUCKS > AMUCK

AMULET n something carried or worn as a protection against evil

AMULETIC > AMULET

AMULETS > AMULET

AMUS > AMU

AMUSABLE adj capable of being amused

AMUSE vb cause to laugh or smile

AMUSEABLE same as **>** AMUSABLE

AMUSED > AMUSE

AMUSEDLY > AMUSE

AMUSEMENT n state of being amused

AMUSER > AMUSE

AMUSERS > AMUSE

AMUSES > AMUSE

AMUSETTE n type of light cannon

AMUSETTES > AMUSETTE

AMUSIA n inability to recognize musical tones

AMUSIAS > AMUSIA

AMUSIC > AMUSIA

AMUSING adj mildly entertaining

AMUSINGLY > AMUSING

AMUSIVE adj deceptive

AMYGDAL n almond

AMYGDALA n almond-shaped part, such as a tonsil or a lobe of the cerebellum

AMYGDALAE > AMYGDALA

AMYGDALE n vesicle in a volcanic rock, formed from a bubble of escaping gas, that has become filled with light-coloured minerals, such as quartz and calcite

AMYGDALES > AMYGDALE

AMYGDALIN n white soluble bitter-tasting crystalline glycoside extracted from bitter almonds

AMYGDALS > AMYGDAL

AMYGDULE same as **>** AMYGDALE

AMYGDULES > AMYGDULE

AMYL n chemical compound

AMYLASE n enzyme

AMYLASES > AMYLASE

AMYLENE another name (no longer in technical usage) for **>** PENTENE

AMYLENES > AMYLENE

AMYLIC adj of or derived from amyl

AMYLOGEN n soluble part of starch

AMYLOGENS > AMYLOGEN

AMYLOID n complex protein ▷ adj starchlike

AMYLOIDAL > AMYLOID

AMYLOIDS > AMYLOID

AMYLOPSIN n enzyme of the pancreatic juice that converts starch into sugar

AMYLOSE n type of chemical

AMYLOSES > AMYLOSE

AMYLS > AMYL

AMYLUM another name for **>** STARCH

AMYLUMS > AMYLUM

AMYOTONIA another name for **>** MYOTONIA

AMYTAL n as in sodium amytal type of sedative

AMYTALS > AMYTAL

AN adj form of **a** used before vowels ▷ n additional condition

ANA adv in equal quantities ▷ n collection of reminiscences

ANABAENA n type of freshwater alga sometimes found in drinking water, giving it a fishy taste and smell

ANABAENAS > ANABAENA

ANABANTID n type of spiny-finned fish of the family which includes the fighting fish, climbing perch, and gourami

ANABAS n type of fish

ANABASES > ANABASIS

ANABASIS n march of Cyrus the Younger and his Greek mercenaries from Sardis to Cunaxa in Babylonia in 401 BC

ANABATIC adj (of air currents) rising upwards, esp up slopes

ANABIOSES > ANABIOSIS

ANABIOSIS n ability to return to life after apparent death

ANABIOTIC > ANABIOSIS

ANABLEPS n type of tropical freshwater fish with eyes adapted for seeing both in air and water

ANABOLIC adj of or relating to anabolism

ANABOLISM n metabolic process in which body tissues are synthesized from food

ANABOLITE n product of anabolism

ANABRANCH n stream that leaves a river and enters it again further downstream

ANACHARIS n water plant

ANACLINAL adj (of valleys and similar formations) progressing in a direction opposite to the dip of the surrounding rock strata

ANACLISES > ANACLITIC

ANACLISIS > ANACLITIC

ANACLITIC adj of or relating to relationships that are characterized by the strong dependence of one person on others or another

ANACONDA n large S American snake which kills by constriction

ANACONDAS > ANACONDA

ANACRUSES > ANACRUSIS

ANACRUSIS n one or more unstressed syllables

at the beginning of a line of verse

ANADEM n garland for the head

ANADEMS > ANADEM

ANAEMIA n deficiency in the number of red blood cells

ANAEMIAS > ANAEMIA

ANAEMIC adj having anaemia

ANAEROBE n organism that does not require oxygen

ANAEROBES > ANAEROBE

ANAEROBIA same as > ANAEROBES

ANAEROBIC adj not requiring oxygen

ANAGLYPH n stereoscopic picture consisting of two images of the same object, taken from slightly different angles

ANAGLYPHS > ANAGLYPH

ANAGLYPHY > ANAGLYPH

ANAGOGE n allegorical interpretation

ANAGOGES > ANAGOGE

ANAGOGIC > ANAGOGE

ANAGOGIES > ANAGOGY

ANAGOGY same as > ANAGOGE

ANAGRAM n word or phrase made by rearranging the letters of another word or phrase

ANAGRAMS > ANAGRAM

ANAL adj of the anus

ANALCIME same as > ANALCITE

ANALCIMES > ANALCIME

ANALCIMIC > ANALCIME

ANALCITE n white, grey, or colourless zeolite mineral

ANALCITES > ANALCITE

ANALECTA same as > ANALECTS

ANALECTIC > ANALECTS

ANALECTS pl n selected literary passages from one or more works

ANALEMMA n graduated scale shaped like a figure of eight that indicates the daily declination of the sun

ANALEMMAS > ANALEMMA

ANALEPTIC adj (of a drug, etc) stimulating the central nervous system ▷ n any drug, such as doxapram, that stimulates the central nervous system

ANALGESIA n absence of pain

ANALGESIC adj (drug) relieving pain ▷ n drug that relieves pain

ANALGETIC n painkilling drug

ANALGIA same as > ANALGESIA

ANALGIAS > ANALGIA

ANALITIES > ANALITY

ANALITY n quality of being psychologically anal

ANALLY > ANAL

ANALOG same as > ANALOGUE

ANALOGA > ANALOGON

ANALOGIC > ANALOGY

ANALOGIES > ANALOGY

ANALOGISE same as > ANALOGIZE

ANALOGISM > ANALOGIZE

ANALOGIST > ANALOGY

ANALOGIZE vb use analogy

ANALOGON n analogue

ANALOGONS > ANALOGON

ANALOGOUS adj similar in some respects

ANALOGS > ANALOG

ANALOGUE n something that is similar in some respects to something else ▷ adj displaying information by means of a dial

ANALOGUES > ANALOGUE

ANALOGY n similarity in some respects

ANALYSAND n any person who is undergoing psychoanalysis

ANALYSE vb make an analysis of (something)

ANALYSED > ANALYSE

ANALYSER > ANALYSE

ANALYSERS > ANALYSE

ANALYSES > ANALYSIS

ANALYSING > ANALYSE

ANALYSIS n separation of a whole into its parts for study and interpretation

ANALYST n person skilled in analysis

ANALYSTS > ANALYST

ANALYTE n substance that is being analyzed

ANALYTES > ANALYTE

ANALYTIC adj relating to analysis ▷ n analytical logic

ANALYTICS > ANALYTIC

ANALYZE same as > ANALYSE

ANALYZED > ANALYZE

ANALYZER > ANALYZE

ANALYZERS > ANALYZE

ANALYZES > ANALYZE

ANALYZING > ANALYZE

ANAMNESES > ANAMNESIS

ANAMNESIS n ability to recall past events

ANAMNIOTE n any vertebrate animal, such as a fish or amphibian, that lacks an amnion, chorion, and allantois during embryonic development

ANAN interj expression of failure to understand

ANANA n pineapple

ANANAS n plant related to the pineapple

ANANASES > ANANAS

ANANDA n Buddhist principle of extreme happiness

ANANDAS > ANANDA

ANANDROUS adj (of flowers) having no stamens

ANANKE n unalterable necessity

ANANKES > ANANKE

ANANTHOUS adj (of higher plants) having no flowers

ANAPAEST n metrical foot of three syllables, the first two short, the last long

ANAPAESTS > ANAPAEST

ANAPEST same as > ANAPAEST

ANAPESTIC > ANAPEST

ANAPESTS > ANAPEST

ANAPHASE n third stage of mitosis, during which the chromatids separate and migrate towards opposite ends of the spindle

ANAPHASES > ANAPHASE

ANAPHASIC > ANAPHASE

ANAPHOR n word referring back to a previous word

ANAPHORA n use of a word such as a pronoun that has the same reference as a word previously used in the same discourse

ANAPHORAL > ANAPHORA

ANAPHORAS > ANAPHORA

ANAPHORIC adj of or relating to anaphorism

ANAPHORS > ANAPHOR

ANAPLASIA n reversion of plant or animal cells to a simpler less differentiated form

ANAPLASTY n plastic surgery

ANAPTYXES > ANAPTYXIS

ANAPTYXIS n insertion of a short vowel between consonants in order to make a word more easily pronounceable

ANARCH n instigator or personification of anarchy

ANARCHAL > ANARCHY

ANARCHIAL > ANARCHY

ANARCHIC > ANARCHY

ANARCHIES > ANARCHY

ANARCHISE vb make anarchic

ANARCHISM n doctrine advocating the abolition of government

ANARCHIST n person who advocates the abolition of government

ANARCHIZE vb make anarchic

ANARCHS > ANARCH

ANARCHY n lawlessness and disorder

ANARTHRIA n loss of the ability to speak coherently

ANARTHRIC > ANARTHRIA

ANAS > ANA

ANASARCA n generalized accumulation of serous fluid within the subcutaneous connective tissue, resulting in oedema

ANASARCAS > ANASARCA

ANASTASES > ANASTASIS

ANASTASIS n Christ's harrowing of hell

ANASTATIC > ANASTASIS

ANATA n Buddhist belief

ANATAS > ANATA

ANATASE n rare blue or black mineral

ANATASES > ANATASE

ANATEXES > ANATEXIS

ANATEXIS n partial melting of rocks

ANATHEMA n detested person or thing

ANATHEMAS > ANATHEMA

ANATMAN same as > ANATA

ANATMANS > ANATMAN

ANATOMIC > ANATOMY

ANATOMIES > ANATOMY

ANATOMISE same as > ANATOMIZE

ANATOMIST n expert in anatomy

ANATOMIZE vb dissect (an animal or plant)

ANATOMY n science of the structure of the body

ANATOXIN n bacterial toxin used in inoculation

ANATOXINS > ANATOXIN

ANATROPY n (of a plant ovule) condition of being inverted during development by a bending of the stalk (funicle) attaching it to the carpel

ANATTA n annatto

ANATTAS > ANATTA

ANATTO same as > ANNATTO

ANATTOS > ANNATTO

ANAXIAL adj asymmetrical

ANBURIES > ANBURY

ANBURY n soft spongy tumour occurring in horses and oxen

ANCE dialect form of > ONCE

ANCESTOR n person from whom one is descended

ANCESTORS > ANCESTOR

ANCESTRAL adj of or inherited from ancestors ▷ n relation that holds between x and y if there is a chain of instances of a given relation leading from x to y

ANCESTRY n lineage or descent

ANCHO *n* chili pepper
ANCHOR *n* heavy hooked device attached to a boat by a cable and dropped overboard to fasten the ship to the sea bottom ▷ *vb* fasten with or as if with an anchor
ANCHORAGE *n* place where boats can be anchored
ANCHORED > ANCHOR
ANCHORESS > ANCHORITE
ANCHORET *n* anchorite
ANCHORETS > ANCHORET
ANCHORING > ANCHOR
ANCHORITE *n* religious recluse
ANCHORMAN *n* broadcaster in a central studio who links up and presents items from outside camera units and other studios
ANCHORMEN > ANCHORMAN
ANCHORS *pl n* brakes of a motor vehicle
ANCHOS > ANCHO
ANCHOVETA *n* type of small anchovy of the American Pacific, used as bait by tuna fishermen
ANCHOVIES > ANCHOVY
ANCHOVY *n* small strong-tasting fish
ANCHUSA *n* Eurasian plant
ANCHUSAS > ANCHUSA
ANCHUSIN *same as* > ALKANET
ANCHUSINS > ANCHUSIN
ANCHYLOSE *same as* > ANKYLOSE
ANCIENT *adj* dating from very long ago ▷ *n* member of a civilized nation in the ancient world, esp a Greek, Roman, or Hebrew
ANCIENTER > ANCIENT
ANCIENTLY *adv* in ancient times
ANCIENTRY *n* quality of being ancient
ANCIENTS > ANCIENT
ANCILE *n* mythical Roman shield
ANCILIA > ANCILE
ANCILLA *n* Latin word for servant
ANCILLAE > ANCILLA
ANCILLARY *adj* supporting the main work of an organization ▷ *n* subsidiary or auxiliary thing or person
ANCILLAS > ANCILLA
ANCIPITAL *adj* flattened and having two edges
ANCLE *old spelling of* > ANKLE
ANCLES > ANCLE
ANCOME *n* inflammation
ANCOMES > ANCOME

ANCON *n* projecting bracket
ANCONAL > ANCON
ANCONE *same as* > ANCON
ANCONEAL > ANCON
ANCONES > ANCONE
ANCONOID > ANCON
ANCORA *adv* Italian for encore
ANCRESS *n* female anchorite
ANCRESSES > ANCRESS
AND *n* additional matter or problem
ANDANTE *adv* (piece to be played) moderately slowly ▷ *n* passage or piece to be performed moderately slowly
ANDANTES > ANDANTE
ANDANTINI > ANDANTINO
ANDANTINO *adv* slightly faster or slower than andante ▷ *n* passage or piece to be performed in this way
ANDESINE *n* feldspar mineral of the plagioclase series
ANDESINES > ANDESINE
ANDESITE *n* fine-grained tan or grey volcanic rock
ANDESITES > ANDESITE
ANDESITIC > ANDESITE
ANDESYTE *n* andesite
ANDESYTES > ANDESYTE
ANDIRON *n* iron stand for supporting logs in a fireplace
ANDIRONS > ANDIRON
ANDOUILLE *n* spicy smoked pork sausage with a blackish skin
ANDRADITE *n* yellow, green, or brownish-black garnet
ANDRO *n* type of sex hormone
ANDROECIA *n* stamens of flowering plants collectively
ANDROGEN *n* any of several steroids, produced as hormones by the testes or made synthetically, that promote development of male sexual organs and male secondary sexual characteristics
ANDROGENS > ANDROGEN
ANDROGYNE *n* person having both male and female sexual characteristics and genital tissues
ANDROGYNY *n* condition of having male and female characteristics
ANDROID *n* robot resembling a human ▷ *adj* resembling a human being
ANDROIDS > ANDROID

ANDROLOGY *n* branch of medicine concerned with diseases and conditions specific to men
ANDROMEDA *n* type of shrub
ANDROS > ANDRO
ANDS > AND
ANDVILE *old form of* > ANVIL
ANDVILES > ANDVILE
ANE *Scots word for* > ONE
ANEAR *adv* nearly ▷ *vb* approach
ANEARED > ANEAR
ANEARING > ANEAR
ANEARS > ANEAR
ANEATH *Scots word for* > BENEATH
ANECDOTA *n* unpublished writings
ANECDOTAL *adj* containing or consisting exclusively of anecdotes rather than connected discourse or research conducted under controlled conditions
ANECDOTE *n* short amusing account of an incident
ANECDOTES > ANECDOTE
ANECDOTIC > ANECDOTE
ANECDYSES > ANECDYSIS
ANECDYSIS *n* period between moults in arthropods
ANECHOIC *adj* having a low degree of reverberation of sound
ANELACE *same as* > ANLACE
ANELACES > ANELACE
ANELASTIC *adj* not elastic
ANELE *vb* anoint, esp to give extreme unction to
ANELED > ANELE
ANELES > ANELE
ANELING > ANELE
ANELLI *pl n* pasta shaped like small rings
ANEMIA *n* anaemia
ANEMIAS > ANEMIA
ANEMIC *same as* > ANAEMIC
ANEMOGRAM *n* record produced by anemograph
ANEMOLOGY *n* study of winds
ANEMONE *n* plant with white, purple, or red flowers
ANEMONES > ANEMONE
ANEMOSES > ANEMOSIS
ANEMOSIS *n* cracking in timber caused by wind affecting growing tree
ANENST *dialect word for* > AGAINST
ANENT *prep* lying against
ANERGIA *n* anergy
ANERGIAS > ANERGIA

ANERGIC > ANERGY
ANERGIES > ANERGY
ANERGY *n* lack of energy
ANERLY *Scots word for* > ONLY
ANEROID *adj* not containing a liquid ▷ *n* barometer that does not contain liquid
ANEROIDS > ANEROID
ANES > ANE
ANESTRA > ANESTRUS
ANESTRI > ANESTRUS
ANESTROUS > ANESTRUS
ANESTRUM *n* anestrus
ANESTRUS *same as* > ANOESTRUS
ANETHOL *n* substance derived from oil of anise
ANETHOLE *n* white water-soluble crystalline substance with a liquorice-like odour
ANETHOLES > ANETHOLE
ANETHOLS > ANETHOL
ANETIC *adj* medically soothing
ANEUPLOID *adj* (of polyploid cells or organisms) having a chromosome number that is not an exact multiple of the haploid number ▷ *n* cell or individual of this type
ANEURIN *a less common name for* > THIAMINE
ANEURINS > ANEURIN
ANEURISM *same as* > ANEURYSM
ANEURISMS > ANEURISM
ANEURYSM *n* permanent swelling of a blood vessel
ANEURYSMS > ANEURYSM
ANEW *adv* once more
ANGA *n* part in Indian music
ANGAKOK *n* Inuit shaman
ANGAKOKS > ANGAKOK
ANGARIA *n* species of shellfish
ANGARIAS > ANGARIA
ANGARIES > ANGARY
ANGARY *n* right to use the property of a neutral state during a war
ANGAS > ANGA
ANGASHORE *n* miserable person given to complaining
ANGEKKOK *n* Inuit shaman
ANGEKKOKS > ANGEKKOK
ANGEKOK *n* Inuit shaman
ANGEKOKS > ANGEKOK
ANGEL *n* spiritual being believed to be an attendant or messenger of God ▷ *vb* provide financial support for
ANGELED > ANGEL
ANGELFISH *n* South American aquarium fish with large fins

ANGELHOOD n state of being an angel

ANGELIC adj very kind, pure, or beautiful

ANGELICA n aromatic plant

ANGELICAL same as > ANGELIC

ANGELICAS > ANGELICA

ANGELING > ANGEL

ANGELS > ANGEL

ANGELUS n series of prayers

ANGELUSES > ANGELUS

ANGER n fierce displeasure or extreme annoyance ▷ vb make (someone) angry

ANGERED > ANGER

ANGERING > ANGER

ANGERLESS > ANGER

ANGERLY adv old form of angrily

ANGERS > ANGER

ANGICO n South American tree

ANGICOS > ANGICO

ANGINA n heart disorder causing sudden severe chest pains

ANGINAL > ANGINA

ANGINAS > ANGINA

ANGINOSE > ANGINA

ANGINOUS > ANGINA

ANGIOGRAM n X-ray picture obtained by angiography

ANGIOLOGY n branch of medical science concerned with the blood vessels and the lymphatic system

ANGIOMA n tumour consisting of a mass of blood vessels or lymphatic vessels

ANGIOMAS > ANGIOMA

ANGIOMATA > ANGIOMA

ANGKLUNG n Asian musical instrument

ANGKLUNGS > ANGKLUNG

ANGLE n space between or shape formed by two lines or surfaces that meet ▷ vb bend or place (something) at an angle

ANGLED > ANGLE

ANGLEDUG n earthworm

ANGLEDUGS > ANGLEDUG

ANGLEPOD n American wild flower

ANGLEPODS > ANGLEPOD

ANGLER n person who fishes with a hook and line

ANGLERS > ANGLER

ANGLES > ANGLE

ANGLESITE n white or grey secondary mineral

ANGLEWISE > ANGLE

ANGLEWORM n earthworm used as bait by anglers

ANGLICE adv in English

ANGLICISE same as > ANGLICIZE

ANGLICISM n word, phrase, or idiom peculiar to the English language, esp as spoken in England

ANGLICIST n expert in or student of English literature or language

ANGLICIZE vb make or become English in outlook, form, etc

ANGLIFIED > ANGLIFY

ANGLIFIES > ANGLIFY

ANGLIFY same as > ANGLICIZE

ANGLING n art or sport of fishing with a hook and line

ANGLINGS > ANGLING

ANGLIST same as > ANGLICIST

ANGLISTS > ANGLIST

ANGLO n White inhabitant of the US not of Latin extraction

ANGLOPHIL n person having admiration for England or the English

ANGLOS > ANGLO

ANGOLA same as > ANGORA

ANGOPHORA n Australian tree related to the eucalyptus

ANGORA n variety of goat, cat, or rabbit with long silky hair

ANGORAS > ANGORA

ANGOSTURA n bitter aromatic bark

ANGRIER > ANGRY

ANGRIES > ANGRY

ANGRIEST > ANGRY

ANGRILY > ANGRY

ANGRINESS > ANGRY

ANGRY adj full of anger ▷ n angry person

ANGST n feeling of anxiety

ANGSTIER > ANGSTY

ANGSTIEST > ANGSTY

ANGSTROM n unit of length used to measure wavelengths

ANGSTROMS > ANGSTROM

ANGSTS > ANGST

ANGSTY adj displaying angst

ANGUIFORM adj shaped like a snake

ANGUINE adj of, relating to, or similar to a snake

ANGUIPED adj having snakes for legs ▷ n mythological Persian creature with snakes for legs

ANGUIPEDE n Persian mythological creature

ANGUIPEDS > ANGUIPED

ANGUISH n great mental pain ▷ vb afflict or be afflicted with anguish

ANGUISHED adj feeling or showing great mental pain

ANGUISHES > ANGUISH

ANGULAR adj (of a person) lean and bony

ANGULARLY > ANGULAR

ANGULATE adj having angles or an angular shape ▷ vb make or become angular

ANGULATED > ANGULATE

ANGULATES > ANGULATE

ANGULOSE same as > ANGULOUS

ANGULOUS adj having angles

ANHEDONIA n inability to feel pleasure

ANHEDONIC > ANHEDONIA

ANHEDRAL n downward inclination of an aircraft wing in relation to the lateral axis

ANHEDRALS > ANHEDRAL

ANHINGA n type of bird

ANHINGAS > ANHINGA

ANHUNGRED adj very hungry

ANHYDRASE n enzyme that catalyzes the removal of water

ANHYDRIDE n substance that combines with water to form an acid

ANHYDRITE n colourless or greyish-white mineral found in sedimentary rocks

ANHYDROUS adj containing no water

ANI n tropical bird

ANICCA n Buddhism belief

ANICCAS > ANICCA

ANICONIC adj (of images of deities, symbols, etc) not portrayed in a human or animal form

ANICONISM > ANICONIC

ANICONIST > ANICONIC

ANICUT n dam in India

ANICUTS > ANICUT

ANIDROSES > ANIDROSIS

ANIDROSIS n absence of sweating

ANIGH adv near

ANIGHT adv at night

ANIL n West Indian shrub

ANILE adj of or like a feeble old woman

ANILIN n aniline

ANILINE n colourless oily liquid

ANILINES > ANILINE

ANILINGUS n sexual stimulation involving oral contact with the anus

ANILINS > ANILIN

ANILITIES > ANILE

ANILITY > ANILE

ANILS > ANIL

ANIMA n feminine principle as present in the male unconscious

ANIMACIES > ANIMACY

ANIMACY n state of being animate

ANIMAL n living creature with specialized sense organs and capable of voluntary motion, esp one other than a human being ▷ adj of animals

ANIMALIAN > ANIMAL

ANIMALIC > ANIMAL

ANIMALIER n painter or sculptor of animal subjects, esp a member of a group of early 19th-century French sculptors who specialized in realistic figures of animals, usually in bronze

ANIMALISE same as > ANIMALIZE

ANIMALISM n preoccupation with physical matters

ANIMALIST > ANIMALISM

ANIMALITY n animal instincts of human beings

ANIMALIZE vb make (a person) brutal or sensual

ANIMALLY adv physically

ANIMALS > ANIMAL

ANIMAS > ANIMA

ANIMATE vb give life to ▷ adj having life

ANIMATED adj interesting and lively

ANIMATELY > ANIMATE

ANIMATER same as > ANIMATOR

ANIMATERS > ANIMATER

ANIMATES > ANIMATE

ANIMATI > ANIMATO

ANIMATIC n animated film sequence

ANIMATICS > ANIMATIC

ANIMATING > ANIMATE

ANIMATION n technique of making cartoon films

ANIMATISM n belief that inanimate objects have consciousness

ANIMATIST > ANIMATISM

ANIMATO n piece of music performed in a lively manner

ANIMATOR n person who makes animated cartoons

ANIMATORS > ANIMATOR

ANIMATOS > ANIMATO

ANIME n type of Japanese animation

ANIMES > ANIME

ANIMI > ANIMUS

ANIMIS > ANIMI

ANIMISM n belief that natural objects possess souls

ANIMISMS > ANIMISM

ANIMIST > ANIMISM

ANIMISTIC > ANIMISM

ANIMISTS > ANIMISM

ANIMOSITY n hostility, hatred

a

ANIMUS *n* hatred, animosity
ANIMUSES > ANIMUS
ANION *n* ion with negative charge
ANIONIC > ANION
ANIONS > ANION
ANIRIDIA *n* absence of the iris, due to a congenital condition or an injury
ANIRIDIAS > ANIRIDIA
ANIRIDIC > ANIRIDIA
ANIS > ANI
ANISE *n* plant with liquorice-flavoured seeds
ANISEED *n* liquorice-flavoured seeds of the anise plant
ANISEEDS > ANISEED
ANISES > ANISE
ANISETTE *n* liquorice-flavoured liqueur made from aniseed
ANISETTES > ANISETTE
ANISIC > ANISE
ANISOGAMY *n* type of sexual reproduction in which the gametes are dissimilar, either in size alone or in size and form
ANISOLE *n* colourless pleasant-smelling liquid used as a solvent
ANISOLES > ANISOLE
ANKER *n* old liquid measure for wine
ANKERITE *n* greyish to brown mineral that resembles dolomite
ANKERITES > ANKERITE
ANKERS > ANKER
ANKH *n* ancient Egyptian symbol
ANKHS > ANKH
ANKLE *n* joint between the foot and leg ▷ *vb* move
ANKLEBONE the nontechnical name for **>** TALUS
ANKLED > ANKLE
ANKLES > ANKLE
ANKLET *n* ornamental chain worn round the ankle
ANKLETS > ANKLET
ANKLING > ANKLE
ANKLONG *n* Asian musical instrument
ANKLONGS > ANKLONG
ANKLUNG *n* Asian musical instrument
ANKLUNGS > ANKLUNG
ANKUS *n* stick used, esp in India, for goading elephants
ANKUSES > ANKUS
ANKUSH *n* Indian weapon
ANKUSHES > ANKUSH
ANKYLOSE *vb* (of bones in a joint, etc) to fuse or stiffen by ankylosis
ANKYLOSED > ANKYLOSE
ANKYLOSES > ANKYLOSE

ANKYLOSIS *n* abnormal immobility of a joint, caused by a fibrous growth
ANKYLOTIC > ANKYLOSIS
ANLACE *n* medieval short dagger with a broad tapering blade
ANLACES > ANLACE
ANLAGE *n* organ or part in the earliest stage of development
ANLAGEN > ANLAGE
ANLAGES > ANLAGE
ANLAS *same as* **>** ANLACE
ANLASES > ANLAS
ANN *n* old Scots word for a widow's pension
ANNA *n* former Indian coin worth one sixteenth of a rupee
ANNAL *n* recorded events of one year
ANNALISE *vb* record in annals
ANNALISED > ANNALISE
ANNALISES > ANNALISE
ANNALIST > ANNAL
ANNALISTS > ANNAL
ANNALIZE *vb* record in annals
ANNALIZED > ANNALIZE
ANNALIZES > ANNALIZE
ANNALS > ANNAL
ANNAS > ANNA
ANNAT *n* singular of annates
ANNATES *pl n* money paid to the Pope
ANNATS > ANNAT
ANNATTA *n* annatto
ANNATTAS > ANNATTA
ANNATTO *n* tropical tree
ANNATTOS > ANNATTO
ANNEAL *vb* toughen by heating and slow cooling ▷ *n* act of annealing
ANNEALED > ANNEAL
ANNEALER > ANNEAL
ANNEALERS > ANNEAL
ANNEALING > ANNEAL
ANNEALS > ANNEAL
ANNECTENT *adj* connecting
ANNELID *n* type of worm with a segmented body
ANNELIDAN > ANNELID
ANNELIDS > ANNELID
ANNEX *vb* seize (territory)
ANNEXABLE > ANNEX
ANNEXE *n* extension to a building
ANNEXED > ANNEX
ANNEXES > ANNEXE
ANNEXING > ANNEX
ANNEXION *n* old form of annexation
ANNEXIONS > ANNEXION
ANNEXMENT > ANNEX
ANNEXURE *n* something that is added
ANNEXURES > ANNEXURE
ANNICUT *n* dam in India

ANNICUTS > ANNICUT
ANNO *adv* Latin for in the year
ANNONA *n* American tree or shrub
ANNONAS > ANNONA
ANNOTATE *vb* add notes to (a written work)
ANNOTATED > ANNOTATE
ANNOTATES > ANNOTATE
ANNOTATOR > ANNOTATE
ANNOUNCE *vb* make known publicly
ANNOUNCED > ANNOUNCE
ANNOUNCER *n* person who introduces radio or television programmes
ANNOUNCES > ANNOUNCE
ANNOY *vb* irritate or displease
ANNOYANCE *n* feeling of being annoyed
ANNOYED > ANNOY
ANNOYER > ANNOY
ANNOYERS > ANNOY
ANNOYING *adj* causing irritation or displeasure
ANNOYS > ANNOY
ANNS > ANN
ANNUAL *adj* happening once a year ▷ *n* plant that completes its life cycle in a year
ANNUALISE *same as* **>** ANNUALIZE
ANNUALIZE *vb* calculate (a rate) for or as if for a year
ANNUALLY > ANNUAL
ANNUALS > ANNUAL
ANNUITANT *n* person in receipt of or entitled to an annuity
ANNUITIES > ANNUITY
ANNUITY *n* fixed sum paid every year
ANNUL *vb* declare (something, esp a marriage) invalid
ANNULAR *adj* ring-shaped ▷ *n* ring finger
ANNULARLY > ANNULAR
ANNULARS > ANNULAR
ANNULATE *adj* having, composed of, or marked with rings ▷ *n* annelid
ANNULATED > ANNULATE
ANNULATES > ANNULATE
ANNULET *n* moulding in the form of a ring
ANNULETS > ANNULET
ANNULI > ANNULUS
ANNULLED > ANNUL
ANNULLING > ANNUL
ANNULMENT *n* formal declaration that a contract or marriage is invalid
ANNULOSE *adj* (of earthworms, crustaceans, and similar animals) having a body formed of a series of rings
ANNULS > ANNUL
ANNULUS *n* area between two concentric circles

ANNULUSES > ANNULUS
ANOA *n* type of small cattle
ANOAS > ANOA
ANOBIID *n* any type of beetle
ANOBIIDS > ANOBIID
ANODAL > ANODE
ANODALLY > ANODE
ANODE *n* positive electrode in a battery, valve, etc
ANODES > ANODE
ANODIC > ANODE
ANODISE *same as* **>** ANODIZE
ANODISED > ANODISE
ANODISER *same as* **>** ANODIZER
ANODISERS > ANODISER
ANODISES > ANODISE
ANODISING > ANODISE
ANODIZE *vb* coat (metal) with a protective oxide film by electrolysis
ANODIZED > ANODIZE
ANODIZER *n* something that anodizes
ANODIZERS > ANODIZER
ANODIZES > ANODIZE
ANODIZING > ANODIZE
ANODONTIA *n* congenital absence of teeth
ANODYNE *n* something that relieves pain or distress ▷ *adj* relieving pain or distress
ANODYNES > ANODYNE
ANODYNIC > ANODYNE
ANOESES > ANOESIS
ANOESIS *n* feeling without understanding
ANOESTRA > ANOESTRUS
ANOESTRI > ANOESTRUS
ANOESTRUM *same as* **>** ANOESTRUS
ANOESTRUS *n* period of sexual inactivity between two periods of oestrus in many mammals
ANOETIC > ANOESIS
ANOINT *vb* smear with oil as a sign of consecration
ANOINTED > ANOINT
ANOINTER > ANOINT
ANOINTERS > ANOINT
ANOINTING *n* act of anointing
ANOINTS > ANOINT
ANOLE *n* type of lizard
ANOLES > ANOLE
ANOLYTE *n* part of electrolyte around anode
ANOLYTES > ANOLYTE
ANOMALIES > ANOMALY
ANOMALOUS *adj* different from the normal or usual order or type
ANOMALY *n* something that deviates from the normal, irregularity
ANOMIC > ANOMIE
ANOMIE *n* lack of social or moral standards
ANOMIES > ANOMIE

ANOMY same as > ANOMIE

ANON adv in a short time, soon

ANONYM n anonymous person or publication

ANONYMA n promiscuous woman

ANONYMAS > ANONYMA

ANONYMISE same as > ANONYMIZE

ANONYMITY > ANONYMOUS

ANONYMIZE vb organize in a way that preserves anonymity

ANONYMOUS adj by someone whose name is unknown or withheld

ANONYMS > ANONYM

ANOOPSIA n squint in which the eye turns upwards

ANOOPSIAS > ANOOPSIA

ANOPHELES n type of mosquito which transmits the malaria parasite to man

ANOPIA n inability to see

ANOPIAS > ANOPIA

ANOPSIA n squint in which the eye turns upwards

ANOPSIAS > ANOPSIA

ANORAK n light waterproof hooded jacket

ANORAKS > ANORAK

ANORECTAL adj of the anus and rectum

ANORECTIC > ANOREXIA

ANORETIC n anorectic

ANORETICS > ANORETIC

ANOREXIA n psychological disorder characterized by fear of becoming fat and refusal to eat

ANOREXIAS > ANOREXIA

ANOREXIC > ANOREXIA

ANOREXICS > ANOREXIA

ANOREXIES > ANOREXY

ANOREXY old name for > ANOREXIA

ANORTHIC another word for > TRICLINIC

ANORTHITE n white to greyish-white or reddish-white mineral

ANOSMATIC > ANOSMIA

ANOSMIA n loss of the sense of smell

ANOSMIAS > ANOSMIA

ANOSMIC > ANOSMIA

ANOTHER adj one more

ANOUGH adj enough

ANOUROUS adj having no tail

ANOVULANT n drug preventing ovulation

ANOVULAR adj without ovulation

ANOW adj old form of enough

ANOXAEMIA n deficiency in the amount of oxygen in the arterial blood

ANOXAEMIC > ANOXAEMIA

ANOXEMIA same as > ANOXAEMIA

ANOXEMIAS > ANOXEMIA

ANOXEMIC > ANOXEMIA

ANOXIA n lack or absence of oxygen

ANOXIAS > ANOXIA

ANOXIC > ANOXIA

ANS pl n as in ifs and ans things that might have happened, but which did not

ANSA n either end of Saturn's rings

ANSAE > ANSA

ANSAPHONE n telephone answering machine

ANSATE adj having a handle or handle-like part

ANSATED adj ansate

ANSERINE adj of or resembling a goose ▷ n chemical compound

ANSERINES > ANSERINE

ANSEROUS same as > ANSERINE

ANSWER n reply to a question, request, letter, etc ▷ vb give an answer (to)

ANSWERED > ANSWER

ANSWERER > ANSWER

ANSWERERS > ANSWER

ANSWERING > ANSWER

ANSWERS > ANSWER

ANT n small insect living in highly-organized colonies

ANTA n pilaster

ANTACID n substance that counteracts acidity ▷ adj having the properties of this substance

ANTACIDS > ANTACID

ANTAE > ANTA

ANTALGIC n pain-relieving drug

ANTALGICS > ANTALGIC

ANTALKALI n substance that neutralizes alkalis

ANTAR old word for > CAVE

ANTARA n South American panpipes

ANTARAS > ANTARA

ANTARCTIC adj relating to Antarctica

ANTARS > ANTAR

ANTAS > ANTA

ANTBEAR n aardvark

ANTBEARS > ANTBEAR

ANTBIRD n South American bird

ANTBIRDS > ANTBIRD

ANTE n player's stake in poker ▷ vb place (one's stake) in poker

ANTEATER n mammal which feeds on ants by means of a long snout

ANTEATERS > ANTEATER

ANTECEDE vb go before, as in time, order, etc

ANTECEDED > ANTECEDE

ANTECEDES > ANTECEDE

ANTECHOIR n part of a church in front of the choir, usually enclosed by screens, tombs, etc

ANTED > ANTE

ANTEDATE vb precede in time ▷ n earlier date

ANTEDATED > ANTEDATE

ANTEDATES > ANTEDATE

ANTEED > ANTE

ANTEFIX n carved ornament

ANTEFIXA > ANTEFIX

ANTEFIXAE > ANTEFIX

ANTEFIXAL > ANTEFIX

ANTEFIXES > ANTEFIX

ANTEING > ANTE

ANTELOPE n deerlike mammal with long legs and horns

ANTELOPES > ANTELOPE

ANTELUCAN adj before daylight

ANTENATAL adj during pregnancy, before birth ▷ n examination during pregnancy

ANTENATI n people born before certain date

ANTENNA n insect's feeler

ANTENNAE > ANTENNA

ANTENNAL > ANTENNA

ANTENNARY > ANTENNA

ANTENNAS > ANTENNA

ANTENNULE n one of a pair of small mobile appendages on the heads of crustaceans in front of the antennae, usually having a sensory function

ANTEPAST n appetizer

ANTEPASTS > ANTEPAST

ANTERIOR adj the front

ANTEROOM n small room leading into a larger one, often used as a waiting room

ANTEROOMS > ANTEROOM

ANTES > ANTE

ANTETYPE n earlier form

ANTETYPES > ANTETYPE

ANTEVERT vb displace (an organ or part) by tilting it forward

ANTEVERTS > ANTEVERT

ANTHELIA > ANTHELION

ANTHELION n faint halo sometimes seen in polar or high altitude regions around the shadow of an object cast onto a thick cloud bank or fog

ANTHELIX n prominent curved fold of cartilage just inside the outer rim of the external ear

ANTHEM n song of loyalty, esp to a country ▷ vb provide with an anthem

ANTHEMED > ANTHEM

ANTHEMIA > ANTHEMION

ANTHEMIC > ANTHEM

ANTHEMING > ANTHEM

ANTHEMION n floral design, used esp in ancient Greek and Roman architecture and decoration, usually consisting of honeysuckle, lotus, or palmette leaf motifs

ANTHEMIS n genus of herbs of Mediterranean and SW Asia

ANTHEMS > ANTHEM

ANTHER n part of a flower's stamen containing pollen

ANTHERAL > ANTHER

ANTHERID n antheridium

ANTHERIDS > ANTHERID

ANTHERS > ANTHER

ANTHESES > ANTHESIS

ANTHESIS n time when a flower becomes sexually functional

ANTHILL n mound near an ants' nest

ANTHILLS > ANTHILL

ANTHOCARP n fruit developing from many flowers

ANTHOCYAN n any of a class of water-soluble glycosidic pigments

ANTHODIA > ANTHODIUM

ANTHODIUM another name for > CAPITULUM

ANTHOID adj resembling a flower

ANTHOLOGY n collection of poems or other literary pieces by various authors

ANTHOTAXY n arrangement of flowers on a stem or parts on a flower

ANTHOZOAN n type of marine invertebrate with a body in the form of a polyp, such as corals, sea anemones, and sea pens

ANTHOZOIC > ANTHOZOAN

ANTHRACES > ANTHRAX

ANTHRACIC adj of anthrax

ANTHRAX n dangerous disease of cattle and sheep, communicable to humans

ANTHRAXES > ANTHRAX

ANTHRO n short for anthropology

ANTHROPIC adj of or relating to human beings

ANTHROS > ANTHRO

ANTHURIUM n tropical American plant cultivated as a house plant for its showy foliage and flowers

ANTI adj opposed (to) ▷ n opponent of a party, policy, or attitude

ANTIABUSE adj designed to prevent abuse

ANTIACNE adj inhibiting the development of acne

a

ANTIAGING adj resisting the effects of ageing

ANTIAIR adj countering attack by aircraft or missile

ANTIALIEN adj designed to prevent foreign animal or plant species from becoming established

ANTIAR another name for > UPAS

ANTIARIN n poison derived from antiar

ANTIARINS > ANTIARIN

ANTIARMOR adj designed or equipped to combat armoured vehicles

ANTIARS > ANTIAR

ANTIATOM n atom composed of antiparticles, in which the nucleus contains antiprotons with orbiting positrons

ANTIATOMS > ANTIATOM

ANTIAUXIN n substance acting against auxin

ANTIBIAS adj countering bias

ANTIBLACK adj hostile to black people

ANTIBODY n protein produced in the blood, which destroys bacteria

ANTIBOSS adj acting against bosses

ANTIBUG adj acting against computer bugs

ANTIBUSER n person who opposes the policy of transporting students to faraway schools to achieve racial balance

ANTIC n actor in a ludicrous or grotesque part ▷ adj fantastic

ANTICAL adj position of plant parts

ANTICALLY > ANTICAL

ANTICAR n opposed to cars

ANTICHLOR n substance used to remove chlorine from a material after bleaching or to neutralize the chlorine present

ANTICISE same as > ANTICIZE

ANTICISED > ANTICISE

ANTICISES > ANTICISE

ANTICITY adj opposed to cities

ANTICIVIC adj opposed to citizenship

ANTICIZE vb play absurdly

ANTICIZED > ANTICIZE

ANTICIZES > ANTICIZE

ANTICK vb perform antics

ANTICKE archaic form of > ANTIQUE

ANTICKED > ANTICK

ANTICKES > ANTICKE

ANTICKING > ANTICK

ANTICKS > ANTICK

ANTICLINE n fold of rock raised up into a broad arch so that the strata slope down on both sides

ANTICLING adj acting against clinging

ANTICLY adv grotesquely

ANTICODON n element of RNA

ANTICOLD adj preventing or fighting the common cold

ANTICOUS adj on the part of a flower furthest from the stem

ANTICRACK adj protecting a computer against unauthorized access

ANTICRIME adj preventing or fighting crime

ANTICS pl n absurd acts or postures

ANTICULT n organisation that is opposed to religious cults

ANTICULTS > ANTICULT

ANTIDORA > ANTIDORON

ANTIDORON n consecrated bread

ANTIDOTAL > ANTIDOTE

ANTIDOTE n substance that counteracts a poison ▷ vb counteract with an antidote

ANTIDOTED > ANTIDOTE

ANTIDOTES > ANTIDOTE

ANTIDRAFT adj opposed to conscription

ANTIDRUG adj intended to discourage illegal drug use

ANTIDUNE n sand hill or inclined bedding plane that forms a steep slope against the direction of a fast-flowing current

ANTIDUNES > ANTIDUNE

ANTIELITE adj opposed to elitism

ANTIENT old spelling of > ANCIENT

ANTIENTS > ANTIENT

ANTIFAT adj acting to remove or prevent fat

ANTIFLU adj acting against influenza

ANTIFOAM adj allowing gas to escape rather than form foam

ANTIFOG adj preventing the buildup of moisture on a surface

ANTIFRAUD adj acting against fraud

ANTIFUR adj opposed to the wearing of fur garments

ANTIGANG adj designed to restrict the activities of criminal gangs

ANTIGAY adj hostile to homosexuals

ANTIGEN n substance causing the blood to produce antibodies

ANTIGENE n antigen

ANTIGENES > ANTIGENE

ANTIGENIC > ANTIGEN

ANTIGENS > ANTIGEN

ANTIGLARE adj cutting down glare

ANTIGRAFT adj designed to reduce corruption

ANTIGUN adj opposed to the possession of guns

ANTIHELIX same as > ANTHELIX

ANTIHERO n central character in a book, film, etc, who lacks the traditional heroic virtues

ANTIHUMAN adj inhuman

ANTIJAM adj preventing jamming

ANTIKING n rival to an established king

ANTIKINGS > ANTIKING

ANTIKNOCK n substance added to motor fuel to reduce knocking in the engine caused by too rapid combustion

ANTILABOR adj opposed to labor interests

ANTILEAK adj preventing leaks

ANTILEFT adj opposed to the left wing in politics

ANTILIFE adj in favour of abortion

ANTILIFER n person in favour of abortion

ANTILOCK adj designed to prevent overbraking

ANTILOG n number whose logarithm to a given base is a given number

ANTILOGS > ANTILOG

ANTILOGY n contradiction in terms

ANTIMACHO adj opposed to macho attitudes

ANTIMALE adj opposed to men

ANTIMAN adj opposed to men ▷ n derogatory term for a homosexual man

ANTIMASK n interlude in a masque

ANTIMASKS > ANTIMASK

ANTIMEN > ANTIMAN

ANTIMERE n part or organ of a bilaterally or radially symmetrical organism that corresponds to a similar structure on the other side of the axis, such as the right or left limb of a four-legged animal

ANTIMERES > ANTIMERE

ANTIMERIC > ANTIMERE

ANTIMINE adj designed to counteract landmines

ANTIMONIC adj of or containing antimony in the pentavalent state

ANTIMONY n brittle silvery-white metallic element

ANTIMONYL n of, consisting of, or containing the monovalent group SbO-

ANTIMUON n antiparticle of a muon

ANTIMUONS > ANTIMUON

ANTIMUSIC n music intended to overthrow traditional conventions and expectations

ANTIMYCIN n antibiotic drug

ANTING n rubbing of ants by birds on their feathers

ANTINGS > ANTING

ANTINODAL > ANTINODE

ANTINODE n point at which the amplitude of one of the two kinds of displacement in a standing wave has maximum value. Generally the other kind of displacement has its minimum value at this point

ANTINODES > ANTINODE

ANTINOISE n sound generated so that it is out of phase with a noise, such as that made by an engine, in order to reduce the noise level by interference

ANTINOME n opposite

ANTINOMES > ANTINOME

ANTINOMIC > ANTINOMY

ANTINOMY n contradiction between two laws or principles that are reasonable in themselves

ANTINOVEL n type of prose fiction in which conventional elements of the novel are rejected

ANTINUKE same as > ANTINUKER

ANTINUKER n person who is opposed to nuclear weapons or energy

ANTINUKES > ANTINUKE

ANTIPAPAL adj opposed to the pope

ANTIPARTY adj opposed to a political party

ANTIPASTI > ANTIPASTO

ANTIPASTO n appetizer in an Italian meal

ANTIPATHY n dislike, hostility

ANTIPHON n hymn sung in alternate parts by two groups of singers

ANTIPHONS > ANTIPHON

ANTIPHONY n antiphonal singing of a musical composition by two choirs

ANTIPILL adj opposed to the use of the contraceptive pill

ANTIPODAL *adj* of or relating to diametrically opposite points on the earth's surface

ANTIPODE *n* exact or direct opposite

ANTIPODES *pl n* any two places diametrically opposite one another on the earth's surface

ANTIPOLAR > ANTIPOLE

ANTIPOLE *n* opposite pole

ANTIPOLES > ANTIPOLE

ANTIPOPE *n* pope set up in opposition to the one chosen by church laws

ANTIPOPES > ANTIPOPE

ANTIPORN *adj* opposed to pornography

ANTIPOT *adj* opposed to illegal use of marijuana

ANTIPRESS *adj* hostile to the news media

ANTIPYIC *n* drug acting against suppuration

ANTIPYICS > ANTIPYIC

ANTIQUARK *n* antiparticle of a quark

ANTIQUARY *n* student or collector of antiques or ancient works of art

ANTIQUATE *vb* make obsolete or old-fashioned

ANTIQUE *n* object of an earlier period, valued for its beauty, workmanship, or age ▷ *adj* made in an earlier period ▷ *vb* give an antique appearance to

ANTIQUED > ANTIQUE

ANTIQUELY > ANTIQUE

ANTIQUER *n* collector of antiques

ANTIQUERS > ANTIQUE

ANTIQUES > ANTIQUE

ANTIQUEY *adj* having the appearance of an antique

ANTIQUING > ANTIQUE

ANTIQUITY *n* great age

ANTIRADAR *adj* preventing detection by radar

ANTIRAPE *adj* protecting against rape

ANTIRED *adj* of a particular colour of antiquark

ANTIRIOT *adj* (of police officers, equipment, measures, etc) designed for or engaged in the control of crowds

ANTIROCK *adj* designed to prevent a vehicle from rocking

ANTIROLL *adj* designed to prevent a vehicle from tilting

ANTIROYAL *adj* opposed to the monarchy

ANTIRUST *adj* (of a product or procedure) effective against rust

▷ *n* substance or device that prevents rust

ANTIRUSTS > ANTIRUST

ANTIS > ANTI

ANTISAG *adj* preventing sagging

ANTISCIAN *n* person living on other side of equator

ANTISENSE *adj* acting in opposite way to RNA

ANTISERA > ANTISERUM

ANTISERUM *n* blood serum containing antibodies used to treat or provide immunity to a disease

ANTISEX *adj* opposed to sexual activity

ANTISHAKE *adj* (in photography) intended to reduce blurring caused by movement ▷ *n* antishake technology

ANTISHARK *adj* protecting against sharks

ANTISHIP *adj* designed for attacking ships

ANTISHOCK *n* one of a pair of walking poles designed to reduce stress on the knees

ANTISKID *adj* intended to prevent skidding

ANTISLEEP *adj* acting to prevent sleep

ANTISLIP *adj* acting to prevent slipping

ANTISMOG *adj* reducing smog

ANTISMOKE *adj* preventing smoke

ANTISMUT *adj* opposed to obscene material

ANTISNOB *n* person opposed to snobbery

ANTISNOBS > ANTISNOB

ANTISOLAR *adj* opposite to the sun

ANTISPAM *adj* intended to prevent spam

ANTISPAST *n* group of four syllables in poetic metre

ANTISTAT *n* substance preventing static electricity

ANTISTATE *adj* opposed to state authority

ANTISTATS > ANTISTAT

ANTISTICK *adj* preventing things from sticking to a surface

ANTISTORY *n* story without a plot

ANTISTYLE *n* style that rejects traditional aesthetics

ANTITANK *adj* (of weapons) designed to destroy military tanks

ANTITAX *adj* opposed to taxation

ANTITHEFT *adj* (of a device, campaign, system, etc) designed to prevent theft

ANTITHET *n* example of antithesis

ANTITHETS > ANTITHET

ANTITOXIC > ANTITOXIN

ANTITOXIN *n* (serum containing) an antibody that acts against a toxin

ANTITRADE *n* wind blowing in the opposite direction to a trade wind

ANTITRAGI *n* cartilaginous projections of the external ear opposite the tragus

ANTITRUST *adj* (of laws) opposing business monopolies ▷ *n* regulating or opposing trusts, monopolies, cartels, or similar organizations, esp in order to prevent unfair competition

ANTITUMOR *n* drug which acts against tumours

ANTITYPAL > ANTITYPE

ANTITYPE *n* person or thing that is foreshadowed or represented by a type or symbol, esp a character or event in the New Testament prefigured in the Old Testament

ANTITYPES > ANTITYPE

ANTITYPIC > ANTITYPE

ANTIULCER *adj* used to treat ulcers

ANTIUNION *adj* opposed to union

ANTIURBAN *adj* opposed to city life

ANTIVENIN *n* antitoxin that counteracts a specific venom, esp snake venom

ANTIVENOM *n* venom antidote

ANTIVIRAL *adj* inhibiting the growth of viruses ▷ *n* any antiviral drug: used to treat diseases caused by viruses, such as herpes infections and AIDS

ANTIVIRUS *adj* relating to software designed to protect computer files from viruses ▷ *n* such a piece of software

ANTIWAR *adj* opposed to war

ANTIWEAR *adj* preventing wear

ANTIWEED *adj* killing or preventing weeds

ANTIWHITE *adj* hostile to white people

ANTIWOMAN *adj* hostile to women

ANTIWORLD *n* hypothetical or supposed world or

universe composed of antimatter

ANTLER *n* branched horn of a male deer

ANTLERED *adj* having antlers

ANTLERS > ANTLER

ANTLIA *n* butterfly proboscis

ANTLIAE > ANTLIA

ANTLIATE *adj* relating to antlia

ANTLIKE *adj* of or like an ant or ants

ANTLION *n* type of insect resembling a dragonfly

ANTLIONS > ANTLION

ANTONYM *n* word that means the opposite of another

ANTONYMIC > ANTONYM

ANTONYMS > ANTONYM

ANTONYMY *n* use of antonyms

ANTPITTA *n* S American bird whose diet consists mainly of ants

ANTPITTAS > ANTPITTA

ANTRA > ANTRUM

ANTRAL > ANTRUM

ANTRE *n* cavern or cave

ANTRES > ANTRE

ANTRORSE *adj* directed or pointing upwards or forwards

ANTRUM *n* natural cavity, esp in a bone

ANTRUMS > ANTRUM

ANTS > ANT

ANTSIER > ANTSY

ANTSIEST > ANTSY

ANTSINESS > ANTSY

ANTSY *adj* restless, nervous, and impatient

ANTWACKIE *adj* old-fashioned

ANUCLEATE *adj* without a nucleus

ANURA *pl n* order of animals that comprises frogs and toads

ANURAL *adj* without a tail

ANURAN *n* type of amphibian

ANURANS > ANURAN

ANURESES > ANURESIS

ANURESIS *n* inability to urinate even though urine is formed by the kidneys and retained in the urinary bladder

ANURETIC > ANURESIS

ANURIA *n* result of a kidney disorder

ANURIAS > ANURIA

ANURIC > ANURIA

ANUROUS *adj* lacking a tail

ANUS *n* opening at the end of the alimentary canal, through which faeces are discharged

ANUSES > ANUS

ANVIL *n* heavy iron block on which metals are

hammered into particular shapes ▷ vb forge on an anvil

ANVILED > ANVIL

ANVILING > ANVIL

ANVILLED > ANVIL

ANVILLING > ANVIL

ANVILS > ANVIL

ANVILTOP n type of stormcloud formation

ANVILTOPS > ANVILTOP

ANXIETIES > ANXIETY

ANXIETY n state of being anxious

ANXIOUS adj worried and tense

ANXIOUSLY > ANXIOUS

ANY adj one or some, no matter which ▷ adv at all

ANYBODIES > ANYBODY

ANYBODY n any person at random

ANYHOW adv anyway

ANYMORE adv at present

ANYON n (in mathematics) projective representation of a Lie group

ANYONE pron any person ▷ n any person at random

ANYONES > ANYONE

ANYONS > ANYON

ANYPLACE adv in, at, or to any unspecified place

ANYROAD a northern English dialect word for > ANYWAY

ANYTHING pron any object, event, or action whatever ▷ n any thing at random

ANYTHINGS > ANYTHING

ANYTIME adv at any time

ANYWAY adv at any rate, nevertheless

ANYWAYS nonstandard word for > ANYWAY

ANYWHEN adv at any time

ANYWHERE adv in, at, or to any place

ANYWHERES nonstandard word for > ANYWHERE

ANYWISE adv in any way or manner

ANZIANI n Italian word for councillors

AORIST n tense of the verb in classical Greek

AORISTIC > AORIST

AORISTS > AORIST

AORTA n main artery of the body, carrying oxygen-rich blood from the heart

AORTAE > AORTA

AORTAL > AORTA

AORTAS > AORTA

AORTIC > AORTA

AORTITIS n inflammation of the aorta

AOUDAD n wild mountain sheep

AOUDADS > AOUDAD

APACE adv swiftly

APACHE n Parisian gangster or ruffian

APACHES > APACHE

APADANA n ancient Persian palace hall

APADANAS > APADANA

APAGE interj Greek word meaning go away

APAGOGE n reduction to absurdity

APAGOGES > APAGOGE

APAGOGIC > APAGOGE

APAID > APAY

APANAGE same as > APPANAGE

APANAGED adj having apanage

APANAGES > APANAGE

APAREJO n kind of packsaddle made of stuffed leather cushions

APAREJOS > APAREJO

APART adv to pieces or in pieces

APARTHEID n former official government policy of racial segregation in S Africa

APARTMENT n room in a building

APARTNESS > APART

APATETIC adj of or relating to coloration that disguises and protects an animal

APATHATON old word for > EPITHET

APATHETIC adj having or showing little or no emotion

APATHIES > APATHY

APATHY n lack of interest or enthusiasm

APATITE n pale green to purple mineral, found in igneous rocks

APATITES > APATITE

APATOSAUR n long-necked dinosaur

APAY vb old word meaning satisfy

APAYD > APAY

APAYING > APAY

APAYS > APAY

APE n tailless monkey such as the chimpanzee or gorilla ▷ vb imitate

APEAK adj in a vertical or almost vertical position

APED > APE

APEDOM n state of being an ape

APEDOMS > APEDOM

APEEK adv nautical word meaning vertically

APEHOOD n state of being ape

APEHOODS > APEHOOD

APELIKE > APE

APEMAN n primate thought to have been the forerunner of humans

APEMEN > APEMAN

APEPSIA n digestive disorder

APEPSIAS > APEPSIA

APEPSIES > APEPSY

APEPSY n apepsia

APER n person who apes

APERCU n outline

APERCUS > APERCU

APERIENT adj having a mild laxative effect ▷ n mild laxative

APERIENTS > APERIENT

APERIES > APERY

APERIODIC adj not periodic

APERITIF n alcoholic drink taken before a meal

APERITIFS > APERITIF

APERITIVE n laxative

APERS > APER

APERT adj open

APERTNESS > APERT

APERTURAL > APERTURE

APERTURE n opening or hole

APERTURED adj having an aperture

APERTURES > APERTURE

APERY n imitative behaviour

APES > APE

APESHIT adj crazy or furious

APETALIES > APETALOUS

APETALOUS adj (of flowering plants) having no petals

APETALY > APETALOUS

APEX n highest point

APEXES > APEX

APGAR n as in apgar score system for determining the condition of an infant at birth

APHAGIA n refusal or inability to swallow

APHAGIAS > APHAGIA

APHAKIA n absence of the lens of an eye

APHAKIAS > APHAKIA

APHANITE n any fine-grained rock, such as a basalt, containing minerals that cannot be distinguished with the naked eye

APHANITES > APHANITE

APHANITIC > APHANITE

APHASIA n disorder of the central nervous system

APHASIAC > APHASIA

APHASIACS > APHASIA

APHASIAS > APHASIA

APHASIC > APHASIA

APHASICS > APHASIA

APHELIA > APHELION

APHELIAN > APHELION

APHELION n point of a planet's orbit that is farthest from the sun

APHELIONS > APHELION

APHERESES > APHERESIS

APHERESIS n omission of a letter or syllable at the beginning of a word

APHERETIC > APHERESIS

APHESES > APHESIS

APHESIS n gradual disappearance of an unstressed vowel at the beginning of a word

APHETIC > APHESIS

APHETISE vb lose a vowel at the beginning of a word

APHETISED > APHETISE

APHETISES > APHETISE

APHETIZE vb lose a vowel at the beginning of a word

APHETIZED > APHETIZE

APHETIZES > APHETIZE

APHICIDE n substance for killing aphids

APHICIDES > APHICIDE

APHID n small insect which sucks the sap from plants

APHIDES > APHIS

APHIDIAN > APHID

APHIDIANS > APHID

APHIDIOUS > APHID

APHIDS > APHID

APHIS n type of aphid such as the blackfly

APHOLATE n type of pesticide

APHOLATES > APHOLATE

APHONIA n loss of the voice caused by damage to the vocal tract

APHONIAS > APHONIA

APHONIC adj affected with aphonia ▷ n person affected with aphonia

APHONICS > APHONIC

APHONIES > APHONY

APHONOUS > APHONIA

APHONY same as > APHONIA

APHORISE same as > APHORIZE

APHORISED > APHORISE

APHORISER > APHORISE

APHORISES > APHORISE

APHORISM n short clever saying expressing a general truth

APHORISMS > APHORISM

APHORIST > APHORISM

APHORISTS > APHORISM

APHORIZE vb write or speak in aphorisms

APHORIZED > APHORIZE

APHORIZER > APHORIZE

APHORIZES > APHORIZE

APHOTIC adj characterized by or growing in the absence of light

APHRODITE n North American butterfly

APHTHA n small ulceration

APHTHAE > APHTHA

APHTHOUS > APHTHA

APHYLLIES > APHYLLOUS

APHYLLOUS adj (of plants) having no leaves

APHYLLY > APHYLLOUS

APIACEOUS adj parsley-like

APIAN adj of, relating to, or resembling bees

APIARIAN adj of or relating to the breeding and care of bees ▷ n apiarist

APIARIANS > APIARIAN

APIARIES > APIARY

APIARIST n beekeeper

APIARISTS > APIARIST

APIARY n place where bees are kept

APICAL adj of, at, or being an apex ▷ n sound made with the tip of the tongue

APICALLY > APICAL

APICALS > APICAL

APICES plural of > APEX

APICIAN adj of fine or dainty food

APICULATE adj (of leaves) ending in a short sharp point

APICULI > APICULUS

APICULUS n short sharp point

APIECE adv each

APIEZON adj as in apiezon oil oil left by distillation

APIMANIA n extreme enthusiasm for bees

APIMANIAS > APIMANIA

APING > APE

APIOL n substance formerly used to assist menstruation

APIOLOGY n study of bees

APIOLS > APIOL

APISH adj stupid or foolish

APISHLY > APISH

APISHNESS > APISH

APISM n behaviour like an ape

APISMS > APISM

APIVOROUS adj eating bees

APLANAT n aplanatic lens

APLANATIC adj (of a lens or mirror) free from spherical aberration

APLANATS > APLANAT

APLANETIC adj (esp of some algal and fungal spores) nonmotile or lacking a motile stage

APLASIA n congenital absence of an organ

APLASIAS > APLASIA

APLASTIC adj relating to or characterized by aplasia

APLENTY adv in plenty

APLITE n type of igneous rock

APLITES > APLITE

APLITIC > APLITE

APLOMB n calm self-possession

APLOMBS > APLOMB

APLUSTRE n stern ornament on an ancient Greek ship

APLUSTRES > APLUSTRE

APNEA same as > APNOEA

APNEAL > APNEA

APNEAS > APNEA

APNEIC > APNEA

APNEUSES > APNEUSIS

APNEUSIS n protracted gasping inhalation followed by short inefficient exhalation, which can cause asphyxia

APNEUSTIC adj of or relating to apneusis

APNOEA n temporary inability to breathe

APNOEAL > APNOEA

APNOEAS > APNOEA

APNOEIC > APNOEA

APO n type of protein

APOAPSES > APOAPSIS

APOAPSIS n point in an orbit furthest from the object orbited

APOCARP n apocarpous gynoecium or fruit

APOCARPS > APOCARP

APOCARPY n presence of many carpels

APOCOPATE vb omit the final sound or sounds of (a word)

APOCOPE n omission of the final sound or sounds of a word

APOCOPES > APOCOPE

APOCOPIC > APOCOPE

APOCRINE adj denoting a type of glandular secretion in which part of the secreting cell is lost with the secretion, as in mammary glands

APOCRYPHA n writings or statements of uncertain authority

APOD n animal without feet

APODAL adj (of snakes, eels, etc) without feet

APODE n animal without feet

APODES > APODE

APODICTIC adj unquestionably true by virtue of demonstration

APODOSES > APODOSIS

APODOSIS n consequent of a conditional statement

APODOUS same as > APODAL

APODS > APOD

APOENZYME n protein component that together with a coenzyme forms an enzyme

APOGAEIC > APOGEE

APOGAMIC > APOGAMY

APOGAMIES > APOGAMY

APOGAMOUS > APOGAMY

APOGAMY n type of reproduction in some ferns

APOGEAL > APOGEE

APOGEAN > APOGEE

APOGEE n point of moon's orbit

APOGEES > APOGEE

APOGEIC > APOGEE

APOGRAPH n exact copy

APOGRAPHS > APOGRAPH

APOLLO n strikingly handsome youth

APOLLOS > APOLLO

APOLOG same as > APOLOGUE

APOLOGAL > APOLOGUE

APOLOGIA n formal written defence of a cause

APOLOGIAE > APOLOGIA

APOLOGIAS > APOLOGIA

APOLOGIES > APOLOGY

APOLOGISE same as > APOLOGIZE

APOLOGIST n person who formally defends a cause

APOLOGIZE vb make an apology

APOLOGS > APOLOG

APOLOGUE n allegory or moral fable

APOLOGUES > APOLOGUE

APOLOGY n expression of regret for wrongdoing

APOLUNE n point in a lunar orbit

APOLUNES > APOLUNE

APOMICT n organism, esp a plant, produced by apomixis

APOMICTIC > APOMIXIS

APOMICTS > APOMICT

APOMIXES > APOMIXIS

APOMIXIS n (esp in plants) any of several types of asexual reproduction, such as parthenogenesis and apogamy, in which fertilization does not take place

APOOP adv on the poop deck

APOPHASES > APOPHASIS

APOPHASIS n device of mentioning a subject by stating that it will not be mentioned

APOPHATIC adj of theology that says God is indescribable

APOPHONY n change in the quality of vowels

APOPHYGE n outward curve at each end of the shaft of a column, adjoining the base or capital

APOPHYGES > APOPHYGE

APOPHYSES > APOPHYSIS

APOPHYSIS n process, outgrowth, or swelling from part of an animal or plant

APOPLAST n nonprotoplasmic component of a plant, including the cell walls and intercellular material

APOPLASTS > APOPLAST

APOPLEX vb afflict with apoplexy

APOPLEXED > APOPLEX

APOPLEXES > APOPLEX

APOPLEXY n stroke

APOPTOSES > APOPTOSIS

APOPTOSIS n programmed death of some of an organism's cells as part of its natural growth and development

APOPTOTIC > APOPTOSIS

APORETIC > APORIA

APORIA n doubt, real or professed, about what to do or say

APORIAS > APORIA

APORT adj on or towards the port side

APOS > APO

APOSITIA n unwillingness to eat

APOSITIAS > APOSITIA

APOSITIC > APOSITIA

APOSPORIC > APOSPORY

APOSPORY n development of the gametophyte from the sporophyte without the formation of spores

APOSTACY same as > APOSTASY

APOSTASY n abandonment of one's religious faith or other belief

APOSTATE n person who has abandoned his or her religion, political party, or cause ▷ adj guilty of apostasy

APOSTATES > APOSTATE

APOSTATIC > APOSTATE

APOSTIL n marginal note

APOSTILLE n apostil

APOSTILS > APOSTIL

APOSTLE n one of the twelve disciples chosen by Christ to preach his gospel

APOSTLES > APOSTLE

APOSTOLIC adj of or relating to the Apostles or their teachings

APOTHECE n obsolete word for shop

APOTHECES > APOTHECE

APOTHECIA n cup-shaped structures that contain the asci, esp in lichens

APOTHEGM n short cryptic remark containing some general or generally accepted truth; maxim

APOTHEGMS > APOTHEGM

APOTHEM n geometrical term

a

APOTHEMS > APOTHEM

APOZEM *n* medicine dissolved in water

APOZEMS > APOZEM

APP *n* application program

APPAID > APPAY

APPAIR *vb* old form of impair

APPAIRED > APPAIR

APPAIRING > APPAIR

APPAIRS > APPAIR

APPAL *vb* dismay, terrify

APPALL *same as* > APPAL

APPALLED > APPALL

APPALLING *adj* dreadful, terrible

APPALLS > APPALL

APPALOOSA *n* North American horse breed

APPALS > APPAL

APPALTI > APPALTO

APPALTO *n* Italian word for contact

APPANAGE *n* land or other provision granted by a king for the support of a member of the royal family, esp a younger son

APPANAGED *adj* having appanage

APPANAGES > APPANAGE

APPARAT *n* Communist Party organization

APPARATS > APPARAT

APPARATUS *n* equipment for a particular purpose

APPAREL *n* clothing ▷ *vb* clothe, adorn, etc

APPARELED > APPAREL

APPARELS > APPAREL

APPARENCY old word for > APPARENT

APPARENT *adj* readily seen, obvious ▷ *n* heir apparent

APPARENTS > APPARENT

APPARITOR *n* officer who summons witnesses and executes the orders of an ecclesiastical and (formerly) a civil court

APPAY old word for > SATISFY

APPAYD > APPAY

APPAYING > APPAY

APPAYS > APPAY

APPEACH old word for > ACCUSE

APPEACHED > APPEACH

APPEACHES > APPEACH

APPEAL *vb* make an earnest request ▷ *n* earnest request

APPEALED > APPEAL

APPEALER > APPEAL

APPEALERS > APPEAL

APPEALING *adj* attractive or pleasing

APPEALS > APPEAL

APPEAR *vb* become visible or present

APPEARED > APPEAR

APPEARER > APPEAR

APPEARERS > APPEAR

APPEARING > APPEAR

APPEARS > APPEAR

APPEASE *vb* pacify (a person) by yielding to his or her demands

APPEASED > APPEASE

APPEASER > APPEASE

APPEASERS > APPEASE

APPEASES > APPEASE

APPEASING > APPEASE

APPEL *n* stamp of the foot, used to warn of one's intent to attack

APPELLANT *n* person who makes an appeal to a higher court

APPELLATE *adj* of appeals

APPELLEE *n* person who is accused or appealed against

APPELLEES > APPELLEE

APPELLOR *n* person initiating a law case

APPELLORS > APPELLOR

APPELS > APPEL

APPEND *vb* join on, add

APPENDAGE *n* thing joined on or added

APPENDANT *adj* attached, affixed, or added ▷ *n* person or thing attached or added

APPENDED > APPEND

APPENDENT *same as* > APPENDANT

APPENDING > APPEND

APPENDIX *n* separate additional material at the end of a book

APPENDS > APPEND

APPERIL old word for > PERIL

APPERILL old word for > PERIL

APPERILLS > APPERILL

APPERILS > APPERIL

APPERTAIN *vb* belong to

APPESTAT *n* neural control centre within the hypothalamus of the brain that regulates the sense of hunger and satiety

APPESTATS > APPESTAT

APPETENCE *n* craving or desire

APPETENCY *same as* > APPETENCE

APPETENT *adj* eager

APPETIBLE *adj* old word meaning desirable

APPETISE *vb* stimulate the appetite

APPETISED > APPETISE

APPETISER *same as* > APPETIZER

APPETISES > APPETISE

APPETITE *n* desire for food or drink

APPETITES > APPETITE

APPETIZE *vb* stimulate the appetite

APPETIZED > APPETIZE

APPETIZER *n* thing eaten or drunk to stimulate the appetite

APPETIZES > APPETIZE

APPLAUD *vb* show approval of by clapping one's hands

APPLAUDED > APPLAUD

APPLAUDER > APPLAUD

APPLAUDS > APPLAUD

APPLAUSE *n* approval shown by clapping one's hands

APPLAUSES > APPLAUSE

APPLE *n* round firm fleshy fruit that grows on trees

APPLECART *n* cart used to carry apples

APPLEJACK *n* brandy made from apples

APPLES > APPLE

APPLET *n* computing program

APPLETINI *n* apple-flavoured alcoholic cocktail

APPLETS > APPLET

APPLEY *adj* resembling or tasting like an apple

APPLIABLE *adj* applicable

APPLIANCE *n* device with a specific function

APPLICANT *n* person who applies for something

APPLICATE *adj* applied practicably

APPLIED *adj* (of a skill, science, etc) put to practical use

APPLIER > APPLY

APPLIERS > APPLY

APPLIES > APPLY

APPLIEST > APPLEY

APPLIQUE *n* decoration or trimming of one material sewn or otherwise fixed onto another ▷ *vb* sew or fix (a decoration) on as an appliqué

APPLIQUED > APPLIQUE

APPLIQUES > APPLIQUE

APPLY *vb* make a formal request

APPLYING > APPLY

APPOINT *vb* assign to a job or position

APPOINTED > APPOINT

APPOINTEE *n* person who is appointed

APPOINTER > APPOINT

APPOINTOR *n* person to whom a power to nominate persons to take property is given by deed or will

APPOINTS > APPOINT

APPORT *n* production of objects at a seance

APPORTION *vb* divide out in shares

APPORTS > APPORT

APPOSABLE *adj* capable of being apposed or brought into apposition

APPOSE *vb* place side by side or near to each other

APPOSED > APPOSE

APPOSER > APPOSE

APPOSERS > APPOSE

APPOSES > APPOSE

APPOSING > APPOSE

APPOSITE *adj* suitable, apt

APPRAISAL *n* assessment of the worth or quality of a person or thing

APPRAISE *vb* estimate the value or quality of

APPRAISED > APPRAISE

APPRAISEE *n* person being appraised

APPRAISER > APPRAISE

APPRAISES > APPRAISE

APPREHEND *vb* arrest and take into custody

APPRESS *vb* press together

APPRESSED > APPRESS

APPRESSES > APPRESS

APPRISE *vb* make aware (of)

APPRISED > APPRISE

APPRISER > APPRISE

APPRISERS > APPRISE

APPRISES > APPRISE

APPRISING > APPRISE

APPRIZE *same as* > APPRISE

APPRIZED > APPRIZE

APPRIZER > APPRIZE

APPRIZERS > APPRIZE

APPRIZES > APPRIZE

APPRIZING > APPRIZE

APPRO *n* approval

APPROACH *vb* come near or nearer (to) ▷ *n* approaching or means of approaching

APPROBATE *vb* accept as valid

APPROOF old word for > TRIAL

APPROOFS > APPROOF

APPROS > APPRO

APPROVAL *n* consent

APPROVALS > APPROVAL

APPROVE *vb* consider good or right

APPROVED > APPROVE

APPROVER > APPROVE

APPROVERS > APPROVE

APPROVES > APPROVE

APPROVING > APPROVE

APPS > APP

APPUI *n* support

APPUIED > APPUY

APPUIS > APPUI

APPULSE *n* close approach of two celestial bodies

APPULSES > APPULSE

APPULSIVE > APPULSE

APPUY *vb* support

APPUYED > APPUY

APPUYING > APPUY

APPUYS > APPUY

APRACTIC > APRAXIA

APRAXIA *n* disorder of the central nervous system

APRAXIAS > APRAXIA

APRAXIC > APRAXIA

APRES *prep* French word for after

APRICATE *vb* bask in sun

APRICATED > APRICATE

APRICATES > APRICATE

APRICOCK *old word for* > APRICOT

APRICOCKS > APRICOT

APRICOT *n* yellowish-orange juicy fruit like a small peach ▷ *adj* yellowish-orange

APRICOTS > APRICOT

APRIORISM *n* philosophical doctrine that there may be genuine knowledge independent of experience

APRIORIST > APRIORISM

APRIORITY *n* condition of being innate in the mind

APRON *n* garment worn over the front of the body to protect the clothes ▷ *vb* equip with an apron

APRONED > APRON

APRONFUL *n* amount held in an apron

APRONFULS > APRONFUL

APRONING > APRON

APRONLIKE > APRON

APRONS > APRON

APROPOS *adv* appropriate(ly)

APROTIC *adj* (of solvents) neither accepting nor donating hydrogen ions

APSARAS *n* Hindu water sprite

APSARASES > APSARAS

APSE *n* arched or domed recess, esp in a church

APSES > APSE

APSIDAL > APSIS

APSIDES > APSIS

APSIDIOLE *n* small arch

APSIS *n* points in the elliptical orbit of a planet or satellite

APSO *n* Tibetan terrier

APSOS > APSO

APT *adj* having a specified tendency ▷ *vb* be fitting

APTAMER *n* artificially-created DNA or RNA molecule

APTAMERS > APTAMER

APTED > APT

APTER > APT

APTERAL *adj* (esp of a classical temple) not having columns at the sides

APTERIA > APTERIUM

APTERISM > APTEROUS

APTERISMS > APTEROUS

APTERIUM *n* bare patch on the skin of a bird

APTEROUS *adj* (of insects) without wings, as silverfish and springtails

APTERYX *n* kiwi (the bird)

APTERYXES > APTERYX

APTEST > APT

APTING > APT

APTITUDE *n* natural ability

APTITUDES > APTITUDE

APTLY > APT

APTNESS > APT

APTNESSES > APT

APTOTE *n* noun without inflections

APTOTES > APTOTE

APTOTIC > APTOTE

APTS > APT

APYRASE *n* enzyme

APYRASES > APYRASE

APYRETIC > APYREXIA

APYREXIA *n* absence of fever

APYREXIAS > APYREXIA

AQUA *n* water

AQUABATIC *adj* of gymnastic feats in water

AQUABOARD *n* board used to ride on water

AQUACADE *same as* > AQUASHOW

AQUACADES > AQUACADE

AQUADROME *n* venue for water sports

AQUAE > AQUA

AQUAFARM *vb* cultivate fish or shellfish

AQUAFARMS > AQUAFARM

AQUAFER *n* aquifer

AQUAFERS > AQUAFER

AQUAFIT *n* type of aerobic exercise done in water

AQUAFITS > AQUAFIT

AQUALUNG *n* mouthpiece attached to air cylinders, worn for underwater swimming

AQUALUNGS > AQUALUNG

AQUANAUT *n* person who lives and works underwater

AQUANAUTS > AQUANAUT

AQUAPHOBE *n* person afraid of water

AQUAPLANE *n* board on which a person stands to be towed by a motorboat ▷ *vb* ride on an aquaplane

AQUAPORIN *n* any one of a group of proteins in cell membranes that allow the passage of water across the membrane

AQUARELLE *n* method of watercolour painting in transparent washes

AQUARIA > AQUARIUM

AQUARIAL > AQUARIUM

AQUARIAN *n* person who keeps an aquarium

AQUARIANS > AQUARIAN

AQUARIIST *same as* > AQUARIST

AQUARIST *n* curator of an aquarium

AQUARISTS > AQUARIST

AQUARIUM *n* tank in which fish and other underwater creatures are kept

AQUARIUMS > AQUARIUM

AQUAROBIC *adj* pertaining to exercises performed standing up in a swimming pool

AQUAS > AQUA

AQUASCAPE *n* extensive view of a body of water seen from one place

AQUASHOW *n* exhibition of swimming and diving, often accompanied by music

AQUASHOWS > AQUASHOW

AQUATIC *adj* living in or near water ▷ *n* marine or freshwater animal or plant

AQUATICS *pl n* water sports

AQUATINT *n* print like a watercolour, produced by etching copper ▷ *vb* etch (a block, etc) in aquatint

AQUATINTA *n* aquatint

AQUATINTS > AQUATINT

AQUATONE *n* fitness exercise in water

AQUATONES > AQUATONE

AQUAVIT *n* grain- or potato-based spirit

AQUAVITS > AQUAVIT

AQUEDUCT *n* structure carrying water across a valley or river

AQUEDUCTS > AQUEDUCT

AQUEOUS *adj* of, like, or containing water

AQUEOUSLY > AQUEOUS

AQUIFER *n* deposit of rock containing water used to supply wells

AQUIFERS > AQUIFER

AQUILEGIA *another name for* > COLUMBINE

AQUILINE *adj* (of a nose) curved like an eagle's beak

AQUILON *n* name for the north wind

AQUILONS > AQUILON

AQUIVER *adv* quivering

AR *n* letter R

ARAARA *another name for* > TREVALLY

ARAARAS > ARAARA

ARABA *n* Asian carriage

ARABAS > ARABA

ARABESK *same as* > ARABESQUE

ARABESKS > ARABESK

ARABESQUE *n* ballet position in which one leg is raised behind and the arms are extended ▷ *adj* designating, of, or decorated in this style

ARABIC *adj* as in *gum arabic* gum exuded by certain acacia trees

ARABICA *n* high-quality coffee bean

ARABICAS > ARABICA

ARABICISE *same as* > ARABICIZE

ARABICIZE *vb* make or become Arabic

ARABILITY *n* suitability of land for growing crops

ARABIN *n* essence of gum arabic

ARABINOSE *n* pentose sugar in plant gums

ARABINS > ARABIN

ARABIS *n* type of plant

ARABISE *vb* make or become Arab

ARABISED > ARABISE

ARABISES > ARABISE

ARABISING > ARABISE

ARABIZE *vb* make or become Arab

ARABIZED > ARABIZE

ARABIZES > ARABIZE

ARABIZING > ARABIZE

ARABLE *adj* suitable for growing crops on ▷ *n* arable land or farming

ARABLES > ARABLE

ARACEOUS *same as* > AROID

ARACHIS *n* Brazilian plant

ARACHISES > ARACHIS

ARACHNID *n* eight-legged invertebrate, such as a spider, scorpion, tick, or mite

ARACHNIDS > ARACHNID

ARACHNOID *n* middle of the three membranes that cover the brain and spinal cord ▷ *adj* of or relating to the middle of the three meninges

ARAGONITE *n* generally white or grey mineral, found in sedimentary rocks

ARAISE *vb* old form of raise

ARAISED > ARAISE

ARAISES > ARAISE

ARAISING > ARAISE

ARAK *same as* > ARRACK

ARAKS > ARAK

ARALIA *n* type of plant

ARALIAS > ARALIA

ARAME *n* Japanese edible seaweed

ARAMES > ARAME

ARAMID *n* synthetic fibre

ARAMIDS > ARAMID

ARANEID *n* member of the spider family

ARANEIDAN > ARANEID

ARANEIDS > ARANEID

ARANEOUS *adj* like a spider's web

ARAPAIMA *n* very large primitive freshwater teleost fish that occurs in tropical S America

ARAPAIMAS > ARAPAIMA
ARAPONGA n South American bird with a bell-like call
ARAPONGAS > ARAPONGA
ARAPUNGA n South American bird with a bell-like call
ARAPUNGAS > ARAPUNGA
ARAR n African tree
ARAROBA n Brazilian leguminous tree
ARAROBAS > ARAROBA
ARARS > ARAR
ARAUCARIA n type of coniferous tree of S America, Australia, and Polynesia, such as the monkey puzzle and bunya-bunya
ARAYSE vb old form of raise
ARAYSED > ARAYSE
ARAYSES > ARAYSE
ARAYSING > ARAYSE
ARB short for > ARBITRAGE
ARBA n Asian carriage
ARBALEST n large medieval crossbow, usually cocked by mechanical means
ARBALESTS > ARBALEST
ARBALIST same as > ARBALEST
ARBALISTS > ARBALIST
ARBAS > ARBA
ARBELEST n arbalest
ARBELESTS > ARBELEST
ARBITER n person empowered to judge in a dispute
ARBITERS > ARBITER
ARBITRAGE n purchase of currencies, securities, or commodities in one market for immediate resale in others in order to profit from unequal prices
ARBITRAL adj of or relating to arbitration
ARBITRARY adj based on personal choice or chance, rather than reason
ARBITRATE vb settle (a dispute) by arbitration
ARBITRESS n female arbitrator
ARBITRIUM n power to decide
ARBLAST n arbalest
ARBLASTER > ARBLAST
ARBLASTS > ARBLAST
ARBOR n revolving shaft or axle in a machine
ARBOREAL adj of or living in trees
ARBORED adj having arbors
ARBOREOUS adj thickly wooded
ARBORES > ARBOR
ARBORET n old name for an area planted with shrubs

ARBORETA > ARBORETUM
ARBORETS > ARBORET
ARBORETUM n place where rare trees or shrubs are cultivated
ARBORIO n as in arborio rice variety of round-grain rice used for making risotto
ARBORIOS > ARBORIO
ARBORISE same as > ARBORIZE
ARBORISED > ARBORISE
ARBORISES > ARBORISE
ARBORIST n specialist in the cultivation of trees
ARBORISTS > ARBORTST
ARBORIZE vb give or take on a treelike branched appearance
ARBORIZED > ARBORIZE
ARBORIZES > ARBORIZE
ARBOROUS adj of trees
ARBORS > ARBOR
ARBOUR n glade sheltered by trees
ARBOURED adj having arbours
ARBOURS > ARBOUR
ARBOVIRAL > ARBOVIRUS
ARBOVIRUS n any one of a group of viruses that cause such diseases as encephalitis and dengue and are transmitted to humans by arthropods, esp insects and ticks
ARBS > ARB
ARBUSCLE n small tree
ARBUSCLES > ARBUSCLE
ARBUTE old name for > ARBUTUS
ARBUTEAN > ARBUTUS
ARBUTES > ARBUTE
ARBUTUS n evergreen shrub with strawberry-like berries
ARBUTUSES > ARBUTUS
ARC n part of a circle or other curve ▷ vb form an arc
ARCADE n covered passageway lined with shops ▷ vb provide with an arcade
ARCADED > ARCADE
ARCADES > ARCADE
ARCADIA n traditional idealized rural setting
ARCADIAN n person who leads a rural life
ARCADIANS > ARCADIAN
ARCADIAS > ARCADIA
ARCADING > ARCADE
ARCADINGS > ARCADE
ARCANA n either of the two divisions of a pack of tarot cards
ARCANAS > ARCANA
ARCANE adj mysterious and secret
ARCANELY > ARCANE

ARCANIST n person with secret knowledge
ARCANISTS > ARCANIST
ARCANUM n profound secret or mystery known only to initiates
ARCANUMS > ARCANUM
ARCATURE n small-scale arcade
ARCATURES > ARCATURE
ARCCOSINE n trigonometric function
ARCED > ARC
ARCH n curved structure supporting a bridge or roof ▷ vb (cause to) form an arch ▷ adj superior, knowing
ARCHAEA n order of prokaryotic microorganisms
ARCHAEAL same as > ARCHAEAN
ARCHAEAN n type of microorganism
ARCHAEANS > ARCHAEAN
ARCHAEI > ARCHAEUS
ARCHAEON same as > ARCHAEAN
ARCHAEUS n spirit believed to inhabit a living thing
ARCHAIC adj ancient
ARCHAICAL same as > ARCHAIC
ARCHAISE same as > ARCHAIZE
ARCHAISED > ARCHAISE
ARCHAISER > ARCHAISE
ARCHAISES > ARCHAISE
ARCHAISM n archaic word or phrase
ARCHAISMS > ARCHAISM
ARCHAIST > ARCHAISM
ARCHAISTS > ARCHAISM
ARCHAIZE vb give an archaic appearance or character to, as by the use of archaisms
ARCHAIZED > ARCHAIZE
ARCHAIZER > ARCHAIZE
ARCHAIZES > ARCHAIZE
ARCHANGEL n chief angel
ARCHDRUID n chief or principal druid
ARCHDUCAL adj of or relating to an archduke, archduchess, or archduchy
ARCHDUCHY n territory of an archduke or archduchess
ARCHDUKE n duke of specially high rank
ARCHDUKES > ARCHDUKE
ARCHEAN > ARCHAEAN
ARCHED adj provided with or spanned by an arch or arches
ARCHEI > ARCHEUS
ARCHENEMY n chief enemy
ARCHER n person who shoots with a bow and arrow

ARCHERESS n female archer
ARCHERIES > ARCHERY
ARCHERS > ARCHER
ARCHERY n art or sport of shooting with a bow and arrow
ARCHES > ARCH
ARCHEST > ARCH
ARCHETYPE n perfect specimen
ARCHEUS n spirit believed to inhabit a living thing
ARCHFIEND n the chief of fiends or devils
ARCHFOE n chief enemy
ARCHFOES > ARCHFOE
ARCHI > ARCO
ARCHICARP n female reproductive structure in ascomycetous fungi that consists of a cell or hypha and develops into the ascogonium
ARCHIL a variant spelling of > ORCHIL
ARCHILOWE n treat given in return
ARCHILS > ARCHIL
ARCHIMAGE n great magician or wizard
ARCHINE n Russian unit of length equal to about 71 cm
ARCHINES > ARCHINE
ARCHING > ARCH
ARCHINGS > ARCH
ARCHITECT n person qualified to design and supervise the construction of buildings
ARCHITYPE n primitive original from which others derive
ARCHIVAL > ARCHIVE
ARCHIVE n collection of records or documents ▷ vb store (documents, data, etc) in an archive or other repository
ARCHIVED > ARCHIVE
ARCHIVES > ARCHIVE
ARCHIVING > ARCHIVE
ARCHIVIST n person in charge of archives
ARCHIVOLT n moulding around an arch, sometimes decorated
ARCHLET n small arch
ARCHLETS > ARCHLET
ARCHLUTE n old bass lute
ARCHLUTES > ARCHLUTE
ARCHLY > ARCH
ARCHNESS > ARCH
ARCHOLOGY n study of the origins of things
ARCHON n (in ancient Athens) one of the nine chief magistrates
ARCHONS > ARCHON
ARCHONTIC > ARCHON
ARCHOSAUR n early type of dinosaur
ARCHRIVAL n chief rival

ARCHSTONE n wedge-shaped stone forming the curved part of an arch
ARCHWAY n passageway under an arch
ARCHWAYS > ARCHWAY
ARCHWISE adv like an arch
ARCIFORM adj shaped like an arch
ARCING > ARC
ARCINGS > ARC
ARCKED > ARC
ARCKING > ARC
ARCKINGS > ARC
ARCMIN n 1/60 of a degree of an angle
ARCMINS > ARCMIN
ARCMINUTE n unit of angular measurement, 1/60 of a degree
ARCO adv musical direction meaning with bow ▷ n bow of a stringed instrument
ARCOGRAPH n instrument used for drawing arcs without using a central point
ARCOLOGY n architecture blending buildings with the natural environment
ARCOS > ARCO
ARCS > ARC
ARCSEC n 1/3600 of a degree of an angle
ARCSECOND n unit used in astronomy
ARCSECS > ARCSEC
ARCSINE n trigonometrical function
ARCSINES > ARCSINE
ARCTIC adj very cold ▷ n high waterproof overshoe with buckles
ARCTICS > ARCTIC
ARCTIID n type of moth
ARCTIIDS > ARCTIID
ARCTOID adj like a bear
ARCTOPHIL n arctophile
ARCUATE adj shaped or bent like an arc or bow
ARCUATED same as > ARCUATE
ARCUATELY > ARCUATE
ARCUATION n use of arches or vaults in buildings
ARCUS n circle around the cornea of the eye
ARCUSES > ARCUS
ARD n primitive plough
ARDEB n unit of dry measure
ARDEBS > ARDEB
ARDENCIES > ARDENT
ARDENCY > ARDENT
ARDENT adj passionate
ARDENTLY > ARDENT
ARDOR same as > ARDOUR
ARDORS > ARDOR
ARDOUR n passion
ARDOURS > ARDOUR
ARDRI n Irish high king
ARDRIGH n Irish high king

ARDRIGHS > ARDRIGH
ARDRIS > ARDRI
ARDS > ARD
ARDUOUS adj hard to accomplish, strenuous
ARDUOUSLY > ARDUOUS
ARE n unit of measure, 100 square metres ▷ vb used as the singular form with you
AREA n part or region
AREACH vb old form of reach
AREACHED > AREACH
AREACHES > AREACH
AREACHING > AREACH
AREAD vb old word meaning declare
AREADING > AREAD
AREADS > AREAD
AREAE > AREA
AREAL > AREA
AREALLY > AREA
AREAR n old form of arrear
AREARS > AREAR
AREAS > AREA
AREAWAY n passageway
AREAWAYS > AREAWAY
ARECA n type of palm tree
ARECAS > ARECA
ARECOLINE n drug derived from betel nut
ARED > AREAD
AREDD > AREAD
AREDE vb old word meaning declare
AREDES > AREDE
AREDING > AREDE
AREFIED > AREFY
AREFIES > AREFY
AREFY vb dry up
AREFYING > AREFY
AREG a plural of > ERG
AREIC adj relating to area
ARENA n seated enclosure for sports events
ARENAS > ARENA
ARENATION n use of hot sand as a medical poultice
ARENE n aromatic hydrocarbon
ARENES > ARENE
ARENITE n any arenaceous rock
ARENITES > ARENITE
ARENITIC > ARENITE
ARENOSE adj sandy
ARENOUS adj sandy
AREOLA n small circular area, such as the coloured ring around the human nipple
AREOLAE > AREOLA
AREOLAR > AREOLA
AREOLAS > AREOLA
AREOLATE > AREOLA
AREOLATED adj areolate
AREOLE n space outlined on a surface
AREOLES > AREOLE
AREOLOGY n study of the planet Mars

AREOMETER n instrument for measuring the density of liquids
AREOMETRY n use of an araeometer
AREOSTYLE n building with widely-spaced columns
AREPA n Colombian cornmeal cake
AREPAS > AREPA
ARERE adv old word meaning backwards
ARES > ARE
ARET vb old word meaning entrust
ARETE n sharp ridge separating two glacial valleys
ARETES > ARETE
ARETHUSA n N American orchid with one long narrow leaf and one rose-purple flower fringed with yellow
ARETHUSAS > ARETHUSA
ARETS > ARET
ARETT vb old word meaning entrust
ARETTED > ARETT
ARETTING > ARETT
ARETTS > ARETT
AREW adv old word meaning in a row
ARF n barking sound
ARFS > ARF
ARGAL same as > ARGALI
ARGALA n Indian stork
ARGALAS > ARGALA
ARGALI n wild sheep
ARGALIS > ARGALI
ARGALS > ARGAL
ARGAN n Moroccan tree
ARGAND n lamp with a hollow circular wick
ARGANDS > ARGAND
ARGANS > ARGAN
ARGEMONE n prickly poppy
ARGEMONES > ARGEMONE
ARGENT n silver
ARGENTAL adj of or containing silver
ARGENTIC adj of or containing silver in the divalent or trivalent state
ARGENTINE adj of, relating to, or resembling silver ▷ n type of small silver fish
ARGENTITE n dark grey mineral that consists of silver sulphide, usually in cubic crystalline forms, and occurs in veins, often with native silver. It is found esp in Mexico, Nevada, and Saxony and is an important source of silver. Formula: Ag_2S
ARGENTOUS adj of or containing silver in the monovalent state
ARGENTS > ARGENT

ARGENTUM an obsolete name for > SILVER
ARGENTUMS > ARGENTUM
ARGH interj cry of pain
ARGHAN n agave plant
ARGHANS > ARGHAN
ARGIL n clay, esp potters' clay
ARGILLITE n any argillaceous rock, esp a hardened mudstone
ARGILS > ARGIL
ARGINASE n type of enzyme
ARGINASES > ARGINASE
ARGININE n essential amino acid of plant and animal proteins, necessary for nutrition and for the production of excretory urea
ARGININES > ARGININE
ARGLE vb quarrel
ARGLED > ARGLE
ARGLES > ARGLE
ARGLING > ARGLE
ARGOL n chemical compound
ARGOLS > ARGOL
ARGON n inert gas found in the air
ARGONAUT n paper nautilus
ARGONAUTS > ARGONAUT
ARGONON n inert gas
ARGONONS > ARGONON
ARGONS > ARGON
ARGOSIES > ARGOSY
ARGOSY n large merchant ship
ARGOT n slang or jargon
ARGOTIC > ARGOT
ARGOTS > ARGOT
ARGUABLE adj capable of being disputed
ARGUABLY adv it can be argued that
ARGUE vb try to prove by giving reasons
ARGUED > ARGUE
ARGUER > ARGUE
ARGUERS > ARGUE
ARGUES > ARGUE
ARGUFIED > ARGUFY
ARGUFIER > ARGUFY
ARGUFIERS > ARGUFY
ARGUFIES > ARGUFY
ARGUFY vb argue or quarrel, esp over something trivial
ARGUFYING > ARGUFY
ARGUING > ARGUE
ARGULI > ARGULUS
ARGULUS n parasite on fish
ARGUMENT n quarrel
ARGUMENTA n appeals to reason
ARGUMENTS > ARGUMENT
ARGUS n any of various brown butterflies
ARGUSES > ARGUS
ARGUTE adj shrill or keen

ARGUTELY > ARGUTE
ARGYLE adj a diamond-shaped pattern ▷ n sock made of this
ARGYLES > ARGYLE
ARGYLL n sock with diamond pattern
ARGYLLS > ARGYLL
ARGYRIA n staining of skin by exposure to silver
ARGYRIAS > ARGYRIA
ARGYRITE n mineral containing silver sulphide
ARGYRITES > ARGYRITE
ARHAT n Buddhist who has achieved enlightenment
ARHATS > ARHAT
ARHATSHIP > ARHAT
ARHYTHMIA n irregular heartbeat
ARHYTHMIC > ARHYTHMIA
ARIA n elaborate song for solo voice, esp one from an opera
ARIARIES > ARIARY
ARIARY n currency of Madagascar
ARIAS > ARIA
ARID adj parched, dry
ARIDER > ARID
ARIDEST > ARID
ARIDITIES > ARID
ARIDITY > ARID
ARIDLY > ARID
ARIDNESS > ARID
ARIEL n type of Arabian gazelle
ARIELS > ARIEL
ARIETTA n short aria
ARIETTAS > ARIETTA
ARIETTE same as > ARIETTA
ARIETTES > ARIETTE
ARIGHT adv rightly
ARIKI n first-born male or female in a notable family
ARIKIS > ARIKI
ARIL n appendage on certain seeds
ARILED adj having an aril
ARILLARY adj having an aril
ARILLATE > ARILLATED
ARILLATED adj having an aril
ARILLI > ARILLUS
ARILLODE n structure in certain seeds that resembles an aril but is developed from the micropyle of the ovule
ARILLODES > ARILLODE
ARILLOID adj of or like an aril
ARILLUS n aril
ARILS > ARIL
ARIOSE adj songlike
ARIOSI > ARIOSO
ARIOSO n recitative with the lyrical quality of an aria
ARIOSOS > ARIOSO
ARIOT adv riotously

ARIPPLE adv in ripples
ARIS n Cockney slang for buttocks
ARISE vb come about
ARISEN > ARISE
ARISES > ARISE
ARISH n field that has been mown
ARISHES > ARISH
ARISING > ARISE
ARISTA n stiff bristle
ARISTAE > ARISTA
ARISTAS > ARISTA
ARISTATE > ARISTA
ARISTO n aristocrat
ARISTOS > ARISTO
ARISTOTLE n bottle
ARK n boat built by Noah, which survived the Flood ▷ vb place in an ark
ARKED > ARK
ARKING > ARK
ARKITE n passenger in ark
ARKITES > ARKITE
ARKOSE n type of sandstone
ARKOSES > ARKOSE
ARKOSIC > ARKOSE
ARKS > ARK
ARLE vb make downpayment
ARLED > ARLE
ARLES > ARLE
ARLING > ARLE
ARM n limbs from the shoulder to the wrist ▷ vb supply with weapons
ARMADA n large number of warships
ARMADAS > ARMADA
ARMADILLO n small S American mammal covered in strong bony plates
ARMAGNAC n dry brown brandy
ARMAGNACS > ARMAGNAC
ARMAMENT n military weapons
ARMAMENTS > ARMAMENT
ARMATURE n revolving structure in an electric motor or generator, wound with coils carrying the current
ARMATURED > ARMATURE
ARMATURES > ARMATURE
ARMBAND n band worn on the arm
ARMBANDS > ARMBAND
ARMCHAIR n upholstered chair with side supports for the arms ▷ adj taking no active part
ARMCHAIRS > ARMCHAIR
ARMED adj equipped with or supported by arms, armour, etc
ARMER > ARM
ARMERIA n generic name for the plant thrift
ARMERIAS > ARMERIA
ARMERS > ARM

ARMET n close-fitting medieval visored helmet with a neck guard
ARMETS > ARMET
ARMFUL n as much as can be held in the arms
ARMFULS > ARMFUL
ARMGAUNT adj word in Shakespeare of uncertain meaning
ARMGUARD n covering to protect the arm
ARMGUARDS > ARMGUARD
ARMHOLE n opening in a garment through which the arm passes
ARMHOLES > ARMHOLE
ARMIES > ARMY
ARMIGER n person entitled to bear heraldic arms
ARMIGERAL > ARMIGER
ARMIGERO n armiger
ARMIGEROS > ARMIGERO
ARMIGERS > ARMIGER
ARMIL n bracelet
ARMILLA n bracelet
ARMILLAE > ARMILLA
ARMILLARY adj of or relating to bracelets
ARMILLAS > ARMILLA
ARMILS > ARMIL
ARMING n act of taking arms or providing with arms
ARMINGS > ARMING
ARMISTICE n agreed suspension of fighting
ARMLESS > ARM
ARMLET n band worn round the arm
ARMLETS > ARMLET
ARMLIKE > ARM
ARMLOAD n amount carried in the arms
ARMLOADS > ARMLOAD
ARMLOCK vb grip someone's arms
ARMLOCKED > ARMLOCK
ARMLOCKS > ARMLOCK
ARMOIRE n large cabinet
ARMOIRES > ARMOIRE
ARMONICA n glass harmonica
ARMONICAS > ARMONICA
ARMOR same as > ARMOUR
ARMORED same as > ARMOURED
ARMORER same as > ARMOURER
ARMORERS > ARMORER
ARMORIAL adj of or relating to heraldry or heraldic arms ▷ n book of coats of arms
ARMORIALS > ARMORIAL
ARMORIES > ARMORY
ARMORING > ARMOR
ARMORIST n heraldry expert
ARMORISTS > ARMORIST
ARMORLESS > ARMOR

ARMORS > ARMOR
ARMORY same as > ARMOURY
ARMOUR n metal clothing formerly worn to protect the body in battle ▷ vb equip or cover with armour
ARMOURED adj having a protective covering
ARMOURER n maker, repairer, or keeper of arms or armour
ARMOURERS > ARMOURER
ARMOURIES > ARMOURY
ARMOURING > ARMOUR
ARMOURS > ARMOUR
ARMOURY n place where weapons are stored
ARMOZEEN n material used for clerical gowns
ARMOZEENS > ARMOZEEN
ARMOZINE n material used for clerical gowns
ARMOZINES > ARMOZINE
ARMPIT n hollow under the arm at the shoulder
ARMPITS > ARMPIT
ARMREST n part of a chair or sofa that supports the arm
ARMRESTS > ARMREST
ARMS > ARM
ARMSFUL > ARMFUL
ARMURE n silk or wool fabric with a small cobbled pattern
ARMURES > ARMURE
ARMY n military land forces of a nation
ARMYWORM n caterpillar of a widely distributed noctuid moth
ARMYWORMS > ARMYWORM
ARNA n Indian water buffalo
ARNAS > ARNA
ARNATTO n annatto
ARNATTOS > ARNATTO
ARNICA n temperate or arctic plant
ARNICAS > ARNICA
ARNOTTO n annatto
ARNOTTOS > ARNOTTO
ARNUT n plant with edible tubers
ARNUTS > ARNUT
AROBA n Asian carriage
AROBAS > AROBA
AROHA n love, compassion, or affection
AROHAS > AROHA
AROID n type of plant
AROIDS > AROID
AROINT vb drive away
AROINTED > AROINT
AROINTING > AROINT
AROINTS > AROINT
AROLLA n European pine tree
AROLLAS > AROLLA
AROMA n pleasant smell
AROMAS > AROMA

AROMATASE n enzyme involved in the production of oestrogen

AROMATIC adj having a distinctive pleasant smell ▷ n something, such as a plant or drug, that gives off a fragrant smell

AROMATICS > AROMATIC

AROMATISE same as > AROMATIZE

AROMATIZE vb make aromatic

AROSE past tense of > ARISE

AROUND adv on all sides (of)

AROUSABLE > AROUSE

AROUSAL > AROUSE

AROUSALS > AROUSE

AROUSE vb stimulate, make active

AROUSED > AROUSE

AROUSER > AROUSE

AROUSERS > AROUSE

AROUSES > AROUSE

AROUSING > AROUSE

AROW adv in a row

AROYNT vb old word meaning to drive away

AROYNTED > AROYNT

AROYNTING > AROYNT

AROYNTS > AROYNT

ARPA n website concerned with structure of the internet

ARPAS > ARPA

ARPEGGIO n notes of a chord played or sung in quick succession

ARPEGGIOS > ARPEGGIO

ARPEN n old French measure of land

ARPENS > ARPEN

ARPENT n former French unit of length

ARPENTS > ARPENT

ARPILLERA n Peruvian wall-hanging

ARQUEBUS n portable long-barrelled gun dating from the 15th century

ARRACACHA n S American plant

ARRACK n alcoholic drink distilled from grain or rice

ARRACKS > ARRACK

ARRAH interj Irish exclamation

ARRAIGN vb bring (a prisoner) before a court to answer a charge

ARRAIGNED > ARRAIGN

ARRAIGNER > ARRAIGN

ARRAIGNS > ARRAIGN

ARRANGE vb plan

ARRANGED > ARRANGE

ARRANGER > ARRANGE

ARRANGERS > ARRANGE

ARRANGES > ARRANGE

ARRANGING > ARRANGE

ARRANT adj utter, downright

ARRANTLY > ARRANT

ARRAS n tapestry wall-hanging

ARRASED adj having an arras

ARRASENE n material used in embroidery

ARRASENES > ARRASENE

ARRASES > ARRAS

ARRAUGHT > AREACH

ARRAY n impressive display or collection ▷ vb arrange in order

ARRAYAL > ARRAY

ARRAYALS > ARRAY

ARRAYED > ARRAY

ARRAYER > ARRAY

ARRAYERS > ARRAY

ARRAYING > ARRAY

ARRAYMENT n act of arraying

ARRAYS > ARRAY

ARREAR n singular of arrears

ARREARAGE same as > ARREARS

ARREARS pl n money owed

ARRECT adj pricked up

ARREEDE vb old word meaning declare

ARREEDES > ARREEDE

ARREEDING > ARREEDE

ARREST vb take (a person) into custody ▷ n act of taking a person into custody

ARRESTANT n substance that stops a chemical reaction

ARRESTED > ARREST

ARRESTEE n arrested person

ARRESTEES > ARRESTEE

ARRESTER n person who arrests

ARRESTERS > ARRESTER

ARRESTING adj attracting attention, striking

ARRESTIVE adj making something stop

ARRESTOR n person or thing that arrests

ARRESTORS > ARRESTOR

ARRESTS > ARREST

ARRET n judicial decision

ARRETS > ARRET

ARRHIZAL adj without roots

ARRIAGE n Scottish feudal service

ARRIAGES > ARRIAGE

ARRIBA interj exclamation of pleasure or approval

ARRIDE vb old word meaning gratify

ARRIDED > ARRIDE

ARRIDES > ARRIDE

ARRIDING > ARRIDE

ARRIERE adj French word meaning old-fashioned

ARRIERO n Spanish word for mule driver

ARRIEROS > ARRIERO

ARRIS n sharp edge at the meeting of two surfaces

ARRISES > ARRIS

ARRISH n corn stubble

ARRISHES > ARRISH

ARRIVAL n arriving

ARRIVALS > ARRIVAL

ARRIVANCE n old word meaning people who have arrived

ARRIVANCY n arrivance

ARRIVE vb reach a place or destination

ARRIVED > ARRIVE

ARRIVER > ARRIVE

ARRIVERS > ARRIVE

ARRIVES > ARRIVE

ARRIVING > ARRIVE

ARRIVISME n unscrupulous ambition

ARRIVISTE n person who is unscrupulously ambitious

ARROBA n unit of weight in Spanish-speaking countries

ARROBAS > ARROBA

ARROCES > ARROZ

ARROGANCE > ARROGANT

ARROGANCY > ARROGANT

ARROGANT adj proud and overbearing

ARROGATE vb claim or seize without justification

ARROGATED > ARROGATE

ARROGATES > ARROGATE

ARROGATOR > ARROGATE

ARROW n pointed shaft shot from a bow

ARROWED adj having an arrow pattern

ARROWHEAD n pointed tip of an arrow

ARROWING > ARROW

ARROWLESS > ARROW

ARROWLIKE > ARROW

ARROWROOT n nutritious starch obtained from the root of a W Indian plant

ARROWS > ARROW

ARROWWOOD n any of various trees or shrubs, esp certain viburnums, having long straight tough stems formerly used by North American Indians to make arrows

ARROWWORM n type of small marine invertebrate with an elongated transparent body

ARROWY adj like an arrow

ARROYO n usually dry stream bed

ARROYOS > ARROYO

ARROZ n Spanish word for rice, used in name of various dishes

ARROZES > ARROZ

ARS > AR

ARSE n buttocks or anus ▷ vb play the fool

ARSED > ARSE

ARSEHOLE n anus

ARSEHOLED adj very drunk

ARSEHOLES > ARSEHOLE

ARSENAL n place where arms and ammunition are made or stored

ARSENALS > ARSENAL

ARSENATE n salt or ester of arsenic acid

ARSENATES > ARSENATE

ARSENIATE n arsenate

ARSENIC n toxic grey element ▷ adj of or containing arsenic

ARSENICAL adj of or containing arsenic ▷ n drug or insecticide containing arsenic

ARSENICS > ARSENIC

ARSENIDE n compound in which arsenic is the most electronegative element

ARSENIDES > ARSENIDE

ARSENIOUS adj of or containing arsenic in the trivalent state

ARSENITE n salt or ester of arsenous acid, esp a salt containing the ion $A_sO_3^{3-}$

ARSENITES > ARSENITE

ARSENO adj containing arsenic

ARSENOUS same as > ARSENIOUS

ARSES > ARSIS

ARSEY adj aggressive, irritable, or argumentative

ARSHEEN n old measure of length in Russia

ARSHEENS > ARSHEEN

ARSHIN n old measure of length in Russia

ARSHINE n old measure of length in Russia

ARSHINES > ARSHINE

ARSHINS > ARSHIN

ARSIER > ARSY

ARSIEST > ARSY

ARSINE n colourless poisonous gas

ARSINES > ARSINE

ARSING > ARSE

ARSINO adj containing arsine

ARSIS n long or stressed syllable in a metrical foot

ARSON n crime of intentionally setting property on fire

ARSONIST > ARSON

ARSONISTS > ARSON

ARSONITE n person committing arson

ARSONITES > ARSONITE

ARSONOUS adj of arson

ARSONS > ARSON

ARSY same as > ARSEY

ART n creation of works of beauty, esp paintings or sculpture

ARTAL a plural of > ROTL

ARTEFACT n something made by human beings

ARTEFACTS > ARTEFACT

ARTEL n cooperative union

ARTELS > ARTEL

ARTEMISIA n type of herbaceous plant of the N hemisphere, such as mugwort, sagebrush, and wormwood

ARTERIAL adj of an artery ▷ n major road

ARTERIALS > ARTERIAL

ARTERIES > ARTERY

ARTERIOLE n any of the small subdivisions of an artery that form thin-walled vessels ending in capillaries

ARTERITIS n inflammation of an artery

ARTERY n one of the tubes carrying blood from the heart

ARTESIAN adj as in artesian well well sunk through impermeable strata receiving water from an area at a higher altitude than that of the well

ARTFUL adj cunning, wily

ARTFULLY > ARTFUL

ARTHOUSE n cinema which shows artistic films

ARTHOUSES > ARTHOUSE

ARTHRITIC > ARTHRITIS

ARTHRITIS n painful inflammation of a joint or joints

ARTHRODIA n joint

ARTHROPOD n animal, such as a spider or insect, with jointed limbs and a segmented body

ARTHROSES > ARTHROSIS

ARTHROSIS n disease of joint

ARTI n ritual performed in homes and temples

ARTIC n articulated vehicle

ARTICHOKE n flower head of a thistle-like plant, cooked as a vegetable

ARTICLE n written piece in a magazine or newspaper ▷ vb bind by a written contract

ARTICLED > ARTICLE

ARTICLES > ARTICLE

ARTICLING > ARTICLE

ARTICS > ARTIC

ARTICULAR adj of or relating to joints

ARTIER > ARTY

ARTIES > ARTY

ARTIEST > ARTY

ARTIFACT same as > ARTEFACT

ARTIFACTS > ARTIFACT

ARTIFICE n clever trick

ARTIFICER n craftsman

ARTIFICES > ARTIFICE

ARTIGI n kind of hooded coat worn in Canada

ARTIGIS > ARTIGI

ARTILLERY n large-calibre guns

ARTILY > ARTY

ARTINESS > ARTY

ARTIS > ARTI

ARTISAN n skilled worker, craftsman

ARTISANAL > ARTISAN

ARTISANS > ARTISAN

ARTIST n person who produces works of art, esp paintings or sculpture

ARTISTE n professional entertainer such as a singer or dancer

ARTISTES > ARTISTE

ARTISTIC adj of or characteristic of art or artists

ARTISTRY n artistic skill

ARTISTS > ARTIST

ARTLESS adj free from deceit or cunning

ARTLESSLY > ARTLESS

ARTMAKER n person who creates art

ARTMAKERS > ARTMAKER

ARTS > ART

ARTSIE n arts student

ARTSIER > ARTSY

ARTSIES > ARTSY

ARTSIEST > ARTSY

ARTSINESS > ARTSY

ARTSMAN old word for > CRAFTSMAN

ARTSMEN > ARTSMAN

ARTSY adj interested in the arts ▷ n person interested in the arts

ARTWORK n all the photographs and illustrations in a publication

ARTWORKS > ARTWORK

ARTY adj having an affected interest in art ▷ n person interested in art

ARUGOLA n salad plant

ARUGOLAS > ARUGOLA

ARUGULA another name for > ROCKET

ARUGULAS > ARUGULA

ARUHE n edible root of a fern

ARUHES > ARUHE

ARUM n type of plant

ARUMS > ARUM

ARUSPEX variant spelling of > HARUSPEX

ARUSPICES > ARUSPEX

ARVAL adj of ploughed land

ARVEE n short for recreational vehicle (RV)

ARVEES > ARVEE

ARVICOLE n water rat

ARVICOLES > ARVICOLE

ARVO n afternoon

ARVOS > ARVO

ARY dialect form of > ANY

ARYBALLOS n ancient Greek flask

ARYL n of, consisting of, or containing an aromatic group

ARYLS > ARYL

ARYTENOID adj denoting either of two small cartilages of the larynx that are attached to the vocal cords ▷ n arytenoid cartilage or muscle

ARYTHMIA n any variation

ARYTHMIAS > ARYTHMIA

ARYTHMIC > ARYTHMIA

AS adv used to indicate amount or extent in comparisons ▷ n ancient Roman unit of weight

ASAFETIDA n bitter resin with an unpleasant onion-like smell

ASANA n any of various postures in yoga

ASANAS > ASANA

ASAR > AS

ASARUM n dried strong-scented root

ASARUMS > ASARUM

ASBESTIC > ASBESTOS

ASBESTINE > ASBESTOS

ASBESTOS n fibrous mineral which does not burn

ASBESTOUS > ASBESTOS

ASBESTUS n asbestos

ASCARED adj afraid

ASCARID n type of parasitic nematode

ASCARIDES > ASCARID

ASCARIDS > ASCARID

ASCARIS n ascarid

ASCARISES > ASCARIS

ASCAUNT adv old word meaning slantwise

ASCEND vb go or move up

ASCENDANT adj dominant or influential

ASCENDED > ASCEND

ASCENDENT same as > ASCENDANT

ASCENDER n part of certain lower-case letters, such as b or h, that extends above the body of the letter

ASCENDERS > ASCENDER

ASCENDEUR n metal grip that is threaded on a rope and can be alternately tightened and slackened as an aid to climbing the rope: used attached to slings for the feet and waist

ASCENDING adj moving upwards

ASCENDS > ASCEND

ASCENSION n act of ascending

ASCENSIVE adj moving upwards

ASCENT n ascending

ASCENTS > ASCENT

ASCERTAIN vb find out definitely

ASCESES > ASCESIS

ASCESIS n exercise of self-discipline

ASCETIC adj (person) abstaining from worldly pleasures and comforts ▷ n person who abstains from worldly comforts and pleasures

ASCETICAL adj ascetic

ASCETICS > ASCETIC

ASCI > ASCUS

ASCIAN n person living in the tropics

ASCIANS > ASCIAN

ASCIDIA > ASCIDIUM

ASCIDIAN n type of minute marine invertebrate, such as the sea squirt

ASCIDIANS > ASCIDIAN

ASCIDIATE > ASCIDIUM

ASCIDIUM n part of a plant that is shaped like a pitcher, such as the modified leaf of the pitcher plant

ASCITES n accumulation of serous fluid in the peritoneal cavity

ASCITIC > ASCITES

ASCITICAL > ASCITES

ASCLEPIAD n Greek verse form

ASCLEPIAS n type of plant often grown as a garden or greenhouse plant for its showy orange-scarlet or purple flowers

ASCOCARP n (in some ascomycetous fungi) a globular structure containing the asci

ASCOCARPS > ASCOCARP

ASCOGONIA n female reproductive bodies in some fungi

ASCON n type of sponge having an oval shape and a thin body wall

ASCONCE adv old form of askance

ASCONOID adj like an ascon

ASCONS > ASCON

ASCORBATE n salt of ascorbic acid

ASCORBIC adj as in ascorbic acid white crystalline vitamin present in plants, esp citrus fruits, tomatoes, and green vegetables

ASCOSPORE n one of the spores (usually eight in number) that are produced in an ascus

ASCOT n type of cravat

ASCOTS > ASCOT

ASCRIBE vb attribute, as to a particular origin
ASCRIBED > ASCRIBE
ASCRIBES > ASCRIBE
ASCRIBING > ASCRIBE
ASCUS n saclike structure in fungi
ASDIC an early form of > SONAR
ASDICS > ASDIC
ASEA adv towards the sea
ASEISMIC adj denoting a region free of earthquakes
ASEITIES > ASEITY
ASEITY n existence derived from itself, having no other source
ASEMANTIC adj not semantic
ASEPALOUS adj (of a plant or flower) having no sepals
ASEPSES > ASEPSIS
ASEPSIS n aseptic condition
ASEPTATE adj not divided into cells or sections by septa
ASEPTIC adj free from harmful bacteria ▷ n aseptic substance
ASEPTICS > ASEPTIC
ASEXUAL adj without sex
ASEXUALLY > ASEXUAL
ASH n powdery substance left when something is burnt ▷ vb reduce to ashes
ASHAKE adv shaking
ASHAME vb make ashamed
ASHAMED adj feeling shame
ASHAMEDLY > ASHAMED
ASHAMES > ASHAME
ASHAMING > ASHAME
ASHCAKE n cornmeal bread
ASHCAKES > ASHCAKE
ASHCAN n large metal dustbin
ASHCANS > ASHCAN
ASHED > ASH
ASHEN adj pale with shock
ASHERIES > ASHERY
ASHERY n place where ashes are made
ASHES > ASH
ASHET n shallow oval dish or large plate
ASHETS > ASHET
ASHFALL n dropping of ash from a volcano
ASHFALLS > ASHFALL
ASHIER > ASHY
ASHIEST > ASHY
ASHINE adv old word meaning shining
ASHINESS > ASHY
ASHING > ASH
ASHIVER adv shivering
ASHKEY n winged fruit of the ash
ASHKEYS > ASHKEY

ASHLAR n block of hewn stone ▷ vb build with ashlars
ASHLARED > ASHLAR
ASHLARING > ASHLAR
ASHLARS > ASHLAR
ASHLER same as > ASHLAR
ASHLERED > ASHLER
ASHLERING > ASHLER
ASHLERS > ASHLER
ASHLESS > ASH
ASHMAN n man who shovels ashes
ASHMEN > ASHMAN
ASHORE adv towards or on land ▷ adj on land, having come from the water
ASHPAN n pan or tray to catch ashes
ASHPANS > ASHPAN
ASHPLANT n walking stick made from an ash sapling
ASHPLANTS > ASHPLANT
ASHRAF > SHERIF
ASHRAM n religious retreat where a Hindu holy man lives
ASHRAMA n stage in Hindu spiritual life
ASHRAMAS > ASHRAMA
ASHRAMITE n person living in an ashram
ASHRAMS > ASHRAM
ASHTANGA n type of yoga
ASHTANGAS > ASHTANGA
ASHTRAY n receptacle for tobacco ash and cigarette butts
ASHTRAYS > ASHTRAY
ASHY adj pale greyish
ASIAGO n type of cheese
ASIAGOS > ASIAGO
ASIDE adv one side ▷ n remark not meant to be heard by everyone present
ASIDES > ASIDE
ASINICO n old Spanish word for fool
ASINICOS > ASINICO
ASININE adj stupid, idiotic
ASININELY > ASININE
ASININITY > ASININE
ASK vb say (something) in a form that requires an answer
ASKANCE adv with an oblique glance ▷ vb turn aside
ASKANCED > ASKANCE
ASKANCES > ASKANCE
ASKANCING > ASKANCE
ASKANT same as > ASKANCE
ASKANTED > ASKANT
ASKANTING > ASKANT
ASKANTS > ASKANT
ASKARI n (in East Africa) a soldier or policeman
ASKARIS > ASKARI
ASKED > ASK
ASKER > ASK

ASKERS > ASK
ASKESES > ASKESIS
ASKESIS n practice of self-discipline
ASKEW adj one side, crooked
ASKEWNESS > ASKEW
ASKING > ASK
ASKINGS > ASK
ASKLENT Scots word for > ASLANT
ASKOI > ASKOS
ASKOS n ancient Greek vase
ASKS > ASK
ASLAKE vb slake
ASLAKED > ASLAKE
ASLAKES > ASLAKE
ASLAKING > ASLAKE
ASLANT adv at a slant (to), slanting (across)
ASLEEP adj sleeping
ASLOPE adj sloping
ASLOSH adj awash
ASMEAR adj smeared
ASMOULDER adv old word meaning smouldering
ASOCIAL n person who avoids social contact
ASOCIALS > ASOCIAL
ASP n small poisonous snake
ASPARAGUS n plant whose shoots are cooked as a vegetable
ASPARKLE adv sparkling
ASPARTAME n artificial sweetener
ASPARTATE n enzyme found in blood
ASPARTIC adj as in aspartic acid nonessential amino acid that is a component of proteins and acts as a neurotransmitter
ASPECT n feature or element ▷ vb look at
ASPECTED > ASPECT
ASPECTING > ASPECT
ASPECTS > ASPECT
ASPECTUAL adj of or relating to grammatical aspect
ASPEN n kind of poplar tree ▷ adj trembling
ASPENS > ASPEN
ASPER n former Turkish monetary unit
ASPERATE adj (of plant parts) having a rough surface due to a covering of short stiff hairs ▷ vb make rough
ASPERATED > ASPERATE
ASPERATES > ASPERATE
ASPERGE vb sprinkle
ASPERGED > ASPERGE
ASPERGER > ASPERGE
ASPERGERS > ASPERGE
ASPERGES > ASPERGE
ASPERGILL n perforated instrument used to sprinkle holy water

ASPERGING > ASPERGE
ASPERITY n roughness of temper
ASPERMIA n failure to form or emit semen
ASPERMIAS > ASPERMIA
ASPEROUS same as > ASPERATE
ASPERS > ASPER
ASPERSE vb spread false rumours about
ASPERSED > ASPERSE
ASPERSER > ASPERSE
ASPERSERS > ASPERSE
ASPERSES > ASPERSE
ASPERSING > ASPERSE
ASPERSION n disparaging or malicious remark
ASPERSIVE > ASPERSE
ASPERSOIR n sprinkler for holy water
ASPERSOR > ASPERSE
ASPERSORS > ASPERSE
ASPERSORY n sprinkler for holy water
ASPHALT n black hard tarlike substance used for road surfaces etc ▷ vb cover with asphalt
ASPHALTED > ASPHALT
ASPHALTER n person who lays asphalt
ASPHALTIC > ASPHALT
ASPHALTS > ASPHALT
ASPHALTUM n asphalt
ASPHERIC adj not spherical ▷ n lens that is not completely spherical
ASPHERICS > ASPHERIC
ASPHODEL n plant with clusters of yellow or white flowers
ASPHODELS > ASPHODEL
ASPHYXIA n suffocation
ASPHYXIAL > ASPHYXIA
ASPHYXIAS > ASPHYXIA
ASPHYXIES > ASPHYXY
ASPHYXY same as > ASPHYXIA
ASPIC n savoury jelly used to coat meat, eggs, fish, etc
ASPICK old word for > ASP
ASPICKS > ASPICK
ASPICS > ASPIC
ASPIDIA > ASPIDIUM
ASPIDIOID > ASPIDIUM
ASPIDIUM n variety of fern
ASPINE old word for > ASPEN
ASPINES > ASPINE
ASPIRANT n person who aspires ▷ adj aspiring or striving
ASPIRANTS > ASPIRANT
ASPIRATA n rough stop
ASPIRATAE > ASPIRATA
ASPIRATE vb pronounce with an h sound ▷ n h sound ▷ adj (of a stop) pronounced with a forceful and audible expulsion of breath

ASPIRATED > ASPIRATE
ASPIRATES > ASPIRATE
ASPIRATOR n device for removing fluids from a body cavity by suction
ASPIRE vb yearn (for), hope (to do or be)
ASPIRED > ASPIRE
ASPIRER > ASPIRE
ASPIRERS > ASPIRE
ASPIRES > ASPIRE
ASPIRIN n drug used to relieve pain and fever
ASPIRING > ASPIRE
ASPIRINS > ASPIRIN
ASPIS n horned viper
ASPISES > ASPIS
ASPISH adj like an asp
ASPLENIUM n type of fern
ASPORT vb old word meaning take away
ASPORTED > ASPORT
ASPORTING > ASPORT
ASPORTS > ASPORT
ASPOUT adv spouting
ASPRAWL adv sprawling
ASPREAD adv spreading
ASPRO n associate professor at an academic institution
ASPROS > ASPRO
ASPROUT adv sprouting
ASPS > ASP
ASQUAT adv squatting
ASQUINT adj with a glance from the corner of the eye
ASRAMA n stage in Hindu spiritual life
ASRAMAS > ASRAMA
ASS n donkey
ASSAGAI same as
> ASSEGAI
ASSAGAIED > ASSAGAI
ASSAGAIS > ASSAGAI
ASSAI adv (usually preceded by a musical direction) very ▷ n Brazilian palm tree
ASSAIL vb attack violently
ASSAILANT n person who attacks another, either physically or verbally
ASSAILED > ASSAIL
ASSAILER > ASSAIL
ASSAILERS > ASSAIL
ASSAILING > ASSAIL
ASSAILS > ASSAIL
ASSAIS > ASSAI
ASSAM n (in Malaysia) tamarind as used in cooking
ASSAMS > ASSAM
ASSART vb clear ground for cultivation
ASSARTED > ASSART
ASSARTING > ASSART
ASSARTS > ASSART
ASSASSIN n person who murders a prominent person
ASSASSINS > ASSASSIN

ASSAULT n violent attack ▷ vb attack violently
ASSAULTED > ASSAULT
ASSAULTER > ASSAULT
ASSAULTS > ASSAULT
ASSAY n analysis of a substance ▷ vb make such an analysis
ASSAYABLE > ASSAY
ASSAYED > ASSAY
ASSAYER > ASSAY
ASSAYERS > ASSAY
ASSAYING > ASSAY
ASSAYINGS > ASSAY
ASSAYS > ASSAY
ASSEGAAI same as
> ASSEGAI
ASSEGAAIS > ASSEGAI
ASSEGAI n slender spear used in S Africa ▷ vb spear with an assegai
ASSEGAIED > ASSEGAI
ASSEGAIS > ASSEGAI
ASSEMBLE vb collect or congregate
ASSEMBLED > ASSEMBLE
ASSEMBLER n person or thing that assembles
ASSEMBLES > ASSEMBLE
ASSEMBLY n assembled group
ASSENT n agreement or consent ▷ vb agree or consent
ASSENTED > ASSENT
ASSENTER n person supporting another's nomination
ASSENTERS > ASSENTER
ASSENTING > ASSENT
ASSENTIVE > ASSENT
ASSENTOR n any of the eight voters legally required to endorse the nomination of a candidate in a parliamentary or local election in addition to the nominator and seconder
ASSENTORS > ASSENTOR
ASSENTS > ASSENT
ASSERT vb declare forcefully
ASSERTED > ASSERT
ASSERTER > ASSERT
ASSERTERS > ASSERT
ASSERTING > ASSERT
ASSERTION n positive statement, usu made without evidence
ASSERTIVE adj confident and direct in dealing with others
ASSERTOR > ASSERT
ASSERTORS > ASSERT
ASSERTORY adj making affirmation
ASSERTS > ASSERT
ASSES > ASS
ASSESS vb judge the worth or importance of
ASSESSED > ASSESS
ASSESSES > ASSESS
ASSESSING > ASSESS

ASSESSOR n person who values property for taxation or insurance purposes
ASSESSORS
> ASSESSOR
ASSET n valuable or useful person or thing
ASSETLESS > ASSET
ASSETS > ASSET
ASSEVER vb old form of asseverate
ASSEVERED > ASSEVER
ASSEVERS > ASSEVER
ASSEZ adv (as part of a musical direction) fairly
ASSHOLE same as
> ARSEHOLE
ASSHOLES > ASSHOLE
ASSIDUITY n constant and close application
ASSIDUOUS adj hard-working
ASSIEGE vb old form of besiege
ASSIEGED > ASSIEGE
ASSIEGES > ASSIEGE
ASSIEGING > ASSIEGE
ASSIENTO n slave trade treaty between Britain and Spain
ASSIENTOS > ASSIENTO
ASSIGN vb appoint (someone) to a job or task ▷ n person to whom property is assigned
ASSIGNAT n paper money issued by the Constituent Assembly in 1789, backed by the confiscated land of the Church and the émigrés
ASSIGNATS > ASSIGNAT
ASSIGNED > ASSIGN
ASSIGNEE n person to whom some right, interest, or property is transferred
ASSIGNEES > ASSIGNEE
ASSIGNER > ASSIGN
ASSIGNERS > ASSIGN
ASSIGNING > ASSIGN
ASSIGNOR n person who transfers or assigns property
ASSIGNORS > ASSIGNOR
ASSIGNS > ASSIGN
ASSIST vb give help or support ▷ n pass by a player which enables another player to score a goal
ASSISTANT n helper ▷ adj junior or deputy
ASSISTED > ASSIST
ASSISTER > ASSIST
ASSISTERS > ASSIST
ASSISTING > ASSIST
ASSISTIVE adj providing a means of reducing a physical impairment
ASSISTOR > ASSIST
ASSISTORS > ASSIST
ASSISTS > ASSIST

ASSIZE n sitting of a legislative assembly
ASSIZED > ASSIZE
ASSIZER n weights and measures official
ASSIZERS > ASSIZER
ASSIZES > ASSIZE
ASSIZING > ASSIZE
ASSLIKE > ASS
ASSOCIATE vb connect in the mind ▷ n partner in business ▷ adj having partial rights or subordinate status
ASSOIL vb absolve
ASSOILED > ASSOIL
ASSOILING > ASSOIL
ASSOILS > ASSOIL
ASSOILZIE vb old Scots word meaning absolve
ASSONANCE n rhyming of vowel sounds but not consonants
ASSONANT > ASSONANCE
ASSONANTS
> ASSONANCE
ASSONATE vb show assonance
ASSONATED > ASSONATE
ASSONATES > ASSONATE
ASSORT vb arrange or distribute equally
ASSORTED adj consisting of various types mixed together
ASSORTER > ASSORT
ASSORTERS > ASSORT
ASSORTING > ASSORT
ASSORTIVE > ASSORT
ASSORTS > ASSORT
ASSOT vb old word meaning make infatuated
ASSOTS > ASSOT
ASSOTT vb besot
ASSOTTED > ASSOT
ASSOTTING > ASSOT
ASSUAGE vb relieve (pain, grief, thirst, etc)
ASSUAGED > ASSUAGE
ASSUAGER > ASSUAGE
ASSUAGERS > ASSUAGE
ASSUAGES > ASSUAGE
ASSUAGING > ASSUAGE
ASSUASIVE > ASSUAGE
ASSUETUDE n state of being accustomed
ASSUMABLE > ASSUME
ASSUMABLY > ASSUME
ASSUME vb take to be true without proof
ASSUMED adj false
ASSUMEDLY > ASSUME
ASSUMER > ASSUME
ASSUMERS > ASSUME
ASSUMES > ASSUME
ASSUMING adj expecting too much ▷ n action of one who assumes
ASSUMINGS > ASSUMING
ASSUMPSIT n (before 1875) an action to recover damages for breach of an express or implied

contract or agreement that was not under seal

ASSURABLE > ASSURE

ASSURANCE n assuring or being assured

ASSURE vb promise or guarantee

ASSURED adj confident ▷ n beneficiary under a life assurance policy

ASSUREDLY > ASSURED

ASSUREDS > ASSURED

ASSURER > ASSURE

ASSURERS > ASSURE

ASSURES > ASSURE

ASSURGENT adj (of leaves, stems, etc) curving or growing upwards

ASSURING > ASSURE

ASSUROR > ASSURE

ASSURORS > ASSURE

ASSWAGE old spelling of > ASSUAGE

ASSWAGED > ASSWAGE

ASSWAGES > ASSWAGE

ASSWAGING > ASSWAGE

ASSWIPE n contemptible person

ASSWIPES > ASSWIPE

ASTABLE adj not stable

ASTANGA same as > ASHTANGA

ASTANGAS > ASTANGA

ASTARE adv staring

ASTART old word for > START

ASTARTED > ASTART

ASTARTING > ASTART

ASTARTS > ASTART

ASTASIA n inability to stand

ASTASIAS > ASTASIA

ASTATIC adj not static

ASTATIDE n binary compound of astatine with a more electropositive element

ASTATIDES > ASTATIDE

ASTATINE n radioactive nonmetallic element

ASTATINES > ASTATINE

ASTATKI n fuel derived from petroleum

ASTATKIS > ASTATKI

ASTEISM n use of irony

ASTEISMS > ASTEISM

ASTELIC > ASTELY

ASTELIES > ASTELY

ASTELY n lack of central cylinder in plants

ASTER n plant with daisy-like flowers

ASTERIA n gemstone with starlike light effect

ASTERIAS > ASTERIA

ASTERID n variety of flowering plant

ASTERIDS > ASTERID

ASTERISK n star-shaped symbol (*) used in printing or writing to indicate a footnote, etc ▷ vb mark with an asterisk

ASTERISKS > ASTERISK

ASTERISM n three asterisks arranged in a triangle to draw attention to the text that follows

ASTERISMS > ASTERISM

ASTERN adv at or towards the stern of a ship ▷ adj at or towards the stern of a ship

ASTERNAL adj not connected or joined to the sternum

ASTEROID n any of the small planets that orbit the sun between Mars and Jupiter ▷ adj of, relating to, or belonging to the class Asteroidea

ASTEROIDS > ASTEROID

ASTERS > ASTER

ASTERT vb start

ASTERTED > ASTERT

ASTERTING > ASTERT

ASTERTS > ASTERT

ASTHANGA n type of yoga

ASTHANGAS > ASTHANGA

ASTHENIA n abnormal loss of strength

ASTHENIAS > ASTHENIA

ASTHENIC adj of, relating to, or having asthenia ▷ n person having long limbs and a small trunk

ASTHENICS > ASTHENIC

ASTHENIES > ASTHENY

ASTHENY same as > ASTHENIA

ASTHMA n illness causing difficulty in breathing

ASTHMAS > ASTHMA

ASTHMATIC adj of, relating to, or having asthma ▷ n person who has asthma

ASTHORE n Irish endearment

ASTHORES > ASTHORE

ASTICHOUS adj not arranged in rows

ASTIGMIA n defect of a lens resulting in the formation of distorted images

ASTIGMIAS > ASTIGMIA

ASTILBE n type of plant

ASTILBES > ASTILBE

ASTIR adj out of bed

ASTOMATAL adj having no stomata

ASTOMOUS adj having no mouth

ASTONE same as > ASTONISH

ASTONED > ASTONE

ASTONES > ASTONE

ASTONIED adj stunned

ASTONIES > ASTONY

ASTONING > ASTONE

ASTONISH vb surprise greatly

ASTONY same as > ASTONISH

ASTONYING > ASTONY

ASTOOP adv stooping

ASTOUND vb overwhelm with amazement

ASTOUNDED > ASTOUND

ASTOUNDS > ASTOUND

ASTRACHAN same as > ASTRAKHAN

ASTRADDLE adj with a leg on either side of something

ASTRAGAL n small convex moulding, usually with a semicircular cross section

ASTRAGALI n bones of the ankles that articulate with the leg bones to form ankle joints

ASTRAGALS > ASTRAGAL

ASTRAKHAN n dark curly fleece of lambs from Astrakhan in Russia

ASTRAL adj of stars ▷ n oil lamp

ASTRALLY > ASTRAL

ASTRALS > ASTRAL

ASTRAND adv on shore

ASTRANTIA n flowering plant

ASTRAY adv off the right path

ASTRICT vb bind, confine, or constrict

ASTRICTED > ASTRICT

ASTRICTS > ASTRICT

ASTRIDE adv with a leg on either side (of) ▷ adj with a leg on either side

ASTRINGE vb cause contraction

ASTRINGED > ASTRINGE

ASTRINGER n person who keeps goshawks

ASTRINGES > ASTRINGE

ASTROCYTE n any of the star-shaped cells in the tissue supporting the brain and spinal cord (neuroglia)

ASTRODOME n transparent dome on the top of an aircraft, through which observations can be made, esp of the stars

ASTROFELL n plant in Spenser's poetry

ASTROID n hypocycloid having four cusps

ASTROIDS > ASTROID

ASTROLABE n instrument formerly used to measure the altitude of stars and planets

ASTROLOGY n study of the alleged influence of the stars, planets, and moon on human affairs

ASTRONAUT n person trained for travelling in space

ASTRONOMY n scientific study of heavenly bodies

ASTROPHEL n plant in Spenser's poetry

ASTRUT adv old word meaning in a protruding way

ASTUCIOUS adj old form of astute

ASTUCITY n quality of being astute

ASTUN vb old form of astonish

ASTUNNED > ASTUN

ASTUNNING > ASTUN

ASTUNS > ASTUN

ASTUTE adj perceptive or shrewd

ASTUTELY > ASTUTE

ASTUTER > ASTUTE

ASTUTEST > ASTUTE

ASTYLAR adj without columns or pilasters

ASUDDEN adv old form of suddenly

ASUNDER adv into parts or pieces ▷ adj into parts or pieces

ASURA n demon in Hindu mythology

ASURAS > ASURA

ASWARM adj filled, esp with moving things

ASWAY adv swaying

ASWIM adv floating

ASWING adv swinging

ASWIRL adv swirling

ASWOON adv swooning

ASYLA > ASYLUM

ASYLEE n person who is granted asylum

ASYLEES > ASYLEE

ASYLLABIC adj not functioning in the manner of a syllable

ASYLUM n refuge or sanctuary

ASYLUMS > ASYLUM

ASYMMETRY n lack of symmetry

ASYMPTOTE n straight line closely approached but never met by a curve

ASYNAPSES > ASYNAPSIS

ASYNAPSIS n failure of pairing of chromosomes at meiosis

ASYNDETA > ASYNDETON

ASYNDETIC adj (of a catalogue or index) without cross references

ASYNDETON n omission of a conjunction between the parts of a sentence

ASYNERGIA n lack of coordination between muscles or parts, as occurs in cerebellar disease

ASYNERGY same as > ASYNERGIA

ASYSTOLE n absence of heartbeat

ASYSTOLES > ASYSTOLE

ASYSTOLIC > ASYSTOLE

AT n Laotian monetary unit worth one hundredth of a kip

ATAATA n grazing marine gastropod

ATAATAS > ATAATA

ATABAL n N African drum

ATABALS > ATABAL

ATABEG n Turkish ruler

ATABEGS > ATABEG

ATABEK n Turkish ruler

ATABEKS > ATABEK

ATABRIN n drug formerly used for treating malaria

ATABRINE same as > ATABRIN

ATABRINES > ATABRINE

ATABRINS > ATABRIN

ATACAMITE n mineral containing copper

ATACTIC adj attribute of a polymer

ATAGHAN a variant of > YATAGHAN

ATAGHANS > ATAGHAN

ATALAYA n watchtower in Spain

ATALAYAS > ATALAYA

ATAMAN n elected leader of the Cossacks

ATAMANS > ATAMAN

ATAMASCO n N American lily

ATAMASCOS > ATAMASCO

ATAP n palm tree of S Asia

ATAPS > ATAP

ATARACTIC adj able to calm or tranquillize ▷ n ataractic drug

ATARAXIA n calmness or peace of mind

ATARAXIAS > ATARAXIA

ATARAXIC same as > ATARACTIC

ATARAXICS > ATARAXIC

ATARAXIES > ATARAXY

ATARAXY same as > ATARAXIA

ATAVIC > ATAVISM

ATAVISM n recurrence of a trait present in distant ancestors

ATAVISMS > ATAVISM

ATAVIST > ATAVISM

ATAVISTIC adj of or relating to reversion to a former or more primitive type

ATAVISTS > ATAVISM

ATAXIA n lack of muscular coordination

ATAXIAS > ATAXIA

ATAXIC > ATAXIA

ATAXICS > ATAXIA

ATAXIES > ATAXY

ATAXY same as > ATAXIA

ATCHIEVE same as > ACHIEVE

ATCHIEVED > ATCHIEVE

ATCHIEVES > ATCHIEVE

ATE past tense of > EAT

ATEBRIN n drug formerly used to treat malaria

ATEBRINS > ATEBRIN

ATECHNIC adj without technical ability ▷ n

person with no technical ability

ATECHNICS > ATECHNIC

ATELIC adj of action without end

ATELIER n workshop, artist's studio

ATELIERS > ATELIER

ATEMOYA n tropical fruit tree

ATEMOYAS > ATEMOYA

ATEMPORAL adj not governed by time

ATENOLOL n type of beta-blocker

ATENOLOLS > ATENOLOL

ATES n shop selling confectionery

ATHAME n witch's ceremonial knife

ATHAMES > ATHAME

ATHANASY n absence of death

ATHANOR n alchemist's furnace

ATHANORS > ATHANOR

ATHEISE vb speak atheistically

ATHEISED > ATHEISE

ATHEISES > ATHEISE

ATHEISING > ATHEISE

ATHEISM n belief that there is no God

ATHEISMS > ATHEISM

ATHEIST > ATHEISM

ATHEISTIC > ATHEISM

ATHEISTS > ATHEISM

ATHEIZE vb speak atheistically

ATHEIZED > ATHEIZE

ATHEIZES > ATHEIZE

ATHEIZING > ATHEIZE

ATHELING n (in Anglo-Saxon England) a prince of any of the royal dynasties

ATHELINGS > ATHELING

ATHEMATIC adj not based on themes

ATHENAEUM n institution for the promotion of learning

ATHENAEUMS same as > ATHENAEUM

ATHENEUM same as > ATHENAEUM

ATHENEUMS > ATHENEUM

ATHEOLOGY n opposition to theology

ATHEOUS adj without a belief in god

ATHERINE n small fish

ATHERINES > ATHERINE

ATHEROMA n fatty deposit on or within the inner lining of an artery, often causing an obstruction to the blood flow

ATHEROMAS > ATHEROMA

ATHETESES > ATHETESIS

ATHETESIS n dismissal of a text as not genuine

ATHETISE vb reject as not genuine

ATHETISED > ATHETISE

ATHETISES > ATHETISE

ATHETIZE vb reject as not genuine

ATHETIZED > ATHETIZE

ATHETIZES > ATHETIZE

ATHETOID > ATHETOSIS

ATHETOSES > ATHETOSIS

ATHETOSIC > ATHETOSIS

ATHETOSIS n condition characterized by uncontrolled rhythmic writhing movement, esp of fingers, hands, head, and tongue, caused by cerebral lesion

ATHETOTIC > ATHETOSIS

ATHIRST adj having an eager desire

ATHLETA same as > ATHLETE

ATHLETAS > ATHLETA

ATHLETE n person trained in or good at athletics

ATHLETES > ATHLETE

ATHLETIC adj physically fit or strong

ATHLETICS n track and field events

ATHODYD another name for > RAMJET

ATHODYDS > ATHODYD

ATHRILL adv feeling thrills

ATHROB adv throbbing

ATHROCYTE n cell able to store matter

ATHWART adv transversely

ATIGI n type of parka worn by the Inuit in Canada

ATIGIS > ATIGI

ATILT adj in a tilted or inclined position

ATIMIES > ATIMY

ATIMY n loss of honour

ATINGLE adv tingling

ATISHOO n sound of a sneeze

ATISHOOS > ATISHOO

ATLANTES > ATLAS

ATLAS n book of maps

ATLASES > ATLAS

ATLATL n Native American throwing stick

ATLATLS > ATLATL

ATMA same as > ATMAN

ATMAN n personal soul or self

ATMANS > ATMAN

ATMAS > ATMA

ATMOLOGY n study of aqueous vapour

ATMOLYSE vb separate gases by filtering

ATMOLYSED > ATMOLYSE

ATMOLYSES > ATMOLYSIS

ATMOLYSIS n method of separating gases that depends on their differential rates of

diffusion through a porous substance

ATMOLYZE vb separate gases by filtering

ATMOLYZED > ATMOLYZE

ATMOLYZES > ATMOLYZE

ATMOMETER n instrument for measuring the rate of evaporation of water into the atmosphere

ATMOMETRY > ATMOMETER

ATMOS n (short for) atmosphere

ATMOSES > ATMOS

ATOC n skunk

ATOCIA n inability to have children

ATOCIAS > ATOCIA

ATOCS > ATOC

ATOK n skunk

ATOKAL adj having no children

ATOKE n part of a worm

ATOKES > ATOKE

ATOKOUS adj having no children

ATOKS > ATOK

ATOLL n ring-shaped coral reef enclosing a lagoon

ATOLLS > ATOLL

ATOM n smallest unit of matter which can take part in a chemical reaction

ATOMIC adj of or using atomic bombs or atomic energy

ATOMICAL > ATOMIC

ATOMICITY n state of being made up of atoms

ATOMICS n science of atoms

ATOMIES > ATOMY

ATOMISE same as > ATOMIZE

ATOMISED > ATOMISE

ATOMISER same as > ATOMIZER

ATOMISERS > ATOMISER

ATOMISES > ATOMISE

ATOMISING > ATOMISE

ATOMISM n ancient philosophical theory

ATOMISMS > ATOMISM

ATOMIST > ATOMISM

ATOMISTIC > ATOMISM

ATOMISTS > ATOMISM

ATOMIZE vb reduce to atoms or small particles

ATOMIZED > ATOMISE

ATOMIZER n device for discharging a liquid in a fine spray

ATOMIZERS > ATOMIZER

ATOMIZES > ATOMIZE

ATOMIZING > ATOMIZE

ATOMS > ATOM

ATOMY n atom or minute particle

ATONABLE > ATONE

ATONAL adj (of music) not written in an established key

ATONALISM > ATONAL
ATONALIST > ATONAL
ATONALITY n absence of or disregard for an established musical key in a composition
ATONALLY > ATONAL
ATONE vb make amends (for sin or wrongdoing)
ATONEABLE > ATONE
ATONED > ATONE
ATONEMENT n something done to make amends for wrongdoing
ATONER > ATONE
ATONERS > ATONE
ATONES > ATONE
ATONIA n lack of normal muscle tone
ATONIAS > ATONIA
ATONIC adj carrying no stress ▷ n unaccented or unstressed syllable
ATONICITY > ATONIC
ATONICS > ATONIC
ATONIES > ATONY
ATONING > ATONE
ATONINGLY > ATONE
ATONY n lack of normal tone or tension, as in muscles
ATOP adv on top
ATOPIC adj of or relating to hypersensitivity to certain allergens
ATOPIES > ATOPY
ATOPY n tendency to be hypersensitive to certain allergens
ATRAMENT n old word meaning black liquid
ATRAMENTS > ATRAMENT
ATRAZINE n white crystalline compound
ATRAZINES > ATRAZINE
ATREMBLE adv trembling
ATRESIA n absence of or unnatural narrowing of a body channel
ATRESIAS > ATRESIA
ATRESIC > ATRESIA
ATRETIC > ATRESIA
ATRIA > ATRIUM
ATRIAL > ATRIUM
ATRIP adj (of an anchor) no longer caught on the bottom
ATRIUM n upper chamber of either half of the heart
ATRIUMS > ATRIUM
ATROCIOUS adj extremely cruel or wicked
ATROCITY n wickedness
ATROPHIA n wasting disease
ATROPHIAS > ATROPHIA
ATROPHIC > ATROPHY
ATROPHIED > ATROPHY
ATROPHIES > ATROPHY
ATROPHY n wasting away of an organ or part ▷ vb (cause to) waste away
ATROPIA n atropine
ATROPIAS > ATROPIA

ATROPIN same as > ATROPINE
ATROPINE n poisonous alkaloid obtained from deadly nightshade
ATROPINES > ATROPINE
ATROPINS > ATROPIN
ATROPISM n condition caused by using belladonna
ATROPISMS > ATROPISM
ATROPOUS adj growing straight
ATS > AT
ATT n old Siamese coin
ATTABOY sentence substitute expression of approval or exhortation
ATTABOYS > ATTABOY
ATTACH vb join, fasten, or connect
ATTACHE n specialist attached to a diplomatic mission
ATTACHED adj fond of
ATTACHER > ATTACH
ATTACHERS > ATTACH
ATTACHES > ATTACH
ATTACHING > ATTACH
ATTACK vb launch a physical assault (against) ▷ n act of attacking
ATTACKED > ATTACK
ATTACKER > ATTACK
ATTACKERS > ATTACK
ATTACKING > ATTACK
ATTACKMAN n attacking player in sport
ATTACKMEN > ATTACKMAN
ATTACKS > ATTACK
ATTAGIRL humorous feminine version of > ATTABOY
ATTAIN vb achieve or accomplish (a task or aim)
ATTAINDER n (formerly) the extinction of a person's civil rights resulting from a sentence of death or outlawry on conviction for treason or felony
ATTAINED > ATTAIN
ATTAINER > ATTAIN
ATTAINERS > ATTAIN
ATTAINING > ATTAIN
ATTAINS > ATTAIN
ATTAINT vb pass judgment of death ▷ n dishonour
ATTAINTED > ATTAINT
ATTAINTS > ATTAINT
ATTAP n palm tree of South Asia
ATTAPS > ATTAP
ATTAR n fragrant oil made from roses
ATTARS > ATTAR
ATTASK old word for > CRITICIZE
ATTASKED > ATTASK
ATTASKING > ATTASK
ATTASKS > ATTASK
ATTASKT > ATTASK

ATTEMPER vb modify by blending
ATTEMPERS > ATTEMPER
ATTEMPT vb try, make an effort ▷ n effort or endeavour
ATTEMPTED > ATTEMPT
ATTEMPTER > ATTEMPT
ATTEMPTS > ATTEMPT
ATTEND vb be present at
ATTENDANT n person who assists, guides, or provides a service ▷ adj accompanying
ATTENDED > ATTEND
ATTENDEE n person who is present at a specified event
ATTENDEES > ATTENDEE
ATTENDER > ATTEND
ATTENDERS > ATTEND
ATTENDING > ATTEND
ATTENDS > ATTEND
ATTENT old word for > ATTENTION
ATTENTAT n attempt
ATTENTATS > ATTENTAT
ATTENTION n concentrated direction of the mind
ATTENTIVE adj giving attention
ATTENTS > ATTENT
ATTENUANT adj causing dilution or thinness, esp of the blood ▷ n attenuant drug or agent
ATTENUATE vb weaken or become weak ▷ adj diluted, weakened, slender, or reduced
ATTERCOP n spider
ATTERCOPS > ATTERCOP
ATTEST vb affirm the truth of, be proof of
ATTESTANT > ATTEST
ATTESTED adj (of cattle) certified to be free from a disease, such as tuberculosis
ATTESTER > ATTEST
ATTESTERS > ATTEST
ATTESTING > ATTEST
ATTESTOR > ATTEST
ATTESTORS > ATTEST
ATTESTS > ATTEST
ATTIC n space or room within the roof of a house
ATTICISE same as > ATTICIZE
ATTICISED > ATTICISE
ATTICISES > ATTICISE
ATTICISM n elegant, simple, and clear expression
ATTICISMS > ATTICISM
ATTICIST > ATTICISM
ATTICISTS > ATTICISM
ATTICIZE vb conform or adapt to the norms of Attica
ATTICIZED > ATTICIZE
ATTICIZES > ATTICIZE
ATTICS > ATTIC

ATTIRE n fine or formal clothes ▷ vb dress, esp in fine elegant clothes
ATTIRED > ATTIRE
ATTIRES > ATTIRE
ATTIRING > ATTIRE
ATTIRINGS > ATTIRE
ATTITUDE n way of thinking and behaving
ATTITUDES > ATTITUDE
ATTOLASER n high-power laser capable of producing laser pulses with a duration measured in attoseconds
ATTOLLENS adj (of muscle) used to lift
ATTOLLENT adj muscle used in lifting
ATTONCE adv old word for at once
ATTONE vb old word meaning appease
ATTONED > ATTONE
ATTONES > ATTONE
ATTONING > ATTONE
ATTORN vb acknowledge a new owner of land as one's landlord
ATTORNED > ATTORN
ATTORNEY n person legally appointed to act for another
ATTORNEYS > ATTORNEY
ATTORNING > ATTORN
ATTORNS > ATTORN
ATTRACT vb arouse the interest or admiration of
ATTRACTED > ATTRACT
ATTRACTER > ATTRACT
ATTRACTOR > ATTRACT
ATTRACTS > ATTRACT
ATTRAHENS adj (of muscle) drawing towards
ATTRAHENT adj something that attracts
ATTRAP vb adorn
ATTRAPPED > ATTRAP
ATTRAPS > ATTRAP
ATTRIBUTE vb regard as belonging to or produced by ▷ n quality or feature representative of a person or thing
ATTRIST vb old word meaning to sadden
ATTRISTED > ATTRIST
ATTRISTS > ATTRIST
ATTRIT vb wear down or dispose of gradually
ATTRITE vb wear down
ATTRITED > ATTRITE
ATTRITES > ATTRITE
ATTRITING > ATTRITE
ATTRITION n constant wearing down to weaken or destroy
ATTRITIVE > ATTRITION
ATTRITS > ATTRIT
ATTRITTED > ATTRIT
ATTUENT adj carrying out attuition

ATTUITE vb perceive by attuition

ATTUITED > ATTUITE

ATTUITES > ATTUITE

ATTUITING > ATTUITE

ATTUITION n way of mentally perceiving something

ATTUITIVE > ATTUITION

ATTUNE vb adjust or accustom (a person or thing)

ATTUNED > ATTUNE

ATTUNES > ATTUNE

ATTUNING > ATTUNE

ATUA n spirit or demon

ATUAS > ATUA

ATWAIN adv old word meaning into two parts

ATWEEL Scots word for > WELL

ATWEEN an archaic or Scots word for > BETWEEN

ATWITTER adv twittering

ATWIXT old word for > BETWEEN

ATYPIC adj not typical

ATYPICAL adj not typical

AUA n yellow-eye mullet

AUAS > AUA

AUBADE n song or poem greeting the dawn

AUBADES > AUBADE

AUBERGE n inn or tavern

AUBERGES > AUBERGE

AUBERGINE n dark purple tropical fruit, cooked and eaten as a vegetable

AUBRETIA same as > AUBRIETIA

AUBRETIAS > AUBRETIA

AUBRIETA same as > AUBRIETIA

AUBRIETAS > AUBRIETA

AUBRIETIA n trailing plant with purple flowers

AUBURN adj (of hair) reddish-brown ▷ n moderate reddish-brown colour

AUBURNS > AUBURN

AUCEPS n old word meaning person who catches hawks

AUCEPSES > AUCEPS

AUCTION n public sale in which articles are sold to the highest bidder ▷ vb sell by auction

AUCTIONED > AUCTION

AUCTIONS > AUCTION

AUCTORIAL adj of or relating to an author

AUCUBA n Japanese laurel

AUCUBAS > AUCUBA

AUDACIOUS adj recklessly bold or daring

AUDACITY > AUDACIOUS

AUDAD n wild African sheep

AUDADS > AUDAD

AUDIAL adj of sound

AUDIBLE adj loud enough to be heard ▷ n change of playing tactics called by the quarterback when the offence is lined up at the line of scrimmage ▷ vb call an audible

AUDIBLED > AUDIBLE

AUDIBLES > AUDIBLE

AUDIBLING > AUDIBLE

AUDIBLY > AUDIBLE

AUDIENCE n group of spectators or listeners

AUDIENCES > AUDIENCE

AUDIENCIA n court in South America

AUDIENT n person who hears

AUDIENTS > AUDIENT

AUDILE n person with a faculty for auditory imagery ▷ adj of or relating to such a person

AUDILES > AUDILE

AUDING n practice of listening to try to understand

AUDINGS > AUDING

AUDIO adj of sound or hearing ▷ n of or relating to sound or hearing

AUDIOBOOK n recorded reading of a book

AUDIOGRAM n graphic record of the acuity of hearing of a person obtained by means of an audiometer

AUDIOLOGY n scientific study of hearing, often including the treatment of persons with hearing defects

AUDIOPHIL n audiophile

AUDIOS > AUDIO

AUDIOTAPE n tape for recording sound

AUDIPHONE n type of hearing aid consisting of a diaphragm that, when placed against the upper teeth, conveys sound vibrations to the inner ear

AUDIT n official examination of business accounts ▷ vb examine (business accounts) officially

AUDITABLE > AUDIT

AUDITED > AUDIT

AUDITEE n one who is audited

AUDITEES > AUDITEE

AUDITING n act of auditing

AUDITINGS > AUDITING

AUDITION n test of a performer's ability for a particular role or job ▷ vb test or be tested in an audition

AUDITIONS > AUDITION

AUDITIVE n person who learns primarily by listening

AUDITIVES > AUDITIVE

AUDITOR n person qualified to audit accounts

AUDITORIA n areas of concert halls, theatres, schools, etc, in which audiences sit

AUDITORS > AUDITOR

AUDITORY adj of or relating to hearing

AUDITRESS n female auditor

AUDITS > AUDIT

AUE interj Maori exclamation

AUF old word for > OAF

AUFGABE n word used in psychology to mean task

AUFGABES > AUFGABE

AUFS > AUF

AUGEND n number to which a number is added

AUGENDS > AUGEND

AUGER n tool for boring holes

AUGERS > AUGER

AUGH interj expressing frustration

AUGHT adv in any least part ▷ n less common word for nought

AUGHTS > AUGHT

AUGITE n black or greenish-black mineral

AUGITES > AUGITE

AUGITIC > AUGITE

AUGMENT vb increase or enlarge ▷ n (in Greek and Sanskrit grammar) a vowel or diphthong prefixed to a verb to form a past tense

AUGMENTED > AUGMENT

AUGMENTER > AUGMENT

AUGMENTOR > AUGMENT

AUGMENTS > AUGMENT

AUGUR vb be a sign of (future events) ▷ n (in ancient Rome) a religious official who observed and interpreted omens and signs to help guide the making of public decisions

AUGURAL > AUGUR

AUGURED > AUGUR

AUGURER old word for > AUGUR

AUGURERS > AUGURER

AUGURIES > AUGURY

AUGURING > AUGUR

AUGURS > AUGUR

AUGURSHIP > AUGUR

AUGURY n foretelling of the future

AUGUST adj dignified and imposing ▷ n auguste

AUGUSTE n type of circus clown

AUGUSTER > AUGUST

AUGUSTES > AUGUSTE

AUGUSTEST > AUGUST

AUGUSTLY > AUGUST

AUGUSTS > AUGUST

AUK n sea bird with short wings

AUKLET n type of small auk

AUKLETS > AUKLET

AUKS > AUK

AULA n hall

AULARIAN n Oxford University student belonging to hall

AULARIANS > AULARIAN

AULAS > AULA

AULD a Scots word for > OLD

AULDER > AULD

AULDEST > AULD

AULIC adj relating to a royal court

AULNAGE n measurement in ells

AULNAGER n inspector of cloth

AULNAGERS > AULNAGER

AULNAGES > AULNAGE

AULOI > AULOS

AULOS n ancient Greek pipes

AUMAIL old word for > ENAMEL

AUMAILED > AUMAIL

AUMAILING > AUMAIL

AUMAILS > AUMAIL

AUMBRIES > AUMBRY

AUMBRY same as > AMBRY

AUMIL n manager in India

AUMILS > AUMIL

AUNE n old French measure of length

AUNES > AUNE

AUNT n father's or mother's sister

AUNTER old word for > ADVENTURE

AUNTERS > AUNTER

AUNTHOOD > AUNT

AUNTHOODS > AUNT

AUNTIE n aunt

AUNTIES > AUNTY

AUNTLIER > AUNTLY

AUNTLIEST > AUNTLY

AUNTLIKE > AUNT

AUNTLY adj of or like an aunt

AUNTS > AUNT

AUNTY same as > AUNTIE

AURA n distinctive air or quality of a person or thing

AURAE > AURA

AURAL adj of or using the ears or hearing

AURALITY > AURAL

AURALLY > AURAL

AURAR plural of > EYRIR

AURAS > AURA

AURATE n salt of auric acid

AURATED adj combined with auric acid

AURATES > AURATE

AUREATE adj covered with gold, gilded

AUREATELY > AUREATE

AUREI > AUREUS

AUREITIES > AUREITY

AUREITY n attributes of gold

AURELIA n large jellyfish

AURELIAN n person who studies butterflies and moths

AURELIANS > AURELIAN

AURELIAS > AURELIA

AUREOLA same as > AUREOLE

AUREOLAE > AUREOLA

AUREOLAS > AUREOLA

AUREOLE n halo

AUREOLED > AUREOLE

AUREOLES > AUREOLE

AUREOLING > AUREOLE

AURES > AURIS

AUREUS n gold coin of the Roman Empire

AURIC adj of or containing gold in the trivalent state

AURICLE n upper chamber of the heart

AURICLED > AURICLE

AURICLES > AURICLE

AURICULA n alpine primrose with leaves shaped like a bear's ear

AURICULAE > AURICULA

AURICULAR adj of, relating to, or received by the sense or organs of hearing ▷ n auricular feather

AURICULAS > AURICULA

AURIFIED > AURIFY

AURIFIES > AURIFY

AURIFORM adj shaped like an ear

AURIFY vb turn into gold

AURIFYING > AURIFY

AURIS n medical word for ear

AURISCOPE n medical instrument for examining the external ear

AURIST a former name for > AUDIOLOGY

AURISTS > AURIST

AUROCHS n recently extinct European wild ox

AUROCHSES > AUROCHS

AURORA n bands of light seen in the sky

AURORAE > AURORA

AURORAL > AURORA

AURORALLY > AURORA

AURORAS > AURORA

AUROREAN adj of dawn

AUROUS adj of or containing gold, esp in the monovalent state

AURUM n gold

AURUMS > AURUM

AUSFORM vb temper steel

AUSFORMED > AUSFORM

AUSFORMS > AUSFORM

AUSLANDER n German word meaning foreigner

AUSPEX same as > AUGUR

AUSPICATE vb inaugurate with a ceremony intended to bring good fortune

AUSPICE n patronage or guidance

AUSPICES > AUSPICE

AUSTENITE n solid solution of carbon in face-centred-cubic gamma iron, usually existing above 723°C

AUSTERE adj stern or severe

AUSTERELY > AUSTERE

AUSTERER > AUSTERE

AUSTEREST > AUSTERE

AUSTERITY n state of being austere

AUSTRAL adj southern ▷ n former monetary unit of Argentina

AUSTRALES > AUSTRAL

AUSTRALIS adj Australian

AUSTRALS > AUSTRAL

AUSUBO n tropical tree

AUSUBOS > AUSUBO

AUTACOID n any natural internal secretion, esp one that exerts an effect similar to a drug

AUTACOIDS > AUTACOID

AUTARCH n absolute ruler

AUTARCHIC > AUTARCHY

AUTARCHS > AUTARCH

AUTARCHY n absolute power or autocracy

AUTARKIC > AUTARKY

AUTARKIES > AUTARKY

AUTARKIST > AUTARKY

AUTARKY n policy of economic self-sufficiency

AUTECIOUS adj (of parasites, esp the rust fungi) completing the entire life cycle on a single species of host

AUTECISM > AUTECIOUS

AUTECISMS > AUTECISM

AUTEUR n director

AUTEURISM > AUTEUR

AUTEURIST > AUTEUR

AUTEURS > AUTEUR

AUTHENTIC adj known to be real, genuine

AUTHOR n writer of a book etc ▷ vb write or originate

AUTHORED > AUTHOR

AUTHORESS n female author

AUTHORIAL > AUTHOR

AUTHORING n creation of documents, esp multimedia documents

AUTHORISE same as > AUTHORIZE

AUTHORISH > AUTHOR

AUTHORISM n condition of being author

AUTHORITY n power to command or control others

AUTHORIZE vb give authority to

AUTHORS > AUTHOR

AUTISM n disorder characterized by lack of response to people and limited ability to communicate

AUTISMS > AUTISM

AUTIST n autistic person

AUTISTIC > AUTISM

AUTISTICS > AUTISM

AUTISTS > AUTIST

AUTO n automobile ▷ vb travel in an automobile

AUTOBAHN n German motorway

AUTOBAHNS > AUTOBAHN

AUTOBANK n automated teller machine

AUTOBANKS > AUTOBANK

AUTOBODY n body of a motor vehicle

AUTOBUS n motor bus

AUTOBUSES > AUTOBUS

AUTOCADE another name for > MOTORCADE

AUTOCADES > AUTOCADE

AUTOCAR n motor car

AUTOCARP n fruit produced through self-fertilization

AUTOCARPS > AUTOCARP

AUTOCARS > AUTOCAR

AUTOCIDAL adj (of insect pest control) effected by the introduction of sterile or genetically altered individuals into the wild population

AUTOCLAVE n apparatus for sterilizing objects by steam under pressure ▷ vb put in or subject to the action of an autoclave

AUTOCOID n hormone

AUTOCOIDS > AUTOCOID

AUTOCRACY n government by an autocrat

AUTOCRAT n ruler with absolute authority

AUTOCRATS > AUTOCRAT

AUTOCRIME n crime of stealing a car

AUTOCRINE adj relating to self-stimulation through production of a factor and its receptor

AUTOCROSS n motor-racing over a rough course

AUTOCUE n electronic television prompting device

AUTOCUES > AUTOCUE

AUTOCUTIE n young and attractive but inexperienced female television presenter

AUTOCYCLE n bicycle powered or assisted by a small engine

AUTODIAL vb dial a telephone number automatically

AUTODIALS > AUTODIAL

AUTODROME n track for motor racing

AUTODYNE adj denoting or relating to an electrical circuit in which the same elements and valves are used as oscillator and detector ▷ n autodyne circuit

AUTODYNES > AUTODYNE

AUTOECISM n (of a parasite) completion of an entire life cycle on a single species of host

AUTOED > AUTO

AUTOFLARE n automatic landing system in aircraft

AUTOFOCUS n camera system in which the lens is focused automatically

AUTOGAMIC > AUTOGAMY

AUTOGAMY n self-fertilization in flowering plants

AUTOGENIC adj produced from within

AUTOGENY n hypothetical process by which living organisms first arose on earth from nonliving matter

AUTOGIRO n self-propelled aircraft resembling a helicopter but with an unpowered rotor

AUTOGIROS > AUTOGIRO

AUTOGRAFT n tissue graft obtained from one part of a patient's body for use on another part

AUTOGRAPH n handwritten signature of a (famous) person ▷ vb write one's signature on or in

AUTOGUIDE n traffic information transmission system

AUTOGYRO same as > AUTOGIRO

AUTOGYROS > AUTOGYRO

AUTOHARP n zither-like musical instrument

AUTOHARPS > AUTOHARP

AUTOICOUS adj (of plants, esp mosses) having male and female reproductive organs on the same plant

AUTOING > AUTO

AUTOLATRY n self-worship

AUTOLOAD vb load automatically

AUTOLOADS > AUTOLOAD

AUTOLOGY n study of oneself

AUTOLYSE vb undergo or cause to undergo autolysis

AUTOLYSED > AUTOLYSE

AUTOLYSES > AUTOLYSE

AUTOLYSIN n any agent that produces autolysis

AUTOLYSIS n destruction of cells and tissues of an organism by enzymes produced by the cells themselves

AUTOLYTIC > AUTOLYSIS

AUTOLYZE same as > AUTOLYSE

AUTOLYZED > AUTOLYZE

AUTOLYZES > AUTOLYZE

AUTOMAGIC adj done with such ease and speed that it seems like magic

AUTOMAKER n car manufacturer

AUTOMAN n car manufacturer

AUTOMAT n vending machine

AUTOMATA > AUTOMATON

AUTOMATE vb make (a manufacturing process) automatic

AUTOMATED > AUTOMATE

AUTOMATES > AUTOMATE

AUTOMATIC adj (of a device) operating mechanically by itself ▷ n self-loading firearm

AUTOMATON n robot

AUTOMATS > AUTOMAT

AUTOMEN > AUTOMAN

AUTOMETER n small device inserted in a photocopier to enable the process of copying to begin and to record the number of copies made

AUTONOMIC adj occurring involuntarily or spontaneously

AUTONOMY n self-government

AUTONYM n writing published under the real name of an author

AUTONYMS > AUTONYM

AUTOPEN n mechanical device used to produce imitation signatures

AUTOPENS > AUTOPEN

AUTOPHAGY n consumption of one's own tissue

AUTOPHOBY n reluctance to refer to oneself

AUTOPHONY n medical diagnosis by listening to vibration of one's own voice in patient

AUTOPHYTE n autotrophic plant, such as any green plant

AUTOPILOT n automatic pilot

AUTOPISTA n Spanish motorway

AUTOPOINT n point-to-point race in cars

AUTOPSIA n autopsy

AUTOPSIAS > AUTOPSIA

AUTOPSIC > AUTOPSY

AUTOPSIED > AUTOPSY

AUTOPSIES > AUTOPSY

AUTOPSIST > AUTOPSY

AUTOPSY n examination of a corpse to determine the cause of death

AUTOPTIC > AUTOPSY

AUTOPUT n motorway in the former Yugoslavia

AUTOPUTS > AUTOPUT

AUTOREPLY n email facility for sending automatic replies

AUTOROUTE n French motorway

AUTOS > AUTO

AUTOSAVE n computer facility for automatically saving data ▷ vb save (computer data) automatically

AUTOSAVED > AUTOSAVE

AUTOSAVES > AUTOSAVE

AUTOSCOPY n hallucination in which one sees oneself

AUTOSOMAL > AUTOSOME

AUTOSOME n any chromosome that is not a sex chromosome

AUTOSOMES > AUTOSOME

AUTOSPORE n nonmotile algal spore that develops adult characteristics before being released

AUTOTELIC adj justifying itself

AUTOTEST n motor race in which standard cars are driven round a circuit

AUTOTESTS > AUTOTEST

AUTOTIMER n device for turning a system on and off automatically at times predetermined by advance setting

AUTOTOMIC > AUTOTOMY

AUTOTOMY n casting off by an animal of a part of its body, to facilitate escape when attacked

AUTOTOXIC > AUTOTOXIN

AUTOTOXIN n any poison or toxin formed in the organism upon which it acts

AUTOTROPH n organism capable of manufacturing complex organic nutritive compounds from simple inorganic sources

AUTOTUNE n software package that automatically manipulates a recording of a vocal track until it is in tune regardless of whether or not the original performance was in tune

AUTOTUNES > AUTOTUNE

AUTOTYPE n photographic process for producing prints in black and white, using a carbon pigment ▷ vb process using autotype

AUTOTYPED > AUTOTYPE

AUTOTYPES > AUTOTYPE

AUTOTYPIC > AUTOTYPE

AUTOTYPY > AUTOTYPE

AUTOVAC n vacuum pump in a car petrol tank

AUTOVACS > AUTOVAC

AUTUMN n season between summer and winter

AUTUMNAL adj of, occurring in, or characteristic of autumn

AUTUMNS > AUTUMN

AUTUMNY adj like autumn

AUTUNITE n yellowish fluorescent radioactive mineral

AUTUNITES > AUTUNITE

AUXESES > AUXESIS

AUXESIS n increase in cell size without division

AUXETIC n something that promotes growth

AUXETICS > AUXETIC

AUXILIAR old word for > AUXILIARY

AUXILIARS > AUXILIAR

AUXILIARY adj secondary or supplementary ▷ n person or thing that supplements or supports

AUXIN n plant hormone that promotes growth

AUXINIC > AUXIN

AUXINS > AUXIN

AUXOCYTE n any cell undergoing meiosis, esp an oocyte or spermatocyte

AUXOCYTES > AUXOCYTE

AUXOMETER n instrument for measuring magnification

AUXOSPORE n diatom cell before its silicaceous cell wall is formed

AUXOTONIC adj (of muscle contraction) occurring against increasing force

AUXOTROPH n mutant strain of microorganism having nutritional requirements additional to those of the normal organism

AVA adv at all ▷ n Polynesian shrub

AVADAVAT n Asian weaverbird with usu red plumage, often kept as a cagebird

AVADAVATS > AVADAVAT

AVAIL vb be of use or advantage (to) ▷ n use or advantage

AVAILABLE adj obtainable or accessible

AVAILABLY > AVAILABLE

AVAILE old word for > LOWER

AVAILED > AVAIL

AVAILES > AVAILE

AVAILFUL old word for > USEFUL

AVAILING > AVAIL

AVAILS > AVAIL

AVAL adj of a grandparent

AVALANCHE n mass of snow or ice falling down a mountain ▷ vb come down overwhelmingly (upon)

AVALE old word for > LOWER

AVALED > AVALE

AVALEMENT n skiing technique where the knees are kept flexible

AVALES > AVALE

AVALING > AVALE

AVANT prep before

AVANTI interj forward!

AVANTIST n proponent of the avant-garde

AVANTISTS > AVANTIST

AVARICE n greed for wealth

AVARICES > AVARICE

AVAS > AVA

AVASCULAR adj (of certain tissues, such as cartilage) lacking blood vessels

AVAST sentence substitute stop! cease!

AVATAR n appearance of a god in animal or human form

AVATARS > AVATAR

AVAUNT sentence substitute go away! depart! ▷ vb go away; depart

AVAUNTED > AVAUNT

AVAUNTING > AVAUNT

AVAUNTS > AVAUNT

AVE n expression of welcome or farewell

AVEL a variant of > OVEL

AVELLAN adj of hazelnuts

AVELLANE same as > AVELLAN

AVELS > AVEL

AVENGE vb take revenge in retaliation for (harm done) or on behalf of (a person harmed)

AVENGED > AVENGE

AVENGEFUL > AVENGE

AVENGER > AVENGE

AVENGERS > AVENGE

AVENGES > AVENGE

AVENGING > AVENGE

AVENIR n future

AVENIRS > AVENIR

AVENS n any of several temperate or arctic rosaceous plants

AVENSES > AVENS

AVENTAIL n front flap of a helmet

AVENTAILE n aventail

AVENTAILS > AVENTAIL

AVENTRE old word for > THRUST

AVENTRED > AVENTRE

AVENTRES > AVENTRE

AVENTRING > AVENTRE

AVENTURE old form of > ADVENTURE

AVENTURES > AVENTURE

AVENTURIN n dark-coloured glass, usually green or brown, spangled with fine particles of gold, copper, or some other metal

AVENUE n wide street

AVENUES > AVENUE

AVER vb state to be true

AVERAGE n typical or normal amount or quality ▷ adj usual or typical ▷ vb calculate the average of

AVERAGED > AVERAGE

AVERAGELY > AVERAGE

AVERAGER n average adjuster

AVERAGERS > AVERAGER

AVERAGES > AVERAGE

AVERAGING > AVERAGE

AVERMENT > AVER

AVERMENTS > AVER

AVERRABLE > AVER

AVERRED > AVER

AVERRING > AVER

AVERS > AVER

AVERSE adj disinclined or unwilling

AVERSELY > AVERSE

AVERSION n strong dislike

AVERSIONS > AVERSION

AVERSIVE n tool or technique intended to repel animals etc

AVERSIVES > AVERSIVE

AVERT vb turn away

AVERTABLE > AVERT

AVERTED > AVERT

AVERTEDLY > AVERT

AVERTER > AVERT

AVERTERS > AVERT

AVERTIBLE > AVERT

AVERTING > AVERT

AVERTS > AVERT

AVES > AVE

AVGAS n aviation fuel

AVGASES > AVGAS

AVGASSES > AVGAS

AVIAN adj of or like a bird ▷ n bird

AVIANISE same as > AVIANIZE

AVIANISED > AVIANISE

AVIANISES > AVIANISE

AVIANIZE vb modify microorganisms in a chicken embryo

AVIANIZED > AVIANIZE

AVIANIZES > AVIANIZE

AVIANS > AVIAN

AVIARIES > AVIARY

AVIARIST n person who keeps an aviary

AVIARISTS > AVIARIST

AVIARY n large cage or enclosure for birds

AVIATE vb pilot or fly in an aircraft

AVIATED > AVIATE

AVIATES > AVIATE

AVIATIC adj pertaining to aviation

AVIATING > AVIATE

AVIATION n art of flying aircraft

AVIATIONS > AVIATION

AVIATOR n pilot of an aircraft

AVIATORS > AVIATOR

AVIATRESS > AVIATOR

AVIATRICE > AVIATOR

AVIATRIX > AVIATOR

AVICULAR adj of small birds

AVID adj keen or enthusiastic

AVIDER > AVID

AVIDEST > AVID

AVIDIN n protein found in egg-white

AVIDINS > AVIDIN

AVIDITIES > AVIDITY

AVIDITY n quality or state of being avid

AVIDLY > AVID

AVIDNESS > AVID

AVIETTE n aeroplane driven by human strength

AVIETTES > AVIETTE

AVIFAUNA n all the birds in a particular region

AVIFAUNAE > AVIFAUNA

AVIFAUNAL > AVIFAUNA

AVIFAUNAS > AVIFAUNA

AVIFORM adj like a bird

AVIGATOR another word for > AVIATOR

AVIGATORS > AVIGATOR

AVINE adj of birds

AVION n aeroplane

AVIONIC > AVIONICS

AVIONICS n science and technology of electronics applied to aeronautics and astronautics

AVIONS > AVION

AVIRULENT adj (esp of bacteria) not virulent

AVISANDUM n consideration of a law case by a judge

AVISE old word for > ADVISE

AVISED > AVISE

AVISEMENT > AVISE

AVISES > AVISE

AVISING > AVISE

AVISO n boat carrying messages

AVISOS > AVISO

AVITAL adj of a grandfather

AVIZANDUM n judge's or court's decision to consider a case privately before giving judgment

AVIZE old word for > ADVISE

AVIZED > AVIZE

AVIZEFULL > AVIZE

AVIZES > AVIZE

AVIZING > AVIZE

AVO n Macao currency unit

AVOCADO n pear-shaped tropical fruit with a leathery green skin and yellowish-green flesh

AVOCADOES > AVOCADO

AVOCADOS > AVOCADO

AVOCATION n occupation

AVOCET n long-legged wading bird

AVOCETS > AVOCET

AVODIRE n African tree

AVODIRES > AVODIRE

AVOID vb prevent from happening

AVOIDABLE > AVOID

AVOIDABLY > AVOID

AVOIDANCE n act of keeping away from or preventing from happening

AVOIDANT adj (of behaviour) demonstrating a tendency to avoid intimacy or interaction with others

AVOIDED > AVOID

AVOIDER > AVOID

AVOIDERS > AVOID

AVOIDING > AVOID

AVOIDS > AVOID

AVOISION n nonpayment of tax

AVOISIONS > AVOISION

AVOPARCIN n type of antibiotic

AVOS > AVO

AVOSET n avocet

AVOSETS > AVOSET

AVOUCH vb vouch for

AVOUCHED > AVOUCH

AVOUCHER > AVOUCH

AVOUCHERS > AVOUCH

AVOUCHES > AVOUCH

AVOUCHING > AVOUCH

AVOURE old word for > AVOWAL

AVOURES > AVOURE

AVOUTERER old word for > ADULTERER

AVOUTRER old word for > ADULTERER

AVOUTRERS > AVOUTRER

AVOUTRIES > AVOUTRY

AVOUTRY old word for > ADULTERY

AVOW vb state or affirm

AVOWABLE > AVOW

AVOWABLY > AVOW

AVOWAL > AVOW

AVOWALS > AVOW

AVOWED > AVOW

AVOWEDLY > AVOW

AVOWER > AVOW

AVOWERS > AVOW

AVOWING > AVOW

AVOWRIES > AVOWRY

AVOWRY old word for > AVOWAL

AVOWS > AVOW

AVOYER n former Swiss magistrate

AVOYERS > AVOYER

AVRUGA n herring roe

AVRUGAS > AVRUGA

AVULSE vb take away by force

AVULSED > AVULSE

AVULSES > AVULSE

AVULSING > AVULSE

AVULSION n forcible tearing away or separation of a bodily structure or part, either as the result of injury or as an intentional surgical procedure

AVULSIONS > AVULSION

AVUNCULAR adj (of a man) friendly, helpful, and caring towards someone younger

AVYZE old word for > ADVISE

AVYZED > AVYZE

AVYZES > AVYZE

AVYZING > AVYZE

AW variant of > ALL

AWA adv away

AWAIT vb wait for

AWAITED > AWAIT

AWAITER > AWAIT

AWAITERS > AWAIT

AWAITING > AWAIT

AWAITS > AWAIT

AWAKE vb emerge or rouse from sleep ▷ adj not sleeping

AWAKED > AWAKE

AWAKEN vb awake

AWAKENED > AWAKEN

AWAKENER > AWAKEN

AWAKENERS > AWAKEN

AWAKENING n start of a feeling or awareness in someone

AWAKENS > AWAKEN

AWAKES > AWAKE

AWAKING > AWAKE

AWAKINGS > AWAKE

AWANTING adj missing

AWARD vb give (something, such as a prize) formally ▷ n something awarded, such as a prize

AWARDABLE > AWARD

AWARDED > AWARD

AWARDEE > AWARD

AWARDEES > AWARD

AWARDER > AWARD

AWARDERS > AWARD

AWARDING > AWARD

AWARDS > AWARD

AWARE adj having knowledge, informed

AWARENESS > AWARE

AWARER > AWARE

AWAREST > AWARE

AWARN vb old form of warn

AWARNED > AWARN

AWARNING > AWARN

AWARNS > AWARN

AWASH adv washed over by water ▷ adj washed over by water

AWATCH adv watching

AWATO n New Zealand caterpillar

AWATOS > AWATO

AWAVE adv in waves

AWAY adv from a place ▷ adj not present ▷ n game played or won at an opponent's ground

AWAYDAY n day trip taken for pleasure

AWAYDAYS > AWAYDAY

AWAYES old word for > AWAY

AWAYNESS > AWAY

AWAYS > AWAY

AWDL n traditional Welsh poem

AWDLS > AWDL

AWE n wonder and respect mixed with dread ▷ vb fill with awe

AWEARIED old word for > WEARY

AWEARY old form of > WEARY

AWEATHER adj towards the weather

AWED > AWE

AWEE adv for a short time

AWEEL interj Scots word meaning well

AWEIGH adj (of an anchor) no longer hooked onto the bottom

AWEING > AWE

AWELESS > AWE

AWES > AWE

AWESOME adj inspiring awe

AWESOMELY > AWESOME

AWESTRIKE vb inspire great awe in

AWESTRUCK adj filled with awe

AWETO n New Zealand caterpillar

AWETOS > AWETO

AWFUL adj very bad or unpleasant ▷ adv very

AWFULLER > AWFUL

AWFULLEST > AWFUL

AWFULLY adv in an unpleasant way

AWFULNESS > AWFUL

AWFY adv (Scots) awfully, extremely

AWHAPE old word for > AMAZE

AWHAPED > AWHAPE

AWHAPES > AWHAPE

AWHAPING > AWHAPE

AWHATO n New Zealand caterpillar

AWHATOS > AWHATO

AWHEEL adv on wheels

AWHEELS same as > AWHEEL

AWHETO n New Zealand caterpillar

AWHETOS > AWHETO

AWHILE adv for a brief time

AWHIRL adv whirling

AWING > AWE

AWK n type of programming language

AWKS > AWK

AWKWARD adj clumsy or ungainly

AWKWARDER > AWKWARD

AWKWARDLY > AWKWARD

AWL n pointed tool for piercing wood, leather, etc

AWLBIRD n woodpecker

AWLBIRDS > AWLBIRD

AWLESS > AWE

AWLS > AWL

AWLWORT n type of aquatic plant

AWLWORTS > AWLWORT

AWMOUS Scots word for > ALMS

AWMRIE n cupboard for church vessels

AWMRIES > AWMRIE

AWMRY n cupboard for church vessels

AWN n bristles on grasses

AWNED > AWN

AWNER n machine for removing awns

AWNERS > AWNER

AWNIER > AWNY

AWNIEST > AWNY

AWNING n canvas roof supported by a frame to give protection against the weather

AWNINGED adj sheltered with awning

AWNINGS > AWNING

AWNLESS > AWN

AWNS > AWN

AWNY adj having awns

AWOKE past tense of > AWAKE

AWOKEN > AWAKE

AWOL n person who is absent without leave

AWOLS > AWOL

AWORK adv old word meaning at work

AWRACK adv in wrecked condition

AWRONG adv old word meaning wrongly

AWRY adj with a twist to one side, askew

AWSOME adj old form of awesome

AX same as > AXE

AXAL adj of an axis

AXE n tool with a sharp blade for felling trees or chopping wood ▷ vb dismiss (employees), restrict (expenditure), or terminate (a project)

AXEBIRD n nightjar

AXEBIRDS > AXEBIRD

AXED > AXE

AXEL n ice-skating movement

AXELIKE adj like an axe in form

AXELS > AXEL

AXEMAN n man who wields an axe, esp to cut down trees

AXEMEN > AXEMAN

AXENIC adj (of a biological culture) free from other microorganisms

AXES > AXIS

AXIAL adj forming or of an axis

AXIALITY > AXIAL

AXIALLY > AXIAL

AXIL n angle where the stalk of a leaf joins a stem

AXILE adj of, relating to, or attached to the axis

AXILEMMA same as > AXOLEMMA

AXILEMMAS > AXILEMMA

AXILLA n area under a bird's wing

AXILLAE > AXILLA

AXILLAR same as > AXILLARY

AXILLARS > AXILLAR

AXILLARY adj of, relating to, or near the armpit ▷ n one of the feathers growing from the axilla of a bird's wing

AXILLAS > AXILLA

AXILS > AXIL

AXING > AXE

AXINITE n crystalline substance

AXINITES > AXINITE

AXIOLOGY n theory of values, moral or aesthetic

AXIOM n generally accepted principle

AXIOMATIC adj containing axioms

AXIOMS > AXIOM

AXION n type of hypothetical elementary particle

AXIONS > AXION

AXIS n (imaginary) line round which a body can rotate or about which an object or geometrical figure is symmetrical

AXISED adj having an axis

AXISES > AXIS

AXITE n type of gunpowder

AXITES > AXITE

AXLE n shaft on which a wheel or pair of wheels turns

AXLED adj having an axle

AXLES > AXLE

AXLETREE n bar fixed across the underpart of a wagon or carriage that has rounded ends on which the wheels revolve

AXLETREES > AXLETREE

AXLIKE > AX

AXMAN same as > AXEMAN

AXMEN > AXMAN

AXOID n type of curve

AXOIDS > AXOID

AXOLEMMA n membrane that encloses the axon of a nerve cell

AXOLEMMAS > AXOLEMMA

AXOLOTL n aquatic salamander of central America

AXOLOTLS > AXOLOTL

AXON n threadlike extension of a nerve cell

AXONAL > AXON

AXONE same as > AXON

AXONEMAL > AXONEME

AXONEME n part of cell consisting of proteins

AXONEMES > AXONEME

AXONES > AXONE

AXONIC > AXON

AXONS > AXON

AXOPLASM n part of cell

AXOPLASMS > AXOPLASM

AXSEED n crown vetch

AXSEEDS > AXSEED

AY adv ever ▷ n expression of agreement

AYAH n native maidservant or nursemaid

AYAHS > AYAH

AYAHUASCA n type of Brazilian plant

AYAHUASCO n South American vine

AYATOLLAH n Islamic religious leader in Iran

AYAYA n type of Inuit singing

AYAYAS > AYAYA

AYE n affirmative vote or voter ▷ adv always

AYELP adv yelping

AYENBITE old word for > REMORSE

AYENBITES > AYENBITE

AYES > AYE

AYGRE old word for > EAGER

AYIN n 16th letter in the Hebrew alphabet

AYINS > AYIN

AYONT adv beyond

AYRE old word for > AIR

AYRES > AYRE

AYRIE old word for > EYRIE

AYRIES > AYRIE

AYS > AY

AYU n small Japanese fish

AYURVEDA n ancient medical treatise in the art of healing and prolonging life

AYURVEDAS > AYURVEDA

AYURVEDIC > AYURVEDA

AYUS > AYU

AYWORD n old word meaning byword

AYWORDS > AYWORD

AZALEA n garden shrub grown for its showy flowers

AZALEAS > AZALEA

AZAN n call to prayer

AZANS > AZAN

AZEDARACH n astringent bark of the chinaberry tree, formerly used as an emetic and cathartic

AZEOTROPE n mixture of liquids that boils at a constant temperature, at a given pressure, without a change in composition

AZEOTROPY > AZEOTROPE

AZERTY n European version of keyboard

AZIDE n type of chemical compound

AZIDES > AZIDE

AZIDO adj containing an azide

AZIMUTH n arc of the sky between the zenith and the horizon

AZIMUTHAL > AZIMUTH

AZIMUTHS > AZIMUTH

AZINE n organic compound

AZINES > AZINE

AZIONE n musical drama

AZIONES > AZIONE

AZLON n fibre made from protein

AZLONS > AZLON

AZO adj of the divalent group -N:N-

AZOIC adj without life

AZOLE n organic compound

AZOLES > AZOLE

AZOLLA n tropical water fern

AZOLLAS > AZOLLA

AZON n type of drawing paper

AZONAL adj not divided into zones

AZONIC adj not confined to a zone

AZONS > AZON

AZOTAEMIA a less common name for > URAEMIA

AZOTAEMIC > AZOTAEMIA

AZOTE an obsolete name for > NITROGEN

AZOTED > AZOTE

AZOTEMIA same as > AZOTAEMIA

AZOTEMIAS > AZOTEMIA

AZOTEMIC > AZOTAEMIA

AZOTES > AZOTE

AZOTH n panacea postulated by Paracelsus

AZOTHS > AZOTH

AZOTIC adj of, containing, or concerned with nitrogen

AZOTISE same as > AZOTIZE

AZOTISED > AZOTISE

AZOTISES > AZOTISE

AZOTISING > AZOTISE

AZOTIZE vb combine or treat with nitrogen or a nitrogen compound

AZOTIZED > AZOTIZE

AZOTIZES > AZOTIZE

AZOTIZING > AZOTIZE

AZOTOUS adj containing nitrogen

AZOTURIA n presence of excess nitrogen in urine

AZOTURIAS > AZOTURIA

AZUKI same as > ADZUKI

AZUKIS > AZUKI

AZULEJO n Spanish porcelain tile

AZULEJOS > AZULEJO

AZURE n (of) the colour of a clear blue sky ▷ adj deep blue

AZUREAN adj azure

AZURES > AZURE

AZURIES > AZURY

AZURINE n blue dye

AZURINES > AZURINE

AZURITE n azure-blue mineral associated with copper deposits

AZURITES > AZURITE

AZURN old word for > AZURE

AZURY adj bluish ▷ n bluish colour

AZYGIES > AZYGY

AZYGOS n biological structure not in a pair

AZYGOSES > AZYGOS

AZYGOUS adj developing or occurring singly

AZYGOUSLY > AZYGOUS

AZYGY n state of not being joined in a pair

AZYM n unleavened bread

AZYME same as > AZYM

AZYMES > AZYME

AZYMITE n member of a church using unleavened bread in the Eucharist

AZYMITES > AZYMITE

AZYMOUS adj unleavened

AZYMS > AZYM

Bb

BA n symbol for the soul in Ancient Egyptian religion
BAA vb the characteristic bleating sound of a sheep ▷ n cry made by a sheep
BAAED > BAA
BAAING > BAA
BAAINGS > BAA
BAAL n any false god or idol
BAALEBOS n master of the house
BAALIM > BAAL
BAALISM > BAAL
BAALISMS > BAAL
BAALS > BAAL
BAAS South African word for > BOSS
BAASES > BAAS
BAASKAAP same as > BAASKAP
BAASKAAPS > BAASKAAP
BAASKAP n (in South Africa) control by Whites of non-Whites
BAASKAPS > BAASKAP
BAASSKAP same as > BAASKAP
BAASSKAPS > BAASSKAP
BABA n small cake of leavened dough
BABACO n greenish-yellow egg-shaped fruit
BABACOOTE n large lemur
BABACOS > BABACO
BABACU n type of Brazilian palm tree
BABACUS > BABACU
BABALAS adj drunk
BABAS > BABA
BABASSU n Brazilian palm tree with hard edible nuts
BABASSUS > BABASSU
BABBELAS same as > BABALAS
BABBITRY same as > BABBITT
BABBITT vb line (a bearing) or face (a surface) with a similar soft alloy
BABBITTED > BABBITT
BABBITTRY n narrow-minded materialism
BABBITTS > BABBITT
BABBLE vb talk excitedly or foolishly ▷ n muddled or foolish speech
BABBLED > BABBLE
BABBLER n person who babbles
BABBLERS > BABBLER

BABBLES > BABBLE
BABBLIER > BABBLE
BABBLIEST > BABBLE
BABBLING > BABBLE
BABBLINGS > BABBLE
BABBLY > BABBLE
BABE n baby
BABEL n confused mixture of noises or voices
BABELDOM > BABEL
BABELDOMS > BABEL
BABELISH > BABEL
BABELISM > BABEL
BABELISMS > BABEL
BABELS > BABEL
BABES > BABE
BABESIA n parasite causing infection in cattle
BABESIAS > BABESIA
BABICHE n thongs or lacings of rawhide
BABICHES > BABICHE
BABIED > BABY
BABIER > BABY
BABIES > BABY
BABIEST > BABY
BABIRUSA n Indonesian wild pig with an almost hairless skin and huge curved canine teeth
BABIRUSAS > BABIRUSA
BABIRUSSA same as > BABIRUSA
BABKA n cake
BABKAS > BABKA
BABLAH n type of acacia
BABLAHS > BABLAH
BABOO same as > BABU
BABOOL n type of acacia
BABOOLS > BABOOL
BABOON n large monkey with a pointed face and a long tail
BABOONERY n uncouth behaviour
BABOONISH adj uncouth
BABOONS > BABOON
BABOOS > BABOO
BABOOSH same as > BABOUCHE
BABOOSHES > BABOOSH
BABOUCHE n Middle-Eastern slipper
BABOUCHES > BABOUCHE
BABU n title or form of address used in India
BABUCHE same as > BABOUCHE
BABUCHES > BABUCHE

BABUDOM > BABU
BABUDOMS > BABU
BABUISM > BABU
BABUISMS > BABU
BABUL n N African and Indian tree with small yellow flowers
BABULS > BABUL
BABUS > BABU
BABUSHKA n headscarf tied under the chin, worn by Russian peasant women
BABUSHKAS > BABUSHKA
BABY n very young child or animal ▷ adj comparatively small of its type ▷ vb treat as a baby
BABYCCINO n drink of frothy milk with a chocolate topping, esp for young children
BABYCINO same as > BABYCCINO
BABYCINOS > BABYCINO
BABYDOLL n woman's short nightdress
BABYDOLLS > BABYDOLL
BABYFOOD n puréed food for babies
BABYFOODS > BABYFOOD
BABYHOOD > BABY
BABYHOODS > BABY
BABYING > BABY
BABYISH > BABY
BABYISHLY > BABY
BABYLIKE adj like a baby
BABYPROOF adj safe for babies to handle ▷ vb make babyproof
BABYSAT > BABYSIT
BABYSIT vb look after a child in its parents' absence
BABYSITS > BABYSIT
BAC n baccalaureate
BACALAO n dried salt cod
BACALAOS > BACALAO
BACALHAU same as > BACALAO
BACALHAUS > BACALHAU
BACCA n berry
BACCAE > BACCA
BACCALA same as > BACALAO
BACCALAS > BACCALA
BACCARA same as > BACCARAT
BACCARAS > BACCARA

BACCARAT n card game involving gambling
BACCARATS > BACCARAT
BACCARE same as > BACKARE
BACCAS > BACCA
BACCATE adj like a berry in form, texture, etc
BACCATED > BACCATE
BACCHANAL n follower of Bacchus ▷ adj of or relating to Bacchus
BACCHANT n priest or votary of Bacchus
BACCHANTE n priestess or female votary of Bacchus
BACCHANTS > BACCHANT
BACCHIAC > BACCHIUS
BACCHIAN same as > BACCHIC
BACCHIC adj riotously drunk
BACCHII > BACCHIUS
BACCHIUS n metrical foot of one short syllable followed by two long ones
BACCIES > BACCY
BACCIFORM adj shaped like a berry
BACCO n tobacco
BACCOES > BACCO
BACCOS > BACCO
BACCY n tobacco
BACH same as > BATCH
BACHA n Indian English word for young child
BACHARACH n German wine
BACHAS > BACHA
BACHATA n type of dance music originating in the Dominican Republic
BACHATAS > BACHATA
BACHCHA n Indian English word for young child
BACHCHAS > BACHCHA
BACHED > BACH
BACHELOR n unmarried man
BACHELORS > BACHELOR
BACHES > BACH
BACHING > BACH
BACHS > BACH
BACILLAR same as > BACILLARY
BACILLARY adj of or caused by bacilli
BACILLI > BACILLUS
BACILLUS n rod-shaped bacterium

BACK n rear part of the human body, from the neck to the pelvis ▷ vb (cause to) move backwards ▷ adj situated behind ▷ adv at, to, or towards the rear

BACKACHE n ache or pain in one's back

BACKACHES > BACKACHE

BACKACTER n mechanical excavator

BACKARE interj instruction to keep one's distance; back off

BACKBAND n back support

BACKBANDS > BACKBAND

BACKBAR n area behind a bar where bottles are stored

BACKBARS > BACKBAR

BACKBEAT n second and fourth beats in music written in even time or, in more complex time signatures, the last beat of the bar

BACKBEATS > BACKBEAT

BACKBENCH n lower-ranking seats in Parliament

BACKBEND n gymnastic exercise in which the trunk is bent backwards until the hands touch the floor

BACKBENDS > BACKBEND

BACKBIT > BACKBITE

BACKBITE vb talk spitefully about an absent person

BACKBITER > BACKBITE

BACKBITES > BACKBITE

BACKBLOCK n singular of backblock: bush or remote farming area

BACKBOARD n board that is placed behind something to form or support its back

BACKBOND n legal document

BACKBONDS > BACKBOND

BACKBONE n spinal column

BACKBONED > BACKBONE

BACKBONES > BACKBONE

BACKBURN vb clear (an area of bush) by creating a fire that burns in the opposite direction from the wind ▷ n act or result of backburning

BACKBURNS > BACKBURN

BACKCAST n backward casting of fishing rod ▷ vb cast a fishing rod backwards

BACKCASTS > BACKCAST

BACKCHAT n impudent replies

BACKCHATS > BACKCHAT

BACKCHECK vb (in ice hockey) return from attack to defence

BACKCLOTH n painted curtain at the back of a stage set

BACKCOMB vb comb (the hair) towards the roots to give more bulk to a hairstyle

BACKCOMBS > BACKCOMB

BACKCOURT n part of the court between the service line and the baseline

BACKCROSS vb mate (a hybrid of the first generation) with one of its parents ▷ n offspring so produced

BACKDATE vb make (a document) effective from a date earlier than its completion

BACKDATED > BACKDATE

BACKDATES > BACKDATE

BACKDOOR adj secret, underhand, or obtained through influence

BACKDOWN n abandonment of an earlier claim

BACKDOWNS > BACKDOWN

BACKDRAFT n reverse movement of air

BACKDROP vb provide a backdrop to (something)

BACKDROPS > BACKDROP

BACKDROPT > BACKDROP

BACKED adj having a back or backing

BACKER n person who gives financial support

BACKERS > BACKER

BACKET n shallow box

BACKETS > BACKET

BACKFALL n fall onto the back

BACKFALLS > BACKFALL

BACKFAT n layer of fat in animals between the skin and muscle

BACKFATS > BACKFAT

BACKFIELD n quarterback and running backs in a team

BACKFILE n archives of a newspaper or magazine

BACKFILES > BACKFILE

BACKFILL vb refill an excavated trench, esp (in archaeology) at the end of an investigation ▷ n soil used to do this

BACKFILLS > BACKFILL

BACKFIRE vb (of a plan) fail to have the desired effect ▷ n (in an engine) explosion of unburnt gases in the exhaust system

BACKFIRED > BACKFIRE

BACKFIRES > BACKFIRE

BACKFISCH n young girl

BACKFIT vb overhaul nuclear power plant

BACKFITS > BACKFIT

BACKFLIP n backwards somersault

BACKFLIPS > BACKFLIP

BACKFLOW n reverse flow

BACKFLOWS > BACKFLOW

BACKHAND n stroke played with the back of the hand facing the direction of the stroke ▷ adv with a backhand stroke ▷ vb play (a shot) backhand

BACKHANDS > BACKHAND

BACKHAUL vb transmit data

BACKHAULS > BACKHAUL

BACKHOE n digger ▷ vb dig with a backhoe

BACKHOED > BACKHOE

BACKHOES > BACKHOE

BACKHOUSE n toilet

BACKIE n ride on the back of someone's bicycle

BACKIES > BACKIE

BACKING n support

BACKINGS > BACKING

BACKLAND n undeveloped land behind a property

BACKLANDS > BACKLAND

BACKLASH n sudden and adverse reaction ▷ vb create a sudden and adverse reaction

BACKLESS adj (of a dress) low-cut at the back

BACKLIFT n backward movement of bat

BACKLIFTS > BACKLIFT

BACKLIGHT vb illuminate (something) from behind

BACKLINE n defensive players in a sports team as a unit

BACKLINES > BACKLINE

BACKLIST n publisher's previously published books that are still available ▷ vb put on a backlist

BACKLISTS > BACKLIST

BACKLIT adj illuminated from behind

BACKLOAD n load for lorry on return journey ▷ vb load a lorry for a return journey

BACKLOADS > BACKLOAD

BACKLOG n accumulation of things to be dealt with

BACKLOGS > BACKLOG

BACKLOT n area outside a film or television studio used for outdoor filming

BACKLOTS > BACKLOT

BACKMOST adj furthest back

BACKOUT n instance of withdrawing (from an agreement, etc)

BACKOUTS > BACKOUT

BACKPACK n large pack carried on the back ▷ vb go hiking with a backpack

BACKPACKS > BACKPACK

BACKPEDAL vb retract or modify a previous opinion, principle, etc

BACKPIECE n tattoo on the back

BACKPLATE n plate of armour which guards the back

BACKRA n white person

BACKRAS > BACKRA

BACKREST n support for the back of something

BACKRESTS > BACKREST

BACKRONYM n contrived acronym using the initial letters of an existing word

BACKROOM n place where research or planning is done, esp secret research in wartime

BACKROOMS > BACKROOM

BACKRUSH n seaward return of wave

BACKS > BACK

BACKSAW n small handsaw

BACKSAWS > BACKSAW

BACKSEAT n seat at the back, esp of a vehicle

BACKSEATS > BACKSEAT

BACKSET n reversal ▷ vb attack from the rear

BACKSETS > BACKSET

BACKSEY n sirloin

BACKSEYS > BACKSEY

BACKSHISH same as > BAKSHEESH

BACKSHORE n area of beach above high tide mark

BACKSIDE n buttocks

BACKSIDES > BACKSIDE

BACKSIGHT n sight of a rifle nearer the stock

BACKSLAP vb demonstrate effusive joviality

BACKSLAPS > BACKSLAP

BACKSLASH n slash which slopes to the left)

BACKSLID > BACKSLIDE

BACKSLIDE vb relapse into former bad habits

BACKSPACE vb move a typewriter carriage or computer cursor backwards ▷ n typewriter key that effects such movements

BACKSPEER same as > BACKSPEIR

BACKSPEIR vb interrogate

BACKSPIN n backward spin given to a ball to reduce its speed at impact

BACKSPINS > BACKSPIN

BACKSTAB vb attack deceitfully

BACKSTABS > BACKSTAB

BACKSTAGE adj behind the stage in a theatre ▷ adv behind the stage in a theatre ▷ n area behind the stage in a theatre

BACKSTAIR adj underhand

b

BACKSTALL n backward flight of a kite ▷ vb execute a backstall with a kite

BACKSTAMP n mark stamped on the back of an envelope ▷ vb mark with a backstamp

BACKSTAY n stay leading aft from the upper part of a mast to the deck or stern

BACKSTAYS > BACKSTAY

BACKSTOP n screen or fence to prevent balls leaving the playing area ▷ vb provide with backing or support

BACKSTOPS > BACKSTOP

BACKSTORY n events assumed before a story begins

BACKSWEPT adj slanting backwards

BACKSWING n backward movement of a bat, etc

BACKSWORD n broad-bladed sword

BACKTALK n argumentative discourse

BACKTALKS > BACKTALK

BACKTRACK vb return by the same route by which one has come

BACKUP n support or reinforcement

BACKUPS > BACKUP

BACKVELD n (in South Africa) remote sparsely populated area

BACKVELDS > BACKVELD

BACKWARD same as > BACKWARDS

BACKWARDS adv towards the rear

BACKWASH n water washed backwards by the motion of a boat ▷ vb remove oil from (combed wool)

BACKWATER n isolated or backward place or condition ▷ vb reverse the direction of a boat, esp to push the oars of a rowing boat

BACKWIND vb direct airflow into the back of a sail

BACKWINDS > BACKWIND

BACKWOOD > BACKWOODS

BACKWOODS pl n remote sparsely populated area

BACKWORD n act or an instance of failing to keep a promise or commitment

BACKWORDS > BACKWORD

BACKWORK n work carried out under the ground

BACKWORKS > BACKWORK

BACKWRAP n back support

BACKWRAPS > BACKWRAP

BACKYARD n yard at the back of a house, etc

BACKYARDS > BACKYARD

BACLAVA same as > BAKLAVA

BACLAVAS > BACLAVA

BACLOFEN n drug used to treat stroke victims

BACLOFENS > BACLOFEN

BACON n salted or smoked pig meat

BACONER n pig that weighs between 83 and 101 kg, from which bacon is cut

BACONERS > BACONER

BACONS > BACON

BACRONYM same as > BACKRONYM

BACRONYMS > BACRONYM

BACS > BAC

BACTERIA pl n large group of microorganisms

BACTERIAL > BACTERIA

BACTERIAN > BACTERIA

BACTERIAS > BACTERIA

BACTERIC > BACTERIA

BACTERIN n vaccine prepared from bacteria

BACTERINS > BACTERIN

BACTERISE same as > BACTERIZE

BACTERIUM n single bacteria

BACTERIZE vb subject to bacterial action

BACTEROID n type of rodlike bacterium occurring in the gut of man and animals

BACULA > BACULUM

BACULINE adj relating to flogging

BACULITE n fossil

BACULITES > BACULITE

BACULUM n bony support in the penis of certain mammals

BACULUMS > BACULUM

BAD adj not good ▷ n unfortunate or unpleasant events collectively ▷ adv badly

BADASS n tough or aggressive person ▷ adj tough or aggressive

BADASSED > BADASS

BADASSES > BADASS

BADDER > BAD

BADDEST > BAD

BADDIE n bad character in a story, film, etc, esp an opponent of the hero

BADDIES > BADDY

BADDISH > BAD

BADDY same as > BADDIE

BADE > BID

BADGE n emblem worn to show membership, rank, etc ▷ vb put a badge on

BADGED > BADGE

BADGELESS > BADGE

BADGER n nocturnal burrowing mammal ▷ vb pester or harass

BADGERED > BADGER

BADGERING > BADGER

BADGERLY > BADGER

BADGERS > BADGER

BADGES > BADGE

BADGING > BADGE

BADINAGE n playful and witty conversation ▷ vb engage in badinage

BADINAGED > BADINAGE

BADINAGES > BADINAGE

BADINERIE n name given in the 18th century to a type of quick, light movement in a suite

BADIOUS adj chestnut; brownish-red

BADLAND > BADLANDS

BADLANDS pl n any deeply eroded barren area

BADLY adv poorly

BADMAN n hired gunman, outlaw, or criminal

BADMASH n evil-doer ▷ adj naughty or bad

BADMASHES > BADMASH

BADMEN > BADMAN

BADMINTON n game played with rackets and a shuttlecock, which is hit back and forth over a high net

BADMOUTH vb speak unfavourably about (someone or something)

BADMOUTHS > BADMOUTH

BADNESS > BAD

BADNESSES > BAD

BADS > BAD

BADWARE n software designed to harm a computer system

BADWARES > BADWARE

BAEL n type of spiny Indian tree

BAELS > BAEL

BAETYL n magical meteoric stone

BAETYLS > BAETYL

BAFF vb strike ground with golf club

BAFFED > BAFF

BAFFIES pl n slippers

BAFFING > BAFF

BAFFLE vb perplex or puzzle ▷ n device to limit or regulate the flow of fluid, light, or sound

BAFFLED > BAFFLE

BAFFLEGAB n insincere speech

BAFFLER > BAFFLE

BAFFLERS > BAFFLE

BAFFLES > BAFFLE

BAFFLING adj impossible to understand

BAFFS > BAFF

BAFFY n golf club

BAFT n coarse fabric

BAFTS > BAFT

BAG n flexible container with an opening at one end ▷ vb put into a bag

BAGARRE n brawl

BAGARRES > BAGARRE

BAGASS same as > BAGASSE

BAGASSE n pulp of sugar cane or similar plants

BAGASSES > BAGASSE

BAGATELLE n something of little value

BAGEL n hard ring-shaped bread roll ▷ vb win a tennis match by six games to love

BAGELED > BAGEL

BAGELING > BAGEL

BAGELLED > BAGEL

BAGELLING > BAGEL

BAGELS > BAGEL

BAGFUL n amount (of something) that can be held in a bag

BAGFULS > BAGFUL

BAGGAGE n suitcases packed for a journey

BAGGAGES > BAGGAGE

BAGGED > BAG

BAGGER n person who packs groceries

BAGGERS > BAGGER

BAGGIE n plastic bag

BAGGIER > BAGGY

BAGGIES > BAGGY

BAGGIEST > BAGGY

BAGGILY > BAGGY

BAGGINESS > BAGGY

BAGGING > BAG

BAGGINGS > BAG

BAGGIT n unspawned salmon

BAGGITS > BAGGIT

BAGGY same as > BAGIE

BAGH n (in India and Pakistan) a garden

BAGHOUSE n dust-filtering chamber

BAGHOUSES > BAGHOUSE

BAGHS > BAGH

BAGIE n turnip

BAGIES > BAGIE

BAGLESS adj (esp of a vacuum cleaner) not containing a bag

BAGLIKE > BAG

BAGMAN n travelling salesman

BAGMEN > BAGMAN

BAGNETTE variant of > BAGUETTE

BAGNETTES > BAGNETTE

BAGNIO n brothel

BAGNIOS > BAGNIO

BAGPIPE vb play the bagpipes

BAGPIPED > BAGPIPE

BAGPIPER > BAGPIPES

BAGPIPERS > BAGPIPES

BAGPIPES pl n musical wind instrument with reed pipes and an inflatable bag

BAGPIPING > BAGPIPE

BAGS > BAG

BAGSFUL > BAGFUL

BAGUET same as > BAGUETTE

BAGUETS > BAGUET

BAGUETTE n narrow French stick loaf

BAGUETTES > BAGUETTE

BAGUIO n hurricane

BAGUIOS > BAGUIO

BAGWASH n laundry that washes clothes without drying or pressing them

BAGWASHES > BAGWASH

BAGWIG n 18th-century wig with hair pushed back into a bag

BAGWIGS > BAGWIG

BAGWORM n type of moth

BAGWORMS > BAGWORM

BAH interj expression of contempt or disgust

BAHADA same as > BAJADA

BAHADAS > BAHADA

BAHADUR n title formerly conferred by the British on distinguished Indians

BAHADURS > BAHADUR

BAHOOKIE n Scottish informal word for the buttocks

BAHOOKIES > BAHOOKIE

BAHT n standard monetary unit of Thailand, divided into 100 satang

BAHTS > BAHT

BAHU n (in India) daughter-in-law

BAHUS > BAHU

BAHUT n decorative cabinet

BAHUTS > BAHUT

BAHUVRIHI n class of compound words consisting of two elements the first of which is a specific feature of the second

BAIDAR same as > BAIDARKA

BAIDARKA n narrow hunting boat

BAIDARKAS > BAIDARKA

BAIDARS > BAIDAR

BAIGNOIRE n low-level theatre box

BAIL n money deposited with a court as security for a person's reappearance ▷ vb pay bail for (a person)

BAILABLE adj eligible for release on bail

BAILBOND n document in which a prisoner and one or more sureties guarantee that the prisoner will attend the court hearing of the charges against him if he is released on bail

BAILBONDS > BAILBOND

BAILED > BAIL

BAILEE n person to whom the possession of goods is transferred under a bailment

BAILEES > BAILEE

BAILER > BAIL

BAILERS > BAIL

BAILEY n outermost wall or court of a castle

BAILEYS > BAILEY

BAILIE n (in Scotland) a municipal magistrate

BAILIES > BAILIE

BAILIFF n sheriff's officer who serves writs and summonses

BAILIFFS > BAILIFF

BAILING > BAIL

BAILIWICK n area a person is interested in or operates in

BAILLI n magistrate

BAILLIAGE n magistrate's area of authority

BAILLIE variant of > BAILIE

BAILLIES > BAILLIE

BAILLIS > BAILLI

BAILMENT n contractual delivery of goods in trust to a person for a specific purpose

BAILMENTS > BAILMENT

BAILOR n person who retains ownership of goods but entrusts possession of them to another under a bailment

BAILORS > BAILOR

BAILOUT n instance of helping (a person, organization, etc) out of a predicament

BAILOUTS > BAILOUT

BAILS > BAIL

BAILSMAN n one standing bail for another

BAILSMEN > BAILSMAN

BAININ n Irish collarless jacket made of white wool

BAININS > BAININ

BAINITE n mixture of iron and iron carbide found in incompletely hardened steels

BAINITES > BAINITE

BAIRN n child

BAIRNISH > BAIRN

BAIRNLIER > BAIRN

BAIRNLIKE > BAIRN

BAIRNLY > BAIRN

BAIRNS > BAIRN

BAISA n small unit of currency in Oman

BAISAS > BAISA

BAISEMAIN n kissing of the hand

BAIT n piece of food on a hook or in a trap to attract fish or animals ▷ vb put a piece of food on or in (a hook or trap)

BAITED > BAIT

BAITER > BAIT

BAITERS > BAIT

BAITFISH n small fish used as bait

BAITH adj both

BAITING > BAIT

BAITINGS > BAIT

BAITS > BAIT

BAIZA n Omani unit of currency

BAIZAS > BAIZA

BAIZE n woollen fabric used to cover billiard and card tables ▷ vb line or cover with such fabric

BAIZED > BAIZE

BAIZES > BAIZE

BAIZING > BAIZE

BAJADA n sloping surface formed from rock deposits

BAJADAS > BAJADA

BAJAN n freshman at Aberdeen University

BAJANS > BAJAN

BAJILLION n extremely large but unspecified number, quantity, or amount

BAJRA n Indian millet

BAJRAS > BAJRA

BAJREE variant of > BAJRA

BAJREES > BAJREE

BAJRI variant of > BAJRA

BAJRIS > BAJRI

BAJU n Malay jacket

BAJUS > BAJU

BAKE vb cook by dry heat as in an oven ▷ n party at which the main dish is baked

BAKEAPPLE n cloudberry

BAKEBOARD n board for bread-making

BAKED > BAKE

BAKEHOUSE same as > BAKERY

BAKELITE n tradename for any one of a class of thermosetting resins used as electric insulators used for making plastic ware, telephone receivers, etc

BAKELITES > BAKELITE

BAKEMEAT n pie

BAKEMEATS > BAKEMEAT

BAKEN > BAKE

BAKEOFF n baking competition

BAKEOFFS > BAKEOFF

BAKER n person whose business is to make or sell bread, cakes, etc

BAKERIES > BAKERY

BAKERS > BAKER

BAKERY n place where bread, cakes, etc are baked or sold

BAKES > BAKE

BAKESHOP n bakery

BAKESHOPS > BAKESHOP

BAKESTONE n flat stone in an oven

BAKEWARE n dishes for baking

BAKEWARES > BAKEWARE

BAKGAT adj fine, excellent, marvellous

BAKHSHISH same as > BAKSHEESH

BAKING n process of cooking bread, cakes, etc ▷ adj (esp of weather) very hot and dry

BAKINGS > BAKING

BAKKIE n small truck

BAKKIES > BAKKIE

BAKLAVA n rich pastry of Middle Eastern origin

BAKLAVAS > BAKLAVA

BAKLAWA same as > BAKLAVA

BAKLAWAS > BAKLAWA

BAKRA n White person, esp one from Britain ▷ adj (of people) White, esp British

BAKRAS > BAKRA

BAKSHEESH n (in some Eastern countries) money given as a tip ▷ vb give such money to (a person)

BAKSHISH same as > BAKSHEESH

BAL n balmoral

BALACLAVA n close-fitting woollen hood that covers the ears and neck, as originally worn by soldiers in the Crimean War

BALADIN n dancer

BALADINE n female dancer

BALADINES > BALADINE

BALADINS > BALADIN

BALAFON n type of W African xylophone

BALAFONS > BALAFON

BALALAIKA n guitar-like musical instrument with a triangular body

BALANCE n stability of mind or body ▷ vb weigh in a balance

BALANCED adj having weight equally distributed

BALANCER n person or thing that balances

BALANCERS > BALANCER

BALANCES > BALANCE

BALANCING > BALANCE

BALANITIS n inflammation of the glans penis, usually due to infection

BALAS n red variety of spinel, used as a gemstone

BALASES > BALAS

BALATA n tropical American tree yielding a latex-like sap

BALATAS > BALATA

BALAYAGE vb highlight hair by painting dye onto sections

BALAYAGED > BALAYAGE

BALAYAGES > BALAYAGE

BALBOA n standard currency unit of Panama

BALBOAS > BALBOA

BALCONET n small balcony

BALCONETS > BALCONET

BALCONIED > BALCONY

BALCONIES > BALCONY

BALCONY n platform on the outside of a building with a rail along the outer edge

BALD adj having little or no hair on the scalp ▷ vb make bald

b

BALDACHIN n richly ornamented silk and gold brocade

BALDAQUIN same as > BALDACHIN

BALDED > BALD

BALDER > BALD

BALDEST > BALD

BALDFACED same as > BALD

BALDHEAD n person with a bald head

BALDHEADS > BALDHEAD

BALDICOOT another name for > COOT

BALDIE same as > BALDY

BALDIER > BALDY

BALDIES > BALDY

BALDIEST > BALDY

BALDING adj becoming bald

BALDISH > BALD

BALDLY > BALD

BALDMONEY another name for > SPIGNEL

BALDNESS > BALD

BALDPATE n person with a bald head

BALDPATED > BALDPATE

BALDPATES > BALDPATE

BALDRIC n wide silk sash or leather belt worn across the body

BALDRICK same as > BALDRIC

BALDRICKS > BALDRICK

BALDRICS > BALDRIC

BALDS > BALD

BALDY adj bald ▷ n bald person

BALE same as > BAIL

BALECTION same as > BOLECTION

BALED > BALE

BALEEN n whalebone

BALEENS > BALEEN

BALEFIRE n bonfire

BALEFIRES > BALEFIRE

BALEFUL adj vindictive or menacing

BALEFULLY > BALEFUL

BALER > BAIL

BALERS > BAIL

BALES > BALE

BALING n act of baling

BALINGS > BALING

BALISAUR n badger-like animal

BALISAURS > BALISAUR

BALISE n electronic beacon used on a railway

BALISES > BALISE

BALISTA same as > BALLISTA

BALISTAE > BALISTA

BALISTAS > BALISTA

BALK vb stop short, esp suddenly or unexpectedly ▷ n roughly squared heavy timber beam

BALKANISE variant of > BALKANIZE

BALKANIZE vb divide (a territory) into small warring states

BALKED > BALK

BALKER > BALK

BALKERS > BALK

BALKIER > BALKY

BALKIEST > BALKY

BALKILY > BALKY

BALKINESS > BALKY

BALKING > BALK

BALKINGLY > BALK

BALKINGS > BALK

BALKLINE n line delimiting the balk area on a snooker table

BALKLINES > BALKLINE

BALKS > BALK

BALKY adj inclined to stop abruptly and unexpectedly

BALL n round or nearly round object, esp one used in games ▷ vb form into a ball

BALLABILE n part of ballet where all dancers perform

BALLABILI > BALLABILE

BALLAD n narrative poem or song ▷ vb sing or write a ballad

BALLADE n verse form

BALLADED > BALLAD

BALLADEER n singer of ballads ▷ vb perform as a balladeer

BALLADES > BALLADE

BALLADIC > BALLAD

BALLADIN same as > BALADIN

BALLADINE same as > BALADINE

BALLADING > BALLAD

BALLADINS > BALLADIN

BALLADIST > BALLAD

BALLADRY n ballad poetry or songs

BALLADS > BALLAD

BALLAN n species of fish

BALLANS > BALLAN

BALLANT vb write a ballad

BALLANTED > BALLANT

BALLANTS > BALLANT

BALLAST n substance used to stabilize a ship when it is not carrying cargo ▷ vb give stability to

BALLASTED > BALLAST

BALLASTER > BALLAST

BALLASTS > BALLAST

BALLAT vb write a ballad

BALLATED > BALLAT

BALLATING > BALLAT

BALLATS > BALLAT

BALLBOY n boy who retrieves balls during a tennis, football, etc, match

BALLBOYS > BALLBOY

BALLCLAY n clay suitable for ceramics

BALLCLAYS > BALLCLAY

BALLCOCK n device for regulating the flow of a liquid into a tank, cistern, etc, consisting of a floating ball mounted at one end of an arm and a valve on the other end that opens and closes as the ball falls and rises

BALLCOCKS > BALLCOCK

BALLED > BALL

BALLER n ball-game player

BALLERINA n female ballet dancer

BALLERINE > BALLERINA

BALLERS > BALLER

BALLET n classical style of expressive dancing based on conventional steps

BALLETED > BALLAD

BALLETIC > BALLET

BALLETING > BALLAD

BALLETS > BALLET

BALLGAME n any game played with a ball

BALLGAMES > BALLGAME

BALLGIRL n girl who retrieves balls during a tennis, football, etc, match

BALLGIRLS > BALLGIRL

BALLGOWN n long formal dress

BALLGOWNS > BALLGOWN

BALLHAWK n skilled baseball player ▷ vb act as a ballhawk

BALLHAWKS > BALLHAWK

BALLIES > BALLY

BALLING > BALL

BALLINGS > BALL

BALLISTA n ancient catapult for hurling stones, etc

BALLISTAE > BALLISTA

BALLISTAS > BALLISTA

BALLISTIC adj of or relating to ballistics

BALLIUM same as > BAILEY

BALLIUMS > BALLIUM

BALLOCKS same as > BOLLOCKS

BALLON n light, graceful quality

BALLONET n air or gas compartment in a balloon or nonrigid airship, used to control buoyancy and shape

BALLONETS > BALLONET

BALLONNE n bouncing step

BALLONNES > BALLONNE

BALLONS > BALLON

BALLOON n inflatable rubber bag used as a plaything or decoration ▷ vb fly in a balloon

BALLOONED > BALLOON

BALLOONS > BALLOON

BALLOT n method of voting ▷ vb vote or ask for a vote from

BALLOTED > BALLOT

BALLOTEE > BALLOT

BALLOTEES > BALLOT

BALLOTER > BALLOT

BALLOTERS > BALLOT

BALLOTING n act of balloting

BALLOTINI n small glass beads

BALLOTS > BALLOT

BALLOW n heavy club

BALLOWS > BALLOW

BALLPARK n stadium used for baseball games

BALLPARKS > BALLPARK

BALLPEEN adj as in ballpeen hammer type of hammer

BALLPOINT n pen with a tiny ball bearing as a writing point

BALLROOM n large hall for dancing

BALLROOMS > BALLROOM

BALLS vb muddle or botch

BALLSED > BALLS

BALLSES > BALLS

BALLSIER > BALLSY

BALLSIEST > BALLSY

BALLSING > BALLS

BALLSY adj courageous and spirited

BALLUP n something botched or muddled

BALLUPS > BALLUP

BALLUTE n inflatable balloon parachute

BALLUTES > BALLUTE

BALLY another word for > BALLYHOO

BALLYARD n baseball ground

BALLYARDS > BALLYARD

BALLYHOO n exaggerated fuss ▷ vb advertise or publicize by sensational or blatant methods

BALLYHOOS > BALLYHOO

BALLYRAG same as > BULLYRAG

BALLYRAGS > BALLYRAG

BALM n aromatic substance used for healing and soothing ▷ vb apply balm to

BALMACAAN n man's knee-length loose flaring overcoat with raglan sleeves

BALMED > BALM

BALMIER > BALMY

BALMIEST > BALMY

BALMILY > BALMY

BALMINESS > BALMY

BALMING > BALM

BALMLIKE > BALM

BALMORAL n laced walking shoe

BALMORALS > BALMORAL

BALMS > BALM

BALMY adj (of weather) mild and pleasant

BALNEAL *adj* of or relating to baths or bathing

BALNEARY *same as* > BALNEAL

BALONEY *n* foolish talk; nonsense

BALONEYS > BALONEY

BALOO *n* bear

BALOOS > BALOO

BALS > BAL

BALSA *n* very light wood from a tropical American tree

BALSAM *n* type of fragrant balm ▷ *vb* embalm

BALSAMED > BALSAM

BALSAMIC > BALSAM

BALSAMING > BALSAM

BALSAMS > BALSAM

BALSAMY > BALSAM

BALSAS > BALSA

BALSAWOOD *same as* > BALSA

BALTHASAR *same as* > BALTHAZAR

BALTHAZAR *n* wine bottle holding the equivalent of sixteen normal bottles (approximately 12 litres)

BALTI *n* spicy Indian dish served in a metal dish

BALTIC *adj* very cold

BALTIS > BALTI

BALU *same as* > BALOO

BALUN *n* electrical device

BALUNS > BALUN

BALUS > BALU

BALUSTER *n* set of posts supporting a rail ▷ *adj* (of a shape) swelling at the base and rising in a concave curve to a narrow stem or neck

BALUSTERS > BALUSTER

BALZARINE *n* light fabric

BAM *vb* cheat

BAMBI *n* born-again middle-aged biker

BAMBINI > BAMBINO

BAMBINO *n* young child, esp an Italian one

BAMBINOS > BAMBINO

BAMBIS > BAMBI

BAMBOO *n* tall treelike tropical grass with hollow stems

BAMBOOS > BAMBOO

BAMBOOZLE *vb* cheat or mislead

BAMMED > BAM

BAMMER > BAM

BAMMERS > BAM

BAMMING > BAM

BAMPOT *n* fool

BAMPOTS > BAMPOT

BAMS > BAM

BAN *vb* prohibit or forbid officially ▷ *n* official prohibition

BANAK *n* type of Central American tree

BANAKS > BANAK

BANAL *adj* ordinary and unoriginal

BANALER > BANAL

BANALEST > BANAL

BANALISE > BANAL

BANALISED > BANAL

BANALISES > BANAL

BANALITY > BANAL

BANALIZE > BANAL

BANALIZED > BANAL

BANALIZES > BANAL

BANALLY > BANAL

BANANA *n* yellow crescent-shaped fruit

BANANAS *adj* crazy

BANAUSIAN > BANAUSIC

BANAUSIC *adj* merely mechanical

BANC *n* as in *in banc* sitting as a full court

BANCO *n* call made in gambling games

BANCOS > BANCO

BANCS > BANC

BAND *n* group of musicians playing together ▷ *vb* unite

BANDA *n* African thatched hut

BANDAGE *n* piece of material used to cover a wound or wrap an injured limb ▷ *vb* cover with a bandage

BANDAGED > BANDAGE

BANDAGER > BANDAGE

BANDAGERS > BANDAGE

BANDAGES > BANDAGE

BANDAGING *n* act of bandaging

BANDAID *adj* (of a solution or remedy) temporary

BANDALORE *n* old-fashioned type of yo-yo

BANDANA *same as* > BANDANNA

BANDANAS > BANDANA

BANDANNA *n* large brightly coloured handkerchief or neckerchief

BANDANNAS > BANDANNA

BANDAR *n* species of monkey

BANDARI *n* Indian English word for female monkey

BANDARIS > BANDARI

BANDARS > BANDAR

BANDAS > BANDA

BANDBOX *n* lightweight usually cylindrical box for hats

BANDBOXES > BANDBOX

BANDBRAKE *n* type of brake

BANDEAU *n* narrow ribbon worn round the head

BANDEAUS > BANDEAU

BANDEAUX > BANDEAU

BANDED > BAND

BANDEIRA *n* 17th-century Portuguese slave-hunting expedition in Brazil

BANDEIRAS > BANDEIRA

BANDELET *n* moulding round top of column

BANDELETS > BANDELET

BANDELIER *same as* > BANDOLEER

BANDER > BAND

BANDEROL *same as* > BANDEROLE

BANDEROLE *n* narrow flag usually with forked ends

BANDEROLS > BANDEROL

BANDERS > BAND

BANDFISH *n* Mediterranean fish with an elongated body

BANDH *n* (in India) a general strike

BANDHS > BANDH

BANDICOOT *n* ratlike Australian marsupial

BANDIED > BANDY

BANDIER > BANDY

BANDIES > BANDY

BANDIEST > BANDY

BANDINESS > BANDY

BANDING *n* practice of grouping schoolchildren according to ability

BANDINGS > BANDING

BANDIT *n* robber, esp a member of an armed gang

BANDITO *n* Mexican bandit

BANDITOS > BANDITO

BANDITRY > BANDIT

BANDITS > BANDIT

BANDITTI > BANDIT

BANDITTIS > BANDIT

BANDMATE *n* fellow member of band

BANDMATES > BANDMATE

BANDOBAST *same as* > BANDOBUST

BANDOBUST *n* (in India and Pakistan) an arrangement

BANDOG *n* ferocious dog

BANDOGS > BANDOG

BANDOLEER *same as* > BANDOLIER

BANDOLEON *same as* > BANDONEON

BANDOLERO *n* highwayman

BANDOLIER *n* shoulder belt for holding cartridges

BANDOLINE *n* glutinous hair dressing, used (esp formerly) to keep the hair in place

BANDONEON *n* type of square concertina, esp used in Argentina

BANDONION *same as* > BANDONEON

BANDOOK *same as* > BUNDOOK

BANDOOKS > BANDOOK

BANDORA *same as* > BANDORE

BANDORAS > BANDORA

BANDORE *n* 16th-century musical instrument

BANDORES > BANDORE

BANDPASS *n* range of frequencies transmitted through a bandpass filter

BANDROL *same as* > BANDEROLE

BANDROLS > BANDROL

BANDS > BAND

BANDSAW *n* power saw with continuous blade

BANDSAWS > BANDSAW

BANDSHELL *n* bandstand concave at back

BANDSMAN *n* player in a musical band

BANDSMEN > BANDSMAN

BANDSTAND *n* roofed outdoor platform for a band

BANDSTER *n* binder of wheat sheaves

BANDSTERS > BANDSTER

BANDURA *n* type of lute

BANDURAS > BANDURA

BANDWAGON *n* type of wagon

BANDWIDTH *n* range of frequencies within a given waveband used for a particular transmission

BANDY *adj* having legs curved outwards at the knees ▷ *vb* exchange (words) in a heated manner

BANDYING > BANDY

BANDYINGS > BANDY

BANDYMAN *n* carriage or cart

BANDYMEN > BANDYMAN

BANE *n* person or thing that causes misery or distress ▷ *vb* cause harm or distress to (someone)

BANEBERRY *n* type of plant with small white flowers and red or white poisonous berries

BANED > BANE

BANEFUL *adj* destructive, poisonous, or fatal

BANEFULLY > BANEFUL

BANES > BANE

BANG *vb* make a short explosive noise

BANGALAY *n* Australian tree valued for its hard red wood

BANGALAYS > BANGALAY

BANGALORE *adj* as in *bangalore torpedo* explosive device in a long metal tube, used to blow gaps in barbed-wire barriers

BANGALOW *n* Australian palm tree native to New South Wales and Queensland

BANGALOWS > BANGALOW

BANGED > BANG

BANGER *n* old decrepit car

BANGERS > BANGER

BANGING > BANG

BANGKOK *n* type of straw hat

BANGKOKS > BANGKOK

BANGLE *n* bracelet worn round the arm or the ankle

BANGLED > BANGLE
BANGLES > BANGLE
BANGS > BANG
BANGSRING same as
> BANXRING
BANGSTER n ruffian
BANGSTERS > BANGSTER
BANGTAIL n horse's tail
cut straight across but not
through the bone
BANGTAILS > BANGTAIL
BANI > BAN
BANIA same as > BANYAN
BANIAN same as > BANYAN
BANIANS > BANIAN
BANIAS > BANIA
BANING > BANE
BANISH vb send
(someone) into exile
BANISHED > BANISH
BANISHER > BANISH
BANISHERS > BANISH
BANISHES > BANISH
BANISHING > BANISH
BANISTER same as
> BANNISTER
BANISTERS pl n railing
supported by posts on a
staircase
BANJAX vb ruin; destroy
BANJAXED > BANJAX
BANJAXES > BANJAX
BANJAXING > BANJAX
BANJO n guitar-like
musical instrument with a
circular body
BANJOES > BANJO
BANJOIST > BANJO
BANJOISTS > BANJO
BANJOLELE n musical
instrument with a neck
like a ukulele and a body
like a banjo
BANJOS > BANJO
BANJULELE n small banjo
BANK n institution offering
services such as the
safekeeping and lending of
money ▷ vb deposit (cash
or cheques) in a bank
BANKABLE adj likely to
ensure financial success
BANKBOOK n book held by
depositors at certain
banks, in which the bank
enters a record of deposits,
withdrawals, and earned
interest
BANKBOOKS > BANKBOOK
BANKCARD n card
guaranteeing payment of
cheque
BANKCARDS > BANKCARD
BANKED > BANK
BANKER n manager or
owner of a bank
BANKERLY > BANKER
BANKERS > BANKER
BANKET n gold-bearing
conglomerate found in
South Africa
BANKETS > BANKET
BANKING same as > BANK
BANKINGS > BANK

BANKIT same as
> BANQUETTE
BANKITS > BANKIT
BANKNOTE n piece of
paper money
BANKNOTES > BANKNOTE
BANKROLL n roll of
currency notes ▷ vb
provide the capital for
BANKROLLS > BANKROLL
BANKRUPT n person
declared by a court to be
unable to pay his or her
debts ▷ adj financially
ruined ▷ vb make
bankrupt
BANKRUPTS > BANKRUPT
BANKS > BANK
BANKSIA n Australian
evergreen tree or shrub
BANKSIAS > BANKSIA
BANKSIDE n riverside
BANKSIDES > BANKSIDE
BANKSMAN n crane driver's
helper, who signals
instructions to the driver
for the movement of the
crane and its jib
BANKSMEN > BANKSMAN
BANKSTER n banker
whose illegal practices
have been exposed
BANKSTERS > BANKSTER
BANLIEUE n suburb of a
city
BANLIEUES > BANLIEUE
BANNABLE > BAN
BANNED > BAN
BANNER n long strip of
cloth displaying a slogan,
advertisement, etc
▷ vb (of a newspaper
headline) to display (a
story) prominently
▷ adj outstandingly
successful
BANNERALL same as
> BANDEROLE
BANNERED > BANNER
BANNERET n small banner
BANNERETS > BANNERET
BANNERING > BANNER
BANNEROL same as
> BANDEROLE
BANNEROLS > BANNEROL
BANNERS > BANNER
BANNET n bonnet
BANNETS > BANNET
BANNING n act of banning
BANNINGS > BANNING
BANNISTER same as
> BANISTERS
BANNOCK n round flat cake
made from oatmeal or
barley
BANNOCKS > BANNOCK
BANNS pl n public
declaration, esp in a
church, of an intended
marriage
BANOFFEE n filling for a
pie, consisting of toffee
and banana
BANOFFEES > BANOFFEE

BANOFFI same as
> BANOFFEE
BANOFFIS > BANOFFI
BANQUET n elaborate
formal dinner ▷ vb hold or
take part in a banquet
BANQUETED > BANQUET
BANQUETER > BANQUET
BANQUETS > BANQUET
BANQUETTE n
upholstered bench
BANS same as > BANNS
BANSELA same as
> BONSELA
BANSELAS > BANSELA
BANSHEE n (in Irish
folklore) female spirit
whose wailing warns of a
coming death
BANSHEES > BANSHEE
BANSHIE same as
> BANSHEE
BANSHIES > BANSHIE
BANT n string ▷ vb tie with
string
BANTAM n small breed of
chicken
BANTAMS > BANTAM
BANTED > BANT
BANTENG n wild ox
BANTENGS > BANTENG
BANTER vb tease jokingly
▷ n teasing or joking
conversation
BANTERED > BANTER
BANTERER > BANTER
BANTERERS > BANTER
BANTERING > BANTER
BANTERS > BANTER
BANTIES > BANTY
BANTING > BANT
BANTINGS > BANT
BANTLING n young child
BANTLINGS > BANTLING
BANTS > BANT
BANTU n offensive name
for a person who speaks a
Bantu language
BANTUS > BANTU
BANTY n bantam
BANXRING n tree-shrew
BANXRINGS > BANXRING
BANYA n traditional
Russian steam bath
BANYAN n Indian tree
BANYANS > BANYAN
BANYAS > BANYA
BANZAI interj patriotic
cheer, battle cry, or
salutation
BANZAIS > BANZAI
BAOBAB n African tree
with a thick trunk and
angular branches
BAOBABS > BAOBAB
BAP n large soft bread roll
BAPS > BAP
BAPTISE same as
> BAPTIZE
BAPTISED > BAPTISE
BAPTISER > BAPTISE
BAPTISERS > BAPTISE
BAPTISES > BAPTISE

BAPTISIA n species of
wild flower
BAPTISIAS > BAPTISIA
BAPTISING > BAPTISE
BAPTISM n Christian
religious ceremony
BAPTISMAL > BAPTISM
BAPTISMS > BAPTISM
BAPTIST n one who
baptizes
BAPTISTRY n part of a
Christian church in which
baptisms are carried out
BAPTISTS > BAPTIST
BAPTIZE vb perform
baptism on
BAPTIZED > BAPTIZE
BAPTIZERS > BAPTIZE
BAPTIZES > BAPTIZE
BAPTIZING > BAPTIZE
BAPU n spiritual father
BAPUS > BAPU
BAR n rigid usually straight
length of metal, wood,
etc, longer than it is wide
or thick ▷ vb fasten or
secure with a bar
BARACAN same as
> BARRACAN
BARACANS > BARACAN
BARACHOIS n (in the
Atlantic Provinces of
Canada) a shallow lagoon
formed by a sand bar
BARAGOUIN n
incomprehensible
language
BARASINGA n type of deer
BARATHEA n fabric made
of silk and wool or cotton
and rayon, used esp for
coats
BARATHEAS > BARATHEA
BARATHRUM n abyss
BARAZA n place where
public meetings are held
BARAZAS > BARAZA
BARB n cutting remark
▷ vb provide with a barb or
barbs
BARBAL adj of a beard
BARBARIAN n member of
a primitive or uncivilized
people ▷ adj uncivilized or
brutal
BARBARIC adj cruel or
brutal
BARBARISE same as
> BARBARIZE
BARBARISM n condition
of being backward or
ignorant
BARBARITY n state of
being barbaric or barbarous
BARBARIZE vb make or
become barbarous
BARBAROUS adj
uncivilized
BARBASCO n S American
plant
BARBASCOS > BARBASCO
BARBASTEL n
insectivorous forest bat

BARBATE *adj* having tufts of long hairs

BARBATED > BARBATE

BARBE *n* Waldensian missionary

BARBECUE *n* grill on which food is cooked over hot charcoal, usu outdoors ▷ *vb* cook (food) on a barbecue

BARBECUED > BARBECUE

BARBECUER > BARBECUE

BARBECUES > BARBECUE

BARBED > BARB

BARBEL *n* long thin growth that hangs from the jaws of certain fishes, such as the carp

BARBELL *n* long metal rod to which heavy discs are attached at each end for weightlifting

BARBELLS > BARBELL

BARBELS > BARBEL

BARBEQUE *same as* > BARBECUE

BARBEQUED > BARBEQUE

BARBEQUES > BARBEQUE

BARBER *n* person who cuts men's hair and shaves beards ▷ *vb* cut the hair of

BARBERED > BARBER

BARBERING > BARBER

BARBERRY *n* shrub with orange or red berries

BARBERS > BARBER

BARBES > BARBE

BARBET *n* type of small tropical bird

BARBETS > BARBET

BARBETTE *n* (formerly) an earthen platform inside a parapet, from which heavy guns could fire over the top

BARBETTES > BARBETTE

BARBICAN *n* walled defence to protect a gate or drawbridge of a fortification

BARBICANS > BARBICAN

BARBICEL *n* any of the minute hooks on the barbules of feathers that interlock with those of adjacent barbules

BARBICELS > BARBICEL

BARBIE *short for* > BARBECUE

BARBIES > BARBIE

BARBING > BARB

BARBITAL *same as* > BARBITONE

BARBITALS > BARBITAL

BARBITONE *n* long-acting barbiturate used medicinally, usually in the form of the sodium salt, as a sedative or hypnotic

BARBLESS > BARB

BARBOLA *n* small models of flowers, etc made from plastic paste

BARBOLAS > BARBOLA

BARBOT *same as* > BURBOT

BARBOTINE *n* clay used in making decorated pottery

BARBOTS > BARBOT

BARBOTTE *same as* > BURBOT

BARBOTTES > BARBOTTE

BARBS > BARB

BARBULE *n* very small barb

BARBULES > BARBULE

BARBUT *n* open-faced helmet

BARBUTS > BARBUT

BARBWIRE *n* barbed wire

BARBWIRES > BARBWIRE

BARBY *same as* > BARBECUE

BARCA *n* boat

BARCAROLE *n* Venetian boat song

BARCAS > BARCA

BARCHAN *n* crescent-shaped shifting sand dune

BARCHANE *same as* > BARCHAN

BARCHANES > BARCHANE

BARCHANS > BARCHAN

BARCODE *n* machine-readable code printed on goods

BARCODED *adj* having a barcode

BARCODES > BARCODE

BARD *n* poet ▷ *vb* place a piece of pork fat on

BARDASH *n* kept boy in a homosexual relationship

BARDASHES > BARDASH

BARDE *same as* > BARD

BARDED > BARDE

BARDES > BARDE

BARDIC > BARD

BARDIE *n* type of Australian grub

BARDIER > BARD

BARDIES > BARDIE

BARDIEST > BARD

BARDING > BARD

BARDISM > BARD

BARDISMS > BARD

BARDLING *n* inferior poet

BARDLINGS > BARDLING

BARDO *n* (in Tibetan Buddhism) the state of the soul between its death and its rebirth

BARDOS > BARDO

BARDS > BARD

BARDSHIP > BARD

BARDSHIPS > BARD

BARDY > BARD

BARE *adj* unclothed, naked ▷ *vb* uncover

BAREBACK *adv* (of horse-riding) without a saddle ▷ *vb* ride bareback

BAREBACKS > BAREBACK

BAREBOAT *n* boat chartered without crew, provisions, etc

BAREBOATS > BAREBOAT

BAREBONE *n* computer casing containing bare essentials

BAREBONED *adj* short of resources

BAREBONES > BAREBONE

BARED > BARE

BAREFACED *adj* shameless or obvious

BAREFIT *same as* > BAREFOOT

BAREFOOT *adv* with the feet uncovered

BAREGE *n* light silky gauze fabric made of wool ▷ *adj* made of such a fabric

BAREGES > BAREGE

BAREGINE *n* curative ingredient in thermal waters

BAREGINES > BAREGINE

BAREHAND *vb* handle with bare hands

BAREHANDS > BAREHAND

BAREHEAD *adv* with head uncovered

BARELAND *adj* as in *bareland croft* refers to a croft with no croft house

BARELY *adv* only just

BARENESS > BARE

BARER > BARE

BARES > BARE

BARESARK *another word for* > BERSERK

BARESARKS > BARESARK

BAREST > BARE

BARF *vb* vomit ▷ *n* act of vomiting

BARFED > BARF

BARFI *n* type of Indian dessert

BARFING > BARF

BARFIS > BARFI

BARFLIES > BARFLY

BARFLY *n* person who frequents bars

BARFS > BARF

BARFUL *adj* presenting difficulties

BARGAIN *n* agreement establishing what each party will give, receive, or perform in a transaction ▷ *vb* negotiate the terms of an agreement

BARGAINED > BARGAIN

BARGAINER > BARGAIN

BARGAINS > BARGAIN

BARGANDER *same as* > BERGANDER

BARGE *n* flat-bottomed boat used to transport freight ▷ *vb* push violently

BARGED > BARGE

BARGEE *n* person in charge of a barge

BARGEES > BARGEE

BARGEESE > BARGOOSE

BARGELLO *n* zigzag tapestry stitch

BARGELLOS > BARGELLO

BARGEMAN *same as* > BARGEE

BARGEMEN > BARGEMAN

BARGEPOLE *n* long pole used to propel a barge

BARGES > BARGE

BARGEST *same as* > BARGHEST

BARGESTS > BARGEST

BARGHEST *n* mythical goblin in the shape of a dog

BARGHESTS > BARGHEST

BARGING > BARGE

BARGOON *Canadian word for* > BARGAIN

BARGOONS > BARGOON

BARGOOSE *n* type of goose; sheldrake

BARGUEST *same as* > BARGHEST

BARGUESTS > BARGUEST

BARHOP *vb* visit several bars in succession

BARHOPPED > BARHOP

BARHOPS > BARHOP

BARIATRIC *adj* of the treatment of obesity

BARIC *adj* of or containing barium

BARILLA *n* impure mixture of sodium carbonate and sodium sulphate

BARILLAS > BARILLA

BARING > BARE

BARISH *adj* quite thinly covered

BARISTA *n* person who makes and sells coffee in a coffee bar

BARISTAS > BARISTA

BARITE *n* colourless or white mineral

BARITES > BARITE

BARITONAL > BARITONE

BARITONE *n* (singer with) the second lowest adult male voice ▷ *adj* relating to or denoting a baritone

BARITONES > BARITONE

BARIUM *n* soft white metallic element

BARIUMS > BARIUM

BARK *vb* (of a dog) make its typical loud abrupt cry

BARKAN *same as* > BARCHAN

BARKANS > BARKAN

BARKED > BARK

BARKEEP *n* barkeeper

BARKEEPER *another name (esp US) for* > BARTENDER

BARKEEPS > BARKEEP

BARKEN *vb* become dry with a bark-like outer layer

BARKENED > BARKEN

BARKENING > BARKEN

BARKENS > BARKEN

BARKER *n* person at a fairground who calls loudly to passers-by in order to attract customers

BARKERS > BARKER

BARKHAN *same as* > BARCHAN

b

BARKHANS > BARKHAN

BARKIER > BARKY

BARKIEST > BARKY

BARKING adj mad ▷ adv extremely

BARKLESS > BARK

BARKS > BARK

BARKY adj having the texture or appearance of bark

BARLEDUC n French preserve made of currants

BARLEDUCS > BARLEDUC

BARLESS > BAR

BARLEY n tall grasslike plant cultivated for grain ▷ sentence substitute cry for truce or respite from the rules of a game

BARLEYS > BARLEY

BARLOW n type of strong knife

BARLOWS > BARLOW

BARM n yeasty froth on fermenting malt liquors

BARMAID n woman who serves in a pub

BARMAIDS > BARMAID

BARMAN same as > BARTENDER

BARMBRACK n loaf of bread with currants in it

BARMEN > BARMAN

BARMIE same as > BARMY

BARMIER > BARMY

BARMIEST > BARMY

BARMILY > BARMY

BARMINESS > BARMY

BARMKIN n protective wall around castle

BARMKINS > BARMKIN

BARMPOT n foolish or deranged person

BARMPOTS > BARMPOT

BARMS > BARM

BARMY adj insane

BARN n large building on a farm used for storing grain ▷ vb keep in a barn

BARNACLE n shellfish that lives attached to rocks, ship bottoms, etc

BARNACLED > BARNACLE

BARNACLES > BARNACLE

BARNBRACK same as > BARMBRACK

BARNED > BARN

BARNET n hair

BARNETS > BARNET

BARNEY n noisy fight or argument ▷ vb argue or quarrel

BARNEYED > BARNEY

BARNEYING > BARNEY

BARNEYS > BARNEY

BARNIER > BARNY

BARNIEST > BARNY

BARNING > BARN

BARNLIKE > BARN

BARNS > BARN

BARNSTORM vb tour rural districts putting on shows or making speeches in a political campaign

BARNWOOD n aged and weathered boards, esp those salvaged from dismantled barns

BARNWOODS > BARNWOOD

BARNY adj reminiscent of a barn

BARNYARD n yard adjoining a barn

BARNYARDS > BARNYARD

BAROCCO same as > BAROQUE

BAROCCOS > BAROCCO

BAROCK same as > BAROQUE

BAROCKS > BAROCK

BAROGRAM n record of atmospheric pressure traced by a barograph or similar instrument

BAROGRAMS > BAROGRAM

BAROGRAPH n barometer that automatically keeps a record of changes in atmospheric pressure

BAROLO n red Italian wine

BAROLOS > BAROLO

BAROMETER n instrument for measuring atmospheric pressure

BAROMETRY > BAROMETER

BAROMETZ n fern whose woolly rhizoma resemble a lamb

BARON n member of the lowest rank of nobility

BARONAGE n barons collectively

BARONAGES > BARONAGE

BARONESS n woman holding the rank of baron

BARONET n commoner who holds the lowest hereditary British title

BARONETCY n rank, position, or patent of a baronet

BARONETS > BARONET

BARONG n broad-bladed cleaver-like knife used in the Philippines

BARONGS > BARONG

BARONIAL adj of, relating to, or befitting a baron or barons

BARONIES > BARONY

BARONNE n baroness

BARONNES > BARONNE

BARONS > BARON

BARONY n domain or rank of a baron

BAROPHILE n living organism that grows best in conditions of high atmospheric pressure

BAROQUE n highly ornate style of art, architecture, or music from the late 16th to the early 18th century ▷ adj ornate in style

BAROQUELY > BAROQUE

BAROQUES > BAROQUE

BAROSAUR n large dinosaur

BAROSAURS > BAROSAUR

BAROSCOPE n any instrument for measuring atmospheric pressure, esp a manometer with one side open to the atmosphere

BAROSTAT n device for maintaining constant pressure, such as one used in an aircraft cabin

BAROSTATS > BAROSTAT

BAROTITIS n inflammation of the ear caused by a change in air pressure

BAROUCHE n four-wheeled horse-drawn carriage, popular in the 19th century, having a retractable hood over the rear half, seats inside for two couples facing each other, and a driver's seat outside at the front

BAROUCHES > BAROUCHE

BARP n hillock or bank of stones

BARPERSON n person who serves in a pub: used esp in advertisements

BARPS > BARP

BARQUE n sailing ship, esp one with three masts

BARQUES > BARQUE

BARQUETTE n boat-shaped pastry shell

BARRA n barramundi

BARRABLE > BAR

BARRACAN n thick, strong fabric

BARRACANS > BARRACAN

BARRACE n record of teams entering a sports contest

BARRACES > BARRACE

BARRACK vb criticize loudly or shout against (a team or speaker)

BARRACKED > BARRACK

BARRACKER > BARRACK

BARRACKS pl n building used to accommodate military personnel

BARRACOON n (formerly) a temporary place of confinement for slaves or convicts, esp those awaiting transportation

BARRACUDA n tropical sea fish

BARRAGE n continuous delivery of questions, complaints, etc ▷ vb attack or confront with a barrage

BARRAGED > BARRAGE

BARRAGES > BARRAGE

BARRAGING > BARRAGE

BARRANCA n ravine or precipice

BARRANCAS > BARRANCA

BARRANCO same as > BARRANCA

BARRANCOS > BARRANCO

BARRAS > BARRA

BARRAT n fraudulent dealings ▷ vb quarrel

BARRATED > BARRAT

BARRATER same as > BARRATOR

BARRATERS > BARRATER

BARRATING > BARRAT

BARRATOR n person guilty of barratry

BARRATORS > BARRATOR

BARRATRY n (formerly) the vexatious stirring up of quarrels or bringing of lawsuits

BARRATS > BARRAT

BARRE n rail at hip height used for ballet practice ▷ vb execute guitar chords by laying the index finger over some or all of the strings ▷ adv by using the barre

BARRED > BAR

BARREED > BARRE

BARREFULL same as > BARFUL

BARREING > BARRE

BARREL n cylindrical container with rounded sides and flat ends ▷ vb put in a barrel

BARRELAGE > BARREL

BARRELED > BARREL

BARRELFUL same as > BARREL

BARRELING > BARREL

BARRELLED > BARREL

BARRELS > BARREL

BARREN adj (of a woman or female animal) incapable of producing offspring

BARRENER > BARREN

BARRENEST > BARREN

BARRENLY > BARREN

BARRENS pl n (in North America) a stretch of land that is sparsely vegetated

BARRES > BARRE

BARRET n small flat cap resembling a biretta

BARRETOR n quarrelsome person

BARRETORS > BARRETOR

BARRETRY same as > BARRATRY

BARRETS > BARRET

BARRETTE n clasp or pin for holding women's hair in place

BARRETTER same as > BARRETOR

BARRETTES > BARRETTE

BARRICADE n barrier, esp one erected hastily for defence ▷ vb erect a barricade across (an entrance)

BARRICADO same as > BARRICADE

BARRICO n small container for liquids
BARRICOES > BARRICO
BARRICOS > BARRICO
BARRIE adj very good
BARRIER n anything that prevents access, progress, or union ▷ vb create or form a barrier
BARRIERED > BARRIER
BARRIERS > BARRIER
BARRIES > BARRY
BARRIEST > BARRY
BARRING > BAR
BARRINGS > BAR
BARRIO n Spanish-speaking quarter in a town or city, esp in the US
BARRIOS > BARRIO
BARRIQUE n wine barrel made of oak
BARRIQUES > BARRIQUE
BARRISTER n lawyer qualified to plead in a higher court
BARRO adj embarrassing
BARROOM n room or building where alcoholic drinks are served over a counter
BARROOMS > BARROOM
BARROW n wheelbarrow
BARROWFUL same as > BARROW
BARROWS > BARROW
BARRULET n narrow band across heraldic shield
BARRULETS > BARRULET
BARRY n mistake or blunder
BARS > BAR
BARSTOOL n high stool in bar
BARSTOOLS > BARSTOOL
BARTEND vb serve drinks from a bar
BARTENDED > BARTEND
BARTENDER n man who serves in a bar
BARTENDS > BARTEND
BARTER vb trade (goods) in exchange for other goods ▷ n trade by the exchange of goods
BARTERED > BARTER
BARTERER > BARTER
BARTERERS > BARTER
BARTERING > BARTER
BARTERS > BARTER
BARTISAN same as > BARTIZAN
BARTISANS > BARTISAN
BARTIZAN n small turret projecting from a wall, parapet, or tower
BARTIZANS > BARTIZAN
BARTON n farmyard
BARTONS > BARTON
BARTSIA n type of semiparasitic plant
BARTSIAS > BARTSIA
BARWARE n glasses, etc used in a bar
BARWARES > BARWARE

BARWOOD n red wood from small African tree
BARWOODS > BARWOOD
BARYE n unit of pressure
BARYES > BARYE
BARYON n elementary particle that has a mass greater than or equal to that of the proton
BARYONIC adj of or relating to a baryon
BARYONS > BARYON
BARYTA same as > BARITE
BARYTAS > BARYTA
BARYTE same as > BARYTA
BARYTES > BARYTA
BARYTIC > BARYTA
BARYTON n bass viol with sympathetic strings as well as its six main strings
BARYTONE adj having the last syllable unaccented ▷ n word in which the last syllable is unaccented
BARYTONES > BARYTONE
BARYTONS > BARYTON
BAS > BA
BASAL adj of, at, or constituting a base
BASALLY > BASAL
BASALT n dark volcanic rock
BASALTES n unglazed black stoneware
BASALTIC > BASALT
BASALTINE adj resembling basalt ▷ n black or greenish-black mineral of the pyroxene group
BASALTS > BASALT
BASAN n sheepskin tanned in bark
BASANITE n black basaltic rock containing plagioclase, augite, olivine, and nepheline, leucite, or analcite, formerly used as a touchstone
BASANITES > BASANITE
BASANS > BASAN
BASANT n Pakistani spring festival
BASANTS > BASANT
BASCINET same as > BASINET
BASCINETS > BASCINET
BASCULE n drawbridge that operates by a counterbalanced weight
BASCULES > BASCULE
BASE n bottom or supporting part of anything ▷ vb use as a basis (for) ▷ adj dishonourable or immoral
BASEBALL n team game in which runs are scored by hitting a ball with a bat then running round four bases
BASEBALLS > BASEBALL

BASEBAND n transmission technique using a narrow range of frequencies that allows only one message to be telecommunicated at a time
BASEBANDS > BASEBAND
BASEBOARD n board functioning as the base of anything
BASEBORN adj born of humble parents
BASED > BASE
BASEEJ pl n Iranian volunteer militia
BASEHEAD n habitual user of freebased cocaine
BASEHEADS > BASEHEAD
BASELARD n short sword
BASELARDS > BASELARD
BASELESS adj not based on fact
BASELINE n value or starting point on an imaginary scale with which other things are compared
BASELINER n tennis player who plays most of his or her shots from the back of the court
BASELINES > BASELINE
BASELOAD n constant part of an electrical power supply
BASELOADS > BASELOAD
BASELY > BASE
BASEMAN n fielder positioned near a base
BASEMEN > BASEMAN
BASEMENT n partly or wholly underground storey of a building
BASEMENTS > BASEMENT
BASEN Spencerian spelling of > BASIN
BASENESS > BASE
BASENJI n small breed of dog
BASENJIS > BASENJI
BASEPATH n diamond-shaped path between bases on a baseball field
BASEPATHS > BASEPATH
BASEPLATE n flat supporting plate or frame
BASER > BASE
BASES > BASIS
BASEST > BASE
BASH vb hit violently or forcefully ▷ n heavy blow
BASHAW n important or pompous person
BASHAWISM > BASHAW
BASHAWS > BASHAW
BASHED > BASH
BASHER > BASH
BASHERS > BASH
BASHES > BASH
BASHFUL adj shy or modest
BASHFULLY > BASHFUL
BASHING > BASH
BASHINGS > BASH

BASHLESS adj not ashamed
BASHLIK n Caucasian hood
BASHLIKS > BASHLIK
BASHLYK same as > BASHLIK
BASHLYKS > BASHLYK
BASHMENT same as > DANCEHALL
BASHMENTS > BASHMENT
BASHO n grand tournament in sumo wrestling
BASHTAG n (on Twitter) hashtag used for abusive comments
BASHTAGS > BASHTAG
BASIC adj of or forming a base or basis ▷ n fundamental principle, fact, etc
BASICALLY adv in a fundamental or elementary manner
BASICITY n state of being a base
BASICS > BASIC
BASIDIA > BASIDIUM
BASIDIAL > BASIDIUM
BASIDIUM n structure, produced by basidiomycetous fungi after sexual reproduction, in which spores are formed at the tips of projecting slender stalks
BASIFIED > BASIFY
BASIFIER > BASIFY
BASIFIERS > BASIFY
BASIFIES > BASIFY
BASIFIXED adj (of an anther) attached to the filament by its base
BASIFUGAL a less common word for > ACROPETAL
BASIFY vb make basic
BASIFYING > BASIFY
BASIJ same as > BASEEJ
BASIL n aromatic herb used in cooking
BASILAR adj of or situated at a base
BASILARY same as > BASILAR
BASILECT n debased dialect
BASILECTS > BASILECT
BASILIC > BASILICA
BASILICA n rectangular church with a rounded end and two aisles
BASILICAE > BASILICA
BASILICAL > BASILICA
BASILICAN > BASILICA
BASILICAS > BASILICA
BASILICON n healing ointment
BASILISK n legendary serpent said to kill by its breath or glance
BASILISKS > BASILISK
BASILS > BASIL
BASIN n round open container

b

b

BASINAL > BASIN
BASINED > BASIN
BASINET n close-fitting medieval helmet of light steel usually with a visor
BASINETS > BASINET
BASINFUL n amount a basin will hold
BASINFULS > BASINFUL
BASING > BASE
BASINLIKE > BASIN
BASINS > BASIN
BASION n (in anatomy) midpoint on the forward border of the foramen magnum
BASIONS > BASION
BASIPETAL adj (of leaves and flowers) produced in order from the apex downwards so that the youngest are at the base
BASIS n fundamental principles etc from which something is started or developed
BASK vb lie in or be exposed to something, esp pleasant warmth
BASKED > BASK
BASKET n container made of interwoven strips of wood or cane
BASKETFUL n as much as a basket will hold
BASKETRY n art or practice of making baskets
BASKETS > BASKET
BASKING > BASK
BASKS > BASK
BASMATI n variety of long-grain rice with slender aromatic grains
BASMATIS > BASMATI
BASNET same as > BASINET
BASNETS > BASNET
BASOCHE n society of medieval French lawyers who performed comic plays
BASOCHES > BASOCHE
BASON same as > BASIN
BASONS > BASON
BASOPHIL adj (of cells or cell contents) easily stained by basic dyes ▷ n basophil cell, esp a leucocyte
BASOPHILE same as > BASOPHIL
BASOPHILS > BASOPHIL
BASQUE n tight-fitting bodice for women
BASQUED > BASQUE
BASQUES > BASQUE
BASQUINE n tight-fitting bodice
BASQUINES > BASQUINE
BASS vb speak or sing in a low pitch
BASSE same as > BASS
BASSED > BASS
BASSER n someone who plays bass guitar or double bass

BASSERS > BASSER
BASSES > BASS
BASSEST > BASS
BASSET n breed of hound ▷ vb (of rock) protrude through earth's surface
BASSETED > BASSET
BASSETING > BASSET
BASSETS > BASSET
BASSETT same as > BASSET
BASSETTED > BASSET
BASSETTS > BASSET
BASSI > BASSO
BASSIER > BASSY
BASSIEST > BASSY
BASSINET n wickerwork or wooden cradle or pram, usually hooded
BASSINETS > BASSINET
BASSING > BASS
BASSIST n player of a double bass, esp in a jazz band
BASSISTS > BASSIST
BASSLINE n (in jazz, rock, and pop music) part played by the bass guitar
BASSLINES > BASSLINE
BASSLY > BASS
BASSNESS > BASS
BASSO n singer with a bass voice
BASSOON n low-pitched woodwind instrument
BASSOONS > BASSOON
BASSOS > BASSO
BASSWOOD n N American linden tree
BASSWOODS > BASSWOOD
BASSY adj manifesting strong bass tones
BAST n fibrous material used for making rope, matting, etc
BASTA interj enough; stop
BASTARD n offensive term for an obnoxious or despicable person ▷ adj offensive term meaning illegitimate by birth
BASTARDLY > BASTARD
BASTARDRY n malicious or cruel behaviour
BASTARDS > BASTARD
BASTARDY n condition of being a bastard
BASTE vb moisten (meat) during cooking with hot fat
BASTED > BASTE
BASTER > BASTE
BASTERS > BASTE
BASTES > BASTE
BASTI n (in India) a slum inhabited by poor people
BASTIDE n small isolated house in France
BASTIDES > BASTIDE
BASTILE same as > BASTILLE
BASTILES > BASTILE
BASTILLE n prison

BASTILLES > BASTILLE
BASTINADE same as > BASTINADO
BASTINADO n punishment or torture by beating on the soles of the feet with a stick ▷ vb beat (a person) in this way
BASTING n loose temporary stitches
BASTINGS > BASTING
BASTION n projecting part of a fortification
BASTIONED > BASTION
BASTIONS > BASTION
BASTIS > BASTI
BASTLE n fortified house
BASTLES > BASTLE
BASTO n ace of clubs in certain card games
BASTOS > BASTO
BASTS > BAST
BASUCO n cocaine-based drug
BASUCOS > BASUCO
BAT n any of various types of club used to hit the ball in certain sports ▷ vb strike with or as if with a bat
BATABLE > BAT
BATARD n canoe made of birchbark
BATARDS > BATARD
BATATA n sweet potato
BATATAS > BATATA
BATAVIA n variety of lettuce with smooth pale green leaves
BATAVIAS > BATAVIA
BATBOY n boy who works at baseball games
BATBOYS > BATBOY
BATCH n group of people or things dealt with at the same time ▷ vb group (items) for efficient processing
BATCHED > BATCH
BATCHER > BATCH
BATCHERS > BATCH
BATCHES > BATCH
BATCHING > BATCH
BATCHINGS > BATCH
BATE vb (of hawks) to jump violently from a perch or the falconer's fist
BATEAU n light flat-bottomed boat used on rivers in Canada and the northern US
BATEAUX > BATEAU
BATED > BATE
BATELESS > BATE
BATELEUR n African bird of prey with a short tail and long wings
BATELEURS > BATELEUR
BATEMENT n reduction
BATEMENTS > BATEMENT
BATES > BATE
BATFISH n type of angler fish with a flattened scaleless body

BATFISHES > BATFISH
BATFOWL vb catch birds by temporarily blinding them with light
BATFOWLED > BATFOWL
BATFOWLER > BATFOWL
BATFOWLS > BATFOWL
BATGIRL n girl who works at baseball games
BATGIRLS > BATGIRL
BATH n large container in which to wash the body ▷ vb wash in a bath
BATHCUBE n cube of soluble scented material for use in a bath
BATHCUBES > BATHCUBE
BATHE vb swim in open water for pleasure
BATHED > BATHE
BATHER > BATHE
BATHERS pl n swimming costume
BATHES > BATHE
BATHETIC adj containing or displaying bathos
BATHHOUSE n building containing baths, esp for public use
BATHING n act of bathing
BATHINGS > BATHING
BATHLESS > BATH
BATHMAT n mat to stand on after a bath
BATHMATS > BATHMAT
BATHMIC > BATHMISM
BATHMISM n growth-force
BATHMISMS > BATHMISM
BATHOLITE same as > BATHOLITH
BATHOLITH n very large irregular-shaped mass of igneous rock, esp granite, formed from an intrusion of magma at great depth, esp one exposed after erosion of less resistant overlying rocks
BATHORSE n officer's packhorse
BATHORSES > BATHORSE
BATHOS n sudden change from a serious subject to a trivial one
BATHOSES > BATHOS
BATHROBE n loose-fitting garment for wear before or after a bath or swimming
BATHROBES > BATHROBE
BATHROOM n room with a bath, sink, and usu a toilet
BATHROOMS > BATHROOM
BATHS > BATH
BATHTUB n bath, esp one not permanently fixed
BATHTUBS > BATHTUB
BATHWATER n used or unused water in a bathtub
BATHYAL adj relating to an ocean depth of between 200 and 2000 metres

BATHYBIUS *n* gelatinous substance on seabed

BATHYLITE *same as* **> BATHOLITH**

BATHYLITH *same as* **> BATHOLITH**

BATIK *n* process of printing fabric using wax to cover areas not to be dyed ▷ *vb* treat material with this process

BATIKED > BATIK

BATIKING > BATIK

BATIKS > BATIK

BATING > BATE

BATISTE *n* fine plain-weave cotton fabric: used esp for shirts and dresses

BATISTES > BATISTE

BATLER *n* flat piece of wood for beating clothes, etc before washing

BATLERS > BATLER

BATLET *same as* > BATLER

BATLETS > BATLET

BATLIKE > BAT

BATMAN *n* officer's servant in the armed forces

BATMEN > BATMAN

BATOLOGY *n* study of brambles

BATON *n* thin stick used by the conductor of an orchestra ▷ *vb* carry or wave a baton

BATONED > BATON

BATONING > BATON

BATONS > BATON

BATOON *same as* > BATON

BATOONED > BATOON

BATOONING > BATOON

BATOONS > BATOON

BATRACHIA *n* group of amphibians including frogs and toads

BATS > BAT

BATSHIT *adj* eccentric or crazy

BATSMAN *n* person who bats or specializes in batting

BATSMEN > BATSMAN

BATSWING *adj* in the form of the wing of a bat

BATSWOMAN > BATSMAN

BATSWOMEN > BATSMAN

BATT *same as* > BAT

BATTA *n* soldier's allowance

BATTALIA *n* arrangement of army prepared for battle

BATTALIAS > BATTALIA

BATTALION *n* army unit consisting of three or more companies

BATTAS > BATTA

BATTEAU *same as* > BATEAU

BATTEAUX > BATTEAU

BATTED > BAT

BATTEL *vb* make fertile

BATTELED > BATTEL

BATTELER > BATTEL

BATTELERS > BATTEL

BATTELING > BATTEL

BATTELLED > BATTEL

BATTELS > BATTEL

BATTEMENT *n* extension of one leg forwards, sideways, or backwards, either once or repeatedly

BATTEN *n* strip of wood fixed to something, esp to hold it in place ▷ *vb* strengthen or fasten with battens

BATTENED > BATTEN

BATTENER > BATTEN

BATTENERS > BATTEN

BATTENING > BATTEN

BATTENS > BATTEN

BATTER *vb* hit repeatedly ▷ *n* mixture of flour, eggs, and milk, used in cooking

BATTERED *adj* subjected to persistent physical violence, esp by a close relative living in the same house

BATTERER *n* person who batters someone

BATTERERS > BATTERER

BATTERIE *n* movement in ballet involving the legs beating together

BATTERIES > BATTERY

BATTERING *n* act or practice of battering someone

BATTERO *n* heavy club

BATTEROS > BATTERO

BATTERS > BATTER

BATTERY *n* device that produces electricity in a torch, radio, etc ▷ *adj* kept in series of cages for intensive rearing

BATTIER > BATTY

BATTIES > BATTY

BATTIEST > BATTY

BATTIK *same as* > BATIK

BATTIKS > BATTIK

BATTILL *old spelling of* > BATTLE

BATTILLED > BATTILL

BATTILLS > BATTILL

BATTILY *adv* in an eccentric or crazy manner

BATTINESS > BATTY

BATTING > BAT

BATTINGS > BAT

BATTLE *n* fight between large armed forces ▷ *vb* struggle

BATTLEAX *same as* > BATTLEAXE

BATTLEAXE *n* kind of axe formerly used in battle

BATTLEBUS *n* coach that transports politicians and their advisers round the country during an election campaign

BATTLED > BATTLE

BATTLER > BATTLE

BATTLERS > BATTLE

BATTLES > BATTLE

BATTLING > BATTLE

BATTOLOGY *n* unnecessary repetition of words

BATTS > BATT

BATTU *adj* (in ballet) involving a beating movement

BATTUE *n* beating of woodland or cover to force game to flee in the direction of hunters

BATTUES > BATTUE

BATTUTA *n* (in music) a beat

BATTUTAS > BATTUTA

BATTUTO *n* (in Italian cookery) selection of chopped herbs

BATTUTOS > BATTUTO

BATTY *adj* eccentric or crazy ▷ *n* bottom; bum

BATWING *adj* shaped like the wings of a bat, as a black tie, collar, etc

BATWOMAN *n* female servant in any of the armed forces

BATWOMEN > BATWOMAN

BAUBEE *same as* > BAWBEE

BAUBEES > BAUBEE

BAUBLE *n* trinket of little value

BAUBLES > BAUBLE

BAUBLING > BAUBLE

BAUCHLE *vb* shuffle along

BAUCHLED > BAUCHLE

BAUCHLES > BAUCHLE

BAUCHLING > BAUCHLE

BAUD *n* unit used to measure the speed of transmission of electronic data

BAUDEKIN *old variant of* > BALDACHIN

BAUDEKINS > BAUDEKIN

BAUDRIC *same as* > BALDRIC

BAUDRICK *same as* > BALDRIC

BAUDRICKE *same as* > BALDRIC

BAUDRICKS > BAUDRICK

BAUDRICS > BAUDRIC

BAUDRONS *n* name for a cat

BAUDS > BAUD

BAUERA *n* small evergreen Australian shrub

BAUERAS > BAUERA

BAUHINIA *n* type of climbing or shrubby plant of tropical and warm regions, widely cultivated for ornament

BAUHINIAS > BAUHINIA

BAUK *same as* > BALK

BAUKED > BAUK

BAUKING > BAUK

BAUKS > BAUK

BAULK *same as* > BALK

BAULKED > BALK

BAULKER > BALK

BAULKERS > BALK

BAULKIER > BAULKY

BAULKIEST > BAULKY

BAULKILY > BALKY

BAULKING > BALK

BAULKLINE *n* line across a pool table behind which the cue ball is placed at start of a game

BAULKS > BALK

BAULKY *same as* > BALKY

BAUR *n* humorous anecdote; joke

BAURS > BAUR

BAUSOND *adj* (of animal) dappled with white spots

BAUXITE *n* claylike substance that is the chief source of aluminium

BAUXITES > BAUXITE

BAUXITIC > BAUXITE

BAVARDAGE *n* chattering

BAVAROIS *n* cold dessert consisting of a rich custard set with gelatine and flavoured in various ways

BAVIN *n* bundle of brushwood or firewood ▷ *vb* bind (brushwood or firewood) into bavins

BAVINED > BAVIN

BAVINING > BAVIN

BAVINS > BAVIN

BAWBEE *n* former Scottish silver coin

BAWBEES > BAWBEE

BAWBLE *same as* > BAUBLE

BAWBLES > BAWBLE

BAWCOCK *n* fine fellow

BAWCOCKS > BAWCOCK

BAWD *n* person who runs a brothel, esp a woman

BAWDIER > BAWDY

BAWDIES > BAWDY

BAWDIEST > BAWDY

BAWDILY > BAWDY

BAWDINESS > BAWDY

BAWDKIN *same as* > BALDACHIN

BAWDKINS > BAWDKIN

BAWDRIC *n* heavy belt to support sword

BAWDRICS > BAWDRIC

BAWDRIES > BAWDRY

BAWDRY *n* obscene talk or language

BAWDS > BAWD

BAWDY *adj* (of writing etc) containing humorous references to sex ▷ *n* obscenity or eroticism, esp in writing or drama

BAWK *n* type of Atlantic seabird

BAWKS > BAWK

BAWL *vb* shout or weep noisily ▷ *n* loud shout or cry

BAWLED > BAWL

BAWLER > BAWL

BAWLERS > BAWL

BAWLEY *n* small fishing boat

BAWLEYS > BAWLEY

BAWLING > BAWL

BAWLINGS > BAWL
BAWLS > BAWL
BAWN n fortified enclosure
BAWNEEN same as
> BAININ
BAWNEENS > BAWNEEN
BAWNS > BAWN
BAWR same as > BAUR
BAWRS > BAWR
BAWSUNT adj black and white in colour
BAWTIE n name for a dog
BAWTIES > BAWTIE
BAWTY same as > BAWTIE
BAXTER old variant of
> BAKER
BAXTERS > BAXTER
BAY n wide semicircular indentation of a shoreline
▷ vb howl in deep tones
BAYADEER same as
> BAYADERE
BAYADEERS > BAYADEER
BAYADERE n dancing girl, esp one serving in a Hindu temple ▷ adj (of fabric, etc) having horizontal stripes
BAYADERES > BAYADERE
BAYAMO n Cuban strong wind
BAYAMOS > BAYAMO
BAYARD n bay horse
BAYARDS > BAYARD
BAYBERRY n tropical American tree that yields an oil used in making bay rum
BAYE vb bathe
BAYED > BAY
BAYES > BAYE
BAYFRONT n shoreline of a bay
BAYFRONTS > BAYFRONT
BAYING > BAY
BAYLE n barrier
BAYLES > BAYLE
BAYMAN n fisherman
BAYMEN > BAYMAN
BAYNODDY n person who fishes in a bay
BAYONET n sharp blade that can be fixed to the end of a rifle ▷ vb stab with a bayonet
BAYONETED > BAYONET
BAYONETS > BAYONET
BAYOU n (in the southern US) a sluggish marshy tributary of a lake or river
BAYOUS > BAYOU
BAYS > BAY
BAYSIDE n shore of a bay
BAYSIDES > BAYSIDE
BAYT same as > BATE
BAYTED > BAYT
BAYTING > BAYT
BAYTS > BAYT
BAYWOOD n light soft wood of a tropical American mahogany tree
BAYWOODS > BAYWOOD
BAYWOP n (in Newfoundland)

derogatory term for a person from outport communities
BAYWOPS > BAYWOP
BAYYAN n Islamic declaration
BAYYANS > BAYYAN
BAZAAR n sale in aid of charity
BAZAARS > BAZAAR
BAZAR same as > BAZAAR
BAZARS > BAZAR
BAZAZZ same as
> PIZZAZZ
BAZAZZES > BAZAZZ
BAZILLION same as
> GAZILLION
BAZOO a US slang word for
> MOUTH
BAZOOKA n portable rocket launcher that fires an armour-piercing projectile
BAZOOKAS > BAZOOKA
BAZOOM n woman's breast
BAZOOMS > BAZOOM
BAZOUKI same as
> BOUZOUKI
BAZOUKIS > BAZOUKI
BAZZ vb throw (an object)
BAZZAZZ same as
> PIZZAZZ
BAZZAZZES > BAZZAZZ
BAZZED > BAZZ
BAZZES > BAZZ
BAZZING > BAZZ
BDELLIUM n African or W Asian tree that yields a gum resin
BDELLIUMS > BDELLIUM
BE vb exist or live
BEACH n area of sand or pebbles on a shore
▷ vb run or haul (a boat) onto a beach
BEACHBALL n light ball for playing on beach
BEACHBOY n male lifeguard on beach
BEACHBOYS > BEACHBOY
BEACHCOMB vb collect objects, seashells, etc on seashore
BEACHED > BEACH
BEACHES > BEACH
BEACHGOER n person who goes to the beach
BEACHHEAD n beach captured by an attacking army on which troops can be landed
BEACHIER > BEACHY
BEACHIEST > BEACHY
BEACHING > BEACH
BEACHSIDE adj situated near a beach
BEACHWEAR n clothes suitable for the beach
BEACHY adj with gentle sandy slopes
BEACON n fire or light on a hill or tower, used as a warning ▷ vb guide or warn

BEACONED > BEACON
BEACONING > BEACON
BEACONS > BEACON
BEAD n small piece of plastic, wood, etc, pierced for threading ▷ vb decorate with beads
BEADBLAST n jet of small glass beads blown from a nozzle under air or steam pressure ▷ vb clean or treat (a surface) with a beadblast
BEADED > BEAD
BEADER n person making things with beads
BEADERS > BEADER
BEADHOUSE n chapel
BEADIER > BEADY
BEADIEST > BEADY
BEADILY > BEADY
BEADINESS > BEADY
BEADING n strip of moulding used for edging furniture
BEADINGS > BEADING
BEADLE n (formerly) a minor parish official who acted as an usher
BEADLEDOM n petty officialdom
BEADLES > BEADLE
BEADLIKE > BEAD
BEADMAN same as
> BEADSMAN
BEADMEN > BEADMAN
BEADROLL n list of persons for whom prayers are to be offered
BEADROLLS > BEADROLL
BEADS > BEAD
BEADSMAN n person who prays for another's soul, esp one paid or fed for doing so
BEADSMEN > BEADSMAN
BEADWORK same as
> BEADING
BEADWORKS > BEADWORK
BEADY adj small, round, and glittering
BEAGLE n small hound with short legs and drooping ears ▷ vb hunt with beagles, normally on foot
BEAGLED > BEAGLE
BEAGLER n person who hunts with beagles
BEAGLERS > BEAGLER
BEAGLES > BEAGLE
BEAGLING > BEAGLE
BEAGLINGS > BEAGLE
BEAK n projecting horny jaws of a bird ▷ vb strike with the beak
BEAKED > BEAK
BEAKER n large drinking cup
BEAKERFUL n amount of liquid in a full beaker
BEAKERS > BEAKER
BEAKIER > BEAK
BEAKIEST > BEAK

BEAKLESS > BEAK
BEAKLIKE > BEAK
BEAKS > BEAK
BEAKY > BEAK
BEAL n infected sore
BEALING n infected sore
BEALINGS > BEALING
BEALS > BEAL
BEAM n broad smile
▷ vb smile broadly
BEAMED > BEAM
BEAMER n full-pitched ball bowled at the batsman's head
BEAMERS > BEAMER
BEAMIER > BEAM
BEAMIEST > BEAM
BEAMILY > BEAM
BEAMINESS > BEAM
BEAMING > BEAM
BEAMINGLY > BEAM
BEAMINGS > BEAM
BEAMISH adj smiling
BEAMISHLY > BEAMISH
BEAMLESS > BEAM
BEAMLET n small beam
BEAMLETS > BEAMLET
BEAMLIKE > BEAM
BEAMS > BEAM
BEAMY > BEAM
BEAN n seed or pod of various plants, eaten as a vegetable or used to make coffee etc ▷ vb strike on the head
BEANBAG n small cloth bag filled with dried beans and thrown in games
BEANBAGS > BEANBAG
BEANBALL n baseball intended to hit batter's head
BEANBALLS > BEANBALL
BEANED > BEAN
BEANERIES > BEANERY
BEANERY n cheap restaurant
BEANFEAST n any festive or merry occasion
BEANIE n close-fitting woollen hat
BEANIES > BEANY
BEANING > BEAN
BEANLIKE > BEAN
BEANO n celebration or party
BEANOS > BEANO
BEANPOLE n tall thin person
BEANPOLES > BEANPOLE
BEANS > BEAN
BEANSTALK n stem of a bean plant
BEANY same as > BEANIE
BEAR vb support or hold up (something) ▷ n type of omnivorous mammal
BEARABLE adj endurable
BEARABLY > BEARABLE
BEARBERRY n type of shrub
BEARBINE n type of bindweed

BEARBINES > BEARBINE
BEARCAT n lesser panda
BEARCATS > BEARCAT
BEARD n hair growing on the lower parts of a man's face ▷ vb oppose boldly
BEARDED > BEARD
BEARDIE n another name for bearded loach
BEARDIER > BEARDY
BEARDIES > BEARDIE
BEARDIEST > BEARDY
BEARDING > BEARD
BEARDLESS adj without a beard
BEARDS > BEARD
BEARDY adj having a beard
BEARE same as > BEAR
BEARED > BEAR
BEARER n person who carries, presents, or upholds something
BEARERS > BEARER
BEARES > BEARE
BEARGRASS n North American plant
BEARHUG n wrestling hold in which the arms are locked tightly round an opponent's chest and arms ▷ vb hold an opponent in a bearhug
BEARHUGS > BEARHUG
BEARING > BEAR
BEARINGS > BEAR
BEARISH adj like a bear
BEARISHLY > BEARISH
BEARLIKE > BEAR
BEARNAISE n rich sauce made from egg yolks, lemon juice or wine vinegar, butter, shallots, herbs, and seasoning
BEARPAW n paw of a bear
BEARPAWS > BEARPAW
BEARS > BEAR
BEARSKIN n tall fur helmet worn by some British soldiers
BEARSKINS > BEARSKIN
BEARWARD n bear keeper
BEARWARDS > BEARWARD
BEARWOOD another name for > CASCARA
BEARWOODS > BEARWOOD
BEAST n large wild animal ▷ vb torture someone using excessive physical exercise
BEASTED > BEAST
BEASTHOOD > BEAST
BEASTIE n small animal
BEASTIES > BEASTIE
BEASTILY > BESTIAL
BEASTING > BEAST
BEASTINGS same as > BEESTINGS
BEASTLIER > BEASTLY
BEASTLIKE > BEAST
BEASTLY adj unpleasant or disagreeable ▷ adv extremely
BEASTS > BEAST

BEAT vb strike with a series of violent blows ▷ n stroke or blow ▷ adj totally exhausted
BEATABLE > BEAT
BEATBOX n drum machine simulated by a human voice ▷ vb simulate a drum machine with a human voice
BEATBOXED > BEATBOX
BEATBOXER n person who practices beatboxing
BEATBOXES > BEATBOX
BEATEN > BEAT
BEATER n device used for beating
BEATERS > BEATER
BEATH vb dry; heat
BEATHED > BEATH
BEATHING > BEATH
BEATHS > BEATH
BEATIER > BEATY
BEATIEST > BEATY
BEATIFIC adj displaying great happiness
BEATIFIED > BEATIFY
BEATIFIES > BEATIFY
BEATIFY vb take first step towards making (a dead person) a saint
BEATING > BEAT
BEATINGS > BEAT
BEATITUDE n any of the blessings on the poor, meek, etc, in the Sermon on the Mount
BEATLESS > BEAT
BEATNIK n young person in the late 1950s who rebelled against conventional attitudes etc
BEATNIKS > BEATNIK
BEATS > BEAT
BEATY adj (of music) having a strong rhythm
BEAU n boyfriend or admirer
BEAUCOUP n large amount
BEAUCOUPS > BEAUCOUP
BEAUFET same as > BUFFET
BEAUFETS > BEAUFET
BEAUFFET same as > BUFFET
BEAUFFETS > BEAUFFET
BEAUFIN same as > BIFFIN
BEAUFINS > BEAUFIN
BEAUISH adj vain and showy
BEAUS > BEAU
BEAUT n person or thing that is outstanding or distinctive ▷ adj good or excellent ▷ interj exclamation of joy or pleasure
BEAUTEOUS adj beautiful
BEAUTER > BEAUT
BEAUTEST > BEAUT
BEAUTIED > BEAUTY
BEAUTIES > BEAUTY

BEAUTIFUL adj very attractive to look at
BEAUTIFY vb make beautiful
BEAUTS > BEAUT
BEAUTY n combination of all the qualities of a person or thing that delight the senses and mind ▷ interj expression of approval or agreement ▷ vb make beautiful
BEAUTYING > BEAUTY
BEAUX > BEAU
BEAUXITE same as > BAUXITE
BEAUXITES > BEAUXITE
BEAVER n amphibious rodent with a big flat tail ▷ vb work steadily or assiduously
BEAVERED > BEAVER
BEAVERIES > BEAVERY
BEAVERING > BEAVER
BEAVERS > BEAVER
BEAVERY n place for keeping beavers
BEBEERINE n alkaloid, resembling quinine, obtained from the bark of the greenheart and other plants
BEBEERU n tropical American tree
BEBEERUS > BEBEERU
BEBLOOD vb stain with blood
BEBLOODED > BEBLOOD
BEBLOODS > BEBLOOD
BEBOP same as > BOP
BEBOPPED > BEBOP
BEBOPPER > BEBOP
BEBOPPERS > BEBOP
BEBOPPING > BEBOP
BEBOPS > BEBOP
BEBUNG n vibrato effect on clavichord
BEBUNGS > BEBUNG
BECALL vb use insulting words about someone
BECALLED > BECALL
BECALLING > BECALL
BECALLS > BECALL
BECALM vb make calm
BECALMED adj (of a sailing ship) motionless through lack of wind
BECALMING > BECALM
BECALMS > BECALM
BECAME > BECOME
BECAP vb put cap on
BECAPPED > BECAP
BECAPPING > BECAP
BECAPS > BECAP
BECARPET vb lay carpet on
BECARPETS > BECARPET
BECASSE n woodcock
BECASSES > BECASSE
BECAUSE conj on account of the fact that; on account of being; since
BECCACCIA n woodcock
BECCAFICO n European songbird, eaten as a

delicacy in Italy and other countries
BECHALK vb mark with chalk
BECHALKED > BECHALK
BECHALKS > BECHALK
BECHAMEL n thick white sauce flavoured with onion and seasoning
BECHAMELS > BECHAMEL
BECHANCE vb happen (to)
BECHANCED > BECHANCE
BECHANCES > BECHANCE
BECHARM vb delight
BECHARMED > BECHARM
BECHARMS > BECHARM
BECK n stream ▷ vb attract someone's attention by nodding or gesturing
BECKE same as > BEAK
BECKED > BECK
BECKES > BECKE
BECKET n clevis forming part of one end of a sheave
BECKETS > BECKET
BECKING > BECK
BECKON vb summon with a gesture ▷ n summoning gesture
BECKONED > BECKON
BECKONER > BECKON
BECKONERS > BECKON
BECKONING > BECKON
BECKONS > BECKON
BECKS > BECK
BECLAMOR vb clamour excessively
BECLAMORS > BECLAMOR
BECLAMOUR vb make a clamour
BECLASP vb embrace
BECLASPED > BECLASP
BECLASPS > BECLASP
BECLOAK vb dress in cloak
BECLOAKED > BECLOAK
BECLOAKS > BECLOAK
BECLOG vb put clogs on
BECLOGGED > BECLOG
BECLOGS > BECLOG
BECLOTHE vb put clothes on
BECLOTHED > BECLOTHE
BECLOTHES > BECLOTHE
BECLOUD vb cover or obscure with a cloud
BECLOUDED > BECLOUD
BECLOUDS > BECLOUD
BECLOWN vb clown around
BECLOWNED > BECLOWN
BECLOWNS > BECLOWN
BECOME vb come to be
BECOMES > BECOME
BECOMING adj attractive or pleasing ▷ n any process of change
BECOMINGS > BECOMING
BECOWARD vb make cowardly
BECOWARDS > BECOWARD
BECQUEREL n SI unit of activity of a radioactive source
BECRAWL vb crawl all over

BECRAWLED > BECRAWL
BECRAWLS > BECRAWL
BECRIME vb make someone guilty of a crime
BECRIMED > BECRIME
BECRIMES > BECRIME
BECRIMING > BECRIME
BECROWD vb crowd with something
BECROWDED > BECROWD
BECROWDS > BECROWD
BECRUST vb cover with crust
BECRUSTED > BECRUST
BECRUSTS > BECRUST
BECUDGEL vb arm with cudgel
BECUDGELS > BECUDGEL
BECURL vb curl
BECURLED > BECURL
BECURLING > BECURL
BECURLS > BECURL
BECURSE vb curse
BECURSED > BECURSE
BECURSES > BECURSE
BECURSING > BECURSE
BECURST > BECURSE
BED n piece of furniture on which to sleep ▷ vb plant in a bed
BEDABBLE vb dabble; moisten
BEDABBLED > BEDABBLE
BEDABBLES > BEDABBLE
BEDAD interj by God (oath)
BEDAGGLE vb soil by trailing through dirt
BEDAGGLED > BEDAGGLE
BEDAGGLES > BEDAGGLE
BEDAMN vb damn
BEDAMNED > BEDAMN
BEDAMNING > BEDAMN
BEDAMNS > BEDAMN
BEDARKEN vb make dark
BEDARKENS > BEDARKEN
BEDASH vb sprinkle with liquid
BEDASHED > BEDASH
BEDASHES > BEDASH
BEDASHING > BEDASH
BEDAUB vb smear with something sticky or dirty
BEDAUBED > BEDAUB
BEDAUBING > BEDAUB
BEDAUBS > BEDAUB
BEDAWIN same as > BEDOUIN
BEDAWINS > BEDAWIN
BEDAZE vb daze
BEDAZED > BEDAZE
BEDAZES > BEDAZE
BEDAZING > BEDAZE
BEDAZZLE vb dazzle or confuse, as with brilliance
BEDAZZLED > BEDAZZLE
BEDAZZLES > BEDAZZLE
BEDBATH n washing of a sick person in bed
BEDBATHS > BEDBATH
BEDBOARD n base of bed
BEDBOARDS > BEDBOARD
BEDBUG n small blood-sucking wingless

insect that infests dirty houses
BEDBUGS > BEDBUG
BEDCHAIR n adjustable chair to support invalid in bed
BEDCHAIRS > BEDCHAIR
BEDCOVER n cover for bed
BEDCOVERS > BEDCOVER
BEDDABLE adj sexually attractive
BEDDED > BED
BEDDER n (at some universities) a college servant employed to keep students' rooms in order
BEDDERS > BEDDER
BEDDING > BED
BEDDINGS > BED
BEDE n prayer
BEDEAFEN vb deafen
BEDEAFENS > BEDEAFEN
BEDECK vb cover with decorations
BEDECKED > BEDECK
BEDECKING > BEDECK
BEDECKS > BEDECK
BEDEGUAR n growth found on rosebushes
BEDEGUARS > BEDEGUAR
BEDEHOUSE same as > BEADHOUSE
BEDEL archaic spelling of > BEADLE
BEDELL same as > BEADLE
BEDELLS > BEDELL
BEDELS > BEDEL
BEDELSHIP > BEDEL
BEDEMAN same as > BEADSMAN
BEDEMEN > BEDEMAN
BEDERAL same as > BEDRAL
BEDERALS > BEDERAL
BEDES > BEDE
BEDESMAN same as > BEADSMAN
BEDESMEN > BEDESMAN
BEDEVIL vb harass, confuse, or torment
BEDEVILED > BEDEVIL
BEDEVILS > BEDEVIL
BEDEW vb wet or cover with or as if with drops of dew
BEDEWED > BEDEW
BEDEWING > BEDEW
BEDEWS > BEDEW
BEDFAST an archaic word for > BEDRIDDEN
BEDFELLOW n temporary associate
BEDFRAME n framework of bed
BEDFRAMES > BEDFRAME
BEDGOWN n night dress
BEDGOWNS > BEDGOWN
BEDHEAD n untidy state of hair, esp caused by sleeping
BEDHEADS > BEDHEAD
BEDIAPER vb put a nappy on

BEDIAPERS > BEDIAPER
BEDIDE > BEDYE
BEDIGHT vb array or adorn ▷ adj adorned or bedecked
BEDIGHTED > BEDIGHT
BEDIGHTS > BEDIGHT
BEDIM vb make dim or obscure
BEDIMMED > BEDIM
BEDIMMING > BEDIM
BEDIMPLE vb form dimples in
BEDIMPLED > BEDIMPLE
BEDIMPLES > BEDIMPLE
BEDIMS > BEDIM
BEDIRTIED > BEDIRTY
BEDIRTIES > BEDIRTY
BEDIRTY vb make dirty
BEDIZEN vb dress or decorate gaudily or tastelessly
BEDIZENED > BEDIZEN
BEDIZENS > BEDIZEN
BEDLAM n noisy confused situation
BEDLAMER n young harp seal
BEDLAMERS > BEDLAMER
BEDLAMISM > BEDLAM
BEDLAMITE n lunatic
BEDLAMP n bedside light
BEDLAMPS > BEDLAMP
BEDLAMS > BEDLAM
BEDLESS > BED
BEDLIKE adj like a bed
BEDLINER n lining for the bed of a truck
BEDLINERS > BEDLINER
BEDMAKER n person who makes beds
BEDMAKERS > BEDMAKER
BEDMATE n person who shares a bed
BEDMATES > BEDMATE
BEDOTTED adj scattered; strewn
BEDOUIN n member of any of the nomadic tribes of Arabs
BEDOUINS > BEDOUIN
BEDPAN n shallow bowl used as a toilet by bedridden people
BEDPANS > BEDPAN
BEDPLATE n heavy metal platform or frame to which an engine or machine is attached
BEDPLATES > BEDPLATE
BEDPOST n vertical support on a bedstead
BEDPOSTS > BEDPOST
BEDQUILT n padded bed cover
BEDQUILTS > BEDQUILT
BEDRAGGLE vb make (hair, clothing, etc) limp, untidy, or dirty, as with rain or mud
BEDRAIL n rail along the side of a bed connecting the headboard with the footboard

BEDRAILS > BEDRAIL
BEDRAL n minor church official
BEDRALS > BEDRAL
BEDRAPE vb adorn
BEDRAPED > BEDRAPE
BEDRAPES > BEDRAPE
BEDRAPING > BEDRAPE
BEDRENCH vb drench
BEDREST n rest in bed, eg to recover from illness
BEDRESTS > BEDREST
BEDRID same as > BEDRIDDEN
BEDRIDDEN adj confined to bed because of illness or old age
BEDRIGHT n rights expected in the marital bed
BEDRIGHTS > BEDRIGHT
BEDRITE same as > BEDRIGHT
BEDRITES > BEDRITE
BEDRIVEL vb drivel around
BEDRIVELS > BEDRIVEL
BEDROCK n solid rock beneath the surface soil
BEDROCKS > BEDROCK
BEDROLL n portable roll of bedding
BEDROLLS > BEDROLL
BEDROOM n room used for sleeping ▷ adj containing references to sex
BEDROOMED adj containing specified number of bedrooms
BEDROOMS > BEDROOM
BEDROP vb drop on
BEDROPPED > BEDROP
BEDROPS > BEDROP
BEDROPT > BEDROP
BEDRUG vb drug excessively
BEDRUGGED > BEDRUG
BEDRUGS > BEDRUG
BEDS > BED
BEDSHEET n sheet for bed
BEDSHEETS > BEDSHEET
BEDSIDE n area beside a bed ▷ adj placed at or near the side of the bed
BEDSIDES > BEDSIDE
BEDSIT n furnished sitting room with a bed
BEDSITS > BEDSIT
BEDSITTER same as > BEDSIT
BEDSKIRT n drapery round the edge of a bed
BEDSKIRTS > BEDSKIRT
BEDSOCK n sock worn in bed
BEDSOCKS > BEDSOCK
BEDSONIA n bacterium causing diseases such as trachoma
BEDSONIAS > BEDSONIA
BEDSORE n ulcer on the skin, caused by a lengthy period of lying in bed due to illness

BEDSORES > BEDSORE
BEDSPREAD n top cover on a bed
BEDSPRING vb spring supporting mattress on bed
BEDSTAND n bedside table
BEDSTANDS > BEDSTAND
BEDSTEAD n framework of a bed
BEDSTEADS > BEDSTEAD
BEDSTRAW n plant with small white or yellow flowers
BEDSTRAWS > BEDSTRAW
BEDTICK n case containing stuffing in mattress
BEDTICKS > BEDTICK
BEDTIME n time when one usually goes to bed
BEDTIMES > BEDTIME
BEDU adj relating to beduins
BEDUCK vb duck under water
BEDUCKED > BEDUCK
BEDUCKING > BEDUCK
BEDUCKS > BEDUCK
BEDUIN variant of > BEDOUIN
BEDUINS > BEDUIN
BEDUMB vb make dumb
BEDUMBED > BEDUMB
BEDUMBING > BEDUMB
BEDUMBS > BEDUMB
BEDUNCE vb cause to look or feel foolish
BEDUNCED > BEDUNCE
BEDUNCES > BEDUNCE
BEDUNCING > BEDUNCE
BEDUNG vb spread with dung
BEDUNGED > BEDUNG
BEDUNGING > BEDUNG
BEDUNGS > BEDUNG
BEDUST vb cover with dust
BEDUSTED > BEDUST
BEDUSTING > BEDUST
BEDUSTS > BEDUST
BEDWARD adj towards bed
BEDWARDS adv towards bed
BEDWARF vb hamper growth of
BEDWARFED > BEDWARF
BEDWARFS > BEDWARF
BEDWARMER n metal pan containing hot coals, formerly used to warm a bed
BEDWETTER n person who urinates in bed
BEDYDE > BEDYE
BEDYE vb dye
BEDYED > BEDYE
BEDYEING > BEDYE
BEDYES > BEDYE
BEE n insect that makes wax and honey
BEEBEE n air rifle
BEEBEES > BEEBEE
BEEBREAD n mixture of pollen and nectar prepared

by worker bees and fed to the larvae
BEEBREADS > BEEBREAD
BEECH n tree with a smooth greyish bark
BEECHEN > BEECH
BEECHES > BEECH
BEECHIER > BEECH
BEECHIEST > BEECH
BEECHMAST n nuts of beech tree
BEECHNUT n small brown triangular edible nut of the beech tree
BEECHNUTS > BEECHNUT
BEECHWOOD n wood of beech tree
BEECHY > BEECH
BEEDI n Indian cigarette
BEEDIE same as > BEEDI
BEEDIES > BEEDI
BEEF n flesh of a cow, bull, or ox ▷ vb complain
BEEFALO n cross between cow and buffalo
BEEFALOES > BEEFALO
BEEFALOS > BEEFALO
BEEFCAKE n musclemen as displayed in photographs
BEEFCAKES > BEEFCAKE
BEEFEATER n yeoman warder at the Tower of London
BEEFED > BEEF
BEEFIER > BEEFY
BEEFIEST > BEEFY
BEEFILY > BEEFY
BEEFINESS > BEEFY
BEEFING > BEEF
BEEFLESS > BEEF
BEEFS > BEEF
BEEFSTEAK n piece of beef that can be grilled, fried, etc, cut from a lean part of the animal
BEEFWOOD n any of various trees that produce very hard wood
BEEFWOODS > BEEFWOOD
BEEFY adj like beef
BEEGAH same as > BIGHA
BEEGAHS > BEEGAH
BEEHIVE n structure in which bees live
BEEHIVED adj (esp of a hairstyle) shaped like a beehive
BEEHIVES > BEEHIVE
BEEKEEPER n person who keeps bees for their honey
BEELIKE > BEE
BEELINE n most direct route between two places ▷ adj make a beeline for (something)
BEELINED > BEELINE
BEELINES > BEELINE
BEELINING > BEELINE
BEEN > BE
BEENAH n understanding; insight
BEENAHS > BEENAH

BEENTO n person who has resided in Britain ▷ adj of, relating to, or characteristic of such a person
BEENTOS > BEENTO
BEEP n high-pitched sound, like that of a car horn ▷ vb (cause to) make this noise
BEEPED > BEEP
BEEPER > BEEP
BEEPERS > BEEP
BEEPING > BEEP
BEEPS > BEEP
BEER n alcoholic drink brewed from malt and hops
BEERAGE n brewing industry
BEERAGES > BEERAGE
BEERFEST n beer festival
BEERFESTS > BEERFEST
BEERHALL n large public room where beer is consumed
BEERHALLS > BEERHALL
BEERIER > BEERY
BEERIEST > BEERY
BEERILY > BEERY
BEERINESS > BEERY
BEERMAT n small mat put under a glass of beer
BEERMATS > BEERMAT
BEERNUT n coated peanut eaten as a snack
BEERNUTS > BEERNUT
BEERS > BEER
BEERSIES pl n (NZ) beers
BEERY adj smelling or tasting of beer
BEES > BEE
BEESOME same as > BISSON
BEESTING adj as in beesting lips of lips, pouting
BEESTINGS n first milk secreted by the mammary glands of a cow or similar animal immediately after giving birth
BEESTUNG adj as in beestung lips of lips, pouting
BEESWAX n wax secreted by bees, used in polishes etc ▷ vb polish with such wax
BEESWAXED > BEESWAX
BEESWAXES > BEESWAX
BEESWING n light filmy crust of tartar that forms in port and some other wines after long keeping in the bottle
BEESWINGS > BEESWING
BEET n plant with an edible root and leaves ▷ vb improve or make better
BEETED > BEET
BEETFLIES > BEETFLY
BEETFLY n type of fly which is a common pest of

beets and mangel-wurzels
BEETING > BEET
BEETLE n insect with a hard wing cover on its back ▷ vb overhang or jut ▷ vb scuttle or scurry
BEETLED > BEETLE
BEETLER n one who operates a beetling machine
BEETLERS > BEETLER
BEETLES > BEETLE
BEETLING > BEETLE
BEETROOT n type of beet plant with a dark red root
BEETROOTS > BEETROOT
BEETS > BEET
BEEVES > BEEF
BEEYARD n place where bees are kept
BEEYARDS > BEEYARD
BEEZER n person or chap ▷ adj excellent
BEEZERS > BEEZER
BEFALL vb happen to (someone)
BEFALLEN > BEFALL
BEFALLING > BEFALL
BEFALLS > BEFALL
BEFANA n Italian gift-bearing good fairy
BEFANAS > BEFANA
BEFELD > BEFALL
BEFELL > BEFALL
BEFFANA same as > BEFANA
BEFFANAS > BEFFANA
BEFINGER vb mark by handling
BEFINGERS > BEFINGER
BEFINNED adj with fins
BEFIT vb be appropriate or suitable for
BEFITS > BEFIT
BEFITTED > BEFIT
BEFITTING > BEFIT
BEFLAG vb decorate with flags
BEFLAGGED > BEFLAG
BEFLAGS > BEFLAG
BEFLEA vb infest with fleas
BEFLEAED > BEFLEA
BEFLEAING > BEFLEA
BEFLEAS > BEFLEA
BEFLECK vb fleck
BEFLECKED > BEFLECK
BEFLECKS > BEFLECK
BEFLOWER vb decorate with flowers
BEFLOWERS > BEFLOWER
BEFLUM vb fool; deceive
BEFLUMMED > BEFLUM
BEFLUMS > BEFLUM
BEFOAM vb cover with foam
BEFOAMED > BEFOAM
BEFOAMING > BEFOAM
BEFOAMS > BEFOAM
BEFOG vb surround with fog
BEFOGGED > BEFOG
BEFOGGING > BEFOG

BEFOGS > BEFOG
BEFOOL vb make a fool of
BEFOOLED > BEFOOL
BEFOOLING > BEFOOL
BEFOOLS > BEFOOL
BEFORE adv indicating something earlier in time, in front of, or preferred to ▷ prep preceding in space or time
BEFORTUNE vb happen to
BEFOUL vb make dirty or foul
BEFOULED > BEFOUL
BEFOULER > BEFOUL
BEFOULERS > BEFOUL
BEFOULING > BEFOUL
BEFOULS > BEFOUL
BEFRET vb fret about something
BEFRETS > BEFRET
BEFRETTED > BEFRET
BEFRIEND vb become friends with
BEFRIENDS > BEFRIEND
BEFRINGE vb decorate with fringe
BEFRINGED > BEFRINGE
BEFRINGES > BEFRINGE
BEFUDDLE vb confuse, muddle, or perplex
BEFUDDLED > BEFUDDLE
BEFUDDLES > BEFUDDLE
BEG vb solicit (money, food, etc), esp in the street
BEGAD interj emphatic exclamation
BEGALL vb make sore by rubbing
BEGALLED > BEGALL
BEGALLING > BEGALL
BEGALLS > BEGALL
BEGAN > BEGIN
BEGAR n compulsory labour
BEGARS > BEGAR
BEGAT > BEGET
BEGAZE vb gaze about or around
BEGAZED > BEGAZE
BEGAZES > BEGAZE
BEGAZING > BEGAZE
BEGEM vb decorate with gems
BEGEMMED > BEGEM
BEGEMMING > BEGEM
BEGEMS > BEGEM
BEGET vb cause or create
BEGETS > BEGET
BEGETTER > BEGET
BEGETTERS > BEGET
BEGETTING > BEGET
BEGGAR n person who begs, esp one who lives by begging ▷ vb be beyond the resources of
BEGGARDOM > BEGGAR
BEGGARED > BEGGAR
BEGGARIES > BEGGARY
BEGGARING > BEGGAR
BEGGARLY adj meanly inadequate
BEGGARS > BEGGAR

BEGGARY n extreme poverty or need
BEGGED > BEG
BEGGING > BEG
BEGGINGLY > BEG
BEGGINGS > BEG
BEGHARD n member of a 13th century Christian brotherhood
BEGHARDS > BEGHARD
BEGIFT vb give gift or gifts to
BEGIFTED > BEGIFT
BEGIFTING > BEGIFT
BEGIFTS > BEGIFT
BEGILD vb gild
BEGILDED > BEGILD
BEGILDING > BEGILD
BEGILDS > BEGILD
BEGILT > BEGILD
BEGIN vb start
BEGINNE same as > BEGINNING
BEGINNER n person who has just started learning to do something
BEGINNERS > BEGINNER
BEGINNES > BEGINNE
BEGINNING n start
BEGINS > BEGIN
BEGIRD vb surround
BEGIRDED > BEGIRD
BEGIRDING > BEGIRD
BEGIRDLE vb surround with girdle
BEGIRDLED > BEGIRDLE
BEGIRDLES > BEGIRDLE
BEGIRDS > BEGIRD
BEGIRT > BEGIRD
BEGLAD vb make glad
BEGLADDED > BEGLAD
BEGLADS > BEGLAD
BEGLAMOR same as > BEGLAMOUR
BEGLAMORS > BEGLAMOR
BEGLAMOUR vb glamourize
BEGLERBEG n governor in the Ottoman empire
BEGLOOM vb make gloomy
BEGLOOMED > BEGLOOM
BEGLOOMS > BEGLOOM
BEGNAW vb gnaw at
BEGNAWED > BEGNAW
BEGNAWING > BEGNAW
BEGNAWS > BEGNAW
BEGO vb harass; beset
BEGOES > BEGO
BEGOGGLED adj wearing goggles
BEGOING > BEGO
BEGONE > BEGO
BEGONIA n tropical plant with waxy flowers
BEGONIAS > BEGONIA
BEGORAH same as > BEGORRA
BEGORED adj smear with gore
BEGORRA interj emphatic exclamation, regarded as a characteristic utterance of Irishmen

BEGORRAH same as > BEGORRA
BEGOT past participle of > BEGET
BEGOTTEN past participle of > BEGET
BEGRIM same as > BEGRIME
BEGRIME vb make dirty
BEGRIMED > BEGRIME
BEGRIMES > BEGRIME
BEGRIMING > BEGRIME
BEGRIMMED > BEGRIM
BEGRIMS > BEGRIM
BEGROAN vb groan at
BEGROANED > BEGROAN
BEGROANS > BEGROAN
BEGRUDGE vb envy (someone) the possession of something
BEGRUDGED > BEGRUDGE
BEGRUDGER > BEGRUDGE
BEGRUDGES > BEGRUDGE
BEGS > BEG
BEGUILE vb cheat or mislead
BEGUILED > BEGUILE
BEGUILER > BEGUILE
BEGUILERS > BEGUILE
BEGUILES > BEGUILE
BEGUILING adj charming, often in a deceptive way
BEGUIN another name for > BEGHARD
BEGUINAGE n convent for members of beguine sisterhood
BEGUINE n S American dance
BEGUINES > BEGUINE
BEGUINS > BEGUIN
BEGULF vb overwhelm
BEGULFED > BEGULF
BEGULFING > BEGULF
BEGULFS > BEGULF
BEGUM n Muslim woman of high rank
BEGUMS > BEGUM
BEGUN past participle of > BEGIN
BEGUNK vb delude; trick
BEGUNKED > BEGUNK
BEGUNKING > BEGUNK
BEGUNKS > BEGUNK
BEHALF n interest, part, benefit, or respect
BEHALVES > BEHALF
BEHAPPEN vb befall
BEHAPPENS > BEHAPPEN
BEHATTED adj wearing a hat
BEHAVE vb act or function in a particular way
BEHAVED > BEHAVE
BEHAVER > BEHAVE
BEHAVERS > BEHAVE
BEHAVES > BEHAVE
BEHAVING > BEHAVE
BEHAVIOR same as > BEHAVIOUR
BEHAVIORS > BEHAVIOR
BEHAVIOUR n manner of behaving

BEHEAD vb remove the head from
BEHEADAL > BEHEAD
BEHEADALS > BEHEAD
BEHEADED > BEHEAD
BEHEADER > BEHEAD
BEHEADERS > BEHEAD
BEHEADING > BEHEAD
BEHEADS > BEHEAD
BEHELD > BEHOLD
BEHEMOTH n huge person or thing
BEHEMOTHS > BEHEMOTH
BEHEST n order or earnest request
BEHESTS > BEHEST
BEHIGHT vb entrust
BEHIGHTS > BEHIGHT
BEHIND adv indicating position to the rear, lateness, responsibility, etc ▷ n buttocks ▷ prep in or to a position further back than ▷ adj in a position further back
BEHINDS > BEHIND
BEHOLD vb look (at)
BEHOLDEN adj indebted or obliged
BEHOLDER > BEHOLD
BEHOLDERS > BEHOLD
BEHOLDING > BEHOLD
BEHOLDS > BEHOLD
BEHOOF n advantage or profit
BEHOOFS > BEHOOF
BEHOOVE same as > BEHOVE
BEHOOVED > BEHOOVE
BEHOOVES > BEHOOVE
BEHOOVING > BEHOOVE
BEHOTE same as > BEHIGHT
BEHOTES > BEHOTE
BEHOTING > BEHOTE
BEHOVE vb be necessary or fitting for
BEHOVED > BEHOVE
BEHOVEFUL adj useful; of benefit
BEHOVELY adj useful
BEHOVES > BEHOVE
BEHOVING > BEHOVE
BEHOWL vb howl at
BEHOWLED > BEHOWL
BEHOWLING > BEHOWL
BEHOWLS > BEHOWL
BEIGE adj pale brown ▷ n very light brown
BEIGEL same as > BAGEL
BEIGELS > BEIGEL
BEIGER > BEIGE
BEIGES > BEIGE
BEIGEST > BEIGE
BEIGIER > BEIGE
BEIGIEST > BEIGE
BEIGNE variant of > BEIGNET
BEIGNES > BEIGNE
BEIGNET n square deep-fried pastry served hot and sprinkled with icing sugar

BEIGNETS > BEIGNET
BEIGY > BEIGE
BEIN *adj* financially comfortable ▷ *vb* fill
BEINED > BEIN
BEING > BE
BEINGLESS > BE
BEINGNESS > BE
BEINGS > BE
BEINING > BEIN
BEINKED *adj* daubed with ink
BEINNESS > BEIN
BEINS > BEIN
BEJABBERS *same as* > BEJABERS
BEJABERS *interj* by Jesus!
BEJADE *vb* jade; tire
BEJADED > BEJADE
BEJADES > BEJADE
BEJADING > BEJADE
BEJANT *same as* > BAJAN
BEJANTS > BEJANT
BEJASUS *same as* > BEJESUS
BEJASUSES > BEJASUS
BEJEEBERS *same as* > BEJABERS
BEJEEZUS *same as* > BEJESUS
BEJESUIT *vb* convert to Jesuitism
BEJESUITS > BEJESUIT
BEJESUS *interj* exclamation of surprise ▷ *n* as in *the bejesus* mild expletive
BEJESUSES > BEJESUS
BEJEWEL *vb* decorate with or as if with jewels
BEJEWELED *same as* > BEJEWEL
BEJEWELS > BEJEWEL
BEJUMBLE *vb* jumble up
BEJUMBLED > BEJUMBLE
BEJUMBLES > BEJUMBLE
BEKAH *n* half shekel
BEKAHS > BEKAH
BEKISS *vb* smother with kisses
BEKISSED > BEKISS
BEKISSES > BEKISS
BEKISSING > BEKISS
BEKNAVE *vb* treat as a knave
BEKNAVED > BEKNAVE
BEKNAVES > BEKNAVE
BEKNAVING > BEKNAVE
BEKNIGHT *vb* esteem
BEKNIGHTS > BEKNIGHT
BEKNOT *vb* tie a knot or knots in
BEKNOTS > BEKNOT
BEKNOTTED > BEKNOT
BEKNOWN *adj* known about
BEL *n* unit for comparing two power levels or measuring the intensity of a sound
BELABOR *same as* > BELABOUR
BELABORED > BELABOR

BELABORS > BELABOR
BELABOUR *vb* attack verbally or physically
BELABOURS > BELABOUR
BELACE *vb* decorate with lace
BELACED > BELACE
BELACES > BELACE
BELACING > BELACE
BELADIED > BELADY
BELADIES > BELADY
BELADY *vb* call a lady
BELADYING > BELADY
BELAH *n* Australian tree which yields a useful timber
BELAHS > BELAH
BELAMIES > BELAMY
BELAMOUR *n* beloved person
BELAMOURE *n* loved one
BELAMOURS > BELAMOUR
BELAMY *n* close friend
BELAR *same as* > BELAH
BELARS > BELAR
BELATE *vb* cause to be late
BELATED *adj* late or too late
BELATEDLY > BELATED
BELATES > BELATE
BELATING > BELATE
BELAUD *vb* praise highly
BELAUDED > BELAUD
BELAUDING > BELAUD
BELAUDS > BELAUD
BELAY *vb* secure a line to a pin or cleat ▷ *n* attachment (of a climber) to a mountain
BELAYED > BELAY
BELAYER > BELAY
BELAYERS > BELAY
BELAYING > BELAY
BELAYS > BELAY
BELCH *vb* expel wind from the stomach noisily through the mouth ▷ *n* act of belching
BELCHED > BELCH
BELCHER > BELCH
BELCHERS > BELCH
BELCHES > BELCH
BELCHING > BELCH
BELDAM *n* old woman, esp an ugly or malicious one
BELDAME *same as* > BELDAM
BELDAMES > BELDAME
BELDAMS > BELDAM
BELEAGUER *vb* trouble persistently
BELEAP *vb* leap over
BELEAPED > BELEAP
BELEAPING > BELEAP
BELEAPS > BELEAP
BELEAPT > BELEAP
BELEE *vb* put on sheltered side
BELEED > BELEE
BELEEING > BELEE
BELEES > BELEE
BELEMNITE *n* type of extinct marine mollusc related to the cuttlefish

BELEMNOID *adj* shaped like a dart
BELFRIED *adj* with a belfry
BELFRIES > BELFRY
BELFRY *n* part of a tower where bells are hung
BELGA *n* former Belgian monetary unit worth five francs
BELGARD *n* kind gaze
BELGARDS > BELGARD
BELGAS > BELGA
BELGICISM *n* word used by Belgians when speaking French or Dutch
BELIE *vb* show to be untrue
BELIED > BELIE
BELIEF *n* faith or confidence
BELIEFS > BELIEF
BELIER > BELIE
BELIERS > BELIE
BELIES > BELIE
BELIEVE *vb* accept as true or real
BELIEVED > BELIEVE
BELIEVER > BELIEVE
BELIEVERS > BELIEVE
BELIEVES > BELIEVE
BELIEVING > BELIEVE
BELIKE *adv* perhaps
BELIQUOR *vb* cause to be drunk
BELIQUORS > BELIQUOR
BELITTLE *vb* treat as having little value or importance
BELITTLED > BELITTLE
BELITTLER > BELITTLE
BELITTLES > BELITTLE
BELIVE *adv* speedily
BELL *n* hollow cup-shaped instrument that emits a ringing sound when struck ▷ *vb* utter (such a sound)
BELLBIND *n* bindweed-type climber
BELLBINDS > BELLBIND
BELLBIRD *n* Australasian bird with bell-like call
BELLBIRDS > BELLBIRD
BELLBOY *n* man or boy employed in a hotel, club, etc, to carry luggage and answer calls for service
BELLBOYS > BELLBOY
BELLBUOY *n* buoy with a bell
BELLBUOYS > BELLBUOY
BELLCAST *adj* relating to a style of roof with a bell shape
BELLCOTE *n* small roofed structure for bell
BELLCOTES > BELLCOTE
BELLE *n* beautiful woman, esp the most attractive woman at a function
BELLED > BELL
BELLEEK *n* kind of thin fragile porcelain with a lustrous glaze

BELLEEKS > BELLEEK
BELLES > BELLE
BELLETER *n* person who makes bells
BELLETERS > BELLETER
BELLHOP *same as* > BELLBOY
BELLHOPS > BELLHOP
BELLIBONE *n* beautiful and good woman
BELLICOSE *adj* warlike and aggressive
BELLIED > BELLY
BELLIES > BELLY
BELLING > BELL
BELLINGS > BELL
BELLINI *n* Prosecco and peach cocktail
BELLINIS > BELLINI
BELLMAN *n* man who rings a bell, esp (formerly) a town crier
BELLMEN > BELLMAN
BELLOCK *vb* shout
BELLOCKED > BELLOCK
BELLOCKS > BELLOCK
BELLOW *vb* make a low deep cry like that of a bull ▷ *n* loud deep roar
BELLOWED > BELLOW
BELLOWER > BELLOW
BELLOWERS > BELLOW
BELLOWING *n* act of bellowing
BELLOWS *pl n* instrument for pumping a stream of air into something
BELLPULL *n* handle, rope, or cord pulled to operate a doorbell or servant's bell
BELLPULLS > BELLPULL
BELLS > BELL
BELLWORT *n* N American plant with slender bell-shaped yellow flowers
BELLWORTS > BELLWORT
BELLY *n* part of the body of a vertebrate which contains the intestines ▷ *vb* (cause to) swell out
BELLYACHE *n* pain in the abdomen ▷ *vb* complain repeatedly
BELLYBAND *n* strap around the belly of a draught animal, holding the shafts of a vehicle
BELLYFUL *n* more than one can tolerate
BELLYFULS > BELLYFUL
BELLYING > BELLY
BELLYINGS > BELLY
BELLYLIKE > BELLY
BELOMANCY *n* art of divination using arrows
BELON *n* type of oyster
BELONG *vb* be the property of
BELONGED > BELONG
BELONGER *n* native-born Caribbean
BELONGERS > BELONGER
BELONGING *n* secure relationship

b

BELONGS > BELONG

BELONS > BELON

BELOVE vb love

BELOVED adj dearly loved ▷ n person dearly loved

BELOVEDS > BELOVED

BELOVES > BELOVE

BELOVING > BELOVE

BELOW adv at or to a position lower than, under ▷ prep at or to a position lower than

BELOWS same as > BELLOWS

BELS > BEL

BELT n band of cloth, leather, etc, worn usu around the waist ▷ vb fasten with a belt

BELTED > BELT

BELTER n outstanding person or event

BELTERS > BELTER

BELTING n material used to make a belt or belts ▷ adj excellent

BELTINGS > BELTING

BELTLESS > BELT

BELTLINE n line separating car's windows from main body

BELTLINES > BELTLINE

BELTMAN n (formerly) a member of a beach life-saving team

BELTMEN > BELTMAN

BELTS > BELT

BELTWAY n people and institutions located in the area bounded by the Washington Beltway

BELTWAYS > BELTWAY

BELUGA n large white sturgeon

BELUGAS > BELUGA

BELVEDERE n building designed and situated to look out on pleasant scenery

BELYING > BELIE

BEMA n speaker's platform in the assembly in ancient Athens

BEMAD vb cause to become mad

BEMADAM vb call a person madam

BEMADAMED > BEMADAM

BEMADAMS > BEMADAM

BEMADDED > BEMAD

BEMADDEN vb cause to become mad

BEMADDENS > BEMADDEN

BEMADDING > BEMAD

BEMADS > BEMAD

BEMAS > BEMA

BEMATA > BEMA

BEMAUL vb maul

BEMAULED > BEMAUL

BEMAULING > BEMAUL

BEMAULS > BEMAUL

BEMAZED adj amazed

BEMBEX n type of wasp

BEMBEXES > BEMBEX

BEMBIX same as > BEMBEX

BEMBIXES > BEMBIX

BEMEAN a less common word for > DEMEAN

BEMEANED > BEMEAN

BEMEANING > BEMEAN

BEMEANS > BEMEAN

BEMEANT > BEMEAN

BEMEDAL vb decorate with medals

BEMEDALED > BEMEDAL

BEMEDALS > BEMEDAL

BEMETE vb measure

BEMETED > BEMETE

BEMETES > BEMETE

BEMETING > BEMETE

BEMINGLE vb mingle

BEMINGLED > BEMINGLE

BEMINGLES > BEMINGLE

BEMIRE vb soil with or as if with mire

BEMIRED > BEMIRE

BEMIRES > BEMIRE

BEMIRING > BEMIRE

BEMIST vb cloud with mist

BEMISTED > BEMIST

BEMISTING > BEMIST

BEMISTS > BEMIST

BEMIX vb mix thoroughly

BEMIXED > BEMIX

BEMIXES > BEMIX

BEMIXING > BEMIX

BEMIXT > BEMIX

BEMOAN vb express sorrow or dissatisfaction about

BEMOANED > BEMOAN

BEMOANER > BEMOAN

BEMOANERS > BEMOAN

BEMOANING > BEMOAN

BEMOANS > BEMOAN

BEMOCK vb mock

BEMOCKED > BEMOCK

BEMOCKING > BEMOCK

BEMOCKS > BEMOCK

BEMOIL vb soil with mud

BEMOILED > BEMOIL

BEMOILING > BEMOIL

BEMOILS > BEMOIL

BEMONSTER vb treat as monster

BEMOUTH vb endow with a mouth

BEMOUTHED > BEMOUTH

BEMOUTHS > BEMOUTH

BEMUD vb cover with mud

BEMUDDED > BEMUD

BEMUDDING > BEMUD

BEMUDDLE vb confound

BEMUDDLED > BEMUDDLE

BEMUDDLES > BEMUDDLE

BEMUDS > BEMUD

BEMUFFLE vb muffle up

BEMUFFLED > BEMUFFLE

BEMUFFLES > BEMUFFLE

BEMURMUR vb murmur at

BEMURMURS > BEMURMUR

BEMUSE vb confuse

BEMUSED adj puzzled or confused

BEMUSEDLY > BEMUSED

BEMUSES > BEMUSE

BEMUSING > BEMUSE

BEMUZZLE vb put muzzle on

BEMUZZLED > BEMUZZLE

BEMUZZLES > BEMUZZLE

BEN n mountain peak ▷ adv in ▷ adj inner

BENADRYL n tradename of an antihistamine drug used in sleeping tablets

BENADRYLS > BENADRYL

BENAME an archaic word for > NAME

BENAMED > BENAME

BENAMES > BENAME

BENAMING > BENAME

BENCH n long seat ▷ vb put a person on a bench

BENCHED > BENCH

BENCHER n member of the governing body of one of the Inns of Court

BENCHERS > BENCHER

BENCHES > BENCH

BENCHIER > BENCHY

BENCHIEST > BENCHY

BENCHING > BENCH

BENCHLAND n level ground at foot of mountains

BENCHLESS > BENCH

BENCHMARK n criterion by which to measure something ▷ vb measure or test against a benchmark

BENCHTOP adj for use at bench ▷ n flat surface area

BENCHTOPS > BENCHTOP

BENCHY adj (of a hillside) hollowed out in benches

BEND vb (cause to) form a curve ▷ n curved part

BENDABLE > BEND

BENDAY vb (printing) reproduce using Benday technique

BENDAYED > BENDAY

BENDAYING > BENDAY

BENDAYS > BENDAY

BENDED > BEND

BENDEE same as > BENDY

BENDEES > BENDEE

BENDER n drinking bout

BENDERS > BENDER

BENDIER > BENDY

BENDIEST > BENDY

BENDING > BEND

BENDINGLY > BEND

BENDINGS > BEND

BENDLET n narrow diagonal stripe on heraldic shield

BENDLETS > BENDLET

BENDS > BEND

BENDWAYS same as > BENDWISE

BENDWISE adv diagonally

BENDY adj flexible or pliable ▷ n okra

BENDYS > BENDY

BENE n blessing

BENEATH prep below ▷ adv below

BENEDICK n recently-married man

BENEDICKS > BENEDICK

BENEDICT n newly married man

BENEDICTS > BENEDICT

BENEDIGHT adj blessed

BENEFACT vb be benefactor to

BENEFACTS > BENEFACT

BENEFIC adj a rare word for beneficent

BENEFICE n church office providing its holder with an income ▷ vb provide with a benefice

BENEFICED > BENEFICE

BENEFICES > BENEFICE

BENEFIT n something that improves or promotes ▷ vb do or receive good

BENEFITED > BENEFIT

BENEFITER > BENEFIT

BENEFITS > BENEFIT

BENEMPT a past participle of > NAME

BENEMPTED > BENEMPT

BENES > BENE

BENET vb trap (something) in a net

BENETS > BENET

BENETTED > BENET

BENETTING > BENET

BENGA n type of Kenyan popular music featuring guitars

BENGALINE n heavy corded fabric, esp silk with woollen or cotton cord

BENGAS > BENGA

BENI n sesame plant

BENIGHT vb shroud in darkness

BENIGHTED adj ignorant or uncultured

BENIGHTEN same as > BENIGHT

BENIGHTER > BENIGHT

BENIGHTS > BENIGHT

BENIGN adj showing kindliness

BENIGNANT adj kind or gracious

BENIGNER > BENIGN

BENIGNEST > BENIGN

BENIGNITY n kindliness

BENIGNLY > BENIGN

BENIS > BENI

BENISEED n sesame

BENISEEDS > BENISEED

BENISON n blessing, esp a spoken one

BENISONS > BENISON

BENITIER n basin for holy water

BENITIERS > BENITIER

BENJ another word for > BHANG

BENJAMIN same as > BENZOIN

BENJAMINS > BENJAMIN

BENJES > BENJ

BENNE *another name for* > SESAME

BENNES > BENNE

BENNET *n* Eurasian and N African plant with yellow flowers

BENNETS > BENNET

BENNI *n* sesame

BENNIES > BENNY

BENNIS > BENNI

BENNY *n* amphetamine tablet, esp benzedrine: a stimulant

BENOMYL *n* fungicide

BENOMYLS > BENOMYL

BENS > BEN

BENT *adj* not straight ▷ *n* personal inclination, propensity, or aptitude

BENTGRASS *n* variety of grass

BENTHAL > BENTHOS

BENTHIC > BENTHOS

BENTHOAL > BENTHON

BENTHON *same as* > BENTHOS

BENTHONIC > BENTHOS

BENTHONS > BENTHON

BENTHOS *n* animals and plants living at the bottom of a sea or lake

BENTHOSES > BENTHOS

BENTIER > BENTY

BENTIEST > BENTY

BENTO *n* thin lightweight box used in Japanese cuisine

BENTONITE *n* valuable clay, formed by the decomposition of volcanic ash, that swells as it absorbs water: used as a filler in the building, paper, and pharmaceutical industries

BENTOS > BENTO

BENTS > BENT

BENTWOOD *n* wood bent in moulds, used mainly for furniture ▷ *adj* made from such wood

BENTWOODS > BENTWOOD

BENTY *adj* covered with bentgrass

BENUMB *vb* make numb or powerless

BENUMBED > BENUMB

BENUMBING > BENUMB

BENUMBS > BENUMB

BENZAL *n* transparent crystalline substance

BENZALS > BENZAL

BENZENE *n* flammable poisonous liquid used as a solvent, insecticide, etc

BENZENES > BENZENE

BENZENOID *adj* similar to benzene

BENZIDIN *same as* > BENZIDINE

BENZIDINE *n* grey or reddish poisonous crystalline powder

BENZIDINS > BENZIDINE

BENZIL *n* yellow compound radical

BENZILS > BENZIL

BENZIN *same as* > BENZINE

BENZINE *n* volatile liquid used as a solvent

BENZINES > BENZINE

BENZINS > BENZIN

BENZOATE *n* any salt or ester of benzoic acid, containing the group C_6H_5COO- or the ion $C_6H_5COO^-$

BENZOATES > BENZOATE

BENZOIC *adj* of, containing, or derived from benzoic acid or benzoin

BENZOIN *n* gum resin used in ointments, perfume, etc

BENZOINS > BENZOIN

BENZOL *n* crude form of benzene

BENZOLE *same as* > BENZOL

BENZOLES > BENZOLE

BENZOLINE *n* unpurified benzene

BENZOLS > BENZOL

BENZOYL *n* of, consisting of, or containing the monovalent group C_6H_5CO-

BENZOYLS > BENZOYL

BENZYL *n* of, consisting of, or containing the monovalent group $C_6H_5CH_2-$

BENZYLIC > BENZYL

BENZYLS > BENZYL

BEPAINT *vb* dye; paint

BEPAINTED > BEPAINT

BEPAINTS > BEPAINT

BEPAT *vb* pat

BEPATCHED *adj* mended with or covered in patches

BEPATS > BEPAT

BEPATTED > BEPAT

BEPATTING > BEPAT

BEPEARL *vb* decorate with pearls

BEPEARLED > BEPEARL

BEPEARLS > BEPEARL

BEPELT *vb* pelt energetically

BEPELTED > BEPELT

BEPELTING > BEPELT

BEPELTS > BEPELT

BEPEPPER *vb* shower with small missiles

BEPEPPERS > BEPEPPER

BEPESTER *vb* pester persistently

BEPESTERS > BEPESTER

BEPIMPLE *vb* form pimples on

BEPIMPLED > BEPIMPLE

BEPIMPLES > BEPIMPLE

BEPITIED > BEPITY

BEPITIES > BEPITY

BEPITY *vb* feel great pity for

BEPITYING > BEPITY

BEPLASTER *vb* cover in thick plaster

BEPLUMED *adj* decorated with feathers

BEPOMMEL *vb* beat vigorously

BEPOMMELS > BEPOMMEL

BEPOWDER *vb* cover with powder

BEPOWDERS > BEPOWDER

BEPRAISE *vb* praise highly

BEPRAISED > BEPRAISE

BEPRAISES > BEPRAISE

BEPROSE *vb* (of poetry) reduce to prose

BEPROSED > BEPROSE

BEPROSES > BEPROSE

BEPROSING > BEPROSE

BEPUFF *vb* puff up

BEPUFFED > BEPUFF

BEPUFFING > BEPUFF

BEPUFFS > BEPUFF

BEQUEATH *vb* dispose of (property) as in a will

BEQUEATHS > BEQUEATH

BEQUEST *n* legal gift of money or property by someone who has died

BEQUESTS > BEQUEST

BERAKE *vb* rake thoroughly

BERAKED > BERAKE

BERAKES > BERAKE

BERAKING > BERAKE

BERASCAL *vb* accuse of being rascal

BERASCALS > BERASCAL

BERATE *vb* scold harshly

BERATED > BERATE

BERATES > BERATE

BERATING > BERATE

BERAY *vb* soil; defile

BERAYED > BERAY

BERAYING > BERAY

BERAYS > BERAY

BERBER *same as* > BERBERE

BERBERE *n* hot-tasting Ethiopian paste

BERBERES > BERBERE

BERBERIN *same as* > BERBERINE

BERBERINE *n* yellow bitter-tasting alkaloid obtained from barberry

BERBERINS > BERBERIN

BERBERIS *n* shrub with red berries

BERBERS > BERBER

BERBICE *n* as in *berbice chair* large armchair with long arms that can be folded inwards to act as leg rests

BERCEAU *n* arched trellis for climbing plants

BERCEAUX > BERCEAU

BERCEUSE *n* lullaby

BERCEUSES > BERCEUSE

BERDACHE *n* Native American transvestite

BERDACHES > BERDACHE

BERDASH *same as* > BERDACHE

BERDASHES > BERDASH

BERE *n* barley

BEREAVE *vb* deprive (of) something or someone valued, esp through death

BEREAVED *adj* having recently lost a close friend or relative through death

BEREAVEN > BEREAVE

BEREAVER > BEREAVE

BEREAVERS > BEREAVE

BEREAVES > BEREAVE

BEREAVING > BEREAVE

BEREFT *adj* deprived

BERES > BERE

BERET *n* round flat close-fitting brimless cap

BERETS > BERET

BERETTA *n* type of pistol

BERETTAS > BERETTA

BERG *n* iceberg

BERGALI *n* fish of the wrasse family

BERGALIS > BERGALI

BERGAMA *n* type of Turkish rug

BERGAMAS > BERGAMA

BERGAMASK *n* person from Bergamo

BERGAMOT *n* small Asian tree, the fruit of which yields an oil used in perfumery

BERGAMOTS > BERGAMOT

BERGANDER *n* species of duck

BERGEN *n* large rucksack with a capacity of over 50 litres

BERGENIA *n* evergreen ground-covering plant

BERGENIAS > BERGENIA

BERGENS > BERGEN

BERGERE *n* type of French armchair

BERGERES > BERGERE

BERGFALL *n* avalanche

BERGFALLS > BERGFALL

BERGHAAN *same as* > BERGMEHL

BERGHAANS > BERGHAAN

BERGMEHL *n* light powdery variety of calcite

BERGMEHLS > BERGMEHL

BERGOMASK *same as* > BERGAMASK

BERGS > BERG

BERGYLT *n* large northern marine food fish

BERGYLTS > BERGYLT

BERHYME *vb* mention in poetry

BERHYMED > BERHYME

BERHYMES > BERHYME

BERHYMING > BERHYME

BERIBERI *n* disease, endemic in E and S Asia, caused by dietary deficiency of thiamine (vitamin B_1). It affects the

b

nerves to the limbs, producing pain, paralysis, and swelling

BERIBERIS > BERIBERI

BERIMBAU n Brazilian single-stringed bowed instrument, used to accompany capoeira

BERIMBAUS > BERIMBAU

BERIME same as **>** BERHYME

BERIMED > BERIME

BERIMES > BERIME

BERIMING > BERIME

BERINGED adj wearing a ring or rings

BERK n stupid person

BERKELIUM n radioactive element

BERKO adj berserk

BERKS > BERK

BERLEY n bait scattered on water to attract fish ▷ vb scatter (bait) on water

BERLEYED > BERLEY

BERLEYING > BERLEY

BERLEYS > BERLEY

BERLIN n fine wool yarn used for tapestry work, etc

BERLINE same as **>** BERLIN

BERLINES > BERLINE

BERLINS > BERLIN

BERM n narrow grass strip between the road and the footpath in a residential area ▷ vb create a berm

BERME same as **>** BERM

BERMED > BERM

BERMES > BERME

BERMING > BERM

BERMS > BERM

BERMUDAS pl n close-fitting shorts that come down to the knees

BERNICLE n barnacle goose: a N European goose that has a black-and-white head and body and grey wings

BERNICLES > BERNICLE

BEROB vb rob

BEROBBED > BEROB

BEROBBING > BEROB

BEROBED adj wearing a robe

BEROBS > BEROB

BEROUGED adj wearing rouge

BERRET same as **>** BERET

BERRETS > BERRET

BERRETTA same as **>** BIRETTA

BERRETTAS > BERRETTA

BERRIED > BERRY

BERRIES > BERRY

BERRIGAN n Australian tree with hanging branches

BERRIGANS > BERRIGAN

BERRY n small soft stoneless fruit ▷ vb bear or produce berries

BERRYING > BERRY

BERRYINGS > BERRY

BERRYLESS > BERRY

BERRYLIKE > BERRY

BERSEEM n Mediterranean clover grown as a forage crop and to improve the soil

BERSEEMS > BERSEEM

BERSERK adj frenziedly violent or destructive ▷ n fearsome Norse warrior

BERSERKER same as **>** BERSERK

BERSERKLY > BERSERK

BERSERKS > BERSERK

BERTH n bunk in a ship or train ▷ vb dock (a ship)

BERTHA n wide deep capelike collar, often of lace, usually to cover up a low neckline

BERTHAGE n place for mooring boats

BERTHAGES > BERTHAGE

BERTHAS > BERTHA

BERTHE n type of lace collar

BERTHED > BERTH

BERTHES > BERTHE

BERTHING n act of berthing

BERTHINGS > BERTHING

BERTHS > BERTH

BERYL n hard transparent mineral

BERYLINE > BERYL

BERYLLIA n beryllium oxide

BERYLLIAS > BERYLLIA

BERYLLIUM n toxic silvery-white metallic element

BERYLS > BERYL

BES variant of **>** BETH

BESAINT vb give saint status to

BESAINTED > BESAINT

BESAINTS > BESAINT

BESANG > BESING

BESAT > BESIT

BESAW > BESEE

BESCATTER vb strew

BESCORCH vb scorch badly

BESCOUR vb scour thoroughly

BESCOURED > BESCOUR

BESCOURS > BESCOUR

BESCRAWL vb cover with scrawls

BESCRAWLS > BESCRAWL

BESCREEN vb conceal with screen

BESCREENS > BESCREEN

BESEE vb provide for; mind

BESEECH vb ask earnestly

BESEECHED > BESEECH

BESEECHER > BESEECH

BESEECHES > BESEECH

BESEEING > BESEE

BESEEKE same as **>** BESEECH

BESEEKES > BESEEKE

BESEEKING > BESEEKE

BESEEM vb be suitable for

BESEEMED > BESEEM

BESEEMING > BESEEM

BESEEMLY adj becoming; suitable

BESEEMS > BESEEM

BESEEN > BESEE

BESEES > BESEE

BESES > BES

BESET vb trouble or harass constantly

BESETMENT > BESET

BESETS > BESET

BESETTER > BESET

BESETTERS > BESET

BESETTING adj tempting, harassing, or assailing

BESHADOW vb darken with shadow

BESHADOWS > BESHADOW

BESHAME vb cause to feel shame

BESHAMED > BESHAME

BESHAMES > BESHAME

BESHAMING > BESHAME

BESHINE vb illuminate

BESHINES > BESHINE

BESHINING > BESHINE

BESHIVER vb shatter

BESHIVERS > BESHIVER

BESHONE > BESHINE

BESHOUT vb shout about

BESHOUTED > BESHOUT

BESHOUTS > BESHOUT

BESHREW vb wish evil on

BESHREWED > BESHREW

BESHREWS > BESHREW

BESHROUD vb cover with a shroud

BESHROUDS > BESHROUD

BESIDE prep at, by, or to the side of

BESIDES prep in addition ▷ adv in addition

BESIEGE vb surround with military forces

BESIEGED > BESIEGE

BESIEGER > BESIEGE

BESIEGERS > BESIEGE

BESIEGES > BESIEGE

BESIEGING > BESIEGE

BESIGH vb sigh for

BESIGHED > BESIGH

BESIGHING > BESIGH

BESIGHS > BESIGH

BESING vb sing about joyfully

BESINGING > BESING

BESINGS > BESING

BESIT vb suit; fit

BESITS > BESIT

BESITTING > BESIT

BESLAVE vb treat as slave

BESLAVED > BESLAVE

BESLAVER vb fawn over

BESLAVERS > BESLAVER

BESLAVES > BESLAVE

BESLAVING > BESLAVE

BESLIME vb cover with slime

BESLIMED > BESLIME

BESLIMES > BESLIME

BESLIMING > BESLIME

BESLOBBER vb slobber over

BESLUBBER same as **>** BESLOBBER

BESMEAR vb smear over

BESMEARED > BESMEAR

BESMEARER > BESMEAR

BESMEARS > BESMEAR

BESMILE vb smile on

BESMILED > BESMILE

BESMILES > BESMILE

BESMILING > BESMILE

BESMIRCH vb tarnish (someone's name or reputation)

BESMOKE vb blacken with smoke

BESMOKED > BESMOKE

BESMOKES > BESMOKE

BESMOKING > BESMOKE

BESMOOTH vb smooth

BESMOOTHS > BESMOOTH

BESMUDGE vb blacken

BESMUDGED > BESMUDGE

BESMUDGES > BESMUDGE

BESMUT vb blacken with smut

BESMUTCH same as **>** BESMIRCH

BESMUTS > BESMUT

BESMUTTED > BESMUT

BESNOW vb cover with snow

BESNOWED > BESNOW

BESNOWING > BESNOW

BESNOWS > BESNOW

BESOGNIO n worthless person

BESOGNIOS > BESOGNIO

BESOIN n need

BESOINS > BESOIN

BESOM n broom made of twigs ▷ vb sweep with a besom

BESOMED > BESOM

BESOMING > BESOM

BESOMS > BESOM

BESONIAN same as **>** BEZONIAN

BESONIANS > BESONIAN

BESOOTHE vb soothe

BESOOTHED > BESOOTHE

BESOOTHES > BESOOTHE

BESORT vb fit

BESORTED > BESORT

BESORTING > BESORT

BESORTS > BESORT

BESOT vb make stupid or muddled

BESOTS > BESOT

BESOTTED adj infatuated

BESOTTING > BESOT

BESOUGHT a past participle of **>** BESEECH

BESOULED adj having a soul

BESPAKE > BESPOKE

BESPANGLE vb cover or adorn with or as if with spangles

BESPAT > BESPIT

BESPATE > BESPIT

BESPATTER vb splash, eg with dirty water

BESPEAK vb indicate or suggest

BESPEAKS > BESPEAK

BESPECKLE vb mark with speckles

BESPED > BESPEED

BESPEED vb get on with (doing something)

BESPEEDS > BESPEED

BESPICE vb flavour with spices

BESPICED > BESPICE

BESPICES > BESPICE

BESPICING > BESPICE

BESPIT vb cover with spittle

BESPITS > BESPIT

BESPOKE adj (esp of a suit) made to the customer's specifications

BESPOKEN > BESPEAK

BESPORT vb amuse oneself

BESPORTED > BESPORT

BESPORTS > BESPORT

BESPOT vb mark with spots

BESPOTS > BESPOT

BESPOTTED > BESPOT

BESPOUSE vb marry

BESPOUSED > BESPOUSE

BESPOUSES > BESPOUSE

BESPOUT vb speak pretentiously

BESPOUTED > BESPOUT

BESPOUTS > BESPOUT

BESPREAD vb cover (a surface) with something

**BESPREADS
> BESPREAD**

BESPRENT adj sprinkled over

BEST adj most excellent of a particular group etc
▷ adv in a manner surpassing all others
▷ n utmost effort
▷ vb defeat

BESTAD same as
> BESTEAD

BESTADDE same as
> BESTEAD

BESTAIN vb stain

BESTAINED > BESTAIN

BESTAINS > BESTAIN

BESTAR vb decorate with stars

BESTARRED > BESTAR

BESTARS > BESTAR

BESTEAD vb serve; assist

BESTEADED > BESTEAD

BESTEADS > BESTEAD

BESTED > BEST

BESTI Indian English word for **> SHAME**

BESTIAL adj brutal or savage

BESTIALLY > BESTIAL

BESTIALS > BESTIAL

BESTIARY n medieval collection of descriptions of animals

BESTICK vb cover with sharp points

BESTICKS > BESTICK

BESTIE n best friend

BESTIES > BESTIE

BESTILL vb cause to be still

BESTILLED > BESTILL

BESTILLS > BESTILL

BESTING > BEST

BESTIR vb cause (oneself) to become active

BESTIRRED > BESTIR

BESTIRS > BESTIR

BESTIS > BESTI

BESTORM vb assault

BESTORMED > BESTORM

BESTORMS > BESTORM

BESTOW vb present (a gift) or confer (an honour)

BESTOWAL > BESTOW

BESTOWALS > BESTOW

BESTOWED > BESTOW

BESTOWER > BESTOW

BESTOWERS > BESTOW

BESTOWING > BESTOW

BESTOWS > BESTOW

BESTREAK vb streak

BESTREAKS > BESTREAK

BESTREW vb scatter or lie scattered over (a surface)

BESTREWED > BESTREW

BESTREWN > BESTREW

BESTREWS > BESTREW

BESTRID > BESTRIDE

BESTRIDE vb have or put a leg on either side of

**BESTRIDES
> BESTRIDE**

BESTRODE > BESTRIDE

BESTROW same as
> BESTREW

BESTROWED > BESTROW

BESTROWN > BESTROW

BESTROWS > BESTROW

BESTS > BEST

BESTUCK > BESTICK

BESTUD vb set with, or as with studs

BESTUDDED > BESTUD

BESTUDS > BESTUD

BESUITED adj wearing a suit

BESUNG > BESING

BESWARM vb swarm over

BESWARMED > BESWARM

BESWARMS > BESWARM

BET n wager between two parties predicting different outcomes of an event ▷ vb make or place a bet with (a person or persons)

BETA n second letter in the Greek alphabet, a consonant, transliterated as b

BETACISM vb type of speech impediment

BETACISMS > BETACISM

BETAINE n sweet-tasting alkaloid that occurs in the sugar beet

BETAINES > BETAINE

BETAKE vb as in betake oneself go

BETAKEN > BETAKE

BETAKES > BETAKE

BETAKING > BETAKE

BETAS > BETA

BETATOPIC adj (of atoms) differing in proton number by one, theoretically as a result of emission of a beta particle

BETATRON n type of particle accelerator for producing high-energy beams of electrons

BETATRONS > BETATRON

BETATTER vb make ragged

BETATTERS > BETATTER

BETAXED adj burdened with taxes

BETCHA interj bet you

BETE same as **>** BEET

BETED > BETE

BETEEM vb accord

BETEEME same as
> BETEEM

BETEEMED > BETEEM

BETEEMES > BETEEME

BETEEMING > BETEEM

BETEEMS > BETEEM

BETEL n Asian climbing plant, the leaves and nuts of which can be chewed

BETELNUT n seed of the betel palm, chewed with betel leaves and lime by people in S and SE Asia as a digestive stimulant and narcotic

BETELNUTS > BETELNUT

BETELS > BETEL

BETES > BETE

BETH n second letter of the Hebrew alphabet transliterated as b

BETHANK vb thank

BETHANKED > BETHANK

BETHANKIT n grace spoken before meal

BETHANKS > BETHANK

BETHEL n seaman's chapel

BETHELS > BETHEL

BETHESDA n church building of certain Christian denominations

BETHESDAS > BETHESDA

BETHINK vb cause (oneself) to consider or meditate

BETHINKS > BETHINK

BETHORN vb cover with thorns

BETHORNED > BETHORN

BETHORNS > BETHORN

BETHOUGHT > BETHINK

BETHRALL vb make slave of

BETHRALLS > BETHRALL

BETHS > BETH

BETHUMB vb (of books) wear by handling

BETHUMBED > BETHUMB

BETHUMBS > BETHUMB

BETHUMP vb thump hard

BETHUMPED > BETHUMP

BETHUMPS > BETHUMP

BETHWACK vb strike hard with flat object

**BETHWACKS
> BETHWACK**

BETID > BETIDE

BETIDE vb happen (to)

BETIDED > BETIDE

BETIDES > BETIDE

BETIDING > BETIDE

BETIGHT > BETIDE

BETIME vb befall

BETIMED > BETIME

BETIMES > BETIME

BETIMING > BETIME

BETING > BETE

BETISE n folly or lack of perception

BETISES > BETISE

BETITLE vb give title to

BETITLED > BETITLE

BETITLES > BETITLE

BETITLING > BETITLE

BETOIL vb tire through hard work

BETOILED > BETOIL

BETOILING > BETOIL

BETOILS > BETOIL

BETOKEN vb indicate or signify

BETOKENED > BETOKEN

BETOKENS > BETOKEN

BETON n concrete

BETONIES > BETONY

BETONS > BETON

BETONY n North American plant

BETOOK the past tense of
> BETAKE

BETOSS vb toss about

BETOSSED > BETOSS

BETOSSES > BETOSS

BETOSSING > BETOSS

BETRAY vb hand over or expose (one's nation, friend, etc) treacherously to an enemy

BETRAYAL > BETRAY

BETRAYALS > BETRAY

BETRAYED > BETRAY

BETRAYER > BETRAY

BETRAYERS > BETRAY

BETRAYING > BETRAY

BETRAYS > BETRAY

BETREAD vb tread over

BETREADS > BETREAD

BETRIM vb decorate

BETRIMMED > BETRIM

BETRIMS > BETRIM

BETROD > BETREAD

BETRODDEN > BETREAD

BETROTH vb promise to marry or to give in marriage

BETROTHAL n engagement to be married

b

BETROTHED adj engaged to be married ▷ n person to whom one is engaged
BETROTHS > BETROTH
BETS > BET
BETTA n fighting fish
BETTAS > BETTA
BETTED > BET
BETTER adj more excellent than others ▷ adv in a more excellent manner ▷ pl n one's superiors ▷ vb improve upon
BETTERED > BETTER
BETTERING > BETTER
BETTERS > BETTER
BETTIES > BETTY
BETTING > BET
BETTINGS > BET
BETTONG n short-nosed rat kangaroo
BETTONGS > BETTONG
BETTOR n person who bets
BETTORS > BETTOR
BETTY n type of short crowbar
BETUMBLED adj thrown into disorder
BETWEEN adv indicating position in the middle, alternatives, etc ▷ prep at a point intermediate to two other points in space, time, etc
BETWEENS > BETWEEN
BETWIXT adv between
BEUNCLED adj having many uncles
BEURRE n butter
BEURRES > BEURRE
BEVATRON n proton synchrotron at the University of California
BEVATRONS > BEVATRON
BEVEL n slanting edge ▷ vb slope
BEVELED > BEVEL
BEVELER > BEVEL
BEVELERS > BEVEL
BEVELING > BEVEL
BEVELLED > BEVEL
BEVELLER > BEVEL
BEVELLERS > BEVEL
BEVELLING > BEVEL
BEVELMENT > BEVEL
BEVELS > BEVEL
BEVER n snack ▷ vb have a snack
BEVERAGE n drink
BEVERAGES > BEVERAGE
BEVERED > BEVER
BEVERING > BEVER
BEVERS > BEVER
BEVIES > BEVY
BEVOMIT vb vomit over
BEVOMITED > BEVOMIT
BEVOMITS > BEVOMIT
BEVOR n armour protecting lower part of face
BEVORS > BEVOR
BEVUE n careless error

BEVUES > BEVUE
BEVVIED > BEVVY
BEVVIES > BEVVY
BEVVY n alcoholic drink ▷ vb drink alcohol
BEVVYING > BEVVY
BEVY n flock or group
BEWAIL vb express great sorrow over
BEWAILED > BEWAIL
BEWAILER > BEWAIL
BEWAILERS > BEWAIL
BEWAILING > BEWAIL
BEWAILS > BEWAIL
BEWARE vb be on one's guard (against)
BEWARED > BEWARE
BEWARES > BEWARE
BEWARING > BEWARE
BEWEARIED > BEWEARY
BEWEARIES > BEWEARY
BEWEARY vb cause to be weary
BEWEEP vb express grief through weeping
BEWEEPING > BEWEEP
BEWEEPS > BEWEEP
BEWENT > BEGO
BEWEPT > BEWEEP
BEWET vb make wet
BEWETS > BEWET
BEWETTED > BEWET
BEWETTING > BEWET
BEWHORE vb treat as a whore
BEWHORED > BEWHORE
BEWHORES > BEWHORE
BEWHORING > BEWHORE
BEWIG vb adorn with a wig
BEWIGGED > BEWIG
BEWIGGING > BEWIG
BEWIGS > BEWIG
BEWILDER vb confuse utterly
BEWILDERS > BEWILDER
BEWINGED adj having wings
BEWITCH vb attract and fascinate
BEWITCHED > BEWITCH
BEWITCHER > BEWITCH
BEWITCHES > BEWITCH
BEWORM vb fill with worms
BEWORMED > BEWORM
BEWORMING > BEWORM
BEWORMS > BEWORM
BEWORRIED > BEWORRY
BEWORRIES > BEWORRY
BEWORRY vb beset with worry
BEWRAP vb wrap up
BEWRAPPED > BEWRAP
BEWRAPS > BEWRAP
BEWRAPT > BEWRAP
BEWRAY an obsolete word for > BETRAY
BEWRAYED > BEWRAY
BEWRAYER > BEWRAY
BEWRAYERS > BEWRAY
BEWRAYING > BEWRAY
BEWRAYS > BEWRAY
BEY n (in the Ottoman empire) a title given to

senior officers, provincial governors, and certain other officials
BEYLIC n province ruled over by a bey
BEYLICS > BEYLIC
BEYLIK same as > BEYLIC
BEYLIKS > BEYLIK
BEYOND prep at or to a point on the other side of ▷ adv at or to the far side of something ▷ n unknown, esp life after death
BEYONDS > BEYOND
BEYS > BEY
BEZ n part of deer's horn
BEZANT n medieval Byzantine gold coin
BEZANTS > BEZANT
BEZAZZ another word for > PIZZAZZ
BEZAZZES > BEZAZZ
BEZEL n sloping edge of a cutting tool
BEZELS > BEZEL
BEZES > BEZ
BEZIL archaic word for > ALCOHOLIC
BEZILS > BEZIL
BEZIQUE n card game for two or more players
BEZIQUES > BEZIQUE
BEZOAR n hard mass, such as a stone or hairball, in the stomach and intestines of animals
BEZOARDIC adj relating to bezoar
BEZOARS > BEZOAR
BEZONIAN n knave or rascal
BEZONIANS > BEZONIAN
BEZZANT same as > BEZANT
BEZZANTS > BEZZANT
BEZZAZZ same as > BEZAZZ
BEZZAZZES > BEZZAZZ
BEZZIE n best friend
BEZZIES > BEZZIE
BEZZLE vb drink to excess
BEZZLED > BEZZLE
BEZZLES > BEZZLE
BEZZLING > BEZZLE
BEZZY same as > BEZZIE
BHAGEE same as > BHAJI
BHAGEES > BHAGEE
BHAI n Indian form of address for a man
BHAIS > BHAI
BHAJAN n singing of devotional songs and hymns
BHAJANS > BHAJAN
BHAJEE same as > BHAJI
BHAJEES > BHAJEE
BHAJI n Indian deep-fried savoury of chopped vegetables in spiced batter
BHAJIA > BHAJI
BHAJIS > BHAJI
BHAKTA n Hindu term for devotee of God

BHAKTAS > BHAKTA
BHAKTI n loving devotion to God leading to nirvana
BHAKTIS > BHAKTI
BHANG n preparation of Indian hemp used as a narcotic and intoxicant
BHANGRA n Punjabi folk music combined with elements of Western pop music
BHANGRAS > BHANGRA
BHANGS > BHANG
BHARAL n wild Himalayan sheep
BHARALS > BHARAL
BHAT n currency of Thailand
BHAVAN n (in India) a large house or building
BHAVANS > BHAVAN
BHAWAN same as > BHAVAN
BHAWANS > BHAWAN
BHEESTIE same as > BHEESTY
BHEESTIES > BHEESTY
BHEESTY same as > BHISTHI
BHEL same as > BAEL
BHELPURI n Indian dish of puffed rice and vegetables
BHELPURIS > BHELPURI
BHELS > BHEL
BHIKHU n fully ordained Buddhist monk
BHIKHUS > BHIKHU
BHIKKHUNI n fully ordained Buddhist nun
BHINDI same as > BINDHI
BHINDIS > BHINDI
BHISHTI n (formerly in India) a water-carrier
BHISHTIS > BHISHTI
BHISTEE same as > BHISHTI
BHISTEES > BHISTEE
BHISTI same as > BHISHTI
BHISTIE same as > BHISHTI
BHISTIES > BHISTIE
BHISTIS > BHISTI
BHOONA same as > BHUNA
BHOONAS > BHOONA
BHOOT same as > BHUT
BHOOTS > BHOOT
BHUNA n Indian sauce
BHUNAS > BHUNA
BHUT n Hindu term for type of ghost
BHUTS > BHUT
BI short for > BISEXUAL
BIACETYL adj liquid with strong odour
BIACETYLS > BIACETYL
BIACH n slang term for a subordinate or inferior person
BIACHES > BIACH
BIALI same as > BIALY
BIALIES > BIALY
BIALIS > BIALI

BIALY n type of bagel

BIALYS > BIALY

BIANNUAL adj occurring twice a year ▷ n something that happens biannually

BIANNUALS > BIANNUAL

BIAS n mental tendency, esp prejudice ▷ vb cause to have a bias ▷ adj slanting obliquely ▷ adv obliquely

BIASED > BIAS

BIASEDLY > BIAS

BIASES > BIAS

BIASING > BIAS

BIASINGS > BIAS

BIASNESS > BIAS

BIASSED > BIAS

BIASSEDLY > BIAS

BIASSES > BIAS

BIASSING > BIAS

BIATCH same as > BIACH

BIATCHES > BIATCH

BIATHLETE n athlete taking part in biathlon

BIATHLON n contest in which skiers with rifles shoot at four targets along a 20-kilometre (12.5-mile) cross-country course

BIATHLONS > BIATHLON

BIAXAL same as > BIAXIAL

BIAXIAL adj (esp of a crystal) having two axes

BIAXIALLY > BIAXIAL

BIB vb drink

BIBACIOUS adj tending to drink to excess

BIBASIC adj with two bases

BIBATION n drinking to excess

BIBATIONS > BIBATION

BIBB n wooden support on a mast for the trestletrees

BIBBED > BIB

BIBBER n drinker

BIBBERIES > BIBBERY

BIBBERS > BIBBER

BIBBERY n drinking to excess

BIBBING n act of bibbing

BIBBINGS > BIBBING

BIBBLE n pebble

BIBBLES > BIBBLE

BIBBS > BIBB

BIBCOCK n tap with a nozzle bent downwards

BIBCOCKS > BIBCOCK

BIBE n (in Newfoundland folklore) spirit whose wailing warns of a coming death

BIBELOT n attractive or curious trinket

BIBELOTS > BIBELOT

BIBES > BIBE

BIBFUL n as in spill a bibful to divulge secrets

BIBFULS > BIBFUL

BIBLE n any book containing the sacred writings of a religion

BIBLES > BIBLE

BIBLESS > BIB

BIBLICAL adj of, occurring in, or referring to the Bible

BIBLICISM n bible-learning

BIBLICIST > BIBLICISM

BIBLIKE > BIB

BIBLIOTIC n study of books

BIBLIST same as > BIBLICIST

BIBLISTS > BIBLIST

BIBS > BIB

BIBULOUS adj addicted to alcohol

BICAMERAL adj (of a legislature) consisting of two chambers

BICARB n bicarbonate of soda

BICARBS > BICARB

BICAUDAL adj having two tails

BICCIES > BICCY

BICCY n biscuit

BICE n medium blue colour

BICENTRIC adj having two centres

BICEP same as > BICEPS

BICEPS n muscle with two origins, esp the muscle that flexes the forearm

BICEPSES > BICEPS

BICES > BICE

BICHIR n African freshwater fish with an elongated body

BICHIRS > BICHIR

BICHORD adj having two strings for each note

BICHROME adj having two colours

BICIPITAL adj having two heads

BICKER vb argue over petty matters ▷ n petty squabble

BICKERED > BICKER

BICKERER > BICKER

BICKERERS > BICKER

BICKERING > BICKER

BICKERS > BICKER

BICKIE short for > BISCUIT

BICKIES > BICKIE

BICOASTAL adj relating to both the east and west coasts of the US

BICOLOR same as > BICOLOUR

BICOLORED same as > BICOLOUR

BICOLORS > BICOLOR

BICOLOUR adj two-coloured

BICOLOURS > BICOLOUR

BICONCAVE adj (of a lens) having concave faces on both sides

BICONVEX adj (of a lens) having convex faces on both sides

BICORN adj having two horns or hornlike parts

BICORNATE same as > BICORN

BICORNE same as > BICORN

BICORNES > BICORNE

BICORNS > BICORN

BICRON n billionth part of a metre

BICRONS > BICRON

BICUSPID adj having two points ▷ n bicuspid tooth

BICUSPIDS > BICUSPID

BICYCLE n vehicle with two wheels, one behind the other, pedalled by the rider ▷ vb ride a bicycle

BICYCLED > BICYCLE

BICYCLER > BICYCLE

BICYCLERS > BICYCLE

BICYCLES > BICYCLE

BICYCLIC adj of, forming, or formed by two circles, cycles, etc

BICYCLING > BICYCLE

BICYCLIST > BICYCLE

BID vb offer (an amount) in attempting to buy something ▷ n offer of a specified amount, as at an auction

BIDARKA same as > BAIDARKA

BIDARKAS > BIDARKA

BIDARKEE same as > BIDARKA

BIDARKEES > BIDARKEE

BIDDABLE adj obedient

BIDDABLY > BIDDABLE

BIDDEN > BID

BIDDER > BID

BIDDERS > BID

BIDDIES > BIDDY

BIDDING > BID

BIDDINGS > BID

BIDDY n woman, esp an old gossipy one

BIDE vb stay or continue

BIDED > BIDE

BIDENT n instrument with two prongs

BIDENTAL n sacred place where lightning has struck

BIDENTALS > BIDENTAL

BIDENTATE > BIDENT

BIDENTS > BIDENT

BIDER > BIDE

BIDERS > BIDE

BIDES > BIDE

BIDET n low basin for washing the genital area

BIDETS > BIDET

BIDI same as > BEEDI

BIDING > BIDE

BIDINGS > BIDE

BIDIS > BIDI

BIDON n oil drum

BIDONS > BIDON

BIDS > BID

BIELD n shelter ▷ vb shelter or take shelter

BIELDED > BIELD

BIELDIER > BIELDY

BIELDIEST > BIELDY

BIELDING > BIELD

BIELDS > BIELD

BIELDY adj sheltered

BIEN adv well

BIENNALE n event occurring every two years

BIENNALES > BIENNALE

BIENNIA > BIENNIUM

BIENNIAL adj occurring every two years ▷ n plant that completes its life cycle in two years

BIENNIALS > BIENNIAL

BIENNIUM n period of two years

BIENNIUMS > BIENNIUM

BIER n stand on which a corpse or coffin rests before burial

BIERS > BIER

BIESTINGS same as > BEESTINGS

BIFACE n prehistoric stone tool

BIFACES > BIFACE

BIFACIAL adj having two faces or surfaces

BIFARIOUS adj having parts arranged in two rows on either side of a central axis

BIFF n blow with the fist ▷ vb give (someone) such a blow

BIFFED > BIFF

BIFFER n someone, such as a sportsperson, who has a reputation for hitting hard

BIFFERS > BIFFER

BIFFIES > BIFFY

BIFFIN n variety of red cooking apple

BIFFING > BIFF

BIFFINS > BIFFIN

BIFFO n fighting or aggressive behaviour ▷ adj aggressive

BIFFOS > BIFFO

BIFFS > BIFF

BIFFY n outdoor toilet

BIFID adj divided into two by a cleft in the middle

BIFIDA > BIFIDUM

BIFIDITY > BIFID

BIFIDLY > BIFID

BIFIDUM n type of bacterium

BIFIDUMS > BIFIDUM

BIFIDUS n bacterium of the human digestive system

BIFIDUSES > BIFIDUS

BIFILAR adj having two parallel threads, as in the suspension of certain measuring instruments

BIFILARLY > BIFILAR

BIFLEX adj bent or flexed in two places

BIFOCAL adj having two different focuses

BIFOCALED adj wearing bifocals

BIFOCALS pl n spectacles with lenses permitting near and distant vision

BIFOLD n something folded in two places

BIFOLDS > BIFOLD

BIFOLIATE adj having only two leaves

BIFORATE adj having two openings, pores, or perforations

BIFORKED adj two-pronged

BIFORM adj having or combining the characteristics of two forms, as a centaur

BIFORMED same as > BIFORM

BIFTAH same as > BIFTER

BIFTAHS > BIFTAH

BIFTER n cannabis cigarette

BIFTERS > BIFTER

BIFURCATE vb fork into two branches ▷ adj forked into two branches

BIG adj of considerable size, height, number, or capacity ▷ adv on a grand scale ▷ vb build

BIGA n chariot drawn by two horses

BIGAE > BIGA

BIGAMIES > BIGAMY

BIGAMIST > BIGAMY

BIGAMISTS > BIGAMY

BIGAMOUS > BIGAMY

BIGAMY n crime of marrying a person while still legally married to someone else

BIGARADE n Seville orange

BIGARADES > BIGARADE

BIGAROON same as > BIGARREAU

BIGAROONS > BIGAROON

BIGARREAU n any of several heart-shaped varieties of sweet cherry that have firm flesh

BIGEMINAL adj double; twinned

BIGEMINY n heart complaint

BIGENER n hybrid between individuals of different genera

BIGENERIC adj (of a hybrid plant) derived from parents of two different genera

BIGENERS > BIGENER

BIGEYE n type of red marine fish

BIGEYES > BIGEYE

BIGFEET > BIGFOOT

BIGFOOT n yeti ▷ vb throw one's weight around

BIGFOOTED > BIGFOOT

BIGFOOTS > BIGFOOT

BIGG n type of barley

BIGGED > BIG

BIGGER > BIG

BIGGEST > BIG

BIGGETY same as > BIGGITY

BIGGIE n something big or important

BIGGIES > BIGGIE

BIGGIN n plain close-fitting cap

BIGGING > BIG

BIGGINGS > BIG

BIGGINS > BIGGIN

BIGGISH > BIG

BIGGITIER > BIGGITY

BIGGITY adj conceited

BIGGON same as > BIGGIN

BIGGONS > BIGGON

BIGGS > BIGG

BIGGY same as > BIGGIE

BIGHA n in India, unit for measuring land

BIGHAS > BIGHA

BIGHEAD n conceited person

BIGHEADED > BIGHEAD

BIGHEADS > BIGHEAD

BIGHORN n large wild mountain sheep

BIGHORNS > BIGHORN

BIGHT n long curved shoreline ▷ vb fasten or bind with a bight

BIGHTED > BIGHT

BIGHTING > BIGHT

BIGHTS > BIGHT

BIGLY > BIG

BIGMOUTH n noisy, indiscreet, or boastful person

BIGMOUTHS > BIGMOUTH

BIGNESS > BIG

BIGNESSES > BIG

BIGNONIA n tropical American climbing shrub, cultivated for its trumpet-shaped yellow or reddish flowers

BIGNONIAS > BIGNONIA

BIGOS n Polish stew

BIGOSES > BIGOS

BIGOT n person who is intolerant, esp regarding religion or race

BIGOTED > BIGOT

BIGOTEDLY > BIGOT

BIGOTRIES > BIGOTRY

BIGOTRY n attitudes, behaviour, or way of thinking of a bigot

BIGOTS > BIGOT

BIGS > BIG

BIGSTICK adj of or relating to irresistible military strength

BIGTIME adj important

BIGUANIDE n any of a class of compounds some of which are used in the treatment of certain forms of diabetes

BIGUINE same as > BEGUINE

BIGUINES > BIGUINE

BIGWIG n important person

BIGWIGS > BIGWIG

BIHOURLY adj occurring every two hours

BIJECTION n mathematical function or mapping that is both an injection and a surjection and therefore has an inverse

BIJECTIVE adj (of a function, relation, etc) associating two sets in such a way that every member of each set is uniquely paired with a member of the other

BIJOU adj (of a house) small but elegant ▷ n something small and delicately worked

BIJOUS > BIJOU

BIJOUX > BIJOU

BIJUGATE adj (of compound leaves) having two pairs of leaflets

BIJUGOUS same as > BIJUGATE

BIJURAL adj relating to two coexisting legal systems

BIJWONER same as > BYWONER

BIJWONERS > BIJWONER

BIKE same as > BICYCLE

BIKED > BIKE

BIKER n person who rides a motorcycle

BIKERS > BIKER

BIKES > BIKE

BIKEWAY n cycle lane

BIKEWAYS > BIKEWAY

BIKIE n member of a motorcycle gang

BIKIES > BIKIE

BIKING > BIKE

BIKINGS > BIKE

BIKINI n woman's brief two-piece swimming costume

BIKINIED > BIKINI

BIKINIS > BIKINI

BIKKIE slang word for > BISCUIT

BIKKIES > BIKKIE

BILABIAL adj of, relating to, or denoting a speech sound articulated using both lips ▷ n bilabial speech sound

BILABIALS > BILABIAL

BILABIATE adj divided into two lips

BILANDER n small two-masted cargo ship

BILANDERS > BILANDER

BILATERAL adj affecting or undertaken by two parties

BILAYER n part of cell membrane

BILAYERS > BILAYER

BILBERRY n bluish-black edible berry

BILBIES > BILBY

BILBO n (formerly) a sword with a marked temper and elasticity

BILBOA same as > BILBO

BILBOAS > BILBOA

BILBOES > BILBO

BILBOS > BILBO

BILBY n Australian marsupial with long pointed ears and grey fur

BILE n bitter yellow fluid secreted by the liver ▷ vb boil

BILECTION same as > BOLECTION

BILED > BILE

BILES > BILE

BILESTONE another name for > GALLSTONE

BILEVEL n hairstyle with two different lengths

BILEVELS > BILEVEL

BILGE n nonsense ▷ vb (of a vessel) to take in water at the bilge

BILGED > BILGE

BILGES > BILGE

BILGIER > BILGE

BILGIEST > BILGE

BILGING > BILGE

BILGY > BILGE

BILHARZIA n disease caused by infestation of the body with blood flukes

BILIAN n type of tree used for its wood

BILIANS > BILIAN

BILIARIES > BILIARY

BILIARY adj of bile, the ducts that convey bile, or the gall bladder ▷ n disease found in dogs

BILIMBI n type of fruit-bearing tree

BILIMBING same as > BILIMBI

BILIMBIS > BILIMBI

BILINEAR adj of or referring to two lines

BILING > BILE

BILINGUAL adj involving or using two languages ▷ n bilingual person

BILIOUS adj sick, nauseous

BILIOUSLY > BILIOUS

BILIRUBIN n orange-yellow pigment in the bile

BILITERAL adj relating to two letters

BILK vb cheat, esp by not paying ▷ n swindle or cheat

BILKED > BILK

BILKER > BILK

BILKERS > BILK

BILKING > BILK

BILKS > BILK

BILL n money owed for goods or services supplied ▷ vb send or present an account for payment to (a person)

BILLABLE adj that can be charged to a client

BILLABONG n stagnant pool in an intermittent stream

BILLBOARD n large outdoor board for displaying advertisements

BILLBOOK n business record of bills received, paid, etc

BILLBOOKS > BILLBOOK

BILLBUG n type of weevil

BILLBUGS > BILLBUG

BILLED > BILL

BILLER n stem of a plant

BILLERS > BILLER

BILLET vb assign a lodging to (a soldier) ▷ n accommodation for a soldier in civil lodgings

BILLETED > BILLET

BILLETEE > BILLET

BILLETEES > BILLET

BILLETER > BILLET

BILLETERS > BILLET

BILLETING n act of billeting

BILLETS > BILLET

BILLFISH n type of fish with elongated jaws, such as the spearfish and marlin

BILLFOLD n small folding case, usually of leather, for holding paper money, documents, etc

BILLFOLDS > BILLFOLD

BILLHEAD n printed form for making out bills

BILLHEADS > BILLHEAD

BILLHOOK n tool with a hooked blade, used for chopping etc

BILLHOOKS > BILLHOOK

BILLIARD n (modifier) of or relating to billiards

BILLIARDS n game played on a table with balls and a cue

BILLIE same as > BILLY

BILLIES > BILLY

BILLING n prominence given in programmes, advertisements, etc, to performers or acts

BILLINGS > BILLING

BILLION n one thousand million ▷ determiner amounting to a billion

BILLIONS > BILLION

BILLIONTH > BILLION

BILLMAN n person who uses a billhook

BILLMEN > BILLMAN

BILLON n alloy consisting of gold or silver and a base metal

BILLONS > BILLON

BILLOW n large sea wave ▷ vb rise up or swell out

BILLOWED > BILLOW

BILLOWIER > BILLOWY

BILLOWING > BILLOW

BILLOWS > BILLOW

BILLOWY adj full of or forming billows

BILLS > BILL

BILLY n metal can or pot for cooking on a camp fire

BILLYBOY n type of river barge

BILLYBOYS > BILLYBOY

BILLYCAN same as > BILLY

BILLYCANS > BILLYCAN

BILLYCOCK n any of several round-crowned brimmed hats of felt, such as the bowler

BILLYO n as in like billyo phrase used to emphasize or intensify something

BILLYOH same as > BILLYO

BILLYOHS > BILLYOH

BILLYOS > BILLYO

BILOBAR same as > BILOBATE

BILOBATE adj divided into or having two lobes

BILOBATED same as > BILOBATE

BILOBED same as > BILOBATE

BILOBULAR adj having two lobules

BILOCULAR adj divided into two chambers or cavities

BILSTED n American gum tree

BILSTEDS > BILSTED

BILTONG n strips of dried meat

BILTONGS > BILTONG

BIMA same as > BEMA

BIMAH same as > BEMA

BIMAHS > BIMAH

BIMANAL same as > BIMANOUS

BIMANOUS adj (of man and the higher primates) having two hands distinct in form and function from the feet

BIMANUAL adj using or requiring both hands

BIMAS > BIMA

BIMBASHI n Turkish military official

BIMBASHIS > BIMBASHI

BIMBETTE n particularly unintelligent bimbo

BIMBETTES > BIMBETTE

BIMBLE n as in bimble box type of dense Australian tree

BIMBO n attractive but empty-headed young person, esp a woman

BIMBOES > BIMBO

BIMBOS > BIMBO

BIMENSAL adj occurring every two months

BIMESTER n period of two months

BIMESTERS > BIMESTER

BIMETAL n material made from two sheets of metal

BIMETALS > BIMETAL

BIMETHYL another word for > ETHANE

BIMETHYLS > BIMETHYL

BIMINI n type of awning for a yacht

BIMINIS > BIMINI

BIMODAL adj having two modes

BIMONTHLY adj every two months ▷ adv every two months ▷ n periodical published every two months

BIMORPH n assembly of piezoelectric crystals

BIMORPHS > BIMORPH

BIN n container for rubbish or for storing grain, coal, etc ▷ vb put in a rubbish bin

BINAL adj twofold

BINARIES > BINARY

BINARISM n state of being binary

BINARISMS > BINARISM

BINARY adj composed of, relating to, or involving two ▷ n something composed of two parts or things

BINATE adj occurring in two parts or in pairs

BINATELY > BINATE

BINAURAL adj relating to, having, or hearing with both ears

BIND vb make secure with or as if with a rope ▷ n annoying situation

BINDABLE > BIND

BINDER n firm cover for holding loose sheets of paper together

BINDERIES > BINDERY

BINDERS > BINDER

BINDERY n bookbindery

BINDHI same as > BINDI

BINDHIS > BINDHI

BINDI n decorative dot worn in the middle of the forehead, esp by Hindu women

BINDING > BIND

BINDINGLY > BIND

BINDINGS > BIND

BINDIS > BINDI

BINDLE n small packet

BINDLES > BINDLE

BINDS > BIND

BINDWEED n plant that twines around a support

BINDWEEDS > BINDWEED

BINE n climbing or twining stem of various plants

BINER n clip used by climbers

BINERS > BINER

BINERVATE adj having two nerves

BINES > BINE

BING n heap or pile, esp of spoil from a mine

BINGE n bout of excessive indulgence, esp in drink ▷ vb indulge in a binge (esp of eating or drinking)

BINGED > BINGE

BINGEING n act of bingeing

BINGEINGS > BINGEING

BINGER n person who is addicted to crack cocaine

BINGERS > BINGER

BINGES > BINGE

BINGHI n Australian derogatory slang for an Aboriginal person

BINGHIS > BINGHI

BINGIES > BINGY

BINGING n act of binging

BINGINGS > BINGING

BINGLE n minor crash or upset, as in a car or on a surfboard ▷ vb layer (hair)

BINGLED > BINGLE

BINGLES > BINGLE

BINGLING > BINGLE

BINGO n gambling game ▷ sentence substitute cry by the winner of a game of bingo ▷ vb (in Scrabble) play all seven of one's tiles in a single turn

BINGOED > BINGO

BINGOES > BINGO

BINGOING > BINGO

BINGOS > BINGO

BINGS > BING

BINGY Australian slang for > STOMACH

BINIOU n small high-pitched Breton bagpipe

BINIOUS > BINIOU

BINIT n (computing) early form of bit

BINITS > BINIT

BINK n ledge

BINKS > BINK

BINMAN another name for > DUSTMAN

BINMEN > BINMAN

BINNACLE n box holding a ship's compass

BINNACLES > BINNACLE

BINNED > BIN

BINNING > BIN

BINOCLE n binocular-style telescope

BINOCLES > BINOCLE

BINOCS > BINOCULAR

BINOCULAR adj involving both eyes

BINOMIAL adj consisting of two terms ▷ n mathematical expression consisting of two terms, such as $3x + 2y$

BINOMIALS > BINOMIAL

b

BINOMINAL adj of or denoting the binomial nomenclature ▷ n two-part taxonomic name

BINOVULAR adj relating to or derived from two different ova

BINS > BIN

BINT n derogatory term for a girl

BINTS > BINT

BINTURONG n arboreal SE Asian mammal with long shaggy black hair

BINUCLEAR adj having two nuclei

BIO short for > BIOGRAPHY

BIOACTIVE adj able to interact with living system

BIOASSAY n method of determining the concentration, activity, or effect of a change to substance by testing its effect on a living organism and comparing this with the activity of an agreed standard ▷ vb subject to a bioassay

BIOASSAYS > BIOASSAY

BIOBANK n large store of human samples for medical research

BIOBANKS > BIOBANK

BIOBLAST same as > BIOPLAST

BIOBLASTS > BIOBLAST

BIOCENOSE adj living together in mutual dependence

BIOCHEMIC adj of or relating to chemical compounds, reactions, etc, occurring in living organisms

BIOCHIP n small glass or silicon plate containing an array of biochemical molecules or structures

BIOCHIPS > BIOCHIP

BIOCIDAL > BIOCIDE

BIOCIDE n substance used to destroy living things

BIOCIDES > BIOCIDE

BIOCLEAN adj free from harmful bacteria

BIOCYCLE n cycling of chemicals through the biosphere

BIOCYCLES > BIOCYCLE

BIODATA n information regarding an individual's education and work history

BIODIESEL n biofuel intended for use in diesel engines

BIODOT n temperature-sensitive device stuck to the skin in order to monitor stress

BIODOTS > BIODOT

BIOENERGY n energy derived from organic matter

BIOETHIC > BIOETHICS

BIOETHICS n study of ethical problems arising from biological research and its applications in such fields as organ transplantation, genetic engineering, or artificial insemination

BIOFACT n item of biological information

BIOFACTS > BIOFACT

BIOFIBERS same as > BIOFIBRES

BIOFIBRES pl n vegetable, animal, or mineral fibres existing in nature which are used by man

BIOFILM n thin layer of living organisms

BIOFILMS > BIOFILM

BIOFOULER n animal that obstructs or pollutes the environment

BIOFUEL n gaseous, liquid, or solid substance of biological origin used as a fuel ▷ vb fuel (a vehicle, etc) using biofuel

BIOFUELED adj running on biofuel

BIOFUELS > BIOFUEL

BIOG short form of > BIOGRAPHY

BIOGAS n gaseous fuel produced by the fermentation of organic waste

BIOGASES > BIOGAS

BIOGASSES > BIOGAS

BIOGEN n hypothetical protein

BIOGENIC adj originating from a living organism

BIOGENIES > BIOGENY

BIOGENOUS > BIOGENY

BIOGENS > BIOGEN

BIOGENY n principle that a living organism must originate from a parent form similar to itself

BIOGRAPH vb write biography of

BIOGRAPHS > BIOGRAPH

BIOGRAPHY n account of a person's life by another person

BIOGS > BIOG

BIOHAZARD n material of biological origin that is hazardous to humans

BIOHERM n mound of material laid down by sedentary marine organisms

BIOHERMS > BIOHERM

BIOLOGIC adj of or relating to biology ▷ n drug, such as a vaccine, that is derived from a living organism

BIOLOGICS > BIOLOGIC

BIOLOGIES > BIOLOGY

BIOLOGISM n explaining human behaviour through biology

BIOLOGIST > BIOLOGY

BIOLOGY n study of living organisms

BIOLYSES > BIOLYSIS

BIOLYSIS n death and dissolution of a living organism

BIOLYTIC > BIOLYSIS

BIOMARKER n substance, physiological characteristic, gene, etc that indicates, or may indicate, the presence of disease, a physiological abnormality, or a psychological condition

BIOMASS n total number of living organisms in a given area

BIOMASSES > BIOMASS

BIOME n major ecological community

BIOMES > BIOME

BIOMETER n device for measuring natural radiation

BIOMETERS > BIOMETER

BIOMETRIC adj of any automated system using physiological or behavioural traits as a means of identification

BIOMETRY n analysis of biological data using mathematical and statistical methods, especially for purposes of identification

BIOMINING n using plants, etc to collect precious metals for extraction

BIOMORPH n form or pattern resembling living thing

BIOMORPHS > BIOMORPH

BIONIC adj having a part of the body that is operated electronically

BIONICS n study of biological functions to create electronic versions

BIONOMIC > BIONOMICS

BIONOMICS a less common name for > ECOLOGY

BIONOMIES > BIONOMY

BIONOMIST > BIONOMICS

BIONOMY n laws of life

BIONT n living thing

BIONTIC > BIONT

BIONTS > BIONT

BIOPARENT n biological parent

BIOPHILIA n innate love for the natural world, supposed to be felt universally by humankind

BIOPHOR n hypothetical material particle

BIOPHORE same as > BIOPHOR

BIOPHORES > BIOPHORE

BIOPHORS > BIOPHOR

BIOPIC n film based on the life of a famous person

BIOPICS > BIOPIC

BIOPIRACY n use of wild plants by international companies to develop medicines, without recompensing the countries from which they are taken

BIOPIRATE > BIOPIRACY

BIOPLASM n living matter

BIOPLASMS > BIOPLASM

BIOPLAST n very small unit of bioplasm

BIOPLASTS > BIOPLAST

BIOPLAY n play based on the life of a famous person

BIOPLAYS > BIOPLAY

BIOPSIC > BIOPSY

BIOPSIED > BIOPSY

BIOPSIES > BIOPSY

BIOPSY n examination of tissue from a living body ▷ vb perform a biopsy on

BIOPSYING > BIOPSY

BIOPTIC > BIOPSY

BIOREGION n area in which climate and environment are consistent

BIORHYTHM n complex recurring pattern of physiological states, believed to affect physical, emotional, and mental states

BIOS > BIO

BIOSAFETY n precautions taken to control the cultivation and distribution of genetically modified crops and products

BIOSCOPE n kind of early film projector

BIOSCOPES > BIOSCOPE

BIOSCOPY n examination of a body to determine whether it is alive

BIOSENSOR n device used to monitor living systems

BIOSOCIAL adj relating to the interaction of biological and social elements

BIOSOLID n residue from treated sewage

BIOSOLIDS > BIOSOLID

BIOSPHERE n part of the earth's surface and atmosphere inhabited by living things

BIOSTABLE adj resistant to the effects of microorganisms

BIOSTATIC adj of or relating to the branch of biology that deals with the structure of organisms in relation to their function

BIOSTROME *n* rock layer consisting of a deposit of organic material, such as fossils

BIOTA *n* plant and animal life of a particular region or period

BIOTAS > BIOTA

BIOTECH *n* biotechnology

BIOTECHS > BIOTECH

BIOTERROR *n* use of biological weapons by terrorists

BIOTIC *adj* of or relating to living organisms ▷ *n* living organism

BIOTICAL *same as* > BIOTIC

BIOTICS > BIOTIC

BIOTIN *n* vitamin of the B complex, abundant in egg yolk and liver

BIOTINS > BIOTIN

BIOTITE *n* black or dark green mineral of the mica group

BIOTITES > BIOTITE

BIOTITIC > BIOTITE

BIOTOPE *n* small area that supports its own distinctive community

BIOTOPES > BIOTOPE

BIOTOXIN *n* toxic substance produced by a living organism

BIOTOXINS > BIOTOXIN

BIOTRON *n* climate-control chamber

BIOTRONS > BIOTRON

BIOTROPH *n* parasitic organism, esp a fungus

BIOTROPHS > BIOTROPH

BIOTURBED *adj* stirred by organisms

BIOTYPE *n* group of genetically identical plants within a species, produced by apomixis

BIOTYPES > BIOTYPE

BIOTYPIC > BIOTYPE

BIOVULAR *adj* (of twins) from two separate eggs

BIOWASTE *n* organic or biodegradable waste

BIOWASTES > BIOWASTE

BIOWEAPON *n* living organism or a toxic product manufactured from it, used to kill or incapacitate

BIPACK *n* obsolete filming process

BIPACKS > BIPACK

BIPAROUS *adj* producing offspring in pairs

BIPARTED *adj* divided into two parts

BIPARTITE *adj* consisting of two parts

BIPARTY *adj* involving two parties

BIPED *n* animal with two feet ▷ *adj* having two feet

BIPEDAL *adj* having two feet

BIPEDALLY > BIPEDAL

BIPEDS > BIPED

BIPHASIC *adj* having two phases

BIPHENYL *n* white or colourless crystalline solid used as a heat-transfer agent

BIPHENYLS > BIPHENYL

BIPINNATE *adj* (of pinnate leaves) having the leaflets themselves divided into smaller leaflets

BIPLANE *n* aeroplane with two sets of wings, one above the other

BIPLANES > BIPLANE

BIPOD *n* two-legged support or stand

BIPODS > BIPOD

BIPOLAR *adj* having two poles

BIPRISM *n* prism having a highly obtuse angle to facilitate beam splitting

BIPRISMS > BIPRISM

BIPYRAMID *n* geometrical form consisting of two pyramids with a common polygonal base

BIRACIAL *adj* for, representing, or including members of two races, esp White and Black

BIRADIAL *adj* showing both bilateral and radial symmetry, as certain sea anemones

BIRADICAL *n* molecule with two centres

BIRAMOSE *same as* > BIRAMOUS

BIRAMOUS *adj* divided into two parts, as the appendages of crustaceans

BIRCH *n* tree with thin peeling bark ▷ *vb* flog with a birch

BIRCHBARK *n* as in *birchbark biting* Native Canadian craft in which designs are bitten onto bark from birch trees

BIRCHED > BIRCH

BIRCHEN > BIRCH

BIRCHES > BIRCH

BIRCHING *n* act of birching

BIRCHINGS > BIRCHING

BIRCHIR *same as* > BICHIR

BIRCHIRS > BIRCHIR

BIRD *n* creature with feathers and wings, most types of which can fly ▷ *vb* hunt for birds

BIRDBATH *n* small basin or trough for birds to bathe in, usually in a garden

BIRDBATHS > BIRDBATH

BIRDBRAIN *n* stupid person

BIRDCAGE *n* wire or wicker cage in which captive birds are kept

BIRDCAGES > BIRDCAGE

BIRDCALL *n* characteristic call or song of a bird

BIRDCALLS > BIRDCALL

BIRDDOG *n* dog used or trained to retrieve game birds

BIRDDOGS > BIRDDOG

BIRDED > BIRD

BIRDER *n* birdwatcher

BIRDERS > BIRDER

BIRDFARM *n* place where birds are kept

BIRDFARMS > BIRDFARM

BIRDFEED *n* food for birds

BIRDFEEDS > BIRDFEED

BIRDHOUSE *n* small shelter or box for birds to nest in

BIRDIE *n* score of one stroke under par for a hole ▷ *vb* play (a hole) in one stroke under par

BIRDIED > BIRDIE

BIRDIEING > BIRDIE

BIRDIES > BIRDIE

BIRDING > BIRD

BIRDINGS > BIRD

BIRDLIFE *n* birds collectively

BIRDLIFES > BIRDLIFE

BIRDLIKE > BIRD

BIRDLIME *n* sticky substance smeared on twigs to catch small birds ▷ *vb* smear (twigs) with birdlime to catch (small birds)

BIRDLIMED > BIRDLIME

BIRDLIMES > BIRDLIME

BIRDMAN *n* man concerned with birds, such as a fowler or ornithologist

BIRDMEN > BIRDMAN

BIRDS > BIRD

BIRDSEED *n* mixture of various kinds of seeds for feeding cage birds

BIRDSEEDS > BIRDSEED

BIRDSEYE *n* type of primrose

BIRDSEYES > BIRDSEYE

BIRDSFOOT *n* type of plant with pods shaped like a bird's foot

BIRDSHOT *n* small pellets designed for shooting birds

BIRDSHOTS > BIRDSHOT

BIRDSONG *n* musical call of a bird or birds

BIRDSONGS > BIRDSONG

BIRDWATCH *vb* watch birds

BIRDWING *n* type of butterfly

BIRDWINGS > BIRDWING

BIREME *n* ancient galley having two banks of oars

BIREMES > BIREME

BIRETTA *n* stiff square cap worn by the Catholic clergy

BIRETTAS > BIRETTA

BIRIANI *same as* > BIRYANI

BIRIANIS > BIRIANI

BIRIYANI *same as* > BIRIANI

BIRIYANIS > BIRIYANI

BIRK *n* birch tree ▷ *adj* consisting or made of birch

BIRKEN *adj* relating to the birch tree

BIRKIE *n* spirited or lively person ▷ *adj* lively

BIRKIER > BIRKIE

BIRKIES > BIRKIE

BIRKIEST > BIRKIE

BIRKS > BIRK

BIRL *same as* > BURL

BIRLE *same as* > BURL

BIRLED > BIRL

BIRLER > BIRL

BIRLERS > BIRL

BIRLES > BIRLE

BIRLIEMAN *n* judge dealing with local law

BIRLIEMEN > BIRLIEMAN

BIRLING > BIRL

BIRLINGS > BIRL

BIRLINN *n* small Scottish book

BIRLINNS > BIRLINN

BIRLS > BIRL

BIRO *n* tradename of a kind of ballpoint pen

BIROS > BIRO

BIRR *vb* make or cause to make a whirring sound ▷ *n* whirring sound

BIRRED > BIRR

BIRRETTA *same as* > BIRETTA

BIRRETTAS > BIRRETTA

BIRRING > BIRR

BIRROTCH *n* Ethiopian monetary unit

BIRRS > BIRR

BIRSE *n* bristle ▷ *vb* bruise

BIRSED > BIRSE

BIRSES > BIRSE

BIRSIER > BIRSY

BIRSIEST > BIRSY

BIRSING > BIRSE

BIRSLE *vb* roast

BIRSLED > BIRSLE

BIRSLES > BIRSLE

BIRSLING > BIRSLE

BIRSY *adj* bristly

BIRTH *n* process of bearing young ▷ *vb* give birth to

BIRTHDATE *n* date on which a person was born

BIRTHDAY *n* anniversary of the day of one's birth

BIRTHDAYS > BIRTHDAY

BIRTHDOM *n* birthright

BIRTHDOMS > BIRTHDOM

BIRTHED > BIRTH

BIRTHER n person who believes Barack Obama was not born in the USA and is not eligible to be President

BIRTHERS > BIRTHER

BIRTHING > BIRTH

BIRTHINGS > BIRTH

BIRTHMARK n blemish on the skin formed before birth

BIRTHNAME n name person was born with

BIRTHRATE n ratio of live births in a specified area, group, etc, to the population of that area, etc, usually expressed per 1000 population per year

BIRTHROOT n N American plant whose roots were formerly used by the American Indians as an aid in childbirth

BIRTHS > BIRTH

BIRTHWORT n type of climbing plant once believed to ease childbirth

BIRYANI n Indian rice-based dish

BIRYANIS > BIRYANI

BIS adv twice ▷ sentence substitute encore! again!

BISCACHA same as > VISCACHA

BISCACHAS > BISCACHA

BISCOTTI > BISCOTTO

BISCOTTO n small Italian biscuit

BISCUIT n small flat dry sweet or plain cake ▷ adj pale brown

BISCUITS > BISCUIT

BISCUITY adj reminiscent of biscuit

BISE n cold dry northerly wind

BISECT vb divide into two equal parts

BISECTED > BISECT

BISECTING > BISECT

BISECTION > BISECT

BISECTOR n straight line or plane that bisects an angle

BISECTORS > BISECTOR

BISECTRIX n bisector of the angle between the optic axes of a crystal

BISECTS > BISECT

BISERIAL adj in two rows

BISERIATE adj (of plant parts, such as petals) arranged in two whorls, cycles, rows, or series

BISERRATE adj (of leaf margins, etc) having serrations that are themselves serrate

BISES > BISE

BISEXUAL adj sexually attracted to both men and women ▷ n bisexual person

BISEXUALS > BISEXUAL

BISH n mistake

BISHES > BISH

BISHOP n clergyman who governs a diocese ▷ vb make a bishop

BISHOPDOM n jurisdiction of bishop

BISHOPED > BISHOP

BISHOPESS > BISHOP

BISHOPING > BISHOP

BISHOPRIC n diocese or office of a bishop

BISHOPS > BISHOP

BISK a less common spelling of > BISQUE

BISKS > BISK

BISMAR n type of weighing scale

BISMARCK n type of pastry

BISMARCKS > BISMARCK

BISMARS > BISMAR

BISMILLAH interj in the name of Allah, a preface to all except one of the surahs of the Koran, used by Muslims as a blessing before eating or some other action

BISMUTH n pinkish-white metallic element

BISMUTHAL > BISMUTH

BISMUTHIC adj of or containing bismuth in the pentavalent state

BISMUTHS > BISMUTH

BISNAGA n type of cactus

BISNAGAS > BISNAGA

BISOM same as > BESOM

BISOMS > BISOM

BISON same as > BUFFALO

BISONS > BISON

BISONTINE adj relating to bison

BISPHENOL n synthetic organic compound used to make plastics and resins

BISQUE n thick rich soup made from shellfish

BISQUES > BISQUE

BISSON adj blind ▷ vb cause to be blind

BISSONED > BISSON

BISSONING > BISSON

BISSONS > BISSON

BIST a form of the second person singular of > BE

BISTABLE adj (of an electronic system) having two stable states ▷ n bistable system

BISTABLES > BISTABLE

BISTATE adj involving two states

BISTER same as > BESTIR

BISTERED > BISTER

BISTERS > BISTER

BISTORT n Eurasian plant with a spike of small pink flowers

BISTORTS > BISTORT

BISTOURY n long surgical knife with a narrow blade

BISTRE n water-soluble pigment

BISTRED > BISTRE

BISTRES > BISTRE

BISTRO n small restaurant

BISTROIC > BISTRO

BISTROS > BISTRO

BISULCATE adj marked by two grooves

BISULFATE n bisulphate

BISULFIDE n bisulphide

BISULFITE n bisulphite

BIT n small piece, portion, or quantity

BITABLE > BITE

BITCH n female dog, fox, or wolf ▷ vb complain or grumble

BITCHED > BITCH

BITCHEN same as > BITCHING

BITCHERY n spiteful talk

BITCHES > BITCH

BITCHFEST n malicious and spiteful discussion of people, events, etc

BITCHIER > BITCHY

BITCHIEST > BITCHY

BITCHILY > BITCHY

BITCHING adj wonderful or excellent

BITCHY adj spiteful or malicious

BITCOIN n type of digital currency

BITCOINS > BITCOIN

BITE vb grip, tear, or puncture the skin, as with the teeth or jaws ▷ n act of biting

BITEABLE > BITE

BITEPLATE n device used by dentists

BITER > BITE

BITERS > BITE

BITES > BITE

BITESIZE adj small enough to put in the mouth whole

BITEWING n dental x-ray film

BITEWINGS > BITEWING

BITING > BITE

BITINGLY > BITE

BITINGS > BITE

BITLESS adj without a bit

BITMAP n picture created by colour or shading on a visual display unit ▷ vb create a bitmap of

BITMAPPED > BITMAP

BITMAPS > BITMAP

BITO n African and Asian tree

BITONAL adj consisting of black and white tones

BITOS > BITO

BITOU n as in bitou bush type of sprawling woody shrub

BITS > BIT

BITSER n mongrel dog

BITSERS > BITSER

BITSIER > BITSY

BITSIEST > BITSY

BITSTOCK n handle or stock of a tool into which a drilling bit is fixed

BITSTOCKS > BITSTOCK

BITSTREAM n sequence of digital data

BITSY adj very small

BITT n strong post on the deck of a ship for securing lines ▷ vb secure (a line) by means of a bitt

BITTACLE same as > BINNACLE

BITTACLES > BITTACLE

BITTE interj you're welcome

BITTED > BITT

BITTEN > BITE

BITTER adj having a sharp unpleasant taste ▷ n beer with a slightly bitter taste ▷ adv very ▷ vb make or become bitter

BITTERED > BITTER

BITTERER > BITTER

BITTEREST > BITTER

BITTERING > BITTER

BITTERISH > BITTER

BITTERLY > BITTER

BITTERN n wading marsh bird with a booming call

BITTERNS > BITTERN

BITTERNUT n E North American hickory tree with thin-shelled nuts and bitter kernels

BITTERS pl n bitter-tasting spirits flavoured with plant extracts

BITTIE n small piece

BITTIER > BITTY

BITTIES > BITTIE

BITTIEST > BITTY

BITTILY adv in a disjointed way

BITTINESS > BITTY

BITTING > BITT

BITTINGS > BITT

BITTOCK n small amount

BITTOCKS > BITTOCK

BITTOR n bittern

BITTORS > BITTOR

BITTOUR same as > BITTOR

BITTOURS > BITTOUR

BITTS > BITT

BITTUR same as > BITTOR

BITTURS > BITTOR

BITTY adj lacking unity, disjointed

BITUMED adj covered with bitumen

BITUMEN n black sticky substance obtained from tar or petrol

BITUMENS > BITUMEN

BITWISE adj relating to an operator in a programming language that manipulates bits

BIUNIQUE adj one-to-one correspondence

BIVALENCE n semantic principle that there are exactly two truth values, so that every meaningful statement is either true or false

BIVALENCY > BIVALENT

BIVALENT adj (of homologous chromosomes) associated together in pairs ▷ n structure formed during meiosis consisting of two homologous chromosomes associated together

BIVALENTS > BIVALENT

BIVALVATE same as > BIVALVE

BIVALVE adj (marine mollusc) with two hinged segments to its shell ▷ n sea creature that has a shell consisting of two hinged valves and breathes through gills

BIVALVED > BIVALVE

BIVALVES > BIVALVE

BIVARIANT same as > BIVARIATE

BIVARIATE adj (of a distribution) involving two random variables, not necessarily independent of one another

BIVIA > BIVIUM

BIVINYL another word for > BUTADIENE

BIVINYLS > BIVINYL

BIVIOUS adj offering a choice of two different ways

BIVIUM n parting of ways

BIVOUAC n temporary camp in the open air ▷ vb camp in a bivouac

BIVOUACKS > BIVOUAC

BIVOUACS > BIVOUAC

BIVVIED > BIVVY

BIVVIES > BIVVY

BIVVY n small tent or shelter ▷ vb camp in a bivouac

BIVVYING > BIVVY

BIWEEKLY adv every two weeks ▷ n periodical published every two weeks

BIYEARLY adv every two years

BIZ n business

BIZARRE adj odd or unusual ▷ n bizarre thing

BIZARRELY > BIZARRE

BIZARRES > BIZARRE

BIZARRO n bizarre person

BIZARROS > BIZARRO

BIZAZZ same as > PIZAZZ

BIZAZZES > BIZAZZ

BIZCACHA same as > VISCACHA

BIZCACHAS > BIZCACHA

BIZE n dry, cold wind in France

BIZES > BIZE

BIZNAGA same as > BISNAGA

BIZNAGAS > BIZNAGA

BIZONAL > BIZONE

BIZONE n place comprising two zones

BIZONES > BIZONE

BIZZES > BIZ

BIZZIES > BIZZY

BIZZO n empty and irrelevant talk or ideas

BIZZOS > BIZZO

BIZZY n policeman

BLAB vb reveal (secrets) indiscreetly

BLABBED > BLAB

BLABBER vb talk without thinking ▷ n person who blabs

BLABBERED > BLABBER

BLABBERS > BLABBER

BLABBIER > BLABBY

BLABBIEST > BLABBY

BLABBING > BLAB

BLABBINGS > BLAB

BLABBY adj talking too much; indiscreet

BLABS > BLAB

BLACK adj of the darkest colour, like coal ▷ n darkest colour ▷ vb make black

BLACKBALL vb exclude from a group ▷ n hard boiled sweet with black-and-white stripes

BLACKBAND n type of iron ore

BLACKBIRD n common European thrush ▷ vb (formerly) to kidnap and sell into slavery

BLACKBODY n hypothetical body that would be capable of absorbing all the electromagnetic radiation falling on it

BLACKBOY n grass tree

BLACKBOYS > BLACKBOY

BLACKBUCK n Indian antelope, the male of which has spiral horns, a dark back, and a white belly

BLACKBUTT n Australian eucalyptus tree with hard wood used as timber

BLACKCAP n brownish-grey warbler, the male of which has a black crown

BLACKCAPS > BLACKCAP

BLACKCOCK n male of the black grouse

BLACKDAMP n air that is low in oxygen content and high in carbon dioxide as a result of an explosion in a mine

BLACKED > BLACK

BLACKEN vb make or become black

BLACKENED > BLACKEN

BLACKENER > BLACKEN

BLACKENS > BLACKEN

BLACKER > BLACK

BLACKEST > BLACK

BLACKFACE n performer made up to imitate a Black person

BLACKFIN n type of tuna

BLACKFINS > BLACKFIN

BLACKFISH n small dark Australian estuary fish

BLACKFLY n type of black aphid that infests beans, sugar beet, and other plants

BLACKGAME n large N European grouse

BLACKGUM n US tree

BLACKGUMS > BLACKGUM

BLACKHEAD n black-tipped plug of fatty matter clogging a skin pore

BLACKING n preparation for giving a black finish to shoes, metals, etc

BLACKINGS > BLACKING

BLACKISH > BLACK

BLACKJACK n pontoon or a similar card game ▷ vb hit with or as if with a kind of truncheon

BLACKLAND n dark soil

BLACKLEAD n graphite ▷ vb colour with blacklead

BLACKLEG n person who continues to work during a strike ▷ vb refuse to join a strike

BLACKLEGS > BLACKLEG

BLACKLIST n list of people or organizations considered untrustworthy etc ▷ vb put on a blacklist

BLACKLY > BLACK

BLACKMAIL n act of attempting to extort money by threats ▷ vb (attempt to) obtain money by blackmail

BLACKNESS > BLACK

BLACKOUT n extinguishing of all light as a precaution against an air attack

BLACKOUTS > BLACKOUT

BLACKPOLL n N American warbler, the male of which has a black-and-white head

BLACKS > BLACK

BLACKSPOT n as in accident blackspot spot where many accidents occur

BLACKTAIL n variety of mule deer having a black tail

BLACKTOP n bituminous mixture used for paving

BLACKTOPS > BLACKTOP

BLACKWASH n wash for colouring a surface black

BLACKWOOD n tall Australian acacia tree

which yields highly valued black timber

BLAD same as > BLAUD

BLADDED > BLAD

BLADDER n sac in the body where urine is held

BLADDERED adj intoxicated

BLADDERS > BLADDER

BLADDERY > BLADDER

BLADDING > BLAD

BLADE n cutting edge of a weapon or tool

BLADED > BLADE

BLADELESS > BLADE

BLADELIKE > BLADE

BLADER n person skating with in-line skates

BLADERS > BLADER

BLADES > BLADE

BLADEWORK n rowing technique

BLADIER > BLADY

BLADIEST > BLADY

BLADING n act or instance of skating with in-line skates

BLADINGS > BLADING

BLADS > BLAD

BLADY adj as in blady grass coarse leafy Australasian grass

BLAE adj bluish-grey

BLAEBERRY another name for > BILBERRY

BLAER > BLAE

BLAES n hardened clay or shale

BLAEST > BLAE

BLAFF n West Indian stew ▷ vb make a barking noise

BLAFFED > BLAFF

BLAFFING > BLAFF

BLAFFS > BLAFF

BLAG vb obtain by wheedling or cadging ▷ n robbery, esp with violence

BLAGGED > BLAG

BLAGGER > BLAG

BLAGGERS > BLAG

BLAGGING > BLAG

BLAGGINGS > BLAG

BLAGS > BLAG

BLAGUE n pretentious but empty talk

BLAGUER > BLAGUE

BLAGUERS > BLAGUE

BLAGUES > BLAGUE

BLAGUEUR n bluffer

BLAGUEURS > BLAGUEUR

BLAH n worthless or silly talk ▷ adj uninteresting ▷ vb talk nonsense or boringly

BLAHED > BLAH

BLAHER > BLAH

BLAHEST > BLAH

BLAHING > BLAH

BLAHS > BLAH

BLAIN n blister, blotch, or sore on the skin

BLAINS > BLAIN

BLAISE same as > BLAES
BLAIZE same as > BLAES
BLAM n representation of the sound of a bullet being fired ▷ vb make the noise of a bullet being fired
BLAMABLE > BLAME
BLAMABLY > BLAME
BLAME vb consider (someone) responsible ▷ n responsibility for something that is wrong
BLAMEABLE > BLAME
BLAMEABLY > BLAME
BLAMED euphemistic word for > DAMNED
BLAMEFUL adj deserving blame
BLAMELESS adj free from blame
BLAMER > BLAME
BLAMERS > BLAME
BLAMES > BLAME
BLAMING > BLAME
BLAMMED > BLAM
BLAMMING > BLAM
BLAMS > BLAM
BLANCH vb become white or pale
BLANCHED > BLANCH
BLANCHER > BLANCH
BLANCHERS > BLANCH
BLANCHES > BLANCH
BLANCHING > BLANCH
BLANCO n whitening substance ▷ vb whiten (something) with blanco
BLANCOED > BLANCO
BLANCOING > BLANCO
BLANCOS > BLANCO
BLAND adj dull and uninteresting ▷ n bland thing ▷ vb as in bland out to become bland
BLANDED > BLAND
BLANDER > BLAND
BLANDEST > BLAND
BLANDING > BLAND
BLANDISH vb persuade by mild flattery
BLANDLY > BLAND
BLANDNESS > BLAND
BLANDS > BLAND
BLANK adj not written on ▷ n empty space ▷ vb cross out, blot, or obscure
BLANKED > BLANK
BLANKER > BLANK
BLANKEST > BLANK
BLANKET n large thick cloth used as covering for a bed ▷ adj applying to a wide group of people, situations, conditions, etc ▷ vb cover as with a blanket
BLANKETED > BLANKET
BLANKETS > BLANKET
BLANKETY n euphemism for any taboo word
BLANKIE n child's security blanket
BLANKIES > BLANKY
BLANKING > BLANK

BLANKINGS > BLANK
BLANKLY > BLANK
BLANKNESS > BLANK
BLANKS > BLANK
BLANKY n child's blanket
BLANQUET n variety of pear
BLANQUETS > BLANQUET
BLARE vb sound loudly and harshly ▷ n loud harsh noise
BLARED > BLARE
BLARES > BLARE
BLARING > BLARE
BLARNEY n flattering talk ▷ vb cajole with flattery
BLARNEYED > BLARNEY
BLARNEYS > BLARNEY
BLART vb sound loudly and harshly
BLARTED > BLART
BLARTING > BLART
BLARTS > BLART
BLASE adj indifferent or bored through familiarity
BLASH n splash ▷ vb splash (something) with liquid
BLASHED > BLASH
BLASHES > BLASH
BLASHIER > BLASHY
BLASHIEST > BLASHY
BLASHING > BLASH
BLASHY adj windy and rainy
BLASPHEME vb speak disrespectfully of (God or sacred things)
BLASPHEMY n behaviour or language that shows disrespect for God or sacred things
BLAST n explosion ▷ vb blow up (a rock etc) with explosives ▷ interj expression of annoyance
BLASTED adv extreme or extremely ▷ adj blighted or withered
BLASTEMA n mass of undifferentiated animal cells that will develop into an organ or tissue: present at the site of regeneration of a lost part
BLASTEMAL > BLASTEMA
BLASTEMAS > BLASTEMA
BLASTEMIC > BLASTEMA
BLASTER > BLAST
BLASTERS > BLAST
BLASTIE n ugly creature
BLASTIER > BLASTY
BLASTIES > BLASTIE
BLASTIEST > BLASTY
BLASTING n distortion of sound caused by overloading certain components of a radio system
BLASTINGS > BLASTING
BLASTMENT n something that frustrates one's plans
BLASTOFF n launching of a rocket

BLASTOFFS > BLASTOFF
BLASTOID n extinct echinoderm found in fossil form
BLASTOIDS > BLASTOID
BLASTOMA n tumour composed of embryonic tissue that has not yet developed a specialized function
BLASTOMAS > BLASTOMA
BLASTOPOR n opening of the archenteron in the gastrula that develops into the anus of some animals
BLASTS > BLAST
BLASTULA n early form of an animal embryo that develops from a morula, consisting of a sphere of cells with a central cavity
BLASTULAE > BLASTULA
BLASTULAR > BLASTULA
BLASTULAS > BLASTULA
BLASTY adj gusty
BLAT vb cry out or bleat like a sheep
BLATANCY > BLATANT
BLATANT adj glaringly obvious
BLATANTLY > BLATANT
BLATE adj shy; ill at ease ▷ vb babble (something)
BLATED > BLATE
BLATER > BLATE
BLATES > BLATE
BLATEST > BLATE
BLATHER vb speak foolishly ▷ n foolish talk
BLATHERED > BLATHER
BLATHERER > BLATHER
BLATHERS > BLATHER
BLATING > BLATE
BLATS > BLAT
BLATT n newspaper
BLATTANT same as > BLATANT
BLATTED > BLAT
BLATTER n, vb prattle
BLATTERED > BLATTER
BLATTERS > BLATTER
BLATTING > BLAT
BLATTS > BLATT
BLAUBOK n South African antelope
BLAUBOKS > BLAUBOK
BLAUD vb slap
BLAUDED > BLAUD
BLAUDING > BLAUD
BLAUDS > BLAUD
BLAW vb blow
BLAWED > BLAW
BLAWING > BLAW
BLAWN > BLAW
BLAWORT n harebell
BLAWORTS > BLAWORT
BLAWS > BLAW
BLAY n small river fish
BLAYS > BLAY
BLAZAR n type of active galaxy
BLAZARS > BLAZAR

BLAZE n strong fire or flame ▷ vb burn or shine brightly
BLAZED > BLAZE
BLAZER n lightweight jacket, often in the colours of a school etc
BLAZERED > BLAZER
BLAZERS > BLAZER
BLAZES pl n hell
BLAZING > BLAZE
BLAZINGLY > BLAZING
BLAZON vb proclaim publicly ▷ n coat of arms
BLAZONED > BLAZON
BLAZONER > BLAZON
BLAZONERS > BLAZON
BLAZONING > BLAZON
BLAZONRY n art or process of describing heraldic arms in proper form
BLAZONS > BLAZON
BLEACH vb make or become white or colourless ▷ n bleaching agent
BLEACHED > BLEACH
BLEACHER > BLEACH
BLEACHERS pl n tier of seats in a sports stadium, etc, that are unroofed and inexpensive
BLEACHERY n place where bleaching is carried out
BLEACHES > BLEACH
BLEACHING > BLEACH
BLEAK adj exposed and barren ▷ n type of fish found in slow-flowing rivers
BLEAKER > BLEAK
BLEAKEST > BLEAK
BLEAKISH > BLEAK
BLEAKLY > BLEAK
BLEAKNESS > BLEAK
BLEAKS > BLEAK
BLEAKY same as > BLEAK
BLEAR vb make (eyes or sight) dim with or as if with tears ▷ adj bleary
BLEARED > BLEAR
BLEARER > BLEAR
BLEAREST > BLEAR
BLEAREYED adj with eyes blurred, as with old age or after waking
BLEARIER > BLEARY
BLEARIEST > BLEARY
BLEARILY > BLEARY
BLEARING > BLEAR
BLEARS > BLEAR
BLEARY adj with eyes dimmed, as by tears or tiredness
BLEAT vb (of a sheep, goat, or calf) utter its plaintive cry ▷ n cry of sheep, goats, and calves
BLEATED > BLEAT
BLEATER > BLEAT
BLEATERS > BLEAT
BLEATING > BLEAT

BLEATINGS > BLEAT

BLEATS > BLEAT

BLEB n fluid-filled blister on the skin

BLEBBIER > BLEB

BLEBBIEST > BLEB

BLEBBING n formation of bleb

BLEBBINGS > BLEB

BLEBBY > BLEB

BLEBS > BLEB

BLECH interj expressing disgust

BLED > BLEED

BLEE n complexion; hue

BLEED vb lose or emit blood

BLEEDER n despicable person

BLEEDERS > BLEEDER

BLEEDING > BLEED

BLEEDINGS > BLEED

BLEEDS > BLEED

BLEEP n high-pitched signal or beep ▷ vb make such a noise

BLEEPED > BLEEP

BLEEPER n small portable radio receiver that makes a bleeping signal

BLEEPERS > BLEEPER

BLEEPING > BLEEP

BLEEPS > BLEEP

BLEES > BLEE

BLELLUM n babbler; blusterer

BLELLUMS > BLELLUM

BLEMISH n defect or stain ▷ vb spoil or tarnish

BLEMISHED > BLEMISH

BLEMISHER > BLEMISH

BLEMISHES > BLEMISH

BLENCH vb shy away, as in fear

BLENCHED > BLENCH

BLENCHER > BLENCH

BLENCHERS > BLENCH

BLENCHES > BLENCH

BLENCHING > BLENCH

BLEND vb mix or mingle (components or ingredients) ▷ n mixture

BLENDE n mineral consisting mainly of zinc sulphide

BLENDED > BLEND

BLENDER n electrical appliance for puréeing vegetables etc

BLENDERS > BLENDER

BLENDES > BLENDE

BLENDING > BLEND

BLENDINGS > BLEND

BLENDS > BLEND

BLENNIES > BLENNY

BLENNIOID n type of small, mainly marine spiny-finned fish with an elongated body, such as the blennies, butterfish, and gunnel

BLENNY n small fish with a tapering scaleless body

BLENT a past participle of > BLEND

BLEOMYCIN n drug used to treat cancer

BLERT n foolish person

BLERTS > BLERT

BLESBOK n S African antelope

BLESBOKS > BLESBOK

BLESBUCK same as > BLESBOK

BLESBUCKS > BLESBUCK

BLESS vb make holy by means of a religious rite

BLESSED > BLESS

BLESSEDER > BLESS

BLESSEDLY > BLESS

BLESSER > BLESS

BLESSERS > BLESS

BLESSES > BLESS

BLESSING > BLESS

BLESSINGS > BLESS

BLEST > BLESS

BLET n state of decay in certain fruits, due to overripening ▷ vb go soft

BLETHER same as > BLATHER

BLETHERED > BLETHER

BLETHERER > BLETHER

BLETHERS > BLETHER

BLETS > BLET

BLETTED > BLET

BLETTING > BLET

BLEUATRE adj blueish

BLEW > BLOW

BLEWART same as > BLAWORT

BLEWARTS > BLEWART

BLEWIT > BLEWITS

BLEWITS n type of edible fungus with a pale brown cap and a bluish stalk

BLEWITSES > BLEWITS

BLEY same as > BLAY

BLEYS > BLEY

BLIGHT n person or thing that spoils or prevents growth ▷ vb cause to suffer a blight

BLIGHTED > BLIGHT

BLIGHTER n irritating person

BLIGHTERS > BLIGHTER

BLIGHTIES > BLIGHTY

BLIGHTING > BLIGHT

BLIGHTS > BLIGHT

BLIGHTY n home country; home leave

BLIKSEM interj South African expression of surprise

BLIMBING same as > BILIMBI

BLIMBINGS > BLIMBING

BLIMEY interj exclamation of surprise or annoyance

BLIMP n small airship ▷ vb to swell out

BLIMPED > BLIMP

BLIMPERY n complacent or reactionary behaviour

BLIMPING > BLIMP

BLIMPISH adj complacent and reactionary

BLIMPS > BLIMP

BLIMY same as > BLIMEY

BLIN Scots word for > BLIND

BLIND adj unable to see ▷ vb deprive of sight ▷ n covering for a window

BLINDAGE n (esp formerly) a protective screen or structure, as over a trench

BLINDAGES > BLINDAGE

BLINDED > BLIND

BLINDER same as > BLIND

BLINDERS same as > BLIND

BLINDEST > BLIND

BLINDFISH n any of various small fishes, esp the cavefish, that have rudimentary or functionless eyes and occur in subterranean streams

BLINDFOLD vb prevent (a person) from seeing by covering the eyes ▷ n piece of cloth used to cover the eyes ▷ adv with the eyes covered by a cloth

BLINDGUT same as > CAECUM

BLINDGUTS > BLINDGUT

BLINDING n sand or grit spread over a road surface to fill up cracks ▷ adj making one blind or as if blind

BLINDINGS > BLINDING

BLINDLESS > BLIND

BLINDLY > BLIND

BLINDNESS > BLIND

BLINDS > BLIND

BLINDSIDE vb take (someone) by surprise

BLINDWORM same as > SLOWWORM

BLING adj flashy ▷ n ostentatious jewellery ▷ vb make ostentatious or flashy

BLINGED > BLING

BLINGER > BLING

BLINGEST > BLING

BLINGIER > BLINGY

BLINGIEST > BLINGY

BLINGING adj flashy and expensive

BLINGLISH n spoken English mixed with Black slang

BLINGS > BLING

BLINGY same as > BLING

BLINI pl n Russian pancakes made of buckwheat flour and yeast

BLINIS same as > BLINI

BLINK vb close and immediately reopen (the eyes) ▷ n act of blinking

BLINKARD n something that twinkles

BLINKARDS > BLINKARD

BLINKED > BLINK

BLINKER vb provide (a horse) with blinkers ▷ n flashing light for sending messages

BLINKERED adj considering only a narrow point of view

BLINKERS same as > BLIND

BLINKING adv extreme or extremely

BLINKS > BLINK

BLINNED > BLIN

BLINNING > BLIN

BLINS > BLIN

BLINTZ n thin pancake folded over a filling usually of apple, cream cheese, or meat

BLINTZE same as > BLINTZ

BLINTZES > BLINTZE

BLINY same as > BLINI

BLIP n spot of light on a radar screen indicating the position of an object ▷ vb produce such a noise

BLIPPED > BLIP

BLIPPING > BLIP

BLIPS > BLIP

BLIPVERT n very short television advertisement

BLIPVERTS > BLIPVERT

BLISS n perfect happiness ▷ vb make or become perfectly happy

BLISSED > BLISS

BLISSES > BLISS

BLISSFUL adj serenely joyful or glad

BLISSING > BLISS

BLISSLESS > BLISS

BLIST archaic form of > BLESSED

BLISTER n small bubble on the skin ▷ vb (cause to) have blisters

BLISTERED > BLISTER

BLISTERS > BLISTER

BLISTERY > BLISTER

BLIT vb move (a block of data) in a computer's memory

BLITE n type of herb

BLITES > BLITE

BLITHE adj casual and indifferent

BLITHEFUL same as > BLITHE

BLITHELY > BLITHE

BLITHER same as > BLETHER

BLITHERED > BLITHER

BLITHERS > BLITHER

BLITHEST > BLITHE

BLITS > BLIT

BLITTED > BLIT

BLITTER n circuit that transfers large amounts of data within a computer's memory

BLITTERS > BLITTER

BLITTING > BLIT

BLITZ *n* violent and sustained attack by aircraft ▷ *vb* attack suddenly and intensively

BLITZED > BLITZ

BLITZER > BLITZ

BLITZERS > BLITZ

BLITZES > BLITZ

BLITZING > BLITZ

BLIVE *same as* > BELIVE

BLIZZARD *n* blinding storm of wind and snow ▷ *vb* (of weather) be stormy with wind and snow

BLIZZARDS > BLIZZARD

BLIZZARDY > BLIZZARD

BLOAT *vb* cause to swell, as with liquid or air ▷ *n* abnormal distention of the abdomen in cattle, sheep, etc

BLOATED *adj* swollen, as with a liquid, air, or wind

BLOATER *n* salted smoked herring

BLOATERS > BLOATER

BLOATING > BLOAT

BLOATINGS > BLOAT

BLOATS > BLOAT

BLOATWARE *n* software with more features than necessary

BLOB *n* soft mass or drop ▷ *vb* put blobs, as of ink or paint, on

BLOBBED > BLOB

BLOBBIER > BLOB

BLOBBIEST > BLOB

BLOBBING > BLOB

BLOBBY > BLOB

BLOBS > BLOB

BLOC *n* people or countries combined by a common interest

BLOCK *n* large solid piece of wood, stone, etc ▷ *vb* obstruct or impede by introducing an obstacle

BLOCKABLE > BLOCK

BLOCKADE *n* sealing off of a place to prevent the passage of goods ▷ *vb* impose a blockade on

BLOCKADED > BLOCKADE

BLOCKADER > BLOCKADE

BLOCKADES > BLOCKADE

BLOCKAGE *n* act of blocking or state of being blocked

BLOCKAGES > BLOCKAGE

BLOCKBUST *vb* (try to) bring about the sale of property at a bargain price by stirring up fears of racial change in an area

BLOCKED *adj* functionally impeded by amphetamine

BLOCKER *n* person or thing that blocks

BLOCKERS > BLOCKER

BLOCKHEAD *n* stupid person

BLOCKHOLE *n* lines marked near stumps on cricket pitch

BLOCKIE *n* owner of a small property, esp a farm

BLOCKIER > BLOCKY

BLOCKIES > BLOCKIE

BLOCKIEST > BLOCKY

BLOCKING *n* interruption of anode current in a valve because of the application of a high negative voltage to the grid

BLOCKINGS > BLOCKING

BLOCKISH *adj* lacking vivacity or imagination

BLOCKS > BLOCK

BLOCKSHIP *n* ship used to block a river or channel and prevent its being used

BLOCKWORK *n* wall-building style

BLOCKY *adj* like a block, esp in shape and solidity

BLOCS > BLOC

BLOG *n* journal written on-line and accessible to users of the internet ▷ *vb* write a blog

BLOGGABLE *adj* interesting enough to be a topic for a blog

BLOGGED > BLOG

BLOGGER > BLOG

BLOGGERS > BLOG

BLOGGING > BLOG

BLOGGINGS > BLOG

BLOGPOST *n* single posting made as part of a blog

BLOGPOSTS > BLOGPOST

BLOGRING *n* group of blogs joined in a ring

BLOGRINGS > BLOGRING

BLOGROLL *n* list of blogs

BLOGROLLS > BLOGROLL

BLOGS > BLOG

BLOKART *n* single-seat three-wheeled vehicle propelled by the wind

BLOKARTS > BLOKART

BLOKE *n* man

BLOKEDOM *n* state of being a bloke

BLOKEDOMS > BLOKEDOM

BLOKEISH *adj* denoting or exhibiting the characteristics believed typical of an ordinary man

BLOKES > BLOKE

BLOKEY *same as* > BLOKEISH

BLOKIER > BLOKEY

BLOKIEST > BLOKEY

BLOKISH *same as* > BLOKEISH

BLONCKET *adj* blue-grey

BLOND *adj* (of men's hair) of a light colour ▷ *n* person, esp a man, having light-coloured hair and skin

BLONDE *n* fair-haired (person) ▷ *adj* (of hair) fair

BLONDER > BLONDE

BLONDES > BLONDE

BLONDEST > BLONDE

BLONDINE *vb* dye hair blonde

BLONDINED > BLONDINE

BLONDINES > BLONDINE

BLONDING *n* act or an instance of dyeing hair blonde

BLONDINGS > BLONDING

BLONDISH > BLOND

BLONDNESS > BLOND

BLONDS > BLOND

BLOOD *n* red fluid that flows around the body ▷ *vb* initiate (a person) to war or hunting

BLOODBATH *n* massacre

BLOODED *adj* (of horses, cattle, etc) of good breeding

BLOODFIN *n* silvery red-finned S American freshwater fish, popular in aquariums

BLOODFINS > BLOODFIN

BLOODIED > BLOODY

BLOODIER > BLOODY

BLOODIES > BLOODY

BLOODIEST > BLOODY

BLOODILY > BLOODY

BLOODING > BLOOD

BLOODINGS > BLOOD

BLOODLESS *adj* without blood or bloodshed

BLOODLIKE > BLOOD

BLOODLINE *n* all the members of a family group over generations, esp regarding characteristics common to that group

BLOODLUST *n* desire to see bloodshed

BLOODRED *adj* having a deep red colour

BLOODROOT *n* N American plant with a single whitish flower and a fleshy red root that yields a red dye

BLOODS > BLOOD

BLOODSHED *n* slaughter or killing

BLOODSHOT *adj* (of an eye) inflamed

BLOODWOOD *n* any of several species of Australian eucalyptus that exude a red sap

BLOODWORM *n* red wormlike aquatic larva of the midge

BLOODWORT *n* plant with red dye in roots

BLOODY *adj* covered with blood ▷ *adv* extreme or extremely ▷ *vb* stain with blood

BLOODYING > BLOODY

BLOOEY *adj* out of order; faulty

BLOOIE *same as* > BLOOEY

BLOOK *n* book published on a blog

BLOOKS > BLOOK

BLOOM *n* blossom on a flowering plant ▷ *vb* (of flowers) open

BLOOMED *adj* (of a lens) coated to reduce light lost by reflection

BLOOMER *n* stupid mistake

BLOOMERS *pl n* woman's baggy knickers

BLOOMERY *n* place in which malleable iron is produced directly from iron ore

BLOOMIER > BLOOMY

BLOOMIEST > BLOOMY

BLOOMING *n* act of blooming

BLOOMINGS > BLOOMING

BLOOMLESS > BLOOM

BLOOMS > BLOOM

BLOOMY *adj* having a fine whitish coating on the surface

BLOOP *vb* (baseball) hit a ball into air beyond infield

BLOOPED > BLOOP

BLOOPER *n* stupid mistake

BLOOPERS > BLOOPER

BLOOPIER > BLOOPY

BLOOPIEST > BLOOPY

BLOOPING > BLOOP

BLOOPS > BLOOP

BLOOPY *adj* (in baseball) relating to a ball hit into the air beyond the infield

BLOOSME *same as* > BLOSSOM

BLOOSMED > BLOOSME

BLOOSMES > BLOOSME

BLOOSMING > BLOOSME

BLOOTERED *adj* drunk

BLOQUISTE *n* supporter of autonomy for Quebec

BLORE *n* strong blast of wind

BLORES > BLORE

BLOSSOM *n* flowers of a plant ▷ *vb* (of plants) flower

BLOSSOMED > BLOSSOM

BLOSSOMS > BLOSSOM

BLOSSOMY > BLOSSOM

BLOT *n* spot or stain ▷ *vb* cause a blemish in or on

BLOTCH *n* discoloured area or stain ▷ *vb* become or cause to become marked by such discoloration

BLOTCHED > BLOTCH

BLOTCHES > BLOTCH

BLOTCHIER > BLOTCHY

BLOTCHILY > BLOTCHY

BLOTCHING > BLOTCH

BLOTCHY *adj* covered in or marked by blotches

BLOTLESS > BLOT

BLOTS > BLOT

BLOTTED > BLOT

BLOTTER *n* sheet of blotting paper

BLOTTERS > BLOTTER

BLOTTIER > BLOTTY

BLOTTIEST > BLOTTY

BLOTTING *n* blot analysis

BLOTTINGS > BLOTTING

BLOTTO *adj* extremely drunk

BLOTTY *adj* covered in blots

BLOUBOK *same as* **>** BLAUBOK

BLOUBOKS > BLOUBOK

BLOUSE *n* woman's shirtlike garment ▷ *vb* hang or cause to hang in full loose folds

BLOUSED > BLOUSE

BLOUSES > BLOUSE

BLOUSIER > BLOUSY

BLOUSIEST > BLOUSY

BLOUSILY > BLOUSY

BLOUSING > BLOUSE

BLOUSON *n* short loose jacket with a tight waist

BLOUSONS > BLOUSON

BLOUSY *adj* loose; blouse-like

BLOVIATE *vb* discourse at length

BLOVIATED > BLOVIATE

BLOVIATES > BLOVIATE

BLOW *vb* (of air, the wind, etc) move ▷ *n* hard hit

BLOWBACK *n* escape to the rear of gases formed during the firing of a weapon or in a boiler, internal-combustion engine, etc

BLOWBACKS > BLOWBACK

BLOWBALL *n* dandelion seed head

BLOWBALLS > BLOWBALL

BLOWBY *n* leakage of gas past the piston of an engine at maximum pressure

BLOWBYS > BLOWBY

BLOWDART *n* dart from a blowpipe

BLOWDARTS > BLOWDART

BLOWDOWN *n* accident in a nuclear reactor in which a cooling pipe bursts causing the loss of essential coolant

BLOWDOWNS > BLOWDOWN

BLOWED > BLOW

BLOWER *n* mechanical device, such as a fan, that blows

BLOWERS > BLOWER

BLOWFISH *a popular name for* **>** PUFFER

BLOWFLIES > BLOWFLY

BLOWFLY *n* fly that lays its eggs in meat

BLOWGUN *same as* **>** BLOWPIPE

BLOWGUNS > BLOWGUN

BLOWHARD *n* boastful person ▷ *adj* blustering or boastful

BLOWHARDS > BLOWHARD

BLOWHOLE *n* nostril of a whale

BLOWHOLES > BLOWHOLE

BLOWIE *n* bluebottle

BLOWIER > BLOWY

BLOWIES > BLOWIE

BLOWIEST > BLOWY

BLOWINESS > BLOWY

BLOWING *n* moving of air

BLOWINGS > BLOWING

BLOWJOB *slang term for* **>** FELLATIO

BLOWJOBS > BLOWJOB

BLOWKART *n* land vehicle with a sail

BLOWKARTS > BLOWKART

BLOWLAMP *another name for* **>** BLOWTORCH

BLOWLAMPS > BLOWLAMP

BLOWN > BLOW

BLOWOFF *n* discharge of a surplus fluid

BLOWOFFS > BLOWOFF

BLOWOUT *n* sudden loss of air in a tyre

BLOWOUTS > BLOWOUT

BLOWPIPE *n* long tube from which darts etc are shot by blowing

BLOWPIPES > BLOWPIPE

BLOWS > BLOW

BLOWSE *n* large, red-faced woman

BLOWSED *same as* **>** BLOWSY

BLOWSES > BLOWSE

BLOWSIER > BLOWSY

BLOWSIEST > BLOWSY

BLOWSILY > BLOWSY

BLOWSY *adj* fat, untidy, and red-faced

BLOWTORCH *n* small burner producing a very hot flame

BLOWTUBE *n* tube for blowing air or oxygen into a flame to intensify its heat

BLOWTUBES > BLOWTUBE

BLOWUP *n* fit of temper

BLOWUPS > BLOWUP

BLOWY *adj* windy

BLOWZE *variant of* **>** BLOWSE

BLOWZED *same as* **>** BLOWSY

BLOWZES > BLOWZE

BLOWZIER > BLOWZY

BLOWZIEST > BLOWZY

BLOWZILY > BLOWZY

BLOWZY *same as* **>** BLOWSY

BLUB *a slang word for* **>** BLUBBER

BLUBBED > BLUB

BLUBBER *n, vb* sob without restraint ▷ *adj* swollen or fleshy ▷ *n* fat of whales, seals, etc

BLUBBERED > BLUBBER

BLUBBERER > BLUBBER

BLUBBERS > BLUBBER

BLUBBERY *adj* of, containing, or like blubber

BLUBBING > BLUB

BLUBS > BLUB

BLUCHER *n* high shoe with laces over the tongue

BLUCHERS > BLUCHER

BLUDE *Scots form of* **>** BLOOD

BLUDES > BLUDE

BLUDGE *vb* evade work ▷ *n* easy task

BLUDGED > BLUDGE

BLUDGEON *n* short thick club ▷ *vb* hit with a bludgeon

BLUDGEONS > BLUDGEON

BLUDGER *n* person who scrounges

BLUDGERS > BLUDGER

BLUDGES > BLUDGE

BLUDGING > BLUDGE

BLUDIE *Scots form of* **>** BLOODY

BLUDIER > BLUDIE

BLUDIEST > BLUDIE

BLUDY *same as* **>** BLUDIE

BLUE *n* colour of a clear unclouded sky ▷ *adj* of the colour blue ▷ *vb* make or become blue

BLUEBACK *n* type of salmon

BLUEBACKS > BLUEBACK

BLUEBALL *n* type of European herb

BLUEBALLS > BLUEBALL

BLUEBEARD *n* any man who murders his wife or wives

BLUEBEAT *n* type of West Indian pop music of the 1960s

BLUEBEATS > BLUEBEAT

BLUEBELL *n* flower with blue bell-shaped flowers

BLUEBELLS > BLUEBELL

BLUEBERRY *n* very small blackish edible fruit that grows on a North American shrub

BLUEBILL *another name for* **>** SCAUP

BLUEBILLS > BLUEBILL

BLUEBIRD *n* North American songbird with a blue plumage

BLUEBIRDS > BLUEBIRD

BLUEBLOOD *n* royal or aristocratic person

BLUEBOOK *n* (in Britain) a government publication, usually the report of a commission

BLUEBOOKS > BLUEBOOK

BLUEBUCK *same as* **>** BLAUBOK

BLUEBUCKS > BLUEBUCK

BLUEBUSH *n* blue-grey herbaceous Australian shrub

BLUECAP *another name for* **>** BLUETIT

BLUECAPS > BLUECAP

BLUECOAT *n* person who wears blue uniform

BLUECOATS > BLUECOAT

BLUECURLS *n* North American plant

BLUED > BLUE

BLUEFIN *another name for* **>** TUNNY

BLUEFINS > BLUEFIN

BLUEFISH *n* type of bluish marine food and game fish

BLUEGILL *n* common N American sunfish, an important freshwater food and game fish

BLUEGILLS > BLUEGILL

BLUEGOWN *n* in past, pauper, recipient of blue gown on King's birthday

BLUEGOWNS > BLUEGOWN

BLUEGRASS *n* any of several North American bluish-green grasses

BLUEGUM *n* widely cultivated Australian tree

BLUEGUMS > BLUEGUM

BLUEHEAD *n* type of fish

BLUEHEADS > BLUEHEAD

BLUEING > BLUE

BLUEINGS > BLUE

BLUEISH *same as* **>** BLUISH

BLUEJACK *n* type of oak tree

BLUEJACKS > BLUEJACK

BLUEJAY *n* N American jay

BLUEJAYS > BLUEJAY

BLUEJEANS *n* blue denim jeans

BLUELINE *n* blue-toned photographic proof

BLUELINER *n* machine for making blueprints

BLUELINES > BLUELINE

BLUELY > BLUE

BLUEMOUTH *n* type of deepwater fish

BLUENESS > BLUE

BLUENOSE *n* puritanical or prudish person

BLUENOSED > BLUENOSE

BLUENOSES > BLUENOSE

BLUEPOINT *n* type of small oyster

BLUEPRINT *n* photographic print of a plan ▷ *vb* make a blueprint of (a plan)

BLUER > BLUE

BLUES *pl n* type of music

BLUESHIFT *n* shift in the spectral lines of a stellar spectrum

BLUESIER > BLUES

BLUESIEST > BLUES

BLUESMAN *n* blues musician

BLUESMEN > BLUESMAN

BLUEST > BLUE

BLUESTEM *n* type of tall grass

BLUESTEMS > BLUESTEM

BLUESTONE *n* blue-grey sandstone containing much clay, used for building and paving

BLUESY > BLUES

b

BLUET n N American plant with small four-petalled blue flowers
BLUETICK n fast-running dog
BLUETICKS > BLUETICK
BLUETIT n small European bird
BLUETITS > BLUETIT
BLUETS > BLUET
BLUETTE n short, brilliant piece of music
BLUETTES > BLUETTE
BLUEWEED n Eurasian weed with blue flowers and pink buds
BLUEWEEDS > BLUEWEED
BLUEWING n type of duck
BLUEWINGS > BLUEWING
BLUEWOOD n type of Mexican shrub
BLUEWOODS > BLUEWOOD
BLUEY adj bluish ▷ n informal Australian word meaning blanket
BLUEYS > BLUEY
BLUFF vb pretend to be confident in order to influence (someone) ▷ n act of bluffing ▷ adj good-naturedly frank and hearty
BLUFFABLE > BLUFF
BLUFFED > BLUFF
BLUFFER > BLUFF
BLUFFERS > BLUFF
BLUFFEST > BLUFF
BLUFFING > BLUFF
BLUFFLY > BLUFF
BLUFFNESS > BLUFF
BLUFFS > BLUFF
BLUGGIER > BLUGGY
BLUGGIEST > BLUGGY
BLUGGY same as > BLOODY
BLUID Scots word for > BLOOD
BLUIDIER > BLUID
BLUIDIEST > BLUID
BLUIDS > BLUID
BLUIDY > BLUID
BLUIER > BLUEY
BLUIEST > BLUEY
BLUING same as > BLUE
BLUINGS > BLUE
BLUISH adj slightly blue
BLUME Scots word for > BLOOM
BLUMED > BLUME
BLUMES > BLUME
BLUMING > BLUME
BLUNDER n clumsy mistake ▷ vb make a blunder
BLUNDERED > BLUNDER
BLUNDERER > BLUNDER
BLUNDERS > BLUNDER
BLUNGE vb mix clay with water
BLUNGED > BLUNGE
BLUNGER n large vat in which the contents are mixed by rotating arms
BLUNGERS > BLUNGER
BLUNGES > BLUNGE

BLUNGING > BLUNGE
BLUNK vb ruin; botch
BLUNKED > BLUNK
BLUNKER > BLUNK
BLUNKERS > BLUNK
BLUNKING > BLUNK
BLUNKS > BLUNK
BLUNT adj not having a sharp edge or point ▷ vb make less sharp ▷ n cannabis cigarette
BLUNTED > BLUNT
BLUNTER > BLUNT
BLUNTEST > BLUNT
BLUNTHEAD n frequent user of marijuana
BLUNTING > BLUNT
BLUNTISH > BLUNT
BLUNTLY > BLUNT
BLUNTNESS > BLUNT
BLUNTS > BLUNT
BLUR vb make or become vague or less distinct ▷ n something vague, hazy, or indistinct
BLURB n promotional description, as on the jacket of a book ▷ vb describe or recommend in a blurb
BLURBED > BLURB
BLURBING > BLURB
BLURBIST n writer of blurbs
BLURBISTS > BLURBIST
BLURBS > BLURB
BLURRED > BLUR
BLURREDLY > BLUR
BLURRIER > BLUR
BLURRIEST > BLUR
BLURRILY > BLUR
BLURRING > BLUR
BLURRY > BLUR
BLURS > BLUR
BLURT vb utter suddenly and involuntarily
BLURTED > BLURT
BLURTER > BLURT
BLURTERS > BLURT
BLURTING > BLURT
BLURTINGS > BLURT
BLURTS > BLURT
BLUSH vb become red in the face, esp from embarrassment or shame ▷ n reddening of the face
BLUSHED > BLUSH
BLUSHER n cosmetic for giving the cheeks a rosy colour
BLUSHERS > BLUSHER
BLUSHES > BLUSH
BLUSHET n modest young woman
BLUSHETS > BLUSHET
BLUSHFUL > BLUSH
BLUSHING > BLUSH
BLUSHINGS > BLUSH
BLUSHLESS > BLUSH
BLUSTER vb speak loudly or in a bullying way ▷ n empty threats or protests

BLUSTERED > BLUSTER
BLUSTERER > BLUSTER
BLUSTERS > BLUSTER
BLUSTERY > BLUSTER
BLUSTROUS adj inclined to bluster
BLUTWURST n blood sausage
BLYPE n piece of skin peeled off after sunburn
BLYPES > BLYPE
BO interj exclamation uttered to startle or surprise someone ▷ n fellow, buddy
BOA n large nonvenomous snake
BOAB short for > BAOBAB
BOABS > BOAB
BOAK same as > BOKE
BOAKED > BOAK
BOAKING > BOAK
BOAKS > BOAK
BOAR n uncastrated male pig
BOARD n long flat piece of sawn timber ▷ vb go aboard (a train, aeroplane, etc)
BOARDABLE > BOARD
BOARDED > BOARD
BOARDER n person who pays rent for accommodation in someone else's home
BOARDERS > BOARDER
BOARDING n act of embarking on an aircraft, train, ship, etc
BOARDINGS > BOARDING
BOARDLIKE > BOARD
BOARDMAN n man who carries a sandwich board
BOARDMEN > BOARDMAN
BOARDROOM n room where the board of a company meets
BOARDS > BOARD
BOARDWALK n promenade, esp along a beach, usually made of planks
BOARFISH n type of spiny-finned marine fish with a compressed body, a long snout, and large eyes
BOARHOUND n dog used to hunt boar
BOARISH adj coarse, cruel, or sensual
BOARISHLY > BOARISH
BOARS > BOAR
BOART same as > BORT
BOARTS > BOART
BOAS > BOA
BOAST vb speak too proudly about one's talents etc ▷ n bragging statement
BOASTED > BOAST
BOASTER > BOAST
BOASTERS > BOAST
BOASTFUL adj tending to boast

BOASTING > BOAST
BOASTINGS > BOAST
BOASTLESS > BOAST
BOASTS > BOAST
BOAT n small vehicle for travelling across water ▷ vb travel in a boat
BOATABLE adj able to be carried by boat
BOATBILL n nocturnal tropical American wading bird with a broad flattened bill
BOATBILLS > BOATBILL
BOATED > BOAT
BOATEL n waterside hotel catering for boating people
BOATELS > BOATEL
BOATER n flat straw hat
BOATERS > BOATER
BOATFUL > BOAT
BOATFULS > BOAT
BOATHOOK n pole with a hook at one end, used aboard a vessel for fending off other vessels or obstacles or for catching a line or mooring buoy
BOATHOOKS > BOATHOOK
BOATHOUSE n shelter by the edge of a river, lake, etc, for housing boats
BOATIE n boating enthusiast
BOATIES > BOATIE
BOATING n rowing, sailing, or cruising in boats as a form of recreation
BOATINGS > BOATING
BOATLIFT n evacuation by boat
BOATLIFTS > BOATLIFT
BOATLIKE > BOAT
BOATLOAD n amount of cargo or number of people held by a boat or ship
BOATLOADS > BOATLOAD
BOATMAN n man who works on, hires out, or repairs boats
BOATMEN > BOATMAN
BOATNECK n wide open neck on garment
BOATNECKS > BOATNECK
BOATPORT n enclosure for boats
BOATPORTS > BOATPORT
BOATS > BOAT
BOATSMAN same as > BOATMAN
BOATSMEN > BOATSMAN
BOATSWAIN n petty officer on a merchant ship or a warrant officer on a warship who is responsible for the maintenance of the ship and its equipment
BOATTAIL n type of blackbird
BOATTAILS > BOATTAIL
BOATYARD n place where boats are kept, repaired, etc

BOATYARDS > BOATYARD

BOB vb move or cause to move up and down repeatedly ▷ n short abrupt movement, as of the head

BOBA n type of Chinese tea

BOBAC same as > BOBAK

BOBACS > BOBAC

BOBAK n type of marmot

BOBAKS > BOBAK

BOBAS > BOBA

BOBBED > BOB

BOBBEJAAN n baboon

BOBBER n type of float for fishing

BOBBERIES > BOBBERY

BOBBERS > BOBBER

BOBBERY n mixed pack of hunting dogs ▷ adj noisy or excitable

BOBBIES > BOBBY

BOBBIN n reel on which thread is wound

BOBBINET n netted fabric of hexagonal mesh, made on a lace machine

BOBBINETS > BOBBINET

BOBBING > BOB

BOBBINS > BOBBIN

BOBBISH adj cheery

BOBBITT vb sever the penis of

BOBBITTED > BOBBITT

BOBBITTS > BOBBITT

BOBBLE n small ball of material, usu for decoration ▷ vb (of a ball) to bounce erratically because of an uneven playing surface

BOBBLED > BOBBLE

BOBBLES > BOBBLE

BOBBLIER > BOBBLY

BOBBLIEST > BOBBLY

BOBBLING > BOBBLE

BOBBLY adj (of fabric) covered in small balls; worn

BOBBY n policeman

BOBBYSOCK n anklelength sock worn esp by teenage girls

BOBBYSOX pl n bobbysocks

BOBCAT n N American feline

BOBCATS > BOBCAT

BOBECHE n candle drip-catcher

BOBECHES > BOBECHE

BOBFLOAT n small buoyant float, usually consisting of a quill stuck through a piece of cork

BOBFLOATS > BOBFLOAT

BOBLET n two-man bobsleigh

BOBLETS > BOBLET

BOBO n rich person who holds bohemian values

BOBOL n type of fraud ▷ vb commit a bobol

BOBOLINK n American songbird, the male of which has a white back and black underparts in the breeding season

BOBOLINKS > BOBOLINK

BOBOLLED > BOBOL

BOBOLLING > BOBOL

BOBOLS > BOBOL

BOBOS > BOBO

BOBOTIE n dish of curried mince

BOBOTIES > BOBOTIE

BOBOWLER n large moth

BOBOWLERS > BOBOWLER

BOBS > BOB

BOBSKATE n child's skate with two parallel blades

BOBSKATES > BOBSKATE

BOBSLED same as > BOBSLEIGH

BOBSLEDS > BOBSLED

BOBSLEIGH n sledge for racing down an icy track ▷ vb ride on a bobsleigh

BOBSTAY n stay between a bowsprit and the stem of a vessel

BOBSTAYS > BOBSTAY

BOBTAIL n docked tail ▷ adj having the tail cut short ▷ vb dock the tail of

BOBTAILED > BOBTAIL

BOBTAILS > BOBTAIL

BOBWEIGHT n balance weight

BOBWHEEL n poetic device

BOBWHEELS > BOBWHEEL

BOBWHITE n brown N American quail, a popular game bird, the male of which has white markings on the head

BOBWHITES > BOBWHITE

BOBWIG n type of short wig

BOBWIGS > BOBWIG

BOCACCIO n edible American fish

BOCACCIOS > BOCACCIO

BOCAGE n wooded countryside characteristic of northern France

BOCAGES > BOCAGE

BOCCA n mouth

BOCCAS > BOCCA

BOCCE same as > BOCCIE

BOCCES > BOCCE

BOCCI same as > BOCCIE

BOCCIA same as > BOCCIE

BOCCIAS > BOCCIA

BOCCIE n Italian version of bowls

BOCCIES > BOCCIE

BOCCIS > BOCCI

BOCHE n derogatory slang for a German soldier

BOCHES > BOCHE

BOCK a variant spelling of > BOKE

BOCKED > BOCK

BOCKEDY adj (of a structure, piece of furniture, etc) unsteady

BOCKING > BOCK

BOCKS > BOCK

BOCONCINI pl n small pieces of mozzarella

BOD n person

BODACH n old man

BODACHS > BODACH

BODACIOUS adj impressive or remarkable

BODDLE same as > BODLE

BODDLES > BODDLE

BODE vb portend or presage

BODED > BODE

BODEFUL adj portentous

BODEGA n shop in a Spanish-speaking country that sells wine

BODEGAS > BODEGA

BODEGUERO n wine seller or grocer

BODEMENT > BODE

BODEMENTS > BODE

BODES > BODE

BODGE vb make a mess of

BODGED > BODGE

BODGER adj worthless or second-rate

BODGERS > BODGER

BODGES > BODGE

BODGIE n unruly or uncouth young man, esp in the 1950s ▷ adj inferior

BODGIER > BODGIE

BODGIES > BODGIE

BODGIEST > BODGIE

BODGING > BODGE

BODHI n as in bodhi tree holy tree of Buddhists

BODHRAN n shallow one-handed drum popular in Irish and Scottish folk music

BODHRANS > BODHRAN

BODICE n upper part of a dress

BODICES > BODICE

BODIED > BODY

BODIES > BODY

BODIKIN n little body

BODIKINS > BODIKIN

BODILESS adj having no body or substance

BODILY adj relating to the body ▷ adv by taking hold of the body

BODING > BODE

BODINGLY > BODE

BODINGS > BODE

BODKIN n blunt large-eyed needle

BODKINS > BODKIN

BODLE n small obsolete Scottish coin

BODLES > BODLE

BODRAG n enemy attack

BODRAGS > BODRAG

BODS > BOD

BODY n entire physical structure of an animal or human

BODYBOARD n surfboard that is shorter and blunter than the standard board and on which the surfer lies rather than stands

BODYCHECK n obstruction of another player ▷ vb deliver a bodycheck to (an opponent)

BODYGUARD n person or group of people employed to protect someone

BODYING > BODY

BODYLINE n (in cricket) fast bowling aimed at the batsman's body

BODYLINES > BODYLINE

BODYMAN n person who repairs car bodies

BODYMEN > BODYMAN

BODYSHELL n external shell of a motor vehicle

BODYSIDE n side of a body of a vehicle

BODYSIDES > BODYSIDE

BODYSUIT n one-piece undergarment for a baby

BODYSUITS > BODYSUIT

BODYSURF vb ride a wave by lying on it without a surfboard

BODYSURFS > BODYSURF

BODYWASH n liquid soap for use in the shower or bath

BODYWORK n outer shell of a motor vehicle

BODYWORKS > BODYWORK

BOEHMITE n grey, red, or brown mineral that consists of alumina in rhombic crystalline form and occurs in bauxite

BOEHMITES > BOEHMITE

BOEP n South African word for a big belly

BOEPS > BOEP

BOERBUL n crossbred mastiff used esp as a watchdog

BOERBULL same as > BOERBUL

BOERBULLS > BOERBULL

BOERBULS > BOERBUL

BOEREWORS n spiced sausage

BOERTJIE South African word for > FRIEND

BOERTJIES > BOERTJIE

BOET n brother

BOETS > BOET

BOEUF n as in boeuf bourguignon casserole of beef, vegetables, herbs, etc, cooked in red wine

BOEUFS > BOEUF

BOFF n boffin ▷ vb hit

BOFFED > BOFF

BOFFIN n scientist or expert

BOFFING > BOFF

BOFFINS > BOFFIN

BOFFINY adj like a boffin

b

BOFFO adj very good
BOFFOLA n great success
BOFFOLAS > BOFFOLA
BOFFOS > BOFFO
BOFFS > BOFF
BOG n wet spongy ground ▷ vb mire or delay
BOGAN n youth who dresses and behaves rebelliously
BOGANS > BOGAN
BOGART vb monopolize or keep to oneself selfishly
BOGARTED > BOGART
BOGARTING > BOGART
BOGARTS > BOGART
BOGBEAN same as > BUCKBEAN
BOGBEANS > BOGBEAN
BOGEY n evil or mischievous spirit ▷ vb play (a hole) in one stroke over par
BOGEYED > BOGEY
BOGEYING > BOGEY
BOGEYISM n demonization
BOGEYISMS > BOGEYISM
BOGEYMAN n frightening person, real or imaginary, used as a threat, esp to children
BOGEYMEN > BOGEYMAN
BOGEYS > BOGEY
BOGGARD same as > BOGGART
BOGGARDS > BOGGARD
BOGGART n ghost or poltergeist
BOGGARTS > BOGGART
BOGGED > BOG
BOGGER n lavatory
BOGGERS > BOGGER
BOGGIER > BOG
BOGGIEST > BOG
BOGGINESS > BOG
BOGGING > BOG
BOGGISH > BOG
BOGGLE vb be surprised, confused, or alarmed
BOGGLED > BOGGLE
BOGGLER > BOGGLE
BOGGLERS > BOGGLE
BOGGLES > BOGGLE
BOGGLING > BOGGLE
BOGGY > BOG
BOGHEAD adj relating to variety of coal from which paraffin can be derived
BOGHOLE n natural hole of wet spongy ground
BOGHOLES > BOGHOLE
BOGIE same as > BOGEY
BOGIED > BOGIE
BOGIEING > BOGIE
BOGIES > BOGY
BOGLAND n area of wetland
BOGLANDS > BOGLAND
BOGLE n rhythmic dance performed to ragga music ▷ vb perform such a dance
BOGLED > BOGLE

BOGLES > BOGLE
BOGLING > BOGLE
BOGMAN n body of a person found preserved in a peat bog
BOGMEN > BOGMAN
BOGOAK n oak or other wood found preserved in peat bogs; bogwood
BOGOAKS > BOGOAK
BOGONG n large nocturnal Australian moth
BOGONGS > BOGONG
BOGS > BOG
BOGUE n type of Mediterranean fish
BOGUES > BOGUE
BOGUS adj not genuine
BOGUSLY > BOGUS
BOGUSNESS > BOGUS
BOGWOOD same as > BOGOAK
BOGWOODS > BOGWOOD
BOGY same as > BOGEY
BOGYISM same as > BOGEYISM
BOGYISMS > BOGYISM
BOGYMAN same as > BOGEYMAN
BOGYMEN > BOGYMAN
BOH same as > BO
BOHEA n black Chinese tea
BOHEAS > BOHEA
BOHEMIA n area frequented by unconventional (esp creative) people
BOHEMIAN adj unconventional in lifestyle or appearance ▷ n person, esp an artist or writer, who lives an unconventional life
BOHEMIANS > BOHEMIAN
BOHEMIAS > BOHEMIA
BOHO short for > BOHEMIAN
BOHOS > BOHO
BOHRIUM n element artificially produced in minute quantities
BOHRIUMS > BOHRIUM
BOHS > BOH
BOHUNK n derogatory name for a labourer from east or central Europe
BOHUNKS > BOHUNK
BOI n lesbian who dresses like a boy
BOIL vb change from a liquid to a vapour so quickly that bubbles are formed ▷ n state or action of boiling
BOILABLE > BOIL
BOILED > BOIL
BOILER n piece of equipment which provides hot water
BOILERIES > BOILERY
BOILERMAN n man who looks after boilers
BOILERMEN > BOILERMAN
BOILERS > BOILER

BOILERY n place where water is boiled to extract salt
BOILING adj very hot ▷ n sweet
BOILINGLY > BOILING
BOILINGS > BOILING
BOILOFF n quantity of liquefied gases lost in evaporation
BOILOFFS > BOILOFF
BOILOVER n surprising result in a sporting event, esp in a horse race
BOILOVERS > BOILOVER
BOILS > BOIL
BOING vb rebound making a noise
BOINGED > BOING
BOINGING > BOING
BOINGS > BOING
BOINK same as > BOING
BOINKED > BOINK
BOINKING > BOINK
BOINKS > BOINK
BOIS > BOI
BOISERIE n finely crafted wood-carving
BOISERIES > BOISERIE
BOITE n artist's portfolio
BOITES > BOITE
BOK n S African antelope
BOKE vb retch or vomit ▷ n retch
BOKED > BOKE
BOKES > BOKE
BOKING > BOKE
BOKKEN n wooden practice sword in kendo
BOKKENS > BOKKEN
BOKO slang word for > NOSE
BOKOS > BOKO
BOKS > BOK
BOLA n missile used by gauchos and Indians of South America
BOLAR adj relating to clay
BOLAS same as > BOLA
BOLASES > BOLAS
BOLD adj confident and fearless ▷ n boldface ▷ vb be or make bold
BOLDED > BOLD
BOLDEN vb make bold
BOLDENED > BOLDEN
BOLDENING > BOLDEN
BOLDENS > BOLDEN
BOLDER > BOLD
BOLDEST > BOLD
BOLDFACE n weight of type characterized by thick heavy lines ▷ vb print in boldface
BOLDFACED > BOLDFACE
BOLDFACES > BOLDFACE
BOLDING > BOLD
BOLDLY > BOLD
BOLDNESS > BOLD
BOLDS > BOLD
BOLE n tree trunk
BOLECTION n stepped moulding covering and projecting beyond the

joint between two members having surfaces at different levels
BOLERO n (music for) traditional Spanish dance
BOLEROS > BOLERO
BOLES > BOLE
BOLETE same as > BOLETUS
BOLETES > BOLETE
BOLETI > BOLETUS
BOLETUS n type of fungus
BOLETUSES > BOLETUS
BOLIDE n large exceptionally bright meteor that often explodes
BOLIDES > BOLIDE
BOLINE n (in Wicca) a knife
BOLINES > BOLINE
BOLIVAR n standard monetary unit of Venezuela, equal to 100 céntimos
BOLIVARES > BOLIVAR
BOLIVARS > BOLIVAR
BOLIVIA n type of woollen fabric
BOLIVIANO n (until 1963 and from 1987) the standard monetary unit of Bolivia, equal to 100 centavos
BOLIVIAS > BOLIVIA
BOLIX same as > BOLLOCKS
BOLIXED > BOLIX
BOLIXES > BOLIX
BOLIXING > BOLIX
BOLL n rounded seed capsule of cotton, flax, etc ▷ vb form into a boll
BOLLARD n short thick post used to prevent the passage of motor vehicles
BOLLARDS > BOLLARD
BOLLED > BOLL
BOLLEN > BOLL
BOLLETRIE n type of W Indian tree
BOLLING > BOLL
BOLLIX same as > BOLLOCKS
BOLLIXED > BOLLIX
BOLLIXES > BOLLIX
BOLLIXING > BOLLIX
BOLLOCK vb rebuke severely
BOLLOCKED > BOLLOCK
BOLLOCKS pl n testicles ▷ interj exclamation of annoyance, disbelief, etc ▷ vb rebuke severely
BOLLOX same as > BOLLOCKS
BOLLOXED > BOLLOX
BOLLOXES > BOLLOX
BOLLOXING > BOLLOX
BOLLS > BOLL
BOLLWORM n any of various moth caterpillars that feed on and destroy cotton bolls

b

BOLLWORMS > BOLLWORM
BOLO n large single-edged knife, originating in the Philippines
BOLOGNA n type of sausage
BOLOGNAS > BOLOGNA
BOLOGNESE n Italian meat and tomato sauce
BOLOGRAPH n record made by a bolometer
BOLOMETER n sensitive instrument for measuring radiant energy by the increase in the resistance of an electrical conductor
BOLOMETRY > BOLOMETER
BOLONEY a variant spelling of > BALONEY
BOLONEYS > BOLONEY
BOLOS > BOLO
BOLSHEVIK n any political radical
BOLSHIE adj difficult or rebellious ▷ n any political radical
BOLSHIER > BOLSHIE
BOLSHIES > BOLSHY
BOLSHIEST > BOLSHIE
BOLSHY same as > BOLSHIE
BOLSON n desert valley surrounded by mountains, with a shallow lake at the centre
BOLSONS > BOLSON
BOLSTER vb support or strengthen ▷ n long narrow pillow
BOLSTERED > BOLSTER
BOLSTERER > BOLSTER
BOLSTERS > BOLSTER
BOLT n sliding metal bar for locking a door etc ▷ vb run away suddenly
BOLTED > BOLT
BOLTER > BOLT
BOLTERS > BOLT
BOLTHEAD n glass receptacle used in chemistry
BOLTHEADS > BOLTHEAD
BOLTHOLE n place of escape from danger
BOLTHOLES > BOLTHOLE
BOLTING > BOLT
BOLTINGS > BOLT
BOLTLESS > BOLT
BOLTLIKE > BOLT
BOLTONIA n N American plant with daisy-like flowers with white, violet, or pinkish rays
BOLTONIAS > BOLTONIA
BOLTROPE n rope sewn to the foot or luff of a sail to strengthen it
BOLTROPES > BOLTROPE
BOLTS > BOLT
BOLUS same as > BOLE
BOLUSES > BOLUS
BOMA n enclosure set up to protect a camp, herd

of animals, etc
BOMAS > BOMA
BOMB n container fitted with explosive material ▷ vb attack with bombs
BOMBABLE > BOMB
BOMBARD vb attack with heavy gunfire or bombs ▷ n ancient type of cannon that threw stone balls
BOMBARDE n alto wind instrument similar to the oboe or medieval shawm, used mainly in Breton traditional music
BOMBARDED > BOMBARD
BOMBARDER > BOMBARD
BOMBARDES > BOMBARDE
BOMBARDON n brass instrument of the tuba type, similar to a sousaphone
BOMBARDS > BOMBARD
BOMBASINE same as > BOMBAZINE
BOMBAST n pompous language ▷ vb speak pompous language
BOMBASTED > BOMBAST
BOMBASTER > BOMBAST
BOMBASTIC > BOMBAST
BOMBASTS > BOMBAST
BOMBAX n type of S American tree
BOMBAXES > BOMBAX
BOMBAZINE n twill fabric, usually of silk and worsted, formerly worn dyed black for mourning
BOMBE n dessert of ice cream lined or filled with custard, cake crumbs, etc ▷ adj (of furniture) having a projecting swollen shape
BOMBED > BOMB
BOMBER n aircraft that drops bombs
BOMBERS > BOMBER
BOMBES > BOMBE
BOMBESIN n hormone found in the body
BOMBESINS > BOMBESIN
BOMBILATE same as > BOMBINATE
BOMBINATE vb make a buzzing noise
BOMBING > BOMB
BOMBINGS > BOMB
BOMBLET n small bomb
BOMBLETS > BOMBLET
BOMBLOAD n quantity of bombs carried at one time
BOMBLOADS > BOMBLOAD
BOMBO n inferior wine
BOMBORA n submerged reef
BOMBORAS > BOMBORA
BOMBOS > BOMBO
BOMBPROOF adj able to withstand the impact of a bomb
BOMBS > BOMB
BOMBSHELL n shocking or unwelcome surprise

BOMBSIGHT n mechanical or electronic device in an aircraft for aiming bombs
BOMBSITE n area where the buildings have been destroyed by bombs
BOMBSITES > BOMBSITE
BOMBYCID n type of moth of the family which includes the silkworm moth, found mostly in Africa and SE Asia
BOMBYCIDS > BOMBYCID
BOMBYCOID adj of or like bombycids
BOMBYX n type of moth
BOMBYXES > BOMBYX
BOMMIE n outcrop of coral reef
BOMMIES > BOMMIE
BON adj good
BONA n goods
BONACI n type of fish
BONACIS > BONACI
BONAMANI > BONAMANO
BONAMANO n gratuity
BONAMIA n parasite
BONAMIAS > BONAMIA
BONANZA n sudden good luck or wealth
BONANZAS > BONANZA
BONASSUS same as > BONASUS
BONASUS n European bison
BONASUSES > BONASUS
BONBON n sweet
BONBONS > BONBON
BONCE n head
BONCES > BONCE
BOND n something that binds, fastens or holds together ▷ vb bind
BONDABLE > BOND
BONDAGE n slavery
BONDAGER > BONDAGE
BONDAGERS > BONDAGE
BONDAGES > BONDAGE
BONDED adj consisting of, secured by, or operating under a bond or bonds
BONDER same as > BONDSTONE
BONDERS > BONDER
BONDING n process by which individuals become emotionally attached to one another
BONDINGS > BONDING
BONDLESS > BOND
BONDMAID n unmarried female serf or slave
BONDMAIDS > BONDMAID
BONDMAN same as > BONDSMAN
BONDMEN > BONDMAN
BONDS > BOND
BONDSMAN n person bound by bond to act as surety for another
BONDSMEN > BONDSMAN
BONDSTONE n long stone or brick laid in a wall as a header

BONDUC n type of North American tree
BONDUCS > BONDUC
BONDWOMAN n female slave
BONDWOMEN > BONDWOMAN
BONE n any of the hard parts in the body that form the skeleton ▷ vb remove the bones from (meat for cooking etc)
BONEBED n site where dinosaur fossils are found
BONEBEDS > BONEBED
BONEBLACK n black residue from the destructive distillation of bones, containing about 10 per cent carbon and 80 per cent calcium phosphate, used as a decolorizing agent and pigment
BONED > BONE
BONEFISH n type of silvery marine game fish occurring in warm shallow waters
BONEHEAD n stupid or obstinate person
BONEHEADS > BONEHEAD
BONELESS > BONE
BONEMEAL n product of dried and ground animal bones, used as a fertilizer or in stock feeds
BONEMEALS > BONEMEAL
BONER n blunder
BONERS > BONER
BONES > BONE
BONESET n N American plant with flat clusters of small white flowers
BONESETS > BONESET
BONETIRED adj completely exhausted
BONEY same as > BONY
BONEYARD an informal name for a > CEMETERY
BONEYARDS > BONEYARD
BONEYER > BONEY
BONEYEST > BONEY
BONFIRE n large outdoor fire
BONFIRES > BONFIRE
BONG n deep reverberating sound, as of a large bell ▷ vb make a deep reverberating sound
BONGED > BONG
BONGING > BONG
BONGO n small drum played with the fingers
BONGOES > BONGO
BONGOIST n bongo player
BONGOISTS > BONGOIST
BONGOS > BONGO
BONGRACE n shade for face
BONGRACES > BONGRACE
BONGS > BONG
BONHAM n piglet
BONHAMS > BONHAM

BONHOMIE n cheerful friendliness
BONHOMIES > BONHOMIE
BONHOMMIE same as > BONHOMIE
BONHOMOUS adj exhibiting bonhomie
BONIATO n sweet potato
BONIATOS > BONIATO
BONIBELL same as > BONNIBELL
BONIBELLS > BONIBELL
BONIE same as > BONNY
BONIER > BONY
BONIEST > BONY
BONIFACE n pub landlord
BONIFACES > BONIFACE
BONILASSE n attractive young woman
BONINESS > BONY
BONING > BONE
BONINGS > BONE
BONISM n doctrine that the world is good, although not the best of all possible worlds
BONISMS > BONISM
BONIST > BONISM
BONISTS > BONISM
BONITA slang term for > HEROIN
BONITAS > BONITA
BONITO n small tunny-like marine food fish
BONITOES > BONITO
BONITOS > BONITO
BONJOUR interj hello
BONK vb have sex with
BONKED > BONK
BONKERS adj crazy
BONKING > BONK
BONKINGS > BONK
BONKS > BONK
BONNE n housemaid or female servant
BONNES > BONNE
BONNET n metal cover over a vehicle's engine ▷ vb place a bonnet on
BONNETED > BONNET
BONNETING > BONNET
BONNETS > BONNET
BONNIBELL n beautiful girl
BONNIE same as > BONNY
BONNIER > BONNY
BONNIES > BONNY
BONNIEST > BONNY
BONNILY > BONNY
BONNINESS > BONNY
BONNOCK n thick oatmeal cake
BONNOCKS > BONNOCK
BONNY adj beautiful ▷ adv agreeably or well
BONOBO n type of anthropoid ape of central W Africa
BONOBOS > BONOBO
BONSAI n ornamental miniature tree or shrub
BONSELA n small gift of money

BONSELAS > BONSELA
BONSELLA same as > BONSELA
BONSELLAS > BONSELLA
BONSOIR interj good evening
BONSPELL same as > BONSPIEL
BONSPELLS > BONSPIEL
BONSPIEL n curling match
BONSPIELS > BONSPIEL
BONTBOK n antelope found in S Africa
BONTBOKS > BONTBOK
BONTEBOK n S African antelope with a deep reddish-brown coat with a white blaze, tail, and rump patch
BONTEBOKS > BONTEBOK
BONUS n something given, paid, or received above what is due or expected ▷ vb give or receive bonus
BONUSED > BONUS
BONUSES > BONUS
BONUSING n (in Scrabble) act of playing all seven of one's tiles in a single turn
BONUSINGS > BONUSING
BONUSSED > BONUS
BONUSSES > BONUS
BONUSSING > BONUS
BONXIE n great skua
BONXIES > BONXIE
BONY adj having many bones
BONZA same as > BONZER
BONZE n Chinese or Japanese Buddhist priest or monk
BONZER adj excellent
BONZES > BONZE
BOO interj shout of disapproval ▷ vb shout 'boo' to show disapproval
BOOAI same as > BOOHAI
BOOAIS > BOOAI
BOOAY same as > BOOHAI
BOOAYS > BOOAY
BOOB n foolish mistake ▷ vb make a foolish mistake ▷ adj of poor quality, similar to that provided in prison
BOOBED > BOOB
BOOBHEAD n repeat offender in a prison
BOOBHEADS > BOOBHEAD
BOOBIALLA n type of tree or shrub
BOOBIE same as > BOOBY
BOOBIES > BOOBY
BOOBING > BOOB
BOOBIRD n person who boos
BOOBIRDS > BOOBIRD
BOOBISH adj doltish
BOOBOISIE n group of people considered as (stupid

BOOBOO n blunder
BOOBOOK n small spotted Australian brown owl
BOOBOOKS > BOOBOOK
BOOBOOS > BOOBOO
BOOBS > BOOB
BOOBY n foolish person
BOOBYISH > BOOBY
BOOBYISM > BOOBY
BOOBYISMS > BOOBY
BOOCOO same as > BEAUCOUP
BOOCOOS > BOOCOO
BOODIE n type of kangaroo
BOODIED > BOODY
BOODIES > BOODY
BOODLE n money or valuables that are counterfeit or used as a bribe ▷ vb give or receive money corruptly or illegally
BOODLED > BOODLE
BOODLER > BOODLE
BOODLERS > BOODLE
BOODLES > BOODLE
BOODLING > BOODLE
BOODY vb sulk
BOODYING > BOODY
BOOED > BOO
BOOFHEAD n stupid person
BOOFHEADS > BOOFHEAD
BOOFIER > BOOFY
BOOFIEST > BOOFY
BOOFY adj muscular and strong but stupid
BOOGALOO n type of dance performed to rock and roll music ▷ vb dance a boogaloo
BOOGALOOS > BOOGALOO
BOOGER n dried mucus from the nose
BOOGERMAN American form of > BOGEYMAN
BOOGERMEN > BOOGERMAN
BOOGERS > BOOGER
BOOGEY same as > BOOGIE
BOOGEYED > BOOGEY
BOOGEYING > BOOGEY
BOOGEYMAN same as > BOGEYMAN
BOOGEYMEN > BOOGEYMAN
BOOGEYS > BOOGEY
BOOGIE vb dance to fast pop music ▷ n session of dancing to pop music
BOOGIED > BOOGIE
BOOGIEING > BOOGIE
BOOGIEMAN same as > BOGEYMAN
BOOGIEMEN > BOOGIEMAN
BOOGIES > BOOGIE
BOOGY same as > BOOGIE
BOOGYING > BOOGY
BOOGYMAN same as > BOGEYMAN
BOOGYMEN > BOOGYMAN
BOOH same as > BOO

BOOHAI n as in up the boohai thoroughly lost
BOOHAIS > BOOHAI
BOOHED > BOOH
BOOHING > BOOH
BOOHOO vb sob or pretend to sob noisily ▷ n distressed or pretended sobbing
BOOHOOED > BOOHOO
BOOHOOING > BOOHOO
BOOHOOS > BOOHOO
BOOHS > BOOH
BOOING n act of booing
BOOINGS > BOOING
BOOJUM n American tree
BOOJUMS > BOOJUM
BOOK n number of pages bound together between covers ▷ vb reserve (a place, passage, etc) in advance
BOOKABLE > BOOK
BOOKBAG n bag for books
BOOKBAGS > BOOKBAG
BOOKCASE n piece of furniture containing shelves for books
BOOKCASES > BOOKCASE
BOOKED > BOOK
BOOKEND n one of a pair of supports for holding books upright ▷ vb occur or be located on either side (of something)
BOOKENDED > BOOKEND
BOOKENDS > BOOKEND
BOOKER > BOOK
BOOKERS > BOOK
BOOKFUL > BOOK
BOOKFULS > BOOK
BOOKIE short for > BOOKMAKER
BOOKIER > BOOKY
BOOKIES > BOOKIE
BOOKIEST > BOOKY
BOOKING n reservation, as of a table or seat
BOOKINGS > BOOKING
BOOKISH adj fond of reading
BOOKISHLY > BOOKISH
BOOKLAND n common land given to private owner
BOOKLANDS > BOOKLAND
BOOKLESS > BOOK
BOOKLET n thin book with paper covers
BOOKLETS > BOOKLET
BOOKLICE > BOOKLOUSE
BOOKLIGHT n small light that can be clipped onto a book for reading by
BOOKLORE n knowledge or beliefs gleaned from books
BOOKLORES > BOOKLORE
BOOKLOUSE n wingless insect that feeds on bookbinding paste, etc
BOOKMAKER n person whose occupation is taking bets
BOOKMAN n learned person

BOOKMARK n person whose occupation is taking bets ▷ vb identify and store (a website) so that one can return to it quickly and easily

BOOKMARKS > BOOKMARK

BOOKMEN > BOOKMAN

BOOKOO same as > BOOCOO

BOOKOOS > BOOKOO

BOOKPLATE n label bearing the owner's name and an individual design or coat of arms, pasted into a book

BOOKRACK n rack for holding books

BOOKRACKS > BOOKRACK

BOOKREST n stand for supporting open book

BOOKRESTS > BOOKREST

BOOKS > BOOK

BOOKSHELF n shelf for books

BOOKSHOP n shop where books are sold

BOOKSHOPS > BOOKSHOP

BOOKSIE same as > BOOKSY

BOOKSIER > BOOKSY

BOOKSIEST > BOOKSY

BOOKSTALL n stall or stand where periodicals, newspapers, or books are sold

BOOKSTAND n support for open book

BOOKSTORE same as > BOOKSHOP

BOOKSY adj inclined to be bookish or literary

BOOKWORK n academic study

BOOKWORKS > BOOKWORK

BOOKWORM n person devoted to reading

BOOKWORMS > BOOKWORM

BOOKY adj bookish

BOOL n bowling bowl ▷ vb play bowls

BOOLED > BOOL

BOOLING > BOOL

BOOLS > BOOL

BOOM vb make a loud deep echoing sound ▷ n loud deep echoing sound

BOOMBOX n portable stereo system

BOOMBOXES > BOOMBOX

BOOMBURB n large suburb that is growing quickly

BOOMBURBS > BOOMBURB

BOOMED > BOOM

BOOMER n large male kangaroo

BOOMERANG n curved wooden missile which can be made to return to the thrower ▷ vb (of a plan) recoil unexpectedly

BOOMERS > BOOMER

BOOMIER > BOOMY

BOOMIEST > BOOMY

BOOMING > BOOM

BOOMINGLY > BOOM

BOOMINGS > BOOM

BOOMKIN n short boom projecting from the deck of a ship

BOOMKINS > BOOMKIN

BOOMLET n small boom in business, birth rate, etc

BOOMLETS > BOOMLET

BOOMS > BOOM

BOOMSLANG n large greenish venomous tree-living snake of southern Africa

BOOMTOWN n town that is enjoying sudden prosperity or has grown rapidly

BOOMTOWNS > BOOMTOWN

BOOMY adj characterized by heavy bass sound

BOON n something extremely useful, helpful, or beneficial

BOONDOCK > BOONDOCKS

BOONDOCKS n remote rural area

BOONER n young working-class person from Canberra

BOONERS > BOONER

BOONG n offensive term for a Black person

BOONGA n offensive term for a Pacific Islander

BOONGARY n tree kangaroo of NE Queensland, Australia

BOONGAS > BOONGA

BOONGS > BOONG

BOONIES short form of > BOONDOCKS

BOONLESS > BOON

BOONS > BOON

BOOR n rude or insensitive person

BOORD obsolete spelling of > BOARD

BOORDE obsolete spelling of > BOARD

BOORDES > BOORDE

BOORDS > BOORD

BOORISH adj ill-mannered, clumsy, or insensitive

BOORISHLY > BOORISH

BOORKA same as > BURKA

BOORKAS > BOORKA

BOORS > BOOR

BOORTREE same as > BOURTREE

BOORTREES > BOORTREE

BOOS > BOO

BOOSE same as > BOOZE

BOOSED > BOOSE

BOOSES > BOOSE

BOOSHIT adj very good

BOOSING > BOOSE

BOOST n encouragement or help ▷ vb improve

BOOSTED > BOOST

BOOSTER n small additional injection of a vaccine

BOOSTERS > BOOSTER

BOOSTING > BOOST

BOOSTS > BOOST

BOOT n outer covering for the foot that extends above the ankle ▷ vb kick

BOOTABLE > BOOT

BOOTBLACK another word for > SHOEBLACK

BOOTCUT adj (of trousers) slightly flared at the bottom of the legs

BOOTED adj wearing boots

BOOTEE n baby's soft shoe

BOOTEES > BOOTEE

BOOTERIES > BOOTERY

BOOTERY n shop where boots and shoes are sold

BOOTH n small partly enclosed cubicle

BOOTHOSE n stocking worn with boots

BOOTHS > BOOTH

BOOTIE n Royal Marine

BOOTIES > BOOTY

BOOTIKIN n small boot

BOOTIKINS > BOOTIKIN

BOOTING > BOOT

BOOTJACK n device that grips the heel of a boot to enable the foot to be withdrawn easily

BOOTJACKS > BOOTJACK

BOOTLACE n strong lace for fastening a boot

BOOTLACES > BOOTLACE

BOOTLAST n foot shape placed in boots or shoes to keep their shape

BOOTLASTS > BOOTLAST

BOOTLEG adj produced, distributed, or sold illicitly ▷ vb make, carry, or sell (illicit goods) ▷ n something made or sold illicitly

BOOTLEGS > BOOTLEG

BOOTLESS adj of little or no use

BOOTLICK vb seek favour by servile or ingratiating behaviour towards (someone, esp someone in authority)

BOOTLICKS > BOOTLICK

BOOTMAKER n person who makes boots and shoes

BOOTS > BOOT

BOOTSTRAP n leather or fabric loop on the back or side of a boot

BOOTY n valuable articles obtained as plunder

BOOZE n (consume) alcoholic drink ▷ vb drink alcohol, esp in excess

BOOZED > BOOZE

BOOZER n person who is fond of drinking

BOOZERS > BOOZER

BOOZES > BOOZE

BOOZEY same as > BOOZY

BOOZIER > BOOZY

BOOZIEST > BOOZY

BOOZILY > BOOZY

BOOZINESS > BOOZY

BOOZING > BOOZE

BOOZINGS > BOOZE

BOOZY adj inclined to or involving excessive drinking of alcohol

BOP vb dance to pop music ▷ n form of jazz with complex rhythms and harmonies

BOPEEP n quick look; peek

BOPEEPS > BOPEEP

BOPPED > BOP

BOPPER > BOP

BOPPERS > BOP

BOPPIER > BOPPY

BOPPIEST > BOPPY

BOPPING > BOP

BOPPISH same as > BOPPY

BOPPY adj resembling or suggesting bebop

BOPS > BOP

BOR n neighbour

BORA n Aboriginal ceremony

BORACES > BORAX

BORACHIO n pig's skin wine carrier

BORACHIOS > BORACHIO

BORACIC same as > BORIC

BORACITE n white mineral that forms salt deposits of magnesium borate

BORACITES > BORACITE

BORAGE n Mediterranean plant with star-shaped blue flowers

BORAGES > BORAGE

BORAK n rubbish

BORAKS > BORAK

BORAL n type of fine powder

BORALS > BORAL

BORANE n any compound of boron and hydrogen

BORANES > BORANE

BORAS > BORA

BORATE n salt or ester of boric acid ▷ vb treat with borax, boric acid, or borate

BORATED > BORATE

BORATES > BORATE

BORATING > BORATE

BORAX n soluble white mineral occurring in alkaline soils and salt deposits

BORAXES > BORAX

BORAZON n extremely hard form of boron nitride

BORAZONS > BORAZON

BORD obsolete spelling of > BOARD

BORDAR n smallholder who held cottage in return for menial work

BORDARS > BORDAR

BORDE obsolete spelling of > BOARD

BORDEAUX adj any of several wines produced around Bordeaux

b

BORDEL same as > BORDELLO

BORDELLO n brothel

BORDELLOS > BORDELLO

BORDELS > BORDEL

BORDER n dividing line between political or geographical regions ▷ vb provide with a border

BORDEREAU n memorandum or invoice prepared for a company by an underwriter, containing a list of reinsured risks

BORDERED > BORDER

BORDERER n person who lives in a border area, esp the border between England and Scotland

BORDERERS > BORDERER

BORDERING > BORDER

BORDERS > BORDER

BORDES > BORDE

BORDS > BORD

BORDURE n outer edge of a shield, esp when decorated distinctively

BORDURES > BORDURE

BORE vb make (someone) weary by being dull

BOREAL adj of or relating to the north or the north wind

BOREALIS adj as in aurora borealis lights seen around the North Pole

BOREAS n name for the north wind

BOREASES > BOREAS

BORECOLE another name for > KALE

BORECOLES > BORECOLE

BORED > BORE

BOREDOM n state of being bored

BOREDOMS > BOREDOM

BOREE same as > MYALL

BOREEN n country lane or narrow road

BOREENS > BOREEN

BOREES > BOREE

BOREHOLE n hole driven into the ground to obtain geological information, release water, etc

BOREHOLES > BOREHOLE

BOREL adj unlearned ▷ n boring tool

BORELS > BOREL

BORER n machine or hand tool for boring holes

BORERS > BORER

BORES > BEAR

BORESCOPE n long narrow device for inspection of, eg, bore

BORESOME adj boring

BORGHETTO n settlement outside city walls

BORGO n small attractive medieval village

BORGOS > BORGO

BORIC adj of or containing boron

BORIDE n compound in which boron is the most electronegative element

BORIDES > BORIDE

BORING n act or process of making or enlarging a hole ▷ adj dull

BORINGLY > BORING

BORINGS > BORING

BORK vb dismiss from job unfairly

BORKED > BORK

BORKING n act of incorrectly configuring a device

BORKINGS > BORKING

BORKS > BORK

BORLOTTI pl n as in borlotti bean variety of kidney bean

BORM vb smear with paint, oil, etc

BORMED > BORM

BORMING > BORM

BORMS > BORM

BORN adj possessing certain qualities from birth

BORNA n as in borna disease viral disease found in mammals, esp horses

BORNE > BEAR

BORNEOL n white solid terpene alcohol

BORNEOLS > BORNEOL

BORNITE n type of mineral

BORNITES > BORNITE

BORNITIC > BORNITE

BORNYL n as in bornyl alcohol white solid alcohol from a Malaysian tree

BORNYLS > BORNYL

BORON n element used in hardening steel

BORONIA n Australian aromatic flowering shrub

BORONIAS > BORONIA

BORONIC > BORON

BORONS > BORON

BOROUGH n town or district with its own council

BOROUGHS > BOROUGH

BORREL adj ignorant

BORRELIA n type of bacterium

BORRELIAS > BORRELIA

BORRELL same as > BORREL

BORROW vb obtain (something) temporarily

BORROWED > BORROW

BORROWER > BORROW

BORROWERS > BORROW

BORROWING > BORROW

BORROWS > BORROW

BORS > BORS

BORSCH same as > BORSCHT

BORSCHES > BORSCH

BORSCHT n Russian soup based on beetroot

BORSCHTS > BORSCHT

BORSHCH same as > BORSCHT

BORSHCHES > BORSHCH

BORSHT same as > BORSCHT

BORSHTS > BORSHT

BORSIC n composite material used in aviation

BORSICS > BORSIC

BORSTAL n (formerly in Britain) prison for young criminals

BORSTALL same as > BORSTAL

BORSTALLS > BORSTALL

BORSTALS > BORSTAL

BORT n inferior grade of diamond used for cutting and drilling or, in powdered form, as an industrial abrasive

BORTIER > BORT

BORTIEST > BORT

BORTS > BORT

BORTSCH same as > BORSCHT

BORTSCHES > BORTSCH

BORTY > BORT

BORTZ same as > BORT

BORTZES > BORTZ

BORZOI n tall dog with a long silky coat

BORZOIS > BORZOI

BOS > BO

BOSBERAAD n meeting in an isolated venue to break a political deadlock

BOSBOK same as > BUSHBUCK

BOSBOKS > BOSBOK

BOSCAGE n mass of trees and shrubs

BOSCAGES > BOSCAGE

BOSCHBOK same as > BUSHBUCK

BOSCHBOKS > BOSCHBOK

BOSCHE same as > BOCHE

BOSCHES > BOSCHE

BOSCHVARK same as > BUSHPIG

BOSCHVELD same as > BUSHVELD

BOSH n empty talk, nonsense

BOSHBOK same as > BUSHBUCK

BOSHBOKS > BOSHBOK

BOSHES > BOSH

BOSHTA same as > BOSHTER

BOSHTER adj excellent

BOSHVARK same as > BOSCHVARK

BOSHVARKS > BOSCHVARK

BOSIE n (in cricket) another term for googly

BOSIES > BOSIE

BOSK n small wood of bushes and small trees

BOSKAGE same as > BOSCAGE

BOSKAGES > BOSKAGE

BOSKER adj excellent

BOSKET n clump of small trees or bushes

BOSKETS > BOSKET

BOSKIER > BOSKY

BOSKIEST > BOSKY

BOSKINESS > BOSKY

BOSKS > BOSK

BOSKY adj containing or consisting of bushes or thickets

BOSOM n chest of a person, esp the female breasts ▷ adj very dear ▷ vb embrace

BOSOMED > BOSOM

BOSOMIER > BOSOMY

BOSOMIEST > BOSOMY

BOSOMING > BOSOM

BOSOMS > BOSOM

BOSOMY adj (of a woman) having large breasts

BOSON n type of elementary particle

BOSONIC > BOSON

BOSONS > BOSON

BOSQUE same as > BOSK

BOSQUES > BOSQUE

BOSQUET same as > BOSKET

BOSQUETS > BOSQUET

BOSS n raised knob or stud ▷ vb employ, supervise, or be in charge of ▷ adj excellent

BOSSBOY n Black African foreman of a gang of workers

BOSSBOYS > BOSSBOY

BOSSDOM n bosses collectively

BOSSDOMS > BOSSDOM

BOSSED > BOSS

BOSSER > BOSS

BOSSES > BOSS

BOSSEST > BOSS

BOSSET n either of the rudimentary antlers found in young deer

BOSSETS > BOSSET

BOSSIER > BOSSY

BOSSIES > BOSSY

BOSSIEST > BOSSY

BOSSILY > BOSSY

BOSSINESS > BOSSY

BOSSING n act of shaping malleable metal

BOSSINGS > BOSSING

BOSSISM n domination of political organizations by bosses

BOSSISMS > BOSSISM

BOSSY same as > BOSS

BOSTANGI n imperial Turkish guard

BOSTANGIS > BOSTANGI

BOSTHOON n boor

BOSTHOONS > BOSTHOON

BOSTON n card game for four, played with two packs

BOSTONS > BOSTON

BOSTRYX n phenomenon in which flowers develop on one side only

BOSTRYXES > BOSTRYX
BOSUN same as
> BOATSWAIN
BOSUNS > BOSUN
BOT n larva of a botfly
BOTA n leather container
BOTANIC same as
> BOTANICAL
BOTANICA n botany
BOTANICAL adj of or
relating to botany or
plants ▷ n any drug or
pesticide that is made
from parts of a plant
BOTANICAS > BOTANICA
BOTANICS > BOTANIC
BOTANIES > BOTANY
BOTANISE same as
> BOTANIZE
BOTANISED > BOTANISE
BOTANISER > BOTANIZE
BOTANISES > BOTANISE
BOTANIST > BOTANY
BOTANISTS > BOTANY
BOTANIZE vb collect or
study plants
BOTANIZED > BOTANIZE
BOTANIZER > BOTANIZE
BOTANIZES > BOTANIZE
BOTANY n study of plants
BOTARGO n relish
consisting of the roe of
mullet or tunny, salted and
pressed into rolls
BOTARGOES > BOTARGO
BOTARGOS > BOTARGO
BOTAS > BOTA
BOTCH vb spoil through
clumsiness ▷ n badly done
piece of work or repair
BOTCHED > BOTCH
BOTCHEDLY > BOTCH
BOTCHER > BOTCH
BOTCHERS > BOTCH
BOTCHERY n instance of
botching
BOTCHES > BOTCH
BOTCHIER > BOTCHY
BOTCHIEST > BOTCHY
BOTCHILY > BOTCHY
BOTCHING > BOTCH
BOTCHINGS > BOTCH
BOTCHY adj clumsily done
or made
BOTE n compensation
given for injury or damage
to property
BOTEL same as **>** BOATEL
BOTELS > BOTEL
BOTES > BOTE
BOTFLIES > BOTFLY
BOTFLY n type of
stout-bodied hairy fly
BOTH pron two considered
together ▷ adj two
considered together
▷ determiner two
BOTHAN n unlicensed
drinking house
BOTHANS > BOTHAN
BOTHER vb take the time
or trouble ▷ n trouble,
fuss, or difficulty

▷ interj exclamation of
slight annoyance
BOTHERED > BOTHER
BOTHERING > BOTHER
BOTHERS > BOTHER
BOTHIE same as **>** BOTHY
BOTHIES > BOTHY
BOTHOLE n hole made by
the larva of the botfly
BOTHOLES > BOTHOLE
BOTHRIA > BOTHRIUM
BOTHRIUM n groove-
shaped sucker on
tapeworm
BOTHRIUMS > BOTHRIUM
BOTHY n hut used for
temporary shelter
BOTHYMAN n man who
lives in bothy
BOTHYMEN > BOTHYMAN
BOTNET n network of
infected computers
BOTNETS > BOTNET
BOTONE adj having lobes
at the ends
BOTONEE same as
> BOTONE
BOTONNEE same as
> BOTONE
BOTOXED adj indicating
someone who has had
Botox treatment
BOTRYOID adj shaped like
a bunch of grapes
BOTRYOSE same as
> BOTRYOID
BOTRYTIS n type of
fungus which causes plant
diseases
BOTS n digestive disease of
horses and some other
animals
BOTT same as **>** BOT
BOTTARGA same as
> BOTARGO
BOTTARGAS > BOTTARGA
BOTTE n thrust or hit
BOTTED > BOT
BOTTEGA n workshop;
studio
BOTTEGAS > BOTTEGA
BOTTES > BOTTE
BOTTIES > BOTTY
BOTTINE n light boot for
women or children
BOTTINES > BOTTINE
BOTTING > BOT
BOTTLE n container for
holding liquids ▷ vb put in
a bottle
BOTTLED > BOTTLE
BOTTLEFUL same as
> BOTTLE
BOTTLER n exceptional
person or thing
BOTTLERS > BOTTLER
BOTTLES > BOTTLE
BOTTLING > BOTTLE
BOTTLINGS > BOTTLE
BOTTOM n lowest, deepest,
or farthest removed part
of a thing ▷ adj lowest or
last ▷ vb provide with a
bottom

BOTTOMED > BOTTOM
BOTTOMER n pit worker
BOTTOMERS > BOTTOMER
BOTTOMING n lowest level
of foundation material for
a road or other structure
BOTTOMRY n contract
whereby the owner of a
ship borrows money to
enable the vessel to
complete the voyage and
pledges the ship as
security for the loan
BOTTOMS > BOTTOM
BOTTOMSET adj as in
bottomset bed fine
sediment deposited at the
front of a growing delta
BOTTONY same as
> BOTONE
BOTTS > BOTT
BOTTY n diminutive for
bottom
BOTULIN n potent toxin
which causes botulism
BOTULINAL > BOTULIN
BOTULINS > BOTULIN
BOTULINUM n botulin-
secreting bacterium
BOTULINUS n type of
bacterium whose toxins
(botulins) cause botulism
BOTULISM n severe food
poisoning
BOTULISMS > BOTULISM
BOUBOU n long flowing
garment
BOUBOUS > BOUBOU
BOUCHE n notch cut in top
corner of shield
BOUCHEE n small pastry
case filled with a savoury
mixture
BOUCHEES > BOUCHEE
BOUCHES > BOUCHE
BOUCLE n looped yarn
giving a knobbly effect
▷ adj of or designating
such a yarn or fabric
BOUCLEE n support for a
cue in billiards using the
hand
BOUCLEES > BOUCLEE
BOUCLES > BOUCLE
BOUDERIE n sulkiness
BOUDERIES > BOUDERIE
BOUDIN n French version
of a black pudding
BOUDINS > BOUDIN
BOUDOIR n woman's
bedroom or private sitting
room
BOUDOIRS > BOUDOIR
BOUFFANT adj (of a
hairstyle) having extra
height through
backcombing ▷ n bouffant
hair style
BOUFFANTS > BOUFFANT
BOUFFE n type of light or
satirical opera common in
France during the 19th
century
BOUFFES > BOUFFE

BOUGE vb move
BOUGED > BOUGE
BOUGES > BOUGE
BOUGET n budget
BOUGETS > BOUGET
BOUGH n large branch of
a tree
BOUGHED > BOUGH
BOUGHLESS > BOUGH
BOUGHPOT n container for
displaying boughs
BOUGHPOTS > BOUGHPOT
BOUGHS > BOUGH
BOUGHT > BUY
BOUGHTEN a dialect word
for **>** BUY
BOUGHTS > BUY
BOUGIE n medical
instrument
BOUGIES > BOUGIE
BOUGING > BOUGE
BOUILLI n stew
BOUILLIS > BOUILLI
BOUILLON n thin clear
broth or stock
BOUILLONS > BOUILLON
BOUK n bulk; volume
BOUKS > BOUK
BOULDER n large rounded
rock ▷ vb convert into
boulders
BOULDERED > BOULDER
BOULDERER > BOULDER
BOULDERS > BOULDER
BOULDERY > BOULDER
BOULE same as **>** BOULLE
BOULES n game popular in
France
BOULEVARD n wide, usu
tree-lined, street
BOULLE adj relating to a
type of marquetry much
used on French furniture
from the 17th century
▷ n something
ornamented with such
marquetry
BOULLES > BOULLE
BOULT same as **>** BOLT
BOULTED > BOULT
BOULTER > BOLT
BOULTERS > BOLT
BOULTING > BOULT
BOULTINGS > BOULT
BOULTS > BOULT
BOUN vb prepare to go out
BOUNCE vb (of a ball etc)
rebound from an impact
▷ n act of rebounding
BOUNCED > BOUNCE
BOUNCER n person
employed at a disco etc to
remove unwanted people
BOUNCERS > BOUNCER
BOUNCES > BOUNCE
BOUNCIER > BOUNCY
BOUNCIEST > BOUNCY
BOUNCILY > BOUNCY
BOUNCING adj vigorous
and robust
BOUNCY adj lively,
exuberant, or
self-confident

BOUND > BIND

BOUNDABLE > BIND

BOUNDARY *n* dividing line that indicates the farthest limit

BOUNDED *adj* (of a set) having a bound

BOUNDEN *adj* morally obligatory

BOUNDER *n* morally reprehensible person

BOUNDERS > BOUNDER

BOUNDING > BIND

BOUNDLESS *adj* unlimited

BOUNDNESS > BIND

BOUNDS *pl n* limit

BOUNED > BOUN

BOUNING > BOUN

BOUNS > BOUN

BOUNTEOUS *adj* giving freely

BOUNTIED > BOUNTY

BOUNTIES > BOUNTY

BOUNTIFUL *adj* plentiful

BOUNTREE *another name for* > BOUNTREE

BOUNTREES > BOUNTREE

BOUNTY *n* generosity

BOUNTYHED *n* generosity

BOUQUET *n* bunch of flowers

BOUQUETS > BOUQUET

BOURASQUE *n* violent storm

BOURBON *n* whiskey made from maize

BOURBONS > BOURBON

BOURD *n* prank ▷ *vb* jest or joke

BOURDED > BOURD

BOURDER *n* prankster

BOURDERS > BOURDER

BOURDING > BOURD

BOURDON *n* 16-foot organ stop of the stopped diapason type

BOURDONS > BOURDON

BOURDS > BOURD

BOURG *n* French market town, esp one beside a castle

BOURGEOIS *n* middle-class (person) ▷ *adj* characteristic of or comprising the middle class

BOURGEON *same as* > BURGEON

BOURGEONS > BOURGEON

BOURGS > BOURG

BOURKHA *same as* > BURKA

BOURKHAS > BOURKHA

BOURLAW *same as* > BYRLAW

BOURLAWS > BOURLAW

BOURN *n* (in S Britain) stream

BOURNE *same as* > BOURN

BOURNES > BOURNE

BOURNS > BOURN

BOURREE *n* traditional French dance in fast duple time

BOURREES > BOURREE

BOURRIDE *n* Mediterranean fish soup

BOURRIDES > BOURRIDE

BOURSE *n* stock exchange of continental Europe, esp Paris

BOURSES > BOURSE

BOURSIER *n* stock-exchange worker

BOURSIERS > BOURSIER

BOURSIN *n* tradename of a smooth white creamy cheese, often flavoured with garlic

BOURSINS > BOURSIN

BOURTREE *n* elder tree

BOURTREES > BOURTREE

BOUSE *vb* raise or haul with a tackle

BOUSED > BOUSE

BOUSES > BOUSE

BOUSIER > BOUSY

BOUSIEST > BOUSY

BOUSING > BOUSE

BOUSOUKI *same as* > BOUZOUKI

BOUSOUKIA > BOUSOUKI

BOUSOUKIS > BOUSOUKI

BOUSY *adj* drunken; boozy

BOUT *n* period of activity or illness

BOUTADE *n* outburst

BOUTADES > BOUTADE

BOUTIQUE *n* small clothes shop

BOUTIQUES > BOUTIQUE

BOUTIQUEY *adj* typical of boutiques

BOUTON *n* knob-shaped contact between nerve fibres

BOUTONNE *adj* reserved or inhibited

BOUTONNEE *same as* > BOUTONNE

BOUTONS > BOUTON

BOUTS > BOUT

BOUVARDIA *n* flowering plant

BOUVIER *n* large powerful dog

BOUVIERS > BOUVIER

BOUZOUKI *n* Greek stringed musical instrument

BOUZOUKIA > BOUZOUKI

BOUZOUKIS > BOUZOUKI

BOVATE *n* obsolete measure of land

BOVATES > BOVATE

BOVID *n* type of ruminant

BOVIDS > BOVID

BOVINE *n* domesticated bovine mammal

BOVINELY > BOVINE

BOVINES > BOVINE

BOVINITY > BOVINE

BOVVER *n* rowdiness, esp caused by gangs of teenage youths

BOVVERS > BOVVER

BOW *vb* lower (one's head) or bend (one's knee or body) as a sign of respect or shame ▷ *n* movement made when bowing

BOWAT *n* lamp

BOWATS > BOWAT

BOWBENT *adj* bent; bow-like

BOWED *adj* lowered, bent forward, or curved

BOWEL *n* intestine, esp the large intestine ▷ *vb* remove the bowels

BOWELED > BOWEL

BOWELING > BOWEL

BOWELLED > BOWEL

BOWELLESS > BOWEL

BOWELLING > BOWEL

BOWELS > BOWEL

BOWER *n* shady leafy shelter ▷ *vb* surround as with a bower

BOWERBIRD *n* songbird of Australia and New Guinea, the males of which build bower-like display grounds to attract females

BOWERED > BOWER

BOWERIES > BOWER

BOWERING > BOWER

BOWERS > BOWER

BOWERY > BOWER

BOWES > BOUGH

BOWET *same as* > BOWAT

BOWETS > BOWET

BOWFIN *n* N American freshwater fish

BOWFINS > BOWFIN

BOWFRONT *adj* having a front that curves outwards

BOWGET *obsolete variant of* > BUDGET

BOWGETS > BOWGET

BOWHEAD *n* type of large-mouthed arctic whale

BOWHEADS > BOWHEAD

BOWHUNT *vb* hunt using a bow and arrows

BOWHUNTED > BOWHUNT

BOWHUNTER *n* person hunting with bow and arrows

BOWHUNTS > BOWHUNT

BOWIE *n* as in *bowie knife* type of hunting knife

BOWING *n* musical technique

BOWINGLY > BOWING

BOWINGS > BOWING

BOWKNOT *n* decorative knot usually having two loops and two loose ends

BOWKNOTS > BOWKNOT

BOWL *n* round container with an open top ▷ *vb* roll smoothly along the ground

BOWLDER *same as* > BOULDER

BOWLDERS > BOWLDER

BOWLED > BOWL

BOWLEG *n* leg curving outwards like a bow between the ankle and the thigh

BOWLEGGED *adj* having legs that curve outwards like a bow

BOWLEGS > BOWLEG

BOWLER *n* player who sends (a ball) towards the batsman

BOWLERS > BOWLER

BOWLESS > BOW

BOWLFUL *same as* > BOWL

BOWLFULS > BOWLFUL

BOWLIKE > BOW

BOWLINE *n* line used to keep the sail taut against the wind

BOWLINES > BOWLINE

BOWLING *n* game in which bowls are rolled at a group of pins

BOWLINGS > BLOW

BOWLLIKE > BOWL

BOWLS *n* game involving biased wooden bowls and a small bowl (the jack)

BOWMAN *n* archer

BOWMEN > BOWMAN

BOWNE *same as* > BOUN

BOWNED > BOWNE

BOWNES > BOWNE

BOWNING > BOWNE

BOWPOT *same as* > BOUGHPOT

BOWPOTS > BOWPOT

BOWR *n* muscle

BOWRS > BOWR

BOWS > BOW

BOWSAW *n* saw with a thin blade in a bow-shaped frame

BOWSAWS > BOWSAW

BOWSE *same as* > BOUSE

BOWSED > BOWSE

BOWSER *n* tanker containing fuel for aircraft, military vehicles, etc

BOWSERS > BOWSER

BOWSES > BOWSE

BOWSEY *same as* > BOWSIE

BOWSEYS > BOWSEY

BOWSHOT *n* distance an arrow travels from the bow

BOWSHOTS > BOWSHOT

BOWSIE *n* low-class, mean or obstreperous person

BOWSIES > BOWSIE

BOWSING > BOWSE

BOWSMAN *n* man who hunts using a bow and arrows

BOWSMEN > BOWMAN

BOWSPRIT *n* spar projecting from the bow of a sailing ship

BOWSPRITS > BOWSPRIT

BOWSTRING *n* string of an archer's bow

BOWSTRUNG > BOWSTRING

BOWWOOD n tree of the mulberry family, native to south-central US

BOWWOODS > BOWWOOD

BOWWOW n imitation of the bark of a dog ▷ vb make a noise like a dog

BOWWOWED > BOWWOW

BOWWOWING > BOWWOW

BOWWOWS > BOWWOW

BOWYANG n band worn round trouser leg below knee

BOWYANGS > BOWYANG

BOWYER n person who makes or sells archery bows

BOWYERS > BOWYER

BOX n container with a firm flat base and sides ▷ vb put into a box

BOXBALL n street ball game

BOXBALLS > BOXBALL

BOXBERRY n fruit of the partridgeberry or wintergreen

BOXBOARD n tough paperboard made from wood and wastepaper pulp: used for making boxes, etc

BOXBOARDS > BOXBOARD

BOXCAR n closed railway freight van

BOXCARS > BOXCAR

BOXED > BOX

BOXEN adj made of boxwood

BOXER n person who participates in the sport of boxing

BOXERCISE n system of sustained exercises combining boxing movements with aerobic activities

BOXERS > BOXER

BOXES > BOX

BOXFISH another name for **>** TRUNKFISH

BOXFISHES > BOXFISH

BOXFUL same as **>** BOX

BOXFULS > BOX

BOXHAUL vb bring (a square-rigger) onto a new tack by backwinding the foresails and steering hard round

BOXHAULED > BOXHAUL

BOXHAULS > BOXHAUL

BOXIER > BOXY

BOXIEST > BOXY

BOXILY > BOXY

BOXINESS > BOXY

BOXING n sport of fighting with the fists

BOXINGS > BOXING

BOXKEEPER n person responsible for theatre boxes

BOXLA n type of lacrosse played indoors

BOXLAS > BOXLA

BOXLIKE > BOX

BOXPLOT n (in statistics) type of graph

BOXPLOTS > BOXPLOT

BOXROOM n small room in which boxes, cases, etc may be stored

BOXROOMS > BOXROOM

BOXTHORN n matrimony vine

BOXTHORNS > BOXTHORN

BOXTIES n Irish potato cakes

BOXTY n type of Irish potato pancake

BOXWALLAH n salesman

BOXWOOD n hard yellow wood of the box tree, used to make tool handles, etc

BOXWOODS > BOXWOOD

BOXY adj squarish or chunky

BOY n male child ▷ vb act the part of a boy in a play

BOYAR n member of an old order of Russian nobility

BOYARD same as **>** BOYAR

BOYARDS > BOYARD

BOYARISM n BOYAR

BOYARISMS > BOYAR

BOYARS > BOYAR

BOYAU n connecting trench

BOYAUX > BOYAU

BOYCHICK same as **>** BOYCHIK

BOYCHICKS > BOYCHICK

BOYCHIK n young boy

BOYCHIKS > BOYCHIK

BOYCOTT vb refuse to deal with (an organization or country) ▷ n instance of boycotting

BOYCOTTED > BOYCOTT

BOYCOTTER > BOYCOTT

BOYCOTTS > BOYCOTT

BOYED > BOY

BOYF n boyfriend

BOYFRIEND n male friend with whom a person is romantically or sexually involved

BOYFS > BOYF

BOYG n troll-like mythical creature

BOYGS > BOYG

BOYHOOD n state or time of being a boy

BOYHOODS > BOYHOOD

BOYING > BOY

BOYISH adj of or like a boy in looks, behaviour, or character

BOYISHLY > BOYISH

BOYKIE n chap or fellow

BOYKIES > BOYKIE

BOYLA n Australian Aboriginal word for magician

BOYLAS > BOYLA

BOYO n boy or young man: often used in direct address

BOYOS > BOYO

BOYS > BOY

BOYSHORTS pl n women's underpants resembling close-fitting shorts

BOYSIER > BOYSY

BOYSIEST > BOYSY

BOYSY adj suited to or typical of boys or young men

BOZO n man, esp a stupid one

BOZOS > BOZO

BOZZETTI > BOZZETTO

BOZZETTO n small sketch of planned work

BRA same as **>** BRASSIERE

BRAAI vb grill or roast (meat) over open coals

BRAAIED > BRAAI

BRAAIING > BRAAI

BRAAIS > BRAAI

BRAATA n small portion added to a purchase to encourage the customer to return

BRAATAS same as **>** BRAATA

BRAATASES > BRAATAS

BRABBLE rare word for **>** SQUABBLE

BRABBLED > BRABBLE

BRABBLER > BRABBLE

BRABBLERS > BRABBLE

BRABBLES > BRABBLE

BRABBLING > BRABBLE

BRACCATE adj (of birds) having feathered legs

BRACCIA > BRACCIO

BRACCIO n former unit of measurement; length of man's arm

BRACE n object fastened to something to straighten or support it ▷ vb steady or prepare (oneself) for something unpleasant

BRACED > BRACE

BRACELET n ornamental chain or band for the wrist

BRACELETS pl n handcuffs

BRACER n person or thing that braces

BRACERO n Mexican World War II labourer

BRACEROS > BRACERO

BRACERS > BRACER

BRACES pl n pair of straps worn over the shoulders for holding up the trousers

BRACH n bitch hound

BRACHAH n blessing

BRACHAHS > BRACHAH

BRACHES > BRACH

BRACHET same as **>** BRACH

BRACHETS > BRACHET

BRACHIA > BRACHIUM

BRACHIAL adj of or relating to the arm or to an armlike part or structure ▷ n brachial part or structure

BRACHIALS > BRACHIAL

BRACHIATE adj having widely divergent paired branches ▷ vb (of some arboreal apes and monkeys) swing by the arms from one hold to the next

BRACHIUM n arm, esp the upper part

BRACHIUMS > BRACHIUM

BRACHOT > BRACHAH

BRACHS > BRACH

BRACING adj refreshing and invigorating ▷ n system of braces used to strengthen or support

BRACINGLY > BRACING

BRACINGS > BRACING

BRACIOLA n Italian meat roulade

BRACIOLAS > BRACIOLA

BRACIOLE > BRACIOLA

BRACIOLES > BRACIOLE

BRACK same as **>** BARMBRACK

BRACKEN n large fern

BRACKENS > BRACKEN

BRACKET n pair of characters used to enclose a section of writing ▷ vb put in brackets

BRACKETED > BRACKET

BRACKETS > BRACKET

BRACKISH adj (of water) slightly salty

BRACKS > BRACK

BRACONID n type of fly with parasitic larva

BRACONIDS > BRACONID

BRACT n leaf at the base of a flower

BRACTEAL > BRACT

BRACTEATE adj (of a plant) having bracts ▷ n fine decorated dish or plate of precious metal

BRACTED > BRACT

BRACTEOLE n secondary bract subtending a flower within an inflorescence

BRACTLESS > BRACT

BRACTLET variant of **>** BRACTEOLE

BRACTLETS > BRACTLET

BRACTS > BRACT

BRAD n small tapered nail with a small head

BRADAWL n small boring tool

BRADAWLS > BRADAWL

BRADDED > BRAD

BRADDING > BRAD

BRADOON same as **>** BRIDOON

BRADOONS > BRADOON

BRADS > BRAD

BRAE n hill or slope

BRAEHEID n summit of a hill or slope

BRAEHEIDS > BRAEHEID

BRAES > BRAE

BRAG vb speak arrogantly and boastfully ▷ n boastful talk or behaviour

BRAGGART n person who boasts loudly ▷ adj boastful

BRAGGARTS > BRAGGART

BRAGGED > BRAG

BRAGGER > BRAG

BRAGGERS > BRAG

BRAGGEST > BRAG

BRAGGIER > BRAGGY

BRAGGIEST > BRAGGY

BRAGGING > BRAG

BRAGGINGS > BRAG

BRAGGY adj boastful

BRAGLY > BRAG

BRAGS > BRAG

BRAHMA n breed of domestic fowl

BRAHMAN n member of highest Hindu caste

BRAHMANI n woman of the highest Hindu caste

BRAHMANIS > BRAHMANI

BRAHMANS > BRAHMAN

BRAHMAS > BRAHMA

BRAHMIN same as > BRAHMAN

BRAHMINS > BRAHMIN

BRAID vb interweave (hair, thread, etc) ▷ n length of hair etc that has been braided ▷ adj broad ▷ adv broadly

BRAIDE adj given to deceit

BRAIDED adj (of a river or stream) flowing in several shallow interconnected channels separated by banks of deposited material

BRAIDER > BRAID

BRAIDERS > BRAID

BRAIDEST > BRAID

BRAIDING n braids collectively

BRAIDINGS > BRAIDING

BRAIDS > BRAID

BRAIL n one of several lines fastened to a fore-and-aft sail to aid in furling it ▷ vb furl (a fore-and-aft sail) using brails

BRAILED > BRAIL

BRAILING > BRAIL

BRAILLE n system of writing for the blind ▷ vb print or write using this method

BRAILLED > BRAILLE

BRAILLER n device for producing text in braille

BRAILLERS > BRAILLER

BRAILLES > BRAILLE

BRAILLING > BRAILLE

BRAILLIST n braille transcriber

BRAILS > BRAIL

BRAIN n soft mass of nervous tissue in the head ▷ vb hit (someone) hard on the head

BRAINBOX n skull

BRAINCASE n part of cranium that covers brain

BRAINDEAD adj having suffered irreversible stoppage of breathing due to brain damage

BRAINED > BRAIN

BRAINFART n idea expressed without much previous thought

BRAINFOOD n food containing nutrients that promote brain function

BRAINIAC n highly intelligent person

BRAINIACS > BRAINIAC

BRAINIER > BRAINY

BRAINIEST > BRAINY

BRAINILY > BRAINY

BRAINING > BRAIN

BRAINISH adj impulsive

BRAINLESS adj stupid

BRAINPAN n skull

BRAINPANS > BRAINPAN

BRAINS > BRAIN

BRAINSICK adj relating to or caused by insanity

BRAINSTEM n stalklike part of the brain consisting of the medulla oblongata, the midbrain, and the pons Varolii

BRAINWASH vb cause (a person) to alter his or her beliefs, esp by methods based on isolation, sleeplessness, etc

BRAINWAVE n sudden idea

BRAINWORK n work done with the brain

BRAINY adj clever

BRAIRD vb appear as shoots

BRAIRDED > BRAIRD

BRAIRDING > BRAIRD

BRAIRDS > BRAIRD

BRAISE vb cook slowly in a covered pan with a little liquid

BRAISED > BRAISE

BRAISES > BRAISE

BRAISING > BRAISE

BRAIZE same as > BRAISE

BRAIZES > BRAIZE

BRAK n crossbred dog ▷ adj (of water) slightly salty

BRAKE same as > BRACKEN

BRAKEAGE > BRAKE

BRAKEAGES > BRAKE

BRAKED > BRAKE

BRAKELESS > BRAKE

BRAKEMAN n crew member of a goods or passenger train. His duties include controlling auxiliary braking power and inspecting the train

BRAKEMEN > BRAKEMAN

BRAKES > BRAKE

BRAKESMAN n pithead winch operator

BRAKESMEN > BRAKESMAN

BRAKIER > BRAKY

BRAKIEST > BRAKY

BRAKING n act of braking

BRAKINGS > BRAKING

BRAKS > BRAK

BRAKY adj brambly

BRALESS > BRA

BRAMBLE n Scots word for blackberry

BRAMBLED > BRAMBLE

BRAMBLES > BRAMBLE

BRAMBLIER > BRAMBLE

BRAMBLING n Eurasian finch with a speckled head and back and, in the male, a reddish brown breast and darker wings and tail

BRAMBLY > BRAMBLE

BRAME n powerful feeling of emotion

BRAMES > BRAME

BRAN n husks of cereal grain

BRANCARD n couch on shafts, carried between two horses

BRANCARDS > BRANCARD

BRANCH n secondary stem of a tree ▷ vb (of stems, roots, etc) divide, then develop in different directions

BRANCHED > BRANCH

BRANCHER n young bird learning to fly

BRANCHERS > BRANCHER

BRANCHERY n branches

BRANCHES > BRANCH

BRANCHIA n gill in aquatic animals

BRANCHIAE > BRANCHIA

BRANCHIAL adj of or relating to the gills of an aquatic animal, esp a fish

BRANCHIER > BRANCH

BRANCHING > BRANCH

BRANCHLET n small branch

BRANCHY > BRANCH

BRAND n particular product ▷ vb mark with a brand

BRANDADE n French puréed fish dish

BRANDADES > BRANDADE

BRANDED adj identifiable as being the product of a particular company

BRANDER > BRAND

BRANDERED > BRAND

BRANDERS > BRAND

BRANDIED > BRANDY

BRANDIES > BRANDY

BRANDING > BRAND

BRANDINGS > BRAND

BRANDISE n three-legged metal stand for cooking pots

BRANDISES > BRANDISE

BRANDISH vb wave (a weapon etc) in a threatening way ▷ n threatening or defiant flourish

BRANDLESS > BRAND

BRANDLING n type of small red earthworm found in manure and used as bait by anglers

BRANDRETH n framework of bars used for cooking meat over fire

BRANDS > BRAND

BRANDY n alcoholic spirit distilled from wine ▷ vb give brandy to

BRANDYING > BRANDY

BRANE n hypothetical component of string theory

BRANES > BRANE

BRANGLE vb quarrel noisily

BRANGLED > BRANGLE

BRANGLES > BRANGLE

BRANGLING > BRANGLE

BRANK vb walk with swaggering gait

BRANKED > BRANK

BRANKIER > BRANKY

BRANKIEST > BRANKY

BRANKING > BRANK

BRANKS pl n (formerly) iron bridle used to restrain scolding women

BRANKY adj ostentatious

BRANLE n old French country dance performed in a linked circle

BRANLES > BRANLE

BRANNED > BRAN

BRANNER n person or machine that treats metal with bran

BRANNERS > BRANNER

BRANNIER > BRANNY

BRANNIEST > BRANNY

BRANNIGAN n noisy quarrel

BRANNING > BRAN

BRANNY adj having the appearance or texture of bran

BRANS > BRAN

BRANSLE another word for > BRANTLE

BRANSLES > BRANSLE

BRANT n type of small goose

BRANTAIL n singing bird with red tail

BRANTAILS > BRANTAIL

BRANTLE n French country dance

BRANTLES > BRANTLE

BRANTS > BRANT

BRAP interj exclamation used to imitate a burst of gunfire

BRAS > BRA

BRASCO n lavatory

BRASCOS > BRASCO

BRASERO n metal grid for burning coals

BRASEROS > BRASERO

BRASES > BRA

BRASH adj offensively loud, showy, or self-confident ▷ n loose rubbish, such as

broken rock, hedge clippings, etc ▷ vb assault
BRASHED > BRASH
BRASHER > BRASH
BRASHES > BRASH
BRASHEST > BRASH
BRASHIER > BRASHY
BRASHIEST > BRASHY
BRASHING > BRASH
BRASHLY > BRASH
BRASHNESS > BRASH
BRASHY adj loosely fragmented
BRASIER same as > BRAZIER
BRASIERS > BRASIER
BRASIL same as > BRAZIL
BRASILEIN same as > BRAZILEIN
BRASILIN same as > BRAZILIN
BRASILINS > BRASILIN
BRASILS > BRASIL
BRASS n alloy of copper and zinc ▷ vb make irritated or annoyed
BRASSAGE n amount charged by government for making coins
BRASSAGES > BRASSAGE
BRASSARD n identifying armband or badge
BRASSARDS > BRASSARD
BRASSART same as > BRASSARD
BRASSARTS > BRASSART
BRASSED > BRASS
BRASSERIE n restaurant serving drinks and cheap meals
BRASSES > BRASS
BRASSET same as > BRASSART
BRASSETS > BRASSET
BRASSICA n any plant of the cabbage and turnip family
BRASSICAS > BRASSICA
BRASSIE n former name for a golf club
BRASSIER > BRASSY
BRASSIERE n bra
BRASSIES > BRASSIE
BRASSIEST > BRASSY
BRASSILY > BRASSY
BRASSING > BRASS
BRASSISH > BRASS
BRASSWARE n items made of brass
BRASSY same as > BRASSIE
BRAST same as > BURST
BRASTING > BRAST
BRASTS > BRAST
BRAT n unruly child
BRATCHET n hunting dog
BRATCHETS > BRATCHET
BRATLING n small badly-behaved child
BRATLINGS > BRATLING
BRATPACK n group of precocious and successful young actors, writers, etc

BRATPACKS > BRATPACK
BRATS > BRAT
BRATTICE n partition of wood or treated cloth used to control ventilation in a mine ▷ vb fit with a brattice
BRATTICED > BRATTICE
BRATTICES > BRATTICE
BRATTIER > BRAT
BRATTIEST > BRAT
BRATTISH same as > BRATTICE
BRATTLE vb make a rattling sound
BRATTLED > BRATTLE
BRATTLES > BRATTLE
BRATTLING > BRATTLE
BRATTY > BRAT
BRATWURST n type of small pork sausage
BRAUNCH old variant of > BRANCH
BRAUNCHED > BRAUNCH
BRAUNCHES > BRAUNCH
BRAUNITE n brown or black mineral
BRAUNITES > BRAUNITE
BRAVA n professional assassin
BRAVADO n showy display of self-confidence ▷ vb behave with bravado
BRAVADOED > BRAVADO
BRAVADOES > BRAVADO
BRAVADOS > BRAVADO
BRAVAS > BRAVA
BRAVE adj having or showing courage, resolution, and daring ▷ n Native American warrior ▷ vb confront with resolution or courage
BRAVED > BRAVE
BRAVELY > BRAVE
BRAVENESS > BRAVE
BRAVER > BRAVE
BRAVERIES > BRAVE
BRAVERS > BRAVE
BRAVERY > BRAVE
BRAVES > BRAVE
BRAVEST > BRAVE
BRAVI > BRAVO
BRAVING > BRAVE
BRAVO interj well done! ▷ n cry of 'bravo' ▷ vb cry or shout 'bravo'
BRAVOED > BRAVO
BRAVOES > BRAVO
BRAVOING > BRAVO
BRAVOS > BRAVO
BRAVURA n display of boldness or daring
BRAVURAS > BRAVURA
BRAVURE > BRAVURA
BRAW adj fine or excellent, esp in appearance or dress ▷ pl n best clothes
BRAWER > BRAW
BRAWEST > BRAW
BRAWL n noisy fight ▷ vb fight noisily
BRAWLED > BRAWL

BRAWLER > BRAWL
BRAWLERS > BRAWL
BRAWLIE adj in good health
BRAWLIER > BRAWLIE
BRAWLIEST > BRAWLIE
BRAWLING > BRAWL
BRAWLINGS > BRAWL
BRAWLS > BRAWL
BRAWLY > BRAW
BRAWN n physical strength
BRAWNED > BRAWN
BRAWNIER > BRAWNY
BRAWNIEST > BRAWNY
BRAWNILY > BRAWNY
BRAWNS > BRAWN
BRAWNY adj muscular and strong
BRAWS n fine apparel
BRAXIES > BRAXY
BRAXY n acute and usually fatal bacterial disease of sheep
BRAY vb (of a donkey) utter its loud harsh sound ▷ n donkey's loud harsh sound
BRAYED > BRAY
BRAYER > BRAY
BRAYERS > BRAY
BRAYING > BRAY
BRAYS > BRAY
BRAZA n Spanish unit of measurement
BRAZAS > BRAZA
BRAZE vb join (two metal surfaces) with brass ▷ n high-melting solder or alloy used in brazing
BRAZED > BRAZE
BRAZELESS > BRAZE
BRAZEN adj shameless and bold ▷ vb face and overcome boldly or shamelessly
BRAZENED > BRAZEN
BRAZENING > BRAZEN
BRAZENLY > BRAZEN
BRAZENRY adj audacity
BRAZENS > BRAZEN
BRAZER > BRAZE
BRAZERS > BRAZE
BRAZES > BRAZE
BRAZIER n portable container for burning charcoal or coal
BRAZIERS > BRAZIER
BRAZIERY > BRAZIER
BRAZIL n red wood used for cabinetwork
BRAZILEIN n red crystalline solid
BRAZILIN n pale yellow soluble crystalline solid
BRAZILINS > BRAZILIN
BRAZILS > BRAZIL
BRAZING > BRAZE
BREACH n breaking of a promise, obligation, etc ▷ vb break (a promise, law, etc)
BREACHED > BREACH
BREACHER > BREACH

BREACHERS > BREACH
BREACHES > BREACH
BREACHING > BREACH
BREAD n food made by baking a mixture of flour and water or milk ▷ vb cover (food) with breadcrumbs before cooking
BREADBIN n container for bread
BREADBINS > BREADBIN
BREADBOX n airtight container for bread, cakes, etc
BREADED > BREAD
BREADHEAD n person solely concerned with money
BREADIER > BREADY
BREADIEST > BREADY
BREADING > BREAD
BREADLESS > BREAD
BREADLINE n queue of people waiting for free food given as charity
BREADNUT n type of Central American and Caribbean tree
BREADNUTS > BREADNUT
BREADROOM n place where bread is kept on ship
BREADROOT n central N American leguminous plant with an edible starchy root
BREADS > BREAD
BREADTH n extent of something from side to side
BREADTHS > BREADTH
BREADY adj having the appearance or texture of bread
BREAK > BRACKEN
BREAKABLE adj capable of being broken ▷ n fragile easily broken article
BREAKAGE n act or result of breaking
BREAKAGES > BREAKAGE
BREAKAWAY n (consisting of) a dissenting group who have left a larger unit ▷ adj dissenting ▷ vb leave hastily or escape
BREAKBACK adj backbreaking; arduous
BREAKBEAT n type of electronic dance music
BREAKBONE adj as in breakbone fever dengue
BREAKDOWN n act or instance of breaking down
BREAKER n large wave
BREAKERS > BREAKER
BREAKEVEN n the level of commercial activity at which the total cost and total revenue of a business enterprise are equal
BREAKFAST n first meal of the day ▷ vb eat breakfast

b

BREAKING > BRACKEN

BREAKINGS > BRACKEN

BREAKNECK *adj* fast and dangerous

BREAKOFF *n* act or an instance of breaking off or stopping

BREAKOFFS > BREAKOFF

BREAKOUT *n* escape, esp from prison or confinement

BREAKOUTS > BREAKOUT

BREAKS > BRACKEN

BREAKTIME *n* period of rest or recreation, esp at school

BREAKUP *n* separation or disintegration

BREAKUPS > BREAKUP

BREAKWALL *n* breakwater

BREAM *n* Eurasian freshwater fish ▷ *vb* clean debris (from the bottom of a vessel)

BREAMED > BREAM

BREAMING > BREAM

BREAMS > BREAM

BREARE *same as* > BRIER

BREARES > BREARE

BREASKIT *same as* > BRISKET

BREASKITS > BREASKIT

BREAST *n* either of the milk-secreting glands on a woman's chest ▷ *vb* reach the summit of

BREASTED > BREAST

BREASTFED *adj* fed at mother's breast

BREASTING > BREAST

BREASTPIN *n* brooch worn on the breast, esp to close a garment

BREASTS > BREAST

BREATH *n* taking in and letting out of air during breathing

BREATHE *vb* take in oxygen and give out carbon dioxide

BREATHED *adj* relating to or denoting a speech sound for whose articulation the vocal cords are not made to vibrate

BREATHER *n* short rest

BREATHERS > BREATHER

BREATHES > BREATHE

BREATHFUL > BREATH

BREATHIER > BREATHY

BREATHILY > BREATHY

BREATHING *n* passage of air into and out of the lungs to supply the body with oxygen

BREATHS > BREATH

BREATHY *adj* (of the speaking voice) accompanied by an audible emission of breath

BRECCIA *n* type of rock

BRECCIAL > BRECCIA

BRECCIAS > BRECCIA

BRECCIATE > BRECCIA

BRECHAM *n* straw horse-collar

BRECHAMS > BRECHAM

BRECHAN *same as* > BRECHAM

BRECHANS > BRECHAN

BRED *n* person who lives in a small remote place

BREDE *archaic spelling of* > BRAID

BREDED > BREDE

BREDES > BREDE

BREDIE *n* meat and vegetable stew

BREDIES > BREDIE

BREDING > BREDE

BREDREN *same as* > BRETHREN

BREDRENS > BREDREN

BREDRIN *same as* > BRETHREN

BREDRINS > BREDRIN

BREDS > BRED

BREE *n* broth, stock, or juice

BREECH *n* buttocks ▷ *vb* fit (a gun) with a breech

BREECHED > BREECH

BREECHES *pl n* trousers extending to just below the knee

BREECHING *n* strap of a harness that passes behind a horse's haunches

BREED *vb* produce new or improved strains of (domestic animals or plants) ▷ *n* group of animals etc within a (species) that have certain clearly defined characteristics

BREEDER *n* person who breeds plants or animals

BREEDERS > BREEDER

BREEDING > BREED

BREEDINGS > BREED

BREEDS > BREED

BREEKS *pl n* trousers

BREEM *same as* > BREME

BREENGE *vb* lunge forward ▷ *n* violent movement

BREENGED > BREENGE

BREENGES > BREENGE

BREENGING > BREENGE

BREER *another word for* > BRAIRD

BREERED > BREER

BREERING > BREER

BREERS > BREER

BREES > BREE

BREESE *same as* > BREEZE

BREESES > BREESE

BREEST *same as* > BREAST

BREESTS > BREAST

BREEZE *n* gentle wind ▷ *vb* move quickly or casually

BREEZED > BREEZE

BREEZES > BREEZE

BREEZEWAY *n* roofed passageway connecting

two buildings, sometimes with the sides enclosed

BREEZIER > BREEZY

BREEZIEST > BREEZY

BREEZILY > BREEZY

BREEZING > BREEZE

BREEZY *adj* windy

BREGMA *n* point on the top of the skull

BREGMAS > BREGMA

BREGMATA > BREGMA

BREGMATE > BREGMA

BREGMATIC > BREGMA

BREHON *n* (formerly) judge in Ireland

BREHONS > BREHON

BREI *vb* speak with a uvular r, esp in Afrikaans

BREID *n* bread

BREIDS > BREID

BREIING > BREI

BREINGE *same as* > BREENGE

BREINGED > BREINGE

BREINGES > BREINGE

BREINGING > BREINGE

BREIS > BREI

BREIST *Scot word for* > BREAST

BREISTS > BREIST

BREKKIE *same as* > BREKKY

BREKKIES > BREKKY

BREKKY *slang word for* > BREAKFAST

BRELOQUE *n* charm attached to watch chain

BRELOQUES > BRELOQUE

BREME *adj* well-known

BREN *n* type of machine gun

BRENNE *vb* burn

BRENNES > BRENNE

BRENNING > BREN

BRENS > BREN

BRENT *n* type of goose ▷ *adj* steep

BRENTER > BRENT

BRENTEST > BRENT

BRENTS > BRENT

BRER *n* brother: usually prefixed to a name

BRERE *same as* > BRIER

BRERES > BRERE

BRERS > BRER

BRESAOLA *n* (in Italian cookery) air-dried, salted beef

BRESAOLAS > BRESAOLA

BRETASCHE *another word for* > BRATTICE

BRETESSE *another word for* > BRATTICE

BRETESSES > BRETESSE

BRETHREN > BROTHER

BRETON *n* hat with an upturned brim and a rounded crown

BRETONS > BRETON

BRETTICE *same as* > BRATTICE

BRETTICED > BRETTICE

BRETTICES > BRETTICE

BREVE *n* accent placed over a vowel to indicate shortness

BREVES > BREVE

BREVET *n* document entitling a commissioned officer to hold temporarily a higher military rank ▷ *vb* promote by brevet

BREVETCY > BREVET

BREVETE *adj* patented

BREVETED > BREVET

BREVETING > BREVET

BREVETS > BREVET

BREVETTED > BREVET

BREVIARY *n* book of prayers to be recited daily by a Roman Catholic priest

BREVIATE *n* summary

BREVIATES > BREVIATE

BREVIER *n* (formerly) size of printer's type approximately equal to 8 point

BREVIERS > BREVIER

BREVIS *same as* > BREWIS

BREVISES > BREVIS

BREVITIES > BREVITY

BREVITY *n* shortness

BREW *vb* make (beer etc) by steeping, boiling, and fermentation ▷ *n* beverage produced by brewing

BREWAGE *n* product of brewing

BREWAGES > BREWAGE

BREWED > BREW

BREWER > BREW

BREWERIES > BREWERY

BREWERS > BREW

BREWERY *n* place where beer etc is brewed

BREWHOUSE *n* brewery

BREWING *n* quantity of a beverage brewed at one time

BREWINGS > BREWING

BREWIS *n* bread soaked in broth, gravy, etc

BREWISES > BREWIS

BREWPUB *n* pub that incorporates a brewery on its premises

BREWPUBS > BREWPUB

BREWS > BREW

BREWSKI *n* beer

BREWSKIES > BREWSKI

BREWSKIS > BREWSKI

BREWSTER *n* person, particularly a woman, who brews

BREWSTERS > BREWSTER

BREY *same as* > BREI

BREYED > BREY

BREYING > BREY

BREYS > BREY

BRIAR *n* S European shrub with a hard woody root (briarroot)

BRIARD *n* medium-sized dog

BRIARDS > BRIARD

BRIARED > BRIAR
BRIARIER > BRIARY
BRIARIEST > BRIARY
BRIARROOT n hard woody root of the briar, used for making tobacco pipes
BRIARS > BRIAR
BRIARWOOD same as > BRIARROOT
BRIARY adj resembling or containing briar
BRIBABLE > BRIBE
BRIBE vb offer or give something to someone to gain favour, influence, etc ▷ n something given or offered as a bribe
BRIBEABLE > BRIBE
BRIBED > BRIBE
BRIBEE n one who is bribed
BRIBEES > BRIBE
BRIBER > BRIBE
BRIBERIES > BRIBERY
BRIBERS > BRIBE
BRIBERY n process of giving or taking bribes
BRIBES > BRIBE
BRIBING > BRIBE
BRICABRAC n miscellaneous small objects, esp furniture and curios, kept because they are ornamental or rare
BRICHT Scot word for > BRIGHT
BRICHTER > BRICHT
BRICHTEST > BRICHT
BRICK n (rectangular block of) baked clay used in building ▷ vb build, enclose, or fill with bricks
BRICKBAT n blunt criticism
BRICKBATS > BRICKBAT
BRICKCLAY n clay for making bricks
BRICKED > BRICK
BRICKEN adj made of brick
BRICKIE n bricklayer
BRICKIER > BRICKY
BRICKIES > BRICKIE
BRICKIEST > BRICKY
BRICKING > BRICK
BRICKINGS > BRICK
BRICKKILN n kiln for making bricks
BRICKLE variant of > BRITTLE
BRICKLES > BRICKLE
BRICKLIKE > BRICK
BRICKS > BRICK
BRICKWALL same as > BRICOLE
BRICKWORK n structure, such as a wall, built of bricks
BRICKY same as > BRICKIE
BRICKYARD n place in which bricks are made, stored, or sold

BRICOLAGE n jumbled effect produced by the close proximity of buildings from different periods and in different architectural styles
BRICOLE n billiards shot
BRICOLES > BRICOLE
BRICOLEUR n person who practises bricolage
BRIDAL adj of a bride or a wedding ▷ n wedding or wedding feast
BRIDALLY > BRIDAL
BRIDALS > BRIDAL
BRIDE n woman who has just been or is about to be married
BRIDECAKE n wedding cake
BRIDED > BRIDE
BRIDEMAID n old form of bridesmaid
BRIDEMAN n bridegroom's attendant
BRIDEMEN > BRIDEMAN
BRIDES > BRIDE
BRIDESMAN same as > BRIDEMAN
BRIDESMEN > BRIDESMAN
BRIDEWELL n house of correction
BRIDGABLE > BRIDGE
BRIDGE n structure for crossing a river etc ▷ vb build a bridge over (something)
BRIDGED > BRIDGE
BRIDGES > BRIDGE
BRIDGING n one or more timber struts fixed between floor or roof joists to stiffen the construction and distribute the loads
BRIDGINGS > BRIDGING
BRIDIE n semicircular pie containing meat and onions
BRIDIES > BRIDIE
BRIDING > BRIDE
BRIDLE n headgear for controlling a horse ▷ vb show anger or indignation
BRIDLED > BRIDLE
BRIDLER > BRIDLE
BRIDLERS > BRIDLE
BRIDLES > BRIDLE
BRIDLEWAY n path for riding horses
BRIDLING > BRIDLE
BRIDOON n horse's bit: small snaffle used in double bridles
BRIDOONS > BRIDOON
BRIE same as > BREE
BRIEF adj short in duration ▷ n condensed statement or written synopsis ▷ vb give information and instructions to (a person)

BRIEFCASE n small flat case for carrying papers, books, etc
BRIEFED > BRIEF
BRIEFER > BRIEF
BRIEFERS > BRIEF
BRIEFEST > BRIEF
BRIEFING n meeting at which detailed information or instructions are given, as for military operations, etc
BRIEFINGS > BRIEFING
BRIEFLESS adj (said of a barrister) without clients
BRIEFLY > BRIEF
BRIEFNESS > BRIEF
BRIEFS pl n men's or women's underpants without legs
BRIER same as > BRIAR
BRIERED > BRIER
BRIERIER > BRIER
BRIERIEST > BRIER
BRIERROOT same as > BRIARROOT
BRIERS > BRIER
BRIERWOOD same as > BRIARROOT
BRIERY > BRIER
BRIES > BRIE
BRIG n two-masted square-rigged ship
BRIGADE n army unit smaller than a division ▷ vb organize into a brigade
BRIGADED > BRIGADE
BRIGADES > BRIGADE
BRIGADIER n high-ranking army officer
BRIGADING > BRIGADE
BRIGALOW n type of acacia tree
BRIGALOWS > BRIGALOW
BRIGAND n bandit
BRIGANDRY > BRIGAND
BRIGANDS > BRIGAND
BRIGHT adj emitting or reflecting much light ▷ adv brightly
BRIGHTEN vb make or become bright or brighter
BRIGHTENS > BRIGHTEN
BRIGHTER > BRIGHT
BRIGHTEST > BRIGHT
BRIGHTISH > BRIGHT
BRIGHTLY > BRIGHT
BRIGHTS pl n high beam of the headlights of a motor vehicle
BRIGS > BRIG
BRIGUE vb solicit
BRIGUED > BRIGUE
BRIGUES > BRIGUE
BRIGUING > BRIGUE
BRIGUINGS > BRIGUE
BRIK n Tunisian pastry
BRIKI same as > CEZVE
BRIKIS > BRIKI
BRIKS > BRIK
BRILL n type of European flatfish popular as a food fish

BRILLER > BRILL
BRILLEST > BRILL
BRILLIANT adj shining with light ▷ n popular circular cut for diamonds and other gemstones in the form of two many-faceted pyramids (the top one truncated) joined at their bases
BRILLO n tradename for a type of scouring pad impregnated with a detergent
BRILLOS > BRILLO
BRILLS > BRILL
BRIM n upper rim of a vessel ▷ vb fill or be full to the brim
BRIMFUL adj completely filled with
BRIMFULL same as > BRIMFUL
BRIMFULLY > BRIMFUL
BRIMING n phosphorescence of sea
BRIMINGS > BRIMING
BRIMLESS > BRIM
BRIMMED > BRIM
BRIMMER n vessel, such as a glass or bowl, filled to the brim
BRIMMERS > BRIMMER
BRIMMING > BRIM
BRIMS > BRIM
BRIMSTONE n sulphur
BRIMSTONY > BRIMSTONE
BRIN n thread of silk from silkworm
BRINDED adj streaky or patchy
BRINDISI n song sung in celebration
BRINDISIS > BRINDISI
BRINDLE n brindled animal
BRINDLED adj brown or grey streaked with a darker colour
BRINDLES > BRINDLE
BRINE n salt water ▷ vb soak in or treat with brine
BRINED > BRINE
BRINELESS > BRINE
BRINER > BRINE
BRINERS > BRINE
BRINES > BRINE
BRING vb carry, convey, or take to a designated place or person
BRINGDOWN n comedown
BRINGER > BRING
BRINGERS > BRING
BRINGING > BRING
BRINGINGS > BRING
BRINGS > BRING
BRINIER > BRINY
BRINIES > BRINY
BRINIEST > BRINY
BRININESS > BRINY
BRINING > BRINE
BRINISH > BRINE

BRINJAL n dark purple tropical fruit, cooked and eaten as a vegetable

BRINJALS > BRINJAL

BRINJARRY n grain trader

BRINK n edge of a steep place

BRINKMAN n one who goes in for brinkmanship

BRINKMEN > BRINKMAN

BRINKS > BRINK

BRINNIES > BRINNY

BRINNY n stone, esp when thrown

BRINS > BRIN

BRINY adj very salty

BRIO n liveliness

BRIOCHE n soft roll or loaf made from a very light yeast dough, sometimes mixed with currants

BRIOCHES > BRIOCHE

BRIOLETTE n pear-shaped gem cut with long triangular facets

BRIONIES > BRIONY

BRIONY same as > BRYONY

BRIOS > BRIO

BRIQUET same as > BRIQUETTE

BRIQUETS > BRIQUET

BRIQUETTE n block of compressed coal dust ▷ vb make into the form of a brick or bricks

BRIS n ritual circumcision of male babies

BRISANCE n shattering effect or power of an explosion or explosive

BRISANCES > BRISANCE

BRISANT > BRISANCE

BRISE n type of jump

BRISES > BRIS

BRISK adj lively and quick ▷ vb enliven

BRISKED > BRISK

BRISKEN vb make or become more lively or brisk

BRISKENED > BRISKEN

BRISKENS > BRISKEN

BRISKER > BRISK

BRISKEST > BRISK

BRISKET n beef from the breast of a cow

BRISKETS > BRISKET

BRISKIER same as > BRISKY

BRISKIEST > BRISKY

BRISKING > BRISK

BRISKISH > BRISK

BRISKLY > BRISK

BRISKNESS > BRISK

BRISKS > BRISK

BRISKY another word for > BRISK

BRISLING same as > SPRAT

BRISLINGS > BRISLING

BRISS same as > BRIS

BRISSES > BRIS

BRISTLE n short stiff hair ▷ vb (cause to) stand up like bristles

BRISTLED > BRISTLE

BRISTLES > BRISTLE

BRISTLIER > BRISTLE

BRISTLING > BRISTLE

BRISTLY > BRISTLE

BRISTOL n as in bristol board type of heavy cardboard

BRISTOLS pl n woman's breasts

BRISURE n mark of cadency in heraldry

BRISURES > BRISURE

BRIT n young of a herring, sprat, or similar fish

BRITANNIA n coin bearing figure of Britannia

BRITCHES same as > BREECHES

BRITH same as > BRIS

BRITHS > BRITH

BRITS > BRIT

BRITSCHKA n light open carriage

BRITSKA same as > BRITZKA

BRITSKAS > BRITSKA

BRITT n young herring or sprat

BRITTANIA variant spelling of > BRITANNIA

BRITTLE adj hard but easily broken ▷ n crunchy sweet made with treacle and nuts

BRITTLED > BRITTLE

BRITTLELY > BRITTLE

BRITTLER > BRITTLE

BRITTLES > BRITTLE

BRITTLEST > BRITTLE

BRITTLING > BRITTLE

BRITTLY > BRITTLE

BRITTS > BRITT

BRITZKA n long horse-drawn carriage

BRITZKAS > BRITZKA

BRITZSKA same as > BRITZKA

BRITZSKAS > BRITZSKAS

BRIZE same as > BREEZE

BRIZES > BRIZE

BRO n family member

BROACH vb introduce (a topic) for discussion ▷ n spit for roasting meat

BROACHED > BROACH

BROACHER > BROACH

BROACHERS > BROACH

BROACHES > BROACH

BROACHING > BROACH

BROAD adj having great breadth or width ▷ n woman

BROADAX same as > BROADAXE

BROADAXE n broad-bladed axe

BROADAXES > BROADAXE

BROADBAND n telecommunication transmission technique using a wide range of frequencies

BROADBEAN n variety of bean

BROADBILL n tropical African and Asian bird with bright plumage and a short wide bill

BROADBRIM n broad-brimmed hat, esp one worn by the Quakers in the 17th century

BROADCAST n programme or announcement on radio or television ▷ vb transmit (a programme or announcement) on radio or television ▷ adj dispersed over a wide area ▷ adv far and wide

BROADEN vb make or become broad or broader

BROADENED > BROADEN

BROADENER > BROADEN

BROADENS > BROADEN

BROADER > BROAD

BROADEST > BROAD

BROADISH > BROAD

BROADLEAF n any tobacco plant having broad leaves, used esp in making cigars

BROADLINE n company dealing in large volumes of cheap products

BROADLOOM adj of or designating carpets woven on a wide loom ▷ n of or designating carpets or carpeting woven on a wide loom to obviate the need for seams

BROADLY > BROAD

BROADNESS > BROAD

BROADS > BROAD

BROADSIDE n strong verbal or written attack ▷ adv with a broader side facing an object

BROADTAIL n highly valued black wavy fur obtained from the skins of newly born karakul lambs

BROADWAY n wide road

BROADWAYS > BROADWAY

BROADWISE adv rare form of breadthwise

BROAST vb cook by broiling and roasting

BROASTED > BROAST

BROASTING > BROAST

BROASTS > BROAST

BROCADE n rich fabric woven with a raised design ▷ vb weave with such a design

BROCADED > BROCADE

BROCADES > BROCADE

BROCADING > BROCADE

BROCAGE another word for > BROKERAGE

BROCAGES > BROCAGE

BROCARD n basic principle of civil law

BROCARDS > BROCARD

BROCATEL n heavy upholstery brocade

BROCATELS > BROCATEL

BROCCOLI n type of cabbage with greenish flower heads

BROCCOLIS > BROCCOLI

BROCH n (in Scotland) a circular dry-stone tower large enough to serve as a fortified home

BROCHAN n type of thin porridge

BROCHANS > BROCHAN

BROCHE adj woven with a raised design, as brocade

BROCHED > BROCHE

BROCHES > BROCHE

BROCHETTE n skewer used for holding pieces of meat or vegetables while grilling

BROCHING > BROCHE

BROCHO same as > BRACHAH

BROCHOS > BROCHO

BROCHS > BROCH

BROCHURE n booklet that contains information about a product or service

BROCHURES > BROCHURE

BROCK n badger

BROCKAGE same as > BROKERAGE

BROCKAGES > BROCKAGE

BROCKED adj having different colours

BROCKET n small tropical American deer with small unbranched antlers

BROCKETS > BROCKET

BROCKIT same as > BROCKED

BROCKRAM another word for > BRECCIA

BROCKRAMS > BROCKRAM

BROCKS > BROCK

BROCOLI same as > BROCCOLI

BROCOLIS > BROCOLI

BROD vb prod

BRODDED > BROD

BRODDING > BROD

BRODDLE vb poke or pierce (something)

BRODDLED > BRODDLE

BRODDLES > BRODDLE

BRODDLING > BRODDLE

BRODEKIN another word for > BUSKIN

BRODEKINS > BRODEKIN

BRODKIN same as > BRODEKIN

BRODKINS > BRODKIN

BRODS > BROD

BROEKIES pl n underpants

BROG vb prick with an awl

BROGAN n heavy laced, usually ankle-high, work boot

BROGANS > BROGAN
BROGGED > BROG
BROGGING > BROG
BROGH same as > BROCH
BROGHS > BROGH
BROGS > BROG
BROGUE n sturdy walking shoe
BROGUEISH > BROGUE
BROGUERY > BROGUE
BROGUES > BROGUE
BROGUISH > BROGUE
BROIDER archaic word for > EMBROIDER
BROIDERED > BROIDER
BROIDERER > BROIDER
BROIDERS > BROIDER
BROIDERY n old form of embroidery
BROIL vb cook by direct heat under a grill ▷ n process of broiling
BROILED > BROIL
BROILER n young tender chicken for roasting
BROILERS > BROILER
BROILING > BROIL
BROILS > BROIL
BROKAGE another word for > BROKERAGE
BROKAGES > BROKAGE
BROKE vb negotiate or deal
BROKED > BROKE
BROKEN > BRACKEN
BROKENLY > BRACKEN
BROKER n agent who buys or sells goods, securities, etc ▷ vb act as a broker (in)
BROKERAGE n commission charged by a broker
BROKERED > BROKER
BROKERIES > BROKERY
BROKERING > BROKER
BROKERS > BROKER
BROKERY n work done by a broker
BROKES > BROKE
BROKING > BROKE
BROKINGS > BROKE
BROLGA n large grey Australian crane with a trumpeting call
BROLGAS > BROLGA
BROLLIES > BROLLY
BROLLY n umbrella
BROMAL n synthetic liquid formerly used medicinally
BROMALS > BROMAL
BROMANCE n close but non-sexual relationship between two men
BROMANCES > BROMANCE
BROMANTIC adj pertaining to or indicating a bromance
BROMATE same as > BROMINATE
BROMATED > BROMATE
BROMATES > BROMATE
BROMATING > BROMATE
BROME n type of grass

BROMELAIN n enzyme in pineapples
BROMELIA n type of plant
BROMELIAD n tropical American plant with a rosette of fleshy leaves
BROMELIAS > BROMELIA
BROMELIN n protein-digesting enzyme found in pineapple and extracted for use in treating joint pain and inflammation, hay fever, and various other conditions
BROMELINS > BROMELIN
BROMEOSIN another name for > EOSIN
BROMES > BROME
BROMIC adj of or containing bromine in the trivalent or pentavalent state
BROMID same as > BROMIDE
BROMIDE n chemical compound used in medicine and photography
BROMIDES > BROMIDE
BROMIDIC adj ordinary
BROMIDS > BROMID
BROMIN same as > BROMINE
BROMINATE vb treat or react with bromine
BROMINE n dark red liquid element that gives off a pungent vapour
BROMINES > BROMINE
BROMINISM same as > BROMISM
BROMINS > BROMIN
BROMISE same as > BROMIZE
BROMISED > BROMIZE
BROMISES > BROMIZE
BROMISING > BROMIZE
BROMISM n bromine poisoning
BROMISMS > BROMISM
BROMIZE vb treat with bromine
BROMIZED > BROMIZE
BROMIZES > BROMIZE
BROMIZING > BROMIZE
BROMMER n S African word for bluebottle
BROMMERS > BROMMER
BROMO n something that contains bromide
BROMOFORM n heavy colourless liquid substance with a sweetish taste
BROMOS > BROMO
BRONC same as > BRONCO
BRONCHI > BRONCHUS
BRONCHIA pl n bronchial tubes
BRONCHIAL adj of the bronchi
BRONCHIUM n medium-sized bronchial tube

BRONCHO same as > BRONCO
BRONCHOS > BRONCHO
BRONCHUS n either of the two branches of the windpipe
BRONCO n (in the US) wild or partially tamed pony
BRONCOS > BRONCO
BRONCS > BRONC
BROND n old form of brand
BRONDS > BROND
BRONDYRON n sword
BRONZE n alloy of copper and tin ▷ adj made of, or coloured like, bronze ▷ vb (esp of the skin) make or become brown
BRONZED > BRONZE
BRONZEN adj made of or the colour of bronze
BRONZER n cosmetic applied to the skin to simulate a sun tan
BRONZERS > BRONZER
BRONZES > BRONZE
BRONZIER > BRONZE
BRONZIEST > BRONZE
BRONZIFY vb cause to become colour of bronze
BRONZING n blue pigment producing a metallic lustre when ground into paint media at fairly high concentrations
BRONZINGS > BRONZING
BRONZITE n type of orthopyroxene often having a metallic or pearly sheen
BRONZITES > BRONZITE
BRONZY > BRONZE
BROO n brow of hill
BROOCH n ornament with a pin, worn fastened to clothes ▷ vb decorate with a brooch
BROOCHED > BROOCH
BROOCHES > BROOCH
BROOCHING > BROOCH
BROOD n number of birds produced at one hatching ▷ vb (of a bird) sit on or hatch eggs
BROODED > BROOD
BROODER n structure used for rearing young chickens or other fowl
BROODERS > BROODER
BROODIER > BROODY
BROODIEST > BROODY
BROODILY > BROODY
BROODING > BROOD
BROODINGS > BROOD
BROODLESS > BROOD
BROODMARE n mare for breeding
BROODS > BROOD
BROODY adj moody and sullen
BROOK n small stream ▷ vb bear or tolerate
BROOKABLE > BROOK
BROOKED > BROOK

BROOKIE n brook trout
BROOKIES > BROOKIE
BROOKING > BROOK
BROOKITE n reddish-brown to black mineral
BROOKITES > BROOKITE
BROOKLET n small brook
BROOKLETS > BROOKLET
BROOKLIKE > BROOK
BROOKLIME n type of blue-flowered trailing plant of N America, Europe or Asia, which grows in moist places
BROOKS > BROOK
BROOKWEED n type of white-flowered plant of Europe or North America, growing in moist places
BROOL n low roar
BROOLS > BROOL
BROOM n long-handled sweeping brush ▷ vb sweep with a broom
BROOMBALL n type of ice hockey played with broom
BROOMCORN n variety of sorghum, the long stiff flower stalks of which can be used to make brooms
BROOMED > BROOM
BROOMIER > BROOMY
BROOMIEST > BROOMY
BROOMING > BROOM
BROOMRAPE n type of plant which grows as brownish small-flowered leafless parasites on the roots of other plants
BROOMS > BROOM
BROOMY adj covered with growth of broom
BROOS > BROO
BROOSE n race at country wedding
BROOSES > BROOSE
BROS > BRO
BROSE n oatmeal or pease porridge, sometimes with butter or fat added
BROSES > BROSE
BROSIER > BROSY
BROSIEST > BROSY
BROSY adj smeared with porridge
BROTH n soup, usu containing vegetables
BROTHA n informal term for an African-American man
BROTHAS > BROTHA
BROTHEL n house where men pay to have sex with prostitutes
BROTHELS > BROTHEL
BROTHER n boy or man with the same parents as another person ▷ interj exclamation of amazement, disgust, surprise, disappointment, etc ▷ vb treat someone like a brother
BROTHERED > BROTHER

b

b

BROTHERLY *adj* of or like a brother, esp in showing loyalty and affection ▷ *adv* in a brotherly way

BROTHERS > BROTHER

BROTHIER > BROTHY

BROTHIEST > BROTHY

BROTHS > BROTH

BROTHY *adj* having appearance or texture of broth

BROUGH *same as* > BROCH

BROUGHAM *n* horse-drawn closed carriage with a raised open driver's seat in front

BROUGHAMS > BROUGHAM

BROUGHS > BROUGH

BROUGHT > BRING

BROUGHTA *same as* > BRAATA

BROUGHTAS *same as* > BRAATA

BROUHAHA *n* loud confused noise

BROUHAHAS > BROUHAHA

BROUZE *same as* > BROOSE

BROUZES > BROUZE

BROW *n* part of the face (from the eyes to the hairline)

BROWALLIA *n* flowering plant

BROWBAND *n* strap of a horse's bridle that goes across the forehead

BROWBANDS > BROWBAND

BROWBEAT *vb* frighten (someone) with threats

BROWBEATS > BROWBEAT

BROWBONE *n* bone of the brow

BROWBONES > BROWBONE

BROWED *adj* having a brow

BROWLESS > BROW

BROWN *n* colour of earth or wood ▷ *adj* (of bread) made from wheatmeal or wholemeal flour ▷ *vb* make or become brown

BROWNED > BROWN

BROWNER *n* brown object

BROWNERS > BROWNER

BROWNEST > BROWN

BROWNIE *n* small square nutty chocolate cake

BROWNIER > BROWN

BROWNIES > BROWNIE

BROWNIEST > BROWN

BROWNING *n* substance used to darken gravies

BROWNINGS > BROWNING

BROWNISH > BROWN

BROWNNESS > BROWN

BROWNNOSE *vb* be abjectly subservient

BROWNOUT *n* dimming or reduction in the use of electric lights in a city, esp to conserve electric power or as a defensive precaution in wartime

BROWNOUTS > BROWNOUT

BROWNS > BROWN

BROWNTAIL *adj* as in *browntail moth* kind of moth

BROWNY > BROWN

BROWRIDGE *n* ridge of bone over eyes

BROWS > BROW

BROWSABLE > BROWSE

BROWSE *vb* look through in a casual manner ▷ *n* instance of browsing

BROWSED > BROWSE

BROWSER *n* software package that enables a user to read hypertext, esp on the Internet

BROWSERS > BROWSER

BROWSES > BROWSE

BROWSIER > BROWSE

BROWSIEST > BROWSE

BROWSING > BROWSE

BROWSINGS > BROWSE

BROWST *n* brewing (of ale, tea)

BROWSTS > BROWST

BROWSY > BROWSE

BRR *same as* > BRRR

BRRR *interj* used to suggest shivering

BRU South African word for > FRIEND

BRUCELLA *n* type of bacterium

BRUCELLAE > BRUCELLA

BRUCELLAS > BRUCELLA

BRUCHID *n* type of beetle

BRUCHIDS > BRUCHID

BRUCIN *same as* > BRUCINE

BRUCINE *n* bitter poisonous alkaloid resembling strychnine

BRUCINES > BRUCINE

BRUCINS > BRUCIN

BRUCITE *n* white translucent mineral

BRUCITES > BRUCITE

BRUCKLE *adj* brittle

BRUGH *n* large house

BRUGHS > BRUGH

BRUHAHA *same as* > BROUHAHA

BRUHAHAS > BRUHAHA

BRUILZIE *same as* > BRULZIE

BRUILZIES > BRUILZIE

BRUIN *n* name for a bear, used in children's tales, fables, etc

BRUINS > BRUIN

BRUISE *n* discoloured area on the skin caused by an injury ▷ *vb* cause a bruise on

BRUISED > BRUISE

BRUISER *n* strong tough person

BRUISERS > BRUISER

BRUISES > BRUISE

BRUISING *adj* causing bruises, as by a blow ▷ *n* bruise or bruises

BRUISINGS > BRUISING

BRUIT *vb* report ▷ *n* abnormal sound heard within the body

BRUITED > BRUIT

BRUITER > BRUIT

BRUITERS > BRUIT

BRUITING > BRUIT

BRUITS > BRUIT

BRULE *n* shortened form of the archaic word for a mixed-race person of Canadian Indian and White (usually French-Canadian) ancestry

BRULES > BRULE

BRULOT *n* coffee-based alcoholic drink, served flaming

BRULOTS > BRULOT

BRULYIE *same as* > BRULYIE

BRULYIES > BRULYIE

BRULZIE *n* noisy dispute

BRULZIES > BRULZIE

BRUMAL *adj* of, characteristic of, or relating to winter

BRUMBIES > BRUMBY

BRUMBY *n* wild horse

BRUME *n* heavy mist or fog

BRUMES > BRUME

BRUMMAGEM *n* something that is cheap and flashy, esp imitation jewellery

BRUMMER *same as* > BROMMER

BRUMMERS > BRUMMER

BRUMOUS > BRUME

BRUNCH *n* breakfast and lunch combined ▷ *vb* eat brunch

BRUNCHED > BRUNCH

BRUNCHER > BRUNCH

BRUNCHERS > BRUNCH

BRUNCHES > BRUNCH

BRUNCHING > BRUNCH

BRUNET *adj* dark brown

BRUNETS > BRUNET

BRUNETTE *n* girl or woman with dark brown hair ▷ *adj* dark brown

BRUNETTES > BRUNETTE

BRUNG > BRING

BRUNIZEM *n* prairie soil

BRUNIZEMS > BRUNIZEM

BRUNT *n* main force or shock of a blow, attack, etc ▷ *vb* suffer the main force or shock of a blow, attack, etc

BRUNTED > BRUNT

BRUNTING > BRUNT

BRUNTS > BRUNT

BRUS > BRU

BRUSH *n* device made of bristles, wires, etc ▷ *vb* clean, scrub, or paint with a brush

BRUSHBACK *n* (baseball) ball intended to hit the batter

BRUSHED *adj* treated with a brushing process

BRUSHER > BRUSH

BRUSHERS > BRUSH

BRUSHES > BRUSH

BRUSHFIRE *n* fire in bushes and scrub

BRUSHIER > BRUSHY

BRUSHIEST > BRUSHY

BRUSHING > BRUSH

BRUSHINGS > BRUSH

BRUSHLAND *n* land characterized by patchy shrubs

BRUSHLESS > BRUSH

BRUSHLIKE > BRUSH

BRUSHMARK *n* indented lines sometimes left by the bristles of a brush on a painted surface

BRUSHOFF *n* abrupt dismissal or rejection

BRUSHOFFS > BRUSHOFF

BRUSHUP *n* the act or an instance of tidying one's appearance

BRUSHUPS > BRUSHUP

BRUSHWOOD *n* cut or broken-off tree branches and twigs

BRUSHWORK *n* characteristic manner of applying paint with a brush

BRUSHY *adj* like a brush

BRUSK *same as* > BRUSQUE

BRUSKER > BRUSK

BRUSKEST > BRUSK

BRUSQUE *adj* blunt or curt in manner or speech

BRUSQUELY > BRUSQUE

BRUSQUER > BRUSQUE

BRUSQUEST > BRUSQUE

BRUSSELS *adj* as in *brussels sprout* small cabbage-like vegetable

BRUSSEN *adj* bold

BRUST *same as* > BURST

BRUSTING > BRUST

BRUSTS > BRUST

BRUT *adj* (of champagne or sparkling wine) very dry ▷ *n* very dry champagne

BRUTAL *adj* cruel and vicious

BRUTALISE *same as* > BRUTALIZE

BRUTALISM *n* austere architectural style of the 1950s on, characterized by the use of exposed concrete and angular shapes

BRUTALIST > BRUTALISM

BRUTALITY > BRUTAL

BRUTALIZE *vb* make or become brutal

BRUTALLY > BRUTAL

BRUTE *n* brutal person ▷ *adj* wholly instinctive or physical, like an animal

BRUTED > BRUTE

BRUTELIKE > BRUTE

BRUTELY > BRUTE

BRUTENESS > BRUTE

BRUTER n diamond cutter
BRUTERS > BRUTER
BRUTES > BRUTE
BRUTEST > BRUTE
BRUTIFIED > BRUTIFY
BRUTIFIES > BRUTIFY
BRUTIFY less common word for > BRUTALIZE
BRUTING n diamond cutting
BRUTINGS > BRUTING
BRUTISH adj of or like an animal
BRUTISHLY > BRUTISH
BRUTISM n stupidity; vulgarity
BRUTISMS > BRUTISM
BRUTS > BRUT
BRUX vb grind one's teeth
BRUXED > BRUX
BRUXES > BRUX
BRUXING > BRUX
BRUXISM n habit of grinding the teeth, esp unconsciously
BRUXISMS > BRUXISM
BRYOLOGY n branch of botany concerned with the study of bryophytes
BRYONIES > BRYONY
BRYONY n wild climbing hedge plant
BRYOPHYTE n type of plant such as mosses, liverworts, or hornworts, which has stems and leaves but lacks roots and reproduces by spores
BRYOZOAN n type of aquatic invertebrate which forms colonies of polyps
BRYOZOANS > BRYOZOAN
BUAT same as > BOWAT
BUATS > BUAT
BUAZE n fibrous African plant
BUAZES > BUAZE
BUB n youngster
BUBA another name for > YAWS
BUBAL n any of various antelopes
BUBALE n large antelope
BUBALES > BUBALE
BUBALINE adj (of antelopes) related to or resembling the bubal
BUBALIS same as > BUBAL
BUBALISES > BUBALIS
BUBALS > BUBAL
BUBAS > BUBA
BUBBA n ordinary American person
BUBBAS > BUBBA
BUBBE n Yiddish word for grandmother
BUBBES > BUBBE
BUBBIE same as > BUBBE
BUBBIES > BUBBY
BUBBLE n ball of air in a liquid or solid ▷ vb form bubbles
BUBBLED > BUBBLE

BUBBLEGUM n type of chewing gum that can be blown into large bubbles
BUBBLER n drinking fountain
BUBBLERS > BUBBLER
BUBBLES > BUBBLE
BUBBLIER > BUBBLY
BUBBLIES > BUBBLY
BUBBLIEST > BUBBLY
BUBBLING > BUBBLE
BUBBLY adj excited and lively ▷ n champagne
BUBBY n old word for woman's breast
BUBINGA n reddish-brown wood from African tree
BUBINGAS > BUBINGA
BUBKES n very small amount
BUBKIS n nothing
BUBO n inflammation and swelling of a lymph node, esp in the armpit or groin
BUBOED > BUBO
BUBOES > BUBO
BUBONIC > BUBO
BUBS > BUB
BUBU same as > BOUBOU
BUBUKLE n red spot on skin
BUBUKLES > BUBUKLE
BUBUS > BUBU
BUCARDO n type of Spanish mountain goat, recently extinct
BUCARDOS > BUCARDO
BUCATINI pl n pasta in the shape of long tubes
BUCCAL adj of or relating to the cheek
BUCCALLY > BUCCAL
BUCCANEER n pirate ▷ vb be or act like a buccaneer
BUCCANIER same as > BUCCANEER
BUCCINA n curved Roman horn
BUCCINAS > BUCCINA
BUCELLAS n type of Portuguese white wine
BUCENTAUR n state barge of Venice from which the doge and other officials dropped a ring into the sea on Ascension Day to symbolize the ceremonial marriage of the state with the Adriatic
BUCHU n S African shrub whose leaves are used as an antiseptic and diuretic
BUCHUS > BUCHU
BUCK n male of the goat, hare, kangaroo, rabbit, and reindeer ▷ vb (of a horse etc) jump with legs stiff and back arched
BUCKAROO n cowboy
BUCKAROOS > BUCKAROO
BUCKAYRO same as > BUCKAROO
BUCKAYROS > BUCKAYRO

BUCKBEAN n type of marsh plant with white or pink flowers
BUCKBEANS > BUCKBEAN
BUCKBOARD n open four-wheeled horse-drawn carriage with the seat attached to a flexible board between the front and rear axles
BUCKBRUSH n American shrub
BUCKED > BUCK
BUCKEEN n (in Ireland) poor young man who aspires to the habits and dress of the wealthy
BUCKEENS > BUCKEEN
BUCKER > BUCK
BUCKEROO same as > BUCKAROO
BUCKEROOS > BUCKEROO
BUCKERS > BUCK
BUCKET vb open-topped roughly cylindrical container ▷ vb rain heavily
BUCKETED > BUCKET
BUCKETFUL same as > BUCKET
BUCKETING > BUCKET
BUCKETS > BUCKET
BUCKEYE n N American tree with erect clusters of white or red flowers and prickly fruits
BUCKEYES > BUCKEYE
BUCKHORN n horn from a buck, used for knife handles, etc
BUCKHORNS > BUCKHORN
BUCKHOUND n hound, smaller than a staghound, used for hunting the smaller breeds of deer, esp fallow deer
BUCKIE n whelk or its shell
BUCKIES > BUCKIE
BUCKING > BUCK
BUCKINGS > BUCK
BUCKISH > BUCK
BUCKISHLY > BUCK
BUCKLE n clasp for fastening a belt or strap ▷ vb fasten or be fastened with a buckle
BUCKLED > BUCKLE
BUCKLER n small round shield worn on the forearm ▷ vb defend
BUCKLERED > BUCKLER
BUCKLERS > BUCKLER
BUCKLES > BUCKLE
BUCKLING another name for > BLOATER
BUCKLINGS > BUCKLING
BUCKO n lively young fellow: often a term of address
BUCKOES > BUCKO
BUCKOS > BUCKO
BUCKRA n (used contemptuously by Black people, esp in the US) White man

BUCKRAKE n large rake attached to tractor
BUCKRAKES > BUCKRAKE
BUCKRAM n cotton or linen cloth stiffened with size, etc ▷ vb stiffen with buckram
BUCKRAMED > BUCKRAM
BUCKRAMS > BUCKRAM
BUCKRAS > BUCKRA
BUCKS > BUCK
BUCKSAW n woodcutting saw
BUCKSAWS > BUCKSAW
BUCKSHEE adj free
BUCKSHEES > BUCKSHEE
BUCKSHISH n tip, present or gift
BUCKSHOT n large lead pellets used for shooting game
BUCKSHOTS > BUCKSHOT
BUCKSKIN n skin of a male deer ▷ adj greyish-yellow
BUCKSKINS pl n (in the US and Canada) breeches, shoes, or a suit of buckskin
BUCKSOM same as > BUXOM
BUCKTAIL n in fishing, fly with appearance of minnow
BUCKTAILS > BUCKTAIL
BUCKTEETH > BUCKTOOTH
BUCKTHORN n thorny shrub whose berries were formerly used as a purgative
BUCKTOOTH n projecting upper front tooth
BUCKU same as > BUCHU
BUCKUS > BUCKU
BUCKWHEAT n small black grain used for making flour
BUCKYBALL n ball-like polyhedral carbon molecule of the type found in buckminsterfullerene and other fullerenes
BUCKYTUBE n tube of carbon atoms structurally similar to buckminsterfullerene
BUCOLIC adj of the countryside or country life ▷ n pastoral poem
BUCOLICAL > BUCOLIC
BUCOLICS > BUCOLIC
BUD n swelling on a plant that develops into a leaf or flower ▷ vb produce buds
BUDA n derogatory Indian English word for an old man
BUDAS > BUDA
BUDDED > BUD
BUDDER > BUD
BUDDERS > BUD
BUDDHA n person who has achieved a state of perfect enlightenment
BUDDHAS > BUDDHA
BUDDIED > BUDDY

BUDDIER > BUDDY
BUDDIES > BUDDY
BUDDIEST > BUDDY
BUDDING > BUDDY
BUDDINGS > BUDDY
BUDDLE *n* sloping trough in which ore is washed ▷ *vb* wash (ore) in a buddle
BUDDLED > BUDDLE
BUDDLEIA *n* shrub with long spikes of purple flowers
BUDDLEIAS > BUDDLEIA
BUDDLES > BUDDLE
BUDDLING > BUDDLE
BUDDY *n* friend ▷ *vb* act as a friend to ▷ *adj* friendly
BUDDYING > BUDDY
BUDGE *vb* move slightly ▷ *n* lambskin dressed for the fur to be worn on the outer side
BUDGED > BUDGE
BUDGER > BUDGE
BUDGEREE *adj* good
BUDGERO *same as* **>** BUDGEROW
BUDGEROS > BUDGERO
BUDGEROW *n* barge use on Ganges
BUDGEROWS > BUDGEROW
BUDGERS > BUDGE
BUDGES > BUDGE
BUDGET *n* financial plan for a period of time ▷ *vb* plan the expenditure of (money or time) ▷ *adj* cheap
BUDGETARY > BUDGET
BUDGETED > BUDGET
BUDGETEER *n* one who prepares a budget
BUDGETER > BUDGET
BUDGETERS > BUDGET
BUDGETING *n* act of budgeting
BUDGETS > BUDGET
BUDGIE *n* short form of budgerigar
BUDGIES > BUDGIE
BUDGING > BUDGE
BUDI *n* derogatory Indian English word an for old woman
BUDIS > BUDI
BUDLESS > BUD
BUDLIKE > BUD
BUDMASH *same as* **>** BADMASH
BUDMASHES > BUDMASH
BUDO *n* combat and spirit in martial arts
BUDOS > BUDO
BUDS > BUD
BUDWOOD *n* branch with buds that is used for grafting
BUDWOODS > BUDWOOD
BUDWORM *n* pest that eats tree leaves and buds
BUDWORMS > BUDWORM
BUFF *n* soft flexible undyed leather ▷ *adj* dull

yellowish-brown ▷ *vb* clean or polish with soft material
BUFFA > BUFFO
BUFFABLE > BUFF
BUFFALO *n* member of the cattle tribe ▷ *vb* confuse
BUFFALOED > BUFFALO
BUFFALOES > BUFFALO
BUFFALOS > BUFFALO
BUFFE > BUFFO
BUFFED > BUFF
BUFFEL *adj* as in *buffel grass* grass used for pasture in Africa, India, and Australia
BUFFER *same as* **>** BUFF
BUFFERED > BUFFER
BUFFERING *n* act of buffering
BUFFERS > BUFFER
BUFFEST > BUFF
BUFFET *n* counter where drinks and snacks are served ▷ *vb* knock against or about
BUFFETED > BUFFET
BUFFETER > BUFFET
BUFFETERS > BUFFET
BUFFETING *n* response of an aircraft structure to buffet, esp an irregular oscillation of the tail
BUFFETS > BUFFET
BUFFI > BUFFO
BUFFIER > BUFFY
BUFFIEST > BUFFY
BUFFING > BUFF
BUFFINGS > BUFFING
BUFFO *n* (in Italian opera of the 18th century) comic part, esp one for a bass
BUFFOON *n* clown or fool
BUFFOONS > BUFFOON
BUFFOS > BUFFO
BUFFS > BUFF
BUFFY *adj* having appearance or texture of buff
BUFO *n* type of toad
BUFOS > BUFO
BUFOTALIN *n* principal poisonous substance in the skin and saliva of the common European toad
BUFTIE *n* homosexual man
BUFTIES > BUFTIE
BUFTY *same as* **>** BUFTIE
BUG *n* insect ▷ *vb* irritate
BUGABOO *n* imaginary source of fear
BUGABOOS > BUGABOO
BUGBANE *n* European plant whose flowers are reputed to repel insects
BUGBANES > BUGBANE
BUGBEAR *n* thing that causes obsessive anxiety
BUGBEARS > BUGBEAR
BUGEYE *n* oyster-dredging boat
BUGEYES > BUGEYE

BUGGAN *n* evil spirit
BUGGANE *same as* **>** BUGGAN
BUGGANES > BUGGANE
BUGGANS > BUGGAN
BUGGED > BUG
BUGGER *n* unpleasant or difficult person or thing ▷ *vb* tire ▷ *interj* exclamation of annoyance or disappointment
BUGGERED > BUGGER
BUGGERIES > BUGGERY
BUGGERING > BUGGER
BUGGERS > BUGGER
BUGGERY *n* anal intercourse
BUGGIER > BUGGY
BUGGIES > BUGGY
BUGGIEST > BUGGY
BUGGIN *same as* **>** BUGGAN
BUGGINESS > BUGGY
BUGGING > BUG
BUGGINGS > BUG
BUGGINS > BUGGIN
BUGGY *n* light horse-drawn carriage ▷ *adj* infested with bugs
BUGHOUSE *n* offensive name for a mental hospital or asylum ▷ *adj* offensive word for insane
BUGHOUSES > BUGHOUSE
BUGLE *n* instrument like a small trumpet ▷ *vb* play or sound (on) a bugle
BUGLED > BUGLE
BUGLER > BUGLE
BUGLERS > BUGLE
BUGLES > BUGLE
BUGLET *n* small bugle
BUGLETS > BUGLET
BUGLEWEED *same as* **>** BUGLE
BUGLING > BUGLE
BUGLOSS *n* hairy Eurasian plant with clusters of blue flowers
BUGLOSSES > BUGLOSS
BUGONG *same as* **>** BOGONG
BUGONGS > BUGONG
BUGOUT *n* act of running away
BUGOUTS > BUGOUT
BUGS > BUG
BUGSEED *n* form of tumbleweed
BUGSEEDS > BUGSEED
BUGSHA *same as* **>** BUQSHA
BUGSHAS > BUGSHA
BUGWORT *another name for* **>** BUGBANE
BUGWORTS > BUGWORT
BUHL *same as* **>** BOULLE
BUHLS > BUHL
BUHLWORK *n* woodwork with decorative inlay
BUHLWORKS > BUHLWORK
BUHR *same as* **>** BURR
BUHRS > BURR
BUHRSTONE *n* hard tough rock containing silica, fossils, and cavities,

formerly used as a grindstone
BUHUND *n* type of Norwegian dog
BUHUNDS > BUHUND
BUIBUI *n* black cloth worn as a shawl by Muslim women
BUIBUIS > BUIBUI
BUIK *same as* **>** BOOK
BUIKS > BUIK
BUILD *vb* make, construct, or form by joining parts or materials ▷ *n* shape of the body
BUILDABLE *adj* suitable for building on
BUILDDOWN *n* planned reduction
BUILDED > BUILD
BUILDER *n* person who constructs houses and other buildings
BUILDERS > BUILDER
BUILDING > BUILD
BUILDINGS > BUILD
BUILDOUT *n* expansion, development, or growth
BUILDOUTS > BUILDOUT
BUILDS > BUILD
BUILDUP *n* gradual approach to a climax or critical point
BUILDUPS > BUILDUP
BUILT > BUILD
BUIRDLIER > BUIRDLY
BUIRDLY *adj* well-built
BUIST *vb* brand sheep with identification mark
BUISTED > BUIST
BUISTING > BUIST
BUISTS > BUIST
BUKE *same as* **>** BOOK
BUKES > BUKE
BUKKAKE *n* type of sexual practice
BUKKAKES > BUKKAKE
BUKSHEE *n* person in charge of paying wages
BUKSHEES > BUKSHEE
BUKSHI *same as* **>** BUKSHEE
BUKSHIS > BUKSHI
BULB *n* onion-shaped root which grows into a flower or plant ▷ *vb* form into the shape of a bulb
BULBAR *adj* of or relating to a bulb, esp the medulla oblongata
BULBED > BULB
BULBEL *same as* **>** BULBIL
BULBELS > BULBEL
BULBIL *n* small bulblike organ growing on plants such as the onion and tiger lily
BULBILS > BULBIL
BULBING > BULB
BULBLET *n* small bulb at base of main bulb
BULBLETS > BULBLET
BULBOSITY > BULBOUS

BULBOUS adj round and fat
BULBOUSLY > BULBOUS
BULBS > BULB
BULBUL n songbird of tropical Africa and Asia
BULBULS > BULBUL
BULGAR same as > BULGUR
BULGARS > BULGAR
BULGE n swelling on a normally flat surface ▷ vb swell outwards
BULGED > BULGE
BULGER > BULGE
BULGERS > BULGE
BULGES > BULGE
BULGHUR same as > BULGUR
BULGHURS > BULGHUR
BULGIER > BULGE
BULGIEST > BULGE
BULGINE same as > BULLGINE
BULGINES > BULGINE
BULGINESS > BULGE
BULGING > BULGE
BULGINGLY > BULGE
BULGUR n kind of dried cracked wheat
BULGURS > BULGUR
BULGY > BULGE
BULIMIA n eating disorder
BULIMIAC > BULIMIA
BULIMIAS > BULIMIA
BULIMIC > BULIMIA
BULIMICS > BULIMIA
BULIMIES > BULIMIA
BULIMUS > BULIMIA
BULIMUSES > BULIMIA
BULIMY same as > BULIMIA
BULK n volume, size, or magnitude of something ▷ vb cohere or cause to cohere in a mass
BULKAGE > BULK
BULKAGES > BULK
BULKED > BULK
BULKER n ship that carries bulk cargo
BULKERS > BULKER
BULKHEAD n partition in a ship or aeroplane
BULKHEADS > BULKHEAD
BULKIER > BULKY
BULKIEST > BULKY
BULKILY > BULKY
BULKINESS > BULKY
BULKING n expansion of excavated material to a volume greater than that of the excavation from which it came
BULKINGS > BULKING
BULKS > BULK
BULKY adj very large and massive, esp so as to be unwieldy
BULL n any male bovine animal, esp one that is sexually mature
BULLA n leaden seal affixed to a papal bull

BULLACE n small Eurasian tree of which the damson is the cultivated form
BULLACES > BULLACE
BULLAE > BULLA
BULLARIES > BULLARY
BULLARY n boilery for preparing salt
BULLATE adj puckered or blistered in appearance
BULLBARS n large protective metal grille on the front of some vehicles, esp four-wheel-drive vehicles
BULLBAT another name for > NIGHTHAWK
BULLBATS > BULLBAT
BULLBRIER n prickly American vine
BULLCOOK n casual or odd job worker in a camp
BULLCOOKS > BULLCOOK
BULLDIKE same as > BULLDYKE
BULLDIKES > BULLDIKE
BULLDOG n thickset dog with a broad head and a muscular body
BULLDOGS > BULLDOG
BULLDOZE vb demolish or flatten with a bulldozer
BULLDOZED > BULLDOZE
BULLDOZER n powerful tractor for moving earth
BULLDOZES > BULLDOZE
BULLDUST n fine dust
BULLDUSTS > BULLDUST
BULLDYKE n mannish lesbian
BULLDYKES > BULLDYKE
BULLED > BULL
BULLER vb make bubbling sound
BULLERED > BULLER
BULLERING > BULLER
BULLERS > BULLER
BULLET n small piece of metal fired from a gun ▷ vb move extremely quickly
BULLETED > BULLET
BULLETIN n short official report or announcement ▷ vb make known by bulletin
BULLETING > BULLET
BULLETINS > BULLETIN
BULLETRIE n W Indian fruit tree
BULLETS > BULLET
BULLEY n fishing boat with two masts
BULLEYS > BULLEY
BULLFIGHT n public show in which a matador kills a bull
BULLFINCH n common European songbird
BULLFROG n large American frog with a deep croak
BULLFROGS > BULLFROG

BULLGINE n steam locomotive
BULLGINES > BULLGINE
BULLHEAD n type of small northern mainly marine fish with a large head covered with bony plates and spines
BULLHEADS > BULLHEAD
BULLHORN n portable loudspeaker having a built-in amplifier and microphone
BULLHORNS > BULLHORN
BULLIED > BULLY
BULLIER > BULLY
BULLIES > BULLY
BULLIEST > BULLY
BULLING > BULL
BULLINGS > BULL
BULLION n gold or silver in the form of bars
BULLIONS > BULLION
BULLISH adj like a bull
BULLISHLY > BULLISH
BULLNECK n enlarged neck
BULLNECKS > BULLNECK
BULLNOSE n rounded exterior angle, as where two walls meet
BULLNOSED adj having a rounded end
BULLNOSES > BULLNOSE
BULLOCK n castrated bull ▷ vb work hard and long
BULLOCKED > BULLOCK
BULLOCKS > BULLOCK
BULLOCKY n driver of a team of bullocks
BULLOSA adj as in epidermolysis bullosa type of genetic skin disorder
BULLOUS adj blistered
BULLPEN n large cell where prisoners are confined together temporarily
BULLPENS > BULLPEN
BULLPOUT n type of fish
BULLPOUTS > BULLPOUT
BULLRING n arena for staging bullfights
BULLRINGS > BULLRING
BULLRUSH same as > BULRUSH
BULLS > BULL
BULLSEYE n central disc of a target
BULLSEYES > BULLSEYE
BULLSHAT > BULLSHIT
BULLSHIT n exaggerated or foolish talk ▷ vb talk bullshit to
BULLSHITS > BULLSHIT
BULLSHOT n cocktail of vodka and beef stock
BULLSHOTS > BULLSHOT
BULLSNAKE n American burrowing snake
BULLWADDY n N Australian tree which grows in dense thickets
BULLWEED n knapweed

BULLWEEDS > BULLWEED
BULLWHACK vb flog with short whip
BULLWHIP n long tapering heavy whip, esp one of plaited rawhide ▷ vb whip with a bullwhip
BULLWHIPS > BULLWHIP
BULLY n person who hurts, persecutes, or intimidates weaker people ▷ vb hurt, intimidate, or persecute (a weaker or smaller person) ▷ adj dashing
BULLYBOY n ruffian or tough, esp a hired one
BULLYBOYS > BULLYBOY
BULLYCIDE n suicide as a result of bullying
BULLYING > BULLY
BULLYISM > BULLY
BULLYISMS > BULLY
BULLYRAG vb bully, esp by means of cruel practical jokes
BULLYRAGS > BULLYRAG
BULNBULN another name for > LYREBIRD
BULNBULNS > BULNBULN
BULRUSH n tall stiff reed
BULRUSHES > BULRUSH
BULRUSHY > BULRUSH
BULSE n purse or bag for diamonds
BULSES > BULSE
BULWADDEE same as > BULLWADDY
BULWADDY same as > BULLWADDY
BULWARK n wall used as a fortification ▷ vb defend or fortify with or as if with a bulwark
BULWARKED > BULWARK
BULWARKS > BULWARK
BUM n buttocks or anus ▷ vb get by begging ▷ adj of poor quality
BUMALO same as > BUMMALO
BUMALOTI same as > BUMMALOTI
BUMALOTIS > BUMALOTI
BUMBAG n small bag attached to a belt and worn round the waist
BUMBAGS > BUMBAG
BUMBAZE vb confuse; bewilder
BUMBAZED > BUMBAZE
BUMBAZES > BUMBAZE
BUMBAZING > BUMBAZE
BUMBLE vb speak, do, or move in a clumsy way ▷ n blunder or botch
BUMBLEBEE n large hairy bee
BUMBLED > BUMBLE
BUMBLEDOM n self-importance in a minor office
BUMBLER > BUMBLE
BUMBLERS > BUMBLE

b

BUMBLES > BUMBLE
BUMBLING > BUMBLE
BUMBLINGS > BUMBLE
BUMBO *n* drink with gin or rum, nutmeg, lemon juice, etc
BUMBOAT *n* any small boat used for ferrying goods to a ship at anchor or at a mooring
BUMBOATS > BUMBOAT
BUMBOS > BUMBO
BUMBOY *n* derogatory term for a young male homosexual
BUMBOYS > BUMBOY
BUMELIA *n* thorny shrub
BUMELIAS > BUMELIA
BUMF *n* official documents or forms
BUMFLUFF *n* soft and fluffy growth of hair on the chin of an adolescent
BUMFLUFFS > BUMFLUFF
BUMFS > BUMF
BUMFUCK *n* remote or insignificant place
BUMFUCKS > BUMFUCK
BUMFUZZLE *vb* confuse
BUMKIN *same as* > BUMPKIN
BUMKINS > BUMKIN
BUMMALO *n* Bombay duck
BUMMALOS > BUMMALO
BUMMALOTI *another word for* > BUMMALO
BUMMAREE *n* dealer at Billingsgate fish market
BUMMAREES > BUMMAREE
BUMMED > BUM
BUMMEL *n* stroll
BUMMELS > STROLL
BUMMER *n* unpleasant or disappointing experience
BUMMERS > BUMMER
BUMMEST > BUM
BUMMING > BUM
BUMMLE *Scots variant of* > BUMBLE
BUMMLED > BUMMLE
BUMMLES > BUMMLE
BUMMLING > BUMMLE
BUMMOCK *n* submerged mass of ice projecting downwards
BUMMOCKS > BUMMOCK
BUMP *vb* knock or strike with a jolt ▷ *n* dull thud from an impact or collision
BUMPED > BUMP
BUMPER *n* bar on the front and back of a vehicle ▷ *adj* unusually large or abundant ▷ *vb* toast with a bumper
BUMPERED > BUMPER
BUMPERING > BUMPER
BUMPERS > BUMPER
BUMPH *same as* > BUMF
BUMPHS > BUMPH
BUMPIER > BUMPY
BUMPIEST > BUMPY
BUMPILY > BUMPY

BUMPINESS > BUMPY
BUMPING > BUMP
BUMPINGS > BUMP
BUMPKIN *n* awkward simple country person
BUMPKINLY > BUMPKIN
BUMPKINS > BUMPKIN
BUMPOLOGY *n* humorous word for phrenology
BUMPS > BUMP
BUMPTIOUS *adj* offensively self-assertive
BUMPY *adj* having an uneven surface
BUMS > BUM
BUMSTER *adj* (of trousers) cut low so as to reveal the top part of the buttocks
BUMSTERS *pl n* trousers cut so that the top lies just above the cleft of the buttocks
BUMSUCKER *n* toady
BUMWAD *n* type of sketching paper
BUMWADS > BUMWAD
BUN *n* small sweet bread roll or cake
BUNA *n* synthetic rubber
BUNAS > BUNA
BUNBURIED > BUNBURY
BUNBURIES > BUNBURY
BUNBURY *vb* make up a story to avoid an unwanted engagement
BUNCE *n* windfall; boom ▷ *vb* charge someone too much money
BUNCED > BUNCE
BUNCES > BUNCE
BUNCH *n* number of things growing, fastened, or grouped together ▷ *vb* group or be grouped together in a bunch
BUNCHED > BUNCH
BUNCHER *n* person who groups things together
BUNCHERS > BUNCHER
BUNCHES *pl n* hair tied into two sections
BUNCHIER > BUNCHY
BUNCHIEST > BUNCHY
BUNCHILY > BUNCHY
BUNCHING > BUNCH
BUNCHINGS > BUNCH
BUNCHY *adj* composed of or resembling bunches
BUNCING > BUNCE
BUNCO *n* swindle, esp one by confidence tricksters ▷ *vb* swindle
BUNCOED > BUNCO
BUNCOES > BUNCO
BUNCOING > BUNCO
BUNCOMBE *same as* > BUNKUM
BUNCOMBES > BUNCOMBE
BUNCOS > BUNCO
BUND *n* embankment or German federation ▷ *vb* form into an embankment

BUNDE > BUND
BUNDED > BUND
BUNDH *same as* > BANDH
BUNDHS > BUNDH
BUNDIED > BUNDY
BUNDIES > BUNDY
BUNDING > BUND
BUNDIST > BUND
BUNDISTS > BUND
BUNDLE *n* number of things gathered loosely together ▷ *vb* cause to go roughly or unceremoniously
BUNDLED > BUNDLE
BUNDLER > BUNDLE
BUNDLERS > BUNDLE
BUNDLES > BUNDLE
BUNDLING > BUNDLE
BUNDLINGS > BUNDLE
BUNDOBUST *same as* > BANDOBUST
BUNDOOK *n* rifle
BUNDOOKS > BUNDOOK
BUNDS > BUND
BUNDT *n* type of sweet cake
BUNDTS > BUNDT
BUNDU *n* largely uninhabited wild region far from towns
BUNDUS > BUNDU
BUNDWALL *n* concrete or earth wall surrounding a storage tank containing crude oil or its refined product, designed to hold the contents of the tank in the event of a rupture or leak
BUNDWALLS > BUNDWALL
BUNDY *n* time clock at work ▷ *vb* register arrival or departure from work on a time clock
BUNDYING > BUNDY
BUNFIGHT *n* tea party
BUNFIGHTS > BUNFIGHT
BUNG *n* stopper for a cask etc ▷ *vb* close with a bung
BUNGALOID *n* bungalow-type house
BUNGALOW *n* one-storey house
BUNGALOWS > BUNGALOW
BUNGED > BUNG
BUNGEE *n* strong elastic cable
BUNGEES > BUNGEE
BUNGER *n* firework
BUNGERS > BUNGER
BUNGEY *same as* > BUNGEE
BUNGEYS > BUNGEY
BUNGHOLE *n* hole in a cask or barrel through which liquid can be drained
BUNGHOLES > BUNGHOLE
BUNGIE *same as* > BUNGEE
BUNGIES > BUNGY
BUNGING > BUNG
BUNGLE *vb* spoil through incompetence ▷ *n* blunder or muddle
BUNGLED > BUNGLE

BUNGLER > BUNGLE
BUNGLERS > BUNGLE
BUNGLES > BUNGLE
BUNGLING > BUNGLE
BUNGLINGS > BUNGLE
BUNGS > BUNG
BUNGWALL *n* Australian fern with an edible rhizome
BUNGWALLS > BUNGWALL
BUNGY *same as* > BUNGEE
BUNHEAD *n* ballerina
BUNHEADS > BUNHEAD
BUNIA *same as* > BUNNIA
BUNIAS > BUNIA
BUNION *n* inflamed swelling on the big toe
BUNIONS > BUNION
BUNJE *same as* > BUNGEE
BUNJEE *same as* > BUNGEE
BUNJEES > BUNJEE
BUNJES > BUNJE
BUNJIE *same as* > BUNGEE
BUNJIES > BUNJIE
BUNJY *same as* > BUNGEE
BUNK *n* narrow shelflike bed ▷ *vb* prepare to sleep
BUNKED > BUNK
BUNKER *n* sand-filled hollow forming an obstacle on a golf course ▷ *vb* drive (the ball) into a bunker
BUNKERED > BUNKER
BUNKERING > BUNKER
BUNKERS > BUNKER
BUNKHOUSE *n* (in the US and Canada) building containing the sleeping quarters of workers on a ranch
BUNKIE *n* short for bunkhouse
BUNKIES > BUNKIE
BUNKING > BUNK
BUNKMATE *n* person who sleeps in the same quarters as another
BUNKMATES > BUNKMATE
BUNKO *same as* > BUNCO
BUNKOED > BUNKO
BUNKOING > BUNKO
BUNKOS > BUNKO
BUNKS > BUNK
BUNKUM *n* nonsense
BUNKUMS > BUNKUM
BUNN *same as* > BUN
BUNNET *same as* > BONNET
BUNNETS > BUNNET
BUNNIA *n* Hindu shopkeeper
BUNNIAS > BUNNIA
BUNNIES > BUNNY
BUNNS > BUNN
BUNNY *n* child's word for a rabbit
BUNODONT *adj* (of the teeth of certain mammals) having cusps that are separate and rounded
BUNRAKU *n* Japanese puppet theatre
BUNRAKUS > BUNRAKU

BUNS pl n buttocks

BUNSEN n as in bunsen burner gas burner used in scientific labs

BUNSENS > BUNSEN

BUNT vb (of an animal) butt (something) with the head or horns ▷ n act or an instance of bunting

BUNTAL n straw obtained from leaves of the talipot palm

BUNTALS > BUNTAL

BUNTED > BUNT

BUNTER n batter who deliberately taps ball lightly

BUNTERS > BUNTER

BUNTIER > BUNT

BUNTIEST > BUNT

BUNTING n decorative flags

BUNTINGS > BUNTING

BUNTLINE n one of several lines fastened to the foot of a square sail for hauling it up to the yard when furling

BUNTLINES > BUNTLINE

BUNTS > BUNT

BUNTY > BUNT

BUNYA n tall dome-shaped Australian coniferous tree

BUNYAS > BUNYA

BUNYIP n legendary monster said to live in swamps and lakes

BUNYIPS > BUNYIP

BUOY n floating marker anchored in the sea ▷ vb prevent from sinking

BUOYAGE n system of buoys

BUOYAGES > BUOYAGE

BUOYANCE same as > BUOYANCY

BUOYANCES > BUOYANCE

BUOYANCY n ability to float in a liquid or to rise in a fluid

BUOYANT adj able to float

BUOYANTLY > BUOYANT

BUOYED > BUOY

BUOYING > BUOY

BUOYS > BUOY

BUPKES same as > BUBKES

BUPKIS same as > BUBKIS

BUPKUS same as > BUBKES

BUPLEVER n type of plant

BUPLEVERS > BUPLEVER

BUPPIE n affluent young Black person

BUPPIES > BUPPY

BUPPY variant of > BUPPIE

BUPRESTID n type of mainly tropical beetle, the adults of which are brilliantly coloured

BUPROPION n antidepressant drug used to help people stop smoking

BUQSHA n former Yemeni coin

BUQSHAS > BUQSHA

BUR same as > BURR

BURA same as > BURAN

BURAN n blizzard, with the wind blowing from the north and reaching gale force

BURANS > BURAN

BURAS > BURA

BURB n suburb

BURBLE vb make a bubbling sound ▷ n bubbling or gurgling sound

BURBLED > BURBLE

BURBLER > BURBLE

BURBLERS > BURBLE

BURBLES > BURBLE

BURBLIER > BURBLY

BURBLIEST > BURBLY

BURBLING > BURBLE

BURBLINGS > BURBLE

BURBLY adj burbling

BURBOT n freshwater fish of the cod family that has barbels around its mouth

BURBOTS > BURBOT

BURBS > BURB

BURD Scots form of > BIRD

BURDASH n fringed sash worn over coat

BURDASHES > BURDASH

BURDEN n heavy load ▷ vb put a burden on

BURDENED > BURDEN

BURDENER > BURDEN

BURDENERS > BURDEN

BURDENING > BURDEN

BURDENOUS > BURDEN

BURDENS > BURDEN

BURDIE Scots form of > BIRDIE

BURDIES > BURDIE

BURDIZZO n surgical instrument used to castrate animals

BURDIZZOS > BURDIZZO

BURDOCK n weed with prickly burrs

BURDOCKS > BURDOCK

BURDS > BURD

BUREAU n office that provides a service

BUREAUS > BUREAU

BUREAUX > BUREAU

BURET same as > BURETTE

BURETS > BURET

BURETTE n glass tube for dispensing known volumes of fluids

BURETTES > BURETTE

BURFI same as > BARFI

BURFIS > BURFI

BURG n fortified town

BURGAGE n (in England) tenure of land or tenement in a town or city, which originally involved a fixed money rent

BURGAGES > BURGAGE

BURGANET same as > BURGONET

BURGANETS > BURGANET

BURGEE n triangular or swallow-tailed flag flown from the mast of a merchant ship

BURGEES > BURGEE

BURGEON vb develop or grow rapidly ▷ n bud of a plant

BURGEONED > BURGEON

BURGEONS > BURGEON

BURGER n hamburger

BURGERS > BURGER

BURGESS n (in England) citizen or freeman of a borough

BURGESSES > BURGESS

BURGH n Scottish borough

BURGHAL > BURGH

BURGHER n citizen

BURGHERS > BURGHER

BURGHS > BURGH

BURGHUL same as > BULGUR

BURGHULS > BURGHUL

BURGLAR n person who enters a building to commit a crime, esp theft ▷ vb burgle

BURGLARED > BURGLAR

BURGLARS > BURGLAR

BURGLARY n crime of entering a building as a trespasser to commit theft or another offence

BURGLE vb break into (a house, shop, etc)

BURGLED > BURGLE

BURGLES > BURGLE

BURGLING > BURGLE

BURGONET n light 16th-century helmet, usually made of steel, with hinged cheekpieces

BURGONETS > BURGONET

BURGOO n porridge

BURGOOS > BURGOO

BURGOUT same as > BURGOO

BURGOUTS > BURGOUT

BURGRAVE n military governor of a German town or castle, esp in the 12th and 13th centuries

BURGRAVES > BURGRAVE

BURGS > BURG

BURGUNDY adj dark-purplish red

BURHEL same as > BHARAL

BURHELS > BURHEL

BURIAL n burying of a dead body

BURIALS > BURIAL

BURIED > BURY

BURIER n person or thing that buries

BURIERS > BURIER

BURIES > BURY

BURIN n steel chisel used for engraving metal, wood, or marble

BURINIST > BURIN

BURINISTS > BURIN

BURINS > BURIN

BURITI n type of palm tree

BURITIS > BURITI

BURK same as > BERK

BURKA same as > BURQA

BURKAS > BURKA

BURKE vb murder in such a way as to leave no marks on the body, usually by suffocation

BURKED > BURKE

BURKER > BURKE

BURKERS > BURKE

BURKES > BURKE

BURKHA n all-enveloping garment worn by Muslim women

BURKHAS > BURKHA

BURKING > BURKE

BURKINI n swimming costume covering the whole body apart from the face, hands, and feet

BURKINIS > BURKINI

BURKITE > BURKE

BURKITES > BURKE

BURKS > BURK

BURL n small knot or lump in wool ▷ vb remove the burls from (cloth)

BURLADERO n safe area for bull-fighter in bull ring

BURLAP n coarse fabric woven from jute, hemp, or the like

BURLAPS > BURLAP

BURLED > BURL

BURLER > BURL

BURLERS > BURL

BURLESK same as > BURLESQUE

BURLESKS > BURLESK

BURLESQUE n artistic work which satirizes a subject by caricature ▷ adj of or characteristic of a burlesque ▷ vb represent or imitate (a person or thing) in a ludicrous way

BURLETTA n type of comic opera

BURLETTAS > BURLETTA

BURLEY same as > BERLEY

BURLEYCUE same as > BURLESQUE

BURLEYED > BURLEY

BURLEYING > BURLEY

BURLEYS > BURLEY

BURLIER > BURLY

BURLIEST > BURLY

BURLILY > BURLY

BURLINESS > BURLY

BURLING > BURL

BURLS > BURL

BURLY adj (of a person) broad and muscular

BURN vb be or set on fire ▷ n injury or mark caused by fire or exposure to heat

BURNABLE > BURN

BURNABLES > BURN

BURNED > BURN

BURNER n part of a stove or lamp that produces the flame

BURNERS > BURNER
BURNET n type of rose
BURNETS > BURNET
BURNIE n sideburn
BURNIES > BURNIE
BURNING > BURN
BURNINGLY > BURN
BURNINGS > BURN
BURNISH vb make smooth and shiny by rubbing ▷ n shiny finish
BURNISHED > BURNISH
BURNISHER > BURNISH
BURNISHES > BURNISH
BURNOOSE same as > BURNOUS
BURNOOSED > BURNOUS
BURNOOSES > BURNOOSE
BURNOUS n long circular cloak with a hood, worn esp by Arabs
BURNOUSE same as > BURNOUS
BURNOUSED > BURNOUS
BURNOUSES > BURNOUSE
BURNOUT n failure of a mechanical device from excessive heating
BURNOUTS > BURNOUT
BURNS > BURN
BURNSIDE n land along side of burn
BURNSIDES > BURNSIDE
BURNT > BURN
BUROO n government office from which unemployment benefit is distributed
BUROOS > BUROO
BURP n belch ▷ vb belch
BURPED > BURP
BURPEE n type of physical exercise movement
BURPEES > BURPEE
BURPING > BURP
BURPS > BURP
BURQA n garment worn by Muslim women in public
BURQAS > BURQA
BURR n small rotary file ▷ vb form a rough edge on (a workpiece)
BURRAMYS n very rare Australian mountain pigmy possum
BURRATA n type of Italian cheese
BURRATAS > BURRATA
BURRAWANG n Australian plant with fernlike leaves and an edible nut
BURRED > BURR
BURREL same as > BHARAL
BURRELL variant of > BHARAL
BURRELLS > BURRELL
BURRELS > BURREL
BURRER n person who removes burrs
BURRERS > BURRER
BURRFISH n type of fish with sharp spines

BURRHEL same as > BURREL
BURRHELS > BURRHEL
BURRIER > BURRY
BURRIEST > BURRY
BURRING > BURR
BURRITO n tortilla folded over a filling of minced beef, chicken, cheese, or beans
BURRITOS > BURRITO
BURRO n donkey, esp one used as a pack animal
BURROS > BURRO
BURROW n hole dug in the ground by a rabbit etc ▷ vb dig holes in the ground
BURROWED > BURROW
BURROWER > BURROW
BURROWERS > BURROW
BURROWING > BURROW
BURROWS > BURROW
BURRS > BURR
BURRSTONE same as > BUHRSTONE
BURRY adj full of or covered in burs
BURS > BURR
BURSA n small fluid-filled sac that reduces friction between movable parts of the body
BURSAE > BURSA
BURSAL > BURSA
BURSAR n treasurer of a school, college, or university
BURSARIAL adj of, relating to, or paid by a bursar or bursary
BURSARIES > BURSARY
BURSARS > BURSAR
BURSARY n scholarship
BURSAS > BURSA
BURSATE > BURSA
BURSE n flat case used at Mass as a container for the corporal
BURSEED n type of plant
BURSEEDS > BURSEED
BURSERA adj of a type of gum tree
BURSES > BURSE
BURSICON n hormone, produced by the insect brain, that regulates processes associated with ecdysis, such as darkening of the cuticle
BURSICONS > BURSICON
BURSIFORM adj shaped like a pouch or sac
BURSITIS n inflammation of a bursa, esp one in the shoulder joint
BURST vb break or cause to break open or apart suddenly and noisily ▷ n sudden breaking open or apart ▷ adj broken apart
BURSTED > BURST

BURSTEN > BURST
BURSTER > BURST
BURSTERS > BURST
BURSTIER > BURSTY
BURSTIEST > BURSTY
BURSTING > BURST
BURSTONE same as > BUHRSTONE
BURSTONES > BURSTONE
BURSTS > BURST
BURSTY adj occurring or happening in sudden bursts; irregular
BURTHEN archaic word for > BURDEN
BURTHENED > BURTHEN
BURTHENS > BURTHEN
BURTON n type of hoisting tackle
BURTONS > BURTON
BURWEED n any of various plants that bear burs, such as the burdock
BURWEEDS > BURWEED
BURY vb place in a grave
BURYING > BURY
BUS n large motor vehicle for carrying passengers between stops ▷ vb travel by bus
BUSBAR n electrical conductor
BUSBARS > BUSBAR
BUSBIES > BUSBY
BUSBOY n waiter's assistant
BUSBOYS > BUSBOY
BUSBY n tall fur hat worn by some soldiers
BUSED > BUS
BUSERA n Ugandan alcoholic drink made from millet: sometimes mixed with honey
BUSERAS > BUSERA
BUSES > BUS
BUSGIRL n waiter's assistant
BUSGIRLS > BUSGIRL
BUSH n dense woody plant, smaller than a tree ▷ vb fit a bush to (a casing or bearing)
BUSHBABY n small African tree-living mammal with large eyes
BUSHBUCK n small nocturnal spiral-horned antelope of Africa, with a reddish-brown coat with a few white markings
BUSHBUCKS > BUSHBUCK
BUSHCRAFT n ability and experience in matters concerned with living in the bush
BUSHED adj extremely tired
BUSHEL n obsolete unit of measure equal to 8 gallons ▷ vb alter or mend (a garment)
BUSHELED > BUSHEL
BUSHELER > BUSHEL

BUSHELERS > BUSHEL
BUSHELING > BUSHEL
BUSHELLED > BUSHEL
BUSHELLER > BUSHEL
BUSHELMAN > BUSHEL
BUSHELMEN > BUSHEL
BUSHELS > BUSHEL
BUSHER > BUSH
BUSHERS > BUSH
BUSHES > BUSH
BUSHFIRE n uncontrolled fire in the bush
BUSHFIRES > BUSHFIRE
BUSHFLIES > BUSHFLY
BUSHFLY n small black Australian fly that breeds in faeces and dung
BUSHGOAT n S African antelope
BUSHGOATS > BUSHGOAT
BUSHIDO n feudal code of the Japanese samurai
BUSHIDOS > BUSHIDO
BUSHIE same as > BUSHY
BUSHIER > BUSHY
BUSHIES > BUSHY
BUSHIEST > BUSHY
BUSHILY > BUSHY
BUSHINESS > BUSHY
BUSHING same as > BUSH
BUSHINGS > BUSHING
BUSHLAND n land characterized by natural vegetation
BUSHLANDS > BUSHLAND
BUSHLESS > BUSH
BUSHLIKE > BUSH
BUSHLOT n small wooded area of land
BUSHLOTS > BUSHLOT
BUSHMAN n person who lives or travels in the bush
BUSHMEAT n meat taken from any animal native to African forests, including species that may be endangered or not usually eaten outside Africa
BUSHMEATS > BUSHMEAT
BUSHMEN > BUSHMAN
BUSHPIG n wild brown or black forest pig of tropical Africa and Madagascar
BUSHPIGS > BUSHPIG
BUSHTIT n small grey active North American songbird
BUSHTITS > BUSHTIT
BUSHVELD n bushy countryside
BUSHVELDS > BUSHVELD
BUSHWA n nonsense
BUSHWAH same as > BUSHWA
BUSHWAHS > BUSHWAH
BUSHWALK vb walk through bushland
BUSHWALKS > BUSHWALK
BUSHWAS > BUSHWA
BUSHWHACK vb ambush
BUSHWOMAN > BUSHMAN
BUSHWOMEN > BUSHMAN

BUSHY adj (of hair) thick and shaggy ▷ n person who lives in the bush
BUSIED > BUSY
BUSIER > BUSY
BUSIES > BUSY
BUSIEST > BUSY
BUSILY adv in a busy manner
BUSINESS n purchase and sale of goods and services
BUSINESSY adj of, relating to, typical of, or suitable for the world of commercial or industrial business
BUSING > BUS
BUSINGS > BUS
BUSK vb act as a busker ▷ n strip of whalebone, wood, steel, etc, inserted into the front of a corset
BUSKED > BUSK
BUSKER > BUSK
BUSKERS > BUSK
BUSKET n bouquet
BUSKETS > BUSKET
BUSKIN n (formerly) sandal-like covering
BUSKINED adj relating to tragedy
BUSKING > BUSK
BUSKINGS > BUSK
BUSKINS > BUSKIN
BUSKS > BUSK
BUSKY same as > BOSKY
BUSLOAD n number of people bus carries
BUSLOADS > BUSLOAD
BUSMAN n person who drives a bus
BUSMEN > BUSMAN
BUSS archaic or dialect word for > KISS
BUSSED > BUS
BUSSES > BUS
BUSSING > BUS
BUSSINGS > BUS
BUSSU n type of palm tree
BUSSUS > BUSSU
BUST n chest of a human being, esp a woman's bosom ▷ adj broken ▷ vb burst or break
BUSTARD n type of bird
BUSTARDS > BUSTARD
BUSTED > BUST
BUSTEE same as > BASTI
BUSTEES > BUSTEE
BUSTER n person or thing destroying something as specified
BUSTERS > BUSTER
BUSTI same as > BASTI
BUSTIC n type of small American tree
BUSTICATE vb break
BUSTICS > BUSTIC
BUSTIER n close-fitting strapless women's top
BUSTIERS > BUSTIER
BUSTIEST > BUSTY

BUSTINESS > BUSTY
BUSTING > BUST
BUSTINGS > BUST
BUSTIS > BUSTI
BUSTLE vb hurry with a show of activity or energy ▷ n energetic and noisy activity
BUSTLED > BUSTLE
BUSTLER > BUSTLE
BUSTLERS > BUSTLE
BUSTLES > BUSTLE
BUSTLINE n shape or size of woman's bust
BUSTLINES > BUSTLINE
BUSTLING > BUSTLE
BUSTS > BUST
BUSTY adj (of a woman) having a prominent bust
BUSULFAN n drug used to treat cancer
BUSULFANS > BUSULFAN
BUSUUTI n garment worn by Ugandan women
BUSUUTIS > BUSUUTI
BUSY adj actively employed ▷ vb keep (someone, esp oneself) busy
BUSYBODY n meddlesome or nosy person
BUSYING > BUSY
BUSYNESS > BUSY
BUSYWORK n unproductive work
BUSYWORKS > BUSYWORK
BUT prep except ▷ adv only ▷ n outer room of a two-roomed cottage: usually the kitchen
BUTADIENE n colourless easily liquefiable flammable gas
BUTANE n gas used for fuel
BUTANES > BUTANE
BUTANOIC adj as in butanoic acid kind of acid
BUTANOL n colourless substance
BUTANOLS > BUTANOL
BUTANONE n colourless soluble flammable liquid used mainly as a solvent for resins
BUTANONES > BUTANONE
BUTCH adj markedly or aggressively masculine ▷ n lesbian who is noticeably masculine
BUTCHER n person who slaughters animals or sells their meat ▷ vb kill and prepare (animals) for meat
BUTCHERED > BUTCHER
BUTCHERER > BUTCHER
BUTCHERLY > BUTCHER
BUTCHERS > BUTCHER
BUTCHERY n senseless slaughter
BUTCHES > BUTCH
BUTCHEST > BUTCH
BUTCHING > BUTCH
BUTCHINGS > BUTCH
BUTCHNESS > BUTCH

BUTE n drug used illegally to dope horses
BUTENE n pungent colourless gas
BUTENES > BUTENE
BUTEO n type of American hawk
BUTEONINE adj of hawks
BUTEOS > BUTEO
BUTES > BUTE
BUTLE vb act as butler
BUTLED > BUTLE
BUTLER n chief male servant ▷ vb act as a butler
BUTLERAGE > BUTLER
BUTLERED > BUTLER
BUTLERIES > BUTLERY
BUTLERING > BUTLER
BUTLERS > BUTLER
BUTLERY n butler's room
BUTLES > BUTLE
BUTLING > BUTLE
BUTMENT same as > ABUTMENT
BUTMENTS > BUTMENT
BUTOH n style of contemporary Japanese dance
BUTOHS > BUTOH
BUTS > BUT
BUTSUDAN n (in Buddhism) small household altar
BUTSUDANS > BUTSUDAN
BUTT n thicker or blunt end of something, such as the end of the stock of a rifle ▷ vb strike or push with the head or horns
BUTTALS n abuttal
BUTTE n isolated steep flat-topped hill
BUTTED > BUTT
BUTTER n edible fatty yellow solid made from cream ▷ vb put butter on
BUTTERBUR n Eurasian plant with fragrant whitish or purple flowers and woolly stems
BUTTERCUP n small yellow flower
BUTTERED > BUTTER
BUTTERFAT n fatty substance of milk from which butter is made, consisting of a mixture of glycerides, mainly butyrin, olein, and palmitin
BUTTERFLY n insect with brightly coloured wings
BUTTERIER > BUTTERY
BUTTERIES > BUTTERY
BUTTERINE n artificial butter made partly from milk
BUTTERING > BUTTER
BUTTERNUT n E North American walnut tree
BUTTERS > BUTTER
BUTTERY n (in some universities) room in which food and drink are sold to students

▷ adj containing, like, or coated with butter
BUTTES > BUTTE
BUTTHEAD n stupid person
BUTTHEADS > BUTTHEAD
BUTTIES > BUTTY
BUTTING > BUTT
BUTTINSKI same as > BUTTINSKY
BUTTINSKY n busybody
BUTTLE vb act as butler
BUTTLED > BUTTLE
BUTTLES > BUTTLE
BUTTLING > BUTTLE
BUTTOCK n either of the two fleshy masses that form the human rump ▷ vb perform a kind of wrestling manoeuvre on a person
BUTTOCKED > BUTTOCK
BUTTOCKS > BUTTOCK
BUTTON n small disc or knob sewn to clothing ▷ vb fasten with buttons
BUTTONED > BUTTON
BUTTONER > BUTTON
BUTTONERS > BUTTON
BUTTONING > BUTTON
BUTTONS n page boy
BUTTONY > BUTTON
BUTTRESS n structure to support a wall ▷ vb support with, or as if with, a buttress
BUTTS > BUTT
BUTTSTOCK n part of gun
BUTTY n sandwich
BUTTYMAN n coalmine worker
BUTTYMEN > BUTTYMAN
BUTUT n Gambian monetary unit worth one hundredth of a dalasi
BUTUTS > BUTUT
BUTYL adj of or containing any of four isomeric forms of the group C_4H_9– ▷ n of, consisting of, or containing any of four isomeric forms of the group C_4H_9–
BUTYLATE vb introduce butyl into (compound)
BUTYLATED > BUTYLATE
BUTYLATES > BUTYLATE
BUTYLENE same as > BUTENE
BUTYLENES > BUTYLENE
BUTYLS > BUTYL
BUTYRAL n type of resin
BUTYRALS > BUTYRAL
BUTYRATE n any salt or ester of butyric acid
BUTYRATES > BUTYRATE
BUTYRIC adj as in butyric acid type of acid
BUTYRIN n colourless liquid found in butter
BUTYRINS > BUTYRIN
BUTYROUS adj butyraceous

b

BUTYRYL n radical of butyric acid

BUTYRYLS > BUTYRYL

BUVETTE n roadside café

BUVETTES > BUVETTE

BUXOM adj (of a woman) healthily plump and full-bosomed

BUXOMER > BUXOM

BUXOMEST > BUXOM

BUXOMLY > BUXOM

BUXOMNESS > BUXOM

BUY vb acquire by paying money for ▷ n thing acquired through payment

BUYABLE > BUY

BUYABLES > BUY

BUYBACK n repurchase by a company of some or all of its shares from an early investor

BUYBACKS > BUYBACK

BUYER n customer

BUYERS > BUYER

BUYING n as in panic buying the buying up of large quantities of something feared to be scarce

BUYINGS > BUYING

BUYOFF n purchase

BUYOFFS > BUYOFF

BUYOUT n purchase of a company

BUYOUTS > BUYOUT

BUYS > BUY

BUZKASHI n game played in Afghanistan, in which opposing teams of horsemen strive for possession of the headless carcass of a goat

BUZKASHIS > BUZKASHI

BUZUKI same as **>** BOUZOUKI

BUZUKIA > BUZUKI

BUZUKIS > BUZUKI

BUZZ n rapidly vibrating humming sound ▷ vb make a humming sound

BUZZARD n bird of prey of the hawk family

BUZZARDS > BUZZARD

BUZZBAIT n fishing lure with small blades that stir the water

BUZZBAITS > BUZZBAIT

BUZZCUT n very short haircut

BUZZCUTS > BUZZCUT

BUZZED > BUZZ

BUZZER n electronic device that produces a buzzing sound as a signal

BUZZERS > BUZZER

BUZZES > BUZZ

BUZZIER > BUZZY

BUZZIEST > BUZZY

BUZZING > BUZZ

BUZZINGLY > BUZZ

BUZZINGS > BUZZ

BUZZKILL n someone or something that spoils the enjoyment of others

BUZZKILLS > BUZZKILL

BUZZSAW n power-operated circular saw

BUZZSAWS > BUZZSAW

BUZZWIG n bushy wig

BUZZWIGS > BUZZWIG

BUZZWORD n word, often originating in a particular jargon, that becomes a vogue word in the community as a whole or among a particular group

BUZZWORDS > BUZZWORD

BUZZY adj making a buzzing sound

BWANA n (in E Africa) master, often used as a respectful form of address

BWANAS > BWANA

BWAZI same as **>** BUAZE

BWAZIS > BWAZI

BY prep indicating the doer of an action, nearness, movement past, time before or during which, etc ▷ adv near ▷ n pass to the next round (of a competition, etc)

BYCATCH n unwanted fish and sea animals caught along with the desired kind

BYCATCHES > BYCATCH

BYCOKET n former Italian high-crowned hat

BYCOKETS > BYCOKET

BYDE same as **>** BIDE

BYDED > BYDE

BYDES > BYDE

BYDING > BYDE

BYE n situation where a player or team wins a round by having no opponent ▷ interj goodbye ▷ sentence substitute goodbye

BYELAW n rule made by a local authority

BYELAWS > BYELAW

BYES > BYE

BYGONE adj past

BYGONES > BYGONE

BYKE same as **>** BICYCLE

BYKED > BICYCLE

BYKES > BICYCLE

BYKING > BICYCLE

BYLANDER same as **>** BILANDER

BYLANDERS > BYLANDER

BYLANE n side lane or alley off a road

BYLANES > BYLANE

BYLAW n rule made by a local authority

BYLAWS > BYLAW

BYLINE n line under the title of a newspaper or magazine article giving the author's name ▷ vb give a byline to

BYLINED > BYLINE

BYLINER > BYLINE

BYLINERS > BYLINE

BYLINES > BYLINE

BYLINING > BYLINE

BYLIVE same as **>** BELIVE

BYNAME n nickname

BYNAMES > BYNAME

BYNEMPT > BENAME

BYPASS n main road built to avoid a city ▷ vb go round or avoid

BYPASSED > BYPASS

BYPASSES > BYPASS

BYPASSING > BYPASS

BYPAST > BYPASS

BYPATH n little-used path or track, esp in the country

BYPATHS > BYPATH

BYPLACE n private place

BYPLACES > BYPLACE

BYPLAY n secondary action or talking carried on apart while the main action proceeds

BYPLAYS > BYPLAY

BYPRODUCT n secondary product

BYRE n shelter for cows

BYREMAN n man who works in byre

BYREMEN > BYREMAN

BYRES > BYRE

BYREWOMAN n woman who works in a byre

BYREWOMEN > BYREWOMAN

BYRL same as **>** BIRL

BYRLADY interj short for By Our Lady

BYRLAKIN interj By Our Ladykin

BYRLAW same as **>** BYLAW

BYRLAWS > BYRLAW

BYRLED > BYRL

BYRLING > BYRL

BYRLS > BYRL

BYRNIE n archaic word for coat of mail

BYRNIES > BYRNIE

BYROAD n secondary or side road

BYROADS > BYROAD

BYROOM n private room

BYROOMS > BYROOM

BYS > BY

BYSSAL adj of mollusc's byssus

BYSSI > BYSSUS

BYSSINE adj made from flax

BYSSOID adj consisting of fine fibres

BYSSUS n mass of threads that attaches an animal to a hard surface

BYSSUSES > BYSSUS

BYSTANDER n person present but not involved

BYSTREET n obscure or secondary street

BYSTREETS > BYSTREET

BYTALK n trivial conversation

BYTALKS > BYTALK

BYTE n group of bits processed as one unit of data

BYTES > BYTE

BYTOWNITE n rare mineral

BYWAY n minor road

BYWAYS > BYWAY

BYWONER n poor tenant-farmer

BYWONERS > BYWONER

BYWORD n person or thing regarded as a perfect example of something

BYWORDS > BYWORD

BYWORK n work done outside usual working hours

BYWORKS > BYWORK

BYZANT same as **>** BEZANT

BYZANTINE adj of, characteristic of, or relating to Byzantium or the Byzantine Empire

BYZANTS > BYZANT

Cc

CAA *a Scot word for* > CALL
CAAED > CAA
CAAING > CAA
CAAS > CAA
CAATINGA *n* Brazilian semi-arid scrub forest
CAATINGAS > CAATINGA
CAB *n* taxi ▷ *vb* take a taxi
CABA *same as* > CABAS
CABAL *n* small group of political plotters ▷ *vb* form a cabal
CABALA *a variant spelling of* > KABBALAH
CABALAS > CABALA
CABALETTA *n* final section of an aria
CABALETTE > CABALETTA
CABALISM > CABALA
CABALISMS > CABALA
CABALIST > CABALA
CABALISTS > CABALA
CABALLED > CABAL
CABALLER > CABAL
CABALLERO *n* Spanish gentleman
CABALLERS > CABAL
CABALLINE *adj* pertaining to a horse
CABALLING > CABAL
CABALS > CABAL
CABANA *n* tent used as a dressing room by the sea
CABANAS > CABANA
CABARET *n* dancing and singing show in a nightclub
CABARETS > CABARET
CABAS *n* reticule
CABBAGE *n* vegetable with a large head of green leaves ▷ *vb* steal
CABBAGED > CABBAGE
CABBAGES > CABBAGE
CABBAGEY > CABBAGE
CABBAGING > CABBAGE
CABBAGY > CABBAGE
CABBALA *a variant spelling of* > KABBALAH
CABBALAH *same as* > CABBALA
CABBALAHS > CABBALA
CABBALAS > CABBALA
CABBALISM > CABBALA
CABBALIST > CABBALA
CABBED > CAB
CABBIE *n* taxi driver
CABBIES > CABBIE
CABBING > CAB

CABBY *same as* > CABBIE
CABDRIVER *n* taxi-driver
CABER *n* tree trunk tossed in competition at Highland games
CABERNET *n* type of grape, or the red wine made from it
CABERNETS > CABERNET
CABERS > CABER
CABESTRO *n* halter made from horsehair
CABESTROS > CABESTRO
CABEZON *n* large fish
CABEZONE *same as* > CABEZON
CABEZONES > CABEZON
CABEZONS > CABEZON
CABILDO *n* Spanish municipal council
CABILDOS > CABILDO
CABIN *n* compartment in a ship or aircraft ▷ *vb* confine in a small space
CABINED > CABIN
CABINET *n* piece of furniture with drawers or shelves
CABINETRY *n* cabinetmaking
CABINETS > CABINET
CABINING > CABIN
CABINMATE *n* sharer of cabin
CABINS > CABIN
CABLE *n* strong thick rope; a wire or bundle of wires that conduct electricity ▷ *vb* send (someone) a message by cable
CABLECAST *n* broadcast on cable
CABLED > CABLE
CABLEGRAM *n* message sent by cable
CABLER *n* cable broadcasting company
CABLERS > CABLER
CABLES > CABLE
CABLET *n* small cable
CABLETS > CABLET
CABLEWAY *n* system for moving people or bulk materials in which suspended cars, buckets, etc, run on cables that extend between terminal towers
CABLEWAYS > CABLEWAY
CABLING > CABLE

CABLINGS > CABLE
CABMAN *n* driver of a cab
CABMEN > CABMAN
CABOB *vb* roast on a skewer
CABOBBED > CABOB
CABOBBING > CABOB
CABOBS > CABOB
CABOC *n* type of Scottish cheese
CABOCEER *n* in African history, indigenous representative appointed by his leader to deal with European slave traders
CABOCEERS > CABOCEER
CABOCHED *adj* in heraldry, with the face exposed, but neck concealed
CABOCHON *n* smooth domed gem, polished but unfaceted
CABOCHONS > CABOCHON
CABOCS > CABOC
CABOMBA *n* type of aquatic plant
CABOMBAS > CABOMBA
CABOODLE *n* lot, bunch, or group
CABOODLES > CABOODLE
CABOOSE *n* guard's van on a train
CABOOSES > CABOOSE
CABOSHED *same as* > CABOCHED
CABOTAGE *n* coastal navigation or shipping, esp within the borders of one country
CABOTAGES > CABOTAGE
CABOVER *n* truck or lorry in which the cab is over the engine
CABOVERS > CABOVER
CABRE *adj* heraldic term designating an animal rearing
CABRESTA *variant of* > CABESTRO
CABRESTAS > CABRESTA
CABRESTO *variant of* > CABESTRO
CABRESTOS > CABRESTO
CABRETTA *n* soft leather obtained from the skins of certain South American or African sheep
CABRETTAS > CABRETTA
CABRIE *n* pronghorn antelope

CABRIES > CABRIE
CABRILLA *n* type of food fish occurring in warm seas around Florida and the Caribbean
CABRILLAS > CABRILLA
CABRIO *short for* > CABRIOLET
CABRIOLE *n* type of furniture leg, popular in the first half of the 18th century, in which an upper convex curve descends tapering to a concave curve
CABRIOLES > CABRIOLE
CABRIOLET *n* small horse-drawn carriage with a folding hood
CABRIOS > CABRIO
CABRIT *n* pronghorn antelope
CABRITS > CABRIT
CABS > CAB
CABSTAND *n* taxi-rank
CABSTANDS > CABSTAND
CACA *n* heroin
CACAFOGO *same as* > CACAFUEGO
CACAFOGOS > CACAFUEGO
CACAFUEGO *n* spitfire
CACAO *same as* > COCOA
CACAOS > COCOA
CACAS > CACA
CACHACA *n* white Brazilian rum made from sugar cane
CACHACAS > CACHACA
CACHAEMIA *n* poisoned condition of the blood
CACHAEMIC > CACHAEMIA
CACHALOT *n* sperm whale
CACHALOTS > CACHALOT
CACHE *n* hidden store of weapons or treasure ▷ *vb* store in a cache
CACHECTIC > CACHEXIA
CACHED > CACHE
CACHEPOT *n* ornamental container for a flowerpot
CACHEPOTS > CACHEPOT
CACHES > CACHE
CACHET *n* prestige, distinction ▷ *vb* apply a commemorative design to an envelope, as a first-day cover
CACHETED > CACHET

CACHETING > CACHET
CACHETS > CACHET
CACHEXIA *n* generally weakened condition of body or mind resulting from any debilitating chronic disease
CACHEXIAS > CACHEXIA
CACHEXIC > CACHEXIA
CACHEXIES > CACHEXIA
CACHEXY *same as* **>** CACHEXIA
CACHING > CACHE
CACHOLONG *n* type of opal
CACHOLOT *same as* **>** CACHALOT
CACHOLOTS > CACHALOT
CACHOU *same as* **>** CATECHU
CACHOUS > CATECHU
CACHUCHA *n* graceful Spanish solo dance in triple time
CACHUCHAS > CACHUCHA
CACIQUE *n* American Indian chief in a Spanish-speaking region
CACIQUES > CACIQUE
CACIQUISM *n* (esp in Spanish America) government by local political bosses
CACK *n* excrement **>** *vb* defecate
CACKED > CACK
CACKIER > CACKY
CACKIEST > CACKY
CACKING > CACK
CACKLE *vb* laugh shrilly **>** *n* cackling noise
CACKLED > CACKLE
CACKLER > CACKLE
CACKLERS > CACKLE
CACKLES > CACKLE
CACKLING > CACKLE
CACKS > CACK
CACKY *adj* of or like excrement
CACODEMON *n* evil spirit or devil
CACODOXY *n* heterodoxy
CACODYL *n* oily poisonous liquid with a strong garlic smell
CACODYLIC > CACODYL
CACODYLS > CACODYL
CACOEPIES > CACOEPY
CACOEPY *n* bad or mistaken pronunciation
CACOETHES *n* uncontrollable urge or desire, esp for something harmful
CACOETHIC > CACOETHES
CACOGENIC *adj* reducing the quality of a race
CACOLET *n* seat fitted to the back of a mule
CACOLETS > CACOLET
CACOLOGY *n* bad choice of words
CACOMIXL *n* carnivorous mammal

CACOMIXLE *same as* **>** CACOMIXL
CACOMIXLS > CACOMIXL
CACONYM *n* erroneous name
CACONYMS > CACONYM
CACONYMY > CACONYM
CACOON *n* large seed of the sword-bean
CACOONS > CACOON
CACOPHONY *n* harsh discordant sound
CACOTOPIA *n* dystopia, the opposite of utopia
CACTI > CACTUS
CACTIFORM *adj* cactus-like
CACTOID *adj* resembling a cactus
CACTUS *n* fleshy desert plant with spines but no leaves
CACTUSES > CACTUS
CACUMEN *n* apex
CACUMENS > CACUMEN
CACUMINA > CACUMEN
CACUMINAL *adj* relating to or denoting a consonant articulated with the tip of the tongue turned back towards the hard palate **>** *n* consonant articulated in this manner
CAD *n* dishonourable man
CADAGA *n* eucalyptus tree
CADAGAS > CADAGA
CADAGI *same as* **>** CADAGA
CADAGIS > CADAGI
CADASTER *n* official register showing details of ownership, boundaries, and value of real property in a district, made for taxation purposes
CADASTERS > CADASTER
CADASTRAL > CADASTER
CADASTRE *same as* **>** CADASTER
CADASTRES > CADASTER
CADAVER *n* corpse
CADAVERIC > CADAVER
CADAVERS > CADAVER
CADDICE *same as* **>** CADDIS
CADDICES > CADDIS
CADDIE *n* person who carries a golfer's clubs **>** *vb* act as a caddie
CADDIED > CADDIE
CADDIES > CADDIE
CADDIS *n* type of coarse woollen yarn, braid, or fabric
CADDISED *adj* trimmed with a type of ribbon
CADDISES > CADDIS
CADDISFLY *n* small fly
CADDISH > CAD
CADDISHLY > CAD
CADDY *same as* **>** CADDIE
CADDYING > CADDIE
CADDYSS *same as* **>** CADDIS
CADDYSSES > CADDIS

CADE *n* juniper tree **>** *adj* (of a young animal) left by its mother and reared by humans
CADEAU *n* present
CADEAUX > CADEAU
CADEE *old form of* **>** CADET
CADEES > CADEE
CADELLE *n* type of beetle that feeds on flour, grain, and other stored foods
CADELLES > CADELLE
CADENCE *n* rise and fall in the pitch of the voice **>** *vb* modulate musically
CADENCED > CADENCE
CADENCES > CADENCE
CADENCIES > CADENCY
CADENCING > CADENCE
CADENCY *same as* **>** CADENCE
CADENT *adj* having cadence
CADENTIAL > CADENT
CADENZA *n* complex solo passage in a piece of music
CADENZAS > CADENZA
CADES > CADE
CADET *n* young person training for the armed forces or police
CADETS > CADET
CADETSHIP > CADET
CADGE *vb* get (something) by taking advantage of someone's generosity
CADGED > CADGE
CADGER *n* person who cadges
CADGERS > CADGER
CADGES > CADGE
CADGIER > CADGY
CADGIEST > CADGY
CADGING > CADGE
CADGY *adj* cheerful
CADI *n* judge in a Muslim community
CADIE *n* messenger
CADIES > CADIE
CADIS > CADI
CADMIC > CADMIUM
CADMIUM *n* bluish-white metallic element used in alloys
CADMIUMS > CADMIUM
CADRANS *n* instrument used in gem cutting
CADRANSES > CADRANS
CADRE *n* group of people trained to form the core of a political or military unit
CADRES > CADRE
CADS > CAD
CADUAC *n* windfall
CADUACS > CADUAC
CADUCEAN > CADUCEUS
CADUCEI > CADUCEUS
CADUCEUS *n* staff entwined with two serpents and bearing a pair of wings at the top, carried by Hermes (Mercury) as messenger of the gods

CADUCITY *n* perishableness
CADUCOUS *adj* (of parts of a plant or animal) shed during the life of the organism
CAECA > CAECUM
CAECAL > CAECUM
CAECALLY > CAECUM
CAECILIAN *n* type of tropical limbless amphibian resembling an earthworm
CAECITIS *n* inflammation of the caecum
CAECUM *n* pouch at the beginning of the large intestine
CAEOMA *n* aecium in some rust fungi that has no surrounding membrane
CAEOMAS > CAEOMA
CAERULE *same as* **>** CERULE
CAERULEAN *same as* **>** CERULEAN
CAESAR *n* any emperor, autocrat, dictator, or other powerful ruler
CAESAREAN *n* surgical incision through the abdominal and uterine walls in order to deliver a baby
CAESARIAN *variant spelling of* **>** CAESAREAN
CAESARISM *n* imperialism
CAESARS > CAESAR
CAESE *interj* Shakespearean interjection
CAESIOUS *adj* having a waxy bluish-grey coating
CAESIUM *n* silvery-white metallic element used in photocells
CAESIUMS > CAESIUM
CAESTUS *same as* **>** CESTUS
CAESTUSES > CAESTUS
CAESURA *n* pause in a line of verse
CAESURAE > CAESURA
CAESURAL > CAESURA
CAESURAS > CAESURA
CAESURIC > CAESURA
CAF *n* short for cafeteria
CAFARD *n* feeling of severe depression
CAFARDS > CAFARD
CAFE *n* small or inexpensive restaurant serving light refreshments
CAFES > CAFE
CAFETERIA *n* self-service restaurant
CAFETIERE *n* kind of coffeepot in which boiling water is poured onto ground coffee and a plunger fitted with a metal filter is pressed down,

forcing the grounds to the bottom

CAFETORIA variant of > CAFETERIA

CAFF n café

CAFFEIN same as > CAFFEINE

CAFFEINE n stimulant found in tea and coffee

CAFFEINES > CAFFEINE

CAFFEINIC adj of or containing caffeine

CAFFEINS > CAFFEINE

CAFFEISM n addiction to caffeine

CAFFEISMS > CAFFEISM

CAFFILA n caravan train

CAFFILAS > CAFFILA

CAFFS > CAFF

CAFILA same as > CAFFILA

CAFILAS > CAFILA

CAFS > CAF

CAFTAN same as > KAFTAN

CAFTANED adj wearing caftan

CAFTANS > CAFTAN

CAG same as > CAGOULE

CAGANER n figure of a squatting defecating person

CAGANERS > CAGANER

CAGE n enclosure of bars or wires, for keeping animals or birds ▷ vb confine in a cage

CAGED > CAGE

CAGEFUL n amount which fills a cage to capacity

CAGEFULS > CAGEFUL

CAGELIKE > CAGE

CAGELING n bird kept in a cage

CAGELINGS > CAGELING

CAGER n basketball player

CAGERS > CAGER

CAGES > CAGE

CAGEWORK n something constructed as if from the bars of a cage

CAGEWORKS > CAGEWORK

CAGEY adj reluctant to go into details

CAGEYNESS > CAGEY

CAGIER > CAGEY

CAGIEST > CAGEY

CAGILY > CAGEY

CAGINESS > CAGY

CAGING > CAGE

CAGMAG adj done shoddily ▷ vb chat idly

CAGMAGGED > CAGMAG

CAGMAGS > CAGMAG

CAGOT n member of a class of French outcasts

CAGOTS > CAGOT

CAGOUL same as > CAGOULE

CAGOULE n lightweight hooded waterproof jacket

CAGOULES > CAGOULE

CAGOULS > CAGOUL

CAGS > CAG

CAGY same as > CAGEY

CAGYNESS > CAGY

CAHIER n notebook

CAHIERS > CAHIER

CAHOOT n partnership

CAHOOTS > CAHOOT

CAHOUN n type of S American palm tree

CAHOUNS > CAHOUN

CAHOW n Bermuda petrel

CAHOWS > CAHOW

CAID n Moroccan district administrator

CAIDS > CAID

CAILLACH same as > CAILLEACH

CAILLACHS > CAILLACH

CAILLE n quail

CAILLEACH n old woman

CAILLES > CAILLE

CAILLIACH same as > CAILLEACH

CAIMAC same as > CAIMACAM

CAIMACAM n Turkish governor of a sanjak

CAIMACAMS > CAIMACAM

CAIMACS > CAIMAC

CAIMAN same as > CAYMAN

CAIMANS > CAIMAN

CAIN n (in Scotland and Ireland) payment in kind

CAINS > CAIN

CAIQUE n long narrow light rowing skiff used on the Bosporus

CAIQUES > CAIQUE

CAIRD n travelling tinker

CAIRDS > CAIRD

CAIRN n mound of stones erected as a memorial or marker

CAIRNED adj marked by a cairn

CAIRNGORM n yellow or brownish quartz gemstone

CAIRNIER > CAIRNY

CAIRNIEST > CAIRNY

CAIRNS > CAIRN

CAIRNY adj covered with cairns

CAISSON same as > COFFERDAM

CAISSONS > CAISSON

CAITIFF n cowardly or base person ▷ adj cowardly

CAITIFFS > CAITIFF

CAITIVE n captive

CAITIVES > CAITIVE

CAJAPUT same as > CAJUPUT

CAJAPUTS > CAJAPUT

CAJEPUT same as > CAJUPUT

CAJEPUTS > CAJEPUT

CAJOLE vb persuade by flattery

CAJOLED > CAJOLE

CAJOLER > CAJOLE

CAJOLERS > CAJOLE

CAJOLERY > CAJOLE

CAJOLES > CAJOLE

CAJOLING > CAJOLE

CAJON n Peruvian wooden box used as a drum

CAJONES > CAJON

CAJUN n music of the Cajun people

CAJUPUT n small tree or shrub

CAJUPUTS > CAJUPUT

CAKE n sweet food baked from a mixture of flour, eggs, etc ▷ vb form into a hardened mass or crust

CAKEAGE n charge in a restaurant for serving cake brought in from outside

CAKEAGES > CAKEAGE

CAKEBOX n box for a cake

CAKEBOXES > CAKEBOX

CAKED > CAKE

CAKEHOLE n mouth

CAKEHOLES > CAKEHOLE

CAKES > CAKE

CAKEWALK n dance based on a march with intricate steps, originally performed by African-Americans with the prize of a cake for the best performers ▷ vb perform the cakewalk

CAKEWALKS > CAKEWALK

CAKEY > CAKE

CAKIER > CAKE

CAKIEST > CAKE

CAKINESS > CAKE

CAKING > CAKE

CAKINGS > CAKE

CAKY > CAKE

CAL adj short for calorie

CALABASH n type of large round gourd

CALABAZA n variety of squash

CALABAZAS > CALABAZA

CALABOGUS n mixed drink containing rum, spruce beer, and molasses

CALABOOSE n prison

CALABRESE n kind of green sprouting broccoli

CALADIUM n type of tropical plant widely cultivated as a potted plant for its colourful variegated foliage

CALADIUMS > CALADIUM

CALALOO same as > CALALU

CALALOOS > CALALOO

CALALU n edible leaves of various plants

CALALUS > CALALU

CALAMANCO n glossy woollen fabric woven with a checked design that shows on one side only

CALAMAR n any member of the squid family

CALAMARI n squid cooked for eating, esp cut into rings and fried in batter

CALAMARIS > CALAMARI

CALAMARS > CALAMAR

CALAMARY variant of > CALAMARI

CALAMATA same as > KALAMATA

CALAMATAS > CALAMATA

CALAMI > CALAMUS

CALAMINE n pink powder consisting chiefly of zinc oxide, used in skin lotions and ointments ▷ vb apply calamine

CALAMINED > CALAMINE

CALAMINES > CALAMINE

CALAMINT n aromatic Eurasian plant with clusters of purple or pink flowers

CALAMINTS > CALAMINT

CALAMITE n type of extinct treelike plant related to the horsetails

CALAMITES > CALAMITE

CALAMITY n disaster

CALAMUS n tropical Asian palm

CALAMUSES > CALAMUS

CALANDO adv (to be performed) with gradually decreasing tone and speed

CALANDRIA n cylindrical vessel through which vertical tubes pass, esp one forming part of an evaporator, heat exchanger, or nuclear reactor

CALANTHE n type of orchid

CALANTHES > CALANTHE

CALASH n horse-drawn carriage with low wheels and a folding top

CALASHES > CALASH

CALATHEA n S American plant often grown as a greenhouse or house plant for its variegated leaves

CALATHEAS > CALATHEA

CALATHI > CALATHUS

CALATHOS same as > CALATHUS

CALATHUS n vase-shaped basket represented in ancient Greek art, used as a symbol of fruitfulness

CALAVANCE n type of pulse

CALCANEA > CALCANEUS

CALCANEAL > CALCANEUS

CALCANEAN > CALCANEUS

CALCANEI > CALCANEUS

CALCANEUM same as > CALCANEUS

CALCANEUS n largest tarsal bone, forming the heel in man

CALCAR n spur or spurlike process

CALCARATE > CALCAR

CALCARIA > CALCAR

CALCARINE > CALCAR

CALCARS > CALCAR
CALCEATE *vb* to shoe
CALCEATED > CALCEATE
CALCEATES > CALCEATE
CALCED *adj* wearing shoes
CALCEDONY *n*
microcrystalline often greyish form of quartz with crystals arranged in parallel fibres: a gemstone
CALCES > CALX
CALCIC *adj* of, containing, or concerned with lime or calcium
CALCICOLE *n* any plant that thrives in lime-rich soils
CALCIFIC *adj* forming or causing to form lime or chalk
CALCIFIED > CALCIFY
CALCIFIES > CALCIFY
CALCIFUGE *n* any plant that thrives in acid soils but not in lime-rich soils
CALCIFY *vb* harden by the depositing of calcium salts
CALCIMINE *n* white or pale tinted wash for walls ▷ *vb* cover with calcimine
CALCINE *vb* oxidize (a substance) by heating
CALCINED > CALCINE
CALCINES > CALCINE
CALCINING > CALCINE
CALCITE *n* colourless or white form of calcium carbonate
CALCITES > CALCITE
CALCITIC > CALCITE
CALCIUM *n* silvery-white metallic element
CALCIUMS > CALCIUM
CALCRETE *another name* for > CALICHE
CALCRETES > CALCRETE
CALCSPAR *another name* for > CALCITE
CALCSPARS > CALCSPAR
CALCTUFA *another name* for > TUFA
CALCTUFAS > CALCTUFA
CALCTUFF *another name* for > TUFA
CALCTUFFS > CALCTUFF
CALCULAR *adj* relating to calculus
CALCULARY *adj* relating to stone
CALCULATE *vb* solve or find out by a mathematical procedure or by reasoning
CALCULI > CALCULUS
CALCULOSE *adj* relating to calculi
CALCULOUS *adj* of or suffering from a stonelike accretion of minerals and salts found in ducts or hollow organs of the body
CALCULUS *n* branch of mathematics dealing with infinitesimal changes to a variable number or quantity

CALDARIA > CALDARIUM
CALDARIUM *n* (in ancient Rome) a room for taking hot baths
CALDERA *n* large basin-shaped crater at the top of a volcano
CALDERAS > CALDERA
CALDRON *same as* > CAULDRON
CALDRONS > CALDRON
CALECHE *a variant of* > CALASH
CALECHES > CALECHE
CALEFIED > CALEFY
CALEFIES > CALEFY
CALEFY *vb* make warm
CALEFYING > CALEFY
CALEMBOUR *n* pun
CALENDAL > CALENDS
CALENDAR *n* chart showing a year divided up into months, weeks, and days ▷ *vb* enter in a calendar
CALENDARS > CALENDAR
CALENDER *n* machine in which paper or cloth is smoothed by passing it between rollers ▷ *vb* smooth in such a machine
CALENDERS > CALENDER
CALENDRER > CALENDER
CALENDRIC > CALENDAR
CALENDRY *n* place where calendering is carried out
CALENDS *pl n* first day of each month in the ancient Roman calendar
CALENDULA *n* marigold
CALENTURE *n* mild fever of tropical climates, similar in its symptoms to sunstroke
CALESA *n* horse-drawn buggy
CALESAS > CALESA
CALESCENT *adj* increasing in heat
CALF *n* young cow, bull, elephant, whale, or seal
CALFDOZER *n* small bulldozer
CALFHOOD *n* state of being a calf
CALFHOODS > CALFHOOD
CALFLESS > CALF
CALFLICK *another word for* > COWLICK
CALFLICKS > CALFLICK
CALFLIKE > CALF
CALFS > CALF
CALFSKIN *n* fine leather made from the skin of a calf
CALFSKINS > CALFSKIN
CALIATOUR *n* red sandalwood
CALIBER *same as* > CALIBRE
CALIBERED > CALIBER
CALIBERS > CALIBER

CALIBRATE *vb* mark the scale or check the accuracy of (a measuring instrument)
CALIBRE *n* person's ability or worth
CALIBRED > CALIBRE
CALIBRES > CALIBRE
CALICES > CALIX
CALICHE *n* bed of sand or clay in arid regions
CALICHES > CALICHE
CALICLE *same as* > CALYCLE
CALICLES > CALICLE
CALICO *n* white cotton fabric
CALICOES > CALICO
CALICOS > CALICO
CALICULAR > CALYCLE
CALID *adj* warm
CALIDITY > CALID
CALIF *same as* > CALIPH
CALIFATE *same as* > CALIPHATE
CALIFATES > CALIFATE
CALIFONT *n* gas water heater
CALIFONTS > CALIFONT
CALIFS > CALIF
CALIGO *n* speck on the cornea causing poor vision
CALIGOES > CALIGO
CALIGOS > CALIGO
CALIMA *n* Saharan dust-storm
CALIMAS > CALIMA
CALIMOCHO *n* Spanish cocktail consisting of cola and red wine
CALIOLOGY *n* the study of birds' nests
CALIPASH *n* greenish glutinous edible part of the turtle found next to the upper shell, considered a delicacy
CALIPEE *n* edible part of the turtle found next to the lower shell
CALIPEES > CALIPEE
CALIPER *same as* > CALLIPER
CALIPERED > CALLIPER
CALIPERS > CALIPER
CALIPH *n* Muslim ruler
CALIPHAL > CALIPH
CALIPHATE *n* office, jurisdiction, or reign of a caliph
CALIPHS > CALIPH
CALISAYA *n* bark of a type of tropical tree from which quinine is extracted
CALISAYAS > CALISAYA
CALIVER *n* type of musket
CALIVERS > CALIVER
CALIX *n* cup
CALIXES > CALIX
CALK *same as* > CAULK
CALKED > CALK
CALKER > CALK
CALKERS > CALK

CALKIN *same as* > CALK
CALKING > CALK
CALKINGS > CALK
CALKINS > CALK
CALKS > CALK
CALL *vb* name ▷ *n* cry, shout
CALLA *n* S African plant with a white funnel-shaped spathe enclosing a yellow spadix
CALLABLE *adj* (of a security) subject to redemption before maturity
CALLAIDES > CALLAIS
CALLAIS *n* type of green stone
CALLALOO *n* leafy green vegetable
CALLALOOS > CALLALOO
CALLALOU *n* crabmeat soup
CALLALOUS > CALLALOU
CALLAN *same as* > CALLANT
CALLANS > CALLAN
CALLANT *n* youth
CALLANTS > CALLANT
CALLAS > CALLA
CALLBACK *n* telephone call made in response to an earlier call
CALLBACKS > CALLBACK
CALLBOARD *n* notice board listing opportunities for performers
CALLBOY *n* person who notifies actors when it is time to go on stage
CALLBOYS > CALLBOY
CALLED > CALL
CALLEE *n* computer function being used
CALLEES > CALLEE
CALLER *n* person or thing that calls, esp a person who makes a brief visit ▷ *adj* (of food, esp fish) fresh
CALLERS > CALLER
CALLET *n* scold
CALLETS > CALLET
CALLID *adj* cunning
CALLIDITY > CALLID
CALLIGRAM *n* poem in which words are positioned so as to create a visual image of the subject on the page
CALLING *n* vocation, profession
CALLINGS > CALLING
CALLIOPE *n* steam organ
CALLIOPES > CALLIOPE
CALLIPASH *same as* > CALIPASH
CALLIPEE *same as* > CALIPEE
CALLIPEES > CALLIPEE
CALLIPER *n* metal splint for supporting the leg ▷ *vb* measure the dimensions of (an object) with callipers

CALLIPERS > CALLIPER

CALLOP n edible Australian freshwater fish

CALLOPS > CALLOP

CALLOSE n carbohydrate found in plants

CALLOSES > CALLOSE

CALLOSITY same as > CALLUS

CALLOUS adj showing no concern for other people's feelings ▷ vb make or become callous

CALLOUSED > CALLOUS

CALLOUSES > CALLOUS

CALLOUSLY > CALLOUS

CALLOUT n inset text within a printed article

CALLOUTS > CALLOUT

CALLOW adj young and inexperienced ▷ n someone young and inexperienced

CALLOWER > CALLOW

CALLOWEST > CALLOW

CALLOWLY adj in a manner suggesting immaturity or inexperience

CALLOWS > CALLOW

CALLS > CALL

CALLTIME n time available for making calls on a mobile phone

CALLTIMES > CALLTIME

CALLUNA n type of heather

CALLUNAS > CALLUNA

CALLUS n area of thick hardened skin ▷ vb produce or cause to produce a callus

CALLUSED > CALLUS

CALLUSES > CALLUS

CALLUSING > CALLUS

CALM adj not agitated or excited ▷ n peaceful state ▷ vb make or become calm

CALMANT n sedative

CALMANTS > CALMANT

CALMATIVE adj (of a remedy or agent) sedative ▷ n sedative remedy or drug

CALMED > CALM

CALMER > CALM

CALMEST > CALM

CALMIER > CALMY

CALMIEST > CALMY

CALMING > CALM

CALMINGLY > CALM

CALMINGS > CALM

CALMLY > CALM

CALMNESS > CALM

CALMS > CALM

CALMSTANE same as > CAMSTONE

CALMSTONE same as > CAMSTONE

CALMY adj tranquil

CALO n military servant

CALOMEL n colourless tasteless powder

CALOMELS > CALOMEL

CALORIC adj of heat or calories ▷ n hypothetical fluid formerly postulated as the embodiment of heat

CALORICS > CALORIC

CALORIE n unit of measurement for the energy value of food

CALORIES > CALORIE

CALORIFIC adj of calories or heat

CALORISE same as > CALORIZE

CALORISED > CALORISE

CALORISES > CALORISE

CALORIST n believer in caloric theory

CALORISTS > CALORIST

CALORIZE vb coat (a ferrous metal) by spraying with aluminium powder and then heating

CALORIZED > CALORIZE

CALORIZES > CALORIZE

CALORY same as > CALORIE

CALOS > CALO

CALOTTE n skullcap worn by Roman Catholic clergy

CALOTTES > CALOTTE

CALOTYPE n early photographic process invented by W. H. Fox Talbot, in which the image was produced on paper treated with silver iodide and developed by sodium thiosulphite

CALOTYPES > CALOTYPE

CALOYER n monk of the Greek Orthodox Church, esp of the Basilian Order

CALOYERS > CALOYER

CALP n type of limestone

CALPA n Hindu unit of time

CALPAC n large black brimless hat

CALPACK same as > CALPAC

CALPACKS > CALPACK

CALPACS > CALPAC

CALPAIN n type of enzyme

CALPAINS > CALPAIN

CALPAS > CALPA

CALPS > CALP

CALQUE same as > CAULK

CALQUED > CALQUE

CALQUES > CALQUE

CALQUING > CALQUE

CALTHA n marsh marigold

CALTHAS > CALTHA

CALTHROP same as > CALTHROP

CALTHROPS > CALTROP

CALTRAP same as > CALTROP

CALTRAPS > CALTRAP

CALTROP n floating Asian plant

CALTROPS > CALTROP

CALUMBA n Mozambiquan root used for medicinal purposes

CALUMBAS > CALUMBA

CALUMET n peace pipe

CALUMETS > CALUMET

CALUMNIED > CALUMNY

CALUMNIES > CALUMNY

CALUMNY n false or malicious statement ▷ vb make a false or malicious statement about (a person)

CALUTRON n device used for the separation of isotopes

CALUTRONS > CALUTRON

CALVADOS n type of apple brandy

CALVARIA n top part of the skull of vertebrates

CALVARIAL > CALVARIUM

CALVARIAN > CALVARIUM

CALVARIAS > CALVARIA

CALVARIES > CALVARY

CALVARIUM same as > CALVARIA

CALVARY n representation of Christ's crucifixion

CALVE vb give birth to a calf

CALVED > CALVE

CALVER vb prepare fish for cooking

CALVERED > CALVER

CALVERING > CALVER

CALVERS > CALVER

CALVES > CALF

CALVING > CALVE

CALVITIES n baldness

CALX n powdery metallic oxide formed when an ore or mineral is roasted

CALXES > CALX

CALYCATE > CALYX

CALYCEAL adj resembling a calyx

CALYCES > CALYX

CALYCINAL same as > CALYCINE

CALYCINE adj relating to, belonging to, or resembling a calyx

CALYCLE n cup-shaped structure, as in the coral skeleton

CALYCLED > CALYCLE

CALYCLES > CALYCLE

CALYCOID adj resembling a calyx

CALYCULAR > CALYCLE

CALYCULE n bracts surrounding the base of the calyx

CALYCULES > CALYCULE

CALYCULI > CALYCULUS

CALYCULUS same as > CALYCLE

CALYPSO n West Indian song with improvised topical lyrics

CALYPSOES > CALYPSO

CALYPSOS > CALYPSO

CALYPTER n alula

CALYPTERA same as > CALYPTRA

CALYPTERS > CALYPTER

CALYPTRA n membranous hood covering the spore-bearing capsule of mosses and liverworts

CALYPTRAS > CALYPTRA

CALYX n outer leaves that protect a flower bud

CALYXES > CALYX

CALZONE n folded pizza filled with cheese, tomatoes, etc

CALZONES > CALZONE

CALZONI > CALZONE

CAM n device that converts a circular motion to a to-and-fro motion ▷ vb furnish (a machine) with a cam

CAMA n hybrid offspring of a camel and a llama

CAMAIEU n cameo

CAMAIEUX > CAMAIEU

CAMAIL n covering of chain mail

CAMAILED > CAMAIL

CAMAILS > CAMAIL

CAMAN n wooden stick used to hit the ball in shinty

CAMANACHD n shinty

CAMANS > CAMAN

CAMARILLA n group of confidential advisers, esp formerly, to the Spanish kings

CAMARON n shrimp

CAMARONS > CAMARON

CAMAS same as > CAMASS

CAMASES > CAMAS

CAMASH same as > CAMASS

CAMASHES > CAMASH

CAMASS n type of North American plant

CAMASSES > CAMASS

CAMBER n slight upward curve to the centre of a surface ▷ vb form or be formed with a surface that curves upwards to its centre

CAMBERED > CAMBER

CAMBERING > CAMBER

CAMBERS > CAMBER

CAMBIA > CAMBIUM

CAMBIAL > CAMBIUM

CAMBIFORM > CAMBIUM

CAMBISM > CAMBIST

CAMBISMS > CAMBIST

CAMBIST n dealer or expert in foreign exchange

CAMBISTRY > CAMBIST

CAMBISTS > CAMBIST

CAMBIUM n meristem that increases the girth of stems and roots

CAMBIUMS > CAMBIUM

CAMBOGE n type of gum resin

CAMBOGES > CAMBOGE
CAMBOGIA another name for > GAMBOGE
CAMBOGIAS > CAMBOGIA
CAMBOOSE n cabin built as living quarters for a gang of lumbermen
CAMBOOSES > CAMBOOSE
CAMBREL a variant of > GAMBREL
CAMBRELS > CAMBREL
CAMBRIC n fine white linen fabric
CAMBRICS > CAMBRIC
CAMCORD vb film with a camcorder
CAMCORDED > CAMCORD
CAMCORDER n combined portable video camera and recorder
CAMCORDS > CAMCORD
CAME > COME
CAMEL n humped mammal
CAMELBACK n type of locomotive
CAMELEER n camel-driver
CAMELEERS > CAMELEER
CAMELEON same as > CHAMELEON
CAMELEONS > CAMELEON
CAMELHAIR n hair of camel
CAMELIA same as > CAMELLIA
CAMELIAS > CAMELIA
CAMELID adj of or relating to camels ▷ n any animal of the camel family
CAMELIDS > CAMELID
CAMELINE n material made from camel hair
CAMELINES > CAMELINE
CAMELISH > CAMEL
CAMELLIA n evergreen ornamental shrub with white, pink, or red flowers
CAMELLIAS > CAMELLIA
CAMELLIKE > CAMEL
CAMELOID n member of the camel family
CAMELOIDS > CAMELOID
CAMELOT n supposedly idyllic period or age
CAMELOTS > CAMELOT
CAMELRIES > CAMELRY
CAMELRY n troops mounted on camels
CAMELS > CAMEL
CAMEO n brooch or ring with a profile head carved in relief ▷ vb appear in a brief role
CAMEOED > CAMEO
CAMEOING > CAMEO
CAMEOS > CAMEO
CAMERA n apparatus used for taking still or moving images
CAMERAE > CAMERA
CAMERAL adj of or relating to a judicial or legislative chamber
CAMERAMAN n man who operates a camera for television or cinema

CAMERAMEN > CAMERAMAN
CAMERAS > CAMERA
CAMERATED adj vaulted
CAMES same as > CANVAS
CAMESE same as > CAMISE
CAMESES > CAMESE
CAMI n camisole
CAMION n lorry, or, esp formerly, a large dray
CAMIONS > CAMION
CAMIS n light robe
CAMISA n smock
CAMISADE same as > CAMISADO
CAMISADES n > CAMISADE
CAMISADO n (formerly) an attack made under cover of darkness
CAMISADOS > CAMISADO
CAMISAS > CAMISA
CAMISE n loose light shirt, smock, or tunic originally worn in the Middle Ages
CAMISES > CAMISE
CAMISIA n surplice
CAMISIAS > CAMISIA
CAMISOLE n woman's bodice-like garment
CAMISOLES > CAMISOLE
CAMLET n tough waterproof cloth
CAMLETS > CAMLET
CAMMED > CAM
CAMMIE n webcam award
CAMMIES > CAMMIE
CAMMING > CAM
CAMO n short for camouflage
CAMOGIE n form of hurling played by women
CAMOGIES > CAMOGIE
CAMOMILE n aromatic plant, used to make herbal tea
CAMOMILES > CAMOMILE
CAMOODI a Caribbean name for > ANACONDA
CAMOODIS > CAMOODI
CAMORRA n secret criminal group
CAMORRAS > CAMORRA
CAMORRIST > CAMORRA
CAMOS > CAMO
CAMOTE n type of sweet potato
CAMOTES > CAMOTE
CAMOUFLET n type of bomb used in a siege to collapse an enemy's tunnel
CAMP vb stay in a camp ▷ adj effeminate or homosexual ▷ adj (place for) temporary lodgings consisting of tents, huts, or cabins
CAMPAGNA same as > CHAMPAIGN
CAMPAGNAS > CAMPAGNA
CAMPAGNE > CAMPAGNA
CAMPAIGN n series of coordinated activities designed to achieve a goal ▷ vb take part in a campaign

CAMPAIGNS > CAMPAIGN
CAMPANA n bell or bell shape
CAMPANAS > CAMPANA
CAMPANERO n South American bellbird
CAMPANILE n bell tower, usu one not attached to another building
CAMPANILI > CAMPANILE
CAMPANIST n expert on bells
CAMPANULA n plant with blue or white bell-shaped flowers
CAMPCRAFT n skills required when camping
CAMPEACHY adj as in campeachy wood kind of wood
CAMPEADOR n champion; term applied especially to El Cid
CAMPED > CAMP
CAMPER n person who lives or temporarily stays in a tent, cabin, etc
CAMPERIES > CAMPERY
CAMPERS > CAMPER
CAMPERY n campness
CAMPESINO n Latin American rural peasant
CAMPEST > CAMP
CAMPFIRE n outdoor fire in a camp, esp one used for cooking or as a focal point for community events
CAMPFIRES > CAMPFIRE
CAMPHANE n one of the terpene hydrocarbons
CAMPHANES > CAMPHANE
CAMPHENE n colourless crystalline insoluble terpene
CAMPHENES > CAMPHENE
CAMPHINE n type of solvent
CAMPHINES > CAMPHINE
CAMPHIRE an archaic name for > HENNA
CAMPHIRES > CAMPHIRE
CAMPHOL another word for > BORNEOL
CAMPHOLS > CAMPHOL
CAMPHONE n combined mobile phone and digital camera
CAMPHONES > CAMPHONE
CAMPHOR n aromatic crystalline substance
CAMPHORIC > CAMPHOR
CAMPHORS > CAMPHOR
CAMPI > CAMPO
CAMPIER > CAMPY
CAMPIEST > CAMPY
CAMPILY > CAMPY
CAMPINESS > CAMPY
CAMPING > CAMP
CAMPINGS > CAMP
CAMPION n red, pink, or white wild flower
CAMPIONS > CAMPION
CAMPLE vb argue

CAMPLED > CAMPLE
CAMPLES > CAMPLE
CAMPLING > CAMPLE
CAMPLY > CAMP
CAMPNESS > CAMP
CAMPO n level or undulating savanna country
CAMPODEID n member of the Campodea genus of bristle-tails
CAMPONG n in Malaysia, a village
CAMPONGS > CAMPONG
CAMPOREE n local meeting or assembly of Scouts
CAMPOREES > CAMPOREE
CAMPOS > CAMPO
CAMPOUT n camping trip
CAMPOUTS > CAMPOUT
CAMPS > CAMP
CAMPSHIRT n short-sleeved shirt
CAMPSITE n area on which holiday makers may pitch a tent
CAMPSITES > CAMPSITE
CAMPSTOOL n folding stool
CAMPUS n grounds of a university or college ▷ vb restrict a student to campus, as a punishment
CAMPUSED > CAMPUS
CAMPUSES > CAMPUS
CAMPUSING > CAMPUS
CAMPY adj effeminate
CAMS > CAM
CAMSHAFT n part of an engine consisting of a rod to which cams are fixed
CAMSHAFTS > CAMSHAFT
CAMSHO adj crooked
CAMSHOCH same as > CAMSHO
CAMSTAIRY adj perverse
CAMSTANE same as > CAMSTONE
CAMSTANES > CAMSTONE
CAMSTEARY same as > CAMSTAIRY
CAMSTONE n limestone used for whitening stone doorsteps
CAMSTONES > CAMSTONE
CAMUS n type of loose robe
CAMUSES > CAMUS
CAMWHORE vb perform sexual acts in front of a webcam for money
CAMWHORED > CAMWHORE
CAMWHORES > CAMWHORE
CAMWOOD n W African leguminous tree
CAMWOODS > CAMWOOD
CAN vb be able to ▷ n metal container for food or liquids
CANADA n canada goose
CANADAS > CANADA
CANAIGRE n southern US dock, the root of which yields a substance used in tanning

CANAIGRES > CANAIGRE
CANAILLE n masses or rabble
CANAILLES > CANAILLE
CANAKIN same as > CANNIKIN
CANAKINS > CANAKIN
CANAL n artificial waterway ▷ vb dig a canal through
CANALBOAT n boat made for canals
CANALED > CANAL
CANALING > CANAL
CANALISE same as > CANALIZE
CANALISED > CANALIZE
CANALISES > CANALIZE
CANALIZE vb give direction to
CANALIZED > CANALIZE
CANALIZES > CANALIZE
CANALLED > CANAL
CANALLER n canal boat worker
CANALLERS > CANALLER
CANALLING > CANAL
CANALS > CANAL
CANAPE n small piece of bread or toast with a savoury topping
CANAPES > CANAPE
CANARD n false report
CANARDS > CANARD
CANARIED > CANARY
CANARIES > CANARY
CANARY n small yellow songbird often kept as a pet ▷ vb perform a dance called the canary
CANARYING > CANARY
CANASTA n card game like rummy, played with two packs
CANASTAS > CANASTA
CANASTER n coarsely broken dried tobacco leaves
CANASTERS > CANASTER
CANBANK n container for receiving cans for recycling
CANBANKS > CANBANK
CANCAN n lively high-kicking dance performed by a female group
CANCANS > CANCAN
CANCEL vb stop (something that has been arranged) from taking place ▷ n new leaf or section of a book replacing a defective one
CANCELBOT n computer program that deletes unwanted mailings to Internet usergroups
CANCELED > CANCEL
CANCELEER vb (of a hawk) to turn in flight when a stoop fails, in order to re-attempt it
CANCELER > CANCEL
CANCELERS > CANCEL

CANCELIER a variant of > CANCELEER
CANCELING > CANCEL
CANCELLED > CANCEL
CANCELLER > CANCEL
CANCELLI n any lattice-like structures
CANCELS > CANCEL
CANCER n serious disease resulting from a malignant growth or tumour
CANCERATE vb become cancerous
CANCERED adj affected by cancer
CANCEROUS > CANCER
CANCERS > CANCER
CANCHA n toasted maize
CANCHAS > CANCHA
CANCRINE adj crab-like
CANCROID adj resembling a cancerous growth ▷ n skin cancer, esp one of only moderate malignancy
CANCROIDS > CANCROID
CANDELA n unit of luminous intensity
CANDELAS > CANDELA
CANDENT adj emitting light as a result of being heated to a high temperature
CANDID adj honest and straightforward ▷ n unposed photograph
CANDIDA n yeastlike parasitic fungus which causes thrush
CANDIDACY > CANDIDATE
CANDIDAL > CANDIDA
CANDIDAS > CANDIDA
CANDIDATE n person seeking a job or position
CANDIDER > CANDID
CANDIDEST > CANDID
CANDIDLY > CANDID
CANDIDS > CANDID
CANDIE n South Indian unit of weight
CANDIED adj coated with sugar
CANDIES > CANDY
CANDIRU n parasitic freshwater catfish of the Amazon region
CANDIRUS > CANDIRU
CANDLE n stick of wax enclosing a wick, burned to produce light ▷ vb test by holding up to a candle
CANDLED > CANDLE
CANDLELIT adj lit by the light of candles
CANDLENUT n tropical Asian and Polynesian tree
CANDLEPIN n bowling pin, as used in skittles, tenpin bowling, candlepins, etc
CANDLER > CANDLE
CANDLERS > CANDLE
CANDLES > CANDLE
CANDLING > CANDLE

CANDOCK n type of water lily, or horsetail
CANDOCKS > CANDOCK
CANDOR same as > CANDOUR
CANDORS > CANDOR
CANDOUR n honesty and straightforwardness
CANDOURS > CANDOUR
CANDY n sweet or sweets ▷ vb make sweet
CANDYGRAM n message accompanied by sweets
CANDYING > CANDY
CANDYMAN n drug-dealer, esp one who targets young people
CANDYMEN > CANDYMAN
CANDYTUFT n garden plant with clusters of white, pink, or purple flowers
CANE n stem of the bamboo or similar plant ▷ vb beat with a cane
CANEBRAKE n thicket of canes
CANED > CANE
CANEFRUIT n fruit, like the raspberry, which grows on woody-stemmed plants
CANEGRUB n Australian grub that feeds on sugarcane
CANEGRUBS > CANEGRUB
CANEH n Hebrew unit of length
CANEHS > CANEH
CANELLA n fragrant cinnamon-like inner bark of a W Indian tree, used as a spice and in medicine
CANELLAS > CANELLA
CANELLINI n white kidney bean
CANEPHOR n sculpted figure carrying a basket on its head
CANEPHORA same as > CANEPHOR
CANEPHORE same as > CANEPHOR
CANEPHORS > CANEPHOR
CANER > CANE
CANERS > CANE
CANES > CANE
CANESCENT adj white or greyish due to the presence of numerous short white hairs
CANEWARE n type of unglazed stoneware
CANEWARES > CANEWARE
CANFIELD n gambling game adapted from a type of patience
CANFIELDS > CANFIELD
CANFUL n amount a can will hold
CANFULS > CANFUL
CANG same as > CANGUE
CANGLE vb wrangle
CANGLED > CANGLE

CANGLES > CANGLE
CANGLING > CANGLE
CANGS > CANG
CANGUE n (formerly in China) a wooden collar worn as a punishment
CANGUES > CANGUE
CANICULAR adj of or relating to the star Sirius or its rising
CANID n animal of the dog family
CANIDS > CANID
CANIER > CANY
CANIEST > CANY
CANIKIN same as > CANNIKIN
CANIKINS > CANIKIN
CANINE adj of or like a dog ▷ n sharp pointed tooth between the incisors and the molars
CANINES > CANINE
CANING n beating with a cane as a punishment
CANINGS > CANING
CANINITY > CANINE
CANISTEL n Caribbean fruit
CANISTELS > CANISTEL
CANISTER n metal container ▷ vb to put into canisters
CANISTERS > CANISTER
CANITIES n grey hair
CANKER n ulceration, ulcerous disease ▷ vb infect or become infected with or as if with canker
CANKERED > CANKER
CANKERING > CANKER
CANKEROUS adj having cankers
CANKERS > CANKER
CANKERY adj like a canker
CANKLE n thickened calf on an overweight person
CANKLES > CANKLE
CANN vb direct a ship's steering
CANNA n type of tropical plant
CANNABIC > CANNABIS
CANNABIN n greenish-black poisonous resin obtained from the Indian hemp plant
CANNABINS > CANNABIN
CANNABIS n Asian plant with tough fibres
CANNACH n cotton grass
CANNACHS > CANNACH
CANNAE vb can not
CANNAS > CANNA
CANNED > CAN
CANNEL n type of dull coal
CANNELON n type of meat loaf
CANNELONI pl n pasta in the shape of tubes, which are usually stuffed
CANNELONS > CANNELON
CANNELS > CANNEL

CANNELURE n groove or fluting, esp one around the cylindrical part of a bullet

CANNER n person or organization whose job is to can foods

CANNERIES > CANNERY

CANNERS > CANNER

CANNERY n factory where food is canned

CANNIBAL n person who eats human flesh

CANNIBALS > CANNIBAL

CANNIE same as > CANNY

CANNIER > CANNY

CANNIEST > CANNY

CANNIKIN n small can, esp one used as a drinking vessel

CANNIKINS > CANNIKIN

CANNILY > CANNY

CANNINESS > CANNY

CANNING > CAN

CANNINGS > CAN

CANNISTER same as > CANISTER

CANNOLI n Sicilian pudding of pasta shells filled with sweetened ricotta

CANNOLIS > CANNOLI

CANNON n gun of large calibre ▷ vb collide (with)

CANNONADE n continuous heavy gunfire ▷ vb attack (a target) with cannon

CANNONED > CANNON

CANNONEER n (formerly) a soldier who served and fired a cannon

CANNONIER same as > CANNONEER

CANNONING > CANNON

CANNONRY n volley of artillery fire

CANNONS > CANNON

CANNOT vb can not

CANNS > CANN

CANNULA n narrow tube for insertion into a bodily cavity

CANNULAE > CANNULA

CANNULAR adj shaped like a cannula

CANNULAS > CANNULA

CANNULATE vb insert a cannula into ▷ adj shaped like a cannula

CANNY adj shrewd, cautious ▷ adv quite

CANOE n light narrow open boat propelled by a paddle or paddles ▷ vb use a canoe

CANOEABLE > CANOE

CANOED > CANOE

CANOEING > CANOE

CANOEINGS > CANOE

CANOEIST > CANOE

CANOEISTS > CANOE

CANOEMAN n man who canoes

CANOEMEN > CANOEMAN

CANOER > CANOE

CANOERS > CANOE

CANOES > CANOE

CANOEWOOD n type of tree

CANOLA n cooking oil extracted from a variety of rapeseed

CANOLAS > CANOLA

CANON n priest serving in a cathedral

CANONESS n woman belonging to any one of several religious orders and living under a rule but not under a vow

CANONIC same as > CANONICAL

CANONICAL adj conforming with canon law

CANONISE same as > CANONIZE

CANONISED > CANONISE

CANONISER > CANONISE

CANONISES > CANONISE

CANONIST n specialist in canon law

CANONISTS > CANONIST

CANONIZE vb declare (a person) officially to be a saint

CANONIZED > CANONIZE

CANONIZER > CANONIZE

CANONIZES > CANONIZE

CANONRIES > CANONRY

CANONRY n office, benefice, or status of a canon

CANONS > CANON

CANOODLE vb kiss and cuddle

CANOODLED > CANOODLE

CANOODLER > CANOODLE

CANOODLES > CANOODLE

CANOPIC adj of ancient Egyptian vase

CANOPIED > CANOPY

CANOPIES > CANOPY

CANOPY n covering above a bed, door, etc ▷ vb cover with or as if with a canopy

CANOPYING > CANOPY

CANOROUS adj tuneful

CANS > CAN

CANSFUL > CANFUL

CANSO n love song

CANSOS > CANSO

CANST vb form of 'can' used with the pronoun thou or its relative form

CANSTICK n candlestick

CANSTICKS > CANSTICK

CANT n insincere talk ▷ vb use cant ▷ adj oblique

CANTABANK n itinerant singer

CANTABILE adv flowing and melodious ▷ n piece or passage performed in this way

CANTAL n French cheese

CANTALA n tropical American plant, the agave

CANTALAS > CANTALA

CANTALOUP n type of melon

CANTALS > CANTAL

CANTAR variant form of > KANTAR

CANTARS > CANTAR

CANTATA n musical work consisting of arias, duets, and choruses

CANTATAS > CANTATA

CANTATE n 98th psalm sung as a nonmetrical hymn

CANTATES > CANTATE

CANTDOG same as > CANTHOOK

CANTDOGS > CANTDOG

CANTED > CANT

CANTEEN n restaurant attached to a workplace or school

CANTEENS > CANTEEN

CANTER vb move at gait between trot and gallop

CANTERED > CANTER

CANTERING > CANTER

CANTERS > CANTER

CANTEST > CANT

CANTHAL > CANTHUS

CANTHARI > CANTHARUS

CANTHARID n type of beetle with a soft elongated body

CANTHARIS n type of soldier beetle

CANTHARUS n large two-handled pottery cup

CANTHI > CANTHUS

CANTHIC adj relating to the canthus

CANTHITIS n inflammation of canthus

CANTHOOK n wooden pole with a hook used for handling logs

CANTHOOKS > CANTHOOK

CANTHUS n inner or outer corner or angle of the eye

CANTIC > CANT

CANTICLE n short hymn with words from the Bible

CANTICLES > CANTICLE

CANTICO vb dance as part of an act of worship

CANTICOED > CANTICO

CANTICOS > CANTICO

CANTICOY same as > CANTICO

CANTICOYS > CANTICOY

CANTICUM n canticle

CANTICUMS > CANTICUM

CANTIER > CANTY

CANTIEST > CANTY

CANTILENA n smooth flowing style in the writing of vocal music

CANTILY > CANTY

CANTINA n bar or wine shop, esp in a Spanish-speaking country

CANTINAS > CANTINA

CANTINESS > CANTY

CANTING > CANT

CANTINGLY > CANT

CANTINGS > CANT

CANTION n song

CANTIONS > CANTION

CANTLE n back part of a saddle that slopes upwards ▷ vb set up, or stand, on high

CANTLED > CANTLE

CANTLES > CANTLE

CANTLET n piece

CANTLETS > CANTLET

CANTLING > CANTLE

CANTO same as > CANTUS

CANTON n political division of a country, esp Switzerland ▷ vb divide into cantons

CANTONAL > CANTON

CANTONED > CANTON

CANTONING > CANTON

CANTONISE vb divide into cantons

CANTONIZE same as > CANTONISE

CANTONS > CANTON

CANTOR n man employed to lead services in a synagogue

CANTORIAL adj of or relating to a precentor

CANTORIS adj (in antiphonal music) to be sung by the cantorial side of a choir

CANTORS > CANTOR

CANTOS > CANTO

CANTRAIP n witch's spell or charm

CANTRAIPS > CANTRAIP

CANTRAP same as > CANTRAIP

CANTRAPS > CANTRAP

CANTRED n district comprising a hundred villages

CANTREDS > CANTRED

CANTREF same as > CANTRED

CANTREFS > CANTREF

CANTRIP n magic spell ▷ adj (of an effect) produced by black magic

CANTRIPS > CANTRIP

CANTS > CANT

CANTUS n medieval form of church singing

CANTUSES > CANTUS

CANTY adj lively

CANULA same as > CANNULA

CANULAE > CANULA

CANULAR adj shaped like a cannula

CANULAS > CANULA

CANULATE same as > CANNULATE

CANULATED > CANULATE

CANULATES > CANULATE

CANVAS n heavy coarse cloth ▷ vb cover with, or be applied to, canvas

CANVASED > CANVAS

CANVASER > CANVAS

CANVASERS > CANVAS

CANVASES > CANVAS

CANVASING > CANVAS

CANVASS *vb* try to get votes or support (from) ▷ *n* canvassing

CANVASSED > CANVASS

CANVASSER > CANVASS

CANVASSES > CANVASS

CANY *adj* cane-like

CANYON *n* deep narrow valley

CANYONEER *n* canyon explorer

CANYONING *n* sport of going down a canyon river by any of various means

CANYONS > CANYON

CANZONA *n* type of 16th- or 17th-century contrapuntal music

CANZONAS > CANZONA

CANZONE *n* Provençal or Italian lyric, often in praise of love or beauty

CANZONES > CANZONE

CANZONET *n* short, cheery, or lively Italian song

CANZONETS > CANZONET

CANZONI > CANZONE

CAP *n* soft close-fitting covering for the head ▷ *vb* cover or top with something

CAPA *n* type of Spanish cloak

CAPABLE *adj* having the ability (for)

CAPABLER > CAPABLE

CAPABLEST > CAPABLE

CAPABLY > CAPABLE

CAPACIOUS *adj* roomy

CAPACITOR *n* device for storing electrical charge

CAPACITY *n* ability to contain, absorb, or hold ▷ *adj* of the maximum amount or number possible

CAPARISON *n* decorated covering for a horse or other animal, esp (formerly) for a warhorse ▷ *vb* put a caparison on

CAPAS > CAPA

CAPE *n* short cloak ▷ *vb* cut and remove the hide of an animal

CAPED > CAPE

CAPEESH *same as* > CAPISCE

CAPELAN *another word for* > CAPELIN

CAPELANS > CAPELAN

CAPELET *n* small cape

CAPELETS > CAPELET

CAPELIN *n* type of small marine food fish

CAPELINE *n* cap-shaped bandage to cover the head or an amputation stump

CAPELINES > CAPELINE

CAPELINS > CAPELIN

CAPELLET *n* wen-like swelling on a horse

CAPELLETS > CAPELLET

CAPELLINE *same as* > CAPELINE

CAPELLINI *n* type of pasta

CAPER *n* high-spirited prank ▷ *vb* skip about

CAPERED > CAPER

CAPERER > CAPER

CAPERERS > CAPER

CAPERING > CAPER

CAPERS *pl n* pickled flower buds of a Mediterranean shrub used in sauces

CAPES > CAPE

CAPESKIN *n* soft leather obtained from the skins of a type of lamb or sheep having hairlike wool ▷ *adj* made of this leather

CAPESKINS > CAPESKIN

CAPEWORK *n* use of the cape by the matador in bullfighting

CAPEWORKS > CAPEWORK

CAPEX *n* capital expenditure

CAPEXES > CAPEX

CAPFUL *n* quantity held by a (usually bottle) cap

CAPFULS > CAPFUL

CAPH *n* letter of the Hebrew alphabet

CAPHS > CAPH

CAPI > CAPO

CAPIAS *n* (formerly) a writ directing the arrest of a named person

CAPIASES > CAPIAS

CAPILLARY *n* very fine blood vessel ▷ *adj* (of a tube) having a fine bore

CAPING > CAPE

CAPISCE *interj* expression meaning *do you understand?*

CAPITA > CAPUT

CAPITAL *n* chief city of a country ▷ *adj* involving or punishable by death

CAPITALLY *adv* in an excellent manner

CAPITALS > CAPITAL

CAPITAN *another name for* > HOGFISH

CAPITANI > CAPITANO

CAPITANO *n* chief; captain

CAPITANOS > CAPITANO

CAPITANS > CAPITAN

CAPITATE *n* largest of the bones of the human wrist

CAPITATED *adj* having fixed upper limit

CAPITATES > CAPITATE

CAPITAYN *n* captain

CAPITAYNS > CAPITAYN

CAPITELLA *n* plural form of singular: capitellum, an enlarged knoblike structure at the end of a bone that forms an articulation with another bone

CAPITOL *n* (in America) building housing the state legislature

CAPITOLS > CAPITOL

CAPITULA > CAPITULUM

CAPITULAR *adj* of or associated with a cathedral chapter ▷ *n* member of a cathedral chapter

CAPITULUM *n* racemose inflorescence in the form of a disc of sessile flowers, the youngest at the centre. It occurs in the daisy and related plants

CAPIZ *n* bivalve shell of a mollusc

CAPIZES > CAPIZ

CAPLE *n* horse

CAPLES > CAPLE

CAPLESS > CAP

CAPLET *n* medicinal tablet, usually oval in shape, coated in a soluble substance

CAPLETS > CAPLET

CAPLIN *same as* > CAPELIN

CAPLINS > CAPLIN

CAPMAKER > CAP

CAPMAKERS > CAP

CAPO *n* device used to raise the pitch of a stringed instrument

CAPOCCHIA *n* fool

CAPOEIRA *n* combination of martial art and dance, which originated among African slaves in 19th-century Brazil

CAPOEIRAS > CAPOEIRA

CAPON *n* castrated cock fowl fattened for eating

CAPONATA *n* Sicilian antipasto relish

CAPONATAS > CAPONATA

CAPONIER *n* covered passageway built across a ditch as a military defence

CAPONIERE *same as* > CAPONIER

CAPONIERS > CAPONIER

CAPONISE *same as* > CAPONIZE

CAPONISED > CAPONISE

CAPONISES > CAPONISE

CAPONIZE *vb* make (a cock) into a capon

CAPONIZED > CAPONIZE

CAPONIZES > CAPONIZE

CAPONS > CAPON

CAPORAL *n* strong coarse dark tobacco

CAPORALS > CAPORAL

CAPOS > CAPO

CAPOT *n* winning of all the tricks by one player ▷ *vb* score a capot (against)

CAPOTASTO *same as* > CAPO

CAPOTE *n* long cloak or soldier's coat, usually with a hood

CAPOTES > CAPOTE

CAPOTS > CAPOT

CAPOTTED > CAPOT

CAPOTTING > CAPOT

CAPOUCH *same as* > CAPUCHE

CAPOUCHES > CAPOUCH

CAPPED > CAP

CAPPER > CAP

CAPPERS > CAP

CAPPING > CAP

CAPPINGS > CAP

CAPRATE *n* any salt of capric acid

CAPRATES > CAPRATE

CAPRESE *n* salad of mozzarella, basil, and tomatoes

CAPRESES > CAPRESE

CAPRI *adj* as in *capri pants* women's tight-fitting trousers

CAPRIC *adj* (of a type of acid) smelling of goats

CAPRICCI > CAPRICCIO

CAPRICCIO *n* lively piece composed freely and without adhering to the rules for any specific musical form

CAPRICE *same as* > CAPRICCIO

CAPRICES > CAPRICE

CAPRID *n* any member of the goat family

CAPRIDS > CAPRID

CAPRIFIED > CAPRIFY

CAPRIFIES > CAPRIFY

CAPRIFIG *n* wild variety of fig of S Europe and SW Asia

CAPRIFIGS > CAPRIFIG

CAPRIFOIL *variant of* > CAPRIFOLE

CAPRIFOLE *n* honeysuckle

CAPRIFORM *adj* goatlike

CAPRIFY *vb* induce figs to ripen

CAPRINE *adj* of or resembling a goat

CAPRIOLE *n* upward but not forward leap made by a horse ▷ *vb* perform a capriole

CAPRIOLED > CAPRIOLE

CAPRIOLES > CAPRIOLE

CAPRIS > CAPRI

CAPROATE *n* any salt of caproic acid

CAPROATES > CAPROATE

CAPROCK *n* layer of rock that overlies a salt dome

CAPROCKS > CAPROCK

CAPROIC *adj* as in *caproic acid* oily acid found in milk

CAPRYLATE *n* any salt of caprylic acid

CAPRYLIC *variant of* > CAPRIC

CAPS > CAP

CAPSAICIN *n* colourless crystalline bitter alkaloid

CAPSICIN n liquid or resin extracted from capsicum

CAPSICINS > CAPSICIN

CAPSICUM n kind of pepper used as a vegetable or as a spice

CAPSICUMS > CAPSICUM

CAPSID n outer protein coat of a mature virus

CAPSIDAL > CAPSID

CAPSIDS > CAPSID

CAPSIZAL > CAPSIZE

CAPSIZALS > CAPSIZE

CAPSIZE vb (of a boat) overturn accidentally

CAPSIZED > CAPSIZE

CAPSIZES > CAPSIZE

CAPSIZING > CAPSIZE

CAPSOMER n one of the units making up a viral capsid

CAPSOMERE n any of the protein units that together form the capsid of a virus

CAPSOMERS > CAPSOMER

CAPSTAN n rotating cylinder round which a ship's rope is wound

CAPSTANS > CAPSTAN

CAPSTONE n one of a set of slabs on the top of a wall, building, etc

CAPSTONES > CAPSTONE

CAPSULAR adj relating to a capsule

CAPSULARY same as > CAPSULAR

CAPSULATE adj within or formed into a capsule

CAPSULE n soluble gelatine case containing a dose of medicine ▷ adj very concise ▷ vb contain within a capsule

CAPSULED > CAPSULE

CAPSULES > CAPSULE

CAPSULING > CAPSULE

CAPSULISE same as > CAPSULIZE

CAPSULIZE vb state (information) in a highly condensed form

CAPTAIN n commander of a ship or civil aircraft ▷ vb be captain of

CAPTAINCY > CAPTAIN

CAPTAINED > CAPTAIN

CAPTAINRY n condition or skill of being a captain

CAPTAINS > CAPTAIN

CAPTAN n type of fungicide

CAPTANS > CAPTAN

CAPTCHA n test in which the user of a website has to decipher a distorted image

CAPTCHAS > CAPTCHA

CAPTION n title or explanation accompanying an illustration ▷ vb provide with a caption

CAPTIONED > CAPTION

CAPTIONS > CAPTION

CAPTIOUS adj tending to make trivial criticisms

CAPTIVATE vb attract and hold the attention of

CAPTIVE n person kept in confinement ▷ adj kept in confinement ▷ vb take prisoner

CAPTIVED > CAPTIVE

CAPTIVES > CAPTIVE

CAPTIVING > CAPTIVE

CAPTIVITY n state of being kept in confinement

CAPTOPRIL n drug used to treat high blood pressure and congestive heart failure

CAPTOR n person who captures a person or animal

CAPTORS > CAPTOR

CAPTURE vb take by force ▷ n capturing

CAPTURED > CAPTURE

CAPTURER > CAPTURE

CAPTURERS > CAPTURE

CAPTURES > CAPTURE

CAPTURING > CAPTURE

CAPUCCIO n hood

CAPUCCIOS > CAPUCCIO

CAPUCHE n large hood or cowl, esp that worn by Capuchin friars

CAPUCHED adj hooded

CAPUCHES > CAPUCHE

CAPUCHIN n S American monkey with thick hair on the top of its head

CAPUCHINS > CAPUCHIN

CAPUERA variant of > CAPOEIRA

CAPUERAS > CAPUERA

CAPUL same as > CAPLE

CAPULS > CAPUL

CAPUT n main or most prominent part of an organ or structure

CAPYBARA n very large S American rodent

CAPYBARAS > CAPYBARA

CAR n motor vehicle designed to carry a small number of people

CARABAO n water buffalo

CARABAOS > CARABAO

CARABID n type of beetle

CARABIDS > CARABID

CARABIN same as > CARBINE

CARABINE same as > CARBINE

CARABINER a variant spelling of > KARABINER

CARABINES > CARABINE

CARABINS > CARABIN

CARACAL n lynx with reddish fur, which inhabits deserts of N Africa and S Asia

CARACALS > CARACAL

CARACARA n type of large carrion-eating bird of prey of S North, Central, and S America, with long legs and a naked face

CARACARAS > CARACARA

CARACK same as > CARRACK

CARACKS > CARACK

CARACOL same as > CARACOLE

CARACOLE n half turn to the right or left ▷ vb execute a half turn to the right or left

CARACOLED > CARACOLE

CARACOLER > CARACOLE

CARACOLES > CARACOLE

CARACOLS > CARACOL

CARACT n sign or symbol

CARACTS > CARACT

CARACUL n fur from the skins of newly born lambs of the karakul sheep

CARACULS > CARACUL

CARAFE n glass bottle for serving water or wine

CARAFES > CARAFE

CARAGANA n pea tree

CARAGANAS > CARAGANA

CARAGEEN same as > CARRAGEEN

CARAGEENS > CARAGEEN

CARAMBA n Spanish interjection similar to 'wow!'

CARAMBOLA n yellow edible star-shaped fruit that grows on a Brazilian tree

CARAMBOLE vb make a carom or carambola (shot in billiards)

CARAMEL n chewy sweet made from sugar and milk ▷ vb turn into caramel

CARAMELS > CARAMEL

CARANGID n type of marine fish with a compressed body and deeply forked tail, such as the horse mackerel, pompano, and pilot fish

CARANGIDS > CARANGID

CARANGOID same as > CARANGID

CARANNA n gumlike substance

CARANNAS > CARANNA

CARAP n crabwood

CARAPACE n hard upper shell of tortoises and crustaceans

CARAPACED adj having carapace

CARAPACES > CARAPACE

CARAPAX n carapace

CARAPAXES > CARAPAX

CARAPS > CARAP

CARASSOW same as > CURASSOW

CARASSOWS > CARASSOW

CARAT n unit of weight of precious stones

CARATE n tropical disease

CARATES > CARATE

CARATS > CARAT

CARAUNA same as > CARANNA

CARAUNAS > CARAUNA

CARAVAN n large enclosed vehicle for living in ▷ vb travel or have a holiday in a caravan

CARAVANCE same as > CALAVANCE

CARAVANED > CARAVAN

CARAVANER n person who holidays in a caravan

CARAVANS > CARAVAN

CARAVEL n two- or three-masted sailing ship

CARAVELLE variant of > CARAVEL

CARAVELS > CARAVEL

CARAWAY n plant whose seeds are used as a spice

CARAWAYS > CARAWAY

CARB n carbohydrate

CARBACHOL n cholinergic agent

CARBAMATE n salt or ester of carbamic acid

CARBAMIC adj as in carbamic acid hypothetical compound known only in carbamate salts

CARBAMIDE another name for > UREA

CARBAMINO adj relating to the compound produced when carbon dioxide reacts with an amino group

CARBAMOYL same as > CARBAMYL

CARBAMYL n radical from carbamic acid

CARBAMYLS > CARBAMYL

CARBANION n negatively charged organic ion in which most of the negative charge is localized on a carbon atom

CARBARN n streetcar depot

CARBARNS > CARBARN

CARBARYL n organic compound of the carbamate group

CARBARYLS > CARBARYL

CARBAZOLE n colourless insoluble solid obtained from coal tar

CARBEEN n Australian eucalyptus tree

CARBEENS > CARBEEN

CARBENE n neutral divalent free radical, such as methylene: CH_2

CARBENES > CARBENE

CARBIDE n compound of carbon with a metal

CARBIDES > CARBIDE

CARBIES > CARBY

CARBINE n light automatic rifle

CARBINEER *n* (formerly) a soldier equipped with a carbine

CARBINES > CARBINE

CARBINIER *same as* > CARBINEER

CARBINOL *same as* > METHANOL

CARBINOLS > CARBINOL

CARBO *n* carbohydrate

CARBOLIC *adj* as in *carbolic acid* phenol, when it is used as a disinfectant

CARBOLICS > CARBOLIC

CARBOLISE *same as* > CARBOLIZE

CARBOLIZE *another word for* > PHENOLATE

CARBON *n* nonmetallic element

CARBONADE *n* stew of beef and onions cooked in beer

CARBONADO *n* piece of meat, fish, etc, scored and grilled ▷ *vb* score and grill (meat, fish, etc)

CARBONARA *n* pasta sauce containing cream, bacon and cheese

CARBONATE *n* salt or ester of carbonic acid ▷ *vb* form or turn into a carbonate

CARBONIC *adj* containing carbon

CARBONISE *same as* > CARBONIZE

CARBONIUM *n* as in *carbonium ion* type of positively charged organic ion

CARBONIZE *vb* turn into carbon as a result of heating

CARBONOUS > CARBON

CARBONS > CARBON

CARBONYL *n* of, consisting of, or containing the divalent group =CO

CARBONYLS > CARBONYL

CARBORA *n* former name for the koala

CARBORAS > CARBORA

CARBORNE *adj* travelling by car

CARBOS > CARBO

CARBOXYL *adj* as in *carboxyl group* functional group in organic acids

CARBOXYLS > CARBOXYL

CARBOY *n* large bottle with a protective casing

CARBOYED > CARBOY

CARBOYS > CARBOY

CARBS > CARB

CARBUNCLE *n* inflamed boil

CARBURATE *same as* > CARBURET

CARBURET *vb* combine or mix (a gas) with carbon or carbon compounds ▷ *vb* to combine with carbon

CARBURETS > CARBURET

CARBURISE *same as* > CARBONIZE

CARBURIZE *same as* > CARBONIZE

CARBY *n* short for carburettor

CARCAJOU *a North American name for* > WOLVERINE

CARCAJOUS > CARCAJOU

CARCAKE *n* (formerly, in Scotland) a cake traditionally made for Shrove Tuesday

CARCAKES > CARCAKE

CARCANET *n* jewelled collar or necklace

CARCANETS > CARCANET

CARCASE *same as* > CARCASS

CARCASED > CARCASE

CARCASES > CARCASE

CARCASING > CARCASE

CARCASS *n* dead body of an animal ▷ *vb* make a carcass of

CARCASSED > CARCASS

CARCASSES > CARCASS

CARCEL *n* French unit of light

CARCELS > CARCEL

CARCERAL *adj* relating to prison

CARCINOID *n* small serotonin-secreting tumour

CARCINOMA *n* malignant tumour

CARD *n* piece of thick stiff paper or cardboard ▷ *vb* comb out fibres of wool or cotton before spinning

CARDAMINE *n* bittercress

CARDAMOM *n* spice obtained from the seeds of a tropical plant

CARDAMOMS > CARDAMOM

CARDAMON *same as* > CARDAMOM

CARDAMONS > CARDAMON

CARDAMUM *same as* > CARDAMOM

CARDAMUMS > CARDAMUM

CARDAN *n* as in *cardan joint* type of universal joint

CARDBOARD *n* thin stiff board made from paper pulp ▷ *adj* without substance

CARDCASE *n* small case for holding business cards

CARDCASES > CARDCASE

CARDECU *n* old French coin (a quarter of a crown)

CARDECUE *same as* > CARDECU

CARDECUES > CARDECUE

CARDECUS > CARDECU

CARDED > CARD

CARDER > CARD

CARDERS > CARD

CARDI *n* cardigan

CARDIA *n* lower oesophageal sphincter

CARDIAC *adj* of the heart ▷ *n* person with a heart disorder

CARDIACAL > CARDIAC

CARDIACS > CARDIAC

CARDIAE > CARDIA

CARDIALGY *n* pain in or near the heart

CARDIAS > CARDIA

CARDIE *short for* > CARDIGAN

CARDIES > CARDIE

CARDIGAN *n* knitted jacket

CARDIGANS > CARDIGAN

CARDINAL *n* any of the high-ranking clergymen of the RC Church who elect the Pope and act as his counsellors ▷ *adj* fundamentally important

CARDINALS > CARDINAL

CARDING > CARD

CARDINGS > CARD

CARDIO *adj* exercising heart ▷ *n* cardiovascular exercise

CARDIOID *n* heart-shaped curve generated by a fixed point on a circle as it rolls around another fixed circle of equal radius

CARDIOIDS > CARDIOID

CARDIOS > CARDIO

CARDIS > CARDI

CARDITIC > CARDITIS

CARDITIS *n* inflammation of the heart

CARDON *n* variety of cactus

CARDONS > CARDON

CARDOON *n* thistle-like S European plant

CARDOONS > CARDOON

CARDPHONE *n* public telephone operated by the insertion of a phonecard instead of coins

CARDPUNCH *n* device for putting data from a CPU onto punched cards

CARDS > CARD

CARDSHARP *n* professional card player who cheats

CARDUUS *n* thistle

CARDUUSES > CARDUUS

CARDY *same as* > CARDIE

CARE *vb* be concerned ▷ *n* careful attention, caution

CARED > CARE

CAREEN *vb* tilt over to one side

CAREENAGE > CAREEN

CAREENED > CAREEN

CAREENER > CAREEN

CAREENERS > CAREEN

CAREENING > CAREEN

CAREENS > CAREEN

CAREER *n* series of jobs that a person has through their life ▷ *vb* rush in an uncontrolled way ▷ *adj* having chosen to dedicate his or her life to a particular occupation

CAREERED > CAREER

CAREERER > CAREER

CAREERERS > CAREER

CAREERING > CAREER

CAREERISM > CAREERIST

CAREERIST *n* person who seeks advancement by any possible means

CAREERS > CAREER

CAREFREE *adj* without worry or responsibility

CAREFUL *adj* cautious in attitude or action

CAREFULLY > CAREFUL

CAREGIVER *same as* > CARER

CARELESS *adj* done or acting with insufficient attention

CARELINE *n* telephone service set up by a company or other organization to provide its customers or clients with information about its products or services

CARELINES > CARELINE

CAREME *n* period of Lent

CAREMES > CAREME

CARER *n* person who looks after someone who is ill or old, often a relative

CARERS > CARER

CARES > CARE

CARESS *n* gentle affectionate touch or embrace ▷ *vb* touch gently and affectionately

CARESSED > CARESS

CARESSER > CARESS

CARESSERS > CARESS

CARESSES > CARESS

CARESSING > CARESS

CARESSIVE *adj* caressing

CARET *n* proofreading symbol

CARETAKE *vb* to work as a caretaker

CARETAKEN > CARETAKE

CARETAKER *n* person employed to look after a place ▷ *adj* performing the duties of an office temporarily

CARETAKES > CARETAKE

CARETOOK > CARETAKE

CARETS > CARET

CAREWARE *n* computer software licensed in exchange for a donation to charity

CAREWARES > CAREWARE

CAREWORN *adj* showing signs of worry

CAREX *n* any member of the sedge family

CARFARE *n* fare that a passenger is charged for a ride on a bus, etc

CARFARES > CARFARE

CARFAX *n* place where principal roads or streets intersect

CARFAXES > CARFAX

CARFOX *same as* **>** CARFAX

CARFOXES > CARFOX

CARFUFFLE *a variant spelling of* **>** KERFUFFLE

CARFUL *n* maximum number of people a car will hold

CARFULS > CARFUL

CARGEESE > CARGOOSE

CARGO *n* goods carried by a ship, aircraft, etc ▷ *vb* load

CARGOED > CARGO

CARGOES > CARGO

CARGOING > CARGO

CARGOOSE *n* crested grebe

CARGOS > CARGO

CARHOP *n* waiter or waitress at a drive-in restaurant ▷ *vb* work as a carhop

CARHOPPED > CARHOP

CARHOPS > CARHOP

CARIACOU *n* type of deer

CARIACOUS > CARIACOU

CARIAMA *another word for* **>** SERIEMA

CARIAMAS > CARIAMA

CARIBE *n* piranha

CARIBES > CARIBE

CARIBOO *same as* **>** CARIBOU

CARIBOOS > CARIBOO

CARIBOU *n* large N American reindeer

CARIBOUS > CARIBOU

CARICES > CAREX

CARIED *adj* (of teeth) decayed

CARIERE *obsolete word for* **>** CAREER

CARIERES > CARIERE

CARIES *n* tooth decay

CARILLON *n* set of bells played by keyboard or mechanically ▷ *vb* play a carillon

CARILLONS > CARILLON

CARINA *n* keel-like part or ridge

CARINAE > CARINA

CARINAL *adj* keel-like

CARINAS > CARINA

CARINATE *adj* having a keel or ridge

CARINATED *same as* **>** CARINATE

CARING *adj* feeling or showing care and compassion for other people ▷ *n* practice or profession of providing social or medical care

CARINGLY > CARING

CARINGS > CARING

CARIOCA *n* Brazilian dance similar to the samba

CARIOCAS > CARIOCA

CARIOLE *n* small open two-wheeled horse-drawn vehicle

CARIOLES > CARIOLE

CARIOSE *same as* **>** CARIOUS

CARIOSITY > CARIOUS

CARIOUS *adj* (of teeth or bone) affected with caries

CARITAS *n* divine love; charity

CARITASES > CARITAS

CARITATES > CARITAS

CARJACK *vb* attack (a car driver) to rob them or to steal the car ▷ *vb* steal a car, by force, from a person who is present

CARJACKED > CARJACK

CARJACKER > CARJACK

CARJACKS > CARJACK

CARJACOU *variation of* **>** CARIACOU

CARJACOUS > CARJACOU

CARK *vb* break down

CARKED > CARK

CARKING > CARK

CARKS > CARK

CARL *another word for* **>** CHURL

CARLE *same as* **>** CARL

CARLES > CARLE

CARLESS > CAR

CARLIN *same as* **>** CARLING

CARLINE *same as* **>** CARLING

CARLINES > CARLINE

CARLING *n* fore-and-aft beam in a vessel

CARLINGS > CARLING

CARLINS > CARLING

CARLISH *adj* churlish

CARLOAD *n* amount that can be carried by a car

CARLOADS > CARLOAD

CARLOCK *n* type of Russian isinglass

CARLOCKS > CARLOCK

CARLOT *n* boor

CARLOTS > CARLOT

CARLS > CARL

CARMAKER *n* car manufacturing company

CARMAKERS > CARMAKER

CARMAN *n* man who drives a car or cart

CARMELITE *n* member of an order of mendicant friars

CARMEN > CARMAN

CARMINE *adj* vivid red ▷ *n* vivid red colour, sometimes with a purplish tinge

CARMINES > CARMINE

CARN *n* cairn

CARNAGE *n* extensive slaughter of people

CARNAGES > CARNAGE

CARNAHUBA *same as* **>** CARNAUBA

CARNAL *adj* of a sexual or sensual nature ▷ *vb* act in a carnal manner

CARNALISE *vb* sensualise

CARNALISM **>** CARNALISE

CARNALIST **>** CARNALISE

CARNALITY > CARNAL

CARNALIZE *same as* **>** CARNALISE

CARNALLED > CARNAL

CARNALLY > CARNAL

CARNALS > CARNAL

CARNAROLI *n* variety of short-grain rice used for risotto

CARNATION *n* cultivated plant with fragrant white, pink, or red flowers

CARNAUBA *n* Brazilian fan palm tree

CARNAUBAS > CARNAUBA

CARNELIAN *n* reddish-yellow gemstone

CARNEOUS *adj* fleshy

CARNET *n* type of customs licence

CARNETS > CARNET

CARNEY *same as* **>** CARNY

CARNEYED > CARNEY

CARNEYING > CARNEY

CARNEYS > CARNEY

CARNIE *same as* **>** CARNY

CARNIED > CARNY

CARNIER > CARNY

CARNIES > CARNY

CARNIEST > CARNY

CARNIFEX *n* executioner

CARNIFIED > CARNIFY

CARNIFIES > CARNIFY

CARNIFY *vb* be altered so as to resemble skeletal muscle

CARNITINE *n* type of white betaine

CARNIVAL *n* festive period with processions, music, and dancing in the street

CARNIVALS > CARNIVAL

CARNIVORA *n* members of a group of carnivorous mammals

CARNIVORE *n* meat-eating animal

CARNIVORY *n* state of being carnivore

CARNOSAUR *n* meat-eating dinosaur

CARNOSE *adj* fleshy

CARNOSITY *n* fleshy protrusion

CARNOTITE *n* radioactive yellow mineral

CARNS > CARN

CARNY *vb* coax or cajole or act in a wheedling manner ▷ *n* person who works in a carnival ▷ *adj* sly

CARNYING > CARNY

CARNYX *n* bronze Celtic war trumpet

CARNYXES > CARNYX

CAROACH *same as* **>** CAROCHE

CAROACHES > CAROACH

CAROB *n* pod of a Mediterranean tree, used as a chocolate substitute

CAROBS > CAROB

CAROCH *same as* **>** CAROCHE

CAROCHE *n* stately ceremonial carriage used in the 16th and 17th centuries

CAROCHES > CAROCHE

CAROL *n* joyful Christmas hymn ▷ *vb* sing carols

CAROLED > CAROL

CAROLER > CAROL

CAROLERS > CAROL

CAROLI > CAROLUS

CAROLING > CAROL

CAROLINGS > CAROL

CAROLLED > CAROL

CAROLLER > CAROL

CAROLLERS > CAROL

CAROLLING > CAROL

CAROLS > CAROL

CAROLUS *n* any of several coins struck in the reign of a king called Charles

CAROLUSES > CAROLUS

CAROM *n* shot in which the cue ball is caused to contact one object ball after another ▷ *vb* carambole

CAROMED > CAROM

CAROMEL *vb* turn into caramel

CAROMELS > CAROMEL

CAROMING > CAROM

CAROMS > CAROM

CARON *n* inverted circumflex

CARONS > CARON

CAROTENE *n* any of four orange-red hydrocarbons, found in many plants, converted to vitamin A in the liver

CAROTENES > CAROTENE

CAROTID *n* either of the two arteries supplying blood to the head ▷ *adj* of either of these arteries

CAROTIDAL > CAROTID

CAROTIDS > CAROTID

CAROTIN *same as* **>** CAROTENE

CAROTINS > CAROTIN

CAROUSAL *n* merry drinking party

CAROUSALS > CAROUSAL

CAROUSE *vb* have a merry drinking party

CAROUSED > CAROUSE

CAROUSEL *n* revolving conveyor belt for luggage or photographic slides

CAROUSELS > CAROUSEL

CAROUSER > CAROUSE

CAROUSERS > CAROUSE

CAROUSES > CAROUSE

CAROUSING *same as* **>** CAROUSE

CARP *n* large freshwater fish ▷ *vb* complain, find fault

CARPACCIO *n* Italian dish of thin slices of raw meat or fish

CARPAL *n* wrist bone

CARPALE *same as* > CARPAL

CARPALES > CARPAL

CARPALIA > CARPAL

CARPALS > CARPAL

CARPED > CARP

CARPEL *n* female reproductive organ of a flowering plant

CARPELS > CARPEL

CARPENTER *n* person who makes or repairs wooden structures ▷ *vb* do the work of a carpenter

CARPENTRY *n* skill or work of a carpenter

CARPER > CARP

CARPERS > CARP

CARPET *n* heavy fabric for covering floors ▷ *vb* cover with a carpet

CARPETBAG *n* travelling bag made of carpeting

CARPETED > CARPET

CARPETING *n* carpet material or carpets in general

CARPETS > CARPET

CARPHONE *n* phone designed for use in a car

CARPHONES > CARPHONE

CARPI > CARPUS

CARPING *adj* tending to make petty complaints ▷ *n* petty complaint

CARPINGLY > CARPING

CARPINGS > CARPING

CARPOLOGY *n* branch of botany concerned with the study of fruits and seeds

CARPOOL *vb* share the use of a single car to travel to work or school

CARPOOLED > CARPOOL

CARPOOLER > CARPOOL

CARPOOLS > CARPOOL

CARPORT *n* shelter for a car, consisting of a roof supported by posts

CARPORTS > CARPORT

CARPS > CARP

CARPUS *n* set of eight bones of the wrist

CARR *n* area of bog or fen in which scrub has become established

CARRACK *n* galleon used as a merchantman

CARRACKS > CARRACK

CARRACT *same as* > CARRACK

CARRACTS > CARRACT

CARRAGEEN *n* edible red seaweed of North America and N Europe

CARRAT *same as* > CARAT

CARRATS > CARRAT

CARRAWAY *same as* > CARAWAY

CARRAWAYS > CARRAWAY

CARRECT *same as* > CARRACK

CARRECTS > CARRECT

CARREFOUR *n* public square, esp one at the intersection of several roads

CARREL *n* small individual study room or private desk

CARRELL *same as* > CARREL

CARRELLS > CARRELL

CARRELS > CARREL

CARRIAGE *n* one of the sections of a train for passengers

CARRIAGES > CARRIAGE

CARRICK *n* as in *carrick bend* type of knot

CARRIED > CARRY

CARRIER *n* person or thing that carries something

CARRIERS > CARRIER

CARRIES > CARRY

CARRIOLE *same as* > CARIOLE

CARRIOLES > CARRIOLE

CARRION *n* dead and rotting flesh

CARRIONS > CARRION

CARRITCH *n* catechism

CARROCH *variant of* > CAROCHE

CARROCHES > CAROCHE

CARROM *same as* > CAROM

CARROMED > CARROM

CARROMING > CARROM

CARROMS > CARROM

CARRON *n* as in *carron oil* ointment of limewater and linseed oil

CARRONADE *n* obsolete naval gun of short barrel and large bore

CARROT *n* long tapering orange root vegetable

CARROTIER > CARROTY

CARROTIN *n* carotene

CARROTINS > CARROTIN

CARROTS > CARROT

CARROTTOP *n* facetious term for a person with red hair

CARROTY *adj* (of hair) reddish-orange

CARROUSEL *a variant spelling of* > CAROUSEL

CARRS > CARR

CARRY *vb* take from one place to another

CARRYALL *n* light four-wheeled horse-drawn carriage usually designed to carry four passengers

CARRYALLS > CARRYALL

CARRYBACK *n* amount carried back in accounting

CARRYCOT *n* light portable bed for a baby, with handles and a hood

CARRYCOTS > CARRYCOT

CARRYING > CARRY

CARRYON *n* fuss or commotion

CARRYONS > CARRYON

CARRYOUT *n* hot cooked food bought in a shop for consumption elsewhere

CARRYOUTS > CARRYOUT

CARRYOVER *n* sum or balance carried forward in accounting

CARRYTALE *n* gossip

CARS > CAR

CARSE *n* riverside area of flat fertile alluvium

CARSES > CARSE

CARSEY *slang word for* > TOILET

CARSEYS > CARSEY

CARSHARE *same as* > CARPOOL

CARSHARED > CARSHARE

CARSHARES > CARSHARE

CARSICK *adj* nauseated from riding in a car

CARSPIEL *n* curling match which has a car as a prize

CARSPIELS > CARSPIEL

CART *n* open two-wheeled horse-drawn vehicle ▷ *vb* carry, usu with some effort

CARTA *n* charter

CARTABLE > CART

CARTAGE *n* process or cost of carting

CARTAGES > CARTAGE

CARTAS > CARTA

CARTE *n* fencing position

CARTED > CART

CARTEL *n* association of competing firms formed to fix prices

CARTELISE *same as* > CARTELIZE

CARTELISM > CARTEL

CARTELIST > CARTEL

CARTELIZE *vb* form or be formed into a cartel

CARTELS > CARTEL

CARTER > CART

CARTERS > CART

CARTES > CARTE

CARTFUL *n* amount a cart can hold

CARTFULS > CARTFUL

CARTHORSE *n* large heavily built horse

CARTILAGE *n* strong flexible tissue forming part of the skeleton

CARTING > CART

CARTLOAD *n* amount a cart can hold

CARTLOADS > CARTLOAD

CARTOGRAM *n* map showing statistical information in diagrammatic form

CARTOLOGY *n* theory of mapmaking

CARTON *n* container made of cardboard or waxed paper ▷ *vb* enclose (goods) in a carton

CARTONAGE *n* material from which mummy masks and coffins were made

CARTONED > CARTON

CARTONING > CARTON

CARTONS > CARTON

CARTOON *n* humorous or satirical drawing ▷ *vb* depict in a cartoon

CARTOONED > CARTOON

CARTOONS > CARTOON

CARTOONY *adj* of or like a cartoon

CARTOP *adj* designed to be transported on top of a vehicle

CARTOPPER *n* anything designed to be transported on top of a vehicle

CARTOUCH *same as* > CARTOUCHE

CARTOUCHE *n* ornamental tablet or panel in the form of a scroll

CARTRIDGE *n* casing containing an explosive charge and bullet for a gun

CARTROAD *n* road for carts to drive on

CARTROADS > CARTROAD

CARTS > CART

CARTULARY *n* collection of charters or records, esp relating to the title to an estate or monastery

CARTWAY *n* way by which carts travel

CARTWAYS > CARTWAY

CARTWHEEL *n* sideways somersault supported by the hands with legs outstretched ▷ *vb* perform a cartwheel movement

CARUCAGE *n* tax due on a carucate

CARUCAGES > CARUCAGE

CARUCATE *n* area of land an oxen team could plough in a year

CARUCATES > CARUCATE

CARUNCLE *n* fleshy outgrowth on the heads of certain birds, such as a cock's comb

CARUNCLES > CARUNCLE

CARVACROL *n* aromatic phenol found in oregano

CARVE *vb* cut to form an object

CARVED > CARVE

CARVEL *same as* > CARAVEL

CARVELS > CARVEL

CARVEN *an archaic or literary past participle of* > CARVE

CARVER n carving knife
CARVERIES > CARVERY
CARVERS > CARVER
CARVERY n restaurant where customers pay a set price for unrestricted helpings
CARVES > CARVE
CARVIES > CARVY
CARVING n figure or design produced by carving stone or wood
CARVINGS > CARVING
CARVY n caraway seed
CARWASH n drive-through structure containing automated equipment for washing cars
CARWASHES > CARWASH
CARYATIC > CARYATID
CARYATID n supporting column in the shape of a female figure
CARYATIDS > CARYATID
CARYOPSES > CARYOPSIS
CARYOPSIS n dry seedlike fruit having the pericarp fused to the seed coat of the single seed: produced by the grasses
CARYOTIN variant of > KARYOTIN
CARYOTINS > CARYOTIN
CASA n house
CASABA n kind of winter muskmelon
CASABAS > CASABA
CASAS > CASA
CASAVA same as > CASSAVA
CASAVAS > CASAVA
CASBAH n citadel of a N African city
CASBAHS > CASBAH
CASCABEL n knoblike protrusion on the rear part of the breech of an obsolete muzzle-loading cannon
CASCABELS > CASCABEL
CASCABLE same as > CASCABEL
CASCABLES > CASCABLE
CASCADE n waterfall ▷ vb flow or fall in a cascade
CASCADED > CASCADE
CASCADES > CASCADE
CASCADING > CASCADE
CASCADURA n Trinidadian fish
CASCARA n bark of a N American shrub, used as a laxative
CASCARAS > CASCARA
CASCHROM n wooden hand-plough
CASCHROMS > CASCHROM
CASCO n Argentinian homestead
CASCOS > CASCO
CASE n instance, example ▷ vb inspect (a building)

with the intention of burgling it
CASEASE n proteolytic enzyme
CASEASES > CASEASE
CASEATE vb undergo caseation
CASEATED > CASEATE
CASEATES > CASEATE
CASEATING > CASEATE
CASEATION n formation of cheese from casein during the coagulation of milk
CASEBOOK n book in which records of legal or medical cases are kept
CASEBOOKS > CASEBOOK
CASEBOUND another word for > HARDBACK
CASED > CASE
CASEFIED > CASEFY
CASEFIES > CASEFY
CASEFY vb make or become similar to cheese
CASEFYING > CASEFY
CASEIC adj relating to cheese
CASEIN n phosphoprotein forming the basis of cheese
CASEINATE n protein found in milk
CASEINS > CASEIN
CASELAW n law established by previous cases
CASELAWS > CASELAW
CASELOAD n number of cases that someone like a doctor or social worker deals with at any one time
CASELOADS > CASELOAD
CASEMAKER n in bookbinding, machine that makes stiff covers for hardbacks
CASEMAN n in printing, a person who sets and corrects type
CASEMATE n armoured compartment in a ship or fortification in which guns are mounted
CASEMATED > CASEMATE
CASEMATES > CASEMATE
CASEMEN > CASEMAN
CASEMENT n window that is hinged on one side
CASEMENTS > CASEMENT
CASEMIX n mix or type of patients treated by a hospital or medical unit
CASEMIXES > CASEMIX
CASEOSE n peptide produced by the peptic digestion of casein
CASEOSES > CASEOSE
CASEOUS adj of or like cheese
CASERN n (formerly) a billet or accommodation for soldiers in a town
CASERNE same as > CASERN

CASERNES > CASERNE
CASERNS > CASERN
CASES > CASE
CASETTE variant of > CASSETTE
CASETTES > CASETTE
CASEVAC vb evacuate (a casualty) from a combat zone, usu by air
CASEVACED > CASEVAC
CASEVACS > CASEVAC
CASEWORK n social work based on close study of the personal histories and circumstances of individuals and families
CASEWORKS > CASEWORK
CASEWORM n caddis worm
CASEWORMS > CASEWORM
CASH n banknotes and coins ▷ adj of, for, or paid in cash ▷ vb obtain cash for
CASHABLE > CASH
CASHAW n winter squash
CASHAWS > CASHAW
CASHBACK n discount offered in return for immediate payment
CASHBACKS > CASHBACK
CASHBOOK n journal in which cash receipts and payments are recorded
CASHBOOKS > CASHBOOK
CASHBOX n box for holding cash
CASHBOXES > CASHBOX
CASHED > CASH
CASHES > CASH
CASHEW n edible kidney-shaped nut
CASHEWS > CASHEW
CASHIER n person responsible for handling cash in a bank, shop, etc ▷ vb dismiss with dishonour from the armed forces
CASHIERED > CASHIER
CASHIERER > CASHIER
CASHIERS > CASHIER
CASHING > CASH
CASHLESS adj functioning, operated, or performed without using coins or banknotes for money transactions but instead using credit cards or electronic transfer of funds
CASHMERE n fine soft wool obtained from goats
CASHMERES > CASHMERE
CASHOO n catechu
CASHOOS > CASHOO
CASHPOINT n cash dispenser
CASIMERE same as > CASSIMERE
CASIMERES > CASIMERE
CASIMIRE variant of > CASSIMERE
CASIMIRES > CASIMIRE
CASING n protective case, covering

CASINGS > CASING
CASINI > CASINO
CASINO n public building or room where gambling games are played
CASINOS > CASINO
CASITA n small house
CASITAS > CASITA
CASK n barrel used to hold alcoholic drink ▷ vb put into a cask
CASKED > CASK
CASKET n small box for valuables ▷ vb put into a casket
CASKETED > CASKET
CASKETING > CASKET
CASKETS > CASKET
CASKIER > CASKY
CASKIEST > CASKY
CASKING > CASK
CASKS > CASK
CASKSTAND n frame on which a cask rests
CASKY adj (of wine) having a musty smell due to resting too long in the cask
CASPASE n type of enzyme
CASPASES > CASPASE
CASQUE n helmet or a helmet-like process or structure
CASQUED > CASQUE
CASQUES > CASQUE
CASSABA same as > CASABA
CASSABAS > CASSABA
CASSAREEP n juice of the bitter cassava root, boiled down to a syrup and used as a flavouring, esp in West Indian cookery
CASSATA n ice cream usually containing nuts and candied fruit
CASSATAS > CASSATA
CASSATION n (esp in France) annulment, as of a judicial decision by a higher court
CASSAVA n starch obtained from the roots of a tropical American plant, used to make tapioca
CASSAVAS > CASSAVA
CASSENA same as > CASSINA
CASSENAS > CASSENA
CASSENE same as > CASSINA
CASSENES > CASSENE
CASSEROLE n covered dish in which food is cooked slowly, usu in an oven ▷ vb cook in a casserole
CASSETTE n plastic container for magnetic tape
CASSETTES > CASSETTE
CASSIA n tropical plant whose pods yield a mild laxative

CASSIAS > CASSIA
CASSIE n type of thorny shrub
CASSIES > CASSIA
CASSIMERE n woollen suiting cloth of plain or twill weave
CASSINA n American tree
CASSINAS > CASSINA
CASSINE same as > CASSINA
CASSINES > CASSINE
CASSINGLE n cassette single
CASSINO n card game for two to four players
CASSINOS > CASSINO
CASSIOPE n type of evergreen shrub
CASSIOPES > CASSIOPE
CASSIS n blackcurrant cordial
CASSISES > CASSIS
CASSOCK n long tunic, usu black, worn by priests
CASSOCKED > CASSOCK
CASSOCKS > CASSOCK
CASSONADE n raw sugar
CASSONE n highly-decorated Italian dowry chest
CASSONES > CASSONE
CASSOULET n stew originating from France, made from haricot beans and goose, duck, pork, etc
CASSOWARY n large flightless bird of Australia and New Guinea
CASSPIR n armoured military vehicle
CASSPIRS > CASSPIR
CAST n actors in a play or film collectively ▷ vb select (an actor) to play a part in a play or film
CASTABLE adj able to be cast
CASTANET > CASTANETS
CASTANETS pl n musical instrument, used by Spanish dancers, consisting of curved pieces of hollow wood clicked together in the hand
CASTAWAY n shipwrecked person ▷ adj shipwrecked or put adrift ▷ vb cause (a ship, person, etc) to be shipwrecked or abandoned
CASTAWAYS > CASTAWAY
CASTE n any of the hereditary classes into which Hindu society is divided
CASTED adj having a caste
CASTEISM n belief in, and adherence to, the caste system
CASTEISMS > CASTEISM
CASTELESS adj having no caste
CASTELLA > CASTELLUM

CASTELLAN n keeper or governor of a castle
CASTELLUM n fort
CASTER n person or thing that casts
CASTERED adj having casters
CASTERS > CASTER
CASTES > CASTE
CASTIGATE vb reprimand severely
CASTING > CAST
CASTINGS > CAST
CASTLE n large fortified building ▷ vb (in chess) make a move involving king and rook
CASTLED adj like a castle in construction
CASTLES > CASTLE
CASTLING n (in chess) act of castling
CASTLINGS > CASTLING
CASTOCK n kale stalk
CASTOCKS > CASTOCK
CASTOFF n person or thing that has been discarded or abandoned
CASTOFFS > CASTOFF
CASTOR same as > CASTER
CASTOREUM n oil secreted from the beaver, used as bait by trappers
CASTORIES > CASTORY
CASTORS > CASTOR
CASTORY n dye derived from beaver pelts
CASTRAL adj relating to camps
CASTRATE vb remove the testicles of
CASTRATED > CASTRATE
CASTRATER > CASTRATE
CASTRATES > CASTRATE
CASTRATI > CASTRATO
CASTRATO n (in 17th- and 18th-century opera) a male singer whose testicles were removed before puberty, allowing the retention of a soprano or alto voice
CASTRATOR > CASTRATE
CASTRATOS > CASTRATO
CASTS > CAST
CASUAL adj careless, nonchalant ▷ n occasional worker
CASUALISE vb make (a regular employee) into a casual worker
CASUALISM > CASUALISE
CASUALIZE same as > CASUALISE
CASUALLY > CASUAL
CASUALS > CASUAL
CASUALTY n person killed or injured in an accident or war
CASUARINA n Australian tree with jointed green branches

CASUIST n person who attempts to resolve moral dilemmas
CASUISTIC > CASUIST
CASUISTRY n reasoning that is misleading or oversubtle
CASUISTS > CASUIST
CASUS n event
CAT n small domesticated furry mammal ▷ vb flog with a cat-'o-nine-tails
CATABASES > CATABASIS
CATABASIS n descent or downward movement
CATABATIC > CATABASIS
CATABOLIC adj of a metabolic process in which complex molecules are broken down into simple ones with the release of energy
CATACLASM n breaking down
CATACLYSM n violent upheaval
CATACOMB n underground burial place, esp the galleries at Rome, consisting of tunnels with vaults or niches leading off them for tombs
CATACOMBS > CATACOMB
CATAFALCO n temporary raised platform on which a body lies in state before or during a funeral
CATALASE n enzyme that catalyses the decomposition of hydrogen peroxide
CATALASES > CATALASE
CATALATIC adj relating to catalase
CATALEPSY n trancelike state in which the body is rigid
CATALEXES > CATALEXIS
CATALEXIS n the state of lacking a syllable in the last foot of a line of poetry
CATALO same as > CATTALO
CATALOES > CATALO
CATALOG same as > CATALOGUE
CATALOGED > CATALOGUE
CATALOGER > CATALOGUE
CATALOGIC > CATALOG
CATALOGS > CATALOG
CATALOGUE n book containing details of items for sale ▷ vb enter (an item) in a catalogue
CATALOS > CATALO
CATALPA n tree of N America and Asia with bell-shaped whitish flowers
CATALPAS > CATALPA

CATALYSE vb speed up (a chemical reaction) by a catalyst
CATALYSED > CATALYSE
CATALYSER > CATALYSE
CATALYSES > CATALYSIS
CATALYSIS n acceleration of a chemical reaction by the action of a catalyst
CATALYST n substance that speeds up a chemical reaction without itself changing
CATALYSTS > CATALYST
CATALYTIC adj of or relating to catalysis
CATALYZE same as > CATALYSE
CATALYZED > CATALYZE
CATALYZER > CATALYZE
CATALYZES > CATALYZE
CATAMARAN n boat with twin parallel hulls
CATAMENIA another word for > MENSES
CATAMITE n boy kept as a homosexual partner
CATAMITES > CATAMITE
CATAMOUNT n any of various medium-sized felines, such as the puma or lynx
CATAPAN n governor in the Byzantine Empire
CATAPANS > CATAPAN
CATAPHOR n word that refers to or stands for another word used later
CATAPHORA n use of a word such as a pronoun that has the same reference as a word used subsequently in the same discourse
CATAPHORS > CATAPHOR
CATAPHYLL n simplified form of plant leaf, such as a scale leaf or cotyledon
CATAPLASM another name for > POULTICE
CATAPLEXY n sudden temporary paralysis, brought on by severe shock
CATAPULT n Y-shaped device with a loop of elastic, used by children for firing stones ▷ vb shoot forwards or upwards violently
CATAPULTS > CATAPULT
CATARACT n eye disease in which the lens becomes opaque
CATARACTS > CATARACT
CATARHINE n ape with nostrils close together
CATARRH n excessive mucus in the nose and throat, during or following a cold
CATARRHAL > CATARRH
CATARRHS > CATARRH

CATASTA n platform on which slaves were presented for sale

CATASTAS > CATASTA

CATATONIA n form of schizophrenia characterized by stupor, with outbreaks of excitement

CATATONIC > CATATONIA

CATATONY another word for > CATATONIA

CATAWBA n type of red North American grape

CATAWBAS > CATAWBA

CATBIRD n North American songbird

CATBIRDS > CATBIRD

CATBOAT n sailing vessel

CATBOATS > CATBOAT

CATBRIAR same as > CATBRIER

CATBRIARS same as > CATBRIERS

CATBRIER n greenbrier

CATBRIERS > CATBRIER

CATCALL n derisive whistle or cry ▷ vb utter such a call (at)

CATCALLED > CATCALL

CATCALLER > CATCALL

CATCALLS > CATCALL

CATCH vb seize, capture ▷ n device for fastening a door, window, etc

CATCHABLE > CATCH

CATCHALL n something designed to cover a variety of situations

CATCHALLS > CATCHALL

CATCHCRY n well-known much-used phrase, perhaps associated with a particular group

CATCHED rarely used past tense of > CATCH

CATCHEN same as > CATCH

CATCHER n person or thing that catches, esp in a game or sport

CATCHERS > CATCHER

CATCHES > CATCH

CATCHFLY n type of plant with sticky calyxes and stems on which insects are trapped

CATCHIER > CATCHY

CATCHIEST > CATCHY

CATCHILY adv in a pleasant or catchy way

CATCHING > CATCH

CATCHINGS > CATCH

CATCHLINE n political or advertising slogan

CATCHMENT n structure in which water is collected

CATCHPOLE n (in medieval England) a sheriff's officer who arrested debtors

CATCHPOLL same as > CATCHPOLE

CATCHT same as > CATCHED

CATCHUP a variant spelling (esp US) of > KETCHUP

CATCHUPS > CATCHUP

CATCHWEED n goosegrass

CATCHWORD n well-known and frequently used phrase

CATCHY adj (of a tune) pleasant and easily remembered

CATCLAW n type of shrub; black bead

CATCLAWS > CATCLAW

CATCON n catalytic converter

CATCONS > CATCON

CATE n delicacy

CATECHIN n soluble yellow solid substance found in mahogany wood

CATECHINS > CATECHIN

CATECHISE same as > CATECHIZE

CATECHISM n instruction on the doctrine of a Christian Church in a series of questions and answers

CATECHIST > CATECHIZE

CATECHIZE vb instruct by using a catechism

CATECHOL n colourless crystalline phenol found in resins and lignins

CATECHOLS > CATECHOL

CATECHU n astringent resinous substance

CATECHUS > CATECHU

CATEGORIC adj unqualified

CATEGORY n class, group

CATELOG obsolete word for > CATALOGUE

CATELOGS > CATELOG

CATENA n connected series, esp of patristic comments on the Bible

CATENAE > CATENA

CATENANE n type of chemical compound in which the molecules have two or more rings that are interlocked like the links of a chain

CATENANES > CATENANE

CATENARY n curve assumed by a heavy uniform flexible cord hanging freely from two points ▷ adj of, resembling, relating to, or constructed using a catenary or suspended chain

CATENAS > CATENA

CATENATE vb arrange or be arranged in a series of chains or rings

CATENATED > CATENATE

CATENATES > CATENATE

CATENOID n geometrical surface generated by rotating a catenary about its axis

CATENOIDS > CATENOID

CATER vb provide what is needed or wanted, esp food or services

CATERAN n (formerly) a member of a band of brigands in the Scottish highlands

CATERANS > CATERAN

CATERED > CATER

CATERER n person whose job is to provide food for social events

CATERERS > CATERER

CATERESS n female caterer

CATERING n supplying of food for a social event

CATERINGS > CATERING

CATERS > CATER

CATERWAUL n wail, yowl ▷ vb make a yowling noise like a cat

CATES pl n choice dainty food

CATFACE n deformity of the surface of a tree trunk, caused by fire or disease

CATFACES > CATFACE

CATFACING n disorder that affects tomatoes, causing scarring of the fruit

CATFALL n line used as a tackle for hoisting an anchor to the cathead

CATFALLS > CATFALL

CATFIGHT n fight between two women

CATFIGHTS > CATFIGHT

CATFISH n fish with whisker-like barbels round the mouth

CATFISHES > CATFISH

CATFLAP n small flap in a door to let a cat go through

CATFLAPS > CATFLAP

CATFOOD n food for cats

CATFOODS > CATFOOD

CATGUT n strong cord used to string musical instruments and sports rackets

CATGUTS > CATGUT

CATHARISE vb purify

CATHARIZE same as > CATHARISE

CATHARSES > CATHARSIS

CATHARSIS n relief of strong suppressed emotions

CATHARTIC adj causing catharsis ▷ n drug that causes catharsis

CATHEAD n fitting at the bow of a vessel for securing the anchor when raised

CATHEADS > CATHEAD

CATHECT vb invest mental or emotional energy in

CATHECTED > CATHECT

CATHECTIC adj of or relating to cathexis

CATHECTS > CATHECT

CATHEDRA n bishop's throne

CATHEDRAE > CATHEDRA

CATHEDRAL n principal church of a diocese

CATHEDRAS > CATHEDRA

CATHEPSIN n proteolytic enzyme responsible for the autolysis of cells after death

CATHEPTIC > CATHEPSIN

CATHETER n tube inserted into a body cavity to drain fluid

CATHETERS > CATHETER

CATHETUS n straight line or radius perpendicular to another line or radius

CATHEXES > CATHEXIS

CATHEXIS n concentration of psychic energy on a single goal

CATHINONE n synthetic alkaloid compound found in certain stimulants

CATHISMA n short hymn used as a response

CATHISMAS > CATHISMA

CATHODAL > CATHODE

CATHODE n negative electrode, by which electrons leave a circuit

CATHODES > CATHODE

CATHODIC > CATHODE

CATHOLE n hole in a ship through which ropes are passed

CATHOLES > CATHOLE

CATHOLIC adj (of tastes or interests) covering a wide range ▷ n member of the Roman Catholic Church

CATHOLICS > CATHOLIC

CATHOLYTE same as > CATOLYTE

CATHOOD n state of being a cat

CATHOODS > CATHOOD

CATHOUSE a slang word for > BROTHEL

CATHOUSES > CATHOUSE

CATION n positively charged ion

CATIONIC > CATION

CATIONS > CATION

CATJANG n tropical shrub

CATJANGS > CATJANG

CATKIN n drooping flower spike of certain trees

CATKINATE adj like catkin

CATKINS > CATKIN

CATLIKE > CAT

CATLIN same as > CATLING

CATLING n long double-edged surgical knife for amputations

CATLINGS > CATLING

CATLINS > CATLIN

CATMINT n Eurasian plant with scented leaves that attract cats

CATMINTS > CATMINT

CATNAP vb doze ▷ n short sleep or doze

CATNAPER > CATNAP

CATNAPERS > CATNAP

CATNAPPED > CATNAP

CATNAPPER > CATNAP

CATNAPS > CATNAP

CATNEP same as > CATMINT

CATNEPS > CATNEP

CATNIP same as > CATMINT

CATNIPS > CATMINT

CATOLYTE n part of the electrolyte that surrounds the cathode in an electrolytic cell

CATOLYTES > CATOLYTE

CATOPTRIC adj relating to reflection

CATRIGGED adj rigged like a catboat

CATS > CAT

CATSKIN n skin and/or fur of a cat

CATSKINS > CATSKIN

CATSPAW n person used by another as a tool

CATSPAWS > CATSPAW

CATSUIT n one-piece usually close-fitting trouser suit

CATSUITS > CATSUIT

CATSUP a variant (esp US) of > KETCHUP

CATSUPS > CATSUP

CATTABU n cross between common cattle and zebu

CATTABUS > CATTABU

CATTAIL n reed mace

CATTAILS > CATTAIL

CATTALO n hardy breed of cattle

CATTALOES > CATTALO

CATTALOS > CATTALO

CATTED > CAT

CATTERIES > CATTERY

CATTERY n place where cats are bred or looked after

CATTIE same as > CATTY

CATTIER > CATTY

CATTIES > CATTY

CATTIEST > CATTY

CATTILY > CATTY

CATTINESS > CATTY

CATTING > CAT

CATTISH > CAT

CATTISHLY > CAT

CATTLE pl n domesticated cows and bulls

CATTLEMAN n person who breeds, rears, or tends cattle

CATTLEMEN > CATTLEMAN

CATTLEYA n tropical American orchid

cultivated for its purplish-pink or white showy flowers

CATTLEYAS > CATTLEYA

CATTY adj spiteful ▷ n unit of weight, used esp in China

CATWALK n narrow pathway or platform

CATWALKS > CATWALK

CATWORKS n machinery on a drilling platform

CATWORM n type of carnivorous worm

CATWORMS > CATWORM

CAUCHEMAR n nightmare

CAUCUS n local committee or faction of a political party ▷ vb hold a caucus

CAUCUSED > CAUCUS

CAUCUSES > CAUCUS

CAUCUSING > CAUCUS

CAUCUSSED > CAUCUS

CAUCUSSES > CAUCUS

CAUDA n area behind the anus of an animal

CAUDAD adv towards the tail or posterior part

CAUDAE > CAUDA

CAUDAL adj at or near an animal's tail

CAUDALLY > CAUDAL

CAUDATE adj having a tail or a tail-like appendage ▷ n lizard-like amphibian

CAUDATED same as > CAUDATE

CAUDATES > CAUDATE

CAUDATION > CAUDATE

CAUDEX n thickened persistent stem base of some herbaceous perennial plants

CAUDEXES > CAUDEX

CAUDICES > CAUDEX

CAUDICLE n stalk to which an orchid's pollen masses are attached

CAUDICLES > CAUDICLE

CAUDILLO n (in Spanish-speaking countries) a military or political leader

CAUDILLOS > CAUDILLO

CAUDLE n hot spiced wine drink made with gruel, formerly used medicinally ▷ vb make such a drink

CAUDLED > CAUDLE

CAUDLES > CAUDLE

CAUDLING > CAUDLE

CAUDRON Spenserian spelling of > CAULDRON

CAUDRONS > CAUDRON

CAUF n cage for holding live fish in the water

CAUGHT > CATCH

CAUK n type of barite

CAUKER n one who caulks

CAUKERS > CAUKER

CAUKS > CAUK

CAUL n membrane sometimes covering a child's head at birth

CAULD a Scot word for > COLD

CAULDER > CAULD

CAULDEST > CAULD

CAULDRIFE adj susceptible to cold

CAULDRON n large pot used for boiling

CAULDRONS > CAULDRON

CAULDS > CAULD

CAULES > CAULIS

CAULICLE n small stalk or stem

CAULICLES > CAULICLE

CAULICULI n plural form of singular cauliculus: another word for caulicle

CAULIFORM adj resembling a caulis

CAULINARY another word for > CAULINE

CAULINE adj relating to or growing from a plant stem

CAULIS n main stem of a plant

CAULK vb fill in (cracks) with paste etc

CAULKED > CAULK

CAULKER > CAULK

CAULKERS > CAULK

CAULKING > CAULK

CAULKINGS > CAULK

CAULKS > CAULK

CAULOME n plant's stem structure, considered as a whole

CAULOMES > CAULOME

CAULS > CAUL

CAUM same as > CAM

CAUMED > CAUM

CAUMING > CAUM

CAUMS > CAUM

CAUMSTANE same as > CAMSTANE

CAUMSTONE same as > CAMSTONE

CAUP n type of quaich

CAUPS > CAUP

CAURI n former coin of Guinea

CAURIS > CAURI

CAUSA n reason or cause

CAUSABLE > CAUSE

CAUSAE > CAUSA

CAUSAL adj of or being a cause ▷ n something that suggests a cause

CAUSALGIA n burning sensation along the course of a peripheral nerve together with local changes in the appearance of the skin

CAUSALGIC > CAUSALGIA

CAUSALITY n relationship of cause and effect

CAUSALLY > CAUSAL

CAUSALS > CAUSAL

CAUSATION n relationship of cause and effect

CAUSATIVE adj producing an effect ▷ n causative form or class of verbs

CAUSE n something that produces a particular effect ▷ vb be the cause of

CAUSED > CAUSE

CAUSELESS > CAUSE

CAUSEN old infinitive of > CAUSE

CAUSER > CAUSE

CAUSERIE n informal talk or conversational piece of writing

CAUSERIES > CAUSERIE

CAUSERS > CAUSE

CAUSES > CAUSE

CAUSEWAY n raised path or road across water or marshland

CAUSEWAYS > CAUSEWAY

CAUSEY n cobbled street ▷ vb cobble

CAUSEYED > CAUSEY

CAUSEYS > CAUSEY

CAUSING > CAUSE

CAUSTIC adj capable of burning by chemical action ▷ n caustic substance

CAUSTICAL > CAUSTIC

CAUSTICS > CAUSTIC

CAUTEL n craftiness

CAUTELOUS > CAUTEL

CAUTELS > CAUTEL

CAUTER n cauterising instrument

CAUTERANT same as > CAUTERY

CAUTERIES > CAUTERY

CAUTERISE same as > CAUTERIZE

CAUTERISM > CAUTERIZE

CAUTERIZE vb burn (a wound) with heat or a caustic agent to prevent infection

CAUTERS > CAUTER

CAUTERY n coagulation of blood or destruction of body tissue by cauterizing

CAUTION n care, esp in the face of danger ▷ vb warn, advise

CAUTIONED > CAUTION

CAUTIONER > CAUTION

CAUTIONRY n in Scots law, standing surety

CAUTIONS > CAUTION

CAUTIOUS adj showing caution

CAUVES > CAUF

CAVA n Spanish sparkling wine

CAVALCADE n procession of people on horseback or in cars

CAVALERO n cavalier

CAVALEROS > CAVALERO

CAVALETTI n bars supported on low stands used in dressage and horse jumping

CAVALIER adj showing haughty disregard ▷ n gallant gentleman

CAVALIERS > CAVALIER

CAVALLA n type of tropical fish

CAVALLAS > CAVALLA

CAVALLIES > CAVALLY

CAVALLY same as > CAVALLA

CAVALRIES > CAVALRY

CAVALRY n part of the army

CAVAS > CAVA

CAVASS n Turkish armed police officer

CAVASSES > CAVASS

CAVATINA n solo song resembling a simple aria

CAVATINAS > CAVATINA

CAVATINE > CAVATINA

CAVE n hollow in the side of a hill or cliff ▷ vb hollow out

CAVEAT n warning ▷ vb introduce a caveat

CAVEATED > CAVEAT

CAVEATING > CAVEAT

CAVEATOR n person who enters a caveat

CAVEATORS > CAVEATOR

CAVEATS > CAVEAT

CAVED > CAVE

CAVEFISH n type of small freshwater fish living in subterranean and other waters in S North America

CAVEL n drawing of lots among miners for an easy and profitable place at the coalface

CAVELIKE adj resembling a cave

CAVELS > CAVEL

CAVEMAN n prehistoric cave dweller

CAVEMEN > CAVEMAN

CAVENDISH n tobacco that has been sweetened and pressed into moulds to form bars

CAVER > CAVING

CAVERN n large cave ▷ vb shut in or as if in a cavern

CAVERNED > CAVERN

CAVERNING > CAVERN

CAVERNOUS adj like a cavern in vastness, depth, or hollowness

CAVERNS > CAVERN

CAVERS > CAVING

CAVES > CAVE

CAVESSON n kind of hard noseband, used (esp formerly) in breaking a horse in

CAVESSONS > CAVESSON

CAVETTI > CAVETTO

CAVETTO n concave moulding, shaped to a quarter circle in cross section

CAVETTOS > CAVETTO

CAVIAR n salted sturgeon roe, regarded as a delicacy

CAVIARE same as > CAVIAR

CAVIARES > CAVIARE

CAVIARIE same as > CAVIAR

CAVIARIES > CAVIARIE

CAVIARS > CAVIAR

CAVICORN adj (of sheep, goats, etc) having hollow horns as distinct from the solid antlers of deer ▷ n sheep, goats, etc with hollow horns as distinct from the solid antlers of deer

CAVICORNS > CAVICORN

CAVIE n hen coop

CAVIER same as > CAVIAR

CAVIERS > CAVIER

CAVIES > CAVY

CAVIL vb make petty objections ▷ n petty objection

CAVILED > CAVIL

CAVILER > CAVIL

CAVILERS > CAVIL

CAVILING > CAVIL

CAVILLED > CAVIL

CAVILLER > CAVIL

CAVILLERS > CAVIL

CAVILLING > CAVIL

CAVILS > CAVIL

CAVING n sport of exploring caves

CAVINGS > CAVING

CAVITARY adj containing cavities

CAVITATE vb to form cavities or bubbles

CAVITATED > CAVITATE

CAVITATES > CAVITATE

CAVITIED > CAVITY

CAVITIES > CAVITY

CAVITY n hollow space

CAVORT vb skip about

CAVORTED > CAVORT

CAVORTER > CAVORT

CAVORTERS > CAVORT

CAVORTING > CAVORT

CAVORTS > CAVORT

CAVY n type of small rodent

CAW n cry of a crow, rook, or raven ▷ vb make this cry

CAWED > CAW

CAWING > CAW

CAWINGS > CAW

CAWK same as > CAUK

CAWKER n metal projection on a horse's shoe to prevent slipping

CAWKERS > CAWKER

CAWKS > CAWK

CAWS > CAW

CAXON n type of wig

CAXONS > CAXON

CAY n low island or bank composed of sand and coral fragments

CAYENNE n very hot condiment

CAYENNED adj seasoned with cayenne

CAYENNES > CAYENNE

CAYMAN n S American reptile similar to an alligator

CAYMANS > CAYMAN

CAYS > CAY

CAYUSE n small American Indian pony used by cowboys

CAYUSES > CAYUSE

CAZ short for > CASUAL

CAZH adj casual

CAZIQUE same as > CACIQUE

CAZIQUES > CAZIQUE

CEANOTHUS n N American shrub grown for its ornamental, often blue, flower clusters

CEAS same as > CAESE

CEASE vb bring or come to an end

CEASED > CEASE

CEASEFIRE n temporary truce

CEASELESS adj without stopping

CEASES > CEASE

CEASING > CEASE

CEASINGS > CEASE

CEAZE obsolete spelling of > SEIZE

CEAZED > CEAZE

CEAZES > CEAZE

CEAZING > CEAZE

CEBADILLA same as > SABADILLA

CEBID n any member of the Cebidae family of New World monkeys

CEBIDS > CEBID

CEBOID same as > CEBID

CEBOIDS > CEBOID

CECA > CECUM

CECAL > CECUM

CECALLY > CECUM

CECILS pl n fried meatballs

CECITIES > CECITY

CECITIS n inflammation of the c(a)ecum

CECITISES > CECITIS

CECITY n rare word for blindness

CECROPIA n large North American moth

CECROPIAS > CECROPIA

CECROPIN n antimicrobial peptide originally derived from the cecropia moth

CECROPINS > CECROPIN

CECUM same as > CAECUM

CEDAR n evergreen coniferous tree ▷ adj made of the wood of a cedar tree

CEDARBIRD n type of waxwing

CEDARED adj covered with cedars

CEDARN adj relating to cedar

CEDARS > CEDAR

CEDARWOOD n wood of any of the cedar trees

CEDARY adj like cedar

CEDE vb surrender (territory or legal rights)

CEDED > CEDE

CEDER > CEDE

CEDERS > CEDE

CEDES > CEDE

CEDI n standard monetary unit of Ghana, divided into 100 pesewas

CEDILLA n character placed under a c in some languages

CEDILLAS > CEDILLA

CEDING > CEDE

CEDIS > CEDI

CEDRATE n citron

CEDRATES > CEDRATE

CEDRINE adj relating to cedar

CEDULA n form of identification in Spanish-speaking countries

CEDULAS > CEDULA

CEE n third letter of the alphabet

CEES > CEE

CEIBA n type of tropical tree

CEIBAS > CEIBA

CEIL vb line (a ceiling) with plaster, boarding, etc

CEILED > CEIL

CEILER > CEIL

CEILERS > CEIL

CEILI variant spelling of > CEILIDH

CEILIDH n social gathering for singing and dancing

CEILIDHS > CEILIDH

CEILING n inner upper surface of a room ▷ vb make a ceiling

CEILINGED > CEILING

CEILINGS > CEILING

CEILIS > CEILI

CEILS > CEIL

CEINTURE n belt

CEINTURES > CEINTURE

CEL short for > CELLULOID

CELADON n type of porcelain having a greyish-green glaze: mainly Chinese

CELADONS > CELADON

CELANDINE n wild plant with yellow flowers

CELEB n celebrity

CELEBRANT n person who performs a religious ceremony

CELEBRATE vb hold festivities to mark (a happy event, anniversary, etc)

CELEBRITY n famous person

CELEBS > CELEB

CELECOXIB n type of anti-inflammatory drug

CELERIAC n variety of celery with a large turnip-like root

CELERIACS > CELERIAC

CELERIES > CELERY

CELERITY n swiftness

CELERY n vegetable with long green crisp edible stalks

CELESTA n instrument like a small piano

CELESTAS > CELESTA

CELESTE same as > CELESTA

CELESTES > CELESTE

CELESTIAL adj heavenly, divine

CELESTINE same as > CELESTITE

CELESTITE n white, red, or blue mineral

CELIAC same as > COELIAC

CELIACS > CELIAC

CELIBACY > CELIBATE

CELIBATE adj unmarried or abstaining from sex, esp because of a religious vow of chastity ▷ n celibate person

CELIBATES > CELIBATE

CELIBATIC adj celibate

CELL n smallest unit of an organism that is able to function independently

CELLA n inner room of a classical temple

CELLAE > CELLA

CELLAR n underground room for storage ▷ vb store in a cellar

CELLARAGE n area of a cellar

CELLARED > CELLAR

CELLARER n monastic official responsible for food, drink, etc

CELLARERS > CELLARER

CELLARET n case, cabinet, or sideboard with compartments for holding wine bottles

CELLARETS > CELLARET

CELLARING > CELLAR

CELLARIST same as > CELLARER

CELLARMAN n person in charge of a cellar

CELLARMEN > CELLARMAN

CELLAROUS adj relating to a cellar

CELLARS > CELLAR

CELLARWAY n way into cellar

CELLBLOCK n group of prison cells

CELLED adj cellular

CELLI > CELLO

CELLING n formation of cells

CELLINGS > CELLING

CELLIST > CELLO

CELLISTS > CELLO

CELLMATE n person with whom a prisoner shares a prison cell

CELLMATES > CELLMATE

CELLO n large low-pitched instrument of the violin family

CELLOIDIN n nitrocellulose compound derived from pyroxylin, used in a solution of alcohol and ether for embedding specimens before cutting sections for microscopy

CELLOS > CELLO

CELLOSE n disaccharide obtained by the hydrolysis of cellulose by cellulase

CELLOSES > CELLOSE

CELLPHONE n portable telephone operated by cellular radio

CELLS > CELL

CELLULAR adj of or consisting of cells ▷ n cellular phone

CELLULARS > CELLULAR

CELLULASE n any enzyme that converts cellulose to the disaccharide cellobiose

CELLULE n very small cell

CELLULES > CELLULE

CELLULITE n fat deposits under the skin alleged to resist dieting

CELLULOID n kind of plastic used to make toys and, formerly, photographic film

CELLULOSE n main constituent of plant cell walls, used in making paper, plastics, etc

CELLULOUS > CELLULOSE

CELOM same as > COELOM

CELOMATA > CELOM

CELOMIC > CELOM

CELOMS > CELOM

CELOSIA same as > COCKSCOMB

CELOSIAS > CELOSIA

CELOTEX n tradename for a type of insulation board

CELOTEXES > CELOTEX

CELS > CEL

CELSITUDE n loftiness

CELT n stone or metal axelike instrument with a bevelled edge

CELTS > CELT

CEMBALI > CEMBALO

CEMBALIST > CEMBALO

CEMBALO n harpsichord

CEMBALOS > CEMBALO

CEMBRA n Swiss pine

CEMBRAS > CEMBRA

CEMENT n powder mixed with water and sand to make mortar or concrete ▷ vb join, bind, or cover with cement

CEMENTA > CEMENTUM

CEMENTED > CEMENT

CEMENTER > CEMENT

CEMENTERS > CEMENT

CEMENTING > CEMENT

CEMENTITE n hard brittle compound of iron and carbon

CEMENTS > CEMENT

CEMENTUM n thin bonelike tissue that covers the dentine in the root of a tooth

CEMENTUMS > CEMENTUM

CEMETERY n place where dead people are buried

CEMITARE obsolete spelling of > SCIMITAR

CEMITARES > CEMITARE

CENACLE n supper room, esp one on an upper floor

CENACLES > CENACLE

CENDRE adj ash-blond

CENOBITE same as > COENOBITE

CENOBITES > CENOBITE

CENOBITIC > CENOBITE

CENOTAPH n monument honouring soldiers who died in a war

CENOTAPHS > CENOTAPH

CENOTE n natural well formed by the collapse of an overlying limestone crust

CENOTES > CENOTE

CENOZOIC adj of or relating to the most recent geological era, characterized by the development and increase of the mammals

CENS n type of annual property rent

CENSE vb burn incense near or before (an altar, shrine, etc)

CENSED > CENSE

CENSER n container for burning incense

CENSERS > CENSER

CENSES > CENSE

CENSING > CENSE

CENSOR n person authorized to prohibit anything considered obscene or objectionable ▷ vb ban or cut parts of (a film, book, etc)

CENSORED > CENSOR

CENSORIAL > CENSOR

CENSORIAN > CENSOR

CENSORING > CENSOR

CENSORS > CENSOR

CENSUAL > CENSUS

CENSURE n severe disapproval ▷ vb criticize severely

CENSURED > CENSURE

CENSURER > CENSURE

CENSURERS > CENSURE

CENSURES > CENSURE

CENSURING > CENSURE

CENSUS n official count of a population ▷ vb conduct a census

CENSUSED > CENSUS

CENSUSES > CENSUS

CENSUSING > CENSUS

CENT n hundredth part of a monetary unit such as the dollar or euro

CENTAGE n rate per hundred

CENTAGES > CENTAGE

CENTAI > CENTAS

CENTAL n unit of weight equal to 100 pounds (45.3 kilograms)

CENTALS > CENTAL

CENTARE same as > CENTIARE

CENTARES > CENTARE

CENTAS n monetary unit of Lithuania

CENTAUR n mythical creature

CENTAUREA n type of plant of the genus which includes the cornflower and knapweed

CENTAURIC adj integrating mind and body

CENTAURS > CENTAUR

CENTAURY n Eurasian plant with purplish-pink flowers, formerly believed to have medicinal properties

CENTAVO n monetary unit in many Latin American countries

CENTAVOS > CENTAVO

CENTENARY n 100th anniversary or its celebration ▷ adj of or relating to a period of 100 years

CENTENIER n in Jersey, a local police officer

CENTER same as > CENTRE

CENTERED > CENTER

CENTERING same as > CENTRING

CENTERS > CENTER

CENTESES > CENTESIS

CENTESIMI > CENTESIMO

CENTESIMO n former monetary unit of Italy, San Marino, and the Vatican City worth one hundredth of a lira

CENTESIS n surgical puncturing of part of the body with a hollow needle, to extract fluid

CENTIARE n unit of area equal to one square metre

CENTIARES > CENTIARE

CENTIGRAM n one hundredth of a gram

CENTILE n (in statistics) another word for percentile

CENTILES > CENTILE

CENTIME n monetary unit worth one hundredth of a franc

CENTIMES > CENTIME

CENTIMO n monetary unit of Costa Rica, Paraguay, Peru, and Venezuela

CENTIMOS > CENTIMO

CENTINEL obsolete variant of > SENTINEL

CENTINELL obsolete variant of > SENTINEL

CENTINELS > CENTINEL

CENTIPEDE n small wormlike creature with many legs

CENTNER n unit of weight equivalent to 100 pounds (45.3 kilograms)

CENTNERS > CENTNER

CENTO n piece of writing composed of quotations from other authors

CENTOIST n one who composes centos

CENTOISTS > CENTOIST

CENTONATE adj having many patches ▷ n Gregorian chant comprised of a patchwork of texts and melodies

CENTONEL obsolete variant of > SENTINEL

CENTONELL obsolete variant of > SENTINEL

CENTONELS > CENTONEL

CENTONES > CENTO

CENTONIST same as > CENTOIST

CENTOS > CENTO

CENTRA > CENTRUM

CENTRAL adj of, at, or forming the centre ▷ n workplace serving as a telecommunications facility

CENTRALER > CENTRAL

CENTRALLY > CENTRAL

CENTRALS > CENTRAL

CENTRE n middle point or part ▷ vb put in the centre of something

CENTRED adj mentally and emotionally confident, focused, and well-balanced

CENTREING same as > CENTRING

CENTRES > CENTRE

CENTRIC adj being central or having a centre

CENTRICAL same as > CENTRIC

CENTRIES > CENTRY

CENTRING n temporary structure, esp one made of timber, used to support an arch during construction

CENTRINGS > CENTRING

CENTRIOLE n either of two rodlike bodies in most animal cells that form the poles of the spindle during mitosis

CENTRISM > CENTRIST

CENTRISMS > CENTRIST

CENTRIST n person favouring political moderation

CENTRISTS > CENTRIST

CENTRODE n locus produced by plotting course of the instantaneous centre of two bodies in relative motion

CENTRODES > CENTRODE

CENTROID n centre of mass of an object of uniform density, esp a geometric figure

CENTROIDS > CENTROID

CENTRUM n main part or body of a vertebra

CENTRUMS > CENTRUM

CENTRY obsolete variant of > SENTRY

CENTS > CENT

CENTU n Lithuanian money unit

CENTUM adj denoting or belonging to the Indo-European languages in which original velar stops (k) were not palatalized ▷ n hundred

CENTUMS > CENTUM

CENTUMVIR n one of the Roman judges who sat in civil cases

CENTUPLE n one hundredfold

CENTUPLED > CENTUPLE

CENTUPLES > CENTUPLE

CENTURIAL adj of or relating to a Roman century

CENTURIES > CENTURY

CENTURION n (in ancient Rome) officer commanding 100 men

CENTURY n period of 100 years

CEORL n freeman of the lowest class in Anglo-Saxon England

CEORLISH > CEORL

CEORLS > CEORL

CEP another name for > PORCINO

CEPACEOUS adj having an onion-like smell or taste

CEPAGE n grape variety or type of wine

CEPAGES > CEPAGE

CEPE another spelling of > CEP

CEPES > CEPE

CEPHALAD adv towards the head or anterior part

CEPHALATE adj possessing a head

CEPHALIC adj of or relating to the head ▷ n remedy for pains in the head

CEPHALICS > CEPHALIC

CEPHALIN n phospholipid, similar to lecithin, that occurs in the nerve tissue and brain

CEPHALINS > CEPHALIN

CEPHALOUS adj with a head

CEPHEID n type of variable star with a regular cycle of variations in luminosity

CEPHEIDS > CEPHEID

CEPS > CEP

CERACEOUS adj waxlike or waxy

CERAMAL same as > CERMET

CERAMALS > CERAMAL

CERAMIC n hard brittle material ▷ adj made of ceramic

CERAMICS n art of producing ceramic objects

CERAMIDE n any of a class of biologically important compounds used as moisturizers in skin-care preparations

CERAMIDES > CERAMIDE

CERAMIST > CERAMICS

CERAMISTS > CERAMICS

CERASIN n meta-arabinic acid

CERASINS > CERASIN

CERASTES n type of venomous snake, esp the horned viper

CERASTIUM n mouse-eared chickweed

CERATE n hard ointment or medicated paste

CERATED adj (of certain birds, such as the falcon) having a cere

CERATES > CERATE

CERATIN same as > KERATIN

CERATINS > CERATIN

CERATITIS same as > KERATITIS

CERATODUS n type of extinct lungfish common in Cretaceous and Triassic times

CERATOID adj having the shape or texture of animal horn

CERBEREAN adj of or resembling Cerberus, the three-headed dog that guarded the entrance to Hades in Greek mythology

CERBERIAN same as > CERBEREAN

CERCAL adj of or relating to a tail

CERCARIA n one of the larval forms of trematode worms. It has a short forked tail and resembles an immature adult

CERCARIAE > CERCARIA

CERCARIAL > CERCARIA

CERCARIAN > CERCARIA

CERCARIAS > CERCARIA

CERCI > CERCUS

CERCIS n type of tree or shrub

CERCISES > CERCIS

CERCLAGE n treatment of a malfunctioning cervix by means of a suture in early pregnancy

CERCLAGES > CERCLAGE

CERCOPID n froghopper or spittlebug

CERCOPIDS > CERCOPID

CERCUS n one of a pair of sensory appendages on some insects and other arthropods

CERE n soft waxy swelling at the base of the upper beak of a parrot ▷ vb wrap (a corpse) in a cerecloth

CEREAL n grass plant with edible grain, such as oat or wheat

CEREALIST n expert in cereals

CEREALS > CEREAL

CEREBELLA n plural of singular cerebellum: one of the major divisions of the vertebrate brain

CEREBRA > CEREBRUM

CEREBRAL same as > CACUMINAL

CEREBRALS > CEREBRAL

CEREBRATE vb use the mind

CEREBRIC > CEREBRUM

CEREBROID > CEREBRUM

CEREBRUM n main part of the brain

CEREBRUMS > CEREBRUM

CERECLOTH n waxed waterproof cloth of a kind formerly used as a shroud

CERED > CERE

CEREMENT n any burial clothes

CEREMENTS > CEREMENT

CEREMONY n formal act or ritual

CEREOUS adj waxlike

CERES > CERE

CERESIN n white wax extracted from ozocerite

CERESINE same as > CERESIN

CERESINES > CERESINE

CERESINS > CERESIN

CEREUS n type of tropical American cactus

CEREUSES > CEREUS

CERGE n large altar candle

CERGES > CERGE

CERIA n ceric oxide

CERIAS > CERIA

CERIC adj of or containing cerium in the tetravalent state

CERING > CERE

CERIPH same as > SERIF

CERIPHS > CERIPH

CERISE adj cherry-red ▷ n moderate to dark red colour

CERISES > CERISE
CERITE n hydrous silicate of cerium
CERITES > CERITE
CERIUM n steel-grey metallic element
CERIUMS > CERIUM
CERMET n materials consisting of a metal matrix with ceramic particles disseminated through it
CERMETS > CERMET
CERNE obsolete variant of > ENCIRCLE
CERNED > CERNE
CERNES > CERNE
CERNING > CERNE
CERNUOUS adj (of some flowers or buds) drooping
CERO n type of large food fish
CEROGRAPH n writing on wax
CEROMANCY n divination by interpreting significance of shapes formed when melted wax is dropped into water
CEROON n hide-covered bale
CEROONS > CEROON
CEROS > CERO
CEROTIC adj as in cerotic acid white insoluble odourless wax
CEROTYPE n process for preparing a printing plate by engraving a wax-coated copper plate and then using this as a mould for an electrotype
CEROTYPES > CEROTYPE
CEROUS adj of or containing cerium in the trivalent state
CERRADO n vast area of tropical savanna in Brazil
CERRADOS > CERRADO
CERRIAL adj relating to the cerris
CERRIS n Turkey oak
CERRISES > CERRIS
CERT n certainty
CERTAIN adj positive and confident
CERTAINER > CERTAIN
CERTAINLY adv without doubt ▷ sentence substitute by all means
CERTAINTY n state of being sure
CERTES adv with certainty
CERTIE n as in by my certie assuredly
CERTIFIED > CERTIFY
CERTIFIER > CERTIFY
CERTIFIES > CERTIFY
CERTIFY vb confirm, attest to
CERTITUDE n confidence, certainty
CERTS > CERT

CERTY n as in by my certy assuredly
CERULE adj sky-blue
CERULEAN n deep blue colour ▷ n light shade of blue
CERULEANS > CERULEAN
CERULEIN n type of dyestuff
CERULEINS > CERULEIN
CERULEOUS adj sky-blue
CERUMEN n wax secreted by glands in the external ear
CERUMENS > CERUMEN
CERUSE n white lead
CERUSES > CERUSE
CERUSITE same as > CERUSSITE
CERUSITES > CERUSITE
CERUSSITE n usually white mineral, found in veins
CERVELAS n French garlicky pork sausage
CERVELAT n smoked sausage made from pork and beef
CERVELATS > CERVELAT
CERVEZA n Spanish word for beer
CERVEZAS > CERVEZA
CERVICAL adj of or relating to the neck or cervix
CERVICES > CERVIX
CERVICUM n flexible region between the prothorax and head in insects
CERVICUMS > CERVICUM
CERVID n type of ruminant mammal characterized by the presence of antlers
CERVIDS > CERVID
CERVINE adj resembling or relating to a deer
CERVIX n narrow entrance of the womb
CERVIXES > CERVIX
CESAREAN variant of > CAESAREAN
CESAREANS > CESAREAN
CESAREVNA n wife of a Russian tsar's eldest son
CESARIAN US variant of > CAESAREAN
CESARIANS > CESARIAN
CESIOUS same as > CAESIOUS
CESIUM same as > CAESIUM
CESIUMS > CESIUM
CESPITOSE adj growing in dense tufts
CESS n any of several special taxes, such as a land tax in Scotland ▷ vb tax or assess for taxation
CESSATION n ceasing
CESSE obsolete variant of > CEASE

CESSED > CESS
CESSER n coming to an end of a term interest or annuity
CESSERS > CESSER
CESSES > CESS
CESSING > CESS
CESSION n ceding
CESSIONS > CESSION
CESSPIT same as > CESSPOOL
CESSPITS > CESSPIT
CESSPOOL n covered tank or pit for collecting and storing sewage or waste water
CESSPOOLS > CESSPOOL
CESTA n in jai alai, the basket used to throw and catch the pelota
CESTAS > CESTA
CESTI > CESTUS
CESTODE n type of parasitic flatworm such as the tapeworms
CESTODES > CESTODE
CESTOI > CESTOS
CESTOID adj (esp of tapeworms and similar animals) ribbon-like in form ▷ n ribbon-like worm
CESTOIDS > CESTOID
CESTOS same as > CESTUS
CESTOSES > CESTOS
CESTUI n legal term to designate a person
CESTUIS > CESTUI
CESTUS n girdle of Aphrodite (Venus) decorated to cause amorousness
CESTUSES > CESTUS
CESURA a variant spelling of > CAESURA
CESURAE > CESURA
CESURAL > CESURA
CESURAS > CESURA
CESURE same as > CAESURA
CESURES > CESURE
CETACEAN n fish-shaped sea mammal such as a whale or dolphin ▷ adj relating to these mammals
CETACEANS > CETACEAN
CETACEOUS same as > CETACEAN
CETANE n colourless liquid hydrocarbon, used as a solvent
CETANES > CETANE
CETE n group of badgers
CETERACH n scale-fern
CETERACHS > CETERACH
CETES > CETE
CETOLOGY n branch of zoology concerned with the study of whales (cetaceans)
CETRIMIDE n quaternary ammonium compound used as a detergent

CETUXIMAB n monoclonal antibody used to treat cancer
CETYL n univalent alcohol radical
CETYLS > CETYL
CETYWALL n valerian
CETYWALLS > CETYWALL
CEVADILLA same as > SABADILLA
CEVAPCICI n sausages made with beef and paprika
CEVICHE n Peruvian seafood dish
CEVICHES > CEVICHE
CEVITAMIC adj as in cevitamic acid ascorbic (acid)
CEYLANITE same as > CEYLONITE
CEYLONITE n pleonaste
CEZVE n small metal pot for brewing coffee
CEZVES > CEZVE
CH pron obsolete form of I
CHA n tea
CHABAZITE n pink, white, or colourless zeolite mineral
CHABLIS n dry white French wine
CHABOUK n type of whip
CHABOUKS > CHABOUK
CHABUK same as > CHABOUK
CHABUKS > CHABUK
CHACE obsolete variant of > CHASE
CHACED > CHACE
CHACES > CHACE
CHACHKA n cheap trinket
CHACHKAS > CHACHKA
CHACING > CHACE
CHACK vb bite
CHACKED > CHACK
CHACKING > CHACK
CHACKS > CHACK
CHACMA n type of baboon with coarse greyish hair, occurring in S and E Africa
CHACMAS > CHACMA
CHACO same as > SHAKO
CHACOES > CHACO
CHACONINE n toxic substance found in potatoes
CHACONNE n musical form consisting of a set of variations on a repeated melodic bass line
CHACONNES > CHACONNE
CHACOS > CHACO
CHAD n small pieces removed during the punching of holes in punch cards, printer paper, etc
CHADAR same as > CHUDDAR
CHADARIM > CHEDER
CHADARS > CHADAR
CHADDAR same as > CHUDDAR
CHADDARS > CHADDAR

CHADDOR same as > CHUDDAR

CHADDORS > CHADDOR

CHADLESS adj (of a keypunch) not producing chads

CHADO n Japanese tea ceremony

CHADOR same as > CHUDDAR

CHADORS > CHADOR

CHADOS > CHADO

CHADRI n shroud which covers the body from head to foot

CHADS > CHAD

CHAEBOL n large, usually family-owned, business group in South Korea

CHAEBOLS > CHAEBOL

CHAETA n the chitinous bristles on the body of annelids

CHAETAE > CHAETA

CHAETAL > CHAETA

CHAETODON n butterfly fish

CHAETOPOD n type of annelid worm

CHAFE vb make sore or worn by rubbing

CHAFED > CHAFE

CHAFER n large beetle

CHAFERS > CHAFER

CHAFES > CHAFE

CHAFF n grain husks ▷ vb tease good-naturedly

CHAFFED > CHAFF

CHAFFER vb haggle

CHAFFERED > CHAFFER

CHAFFERER > CHAFFER

CHAFFERS > CHAFFER

CHAFFERY n bargaining

CHAFFIER > CHAFF

CHAFFIEST > CHAFF

CHAFFINCH n small European songbird

CHAFFING > CHAFF

CHAFFINGS > CHAFF

CHAFFRON same as > CHAMFRON

CHAFFRONS > CHAFFRON

CHAFFS > CHAFF

CHAFFY > CHAFF

CHAFING > CHAFE

CHAFT n jaw

CHAFTS > CHAFT

CHAGAN n Mongolian royal or imperial title

CHAGANS > CHAGAN

CHAGRIN n annoyance and disappointment ▷ vb embarrass and annoy

CHAGRINED > CHAGRIN

CHAGRINS > CHAGRIN

CHAI n tea, esp as made in India with added spices

CHAIN n flexible length of connected metal links ▷ vb restrict or fasten with or as if with a chain

CHAINE adj (of a dance turn) producing a full rotation for every two

steps taken ▷ vb produce a full rotation for every two steps taken

CHAINED > CHAIN

CHAINER n person who chains

CHAINERS > CHAINER

CHAINES > CHAINE

CHAINFALL n type of hoist

CHAINING > CHAIN

CHAINLESS adj having no chain

CHAINLET n small chain

CHAINLETS > CHAINLET

CHAINMAN n person who does the chaining in a survey

CHAINMEN > CHAINMAN

CHAINS > CHAIN

CHAINSAW n motor-driven saw with teeth linked in a continuous chain ▷ vb operate a chainsaw

CHAINSAWS > CHAINSAW

CHAINSHOT n cannon shot of two balls joined by a chain

CHAINWORK n work linked or looped in the manner of a chain

CHAIR n seat with a back, for one person ▷ vb preside over (a meeting)

CHAIRBACK n back part of a chair

CHAIRDAYS n old age

CHAIRED > CHAIR

CHAIRING > CHAIR

CHAIRLIFT n series of chairs suspended from a moving cable for carrying people up a slope

CHAIRMAN n person in charge of a company's board of directors or a meeting ▷ vb to act as chairman of

CHAIRMANS > CHAIRMAN

CHAIRMEN > CHAIRMAN

CHAIRS > CHAIR

CHAIS > CHAI

CHAISE n light horse-drawn carriage

CHAISES > CHAISE

CHAKALAKA n relish made from tomatoes, onions, and spices

CHAKRA n (in yoga) any of the seven major energy centres in the body

CHAKRAS > CHAKRA

CHAL n in Romany, person or fellow

CHALAH same as > CHALLAH

CHALAHS > CHALAH

CHALAN vb (in India) to cause an accused person to appear before a magistrate ▷ n invoice, pass, or voucher

CHALANED > CHALAN

CHALANING > CHALAN

CHALANNED same as > CHALANED

CHALANS > CHALAN

CHALAZA n one of a pair of spiral threads holding the yolk of a bird's egg in position

CHALAZAE > CHALAZA

CHALAZAL > CHALAZA

CHALAZAS > CHALAZA

CHALAZIA > CHALAZION

CHALAZION n small cyst on the eyelid resulting from chronic inflammation of a meibomian gland

CHALCID n type of tiny insect

CHALCIDS > CHALCID

CHALCOGEN n any of the elements oxygen, sulphur, selenium, tellurium, or polonium, of group 6A of the periodic table

CHALDER n former Scottish dry measure

CHALDERS > CHALDER

CHALDRON n unit of capacity equal to 36 bushels. Formerly used in the US for the measurement of solids, being equivalent to 1.268 cubic metres. Used in Britain for both solids and liquids, it is equivalent to 1.309 cubic metres

CHALDRONS > CHALDRON

CHALEH same as > CHALLAH

CHALEHS > CHALEH

CHALET n kind of Swiss wooden house with a steeply sloping roof

CHALETS > CHALET

CHALICE n large goblet

CHALICED adj (of plants) having cup-shaped flowers

CHALICES > CHALICE

CHALK n soft white rock consisting of calcium carbonate ▷ vb draw or mark with chalk

CHALKED > CHALK

CHALKFACE n work or art of teaching in a school

CHALKIER > CHALK

CHALKIEST > CHALK

CHALKING > CHALK

CHALKLIKE > CHALK

CHALKMARK n as in walk the chalkmark straight line drawn with chalk, used as a sobriety test

CHALKPIT n quarry for chalk

CHALKPITS > CHALKPIT

CHALKS > CHALK

CHALKY > CHALK

CHALLA same as > CHALLAH

CHALLAH n type of bread

CHALLAHS > CHALLAH

CHALLAN same as > CHALAN

CHALLANS > CHALLAN

CHALLAS > CHALLA

CHALLENGE n demanding or stimulating situation ▷ vb issue a challenge to

CHALLIE same as > CHALLIS

CHALLIES > CHALLIE

CHALLIS n lightweight plain-weave fabric

CHALLISES > CHALLIS

CHALLOT > CHALLAH

CHALLOTH > CHALLAH

CHALLY same as > CHALLIS

CHALONE n any internal secretion that inhibits a physiological process or function

CHALONES > CHALONE

CHALONIC > CHALONE

CHALOT > CHALAH

CHALOTH > CHALAH

CHALS > CHAL

CHALUMEAU n early type of reed instrument, precursor of the clarinet

CHALUPA n Mexican dish

CHALUPAS > CHALUPA

CHALUTZ n member of an organization of immigrants to Israeli agricultural settlements

CHALUTZES > CHALUTZ

CHALUTZIM > CHALUTZ

CHALYBEAN adj (of steel) of superior quality

CHALYBITE another name for > SIDERITE

CHAM an archaic word for > KHAN

CHAMADE n (formerly) a signal by drum or trumpet inviting an enemy to a parley

CHAMADES > CHAMADE

CHAMBER n hall used for formal meetings ▷ vb act lasciviously

CHAMBERED > CHAMBER

CHAMBERER n lascivious person

CHAMBERS pl n judge's room for hearing private cases not taken in open court

CHAMBRAY n smooth light fabric of cotton, linen, etc, with white weft and a coloured warp

CHAMBRAYS > CHAMBRAY

CHAMBRE adj (of wine) at room temperature

CHAMELEON n small lizard that changes colour to blend in with its surroundings

CHAMELOT same as > CAMLET

CHAMELOTS > CHAMELOT

CHAMETZ n leavened food which may not be eaten during Passover

CHAMETZES > CHAMETZ
CHAMFER same as > CHASE
CHAMFERED > CHAMFER
CHAMFERER > CHAMFER
CHAMFERS > CHAMFER
CHAMFRAIN same as > CHAMFRON
CHAMFRON n piece of armour for a horse's head
CHAMFRONS > CHAMFRON
CHAMISA n American shrub
CHAMISAL n place overgrown with chamiso
CHAMISALS > CHAMISAL
CHAMISAS > CHAMISA
CHAMISE same as > CHAMISO
CHAMISES > CHAMISE
CHAMISO n four-wing saltbush
CHAMISOS > CHAMISO
CHAMLET same as > CAMLET
CHAMLETS > CHAMLET
CHAMMIED > CHAMMY
CHAMMIES > CHAMMY
CHAMMY same as > CHAMOIS
CHAMMYING > CHAMMY
CHAMOIS n small mountain antelope or a pice of leather from its skin, used for polishing ▷ vb polish with a chamois
CHAMOISED > CHAMOIS
CHAMOISES > CHAMOIS
CHAMOIX same as > CHAMOIS
CHAMOMILE same as > CAMOMILE
CHAMP vb chew noisily
CHAMPAC n type of tree
CHAMPACA same as > CHAMPAC
CHAMPACAS > CHAMPACA
CHAMPACS > CHAMPAC
CHAMPAGNE n sparkling white French wine ▷ adj denoting a luxurious lifestyle
CHAMPAIGN n expanse of open level or gently undulating country
CHAMPAK same as > CHAMPAC
CHAMPAKS > CHAMPAK
CHAMPART n granting of land to a person, on condition that a portion of the crops will be given to the seller
CHAMPARTS > CHAMPART
CHAMPED > CHAMP
CHAMPER > CHAMP
CHAMPERS n champagne
CHAMPERTY n (formerly) an illegal bargain between a party to litigation and an outsider whereby the latter agrees to pay for the action and thereby share in any proceeds recovered
CHAMPIER > CHAMPY

CHAMPIEST > CHAMPY
CHAMPING > CHAMP
CHAMPION n overall winner of a competition ▷ vb support ▷ adj excellent ▷ adv very well
CHAMPIONS > CHAMPION
CHAMPLEVE adj of or relating to a process of enamelling by which grooves are cut into a metal base and filled with enamel colours ▷ n object enamelled by this process
CHAMPS > CHAMP
CHAMPY adj (of earth) churned up (by cattle, for example)
CHAMS > CHAM
CHANA n (in Indian cookery) chickpeas
CHANAS > CHANA
CHANCE n likelihood, probability ▷ vb risk, hazard
CHANCED > CHANCE
CHANCEFUL > CHANCE
CHANCEL n part of a church containing the altar and choir
CHANCELS > CHANCEL
CHANCER n unscrupulous or dishonest opportunist
CHANCERS > CHANCER
CHANCERY n Lord Chancellor's court, now a division of the High Court of Justice
CHANCES > CHANCE
CHANCEY same as > CHANCY
CHANCIER > CHANCY
CHANCIEST > CHANCY
CHANCILY > CHANCY
CHANCING > CHANCE
CHANCRE n small hard growth which is the first sign of syphilis
CHANCRES > CHANCRE
CHANCROID n soft venereal ulcer, esp of the male genitals, caused by a bacterial infection ▷ adj relating to or resembling a chancroid or chancre
CHANCROUS > CHANCRE
CHANCY adj uncertain, risky
CHANDELLE n abrupt climbing turn almost to the point of stalling, in which an aircraft's momentum is used to increase its rate of climb ▷ vb carry out a chandelle
CHANDLER n dealer, esp in ships' supplies
CHANDLERS > CHANDLER
CHANDLERY n business, warehouse, or merchandise of a chandler
CHANFRON same as > CHAMFRON

CHANFRONS > CHANFRON
CHANG n loud discordant noise
CHANGA interj in Indian English, an expression of approval or agreement
CHANGE n becoming different ▷ vb make or become different
CHANGED > CHANGE
CHANGEFUL adj often changing
CHANGER > CHANGE
CHANGERS > CHANGE
CHANGES > CHANGE
CHANGEUP n type of baseball pitch
CHANGEUPS > CHANGEUP
CHANGING > CHANGE
CHANGS > CHANG
CHANK n shell of several types of sea conch, used to make bracelets
CHANKS > CHANK
CHANNEL n band of broadcasting frequencies ▷ vb direct or convey through a channel
CHANNELED > CHANNEL
CHANNELER > CHANNEL
CHANNELS > CHANNEL
CHANNER n gravel
CHANNERS > CHANNER
CHANOYO a variant of > CHADO
CHANOYOS > CHANOYO
CHANOYU same as > CHADO
CHANOYUS > CHADO
CHANSON n song
CHANSONS > CHANSON
CHANT vb utter or sing (a slogan or psalm) ▷ n rhythmic or repetitious slogan
CHANTABLE > CHANT
CHANTAGE n blackmail
CHANTAGES > CHANTAGE
CHANTED > CHANT
CHANTER n (on bagpipes) pipe on which the melody is played
CHANTERS > CHANTER
CHANTEUSE n female singer, esp in a nightclub or cabaret
CHANTEY the usual US spelling of > SHANTY
CHANTEYS > CHANTEY
CHANTIE n chamber pot
CHANTIES > CHANTY
CHANTILLY n as in chantilly lace delicate ornamental lace
CHANTING > CHANT
CHANTINGS > CHANTING
CHANTOR same as > CHANTER
CHANTORS > CHANTOR
CHANTRESS n female chanter
CHANTRIES > CHANTRY
CHANTRY n endowment for the singing of Masses for the soul of the founder

or others designated by him
CHANTS > CHANT
CHANTY same as > SHANTY
CHANUKIAH a variant spelling of > HANUKIAH
CHAO n Vietnamese rice porridge
CHAOLOGY n study of chaos theory
CHAORDIC adj combining elements of chaos and order
CHAOS n complete disorder or confusion
CHAOSES > CHAOS
CHAOTIC > CHAOS
CHAP n man or boy ▷ vb (of the skin) to make or become raw and cracked, esp by exposure to cold
CHAPARRAL n (in the southwestern US) a dense growth of shrubs and trees, esp evergreen oaks
CHAPATI n (in Indian cookery) flat thin unleavened bread
CHAPATIES > CHAPATI
CHAPATIS > CHAPATI
CHAPATTI same as > CHAPATI
CHAPATTIS > CHAPATTI
CHAPBOOK n book of popular ballads, stories, etc, formerly sold by chapmen or pedlars
CHAPBOOKS > CHAPBOOK
CHAPE n metal tip or trimming for a scabbard
CHAPEAU n hat
CHAPEAUS > CHAPEAU
CHAPEAUX > CHAPEAU
CHAPEL n place of worship with its own altar, within a church
CHAPELESS > CHAPE
CHAPELRY n district legally assigned to and served by an Anglican chapel
CHAPELS > CHAPEL
CHAPERON n (esp formerly) an older or married woman who accompanies or supervises a young unmarried woman on social occasions ▷ vb act as a chaperon to
CHAPERONE same as > CHAPERON
CHAPERONS > CHAPERON
CHAPES > CHAPE
CHAPESS n woman
CHAPESSES > CHAPESS
CHAPITER same as > CAPITAL
CHAPITERS > CHAPITER
CHAPKA same as > CZAPKA
CHAPKAS > CHAPKA
CHAPLAIN n clergyman attached to a chapel, military body, or institution

CHAPLAINS > CHAPLAIN
CHAPLESS *adj* lacking a lower jaw
CHAPLET *n* garland for the head ▷ *vb* create a garland
CHAPLETED > CHAPLET
CHAPLETS > CHAPLET
CHAPMAN *n* travelling pedlar
CHAPMEN > CHAPMAN
CHAPPAL *n* one of a pair of sandals, usually of leather, worn in India
CHAPPALS > CHAPPAL
CHAPPATI *same as* > CHAPATI
CHAPPATIS > CHAPPATI
CHAPPED > CHAP
CHAPPESS *same as* > CHAPESS
CHAPPIE *n* man or boy
CHAPPIER > CHAPPY
CHAPPIES > CHAPPIE
CHAPPIEST > CHAPPY
CHAPPING > CHAP
CHAPPY *adj* (of skin) chapped
CHAPRASSI *n* in India, during the British Empire, an office messenger
CHAPS > CHAP
CHAPSTICK *n* cylinder of a substance for preventing or soothing chapped lips
CHAPT *adj* chapped
CHAPTER *n* division of a book ▷ *vb* divide into chapters
CHAPTERAL > CHAPTER
CHAPTERED > CHAPTER
CHAPTERS > CHAPTER
CHAPTREL *n* capital of a pillar supporting an arch
CHAPTRELS > CHAPTREL
CHAQUETA *n* South American cowboy jacket
CHAQUETAS > CHAQUETA
CHAR *vb* blacken by partial burning ▷ *n* charwoman
CHARA *n* type of green freshwater algae
CHARABANC *n* coach for sightseeing
CHARACID *same as* > CHARACIN
CHARACIDS > CHARACIN
CHARACIN *n* type of small carnivorous freshwater fish of Central and S America and Africa
CHARACINS > CHARACIN
CHARACT *n* distinctive mark
CHARACTER *n* combination of qualities distinguishing a person, group, or place
CHARACTS > CHARACT
CHARADE *n* absurd pretence
CHARADES *n* game in which one team acts out each syllable of a word or

phrase, which the other team has to guess
CHARANGA *n* type of orchestra used in performing traditional Cuban music
CHARANGAS > CHARANGA
CHARANGO *n* Andean ten-stringed mandolin
CHARANGOS > CHARANGO
CHARAS *another name for* > HASHISH
CHARASES > CHARAS
CHARBROIL *vb* grill over charcoal
CHARCOAL *n* black substance formed by partially burning wood ▷ *adj* very dark grey ▷ *vb* write, draw, or blacken with charcoal
CHARCOALS > CHARCOAL
CHARCOALY > CHARCOAL
CHARD *n* variety of beet
CHARDS > CHARD
CHARE *same as* > CHAR
CHARED > CHAR
CHARES > CHAR
CHARET *obsolete variant of* > CHARIOT
CHARETS > CHARET
CHARETTE *n* public brainstorming session
CHARETTES > CHARETTE
CHARGE *vb* ask as a price ▷ *n* price charged
CHARGED > CHARGE
CHARGEFUL *adj* expensive
CHARGER *n* device for charging an accumulator
CHARGERS > CHARGER
CHARGES > CHARGE
CHARGING *n* act of charging
CHARGINGS > CHARGING
CHARGRILL *vb* grill over charcoal
CHARIDEE *n* jocular spelling of charity, as pronounced in a mid-Atlantic accent
CHARIDEES > CHARIDEE
CHARIER > CHARY
CHARIEST > CHARY
CHARILY *adv* cautiously
CHARINESS *n* state of being chary
CHARING > CHAR
CHARIOT *n* two-wheeled horse-drawn vehicle ▷ *vb* ride in a chariot
CHARIOTED > CHARIOT
CHARIOTS > CHARIOT
CHARISM *same as* > CHARISMA
CHARISMA *n* person's power to attract or influence people
CHARISMAS > CHARISMA
CHARISMS > CHARISM
CHARITIES > CHARITY
CHARITY *n* organization that gives help, such as

money or food, to those in need
CHARIVARI *n* discordant mock serenade to newlyweds, made with pans, kettles, etc ▷ *vb* make such a serenade
CHARK *vb* char
CHARKA *same as* > CHARKHA
CHARKAS > CHARKA
CHARKED > CHARK
CHARKHA *n* (in India) a spinning wheel, esp for cotton
CHARKHAS > CHARKHA
CHARKING > CHARK
CHARKS > CHARK
CHARLADY *same as* > CHARWOMAN
CHARLATAN *n* person who claims expertise that he or she does not have
CHARLEY *n* as in *charley horse* muscle stiffness after strenuous exercise
CHARLEYS > CHARLEY
CHARLIE *n* fool
CHARLIER *n* as in *charlier shoe* special light horseshoe
CHARLIES > CHARLIE
CHARLOCK *n* weed with hairy leaves and yellow flowers
CHARLOCKS > CHARLOCK
CHARLOTTE *n* dessert made with fruit and bread or cake crumbs
CHARM *n* attractive quality ▷ *vb* attract, delight
CHARMED *adj* delighted or fascinated
CHARMER *n* attractive person
CHARMERS > CHARMER
CHARMEUSE *n* trademark for a lightweight fabric with a satin-like finish
CHARMFUL *adj* highly charming or enchanting
CHARMING *adj* attractive
CHARMLESS *adj* devoid of charm
CHARMONIA *pl n* elementary particles containing an antiquark and a charm quark
CHARMS > CHARM
CHARNECO *n* type of sweet wine
CHARNECOS > CHARNECO
CHARNEL *adj* ghastly ▷ *n* ghastly thing
CHARNELS > CHARNEL
CHAROSET *n* dish of chopped fruit, nuts and wine, eaten at Passover
CHAROSETH *same as* > CHAROSET
CHAROSETS > CHAROSET
CHARPAI *same as* > CHARPOY
CHARPAIS > CHARPAI

CHARPIE *n* lint pieces used to make surgical dressings
CHARPIES > CHARPIE
CHARPOY *n* type of bedstead
CHARPOYS > CHARPOY
CHARQUI *n* meat, esp beef, cut into strips and dried
CHARQUID > CHARQUI
CHARQUIS > CHARQUI
CHARR *same as* > CHAR
CHARREADA *n* Mexican display of skills similar to a rodeo
CHARRED > CHAR
CHARRIER > CHARRY
CHARRIEST > CHARRY
CHARRING > CHAR
CHARRO *n* Mexican cowboy
CHARROS > CHARRO
CHARRS > CHARR
CHARRY *adj* of or relating to charcoal
CHARS > CHAR
CHART *n* graph, table, or diagram showing information ▷ *vb* plot the course of
CHARTA *n* charter
CHARTABLE > CHART
CHARTAS > CHARTA
CHARTED > CHART
CHARTER *n* document granting or demanding certain rights ▷ *vb* hire by charter
CHARTERED *adj* officially qualified to practise a profession
CHARTERER > CHARTER
CHARTERS > CHARTER
CHARTING > CHART
CHARTISM *n* historical reform movement in Britain
CHARTISMS > CHARTISM
CHARTIST *n* supporter of chartism
CHARTISTS > CHARTIST
CHARTLESS *adj* not mapped
CHARTS > CHART
CHARVER *n* derogatory term for a young woman
CHARVERS > CHARVER
CHARWOMAN *n* woman whose job is to clean other people's homes
CHARWOMEN > CHARWOMAN
CHARY *adj* wary, careful
CHAS > CHA
CHASE *vb* run after quickly in order to catch or drive away ▷ *n* chasing, pursuit
CHASEABLE > CHASE
CHASED > CHASE
CHASEPORT *n* porthole through which a chase gun is fired
CHASER *n* milder drink drunk after another stronger one

CHASERS > CHASER
CHASES > CHASE
CHASING > CHASE
CHASINGS > CHASE
CHASM *n* deep crack in the earth ▷ *vb* create a chasm
CHASMAL > CHASM
CHASMED > CHASM
CHASMIC > CHASM
CHASMIER > CHASMY
CHASMIEST > CHASMY
CHASMS > CHASM
CHASMY *adj* full of chasms
CHASSE *n* one of a series of gliding steps in ballet ▷ *vb* perform either of these steps
CHASSED > CHASSE
CHASSEED > CHASSE
CHASSEING > CHASSE
CHASSEPOT *n* breech-loading bolt-action rifle formerly used by the French Army
CHASSES > CHASSE
CHASSEUR *n* member of a unit specially trained and equipped for swift deployment ▷ *adj* designating or cooked in a sauce consisting of white wine and mushrooms
CHASSEURS > CHASSEUR
CHASSIS *n* frame, wheels, and mechanical parts of a vehicle
CHASTE *adj* abstaining from sex outside marriage or altogether
CHASTELY > CHASTE
CHASTEN *vb* subdue by criticism
CHASTENED > CHASTEN
CHASTENER > CHASTEN
CHASTENS > CHASTEN
CHASTER > CHASTE
CHASTEST > CHASTE
CHASTISE *vb* scold severely
CHASTISED > CHASTISE
CHASTISER > CHASTISE
CHASTISES > CHASTISE
CHASTITY *n* state of being chaste
CHASUBLE *n* long sleeveless robe worn by a priest when celebrating Mass
CHASUBLES > CHASUBLE
CHAT *n* informal conversation ▷ *vb* have an informal conversation
CHATBOT *n* computer program
CHATBOTS > CHATBOT
CHATCHKA *variant of* **>** TCHOTCHKE
CHATCHKAS > CHATCHKA
CHATCHKE *same as* **>** TCHOTCHKE
CHATCHKES > CHATCHKE
CHATEAU *n* French castle
CHATEAUS > CHATEAU

CHATEAUX > CHATEAU
CHATELAIN *same as* **>** CASTELLAN
CHATLINE *n* telephone service enabling callers to join in general conversation with each other
CHATLINES > CHATLINE
CHATON *n* in jewellery, a stone with a reflective metal foil backing
CHATONS > CHATON
CHATOYANT *adj* having changeable lustre ▷ *n* gemstone with a changeable lustre
CHATROOM *n* site on the Internet where users have group discussions by e-mail
CHATROOMS > CHATROOM
CHATS > CHAT
CHATTA *n* umbrella
CHATTAS > CHATTA
CHATTED > CHAT
CHATTEL *n* item of movable personal property
CHATTELS > CHATTEL
CHATTER *vb* speak quickly and continuously about unimportant things ▷ *n* idle talk
CHATTERED > CHATTER
CHATTERER *same as* **>** COTINGA
CHATTERS > CHATTER
CHATTERY > CHATTER
CHATTI *n* (in India) an earthenware pot
CHATTIER > CHATTY
CHATTIES > CHATTI
CHATTIEST > CHATTY
CHATTILY > CHATTY
CHATTING > CHAT
CHATTIS > CHATTI
CHATTY *adj* (of a person) fond of friendly, informal conversation
CHAUFE *obsolete variant of* **>** CHAFE
CHAUFED > CHAUFE
CHAUFER *same as* **>** CHAUFFER
CHAUFERS > CHAUFER
CHAUFES > CHAUFE
CHAUFF *obsolete variant of* **>** CHAFE
CHAUFFED > CHAUFF
CHAUFFER *n* small portable heater or stove
CHAUFFERS > CHAUFFER
CHAUFFEUR *n* person employed to drive a car for someone ▷ *vb* act as driver for (someone)
CHAUFFING > CHAUFF
CHAUFFS > CHAUFF
CHAUFING > CHAUFE
CHAUMER *n* chamber
CHAUMERS > CHAUMER
CHAUNCE *archaic variant of* **>** CHANCE

CHAUNCED > CHAUNCE
CHAUNCES > CHAUNCE
CHAUNCING > CHAUNCE
CHAUNGE *archaic variant of* **>** CHANGE
CHAUNGED > CHAUNGE
CHAUNGES > CHAUNGE
CHAUNGING > CHAUNGE
CHAUNT *a less common variant of* **>** CHANT
CHAUNTED > CHAUNT
CHAUNTER > CHAUNT
CHAUNTERS > CHAUNT
CHAUNTING > CHAUNT
CHAUNTRY *same as* **>** CHANTRY
CHAUNTS > CHAUNT
CHAUSSES *n* tight-fitting medieval garment covering the feet and legs, usually made of chain mail
CHAUSSURE *n* any type of footwear
CHAUVIN *n* chauvinist
CHAUVINS > CHAUVIN
CHAV *n* informal derogatory word for a young working-class person who wears casual sports clothes
CHAVE *vb* old dialect term for "I have"
CHAVENDER *n* chub
CHAVETTE *n* informal derogatory word for a young working-class female who wears casual sports clothes
CHAVETTES > CHAVETTE
CHAVISH > CHAV
CHAVS > CHAV
CHAVVIER > CHAVVY
CHAVVIEST > CHAVVY
CHAVVY *adj* relating to or like a chav
CHAW *vb* chew (tobacco), esp without swallowing it ▷ *n* something chewed, esp a plug of tobacco
CHAWBACON *n* bumpkin
CHAWDRON *n* entrails
CHAWDRONS > CHAWDRON
CHAWED > CHAW
CHAWER > CHAW
CHAWERS > CHAW
CHAWING > CHAW
CHAWK *n* jackdaw
CHAWKS > CHAWK
CHAWS > CHAW
CHAY *n* plant of the madder family
CHAYA *same as* **>** CHAY
CHAYAS > CHAYA
CHAYOTE *n* tropical climbing plant
CHAYOTES > CHAYOTE
CHAYROOT *n* root of the chay plant
CHAYROOTS > CHAYROOT
CHAYS > CHAY
CHAZAN *same as* **>** CANTOR
CHAZANIM > CHAZAN
CHAZANS > CHAZAN

CHAZZAN *variant of* **>** CHAZAN
CHAZZANIM > CHAZZAN
CHAZZANS > CHAZZAN
CHAZZEN *same as* **>** CHAZZAN
CHAZZENIM > CHAZZEN
CHAZZENS > CHAZZEN
CHE *pron* dialectal form meaning "I"
CHEAP *adj* costing relatively little ▷ *adv* at very little cost ▷ *n* bargain ▷ *vb* take the cheapest option
CHEAPED > CHEAP
CHEAPEN *vb* lower the reputation of
CHEAPENED > CHEAPEN
CHEAPENER > CHEAPEN
CHEAPENS > CHEAPEN
CHEAPER > CHEAP
CHEAPEST > CHEAP
CHEAPIE *n* something inexpensive
CHEAPIES > CHEAPIE
CHEAPING > CHEAP
CHEAPISH > CHEAP
CHEAPJACK *n* person who sells cheap and shoddy goods ▷ *adj* shoddy or inferior
CHEAPLY > CHEAP
CHEAPNESS > CHEAP
CHEAPO *n* very cheap and possibly shoddy thing
CHEAPOS > CHEAPO
CHEAPS > CHEAP
CHEAPSHOT *n* abusive remark
CHEAPY *same as* **>** CHEAPIE
CHEAT *vb* act dishonestly to gain profit or advantage ▷ *n* person who cheats
CHEATABLE > CHEAT
CHEATED > CHEAT
CHEATER > CHEAT
CHEATERS > CHEAT
CHEATERY *n* cheating
CHEATING > CHEAT
CHEATINGS > CHEAT
CHEATS > CHEAT
CHEBEC *n* type of boat
CHEBECS > CHEBEC
CHECHAKO *same as* **>** CHEECHAKO
CHECHAKOS > CHECHAKO
CHECHAQUO *same as* **>** CHEECHAKO
CHECHIA *n* Berber skullcap
CHECHIAS > CHECHIA
CHECK *vb* examine or investigate ▷ *n* control designed to ensure accuracy
CHECKABLE > CHECK
CHECKBOOK *n* American word for chequebook
CHECKBOX *n* small clickable box on a computer screen
CHECKED > CHECK

CHECKER same as
> CHEQUER
CHECKERED same as
> CHEQUERED
CHECKERS n game for
two players using a
checkerboard and 12
checkers each. The object
is to jump over and
capture the opponent's
pieces
CHECKIER > CHECKY
CHECKIEST > CHECKY
CHECKING n act of
checking
CHECKINGS > CHECKING
CHECKLESS adj without
check or restraint
CHECKLIST vb check
items, facts, etc, against
those in a list used for
verification
CHECKMARK vb make a
mark of approval or
verification
CHECKMATE n winning
position in which an
opponent's king is under
attack and unable to
escape ▷ vb place the king
of (one's opponent) in
checkmate ▷ interj call
made when placing an
opponent's king in
checkmate
CHECKOFF n procedure
where an employer pays
the employee's union dues
straight from his or her
salary
CHECKOFFS > CHECKOFF
CHECKOUT n counter in a
supermarket, where
customers pay
CHECKOUTS > CHECKOUT
CHECKRAIL another word
for > GUARDRAIL
CHECKREIN n bearing
rein
CHECKROOM n place at a
railway station, airport,
etc, where luggage may be
left for a small charge with
an attendant for
safekeeping
CHECKROW n row of
plants, esp corn, in which
the spaces between
adjacent plants are equal
to those between adjacent
rows to facilitate
cultivation ▷ vb plant in
checkrows
CHECKROWS > CHECKROW
CHECKS > CHECK
CHECKSUM n digit
representing the number
of bits of information
transmitted, attached to
the end of a message, to
verify the integrity of data
CHECKSUMS > CHECKSUM
CHECKUP n thorough
medical examination
CHECKUPS > CHECKUP

CHECKY adj having
squares of alternating
tinctures or furs
CHEDARIM same as
> CHADARIM
CHEDDAR n type of
smooth hard yellow or
whitish cheese
CHEDDARS > CHEDDAR
CHEDDARY > CHEDDAR
CHEDDITE n explosive
made by mixing a
powdered chlorate or
perchlorate with a fatty
substance, such as
castor oil
CHEDDITES > CHEDDITE
CHEDER n Jewish religious
education
CHEDERS > CHEDER
CHEDITE same as
> CHEDDITE
CHEDITES > CHEDITE
CHEECHAKO n local name
for a newcomer to Alaska
CHEEK n either side of the
face below the eye
▷ vb speak impudently to
CHEEKBONE n bone at the
top of the cheek, just
below the eye
CHEEKED > CHEEK
CHEEKFUL n quantity
that can be held in a cheek
CHEEKFULS > CHEEKFUL
CHEEKIER > CHEEKY
CHEEKIEST > CHEEKY
CHEEKILY > CHEEKY
CHEEKING > CHEEK
CHEEKLESS > CHEEK
CHEEKS > CHEEK
CHEEKY adj impudent,
disrespectful
CHEEP n young bird's
high-pitched cry ▷ vb utter
a cheep
CHEEPED > CHEEP
CHEEPER > CHEEP
CHEEPERS > CHEEP
CHEEPING > CHEEP
CHEEPS > CHEEP
CHEER vb applaud or
encourage with shouts
▷ n shout of applause or
encouragement
CHEERED > CHEER
CHEERER > CHEER
CHEERERS > CHEER
CHEERFUL adj having a
happy disposition
CHEERIER > CHEERY
CHEERIEST > CHEERY
CHEERILY > CHEERY
CHEERING n act of
cheering
CHEERINGS > CHEERING
CHEERIO interj goodbye
▷ n small red cocktail
sausage ▷ sentence
substitute farewell greeting
CHEERIOS > CHEERIO
CHEERLEAD vb lead a
crowd in formal cheers at
sports events

CHEERLED > CHEERLEAD
CHEERLESS adj dreary,
gloomy
CHEERLY adv cheerful or
cheerfully
CHEERO same as
> CHEERIO
CHEEROS > CHEERO
CHEERS interj drinking
toast ▷ sentence substitute
drinking toast
CHEERY adj cheerful
CHEESE n food made from
coagulated milk curd
▷ vb stop
CHEESED > CHEESE
CHEESES > CHEESE
CHEESEVAT n in
cheese-making, vat in
which curds are formed
and cut
CHEESIER > CHEESY
CHEESIEST > CHEESY
CHEESILY > CHEESY
CHEESING > CHEESE
CHEESY adj like cheese
CHEETAH n large
fast-running spotted
African wild cat
CHEETAHS > CHEETAH
CHEEWINK same as
> CHEWINK
CHEEWINKS > CHEEWINK
CHEF n cook in a
restaurant ▷ vb work as
a chef
CHEFDOM n state or
condition of being a chef
CHEFDOMS > CHEFDOM
CHEFED > CHEF
CHEFFED > CHEF
CHEFFIER > CHEFFY
CHEFFIEST > CHEFFY
CHEFFING > CHEF
CHEFFY adj relating to or
characteristic of chefs
CHEFING > CHEF
CHEFS > CHEF
CHEGOE same as
> CHIGGER
CHEGOES > CHIGGER
CHEILITIS n
inflammation of the
lip(s)
CHEKA n secret police set
up in Russia in 1917
CHEKAS > CHEKA
CHEKIST n member of the
cheka
CHEKISTS > CHEKIST
CHELA n disciple of a
religious teacher
CHELAE > CHELA
CHELAS > CHELA
CHELASHIP > CHELA
CHELATE n coordination
compound ▷ adj of or
possessing chelae
▷ vb form a chelate
CHELATED > CHELATE
CHELATES > CHELATE
CHELATING > CHELATE
CHELATION n process by
which a chelate is formed

CHELATOR > CHELATE
CHELATORS > CHELATE
CHELICERA n one of a
pair of appendages on the
head of spiders and other
arachnids: often modified
as food-catching claws
CHELIFORM adj shaped
like a chela
CHELIPED n (on a
arthropod) either of two
legs which each carry a
claw
CHELIPEDS > CHELIPED
CHELLUP n noise
CHELLUPS > CHELLUP
CHELOID a variant spelling
of > KELOID
CHELOIDAL > CHELOID
CHELOIDS > CHELOID
CHELONE n hardy N
American plant
CHELONES > CHELONE
CHELONIAN n type of
reptile such as the
tortoises and turtles, in
which most of the body is
enclosed in a protective
bony capsule
CHELP vb (esp of women
or children) to chatter or
speak out of turn
CHELPED > CHELP
CHELPING > CHELP
CHELPS > CHELP
CHEM n chemistry
CHEMIC vb bleach
▷ n chemist
CHEMICAL n substance
used in or resulting from a
reaction involving changes
to atoms or molecules
▷ adj of chemistry or
chemicals
CHEMICALS > CHEMICAL
CHEMICKED > CHEMIC
CHEMICS > CHEMIC
CHEMISE n woman's
loose-fitting slip
CHEMISES > CHEMISE
CHEMISM n chemical
action
CHEMISMS > CHEMISM
CHEMISORB vb take up (a
substance) by
chemisorption
CHEMIST n shop selling
medicines and cosmetics
CHEMISTRY n science of
the composition,
properties, and reactions
of substances
CHEMISTS > CHEMIST
CHEMITYPE n process by
which a relief impression is
obtained from an
engraving
CHEMITYPY
> CHEMITYPE
CHEMMIES > CHEMMY
CHEMMY n gambling card
game
CHEMO n short form of
chemotherapy

CHEMOKINE n type of protein

CHEMOS > CHEMO

CHEMOSORB same as **>** CHEMISORB

CHEMOSTAT n apparatus for growing bacterial cultures at a constant rate by controlling the supply of nutrient medium

CHEMPADUK n Malaysian evergreen tree

CHEMS > CHEM

CHEMTRAIL n supposed vapour trail containing toxic chemicals

CHEMURGIC > CHEMURGY

CHEMURGY n branch of chemistry concerned with the industrial use of organic raw materials, esp materials of agricultural origin

CHENAR n oriental plane tree

CHENARS > CHENAR

CHENET another word for **>** GENIP

CHENETS > CHENET

CHENILLE n (fabric of) thick tufty yarn

CHENILLES > CHENILLE

CHENIX n ancient measure, slightly more than a quart

CHENIXES > CHENIX

CHENOPOD n type of plant of the family which includes the beet, mangel-wurzel, spinach, and goosefoot

CHENOPODS > CHENOPOD

CHEONGSAM n straight dress, usually of silk or cotton, with a stand-up collar and a slit in one side of the skirt, worn by Chinese women

CHEQUE n written order to one's bank to pay money from one's account

CHEQUER n piece used in Chinese chequers ▷ vb make irregular in colour or character

CHEQUERED adj marked by varied fortunes

CHEQUERS n game of draughts

CHEQUES > CHEQUE

CHEQUIER > CHEQUY

CHEQUIEST > CHEQUY

CHEQUING adj as in chequing account (in Canada) account against which cheques can be drawn

CHEQUY same as **>** CHECKY

CHER adj dear or expensive

CHERALITE n rare phosphate-silicate of Thorium and Calcium

CHERE feminine variant of **>** CHER

CHERIMOYA n large tropical fruit with custardlike flesh

CHERISH vb cling to (an idea or feeling)

CHERISHED > CHERISH

CHERISHER > CHERISH

CHERISHES > CHERISH

CHERMOULA n type of marinade used in N African cookery

CHERNOZEM n black soil, rich in humus and carbonates, in cool or temperate semiarid regions, as the grasslands of Russia

CHEROOT n cigar with both ends cut flat

CHEROOTS > CHEROOT

CHERRIED > CHERRY

CHERRIER > CHERRY

CHERRIES > CHERRY

CHERRIEST > CHERRY

CHERRY n small red or black fruit with a stone ▷ adj deep red ▷ vb cheer

CHERRYING > CHERRY

CHERT n microcrystalline form of silica

CHERTIER > CHERT

CHERTIEST > CHERT

CHERTS > CHERT

CHERTY > CHERT

CHERUB n angel, often represented as a winged child

CHERUBIC > CHERUB

CHERUBIM > CHERUB

CHERUBIMS > CHERUB

CHERUBIN n cherub ▷ adj cherubic

CHERUBINS > CHERUBIN

CHERUBS > CHERUB

CHERUP same as **>** CHIRRUP

CHERUPED > CHERUP

CHERUPING > CHERUP

CHERUPS > CHERUP

CHERVIL n aniseed-flavoured herb

CHERVILS > CHERVIL

CHESHIRE n breed of American pig

CHESHIRES > CHESHIRE

CHESIL n gravel or shingle

CHESILS > CHESIL

CHESNUT rare variant of **>** CHESTNUT

CHESNUTS > CHESTNUT

CHESS n board game for two players

CHESSEL n mould used in cheese-making

CHESSELS > CHESSEL

CHESSES > CHESS

CHESSMAN n piece used in chess

CHESSMEN > CHESSMAN

CHEST n front of the body, from neck to waist ▷ vb hit with the chest, as with a ball in football

CHESTED > CHEST

CHESTFUL n amount a chest will hold

CHESTFULS > CHESTFUL

CHESTIER > CHESTY

CHESTIEST > CHESTY

CHESTILY > CHESTY

CHESTING > CHEST

CHESTNUT n reddish-brown edible nut ▷ adj (of hair or a horse) reddish-brown

CHESTNUTS > CHESTNUT

CHESTS > CHEST

CHESTY adj symptomatic of chest disease

CHETAH same as **>** CHEETAH

CHETAHS > CHETAH

CHETH same as **>** HETH

CHETHS > CHETH

CHETNIK n member of a Serbian nationalist paramilitary group

CHETNIKS > CHETNIK

CHETRUM n monetary unit in Bhutan

CHETRUMS > CHETRUM

CHEVAL n as in cheval glass full-length mirror that can swivel

CHEVALET n bridge of a stringed musical instrument

CHEVALETS > CHEVALET

CHEVALIER n member of the French Legion of Honour

CHEVELURE n nebulous part of the tail of a comet

CHEVEN n chub

CHEVENS > CHEVEN

CHEVEREL n kid or goatskin leather

CHEVERELS > CHEVEREL

CHEVERILS same as **>** CHEVEREL

CHEVERILS > CHEVERIL

CHEVERON same as **>** CHEVRON

CHEVERONS > CHEVERON

CHEVERYE same as **>** CHIEFERY

CHEVERYES > CHEVERYE

CHEVET n semicircular or polygonal east end of a church

CHEVETS > CHEVET

CHEVIED > CHEVY

CHEVIES > CHEVY

CHEVILLE n peg of a stringed musical instrument

CHEVILLES > CHEVILLE

CHEVIN same as **>** CHEVEN

CHEVINS > CHEVIN

CHEVIOT n type of British sheep reared for its wool

CHEVIOTS > CHEVIOT

CHEVRE n any cheese made from goats' milk

CHEVRES > CHEVRE

CHEVRET n type of goats' cheese

CHEVRETS > CHEVRET

CHEVRETTE n skin of a young goat

CHEVRON n V-shaped pattern ▷ vb make a chevron

CHEVRONED > CHEVRON

CHEVRONS > CHEVRON

CHEVRONY adj in heraldry, bearing chevrons

CHEVY same as **>** CHIVY

CHEVYING > CHEVY

CHEW vb grind (food) between the teeth ▷ n act of chewing

CHEWABLE > CHEW

CHEWED > CHEW

CHEWER > CHEW

CHEWERS > CHEW

CHEWET n type of meat pie

CHEWETS > CHEWET

CHEWIE n chewing gum

CHEWIER > CHEWY

CHEWIES > CHEWY

CHEWIEST > CHEWY

CHEWINESS > CHEWY

CHEWING > CHEW

CHEWINK n towhee

CHEWINKS > CHEWINK

CHEWS > CHEW

CHEWY adj requiring a lot of chewing ▷ n dog's rubber toy

CHEZ prep at the home of

CHI n 22nd letter of the Greek alphabet

CHIA n plant of the mint family

CHIACK vb tease or banter ▷ n good-humoured banter

CHIACKED > CHIACK

CHIACKING > CHIACK

CHIACKS > CHIACK

CHIANTI n dry red Italian wine

CHIANTIS > CHIANTI

CHIAO n Chinese coin equal to one tenth of one yuan

CHIAREZZA n (in music) clarity

CHIAREZZE > CHIAREZZA

CHIAS > CHIA

CHIASM same as **>** CHIASMA

CHIASMA n biological term

CHIASMAL > CHIASMA

CHIASMAS > CHIASMA

CHIASMATA > CHIASMA

CHIASMI > CHIASMUS

CHIASMIC > CHIASMA

CHIASMS > CHIASMA

CHIASMUS n reversal of the order of words in the second of two parallel phrases

CHIASTIC > CHIASMUS

CHIAUS same as **>** CHOUSE

CHIAUSED > CHIAUS

CHIAUSES > CHIAUS

CHIAUSING > CHIAUS

CHIB vb in Scots English, stab or slash with a sharp weapon ▷ n sharp weapon

CHIBBED > CHIB
CHIBBING > CHIB
CHIBOL n spring onion
CHIBOLS > CHIBOL
CHIBOUK n Turkish tobacco pipe with an extremely long stem
CHIBOUKS > CHIBOUK
CHIBOUQUE same as > CHIBOUK
CHIBS > CHIB
CHIC adj stylish, elegant ▷ n stylishness, elegance
CHICA n Spanish young girl
CHICALOTE n type of poppy of the southwestern US and Mexico with prickly leaves and white or yellow flowers
CHICANA n female chicano
CHICANAS > CHICANA
CHICANE n obstacle in a motor-racing circuit ▷ vb deceive or trick by chicanery
CHICANED > CHICANE
CHICANER > CHICANE
CHICANERS > CHICANE
CHICANERY n trickery, deception
CHICANES > CHICANE
CHICANING > CHICANE
CHICANO n American citizen of Mexican origin
CHICANOS > CHICANO
CHICAS > CHICA
CHICCORY a variant spelling of > CHICORY
CHICER > CHIC
CHICEST > CHIC
CHICH another word for > CHICKPEA
CHICHA n Andean drink made from fermented maize
CHICHAS > CHICHA
CHICHES > CHICKPEA
CHICHI adj affectedly pretty or stylish ▷ n quality of being affectedly pretty or stylish
CHICHIER > CHICHI
CHICHIEST > CHICHI
CHICHIS > CHICHI
CHICK n baby bird
CHICKADEE n small North American songbird
CHICKAREE n American red squirrel
CHICKEE n open-sided, thatched building on stilts
CHICKEES > CHICKEE
CHICKEN n domestic fowl ▷ adj cowardly ▷ vb lose one's nerve
CHICKENED > CHICKEN
CHICKENS > CHICKEN
CHICKLING n small chick
CHICKORY same as > CHICORY

CHICKPEA n edible yellow pealike seed
CHICKPEAS > CHICKPEA
CHICKS > CHICK
CHICKWEED n weed with small white flowers
CHICLE n gumlike substance obtained from the sapodilla
CHICLES > CHICLE
CHICLY > CHIC
CHICNESS > CHIC
CHICO n spiny chenopodiaceous shrub
CHICON same as > CHICORY
CHICONS > CHICON
CHICORIES > CHICORY
CHICORY n plant whose leaves are used in salads
CHICOS > CHICO
CHICOT n dead tree
CHICOTS > CHICOT
CHICS > CHIC
CHID > CHIDE
CHIDDEN > CHIDE
CHIDE vb rebuke, scold
CHIDED > CHIDE
CHIDER > CHIDE
CHIDERS > CHIDE
CHIDES > CHIDE
CHIDING > CHIDE
CHIDINGLY > CHIDE
CHIDINGS > CHIDE
CHIDLINGS n intestines of a pig prepared as a dish
CHIEF n head of a group of people ▷ adj most important
CHIEFDOM n any tribal social group led by a chief
CHIEFDOMS > CHIEFDOM
CHIEFER > CHIEF
CHIEFERY n lands belonging to a chief
CHIEFESS n female chief
CHIEFEST > CHIEF
CHIEFLESS adj lacking a chief
CHIEFLING n petty chief
CHIEFLY adv especially ▷ adj of or relating to a chief or chieftain
CHIEFRIES > CHIEFRY
CHIEFRY same as > CHIEFERY
CHIEFS > CHIEF
CHIEFSHIP n state of being a chief
CHIEFTAIN n leader of a tribe
CHIEL n young man
CHIELD same as > CHIEL
CHIELDS > CHIEL
CHIELS > CHIEL
CHIFFON n fine see-through fabric ▷ adj made of chiffon
CHIFFONS > CHIFFON
CHIFFONY > CHIFFON
CHIGETAI n variety of the Asiatic wild ass of Mongolia

CHIGETAIS > CHIGETAI
CHIGGA n informal Australian derogatory word for a young working-class person from Hobart, Tasmania
CHIGGAS > CHIGGA
CHIGGER n parasitic larva of various mites
CHIGGERS > CHIGGER
CHIGNON n knot of hair pinned up at the back of the head ▷ vb make a chignon
CHIGNONED > CHIGNON
CHIGNONS > CHIGNON
CHIGOE same as > CHIGGER
CHIGOES > CHIGOE
CHIGRE same as > CHIGGER
CHIGRES > CHIGRE
CHIHUAHUA n tiny short-haired dog
CHIK n slatted blind
CHIKARA n Indian seven-stringed musical instrument
CHIKARAS > CHIKARA
CHIKHOR same as > CHUKAR
CHIKHORS > CHIKHOR
CHIKOR same as > CHUKAR
CHIKORS > CHIKOR
CHIKS > CHIK
CHILBLAIN n inflammation of the fingers or toes, caused by exposure to cold
CHILD n young human being, boy or girl ▷ vb give birth
CHILDBED n condition of giving birth to a child
CHILDBEDS > CHILDBED
CHILDCARE n care provided for children without homes (or with a seriously disturbed home life) by a local authority
CHILDE n young man of noble birth
CHILDED > CHILD
CHILDER dialect variant of > CHILDREN
CHILDES > CHILDE
CHILDHOOD n time or condition of being a child
CHILDING > CHILD
CHILDISH adj immature, silly
CHILDLESS > CHILD
CHILDLIER > CHILD
CHILDLIKE adj innocent, trustful
CHILDLY > CHILD
CHILDNESS n nature of a child
CHILDREN > CHILD
CHILDS > CHILD
CHILE a variant spelling of > CHILLI
CHILES > CHILE
CHILI same as > CHILLI

CHILIAD n group of one thousand
CHILIADAL > CHILIAD
CHILIADIC > CHILIAD
CHILIADS > CHILIAD
CHILIAGON n thousand-sided polygon
CHILIARCH n commander of a thousand men
CHILIASM n belief in the Second Coming of Christ
CHILIASMS > CHILIASM
CHILIAST > CHILIASM
CHILIASTS > CHILIASM
CHILIDOG n hot dog served with chilli sauce
CHILIDOGS > CHILIDOG
CHILIES > CHILI
CHILIS > CHILI
CHILL n feverish cold ▷ vb make (something) cool or cold ▷ adj unpleasantly cold
CHILLADA n spicy Mexican dish made of fried vegetables and pulses
CHILLADAS > CHILLADA
CHILLAX vb take rest or recreation, as from work
CHILLAXED > CHILLAX
CHILLAXES > CHILLAX
CHILLED > CHILL
CHILLER n cooling or refrigerating device
CHILLERS > CHILLER
CHILLEST > CHILL
CHILLI n small red or green hot-tasting capsicum pod, used in cooking
CHILLIER > CHILLY
CHILLIES > CHILLI
CHILLIEST > CHILLY
CHILLILY > CHILLY
CHILLING > CHILL
CHILLINGS > CHILL
CHILLIS > CHILLI
CHILLNESS > CHILL
CHILLS > CHILL
CHILLUM n short pipe, usually of clay, used esp for smoking cannabis
CHILLUMS > CHILLUM
CHILLY adj moderately cold
CHILOPOD n type of arthropod of the class which includes the centipedes
CHILOPODS > CHILOPOD
CHILTEPIN n variety of chilli pepper
CHIMAERA same as > CHIMERA
CHIMAERAS > CHIMAERA
CHIMAERIC > CHIMAERA
CHIMAR same as > CHIMERE
CHIMARS > CHIMAR
CHIMB same as > CHIME
CHIMBLEY same as > CHIMNEY
CHIMBLEYS > CHIMBLEY

CHIMBLIES > CHIMBLY
CHIMBLY same as > CHIMNEY
CHIMBS > CHIME
CHIME n musical ringing sound of a bell or clock ▷ vb make a musical ringing sound
CHIMED > CHIME
CHIMENEA n freestanding outdoor fireplace
CHIMENEAS > CHIMENEA
CHIMER > CHIME
CHIMERA n unrealistic hope or idea
CHIMERAS > CHIMERA
CHIMERE n gown worn by bishops
CHIMERES > CHIMERE
CHIMERIC same as > CHIMERA
CHIMERID n fish of the genus Chimaera
CHIMERIDS > CHIMERID
CHIMERISM n medical condition in which a person possesses two genetically distinct sets of cells
CHIMERS > CHIME
CHIMES > CHIME
CHIMINEA n freestanding outdoor fireplace with a rounded body
CHIMINEAS > CHIMINEA
CHIMING > CHIME
CHIMLA same as > CHIMNEY
CHIMLAS > CHIMLA
CHIMLEY same as > CHIMNEY
CHIMLEYS > CHIMLEY
CHIMNEY n hollow vertical structure for carrying away smoke from a fire ▷ vb climb two vertical, parallel, chimney-like rock faces
CHIMNEYED > CHIMNEY
CHIMNEYS > CHIMNEY
CHIMO interj Inuit greeting and toast
CHIMP n chimpanzee
CHIMPS > CHIMP
CHIN n part of the face below the mouth ▷ vb hit someone in the chin
CHINA n fine earthenware or porcelain
CHINAMAN n in cricket, a ball bowled by a left-handed bowler to a right-handed batsman that spins from off to leg
CHINAMEN > CHINAMAN
CHINAMPA n in Mesoamerican agriculture, an artificially created island used for growing crops
CHINAMPAS > CHINAMPA
CHINAR same as > CHINAR
CHINAROOT n bristly greenbrier

CHINARS > CHENAR
CHINAS > CHINA
CHINAWARE n articles made of china, esp those made for domestic use
CHINBONE n front part of the mandible which forms the chin
CHINBONES > CHINBONE
CHINCAPIN n dwarf chestnut tree
CHINCH n (S US) bedbug ▷ vb be frugal or miserly
CHINCHED > CHINCH
CHINCHES > CHINCH
CHINCHIER > CHINCHY
CHINCHING > CHINCH
CHINCHY adj tightfisted
CHINCOUGH n whooping cough
CHINDIT n Allied soldier fighting behind the Japanese lines in Burma during World War II
CHINDITS > CHINDIT
CHINE same as > CHIME
CHINED > CHINE
CHINES > CHINE
CHINESE adj of or relating to China
CHING n high-pitched ring or chime
CHINGS > CHING
CHINING > CHINE
CHINK n small narrow opening ▷ vb make a light ringing sound
CHINKAPIN same as > CHINCAPIN
CHINKARA n Indian gazelle
CHINKARAS > CHINKARA
CHINKED > CHINK
CHINKIE n offensive term for a (takeaway) meal of Chinese food
CHINKIER > CHINK
CHINKIES > CHINKIE
CHINKIEST > CHINK
CHINKING > CHINK
CHINKS > CHINK
CHINKY > CHINK
CHINLESS adj having a receding chin
CHINNED > CHIN
CHINNING > CHIN
CHINO n durable cotton twill cloth
CHINOIS n conical sieve
CHINOISES > CHINOIS
CHINONE n benzoquinone
CHINONES > CHINONE
CHINOOK n wind found in the Rocky Mountains
CHINOOKS > CHINOOK
CHINOS pl n trousers made of a kind of hard-wearing cotton
CHINOVNIK n Russian official or bureaucrat
CHINS > CHIN
CHINSE vb fill the seams of a boat

CHINSED > CHINSE
CHINSES > CHINSE
CHINSING > CHINSE
CHINSTRAP n strap on a helmet which fastens under the chin
CHINTS obsolete variant of > CHINTZ
CHINTSES > CHINTS
CHINTZ n printed cotton fabric with a glazed finish
CHINTZES > CHINTZ
CHINTZIER > CHINTZY
CHINTZY adj of or covered with chintz
CHINWAG n chat
CHINWAGS > CHINWAG
CHIP n strip of potato, fried in deep fat ▷ vb break small pieces from
CHIPBOARD n thin board made of compressed wood particles
CHIPMUCK another word for > CHIPMUNK
CHIPMUCKS > CHIPMUCK
CHIPMUNK n small squirrel-like N American rodent with a striped back
CHIPMUNKS > CHIPMUNK
CHIPOCHIA same as > CAPOCCHIA
CHIPOLATA n small sausage
CHIPOTLE n dried chilli pepper
CHIPOTLES > CHIPOTLE
CHIPPABLE > CHIP
CHIPPED > CHIP
CHIPPER vb chirp or chatter
CHIPPERED > CHIPPER
CHIPPERS > CHIPPER
CHIPPIE same as > CHIPPY
CHIPPIER > CHIPPY
CHIPPIES > CHIPPY
CHIPPIEST > CHIPPY
CHIPPING > CHIP
CHIPPINGS > CHIP
CHIPPY n fish-and-chip shop ▷ adj resentful or oversensitive about being perceived as inferior
CHIPS > CHIP
CHIPSET n highly integrated circuit on the motherboard of a computer
CHIPSETS > CHIPSET
CHIRAGRA n gout occurring in the hands
CHIRAGRAS > CHIRAGRA
CHIRAGRIC > CHIRAGRA
CHIRAL > CHIRALITY
CHIRALITY n configuration or handedness (left or right) of an asymmetric, optically active chemical compound
CHIRIMOYA same as > CHERIMOYA

▷ adj spritely; high-spirited
CHIRKED > CHIRK
CHIRKER > CHIRK
CHIRKEST > CHIRK
CHIRKING > CHIRK
CHIRKS > CHIRK
CHIRL vb warble
CHIRLED > CHIRL
CHIRLING > CHIRL
CHIRLS > CHIRL
CHIRM n chirping of birds ▷ vb (esp of a bird) to chirp
CHIRMED > CHIRM
CHIRMING > CHIRM
CHIRMS > CHIRM
CHIRO n informal name for chiropractor
CHIROLOGY n palmistry
CHIRONOMY n art of hand movement in oratory or theatrical performance
CHIROPODY n treatment of the feet, esp the treatment of corns, verrucas, etc
CHIROPTER n type of bat
CHIROS > CHIRO
CHIRP vb (of a bird or insect) make a short high-pitched sound ▷ n chirping sound
CHIRPED > CHIRP
CHIRPER > CHIRP
CHIRPERS > CHIRP
CHIRPIER > CHIRPY
CHIRPIEST > CHIRPY
CHIRPILY > CHIRPY
CHIRPING n act of chirping
CHIRPINGS > CHIRPING
CHIRPS > CHIRP
CHIRPY adj lively and cheerful
CHIRR vb (esp of certain insects, such as crickets) to make a shrill trilled sound ▷ n sound of chirring
CHIRRE same as > CHIRR
CHIRRED > CHIRR
CHIRREN n dialect form of children
CHIRRES > CHIRRE
CHIRRING > CHIRR
CHIRRS > CHIRR
CHIRRUP vb (of some birds) to chirp repeatedly ▷ n chirruping sound
CHIRRUPED > CHIRRUP
CHIRRUPER > CHIRRUP
CHIRRUPS > CHIRRUP
CHIRRUPY > CHIRRUP
CHIRT vb squirt
CHIRTED > CHIRT
CHIRTING > CHIRT
CHIRTS > CHIRT
CHIRU n Tibetan antelope
CHIRUS > CHIRU
CHIS > CHI
CHISEL n metal tool with a sharp end for shaping wood or stone ▷ vb carve or form with a chisel

CHISELED same as
> CHISELLED
CHISELER > CHISEL
CHISELERS > CHISEL
CHISELING > CHISEL
CHISELLED adj finely or
sharply formed
CHISELLER n person
who uses a chisel
CHISELS > CHISEL
CHIT n short official note,
such as a receipt ▷ vb
sprout
CHITAL n type of deer
CHITALS > CHITAL
CHITCHAT n chat, gossip
▷ vb gossip
CHITCHATS > CHITCHAT
CHITIN n outer layer of
the bodies of arthropods
CHITINOID > CHITIN
CHITINOUS > CHITIN
CHITINS > CHITIN
CHITLIN n pig intestine
cooked and served as a dish
CHITLING > CHITLINGS
CHITLINGS same as
> CHIDLINGS
CHITLINS > CHIDLINGS
CHITON n (in ancient
Greece and Rome) a loose
woollen tunic
CHITONS > CHITON
CHITOSAN n
polysaccharide derived
from chitin
CHITOSANS > CHITOSAN
CHITS > CHIT
CHITTED > CHIT
CHITTER vb twitter or
chirp
CHITTERED > CHITTER
CHITTERS > CHITTER
CHITTIER > CHITTY
CHITTIES > CHITTY
CHITTIEST > CHITTY
CHITTING > CHIT
CHITTY adj childish
▷ vb sprout
CHIV n knife ▷ vb stab
(someone)
CHIVALRIC > CHIVALRY
CHIVALRY n courteous
behaviour, esp by men
towards women
CHIVAREE n charivari
▷ vb to perform a chivaree
CHIVAREED > CHIVAREE
CHIVAREES > CHIVAREE
CHIVARI same as
> CHARIVARI
CHIVARIED > CHIVARI
CHIVARIES > CHIVARI
CHIVE n small Eurasian
plant ▷ vb file or cut off
CHIVED > CHIVE
CHIVES same as > CHIVE
CHIVIED > CHIVY
CHIVIES > CHIVY
CHIVING > CHIVE
CHIVS > CHIV
CHIVVED > CHIV
CHIVVIED > CHIVVY

CHIVVIES > CHIVVY
CHIVVING > CHIV
CHIVVY same as > CHIVY
CHIVVYING > CHIVVY
CHIVY vb harass or nag
▷ n hunt
CHIVYING > CHIVY
CHIYOGAMI n type of
highly decorated Japanese
craft paper
CHIZ n cheat ▷ vb cheat
CHIZZ same as > CHIZ
CHIZZED > CHIZ
CHIZZES > CHIZ
CHIZZING > CHIZ
CHLAMYDES > CHLAMYS
CHLAMYDIA n type of
bacteria responsible for
some sexually transmitted
diseases
CHLAMYS n woollen cloak
worn by ancient Greek
soldiers
CHLAMYSES > CHLAMYS
CHLOASMA n appearance
on a person's skin, esp of
the face, of patches of
darker colour: associated
with hormonal changes
caused by liver disease or
the use of oral
contraceptives
CHLOASMAS > CHLOASMA
CHLORACNE n disfiguring
skin disease that results
from contact with or
ingestion or inhalation of
certain chlorinated
aromatic hydrocarbons
CHLORAL n colourless oily
liquid with a pungent
odour
CHLORALS > CHLORAL
CHLORATE n type of
chemical salt
CHLORATES > CHLORATE
CHLORDAN same as
> CHLORDANE
CHLORDANE n white
insoluble toxic solid
CHLORDANS > CHLORDAN
CHLORELLA n type of
microscopic unicellular
green alga, some species
of which are used in the
preparation of human
food
CHLORIC adj of or
containing chlorine in the
pentavalent state
CHLORID n type of
chlorine compound
CHLORIDE n compound
of chlorine and another
substance
CHLORIDES > CHLORIDE
CHLORIDIC > CHLORIDE
CHLORIDS > CHLORID
CHLORIN same as
> CHLORINE
CHLORINE n strong-
smelling greenish-yellow
gaseous element, used to
disinfect water

CHLORINES > CHLORINE
CHLORINS > CHLORIN
CHLORITE n any of a
group of green soft
secondary minerals
consisting of the hydrated
silicates of aluminium,
iron, and magnesium in
monoclinic crystalline
form: common in
metamorphic rocks
CHLORITES > CHLORITE
CHLORITIC > CHLORITE
CHLOROSES
> CHLOROSIS
CHLOROSIS n disorder,
formerly common in
adolescent girls,
characterized by pale
greenish-yellow skin,
weakness, and palpitation
and caused by insufficient
iron in the body
CHLOROTIC
> CHLOROSIS
CHLOROUS adj of or
containing chlorine in the
trivalent state
CHOANA n posterior nasal
aperture
CHOANAE > CHOANA
CHOBDAR n in India and
Nepal, king's macebearer
or attendant
CHOBDARS > CHOBDAR
CHOC short form of
> CHOCOLATE
CHOCCIER > CHOCCY
CHOCCIES > CHOCCY
CHOCCIEST > CHOCCY
CHOCCY n chocolate
▷ adj made of, tasting of,
smelling of, or resembling
chocolate
CHOCHO same as
> CHAYOTE
CHOCHOS > CHOCHO
CHOCK n block or wedge
used to prevent a heavy
object from moving
▷ vb secure by a chock
▷ adv as closely or tightly
as possible
CHOCKED > CHOCK
CHOCKER adj full up
CHOCKFUL adj filled to
capacity
CHOCKFULL variant of
> CHOCKFUL
CHOCKING > CHOCK
CHOCKO same as > CHOCO
CHOCKOS > CHOCKO
CHOCKS > CHOCK
CHOCO n member of the
Australian army
CHOCOLATE n sweet food
made from cacao seeds
▷ adj dark brown
CHOCOLATY
> CHOCOLATE
CHOCOS > CHOCO
CHOCS > CHOC
CHOCTAW n movement in
ice-skating

CHOCTAWS > CHOCTAW
CHODE > CHIDE
CHOENIX same as
> CHENIX
CHOENIXES > CHOENIX
CHOG n core of a piece of
fruit
CHOGS > CHOG
CHOICE n choosing
▷ adj of high quality
CHOICEFUL adj fickle
CHOICELY > CHOICE
CHOICER > CHOICE
CHOICES > CHOICE
CHOICEST > CHOICE
CHOIL n end of a knife
blade next to the handle
CHOILS > CHOIL
CHOIR n organized group
of singers, esp in church
▷ vb sing in chorus
CHOIRBOY n boy who
sings in a church choir
CHOIRBOYS > CHOIRBOY
CHOIRED > CHOIR
CHOIRGIRL n girl who
sings in a choir
CHOIRING > CHOIR
CHOIRLIKE > CHOIR
CHOIRMAN n man who
sings in a choir
CHOIRMEN > CHOIRMAN
CHOIRS > CHOIR
CHOKE vb hinder or stop
the breathing of (a person)
by strangling or
smothering ▷ n device
found in a petrol engine
CHOKEABLE > CHOKE
CHOKEBORE n shotgun
bore that becomes
narrower towards the
muzzle so that the shot is
not scattered
CHOKECOIL n type of
electronic inductor
CHOKED adj disappointed
or angry
CHOKEDAMP another word
for > BLACKDAMP
CHOKEHOLD n act of
holding a person's neck
across the windpipe, esp
from behind
CHOKER n tight-fitting
necklace
CHOKERS > CHOKER
CHOKES > CHOKE
CHOKEY n slang word for
prison ▷ adj involving,
caused by, or causing
choking
CHOKEYS > CHOKEY
CHOKIDAR n in India, a
gatekeeper
CHOKIDARS > CHOKIDAR
CHOKIER > CHOKEY
CHOKIES > CHOKEY
CHOKIEST > CHOKEY
CHOKING > CHOKE
CHOKINGLY > CHOKE
CHOKO n pear-shaped fruit
of a tropical American
vine, eaten as a vegetable

CHOKOS > CHOKO
CHOKRA n in India, a boy or young man
CHOKRAS > CHOKRA
CHOKRI n in India, a girl or young woman
CHOKRIS > CHOKRI
CHOKY same as **>** CHOKEY
CHOLA n Hispanic girl
CHOLAEMIA n toxic medical condition indicated by the presence of bile in the blood
CHOLAEMIC > CHOLAEMIA
CHOLAS > CHOLA
CHOLATE n salt of cholic acid
CHOLATES > CHOLATE
CHOLECYST n gall bladder
CHOLELITH n gallstone
CHOLEMIA same as **>** CHOLAEMIA
CHOLEMIAS > CHOLEMIA
CHOLENT n meal prepared on Friday and left to cook until eaten for Sabbath lunch
CHOLENTS > CHOLENT
CHOLER n bad temper
CHOLERA n serious infectious disease
CHOLERAIC > CHOLERA
CHOLERAS > CHOLERA
CHOLERIC adj bad-tempered
CHOLEROID > CHOLERA
CHOLERS > CHOLER
CHOLI n short-sleeved bodice, as worn by Indian women
CHOLIAMB n imperfect iambic trimeter, with a spondee as the last foot
CHOLIAMBS > CHOLIAMB
CHOLIC adj as in cholic acid crystalline acid found in bile
CHOLINE n colourless viscous soluble alkaline substance present in animal tissues
CHOLINES > CHOLINE
CHOLIS > CHOLI
CHOLLA n type of spiny cactus
CHOLLAS > CHOLLA
CHOLLERS pl n jowls or cheeks
CHOLO n chicano gangster
CHOLOS > CHOLO
CHOLTRIES > CHOLTRY
CHOLTRY n caravanserai
CHOMETZ same as **>** CHAMETZ
CHOMETZES > CHOMETZ
CHOMMIE n (in informal South African English) friend
CHOMMIES > CHOMMIE
CHOMP vb chew noisily **>** n act or sound of chewing in this manner
CHOMPED > CHOMP

CHOMPER > CHOMP
CHOMPERS > CHOMP
CHOMPING > CHOMP
CHOMPS > CHOMP
CHON n North and South Korean monetary unit
CHONDRAL adj of or relating to cartilage
CHONDRE another word for **>** CHONDRULE
CHONDRES > CHONDRE
CHONDRI > CHONDRUS
CHONDRIFY vb become or convert into cartilage
CHONDRIN n resilient translucent bluish-white substance that forms the matrix of cartilage
CHONDRINS > CHONDRIN
CHONDRITE n stony meteorite consisting mainly of silicate minerals in the form of chondrules
CHONDROID adj resembling cartilage
CHONDROMA n benign cartilaginous growth or neoplasm
CHONDRULE n one of the small spherical masses of mainly silicate minerals present in chondrites
CHONDRUS n cartilage
CHONS > CHON
CHOOF vb go away
CHOOFED > CHOOF
CHOOFING > CHOOF
CHOOFS > CHOOF
CHOOK n hen or chicken **>** vb make the sound of a hen of chicken
CHOOKED > CHOOK
CHOOKIE same as **>** CHOOK
CHOOKIES > CHOOK
CHOOKING > CHOOK
CHOOKS > CHOOK
CHOOM n Englishman
CHOOMS > CHOOM
CHOON n slang term for music that one likes
CHOONS > CHOON
CHOOSE vb select from a number of alternatives
CHOOSER > CHOOSE
CHOOSERS > CHOOSE
CHOOSES > CHOOSE
CHOOSEY same as **>** CHOOSY
CHOOSIER > CHOOSY
CHOOSIEST > CHOOSY
CHOOSILY adv in a fussy or choosy way
CHOOSING > CHOOSE
CHOOSY adj fussy, hard to please
CHOP vb cut with a blow from an axe or knife **>** n cutting or sharp blow
CHOPHOUSE n restaurant specializing in steaks, grills, chops, etc
CHOPIN same as **>** CHOPINE

CHOPINE n sandal-like shoe popular in the 18th century
CHOPINES > CHOPINE
CHOPINS > CHOPIN
CHOPLOGIC n person who uses excessively subtle or involved logic
CHOPPED > CHOP
CHOPPER n helicopter **>** vb travel by helicopter
CHOPPERED > CHOPPER
CHOPPERS > CHOPPER
CHOPPIER > CHOPPY
CHOPPIEST > CHOPPY
CHOPPILY > CHOPPY
CHOPPING > CHOP
CHOPPINGS > CHOP
CHOPPY adj (of the sea) fairly rough
CHOPS > CHOP
CHOPSOCKY n genre of martial arts film
CHOPSTICK n one of a pair of thin sticks used as eating utensils
CHORAGI > CHORAGUS
CHORAGIC > CHORAGUS
CHORAGUS n leader of a chorus
CHORAL adj of a choir
CHORALE n slow stately hymn tune
CHORALES > CHORALE
CHORALIST n singer or composer of chorals
CHORALLY > CHORAL
CHORALS > CHORAL
CHORD n straight line joining two points on a curve **>** vb provide (a melodic line) with chords
CHORDA n in anatomy, a cord
CHORDAE > CHORDA
CHORDAL > CHORD
CHORDATE n type of animal with a long fibrous rod just above the gut to support the body, such as the vertebrates
CHORDATES > CHORDATE
CHORDED > CHORD
CHORDEE n painful penile erection, a symptom of gonorrhoea
CHORDEES > CHORDEE
CHORDING n distribution of chords throughout a piece of harmony
CHORDINGS > CHORDING
CHORDS > CHORD
CHORDWISE adv in the direction of an aerofoil chord **>** adj moving in this direction
CHORE n routine task **>** vb carry out chores
CHOREA n disorder of the nervous system
CHOREAL > CHOREA
CHOREAS > CHOREA
CHOREATIC > CHOREA

CHOREBOY n boy who does chores
CHOREBOYS > CHOREBOY
CHORED > CHORE
CHOREE n trochee
CHOREES > CHOREE
CHOREGI > CHOREGUS
CHOREGIC > CHOREGUS
CHOREGUS n in ancient Greece, the producer/financier of a dramatist's works
CHOREIC > CHOREA
CHOREMAN n handyman
CHOREMEN > CHOREMAN
CHOREOID adj resembling chorea
CHORES > CHORE
CHOREUS same as **>** CHOREE
CHOREUSES > CHOREUS
CHORIA > CHORION
CHORIAL > CHORION
CHORIAMB n metrical foot used in classical verse consisting of four syllables, two short ones between two long ones
CHORIAMBI > CHORIAMB
CHORIAMBS > CHORIAMB
CHORIC adj in the manner of a chorus
CHORINE n chorus girl
CHORINES > CHORINE
CHORING > CHORE
CHORIOID same as **>** CHOROID
CHORIOIDS > CHORIOID
CHORION n outer membrane forming a sac around an embryo
CHORIONIC > CHORION
CHORIONS > CHORION
CHORISES > CHORISIS
CHORISIS n multiplication of leaves etc by branching or splitting
CHORISM > CHORISIS
CHORISMS > CHORISIS
CHORIST n choir member
CHORISTER n singer in a choir
CHORISTS > CHORIST
CHORIZO n kind of highly seasoned pork sausage of Spain or Mexico
CHORIZONT n person who challenges the authorship of a work
CHORIZOS > CHORIZO
CHOROID adj resembling the chorion, esp in being vascular **>** n vascular membrane of the eyeball
CHOROIDAL > CHOROID
CHOROIDS > CHOROID
CHOROLOGY n study of the causal relations between geographical phenomena occurring within a particular region
CHORRIE n dilapidated old car

CHORRIES > CHORRIE
CHORTEN n Buddhist shrine
CHORTENS > CHORTEN
CHORTLE vb chuckle in amusement ▷ n amused chuckle
CHORTLED > CHORTLE
CHORTLER > CHORTLE
CHORTLERS > CHORTLE
CHORTLES > CHORTLE
CHORTLING > CHORTLE
CHORUS n large choir ▷ vb sing or say together
CHORUSED > CHORUS
CHORUSES > CHORUS
CHORUSING > CHORUS
CHORUSSED > CHORUS
CHORUSSES > CHORUS
CHOSE > CHOOSE
CHOSEN > CHOOSE
CHOSES > CHOOSE
CHOTA adj (in British Empire Indian usage) small
CHOTT a variant spelling of > SHOTT
CHOTTS > CHOTT
CHOU n type of cabbage
CHOUGH n large black Eurasian and N African bird of the crow family
CHOUGHS > CHOUGH
CHOULTRY same as > CHOLTRY
CHOUNTER same as > CHUNTER
CHOUNTERS > CHOUNTER
CHOUSE vb to cheat
CHOUSED > CHOUSE
CHOUSER > CHOUSE
CHOUSERS > CHOUSE
CHOUSES > CHOUSE
CHOUSH n Turkish messenger
CHOUSHES > CHOUSH
CHOUSING > CHOUSE
CHOUT n blackmail
CHOUTS > CHOUT
CHOUX > CHOU
CHOW n thick-coated dog with a curled tail, orig. from China ▷ vb eat
CHOWCHOW same as > CHOW
CHOWCHOWS > CHOWCHOW
CHOWDER n thick soup containing clams or fish ▷ vb to make a chowder of
CHOWDERED > CHOWDER
CHOWDERS > CHOWDER
CHOWDOWN n act of eating a lot of food
CHOWDOWNS > CHOWDOWN
CHOWED > CHOW
CHOWHOUND n person who loves eating
CHOWING > CHOW
CHOWK n marketplace or market area
CHOWKIDAR same as > CHOKIDAR
CHOWKS > CHOWK

CHOWRI n fly-whisk
CHOWRIES > CHOWRI
CHOWRIS > CHOWRI
CHOWRY same as > CHOWRI
CHOWS > CHOW
CHOWSE same as > CHOUSE
CHOWSED > CHOWSE
CHOWSES > CHOWSE
CHOWSING > CHOWSE
CHOWTIME n mealtime
CHOWTIMES > CHOWTIME
CHRESARD n amount of water present in the soil that is available to plants
CHRESARDS > CHRESARD
CHRISM n consecrated oil used for anointing in some churches
CHRISMA > CHRISMON
CHRISMAL n chrism container
CHRISMALS > CHRISMAL
CHRISMON n monogram and symbol of Christ's name
CHRISMONS > CHRISMON
CHRISMS > CHRISM
CHRISOM same as > CHRISM
CHRISOMS > CHRISOM
CHRISTEN vb baptize
CHRISTENS > CHRISTEN
CHRISTIAN adj exhibiting kindness or goodness
CHRISTIE same as > CHRISTY
CHRISTIES > CHRISTIE
CHRISTOM same as > CHRISOM
CHRISTOMS > CHRISTOM
CHRISTY n skiing turn for stopping or changing direction quickly
CHROMA n attribute of a colour
CHROMAKEY n (in colour television) a special effect in which a coloured background can be eliminated and a different background substituted
CHROMAS > CHROMA
CHROMATE n any salt or ester of chromic acid
CHROMATES > CHROMATE
CHROMATIC adj of colour or colours
CHROMATID n either of the two strands into which a chromosome divides during mitosis. They separate to form daughter chromosomes at anaphase
CHROMATIN n part of the nucleus of a cell that forms the chromosomes and can easily be dyed
CHROME n anything plated with chromium ▷ vb plate with chromium ▷ vb to chromium-plate ▷ adj of or having the appearance of chrome

CHROMED > CHROME
CHROMEL n nickel-based alloy
CHROMELS > CHROMEL
CHROMENE n chemical compound
CHROMENES > CHROMENE
CHROMES > CHROME
CHROMIC adj of or containing chromium in the trivalent state
CHROMIDE n any member of the cichlid family of fish
CHROMIDES > CHROMIDE
CHROMIDIA n chromatins in cell cytoplasm
CHROMIER > CHROME
CHROMIEST > CHROMY
CHROMING > CHROME
CHROMINGS > CHROME
CHROMISE same as > CHROMIZE
CHROMISED > CHROMISE
CHROMISES > CHROMISE
CHROMITE n brownish-black mineral which is the only commercial source of chromium
CHROMITES > CHROMITE
CHROMIUM n grey metallic element used in steel alloys and for electroplating
CHROMIUMS > CHROMIUM
CHROMIZE vb chrome-plate
CHROMIZED > CHROMIZE
CHROMIZES > CHROMIZE
CHROMO n picture produced by lithography
CHROMOGEN n compound that forms coloured compounds on oxidation
CHROMOLY n type of steel alloy
CHROMOS > CHROMO
CHROMOUS adj of or containing chromium in the divalent state
CHROMY > CHROME
CHROMYL n of, consisting of, or containing the divalent radical CrO_2
CHROMYLS > CHROMYL
CHRONAXIE n minimum time required for excitation of a nerve or muscle when the stimulus is double the minimum (threshold) necessary to elicit a basic response
CHRONAXY same as > CHRONAXIE
CHRONIC adj (of an illness) lasting a long time ▷ n chronically-ill patient
CHRONICAL > CHRONIC
CHRONICLE n record of events in order of occurrence ▷ vb record in or as if in a chronicle
CHRONICS > CHRONIC
CHRONON n unit of time
CHRONONS > CHRONON

CHRYSALID adj of or relating to a chrysalis
CHRYSALIS n insect in the stage between larva and adult, when it is in a cocoon
CHRYSANTH n chrysanthemum
CHTHONIAN adj of or relating to the underworld
CHTHONIC same as > CHTHONIAN
CHUB n European freshwater fish of the carp family
CHUBASCO n in Mexico, a hurricane
CHUBASCOS > CHUBASCO
CHUBBIER > CHUBBY
CHUBBIEST > CHUBBY
CHUBBILY > CHUBBY
CHUBBY adj plump and round
CHUBS > CHUB
CHUCK vb throw ▷ n cut of beef from the neck to the shoulder
CHUCKED > CHUCK
CHUCKER n person who throws something
CHUCKERS > CHUCKER
CHUCKHOLE n pothole
CHUCKIE n small stone
CHUCKIES > CHUCKIE
CHUCKING > CHUCK
CHUCKLE vb laugh softly ▷ n soft laugh
CHUCKLED > CHUCKLE
CHUCKLER > CHUCKLE
CHUCKLERS > CHUCKLE
CHUCKLES > CHUCKLE
CHUCKLING > CHUCKLE
CHUCKS > CHUCK
CHUCKY same as > CHUCKIE
CHUDDAH same as > CHUDDAR
CHUDDAHS > CHUDDAH
CHUDDAR n large shawl or veil
CHUDDARS > CHUDDAR
CHUDDER same as > CHUDDAR
CHUDDERS > CHUDDER
CHUDDIES pl n underpants
CHUDDY n chewing gum
CHUFA n type of sedge
CHUFAS > CHUFA
CHUFF vb (of a steam engine) move while making a puffing sound ▷ n puffing sound of or as if of a steam engine ▷ adj boorish
CHUFFED adj very pleased
CHUFFER > CHUFF
CHUFFEST > CHUFF
CHUFFIER > CHUFFY
CHUFFIEST > CHUFFY
CHUFFING > CHUFF
CHUFFS > CHUFF
CHUFFY adj boorish and surly

CHUG *n* short dull sound like the noise of an engine ▷ *vb* operate or move with this sound

CHUGALUG *vb* to gulp down a drink in one go

CHUGALUGS > CHUGALUG

CHUGGED > CHUG

CHUGGER > CHUG

CHUGGERS > CHUG

CHUGGING > CHUG

CHUGS > CHUG

CHUKAR *n* common Indian partridge

CHUKARS > CHUKAR

CHUKKA *n* period of play in polo

CHUKKAR *same as* **>** CHUKKA

CHUKKARS > CHUKKAR

CHUKKAS > CHUKKA

CHUKKER *same as* **>** CHUKKA

CHUKKERS > CHUKKER

CHUKOR *same as* **>** CHUKAR

CHUKORS > CHUKOR

CHUM *n* close friend ▷ *vb* be or become an intimate friend (of)

CHUMASH *n* printed book containing one of the Five Books of Moses

CHUMASHES > CHUMASH

CHUMASHIM > CHUMASH

CHUMLEY *same as* **>** CHIMNEY

CHUMLEYS > CHUMLEY

CHUMMAGE *n* formerly, fee paid by a prisoner for sole occupancy of a cell

CHUMMAGES > CHUMMAGE

CHUMMED > CHUM

CHUMMIER > CHUMMY

CHUMMIES > CHUMMY

CHUMMIEST > CHUMMY

CHUMMILY > CHUMMY

CHUMMING > CHUM

CHUMMY *adj* friendly ▷ *n* chum

CHUMP *n* stupid person ▷ *vb* chew noisily

CHUMPED > CHUMP

CHUMPING *n* collecting wood for bonfires on Guy Fawkes Day

CHUMPINGS > CHUMPING

CHUMPS > CHUMP

CHUMS > CHUM

CHUMSHIP *n* friendship

CHUMSHIPS > CHUMSHIP

CHUNDER *vb* vomit ▷ *n* vomit

CHUNDERED > CHUNDER

CHUNDERS > CHUNDER

CHUNK *n* thick solid piece ▷ *vb* to break up into chunks

CHUNKED > CHUNK

CHUNKIER > CHUNKY

CHUNKIEST > CHUNKY

CHUNKILY > CHUNKY

CHUNKING *n* grouping together of a number of items by the mind, after

which they can be remembered as a single item, such as a word or a musical phrase

CHUNKINGS > CHUNKING

CHUNKS > CHUNK

CHUNKY *adj* (of a person) broad and heavy

CHUNNEL *n* rail tunnel linking England and France

CHUNNELS > CHUNNEL

CHUNNER *same as* **>** CHUNTER

CHUNNERED > CHUNNER

CHUNNERS > CHUNNER

CHUNTER *vb* mutter or grumble incessantly in a meaningless fashion

CHUNTERED > CHUNTER

CHUNTERS > CHUNTER

CHUPATI *same as* **>** CHUPATTI

CHUPATIS > CHUPATI

CHUPATTI *variant spellings of* **>** CHAPATI

CHUPATTIS > CHUPATTI

CHUPATTY *same as* **>** CHUPATTI

CHUPPA *variant of* **>** CHUPPAH

CHUPPAH *n* canopy under which a marriage is performed

CHUPPAHS > CHUPPAH

CHUPPAS > CHUPPA

CHUPPOT > CHUPPAH

CHUPPOTH *same as* **>** CHUPPOT

CHUPRASSY *same as* **>** CHAPRASSI

CHUR *interj* expression of agreement

CHURCH *n* building for public Christian worship ▷ *vb* bring someone to church for special ceremonies

CHURCHED > CHURCH

CHURCHES > CHURCH

CHURCHIER > CHURCHY

CHURCHING > CHURCH

CHURCHISM *n* adherence to the principles of an established church

CHURCHLY *adj* appropriate to, associated with, or suggestive of church life and customs

CHURCHMAN *n* clergyman

CHURCHMEN > CHURCHMAN

CHURCHWAY *n* way or road that leads to a church

CHURCHY *adj* like a church, church service, etc

CHURIDAR *n* as in *churidar pyjamas* long tight-fitting trousers, worn by Indian men and women

CHURIDARS > CHURIDAR

CHURINGA *n* sacred amulet of the native Australians

CHURINGAS > CHURINGA

CHURL *n* surly ill-bred person

CHURLISH *adj* surly and rude

CHURLS > CHURL

CHURN *n* machine in which cream is shaken to make butter ▷ *vb* stir (cream) vigorously to make butter

CHURNED > CHURN

CHURNER > CHURN

CHURNERS > CHURN

CHURNING *n* quantity of butter churned at any one time

CHURNINGS > CHURNING

CHURNMILK *n* buttermilk

CHURNS > CHURN

CHURR *same as* **>** CHIRR

CHURRED > CHURR

CHURRING > CHURR

CHURRO *n* Spanish dough stick snack

CHURROS > CHURRO

CHURRS > CHURR

CHURRUS *n* hemp resin

CHURRUSES > CHURRUS

CHUSE *obsolete variant of* **>** CHOOSE

CHUSED > CHUSE

CHUSES > CHUSE

CHUSING > CHUSE

CHUT *interj* expression of surprise or annoyance ▷ *vb* make such an expression

CHUTE *n* steep slope down which things may be slid ▷ *vb* to descend by a chute

CHUTED > CHUTE

CHUTES > CHUTE

CHUTING > CHUTE

CHUTIST > CHUTE

CHUTISTS > CHUTE

CHUTNEE *same as* **>** CHUTNEY

CHUTNEES > CHUTNEE

CHUTNEY *n* pickle made from fruit, vinegar, spices, and sugar

CHUTNEYS > CHUTNEY

CHUTS > CHUT

CHUTZPA *same as* **>** CHUTZPAH

CHUTZPAH *n* unashamed self-confidence

CHUTZPAHS > CHUTZPAH

CHUTZPAS > CHUTZPA

CHYACK *same as* **>** CHIACK

CHYACKED > CHYACK

CHYACKING > CHYACK

CHYACKS > CHYACK

CHYLDE *archaic word for* **>** CHILD

CHYLE *n* milky fluid formed in the small intestine during digestion

CHYLES > CHYLE

CHYLIFIED > CHYLIFY

CHYLIFIES > CHYLIFY

CHYLIFY *vb* to be turned into chyle

CHYLOUS > CHYLE

CHYLURIA *n* presence of chyle in urine

CHYLURIAS > CHYLURIA

CHYME *n* partially digested food that leaves the stomach

CHYMES > CHYME

CHYMIC *same as* **>** CHEMIC

CHYMICS > CHYMIC

CHYMIFIED > CHYMIFY

CHYMIFIES > CHYMIFY

CHYMIFY *vb* to form into chyme

CHYMIST *same as* **>** CHEMIST

CHYMISTRY *same as* **>** CHEMISTRY

CHYMISTS > CHYMIST

CHYMOSIN *another name for* **>** RENNIN

CHYMOSINS > CHYMOSIN

CHYMOUS > CHYME

CHYND *adj* chined

CHYPRE *n* perfume made from sandalwood

CHYPRES > CHYPRE

CHYTRID *n* variety of fungus

CHYTRIDS > CHYTRID

CIABATTA *n* type of bread made with olive oil

CIABATTAS > CIABATTA

CIABATTE > CIABATTA

CIAO *an informal word for* **>** HELLO

CIBATION *n* feeding

CIBATIONS > CIBATION

CIBOL *same as* **>** CHIBOL

CIBOLS > CIBOL

CIBORIA > CIBORIUM

CIBORIUM *n* goblet-shaped lidded vessel used to hold consecrated wafers in Holy Communion

CIBOULE *same as* **>** CHIBOL

CIBOULES > CIBOULE

CICADA *n* large insect that makes a high-pitched drone

CICADAE > CICADA

CICADAS > CICADA

CICALA *same as* **>** CICADA

CICALAS > CICALA

CICALE > CICALA

CICATRICE *n* scar

CICATRISE *same as* **>** CICATRIZE

CICATRIX *n* scar

CICATRIZE *vb* (of a wound or defect in tissue) to close or be closed by scar formation

CICELIES > CICELY

CICELY *n* type of plant

CICERO *n* measure for type that is somewhat larger than the pica

CICERONE *n* person who guides and informs sightseers ▷ *vb* to act as a cicerone

CICERONED > CICERONE
CICERONES > CICERONE
CICERONI > CICERONE
CICEROS > CICERO
CICHLID n type of tropical freshwater fish popular in aquariums
CICHLIDAE n cichlids
CICHLIDS > CICHLID
CICHLOID > CICHLID
CICINNUS n scorpioid cyme
CICISBEI > CICISBEO
CICISBEO n escort or lover of a married woman, esp in 18th-century Italy
CICISBEOS > CICISBEO
CICLATON n rich material of silk and gold
CICLATONS > CICLATON
CICLATOUN same as **>** CICLATON
CICOREE same as **>** CHICORY
CICOREES > CICOREE
CICUTA n spotted hemlock
CICUTAS > CICUTA
CICUTINE same as **>** CONIINE
CICUTINES > CICUTINE
CID n leader
CIDARIS n sea urchin
CIDARISES > CIDARIS
CIDE Shakespearean variant of **>** DECIDE
CIDED > CIDE
CIDER n alcoholic drink made from fermented apple juice
CIDERKIN n weak type of cider
CIDERKINS > CIDERKIN
CIDERS > CIDER
CIDERY > CIDER
CIDES > CIDE
CIDING > CIDE
CIDS > CID
CIEL same as **>** CEIL
CIELED > CIEL
CIELING > CIEL
CIELINGS > CIEL
CIELS > CIEL
CIERGE same as **>** CERGE
CIERGES > CIERGE
CIG same as **>** CIGARETTE
CIGAR n roll of cured tobacco leaves for smoking
CIGARET same as **>** CIGARETTE
CIGARETS > CIGARET
CIGARETTE n thin roll of shredded tobacco in thin paper, for smoking
CIGARILLO n small cigar often only slightly larger than a cigarette
CIGARLIKE > CIGAR
CIGARS > CIGAR
CIGGIE same as **>** CIGARETTE
CIGGIES > CIGGIE

CIGGY same as **>** CIGARETTE
CIGS > CIG
CIGUATERA n food poisoning caused by a toxin in seafood
CILANTRO same as **>** CORIANDER
CILANTROS > CILANTRO
CILIA > CILIUM
CILIARY adj of or relating to cilia
CILIATE n type of protozoan
CILIATED > CILIATE
CILIATELY > CILIATE
CILIATES > CILIATE
CILIATION > CILIATE
CILICE n haircloth fabric or garment
CILICES > CILICE
CILICIOUS adj made of hair
CILIOLATE adj covered with minute hairs, as some plants
CILIUM n short thread projecting from a cell that causes movement
CILL a variant spelling (used in the building industry) for **>** SILL
CILLS > CILL
CIMAR same as **>** CYMAR
CIMARS > CIMAR
CIMBALOM n type of dulcimer, esp of Hungary
CIMBALOMS > CIMBALOM
CIMELIA n (especially, ecclesiastical) treasures
CIMEX n type of heteropterous insect, esp the bedbug
CIMICES > CIMEX
CIMIER n crest of a helmet
CIMIERS > CIMIER
CIMINITE n type of igneous rock
CIMINITES > CIMINITE
CIMMERIAN adj very dark or gloomy
CIMOLITE n clayey, whitish mineral
CIMOLITES > CIMOLITE
CINCH n easy task ▷ vb fasten a girth around (a horse)
CINCHED > CINCH
CINCHES > CINCH
CINCHING > CINCH
CINCHINGS > CINCH
CINCHONA same as **>** CALISAYA
CINCHONAS > CINCHONA
CINCHONIC > CINCHONA
CINCINNUS same as **>** CICINNUS
CINCT adj encircled
CINCTURE n something, such as a belt or girdle, that goes around another thing ▷ vb to encircle
CINCTURED > CINCTURE
CINCTURES > CINCTURE

CINDER n piece of material that will not burn, left after burning coal ▷ vb burn to cinders
CINDERED > CINDER
CINDERING > CINDER
CINDEROUS > CINDER
CINDERS > CINDER
CINDERY > CINDER
CINE n as in cine camera camera able to film moving pictures
CINEAST same as **>** CINEASTE
CINEASTE n enthusiast for films
CINEASTES > CINEASTE
CINEASTS > CINEAST
CINEMA n place for showing films
CINEMAS > CINEMA
CINEMATIC > CINEMA
CINEOL n colourless oily liquid with a camphor-like odour and a spicy taste
CINEOLE same as **>** CINEOL
CINEOLES > CINEOLE
CINEOLS > CINEOL
CINEPHILE n film enthusiast
CINEPLEX n (tradename for) a large cinema complex
CINERAMIC adj relating to a cinematic process producing widescreen images
CINERARIA n garden plant with daisy-like flowers
CINERARY adj of (someone's) ashes
CINERATOR same as **>** CREMATOR
CINEREA n grey matter of the brain and nervous system
CINEREAL adj ashy
CINEREAS > CINEREA
CINEREOUS adj of a greyish colour
CINERIN n either of two organic compounds used as insecticides
CINERINS > CINERIN
CINES > CINE
CINGULA > CINGULUM
CINGULAR adj ring-shaped
CINGULATE > CINGULUM
CINGULUM n girdle-like part, such as the ridge round the base of a tooth or the band of fibres connecting parts of the cerebrum
CINNABAR n heavy red mineral containing mercury
CINNABARS > CINNABAR
CINNAMIC > CINNAMON
CINNAMON n spice obtained from the bark of an Asian tree

CINNAMONS > CINNAMON
CINNAMONY > CINNAMON
CINNAMYL n univalent radical of cinnamic compounds
CINNAMYLS > CINNAMYL
CINQ n number five
CINQS > CINQ
CINQUAIN n stanza of five lines
CINQUAINS > CINQUAIN
CINQUE n number five in cards, dice, etc
CINQUES > CINQUE
CION same as **>** SCION
CIONS > CION
CIOPPINO n Italian rich fish stew
CIOPPINOS > CIOPPINO
CIPAILLE n type of pie traditional in Quebec
CIPAILLES > CIPAILLE
CIPHER n system of secret writing ▷ vb put (a message) into secret writing
CIPHERED > CIPHER
CIPHERER > CIPHER
CIPHERERS > CIPHER
CIPHERING > CIPHER
CIPHERS > CIPHER
CIPHONIES > CIPHONY
CIPHONY n ciphered telephony
CIPOLIN n Italian marble with alternating white and green streaks
CIPOLINS > CIPOLIN
CIPOLLINO same as **>** CIPOLIN
CIPPI > CIPPUS
CIPPUS n pillar bearing an inscription
CIRCA prep approximately, about
CIRCADIAN adj of biological processes that occur regularly at 24-hour intervals
CIRCAR n in India, part of a province
CIRCARS > CIRCAR
CIRCINATE adj (of part of a plant, such as a young fern) coiled so that the tip is at the centre
CIRCITER prep around, about
CIRCLE n perfectly round geometric figure, line, or shape ▷ vb move in a circle (round)
CIRCLED > CIRCLE
CIRCLER > CIRCLE
CIRCLERS > CIRCLE
CIRCLES > CIRCLE
CIRCLET n circular ornament worn on the head
CIRCLETS > CIRCLET
CIRCLING > CIRCLE
CIRCLINGS > CIRCLE
CIRCLIP n type of fastener

CIRCLIPS > CIRCLIP
CIRCS pl n circumstances
CIRCUIT n complete route or course, esp a circular one ▷ vb make or travel in a circuit around (something)
CIRCUITAL > CIRCUIT
CIRCUITED > CIRCUIT
CIRCUITRY n electrical circuit(s)
CIRCUITS > CIRCUIT
CIRCUITY n (of speech, reasoning, etc) a roundabout or devious quality
CIRCULAR adj in the shape of a circle ▷ n letter for general distribution
CIRCULARS > CIRCULAR
CIRCULATE vb send, go, or pass from place to place or person to person
CIRCUS n travelling company of acrobats, clowns, performing animals, etc
CIRCUSES > CIRCUS
CIRCUSSY > CIRCUS
CIRCUSY > CIRCUS
CIRE adj (of fabric) treated with a heat or wax process to make it smooth ▷ n such a surface on a fabric
CIRES > CIRE
CIRL n bird belonging to the bunting family
CIRLS > CIRL
CIRQUE n steep-sided semicircular hollow found in mountainous areas
CIRQUES > CIRQUE
CIRRATE adj bearing or resembling cirri
CIRRHOSED
> CIRRHOSIS
CIRRHOSES
> CIRRHOSIS
CIRRHOSIS n serious liver disease, often caused by drinking too much alcohol
CIRRHOTIC
> CIRRHOSIS
CIRRI > CIRRUS
CIRRIFORM adj cirrus-like
CIRRIPED same as
> CIRRIPEDE
CIRRIPEDE n type of marine crustacean of the subclass including the barnacles
CIRRIPEDS > CIRRIPED
CIRROSE same as
> CIRRATE
CIRROUS same as
> CIRRATE
CIRRUS n high wispy cloud
CIRRUSES > CIRRUS
CIRSOID adj resembling a varix

CIS adj having two groups of atoms on the same side of a double bond
CISALPINE adj on this (the southern) side of the Alps, as viewed from Rome
CISCO n whitefish, esp the lake herring of the deep lakes of North America
CISCOES > CISCO
CISCOS > CISCO
CISELEUR n person who is expert in ciselure
CISELEURS > CISELEUR
CISELURE n art or process of chasing metal
CISELURES > CISELURE
CISLUNAR adj of or relating to the space between the earth and the moon
CISPADANE adj on this (the southern) side of the River Po, as viewed from Rome
CISPLATIN n cytotoxic drug that acts by preventing DNA replication and hence cell division, used in the treatment of tumours, esp of the ovary and testis
CISSIER > CISSY
CISSIES > CISSY
CISSIEST > CISSY
CISSIFIED another word for > SISSY
CISSING n appearance of pinholes, craters, etc, in paintwork
CISSINGS > CISSING
CISSOID n geometric curve whose two branches meet in a cusp at the origin and are asymptotic to a line parallel to the y-axis
CISSOIDS > CISSOID
CISSUS n type of climbing plant
CISSUSES > CISSUS
CISSY same as > SISSY
CIST n wooden box for holding ritual objects used in ancient Rome and Greece ▷ vb make a cist
CISTED > CIST
CISTERN n water tank, esp one that holds water for flushing a toilet
CISTERNA n sac or partially closed space containing body fluid, esp lymph or cerebrospinal fluid
CISTERNAE > CISTERNA
CISTERNAL > CISTERN
CISTERNS > CISTERN
CISTIC adj cist-like
CISTRON n section of a chromosome that encodes a single polypeptide chain
CISTRONIC > CISTRON
CISTRONS > CISTRON

CISTS > CIST
CISTUS n type of plant
CISTUSES > CISTUS
CISTVAEN n pre-Christian stone coffin or burial chamber
CISTVAENS > CISTVAEN
CIT n pejorative term for a town dweller
CITABLE > CITE
CITADEL n fortress in a city
CITADELS > CITADEL
CITAL n court summons
CITALS > CITAL
CITATION n commendation for bravery
CITATIONS > CITATION
CITATOR n legal publication
CITATORS > CITATOR
CITATORY > CITATION
CITE vb quote, refer to
CITEABLE > CITE
CITED > CITE
CITER > CITE
CITERS > CITE
CITES > CITE
CITESS n female cit
CITESSES > CITESS
CITHARA n ancient stringed musical instrument
CITHARAS > CITHARA
CITHARIST n player of the cithara
CITHER same as
> CITTERN
CITHERN same as
> CITTERN
CITHERNS > CITHERN
CITHERS > CITHER
CITHREN same as
> CITHARA
CITHRENS > CITHREN
CITIED adj having cities
CITIES > CITY
CITIFIED > CITIFY
CITIFIES > CITIFY
CITIFY vb cause to conform to or adopt the customs, habits, or dress of city people
CITIFYING > CITIFY
CITIGRADE adj relating to (fast-moving) wolf spiders
CITING > CITE
CITIZEN n native or naturalized member of a state or nation
CITIZENLY > CITIZEN
CITIZENRY n citizens collectively
CITIZENS > CITIZEN
CITO adv swiftly
CITOLA n type of medieval stringed instrument
CITOLAS > CITOLA
CITOLE a rare word for
> CITTERN
CITOLES > CITOLE

CITRAL n volatile liquid with a lemon-like odour
CITRALS > CITRAL
CITRANGE n type of acidic and aromatic orange
CITRANGES > CITRANGE
CITRATE n any salt or ester of citric acid
CITRATED adj treated with a citrate
CITRATES > CITRATE
CITREOUS adj of a greenish-yellow colour
CITRIC adj of or derived from citrus fruits or citric acid
CITRIN n vitamin P
CITRINE n brownish-yellow variety of quartz: a gemstone
CITRINES > CITRINE
CITRININ n type of mycotoxin
CITRININS > CITRININ
CITRINS > CITRIN
CITRON n lemon-like fruit of a small Asian tree
CITRONS > CITRON
CITROUS same as
> CITRUS
CITRUS n type of tropical or subtropical tree or shrub
CITRUSES > CITRUS
CITRUSSY adj having or resembling the taste or colour of a citrus fruit
CITRUSY same as
> CITRUSSY
CITS > CIT
CITTERN n medieval stringed instrument
CITTERNS > CITTERN
CITY n large or important town
CITYFIED > CITYFY
CITYFIES > CITYFY
CITYFY same as > CITIFY
CITYFYING > CITYFY
CITYSCAPE n urban landscape
CITYWARD adv towards a city
CITYWIDE adj occurring throughout a city
CIVE same as > CHIVE
CIVES > CIVE
CIVET n spotted catlike African mammal
CIVETLIKE > CIVET
CIVETS > CIVET
CIVIC adj of a city or citizens
CIVICALLY > CIVIC
CIVICISM n principle of civil government
CIVICISMS > CIVICISM
CIVICS n study of the rights and responsibilities of citizenship
CIVIE same as > CIVVY
CIVIES > CIVIE
CIVIL adj relating to the citizens of a state

CIVILIAN adj not belonging to the armed forces ▷ n person who is not a member of the armed forces or police
CIVILIANS > CIVILIAN
CIVILISE same as > CIVILIZE
CIVILISED same as > CIVILIZED
CIVILISER > CIVILISE
CIVILISES > CIVILISE
CIVILIST n civilian
CIVILISTS > CIVILIST
CIVILITY n polite or courteous behaviour
CIVILIZE vb refine or educate (a person)
CIVILIZED adj having a high state of culture and social development
CIVILIZER > CIVILIZE
CIVILIZES > CIVILIZE
CIVILLY > CIVIL
CIVILNESS > CIVIL
CIVILS > CIVIL
CIVISM n good citizenship
CIVISMS > CIVISM
CIVVIES > CIVVY
CIVVY n civilian
CIZERS archaic spelling of > SCISSORS
CLABBER vb to cover with mud
CLABBERED > CLABBER
CLABBERS > CLABBER
CLACH n stone ▷ vb kill by stoning
CLACHAN n small village
CLACHANS > CLACHAN
CLACHED > CLACH
CLACHES > CLACH
CLACHING > CLACH
CLACHS > CLACH
CLACK n sound made by two hard objects striking each other ▷ vb make this sound
CLACKBOX n casing enclosing a clack
CLACKDISH n formerly, a dish carried by a beggar
CLACKED > CLACK
CLACKER n object that makes a clacking sound
CLACKERS > CLACKER
CLACKING > CLACK
CLACKS > CLACK
CLAD vb bond a metal to (another metal), esp to form a protective coat
CLADDAGH n Irish ring
CLADDAGHS > CLADDAGH
CLADDED adj covered with cladding
CLADDER > CLAD
CLADDERS > CLAD
CLADDIE another name for > KORARI
CLADDIES > CLADDIE
CLADDING > CLOTHE
CLADDINGS > CLOTHE

CLADE n group of organisms sharing a common ancestor
CLADES > CLADE
CLADISM > CLADIST
CLADISMS > CLADIST
CLADIST n proponent of cladistics
CLADISTIC > CLADIST
CLADISTS > CLADIST
CLADODE n stem resembling and functioning as a leaf
CLADODES > CLADODE
CLADODIAL > CLADODE
CLADOGRAM n treelike diagram illustrating the development of a clade
CLADS > CLAD
CLAES Scots word for > CLOTHES
CLAFOUTI same as > CLAFOUTIS
CLAFOUTIS n French baked pudding
CLAG n sticky mud ▷ vb stick, as mud
CLAGGED > CLAG
CLAGGIER > CLAGGY
CLAGGIEST > CLAGGY
CLAGGING > CLAG
CLAGGY adj stickily clinging, as mud
CLAGS > CLAG
CLAIM vb assert as a fact ▷ n assertion that something is true
CLAIMABLE > CLAIM
CLAIMANT n person who makes a claim
CLAIMANTS > CLAIMANT
CLAIMED > CLAIM
CLAIMER > CLAIM
CLAIMERS > CLAIM
CLAIMING > CLAIM
CLAIMS > CLAIM
CLAM n edible shellfish with a hinged shell ▷ vb gather clams
CLAMANCY n urgency
CLAMANT adj noisy
CLAMANTLY > CLAMANT
CLAMBAKE n picnic, often by the sea, at which clams, etc, are baked
CLAMBAKES > CLAMBAKE
CLAMBE old variant of > CLIMB
CLAMBER vb climb awkwardly ▷ n climb performed in this manner
CLAMBERED > CLAMBER
CLAMBERER > CLAMBER
CLAMBERS > CLAMBER
CLAME archaic variant of > CLAIM
CLAMES > CLAIM
CLAMLIKE > CLAM
CLAMMED > CLAM
CLAMMER n person who gathers clams
CLAMMERS > CLAMMER
CLAMMIER > CLAMMY

CLAMMIEST > CLAMMY
CLAMMILY > CLAMMY
CLAMMING > CLAM
CLAMMY adj unpleasantly moist and sticky
CLAMOR same as > CLAMOUR
CLAMORED > CLAMOR
CLAMORER > CLAMOR
CLAMORERS > CLAMOR
CLAMORING > CLAMOR
CLAMOROUS > CLAMOR
CLAMORS > CLAMOR
CLAMOUR n loud protest ▷ vb make a loud noise or outcry
CLAMOURED > CLAMOUR
CLAMOURER > CLAMOUR
CLAMOURS > CLAMOUR
CLAMP n tool with movable jaws for holding things together tightly ▷ vb fasten with a clamp
CLAMPDOWN n sudden restrictive measure
CLAMPED > CLAMP
CLAMPER n spiked metal frame fastened to the sole of a shoe ▷ vb to tread heavily
CLAMPERED > CLAMPER
CLAMPERS > CLAMPER
CLAMPING n act of clamping
CLAMPINGS > CLAMPING
CLAMPS > CLAMP
CLAMS > CLAM
CLAMSHELL n dredging bucket that is hinged like the shell of a clam
CLAMWORM the US name for the > RAGWORM
CLAMWORMS > CLAMWORM
CLAN n group of families with a common ancestor
CLANG vb make a loud ringing metallic sound ▷ n ringing metallic sound
CLANGBOX n device fitted to a jet-engine to change the direction of thrust
CLANGED > CLANG
CLANGER n obvious mistake
CLANGERS > CLANGER
CLANGING > CLANG
CLANGINGS > CLANG
CLANGOR same as > CLANGOUR
CLANGORED > CLANGOR
CLANGORS > CLANGOR
CLANGOUR n loud continuous clanging sound ▷ vb make or produce a loud resonant noise
CLANGOURS > CLANGOUR
CLANGS > CLANG
CLANK n harsh metallic sound ▷ vb make such a sound
CLANKED > CLANK
CLANKIER > CLANKY
CLANKIEST > CLANKY

CLANKING > CLANK
CLANKINGS > CLANK
CLANKS > CLANK
CLANKY adj making clanking sounds
CLANNISH adj (of a group) tending to exclude outsiders
CLANS > CLAN
CLANSHIP n association of families under the leadership of a chieftain
CLANSHIPS > CLANSHIP
CLANSMAN n man belonging to a clan
CLANSMEN > CLANSMAN
CLAP vb applaud by hitting the palms of one's hands sharply together ▷ n act or sound of clapping
CLAPBOARD n long thin timber board with one edge thicker than the other, used esp in the US and Canada in wood-frame construction by lapping each board over the one below ▷ vb cover with such boards
CLAPBREAD n type of cake made from oatmeal
CLAPDISH same as > CLACKDISH
CLAPNET n net that can be closed instantly by pulling a string
CLAPNETS > CLAPNET
CLAPPED > CLAP
CLAPPER n piece of metal inside a bell ▷ vb make a sound like a clapper
CLAPPERED > CLAPPER
CLAPPERS > CLAPPER
CLAPPING > CLAP
CLAPPINGS > CLAP
CLAPS > CLAP
CLAPT > CLAP
CLAPTRAP n foolish or pretentious talk
CLAPTRAPS > CLAPTRAP
CLAQUE n group of people hired to applaud
CLAQUER same as > CLAQUEUR
CLAQUERS > CLAQUEUR
CLAQUES > CLAQUE
CLAQUEUR n member of a claque
CLAQUEURS > CLAQUEUR
CLARAIN n one of the four major lithotypes of banded coal
CLARAINS > CLARAIN
CLARENCE n closed four-wheeled horse-drawn carriage, having a glass front
CLARENCES > CLARENCE
CLARENDON n style of boldface roman type
CLARET n dry red wine from Bordeaux ▷ adj purplish-red ▷ vb to drink claret

CLARETED > CLARET
CLARETING > CLARET
CLARETS > CLARET
CLARIES > CLARY
CLARIFIED > CLARIFY
CLARIFIER > CLARIFY
CLARIFIES > CLARIFY
CLARIFY *vb* make (a matter) clear and unambiguous
CLARINET *n* keyed woodwind instrument with a single reed
CLARINETS > CLARINET
CLARINI > CLARINO
CLARINO *adj* relating to a high passage for the trumpet in 18th-century music ▷ *n* high register of the trumpet
CLARINOS > CLARINO
CLARION *n* obsolete high-pitched trumpet ▷ *adj* clear and ringing ▷ *vb* proclaim loudly
CLARIONED > CLARION
CLARIONET *same as* > CLARINET
CLARIONS > CLARION
CLARITIES > CLARITY
CLARITY *n* clearness
CLARKIA *n* N American plant cultivated for its red, purple, or pink flowers
CLARKIAS > CLARKIA
CLARO *n* mild light-coloured cigar
CLAROES > CLARO
CLAROS > CLARO
CLARSACH *n* Celtic harp of Scotland and Ireland
CLARSACHS > CLARSACH
CLART *vb* to dirty
CLARTED > CLART
CLARTHEAD *n* slow-witted or stupid person
CLARTIER > CLARTY
CLARTIEST > CLARTY
CLARTING > CLART
CLARTS *pl n* lumps of mud, esp on shoes
CLARTY *adj* dirty, esp covered in mud
CLARY *n* European plant with aromatic leaves and blue flowers
CLASH *vb* come into conflict ▷ *n* fight, argument
CLASHED > CLASH
CLASHER > CLASH
CLASHERS > CLASH
CLASHES > CLASH
CLASHING > CLASH
CLASHINGS > CLASH
CLASP *n* device for fastening things ▷ *vb* grasp or embrace firmly
CLASPED > CLASP
CLASPER > CLASP
CLASPERS *pl n* paired organ of male insects, used to clasp the female during copulation

CLASPING > CLASP
CLASPINGS > CLASP
CLASPS > CLASP
CLASPT *old inflection of* > CLASP
CLASS *n* group of people sharing a similar social position ▷ *vb* place in a class
CLASSABLE > CLASS
CLASSED > CLASS
CLASSER > CLASS
CLASSES > CLASSIS
CLASSIBLE *adj* able to be classed
CLASSIC *adj* being a typical example of something ▷ *n* author, artist, or work of art of recognized excellence
CLASSICAL *adj* of or in a restrained conservative style
CLASSICO *adj* (of Italian wines) coming from the centre of a specific wine-growing region
CLASSICS *pl n* the. a body of literature regarded as great or lasting, esp that of ancient Greece or Rome
CLASSIER > CLASSY
CLASSIEST > CLASSY
CLASSIFIC *adj* relating to classification
CLASSIFY *vb* divide into groups with similar characteristics
CLASSILY > CLASSY
CLASSING > CLASS
CLASSINGS > CLASS
CLASSIS *n* governing body of elders or pastors
CLASSISM *n* belief that people from certain social or economic classes are superior to others
CLASSISMS > CLASSISM
CLASSIST > CLASSISM
CLASSISTS > CLASSISM
CLASSLESS *adj* not belonging to a class
CLASSMAN *n* graduate of Oxford University with a classed honours degree
CLASSMATE *n* friend or contemporary in the same class of a school
CLASSMEN > CLASSMAN
CLASSON *n* elementary atomic particle
CLASSONS > CLASSON
CLASSROOM *n* room in a school where lessons take place
CLASSWORK *n* school work done in class
CLASSY *adj* stylish and elegant
CLAST *n* fragment of a clastic rock
CLASTIC *adj* composed of fragments ▷ *n* clast

CLASTICS > CLASTIC
CLASTS > CLAST
CLAT *n* irksome or troublesome task ▷ *vb* to scrape
CLATCH *vb* to move making a squelching sound
CLATCHED > CLATCH
CLATCHES > CLATCH
CLATCHING > CLATCH
CLATHRATE *adj* resembling a net or lattice ▷ *n* solid compound in which molecules of one substance are physically trapped in the crystal lattice of another
CLATS > CLAT
CLATTED > CLAT
CLATTER *n* (make) a rattling noise ▷ *vb* make a rattling noise, as when hard objects hit each other
CLATTERED > CLATTER
CLATTERER > CLATTER
CLATTERS > CLATTER
CLATTERY > CLATTER
CLATTING > CLAT
CLAUCHT *vb* to seize by force
CLAUCHTED > CLAUCHT
CLAUCHTS > CLAUCHT
CLAUGHT *same as* > CLAUCHT
CLAUGHTED > CLAUGHT
CLAUGHTS > CLAUGHT
CLAUSAL > CLAUSE
CLAUSE *n* section of a legal document
CLAUSES > CLAUSE
CLAUSTRA > CLAUSTRUM
CLAUSTRAL *same as* > CLOISTRAL
CLAUSTRUM *n* thin layer of grey matter in the brain
CLAUSULA *n* type of cadence in polyphony
CLAUSULAE > CLAUSULA
CLAUSULAR > CLAUSE
CLAUT *same as* > CLAT
CLAUTED > CLAUT
CLAUTING > CLAUT
CLAUTS > CLAUT
CLAVATE *adj* shaped like a club with the thicker end uppermost
CLAVATED *same as* > CLAVATE
CLAVATELY > CLAVATE
CLAVATION > CLAVATE
CLAVE *n* one of a pair of hardwood sticks struck together to make a hollow sound
CLAVECIN *n* harpsichord
CLAVECINS > CLAVECIN
CLAVER *vb* talk idly ▷ *n* idle talk
CLAVERED > CLAVER
CLAVERING > CLAVER
CLAVERS > CLAVER
CLAVES > CLAVE
CLAVI > CLAVUS

CLAVICLE *n* either of the two bones connecting the shoulder blades with the upper part of the breastbone
CLAVICLES > CLAVICLE
CLAVICORN *n* type of beetle such as the ladybirds, characterized by club-shaped antennae
CLAVICULA *n* clavicle
CLAVIE *n* tar-barrel traditionally set alight in Moray in Scotland on Hogmanay
CLAVIER *n* any keyboard instrument
CLAVIERS > CLAVIER
CLAVIES > CLAVIE
CLAVIFORM *same as* > CLAVATE
CLAVIGER *n* key- or club-bearer
CLAVIGERS > CLAVIGER
CLAVIS *n* key
CLAVULATE *adj* club-shaped
CLAVUS *n* corn on the toe
CLAW *n* sharp hooked nail of a bird or beast ▷ *vb* tear with claws or nails
CLAWBACK *n* recovery of a sum of money
CLAWBACKS > CLAWBACK
CLAWED > CLAW
CLAWER > CLAW
CLAWERS > CLAW
CLAWING > CLAW
CLAWLESS > CLAW
CLAWLIKE *adj* resembling a claw or claws
CLAWS > CLAW
CLAXON *same as* > KLAXON
CLAXONS > CLAXON
CLAY *n* fine-grained earth used to make bricks and pottery ▷ *vb* cover or mix with clay
CLAYBANK *n* dull brownish-orange colour
CLAYBANKS > CLAYBANK
CLAYED > CLAY
CLAYEY > CLAY
CLAYIER > CLAY
CLAYIEST > CLAY
CLAYING > CLAY
CLAYISH > CLAY
CLAYLIKE > CLAY
CLAYMORE *n* large two-edged sword formerly used by Scottish Highlanders
CLAYMORES > CLAYMORE
CLAYPAN *n* layer of stiff impervious clay situated just below the surface of the ground
CLAYPANS > CLAYPAN
CLAYS > CLAY
CLAYSTONE *n* compact very fine-grained rock consisting of consolidated clay particles

C

CLAYTONIA n low-growing N American succulent plant

CLAYWARE n pottery

CLAYWARES > CLAYWARE

CLEAN adj free from dirt or impurities ▷ vb make (something) free from dirt ▷ adv completely

CLEANABLE > CLEAN

CLEANED > CLEAN

CLEANER n person or thing that removes dirt

CLEANERS > CLEANER

CLEANEST > CLEAN

CLEANING n act of cleaning something

CLEANINGS > CLEANING

CLEANISH adj quite clean

CLEANLIER > CLEANLY

CLEANLILY > CLEANLY

CLEANLY adv easily or smoothly ▷ adj habitually clean or neat

CLEANNESS > CLEAN

CLEANOUT n act or instance of cleaning (something) out

CLEANOUTS > CLEANOUT

CLEANS > CLEAN

CLEANSE vb make clean

CLEANSED > CLEANSE

CLEANSER n cleansing agent, such as a detergent

CLEANSERS > CLEANSER

CLEANSES > CLEANSE

CLEANSING > CLEANSE

CLEANSKIN n unbranded animal

CLEANUP n process of cleaning up or eliminating something

CLEANUPS > CLEANUP

CLEAR adj free from doubt or confusion ▷ adv in a clear or distinct manner ▷ vb make or become clear

CLEARABLE > CLEAR

CLEARAGE n clearance

CLEARAGES > CLEARAGE

CLEARANCE n clearing

CLEARCOLE n type of size containing whiting ▷ vb paint (a wall) with this size

CLEARCUT n act of felling all trees in area

CLEARCUTS > CLEARCUT

CLEARED > CLEAR

CLEARER > CLEAR

CLEARERS > CLEAR

CLEAREST > CLEAR

CLEAREYED adj having good judgment

CLEARING n treeless area in a wood

CLEARINGS > CLEARING

CLEARLY adv in a clear, distinct, or obvious manner

CLEARNESS > CLEAR

CLEAROUT n act or instance of removing (things or material)

CLEAROUTS > CLEAROUT

CLEARS > CLEAR

CLEARSKIN same as > CLEANSKIN

CLEARWAY n stretch of road on which motorists may stop in an emergency

CLEARWAYS > CLEARWAY

CLEARWEED n plant like nettle

CLEARWING n type of moth

CLEAT n wedge ▷ vb supply or support with a cleat or cleats

CLEATED > CLEAT

CLEATING > CLEAT

CLEATS > CLEAT

CLEAVABLE > CLEAVE

CLEAVAGE n space between a woman's breasts, as revealed by a low-cut dress

CLEAVAGES > CLEAVAGE

CLEAVE vb split apart ▷ n split

CLEAVED > CLEAVE

CLEAVER n butcher's heavy knife with a square blade

CLEAVERS n plant with small white flowers and sticky fruits

CLEAVES > CLEAVE

CLEAVING > CLEAVE

CLEAVINGS > CLEAVE

CLECHE adj (in heraldry) voided so that only a narrow border is visible

CLECK vb (of birds) to hatch ▷ n piece of gossip

CLECKED > CLECK

CLECKIER > CLECK

CLECKIEST > CLECK

CLECKING > CLECK

CLECKINGS > CLECK

CLECKS > CLECK

CLECKY > CLECK

CLEEK n large hook, such as one used to land fish ▷ vb to seize

CLEEKED > CLEEK

CLEEKING > CLEEK

CLEEKIT > CLEEK

CLEEKS > CLEEK

CLEEP same as > CLEPE

CLEEPED > CLEEP

CLEEPING > CLEEP

CLEEPS > CLEEP

CLEEVE n cliff

CLEEVES > CLEEVE

CLEF n symbol at the beginning of a stave to show the pitch

CLEFS > CLEF

CLEFT > CLEAVE

CLEFTED > CLEAVE

CLEFTING > CLEAVE

CLEFTS > CLEAVE

CLEG another name for a > HORSEFLY

CLEGS > CLEG

CLEIDOIC adj as in cleidoic egg egg of birds and insects

CLEIK same as > CLEEK

CLEIKS > CLEEK

CLEITHRAL adj covered with a roof

CLEM vb be hungry or cause to be hungry

CLEMATIS n climbing plant with large colourful flowers

CLEMENCY n kind or lenient treatment

CLEMENT adj (of weather) mild

CLEMENTLY > CLEMENT

CLEMMED > CLEM

CLEMMING > CLEM

CLEMS > CLEM

CLENCH vb close or squeeze (one's teeth or fist) tightly ▷ n firm grasp or grip

CLENCHED > CLENCH

CLENCHER > CLENCH

CLENCHERS > CLENCH

CLENCHES > CLENCH

CLENCHING > CLENCH

CLEOME n type of herbaceous or shrubby plant

CLEOMES > CLEOME

CLEOPATRA n type of yellow butterfly, the male of which has its wings flushed with orange

CLEPE vb call by the name of

CLEPED > CLEPE

CLEPES > CLEPE

CLEPING > CLEPE

CLEPSYDRA n ancient device for measuring time by the flow of water or mercury through a small aperture

CLEPT > CLEPE

CLERGIES > CLERGY

CLERGY n priests and ministers as a group

CLERGYMAN n member of the clergy

CLERGYMEN > CLERGYMAN

CLERIC n member of the clergy

CLERICAL adj of clerks or office work

CLERICALS pl n distinctive dress of a clergyman

CLERICATE n clerical post

CLERICITY n condition of being a clergyman

CLERICS > CLERIC

CLERID n beetle that preys on other insects

CLERIDS > CLERID

CLERIHEW n form of comic or satiric verse, consisting of two couplets and containing the name of a well-known person

CLERIHEWS > CLERIHEW

CLERISIES > CLERISY

CLERISY n learned or educated people

CLERK n employee who keeps records, files, and accounts ▷ vb work as a clerk

CLERKDOM > CLERK

CLERKDOMS > CLERK

CLERKED > CLERK

CLERKESS n female office clerk

CLERKING > CLERK

CLERKISH > CLERK

CLERKLIER > CLERKLY

CLERKLIKE adj acting in a scholarly manner

CLERKLING n young or inexperienced clerk

CLERKLY adj of or like a clerk ▷ adv in the manner of a clerk

CLERKS > CLERK

CLERKSHIP > CLERK

CLERUCH n settler in a cleruchy

CLERUCHIA same as > CLERUCHY

CLERUCHS > CLERUCH

CLERUCHY n (in the ancient world) a special type of Athenian colony, in which settlers retained their Athenian citizenship and the community remained a political dependency of Athens

CLEUCH same as > CLOUGH

CLEUCHS > CLEUCH

CLEUGH same as > CLOUGH

CLEUGHS > CLEUGH

CLEVE same as > CLEEVE

CLEVEITE n crystalline variety of the mineral uraninite

CLEVEITES > CLEVEITE

CLEVER adj intelligent, quick at learning

CLEVERER > CLEVER

CLEVEREST > CLEVER

CLEVERISH > CLEVER

CLEVERLY > CLEVER

CLEVES > CLEEVE

CLEVIS n type of fastening used in agriculture

CLEVISES > CLEVIS

CLEW n ball of thread, yarn, or twine ▷ vb coil or roll into a ball

CLEWED > CLEW

CLEWING > CLEW

CLEWS > CLEW

CLIANTHUS n Australian or NZ plant with slender scarlet flowers

CLICHE n expression or idea that is no longer effective because of overuse ▷ vb use a cliché (in speech or writing)

CLICHED > CLICHE

CLICHEED > CLICHE

CLICHES > CLICHE

CLICK n short sharp sound ▷ vb make this sound
CLICKABLE adj (of a website) having links that can be accessed by clicking a computer mouse
CLICKBAIT n hyperlink that entices one to click through to a new website
CLICKED > CLICK
CLICKER > CLICK
CLICKERS > CLICK
CLICKET vb make a click
CLICKETED > CLICKET
CLICKETS > CLICKET
CLICKING > CLICK
CLICKINGS > CLICK
CLICKLESS > CLICK
CLICKS > CLICK
CLICKWRAP adj (of agreement) consented to by user clicking computer button
CLIED > CLY
CLIENT n person who uses the services of a professional person or company
CLIENTAGE same as > CLIENTELE
CLIENTAL > CLIENT
CLIENTELE n clients collectively
CLIENTS > CLIENT
CLIES > CLY
CLIFF n steep rock face, esp along the sea shore ▷ vb scale a cliff
CLIFFED > CLIFF
CLIFFHANG vb (of a serial or film) to end on a note of suspense
CLIFFHUNG > CLIFFHANG
CLIFFIER > CLIFF
CLIFFIEST > CLIFF
CLIFFLIKE > CLIFF
CLIFFS > CLIFF
CLIFFSIDE n side of a cliff
CLIFFTOP n top of a cliff
CLIFFTOPS > CLIFFTOP
CLIFFY > CLIFF
CLIFT same as > CLIFF
CLIFTED > CLIFF
CLIFTIER > CLIFF
CLIFTIEST > CLIFF
CLIFTS > CLIFF
CLIFTY > CLIFF
CLIMACTIC adj consisting of, involving, or causing a climax
CLIMATAL > CLIMATE
CLIMATE n typical weather conditions of an area ▷ vb acclimatize
CLIMATED > CLIMATE
CLIMATES > CLIMATE
CLIMATIC > CLIMATE
CLIMATING > CLIMATE
CLIMATISE vb in Australia, adapt or

become accustomed to a new climate or environment
CLIMATIZE same as > CLIMATISE
CLIMATURE n clime
CLIMAX n most intense point of an experience, series of events, or story ▷ vb reach a climax
CLIMAXED > CLIMAX
CLIMAXES > CLIMAX
CLIMAXING > CLIMAX
CLIMB vb go up, ascend ▷ n climbing
CLIMBABLE > CLIMB
CLIMBDOWN n act of backing down from opinion
CLIMBED > CLIMB
CLIMBER n person or thing that climbs
CLIMBERS > CLIMBER
CLIMBING > CLIMB
CLIMBINGS > CLIMB
CLIMBS > CLIMB
CLIME n place or its climate
CLIMES > CLIME
CLINAL > CLINE
CLINALLY > CLINE
CLINAMEN n bias
CLINAMENS > CLINAMEN
CLINCH vb settle (an argument or agreement) decisively ▷ n movement in which one competitor holds on to the other to avoid punches
CLINCHED > CLINCH
CLINCHER n something decisive
CLINCHERS > CLINCHER
CLINCHES > CLINCH
CLINCHING > CLINCH
CLINE n variation within a species
CLINES > CLINE
CLING vb hold tightly or stick closely ▷ n tendency of cotton fibres in a sample to stick to each other
CLINGED > CLING
CLINGER > CLING
CLINGERS > CLING
CLINGFILM n thin polythene material for wrapping food
CLINGFISH n type of small marine fish with a flattened elongated body and a sucking disc beneath the head for clinging to rocks, etc
CLINGIER > CLING
CLINGIEST > CLING
CLINGING > CLING
CLINGS > CLING
CLINGWRAP same as > CLINGFILM
CLINGY > CLING
CLINIC n building where outpatients receive medical treatment or advice

CLINICAL adj of a clinic
CLINICIAN n physician, psychiatrist, etc, who specializes in clinical work as opposed to one engaged in laboratory or experimental studies
CLINICS > CLINIC
CLINIQUE same as > CLINIC
CLINIQUES > CLINIC
CLINK n (make) a light sharp metallic sound ▷ vb make a light sharp metallic sound
CLINKED > CLINK
CLINKER n fused coal left over in a fire or furnace ▷ vb form clinker during burning
CLINKERED > CLINKER
CLINKERS > CLINKER
CLINKING > CLINK
CLINKS > CLINK
CLINOAXES > CLINOAXIS
CLINOAXIS n in a monoclinic crystal, the lateral axis which forms an oblique angle with the vertical axis
CLINOSTAT n apparatus for studying tropisms in plants, usually a rotating disc to which the plant is attached so that it receives an equal stimulus on all sides
CLINQUANT adj glittering, esp with tinsel ▷ n tinsel or imitation gold leaf
CLINT n section of a limestone pavement separated from others by fissures
CLINTONIA n type of temperate plant with white, greenish-yellow, or purplish flowers, broad ribbed leaves, and blue berries
CLINTS > CLINT
CLIP vb cut with shears or scissors ▷ n short extract of a film
CLIPART n large collection of simple drawings stored in a computer
CLIPARTS > CLIPART
CLIPBOARD n portable writing board with a clip at the top for holding paper
CLIPE same as > CLYPE
CLIPED > CLIPE
CLIPES > CLIPE
CLIPING > CLIPE
CLIPPABLE > CLIP
CLIPPED > CLIP
CLIPPER n fast commercial sailing ship
CLIPPERS pl n tool for clipping
CLIPPIE n bus conductress

CLIPPIES > CLIPPIE
CLIPPING same as > CLIP
CLIPPINGS > CLIP
CLIPS > CLIP
CLIPSHEAR n earwig
CLIPSHEET n sheet of paper with text printed on one side only
CLIPT old inflection of > CLIP
CLIQUE n small exclusive group ▷ vb to form a clique
CLIQUED > CLIQUE
CLIQUES > CLIQUE
CLIQUEY adj exclusive, confined to a small group
CLIQUIER > CLIQUEY
CLIQUIEST > CLIQUEY
CLIQUING > CLIQUE
CLIQUISH > CLIQUE
CLIQUISM > CLIQUE
CLIQUISMS > CLIQUE
CLIQUY same as > CLIQUEY
CLIT same as > CLITORIS
CLITELLA > CLITELLUM
CLITELLAR > CLITELLUM
CLITELLUM n thickened saddle-like region of epidermis in earthworms and leeches whose secretions bind copulating worms together and later form a cocoon around the eggs
CLITHRAL same as > CLEITHRAL
CLITIC adj (of a word) incapable of being stressed ▷ n clitic word
CLITICISE same as > CLITICIZE
CLITICIZE vb pronounce as part of following or preceding word
CLITICS > CLITIC
CLITORAL > CLITORIS
CLITORIC > CLITORIS
CLITORIS n small sexually sensitive organ at the front of the vulva
CLITS > CLIT
CLITTER vb to stridulate
CLITTERED > CLITTER
CLITTERS > CLITTER
CLIVERS same as > CLEAVERS
CLIVIA n plant belonging to the Amaryllid family
CLIVIAS > CLIVIA
CLOACA n cavity in most animals into which the alimentary canal and the genital and urinary ducts open
CLOACAE > CLOACA
CLOACAL > CLOACA
CLOACAS > CLOACA
CLOACINAL > CLOACA
CLOACITIS n inflammation of the cloaca in birds, including

domestic fowl, and other animals with a common opening of the urinary and gastrointestinal tracts

CLOAK n loose sleeveless outer garment ▷ vb cover or conceal

CLOAKED > CLOAK

CLOAKING > CLOAK

CLOAKROOM n room where coats may be left temporarily

CLOAKS > CLOAK

CLOAM adj made of clay or earthenware ▷ n clay or earthenware pots, dishes, etc, collectively

CLOAMS > CLOAM

CLOBBER vb hit ▷ n belongings, esp clothes

CLOBBERED > CLOBBER

CLOBBERS > CLOBBER

CLOCHARD n tramp

CLOCHARDS > CLOCHARD

CLOCHE n cover to protect young plants

CLOCHES > CLOCHE

CLOCK n instrument for showing the time ▷ vb record (time) with a stopwatch

CLOCKED > CLOCK

CLOCKER > CLOCK

CLOCKERS > CLOCK

CLOCKING > CLOCK

CLOCKINGS > CLOCK

CLOCKLIKE > CLOCK

CLOCKS > CLOCK

CLOCKWISE adj in the direction in which the hands of a clock rotate

CLOCKWORK n mechanism similar to the kind in a clock, used in wind-up toys

CLOD n lump of earth ▷ vb pelt with clods

CLODDED > CLOD

CLODDIER > CLOD

CLODDIEST > CLOD

CLODDING > CLOD

CLODDISH > CLOD

CLODDY > CLOD

CLODLY > CLOD

CLODPATE n dull or stupid person

CLODPATED adj stupid

CLODPATES > CLODPATE

CLODPOLE same as > CLODPATE

CLODPOLES > CLODPOLE

CLODPOLL same as > CLODPATE

CLODPOLLS > CLODPOLL

CLODS > CLOD

CLOFF n cleft of a tree

CLOFFS > CLOFF

CLOG vb obstruct ▷ n wooden or wooden-soled shoe

CLOGDANCE n dance performed in clogs

CLOGGED > CLOG

CLOGGER n clogmaker

CLOGGERS > CLOGGER

CLOGGIER > CLOG

CLOGGIEST > CLOG

CLOGGILY > CLOG

CLOGGING > CLOG

CLOGGINGS > CLOG

CLOGGY > CLOG

CLOGS > CLOG

CLOISON n partition

CLOISONNE n design made by filling in a wire outline with coloured enamel ▷ adj of, relating to, or made by cloisonné

CLOISONS > CLOISON

CLOISTER n covered pillared arcade, usu in a monastery ▷ vb confine or seclude in or as if in a monastery

CLOISTERS > CLOISTER

CLOISTRAL adj of, like, or characteristic of a cloister

CLOKE same as > CLOAK

CLOKED > CLOKE

CLOKES > CLOKE

CLOKING > CLOKE

CLOMB a past tense and past participle of > CLIMB

CLOMP same as > CLUMP

CLOMPED > CLOMP

CLOMPING > CLOMP

CLOMPS > CLOMP

CLON same as > CLONE

CLONAL > CLONE

CLONALLY > CLONE

CLONE n animal or plant produced artificially from the cells of another animal or plant ▷ vb produce as a clone

CLONED > CLONE

CLONER > CLONE

CLONERS > CLONE

CLONES > CLONE

CLONIC > CLONUS

CLONICITY > CLONUS

CLONIDINE n anti-hypertensive drug

CLONING > CLONE

CLONINGS > CLONE

CLONISM n series of clonic spasms

CLONISMS > CLONISM

CLONK vb make a dull thud ▷ n loud thud

CLONKED > CLONK

CLONKIER > CLONKY

CLONKIEST > CLONKY

CLONKING > CLONK

CLONKS > CLONK

CLONKY same as > CLUNKY

CLONS > CLON

CLONUS n type of convulsion

CLONUSES > CLONUS

CLOOP n sound made when a cork is drawn from a bottle

CLOOPS > CLOOP

CLOOT n hoof

CLOOTIE adj as in clootie dumpling kind of dumpling

CLOOTS > CLOOT

CLOP vb make a sound as of a horse's hooves ▷ n sound of this nature

CLOPPED > CLOP

CLOPPING > CLOP

CLOPS > CLOP

CLOQUE n fabric with an embossed surface

CLOQUES > CLOQUE

CLOSABLE > CLOSE

CLOSE vb shut ▷ n end, conclusion ▷ adj near ▷ adv closely, tightly

CLOSEABLE > CLOSE

CLOSED > CLOSE

CLOSEDOWN n closure or stoppage of operations

CLOSEHEAD n entrance to a close

CLOSELY > CLOSE

CLOSENESS > CLOSE

CLOSEOUT n termination of an account on which the margin is exhausted

CLOSEOUTS > CLOSEOUT

CLOSER > CLOSE

CLOSERS > CLOSE

CLOSES > CLOSE

CLOSEST > CLOSE

CLOSET n cupboard ▷ adj private, secret ▷ vb shut (oneself) away in private

CLOSETED > CLOSET

CLOSETFUL n quantity that may be contained in a closet

CLOSETING > CLOSET

CLOSETS > CLOSET

CLOSEUP n photo taken close to subject

CLOSEUPS > CLOSEUP

CLOSING > CLOSE

CLOSINGS > CLOSE

CLOSURE n closing ▷ vb (in a deliberative body) to end (debate) by closure

CLOSURED > CLOSURE

CLOSURES > CLOSURE

CLOSURING > CLOSURE

CLOT n soft thick lump formed from liquid ▷ vb form soft thick lumps

CLOTBUR n burdock

CLOTBURS > CLOTBUR

CLOTE n burdock

CLOTES > CLOTE

CLOTH n (piece of) woven fabric

CLOTHE vb put clothes on

CLOTHED > CLOTHE

CLOTHES pl n garments

CLOTHIER n maker or seller of clothes or cloth

CLOTHIERS > CLOTHIER

CLOTHING > CLOTHE

CLOTHINGS > CLOTHE

CLOTHLIKE > CLOTH

CLOTHS > CLOTH

CLOTPOLL same as > CLODPOLL

CLOTPOLLS > CLOTPOLL

CLOTS > CLOT

CLOTTED > CLOT

CLOTTER vb to clot

CLOTTERED > CLOTTER

CLOTTERS > CLOTTER

CLOTTIER > CLOTTY

CLOTTIEST > CLOTTY

CLOTTING > CLOT

CLOTTINGS > CLOT

CLOTTISH > CLOT

CLOTTY adj full of clots

CLOTURE n closure in the US Senate ▷ vb end (debate) in the US Senate by cloture

CLOTURED > CLOTURE

CLOTURES > CLOTURE

CLOTURING > CLOTURE

CLOU n crux; focus

CLOUD n mass of condensed water vapour floating in the sky ▷ vb become cloudy

CLOUDAGE n mass of clouds

CLOUDAGES > CLOUDAGE

CLOUDED > CLOUD

CLOUDIER > CLOUDY

CLOUDIEST > CLOUDY

CLOUDILY > CLOUDY

CLOUDING > CLOUD

CLOUDINGS > CLOUD

CLOUDLAND n realm or fantasy or impractical notions

CLOUDLESS > CLOUD

CLOUDLET n small cloud

CLOUDLETS > CLOUDLET

CLOUDLIKE > CLOUD

CLOUDS > CLOUD

CLOUDTOWN n cloudland

CLOUDY adj having a lot of clouds

CLOUGH n gorge or narrow ravine

CLOUGHS > CLOUGH

CLOUR vb to thump or dent

CLOURED > CLOUR

CLOURING > CLOUR

CLOURS > CLOUR

CLOUS > CLOU

CLOUT n hard blow ▷ vb hit hard

CLOUTED > CLOUT

CLOUTER > CLOUT

CLOUTERLY adj clumsy

CLOUTERS > CLOUT

CLOUTING > CLOUT

CLOUTS > CLOUT

CLOVE n tropical evergreen myrtaceous tree

CLOVEN > CLEAVE

CLOVER n plant with three-lobed leaves

CLOVERED adj covered with clover

CLOVERS > CLOVER

CLOVERY > CLOVER

CLOVES > CLOVE

CLOVIS n as in clovis point flint projectile dating from the 10th millennium bc

CLOW n clove ▷ vb rake with a clow

CLOWDER n collective term for a group of cats

CLOWDERS > CLOWDER

CLOWED > CLOW

CLOWING > CLOW

CLOWN n comic entertainer in a circus ▷ vb behave foolishly

CLOWNED > CLOWN

CLOWNERY > CLOWN

CLOWNFISH n small, brightly-coloured tropical fish

CLOWNING > CLOWN

CLOWNINGS > CLOWN

CLOWNISH > CLOWN

CLOWNS > CLOWN

CLOWS > CLOW

CLOY vb cause weariness through an excess of something initially pleasurable

CLOYE vb to claw

CLOYED > CLOYE

CLOYES > CLOYE

CLOYING adj sickeningly sweet

CLOYINGLY > CLOYING

CLOYLESS adj not cloying

CLOYMENT n satiety

CLOYMENTS > CLOYMENT

CLOYS > CLOY

CLOYSOME adj cloying

CLOZAPINE n drug used to treat mental illness

CLOZE adj as in cloze test test of the ability to understand text

CLOZES > CLOZE

CLUB n association of people with common interests ▷ vb hit with a club

CLUBABLE same as > CLUBBABLE

CLUBBABLE adj suitable to be a member of a club

CLUBBED > CLUB

CLUBBER n person who regularly frequents nightclubs

CLUBBERS > CLUBBER

CLUBBIER > CLUBBY

CLUBBIEST > CLUBBY

CLUBBILY > CLUBBY

CLUBBING > CLUB

CLUBBINGS > CLUB

CLUBBISH adj clubby

CLUBBISM n advantage gained through membership of a club or clubs

CLUBBISMS > CLUBBISM

CLUBBIST > CLUBBISM

CLUBBISTS > CLUBBISM

CLUBBY adj sociable, esp effusively so

CLUBFACE n face of golf club

CLUBFACES > CLUBFACE

CLUBFEET > CLUBFOOT

CLUBFOOT n congenital deformity of the foot

CLUBHAND n congenital deformity of the hand

CLUBHANDS > CLUBHAND

CLUBHAUL vb force (a sailing vessel) onto a new tack, esp in an emergency

CLUBHAULS > CLUBHAUL

CLUBHEAD n head of golf club

CLUBHEADS > CLUBHEAD

CLUBHOUSE n premises of a sports or other club, esp a golf club

CLUBLAND n (in Britain) the area of London around St. James's, which contains most of the famous London clubs

CLUBLANDS > CLUBLAND

CLUBMAN n man who is an enthusiastic member of a club or clubs

CLUBMATE n friend or contemporary in the same club

CLUBMATES > CLUBMATE

CLUBMEN > CLUBMAN

CLUBMOSS n type of green moss-like plant

CLUBROOM n room in which a club meets

CLUBROOMS > CLUBROOM

CLUBROOT n disease of cabbages

CLUBROOTS > CLUBROOT

CLUBRUSH n any rush of the genus Scirpus

CLUBS > CLUB

CLUBWOMAN n woman who is an enthusiastic member of a club or clubs

CLUBWOMEN > CLUBWOMAN

CLUCK n low clicking noise made by a hen ▷ vb make this noise

CLUCKED > CLUCK

CLUCKER n chicken

CLUCKERS > CLUCKER

CLUCKIER > CLUCKY

CLUCKIEST > CLUCKY

CLUCKING > CLUCK

CLUCKS > CLUCK

CLUCKY adj wishing to have a baby

CLUDGIE n toilet

CLUDGIES > CLUDGIE

CLUE n something that helps to solve a mystery or puzzle ▷ vb help solve a mystery or puzzle

CLUED > CLUE

CLUEING > CLUE

CLUELESS adj stupid

CLUES > CLUE

CLUEY adj (Australian) well-informed and adroit

CLUIER > CLUEY

CLUIEST > CLUEY

CLUING > CLUE

CLUMBER n type of thickset spaniel

CLUMBERS > CLUMBER

CLUMP n small group of things or people ▷ vb walk heavily

CLUMPED > CLUMP

CLUMPER > CLUMP

CLUMPERS > CLUMP

CLUMPET n large chunk of floating ice

CLUMPETS > CLUMPET

CLUMPIER > CLUMP

CLUMPIEST > CLUMP

CLUMPING > CLUMP

CLUMPISH > CLUMP

CLUMPLIKE > CLUMP

CLUMPS > CLUMP

CLUMPY > CLUMP

CLUMSIER > CLUMSY

CLUMSIEST > CLUMSY

CLUMSILY > CLUMSY

CLUMSY adj lacking skill or physical coordination

CLUNCH n hardened clay

CLUNCHES > CLUNCH

CLUNG > CLING

CLUNK n dull metallic sound ▷ vb make such a sound

CLUNKED > CLUNK

CLUNKER n dilapidated old car or other machine

CLUNKERS > CLUNKER

CLUNKIER > CLUNKY

CLUNKIEST > CLUNKY

CLUNKING > CLUNK

CLUNKS > CLUNK

CLUNKY adj making a clunking noise

CLUPEID n type of fish

CLUPEIDS > CLUPEID

CLUPEOID n type of soft-finned fish belonging to the order which includes the herrings, salmon, and tarpon

CLUPEOIDS > CLUPEOID

CLUSIA n tree of the tropical American genus Clusia

CLUSIAS > CLUSIA

CLUSTER n small close group ▷ vb gather in clusters

CLUSTERED > CLUSTER

CLUSTERS > CLUSTER

CLUSTERY > CLUSTER

CLUTCH vb grasp tightly ▷ n mechanical device

CLUTCHED > CLUTCH

CLUTCHES > CLUTCH

CLUTCHIER > CLUTCHY

CLUTCHING > CLUTCH

CLUTCHY adj (of a person) tending to cling

CLUTTER vb scatter objects about (a place) untidily ▷ n untidy mess

CLUTTERED > CLUTTER

CLUTTERS > CLUTTER

CLUTTERY adj full of clutter

CLY vb to steal or seize

CLYING > CLY

CLYPE vb tell tales ▷ n person who tells tales

CLYPEAL > CLYPEUS

CLYPEATE > CLYPEUS

CLYPED > CLYPE

CLYPEI > CLYPEUS

CLYPES > CLYPE

CLYPEUS n cuticular plate on the head of some insects

CLYPING > CLYPE

CLYSTER a former name for an > ENEMA

CLYSTERS > CLYSTER

CNEMIAL > CNEMIS

CNEMIDES > CNEMIS

CNEMIS n shin or tibia

CNIDA n nematocyst

CNIDAE > CNIDA

CNIDARIAN n type of invertebrate of the phylum which comprises the coelenterates

COACH n long-distance bus ▷ vb train, teach

COACHABLE adj capable of being coached

COACHDOG n Dalmatian dog

COACHDOGS > COACHDOG

COACHED > COACH

COACHEE n person who receives training from a coach

COACHEES > COACHEE

COACHER > COACH

COACHERS > COACH

COACHES > COACH

COACHIER > COACHY

COACHIES > COACHY

COACHIEST > COACHY

COACHING > COACH

COACHINGS > COACH

COACHLINE n decorative line on the bodywork of a vehicle

COACHLOAD n quantity that a coach can carry

COACHMAN n driver of a horse-drawn coach or carriage

COACHMEN > COACHMAN

COACHWHIP n whipsnake

COACHWOOD n Australian tree yielding light aromatic wood used for furniture etc

COACHWORK n body of a car

COACHY n coachman ▷ adj resembling or pertaining to a coach

COACT vb to act together

COACTED > COACT

COACTING > COACT

COACTION n any relationship between organisms within a community

COACTIONS > COACTION

COACTIVE > COACTION

COACTOR > COACT

COACTORS > COACT

COACTS > COACT

COADAPTED adj adapted to one another

COADIES > COADY

COADJUTOR n bishop appointed as assistant to a diocesan bishop

COADMIRE vb to admire together

COADMIRED > COADMIRE

COADMIRES > COADMIRE

COADMIT vb to admit together

COADMITS > COADMIT

COADUNATE same as > CONNATE

COADY n sauce made from molasses

COAEVAL n contemporary

COAEVALS > COAEVAL

COAGENCY n joint agency

COAGENT > COAGENCY

COAGENTS > COAGENCY

COAGULA > COAGULUM

COAGULANT n substance causing coagulation

COAGULASE n any enzyme that causes coagulation of blood

COAGULATE vb change from a liquid to a semisolid mass ⊳ n solid or semisolid substance produced by coagulation

COAGULUM n any coagulated mass

COAGULUMS > COAGULUM

COAITA n spider monkey

COAITAS > COAITA

COAL n black rock consisting mainly of carbon, used as fuel ⊳ vb take in, or turn into coal

COALA same as > KOALA

COALAS > COALA

COALBALL n in coal, nodule containing petrified plant or animal remains

COALBALLS > COALBALL

COALBIN n bin for holding coal

COALBINS > COALBIN

COALBOX n box for holding coal

COALBOXES > COALBOX

COALDUST n dust from coal

COALDUSTS > COALDUST

COALED > COAL

COALER n ship, train, etc, used to carry or supply coal

COALERS > COALER

COALESCE vb come together, merge

COALESCED > COALESCE

COALESCES > COALESCE

COALFACE n exposed seam of coal in a mine

COALFACES > COALFACE

COALFIELD n area with coal under the ground

COALFISH n type of dark-coloured food fish occurring in northern seas

COALHOLE n small coal cellar

COALHOLES > COALHOLE

COALHOUSE n shed or building for storing coal

COALIER > COAL

COALIEST > COAL

COALIFIED > COALIFY

COALIFIES > COALIFY

COALIFY vb to turn into coal

COALING > COAL

COALISE vb to form a coalition

COALISED > COALISE

COALISES > COALISE

COALISING > COALISE

COALITION n temporary alliance, esp between political parties

COALIZE same as > COALISE

COALIZED > COALIZE

COALIZES > COALIZE

COALIZING > COALIZE

COALLESS adj without coal

COALMAN n man who delivers coal

COALMEN > COALMAN

COALMINE n mine from which coal is extracted

COALMINER > COALMINE

COALMINES > COALMINE

COALPIT n pit from which coal is extracted

COALPITS > COALPIT

COALS > COAL

COALSACK n dark nebula near the constellation Cygnus

COALSACKS > COALSACK

COALSHED n shed in which coal is stored

COALSHEDS > COALSHED

COALY > COAL

COALYARD n yard in which coal is stored

COALYARDS > COALYARD

COAMING n raised frame round a ship's hatchway for keeping out water

COAMINGS > COAMING

COANCHOR vb to co-present a TV programme

COANCHORS > COANCHOR

COANNEX vb to annex with something else

COANNEXED > COANNEX

COANNEXES > COANNEX

COAPPEAR vb to appear jointly

COAPPEARS > COAPPEAR

COAPT vb to secure

COAPTED > COAPT

COAPTING > COAPT

COAPTS > COAPT

COARB n spiritual successor

COARBS > COARB

COARCTATE adj (of a pupa) enclosed in a hard barrel-shaped case (puparium), as in the housefly ⊳ vb (esp of the aorta) to become narrower

COARSE adj rough in texture

COARSELY > COARSE

COARSEN vb make or become coarse

COARSENED > COARSEN

COARSENS > COARSEN

COARSER > COARSE

COARSEST > COARSE

COARSISH > COARSE

COASSIST vb to assist jointly

COASSISTS > COASSIST

COASSUME vb to assume jointly

COASSUMED > COASSUME

COASSUMES > COASSUME

COAST n place where the land meets the sea ⊳ vb move by momentum, without the use of power

COASTAL > COAST

COASTALLY > COAST

COASTED > COAST

COASTER n small mat placed under a glass

COASTERS > COASTER

COASTING > COAST

COASTINGS > COAST

COASTLAND n land fringing a coast

COASTLINE n outline of a coast

COASTS > COAST

COASTWARD adv towards the coast

COASTWISE adv along the coast

COAT n outer garment with long sleeves ⊳ vb cover with a layer

COATDRESS n garment that can be worn as a coat or a dress

COATE same as > QUOTE

COATED adj covered with an outer layer, film, etc

COATEE n short coat, esp for a baby

COATEES > COATEE

COATER n machine that applies a coating to something

COATERS > COATER

COATES > COATE

COATI n type of omnivorous mammal

COATING n covering layer

COATINGS > COATING

COATIS > COATI

COATLESS adj without a coat

COATRACK n rack for hanging coats on

COATRACKS > COATRACK

COATROOM n cloakroom

COATROOMS > COATROOM

COATS > COAT

COATSTAND n stand for hanging coats on

COATTAIL n long tapering tail at the back of a man's tailored coat

COATTAILS > COATTAIL

COATTEND vb to attend jointly

COATTENDS > COATTEND

COATTEST vb to attest jointly

COATTESTS > COATTEST

COAUTHOR n person who shares the writing of a book, article, etc, with another ⊳ vb be the joint author of (a book, article, etc)

COAUTHORS > COAUTHOR

COAX vb persuade gently

COAXAL same as > COAXIAL

COAXED > COAX

COAXER > COAX

COAXERS > COAX

COAXES > COAX

COAXIAL adj (of a cable) transmitting by means of two concentric conductors separated by an insulator

COAXIALLY > COAXIAL

COAXING n act of coaxing

COAXINGLY > COAX

COAXINGS > COAXING

COB n stalk of an ear of maize ⊳ vb beat, esp on the buttocks

COBAEA n tropical climbing shrub

COBAEAS > COBAEA

COBALAMIN n vitamin B12

COBALT n brittle silvery-white metallic element

COBALTIC adj of or containing cobalt, esp in the trivalent state

COBALTINE same as > COBALTITE

COBALTITE n rare silvery-white mineral

COBALTOUS adj of or containing cobalt in the divalent state

COBALTS > COBALT

COBB same as > COB

COBBED > COB

COBBER n friend

COBBERS > COBBER

COBBIER > COBBY

COBBIEST > COBBY

COBBING > COB

COBBLE n cobblestone ⊳ vb pave (a road) with cobblestones

COBBLED > COBBLE

COBBLER n shoe mender

COBBLERS pl n nonsense ⊳ interj exclamation of strong disagreement

COBBLERY n shoemaking or shoemending

COBBLES pl n coal in small rounded lumps
COBBLING > COBBLE
COBBLINGS > COBBLE
COBBS > COBB
COBBY adj short and stocky
COBIA n large dark-striped game fish
COBIAS > COBIA
COBLE n small single-masted flat-bottomed fishing boat
COBLES > COBLE
COBLOAF n round loaf of bread
COBLOAVES > COBLOAF
COBNUT another name for > HAZELNUT
COBNUTS > COBNUT
COBRA n venomous hooded snake of Asia and Africa
COBRAS > COBRA
COBRIC > COBRA
COBRIFORM adj cobra-like
COBS > COB
COBURG n rounded loaf with a cross cut on the top
COBURGS > COBURG
COBWEB n spider's web
COBWEBBED > COBWEB
COBWEBBY > COBWEB
COBWEBS > COBWEB
COBZA n Romanian lute
COBZAS > COBZA
COCA n dried leaves of a S American shrub which contain cocaine
COCAIN same as > COCAINE
COCAINE n addictive drug used as a narcotic and as an anaesthetic
COCAINES > COCAINE
COCAINISE same as > COCAINIZE
COCAINISM n use of cocaine
COCAINIST n cocaine addict
COCAINIZE vb anaesthetize with cocaine
COCAINS > COCAIN
COCAPTAIN vb to captain jointly
COCAS > COCA
COCCAL > COCCUS
COCCI > COCCUS
COCCIC > COCCUS
COCCID n type of homopterous insect
COCCIDIA > COCCIDIUM
COCCIDIUM n any parasitic protozoan of the order Coccidia
COCCIDS > COCCID
COCCO n taro
COCCOID > COCCUS
COCCOIDAL > COCCUS
COCCOIDS > COCCUS
COCCOLITE n variety of pyroxene

COCCOLITH n any of the round calcareous plates in chalk formations: formed the outer layer of unicellular plankton
COCCOS > COCCO
COCCOUS > COCCUS
COCCUS n any spherical or nearly spherical bacterium
COCCYGEAL > COCCYX
COCCYGES > COCCYX
COCCYGIAN > COCCYX
COCCYX n bone at the base of the spinal column
COCCYXES > COCCYX
COCH obsolete variant of > COACH
COCHAIR vb to chair jointly
COCHAIRED > COCHAIR
COCHAIRS > COCHAIR
COCHES > COCH
COCHIN n large breed of domestic fowl
COCHINEAL n red dye obtained from a Mexican insect, used for food colouring
COCHINS > COCHIN
COCHLEA n spiral tube in the internal ear
COCHLEAE > COCHLEA
COCHLEAR adj of or relating to the cochlea ▷ n spoonful
COCHLEARE variant of > COCHLEAR
COCHLEARS > COCHLEAR
COCHLEAS > COCHLEA
COCHLEATE adj shaped like a snail's shell
COCINERA n in Mexico, a female cook
COCINERAS > COCINERA
COCK n male bird, esp of domestic fowl ▷ vb draw back (the hammer of a gun) to firing position
COCKADE n feather or rosette worn on a hat as a badge
COCKADED > COCKADE
COCKADES > COCKADE
COCKAMAMY adj ridiculous or nonsensical
COCKAPOO n cross between a cocker spaniel and a poodle
COCKAPOOS > COCKAPOO
COCKATEEL same as > COCKATIEL
COCKATIEL n crested Australian parrot with a greyish-brown and yellow plumage
COCKATOO n crested parrot of Australia or the East Indies
COCKATOOS > COCKATOO
COCKBILL vb to tilt up one end of
COCKBILLS > COCKBILL
COCKBIRD n male bird
COCKBIRDS > COCKBIRD

COCKBOAT n any small boat
COCKBOATS > COCKBOAT
COCKCROW n daybreak
COCKCROWS > COCKCROW
COCKED > COCK
COCKER n devotee of cockfighting ▷ vb pamper or spoil by indulgence
COCKERED > COCKER
COCKEREL n young domestic cock
COCKERELS > COCKEREL
COCKERING > COCKER
COCKERS > COCKER
COCKET n document issued by a customs officer
COCKETS > COCKET
COCKEYE n eye affected with strabismus or one that squints
COCKEYED adj crooked, askew
COCKEYES > COCKEYE
COCKFIGHT n fight between two gamecocks fitted with sharp metal spurs
COCKHORSE n rocking horse
COCKIER > COCKY
COCKIES > COCKY
COCKIEST > COCKY
COCKILY > COCKY
COCKINESS n conceited self-assurance
COCKING > COCK
COCKISH adj wanton
COCKLE n edible shellfish ▷ vb fish for cockles
COCKLEBUR n type of coarse weed with spiny burs
COCKLED > COCKLE
COCKLEERT a Southwest English dialect variant of > COCKCROW
COCKLEMAN n man who collects cockles
COCKLEMEN > COCKLEMAN
COCKLER n person employed to gather cockles
COCKLERS > COCKLER
COCKLES > COCKLE
COCKLIKE adj resembling a cock
COCKLING > COCKLE
COCKLINGS > COCKLING
COCKLOFT n small loft, garret, or attic
COCKLOFTS > COCKLOFT
COCKMATCH n cockfight
COCKNEY n native of London, esp of its East End ▷ adj characteristic of cockneys or their dialect
COCKNEYFY vb cause (one's speech, manners, etc) to fit the stereotyped idea of a cockney
COCKNEYS > COCKNEY
COCKNIFY same as > COCKNEYFY

COCKPIT n pilot's compartment in an aircraft
COCKPITS > COCKPIT
COCKROACH n beetle-like insect which is a household pest
COCKS > COCK
COCKSCOMB n comb of a domestic cock
COCKSFOOT n type of Eurasian grass, cultivated as a pasture grass in N America and S Africa
COCKSHIES > COCKSHY
COCKSHOT another name for > COCKSHY
COCKSHOTS > COCKSHOT
COCKSHUT n dusk
COCKSHUTS > COCKSHUT
COCKSHY n target aimed at in throwing games
COCKSIER > COCKSY
COCKSIEST > COCKSY
COCKSMAN n man reputed to be sexually accomplished
COCKSMEN > COCKSMAN
COCKSPUR n spur on the leg of a cock
COCKSPURS > COCKSPUR
COCKSURE adj overconfident, arrogant
COCKSWAIN same as > COXSWAIN
COCKSY adj cocky
COCKTAIL n mixed alcoholic drink
COCKTAILS > COCKTAIL
COCKUP n something done badly ▷ vb ruin or spoil
COCKUPS > COCKUP
COCKY adj conceited and overconfident ▷ n farmer whose farm is regarded as small or of little account
COCO n coconut palm
COCOA n powder made from the seed of the cacao tree
COCOANUT same as > COCONUT
COCOANUTS > COCONUT
COCOAS > COCOA
COCOBOLA n type of rosewood
COCOBOLAS > COCOBOLA
COCOBOLO same as > COCOBOLA
COCOBOLOS > COCOBOLO
COCOMAT n mat made from coconut fibre
COCOMATS > COCOMAT
COCONUT n large hard fruit of a type of palm tree
COCONUTS > COCONUT
COCOON n silky protective covering of a silkworm ▷ vb wrap up tightly for protection
COCOONED > COCOON
COCOONER n person who retreats to a secure family environment

COCOONERS > COCOONER

COCOONERY n place where silkworms feed and make cocoons

COCOONING > COCOON

COCOONS > COCOON

COCOPAN n (in South Africa) a small wagon running on narrow-gauge railway lines used in mines

COCOPANS > COCOPAN

COCOPLUM n tropical shrub or its fruit

COCOPLUMS > COCOPLUM

COCOS > COCO

COCOTTE n small fireproof dish in which individual portions of food are cooked

COCOTTES > COCOTTE

COCOUNSEL vb to counsel jointly

COCOYAM n food plant of West Africa with edible underground stem

COCOYAMS > COCOYAM

COCOZELLE n variety of squash

COCREATE vb to create jointly

COCREATED > COCREATE

COCREATES > COCREATE

COCREATOR > COCREATE

COCTILE adj made by exposing to heat

COCTION n boiling

COCTIONS > COCTION

COCULTURE vb to culture together

COCURATOR n joint curator

COCUSWOOD n wood from a tropical American leguminous tree, used for inlaying, musical instruments, etc

COD n large food fish of the North Atlantic ▷ adj having the character of an imitation or parody ▷ vb make fun of

CODA n final part of a musical composition

CODABLE adj capable of being coded

CODAS > CODA

CODDED > COD

CODDER n cod fisherman or his boat

CODDERS > CODDER

CODDING > COD

CODDLE vb pamper, overprotect ▷ n stew made from ham and bacon scraps

CODDLED > CODDLE

CODDLER > CODDLE

CODDLERS > CODDLE

CODDLES > CODDLE

CODDLING > CODDLE

CODE n system by which messages can be communicated secretly or briefly ▷ vb put into code

CODEBOOK n book containing the means to decipher a code

CODEBOOKS > CODEBOOK

CODEBTOR n fellow debtor

CODEBTORS > CODEBTOR

CODEC n set of electrical equipment

CODECS > CODEC

CODED > CODE

CODEIA n codeine

CODEIAS > CODEIA

CODEIN same as > CODEINE

CODEINA obsolete variant of > CODEINE

CODEINAS > CODEINA

CODEINE n drug used as a painkiller

CODEINES > CODEINE

CODEINS > CODEIN

CODELESS adj lacking a code

CODEN n identification code assigned to a publication

CODENAME same as > CODEWORD

CODENAMES > CODEWORD

CODENS > CODEN

CODER n person or thing that codes

CODERIVE vb to derive jointly

CODERIVED > CODERIVE

CODERIVES > CODERIVE

CODERS > CODER

CODES > CODE

CODESIGN vb to design jointly

CODESIGNS > CODESIGN

CODETTA n short coda

CODETTAS > CODETTA

CODEVELOP vb to develop jointly

CODEWORD n (esp in military use) a word used to identify a classified plan, operation, etc

CODEWORDS > CODEWORD

CODEX n volume of manuscripts of an ancient text

CODEXES > CODEX

CODFISH n cod

CODFISHES > CODFISH

CODGER n old man

CODGERS > CODGER

CODICES > CODEX

CODICIL n addition to a will

CODICILS > CODICIL

CODIFIED > CODIFY

CODIFIER > CODIFY

CODIFIERS > CODIFY

CODIFIES > CODIFY

CODIFY vb organize (rules or procedures) systematically

CODIFYING > CODIFY

CODILLA n coarse tow of hemp and flax

CODILLAS > CODILLA

CODILLE n in the card game ombre, term indicating that the game is won

CODILLES > CODILLE

CODING > CODE

CODINGS > CODE

CODIRECT vb to direct jointly

CODIRECTS > CODIRECT

CODIST n codifier

CODISTS > CODIST

CODLIN same as > CODLING

CODLING n young cod

CODLINGS > CODLING

CODLINS > CODLIN

CODOLOGY n art or practice of bluffing or deception

CODOMAIN n set of values that a function is allowed to take

CODOMAINS > CODOMAIN

CODON n part of a DNA molecule

CODONS > CODON

CODPIECE n bag covering the male genitals, attached to the breeches

CODPIECES > CODPIECE

CODRIVE vb take alternate turns driving a car with another person

CODRIVEN > CODRIVE

CODRIVER n one of two drivers who take turns to drive a car

CODRIVERS > CODRIVER

CODRIVES > CODRIVE

CODRIVING > CODRIVE

CODROVE > CODRIVE

CODS > COD

COED adj educating both sexes together ▷ n school or college that educates both sexes together

COEDIT vb edit (a book, newspaper, etc) jointly

COEDITED > COEDIT

COEDITING > COEDIT

COEDITOR > COEDIT

COEDITORS > COEDIT

COEDITS > COEDIT

COEDS > COED

COEFFECT n secondary effect

COEFFECTS > COEFFECT

COEHORN n type of small artillery mortar

COEHORNS > COEHORN

COELIAC adj of or relating to the abdomen ▷ n person who has coeliac disease

COELIACS > COELIAC

COELOM n body cavity of many multicellular animals

COELOMATA n animals possessing a coelom

COELOMATE adj possessing a coelom

COELOME same as > COELOM

COELOMES > COELOME

COELOMIC > COELOM

COELOMS > COELOM

COELOSTAT n astronomical instrument consisting of a plane mirror mounted parallel to the earth's axis and rotated about this axis once every two days so that light from a celestial body, esp the sun, is reflected onto a second mirror, which reflects the beam into a telescope

COEMBODY vb to embody jointly

COEMPLOY vb to employ together

COEMPLOYS > COEMPLOY

COEMPT vb buy up something in its entirety

COEMPTED > COEMPT

COEMPTING > COEMPT

COEMPTION n buying up of the complete supply of a commodity

COEMPTS > COEMPT

COENACLE same as > CENACLE

COENACLES > COENACLE

COENACT vb to enact jointly

COENACTED > COENACT

COENACTS > COENACT

COENAMOR vb enamour jointly

COENAMORS > COENAMOR

COENAMOUR vb enamour jointly

COENDURE vb to endure together

COENDURED > COENDURE

COENDURES > COENDURE

COENOBIA > COENOBIUM

COENOBITE n member of a religious order in a monastic community

COENOBIUM n monastery or convent

COENOCYTE n mass of protoplasm containing many nuclei and enclosed by a cell wall: occurs in many fungi and some algae

COENOSARC n system of protoplasmic branches connecting the polyps of colonial organisms such as corals

COENURE variant form of > COENURUS

COENURES > COENURE

COENURI > COENURUS

COENURUS n encysted larval form of a type of tapeworm with many encapsulated heads

COENZYME n nonprotein organic molecule that forms a complex with certain enzymes and is essential for their activity

COENZYMES > COENZYME
COEQUAL n equal ▷ adj of the same size, rank, etc
COEQUALLY > COEQUAL
COEQUALS > COEQUAL
COEQUATE vb to equate together
COEQUATED > COEQUATE
COEQUATES > COEQUATE
COERCE vb compel, force
COERCED > COERCE
COERCER > COERCE
COERCERS > COERCE
COERCES > COERCE
COERCIBLE > COERCE
COERCIBLY > COERCE
COERCING > COERCE
COERCION n act or power of coercing
COERCIONS > COERCION
COERCIVE > COERCE
COERECT vb to erect together
COERECTED > COERECT
COERECTS > COERECT
COESITE n polymorph of silicon dioxide
COESITES > COESITE
COETERNAL adj existing together eternally
COEVAL n contemporary ▷ adj contemporary
COEVALITY > COEVAL
COEVALLY > COEVAL
COEVALS > COEVAL
COEVOLVE vb to evolve together
COEVOLVED > COEVOLVE
COEVOLVES > COEVOLVE
COEXERT vb to exert together
COEXERTED > COEXERT
COEXERTS > COEXERT
COEXIST vb exist together, esp peacefully despite differences
COEXISTED > COEXIST
COEXISTS > COEXIST
COEXTEND vb extend or cause to extend equally in space or time
COEXTENDS > COEXTEND
COFACTOR n number associated with an element in a square matrix, equal to the determinant of the matrix formed by removing the row and column in which the element appears from the given determinant
COFACTORS > COFACTOR
COFEATURE vb to feature together
COFF vb buy
COFFED > COFF
COFFEE n drink made from the roasted and ground seeds of a tropical shrub ▷ adj medium-brown
COFFEEPOT n pot in which coffee is brewed or served

COFFEES > COFFEE
COFFER n chest, esp for storing valuables ▷ vb store
COFFERDAM n watertight enclosure pumped dry to enable construction work to be done
COFFERED > COFFERDAM
COFFERING > COFFERDAM
COFFERS > COFFERDAM
COFFIN n box in which a corpse is buried or cremated ▷ vb place in or as in a coffin
COFFINED > COFFIN
COFFING > COFF
COFFINING > COFFIN
COFFINITE n uranium-bearing silicate mineral
COFFINS > COFFIN
COFFLE n (esp formerly) a line of slaves, beasts, etc, fastened together ▷ vb to fasten together in a coffle
COFFLED > COFFLE
COFFLES > COFFLE
COFFLING > COFFLE
COFFRET n small coffer
COFFRETS > COFFRET
COFFS > COFF
COFINANCE vb to finance jointly
COFIRING n combustion of two different types of fuel at the same time
COFIRINGS > COFIRING
COFOUND vb to found jointly
COFOUNDED > COFOUND
COFOUNDER > COFOUND
COFOUNDS > COFOUND
COFT > COFF
COG n one of the teeth on the rim of a gearwheel ▷ vb roll (cast-steel ingots) to convert them into blooms
COGENCE > COGENT
COGENCES > COGENT
COGENCIES > COGENT
COGENCY > COGENT
COGENER n thing of the same kind
COGENERS > COGENER
COGENT adj forcefully convincing
COGENTLY > COGENT
COGGED > COG
COGGER n deceiver
COGGERS > COGGER
COGGIE n quaich or drinking cup
COGGIES > COGGIE
COGGING > COG
COGGINGS > COG
COGGLE vb wobble or rock
COGGLED > COGGLE
COGGLES > COGGLE
COGGLIER > COGGLE
COGGLIEST > COGGLE
COGGLING > COGGLE
COGGLY > COGGLE

COGIE same as > COGGIE
COGIES > COGIE
COGITABLE adj conceivable
COGITATE vb think deeply about
COGITATED > COGITATE
COGITATES > COGITATE
COGITATOR > COGITATE
COGITO n philosophical theory
COGITOS > COGITO
COGNAC n French brandy
COGNACS > COGNAC
COGNATE adj derived from a common original form ▷ n cognate word or language
COGNATELY > COGNATE
COGNATES > COGNATE
COGNATION > COGNATE
COGNISANT same as > COGNIZANT
COGNISE same as > COGNIZE
COGNISED > COGNISE
COGNISER > COGNISE
COGNISERS > COGNISE
COGNISES > COGNISE
COGNISING > COGNISE
COGNITION n act or experience of knowing or acquiring knowledge
COGNITIVE adj of or relating to cognition
COGNIZANT adj aware
COGNIZE vb perceive, become aware of, or know
COGNIZED > COGNIZE
COGNIZER > COGNIZE
COGNIZERS > COGNIZE
COGNIZES > COGNIZE
COGNIZING > COGNIZE
COGNOMEN n nickname
COGNOMENS > COGNOMEN
COGNOMINA > COGNOMEN
COGNOSCE vb in Scots law, to give judgment upon
COGNOSCED > COGNOSCE
COGNOSCES > COGNOSCE
COGNOVIT n in law, a defendant's confession that the case against him is just
COGNOVITS > COGNOVIT
COGON n type of coarse tropical grass used for thatching
COGONS > COGON
COGS > COG
COGUE n wooden pail or drinking vessel
COGUES > COGUE
COGWAY n rack railway
COGWAYS > COGWAY
COGWHEEL same as > GEARWHEEL
COGWHEELS > COGWHEEL
COHAB n cohabitor
COHABIT vb live together as husband and wife without being married
COHABITED > COHABIT

COHABITEE > COHABIT
COHABITER > COHABIT
COHABITOR n one who cohabits
COHABITS > COHABIT
COHABS > COHAB
COHEAD vb to head jointly
COHEADED > COHEAD
COHEADING > COHEAD
COHEADS > COHEAD
COHEIR n person who inherits jointly with others
COHEIRESS > COHEIR
COHEIRS > COHEIR
COHEN same as > KOHEN
COHENS > COHEN
COHERE vb hold or stick together
COHERED > COHERE
COHERENCE n logical or natural connection or consistency
COHERENCY same as > COHERENCE
COHERENT adj logical and consistent
COHERER n electrical component
COHERERS > COHERER
COHERES > COHERE
COHERING > COHERE
COHERITOR n coheir
COHESIBLE adj capable of cohesion
COHESION n sticking together
COHESIONS > COHESION
COHESIVE adj sticking together to form a whole
COHIBIT vb to restrain
COHIBITED > COHIBIT
COHIBITS > COHIBIT
COHO n type of Pacific salmon
COHOBATE vb redistil (a distillate), esp by allowing it to mingle with the remaining matter
COHOBATED > COHOBATE
COHOBATES > COHOBATE
COHOE same as > COHO
COHOES > COHO
COHOG n quahog, an edible clam
COHOGS > COHOG
COHOLDER n joint holder
COHOLDERS > COHOLDER
COHORN same as > COEHORN
COHORNS > COEHORN
COHORT n band of associates
COHORTS > COHORT
COHOS > COHO
COHOSH n type of North American plant
COHOSHES > COHOSH
COHOST vb to host jointly
COHOSTED > COHOST
COHOSTESS vb (of a woman) to host jointly
COHOSTING > COHOST
COHOSTS > COHOST

COHOUSING n type of housing with some shared facilities

COHUNE n tropical feather palm

COHUNES > COHUNE

COHYPONYM n word which is one of multiple hyponyms of another word

COIF vb arrange the hair of ▷ n close-fitting cap worn in the Middle Ages

COIFED adj wearing a coif

COIFFE vb to coiffure

COIFFED > COIF

COIFFES > COIFFE

COIFFEUR n hairdresser

COIFFEURS > COIFFEUR

COIFFEUSE > COIFFEUR

COIFFING > COIF

COIFFURE n hairstyle ▷ vb dress or arrange (the hair)

COIFFURED > COIFFURE

COIFFURES > COIFFURE

COIFING > COIF

COIFS > COIF

COIGN vb wedge ▷ n quoin

COIGNE same as > COIGN

COIGNED > COIGN

COIGNES > COIGNE

COIGNING > COIGN

COIGNS > COIGN

COIL vb wind in loops ▷ n something coiled

COILED > COIL

COILER > COIL

COILERS > COIL

COILING > COIL

COILS > COIL

COIN n piece of metal money ▷ vb invent (a word or phrase)

COINABLE > COIN

COINAGE n coins collectively

COINAGES > COINAGE

COINCIDE vb happen at the same time

COINCIDED > COINCIDE

COINCIDES > COINCIDE

COINED > COIN

COINER > COIN

COINERS > COIN

COINFECT vb infect at same time as other infection

COINFECTS > COINFECT

COINFER vb infer jointly

COINFERS > COINFER

COINHERE vb to inhere together

COINHERED > COINHERE

COINHERES > COINHERE

COINING > COIN

COININGS > COIN

COINMATE n fellow inmate

COINMATES > COINMATE

COINOP adj (of a machine) operated by putting a coin in a slot

COINS > COIN

COINSURE vb insure jointly

COINSURED > COINSURE

COINSURER > COINSURE

COINSURES > COINSURE

COINTER vb to inter together

COINTERS > COINTER

COINTREAU n tradename for a French orange liqueur

COINVENT vb to invent jointly

COINVENTS > COINVENT

COIR n coconut fibre, used for matting

COIRS > COIR

COISTREL n knave

COISTRELS > COISTREL

COISTRIL same as > COISTREL

COISTRILS > COISTRIL

COIT n buttocks

COITAL > COITUS

COITALLY > COITUS

COITION same as > COITUS

COITIONAL > COITION

COITIONS > COITION

COITS > COIT

COITUS n sexual intercourse

COITUSES > COITUS

COJOIN vb to conjoin

COJOINED > COJOIN

COJOINING > COJOIN

COJOINS > COJOIN

COJONES pl n testicles

COKE n solid fuel left after gas has been distilled from coal ▷ vb become or convert into coke

COKED > COKE

COKEHEAD n cocaine addict

COKEHEADS > COKEHEAD

COKELIKE > COKE

COKERNUT same as > COCONUT

COKERNUTS > COKERNUT

COKES n fool

COKESES > COKES

COKIER > COKY

COKIEST > COKY

COKING n act of coking

COKINGS > COKING

COKULORIS n palette with irregular holes, placed between lighting and camera to prevent glare

COKY adj like coke

COL n high mountain pass

COLA n dark brown fizzy soft drink

COLANDER n perforated bowl for straining or rinsing foods

COLANDERS > COLANDER

COLAS > COLA

COLBIES > COLBY

COLBY n type of mild-tasting hard cheese

COLBYS > COLBY

COLCANNON n dish, originating in Ireland, of potatoes and cabbage or other greens boiled and mashed together

COLCHICA > COLCHICUM

COLCHICUM n type of Eurasian liliaceous plant, such as the autumn crocus

COLCOTHAR n finely powdered form of ferric oxide produced by heating ferric sulphate and used as a pigment and as jewellers' rouge

COLD adj lacking heat ▷ n lack of heat

COLDBLOOD n any heavy draught-horse

COLDCOCK vb to knock to the ground

COLDCOCKS > COLDCOCK

COLDER > COLD

COLDEST > COLD

COLDHOUSE n unheated greenhouse

COLDIE n cold can or bottle of beer

COLDIES > COLDIE

COLDISH > COLD

COLDLY > COLD

COLDNESS > COLD

COLDS > COLD

COLE same as > CABBAGE

COLEAD vb to lead together

COLEADER > COLEAD

COLEADERS > COLEAD

COLEADING > COLEAD

COLEADS > COLEAD

COLECTOMY n surgical removal of part or all of the colon

COLED > COLEAD

COLEOPTER n aircraft that has an annular wing with the fuselage and engine on the centre line

COLES > COLE

COLESEED n common rape or cole

COLESEEDS > COLESEED

COLESLAW n salad dish of shredded raw cabbage in a dressing

COLESLAWS > COLESLAW

COLESSEE n joint lessee

COLESSEES > COLESSEE

COLESSOR n joint lessor

COLESSORS > COLESSOR

COLETIT n coal tit

COLETITS > COLETIT

COLEUS n Old World plant

COLEUSES > COLEUS

COLEWORT same as > CABBAGE

COLEWORTS > CABBAGE

COLEY same as > COALFISH

COLEYS > COLEY

COLIBRI n hummingbird

COLIBRIS > COLIBRI

COLIC n severe pains in the stomach and bowels

COLICIN n bactericidal protein

COLICINE n antibacterial protein

COLICINES > COLICINE

COLICINS > COLICIN

COLICKIER > COLICKY

COLICKY adj relating to or suffering from colic

COLICROOT n N American plant with tubular white or yellow flowers and a bitter root formerly used to relieve colic

COLICS > COLIC

COLICWEED n type of plant such as the squirrel corn and Dutchman's-breeches

COLIES > COLY

COLIFORM n type of bacteria of the intestinal tract

COLIFORMS > COLIFORM

COLIN n quail

COLINEAR same as > COLLINEAR

COLINS > COLIN

COLIPHAGE n bacteriophage

COLISEUM n large building, such as a stadium or theatre, used for entertainments, sports, etc

COLISEUMS > COLISEUM

COLISTIN n polymyxin antibiotic

COLISTINS > COLISTIN

COLITIC > COLITIS

COLITIS n inflammation of the colon

COLITISES > COLITIS

COLL vb to embrace

COLLAGE n type of art form ▷ vb to make a collage

COLLAGED > COLLAGE

COLLAGEN n protein found in cartilage and bone that yields gelatine when boiled

COLLAGENS > COLLAGEN

COLLAGES > COLLAGE

COLLAGING > COLLAGE

COLLAGIST > COLLAGE

COLLAPSAR n collapsed star, either a white dwarf, neutron star, or black hole

COLLAPSE vb fall down suddenly ▷ n collapsing

COLLAPSED > COLLAPSE

COLLAPSES > COLLAPSE

COLLAR n part of a garment round the neck ▷ vb seize, arrest

COLLARD n variety of the cabbage with a crown of edible leaves

COLLARDS > COLLARD

COLLARED > COLLAR

COLLARET n small collar

COLLARETS > COLLARET

COLLARING > COLLAR

COLLARS > COLLAR

COLLATE *vb* gather together, examine, and put in order

COLLATED > COLLATE

COLLATES > COLLATE

COLLATING > COLLATE

COLLATION *n* collating

COLLATIVE *adj* involving collation

COLLATOR *n* person or machine that collates texts or manuscripts

COLLATORS > COLLATOR

COLLEAGUE *n* fellow worker, esp in a profession

COLLECT *vb* gather together ▷ *n* short prayer

COLLECTED *adj* calm and controlled

COLLECTOR *n* person who collects objects as a hobby

COLLECTS > COLLECT

COLLED > COLL

COLLEEN *n* girl

COLLEENS > COLLEEN

COLLEGE *n* place of higher education

COLLEGER *n* member of a college

COLLEGERS > COLLEGER

COLLEGES > COLLEGE

COLLEGIA > COLLEGIUM

COLLEGIAL *adj* of or relating to a college

COLLEGIAN *n* member of a college

COLLEGIUM *n* (in the former Soviet Union) a board in charge of a department

COLLET *n* (in a jewellery setting) a band or coronet-shaped claw that holds an individual stone ▷ *vb* mount in a collet

COLLETED > COLLET

COLLETING > COLLET

COLLETS > COLLET

COLLICULI *n* plural form of singular colliculus: small elevation, as on the surface of the optic lobe of the brain

COLLIDE *vb* crash together violently

COLLIDED > COLLIDE

COLLIDER *n* particle accelerator in which beams of particles are made to collide

COLLIDERS > COLLIDER

COLLIDES > COLLIDE

COLLIDING > COLLIDE

COLLIE *n* silky-haired sheepdog

COLLIED > COLLY

COLLIER *n* coal miner

COLLIERS > COLLIER

COLLIERY *n* coal mine

COLLIES > COLLY

COLLIGATE *vb* connect or link together

COLLIMATE *vb* adjust the line of sight of (an optical instrument)

COLLINEAR *adj* lying on the same straight line

COLLING *n* embrace

COLLINGS > COLLING

COLLINS *n* type of cocktail

COLLINSES > COLLINS

COLLINSIA *n* N American plant with blue, white, or purple flowers

COLLISION *n* violent crash between moving objects

COLLOCATE *vb* (of words) occur together regularly

COLLODION *n* colourless or yellow syrupy liquid that consists of a solution of pyroxylin in ether and alcohol: used in medicine and in the manufacture of photographic plates, lacquers, etc

COLLODIUM *same as* > COLLODION

COLLOGUE *vb* confer confidentially

COLLOGUED > COLLOGUE

COLLOGUES > COLLOGUE

COLLOID *n* suspension of particles in a solution ▷ *adj* of or relating to the gluelike translucent material found in certain degenerating tissues

COLLOIDAL *adj* of, denoting, or having the character of a colloid

COLLOIDS > COLLOID

COLLOP *n* small slice of meat

COLLOPS > COLLOP

COLLOQUE *vb* to converse

COLLOQUED > COLLOQUE

COLLOQUES > COLLOQUE

COLLOQUIA *n* plural form of singular colloquium: informal gathering

COLLOQUY *n* conversation or conference

COLLOTYPE *n* method of lithographic printing from a flat surface of hardened gelatine: used mainly for fine-detail reproduction in monochrome or colour

COLLOTYPY > COLLOTYPE

COLLS > COLL

COLLUDE *vb* act in collusion

COLLUDED > COLLUDE

COLLUDER > COLLUDE

COLLUDERS > COLLUDE

COLLUDES > COLLUDE

COLLUDING > COLLUDE

COLLUSION *n* secret or illegal cooperation

COLLUSIVE > COLLUSION

COLLUVIA > COLLUVIUM

COLLUVIAL > COLLUVIUM

COLLUVIES *n* offscourings

COLLUVIUM *n* mixture of rock fragments from the bases of cliffs

COLLY *n* soot or grime, such as coal dust ▷ *vb* begrime

COLLYING > COLLY

COLLYRIA > COLLYRIUM

COLLYRIUM *a technical name for an* > EYEWASH

COLOBI > COLOBUS

COLOBID > COLOBUS

COLOBOMA *n* structural defect of the eye, esp in the choroid, retina, or iris

COLOBOMAS > COLOBOMA

COLOBUS *n* type of Old World monkey

COLOBUSES > COLOBUS

COLOCATE *vb* to locate together

COLOCATED > COLOCATE

COLOCATES > COLOCATE

COLOCYNTH *n* type of Mediterranean and Asian climbing plant with bitter-tasting fruit .

COLOG *n* logarithm of the reciprocal of a number

COLOGNE *n* mild perfume

COLOGNED > COLOGNE

COLOGNES > COLOGNE

COLOGS > COLOG

COLOMBARD *n* grape used to make wine

COLON *n* punctuation mark (:)

COLONE *variant of* > COLON

COLONEL *n* senior commissioned army or air-force officer

COLONELCY > COLONEL

COLONELS > COLONEL

COLONES > COLONE

COLONI > COLONUS

COLONIAL *n* inhabitant of a colony ▷ *adj* of or inhabiting a colony or colonies

COLONIALS > COLONIAL

COLONIC *adj* of or relating to the colon ▷ *n* irrigation of the colon

COLONICS > COLONIC

COLONIES > COLONY

COLONISE *same as* > COLONIZE

COLONISED > COLONISE

COLONISER > COLONISE

COLONISES > COLONISE

COLONIST *n* settler in a colony

COLONISTS > COLONIST

COLONITIS *same as* > COLITIS

COLONIZE *vb* make into a colony

COLONIZED > COLONIZE

COLONIZER > COLONIZE

COLONIZES > COLONIZE

COLONNADE *n* row of columns

COLONS > COLON

COLONUS *n* ancient Roman farmer

COLONY *n* people who settle in a new country but remain ruled by their homeland

COLOPHON *n* publisher's symbol on a book

COLOPHONS > COLOPHON

COLOPHONY *another name for* > ROSIN

COLOR *same as* > COLOUR

COLORABLE > COLOR

COLORABLY > COLOR

COLORADO *adj* (of a cigar) of middling colour and strength

COLORANT *n* any substance that imparts colour, such as a pigment, dye, or ink

COLORANTS > COLORANT

COLORBRED *adj* (of animals) bred for their colour

COLORCAST *vb* broadcast in colour

COLORED *US spelling of* > COLOURED

COLOREDS > COLORED

COLORER > COLOR

COLORERS > COLOR

COLORFAST *adj* variant of colourfast: (of a fabric) having a colour that does not run when washed

COLORFUL > COLOR

COLORIFIC *adj* producing, imparting, or relating to colour

COLORING > COLOUR

COLORINGS > COLOUR

COLORISE *same as* > COLOURIZE

COLORISED > COLORISE

COLORISER > COLORISE

COLORISES > COLORISE

COLORISM > COLOR

COLORISMS > COLOR

COLORIST > COLOR

COLORISTS > COLOR

COLORIZE *same as* > COLOURIZE

COLORIZED > COLOURIZE

COLORIZER > COLORIZE

COLORIZES > COLORIZE

COLORLESS > COLOR

COLORMAN *same as* > COLOURMAN

COLORMEN > COLORMAN

COLORS > COLOR

COLORWASH *n* cheap form of distemper ▷ *vb* paint with this

COLORWAY *variant of* > COLOURWAY

COLORWAYS > COLORWAY

COLORY same as > COLOURY

COLOSSAL adj very large

COLOSSEUM same as > COLISEUM

COLOSSI > COLOSSUS

COLOSSUS n huge statue

COLOSTOMY n operation to form an opening from the colon onto the surface of the body, for emptying the bowel

COLOSTRAL > COLOSTRUM

COLOSTRIC > COLOSTRUM

COLOSTRUM n thin milky secretion from the nipples that precedes and follows true lactation. It consists largely of serum and white blood cells

COLOTOMY n colonic incision

COLOUR n appearance of things as a result of reflecting light ▷ vb apply colour to

COLOURANT same as > COLORANT

COLOURED adj having colour ▷ n person who is not white

COLOUREDS > COLOURED

COLOURER > COLOUR

COLOURERS > COLOUR

COLOURFUL adj with bright or varied colours

COLOURING n application of colour

COLOURISE same as > COLOURIZE

COLOURISM n discrimination in which people are judged on the basis of their skin colour

COLOURIST n person who uses colour, esp an artist

COLOURIZE vb add colour electronically to (an old black-and-white film)

COLOURMAN n person who deals in paints

COLOURMEN > COLOURMAN

COLOURS > COLOUR

COLOURWAY n one of several different combinations of colours in which a given pattern is printed on fabrics, wallpapers, etc

COLOURY adj possessing colour

COLPITIS another name for > VAGINITIS

COLPOTOMY n surgical incision into the wall of the vagina

COLS > COL

COLT n young male horse ▷ vb to fool

COLTAN n metallic ore

COLTANS > COLTAN

COLTED > COLT

COLTER same as > COULTER

COLTERS > COULTER

COLTHOOD n state of being a colt

COLTHOODS > COLTHOOD

COLTING > COLT

COLTISH adj inexperienced

COLTISHLY > COLTISH

COLTS > COLT

COLTSFOOT n weed with yellow flowers and heart-shaped leaves

COLTWOOD n plant mentioned in Spenser's Faerie Queene

COLTWOODS > COLTWOOD

COLUBRIAD n epic poem about a snake

COLUBRID n type of snake such as the grass snake and whip snakes

COLUBRIDS > COLUBRID

COLUBRINE adj of or resembling a snake

COLUGO n flying lemur

COLUGOS > COLUGO

COLUMBARY n dovecote

COLUMBATE n niobate

COLUMBIC another word for > NIOBIC

COLUMBINE n garden flower with five petals ▷ adj of, relating to, or resembling a dove

COLUMBITE n black mineral occurring in coarse granite

COLUMBIUM the former name of > NIOBIUM

COLUMBOUS another word for > NIOBOUS

COLUMEL n in botany, the central column in a capsule

COLUMELLA n central part of the spore-producing body of some fungi and mosses

COLUMELS > COLUMEL

COLUMN n pillar ▷ vb create a column

COLUMNAL > COLUMN

COLUMNAR > COLUMN

COLUMNEA n flowering plant

COLUMNEAS > COLUMNEA

COLUMNED > COLUMN

COLUMNIST n journalist who writes a regular feature in a newspaper

COLUMNS > COLUMN

COLURE n either of two great circles on the celestial sphere

COLURES > COLURE

COLY n S African arboreal bird

COLZA n oilseed rape, a Eurasian plant with bright yellow flowers

COLZAS > COLZA

COMA n state of deep unconsciousness

COMADE > COMAKE

COMAE > COMA

COMAKE vb to make together

COMAKER > COMAKE

COMAKERS > COMAKE

COMAKES > COMAKE

COMAKING > COMAKE

COMAL > COMA

COMANAGE vb to manage jointly

COMANAGED > COMANAGE

COMANAGER > COMANAGE

COMANAGES > COMANAGE

COMARB same as > COARB

COMARBS > COMARB

COMART n covenant

COMARTS > COMART

COMAS > COMA

COMATE adj having tufts of hair ▷ n companion

COMATES > COMATE

COMATIC > COMA

COMATIK variant of > KOMATIK

COMATIKS > COMATIK

COMATOSE adj in a coma

COMATULA same as > COMATULID

COMATULAE > COMATULID

COMATULID n any of a group of crinoid echinoderms, including the feather stars, in which the adults are free-swimming

COMB n toothed implement for arranging the hair ▷ vb use a comb on

COMBAT vb fight, struggle ▷ n fight or struggle

COMBATANT n fighter ▷ adj fighting

COMBATED > COMBAT

COMBATER > COMBAT

COMBATERS > COMBAT

COMBATING > COMBAT

COMBATIVE adj eager or ready to fight, argue, etc

COMBATS > COMBAT

COMBATTED > COMBAT

COMBE same as > COMB

COMBED > COMB

COMBER n long curling wave

COMBERS > COMBER

COMBES > COMBE

COMBI n combination boiler

COMBIER > COMBY

COMBIES > COMBY

COMBIEST > COMBY

COMBINATE adj betrothed

COMBINE vb join together ▷ n association of people or firms for a common purpose

COMBINED n competitive event consisting of two skiing competitions

COMBINEDS > COMBINE

COMBINER > COMBINE

COMBINERS > COMBINE

COMBINES > COMBINE

COMBING > COMB

COMBINGS pl n loose hair or fibres removed by combing, esp from animals

COMBINING > COMBINE

COMBIS > COMBI

COMBLE n apex; zenith

COMBLES > COMBLE

COMBLESS adj without a comb

COMBLIKE adj resembling a comb

COMBO n small group of jazz musicians

COMBOS > COMBO

COMBOVER n hairstyle in which thinning hair is combed over the scalp

COMBOVERS > COMBOVER

COMBRETUM n any tree or shrub belonging to the genus Combretum

COMBS > COMB

COMBUST adj invisible due to proximity to the sun ▷ vb burn

COMBUSTED > COMBUST

COMBUSTOR n combustion system of a jet engine or ramjet, comprising the combustion chamber, the fuel injection apparatus, and the igniter

COMBUSTS > COMBUST

COMBWISE adv in the manner of a comb

COMBY adj comb-like ▷ n combination boiler

COME vb move towards a place, arrive

COMEBACK n return to a former position ▷ vb return, esp to the memory

COMEBACKS > COMEBACK

COMEDDLE vb mix

COMEDDLED > COMEDDLE

COMEDDLES > COMEDDLE

COMEDIAN n entertainer who tells jokes

COMEDIANS > COMEDIAN

COMEDIC adj of or relating to comedy

COMEDIES > COMEDY

COMEDIST n writer of comedies

COMEDISTS > COMEDIST

COMEDO the technical name for > BLACKHEAD

COMEDONES > COMEDO

COMEDOS > COMEDO

COMEDOWN n decline in status ▷ vb come to a place regarded as lower

COMEDOWNS > COMEDOWN

COMEDY n humorous play, film, or programme

COMELIER > COMELY

COMELIEST > COMELY

COMELILY > COMELY

COMELY adj nice-looking

COMEMBER n fellow member

COMEMBERS > COMEMBER

COMEOVER n person who has come from Britain to the Isle of Man to settle

COMEOVERS > COMEOVER

COMER n person who comes

COMERS > COMER

COMES > COME

COMET n heavenly body with a long luminous tail

COMETARY > COMET

COMETH > COME

COMETHER n coaxing; allure

COMETHERS > COMETHER

COMETIC > COMET

COMETS > COMET

COMFIER > COMFY

COMFIEST > COMFY

COMFILY adv in a manner suggestive of or promoting comfort

COMFINESS > COMFY

COMFIT n sugar-coated sweet

COMFITS > COMFIT

COMFITURE n confiture

COMFORT n physical ease or wellbeing ▷ vb soothe, console

COMFORTED > COMFORT

COMFORTER n person or thing that comforts

COMFORTS > COMFORT

COMFREY n tall plant with bell-shaped flowers

COMFREYS > COMFREY

COMFY adj comfortable

COMIC adj humorous, funny ▷ n comedian

COMICAL adj amusing

COMICALLY > COMICAL

COMICE n kind of pear

COMICES > COMICE

COMICS > COMIC

COMING > COME

COMINGLE same as > COMMINGLE

COMINGLED > COMMINGLE

COMINGLES > COMINGLE

COMINGS > COME

COMIQUE n comic actor

COMIQUES > COMIQUE

COMITADJI n Balkan guerrilla fighter

COMITAL adj relating to a count or earl

COMITATUS n leader's retinue

COMITIA n ancient Roman assembly

COMITIAL > COMITIA

COMITIAS > COMITIA

COMITIES > COMITY

COMITY n friendly politeness, esp between different countries

COMIX n comic books in general

COMM n as in comm badge small wearable badge-shaped radio transmitter and receiver

COMMA n punctuation mark (,)

COMMAND vb order ▷ n authoritative instruction that something must be done

COMMANDED > COMMAND

COMMANDER n military officer in command of a group or operation

COMMANDO n (member of) a military unit trained for swift raids in enemy territory

COMMANDOS > COMMANDO

COMMANDS > COMMAND

COMMAS > COMMA

COMMATA > COMMA

COMMENCE vb begin

COMMENCED > COMMENCE

COMMENCER > COMMENCE

COMMENCES > COMMENCE

COMMEND vb praise

COMMENDAM n temporary holding of an ecclesiastical benefice

COMMENDED > COMMEND

COMMENDER > COMMEND

COMMENDS > COMMEND

COMMENSAL adj (of two different species of plant or animal) living in close association, such that one species benefits without harming the other ▷ n commensal plant or animal

COMMENT n remark ▷ vb make a comment

COMMENTED > COMMENT

COMMENTER > COMMENT

COMMENTOR > COMMENT

COMMENTS > COMMENT

COMMER same as > COMER

COMMERCE n buying and selling, trade ▷ vb to trade

COMMERCED > COMMERCE

COMMERCES > COMMERCE

COMMERE n female compere

COMMERES > COMMERE

COMMERGE vb to merge together

COMMERGED > COMMERGE

COMMERGES > COMMERGE

COMMERS > COMMER

COMMIE adj communist

COMMIES > COMMIE

COMMINATE vb to anathematise

COMMINGLE vb mix or be mixed

COMMINUTE vb break (a bone) into several small fragments

COMMIS n apprentice waiter or chef ▷ adj (of a waiter or chef) apprentice

COMMISH n commissioner

COMMISHES > COMMISH

COMMISSAR n (formerly) official responsible for political education in Communist countries

COMMIT vb perform (a crime or error)

COMMITS > COMMIT

COMMITTAL n act of committing or pledging

COMMITTED > COMMIT

COMMITTEE n group of people appointed to perform a specified service or function

COMMITTER > COMMIT

COMMIX a rare word for > MIX

COMMIXED > COMMIX

COMMIXES > COMMIX

COMMIXING > COMMIX

COMMIXT > COMMIX

COMMO short for > COMMUNIST

COMMODE n seat with a hinged flap concealing a chamber pot

COMMODES > COMMODE

COMMODIFY vb to make into a commodity

COMMODITY n something that can be bought or sold

COMMODO same as > COMODO

COMMODORE n senior commissioned officer in the navy

COMMON adj occurring often ▷ n area of grassy land belonging to a community ▷ vb sit at table with strangers

COMMONAGE n use of something, esp a pasture, in common with others

COMMONED > COMMON

COMMONER n person who does not belong to the nobility

COMMONERS > COMMONER

COMMONEST > COMMON

COMMONEY n playing marble of a common sort

COMMONEYS > COMMONEY

COMMONING > COMMON

COMMONLY adv usually

COMMONS n people not of noble birth viewed as forming a political order

COMMORANT n resident

COMMOS > COMMO

COMMOT n in medieval Wales, a division of land

COMMOTE same as > COMMOT

COMMOTES > COMMOTE

COMMOTION n noisy disturbance

COMMOTS > COMMOT

COMMOVE vb disturb

COMMOVED > COMMOVE

COMMOVES > COMMOVE

COMMOVING > COMMOVE

COMMS pl n communications

COMMUNAL adj shared

COMMUNARD n member of a commune

COMMUNE n group of people who live together and share everything ▷ vb feel very close (to)

COMMUNED > COMMUNE

COMMUNER > COMMUNE

COMMUNERS > COMMUNE

COMMUNES > COMMUNE

COMMUNING > COMMUNE

COMMUNION n sharing of thoughts or feelings

COMMUNISE same as > COMMUNIZE

COMMUNISM n belief that all property and means of production should be shared by the community

COMMUNIST n supporter of any form of communism ▷ adj of, characterized by, favouring, or relating to communism

COMMUNITY n all the people living in one district

COMMUNIZE vb make (property) public

COMMUTATE vb reverse the direction of (an electric current)

COMMUTE vb travel daily to and from work ▷ n journey made by commuting

COMMUTED > COMMUTE

COMMUTER n person who commutes to and from work

COMMUTERS > COMMUTER

COMMUTES > COMMUTE

COMMUTING n act of commuting

COMMUTUAL adj mutual

COMMY same as > COMMIE

COMODO adv (to be performed) at a convenient relaxed speed

COMONOMER n monomer that, with another, constitutes a copolymer

COMORBID adj (of illness) happening at same time as other illness

COMOSE another word for > COMATE

COMOUS adj hairy

COMP n person who sets and corrects type ▷ vb set or correct type

COMPACT adj closely packed ▷ n small flat case containing a mirror and face powder ▷ vb pack closely together

COMPACTED > COMPACT

COMPACTER > COMPACT

COMPACTLY > COMPACT

COMPACTOR n machine which compresses waste material for easier disposal

COMPACTS > COMPACT

COMPADRE n masculine friend
COMPADRES > COMPADRE
COMPAGE obsolete form of > COMPAGES
COMPAGES n structure or framework
COMPAND vb (of a transmitter signal) to compress before, and expand after, transmission
COMPANDED > COMPAND
COMPANDER n system for improving the signal-to-noise ratio of a signal at a transmitter or recorder by first compressing the volume range of the signal and then restoring it to its original amplitude level at the receiving or reproducing apparatus
COMPANDOR same as > COMPANDER
COMPANDS > COMPAND
COMPANIED > COMPANY
COMPANIES > COMPANY
COMPANING > COMPANY
COMPANION n person who associates with or accompanies someone ▷ vb accompany or be a companion to
COMPANY n business organization ▷ vb associate or keep company with someone
COMPARE vb examine (things) and point out the resemblances or differences
COMPARED > COMPARE
COMPARER > COMPARE
COMPARERS > COMPARE
COMPARES > COMPARE
COMPARING > COMPARE
COMPART vb to divide into parts
COMPARTED > COMPART
COMPARTS > COMPART
COMPAS n rhythm in flamenco
COMPASS n instrument for showing direction ▷ vb encircle or surround
COMPASSED > COMPASS
COMPASSES > COMPASS
COMPAST adj rounded
COMPEAR vb in Scots law, to appear in court
COMPEARED > COMPEAR
COMPEARS > COMPEAR
COMPED > COMP
COMPEER n person of equal rank, status, or ability ▷ vb to equal
COMPEERED > COMPEER
COMPEERS > COMPEER
COMPEL vb force (to be or do)
COMPELLED > COMPEL
COMPELLER > COMPEL
COMPELS > COMPEL
COMPEND n compendium

COMPENDIA n plural form of singular compendium: book containing a collection of useful hints
COMPENDS > COMPEND
COMPER n person who regularly enters competitions
COMPERE n person who presents a stage, radio, or television show ▷ vb be the compere of
COMPERED > COMPERE
COMPERES > COMPERE
COMPERING > COMPERE
COMPERS > COMPER
COMPESCE vb to curb
COMPESCED > COMPESCE
COMPESCES > COMPESCE
COMPETE vb try to win or achieve (a prize, profit, etc)
COMPETED > COMPETE
COMPETENT adj having the skill or knowledge to do something well
COMPETES > COMPETE
COMPETING > COMPETE
COMPILE vb collect and arrange (information), esp to make a book
COMPILED > COMPILE
COMPILER n person who compiles information
COMPILERS > COMPILER
COMPILES > COMPILE
COMPILING > COMPILE
COMPING n act of comping
COMPINGS > COMPING
COMPITAL adj pertaining to crossroads
COMPLAIN vb express resentment or displeasure
COMPLAINS > COMPLAIN
COMPLAINT n complaining
COMPLEAT an archaic spelling of > COMPLETE
COMPLEATS > COMPLEAT
COMPLECT vb interweave or entwine
COMPLECTS > COMPLECT
COMPLETE adj thorough, absolute ▷ vb finish
COMPLETED > COMPLETE
COMPLETER > COMPLETE
COMPLETES > COMPLETE
COMPLEX adj made up of parts ▷ n whole made up of parts ▷ vb to form a complex
COMPLEXED > COMPLEX
COMPLEXER > COMPLEX
COMPLEXES > COMPLEX
COMPLEXLY > COMPLEX
COMPLEXUS n complex
COMPLIANT adj complying, obliging, or yielding
COMPLICE n associate or accomplice
COMPLICES > COMPLICE
COMPLICIT adj involved in a crime or questionable act

COMPLIED > COMPLY
COMPLIER > COMPLY
COMPLIERS > COMPLY
COMPLIES > COMPLY
COMPLIN same as > COMPLINE
COMPLINE n last service of the day in the Roman Catholic Church
COMPLINES > COMPLINE
COMPLINS > COMPLIN
COMPLISH vb accomplish
COMPLOT n plot or conspiracy ▷ vb plot together
COMPLOTS > COMPLOT
COMPLUVIA n plural form of singular compluvium: an unroofed space over the atrium in a Roman house, though which rain fell and was collected
COMPLY vb act in accordance (with)
COMPLYING > COMPLY
COMPO n mixture of materials, such as mortar, plaster, etc ▷ adj intended to last for several days
COMPONE same as > COMPONY
COMPONENT adj (being) part of a whole ▷ n constituent part or feature of a whole
COMPONY adj made up of alternating metal and colour, colour and fur, or fur and metal
COMPORT vb behave (oneself) in a specified way
COMPORTED > COMPORT
COMPORTS > COMPORT
COMPOS > COMPO
COMPOSE vb put together
COMPOSED adj calm
COMPOSER n person who writes music
COMPOSERS > COMPOSER
COMPOSES > COMPOSE
COMPOSING > COMPOSE
COMPOSITE adj made up of separate parts ▷ n something composed of separate parts ▷ vb merge related motions from local branches of (a political party, trade union, etc) so as to produce a manageable number of proposals for discussion at national level
COMPOST n decayed plants used as a fertilizer ▷ vb make (vegetable matter) into compost
COMPOSTED > COMPOST
COMPOSTER n bin or other container used to turn garden waste into compost
COMPOSTS > COMPOST
COMPOSURE n calmness

COMPOT same as > COMPOTE
COMPOTE n fruit stewed with sugar
COMPOTES > COMPOTE
COMPOTIER n dish for holding compote
COMPOTS > COMPOT
COMPOUND adj (thing, esp chemical) made up of two or more combined parts or elements ▷ vb combine or make by combining ▷ n fenced enclosure containing buildings
COMPOUNDS > COMPOUND
COMPRADOR n (formerly in China and some other Asian countries) a native agent of a foreign enterprise
COMPRESS vb squeeze together ▷ n pad applied to stop bleeding or cool inflammation
COMPRINT vb to print jointly
COMPRINTS > COMPRINT
COMPRISAL > COMPRISE
COMPRISE vb be made up of or make up
COMPRISED > COMPRISE
COMPRISES > COMPRISE
COMPRIZE same as > COMPRISE
COMPRIZED > COMPRIZE
COMPRIZES > COMPRIZE
COMPS > COMP
COMPT obsolete variant of > COUNT
COMPTABLE n countable
COMPTED > COMPT
COMPTER n formerly, a prison
COMPTERS > COMPT
COMPTIBLE same as > COMPTABLE
COMPTING > COUNT
COMPTROLL obsolete variant of > CONTROL
COMPTS > COUNT
COMPULSE vb to compel
COMPULSED > COMPULSE
COMPULSES > COMPULSE
COMPUTANT n calculator
COMPUTE vb calculate, esp using a computer ▷ n calculation
COMPUTED > COMPUTE
COMPUTER n electronic machine that stores and processes data
COMPUTERS > COMPUTER
COMPUTES > COMPUTE
COMPUTING n activity of using computers and writing programs for them ▷ adj of or relating to computers
COMPUTIST n one who computes
COMRADE n fellow member of a union or socialist political party

COMRADELY > COMRADE
COMRADERY n comradeship
COMRADES > COMRADE
COMS pl n one-piece woollen undergarment with long sleeves and legs
COMSAT n communications satellite
COMSATS > COMSAT
COMSYMP n Communist Party sympathizer
COMSYMPS > COMSYMP
COMTE n European nobleman
COMTES > COMTE
COMUS n wild party
COMUSES > COMUS
CON vb deceive, swindle ▷ n convict ▷ prep with
CONACRE n farming land let for a season or for eleven months ▷ vb to let conacre
CONACRED > CONACRE
CONACRES > CONACRE
CONACRING > CONACRE
CONARIA > CONARIUM
CONARIAL > CONARIUM
CONARIUM n pineal gland
CONATION n element in psychological processes that tends towards activity or change and appears as desire, volition, and striving
CONATIONS > CONATION
CONATIVE adj denoting an aspect of verbs in some languages used to indicate the effort of the agent in performing the activity described by the verb
CONATUS n effort or striving of natural impulse
CONCAUSE n shared cause
CONCAUSES > CONCAUSE
CONCAVE adj curving inwards ▷ vb make concave
CONCAVED > CONCAVE
CONCAVELY > CONCAVE
CONCAVES > CONCAVE
CONCAVING > CONCAVE
CONCAVITY n state or quality of being concave
CONCEAL vb cover and hide
CONCEALED > CONCEAL
CONCEALER > CONCEAL
CONCEALS > CONCEAL
CONCEDE vb admit to be true
CONCEDED > CONCEDE
CONCEDER > CONCEDE
CONCEDERS > CONCEDE
CONCEDES > CONCEDE
CONCEDING > CONCEDE
CONCEDO interj I allow; I concede (a point)
CONCEIT n too high an opinion of oneself ▷ vb like or be able to bear

(something, such as food or drink)
CONCEITED adj having an excessively high opinion of oneself
CONCEITS > CONCEIT
CONCEITY adj full of conceit
CONCEIVE vb imagine, think
CONCEIVED > CONCEIVE
CONCEIVER > CONCEIVE
CONCEIVES > CONCEIVE
CONCENT n concord, as of sounds, voices, etc
CONCENTER same as > CONCENTRE
CONCENTRE vb converge or cause to converge on a common centre
CONCENTS > CONCENT
CONCENTUS n vocal harmony
CONCEPT n abstract or general idea
CONCEPTI > CONCEPTUS
CONCEPTS > CONCEPT
CONCEPTUS n any product of conception, including the embryo, foetus and surrounding tissue
CONCERN n anxiety, worry ▷ vb worry (someone)
CONCERNED adj interested, involved
CONCERNS > CONCERN
CONCERT n musical entertainment
CONCERTED adj done together
CONCERTI > CONCERTO
CONCERTO n large-scale composition for a solo instrument and orchestra
CONCERTOS > CONCERTO
CONCERTS > CONCERT
CONCETTI > CONCETTO
CONCETTO n conceit, ingenious thought
CONCH same as > CONCHA
CONCHA n any bodily organ or part resembling a shell in shape
CONCHAE > CONCHA
CONCHAL > CONCHA
CONCHAS > CONCHA
CONCHATE adj shell-shaped
CONCHE vb (in chocolate-making) to use a conche
CONCHED > CONCHE
CONCHES > CONCHE
CONCHIE n conscientious objector
CONCHIES > CONCHIE
CONCHING > CONCHE
CONCHITIS n inflammation of the outer ear
CONCHO n American metal ornament
CONCHOID n type of plane curve

CONCHOIDS > CONCHOID
CONCHOS > CONCHO
CONCHS > CONCH
CONCHY same as > CONCHIE
CONCIERGE n (in France) caretaker in a block of flats
CONCILIAR adj of, from, or by means of a council, esp an ecclesiastical one
CONCISE adj brief and to the point ▷ vb mutilate
CONCISED > CONCISE
CONCISELY > CONCISE
CONCISER > CONCISE
CONCISES > CONCISE
CONCISEST > CONCISE
CONCISING > CONCISE
CONCISION n quality of being concise
CONCLAVE n secret meeting
CONCLAVES > CONCLAVE
CONCLUDE vb decide by reasoning
CONCLUDED > CONCLUDE
CONCLUDER > CONCLUDE
CONCLUDES > CONCLUDE
CONCOCT vb make up (a story or plan)
CONCOCTED > CONCOCT
CONCOCTER > CONCOCT
CONCOCTOR > CONCOCT
CONCOCTS > CONCOCT
CONCOLOR adj of a single colour
CONCORD n state of peaceful agreement, harmony ▷ vb to agree
CONCORDAL > CONCORD
CONCORDAT n pact or treaty
CONCORDED > CONCORD
CONCORDS > CONCORD
CONCOURS n contest
CONCOURSE n large open public place where people can gather
CONCREATE vb to create at the same time
CONCRETE n mixture of cement, sand, stone, and water, used in building ▷ vb cover with concrete ▷ adj made of concrete
CONCRETED > CONCRETE
CONCRETES > CONCRETE
CONCREW vb to grow together
CONCREWED > CONCREW
CONCREWS > CONCREW
CONCUBINE n woman living in a man's house but not married to him and kept for his sexual pleasure
CONCUPIES > CONCUPY
CONCUPY n concupiscence
CONCUR vb agree
CONCURRED > CONCUR
CONCURS > CONCUR
CONCUSS vb injure (the brain) by a fall or blow
CONCUSSED > CONCUSS

CONCUSSES > CONCUSS
CONCYCLIC adj (of a set of geometric points) lying on a common circle
COND old inflection of > CON
CONDEMN vb express disapproval of
CONDEMNED > CONDEMN
CONDEMNER > CONDEMN
CONDEMNOR > CONDEMN
CONDEMNS > CONDEMN
CONDENSE vb make shorter
CONDENSED adj (of printers' type) narrower than usual for a particular height
CONDENSER same as > CAPACITOR
CONDENSES > CONDENSE
CONDER n person who directs the steering of a vessel
CONDERS > CONDER
CONDIDDLE vb to steal
CONDIE n culvert; tunnel
CONDIES > CONDIE
CONDIGN adj (esp of a punishment) fitting
CONDIGNLY > CONDIGN
CONDIMENT n seasoning for food, such as salt or pepper
CONDITION n particular state of being ▷ vb train or influence to behave in a particular way
CONDO n condominium
CONDOES > CONDO
CONDOLE vb express sympathy with someone in grief, pain, etc
CONDOLED > CONDOLE
CONDOLENT adj expressing sympathy with someone in grief
CONDOLER > CONDOLE
CONDOLERS > CONDOLE
CONDOLES > CONDOLE
CONDOLING > CONDOLE
CONDOM n contraceptive
CONDOMS > CONDOM
CONDONE vb overlook or forgive (wrongdoing)
CONDONED > CONDONE
CONDONER > CONDONE
CONDONERS > CONDONE
CONDONES > CONDONE
CONDONING > CONDONE
CONDOR n large vulture of S America
CONDORES > CONDOR
CONDORS > CONDOR
CONDOS > CONDO
CONDUCE vb lead or contribute (to a result)
CONDUCED > CONDUCE
CONDUCER > CONDUCE
CONDUCERS > CONDUCE
CONDUCES > CONDUCE
CONDUCING > CONDUCE
CONDUCIVE adj likely to lead (to)

CONDUCT *n* management of an activity ▷ *vb* carry out (a task)
CONDUCTED > CONDUCT
CONDUCTI > CONDUCTUS
CONDUCTOR *n* person who conducts musicians
CONDUCTS > CONDUCT
CONDUCTUS *n* medieval liturgical composition
CONDUIT *n* channel or tube for fluid or cables
CONDUITS > CONDUIT
CONDYLAR > CONDYLE
CONDYLE *n* rounded projection on the articulating end of a bone
CONDYLES > CONDYLE
CONDYLOID *adj* of or resembling a condyle
CONDYLOMA *n* skin tumour near the anus or genital organs, esp as a result of syphilis
CONE *n* object with a circular base, tapering to a point ▷ *vb* shape like a cone or part of a cone
CONED > CONE
CONELRAD *n* US defence and information system for use in the event of air attack
CONELRADS > CONELRAD
CONENOSE *n* bloodsucking bug of the genus Triatoma
CONENOSES > CONENOSE
CONEPATE *same as* > CONEPATL
CONEPATES > CONEPATE
CONEPATL *n* skunk
CONEPATLS > CONEPATL
CONES > CONE
CONEY *same as* > CONY
CONEYS > CONEY
CONF *n* online forum
CONFAB *n* conversation ▷ *vb* converse
CONFABBED > CONFAB
CONFABS > CONFAB
CONFECT *vb* prepare by combining ingredients
CONFECTED > CONFECT
CONFECTS > CONFECT
CONFER *vb* discuss together
CONFEREE *n* person who takes part in a conference
CONFEREES > CONFEREE
CONFERRAL > CONFER
CONFERRED > CONFER
CONFERREE *same as* > CONFEREE
CONFERRER > CONFER
CONFERS > CONFER
CONFERVA *n* type of threadlike green alga typically occurring in fresh water
CONFERVAE > CONFERVA
CONFERVAL > CONFERVA
CONFERVAS > CONFERVA

CONFESS *vb* admit (a fault or crime)
CONFESSED > CONFESS
CONFESSES > CONFESS
CONFESSOR *n* priest who hears confessions
CONFEST *adj* admitted
CONFESTLY *adv* confessedly
CONFETTI *n* small pieces of coloured paper thrown at weddings
CONFETTO *n* sweetmeat
CONFIDANT *n* person confided in
CONFIDE *vb* tell someone (a secret)
CONFIDED > CONFIDE
CONFIDENT *adj* sure, esp of oneself
CONFIDER > CONFIDE
CONFIDERS > CONFIDE
CONFIDES > CONFIDE
CONFIDING *adj* trusting
CONFIGURE *vb* to design or set up
CONFINE *vb* keep within bounds ▷ *n* limit
CONFINED *adj* enclosed or restricted
CONFINER > CONFINE
CONFINERS > CONFINE
CONFINES > CONFINE
CONFINING > CONFINE
CONFIRM *vb* prove to be true
CONFIRMED *adj* firmly established in a habit or condition
CONFIRMEE *n* person to whom a confirmation is made
CONFIRMER > CONFIRM
CONFIRMOR *n* person who makes a confirmation
CONFIRMS > CONFIRM
CONFISEUR *n* confectioner
CONFIT *n* preserve
CONFITEOR *n* Catholic prayer asking for forgiveness
CONFITS > CONFIT
CONFITURE *n* confection, preserve of fruit, etc
CONFIX *vb* to fasten
CONFIXED > CONFIX
CONFIXES > CONFIX
CONFIXING > CONFIX
CONFLATE *vb* combine or blend into a whole
CONFLATED > CONFLATE
CONFLATES > CONFLATE
CONFLICT *n* disagreement ▷ *vb* be incompatible
CONFLICTS > CONFLICT
CONFLUENT *adj* flowing together or merging ▷ *n* stream that flows into another, usually of approximately equal size
CONFLUX *n* merging or following together, especially of rivers

CONFLUXES > CONFLUX
CONFOCAL *adj* having a common focus or common foci
CONFORM *vb* comply with accepted standards or customs
CONFORMAL *adj* (of a transformation) preserving the angles of the depicted surface
CONFORMED > CONFORM
CONFORMER > CONFORM
CONFORMS > CONFORM
CONFOUND *vb* astound, bewilder
CONFOUNDS > CONFOUND
CONFRERE *n* colleague
CONFRERES > CONFRERE
CONFRERIE *n* brotherhood
CONFRONT *vb* come face to face with
CONFRONTE *adj* in heraldry, (of two animals) face to face
CONFRONTS > CONFRONT
CONFS > CONF
CONFUSE *vb* mix up
CONFUSED *adj* lacking a clear understanding of something
CONFUSES > CONFUSE
CONFUSING *adj* causing bewilderment
CONFUSION *n* mistaking one person or thing for another
CONFUTE *vb* prove wrong
CONFUTED > CONFUTE
CONFUTER > CONFUTE
CONFUTERS > CONFUTE
CONFUTES > CONFUTE
CONFUTING > CONFUTE
CONGA *n* dance performed by a number of people in single file ▷ *vb* dance the conga
CONGAED > CONGA
CONGAING > CONGA
CONGAS > CONGA
CONGE *n* permission to depart or dismissal, esp when formal ▷ *vb* to take one's leave
CONGEAL *vb* (of a liquid) become thick and sticky
CONGEALED > CONGEAL
CONGEALER > CONGEAL
CONGEALS > CONGEAL
CONGED > CONGE
CONGEE *same as* > CONGE
CONGEED > CONGEE
CONGEEING > CONGEE
CONGEES > CONGEE
CONGEING > CONGE
CONGENER *n* member of a class, group, or other category, esp any animal of a specified genus
CONGENERS > CONGENER
CONGENIAL *adj* pleasant, agreeable

CONGENIC *adj* (of inbred animal cells) genetically identical except for a single gene locus
CONGER *n* large sea eel
CONGERIES *n* collection of objects or ideas
CONGERS > CONGER
CONGES > CONGE
CONGEST *vb* crowd or become crowded to excess
CONGESTED *adj* crowded to excess
CONGESTS > CONGEST
CONGIARY *n* Roman emperor's gift to the people or soldiers
CONGII > CONGIUS
CONGIUS *n* unit of liquid measure equal to 1 Imperial gallon
CONGLOBE *vb* to gather into a globe or ball
CONGLOBED > CONGLOBE
CONGLOBES > CONGLOBE
CONGO *same as* > CONGOU
CONGOES > CONGOU
CONGOS > CONGO
CONGOU *n* kind of black tea from China
CONGOUS > CONGOU
CONGRATS *sentence substitute* congratulations
CONGREE *vb* agree
CONGREED > CONGREE
CONGREES > CONGREE
CONGREET *vb* (of two or more people) to greet one another
CONGREETS > CONGREET
CONGRESS *n* formal meeting for discussion
CONGRUE *vb* agree
CONGRUED > CONGRUE
CONGRUENT *adj* similar, corresponding
CONGRUES > CONGRUE
CONGRUING > CONGRUE
CONGRUITY > CONGRUOUS
CONGRUOUS *adj* appropriate or in keeping
CONI > CONUS
CONIA *same as* > CONIINE
CONIAS > CONIINE
CONIC *adj* having the shape of a cone
CONICAL *adj* cone-shaped
CONICALLY > CONIC
CONICINE *same as* > CONIINE
CONICINES > CONICINE
CONICITY > CONICAL
CONICS *n* branch of geometry
CONIDIA > CONIDIUM
CONIDIAL > CONIDIUM
CONIDIAN > CONIDIUM
CONIDIUM *n* asexual spore formed at the tip of a specialized filament in certain types of fungi
CONIES > CONY

CONIFER *n* cone-bearing tree, such as the fir or pine
CONIFERS > CONIFER
CONIFORM *adj* cone-shaped
CONIINE *n* colourless poisonous soluble liquid alkaloid found in hemlock
CONIINES > CONIINE
CONIMA *n* gum resin from the conium hemlock tree
CONIMAS > CONIMA
CONIN *same as* > CONIINE
CONINE *same as* > CONIINE
CONINES > CONINE
CONING > CONE
CONINS > CONIN
CONIOLOGY *a variant spelling of* > KONIOLOGY
CONIOSES > CONIOSIS
CONIOSIS *n* any disease or condition caused by dust inhalation
CONIUM *n* N temperate umbelliferous plant, esp hemlock
CONIUMS > CONIUM
CONJECT *vb* to conjecture
CONJECTED > CONJECT
CONJECTS > CONJECT
CONJEE *vb* prepare as, or in, a conjee (a gruel of boiled rice and water)
CONJEED > CONJEE
CONJEEING > CONJEE
CONJEES > CONJEE
CONJOIN *vb* join or become joined
CONJOINED > CONJOIN
CONJOINER > CONJOIN
CONJOINS > CONJOIN
CONJOINT *adj* united, joint, or associated
CONJUGAL *adj* of marriage
CONJUGANT *n* either of a pair of organisms or gametes undergoing conjugation
CONJUGATE *vb* inflect (a verb) systematically
CONJUNCT *adj* joined ▷ *n* one of the propositions or formulas in a conjunction
CONJUNCTS > CONJUNCT
CONJUNTO *n* style of Mexican music
CONJUNTOS > CONJUNTO
CONJURE *vb* perform tricks that appear to be magic
CONJURED > CONJURE
CONJURER *same as* > CONJUROR
CONJURERS > CONJUROR
CONJURES > CONJURE
CONJURIES > CONJURY
CONJURING *n* performance of tricks that appear to defy natural laws ▷ *adj* denoting or relating to such tricks or entertainment

CONJUROR *n* person who performs magic tricks for people's entertainment
CONJURORS > CONJUROR
CONJURY *n* magic
CONK *n* nose ▷ *vb* strike (someone) on the head or nose
CONKED > CONK
CONKER *n* nut of the horse chestnut
CONKERS *n* game played with conkers tied on strings
CONKIER > CONKY
CONKIEST > CONKY
CONKING > CONK
CONKOUT *n* time when a machine stops working
CONKOUTS > CONKOUT
CONKS > CONK
CONKY *adj* affected by the timber disease, conk
CONMAN *n* person who uses confidence tricks to swindle or defraud
CONMEN > CONMAN
CONN *same as* > CON
CONNATE *adj* existing in a person or thing from birth
CONNATELY > CONNATE
CONNATION *n* joining of similar parts or organs
CONNATURE *n* sharing a common nature or character
CONNE *same as* > CON
CONNECT *vb* join together
CONNECTED *adj* joined or linked together
CONNECTER > CONNECT
CONNECTOR > CONNECT
CONNECTS > CONNECT
CONNED > CON
CONNER *same as* > CONDER
CONNERS > CONNER
CONNES > CONNE
CONNEXION *n* act or state of connecting
CONNEXIVE *adj* connective
CONNIE *n* tram or bus conductor
CONNIES > CONNIE
CONNING > CON
CONNINGS > CON
CONNIVE *vb* allow (wrongdoing) by ignoring it
CONNIVED > CONNIVE
CONNIVENT *adj* (of parts of plants and animals) touching without being fused, as some petals, insect wings, etc
CONNIVER > CONNIVE
CONNIVERS > CONNIVE
CONNIVERY *n* act of conniving
CONNIVES > CONNIVE
CONNIVING > CONNIVE
CONNOR *n* type of saltwater fish
CONNORS > CONNOR

CONNOTATE *vb* to connote
CONNOTE *vb* imply or suggest
CONNOTED > CONNOTE
CONNOTES > CONNOTE
CONNOTING > CONNOTE
CONNOTIVE *adj* act or state of connecting
CONNS > CONN
CONNUBIAL *adj* of marriage
CONODONT *n* any of various small Palaeozoic toothlike fossils derived from an extinct eel-like marine animal
CONODONTS > CONODONT
CONOID *n* geometric surface ▷ *adj* conical, cone-shaped
CONOIDAL *same as* > CONOID
CONOIDIC > CONOID
CONOIDS > CONOID
CONOMINEE *n* joint nominee
CONQUER *vb* defeat
CONQUERED > CONQUER
CONQUERER *variant of* > CONQUEROR
CONQUEROR > CONQUER
CONQUERS > CONQUER
CONQUEST *n* conquering
CONQUESTS > CONQUEST
CONQUIAN *same as* > COONCAN
CONQUIANS > COONCAN
CONS > CON
CONSCIENT *adj* conscious
CONSCIOUS *adj* alert and awake ▷ *n* conscious part of the mind
CONSCRIBE *vb* to enrol compulsorily
CONSCRIPT *n* person enrolled for compulsory military service ▷ *vb* enrol (someone) for compulsory military service
CONSEIL *n* advice
CONSEILS > CONSEIL
CONSENSUS *n* general agreement
CONSENT *n* agreement, permission ▷ *vb* permit, agree to
CONSENTED > CONSENT
CONSENTER > CONSENT
CONSENTS > CONSENT
CONSERVE *vb* protect from harm, decay, or loss ▷ *n* jam containing large pieces of fruit
CONSERVED > CONSERVE
CONSERVER > CONSERVE
CONSERVES > CONSERVE
CONSIDER *vb* regard as
CONSIDERS > CONSIDER
CONSIGN *vb* put somewhere
CONSIGNED > CONSIGN
CONSIGNEE *n* person, agent, organization, etc,

to which merchandise is consigned
CONSIGNER *same as* > CONSIGNOR
CONSIGNOR *n* person, enterprise, etc, that consigns goods
CONSIGNS > CONSIGN
CONSIST *vb* be composed (of)
CONSISTED > CONSIST
CONSISTS > CONSIST
CONSOCIES *n* natural community with a single dominant species
CONSOL *n* consolidated annuity, a British government bond
CONSOLATE *vb* to console
CONSOLE *vb* comfort in distress ▷ *n* panel of controls for electronic equipment
CONSOLED > CONSOLE
CONSOLER > CONSOLE
CONSOLERS > CONSOLE
CONSOLES > CONSOLE
CONSOLING > CONSOLE
CONSOLS *pl n* irredeemable British government securities
CONSOLUTE *adj* (of two or more liquids) mutually soluble in all proportions
CONSOMME *n* thin clear meat soup
CONSOMMES > CONSOMME
CONSONANT *n* speech sound made by partially or completely blocking the breath stream ▷ *adj* agreeing (with)
CONSONOUS *adj* harmonious
CONSORT *vb* keep company (with) ▷ *n* husband or wife of a monarch
CONSORTED > CONSORT
CONSORTER > CONSORT
CONSORTIA *n* plural form of singular consortium: association of financiers, companies etc
CONSORTS > CONSORT
CONSPIRE *vb* plan a crime together in secret
CONSPIRED > CONSPIRE
CONSPIRER > CONSPIRE
CONSPIRES > CONSPIRE
CONSPUE *vb* spit on with contempt
CONSPUED > CONSPUE
CONSPUES > CONSPUE
CONSPUING > CONSPUE
CONSTABLE *n* police officer of the lowest rank
CONSTANCY *n* quality of having a resolute mind, purpose, or affection
CONSTANT *adj* continuous ▷ *n* unvarying quantity
CONSTANTS > CONSTANT
CONSTATE *vb* to affirm

CONSTATED > CONSTATE
CONSTATES > CONSTATE
CONSTER *obsolete variant of* > CONSTRUE
CONSTERED > CONSTRUE
CONSTERS > CONSTRUE
CONSTRAIN *vb* compel, force
CONSTRICT *vb* make narrower by squeezing
CONSTRUAL *n* act of construing
CONSTRUCT *vb* build or put together ▷ *n* complex idea resulting from the combination of simpler ideas
CONSTRUE *vb* interpret ▷ *n* something that is construed, such as a piece of translation
CONSTRUED > CONSTRUE
CONSTRUER > CONSTRUE
CONSTRUES > CONSTRUE
CONSUL *n* official representing a state in a foreign country
CONSULAGE *n* duty paid by merchants for a consul's protection of their goods while abroad
CONSULAR *n* anyone of consular rank
CONSULARS > CONSULAR
CONSULATE *n* workplace or position of a consul
CONSULS > CONSUL
CONSULT *vb* go to for advice or information
CONSULTA *n* official planning meeting
CONSULTAS > CONSULTA
CONSULTED > CONSULT
CONSULTEE *n* person who is consulted
CONSULTER > CONSULT
CONSULTOR > CONSULT
CONSULTS > CONSULT
CONSUME *vb* eat or drink
CONSUMED > CONSUME
CONSUMER *n* person who buys goods or uses services
CONSUMERS > CONSUMER
CONSUMES > CONSUME
CONSUMING > CONSUME
CONSUMPT *n* quantity used up; consumption
CONSUMPTS > CONSUMPT
CONTACT *n* communicating ▷ *vb* get in touch with ▷ *interj* (formerly) call made by the pilot to indicate the engine is ready for starting
CONTACTED > CONTACT
CONTACTEE *n* person contacted by aliens
CONTACTOR *n* type of switch for repeatedly opening and closing an electric circuit. Its operation can be

mechanical, electromagnetic, or pneumatic
CONTACTS > CONTACT
CONTADINA *n* female Italian farmer
CONTADINE > CONTADINA
CONTADINI > CONTADINO
CONTADINO *n* Italian farmer
CONTAGIA > CONTAGIUM
CONTAGION *n* passing on of disease by contact
CONTAGIUM *n* specific virus or other direct cause of any infectious disease
CONTAIN *vb* hold or be capable of holding
CONTAINED > CONTAIN
CONTAINER *n* object used to hold or store things in
CONTAINS > CONTAIN
CONTANGO *n* (formerly, on the London Stock Exchange) postponement of payment for and delivery of stock from one account day to the next ▷ *vb* arrange such a postponement of payment (for)
CONTANGOS > CONTANGO
CONTE *n* tale or short story, esp of adventure
CONTECK *n* contention
CONTECKS > CONTECK
CONTEMN *vb* regard with contempt
CONTEMNED > CONTEMN
CONTEMNER > CONTEMN
CONTEMNOR > CONTEMN
CONTEMNS > CONTEMN
CONTEMPER *vb* to modify
CONTEMPO *adj* contemporary
CONTEMPT *n* dislike and disregard
CONTEMPTS > CONTEMPT
CONTEND *vb* deal with
CONTENDED > CONTEND
CONTENDER > CONTEND
CONTENDS > CONTEND
CONTENT *n* meaning or substance of a piece of writing ▷ *adj* satisfied with things as they are ▷ *vb* make (someone) content
CONTENTED *adj* satisfied with one's situation or life
CONTENTLY > CONTENT
CONTENTS > CONTENT
CONTES > CONTE
CONTESSA *n* Italian countess
CONTESSAS > CONTESSA
CONTEST *n* competition or struggle ▷ *vb* dispute, object to
CONTESTED > CONTEST
CONTESTER > CONTEST
CONTESTS > CONTEST

CONTEXT *n* circumstances of an event or fact
CONTEXTS > CONTEXT
CONTICENT *adj* silent
CONTINENT *n* one of the earth's large masses of land ▷ *adj* able to control one's bladder and bowels
CONTINUA > CONTINUUM
CONTINUAL *adj* constant
CONTINUE *vb* (cause to) remain in a condition or place
CONTINUED > CONTINUE
CONTINUER > CONTINUE
CONTINUES > CONTINUE
CONTINUO *n* continuous bass part, usu played on a keyboard instrument
CONTINUOS > CONTINUO
CONTINUUM *n* continuous series
CONTLINE *n* space between the bilges of stowed casks
CONTLINES > CONTLINE
CONTO *n* former Portuguese monetary unit worth 1000 escudos
CONTORNI > CONTORNO
CONTORNO *n* in Italy, side dish of salad or vegetables
CONTORNOS > CONTORNO
CONTORT *vb* twist out of shape
CONTORTED *adj* twisted out of shape
CONTORTS > CONTORT
CONTOS > CONTO
CONTOUR *n* outline ▷ *vb* shape so as to form or follow the contour of something
CONTOURED > CONTOUR
CONTOURS > CONTOUR
CONTRA *n* counter-argument
CONTRACT *n* (document setting out) a formal agreement ▷ *vb* make a formal agreement (to do something)
CONTRACTS > CONTRACT
CONTRAIL *n* aeroplane's vapour trail
CONTRAILS > CONTRAIL
CONTRAIR *adj* contrary
CONTRALTI > CONTRALTO
CONTRALTO *n* (singer with) the lowest female voice ▷ *adj* of or denoting a contralto
CONTRARY *n* complete opposite ▷ *adj* opposed, completely different ▷ *adv* in opposition
CONTRAS > CONTRA
CONTRAST *n* obvious difference ▷ *vb* compare in order to show differences
CONTRASTS > CONTRAST
CONTRASTY *adj* (of a photograph or subject)

having sharp gradations in tone, esp between light and dark areas
CONTRAT *old form of* > CONTRACT
CONTRATE *adj* (of gears) having teeth set at a right angle to the axis
CONTRATS > CONTRAT
CONTRIST *vb* to make sad
CONTRISTS > CONTRIST
CONTRITE *adj* sorry and apologetic
CONTRIVE *vb* make happen
CONTRIVED *adj* planned or artificial
CONTRIVER > CONTRIVE
CONTRIVES > CONTRIVE
CONTROL *n* power to direct something ▷ *vb* have power over
CONTROLE *adj* officially registered
CONTROLS > CONTROL
CONTROUL *obsolete variant of* > CONTROL
CONTROULS > CONTROUL
CONTUMACY *n* obstinate disobedience
CONTUMELY *n* scornful or insulting treatment
CONTUND *vb* to pummel
CONTUNDED > CONTUND
CONTUNDS > CONTUND
CONTUSE *vb* injure (the body) without breaking the skin
CONTUSED > CONTUSE
CONTUSES > CONTUSE
CONTUSING > CONTUSE
CONTUSION *n* bruise
CONTUSIVE > CONTUSE
CONUNDRUM *n* riddle
CONURBAN *adj* relating to an urban region
CONURBIA *n* conurbations considered collectively
CONURBIAS > CONURBIA
CONURE *n* small American parrot
CONURES > CONURE
CONUS *n* any of several cone-shaped structures
CONVECT *vb* to circulate hot air by convection
CONVECTED > CONVECT
CONVECTOR *n* heater that gives out hot air
CONVECTS > CONVECT
CONVENE *vb* gather or summon for a formal meeting
CONVENED > CONVENE
CONVENER *n* person who calls a meeting
CONVENERS > CONVENER
CONVENES > CONVENE
CONVENING *n* act of convening
CONVENOR *same as* > CONVENER
CONVENORS > CONVENOR

CONVENT *n* building where nuns live ▷ *vb* to summon

CONVENTED > CONVENT

CONVENTS > CONVENT

CONVERGE *vb* meet or join

CONVERGED > CONVERGE

CONVERGES > CONVERGE

CONVERSE *vb* have a conversation ▷ *n* opposite or contrary ▷ *adj* reversed or opposite

CONVERSED > CONVERSE

CONVERSER > CONVERSE

CONVERSES > CONVERSE

CONVERSO *n* medieval Spanish Jew converting to Catholicism

CONVERSOS > CONVERSO

CONVERT *vb* change in form, character, or function ▷ *n* person who has converted to a different belief or religion

CONVERTED > CONVERT

CONVERTER *n* person or thing that converts

CONVERTOR *same as* > CONVERTER

CONVERTS > CONVERT

CONVEX *adj* curving outwards ▷ *vb* make convex

CONVEXED > CONVEX

CONVEXES > CONVEX

CONVEXING > CONVEX

CONVEXITY *n* state or quality of being convex

CONVEXLY > CONVEX

CONVEY *vb* communicate (information)

CONVEYAL *n* act or means of conveying

CONVEYALS > CONVEYAL

CONVEYED > CONVEY

CONVEYER *same as* > CONVEYOR

CONVEYERS > CONVEYER

CONVEYING > CONVEY

CONVEYOR *n* person or thing that conveys

CONVEYORS > CONVEYOR

CONVEYS > CONVEY

CONVICT *vb* declare guilty ▷ *n* person serving a prison sentence ▷ *adj* convicted

CONVICTED > CONVICT

CONVICTS > CONVICT

CONVINCE *vb* persuade by argument or evidence

CONVINCED > CONVINCE

CONVINCER > CONVINCE

CONVINCES > CONVINCE

CONVIVE *vb* to feast together

CONVIVED > CONVIVE

CONVIVES > CONVIVE

CONVIVIAL *adj* sociable, lively

CONVIVING > CONVIVE

CONVO *n* conversation

CONVOCATE *vb* call together

CONVOKE *vb* call together

CONVOKED > CONVOKE

CONVOKER > CONVOKE

CONVOKERS > CONVOKE

CONVOKES > CONVOKE

CONVOKING > CONVOKE

CONVOLUTE *vb* form into a twisted, coiled, or rolled shape ▷ *adj* rolled longitudinally upon itself

CONVOLVE *vb* wind or roll together

CONVOLVED > CONVOLVE

CONVOLVES > CONVOLVE

CONVOS > CONVO

CONVOY *n* group of vehicles or ships travelling together ▷ *vb* escort while in transit

CONVOYED > CONVOY

CONVOYING > CONVOY

CONVOYS > CONVOY

CONVULSE *vb* (of part of the body) undergo violent spasms

CONVULSED > CONVULSE

CONVULSES > CONVULSE

CONWOMAN *n* woman who uses confidence tricks to swindle or defraud

CONWOMEN > CONWOMAN

CONY *n* rabbit

COO *vb* (of a dove or pigeon) make a soft murmuring sound ▷ *n* sound of cooing ▷ *interj* exclamation of surprise, awe, etc

COOCH *n* slang term for vagina

COOCHES > COOCH

COOCOO *old spelling of* > CUCKOO

COOED > COO

COOEE *interj* call to attract attention ▷ *vb* utter this call ▷ *n* calling distance

COOEED > COOEE

COOEEING > COOEE

COOEES > COOEE

COOER > COO

COOERS > COO

COOEY *same as* > COOEE

COOEYED > COOEY

COOEYING > COOEY

COOEYS > COOEY

COOF *n* simpleton

COOFS > COOF

COOING > COO

COOINGLY > COO

COOINGS > COO

COOK *vb* prepare (food) by heating ▷ *n* person who cooks food

COOKABLE *adj* able to be cooked ▷ *n* something that can be cooked

COOKABLES > COOKABLE

COOKBOOK *n* book containing recipes and instructions for cooking

COOKBOOKS > COOKBOOK

COOKED > COOK

COOKER *n* apparatus for cooking heated by gas or electricity

COOKERIES > COOKERY

COOKERS > COOKER

COOKERY *n* art of cooking

COOKEY *same as* > COOKIE

COOKEYS > COOKEY

COOKHOUSE *n* place for cooking, esp a camp kitchen

COOKIE *n* biscuit

COOKIES > COOKIE

COOKING > COOK

COOKINGS > COOK

COOKLESS *adj* devoid of a cook

COOKMAID *n* maid who assists a cook

COOKMAIDS > COOKMAID

COOKOFF *n* cookery competition

COOKOFFS > COOKOFF

COOKOUT *n* party where a meal is cooked and eaten out of doors

COOKOUTS > COOKOUT

COOKROOM *n* room in which food is cooked

COOKROOMS > COOKROOM

COOKS > COOK

COOKSHACK *n* makeshift building in which food is cooked

COOKSHOP *n* shop that sells cookery equipment

COOKSHOPS > COOKSHOP

COOKSTOVE *n* stove for cooking

COOKTOP *n* flat unit for cooking in saucepans or the top part of a stove

COOKTOPS > COOKTOP

COOKWARE *n* cooking utensils

COOKWARES > COOKWARE

COOKY *same as* > COOKIE

COOL *adj* moderately cold ▷ *vb* make or become cool ▷ *n* coolness

COOLABAH *n* Australian tree that grows along rivers, with smooth bark and long narrow leaves

COOLABAHS > COOLABAH

COOLAMON *n* shallow dish of wood or bark, used for carrying water

COOLAMONS > COOLAMON

COOLANT *n* fluid used to cool machinery while it is working

COOLANTS > COOLANT

COOLDOWN *n* gentle stretching exercises after strenuous activity, to allow the heart rate gradually to return to normal

COOLDOWNS > COOLDOWN

COOLED > COOL

COOLER *n* container for making or keeping things cool

COOLERS > COOLER

COOLEST > COOL

COOLHOUSE *n* greenhouse in which a cool temperature is maintained

COOLIBAH *same as* > COOLABAH

COOLIBAHS > COOLIBAH

COOLIBAR *same as* > COOLABAH

COOLIBARS > COOLIBAR

COOLIE *n* unskilled Oriental labourer

COOLIES > COOLIE

COOLING *n* as in *regenerative cooling* method of cooling rocket combustion chambers

COOLINGLY > COOL

COOLINGS > COOLING

COOLISH > COOL

COOLIST *n* person who does not believe in global warming

COOLISTS > COOLIST

COOLLY > COOL

COOLNESS > COOL

COOLS > COOL

COOLTH *n* coolness

COOLTHS > COOLTH

COOLY *same as* > COOLIE

COOM *n* waste material ▷ *vb* to blacken

COOMB *same as* > COMB

COOMBE *same as* > COMB

COOMBES > COOMBE

COOMBS > COOMB

COOMED > COOM

COOMIER > COOMY

COOMIEST > COOMY

COOMING > COOM

COOMS > COOM

COOMY *adj* grimy

COON *n* raccoon

COONCAN *n* card game for two players, similar to rummy

COONCANS > COONCAN

COONDOG *n* dog trained to hunt raccoons

COONDOGS > COONDOG

COONHOUND *n* dog for hunting raccoons

COONS > COON

COONSHIT *n* offensive term for a contemptible person

COONSHITS > COONSHIT

COONSKIN *n* pelt of a raccoon

COONSKINS > COONSKIN

COONTIE *n* evergreen plant of S Florida

COONTIES > COONTIE

COONTY *same as* > COONTIE

COOP *n* cage or pen for poultry ▷ *vb* confine in a restricted area

COOPED > COOP

COOPER *n* person who makes or repairs barrels ▷ *vb* make or mend (barrels, casks, etc)

COOPERAGE *n* craft, place of work, or products of a cooper

COOPERATE vb work or act together
COOPERED > COOPER
COOPERIES > COOPERY
COOPERING > COOPER
COOPERS > COOP
COOPERY same as > COOPERAGE
COOPING > COOP
COOPS > COOP
COOPT vb add (someone) to a group by the agreement of the existing members
COOPTED > COOPT
COOPTING > COOPT
COOPTION > COOPT
COOPTIONS > COOPT
COOPTS > COOPT
COORDINAL adj (of animals or plants) belonging to the same order
COORIE same as > COURIE
COORIED > COORIE
COORIEING > COORIE
COORIES > COORIE
COOS > COO
COOSEN same as > COZEN
COOSENED > COOSEN
COOSENING > COOSEN
COOSENS > COOSEN
COOSER n stallion
COOSERS > COOSER
COOSIN same as > COZEN
COOSINED > COOSIN
COOSINING > COOSIN
COOSINS > COOSIN
COOST Scots form of > CAST
COOT n small black water bird
COOTCH n hiding place ▷ vb hide
COOTCHED > COOTCH
COOTCHES > COOTCH
COOTCHING > COOTCH
COOTER n type of freshwater turtle
COOTERS > COOTER
COOTIE n a body louse
COOTIES > COOTIE
COOTIKIN n gaiter
COOTIKINS > COOTIKIN
COOTS > COOT
COOZE n US and Canadian taboo slang word for the female genitals
COOZES > COOZE
COP same as > COPPER
COPACETIC adj very good
COPAIBA n resin obtained from certain tropical trees
COPAIBAS > COPAIBA
COPAIVA same as > COPAIBA
COPAIVAS > COPAIVA
COPAL n resin used in varnishes
COPALM n aromatic resin
COPALMS > COPALM
COPALS > COPAL
COPARCENY n form of joint ownership of property

COPARENT n fellow parent
COPARENTS > COPARENT
COPARTNER n partner or associate
COPASETIC same as > COPACETIC
COPASTOR n fellow pastor
COPASTORS > COPASTOR
COPATAINE adj (of a hat) high-crowned
COPATRIOT n fellow patriot
COPATRON n fellow patron
COPATRONS > COPATRON
COPAY n amount payable for treatment by person with medical insurance
COPAYMENT n fee paid for medical insurance
COPAYS > COPAY
COPE vb deal successfully (with) ▷ n large ceremonial cloak worn by some Christian priests
COPECK same as > KOPECK
COPECKS > COPECK
COPED > COPE
COPEMATE n partner
COPEMATES > COPEMATE
COPEN n shade of blue
COPENS > COPEN
COPEPOD n type of minute crustacean
COPEPODS > COPEPOD
COPER n horse-dealer ▷ vb smuggle liquor to deep-sea fishermen
COPERED > COPER
COPERING > COPER
COPERS > COPER
COPES > COPE
COPESETIC same as > COPACETIC
COPESTONE same as > CAPSTONE
COPIABLE adj able to be copied
COPIED > COPY
COPIER n machine that copies
COPIERS > COPIER
COPIES > COPY
COPIHUE n Chilean bellflower
COPIHUES > COPIHUE
COPILOT n second pilot of an aircraft ▷ vb act as a copilot
COPILOTED > COPILOT
COPILOTS > COPILOT
COPING n sloping top row of a wall
COPINGS > COPING
COPIOUS adj abundant, plentiful
COPIOUSLY > COPIOUS
COPITA n tulip-shaped sherry glass
COPITAS > COPITA
COPLANAR adj lying in the same plane
COPLOT vb plot together

COPLOTS > COPLOT
COPLOTTED > COPLOT
COPOLYMER n chemical compound of high molecular weight formed by uniting the molecules of two or more different compounds (monomers)
COPOUT n act of avoiding responsibility
COPOUTS > COPOUT
COPPED > COPPER
COPPER n soft reddish-brown metal ▷ adj reddish-brown ▷ vb coat or cover with copper
COPPERAH same as > COPRA
COPPERAHS > COPPERAH
COPPERAS n ferrous sulphate
COPPERED > COPPER
COPPERING > COPPER
COPPERISH adj copper-like
COPPERS > COPPER
COPPERY > COPPER
COPPICE n small group of trees growing close together ▷ vb trim back (trees or bushes) to form a coppice
COPPICED > COPPICE
COPPICES > COPPICE
COPPICING > COPPICE
COPPIES > COPPY
COPPIN n ball of thread
COPPING > COPPER
COPPINS > COPPIN
COPPLE n hill rising to a point
COPPLES > COPPLE
COPPRA same as > COPRA
COPPRAS > COPRA
COPPY n small wooden stool
COPRA n dried oil-yielding kernel of the coconut
COPRAEMIA n type of poisoning caused by faecal matter entering the bloodstream
COPRAEMIC adj relating to or causing copraemia
COPRAH same as > COPRA
COPRAHS > COPRAH
COPRAS > COPRA
COPREMIA same as > COPRAEMIA
COPREMIAS > COPREMIA
COPREMIC same as > COPRAEMIC
COPRESENT vb to present jointly
COPRINCE n fellow prince
COPRINCES > COPRINCE
COPRODUCE vb to produce jointly
COPRODUCT n joint product
COPROLITE n any of various rounded stony nodules thought to be

the fossilized faeces of Palaeozic-Cenozoic vertebrates
COPROLITH n hard stony mass of dried faeces
COPROLOGY n preoccupation with excrement
COPROSMA n Australasian shrub sometimes planted for ornament
COPROSMAS > COPROSMA
COPROZOIC adj (of animals) living in dung
COPS > COPPER
COPSE same as > COPPICE
COPSED > COPSE
COPSES > COPSE
COPSEWOOD n brushwood
COPSHOP n police station
COPSHOPS > COPSHOP
COPSIER > COPSY
COPSIEST > COPSY
COPSING > COPSE
COPSY adj having copses
COPTER n helicopter
COPTERS > COPTER
COPUBLISH vb to publish jointly
COPULA n verb used to link the subject and complement of a sentence
COPULAE > COPULA
COPULAR > COPULA
COPULAS > COPULA
COPULATE vb have sexual intercourse
COPULATED > COPULATE
COPULATES > COPULATE
COPURIFY vb to purify together
COPY n thing made to look exactly like another ▷ vb make a copy of
COPYABLE > COPY
COPYBOOK n book of specimens for imitation
COPYBOOKS > COPYBOOK
COPYBOY n formerly, in journalism, boy who carried copy and ran errands
COPYBOYS > COPYBOY
COPYCAT n person who imitates or copies someone ▷ vb to imitate with great attention to detail
COPYCATS > COPYCAT
COPYDESK n desk where newspaper copy is edited
COPYDESKS > COPYDESK
COPYEDIT vb prepare text for printing by styling, correcting, etc
COPYEDITS > COPYEDIT
COPYFIGHT n legal battle over the use of a copyright
COPYGIRL n female copyboy
COPYGIRLS > COPYGIRL
COPYGRAPH n process for copying type

COPYHOLD n tenure less than freehold of land in England evidenced by a copy of the Court roll

COPYHOLDS > COPYHOLD

COPYING n act of copying

COPYINGS > COPYING

COPYISM n slavish copying

COPYISMS > COPYISM

COPYIST n person who makes written copies

COPYISTS > COPYIST

COPYLEFT n permission to use something free of charge ▷ vb use copyright law to make (work, esp software) free to use

COPYLEFTS > COPYLEFT

COPYREAD vb subedit

COPYREADS > COPYREAD

COPYRIGHT n exclusive legal right to reproduce and control a book, work of art, etc ▷ vb take out a copyright on ▷ adj protected by copyright

COPYTAKER n (esp in a newspaper office) a person employed to type reports as journalists dictate them over the telephone

COQUET vb behave flirtatiously

COQUETRY n flirtation

COQUETS > COQUET

COQUETTE n woman who flirts

COQUETTED > COQUET

COQUETTES > COQUETTE

COQUI n type of tree-dwelling frog

COQUILLA n type of South American nut

COQUILLAS > COQUILLA

COQUILLE n any dish, esp seafood, served in a scallop shell

COQUILLES > COQUILLE

COQUINA n soft limestone

COQUINAS > COQUINA

COQUIS > COQUI

COQUITO n Chilean palm tree yielding edible nuts and a syrup

COQUITOS > COQUITO

COR interj exclamation of surprise, amazement, or admiration

CORACLE n small round boat of wicker covered with skins

CORACLES > CORACLE

CORACOID n paired ventral bone of the pectoral girdle in vertebrates

CORACOIDS > CORACOID

CORAGGIO interj exhortation to hold one's nerve

CORAL n hard substance formed from the skeletons of very small sea animals ▷ adj orange-pink

CORALLA > CORALLUM

CORALLINE n type of red alga impregnated with calcium carbonate

CORALLITE n skeleton of a coral polyp

CORALLOID same as > CORALLINE

CORALLUM n skeleton of any zoophyte

CORALROOT n N temperate leafless orchid with small yellow-green or purple flowers and branched roots resembling coral

CORALS > CORAL

CORALWORT n coralroot or toothwort

CORAM prep before, in the presence of

CORAMINE n type of stimulant

CORAMINES > CORAMINE

CORANACH same as > CORONACH

CORANACHS > CORANACH

CORANTO same as > COURANTE

CORANTOES > CORANTO

CORANTOS > CORANTO

CORBAN n gift to God

CORBANS > CORBAN

CORBE obsolete variant of > CORBEL

CORBEAU n blackish green colour

CORBEAUS > CORBEAU

CORBEIL n carved ornament in the form of a basket of fruit, flowers, etc

CORBEILLE same as > CORBEIL

CORBEILS > CORBEIL

CORBEL n stone or timber support sticking out of a wall ▷ vb lay (a stone or brick) so that it forms a corbel

CORBELED > CORBEL

CORBELING n set of corbels stepped outwards, one above another

CORBELLED > CORBEL

CORBELS > CORBEL

CORBES > CORBE

CORBICULA n pollen basket

CORBIE n raven or crow

CORBIES > CORBIE

CORBINA n type of North American whiting

CORBINAS > CORBINA

CORBY same as > CORBIE

CORCASS n in Ireland, marshland

CORCASSES > CORCASS

CORD n thin rope or thick string ▷ adj (of fabric) ribbed ▷ vb bind or furnish with a cord or cords

CORDAGE n lines and rigging of a vessel

CORDAGES > CORDAGE

CORDATE adj heart-shaped

CORDATELY > CORDATE

CORDED adj tied or fastened with cord

CORDELLE vb to tow

CORDELLED > CORDELLE

CORDELLES > CORDELLE

CORDER > CORD

CORDERS > CORD

CORDGRASS n type of coarse grass

CORDIAL adj warm and friendly ▷ n drink with a fruit base

CORDIALLY > CORDIAL

CORDIALS > CORDIAL

CORDIFORM adj heart-shaped

CORDINER n shoemaker

CORDINERS > CORDINER

CORDING > CORD

CORDINGS > CORD

CORDITE n explosive used in guns and bombs

CORDITES > CORDITE

CORDLESS adj (of an electrical appliance) powered by an internal battery, so that there is no cable connecting the appliance itself to the electrical mains

CORDLIKE > CORD

CORDOBA n standard monetary unit of Nicaragua

CORDOBAS > CORDOBA

CORDON n chain of police, soldiers, etc, guarding an area ▷ vb put or form a cordon (around)

CORDONED > CORDON

CORDONING > CORDON

CORDONNET n type of thread

CORDONS > CORDON

CORDOTOMY n method of pain relief in which nerves are cut

CORDOVAN n fine leather now made principally from horsehide, isolated from the skin layers above and below it and tanned

CORDOVANS > CORDOVAN

CORDS pl n trousers made of corduroy

CORDUROY n cotton fabric with a velvety ribbed surface

CORDUROYS pl n trousers made of corduroy

CORDWAIN an archaic name for > CORDOVAN

CORDWAINS > CORDWAIN

CORDWOOD n wood that has been cut into lengths of four feet so that it can be stacked in cords

CORDWOODS > CORDWOOD

CORDYLINE n any tree of the genus Cordyline

CORE n central part of certain fruits, containing the seeds ▷ vb remove the core from

CORED > CORE

COREDEEM vb to redeem together

COREDEEMS > COREDEEM

COREGENT n joint regent

COREGENTS > COREGENT

COREIGN vb to reign jointly

COREIGNS > COREIGN

CORELATE same as > CORRELATE

CORELATED > CORELATE

CORELATES > CORELATE

CORELESS > CORE

CORELLA n white Australian cockatoo

CORELLAS > CORELLA

COREMIA > COREMIUM

COREMIUM n spore-producing organ of certain fungi

COREOPSIS n American and tropical African plant cultivated for its yellow, brown, or yellow-and-red daisy-like flowers

CORER > CORE

CORERS > CORE

CORES > CORE

COREY n slang word for the penis

COREYS > COREY

CORF n wagon or basket used formerly in mines

CORFHOUSE n shed used for curing salmon and storing nets

CORGI n short-legged sturdy dog

CORGIS > CORGI

CORIA > CORIUM

CORIANDER n plant grown for its aromatic seeds and leaves

CORIES > CORY

CORING > CORE

CORIOUS adj leathery

CORIUM n deep inner layer of the skin

CORIUMS > CORIUM

CORIVAL same as > CORRIVAL

CORIVALRY > CORIVAL

CORIVALS > CORIVAL

CORIXID n type of water bug

CORIXIDS > CORIXID

CORK n thick light bark of a Mediterranean oak ▷ vb seal with a cork ▷ adj made of cork

CORKAGE n restaurant's charge for serving wine bought elsewhere

CORKAGES > CORKAGE

CORKBOARD n thin slab made of granules of cork, used as a floor or wall finish and as an insulator

CORKBORER n tool for cutting a hole in a stopper to insert a glass tube

CORKED adj (of wine) spoiled through having a decayed cork

CORKER n splendid or outstanding person or thing

CORKERS > CORKER

CORKIER > CORKY

CORKIEST > CORKY

CORKINESS > CORKY

CORKING adj excellent

CORKIR n lichen from which red or purple dye is made

CORKIRS > CORKIR

CORKLIKE > CORK

CORKS > CORK

CORKSCREW n spiral metal tool for pulling corks from bottles ▷ adj like a corkscrew in shape ▷ vb move in a spiral or zigzag course

CORKTREE n type of evergreen oak tree

CORKTREES > CORKTREE

CORKWING n type of greenish or bluish European fish

CORKWINGS > CORKWING

CORKWOOD n type of small tree of the southeastern US, with very lightweight porous wood

CORKWOODS > CORKWOOD

CORKY same as > CORKED

CORM n bulblike underground stem of certain plants

CORMEL n new small corm arising from the base of a fully developed one

CORMELS > CORMEL

CORMIDIA > CORMIDIUM

CORMIDIUM n iteration of the repeating zooid pattern in a siphosome

CORMLET n small corm

CORMLETS > CORMLET

CORMLIKE adj resembling a corm

CORMOID adj like a corm

CORMORANT n large dark-coloured long-necked sea bird

CORMOUS > CORM

CORMS > CORM

CORMUS n corm

CORMUSES > CORMUS

CORN n cereal plant such as wheat or oats ▷ vb feed (animals) with corn, esp oats

CORNACRE same as > CONACRE

CORNACRES > CORNACRE

CORNAGE n rent fixed according to the number of horned cattle pastured

CORNAGES > CORNAGE

CORNBALL n person given to mawkish or unsophisticated behaviour

CORNBALLS > CORNBALL

CORNBORER n larva of the pyralid moth

CORNBRAID vb braid hair in cornrows

CORNBRASH n type of limestone which produces good soil for growing corn

CORNBREAD n bread made from maize meal

CORNCAKE n kind of cornmeal flatbread

CORNCAKES > CORNCAKE

CORNCOB n core of an ear of maize, to which the kernels are attached

CORNCOBS > CORNCOB

CORNCRAKE n brown Eurasian bird with a harsh cry

CORNCRIB n ventilated building for the storage of unhusked maize

CORNCRIBS > CORNCRIB

CORNEA n transparent membrane covering the eyeball

CORNEAE > CORNEA

CORNEAL > CORNEA

CORNEAS > CORNEA

CORNED adj preserved in salt or brine

CORNEITIS n inflammation of cornea

CORNEL n type of plant such as the dogwood or dwarf cornel

CORNELIAN same as > CARNELIAN

CORNELS > CORNEL

CORNEMUSE n French bagpipe

CORNEOUS adj horny

CORNER n area or angle where two converging lines or surfaces meet ▷ vb force into a difficult or inescapable position

CORNERED > CORNER

CORNERING n act of cornering

CORNERMAN n in baseball, first baseman

CORNERMEN > CORNERMAN

CORNERS > CORNER

CORNET same as > CORNETT

CORNETCY n commission or rank of a cornet

CORNETIST n person who plays the cornet

CORNETS > CORNET

CORNETT n musical instrument

CORNETTI > CORNETTO

CORNETTO same as > CORNETT

CORNETTOS > CORNETTO

CORNETTS > CORNETT

CORNFED adj fed on corn

CORNFIELD n field planted with cereal crops

CORNFLAG n gladiolus

CORNFLAGS > CORNFLAG

CORNFLAKE n singular form of plural cornflakes: toasted flakes made from cornmeal, sold as a breakfast cereal

CORNFLIES > CORNFLY

CORNFLOUR n fine maize flour

CORNFLY n small fly

CORNHUSK n outer protective covering of an ear of maize

CORNHUSKS > CORNHUSK

CORNI > CORNO

CORNICE n decorative moulding round the top of a wall ▷ vb furnish or decorate with or as if with a cornice

CORNICED > CORNICE

CORNICES > CORNICE

CORNICHE n coastal road, esp one built into the face of a cliff

CORNICHES > CORNICHE

CORNICHON n type of small gherkin

CORNICING n act of cornicing

CORNICLE n wax-secreting organ on an aphid's abdomen

CORNICLES > CORNICLE

CORNICULA n plural form of singular corniculum: small horn

CORNIER > CORNY

CORNIEST > CORNY

CORNIFIC adj producing horns

CORNIFIED > CORNIFY

CORNIFIES > CORNIFY

CORNIFORM adj horn-shaped

CORNIFY vb turn soft tissue hard

CORNILY > CORNY

CORNINESS > CORNY

CORNING > CORN

CORNIST n horn-player

CORNISTS > CORNIST

CORNLAND n land suitable for growing corn or grain

CORNLANDS > CORNLAND

CORNLOFT n loft for storing corn

CORNLOFTS > CORNLOFT

CORNMEAL n meal made from maize

CORNMEALS > CORNMEAL

CORNMILL n flour mill

CORNMILLS > CORNMILL

CORNMOTH n moth whose larvae feed on grain

CORNMOTHS > CORNMOTH

CORNO n French horn

CORNOPEAN n cornet (the brass musical instrument)

CORNPIPE n musical instrument made from a stalk of corn etc

CORNPIPES > CORNPIPE

CORNPONE n American corn bread

CORNPONES > CORNPONE

CORNRENT n rent for land that is paid in corn

CORNRENTS > CORNRENT

CORNROW n hairstyle in which the hair is plaited in close parallel rows ▷ vb style the hair in a cornrow

CORNROWED > CORNROW

CORNROWS > CORNROW

CORNS > CORN

CORNSILK n threads on an ear of maize

CORNSILKS > CORNSILK

CORNSTALK n stalk of stem of corn

CORNSTONE n mottled green and red limestone

CORNU n part or structure resembling a horn or having a hornlike pattern

CORNUA > CORNU

CORNUAL > CORNU

CORNUS n any member of the genus Cornus, such as dogwood

CORNUSES > CORNUS

CORNUTE adj having or resembling cornua ▷ vb to make a cuckold of

CORNUTED same as > CORNUTE

CORNUTES > CORNUTE

CORNUTING > CORNUTE

CORNUTO n cuckold

CORNUTOS > CORNUTO

CORNWORM n cornmoth larva

CORNWORMS > CORNWORM

CORNY adj unoriginal or oversentimental

COROCORE same as > COROCORO

COROCORES > COROCORE

COROCORO n South Asian vessel fitted with outriggers

COROCOROS > COROCORO

CORODIES > CORODY

CORODY n feudal law

COROLLA n petals of a flower collectively

COROLLARY n idea, fact, or proposition which is the natural result of something else ▷ adj consequent or resultant

COROLLAS > COROLLA

COROLLATE adj having a corolla

COROLLINE adj relating to a corolla

CORONA n ring of light round the moon or sun

CORONACH n dirge or lamentation for the dead

CORONACHS > CORONACH

CORONAE > CORONA

CORONAL n circlet for the head ▷ adj of or relating to a corona or coronal

CORONALLY > CORONAL

CORONALS > CORONAL

CORONARY adj of the arteries surrounding the heart ▷ n coronary thrombosis

CORONAS > CORONA

CORONATE vb to crown

CORONATED > CORONATE

CORONATES > CORONATE

CORONEL n iron head of a tilting spear

CORONELS > CORONEL

CORONER n official responsible for the investigation deaths

CORONERS > CORONER

CORONET n small crown

CORONETED adj wearing a coronet

CORONETS > CORONET

CORONIAL adj relating to a coroner

CORONIS n symbol used in Greek writing

CORONISES > CORONIS

CORONIUM n highly-ionized iron and nickel seen as a green line in the solar coronal spectrum

CORONIUMS > CORONIUM

CORONOID adj crown-shaped

COROTATE vb to rotate together

COROTATED > COROTATE

COROTATES > COROTATE

COROZO n tropical American palm whose seeds yield a useful oil

COROZOS > COROZO

CORPORA > CORPUS

CORPORAL n noncommissioned officer in an army ▷ adj of the body

CORPORALE same as > CORPORAL

CORPORALS > CORPORAL

CORPORAS n communion cloth

CORPORATE adj of business corporations

CORPOREAL adj physical or tangible

CORPORIFY vb to embody

CORPOSANT n Saint Elmo's fire

CORPS n military unit with a specific function

CORPSE n dead body ▷ vb laugh or cause to laugh involuntarily or inopportunely while on stage

CORPSED > CORPSE

CORPSES > CORPSE

CORPSING > CORPSE

CORPSMAN n medical orderly or stretcher-bearer

CORPSMEN > CORPSMAN

CORPULENT adj fat or plump

CORPUS n collection of writings, esp by a single author

CORPUSCLE n red or white blood cell

CORPUSES > CORPUS

CORRADE vb to erode by the abrasive action of rock particles

CORRADED > CORRADE

CORRADES > CORRADE

CORRADING > CORRADE

CORRAL n enclosure for cattle or horses ▷ vb put in a corral

CORRALLED > CORRAL

CORRALS > CORRAL

CORRASION n erosion of rocks caused by fragments transported over them by water, wind, or ice

CORRASIVE > CORRASION

CORREA n Australian evergreen shrub with large showy tubular flowers

CORREAS > CORREA

CORRECT adj free from error, true ▷ vb put right

CORRECTED > CORRECT

CORRECTER > CORRECT

CORRECTLY > CORRECT

CORRECTOR > CORRECT

CORRECTS > CORRECT

CORRELATE vb place or be placed in a mutual relationship ▷ n either of two things mutually related ▷ adj having a mutual, complementary, or reciprocal relationship

CORRETTO n espresso containing alcohol

CORRETTOS > CORRETTO

CORRIDA the Spanish word for > BULLFIGHT

CORRIDAS > CORRIDA

CORRIDOR n passage in a building or train

CORRIDORS > CORRIDOR

CORRIE same as > CIRQUE

CORRIES > CORRIE

CORRIGENT n corrective

CORRIVAL a rare word for > RIVAL

CORRIVALS > CORRIVAL

CORRODANT > CORRODE

CORRODE vb eat or be eaten away by chemical action or rust

CORRODED > CORRODE

CORRODENT > CORRODE

CORRODER > CORRODE

CORRODERS > CORRODE

CORRODES > CORRODE

CORRODIES > CORRODY

CORRODING > CORRODE

CORRODY same as > CORODY

CORROSION n process by which something, esp a metal, is corroded

CORROSIVE adj (esp of acids or alkalis) capable of destroying solid materials ▷ n corrosive substance, such as a strong acid or alkali

CORRUGATE vb fold into alternate grooves and ridges ▷ adj folded into furrows and ridges

CORRUPT adj open to or involving bribery ▷ vb make corrupt

CORRUPTED > CORRUPT

CORRUPTER > CORRUPT

CORRUPTLY > CORRUPT

CORRUPTOR > CORRUPT

CORRUPTS > CORRUPT

CORS > COR

CORSAC n type of fox of central Asia

CORSACS > CORSAC

CORSAGE n small bouquet worn on the bodice of a dress

CORSAGES > CORSAGE

CORSAIR n pirate

CORSAIRS > CORSAIR

CORSE n corpse

CORSELET n one-piece undergarment combining a corset and bra

CORSELETS > CORSELET

CORSES > CORSE

CORSET n women's undergarment ▷ vb dress or enclose in, or as in, a corset

CORSETED > CORSET

CORSETIER n man who makes and fits corsets

CORSETING > CORSET

CORSETRY n making of or dealing in corsets

CORSETS > CORSET

CORSEY n pavement or pathway

CORSEYS > CORSEY

CORSITE n type of rock

CORSITES > CORSITE

CORSIVE n corrodent

CORSIVES > CORSIVE

CORSLET same as > CORSELET

CORSLETED > CORSLET

CORSLETS > CORSLET

CORSNED n ordeal to discover innocence or guilt

CORSNEDS > CORSNED

CORSO n promenade

CORSOS > CORSO

CORTEGE n funeral procession

CORTEGES > CORTEGE

CORTEX n outer layer of the brain or other internal organ

CORTEXES > CORTEX

CORTICAL > CORTEX

CORTICATE adj (of plants, seeds, etc) having a bark, husk, or rind

CORTICES > CORTEX

CORTICOID n steroid hormone

CORTICOSE adj consisting of or like bark

CORTILE n open, internal courtyard

CORTILI > CORTILE

CORTIN n adrenal cortex extract

CORTINA n weblike part of certain mushrooms

CORTINAS > CORTINA

CORTINS > CORTIN

CORTISOL n principal glucocorticoid secreted by the adrenal cortex

CORTISOLS > CORTISOL

CORTISONE n steroid hormone used to treat various diseases

CORULER n joint ruler

CORULERS > CORULER

CORUNDUM n hard mineral used as an abrasive

CORUNDUMS > CORUNDUM

CORUSCANT adj giving off flashes of light

CORUSCATE vb sparkle

CORVEE n day's unpaid labour owed by a feudal vassal to his lord

CORVEES > CORVEE

CORVES > CORF

CORVET same as > CURVET

CORVETED > CORVET

CORVETING > CORVET

CORVETS > CORVET

CORVETTE n lightly armed escort warship ▷ vb to participate in social activities with fellow Corvette car enthusiasts

CORVETTED > CORVETTE

CORVETTES > CORVETTE

CORVID n any member of the crow family

CORVIDS > CORVID

CORVINA same as > CORBINA

CORVINAS > CORVINA

CORVINE adj of, relating to, or resembling a crow

CORVUS n type of ancient hook

CORVUSES > CORVUS

CORY n catfish belonging to the South American Corydoras genus

CORYBANT n wild attendant of the goddess Cybele

CORYBANTS > CORYBANT

CORYDALIS n N temperate plant with finely-lobed leaves and spurred yellow or pinkish flowers

CORYLUS n hazel genus

CORYLUSES > CORYLUS

CORYMB n flat-topped flower cluster ▷ vb be corymb-like
CORYMBED > CORYMB
CORYMBOSE > CORYMB
CORYMBOUS > CORYMB
CORYMBS > CORYMB
CORYPHAEI n plural form of singular coryphaeus: leader of the chorus
CORYPHE n coryphaeus
CORYPHEE n leading dancer of a corps de ballet
CORYPHEES > CORYPHEE
CORYPHENE n any fish of the genus Coryphaena
CORYPHES > CORYPHE
CORYZA n acute inflammation in the nose
CORYZAL > CORYZA
CORYZAS > CORYZA
COS same as > COSINE
COSCRIPT vb to script jointly
COSCRIPTS > COSCRIPT
COSE vb get cosy
COSEC same as > COSECANT
COSECANT n (in trigonometry) the ratio of the length of the hypotenuse to that of the opposite side in a right-angled triangle
COSECANTS > COSECANT
COSECH n hyperbolic cosecant
COSECHS > COSECH
COSECS > COSEC
COSED > COSE
COSEISMAL adj of or designating points at which earthquake waves are felt at the same time ▷ n such a line on a map
COSEISMIC same as > COSEISMAL
COSES > COSE
COSET n mathematical set
COSETS > COSET
COSEY n tea cosy
COSEYS > COSEY
COSH n heavy blunt weapon ▷ vb hit with a cosh
COSHED > COSH
COSHER vb pamper or coddle
COSHERED > COSHER
COSHERER > COSHER
COSHERERS > COSHER
COSHERIES > COSHERY
COSHERING > COSHER
COSHERS > COSHER
COSHERY n Irish chief's right to lodge at his tenants' houses
COSHES > COSH
COSHING > COSH
COSIE same as > COSY
COSIED > COSY
COSIER n cobbler
COSIERS > COSIER

COSIES > COSY
COSIEST > COSY
COSIGN vb to sign jointly
COSIGNED > COSIGN
COSIGNER > COSIGN
COSIGNERS > COSIGN
COSIGNING > COSIGN
COSIGNS > COSIGN
COSILY > COSY
COSINE n trigonometric function
COSINES > COSINE
COSINESS > COSY
COSING > COSE
COSMEA n plant of the genus Cosmos
COSMEAS > COSMEA
COSMESES > COSMESIS
COSMESIS n aesthetic covering on a prosthesis to make it look more natural
COSMETIC n preparation used to improve the appearance of a person's skin ▷ adj improving the appearance only
COSMETICS > COSMETIC
COSMIC adj of the whole universe
COSMICAL > COSMIC
COSMID n segment of DNA
COSMIDS > COSMID
COSMIN same as > COSMINE
COSMINE n substance resembling dentine
COSMINES > COSMINE
COSMINS > COSMIN
COSMISM n Russian cultural and philosophical movement
COSMISMS > COSMISM
COSMIST > COSMISM
COSMISTS > COSMISM
COSMOCRAT n ruler of the world
COSMOGENY same as > COSMOGONY
COSMOGONY n study of the origin of the universe
COSMOID adj (of the scales of coelacanths and lungfish) consisting of two inner bony layers and an outer layer of cosmine
COSMOLINE n type of petroleum jelly ▷ vb to apply cosmoline to
COSMOLOGY n study of the origin and nature of the universe
COSMONAUT n Russian name for an astronaut
COSMORAMA n lifelike display, using mirrors and lenses, which shows reflections of various views of parts of the world
COSMOS n universe
COSMOSES > COSMOS
COSMOTRON n large type of particle accelerator
COSPHERED adj sharing the same sphere

COSPLAY n recreational activity in which people interact while dressed as fictional characters
COSPLAYS > COSPLAY
COSPONSOR vb to sponsor jointly
COSS another name for > KOS
COSSACK n Slavonic warrior-peasant
COSSACKS > COSSACK
COSSES > COSS
COSSET vb pamper ▷ n any pet animal, esp a lamb
COSSETED > COSSET
COSSETING > COSSET
COSSETS > COSSET
COSSETTED adj pampered, spoilt
COSSIE n informal name for a swimming costume
COSSIES > COSSIE
COST n amount of money, time, labour, etc, required for something ▷ vb have as its cost
COSTA n riblike part, such as the midrib of a plant leaf
COSTAE > COSTA
COSTAL n strengthening rib of an insect's wing
COSTALGIA n pain in the ribs
COSTALLY > COSTAL
COSTALS > COSTAL
COSTAR n actor who shares the billing with another ▷ vb share the billing with another actor
COSTARD n English variety of apple tree
COSTARDS > COSTARD
COSTARRED > COSTAR
COSTARS > COSTAR
COSTATE adj having ribs
COSTATED same as > COSTATE
COSTE vb to draw near
COSTEAN vb to mine for lodes
COSTEANED > COSTEAN
COSTEANS > COSTEAN
COSTED > COST
COSTER n person who sells fruit, vegetables etc from a barrow
COSTERS > COSTER
COSTES > COSTE
COSTING n as in marginal costing method of cost accounting
COSTINGS > COSTING
COSTIVE adj having or causing constipation
COSTIVELY > COSTIVE
COSTLESS > COST
COSTLIER > COSTLY
COSTLIEST > COSTLY
COSTLY adj expensive
COSTMARY n herbaceous Asian plant whose fragrant leaves were used

as a seasoning and to flavour ale
COSTOTOMY n surgical incision into a rib
COSTREL n flask, usually of earthenware or leather
COSTRELS > COSTREL
COSTS > COST
COSTUME n style of dress of a particular place or time, or for a particular activity ▷ vb provide with a costume
COSTUMED > COSTUME
COSTUMER same as > COSTUMIER
COSTUMERS > COSTUMIER
COSTUMERY n collective term for costumes
COSTUMES > COSTUME
COSTUMEY adj (stage) costume-like; unrealistic
COSTUMIER n maker or seller of costumes
COSTUMING > COSTUME
COSTUS n Himalayan herb with an aromatic root
COSTUSES > COSTUS
COSY adj warm and snug ▷ n cover for keeping things warm ▷ vb to make oneself snug and warm
COSYING > COSY
COT n baby's bed with high sides ▷ vb entangle or become entangled
COTAN same as > COTANGENT
COTANGENT n (in trigonometry) the ratio of the length of the adjacent side to that of the opposite side in a right-angled triangle
COTANS > COTANGENT
COTE same as > COT
COTEAU n hillside
COTEAUS > COTEAU
COTEAUX > COTEAU
COTED > COT
COTELETTE n cutlet
COTELINE n kind of muslin
COTELINES > COTELINE
COTENANCY > COTENANT
COTENANT n person who holds property jointly or in common with others
COTENANTS > COTENANT
COTERIE n exclusive group, clique
COTERIES > COTERIE
COTES > COTE
COTH n hyperbolic cotangent
COTHS > COTH
COTHURN same as > COTHURNUS
COTHURNAL > COTHURNUS
COTHURNI > COTHURNUS
COTHURNS > COTHURNUS

COTHURNUS *n* buskin worn in ancient Greek tragedy

COTICULAR *adj* relating to whetstones

COTIDAL *adj* (of a line on a tidal chart) joining points at which high tide occurs simultaneously

COTILLION *n* French formation dance of the 18th century

COTILLON *same as* > COTILLION

COTILLONS > COTILLON

COTING > COT

COTINGA *n* tropical bird

COTINGAS > COTINGA

COTININE *n* substance used to indicate presence of nicotine

COTININES > COTININE

COTISE *same as* > COTTISE

COTISED > COTISE

COTISES > COTISE

COTISING > COTISE

COTLAND *n* grounds that belong to a cotter

COTLANDS > COTLAND

COTQUEAN *n* coarse woman

COTQUEANS > COTQUEAN

COTRUSTEE *n* fellow trustee

COTS > COT

COTT *same as* > COT

COTTA *n* short form of surplice

COTTABUS *n* ancient Greek game involving throwing wine into a vessel

COTTAE > COTTA

COTTAGE *n* small house in the country ▷ *vb* engage in homosexual activity in a public lavatory

COTTAGED > COTTAGE

COTTAGER *n* person who lives in a cottage

COTTAGERS > COTTAGER

COTTAGES > COTTAGE

COTTAGEY *adj* resembling a cottage

COTTAGING *n* homosexual activity between men in a public lavatory

COTTAR *same as* > COTTER

COTTARS > COTTAR

COTTAS > COTTA

COTTED > COT

COTTER *n* pin or wedge used to secure machine parts ▷ *vb* secure (two parts) with a cotter

COTTERED > COTTER

COTTERING > COTTER

COTTERS > COTTIER

COTTID *n* type of fish typically with a large head, tapering body, and spiny fins

COTTIDS > COTTID

COTTIER *same as* > COTTER

COTTIERS > COTTIER

COTTING > COT

COTTISE *n* type of heraldic decoration ▷ *vb* (in heraldry) decorate with a cottise

COTTISED > COTTISE

COTTISES > COTTISE

COTTISING > COTTISE

COTTOID *adj* resembling a fish of the genus Cottus

COTTON *n* white downy fibre covering the seeds of a tropical plant ▷ *vb* take a liking

COTTONADE *n* coarse fabric of cotton or mixed fibres, used for work clothes, etc

COTTONED > COTTON

COTTONING > COTTON

COTTONS > COTTON

COTTONY > COTTON

COTTOWN *Scots variant of* > COTTON

COTTOWNS > COTTON

COTTS > COTT

COTTUS *n* type of fish with four yellowish knobs on its head

COTTUSES > COTTUS

COTURNIX *n* variety of quail

COTWAL *n* Indian police officer

COTWALS > COTWAL

COTYLAE > COTYLE

COTYLE *n* cuplike cavity

COTYLEDON *n* first leaf of a plant embryo

COTYLES > COTYLE

COTYLOID *adj* shaped like a cup ▷ *n* small bone forming part of the acetabular cavity in some mammals

COTYLOIDS > COTYLOID

COTYPE *n* type specimen in biological study

COTYPES > COTYPE

COUCAL *n* type of ground-living bird of Africa, S Asia, and Australia, with long strong legs

COUCALS > COUCAL

COUCH *n* piece of upholstered furniture for seating more than one person ▷ *vb* express in a particular way

COUCHANT *adj* in a lying position

COUCHE *adj* in heraldry (of a shield), tilted

COUCHED > COUCH

COUCHEE *n* reception held late at night

COUCHEES > COUCHEE

COUCHER > COUCH

COUCHERS > COUCH

COUCHES > COUCH

COUCHETTE *n* bed converted from seats on a train or ship

COUCHING *n* method of embroidery in which the thread is caught down at intervals by another thread passed through the material from beneath

COUCHINGS > COUCHING

COUDE *adj* relating to the construction of a reflecting telescope ▷ *n* type of reflecting telescope

COUDES > COUDE

COUGAN *n* drunk and rowdy person

COUGANS > COUGAN

COUGAR *n* puma

COUGARS > COUGAR

COUGH *vb* expel air from the lungs abruptly and noisily ▷ *n* act or sound of coughing

COUGHED > COUGH

COUGHER > COUGH

COUGHERS > COUGH

COUGHING > COUGH

COUGHINGS > COUGH

COUGHS > COUGH

COUGUAR *same as* > COUGAR

COUGUARS > COUGUAR

COULD > CAN

COULDEST *same as* > COULDST

COULDST *vb* form of 'could' used with the pronoun *thou* or its relative form

COULEE *n* flow of molten lava

COULEES > COULEE

COULIBIAC *n* Russian fish pie

COULIS *n* thin purée of vegetables or fruit

COULISSE *n* timber member grooved to take a sliding panel, such as a sluicegate, portcullis, or stage flat

COULISSES > COULISSE

COULOIR *n* deep gully on a mountain side, esp in the French Alps

COULOIRS > COULOIR

COULOMB *n* SI unit of electric charge

COULOMBIC > COULOMB

COULOMBS > COULOMB

COULTER *n* blade at the front of a ploughshare

COULTERS > COULTER

COUMARIC > COUMARIN

COUMARIN *n* white vanilla-scented crystalline ester, used in perfumes and flavourings and as an anticoagulant

COUMARINS > COUMARIN

COUMARONE *n* colourless insoluble aromatic liquid obtained from coal tar and used in the manufacture of synthetic resins

COUMAROU *n* tonka bean tree, or its seed

COUMAROUS > COUMAROU

COUNCIL *n* group meeting for discussion or consultation ▷ *adj* of or by a council

COUNCILOR *n* member of a council

COUNCILS > COUNCIL

COUNSEL *n* advice or guidance ▷ *vb* give guidance to

COUNSELED > COUNSEL

COUNSELEE *n* one who is counselled

COUNSELOR *n* person who gives counsel

COUNSELS > COUNSEL

COUNT *vb* say numbers in order ▷ *n* counting

COUNTABLE *adj* capable of being counted

COUNTABLY > COUNTABLE

COUNTBACK *n* system of deciding the winner of a tied competition by comparing earlier points or scores

COUNTDOWN *n* counting backwards to zero of the seconds before an event ▷ *vb* count numbers backwards towards zero, esp in timing such a critical operation

COUNTED > COUNT

COUNTER *n* long flat surface in a bank or shop ▷ *vb* oppose, retaliate against ▷ *adv* in the opposite direction

COUNTERED > COUNTER

COUNTERS > COUNTER

COUNTESS *n* woman holding the rank of count or earl

COUNTIAN *n* dweller in a given county

COUNTIANS > COUNTIAN

COUNTIES > COUNTY

COUNTING > COUNT

COUNTLESS *adj* too many to count

COUNTLINE *n* (in confectionery marketing) a chocolate-based bar

COUNTRIES > COUNTRY

COUNTROL *obsolete variant of* > CONTROL

COUNTROLS > COUNTROL

COUNTRY *n* nation

COUNTS > COUNT

COUNTSHIP > COUNT

COUNTY *n* (in some countries) division of a country ▷ *adj* upper-class

COUP *n* successful action ▷ *vb* turn or fall over

COUPE n sports car with two doors and a sloping fixed roof

COUPED > COUP

COUPEE n dance movement

COUPEES > COUPEE

COUPER n dealer

COUPERS > COUPER

COUPES > COUPE

COUPING > COUP

COUPLE n two people who are married or romantically involved ▷ vb connect, associate

COUPLED > COUPLE

COUPLEDOM n state of living as a couple, esp when regarded as being interested in each other to the exclusion of the outside world

COUPLER n mechanical device

COUPLERS > COUPLER

COUPLES > COUPLE

COUPLET n two consecutive lines of verse

COUPLETS > COUPLET

COUPLING n device for connecting things, such as railway carriages

COUPLINGS > COUPLING

COUPON n piece of paper entitling the holder to a discount or gift

COUPONING n in marketing, distribution or redemption of promotional coupons

COUPONS > COUPON

COUPS > COUP

COUPURE n entrenchment made by besieged forces behind a breach

COUPURES > COUPURE

COUR obsolete variant of > COVER

COURAGE n ability to face danger or pain without fear

COURAGES > COURAGE

COURANT n courante ▷ adj (of an animal) running

COURANTE n old dance in quick triple time

COURANTES > COURANTE

COURANTO same as > COURANTE

COURANTOS > COURANTO

COURANTS > COURANT

COURB vb to bend

COURBARIL n tropical American tree whose wood is a useful timber and whose gum is a source of copal

COURBED > COURB

COURBETTE same as > CURVET

COURBING > COURB

COURBS > COURB

COURD obsolete variant of > COVERED

COURE obsolete variant of > COVER

COURED > COURE

COURES > COURE

COURGETTE n type of small vegetable marrow

COURIE vb nestle or snuggle

COURIED > COURIE

COURIEING > COURIE

COURIER n person employed to look after holiday-makers ▷ vb send (a parcel, letter, etc) by courier

COURIERED > COURIER

COURIERS > COURIER

COURIES > COURIE

COURING > COUR

COURLAN another name for > LIMPKIN

COURLANS > COURLAN

COURS > COUR

COURSE n series of lessons or medical treatment ▷ vb (of liquid) run swiftly

COURSED > COURSE

COURSER n swift horse

COURSERS > COURSER

COURSES another word for > MENSES

COURSING n hunting with hounds trained to hunt game by sight

COURSINGS > COURSING

COURT n body which decides legal cases ▷ vb try to gain the love of

COURTED > COURT

COURTEOUS adj polite

COURTER n suitor

COURTERS > COURTER

COURTESAN n mistress or high-class prostitute

COURTESY n politeness, good manners

COURTEZAN same as > COURTESAN

COURTIER n attendant at a royal court

COURTIERS > COURTIER

COURTING > COURT

COURTINGS > COURT

COURTLET n small court

COURTLETS > COURTLET

COURTLIER > COURTLY

COURTLIKE adj courtly

COURTLING n fawning courtier

COURTLY adj ceremoniously polite

COURTROOM n room in which the sittings of a law court are held

COURTS > COURT

COURTSHIP n courting of an intended spouse or mate

COURTSIDE n in sport, area closest to the court

COURTYARD n paved space enclosed by buildings or walls

COUSCOUS n type of semolina used in North African cookery

COUSIN n child of one's uncle or aunt

COUSINAGE n kinship

COUSINLY > COUSIN

COUSINRY n collective term for cousins

COUSINS > COUSIN

COUTA n traditional Australian sailing boat

COUTAS > COUTA

COUTEAU n large two-edged knife used formerly as a weapon

COUTEAUX > COUTEAU

COUTER n armour designed to protect the elbow

COUTERS > COUTER

COUTH adj refined ▷ n refinement

COUTHER > COUTH

COUTHEST > COUTH

COUTHIE adj sociable

COUTHIER > COUTHIE

COUTHIEST > COUTHIE

COUTHS > COUTH

COUTHY same as > COUTHIE

COUTIL n type of tightly-woven twill cloth

COUTILLE same as > COUTIL

COUTILLES > COUTILLE

COUTILS > COUTIL

COUTURE n high-fashion designing and dressmaking ▷ adj relating to high fashion design and dress-making

COUTURES > COUTURE

COUTURIER n person who designs women's fashion clothes

COUVADE n custom in certain cultures relating to childbirth

COUVADES > COUVADE

COUVERT another word for > COVER

COUVERTS > COUVERT

COUZIN n South African word for a friend

COUZINS > COUZIN

COVALENCE same as > COVALENCY

COVALENCY n ability to form a bond in which two atoms share a pair of electrons

COVALENT > COVALENCY

COVARIANT n variant that varies leaving certain mathematical relationships it has with another variant (its covariant) unchanged

COVARIATE n statistical variable

COVARIED > COVARY

COVARIES > COVARY

COVARY vb vary together maintaining a certain mathematical relationship

COVARYING > COVARY

COVE n small bay or inlet ▷ vb form an architectural cove in

COVED > COVE

COVELET n small cove

COVELETS > COVELET

COVELLINE same as > COVELLITE

COVELLITE n indigo copper (blue sulphide of copper)

COVEN n meeting of witches

COVENANT n contract ▷ vb agree by a covenant

COVENANTS > COVENANT

COVENS > COVEN

COVENT same as > CONVENT

COVENTS > COVENT

COVER vb place something over, to protect or conceal ▷ n anything that covers

COVERABLE > COVER

COVERAGE n amount or extent covered

COVERAGES > COVERAGE

COVERALL n thing that covers something entirely

COVERALLS > COVERALL

COVERED > COVER

COVERER > COVER

COVERERS > COVER

COVERING another word for > COVER

COVERINGS > COVERING

COVERLESS > COVER

COVERLET n bed cover

COVERLETS > COVERLET

COVERLID same as > COVERLET

COVERLIDS > COVERLID

COVERS > COVER

COVERSED adj as in coversed sine obsolete function in trigonometry

COVERSINE n function in trigonometry

COVERSLIP n very thin piece of glass placed over a specimen on a glass slide

COVERT adj concealed, secret ▷ n thicket giving shelter to game birds or animals

COVERTLY > COVERT

COVERTS > COVERT

COVERTURE n condition or status of a married woman considered as being under the protection and influence of her husband

COVERUP n concealment of a mistake, crime, etc

COVERUPS > COVERUP

COVES > COVE

COVET vb long to possess (what belongs to someone else)

COVETABLE > COVET
COVETED > COVET
COVETER > COVET
COVETERS > COVET
COVETING > COVET
COVETISE *n* covetousness
COVETISES > COVETISE
COVETOUS *adj* jealously longing to possess something
COVETS > COVET
COVEY *n* small flock of grouse or partridge
COVEYS > COVEY
COVIN *n* conspiracy between two or more persons
COVINE *n* conspiracy between people to injure someone else
COVINES > COVINE
COVING *same as* > COVE
COVINGS > COVING
COVINOUS *adj* deceitful
COVINS > COVIN
COVYNE *same as* > COVIN
COVYNES > COVYNE
COW *n* mature female of certain mammals ▷ *vb* intimidate, subdue
COWAGE *n* tropical climbing plant
COWAGES > COWAGE
COWAL *n* shallow lake or swampy depression supporting vegetation
COWALS > COWAL
COWAN *n* drystone waller
COWANS > COWAN
COWARD *n* person who lacks courage ▷ *vb* show (someone) up to be a coward
COWARDED > COWARD
COWARDICE *n* lack of courage
COWARDING > COWARD
COWARDLY *adj* of or characteristic of a coward
COWARDRY *n* cowardice
COWARDS > COWARD
COWBANE *n* poisonous marsh plant
COWBANES > COWBANE
COWBELL *n* bell hung around a cow's neck
COWBELLS > COWBELL
COWBERRY *n* creeping evergreen shrub of N temperate and arctic regions, with pink or red flowers and edible berries
COWBIND *n* any of various bryony plants, esp the white bryony
COWBINDS > COWBIND
COWBIRD *n* American oriole with a dark plumage and short bill
COWBIRDS > COWBIRD
COWBOY *n* (in the US) ranch worker who herds and tends cattle ▷ *vb* work or behave as a cowboy

COWBOYED > COWBOY
COWBOYING > COWBOY
COWBOYS > COWBOY
COWED > COW
COWEDLY > COW
COWER *vb* cringe in fear
COWERED > COWER
COWERING > COWER
COWERS > COWER
COWFEEDER *n* dairyman
COWFISH *n* type of trunkfish with hornlike spines over the eyes
COWFISHES > COWFISH
COWFLAP *n* cow dung
COWFLAPS > COWFLAP
COWFLOP *n* foxglove
COWFLOPS > COWFLOP
COWGIRL *n* female cowboy
COWGIRLS > COWGIRL
COWGRASS *n* red clover
COWHAGE *same as* > COWAGE
COWHAGES > COWHAGE
COWHAND *same as* > COWBOY
COWHANDS > COWBOY
COWHEARD *same as* > COWHERD
COWHEARDS > COWHEARD
COWHEEL *n* heel of a cow, used as cooking ingredient
COWHEELS > COWHEEL
COWHERB *n* European plant with clusters of pink flowers
COWHERBS > COWHERB
COWHERD *n* person employed to tend cattle
COWHERDS > COWHERD
COWHIDE *n* hide of a cow ▷ *vb* to lash with a cowhide whip
COWHIDED > COWHIDE
COWHIDES > COWHIDE
COWHIDING > COWHIDE
COWHOUSE *n* byre
COWHOUSES > COWHOUSE
COWIER > COWY
COWIEST > COWY
COWING > COW
COWINNER *n* joint winner
COWINNERS > COWINNER
COWISH *adj* cowardly ▷ *n* N American plant with an edible root
COWISHES > COWISH
COWITCH *another name for* > COWAGE
COWITCHES > COWITCH
COWK *vb* retch or feel nauseated
COWKED > COWK
COWKING > COWK
COWKS > COWK
COWL *same as* > COWLING
COWLED *adj* wearing a cowl
COWLICK *n* tuft of hair over the forehead
COWLICKS > COWLICK
COWLIKE *adj* like a cow

COWLING *n* cover on an engine
COWLINGS > COWLING
COWLS > COWL
COWLSTAFF *n* pole, used by two people, for carrying a vessel
COWMAN *n* man who owns cattle
COWMEN > COWMAN
COWORKER *n* fellow worker
COWORKERS > COWORKER
COWP *same as* > COUP
COWPAT *n* pool of cow dung
COWPATS > COWPAT
COWPEA *n* type of tropical climbing plant
COWPEAS > COWPEA
COWPED > COWP
COWPIE *n* cowpat
COWPIES > COWPIE
COWPING > COWP
COWPLOP *n* cow dung
COWPLOPS > COWPLOP
COWPOKE *n* cowboy
COWPOKES > COWPOKE
COWPOX *n* disease of cows
COWPOXES > COWPOX
COWPS > COWP
COWPUNK *n* music that combines country music and punk
COWPUNKS > COWPUNK
COWRIE *n* brightly-marked sea shell
COWRIES > COWRIE
COWRITE *vb* to write jointly
COWRITER > COWRITE
COWRITERS > COWRITE
COWRITES > COWRITE
COWRITING > COWRITE
COWRITTEN > COWRITE
COWROTE > COWRITE
COWRY *same as* > COWRIE
COWS > COW
COWSHED *n* byre
COWSHEDS > COWSHED
COWSKIN *same as* > COWHIDE
COWSKINS > COWSKIN
COWSLIP *n* small yellow wild European flower
COWSLIPS > COWSLIP
COWTOWN *n* rural town in a cattle-raising area
COWTOWNS > COWTOWN
COWTREE *n* South American tree that produces latex
COWTREES > COWTREE
COWY *adj* cowlike
COX *n* coxswain ▷ *vb* act as cox of (a boat)
COXA *n* technical name for the hipbone or hip joint
COXAE > COXA
COXAL > COXA
COXALGIA *n* pain in the hip joint
COXALGIAS > COXALGIA

COXALGIC > COXALGIA
COXALGIES > COXALGIA
COXALGY *same as* > COXALGIA
COXCOMB *same as* > COCKSCOMB
COXCOMBIC > COXCOMB
COXCOMBRY *n* conceited arrogance or foppishness
COXCOMBS > COXCOMB
COXED > COX
COXES > COX
COXIB *n* anti-inflammatory drug
COXIBS > COXIB
COXIER > COXY
COXIEST > COXY
COXINESS > COXY
COXING > COX
COXITIDES > COXITIS
COXITIS *n* inflammation of the hip joint
COXLESS > COX
COXSWAIN *n* person who steers a rowing boat
COXSWAINS > COXSWAIN
COXY *adj* cocky
COY *adj* affectedly shy or modest ▷ *vb* to caress
COYAU *n* type of steep roof
COYAUS > COYAU
COYDOG *n* cross between a coyote and a dog
COYDOGS > COYDOG
COYED > COY
COYER > COY
COYEST > COY
COYING > COY
COYISH > COY
COYISHLY > COY
COYLY > COY
COYNESS > COY
COYNESSES > COY
COYOTE *n* prairie wolf of N America
COYOTES > COYOTE
COYOTILLO *n* thorny poisonous shrub of Mexico and the southwestern US
COYPOU *same as* > COYPU
COYPOUS > COYPOU
COYPU *n* beaver-like aquatic rodent
COYPUS > COYPU
COYS > COY
COYSTREL *same as* > COISTREL
COYSTRELS > COYSTREL
COYSTRIL *same as* > COISTREL
COYSTRILS > COYSTRIL
COZ *archaic word for* > COUSIN
COZE *vb* to chat
COZED > COZE
COZEN *vb* cheat, trick
COZENAGE > COZEN
COZENAGES > COZEN
COZENED > COZEN
COZENER > COZEN
COZENERS > COZEN
COZENING > COZEN
COZENS > COZEN

COZES > COZE

COZEY n tea cosy

COZEYS > COZEY

COZIE same as > COZEY

COZIED > COSY

COZIER n cobbler

COZIERS > COZIER

COZIES > COZEY

COZIEST > COZEY

COZILY > COZY

COZINESS > COZY

COZING > COZE

COZY same as > COSY

COZYING > COZY

COZZES > COZ

COZZIE n swimming costume

COZZIES > COZZIE

CRAAL vb to enclose in a craal (or kraal)

CRAALED > CRAAL

CRAALING > CRAAL

CRAALS > CRAAL

CRAB n edible shellfish with ten legs, the first pair modified into pincers ▷ vb catch crabs

CRABAPPLE n tree bearing small sour apple-like fruit

CRABBED > CRAB

CRABBEDLY > CRAB

CRABBER n crab fisherman

CRABBERS > CRABBER

CRABBIER > CRABBY

CRABBIEST > CRABBY

CRABBILY > CRABBY

CRABBING > CRAB

CRABBIT adj Scots word meaning bad-tempered

CRABBY adj bad-tempered

CRABEATER n species of seal

CRABGRASS n type of coarse weedy grass

CRABLIKE adj resembling a crab

CRABMEAT n edible flesh of a crab

CRABMEATS > CRABMEAT

CRABS > CRAB

CRABSTICK n stick, cane, or cudgel made of crabapple wood

CRABWISE adv (of motion) sideways

CRABWOOD n tropical American tree

CRABWOODS > CRABWOOD

CRACHACH pl n (in Wales) elitists

CRACK vb break or split partially ▷ n sudden sharp noise ▷ adj first-rate, excellent

CRACKA n US derogatory word for a poor White person

CRACKAS > CRACKA

CRACKBACK n in American football, illegal blocking of an opponent

CRACKDOWN n severe disciplinary measures

CRACKED adj damaged by cracking ▷ n sharp noise

CRACKER n thin dry biscuit

CRACKERS adj insane

CRACKET n low stool, often one with three legs

CRACKETS > CRACKET

CRACKHEAD n person addicted to the drug crack

CRACKIE n small mongrel dog

CRACKIER > CRACKY

CRACKIES > CRACKY

CRACKIEST > CRACKY

CRACKING adj very fast

CRACKINGS > CRACKING

CRACKJAW adj difficult to pronounce ▷ n word or phrase that is difficult to pronounce

CRACKJAWS > CRACKJAW

CRACKLE vb make small sharp popping noises ▷ n crackling sound

CRACKLED > CRACKLE

CRACKLES > CRACKLE

CRACKLIER > CRACKLY

CRACKLING n crackle

CRACKLY adj making a cracking sound

CRACKNEL n type of hard plain biscuit

CRACKNELS > CRACKNEL

CRACKPOT adj eccentric ▷ n eccentric person

CRACKPOTS > CRACKPOT

CRACKS > CRACK

CRACKSMAN n burglar, esp a safe-breaker

CRACKSMEN > CRACKSMAN

CRACKUP n physical or mental breakdown

CRACKUPS > CRACKUP

CRACKY adj full of cracks ▷ n something that is full of cracks

CRACOWE n medieval shoe with a sharply pointed toe

CRACOWES > CRACOWE

CRADLE n baby's bed on rockers ▷ vb hold gently as if in a cradle

CRADLED > CRADLE

CRADLER > CRADLE

CRADLERS > CRADLE

CRADLES > CRADLE

CRADLING n framework of iron or wood, esp as used in the construction of a ceiling

CRADLINGS > CRADLING

CRAFT n occupation requiring skill with the hands ▷ vb make skilfully

CRAFTED > CRAFT

CRAFTER n person doing craftwork

CRAFTERS > CRAFTER

CRAFTIER > CRAFTY

CRAFTIEST > CRAFTY

CRAFTILY > CRAFTY

CRAFTING > CRAFT

CRAFTLESS adj guileless

CRAFTS > CRAFT

CRAFTSMAN n skilled worker

CRAFTSMEN > CRAFTSMAN

CRAFTWORK n handicraft

CRAFTY adj skilled in deception

CRAG n steep rugged rock

CRAGFAST adj stranded on a crag

CRAGGED same as > CRAGGY

CRAGGER n member of a carbon reduction action group

CRAGGERS > CRAGGER

CRAGGIER > CRAGGY

CRAGGIEST > CRAGGY

CRAGGILY > CRAGGY

CRAGGY adj having many crags

CRAGS > CRAG

CRAGSMAN n rock climber

CRAGSMEN > CRAGSMAN

CRAIC n Irish word meaning fun

CRAICS > CRAIC

CRAIG a Scot word for > CRAG

CRAIGS > CRAIG

CRAKE n bird of the rail family, such as the corncrake ▷ vb to boast

CRAKED > CRAKE

CRAKES > CRAKE

CRAKING > CRAKE

CRAM vb force into too small a space ▷ n act or condition of cramming

CRAMBE n any plant of the genus Crambe

CRAMBES > CRAMBE

CRAMBO n word game

CRAMBOES > CRAMBO

CRAMBOS > CRAMBO

CRAME n merchant's booth or stall

CRAMES > CRAME

CRAMESIES > CRAMESY

CRAMESY same as > CRAMOISY

CRAMFULL adj very full

CRAMMABLE adj able to be crammed or filled

CRAMMED > CRAM

CRAMMER n person or school that prepares pupils for an examination

CRAMMERS > CRAMMER

CRAMMING n act of cramming

CRAMMINGS > CRAMMING

CRAMOISIE same as > CRAMOISY

CRAMOISY adj of a crimson colour ▷ n crimson cloth

CRAMP n painful muscular contraction ▷ vb affect with a cramp

CRAMPBARK n guelder rose

CRAMPED adj closed in

CRAMPER n spiked metal plate used as a brace for the feet in throwing the stone

CRAMPERS > CRAMPER

CRAMPET n cramp iron

CRAMPETS > CRAMPET

CRAMPFISH n electric ray

CRAMPIER > CRAMPY

CRAMPIEST > CRAMPY

CRAMPING > CRAMP

CRAMPIT same as > CRAMPET

CRAMPITS > CRAMPIT

CRAMPON n spiked plate strapped to a boot for climbing on ice ▷ vb climb using crampons

CRAMPONED > CRAMPON

CRAMPONS > CRAMPON

CRAMPOON same as > CRAMPON

CRAMPOONS > CRAMPOON

CRAMPS > CRAMP

CRAMPY adj affected with cramp

CRAMS > CRAM

CRAN n unit of capacity used for measuring fresh herring, equal to 37.5 gallons

CRANACHAN n Scottish dessert made with oatmeal, cream, and whisky

CRANAGE n use of a crane

CRANAGES > CRANAGE

CRANBERRY n sour edible red berry

CRANCH vb to crunch

CRANCHED > CRANCH

CRANCHES > CRANCH

CRANCHING > CRANCH

CRANE n machine for lifting and moving heavy weights ▷ vb stretch (one's neck) to see something

CRANED > CRANE

CRANEFLY n fly with long legs, slender wings, and a narrow body

CRANES > CRANE

CRANIA > CRANIUM

CRANIAL adj of or relating to the skull

CRANIALLY > CRANIAL

CRANIATE adj having a skull or cranium ▷ n vertebrate

CRANIATES > CRANIATE

CRANING > CRANE

CRANIUM n skull

CRANIUMS > CRANIUM

CRANK n arm projecting at right angles from a shaft ▷ vb turn with a crank ▷ adj (of a sailing vessel) easily keeled over by the wind

CRANKCASE n metal case that encloses the crankshaft in an internal-combustion engine

CRANKED > CRANK

CRANKER > CRANK
CRANKEST > CRANK
CRANKIER > CRANK
CRANKIEST > CRANK
CRANKILY > CRANK
CRANKING > CRANK
CRANKISH adj somewhat eccentric or bad-tempered
CRANKLE vb to bend or wind
CRANKLED > CRANKLE
CRANKLES > CRANKLE
CRANKLING > CRANKLE
CRANKLY adj vigorously
CRANKNESS n (of a vessel) liability to capsize
CRANKOUS adj fretful
CRANKPIN n short cylindrical pin in a crankshaft, to which the connecting rod is attached
CRANKPINS > CRANKPIN
CRANKS > CRANK
CRANKY same as > CRANK
CRANNIED > CRANNY
CRANNIES > CRANNY
CRANNOG n ancient Celtic lake or bog dwelling
CRANNOGE same as > CRANNOG
CRANNOGES > CRANNOGE
CRANNOGS > CRANNOG
CRANNY n narrow opening ▷ vb to become full of crannies
CRANNYING > CRANNY
CRANREUCH n hoarfrost
CRANS > CRAN
CRANTS n garland carried in front of a maiden's bier
CRANTSES > CRANTS
CRAP n rubbish, nonsense ▷ vb defecate
CRAPAUD n frog or toad
CRAPAUDS > CRAPAUD
CRAPE same as > CREPE
CRAPED > CRAPE
CRAPELIKE > CRAPE
CRAPES > CRAPE
CRAPIER > CRAPE
CRAPIEST > CRAPE
CRAPING > CRAPE
CRAPLE same as > GRAPPLE
CRAPLES > CRAPLE
CRAPOLA n rubbish
CRAPOLAS > CRAPOLA
CRAPPED > CRAP
CRAPPER n toilet
CRAPPERS > CRAPPER
CRAPPIE n N American freshwater fish)
CRAPPIER > CRAPPY
CRAPPIES > CRAPPIE
CRAPPIEST > CRAPPY
CRAPPING > CRAP
CRAPPY adj worthless, lousy
CRAPS > CRAP
CRAPSHOOT n dice game
CRAPULENT adj given to or resulting from excessive eating or drinking

CRAPULOUS same as > CRAPULENT
CRAPY > CRAPE
CRARE n type of trading vessel
CRARES > CRARE
CRASES > CRASIS
CRASH n collision involving a vehicle or vehicles ▷ vb (cause to) collide violently with a vehicle, a stationary object, or the ground ▷ adj requiring or using great effort in order to achieve results quickly
CRASHED > CRASH
CRASHER > CRASH
CRASHERS > CRASH
CRASHES > CRASH
CRASHING adj extreme
CRASHPAD n place to sleep or live temporarily
CRASHPADS > CRASHPAD
CRASIS n fusion or contraction of two adjacent vowels into one
CRASS adj stupid and insensitive
CRASSER > CRASS
CRASSEST > CRASS
CRASSLY > CRASS
CRASSNESS > CRASS
CRATCH n rack for holding fodder for cattle, etc
CRATCHES > CRATCH
CRATE n large wooden container for packing goods ▷ vb put in a crate
CRATED > CRATE
CRATEFUL > CRATE
CRATEFULS > CRATE
CRATER n bowl-shaped opening at the top of a volcano ▷ vb make or form craters
CRATERED > CRATER
CRATERING > CRATER
CRATERLET n small crater
CRATEROUS > CRATER
CRATERS > CRATER
CRATES > CRATE
CRATHUR same as > CRATUR
CRATHURS > CRATHUR
CRATING > CRATE
CRATON n stable part of the earth's continental crust
CRATONIC > CRATON
CRATONS > CRATON
CRATUR n whisky or whiskey
CRATURS > CRATUR
CRAUNCH same as > CRUNCH
CRAUNCHED > CRAUNCH
CRAUNCHES > CRAUNCH
CRAUNCHY > CRAUNCH
CRAVAT n man's scarf worn like a tie ▷ vb wear a cravat
CRAVATE same as > CRAVAT

CRAVATES > CRAVATE
CRAVATS > CRAVAT
CRAVATTED > CRAVAT
CRAVE vb desire intensely
CRAVED > CRAVE
CRAVEN adj cowardly ▷ n coward ▷ vb to make cowardly
CRAVENED > CRAVEN
CRAVENING > CRAVEN
CRAVENLY > CRAVEN
CRAVENS > CRAVEN
CRAVER > CRAVE
CRAVERS > CRAVE
CRAVES > CRAVE
CRAVING n intense desire or longing
CRAVINGS > CRAVING
CRAW n pouchlike part of a bird's oesophagus
CRAWDAD n crayfish
CRAWDADDY n crayfish
CRAWDADS > CRAWDAD
CRAWFISH same as > CRAYFISH
CRAWL vb move on one's hands and knees ▷ n crawling motion or pace
CRAWLED > CRAWL
CRAWLER n servile flatterer
CRAWLERS > CRAWLER
CRAWLIER > CRAWLY
CRAWLIEST > CRAWLY
CRAWLING n defect in freshly applied paint or varnish characterized by bare patches and ridging
CRAWLINGS > CRAWLING
CRAWLS > CRAWL
CRAWLWAY n in a mine, low passageway that can only be negotiated by crawling
CRAWLWAYS > CRAWLWAY
CRAWLY adj feeling like creatures are crawling on one's skin
CRAWS > CRAW
CRAY n crayfish
CRAYER same as > CRARE
CRAYERS > CRAYER
CRAYFISH n edible shellfish like a lobster
CRAYON n stick or pencil of coloured wax or clay ▷ vb draw or colour with a crayon
CRAYONED > CRAYON
CRAYONER > CRAYON
CRAYONERS > CRAYON
CRAYONING > CRAYON
CRAYONIST > CRAYON
CRAYONS > CRAYON
CRAYS > CRAY
CRAYTHUR variant of > CRATUR
CRAYTHURS > CRAYTHUR
CRAZE n short-lived fashion or enthusiasm ▷ vb make mad
CRAZED adj wild and uncontrolled

CRAZES > CRAZE
CRAZIER > CRAZY
CRAZIES > CRAZY
CRAZIEST > CRAZY
CRAZILY > CRAZY
CRAZINESS > CRAZY
CRAZING n act of crazing
CRAZINGS > CRAZING
CRAZY adj ridiculous ▷ n crazy person ▷ n crazy person
CRAZYWEED n locoweed
CREACH same as > CREAGH
CREACHS > CREACH
CREAGH n foray
CREAGHS > CREAGH
CREAK n (make) a harsh squeaking sound ▷ vb make or move with a harsh squeaking sound
CREAKED > CREAK
CREAKIER > CREAK
CREAKIEST > CREAK
CREAKILY > CREAK
CREAKING > CREAK
CREAKS > CREAK
CREAKY > CREAK
CREAM n fatty part of milk ▷ adj yellowish-white ▷ vb beat to a creamy consistency
CREAMCUPS n Californian plant with small cream-coloured or yellow flowers on long stalks
CREAMED > CREAM
CREAMER n powdered milk substitute for use in coffee
CREAMERS > CREAMER
CREAMERY n place where dairy products are made or sold
CREAMIER > CREAMY
CREAMIEST > CREAMY
CREAMILY > CREAMY
CREAMING > CREAM
CREAMLAID adj (of laid paper) cream-coloured and of a ribbed appearance
CREAMLIKE > CREAM
CREAMPUFF n puff pastry filled with cream
CREAMS > CREAM
CREAMWARE n type of earthenware with a deep cream body developed about 1720 and widely produced
CREAMWOVE adj (of wove paper) cream-coloured and even-surfaced
CREAMY adj resembling cream in colour, taste, or consistency
CREANCE n long light cord used in falconry
CREANCES > CREANCE
CREANT adj formative
CREASE n line made by folding or pressing ▷ vb crush or line
CREASED > CREASE
CREASER > CREASE

CREASERS > CREASE

CREASES > CREASE

CREASIER > CREASE

CREASIEST > CREASE

CREASING > CREASE

CREASOTE same as > CREOSOTE

CREASOTED > CREASOTE

CREASOTES > CREASOTE

CREASY > CREASE

CREATABLE > CREATE

CREATE vb make, cause to exist

CREATED > CREATE

CREATES > CREATE

CREATIC adj relating to flesh or meat

CREATIN same as > CREATINE

CREATINE n important metabolite involved in many biochemical reactions and present in many types of living cells

CREATINES > CREATINE

CREATING > CREATE

CREATINS > CREATIN

CREATION n creating or being created

CREATIONS > CREATION

CREATIVE adj imaginative or inventive ▷ n person who is creative professionally

CREATIVES > CREATIVE

CREATOR n person who creates

CREATORS > CREATOR

CREATRESS > CREATOR

CREATRIX > CREATOR

CREATURAL > CREATURE

CREATURE n animal, person, or other being

CREATURES n > CREATURE

CRECHE n place where small children are looked after

CRECHES > CRECHE

CRED n short for credibility

CREDAL > CREED

CREDENCE n belief in the truth or accuracy of a statement

CREDENCES > CREDENCE

CREDENDA > CREDENDUM

CREDENDUM n article of faith

CREDENT adj believing or believable

CREDENZA n type of small sideboard

CREDENZAS > CREDENZA

CREDIBLE adj believable

CREDIBLY > CREDIBLE

CREDIT n system of allowing customers to receive goods and pay later ▷ vb enter as a credit in an account

CREDITED > CREDIT

CREDITING > CREDIT

CREDITOR n person to whom money is owed

CREDITORS > CREDITOR

CREDITS pl n list of people responsible for the production of a film, programme, or record

CREDO n creed

CREDOS > CREDO

CREDS > CRED

CREDULITY n willingness to believe something on little evidence

CREDULOUS adj too willing to believe

CREE vb to soften grain by boiling or soaking

CREED n statement or system of (Christian) beliefs or principles

CREEDAL > CREED

CREEDS > CREED

CREEING > CREE

CREEK n narrow inlet or bay

CREEKIER > CREEKY

CREEKIEST > CREEKY

CREEKS > CREEK

CREEKSIDE n side of a creek

CREEKY adj abounding in creeks

CREEL n wicker basket used by anglers ▷ vb to fish using creels

CREELED > CREEL

CREELING > CREEL

CREELS > CREEL

CREEP vb move quietly and cautiously ▷ n creeping movement

CREEPAGE n imperceptible movement

CREEPAGES > CREEPAGE

CREEPED > CREEP

CREEPER n creeping plant ▷ vb train a plant to creep

CREEPERED > CREEPER

CREEPERS > CREEPER

CREEPIE n low stool

CREEPIER > CREEPY

CREEPIES > CREEPIE

CREEPIEST > CREEPY

CREEPILY > CREEPY

CREEPING > CREEP

CREEPMICE n plural form of singular creepmouse: a term of endearment

CREEPS > CREEP

CREEPY adj causing a feeling of fear or disgust

CREES > CREE

CREESE same as > KRIS

CREESED > CREESE

CREESES > CREESE

CREESH vb to lubricate

CREESHED > CREESH

CREESHES > CREESH

CREESHIER > CREESHY

CREESHING > CREESH

CREESHY adj greasy

CREESING > CREESE

CREM n crematorium

CREMAINS n cremated remains of a body

CREMANT adj (of wine) moderately sparkling

CREMASTER n muscle which raises and lowers the scrotum

CREMATE vb burn (a corpse) to ash

CREMATED > CREMATE

CREMATES > CREMATE

CREMATING > CREMATE

CREMATION > CREMATE

CREMATOR n furnace for cremating corpses

CREMATORS > CREMATOR

CREMATORY adj of or relating to cremation or crematoriums

CREME n cream ▷ adj (of a liqueur) rich and sweet

CREMES > CREME

CREMINI n variety of mushroom

CREMINIS > CREMINI

CREMOCARP n any fruit, such as anise or fennel, consisting of two united carpels

CREMONA same as > CROMORNA

CREMONAS > CREMONA

CREMOR n cream

CREMORNE n penis

CREMORNES > CREMORNE

CREMORS > CREMOR

CREMOSIN adj crimson

CREMS > CREM

CREMSIN same as > CREMOSIN

CRENA n cleft or notch

CRENAS > CRENA

CRENATE adj having a scalloped margin, as certain leaves

CRENATED same as > CRENATE

CRENATELY > CRENATE

CRENATION n any of the rounded teeth or the notches between them on a crenate structure

CRENATURE same as > CRENATION

CRENEL n opening formed in the top of a wall having slanting sides ▷ vb crenellate

CRENELATE vb supply with battlements

CRENELED > CRENEL

CRENELING > CRENEL

CRENELLE same as > CRENEL

CRENELLED > CRENEL

CRENELLES > CRENELLE

CRENELS > CRENEL

CRENSHAW n variety of melon

CRENSHAWS > CRENSHAW

CRENULATE adj having a margin very finely notched with rounded projections, as certain leaves

CREODONT n type of extinct Tertiary mammal,

the ancestor of modern carnivores

CREODONTS > CREODONT

CREOLE n language developed from a mixture of languages ▷ adj of or relating to a creole

CREOLES > CREOLE

CREOLIAN n Creole

CREOLIANS > CREOLIAN

CREOLISE vb (of a pidgin language) to become the native language of a speech community

CREOLISED same as > CREOLIZED

CREOLISES > CREOLISE

CREOLIST n student of creole languages

CREOLISTS > CREOLIST

CREOLIZE same as > CREOLISE

CREOLIZED adj (of a language) incorporating a considerable range of features from one or more unrelated languages, as the result of contact between language communities

CREOLIZES > CREOLIZE

CREOPHAGY n act of eating meat

CREOSOL n insoluble oily liquid

CREOSOLS > CREOSOL

CREOSOTE n dark oily liquid made from coal tar and used for preserving wood ▷ vb treat with creosote

CREOSOTED > CREOSOTE

CREOSOTES > CREOSOTE

CREOSOTIC > CREOSOTE

CREPANCE n injury to a horse's hind leg caused by being struck by the shoe of the other hind foot

CREPANCES > CREPANCE

CREPE n fabric or rubber with a crinkled texture ▷ vb cover or drape with crepe ▷ vb to crimp or frizz

CREPED > CREPE

CREPERIE n eating establishment that specializes in pancakes

CREPERIES > CREPERIE

CREPES > CREPE

CREPEY same as > CREPY

CREPIER > CREPY

CREPIEST > CREPY

CREPINESS > CREPY

CREPING > CREPE

CREPITANT > CREPITATE

CREPITATE vb make a rattling or crackling sound

CREPITUS n crackling chest sound heard in pneumonia and other lung diseases

CREPOLINE n light silk material used in dressmaking

CREPON n thin material made of fine wool and/or silk

CREPONS > CREPON

CREPS pl n slang term for training shoes

CREPT > CREEP

CREPUSCLE n twilight

CREPY adj (esp of the skin) having a dry wrinkled appearance like crepe

CRESCENDI > CRESCENDO

CRESCENDO n gradual increase in loudness, esp in music ▷ adv gradually getting louder ▷ vb increase in loudness or force

CRESCENT n (curved shape of) the moon as seen in its first or last quarter ▷ adj crescent-shaped

CRESCENTS > CRESCENT

CRESCIVE adj increasing

CRESOL n aromatic compound

CRESOLS > CRESOL

CRESS n plant with strong-tasting leaves, used in salads

CRESSES > CRESS

CRESSET n metal basket mounted on a pole

CRESSETS > CRESSET

CRESSIER > CRESSY

CRESSIEST > CRESSY

CRESSY > CRESS

CREST n top of a mountain, hill, or wave ▷ vb come to or be at the top of

CRESTA adj as in cresta run high-speed tobogganing down a steep narrow passage

CRESTAL > CRYSTAL

CRESTALS > CRESTAL

CRESTED > CREST

CRESTING same as > CREST

CRESTINGS > CREST

CRESTLESS > CREST

CRESTON n hogback

CRESTONS > CRESTON

CRESTS > CREST

CRESYL n tolyl

CRESYLIC adj of, concerned with, or containing creosote or cresol

CRESYLS > CRESYL

CRETIC n metrical foot

CRETICS > CRETIC

CRETIN n stupid person

CRETINISE vb make (someone) a cretin

CRETINISM n condition arising from a deficiency of thyroid hormone, present from birth, characterized by dwarfism and mental retardation

CRETINIZE same as > CRETINISE

CRETINOID > CRETIN

CRETINOUS > CRETIN

CRETINS > CRETIN

CRETISM n lying

CRETISMS > CRETISM

CRETONNE n heavy printed cotton fabric used in furnishings

CRETONNES > CRETONNE

CRETONS pl n spread made from pork fat and onions

CREUTZER n former copper and silver coin of Germany or Austria

CREUTZERS > CREUTZER

CREVALLE n any fish of the family Carangidae

CREVALLES > CREVALLE

CREVASSE n deep open crack in a glacier ▷ vb make a break or fissure in (a dyke, wall, etc)

CREVASSED > CREVASSE

CREVASSES > CREVASSE

CREVETTE n shrimp

CREVETTES > CREVETTE

CREVICE n narrow crack or gap in rock

CREVICED > CREVICE

CREVICES > CREVICE

CREW n people who work on a ship or aircraft ▷ vb serve as a crew member (on)

CREWCUT n very short haircut

CREWCUTS > CREWCUT

CREWE n type of pot

CREWED > CREW

CREWEL n fine worsted yarn used in embroidery ▷ vb to embroider in crewel

CREWELIST > CREWEL

CREWELLED > CREWEL

CREWELS > CREWEL

CREWES > CREWE

CREWING > CREW

CREWLESS adj lacking a crew

CREWMAN n member of a ship's crew

CREWMATE n colleague on the crew of a boat or ship

CREWMATES > CREWMATE

CREWMEN > CREWMAN

CREWNECK n plain round neckline in sweaters

CREWNECKS > CREWNECK

CREWS > CREW

CRIA n baby llama, alpaca, or vicuna

CRIANT adj garish

CRIAS > CRIA

CRIB n piece of writing stolen from elsewhere ▷ vb copy (someone's work) dishonestly

CRIBBAGE n card game for two to four players

CRIBBAGES > CRIBBAGE

CRIBBED > CRIB

CRIBBER > CRIB

CRIBBERS > CRIB

CRIBBING > CRIB

CRIBBINGS > CRIB

CRIBBLE vb to sift

CRIBBLED > CRIBBLE

CRIBBLES > CRIBBLE

CRIBBLING > CRIBBLE

CRIBELLA > CRIBELLUM

CRIBELLAR > CRIBELLUM

CRIBELLUM n sievelike spinning organ in certain spiders that occurs between the spinnerets

CRIBLE adj dotted

CRIBRATE adj sievelike

CRIBROSE adj pierced with holes

CRIBROUS > CRIBROSE

CRIBS > CRIB

CRIBWORK same as > CRIB

CRIBWORKS > CRIBWORK

CRICETID n any member of the family Cricetidae, such as the hamster and vole

CRICETIDS > CRICETID

CRICK n muscle spasm or cramp in the back or neck ▷ vb cause a crick in

CRICKED > CRICK

CRICKET n outdoor sport ▷ vb play cricket

CRICKETED > CRICKET

CRICKETER > CRICKET

CRICKETS > CRICKET

CRICKEY same as > CRIKEY

CRICKING > CRICK

CRICKS > CRICK

CRICKY same as > CRIKEY

CRICOID adj of or relating to part of the larynx ▷ n this cartilage

CRICOIDS > CRICOID

CRIED > CRY

CRIER n (formerly) official who made public announcements

CRIERS > CRIER

CRIES > CRY

CRIKEY interj expression of surprise

CRIM short for > CRIMINAL

CRIME n unlawful act ▷ vb charge with a crime

CRIMED > CRIME

CRIMEFUL adj criminal

CRIMELESS adj innocent

CRIMEN n crime

CRIMES > CRIME

CRIMEWAVE n period of increased criminal activity

CRIMINA > CRIMEN

CRIMINAL n person guilty of a crime ▷ adj of crime

CRIMINALS > CRIMINAL

CRIMINATE vb charge with a crime

CRIMINE interj expression of surprise

CRIMING > CRIME

CRIMINI > CRIMINE

CRIMINIS n accomplice in crime

CRIMINOUS adj criminal

CRIMINY interj cry of surprise

CRIMMER a variant spelling of > KRIMMER

CRIMMERS > CRIMMER

CRIMP vb fold or press into ridges ▷ n act or result of crimping

CRIMPED > CRIMP

CRIMPER > CRIMP

CRIMPERS > CRIMP

CRIMPIER > CRIMP

CRIMPIEST > CRIMP

CRIMPING > CRIMP

CRIMPLE vb crumple, wrinkle, or curl

CRIMPLED > CRIMPLE

CRIMPLES > CRIMPLE

CRIMPLING > CRIMPLE

CRIMPS > CRIMP

CRIMPY > CRIMP

CRIMS > CRIM

CRIMSON adj deep purplish-red ▷ n deep or vivid red colour ▷ vb make or become crimson

CRIMSONED > CRIMSON

CRIMSONS > CRIMSON

CRINAL adj relating to the hair

CRINATE adj having hair

CRINATED same as > CRINATE

CRINE vb to shrivel

CRINED > CRINE

CRINES > CRINE

CRINGE vb flinch in fear ▷ n act of cringing

CRINGED > CRINGE

CRINGER > CRINGE

CRINGERS > CRINGE

CRINGES > CRINGE

CRINGING > CRINGE

CRINGINGS > CRINGE

CRINGLE n eye at the edge of a sail

CRINGLES > CRINGLE

CRINING > CRINE

CRINITE adj covered with soft hairs or tufts ▷ n sedimentary rock

CRINITES > CRINITE

CRINKLE n wrinkle, crease, or fold ▷ vb become slightly creased or folded

CRINKLED > CRINKLE

CRINKLES > CRINKLE

CRINKLIER > CRINKLY

CRINKLIES > CRINKLY

CRINKLING > CRINKLE

CRINKLY adj wrinkled ▷ n old person

CRINOID n type of primitive echinoderm

CRINOIDAL > CRINOID

CRINOIDS > CRINOID

CRINOLINE n hooped petticoat

CRINOSE adj hairy

CRINUM n type of mostly tropical plant

CRINUMS > CRINUM

CRIOLLO n native or inhabitant of Latin America of European descent ▷ adj of, relating to, or characteristic of a criollo or criollos

CRIOLLOS > CRIOLLO

CRIOS n multicoloured woven woollen belt

CRIOSES > CRIOS

CRIP n offensive word for a person who is lame or disabled

CRIPE variant of > CRIPES

CRIPES interj expression of surprise

CRIPPLE n offensive word for a person who is lame or disabled ▷ vb make lame or disabled

CRIPPLED > CRIPPLE

CRIPPLER > CRIPPLE

CRIPPLERS > CRIPPLE

CRIPPLES > CRIPPLE

CRIPPLING adj damaging or injurious

CRIPS > CRIP

CRIS variant of > KRIS

CRISE n crisis

CRISES > CRISIS

CRISIC adj relating to a crisis

CRISIS n crucial stage, turning point

CRISP adj fresh and firm ▷ n very thin slice of potato fried till crunchy ▷ vb make or become crisp

CRISPATE adj having a curled or waved appearance

CRISPATED same as > CRISPATE

CRISPED same as > CRISPATE

CRISPEN vb to make crisp

CRISPENED > CRISPEN

CRISPENS > CRISPEN

CRISPER n compartment in a refrigerator

CRISPERS > CRISPER

CRISPEST > CRISP

CRISPHEAD n variety of lettuce

CRISPIER > CRISPY

CRISPIES pl n as in rice crispies puffed grains of rice, eaten esp as breakfast cereal

CRISPIEST > CRISPY

CRISPILY > CRISPY

CRISPIN n cobbler

CRISPING > CRISP

CRISPINS > CRISPIN

CRISPLY > CRISP

CRISPNESS > CRISP

CRISPS > CRISP

CRISPY adj hard and crunchy

CRISSA > CRISSUM

CRISSAL > CRISSUM

CRISSUM n area or feathers surrounding the cloaca of a bird

CRISTA n structure resembling a ridge or crest

CRISTAE > CRISTA

CRISTATE adj having a crest

CRISTATED same as > CRISTATE

CRIT abbreviation of > CRITICISM

CRITERIA > CRITERION

CRITERIAL > CRITERION

CRITERIUM n standard of judgment

CRITERIUM n type of bicycle race, involving many laps of a short course

CRITH n unit of weight for gases

CRITHS > CRITH

CRITIC n professional judge of any of the arts

CRITICAL adj very important or dangerous

CRITICISE same as > CRITICIZE

CRITICISM n fault-finding

CRITICIZE vb find fault with

CRITICS > CRITIC

CRITIQUE n critical essay ▷ vb to review critically

CRITIQUED > CRITIQUE

CRITIQUES > CRITIQUE

CRITS > CRIT

CRITTER a dialect word for > CREATURE

CRITTERS > CRITTER

CRITTUR same as > CRITTER

CRITTURS > CRITTUR

CRIVENS interj expression of surprise

CRIVVENS same as > CRIVENS

CROAK vb (of a frog or crow) give a low hoarse cry ▷ n low hoarse sound

CROAKED > CROAK

CROAKER n animal, bird, etc, that croaks

CROAKERS > CROAKER

CROAKIER > CROAK

CROAKIEST > CROAK

CROAKILY > CROAK

CROAKING > CROAK

CROAKINGS > CROAK

CROAKS > CROAK

CROAKY > CROAK

CROC short for > CROCODILE

CROCEATE adj saffron-coloured

CROCEIN n any one of a group of red or orange acid azo dyes

CROCEINE same as > CROCEIN

CROCEINES > CROCEIN

CROCEINS > CROCEIN

CROCEOUS adj saffron-coloured

CROCHE n knob at the top of a deer's horn

CROCHES > CROCHE

CROCHET vb make by looping and intertwining yarn with a hooked needle ▷ n work made in this way

CROCHETED > CROCHET

CROCHETER > CROCHET

CROCHETS > CROCHET

CROCI > CROCUS

CROCINE adj relating to the crocus

CROCK n earthenware pot or jar ▷ vb become or cause to become weak or disabled

CROCKED adj injured

CROCKERY n dishes

CROCKET n carved ornament in the form of a curled leaf or cusp

CROCKETED > CROCKET

CROCKETS > CROCKET

CROCKING > CROCK

CROCKPOT n tradename for a brand of slow cooker

CROCKPOTS > CROCKPOT

CROCKS > CROCK

CROCODILE n large amphibious tropical reptile

CROCOITE n rare orange secondary mineral

CROCOITES > CROCOITE

CROCOSMIA n type of S African plant

CROCS > CROC

CROCUS n flowering plant

CROCUSES > CROCUS

CROFT n small farm worked by one family in Scotland ▷ vb farm land as a croft

CROFTED > CROFT

CROFTER n owner or tenant of a small farm, esp in Scotland or northern England

CROFTERS > CROFTER

CROFTING n system or occupation of working land in crofts

CROFTINGS > CROFTING

CROFTS > CROFT

CROG vb ride on a bicycle as a passenger

CROGGED > CROG

CROGGIES > CROGGY

CROGGING > CROG

CROGGY n ride on a bicycle as a passenger

CROGS > CROG

CROISSANT n rich flaky crescent-shaped roll

CROJIK n triangular sail

CROJIKS > CROJIK

CROKINOLE n board game popular in Canada in which players flick wooden discs

CROMACK same as > CRUMMOCK

CROMACKS > CROMACK

CROMB same as > CROME

CROMBEC n African Old World warbler with colourful plumage

CROMBECS > CROMBEC

CROMBED > CROMB

CROMBING > CROMB

CROMBS > CROMB

CROME n hook ▷ vb use a crome

CROMED > CROME

CROMES > CROME

CROMING > CROME

CROMLECH n circle of prehistoric standing stones

CROMLECHS > CROMLECH

CROMORNA n one of the reed stops in an organ

CROMORNAS > CROMORNA

CROMORNE variant of > CROMORNA

CROMORNES > CROMORNE

CRON n computer application that schedules tasks chronologically

CRONE n witchlike old woman

CRONES > CRONE

CRONET n hair which grows over the top of a horse's hoof

CRONETS > CRONET

CRONIES > CRONY

CRONISH > CRONE

CRONK adj unfit

CRONKER > CRONK

CRONKEST > CRONK

CRONS > CRON

CRONY n close friend

CRONYISM n practice of appointing friends to high-level, esp political, posts regardless of their suitability

CRONYISMS > CRONYISM

CROODLE vb to nestle close

CROODLED > CROODLE

CROODLES > CROODLE

CROODLING > CROODLE

CROOK n dishonest person ▷ vb bend or curve ▷ adj Australian word meaning ill

CROOKBACK a rare word for > HUNCHBACK

CROOKED adj bent or twisted

CROOKEDER > CROOKED

CROOKEDLY > CROOKED

CROOKER > CROOK

CROOKERY n illegal or dishonest activity

CROOKEST > CROOK

CROOKING > CROOK

CROOKNECK n any type of summer squash

CROOKS > CROOK

CROOL vb spoil
CROOLED > CROOL
CROOLING > CROOL
CROOLS > CROOL
CROON vb sing, hum, or speak in a soft low tone ▷ n soft low singing or humming
CROONED > CROON
CROONER > CROON
CROONERS > CROON
CROONIER > CROONY
CROONIEST > CROONY
CROONING > CROON
CROONINGS > CROON
CROONS > CROON
CROONY adj singing like a crooner
CROOVE n animal enclosure
CROOVES > CROOVE
CROP n cultivated plant ▷ vb cut very short
CROPBOUND n poultry disease causing a pendulous crop
CROPFUL n quantity that can be held in the craw
CROPFULL adj satiated ▷ n amount that a crop can take
CROPFULLS > CROPFULL
CROPFULS > CROPFUL
CROPLAND n land on which crops are grown
CROPLANDS > CROPLAND
CROPLESS adj without crops
CROPPED > CROP
CROPPER n person who cultivates or harvests a crop
CROPPERS > CROPPER
CROPPIE same as > CROPPY
CROPPIES > CROPPY
CROPPING > CROP
CROPPINGS > CROP
CROPPY n rebel in the Irish rising of 1798
CROPS > CROP
CROPSICK adj sick from excessive food or drink
CROQUANTE n crisp nut-filled chocolate or cake
CROQUET n game played on a lawn in which balls are hit through hoops ▷ vb drive away a ball by hitting one's own when the two are in contact
CROQUETED > CROQUET
CROQUETS > CROQUET
CROQUETTE n fried cake of potato, meat, or fish
CROQUIS n rough sketch
CRORE n (in Indian English) ten million
CROREPATI n (in India) person whose assets are at least 10 million rupees
CRORES > CRORE

CROSIER n staff carried by bishops as a symbol of pastoral office ▷ vb bear or carry such a cross
CROSIERED > CROSIER
CROSIERS > CROSIER
CROSS vb move or go across (something) ▷ n structure, symbol, or mark of two intersecting lines ▷ adj angry, annoyed
CROSSABLE adj capable of being crossed
CROSSARM n in mining, horizontal bar on which a drill is mounted
CROSSARMS > CROSSARM
CROSSBAND vb to set the grain of layers of wood at right angles to one another
CROSSBAR n horizontal bar across goalposts or on a bicycle ▷ vb provide with crossbars
CROSSBARS > CROSSBAR
CROSSBEAM n beam that spans from one support to another
CROSSBILL n finch that has a bill with crossed tips
CROSSBIT > CROSSBITE
CROSSBITE vb to trick
CROSSBOW n weapon consisting of a bow fixed across a wooden stock
CROSSBOWS > CROSSBOW
CROSSBRED adj bred from two different types of animal or plant ▷ n crossbred plant or animal, esp an animal resulting from a cross between two pure breeds
CROSSBUCK n US roadsign used at railroad crossings
CROSSCUT vb cut across ▷ adj cut across ▷ n transverse cut or course
CROSSCUTS > CROSSCUT
CROSSE n light staff used in playing lacrosse
CROSSED > CROSS
CROSSER > CROSS
CROSSERS > CROSS
CROSSES > CROSS
CROSSEST > CROSS
CROSSETTE n in architecture, return in a corner of the architrave of a window or door
CROSSFALL n camber of a road
CROSSFIRE n gunfire crossing another line of fire
CROSSFISH n starfish
CROSSHAIR n one of two fine wires that cross in the focal plane of a gunsight or other optical instrument, used to define the line of sight

CROSSHEAD n subsection or paragraph heading printed within the body of the text
CROSSING n place where a street may be crossed safely
CROSSINGS > CROSSING
CROSSISH > CROSS
CROSSJACK n square sail on a ship's mizzenmast
CROSSLET n cross having a smaller cross near the end of each arm
CROSSLETS > CROSSLET
CROSSLY > CROSS
CROSSNESS > CROSS
CROSSOVER n place at which a crossing is made ▷ adj (of music, fashion, art, etc) combining two distinct styles
CROSSPLY adj having layers of fabric with cords running diagonally
CROSSROAD n road that crosses another road
CROSSRUFF n alternate trumping of each other's leads by two partners, or by declarer and dummy ▷ vb trump alternately in two hands of a partnership
CROSSTALK n rapid or witty talk
CROSSTIE n railway sleeper
CROSSTIED adj tied with ropes going across
CROSSTIES > CROSSTIE
CROSSTOWN adj going across town
CROSSTREE n either of a pair of wooden or metal braces on the head of a mast to support the topmast, etc
CROSSWALK n place marked where pedestrians may cross a road
CROSSWAY same as > CROSSROAD
CROSSWAYS same as > CROSSWISE
CROSSWIND n wind that blows at right angles to the direction of travel
CROSSWIRE n either of the two lines that cross in a gunsight
CROSSWISE adv across ▷ adj across
CROSSWORD n puzzle in which the solver deduces words suggested by clues and writes them into a grid
CROSSWORT n herbaceous Eurasian plant with pale yellow flowers and whorls of hairy leaves
CROST > CROSS
CROSTATA n type of fruit tart

CROSTATAS > CROSTATA
CROSTINI > CROSTINO
CROSTINIS > CROSTINO
CROSTINO n piece of toasted bread served with a savoury topping
CROTAL n any of various lichens used in dyeing wool
CROTALA > CROTALUM
CROTALE n type of small cymbal
CROTALES > CROTAL
CROTALINE adj relating to rattlesnakes
CROTALISM n poisoning due to ingestion of plants of the genus Crotalaria
CROTALS > CROTAL
CROTALUM n ancient castanet-like percussion instrument
CROTCH n part of the body between the tops of the legs ▷ vb have crotch (usu of a piece of clothing) removed
CROTCHED > CROTCH
CROTCHES > CROTCH
CROTCHET n musical note half the length of a minim
CROTCHETS > CROTCHET
CROTCHETY adj bad-tempered
CROTON n type of shrub or tree, the seeds of which yield croton oil
CROTONBUG n species of cockroach
CROTONIC adj as in crotonic acid type of colourless acid
CROTONS > CROTON
CROTTLE same as > CROTAL
CROTTLES > CROTTLE
CROUCH vb bend low with the legs and body close ▷ n this position
CROUCHED > CROUCH
CROUCHES > CROUCH
CROUCHING > CROUCH
CROUP n throat disease of children, with a cough ▷ vb have croup
CROUPADE n leap by a horse, pulling the hind legs towards the belly
CROUPADES > CROUPADE
CROUPE same as > CROUP
CROUPED > CROUP
CROUPER obsolete variant of > CRUPPER
CROUPERS > CROUPER
CROUPES > CROUPE
CROUPIER n person who collects bets and pays out winnings at a gambling table in a casino
CROUPIERS > CROUPIER
CROUPIEST > CROUP
CROUPILY > CROUP
CROUPING > CROUP

CROUPON n type of highly-polished flexible leather

CROUPONS > CROUPON

CROUPOUS > CROUP

CROUPS > CROUP

CROUPY > CROUP

CROUSE adj lively, confident, or saucy

CROUSELY > CROUSE

CROUSTADE n pastry case in which food is served

CROUT n sauerkraut

CROUTE n small round of toasted bread on which a savoury mixture is served

CROUTES > CROUTE

CROUTON n small piece of fried or toasted bread served in soup

CROUTONS > CROUTON

CROUTS > CROUT

CROW n large black bird with a harsh call ▷ vb (of a cock) make a shrill squawking sound

CROWBAIT n worn-out horse

CROWBAITS > CROWBAIT

CROWBAR n iron bar used as a lever ▷ vb use a crowbar to lever (something)

CROWBARS > CROWBAR

CROWBERRY n low-growing N temperate evergreen shrub with small purplish flowers and black berry-like fruit

CROWBOOT n type of Inuit boot made of fur and leather

CROWBOOTS > CROWBOOT

CROWD n large group of people or things ▷ vb gather together in large numbers

CROWDED > CROWD

CROWDEDLY > CROWD

CROWDER > CROWD

CROWDERS > CROWD

CROWDFUND vb fund a project via a large number of small donations

CROWDIE n porridge of meal and water

CROWDIES > CROWDIE

CROWDING > CROWD

CROWDS > CROWD

CROWDY same as > CROWDIE

CROWEA n Australian shrub with pink flowers

CROWEAS > CROWEA

CROWED > CROW

CROWER > CROW

CROWERS > CROW

CROWFEET > CROWFOOT

CROWFOOT n type of plant

CROWFOOTS > CROWFOOT

CROWING n act of crowing

CROWINGLY > CROW

CROWINGS > CROWING

CROWN n monarch's headdress of gold and jewels ▷ vb put a crown on the head of (someone) to proclaim him or her monarch

CROWNED > CROWN

CROWNER n promotional label

CROWNERS > CROWNER

CROWNET n coronet

CROWNETS > CROWNET

CROWNING n stage of labour when the infant's head is passing through the vaginal opening

CROWNINGS > CROWNING

CROWNLAND n large administrative division of the former empire of Austria-Hungary

CROWNLESS > CROWN

CROWNLET n small crown

CROWNLETS > CROWNLET

CROWNS > CROWN

CROWNWORK n manufacture of artificial crowns for teeth

CROWS > CROW

CROWSFEET > CROWSFOOT

CROWSFOOT n wrinkle at side of eye

CROWSTEP n set of steps to the top of a gable on a building

CROWSTEPS > CROWSTEP

CROZE n recess cut at the end of a barrel or cask to receive the head

CROZER n machine which cuts grooves in cask staves

CROZERS > CROZER

CROZES > CROZE

CROZIER same as > CROSIER

CROZIERS > CROZIER

CROZZLED adj blackened or burnt at the edges

CRU n (in France) a vineyard, group of vineyards, or wine-producing region

CRUBEEN n pig's trotter

CRUBEENS > CRUBEEN

CRUCES > CRUX

CRUCIAL adj very important

CRUCIALLY > CRUCIAL

CRUCIAN n European fish

CRUCIANS > CRUCIAN

CRUCIATE adj shaped or arranged like a cross ▷ n cruciate ligament

CRUCIATES > CRUCIATE

CRUCIBLE n pot in which metals are melted

CRUCIBLES > CRUCIBLE

CRUCIFER n type of plant with a corolla of four petals arranged like a cross, such as the brassicas, mustard, cress, and wallflower

CRUCIFERS > CRUCIFER

CRUCIFIED > CRUCIFY

CRUCIFIER > CRUCIFY

CRUCIFIES > CRUCIFY

CRUCIFIX n model of Christ on the Cross

CRUCIFORM adj cross-shaped ▷ n geometric curve, shaped like a cross, that has four similar branches asymptotic to two mutually perpendicular pairs of lines

CRUCIFY vb put to death by fastening to a cross

CRUCK n wooden timber supporting the end of certain roofs

CRUCKS > CRUCK

CRUD n sticky or encrusted substance ▷ interj expression of disgust, disappointment, etc ▷ vb cover with a sticky or encrusted substance

CRUDDED > CRUD

CRUDDIER > CRUDDY

CRUDDIEST > CRUDDY

CRUDDING > CRUD

CRUDDLE vb to curdle

CRUDDLED > CRUDDLE

CRUDDLES > CRUDDLE

CRUDDLING > CRUDDLE

CRUDDY adj dirty or unpleasant

CRUDE adj rough and simple ▷ n crude oil

CRUDELY > CRUDE

CRUDENESS > CRUDE

CRUDER > CRUDE

CRUDES > CRUDE

CRUDEST > CRUDE

CRUDIER > CRUDY

CRUDIEST > CRUDY

CRUDITES pl n selection of raw vegetables often served with a variety of dips before a meal

CRUDITIES > CRUDE

CRUDITY > CRUDE

CRUDO n sliced raw seafood

CRUDOS > CRUDO

CRUDS > CRUD

CRUDY adj raw

CRUE obsolete variant of > CREW

CRUEL adj delighting in others' pain

CRUELER > CRUEL

CRUELEST > CRUEL

CRUELLER > CRUEL

CRUELLEST > CRUEL

CRUELLS same as > CRUELS

CRUELLY > CRUEL

CRUELNESS > CRUEL

CRUELS n disease of cattle and sheep

CRUELTIES > CRUELTY

CRUELTY n deliberate infliction of pain or suffering

CRUES > CREW

CRUET n small container for salt, pepper, etc, at table

CRUETS > CRUET

CRUFT n redundant technical hardware

CRUFTS > CRUFT

CRUISE n sail for pleasure ▷ vb sail from place to place for pleasure

CRUISED > CRUISE

CRUISER n fast warship

CRUISERS > CRUISER

CRUISES > CRUISE

CRUISEWAY n canal used for recreational purposes

CRUISEY same as > CRUISY

CRUISIE same as > CRUIZIE

CRUISIER > CRUISY

CRUISIES > CRUISIE

CRUISIEST > CRUISY

CRUISING > CRUISE

CRUISINGS > CRUISE

CRUISY adj frequented by homosexuals searching for partners

CRUIVE n animal enclosure

CRUIVES > CRUIVE

CRUIZIE n oil lamp

CRUIZIES > CRUIZIE

CRULLER n light sweet ring-shaped cake, fried in deep fat

CRULLERS > CRULLER

CRUMB n small fragment of bread or other dry food ▷ vb prepare or cover (food) with breadcrumbs ▷ adj (esp of pie crusts) made with a mixture of biscuit crumbs, sugar, etc

CRUMBED > CRUMB

CRUMBER > CRUMB

CRUMBERS > CRUMB

CRUMBIER > CRUMBY

CRUMBIEST > CRUMBY

CRUMBING > CRUMB

CRUMBLE vb break into fragments ▷ n pudding of stewed fruit with a crumbly topping

CRUMBLED > CRUMBLE

CRUMBLES > CRUMBLE

CRUMBLIER > CRUMBLY

CRUMBLIES n elderly people

CRUMBLING > CRUMBLE

CRUMBLY adj easily crumbled or crumbling

CRUMBS interj expression of dismay or surprise

CRUMBUM n rogue

CRUMBUMS > CRUMBUM

CRUMBY adj full of crumbs

CRUMEN n deer's larmier or tear-pit

CRUMENAL n purse

CRUMENALS > CRUMENAL

CRUMENS > CRUMEN

CRUMHORN n medieval woodwind instrument

of bass pitch, consisting of an almost cylindrical tube curving upwards and blown through a double reed covered by a pierced cap

CRUMHORNS > CRUMHORN

CRUMMACK *same as* **> CRUMMOCK**

CRUMMACKS > CRUMMACK

CRUMMIE *n* cow with a crumpled horn

CRUMMIER > CRUMMY

CRUMMIES > CRUMMY

CRUMMIEST > CRUMMY

CRUMMILY *adv* in a manner suggestive of or indicating poor quality

CRUMMOCK *n* stick with a crooked head

CRUMMOCKS > CRUMMOCK

CRUMMY *adj* of poor quality ⊳ *n* lorry that carries loggers to work from their camp

CRUMP *vb* thud or explode with a loud dull sound ⊳ *n* crunching, thudding, or exploding noise ⊳ *adj* crooked

CRUMPED > CRUMP

CRUMPER > CRUMP

CRUMPEST > CRUMP

CRUMPET *n* round soft yeast cake, eaten buttered

CRUMPETS > CRUMPET

CRUMPIER > CRUMPY

CRUMPIEST > CRUMPY

CRUMPING > CRUMP

CRUMPLE *vb* crush, crease ⊳ *n* untidy crease or wrinkle

CRUMPLED > CRUMPLE

CRUMPLES > CRUMPLE

CRUMPLIER > CRUMPLE

CRUMPLING > CRUMPLE

CRUMPLY > CRUMPLE

CRUMPS > CRUMP

CRUMPY *adj* crisp

CRUNCH *vb* bite or chew with a noisy crushing sound ⊳ *n* crunching sound

CRUNCHED > CRUNCH

CRUNCHER > CRUNCH

CRUNCHERS > CRUNCH

CRUNCHES > CRUNCH

CRUNCHIE *n* derogatory word for an Afrikaner

CRUNCHIER > CRUNCH

CRUNCHIES > CRUNCHIE

CRUNCHILY > CRUNCH

CRUNCHING > CRUNCH

CRUNCHY > CRUNCH

CRUNK *n* form of hip-hop music originating in the Southern US

CRUNKED *adj* excited or intoxicated

CRUNKLE *Scots variant of* **> CRINKLE**

CRUNKLED > CRUNKLE

CRUNKLES > CRUNKLE

CRUNKLING > CRUNKLE

CRUNKS > CRUNK

CRUNODAL > CRUNODE

CRUNODE *n* mathematical term

CRUNODES > CRUNODE

CRUOR *n* blood clot

CRUORES > CRUOR

CRUORS > CRUOR

CRUPPER *n* strap that passes from the back of a saddle under a horse's tail

CRUPPERS > CRUPPER

CRURA > CRUS

CRURAL *adj* of or relating to the leg or thigh

CRUS *n* leg, esp from the knee to the foot

CRUSADE *n* medieval Christian war to recover the Holy Land from the Muslims ⊳ *vb* take part in a crusade

CRUSADED > CRUSADE

CRUSADER > CRUSADE

CRUSADERS > CRUSADE

CRUSADES > CRUSADE

CRUSADING > CRUSADE

CRUSADO *n* former gold or silver coin of Portugal

CRUSADOES > CRUSADO

CRUSADOS > CRUSADO

CRUSE *n* small earthenware jug or pot

CRUSES > CRUSE

CRUSET *n* goldsmith's crucible

CRUSETS > CRUSET

CRUSH *vb* compress so as to injure, break, or crumple ⊳ *n* dense crowd

CRUSHABLE > CRUSH

CRUSHED > CRUSH

CRUSHER > CRUSH

CRUSHERS > CRUSH

CRUSHES > CRUSH

CRUSHING > CRUSH

CRUSIAN *variant of* **> CRUCIAN**

CRUSIANS > CRUSIAN

CRUSIE *same as* **> CRUIZIE**

CRUSIES > CRUSIE

CRUSILY *adj* (in heraldry) strewn with crosses

CRUST *n* hard outer part of something, esp bread ⊳ *vb* cover with or form a crust

CRUSTA *n* hard outer layer; type of cocktail

CRUSTACEA *n* members of the Crustacea class of arthropods including the lobster

CRUSTAE > CRUSTA

CRUSTAL *adj* of or relating to the earth's crust

CRUSTAS > CRUSTA

CRUSTATE *adj* covered with a crust

CRUSTATED *same as* **> CRUSTATE**

CRUSTED > CRUST

CRUSTIER > CRUSTY

CRUSTIES > CRUSTY

CRUSTIEST > CRUSTY

CRUSTILY > CRUSTY

CRUSTING > CRUST

CRUSTLESS *adj* lacking a crust

CRUSTOSE *adj* having a crustlike appearance

CRUSTS > CRUST

CRUSTY *adj* having a crust ⊳ *n* dirty type of punk or hippy whose lifestyle involves travelling and squatting

CRUTCH *n* long stick like support with a rest for the armpit ⊳ *vb* support or sustain (a person or thing) as with a crutch

CRUTCHED > CRUTCH

CRUTCHES > CRUTCH

CRUTCHING > CRUTCH

CRUVE *same as* **> CRUIVE**

CRUVES > CRUVE

CRUX *n* crucial or decisive point

CRUXES > CRUX

CRUZADO *same as* **> CRUSADO**

CRUZADOES > CRUZADO

CRUZADOS > CRUZADO

CRUZEIRO *n* former monetary unit of Brazil, replaced by the cruzeiro real

CRUZEIROS > CRUZEIRO

CRUZIE *same as* **> CRUIZIE**

CRUZIES > CRUZIE

CRWTH *n* ancient stringed instrument of Celtic origin

CRWTHS > CRWTH

CRY *vb* shed tears ⊳ *n* fit of weeping

CRYBABIES > CRYBABY

CRYBABY *n* person, esp a child, who cries too readily

CRYER *same as* **> CRIER**

CRYERS > CRYER

CRYING > CRY

CRYINGLY > CRY

CRYINGS > CRY

CRYOBANK *n* place for storing genetic material at low temperature

CRYOBANKS > CRYOBANK

CRYOCABLE *n* highly conducting electrical cable cooled with a refrigerant such as liquid nitrogen

CRYOGEN *n* substance used to produce low temperatures

CRYOGENIC *adj* of the branch of physics concerned with the production of very low temperatures

CRYOGENS > CRYOGEN

CRYOGENY *n* cryogenic science

CRYOLITE *n* white or colourless mineral

CRYOLITES > CRYOLITE

CRYOMETER *n* thermometer for measuring low temperatures

CRYOMETRY **> CRYOMETER**

CRYONIC *adj* relating to or involving cryonics

CRYONICS *n* practice of freezing a human corpse in the hope of restoring it to life in the future

CRYOPHYTE *n* organism, esp an alga or moss, that grows on snow or ice

CRYOPROBE *n* supercooled instrument used in surgery

CRYOSCOPE *n* any instrument used to determine the freezing point of a substance

CRYOSCOPY *n* determination of freezing points, esp for the determination of molecular weights by measuring the lowering of the freezing point of a solvent when a known quantity of solute is added

CRYOSTAT *n* apparatus for maintaining a constant low temperature or a vessel in which a substance is stored at a low temperature

CRYOSTATS > CRYOSTAT

CRYOTRON *n* miniature switch working at the temperature of liquid helium and depending for its action on the production and destruction of superconducting properties in the conductor

CRYOTRONS > CRYOTRON

CRYPT *n* vault under a church, esp one used as a burial place

CRYPTADIA *n* things to be kept hidden

CRYPTAL > CRYPT

CRYPTIC *adj* obscure in meaning, secret

CRYPTICAL *same as* **> CRYPTIC**

CRYPTO *n* person who is a secret member of an organization or sect

CRYPTOGAM *n* plant that reproduces by spores not seeds

CRYPTON *n* krypton

CRYPTONS > CRYPTON

CRYPTONYM *n* code name

CRYPTOS > CRYPTO

CRYPTS > CRYPT

CRYSTAL *n* symmetrically shaped solid formed naturally ⊳ *adj* bright and clear

CRYSTALS > CRYSTAL
CSARDAS n type of Hungarian folk dance
CSARDASES > CSARDAS
CTENE n locomotor organ found in ctenophores (or comb jellies)
CTENES > CTENE
CTENIDIA > CTENIDIUM
CTENIDIUM n one of the comblike respiratory gills of molluscs
CTENIFORM adj comblike
CTENOID adj toothed like a comb, as the scales of perches
CUADRILLA n matador's assistants in a bullfight
CUATRO n four-stringed guitar
CUATROS > CUATRO
CUB n young wild animal such as a bear or fox ▷ adj young or inexperienced ▷ vb give birth to cubs
CUBAGE same as > CUBATURE
CUBAGES > CUBATURE
CUBANE n rare octahedral hydrocarbon
CUBANELLE n variety of pepper
CUBANES > CUBANE
CUBATURE n determination of the cubic contents of something
CUBATURES > CUBATURE
CUBBED > CUB
CUBBIER > CUBBY
CUBBIES > CUBBY
CUBBIEST > CUBBY
CUBBING > CUB
CUBBINGS > CUB
CUBBISH > CUB
CUBBISHLY > CUB
CUBBY n cubbyhole ▷ adj short and plump
CUBBYHOLE n small enclosed space or room
CUBE n object with six equal square sides ▷ vb cut into cubes
CUBEB n SE Asian woody climbing plant with brownish berries
CUBEBS > CUBEB
CUBED > CUBE
CUBER > CUBE
CUBERS > CUBE
CUBES > CUBE
CUBHOOD n state of being a cub
CUBHOODS > CUBHOOD
CUBIC adj having three dimensions ▷ n cubic equation
CUBICA n fine shalloon-like fabric
CUBICAL adj of or related to volume
CUBICALLY > CUBICAL

CUBICAS > CUBICA
CUBICITY n property of being cubelike
CUBICLE n enclosed part of a large room, screened for privacy
CUBICLES > CUBICLE
CUBICLY > CUBIC
CUBICS > CUBIC
CUBICULA > CUBICULUM
CUBICULUM n underground burial chamber in Imperial Rome, such as those found in the catacombs
CUBIFORM adj having the shape of a cube
CUBING > CUBE
CUBISM n style of art in which objects are represented by geometrical shapes
CUBISMS > CUBISM
CUBIST > CUBISM
CUBISTIC > CUBISM
CUBISTS > CUBISM
CUBIT n old measure of length based on the length of the forearm
CUBITAL adj of or relating to the forearm
CUBITI > CUBITUS
CUBITS > CUBIT
CUBITUS n elbow
CUBITUSES > CUBITUS
CUBLESS adj having no cubs
CUBOID n shaped like a cube ▷ n geometric solid whose six faces are rectangles
CUBOIDAL same as > CUBOID
CUBOIDS > CUBOID
CUBS > CUB
CUCKING adj as in cucking stool stool in which suspected witches were tested
CUCKOLD n man whose wife has been unfaithful ▷ vb be unfaithful to (one's husband)
CUCKOLDED > CUCKOLD
CUCKOLDLY adj possessing the qualities of a cuckold
CUCKOLDOM n state of being a cuckold
CUCKOLDRY > CUCKOLD
CUCKOLDS > CUCKOLD
CUCKOO n migratory bird ▷ adj insane or foolish ▷ interj imitation or representation of the call of a cuckoo ▷ vb repeat over and over
CUCKOOED > CUCKOO
CUCKOOING > CUCKOO
CUCKOOS > CUCKOO
CUCULLATE adj shaped like a hood or having a hoodlike part

CUCUMBER n long green-skinned fleshy fruit used in salads
CUCUMBERS > CUCUMBER
CUCURBIT n type of tropical or subtropical creeping plant such as the pumpkin, cucumber, squashes, and gourds
CUCURBITS > CUCURBIT
CUD n partially digested food chewed by a ruminant
CUDBEAR another name for > ORCHIL
CUDBEARS > CUDBEAR
CUDDEN n young coalfish
CUDDENS > CUDDEN
CUDDIE same as > CUDDY
CUDDIES > CUDDY
CUDDIN same as > CUDDEN
CUDDINS > CUDDIN
CUDDLE n hug ▷ vb to hold close
CUDDLED > CUDDLE
CUDDLER > CUDDLE
CUDDLERS > CUDDLE
CUDDLES > CUDDLE
CUDDLIER > CUDDLE
CUDDLIEST > CUDDLE
CUDDLING > CUDDLE
CUDDLY > CUDDLE
CUDDY n small cabin in a boat
CUDGEL n short thick stick used as a weapon ▷ vb use a cudgel
CUDGELED > CUDGEL
CUDGELER > CUDGEL
CUDGELERS > CUDGEL
CUDGELING > CUDGEL
CUDGELLED > CUDGEL
CUDGELLER > CUDGEL
CUDGELS > CUDGEL
CUDGERIE n type of large tropical tree with light-coloured wood
CUDGERIES > CUDGERIE
CUDS > CUD
CUDWEED n type of temperate plant
CUDWEEDS > CUDWEED
CUE n signal to an actor or musician to begin speaking or playing ▷ vb give a cue to
CUED > CUE
CUEING same as > CUE
CUEINGS > CUEING
CUEIST n snooker or billiards player
CUEISTS > CUEIST
CUES > CUE
CUESTA n long low ridge with a steep scarp slope and a gentle back slope
CUESTAS > CUESTA
CUFF n end of a sleeve ▷ vb hit with an open hand
CUFFABLE n able to be folded down at the ankle
CUFFED > CUFF
CUFFIN n man

CUFFING > CUFF
CUFFINS > CUFFIN
CUFFLE vb scuffle
CUFFLED > CUFFLE
CUFFLES > CUFFLE
CUFFLESS adj having no cuff(s)
CUFFLING > CUFFLE
CUFFLINK n detachable fastener for shirt cuff
CUFFLINKS > CUFFLINK
CUFFO adv free of charge
CUFFS > CUFF
CUFFUFFLE same as > KERFUFFLE
CUIF same as > COOF
CUIFS > CUIF
CUING > CUE
CUIRASS n piece of armour, of leather or metal covering the chest and back ▷ vb equip with a cuirass
CUIRASSED > CUIRASS
CUIRASSES > CUIRASS
CUISH same as > CUISSE
CUISHES > CUISH
CUISINART n type of food processor
CUISINE n style of cooking
CUISINES > CUISINE
CUISINIER n cook
CUISSE n piece of armour for the thigh
CUISSER same as > COOSER
CUISSERS > CUISSER
CUISSES > CUISSE
CUIT n ankle
CUITER vb to pamper
CUITERED > CUITER
CUITERING > CUITER
CUITERS > CUITER
CUITIKIN n gaiter
CUITIKINS > CUITIKIN
CUITS > CUIT
CUITTLE vb to wheedle
CUITTLED > CUITTLE
CUITTLES > CUITTLE
CUITTLING > CUITTLE
CUKE n cucumber
CUKES > CUKE
CULCH n the basis of an oyster bed
CULCHES > CULCH
CULCHIE n rough or unsophisticated country-dweller from outside Dublin ▷ adj rough or unsophisticated
CULCHIER > CULCHIE
CULCHIES > CULCHIE
CULCHIEST > CULCHIE
CULET n flat face at the bottom of a gem
CULETS > CULET
CULEX n type of mosquito
CULEXES > CULEX
CULICES > CULEX
CULICID n type of dipterous insect
CULICIDS > CULICID

CULICINE n any member of the genus Culex containing mosquitoes

CULICINES > CULICINE

CULINARY adj of kitchens or cookery

CULL vb choose, gather ▷ n culling

CULLAY n soapbark tree

CULLAYS > CULLAY

CULLED > CULL

CULLENDER same as > COLANDER

CULLER n person employed to cull animals

CULLERS > CULLER

CULLET n waste glass for melting down to be reused

CULLETS > CULLET

CULLIED > CULLY

CULLIES > CULLY

CULLING > CULL

CULLINGS > CULL

CULLION n rascal

CULLIONLY > CULLION

CULLIONS > CULLION

CULLIS same as > COULISSE

CULLISES > CULLIS

CULLS > CULL

CULLY n pal ▷ vb to trick

CULLYING > CULLY

CULLYISM n state of being a dupe

CULLYISMS > CULLYISM

CULM n coal-mine waste ▷ vb to form a culm or grass stem

CULMED > CULM

CULMEN n summit

CULMINA > CULMEN

CULMINANT adj highest or culminating

CULMINATE vb reach the highest point or climax

CULMING > CULM

CULMS > CULM

CULOTTE > CULOTTES

CULOTTES pl n women's knee-length trousers cut to look like a skirt

CULPA n act of neglect

CULPABLE adj deserving blame

CULPABLY > CULPABLE

CULPAE > CULPA

CULPATORY adj expressing blame

CULPRIT n person guilty of an offence or misdeed

CULPRITS > CULPRIT

CULSHIE n rough or unsophisticated country-dweller from outside Dublin ▷ adj rough or unsophisticated

CULSHIER > CULSHIE

CULSHIES > CULSHIE

CULSHIEST > CULSHIE

CULT n specific system of worship ▷ adj very popular among a limited group of people

CULTCH same as > CULTCH

CULTCHES > CULTCH

CULTER same as > COULTER

CULTERS > CULTER

CULTI > CULTUS

CULTIC adj of or relating to a religious cult

CULTIER > CULTY

CULTIEST > CULTY

CULTIGEN n species of plant that is known only as a cultivated form and did not originate from a wild type

CULTIGENS > CULTIGEN

CULTISH adj intended to appeal to a small group of fashionable people

CULTISHLY > CULTISH

CULTISM > CULT

CULTISMS > CULT

CULTIST > CULT

CULTISTS > CULT

CULTIVAR n variety of a plant that was produced from a natural species and is maintained by cultivation

CULTIVARS > CULTIVAR

CULTIVATE vb prepare (land) to grow crops

CULTLIKE adj resembling a cult

CULTRATE adj shaped like a knife blade

CULTRATED same as > CULTRATE

CULTS > CULT

CULTURAL adj of or relating to artistic or social pursuits or events considered to be valuable or enlightened

CULTURATI n people interested in cultural activities

CULTURE n ideas, customs, and art of a particular society ▷ vb grow (bacteria) for study

CULTURED adj showing good taste or manners

CULTURES > CULTURE

CULTURING > CULTURE

CULTURIST > CULTURE

CULTUS another word for > CULT

CULTUSES > CULTUS

CULTY same as > CULTISH

CULVER an archaic or poetic name for > PIGEON

CULVERIN n long-range medium to heavy cannon used during the 15th, 16th, and 17th centuries

CULVERINS > CULVERIN

CULVERS > CULVER

CULVERT n drain under a road or railway ▷ vb direct water through a culvert

CULVERTED > CULVERT

CULVERTS > CULVERT

CUM prep with ▷ n semen ▷ vb ejaculate sperm

CUMACEAN n type of small marine crustacean, mostly dwelling on the sea bed but sometimes found among the plankton

CUMACEANS > CUMACEAN

CUMARIC > CUMARIN

CUMARIN same as > COUMARIN

CUMARINS > CUMARIN

CUMARONE variant spelling of > COUMARONE

CUMARONES > CUMARONE

CUMBENT adj lying down

CUMBER vb obstruct or hinder ▷ n hindrance or burden

CUMBERED > CUMBER

CUMBERER > CUMBER

CUMBERERS > CUMBER

CUMBERING > CUMBER

CUMBERS > CUMBER

CUMBIA n Colombian style of music

CUMBIAS > CUMBIA

CUMBRANCE n burden, obstacle, or hindrance

CUMBROUS adj awkward because of size, weight, or height

CUMBUNGI n type of tall Australian marsh plant

CUMBUNGIS > CUMBUNGI

CUMEC n unit of volumetric rate of flow

CUMECS > CUMEC

CUMIN n sweet-smelling seeds of a Mediterranean plant, used in cooking

CUMINS > CUMIN

CUMMED > CUM

CUMMER n gossip

CUMMERS > CUMMER

CUMMIN same as > CUMIN

CUMMING > CUM

CUMMINS > CUMMIN

CUMQUAT same as > KUMQUAT

CUMQUATS > CUMQUAT

CUMS > CUM

CUMSHAW n (used, esp formerly, by beggars in Chinese ports) a present or tip

CUMSHAWS > CUMSHAW

CUMULATE vb accumulate ▷ adj heaped up

CUMULATED > CUMULATE

CUMULATES > CUMULATE

CUMULET n variety of domestic fancy pigeon

CUMULETS > CUMULET

CUMULI > CUMULUS

CUMULOSE adj full of heaps

CUMULOUS adj resembling or consisting of cumulus clouds

CUMULUS n thick white or dark grey cloud

CUMULUSES > CUMULUS

CUNABULA n cradle

CUNCTATOR n person in habit of being late

CUNDIES > CUNDY

CUNDUM n early form of condom

CUNDUMS > CUNDUM

CUNDY n sewer

CUNEAL same as > CUNEIFORM

CUNEATE adj wedge-shaped: cuneate leaves are attached at the narrow end

CUNEATED same as > CUNEATE

CUNEATELY > CUNEATE

CUNEATIC adj cuneiform

CUNEI > CUNEUS

CUNEIFORM adj (written in) an ancient system of writing using wedge-shaped characters ▷ n ancient system of writing using wedge-shaped characters

CUNETTE n small trench dug in the main ditch of a fortification

CUNETTES > CUNETTE

CUNEUS n small wedge-shaped area of the cerebral cortex

CUNIFORM same as > CUNIFORM

CUNIFORMS > CUNIFORM

CUNIT n one hundred cubic feet

CUNITS > CUNIT

CUNJEVOI n plant of tropical Asia and Australia with small flowers, cultivated for its edible rhizome

CUNJEVOIS > CUNJEVOI

CUNNER n fish of the wrasse family

CUNNERS > CUNNER

CUNNING adj clever at deceiving ▷ n cleverness at deceiving

CUNNINGER > CUNNING

CUNNINGLY > CUNNING

CUNNINGS > CUNNING

CUNT n taboo word for female genitals

CUNTS > CUNT

CUP n small bowl-shaped drinking container with a handle ▷ vb form (one's hands) into the shape of a cup

CUPBEARER n attendant who fills and serves wine cups, as in a royal household

CUPBOARD n piece of furniture or alcove with a door, for storage ▷ vb to store in a cupboard

CUPBOARDS > CUPBOARD

CUPCAKE n small cake baked in a cup-shaped foil or paper case

CUPCAKES > CUPCAKE

CUPEL n refractory pot in which gold or silver is refined ▷ vb refine (gold or silver) by means of cupellation
CUPELED > CUPEL
CUPELER > CUPEL
CUPELERS > CUPEL
CUPELING > CUPEL
CUPELLED > CUPEL
CUPELLER > CUPEL
CUPELLERS > CUPEL
CUPELLING > CUPEL
CUPELS > CUPEL
CUPFERRON n compound used in chemical analysis
CUPFUL n amount a cup will hold
CUPFULS > CUPFUL
CUPGALL n gall found on oakleaves
CUPGALLS > CUPGALL
CUPHEAD n type of bolt or rivet with a cup-shaped head
CUPHEADS > CUPHEAD
CUPID n figure representing the Roman god of love
CUPIDITY n greed for money or possessions
CUPIDS > CUPID
CUPLIKE > CUP
CUPMAN n drinking companion
CUPMEN > CUPMAN
CUPOLA n domed roof or ceiling ▷ vb to provide with a cupola
CUPOLAED > CUPOLA
CUPOLAING > CUPOLA
CUPOLAR > CUPOLA
CUPOLAS > CUPOLA
CUPOLATED > CUPOLA
CUPPA n cup of tea
CUPPAS > CUPPA
CUPPED > CUP
CUPPER same as > CUPPA
CUPPERS > CUPPER
CUPPIER > CUPPY
CUPPIEST > CUPPY
CUPPING > CUP
CUPPINGS > CUP
CUPPY adj cup-shaped
CUPREOUS adj of copper
CUPRESSUS n type of tree
CUPRIC adj of or containing copper in the divalent state
CUPRITE n red secondary mineral
CUPRITES > CUPRITE
CUPROUS adj of or containing copper in the monovalent state
CUPRUM an obsolete name for > COPPER
CUPRUMS > CUPRUM
CUPS > CUP
CUPSFUL > CUPFUL
CUPULA n dome-shaped structure
CUPULAE > CUPULA

CUPULAR same as > CUPULATE
CUPULATE adj shaped like a small cup
CUPULE n cup-shaped part or structure
CUPULES > CUPULE
CUR n mongrel dog
CURABLE adj capable of being cured
CURABLY > CURABLE
CURACAO n orange-flavoured liqueur
CURACAOS > CURACAO
CURACIES > CURACY
CURACOA same as > CURACAO
CURACOAS > CURACOA
CURACY n work or position of a curate
CURAGH same as > CURRACH
CURAGHS > CURAGH
CURANDERA n female faith healer
CURANDERO n male faith healer
CURARA same as > CURARE
CURARAS > CURARA
CURARE n poisonous resin of a S American tree
CURARES > CURARE
CURARI same as > CURARE
CURARINE n alkaloid extracted from curare, used as a muscle relaxant in surgery
CURARINES > CURARINE
CURARIS > CURARI
CURARISE same as > CURARIZE
CURARISED > CURARISE
CURARISES > CURARISE
CURARIZE vb paralyse or treat with curare
CURARIZED > CURARIZE
CURARIZES > CURARIZE
CURASSOW n gallinaceous ground-nesting bird with long legs and tails and, typically, a distinctive crest of curled feathers
CURASSOWS > CURASSOW
CURAT n cuirass
CURATE n clergyman who assists a parish priest ▷ vb be in charge of (an art exhibition or museum)
CURATED > CURATE
CURATES > CURATE
CURATING > CURATE
CURATION n work of a curator
CURATIONS > CURATION
CURATIVE n something able to cure ▷ adj able to cure
CURATIVES > CURATIVE
CURATOR n person in charge of a museum or art gallery
CURATORS > CURATOR
CURATORY > CURATOR
CURATRIX n female curator

CURATS > CURAT
CURB n something that restrains ▷ vb control, restrain
CURBABLE adj capable of being restrained
CURBED > CURB
CURBER > CURB
CURBERS > CURB
CURBING the US spelling of > KERBING
CURBINGS > CURBING
CURBLESS adj having no restraint
CURBS > CURB
CURBSIDE n pavement
CURBSIDES > CURBSIDE
CURBSTONE the US spelling of > KERBSTONE
CURCH n woman's plain cap or kerchief
CURCHEF same as > CURCH
CURCHEFS > CURCHEF
CURCHES > CURCH
CURCULIO n type of American weevil
CURCULIOS > CURCULIO
CURCUMA n type of tropical Asian tuberous plant
CURCUMAS > CURCUMA
CURCUMIN n yellow dye derived from turmeric
CURCUMINE same as > CURCUMIN
CURCUMINS > CURCUMIN
CURD n coagulated milk, used to make cheese ▷ vb turn into or become curd
CURDED > CURD
CURDIER > CURD
CURDIEST > CURD
CURDINESS > CURD
CURDING > CURD
CURDLE vb turn into curd, coagulate
CURDLED > CURDLE
CURDLER > CURDLE
CURDLERS > CURDLE
CURDLES > CURDLE
CURDLING > CURDLE
CURDS > CURD
CURDY > CURD
CURE vb get rid of (an illness or problem) ▷ n (treatment causing) curing of an illness or person
CURED > CURE
CURELESS > CURE
CURER > CURE
CURERS > CURE
CURES > CURE
CURET same as > CURETTE
CURETS > CURET
CURETTAGE n process of using a curette
CURETTE n surgical instrument for scraping tissue from body cavities ▷ vb scrape with a curette
CURETTED > CURETTE

CURETTES > CURETTE
CURETTING > CURETTE
CURF n type of limestone
CURFEW n law ordering people to stay inside after a specific time
CURFEWS > CURFEW
CURFS > CURF
CURFUFFLE vb make a kerfuffle
CURIA n papal court and government of the Roman Catholic Church
CURIAE > CURIA
CURIAL > CURIA
CURIALISM n ultramontanism
CURIALIST > CURIALISM
CURIAS > CURIA
CURIE n standard unit of radioactivity
CURIES > CURIE
CURIET n cuirass
CURIETS > CURIET
CURING n act of curing
CURINGS > CURING
CURIO n rare or unusual object valued as a collector's item
CURIOS > CURIO
CURIOSA n curiosities
CURIOSITY n eagerness to know or find out
CURIOUS adj eager to learn or know
CURIOUSER > CURIOUS
CURIOUSLY > CURIOUS
CURITE n oxide of uranium and lead
CURITES > CURITE
CURIUM n radioactive element artificially produced from plutonium
CURIUMS > CURIUM
CURL n curved piece of hair ▷ vb make (hair) into curls or (of hair) grow in curls
CURLED > CURL
CURLER n pin or small tube for curling hair
CURLERS > CURLER
CURLEW n long-billed wading bird
CURLEWS > CURLEW
CURLI pl n curled hairlike processes on the surface of the E. coli bacterium
CURLICUE n ornamental curl or twist ▷ vb to curl or twist elaborately, as in curlicues
CURLICUED > CURLICUE
CURLICUES > CURLICUE
CURLIER > CURLY
CURLIES pl n as in have by the short and curlies have completely in one's power
CURLIEST > CURLY
CURLILY > CURLY
CURLINESS > CURLY
CURLING n game like bowls, played with heavy stones on ice

CURLINGS > CURLING
CURLPAPER *n* strip of paper used to roll up and set a section of hair, usually wetted, into a curl
CURLS > CURL
CURLY *adj* tending to curl
CURLYCUE *same as* > CURLICUE
CURLYCUES > CURLYCUE
CURN *n* grain (of corn etc)
CURNEY *same as* > CURNY
CURNIER > CURNY
CURNIEST > CURNY
CURNS > CURN
CURNY *adj* granular
CURPEL *same as* > CRUPPER
CURPELS > CURPEL
CURR *vb* to purr
CURRACH *a Scot or Irish name for* > CORACLE
CURRACHS > CURRACH
CURRAGH *same as* > CURRACH
CURRAGHS > CURRAGH
CURRAJONG *same as* > KURRAJONG
CURRAN *n* black bun
CURRANS > CURRAN
CURRANT *n* small dried grape
CURRANTS > CURRANT
CURRANTY > CURRANT
CURRAWONG *n* Australian songbird
CURRED > CURR
CURREJONG *same as* > KURRAJONG
CURRENCY *n* money in use in a particular country
CURRENT *adj* of the immediate present ▷ *n* flow of water or air in one direction
CURRENTLY > CURRENT
CURRENTS > CURRENT
CURRICLE *n* two-wheeled open carriage drawn by two horses side by side
CURRICLES > CURRICLE
CURRICULA *n* plural form of singular curriculum: course of study in one subject at school or college
CURRIE *same as* > CURRY
CURRIED > CURRY
CURRIER *n* person who curries leather
CURRIERS > CURRIER
CURRIERY *n* trade, work, or place of occupation of a currier
CURRIES > CURRY
CURRIJONG *same as* > KURRAJONG
CURRING > CURR
CURRISH *adj* of or like a cur
CURRISHLY > CURRISH
CURRS > CURR
CURRY *n* Indian dish of meat or vegetables in a hot spicy sauce ▷ *vb*

prepare (food) with curry powder
CURRYCOMB *n* ridged comb used for grooming horses
CURRYING > CURRY
CURRYINGS > CURRY
CURS > CUR
CURSAL > CURSUS
CURSE *vb* swear (at) ▷ *n* swearword
CURSED > CURSE
CURSEDER > CURSE
CURSEDEST > CURSE
CURSEDLY > CURSE
CURSENARY *same as* > CURSORARY
CURSER > CURSE
CURSERS > CURSE
CURSES > CURSE
CURSI > CURSUS
CURSILLO *n* short religious retreat
CURSILLOS > CURSILLO
CURSING > CURSE
CURSINGS > CURSE
CURSITOR *n* clerk in the Court of Chancery
CURSITORS > CURSITOR
CURSITORY > CURSITOR
CURSIVE *n* (handwriting) done with joined letters ▷ *adj* of handwriting or print in which letters are joined in a flowing style
CURSIVELY > CURSIVE
CURSIVES > CURSIVE
CURSOR *n* movable point of light that shows a specific position on a visual display unit
CURSORARY *adj* cursory
CURSORES > CURSOR
CURSORIAL *adj* adapted for running
CURSORILY > CURSORY
CURSORS > CURSOR
CURSORY *adj* quick and superficial
CURST *same as* > CURSE
CURSTNESS *n* peevishness
CURSUS *n* Neolithic parallel earthworks
CURT *adj* brief and rather rude
CURTAIL *vb* cut short
CURTAILED > CURTAIL
CURTAILER > CURTAIL
CURTAILS > CURTAIL
CURTAIN *n* piece of cloth hung at a window or opening as a screen ▷ *vb* provide with curtains
CURTAINED > CURTAIN
CURTAINS *pl n* death or ruin
CURTAL *adj* cut short ▷ *n* animal whose tail has been docked
CURTALAX *same as* > CURTALAXE
CURTALAXE *n* cutlass
CURTALS > CURTAL

CURTANA *n* unpointed sword displayed at a coronation as an emblem of mercy
CURTANAS > CURTANA
CURTATE *adj* shortened
CURTATION > CURTATE
CURTAXE *same as* > CURTALAXE
CURTAXES > CURTAXE
CURTER > CURT
CURTESIES > CURTESY
CURTEST > CURT
CURTESY *n* widower's life interest in his wife's estate
CURTILAGE *n* enclosed area of land adjacent to a dwelling house
CURTLY > CURT
CURTNESS > CURT
CURTSEY *same as* > CURTSY
CURTSEYED > CURTSEY
CURTSEYS > CURTSEY
CURTSIED > CURTSY
CURTSIES > CURTSY
CURTSY *n* woman's gesture of respect ▷ *vb* make a curtsy
CURTSYING > CURTSY
CURULE *adj* (in ancient Rome) of the highest rank, esp one entitled to use a curule chair
CURVATE *adj* curved
CURVATED *same as* > CURVATE
CURVATION > CURVATE
CURVATIVE *adj* having curved edges
CURVATURE *n* curved shape
CURVE *n* continuously bending line with no straight parts ▷ *vb* form or move in a curve
CURVEBALL *n* in baseball, a ball pitched in a curving path ▷ *vb* pitch a curveball
CURVED > CURVE
CURVEDLY > CURVE
CURVES > CURVE
CURVESOME *adj* curvaceous
CURVET *n* horse's low leap with all four feet off the ground ▷ *vb* make such a leap
CURVETED > CURVET
CURVETING > CURVET
CURVETS > CURVET
CURVETTED > CURVET
CURVEY *same as* > CURVY
CURVIER > CURVE
CURVIEST > CURVE
CURVIFORM *adj* having a curved form
CURVINESS > CURVY
CURVING > CURVE
CURVITAL *adj* relating to curvature
CURVITIES > CURVITY
CURVITY *n* curvedness
CURVY > CURVE

CUSCUS *n* large Australian nocturnal possum
CUSCUSES > CUSCUS
CUSEC *n* unit of flow equal to 1 cubic foot per second
CUSECS > CUSEC
CUSH *n* cushion
CUSHAT *n* wood pigeon
CUSHATS > CUSHAT
CUSHAW *same as* > CASHAW
CUSHAWS > CUSHAW
CUSHES > CUSH
CUSHIE *same as* > CUSHAT
CUSHIER > CUSHY
CUSHIES > CUSHIE
CUSHIEST > CUSHY
CUSHILY > CUSHY
CUSHINESS > CUSHY
CUSHION *n* bag filled with soft material, to make a seat more comfortable ▷ *vb* lessen the effects of
CUSHIONED > CUSHION
CUSHIONET *n* small cushion
CUSHIONS > CUSHION
CUSHIONY > CUSHION
CUSHTY *interj* exclamation of pleasure, agreement, approval, etc
CUSHY *adj* easy
CUSK *n* type of food fish of northern coastal waters, with a single long dorsal fin
CUSKS > CUSK
CUSP *n* pointed end, esp on a tooth
CUSPAL > CUSP
CUSPATE *adj* having a cusp or cusps
CUSPATED *same as* > CUSPATE
CUSPED *same as* > CUSPATE
CUSPID *n* tooth having one point
CUSPIDAL *same as* > CUSPIDATE
CUSPIDATE *adj* having a cusp or cusps
CUSPIDES > CUSPIS
CUSPIDOR *another word (esp US) for* > SPITTOON
CUSPIDORE *same as* > CUSPIDOR
CUSPIDORS > CUSPIDOR
CUSPIDS > CUSPID
CUSPIER > CUSPY
CUSPIEST > CUSPY
CUSPIS *n* in anatomy, tapering structure
CUSPS > CUSP
CUSPY *adj* (of a computer program) well-designed and user-friendly
CUSS *n* curse, oath ▷ *vb* swear (at)
CUSSED *adj* obstinate
CUSSEDLY > CUSSED
CUSSER *same as* > COOSER
CUSSERS > CUSSER
CUSSES > CUSS

CUSSING > CUSS
CUSSO n tree of the rose family
CUSSOS > CUSSO
CUSSWORD n swearword
CUSSWORDS > CUSSWORD
CUSTARD n sweet yellow sauce made from milk and eggs
CUSTARDS > CUSTARD
CUSTARDY > CUSTARD
CUSTOCK same as **>** CASTOCK
CUSTOCKS > CUSTOCK
CUSTODE n custodian
CUSTODES > CUSTODE
CUSTODIAL > CUSTODY
CUSTODIAN n person in charge of a public building
CUSTODIER n custodian
CUSTODIES > CUSTODY
CUSTODY n protective care
CUSTOM n long-established activity or action ▷ adj made to the specifications of an individual customer
CUSTOMARY adj usual ▷ n statement in writing of customary laws and practices
CUSTOMED adj accustomed
CUSTOMER n person who buys goods or services
CUSTOMERS > CUSTOMER
CUSTOMISE same as **>** CUSTOMIZE
CUSTOMIZE vb make (something) according to a customer's individual requirements
CUSTOMS n duty charged on imports and exports
CUSTOS n superior in the Franciscan religious order
CUSTREL n knave
CUSTRELS > CUSTREL
CUSTUMAL another word for **>** CUSTOMARY
CUSTUMALS > CUSTUMAL
CUSTUMARY n customary
CUSUM n analysis technique used in statistics
CUSUMS > CUSUM
CUT vb open up, penetrate, wound, or divide with a sharp instrument
CUTANEOUS adj of the skin
CUTAWAY adj (of a drawing or model) having part of the outside omitted to reveal the inside ▷ n man's coat cut diagonally from the front waist to the back of the knees
CUTAWAYS > CUTAWAY
CUTBACK n decrease or reduction ▷ vb shorten by cutting
CUTBACKS > CUTBACK

CUTBANK n steep banking at a bend in a river
CUTBANKS > CUTBANK
CUTBLOCK n area where logging is permitted
CUTBLOCKS > CUTBLOCK
CUTCH same as **>** CATECHU
CUTCHA adj crude
CUTCHERRY n (formerly, in India) government offices and law courts collectively
CUTCHERY same as **>** CUTCHERRY
CUTCHES > CUTCH
CUTDOWN n decrease
CUTDOWNS > CUTDOWN
CUTE adj appealing or attractive
CUTELY > CUTE
CUTENESS > CUTE
CUTER > CUTE
CUTES > CUTIS
CUTESIE same as **>** CUTESY
CUTESIER > CUTESY
CUTESIEST > CUTESY
CUTEST > CUTE
CUTESY adj affectedly cute or coy
CUTEY same as **>** CUTIE
CUTEYS > CUTEY
CUTGLASS adj (of an accent) upper-class
CUTGRASS n any grass of the genus Leersia
CUTICLE n skin at the base of a fingernail or toenail
CUTICLES > CUTICLE
CUTICULA n cuticle
CUTICULAE > CUTICULA
CUTICULAR > CUTICLE
CUTIE n person regarded as appealing or attractive, esp a girl or woman
CUTIES > CUTIE
CUTIKIN same as **>** CUTIKIN
CUTIKINS > CUTIKIN
CUTIN n waxy waterproof substance
CUTINISE same as **>** CUTINIZE
CUTINISED > CUTINISE
CUTINISES > CUTINISE
CUTINIZE vb become or cause to become covered or impregnated with cutin
CUTINIZED > CUTINIZE
CUTINIZES > CUTINIZE
CUTINS > CUTIN
CUTIS a technical name for the **>** SKIN
CUTISES > CUTIS
CUTLAS same as **>** CUTLASS
CUTLASES > CUTLAS
CUTLASS n curved one-edged sword formerly used by sailors
CUTLASSES > CUTLASS
CUTLER n maker of cutlery

CUTLERIES > CUTLERY
CUTLERS > CUTLER
CUTLERY n knives, forks, and spoons
CUTLET n small piece of meat like a chop
CUTLETS > CUTLET
CUTLETTE n flat croquette of minced meat
CUTLETTES > CUTLETTE
CUTLINE n caption
CUTLINES > CUTLINE
CUTOFF n limit or termination
CUTOFFS > CUTOFF
CUTOUT n something that has been cut out from something else
CUTOUTS > CUTOUT
CUTOVER n transitional period in IT system changeover
CUTOVERS > CUTOVER
CUTPURSE n pickpocket
CUTPURSES > CUTPURSE
CUTS > CUT
CUTSCENE n non-interactive scene in a computer game
CUTSCENES > CUTSCENE
CUTTABLE adj capable of being cut
CUTTAGE n propagation by using parts taken from growing plants
CUTTAGES > CUTTAGE
CUTTER n person or tool that cuts
CUTTERS > CUTTER
CUTTHROAT n person who cuts throats
CUTTIER > CUTTY
CUTTIES > CUTTY
CUTTIEST > CUTTY
CUTTING > CUT
CUTTINGLY > CUT
CUTTINGS > CUT
CUTTLE vb to whisper
CUTTLED > CUTTLE
CUTTLES > CUTTLE
CUTTLING > CUTTLE
CUTTO n large knife
CUTTOE same as **>** CUTTO
CUTTOES > CUTTO
CUTTY adj short or cut short ▷ n something cut short
CUTUP n joker or prankster
CUTUPS > CUTUP
CUTWATER n forward part of the stem of a vessel, which cuts through the water
CUTWATERS > CUTWATER
CUTWORK n type of openwork embroidery
CUTWORKS > CUTWORK
CUTWORM n caterpillar of various types of moth
CUTWORMS > CUTWORM
CUVEE n individual batch or blend of wine
CUVEES > CUVEE

CUVETTE n shallow dish or vessel for holding liquid
CUVETTES > CUVETTE
CUZ n cousin
CUZES > CUZ
CUZZES > CUZ
CUZZIE n close friend or family member
CUZZIES > CUZZIE
CWM same as **>** CIRQUE
CWMS > CWM
CWTCH vb be snuggled up
CWTCHED > CWTCH
CWTCHES > CWTCH
CWTCHING > CWTCH
CYAN n highly saturated green-blue ▷ adj of this colour
CYANAMID same as **>** CYANAMIDE
CYANAMIDE n white or colourless crystalline soluble weak dibasic acid, which can be hydrolysed to urea
CYANAMIDS > CYANAMID
CYANATE n any salt or ester of cyanic acid
CYANATES > CYANATE
CYANIC adj as in cyanic acid colourless poisonous volatile liquid acid
CYANID same as **>** CYANIDE
CYANIDE n extremely poisonous chemical compound ▷ vb treat with cyanide
CYANIDED > CYANIDE
CYANIDES > CYANIDE
CYANIDING > CYANIDE
CYANIDS > CYANID
CYANIN same as **>** CYANINE
CYANINE n blue dye used in photography
CYANINES > CYANINE
CYANINS > CYANIN
CYANISE vb turn into cyanide
CYANISED > CYANISE
CYANISES > CYANISE
CYANISING > CYANISE
CYANITE a variant spelling of **>** KYANITE
CYANITES > CYANITE
CYANITIC > CYANITE
CYANIZE same as **>** CYANISE
CYANIZED > CYANIZE
CYANIZES > CYANIZE
CYANIZING > CYANIZE
CYANO adj containing cyanogen
CYANOGEN n poisonous colourless flammable gas
CYANOGENS > CYANOGEN
CYANOSE same as **>** CYANOSIS
CYANOSED adj affected by cyanosis
CYANOSES > CYANOSIS
CYANOSIS n blueness of the skin, caused by a

deficiency of oxygen in the blood

CYANOTIC > CYANOSIS

CYANOTYPE another name for **>** BLUEPRINT

CYANS > CYAN

CYANURATE n chemical derived from cyanide

CYANURET n cyanide

CYANURETS > CYANURET

CYATHI > CYATHUS

CYATHIA > CYATHIUM

CYATHIUM n inflorescence of the type found in the poinsettia

CYATHUS n ancient measure of wine

CYBER adj involving computers

CYBERCAFE n café equipped with computer terminals which customers can use to access the internet

CYBERCAST same as **>** WEBCAST

CYBERNATE vb control (a manufacturing process) with a servomechanism or (of a process) to be controlled by a servomechanism

CYBERNAUT n person using internet

CYBERPET n electronic toy that simulates the activities of a pet, requiring the owner to feed, discipline, and entertain it

CYBERPETS > CYBERPET

CYBERPORN n pornography on Internet

CYBERPUNK n genre of science fiction that features rebellious computer hackers and is set in a dystopian society integrated by computer networks

CYBERSEX n exchanging of sexual messages or information via the internet

CYBERWAR n information warfare

CYBERWARS > CYBERWAR

CYBORG n (in science fiction) a living being enhanced by computer implants

CYBORGS > CYBORG

CYBRARIAN n person in charge of computer archives

CYBRID n cytoplasmic hybrid

CYBRIDS > CYBRID

CYCAD n type of tropical or subtropical plant

CYCADEOID n (now extinct) plant with a woody stem and tough leaves

CYCADS > CYCAD

CYCAS n palm tree of the genus Cycas

CYCASES > CYCAS

CYCASIN n glucoside, toxic to mammals, occurring in cycads

CYCASINS > CYCASIN

CYCLAMATE n salt or ester of cyclamic acid. Certain of the salts have a very sweet taste and were formerly used as food additives and sugar substitutes

CYCLAMEN n plant with red, pink, or white flowers ▷ adj of a dark reddish-purple colour

CYCLAMENS > CYCLAMEN

CYCLASE n enzyme which acts as a catalyst in the formation of a cyclic compound

CYCLASES > CYCLASE

CYCLE vb ride a bicycle ▷ n bicycle

CYCLECAR n any light car with an engine capacity of 1100cc or less

CYCLECARS > CYCLECAR

CYCLED > CYCLE

CYCLEPATH n special path for bicycles

CYCLER same as **>** CYCLIST

CYCLERIES > CYCLERY

CYCLERS > CYCLIST

CYCLERY n business dealing in bicycles and bicycle accessories

CYCLES > CYCLE

CYCLEWAY n path or way designed, and reserved for, cyclists

CYCLEWAYS > CYCLEWAY

CYCLIC adj recurring or revolving in cycles

CYCLICAL n short-term trend, of which reversal is expected ▷ adj cyclic

CYCLICALS > CYCLIC

CYCLICISM > CYCLIC

CYCLICITY > CYCLIC

CYCLICLY > CYCLIC

CYCLIN n type of protein

CYCLING > CYCLE

CYCLINGS > CYCLE

CYCLINS > CYCLIN

CYCLISE same as **>** CYCLIZE

CYCLISED > CYCLISE

CYCLISES > CYCLISE

CYCLISING > CYCLISE

CYCLIST n person who rides a bicycle

CYCLISTS > CYCLIST

CYCLITOL n alicyclic compound

CYCLITOLS > CYCLITOL

CYCLIZE vb be cyclical

CYCLIZED > CYCLIZE

CYCLIZES > CYCLIZE

CYCLIZINE n drug used to relieve the symptoms of motion sickness

CYCLIZING > CYCLIZE

CYCLO n type of rickshaw

CYCLOGIRO n aircraft lifted and propelled by pivoted blades rotating parallel to roughly horizontal transverse axes

CYCLOID adj resembling a circle ▷ n mathematical curve

CYCLOIDAL > CYCLOID

CYCLOIDS > CYCLOID

CYCLOLITH n stone circle

CYCLONAL > CYCLONE

CYCLONE n violent wind moving round a central area

CYCLONES > CYCLONE

CYCLONIC > CYCLONE

CYCLONITE n white crystalline insoluble explosive prepared by the action of nitric acid on hexamethylenetetramine

CYCLOPEAN adj of or relating to the Cyclops

CYCLOPES > CYCLOPS

CYCLOPIAN > CYCLOPS

CYCLOPIC > CYCLOPS

CYCLOPS n type of copepod characterized by having one eye

CYCLORAMA n large picture, such as a battle scene, on the interior wall of a cylindrical room, designed to appear in natural perspective to a spectator in the centre

CYCLOS > CYCLO

CYCLOSES > CYCLOSIS

CYCLOSIS n circulation of cytoplasm or cell organelles, such as food vacuoles in some protozoans

CYCLOTRON n apparatus that accelerates charged particles by means of a strong vertical magnetic field

CYCLUS n cycle

CYCLUSES > CYCLUS

CYDER same as **>** CIDER

CYDERS > CYDER

CYESES > CYESIS

CYESIS the technical name for **>** PREGNANCY

CYGNET n young swan

CYGNETS > CYGNET

CYLICES > CYLIX

CYLIKES same as **>** KYLIX

CYLINDER n solid or hollow body with straight sides and circular ends

CYLINDERS > CYLINDER

CYLINDRIC adj shaped like, or characteristic of a cylinder

CYLIX a variant of **>** KYLIX

CYMA n moulding with a double curve, part concave and part convex

CYMAE > CYMA

CYMAGRAPH same as **>** CYMOGRAPH

CYMAR n woman's short fur-trimmed jacket, popular in the 17th and 18th centuries

CYMARS > CYMAR

CYMAS > CYMA

CYMATIA > CYMATIUM

CYMATICS n theory and practice of a therapy whereby sound waves are directed at the body, with the aim of promoting health

CYMATIUM n top moulding of a classical cornice or entablature

CYMBAL n percussion instrument

CYMBALEER > CYMBAL

CYMBALER > CYMBAL

CYMBALERS > CYMBAL

CYMBALIST > CYMBAL

CYMBALO another name for **>** DULCIMER

CYMBALOES > CYMBALO

CYMBALOM same as **>** CIMBALOM

CYMBALOMS > CYMBALOM

CYMBALOS > CYMBALO

CYMBALS > CYMBAL

CYMBIDIA > CYMBIDIUM

CYMBIDIUM n any orchid of the genus Cymbidium

CYMBIFORM adj shaped like a boat

CYMBLING same as **>** CYMLING

CYMBLINGS > CYMLING

CYME n type of flower cluster

CYMENE n colourless insoluble liquid

CYMENES > CYMENE

CYMES > CYME

CYMLIN same as **>** CYMLING

CYMLING n pattypan squash

CYMLINGS > CYMLING

CYMLINS > CYMLIN

CYMOGENE n mixture of volatile flammable hydrocarbons, mainly butane, obtained in the distillation of petroleum

CYMOGENES > CYMOGENE

CYMOGRAPH n instrument for tracing the outline of an architectural moulding

CYMOID adj resembling a cyme or cyma

CYMOL same as **>** CYMENE

CYMOLS > CYMOL

CYMOPHANE n yellow or green opalescent variety of chrysoberyl

CYMOSE adj having the characteristics of a cyme

CYMOSELY > CYMOSE

CYMOUS adj relating to a cyme

CYNANCHE *n* any disease characterised by inflammation and swelling of the throat
CYNANCHES > CYNANCHE
CYNEGETIC *adj* relating to hunting
CYNIC *n* person who believes that people always act selfishly ▷ *adj* of or relating to Sirius, the Dog Star
CYNICAL *adj* believing that people always act selfishly
CYNICALLY > CYNICAL
CYNICISM *n* attitude or beliefs of a cynic
CYNICISMS > CYNICISM
CYNICS > CYNIC
CYNODONT *n* carnivorous mammal-like reptile of the late Permian and Triassic periods, whose specialized teeth were well developed
CYNODONTS > CYNODONT
CYNOMOLGI *n* plural form of singular cynomolgus: type of monkey
CYNOSURAL > CYNOSURE
CYNOSURE *n* centre of attention
CYNOSURES > CYNOSURE
CYPHER *same as* > CIPHER
CYPHERED > CYPHER
CYPHERING > CYPHER
CYPHERS > CYPHER
CYPRES *n* legal doctrine
CYPRESES > CYPRES
CYPRESS *n* evergreen tree with dark green leaves
CYPRESSES > CYPRESS
CYPRIAN *n* prostitute or dancer
CYPRIANS > CYPRIAN
CYPRID *n* cypris
CYPRIDES > CYPRIS
CYPRIDS > CYPRID
CYPRINE *adj* relating to carp ▷ *n* type of silicate mineral
CYPRINES > CYPRINE
CYPRINID *n* type of mainly freshwater fish, usu with toothless jaws and cycloid scales, such as the carp, tench, roach, rudd, and dace
CYPRINIDS > CYPRINID
CYPRINOID *n* type of fish belonging to the suborder which includes cyprinids, electric eels, and loaches
CYPRIS *n* member of the genus Cypris (small bivalve

freshwater crustaceans)
CYPRUS *same as* > CYPRESS
CYPRUSES > CYPRUS
CYPSELA *n* dry one-seeded fruit of the daisy and related plants
CYPSELAE > CYPSELA
CYST *n* (abnormal) sac in the body containing fluid or soft matter
CYSTEIN *same as* > CYSTEINE
CYSTEINE *n* sulphur-containing amino acid
CYSTEINES > CYSTEINE
CYSTEINIC > CYSTEINE
CYSTEINS > CYSTEIN
CYSTIC *adj* of, relating to, or resembling a cyst
CYSTID *n* cystidean
CYSTIDEAN *n* any echinoderm of the class Cystoidea, an extinct order of sea lilies
CYSTIDS > CYSTID
CYSTIFORM *adj* having the form of a cyst
CYSTINE *n* sulphur-containing amino acid
CYSTINES > CYSTINE
CYSTITIS *n* inflammation of the bladder
CYSTOCARP *n* reproductive body in red algae, developed after fertilization and consisting of filaments bearing carpospores
CYSTOCELE *n* hernia of the urinary bladder, esp one protruding into the vagina
CYSTOID *adj* resembling a cyst or bladder ▷ *n* tissue mass that resembles a cyst but lacks an outer membrane
CYSTOIDS > CYSTOID
CYSTOLITH *n* knoblike deposit of calcium carbonate in the epidermal cells of such plants as the stinging nettle
CYSTOTOMY *n* surgical incision into the gall bladder or urinary bladder
CYSTS > CYST
CYTASE *n* cellulose-dissolving enzyme
CYTASES > CYTASE
CYTASTER *another word for* > ASTER

CYTASTERS > CYTASTER
CYTE *n* biological cell
CYTES > CYTE
CYTIDINE *n* nucleoside formed by the condensation of cytosine and ribose
CYTIDINES > CYTIDINE
CYTIDYLIC *adj* as in *cytidylic acid* nucleotide that is found in DNA
CYTISI > CYTISUS
CYTISINE *n* poisonous alkaloid found in laburnum seeds
CYTISINES > CYTISINE
CYTISUS *n* any plant of the broom genus, Cytisus
CYTODE *n* mass of protoplasm without a nucleus
CYTODES > CYTODE
CYTOGENY *n* origin and development of plant cells
CYTOID *adj* resembling a cell
CYTOKINE *n* any of various proteins, secreted by cells, that carry signals to neighbouring cells. Cytokines include interferon
CYTOKINES > CYTOKINE
CYTOKININ *n* any of a group of plant hormones that promote cell division and retard ageing in plants
CYTOLOGIC > CYTOLOGY
CYTOLOGY *n* study of plant and animal cells
CYTOLYSES > CYTOLYSIS
CYTOLYSIN *n* substance that can partially or completely destroy animal cells
CYTOLYSIS *n* dissolution of cells, esp by the destruction of their membranes
CYTOLYTIC > CYTOLYSIS
CYTOMETER *n* glass slide used to count and measure blood cells
CYTOMETRY *n* counting of blood cells using a cytometer
CYTON *n* main part of a neuron
CYTONS > CYTON
CYTOPATHY *n* disease of a cell
CYTOPENIA *n* blood disorder where there is a

deficiency in the blood cells
CYTOPLASM *n* protoplasm of a cell excluding the nucleus
CYTOPLAST *n* intact cytoplasm of a single cell
CYTOSINE *n* white crystalline pyrimidine occurring in nucleic acids
CYTOSINES > CYTOSINE
CYTOSOL *n* solution in a biological cell
CYTOSOLIC > CYTOSOL
CYTOSOLS > CYTOSOL
CYTOSOME *n* body of a cell excluding its nucleus
CYTOSOMES > CYTOSOME
CYTOTAXES > CYTOTAXIS
CYTOTAXIS *n* movement of cells due to external stimulation
CYTOTOXIC *adj* poisonous to living cells: denoting certain drugs used in the treatment of leukaemia and other cancers
CYTOTOXIN *n* any substance that is poisonous to living cells
CZAPKA *n* leather and felt peaked military helmet of Polish origin
CZAPKAS > CZAPKA
CZAR *same as* > TSAR
CZARDAS *n* Hungarian national dance of alternating slow and fast sections
CZARDASES > CZARDAS
CZARDOM > CZAR
CZARDOMS > CZAR
CZAREVICH *n* son of a czar
CZAREVNA *a variant spelling (esp US) of* > TSAREVNA
CZAREVNAS > CZAREVNA
CZARINA *variant spelling (esp US) of* > TSARINA
CZARINAS > CZARINA
CZARISM *a variant spelling (esp US) of* > TSARISM
CZARISMS > CZARISM
CZARIST *n* a supporter of the czar
CZARISTS > CZARISM
CZARITSA *n* Russian empress
CZARITSAS > CZARITSA
CZARITZA *same as* > CZARINA
CZARITZAS > CZARINA
CZARS > CZAR

Dd

DA *n* Burmese knife

DAAL *n* (in Indian cookery) split pulses

DAALS > DAAL

DAB *vb* pat lightly ▷ *n* small amount of something soft or moist

DABBA *n* in Indian cookery, round metal box used to transport hot food

DABBAS > DABBA

DABBED > DAB

DABBER *n* pad used by printers for applying ink by hand

DABBERS > DABBER

DABBING > DAB

DABBITIES > DABBITY

DABBITY *n* temporary tattoo

DABBLE *vb* be involved in something superficially

DABBLED > DABBLE

DABBLER > DABBLE

DABBLERS > DABBLE

DABBLES > DABBLE

DABBLING > DABBLE

DABBLINGS > DABBLE

DABCHICK *n* type of small grebe

DABCHICKS > DABCHICK

DABS > DAB

DABSTER *n* incompetent or amateurish worker

DABSTERS > DABSTER

DACE *n* small European freshwater fish

DACES > DACE

DACHA *n* country cottage in Russia

DACHAS > DACHA

DACHSHUND *n* dog with a long body and short legs

DACITE *n* volcanic rock

DACITES > DACITE

DACK *vb* remove the trousers from (someone) by force

DACKED > DACK

DACKER *vb* walk slowly

DACKERED > DACKER

DACKERING > DACKER

DACKERS > DACKER

DACKING > DACK

DACKS > DACK

DACOIT *n* (in India and Myanmar) a member of a gang of armed robbers

DACOITAGE *n* robbery by armed gang

DACOITIES > DACOITY

DACOITS > DACOIT

DACOITY *n* (in India and Myanmar) robbery by an armed gang

DACQUOISE *n* cake with meringue layers

DACRON *n* US tradename for a synthetic polyester fibre or fabric

DACRONS > DACRON

DACTYL *n* metrical foot of three syllables, one long followed by two short

DACTYLAR *adj* poetry term

DACTYLI > DACTYLUS

DACTYLIC *same as* > DACTYL

DACTYLICS > DACTYLIC

DACTYLIST *n* poet

DACTYLS > DACTYL

DACTYLUS *n* tip of a squid's tentacular club

DAD *n* father ▷ *vb* act or treat as a father

DADA *n* nihilistic artistic movement of the early 20th century

DADAH *n* illegal drugs

DADAHS > DADAH

DADAISM *same as* > DADA

DADAISMS > DADAISM

DADAIST > DADA

DADAISTIC > DADA

DADAISTS > DADA

DADAS > DADA

DADCHELOR *adj* as in *dadchelor party* party held for a prospective father

DADDED > DAD

DADDIES > DADDY

DADDING > DAD

DADDLE *vb* walk unsteadily

DADDLED > DADDLE

DADDLES > DADDLE

DADDLING > DADDLE

DADDOCK *n* core of a dead tree

DADDOCKS > DADDOCK

DADDY *n* father

DADGUM *mild form of* > DAMNED

DADO *n* lower part of an interior wall decorated differently from the upper part ▷ *vb* provide with a dado

DADOED > DADO

DADOES > DADO

DADOING > DADO

DADOS > DADO

DADS > DAD

DAE *a Scot word for* > DO

DAEDAL *adj* skilful or intricate

DAEDALEAN *same as* > DAEDALIAN

DAEDALIAN *adj* of, relating to, or resembling the work of Daedalus, the Athenian architect and inventor of Greek mythology

DAEDALIC *same as* > DAEDALIAN

DAEING > DAE

DAEMON *same as* > DEMON

DAEMONES > DAEMON

DAEMONIC > DAEMON

DAEMONS > DAEMON

DAES > DAE

DAFF *vb* frolic

DAFFED > DAFF

DAFFIER > DAFFY

DAFFIES > DAFFY

DAFFIEST > DAFFY

DAFFILY > DAFFY

DAFFINESS > DAFFY

DAFFING > DAFF

DAFFINGS > DAFF

DAFFODIL *n* yellow trumpet-shaped flower that blooms in spring ▷ *adj* brilliant yellow

DAFFODILS > DAFFODIL

DAFFS > DAFF

DAFFY *another word for* > DAFT

DAFT *adj* foolish or crazy

DAFTAR *Indian word for* > OFFICE

DAFTARS > DAFTAR

DAFTER > DAFT

DAFTEST > DAFT

DAFTIE *n* foolish person

DAFTIES > DAFTIE

DAFTLY > DAFT

DAFTNESS > DAFT

DAG *n* character ▷ *vb* cut daglocks from sheep

DAGABA *n* shrine for Buddhist relics

DAGABAS > DAGABA

DAGGA *n* cannabis

DAGGAS > DAGGA

DAGGED > DAG

DAGGER > DAG

DAGGERED > DAG

DAGGERING > DAG

DAGGERS > DAG

DAGGIER > DAGGY

DAGGIEST > DAGGY

DAGGING > DAG

DAGGINGS > DAG

DAGGLE *vb* trail through water

DAGGLED > DAGGLE

DAGGLES > DAGGLE

DAGGLING > DAGGLE

DAGGY *adj* amusing

DAGLOCK *n* dung-caked lock of wool around the hindquarters of a sheep

DAGLOCKS > DAGLOCK

DAGO *n* offensive term for a member of a Latin race, esp a Spaniard or Portuguese

DAGOBA *n* dome-shaped Buddhist shrine

DAGOBAS > DAGOBA

DAGOES > DAGO

DAGOS > DAGO

DAGS > DAG

DAGWOOD *n* European shrub

DAGWOODS > DAGWOOD

DAH *n* long sound used in combination with the short sound in the spoken representation of Morse and other telegraphic codes

DAHABEAH *n* houseboat used on the Nile

DAHABEAHS > DAHABEAH

DAHABEEAH *n* Egyptian houseboat

DAHABIAH *same as* > DAHABEAH

DAHABIAHS > DAHABIAH

DAHABIEH *n* Egyptian houseboat

DAHABIEHS > DAHABIEH

DAHABIYA *n* Egyptian houseboat

DAHABIYAH *n* Egyptian houseboat

DAHABIYAS > DAHABIYA

DAHABIYEH *n* Egyptian houseboat

DAHL *same as* > DHAL

DAHLIA *n* brightly coloured garden flower

DAHLIAS > DAHLIA

DAHLS > DAHL

DAHOON *n* evergreen shrub

DAHOONS > DAHOON

DAHS > DAH
DAIDLE vb waddle about
DAIDLED > DAIDLE
DAIDLES > DAIDLE
DAIDLING > DAIDLE
DAIDZEIN n type of protein
DAIDZEINS > DAIDZEIN
DAIKER vb walk slowly
DAIKERED > DAIKER
DAIKERING > DAIKER
DAIKERS > DAIKER
DAIKO n Japanese drum
DAIKON another name for > MOOLI
DAIKONS > DAIKON
DAIKOS > DAIKO
DAILIES > DAILY
DAILINESS > DAILY
DAILY adj occurring every day or every weekday ▷ adv every day ▷ n daily newspaper
DAILYNESS > DAILY
DAIMEN adj occasional
DAIMIO same as > DAIMYO
DAIMIOS > DAIMIO
DAIMOKU n Nichiren Buddhist chant
DAIMOKUS > DAIMOKU
DAIMON same as > DEMON
DAIMONES pl n disembodied souls
DAIMONIC > DAIMON
DAIMONS > DAIMON
DAIMYO n magnate in Japan from the 11th to the 19th century
DAIMYOS > DAIMYO
DAINE vb condescend
DAINED > DAINE
DAINES > DAINE
DAINING > DAINE
DAINT adj dainty ▷ n dainty
DAINTIER > DAINTY
DAINTIES > DAINTY
DAINTIEST > DAINTY
DAINTILY > DAINTY
DAINTS > DAINT
DAINTY adj delicate or elegant ▷ n small cake or sweet
DAIQUIRI n iced drink containing rum, lime juice, and sugar
DAIQUIRIS > DAIQUIRI
DAIRIES > DAIRY
DAIRY n place for the processing or sale of milk and its products ▷ adj of milk or its products
DAIRYING n business of producing, processing, and selling dairy products
DAIRYINGS > DAIRYING
DAIRYMAID n (formerly) woman employed to milk cows
DAIRYMAN n man employed to look after cows
DAIRYMEN > DAIRYMAN

DAIS n raised platform in a hall, used by a speaker
DAISES > DAIS
DAISHIKI n upper garment
DAISHIKIS > DAISHIKI
DAISIED > DAISY
DAISIES > DAISY
DAISY n small wild flower with a yellow centre and white petals
DAK n system of mail delivery or passenger transport
DAKER vb walk slowly
DAKERED > DAKER
DAKERHEN n European bird
DAKERHENS > DAKERHEN
DAKERING > DAKER
DAKERS > DAKER
DAKOIT same as > DACOIT
DAKOITI same as > DAKOIT
DAKOITIES > DAKOIT
DAKOITIS > DAKOIT
DAKOITS > DAKOIT
DAKOITY n armed robbery
DAKS an informal name for > TROUSERS
DAL same as > DECALITRE
DALAPON n herbicide
DALAPONS > DALAPON
DALASI n standard monetary unit of The Gambia, divided into 100 bututs
DALASIS > DALASI
DALE n (esp in N England) valley
DALED same as > DALETH
DALEDH n letter of Hebrew alphabet
DALEDHS > DALEDH
DALEDS > DALED
DALES > DALE
DALESMAN n person living in a dale, esp in the dales of N England
DALESMEN > DALESMAN
DALETH n fourth letter of the Hebrew alphabet, transliterated as d or, when final, dh
DALETHS > DALETH
DALGYTE another name for > BILBY
DALGYTES > DALGYTE
DALI n type of tree
DALIS > DALI
DALLE > DALLES
DALLES pl n stretch of a river between high rock walls, with rapids and dangerous currents
DALLIANCE n flirtation
DALLIED > DALLY
DALLIER > DALLY
DALLIERS > DALLY
DALLIES > DALLY
DALLOP n semisolid lump
DALLOPS > DALLOP
DALLY vb waste time

DALLYING > DALLY
DALMAHOY n bushy wig
DALMAHOYS > DALMAHOY
DALMATIAN n breed of dog characterized by its striking spotted markings
DALMATIC n wide-sleeved tunic-like vestment open at the sides, worn by deacons and bishops
DALMATICS > DALMATIC
DALS > DAL
DALT n foster child
DALTON n atomic mass unit
DALTONIAN > DALTON
DALTONIC > DALTONISM
DALTONISM n colour blindness, esp the confusion of red and green
DALTONS > DALTON
DALTS > DALT
DAM n barrier built across a river to create a lake ▷ vb build a dam across (a river)
DAMAGE vb harm, spoil ▷ n harm to a person or thing
DAMAGED > DAMAGE
DAMAGER > DAMAGE
DAMAGERS > DAMAGE
DAMAGES pl n money awarded as compensation for injury or loss
DAMAGING > DAMAGE
DAMAN n the Syrian rock hyrax
DAMANS > DAMAN
DAMAR same as > DAMMAR
DAMARS > DAMMAR
DAMASCENE vb ornament (metal, esp steel) by etching or by inlaying, usually with gold or silver ▷ n design or article produced by this process ▷ adj of or relating to this process
DAMASK n fabric with a pattern woven into it, used for tablecloths etc ▷ vb ornament (metal) by etching or inlaying, usually with gold or silver
DAMASKED > DAMASK
DAMASKEEN vb decorate metal
DAMASKIN vb decorate metal
DAMASKING > DAMASK
DAMASKINS > DAMASKIN
DAMASKS > DAMASK
DAMASQUIN vb decorate metal
DAMASSIN n patterned damask
DAMASSINS > DAMASSIN
DAMBOARD n draughtboard
DAMBOARDS > DAMBOARD
DAMBROD n draughtboard
DAMBRODS > DAMBROD
DAME n woman

DAMES > DAME
DAMEWORT n sweet-scented perennial plant with mauve or white flowers
DAMEWORTS > DAMEWORT
DAMFOOL adj foolish ▷ n foolish person
DAMFOOLS > DAMFOOL
DAMIANA n herbal medicine
DAMIANAS > DAMIANA
DAMMAR n any of various resins obtained from SE Asian trees
DAMMARS > DAMMAR
DAMME interj exclamation of surprise
DAMMED > DAM
DAMMER same as > DAMMAR
DAMMERS > DAMMER
DAMMING > DAM
DAMMIT interj exclamation of surprise
DAMN interj exclamation of annoyance ▷ adj extreme(ly) ▷ vb condemn as bad or worthless
DAMNABLE adj annoying
DAMNABLY adv in a detestable manner
DAMNATION interj exclamation of anger ▷ n eternal punishment
DAMNATORY adj threatening or occasioning condemnation
DAMNDEST n utmost
DAMNDESTS > DAMNDEST
DAMNED adj condemned to hell ▷ adv extreme or extremely
DAMNEDER > DAMNED
DAMNEDEST n utmost
DAMNER n person who damns
DAMNERS > DAMNER
DAMNEST same as > DAMNEDEST
DAMNIFIED > DAMNIFY
DAMNIFIES > DAMNIFY
DAMNIFY vb cause loss or damage to (a person)
DAMNING > DAMN
DAMNINGLY > DAMN
DAMNS > DAMN
DAMOISEL same as > DAMSEL
DAMOISELS > DAMOISEL
DAMOSEL same as > DAMSEL
DAMOSELS > DAMOSEL
DAMOZEL n a young girl or unmarried woman
DAMOZELS > DAMOZEL
DAMP adj slightly wet ▷ n slight wetness, moisture ▷ vb make damp
DAMPED > DAMP
DAMPEN vb reduce the intensity of

DAMPENED > DAMPEN
DAMPENER > DAMPEN
DAMPENERS > DAMPEN
DAMPENING > DAMPEN
DAMPENS > DAMPEN
DAMPER *n* movable plate to regulate the draught in a fire
DAMPERS > DAMPER
DAMPEST > DAMP
DAMPIER > DAMPY
DAMPIEST > DAMPY
DAMPING *n* moistening or wetting
DAMPINGS > DAMPING
DAMPISH > DAMP
DAMPLY > DAMP
DAMPNESS > DAMP
DAMPS > DAMP
DAMPY *adj* damp
DAMS > DAM
DAMSEL *n* young woman
DAMSELFLY *n* type of insect similar to but smaller than a dragonfly
DAMSELS > DAMSEL
DAMSON *n* small blue-black plumlike fruit
DAMSONS > DAMSON
DAN *n* in judo, any of the 10 black-belt grades of proficiency
DANAZOL *n* type of drug
DANAZOLS > DANAZOL
DANCE *vb* move the feet and body rhythmically in time to music ▷ *n* series of steps and movements in time to music
DANCEABLE > DANCE
DANCED > DANCE
DANCEHALL *n* style of dance-oriented reggae
DANCER > DANCE
DANCERS > DANCE
DANCES > DANCE
DANCETTE *another name for* > CHEVRON
DANCETTEE *adj* having a zigzag pattern
DANCETTES > DANCETTE
DANCETTY *adj* having a zigzag pattern
DANCEY *adj* of, relating to, or resembling dance music
DANCICAL *n* type of dance show set to pop music
DANCICALS > DANCICAL
DANCIER > DANCEY
DANCIEST > DANCEY
DANCING > DANCE
DANCINGS > DANCE
DANCY *adj* (of music) appropriate for dancing
DANDELION *n* yellow-flowered wild plant
DANDER *n* stroll ▷ *vb* stroll
DANDERED > DANDER
DANDERING > DANDER
DANDERS > DANDER
DANDIACAL *adj* like a dandy
DANDIER > DANDY

DANDIES > DANDY
DANDIEST > DANDY
DANDIFIED > DANDIFY
DANDIFIES > DANDIFY
DANDIFY *vb* dress like or cause to resemble a dandy
DANDILY > DANDY
DANDIPRAT *n* small English coin minted in the 16th century
DANDLE *vb* move (a child) up and down on one's knee
DANDLED > DANDLE
DANDLER > DANDLE
DANDLERS > DANDLE
DANDLES > DANDLE
DANDLING > DANDLE
DANDRIFF *same as* > DANDRUFF
DANDRIFFS > DANDRIFF
DANDRUFF *n* loose scales of dry dead skin shed from the scalp
DANDRUFFS > DANDRUFF
DANDRUFFY > DANDRUFF
DANDY *n* man who is overconcerned with the elegance of his appearance ▷ *adj* very good
DANDYFUNK *n* ship's biscuit
DANDYISH > DANDY
DANDYISM > DANDY
DANDYISMS > DANDY
DANDYPRAT *n* English coin
DANEGELD *n* tax levied in Anglo-Saxon England to provide protection money for, or to finance forces to oppose, Viking invaders
DANEGELDS > DANEGELD
DANEGELT *same as* > DANEGELD
DANEGELTS > DANEGELT
DANELAGH *same as* > DANELAW
DANELAGHS > DANELAGH
DANELAW *n* Danish law in parts of Anglo-Saxon England
DANELAWS > DANELAW
DANEWEED *n* dwarf elder
DANEWEEDS > DANEWEED
DANEWORT *n* dwarf elder
DANEWORTS > DANEWORT
DANG *a euphemistic word for* > DAMN
DANGED > DANG
DANGER *n* possibility of being injured or killed ▷ *vb* in archaic usage, endanger
DANGERED > DANGER
DANGERING > DANGER
DANGEROUS *adj* likely or able to cause injury or harm
DANGERS > DANGER
DANGING > DANG
DANGLE *vb* hang loosely ▷ *n* act of dangling or something that dangles

DANGLED > DANGLE
DANGLER > DANGLE
DANGLERS > DANGLE
DANGLES > DANGLE
DANGLIER > DANGLE
DANGLIEST > DANGLE
DANGLING > DANGLE
DANGLINGS > DANGLE
DANGLY > DANGLE
DANGS > DANG
DANIO *n* type of tropical freshwater fish
DANIOS > DANIO
DANISH *n* sweet pastry
DANISHES > DANISH
DANK *adj* unpleasantly damp and chilly ▷ *n* unpleasant damp and chilliness
DANKER > DANK
DANKEST > DANK
DANKISH > DANK
DANKLY > DANK
DANKNESS > DANK
DANKS > DANK
DANNEBROG *n* Danish flag
DANNIES > DANNY
DANNY *n* hand (used esp when addressing children)
DANS > DAN
DANSAK *n* type of Indian dish
DANSAKS > DANSAK
DANSEUR *n* male ballet dancer
DANSEURS > DANSEUR
DANSEUSE *n* female ballet dancer
DANSEUSES > DANSEUSE
DANT *vb* intimidate
DANTED > DANT
DANTHONIA *n* type of grass of N temperate regions and S America
DANTING > DANT
DANTON *same as* > DAUNTON
DANTONED > DANTON
DANTONING > DANTON
DANTONS > DANTON
DANTS > DANT
DAP *vb* engage in type of fly fishing
DAPHNE *n* ornamental Eurasian shrub
DAPHNES > DAPHNE
DAPHNIA *n* type of water flea
DAPHNIAS > DAPHNIA
DAPHNID *n* water flea
DAPHNIDS > DAPHNID
DAPPED > DAP
DAPPER *adj* (of a man) neat in appearance ▷ *n* fisherman or -woman who uses a bobbing bait
DAPPERER > DAPPER
DAPPEREST > DAPPER
DAPPERLY > DAPPER
DAPPERS > DAPPER
DAPPING > DAP
DAPPLE *vb* mark or become marked with

spots or patches of a different colour ▷ *n* mottled or spotted markings ▷ *adj* marked with dapples or spots
DAPPLED > DAPPLE
DAPPLES > DAPPLE
DAPPLING > DAPPLE
DAPS > DAP
DAPSONE *n* antimicrobial drug
DAPSONES > DAPSONE
DAQUIRI *n* rum cocktail
DAQUIRIS > DAQUIRI
DARAF *n* unit of elastance equal to a reciprocal farad
DARAFS > DARAF
DARB *n* something excellent
DARBAR *n* hall in Sikh temple
DARBARS > DARBAR
DARBIES *pl n* handcuffs
DARBS > DARB
DARCIES > DARCY
DARCY *n* unit expressing the permeability coefficient of rock
DARCYS > DARCY
DARE *vb* be courageous enough to try (to do something) ▷ *n* challenge to do something risky
DARED > DARE
DAREDEVIL *n* recklessly bold person ▷ *adj* recklessly bold or daring
DAREFUL *adj* daring
DARER > DARE
DARERS > DARE
DARES > DARE
DARESAY *vb* venture to say
DARG *n* day's work
DARGA *n* Muslim shrine
DARGAH *n* tomb of a Muslim saint
DARGAHS > DARGAH
DARGAS > DARGA
DARGLE *n* wooded hollow
DARGLES > DARGLE
DARGS > DARG
DARI *n* variety of sorghum
DARIC *n* gold coin of ancient Persia
DARICS > DARIC
DARING *adj* willing to take risks ▷ *n* courage to do dangerous things
DARINGLY > DARING
DARINGS > DARING
DARIOLE *n* small cup-shaped mould
DARIOLES > DARIOLE
DARIS > DARI
DARK *adj* having little or no light ▷ *n* absence of light ▷ *vb* in archaic usage, darken
DARKED > DARK
DARKEN *vb* make or become dark or darker
DARKENED > DARKEN

DARKENER > DARKEN
DARKENERS > DARKEN
DARKENING > DARKEN
DARKENS > DARKEN
DARKER > DARK
DARKEST > DARK
DARKEY same as > DARKY
DARKEYS > DARKEY
DARKFIELD n as in
darkfield microscope kind of
microscope
DARKIE same as > DARKY
DARKIES > DARKY
DARKING > DARK
DARKISH > DARK
DARKLE vb grow dark
DARKLED > DARKLE
DARKLES > DARKLE
DARKLIER > DARK
DARKLIEST > DARK
DARKLING adj in the dark
or night
DARKLINGS adv in
darkness
DARKLY > DARK
DARKMANS n slang term
for night-time
DARKNESS > DARK
DARKNET n covert
communication network
on the Internet
DARKNETS > DARKNET
DARKROOM n darkened
room for processing
photographic film
DARKROOMS > DARKROOM
DARKS > DARK
DARKSOME adj dark or
darkish
DARKY n offensive word for
a Black person
DARLING n much-loved
person ▷ adj much-loved
DARLINGLY > DARLING
DARLINGS > DARLING
DARN vb mend (a garment)
with a series of interwoven
stitches ▷ n patch of
darned work
DARNATION mild form of
> DAMNATION
DARNDEST n utmost
DARNDESTS > DARNDEST
DARNED adj damned
DARNEDER > DARNED
DARNEDEST a euphemistic
word for > DAMNEDEST
DARNEL n weed that
grows in grain fields
DARNELS > DARNEL
DARNER > DARN
DARNERS > DARN
DARNEST same as
> DARNDEST
DARNESTS > DARNEST
DARNING > DARN
DARNINGS > DARN
DARNS > DARN
DAROGHA n in India,
manager
DAROGHAS > DAROGHA
DARRAIGN same as
> DERAIGN

DARRAIGNE vb clear from
guilt
DARRAIGNS > DARRAIGN
DARRAIN vb clear of guilt
DARRAINE vb clear of guilt
DARRAINED > DARRAINE
DARRAINES > DARRAINE
DARRAINS > DARRAIN
DARRAYN vb clear of guilt
DARRAYNED > DARRAYN
DARRAYNS > DARRAYN
DARRE vb dare
DARRED > DARRE
DARRES > DARRE
DARRING > DARRE
DARSHAN n Hindu
blessing
DARSHANS > DARSHAN
DART n small narrow
pointed missile ▷ vb move
or direct quickly and
suddenly
DARTBOARD n circular
board used as the target in
the game of darts
DARTED > DART
DARTER n type of aquatic
bird
DARTERS > DARTER
DARTING > DART
DARTINGLY > DART
DARTITIS n nervous
twitching while playing
darts
DARTLE vb move swiftly
DARTLED > DARTLE
DARTLES > DARTLE
DARTLING > DARTLE
DARTRE n skin disease
DARTRES > DARTRE
DARTROUS adj having a
skin disease
DARTS n game in which
darts are thrown at a
dartboard
DARZI n tailor in India
DARZIS > DARZI
DAS > DA
DASH vb move quickly
▷ n sudden quick
movement
DASHBOARD n instrument
panel in a vehicle
DASHED > DASH
DASHEEN another name for
> TARO
DASHEENS > DASHEEN
DASHEKI n upper
garment
DASHEKIS > DASHEKI
DASHER n one of the
boards surrounding an
ice-hockey rink
DASHERS > DASHER
DASHES > DASH
DASHI n clear stock made
from dried fish and kelp
DASHIER > DASHY
DASHIEST > DASHY
DASHIKI n large
loose-fitting buttonless
upper garment
DASHIKIS > DASHIKI

DASHING adj stylish and
attractive
DASHINGLY > DASHING
DASHIS > DASHI
DASHLIGHT n light
illuminating the
dashboard of an
automobile
DASHPOT n device for
damping vibrations
DASHPOTS > DASHPOT
DASHY adj showy
DASSIE n type of hoofed
rodent-like animal
DASSIES > DASSIE
DASTARD n contemptible
sneaking coward
DASTARDLY adj wicked
and cowardly
DASTARDS > DASTARD
DASTARDY n cowardice
DASYMETER n device for
measuring density of
gases
DASYPOD n armadillo
DASYPODS > DASYPOD
DASYURE n small
marsupial of Australia,
New Guinea, and adjacent
islands
DASYURES > DASYURE
DATA n information
consisting of
observations,
measurements, or facts
DATABANK n store of a
large amount of
information, esp in a form
that can be handled by a
computer
DATABANKS > DATABANK
DATABASE n store of
information in a form that
can be easily handled by a
computer ▷ vb put data
into a database
DATABASED > DATABASE
DATABASES > DATABASE
DATABLE > DATE
DATABUS n computing
term
DATABUSES > DATABUS
DATACARD n smart card
DATACARDS > DATACARD
DATACOMMS n computing
term
DATAFLOW n as in *dataflow
architecture* means of
arranging computer data
processing in which
operations are governed
by the data present and
the processing it requires
rather than by a
prewritten program that
awaits data to be
processed
DATAGLOVE n computing
term
DATAGRAM n (in
computing) self-contained
unit of data transmitted in
a packet-switched
network

DATAGRAMS > DATAGRAM
DATAL adj slow-witted
▷ n day labour
DATALLER n worker paid
by the day
DATALLERS > DATALLER
DATALS > DATAL
DATARIA n Roman
Catholic office
DATARIAS > DATARIA
DATARIES > DATARY
DATARY n head of the
dataria
DATCHA same as > DACHA
DATCHAS > DATCHA
DATE n specified day of the
month ▷ vb mark with the
date
DATEABLE > DATE
DATEBOOK n list of
forthcoming events
DATEBOOKS > DATEBOOK
DATED adj old-fashioned
DATEDLY > DATED
DATEDNESS > DATED
DATELESS > DATE
DATELINE n information
about the place and time a
story was written, placed
at the top of the article
DATELINED > DATELINE
DATELINES > DATELINE
DATER n person who dates
DATERS > DATER
DATES > DATE
DATING n any of several
techniques for
establishing the age of
objects
DATINGS > DATING
DATIVAL > DATIVE
DATIVE adj denoting a
grammatical case
▷ n grammatical case
DATIVELY > DATIVE
DATIVES > DATIVE
DATO n chief of any of
certain Muslim tribes in
the Philippine Islands
DATOLITE n colourless
mineral
DATOLITES > DATOLITE
DATOS > DATO
DATTO n Datsun car
DATTOS > DATTO
DATUM n single piece of
information in the form of
a fact or statistic
DATUMS > DATUM
DATURA n type of plant
DATURAS > DATURA
DATURIC > DATURA
DATURINE n poisonous
alkaloid
DATURINES > DATURINE
DAUB vb smear or spread
quickly or clumsily ▷ n
crude or badly done
painting
DAUBE n braised meat
stew
DAUBED > DAUB
DAUBER > DAUB

DAUBERIES > DAUBERY
DAUBERS > DAUB
DAUBERY n act or an instance of daubing
DAUBES > DAUBE
DAUBIER > DAUB
DAUBIEST > DAUB
DAUBING > DAUB
DAUBINGLY > DAUB
DAUBINGS > DAUB
DAUBRIES > DAUBRY
DAUBRY n unskilful painting
DAUBS > DAUB
DAUBY > DAUB
DAUD n lump or chunk of something ▷ vb (in dialect) whack
DAUDED > DAUD
DAUDING > DAUD
DAUDS > DAUD
DAUGHTER n female child ▷ adj denoting a cell, chromosome, etc. produced by the division of one of its own kind
DAUGHTERS > DAUGHTER
DAULT n foster child
DAULTS > DAULT
DAUNDER vb stroll
DAUNDERED > DAUNDER
DAUNDERS > DAUNDER
DAUNER vb stroll
DAUNERED > DAUNER
DAUNERING > DAUNER
DAUNERS > DAUNER
DAUNT vb intimidate
DAUNTED > DAUNT
DAUNTER > DAUNT
DAUNTERS > DAUNT
DAUNTING adj intimidating or worrying
DAUNTLESS adj fearless
DAUNTON vb dishearten
DAUNTONED > DAUNTON
DAUNTONS > DAUNTON
DAUNTS > DAUNT
DAUPHIN n (formerly) eldest son of the king of France
DAUPHINE n wife of a dauphin
DAUPHINES > DAUPHINE
DAUPHINS > DAUPHIN
DAUR a Scot word for > DARE
DAURED > DAUR
DAURING > DAUR
DAURS > DAUR
DAUT vb fondle
DAUTED > DAUT
DAUTIE n darling
DAUTIES > DAUTIE
DAUTING > DAUT
DAUTS > DAUT
DAVEN vb pray
DAVENED > DAVEN
DAVENING > DAVEN
DAVENPORT n small writing table with drawers
DAVENS > DAVEN
DAVIDIA n Chinese shrub
DAVIDIAS > DAVIDIA

DAVIES > DAVY
DAVIT n crane, usu one of a pair, at a ship's side, for lowering and hoisting a lifeboat
DAVITS > DAVIT
DAVY n miner's safety lamp
DAW n archaic, dialect, or poetic name for a jackdaw ▷ vb old word for dawn
DAWAH n practice of educating non-Muslims about the message of Islam
DAWAHS > DAWAH
DAWBAKE n foolish or slow-witted person
DAWBAKES > DAWBAKE
DAWBRIES > DAWBRY
DAWBRY n unskilful painting
DAWCOCK n male jackdaw
DAWCOCKS > DAWCOCK
DAWD vb thump
DAWDED > DAWD
DAWDING > DAWD
DAWDLE vb walk slowly, lag behind
DAWDLED > DAWDLE
DAWDLER > DAWDLE
DAWDLERS > DAWDLE
DAWDLES > DAWDLE
DAWDLING > DAWDLE
DAWDS > DAWD
DAWED > DAW
DAWEN > DAW
DAWING > DAW
DAWISH > DAW
DAWK same as > DAK
DAWKS > DAWK
DAWN n daybreak ▷ vb begin to grow light
DAWNED > DAWN
DAWNER vb stroll
DAWNERED > DAWNER
DAWNERING > DAWNER
DAWNERS > DAWNER
DAWNEY adj (of a person) dull or slow
DAWNING > DAWN
DAWNINGS > DAWN
DAWNLIKE > DAWN
DAWNS > DAWN
DAWS > DAW
DAWSONITE n mineral
DAWT vb fondle
DAWTED > DAWT
DAWTIE n darling
DAWTIES > DAWTIE
DAWTING > DAWT
DAWTS > DAWT
DAY n period of 24 hours
DAYAN n senior rabbi, esp one who sits in a religious court
DAYANIM > DAYAN
DAYANS > DAYAN
DAYBED n narrow bed for day use
DAYBEDS > DAYBED
DAYBOAT n small sailing boat with no sleeping accommodation

DAYBOATS > DAYBOAT
DAYBOOK n book in which transactions are recorded as they occur
DAYBOOKS > DAYBOOK
DAYBOY n boy who attends a boarding school but returns home each evening
DAYBOYS > DAYBOY
DAYBREAK n time in the morning when light first appears
DAYBREAKS > DAYBREAK
DAYCARE n care provided during the working day for people who might be at risk if left on their own
DAYCARES > DAYCARE
DAYCATION n day trip to a place
DAYCENTRE n building used for daycare or other welfare services
DAYCH vb thatch
DAYCHED > DAYCH
DAYCHES > DAYCH
DAYCHING > DAYCH
DAYDREAM n pleasant fantasy indulged in while awake ▷ vb indulge in idle fantasy
DAYDREAMS > DAYDREAM
DAYDREAMT > DAYDREAM
DAYDREAMY > DAYDREAM
DAYFLIES > DAYFLY
DAYFLOWER n type of tropical and subtropical plant with narrow pointed leaves and blue or purplish flowers which wilt quickly
DAYFLY another name for > MAYFLY
DAYGIRL n girl who attends a boarding school but returns home each evening
DAYGIRLS > DAYGIRL
DAYGLO n fluorescent colours
DAYGLOW n fluorescent colours
DAYGLOWS > DAYGLOW
DAYLIGHT n light from the sun
DAYLIGHTS pl n consciousness or wits
DAYLILIES > DAYLILY
DAYLILY n any of various plants having lily-like flowers
DAYLIT > DAYLIGHT
DAYLONG adv lasting the entire day
DAYMARE n bad dream during the day
DAYMARES > DAYMARE
DAYMARK n navigation aid
DAYMARKS > DAYMARK
DAYNT adj dainty ▷ n thing or condition that is extravagant or best
DAYNTS > DAYNT

DAYPACK n small rucksack
DAYPACKS > DAYPACK
DAYROOM n communal living room in a residential institution
DAYROOMS > DAYROOM
DAYS adv during the day, esp regularly
DAYSACK n rucksack
DAYSACKS > DAYSACK
DAYSAIL vb day trip on a sailing boat or yacht
DAYSAILED > DAYSAIL
DAYSAILER same as > DAYSAILOR
DAYSAILOR n small sailing boat with no sleeping accommodation
DAYSAILS > DAYSAIL
DAYSHELL n thistle
DAYSHELLS > DAYSHELL
DAYSIDE n side of a planet nearest the sun
DAYSIDES > DAYSIDE
DAYSMAN n umpire
DAYSMEN > DAYSMAN
DAYSPRING a poetic word for > DAWN
DAYSTAR a poetic word for > SUN
DAYSTARS > DAYSTAR
DAYTALE n day labour
DAYTALER n worker paid by the day
DAYTALERS > DAYTALER
DAYTALES > DAYTALE
DAYTIME n time from sunrise to sunset
DAYTIMES > DAYTIME
DAYWEAR n clothes for everyday or informal wear
DAYWEARS > DAYWEAR
DAYWORK n daytime work
DAYWORKER > DAYWORK
DAYWORKS > DAYWORK
DAZE vb stun, by a blow or shock ▷ n state of confusion or shock
DAZED > DAZE
DAZEDLY > DAZE
DAZEDNESS > DAZE
DAZER > DAZE
DAZERS > DAZE
DAZES > DAZE
DAZING > DAZE
DAZZLE vb impress greatly ▷ n bright light that dazzles
DAZZLED > DAZZLE
DAZZLER > DAZZLE
DAZZLERS > DAZZLE
DAZZLES > DAZZLE
DAZZLING > DAZZLE
DAZZLINGS > DAZZLING
DE prep of or from
DEACIDIFY vb removal acid from
DEACON n ordained minister ranking immediately below a priest ▷ vb make a deacon of
DEACONED > DEACON

DEACONESS n (in the early church and in some modern Churches) a female member of the laity with duties similar to those of a deacon

DEACONING > DEACON

DEACONRY n office or status of a deacon

DEACONS > DEACON

DEAD adj no longer alive ▷ n period during which coldness or darkness is most intense ▷ adv extremely ▷ vb in archaic usage, die or kill

DEADBEAT n lazy useless person

DEADBEATS > DEADBEAT

DEADBOLT n bolt operated without a spring

DEADBOLTS > DEADBOLT

DEADBOY same as > DEADMAN

DEADBOYS > DEADBOY

DEADED > DEAD

DEADEN vb make less intense

DEADENED > DEADEN

DEADENER > DEADEN

DEADENERS > DEADEN

DEADENING > DEADEN

DEADENS > DEADEN

DEADER > DEAD

DEADERS > DEAD

DEADEST > DEAD

DEADEYE n either of two disclike blocks used to tighten a shroud on a boat

DEADEYES > DEADEYE

DEADFALL n type of trap, used esp for catching large animals, in which a heavy weight falls to crush the prey

DEADFALLS > DEADFALL

DEADHEAD n person who does not pay on a bus, at a game, etc ▷ vb cut off withered flowers from (a plant)

DEADHEADS > DEADHEAD

DEADHOUSE n mortuary

DEADING > DEAD

DEADLIER > DEADLY

DEADLIEST > DEADLY

DEADLIFT vb weightlifting term

DEADLIFTS > DEADLIFT

DEADLIGHT n bull's-eye let into the deck or hull of a vessel to admit light to a cabin

DEADLINE n time limit ▷ vb put a time limit on an action, decision, etc

DEADLINED > DEADLINE

DEADLINES > DEADLINE

DEADLOCK n point in a dispute at which no agreement can be reached ▷ vb bring or come to a deadlock

DEADLOCKS > DEADLOCK

DEADLY adj likely to cause death ▷ adv extremely.

DEADMAN n item used in construction

DEADMEN > DEADMAN

DEADNESS > DEAD

DEADPAN adv showing no emotion or expression ▷ adj deliberately emotionless ▷ n deadpan expression or manner

DEADPANS > DEADPAN

DEADS > DEAD

DEADSTOCK n farm equipment

DEADWOOD n dead trees or branches

DEADWOODS > DEADWOOD

DEAERATE vb remove air from

DEAERATED > DEAERATE

DEAERATES > DEAERATE

DEAERATOR > DEAERATE

DEAF adj unable to hear

DEAFBLIND adj unable to hear or see

DEAFEN vb make deaf, esp temporarily

DEAFENED > DEAFEN

DEAFENING n excessively loud

DEAFENS > DEAFEN

DEAFER > DEAF

DEAFEST > DEAF

DEAFISH > DEAF

DEAFLY > DEAF

DEAFNESS > DEAF

DEAIR vb remove air from

DEAIRED > DEAIR

DEAIRING > DEAIR

DEAIRS > DEAIR

DEAL n agreement or transaction ▷ vb inflict (a blow) on ▷ adj of fir or pine

DEALATE adj (of insects) having lost their wings after mating ▷ n insect that has shed its wings

DEALATED same as > DEALATE

DEALATES > DEALATE

DEALATION > DEALATE

DEALBATE adj bleached

DEALER n person whose business involves buying and selling

DEALERS > DEALER

DEALFISH n long thin fish

DEALIGN vb fall out of agreement with (a political party)

DEALIGNED > DEALIGN

DEALIGNS > DEALIGN

DEALING > DEAL

DEALINGS pl n transactions or business relations

DEALMAKER n person who makes deals

DEALS > DEAL

DEALT > DEAL

DEAMINASE n enzyme that breaks down amino compounds

DEAMINATE vb remove one or more amino groups from (a molecule)

DEAMINISE same as > DEAMINATE

DEAMINIZE same as > DEAMINATE

DEAN n chief administrative official of a college or university faculty ▷ vb punish (a student) by sending them to the dean

DEANED > DEAN

DEANER n shilling

DEANERIES > DEANERY

DEANERS > DEANER

DEANERY n office or residence of a dean

DEANING > DEAN

DEANS > DEAN

DEANSHIP > DEAN

DEANSHIPS > DEAN

DEAR n someone regarded with affection ▷ adj much-loved

DEARE vb harm

DEARED > DEARE

DEARER > DEAR

DEARES > DEARE

DEAREST > DEAR

DEARESTS > DEAREST

DEARIE same as > DEARY

DEARIES > DEARY

DEARING > DEARE

DEARLING n darling

DEARLINGS > DEARLING

DEARLY adv very much

DEARN vb hide

DEARNED > DEARN

DEARNESS > DEAR

DEARNFUL adj secret

DEARNING > DEARN

DEARNLY > DEARN

DEARNS > DEARN

DEARS > DEAR

DEARTH n inadequate amount, scarcity

DEARTHS > DEARTH

DEARY n term of affection: now often sarcastic or facetious

DEASH vb remove ash from

DEASHED > DEASH

DEASHES > DEASH

DEASHING > DEASH

DEASIL adv in the direction of the apparent course of the sun ▷ n motion in this direction

DEASILS > DEASIL

DEASIUL n motion towards the sun

DEASIULS > DEASIUL

DEASOIL n motion towards the sun

DEASOILS > DEASOIL

DEATH n permanent end of life in a person or animal

DEATHBED n bed where a person is about to die or has just died

DEATHBEDS > DEATHBED

DEATHBLOW n thing or event that destroys hope

DEATHCARE adj relating to services helping arrange funerals

DEATHCUP n poisonous fungus

DEATHCUPS > DEATHCUP

DEATHFUL adj murderous

DEATHIER > DEATH

DEATHIEST > DEATH

DEATHLESS adj everlasting, because of fine qualities

DEATHLIER > DEATHLY

DEATHLIKE > DEATH

DEATHLY adv like death ▷ adj resembling death

DEATHS > DEATH

DEATHSMAN n executioner

DEATHSMEN > DEATHSMAN

DEATHTRAP n building, vehicle, etc, that is considered very unsafe

DEATHWARD adv heading towards death

DEATHY > DEATH

DEAVE vb deafen

DEAVED > DEAVE

DEAVES > DEAVE

DEAVING > DEAVE

DEAW n dew ▷ vb to cover with dew

DEAWED > DEAW

DEAWIE > DEAW

DEAWING > DEAW

DEAWS > DEAW

DEAWY > DEAW

DEB n debutante

DEBACLE n disastrous failure

DEBACLES > DEBACLE

DEBAG vb remove the trousers from (someone) by force

DEBAGGED > DEBAG

DEBAGGING > DEBAG

DEBAGS > DEBAG

DEBAR vb prevent, bar

DEBARK vb remove the bark from (a tree)

DEBARKED > DEBARK

DEBARKER > DEBARK

DEBARKERS > DEBARK

DEBARKING > DEBARK

DEBARKS > DEBARK

DEBARMENT > DEBAR

DEBARRASS vb relieve

DEBARRED > DEBAR

DEBARRING > DEBAR

DEBARS > DEBAR

DEBASE vb lower in value, quality, or character

DEBASED > DEBASE

DEBASER > DEBASE

DEBASERS > DEBASE

DEBASES > DEBASE

DEBASING > DEBASE

DEBATABLE adj not absolutely certain

DEBATABLY > DEBATABLE

DEBATE n discussion
▷ vb discuss formally
DEBATED ▷ DEBATE
DEBATEFUL adj
quarrelsome
DEBATER ▷ DEBATE
DEBATERS ▷ DEBATE
DEBATES ▷ DEBATE
DEBATING n act of
debating
DEBATINGS ▷ DEBATING
DEBAUCH vb make
(someone) bad or corrupt,
esp sexually ▷ n instance
or period of extreme
dissipation
DEBAUCHED ▷ DEBAUCH
DEBAUCHEE n man who
leads a life of reckless
drinking, promiscuity, and
self-indulgence
DEBAUCHER ▷ DEBAUCH
DEBAUCHES ▷ DEBAUCH
DEBBIER ▷ DEBBY
DEBBIES ▷ DEBBY
DEBBIEST ▷ DEBBY
DEBBY n debutante
▷ adj of, or resembling a
debutante
DEBE n tin
DEBEAK vb remove part of
the beak of poultry to
reduce the risk of such
habits as feather-picking
or cannibalism
DEBEAKED ▷ DEBEAK
DEBEAKING ▷ DEBEAK
DEBEAKS ▷ DEBEAK
DEBEARD vb remove beard
from mussel
DEBEARDED ▷ DEBEARD
DEBEARDS ▷ DEBEARD
DEBEL vb beat in war
DEBELLED ▷ DEBEL
DEBELLING ▷ DEBEL
DEBELS ▷ DEBEL
DEBENTURE n long-term
bond bearing fixed
interest, issued by a
company or a government
agency
DEBES ▷ DEBE
DEBILE adj lacking
strength
DEBILITY n weakness,
infirmity
DEBIT n sum owing
entered on the left side of
an account ▷ vb charge
(an account) with a debt
DEBITED ▷ DEBIT
DEBITING ▷ DEBIT
DEBITOR n person in debt
DEBITORS ▷ DEBITOR
DEBITS ▷ DEBIT
DEBONAIR adj (of a man)
charming and refined
DEBONAIRE adj suave and
refined
DEBONE vb remove bones
from
DEBONED ▷ DEBONE
DEBONER ▷ DEBONE
DEBONERS ▷ DEBONE

DEBONES ▷ DEBONE
DEBONING ▷ DEBONE
DEBOSH vb debauch
DEBOSHED ▷ DEBOSH
DEBOSHES ▷ DEBOSH
DEBOSHING ▷ DEBOSH
DEBOSS vb carve a design
into
DEBOSSED ▷ DEBOSS
DEBOSSES ▷ DEBOSS
DEBOSSING ▷ DEBOSS
DEBOUCH vb move out
from a narrow place to a
wider one ▷ n outlet or
passage, as for the exit of
troops
DEBOUCHE same as
▷ DEBOUCH
DEBOUCHED ▷ DEBOUCH
DEBOUCHES ▷ DEBOUCH
DEBRIDE vb remove dead
tissue from
DEBRIDED ▷ DEBRIDE
DEBRIDES ▷ DEBRIDE
DEBRIDING ▷ DEBRIDE
DEBRIEF vb receive a
report from (a soldier,
diplomat, etc) after an
event
DEBRIEFED ▷ DEBRIEF
DEBRIEFER ▷ DEBRIEF
DEBRIEFS ▷ DEBRIEF
DEBRIS n fragments of
something destroyed
DEBRUISE vb (in heraldry)
overlay or partly cover
DEBRUISED ▷ DEBRUISE
DEBRUISES ▷ DEBRUISE
DEBS ▷ DEB
DEBT n something owed,
esp money
DEBTED adj in debt
DEBTEE n person owed a
debt
DEBTEES ▷ DEBTEE
DEBTLESS ▷ DEBT
DEBTOR n person who
owes money
DEBTORS ▷ DEBTOR
DEBTS ▷ DEBT
DEBUD same as ▷ DISBUD
DEBUDDED ▷ DEBUD
DEBUDDING ▷ DEBUD
DEBUDS ▷ DEBUD
DEBUG vb find and remove
defects in (a computer
program) ▷ n something
that locates and removes
defects in a device, system,
etc
DEBUGGED ▷ DEBUG
DEBUGGER ▷ DEBUG
DEBUGGERS ▷ DEBUG
DEBUGGING n act of
debugging
DEBUGS ▷ DEBUG
DEBUNK vb expose the
falseness of
DEBUNKED ▷ DEBUNK
DEBUNKER ▷ DEBUNK
DEBUNKERS ▷ DEBUNK
DEBUNKING ▷ DEBUNK
DEBUNKS ▷ DEBUNK

DEBUR vb remove burs
from (a piece of machined
metal)
DEBURR vb remove burrs
from (a workpiece)
DEBURRED ▷ DEBURR
DEBURRING ▷ DEBURR
DEBURRS ▷ DEBURR
DEBURS ▷ DEBUR
DEBUS vb unload (goods)
or (esp of troops) to alight
from a motor vehicle
DEBUSED ▷ DEBUS
DEBUSES ▷ DEBUS
DEBUSING ▷ DEBUS
DEBUSSED ▷ DEBUS
DEBUSSES ▷ DEBUS
DEBUSSING ▷ DEBUS
DEBUT n first public
appearance of a performer
▷ vb make a debut
DEBUTANT n person who
is making a first
appearance in a particular
capacity, such as a
sportsperson playing in a
first game for a team
DEBUTANTE n young
upper-class woman being
formally presented to
society
DEBUTANTS ▷ DEBUTANT
DEBUTED ▷ DEBUT
DEBUTING ▷ DEBUT
DEBUTS ▷ DEBUT
DEBYE n unit of electric
dipole moment
DEBYES ▷ DEBYE
DECACHORD n instrument
with ten strings
DECAD n ten years
DECADAL ▷ DECADE
DECADE n period of ten
years
DECADENCE n
deterioration in morality
or culture
DECADENCY same as
▷ DECADENCE
DECADENT adj
characterized by decay or
decline, as in being
self-indulgent or morally
corrupt ▷ n decadent
person
DECADENTS ▷ DECADENT
DECADES ▷ DECADE
DECADS ▷ DECAD
DECAF n decaffeinated
coffee ▷ adj decaffeinated
DECAFF n decaffeinated
coffee
DECAFFS ▷ DECAFF
DECAFS ▷ DECAF
DECAGON n geometric
figure with ten faces
DECAGONAL ▷ DECAGON
DECAGONS ▷ DECAGON
DECAGRAM n ten grams
DECAGRAMS ▷ DECAGRAM
DECAHEDRA n plural form
of singular decahedron:
solid figure with ten plane
faces

DECAL vb transfer (a
design) by decalcomania
DECALCIFY vb remove
calcium or lime from
(bones, teeth, etc)
DECALED ▷ DECAL
DECALING ▷ DECAL
DECALITER same as
▷ DECALITRE
DECALITRE n measure of
volume equivalent to 10
litres
DECALLED ▷ DECAL
DECALLING ▷ DECAL
DECALOG same as
▷ DECALOGUE
DECALOGS ▷ DECALOG
DECALOGUE n Ten
Commandments
DECALS ▷ DECAL
DECAMETER same as
▷ DECAMETRE
DECAMETRE n unit of
length equal to ten metres
DECAMP vb depart secretly
or suddenly
DECAMPED ▷ DECAMP
DECAMPING ▷ DECAMP
DECAMPS ▷ DECAMP
DECAN n one of three
divisions of a sign of the
zodiac
DECANAL adj of or relating
to a dean or deanery
DECANALLY ▷ DECANAL
DECANE n liquid alkane
hydrocarbon
DECANES ▷ DECANE
DECANI adv be sung by the
decanal side of a choir
DECANOIC adj as in
decanoic acid white
crystalline insoluble
carboxylic acid with an
unpleasant odour, used in
perfumes and for making
fruit flavours
DECANS ▷ DECAN
DECANT vb pour (a liquid)
from one container to
another
DECANTATE vb decant
DECANTED ▷ DECANT
DECANTER n stoppered
bottle for wine or spirits
DECANTERS ▷ DECANTER
DECANTING ▷ DECANT
DECANTS ▷ DECANT
DECAPOD n creature, such
as a crab, with five pairs of
walking limbs ▷ adj of,
relating to, or belonging to
these creatures
DECAPODAL ▷ DECAPOD
DECAPODAN ▷ DECAPOD
DECAPODS ▷ DECAPOD
DECARB vb decoke
DECARBED ▷ DECARB
DECARBING ▷ DECARB
DECARBS ▷ DECARB
DECARE n ten ares or 1000
square metres
DECARES ▷ DECARE
DECASTERE n ten steres

DECASTICH n poem with ten lines

DECASTYLE n portico consisting of ten columns

DECATHLON n athletic contest with ten events

DECAUDATE vb remove the tail from

DECAY vb become weaker or more corrupt ▷ n process of decaying

DECAYABLE > DECAY

DECAYED > DECAY

DECAYER > DECAY

DECAYERS > DECAY

DECAYING > DECAY

DECAYLESS adj immortal

DECAYS > DECAY

DECCIE n decoration

DECCIES > DECCIE

DECEASE n death

DECEASED adj dead ▷ n dead person

DECEASEDS > DECEASED

DECEASES > DECEASE

DECEASING > DECEASE

DECEDENT n deceased person

DECEDENTS > DECEDENT

DECEIT n behaviour intended to deceive

DECEITFUL adj full of deceit

DECEITS > DECEIT

DECEIVE vb mislead by lying

DECEIVED > DECEIVE

DECEIVER > DECEIVE

DECEIVERS > DECEIVE

DECEIVES > DECEIVE

DECEIVING > DECEIVE

DECELERON n type of aileron

DECEMVIR n (in ancient Rome) a member of a board of ten magistrates, esp either of the two commissions established in 451 and 450 BC to revise the laws

DECEMVIRI > DECEMVIR

DECEMVIRS > DECEMVIR

DECENARY adj of or relating to a tithing

DECENCIES pl n generally accepted standards of good behaviour

DECENCY n conformity to the prevailing standards of what is right

DECENNARY same as > DECENARY

DECENNIA > DECENNIUM

DECENNIAL adj lasting for ten years ▷ n tenth anniversary or its celebration

DECENNIUM a less common word for > DECADE

DECENT adj (of a person) polite and morally acceptable

DECENTER vb put out of centre

DECENTERS > DECENTER

DECENTEST > DECENT

DECENTLY > DECENT

DECENTRE vb put out of centre

DECENTRED > DECENTRE

DECENTRES > DECENTRE

DECEPTION n deceiving

DECEPTIVE adj likely or designed to deceive

DECEPTORY adj deceiving

DECERN vb decree or adjudge

DECERNED > DECERN

DECERNING > DECERN

DECERNS > DECERN

DECERTIFY vb withdraw or remove a certificate or certification from (a person, organization, or country)

DECESSION n departure

DECHEANCE n forfeiting

DECIARE n one tenth of an are or 10 square metres

DECIARES > DECIARE

DECIBEL n unit for measuring the intensity of sound

DECIBELS > DECIBEL

DECIDABLE adj able to be decided

DECIDE vb (cause to) reach a decision

DECIDED adj unmistakable

DECIDEDLY > DECIDED

DECIDER n thing that determines who wins a match or championship

DECIDERS > DECIDER

DECIDES > DECIDE

DECIDING > DECIDE

DECIDUA n membrane lining the uterus of some mammals during pregnancy

DECIDUAE > DECIDUA

DECIDUAL > DECIDUA

DECIDUAS > DECIDUA

DECIDUATE > DECIDUA

DECIDUOUS adj (of a tree) shedding its leaves annually

DECIGRAM n tenth of a gram

DECIGRAMS > DECIGRAM

DECILE n one of nine actual or notional values of a variable dividing its distribution into ten groups with equal frequencies: the ninth decile is the value below which 90% of the population lie

DECILES > DECILE

DECILITER same as > DECILITRE

DECILITRE n measure of volume equivalent to one tenth of a litre

DECILLION n (in Britain, France, and Germany) the number represented as one followed by 60 zeros (10^{60})

DECIMAL n fraction written in the form of a dot followed by one or more numbers ▷ adj relating to or using powers of ten

DECIMALLY > DECIMAL

DECIMALS > DECIMAL

DECIMATE vb destroy or kill a large proportion of

DECIMATED > DECIMATE

DECIMATES > DECIMATE

DECIMATOR > DECIMATE

DECIME n former French coin

DECIMES > DECIME

DECIMETER same as > DECIMETRE

DECIMETRE n unit of length equal to one tenth of a metre

DECIPHER vb work out the meaning of (something illegible or in code)

DECIPHERS > DECIPHER

DECISION n judgment, conclusion, or resolution

DECISIONS > DECISION

DECISIVE adj having a definite influence

DECISORY adj deciding

DECISTERE n tenth of a stere

DECK n area of a ship that forms a floor ▷ vb dress or decorate

DECKCHAIR n folding wooden and canvas chair designed for use outside

DECKED adj having a wooden deck or platform

DECKEL same as > DECKLE

DECKELS > DECKEL

DECKER > DECK

DECKERS > DECK

DECKHAND n seaman assigned various duties, such as mooring and cargo handling, on the deck of a ship

DECKHANDS > DECKHAND

DECKHOUSE n houselike cabin on the deck of a ship

DECKING n wooden platform in a garden

DECKINGS > DECKING

DECKLE n frame used to contain pulp on the mould in the making of handmade paper

DECKLED > DECKLE

DECKLES > DECKLE

DECKLESS adj without a deck

DECKO n look ▷ vb have a look

DECKOED > DECKO

DECKOING > DECKO

DECKOS > DECKO

DECKS > DECK

DECLAIM vb speak loudly and dramatically

DECLAIMED > DECLAIM

DECLAIMER > DECLAIM

DECLAIMS > DECLAIM

DECLARANT n person who makes a declaration

DECLARE vb state firmly and forcefully

DECLARED > DECLARE

DECLARER n person who declares

DECLARERS > DECLARER

DECLARES > DECLARE

DECLARING > DECLARE

DECLASS vb lower in social status or position

DECLASSE adj having lost social standing or status

DECLASSED > DECLASS

DECLASSEE adj (of a woman) having lost social standing or status

DECLASSES > DECLASS

DECLAW vb remove claws from

DECLAWED > DECLAW

DECLAWING > DECLAW

DECLAWS > DECLAW

DECLINAL adj bending down ▷ n action of politely refusing or declining

DECLINALS > DECLINAL

DECLINANT adj heraldry term ▷ n person who is diminishing in luck or wealth

DECLINATE adj (esp of plant parts) descending from the horizontal in a curve

DECLINE vb become smaller, weaker, or less important ▷ n gradual weakening or loss

DECLINED > DECLINE

DECLINER > DECLINE

DECLINERS > DECLINE

DECLINES > DECLINE

DECLINING > DECLINE

DECLINIST n person believing something is in decline

DECLIVITY n downward slope

DECLIVOUS adj steep

DECLUTCH vb disengage the clutch of a motor vehicle

DECLUTTER vb simplify or get rid of mess, disorder, complications, etc

DECO adj as in art deco style of art, jewellery, design, etc

DECOCT vb extract the essence from (a substance) by boiling

DECOCTED > DECOCT

DECOCTING > DECOCT

DECOCTION n extraction by boiling

DECOCTIVE > DECOCT

DECOCTS > DECOCT

DECOCTURE n substance obtained by decoction
DECODE vb convert from code into ordinary language
DECODED > DECODE
DECODER > DECODE
DECODERS > DECODE
DECODES > DECODE
DECODING n act of decoding
DECODINGS > DECODING
DECOHERER n electrical device
DECOKE n decarbonize
DECOKED > DECOKE
DECOKES > DECOKE
DECOKING > DECOKE
DECOLLATE vb separate (continuous stationery, etc) into individual forms
DECOLLETE adj (of a woman's garment) low-cut ▷ n low-cut neckline
DECOLOR vb bleach
DECOLORED > DECOLOR
DECOLORS > DECOLOR
DECOLOUR vb deprive of colour, as by bleaching
DECOLOURS > DECOLOUR
DECOMMIT vb withdraw from a commitment or agreed course of action
DECOMMITS > DECOMMIT
DECOMPLEX adj repeatedly compound
DECOMPOSE vb be broken down through chemical or bacterial action
DECONGEST vb relieve congestion in
DECONTROL vb free of restraints or controls, esp government controls
DECOR n style in which a room or house is decorated
DECORATE vb make more attractive by adding something ornamental
DECORATED > DECORATE
DECORATES > DECORATE
DECORATOR n person whose profession is the painting and wallpapering of buildings
DECOROUS adj polite, calm, and sensible in behaviour
DECORS pl n decorations
DECORUM n polite and socially correct behaviour
DECORUMS > DECORUM
DECOS pl n decorations
DECOUPAGE n art or process of decorating a surface with shapes or illustrations cut from paper, card, etc
DECOUPLE vb separate (joined or coupled subsystems) thereby

enabling them to exist and operate separately
DECOUPLED > DECOUPLE
DECOUPLER > DECOUPLE
DECOUPLES > DECOUPLE
DECOY n person or thing used to lure someone into danger ▷ vb lure away by means of a trick
DECOYED > DECOY
DECOYER > DECOY
DECOYERS > DECOY
DECOYING > DECOY
DECOYS > DECOY
DECREASE vb make or become less ▷ n lessening, reduction
DECREASED > DECREASE
DECREASES > DECREASE
DECREE n law made by someone in authority ▷ vb order by decree
DECREED > DECREE
DECREEING > DECREE
DECREER > DECREE
DECREERS > DECREE
DECREES > DECREE
DECREET n final judgment or sentence of a court
DECREETS > DECREET
DECREMENT n act of decreasing
DECREPIT adj weakened or worn out by age or long use
DECRETAL n papal decree ▷ adj of or relating to a decretal or a decree
DECRETALS > DECRETAL
DECRETIST n law student
DECRETIVE adj of a decree
DECRETORY adj of a decree
DECREW vb decrease
DECREWED > DECREW
DECREWING > DECREW
DECREWS > DECREW
DECRIAL > DECRY
DECRIALS > DECRY
DECRIED > DECRY
DECRIER > DECRY
DECRIERS > DECRY
DECRIES > DECRY
DECROWN vb depose
DECROWNED > DECROWN
DECROWNS > DECROWN
DECRY vb express disapproval of
DECRYING > DECRY
DECRYPT vb decode (a message)
DECRYPTED > DECRYPT
DECRYPTS > DECRYPT
DECTET n ten musicians
DECTETS > DECTET
DECUBITAL > DECUBITUS
DECUBITI > DECUBITUS
DECUBITUS n posture adopted when lying down
DECUMAN n large wave

DECUMANS > DECUMAN
DECUMBENT adj lying down or lying flat
DECUPLE vb increase by ten times ▷ n amount ten times as large as a given reference ▷ adj increasing tenfold
DECUPLED > DECUPLE
DECUPLES > DECUPLE
DECUPLING > DECUPLE
DECURIA n group of ten
DECURIAS > DECURIA
DECURIES > DECURY
DECURION n local councillor
DECURIONS > DECURION
DECURRENT adj extending down the stem, esp (of a leaf) having the base of the blade extending down the stem as two wings
DECURSION n state of being decurrent
DECURSIVE adj extending downwards
DECURVE vb curve downwards
DECURVED adj bent or curved downwards
DECURVES > DECURVE
DECURVING > DECURVE
DECURY n (in ancient Rome) a body of ten men
DECUSSATE vb cross or cause to cross in the form of the letter X ▷ adj in the form of the letter X
DEDAL same as > DAEDAL
DEDALIAN adj of Daedalus
DEDANS n open gallery at the server's end of the court
DEDENDA > DEDENDUM
DEDENDUM n radial distance between the pitch circle and root of a gear tooth
DEDENDUMS > DEDENDUM
DEDICANT n person who dedicates
DEDICANTS > DEDICANT
DEDICATE vb commit (oneself or one's time) wholly to a special purpose or cause
DEDICATED adj devoted to a particular purpose or cause
DEDICATEE > DEDICATE
DEDICATES > DEDICATE
DEDICATOR > DEDICATE
DEDIMUS n legal term
DEDIMUSES > DEDIMUS
DEDUCE vb reach (a conclusion) by reasoning from evidence
DEDUCED > DEDUCE
DEDUCES > DEDUCE
DEDUCIBLE > DEDUCE
DEDUCIBLY > DEDUCE
DEDUCING > DEDUCE
DEDUCT vb subtract

DEDUCTED > DEDUCT
DEDUCTING > DEDUCT
DEDUCTION n deducting
DEDUCTIVE adj of or relating to deduction
DEDUCTS > DEDUCT
DEE a Scot word for > DIE
DEED n something that is done ▷ vb convey or transfer (property) by deed ▷ adj Scots form of dead
DEEDED > DEED
DEEDER > DEED
DEEDEST > DEED
DEEDFUL adj full of exploits
DEEDIER > DEEDY
DEEDIEST > DEEDY
DEEDILY > DEEDY
DEEDING > DEED
DEEDLESS adj without exploits
DEEDS > DEED
DEEDY adj hard-working
DEEING > DEE
DEEJAY n disc jockey ▷ vb work or act as a disc jockey
DEEJAYED > DEEJAY
DEEJAYING n act of deejaying
DEEJAYS > DEEJAY
DEEK vb look at
DEELY adj as in deely boppers hairband with two bobbing antennae-like attachments
DEEM vb consider, judge
DEEMED > DEEM
DEEMING > DEEM
DEEMS > DEEM
DEEMSTER n title of one of the two justices in the Isle of Man
DEEMSTERS > DEEMSTER
DEEN n din
DEENS > DEEN
DEEP adj extending or situated far down, inwards, backwards, or sideways ▷ n any deep place on land or under water
DEEPEN vb make or become deeper or more intense
DEEPENED > DEEPEN
DEEPENER > DEEPEN
DEEPENERS > DEEPEN
DEEPENING n act of deepening
DEEPENS > DEEPEN
DEEPER > DEEP
DEEPEST > DEEP
DEEPFELT adj sincere
DEEPFROZE vb froze in a freezer
DEEPIE n 3D film
DEEPIES > DEEPIE
DEEPLY > DEEP
DEEPMOST adj deepest
DEEPNESS > DEEP
DEEPS > DEEP

DEEPWATER adj seagoing

DEER n large wild animal, the male of which has antlers

DEERBERRY n huckleberry

DEERE adj serious ▷ n deer

DEERES > DEERE

DEERFLIES > DEERFLY

DEERFLY n insect related to the horsefly

DEERGRASS n type of plant that grows in dense tufts in peat bogs of temperate regions

DEERHORN n horn of a deer

DEERHORNS > DEERHORN

DEERHOUND n very large rough-coated breed of dog of the greyhound type

DEERLET n ruminant mammal

DEERLETS > DEERLET

DEERLIKE adj like a deer

DEERS > DEER

DEERSKIN n hide of a deer

DEERSKINS > DEERSKIN

DEERWEED n forage plant

DEERWEEDS > DEERWEED

DEERYARD n gathering place for deer

DEERYARDS > DEERYARD

DEES > DEE

DEET n insect-repellent

DEETS > DEET

DEEV n mythical monster

DEEVE vb deafen

DEEVED > DEEVE

DEEVES > DEEVE

DEEVING > DEEVE

DEEVS > DEEV

DEEWAN n chief of a village in India

DEEWANS > DEEWAN

DEF adj very good

DEFACE vb deliberately spoil the appearance of

DEFACED > DEFACE

DEFACER > DEFACE

DEFACERS > DEFACE

DEFACES > DEFACE

DEFACING > DEFACE

DEFAECATE same as > DEFECATE

DEFALCATE vb make wrong use of funds entrusted to one

DEFAME vb attack the good reputation of

DEFAMED > DEFAME

DEFAMER > DEFAME

DEFAMERS > DEFAME

DEFAMES > DEFAME

DEFAMING > DEFAME

DEFAMINGS > DEFAME

DEFANG vb remove the fangs of

DEFANGED > DEFANG

DEFANGING > DEFANG

DEFANGS > DEFANG

DEFAST adj defaced

DEFASTE adj defaced

DEFAT vb remove fat from

DEFATS > DEFAT

DEFATTED > DEFAT

DEFATTING > DEFAT

DEFAULT n failure to do something ▷ vb fail to fulfil an obligation

DEFAULTED > DEFAULT

DEFAULTER n person who defaults

DEFAULTS > DEFAULT

DEFEAT vb win a victory over ▷ n defeating

DEFEATED > DEFEAT

DEFEATER > DEFEAT

DEFEATERS > DEFEAT

DEFEATING > DEFEAT

DEFEATISM n ready acceptance or expectation of defeat

DEFEATIST > DEFEATISM

DEFEATS > DEFEAT

DEFEATURE vb deform

DEFECATE vb discharge waste from the body through the anus

DEFECATED > DEFECATE

DEFECATES > DEFECATE

DEFECATOR > DEFECATE

DEFECT n imperfection, blemish ▷ vb desert one's cause or country to join the opposing forces

DEFECTED > DEFECT

DEFECTING > DEFECT

DEFECTION n act or an instance of defecting

DEFECTIVE adj imperfect, faulty

DEFECTOR > DEFECT

DEFECTORS > DEFECT

DEFECTS > DEFECT

DEFENCE n resistance against attack

DEFENCED > DEFENCE

DEFENCES > DEFENCE

DEFENCING > DEFENCE

DEFEND vb protect from harm or danger

DEFENDANT n person accused of a crime ▷ adj making a defence

DEFENDED > DEFEND

DEFENDER > DEFEND

DEFENDERS > DEFEND

DEFENDING > DEFEND

DEFENDS > DEFEND

DEFENSE same as > DEFENCE

DEFENSED > DEFENSE

DEFENSES > DEFENSE

DEFENSING > DEFENSE

DEFENSIVE adj intended for defence

DEFER vb delay (something) until a future time

DEFERABLE > DEFER

DEFERENCE n polite and respectful behaviour

DEFERENT adj (esp of a bodily nerve, vessel, or duct) conveying an impulse, fluid, etc, outwards, down, or away ▷ n (in the Ptolemaic system) a circle centred on the earth around which the centre of the epicycle was thought to move

DEFERENTS > DEFERENT

DEFERMENT n act of deferring or putting off until another time

DEFERRAL same as > DEFERMENT

DEFERRALS > DEFERRAL

DEFERRED adj withheld over a certain period

DEFERRER > DEFER

DEFERRERS > DEFER

DEFERRING > DEFER

DEFERS > DEFER

DEFFER > DEF

DEFFEST > DEF

DEFFLY archaic word > DEFTLY

DEFFO interj definitely: an expression of agreement or consent

DEFI n challenge

DEFIANCE n open resistance or disobedience

DEFIANCES > DEFIANCE

DEFIANT adj marked by resistance or bold opposition, as to authority

DEFIANTLY > DEFIANT

DEFICIENT adj lacking some essential thing or quality

DEFICIT n amount by which a sum of money is too small

DEFICITS > DEFICIT

DEFIED > DEFY

DEFIER > DEFY

DEFIERS > DEFY

DEFIES > DEFY

DEFILADE n protection provided by obstacles against enemy crossfire from the rear, or observation ▷ vb provide protection for by defilade

DEFILADED > DEFILADE

DEFILADES > DEFILADE

DEFILE vb treat (something sacred or important) without respect ▷ n narrow valley or pass

DEFILED > DEFILE

DEFILER > DEFILE

DEFILERS > DEFILE

DEFILES > DEFILE

DEFILING > DEFILE

DEFINABLE > DEFINE

DEFINABLY > DEFINE

DEFINE vb state precisely the meaning of

DEFINED > DEFINE

DEFINER > DEFINE

DEFINERS > DEFINE

DEFINES > DEFINE

DEFINIENS n word or words used to define or give an account of the meaning of another word, as in a dictionary entry

DEFINING > DEFINE

DEFINITE adj firm, clear, and precise ▷ n something that is firm, clear, and precise

DEFINITES > DEFINITE

DEFIS > DEFI

DEFLATE vb (cause to) collapse through the release of air

DEFLATED > DEFLATE

DEFLATER > DEFLATE

DEFLATERS > DEFLATE

DEFLATES > DEFLATE

DEFLATING > DEFLATE

DEFLATION n reduction in economic activity resulting in lower output and investment

DEFLATOR > DEFLATE

DEFLATORS > DEFLATE

DEFLEA vb remove fleas from

DEFLEAED > DEFLEA

DEFLEAING > DEFLEA

DEFLEAS > DEFLEA

DEFLECT vb (cause to) turn aside from a course

DEFLECTED > DEFLECT

DEFLECTOR > DEFLECT

DEFLECTS > DEFLECT

DEFLEX vb turn downwards

DEFLEXED > DEFLEX

DEFLEXES > DEFLEX

DEFLEXING > DEFLEX

DEFLEXION n deflection

DEFLEXURE n act of deflecting

DEFLORATE vb deflower

DEFLOWER vb deprive (a woman) of her virginity

DEFLOWERS > DEFLOWER

DEFLUENT adj running downwards

DEFLUXION n discharge

DEFO interj (slang) definitely

DEFOAM vb remove foam from

DEFOAMED > DEFOAM

DEFOAMER > DEFOAM

DEFOAMERS > DEFOAM

DEFOAMING > DEFOAM

DEFOAMS > DEFOAM

DEFOCUS vb put out of focus

DEFOCUSED > DEFOCUS

DEFOCUSES > DEFOCUS

DEFOG vb clear of vapour

DEFOGGED > DEFOG

DEFOGGER > DEFOG

DEFOGGERS > DEFOG

DEFOGGING > DEFOG

DEFOGS > DEFOG

DEFOLIANT n chemical sprayed or dusted onto trees to cause their leaves to fall, esp to remove cover from an enemy in warfare

DEFOLIATE *vb* deprive (a plant) of its leaves ▷ *adj* (of a plant) having shed its leaves

DEFORCE *vb* withhold (property, esp land) wrongly or by force from the rightful owner

DEFORCED > DEFORCE

DEFORCER > DEFORCE

DEFORCERS > DEFORCE

DEFORCES > DEFORCE

DEFORCING > DEFORCE

DEFOREST *vb* clear of trees

DEFORESTS > DEFOREST

DEFORM *vb* put out of shape or spoil the appearance of

DEFORMED *adj* disfigured or misshapen

DEFORMER > DEFORM

DEFORMERS > DEFORM

DEFORMING > DEFORM

DEFORMITY *n* distortion of a body part

DEFORMS > DEFORM

DEFOUL *vb* defile

DEFOULED > DEFOUL

DEFOULING > DEFOUL

DEFOULS > DEFOUL

DEFRAG *vb* defragment

DEFRAGGED > DEFRAG

DEFRAGGER > DEFRAG

DEFRAGS > DEFRAG

DEFRAUD *vb* cheat out of money, property, etc

DEFRAUDED > DEFRAUD

DEFRAUDER > DEFRAUD

DEFRAUDS > DEFRAUD

DEFRAY *vb* provide money for (costs or expenses)

DEFRAYAL > DEFRAY

DEFRAYALS > DEFRAY

DEFRAYED > DEFRAY

DEFRAYER > DEFRAY

DEFRAYERS > DEFRAY

DEFRAYING > DEFRAY

DEFRAYS > DEFRAY

DEFREEZE *vb* defrost

DEFREEZES > DEFREEZE

DEFRIEND *vb* remove (a person) from the list of one's friends on a social networking website

DEFRIENDS > DEFRIEND

DEFROCK *vb* deprive (a priest) of priestly status

DEFROCKED > DEFROCK

DEFROCKS > DEFROCK

DEFROST *vb* make or become free of ice

DEFROSTED > DEFROST

DEFROSTER *n* device by which the de-icing process of a refrigerator is accelerated, usually by circulating the refrigerant without the expansion process

DEFROSTS > DEFROST

DEFROZE > DEFREEZE

DEFROZEN > DEFREEZE

DEFT *adj* quick and skilful in movement

DEFTER > DEFT

DEFTEST > DEFT

DEFTLY > DEFT

DEFTNESS > DEFT

DEFUEL *vb* remove fuel from

DEFUELED > DEFUEL

DEFUELING > DEFUEL

DEFUELLED > DEFUEL

DEFUELS > DEFUEL

DEFUNCT *adj* no longer existing or operative ▷ *n* deceased person

DEFUNCTS > DEFUNCT

DEFUND *vb* stop funds to

DEFUNDED > DEFUND

DEFUNDING > DEFUND

DEFUNDS > DEFUND

DEFUSE *vb* remove the fuse of (an explosive device)

DEFUSED > DEFUSE

DEFUSER > DEFUSE

DEFUSERS > DEFUEL

DEFUSES > DEFUSE

DEFUSING > DEFUSE

DEFUZE *same as* > DEFUSE

DEFUZED > DEFUZE

DEFUZES > DEFUZE

DEFUZING > DEFUZE

DEFY *vb* resist openly and boldly

DEFYING > DEFY

DEG *vb* water (a plant, etc)

DEGAGE *adj* unconstrained in manner

DEGAME *n* tree of South and Central America

DEGAMES > DEGAME

DEGAMI *same as* > DEGAME

DEGAMIS > DEGAMI

DEGARNISH *vb* remove ornament from

DEGAS *vb* remove gas from (a container, vacuum tube, liquid, adsorbent, etc)

DEGASES > DEGAS

DEGASSED > DEGAS

DEGASSER > DEGAS

DEGASSERS > DEGAS

DEGASSES > DEGAS

DEGASSING > DEGAS

DEGAUSS *n* demagnetize

DEGAUSSED > DEGAUSS

DEGAUSSER > DEGAUSS

DEGAUSSES > DEGAUSS

DEGEARING *n* process in which a company replaces some or all of its fixed-interest loan stock with ordinary shares

DEGENDER *vb* remove reference to gender from

DEGENDERS > DEGENDER

DEGERM *vb* remove germs from

DEGERMED > DEGERM

DEGERMING > DEGERM

DEGERMS > DEGERM

DEGGED > DEG

DEGGING > DEG

DEGLAZE *vb* dilute meat sediments in (a pan) in order to make a sauce or gravy

DEGLAZED > DEGLAZE

DEGLAZES > DEGLAZE

DEGLAZING > DEGLAZE

DEGOUT *n* disgust ▷ *vb* cover (something) with gouts or drops of something

DEGOUTED > DEGOUT

DEGOUTING > DEGOUT

DEGOUTS > DEGOUT

DEGRADE *vb* reduce to dishonour or disgrace

DEGRADED > DEGRADE

DEGRADER > DEGRADE

DEGRADERS > DEGRADE

DEGRADES > DEGRADE

DEGRADING *adj* causing humiliation

DEGRAS *n* emulsion used for dressing hides

DEGREASE *vb* remove grease from

DEGREASED > DEGREASE

DEGREASER > DEGREASE

DEGREASES > DEGREASE

DEGREE *n* stage in a scale of relative amount or intensity

DEGREED *adj* having a degree

DEGREES > DEGREE

DEGS > DEG

DEGU *n* small S American rodent

DEGUM *vb* remove gum from

DEGUMMED > DEGUM

DEGUMMING > DEGUM

DEGUMS > DEGUM

DEGUS > DEGU

DEGUST *vb* taste, esp with care or relish

DEGUSTATE *same as* > DEGUST

DEGUSTED > DEGUST

DEGUSTING > DEGUST

DEGUSTS > DEGUST

DEHAIR *vb* remove hair

DEHAIRED > DEHAIR

DEHAIRING > DEHAIR

DEHAIRS > DEHAIR

DEHISCE *vb* (of the seed capsules of some plants) to burst open spontaneously

DEHISCED > DEHISCE

DEHISCENT *adj* (of fruits, anthers, etc) opening spontaneously to release seeds or pollen

DEHISCES > DEHISCE

DEHISCING > DEHISCE

DEHORN *vb* remove or prevent the growth of the horns of (cattle, sheep, or goats)

DEHORNED > DEHORN

DEHORNER > DEHORN

DEHORNERS > DEHORN

DEHORNING > DEHORN

DEHORNS > DEHORN

DEHORS *prep* apart from

DEHORT *vb* dissuade

DEHORTED > DEHORT

DEHORTER > DEHORT

DEHORTERS > DEHORT

DEHORTING > DEHORT

DEHORTS > DEHORT

DEHYDRATE *vb* remove water from (food) to preserve it

DEI > DEUS

DEICE *vb* free or be freed of ice

DEICED > DEICE

DEICER > DEICE

DEICERS > DEICE

DEICES > DEICE

DEICIDAL > DEICIDE

DEICIDE *n* act of killing a god

DEICIDES > DEICIDE

DEICING > DEICE

DEICTIC *adj* proving by direct argument

DEICTICS > DEICTIC

DEID *a Scot word for* > DEAD

DEIDER > DEID

DEIDEST > DEID

DEIDS > DEID

DEIF *a Scot word for* > DEAF

DEIFER > DEIF

DEIFEST > DEIF

DEIFIC *adj* making divine or exalting to the position of a god

DEIFICAL *adj* divine

DEIFIED > DEIFY

DEIFIER > DEIFY

DEIFIERS > DEIFY

DEIFIES > DEIFY

DEIFORM *adj* having the form or appearance of a god

DEIFY *vb* treat or worship as a god

DEIFYING > DEIFY

DEIGN *vb* agree (to do something), but as if doing someone a favour

DEIGNED > DEIGN

DEIGNING > DEIGN

DEIGNS > DEIGN

DEIL *a Scot word for* > DEVIL

DEILS > DEIL

DEINDEX *vb* cause to become no longer index-linked

DEINDEXED > DEINDEX

DEINDEXES > DEINDEX

DEINOSAUR *n* dinosaur

DEIONISE *same as* > DEIONIZE

DEIONISED > DEIONISE

DEIONISER > DEIONISE

DEIONISES > DEIONISE

DEIONIZE *vb* to remove ions from (water, etc), esp by ion exchange

DEIONIZED > DEIONIZE

DEIONIZER > DEIONIZE
DEIONIZES > DEIONIZE
DEIPAROUS adj giving birth to a god
DEISEAL n clockwise motion
DEISEALS > DEISEAL
DEISHEAL n clockwise motion
DEISHEALS > DEISHEAL
DEISM n belief in God but not in divine revelation
DEISMS > DEISM
DEIST > DEISM
DEISTIC > DEISM
DEISTICAL > DEISM
DEISTS > DEISM
DEITIES > DEITY
DEITY n god or goddess
DEIXES > DEIXIS
DEIXIS n use or reference of a deictic word
DEIXISES > DEIXIS
DEJECT vb have a depressing effect on ▷ adj downcast
DEJECTA pl n waste products excreted through the anus
DEJECTED adj unhappy
DEJECTING > DEJECT
DEJECTION n lowness of spirits
DEJECTORY adj causing dejection
DEJECTS > DEJECT
DEJEUNE n lunch
DEJEUNER n lunch
DEJEUNERS > DEJEUNER
DEJEUNES > DEJEUNE
DEKAGRAM n ten grams
DEKAGRAMS > DEKAGRAM
DEKALITER n ten litres
DEKALITRE n ten litres
DEKALOGY n series of ten related works
DEKAMETER n ten meters
DEKAMETRE n ten metres
DEKARE n unit of measurement equal to ten ares
DEKARES > DEKARE
DEKE vb make a deceptive movement ▷ n such a movement
DEKED > DEKE
DEKEING > DEKE
DEKES > DEKE
DEKING > DEKE
DEKKO n look ▷ vb have a look
DEKKOED > DEKKO
DEKKOING > DEKKO
DEKKOS > DEKKO
DEL n differential operator
DELAINE n sheer wool or wool and cotton fabric
DELAINES > DELAINE
DELAPSE vb be inherited
DELAPSED > DELAPSE
DELAPSES > DELAPSE
DELAPSING > DELAPSE

DELAPSION n falling down
DELATE vb (formerly) to bring a charge against
DELATED > DELATE
DELATES > DELATE
DELATING > DELATE
DELATION > DELATE
DELATIONS > DELATE
DELATOR > DELATE
DELATORS > DELATE
DELAY vb put off to a later time ▷ n act of delaying
DELAYABLE > DELAY
DELAYED > DELAY
DELAYER > DELAY
DELAYERS > DELAY
DELAYING > DELAY
DELAYS > DELAY
DELE n sign indicating that typeset matter is to be deleted ▷ vb mark (matter to be deleted) with a dele
DELEAD vb remove lead from
DELEADED > DELEAD
DELEADING > DELEAD
DELEADS > DELEAD
DELEAVE vb separate copies
DELEAVED > DELEAVE
DELEAVES > DELEAVE
DELEAVING > DELEAVE
DELEBLE adj able to be deleted
DELECTATE vb delight
DELED > DELE
DELEGABLE > DELEGATE
DELEGACY n elected standing committee at some British universities
DELEGATE n person chosen to represent others, esp at a meeting ▷ vb entrust (duties or powers) to someone
DELEGATED > DELEGATE
DELEGATEE > DELEGATE
DELEGATES > DELEGATE
DELEGATOR > DELEGATE
DELEING > DELE
DELENDA pl n items for deleting
DELES > DELE
DELETABLE > DELETE
DELETE vb remove (something written or printed)
DELETED > DELETE
DELETES > DELETE
DELETING > DELETE
DELETION n act of deleting or fact of being deleted
DELETIONS > DELETION
DELETIVE > DELETE
DELETORY > DELETE
DELF n kind of earthenware
DELFS > DELF
DELFT n tin-glazed earthenware, typically

having blue designs on white
DELFTS > DELFT
DELFTWARE same as > DELFT
DELI n delicatessen
DELIBATE vb taste
DELIBATED > DELIBATE
DELIBATES > DELIBATE
DELIBLE adj able to be deleted
DELICACY n being delicate
DELICATE adj fine or subtle in quality or workmanship ▷ n delicacy
DELICATES > DELICATE
DELICE n delicacy
DELICES > DELICE
DELICIOUS adj very appealing to taste or smell
DELICT n wrongful act for which the person injured has the right to a civil remedy
DELICTS > DELICT
DELIGHT n (source of) great pleasure ▷ vb please greatly
DELIGHTED adj greatly pleased ▷ sentence substitute I should be delighted to!
DELIGHTER > DELIGHT
DELIGHTS > DELIGHT
DELIME vb remove lime from
DELIMED > DELIME
DELIMES > DELIME
DELIMING > DELIME
DELIMIT vb mark or lay down the limits of
DELIMITED > DELIMIT
DELIMITER > DELIMIT
DELIMITS > DELIMIT
DELINEATE vb show by drawing
DELINK vb remove or break a link
DELINKED > DELINK
DELINKING > DELINK
DELINKS > DELINK
DELIQUIUM n loss of consciousness
DELIRIA > DELIRIUM
DELIRIANT > DELIRIUM
DELIRIOUS adj suffering from delirium
DELIRIUM n state of excitement and mental confusion, often with hallucinations
DELIRIUMS > DELIRIUM
DELIS > DELI
DELISH adj delicious
DELIST vb remove from a list
DELISTED > DELIST
DELISTING > DELIST
DELISTS > DELIST
DELIVER vb carry (goods etc) to a destination
DELIVERED > DELIVER
DELIVERER > DELIVER

DELIVERLY adv quickly
DELIVERS > DELIVER
DELIVERY n delivering
DELL n small wooded hollow
DELLIER > DELLY
DELLIES > DELLY
DELLIEST > DELLY
DELLS > DELL
DELLY n delicatessen ▷ adj full of dells
DELO an informal word for > DELEGATE
DELOPE vb shoot into the air
DELOPED > DELOPE
DELOPES > DELOPE
DELOPING > DELOPE
DELOS > DELO
DELOUSE vb rid (a person or animal) of lice
DELOUSED > DELOUSE
DELOUSER > DELOUSE
DELOUSERS > DELOUSE
DELOUSES > DELOUSE
DELOUSING > DELOUSE
DELPH n kind of earthenware
DELPHIC adj obscure or ambiguous
DELPHIN n fatty substance from dolphin oil
DELPHINIA n plural form of singular delphinium: garden plant with blue, white or pink flowers
DELPHINS > DELPHIN
DELPHS > DELPH
DELS > DEL
DELT n deltoid muscle
DELTA n fourth letter in the Greek alphabet
DELTAIC > DELTA
DELTAS > DELTA
DELTIC > DELTA
DELTOID n muscle acting to raise the arm ▷ adj shaped like a Greek capital delta
DELTOIDEI n deltoid
DELTOIDS > DELTOID
DELTS > DELT
DELUBRUM n shrine
DELUBRUMS > DELUBRUM
DELUDABLE > DELUDE
DELUDE vb deceive
DELUDED > DELUDE
DELUDER > DELUDE
DELUDERS > DELUDE
DELUDES > DELUDE
DELUDING > DELUDE
DELUGE n great flood ▷ vb flood
DELUGED > DELUGE
DELUGES > DELUGE
DELUGING > DELUGE
DELUNDUNG n spotted mammal
DELUSION n mistaken idea or belief
DELUSIONS > DELUSION
DELUSIVE > DELUSION
DELUSORY > DELUSION

DELUSTER same as > DELUSTRE

DELUSTERS > DELUSTER

DELUSTRE vb remove the lustre from

DELUSTRED > DELUSTRE

DELUSTRES > DELUSTRE

DELUXE adj rich, elegant, superior, or sumptuous

DELVE vb research deeply (for information)

DELVED > DELVE

DELVER > DELVE

DELVERS > DELVE

DELVES > DELVE

DELVING > DELVE

DEMAGOG same as > DEMAGOGUE

DEMAGOGED > DEMAGOG

DEMAGOGIC adj of, characteristic of, relating to, or resembling a demagogue

DEMAGOGS > DEMAGOG

DEMAGOGUE n political agitator who appeals to the prejudice and passions of the mob

DEMAGOGY n demagoguery

DEMAIN n demesne

DEMAINE n demesne

DEMAINES > DEMAINE

DEMAINS > DEMAIN

DEMAN vb reduce the workforce of (a plant, industry, etc)

DEMAND vb request forcefully ▷ n forceful request

DEMANDANT n (formerly) the plaintiff in an action relating to real property

DEMANDED > DEMAND

DEMANDER > DEMAND

DEMANDERS > DEMAND

DEMANDING adj requiring a lot of time or effort

DEMANDS > DEMAND

DEMANNED > DEMAN

DEMANNING > DEMAN

DEMANS > DEMAN

DEMANTOID n bright green variety of andradite garnet

DEMARCATE vb mark, fix, or draw the boundaries, limits, etc, of

DEMARCHE n move, step, or manoeuvre, esp in diplomatic affairs

DEMARCHES > DEMARCHE

DEMARK vb demarcate

DEMARKED > DEMARK

DEMARKET vb discourage consumers from buying (a particular product), either because it is faulty or because it could jeopardize the seller's reputation

DEMARKETS > DEMARKET

DEMARKING > DEMARK

DEMARKS > DEMARK

DEMAST vb remove the mast from

DEMASTED > DEMAST

DEMASTING > DEMAST

DEMASTS > DEMAST

DEMAYNE n demesne

DEMAYNES > DEMAYNE

DEME n (in preclassical Greece) the territory inhabited by a tribe

DEMEAN vb lower (oneself) in dignity, status, or character

DEMEANE n demesne

DEMEANED > DEMEAN

DEMEANES n demesne

DEMEANING > DEMEAN

DEMEANOR same as > DEMEANOUR

DEMEANORS > DEMEANOR

DEMEANOUR n way a person behaves

DEMEANS > DEMEAN

DEMENT vb deteriorate mentally, esp because of old age

DEMENTATE vb deteriorate mentally

DEMENTED adj mad

DEMENTI n denial

DEMENTIA n state of serious mental deterioration

DEMENTIAL > DEMENTIA

DEMENTIAS > DEMENTIA

DEMENTING > DEMENT

DEMENTIS > DEMENTI

DEMENTS > DEMENT

DEMERARA n brown crystallized cane sugar from the Caribbean and nearby countries

DEMERARAN adj from Demerara

DEMERARAS > DEMERARA

DEMERGE vb separate a company from another

DEMERGED > DEMERGE

DEMERGER n separation of two or more companies which have previously been merged

DEMERGERS > DEMERGER

DEMERGES > DEMERGE

DEMERGING > DEMERGE

DEMERIT n fault, disadvantage ▷ vb deserve

DEMERITED > DEMERIT

DEMERITS > DEMERIT

DEMERSAL adj living or occurring on the bottom of a sea or a lake

DEMERSE vb immerse

DEMERSED > DEMERSE

DEMERSES > DEMERSE

DEMERSING > DEMERSE

DEMERSION > DEMERSE

DEMES > DEME

DEMESNE n land surrounding a house

DEMESNES > DEMESNE

DEMETON n insecticide

DEMETONS > DEMETON

DEMIC adj of population

DEMIES > DEMY

DEMIGOD n being who is part mortal, part god

DEMIGODS > DEMIGOD

DEMIJOHN n large bottle with a short neck, often encased in wicker

DEMIJOHNS > DEMIJOHN

DEMILUNE n outwork in front of a fort, shaped like a crescent moon

DEMILUNES > DEMILUNE

DEMIMONDE n (esp in the 19th century) class of women considered to be outside respectable society because of promiscuity

DEMINER n person who removes mines

DEMINERS > DEMINER

DEMINING n act of removing mines

DEMININGS > DEMINING

DEMIPIQUE n low pique on a saddle

DEMIREP n woman of bad repute, esp a prostitute

DEMIREPS > DEMIREP

DEMISABLE > DEMISE

DEMISE n eventual failure (of something successful) ▷ vb transfer for a limited period

DEMISED > DEMISE

DEMISES > DEMISE

DEMISING > DEMISE

DEMISS adj humble

DEMISSION n relinquishment of or abdication from an office, responsibility, etc

DEMISSIVE adj humble

DEMISSLY > DEMISS

DEMIST vb remove condensation from (a windscreen)

DEMISTED > DEMIST

DEMISTER n device incorporating a heater and/or blower used in a motor vehicle to free the windscreen of condensation

DEMISTERS > DEMISTER

DEMISTING > DEMIST

DEMISTS > DEMIST

DEMIT vb resign (an office, position, etc)

DEMITASSE n small cup used to serve coffee, esp after a meal

DEMITS > DEMIT

DEMITTED > DEMIT

DEMITTING > DEMIT

DEMIURGE n (in the philosophy of Plato) the creator of the universe

DEMIURGES > DEMIURGE

DEMIURGIC > DEMIURGE

DEMIURGUS n demiurge

DEMIVEG n person who eats poultry and fish, but no red meat ▷ adj denoting a person who eats poultry and fish, but no red meat

DEMIVEGES > DEMIVEG

DEMIVOLT n half turn on the hind legs

DEMIVOLTE same as > DEMIVOLT

DEMIVOLTS > DEMIVOLT

DEMIWORLD n demimonde

DEMO n demonstration, organized expression of public opinion ▷ vb demonstrate

DEMOB vb demobilize

DEMOBBED > DEMOB

DEMOBBING > DEMOB

DEMOBS > DEMOB

DEMOCRACY n government by the people or their elected representatives

DEMOCRAT n advocate of democracy

DEMOCRATS > DEMOCRAT

DEMOCRATY n democracy

DEMODE adj out of fashion

DEMODED adj out of fashion

DEMOED > DEMO

DEMOI > DEMOS

DEMOING > DEMO

DEMOLISH vb knock down or destroy (a building)

DEMOLOGY n demography

DEMON n evil spirit

DEMONESS n female demon

DEMONIAC adj appearing to be possessed by a devil ▷ n person possessed by an evil spirit or demon

DEMONIACS > DEMONIAC

DEMONIAN adj of a demon

DEMONIC adj evil

DEMONICAL adj demonic

DEMONISE same as > DEMONIZE

DEMONISED > DEMONISE

DEMONISES > DEMONISE

DEMONISM n study of demons

DEMONISMS > DEMONISM

DEMONIST > DEMONISM

DEMONISTS > DEMONISM

DEMONIZE vb make into a demon

DEMONIZED > DEMONIZE

DEMONIZES > DEMONIZE

DEMONRIES > DEMONRY

DEMONRY > DEMON

DEMONS > DEMON

DEMOS n people of a nation regarded as a political unit

DEMOSCENE n computer art subculture

DEMOSES > DEMOS

DEMOTE vb reduce in status or rank

DEMOTED > DEMOTE

DEMOTES ▷ DEMOTE

DEMOTIC adj of the common people ▷ n demotic script of ancient Egypt

DEMOTICS ▷ DEMOTIC

DEMOTING ▷ DEMOTE

DEMOTION ▷ DEMOTE

DEMOTIONS ▷ DEMOTE

DEMOTIST ▷ DEMOTIC

DEMOTISTS ▷ DEMOTIC

DEMOUNT vb remove (a motor, gun, etc) from its mounting or setting

DEMOUNTED ▷ DEMOUNT

DEMOUNTS ▷ DEMOUNT

DEMPSTER same as ▷ DEEMSTER

DEMPSTERS ▷ DEMPSTER

DEMPT ▷ DEEM

DEMULCENT adj soothing ▷ n drug or agent that soothes the irritation of inflamed or injured skin surfaces

DEMULSIFY vb undergo or cause to undergo a process in which an emulsion is permanently broken down into its constituents

DEMUR vb raise objections or show reluctance ▷ n act of demurring

DEMURE adj quiet, reserved, and rather shy ▷ vb archaic for look demure ▷ n archaic for demure look

DEMURED ▷ DEMURE

DEMURELY ▷ DEMURE

DEMURER ▷ DEMURE

DEMURES ▷ DEMURE

DEMUREST ▷ DEMURE

DEMURING ▷ DEMURE

DEMURRAGE n delaying of a ship, railway wagon, etc, caused by the charterer's failure to load, unload, etc, before the time of scheduled departure

DEMURRAL n act of demurring

DEMURRALS ▷ DEMURRAL

DEMURRED ▷ DEMUR

DEMURRER n pleading that admits an opponent's point but denies that it is a relevant or valid argument

DEMURRERS ▷ DEMURRER

DEMURRING ▷ DEMUR

DEMURS ▷ DEMUR

DEMY n size of printing paper, 17½ by 22½ inches (444.5 × 571.5 mm)

DEMYSHIP ▷ DEMY

DEMYSHIPS ▷ DEMY

DEMYSTIFY vb remove the mystery from

DEMYTHIFY vb remove the mythical characteristics from

DEN n home of a wild animal ▷ vb live in or as if in a den

DENAR n standard monetary unit of Macedonia, divided into 100 deni

DENARI ▷ DENAR

DENARIES ▷ DENARIUS

DENARII ▷ DENARIUS

DENARIUS n ancient Roman silver coin, often called a penny in translation

DENARS ▷ DENAR

DENARY adj calculated by tens

DENATURE vb change the nature of

DENATURED ▷ DENATURE

DENATURES ▷ DENATURE

DENAY vb deny

DENAYED ▷ DENAY

DENAYING ▷ DENAY

DENAYS ▷ DENAY

DENAZIFY vb free or declare (people, institutions, etc) freed from Nazi influence or ideology

DENCH adj excellent

DENDRIMER n chemical compound with treelike molecular structure

DENDRITE n any of the short branched threadlike extensions of a nerve cell, which conduct impulses towards the cell body

DENDRITES ▷ DENDRITE

DENDRITIC ▷ DENDRITE

DENDROID adj freely branching ▷ n something that branches freely

DENDROIDS ▷ DENDROID

DENDRON same as ▷ DENDRITE

DENDRONS ▷ DENDRON

DENE n narrow wooded valley

DENERVATE vb deprive (a tissue or organ) of its nerve supply

DENES ▷ DENE

DENET vb remove from the Net Book Agreement

DENETS ▷ DENET

DENETTED ▷ DENET

DENETTING ▷ DENET

DENGUE n viral disease transmitted by mosquitoes

DENGUES ▷ DENGUE

DENI n monetary unit of the Former Yugoslav Republic of Macedonia, worth one hundredth of a denar

DENIABLE adj able to be denied

DENIABLY ▷ DENIABLE

DENIAL n statement that something is not true

DENIALIST n person who refuses to believe an established fact

DENIALS ▷ DENIAL

DENIED ▷ DENY

DENIER n unit of weight used to measure the fineness of nylon or silk

DENIERS ▷ DENIER

DENIES ▷ DENY

DENIGRATE vb criticize unfairly

DENIM n hard-wearing cotton fabric, usu blue

DENIMED adj wearing denim

DENIMS pl n jeans or overalls made of denim

DENIS ▷ DENI

DENITRATE vb undergo or cause to undergo a process in which a compound loses a nitro or nitrate group, nitrogen dioxide, or nitric acid

DENITRIFY vb undergo or cause to undergo loss or removal of nitrogen compounds or nitrogen

DENIZEN n inhabitant ▷ vb make a denizen

DENIZENED ▷ DENIZEN

DENIZENS ▷ DENIZEN

DENNED ▷ DEN

DENNET n carriage for one horse

DENNETS ▷ DENNET

DENNING ▷ DEN

DENOMINAL adj formed from a noun

DENOTABLE ▷ DENOTE

DENOTATE vb denote

DENOTATED ▷ DENOTATE

DENOTATES ▷ DENOTATE

DENOTE vb be a sign of

DENOTED ▷ DENOTE

DENOTES ▷ DENOTE

DENOTING ▷ DENOTE

DENOTIVE ▷ DENOTE

DENOUNCE vb speak vehemently against

DENOUNCED ▷ DENOUNCE

DENOUNCER ▷ DENOUNCE

DENOUNCES ▷ DENOUNCE

DENS ▷ DEN

DENSE adj closely packed

DENSELY ▷ DENSE

DENSENESS ▷ DENSE

DENSER ▷ DENSE

DENSEST ▷ DENSE

DENSIFIED ▷ DENSIFY

DENSIFIER ▷ DENSIFY

DENSIFIES ▷ DENSIFY

DENSIFY vb make or become dense

DENSITIES ▷ DENSITY

DENSITY n degree to which something is filled or occupied

DENT n hollow in the surface of something, made by hitting it ▷ vb make a dent in

DENTAL adj of teeth or dentistry ▷ n dental consonant

DENTALIA ▷ DENTALIUM

DENTALITY n use of teeth in pronouncing words

DENTALIUM n type of mollusc

DENTALLY ▷ DENTAL

DENTALS ▷ DENTAL

DENTARIA n botanical term

DENTARIAS ▷ DENTARIA

DENTARIES ▷ DENTARY

DENTARY n lower jawbone with teeth

DENTATE adj having teeth or teethlike notches

DENTATED adj having teeth

DENTATELY ▷ DENTATE

DENTATION n state or condition of being dentate

DENTED ▷ DENT

DENTEL n architectural term

DENTELLE n bookbinding term

DENTELLES ▷ DENTELLE

DENTELS ▷ DENTEL

DENTEX n large predatory fish

DENTEXES ▷ DENTEX

DENTICLE n small tooth or toothlike part, such as any of the placoid scales of sharks

DENTICLES ▷ DENTICLE

DENTIFORM adj shaped like a tooth

DENTIL n architectural ornament

DENTILED ▷ DENTIL

DENTILS ▷ DENTIL

DENTIN same as ▷ DENTINE

DENTINAL ▷ DENTINE

DENTINE n hard dense tissue forming the bulk of a tooth

DENTINES ▷ DENTINE

DENTING ▷ DENT

DENTINS ▷ DENTIN

DENTIST n person qualified to practise dentistry

DENTISTRY n branch of medicine concerned with the teeth and gums

DENTISTS ▷ DENTIST

DENTITION n typical arrangement of teeth in a species

DENTOID adj resembling a tooth

DENTS ▷ DENT

DENTULOUS adj having teeth

DENTURAL ▷ DENTURE

DENTURE n false tooth

DENTURES ▷ DENTURE

DENTURIST n person who makes dentures

DENUDATE adj denuded ▷ vb denude

DENUDATED > DENUDATE

DENUDATES > DENUDATE

DENUDE vb remove the covering or protection from

DENUDED > DENUDE

DENUDER > DENUDE

DENUDERS > DENUDE

DENUDES > DENUDE

DENUDING > DENUDE

DENY vb declare to be untrue

DENYING > DENY

DENYINGLY > DENY

DEODAND n (formerly) a thing that had caused a death and was forfeited to the crown for a charitable purpose

DEODANDS > DEODAND

DEODAR n Himalayan cedar with drooping branches

DEODARA same as > DEODAR

DEODARAS > DEODARA

DEODARS > DEODAR

DEODATE n offering to God

DEODATES > DEODATE

DEODORANT n substance applied to the body to mask the smell of perspiration

DEODORISE same as > DEODORIZE

DEODORIZE vb remove or disguise the smell of

DEONTIC adj of or relating to such ethical concepts as obligation and permissibility

DEONTICS > DEONTIC

DEORBIT vb go out of orbit

DEORBITED > DEORBIT

DEORBITS > DEORBIT

DEOXIDATE vb remove oxygen atoms from

DEOXIDISE same as > DEOXIDIZE

DEOXIDIZE vb remove oxygen atoms from (a compound, molecule, etc)

DEOXY adj having less oxygen than a specified related compound

DEP n small shop where newspapers, sweets, soft drinks, etc are sold

DEPAINT vb depict

DEPAINTED > DEPAINT

DEPAINTS > DEPAINT

DEPANNEUR n (in Quebec) a convenience store

DEPART vb leave

DEPARTED adj dead ▷ n dead person

DEPARTEDS > DEPARTED

DEPARTEE > DEPART

DEPARTEES > DEPART

DEPARTER > DEPART

DEPARTERS > DEPART

DEPARTING > DEPART

DEPARTS > DEPART

DEPARTURE n act of departing

DEPASTURE vb graze or denude by grazing (a pasture, esp a meadow specially grown for the purpose)

DEPECHE n message ▷ vb dispatch; rid oneself of

DEPECHED > DEPECHE

DEPECHES > DEPECHE

DEPECHING > DEPECHE

DEPEINCT vb paint

DEPEINCTS > DEPEINCT

DEPEND vb put trust (in)

DEPENDANT same as > DEPENDENT

DEPENDED > DEPEND

DEPENDENT adj depending on someone or something ▷ n element in a phrase or clause that is not the governor

DEPENDING > DEPEND

DEPENDS > DEPEND

DEPEOPLE vb reduce population

DEPEOPLED > DEPEOPLE

DEPEOPLES > DEPEOPLE

DEPERM vb demagnetize

DEPERMED > DEPERM

DEPERMING > DEPERM

DEPERMS > DEPERM

DEPICT vb produce a picture of

DEPICTED > DEPICT

DEPICTER > DEPICT

DEPICTERS > DEPICT

DEPICTING > DEPICT

DEPICTION > DEPICT

DEPICTIVE > DEPICT

DEPICTOR > DEPICT

DEPICTORS > DEPICT

DEPICTS > DEPICT

DEPICTURE a less common word for > DEPICT

DEPIGMENT vb reduce or remove the normal pigmentation of (the skin)

DEPILATE vb remove the hair from

DEPILATED > DEPILATE

DEPILATES > DEPILATE

DEPILATOR > DEPILATE

DEPLANE vb disembark from an aeroplane

DEPLANED > DEPLANE

DEPLANES > DEPLANE

DEPLANING > DEPLANE

DEPLENISH vb deprive of contents, such as furniture, stock, etc

DEPLETE vb use up

DEPLETED > DEPLETE

DEPLETER > DEPLETE

DEPLETERS > DEPLETE

DEPLETES > DEPLETE

DEPLETING > DEPLETE

DEPLETION > DEPLETE

DEPLETIVE > DEPLETE

DEPLETORY > DEPLETE

DEPLORE vb condemn strongly

DEPLORED > DEPLORE

DEPLORER > DEPLORE

DEPLORERS > DEPLORE

DEPLORES > DEPLORE

DEPLORING > DEPLORE

DEPLOY vb get (troops or resources) ready for immediate action

DEPLOYED > DEPLOY

DEPLOYER > DEPLOY

DEPLOYERS > DEPLOY

DEPLOYING > DEPLOY

DEPLOYS > DEPLOY

DEPLUME vb deprive of feathers

DEPLUMED > DEPLUME

DEPLUMES > DEPLUME

DEPLUMING > DEPLUME

DEPOLISH vb remove the polish from

DEPONE vb declare (something) under oath

DEPONED > DEPONE

DEPONENT n person who makes a statement on oath ▷ adj (of a verb, esp in Latin) having the inflectional endings of a passive verb but the meaning of an active verb

DEPONENTS > DEPONENT

DEPONES > DEPONE

DEPONING > DEPONE

DEPORT vb remove forcibly from a country

DEPORTED > DEPORT

DEPORTEE n person deported or awaiting deportation

DEPORTEES > DEPORTEE

DEPORTER > DEPORT

DEPORTERS > DEPORT

DEPORTING > DEPORT

DEPORTS > DEPORT

DEPOSABLE > DEPOSE

DEPOSAL n deposition; giving of testimony under oath

DEPOSALS > DEPOSAL

DEPOSE vb remove from an office or position of power

DEPOSED > DEPOSE

DEPOSER > DEPOSE

DEPOSERS > DEPOSE

DEPOSES > DEPOSE

DEPOSING > DEPOSE

DEPOSIT vb put down ▷ n sum of money paid into a bank account

DEPOSITED > DEPOSIT

DEPOSITOR n person who places or has money on deposit in a bank or similar organization

DEPOSITS > DEPOSIT

DEPOT n building where goods or vehicles are kept when not in use ▷ adj (of a

drug) designed for gradual release

DEPOTS > DEPOT

DEPRAVE vb make morally bad

DEPRAVED adj morally bad

DEPRAVER > DEPRAVE

DEPRAVERS > DEPRAVE

DEPRAVES > DEPRAVE

DEPRAVING > DEPRAVE

DEPRAVITY n moral corruption

DEPRECATE vb express disapproval of

DEPREDATE vb plunder or destroy

DEPREHEND vb apprehend

DEPRENYL n drug combating effects of ageing

DEPRENYLS > DEPRENYL

DEPRESS vb make sad

DEPRESSED adj low in spirits

DEPRESSES > DEPRESS

DEPRESSOR n person or thing that depresses

DEPRIVAL > DEPRIVE

DEPRIVALS > DEPRIVE

DEPRIVE vb prevent from (having or enjoying)

DEPRIVED adj lacking adequate living conditions, education, etc

DEPRIVER > DEPRIVE

DEPRIVERS > DEPRIVE

DEPRIVES > DEPRIVE

DEPRIVING > DEPRIVE

DEPROGRAM vb free someone from indoctrination

DEPS > DEP

DEPSIDE n organic chemical compound

DEPSIDES > DEPSIDE

DEPTH n distance downwards, backwards, or inwards

DEPTHLESS adj immeasurably deep

DEPTHS > DEPTH

DEPURANT adj purifying

DEPURANTS > DEPURANT

DEPURATE vb cleanse or purify or to be cleansed or purified

DEPURATED > DEPURATE

DEPURATES > DEPURATE

DEPURATOR > DEPURATE

DEPUTABLE > DEPUTE

DEPUTE vb appoint (someone) to act on one's behalf ▷ n deputy

DEPUTED > DEPUTE

DEPUTES > DEPUTE

DEPUTIES > DEPUTY

DEPUTING > DEPUTE

DEPUTISE same as > DEPUTIZE

DEPUTISED > DEPUTISE

DEPUTISES > DEPUTISE

DEPUTIZE vb act as deputy

DEPUTIZED > DEPUTIZE

DEPUTIZES > DEPUTIZE

DEPUTY n person appointed to act on behalf of another

DEQUEUE vb remove (an item) from a queue of computing tasks

DEQUEUED > DEQUEUE

DEQUEUES > DEQUEUE

DEQUEUING > DEQUEUE

DERACINE adj uprooted from their usual environment ▷ n person who has been uprooted from their usual environment

DERACINES > DERACINE

DERAIGN vb contest (a claim, suit, etc)

DERAIGNED > DERAIGN

DERAIGNS > DERAIGN

DERAIL vb cause (a train) to go off the rails ▷ n device to make locomotives leave the rails to avoid a collision or accident

DERAILED > DERAIL

DERAILER same as > DERAIL

DERAILERS > DERAILER

DERAILING > DERAIL

DERAILS > DERAIL

DERANGE vb disturb the order or arrangement of

DERANGED > DERANGE

DERANGER > DERANGE

DERANGERS > DERANGE

DERANGES > DERANGE

DERANGING > DERANGE

DERAT vb remove rats from

DERATE vb assess the value of some types of property at a lower rate than others for local taxation

DERATED > DERATE

DERATES > DERATE

DERATING > DERATE

DERATINGS > DERATE

DERATION vb end rationing of (food, petrol, etc)

DERATIONS > DERATION

DERATS > DERAT

DERATTED > DERAT

DERATTING > DERAT

DERAY vb go mad

DERAYED > DERAY

DERAYING > DERAY

DERAYS > DERAY

DERBIES > DERBY

DERBY n bowler hat

DERE vb injure

DERECHO n long, fast-moving line of severe storms

DERECHOS > DERECHO

DERED > DERE

DERELICT adj unused and falling into ruins ▷ n social outcast, vagrant

DERELICTS > DERELICT

DEREPRESS vb induce operation of gene

DERES > DERE

DERHAM same as > DIRHAM

DERHAMS > DERHAM

DERIDE vb treat with contempt or ridicule

DERIDED > DERIDE

DERIDER > DERIDE

DERIDERS > DERIDE

DERIDES > DERIDE

DERIDING > DERIDE

DERIG vb remove equipment, eg from stage set

DERIGGED > DERIG

DERIGGING > DERIG

DERIGS > DERIG

DERING > DERE

DERINGER same as > DERRINGER

DERINGERS > DERINGER

DERISIBLE adj subject to or deserving of derision

DERISION n act of deriding

DERISIONS > DERISION

DERISIVE adj mocking, scornful

DERISORY adj too small or inadequate to be considered seriously

DERIVABLE > DERIVE

DERIVABLY > DERIVE

DERIVATE n derivative ▷ vb derive (something)

DERIVATED > DERIVATE

DERIVATES > DERIVATE

DERIVE vb take or develop (from)

DERIVED > DERIVE

DERIVER > DERIVE

DERIVERS > DERIVE

DERIVES > DERIVE

DERIVING > DERIVE

DERM same as > DERMA

DERMA n beef or fowl intestine used as a casing for certain dishes, esp kishke

DERMAL adj of or relating to the skin

DERMAS > DERMA

DERMATIC adj of skin

DERMATOID adj resembling skin

DERMATOME n surgical instrument for cutting thin slices of skin, esp for grafting

DERMESTID n type of beetle whose larva and adult is destructive to many stored organic materials, such as wool and meat

DERMIC > DERMIS

DERMIS another name for > CORIUM

DERMISES > DERMIS

DERMOID adj of or resembling skin ▷ n congenital cystic tumour whose walls are lined with epithelium

DERMOIDS > DERMOID

DERMS > DERM

DERN n concealment ▷ vb keep hidden

DERNED > DERN

DERNFUL adj sorrowful

DERNIER adj last

DERNING > DERN

DERNLY adv sorrowfully

DERNS > DERN

DERO n tramp or derelict

DEROGATE vb detract from ▷ adj debased or degraded

DEROGATED > DEROGATE

DEROGATES > DEROGATE

DEROS > DERO

DERRICK n simple crane ▷ vb raise or lower the jib of (a crane)

DERRICKED > DERRICK

DERRICKS > DERRICK

DERRIERE n backside

DERRIERES > DERRIERE

DERRIES > DERRY

DERRINGER n small large-bored pistol

DERRIS n E Indian woody climbing plant

DERRISES > DERRIS

DERRO n vagrant

DERROS > DERRO

DERRY n derelict house, esp one used by tramps, drug addicts, etc

DERTH same as > DEARTH

DERTHS > DERTH

DERV n diesel oil, when used for road transport

DERVISH n member of a Muslim religious order noted for a frenzied whirling dance

DERVISHES > DERVISH

DERVS > DERV

DESALT vb desalinate

DESALTED > DESALT

DESALTER > DESALT

DESALTERS > DESALT

DESALTING > DESALT

DESALTS > DESALT

DESAND vb remove sand from

DESANDED > DESAND

DESANDING > DESAND

DESANDS > DESAND

DESCALE vb remove a hard coating from inside (a kettle or pipe)

DESCALED > DESCALE

DESCALER n something that removes limescale

DESCALERS > DESCALER

DESCALES > DESCALE

DESCALING > DESCALE

DESCANT n tune played or sung above a basic melody ▷ adj denoting the highest member in a family of musical instruments ▷ vb compose or perform a descant (for a piece of music)

DESCANTED > DESCANT

DESCANTER > DESCANT

DESCANTS > DESCANT

DESCEND vb move down (a slope etc)

DESCENDED > DESCEND

DESCENDER same as > DESCEND

DESCENDS > DESCEND

DESCENT n descending

DESCENTS > DESCENT

DESCHOOL vb separate education from the institution of school and operate through the pupil's life experience as opposed to a set curriculum

DESCHOOLS > DESCHOOL

DESCRIBE vb give an account of (something or someone) in words

DESCRIBED > DESCRIBE

DESCRIBER > DESCRIBE

DESCRIBES > DESCRIBE

DESCRIED > DESCRY

DESCRIER > DESCRY

DESCRIERS > DESCRY

DESCRIES > DESCRY

DESCRIVE vb describe

DESCRIVED > DESCRIVE

DESCRIVES > DESCRIVE

DESCRY vb catch sight of

DESCRYING > DESCRY

DESECRATE vb damage or insult (something sacred)

DESEED vb remove the seeds from (eg a fruit)

DESEEDED > DESEED

DESEEDER n person who deseeds

DESEEDERS > DESEEDER

DESEEDING > DESEED

DESEEDS > DESEED

DESELECT vb refuse to select (an MP) for re-election

DESELECTS > DESELECT

DESERT n region with little or no vegetation because of low rainfall ▷ vb abandon (a person or place) without intending to return

DESERTED > DESERT

DESERTER > DESERT

DESERTERS > DESERT

DESERTIC adj (of soil) developing in hot climates

DESERTIFY vb turn into desert

DESERTING > DESERT

DESERTION n act of deserting or abandoning or the state of being deserted or abandoned

DESERTS > DESERT

DESERVE vb be entitled to or worthy of

DESERVED > DESERVE

DESERVER > DESERVE

DESERVERS > DESERVE

DESERVES > DESERVE

DESERVING adj worthy of help, praise, or reward ▷ n merit or demerit

DESEX vb desexualize

DESEXED > DESEX

DESEXES > DESEX

DESEXING > DESEX

DESHI same as > DESI

DESHIS > DESHI

DESI adj (in Indian English) indigenous or local ▷ n (in Indian English) indigenous or local person

DESICCANT adj desiccating or drying ▷ n substance, such as calcium oxide, that absorbs water and is used to remove moisture

DESICCATE vb remove most of the water from

DESIGN vb work out the structure or form of (something), by making a sketch or plans ▷ n preliminary drawing

DESIGNATE vb give a name to ▷ adj appointed but not yet in office

DESIGNED > DESIGN

DESIGNEE n person designated to do something

DESIGNEES > DESIGNEE

DESIGNER n person who draws up original sketches or plans from which things are made ▷ adj designed by a well-known designer

DESIGNERS > DESIGNER

DESIGNFUL adj scheming

DESIGNING adj cunning and scheming

DESIGNS > DESIGN

DESILVER vb remove silver from

DESILVERS > DESILVER

DESINE same as > DESIGN

DESINED > DESINE

DESINENCE n ending or termination, esp an inflectional ending of a word

DESINENT > DESINENCE

DESINES > DESINE

DESINING > DESINE

DESIPIENT adj foolish

DESIRABLE adj worth having ▷ n person or thing that is the object of desire

DESIRABLY > DESIRABLE

DESIRE vb want very much ▷ n wish, longing

DESIRED > DESIRE

DESIRER > DESIRE

DESIRERS > DESIRE

DESIRES > DESIRE

DESIRING > DESIRE

DESIROUS adj having a desire for

DESIS > DESI

DESIST vb stop (doing something)

DESISTED > DESIST

DESISTING > DESIST

DESISTS > DESIST

DESK n piece of furniture with a writing surface and drawers

DESKBOUND adj engaged in or involving sedentary work, as at an office desk

DESKFAST n breakfast eaten at one's desk at work

DESKFASTS > DESKFAST

DESKILL vb mechanize or computerize (a job) thereby reducing the skill required to do it

DESKILLED > DESKILL

DESKILLS > DESKILL

DESKING n desks and related furnishings in a given space, eg an office

DESKINGS > DESKING

DESKMAN n police officer in charge in police station

DESKMEN > DESKMAN

DESKNOTE n small computer

DESKNOTES > DESKNOTE

DESKS > DESK

DESKTOP adj (of a computer) small enough to use at a desk ▷ n a computer small enough to use at a desk

DESKTOPS > DESKTOP

DESMAN n either of two molelike amphibious mammals

DESMANS > DESMAN

DESMID n type of mainly unicellular freshwater green alga

DESMIDIAN > DESMID

DESMIDS > DESMID

DESMINE n type of mineral

DESMINES > DESMINE

DESMODIUM n type of plant

DESMOID adj resembling a tendon or ligament ▷ n very firm tumour of connective tissue

DESMOIDS > DESMOID

DESMOSOME n structure in the cell membranes of adjacent cells that binds them together

DESNOOD vb remove the snood of a turkey poult to reduce the risk of cannibalism

DESNOODED > DESNOOD

DESNOODS > DESNOOD

DESOEUVRE adj with nothing to do

DESOLATE adj uninhabited and bleak ▷ vb deprive of inhabitants

DESOLATED > DESOLATE

DESOLATER > DESOLATE

DESOLATES > DESOLATE

DESOLATOR > DESOLATE

DESORB vb change from an adsorbed state to a gaseous or liquid state

DESORBED > DESORB

DESORBER n something that desorbs

DESORBERS > DESORBER

DESORBING > DESORB

DESORBS > DESORB

DESOXY same as > DEOXY

DESPAIR n total loss of hope ▷ vb lose hope

DESPAIRED > DESPAIR

DESPAIRER n one who despairs

DESPAIRS > DESPAIR

DESPATCH same as > DISPATCH

DESPERADO n reckless person ready to commit any violent illegal act

DESPERATE adj in despair and reckless

DESPIGHT obsolete form of > DESPITE

DESPIGHTS > DESPIGHT

DESPISAL > DESPISE

DESPISALS > DESPISE

DESPISE vb regard with contempt

DESPISED > DESPISE

DESPISER > DESPISE

DESPISERS > DESPISE

DESPISES > DESPISE

DESPISING > DESPISE

DESPITE prep in spite of ▷ n contempt ▷ vb show contempt for

DESPITED > DESPITE

DESPITES > DESPITE

DESPITING > DESPITE

DESPOIL vb plunder

DESPOILED > DESPOIL

DESPOILER > DESPOIL

DESPOILS > DESPOIL

DESPOND vb lose heart or hope

DESPONDED > DESPOND

DESPONDS > DESPOND

DESPOT n person in power who acts unfairly or cruelly

DESPOTAT n despot's domain

DESPOTATE same as > DESPOTAT

DESPOTATS > DESPOTAT

DESPOTIC > DESPOT

DESPOTISM n unfair or cruel government or behaviour

DESPOTS > DESPOT

DESPUMATE vb clarify or purify (a liquid) by skimming a scum from its surface

DESSE n desk

DESSERT n sweet course served at the end of a meal

DESSERTS > DESSERT

DESSES > DESSE

DESSYATIN n Russian measure of land

DESTAIN vb remove stain from

DESTAINED > DESTAIN

DESTAINS > DESTAIN

DESTEMPER same as > DISTEMPER

DESTINATE same as > DESTINE

DESTINE vb set apart or appoint

DESTINED adj certain to be or to do something

DESTINES > DESTINE

DESTINIES > DESTINY

DESTINING > DESTINE

DESTINY n future marked out for a person or thing

DESTITUTE adj having no money or possessions

DESTOCK vb reduce the amount of stock

DESTOCKED > DESTOCK

DESTOCKS > DESTOCK

DESTREAM vb take (pupils) out of classes that are organized by ability

DESTREAMS > DESTREAM

DESTRESS vb make or become less stressed

DESTRIER an archaic word for > WARHORSE

DESTRIERS > DESTRIER

DESTROY vb ruin, demolish

DESTROYED > DESTROY

DESTROYER n small heavily armed warship

DESTROYS > DESTROY

DESTRUCT vb destroy (one's own missile or rocket) for safety ▷ n act of destructing ▷ adj designed to be capable of destroying itself or the object, system, or installation containing it

DESTRUCTO n person who causes havoc or destruction

DESTRUCTS > DESTRUCT

DESUETUDE n condition of not being in use

DESUGAR vb remove sugar from

DESUGARED > DESUGAR

DESUGARS > DESUGAR

DESULFUR same as > DESULPHUR

DESULFURS > DESULFUR

DESULPHUR vb remove sulphur from

DESULTORY adj jumping from one thing to another, disconnected

DESYATIN n Russian unit of area

DESYATINS > DESYATIN

DESYNE same as > DESIGN

DESYNED > DESYNE

DESYNES > DESYNE

DESYNING > DESYNE

d

DETACH vb disengage and separate

DETACHED adj (of a house) not joined to another house

DETACHER > DETACH

DETACHERS > DETACH

DETACHES > DETACH

DETACHING > DETACH

DETAIL n individual piece of information ▷ vb list fully

DETAILED adj having many details

DETAILER > DETAIL

DETAILERS > DETAIL

DETAILING > DETAIL

DETAILS > DETAIL

DETAIN vb delay (someone)

DETAINED > DETAIN

DETAINEE > DETAIN

DETAINEES > DETAIN

DETAINER n wrongful withholding of the property of another person

DETAINERS > DETAINER

DETAINING > DETAIN

DETAINS > DETAIN

DETANGLE vb remove tangles from (esp hair)

DETANGLED > DETANGLE

DETANGLER n cosmetic product used to detangle hair

DETANGLES > DETANGLE

DETASSEL vb remove top part of corn plant

DETASSELS > DETASSEL

DETECT vb notice

DETECTED > DETECT

DETECTER > DETECT

DETECTERS > DETECT

DETECTING > DETECT

DETECTION n act of noticing, discovering, or sensing something

DETECTIVE n police officer or private agent who investigates crime ▷ adj used in or serving for detection

DETECTOR n instrument used to find something

DETECTORS > DETECTOR

DETECTS > DETECT

DETENT n locking piece of a mechanism, often spring-loaded to check the movement of a wheel in one direction only

DETENTE n easing of tension between nations

DETENTES > DETENTE

DETENTION n imprisonment

DETENTIST n supporter of detente

DETENTS > DETENT

DETENU n prisoner

DETENUE n female prisoner

DETENUES > DETENUE

DETENUS > DETENU

DETER vb discourage (someone) from doing something by instilling fear or doubt

DETERGE vb wash or wipe away

DETERGED > DETERGE

DETERGENT n chemical substance for washing clothes or dishes ▷ adj having cleansing power

DETERGER n detergent

DETERGERS > DETERGER

DETERGES > DETERGE

DETERGING > DETERGE

DETERMENT > DETER

DETERMINE vb settle (an argument or a question) conclusively

DETERRED > DETER

DETERRENT n something that deters ▷ adj tending to deter

DETERRER > DETER

DETERRERS > DETERRER

DETERRING > DETER

DETERS > DETER

DETERSION n act of cleansing

DETERSIVE same as > DETERGENT

DETEST vb dislike intensely

DETESTED > DETEST

DETESTER > DETEST

DETESTERS > DETEST

DETESTING > DETEST

DETESTS > DETEST

DETHATCH vb remove dead grass from lawn

DETHRONE vb remove from a throne or position of power

DETHRONED > DETHRONE

DETHRONER > DETHRONE

DETHRONES > DETHRONE

DETICK vb remove ticks from

DETICKED > DETICK

DETICKER > DETICK

DETICKERS > DETICK

DETICKING > DETICK

DETICKS > DETICK

DETINUE n action brought by a plaintiff to recover goods wrongfully detained

DETINUES > DETINUE

DETONABLE adj that can be detonated

DETONATE vb explode

DETONATED > DETONATE

DETONATES > DETONATE

DETONATOR n small amount of explosive, or a device, used to set off an explosion

DETORSION > DETORT

DETORT vb pervert

DETORTED > DETORT

DETORTING > DETORT

DETORTION > DETORT

DETORTS > DETORT

DETOUR n route that is not the most direct one ▷ vb deviate or cause to deviate from a direct route or course of action

DETOURED > DETOUR

DETOURING > DETOUR

DETOURS > DETOUR

DETOX n treatment to rid the body of poisonous substances ▷ vb undergo treatment to rid the body of poisonous substances

DETOXED > DETOX

DETOXES > DETOX

DETOXIFY vb remove poison from

DETOXING > DETOX

DETRACT vb make (something) seem less good

DETRACTED > DETRACT

DETRACTOR > DETRACT

DETRACTS > DETRACT

DETRAIN vb leave or cause to leave a railway train, as passengers, etc

DETRAINED > DETRAIN

DETRAINS > DETRAIN

DETRAQUE n insane person

DETRAQUEE n female insane person

DETRAQUES > DETRAQUE

DETRIMENT n disadvantage or damage

DETRITAL > DETRITUS

DETRITION n act of rubbing or wearing away by friction

DETRITUS n loose mass of stones and silt worn away from rocks

DETRUDE vb force down or thrust away or out

DETRUDED > DETRUDE

DETRUDES > DETRUDE

DETRUDING > DETRUDE

DETRUSION > DETRUDE

DETRUSOR n muscle in the wall of the bladder

DETRUSORS > DETRUSOR

DETUNE vb change pitch of (stringed instrument)

DETUNED > DETUNE

DETUNES > DETUNE

DETUNING > DETUNE

DEUCE vb score deuce in tennis ▷ n score of forty all

DEUCED adj damned

DEUCEDLY > DEUCED

DEUCES > DEUCE

DEUCING > DEUCE

DEUDDARN n two-tiered Welsh dresser

DEUDDARNS > DEUDDARN

DEUS n god

DEUTERATE vb treat or combine with deuterium

DEUTERIC adj (of mineral) formed by metasomatic changes

DEUTERIDE n compound of deuterium with some other element. It is analogous to a hydride

DEUTERIUM n isotope of hydrogen twice as heavy as the normal atom

DEUTERON n nucleus of a deuterium atom, consisting of one proton and one neutron

DEUTERONS > DEUTERON

DEUTON old form of > DEUTERON

DEUTONS > DEUTON

DEUTZIA n shrub with clusters of pink or white flowers

DEUTZIAS > DEUTZIA

DEV same as > DEVA

DEVA n (in Hinduism and Buddhism) divine being or god

DEVALL vb stop

DEVALLED > DEVALL

DEVALLING > DEVALL

DEVALLS > DEVALL

DEVALUATE same as > DEVALUE

DEVALUE vb reduce the exchange value of (a currency)

DEVALUED > DEVALUE

DEVALUES > DEVALUE

DEVALUING > DEVALUE

DEVAS > DEVA

DEVASTATE vb destroy

DEVEIN vb remove vein from

DEVEINED > DEVEIN

DEVEINING > DEVEIN

DEVEINS > DEVEIN

DEVEL same as > DEVVEL

DEVELED > DEVEL

DEVELING > DEVEL

DEVELLED > DEVEL

DEVELLING > DEVEL

DEVELOP vb grow or bring to a later, more elaborate, or more advanced stage

DEVELOPE old form of > DEVELOP

DEVELOPED > DEVELOP

DEVELOPER n person who develops property

DEVELOPES > DEVELOPE

DEVELOPPE n ballet position

DEVELOPS > DEVELOP

DEVELS > DEVEL

DEVERBAL n word deriving from verb

DEVERBALS > DEVERBAL

DEVEST variant spelling of > DIVEST

DEVESTED > DEVEST

DEVESTING > DEVEST

DEVESTS > DEVEST

DEVI n Hindu goddess

DEVIANCE n act or state of being deviant

DEVIANCES > DEVIANCE

DEVIANCY same as > DEVIANCE

DEVIANT adj (person) deviating from what is considered acceptable behaviour ▷ n person whose behaviour deviates from what is considered to be acceptable

DEVIANTS > DEVIANT

DEVIATE vb differ from others in belief or thought

DEVIATED > DEVIATE

DEVIATES > DEVIATE

DEVIATING > DEVIATE

DEVIATION n act or result of deviating

DEVIATIVE adj tending to deviate

DEVIATOR > DEVIATE

DEVIATORS > DEVIATE

DEVIATORY > DEVIATE

DEVICE n machine or tool used for a specific task

DEVICEFUL adj full of devices

DEVICES > DEVICE

DEVIL n evil spirit ▷ vb prepare (food) with a highly flavoured spiced mixture

DEVILDOM n domain of evil spirits

DEVILDOMS > DEVILDOM

DEVILED > DEVIL

DEVILESS n female devil

DEVILET n young devil

DEVILETS > DEVILET

DEVILFISH n manta fish

DEVILING > DEVIL

DEVILINGS > DEVIL

DEVILISH adj cruel or unpleasant ▷ adv extremely

DEVILISM n doctrine of devil

DEVILISMS > DEVILISM

DEVILKIN n small devil

DEVILKINS > DEVILKIN

DEVILLED > DEVIL

DEVILLING > DEVIL

DEVILMENT n mischievous conduct

DEVILRIES > DEVILRY

DEVILRY n mischievousness

DEVILS > DEVIL

DEVILSHIP n character of devil

DEVILTRY same as > DEVILRY

DEVILWOOD n small US tree

DEVIOUS adj insincere and dishonest

DEVIOUSLY > DEVIOUS

DEVIS > DEVI

DEVISABLE adj (of property, esp realty) capable of being transferred by will

DEVISAL n act of inventing, contriving, or devising

DEVISALS > DEVISAL

DEVISE vb work out (something) in one's mind ▷ n disposition of property by will

DEVISED > DEVISE

DEVISEE n person to whom property, esp realty, is devised by will

DEVISEES > DEVISEE

DEVISER > DEVISE

DEVISERS > DEVISE

DEVISES > DEVISE

DEVISING > DEVISE

DEVISOR n person who devises property, esp realty, by will

DEVISORS > DEVISOR

DEVITRIFY vb change from a vitreous state to a crystalline state

DEVLING n young devil

DEVLINGS > DEVLING

DEVO n short for devolution

DEVOICE vb make (a voiced speech sound) voiceless

DEVOICED > DEVOICE

DEVOICES > DEVOICE

DEVOICING n act of devoicing

DEVOID adj completely lacking (in)

DEVOIR n duty

DEVOIRS > DEVOIR

DEVOLVE vb pass to a successor or substitute

DEVOLVED > DEVOLVE

DEVOLVES > DEVOLVE

DEVOLVING > DEVOLVE

DEVON n bland processed meat in sausage form, eaten cold in slices

DEVONIAN adj of, denoting, or formed in the fourth period of the Palaeozoic era, between the Silurian and Carboniferous periods

DEVONPORT same as > DAVENPORT

DEVONS > DEVON

DEVORE n velvet fabric with a raised pattern

DEVORES > DEVORE

DEVOS > DEVO

DEVOT n devotee

DEVOTE vb apply or dedicate to a particular purpose

DEVOTED adj showing loyalty or devotion

DEVOTEDLY > DEVOTED

DEVOTEE n person who is very enthusiastic about something

DEVOTEES > DEVOTEE

DEVOTES > DEVOTE

DEVOTING > DEVOTE

DEVOTION n strong affection for or loyalty to someone or something

DEVOTIONS > DEVOTION

DEVOTS > DEVOT

DEVOUR vb eat greedily

DEVOURED > DEVOUR

DEVOURER > DEVOUR

DEVOURERS > DEVOUR

DEVOURING > DEVOUR

DEVOURS > DEVOUR

DEVOUT adj deeply religious

DEVOUTER > DEVOUT

DEVOUTEST > DEVOUT

DEVOUTLY > DEVOUT

DEVS > DEV

DEVVEL vb strike with blow

DEVVELLED > DEVVEL

DEVVELS > DEVVEL

DEW n drops of water that form on the ground at night from vapour in the air ▷ vb moisten with or as with dew

DEWAN n (formerly in India) the chief or finance minister of a state ruled by an Indian prince

DEWANI n post of dewan

DEWANIS > DEWANI

DEWANNIES > DEWANNY

DEWANNY same as > DEWANI

DEWANS > DEWAN

DEWAR n as in dewar flask type of vacuum flask

DEWARS > DEWAR

DEWATER vb remove water from

DEWATERED > DEWATER

DEWATERER > DEWATER

DEWATERS > DEWATER

DEWAX vb remove wax from

DEWAXED > DEWAX

DEWAXES > DEWAX

DEWAXING > DEWAX

DEWBERRY n type of bramble with blue-black fruits

DEWCLAW n nonfunctional claw on a dog's leg

DEWCLAWED > DEWCLAW

DEWCLAWS > DEWCLAW

DEWDROP n drop of dew

DEWDROPS > DEWDROP

DEWED > DEW

DEWFALL n formation of dew

DEWFALLS > DEWFALL

DEWFULL obsolete form of > DUE

DEWIER > DEWY

DEWIEST > DEWY

DEWILY > DEWY

DEWINESS > DEWY

DEWING > DEW

DEWITT vb kill, esp hang unlawfully

DEWITTED > DEWITT

DEWITTING > DEWITT

DEWITTS > DEWITT

DEWLAP n loose fold of skin hanging under the throat in dogs, cattle, etc

DEWLAPPED > DEWLAP

DEWLAPS > DEWLAP

DEWLAPT > DEWLAP

DEWLESS > DEW

DEWOOL vb remove wool from

DEWOOLED > DEWOOL

DEWOOLING > DEWOOL

DEWOOLS > DEWOOL

DEWORM vb rid of worms

DEWORMED > DEWORM

DEWORMER > DEWORM

DEWORMERS > DEWORM

DEWORMING > DEWORM

DEWORMS > DEWORM

DEWPOINT n temperature at which water vapour in the air becomes saturated and water droplets begin to form

DEWPOINTS > DEWPOINT

DEWS > DEW

DEWY adj moist with or as with dew

DEX n dextroamphetamine

DEXES > DEX

DEXIE n pill containing dextroamphetamine

DEXIES > DEXIE

DEXTER adj of or on the right side of a shield, etc, from the bearer's point of view ▷ n small breed of beef cattle

DEXTERITY n skill in using one's hands

DEXTEROUS adj possessing or done with dexterity

DEXTERS > DEXTER

DEXTRAL n right-handed person

DEXTRALLY > DEXTRAL

DEXTRALS > DEXTRAL

DEXTRAN n polysaccharide compound

DEXTRANS > DEXTRAN

DEXTRIN n sticky substance obtained from starch

DEXTRINE same as > DEXTRIN

DEXTRINES > DEXTRINE

DEXTRINS > DEXTRIN

DEXTRO adj dextrorotatory or rotating to the right

DEXTRORSE adj (of some climbing plants) growing upwards in a helix from left to right or anticlockwise

DEXTROSE n glucose occurring in fruit, honey, and the blood of animals

DEXTROSES > DEXTROSE

DEXTROUS same as > DEXTEROUS

DEXY same as > DEXIE

DEY n title given to commanders or governors of the Janissaries of Algiers

DEYS > DEY

DEZINC vb remove zinc from

DEZINCED > DEZINC

DEZINCING > DEZINC
DEZINCKED > DEZINC
DEZINCS > DEZINC
DHAK n tropical Asian tree
DHAKS > DHAK
DHAL n curry made from lentils or beans
DHALS > DHAL
DHAMMA variant of **>** DHARMA
DHAMMAS > DHAMMA
DHANSAK n any of a variety of Indian dishes
DHANSAKS > DHANSAK
DHARMA n moral law or behaviour
DHARMAS > DHARMA
DHARMIC > DHARMA
DHARMSALA n Indian hostel
DHARNA n (in India) a method of obtaining justice
DHARNAS > DHARNA
DHIKR n Sufi religious ceremony
DHIKRS > DHIKR
DHIMMI n non-Muslim living in a state governed by sharia law
DHIMMIS > DHIMMI
DHOBI n (in India, Malaya, East Africa, etc, esp formerly) a washerman
DHOBIS > DHOBI
DHOL n type of Indian drum
DHOLAK n type of two-headed drum
DHOLAKS > DHOLAK
DHOLE n fierce canine mammal
DHOLES > DHOLE
DHOLL same as **>** DHAL
DHOLLS > DHOLL
DHOLS > DHOL
DHOOLIES > DHOOLY
DHOOLY same as **>** DOOLIE
DHOORA same as **>** DURRA
DHOORAS > DHOORA
DHOOTI same as **>** DHOTI
DHOOTIE same as **>** DHOTI
DHOOTIES > DHOOTIE
DHOOTIS > DHOOTI
DHOTI n long loincloth worn by men in India
DHOTIS > DHOTI
DHOURRA same as **>** DURRA
DHOURRAS > DHOURRA
DHOW n Arab sailing ship
DHOWS > DHOW
DHURNA same as **>** DHARNA
DHURNAS > DHURNA
DHURRA same as **>** DURRA
DHURRAS > DHURRA
DHURRIE same as **>** DURRIE
DHURRIES > DHURRIE
DHUTI same as **>** DHOTI
DHUTIS > DHUTI
DHYANA n type of Hindu meditation
DHYANAS > DHYANA
DI > DEUS

DIABASE n altered dolerite
DIABASES > DIABASE
DIABASIC > DIABASE
DIABETES n disorder in which an abnormal amount of urine containing an excess of sugar is excreted
DIABETIC n person who has diabetes **>** adj of or having diabetes
DIABETICS > DIABETIC
DIABLE n type of sauce
DIABLERIE n magic or witchcraft connected with devils
DIABLERY same as **>** DIABLERIE
DIABLES > DIABLE
DIABOLIC adj of the Devil
DIABOLISE same as **>** DIABOLIZE
DIABOLISM n witchcraft, devil worship
DIABOLIST > DIABOLISM
DIABOLIZE vb make (someone or something) diabolical
DIABOLO n game using a spinning top and a cord fastened to two sticks
DIABOLOGY n study of devils
DIABOLOS > DIABOLO
DIACETYL n aromatic compound
DIACETYLS > DIACETYL
DIACHRONY n change over time
DIACHYLON n acid or salt that contains two acidic hydrogen atoms
DIACHYLUM n plaster containing glycerin with lead salts
DIACID n lead plaster
DIACIDIC adj (of a base, such as calcium hydroxide $Ca(OH)_2$) capable of neutralizing two protons with one of its molecules
DIACIDS > DIACID
DIACODION n herbal remedy aiding sleep
DIACODIUM n syrup of poppies
DIACONAL adj of or associated with a deacon or the diaconate
DIACONATE n position or period of office of a deacon
DIACRITIC n sign above or below a character to indicate phonetic value or stress
DIACT same as **>** DIACTINE
DIACTINAL adj having two pointed ends
DIACTINE adj two-rayed **>** n sponge spicule having two rays that develop in

different directions from a single point of origin
DIACTINES > DIACTINE
DIACTINIC adj able to transmit photochemically active radiation
DIACTS > DIACT
DIADEM n crown **>** vb adorn or crown with or as with a diadem
DIADEMED > DIADEM
DIADEMING > DIADEM
DIADEMS > DIADEM
DIADOCHI pl n the six Macedonian generals who, after the death of Alexander the Great, fought for control of his empire
DIADOCHY n replacement of one element in a crystal by another
DIADROM n complete course of pendulum
DIADROMS > DIADROM
DIAERESES > DIAERESIS
DIAERESIS n mark placed over a vowel to show that it is pronounced separately from the preceding one, for example in Noël
DIAERETIC > DIAERESIS
DIAGLYPH n figure cut into stone
DIAGLYPHS > DIAGLYPH
DIAGNOSE vb determine by diagnosis
DIAGNOSED > DIAGNOSE
DIAGNOSES > DIAGNOSIS
DIAGNOSIS n discovery and identification of diseases from the examination of symptoms
DIAGONAL adj from corner to corner **>** n diagonal line
DIAGONALS > DIAGONAL
DIAGRAM n sketch showing the form or workings of something **>** vb show in or as if in a diagram
DIAGRAMED > DIAGRAM
DIAGRAMS > DIAGRAM
DIAGRAPH n device for enlarging or reducing maps, plans, etc
DIAGRAPHS > DIAGRAPH
DIAGRID n diagonal structure network
DIAGRIDS > DIAGRID
DIAL n face of a clock or watch **>** vb operate the dial or buttons on a telephone in order to contact (a number)
DIALECT n form of a language spoken in a particular area
DIALECTAL > DIALECT

DIALECTIC n logical debate by question and answer to resolve differences between two views **>** adj of or relating to logical disputation
DIALECTS > DIALECT
DIALED > DIAL
DIALER > DIAL
DIALERS > DIAL
DIALING > DIAL
DIALINGS > DIAL
DIALIST n dial-maker
DIALISTS > DIALIST
DIALLAGE n green or brownish-black variety of the mineral augite in the form of layers of platelike crystals
DIALLAGES > DIALLAGE
DIALLAGIC > DIALLAGE
DIALLED > DIAL
DIALLEL n interbreeding among a group of parents **>** adj (of lines) not parallel, meeting, or intersecting
DIALLELS > DIALLEL
DIALLER > DIAL
DIALLERS > DIAL
DIALLING > DIAL
DIALLINGS > DIAL
DIALLIST same as **>** DIALIST
DIALLISTS > DIALLIST
DIALOG same as **>** DIALOGUE
DIALOGED > DIALOG
DIALOGER > DIALOG
DIALOGERS > DIALOG
DIALOGIC > DIALOGUE
DIALOGING > DIALOG
DIALOGISE same as **>** DIALOGIZE
DIALOGISM n deduction with one premise and a disjunctive conclusion
DIALOGIST n person who writes or takes part in a dialogue
DIALOGITE n carbonate mineral
DIALOGIZE vb carry on a dialogue
DIALOGS > DIALOG
DIALOGUE n conversation between two people, esp in a book, film, or play **>** vb put into the form of a dialogue
DIALOGUED > DIALOGUE
DIALOGUER > DIALOGUE
DIALOGUES > DIALOGUE
DIALS > DIAL
DIALYSATE n liquid used in dialysis
DIALYSE vb separate by dialysis
DIALYSED > DIALYSE
DIALYSER n machine that performs dialysis, esp one that removes impurities from the blood of patients with malfunctioning kidneys

DIALYSERS > DIALYSER
DIALYSES > DIALYSIS
DIALYSING > DIALYSE
DIALYSIS n filtering of blood through a membrane to remove waste products
DIALYTIC > DIALYSIS
DIALYZATE same as > DIALYSATE
DIALYZE same as > DIALYSE
DIALYZED > DIALYZE
DIALYZER same as > DIALYSER
DIALYZERS > DIALYZER
DIALYZES > DIALYZE
DIALYZING > DIALYZE
DIAMAGNET n substance exhibiting diamagnetism
DIAMANTE adj decorated with artificial jewels or sequins ⊳ n fabric so covered
DIAMANTES > DIAMANTE
DIAMETER n (length of) a straight line through the centre of a circle or sphere
DIAMETERS > DIAMETER
DIAMETRAL same as > DIAMETRIC
DIAMETRIC adj of a diameter
DIAMIDE n compound containing two amido groups
DIAMIDES > DIAMIDE
DIAMIN same as > DIAMINE
DIAMINE n any chemical compound containing two amino groups in its molecules
DIAMINES > DIAMINE
DIAMINS > DIAMIN
DIAMOND n exceptionally hard precious stone ⊳ adj (of an anniversary) the sixtieth ⊳ vb stud or decorate with diamonds
DIAMONDED > DIAMOND
DIAMONDS > DIAMOND
DIAMYL adj with two amyl groups
DIANDRIES > DIANDRY
DIANDROUS adj (of some flowers or flowering plants) having two stamens
DIANDRY n practice of having two husbands
DIANE adj as in steak diane kind of steak
DIANODAL adj going through a node
DIANOETIC adj of or relating to thought, esp to discursive reasoning rather than intuition
DIANOIA n perception and experience regarded as lower modes of knowledge
DIANOIAS > DIANOIA

DIANTHUS n type of widely cultivated Eurasian plant, such as the carnation, pink, and sweet william
DIAPASE same as > DIAPASON
DIAPASES > DIAPASE
DIAPASON n either of two stops found throughout the range of a pipe organ
DIAPASONS > DIAPASON
DIAPAUSE vb undergo diapause ⊳ n period of suspended development and growth accompanied by decreased metabolism in insects and some other animals. It is correlated with seasonal changes
DIAPAUSED > DIAPAUSE
DIAPAUSES > DIAPAUSE
DIAPENTE n (in classical Greece) the interval of a perfect fifth
DIAPENTES > DIAPENTE
DIAPER n nappy ⊳ vb decorate with a geometric pattern
DIAPERED > DIAPER
DIAPERING > DIAPER
DIAPERS > DIAPER
DIAPHONE n set of all realizations of a given phoneme in a language
DIAPHONES > DIAPHONE
DIAPHONIC > DIAPHONY
DIAPHONY n style of two-part polyphonic singing
DIAPHRAGM n muscular partition that separates the abdominal cavity and chest cavity
DIAPHYSES > DIAPHYSIS
DIAPHYSIS n shaft of a long bone
DIAPIR n anticlinal fold in which the brittle overlying rock has been pierced by material, such as salt, from beneath
DIAPIRIC > DIAPIR
DIAPIRISM > DIAPIR
DIAPIRS > DIAPIR
DIAPSID n reptile with two holes in rear of skull
DIAPSIDS > DIAPSID
DIAPYESES > DIAPYESIS
DIAPYESIS n discharge of pus
DIAPYETIC > DIAPYESIS
DIARCH adj (of a vascular bundle) having two strands of xylem
DIARCHAL > DIARCHY
DIARCHIC > DIARCHY
DIARCHIES > DIARCHY
DIARCHY n government by two states, individuals, etc

DIARIAL > DIARY
DIARIAN > DIARY
DIARIES > DIARY
DIARISE same as > DIARIZE
DIARISED > DIARISE
DIARISES > DIARISE
DIARISING > DIARISE
DIARIST n person who writes a diary
DIARISTIC > DIARIST
DIARISTS > DIARIST
DIARIZE vb record in diary
DIARIZED > DIARIZE
DIARIZES > DIARIZE
DIARIZING > DIARIZE
DIARRHEA same as > DIARRHOEA
DIARRHEAL > DIARRHEA
DIARRHEAS > DIARRHEA
DIARRHEIC > DIARRHEA
DIARRHOEA n frequent discharge of abnormally liquid faeces
DIARY n (book for) a record of daily events, appointments, or observations
DIASCIA n S African plant, usu with pink flowers
DIASCIAS > DIASCIA
DIASCOPE n optical projector used to display transparencies
DIASCOPES > DIASCOPE
DIASPORA n dispersion or spreading, as of people originally belonging to one nation or having a common culture
DIASPORAS > DIASPORA
DIASPORE n white, yellowish, or grey mineral
DIASPORES > DIASPORE
DIASPORIC > DIASPORA
DIASTASE n enzyme that converts starch into sugar
DIASTASES > DIASTASIS
DIASTASIC > DIASTASE
DIASTASIS n separation of an epiphysis from the long bone to which it is normally attached without fracture of the bone
DIASTATIC > DIASTASIS
DIASTEM same as > DIASTEMA
DIASTEMA n abnormal space, fissure, or cleft in a bodily organ or part
DIASTEMAS > DIASTEMA
DIASTEMS > DIASTEM
DIASTER n stage in cell division
DIASTERS > DIASTER
DIASTOLE n dilation of the chambers of the heart
DIASTOLES > DIASTOLE
DIASTOLIC > DIASTOLE

DIASTRAL > DIASTER
DIASTYLE adj having columns about three diameters apart ⊳ n diastyle building
DIASTYLES > DIASTYLE
DIATHERMY n local heating of the body tissues with an electric current for medical or surgical purposes
DIATHESES > DIATHESIS
DIATHESIS n hereditary or acquired susceptibility of the body to one or more diseases
DIATHETIC > DIATHESIS
DIATOM n microscopic unicellular alga
DIATOMIC adj containing two atoms
DIATOMIST n specialist in diatoms
DIATOMITE n soft very fine-grained whitish rock consisting of the siliceous remains of diatoms deposited in the ocean or in ponds or lakes. It is used as an absorbent, filtering medium, insulator, filler, etc
DIATOMS > DIATOM
DIATONIC adj of a regular major or minor scale
DIATREME n volcanic vent produced by an eruption of gas
DIATREMES > DIATREME
DIATRETA > DIATRETUM
DIATRETUM n Roman glass bowl
DIATRIBE n bitter critical attack
DIATRIBES > DIATRIBE
DIATRON n circuit that uses diodes
DIATRONS > DIATRON
DIATROPIC adj relating to a type of response in plants to an external stimulus
DIAXON n bipolar cell
DIAXONS > DIAXON
DIAZEPAM n chemical compound used as a minor tranquillizer and muscle relaxant and to treat acute epilepsy
DIAZEPAMS > DIAZEPAM
DIAZEUXES > DIAZEUXIS
DIAZEUXIS n separation of two tetrachords by interval of a tone
DIAZIN same as > DIAZINE
DIAZINE n organic compound
DIAZINES > DIAZINE
DIAZINON n type of insecticide
DIAZINONS > DIAZINON

DIAZINS > DIAZIN

DIAZO adj relating to a method for reproducing documents ▷ n document produced by this method

DIAZOES > DIAZO

DIAZOLE n type of organic compound

DIAZOLES > DIAZOLE

DIAZONIUM n type of chemical group

DIAZOS > DIAZO

DIAZOTISE same as > DIAZOTIZE

DIAZOTIZE vb cause (an aryl amine) to react with nitrous acid to produce a diazonium salt

DIB vb fish by allowing the bait to bob and dip on the surface

DIBASIC adj (of an acid) containing two acidic hydrogen atoms

DIBBED > DIB

DIBBER same as > DIBBLE

DIBBERS > DIBBER

DIBBING > DIB

DIBBLE n small gardening tool ▷ vb make a hole in (the ground) with a dibble

DIBBLED > DIBBLE

DIBBLER > DIBBLE

DIBBLERS > DIBBLE

DIBBLES > DIBBLE

DIBBLING > DIBBLE

DIBBS n money

DIBBUK variant spelling of > DYBBUK

DIBBUKIM > DIBBUK

DIBBUKKIM > DIBBUK

DIBBUKS > DIBBUK

DIBROMIDE n chemical compound that contains two bromine atoms per molecule

DIBS > DIB

DIBUTYL adj with two butyl groups

DICACIOUS adj teasing

DICACITY n playful teasing

DICACODYL n oily slightly water-soluble poisonous liquid with garlic-like odour

DICAMBA n type of weedkiller

DICAMBAS > DICAMBA

DICAST n juror in ancient Athens

DICASTERY n congregation

DICASTIC > DICAST

DICASTS > DICAST

DICE n small cube with numbered sides ▷ vb cut (food) into small cubes

DICED > DICE

DICENTRA n Asian or N American plant with finely divided leaves and ornamental clusters of drooping flowers

DICENTRAS > DICENTRA

DICENTRIC n abnormal chromosome with two centromeres

DICER > DICE

DICERS > DICE

DICES > DICE

DICEY adj dangerous or risky

DICH interj archaic expression meaning "may it do"

DICHASIA > DICHASIUM

DICHASIAL > DICHASIUM

DICHASIUM n cymose inflorescence in which each branch bearing a flower gives rise to two other flowering branches, as in the stitchwort

DICHOGAMY n maturation of male and female parts of a flower at different times, preventing automatic self-pollination

DICHONDRA n creeping perennial herb

DICHOPTIC adj having the eyes distinctly separate

DICHORD n two-stringed musical instrument

DICHORDS > DICHORD

DICHOTIC adj relating to or involving the stimulation of each ear simultaneously by different sounds

DICHOTOMY n division into two opposed groups or parts

DICHROIC adj having or consisting of only two colours

DICHROISM n property of a uniaxial crystal, such as tourmaline, of showing a perceptible difference in colour when viewed along two different axes in transmitted white light

DICHROITE n grey or violet-blue dichroic material

DICHROMAT n person able to distinguish only two colours

DICHROMIC adj of or involving only two colours

DICHT vb wipe

DICHTED > DICHT

DICHTING > DICHT

DICHTS > DICHT

DICIER > DICEY

DICIEST > DICEY

DICING > DICE

DICINGS > DICE

DICK n penis ▷ vb penetrate with a penis

DICKED > DICK

DICKENS n euphemism for devil

DICKENSES > DICKENS

DICKER vb trade (goods) by bargaining ▷ n petty bargain or barter

DICKERED > DICKER

DICKERER n person who dickers

DICKERERS > DICKERER

DICKERING > DICKER

DICKERS > DICKER

DICKEY same as > DICKY

DICKEYS > DICKEY

DICKHEAD n stupid or despicable man or boy

DICKHEADS > DICKHEAD

DICKIE same as > DICKY

DICKIER > DICKY

DICKIES > DICKY

DICKIEST > DICKY

DICKING > DICK

DICKINGS > DICKING

DICKS > DICK

DICKTIER > DICKTY

DICKTIEST > DICKTY

DICKTY same as > DICTY

DICKY n false shirt front ▷ adj shaky or weak

DICKYBIRD See > DICKY

DICLINIES > DICLINOUS

DICLINISM > DICLINOUS

DICLINOUS adj (of flowering plants) bearing unisexual flowers

DICLINY > DICLINOUS

DICOT n type of flowering plant

DICOTS > DICOT

DICOTYL n type of flowering plant

DICOTYLS > DICOTYL

DICROTAL same as > DICROTIC

DICROTIC adj having or relating to a double pulse for each heartbeat

DICROTISM > DICROTIC

DICROTOUS same as > DICROTIC

DICT vb dictate

DICTA > DICTUM

DICTATE vb say aloud for someone else to write down ▷ n authoritative command

DICTATED > DICTATE

DICTATES > DICTATE

DICTATING > DICTATE

DICTATION n act of dictating words to be taken down in writing

DICTATOR n ruler who has complete power

DICTATORS > DICTATOR

DICTATORY adj tending to dictate

DICTATRIX > DICTATOR

DICTATURE n dictatorship

DICTED > DICT

DICTIER > DICTY

DICTIEST > DICTY

DICTING > DICT

DICTION n manner of pronouncing words and sounds

DICTIONAL > DICTION

DICTIONS > DICTION

DICTS > DICT

DICTUM n formal statement

DICTUMS > DICTUM

DICTY adj conceited; snobbish

DICTYOGEN n plant with net-veined leaves

DICUMAROL n anticoagulant drug

DICYCLIC adj having the perianth arranged in two whorls

DICYCLIES > DICYCLIC

DICYCLY > DICYCLIC

DID > DO

DIDACT n instructive person

DIDACTIC adj intended to instruct

DIDACTICS n art or science of teaching

DIDACTS > DIDACT

DIDACTYL adj having only two toes on each foot ▷ n animal with only two toes on each foot

DIDACTYLS > DIDACTYL

DIDAKAI same as > DIDICOY

DIDAKAIS > DIDAKAI

DIDAKEI same as > DIDICOY

DIDAKEIS > DIDAKEI

DIDAPPER n small grebe

DIDAPPERS > DIDAPPER

DIDDER vb shake with fear

DIDDERED > DIDDER

DIDDERING > DIDDER

DIDDERS > DIDDER

DIDDICOY same as > DIDICOY

DIDDICOYS > DIDDICOY

DIDDIER > DIDDY

DIDDIES > DIDDY

DIDDIEST > DIDDY

DIDDLE vb swindle

DIDDLED > DIDDLE

DIDDLER > DIDDLE

DIDDLERS > DIDDLE

DIDDLES > DIDDLE

DIDDLEY n worthless amount

DIDDLEYS > DIDDLEY

DIDDLIES > DIDDLY

DIDDLING > DIDDLE

DIDDLY n worthless amount

DIDDUMS interj expression of sympathy, esp to a child

DIDDY n female breast or nipple ▷ adj of or relating to a diddy

DIDELPHIC adj with two genital tubes or ovaries

DIDELPHID n marsupial

DIDICOI same as > DIDICOY
DIDICOIS > DIDICOI
DIDICOY n (in Britain) a person who lives like a Gypsy but is not a true Romany
DIDICOYS > DIDICOY
DIDIE same as > DIDY
DIDIES > DIDY
DIDJERIDU n Australian Aboriginal wind instrument
DIDO n antic
DIDOES > DIDO
DIDOS > DIDO
DIDRACHM n two-drachma piece
DIDRACHMA same as > DIDRACHM
DIDRACHMS > DIDRACHM
DIDST form of the past tense of > DO
DIDY n woman's breast
DIDYMIUM n mixture of the metallic rare earths neodymium and praseodymium, once thought to be an element
DIDYMIUMS > DIDYMIUM
DIDYMOUS adj in pairs or in two parts
DIDYNAMY n (of stamens) being in two unequal pairs
DIE vb cease all biological activity permanently ▷ n shaped block used to cut or form metal
DIEB n N African jackal
DIEBACK n disease of trees and shrubs ▷ vb (of plants) to suffer from dieback
DIEBACKS > DIEBACK
DIEBS > DIEB
DIECIOUS same as > DIOECIOUS
DIED > DIE
DIEDRAL same as > DIHEDRAL
DIEDRALS > DIEDRAL
DIEDRE n large shallow groove or corner in a rock face
DIEDRES > DIEDRE
DIEGESES > DIEGESIS
DIEGESIS n utterance of fact
DIEGETIC adj relating to a factual narrative
DIEHARD n person who resists change
DIEHARDS > DIEHARD
DIEING > DIE
DIEL n 24-hour period ▷ adj of or lasting for any 24-hour period
DIELDRIN n highly toxic insecticide
DIELDRINS > DIELDRIN
DIELS > DIEL
DIELYTRA n genus of herbaceous plants
DIELYTRAS > DIELYTRA

DIEMAKER n one who makes dies
DIEMAKERS > DIEMAKER
DIENE n type of hydrocarbon
DIENES > DIENE
DIEOFF n process of dying in large numbers
DIEOFFS > DIEOFF
DIERESES > DIERESIS
DIERESIS same as > DIAERESIS
DIERETIC > DIERESIS
DIES > DIE
DIESEL vb drive diesel-fueled vehicle ▷ n diesel engine
DIESELED > DIESEL
DIESELING > DIESEL
DIESELISE same as > DIESELIZE
DIESELIZE vb be equipped with diesel engine
DIESELS > DIESEL
DIESES > DIESIS
DIESINKER n person who engraves dies
DIESIS n (in ancient Greek theory) any interval smaller than a whole tone
DIESTER n synthetic lubricant
DIESTERS > DIESTER
DIESTOCK n device holding the dies used to cut an external screw thread
DIESTOCKS > DIESTOCK
DIESTROUS same as > DIOESTRUS
DIESTRUM another word for > DIESTROUS
DIESTRUMS > DIESTRUM
DIESTRUS same as > DIOESTRUS
DIET n food that a person or animal regularly eats ▷ vb follow a special diet so as to lose weight ▷ adj (of food) suitable for a weight-reduction diet
DIETARIAN n dieter
DIETARIES > DIETARY
DIETARILY > DIETARY
DIETARY adj of or relating to a diet ▷ n regulated diet
DIETED > DIET
DIETER > DIET
DIETERS > DIET
DIETETIC adj prepared for special dietary requirements
DIETETICS n study of diet and nutrition
DIETHER n chemical compound
DIETHERS > DIETHER
DIETHYL adj as in diethyl ether ether
DIETHYLS > DIETHYL
DIETICIAN n person who specializes in dietetics

DIETINE n low-ranking diet
DIETINES > DIETINE
DIETING > DIET
DIETINGS > DIET
DIETIST another word for > DIETITIAN
DIETISTS > DIETIST
DIETITIAN same as > DIETICIAN
DIETS > DIET
DIF same as > DIFF
DIFF n (slang) difference
DIFFER vb be unlike
DIFFERED > DIFFER
DIFFERENT adj unlike
DIFFERING > DIFFER
DIFFERS > DIFFER
DIFFICILE adj difficult
DIFFICULT adj requiring effort or skill to do or understand
DIFFIDENT adj lacking self-confidence
DIFFLUENT adj flowing; not fixed
DIFFORM adj irregular in form
DIFFRACT vb cause to undergo diffraction
DIFFRACTS > DIFFRACT
DIFFS > DIFF
DIFFUSE vb spread over a wide area ▷ adj widely spread
DIFFUSED > DIFFUSE
DIFFUSELY > DIFFUSE
DIFFUSER n person or thing that diffuses
DIFFUSERS > DIFFUSER
DIFFUSES > DIFFUSE
DIFFUSING > DIFFUSE
DIFFUSION n act of diffusing or the fact of being diffused
DIFFUSIVE adj characterized by diffusion
DIFFUSOR same as > DIFFUSER
DIFFUSORS > DIFFUSOR
DIFS > DIF
DIG vb cut into, break up, and turn over or remove (earth), esp with a spade ▷ n digging
DIGAMIES > DIGAMY
DIGAMIST > DIGAMY
DIGAMISTS > DIGAMY
DIGAMMA n letter of the Greek alphabet
DIGAMMAS > DIGAMMA
DIGAMOUS > DIGAMY
DIGAMY n second marriage
DIGASTRIC adj (of certain muscles) having two fleshy portions joined by a tendon ▷ n muscle of the mandible that assists in lowering the lower jaw
DIGENESES > DIGENESIS

DIGENESIS n ability to alternate sexual and asexual means of reproduction
DIGENETIC adj of or relating to digenesis
DIGERATI pl n people who earn large amounts of money through internet-related business
DIGEST vb subject to a process of digestion ▷ n shortened version of a book, report, or article
DIGESTANT same as > DIGESTIVE
DIGESTED > DIGEST
DIGESTER n apparatus or vessel, such as an autoclave, in which digestion is carried out
DIGESTERS > DIGESTER
DIGESTIF n something, esp a drink, taken as an aid to digestion, either before or after a meal
DIGESTIFS > DIGESTIF
DIGESTING > DIGEST
DIGESTION n (body's system for) breaking down food into easily absorbed substances
DIGESTIVE adj relating to digestion
DIGESTOR same as > DIGESTER
DIGESTORS > DIGESTOR
DIGESTS > DIGEST
DIGGABLE adj that can be dug
DIGGED a past tense of > DIG
DIGGER n machine used for digging
DIGGERS > DIGGER
DIGGING > DIG
DIGGINGS pl n material that has been dug out
DIGHT vb adorn or equip, as for battle
DIGHTED > DIGHT
DIGHTING > DIGHT
DIGHTS > DIGHT
DIGICAM n digital camera
DIGICAMS > DIGICAM
DIGIPACK n type of packaging for a CD or DVD
DIGIPACKS > DIGIPACK
DIGIT n finger or toe
DIGITAL adj displaying information as numbers ▷ n one of the keys on the manuals of an organ or piano, etc
DIGITALIN n poisonous amorphous crystalline mixture of glycosides extracted from digitalis leaves and formerly used in treating heart disease
DIGITALIS n drug made from foxglove leaves, used as a heart stimulant
DIGITALLY > DIGITAL

DIGITALS > DIGITAL

DIGITATE adj (of leaves) having leaflets in the form of a spread hand

DIGITATED same as > DIGITATE

DIGITISE same as > DIGITIZE

DIGITISED > DIGITISE

DIGITISER > DIGITIZE

DIGITISES > DIGITISE

DIGITIZE vb transcribe (data) into a digital form for processing by a computer

DIGITIZED adj recorded or stored in digital form

DIGITIZER > DIGITIZE

DIGITIZES > DIGITIZE

DIGITONIN n type of glycoside

DIGITOXIN same as > DIGOXIN

DIGITRON n type of tube, for displaying information, having a common anode and several cathodes shaped in the form of characters, which can be lit by a glow discharge

DIGITRONS > DIGITRON

DIGITS > DIGIT

DIGITULE n any small finger-like process

DIGITULES > DIGITULE

DIGLOSSIA n existence in a language of a high, or socially prestigious, and a low, or everyday, form, as German and Swiss German in Switzerland

DIGLOSSIC > DIGLOSSIA

DIGLOT n bilingual book

DIGLOTS > DIGLOT

DIGLOTTIC > DIGLOT

DIGLYPH n ornament in Doric frieze with two grooves

DIGLYPHS > DIGLYPH

DIGNIFIED adj calm, impressive, and worthy of respect

DIGNIFIES > DIGNIFY

DIGNIFY vb add distinction to

DIGNITARY n person of high official position

DIGNITIES > DIGNITY

DIGNITY n serious, calm, and controlled behaviour or manner

DIGONAL adj of or relating to a symmetry operation

DIGOXIN n glycoside extracted from the leaves of the woolly foxglove

DIGOXINS > DIGOXIN

DIGRAPH n two letters used to represent a single sound

DIGRAPHIC > DIGRAPH

DIGRAPHS > DIGRAPH

DIGRESS vb depart from the main subject in speech or writing

DIGRESSED > DIGRESS

DIGRESSER > DIGRESS

DIGRESSES > DIGRESS

DIGS > DIG

DIGYNIAN adj relating to plant class Digynia

DIGYNOUS another word for > DIGYNIAN

DIHEDRA > DIHEDRON

DIHEDRAL adj having or formed by two intersecting planes ▷ n figure formed by two intersecting planes

DIHEDRALS > DIHEDRAL

DIHEDRON same as > DIHEDRAL

DIHEDRONS > DIHEDRON

DIHYBRID n offspring of two individuals that differ with respect to two pairs of genes

DIHYBRIDS > DIHYBRID

DIHYDRIC adj (of an alcohol) containing two hydroxyl groups per molecule

DIKA n wild mango

DIKAS > DIKA

DIKAST same as > DICAST

DIKASTS > DIKAST

DIKDIK n small African antelope

DIKDIKS > DIKDIK

DIKE same as > DYKE

DIKED > DIKE

DIKER n builder of dikes

DIKERS > DIKER

DIKES > DIKE

DIKETONE n as in diphenylene diketone a compound used in dye manufacture, aka anthraquinone

DIKETONES > DIKETONE

DIKEY adj (of a lesbian) masculine

DIKIER > DIKEY

DIKIEST > DIKEY

DIKING > DIKE

DIKKOP n type of brownish shore bird with a large head and eyes

DIKKOPS > DIKKOP

DIKTAT n dictatorial decree

DIKTATS > DIKTAT

DILATABLE > DILATE

DILATABLY > DILATE

DILATANCY n phenomenon caused by the nature of the stacking or fitting together of particles or granules in a heterogeneous system, such as the solidification of certain sols under pressure, and the thixotropy of certain gels

DILATANT adj tending to dilate ▷ n something, such as a catheter, that causes dilation

DILATANTS > DILATANT

DILATATE same as > DILATE

DILATATOR same as > DILATOR

DILATE vb make or become wider or larger

DILATED > DILATE

DILATER same as > DILATOR

DILATERS > DILATER

DILATES > DILATE

DILATING > DILATE

DILATION > DILATE

DILATIONS > DILATE

DILATIVE > DILATE

DILATOR n something that dilates an object

DILATORS > DILATOR

DILATORY adj tending or intended to waste time

DILDO n object used as a substitute for an erect penis

DILDOE same as > DILDO

DILDOES > DILDOE

DILDOS > DILDO

DILEMMA n situation offering a choice between two undesirable alternatives

DILEMMAS > DILEMMA

DILEMMIC > DILEMMA

DILIGENCE n steady and careful application

DILIGENT adj careful and persevering in carrying out duties

DILL vb flavour with dill ▷ n sweet-smelling herb

DILLED > DILL

DILLI n dilly bag; small bag, esp one made of plaited grass and used for carrying food

DILLIER > DILLY

DILLIES > DILLY

DILLIEST > DILLY

DILLING > DILL

DILLINGS > DILL

DILLIS > DILLI

DILLS > DILL

DILLWEED n dill plant or its foliage

DILLWEEDS > DILLWEED

DILLY adj foolish ▷ n person or thing that is remarkable

DILSCOOP n type of shot in cricket in which the ball goes over the wicketkeeper's head

DILSCOOPS > DILSCOOP

DILTIAZEM n drug used to treat angina

DILUENT adj causing dilution or serving to dilute ▷ n substance used for or causing dilution

DILUENTS > DILUENT

DILUTABLE > DILUTE

DILUTE vb make (a liquid) less concentrated, esp by adding water ▷ adj (of a liquid) thin and watery

DILUTED > DILUTE

DILUTEE > DILUTE

DILUTEES > DILUTE

DILUTER > DILUTE

DILUTERS > DILUTE

DILUTES > DILUTE

DILUTING > DILUTE

DILUTION n act of diluting or state of being diluted

DILUTIONS > DILUTION

DILUTIVE adj having effect of decreasing earnings per share

DILUTOR n thing intended to have a diluting effect

DILUTORS > DILUTOR

DILUVIA > DILUVIUM

DILUVIAL adj of a flood, esp the great Flood described in the Old Testament

DILUVIAN same as > DILUVIAL

DILUVION same as > DILUVIUM

DILUVIONS > DILUVION

DILUVIUM n glacial drift

DILUVIUMS > DILUVIUM

DIM adj badly lit ▷ vb make or become dim

DIMBLE n wooded hollow; dingle

DIMBLES > DIMBLE

DIMBO n unintelligent person

DIMBOES > DIMBO

DIMBOS > DIMBO

DIME n coin of the US and Canada, worth ten cents

DIMENSION n measurement of the size of something in a particular direction ▷ vb shape or cut to specified dimensions

DIMER n type of molecule

DIMERIC adj of a dimer

DIMERISE same as > DIMERIZE

DIMERISED > DIMERISE

DIMERISES > DIMERISE

DIMERISM > DIMEROUS

DIMERISMS > DIMEROUS

DIMERIZE vb react or cause to react to form a dimer

DIMERIZED > DIMERIZE

DIMERIZES > DIMERIZE

DIMEROUS adj consisting of or divided into two segments, as the tarsi of some insects

DIMERS > DIMER

DIMES > DIME

DIMETER n type of verse

DIMETERS > DIMETER

DIMETHYL n ethane

DIMETHYLS > DIMETHYL

DIMETRIC adj of, relating to, or shaped like a quadrilateral

DIMIDIATE adj divided in halves ▷ vb halve (two bearings) so that they can be represented on the same shield

DIMINISH vb make or become smaller, fewer, or less

DIMISSORY adj granting permission to be ordained

DIMITIES > DIMITY

DIMITY n light strong cotton fabric with woven stripes or squares

DIMLY > DIM

DIMMABLE adj that can be dimmed

DIMMED > DIM

DIMMER > DIM

DIMMERS > DIM

DIMMEST > DIM

DIMMING n as in global dimming decrease in the amount of sunlight reaching the earth

DIMMINGS > DIMMING

DIMMISH > DIM

DIMNESS > DIM

DIMNESSES > DIM

DIMORPH n either of two forms of a substance that exhibits dimorphism

DIMORPHIC adj having two distinct forms

DIMORPHS > DIMORPH

DIMOUT n reduction of lighting

DIMOUTS > DIMOUT

DIMP n in Northern English dialect, a cigarette butt

DIMPLE n small natural dent, esp in the cheeks or chin ▷ vb produce dimples by smiling

DIMPLED > DIMPLE

DIMPLES > DIMPLE

DIMPLIER > DIMPLE

DIMPLIEST > DIMPLE

DIMPLING > DIMPLE

DIMPLY > DIMPLE

DIMPS > DIMP

DIMPSIES > DIMPSY

DIMPSY n twilight

DIMS > DIM

DIMWIT n stupid person

DIMWITS > DIMWIT

DIMWITTED > DIMWIT

DIMYARIAN adj with two adductor muscles

DIMYARY adj with two adductor muscles

DIN n loud unpleasant confused noise ▷ vb instil (something) into someone by constant repetition

DINAR n monetary unit

DINARCHY same as > DIARCHY

DINARS > DINAR

DINDLE another word for > DINNLE

DINDLED > DINDLE

DINDLES > DINDLE

DINDLING > DINDLE

DINE vb eat dinner

DINED > DINE

DINER n person eating a meal

DINERIC adj of or concerned with the interface between immiscible liquids

DINERO n money

DINEROS > DINERO

DINERS > DINER

DINES > DINE

DINETTE n alcove or small area for use as a dining room

DINETTES > DINETTE

DINFUL adj noisy

DING n small dent in a vehicle ▷ vb ring or cause to ring, esp with tedious repetition

DINGBAT n any unnamed object

DINGBATS > DINGBAT

DINGDONG n sound of a bell or bells ▷ vb make such a sound

DINGDONGS > DINGDONG

DINGE n dent ▷ vb make a dent in (something)

DINGED > DINGE

DINGER n (in baseball) home run

DINGERS > DINGER

DINGES n jocular word for something whose name is unknown or forgotten

DINGESES > DINGES

DINGEY same as > DINGHY

DINGEYS > DINGEY

DINGHIES > DINGHY

DINGHY n small boat, powered by sails, oars, or a motor ▷ vb ignore or avoid a person or event

DINGIED > DINGEY

DINGIER > DINGY

DINGIES > DINGY

DINGIEST > DINGY

DINGILY > DINGY

DINGINESS > DINGY

DINGING > DINGE

DINGLE n small wooded hollow or valley

DINGLES > DINGLE

DINGO n Australian wild dog ▷ vb act in a cowardly manner

DINGOED > DINGO

DINGOES > DINGO

DINGOING > DINGO

DINGOS > DINGO

DINGS > DING

DINGUS same as > DINGES

DINGUSES > DINGUS

DINGY adj lacking light ▷ vb ignore or avoid a person or event

DINGYING > DINGY

DINIC n remedy for vertigo

DINICS > DINIC

DINING n act of dining

DININGS > DINING

DINITRO adj containing two nitro groups

DINK adj neat or neatly dressed ▷ vb carry (a second person) on a horse, bicycle, etc ▷ n ball struck delicately

DINKED > DINK

DINKER > DINK

DINKEST > DINK

DINKEY n small locomotive

DINKEYS > DINKEY

DINKIE n affluent married childless person ▷ adj designed for or appealing to dinkies

DINKIER > DINKY

DINKIES > DINKIE

DINKIEST > DINKY

DINKING > DINK

DINKLIER > DINKLY

DINKLIEST > DINKLY

DINKLY adj neat

DINKS > DINK

DINKUM n truth or genuineness

DINKUMS > DINKUM

DINKY adj small and neat

DINMONT n neutered sheep

DINMONTS > DINMONT

DINNA vb a Scots word for do not

DINNAE vb (Scots) do not

DINNED > DIN

DINNER vb dine ▷ n main meal of the day

DINNERED > DINNER

DINNERING > DINNER

DINNERS > DINNER

DINNING > DIN

DINNLE vb shake

DINNLED > DINNLE

DINNLES > DINNLE

DINNLING > DINNLE

DINO n dinosaur

DINOCERAS n uintathere, a gigantic fossil ungulate

DINOMANIA n strong interest in dinosaurs

DINOS > DINO

DINOSAUR n type of extinct prehistoric reptile, many of which were of gigantic size

DINOSAURS > DINOSAUR

DINOTHERE n type of extinct elephant-like mammal with tusks curving downwards and backwards

DINS > DIN

DINT variant of > DENT

DINTED > DINT

DINTING > DINT

DINTLESS > DINT

DINTS > DINT

DIOBOL n ancient Greek coin

DIOBOLON same as > DIOBOL

DIOBOLONS > DIOBOLON

DIOBOLS > DIOBOL

DIOCESAN adj of or relating to a diocese ▷ n bishop of a diocese

DIOCESANS > DIOCESAN

DIOCESE n district over which a bishop has control

DIOCESES > DIOCESE

DIODE n semiconductor device

DIODES > DIODE

DIOECIES > DIOECY

DIOECIOUS adj (of plants) having the male and female reproductive organs on separate plants

DIOECISM > DIOECIOUS

DIOECISMS > DIOECIOUS

DIOECY n state of being dioecious

DIOESTRUS n period in mammal's oestral cycle

DIOICOUS same as > DIOECIOUS

DIOL n any of a class of alcohols that have two hydroxyl groups in each molecule

DIOLEFIN n type of polymer

DIOLEFINS > DIOLEFIN

DIOLS > DIOL

DIONYSIAC same as > DIONYSIAN

DIONYSIAN adj wild or orgiastic

DIOPSIDE n colourless or pale-green pyroxene mineral

DIOPSIDES > DIOPSIDE

DIOPSIDIC > DIOPSIDE

DIOPTASE n green glassy mineral

DIOPTASES > DIOPTASE

DIOPTER same as > DIOPTRE

DIOPTERS > DIOPTER

DIOPTRAL > DIOPTRE

DIOPTRATE adj (of compound eye) divided by transverse line

DIOPTRE n unit for measuring the refractive power of a lens

DIOPTRES > DIOPTRE

DIOPTRIC adj of or concerned with dioptrics

DIOPTRICS n branch of geometrical optics concerned with the formation of images by lenses

DIORAMA n miniature three-dimensional scene

DIORAMAS > DIORAMA

DIORAMIC > DIORAMA

DIORISM n definition; clarity

DIORISMS > DIORISM

DIORISTIC > DIORISM

d

DIORITE n dark coarse-grained igneous plutonic rock
DIORITES > DIORITE
DIORITIC > DIORITE
DIOSGENIN n yam-based substance used in hormone therapy
DIOTA n type of ancient vase
DIOTAS > DIOTA
DIOXAN n colourless insoluble toxic liquid
DIOXANE same as > DIOXAN
DIOXANES > DIOXANE
DIOXANS > DIOXAN
DIOXID same as > DIOXIDE
DIOXIDE n oxide containing two oxygen atoms per molecule
DIOXIDES > DIOXIDE
DIOXIDS > DIOXID
DIOXIN n poisonous chemical by-products of certain weedkillers
DIOXINS > DIOXIN
DIP vb plunge quickly or briefly into a liquid ▷ n dipping
DIPCHICK same as > DABCHICK
DIPCHICKS > DIPCHICK
DIPEPTIDE n compound consisting of two linked amino acids
DIPHASE adj of, having, or concerned with two phases
DIPHASIC same as > DIPHASE
DIPHENYL another name for > BIPHENYL
DIPHENYLS > DIPHENYL
DIPHONE n combination of two speech sounds
DIPHONES > DIPHONE
DIPHTHONG n union of two vowel sounds in a single compound sound
DIPHYSITE n belief in Christ having both divine and human natures
DIPLEGIA n paralysis of corresponding parts on both sides of the body
DIPLEGIAS > DIPLEGIA
DIPLEGIC > DIPLEGIA
DIPLEX adj (in telecommunications) permitting the transmission of simultaneous signals in both directions
DIPLEXER n device that enables the simultaneous transmission of more than one signal
DIPLEXERS > DIPLEXER
DIPLOE n spongy bone separating the two layers of compact bone of the skull

DIPLOES > DIPLOE
DIPLOGEN n heavy hydrogen
DIPLOGENS > DIPLOGEN
DIPLOIC adj relating to diploe
DIPLOID adj denoting a cell or organism with pairs of homologous chromosomes ▷ n diploid cell or organism
DIPLOIDIC > DIPLOID
DIPLOIDS > DIPLOID
DIPLOIDY > DIPLOID
DIPLOMA vb bestow diploma on ▷ n qualification awarded by a college on successful completion of a course
DIPLOMACY n conduct of the relations between nations by peaceful means
DIPLOMAED > DIPLOMA
DIPLOMAS > DIPLOMA
DIPLOMAT n official engaged in diplomacy
DIPLOMATA > DIPLOMA
DIPLOMATE n any person who has been granted a diploma, esp a physician certified as a specialist
DIPLOMATS > DIPLOMAT
DIPLON another name for > DEUTERON
DIPLONEMA a less common name for > DIPLOTENE
DIPLONS > DIPLON
DIPLONT n animal or plant that has the diploid number of chromosomes in its somatic cells
DIPLONTIC > DIPLONT
DIPLONTS > DIPLONT
DIPLOPIA n visual defect in which a single object is seen in duplicate
DIPLOPIAS > DIPLOPIA
DIPLOPIC > DIPLOPIA
DIPLOPOD n type of arthropod such as the millipede
DIPLOPODS > DIPLOPOD
DIPLOSES > DIPLOSIS
DIPLOSIS n doubling of the haploid number of chromosomes that occurs during fusion of gametes to form a diploid zygote
DIPLOTENE n fourth stage of the prophase of meiosis, during which the paired homologous chromosomes separate except at the places where genetic exchange has occurred
DIPLOZOA n type of parasitic worm
DIPLOZOIC adj (of certain animals) bilaterally symmetrical
DIPLOZOON n type of parasitic worm

DIPNET vb fish using fishing net on pole
DIPNETS > DIPNET
DIPNETTED > DIPNET
DIPNOAN n lungfish
DIPNOANS > DIPNOAN
DIPNOOUS adj having lungs and gills
DIPODIC > DIPODY
DIPODIES > DIPODY
DIPODY n metrical unit consisting of two feet
DIPOLAR > DIPOLE
DIPOLE n two equal but opposite electric charges or magnetic poles separated by a small distance
DIPOLES > DIPOLE
DIPPABLE > DIP
DIPPED > DIP
DIPPER n ladle used for dipping
DIPPERFUL n amount held by scoop
DIPPERS > DIPPER
DIPPIER > DIPPY
DIPPIEST > DIPPY
DIPPINESS > DIPPY
DIPPING > DIP
DIPPINGS > DIP
DIPPY adj odd, eccentric, or crazy
DIPROTIC adj having two hydrogen atoms
DIPS > DIP
DIPSADES > DIPSAS
DIPSAS n type of snake
DIPSHIT n stupid person
DIPSHITS > DIPSHIT
DIPSO n (slang) dipsomaniac or alcoholic
DIPSOS > DIPSO
DIPSTICK n notched rod dipped into a container to measure the level of a liquid
DIPSTICKS > DIPSTICK
DIPSWITCH n switch for dipping a vehicle's headlights
DIPT > DIP
DIPTERA n order of insects with two wings
DIPTERAL adj having a double row of columns
DIPTERAN n dipterous insect ▷ adj having two wings or winglike parts
DIPTERANS > DIPTERAN
DIPTERAS > DIPTERA
DIPTERIST n fly expert
DIPTEROI > DIPTEROS
DIPTERON same as > DIPTERAN
DIPTERONS > DIPTERON
DIPTEROS n Greek building with double columns
DIPTEROUS adj having two wings or winglike parts
DIPTYCA same as > DIPTYCH

DIPTYCAS > DIPTYCA
DIPTYCH n painting on two hinged panels
DIPTYCHS > DIPTYCH
DIQUARK n particle in physics
DIQUARKS > DIQUARK
DIQUAT n type of herbicide
DIQUATS > DIQUAT
DIRAM n money unit of Tajikistan
DIRAMS > DIRAM
DIRDAM same as > DIRDUM
DIRDAMS > DIRDAM
DIRDUM n tumult
DIRDUMS > DIRDUM
DIRE adj disastrous, urgent, or terrible
DIRECT adj (of a route) shortest, straight ▷ adv in a direct manner ▷ vb lead and organize
DIRECTED adj (of a number, line, or angle) having either a positive or negative sign to distinguish measurement in one direction or orientation from that in the opposite direction or orientation
DIRECTER > DIRECT
DIRECTEST > DIRECT
DIRECTING > DIRECT
DIRECTION n course or line along which a person or thing moves, points, or lies
DIRECTIVE n instruction, order ▷ adj tending to direct
DIRECTLY adv in a direct manner
DIRECTOR n person or thing that directs or controls
DIRECTORS > DIRECTOR
DIRECTORY n book listing names, addresses, and telephone numbers ▷ adj directing
DIRECTRIX n fixed reference line, situated on the convex side of a conic section, that is used when defining or calculating its eccentricity
DIRECTS > DIRECT
DIREFUL same as > DIRE
DIREFULLY > DIREFUL
DIRELY > DIRE
DIREMPT vb separate with force
DIREMPTED > DIREMPT
DIREMPTS > DIREMPT
DIRENESS > DIRE
DIRER > DIRE
DIREST > DIRE
DIRGE n slow sad song of mourning
DIRGEFUL > DIRGE
DIRGELIKE > DIRGE
DIRGES > DIRGE

DIRHAM n standard monetary unit of Morocco

DIRHAMS > DIRHAM

DIRHEM same as > DIRHAM

DIRHEMS > DIRHEM

DIRIGE n dirge

DIRIGENT adj directing

DIRIGES > DIRIGE

DIRIGIBLE adj able to be steered ▷ n airship

DIRIGISM same as > DIRIGISME

DIRIGISME n control by the state of economic and social matters

DIRIGISMS > DIRIGISM

DIRIGISTE > DIRIGISME

DIRIMENT adj (of an impediment to marriage in canon law) totally invalidating

DIRK n dagger, formerly worn by Scottish Highlanders ▷ vb stab with a dirk

DIRKE variant of > DIRK

DIRKED > DIRK

DIRKES > DIRKE

DIRKING > DIRK

DIRKS > DIRK

DIRL vb tingle; vibrate

DIRLED > DIRL

DIRLING > DIRL

DIRLS > DIRL

DIRNDL n full gathered skirt

DIRNDLS > DIRNDL

DIRT vb soil ▷ n unclean substance, filth

DIRTBAG n filthy person

DIRTBAGS > DIRTBAG

DIRTBALL n contemptible person

DIRTBALLS > DIRTBALL

DIRTED > DIRT

DIRTIED > DIRTY

DIRTIER > DIRTY

DIRTIES > DIRTY

DIRTIEST > DIRTY

DIRTILY > DIRTY

DIRTINESS > DIRTY

DIRTING > DIRT

DIRTS > DIRT

DIRTY adj covered or marked with dirt ▷ vb make dirty

DIRTYING > DIRTY

DIS same as > DISS

DISA n type of orchid

DISABLE vb make ineffective, unfit, or incapable

DISABLED adj lacking a physical power, such as the ability to walk

DISABLER > DISABLE

DISABLERS > DISABLE

DISABLES > DISABLE

DISABLING > DISABLE

DISABLISM n discrimination against disabled people

DISABLIST > DISABLISM

DISABUSAL > DISABUSE

DISABUSE vb rid (someone) of a mistaken idea

DISABUSED > DISABUSE

DISABUSES > DISABUSE

DISACCORD n lack of agreement or harmony ▷ vb be out of agreement

DISADORN vb deprive of ornamentation

DISADORNS > DISADORN

DISAFFECT vb cause to lose loyalty or affection

DISAFFIRM vb deny or contradict (a statement)

DISAGREE vb argue or have different opinions

DISAGREED > DISAGREE

DISAGREES > DISAGREE

DISALLIED > DISALLY

DISALLIES > DISALLY

DISALLOW vb reject as untrue or invalid

DISALLOWS > DISALLOW

DISALLY vb separate

DISANCHOR vb raise anchor of

DISANNEX vb disunite

DISANNUL vb cancel

DISANNULS > DISANNUL

DISANOINT vb invalidate anointment of

DISAPPEAR vb cease to be visible

DISAPPLY vb make (law) invalid

DISARM vb deprive of weapons

DISARMED > DISARM

DISARMER > DISARM

DISARMERS > DISARM

DISARMING adj removing hostility or suspicion

DISARMS > DISARM

DISARRAY n confusion and lack of discipline ▷ vb throw into confusion

DISARRAYS > DISARRAY

DISAS > DISA

DISASTER n occurrence that causes great distress or destruction

DISASTERS > DISASTER

DISATTIRE vb remove clothes from

DISATTUNE vb render out of tune

DISAVOUCH archaic form of > DISAVOW

DISAVOW vb deny connection with or responsibility for

DISAVOWAL > DISAVOW

DISAVOWED > DISAVOW

DISAVOWER > DISAVOW

DISAVOWS > DISAVOW

DISBAND vb (cause to) cease to function as a group

DISBANDED > DISBAND

DISBANDS > DISBAND

DISBAR vb deprive (a barrister) of the right to practise

DISBARK same as > DISEMBARK

DISBARKED > DISBARK

DISBARKS > DISBARK

DISBARRED > DISBAR

DISBARS > DISBAR

DISBELIEF n refusal or reluctance to believe

DISBENCH vb remove from bench

DISBODIED adj disembodied

DISBOSOM vb disclose

DISBOSOMS > DISBOSOM

DISBOUND adj unbound

DISBOWEL vb disembowel

DISBOWELS > DISBOWEL

DISBRANCH vb remove or cut a branch or branches from (a tree)

DISBUD vb remove superfluous buds from (a plant, esp a fruit tree)

DISBUDDED > DISBUD

DISBUDS > DISBUD

DISBURDEN vb remove a load from (a person or animal)

DISBURSAL > DISBURSE

DISBURSE vb pay out

DISBURSED > DISBURSE

DISBURSER > DISBURSE

DISBURSES > DISBURSE

DISC n flat circular object ▷ vb work (land) with a disc harrow

DISCAGE vb release from cage

DISCAGED > DISCAGE

DISCAGES > DISCAGE

DISCAGING > DISCAGE

DISCAL adj relating to or resembling a disc

DISCALCED adj barefooted: used to denote friars and nuns who wear sandals

DISCANDIE same as > DISCANDY

DISCANDY vb melt; dissolve

DISCANT same as > DESCANT

DISCANTED > DISCANT

DISCANTER > DISCANT

DISCANTS > DISCANT

DISCARD vb get rid of (something or someone) as useless or undesirable ▷ n person or thing that has been cast aside

DISCARDED > DISCARD

DISCARDER > DISCARD

DISCARDS > DISCARD

DISCASE vb remove case from

DISCASED > DISCASE

DISCASES > DISCASE

DISCASING > DISCASE

DISCED > DISC

DISCEPT vb discuss

DISCEPTED > DISCEPT

DISCEPTS > DISCEPT

DISCERN vb see or be aware of (something) clearly

DISCERNED > DISCERN

DISCERNER > DISCERN

DISCERNS > DISCERN

DISCERP vb divide

DISCERPED > DISCERP

DISCERPS > DISCERP

DISCHARGE vb release, allow to go ▷ n substance that comes out from a place

DISCHURCH vb deprive of church membership

DISCI > DISCUS

DISCIDE vb split

DISCIDED > DISCIDE

DISCIDES > DISCIDE

DISCIDING > DISCIDE

DISCIFORM adj disc-shaped

DISCINCT adj loosely dressed, without belt

DISCING > DISC

DISCIPLE vb teach ▷ n follower of the doctrines of a teacher, esp Jesus Christ

DISCIPLED > DISCIPLE

DISCIPLES > DISCIPLE

DISCLAIM vb deny (responsibility for or knowledge of something)

DISCLAIMS > DISCLAIM

DISCLESS adj having no disc

DISCLIKE > DISC

DISCLIMAX n climax community resulting from the activities of man or domestic animals in climatic and other conditions that would otherwise support a different type of community

DISCLOSE vb make known

DISCLOSED > DISCLOSE

DISCLOSER > DISCLOSE

DISCLOSES > DISCLOSE

DISCLOST > DISCLOSE

DISCO vb go to a disco ▷ n nightclub where people dance to amplified pop records

DISCOBOLI pl n discus throwers

DISCOED > DISCO

DISCOER > DISCO

DISCOERS > DISCO

DISCOES > DISCO

DISCOID adj like a disc ▷ n disclike object

DISCOIDAL adj like a disc

DISCOIDS > DISCOID

DISCOING > DISCO

DISCOLOGY n study of gramophone records

DISCOLOR same as > DISCOLOUR

DISCOLORS > DISCOLOR

DISCOLOUR vb change in colour, fade

DISCOMFIT vb make uneasy or confused

DISCOMMON vb deprive (land) of the character and status of common, as by enclosure

DISCORD n lack of agreement or harmony between people ▷ vb disagree

DISCORDED > DISCORD

DISCORDS > DISCORD

DISCOS > DISCO

DISCOUNT vb take no account of (something) because it is considered to be unreliable, prejudiced, or irrelevant ▷ n deduction from the full price of something

DISCOUNTS > DISCOUNT

DISCOURE vb discover

DISCOURED > DISCOURE

DISCOURES > DISCOURE

DISCOURSE n conversation ▷ vb speak or write (about) at length

DISCOVER vb be the first to find or to find out about

DISCOVERS > DISCOVER

DISCOVERT adj (of a woman) not under the protection of a husband

DISCOVERY n discovering

DISCREDIT vb damage the reputation of ▷ n damage to someone's reputation

DISCREET adj careful to avoid embarrassment, esp by keeping confidences secret

DISCRETE adj separate, distinct

DISCRETER > DISCRETE

DISCROWN vb deprive of a crown

DISCROWNS > DISCROWN

DISCS > DISC

DISCUMBER vb disencumber

DISCURE old form of > DISCOVER

DISCURED > DISCURE

DISCURES > DISCURE

DISCURING > DISCURE

DISCURSUS n discursive reasoning

DISCUS n object thrown in sports competitions

DISCUSES > DISCUS

DISCUSS vb consider (something) by talking it over

DISCUSSED > DISCUSS

DISCUSSER > DISCUSS

DISCUSSES > DISCUSS

DISDAIN n feeling of superiority and dislike ▷ vb refuse with disdain

DISDAINED > DISDAIN

DISDAINS > DISDAIN

DISEASE vb make uneasy ▷ n illness, sickness

DISEASED adj having or affected with disease

DISEASES > DISEASE

DISEASING > DISEASE

DISEDGE vb render blunt

DISEDGED > DISEDGE

DISEDGES > DISEDGE

DISEDGING > DISEDGE

DISEMBARK vb get off a ship, aircraft, or bus

DISEMBODY vb free from the body or from physical form

DISEMPLOY vb dismiss from employment

DISENABLE vb cause to become incapable

DISENDOW vb take away an endowment from

DISENDOWS > DISENDOW

DISENGAGE vb release from a connection

DISENROL vb remove from register

DISENROLS > DISENROL

DISENTAIL vb free (an estate) from entail ▷ n act of disentailing

DISENTOMB vb disinter

DISESTEEM vb think little of ▷ n lack of esteem

DISEUR same as > DISEUSE

DISEURS > DISEUR

DISEUSE n (esp formerly) an actress who presents dramatic recitals

DISEUSES > DISEUSE

DISFAME n discredit ▷ vb throw into disrepute or remove fame (from)

DISFAMED > DISFAME

DISFAMES > DISFAME

DISFAMING > DISFAME

DISFAVOR same as > DISFAVOUR

DISFAVORS > DISFAVOR

DISFAVOUR n disapproval or dislike ▷ vb regard or treat with disapproval or dislike

DISFIGURE vb spoil the appearance of

DISFLESH vb reduce flesh of

DISFLUENT adj lacking fluency in speech

DISFOREST same as > DEFOREST

DISFORM vb change form of

DISFORMED > DISFORM

DISFORMS > DISFORM

DISFROCK another word for > UNFROCK

DISFROCKS > DISFROCK

DISGAVEL vb deprive of quality of gavelkind

DISGAVELS > DISGAVEL

DISGEST vb digest

DISGESTED > DISGEST

DISGESTS > DISGEST

DISGODDED adj deprived of religion

DISGORGE vb empty out, discharge

DISGORGED > DISGORGE

DISGORGER n thin notched metal implement for removing hooks from a fish

DISGORGES > DISGORGE

DISGOWN vb remove gown from

DISGOWNED > DISGOWN

DISGOWNS > DISGOWN

DISGRACE n condition of shame, loss of reputation, or dishonour ▷ vb bring shame upon (oneself or others)

DISGRACED > DISGRACE

DISGRACER > DISGRACE

DISGRACES > DISGRACE

DISGRADE vb degrade

DISGRADED > DISGRADE

DISGRADES > DISGRADE

DISGUISE vb change the appearance or manner in order to conceal the identity of (someone or something) ▷ n mask, costume, or manner that disguises

DISGUISED > DISGUISE

DISGUISER > DISGUISE

DISGUISES > DISGUISE

DISGUST n great loathing or distaste ▷ vb sicken, fill with loathing

DISGUSTED > DISGUST

DISGUSTS > DISGUST

DISH n shallow container used for holding or serving food ▷ vb put into a dish

DISHABIT vb dislodge

DISHABITS > DISHABIT

DISHABLE obsolete form of > DISABLE

DISHABLED > DISHABLE

DISHABLES > DISHABLE

DISHALLOW vb make unholy

DISHCLOTH n cloth for washing dishes

DISHCLOUT same as > DISHCLOTH

DISHDASH same as > DISHDASHA

DISHDASHA n long-sleeved collarless white garment worn by some Muslim men

DISHED adj shaped like a dish

DISHELM vb remove helmet from

DISHELMED > DISHELM

DISHELMS > DISHELM

DISHERIT vb disinherit

DISHERITS > DISHERIT

DISHES > DISH

DISHEVEL vb disarrange (the hair or clothes) of (someone)

DISHEVELS > DISHEVEL

DISHFUL n the amount that a dish is able to hold

DISHFULS > DISHFUL

DISHIER > DISHY

DISHIEST > DISHY

DISHING > DISH

DISHINGS > DISH

DISHLIKE > DISH

DISHMOP n mop for cleaning dishes

DISHMOPS > DISHMOP

DISHOARD vb put previously withheld (money) into circulation

DISHOARDS > DISHOARD

DISHOME vb deprive of home

DISHOMED > DISHOME

DISHOMES > DISHOME

DISHOMING > DISHOME

DISHONEST adj not honest or fair

DISHONOR same as > DISHONOUR

DISHONORS > DISHONOR

DISHONOUR vb treat with disrespect ▷ n lack of respect

DISHORN vb remove horns from

DISHORNED > DISHORN

DISHORNS > DISHORN

DISHORSE vb dismount

DISHORSED > DISHORSE

DISHORSES > DISHORSE

DISHOUSE vb deprive of home

DISHOUSED > DISHOUSE

DISHOUSES > DISHOUSE

DISHPAN n large pan for washing dishes, pots, etc

DISHPANS > DISHPAN

DISHRAG n dishcloth

DISHRAGS > DISHRAG

DISHTOWEL n towel for drying dishes and kitchen utensils

DISHUMOUR vb upset; offend

DISHWARE n tableware

DISHWARES > DISHWARE

DISHWATER n water in which dishes and kitchen utensils are or have been washed

DISHY adj good-looking

DISILLUDE vb remove illusions from

DISIMMURE vb release

DISINFECT vb rid of harmful germs, chemically

DISINFEST vb rid of vermin

DISINFORM vb give wrong information

DISINHUME vb dig up

DISINTER vb dig up

DISINTERS > DISINTER

DISINURE vb render unaccustomed

DISINURED > DISINURE

DISINURES > DISINURE

DISINVENT *vb* undo the invention or existence of
DISINVEST *vb* remove investment (from)
DISINVITE *vb* retract invitation to
DISJASKIT *adj* fatigued
DISJECT *vb* break apart
DISJECTED > DISJECT
DISJECTS > DISJECT
DISJOIN *vb* disconnect or become disconnected
DISJOINED > DISJOIN
DISJOINS > DISJOIN
DISJOINT *vb* take apart or come apart at the joints ▷ *adj* (of two sets) having no members in common
DISJOINTS > DISJOINT
DISJUNCT *adj* not united or joined ▷ *n* one of the propositions or formulas in a disjunction
DISJUNCTS > DISJUNCT
DISJUNE *n* breakfast ▷ *vb* breakfast
DISJUNED > DISJUNE
DISJUNES > DISJUNE
DISJUNING > DISJUNE
DISK *same as* **>** DISC
DISKED > DISK
DISKER *n* person who breaks up earth with a type of farm implement
DISKERS > DISKER
DISKETTE *n* floppy disk
DISKETTES > DISKETTE
DISKING > DISK
DISKLESS > DISK
DISKLIKE > DISK
DISKS > DISK
DISLEAF *vb* remove leaf or leaves from
DISLEAFED > DISLEAF
DISLEAFS > DISLEAF
DISLEAL *archaic form of* **>** DISLOYAL
DISLEAVE *variant of* **>** DISLEAF
DISLEAVED > DISLEAVE
DISLEAVES > DISLEAVE
DISLIKE *vb* consider unpleasant or disagreeable ▷ *n* feeling of not liking something or someone
DISLIKED > DISLIKE
DISLIKEN *vb* render dissimilar to
DISLIKENS > DISLIKEN
DISLIKER > DISLIKE
DISLIKERS > DISLIKE
DISLIKES > DISLIKE
DISLIKING > DISLIKE
DISLIMB *vb* remove limbs from
DISLIMBED > DISLIMB
DISLIMBS > DISLIMB
DISLIMN *vb* efface
DISLIMNED > DISLIMN
DISLIMNS > DISLIMN
DISLINK *vb* disunite
DISLINKED > DISLINK

DISLINKS > DISLINK
DISLOAD *vb* unload
DISLOADED > DISLOAD
DISLOADS > DISLOAD
DISLOCATE *vb* displace (a bone or joint) from its normal position
DISLODGE *vb* remove (something) from a previously fixed position
DISLODGED > DISLODGE
DISLODGES > DISLODGE
DISLOIGN *vb* put at a distance
DISLOIGNS > DISLOIGN
DISLOYAL *adj* not loyal, deserting one's allegiance
DISLUSTRE *vb* remove lustre from
DISMAL *adj* gloomy and depressing
DISMALER > DISMAL
DISMALEST > DISMAL
DISMALITY > DISMAL
DISMALLER > DISMAL
DISMALLY > DISMAL
DISMALS *pl n* gloomy state of mind
DISMAN *vb* remove men from
DISMANNED > DISMAN
DISMANS > DISMAN
DISMANTLE *vb* take apart piece by piece
DISMASK *vb* remove mask from
DISMASKED > DISMASK
DISMASKS > DISMASK
DISMAST *vb* break off the mast or masts of (a sailing vessel)
DISMASTED > DISMAST
DISMASTS > DISMAST
DISMAY *vb* fill with alarm or depression ▷ *n* alarm mixed with sadness
DISMAYD > DISMAY
DISMAYED > DISMAY
DISMAYFUL > DISMAY
DISMAYING > DISMAY
DISMAYL *vb* remove a coat of mail from
DISMAYLED > DISMAYL
DISMAYLS > DISMAYL
DISMAYS > DISMAY
DISME *old form of* **>** DIME
DISMEMBER *vb* remove the limbs of
DISMES > DISME
DISMISS *vb* remove (an employee) from a job ▷ *sentence substitute* order to end an activity or give permission to disperse
DISMISSAL *n* official notice of discharge from employment or service
DISMISSED > DISMISS
DISMISSES > DISMISS
DISMODED *adj* no longer fashionable
DISMOUNT *vb* get off a horse or bicycle ▷ *n* act of dismounting

DISMOUNTS > DISMOUNT
DISNATURE *vb* cause to be in an unnatural condition
DISNEST *vb* remove from nest
DISNESTED > DISNEST
DISNESTS > DISNEST
DISOBEY *vb* neglect or refuse to obey
DISOBEYED > DISOBEY
DISOBEYER > DISOBEY
DISOBEYS > DISOBEY
DISOBLIGE *vb* disregard the desires of
DISODIUM *n* compound containing two sodium atoms
DISOMIC *adj* having an extra chromosome in the haploid state
DISOMIES > DISOMIC
DISOMY > DISOMIC
DISORBED *adj* thrown out of orbit
DISORDER *n* state of untidiness and disorganization ▷ *vb* upset the order of
DISORDERS > DISORDER
DISORIENT *vb* cause (someone) to lose their bearings
DISOWN *vb* deny any connection with (someone)
DISOWNED > DISOWN
DISOWNER > DISOWN
DISOWNERS > DISOWN
DISOWNING > DISOWN
DISOWNS > DISOWN
DISPACE *vb* move or travel about
DISPACED > DISPACE
DISPACES > DISPACE
DISPACING > DISPACE
DISPARAGE *vb* speak contemptuously of
DISPARATE *adj* completely different ▷ *n* unlike things or people
DISPARITY *n* inequality or difference
DISPARK *vb* release
DISPARKED > DISPARK
DISPARKS > DISPARK
DISPART *vb* separate
DISPARTED > DISPART
DISPARTS > DISPART
DISPATCH *vb* send off to a destination or to perform a task ▷ *n* official communication or report, sent in haste
DISPATHY *obsolete spelling of* **>** DYSPATHY
DISPAUPER *vb* state that someone is no longer a pauper
DISPEACE *n* absence of peace
DISPEACES > DISPEACE
DISPEL *vb* destroy or remove

DISPELLED > DISPEL
DISPELLER > DISPEL
DISPELS > DISPEL
DISPENCE *same as* **>** DISPENSE
DISPENCED > DISPENCE
DISPENCES > DISPENCE
DISPEND *vb* spend
DISPENDED > DISPEND
DISPENDS > DISPEND
DISPENSE *vb* distribute in portions
DISPENSED > DISPENSE
DISPENSER *n* device, such as a vending machine, that automatically dispenses a single item or a measured quantity
DISPENSES > DISPENSE
DISPEOPLE *vb* remove inhabitants from
DISPERSAL *n* act of dispersing or the condition of being dispersed
DISPERSE *vb* scatter over a wide area ▷ *adj* of or consisting of the particles in a colloid or suspension
DISPERSED > DISPERSE
DISPERSER > DISPERSE
DISPERSES > DISPERSE
DISPIRIT *vb* make downhearted
DISPIRITS > DISPIRIT
DISPLACE *vb* move from the usual location
DISPLACED > DISPLACE
DISPLACER > DISPLACE
DISPLACES > DISPLACE
DISPLANT *vb* displace
DISPLANTS > DISPLANT
DISPLAY *vb* make visible or noticeable ▷ *n* displaying
DISPLAYED > DISPLAY
DISPLAYER > DISPLAY
DISPLAYS > DISPLAY
DISPLE *vb* punish
DISPLEASE *vb* annoy or upset
DISPLED > DISPLE
DISPLES > DISPLE
DISPLING > DISPLE
DISPLODE *obsolete word for* **>** EXPLODE
DISPLODED > DISPLODE
DISPLODES > DISPLODE
DISPLUME *vb* remove feathers from
DISPLUMED > DISPLUME
DISPLUMES > DISPLUME
DISPONDEE *n* (poetry) double foot of two long syllables
DISPONE *vb* transfer ownership
DISPONED > DISPONE
DISPONEE *n* person whom something is disponed to
DISPONEES > DISPONEE
DISPONER > DISPONE

DISPONERS > DISPONE
DISPONES > DISPONE
DISPONGE same as
> DISPUNGE
DISPONGED > DISPONGE
DISPONGES > DISPONGE
DISPONING > DISPONE
DISPORT vb indulge
(oneself) in pleasure
▷ n amusement
DISPORTED > DISPORT
DISPORTS > DISPORT
DISPOSAL n getting rid of
something
DISPOSALS > DISPOSAL
DISPOSE vb place in a
certain order
DISPOSED adj willing or
eager
DISPOSER > DISPOSE
DISPOSERS > DISPOSE
DISPOSES > DISPOSE
DISPOSING > DISPOSE
DISPOST vb remove from
post
DISPOSTED > DISPOST
DISPOSTS > DISPOST
DISPOSURE a rare word for
> DISPOSAL
DISPRAD old form of
> DISPREAD
DISPRAISE vb express
disapproval or
condemnation of ▷ n
disapproval, etc,
expressed
DISPREAD vb spread out
DISPREADS > DISPREAD
DISPRED old spelling of
> DISPREAD
DISPREDS > DISPRED
DISPRISON vb release
from captivity
DISPRIZE vb scorn
DISPRIZED > DISPRIZE
DISPRIZES > DISPRIZE
DISPROFIT n loss ▷ vb
(cause to) fail to profit
DISPROOF n facts that
disprove something
DISPROOFS > DISPROOF
DISPROOVE vb
disapprove of
DISPROVAL > DISPROVE
DISPROVE vb show (an
assertion or claim) to be
incorrect
DISPROVED > DISPROVE
DISPROVEN > DISPROVE
DISPROVER > DISPROVE
DISPROVES > DISPROVE
DISPUNGE vb expunge
DISPUNGED > DISPUNGE
DISPUNGES > DISPUNGE
DISPURSE another word for
> DISBURSE
DISPURSED > DISPURSE
DISPURSES > DISPURSE
DISPURVEY vb strip of
equipment, provisions, etc
DISPUTANT n person
who argues ▷ adj engaged
in argument

DISPUTE n disagreement,
argument ▷ vb argue
about (something)
DISPUTED > DISPUTE
DISPUTER > DISPUTE
DISPUTERS > DISPUTE
DISPUTES > DISPUTE
DISPUTING > DISPUTE
DISQUIET n feeling of
anxiety ▷ vb make
(someone) anxious ▷ adj
uneasy or anxious
DISQUIETS > DISQUIET
DISRANK vb demote
DISRANKED > DISRANK
DISRANKS > DISRANK
DISRATE vb punish (an
officer) by lowering in rank
DISRATED > DISRATE
DISRATES > DISRATE
DISRATING > DISRATE
DISREGARD vb give little
or no attention to ▷ n lack
of attention or respect
DISRELISH vb have a
feeling of aversion for
▷ n such a feeling
DISREPAIR n condition
of being worn out or in
poor working order
DISREPUTE n loss or lack
of good reputation
DISROBE vb undress
DISROBED > DISROBE
DISROBER > DISROBE
DISROBERS > DISROBE
DISROBES > DISROBE
DISROBING > DISROBE
DISROOT vb uproot
DISROOTED > DISROOT
DISROOTS > DISROOT
DISRUPT vb interrupt the
progress of
DISRUPTED > DISRUPT
DISRUPTER > DISRUPT
DISRUPTOR > DISRUPT
DISRUPTS > DISRUPT
DISS vb treat (a person)
with contempt
DISSAVE vb spend savings
DISSAVED > DISSAVE
DISSAVER n person who
dissaves
DISSAVERS > DISSAVER
DISSAVES > DISSAVE
DISSAVING > DISSAVE
DISSEAT vb unseat
DISSEATED > DISSEAT
DISSEATS > DISSEAT
DISSECT vb cut open (a
corpse) to examine it
DISSECTED adj in the
form of narrow lobes or
segments
DISSECTOR > DISSECT
DISSECTS > DISSECT
DISSED > DISS
DISSEISE vb deprive of
seisin
DISSEISED > DISSEISE
DISSEISEE n person
who is disseised
DISSEISES > DISSEISE

DISSEISIN n act of
disseising or state of being
disseised
DISSEISOR > DISSEISE
DISSEIZE same as
> DISSEISE
DISSEIZED > DISSEIZE
DISSEIZEE n person
who is disseized
DISSEIZES > DISSEIZE
DISSEIZIN same as
> DISSEISIN
DISSEIZOR > DISSEIZE
DISSEMBLE vb conceal
one's real motives or
emotions by pretence
DISSEMBLY n
dismantling
DISSENSUS n
disagreement within
group
DISSENT vb disagree
▷ n disagreement
DISSENTED > DISSENT
DISSENTER > DISSENT
DISSENTS > DISSENT
DISSERT n give or make a
dissertation; dissertate
DISSERTED > DISSERT
DISSERTS > DISSERT
DISSERVE vb do a
disservice to
DISSERVED > DISSERVE
DISSERVES > DISSERVE
DISSES > DISS
DISSEVER vb break off or
become broken off
DISSEVERS > DISSEVER
DISSHIVER vb break in
pieces
DISSIDENT n person
who disagrees with and
criticizes the government
▷ adj disagreeing with the
government
DISSIGHT n eyesore
DISSIGHTS > DISSIGHT
DISSIMILE n
comparison using
contrast
DISSING > DISS
DISSIPATE vb waste or
squander
DISSOCIAL adj
incongruous or
irreconcilable
DISSOLUTE adj leading
an immoral life
DISSOLVE vb (cause to)
become liquid ▷ n scene
filmed or televised by
dissolving
DISSOLVED > DISSOLVE
DISSOLVER > DISSOLVE
DISSOLVES > DISSOLVE
DISSONANT adj
discordant
DISSUADE vb deter
(someone) by persuasion
from doing something
DISSUADED > DISSUADE
DISSUADER > DISSUADE
DISSUADES > DISSUADE
DISSUNDER vb separate

DISTAFF n rod on which
wool etc is wound for
spinning
DISTAFFS > DISTAFF
DISTAIN vb stain; tarnish
DISTAINED > DISTAIN
DISTAINS > DISTAIN
DISTAL adj (of a bone, limb,
etc) situated farthest from
the point of attachment
DISTALLY > DISTAL
DISTANCE n space
between two points
DISTANCED > DISTANCE
DISTANCES > DISTANCE
DISTANT adj far apart
DISTANTLY > DISTANT
DISTASTE n dislike,
disgust
DISTASTED > DISTASTE
DISTASTES > DISTASTE
DISTAVES > DISTAFF
DISTEMPER n highly
contagious viral disease of
dogs ▷ vb paint with
distemper
DISTEND vb (of part of the
body) swell
DISTENDED > DISTEND
DISTENDER > DISTEND
DISTENDS > DISTEND
DISTENT adj bloated;
swollen ▷ n breadth;
distension
DISTENTS > DISTENT
DISTHENE n bluish-green
mineral
DISTHENES > DISTHENE
DISTHRONE vb remove
from throne
DISTICH n unit of two
verse lines
DISTICHAL > DISTICH
DISTICHS > DISTICH
DISTIL vb subject to or
obtain by distillation
DISTILL same as
> DISTIL
DISTILLED > DISTIL
DISTILLER n person or
company that makes
strong alcoholic drink, esp
whisky
DISTILLS > DISTILL
DISTILS > DISTIL
DISTINCT adj not the
same
DISTINGUE adj
distinguished or noble
DISTOME n parasitic
flatworm
DISTOMES > DISTOME
DISTORT vb misrepresent
(the truth or facts)
DISTORTED > DISTORT
DISTORTER > DISTORT
DISTORTS > DISTORT
DISTRACT vb draw the
attention of (a person)
away from something
DISTRACTS > DISTRACT
DISTRAIL n trail made by
aircraft flying through
cloud

DISTRAILS > DISTRAIL
DISTRAIN vb seize (personal property) to enforce payment of a debt
DISTRAINS > DISTRAIN
DISTRAINT n act or process of distraining
DISTRAIT adj absent-minded or preoccupied
DISTRAITE feminine form of **>** DISTRAIT
DISTRESS n extreme unhappiness **>** vb upset badly
DISTRICT n area of land regarded as an administrative or geographical unit **>** vb divide into districts
DISTRICTS > DISTRICT
DISTRIX n splitting of the ends of hairs
DISTRIXES > DISTRIX
DISTRUST vb regard as untrustworthy **>** n feeling of suspicion or doubt
DISTRUSTS > DISTRUST
DISTUNE vb cause to be out of tune
DISTUNED > DISTUNE
DISTUNES > DISTUNE
DISTUNING > DISTUNE
DISTURB vb intrude on
DISTURBED adj emotionally upset or maladjusted
DISTURBER > DISTURB
DISTURBS > DISTURB
DISTYLE n temple with two columns
DISTYLES > DISTYLE
DISULFATE n chemical compound containing two sulfate ions
DISULFID same as **>** DISULFIDE
DISULFIDE n compound of a base with two atoms of sulfur
DISULFIDS > DISULFID
DISUNION > DISUNITE
DISUNIONS > DISUNITE
DISUNITE vb cause disagreement among
DISUNITED > DISUNITE
DISUNITER > DISUNITE
DISUNITES > DISUNITE
DISUNITY n dissension or disagreement
DISUSAGE n disuse
DISUSAGES > DISUSAGE
DISUSE vb stop using **>** n state of being no longer used
DISUSED adj no longer used
DISUSES > DISUSE
DISUSING > DISUSE
DISVALUE vb belittle
DISVALUED > DISVALUE
DISVALUES > DISVALUE
DISVOUCH vb dissociate oneself from
DISYOKE vb unyoke

DISYOKED > DISYOKE
DISYOKES > DISYOKE
DISYOKING > DISYOKE
DIT vb stop something happening **>** n short sound used in the spoken representation of telegraphic codes
DITA n tropical shrub
DITAL n key for raising pitch of lute string
DITALS > DITAL
DITAS > DITA
DITCH n narrow channel dug in the earth for drainage or irrigation **>** vb abandon
DITCHED > DITCH
DITCHER > DITCH
DITCHERS > DITCH
DITCHES > DITCH
DITCHING > DITCH
DITCHLESS > DITCH
DITE vb set down in writing
DITED > DITE
DITES > DITE
DITHECAL adj having two thecae
DITHECOUS another word for **>** DITHECAL
DITHEISM n belief in two equal gods
DITHEISMS > DITHEISM
DITHEIST > DITHEISM
DITHEISTS > DITHEISM
DITHELETE n one believing that Christ had two wills
DITHELISM n belief that Christ had two wills
DITHER vb be uncertain or indecisive **>** n state of indecision or agitation
DITHERED > DITHER
DITHERER > DITHER
DITHERERS > DITHER
DITHERIER > DITHER
DITHERING > DITHER
DITHERS > DITHER
DITHERY > DITHER
DITHIOL n chemical compound
DITHIOLS > DITHIOL
DITHIONIC adj as in dithionic acid type of acid
DITHYRAMB n (in ancient Greece) a passionate choral hymn in honour of Dionysus
DITING > DITE
DITOKOUS adj producing two eggs
DITONE n interval of two tones
DITONES > DITONE
DITROCHEE n double metrical foot
DITS > DIT
DITSIER > DITSY
DITSIEST > DITSY
DITSINESS > DITSY
DITSY same as **>** DITZY

DITT same as **>** DIT
DITTANDER n type of plant of coastal Europe, N Africa, and SW Asia, with clusters of small white flowers
DITTANIES > DITTANY
DITTANY n aromatic plant
DITTAY n accusation; charge
DITTAYS > DITTAY
DITTED > DIT
DITTIED > DITTY
DITTIES > DITTY
DITTING > DIT
DITTIT > DIT
DITTO n same **>** adv in the same way **>** sentence substitute used to avoid repeating or to confirm agreement with an immediately preceding sentence **>** vb copy
DITTOED > DITTO
DITTOING > DITTO
DITTOLOGY n interpretation in two ways
DITTOS > DITTO
DITTS > DITT
DITTY vb set to music **>** n short simple poem or song
DITTYING > DITTY
DITZ n silly scatterbrained person
DITZES > DITZ
DITZIER > DITZY
DITZIEST > DITZY
DITZINESS > DITZY
DITZY adj silly and scatterbrained
DIURESES > DIURESIS
DIURESIS n excretion of an unusually large quantity of urine
DIURETIC n drug that increases the flow of urine **>** adj acting to increase the flow of urine
DIURETICS > DIURETIC
DIURNAL adj happening during the day or daily **>** n service book containing all the canonical hours except matins
DIURNALLY > DIURNAL
DIURNALS > DIURNAL
DIURON n type of herbicide
DIURONS > DIURON
DIUTURNAL adj long-lasting
DIV n stupid or foolish person
DIVA n distinguished female singer
DIVAGATE vb digress or wander
DIVAGATED > DIVAGATE
DIVAGATES > DIVAGATE
DIVALENCE > DIVALENT
DIVALENCY > DIVALENT

DIVALENT n element that can unite with two atoms **>** adj having two valencies or a valency of two
DIVALENTS > DIVALENT
DIVAN n low backless bed
DIVANS > DIVAN
DIVAS > DIVA
DIVE vb plunge headfirst into water **>** n diving
DIVEBOMB vb bomb while making steep dives
DIVEBOMBS > DIVEBOMB
DIVED > DIVE
DIVELLENT adj separating
DIVER n person who works or explores underwater
DIVERGE vb separate and go in different directions
DIVERGED > DIVERGE
DIVERGENT adj diverging or causing divergence
DIVERGES > DIVERGE
DIVERGING > DIVERGE
DIVERS adj various **>** determiner various
DIVERSE vb turn away **>** adj having variety, assorted
DIVERSED > DIVERSE
DIVERSELY > DIVERSE
DIVERSES > DIVERSE
DIVERSIFY vb create different forms of
DIVERSING > DIVERSE
DIVERSION n official detour used by traffic when a main route is closed
DIVERSITY n quality of being different or varied
DIVERSLY > DIVERS
DIVERT vb change the direction of
DIVERTED > DIVERT
DIVERTER > DIVERT
DIVERTERS > DIVERT
DIVERTING > DIVERT
DIVERTIVE > DIVERT
DIVERTS > DIVERT
DIVES > DIVE
DIVEST vb strip (of clothes)
DIVESTED > DIVEST
DIVESTING > DIVEST
DIVESTS > DIVEST
DIVESTURE > DIVEST
DIVI alternative spelling of **>** DIVVY
DIVIDABLE > DIVIDE
DIVIDANT adj distinct
DIVIDE vb separate into parts **>** n division, split
DIVIDED adj split
DIVIDEDLY > DIVIDED
DIVIDEND n sum of money representing part of the profit made, paid by a company to its shareholders
DIVIDENDS > DIVIDEND

d

d

DIVIDER n screen used to divide a room into separate areas

DIVIDERS pl n compasses with two pointed arms, used for measuring or dividing lines

DIVIDES > DIVIDE

DIVIDING > DIVIDE

DIVIDINGS > DIVIDE

DIVIDIVI n tropical tree

DIVIDIVIS > DIVIDIVI

DIVIDUAL adj divisible

DIVIDUOUS adj divided

DIVIED same as > DIVVIED

DIVINABLE > DIVINE

DIVINATOR n diviner

DIVINE adj of God or a god ▷ vb discover (something) by intuition or guessing ▷ n priest who is learned in theology

DIVINED > DIVINE

DIVINELY > DIVINE

DIVINER > DIVINE

DIVINERS > DIVINE

DIVINES > DIVINE

DIVINEST > DIVINE

DIVING > DIVE

DIVINGS > DIVE

DIVINIFY vb give divine status to

DIVINING > DIVINE

DIVINISE same as > DIVINIZE

DIVINISED > DIVINISE

DIVINISES > DIVINISE

DIVINITY n study of religion

DIVINIZE vb make divine

DIVINIZED > DIVINIZE

DIVINIZES > DIVINIZE

DIVIS > DIVI

DIVISIBLE adj capable of being divided

DIVISIBLY > DIVISIBLE

DIVISIM adv separately

DIVISION n dividing, sharing out

DIVISIONS > DIVISION

DIVISIVE adj tending to cause disagreement

DIVISOR n number to be divided into another number

DIVISORS > DIVISOR

DIVNA vb do not

DIVO n male diva

DIVORCE n legal ending of a marriage ▷ vb legally end one's marriage (to)

DIVORCED > DIVORCE

DIVORCEE n person who is divorced

DIVORCEES > DIVORCEE

DIVORCER > DIVORCE

DIVORCERS > DIVORCE

DIVORCES > DIVORCE

DIVORCING > DIVORCE

DIVORCIVE > DIVORCE

DIVOS > DIVO

DIVOT n small piece of turf

DIVOTS > DIVOT

DIVS > DIV

DIVULGATE vb make publicly known

DIVULGE vb make known, disclose

DIVULGED > DIVULGE

DIVULGER > DIVULGE

DIVULGERS > DIVULGE

DIVULGES > DIVULGE

DIVULGING > DIVULGE

DIVULSE vb tear apart

DIVULSED > DIVULSE

DIVULSES > DIVULSE

DIVULSING > DIVULSE

DIVULSION n tearing or pulling apart

DIVULSIVE > DIVULSION

DIVVIED > DIVVY

DIVVIER > DIVVY

DIVVIES > DIVVY

DIVVIEST > DIVVY

DIVVY vb divide and share ▷ adj stupid ▷ n stupid person

DIVVYING > DIVVY

DIVYING same as > DIVVYING

DIWAN same as > DEWAN

DIWANS > DIWAN

DIXI interj I have spoken

DIXIE n large metal pot for cooking, brewing tea, etc

DIXIES > DIXIE

DIXIT n statement

DIXITS > DIXIT

DIXY same as > DIXIE

DIYA n small oil lamp, usu made from clay

DIYAS > DIYA

DIZAIN n ten-line poem

DIZAINS > DIZAIN

DIZEN archaic word for > BEDIZEN

DIZENED > DIZEN

DIZENING > DIZEN

DIZENMENT > DIZEN

DIZENS > DIZEN

DIZYGOTIC adj developed from two separately fertilized eggs

DIZYGOUS another word for > DIZYGOTIC

DIZZARD n dunce

DIZZARDS > DIZZARD

DIZZIED > DIZZY

DIZZIER > DIZZY

DIZZIES > DIZZY

DIZZIEST > DIZZY

DIZZILY > DIZZY

DIZZINESS > DIZZY

DIZZY adj having or causing a whirling sensation ▷ vb make dizzy

DIZZYING > DIZZY

DJEBEL a variant spelling of > JEBEL

DJEBELS > DJEBEL

DJELLABA n kind of loose cloak with a hood, worn by men esp in North Africa and the Middle East

DJELLABAH same as > DJELLABA

DJELLABAS > DJELLABA

DJEMBE n W African drum

DJEMBES > DJEMBE

DJIBBA same as > JUBBAH

DJIBBAH same as > JUBBAH

DJIBBAHS > DJIBBAH

DJIBBAS > DJIBBA

DJIN same as > JINN

DJINN > DJINN

DJINNI same as > JINNI

DJINNS > DJINN

DJINNY same as > JINNI

DJINS > DJIN

DO vb perform or complete (a deed or action) ▷ n party, celebration

DOAB n alluvial land between two converging rivers

DOABLE adj capable of being done

DOABS > DOAB

DOAT same as > DOTE

DOATED > DOAT

DOATER > DOAT

DOATERS > DOAT

DOATING > DOAT

DOATINGS > DOAT

DOATS > DOAT

DOB vb as in dob in inform against or report

DOBBED > DOB

DOBBER n informant or traitor

DOBBERS > DOBBER

DOBBIE same as > DOBBY

DOBBIES > DOBBY

DOBBIN n name for a horse

DOBBING > DOB

DOBBINS > DOBBIN

DOBBY n attachment to a loom, used in weaving small figures

DOBCHICK same as > DABCHICK

DOBCHICKS > DOBCHICK

DOBE same as > ADOBE

DOBES > DOBE

DOBHASH n interpreter

DOBHASHES > DOBHASH

DOBIE n cannabis

DOBIES > DOBIE

DOBLA n medieval Spanish gold coin, probably worth 20 maravedis

DOBLAS > DOBLA

DOBLON a variant spelling of > DOUBLOON

DOBLONES > DOBLON

DOBLONS > DOBLON

DOBRA n standard monetary unit of São Tomé e Principe

DOBRAS > DOBRA

DOBRO n type of acoustic guitar

DOBROS > DOBRO

DOBS > DOB

DOBSON n larva of dobsonfly

DOBSONFLY n large North American insect

DOBSONS > DOBSON

DOBY same as > DOBIE

DOC same as > DOCTOR

DOCENT n voluntary worker who acts as a guide

DOCENTS > DOCENT

DOCETIC adj believing that the humanity of Christ was apparent and not real

DOCHMIAC > DOCHMIUS

DOCHMII > DOCHMIUS

DOCHMIUS n five-syllable foot

DOCHT > DOW

DOCIBLE adj easily tamed

DOCILE adj (of a person or animal) easily controlled

DOCILELY > DOCILE

DOCILER > DOCILE

DOCILEST > DOCILE

DOCILITY > DOCILE

DOCIMASY n close examination

DOCK n enclosed area of water where ships are loaded, unloaded, or repaired ▷ vb bring or be brought into dock

DOCKAGE n charge levied upon a vessel for using a dock

DOCKAGES > DOCKAGE

DOCKED > DOCK

DOCKEN n something of no value or importance

DOCKENS > DOCKEN

DOCKER n person employed to load and unload ships

DOCKERS > DOCKER

DOCKET n label on a delivery, stating contents, delivery instructions, etc ▷ vb fix a docket to (a package or other delivery)

DOCKETED > DOCKET

DOCKETING > DOCKET

DOCKETS > DOCKET

DOCKHAND n dock labourer

DOCKHANDS > DOCKHAND

DOCKING > DOCK

DOCKINGS > DOCK

DOCKISE same as > DOCKIZE

DOCKISED > DOCKISE

DOCKISES > DOCKISE

DOCKISING > DOCKISE

DOCKIZE vb convert into docks

DOCKIZED > DOCKIZE

DOCKIZES > DOCKIZE

DOCKIZING > DOCKIZE

DOCKLAND n area around the docks

DOCKLANDS > DOCKLAND

DOCKS > DOCK

DOCKSIDE *n* area next to dock
DOCKSIDES > DOCKSIDE
DOCKYARD *n* place where ships are built or repaired
DOCKYARDS > DOCKYARD
DOCO *n* (slang) documentary
DOCOS > DOCO
DOCQUET *same as* > DOCKET
DOCQUETED > DOCQUET
DOCQUETS > DOCQUET
DOCS > DOC
DOCTOR *n* person licensed to practise medicine ▷ *vb* alter in order to deceive
DOCTORAL > DOCTOR
DOCTORAND *n* student working towards doctorate
DOCTORATE *n* highest academic degree in any field of knowledge
DOCTORED > DOCTOR
DOCTORESS *n* female doctor
DOCTORIAL > DOCTOR
DOCTORING *n* act of doctoring
DOCTORLY > DOCTOR
DOCTORS > DOCTOR
DOCTRESS *same as* > DOCTORESS
DOCTRINAL > DOCTRINE
DOCTRINE *n* body of teachings of a religious, political, or philosophical group
DOCTRINES > DOCTRINE
DOCU *n* documentary film
DOCUDRAMA *n* film or television programme based on true events, presented in a dramatized form
DOCUMENT *n* piece of paper providing an official record of something ▷ *vb* record or report (something) in detail
DOCUMENTS > DOCUMENT
DOCUS > DOCU
DOCUSOAP *n* reality television programme in the style of a documentary
DOCUSOAPS > DOCUSOAP
DOD *vb* clip
DODDARD *adj* archaic word for missing branches; rotten ▷ *n* tree missing its top branches through rot
DODDARDS > DODDARD
DODDED > DOD
DODDER *vb* move unsteadily ▷ *n* type of rootless parasitic plant
DODDERED > DODDER
DODDERER > DODDER
DODDERERS > DODDER
DODDERIER > DODDER
DODDERING *adj* shaky, feeble, or infirm, esp from old age

DODDERS > DODDER
DODDERY > DODDER
DODDIER > DODDY
DODDIES > DODDY
DODDIEST > DODDY
DODDING > DOD
DODDIPOLL *same as* > DODDYPOLL
DODDLE *n* something easily accomplished
DODDLES > DODDLE
DODDY *n* bad mood ▷ *adj* sulky
DODDYPOLL *n* dunce
DODECAGON *n* geometric figure with twelve sides
DODGE *vb* avoid (a blow, being seen, etc) by moving suddenly ▷ *n* cunning or deceitful trick
DODGEBALL *n* game in which the players form a circle and try to hit opponents in the circle with a large ball
DODGED > DODGE
DODGEM *n* bumper car
DODGEMS > DODGEM
DODGER *n* person who evades a responsibility or duty
DODGERIES > DODGERY
DODGERS > DODGER
DODGERY *n* deception
DODGES > DODGE
DODGIER > DODGY
DODGIEST > DODGY
DODGINESS > DODGY
DODGING > DODGE
DODGINGS > DODGE
DODGY *adj* dangerous, risky
DODKIN *n* coin of little value
DODKINS > DODKIN
DODMAN *n* snail
DODMANS > DODMAN
DODO *n* large flightless extinct bird
DODOES > DODO
DODOISM > DODO
DODOISMS > DODO
DODOS > DODO
DODS > DOD
DOE *n* female deer, hare, or rabbit
DOEK *n* square of cloth worn on the head by women
DOEKS > DOEK
DOEN > DO
DOER *n* active or energetic person
DOERS > DO
DOES > DO
DOESKIN *n* skin of a deer, lamb, or sheep
DOESKINS > DOESKIN
DOEST > DO
DOETH > DO
DOF *informal South African word for* > STUPID

DOFF *vb* take off or lift (one's hat) in polite greeting
DOFFED > DOFF
DOFFER > DOFF
DOFFERS > DOFF
DOFFING > DOFF
DOFFS > DOFF
DOG *n* domesticated four-legged mammal ▷ *vb* follow (someone) closely
DOGAN *n* offensive word for a Catholic
DOGANS > DOGAN
DOGARESSA *n* wife of doge
DOGATE *n* office of doge
DOGATES > DOGATE
DOGBANE *n* N American plant
DOGBANES > DOGBANE
DOGBERRY *n* any of certain plants that have berry-like fruits, such as the European dogwood or the bearberry
DOGBOLT *n* bolt on cannon
DOGBOLTS > DOGBOLT
DOGCART *n* light horse-drawn two-wheeled cart
DOGCARTS > DOGCART
DOGDOM *n* world of dogs
DOGDOMS > DOGDOM
DOGE *n* (formerly) chief magistrate of Venice or Genoa
DOGEAR *vb* fold down the corner of (a page) ▷ *n* folded-down corner of a page
DOGEARED > DOGEAR
DOGEARING > DOGEAR
DOGEARS > DOGEAR
DOGEATE *n* office of doge
DOGEATES > DOGEATE
DOGEDOM *n* domain of doge
DOGEDOMS > DOGEDOM
DOGES > DOGE
DOGESHIP > DOGE
DOGESHIPS > DOGE
DOGEY *same as* > DOGIE
DOGEYS > DOGEY
DOGFACE *n* WW2 US soldier
DOGFACES > DOGFACE
DOGFIGHT *vb* fight in confused way ▷ *n* close-quarters combat between fighter aircraft
DOGFIGHTS > DOGFIGHT
DOGFISH *n* small shark
DOGFISHES > DOGFISH
DOGFOOD *n* food for a dog
DOGFOODS > DOGFOOD
DOGFOUGHT > DOGFIGHT
DOGFOX *n* male fox
DOGFOXES > DOGFOX
DOGGED > DOG
DOGGEDER > DOG

DOGGEDEST > DOG
DOGGEDLY > DOG
DOGGER *n* Dutch fishing vessel with two masts
DOGGEREL *n* poorly written poetry, usu comic
DOGGERELS > DOGGEREL
DOGGERIES > DOGGERY
DOGGERMAN *n* sailor on dogger
DOGGERMEN > DOGGERMAN
DOGGERS > DOGGER
DOGGERY *n* surly behaviour
DOGGESS *n* female dog
DOGGESSES > DOGGESS
DOGGIE *same as* > DOGGY
DOGGIER > DOGGY
DOGGIES > DOGGY
DOGGIEST > DOGGY
DOGGINESS > DOGGY
DOGGING > DOG
DOGGINGS > DOG
DOGGISH *adj* of or like a dog
DOGGISHLY > DOGGISH
DOGGO *adv* in hiding and keeping quiet
DOGGONE *interj* exclamation of annoyance, disappointment, etc ▷ *vb* damn ▷ *adj* damnedest
DOGGONED > DOGGONE
DOGGONER > DOGGONE
DOGGONES > DOGGONE
DOGGONEST > DOGGONE
DOGGONING > DOGGONE
DOGGREL *same as* > DOGGEREL
DOGGRELS > DOGGREL
DOGGY *n* child's word for a dog ▷ *adj* of or like a dog
DOGHANGED *same as* > HANGDOG
DOGHOLE *n* squalid dwelling place
DOGHOLES > DOGHOLE
DOGHOUSE *n* kennel
DOGHOUSES > DOGHOUSE
DOGIE *n* motherless calf
DOGIES > DOGY
DOGLEG *n* sharp bend ▷ *vb* go off at an angle ▷ *adj* of or with the shape of a dogleg
DOGLEGGED > DOGLEG
DOGLEGS > DOGLEG
DOGLIKE > DOG
DOGMA *n* doctrine or system of doctrines proclaimed by authority as true
DOGMAN *n* person who directs a crane whilst riding on an object being lifted by it
DOGMAS > DOGMA
DOGMATA > DOGMA
DOGMATIC *adj* habitually stating one's opinions forcefully or arrogantly

DOGMATICS n study of religious dogmas and doctrines

DOGMATISE same as > DOGMATIZE

DOGMATISM > DOGMATIZE

DOGMATIST n dogmatic person

DOGMATIZE vb say or state (something) in a dogmatic manner

DOGMATORY > DOGMA

DOGMEN > DOGMAN

DOGNAP vb carry off and hold (a dog), usually for ransom

DOGNAPED > DOGNAP

DOGNAPER > DOGNAP

DOGNAPERS > DOGNAP

DOGNAPING > DOGNAP

DOGNAPPED > DOGNAP

DOGNAPPER > DOGNAP

DOGNAPS > DOGNAP

DOGPILE n practice of people jumping on top of each other to form a pile of bodies, usu in celebration or for amusement

DOGPILES > DOGPILE

DOGREL n doggerel

DOGRELS > DOGREL

DOGROBBER n army cook

DOGS > DOG

DOGSBODY n person who carries out boring tasks for others ▷ vb act as a dogsbody

DOGSHIP n condition of being a dog

DOGSHIPS > DOGSHIP

DOGSHORES n pieces of wood to prop up boat

DOGSHOW n competition in which dogs are judged

DOGSHOWS > DOGSHOW

DOGSKIN n leather from dog's skin

DOGSKINS > DOGSKIN

DOGSLED n sleigh drawn by dogs

DOGSLEDS > DOGSLED

DOGSLEEP n feigned sleep

DOGSLEEPS > DOGSLEEP

DOGSTAIL n type of grass

DOGSTAILS > DOGSTAIL

DOGTAIL same as > DOGSTAIL

DOGTAILS > DOGSTAIL

DOGTEETH > DOGTOOTH

DOGTOOTH n carved ornament in the form of four leaflike projections radiating from a raised centre, used in England in the 13th century

DOGTOWN n community of prairie dogs

DOGTOWNS > DOGTOWN

DOGTROT n gently paced trot

DOGTROTS > DOGTROT

DOGVANE n light windvane mounted on the side of a vessel

DOGVANES > DOGVANE

DOGWATCH n either of two watches aboard ship, from four to six pm or from six to eight pm

DOGWOOD n type of tree or shrub

DOGWOODS > DOGWOOD

DOGY same as > DOGIE

DOH n in tonic sol-fa, first degree of any major scale ▷ interj exclamation of annoyance when something goes wrong

DOHS > DOH

DOHYO n sumo wrestling ring

DOHYOS > DOHYO

DOILED same as > DOILT

DOILIED adj having a doily

DOILIES > DOILY

DOILT adj foolish

DOILTER > DOILT

DOILTEST > DOILT

DOILY n decorative lacy paper mat, laid on a plate

DOING > DO

DOINGS pl n deeds or actions

DOIT n former small copper coin of the Netherlands

DOITED adj foolish or childish, as from senility

DOITIT same as > DOITED

DOITKIN same as > DOIT

DOITKINS > DOITKIN

DOITS > DOIT

DOJO n room or hall for the practice of martial arts

DOJOS > DOJO

DOL n unit of pain intensity, as measured by dolorimetry

DOLABRATE adj shaped like a hatchet or axe head

DOLCE n dessert ▷ adv (to be performed) gently and sweetly

DOLCES > DOLCE

DOLCETTO n variety of grape for making wine

DOLCETTOS > DOLCETTO

DOLCI > DOLCE

DOLDRUMS pl n depressed state of mind

DOLE n money received from the state while unemployed ▷ vb distribute in small quantities

DOLED > DOLE

DOLEFUL adj dreary, unhappy

DOLEFULLY > DOLEFUL

DOLENT adj sad

DOLENTE adv (to be performed) in a sorrowful manner

DOLERITE n dark basic intrusive igneous rock consisting of plagioclase feldspar and a pyroxene, such as augite

DOLERITES > DOLERITE

DOLERITIC > DOLERITE

DOLES > DOLE

DOLESOME same as > DOLEFUL

DOLIA > DOLIUM

DOLICHOS n tropical vines

DOLICHURI n poetic term

DOLINA same as > DOLINE

DOLINAS > DOLINA

DOLINE n depression of the ground surface formed in limestone regions

DOLINES > DOLINE

DOLING > DOLE

DOLIUM n genus of molluscs

DOLL n small model of a human being, used as a toy ▷ vb as in doll up dress up

DOLLAR n standard monetary unit of many countries

DOLLARED adj flagged with a dollar sign

DOLLARISE same as > DOLLARIZE

DOLLARIZE vb replace a country's currency with US dollar

DOLLARS > DOLLAR

DOLLDOM > DOLL

DOLLDOMS > DOLL

DOLLED > DOLL

DOLLHOOD > DOLL

DOLLHOODS > DOLL

DOLLHOUSE n toy house in which dolls and miniature furniture can be put

DOLLIED > DOLLY

DOLLIER n person who operates a dolly

DOLLIERS > DOLLIER

DOLLIES > DOLLY

DOLLINESS > DOLLY

DOLLING > DOLL

DOLLISH > DOLL

DOLLISHLY > DOLL

DOLLOP n lump (of food) ▷ vb serve out (food)

DOLLOPED > DOLLOP

DOLLOPING > DOLLOP

DOLLOPS > DOLLOP

DOLLS > DOLL

DOLLY adj attractive and unintelligent ▷ n wheeled support on which a camera may be mounted; shaped block of lead used to hammer dents out of sheet metal ▷ vb wheel (a camera) backwards or forwards on a dolly

DOLLYBIRD n pretty and fashionable young woman

DOLLYING > DOLLY

DOLMA n vine leaf stuffed with a filling of meat and rice

DOLMADES > DOLMA

DOLMAN n long Turkish outer robe

DOLMANS > DOLMAN

DOLMAS > DOLMA

DOLMEN n prehistoric monument

DOLMENIC > DOLMEN

DOLMENS > DOLMEN

DOLOMITE n mineral consisting of calcium magnesium carbonate

DOLOMITES > DOLOMITE

DOLOMITIC > DOLOMITE

DOLOR same as > DOLOUR

DOLORIFIC adj causing pain or sadness

DOLOROSO adv (to be performed) in a sorrowful manner

DOLOROUS adj sad, mournful

DOLORS > DOLOR

DOLOS n knucklebone of a sheep, buck, etc, used esp by diviners

DOLOSSE > DOLOS

DOLOSTONE n rock composed of the mineral dolomite

DOLOUR n grief or sorrow

DOLOURS > DOLOUR

DOLPHIN n sea mammal of the whale family

DOLPHINET n female dolphin

DOLPHINS > DOLPHIN

DOLS > DOL

DOLT n stupid person

DOLTISH > DOLT

DOLTISHLY > DOLT

DOLTS > DOLT

DOM n title given to various monks and to certain of the canons regular

DOMAIN n field of knowledge or activity

DOMAINAL > DOMAIN

DOMAINE n French estate where wine is made

DOMAINES > DOMAINE

DOMAINS > DOMAIN

DOMAL adj of a house

DOMANIAL > DOMAIN

DOMATIA > DOMATIUM

DOMATIUM n plant cavity inhabited by commensal insects or mites or, occasionally, microorganisms

DOME n rounded roof built on a circular base ▷ vb cover with or as if with a dome

DOMED > DOME

DOMELIKE > DOME

DOMES > DOME

DOMESDAY same as > DOOMSDAY

DOMESDAYS > DOMESDAY

DOMESTIC adj of one's own country or a specific country ▷ n person whose job is to do housework in someone else's house

DOMESTICS > DOMESTIC

DOMETT n wool and cotton cloth

DOMETTS > DOMETT

DOMIC adj dome-shaped

DOMICAL > DOME

DOMICALLY > DOME

DOMICIL same as > DOMICILE

DOMICILE n place where one lives ▷ vb establish or be established in a dwelling place

DOMICILED > DOMICILE

DOMICILES > DOMICILE

DOMICILS > DOMICIL

DOMIER > DOMY

DOMIEST > DOMY

DOMINANCE n control

DOMINANCY > DOMINANCE

DOMINANT adj having authority or influence ▷ n dominant allele or character

DOMINANTS > DOMINANT

DOMINATE vb control or govern

DOMINATED > DOMINATE

DOMINATES > DOMINATE

DOMINATOR > DOMINATE

DOMINE n clergyman

DOMINEE n minister of the Dutch Reformed Church

DOMINEER vb act with arrogance or tyranny

DOMINEERS > DOMINEER

DOMINEES > DOMINEE

DOMINES > DOMINE

DOMING > DOME

DOMINICAL adj of, relating to, or emanating from Jesus Christ as Lord

DOMINICK n breed of chicken

DOMINICKS > DOMINICK

DOMINIE n minister or clergyman: also used as a term of address

DOMINIES > DOMINIE

DOMINION same as > DOMINIUM

DOMINIONS same as > DOMINION

DOMINIQUE n type of chicken

DOMINIUM n ownership or right to possession of property, esp realty

DOMINIUMS > DOMINIUM

DOMINO n small rectangular block marked with dots, used in dominoes

DOMINOES n game in which dominoes with matching halves are laid together

DOMINOS > DOMINO

DOMOIC adj as in domoic acid kind of amino acid

DOMS > DOM

DOMY adj having a dome or domes

DON vb put on (clothing) ▷ n member of the teaching staff at a university or college

DONA n Spanish lady

DONAH n woman

DONAHS > DONAH

DONAIR same as > DONER

DONAIRS > DONAIR

DONARIES > DONARY

DONARY n thing given for holy use

DONAS > DONA

DONATARY n recipient

DONATE vb give, esp to a charity or organization

DONATED > DONATE

DONATES > DONATE

DONATING > DONATE

DONATION n donating

DONATIONS > DONATION

DONATISM n doctrine and beliefs relating to a schismatic heretical Christian sect originating in N Africa in 311 AD

DONATISMS > DONATISM

DONATIVE n gift or donation ▷ adj of or like a donation

DONATIVES > DONATIVE

DONATOR > DONATE

DONATORS > DONATE

DONATORY n recipient

DONDER vb beat (someone) up ▷ n wretch

DONDERED > DONDER

DONDERING > DONDER

DONDERS > DONDER

DONE > DO

DONEE n person who receives a gift

DONEES > DONEE

DONEGAL n type of tweed

DONEGALS > DONEGAL

DONENESS n extent to which something is cooked

DONEPEZIL n drug used to treat dementia

DONER n as in doner kebab grilled meat and salad served in pitta bread with chilli sauce

DONG n deep reverberating sound of a large bell ▷ vb (of a bell) to make a deep reverberating sound

DONGA n steep-sided gully created by soil erosion

DONGAS > DONGA

DONGED > DONG

DONGING > DONG

DONGLE n electronic device

DONGLES > DONGLE

DONGOLA n leather tanned using a particular method

DONGOLAS > DONGOLA

DONGS > DONG

DONING n act of giving blood

DONINGS > DONING

DONJON n heavily fortified central tower of a castle

DONJONS > DONJON

DONKEY n long-eared member of the horse family

DONKEYS > DONKEY

DONKO n tearoom or cafeteria in a factory, wharf area, etc

DONKOS > DONKO

DONNA n Italian lady

DONNARD same as > DONNERT

DONNART same as > DONNERT

DONNAS > DONNA

DONNAT n lazy person

DONNATS > DONNAT

DONNE same as > DONNEE

DONNED > DON

DONNEE n subject or theme

DONNEES > DONNEE

DONNERD adj stupid

DONNERED same as > DONNERT

DONNERT adj stunned

DONNES > DONNE

DONNICKER n toilet

DONNIES > DONNY

DONNIKER same as > DONNICKER

DONNIKERS > DONNIKER

DONNING > DON

DONNISH adj serious and academic

DONNISHLY > DONNISH

DONNISM n loftiness

DONNISMS > DONNISM

DONNOT n lazy person

DONNOTS > DONNOT

DONNY same as > DANNY

DONOR n person who gives blood or organs for medical use

DONORS > DONOR

DONORSHIP > DONOR

DONS > DON

DONSHIP n state or condition of being a don

DONSHIPS > DONSHIP

DONSIE adj rather unwell

DONSIER > DONSIE

DONSIEST > DONSIE

DONSY same as > DONSIE

DONUT same as > DOUGHNUT

DONUTS > DONUT

DONUTTED > DONUT

DONUTTING > DONUT

DONZEL n man of high birth

DONZELS > DONZEL

DOO a Scot word for > DOVE

DOOB n cannabis cigarette

DOOBIE same as > DOOB

DOOBIES > DOOBIE

DOOBREY n thingumabob

DOOBREYS > DOOBREY

DOOBRIE same as > DOOBREY

DOOBRIES > DOOBRIE

DOOBRY n thing whose name is unknown or forgotten

DOOBS > DOOB

DOOCE vb dismiss (an employee) because of comments they have posted on the Internet

DOOCED > DOOCE

DOOCES > DOOCE

DOOCING > DOOCE

DOOCOT n dovecote

DOOCOTS > DOOCOT

DOODAD same as > DOODAH

DOODADS > DOODAD

DOODAH n unnamed thing

DOODAHS > DOODAH

DOODIES > DOODY

DOODLE vb scribble or draw aimlessly ▷ n shape or picture drawn aimlessly

DOODLEBUG n diviner's rod

DOODLED > DOODLE

DOODLER > DOODLE

DOODLERS > DOODLE

DOODLES > DOODLE

DOODLING > DOODLE

DOODOO n excrement

DOODOOS > DOODOO

DOODY same as > DOODOO

DOOFER n thingamajig

DOOFERS > DOOFER

DOOFUS n slow-witted or stupid person

DOOFUSES > DOOFUS

DOOHICKEY another name for > DOODAH

DOOK n wooden plug driven into a wall to hold a nail, screw, etc ▷ vb dip or plunge

DOOKED > DOOK

DOOKET n dovecote

DOOKETS > DOOKET

DOOKING > DOOK

DOOKS > DOOK

DOOL n boundary marker

DOOLALLY adj out of one's mind

DOOLAN n Roman Catholic

DOOLANS > DOOLAN

DOOLE same as > DOOL

DOOLEE same as > DOOLIE

DOOLEES > DOOLEE

DOOLES > DOOLE

DOOLIE n enclosed couch on poles for carrying passengers

DOOLIES > DOOLIE

DOOLS > DOOL

DOOLY same as > DOOLIE

DOOM n death or a terrible fate ▷ vb destine or condemn to death or a terrible fate

DOOMED > DOOM

DOOMFUL > DOOM

DOOMFULLY > DOOM

DOOMIER > DOOMY

DOOMIEST > DOOMY

DOOMILY > DOOMY

DOOMING > DOOM

DOOMS > DOOM
DOOMSAYER n pessimist
DOOMSDAY n day on which the Last Judgment will occur
DOOMSDAYS > DOOMSDAY
DOOMSMAN n pessimist
DOOMSMEN > DOOMSMAN
DOOMSTER n person habitually given to predictions of impending disaster or doom
DOOMSTERS > DOOMSTER
DOOMWATCH n surveillance of the environment to warn of and prevent harm to it from human factors such as pollution or overpopulation
DOOMY adj despondent or pessimistic
DOON same as > DOWN
DOONA n large quilt used as a bed cover
DOONAS > DOONA
DOOR n hinged or sliding panel for closing the entrance to a building, room, etc
DOORBELL n device for visitors to announce presence at a door
DOORBELLS > DOORBELL
DOORCASE same as > DOORFRAME
DOORCASES > DOORCASE
DOORED adj having a door
DOORFRAME n frame that supports a door
DOORJAMB n vertical post forming one side of a door frame
DOORJAMBS > DOORJAMB
DOORKNOB n knob for opening and closing a door
DOORKNOBS > DOORKNOB
DOORKNOCK n fund-raising campaign for charity conducted by seeking donations from door to door
DOORLESS > DOOR
DOORMAN n man employed to be on duty at the entrance to a large public building
DOORMAT n mat for wiping dirt from shoes before going indoors
DOORMATS > DOORMAT
DOORMEN > DOORMAN
DOORN n thorn
DOORNAIL n as in dead as a doornail dead beyond any doubt
DOORNAILS > DOORNAIL
DOORNBOOM n S African tree with yellow or white flowers
DOORNS > DOORN
DOORPLATE n nameplate on door

DOORPOST same as > DOORJAMB
DOORPOSTS > DOORPOST
DOORS > DOOR
DOORSILL n horizontal member of wood, stone, etc, forming the bottom of a doorframe
DOORSILLS > DOORSILL
DOORSMAN n doorkeeper
DOORSMEN > DOORSMAN
DOORSTEP n step in front of a door
DOORSTEPS > DOORSTEP
DOORSTONE n stone of threshold
DOORSTOP n heavy object or one fixed to the floor, which prevents a door from closing or from striking a wall
DOORSTOPS > DOORSTOP
DOORWAY n opening into a building or room
DOORWAYS > DOORWAY
DOORWOMAN n female doorman
DOORWOMEN > DOORWOMAN
DOORYARD n yard in front of the front or back door of a house
DOORYARDS > DOORYARD
DOOS > DOO
DOOSRA n delivery in cricket
DOOSRAS > DOOSRA
DOOWOP n style of singing in harmony
DOOWOPS > DOOWOP
DOOZER same as > DOOZY
DOOZERS > DOOZER
DOOZIE same as > DOOZY
DOOZIES > DOOZIE
DOOZY n something excellent
DOP vb curtsy ▷ n tot or small drink, usually alcoholic ▷ vb fail to reach the required standard in (an examination, course, etc)
DOPA n precursor to dopamine
DOPAMINE n chemical found in the brain that acts as a neurotransmitter
DOPAMINES > DOPAMINE
DOPANT n element or compound used to dope a semiconductor
DOPANTS > DOPANT
DOPAS > DOPA
DOPATTA n headscarf
DOPATTAS > DOPATTA
DOPE n illegal drug, usu cannabis ▷ vb give a drug to, esp in order to improve performance in a race ▷ adj excellent
DOPED > DOPE
DOPEHEAD n habitual drug user
DOPEHEADS > DOPEHEAD

DOPER n person who administers dope
DOPERS > DOPER
DOPES > DOPE
DOPESHEET n document giving information on horse races
DOPEST > DOPE
DOPESTER n person who makes predictions, esp in sport or politics
DOPESTERS > DOPESTER
DOPEY adj half-asleep, drowsy
DOPEYNESS > DOPEY
DOPIAZA n Indian meat or fish dish cooked in onion sauce
DOPIAZAS > DOPIAZA
DOPIER > DOPY
DOPIEST > DOPY
DOPILY > DOPEY
DOPINESS > DOPEY
DOPING > DOPE
DOPINGS > DOPE
DOPPED > DOP
DOPPER n member of an Afrikaner church who practises a strict Calvinism
DOPPERS > DOPPER
DOPPIE n cartridge case
DOPPIES > DOPPIE
DOPPING > DOP
DOPPINGS > DOP
DOPPIO n double measure, esp of espresso coffee
DOPPIOS > DOPPIO
DOPS > DOP
DOPY same as > DOPEY
DOR n European dung beetle
DORAD n South American river fish
DORADO n large marine percoid fish
DORADOS > DORADO
DORADS > DORAD
DORB same as > DORBA
DORBA n stupid, inept, or clumsy person
DORBAS > DORBA
DORBEETLE same as > DOR
DORBS > DORB
DORBUG n type of beetle
DORBUGS > DORBUG
DORE n walleye fish
DOREE n type of fish
DOREES > DOREE
DORES > DORE
DORHAWK n nightjar
DORHAWKS > DORHAWK
DORIC adj rustic
DORIDOID n shell-less mollusc
DORIDOIDS > DORIDOID
DORIES > DORY
DORIS n woman
DORISE same as > DORIZE
DORISED > DORISE
DORISES > DORISE
DORISING > DORISE

DORIZE vb become Doric
DORIZED > DORIZE
DORIZES > DORIZE
DORIZING > DORIZE
DORK n stupid person
DORKIER > DORK
DORKIEST > DORK
DORKINESS > DORK
DORKISH adj stupid or contemptible
DORKS > DORK
DORKY > DORK
DORLACH n quiver of arrows
DORLACHS > DORLACH
DORM same as > DORMITORY
DORMANCY > DORMANT
DORMANT adj supporting beam ▷ adj temporarily quiet, inactive, or not being used
DORMANTS > DORMANT
DORMER n window that sticks out from a sloping roof
DORMERED adj having dormer windows
DORMERS > DORMER
DORMICE > DORMOUSE
DORMIE adj (in golf) leading by as many holes as there are left
DORMIENT adj dormant
DORMIN n hormone found in plants
DORMINS > DORMIN
DORMITION n Mary's assumption to heaven
DORMITIVE adj sleep-inducing
DORMITORY n large room, esp at a school, containing several beds ▷ adj (of a town or suburb) having many inhabitants who travel to work in a nearby city
DORMOUSE n small mouselike rodent with a furry tail
DORMS > DORM
DORMY same as > DORMIE
DORNECK same as > DORNICK
DORNECKS > DORNECK
DORNICK n heavy damask cloth
DORNICKS > DORNICK
DORNOCK n type of coarse fabric
DORNOCKS > DORNOCK
DORONICUM n Eurasian and N African plant with yellow daisy-like flowers
DORP n small town
DORPER n breed of sheep
DORPERS > DORPER
DORPS > DORP
DORR same as > DOR
DORRED > DOR
DORRING > DOR
DORRS > DORR
DORS > DOR

DORSA > DORSUM

DORSAD *adj* towards the back or dorsal aspect

DORSAL *adj* of or on the back ▷ *n* dorsal fin

DORSALLY > DORSAL

DORSALS > DORSAL

DORSE *n* type of small fish

DORSEL *another word for* > DOSSAL

DORSELS > DORSEL

DORSER *n* hanging tapestry

DORSERS > DORSER

DORSES > DORSE

DORSIFLEX *adj* bending towards the back ▷ *vb* bend towards the back or dorsal

DORSUM *n* the back

DORT *vb* sulk

DORTED > DORT

DORTER *n* dormitory

DORTERS > DORTER

DORTIER > DORTY

DORTIEST > DORTY

DORTINESS > DORTY

DORTING > DORT

DORTOUR *same as* > DORTER

DORTOURS > DORTOUR

DORTS > DORT

DORTY *adj* haughty, or sullen

DORY *n* spiny-finned edible sea fish

DORYMAN *n* person who fishes from a small boat called a dory

DORYMEN > DORYMAN

DOS > DO

DOSA *n* an Indian pancake made from rice flour

DOSAGE *same as* > DOSE

DOSAGES > DOSAGE

DOSAI > DOSA

DOSAS > DOSA

DOSE *n* specific quantity of a medicine taken at one time ▷ *vb* give a dose to

DOSED > DOSE

DOSEH *n* former Egyptian religious ceremony

DOSEHS > DOSEH

DOSEMETER *same as* > DOSIMETER

DOSER > DOSE

DOSERS > DOSE

DOSES > DOSE

DOSH *n* money

DOSHA *n* (in Hinduism) any of the three energies believed to be in the body

DOSHAS > DOSHA

DOSHES > DOSH

DOSIMETER *n* instrument for measuring the dose of X-rays or other radiation absorbed by matter or the intensity of a source of radiation

DOSIMETRY > DOSIMETER

DOSING > DOSE

DOSIOLOGY *n* study of doses

DOSOLOGY *same as* > DOSIOLOGY

DOSS *vb* sleep, esp in a dosshouse ▷ *n* bed, esp in a dosshouse

DOSSAL *n* ornamental hanging used in churches

DOSSALS > DOSSAL

DOSSED > DOSS

DOSSEL *same as* > DOSSAL

DOSSELS > DOSSEL

DOSSER *n* bag or basket for carrying objects on the back

DOSSERET *n* stone above column supporting an arch

DOSSERETS > DOSSERET

DOSSERS > DOSSER

DOSSES > DOSS

DOSSHOUSE *n* cheap lodging house for homeless people

DOSSIER *n* collection of documents about a subject or person

DOSSIERS > DOSSIER

DOSSIL *n* lint for dressing wound

DOSSILS > DOSSIL

DOSSING > DOSS

DOST *a singular form of the present tense (indicative mood) of* > DO

DOT *n* small round mark ▷ *vb* mark with a dot

DOTAGE *n* weakness as a result of old age

DOTAGES > DOTAGE

DOTAL > DOT

DOTANT *another word for* > DOTARD

DOTANTS > DOTANT

DOTARD *n* person who is feeble-minded through old age

DOTARDLY > DOTARD

DOTARDS > DOTARD

DOTATION *n* act of giving a dowry

DOTATIONS > DOTATION

DOTCOM *n* company that does most of its business on the Internet

DOTCOMMER *n* person who carries out business on the internet

DOTCOMS > DOTCOM

DOTE *vb* love to an excessive or foolish degree

DOTED > DOTE

DOTER > DOTE

DOTERS > DOTE

DOTES > DOTE

DOTH *a singular form of the present tense of* > DO

DOTIER > DOTY

DOTIEST > DOTY

DOTING > DOTE

DOTINGLY > DOTE

DOTINGS > DOTE

DOTISH *adj* foolish

DOTS > DOT

DOTTED > DOT

DOTTEL *same as* > DOTTLE

DOTTELS > DOTTEL

DOTTER > DOT

DOTTEREL *n* rare kind of plover

DOTTERELS > DOTTEREL

DOTTERS > DOT

DOTTIER > DOTTY

DOTTIEST > DOTTY

DOTTILY > DOTTY

DOTTINESS > DOTTY

DOTTING > DOT

DOTTLE *n* tobacco left in a pipe after smoking ▷ *adj* relating to dottle

DOTTLED *adj* foolish

DOTTLER > DOTTLE

DOTTLES > DOTTLE

DOTTLEST > DOTTLE

DOTTREL *same as* > DOTTEREL

DOTTRELS > DOTTREL

DOTTY *adj* rather eccentric

DOTY *adj* (of wood) rotten

DOUANE *n* customs house

DOUANES > DOUANE

DOUANIER *n* customs officer

DOUANIERS > DOUANIER

DOUAR *same as* > DUAR

DOUARS > DOUAR

DOUBLE *adj* as much again in number, amount, size, etc ▷ *adv* twice over ▷ *n* twice the number, amount, size, etc ▷ *vb* make or become twice as much or as many

DOUBLED > DOUBLE

DOUBLER > DOUBLE

DOUBLERS > DOUBLE

DOUBLES *n* game between two pairs of players

DOUBLET *n* man's close-fitting jacket, with or without sleeves

DOUBLETON *n* original holding of two cards only in a suit

DOUBLETS > DOUBLET

DOUBLING > DOUBLE

DOUBLINGS > DOUBLE

DOUBLOON *n* former Spanish gold coin

DOUBLOONS > DOUBLOON

DOUBLURE *n* decorative lining of vellum or leather, etc, on the inside of a book cover

DOUBLURES > DOUBLURE

DOUBLY *adv* in a greater degree, quantity, or measure

DOUBT *n* uncertainty about the truth, facts, or existence of something ▷ *vb* question the truth of

DOUBTABLE > DOUBT

DOUBTABLY > DOUBT

DOUBTED > DOUBT

DOUBTER > DOUBT

DOUBTERS > DOUBT

DOUBTFUL *adj* unlikely ▷ *n* person who is undecided or uncertain about an issue

DOUBTFULS > DOUBTFUL

DOUBTING > DOUBT

DOUBTINGS > DOUBT

DOUBTLESS *adv* probably or certainly ▷ *adj* certain

DOUBTS > DOUBT

DOUC *n* Old World monkey

DOUCE *adj* quiet

DOUCELY > DOUCE

DOUCENESS > DOUCE

DOUCEPERE *same as* > DOUZEPER

DOUCER > DOUCE

DOUCEST > DOUCE

DOUCET *n* former flute-like instrument

DOUCETS > DOUCET

DOUCEUR *n* gratuity, tip, or bribe

DOUCEURS > DOUCEUR

DOUCHE *n* stream of water onto or into the body ▷ *vb* cleanse or treat by means of a douche

DOUCHEBAG *n* despicable person

DOUCHED > DOUCHE

DOUCHES > DOUCHE

DOUCHING *n* act of douching

DOUCHINGS > DOUCHING

DOUCINE *n* type of moulding for cornice

DOUCINES > DOUCINE

DOUCS > DOUC

DOUGH *n* thick mixture used for making bread etc

DOUGHBALL *n* ball of bread used as bait in carp fishing

DOUGHBOY *n* infantryman, esp in World War I

DOUGHBOYS > DOUGHBOY

DOUGHFACE *n* Northern Democrat who sided with the South in the American Civil War

DOUGHIER > DOUGHY

DOUGHIEST > DOUGHY

DOUGHLIKE > DOUGH

DOUGHNUT *n* small cake of sweetened dough fried in deep fat ▷ *vb* (of Members of Parliament) to surround (a speaker) during the televising of Parliament to give the impression that the chamber is crowded or the speaker is well supported

DOUGHNUTS > DOUGHNUT

DOUGHS > DOUGH

DOUGHT > DOW

DOUGHTIER > DOUGHTY

DOUGHTILY > DOUGHTY

DOUGHTY *adj* brave and determined

DOUGHY adj resembling dough in consistency, colour, etc

DOUK same as > DOOK

DOUKED > DOUK

DOUKING > DOUK

DOUKS > DOUK

DOULA n woman trained to provide support to families during pregnancy, childbirth, and time following the birth

DOULAS > DOULA

DOULEIA same as > DULIA

DOULEIAS > DOULEIA

DOUM n as in doum palm variety of palm tree

DOUMA same as > DUMA

DOUMAS > DOUMA

DOUMS > DOUM

DOUN same as > DOWN

DOUP n bottom

DOUPIONI n type of fabric

DOUPIONIS > DOUPIONI

DOUPPIONI n type of silk yarn

DOUPS > DOUP

DOUR adj sullen and unfriendly

DOURA same as > DURRA

DOURAH same as > DURRA

DOURAHS > DOURAH

DOURAS > DOURA

DOURER > DOUR

DOUREST > DOUR

DOURINE n infectious venereal disease of horses

DOURINES > DOURINE

DOURLY > DOUR

DOURNESS > DOUR

DOUSE vb drench with water or other liquid ▷ n immersion

DOUSED > DOUSE

DOUSER > DOUSE

DOUSERS > DOUSE

DOUSES > DOUSE

DOUSING > DOUSE

DOUT vb extinguish

DOUTED > DOUT

DOUTER > DOUT

DOUTERS > DOUT

DOUTING > DOUT

DOUTS > DOUT

DOUX adj sweet

DOUZEPER n distinguished person

DOUZEPERS > DOUZEPER

DOVE vb be semi-conscious ▷ n bird with a heavy body, small head, and short legs

DOVECOT same as > DOVECOTE

DOVECOTE n structure for housing pigeons

DOVECOTES > DOVECOTE

DOVECOTS > DOVECOT

DOVED > DOVE

DOVEISH adj dovelike

DOVEKEY same as > DOVEKIE

DOVEKEYS > DOVEKEY

DOVEKIE n small short-billed auk

DOVEKIES > DOVEKIE

DOVELET n small dove

DOVELETS > DOVELET

DOVELIKE > DOVE

DOVEN vb pray

DOVENED > DOVEN

DOVENING > DOVEN

DOVENS > DOVEN

DOVER vb doze ▷ n doze

DOVERED > DOVER

DOVERING > DOVER

DOVERS > DOVER

DOVES > DOVE

DOVETAIL n joint containing wedge-shaped tenons ▷ vb fit together neatly

DOVETAILS > DOVETAIL

DOVIE Scots word for > STUPID

DOVIER > DOVIE

DOVIEST > DOVIE

DOVING > DOVE

DOVISH > DOVE

DOW vb archaic word meaning be of worth

DOWABLE adj capable of being endowed

DOWAGER n widow possessing property or a title obtained from her husband

DOWAGERS > DOWAGER

DOWAR same as > DUAR

DOWARS > DOWAR

DOWD n woman who wears unfashionable clothes

DOWDIER > DOWDY

DOWDIES > DOWDY

DOWDIEST > DOWDY

DOWDILY > DOWDY

DOWDINESS > DOWDY

DOWDS > DOWD

DOWDY adj dull and old-fashioned ▷ n dowdy woman

DOWDYISH > DOWDY

DOWDYISM > DOWD

DOWDYISMS > DOWD

DOWED > DOW

DOWEL n wooden or metal peg used as a fastener ▷ vb join pieces of wood using dowels

DOWELED > DOWEL

DOWELING n joining of two pieces of wood using dowels

DOWELINGS > DOWELING

DOWELLED > DOWEL

DOWELLING same as > DOWELING

DOWELS > DOWEL

DOWER n life interest in a part of her husband's estate allotted to a widow by law ▷ vb endow

DOWERED > DOWER

DOWERIES > DOWERY

DOWERING > DOWER

DOWERLESS > DOWER

DOWERS > DOWER

DOWERY same as > DOWRY

DOWF adj dull; listless

DOWFNESS > DOWF

DOWIE adj dull and dreary

DOWIER > DOWIE

DOWIEST > DOWIE

DOWING > DOW

DOWITCHER n type of snipelike shore bird of arctic and subarctic N America

DOWL n fluff

DOWLAS n coarse fabric

DOWLASES > DOWLAS

DOWLE same as > DOWL

DOWLES > DOWLE

DOWLIER > DOWLY

DOWLIEST > DOWLY

DOWLNE obsolete form of > DOWN

DOWLNES > DOWLNE

DOWLNEY > DOWLNE

DOWLS > DOWL

DOWLY adj dull

DOWN adv indicating movement to or position in a lower place ▷ adj depressed, unhappy ▷ vb drink quickly ▷ n soft fine feathers

DOWNA obsolete Scots form of > CANNOT

DOWNBEAT adj gloomy ▷ n first beat of a bar

DOWNBEATS > DOWNBEAT

DOWNBOW n (in music) a downward stroke of the bow across the strings

DOWNBOWS > DOWNBOW

DOWNBURST n very high-speed downward movement of turbulent air in a limited area for a short time. Near the ground it spreads out from its centre with high horizontal velocities

DOWNCAST adj sad, dejected ▷ n ventilation shaft

DOWNCASTS > DOWNCAST

DOWNCOME same as > DOWNCOMER

DOWNCOMER n pipe that connects a cistern to a WC, wash basin, etc

DOWNCOMES > DOWNCOME

DOWNCOURT adj in far end a of court

DOWNCRIED > DOWNCRY

DOWNCRIES > DOWNCRY

DOWNCRY vb denigrate or disparage

DOWNDRAFT n downward air current

DOWNED > DOWN

DOWNER n barbiturate, tranquillizer, or narcotic

DOWNERS > DOWNER

DOWNFALL same as > DEADFALL

DOWNFALLS > DOWNFALL

DOWNFIELD adj at far end of field

DOWNFLOW n something that flows down

DOWNFLOWS > DOWNFLOW

DOWNFORCE n force produced by air resistance plus gravity that increases the stability of an aircraft or motor vehicle by pressing it downwards

DOWNGRADE n reduce in importance or value

DOWNHAUL n line for hauling down a sail or for increasing the tension at its luff

DOWNHAULS > DOWNHAUL

DOWNHILL adj going or sloping down ▷ adv towards the bottom of a hill ▷ n downward slope

DOWNHILLS > DOWNHILL

DOWNHOLE adj (in the oil industry) denoting any piece of equipment that is used in the well itself

DOWNIER > DOWNY

DOWNIES > DOWNY

DOWNIEST > DOWNY

DOWNILY adv in a manner resembling or indicating a layer of soft fine feathers or hairs

DOWNINESS > DOWNY

DOWNING > DOWN

DOWNLAND same as > DOWNS

DOWNLANDS > DOWNLAND

DOWNLESS > DOWN

DOWNLIGHT n lamp shining downwards

DOWNLIKE > DOWN

DOWNLINK n satellite transmission channel

DOWNLINKS > DOWNLINK

DOWNLOAD vb transfer (data) from the memory of one computer to that of another, especially over the Internet ▷ n file transferred in such a way

DOWNLOADS > DOWNLOAD

DOWNLOW n as in on the downlow not widely known

DOWNLOWS > DOWNLOW

DOWNMOST adj lowest

DOWNPIPE n pipe for carrying rainwater from a roof gutter to the ground or to a drain

DOWNPIPES > DOWNPIPE

DOWNPLAY vb play down

DOWNPLAYS > DOWNPLAY

DOWNPOUR n heavy fall of rain

DOWNPOURS > DOWNPOUR

DOWNRANGE adv in the direction of the intended flight path of a rocket or missile

DOWNRATE vb reduce in value or importance

DOWNRATED > DOWNRATE
DOWNRATES > DOWNRATE
DOWNRIGHT adv extreme(ly) ⊳ adj absolute
DOWNRIVER adv in direction of current
DOWNRUSH n instance of rushing down
DOWNS pl n low grassy hills, esp in S England
DOWNSCALE vb reduce in scale
DOWNSHIFT vb reduce work hours
DOWNSIDE n disadvantageous aspect of a situation
DOWNSIDES > DOWNSIDE
DOWNSIZE vb reduce the number of people employed by (a company)
DOWNSIZED > DOWNSIZE
DOWNSIZER > DOWNSIZE
DOWNSIZES > DOWNSIZE
DOWNSLIDE n downward trend
DOWNSLOPE adv towards the bottom of a slope ⊳ n downward slope
DOWNSPIN n sudden downturn
DOWNSPINS > DOWNSPIN
DOWNSPOUT same as **>** DOWNPIPE
DOWNSTAGE adj or at the front part of the stage ⊳ adv at or towards the front of the stage ⊳ n front half of the stage
DOWNSTAIR adj situated on lower floor
DOWNSTATE adj in, or relating to the part of the state away from large cities, esp the southern part ⊳ adv towards the southern part of a state ⊳ n southern part of a state
DOWNSWEPT adj curved downwards
DOWNSWING n statistical downward trend in business activity, the death rate, etc
DOWNTHROW n state of throwing down or being thrown down
DOWNTICK n small decrease
DOWNTICKS > DOWNTICK
DOWNTIME n time during which a computer or other machine is not working
DOWNTIMES > DOWNTIME
DOWNTOWN n central or lower part of a city, esp the main commercial area ⊳ adv towards, to, or into this area ⊳ adj of, relating to, or situated in the downtown area
DOWNTOWNS > DOWNTOWN

DOWNTREND n downward trend
DOWNTROD adj downtrodden
DOWNTURN n drop in the success of an economy or a business
DOWNTURNS > DOWNTURN
DOWNWARD same as **>** DOWNWARDS
DOWNWARDS adv from a higher to a lower level, condition, or position
DOWNWARP n wide depression in the earth's surface
DOWNWARPS > DOWNWARP
DOWNWASH n downward deflection of an airflow, esp one caused by an aircraft wing
DOWNWIND adj in the same direction towards which the wind is blowing
DOWNY adj covered with soft fine hair or feathers ⊳ n as in the downy bed
DOWNZONE vb reduce density of housing in area
DOWNZONED > DOWNZONE
DOWNZONES > DOWNZONE
DOWP same as **>** DOUP
DOWPS > DOWP
DOWRIES > DOWRY
DOWRY n property brought by a woman to her husband at marriage
DOWS > DOW
DOWSABEL n sweetheart
DOWSABELS > DOWSABEL
DOWSE same as **>** DOUSE
DOWSED > DOWSE
DOWSER > DOWSE
DOWSERS > DOWSE
DOWSES > DOWSE
DOWSET same as **>** DOUCET
DOWSETS > DOWSET
DOWSING n act of dowsing
DOWSINGS > DOWSING
DOWT n cigarette butt
DOWTS > DOWT
DOXAPRAM n drug used to stimulate the respiration
DOXAPRAMS > DOXAPRAM
DOXASTIC adj of or relating to belief ⊳ n branch of logic that studies the concept of belief
DOXASTICS > DOXASTIC
DOXIE same as **>** DOXY
DOXIES > DOXY
DOXOLOGY n short hymn of praise to God
DOXY n opinion or doctrine, esp concerning religious matters
DOY n beloved person: used esp as an endearment
DOYEN n senior member of a group, profession, or society
DOYENNE > DOYEN

DOYENNES > DOYEN
DOYENS > DOYEN
DOYLEY same as **>** DOILY
DOYLEYS > DOYLEY
DOYLIES > DOYLY
DOYLY same as **>** DOILY
DOYS > DOY
DOZE vb sleep lightly or briefly ⊳ n short sleep
DOZED adj (of timber or rubber) rotten or decayed
DOZEN vb stun
DOZENED > DOZEN
DOZENING > DOZEN
DOZENS > DOZEN
DOZENTH > DOZEN
DOZENTHS > DOZEN
DOZER > DOZE
DOZERS > DOZE
DOZES > DOZE
DOZIER > DOZY
DOZIEST > DOZY
DOZILY > DOZY
DOZINESS > DOZY
DOZING > DOZE
DOZINGS > DOZE
DOZY adj feeling sleepy
DRAB adj dull and dreary ⊳ n light olive-brown colour ⊳ vb consort with prostitutes
DRABBED > DRAB
DRABBER n one who frequents low women
DRABBERS > DRABBER
DRABBEST > DRAB
DRABBET n yellowish-brown fabric of coarse linen
DRABBETS > DRABBET
DRABBIER > DRABBY
DRABBIEST > DRABBY
DRABBING > DRAB
DRABBISH adj promiscuous
DRABBLE vb make or become wet or dirty
DRABBLED > DRABBLE
DRABBLER n part fixed to bottom of sail
DRABBLERS > DRABBLER
DRABBLES > DRABBLE
DRABBLING > DRABBLE
DRABBY adj promiscuous
DRABETTE n type of rough linen fabric
DRABETTES > DRABETTE
DRABLER same as **>** DRABBLE
DRABLERS > DRABLER
DRABLY > DRAB
DRABNESS > DRAB
DRABS > DRAB
DRAC same as **>** DRACK
DRACAENA n type of tropical plant often cultivated as a house plant for its decorative foliage
DRACAENAS > DRACAENA
DRACENA same as **>** DRACAENA
DRACENAS > DRACENA
DRACHM same as **>** DRAM

DRACHMA n former monetary unit of Greece
DRACHMAE > DRACHMA
DRACHMAI > DRACHMA
DRACHMAS > DRACHMA
DRACHMS > DRACHM
DRACK adj (esp of a woman) unattractive
DRACO n as in draco lizard flying lizard
DRACONE n large container towed by a ship
DRACONES > DRACONE
DRACONIAN adj severe, harsh
DRACONIC same as **>** DRACONIAN
DRACONISM > DRACONIAN
DRACONTIC same as **>** DRACONIC
DRAD > DREAD
DRAFF n residue of husks used as a food for cattle
DRAFFIER > DRAFF
DRAFFIEST > DRAFF
DRAFFISH adj worthless
DRAFFS > DRAFF
DRAFFY > DRAFF
DRAFT same as **>** DRAUGHT
DRAFTABLE > DRAFT
DRAFTED > DRAFT
DRAFTEE n conscript
DRAFTEES > DRAFTEE
DRAFTER > DRAFT
DRAFTERS > DRAFT
DRAFTIER > DRAFTY
DRAFTIEST > DRAFTY
DRAFTILY > DRAFTY
DRAFTING > DRAFT
DRAFTINGS > DRAFT
DRAFTS > DRAFT
DRAFTSMAN adj person skilled in drawing
DRAFTSMEN > DRAFTSMAN
DRAFTY same as **>** DRAUGHTY
DRAG vb pull with force, esp along the ground ⊳ n person or thing that slows up progress
DRAGEE n sweet made of a nut, fruit, etc, coated with a hard sugar icing
DRAGEES > DRAGEE
DRAGGED > DRAG
DRAGGER > DRAG
DRAGGERS > DRAG
DRAGGIER > DRAGGY
DRAGGIEST > DRAGGY
DRAGGING > DRAG
DRAGGINGS > DRAGGING
DRAGGLE vb make or become wet or dirty by trailing on the ground
DRAGGLED > DRAGGLE
DRAGGLES > DRAGGLE
DRAGGLING > DRAGGLE
DRAGGY adj slow or boring
DRAGHOUND n hound used to follow an artificial trail of scent in a drag hunt

DRAGLINE same as
> DRAGROPE
DRAGLINES > DRAGLINE
DRAGNET n net used to
scour the bottom of a
pond or river
DRAGNETS > DRAGNET
DRAGOMAN n (in some
Middle Eastern countries)
professional interpreter or
guide
DRAGOMANS > DRAGOMAN
DRAGOMEN > DRAGOMAN
DRAGON n mythical
fire-breathing monster
like a huge lizard
DRAGONESS > DRAGON
DRAGONET n type of small
spiny-finned fish with a
flat head and a slender
brightly coloured body
DRAGONETS > DRAGONET
DRAGONFLY n brightly
coloured insect with a long
slender body and two pairs
of wings
DRAGONISE same as
> DRAGONIZE
DRAGONISH > DRAGON
DRAGONISM n vigilance
DRAGONIZE vb turn into
dragon
DRAGONNE adj dragonlike
DRAGONS > DRAGON
DRAGOON n heavily armed
cavalryman ▷ vb coerce,
force
DRAGOONED > DRAGOON
DRAGOONS > DRAGOON
DRAGROPE n rope used to
drag military equipment,
esp artillery
DRAGROPES > DRAGROPE
DRAGS > DRAG
DRAGSMAN n carriage
driver
DRAGSMEN > DRAGSMAN
DRAGSTER n car specially
built or modified for drag
racing
DRAGSTERS > DRAGSTER
DRAGSTRIP n track for
drag racing
DRAGWAY n race course for
drag racing
DRAGWAYS > DRAGWAY
DRAIL n weighted hook
used in trolling ▷ vb fish
with a drail
DRAILED > DRAIL
DRAILING > DRAIL
DRAILS > DRAIL
DRAIN n pipe or channel
that carries off water or
sewage ▷ vb draw off or
remove liquid from
DRAINABLE > DRAIN
DRAINAGE n system of
drains
DRAINAGES > DRAINAGE
DRAINED > DRAIN
DRAINER n person or
thing that drains
DRAINERS > DRAINER

DRAINING > DRAIN
DRAINPIPE same as
> DOWNPIPE
DRAINS > DRAIN
DRAISENE same as
> DRAISINE
DRAISENES > DRAISENE
DRAISINE n light rail
vehicle
DRAISINES > DRAISINE
DRAKE n male duck
DRAKES > DRAKE
DRAM n small amount of a
strong alcoholic drink, esp
whisky ▷ vb drink a dram
DRAMA n serious play for
theatre, television, or radio
DRAMADIES > DRAMEDY
DRAMADY same as
> DRAMEDY
DRAMAS > DRAMA
DRAMATIC adj of or like
drama
DRAMATICS n art of
acting or producing plays
DRAMATISE same as
> DRAMATIZE
DRAMATIST n person
who writes plays
DRAMATIZE vb rewrite (a
book) in the form of a play
DRAMATURG n literary
adviser at a theatre
DRAMEDIES > DRAMEDY
DRAMEDY n television or
film drama in which there
are important elements of
comedy
DRAMMACH n oatmeal
mixed with cold water
DRAMMACHS > DRAMMACH
DRAMMED > DRAM
DRAMMING > DRAM
DRAMMOCK same as
> DRAMMACH
DRAMMOCKS > DRAMMOCK
DRAMS > DRAM
DRAMSHOP n bar
DRAMSHOPS > DRAMSHOP
DRANGWAY n narrow lane
DRANGWAYS > DRANGWAY
DRANK > DRINK
DRANT vb drone
DRANTED > DRANT
DRANTING > DRANT
DRANTS > DRANT
DRAP a Scot word for > DROP
DRAPABLE > DRAPE
DRAPE vb cover with
material, usu in folds ▷ n
piece of cloth hung at a
window or opening as a
screen
DRAPEABLE > DRAPE
DRAPED > DRAPE
DRAPER n person who
sells fabrics and sewing
materials
DRAPERIED > DRAPERY
DRAPERIES > DRAPERY
DRAPERS > DRAPER
DRAPERY n fabric or
clothing arranged and
draped

DRAPES pl n material hung
at an opening or window
to shut out light or to
provide privacy
DRAPET n cloth
DRAPETS > DRAPET
DRAPEY adj hanging in
loose folds
DRAPIER n draper
DRAPIERS > DRAPIER
DRAPIEST > DRAPEY
DRAPING > DRAPE
DRAPPED > DRAP
DRAPPIE n little drop, esp
a small amount of spirits
DRAPPIES > DRAPPIE
DRAPPING > DRAP
DRAPPY n drop (of liquid)
DRAPS > DRAP
DRASTIC n strong
purgative ▷ adj strong and
severe
DRASTICS > DRASTIC
DRAT interj exclamation of
annoyance ▷ vb curse
DRATCHELL n low
woman
DRATS > DRAT
DRATTED adj wretched
DRATTING > DRAT
DRAUGHT vb make
preliminary plan
▷ n current of cold air, esp
in an enclosed space
▷ adj (of an animal) used
for pulling heavy loads
DRAUGHTED > DRAUGHT
DRAUGHTER > DRAUGHT
DRAUGHTS n game for
two players using a
draughtboard and 12
draughtsmen each
DRAUGHTY adj exposed to
draughts of air
DRAUNT same as > DRANT
DRAUNTED > DRAUNT
DRAUNTING > DRAUNT
DRAUNTS > DRAUNT
DRAVE archaic past of
> DRIVE
DRAW vb sketch (a figure,
picture, etc) with a pencil
or pen ▷ n raffle or lottery
DRAWABLE > DRAW
DRAWBACK n
disadvantage ▷ vb move
backwards
DRAWBACKS > DRAWBACK
DRAWBAR n strong metal
bar on a tractor,
locomotive, etc
DRAWBARS > DRAWBAR
DRAWBORE n hole bored
through tenon
DRAWBORES > DRAWBORE
DRAWCORD n cord for
drawing tight eg round a
hood
DRAWCORDS > DRAWCORD
DRAWDOWN n decrease
DRAWDOWNS > DRAWDOWN
DRAWEE n person or
organization on which
payment is drawn

DRAWEES > DRAWEE
DRAWER n sliding box-
shaped part of a piece of
furniture, used for storage
DRAWERFUL n amount
contained in drawer
DRAWERS pl n
undergarment worn on
the lower part of the body
DRAWING > DRAW
DRAWINGS > DRAW
DRAWKNIFE n
woodcutting tool with
two handles at right
angles to the blade, used
to shave wood
DRAWL vb speak slowly,
with long vowel sounds
▷ n drawling manner of
speech
DRAWLED > DRAWL
DRAWLER > DRAWL
DRAWLERS > DRAWL
DRAWLIER > DRAWL
DRAWLIEST > DRAWL
DRAWLING > DRAWL
DRAWLS > DRAWL
DRAWLY > DRAWL
DRAWN > DRAW
DRAWNWORK n type of
ornamental needlework
DRAWPLATE n plate used
to reduce the diameter of
wire by drawing it through
conical holes
DRAWS > DRAW
DRAWSHAVE same as
> DRAWKNIFE
DRAWTUBE n tube, such as
one of the component
tubes of a telescope,
fitting coaxially within
another tube through
which it can slide
DRAWTUBES > DRAWTUBE
DRAY vb pull using cart
▷ n low cart used for
carrying heavy loads
DRAYAGE n act of
transporting something a
short distance
DRAYAGES > DRAYAGE
DRAYED > DRAY
DRAYHORSE n large
powerful horse used for
drawing a dray
DRAYING > DRAY
DRAYMAN n driver of a dray
DRAYMEN > DRAYMAN
DRAYS > DRAY
DRAZEL n low woman
DRAZELS > DRAZEL
DREAD vb anticipate with
apprehension or fear
▷ n great fear ▷ adj
awesome
DREADED > DREAD
DREADER > DREAD
DREADERS > DREAD
DREADEST > DREAD
DREADFUL n cheap, often
lurid or sensational book
or magazine ▷ adj very
disagreeable or shocking

DREADFULS > DREADFUL
DREADING > DREAD
DREADLESS > DREAD
DREADLOCK n Rastafarian hair braid
DREADLY > DREAD
DREADS > DREAD
DREAM n imagined events experienced while asleep ▷ vb see imaginary pictures in the mind while asleep ▷ adj ideal
DREAMBOAT n exceptionally attractive person or thing, esp a person of the opposite sex
DREAMED > DREAM
DREAMER n person who dreams habitually
DREAMERS > DREAMER
DREAMERY n dream world
DREAMFUL > DREAM
DREAMHOLE n light-admitting hole in a tower
DREAMIER > DREAMY
DREAMIEST > DREAMY
DREAMILY > DREAMY
DREAMING > DREAM
DREAMINGS > DREAM
DREAMLAND n ideal land existing in dreams or in the imagination
DREAMLESS > DREAM
DREAMLIKE > DREAM
DREAMS > DREAM
DREAMT > DREAM
DREAMTIME n time when the world was new and fresh
DREAMY adj vague or impractical
DREAR same as > DREARY
DREARE obsolete form of > DREAR
DREARER > DREAR
DREARES > DREARE
DREAREST > DREAR
DREARIER > DREARY
DREARIES > DREARY
DREARIEST > DREARY
DREARILY > DREARY
DREARING n sorrow
DREARINGS > DREARING
DREARS > DREAR
DREARY adj dull, boring ▷ n dreary thing or person
DRECK n rubbish
DRECKIER > DRECK
DRECKIEST > DRECK
DRECKISH adj like rubbish
DRECKS > DRECK
DRECKSILL n doorstep
DRECKY > DRECK
DREDGE vb clear or search (a river bed or harbour) by removing silt or mud ▷ n machine used to remove mud from a river bed or harbour
DREDGED > DREDGE
DREDGER same as > DREDGE
DREDGERS > DREDGER

DREDGES > DREDGE
DREDGING > DREDGE
DREDGINGS > DREDGE
DREE vb endure ▷ adj dreary
DREED > DREE
DREEING > DREE
DREER > DREE
DREES > DREE
DREEST > DREE
DREG n small quantity
DREGGIER > DREGGY
DREGGIEST > DREGGY
DREGGISH adj foul
DREGGY adj like or full of dregs
DREGS pl n solid particles that settle at the bottom of some liquids
DREICH adj dreary
DREICHER > DREICH
DREICHEST > DREICH
DREIDEL n spinning top
DREIDELS > DREIDEL
DREIDL same as > DREIDEL
DREIDLS > DREIDL
DREIGH same as > DREICH
DREIGHER > DREIGH
DREIGHEST > DREIGH
DREK same as > DRECK
DREKKIER > DREKKY
DREKKIEST > DREKKY
DREKKISH same as > DRECKISH
DREKKY > DREK
DREKS > DREK
DRENCH vb make completely wet ▷ n act or an instance of drenching
DRENCHED > DRENCH
DRENCHER > DRENCH
DRENCHERS > DRENCH
DRENCHES > DRENCH
DRENCHING > DRENCH
DRENT > DRENCH
DREPANID n type of moth of the superfamily which comprises the hook-tip moths
DREPANIDS > DREPANID
DREPANIUM n type of flower cluster
DRERE obsolete form of > DREAR
DRERES > DRERE
DRERIHEAD n obsolete word for dreary
DRESS n one-piece garment for a woman or girl ▷ vb put clothes on ▷ adj suitable for a formal occasion
DRESSAGE n training of a horse to perform manoeuvres in response to the rider's body signals
DRESSAGES > DRESSAGE
DRESSED > DRESS
DRESSER n piece of furniture with shelves and with cupboards
DRESSERS > DRESSER

DRESSES > DRESS
DRESSIER > DRESSY
DRESSIEST > DRESSY
DRESSILY > DRESSY
DRESSING n sauce for salad
DRESSINGS pl n dressed stonework, mouldings, and carved ornaments used to form quoins, keystones, sills, and similar features
DRESSMADE > DRESSMAKE
DRESSMAKE vb make clothes
DRESSY adj (of clothes) elegant
DREST > DRESS
DREVILL n offensive person
DREVILLS > DREVILL
DREW > DRAW
DREY n squirrel's nest
DREYS > DREY
DRIB vb flow in drops
DRIBBED > DRIB
DRIBBER > DRIB
DRIBBERS > DRIB
DRIBBING > DRIB
DRIBBLE vb (allow to) flow in drops ▷ n small quantity of liquid falling in drops
DRIBBLED > DRIBBLE
DRIBBLER > DRIBBLE
DRIBBLERS > DRIBBLE
DRIBBLES > DRIBBLE
DRIBBLET same as > DRIBLET
DRIBBLETS > DRIBBLET
DRIBBLIER > DRIBBLE
DRIBBLING n act of dribbling
DRIBBLY > DRIBBLE
DRIBLET n small amount
DRIBLETS > DRIBLET
DRIBS > DRIB
DRICE n pellets of frozen carbon dioxide
DRICES > DRICE
DRICKSIE same as > DRUXY
DRICKSIER > DRICKSIE
DRIED > DRY
DRIEGH adj tedious
DRIER > DRY
DRIERS > DRY
DRIES > DRY
DRIEST > DRY
DRIFT vb be carried along by currents of air or water ▷ n something piled up by the wind or current
DRIFTAGE n act of drifting
DRIFTAGES > DRIFTAGE
DRIFTED > DRIFT
DRIFTER n person who moves aimlessly from place to place or job to job
DRIFTERS > DRIFTER
DRIFTIER > DRIFT

DRIFTIEST > DRIFT
DRIFTING n act of drifting
DRIFTINGS > DRIFTING
DRIFTLESS > DRIFT
DRIFTNET n fishing net that drifts with the tide
DRIFTNETS > DRIFTNET
DRIFTPIN same as > DRIFT
DRIFTPINS > DRIFTPIN
DRIFTS > DRIFT
DRIFTWOOD n wood floating on or washed ashore by the sea
DRIFTY > DRIFT
DRILL n tool or machine for boring holes ▷ vb bore a hole in (something) with or as if with a drill
DRILLABLE > DRILL
DRILLED > DRILL
DRILLER > DRILL
DRILLERS > DRILL
DRILLHOLE n hole drilled in the ground, usu for exploratory purposes
DRILLING same as > DRILL
DRILLINGS > DRILL
DRILLS > DRILL
DRILLSHIP n floating drilling platform
DRILY adv in a dry manner
DRINK vb swallow (a liquid) ▷ n (portion of) a liquid suitable for drinking
DRINKABLE > DRINK
DRINKABLY > DRINK
DRINKER n person who drinks
DRINKERS > DRINKER
DRINKING > DRINK
DRINKINGS > DRINK
DRINKS > DRINK
DRIP vb (let) fall in drops ▷ n falling of drops of liquid
DRIPLESS > DRIP
DRIPPED > DRIP
DRIPPER > DRIP
DRIPPERS > DRIP
DRIPPIER > DRIPPY
DRIPPIEST > DRIPPY
DRIPPILY > DRIPPY
DRIPPING > DRIP
DRIPPINGS > DRIP
DRIPPY adj mawkish, insipid, or inane
DRIPS > DRIP
DRIPSTONE n form of calcium carbonate existing in stalactites or stalagmites
DRIPT > DRIP
DRISHEEN n pudding made of sheep's intestines filled with meal and sheep's blood
DRISHEENS > DRISHEEN
DRIVABLE > DRIVE
DRIVE vb guide the movement of (a vehicle) ▷ n journey by car, van, etc

DRIVEABLE > DRIVE
DRIVEL n foolish talk
▷ vb speak foolishly
DRIVELED > DRIVEL
DRIVELER > DRIVEL
DRIVELERS > DRIVEL
DRIVELINE n
transmission line from
engine to wheels of vehicle
DRIVELING > DRIVEL
DRIVELLED > DRIVEL
DRIVELLER > DRIVEL
DRIVELS > DRIVEL
DRIVEN > DRIVE
DRIVER n person who
drives a vehicle
DRIVERS > DRIVER
DRIVES > DRIVE
DRIVEWAY n path for
vehicles connecting a
building to a public road
DRIVEWAYS > DRIVEWAY
DRIVING > DRIVE
DRIVINGLY > DRIVE
DRIVINGS > DRIVE
DRIZZLE n very light rain
▷ vb rain lightly
DRIZZLED > DRIZZLE
DRIZZLES > DRIZZLE
DRIZZLIER > DRIZZLE
DRIZZLING > DRIZZLE
DRIZZLY > DRIZZLE
DROGER n W Indian boat
DROGERS > DROGER
DROGHER same as
> DROGER
DROGHERS > DROGHER
DROGUE n any funnel-like
device used as a sea
anchor
DROGUES > DROGUE
DROGUET n woollen fabric
DROGUETS > DROGUET
DROICH n dwarf
DROICHIER > DROICHY
DROICHS > DROICH
DROICHY adj dwarfish
DROID same as > ANDROID
DROIDS > DROID
DROIL vb carry out boring
menial work
DROILED > DROIL
DROILING > DROIL
DROILS > DROIL
DROIT n legal or moral
right or claim
DROITS > DROIT
DROKE n small group of
trees
DROKES > DROKE
DROLE adj amusing
▷ n scoundrel
DROLER > DROLE
DROLES > DROLE
DROLEST > DROLE
DROLL vb speak wittily
▷ adj quaintly amusing
DROLLED > DROLL
DROLLER > DROLL
DROLLERY n humour
DROLLEST > DROLL
DROLLING > DROLL
DROLLINGS > DROLL

DROLLISH adj somewhat
droll
DROLLNESS > DROLL
DROLLS > DROLL
DROLLY > DROLL
DROME same as
> AERODROME
DROMEDARE obsolete form
of > DROMEDARY
DROMEDARY n camel with
a single hump
DROMES > DROME
DROMIC adj relating to
running track
DROMICAL same as
> DROMIC
DROMOI > DROMOS
DROMON same as
> DROMOND
DROMOND n sailing vessel
of the 12th to 15th
centuries
DROMONDS > DROMOND
DROMONS > DROMON
DROMOS n Greek
passageway
DRONE n male bee ▷ vb
make a monotonous low
dull sound
DRONED > DRONE
DRONER > DRONE
DRONERS > DRONE
DRONES > DRONE
DRONGO n tropical
songbird
DRONGOES > DRONGO
DRONGOS > DRONGO
DRONIER > DRONY
DRONIEST > DRONY
DRONING > DRONE
DRONINGLY > DRONE
DRONISH > DRONE
DRONISHLY > DRONE
DRONKLAP n South
African word for a
drunkard
DRONKLAPS
> DRONKLAP
DRONY adj monotonous
DROOB n pathetic person
DROOBS > DROOB
DROOG n ruffian
DROOGISH > DROOG
DROOGS > DROOG
DROOK same as > DROUK
DROOKED > DROOK
DROOKING > DROOK
DROOKINGS > DROOK
DROOKIT same as
> DROUKIT
DROOKS > DROOK
DROOL vb show excessive
enthusiasm (for)
DROOLED > DROOL
DROOLIER > DROOLY
DROOLIEST > DROOLY
DROOLING > DROOL
DROOLS > DROOL
DROOLY adj tending to
drool
DROOME obsolete form of
> DRUM
DROOMES > DRUM

DROOP vb hang
downwards loosely ▷ n
act or state of drooping
DROOPED > DROOP
DROOPIER > DROOPY
DROOPIEST > DROOPY
DROOPILY > DROOPY
DROOPING > DROOP
DROOPS > DROOP
DROOPY adj hanging or
sagging downwards
DROP vb (allow to) fall
vertically ▷ n small
quantity of liquid forming
a round shape
DROPCLOTH n cloth
spread on floor to catch
drips while painting
DROPFLIES > DROPFLY
DROPFLY n (angling)
artificial fly
DROPFORGE vb forge
metal between two dies
DROPHEAD adj as in
drophead coupe two-door
car with a folding roof and
sloping back
DROPHEADS > DROPHEAD
DROPKICK n (in certain
ball games) a kick in which
the ball is first dropped
then kicked as it bounces
from the ground
DROPKICKS > DROPKICK
DROPLET n very small
drop of liquid
DROPLETS > DROPLET
DROPLIGHT n electric
light that may be raised or
lowered by means of a
pulley or other mechanism
DROPLOCK adj as in
droplock loan type of bank
loan ▷ n type of bank loan
DROPLOCKS > DROPLOCK
DROPOUT n person who
rejects conventional
society ▷ vb abandon or
withdraw (from an
institution or group)
DROPOUTS > DROPOUT
DROPPABLE > DROP
DROPPED > DROP
DROPPER n small tube
with a rubber part at one
end
DROPPERS > DROPPER
DROPPING > DROP
DROPPINGS pl n faeces of
certain animals, such as
rabbits or birds
DROPPLE n trickle
DROPPLES > DROPPLE
DROPS > DROP
DROPSEED n type of grass
DROPSEEDS > DROPSEED
DROPSHOT n (in tennis)
shot in which a softly
returned ball just clears
the net before falling
abruptly
DROPSHOTS > DROPSHOT
DROPSICAL > DROPSY
DROPSIED > DROPSY

DROPSIES > DROPSY
DROPSONDE n radiosonde
dropped by parachute
DROPSTONE n calcium
carbonate in stalactites
DROPSY n illness in which
watery fluid collects in the
body
DROPT > DROP
DROPTOP n convertible car
DROPTOPS > DROPTOP
DROPWISE adv in form of a
drop
DROPWORT n Eurasian
plant with cream-coloured
flowers, related to the rose
DROPWORTS > DROPWORT
DROSERA n insectivorous
plant
DROSERAS > DROSERA
DROSHKIES > DROSHKY
DROSHKY n four-wheeled
carriage, formerly used in
Russia
DROSKIES > DROSKY
DROSKY same as
> DROSHKY
DROSS n scum formed on
the surfaces of molten
metals
DROSSES > DROSS
DROSSIER > DROSS
DROSSIEST > DROSS
DROSSY > DROSS
DROSTDIES > DROSTDY
DROSTDY n office of
landdrost
DROSTDYS > DROSTDY
DROUGHT n prolonged
shortage of rainfall
DROUGHTS > DROUGHT
DROUGHTY > DROUGHT
DROUK vb drench
DROUKED > DROUK
DROUKING > DROUK
DROUKINGS > DROUK
DROUKIT adj drenched
DROUKS > DROUK
DROUTH same as
> DROUGHT
DROUTHIER > DROUTHY
DROUTHS > DROUTH
DROUTHY adj thirsty or dry
DROVE > DRIVE
DROVED > DRIVE
DROVER n person who
drives sheep or cattle
DROVERS > DROVER
DROVES > DRIVE
DROVING > DRIVE
DROVINGS > DRIVE
DROW n sea fog
DROWN vb die or kill by
immersion in liquid
DROWND dialect form of
> DROWN
DROWNDED > DROWND
DROWNDING > DROWND
DROWNDS > DROWND
DROWNED > DROWN
DROWNER > DROWN
DROWNERS > DROWN
DROWNING > DROWN

DROWNINGS > DROWN
DROWNS > DROWN
DROWS > DROW
DROWSE vb be sleepy, dull, or sluggish ▷ n state of being drowsy
DROWSED > DROWSE
DROWSES > DROWSE
DROWSIER > DROWSY
DROWSIEST > DROWSY
DROWSIHED adj old form of drowsy
DROWSILY > DROWSY
DROWSING > DROWSE
DROWSY adj feeling sleepy
DRUB vb beat as with a stick ▷ n blow, as from a stick
DRUBBED > DRUB
DRUBBER > DRUB
DRUBBERS > DRUB
DRUBBING > DRUB
DRUBBINGS > DRUB
DRUBS > DRUB
DRUCKEN adj drunken
DRUDGE n person who works hard at uninteresting tasks ▷ vb work at such tasks
DRUDGED > DRUDGE
DRUDGER > DRUDGE
DRUDGERS > DRUDGE
DRUDGERY n uninteresting work that must be done
DRUDGES > DRUDGE
DRUDGING > DRUDGE
DRUDGISM > DRUDGE
DRUDGISMS > DRUDGE
DRUG n substance used in the treatment or prevention of disease ▷ vb give a drug to (a person or animal) to cause sleepiness or unconsciousness
DRUGGED > DRUG
DRUGGER n druggist
DRUGGERS > DRUGGER
DRUGGET n coarse fabric used as a protective floor-covering, etc
DRUGGETS > DRUGGET
DRUGGIE n drug addict
DRUGGIER > DRUG
DRUGGIES > DRUGGIE
DRUGGIEST > DRUG
DRUGGING > DRUG
DRUGGIST n pharmacist
DRUGGISTS > DRUGGIST
DRUGGY > DRUG
DRUGLESS adj having no drugs
DRUGLORD n criminal who controls the distribution and sale of large quantities of illegal drugs
DRUGLORDS > DRUGLORD
DRUGMAKER n manufacturer of drugs
DRUGS > DRUG
DRUGSTER n drug addict
DRUGSTERS > DRUGSTER

DRUGSTORE n pharmacy where a wide range of goods are available
DRUID n member of an ancient order of priests in the pre-Christian era
DRUIDESS > DRUID
DRUIDIC > DRUID
DRUIDICAL > DRUID
DRUIDISM > DRUID
DRUIDISMS > DRUID
DRUIDRIES > DRUID
DRUIDRY > DRUID
DRUIDS > DRUID
DRUM n percussion instrument ▷ vb play (music) on a drum
DRUMBEAT n sound made by beating a drum
DRUMBEATS > DRUMBEAT
DRUMBLE vb be inactive
DRUMBLED > DRUMBLE
DRUMBLES > DRUMBLE
DRUMBLING > DRUMBLE
DRUMFIRE n heavy, rapid, and continuous gunfire, the sound of which resembles rapid drumbeats
DRUMFIRES > DRUMFIRE
DRUMFISH n one of several types of fish that make a drumming sound
DRUMHEAD n part of a drum that is struck
DRUMHEADS > DRUMHEAD
DRUMLIER > DRUMLY
DRUMLIEST > DRUMLY
DRUMLIKE > DRUM
DRUMLIN n streamlined mound of glacial drift
DRUMLINS > DRUMLIN
DRUMLY adj dismal; dreary
DRUMMED > DRUM
DRUMMER n person who plays a drum or drums
DRUMMERS > DRUMMER
DRUMMIES > DRUMMY
DRUMMING n act of drumming
DRUMMINGS > DRUMMING
DRUMMOCK same as > DRAMMOCK
DRUMMOCKS > DRUMMOCK
DRUMMY n (in South Africa) drum majorette
DRUMROLL n continued repeated sound of drum
DRUMROLLS > DRUMROLL
DRUMS > DRUM
DRUMSTICK n stick used for playing a drum
DRUNK > DRINK
DRUNKARD n person who frequently gets drunk
DRUNKARDS > DRUNKARD
DRUNKEN adj drunk or frequently drunk
DRUNKENLY > DRUNKEN
DRUNKER > DRINK
DRUNKEST > DRINK
DRUNKISH adj rather drunk

DRUNKS > DRINK
DRUPE n fleshy fruit with a stone, such as the peach or cherry
DRUPEL same as > DRUPELET
DRUPELET n small drupe, usually one of a number forming a compound fruit
DRUPELETS > DRUPELET
DRUPELS > DRUPEL
DRUPES > DRUPE
DRUSE n aggregate of small crystals within a cavity
DRUSEN pl n small deposits of material on the retina
DRUSES > DRUSE
DRUSIER > DRUSY
DRUSIEST > DRUSY
DRUSY adj made of tiny crystals
DRUTHER n preference
DRUTHERS n preference
DRUXIER > DRUXY
DRUXIEST > DRUXY
DRUXY adj (of wood) having decayed white spots
DRY adj lacking moisture ▷ vb make or become dry
DRYABLE > DRY
DRYAD n wood nymph
DRYADES > DRYAD
DRYADIC > DRYAD
DRYADS > DRYAD
DRYAS n alpine plant with white flowers
DRYASDUST adj boringly bookish
DRYBEAT vb beat severely
DRYBEATEN > DRYBEAT
DRYBEATS > DRYBEAT
DRYER > DRY
DRYERS > DRY
DRYEST > DRY
DRYING > DRY
DRYINGS > DRY
DRYISH adj fairly dry
DRYLAND n arid area
DRYLANDS > DRYLAND
DRYLOT n livestock enclosure
DRYLOTS > DRYLOT
DRYLY same as > DRILY
DRYMOUTH n condition of insufficient saliva
DRYMOUTHS > DRYMOUTH
DRYNESS > DRY
DRYNESSES > DRY
DRYPOINT n copper engraving technique using a hard steel needle
DRYPOINTS > DRYPOINT
DRYS > DRY
DRYSALTER n dealer in certain chemical products, such as dyestuffs and gums, and in dried, tinned, or salted foods and edible oils
DRYSTONE adj (of a wall) made without mortar

DRYSUIT n waterproof rubber suit for wearing in esp cold water
DRYSUITS > DRYSUIT
DRYWALL n wall built without mortar ▷ vb build a wall without mortar
DRYWALLED > DRYWALL
DRYWALLS > DRYWALL
DRYWELL n type of sewage disposal system
DRYWELLS > DRYWELL
DSO same as > ZHO
DSOBO same as > ZOBO
DSOBOS > DSOBO
DSOMO same as > ZHOMO
DSOMOS > DSOMO
DSOS > DSO
DUAD a rare word for > PAIR
DUADS > DUAD
DUAL adj having two parts, functions, or aspects ▷ n dual number ▷ vb make (a road) into a dual carriageway
DUALIN n explosive substance
DUALINS > DUALIN
DUALISE same as > DUALIZE
DUALISED > DUALISE
DUALISES > DUALISE
DUALISING > DUALISE
DUALISM n state of having two distinct parts
DUALISMS > DUALISM
DUALIST > DUALISM
DUALISTIC > DUALISM
DUALISTS > DUALISM
DUALITIES > DUALITY
DUALITY n state or quality of being two or in two parts
DUALIZE vb cause to have two parts
DUALIZED > DUALIZE
DUALIZES > DUALIZE
DUALIZING > DUALIZE
DUALLED > DUAL
DUALLIE n pickup truck with dual rear tyres
DUALLIES > DUALLIE
DUALLING > DUAL
DUALLY > DUAL
DUALS > DUAL
DUAN n poem
DUANS > DUAN
DUAR n Arab camp
DUARCHIES > DUARCHY
DUARCHY same as > DIARCHY
DUARS > DUAR
DUATHLETE n athlete who competes in duathlons
DUATHLON n athletic contest in which each athlete competes in running and cycling events
DUATHLONS > DUATHLON
DUB vb give (a person or place) a name or nickname ▷ n style of reggae record production

d

DUBBED > DUB

DUBBER > DUB

DUBBERS > DUB

DUBBIN n thick grease applied to leather to soften and waterproof it ▷ vb apply dubbin to

DUBBINED > DUBBIN

DUBBING > DUB

DUBBINGS > DUB

DUBBINING > DUBBIN

DUBBINS > DUBBIN

DUBBO adj stupid ▷ n stupid person

DUBBOS > DUBBO

DUBIETIES > DUBIETY

DUBIETY n state of being doubtful

DUBIOSITY same as > DUBIETY

DUBIOUS adj feeling or causing doubt

DUBIOUSLY > DUBIOUS

DUBITABLE adj open to doubt

DUBITABLY > DUBITABLE

DUBITANCY > DUBITATE

DUBITATE vb doubt

DUBITATED > DUBITATE

DUBITATES > DUBITATE

DUBNIUM n chemical element

DUBNIUMS > DUBNIUM

DUBONNET n dark purplish-red colour

DUBONNETS > DUBONNET

DUBS > DUB

DUBSTEP n genre of electronic music

DUBSTEPS > DUBSTEP

DUCAL adj of a duke

DUCALLY > DUCAL

DUCAT n former European gold or silver coin

DUCATOON n former silver coin

DUCATOONS > DUCATOON

DUCATS > DUCAT

DUCDAME interj Shakespearean nonsense word

DUCE n leader

DUCES > DUCE

DUCHESS n woman who holds the rank of duke ▷ vb overwhelm with flattering attention

DUCHESSE n type of satin

DUCHESSED > DUCHESS

DUCHESSES > DUCHESS

DUCHIES > DUCHY

DUCHY n territory of a duke or duchess

DUCI > DUCE

DUCK n water bird ▷ vb move (the head or body) quickly downwards

DUCKBILL n duckbilled platypus

DUCKBILLS > DUCKBILL

DUCKBOARD n board or boards laid so as to form a floor or path over wet or muddy ground

DUCKED > DUCK

DUCKER > DUCK

DUCKERS > DUCK

DUCKFOOT adj as in duckfoot quote chevron-shaped quotation mark

DUCKIE same as > DUCKY

DUCKIER > DUCKY

DUCKIES > DUCKY

DUCKIEST > DUCKY

DUCKING > DUCK

DUCKINGS > DUCK

DUCKISH n twilight

DUCKISHES > DUCKISH

DUCKLING n baby duck

DUCKLINGS > DUCKLING

DUCKMOLE another word for > DUCKBILL

DUCKMOLES > DUCKMOLE

DUCKPIN n short bowling pin

DUCKPINS > DUCKPIN

DUCKS > DUCK

DUCKSHOVE vb evade responsibility

DUCKTAIL n Teddy boy's hairstyle

DUCKTAILS > DUCKTAIL

DUCKWALK vb walk in a squatting posture

DUCKWALKS > DUCKWALK

DUCKWEED n type of small stemless aquatic plant with rounded leaves, which floats on still water in temperate regions

DUCKWEEDS > DUCKWEED

DUCKY n darling or dear ▷ adj delightful

DUCT vb convey via a duct ▷ n tube, pipe, or channel through which liquid or gas is conveyed

DUCTAL > DUCT

DUCTED > DUCT

DUCTILE adj (of a metal) able to be shaped into sheets or wires

DUCTILELY > DUCTILE

DUCTILITY > DUCTILE

DUCTING > DUCT

DUCTINGS > DUCT

DUCTLESS > DUCT

DUCTS > DUCT

DUCTULE n small duct

DUCTULES > DUCTULE

DUCTWORK n system of ducts

DUCTWORKS > DUCTWORK

DUD n ineffectual person or thing ▷ adj bad or useless

DUDDER n door-to-door salesman ▷ vb tremble or shudder

DUDDERED > DUDDER

DUDDERIES > DUDDERY

DUDDERING > DUDDER

DUDDERS > DUDDER

DUDDERY n place where old clothes are sold

DUDDIE adj ragged ▷ n friend or a chum

DUDDIER > DUDDIE

DUDDIES > DUDDIE

DUDDIEST > DUDDIE

DUDDY same as > DUDDIE

DUDE vb dress fashionably ▷ n man

DUDED > DUDE

DUDEEN n clay pipe with a short stem

DUDEENS > DUDEEN

DUDENESS n state of being a dude

DUDES > DUDE

DUDETTE n woman who behaves like a dude

DUDETTES > DUDETTE

DUDGEON n anger or resentment

DUDGEONS > DUDGEON

DUDHEEN n type of pipe

DUDHEENS > DUDHEEN

DUDING > DUDE

DUDISH > DUDE

DUDISHLY > DUDE

DUDISM n being a dude

DUDISMS > DUDISM

DUDS > DUD

DUE vb supply with ▷ adj expected or scheduled to be present or arrive ▷ n something that is owed or required ▷ adv directly or exactly

DUECENTO n thirteenth century (in Italian art)

DUECENTOS > DUECENTO

DUED > DUE

DUEFUL adj proper

DUEL n formal fight with deadly weapons between two people ▷ vb fight in a duel

DUELED > DUEL

DUELER > DUEL

DUELERS > DUEL

DUELING n act of dueling

DUELINGS > DUELING

DUELIST > DUEL

DUELISTS > DUEL

DUELLED > DUEL

DUELLER > DUEL

DUELLERS > DUEL

DUELLI > DUELLO

DUELLING > DUEL

DUELLINGS > DUEL

DUELLIST > DUEL

DUELLISTS > DUEL

DUELLO n art of duelling

DUELLOS > DUELLO

DUELS > DUEL

DUELSOME adj given to duelling

DUENDE n Spanish goblin

DUENDES > DUENDE

DUENESS > DUE

DUENESSES > DUE

DUENNA n (esp in Spain) elderly woman acting as chaperone to a young woman

DUENNAS > DUENNA

DUES pl n membership fees

DUET n piece of music for two performers ▷ vb perform a duet

DUETED > DUET

DUETING > DUET

DUETS > DUET

DUETT same as > DUET

DUETTED > DUET

DUETTI > DUETTO

DUETTING > DUET

DUETTINO n simple duet

DUETTINOS > DUETTINO

DUETTIST > DUET

DUETTISTS > DUET

DUETTO same as > DUET

DUETTOS > DUETTO

DUETTS > DUETT

DUFF adj broken or useless ▷ vb change the appearance of or give a false appearance to (old or stolen goods) ▷ n rump or buttocks

DUFFED > DUFF

DUFFEL n heavy woollen cloth with a thick nap

DUFFELS > DUFFEL

DUFFER n dull or incompetent person

DUFFERDOM n condition of being a duffer

DUFFERISM same as > DUFFERDOM

DUFFERS > DUFFER

DUFFEST > DUFF

DUFFING > DUFF

DUFFINGS > DUFF

DUFFLE same as > DUFFEL

DUFFLES > DUFFLE

DUFFS > DUFF

DUFUS same as > DOOFUS

DUFUSES > DUFUS

DUG > DIG

DUGITE n medium-sized Australian venomous snake

DUGITES > DUGITE

DUGONG n whalelike mammal of tropical waters

DUGONGS > DUGONG

DUGOUT n (at a sports ground) covered bench where managers and substitutes sit

DUGOUTS > DUGOUT

DUGS > DIG

DUH interj ironic response to a question or statement

DUHKHA same as > DUKKHA

DUHKHAS > DUHKHA

DUI > DUO

DUIKER n small African antelope

DUIKERBOK same as > DUIKER

DUIKERS > DUIKER

DUING > DUE

DUIT n former Dutch coin

DUITS > DUIT

DUKA n shop

DUKAS > DUKA

DUKE vb fight with fists ▷ n nobleman of the highest rank
DUKED > DUKE
DUKEDOM n title, rank, or position of a duke
DUKEDOMS > DUKEDOM
DUKELING n low-ranking duke
DUKELINGS > DUKELING
DUKERIES > DUKERY
DUKERY n duke's domain
DUKES pl n fists
DUKESHIP > DUKE
DUKESHIPS > DUKE
DUKING > DUKE
DUKKA n mix of ground roast nuts and spices
DUKKAH same as > DUKKA
DUKKAHS > DUKKAH
DUKKAS > DUKKA
DUKKHA n Buddhist belief that all things are suffering
DUKKHAS > DUKKHA
DULCAMARA n orange-fruited vine
DULCE n sweet food or drink
DULCES > DULCE
DULCET adj (of a sound) soothing or pleasant ▷ n soft organ stop
DULCETLY > DULCET
DULCETS > DULCET
DULCIAN n precursor to the bassoon
DULCIANA n sweet-toned organ stop, controlling metal pipes of narrow scale
DULCIANAS > DULCIANA
DULCIANS > DULCIAN
DULCIFIED > DULCIFY
DULCIFIES > DULCIFY
DULCIFY vb make pleasant or agreeable
DULCIMER n tuned percussion instrument consisting of a set of strings stretched over a sounding board and struck with hammers
DULCIMERS > DULCIMER
DULCIMORE former name for > DULCIMER
DULCINEA n man's sweetheart
DULCINEAS > DULCINEA
DULCITE n sweet substance
DULCITES > DULCITE
DULCITOL another word for > DULCITE
DULCITOLS > DULCITOL
DULCITUDE n sweetness
DULCOSE another word for > DULCITE
DULCOSES > DULCOSE
DULE n suffering; misery
DULES > DULE
DULIA n veneration accorded to saints
DULIAS > DULIA
DULL adj not interesting ▷ vb make or become dull

DULLARD n dull or stupid person
DULLARDS > DULLARD
DULLED > DULL
DULLER > DULL
DULLEST > DULL
DULLIER > DULL
DULLIEST > DULL
DULLING > DULL
DULLISH > DULL
DULLISHLY > DULL
DULLNESS > DULL
DULLS > DULL
DULLY > DULL
DULNESS > DULL
DULNESSES > DULL
DULOCRACY n rule by slaves
DULOSES > DULOSIS
DULOSIS n behaviour where one species of ant forces members of another to work for them
DULOTIC > DULOSIS
DULSE n seaweed with large red edible fronds
DULSES > DULSE
DULY adv in a proper manner
DUM adj steamed
DUMA n elective legislative assembly established by Tsar Nicholas II
DUMAIST n member of duma
DUMAISTS > DUMAIST
DUMAS > DUMA
DUMB vb silence ▷ adj lacking the power to speak
DUMBBELL n short bar with a heavy ball or disc at each end, used for physical exercise
DUMBBELLS > DUMBBELL
DUMBCANE n West Indian aroid plant
DUMBCANES > DUMBCANE
DUMBED > DUMB
DUMBER > DUMB
DUMBEST > DUMB
DUMBFOUND vb strike dumb with astonishment
DUMBHEAD n dunce
DUMBHEADS > DUMBHEAD
DUMBING > DUMB
DUMBLY > DUMB
DUMBNESS > DUMB
DUMBO n slow-witted unintelligent person
DUMBOS > DUMBO
DUMBS > DUMB
DUMBSHIT n taboo slang word for a stupid person
DUMBSHITS > DUMBSHIT
DUMBSHOW n actions performed without words in a play
DUMBSHOWS > DUMBSHOW
DUMBSIZE vb reduce the number in a workforce to the point it becomes ineffective

DUMBSIZED > DUMBSIZE
DUMBSIZES > DUMBSIZE
DUMDUM n soft-nosed bullet
DUMDUMS > DUMDUM
DUMELA sentence substitute hello
DUMFOUND same as > DUMBFOUND
DUMFOUNDS > DUMFOUND
DUMKA n Slavonic lyrical song
DUMKAS > DUMKA
DUMKY > DUMKA
DUMMERER n person who pretends to be dumb
DUMMERERS > DUMMERER
DUMMIED > DUMMY
DUMMIER > DUMMY
DUMMIES > DUMMY
DUMMIEST > DUMMY
DUMMINESS > DUMMY
DUMMKOPF n stupid person
DUMMKOPFS > DUMMKOPF
DUMMY adj sham ▷ n figure representing the human form ▷ adj imitation, substitute ▷ vb prepare a dummy of (a proposed book, page, etc)
DUMMYING > DUMMY
DUMOSE adj bushlike
DUMOSITY > DUMOSE
DUMOUS same as > DUMOSE
DUMP vb drop or let fall in a careless manner ▷ n place where waste materials are left
DUMPBIN n unit in a bookshop displaying a particular publisher's books
DUMPBINS > DUMPBIN
DUMPCART n cart for dumping without handling
DUMPCARTS > DUMPCART
DUMPED > DUMP
DUMPEE n person dumped from a relationship
DUMPEES > DUMPEE
DUMPER > DUMP
DUMPERS > DUMP
DUMPIER > DUMPY
DUMPIES > DUMPY
DUMPIEST > DUMPY
DUMPILY > DUMPY
DUMPINESS > DUMPY
DUMPING > DUMP
DUMPINGS > DUMP
DUMPISH same as > DUMPY
DUMPISHLY > DUMPISH
DUMPLE vb form into dumpling shape
DUMPLED > DUMPLE
DUMPLES > DUMPLE
DUMPLING n small ball of dough cooked and served with stew
DUMPLINGS > DUMPLING
DUMPS pl n state of melancholy or depression

DUMPSITE n location of dump
DUMPSITES > DUMPSITE
DUMPSTER n refuse skip
DUMPSTERS > DUMPSTER
DUMPTRUCK n lorry with a tipping container
DUMPY n dumpy person ▷ adj short and plump
DUN adj brownish-grey ▷ vb demand payment from (a debtor) ▷ n demand for payment
DUNAM n unit of area measurement
DUNAMS > DUNAM
DUNCE n person who is stupid or slow to learn
DUNCEDOM > DUNCE
DUNCEDOMS > DUNCE
DUNCELIKE > DUNCE
DUNCERIES > DUNCERY
DUNCERY n duncelike behaviour
DUNCES > DUNCE
DUNCH vb push against gently
DUNCHED > DUNCH
DUNCHES > DUNCH
DUNCHING > DUNCH
DUNCICAL adj duncelike
DUNCISH adj duncelike
DUNCISHLY > DUNCE
DUNDER n cane juice lees
DUNDERS > DUNDER
DUNE n mound or ridge of drifted sand
DUNELAND n land characterized by dunes
DUNELANDS > DUNELAND
DUNELIKE > DUNE
DUNES > DUNE
DUNG n faeces from animals such as cattle ▷ vb cover (ground) with manure
DUNGAREE n coarse cotton fabric used chiefly for work clothes, etc
DUNGAREED adj wearing dungarees
DUNGAREES > DUNGAREE
DUNGED > DUNG
DUNGEON vb hold captive in dungeon ▷ n underground prison cell
DUNGEONED > DUNGEON
DUNGEONER n jailer
DUNGEONS > DUNGEON
DUNGER n old decrepit car
DUNGERS > DUNGER
DUNGHEAP n pile of dung
DUNGHEAPS > DUNGHEAP
DUNGHILL n heap of dung
DUNGHILLS > DUNGHILL
DUNGIER > DUNG
DUNGIEST > DUNG
DUNGING > DUNG
DUNGMERE n cesspool
DUNGMERES > DUNGMERE
DUNGS > DUNG
DUNGY > DUNG

DUNITE n ultrabasic igneous rock
DUNITES > DUNITE
DUNITIC > DUNITE
DUNK vb dip (a biscuit or bread) in a drink or soup before eating it
DUNKED > DUNK
DUNKER > DUNK
DUNKERS > DUNK
DUNKING n act of dunking
DUNKINGS > DUNKING
DUNKS > DUNK
DUNLIN n small sandpiper
DUNLINS > DUNLIN
DUNNAGE n loose material used for packing cargo
DUNNAGES > DUNNAGE
DUNNAKIN n lavatory
DUNNAKINS > DUNNAKIN
DUNNART n type of insectivorous marsupial
DUNNARTS > DUNNART
DUNNED > DUN
DUNNER > DUN
DUNNESS > DUN
DUNNESSES > DUN
DUNNEST > DUN
DUNNIER > DUNNY
DUNNIES > DUNNY
DUNNIEST > DUNNY
DUNNING > DUN
DUNNINGS > DUN
DUNNISH > DUN
DUNNITE n explosive containing ammonium picrate
DUNNITES > DUNNITE
DUNNO vb slang for don't know
DUNNOCK n hedge sparrow
DUNNOCKS > DUNNOCK
DUNNY n in Australia, toilet ▷ adj relating to dunny
DUNS > DUN
DUNSH same as > DUNCH
DUNSHED > DUNSH
DUNSHES > DUNSH
DUNSHING > DUNSH
DUNT n blow ▷ vb strike or hit
DUNTED > DUNT
DUNTING > DUNT
DUNTS > DUNT
DUO same as > DUET
DUOBINARY adj denoting a communications system for coding digital data in which three data bands are used, 0, +1, −1
DUODECIMO n book size resulting from folding a sheet of paper into twelve leaves
DUODENA > DUODENUM
DUODENAL > DUODENUM
DUODENARY adj of or relating to the number 12
DUODENUM n first part of the small intestine, just below the stomach
DUODENUMS > DUODENUM

DUOLOG same as > DUOLOGUE
DUOLOGS > DUOLOG
DUOLOGUE n (in drama) conversation between only two speakers
DUOLOGUES > DUOLOGUE
DUOMI > DUOMO
DUOMO n cathedral in Italy
DUOMOS > DUOMO
DUOPOLIES > DUOPOLY
DUOPOLY n situation when control of a commodity is vested in two producers or suppliers
DUOPSONY n two rival buyers controlling sellers
DUOS > DUO
DUOTONE n process for producing halftone illustrations
DUOTONES > DUOTONE
DUP vb open
DUPABLE > DUPE
DUPATTA n scarf worn in India
DUPATTAS > DUPATTA
DUPE vb deceive or cheat ▷ n person who is easily deceived
DUPED > DUPE
DUPER > DUPE
DUPERIES > DUPE
DUPERS > DUPE
DUPERY > DUPE
DUPES > DUPE
DUPING n act of duping
DUPINGS > DUPING
DUPION n silk fabric made from the threads of double cocoons
DUPIONS > DUPION
DUPLE adj having two beats in a bar
DUPLET n pair of electrons shared between two atoms in a covalent bond
DUPLETS > DUPLET
DUPLEX vb duplicate ▷ n apartment on two floors ▷ adj having two parts
DUPLEXED > DUPLEX
DUPLEXER n telecommunications system
DUPLEXERS > DUPLEXER
DUPLEXES > DUPLEX
DUPLEXING > DUPLEX
DUPLEXITY > DUPLEX
DUPLICAND n feu duty doubled
DUPLICATE adj copied exactly from an original ▷ n exact copy ▷ vb make an exact copy of
DUPLICITY n deceitful behaviour
DUPLIED > DUPLY
DUPLIES > DUPLY
DUPLY vb give a second reply
DUPLYING > DUPLY
DUPONDII > DUPONDIUS

DUPONDIUS n brass coin of ancient Rome worth half a sesterce
DUPPED > DUP
DUPPIES > DUPPY
DUPPING > DUP
DUPPY n spirit or ghost
DUPS > DUP
DURA same as > DURRA
DURABLE adj long-lasting
DURABLES pl n goods that require infrequent replacement
DURABLY > DURABLE
DURAL n alloy of aluminium and copper
DURALS > DURAL
DURALUMIN n light and strong aluminium alloy containing copper, silicon, magnesium, and manganese
DURAMEN another name for > HEARTWOOD
DURAMENS > DURAMEN
DURANCE n imprisonment
DURANCES > DURANCE
DURANT n tough, leathery cloth
DURANTS > DURANT
DURAS > DURA
DURATION n length of time that something lasts
DURATIONS > DURATION
DURATIVE adj denoting an aspect of verbs that includes the imperfective and the progressive ▷ n durative aspect of a verb
DURATIVES > DURATIVE
DURBAR n (formerly) the court of a native ruler or a governor in India
DURBARS > DURBAR
DURDUM same as > DIRDUM
DURDUMS > DURDUM
DURE vb endure
DURED > DURE
DUREFUL adj lasting
DURES > DURE
DURESS n compulsion by use of force or threats
DURESSE same as > DURESS
DURESSES > DURESS
DURGAH same as > DARGAH
DURGAHS > DURGAH
DURGAN n dwarf
DURGANS > DURGAN
DURGIER > DURGY
DURGIEST > DURGY
DURGY adj dwarflike
DURIAN n SE Asian tree whose very large oval fruits have a hard spiny rind and an evil smell
DURIANS > DURIAN
DURICRUST another name for > CALICHE
DURING prep throughout or within the limit of (a period of time)
DURION same as > DURIAN

DURIONS > DURION
DURMAST n large Eurasian oak tree with lobed leaves
DURMASTS > DURMAST
DURN same as > DARN
DURNDEST same as > DARNEDEST
DURNED > DURN
DURNEDER > DURN
DURNEDEST > DURN
DURNING > DURN
DURNS > DURN
DURO n silver peso of Spain or Spanish America
DUROC n breed of pig
DUROCS > DUROC
DUROMETER n instrument for measuring hardness
DUROS > DURO
DUROY n coarse woollen fabric
DUROYS > DUROY
DURR same as > DURRA
DURRA n Old World variety of sorghum with hairy flower spikes and round seeds, cultivated for grain and fodder
DURRAS > DURRA
DURRIE n cotton carpet made in India, often in rectangular pieces fringed at the ends
DURRIES > DURRY
DURRS > DURR
DURRY n cigarette
DURST a past tense of > DARE
DURUKULI n S American monkey
DURUKULIS > DURUKULI
DURUM n variety of wheat cultivated mainly in the Mediterranean region, used chiefly to make pastas
DURUMS > DURUM
DURZI n Indian tailor
DURZIS > DURZI
DUSH vb strike hard
DUSHED > DUSH
DUSHES > DUSH
DUSHING > DUSH
DUSK n time just before nightfall, when it is almost dark ▷ adj shady ▷ vb make or become dark
DUSKED > DUSK
DUSKEN vb grow dark
DUSKENED > DUSKEN
DUSKENING > DUSKEN
DUSKENS > DUSKEN
DUSKER > DUSK
DUSKEST > DUSK
DUSKIER > DUSKY
DUSKIEST > DUSKY
DUSKILY > DUSKY
DUSKINESS > DUSKY
DUSKING > DUSK
DUSKISH > DUSK
DUSKISHLY > DUSK
DUSKLY > DUSK

DUSKNESS > DUSK
DUSKS > DUSK
DUSKY adj dark in colour
DUST n small dry particles of earth, sand, or dirt ▷ vb remove dust from (furniture) by wiping
DUSTBALL n ball of dust
DUSTBALLS > DUSTBALL
DUSTBIN n large container for household rubbish
DUSTBINS > DUSTBIN
DUSTCART n truck for collecting household rubbish
DUSTCARTS > DUSTCART
DUSTCLOTH n cloth used for dusting
DUSTCOAT n light, loose-fitting long coat
DUSTCOATS > DUSTCOAT
DUSTCOVER same as **>** DUSTSHEET
DUSTED > DUST
DUSTER n cloth used for dusting
DUSTERS > DUSTER
DUSTHEAP n accumulation of refuse
DUSTHEAPS > DUSTHEAP
DUSTIER > DUSTY
DUSTIEST > DUSTY
DUSTILY > DUSTY
DUSTINESS > DUSTY
DUSTING > DUST
DUSTINGS > DUST
DUSTLESS > DUST
DUSTLIKE > DUST
DUSTMAN n man whose job is to collect household rubbish
DUSTMEN > DUSTMAN
DUSTOFF n casualty evacuation helicopter
DUSTOFFS > DUSTOFF
DUSTPAN n short-handled shovel
DUSTPANS > DUSTPAN
DUSTPROOF adj repelling dust
DUSTRAG n cloth for dusting
DUSTRAGS > DUSTRAG
DUSTS > DUST
DUSTSHEET n large cloth cover to protect furniture from dust
DUSTSTORM n storm with whirling column of dust
DUSTUP n quarrel, fight, or argument
DUSTUPS > DUSTUP
DUSTY adj covered with dust
DUTCH n wife
DUTCHES > DUTCH
DUTCHMAN n piece of wood, metal, etc, used to repair or patch faulty workmanship
DUTCHMEN > DUTCHMAN
DUTEOUS adj dutiful or obedient

DUTEOUSLY > DUTEOUS
DUTIABLE adj (of goods) requiring payment of duty
DUTIED adj liable for duty
DUTIES > DUTY
DUTIFUL adj doing what is expected
DUTIFULLY > DUTIFUL
DUTY n work or a task performed as part of one's job
DUUMVIR n one of two coequal magistrates or officers
DUUMVIRAL > DUUMVIR
DUUMVIRI > DUUMVIR
DUUMVIRS > DUUMVIR
DUVET same as **>** DOONA
DUVETINE same as **>** DUVETYN
DUVETINES > DUVETINE
DUVETS > DUVET
DUVETYN n soft napped velvety fabric of cotton, silk, wool, or rayon
DUVETYNE same as **>** DUVETYN
DUVETYNES > DUVETYNE
DUVETYNS > DUVETYN
DUX n (in Scottish and certain other schools) the top pupil in a class or school
DUXELLES n paste of mushrooms and onions
DUXES > DUX
DUYKER same as **>** DUIKER
DUYKERS > DUYKER
DVANDVA n class of compound words
DVANDVAS > DVANDVA
DVORNIK n Russian doorkeeper
DVORNIKS > DVORNIK
DWAAL n state of absent-mindedness
DWAALS > DWAAL
DWALE n deadly nightshade
DWALES > DWALE
DWALM vb faint
DWALMED > DWALM
DWALMING > DWALM
DWALMS > DWALM
DWAM n stupor or daydream ▷ vb faint or fall ill
DWAMMED > DWAM
DWAMMING > DWAM
DWAMS > DWAM
DWANG n short piece of wood inserted in a timber-framed wall
DWANGS > DWANG
DWARF adj undersized ▷ n person who is smaller than average ▷ adj (of an animal or plant) much smaller than the usual size for the species ▷ vb cause (someone or something) to seem small by being much larger
DWARFED > DWARF
DWARFER > DWARF

DWARFEST > DWARF
DWARFING > DWARF
DWARFISH > DWARF
DWARFISM n condition of being a dwarf
DWARFISMS > DWARFISM
DWARFLIKE > DWARF
DWARFNESS > DWARF
DWARFS > DWARF
DWARVES > DWARF
DWAUM same as **>** DWAM
DWAUMED > DWAUM
DWAUMING > DWAUM
DWAUMS > DWAUM
DWEEB n stupid or uninteresting person
DWEEBIER > DWEEBY
DWEEBIEST > DWEEBY
DWEEBISH > DWEEB
DWEEBS > DWEEB
DWEEBY adj like or typical of a dweeb
DWELL vb live, reside ▷ n regular pause in the operation of a machine
DWELLED > DWELL
DWELLER > DWELL
DWELLERS > DWELL
DWELLING > DWELL
DWELLINGS > DWELL
DWELLS > DWELL
DWELT > DWELL
DWILE n floor cloth
DWILES > DWILE
DWINDLE vb grow less in size, strength, or number
DWINDLED > DWINDLE
DWINDLES > DWINDLE
DWINDLING > DWINDLE
DWINE vb languish
DWINED > DWINE
DWINES > DWINE
DWINING > DWINE
DYABLE > DYE
DYAD n operator that is the unspecified product of two vectors
DYADIC adj of or relating to a dyad ▷ n sum of a particular number of dyads
DYADICS > DYADIC
DYADS > DYAD
DYARCHAL > DIARCHY
DYARCHIC > DYARCHY
DYARCHIES > DYARCHY
DYARCHY same as **>** DIARCHY
DYBBUK n (in Jewish folklore) the body of a person possessed by the soul of a dead sinner
DYBBUKIM > DYBBUK
DYBBUKKIM > DYBBUK
DYBBUKS > DYBBUK
DYE n colouring substance ▷ vb colour (hair or fabric) by applying a dye
DYEABLE > DYE
DYED > DYE
DYEING > DYE
DYEINGS > DYE
DYELINE same as **>** DIAZO

DYELINES > DYELINE
DYER > DYE
DYERS > DYE
DYES > DYE
DYESTER n dyer
DYESTERS > DYESTER
DYESTUFF n substance that can be used as a dye or from which a dye can be obtained
DYESTUFFS > DYESTUFF
DYEWEED n plant that produces dye
DYEWEEDS > DYEWEED
DYEWOOD n any wood from which dyes and pigments can be obtained
DYEWOODS > DYEWOOD
DYEWORKS n place where dye is made
DYING > DIE
DYINGLY > DIE
DYINGNESS > DIE
DYINGS > DIE
DYKE n wall built to prevent flooding ▷ vb embankment or wall built to confine a river to a particular course
DYKED > DYKE
DYKES > DYKE
DYKEY same as **>** DIKEY
DYKIER > DYKEY
DYKIEST > DYKEY
DYKING > DYKE
DYKON n celebrity admired by lesbians
DYKONS > DYKON
DYNAMETER n instrument for determining the magnifying power of telescopes
DYNAMIC adj full of energy, ambition, and new ideas ▷ n energetic or driving force
DYNAMICAL same as **>** DYNAMIC
DYNAMICS n branch of mechanics concerned with the forces that change or produce the motions of bodies
DYNAMISE same as **>** DYNAMIZE
DYNAMISED > DYNAMISE
DYNAMISES > DYNAMISE
DYNAMISM n great energy and enthusiasm
DYNAMISMS > DYNAMISM
DYNAMIST > DYNAMISM
DYNAMISTS > DYNAMISM
DYNAMITE n explosive made of nitroglycerine ▷ vb blow (something) up with dynamite
DYNAMITED > DYNAMITE
DYNAMITER > DYNAMITE
DYNAMITES > DYNAMITE
DYNAMITIC > DYNAMITE
DYNAMIZE vb cause to be dynamic
DYNAMIZED > DYNAMIZE
DYNAMIZES > DYNAMIZE

d

DYNAMO n device for converting mechanical energy into electrical energy

DYNAMOS > DYNAMO

DYNAMOTOR n electrical machine having a single magnetic field and two independent armature windings of which one acts as a motor and the other a generator: used to convert direct current from a battery into alternating current

DYNAST n hereditary ruler

DYNASTIC > DYNASTY

DYNASTIES > DYNASTY

DYNASTS > DYNAST

DYNASTY n sequence of hereditary rulers

DYNATRON n as in *dynatron oscillator* type of oscillator

DYNATRONS > DYNATRON

DYNE n cgs unit of force

DYNEIN n class of proteins

DYNEINS > DYNEIN

DYNEL n trade name for synthetic fibre

DYNELS > DYNEL

DYNES > DYNE

DYNODE n electrical component

DYNODES > DYNODE

DYNORPHIN n drug used to treat cocaine addiction

DYSBINDIN n gene associated with schizophrenia

DYSCHROA n discolouration of skin

DYSCHROAS > DYSCHROA

DYSCHROIA same as > DYSCHROA

DYSCRASIA n any abnormal physiological condition, esp of the blood

DYSCRASIC > DYSCRASIA

DYSCRATIC > DYSCRASIA

DYSENTERY n infection of the intestine causing severe diarrhoea

DYSGENIC adj of, relating to, or contributing to

a degeneration or deterioration in the fitness and quality of a race or strain

DYSGENICS n study of factors capable of reducing the quality of a race or strain, esp the human race

DYSLALIA n defective speech characteristic of those affected by aphasia

DYSLALIAS > DYSLALIA

DYSLECTIC > DYSLEXIA

DYSLEXIA n disorder causing impaired ability to read

DYSLEXIAS > DYSLEXIA

DYSLEXIC > DYSLEXIA

DYSLEXICS > DYSLEXIA

DYSLOGIES > DYSLOGY

DYSLOGY n uncomplimentary remarks

DYSMELIA n condition of missing or stunted limbs

DYSMELIAS > DYSMELIA

DYSMELIC > DYSMELIA

DYSODIL n yellow or green mineral

DYSODILE same as > DYSODIL

DYSODILES > DYSODILE

DYSODILS > DYSODIL

DYSODYLE same as > DYSODYL

DYSODYLES > DYSODYLE

DYSPATHY n dislike

DYSPEPSIA n indigestion

DYSPEPSY same as > DYSPEPSIA

DYSPEPTIC adj relating to or suffering from dyspepsia ▷ n person suffering from dyspepsia

DYSPHAGIA n difficulty in swallowing, caused by obstruction or spasm of the oesophagus

DYSPHAGIC > DYSPHAGIA

DYSPHAGY same as > DYSPHAGIA

DYSPHASIA n disorder of language caused by a brain lesion

DYSPHASIC > DYSPHASIA

DYSPHONIA n any impairment in the ability to speak normally, as from spasm or strain of the vocal cords

DYSPHONIC > DYSPHONIA

DYSPHORIA n feeling of being ill at ease

DYSPHORIC > DYSPHORIA

DYSPLASIA n abnormal development of an organ or part of the body, including congenital absence

DYSPNEA same as > DYSPNOEA

DYSPNEAL > DYSPNEA

DYSPNEAS > DYSPNEA

DYSPNEIC > DYSPNEA

DYSPNOEA n difficulty in breathing or in catching the breath

DYSPNOEAL > DYSPNOEA

DYSPNOEAS > DYSPNOEA

DYSPNOEIC > DYSPNOEA

DYSPNOIC > DYSPNOEA

DYSPRAXIA n impairment in the control of the motor system

DYSPRAXIC adj suffering from dyspraxia

DYSTAXIA n lack of muscular coordination resulting in shaky limb movements and unsteady gait

DYSTAXIAS > DYSTAXIA

DYSTAXIC adj relating to or affected by dystaxia

DYSTECTIC adj difficult to fuse together

DYSTHESIA n unpleasant skin sensation

DYSTHETIC > DYSTHESIA

DYSTHYMIA n characteristics of the neurotic and introverted, including anxiety, depression, and compulsive behaviour

DYSTHYMIC > DYSTHYMIA

DYSTOCIA n abnormal, slow, or difficult childbirth, usually because of disordered or ineffective contractions of the uterus

DYSTOCIAL > DYSTOCIA

DYSTOCIAS > DYSTOCIA

DYSTONIA n neurological disorder, caused by disease of the basal ganglia, in which the muscles of the trunk, shoulders, and neck go into spasm, so that the head and limbs are held in unnatural positions

DYSTONIAS > DYSTONIA

DYSTONIC > DYSTONIA

DYSTOPIA n imaginary place where everything is as bad as it can be

DYSTOPIAN > DYSTOPIA

DYSTOPIAS > DYSTOPIA

DYSTROPHY n any of various bodily disorders, characterized by wasting of tissues

DYSURIA n difficult or painful urination

DYSURIAS > DYSURIA

DYSURIC > DYSURIA

DYSURIES > DYSURY

DYSURY same as > DYSURIA

DYTISCID n type of carnivorous aquatic beetle with large flattened back legs used for swimming

DYTISCIDS > DYTISCID

DYVOUR n debtor

DYVOURIES > DYVOURY

DYVOURS > DYVOUR

DYVOURY n bankruptcy

DZEREN n Chinese yellow antelope

DZERENS > DZEREN

DZHO same as > ZHO

DZHOS > DZHO

DZIGGETAI a variant of > CHIGETAI

DZO a variant spelling of > ZO

DZOS > ZO

Ee

EA *n* river
EACH *pron* every (one) taken separately ▷ *determiner* every (one) of two or more considered individually ▷ *adv* for, to, or from each one
EACHWHERE *adv* everywhere
EADISH *n* aftermath
EADISHES > EADISH
EAGER *adj* showing or feeling great desire, keen ▷ *n* eagre
EAGERER > EAGER
EAGEREST > EAGER
EAGERLY > EAGER
EAGERNESS > EAGER
EAGERS > EAGER
EAGLE *n* bird of prey ▷ *vb* in golf, score two strokes under par for a hole
EAGLED > EAGLE
EAGLEHAWK *n* large Australian eagle
EAGLES > EAGLE
EAGLET *n* young eagle
EAGLETS > EAGLET
EAGLEWOOD *n* Asian thymelaeaceous tree with fragrant wood that yields a resin used as a perfume
EAGLING > EAGLE
EAGRE *n* tidal bore, esp of the Humber or Severn estuaries
EAGRES > EAGRE
EALDORMAN *n* official of Anglo-Saxon England, appointed by the king, who was responsible for law, order, and justice in his shire and for leading his local fyrd in battle
EALDORMEN > EALDORMAN
EALE *n* beast in Roman legend ▷ *vb* to ail
EALED > EALE
EALES > EALE
EALING > EALE
EAN *vb* give birth
EANED > EAN
EANING > EAN
EANLING *n* newborn lamb
EANLINGS > EANLING
EANS > EAN
EAR *n* organ of hearing, esp the external part of it

▷ *vb* (of cereal plants) to develop such parts
EARACHE *n* pain in the ear
EARACHES > EARACHE
EARBALL *n* device used in acupressure
EARBALLS > EARBALL
EARBASH *vb* talk incessantly
EARBASHED > EARBASH
EARBASHER > EARBASH
EARBASHES > EARBASH
EARBOB *n* earring
EARBOBS > EARBOB
EARBUD *n* small earphone
EARBUDS > EARBUD
EARCON *n* sound representing object or event
EARCONS > EARCON
EARD *vb* bury
EARDED > EARD
EARDING > EARD
EARDROP *n* pendant earring
EARDROPS *pl n* liquid medication for inserting into the external ear
EARDRUM *n* part of the ear which enables one to hear sounds
EARDRUMS > EARDRUM
EARDS > EARD
EARED *adj* having an ear or ears
EARFLAP *n* either of two pieces of fabric or fur attached to a cap
EARFLAPS > EARFLAP
EARFUL *n* scolding or telling-off
EARFULS > EARFUL
EARHOLE *n* the external opening of the ear
EARHOLES > EARHOLE
EARING *n* line fastened to a corner of a sail for reefing
EARINGS > EARING
EARL *n* British nobleman ranking next below a marquess
EARLAP *same as* > EARFLAP
EARLAPS > EARLAP
EARLDOM *n* rank, title, or dignity of an earl or countess
EARLDOMS > EARLDOM
EARLESS > EAR
EARLIER > EARLY

EARLIES > EARLY
EARLIEST > EARLY
EARLIKE > EAR
EARLINESS > EARLY
EARLOBE *n* fleshy lower part of the outer ear
EARLOBES > EARLOBE
EARLOCK *n* curl of hair close to ear
EARLOCKS > EARLOCK
EARLS > EARL
EARLSHIP *n* title or position of earl
EARLSHIPS > EARLSHIP
EARLY *adv* before the expected or usual time ▷ *adj* occurring or arriving before the correct or expected time ▷ *n* something which is early
EARLYWOOD *n* light wood made by tree in spring
EARMARK *vb* set (something) aside for a specific purpose ▷ *n* distinguishing mark
EARMARKED > EARMARK
EARMARKS > EARMARK
EARMUFF *n* item of clothing for keeping the ears warm
EARMUFFS > EARMUFF
EARN *vb* obtain by work or merit
EARNED > EARN
EARNER > EARN
EARNERS > EARN
EARNEST *adj* serious and sincere ▷ *n* part payment given in advance
EARNESTLY > EARNEST
EARNESTS > EARNEST
EARNING > EARN
EARNINGS *pl n* money earned
EARNS > EARN
EARPHONE *n* receiver for a radio etc, held to or put in the ear
EARPHONES > EARPHONE
EARPICK *n* instrument for removing ear wax
EARPICKS > EARPICK
EARPIECE *n* earphone in a telephone receiver
EARPIECES > EARPIECE
EARPLUG *n* piece of soft material placed in the ear to keep out water or noise

EARPLUGS > EARPLUG
EARRING *n* ornament for the lobe of the ear
EARRINGED *adj* wearing earrings
EARRINGS > EARRING
EARS > EAR
EARSHOT *n* hearing range
EARSHOTS > EARSHOT
EARST *adv* first; previously
EARSTONE *n* calcium carbonate crystal in the ear
EARSTONES > EARSTONE
EARTH *n* planet that we live on ▷ *vb* connect (a circuit) to earth
EARTHBORN *adj* of earthly origin
EARTHED > EARTH
EARTHEN *adj* made of baked clay or earth
EARTHFALL *n* landslide
EARTHFAST *adj* method of building
EARTHFLAX *n* type of asbestos
EARTHIER > EARTHY
EARTHIEST > EARTHY
EARTHILY > EARTHY
EARTHING > EARTH
EARTHLIER > EARTHLY
EARTHLIES > EARTHLY
EARTHLIKE > EARTH
EARTHLING *n* (esp in poetry or science fiction) an inhabitant of the earth
EARTHLY *adj* conceivable or possible ▷ *n* chance
EARTHMAN *n* (esp in science fiction) an inhabitant or native of the earth
EARTHMEN > EARTHMAN
EARTHNUT *n* perennial umbelliferous plant of Europe and Asia, with edible dark brown tubers
EARTHNUTS > EARTHNUT
EARTHPEA *n* peanut; groundnut
EARTHPEAS > EARTHPEA
EARTHRISE *n* rising of the earth above the lunar horizon, as seen from a spacecraft emerging from the lunar farside
EARTHS > EARTH
EARTHSET *n* setting of the earth below the lunar

horizon, as seen from a spacecraft emerging from the lunar farside

EARTHSETS > EARTHSET

EARTHSTAR n type of woodland fungus

EARTHWARD adv towards the earth

EARTHWAX n ozocerite

EARTHWOLF n aardvark

EARTHWORK n fortification made of earth

EARTHWORM n worm which burrows in the soil

EARTHY adj coarse or crude

EARWAX nontechnical name for > CERUMEN

EARWAXES > EARWAX

EARWIG n small insect with a pincer-like tail ▷ vb eavesdrop

EARWIGGED > EARWIG

EARWIGGY > EARWIG

EARWIGS > EARWIG

EARWORM n irritatingly catchy tune

EARWORMS > EARWORM

EAS > EA

EASE n freedom from difficulty, discomfort, or worry ▷ vb give bodily or mental ease to

EASED > EASE

EASEFUL adj characterized by or bringing ease

EASEFULLY > EASEFUL

EASEL n frame to support an artist's canvas or a blackboard

EASELED adj mounted on easel

EASELESS > EASE

EASELS > EASEL

EASEMENT n right enjoyed by a landowner of making limited use of his neighbour's land, as by crossing it to reach his own property

EASEMENTS > EASEMENT

EASER > EASE

EASERS > EASE

EASES > EASE

EASIED > EASY

EASIER > EASY

EASIES > EASY

EASIEST > EASY

EASILY adv without difficulty

EASINESS n quality or condition of being easy to accomplish, do, obtain, etc

EASING n as in quantitative easing increasing the supply of money to stimulate the economy

EASINGS > EASING

EASLE n hot ash

EASLES > EASLE

EASSEL adv easterly

EASSIL adv easterly

EAST n (direction towards) the part of the horizon where the sun rises ▷ adj in the east ▷ adv in, to, or towards the east ▷ vb move or turn east

EASTABOUT adv in, to, or towards the east

EASTBOUND adj going towards the east

EASTED > EAST

EASTER n most important festival of the Christian Church

EASTERLY adj of or in the east ▷ adv towards the east ▷ n wind from the east

EASTERN adj situated in or towards the east

EASTERNER n person from the east of a country or area

EASTERS > EASTER

EASTING n net distance eastwards made by a vessel moving towards the east

EASTINGS > EASTING

EASTLAND adj, n (of or relating to) land in east

EASTLANDS > EASTLAND

EASTLIN adj easterly

EASTLING adj easterly

EASTLINGS adv eastward

EASTLINS adv eastward

EASTMOST adj furthest east

EASTS > EAST

EASTWARD same as > EASTWARDS

EASTWARDS adv towards the east

EASY adj not needing much work or effort ▷ vb stop rowing

EASYGOING adj relaxed in manner

EASYING > EASY

EAT vb take (food) into the mouth and swallow it

EATABLE adj fit or suitable for eating

EATABLES pl n food

EATAGE n grazing rights

EATAGES > EATAGE

EATCHE n adze

EATCHES > EATCHE

EATEN > EAT

EATER > EAT

EATERIE same as > EATERY

EATERIES > EATERY

EATERS > EAT

EATERY n restaurant or eating house

EATH adj easy

EATHE same as > EATH

EATHLY > EATH

EATING > EAT

EATINGS > EAT

EATS > EAT

EAU same as > EA

EAUS > EAU

EAUX > EAU

EAVE n overhanging edge of a roof

EAVED adj having eaves

EAVES > EAVE

EAVESDRIP n water dropping from eaves

EAVESDROP vb listen secretly to a private conversation

EBAUCHE n rough sketch

EBAUCHES > EBAUCHE

EBAYER n any person who uses eBay

EBAYERS > EBAYER

EBAYING n buying or selling using eBay

EBAYINGS > EBAYING

EBB vb (of tide water) flow back ▷ n flowing back of the tide

EBBED > EBB

EBBET n type of newt

EBBETS > EBBET

EBBING > EBB

EBBLESS > EBB

EBBS > EBB

EBENEZER n chapel

EBENEZERS > EBENEZER

EBENISTE n cabinetmaker

EBENISTES > EBENISTE

EBIONISE same as > EBIONIZE

EBIONISED > EBIONISE

EBIONISES > EBIONISE

EBIONISM n doctrine that the poor shall be saved

EBIONISMS > EBIONISM

EBIONITIC > EBIONISM

EBIONIZE vb preach ebionism

EBIONIZED > EBIONIZE

EBIONIZES > EBIONIZE

EBON poetic word for > EBONY

EBONICS n dialect used by African-Americans

EBONIES > EBONY

EBONISE same as > EBONIZE

EBONISED > EBONISE

EBONISES > EBONISE

EBONISING > EBONISE

EBONIST n carver of ebony

EBONISTS > EBONIST

EBONITE another name for > VULCANITE

EBONITES > EBONITE

EBONIZE vb stain or otherwise finish in imitation of ebony

EBONIZED > EBONIZE

EBONIZES > EBONIZE

EBONIZING > EBONIZE

EBONS > EBON

EBONY n hard black wood ▷ adj deep black

EBOOK n book in electronic form

EBOOKS > EBOOK

EBRIATE adj drunk

EBRIATED > EBRIATE

EBRIETIES > EBRIETY

EBRIETY n drunkenness

EBRILLADE n jerk on rein, when horse refuses to turn

EBRIOSE adj drunk

EBRIOSITY > EBRIOSE

EBULLIENT adj full of enthusiasm or excitement

EBURNEAN adj made of ivory

EBURNEOUS adj like ivory

ECAD n organism whose form has been affected by its environment

ECADS > ECAD

ECARINATE adj having no carina or keel

ECARTE n card game for two, played with 32 cards and king high

ECARTES > ECARTE

ECAUDATE adj tailless

ECBOLE n digression

ECBOLES > ECBOLE

ECBOLIC adj hastening labour or abortion ▷ n drug or agent that hastens labour or abortion

ECBOLICS > ECBOLIC

ECCE interj behold

ECCENTRIC adj odd or unconventional ▷ n eccentric person

ECCLESIA n (in informal Church usage) a congregation

ECCLESIAE > ECCLESIA

ECCLESIAL adj ecclesiastical

ECCO interj look there

ECCRINE adj of or denoting glands that secrete externally

ECCRISES > ECCRISIS

ECCRISIS n excrement

ECCRITIC n purgative

ECCRITICS > ECCRITIC

ECDEMIC adj not indigenous or endemic

ECDYSES > ECDYSIS

ECDYSIAL > ECDYSIS

ECDYSIAST facetious word for > STRIPPER

ECDYSIS n shedding of the cuticle in arthropods or the outer epidermal layer in reptiles

ECDYSISES > ECDYSIS

ECDYSON same as > ECDYSONE

ECDYSONE n hormone secreted by the prothoracic gland of insects that controls ecdysis and stimulates metamorphosis

ECDYSONES > ECDYSONE

ECDYSONS > ECDYSON

ECESIC > ECESIS

ECESIS n establishment of a plant in a new environment

ECESISES > ECESIS
ECH same as > ECHE
ECHAPPE n leap in ballet
ECHAPPES > ECHAPPE
ECHARD n water that is present in the soil but cannot be utilized by plants
ECHARDS > ECHARD
ECHE vb eke out
ECHED > ECHE
ECHELLE n ladder; scale
ECHELLES > ECHELLE
ECHELON n level of power or responsibility ▷ vb assemble in echelon
ECHELONED > ECHELON
ECHELONS > ECHELON
ECHES > ECHE
ECHEVERIA n tropical American plant cultivated for its colourful foliage
ECHIDNA n Australian spiny egg-laying mammal
ECHIDNAE > ECHIDNA
ECHIDNAS > ECHIDNA
ECHIDNINE n snake poison
ECHINACEA n N American plant with purple and black flowers
ECHINATE adj covered with spines, bristles, or bristle-like outgrowths
ECHINATED same as > ECHINATE
ECHING > ECHE
ECHINI > ECHINUS
ECHINOID n type of echinoderm of the class which includes the sea urchins and sand dollars
ECHINOIDS > ECHINOID
ECHINUS n ovolo moulding between the shaft and the abacus of a Doric column
ECHINUSES > ECHINUS
ECHIUM n type of Eurasian and African plant
ECHIUMS > ECHIUM
ECHIURAN n spoonworm
ECHIURANS > ECHIURAN
ECHIUROID n marine worm
ECHO n repetition of sounds by reflection of sound waves off a surface ▷ vb repeat or be repeated as an echo
ECHOED > ECHO
ECHOER > ECHO
ECHOERS > ECHO
ECHOES > ECHO
ECHOEY adj producing echoes
ECHOGRAM n record made by echography
ECHOGRAMS > ECHOGRAM
ECHOGRAPH n device that uses sonic waves to measure the depth of water

ECHOIC adj characteristic of or resembling an echo
ECHOIER > ECHOEY
ECHOIEST > ECHOEY
ECHOING > ECHO
ECHOISE same as > ECHOIZE
ECHOISED > ECHOISE
ECHOISES > ECHOISE
ECHOISING > ECHOISE
ECHOISM n onomatopoeia as a source of word formation
ECHOISMS > ECHOISM
ECHOIST > ECHOISM
ECHOISTS > ECHOISM
ECHOIZE vb repeat like echo
ECHOIZED > ECHOIZE
ECHOIZES > ECHOIZE
ECHOIZING > ECHOIZE
ECHOLALIA n tendency to repeat mechanically words just spoken by another person: can occur in cases of brain damage, mental retardation, and schizophrenia
ECHOLALIC > ECHOLALIA
ECHOLESS > ECHO
ECHOS > ECHO
ECHOVIRUS n any of a group of viruses that can cause symptoms of mild meningitis, the common cold, or infections of the intestinal and respiratory tracts
ECHT adj real
ECLAIR n finger-shaped pastry filled with cream and covered with chocolate
ECLAIRS > ECLAIR
ECLAMPSIA n serious condition that can develop towards the end of a pregnancy, causing high blood pressure, swelling, and convulsions
ECLAMPSY same as > ECLAMPSIA
ECLAMPTIC > ECLAMPSIA
ECLAT n brilliant success
ECLATS > ECLAT
ECLECTIC adj selecting from various styles, ideas, or sources ▷ n person who takes an eclectic approach
ECLECTICS > ECLECTIC
ECLIPSE n temporary obscuring of one star or planet by another ▷ vb surpass or outclass
ECLIPSED > ECLIPSE
ECLIPSER > ECLIPSE
ECLIPSERS > ECLIPSE
ECLIPSES > ECLIPSIS
ECLIPSING > ECLIPSE
ECLIPSIS same as > ELLIPSIS

ECLIPTIC n apparent path of the sun ▷ adj of or relating to an eclipse
ECLIPTICS > ECLIPTIC
ECLOGITE n rare coarse-grained basic rock consisting principally of garnet and pyroxene. Quartz, feldspar, etc, may also be present. It is thought to originate by metamorphism or igneous crystallization at extremely high pressure
ECLOGITES > ECLOGITE
ECLOGUE n pastoral or idyllic poem, usually in the form of a conversation or soliloquy
ECLOGUES > ECLOGUE
ECLOSE vb emerge
ECLOSED > ECLOSE
ECLOSES > ECLOSE
ECLOSING > ECLOSE
ECLOSION n emergence of an insect larva from the egg or an adult from the pupal case
ECLOSIONS > ECLOSION
ECO n ecology activist
ECOCIDAL > ECOCIDE
ECOCIDE n total destruction of an area of the natural environment
ECOCIDES > ECOCIDE
ECOD same as > EGAD
ECOFREAK n environmentalist
ECOFREAKS > ECOFREAK
ECOGIFT n donation of land for environmental purposes
ECOGIFTS > ECOGIFT
ECOLODGE n eco-friendly tourist accommodation
ECOLODGES > ECOLODGE
ECOLOGIC > ECOLOGY
ECOLOGIES > ECOLOGY
ECOLOGIST > ECOLOGY
ECOLOGY n study of the links between living things and their environment
ECOMAP n diagram showing the links between an individual and their community
ECOMAPS > ECOMAP
ECOMMERCE n business transactions conducted on the internet
ECONOBOX n fuel efficient utility vehicle
ECONOMIC adj of economics
ECONOMICS n social science concerned with the production and consumption of goods and services
ECONOMIES > ECONOMY
ECONOMISE same as > ECONOMIZE
ECONOMISM n political theory that regards

economics as the main factor in society, ignoring or reducing to simplistic economic terms other factors such as culture, nationality, etc
ECONOMIST n specialist in economics
ECONOMIZE vb reduce expense or waste
ECONOMY n system of interrelationship of money, industry, and employment in a country ▷ adj denoting a class of air travel that is cheaper than first-class
ECONUT n environmentalist
ECONUTS > ECONUT
ECOPHOBIA n fear of home
ECORCHE n anatomical figure without the skin
ECORCHES > ECORCHE
ECOREGION n area defined by its environmental conditions, esp climate, landforms, and soil characteristics
ECOS > ECO
ECOSPHERE n planetary ecosystem, consisting of all living organisms and their environment
ECOSSAISE n lively dance in two-four time
ECOSTATE adj with no ribs or nerves
ECOSYSTEM n system involving interactions between a community and its environment
ECOTAGE n sabotage for ecological motives
ECOTAGES > ECOTAGE
ECOTARIAN n person who eats only eco-friendly food
ECOTONAL > ECOTONE
ECOTONE n zone between two major ecological communities
ECOTONES > ECOTONE
ECOTOPIA n ecologically ideal area or society
ECOTOPIAS > ECOTOPIA
ECOTOUR n holiday taking care not to damage environment ▷ vb take an ecotour
ECOTOURED > ECOTOUR
ECOTOURS > ECOTOUR
ECOTOXIC adj harmful to animals, plants or the environment
ECOTYPE n organisms within a species that have adapted to a particular environment
ECOTYPES > ECOTYPE
ECOTYPIC > ECOTYPE
ECOZONE n large area with an ecosystem
ECOZONES > ECOZONE

e

ECPHRASES
> ECPHRASIS

ECPHRASIS *same as*
> EKPHRASIS

ECRASEUR *n* surgical device consisting of a heavy wire loop placed around a part to be removed and tightened until it cuts through

ECRASEURS
> ECRASEUR

ECRITOIRE *n* writing desk with compartments and drawers

ECRU *adj* pale creamy-brown ▷ *n* greyish-yellow to a light greyish colour

ECRUS > ECRU

ECSTASES > ECSTASIS

ECSTASIED > ECSTASY

ECSTASIES > ECSTASY

ECSTASIS *same as*
> ECSTASY

ECSTASISE *same as*
> ECSTASIZE

ECSTASIZE *vb* make or become ecstatic

ECSTASY *n* state of intense delight

ECSTATIC *adj* in a trancelike state of great rapture or delight ▷ *n* person who has periods of intense trancelike joy

ECSTATICS *pl n* fits of delight or rapture

ECTASES > ECTASIS

ECTASIA *n* distension or dilation of a duct, vessel, or hollow viscus

ECTASIAS > ECTASIA

ECTASIS *same as*
> ECTASIA

ECTATIC > ECTASIA

ECTHYMA *n* local inflammation of the skin

ECTHYMAS > ECTHYMA

ECTHYMATA > ECTHYMA

ECTOBLAST *same as*
> EPIBLAST

ECTOCRINE *n* substance that is released by an organism into the external environment and influences the development, behaviour, etc, of members of the same or different species

ECTODERM *n* outer germ layer of an animal embryo, which gives rise to epidermis and nervous tissue

ECTODERMS > ECTODERM

ECTOGENE *n* type of gene

ECTOGENES > ECTOGENE

ECTOGENIC *adj* capable of developing outside the host

ECTOGENY *n* (of bacteria, etc) development outside the host

ECTOMERE *n* any of the blastomeres that later develop into ectoderm

ECTOMERES > ECTOMERE

ECTOMERIC > ECTOMERE

ECTOMORPH *n* person with a thin body build: said to be correlated with cerebrotonia

ECTOPHYTE *n* parasitic plant that lives on the surface of its host

ECTOPIA *n* congenital displacement of an organ or part

ECTOPIAS > ECTOPIA

ECTOPIC > ECTOPIA

ECTOPIES > ECTOPY

ECTOPLASM *n* substance that supposedly is emitted from the body of a medium during a trance

ECTOPROCT *another word* for > BRYOZOAN

ECTOPY *same as*
> ECTOPIA

ECTOSARC *n* ectoplasm of an amoeba or any other protozoan

ECTOSARCS > ECTOSARC

ECTOTHERM *n* animal whose body temperature is determined by ambient temperature

ECTOZOA > ECTOZOON

ECTOZOAN *same as*
> ECTOZOON

ECTOZOANS > ECTOZOAN

ECTOZOIC > ECTOZOON

ECTOZOON *n* parasitic organism that lives on the outside of its host

ECTROPIC > ECTROPION

ECTROPION *n* condition in which the eyelid turns over exposing some of the inner lid

ECTROPIUM *same as*
> ECTROPION

ECTYPAL > ECTYPE

ECTYPE *n* copy as distinguished from a prototype

ECTYPES > ECTYPE

ECU *n* any of various former French gold or silver coins

ECUELLE *n* covered soup bowl with handles

ECUELLES > ECUELLE

ECUMENE *n* inhabited area of the world

ECUMENES > ECUMENE

ECUMENIC *adj* tending to promote unity among Churches

ECUMENICS > ECUMENIC

ECUMENISM *n* aim of unity among Christian churches throughout the world

ECUMENIST *n* believer in ecumenicism

ECURIE *n* team of motor-racing cars

ECURIES > ECURIE

ECUS > ECU

ECZEMA *n* skin disease causing intense itching

ECZEMAS > ECZEMA

ED *n* education

EDACIOUS *adj* devoted to eating

EDACITIES > EDACIOUS

EDACITY > EDACIOUS

EDAMAME *n* immature soybeans boiled in the pod

EDAMAMES > EDAMAME

EDAPHIC *adj* of or relating to the physical and chemical conditions of the soil

EDDIED > EDDY

EDDIES > EDDY

EDDISH *n* pasture grass

EDDISHES > EDDISH

EDDO *same as* > TARO

EDDOES > EDDO

EDDY *n* circular movement of air, water, etc ▷ *vb* move with a circular motion

EDDYING > EDDY

EDELWEISS *n* alpine plant with white flowers

EDEMA *same as* > OEDEMA

EDEMAS > EDEMA

EDEMATA > EDEMA

EDEMATOSE > EDEMA

EDEMATOUS > EDEMA

EDENIC *adj* delightful, like the Garden of Eden

EDENTAL *adj* having few or no teeth

EDENTATE *n* mammal with few or no teeth, such as an armadillo or a sloth ▷ *adj* denoting such a mammal

EDENTATES > EDENTATE

EDGE *n* border or line where something ends or begins ▷ *vb* provide an edge or border for

EDGEBONE *n* aitchbone

EDGEBONES > EDGEBONE

EDGED > EDGE

EDGELESS > EDGE

EDGER > EDGE

EDGERS > EDGE

EDGES > EDGE

EDGEWAYS *adv* with the edge forwards or uppermost

EDGEWISE *same as*
> EDGEWAYS

EDGIER > EDGY

EDGIEST > EDGY

EDGILY > EDGY

EDGINESS > EDGY

EDGING *n* anything placed along an edge to finish it ▷ *adj* relating to or used for making an edge

EDGINGS > EDGING

EDGY *adj* nervous or irritable

EDH *n* character of the runic alphabet

EDHS > EDH

EDIBILITY > EDIBLE

EDIBLE *adj* fit to be eaten

EDIBLES *pl n* articles fit to eat

EDICT *n* order issued by an authority

EDICTAL > EDICT

EDICTALLY > EDICT

EDICTS > EDICT

EDIFICE *n* large building

EDIFICES > EDIFICE

EDIFICIAL > EDIFICE

EDIFIED > EDIFY

EDIFIER > EDIFY

EDIFIERS > EDIFY

EDIFIES > EDIFY

EDIFY *vb* improve morally by instruction

EDIFYING > EDIFY

EDILE *variant spelling of*
> AEDILE

EDILES > EDILE

EDIT *vb* prepare (a book, film, etc) for publication or broadcast ▷ *n* act of editing

EDITABLE > EDIT

EDITED > EDIT

EDITING > EDIT

EDITINGS > EDIT

EDITION *n* number of copies of a new publication printed at one time ▷ *vb* produce multiple copies of (an original work of art)

EDITIONED > EDITION

EDITIONS > EDITION

EDITOR *n* person who edits

EDITORIAL *n* newspaper article stating the opinion of the editor ▷ *adj* of editing or editors

EDITORS > EDITOR

EDITRESS *n* female editor

EDITRICES > EDITRIX

EDITRIX *n* female editor

EDITRIXES > EDITRIX

EDITS > EDIT

EDS > ED

EDUCABLE *adj* capable of being trained or educated ▷ *n* mentally retarded person who is capable of being educated

EDUCABLES > EDUCABLE

EDUCATE *vb* teach

EDUCATED *adj* having an education, esp a good one

EDUCATES > EDUCATE

EDUCATING > EDUCATE

EDUCATION *n* process of acquiring knowledge and understanding

EDUCATIVE *adj* educating

EDUCATOR *n* person who educates

EDUCATORS > EDUCATOR

EDUCATORY *adj* educative or educational

EDUCE *vb* evolve or develop

EDUCED > EDUCE

EDUCEMENT > EDUCE

EDUCES > EDUCE

EDUCIBLE > EDUCE

EDUCING > EDUCE

EDUCT n substance separated from a mixture without chemical change

EDUCTION n something educed

EDUCTIONS > EDUCTION

EDUCTIVE > EDUCE

EDUCTOR > EDUCE

EDUCTORS > EDUCE

EDUCTS > EDUCT

EE Scots word for > EYE

EECH same as > ECHE

EECHED > EECH

EECHES > EECH

EECHING > EECH

EEEW interj exclamation of disgust

EEJIT Scots and Irish word for > IDIOT

EEJITS > EEJIT

EEK interj indicating shock or fright

EEL n snakelike fish

EELFARE n young eel

EELFARES > EELFARE

EELGRASS n type of submerged marine plant with grasslike leaves

EELIER > EEL

EELIEST > EEL

EELLIKE adj resembling an eel

EELPOUT n marine eel-like blennioid fish

EELPOUTS > EELPOUT

EELS > EEL

EELWORM n any of various nematode worms

EELWORMS > EELWORM

EELWRACK n grasslike plant growing in seawater

EELWRACKS > EELWRACK

EELY > EEL

EEN > EE

EENSIER > EENSY

EENSIEST > EENSY

EENSY adj very small

EERIE adj uncannily frightening or disturbing

EERIER > EERIE

EERIEST > EERIE

EERILY > EERIE

EERINESS > EERIE

EERY same as > EERIE

EEVEN n evening

EEVENS > EEVEN

EEVN n evening

EEVNING n evening

EEVNINGS > EEVNING

EEVNS > EEVN

EEW interj exclamation of disgust

EF n the letter F

EFF vb say the word 'fuck'

EFFABLE adj capable of being expressed in words

EFFACE vb remove by rubbing

EFFACED > EFFACE

EFFACER > EFFACE

EFFACERS > EFFACE

EFFACES > EFFACE

EFFACING > EFFACE

EFFECT n change or result caused by someone or something ▷ vb cause to happen, accomplish

EFFECTED > EFFECT

EFFECTER > EFFECT

EFFECTERS > EFFECT

EFFECTING > EFFECT

EFFECTIVE adj producing a desired result ▷ n serviceman who is equipped and prepared for action

EFFECTOR n nerve ending that terminates in a muscle or gland and provides neural stimulation causing contraction or secretion

EFFECTORS > EFFECTOR

EFFECTS pl n personal belongings

EFFECTUAL adj producing the intended result

EFFED > EFF

EFFEIR vb suit

EFFEIRED > EFFEIR

EFFEIRING > EFFEIR

EFFEIRS > EFFEIR

EFFENDI n (in the Ottoman Empire) a title of respect

EFFENDIS > EFFENDI

EFFERE same as > EFFEIR

EFFERED > EFFERE

EFFERENCE > EFFERENT

EFFERENT adj carrying or conducting outwards from a part or an organ of the body, esp from the brain or spinal cord ▷ n nerve that carries impulses outwards from the brain or spinal cord

EFFERENTS > EFFERENT

EFFERES > EFFERE

EFFERING > EFFERE

EFFETE adj powerless, feeble

EFFETELY > EFFETE

EFFICACY n quality of being successful in producing an intended result

EFFICIENT adj functioning effectively with little waste of effort

EFFIERCE vb archaic word meaning make fierce

EFFIERCED > EFFIERCE

EFFIERCES > EFFIERCE

EFFIGIAL > EFFIGY

EFFIGIES > EFFIGY

EFFIGY n image or likeness of a person

EFFING > EFF

EFFINGS > EFF

EFFLUENCE n act or process of flowing out

EFFLUENT n liquid discharged as waste ▷ adj flowing out or forth

EFFLUENTS > EFFLUENT

EFFLUVIA > EFFLUVIUM

EFFLUVIAL > EFFLUVIUM

EFFLUVIUM n unpleasant smell, as of decaying matter or gaseous waste

EFFLUX same as > EFFLUENCE

EFFLUXES > EFFLUX

EFFLUXION same as > EFFLUX

EFFORCE vb force

EFFORCED > EFFORCE

EFFORCES > EFFORCE

EFFORCING > EFFORCE

EFFORT n physical or mental exertion

EFFORTFUL > EFFORT

EFFORTS > EFFORT

EFFRAIDE same as > AFRAID

EFFRAY same as > AFFRAY

EFFRAYS > EFFRAY

EFFS > EFF

EFFULGE vb radiate

EFFULGED > EFFULGE

EFFULGENT adj radiant

EFFULGES > EFFULGE

EFFULGING > EFFULGE

EFFUSE vb pour or flow out ▷ adj (esp of an inflorescence) spreading out loosely

EFFUSED > EFFUSE

EFFUSES > EFFUSE

EFFUSING > EFFUSE

EFFUSION n unrestrained outburst

EFFUSIONS > EFFUSION

EFFUSIVE adj openly emotional, demonstrative

EFS > EF

EFT n dialect or archaic name for a newt ▷ adv again

EFTEST adj nearest at hand

EFTS > EFT

EFTSOON > EFTSOONS

EFTSOONS adv soon afterwards

EGAD n mild oath or expression of surprise

EGADS > EGAD

EGAL adj equal

EGALITE n equality

EGALITES > EGALITY

EGALITIES > EGALITY

EGALITY n equality

EGALLY > EGAL

EGAREMENT n confusion

EGENCE n need

EGENCES > EGENCE

EGENCIES > EGENCY

EGENCY same as > EGENCE

EGER same as > EAGRE

EGERS > EGER

EGEST vb excrete (waste material)

EGESTA pl n anything egested, as waste material from the body

EGESTED > EGEST

EGESTING > EGEST

EGESTION > EGEST

EGESTIONS > EGEST

EGESTIVE > EGEST

EGESTS > EGEST

EGG n object laid by birds and other creatures, containing a developing embryo ▷ vb urge or incite, esp to daring or foolish acts

EGGAR same as > EGGER

EGGARS > EGGAR

EGGBEATER n kitchen utensil for beating eggs, whipping cream, etc

EGGCORN n misspelling caused by the mishearing of a word

EGGCORNS > EGGCORN

EGGCUP n cup for holding a boiled egg

EGGCUPS > EGGCUP

EGGED > EGG

EGGER n moth with brown body and wings

EGGERIES > EGGERY

EGGERS > EGGER

EGGERY n place where eggs are laid

EGGFRUIT n fruit of eggplant

EGGFRUITS > EGGFRUIT

EGGHEAD n intellectual person

EGGHEADED > EGGHEAD

EGGHEADS > EGGHEAD

EGGIER > EGGY

EGGIEST > EGGY

EGGING > EGG

EGGLER n egg dealer: sometimes itinerant

EGGLERS > EGGLER

EGGLESS > EGG

EGGMASS n intelligentsia

EGGMASSES > EGGMASS

EGGNOG n drink made of raw eggs, milk, sugar, spice, and brandy or rum

EGGNOGS > EGGNOG

EGGPLANT n dark purple tropical fruit, cooked and eaten as a vegetable

EGGPLANTS > EGGPLANT

EGGS > EGG

EGGSHELL n hard covering round the egg of a bird or animal ▷ adj (of paint) having a very slight sheen

EGGSHELLS > EGGSHELL

EGGWASH n beaten egg for brushing on pastry

EGGWASHES > EGGWASH

EGGWHISK same as > EGGBEATER

EGGWHISKS > EGGWHISK

EGGY adj soaked in or tasting of egg

EGIS rare spelling of > AEGIS

EGISES > EGIS
EGLANTINE n Eurasian rose
EGLATERE archaic name for > EGLANTINE
EGLATERES > EGLATERE
EGLOMISE n gilding
EGLOMISES > EGLOMISE
EGMA mispronunciation of > ENIGMA
EGMAS > EGMA
EGO n conscious mind of an individual
EGOISM n excessive concern for one's own interests
EGOISMS > EGOISM
EGOIST n person who is preoccupied with his own interests
EGOISTIC > EGOIST
EGOISTS > EGOIST
EGOITIES > EGOITY
EGOITY n essence of the ego
EGOLESS adj without an ego
EGOMANIA n obsessive concern with fulfilling one's own needs and desires, regardless of the effect on other people
EGOMANIAC > EGOMANIA
EGOMANIAS > EGOMANIA
EGOS > EGO
EGOSURF vb search for one's own name on the internet
EGOSURFED > EGOSURF
EGOSURFS > EGOSURF
EGOTHEISM n making god of oneself
EGOTISE same as > EGOTIZE
EGOTISED > EGOTISE
EGOTISES > EGOTISE
EGOTISING > EGOTISE
EGOTISM n concern only for one's own interests and feelings
EGOTISMS > EGOTISM
EGOTIST n conceited boastful person
EGOTISTIC > EGOTIST
EGOTISTS > EGOTIST
EGOTIZE vb talk or write in self-important way
EGOTIZED > EGOTIZE
EGOTIZES > EGOTIZE
EGOTIZING > EGOTIZE
EGREGIOUS adj outstandingly bad
EGRESS same as > EMERSION
EGRESSED > EGRESS
EGRESSES > EGRESS
EGRESSING > EGRESS
EGRESSION same as > EGRESS
EGRESSIVE n speech sound produced with an exhalation of breath
EGRET n lesser white heron

EGRETS > EGRET
EGYPTIAN n type of typeface
EGYPTIANS > EGYPTIAN
EH interj exclamation of surprise or inquiry ▷ vb say 'eh'
EHED > EH
EHING > EH
EHS > EH
EIDE > EIDOS
EIDENT adj diligent
EIDER n Arctic duck
EIDERDOWN n quilt (orig. stuffed with eider feathers)
EIDERS > EIDER
EIDETIC adj (of images) exceptionally vivid, allowing detailed recall of something ▷ n person with eidetic ability
EIDETICS > EIDETIC
EIDOGRAPH n device for copying drawings
EIDOLA > EIDOLON
EIDOLIC > EIDOLON
EIDOLON n unsubstantial image
EIDOLONS > EIDOLON
EIDOS n intellectual character of a culture or a social group
EIGENMODE n characteristic vibration pattern
EIGENTONE n characteristic acoustic resonance frequency of a system
EIGHT n one more than seven ▷ adj amounting to eight
EIGHTBALL n black ball in pool
EIGHTEEN n eight and ten ▷ adj amounting to eighteen ▷ determiner amounting to eighteen
EIGHTEENS > EIGHTEEN
EIGHTFOIL n eight leaved flower shape in heraldry
EIGHTFOLD adj having eight times as many or as much ▷ adv by eight times as many or as much
EIGHTFOOT adj measuring eight feet
EIGHTH n number eight in a series ▷ adj coming after the seventh and before the ninth ▷ adv after the seventh person, position, event, etc
EIGHTHLY same as > EIGHTH
EIGHTHS > EIGHTH
EIGHTIES > EIGHTY
EIGHTIETH n one of 80 approximately equal parts of something

EIGHTS > EIGHT
EIGHTSMAN n member of an eight-man team
EIGHTSMEN > EIGHTSMAN
EIGHTSOME n group of eight people
EIGHTVO another word for > OCTAVO
EIGHTVOS > EIGHTVO
EIGHTY n eight times ten ▷ adj amounting to eighty ▷ determiner amounting to eighty
EIGNE adj firstborn
EIK variant form of > EKE
EIKED > EIK
EIKING > EIK
EIKON variant spelling of > ICON
EIKONES > EIKON
EIKONS > EIKON
EIKS > EIK
EILD n old age
EILDING n fuel
EILDINGS > EILDING
EILDS > EILD
EINA interj exclamation of pain
EINE pl n eyes
EINKORN n variety of wheat of Greece and SW Asia
EINKORNS > EINKORN
EINSTEIN n scientific genius
EINSTEINS > EINSTEIN
EIRACK n young hen
EIRACKS > EIRACK
EIRENIC variant spelling of > IRENIC
EIRENICAL same as > IRENIC
EIRENICON n proposition that attempts to harmonize conflicting viewpoints
EIRENICS n theology concerned with unity among churches
EISEGESES > EISEGESIS
EISEGESIS n interpretation of a text, esp a biblical text, using one's own ideas
EISEL n vinegar
EISELL same as > EISEL
EISELLS > EISELL
EISELS > EISEL
EISH interj South African exclamation
EISWEIN n wine made from grapes frozen on the vine
EISWEINS > EISWEIN
EITHER pron one or the other (of two) ▷ adv likewise ▷ determiner one or the other (of two)
EJACULATE vb eject (semen)
EJECT vb force out, expel

EJECTA pl n matter thrown out by a volcano or during a meteorite impact
EJECTABLE > EJECT
EJECTED > EJECT
EJECTING > EJECT
EJECTION > EJECT
EJECTIONS > EJECT
EJECTIVE adj relating to or causing ejection ▷ n ejective consonant
EJECTIVES > EJECTIVE
EJECTMENT n (formerly) an action brought by a wrongfully dispossessed owner seeking to recover possession of his land
EJECTOR n person or thing that ejects
EJECTORS > EJECTOR
EJECTS > EJECT
EJIDO n communal farmland in Mexico
EJIDOS > EJIDO
EKE vb increase, enlarge, or lengthen
EKED > EKE
EKES > EKE
EKING > EKE
EKISTIC > EKISTICS
EKISTICAL > EKISTICS
EKISTICS n science or study of human settlements
EKKA n type of one-horse carriage
EKKAS > EKKA
EKLOGITE same as > ECLOGITE
EKLOGITES > EKLOGITE
EKPHRASES > EKPHRASIS
EKPHRASIS n description of a visual work of art
EKPWELE n former monetary unit of Equatorial Guinea
EKPWELES > EKPWELE
EKTEXINE n in pollen and spores, the outer of the two layers that make up the exine
EKTEXINES > EKTEXINE
EKUELE same as > EKPWELE
EL n American elevated railway
ELABORATE adj with a lot of fine detail ▷ vb expand upon
ELAEOLITE n nephelite
ELAIN same as > TRIOLEIN
ELAINS > ELAIN
ELAIOSOME n oil-rich body on seeds or fruits that attracts ants, which act as dispersal agents
ELAN n style and vigour
ELANCE vb throw a lance
ELANCED > ELANCE
ELANCES > ELANCE
ELANCING > ELANCE

ELAND n large antelope of southern Africa

ELANDS > ELAND

ELANET n bird of prey

ELANETS > ELANET

ELANS > ELAN

ELAPHINE adj of or like a red deer

ELAPID n mostly tropical type of venomous snake

ELAPIDS > ELAPID

ELAPINE adj of or like an elapid

ELAPSE vb (of time) pass by

ELAPSED > ELAPSE

ELAPSES > ELAPSE

ELAPSING > ELAPSE

ELASTANCE n reciprocal of capacitance

ELASTANE n synthetic fibre that is able to return to its original shape after being stretched

ELASTANES > ELASTANE

ELASTASE n enzyme that digests elastin

ELASTASES > ELASTASE

ELASTIC adj resuming normal shape after distortion ▷ n tape or fabric containing interwoven strands of flexible rubber

ELASTICS > ELASTIC

ELASTIN n fibrous scleroprotein

ELASTINS > ELASTIN

ELASTOMER n any material, such as natural or synthetic rubber, that is able to resume its original shape when a deforming force is removed

ELATE vb fill with high spirits, exhilaration, pride or optimism

ELATED adj extremely happy and excited

ELATEDLY > ELATED

ELATER n elaterid beetle

ELATERID n type of beetle of the family which constitutes the click beetles

ELATERIDS > ELATERID

ELATERIN n white crystalline substance found in elaterium, used as a purgative

ELATERINS > ELATERIN

ELATERITE n dark brown naturally occurring bitumen resembling rubber

ELATERIUM n greenish sediment prepared from the juice of the squirting cucumber, used as a purgative

ELATERS > ELATER

ELATES > ELATE

ELATING > ELATE

ELATION n feeling of great happiness and excitement

ELATIONS > ELATION

ELATIVE adj denoting a grammatical case in Finnish and other languages ▷ n elative case

ELATIVES > ELATIVE

ELBOW n joint between the upper arm and the forearm ▷ vb shove or strike with the elbow

ELBOWED > ELBOW

ELBOWING n act of elbowing

ELBOWINGS > ELBOWING

ELBOWROOM n sufficient scope to move or function

ELBOWS > ELBOW

ELCHEE n ambassador

ELCHEES > ELCHEE

ELCHI same as > ELCHEE

ELCHIS > ELCHI

ELD n old age

ELDER adj older ▷ n older person

ELDERCARE n care of elderly

ELDERLIES > ELDERLY

ELDERLY adj (fairly) old

ELDERS > ELDER

ELDERSHIP > ELDER

ELDEST adj, n oldest (child)

ELDESTS > ELDEST

ELDIN n fuel

ELDING same as > ELDIN

ELDINGS > ELDING

ELDINS > ELDIN

ELDORADO n place of great riches or fabulous opportunity

ELDORADOS > ELDORADO

ELDRESS n woman elder

ELDRESSES > ELDRESS

ELDRICH same as > ELDRITCH

ELDRITCH adj weird, uncanny

ELDS > ELD

ELECT vb choose by voting ▷ adj appointed but not yet in office

ELECTABLE > ELECT

ELECTED > ELECT

ELECTEE n someone who is elected

ELECTEES > ELECTEE

ELECTING > ELECT

ELECTION n choosing of representatives by voting

ELECTIONS > ELECTION

ELECTIVE adj chosen by election ▷ n optional course or hospital placement undertaken by a medical student

ELECTIVES > ELECTIVE

ELECTOR n someone who has the right to vote in an election

ELECTORAL adj of or relating to elections

ELECTORS > ELECTOR

ELECTRESS n female elector

ELECTRET n permanently polarized dielectric material

ELECTRETS > ELECTRET

ELECTRIC adj produced by, transmitting, or powered by electricity ▷ n electric train, car, etc

ELECTRICS > ELECTRIC

ELECTRIFY vb adapt for operation by electric power

ELECTRISE same as > ELECTRIZE

ELECTRIZE vb electrify

ELECTRO vb (in printing) make a metallic copy of a page

ELECTRODE n conductor through which an electric current enters or leaves a battery, vacuum tube, etc

ELECTROED > ELECTRO

ELECTRON n elementary particle in all atoms that has a negative electrical charge

ELECTRONS > ELECTRON

ELECTROS > ELECTRO

ELECTRUM n alloy of gold (55–88 per cent) and silver used for jewellery and ornaments

ELECTRUMS > ELECTRUM

ELECTS > ELECT

ELECTUARY n paste taken orally, containing a drug mixed with syrup or honey

ELEDOISIN n substance extracted from the salivary glands of a small octopus for medical applications

ELEGANCE n dignified grace in appearance, movement, or behaviour

ELEGANCES > ELEGANCE

ELEGANCY same as > ELEGANCE

ELEGANT adj pleasing or graceful in dress, style, or design

ELEGANTLY > ELEGANT

ELEGIAC adj mournful or plaintive ▷ n elegiac couplet or stanza

ELEGIACAL > ELEGIAC

ELEGIACS > ELEGIAC

ELEGIAST n writer of elegies

ELEGIASTS > ELEGIAST

ELEGIES > ELEGY

ELEGISE same as > ELEGIZE

ELEGISED > ELEGISE

ELEGISES > ELEGISE

ELEGISING > ELEGISE

ELEGIST > ELEGIZE

ELEGISTS > ELEGIZE

ELEGIT n writ delivering debtor's property to plaintiff

ELEGITS > ELEGIT

ELEGIZE vb compose an elegy or elegies (in memory of)

ELEGIZED > ELEGIZE

ELEGIZES > ELEGIZE

ELEGIZING > ELEGIZE

ELEGY n mournful poem, esp a lament for the dead

ELEMENT n component part

ELEMENTAL adj of primitive natural forces or passions ▷ n spirit or force that is said to appear in physical form

ELEMENTS > ELEMENT

ELEMI n fragrant resin obtained from various tropical trees

ELEMIS > ELEMI

ELENCH n refutation in logic

ELENCHI > ELENCHUS

ELENCHIC > ELENCHUS

ELENCHS > ELENCH

ELENCHTIC same as > ELENCTIC

ELENCHUS n refutation of an argument by proving the contrary of its conclusion, esp syllogistically

ELENCTIC adj refuting an argument by proving the falsehood of its conclusion

ELEOPTENE n liquid part of a volatile oil

ELEPHANT n huge four-footed thick-skinned animal with ivory tusks and a long trunk

ELEPHANTS adj in Australia, a slang word for drunk

ELEUTHERI pl n secret society

ELEVATE vb raise in rank or status

ELEVATED adj higher than normal ▷ n railway that runs on an elevated structure

ELEVATEDS > ELEVATED

ELEVATES > ELEVATE

ELEVATING > ELEVATE

ELEVATION n raising

ELEVATOR n lift for carrying people

ELEVATORS > ELEVATOR

ELEVATORY > ELEVATE

ELEVEN n one more than ten ▷ adj amounting to eleven ▷ determiner amounting to eleven

ELEVENS > ELEVEN

ELEVENSES n mid-morning snack

ELEVENTH n (of) number eleven in a series ▷ adj coming after the tenth in numbering or counting order, position, time, etc

ELEVENTHS > ELEVENTH
ELEVON n aircraft control surface usually fitted to tailless or delta-wing aircraft
ELEVONS > ELEVON
ELF n (In folklore) small mischievous fairy ▷ vb entangle (esp hair)
ELFED > ELF
ELFHOOD > ELF
ELFHOODS > ELF
ELFIN adj small and delicate ▷ n young elf
ELFING > ELF
ELFINS > ELFIN
ELFISH adj of, relating to, or like an elf or elves ▷ n supposed language of elves
ELFISHLY > ELFISH
ELFLAND another name for > FAIRYLAND
ELFLANDS > ELFLAND
ELFLIKE > ELF
ELFLOCK n lock of hair
ELFLOCKS > ELFLOCK
ELFS > ELF
ELHI adj informal word for or relating to elementary high school
ELIAD n glance
ELIADS > ELIAD
ELICHE n pasta in the form of spirals
ELICHES > ELICHE
ELICIT vb bring about (a response or reaction)
ELICITED > ELICIT
ELICITING > ELICIT
ELICITOR > ELICIT
ELICITORS > ELICIT
ELICITS > ELICIT
ELIDE vb omit (a vowel or syllable) from a spoken word
ELIDED > ELIDE
ELIDES > ELIDE
ELIDIBLE > ELIDE
ELIDING > ELIDE
ELIGIBLE adj meeting the requirements or qualifications needed ▷ n eligible person or thing
ELIGIBLES > ELIGIBLE
ELIGIBLY > ELIGIBLE
ELIMINANT > ELIMINATE
ELIMINATE vb get rid of
ELINT n electronic intelligence
ELINTS > ELINT
ELISION n omission of a syllable or vowel from a spoken word
ELISIONS > ELISION
ELITE n most powerful, rich, or gifted members of a group ▷ adj of, relating to, or suitable for an elite
ELITES > ELITE
ELITISM n belief that society should be ruled by a small group of superior people

ELITISMS > ELITISM
ELITIST > ELITISM
ELITISTS > ELITISM
ELIXIR n legendary liquid
ELIXIRS > ELIXIR
ELK n large deer of N Europe and Asia
ELKHORN n as in elkhorn fern fern with a large leaf like an elk's horn
ELKHOUND n powerful breed of dog of the spitz type with a thick grey coat and tightly curled tail
ELKHOUNDS > ELKHOUND
ELKS > ELK
ELL n obsolete unit of length
ELLAGIC adj of an acid derived from gallnuts
ELLIPSE n oval shape
ELLIPSES > ELLIPSIS
ELLIPSIS n omission of letters or words in a sentence
ELLIPSOID n surface whose plane sections are ellipses or circles
ELLIPTIC adj relating to or having the shape of an ellipse
ELLOPS same as > ELOPS
ELLOPSES > ELLOPS
ELLS > ELL
ELLWAND n stick for measuring lengths
ELLWANDS > ELLWAND
ELM n tree with serrated leaves
ELMEN adj of or relating to elm trees
ELMIER > ELMY
ELMIEST > ELMY
ELMS > ELM
ELMWOOD n wood from an elm tree
ELMWOODS > ELMWOOD
ELMY adj of or relating to elm trees
ELOCUTE vb speak as if practising elocution
ELOCUTED > ELOCUTE
ELOCUTES > ELOCUTE
ELOCUTING > ELOCUTE
ELOCUTION n art of speaking clearly in public
ELOCUTORY > ELOCUTION
ELODEA n type of American plant
ELODEAS > ELODEA
ELOGE same as > EULOGY
ELOGES > ELOGE
ELOGIES > ELOGY
ELOGIST > ELOGY
ELOGISTS > ELOGY
ELOGIUM same as > EULOGY
ELOGIUMS > ELOGIUM
ELOGY same as > EULOGY
ELOIGN vb remove (oneself, one's property, etc) to a distant place
ELOIGNED > ELOIGN

ELOIGNER > ELOIGN
ELOIGNERS > ELOIGN
ELOIGNING > ELOIGN
ELOIGNS > ELOIGN
ELOIN same as > ELOIGN
ELOINED > ELOIN
ELOINER > ELOIN
ELOINERS > ELOIGN
ELOINING > ELOIN
ELOINMENT > ELOIGN
ELOINS > ELOIN
ELONGATE vb make or become longer ▷ adj long and narrow
ELONGATED > ELONGATE
ELONGATES > ELONGATE
ELOPE vb (of two people) run away secretly to get married
ELOPED > ELOPE
ELOPEMENT > ELOPE
ELOPER > ELOPE
ELOPERS > ELOPE
ELOPES > ELOPE
ELOPING > ELOPE
ELOPS n type of fish
ELOPSES > ELOPS
ELOQUENCE n fluent powerful use of language
ELOQUENT adj (of speech or writing) fluent and persuasive
ELPEE n LP, long-playing record
ELPEES > ELPEE
ELS > EL
ELSE adv in addition or more
ELSEWHERE adv in or to another place
ELSEWISE adv otherwise
ELSHIN n cobbler's awl
ELSHINS > ELSHIN
ELSIN variant of > ELSHIN
ELSINS > ELSIN
ELT n young female pig
ELTCHI variant of > ELCHEE
ELTCHIS > ELTCHI
ELTS > ELT
ELUANT same as > ELUENT
ELUANTS > ELUANT
ELUATE n solution of adsorbed material obtained during the process of elution
ELUATES > ELUATE
ELUCIDATE vb make (something difficult) clear
ELUDE vb escape from by cleverness or quickness
ELUDED > ELUDE
ELUDER > ELUDE
ELUDERS > ELUDE
ELUDES > ELUDE
ELUDIBLE adj able to be eluded
ELUDING > ELUDE
ELUENT n solvent used for eluting
ELUENTS > ELUENT
ELUSION > ELUDE
ELUSIONS > ELUDE

ELUSIVE adj difficult to catch or remember
ELUSIVELY > ELUSIVE
ELUSORY adj avoiding the issue
ELUTE vb wash out (a substance) by the action of a solvent
ELUTED > ELUTE
ELUTES > ELUTE
ELUTING > ELUTE
ELUTION > ELUTE
ELUTIONS > ELUTE
ELUTOR > ELUTE
ELUTORS > ELUTE
ELUTRIATE vb purify or separate (a substance or mixture) by washing and straining or decanting
ELUVIA > ELUVIUM
ELUVIAL > ELUVIUM
ELUVIATE vb remove material suspended in water in a layer of soil by the action of rainfall
ELUVIATED > ELUVIATE
ELUVIATES > ELUVIATE
ELUVIUM n mass of sand, silt, etc
ELUVIUMS > ELUVIUM
ELVAN n type of rock
ELVANITE variant of > ELVAN
ELVANITES > ELVANITE
ELVANS > ELVAN
ELVEN adj like an elf
ELVER n young eel
ELVERS > ELVER
ELVES > ELF
ELVISH same as > ELFISH
ELVISHLY > ELVISH
ELYSIAN adj delightful, blissful
ELYTRA > ELYTRUM
ELYTRAL > ELYTRON
ELYTROID > ELYTRON
ELYTRON n either of the horny front wings of beetles and some other insects
ELYTROUS > ELYTRON
ELYTRUM same as > ELYTRON
EM n square of a body of any size of type, used as a unit of measurement
EMACIATE vb become or cause to become abnormally thin
EMACIATED adj abnormally thin
EMACIATES > EMACIATE
EMACS n powerful computer program
EMACSEN > EMACS
EMAIL n electronic mail ▷ vb send a message by electronic mail
EMAILED > EMAIL
EMAILER > EMAIL
EMAILERS > EMAILER
EMAILING > EMAIL
EMAILINGS > EMAILING

EMAILS > EMAIL

EMANANT > EMANATE

EMANATE vb issue, proceed from a source

EMANATED > EMANATE

EMANATES > EMANATE

EMANATING > EMANATE

EMANATION n act or instance of emanating

EMANATIST > EMANATE

EMANATIVE > EMANATE

EMANATOR > EMANATE

EMANATORS > EMANATE

EMANATORY > EMANATE

EMBACE variant of > EMBASE

EMBACES > EMBACE

EMBACING > EMBACE

EMBAIL vb enclose in a circle

EMBAILED > EMBAIL

EMBAILING > EMBAIL

EMBAILS > EMBAIL

EMBALE vb bind

EMBALED > EMBALE

EMBALES > EMBALE

EMBALING > EMBALE

EMBALL vb enclose in a circle

EMBALLED > EMBALL

EMBALLING > EMBALL

EMBALLS > EMBALL

EMBALM vb preserve (a corpse) from decay by the use of chemicals etc

EMBALMED > EMBALM

EMBALMER > EMBALM

EMBALMERS > EMBALM

EMBALMING > EMBALM

EMBALMS > EMBALM

EMBANK vb protect, enclose, or confine with an embankment

EMBANKED > EMBANK

EMBANKER > EMBANK

EMBANKERS > EMBANK

EMBANKING > EMBANK

EMBANKS > EMBANK

EMBAR vb close in with bars

EMBARGO n order by a government prohibiting trade with a country ▷ vb put an embargo on

EMBARGOED > EMBARGO

EMBARGOES > EMBARGO

EMBARK vb board a ship or aircraft

EMBARKED > EMBARK

EMBARKING > EMBARK

EMBARKS > EMBARK

EMBARRAS n embarrassment

EMBARRASS vb cause to feel self-conscious or ashamed

EMBARRED > EMBAR

EMBARRING > EMBAR

EMBARS > EMBAR

EMBASE vb degrade or debase

EMBASED > EMBASE

EMBASES > EMBASE

EMBASING > EMBASE

EMBASSADE n embassy

EMBASSAGE n work of an embassy

EMBASSIES > EMBASSY

EMBASSY n offices or official residence of an ambassador

EMBASTE > EMBASE

EMBATHE vb bathe with water

EMBATHED > EMBATHE

EMBATHES > EMBATHE

EMBATHING > EMBATHE

EMBATTLE vb deploy (troops) for battle

EMBATTLED adj having a lot of difficulties

EMBATTLES > EMBATTLE

EMBAY vb form into a bay

EMBAYED > EMBAY

EMBAYING > EMBAY

EMBAYLD > EMBAIL

EMBAYMENT n shape resembling a bay

EMBAYS > EMBAY

EMBED vb fix firmly in something solid ▷ n journalist accompanying an active military unit

EMBEDDED > EMBED

EMBEDDING n practice of assigning or being assigned a journalist to accompany an active military unit

EMBEDMENT > EMBED

EMBEDS > EMBED

EMBELLISH vb decorate

EMBER n glowing piece of wood or coal in a dying fire

EMBERS > EMBER

EMBEZZLE vb steal money that has been entrusted to one

EMBEZZLED > EMBEZZLE

EMBEZZLER > EMBEZZLE

EMBEZZLES > EMBEZZLE

EMBITTER vb make (a person) resentful or bitter

EMBITTERS > EMBITTER

EMBLAZE vb cause to light up

EMBLAZED > EMBLAZE

EMBLAZER > EMBLAZE

EMBLAZERS > EMBLAZE

EMBLAZES > EMBLAZE

EMBLAZING > EMBLAZE

EMBLAZON vb decorate with bright colours

EMBLAZONS > EMBLAZON

EMBLEM n object or design that symbolizes a quality, type, or group ▷ vb represent or signify

EMBLEMA n mosaic decoration

EMBLEMATA > EMBLEMA

EMBLEMED > EMBLEM

EMBLEMING > EMBLEM

EMBLEMISE same as > EMBLEMIZE

EMBLEMIZE vb function as an emblem of

EMBLEMS > EMBLEM

EMBLIC n type of Indian tree

EMBLICS > EMBLIC

EMBLOOM vb adorn with blooms

EMBLOOMED > EMBLOOM

EMBLOOMS > EMBLOOM

EMBLOSSOM vb adorn with blossom

EMBODIED > EMBODY

EMBODIER > EMBODY

EMBODIERS > EMBODY

EMBODIES > EMBODY

EMBODY vb be an example or expression of

EMBODYING > EMBODY

EMBOG vb sink down into a bog

EMBOGGED > EMBOG

EMBOGGING > EMBOG

EMBOGS > EMBOG

EMBOGUE vb go out through a narrow channel or passage

EMBOGUED > EMBOGUE

EMBOGUES > EMBOGUE

EMBOGUING > EMBOGUE

EMBOIL vb enrage or be enraged

EMBOILED > EMBOIL

EMBOILING > EMBOIL

EMBOILS > EMBOIL

EMBOLDEN vb encourage (someone)

EMBOLDENS > EMBOLDEN

EMBOLI > EMBOLUS

EMBOLIC adj of or relating to an embolus or embolism

EMBOLIES > EMBOLY

EMBOLISE same as > EMBOLIZE

EMBOLISED > EMBOLISE

EMBOLISES > EMBOLISE

EMBOLISM n blocking of a blood vessel by a blood clot or air bubble

EMBOLISMS > EMBOLISM

EMBOLIZE vb cause embolism in (a blood vessel)

EMBOLIZED > EMBOLIZE

EMBOLIZES > EMBOLIZE

EMBOLUS n material that blocks a blood vessel

EMBOLUSES > EMBOLUS

EMBOLY n infolding of an outer layer of cells so as to form a pocket in the surface

EMBORDER vb edge or border

EMBORDERS > EMBORDER

EMBOSCATA n sudden attack or raid

EMBOSK vb hide or cover

EMBOSKED > EMBOSK

EMBOSKING > EMBOSK

EMBOSKS > EMBOSK

EMBOSOM vb enclose or envelop, esp protectively

EMBOSOMED > EMBOSOM

EMBOSOMS > EMBOSOM

EMBOSS vb create a decoration that stands out on (a surface)

EMBOSSED adj (of a design or pattern) standing out from a surface

EMBOSSER > EMBOSS

EMBOSSERS > EMBOSS

EMBOSSES > EMBOSS

EMBOSSING > EMBOSS

EMBOST > EMBOSS

EMBOUND vb surround or encircle

EMBOUNDED > EMBOUND

EMBOUNDS > EMBOUND

EMBOW vb design or create (a structure) in the form of an arch or vault

EMBOWED > EMBOW

EMBOWEL vb bury or embed deeply

EMBOWELED > EMBOWEL

EMBOWELS > EMBOWEL

EMBOWER vb enclose in or as in a bower

EMBOWERED > EMBOWER

EMBOWERS > EMBOWER

EMBOWING > EMBOW

EMBOWMENT > EMBOW

EMBOWS > EMBOW

EMBOX vb put in a box

EMBOXED > EMBOX

EMBOXES > EMBOX

EMBOXING > EMBOX

EMBRACE vb clasp in the arms, hug ▷ n act of embracing

EMBRACED > EMBRACE

EMBRACEOR n person guilty of embracery

EMBRACER > EMBRACE

EMBRACERS > EMBRACE

EMBRACERY n offence of attempting by corrupt means to influence a jury or juror, as by bribery or threats

EMBRACES > EMBRACE

EMBRACING > EMBRACE

EMBRACIVE > EMBRACE

EMBRAID vb braid or interweave

EMBRAIDED > EMBRAID

EMBRAIDS > EMBRAID

EMBRANGLE vb confuse or entangle

EMBRASOR n one who embraces

EMBRASORS > EMBRASOR

EMBRASURE n door or window having splayed sides so that the opening is larger on the inside

EMBRAVE vb adorn or decorate

EMBRAVED > EMBRAVE

EMBRAVES > EMBRAVE

EMBRAVING > EMBRAVE

EMBRAZURE *variant of* > EMBRASURE

EMBREAD *vb* braid

EMBREADED > EMBREAD

EMBREADS > EMBREAD

EMBREATHE *vb* breathe in air

EMBRITTLE *vb* become brittle

EMBROCATE *vb* apply a liniment or lotion to (a part of the body)

EMBROGLIO *same as* > IMBROGLIO

EMBROIDER *vb* decorate with needlework

EMBROIL *vb* involve (a person) in problems

EMBROILED > EMBROIL

EMBROILER > EMBROIL

EMBROILS > EMBROIL

EMBROWN *vb* make or become brown

EMBROWNED > EMBROWN

EMBROWNS > EMBROWN

EMBRUE *variant spelling of* > IMBRUE

EMBRUED > EMBRUE

EMBRUES > EMBRUE

EMBRUING > EMBRUE

EMBRUTE *variant of* > IMBRUTE

EMBRUTED > EMBRUTE

EMBRUTES > EMBRUTE

EMBRUTING > EMBRUTE

EMBRYO *n* unborn creature in the early stages of development

EMBRYOID > EMBRYO

EMBRYOIDS > EMBRYO

EMBRYON *variant of* > EMBRYO

EMBRYONAL *same as* > EMBRYONIC

EMBRYONIC *adj* at an early stage

EMBRYONS > EMBRYO

EMBRYOS > EMBRYO

EMBRYOTIC *variant of* > EMBRYONIC

EMBUS *vb* cause (troops) to board a transport vehicle

EMBUSED > EMBUS

EMBUSES > EMBUS

EMBUSIED > EMBUSY

EMBUSIES > EMBUSY

EMBUSING > EMBUS

EMBUSQUE *n* man who avoids military conscription by obtaining a government job

EMBUSQUES > EMBUSQUE

EMBUSSED > EMBUS

EMBUSSES > EMBUS

EMBUSSING > EMBUS

EMBUSY *vb* keep occupied

EMBUSYING > EMBUSY

EMCEE *n* master of ceremonies ▷ *vb* act as master of ceremonies (for or at)

EMCEED > EMCEE

EMCEEING > EMCEE

EMCEES > EMCEE

EMDASH *n* long dash in punctuation

EMDASHES > EMDASH

EME *n* uncle

EMEER *variant of* > EMIR

EMEERATE *variant of* > EMIRATE

EMEERATES > EMEERATE

EMEERS > EMEER

EMEND *vb* remove errors from

EMENDABLE > EMEND

EMENDALS *pl n* funds put aside for repairs

EMENDATE *vb* make corrections

EMENDATED > EMENDATE

EMENDATES > EMENDATE

EMENDATOR *n* one who emends a text

EMENDED > EMEND

EMENDER > EMEND

EMENDERS > EMEND

EMENDING > EMEND

EMENDS > EMEND

EMERALD *n* bright green precious stone ▷ *adj* bright green

EMERALDS > EMERALD

EMERAUDE *archaic variant of* > EMERALD

EMERAUDES > EMERAUDE

EMERG *n* part of a hospital dealing with emergencies

EMERGE *vb* come into view

EMERGED > EMERGE

EMERGENCE *n* act or process of emerging

EMERGENCY *n* sudden unforeseen occurrence needing immediate action

EMERGENT *adj* coming into being or notice ▷ *n* aquatic plant with stem and leaves above the water

EMERGENTS > EMERGENT

EMERGES > EMERGE

EMERGING > EMERGE

EMERGS > EMERG

EMERIED > EMERY

EMERIES > EMERY

EMERITA *adj* retired, but retaining an honorary title ▷ *n* woman who is retired, but retains an honorary title

EMERITAE > EMERITA

EMERITAS > EMERITA

EMERITI > EMERITUS

EMERITUS *adj* retired, but retaining an honorary title ▷ *n* man who is retired, but retains an honorary title

EMEROD *n* haemorrhoid

EMERODS > EMEROD

EMEROID *variant of* > EMEROD

EMEROIDS > EMEROID

EMERSE *same as* > EMERSED

EMERSED *adj* protruding above the surface of the water

EMERSION *n* act or an instance of emerging

EMERSIONS > EMERSION

EMERY *n* hard mineral used for smoothing and polishing ▷ *vb* apply emery to

EMERYING > EMERY

EMES > EME

EMESES > EMESIS

EMESIS *technical name for* > VOMITING

EMESISES > EMESIS

EMETIC *n* substance that causes vomiting ▷ *adj* causing vomiting

EMETICAL *same as* > EMETIC

EMETICS > EMETIC

EMETIN *same as* > EMETINE

EMETINE *n* white bitter poisonous alkaloid

EMETINES > EMETINE

EMETINS > EMETIN

EMEU *variant of* > EMU

EMEUS > EMEU

EMEUTE *n* uprising or rebellion

EMEUTES > EMEUTE

EMIC *adj* of or relating to a significant linguistic unit ▷ *n* emic viewpoint or approach

EMICANT > EMICATE

EMICATE *vb* twinkle

EMICATED > EMICATE

EMICATES > EMICATE

EMICATING > EMICATE

EMICATION > EMICATE

EMICS > EMIC

EMICTION *n* passing of urine

EMICTIONS > EMICTION

EMICTORY > EMICTION

EMIGRANT *n* person who leaves one place or country, esp a native country, to settle in another

EMIGRANTS > EMIGRANT

EMIGRATE *vb* go and settle in another country

EMIGRATED > EMIGRATE

EMIGRATES > EMIGRATE

EMIGRE *n* someone who has left his native country for political reasons

EMIGRES > EMIGRE

EMINENCE *n* position of superiority or fame

EMINENCES > EMINENCE

EMINENCY *same as* > EMINENCE

EMINENT *adj* distinguished, well-known

EMINENTLY > EMINENT

EMIR *n* Muslim ruler

EMIRATE *n* emir's country

EMIRATES > EMIRATE

EMIRS > EMIR

EMISSARY *n* agent sent on a mission by a government ▷ *adj* (of veins) draining blood from sinuses in the dura mater to veins outside the skull

EMISSILE *adj* able to be emitted

EMISSION *n* act of giving out heat, light, a smell, etc

EMISSIONS > EMISSION

EMISSIVE > EMISSION

EMIT *vb* give out

EMITS > EMIT

EMITTANCE > EMIT

EMITTED > EMIT

EMITTER *n* person or thing that emits

EMITTERS > EMITTER

EMITTING > EMIT

EMLETS *pl n* as in blood-drop emlets Chilean plant

EMMA *n* former communications code for the letter A

EMMARBLE *vb* decorate with marble

EMMARBLED > EMMARBLE

EMMARBLES > EMMARBLE

EMMAS > EMMA

EMMER *n* variety of wheat

EMMERS > EMMER

EMMESH *variant of* > ENMESH

EMMESHED > EMMESH

EMMESHES > EMMESH

EMMESHING > EMMESH

EMMET *n* tourist or holiday-maker

EMMETROPE *n* person whose vision is normal

EMMETS > EMMET

EMMEW *vb* restrict

EMMEWED > EMMEW

EMMEWING > EMMEW

EMMEWS > EMMEW

EMMOVE *vb* cause emotion in

EMMOVED > EMMOVE

EMMOVES > EMMOVE

EMMOVING > EMMOVE

EMMY *n* award for outstanding television performances and productions

EMMYS > EMMY

EMO *n* type of music

EMOCORE *n* punk rock with lyrics that deal with emotional subjects

EMOCORES > EMOCORE

EMODIN *n* type of chemical compound

EMODINS > EMODIN

EMOJI *n* digital icon used in electronic communication

EMOJIS > EMOJI

EMOLLIATE *vb* make soft or smooth

EMOLLIENT *adj* softening, soothing

▷ *n* substance which softens or soothes the skin

EMOLUMENT *n* fees or wages from employment

EMONG variant of > AMONG

EMONGES variant of > AMONG

EMONGEST variant of > AMONGST

EMONGST variant of > AMONGST

EMOS > EMO

EMOTE *vb* display exaggerated emotion, as if acting

EMOTED > EMOTE

EMOTER > EMOTE

EMOTERS > EMOTE

EMOTES > EMOTE

EMOTICON *n* any of several combinations of symbols used in electronic mail and text messaging to indicate the state of mind of the writer, such as :-) to express happiness

EMOTICONS > EMOTICON

EMOTING > EMOTE

EMOTION *n* strong feeling

EMOTIONAL *adj* readily affected by or appealing to the emotions

EMOTIONS > EMOTION

EMOTIVE *adj* tending to arouse emotion

EMOTIVELY > EMOTIVE

EMOTIVISM *n* theory that moral utterances do not have a truth value but express the feelings of the speaker, so that *murder is wrong* is equivalent to *down with murder*

EMOTIVITY > EMOTIVE

EMOVE *vb* cause to feel emotion

EMOVED > EMOVE

EMOVES > EMOVE

EMOVING > EMOVE

EMPACKET *vb* wrap up

EMPACKETS > EMPACKET

EMPAESTIC *adj* embossed

EMPAIRE variant of > IMPAIR

EMPAIRED > EMPAIRE

EMPAIRES > EMPAIRE

EMPAIRING > EMPAIRE

EMPALE less common spelling of > IMPALE

EMPALED > EMPALE

EMPALER > EMPALE

EMPALERS > EMPALE

EMPALES > EMPALE

EMPALING > EMPALE

EMPANADA *n* Spanish meat-filled pastry

EMPANADAS > EMPANADA

EMPANEL *vb* enter on a list (names of persons to be summoned for jury service)

EMPANELED > EMPANEL

EMPANELS > EMPANEL

EMPANOPLY *vb* put armour on

EMPARE variant of > IMPAIR

EMPARED > EMPARE

EMPARES > EMPARE

EMPARING > EMPARE

EMPARL variant of > IMPARL

EMPARLED > EMPARL

EMPARLING > EMPARL

EMPARLS > EMPARL

EMPART variant of > IMPART

EMPARTED > EMPART

EMPARTING > EMPART

EMPARTS > EMPART

EMPATHIC *adj* of or relating to empathy

EMPATHIES > EMPATHY

EMPATHISE same as > EMPATHIZE

EMPATHIST > EMPATHY

EMPATHIZE *vb* sense and understand someone else's feelings as if they were one's own

EMPATHY *n* ability to understand someone else's feelings

EMPATRON *vb* treat in the manner of a patron

EMPATRONS > EMPATRON

EMPAYRE variant of > IMPAIR

EMPAYRED > EMPAYRE

EMPAYRES > EMPAYRE

EMPAYRING > EMPAYRE

EMPEACH variant of > IMPEACH

EMPEACHED > EMPEACH

EMPEACHES > EMPEACH

EMPENNAGE *n* rear part of an aircraft, comprising the fin, rudder, and tailplane

EMPEOPLE *vb* bring people into

EMPEOPLED > EMPEOPLE

EMPEOPLES > EMPEOPLE

EMPERCE variant of > EMPIERCE

EMPERCED > EMPERCE

EMPERCES > EMPERCE

EMPERCING > EMPERCE

EMPERIES > EMPERY

EMPERISE variant of > EMPERIZE

EMPERISED > EMPERISE

EMPERISES > EMPERISE

EMPERISH *vb* damage or harm

EMPERIZE *vb* act like an emperor

EMPERIZED > EMPERIZE

EMPERIZES > EMPERIZE

EMPEROR *n* ruler of an empire

EMPERORS > EMPEROR

EMPERY *n* dominion or power

EMPHASES > EMPHASIS

EMPHASIS *n* special importance or significance

EMPHASISE same as > EMPHASIZE

EMPHASIZE *vb* give emphasis or prominence to

EMPHATIC *adj* showing emphasis ▷ *n* emphatic consonant, as used in Arabic

EMPHATICS > EMPHATIC

EMPHLYSES > EMPHLYSIS

EMPHLYSIS *n* outbreak of blisters on the body

EMPHYSEMA *n* condition in which the air sacs of the lungs are grossly enlarged, causing breathlessness

EMPIERCE *vb* pierce or cut

EMPIERCED > EMPIERCE

EMPIERCES > EMPIERCE

EMPIGHT *adj* attached or positioned ▷ *vb* attach or position

EMPIGHTED > EMPIGHT

EMPIGHTS > EMPIGHT

EMPIRE *n* group of territories under the rule of one state or person

EMPIRES > EMPIRE

EMPIRIC *n* person who relies on empirical methods

EMPIRICAL *adj* relying on experiment or experience, not on theory ▷ *n* posterior probability of an event derived on the basis of its observed frequency in a sample

EMPIRICS > EMPIRIC

EMPLACE *vb* put in place or position

EMPLACED > EMPLACE

EMPLACES > EMPLACE

EMPLACING > EMPLACE

EMPLANE *vb* board or put on board an aeroplane

EMPLANED > EMPLANE

EMPLANES > EMPLANE

EMPLANING > EMPLANE

EMPLASTER *vb* cover with plaster

EMPLASTIC *adj* sticky

EMPLEACH variant of > IMPLEACH

EMPLECTON *n* type of masonry filled with rubbish

EMPLECTUM variant of > EMPLECTON

EMPLONGE variant of > IMPLUNGE

EMPLONGED > EMPLONGE

EMPLONGES > EMPLONGE

EMPLOY *vb* engage or make use of the services of (a person) in return for money ▷ *n* state of being employed

EMPLOYE same as > EMPLOYEE

EMPLOYED > EMPLOY

EMPLOYEE *n* person who is hired to work for someone in return for payment

EMPLOYEES > EMPLOYEE

EMPLOYER *n* person or organization that employs someone

EMPLOYERS > EMPLOYER

EMPLOYES > EMPLOYE

EMPLOYING > EMPLOY

EMPLOYS > EMPLOY

EMPLUME *vb* put a plume on

EMPLUMED > EMPLUME

EMPLUMES > EMPLUME

EMPLUMING > EMPLUME

EMPOISON *vb* embitter or corrupt

EMPOISONS > EMPOISON

EMPOLDER variant spelling of > IMPOLDER

EMPOLDERS > EMPOLDER

EMPORIA > EMPORIUM

EMPORIUM *n* large general shop

EMPORIUMS > EMPORIUM

EMPOWER *vb* enable, authorize

EMPOWERED > EMPOWER

EMPOWERS > EMPOWER

EMPRESS *n* woman who rules an empire

EMPRESSE *adj* keen; zealous

EMPRESSES > EMPRESS

EMPRISE *n* chivalrous or daring enterprise

EMPRISES > EMPRISE

EMPRIZE variant of > EMPRISE

EMPRIZES > EMPRIZE

EMPT *vb* empty

EMPTED > EMPT

EMPTIABLE > EMPTY

EMPTIED > EMPTY

EMPTIER > EMPTY

EMPTIERS > EMPTY

EMPTIES > EMPTY

EMPTIEST > EMPTY

EMPTILY > EMPTY

EMPTINESS > EMPTY

EMPTING > EMPT

EMPTINGS variant of > EMPTINS

EMPTINS *pl n* liquid leavening agent made from potatoes

EMPTION *n* process of buying something

EMPTIONAL > EMPTION

EMPTIONS > EMPTION

EMPTS > EMPT

EMPTY *adj* containing nothing ▷ *vb* make or become empty ▷ *n* empty container, esp a bottle

EMPTYING > EMPTY

EMPTYINGS > EMPTY

EMPTYSES > EMPTYSIS

EMPTYSIS *n* act of spitting up blood**

EMPURPLE vb make or become purple
EMPURPLED > EMPURPLE
EMPURPLES > EMPURPLE
EMPUSA n goblin in Greek mythology
EMPUSAS > EMPUSA
EMPUSE variant of > EMPUSA
EMPUSES > EMPUSE
EMPYEMA n collection of pus in a body cavity
EMPYEMAS > EMPYEMA
EMPYEMATA > EMPYEMA
EMPYEMIC > EMPYEMA
EMPYESES > EMPYESIS
EMPYESIS n pus-filled boil on the skin
EMPYREAL variant of > EMPYREAN
EMPYREAN n heavens or sky ▷ adj of or relating to the sky or the heavens
EMPYREANS > EMPYREAN
EMPYREUMA n smell and taste associated with burning vegetable and animal matter
EMS > EM
EMU n large Australian flightless bird with long legs
EMULATE vb attempt to equal or surpass by imitating
EMULATED > EMULATE
EMULATES > EMULATE
EMULATING > EMULATE
EMULATION n act of emulating or imitating
EMULATIVE > EMULATE
EMULATOR > EMULATE
EMULATORS > EMULATE
EMULE variant of > EMULATE
EMULED > EMULE
EMULES > EMULE
EMULGE vb remove liquid from
EMULGED > EMULGE
EMULGENCE > EMULGE
EMULGENT > EMULGE
EMULGES > EMULGE
EMULGING > EMULGE
EMULING > EMULE
EMULOUS adj desiring or aiming to equal or surpass another
EMULOUSLY > EMULOUS
EMULSIBLE > EMULSIFY
EMULSIFY vb (of two liquids) join together
EMULSIN n enzyme that is found in almonds
EMULSINS > EMULSIN
EMULSION n light-sensitive coating on photographic film ▷ vb paint with emulsion paint
EMULSIONS > EMULSION
EMULSIVE > EMULSION
EMULSOID n sol with a liquid disperse phase

EMULSOIDS > EMULSOID
EMULSOR n device that emulsifies
EMULSORS > EMULSOR
EMUNCTION > EMUNCTORY
EMUNCTORY adj of or relating to a bodily organ or duct having an excretory function ▷ n excretory organ or duct, such as a skin pore
EMUNGE vb clean or clear out
EMUNGED > EMUNGE
EMUNGES > EMUNGE
EMUNGING > EMUNGE
EMURE variant of > IMMURE
EMURED > EMURE
EMURES > EMURE
EMURING > EMURE
EMUS > EMU
EMYD n freshwater tortoise or terrapin
EMYDE same as > EMYD
EMYDES > EMYDE
EMYDS > EMYD
EMYS n freshwater tortoise or terrapin
EN n unit of measurement, half the width of an em
ENABLE vb provide (a person) with the means (to do something)
ENABLED > ENABLE
ENABLER > ENABLE
ENABLERS > ENABLE
ENABLES > ENABLE
ENABLING > ENABLE
ENACT vb establish by law
ENACTABLE > ENACT
ENACTED > ENACT
ENACTING > ENACT
ENACTION > ENACT
ENACTIONS > ENACT
ENACTIVE > ENACT
ENACTMENT > ENACT
ENACTOR > ENACT
ENACTORS > ENACT
ENACTORY > ENACT
ENACTS > ENACT
ENACTURE > ENACT
ENACTURES > ENACT
ENALAPRIL n ACE inhibitor used to treat high blood pressure and congestive heart failure
ENALLAGE n act of using one grammatical form in the place of another
ENALLAGES > ENALLAGE
ENAMEL n glasslike coating applied to metal etc to preserve the surface ▷ vb cover with enamel
ENAMELED > ENAMEL
ENAMELER > ENAMEL
ENAMELERS > ENAMEL
ENAMELING > ENAMEL
ENAMELIST > ENAMEL
ENAMELLED > ENAMEL
ENAMELLER > ENAMEL
ENAMELS > ENAMEL

ENAMINE n type of unsaturated compound
ENAMINES > ENAMINE
ENAMOR same as > ENAMOUR
ENAMORADO n beloved one, lover
ENAMORED same as > ENAMOURED
ENAMORING > ENAMOR
ENAMORS > ENAMOR
ENAMOUR vb inspire with love
ENAMOURED adj inspired with love
ENAMOURS > ENAMOUR
ENANTHEMA n ulcer on a mucous membrane
ENARCH variant of > INARCH
ENARCHED > ENARCH
ENARCHES > ENARCH
ENARCHING > ENARCH
ENARGITE n sulphide of copper and arsenic
ENARGITES > ENARGITE
ENARM vb provide with arms
ENARMED > ENARM
ENARMING > ENARM
ENARMS > ENARM
ENATE adj growing out or outwards ▷ n relative on the mother's side
ENATES > ENATE
ENATIC adj related on one's mother's side
ENATION > ENATE
ENATIONS > ENATE
ENAUNTER conj in case that
ENCAENIA n festival of dedication or commemoration
ENCAENIAS > ENCAENIA
ENCAGE vb confine in or as in a cage
ENCAGED > ENCAGE
ENCAGES > ENCAGE
ENCAGING > ENCAGE
ENCALM vb becalm, settle
ENCALMED > ENCALM
ENCALMING > ENCALM
ENCALMS > ENCALM
ENCAMP vb set up in a camp
ENCAMPED > ENCAMP
ENCAMPING > ENCAMP
ENCAMPS > ENCAMP
ENCANTHIS n tumour of the eye
ENCAPSULE vb enclose or be enclosed in or as if in a capsule
ENCARPUS n decoration of fruit or flowers in a frieze
ENCASE vb enclose or cover completely
ENCASED > ENCASE
ENCASES > ENCASE
ENCASH vb exchange (a cheque) for cash

ENCASHED > ENCASH
ENCASHES > ENCASH
ENCASHING > ENCASH
ENCASING > ENCASE
ENCASTRE adj (of a beam) fixed at the ends
ENCAUSTIC adj decorated by any process involving burning in colours, esp by inlaying coloured clays and baking or by fusing wax colours to the surface ▷ n process of burning in colours
ENCAVE variant of > INCAVE
ENCAVED > ENCAVE
ENCAVES > ENCAVE
ENCAVING > ENCAVE
ENCEINTE n boundary wall enclosing a defended area
ENCEINTES > ENCEINTE
ENCEPHALA n brains
ENCHAFE vb heat up
ENCHAFED > ENCHAFE
ENCHAFES > ENCHAFE
ENCHAFING > ENCHAFE
ENCHAIN vb bind with chains
ENCHAINED > ENCHAIN
ENCHAINS > ENCHAIN
ENCHANT vb delight and fascinate
ENCHANTED > ENCHANT
ENCHANTER > ENCHANT
ENCHANTS > ENCHANT
ENCHARGE vb give into the custody of
ENCHARGED > ENCHARGE
ENCHARGES > ENCHARGE
ENCHARM vb enchant
ENCHARMED > ENCHARM
ENCHARMS > ENCHARM
ENCHASE less common word for > CHASE
ENCHASED > ENCHASE
ENCHASER > ENCHASE
ENCHASERS > ENCHASE
ENCHASES > ENCHASE
ENCHASING > ENCHASE
ENCHEASON n reason
ENCHEER vb cheer up
ENCHEERED > ENCHEER
ENCHEERS > ENCHEER
ENCHILADA n Mexican dish of a tortilla filled with meat, served with chilli sauce
ENCHORIAL adj of or used in a particular country: used esp of the popular (demotic) writing of the ancient Egyptians
ENCHORIC same as > ENCHORIAL
ENCIERRO n Spanish bull run
ENCIERROS > ENCIERRO
ENCINA n type of oak
ENCINAL > ENCINA
ENCINAS > ENCINA

ENCIPHER vb convert (a message, document, etc) from plain text into code or cipher
ENCIPHERS > ENCIPHER
ENCIRCLE vb form a circle around
ENCIRCLED > ENCIRCLE
ENCIRCLES > ENCIRCLE
ENCLASP vb clasp
ENCLASPED > ENCLASP
ENCLASPS > ENCLASP
ENCLAVE n part of a country entirely surrounded by another ▷ vb hold in an enclave
ENCLAVED > ENCLAVE
ENCLAVES > ENCLAVE
ENCLAVING > ENCLAVE
ENCLISES > ENCLISIS
ENCLISIS n state of being enclitic
ENCLITIC adj denoting or relating to a monosyllabic word or form that is treated as a suffix of the preceding word ▷ n enclitic word or linguistic form
ENCLITICS > ENCLITIC
ENCLOSE vb surround completely
ENCLOSED > ENCLOSE
ENCLOSER > ENCLOSE
ENCLOSERS > ENCLOSE
ENCLOSES > ENCLOSE
ENCLOSING > ENCLOSE
ENCLOSURE n area of land enclosed by a fence, wall, or hedge
ENCLOTHE vb clothe
ENCLOTHED > ENCLOTHE
ENCLOTHES > ENCLOTHE
ENCLOUD vb hide with clouds
ENCLOUDED > ENCLOUD
ENCLOUDS > ENCLOUD
ENCODABLE > ENCODE
ENCODE vb convert (a message) into code
ENCODED > ENCODE
ENCODER > ENCODE
ENCODERS > ENCODE
ENCODES > ENCODE
ENCODING n act of encoding
ENCODINGS > ENCODING
ENCOLOUR vb give a colour to
ENCOLOURS > ENCOLOUR
ENCOLPION n religious symbol worn on the breast
ENCOLPIUM variant of > ENCOLPION
ENCOLURE n mane of a horse
ENCOLURES > ENCOLURE
ENCOMIA > ENCOMIUM
ENCOMIAST n person who speaks or writes an encomium
ENCOMION variant of > ENCOMIUM

ENCOMIUM n formal expression of praise
ENCOMIUMS > ENCOMIUM
ENCOMPASS vb surround
ENCORE interj again, once more ▷ n extra performance due to enthusiastic demand ▷ vb demand an extra or repeated performance
ENCORED > ENCORE
ENCORES > ENCORE
ENCORING > ENCORE
ENCOUNTER vb meet unexpectedly ▷ n unexpected meeting
ENCOURAGE vb inspire with confidence
ENCRADLE vb put in a cradle
ENCRADLED > ENCRADLE
ENCRADLES > ENCRADLE
ENCRATIES > ENCRATY
ENCRATY n control of one's desires, actions, etc
ENCREASE variant form of > INCREASE
ENCREASED > ENCREASE
ENCREASES > ENCREASE
ENCRIMSON vb make crimson
ENCRINAL > ENCRINITE
ENCRINIC > ENCRINITE
ENCRINITE n sedimentary rock formed almost exclusively from the skeletal plates of crinoids
ENCROACH vb intrude gradually on a person's rights or land
ENCRUST vb cover with a layer of something
ENCRUSTED > ENCRUST
ENCRUSTS > ENCRUST
ENCRYPT vb put (a message) into code
ENCRYPTED > ENCRYPT
ENCRYPTS > ENCRYPT
ENCUMBER vb hinder or impede
ENCUMBERS > ENCUMBER
ENCURTAIN vb cover or surround with curtains
ENCYCLIC n letter sent by the Pope to all bishops
ENCYCLICS > ENCYCLIC
ENCYST vb enclose or become enclosed by a cyst, thick membrane, or shell
ENCYSTED > ENCYST
ENCYSTING > ENCYST
ENCYSTS > ENCYST
END n furthest point or part ▷ vb bring or come to a finish
ENDAMAGE vb cause injury to
ENDAMAGED > ENDAMAGE
ENDAMAGES > ENDAMAGE
ENDAMEBA same as > ENDAMOEBA
ENDAMEBAE > ENDAMEBA
ENDAMEBAS > ENDAMEBA

ENDAMEBIC > ENDAMEBA
ENDAMOEBA same as > ENTAMOEBA
ENDANGER vb put in danger
ENDANGERS > ENDANGER
ENDARCH adj having the first-formed xylem internal to that formed later
ENDARCHY n state of being endarch
ENDART variant of > INDART
ENDARTED > ENDART
ENDARTING > ENDART
ENDARTS > ENDART
ENDASH n short dash in punctuation
ENDASHES > ENDASH
ENDBRAIN n part of the brain
ENDBRAINS > ENDBRAIN
ENDCAP n display placed at the end of a shop aisle
ENDCAPS > ENDCAP
ENDEAR vb cause to be liked
ENDEARED > ENDEAR
ENDEARING adj giving rise to love or esteem
ENDEARS > ENDEAR
ENDEAVOR same as > ENDEAVOUR
ENDEAVORS > ENDEAVOR
ENDEAVOUR vb try ▷ n effort
ENDECAGON n figure with eleven sides
ENDED > END
ENDEICTIC > ENDEIXIS
ENDEIXES > ENDEIXIS
ENDEIXIS n sign or mark
ENDEMIAL same as > ENDEMIC
ENDEMIC adj present within a particular area or group of people ▷ n endemic disease or plant
ENDEMICAL adj endemic
ENDEMICS > ENDEMIC
ENDEMISM > ENDEMIC
ENDEMISMS > ENDEMIC
ENDENIZEN vb make a denizen
ENDER > END
ENDERMIC adj (of a medicine) acting by absorption through the skin
ENDERON variant of > ANDIRON
ENDERONS > ENDERON
ENDERS > END
ENDEW variant of > ENDUE
ENDEWED > ENDEW
ENDEWING > ENDEW
ENDEWS > ENDEW
ENDEXINE n inner layer of an exine
ENDEXINES > ENDEXINE
ENDGAME n closing stage of a game of chess

ENDGAMES > ENDGAME
ENDGATE n tailboard of a vehicle
ENDGATES > ENDGATE
ENDING n last part or conclusion of something
ENDINGS > ENDING
ENDIRON variant of > ANDIRON
ENDIRONS > ENDIRON
ENDITE variant of > INDICT
ENDITED > ENDITE
ENDITES > ENDITE
ENDITING > ENDITE
ENDIVE n curly-leaved plant used in salads
ENDIVES > ENDIVE
ENDLANG variant of > ENDLONG
ENDLEAF n endpaper in a book
ENDLEAFS > ENDLEAF
ENDLEAVES > ENDLEAF
ENDLESS adj having no end
ENDLESSLY > ENDLESS
ENDLONG adv lengthways or on end
ENDMOST adj nearest the end
ENDNOTE n note at the end of a section of writing
ENDNOTES > ENDNOTE
ENDOBLAST less common name for > ENDODERM
ENDOCARP n inner, usually woody, layer of the pericarp of a fruit, such as the stone of a peach or cherry
ENDOCARPS > ENDOCARP
ENDOCAST n cast made of the inside of a cranial cavity to show the size and shape of a brain
ENDOCASTS > ENDOCAST
ENDOCRINE adj relating to the glands which secrete hormones directly into the bloodstream ▷ n endocrine gland
ENDOCYTIC adj involving absorption of cells
ENDODERM n inner germ layer of an animal embryo, which gives rise to the lining of the digestive and respiratory tracts
ENDODERMS > ENDODERM
ENDODYNE same as > AUTODYNE
ENDOERGIC adj (of a nuclear reaction) occurring with absorption of energy
ENDOGAMIC > ENDOGAMY
ENDOGAMY n marriage within one's own tribe or similar unit
ENDOGEN n plant that increases in size by internal growth

ENDOGENIC *adj* formed or occurring inside the earth

ENDOGENS > ENDOGEN

ENDOGENY *n* development by internal growth

ENDOLYMPH *n* fluid that fills the membranous labyrinth of the internal ear

ENDOMIXES > ENDOMIXIS

ENDOMIXIS *n* reorganization of certain nuclei with some protozoa

ENDOMORPH *n* person with a fat and heavy body build: said to be correlated with viscerotonia

ENDOPHAGY *n* cannibalism within the same group or tribe

ENDOPHYTE *n* fungus, or occasionally an alga or other organism, that lives within a plant

ENDOPLASM *n* inner cytoplasm in some cells, esp protozoa, which is more granular and fluid than the outer cytoplasm

ENDOPOD *n* inner branch of a two-branched crustacean

ENDOPODS > ENDOPOD

ENDOPROCT *n* small animal living in water

ENDORPHIN *n* chemical occurring in the brain, which has a similar effect to morphine

ENDORSE *vb* give approval to

ENDORSED > ENDORSE

ENDORSEE *n* person in whose favour a negotiable instrument is endorsed

ENDORSEES > ENDORSEE

ENDORSER > ENDORSE

ENDORSERS > ENDORSE

ENDORSES > ENDORSE

ENDORSING > ENDORSE

ENDORSIVE > ENDORSE

ENDORSOR > ENDORSE

ENDORSORS > ENDORSE

ENDOSARC *same as* > ENDOPLASM

ENDOSARCS > ENDOSARC

ENDOSCOPE *n* long slender medical instrument used for examining the interior of hollow organs including the lung, stomach, bladder and bowel

ENDOSCOPY > ENDOSCOPE

ENDOSMOS *same as* > ENDOSMOSE

ENDOSMOSE *n* osmosis in which water enters a cell or organism from the surrounding solution

ENDOSOME *n* sac within a biological cell

ENDOSOMES > ENDOSOME

ENDOSPERM *n* tissue within the seed of a flowering plant that surrounds and nourishes the developing embryo

ENDOSPORE *n* small asexual spore produced by some bacteria and algae

ENDOSS *vb* endorse

ENDOSSED > ENDOSS

ENDOSSES > ENDOSS

ENDOSSING > ENDOSS

ENDOSTEA > ENDOSTEUM

ENDOSTEAL > ENDOSTEUM

ENDOSTEUM *n* highly vascular membrane lining the marrow cavity of long bones, such as the femur and humerus

ENDOSTYLE *n* groove or fold in the pharynx of various chordates

ENDOTHERM *n* animal with warm blood

ENDOTOXIC > ENDOTOXIN

ENDOTOXIN *n* toxin contained within the protoplasm of an organism, esp a bacterium, and liberated only at death

ENDOW *vb* provide permanent income for

ENDOWED > ENDOW

ENDOWER > ENDOW

ENDOWERS > ENDOW

ENDOWING > ENDOW

ENDOWMENT *n* money given to an institution, such as a hospital

ENDOWS > ENDOW

ENDOZOA > ENDOZOON

ENDOZOIC *adj* (of a plant) living within an animal

ENDOZOON *variant of* > ENTOZOON

ENDPAPER *n* either of two leaves at the front and back of a book pasted to the inside of the cover

ENDPAPERS > ENDPAPER

ENDPLATE *n* any usually flat platelike structure at the end of something

ENDPLATES > ENDPLATE

ENDPLAY *n* technique in card games ▷ *vb* force (an opponent) to make a particular lead near the end of a hand

ENDPLAYED > ENDPLAY

ENDPLAYS > ENDPLAY

ENDPOINT *n* point at which anything is complete

ENDPOINTS > ENDPOINT

ENDRIN *n* type of insecticide

ENDRINS > ENDRIN

ENDS > END

ENDSHIP *n* small village

ENDSHIPS > ENDSHIP

ENDUE *vb* invest or provide, as with some quality or trait

ENDUED > ENDUE

ENDUES > ENDUE

ENDUING > ENDUE

ENDUNGEON *vb* put in a dungeon

ENDURABLE > ENDURE

ENDURABLY > ENDURE

ENDURANCE *n* act or power of enduring

ENDURE *vb* bear (hardship) patiently

ENDURED > ENDURE

ENDURER > ENDURE

ENDURERS > ENDURE

ENDURES > ENDURE

ENDURING *adj* long-lasting

ENDURO *n* long-distance race for vehicles

ENDUROS > ENDURO

ENDWAYS *adv* having the end forwards or upwards ▷ *adj* vertical or upright

ENDWISE *same as* > ENDWAYS

ENDYSES > ENDYSIS

ENDYSIS *n* formation of new layers of integument after ecdysis

ENDZONE *n* (in American football) area at either end of the playing field

ENDZONES > ENDZONE

ENE *variant of* > EVEN

ENEMA *n* medicine injected into the rectum to empty the bowels

ENEMAS > ENEMA

ENEMATA > ENEMA

ENEMIES > ENEMY

ENEMY *n* hostile person or nation, opponent ▷ *adj* of or belonging to an enemy

ENERGETIC *adj* having or showing energy and enthusiasm

ENERGIC > ENERGY

ENERGID *n* nucleus and cytoplasm in a syncytium

ENERGIDS > ENERGID

ENERGIES > ENERGY

ENERGISE *same as* > ENERGIZE

ENERGISED > ENERGISE

ENERGISER > ENERGISE

ENERGISES > ENERGISE

ENERGIZE *vb* give vigour to

ENERGIZED > ENERGIZE

ENERGIZER > ENERGIZE

ENERGIZES > ENERGIZE

ENERGUMEN *n* person thought to be possessed by an evil spirit

ENERGY *n* capacity for intense activity

ENERVATE *vb* deprive of strength or vitality ▷ *adj* deprived of strength or vitality

ENERVATED > ENERVATE

ENERVATES > ENERVATE

ENERVATOR > ENERVATE

ENERVE *vb* enervate

ENERVED > ENERVE

ENERVES > ENERVE

ENERVING > ENERVE

ENES > ENE

ENEW *vb* force a bird into water

ENEWED > ENEW

ENEWING > ENEW

ENEWS > ENEW

ENFACE *vb* write, print, or stamp (something) on the face of (a document)

ENFACED > ENFACE

ENFACES > ENFACE

ENFACING > ENFACE

ENFANT *n* French child

ENFANTS > ENFANT

ENFEEBLE *vb* weaken

ENFEEBLED > ENFEEBLE

ENFEEBLER > ENFEEBLE

ENFEEBLES > ENFEEBLE

ENFELON *vb* infuriate

ENFELONED > ENFELON

ENFELONS > ENFELON

ENFEOFF *vb* invest (a person) with possession of a freehold estate in land

ENFEOFFED > ENFEOFF

ENFEOFFS > ENFEOFF

ENFESTED *adj* made bitter

ENFETTER *vb* fetter

ENFETTERS > ENFETTER

ENFEVER *vb* make feverish

ENFEVERED > ENFEVER

ENFEVERS > ENFEVER

ENFIERCE *vb* make ferocious

ENFIERCED > ENFIERCE

ENFIERCES > ENFIERCE

ENFILADE *n* burst of gunfire sweeping from end to end along a line of troops ▷ *vb* attack along an enfilade

ENFILADED > ENFILADE

ENFILADES > ENFILADE

ENFILED *adj* passed through

ENFIRE *vb* set alight

ENFIRED > ENFIRE

ENFIRES > ENFIRE

ENFIRING > ENFIRE

ENFIX *variant of* > INFIX

ENFIXED > ENFIX

ENFIXES > ENFIX

ENFIXING > ENFIX

ENFLAME *variant of* > INFLAME

ENFLAMED > ENFLAME

ENFLAMES > ENFLAME

ENFLAMING > ENFLAME

ENFLESH *vb* make flesh

ENFLESHED > ENFLESH

ENFLESHES > ENFLESH

ENFLOWER *vb* put flowers on

ENFLOWERS > ENFLOWER

ENFOLD *vb* cover by wrapping something around

ENFOLDED > ENFOLD

ENFOLDER > ENFOLD

ENFOLDERS > ENFOLD

ENFOLDING > ENFOLD

ENFOLDS > ENFOLD

ENFORCE *vb* impose obedience (to a law etc)

ENFORCED > ENFORCE

ENFORCER > ENFORCE

ENFORCERS > ENFORCE

ENFORCES > ENFORCE

ENFORCING > ENFORCE

ENFOREST *vb* make into a forest

ENFORESTS > ENFOREST

ENFORM *variant of* > INFORM

ENFORMED > ENFORM

ENFORMING > ENFORM

ENFORMS > ENFORM

ENFRAME *vb* put inside a frame

ENFRAMED > ENFRAME

ENFRAMES > ENFRAME

ENFRAMING > ENFRAME

ENFREE *vb* release, make free

ENFREED > ENFREE

ENFREEDOM *variant of* > ENFREE

ENFREEING > ENFREE

ENFREES > ENFREE

ENFREEZE *vb* freeze

ENFREEZES > ENFREEZE

ENFROSEN > ENFREEZE

ENFROZE > ENFREEZE

ENFROZEN > ENFREEZE

ENG *another name for* > AGMA

ENGAGE *vb* take part, participate ▷ *adj* (of an artist) morally or politically committed to some ideology

ENGAGED *adj* pledged to be married

ENGAGEDLY > ENGAGED

ENGAGEE *adj* (of a female artist) morally or politically committed to some ideology

ENGAGER > ENGAGE

ENGAGERS > ENGAGE

ENGAGES > ENGAGE

ENGAGING *adj* charming

ENGAOL *vb* put into gaol

ENGAOLED > ENGAOL

ENGAOLING > ENGAOL

ENGAOLS > ENGAOL

ENGARLAND *vb* cover with garlands

ENGENDER *vb* produce, cause to occur

ENGENDERS > ENGENDER

ENGENDURE > ENGENDER

ENGILD *vb* cover with or as if with gold

ENGILDED > ENGILD

ENGILDING > ENGILD

ENGILDS > ENGILD

ENGILT > ENGILD

ENGINE *n* any machine which converts energy into mechanical work ▷ *vb* put an engine in

ENGINED > ENGINE

ENGINEER *n* person trained in any branch of engineering ▷ *vb* plan in a clever manner

ENGINEERS > ENGINEER

ENGINER > ENGINE

ENGINERS > ENGINE

ENGINERY *n* collection or assembly of engines

ENGINES > ENGINE

ENGINING > ENGINE

ENGINOUS *adj* ingenious or clever

ENGIRD *vb* surround

ENGIRDED > ENGIRD

ENGIRDING > ENGIRD

ENGIRDLE *variant of* > ENGIRD

ENGIRDLED > ENGIRDLE

ENGIRDLES > ENGIRDLE

ENGIRDS > ENGIRD

ENGIRT > ENGIRD

ENGLACIAL *adj* embedded in, carried by, or running through a glacier

ENGLISH *vb* put spin on a billiard ball

ENGLISHED > ENGLISH

ENGLISHES > ENGLISH

ENGLOBE *vb* surround as if in a globe

ENGLOBED > ENGLOBE

ENGLOBES > ENGLOBE

ENGLOBING > ENGLOBE

ENGLOOM *vb* make dull or dismal

ENGLOOMED > ENGLOOM

ENGLOOMS > ENGLOOM

ENGLUT *vb* devour ravenously

ENGLUTS > ENGLUT

ENGLUTTED > ENGLUT

ENGOBE *n* liquid put on pottery before glazing

ENGOBES > ENGOBE

ENGORE *vb* pierce or wound

ENGORED > ENGORE

ENGORES > ENGORE

ENGORGE *vb* clog with blood

ENGORGED > ENGORGE

ENGORGES > ENGORGE

ENGORGING > ENGORGE

ENGORING > ENGORE

ENGOULED *adj* (in heraldry) with ends coming from the mouths of animals

ENGOUMENT *n* obsessive liking

ENGRACE *vb* give grace to

ENGRACED > ENGRACE

ENGRACES > ENGRACE

ENGRACING > ENGRACE

ENGRAFF *variant of* > ENGRAFT

ENGRAFFED > ENGRAFF

ENGRAFFS > ENGRAFF

ENGRAFT *vb* graft (a shoot, bud, etc) onto a stock

ENGRAFTED > ENGRAFT

ENGRAFTS > ENGRAFT

ENGRAIL *vb* decorate or mark with small carved notches

ENGRAILED > ENGRAIL

ENGRAILS > ENGRAIL

ENGRAIN *variant spelling of* > INGRAIN

ENGRAINED > ENGRAIN

ENGRAINER > ENGRAIN

ENGRAINS > ENGRAIN

ENGRAM *n* physical basis of an individual memory in the brain

ENGRAMMA *variant of* > ENGRAM

ENGRAMMAS > ENGRAMMA

ENGRAMME *variant of* > ENGRAM

ENGRAMMES > ENGRAMME

ENGRAMMIC > ENGRAM

ENGRAMS > ENGRAM

ENGRASP *vb* grasp or seize

ENGRASPED > ENGRASP

ENGRASPS > ENGRASP

ENGRAVE *vb* carve (a design) onto a hard surface

ENGRAVED > ENGRAVE

ENGRAVEN > ENGRAVE

ENGRAVER > ENGRAVE

ENGRAVERS > ENGRAVE

ENGRAVERY > ENGRAVE

ENGRAVES > ENGRAVE

ENGRAVING *n* print made from an engraved plate

ENGRENAGE *n* act of putting into gear

ENGRIEVE *vb* grieve

ENGRIEVED > ENGRIEVE

ENGRIEVES > ENGRIEVE

ENGROOVE -*vb* put a groove in

ENGROOVED > ENGROOVE

ENGROOVES > ENGROOVE

ENGROSS *vb* occupy the attention of (a person) completely

ENGROSSED > ENGROSS

ENGROSSER > ENGROSS

ENGROSSES > ENGROSS

ENGS > ENG

ENGUARD *vb* protect or defend

ENGUARDED > ENGUARD

ENGUARDS > ENGUARD

ENGULF *vb* cover or surround completely

ENGULFED > ENGULF

ENGULFING > ENGULF

ENGULFS > ENGULF

ENGULPH *variant of* > ENGULF

ENGULPHED > ENGULPH

ENGULPHS > ENGULPH

ENGYSCOPE *n* microscope

ENHALO *vb* surround with or as if with a halo

ENHALOED > ENHALO

ENHALOES > ENHALO

ENHALOING > ENHALO

ENHALOS > ENHALO

ENHANCE *vb* increase in quality, value, or attractiveness

ENHANCED > ENHANCE

ENHANCER > ENHANCE

ENHANCERS > ENHANCE

ENHANCES > ENHANCE

ENHANCING > ENHANCE

ENHANCIVE > ENHANCE

ENHEARSE *variant of* > INHEARSE

ENHEARSED > ENHEARSE

ENHEARSES > ENHEARSE

ENHEARTEN *vb* give heart to, encourage

ENHUNGER *vb* cause to be hungry

ENHUNGERS > ENHUNGER

ENHYDRITE *n* type of mineral

ENHYDROS *n* piece of chalcedony that contains water

ENHYDROUS > ENHYDROS

ENIAC *n* early type of computer built in the 1940s

ENIACS > ENIAC

ENIGMA *n* puzzling thing or person

ENIGMAS > ENIGMA

ENIGMATA > ENIGMA

ENIGMATIC > ENIGMA

ENISLE *vb* put on or make into an island

ENISLED > ENISLE

ENISLES > ENISLE

ENISLING > ENISLE

ENJAMB *vb* (of a line of verse) run over into the next line

ENJAMBED > ENJAMB

ENJAMBING > ENJAMB

ENJAMBS > ENJAMB

ENJOIN *vb* order (someone) to do something

ENJOINDER *n* order

ENJOINED > ENJOIN

ENJOINER > ENJOIN

ENJOINERS > ENJOIN

ENJOINING > ENJOIN

ENJOINS > ENJOIN

ENJOY *vb* take joy in

ENJOYABLE > ENJOY

ENJOYABLY > ENJOY

ENJOYED > ENJOY

ENJOYER > ENJOY

ENJOYERS > ENJOY

ENJOYING > ENJOY

ENJOYMENT *n* act or condition of receiving pleasure from something

ENJOYS > ENJOY

ENKERNEL *vb* put inside a kernel

ENKERNELS > ENKERNEL
ENKINDLE vb set on fire
ENKINDLED > ENKINDLE
ENKINDLER > ENKINDLE
ENKINDLES > ENKINDLE
ENLACE vb bind or encircle with or as with laces
ENLACED > ENLACE
ENLACES > ENLACE
ENLACING > ENLACE
ENLARD vb put lard on
ENLARDED > ENLARD
ENLARDING > ENLARD
ENLARDS > ENLARD
ENLARGE vb make or grow larger
ENLARGED > ENLARGE
ENLARGEN variant of > ENLARGE
ENLARGENS > ENLARGE
ENLARGER n optical instrument for making enlarged photographic prints in which a negative is brightly illuminated and its enlarged image is focused onto a sheet of sensitized paper
ENLARGERS > ENLARGER
ENLARGES > ENLARGE
ENLARGING > ENLARGE
ENLEVE adj having been abducted
ENLIGHT vb light up
ENLIGHTED > ENLIGHT
ENLIGHTEN vb give information to
ENLIGHTS > ENLIGHT
ENLINK vb link together
ENLINKED > ENLINK
ENLINKING > ENLINK
ENLINKS > ENLINK
ENLIST vb enter the armed forces
ENLISTED > ENLIST
ENLISTEE > ENLIST
ENLISTEES > ENLIST
ENLISTER > ENLIST
ENLISTERS > ENLIST
ENLISTING > ENLIST
ENLISTS > ENLIST
ENLIT > ENLIGHT
ENLIVEN vb make lively or cheerful
ENLIVENED > ENLIVEN
ENLIVENER > ENLIVEN
ENLIVENS > ENLIVEN
ENLOCK vb lock or secure
ENLOCKED > ENLOCK
ENLOCKING > ENLOCK
ENLOCKS > ENLOCK
ENLUMINE vb illuminate
ENLUMINED > ENLUMINE
ENLUMINES > ENLUMINE
ENMESH vb catch or involve in or as if in a net or snare
ENMESHED > ENMESH
ENMESHES > ENMESH
ENMESHING > ENMESH
ENMEW variant of > EMMEW
ENMEWED > ENMEW

ENMEWING > ENMEW
ENMEWS > ENMEW
ENMITIES > ENMITY
ENMITY n ill will, hatred
ENMOSSED adj having a covering of moss
ENMOVE variant of > EMMOVE
ENMOVED > ENMOVE
ENMOVES > ENMOVE
ENMOVING > ENMOVE
ENNAGE n number of ens in printed matter
ENNAGES > ENNAGE
ENNEAD n group or series of nine
ENNEADIC > ENNEAD
ENNEADS > ENNEAD
ENNEAGON another name for > NONAGON
ENNEAGONS > ENNEAGON
ENNEAGRAM n personality system involving nine distinct but interconnected personality types
ENNOBLE vb make noble, elevate
ENNOBLED > ENNOBLE
ENNOBLER > ENNOBLE
ENNOBLERS > ENNOBLE
ENNOBLES > ENNOBLE
ENNOBLING > ENNOBLE
ENNOG n back alley
ENNOGS > ENNOG
ENNUI n boredom, dissatisfaction ▷ vb bore
ENNUIED > ENNUI
ENNUIS > ENNUI
ENNUYE adj bored
ENNUYED > ENNUI
ENNUYEE same as > ENNUYE
ENNUYING > ENNUI
ENODAL adj having no nodes
ENOKI variant of > ENOKITAKE
ENOKIDAKE variant of > ENOKITAKE
ENOKIS > ENOKI
ENOKITAKE n Japanese mushroom
ENOL n type of organic compound
ENOLASE n type of enzyme
ENOLASES > ENOLASE
ENOLIC > ENOL
ENOLOGIES > ENOLOGY
ENOLOGIST n wine expert
ENOLOGY usual US spelling of > OENOLOGY
ENOLS > ENOL
ENOMOTIES > ENOMOTY
ENOMOTY n division of the Spartan army in ancient Greece
ENOPHILE n lover of wine
ENOPHILES > ENOPHILE
ENORM variant of > ENORMOUS

ENORMITY n great wickedness
ENORMOUS adj very big, vast
ENOSES > ENOSIS
ENOSIS n union of Greece and Cyprus
ENOSISES > ENOSIS
ENOUGH adj as much or as many as necessary ▷ n sufficient quantity ▷ adv sufficiently
ENOUGHS > ENOUGH
ENOUNCE vb enunciate
ENOUNCED > ENOUNCE
ENOUNCES > ENOUNCE
ENOUNCING > ENOUNCE
ENOW archaic word for > ENOUGH
ENOWS > ENOW
ENPLANE vb board an aircraft
ENPLANED > ENPLANE
ENPLANES > ENPLANE
ENPLANING > ENPLANE
ENPRINT n standard photographic print
ENPRINTS > ENPRINT
ENQUEUE vb add (an item) to a queue of computing tasks
ENQUEUED > ENQUEUE
ENQUEUES > ENQUEUE
ENQUEUING > ENQUEUE
ENQUIRE same as > INQUIRE
ENQUIRED > ENQUIRE
ENQUIRER > ENQUIRE
ENQUIRERS > ENQUIRE
ENQUIRES > ENQUIRE
ENQUIRIES > ENQUIRE
ENQUIRING > ENQUIRE
ENQUIRY > ENQUIRE
ENRACE vb bring in a race of people
ENRACED > ENRACE
ENRACES > ENRACE
ENRACING > ENRACE
ENRAGE vb make extremely angry
ENRAGED > ENRAGE
ENRAGEDLY > ENRAGE
ENRAGES > ENRAGE
ENRAGING > ENRAGE
ENRANCKLE vb upset, make irate
ENRANGE vb arrange, organize
ENRANGED > ENRANGE
ENRANGES > ENRANGE
ENRANGING > ENRANGE
ENRANK vb put in a row
ENRANKED > ENRANK
ENRANKING > ENRANK
ENRANKS > ENRANK
ENRAPT > ENRAPTURE
ENRAPTURE vb fill with delight
ENRAUNGE variant of > ENRANGE
ENRAUNGED > ENRAUNGE
ENRAUNGES > ENRAUNGE
ENRAVISH vb enchant

ENRHEUM vb pass a cold on to
ENRHEUMED > ENRHEUM
ENRHEUMS > ENRHEUM
ENRICH vb improve in quality
ENRICHED > ENRICH
ENRICHER > ENRICH
ENRICHERS > ENRICH
ENRICHES > ENRICH
ENRICHING > ENRICH
ENRIDGED adj ridged
ENRING vb put a ring round
ENRINGED > ENRING
ENRINGING > ENRING
ENRINGS > ENRING
ENRIVEN adj ripped
ENROBE vb dress in or as if in a robe
ENROBED > ENROBE
ENROBER > ENROBE
ENROBERS > ENROBE
ENROBES > ENROBE
ENROBING > ENROBE
ENROL vb (cause to) become a member
ENROLL same as > ENROL
ENROLLED > ENROLL
ENROLLEE > ENROL
ENROLLEES > ENROL
ENROLLER > ENROL
ENROLLERS > ENROL
ENROLLING > ENROLL
ENROLLS > ENROLL
ENROLMENT n act of enrolling or state of being enrolled
ENROLS > ENROL
ENROOT vb establish (plants) by fixing their roots in the earth
ENROOTED > ENROOT
ENROOTING > ENROOT
ENROOTS > ENROOT
ENROUGH vb roughen
ENROUGHED > ENROUGH
ENROUGHS > ENROUGH
ENROUND vb encircle
ENROUNDED > ENROUND
ENROUNDS > ENROUND
ENS n being or existence in the most general abstract sense
ENSAMPLE n example ▷ vb make an example
ENSAMPLED > ENSAMPLE
ENSAMPLES > ENSAMPLE
ENSATE adj shaped like a sword
ENSCONCE vb settle firmly or comfortably
ENSCONCED > ENSCONCE
ENSCONCES > ENSCONCE
ENSCROLL variant of > INSCROLL
ENSCROLLS > ENSCROLL
ENSEAL vb seal up
ENSEALED > ENSEAL
ENSEALING > ENSEAL
ENSEALS > ENSEAL
ENSEAM vb put a seam on
ENSEAMED > ENSEAM

ENSEAMING > ENSEAM
ENSEAMS > ENSEAM
ENSEAR vb dry
ENSEARED > ENSEAR
ENSEARING > ENSEAR
ENSEARS > ENSEAR
ENSEMBLE n all the parts of something taken together ▷ adv all together or at once ▷ adj (of a film or play) involving several separate but often interrelated story lines
ENSEMBLES > ENSEMBLE
ENSERF vb enslave
ENSERFED > ENSERF
ENSERFING > ENSERF
ENSERFS > ENSERF
ENSEW variant of > ENSUE
ENSEWED > ENSEW
ENSEWING > ENSEW
ENSEWS > ENSEW
ENSHEATH variant of > INSHEATHE
ENSHEATHE variant of > INSHEATHE
ENSHEATHS > ENSHEATH
ENSHELL variant of > INSHELL
ENSHELLED > ENSHELL
ENSHELLS > ENSHELL
ENSHELTER vb shelter
ENSHIELD vb protect
ENSHIELDS > ENSHIELD
ENSHRINE vb cherish or treasure
ENSHRINED > ENSHRINE
ENSHRINEE > ENSHRINE
ENSHRINES > ENSHRINE
ENSHROUD vb cover or hide as with a shroud
ENSHROUDS > ENSHROUD
ENSIFORM adj shaped like a sword blade
ENSIGN n naval flag ▷ vb mark with a sign
ENSIGNCY > ENSIGN
ENSIGNED > ENSIGN
ENSIGNING > ENSIGN
ENSIGNS > ENSIGN
ENSILAGE n process of ensiling green fodder ▷ vb make into silage
ENSILAGED > ENSILAGE
ENSILAGES > ENSILAGE
ENSILE vb store and preserve (green fodder) in an enclosed pit or silo
ENSILED > ENSILE
ENSILES > ENSILE
ENSILING > ENSILE
ENSKIED > ENSKY
ENSKIES > ENSKY
ENSKY vb put in the sky
ENSKYED > ENSKY
ENSKYING > ENSKY
ENSLAVE vb make a slave of (someone)
ENSLAVED > ENSLAVE
ENSLAVER > ENSLAVE
ENSLAVERS > ENSLAVE
ENSLAVES > ENSLAVE

ENSLAVING > ENSLAVE
ENSNARE vb catch in or as if in a snare
ENSNARED > ENSNARE
ENSNARER > ENSNARE
ENSNARERS > ENSNARE
ENSNARES > ENSNARE
ENSNARING > ENSNARE
ENSNARL vb become tangled in
ENSNARLED > ENSNARL
ENSNARLS > ENSNARL
ENSORCEL vb enchant
ENSORCELL variant of > ENSORCEL
ENSORCELS > ENSORCEL
ENSOUL vb endow with a soul
ENSOULED > ENSOUL
ENSOULING > ENSOUL
ENSOULS > ENSOUL
ENSPHERE vb enclose in or as if in a sphere
ENSPHERED > ENSPHERE
ENSPHERES > ENSPHERE
ENSTAMP vb imprint with a stamp
ENSTAMPED > ENSTAMP
ENSTAMPS > ENSTAMP
ENSTATITE n grey, green, yellow, or brown pyroxene mineral consisting of magnesium silicate in orthorhombic crystalline form
ENSTEEP vb soak in water
ENSTEEPED > ENSTEEP
ENSTEEPS > ENSTEEP
ENSTYLE vb give a name to
ENSTYLED > ENSTYLE
ENSTYLES > ENSTYLE
ENSTYLING > ENSTYLE
ENSUE vb come next, result
ENSUED > ENSUE
ENSUES > ENSUE
ENSUING adj following subsequently or in order
ENSUITE n bathroom attached to another room
ENSUITES > ENSUITE
ENSURE vb make certain or sure
ENSURED > ENSURE
ENSURER > ENSURE
ENSURERS > ENSURE
ENSURES > ENSURE
ENSURING > ENSURE
ENSWATHE vb bind or wrap
ENSWATHED > ENSWATHE
ENSWATHES > ENSWATHE
ENSWEEP vb sweep across
ENSWEEPS > ENSWEEP
ENSWEPT > ENSWEEP
ENTAIL vb bring about or impose inevitably ▷ n restriction imposed by entailing an estate
ENTAILED > ENTAIL
ENTAILER > ENTAIL
ENTAILERS > ENTAIL

ENTAILING > ENTAIL
ENTAILS > ENTAIL
ENTAME vb make tame
ENTAMEBA same as > ENTAMOEBA
ENTAMEBAE > ENTAMEBA
ENTAMEBAS > ENTAMEBA
ENTAMED > ENTAME
ENTAMES > ENTAME
ENTAMING > ENTAME
ENTAMOEBA n parasitic amoeba that lives in the intestines of man and causes amoebic dysentery
ENTANGLE vb catch or involve in or as if in a tangle
ENTANGLED > ENTANGLE
ENTANGLER > ENTANGLE
ENTANGLES > ENTANGLE
ENTASES > ENTASIS
ENTASIA same as > ENTASIS
ENTASIAS > ENTASIA
ENTASIS n slightly convex curve given to the shaft of a structure
ENTASTIC adj (of a disease) characterized by spasms
ENTAYLE variant of > ENTAIL
ENTAYLED > ENTAYLE
ENTAYLES > ENTAYLE
ENTAYLING > ENTAYLE
ENTELECHY n (in the philosophy of Aristotle) actuality as opposed to potentiality
ENTELLUS n langur of S Asia
ENTENDER vb make more tender
ENTENDERS > ENTENDER
ENTENTE n friendly understanding between nations
ENTENTES > ENTENTE
ENTER vb come or go in
ENTERA > ENTERON
ENTERABLE > ENTER
ENTERAL same as > ENTERIC
ENTERALLY > ENTERIC
ENTERATE adj with an intestine separate from the outer wall of the body
ENTERED > ENTER
ENTERER > ENTER
ENTERERS > ENTER
ENTERIC adj intestinal ▷ n infectious disease of the intestines
ENTERICS > ENTERIC
ENTERING > ENTER
ENTERINGS > ENTER
ENTERITIS n inflammation of the intestine, causing diarrhoea
ENTERON n alimentary canal
ENTERONS > ENTERON
ENTERS > ENTER

ENTERTAIN vb amuse
ENTERTAKE vb entertain
ENTERTOOK > ENTERTAKE
ENTETE adj obsessed
ENTETEE variant of > ENTETE
ENTHALPY n thermodynamic property of a system equal to the sum of its internal energy and the product of its pressure and volume
ENTHETIC adj (esp of infectious diseases) introduced into the body from without
ENTHRAL vb hold the attention of
ENTHRALL same as > ENTHRAL
ENTHRALLS > ENTHRALL
ENTHRALS > ENTHRAL
ENTHRONE vb place (someone) on a throne
ENTHRONED > ENTHRONE
ENTHRONES > ENTHRONE
ENTHUSE vb (cause to) show enthusiasm
ENTHUSED > ENTHUSE
ENTHUSES > ENTHUSE
ENTHUSING > ENTHUSE
ENTHYMEME n incomplete syllogism, in which one or more premises are unexpressed as their truth is considered to be self-evident
ENTIA > ENS
ENTICE vb attract by exciting hope or desire, tempt
ENTICED > ENTICE
ENTICER > ENTICE
ENTICERS > ENTICE
ENTICES > ENTICE
ENTICING > ENTICE
ENTICINGS > ENTICE
ENTIRE adj including every detail, part, or aspect of something ▷ n state of being entire
ENTIRELY adv without reservation or exception
ENTIRES > ENTIRE
ENTIRETY n state of being entire or whole
ENTITIES > ENTITY
ENTITLE vb give a right to
ENTITLED > ENTITLE
ENTITLES > ENTITLE
ENTITLING > ENTITLE
ENTITY n separate distinct thing
ENTOBLAST less common name for > ENDODERM
ENTODERM same as > ENDODERM
ENTODERMS > ENTODERM
ENTOIL archaic word for > ENSNARE
ENTOILED > ENTOIL
ENTOILING > ENTOIL
ENTOILS > ENTOIL

ENTOMB vb place (a corpse) in a tomb
ENTOMBED > ENTOMB
ENTOMBING > ENTOMB
ENTOMBS > ENTOMB
ENTOMIC adj denoting or relating to insects
ENTOPHYTE variant of > ENDOPHYTE
ENTOPIC adj situated in its normal place or position
ENTOPROCT n type of marine animal
ENTOPTIC adj (of visual sensation) resulting from structures within the eye itself
ENTOPTICS n study of entoptic visions
ENTOTIC adj of or relating to the inner ear
ENTOURAGE n group of people who assist an important person
ENTOZOA > ENTOZOON
ENTOZOAL > ENTOZOON
ENTOZOAN same as > ENTOZOON
ENTOZOANS > ENTOZOAN
ENTOZOIC adj of or relating to an entozoon
ENTOZOON n internal parasite
ENTRAIL vb twist or entangle
ENTRAILED > ENTRAIL
ENTRAILS pl n intestines
ENTRAIN vb board or put aboard a train
ENTRAINED > ENTRAIN
ENTRAINER > ENTRAIN
ENTRAINS > ENTRAIN
ENTRALL variant of > ENTRAILS
ENTRALLES variant of > ENTRAILS
ENTRAMMEL vb hamper or obstruct by entangling
ENTRANCE n way into a place ▷ vb delight ▷ adj necessary in order to enter something
ENTRANCED > ENTRANCE
ENTRANCES > ENTRANCE
ENTRANT n person who enters a university, contest, etc
ENTRANTS > ENTRANT
ENTRAP vb trick into difficulty etc
ENTRAPPED > ENTRAP
ENTRAPPER > ENTRAP
ENTRAPS > ENTRAP
ENTREAT vb ask earnestly
ENTREATED > ENTREAT
ENTREATS > ENTREAT
ENTREATY n earnest request
ENTRECHAT n leap in ballet during which the dancer repeatedly crosses his feet or beats them together

ENTRECOTE n beefsteak cut from between the ribs
ENTREE n dish served before a main course
ENTREES > ENTREE
ENTREMES variant of > ENTREMETS
ENTREMETS n dessert
ENTRENCH vb establish firmly
ENTREPOT n warehouse for commercial goods
ENTREPOTS > ENTREPOT
ENTRESOL another name for > MEZZANINE
ENTRESOLS > ENTRESOL
ENTREZ interj enter
ENTRIES > ENTRY
ENTRISM variant of > ENTRYISM
ENTRISMS > ENTRISM
ENTRIST > ENTRYISM
ENTRISTS > ENTRYISM
ENTROLD adj surrounded
ENTROPIC > ENTROPY
ENTROPIES > ENTROPY
ENTROPION n turning inwards of the edge of the eyelid
ENTROPIUM variant of > ENTROPION
ENTROPY n lack of organization
ENTRUST vb put into the care or protection of
ENTRUSTED > ENTRUST
ENTRUSTS > ENTRUST
ENTRY n entrance ▷ adj necessary in order to enter something
ENTRYISM n policy or practice of members of a particular political group joining an existing political party with the intention of changing its principles and policies, instead of forming a new party
ENTRYISMS > ENTRYISM
ENTRYIST > ENTRYISM
ENTRYISTS > ENTRYISM
ENTRYWAY n entrance passage
ENTRYWAYS > ENTRYWAY
ENTS pl n (coll.) entertainments
ENTWINE vb twist together or around
ENTWINED > ENTWINE
ENTWINES > ENTWINE
ENTWINING > ENTWINE
ENTWIST vb twist together or around
ENTWISTED > ENTWIST
ENTWISTS > ENTWIST
ENUCLEATE vb remove the nucleus from (a cell) ▷ adj (of cells) deprived of their nuclei
ENUF common intentional literary misspelling of > ENOUGH
ENUMERATE vb name one by one

ENUNCIATE vb pronounce clearly
ENURE variant spelling of > INURE
ENURED > ENURE
ENUREMENT > ENURE
ENURES > ENURE
ENURESES > ENURESIS
ENURESIS n involuntary discharge of urine, esp during sleep
ENURETIC > ENURESIS
ENURETICS > ENURESIS
ENURING > ENURE
ENURN same as > INURN
ENURNED same as > INURNED
ENURNING same as > INURNING
ENURNS same as > INURNS
ENVASSAL vb make a vassal of
ENVASSALS > ENVASSAL
ENVAULT vb enclose in a vault; entomb
ENVAULTED > ENVAULT
ENVAULTS > ENVAULT
ENVEIGLE same as > INVEIGLE
ENVEIGLED > ENVEIGLE
ENVEIGLES > ENVEIGLE
ENVELOP vb wrap up, enclose
ENVELOPE n folded gummed paper cover for a letter
ENVELOPED > ENVELOP
ENVELOPER > ENVELOP
ENVELOPES > ENVELOPE
ENVELOPS > ENVELOP
ENVENOM vb fill or impregnate with venom
ENVENOMED > ENVENOM
ENVENOMS > ENVENOM
ENVERMEIL vb dye vermilion
ENVIABLE adj arousing envy, fortunate
ENVIABLY > ENVIABLE
ENVIED > ENVY
ENVIER > ENVY
ENVIERS > ENVY
ENVIES > ENVY
ENVIOUS adj full of envy
ENVIOUSLY > ENVIOUS
ENVIRO n environmentalist
ENVIRON vb encircle or surround
ENVIRONED > ENVIRON
ENVIRONS pl n surrounding area, esp of a town
ENVIROS > ENVIRO
ENVISAGE vb conceive of as a possibility
ENVISAGED > ENVISAGE
ENVISAGES > ENVISAGE
ENVISION vb conceive of as a possibility, esp in the future
ENVISIONS > ENVISION
ENVOI same as > ENVOY

ENVOIS > ENVOI
ENVOY n messenger
ENVOYS > ENVOY
ENVOYSHIP > ENVOY
ENVY n feeling of discontent aroused by another's good fortune ▷ vb grudge (another's good fortune, success, or qualities)
ENVYING > ENVY
ENVYINGLY > ENVY
ENVYINGS > ENVY
ENWALL vb wall in
ENWALLED > ENWALL
ENWALLING > ENWALL
ENWALLOW vb sink or plunge
ENWALLOWS > ENWALLOW
ENWALLS > ENWALL
ENWHEEL archaic word for > ENCIRCLE
ENWHEELED > ENWHEEL
ENWHEELS > ENWHEEL
ENWIND vb wind or coil around
ENWINDING > ENWIND
ENWINDS > ENWIND
ENWOMB vb enclose in or as if in a womb
ENWOMBED > ENWOMB
ENWOMBING > ENWOMB
ENWOMBS > ENWOMB
ENWOUND > ENWIND
ENWRAP vb wrap or cover up
ENWRAPPED > ENWRAP
ENWRAPS > ENWRAP
ENWREATH vb surround or encircle with or as with a wreath or wreaths
ENWREATHE same as > ENWREATH
ENWREATHS > ENWREATH
ENZIAN n gentian violet
ENZIANS > ENZIAN
ENZONE vb enclose in a zone
ENZONED > ENZONE
ENZONES > ENZONE
ENZONING > ENZONE
ENZOOTIC adj (of diseases) affecting animals within a limited region ▷ n enzootic disease
ENZOOTICS > ENZOOTIC
ENZYM same as > ENZYME
ENZYMATIC > ENZYME
ENZYME n complex protein that acts as a catalyst
ENZYMES > ENZYME
ENZYMIC > ENZYME
ENZYMS > ENZYM
EOAN adj of or relating to the dawn
EOBIONT n hypothetical chemical precursor of a living cell
EOBIONTS > EOBIONT
EOCENE adj of, denoting, or formed in the second epoch of the Tertiary period

EOHIPPUS *n* earliest horse: an extinct Eocene dog-sized animal of the genus with four-toed forelegs, three-toed hindlegs, and teeth specialized for browsing

EOLIAN *adj* of or relating to the wind

EOLIENNE *n* type of fine cloth

EOLIENNES > EOLIENNE

EOLIPILE *variant of* > AEOLIPILE

EOLIPILES > EOLIPILE

EOLITH *n* stone used as a primitive tool in Eolithic times

EOLITHIC > EOLITH

EOLITHS > EOLITH

EOLOPILE *variant of* > AEOLIPILE

EOLOPILES > EOLOPILE

EON *n* two or more eras

EONIAN *adj* of or relating to an eon

EONISM *n* adoption of female dress and behaviour by a male

EONISMS > EONISM

EONS > EON

EORL *n* Anglo-Saxon nobleman

EORLS > EORL

EOSIN *n* red crystalline water-insoluble derivative of fluorescein

EOSINE *same as* > EOSIN

EOSINES > EOSINE

EOSINIC > EOSIN

EOSINS > EOSIN

EOTHEN *adv* from the East

EPACRID *n* type of heath-like plant

EPACRIDS > EPACRID

EPACRIS *n* genus of the epacrids

EPACRISES > EPACRIS

EPACT *n* difference in time between the solar year and the lunar year

EPACTS > EPACT

EPAENETIC *adj* eulogistic

EPAGOGE *n* inductive reasoning

EPAGOGES > EPAGOGE

EPAGOGIC > EPAGOGE

EPANODOS *n* return to main theme after a digression

EPARCH *n* bishop or metropolitan in charge of an eparchy

EPARCHATE *same as* > EPARCHY

EPARCHIAL > EPARCHY

EPARCHIES > EPARCHY

EPARCHS > EPARCH

EPARCHY *n* diocese of the Eastern Christian Church

EPATANT *adj* startling or shocking

EPATER *vb* shock conventional people

EPATERED > EPATER

EPATERING > EPATER

EPATERS > EPATER

EPAULE *n* shoulder of a fortification

EPAULES > EPAULE

EPAULET *same as* > EPAULETTE

EPAULETED *adj* wearing an epaulet

EPAULETS > EPAULET

EPAULETTE *n* shoulder ornament on a uniform

EPAXIAL *adj* above the axis

EPAZOTE *n* type of herb

EPAZOTES > EPAZOTE

EPEDAPHIC *adj* of or relating to atmospheric conditions

EPEE *n* straight-bladed sword used in fencing

EPEEIST *n* one who uses or specializes in using an epee

EPEEISTS > EPEEIST

EPEES > EPEE

EPEIRA *same as* > EPEIRID

EPEIRAS > EPEIRA

EPEIRIC *adj* in, of, or relating to a continent

EPEIRID *n* type of spider

EPEIRIDS > EPEIRID

EPENDYMA *n* membrane lining the ventricles of the brain and the central canal of the spinal cord

EPENDYMAL > EPENDYMA

EPENDYMAS > EPENDYMA

EPEOLATRY *n* worship of words

EPERDU *adj* distracted

EPERDUE *adj* distracted

EPERGNE *n* ornamental centrepiece for a table

EPERGNES > EPERGNE

EPHA *same as* > EPHAH

EPHAH *n* Hebrew unit of dry measure

EPHAHS > EPHAH

EPHAS > EPHA

EPHEBE *n* (in ancient Greece) youth about to enter full citizenship

EPHEBES > EPHEBE

EPHEBI > EPHEBE

EPHEBIC > EPHEBE

EPHEBOI > EPHEBOS

EPHEBOS *same as* > EPHEBE

EPHEBUS *same as* > EPHEBE

EPHEDRA *n* gymnosperm shrub

EPHEDRAS > EPHEDRA

EPHEDRIN *same as* > EPHEDRINE

EPHEDRINE *n* alkaloid used for treatment of asthma and hay fever

EPHEDRINS > EPHEDRIN

EPHELIDES > EPHELIS

EPHELIS *n* freckle

EPHEMERA *n* something transitory or short-lived

EPHEMERAE > EPHEMERA

EPHEMERAL *adj* short-lived ▷ *n* short-lived organism, such as the mayfly

EPHEMERAS > EPHEMERA

EPHEMERID *n* mayfly

EPHEMERIS *n* table giving the future positions of a planet, comet, or satellite

EPHEMERON *n* an insect that lives for only one day; anything short-lived

EPHIALTES *n* incubus

EPHOD *n* embroidered vestment worn by priests

EPHODS > EPHOD

EPHOR *n* (in ancient Greece) one of a board of senior magistrates in any of several Dorian states

EPHORAL > EPHOR

EPHORALTY > EPHOR

EPHORATE > EPHOR

EPHORATES > EPHOR

EPHORI > EPHOR

EPHORS > EPHOR

EPIBIOSES > EPIBIOSIS

EPIBIOSIS *n* any relationship between two organisms in which one grows on the other but is not parasitic on it

EPIBIOTIC > EPIBIOSIS

EPIBLAST *n* outermost layer of an embryo, which becomes the ectoderm at gastrulation

EPIBLASTS > EPIBLAST

EPIBLEM *n* outermost cell layer of a root

EPIBLEMS > EPIBLEM

EPIBOLIC > EPIBOLY

EPIBOLIES > EPIBOLY

EPIBOLY *n* process that occurs during gastrulation in vertebrates

EPIC *n* long poem, book, or film about heroic events or actions ▷ *adj* very impressive or ambitious

EPICAL > EPIC

EPICALLY > EPIC

EPICALYX *n* series of small sepal-like bracts forming an outer calyx beneath the true calyx in some flowers

EPICANTHI *n* folds of skin extending vertically over the inner angles of the eyes

EPICARDIA *n* layers of pericardia in direct contact with the heart

EPICARP *n* outermost layer of the pericarp of fruits

EPICARPS > EPICARP

EPICEDE *same as* > EPICEDIUM

EPICEDES > EPICEDE

EPICEDIA > EPICEDIUM

EPICEDIAL > EPICEDIUM

EPICEDIAN > EPICEDIUM

EPICEDIUM *n* funeral ode

EPICENE *adj* having the characteristics of both sexes; hermaphroditic ▷ *n* epicene person or creature

EPICENES > EPICENE

EPICENISM > EPICENE

EPICENTER *same as* > EPICENTRE

EPICENTRA *n* epicentres

EPICENTRE *n* point on the earth's surface immediately above the origin of an earthquake

EPICIER *n* grocer

EPICIERS > EPICIER

EPICISM *n* style or trope characteristic of epics

EPICISMS > EPIC

EPICIST *n* writer of epics

EPICISTS > EPIC

EPICLESES > EPICLESIS

EPICLESIS *n* invocation of the Holy Spirit to consecrate the bread and wine of the Eucharist

EPICLIKE *adj* resembling or reminiscent of an epic

EPICORMIC *adj* (of a tree shoot or branch) growing from a dormant bud below the bark

EPICOTYL *n* part of an embryo plant stem above the cotyledons but beneath the terminal bud

EPICOTYLS > EPICOTYL

EPICRANIA *n* tissue covering the cranium

EPICRISES > EPICRISIS

EPICRISIS *n* secondary crisis occurring in the course of a disease

EPICRITIC *adj* (of certain nerve fibres of the skin) serving to perceive and distinguish fine variations of temperature or touch

EPICS > EPIC

EPICURE *n* person who enjoys good food and drink

EPICUREAN *adj* devoted to sensual pleasures, esp food and drink ▷ *n* epicure

EPICURES > EPICURE

EPICURISE *same as* > EPICURIZE

EPICURISM > EPICURE

EPICURIZE *vb* act as an epicure

EPICYCLE n (in the Ptolemaic system) a small circle, around which a planet was thought to revolve
EPICYCLES > EPICYCLE
EPICYCLIC > EPICYCLE
EPIDEMIC n widespread occurrence of a disease ▷ adj (esp of a disease) affecting many people in an area
EPIDEMICS > EPIDEMIC
EPIDERM same as > EPIDERMIS
EPIDERMAL > EPIDERMIS
EPIDERMIC > EPIDERMIS
EPIDERMIS n outer layer of the skin
EPIDERMS > EPIDERM
EPIDICTIC adj designed to display something, esp the skill of the speaker in rhetoric
EPIDOSITE n rock formed of quartz and epidote
EPIDOTE n green mineral
EPIDOTES > EPIDOTE
EPIDOTIC > EPIDOTE
EPIDURAL n spinal anaesthetic injected to relieve pain during childbirth ▷ adj on or over the outermost membrane covering the brain and spinal cord
EPIDURALS > EPIDURAL
EPIFAUNA n animals that live on the surface of the seabed
EPIFAUNAE > EPIFAUNA
EPIFAUNAL > EPIFAUNA
EPIFAUNAS > EPIFAUNA
EPIFOCAL adj situated or occurring at an epicentre
EPIGAEAL same as > EPIGEAL
EPIGAEAN same as > EPIGEAL
EPIGAEOUS same as > EPIGEAL
EPIGAMIC adj attractive to the opposite sex
EPIGEAL adj of or relating to a form of seed germination
EPIGEAN same as > EPIGEAL
EPIGEIC same as > EPIGEAL
EPIGENE adj formed or taking place at or near the surface of the earth
EPIGENIC adj pertaining to the theory of the gradual development of the embryo
EPIGENIST n one who studies or espouses the theory of the gradual development of the embryo

EPIGENOUS adj growing on the surface, esp the upper surface, of an organism or part
EPIGEOUS same as > EPIGEAL
EPIGON same as > EPIGONE
EPIGONE n inferior follower or imitator
EPIGONES > EPIGONE
EPIGONI > EPIGONE
EPIGONIC > EPIGONE
EPIGONISM > EPIGONE
EPIGONOUS > EPIGONE
EPIGONS > EPIGON
EPIGONUS same as > EPIGONE
EPIGRAM n short witty remark or poem
EPIGRAMS > EPIGRAM
EPIGRAPH n quotation at the start of a book
EPIGRAPHS > EPIGRAPH
EPIGRAPHY n study of ancient inscriptions
EPIGYNIES > EPIGYNOUS
EPIGYNOUS adj (of flowers) having the receptacle enclosing and fused with the gynoecium so that the other floral parts arise above it
EPIGYNY > EPIGYNOUS
EPILATE vb remove hair from
EPILATED > EPILATE
EPILATES > EPILATE
EPILATING > EPILATE
EPILATION > EPILATE
EPILATOR n electrical appliance consisting of a metal spiral head that rotates at high speed, plucking unwanted hair
EPILATORS > EPILATOR
EPILEPSY n disorder of the nervous system causing loss of consciousness and sometimes convulsions
EPILEPTIC adj of or having epilepsy ▷ n person who has epilepsy
EPILIMNIA n upper layers of water in lakes
EPILITHIC adj (of plants) growing on the surface of rock
EPILOBIUM n willow-herb
EPILOG same as > EPILOGUE
EPILOGIC > EPILOGUE
EPILOGISE same as > EPILOGIZE
EPILOGIST > EPILOGUE
EPILOGIZE vb write or deliver epilogues
EPILOGS > EPILOG
EPILOGUE n short speech or poem at the end of a literary work, esp a play

EPILOGUED adj followed by an epilogue
EPILOGUES > EPILOGUE
EPIMER n isomer
EPIMERASE n enzyme that interconverts epimers
EPIMERE n dorsal part of the mesoderm of a vertebrate embryo
EPIMERES > EPIMERE
EPIMERIC > EPIMERISM
EPIMERISE same as > EPIMERIZE
EPIMERISM n optical isomerism in which isomers can form about asymmetric atoms within the molecule
EPIMERIZE vb change (a chemical compound) into an epimer
EPIMERS > EPIMER
EPIMYSIA > EPIMYSIUM
EPIMYSIUM n sheath of connective tissue that encloses a skeletal muscle
EPINAOI > EPINAOS
EPINAOS n rear vestibule
EPINASTIC > EPINASTY
EPINASTY n increased growth of the upper surface of a plant part, such as a leaf, resulting in a downward bending of the part
EPINEURAL adj outside a nerve trunk
EPINEURIA n sheaths of connective tissue around bundles of nerve fibres
EPINICIAN > EPINICION
EPINICION n victory song
EPINIKIAN > EPINICION
EPINIKION same as > EPINICION
EPINOSIC adj unhealthy
EPIPHANIC > EPIPHANY
EPIPHANY n moment of great or sudden revelation
EPIPHRAGM n disc of calcium phosphate and mucilage secreted by snails across the aperture of their shells before hibernation
EPIPHYSES > EPIPHYSIS
EPIPHYSIS n end of a long bone, initially separated from the shaft (diaphysis) by a section of cartilage that eventually ossifies so that the two portions fuse together
EPIPHYTAL > EPIPHYTE
EPIPHYTE n plant that grows on another plant but is not parasitic on it
EPIPHYTES > EPIPHYTE
EPIPHYTIC > EPIPHYTE
EPIPLOIC > EPIPLOON

EPIPLOON n greater omentum
EPIPLOONS > EPIPLOON
EPIPOLIC > EPIPOLISM
EPIPOLISM n fluorescence
EPIROGENY n formation and submergence of continents by broad, relatively slow, displacements of the earth's crust
EPIRRHEMA n address in Greek comedy
EPISCIA n creeping plant
EPISCIAS > EPISCIA
EPISCOPAL adj of or governed by bishops
EPISCOPE n optical device that projects an enlarged image of an opaque object, such as a printed page or photographic print, onto a screen by means of reflected light
EPISCOPES > EPISCOPE
EPISCOPY n area overseen
EPISEMON n emblem
EPISEMONS > EPISEMON
EPISODAL same as > EPISODIC
EPISODE n incident in a series of incidents
EPISODES > EPISODE
EPISODIAL same as > EPISODIC
EPISODIC adj occurring at irregular intervals
EPISOMAL adj of or like an episome
EPISOME n unit of genetic material (DNA) in bacteria that can be replicated
EPISOMES > EPISOME
EPISPERM n protective outer layer of certain seeds
EPISPERMS > EPISPERM
EPISPORE n outer layer of certain spores
EPISPORES > EPISPORE
EPISTASES > EPISTASIS
EPISTASIS n scum on the surface of a liquid, esp on an old specimen of urine
EPISTASY same as > EPISTASIS
EPISTATIC > EPISTASIS
EPISTAXES > EPISTAXIS
EPISTAXIS technical name for > NOSEBLEED
EPISTEMIC adj of or relating to knowledge or epistemology
EPISTERNA n parts of the sternums of mammals
EPISTLE n letter, esp of an apostle ▷ vb preface
EPISTLED > EPISTLE

EPISTLER n writer of an epistle or epistles

EPISTLERS > EPISTLER

EPISTLES > EPISTLE

EPISTLING > EPISTLE

EPISTOLER same as > EPISTLER

EPISTOLET n short letter

EPISTOLIC > EPISTLE

EPISTOME n area between the mouth and antennae of crustaceans

EPISTOMES > EPISTOME

EPISTYLE n lowest part of an entablature that bears on the columns

EPISTYLES > EPISTYLE

EPITAPH n commemorative inscription on a tomb ▷ vb compose an epitaph

EPITAPHED > EPITAPH

EPITAPHER > EPITAPH

EPITAPHIC > EPITAPH

EPITAPHS > EPITAPH

EPITASES > EPITASIS

EPITASIS n (in classical drama) part of a play in which the main action develops

EPITAXES > EPITAXIS

EPITAXIAL > EPITAXY

EPITAXIC > EPITAXY

EPITAXIES > EPITAXY

EPITAXIS same as > EPITAXY

EPITAXY n growth of a thin layer on the surface of a crystal

EPITHECA n outer and older layer of the cell wall of a diatom

EPITHECAE > EPITHECA

EPITHELIA n animal tissues consisting of one or more layers of closely packed cells covering the external and internal surfaces of the body

EPITHEM n external topical application

EPITHEMA > EPITHEM

EPITHEMS > EPITHEM

EPITHESES > EPITHESIS

EPITHESIS n addition of a letter to the end of a word, so that its sense does not change

EPITHET n descriptive word or name ▷ vb name

EPITHETED > EPITHET

EPITHETIC > EPITHET

EPITHETON same as > EPITHET

EPITHETS > EPITHET

EPITOME n typical example

EPITOMES > EPITOME

EPITOMIC > EPITOME

EPITOMISE same as > EPITOMIZE

EPITOMIST > EPITOMIZE

EPITOMIZE vb be the epitome of

EPITONIC adj undergoing too great a strain

EPITOPE n site on an antigen at which a specific antibody becomes attached

EPITOPES > EPITOPE

EPITRITE n metrical foot with three long syllables and one short one

EPITRITES > EPITRITE

EPIZEUXES > EPIZEUXIS

EPIZEUXIS n deliberate repetition of a word

EPIZOA > EPIZOON

EPIZOAN same as > EPIZOON

EPIZOANS > EPIZOAN

EPIZOIC adj (of an animal or plant) growing or living on the exterior of a living animal

EPIZOISM > EPIZOIC

EPIZOISMS > EPIZOIC

EPIZOITE n organism that lives on an animal but is not parasitic on it

EPIZOITES > EPIZOITE

EPIZOON n animal that lives on the body of another animal

EPIZOOTIC adj (of a disease) suddenly and temporarily affecting a large number of animals over a large area ▷ n epizootic disease

EPIZOOTY n animal disease

EPOCH n period of notable events

EPOCHA same as > EPOCH

EPOCHAL > EPOCH

EPOCHALLY > EPOCH

EPOCHAS > EPOCHA

EPOCHS > EPOCH

EPODE n part of a lyric ode that follows the strophe and the antistrophe

EPODES > EPODE

EPODIC > EPODE

EPONYM n name derived from the name of a real or mythical person

EPONYMIC > EPONYM

EPONYMIES > EPONYMY

EPONYMOUS adj after whom a book, play, etc is named

EPONYMS > EPONYM

EPONYMY n derivation of names of places, etc, from those of persons

EPOPEE n epic poem

EPOPEES > EPOPEE

EPOPOEIA same as > EPOPEE

EPOPOEIAS > EPOPOEIA

EPOPT n one initiated into mysteries

EPOPTS > EPOPT

EPOS n body of poetry in which the tradition of a people is conveyed

EPOSES > EPOS

EPOXIDE n chemical compound

EPOXIDES > EPOXIDE

EPOXIDISE same as > EPOXIDIZE

EPOXIDIZE vb form an epoxide

EPOXIED > EPOXY

EPOXIES > EPOXY

EPOXY adj of or containing a specific type of chemical compound ▷ n epoxy resin ▷ vb glue with epoxy resin

EPOXYED > EPOXY

EPOXYING > EPOXY

EPRIS adj enamoured

EPRISE feminine form of > EPRIS

EPSILON n fifth letter of the Greek alphabet

EPSILONIC adj of or relating to an arbitrary small quantity

EPSILONS > EPSILON

EPSOMITE n sulphate of magnesium

EPSOMITES > EPSOMITE

EPUISE adj exhausted

EPUISEE feminine form of > EPUISE

EPULARY adj of or relating to feasting

EPULATION n feasting

EPULIDES > EPULIS

EPULIS n swelling of the gum

EPULISES > EPULIS

EPULOTIC n scarring

EPULOTICS > EPULOTIC

EPURATE vb purify

EPURATED > EPURATE

EPURATES > EPURATE

EPURATING > EPURATE

EPURATION > EPURATE

EPYLLIA > EPYLLION

EPYLLION n miniature epic

EPYLLIONS > EPYLLION

EQUABLE adj even-tempered

EQUABLY > EQUABLE

EQUAL adj identical in size, quantity, degree, etc ▷ n person or thing equal to another ▷ vb be equal to

EQUALED > EQUAL

EQUALI pl n pieces for a group of instruments of the same kind

EQUALING > EQUAL

EQUALISE same as > EQUALIZE

EQUALISED > EQUALISE

EQUALISER same as > EQUALIZER

EQUALISES > EQUALISE

EQUALITY n state of being equal

EQUALIZE vb make or become equal

EQUALIZED > EQUALIZE

EQUALIZER n person or thing that equalizes, esp a device to counterbalance opposing forces

EQUALIZES > EQUALIZE

EQUALLED > EQUAL

EQUALLING > EQUAL

EQUALLY > EQUAL

EQUALNESS n equality

EQUALS > EQUAL

EQUANT n circle in which a planet was formerly believed to move

EQUANTS > EQUANT

EQUATABLE > EQUATE

EQUATE vb make or regard as equivalent

EQUATED > EQUATE

EQUATES > EQUATE

EQUATING > EQUATE

EQUATION n mathematical statement that two expressions are equal

EQUATIONS > EQUATION

EQUATIVE adj (in grammar) denoting the equivalence or identity of two terms

EQUATOR n imaginary circle round the earth

EQUATORS > EQUATOR

EQUERRIES > EQUERRY

EQUERRY n attendant to a member of a royal family

EQUES n (in ancient Rome) horseman

EQUID n any animal of the horse family

EQUIDS > EQUID

EQUIFINAL adj having the same end or result

EQUIMOLAL adj having an equal number of moles

EQUIMOLAR same as > EQUIMOLAL

EQUINAL same as > EQUINE

EQUINE adj of or like a horse ▷ n any animal of the horse family

EQUINELY > EQUINE

EQUINES > EQUINE

EQUINIA n glanders

EQUINIAS > EQUINIA

EQUINITY n horse-like nature

EQUINOX n time of year when day and night are of equal length

EQUINOXES > EQUINOX

EQUIP vb provide with supplies, components, etc

EQUIPAGE n horse-drawn carriage, esp one elegantly equipped and attended by liveried footmen ▷ vb equip

EQUIPAGED > EQUIPAGE

EQUIPAGES > EQUIPAGE

EQUIPE n (esp in motor racing) team
EQUIPES > EQUIPE
EQUIPMENT n set of tools or devices used for a particular purpose
EQUIPOISE n perfect balance ▷ vb offset or balance in weight or force
EQUIPPED > EQUIP
EQUIPPER > EQUIP
EQUIPPERS > EQUIP
EQUIPPING > EQUIP
EQUIPS > EQUIP
EQUISETA > EQUISETUM
EQUISETIC > EQUISETUM
EQUISETUM n type of plant such as the horsetail
EQUITABLE adj fair and reasonable
EQUITABLY > EQUITABLE
EQUITANT adj (of a leaf) having the base folded around the stem so that it overlaps the leaf above and opposite
EQUITES pl n cavalry
EQUITIES > EQUITY
EQUITY n fairness
EQUIVALVE adj equipped with identical valves
EQUIVOCAL adj ambiguous
EQUIVOKE same as > EQUIVOQUE
EQUIVOKES > EQUIVOKE
EQUIVOQUE n play on words
ER interj sound made when hesitating in speech
ERA n period of time considered as distinctive
ERADIATE less common word for > RADIATE
ERADIATED > ERADIATE
ERADIATES > ERADIATE
ERADICANT > ERADICATE
ERADICATE vb destroy completely
ERAS > ERA
ERASABLE > ERASE
ERASE vb destroy all traces of
ERASED > ERASE
ERASEMENT > ERASE
ERASER n object for erasing something written
ERASERS > ERASER
ERASES > ERASE
ERASING > ERASE
ERASION n act of erasing
ERASIONS > ERASION
ERASURE n erasing
ERASURES > ERASURE
ERATHEM n stratum of rocks representing a specific geological era
ERATHEMS > ERATHEM
ERBIA n oxide of erbium
ERBIAS > ERBIA

ERBIUM n metallic element of the lanthanide series
ERBIUMS > ERBIUM
ERE prep before ▷ vb plough
ERECT vb build ▷ adj upright
ERECTABLE > ERECT
ERECTED > ERECT
ERECTER same as > ERECTOR
ERECTERS > ERECTER
ERECTILE adj capable of becoming erect from sexual excitement
ERECTING > ERECT
ERECTION n act of erecting or the state of being erected
ERECTIONS > ERECTION
ERECTIVE adj producing erections
ERECTLY > ERECT
ERECTNESS > ERECT
ERECTOR n any muscle that raises a part or makes it erect
ERECTORS > ERECTOR
ERECTS > ERECT
ERED > ERE
ERELONG adv before long
EREMIC adj of or relating to deserts
EREMITAL > EREMITE
EREMITE n Christian hermit
EREMITES > EREMITE
EREMITIC > EREMITE
EREMITISH > EREMITE
EREMITISM > EREMITE
EREMURI > EREMURUS
EREMURUS n type of herb
ERENOW adv long before the present
EREPSIN n mixture of proteolytic enzymes secreted by the small intestine
EREPSINS > EREPSIN
ERES > ERE
ERETHIC > ERETHISM
ERETHISM n abnormally high degree of irritability or sensitivity in any part of the body
ERETHISMS > ERETHISM
ERETHITIC > ERETHISM
EREV n day before
EREVS > EREV
EREWHILE adv short time ago
EREWHILES same as > EREWHILE
ERF n plot of land marked off for building purposes
ERG same as > ERGOMETER
ERGASTIC adj consisting of the non-living by-products of protoplasmic activity
ERGATANER n wingless male ant
ERGATE n worker ant

ERGATES > ERGATE
ERGATIVE adj denoting a type of verb that takes the same noun as either direct object or as subject, with equivalent meaning. Thus, "fuse" is an ergative verb: "He fused the lights" and "The lights fused" have equivalent meaning ▷ n ergative verb
ERGATIVES > ERGATIVE
ERGATOID > ERGATE
ERGATOIDS > ERGATOID
ERGO same as > ERGOMETER
ERGODIC adj of or relating to the probability that any state will recur
ERGOGENIC adj giving energy
ERGOGRAM n tracing produced by an ergograph
ERGOGRAMS > ERGOGRAM
ERGOGRAPH n instrument that measures and records the amount of work a muscle does during contraction, its rate of fatigue, etc
ERGOMANIA n excessive desire to work
ERGOMETER n dynamometer
ERGOMETRY n measurement of work done
ERGON n work
ERGONOMIC adj designed to minimize effort
ERGONS > ERGON
ERGOS > ERGO
ERGOT n fungal disease of cereal
ERGOTIC > ERGOT
ERGOTISE same as > ERGOTIZE
ERGOTISED > ERGOTISE
ERGOTISES > ERGOTISE
ERGOTISM n ergot poisoning, producing either burning pains and eventually gangrene in the limbs or itching skin and convulsions
ERGOTISMS > ERGOTISM
ERGOTIZE vb inflict ergotism upon
ERGOTIZED > ERGOTIZE
ERGOTIZES > ERGOTIZE
ERGOTS > ERGOT
ERGS > ERG
ERHU n Chinese two-stringed violin
ERHUS > ERHU
ERIACH same as > ERIC
ERIACHS > ERIACH
ERIC n (in old Irish law) fine paid by a murderer to the family of his victim
ERICA n genus of plants including heathers
ERICAS > ERICA
ERICK same as > ERIC

ERICKS > ERICK
ERICOID adj (of leaves) small and tough, resembling those of heather
ERICS > ERIC
ERIGERON n type of plant
ERIGERONS > ERIGERON
ERING > ERE
ERINGO same as > ERYNGO
ERINGOES > ERINGO
ERINGOS > ERINGO
ERINITE n arsenate of copper
ERINITES > ERINITE
ERINUS n type of plant
ERINUSES > ERINUS
ERIOMETER n device for measuring the diameters of minute particles or fibres
ERIONITE n common form of zeolite
ERIONITES > ERIONITE
ERIOPHYID n type of mite
ERISTIC adj of, relating, or given to controversy or logical disputation ▷ n person who engages in logical disputes
ERISTICAL same as > ERISTIC
ERISTICS > ERISTIC
ERK n aircraftman or naval rating
ERKS > ERK
ERLANG n unit of traffic intensity in a telephone system
ERLANGS > ERLANG
ERLKING n malevolent spirit who carries off children
ERLKINGS > ERLKING
ERM interj expression of hesitation
ERMELIN n ermine
ERMELINS > ERMELIN
ERMINE n stoat in northern regions
ERMINED adj clad in the fur of the ermine
ERMINES > ERMINE
ERN archaic variant of > EARN
ERNE n fish-eating (European) sea eagle
ERNED > ERN
ERNES > ERNE
ERNING > ERN
ERNS > ERN
ERODABLE > ERODE
ERODE vb wear away
ERODED > ERODE
ERODENT > ERODE
ERODENTS > ERODE
ERODES > ERODE
ERODIBLE > ERODE
ERODING > ERODE
ERODIUM n type of geranium

ERODIUMS > ERODIUM

EROGENIC same as
> EROGENOUS

EROGENOUS adj sensitive
to sexual stimulation

EROS n lust .

EROSE adj jagged or
uneven, as though
gnawed or bitten

EROSELY > EROSE

EROSES > EROS

EROSIBLE adj able to be
eroded

EROSION n wearing away
of rocks or soil

EROSIONAL > EROSION

EROSIONS > EROSION

EROSIVE > EROSION

EROSIVITY > EROSION

EROSTRATE adj without a
beak

EROTEMA n rhetorical
question

EROTEMAS > EROTEMA

EROTEME same as
> EROTEMA

EROTEMES > EROTEME

EROTESES > EROTESIS

EROTESIS same as
> EROTEMA

EROTETIC adj pertaining
to a rhetorical question

EROTIC adj relating to
sexual pleasure or desire
▷ n person who has strong
sexual desires

EROTICA n sexual
literature or art

EROTICAL adj erotic

EROTICAS > EROTICA

EROTICISE same as
> EROTICIZE

EROTICISM n erotic
quality or nature

EROTICIST
> EROTICISM

EROTICIZE vb regard or
present in a sexual way

EROTICS > EROTIC

EROTISE same as
> EROTIZE

EROTISED > EROTISE

EROTISES > EROTISE

EROTISING > EROTISE

EROTISM same as
> EROTICISM

EROTISMS > EROTISM

EROTIZE vb make erotic

EROTIZED > EROTIZE

EROTIZES > EROTIZE

EROTIZING > EROTIZE

EROTOLOGY n study of
erotic stimuli and sexual
behaviour

ERR vb make a mistake

ERRABLE adj capable of
making a mistake

ERRANCIES > ERRANCY

ERRANCY n state or an
instance of erring or a
tendency to err

ERRAND n short trip to do
something for someone

ERRANDS > ERRAND

ERRANT adj behaving in a
manner considered to be
unacceptable ▷ n
knight-errant

ERRANTLY > ERRANT

ERRANTRY n way of life of
a knight errant

ERRANTS > ERRANT

ERRATA > ERRATUM

ERRATAS informal variant
of > ERRATA

ERRATIC adj irregular or
unpredictable ▷ n rock
that has been transported
by glacial action

ERRATICAL adj erratic

ERRATICS > ERRATIC

ERRATUM n error in
writing or printing

ERRED > ERR

ERRHINE adj causing
nasal secretion ▷ n errhine
drug or agent

ERRHINES > ERRHINE

ERRING > ERR

ERRINGLY > ERR

ERRINGS > ERR

ERRONEOUS adj incorrect,
mistaken

ERROR n mistake,
inaccuracy, or
misjudgment

ERRORIST n one who
makes errors

ERRORISTS
> ERRORIST

ERRORLESS > ERROR

ERRORS > ERROR

ERRS > ERR

ERS same as > ERVIL

ERSATZ adj made in
imitation ▷ n ersatz
substance or article

ERSATZES > ERSATZ

ERSES > ERS

ERST adv long ago

ERSTWHILE adj former
▷ adv formerly

ERUCIC adj as in erucic acid
crystalline fatty acid

ERUCIFORM adj
resembling a caterpillar

ERUCT vb belch

ERUCTATE same as
> ERUCT

ERUCTATED
> ERUCTATE

ERUCTATES > ERUCTATE

ERUCTED > ERUCT

ERUCTING > ERUCT

ERUCTS > ERUCT

ERUDITE adj having great
academic knowledge
▷ n erudite person

ERUDITELY > ERUDITE

ERUDITES > ERUDITE

ERUDITION > ERUDITE

ERUGO n verdigris

ERUGOS > ERUGO

ERUMPENT adj bursting
out or (esp of plant parts)
developing as though
bursting through an
overlying structure

ERUPT vb eject (steam,
water, or volcanic
material) violently

ERUPTED > ERUPT

ERUPTIBLE > ERUPT

ERUPTING > ERUPT

ERUPTION > ERUPT

ERUPTIONS > ERUPT

ERUPTIVE adj erupting or
tending to erupt ▷ n type
of volcanic rock

ERUPTIVES > ERUPTIVE

ERUPTS > ERUPT

ERUV n area within which
certain activities
forbidden to be done on
the Sabbath are permitted

ERUVIM > ERUV

ERUVIN > ERUV

ERUVS > ERUV

ERVALENTA n health food
made from lentil and
barley flour

ERVEN > ERF

ERVIL n type of vetch

ERVILS > ERVIL

ERYNGIUM n type of
temperate and subtropical
plant

ERYNGIUMS > ERYNGIUM

ERYNGO n type of plant
with toothed or lobed
leaves

ERYNGOES > ERYNGO

ERYNGOS > ERYNGO

ERYTHEMA n patchy
inflammation of the skin

ERYTHEMAL > ERYTHEMA

ERYTHEMAS > ERYTHEMA

ERYTHEMIC > ERYTHEMA

ERYTHRINA n tropical
tree with red flowers

ERYTHRISM n abnormal
red coloration, as in
plumage or hair

ERYTHRITE n sweet
crystalline compound
extracted from certain
algae and lichens

ERYTHROID adj red or
reddish

ERYTHRON n red blood
cells and their related
tissues

ERYTHRONS > ERYTHRON

ES n letter S

ESCABECHE n (in Mexican
cookery) pickled
vegetables and peppers,
served as a condiment for
fish

ESCALADE n assault by
the use of ladders, esp on a
fortification ▷ vb gain
access to (a place) by the
use of ladders

ESCALADED > ESCALADE

ESCALADER > ESCALADE

ESCALADES > ESCALADE

ESCALADO n escalade

ESCALATE vb increase in
extent or intensity

ESCALATED > ESCALATE

ESCALATES > ESCALATE

ESCALATOR n moving
staircase

ESCALIER n staircase

ESCALIERS > ESCALIER

ESCALLOP another word for
> SCALLOP

ESCALLOPS > ESCALLOP

ESCALOP another word for
> SCALLOP

ESCALOPE n thin slice of
meat, esp veal

ESCALOPED > ESCALOP

ESCALOPES > ESCALOPE

ESCALOPS > ESCALOP

ESCAPABLE > ESCAPE

ESCAPADE n mischievous
adventure

ESCAPADES > ESCAPADE

ESCAPADO n escaped
criminal

ESCAPADOS > ESCAPADO

ESCAPE vb get free (of)
▷ n act of escaping

ESCAPED > ESCAPE

ESCAPEE n person who
has escaped

ESCAPEES > ESCAPEE

ESCAPER > ESCAPE

ESCAPERS > ESCAPE

ESCAPES > ESCAPE

ESCAPING > ESCAPE

ESCAPISM n taking
refuge in fantasy to avoid
unpleasant reality

ESCAPISMS > ESCAPISM

ESCAPIST > ESCAPISM

ESCAPISTS > ESCAPISM

ESCAR same as > ESKER

ESCARGOT n variety of
edible snail, usually eaten
with a sauce made of
melted butter and garlic

ESCARGOTS > ESCARGOT

ESCAROLE n variety of
endive with broad leaves,
used in salads

ESCAROLES > ESCAROLE

ESCARP n inner side of the
ditch separating besiegers
and besieged ▷ vb make
into a slope

ESCARPED > ESCARP

ESCARPING > ESCARP

ESCARPS > ESCARP

ESCARS > ESCAR

ESCHALOT another name
for a > SHALLOT

ESCHALOTS > ESCHALOT

ESCHAR n dry scab or
slough

ESCHARS > ESCHAR

ESCHEAT n possessions
that become state
property in the absence of
an heir ▷ vb attain such
property

ESCHEATED > ESCHEAT

ESCHEATOR > ESCHEAT

ESCHEATS > ESCHEAT

ESCHEW vb abstain from,
avoid

ESCHEWAL > ESCHEW

ESCHEWALS > ESCHEW

ESCHEWED > ESCHEW
ESCHEWER > ESCHEW
ESCHEWERS > ESCHEW
ESCHEWING > ESCHEW
ESCHEWS > ESCHEW
ESCLANDRE n scandal or notoriety
ESCOLAR n slender spiny-finned fish
ESCOLARS > ESCOLAR
ESCOPETTE n carbine
ESCORT n people following another person for protection or as an honour ▷ vb act as an escort to
ESCORTAGE > ESCORT
ESCORTED > ESCORT
ESCORTING > ESCORT
ESCORTS > ESCORT
ESCOT vb maintain
ESCOTED > ESCOT
ESCOTING > ESCOT
ESCOTS > ESCOT
ESCOTTED > ESCOT
ESCOTTING > ESCOT
ESCRIBANO n clerk
ESCRIBE vb make a mathematical drawing
ESCRIBED > ESCRIBE
ESCRIBES > ESCRIBE
ESCRIBING > ESCRIBE
ESCROC n conman
ESCROCS > ESCROC
ESCROL same as > ESCROLL
ESCROLL n scroll
ESCROLLS > ESCROLL
ESCROLS > ESCROL
ESCROW n item delivered to a third party pending fulfilment of a condition ▷ vb place (money, a document, etc) in escrow
ESCROWED > ESCROW
ESCROWING > ESCROW
ESCROWS > ESCROW
ESCUAGE (in medieval Europe) another word for > SCUTAGE
ESCUAGES > ESCUAGE
ESCUDO n former monetary unit of Portugal
ESCUDOS > ESCUDO
ESCULENT adj edible ▷ n any edible substance
ESCULENTS > ESCULENT
ESEMPLASY n unification
ESERINE n crystalline alkaloid
ESERINES > ESERINE
ESES > ES
ESILE n vinegar
ESILES > ESILE
ESKAR same as > ESKER
ESKARS > ESKAR
ESKER n long ridge of gravel, sand, etc
ESKERS > ESKER
ESKIES > ESKY
ESKY n portable insulated container
ESLOIN same as > ELOIGN

ESLOINED > ESLOIN
ESLOINING > ESLOIN
ESLOINS > ESLOIN
ESLOYNE same as > ELOIGN
ESLOYNED > ESLOYNE
ESLOYNES > ESLOYNE
ESLOYNING > ESLOYNE
ESNE n household slave
ESNECIES > ESNECY
ESNECY n inheritance law
ESNES > ESNE
ESOPHAGI > ESOPHAGUS
ESOPHAGUS n part of the alimentary canal between the pharynx and the stomach
ESOTERIC adj understood by only a small number of people with special knowledge
ESOTERICA pl n esoteric things
ESOTERIES > ESOTERIC
ESOTERISM > ESOTERIC
ESOTERY > ESOTERIC
ESOTROPIA n condition in which eye turns inwards
ESOTROPIC > ESOTROPIA
ESPADA n sword
ESPADAS > ESPADA
ESPAGNOLE n tomato and sherry sauce
ESPALIER n shrub or fruit tree trained to grow flat ▷ vb train (a plant) on an espalier
ESPALIERS > ESPALIER
ESPANOL n Spanish person
ESPANOLES > ESPANOL
ESPARTO n grass of S Europe and N Africa
ESPARTOS > ESPARTO
ESPECIAL adj special
ESPERANCE n hope or expectation
ESPIAL n act or fact of being seen or discovered
ESPIALS > ESPIAL
ESPIED > ESPY
ESPIEGLE adj playful
ESPIER > ESPY
ESPIERS > ESPY
ESPIES > ESPY
ESPIONAGE n spying
ESPLANADE n wide open road used as a public promenade
ESPOIR n category of wrestler
ESPOIRS > ESPOIR
ESPOUSAL n adoption or support
ESPOUSALS > ESPOUSAL
ESPOUSE vb adopt or give support to (a cause etc)
ESPOUSED > ESPOUSE
ESPOUSER > ESPOUSE
ESPOUSERS > ESPOUSE
ESPOUSES > ESPOUSE
ESPOUSING > ESPOUSE

ESPRESSO n strong coffee made by forcing steam or boiling water through ground coffee beans
ESPRESSOS > ESPRESSO
ESPRIT n spirit, liveliness, or wit
ESPRITS > ESPRIT
ESPUMOSO n sparkling wine
ESPUMOSOS > ESPUMOSO
ESPY vb catch sight of
ESPYING > ESPY
ESQUIRE n courtesy title placed after a man's name ▷ vb escort
ESQUIRED > ESQUIRE
ESQUIRES > ESQUIRE
ESQUIRESS feminine form of > ESQUIRE
ESQUIRING > ESQUIRE
ESQUISSE n sketch
ESQUISSES > ESQUISSE
ESS n letter S
ESSAY n short literary composition ▷ vb attempt
ESSAYED > ESSAY
ESSAYER > ESSAY
ESSAYERS > ESSAY
ESSAYETTE n short essay
ESSAYING > ESSAY
ESSAYISH > ESSAY
ESSAYIST n person who writes essays
ESSAYISTS > ESSAYIST
ESSAYS > ESSAY
ESSE n existence
ESSENCE n most important feature of a thing which determines its identity
ESSENCES > ESSENCE
ESSENTIAL adj vitally important ▷ n something fundamental or indispensable
ESSES > ESS
ESSIVE n grammatical case
ESSIVES > ESSIVE
ESSOIN n excuse ▷ vb excuse for not appearing in court
ESSOINED > ESSOIN
ESSOINER > ESSOIN
ESSOINERS > ESSOIN
ESSOINING > ESSOIN
ESSOINS > ESSOIN
ESSONITE variant spelling of > HESSONITE
ESSONITES > ESSONITE
ESSOYNE same as > ESSOIN
ESSOYNES > ESSOYNE
EST n treatment intended to help people towards psychological growth
ESTABLISH vb set up on a permanent basis
ESTACADE n defensive arrangement of stakes
ESTACADES > ESTACADE
ESTAFETTE n mounted courier

ESTAMINET n small café, bar, or bistro, esp a shabby one
ESTANCIA n (in Spanish America) a large estate or cattle ranch
ESTANCIAS > ESTANCIA
ESTATE n landed property ▷ vb provide with an estate
ESTATED > ESTATE
ESTATES > ESTATE
ESTATING > ESTATE
ESTEEM n high regard ▷ vb think highly of
ESTEEMED > ESTEEM
ESTEEMING > ESTEEM
ESTEEMS > ESTEEM
ESTER n chemical compound
ESTERASE n any of a group of enzymes that hydrolyse esters into alcohols and acids
ESTERASES > ESTERASE
ESTERIFY vb change or cause to change into an ester
ESTERS > ESTER
ESTHESES > ESTHESIS
ESTHESIA US spelling of > AESTHESIA
ESTHESIAS > ESTHESIA
ESTHESIS n esthesia
ESTHETE US spelling of > AESTHETE
ESTHETES > ESTHETE
ESTHETIC > ESTHETE
ESTHETICS > ESTHETE
ESTIMABLE adj worthy of respect
ESTIMABLY > ESTIMABLE
ESTIMATE vb calculate roughly ▷ n approximate calculation
ESTIMATED > ESTIMATE
ESTIMATES > ESTIMATE
ESTIMATOR n person or thing that estimates
ESTIVAL usual US spelling of > AESTIVAL
ESTIVATE usual US spelling of > AESTIVATE
ESTIVATED > ESTIVATE
ESTIVATES > ESTIVATE
ESTIVATOR > ESTIVATE
ESTOC n short stabbing sword
ESTOCS > ESTOC
ESTOILE n heraldic star with wavy points
ESTOILES > ESTOILE
ESTOP vb preclude by estoppel
ESTOPPAGE > ESTOP
ESTOPPED > ESTOP
ESTOPPEL n rule of evidence whereby a person is precluded from denying the truth of a statement of facts he has previously asserted
ESTOPPELS > ESTOPPEL
ESTOPPING > ESTOP

ESTOPS > ESTOP
ESTOVER *same as* **>** ESTOVERS
ESTOVERS *pl n* right allowed by law to tenants of land to cut timber, esp for fuel and repairs
ESTRADE *n* dais or raised platform
ESTRADES > ESTRADE
ESTRADIOL *n* most potent estrogenic hormone secreted by the mammalian ovary
ESTRAGON *another name for* **>** TARRAGON
ESTRAGONS > ESTRAGON
ESTRAL *US spelling of* **>** OESTRAL
ESTRANGE *vb* separate and live apart from (one's spouse)
ESTRANGED *adj* no longer living with one's spouse
ESTRANGER > ESTRANGE
ESTRANGES > ESTRANGE
ESTRAPADE *n* attempt by a horse to throw its rider
ESTRAY *n* stray domestic animal of unknown ownership ▷ *vb* stray
ESTRAYED > ESTRAY
ESTRAYING > ESTRAY
ESTRAYS > ESTRAY
ESTREAT *n* true copy of or extract from a court record ▷ *vb* send an extract of the court record
ESTREATED > ESTREAT
ESTREATS > ESTREAT
ESTREPE *vb* lay waste
ESTREPED > ESTREPE
ESTREPES > ESTREPE
ESTREPING > ESTREPE
ESTRICH *n* ostrich
ESTRICHES > ESTRICH
ESTRIDGE *n* ostrich
ESTRIDGES > ESTRIDGE
ESTRILDID *n* weaver finch
ESTRIN *US spelling of* **>** OESTRIN
ESTRINS > ESTRIN
ESTRIOL *usual US spelling of* **>** OESTRIOL
ESTRIOLS > ESTRIOL
ESTRO *n* poetic inspiration
ESTROGEN *usual US spelling of* **>** OESTROGEN
ESTROGENS > ESTROGEN
ESTRONE *usual US spelling of* **>** OESTRONE
ESTRONES > ESTRONE
ESTROS > ESTRO
ESTROUS > ESTRUS
ESTRUAL > ESTRUS
ESTRUM *usual US spelling of* **>** OESTRUM
ESTRUMS > ESTRUM
ESTRUS *usual US spelling of* **>** OESTRUS
ESTRUSES > ESTRUS
ESTS > EST
ESTUARIAL > ESTUARY

ESTUARIAN > ESTUARY
ESTUARIES > ESTUARY
ESTUARINE *adj* formed or deposited in an estuary
ESTUARY *n* mouth of a river
ESURIENCE > ESURIENT
ESURIENCY > ESURIENT
ESURIENT *adj* greedy
ET *dialect past tense of* **>** EAT
ETA *n* seventh letter in the Greek alphabet
ETACISM *n* pronunciation of eta as a long vowel sound
ETACISMS > ETACISM
ETAERIO *n* aggregate fruit
ETAERIOS > ETAERIO
ETAGE *n* floor in a multi-storey building
ETAGERE *n* stand with open shelves for displaying ornaments, etc
ETAGERES > ETAGERE
ETAGES > ETAGE
ETALAGE *n* display
ETALAGES > ETALAGE
ETALON *n* device used in spectroscopy
ETALONS > ETALON
ETAMIN *same as* **>** ETAMINE
ETAMINE *n* cotton or worsted fabric of loose weave
ETAMINES > ETAMINE
ETAMINS > ETAMIN
ETAPE *n* public storehouse
ETAPES > ETAPE
ETAS > ETA
ETAT *n* state
ETATISM *same as* **>** ETATISME
ETATISME *n* authoritarian control by the state
ETATISMES > ETATISME
ETATISMS > ETATISM
ETATIST > ETATISME
ETATISTE > ETATISME
ETATISTES > ETATISME
ETATS > ETAT
ETCETERA *n* number of other items
ETCETERAS *pl n* miscellaneous extra things or people
ETCH *vb* wear away or cut the surface of (metal, glass, etc) with acid
ETCHANT *n* any acid or corrosive used for etching
ETCHANTS > ETCHANT
ETCHED > ETCH
ETCHER > ETCH
ETCHERS > ETCH
ETCHES > ETCH
ETCHING *n* picture printed from an etched metal plate
ETCHINGS > ETCHING
ETEN *n* giant

ETENS > ETEN
ETERNAL *adj* without beginning or end ▷ *n* eternal thing
ETERNALLY > ETERNAL
ETERNALS > ETERNAL
ETERNE *archaic or poetic word for* **>** ETERNAL
ETERNISE *same as* **>** ETERNIZE
ETERNISED > ETERNISE
ETERNISES > ETERNISE
ETERNITY *n* infinite time
ETERNIZE *vb* make eternal
ETERNIZED > ETERNIZE
ETERNIZES > ETERNIZE
ETESIAN *adj* (of NW winds) recurring annually in the summer in the E Mediterranean ▷ *n* etesian wind
ETESIANS > ETESIAN
ETH *same as* **>** EDH
ETHAL *n* cetyl alcohol
ETHALS > ETHAL
ETHANAL *n* colourless volatile pungent liquid
ETHANALS > ETHANAL
ETHANE *n* odourless flammable gas
ETHANES > ETHANE
ETHANOATE *same as* **>** ACETATE
ETHANOIC *adj* as in ethanoic acid acetic acid
ETHANOL *same as* **>** ALCOHOL
ETHANOLS > ETHANOL
ETHANOYL *n* substance consisting of or containing the monovalent group CH_3CO-
ETHANOYLS > ETHANOYL
ETHE *adj* easy
ETHENE *same as* **>** ETHYLENE
ETHENES > ETHENE
ETHEPHON *n* synthetic plant-growth regulator
ETHEPHONS > ETHEPHON
ETHER *n* colourless anaesthetic
ETHERCAP *n* spider
ETHERCAPS > ETHERCAP
ETHEREAL *adj* extremely delicate
ETHEREOUS *same as* **>** ETHEREAL
ETHERIAL *same as* **>** ETHEREAL
ETHERIC > ETHER
ETHERICAL > ETHER
ETHERIFY *vb* change (a compound, such as an alcohol) into an ether
ETHERION *n* gas formerly believed to exist in air
ETHERIONS > ETHERION
ETHERISE *same as* **>** ETHERIZE
ETHERISED > ETHERISE
ETHERISER > ETHERISE
ETHERISES > ETHERISE

ETHERISH > ETHER
ETHERISM *n* addiction to ether
ETHERISMS > ETHERISM
ETHERIST > ETHERISM
ETHERISTS > ETHERISM
ETHERIZE *vb* subject (a person) to the anaesthetic influence of ether fumes
ETHERIZED > ETHERIZE
ETHERIZER > ETHERIZE
ETHERIZES > ETHERIZE
ETHERS > ETHER
ETHIC *n* moral principle
ETHICAL *adj* of or based on a system of moral beliefs ▷ *n* drug available only by prescription
ETHICALLY > ETHICAL
ETHICALS > ETHICAL
ETHICIAN > ETHICS
ETHICIANS > ETHICS
ETHICISE *same as* **>** ETHICIZE
ETHICISED > ETHICISE
ETHICISES > ETHICISE
ETHICISM > ETHICS
ETHICISMS > ETHICS
ETHICIST > ETHICS
ETHICISTS > ETHICS
ETHICIZE *vb* make or consider as ethical
ETHICIZED > ETHICIZE
ETHICIZES > ETHICIZE
ETHICS *n* code of behaviour
ETHINYL *same as* **>** ETHYNYL
ETHINYLS > ETHINYL
ETHION *n* type of pesticide
ETHIONINE *n* type of amino acid
ETHIONS > ETHION
ETHIOPS *n* dark-coloured chemical compound
ETHIOPSES > ETHIOPS
ETHMOID *adj* denoting or relating to a specific bone of the skull ▷ *n* ethmoid bone
ETHMOIDAL *same as* **>** ETHMOID
ETHMOIDS > ETHMOID
ETHNARCH *n* ruler of a people or province, as in parts of the Roman and Byzantine Empires
ETHNARCHS > ETHNARCH
ETHNARCHY > ETHNARCH
ETHNE > ETHNOS
ETHNIC *adj* relating to a people or group that shares a culture, religion, or language ▷ *n* member of an ethnic group, esp a minority group
ETHNICAL *same as* **>** ETHNIC
ETHNICISM *n* paganism
ETHNICITY > ETHNIC
ETHNICS > ETHNIC
ETHNOCIDE *n* extermination of a race

ETHNOGENY *n* branch of ethnology that deals with the origin of races or peoples

ETHNOLOGY *n* study of human races

ETHNONYM *n* name of ethnic group

ETHNONYMS > ETHNONYM

ETHNOS *n* ethnic group

ETHNOSES > ETHNOS

ETHOGRAM *n* description of animal's behaviour

ETHOGRAMS > ETHOGRAM

ETHOLOGIC > ETHOLOGY

ETHOLOGY *n* study of the behaviour of animals in their normal environment

ETHONONE another name for > KETENE

ETHONONES > ETHONONE

ETHOS *n* distinctive spirit and attitudes of a people, culture, etc

ETHOSES > ETHOS

ETHOXIDE *n* any of a class of saltlike compounds

ETHOXIDES > ETHOXIDE

ETHOXIES > ETHOXY

ETHOXY same as > ETHOXYL

ETHOXYL *n* univalent radical

ETHOXYLS > ETHOXYL

ETHS > ETH

ETHYL *adj* type of chemical hydrocarbon group

ETHYLATE same as > ETHOXIDE

ETHYLATED > ETHYLATE

ETHYLATES > ETHYLATE

ETHYLENE *n* poisonous gas used as an anaesthetic and as fuel

ETHYLENES > ETHYLENE

ETHYLENIC > ETHYLENE

ETHYLIC > ETHYL

ETHYLS > ETHYL

ETHYNE another name for > ACETYLENE

ETHYNES > ETHYNE

ETHYNYL *n* univalent radical

ETHYNYLS > ETHYNYL

ETIC *adj* relating to linguistic terms analysed without regard to structural function ▷ *n* etic approach or viewpoint

ETICS > ETIC

ETIOLATE *vb* become pale and weak

ETIOLATED > ETIOLATE

ETIOLATES > ETIOLATE

ETIOLIN *n* yellow pigment

ETIOLINS > ETIOLIN

ETIOLOGIC > ETIOLOGY

ETIOLOGY *n* study of the causes of diseases

ETIQUETTE *n* conventional code of conduct

ETNA *n* container used to heat liquids

ETNAS > ETNA

ETOILE *n* star

ETOILES > ETOILE

ETOUFFEE *n* spicy Cajun stew

ETOUFFEES > ETOUFFEE

ETOURDI *adj* foolish

ETOURDIE feminine form of > ETOURDI

ETRANGER *n* foreigner

ETRANGERE feminine form of > ETRANGER

ETRANGERS > ETRANGER

ETRENNE *n* New Year's gift

ETRENNES > ETRENNE

ETRIER *n* short portable ladder or set of webbing loops

ETRIERS > ETRIER

ETTERCAP *n* spider

ETTERCAPS > ETTERCAP

ETTIN *n* giant

ETTINS > ETTIN

ETTLE *vb* intend

ETTLED > ETTLE

ETTLES > ETTLE

ETTLING > ETTLE

ETUDE *n* short musical composition for a solo instrument

ETUDES > ETUDE

ETUI *n* small usually ornamented case

ETUIS > ETUI

ETWEE same as > ETUI

ETWEES > ETUI

ETYMA > ETYMON

ETYMIC > ETYMON

ETYMOLOGY *n* study of the sources and development of words

ETYMON *n* earliest form of a word or morpheme from which another is derived

ETYMONS > ETYMON

ETYPIC *adj* unable to conform to type

ETYPICAL same as > ETYPIC

EUCAIN same as > EUCAINE

EUCAINE *n* crystalline optically active substance

EUCAINES > EUCAINE

EUCAINS > EUCAIN

EUCALYPT *n* myrtaceous tree

EUCALYPTI *n* eucalypts

EUCALYPTS > EUCALYPT

EUCARYON same as > EUKARYOTE

EUCARYONS > EUCARYON

EUCARYOT same as > EUKARYOTE

EUCARYOTE same as > EUKARYOTE

EUCARYOTS > EUCARYOT

EUCHARIS *n* S American plant cultivated for its large white fragrant flowers

EUCHLORIC > EUCHLORIN

EUCHLORIN *n* explosive gaseous mixture of chlorine and chlorine dioxide

EUCHOLOGY *n* prayer formulary

EUCHRE *n* US and Canadian card game ▷ *vb* prevent (a player) from making his contracted tricks

EUCHRED > EUCHRE

EUCHRES > EUCHRE

EUCHRING > EUCHRE

EUCLASE *n* brittle green gem

EUCLASES > EUCLASE

EUCLIDEAN *adj* of or relating to Euclid (Greek mathematician of Alexandria, 3rd century BC), esp his system of geometry

EUCLIDIAN same as > EUCLIDEAN

EUCRITE *n* type of stony meteorite

EUCRITES > EUCRITE

EUCRITIC > EUCRITE

EUCRYPHIA *n* Australian and S American tree or shrub, mostly evergreen, with dark lustrous green leaves and white flowers

EUCYCLIC *adj* (of plants) having the same number of leaves in each whorl

EUDAEMON same as > EUDEMON

EUDAEMONS > EUDAEMON

EUDAEMONY same as > EUDEMONIA

EUDAIMON same as > EUDAEMON

EUDAIMONS > EUDAIMON

EUDEMON *n* benevolent spirit or demon

EUDEMONIA *n* happiness, esp (in the philosophy of Aristotle) that resulting from a rational active life

EUDEMONIC > EUDEMONIA

EUDEMONS > EUDEMON

EUDIALYTE *n* brownish-red mineral

EUGARIE another name for > PIPI

EUGARIES > EUGARIE

EUGE *interj* well done!

EUGENIA *n* plant of the clove family

EUGENIAS > EUGENIA

EUGENIC > EUGENICS

EUGENICAL > EUGENICS

EUGENICS *n* study of methods of improving the human race

EUGENISM > EUGENICS

EUGENISMS > EUGENICS

EUGENIST > EUGENICS

EUGENISTS > EUGENICS

EUGENOL *n* oily liquid used in perfumery

EUGENOLS > EUGENOL

EUGH archaic form of > YEW

EUGHEN archaic form of > YEW

EUGHS > EUGH

EUGLENA *n* type of freshwater unicellular organism

EUGLENAS > EUGLENA

EUGLENID same as > EUGLENA

EUGLENIDS > EUGLENID

EUGLENOID > EUGLENA

EUK *vb* itch

EUKARYON same as > EUKARYOTE

EUKARYONS > EUKARYON

EUKARYOT same as > EUKARYOTE

EUKARYOTE *n* type of organism whose cells each have a distinct nucleus within which the genetic material is contained

EUKARYOTS > EUKARYOT

EUKED > EUK

EUKING > EUK

EUKS > EUK

EULACHAN same as > EULACHON

EULACHANS > EULACHAN

EULACHON *n* salmonoid food fish

EULACHONS > EULACHON

EULOGIA *n* blessed bread

EULOGIAE > EULOGIA

EULOGIAS > EULOGIA

EULOGIES > EULOGY

EULOGISE same as > EULOGIZE

EULOGISED > EULOGISE

EULOGISER > EULOGISE

EULOGISES > EULOGISE

EULOGIST > EULOGIZE

EULOGISTS > EULOGIZE

EULOGIUM same as > EULOGY

EULOGIUMS > EULOGIUM

EULOGIZE *vb* praise (a person or thing) highly in speech or writing

EULOGIZED > EULOGIZE

EULOGIZER > EULOGIZE

EULOGIZES > EULOGIZE

EULOGY *n* speech or writing in praise of a person

EUMELANIN *n* dark melanin

EUMERISM *n* collection of similar parts

EUMERISMS > EUMERISM

EUMONG same as > EUMUNG

EUMONGS > EUMONG

EUMUNG *n* any of various Australian acacias

EUMUNGS > EUMUNG

EUNUCH *n* castrated man

EUNUCHISE same as > EUNUCHIZE

EUNUCHISM > EUNUCH

EUNUCHIZE *vb* castrate

EUNUCHOID *n* one suffering from deficient sexual development

EUNUCHS > EUNUCH

EUOI *n* cry of Bacchic frenzy

EUONYMIN *n* extract derived from the bark of the euonymus

EUONYMINS > EUONYMIN

EUONYMUS *n* type of N temperate tree or shrub

EUOUAE *n* musical term

EUOUAES > EUOUAE

EUPAD *n* antiseptic powder

EUPADS > EUPAD

EUPATRID *n* (in ancient Greece) hereditary noble or landowner

EUPATRIDS > EUPATRID

EUPEPSIA *n* good digestion

EUPEPSIAS > EUPEPSIA

EUPEPSIES > EUPEPSY

EUPEPSY *same as* > EUPEPSIA

EUPEPTIC > EUPEPSIA

EUPHAUSID *n* small pelagic shrimplike crustacean

EUPHEMISE *same as* > EUPHEMIZE

EUPHEMISM *n* inoffensive word or phrase substituted for one considered offensive or upsetting

EUPHEMIST > EUPHEMISM

EUPHEMIZE *vb* speak in euphemisms or refer to by means of a euphemism

EUPHENIC *n* of or pertaining to biological improvement

EUPHENICS *n* science of biological improvement

EUPHOBIA *n* fear of good news

EUPHOBIAS > EUPHOBIA

EUPHON *n* glass harmonica

EUPHONIA *same as* > EUPHONY

EUPHONIAS > EUPHONIA

EUPHONIC *adj* denoting or relating to euphony

EUPHONIES > EUPHONY

EUPHONISE *same as* > EUPHONIZE

EUPHONISM *n* use of pleasant-sounding words

EUPHONIUM *n* brass musical instrument, tenor tuba

EUPHONIZE *vb* make pleasant to hear

EUPHONS > EUPHON

EUPHONY *n* pleasing sound

EUPHORBIA *n* type of plant such as the spurge or poinsettia

EUPHORIA *n* sense of elation

EUPHORIAS > EUPHORIA

EUPHORIC > EUPHORIA

EUPHORIES > EUPHORY

EUPHORY *same as* > EUPHORIA

EUPHOTIC *adj* denoting or relating to the uppermost part of a sea or lake down to about 100 metres depth, which receives enough light to enable photosynthesis to take place

EUPHRASIA *n* eyebright

EUPHRASY *same as* > EYEBRIGHT

EUPHROE *n* wooden block through which the lines of a crowfoot are rove

EUPHROES > EUPHROE

EUPHUISE *same as* > EUPHUIZE

EUPHUISED > EUPHUISE

EUPHUISES > EUPHUISE

EUPHUISM *n* artificial prose style of the Elizabethan period, marked by extreme use of antithesis, alliteration, and extended similes and allusions

EUPHUISMS > EUPHUISM

EUPHUIST > EUPHUISM

EUPHUISTS > EUPHUISM

EUPHUIZE *vb* write in euphuism

EUPHUIZED > EUPHUIZE

EUPHUIZES > EUPHUIZE

EUPLASTIC *adj* healing quickly and well

EUPLOID *adj* having chromosomes in an exact multiple of the haploid number ⊳ *n* euploid cell or individual

EUPLOIDS > EUPLOID

EUPLOIDY > EUPLOID

EUPNEA *same as* > EUPNOEA

EUPNEAS > EUPNEA

EUPNEIC > EUPNOEA

EUPNOEA *n* normal relaxed breathing

EUPNOEAS > EUPNOEA

EUPNOEIC > EUPNOEA

EUREKA *n* exclamation of triumph at finding something

EUREKAS > EUREKA

EURHYTHMY *n* rhythmic movement

EURIPI > EURIPUS

EURIPUS *n* strait or channel with a strong current or tide

EURIPUSES > EURIPUS

EURO *n* unit of the single currency of the European Union

EUROBOND *n* bond issued in a eurocurrency

EUROBONDS > EUROBOND

EUROCRAT *n* member, esp a senior member, of the administration of the European Union

EUROCRATS > EUROCRAT

EUROCREEP *n* gradual introduction of the euro into use in Britain

EUROKIES > EUROKY

EUROKOUS > EUROKY

EUROKY *n* ability of an organism to live under different conditions

EUROLAND *n* area containing the countries using the euro

EUROLANDS > EUROLAND

EURONOTE *n* form of euro-commercial paper consisting of short-term negotiable bearer notes

EURONOTES > EURONOTE

EUROPHILE *n* person who admires Europe, Europeans, or the European Union

EUROPIUM *n* silvery-white element of the lanthanide series

EUROPIUMS > EUROPIUM

EUROPOP *n* type of pop music by European artists

EUROPOPS > EUROPOP

EUROS > EURO

EUROZONE *n* area containing the countries using the euro

EUROZONES > EUROZONE

EURYBATH *n* organism that can live at different depths underwater

EURYBATHS > EURYBATH

EURYOKIES > EURYOKY

EURYOKOUS > EURYOKY

EURYOKY *same as* > EUROKY

EURYTHERM *n* organism that can tolerate widely differing temperatures

EURYTHMIC *adj* having a pleasing and harmonious rhythm, order, or structure

EURYTHMY *n* dancing style in which the rhythm of music is expressed through body movements

EURYTOPIC *adj* (of a species) able to tolerate a wide range of environments

EUSOCIAL *adj* using division of labour

EUSOL *n* solution of eupad in water

EUSOLS > EUSOL

EUSTACIES > EUSTATIC

EUSTACY > EUSTATIC

EUSTASIES > EUSTATIC

EUSTASY > EUSTATIC

EUSTATIC *adj* denoting or relating to worldwide changes in sea level, caused by the melting of ice sheets, movements of

the ocean floor, sedimentation, etc

EUSTELE *n* central cylinder of a seed plant

EUSTELES > EUSTELE

EUSTYLE *n* building with columns optimally spaced

EUSTYLES > EUSTYLE

EUTAXIA *n* condition of being easily melted

EUTAXIAS > EUTAXIA

EUTAXIES > EUTAXY

EUTAXITE *n* banded volcanic rock

EUTAXITES > EUTAXITE

EUTAXITIC > EUTAXITE

EUTAXY *n* good order

EUTECTIC *adj* (of a mixture of substances, esp an alloy) having the lowest freezing point of all possible mixtures of the substances ⊳ *n* eutectic mixture

EUTECTICS > EUTECTIC

EUTECTOID *n* mixture of substances similar to a eutectic, but forming two or three constituents from a solid instead of from a melt ⊳ *adj* concerned with or suitable for eutectoid mixtures

EUTEXIA *same as* > EUTAXIA

EUTEXIAS > EUTEXIA

EUTHANASE *same as* > EUTHANIZE

EUTHANASY *n* the act of killing someone painlessly

EUTHANAZE *same as* > EUTHANIZE

EUTHANISE *same as* > EUTHANIZE

EUTHANIZE *vb* put (someone, esp one suffering from a terminal illness) to death painlessly

EUTHENICS *n* study of the control of the environment, esp with a view to improving the health and living standards of the human race

EUTHENIST > EUTHENICS

EUTHERIAN *n* type of mammal with a placenta, whose young reach an advanced state of development before birth

EUTHYMIA *n* pleasant state of mind

EUTHYMIAS > EUTHYMIA

EUTHYROID *n* condition of having thyroid glands that function normally

EUTRAPELY *n* conversational skill

EUTROPHIC *adj* (of lakes and similar habitats) rich in organic and mineral nutrients and supporting an abundant plant life, which in the process of

e

decaying depletes the oxygen supply for animal life

EUTROPHY > EUTROPHIC

EUTROPIC > EUTROPY

EUTROPIES > EUTROPY

EUTROPOUS > EUTROPY

EUTROPY *n* chemical structure

EUXENITE *n* rare brownish-black mineral containing erbium, cerium, uranium, columbium, and yttrium

EUXENITES > EUXENITE

EVACUANT *adj* serving to promote excretion, esp of the bowels ▷ *n* evacuant agent

EVACUANTS > EVACUANT

EVACUATE *vb* send (someone) away from a place of danger

EVACUATED > EVACUATE

EVACUATES > EVACUATE

EVACUATOR > EVACUATE

EVACUEE *n* person evacuated from a place of danger

EVACUEES > EVACUEE

EVADABLE > EVADE

EVADE *vb* get away from or avoid

EVADED > EVADE

EVADER > EVADE

EVADERS > EVADE

EVADES > EVADE

EVADIBLE > EVADE

EVADING > EVADE

EVADINGLY > EVADE

EVAGATION *n* digression

EVAGINATE *vb* turn (an organ or part) inside out

EVALUABLE > EVALUATE

EVALUATE *vb* find or judge the value of

EVALUATED > EVALUATE

EVALUATES > EVALUATE

EVALUATOR > EVALUATE

EVANESCE *vb* fade gradually from sight

EVANESCED > EVANESCE

EVANESCES > EVANESCE

EVANGEL *n* gospel of Christianity

EVANGELIC *adj* of, based upon, or following from the gospels

EVANGELS > EVANGEL

EVANGELY *n* gospel

EVANISH *poetic word for* > VANISH

EVANISHED > EVANISH

EVANISHES > EVANISH

EVANITION > EVANISH

EVAPORATE *vb* change from a liquid or solid to a vapour

EVAPORITE *n* any sedimentary rock, such as rock salt, gypsum, or anhydrite, formed by evaporation of former seas or salt-water lakes

EVASIBLE > EVASION

EVASION *n* act of evading something by cunning or illegal means

EVASIONAL > EVASION

EVASIONS > EVASION

EVASIVE *adj* not straightforward

EVASIVELY > EVASIVE

EVE *n* evening or day before some special event

EVECTION *n* irregularity in the moon's motion caused by perturbations of the sun and planets

EVECTIONS > EVECTION

EVEJAR *n* nightjar

EVEJARS > EVEJAR

EVEN *adj* flat or smooth ▷ *adv* equally ▷ *vb* make even ▷ *n* eve

EVENED > EVEN

EVENEMENT *n* event

EVENER > EVEN

EVENERS > EVEN

EVENEST > EVEN

EVENFALL *n* early evening

EVENFALLS > EVENFALL

EVENING *n* end of the day or early part of the night ▷ *adj* of or in the evening

EVENINGS *adv* in the evening, esp regularly

EVENLY > EVEN

EVENNESS > EVEN

EVENS *adv* (of a bet) winning the same as the amount staked if successful

EVENSONG *n* evening prayer

EVENSONGS > EVENSONG

EVENT *n* anything that takes place ▷ *vb* take part or ride (a horse) in eventing

EVENTED > EVENT

EVENTER > EVENTING

EVENTERS > EVENTING

EVENTFUL *adj* full of exciting incidents

EVENTIDE *n* evening

EVENTIDES > EVENTIDE

EVENTING *n* riding competitions, usu involving cross-country, jumping, and dressage

EVENTINGS > EVENTING

EVENTIVE *adj* relating to an event

EVENTLESS > EVENT

EVENTRATE *vb* open the belly of

EVENTS > EVENT

EVENTUAL *adj* ultimate

EVENTUATE *vb* result ultimately (in)

EVER *adv* at any time

EVERGLADE *n* large area of submerged marshland

EVERGREEN *adj* (tree or shrub) having leaves throughout the year ▷ *n* evergreen tree or shrub

EVERMORE *adv* for all time to come

EVERNET *n* hypothetical form of internet

EVERNETS > EVERNET

EVERSIBLE > EVERT

EVERSION > EVERT

EVERSIONS > EVERT

EVERT *vb* turn (some bodily part) outwards or inside out

EVERTED > EVERT

EVERTING > EVERT

EVERTOR *n* any muscle that turns a part outwards

EVERTORS > EVERTOR

EVERTS > EVERT

EVERWHERE *adv* to or in all parts or places

EVERWHICH *dialect version of* > WHICHEVER

EVERY *adj* each without exception

EVERYBODY *pron* every person

EVERYDAY *adj* usual or ordinary ▷ *n* ordinary day

EVERYDAYS > EVERYDAY

EVERYMAN *n* ordinary person; common man

EVERYMEN > EVERYMAN

EVERYONE *pron* every person

EVERYWAY *adv* in every way

EVERYWHEN *adv* to or in all parts or places

EVES > EVE

EVET *n* eft

EVETS > EVET

EVHOE *interj* cry of Bacchic frenzy

EVICT *vb* legally expel (someone) from his or her home

EVICTED > EVICT

EVICTEE > EVICT

EVICTEES > EVICT

EVICTING > EVICT

EVICTION > EVICT

EVICTIONS > EVICT

EVICTOR > EVICT

EVICTORS > EVICT

EVICTS > EVICT

EVIDENCE *n* ground for belief ▷ *vb* demonstrate, prove

EVIDENCED > EVIDENCE

EVIDENCES > EVIDENCE

EVIDENT *adj* easily seen or understood ▷ *n* item of evidence

EVIDENTLY *adv* without question

EVIDENTS > EVIDENT

EVIL *n* wickedness ▷ *adj* harmful ▷ *adv* in an evil manner

EVILDOER *n* wicked person

EVILDOERS > EVILDOER

EVILDOING > EVILDOER

EVILER > EVIL

EVILEST > EVIL

EVILLER > EVIL

EVILLEST > EVIL

EVILLY > EVIL

EVILNESS > EVIL

EVILS > EVIL

EVINCE *vb* make evident

EVINCED > EVINCE

EVINCES > EVINCE

EVINCIBLE > EVINCE

EVINCIBLY > EVINCE

EVINCING > EVINCE

EVINCIVE > EVINCE

EVIRATE *vb* castrate

EVIRATED > EVIRATE

EVIRATES > EVIRATE

EVIRATING > EVIRATE

EVITABLE *adj* able to be avoided

EVITATE *archaic word for* > AVOID

EVITATED > EVITATE

EVITATES > EVITATE

EVITATING > EVITATE

EVITATION > EVITATE

EVITE *archaic word for* > AVOID

EVITED > EVITE

EVITERNAL *adj* eternal

EVITES > EVITE

EVITING > EVITE

EVO *informal word for* > EVENING

EVOCABLE > EVOKE

EVOCATE *vb* evoke

EVOCATED > EVOCATE

EVOCATES > EVOCATE

EVOCATING > EVOCATE

EVOCATION *n* act of evoking

EVOCATIVE *adj* tending or serving to evoke

EVOCATOR *n* person or thing that evokes

EVOCATORS > EVOCATOR

EVOCATORY *adj* evocative

EVOE *interj* cry of Bacchic frenzy

EVOHE *interj* cry of Bacchic frenzy

EVOKE *vb* call or summon up (a memory, feeling, etc)

EVOKED > EVOKE

EVOKER > EVOKE

EVOKERS > EVOKE

EVOKES > EVOKE

EVOKING > EVOKE

EVOLUE *n* colonial term for an African educated according to European principles

EVOLUES > EVOLUE

EVOLUTE *n* geometric curve ▷ *adj* having the margins rolled outwards ▷ *vb* evolve

EVOLUTED > EVOLUTE

EVOLUTES > EVOLUTE

EVOLUTING > EVOLUTE

EVOLUTION *n* gradual change in the characteristics of living things over successive generations, esp to a more complex form

EVOLUTIVE adj relating to, tending to, or promoting evolution

EVOLVABLE > EVOLVE

EVOLVE vb develop gradually

EVOLVED > EVOLVE

EVOLVENT adj evolving ▷ n involute curve

EVOLVENTS > EVOLVENT

EVOLVER > EVOLVE

EVOLVERS > EVOLVE

EVOLVES > EVOLVE

EVOLVING > EVOLVE

EVONYMUS same as > EUONYMUS

EVOS > EVO

EVOVAE n mnemonic used in sacred music

EVOVAES > EVOVAE

EVULGATE vb make public

EVULGATED > EVULGATE

EVULGATES > EVULGATE

EVULSE vb extract by force

EVULSED > EVULSE

EVULSES > EVULSE

EVULSING > EVULSE

EVULSION n act of extracting by force

EVULSIONS > EVULSION

EVZONE n soldier in an elite Greek infantry regiment

EVZONES > EVZONE

EWE n female sheep

EWER n large jug with a wide mouth

EWERS > EWER

EWES > EWE

EWEST Scots word for > NEAR

EWFTES Spenserian plural of > EFT

EWGHEN archaic form of > YEW

EWHOW interj expression of pity or regret

EWK vb itch

EWKED > EWK

EWKING > EWK

EWKS > EWK

EWT archaic form of > NEWT

EWTS > EWT

EX prep not including ▷ n former husband, wife etc ▷ vb cross out or delete

EXABYTE n very large unit of computer memory

EXABYTES > EXABYTE

EXACT adj correct and complete in every detail ▷ vb demand (payment or obedience)

EXACTA n horse-racing bet

EXACTABLE > EXACT

EXACTAS > EXACTA

EXACTED > EXACT

EXACTER > EXACT

EXACTERS > EXACT

EXACTEST > EXACT

EXACTING adj making rigorous or excessive demands

EXACTION n act of obtaining or demanding money as a right

EXACTIONS > EXACTION

EXACTLY adv precisely, in every respect ▷ interj just so! precisely!

EXACTMENT n condition of being exact

EXACTNESS > EXACT

EXACTOR > EXACT

EXACTORS > EXACT

EXACTRESS > EXACT

EXACTS > EXACT

EXACUM n type of tropical plant

EXACUMS > EXACUM

EXAHERTZ n very large unit of frequency

EXALT vb praise highly

EXALTED adj high or elevated in rank, position, dignity, etc

EXALTEDLY > EXALTED

EXALTER > EXALT

EXALTERS > EXALT

EXALTING > EXALT

EXALTS > EXALT

EXAM n examination

EXAMEN n examination of conscience

EXAMENS > EXAMEN

EXAMINANT n examiner

EXAMINATE n examinee

EXAMINE vb look at closely

EXAMINED > EXAMINE

EXAMINEE n person who sits an exam

EXAMINEES > EXAMINEE

EXAMINER > EXAMINE

EXAMINERS > EXAMINE

EXAMINES > EXAMINE

EXAMINING > EXAMINE

EXAMPLAR archaic form of > EXEMPLAR

EXAMPLARS > EXAMPLAR

EXAMPLE n specimen typical of its group

EXAMPLED > EXAMPLE

EXAMPLES > EXAMPLE

EXAMPLING > EXAMPLE

EXAMS > EXAM

EXANIMATE adj lacking life

EXANTHEM same as > EXANTHEMA

EXANTHEMA n skin eruption or rash occurring as a symptom in a disease such as measles or scarlet fever

EXANTHEMS > EXANTHEM

EXAPTED adj biologically adapted

EXAPTIVE adj involving biological adaptation

EXARATE adj (of the pupa of some insects) having legs, wings, antennae, etc, free and movable

EXARATION n writing

EXARCH n head of certain autonomous Orthodox Christian Churches ▷ adj (of a xylem strand) having the first-formed xylem external to that formed later

EXARCHAL > EXARCH

EXARCHATE n office, rank, or jurisdiction of an exarch

EXARCHIES > EXARCHY

EXARCHIST n supporter of an exarch

EXARCHS > EXARCH

EXARCHY same as > EXARCHATE

EXCAMB vb exchange

EXCAMBED > EXCAMB

EXCAMBING > EXCAMB

EXCAMBION n exchange, esp of land

EXCAMBIUM same as > EXCAMBION

EXCAMBS > EXCAMB

EXCARNATE vb remove flesh from

EXCAUDATE adj having no tail or tail-like process

EXCAVATE vb unearth buried objects from (a piece of land) methodically to learn about the past

EXCAVATED > EXCAVATE

EXCAVATES > EXCAVATE

EXCAVATOR n large machine used for digging

EXCEED vb be greater than

EXCEEDED > EXCEED

EXCEEDER > EXCEED

EXCEEDERS > EXCEED

EXCEEDING adj very great

EXCEEDS > EXCEED

EXCEL vb be superior to

EXCELLED > EXCEL

EXCELLENT adj exceptionally good

EXCELLING > EXCEL

EXCELS > EXCEL

EXCELSIOR n excellent: used as a motto and as a trademark for various products, esp in the US for fine wood shavings used for packing breakable objects

EXCENTRIC same as > ECCENTRIC

EXCEPT prep other than, not including ▷ vb leave out; omit; exclude

EXCEPTANT n person taking exception

EXCEPTED > EXCEPT

EXCEPTING prep except

EXCEPTION n excepting

EXCEPTIVE adj relating to or forming an exception

EXCEPTOR > EXCEPT

EXCEPTORS > EXCEPT

EXCEPTS > EXCEPT

EXCERPT n passage taken from a book, speech, etc

▷ vb take a passage from a book, speech, etc

EXCERPTA > EXCERPTUM

EXCERPTED > EXCERPT

EXCERPTER > EXCERPT

EXCERPTOR > EXCERPT

EXCERPTS > EXCERPT

EXCERPTUM n excerpt

EXCESS n state or act of exceeding the permitted limits ▷ vb make (a position) redundant

EXCESSED > EXCESS

EXCESSES > EXCESS

EXCESSING > EXCESS

EXCESSIVE adj exceeding the normal or permitted extents or limits

EXCHANGE vb give or receive (something) in return for something else ▷ n act of exchanging

EXCHANGED > EXCHANGE

EXCHANGER n person or thing that exchanges

EXCHANGES > EXCHANGE

EXCHEAT same as > ESCHEAT

EXCHEATS > EXCHEAT

EXCHEQUER n (in Britain and certain other countries) accounting department of the Treasury, responsible for receiving and issuing funds

EXCIDE vb cut out

EXCIDED > EXCIDE

EXCIDES > EXCIDE

EXCIDING > EXCIDE

EXCIMER n excited dimer which would remain dissociated in the ground state

EXCIMERS > EXCIMER

EXCIPIENT n substance, such as sugar or gum, used to prepare a drug or drugs in a form suitable for administration

EXCIPLE n part of a lichen

EXCIPLES > EXCIPLE

EXCISABLE > EXCISE

EXCISE n tax on goods produced for the home market ▷ vb cut out or away

EXCISED > EXCISE

EXCISEMAN n (formerly) a government agent who collected excise and prevented smuggling

EXCISEMEN > EXCISEMAN

EXCISES > EXCISE

EXCISING > EXCISE

EXCISION > EXCISE

EXCISIONS > EXCISE

EXCITABLE adj easily excited

EXCITABLY > EXCITABLE

EXCITANCY n ability to excite

EXCITANT adj able to excite or stimulate ▷ n something, such as a drug or other agent, able to excite

EXCITANTS > EXCITANT

EXCITE vb arouse to strong emotion

EXCITED adj emotionally aroused, esp to pleasure or agitation

EXCITEDLY > EXCITED

EXCITER n person or thing that excites

EXCITERS > EXCITER

EXCITES > EXCITE

EXCITING adj causing excitement

EXCITON n excited electron bound to the hole produced by its excitation

EXCITONIC > EXCITON

EXCITONS > EXCITON

EXCITOR n type of nerve

EXCITORS > EXCITOR

EXCLAIM vb speak suddenly, cry out

EXCLAIMED > EXCLAIM

EXCLAIMER > EXCLAIM

EXCLAIMS > EXCLAIM

EXCLAVE n territory owned by a country, but surrounded by another

EXCLAVES > EXCLAVE

EXCLOSURE n area of land, esp in a forest, fenced round to keep out unwanted animals

EXCLUDE vb keep out, leave out

EXCLUDED > EXCLUDE

EXCLUDEE > EXCLUDE

EXCLUDEES > EXCLUDE

EXCLUDER > EXCLUDE

EXCLUDERS > EXCLUDE

EXCLUDES > EXCLUDE

EXCLUDING prep excepting

EXCLUSION n act or an instance of excluding or the state of being excluded

EXCLUSIVE adj excluding everything else ▷ n story reported in only one newspaper

EXCLUSORY > EXCLUDE

EXCORIATE vb censure severely

EXCREMENT n waste matter discharged from the body

EXCRETA n excrement

EXCRETAL > EXCRETA

EXCRETE vb discharge (waste matter) from the body

EXCRETED > EXCRETE

EXCRETER > EXCRETE

EXCRETERS > EXCRETE

EXCRETES > EXCRETE

EXCRETING > EXCRETE

EXCRETION > EXCRETE

EXCRETIVE > EXCRETE

EXCRETORY > EXCRETE

EXCUBANT adj keeping guard

EXCUDIT sentence substitute (named person) made this

EXCULPATE vb free from blame or guilt

EXCURRENT adj having an outward flow, as certain pores in sponges, ducts, etc

EXCURSE vb wander

EXCURSED > EXCURSE

EXCURSES > EXCURSE

EXCURSING > EXCURSE

EXCURSION n short journey, esp for pleasure

EXCURSIVE adj tending to digress

EXCURSUS n incidental digression from the main topic under discussion or from the main story in a narrative

EXCUSABLE > EXCUSE

EXCUSABLY > EXCUSE

EXCUSAL > EXCUSE

EXCUSALS > EXCUSE

EXCUSE n explanation offered to justify (a fault etc) ▷ vb put forward a reason or justification for (a fault etc)

EXCUSED > EXCUSE

EXCUSER > EXCUSE

EXCUSERS > EXCUSE

EXCUSES > EXCUSE

EXCUSING > EXCUSE

EXCUSIVE adj excusing

EXEAT n leave of absence from school or some other institution

EXEATS > EXEAT

EXEC n executive

EXECRABLE adj of very poor quality

EXECRABLY > EXECRABLE

EXECRATE vb feel and express loathing and hatred of (someone or something)

EXECRATED > EXECRATE

EXECRATES > EXECRATE

EXECRATOR > EXECRATE

EXECS > EXEC

EXECUTANT n performer, esp of musical works

EXECUTARY n person whose job comprises tasks appropriate to a middle-management executive as well as those traditionally carried out by a secretary

EXECUTE vb put (a condemned person) to death

EXECUTED > EXECUTE

EXECUTER > EXECUTE

EXECUTERS > EXECUTE

EXECUTES > EXECUTE

EXECUTING > EXECUTE

EXECUTION n act of executing

EXECUTIVE n person or group in an administrative position ▷ adj having the function of carrying out plans, orders, laws, etc

EXECUTOR n person appointed to perform the instructions of a will

EXECUTORS > EXECUTOR

EXECUTORY adj (of a law, agreement, etc) coming into operation at a future date

EXECUTRIX n female executor

EXECUTRY n condition of being an executor

EXED > EX

EXEDRA n building, room, portico, or apse containing a continuous bench

EXEDRAE > EXEDRA

EXEDRAS > EXEDRA

EXEEM same as > EXEME

EXEEMED > EXEEM

EXEEMING > EXEEM

EXEEMS > EXEEM

EXEGESES > EXEGESIS

EXEGESIS n explanation of a text, esp of the Bible

EXEGETE n person who practises exegesis

EXEGETES > EXEGETE

EXEGETIC adj of or relating to exegesis

EXEGETICS n scientific study of exegesis and exegetical methods

EXEGETIST same as > EXEGETE

EXEME vb set free

EXEMED > EXEME

EXEMES > EXEME

EXEMING > EXEME

EXEMPLA > EXEMPLUM

EXEMPLAR n person or thing to be copied, model

EXEMPLARS > EXEMPLAR

EXEMPLARY adj being a good example

EXEMPLE same as > EXAMPLE

EXEMPLES > EXEMPLE

EXEMPLIFY vb show an example of

EXEMPLUM n anecdote that supports a moral point or sustains an argument, used esp in medieval sermons

EXEMPT adj not subject to an obligation etc ▷ vb release from an obligation etc ▷ n person who is exempt from an obligation, tax, etc

EXEMPTED > EXEMPT

EXEMPTING > EXEMPT

EXEMPTION > EXEMPT

EXEMPTIVE > EXEMPT

EXEMPTS > EXEMPT

EXEQUATUR n official authorization issued by a host country to a consular agent, permitting him to perform his official duties

EXEQUIAL > EXEQUY

EXEQUIES > EXEQUY

EXEQUY n funeral rite

EXERCISE n activity to train the body or mind ▷ vb make use of

EXERCISED > EXERCISE

EXERCISER n device with springs or elasticated cords for muscular exercise

EXERCISES > EXERCISE

EXERCYCLE n exercise bicycle

EXERGIES > EXERGY

EXERGONIC adj (of a biochemical reaction) producing energy and therefore occurring spontaneously

EXERGUAL > EXERGUE

EXERGUE n space on the reverse of a coin or medal

EXERGUES > EXERGUE

EXERGY n maximum amount of useful work obtainable from a system

EXERT vb use (influence, authority, etc) forcefully or effectively

EXERTED > EXERT

EXERTING > EXERT

EXERTION > EXERT

EXERTIONS > EXERT

EXERTIVE > EXERT

EXERTS > EXERT

EXES > EX

EXEUNT vb (they) go out

EXFIL vb exfiltrate

EXFILLED > EXFIL

EXFILLING > EXFIL

EXFILS > EXFIL

EXFOLIANT n cosmetic removing dead skin

EXFOLIATE vb peel in scales or layers

EXHALABLE > EXHALE

EXHALANT adj emitting a vapour or liquid ▷ n organ or vessel that emits a vapour or liquid

EXHALANTS > EXHALANT

EXHALE vb breathe out

EXHALED > EXHALE

EXHALENT same as > EXHALANT

EXHALENTS > EXHALENT

EXHALES > EXHALE

EXHALING > EXHALE

EXHAUST vb tire out ▷ n gases ejected from an engine as waste products

EXHAUSTED > EXHAUST

EXHAUSTER > EXHAUST

EXHAUSTS > EXHAUST

EXHEDRA same as > EXEDRA

EXHEDRAE > EXHEDRA

EXHIBIT *vb* display to the public ▷ *n* object exhibited to the public
EXHIBITED > EXHIBIT
EXHIBITER > EXHIBIT
EXHIBITOR *n* person or thing that exhibits
EXHIBITS > EXHIBIT
EXHORT *vb* urge earnestly
EXHORTED > EXHORT
EXHORTER > EXHORT
EXHORTERS > EXHORT
EXHORTING > EXHORT
EXHORTS > EXHORT
EXHUMATE *same as* > EXHUME
EXHUMATED > EXHUMATE
EXHUMATES > EXHUMATE
EXHUME *vb* dig up (something buried, esp a corpse)
EXHUMED > EXHUME
EXHUMER > EXHUME
EXHUMERS > EXHUME
EXHUMES > EXHUME
EXHUMING > EXHUME
EXIES *n* hysterics
EXIGEANT *adj* exacting
EXIGEANTE *same as* > EXIGEANT
EXIGENCE *same as* > EXIGENCY
EXIGENCES > EXIGENCE
EXIGENCY *n* urgent demand or need
EXIGENT *adj* urgent ▷ *n* emergency
EXIGENTLY > EXIGENT
EXIGENTS > EXIGENT
EXIGIBLE *adj* liable to be exacted or required
EXIGUITY > EXIGUOUS
EXIGUOUS *adj* scanty or meagre
EXILABLE > EXILE
EXILE *n* prolonged, usu enforced, absence from one's country ▷ *vb* expel from one's country
EXILED > EXILE
EXILEMENT *same as* > EXILE
EXILER > EXILE
EXILERS > EXILE
EXILES > EXILE
EXILIAN > EXILE
EXILIC > EXILE
EXILING > EXILE
EXILITIES > EXILITY
EXILITY *n* poverty or meagreness
EXIMIOUS *adj* select and distinguished
EXINE *n* outermost coat of a pollen grain or a spore
EXINES > EXINE
EXING > EX
EXIST *vb* have being or reality
EXISTED > EXIST
EXISTENCE *n* fact or state of being real, live, or actual

EXISTENT *adj* in existence ▷ *n* person or a thing that exists
EXISTENTS > EXISTENT
EXISTING > EXIST
EXISTS > EXIST
EXIT *n* way out ▷ *vb* go out
EXITANCE *n* measure of the ability of a surface to emit radiation
EXITANCES > EXITANCE
EXITED > EXIT
EXITING > EXIT
EXITLESS > EXIT
EXITS > EXIT
EXO *informal word for* > EXCELLENT
EXOCARP *same as* > EPICARP
EXOCARPS > EXOCARP
EXOCRINE *adj* relating to a gland, such as the sweat gland, that secretes externally through a duct ▷ *n* exocrine gland
EXOCRINES > EXOCRINE
EXOCYCLIC *adj* (of a sea urchin) having the anus situated outside the apical disc
EXOCYTIC *adj* outside biological cell
EXOCYTOSE *vb* secrete substance from within cell
EXODE *n* exodus
EXODERM *same as* > ECTODERM
EXODERMAL > EXODERM
EXODERMIS *same as* > ECTODERM
EXODERMS > EXODERM
EXODES > EXODE
EXODIC > EXODE
EXODIST > EXODUS
EXODISTS > EXODUS
EXODOI > EXODOS
EXODONTIA *n* branch of dental surgery concerned with the extraction of teeth
EXODOS *n* processional song performed at the end of a play
EXODUS *n* departure of a large number of people
EXODUSES > EXODUS
EXOENZYME *n* extracellular enzyme
EXOERGIC *adj* (of a nuclear reaction) occurring with evolution of energy
EXOGAMIC > EXOGAMY
EXOGAMIES > EXOGAMY
EXOGAMOUS > EXOGAMY
EXOGAMY *n* act of marrying a person from another tribe, clan, etc
EXOGEN *n* type of plant
EXOGENIC *adj* formed or occurring on the earth's surface

EXOGENISM > EXOGENOUS
EXOGENOUS *adj* having an external origin
EXOGENS > EXOGEN
EXOMION *same as* > EXOMIS
EXOMIONS > EXOMION
EXOMIS *n* sleeveless jacket
EXOMISES > EXOMIS
EXON *n* one of the officers who command the Yeomen of the Guard
EXONERATE *vb* free from blame or a criminal charge
EXONIC > EXON
EXONS > EXON
EXONUMIA *n* objects of interest to numismatists that are not coins, such as medals and tokens
EXONUMIST *n* collector of medals and tokens
EXONYM *n* name given to a place by foreigners
EXONYMS > EXONYM
EXOPHAGY *n* (among cannibals) custom of eating only members of other tribes
EXOPHORIC *adj* denoting or relating to a pronoun such as "I" or "you", the meaning of which is determined by reference outside the discourse rather than by a preceding or following expression
EXOPLANET *n* planet that orbits a star in a solar system other than that of Earth
EXOPLASM *another name for* > ECTOPLASM
EXOPLASMS > EXOPLASM
EXOPOD *same as* > EXOPODITE
EXOPODITE *n* outer projection on the hind legs of some crustaceans
EXOPODS > EXOPOD
EXORABLE *adj* able to be persuaded or moved by pleading
EXORATION *n* plea
EXORCISE *same as* > EXORCIZE
EXORCISED > EXORCISE
EXORCISER > EXORCISE
EXORCISES > EXORCISE
EXORCISM > EXORCIZE
EXORCISMS > EXORCIZE
EXORCIST > EXORCIZE
EXORCISTS > EXORCIZE
EXORCIZE *vb* expel (evil spirits) by prayers and religious rites
EXORCIZED > EXORCIZE
EXORCIZER > EXORCIZE
EXORCIZES > EXORCIZE
EXORDIA > EXORDIUM
EXORDIAL > EXORDIUM
EXORDIUM *n* introductory part or beginning, esp of an oration or discourse

EXORDIUMS > EXORDIUM
EXOSMIC > EXOSMOSIS
EXOSMOSE *same as* > EXOSMOSIS
EXOSMOSES > EXOSMOSIS
EXOSMOSIS *n* osmosis in which water flows from a cell or organism into the surrounding solution
EXOSMOTIC > EXOSMOSIS
EXOSPHERE *n* outermost layer of the earth's atmosphere
EXOSPORAL > EXOSPORE
EXOSPORE *n* outer layer of the spores of some algae and fungi
EXOSPORES > EXOSPORE
EXOSPORIA *n* exospores
EXOSTOSES > EXOSTOSIS
EXOSTOSIS *n* abnormal bony outgrowth from the surface of a bone
EXOTERIC *adj* intelligible to or intended for more than a select or initiated minority
EXOTIC *adj* having a strange allure or beauty ▷ *n* non-native plant
EXOTICA *pl n* (collection of) exotic objects
EXOTICISE *same as* > EXOTICIZE
EXOTICISM > EXOTIC
EXOTICIST > EXOTIC
EXOTICIZE *vb* regard or present as exotic
EXOTICS > EXOTIC
EXOTISM *n* something exotic
EXOTISMS > EXOTIC
EXOTOXIC > EXOTOXIN
EXOTOXIN *n* toxin produced by a microorganism and secreted into the surrounding medium
EXOTOXINS > EXOTOXIN
EXOTROPIA *n* condition in which eye turns outwards
EXOTROPIC > EXOTROPIA
EXPAND *vb* make or become larger
EXPANDED *adj* (of printer's type) wider than usual for a particular height
EXPANDER *n* device for exercising and developing the muscles of the body
EXPANDERS > EXPANDER
EXPANDING > EXPAND
EXPANDOR *same as* > EXPANDER
EXPANDORS > EXPANDOR
EXPANDS > EXPAND
EXPANSE *n* uninterrupted wide area
EXPANSES > EXPANSE

EXPANSILE adj able to expand or cause expansion

EXPANSION n act of expanding

EXPANSIVE adj wide or extensive

EXPAT n short for expatriate

EXPATIATE vb speak or write at great length (on)

EXPATS > EXPAT

EXPECT vb regard as probable

EXPECTANT adj expecting or hopeful ▷ n person who expects something

EXPECTED > EXPECT

EXPECTER n person who expects

EXPECTERS > EXPECTER

EXPECTING adj pregnant

EXPECTS > EXPECT

EXPEDIENT n something that achieves a particular purpose ▷ adj suitable to the circumstances, appropriate

EXPEDITE vb hasten the progress of ▷ adj unimpeded or prompt

EXPEDITED > EXPEDITE

EXPEDITER n person who expedites something, esp a person employed in an industry to ensure that work on each job progresses efficiently

EXPEDITES > EXPEDITE

EXPEDITOR same as > EXPEDITER

EXPEL vb drive out with force

EXPELLANT adj forcing out or having the capacity to force out ▷ n medicine used to expel undesirable substances or organisms from the body, esp worms from the digestive tract

EXPELLED > EXPEL

EXPELLEE > EXPEL

EXPELLEES > EXPEL

EXPELLENT same as > EXPELLANT

EXPELLER > EXPEL

EXPELLERS pl n residue remaining after an oilseed has been crushed to expel the oil, used for animal fodder

EXPELLING > EXPEL

EXPELS > EXPEL

EXPEND vb spend, use up

EXPENDED > EXPEND

EXPENDER > EXPEND

EXPENDERS > EXPEND

EXPENDING > EXPEND

EXPENDS > EXPEND

EXPENSE n cost

EXPENSED > EXPENSE

EXPENSES > EXPENSE

EXPENSING > EXPENSE

EXPENSIVE adj high-priced

EXPERT n person with extensive skill or knowledge in a particular field ▷ adj skilful or knowledgeable ▷ vb experience

EXPERTED > EXPERT

EXPERTING > EXPERT

EXPERTISE same as > EXPERTIZE

EXPERTISM > EXPERTIZE

EXPERTIZE vb act as an expert or give an expert opinion (on)

EXPERTLY > EXPERT

EXPERTS > EXPERT

EXPIABLE adj capable of being expiated or atoned for

EXPIATE vb make amends for

EXPIATED > EXPIATE

EXPIATES > EXPIATE

EXPIATING > EXPIATE

EXPIATION n act, process, or a means of expiating

EXPIATOR > EXPIATE

EXPIATORS > EXPIATE

EXPIATORY adj capable of making expiation

EXPIRABLE > EXPIRE

EXPIRANT n one who expires

EXPIRANTS > EXPIRANT

EXPIRE vb finish or run out

EXPIRED > EXPIRE

EXPIRER > EXPIRE

EXPIRERS > EXPIRE

EXPIRES > EXPIRE

EXPIRIES > EXPIRY

EXPIRING > EXPIRE

EXPIRY n end, esp of a contract period

EXPISCATE vb find; fish out

EXPLAIN vb make clear and intelligible

EXPLAINED > EXPLAIN

EXPLAINER > EXPLAIN

EXPLAINS > EXPLAIN

EXPLANT vb transfer (living tissue) from its natural site to a new site or to a culture medium ▷ n piece of tissue treated in this way

EXPLANTED > EXPLANT

EXPLANTS > EXPLANT

EXPLETIVE n swearword ▷ adj expressing no particular meaning, esp when filling out a line of verse

EXPLETORY adj expletive

EXPLICATE vb explain

EXPLICIT adj precisely and clearly expressed ▷ n word used to indicate the end of a book

EXPLICITS > EXPLICIT

EXPLODE vb burst with great violence, blow up

EXPLODED > EXPLODE

EXPLODER > EXPLODE

EXPLODERS > EXPLODE

EXPLODES > EXPLODE

EXPLODING > EXPLODE

EXPLOIT vb take advantage of for one's own purposes ▷ n notable feat or deed

EXPLOITED > EXPLOIT

EXPLOITER > EXPLOIT

EXPLOITS > EXPLOIT

EXPLORE vb investigate

EXPLORED > EXPLORE

EXPLORER > EXPLORE

EXPLORERS > EXPLORE

EXPLORES > EXPLORE

EXPLORING > EXPLORE

EXPLOSION n exploding

EXPLOSIVE adj tending to explode ▷ n substance that causes explosions

EXPO n exposition, large public exhibition

EXPONENT n person who advocates an idea, cause, etc ▷ adj offering a declaration, explanation, or interpretation

EXPONENTS > EXPONENT

EXPONIBLE adj able to be explained

EXPORT n selling or shipping of goods to a foreign country ▷ vb sell or ship (goods) to a foreign country

EXPORTED > EXPORT

EXPORTER > EXPORT

EXPORTERS > EXPORT

EXPORTING > EXPORT

EXPORTS > EXPORT

EXPOS > EXPO

EXPOSABLE > EXPOSE

EXPOSAL > EXPOSE

EXPOSALS > EXPOSE

EXPOSE vb uncover or reveal ▷ n bringing of a crime, scandal, etc to public notice

EXPOSED adj not concealed

EXPOSER > EXPOSE

EXPOSERS > EXPOSE

EXPOSES > EXPOSE

EXPOSING > EXPOSE

EXPOSIT vb state

EXPOSITED > EXPOSIT

EXPOSITOR n person who expounds

EXPOSITS > EXPOSIT

EXPOSOME n collection of environmental factors which can affect a person's health

EXPOSOMES > EXPOSOME

EXPOSTURE n exposure

EXPOSURE n exposing

EXPOSURES > EXPOSURE

EXPOUND vb explain in detail

EXPOUNDED > EXPOUND

EXPOUNDER > EXPOUND

EXPOUNDS > EXPOUND

EXPRESS vb put into words ▷ adj explicitly stated ▷ n fast train or bus stopping at only a few stations ▷ adv by express delivery

EXPRESSED > EXPRESS

EXPRESSER > EXPRESS

EXPRESSES > EXPRESS

EXPRESSLY adv definitely

EXPRESSO variant of > ESPRESSO

EXPRESSOS > EXPRESSO

EXPUGN vb storm

EXPUGNED > EXPUGN

EXPUGNING > EXPUGN

EXPUGNS > EXPUGN

EXPULSE vb expel

EXPULSED > EXPULSE

EXPULSES > EXPULSE

EXPULSING > EXPULSE

EXPULSION n act of expelling or the fact of being expelled

EXPULSIVE adj tending or serving to expel

EXPUNCT vb expunge

EXPUNCTED > EXPUNCT

EXPUNCTS > EXPUNCT

EXPUNGE vb delete, erase, blot out

EXPUNGED > EXPUNGE

EXPUNGER > EXPUNGE

EXPUNGERS > EXPUNGE

EXPUNGES > EXPUNGE

EXPUNGING > EXPUNGE

EXPURGATE vb remove objectionable parts from (a book etc)

EXPURGE vb purge

EXPURGED > EXPURGE

EXPURGES > EXPURGE

EXPURGING > EXPURGE

EXQUISITE adj of extreme beauty or delicacy ▷ n dandy

EXSCIND vb cut off or out

EXSCINDED > EXSCIND

EXSCINDS > EXSCIND

EXSECANT n trigonometric function

EXSECANTS > EXSECANT

EXSECT vb cut out

EXSECTED > EXSECT

EXSECTING > EXSECT

EXSECTION > EXSECT

EXSECTS > EXSECT

EXSERT vb thrust out ▷ adj protruded or stretched out from (something)

EXSERTED > EXSERT

EXSERTILE > EXSERT

EXSERTING > EXSERT

EXSERTION > EXSERT

EXSERTS > EXSERT

EXSICCANT n medicine which causes drying or desiccation

EXSICCATE vb dry up

EXSTROPHY n congenital eversion of a hollow organ, esp the urinary bladder

EXSUCCOUS adj without sap or juice

EXTANT adj still existing

EXTASIES > EXTASY

EXTASY same as > ECSTASY

EXTATIC same as > ECSTATIC

EXTEMPORE adj without planning or preparation ▷ adv without planning or preparation

EXTEND vb draw out or be drawn out, stretch

EXTENDANT adj (in heraldry) with wings spread

EXTENDED > EXTEND

EXTENDER n person or thing that extends

EXTENDERS > EXTENDER

EXTENDING > EXTEND

EXTENDS > EXTEND

EXTENSE adj extensive ▷ n extension; expanse

EXTENSES > EXTENSE

EXTENSILE adj capable of being extended

EXTENSION n room or rooms added to an existing building ▷ adj denoting something that can be extended or that extends another object

EXTENSITY n that part of sensory perception relating to the spatial aspect of objects

EXTENSIVE adj having a large extent, widespread

EXTENSOR n muscle that extends a part of the body

EXTENSORS > EXTENSOR

EXTENT n range over which something extends, area

EXTENTS > EXTENT

EXTENUATE vb make (an offence or fault) less blameworthy

EXTERIOR n part or surface on the outside ▷ adj of, on, or coming from the outside

EXTERIORS > EXTERIOR

EXTERMINE vb exterminate

EXTERN n person with an official connection to an institution but does not reside in it

EXTERNAL adj of, situated on, or coming from the outside ▷ n external circumstance or aspect, esp one that is superficial or inessential

EXTERNALS > EXTERNAL

EXTERNAT n day school

EXTERNATS > EXTERNAT

EXTERNE same as > EXTERN

EXTERNES > EXTERNE

EXTERNS > EXTERN

EXTINCT adj having died out ▷ vb extinguish

EXTINCTED > EXTINCT

EXTINCTS > EXTINCT

EXTINE same as > EXINE

EXTINES > EXTINE

EXTIRP vb extirpate

EXTIRPATE vb destroy utterly

EXTIRPED > EXTIRP

EXTIRPING > EXTIRP

EXTIRPS > EXTIRP

EXTOL vb praise highly

EXTOLD archaic past participle of > EXTOL

EXTOLL same as > EXTOL

EXTOLLED > EXTOLL

EXTOLLER > EXTOL

EXTOLLERS > EXTOL

EXTOLLING > EXTOLL

EXTOLLS > EXTOLL

EXTOLMENT > EXTOL

EXTOLS > EXTOL

EXTORSIVE adj intended or tending to extort

EXTORT vb get (something) by force or threats

EXTORTED > EXTORT

EXTORTER > EXTORT

EXTORTERS > EXTORT

EXTORTING > EXTORT

EXTORTION n act of securing money, favours, etc by intimidation or violence

EXTORTIVE > EXTORT

EXTORTS > EXTORT

EXTRA adj more than is usual, expected or needed ▷ n additional person or thing ▷ adv unusually or exceptionally

EXTRABOLD n very bold typeface

EXTRACT vb pull out by force ▷ n something extracted, such as a passage from a book etc

EXTRACTED > EXTRACT

EXTRACTOR n person or thing that extracts

EXTRACTS > EXTRACT

EXTRADITE vb send (an accused person) back to his or her own country for trial

EXTRADOS n outer curve or surface of an arch or vault

EXTRAIT n extracts

EXTRAITS > EXTRAIT

EXTRALITY n diplomatic immunity

EXTRANET n intranet that is modified to allow outsiders access to it, esp

one belonging to a business that allows access to customers

EXTRANETS > EXTRANET

EXTRAPOSE vb move (a word or words) to the end of a clause or sentence

EXTRAS > EXTRA

EXTRAUGHT old past participle of > EXTRACT

EXTRAVERT same as > EXTROVERT

EXTREAT n extraction ▷ vb extract or eliminate (something)

EXTREATED > EXTREAT

EXTREATS > EXTREAT

EXTREMA > EXTREMUM

EXTREMAL n clause in a recursive definition that specifies that no items other than those generated by the stated rules fall within the definition

EXTREMALS > EXTREMAL

EXTREME adj of a high or the highest degree or intensity ▷ n either of the two limits of a scale or range

EXTREMELY > EXTREME

EXTREMER > EXTREME

EXTREMES > EXTREME

EXTREMEST > EXTREME

EXTREMISM > EXTREMIST

EXTREMIST n person who favours immoderate methods ▷ adj holding extreme opinions

EXTREMITY n farthest point

EXTREMUM n extreme point

EXTREMUMS > EXTREMUM

EXTRICATE vb free from complication or difficulty

EXTRINSIC adj not contained or included within

EXTROPIES > EXTROPY

EXTROPY n supposition that human life will expand throughout the universe via technology

EXTRORSAL same as > EXTRORSE

EXTRORSE adj turned or opening outwards or away from the axis

EXTROVERT adj lively and outgoing ▷ n extrovert person

EXTRUDE vb squeeze or force out

EXTRUDED > EXTRUDE

EXTRUDER > EXTRUDE

EXTRUDERS > EXTRUDE

EXTRUDES > EXTRUDE

EXTRUDING > EXTRUDE

EXTRUSILE adj being thrust or forced out

EXTRUSION n act or process of extruding

EXTRUSIVE adj tending to extrude

EXTRUSORY > EXTRUDE

EXTUBATE vb remove tube from hollow organ

EXTUBATED > EXTUBATE

EXTUBATES > EXTUBATE

EXUBERANT adj high-spirited

EXUBERATE vb be exuberant

EXUDATE same as > EXUDATION

EXUDATES > EXUDATE

EXUDATION n act of exuding or oozing out

EXUDATIVE > EXUDATION

EXUDE vb (of a liquid or smell) seep or flow out slowly and steadily

EXUDED > EXUDE

EXUDES > EXUDE

EXUDING > EXUDE

EXUL vb exile; banish

EXULLED > EXUL

EXULLING > EXUL

EXULS > EXUL

EXULT vb be joyful or jubilant

EXULTANCE > EXULTANT

EXULTANCY > EXULTANT

EXULTANT adj elated or jubilant, esp because of triumph or success

EXULTED > EXULT

EXULTING > EXULT

EXULTS > EXULT

EXURB n residential area beyond suburbs

EXURBAN > EXURBIA

EXURBIA n region outside the suburbs of a city

EXURBIAS > EXURBIA

EXURBS > EXURB

EXUVIA n cast-off exoskeleton of animal

EXUVIAE > EXUVIA

EXUVIAL > EXUVIA

EXUVIATE vb shed (a skin or similar outer covering)

EXUVIATED > EXUVIATE

EXUVIATES > EXUVIATE

EXUVIUM n cast-off exoskeleton of animal

EYALET n province of Ottoman Empire

EYALETS > EYALET

EYAS n nestling hawk or falcon

EYASES > EYAS

EYASS same as > EYAS

EYASSES > EYASS

EYE n organ of sight ▷ vb look at carefully or warily

EYEABLE adj pleasant to look at

EYEBALL n ball-shaped part of the eye ▷ vb eye

EYEBALLED > EYEBALL

EYEBALLS > EYEBALL
EYEBANK n place in which corneas are stored
EYEBANKS > EYEBANK
EYEBAR n bar with flattened ends with holes for connecting pins
EYEBARS > EYEBAR
EYEBATH same as > EYECUP
EYEBATHS > EYEBATH
EYEBEAM n glance
EYEBEAMS > EYEBEAM
EYEBLACK another name for > MASCARA
EYEBLACKS > EYEBLACK
EYEBLINK n very small amount of time
EYEBLINKS > EYEBLINK
EYEBOLT n type of threaded bolt
EYEBOLTS > EYEBOLT
EYEBRIGHT n type of plant with small white-and-purple flowers, formerly used to treat eye disorders
EYEBROW n line of hair on the bony ridge above the eye ▷ vb equip with artificial eyebrows
EYEBROWED > EYEBROW
EYEBROWS > EYEBROW
EYECUP same as > EYEBATH
EYECUPS > EYECUP
EYED > EYE
EYEDNESS > EYE
EYEDROPS n medicine applied to the eyes in drops
EYEFOLD n fold of skin above eye
EYEFOLDS > EYEFOLD
EYEFUL n view
EYEFULS > EYEFUL

EYEGLASS n lens for aiding defective vision
EYEHOLE n hole through which something is passed
EYEHOLES > EYEHOLE
EYEHOOK n hook attached to a ring at the extremity of a rope or chain
EYEHOOKS > EYEHOOK
EYEING > EYE
EYELASH n short hair that grows out from the eyelid
EYELASHES > EYELASH
EYELESS > EYE
EYELET n small hole for a lace or cord to be passed through ▷ vb supply with an eyelet or eyelets
EYELETED > EYELET
EYELETEER n small bodkin or other pointed tool for making eyelet holes
EYELETING > EYELET
EYELETS > EYELET
EYELETTED > EYELET
EYELEVEL adj level with a person's eyes
EYELIAD same as > OEILLADE
EYELIADS > EYELIAD
EYELID n fold of skin that covers the eye when it is closed
EYELIDS > EYELID
EYELIFT n cosmetic surgery for eyes
EYELIFTS > EYELIFT
EYELIKE > EYE
EYELINER n cosmetic used to outline the eyes
EYELINERS > EYELINER
EYEN pl n eyes
EYEOPENER n something surprising

EYEPATCH n material worn over an injured eye
EYEPIECE n lens in a microscope, telescope, etc, into which the person using it looks
EYEPIECES > EYEPIECE
EYEPOINT n position of a lens at which the sharpest image is obtained
EYEPOINTS > EYEPOINT
EYEPOPPER n something that excites the eye
EYER n someone who eyes
EYERS > EYER
EYES > EYE
EYESHADE n opaque or tinted translucent visor, worn on the head like a cap to protect the eyes from glare
EYESHADES > EYESHADE
EYESHADOW n coloured cosmetic put around the eyes so as to enhance their colour or shape
EYESHINE n reflection of light from animal eye at night
EYESHINES > EYESHINE
EYESHOT n range of vision
EYESHOTS > EYESHOT
EYESIGHT n ability to see
EYESIGHTS > EYESIGHT
EYESOME adj attractive
EYESORE n ugly object
EYESORES > EYESORE
EYESPOT n small area of pigment
EYESPOTS > EYESPOT
EYESTALK n movable stalk bearing a compound eye at its tip: occurs in crustaceans and some molluscs
EYESTALKS > EYESTALK

EYESTONE n device for removing foreign body from eye
EYESTONES > EYESTONE
EYESTRAIN n fatigue or irritation of the eyes, caused by tiredness or a failure to wear glasses
EYETEETH > EYETOOTH
EYETOOTH n either of the two canine teeth in the upper jaw
EYEWASH n nonsense
EYEWASHES > EYEWASH
EYEWATER n lotion for the eyes
EYEWATERS > EYEWATER
EYEWEAR n spectacles; glasses
EYEWEARS > EYEWEAR
EYEWINK n wink of the eye; instant
EYEWINKS > EYEWINK
EYING > EYE
EYLIAD same as > OEILLADE
EYLIADS > EYLIAD
EYNE poetic plural of > EYE
EYOT n island
EYOTS > EYOT
EYRA n reddish-brown variety of the jaguarondi
EYRAS > EYRA
EYRE n obsolete circuit court
EYRES > EYRE
EYRIE n nest of an eagle
EYRIES > EYRIE
EYRIR n Icelandic monetary unit
EYRY same as > EYRIE
EZINE n magazine available only in electronic form
EZINES > EZINE

Ff

FA same as > FAH
FAA Scot word for > FALL
FAAING > FAA
FAAN > FAA
FAAS > FAA
FAB adj excellent ▷ n fabrication
FABACEOUS adj belonging to the legume family of flowering plants which includes peas and beans
FABBER > FAB
FABBEST > FAB
FABBIER > FABBY
FABBIEST > FABBY
FABBY same as > FAB
FABLE n story with a moral ▷ vb relate or tell (fables)
FABLED adj made famous in legend
FABLER > FABLE
FABLERS > FABLE
FABLES > FABLE
FABLET n large smartphone able to perform many of the functions of a tablet computer
FABLETS > FABLET
FABLIAU n comic usually ribald verse tale
FABLIAUX > FABLIAU
FABLING > FABLE
FABLINGS > FABLE
FABRIC n knitted or woven cloth ▷ vb build
FABRICANT n manufacturer
FABRICATE vb make up (a story or lie)
FABRICKED > FABRIC
FABRICS > FABRIC
FABRIQUE n (in Quebec) group of laypersons who hold church property in trust for the parish
FABRIQUES > FABRIQUE
FABS > FAB
FABULAR adj relating to fables
FABULATE vb make up fables
FABULATED > FABULATE
FABULATES > FABULATE
FABULATOR > FABULATE
FABULISE vb make up fables
FABULISED > FABULISE

FABULISES > FABULISE
FABULISM n literary technique of placing fantastical elements in mundane settings
FABULISMS > FABULISM
FABULIST n person who invents or recounts fables
FABULISTS > FABULIST
FABULIZE vb make up fables
FABULIZED > FABULIZE
FABULIZES > FABULIZE
FABULOUS adj excellent
FABURDEN n early form of counterpoint
FABURDENS > FABURDEN
FACADE n front of a building
FACADES > FACADE
FACE n front of the head ▷ vb look or turn towards
FACEABLE > FACE
FACEBAR n wrestling hold
FACEBARS > FACEBAR
FACEBOOK vb search for (someone) on the Facebook website
FACEBOOKS > FACEBOOK
FACECLOTH n small piece of cloth used to wash the face and hands
FACED > FACE
FACEDOWN vb confront and force (someone or something) to back down
FACEDOWNS > FACEDOWN
FACELESS adj impersonal, anonymous
FACELIFT n cosmetic surgery for the face
FACELIFTS > FACELIFT
FACEMAIL n computer program which uses an electronically generated face to deliver messages on screen
FACEMAILS > FACEMAIL
FACEMAN n miner who works at the coalface
FACEMASK n protective mask for the face
FACEMASKS > FACEMASK
FACEMEN > FACEMAN
FACEOFF n when opposing skaters compete for the puck at the start of an ice hockey game
FACEOFFS > FACEOFF

FACEPLATE n perforated circular metal plate that can be attached to the headstock of a lathe in order to hold flat or irregularly shaped workpieces
FACEPRINT n digitally recorded representation of a person's face that can be used for security purposes because it is as individual as a fingerprint
FACER n difficulty or problem
FACERS > FACER
FACES > FACE
FACET n aspect ▷ vb cut facets in (a gemstone)
FACETE adj witty and humorous
FACETED > FACET
FACETELY > FACETE
FACETIAE pl n humorous or witty sayings
FACETIME vb talk with (someone) via the FaceTime application
FACETIMED > FACETIME
FACETIMES > FACETIME
FACETING n act of faceting
FACETINGS > FACETING
FACETIOUS adj funny or trying to be funny, esp at inappropriate times
FACETS > FACET
FACETTED > FACET
FACETTING > FACET
FACEUP adj with the face or surface exposed
FACIA same as > FASCIA
FACIAE > FACIA
FACIAL adj of or relating to the face ▷ n beauty treatment for the face
FACIALIST n beautician who specializes in treatments for the face
FACIALLY > FACIAL
FACIALS > FACIAL
FACIAS > FACIA
FACIEND n multiplicand
FACIENDS > FACIEND
FACIES n general form and appearance
FACILE adj (of a remark, argument, etc) superficial
FACILELY > FACILE
FACILITY n skill

FACING n lining or covering for decoration or reinforcement
FACINGS > FACING
FACONNE adj denoting a fabric with the design woven in ▷ n such a fabric
FACONNES > FACONNE
FACSIMILE n exact copy ▷ vb make an exact copy of
FACT n event or thing known to have happened or existed
FACTA > FACTUM
FACTFUL > FACT
FACTICE n soft rubbery material
FACTICES > FACTICE
FACTICITY n philosophical process
FACTION n (dissenting) minority group within a larger body
FACTIONAL > FACTION
FACTIONS > FACTION
FACTIOUS adj of or producing factions
FACTIS variant of > FACTICE
FACTISES > FACTIS
FACTITIVE adj denoting a verb taking a direct object as well as a noun in apposition, as for example elect in They elected John president, where John is the direct object and president is the complement
FACTIVE adj giving rise to the presupposition that a sentence is true
FACTOID n piece of unreliable information believed to be true
FACTOIDAL > FACTOID
FACTOIDS > FACTOID
FACTOR n element contributing to a result ▷ vb engage in the business of a factor
FACTORAGE n commission payable to a factor
FACTORED > FACTOR
FACTORIAL n product of all the integers from one to a given number ▷ adj of factorials or factors
FACTORIES > FACTORY
FACTORING n business of a factor

FACTORISE *same as*
> FACTORIZE

FACTORIZE *vb* calculate the factors of (a number)

FACTORS > FACTOR

FACTORY *n* building where goods are manufactured

FACTOTUM *n* person employed to do all sorts of work

FACTOTUMS > FACTOTUM

FACTS > FACT

FACTSHEET *n* printed sheet containing information relating to items covered in a television or radio programme

FACTUAL *adj* concerning facts rather than opinions or theories

FACTUALLY > FACTUAL

FACTUM *n* something done, deed

FACTUMS > FACTUM

FACTURE *n* construction

FACTURES > FACTURE

FACULA *n* any of the bright areas on the sun's surface

FACULAE > FACULA

FACULAR > FACULA

FACULTIES > FACULTY

FACULTY *n* physical or mental ability

FACUNDITY *n* eloquence, fluency of speech

FAD *n* short-lived fashion

FADABLE > FADE

FADAISE *n* silly remark

FADAISES > FADAISE

FADDIER > FADDY

FADDIEST > FADDY

FADDINESS *n* excessive fussiness

FADDISH > FAD

FADDISHLY > FAD

FADDISM > FAD

FADDISMS > FAD

FADDIST > FAD

FADDISTS > FAD

FADDLE *vb* mess around, toy with

FADDLED > FADDLE

FADDLES > FADDLE

FADDLING > FADDLE

FADDY *adj* unreasonably fussy, particularly about food

FADE *vb* (cause to) lose brightness, colour, or strength ▷ *n* act or an instance of fading

FADEAWAY *n* fading to the point of disappearance

FADEAWAYS > FADEAWAY

FADED > FADE

FADEDLY > FADE

FADEDNESS > FADE

FADEIN *n* gradual appearance of image on film

FADEINS > FADEIN

FADELESS *adj* not subject to fading

FADEOUT *n* gradual disappearance of image on film

FADEOUTS > FADEOUT

FADER > FADE

FADERS > FADE

FADES > FADE

FADEUR *n* blandness, insipidness

FADEURS > FADEUR

FADGE *vb* agree ▷ *n* package of wool in a wool-bale

FADGED > FADGE

FADGES > FADGE

FADGING > FADGE

FADIER > FADY

FADIEST > FADY

FADING *n* variation in strength of received radio signals

FADINGS > FADING

FADLIKE > FAD

FADO *n* type of melancholy Portuguese folk song

FADOMETER *n* instrument used to determine the resistance to fading of a pigment or dye

FADOS > FADO

FADS > FAD

FADY *adj* faded

FAE *Scot word for* > FROM

FAECAL *adj* of, relating to, or consisting of faeces

FAECES *pl n* waste matter discharged from the anus

FAENA *n* matador's final actions before the kill

FAENAS > FAENA

FAERIE *n* land of fairies

FAERIES > FAERY

FAERY *same as* > FAERIE

FAFF *vb* dither or fuss

FAFFED > FAFF

FAFFIER > FAFFY

FAFFIEST > FAFFY

FAFFING > FAFF

FAFFS > FAFF

FAFFY *adj* awkward and time-consuming to do or use

FAG *same as* > FAGGOT

FAGACEOUS *adj* relating to a family of trees, including beech, oak, and chestnut, whose fruit is enclosed in a husk

FAGGED > FAG

FAGGERIES > FAGGERY

FAGGERY *n* offensive term for homosexuality

FAGGIER > FAG

FAGGIEST > FAG

FAGGING > FAG

FAGGINGS > FAG

FAGGOT *n* ball of chopped liver, herbs, and bread ▷ *vb* collect into a bundle or bundles

FAGGOTED > FAGGOT

FAGGOTING *n* decorative needlework done by tying vertical threads together in bundles

FAGGOTRY *n* offensive term for homosexuality

FAGGOTS > FAGGOT

FAGGOTY > FAGGOT

FAGGY > FAG

FAGIN *n* criminal

FAGINS > FAGIN

FAGOT *same as* > FAGGOT

FAGOTED > FAGOT

FAGOTER > FAGOT

FAGOTERS > FAGOT

FAGOTING *same as* > FAGGOTING

FAGOTINGS > FAGOTING

FAGOTS > FAGOT

FAGOTTI > FAGOTTO

FAGOTTIST *n* bassoon player

FAGOTTO *n* bassoon

FAGOTTOS > FAGOTTO

FAGS > FAG

FAH *n* (in tonic sol-fa) fourth degree of any major scale

FAHLBAND *n* thin bed of schistose rock impregnated with metallic sulphides

FAHLBANDS > FAHLBAND

FAHLERZ *n* copper ore

FAHLERZES > FAHLERZ

FAHLORE *n* copper ore

FAHLORES > FAHLORE

FAHS > FAH

FAIBLE *variant of* > FOIBLE

FAIBLES > FAIBLE

FAIENCE *n* tin-glazed earthenware

FAIENCES > FAIENCE

FAIK *vb* grasp

FAIKED > FAIK

FAIKES > FAIK

FAIKING > FAIK

FAIKS > FAIK

FAIL *vb* be unsuccessful ▷ *n* instance of not passing an exam or test

FAILED > FAIL

FAILING *n* weak point ▷ *prep* in the absence of

FAILINGLY > FAILING

FAILINGS > FAILING

FAILLE *n* soft light ribbed fabric of silk, rayon, or taffeta

FAILLES > FAILLE

FAILOVER *n* automatic transfer to a backup computer system in the event of a primary system failure

FAILOVERS > FAILOVER

FAILS > FAIL

FAILURE *n* act or instance of failing

FAILURES > FAILURE

FAIN *adv* gladly ▷ *adj* willing or eager

FAINE *variant of* > FAIN

FAINEANCE > FAINEANT

FAINEANCY > FAINEANT

FAINEANT *n* lazy person ▷ *adj* indolent

FAINEANTS > FAINEANT

FAINED > FAIN

FAINER > FAIN

FAINES > FAINE

FAINEST > FAIN

FAINING > FAIN

FAINITES *interj* cry for truce or respite from the rules of a game

FAINLY > FAIN

FAINNE *n* badge worn by advocates of the Irish language

FAINNES > FAINNE

FAINNESS > FAIN

FAINS *same as* > FAINITES

FAINT *adj* lacking clarity, brightness, or volume ▷ *vb* lose consciousness temporarily ▷ *n* temporary loss of consciousness

FAINTED > FAINT

FAINTER > FAINT

FAINTERS > FAINT

FAINTEST > FAINT

FAINTIER > FAINTY

FAINTIEST > FAINTY

FAINTING > FAINT

FAINTINGS > FAINT

FAINTISH > FAINT

FAINTLY > FAINT

FAINTNESS > FAINT

FAINTS > FAINT

FAINTY > FAINT

FAIR *adj* unbiased and reasonable ▷ *adv* fairly ▷ *n* travelling entertainment ▷ *vb* join together to form a smooth shape

FAIRED > FAIR

FAIRER > FAIR

FAIREST > FAIR

FAIRFACED *adj* (of brickwork) having a neat smooth unplastered surface

FAIRGOER *n* person attending fair

FAIRGOERS > FAIRGOER

FAIRIER > FAIRY

FAIRIES > FAIRY

FAIRIEST > FAIRY

FAIRILY > FAIRY

FAIRING *n* structure fitted round part of a vehicle to reduce drag

FAIRINGS > FAIRING

FAIRISH *adj* moderately good, well, etc

FAIRISHLY > FAIRISH

FAIRLEAD *n* block or ring through which a line is rove to keep it clear of obstructions, prevent chafing, or maintain it at an angle

FAIRLEADS > FAIRLEAD

FAIRLY *adv* moderately

FAIRNESS > FAIR

FAIRS > FAIR
FAIRWAY *n* area between the tee and the green
FAIRWAYS > FAIRWAY
FAIRY *n* imaginary small creature ▷ *adj* of or relating to a fairy or fairies
FAIRYDOM > FAIRY
FAIRYDOMS > FAIRY
FAIRYHOOD > FAIRY
FAIRYISM > FAIRY
FAIRYISMS > FAIRY
FAIRYLAND *n* imaginary place where fairies live
FAIRYLIKE > FAIRY
FAIRYTALE *n* story about fairies or other mythical or magical beings, esp one of traditional origin told to children
FAITH *n* strong belief, esp without proof
FAITHCURE *n* supposed cure or healing through prayer or faith in God
FAITHED *adj* having faith or a faith
FAITHER *Scot word for* **>** FATHER
FAITHERS > FAITHER
FAITHFUL *adj* loyal
FAITHFULS > FAITHFUL
FAITHING *n* practising a faith
FAITHINGS > FAITHING
FAITHLESS *adj* disloyal or dishonest
FAITHS > FAITH
FAITOR *n* traitor, impostor
FAITORS > FAITOR
FAITOUR *n* impostor
FAITOURS > FAITOUR
FAIX *interj* have faith
FAJITA > FAJITAS
FAJITAS *pl n* Mexican dish
FAKE *vb* cause something not genuine to appear so by fraud ▷ *n* person, thing, or act that is not genuine ▷ *adj* not genuine
FAKED > FAKE
FAKEER *same as* **>** FAKIR
FAKEERS > FAKEER
FAKEMENT *n* something false, counterfeit
FAKEMENTS > FAKEMENT
FAKER > FAKE
FAKERIES > FAKE
FAKERS > FAKE
FAKERY > FAKE
FAKES > FAKE
FAKEY *adj, adv* (of a skateboarding manoeuvre) travelling backwards ▷ *n* skateboarding position in which the skateboarder faces backwards
FAKEYS > FAKEY
FAKIE *same as* **>** FAKEY
FAKIER > FAKEY
FAKIES > FAKIE

FAKIEST > FAKEY
FAKING > FAKE
FAKIR *n* Muslim who spurns worldly possessions
FAKIRISM > FAKIR
FAKIRISMS > FAKIR
FAKIRS > FAKIR
FALAFEL *n* ball or cake made from chickpeas
FALAFELS > FALAFEL
FALAJ *n* kind of irrigation channel in ancient Oman
FALANGISM > FALANGIST
FALANGIST *n* member of the Fascist movement founded in Spain in 1933
FALBALA *n* gathered flounce, frill, or ruffle
FALBALAS > FALBALA
FALCADE *n* movement of a horse
FALCADES > FALCADE
FALCATE *adj* shaped like a sickle
FALCATED > FALCATE
FALCATION > FALCATE
FALCES > FALX
FALCHION *n* short and slightly curved medieval sword broader towards the point
FALCHIONS > FALCHION
FALCIFORM *same as* **>** FALCATE
FALCON *n* small bird of prey
FALCONER *n* person who breeds or trains hawks or who follows the sport of falconry
FALCONERS > FALCONER
FALCONET *n* type of small falcons
FALCONETS > FALCONET
FALCONINE *adj* of, relating to, or resembling a falcon
FALCONOID *n* chemical thought to resist cancer
FALCONRY *n* art of training falcons
FALCONS > FALCON
FALCULA *n* sharp curved claw, esp of a bird
FALCULAE > FALCULA
FALCULAS > FALCULA
FALCULATE > FALCULA
FALDAGE *n* feudal right
FALDAGES > FALDAGE
FALDERAL *n* showy but worthless trifle ▷ *vb* sing nonsense words
FALDERALS > FALDERAL
FALDEROL *same as* **>** FALDERAL
FALDEROLS > FALDEROL
FALDETTA *n* Maltese woman's garment with a stiffened hood
FALDETTAS > FALDETTA
FALDSTOOL *n* backless seat, sometimes capable

of being folded, used by bishops and certain other prelates
FALL *vb* drop through the force of gravity ▷ *n* falling
FALLACIES > FALLACY
FALLACY *n* false belief
FALLAL *n* showy ornament, trinket, or article of dress
FALLALERY > FALLAL
FALLALISH *adj* foppish
FALLALS > FALLAL
FALLAWAY *n* friendship that has been withdrawn
FALLAWAYS > FALLAWAY
FALLBACK *n* something that recedes or retreats
FALLBACKS > FALLBACK
FALLBOARD *n* cover for piano keyboard
FALLEN > FALL
FALLER *n* any device that falls or operates machinery by falling
FALLERS > FALLER
FALLFISH *n* large N American freshwater fish resembling the chub
FALLIBLE *adj* (of a person) liable to make mistakes
FALLIBLY > FALLIBLE
FALLING > FALL
FALLINGS > FALL
FALLOFF *n* decline or drop
FALLOFFS > FALLOFF
FALLOUT *n* radioactive particles spread as a result of a nuclear explosion ▷ *vb* disagree and quarrel ▷ *sentence substitute* order to leave a parade or disciplinary formation
FALLOUTS > FALLOUT
FALLOW *adj* (of land) ploughed but left unseeded to regain fertility ▷ *n* land treated in this way ▷ *vb* leave (land) unseeded after ploughing and harrowing it
FALLOWED > FALLOW
FALLOWER > FALLOW
FALLOWEST > FALLOW
FALLOWING > FALLOW
FALLOWS > FALLOW
FALLS > FALL
FALSE *adj* not true or correct ▷ *adv* in a false or dishonest manner ▷ *vb* falsify
FALSED > FALSE
FALSEFACE *n* mask
FALSEHOOD *n* quality of being untrue
FALSELY > FALSE
FALSENESS > FALSE
FALSER > FALSE
FALSERS *n* colloquial term for false teeth
FALSES > FALSE
FALSEST > FALSE

FALSETTO *n* voice pitched higher than one's natural range
FALSETTOS > FALSETTO
FALSEWORK *n* framework supporting something under construction
FALSIE *n* pad used to enlarge breast shape
FALSIES > FALSIE
FALSIFIED > FALSIFY
FALSIFIER > FALSIFY
FALSIFIES > FALSIFY
FALSIFY *vb* alter fraudulently
FALSING > FALSE
FALSISH > FALSE
FALSISM > FALSE
FALSISMS > FALSE
FALSITIES > FALSITY
FALSITY *n* state of being false
FALTBOAT *n* collapsible boat made of waterproof material stretched over a light framework
FALTBOATS > FALTBOAT
FALTER *vb* be hesitant, weak, or unsure ▷ *n* uncertainty or hesitancy in speech or action
FALTERED > FALTER
FALTERER > FALTER
FALTERERS > FALTER
FALTERING > FALTER
FALTERS > FALTER
FALX *n* sickle-shaped anatomical structure
FAME *n* state of being widely recognized ▷ *vb* make known or famous
FAMED > FAME
FAMELESS > FAME
FAMES > FAME
FAMILIAL *adj* of or relating to the family
FAMILIAR *adj* well-known ▷ *n* demon supposed to attend a witch
FAMILIARS *n* attendant demons
FAMILIES > FAMILY
FAMILISM *n* practice of a mystical Christian religious sect of the 16th and 17th centuries based upon love
FAMILISMS > FAMILISM
FAMILIST *adj* relating to familism
FAMILLE *n* type of Chinese porcelain
FAMILLES > FAMILLE
FAMILY *n* group of parents and their children ▷ *adj* suitable for parents and children together
FAMINE *n* severe shortage of food
FAMINES > FAMINE
FAMING > FAME

FAMISH *vb* be or make very hungry or weak
FAMISHED *adj* very hungry
FAMISHES > FAMISH
FAMISHING > FAMISH
FAMOUS *adj* very well-known ▷ *vb* make famous
FAMOUSED > FAMOUS
FAMOUSES > FAMOUS
FAMOUSING > FAMOUS
FAMOUSLY *adv* excellently
FAMULI > FAMULUS
FAMULUS *n* (formerly) the attendant of a sorcerer or scholar
FAN *n* object used to create a current of air ▷ *vb* blow or cool with a fan
FANAL *n* lighthouse
FANALS > FANAL
FANATIC *n* person who is excessively enthusiastic about something ▷ *adj* excessively enthusiastic
FANATICAL *adj* surpassing what is normal or accepted in enthusiasm for or belief in something
FANATICS > FANATIC
FANBASE *n* body of admirers
FANBASES > FANBASE
FANBOY *n* obsessive fan of a subject or hobby
FANBOYS > FANBOY
FANCIABLE *adj* sexually attractive
FANCIED *adj* imaginary
FANCIER *n* person interested in plants or animals
FANCIERS > FANCIER
FANCIES > FANCY
FANCIEST > FANCY
FANCIFIED > FANCIFY
FANCIFIES > FANCIFY
FANCIFUL *adj* not based on fact
FANCIFY *vb* make more beautiful
FANCILESS > FANCY
FANCILY > FANCY
FANCINESS > FANCY
FANCY *adj* elaborate, not plain ▷ *n* sudden irrational liking or desire ▷ *vb* be sexually attracted to
FANCYING > FANCY
FANCYWORK *n* ornamental needlework
FAND *vb* try
FANDANGLE *n* elaborate ornament
FANDANGO *n* lively Spanish dance
FANDANGOS > FANDANGO
FANDED > FAND
FANDING > FAND
FANDOM *n* collectively, the fans of a sport, pastime or person

FANDOMS > FANDOM
FANDS > FAND
FANE *n* temple or shrine
FANEGA *n* Spanish unit of measurement
FANEGADA *n* Spanish unit of land area
FANEGADAS > FANEGADA
FANEGAS > FANEGA
FANES > FANE
FANFARADE *n* fanfare
FANFARE *n* tune played on brass instruments ▷ *vb* perform a fanfare
FANFARED > FANFARE
FANFARES > FANFARE
FANFARING > FANFARE
FANFARON *n* braggart
FANFARONA *n* gold chain
FANFARONS > FANFARON
FANFIC *n* fiction based on work by other authors
FANFICS > FANFIC
FANFOLD *vb* fold (paper) like a fan
FANFOLDED > FANFOLD
FANFOLDS > FANFOLD
FANG *n* snake's tooth which injects poison ▷ *vb* seize
FANGA *same as* > FANEGA
FANGAS > FANGA
FANGED > FANG
FANGING > FANG
FANGIRL *n* enthusiastic female devotee of something
FANGIRLS > FANGIRL
FANGLE *vb* fashion
FANGLED > FANGLE
FANGLES > FANGLE
FANGLESS > FANG
FANGLIKE > FANG
FANGLING > FANGLE
FANGO *n* mud from thermal springs in Italy
FANGOS > FANGO
FANGS > FANG
FANION *n* small flag used by surveyors
FANIONS > FANION
FANJET *same as* > TURBOFAN
FANJETS > FANJET
FANK *n* sheep pen ▷ *vb* put sheep in a pen
FANKED > FANK
FANKING > FANK
FANKLE *vb* entangle ▷ *n* tangle
FANKLED > FANKLE
FANKLES > FANKLE
FANKLING > FANKLE
FANKS > FANK
FANLIGHT *n* semicircular window over a door or window
FANLIGHTS > FANLIGHT
FANLIKE > FAN
FANNED > FAN
FANNEL *n* ecclesiastical vestment
FANNELL *variant of* > FANNEL

FANNELLS > FANNELL
FANNELS > FANNEL
FANNER > FAN
FANNERS > FAN
FANNIED > FANNY
FANNIES > FANNY
FANNING > FAN
FANNINGS > FAN
FANNY *n* taboo word for female genitals ▷ *vb* waste time; misbehave
FANNYING > FANNY
FANO *same as* > FANON
FANON *n* collar-shaped vestment
FANONS > FANON
FANOS > FANO
FANS > FAN
FANSITE *n* website aimed at fans of a celebrity, film, etc
FANSITES > FANSITE
FANSUB *n* fan-produced subtitling of films
FANSUBS > FANSUB
FANTAD *n* nervous, agitated state
FANTADS > FANTAD
FANTAIL *n* small New Zealand bird with a tail like a fan
FANTAILED *adj* having a tail like a fan
FANTAILS > FANTAIL
FANTASIA *n* musical composition of an improvised nature
FANTASIAS > FANTASIA
FANTASIE *same as* > FANTASY
FANTASIED > FANTASY
FANTASIES > FANTASY
FANTASISE *same as* > FANTASIZE
FANTASIST *n* person who indulges in fantasies
FANTASIZE *vb* indulge in daydreams
FANTASM *archaic spelling of* > PHANTASM
FANTASMAL > FANTASM
FANTASMIC > FANTASM
FANTASMS > FANTASM
FANTASQUE *n* fantasy
FANTAST *n* dreamer or visionary
FANTASTIC *adj* very good ▷ *n* person who dresses or behaves eccentrically
FANTASTRY *n* condition of being fantastic
FANTASTS > FANTAST
FANTASY *n* far-fetched notion ▷ *adj* of a type of competition ▷ *vb* fantasize
FANTEEG *n* nervous, agitated state
FANTEEGS > FANTEEG
FANTIGUE *variant of* > FANTEEG
FANTIGUES > FANTIGUE
FANTOD *n* crotchety or faddish behaviour

FANTODS > FANTOD
FANTOM *archaic spelling of* > PHANTOM
FANTOMS > FANTOM
FANTOOSH *adj* pretentious
FANUM *n* temple
FANUMS > FANUM
FANWISE *adj* like a fan
FANWORT *n* aquatic plant
FANWORTS > FANWORT
FANZINE *n* magazine produced by fans
FANZINES > FANZINE
FAP *adj* drunk
FAQIR *same as* > FAKIR
FAQIRS > FAQIR
FAQUIR *variant of* > FAQIR
FAQUIRS > FAQUIR
FAR *adv* at, to, or from a great distance ▷ *adj* remote in space or time ▷ *vb* go far
FARAD *n* unit of electrical capacitance
FARADAIC *same as* > FARADIC
FARADAY *n* quantity of electricity
FARADAYS > FARADAY
FARADIC *adj* of an intermittent asymmetric alternating current
FARADISE *same as* > FARADIZE
FARADISED > FARADISE
FARADISER > FARADISE
FARADISES > FARADISE
FARADISM *n* therapeutic use of faradic currents
FARADISMS > FARADISM
FARADIZE *vb* treat (an organ or part) with faradic currents
FARADIZED > FARADIZE
FARADIZER > FARADIZE
FARADIZES > FARADIZE
FARADS > FARAD
FARAND *adj* pleasant or attractive in manner or appearance
FARANDINE *n* silk and wool cloth
FARANDOLE *n* lively dance in six-eight or four-four time from Provence
FARAWAY *adj* very distant
FARAWAYS *same as* > FARAWAY
FARCE *n* boisterous comedy ▷ *vb* enliven (a speech, etc) with jokes
FARCEMEAT > FARCE
FARCEMEAT *same as* > FORCEMEAT
FARCER *same as* > FARCEUR
FARCERS > FARCER
FARCES > FARCE
FARCEUR *n* writer of or performer in farces
FARCEURS > FARCEUR
FARCEUSE *n* female farceur**

FARCEUSES > FARCEUSE

FARCI *adj* (of food) stuffed

FARCICAL *adj* ludicrous

FARCIE *same as* > FARCI

FARCIED *adj* afflicted with farcy

FARCIES > FARCY

FARCIFIED > FARCIFY

FARCIFIES > FARCIFY

FARCIFY *vb* turn into a farce

FARCIN *n* equine disease

FARCING > FARCE

FARCINGS > FARCE

FARCINS > FARCIN

FARCY *n* form of glanders, a bacterial disease of horses

FARD *n* paint for the face, esp white paint ▷ *vb* paint (the face) with fard

FARDAGE *n* material laid beneath or between cargo

FARDAGES > FARDAGE

FARDED > FARD

FARDEL *n* bundle or burden

FARDELS > FARDEL

FARDEN *n* farthing

FARDENS > FARDEN

FARDING > FARD

FARDINGS > FARD

FARDS > FARD

FARE *n* charge for a passenger's journey ▷ *vb* get on (as specified)

FAREBOX *n* box where money for bus fares is placed

FAREBOXES > FAREBOX

FARED > FARE

FARER > FARE

FARERS > FARE

FARES > FARE

FAREWELL *interj* goodbye ▷ *n* act of saying goodbye and leaving ▷ *vb* say goodbye ▷ *adj* parting or closing ▷ *sentence substitute* goodbye

FAREWELLS > FAREWELL

FARFAL *same as* > FELAFEL

FARFALLE *n* pasta in bow shapes

FARFALLES > FARFALLE

FARFALS > FARFAL

FARFEL *same as* > FELAFEL

FARFELS *same as* > FARFEL

FARFET *adj* far-fetched

FARINA *n* flour or meal made from any kind of cereal grain

FARINAS > FARINA

FARING > FARE

FARINHA *n* cassava meal

FARINHAS > FARINHA

FARINOSE *adj* similar to or yielding farina

FARL *n* thin cake of oatmeal, often triangular in shape

FARLE *same as* > FARL

FARLES > FARLE

FARLS > FARL

FARM *n* area of land for growing crops or rearing livestock ▷ *vb* cultivate (land)

FARMABLE > FARM

FARMED *adj* (of fish or game) reared on a farm

FARMER *n* person who owns or runs a farm

FARMERESS *n* female farmer

FARMERIES > FARMERY

FARMERS > FARMER

FARMERY *n* farm buildings

FARMHAND *n* person who is hired to work on a farm

FARMHANDS > FARMHAND

FARMHOUSE *n* house attached to a farm

FARMING *n* business or skill of agriculture

FARMINGS > FARMING

FARMLAND *n* land that is used for or suitable for farming

FARMLANDS > FARMLAND

FARMOST *adj* most distant

FARMS > FARM

FARMSTEAD *n* farm and its buildings

FARMWIFE *n* woman who works on a farm

FARMWIVES > FARMWIFE

FARMWORK *n* tasks carried out on a farm

FARMWORKS > FARMWORK

FARMYARD *n* small area of land enclosed by or around the farm buildings

FARMYARDS > FARMYARD

FARNARKEL *vb* spend time or act in a careless or inconsequential manner

FARNESOL *n* colourless aromatic sesquiterpene alcohol found in many essential oils and used in the form of its derivatives in perfumery

FARNESOLS > FARNESOL

FARNESS > FAR

FARNESSES > FAR

FARO *n* gambling game

FAROLITO *n* votive candle

FAROLITOS > FAROLITO

FAROS > FARO

FAROUCHE *adj* sullen or shy

FARRAGO *n* jumbled mixture of things

FARRAGOES > FARRAGO

FARRAGOS > FARRAGO

FARRAND *variant of* > FARAND

FARRANT *variant of* > FARAND

FARRED > FAR

FARREN *n* allotted ground

FARRENS > FARREN

FARRIER *n* person who shoes horses

FARRIERS > FARRIER

FARRIERY *n* art, work, or establishment of a farrier

FARRING > FAR

FARROW *n* litter of piglets ▷ *vb* (of a sow) give birth ▷ *adj* (of a cow) not calving in a given year

FARROWED > FARROW

FARROWING > FARROW

FARROWS > FARROW

FARRUCA *n* flamenco dance performed by men

FARRUCAS > FARRUCA

FARS > FAR

FARSE *vb* insert into

FARSED > FARSE

FARSEEING *adj* having shrewd judgment

FARSES > FARSE

FARSIDE *n* part of the Moon facing away from the Earth

FARSIDES > FARSIDE

FARSING > FARSE

FART *n* emission of gas from the anus ▷ *vb* emit gas from the anus

FARTED > FART

FARTHEL *same as* > FARL

FARTHELS > FARTHEL

FARTHER > FAR

FARTHEST > FAR

FARTHING *n* former British coin equivalent to a quarter of a penny

FARTHINGS > FARTHING

FARTING > FART

FARTLEK *n* in sport, another name for interval training

FARTLEKS > FARTLEK

FARTS > FART

FAS > FA

FASCES *pl n* (in ancient Rome) a bundle of rods containing an axe

FASCI > FASCIO

FASCIA *n* outer surface of a dashboard

FASCIAE > FASCIA

FASCIAL > FASCIA

FASCIAS > FASCIA

FASCIATE *adj* (of stems and branches) abnormally flattened due to coalescence

FASCIATED *same as* > FASCIATE

FASCICLE *same as* > FASCICULE

FASCICLED *adj* in instalments

FASCICLES > FASCICLE

FASCICULE *n* one part of a printed work that is published in instalments

FASCICULI > FASCICULE

FASCIITIS *n* inflammation of the fascia of a muscle

FASCINATE *vb* attract and interest strongly

FASCINE *n* bundle of long sticks used in construction

FASCINES > FASCINE

FASCIO *n* political group

FASCIOLA *n* band

FASCIOLAS > FASCIOLA

FASCIOLE *n* band

FASCIOLES > FASCIOLE

FASCIS > FASCI

FASCISM *n* right-wing totalitarian political system

FASCISMI > FASCISMO

FASCISMO *Italian word for* > FASCISM

FASCISMS > FASCISM

FASCIST *n* adherent or practitioner of fascism ▷ *adj* characteristic of or relating to fascism

FASCISTA *Italian word for* > FASCIST

FASCISTI > FASCISTA

FASCISTIC > FASCIST

FASCISTS > FASCIST

FASCITIS *same as* > FASCIITIS

FASH *n* worry ▷ *vb* trouble

FASHED > FASH

FASHERIES > FASHERY

FASHERY *n* difficulty, trouble

FASHES > FASH

FASHING > FASH

FASHION *n* style popular at a particular time ▷ *vb* form or make into a particular shape

FASHIONED > FASHION

FASHIONER > FASHION

FASHIONS > FASHION

FASHIONY *adj* of or relating to fashion

FASHIOUS *adj* troublesome

FAST *adj* (capable of) acting or moving quickly ▷ *adv* quickly ▷ *vb* go without food, esp for religious reasons ▷ *n* period of fasting

FASTBACK *n* car having a back that forms one continuous slope from roof to rear

FASTBACKS > FASTBACK

FASTBALL *n* ball pitched at the pitcher's top speed

FASTBALLS > FASTBALL

FASTED > FAST

FASTEN *vb* make or become firmly fixed or joined

FASTENED > FASTEN

FASTENER > FASTEN

FASTENERS > FASTEN

FASTENING *n* something that fastens something, such as a clasp or lock

FASTENS > FASTEN

FASTER > FAST

FASTERS > FAST

FASTEST > FAST

FASTI *pl n* in ancient Rome, business days

FASTIE n deceitful act
FASTIES > FASTIE
FASTIGIUM n highest point
FASTING > FAST
FASTINGS > FAST
FASTISH > FAST
FASTLY > FAST
FASTNESS n fortress, safe place
FASTS > FAST
FASTUOUS adj arrogant
FAT adj having excess flesh on the body ▷ n extra flesh on the body
FATAL adj causing death or ruin
FATALISM n belief that all events are predetermined and people are powerless to change their destinies
FATALISMS > FATALISM
FATALIST > FATALISM
FATALISTS > FATALISM
FATALITY n death caused by an accident or disaster
FATALLY adv resulting in death or disaster
FATALNESS > FATAL
FATBACK n fat from the upper part of a side of pork
FATBACKS > FATBACK
FATBIRD n nocturnal bird
FATBIRDS > FATBIRD
FATE n power supposed to predetermine events ▷ vb predetermine
FATED adj destined
FATEFUL adj having important, usu disastrous, consequences
FATEFULLY > FATEFUL
FATES > FATE
FATHEAD n stupid person
FATHEADED adj stupid
FATHEADS > FATHEAD
FATHER n male parent ▷ vb be the father of (offspring)
FATHERED > FATHER
FATHERING > FATHER
FATHERLY adj kind or protective, like a father
FATHERS > FATHER
FATHOM n unit of length ▷ vb understand
FATHOMED > FATHOM
FATHOMER > FATHOM
FATHOMERS > FATHOM
FATHOMING > FATHOM
FATHOMS > FATHOM
FATIDIC adj prophetic
FATIDICAL same as > FATIDIC
FATIGABLE > FATIGUE
FATIGATE vb fatigue
FATIGATED > FATIGATE
FATIGATES > FATIGATE
FATIGUE n extreme physical or mental tiredness ▷ vb tire out
FATIGUED > FATIGUE
FATIGUES > FATIGUE

FATIGUING > FATIGUE
FATING > FATE
FATISCENT adj having the appearance of being cracked
FATLESS > FAT
FATLIKE > FAT
FATLING n young farm animal fattened for killing
FATLINGS > FATLING
FATLY > FAT
FATNESS > FAT
FATNESSES > FAT
FATS > FAT
FATSIA n type of shrub
FATSIAS > FATSIA
FATSO n fat person: used as an insulting or disparaging term of address
FATSOES > FATSO
FATSOS > FATSO
FATSTOCK n livestock fattened and ready for market
FATSTOCKS > FATSTOCK
FATTED > FAT
FATTEN vb (cause to) become fat
FATTENED > FATTEN
FATTENER > FATTEN
FATTENERS > FATTEN
FATTENING > FATTEN
FATTENS > FATTEN
FATTER > FAT
FATTEST > FAT
FATTIER > FATTY
FATTIES > FATTY
FATTIEST > FATTY
FATTILY > FATTY
FATTINESS > FATTY
FATTING > FAT
FATTISH > FAT
FATTISM n discrimination on the basis of weight
FATTISMS > FATTISM
FATTIST > FATTISM
FATTISTS > FATTISM
FATTRELS n ends of ribbon
FATTY adj containing fat ▷ n fat person
FATUITIES > FATUITY
FATUITOUS > FATUITY
FATUITY n foolish thoughtlessness
FATUOUS adj foolish
FATUOUSLY > FATUOUS
FATWA n religious decree issued by a Muslim leader ▷ vb issue a fatwa
FATWAH same as > FATWA
FATWAHED > FATWAH
FATWAHING > FATWAH
FATWAHS > FATWAH
FATWAING > FATWA
FATWAS > FATWA
FATWOOD n wood used for kindling
FATWOODS > FATWOOD
FAUBOURG n suburb or quarter, esp of a French city

FAUBOURGS > FAUBOURG
FAUCAL adj of or relating to the fauces
FAUCALS > FAUCAL
FAUCES n area of the mouth
FAUCET n tap
FAUCETRY n art or practice of making faucets
FAUCETS > FAUCET
FAUCHION n short sword
FAUCHIONS > FAUCHION
FAUCHON variant of > FAUCHION
FAUCHONS > FAUCHON
FAUCIAL same as > FAUCAL
FAUGH interj exclamation of disgust, scorn, etc
FAULCHION variant of > FAUCHION
FAULD n piece of armour
FAULDS > FAULD
FAULT n responsibility for something wrong ▷ vb criticize or blame
FAULTED > FAULT
FAULTFUL > FAULT
FAULTIER > FAULTY
FAULTIEST > FAULTY
FAULTILY > FAULTY
FAULTING > FAULT
FAULTLESS adj without fault
FAULTLINE n surface of a fault fracture
FAULTS > FAULT
FAULTY adj badly designed or not working properly
FAUN n (in Roman legend) mythological creature
FAUNA n animals of a given place or time
FAUNAE > FAUNA
FAUNAL > FAUNA
FAUNALLY > FAUNA
FAUNAS > FAUNA
FAUNIST > FAUNA
FAUNISTIC > FAUNA
FAUNISTS > FAUNA
FAUNLIKE > FAUN
FAUNS > FAUN
FAUNULA n fauna of a small single environment
FAUNULAE > FAUNULA
FAUNULE same as > FAUNULA
FAUNULES > FAUNULE
FAUR Scot word for > FAR
FAURD adj favoured
FAURER > FAUR
FAUREST > FAUR
FAUSTIAN adj of or relating to Faust, esp reminiscent of his bargain with the devil
FAUT Scot word for > FAULT
FAUTED > FAUT
FAUTEUIL n armchair, the sides of which are not upholstered
FAUTEUILS > FAUTEUIL

FAUTING > FAUT
FAUTOR n patron
FAUTORS > FAUTOR
FAUTS > FAUT
FAUVE adj of the style of the Fauve art movement ▷ n member of the Fauve art movement
FAUVES > FAUVE
FAUVETTE n singing bird, warbler
FAUVETTES > FAUVETTE
FAUVISM > FAUVE
FAUVISMS > FAUVISM
FAUVIST n artist following the Fauve style of painting
FAUVISTS > FAUVIST
FAUX adj false
FAUXMANCE n fake romance between two celebrities to gain media coverage
FAVA n type of bean
FAVAS > FAVA
FAVE short for > FAVOURITE
FAVEL adj (of a horse) dun-coloured ▷ n fallow-coloured horse
FAVELA n (in Brazil) a shanty or shantytown
FAVELAS > FAVELA
FAVELL variant of > FAVEL
FAVELLA n group of spores
FAVELLAS > FAVELLA
FAVELS > FAVEL
FAVEOLATE adj pitted with cell-like cavities
FAVER > FAVE
FAVES > FAVE
FAVEST > FAVE
FAVICON n icon displayed before a website's URL
FAVICONS > FAVICON
FAVISM n type of anaemia
FAVISMS > FAVISM
FAVONIAN adj of or relating to the west wind
FAVOR same as > FAVOUR
FAVORABLE adj favourable
FAVORABLY adv favourably
FAVORED > FAVOR
FAVORER > FAVOUR
FAVORERS > FAVOUR
FAVORING > FAVOR
FAVORITE same as > FAVOURITE
FAVORITES > FAVORITE
FAVORLESS > FAVOR
FAVORS same as > FAVOURS
FAVOSE same as > FAVEOLATE
FAVOUR n approving attitude ▷ vb prefer
FAVOURED > FAVOUR
FAVOURER > FAVOUR
FAVOURERS > FAVOUR
FAVOURING > FAVOUR

FAVOURITE adj most liked ▷ n preferred person or thing
FAVOURS pl n sexual intimacy
FAVOUS adj resembling honeycomb
FAVRILE n type of iridescent glass
FAVRILES > FAVRILE
FAVUS n infectious fungal skin disease
FAVUSES > FAVUS
FAW n gypsy
FAWN n young deer ▷ adj light yellowish-brown ▷ vb seek attention from (someone) by insincere flattery
FAWNED > FAWN
FAWNER > FAWN
FAWNERS > FAWN
FAWNIER > FAWNY
FAWNIEST > FAWNY
FAWNING > FAWN
FAWNINGLY > FAWN
FAWNINGS > FAWN
FAWNLIKE > FAWN
FAWNS > FAWN
FAWNY adj of a fawn colour
FAWS > FAW
FAX n electronic system ▷ vb send (a document) by this system
FAXABLE adj able to be faxed
FAXED > FAX
FAXES > FAX
FAXING > FAX
FAY n fairy or sprite ▷ adj of or resembling a fay ▷ vb fit or be fitted closely or tightly
FAYALITE n rare brown or black mineral
FAYALITES > FAYALITE
FAYED > FAY
FAYENCE variant of > FAIENCE
FAYENCES > FAYENCE
FAYER > FAY
FAYEST > FAY
FAYING > FAY
FAYNE vb pretend
FAYNED > FAYNE
FAYNES > FAYNE
FAYNING > FAYNE
FAYRE pseudo-archaic spelling of > FAIR
FAYRES > FAYRE
FAYS > FAY
FAZE vb disconcert or fluster
FAZED adj worried or disconcerted
FAZENDA n large estate or ranch
FAZENDAS > FAZENDA
FAZES > FAZE
FAZING > FAZE
FE n variant of Hebrew letter pe, transliterated as f
FEAGUE vb whip or beat
FEAGUED > FEAGUE

FEAGUES > FEAGUE
FEAGUING > FEAGUE
FEAL vb conceal
FEALED > FEAL
FEALING > FEAL
FEALS > FEAL
FEALTIES > FEALTY
FEALTY n (in feudal society) subordinate's loyalty
FEAR n distress or alarm caused by impending danger or pain ▷ vb be afraid of (something or someone)
FEARE n companion, spouse
FEARED > FEAR
FEARER > FEAR
FEARERS > FEAR
FEARES > FEARE
FEARFUL adj feeling fear
FEARFULLY adv in a fearful manner
FEARING > FEAR
FEARLESS > FEAR
FEARS > FEAR
FEARSOME adj terrifying
FEART adj (Scots) afraid
FEASANCE n performance of an act
FEASANCES > FEASANCE
FEASE vb perform an act
FEASED > FEASE
FEASES > FEASE
FEASIBLE adj able to be done, possible
FEASIBLY > FEASIBLE
FEASING > FEASE
FEAST n lavish meal ▷ vb eat a feast
FEASTED > FEAST
FEASTER > FEAST
FEASTERS > FEAST
FEASTFUL adj festive
FEASTING > FEAST
FEASTINGS > FEAST
FEASTLESS > FEAST
FEASTS > FEAST
FEAT n remarkable, skilful, or daring action
FEATED > FEAT
FEATEOUS adj neat
FEATER > FEAT
FEATEST > FEAT
FEATHER n one of the barbed shafts forming the plumage of birds ▷ vb fit or cover with feathers
FEATHERED > FEATHER
FEATHERS > FEATHER
FEATHERY > FEATHER
FEATING > FEAT
FEATLIER > FEAT
FEATLIEST > FEAT
FEATLY > FEAT
FEATOUS variant of > FEATEOUS
FEATS > FEAT
FEATUOUS variant of > FEATEOUS
FEATURE n part of the face, such as the eyes

▷ vb have as a feature or be a feature in
FEATURED adj having features as specified
FEATURELY adj handsome
FEATURES > FEATURE
FEATURING > FEATURE
FEAZE same as > FEEZE
FEAZED > FEAZE
FEAZES > FEAZE
FEAZING > FEAZE
FEBLESSE n feebleness
FEBLESSES > FEBLESSE
FEBRICITY n condition of having a fever
FEBRICULA n slight transient fever
FEBRICULE variant of > FEBRICULA
FEBRIFIC adj causing or having a fever
FEBRIFUGE n any drug or agent for reducing fever ▷ adj serving to reduce fever
FEBRILE adj very active and nervous
FEBRILITY > FEBRILE
FECAL same as > FAECAL
FECES same as > FAECES
FECHT Scot word for > FIGHT
FECHTER > FECHT
FECHTERS > FECHT
FECHTING > FECHT
FECHTS > FECHT
FECIAL adj heraldic
FECIALS > FECIAL
FECIT vb (he or she) made it
FECK vb euphemism for 'fuck'
FECKED > FECK
FECKIN same as > FECKING
FECKING > FECK
FECKLESS adj ineffectual or irresponsible
FECKLY > FECK
FECKS > FECK
FECULA n type of starch
FECULAE > FECULA
FECULAS > FECULA
FECULENCE > FECULENT
FECULENCY > FECULENT
FECULENT adj filthy, scummy, muddy, or foul
FECUND adj fertile
FECUNDATE vb make fruitful
FECUNDITY n fertility
FED n FBI agent
FEDARIE n accomplice
FEDARIES > FEDARIE
FEDAYEE n (in Arab states) a commando
FEDAYEEN > FEDAYEE
FEDELINI n type of pasta
FEDELINIS > FEDELINI
FEDERACY n alliance
FEDERAL adj of a system of governance

▷ n supporter of federal union or federation
FEDERALLY > FEDERAL
FEDERALS > FEDERAL
FEDERARIE variant of > FEDARIE
FEDERARY variant of > FEDARIE
FEDERATE vb unite in a federation ▷ adj federal
FEDERATED > FEDERATE
FEDERATES > FEDERATE
FEDERATOR > FEDERATE
FEDEX vb send by FedEx
FEDEXED > FEDEX
FEDEXES > FEDEX
FEDEXING > FEDEX
FEDORA n man's soft hat with a brim
FEDORAS > FEDORA
FEDS > FEE
FEE n charge paid to be allowed to do something ▷ vb pay a fee to
FEEB n contemptible person
FEEBLE adj lacking physical or mental power ▷ vb make feeble
FEEBLED > FEEBLE
FEEBLER > FEEBLE
FEEBLES > FEEBLE
FEEBLEST > FEEBLE
FEEBLING > FEEBLE
FEEBLISH > FEEBLE
FEEBLY > FEEBLE
FEEBS > FEEB
FEED vb give food to ▷ n act of feeding
FEEDABLE > FEE
FEEDBACK n information received in response to something done ▷ adv return (part of the output of a system) to its input
FEEDBACKS > FEEDBACK
FEEDBAG n any bag in which feed for livestock is sacked
FEEDBAGS > FEEDBAG
FEEDBOX n trough, manger
FEEDBOXES > FEEDBOX
FEEDER n baby's bib
FEEDERS > FEED
FEEDGRAIN n cereal grown to feed livestock
FEEDHOLE n small hole through which cable etc is inserted
FEEDHOLES > FEEDHOLE
FEEDING > FEED
FEEDINGS > FEED
FEEDLOT n area where livestock are fattened rapidly
FEEDLOTS > FEEDLOT
FEEDPIPE n pipe through which something is supplied to a machine or system
FEEDPIPES > FEEDPIPE
FEEDS > FEED

FEEDSTOCK n main raw material used in the manufacture of a product
FEEDSTUFF n any material used as a food, esp for animals
FEEDWATER n water, previously purified to prevent scale deposit or corrosion, that is fed to boilers for steam generation
FEEDYARD n place where cattle are kept and fed
FEEDYARDS > FEEDYARD
FEEING > FEE
FEEL vb have a physical or emotional sensation of ▷ n act of feeling
FEELBAD n something inducing depression
FEELER n organ of touch in some animals
FEELERS > FEELER
FEELESS > FEE
FEELGOOD adj causing or characterized by a feeling of self-satisfaction
FEELING > FEEL
FEELINGLY > FEEL
FEELINGS > FEEL
FEELS > FEEL
FEEN n in Irish dialect, an informal word for 'man'
FEENS > FEEN
FEER vb make a furrow
FEERED > FEER
FEERIE n fairyland
FEERIES > FEERIE
FEERIN n furrow
FEERING > FEER
FEERINGS > FEER
FEERINS > FEERIN
FEERS > FEER
FEES > FEE
FEESE vb perturb
FEESED > FEESE
FEESES > FEESE
FEESING > FEESE
FEET > FOOT
FEETFIRST adv with the feet coming first
FEETLESS > FOOT
FEEZE vb beat ▷ n rush
FEEZED > FEEZE
FEEZES > FEEZE
FEEZING > FEEZE
FEG same as > FIG
FEGARIES > FEGARY
FEGARY variant of > VAGARY
FEGS > FEG
FEH same as > FE
FEHM n medieval German court
FEHME > FEHM
FEHMIC > FEHM
FEHS > FEH
FEIGN vb pretend
FEIGNED > FEIGN
FEIGNEDLY > FEIGN
FEIGNER > FEIGN
FEIGNERS > FEIGN
FEIGNING > FEIGN

FEIGNINGS > FEIGN
FEIGNS > FEIGN
FEIJOA n evergreen myrtaceous shrub of S America
FEIJOADA n Brazilian stew of black beans, meat and vegetables
FEIJOADAS > FEIJOADA
FEIJOAS > FEIJOA
FEINT n sham attack meant to distract an opponent ▷ vb make a feint ▷ adj printing term meaning ruled with faint lines
FEINTED > FEINT
FEINTER > FEINT
FEINTEST > FEINT
FEINTING > FEINT
FEINTS pl n leavings of the second distillation of Scotch malt whisky
FEIRIE adj nimble
FEIRIER > FEIRIE
FEIRIEST > FEIRIE
FEIS n Irish music and dance festival
FEISEANNA > FEIS
FEIST n small aggressive dog
FEISTIER > FEISTY
FEISTIEST > FEISTY
FEISTILY > FEISTY
FEISTS > FEIST
FEISTY adj showing courage or spirit
FELAFEL same as > FALAFEL
FELAFELS > FELAFEL
FELCH vb suck semen from the vagina or anus of (a sexual partner)
FELCHED > FELCH
FELCHES > FELCH
FELCHING > FELCH
FELDGRAU n ordinary German soldier (from uniform colour)
FELDGRAUS > FELDGRAU
FELDSCHAR same as > FELDSHER
FELDSCHER same as > FELDSHER
FELDSHER n (in Russia) a medical doctor's assistant
FELDSHERS > FELDSHER
FELDSPAR n hard mineral that is the main constituent of igneous rocks
FELDSPARS > FELDSPAR
FELDSPATH variant of > FELDSPAR
FELICIA n type of African herb
FELICIAS > FELICIA
FELICIFIC adj making or tending to make happy
FELICITER adj happily, successfully
FELICITY n happiness
FELID n any animal belonging to the cat family
FELIDS > FELID

FELINE adj of cats ▷ n member of the cat family
FELINELY > FELINE
FELINES > FELINE
FELINITY > FELINE
FELL vb cut or knock down ▷ adj cruel or deadly
FELLA nonstandard variant of > FELLOW
FELLABLE > FALL
FELLAH n peasant in Arab countries
FELLAHEEN > FELLAH
FELLAHIN > FELLAH
FELLAHS > FELLAH
FELLAS > FELLA
FELLATE vb perform fellatio on (a person)
FELLATED > FELLATE
FELLATES > FELLATE
FELLATING > FELLATE
FELLATIO n sexual activity in which the penis is stimulated by the partner's mouth
FELLATION same as > FELLATIO
FELLATIOS > FELLATIO
FELLATOR > FELLATIO
FELLATORS > FELLATIO
FELLATRIX > FELLATIO
FELLED > FELL
FELLER n person or thing that fells
FELLERS > FELLER
FELLEST > FELL
FELLIES > FELLY
FELLING > FELL
FELLINGS > FELLING
FELLNESS > FELL
FELLOE n (segment of) the rim of a wheel
FELLOES > FELLOE
FELLOW n man or boy ▷ adj in the same group or condition
FELLOWED > FELLOW
FELLOWING > FELLOW
FELLOWLY adj friendly, companionable
FELLOWMAN n companion
FELLOWMEN > FELLOWMAN
FELLOWS > FELLOW
FELLS > FELL
FELLY same as > FELLOE
FELON n (formerly) person guilty of a felony ▷ adj evil
FELONIES > FELONY
FELONIOUS adj of, involving, or constituting a felony
FELONOUS adj wicked
FELONRIES > FELONRY
FELONRY n felons collectively
FELONS > FELON
FELONY n serious crime
FELSIC adj relating to igneous rock
FELSITE n any fine-grained igneous rock

FELSITES > FELSITE
FELSITIC > FELSITE
FELSPAR same as > FELDSPAR
FELSPARS > FELSPAR
FELSTONE same as > FELSITE
FELSTONES > FELSTONE
FELT n matted fabric ▷ vb become matted
FELTED > FELT
FELTER vb mat together
FELTERED > FELTER
FELTERING > FELTER
FELTERS > FELTER
FELTIER > FELT
FELTIEST > FELT
FELTING n felted material
FELTINGS > FELTING
FELTLIKE > FEEL
FELTS > FELT
FELTY > FELT
FELUCCA n narrow lateen-rigged vessel
FELUCCAS > FELUCCA
FELWORT n type of plant
FELWORTS > FELWORT
FEM n passive homosexual
FEMAL adj effeminate ▷ n effeminate person
FEMALE adj of the sex which bears offspring ▷ n female person or animal
FEMALES > FEMALE
FEMALITY > FEMALE
FEMALS > FEMAL
FEME n woman or wife
FEMERALL n ventilator or smoke outlet on a roof
FEMERALLS > FEMERALL
FEMERELL n ventilator or smoke outlet in a roof
FEMERELLS > FEMERELL
FEMES > FEME
FEMETARY variant of > FUMITORY
FEMICIDAL > FEMICIDE
FEMICIDE n killing of females because of their gender
FEMICIDES > FEMICIDE
FEMINACY n feminine character
FEMINAL adj feminine, female
FEMINAZI n militant feminist
FEMINAZIS > FEMINAZI
FEMINEITY n quality of being feminine
FEMINIE n women collectively
FEMINIES > FEMINIE
FEMININE adj having qualities traditionally regarded as suitable for, or typical of, women ▷ n short for feminine noun
FEMININES > FEMININE
FEMINISE same as > FEMINIZE

FEMINISED > FEMINISE
FEMINISES > FEMINISE
FEMINISM n advocacy of equal rights for women
FEMINISMS > FEMINISM
FEMINIST n person who advocates equal rights for women ▷ adj of, relating to, or advocating feminism
FEMINISTS > FEMINIST
FEMINITY > FEMINAL
FEMINIZE vb make or become feminine
FEMINIZED > FEMINIZE
FEMINIZES > FEMINIZE
FEMITER variant of > FUMITORY
FEMITERS > FEMITER
FEMME n woman or wife
FEMMES > FEMME
FEMMIER > FEMMY
FEMMIEST > FEMMY
FEMMY adj markedly or exaggeratedly feminine
FEMORA > FEMUR
FEMORAL adj of the thigh
FEMS > FEM
FEMUR n thighbone
FEMURS > FEMUR
FEN n low-lying flat marshy land
FENAGLE variant of > FINAGLE
FENAGLED > FENAGLE
FENAGLES > FENAGLE
FENAGLING > FENAGLE
FENCE n barrier of posts linked by wire or wood ▷ vb enclose with or as if with a fence
FENCED > FENCE
FENCELESS > FENCE
FENCELIKE > FENCE
FENCER n person who fights with a sword
FENCEROW n uncultivated land flanking a fence
FENCEROWS > FENCEROW
FENCERS > FENCER
FENCES > FENCE
FENCIBLE n (formerly) a person who undertook military service in immediate defence of his homeland only
FENCIBLES > FENCIBLE
FENCING n sport of fighting with swords
FENCINGS > FENCING
FEND vb give support (to someone, esp oneself) ▷ n shift or effort
FENDED > FEND
FENDER n low metal frame in front of a fireplace
FENDERED adj having a fender
FENDERS > FENDER
FENDIER > FENDY
FENDIEST > FENDY
FENDING > FEND
FENDS > FEND

FENDY adj thrifty
FENESTRA n small opening in or between bones, esp one of the openings between the middle and inner ears
FENESTRAE > FENESTRA
FENESTRAL > FENESTRA
FENESTRAS > FENESTRA
FENI n Goan alcoholic drink
FENING n small currency unit of Bosnia-Herzegovina
FENINGS > FENING
FENIS > FENI
FENITAR variant of > FUMITORY
FENITARS > FENITAR
FENKS n whale blubber
FENLAND > FEN
FENLANDS > FEN
FENMAN > FEN
FENMEN > FEN
FENNEC n type of nocturnal desert fox
FENNECS > FENNEC
FENNEL n fragrant plant
FENNELS > FENNEL
FENNIER > FENNY
FENNIES > FENNY
FENNIEST > FENNY
FENNING same as > FENING
FENNISH > FEN
FENNY adj boggy or marshy ▷ n feni
FENS > FEN
FENT n piece of waste fabric
FENTANYL n narcotic drug used in medicine to relieve pain
FENTANYLS > FENTANYL
FENTHION n type of pesticide
FENTHIONS > FENTHION
FENTS > FENT
FENUGREEK n Mediterranean plant grown for its heavily scented seeds
FENURON n type of herbicide
FENURONS > FENURON
FEOD same as > FEUD
FEODAL > FEOD
FEODARIES > FEOD
FEODARY > FEOD
FEODS > FEOD
FEOFF same as > FIEF
FEOFFED > FEOFF
FEOFFEE n (in feudal society) a vassal granted a fief by his lord
FEOFFEES > FEOFFEE
FEOFFER > FEOFF
FEOFFERS > FEOFF
FEOFFING > FEOFF
FEOFFMENT n (in medieval Europe) a lord's act of granting a fief to his man

FEOFFOR > FEOFF
FEOFFORS > FEOFF
FEOFFS > FEOFF
FER same as > FAR
FERACIOUS adj fruitful
FERACITY > FERACIOUS
FERAL adj wild ▷ n person who displays such tendencies and appearance
FERALISED same as > FERALIZED
FERALIZED adj once domesticated, but now wild
FERALS > FERAL
FERBAM n powder used as a fungicide
FERBAMS > FERBAM
FERE n companion ▷ adj fierce
FERER > FERE
FERES > FERE
FEREST > FERE
FERETORY n shrine, usually portable, for a saint's relics
FERIA n weekday on which no feast occurs
FERIAE > FERIA
FERIAL adj of or relating to a feria
FERIAS > FERIA
FERINE same as > FERAL
FERITIES > FERAL
FERITY > FERAL
FERLIE same as > FERLY
FERLIED > FERLY
FERLIER > FERLY
FERLIES > FERLY
FERLIEST > FERLY
FERLY adj wonderful ▷ n wonder ▷ vb wonder
FERLYING > FERLY
FERM variant of > FARM
FERMATA another word for > PAUSE
FERMATAS > FERMATA
FERMATE > FERMATA
FERMENT n any agent that causes fermentation ▷ vb (cause to) undergo fermentation
FERMENTED > FERMENT
FERMENTER > FERMENT
FERMENTOR > FERMENT
FERMENTS > FERMENT
FERMI n unit of length
FERMION n type of particle
FERMIONIC > FERMION
FERMIONS > FERMION
FERMIS > FERMI
FERMIUM n chemical element
FERMIUMS > FERMIUM
FERMS > FERM
FERN n flowerless plant with fine fronds
FERNALLY n seedless plant that is not a true fern
FERNBIRD n small brown and white New Zealand

swamp bird with a fernlike tail
FERNBIRDS > FERNBIRD
FERNERIES > FERNERY
FERNERY n place where ferns are grown
FERNIER > FERN
FERNIEST > FERN
FERNING n production of a fern-like pattern
FERNINGS > FERNING
FERNINST same as > FORNENST
FERNLESS > FERN
FERNLIKE > FERN
FERNS > FERN
FERNSHAW n fern thicket
FERNSHAWS > FERNSHAW
FERNTICLE n freckle
FERNY > FERN
FEROCIOUS adj savagely fierce or cruel
FEROCITY > FEROCIOUS
FERRATE n type of salt
FERRATES > FERRATE
FERREL variant of > FERRULE
FERRELED > FERREL
FERRELING > FERREL
FERRELLED > FERREL
FERRELS > FERREL
FERREOUS adj containing or resembling iron
FERRET n tamed polecat ▷ vb hunt with ferrets
FERRETED > FERRET
FERRETER > FERRET
FERRETERS > FERRET
FERRETING > FERRET
FERRETS > FERRET
FERRETY > FERRET
FERRIAGE n transportation by ferry
FERRIAGES > FERRIAGE
FERRIC adj of or containing iron
FERRIED > FERRY
FERRIES > FERRY
FERRITE n type of ceramic compound
FERRITES > FERRITE
FERRITIC > FERRITE
FERRITIN n protein that contains iron and plays a part in the storage of iron in the body. It occurs in the liver and spleen
FERRITINS > FERRITIN
FERROCENE n reddish-orange insoluble crystalline compound
FERROGRAM n slide used to illustrate suspended iron particles in the lubricant of a machine
FERROTYPE n photographic print produced directly in a camera by exposing a sheet of iron or tin coated with a sensitized enamel
FERROUS adj of or containing iron in the divalent state

FERRUGO *n* disease affecting plants
FERRUGOS > FERRUGO
FERRULE *n* metal cap to strengthen the end of a stick ▷ *vb* equip (a stick, etc) with a ferrule
FERRULED > FERRULE
FERRULES > FERRULE
FERRULING > FERRULE
FERRUM *Latin word for* > IRON
FERRUMS > FERRUM
FERRY *n* boat for transporting people and vehicles ▷ *vb* carry by ferry
FERRYBOAT *same as* > FERRY
FERRYING > FERRY
FERRYMAN *n* someone who provides a ferry service
FERRYMEN > FERRYMAN
FERTIGATE *vb* fertilize and irrigate at the same time
FERTILE *adj* capable of producing young, crops, or vegetation
FERTILELY > FERTILE
FERTILER > FERTILE
FERTILEST > FERTILE
FERTILISE *same as* > FERTILIZE
FERTILITY *n* ability to produce offspring, esp abundantly
FERTILIZE *vb* provide (an animal or plant) with sperm or pollen to bring about fertilization
FERULA *n* large Mediterranean plant
FERULAE > FERULA
FERULAS > FERULA
FERULE *same as* > FERRULE
FERULED > FERULE
FERULES > FERULE
FERULING > FERULE
FERVENCY *another word for* > FERVOUR
FERVENT *adj* intensely passionate and sincere
FERVENTER > FERVENT
FERVENTLY > FERVENT
FERVID *same as* > FERVENT
FERVIDER > FERVID
FERVIDEST > FERVID
FERVIDITY > FERVID
FERVIDLY > FERVID
FERVOR *same as* > FERVOUR
FERVOROUS > FERVOUR
FERVORS > FERVOR
FERVOUR *n* intensity of feeling
FERVOURS > FERVOUR
FES > FE
FESCUE *n* pasture and lawn grass with stiff narrow leaves
FESCUES > FESCUE
FESS *same as* > FESSE

FESSE *n* horizontal band across a shield
FESSED > FESS
FESSES > FESSE
FESSING > FESS
FESSWISE *adv* in heraldry, with a horizontal band across the shield
FEST *n* event at which the emphasis is on a particular activity
FESTA *n* festival
FESTAL *adj* festive ▷ *n* festivity
FESTALLY > FESTAL
FESTALS > FESTAL
FESTAS > FESTA
FESTER *vb* grow worse and increasingly hostile ▷ *n* small ulcer or sore containing pus
FESTERED > FESTER
FESTERING > FESTER
FESTERS > FESTER
FESTIER > FESTY
FESTIEST > FESTY
FESTILOGY *n* treatise about church festivals
FESTINATE *vb* hurry
FESTIVAL *n* organized series of special events or performances
FESTIVALS > FESTIVAL
FESTIVE *adj* of or like a celebration
FESTIVELY > FESTIVE
FESTIVITY *n* happy celebration
FESTIVOUS > FESTIVE
FESTOLOGY *variant of* > FESTILOGY
FESTOON *vb* hang decorations in loops ▷ *n* decorative chain
FESTOONED > FESTOON
FESTOONS > FESTOON
FESTS > FEST
FESTY *adj* dirty
FET *vb* fetch
FETA *n* white salty Greek cheese
FETAL *adj* of, relating to, or resembling a fetus
FETAS > FETA
FETATION *n* state of pregnancy
FETATIONS > FETATION
FETCH *vb* go after and bring back ▷ *n* ghost or apparition of a living person
FETCHED > FETCH
FETCHER *n* person or animal that fetches
FETCHERS > FETCHER
FETCHES > FETCH
FETCHING *adj* attractive
FETE *n* gala, bazaar, etc, usu held outdoors ▷ *vb* honour or entertain regally
FETED > FETE
FETERITA *n* type of sorghum

FETERITAS > FETERITA
FETES > FETE
FETIAL *n* ancient Roman herald ▷ *adj* of or relating to the fetiales
FETIALES > FETIAL
FETIALIS *n* priest in ancient Rome
FETIALS > FETIAL
FETICH *same as* > FETISH
FETICHE *variant of* > FETICH
FETICHES > FETICH
FETICHISE *variant of* > FETICHIZE
FETICHISM *same as* > FETISHISM
FETICHIST > FETISHISM
FETICHIZE *vb* be excessively or irrationally devoted to an object, activity, etc
FETICIDAL > FETICIDE
FETICIDE *n* destruction of a fetus in the uterus
FETICIDES > FETICIDE
FETID *adj* stinking
FETIDER > FETID
FETIDEST > FETID
FETIDITY > FETID
FETIDLY > FETID
FETIDNESS > FETID
FETING > FETE
FETISH *n* sexual pleasure derived from an inanimate object
FETISHES > FETISH
FETISHISE *same as* > FETISHIZE
FETISHISM *n* condition in which the handling of an inanimate object or a specific part of the body other than the sexual organs is a source of sexual satisfaction
FETISHIST > FETISHISM
FETISHIZE *vb* be excessively or irrationally devoted to (an object, activity, etc)
FETLOCK *n* projection behind and above a horse's hoof
FETLOCKED *adj* having fetlocks
FETLOCKS > FETLOCK
FETOLOGY *n* branch of medicine concerned with the fetus in the uterus
FETOR *n* offensive stale or putrid odour
FETORS > FETOR
FETOSCOPE *n* fibreoptic instrument that can be passed through the abdomen of a pregnant woman to enable examination of the fetus and withdrawal of blood for sampling in prenatal diagnosis

FETOSCOPY > FETOSCOPE
FETS > FET
FETT *variant of* > FET
FETTA *variant of* > FETA
FETTAS > FETTA
FETTED > FET
FETTER *n* chain or shackle for the foot ▷ *vb* restrict
FETTERED > FETTER
FETTERER > FETTER
FETTERERS > FETTER
FETTERING > FETTER
FETTERS > FETTER
FETTING > FET
FETTLE *same as* > FETTLING
FETTLED > FETTLE
FETTLER *n* person employed to maintain railway tracks
FETTLERS > FETTLER
FETTLES > FETTLE
FETTLING *n* refractory material used to line the hearth of puddling furnaces
FETTLINGS > FETTLING
FETTS > FETT
FETTUCINE *n* type of pasta in the form of narrow ribbons
FETTUCINI *same as* > FETTUCINE
FETUS *n* embryo of a mammal in the later stages of development
FETUSES > FETUS
FETWA *variant of* > FATWA
FETWAS > FETWA
FEU *n* (in Scotland) type of rent
FEUAR *n* tenant of a feu
FEUARS > FEUAR
FEUD *n* long bitter hostility between two people or groups ▷ *vb* carry on a feud
FEUDAL *adj* of or like feudalism
FEUDALISE *same as* > FEUDALIZE
FEUDALISM *n* medieval system in which people held land from a lord, and in return worked and fought for him
FEUDALIST > FEUDALISM
FEUDALITY *n* state or quality of being feudal
FEUDALIZE *vb* make feudal
FEUDALLY > FEUDAL
FEUDARIES > FEUDARY
FEUDARY *n* holder of land through feudal right
FEUDATORY *n* person holding a fief ▷ *adj* relating to or characteristic of the relationship between lord and vassal
FEUDED > FEUD
FEUDING > FEUD
FEUDINGS > FEUD

FEUDIST n person who takes part in a feud or quarrel

FEUDISTS > FEUDIST

FEUDS > FEUD

FEUED > FEU

FEUILLETE n puff pastry

FEUING > FEU

FEUS > FEU

FEUTRE vb place in a resting position

FEUTRED > FEUTRE

FEUTRES > FEUTRE

FEUTRING > FEUTRE

FEVER n (illness causing) high body temperature ▷ vb affect with or as if with fever

FEVERED > FEVER

FEVERFEW n bushy European plant with white flower heads, formerly used medicinally

FEVERFEWS > FEVERFEW

FEVERING > FEVER

FEVERISH adj suffering from fever

FEVERLESS > FEVER

FEVEROUS same as > FEVERISH

FEVERROOT n American wild plant

FEVERS > FEVER

FEVERWEED n plant thought to be medicinal

FEVERWORT n any of several plants considered to have medicinal properties, such as horse gentian and boneset

FEW adj not many ▷ n as in the few small number of people considered as a class

FEWER > FEW

FEWEST > FEW

FEWMET variant of > FUMET

FEWMETS > FEWMET

FEWNESS > FEW

FEWNESSES > FEW

FEWS > FEW

FEWTER variant of > FEUTRE

FEWTERED > FEUTRE

FEWTERING > FEUTRE

FEWTERS > FEUTRE

FEWTRILS n trifles, trivia

FEY adj whimsically strange ▷ vb clean out

FEYED > FEY

FEYER > FEY

FEYEST > FEY

FEYING > FEY

FEYLY > FEY

FEYNESS > FEY

FEYNESSES > FEY

FEYS > FEY

FEZ n brimless tasselled cap, orig. from Turkey

FEZES > FEZ

FEZZED adj wearing a fez

FEZZES > FEZ

FEZZY > FEZ

FIACRE n small four-wheeled horse-drawn carriage

FIACRES > FIACRE

FIANCE n man engaged to be married

FIANCEE n woman who is engaged to be married

FIANCEES > FIANCEE

FIANCES > FIANCE

FIAR n property owner

FIARS n legally fixed price of corn

FIASCHI > FIASCO

FIASCO n ridiculous or humiliating failure

FIASCOES > FIASCO

FIASCOS > FIASCO

FIAT n arbitrary order ▷ vb issue a fiat

FIATED > FIAT

FIATING > FIAT

FIATS > FIAT

FIAUNT n fiat

FIAUNTS > FIAUNT

FIB n trivial lie ▷ vb tell a lie

FIBBED > FIB

FIBBER > FIB

FIBBERIES > FIB

FIBBERS > FIB

FIBBERY > FIB

FIBBING > FIB

FIBER same as > FIBRE

FIBERED > FIBRE

FIBERFILL same as > FIBREFILL

FIBERISE same as > FIBERIZE

FIBERISED > FIBERISE

FIBERISES > FIBERISE

FIBERIZE vb break into fibres

FIBERIZED > FIBERIZE

FIBERIZES > FIBERIZE

FIBERLESS > FIBRE

FIBERLIKE > FIBER

FIBERS > FIBER

FIBRANNE n synthetic fabric

FIBRANNES > FIBRANNE

FIBRATE n drug used to lower fat levels in the body

FIBRATES > FIBRATE

FIBRE n thread that can be spun into yarn

FIBRED > FIBRE

FIBREFILL n synthetic fibre used as a filling for pillows, quilted materials, etc

FIBRELESS > FIBRE

FIBRELIKE adj like a fibre

FIBRES > FIBRE

FIBRIFORM adj having the form of a fibre or fibres

FIBRIL n small fibre

FIBRILAR > FIBRIL

FIBRILLA same as > FIBRIL

FIBRILLAE > FIBRILLA

FIBRILLAR > FIBRIL

FIBRILLIN n kind of protein

FIBRILS > FIBRIL

FIBRIN n white insoluble elastic protein

FIBRINOID > FIBRIN

FIBRINOUS adj of, containing, or resembling fibrin

FIBRINS > FIBRIN

FIBRO n mixture of cement and asbestos fibre

FIBROCYTE n type of fibroblast

FIBROID adj (of structures or tissues) containing or resembling fibres ▷ n benign tumour composed of fibrous connective tissue

FIBROIDS > FIBROID

FIBROIN n tough elastic protein

FIBROINS > FIBROIN

FIBROLINE n type of yarn

FIBROLITE n trademark name for a type of building board containing asbestos and cement

FIBROMA n type of benign tumour

FIBROMAS > FIBROMA

FIBROMATA > FIBROMA

FIBROS > FIBRO

FIBROSE vb become fibrous

FIBROSED > FIBROSE

FIBROSES > FIBROSE

FIBROSING > FIBROSE

FIBROSIS n formation of an abnormal amount of fibrous tissue

FIBROTIC > FIBROSIS

FIBROUS adj consisting of, containing, or resembling fibres

FIBROUSLY > FIBROUS

FIBS > FIB

FIBSTER n fibber

FIBSTERS > FIBSTER

FIBULA n slender outer bone of the lower leg

FIBULAE > FIBULA

FIBULAR > FIBULA

FIBULAS > FIBULA

FICAIN n cysteine proteinase isolated from the latex of figs

FICAINS > FICAIN

FICE n small aggressive dog

FICES > FICE

FICHE n film for storing publications in miniature

FICHES > FICHE

FICHU n woman's shawl or scarf

FICHUS > FICHU

FICIN n enzyme

FICINS > FICIN

FICKLE adj changeable, inconstant ▷ vb puzzle

FICKLED > FICKLE

FICKLER > FICKLE

FICKLES > FICKLE

FICKLEST > FICKLE

FICKLING > FICKLE

FICKLY > FICKLE

FICO n worthless trifle

FICOES > FICO

FICOS > FICO

FICTILE adj moulded or capable of being moulded from clay

FICTION n literary works of the imagination

FICTIONAL > FICTION

FICTIONS > FICTION

FICTIVE adj of, relating to, or able to create fiction

FICTIVELY > FICTIVE

FICTOR n sculptor

FICTORS > FICTOR

FICUS n type of plant

FICUSES > FICUS

FID n spike for separating strands of rope in splicing

FIDDIOUS vb treat someone as Coriolanus, in the eponymous play, dealt with Aufidius

FIDDLE n violin ▷ vb play the violin

FIDDLED > FIDDLE

FIDDLER n person who plays the fiddle

FIDDLERS > FIDDLER

FIDDLES > FIDDLE

FIDDLEY n area of a vessel

FIDDLEYS > FIDDLEY

FIDDLIER > FIDDLY

FIDDLIEST > FIDDLY

FIDDLING adj trivial ▷ n act of fiddling

FIDDLINGS > FIDDLING

FIDDLY adj awkward to do or use

FIDEISM n theological doctrine

FIDEISMS > FIDEISM

FIDEIST > FIDEISM

FIDEISTIC > FIDEISM

FIDEISTS > FIDEISM

FIDELISMO n belief in, adherence to, or advocacy of the principles of Fidel Castro, the Cuban Communist statesman (born 1927)

FIDELISTA n advocate of fidelismo

FIDELITY n faithfulness

FIDES n faith or trust

FIDGE obsolete word for > FIDGET

FIDGED > FIDGE

FIDGES > FIDGE

FIDGET vb move about restlessly ▷ n person who fidgets

FIDGETED > FIDGET

FIDGETER > FIDGET

FIDGETERS > FIDGET

FIDGETIER > FIDGET

FIDGETING > FIDGET

FIDGETS > FIDGET

FIDGETY > FIDGET

FIDGING > FIDGE

FIDIBUS n spill for lighting a candle or pipe

FIDIBUSES > FIDIBUS
FIDO *n* generic term for a dog
FIDOS > FIDO
FIDS > FID
FIDUCIAL *adj* used as a standard of reference or measurement
FIDUCIARY *n* person bound to act for someone else's benefit, as a trustee ▷ *adj* of a trust or trustee
FIE *same as >* FEY
FIEF *n* land granted by a lord in return for war service
FIEFDOM *n* (in Feudal Europe) the property owned by a lord
FIEFDOMS > FIEFDOM
FIEFS > FIEF
FIELD *n* piece of land used for pasture or growing crops ▷ *vb* stop, catch, or return (the ball) as a fielder
FIELDBOOT *n* knee-length boot
FIELDED > FIELD
FIELDER *n* (in certain sports) player whose task is to field the ball
FIELDERS > FIELDER
FIELDFARE *n* type of large Old World thrush
FIELDING > FIELD
FIELDINGS > FIELD
FIELDMICE *pl n* nocturnal mice
FIELDS > FIELD
FIELDSMAN *n* fielder
**FIELDSMEN
>** FIELDSMAN
FIELDVOLE *n* small rodent
FIELDWARD *adv* towards a field or fields
FIELDWORK *n* investigation made in the field as opposed to the classroom or the laboratory
FIEND *n* evil spirit
FIENDISH *adj* of or like a fiend
FIENDLIKE > FIEND
FIENDS > FIEND
FIENT *n* fiend
FIENTS > FIENT
FIER *same as >* FERE
FIERCE *adj* wild or aggressive
FIERCELY > FIERCE
FIERCER > FIERCE
FIERCEST > FIERCE
FIERE *same as >* FERE
FIERES > FERE
FIERIER > FIERY
FIERIEST > FIERY
FIERILY > FIERY
FIERINESS > FIERY
FIERS > FIER
FIERY *adj* consisting of or like fire
FIEST > FIE

FIESTA *n* religious festival, carnival
FIESTAS > FIESTA
FIFE *n* small high-pitched flute ▷ *vb* play (music) on a fife
FIFED > FIFE
FIFER > FIFE
FIFERS > FIFE
FIFES > FIFE
FIFING > FIFE
FIFTEEN *n* five and ten ▷ *adj* amounting to fifteen ▷ *determiner* amounting to fifteen
FIFTEENER *n* fifteen-syllable line of poetry
FIFTEENS > FIFTEEN
FIFTEENTH *adj* coming after the fourteenth in order, position, time, etc. Often written: 15th ▷ *n* one of 15 equal or nearly equal parts of something
FIFTH *n* (of) number five in a series ▷ *adj* of or being number five in a series ▷ *adv* after the fourth person, position, event, etc
FIFTHLY *same as >* FIFTH
FIFTHS > FIFTH
FIFTIES > FIFTY
FIFTIETH *adj* being the ordinal number of *fifty* in order, position, time, etc. Often written: 50th ▷ *n* one of 50 equal or approximately equal parts of something
FIFTIETHS > FIFTIETH
FIFTY *n* five times ten ▷ *adj* amounting to fifty ▷ *determiner* amounting to fifty
FIFTYISH > FIFTY
FIG *n* soft pear-shaped fruit ▷ *vb* dress (up) or rig (out)
FIGEATER *n* large beetle
FIGEATERS > FIGEATER
FIGGED > FIG
FIGGERIES > FIGGERY
FIGGERY *n* adornment, ornament
FIGGING > FIG
FIGHT *vb* struggle (against) in battle or physical combat ▷ *n* aggressive conflict between two (groups of) people
FIGHTABLE > FIGHT
FIGHTBACK *n* act or campaign of resistance
FIGHTER *n* boxer
FIGHTERS > FIGHTER
FIGHTING > FIGHT
FIGHTINGS > FIGHT
FIGHTS > FIGHT
FIGJAM *n* very conceited person
FIGJAMS > FIGJAM

FIGMENT *n* fantastic notion, invention, or fabrication
FIGMENTS > FIGMENT
FIGO *variant of >* FICO
FIGOS > FIGO
FIGS > FIG
FIGTREE *n* tree that produces figs
FIGTREES > FIGTREE
FIGULINE *adj* of or resembling clay ▷ *n* article made of clay
FIGULINES > FIGULINE
FIGURABLE > FIGURE
FIGURAL *adj* composed of or relating to human or animal figures
FIGURALLY > FIGURAL
FIGURANT *n* ballet dancer who does group work but no solo roles
FIGURANTE *n* female figurant
FIGURANTS > FIGURANT
FIGURATE *adj* exhibiting or produced by figuration
FIGURE *n* numerical symbol ▷ *vb* calculate (sums or amounts)
FIGURED *adj* decorated with a design
FIGUREDLY > FIGURED
FIGURER > FIGURE
FIGURERS > FIGURE
FIGURES > FIGURE
FIGURINE *n* statuette
FIGURINES > FIGURINE
FIGURING > FIGURE
FIGURIST *n* user of numbers
FIGURISTS > FIGURIST
FIGWORT *n* N temperate plant
FIGWORTS > FIGWORT
FIKE *vb* fidget
FIKED > FIKE
FIKERIES > FIKERY
FIKERY *n* fuss
FIKES > FIKE
FIKIER > FIKY
FIKIEST > FIKY
FIKING > FIKE
FIKISH *adj* fussy
FIKY *adj* fussy
FIL *same as >* FILS
FILA > FILUM
FILABEG *variant of >* FILIBEG
FILABEGS > FILABEG
FILACEOUS *adj* made of threads
FILACER *n* formerly, English legal officer
FILACERS > FILACER
FILAGGRIN *n* protein found in skin cells
FILAGREE *same as >* FILIGREE
**FILAGREED
>** FILAGREE
**FILAGREES
>** FILAGREE

FILAMENT *n* fine wire in a light bulb that gives out light
FILAMENTS > FILAMENT
FILANDER *n* species of kangaroo
FILANDERS > FILANDER
FILAR *adj* of thread
FILAREE *n* type of storksbill, a weed
FILAREES > FILAREE
FILARIA *n* type of parasitic nematode worm
FILARIAE > FILARIA
FILARIAL > FILARIA
FILARIAN > FILARIA
FILARIID *adj* of or relating to a family of threadlike roundworms
FILARIIDS > FILARIID
FILASSE *n* vegetable fibre such as jute
FILASSES > FILASSE
FILATORY *n* machine for making threads
FILATURE *n* act or process of spinning silk, etc, into threads
FILATURES > FILATURE
FILAZER *variant of
>** FILACER
FILAZERS > FILAZER
FILBERD *variant of
>** FILBERT
FILBERDS > FILBERD
FILBERT *n* hazelnut
FILBERTS > FILBERT
FILCH *vb* steal (small amounts)
FILCHED > FILCH
FILCHER > FILCH
FILCHERS > FILCH
FILCHES > FILCH
FILCHING > FILCH
FILCHINGS > FILCH
FILE *n* box or folder used to keep documents in order ▷ *vb* place (a document) in a file
FILEABLE > FILE
FILECARD *n* type of brush with sharp steel bristles, used for cleaning the teeth of a file
FILECARDS > FILECARD
FILED > FILE
FILEFISH *n* type of tropical triggerfish with a narrow compressed body and a very long dorsal spine
FILEMOT *n* type of brown colour
FILEMOTS > FILEMOT
FILENAME *n* arrangement of characters that enables a computer system to permit the user to have access to a particular file
FILENAMES > FILENAME
FILER > FILE
FILERS > FILE
FILES > FILE
FILET *variant of >* FILLET

FILETED > FILET
FILETING > FILET
FILETS > FILET
FILFOT *variant of*
> FYLFOT
FILFOTS > FILFOT
FILIAL *adj* of or befitting
a son or daughter
FILIALLY > FILIAL
FILIATE *vb* fix judicially
the paternity of (a child)
FILIATED > FILIATE
FILIATES > FILIATE
FILIATING > FILIATE
FILIATION *n* line of
descent
FILIBEG *n* kilt worn by
Scottish Highlanders
FILIBEGS > FILIBEG
FILICIDAL > FILICIDE
FILICIDE *n* act of killing
one's own son or daughter
FILICIDES > FILICIDE
FILIFORM *adj* having the
form of a thread
FILIGRAIN *n* filigree
FILIGRANE *variant of*
> FILIGRAIN
FILIGREE *n* delicate
ornamental work of gold
or silver wire ▷ *adj* made of
filigree ▷ *vb* decorate with
or as if with filigree
FILIGREED > FILIGREE
FILIGREES > FILIGREE
FILII > FILIUS
FILING > FILE
FILINGS *pl n* shavings
removed by a file
FILIOQUE *n* theological
term found in the Nicene
Creed
FILIOQUES > FILIOQUE
FILISTER *same as*
> FILLISTER
FILISTERS > FILISTER
FILIUS *n* son
FILK *n* parodic type of folk
music with science fiction
lyrics
FILKS > FILK
FILL *vb* make or become
full
FILLABLE > FILL
FILLAGREE *same as*
> FILIGREE
FILLE *n* girl
FILLED > FILL
FILLER *n* substance that
fills a gap or increases bulk
FILLERS > FILLER
FILLES > FILLE
FILLESTER *same as*
> FILLISTER
FILLET *n* boneless piece
of meat or fish ▷ *vb*
remove the bones from
FILLETED > FILLET
FILLETER *n* person who
fillets
FILLETERS > FILLETER
FILLETING > FILLET
FILLETS > FILLET

FILLIBEG *same as*
> FILIBEG
FILLIBEGS > FILLIBEG
FILLIES > FILLY
FILLING *n* substance
that fills a gap or cavity
▷ *adj* (of food) substantial
and satisfying
FILLINGS > FILLING
FILLIP *n* something that
adds stimulation or
enjoyment ▷ *vb* stimulate
or excite
FILLIPED > FILLIP
FILLIPEEN *n* philopoena
FILLIPING > FILLIP
FILLIPS > FILLIP
FILLISTER *n* adjustable
plane for cutting rabbets,
grooves, etc
FILLO *variant of* **>** FILO
FILLOS > FILLO
FILLS > FILL
FILLY *n* young female
horse
FILM *n* projected images
creating the illusion of
movement ▷ *vb*
photograph with a movie
or video camera ▷ *adj*
connected with films or
the cinema
FILMABLE > FILM
FILMCARD *n* cinema
loyalty card
FILMCARDS > FILMCARD
FILMDOM *n* cinema
industry
FILMDOMS > FILMDOM
FILMED > FILM
FILMER *n* film-maker
FILMERS > FILMER
FILMFEST *n* film festival
FILMFESTS > FILMFEST
FILMGOER *n* person who
goes regularly to the cinema
FILMGOERS > FILMGOER
FILMGOING *n* activity of
going to see films
FILMI *adj* of or relating to
Indian films
FILMIC *adj* of or
suggestive of films or the
cinema
FILMIER > FILMY
FILMIEST > FILMY
FILMILY > FILMY
FILMINESS > FILMY
FILMING > FILM
FILMIS > FILMI
FILMISH > FILMI
FILMLAND *n* cinema
industry
FILMLANDS > FILMLAND
FILMLESS > FILM
FILMLIKE > FILM
FILMMAKER *n* person
who makes films
FILMS > FILM
FILMSET *vb* set (type
matter) by filmsetting
FILMSETS > FILMSET
FILMSTRIP *n* strip of film
composed of different

images projected
separately as slides
FILMY *adj* very thin,
delicate
FILO *n* type of flaky Greek
pastry in very thin sheets
FILOPLUME *n* any of the
hairlike feathers that lack
vanes and occur between
the contour feathers
FILOPODIA *n* plural form
of singular filopodium:
ectoplasmic
pseudopodium
FILOS > FILO
FILOSE *adj* resembling a
thread or threadlike
process
FILOSELLE *n* soft silk
thread, used esp for
embroidery
FILOVIRUS *n* any
member of a family of
viruses that includes the
agents responsible for
Ebola virus disease and
Marburg disease
FILS *n* monetary unit of
Bahrain, Iraq, Jordan, and
Kuwait
FILTER *n* device
permitting fluid to pass
but retaining solids
▷ *vb* remove impurities
from (a substance) with a
filter
FILTERED > FILTER
FILTERER > FILTER
FILTERERS > FILTER
FILTERING > FILTER
FILTERS > FILTER
FILTH *n* disgusting dirt
FILTHIER > FILTHY
FILTHIEST > FILTHY
FILTHILY > FILTHY
FILTHS > FILTH
FILTHY *adj* characterized
by or full of filth ▷ *adv*
extremely
FILTRABLE *adj* capable
of being filtered
FILTRATE *n* filtered gas
or liquid ▷ *vb* remove
impurities with a filter
FILTRATED > FILTRATE
FILTRATES > FILTRATE
FILTRE *adj* as in *cafe filtre* a
strong black filtered coffee
FILUM *n* any threadlike
structure or part
FIMBLE *n* male plant of
the hemp
FIMBLES > FIMBLE
FIMBRIA *n* fringe or
fringelike margin or border
FIMBRIAE > FIMBRIA
FIMBRIAL > FIMBRIA
FIMBRIATE *adj* having a
fringed margin, as some
petals, antennae, etc
FIN *n* any of the
appendages of some
aquatic animals
▷ *vb* provide with fins

FINABLE *adj* liable to a
fine
FINAGLE *vb* get or achieve
by craftiness or trickery
FINAGLED > FINAGLE
FINAGLER > FINAGLE
FINAGLERS > FINAGLE
FINAGLES > FINAGLE
FINAGLING *n* use of
trickery to achieve aims
FINAL *adj* at the end ▷ *n*
deciding contest
FINALE *n* concluding part
of a performance
FINALES > FINALE
FINALIS *n* musical
finishing note
FINALISE *same as*
> FINALIZE
FINALISED > FINALISE
FINALISER > FINALISE
FINALISES > FINALISE
FINALISM *n* doctrine that
final causes determine the
course of all events
FINALISMS > FINALISM
FINALIST *n* competitor
in a final
FINALISTS > FINALIST
FINALITY *n* condition or
quality of being final or
settled
FINALIZE *vb* put into
final form
FINALIZED > FINALIZE
FINALIZER > FINALIZE
FINALIZES > FINALIZE
FINALLY *adv* after a long
delay
FINALS *pl n* deciding part
of a competition
FINANCE *vb* provide or
obtain funds for ▷ *n*
system of money, credit,
and investment
FINANCED > FINANCE
FINANCES > FINANCE
FINANCIAL *adj* of or
relating to finance,
finances, or people who
manage money
FINANCIER *n* person
involved in large-scale
financial business
FINANCING > FINANCE
FINBACK *another name for*
> RORQUAL
FINBACKS > FINBACK
FINCA *n* Spanish villa
FINCAS > FINCA
FINCH *n* small songbird
with a short strong beak
FINCHED *adj* with streaks
or spots on the back
FINCHES > FINCH
FIND *vb* discover by chance
▷ *n* person or thing found,
esp when valuable
FINDABLE > FIND
FINDER *n* small telescope
fitted to a larger one
FINDERS > FINDER
FINDING > FIND
FINDINGS > FIND

FINDRAM variant of
> FINNAN

FINDRAMS > FINDRAM

FINDS > FIND

FINE adj very good ▷ n
payment imposed as a
penalty ▷ vb impose a
fine on

FINEABLE same as
> FINABLE

FINED > FINE

FINEER variant of
> VENEER

FINEERED > FINEER

FINEERING > FINEER

FINEERS > FINEER

FINEISH > FINE

FINELESS > FINE

FINELY adv into small
pieces

FINENESS n state or
quality of being fine

FINER > FINE

FINERIES > FINERY

FINERS > FINE

FINERY n showy clothing

FINES > FINE

FINESPUN adj spun or
drawn out to a fine thread

FINESSE n delicate skill
▷ vb bring about with
finesse

FINESSED > FINESSE

FINESSER > FINESSE

FINESSERS > FINESSE

FINESSES > FINESSE

FINESSING > FINESSE

FINEST n (in the US)
police of a particular city

FINESTS > FINEST

FINFISH n fish with fins,
as opposed to shellfish

FINFISHES > FINFISH

FINFOOT n type of aquatic
bird

FINFOOTS > FINFOOT

FINGAN variant of
> FINJAN

FINGANS > FINGAN

FINGER n one of the four
long jointed parts of the
hand ▷ vb touch or handle
with the fingers

FINGERED adj marked or
dirtied by handling

FINGERER > FINGER

FINGERERS > FINGER

FINGERING n technique
of using the fingers in
playing a musical
instrument

FINGERS > FINGER

FINGERTIP n end joint or
tip of a finger

FINI n end; finish

FINIAL n ornament at
the apex of a gable or
spire

FINIALED adj having a
finial or finials

FINIALS > FINIAL

FINICAL another word for
> FINICKY

FINICALLY > FINICAL

FINICKETY adj fussy or
tricky

FINICKIER > FINICKY

FINICKIN variant of
> FINICKY

FINICKING same as
> FINICKY

FINICKY adj excessively
particular, fussy

FINIKIN variant of
> FINICKY

FINIKING variant of
> FINICKY

FINING n process of
removing bubbles from
molten glass

FININGS > FINING

FINIS > FINI

FINISES > FINIS

FINISH vb bring to an
end, stop ▷ n end, last
part

FINISHED adj perfected

FINISHER n craftsman
who carries out the final
tasks in a manufacturing
process

FINISHERS > FINISHER

FINISHES > FINISH

FINISHING n act or skill
of goal scoring

FINITE adj having limits
in space, time, or size ▷ n a
verb limited by person,
number, tense or mood

FINITELY > FINITE

FINITES > FINITE

FINITISM n view that
only those entities may be
admitted to mathematics
that can be constructed in
a finite number of steps,
and only those propositions
entertained whose truth
can be proved in a finite
number of steps

FINITISMS > FINITISM

FINITIST n one who
believes in or advocates
finitism

FINITISTS > FINITIST

FINITO adj finished

FINITUDE > FINITE

FINITUDES > FINITE

FINJAN n small,
handleless coffee cup

FINJANS > FINJAN

FINK n strikebreaker ▷ vb
inform (on someone), as to
the police

FINKED > FINK

FINKING > FINK

FINKS > FINK

FINLESS > FIN

FINLIKE > FIN

FINLIT n understanding
of the concepts associated
with finance

FINLITS > FINLIT

FINMARK n monetary unit
of Finland

FINMARKS > FINMARK

FINNAC variant of
> FINNOCK

FINNACK variant of
> FINNOCK

FINNACKS > FINNACK

FINNACS > FINNAC

FINNAN n smoked
haddock

FINNANS > FINNAN

FINNED > FIN

FINNER another name for
> RORQUAL

FINNERS > FINNER

FINNESKO n reindeer-skin
boot

FINNICKY variant of
> FINICKY

FINNIER > FINNY

FINNIEST > FINNY

FINNING > FIN

FINNMARK n Finnish
monetary unit

FINNMARKS > FINNMARK

FINNOCHIO variant of
> FINOCCHIO

FINNOCK n young sea
trout on its first return to
fresh water

FINNOCKS > FINNOCK

FINNSKO variant of
> FINNESKO

FINNY adj relating to or
containing many fishes

FINO n very dry sherry

FINOCCHIO n variety of
fennel with celery-like
stalks which are eaten as a
vegetable

FINOCHIO same as
> FINOCCHIO

FINOCHIOS > FINOCHIO

FINOS > FINO

FINS > FIN

FINSKO variant of
> FINNESKO

FIORATURA same as
> FIORITURA

FIORD same as > FJORD

FIORDS > FIORD

FIORIN n type of
temperate perennial grass

FIORINS > FIORIN

FIORITURA n
embellishment, esp
ornamentation added by
the performer

FIORITURE
> FIORITURA

FIPPENCE n fivepence

FIPPENCES > FIPPENCE

FIPPLE n wooden plug
forming a flue in the end of
a pipe

FIPPLES > FIPPLE

FIQH n Islamic
jurisprudence

FIQHS > FIQH

FIQUE n hemp

FIQUES > FIQUE

FIR n pyramid-shaped tree

FIRE n state of
combustion producing
heat, flames, and smoke
▷ vb operate (a weapon) so
that a bullet or missile is
released

FIREABLE > FIRE

FIREARM n rifle, pistol, or
shotgun

FIREARMED adj carrying
firearm

FIREARMS > FIREARM

FIREBACK n ornamental
iron slab against the back
wall of a hearth

FIREBACKS > FIREBACK

FIREBALL n ball of fire at
the centre of an explosion

FIREBALLS > FIREBALL

FIREBASE n artillery base
from which heavy fire is
directed at the enemy

FIREBASES > FIREBASE

FIREBIRD n any of
various songbirds having a
bright red plumage, esp
the Baltimore oriole

FIREBIRDS > FIREBIRD

FIREBOARD n
mantelpiece

FIREBOAT n motor vessel
with fire-fighting apparatus

FIREBOATS > FIREBOAT

FIREBOMB n bomb that is
designed to cause fires
▷ vb detonate such a bomb

FIREBOMBS > FIREBOMB

FIREBOX n furnace
chamber of a boiler in a
steam locomotive

FIREBOXES > FIREBOX

FIREBRAND n person
who causes unrest

FIREBRAT n type of small
primitive wingless insect

FIREBRATS > FIREBRAT

FIREBREAK n strip of
cleared land to stop the
advance of a fire

FIREBRICK n heat-
resistant brick used for
lining furnaces, fireplaces,
etc

FIREBUG n person who
deliberately sets fire to
property

FIREBUGS > FIREBUG

FIREBUSH n as in Chilean
firebush South American
shrub with scarlet flowers

FIRECLAY n heat-
resistant clay used in the
making of firebricks,
furnace linings, etc

FIRECLAYS > FIRECLAY

FIRECREST n small
European warbler with a
crown striped with yellow,
black, and white

FIRED > FIRE

FIREDAMP n explosive
gas, composed mainly of
methane, formed in mines

FIREDAMPS > FIREDAMP

FIREDOG n either of two
metal stands supporting
logs in a fire

FIREDOGS > FIREDOG

FIREDRAKE n fire-
breathing dragon

FIREFANG *vb* become overheated through decomposition

FIREFANGS > FIREFANG

FIREFIGHT *n* brief small-scale engagement between opposing military ground forces using short-range light weapons

FIREFLIES > FIREFLY

FIREFLOAT *n* boat used for firefighting

FIREFLOOD *n* method of extracting oil from a well by burning some of the oil to increase the rate of flow

FIREFLY *n* beetle that glows in the dark

FIREGUARD *same as* > FIREBREAK

FIREHALL *n* US and Canadian word for fire station

FIREHALLS > FIREHALL

FIREHOSE *n* hose used to extinguish fires

FIREHOSES > FIREHOSE

FIREHOUSE *n* firestation

FIRELESS > FIRE

FIRELIGHT *n* light from a fire

FIRELIT *adj* lit by firelight

FIRELOCK *n* obsolete type of gunlock with a priming mechanism ignited by sparks

FIRELOCKS > FIRELOCK

FIREMAN *n* man who puts out fires and rescues people

FIREMANIC > FIREMAN

FIREMARK *n* plaque indicating that a building is insured

FIREMARKS > FIREMARK

FIREMEN > FIREMAN

FIREPAN *n* metal container for a fire in a room

FIREPANS > FIREPAN

FIREPINK *n* wildflower belonging to the pink family

FIREPINKS > FIREPINK

FIREPIT *n* hole dug in the ground for a fire

FIREPITS > FIREPIT

FIREPLACE *n* recess in a room for a fire

FIREPLUG *n* US and New Zealand name for a fire hydrant

FIREPLUGS > FIREPLUG

FIREPOT *n* Chinese fondue-like cooking pot

FIREPOTS > FIREPOT

FIREPOWER *n* amount of fire that may be delivered by a unit or weapon

FIREPROOF *adj* capable of resisting damage by fire ▷ *vb* make resistant to fire

FIRER > FIRE

FIREREEL *n* fire engine

FIREREELS > FIREREEL

FIREROOM *n* stokehold

FIREROOMS > FIREROOM

FIRERS > FIRE

FIRES > FIRE

FIRESCAPE *vb* arrange a garden so that fire cannot spread easily

FIRESHIP *n* vessel loaded with flammable materials, ignited, and directed among enemy warships to set them alight

FIRESHIPS > FIRESHIP

FIRESIDE *n* hearth

FIRESIDES > FIRESIDE

FIRESTONE *n* sandstone that withstands intense heat, esp one used for lining kilns, furnaces, etc

FIRESTORM *n* uncontrollable blaze sustained by violent winds that are drawn into the column of rising hot air over the burning area: often the result of heavy bombing

FIRETHORN *n* type of evergreen spiny shrub of SE Europe and Asia with bright red or orange fruits, cultivated for ornament

FIRETRAP *n* building that would burn easily or one without fire escapes

FIRETRAPS > FIRETRAP

FIRETRUCK *n* fire engine

FIREWALL *n* appliance that prevents unauthorized access to a computer network from the internet ▷ *vb* protect (a computer system) or block (unwanted access) with a firewall

FIREWALLS > FIREWALL

FIREWATER *n* any alcoholic spirit

FIREWEED *n* any of various plants that appear as first vegetation in burnt-over areas, esp rosebay willowherb

FIREWEEDS > FIREWEED

FIREWOMAN *n* female firefighter

FIREWOMEN > FIREWOMAN

FIREWOOD *n* wood for burning

FIREWOODS > FIREWOOD

FIREWORK *n* device containing chemicals that is ignited to produce spectacular explosions and coloured sparks

FIREWORKS *pl n* show in which fireworks are let off

FIREWORM *n* cranberry worm

FIREWORMS > FIREWORM

FIRIE *n* in Australian English, informal word for a firefighter

FIRIES > FIRIE

FIRING *n* discharge of a firearm

FIRINGS > FIRING

FIRK *vb* beat

FIRKED > FIRK

FIRKIN *n* small wooden barrel or similar container

FIRKING > FIRK

FIRKINS > FIRKIN

FIRKS > FIRK

FIRLOT *n* unit of measurement for grain

FIRLOTS > FIRLOT

FIRM *adj* not soft or yielding ▷ *adv* in an unyielding manner ▷ *vb* make or become firm ▷ *n* business company

FIRMAMENT *n* sky or the heavens

FIRMAN *n* edict of an Oriental sovereign

FIRMANS > FIRMAN

FIRMED > FIRM

FIRMER > FIRM

FIRMERS > FIRM

FIRMEST > FIRM

FIRMING > FIRM

FIRMLESS *adj* unstable

FIRMLY > FIRM

FIRMNESS > FIRM

FIRMS > FIRM

FIRMWARE *n* fixed form of software programmed into a read-only memory

FIRMWARES > FIRMWARE

FIRN *another name for* > NEVE

FIRNS > FIRN

FIRRIER > FIRRY

FIRRIEST > FIRRY

FIRRING *n* wooden battens used in building construction

FIRRINGS > FIRRING

FIRRY *adj* of, relating to, or made from fir trees

FIRS > FIR

FIRST *adj* earliest in time or order ▷ *n* person or thing coming before all others ▷ *adv* before anything else

FIRSTBORN *adj* eldest of the children in a family ▷ *n* eldest child in a family

FIRSTHAND *adj* from the original source

FIRSTLING *n* first, esp the first offspring

FIRSTLY *adv* coming before other points, questions, etc

FIRSTNESS > FIRST

FIRSTS *pl n* saleable goods of the highest quality

FIRTH *n* narrow inlet of the sea, esp in Scotland

FIRTHS → FIRTH

FIRWOOD *n* wood of the fir tree

FIRWOODS > FIRWOOD

FISC *n* state or royal treasury

FISCAL *adj* of government finances, esp taxes ▷ *n* (in some countries) a public prosecutor

FISCALIST > FISCAL

FISCALLY > FISCAL

FISCALS > FISCAL

FISCS > FISC

FISGIG *variant of* > FISHGIG

FISGIGS > FISGIG

FISH *n* cold-blooded vertebrate with gills, that lives in water ▷ *vb* try to catch fish

FISHABLE > FISH

FISHBALL *n* fried ball of flaked fish and mashed potato

FISHBALLS > FISHBALL

FISHBOAT *n* boat used for fishing

FISHBOATS > FISHBOAT

FISHBOLT *n* bolt used for fastening a fishplate to a rail

FISHBOLTS > FISHBOLT

FISHBONE *n* bone of a fish

FISHBONES > FISHBONE

FISHBOWL *n* goldfish bowl

FISHBOWLS > FISHBOWL

FISHCAKE *n* mixture of flaked fish and mashed potatoes formed into a flat circular shape

FISHCAKES > FISHCAKE

FISHED > FISH

FISHER *n* fisherman

FISHERIES > FISHERY

FISHERMAN *n* person who catches fish for a living or for pleasure

FISHERMEN > FISHERMAN

FISHERS > FISHER

FISHERY *n* area of the sea used for fishing

FISHES > FISH

FISHEYE *n* type of lens

FISHEYES > FISHEYE

FISHFUL *adj* teeming with fish

FISHGIG *n* pole with barbed prongs for impaling fish

FISHGIGS > FISHGIG

FISHHOOK *n* sharp hook used in angling, esp one with a barb

FISHHOOKS > FISHHOOK

FISHIER > FISHY

FISHIEST > FISHY

FISHIFIED > FISHIFY

FISHIFIES > FISHIFY

FISHIFY *vb* change into fish

FISHILY > FISHY

FISHINESS > FISHY

FISHING *n* job or pastime of catching fish

FISHINGS > FISHING
FISHKILL n mass killing of fish by pollution
FISHKILLS > FISHKILL
FISHLESS > FISH
FISHLIKE > FISH
FISHLINE n line used on a fishing-rod
FISHLINES > FISHLINE
FISHMEAL n ground dried fish used as feed for farm animals or as a fertilizer
FISHMEALS > FISHMEAL
FISHNET n open mesh fabric resembling netting
FISHNETS > FISHNET
FISHPLATE n metal plate holding rails together
FISHPOLE n boom arm for a microphone
FISHPOLES > FISHPOLE
FISHPOND > FISH
FISHPONDS > FISH
FISHSKIN n skin of a fish
FISHSKINS > FISHSKIN
FISHTAIL n nozzle having a long narrow slot at the top, placed over a Bunsen burner to produce a thin fanlike flame ▷ vb slow an aeroplane by moving the tail from side to side
FISHTAILS > FISHTAIL
FISHWAY n fish ladder
FISHWAYS > FISHWAY
FISHWIFE n coarse scolding woman
FISHWIVES > FISHWIFE
FISHWORM n worm used as fishing bait
FISHWORMS > FISHWORM
FISHY adj of or like fish
FISHYBACK n goods supply chain involving container transfer from lorry to ship
FISK vb frisk
FISKED > FISK
FISKING > FISK
FISKS > FISK
FISNOMIE n physiognomy
FISNOMIES > FISNOMIE
FISSATE > FISSILE
FISSILE adj capable of undergoing nuclear fission
FISSILITY > FISSILE
FISSION n splitting
FISSIONAL > FISSION
FISSIONED adj split or broken into parts
FISSIONS > FISSION
FISSIPED adj having toes that are separated from one another, as dogs, cats, bears, and similar carnivores ▷ n fissiped animal
FISSIPEDS > FISSIPED
FISSIVE > FISSILE
FISSLE vb rustle
FISSLED > FISSLE

FISSLES > FISSLE
FISSLING > FISSLE
FISSURAL > FISSURE
FISSURE n long narrow cleft or crack ▷ vb crack or split apart
FISSURED > FISSURE
FISSURES > FISSURE
FISSURING > FISSURE
FIST n clenched hand ▷ vb hit with the fist
FISTED > FIST
FISTFIGHT n fight using bare fists
FISTFUL n quantity that can be held in a fist or hand
FISTFULS > FISTFUL
FISTIANA n world of boxing
FISTIC adj of or relating to fisticuffs or boxing
FISTICAL > FISTIC
FISTICUFF n cuff or blow ▷ vb fight or strike with the fists
FISTIER > FIST
FISTIEST > FIST
FISTING n act of fisting
FISTINGS > FISTING
FISTMELE n measure of the width of a hand and the extended thumb, used to calculate the approximate height of the string of a braced bow
FISTMELES > FISTMELE
FISTNOTE n note in printed text preceded by the fist symbol
FISTNOTES > FISTNOTE
FISTS > FIST
FISTULA n long narrow ulcer
FISTULAE > FISTULA
FISTULAR same as **>** FISTULOUS
FISTULAS > FISTULA
FISTULATE same as **>** FISTULOUS
FISTULOSE variant of **>** FISTULOUS
FISTULOUS adj containing, relating to, or resembling a fistula
FISTY > FIST
FIT vb be appropriate or suitable for ▷ adj appropriate ▷ n way in which something fits
FITCH n fur of the polecat or ferret
FITCHE adj pointed
FITCHEE variant of **>** FITCHE
FITCHES > FITCH
FITCHET same as **>** FITCH
FITCHETS > FITCHET
FITCHEW archaic name for **>** POLECAT
FITCHEWS > FITCHEW
FITCHY variant of **>** FITCHE
FITFUL adj occurring in irregular spells

FITFULLY > FITFUL
FITLIER > FITLY
FITLIEST > FITLY
FITLY adv in a proper manner or place or at a proper time
FITMENT n accessory attached to a machine
FITMENTS > FITMENT
FITNA n state of trouble or chaos
FITNAS > FITNA
FITNESS n state of being fit
FITNESSES > FITNESS
FITS > FIT
FITT n song
FITTABLE > FIT
FITTE variant of **>** FITT
FITTED > FIT
FITTER > FIT
FITTERS > FIT
FITTES > FITTE
FITTEST > FIT
FITTING > FIT
FITTINGLY > FIT
FITTINGS > FIT
FITTS > FITT
FIVE n one more than four ▷ adj amounting to five ▷ determiner amounting to five
FIVEFOLD adj having five times as many or as much ▷ adv by five times as many or as much
FIVEPENCE n five-penny coin
FIVEPENNY adj (of a nail) one and three-quarters of an inch in length
FIVEPIN > FIVEPINS
FIVEPINS n bowling game played esp in Canada
FIVER n five-pound note
FIVERS > FIVER
FIVES n ball game resembling squash
FIX vb make or become firm, stable, or secure ▷ n difficult situation
FIXABLE > FIX
FIXATE vb become or cause to become fixed
FIXATED > FIXATE
FIXATES > FIXATE
FIXATIF variant of **>** FIXATIVE
FIXATIFS > FIXATIF
FIXATING > FIXATE
FIXATION n obsessive interest in something
FIXATIONS > FIXATION
FIXATIVE n liquid used to preserve or hold things in place ▷ adj serving or tending to fix
FIXATIVES > FIXATIVE
FIXATURE n something that holds an object in place
FIXATURES > FIXATURE

FIXED adj attached or placed so as to be immovable
FIXEDLY > FIXED
FIXEDNESS > FIXED
FIXER n solution used to make a photographic image permanent
FIXERS > FIXER
FIXES > FIX
FIXING n means of attaching one thing to another
FIXINGS pl n apparatus or equipment
FIXIT n solution to a complex problem ▷ adj that fixes things
FIXITIES > FIXITY
FIXITS > FIXIT
FIXITY n state of being fixed
FIXIVE > FIX
FIXT adj fixed
FIXTURE n permanently fitted piece of household equipment
FIXTURES > FIXTURE
FIXURE n firmness
FIXURES > FIXURE
FIZ variant of **>** FIZZ
FIZGIG vb inform on someone to the police
FIZGIGGED > FIZGIG
FIZGIGS > FIZGIG
FIZZ vb make a hissing or bubbling noise ▷ n hissing or bubbling noise
FIZZED > FIZZ
FIZZEN variant of **>** FOISON
FIZZENS > FIZZEN
FIZZER n anything that fizzes
FIZZERS > FIZZER
FIZZES > FIZZ
FIZZGIG variant of **>** FISHGIG
FIZZGIGS > FIZZGIG
FIZZIER > FIZZ
FIZZIEST > FIZZ
FIZZILY adv in a fizzy manner
FIZZINESS > FIZZ
FIZZING > FIZZ
FIZZINGS > FIZZ
FIZZLE vb make a weak hissing or bubbling sound ▷ n hissing or bubbling sound
FIZZLED > FIZZLE
FIZZLES > FIZZLE
FIZZLING > FIZZLE
FIZZY > FIZZ
FJELD n high rocky plateau
FJELDS > FJELD
FJORD n long narrow inlet of the sea between cliffs
FJORDIC > FJORD
FJORDS > FJORD
FLAB n unsightly body fat
FLABBIER > FLABBY

FLABBIEST > FLABBY

FLABBILY > FLABBY

FLABBY adj having flabby flesh

FLABELLA > FLABELLUM

FLABELLUM n fan-shaped organ or part, such as the tip of the proboscis of a honeybee

FLABS > FLAB

FLACCID adj soft and limp

FLACCIDER > FLACCID

FLACCIDLY > FLACCID

FLACK vb flutter

FLACKED > FLACK

FLACKER vb flutter like a bird

FLACKERED > FLACKER

FLACKERS > FLACKER

FLACKERY > FLACK

FLACKET n flagon ▷ vb flap or flutter about

FLACKETED > FLACKET

FLACKETS > FLACKET

FLACKING > FLACK

FLACKS > FLACK

FLACON n small stoppered bottle or flask

FLACONS > FLACON

FLAFF vb flap

FLAFFED > FLAFF

FLAFFER vb flutter

FLAFFERED > FLAFFER

FLAFFERS > FLAFFER

FLAFFING > FLAFF

FLAFFS > FLAFF

FLAG n piece of cloth attached to a pole as an emblem or signal ▷ vb mark with a flag or sticker

FLAGELLA > FLAGELLUM

FLAGELLAR > FLAGELLUM

FLAGELLIN n structural protein of bacterial flagella

FLAGELLUM n whiplike outgrowth from a cell that acts as an organ of movement

FLAGEOLET n small instrument like a recorder

FLAGGED > FLAG

FLAGGER > FLAG

FLAGGERS > FLAG

FLAGGIER > FLAGGY

FLAGGIEST > FLAGGY

FLAGGING > FLAG

FLAGGINGS > FLAG

FLAGGY adj drooping

FLAGITATE vb importune

FLAGLESS > FLAG

FLAGMAN n person who has charge of a flag

FLAGMEN > FLAGMAN

FLAGON n wide bottle for wine or cider

FLAGONS > FLAGON

FLAGPOLE n pole for a flag

FLAGPOLES > FLAGPOLE

FLAGRANCE > FLAGRANT

FLAGRANCY > FLAGRANT

FLAGRANT adj openly outrageous

FLAGS > FLAG

FLAGSHIP n admiral's ship

FLAGSHIPS > FLAGSHIP

FLAGSTAFF same as > FLAGPOLE

FLAGSTICK n in golf, pole used to indicate position of hole

FLAGSTONE n flat slab of hard stone for paving

FLAIL vb wave about wildly ▷ n tool formerly used for threshing grain by hand

FLAILED > FLAIL

FLAILING > FLAIL

FLAILS > FLAIL

FLAIR n natural ability

FLAIRS > FLAIR

FLAK n anti-aircraft fire

FLAKE n small thin piece, esp chipped off something ▷ vb peel off in flakes

FLAKED > FLAKE

FLAKER > FLAKE

FLAKERS > FLAKE

FLAKES > FLAKE

FLAKEY same as > FLAKY

FLAKIER > FLAKY

FLAKIES n dandruff

FLAKIEST > FLAKY

FLAKILY > FLAKY

FLAKINESS > FLAKY

FLAKING > FLAKE

FLAKS > FLAK

FLAKY adj like or made of flakes

FLAM n falsehood, deception, or sham ▷ vb cheat or deceive

FLAMBE vb cook or serve (food) in flaming brandy ▷ adj (of food) served in flaming brandy

FLAMBEAU n burning torch, as used in night processions

FLAMBEAUS > FLAMBEAU

FLAMBEAUX > FLAMBEAU

FLAMBEE same as > FLAMBE

FLAMBEED > FLAMBEE

FLAMBEES > FLAMBEE

FLAMBEING > FLAMBE

FLAMBES > FLAMBE

FLAME n luminous burning gas coming from burning material ▷ vb burn brightly

FLAMED > FLAME

FLAMELESS > FLAME

FLAMELET > FLAME

FLAMELETS > FLAME

FLAMELIKE > FLAME

FLAMEN n (in ancient Rome) type of priest

FLAMENCO n rhythmical Spanish dance accompanied by a guitar and vocalist

FLAMENCOS > FLAMENCO

FLAMENS > FLAMEN

FLAMEOUT n failure of an aircraft jet engine in flight due to extinction of the flame ▷ vb (of a jet engine) to fail in flight or to cause (a jet engine) to fail in flight

FLAMEOUTS > FLAMEOUT

FLAMER > FLAME

FLAMERS > FLAME

FLAMES > FLAME

FLAMFEW n fantastic trifle

FLAMFEWS > FLAMFEW

FLAMIER > FLAME

FLAMIEST > FLAME

FLAMINES > FLAMEN

FLAMING adj burning with flames ▷ adv extremely

FLAMINGLY > FLAMING

FLAMINGO n large pink wading bird with a long neck and legs

FLAMINGOS > FLAMINGO

FLAMM variant of > FLAM

FLAMMABLE adj easily set on fire

FLAMMED > FLAM

FLAMMING > FLAM

FLAMMS > FLAMM

FLAMMULE n small flame

FLAMMULES > FLAMMULE

FLAMS > FLAM

FLAMY > FLAME

FLAN n open sweet or savoury tart

FLANCARD n armour covering a horse's flank

FLANCARDS > FLANCARD

FLANCH variant of > FLAUNCH

FLANCHED > FLANCH

FLANCHES > FLANCH

FLANCHING > FLANCH

FLANE vb walk idly, saunter

FLANED > FLANE

FLANERIE n aimless strolling or lounging

FLANERIES > FLANERIE

FLANES n arrows

FLANEUR n idler or loafer

FLANEURS > FLANEUR

FLANGE n projecting rim or collar ▷ vb attach or provide (a component) with a flange

FLANGED > FLANGE

FLANGER > FLANGE

FLANGERS > FLANGE

FLANGES > FLANGE

FLANGING n act of flanging

FLANGINGS > FLANGING

FLANING > FLANE

FLANK n part of the side between the hips and ribs ▷ vb be at or move along the side of

FLANKED > FLANK

FLANKEN n cut of beef

FLANKENS > FLANKEN

FLANKER n one of a detachment of soldiers guarding the flanks

FLANKERED > FLANKER

FLANKERS > FLANKER

FLANKING > FLANK

FLANKS > FLANK

FLANNEL n small piece of cloth for washing the face ▷ vb talk evasively

FLANNELED > FLANNEL

FLANNELET n cotton imitation of flannel

FLANNELLY > FLANNEL

FLANNELS > FLANNEL

FLANNEN adj made of flannel

FLANNENS > FLANNEN

FLANNIE same as > FLANNY

FLANNIES > FLANNIE

FLANNY n shirt made of flannel

FLANS > FLAN

FLAP vb move back and forwards or up and down ▷ n action or sound of flapping

FLAPERON n control flap on aircraft wing

FLAPERONS > FLAPERON

FLAPJACK n chewy biscuit made with oats

FLAPJACKS > FLAPJACK

FLAPLESS > FLAP

FLAPPABLE > FLAP

FLAPPED > FLAP

FLAPPER n (in the 1920s) an unconventional young woman

FLAPPERS > FLAPPER

FLAPPIER > FLAPPY

FLAPPIEST > FLAPPY

FLAPPING > FLAP

FLAPPINGS > FLAP

FLAPPY adj loose

FLAPS > FLAP

FLAPTRACK n component in an aircraft wing

FLARE vb blaze with a sudden unsteady flame ▷ n sudden unsteady flame

FLAREBACK n flame in the breech of a gun when fired

FLARED > FLARE

FLARES pl n trousers with legs that widen below the knee

FLAREUP n outbreak of something

FLAREUPS > FLAREUP

FLARIER > FLARE

FLARIEST > FLARE

FLARING > FLARE

FLARINGLY > FLARE

FLARY adj flare-like

FLASER n type of sedimentary structure in rock

FLASERS > FLASER

FLASH n sudden burst of light or flame ▷ adj vulgarly showy ▷ vb (cause to) burst into flame

FLASHBACK n scene in a book, play, or film, that shows earlier events ▷ vb return in a novel, film, etc, to a past event
FLASHBANG n stun grenade
FLASHBULB n small light bulb that produces a bright flash of light
FLASHCARD n card shown briefly as a memory test
FLASHCUBE n in photography, a cube with a bulb that is attached to a camera
FLASHED > FLASH
FLASHER n man who exposes himself indecently
FLASHERS > FLASHER
FLASHES > FLASH
FLASHEST > FLASH
FLASHGUN n type of electronic flash, attachable to or sometimes incorporated in a camera, that emits a very brief flash of light when the shutter is open
FLASHGUNS > FLASHGUN
FLASHIER > FLASHY
FLASHIEST > FLASHY
FLASHILY > FLASHY
FLASHING n watertight material used to cover joins in a roof
FLASHINGS > FLASHING
FLASHLAMP n electric lamp producing a flash of intense light
FLASHOVER n electric discharge over or around the surface of an insulator
FLASHTUBE n tube used in a flashlamp
FLASHY adj showy in a vulgar way
FLASK n flat bottle
FLASKET n long shallow basket
FLASKETS > FLASKET
FLASKS > FLASK
FLAT adj level and horizontal ▷ adv in or into a flat position ▷ n flat surface ▷ vb live in a flat
FLATBACK n flat-backed ornament, designed for viewing from front
FLATBACKS > FLATBACK
FLATBED n type of printing machine
FLATBEDS > FLATBED
FLATBOAT n flat-bottomed boat for transporting goods on a canal
FLATBOATS > FLATBOAT
FLATBREAD n type of thin unleavened bread
FLATCAP n Elizabethan man's hat
FLATCAPS > FLATCAP
FLATCAR n flatbed

FLATCARS > FLATCAR
FLATETTE n very small flat
FLATETTES > FLATETTE
FLATFEET > FLATFOOT
FLATFISH n sea fish, such as the sole, which has a flat body
FLATFOOT n condition in which the entire sole of the foot is able to touch the ground because of flattening of the instep arch
FLATFOOTS > FLATFOOT
FLATFORM n thick, level sole on a shoe
FLATFORMS > FLATFORM
FLATHEAD n common Australian flatfish
FLATHEADS > FLATHEAD
FLATIRON n (formerly) an iron for pressing clothes that was heated by being placed on a stove
FLATIRONS > FLATIRON
FLATLAND n land notable for its levelness
FLATLANDS > FLATLAND
FLATLET n small flat
FLATLETS > FLATLET
FLATLINE vb die or be so near death that the display of one's vital signs on medical monitoring equipment shows a flat line rather than peaks and troughs
FLATLINED > FLATLINE
FLATLINER > FLATLINE
FLATLINES > FLATLINE
FLATLING adv in a flat or prostrate position ▷ adj with the flat side, as of a sword
FLATLINGS same as > FLATLING
FLATLONG adv prostrate
FLATLY > FLAT
FLATMATE n person with whom one shares a flat
FLATMATES > FLATMATE
FLATNESS > FLAT
FLATPACK n (of a piece of furniture, equipment, or other construction) supplied in pieces packed into a flat box for assembly by the buyer
FLATPACKS > FLATPACK
FLATPICK vb play (a guitar, etc) by plucking individual strings with a plectrum
FLATPICKS > FLATPICK
FLATS > FLAT
FLATSHARE n state of living in a flat where each occupant shares the facilities and expenses ▷ vb live in a flat with other people who are not relatives
FLATSTICK adv with great speed or effort

FLATTED > FLAT
FLATTEN vb make or become flat or flatter
FLATTENED > FLATTEN
FLATTENER > FLATTEN
FLATTENS > FLATTEN
FLATTER vb praise insincerely
FLATTERED > FLATTER
FLATTERER > FLATTER
FLATTERS > FLATTER
FLATTERY n excessive or insincere praise
FLATTEST > FLAT
FLATTIE n flat tyre
FLATTIES same as > FLATTIE
FLATTING > FLAT
FLATTINGS > FLAT
FLATTISH adj somewhat flat
FLATTOP n informal name for an aircraft carrier
FLATTOPS > FLATTOP
FLATTY n flat shoe
FLATULENT adj suffering from or caused by too much gas in the intestines
FLATUOUS > FLATUS
FLATUS n gas generated in the alimentary canal
FLATUSES > FLATUS
FLATWARE n cutlery
FLATWARES > FLATWARE
FLATWASH n laundry that can be ironed mechanically
FLATWAYS adv with the flat or broad side down or in contact with another surface
FLATWISE same as > FLATWAYS
FLATWORK n laundry that can be ironed mechanically
FLATWORKS > FLATWORK
FLATWORM n worm, such as a tapeworm, with a flattened body
FLATWORMS > FLATWORM
FLAUGHT vb flutter
FLAUGHTED > FLAUGHT
FLAUGHTER vb cut peat
FLAUGHTS > FLAUGHT
FLAUNCH n cement or mortar slope to throw off water ▷ vb cause to slope in this manner
FLAUNCHED > FLAUNCH
FLAUNCHES > FLAUNCH
FLAUNE variant of > FLAM
FLAUNES > FLAUNE
FLAUNT vb display (oneself or one's possessions) arrogantly ▷ n act of flaunting
FLAUNTED > FLAUNT
FLAUNTER > FLAUNT
FLAUNTERS > FLAUNT
FLAUNTIER > FLAUNTY
FLAUNTILY > FLAUNTY
FLAUNTING > FLAUNT

FLAUNTS > FLAUNT
FLAUNTY adj characterized by or inclined to ostentatious display
FLAUTA n tortilla rolled around a filling
FLAUTAS > FLAUTA
FLAUTIST n flute player
FLAUTISTS > FLAUTIST
FLAVA n individual style
FLAVANOL n type of flavonoid
FLAVANOLS > FLAVANOL
FLAVANONE n flavone-derived compound
FLAVAS > FLAVA
FLAVIN n heterocyclic ketone
FLAVINE same as > FLAVIN
FLAVINES > FLAVINE
FLAVINS > FLAVIN
FLAVONE n crystalline compound occurring in plants
FLAVONES > FLAVONE
FLAVONOID n any of a group of organic compounds that occur as pigments in fruit and flowers
FLAVONOL n flavonoid that occurs in red wine and is said to offer protection against heart disease
FLAVONOLS > FLAVONOL
FLAVOR same as > FLAVOUR
FLAVORED > FLAVOR
FLAVORER > FLAVOR
FLAVORERS > FLAVOR
FLAVORFUL adj flavourful
FLAVORING same as > FLAVOURING
FLAVORIST n blender of ingredients, to create or enhance flavours
FLAVOROUS adj having flavour
FLAVORS > FLAVOR
FLAVORY adj flavoursome
FLAVOUR n distinctive taste ▷ vb give flavour to
FLAVOURED > FLAVOUR
FLAVOURER > FLAVOUR
FLAVOURS > FLAVOUR
FLAVOURY adj flavoursome
FLAW n imperfection or blemish ▷ vb make or become blemished, defective, or imperfect
FLAWED > FLAW
FLAWIER > FLAW
FLAWIEST > FLAW
FLAWING > FLAW
FLAWLESS > FLAW
FLAWN variant of > FLAM
FLAWNS > FLAWN
FLAWS > FLAW
FLAWY > FLAW
FLAX n plant grown for its stem fibres and seeds

FLAXEN *adj* (of hair) pale yellow
FLAXES > FLAX
FLAXIER > FLAXY
FLAXIEST > FLAXY
FLAXSEED *n* seed of the flax plant, which yields linseed oil
FLAXSEEDS > FLAXSEED
FLAXY *same as* > FLAXEN
FLAY *same as* > FLEY
FLAYED > FLAY
FLAYER > FLAY
FLAYERS > FLAY
FLAYING > FLAY
FLAYS > FLAY
FLAYSOME *adj* frightening
FLEA *n* small bloodsucking insect
FLEABAG *n* dirty or unkempt person, esp a woman
FLEABAGS > FLEABAG
FLEABANE *n* as in *Canadian fleabane* small plant thought to ward off fleas
FLEABANES > FLEABANE
FLEABITE *n* bite of a flea
FLEABITES > FLEABITE
FLEADH *n* festival of Irish music, dancing, and culture
FLEADHS > FLEADH
FLEAM *n* lancet used for letting blood
FLEAMS > FLEAM
FLEAPIT *n* shabby cinema or theatre
FLEAPITS > FLEAPIT
FLEAS > FLEA
FLEASOME > FLEA
FLEAWORT *n* type of plant, esp a European species with yellow daisy-like flowers and rosettes of downy leaves
FLEAWORTS > FLEAWORT
FLECHE *n* slender spire
FLECHES > FLECHE
FLECHETTE *n* steel dart or missile dropped from an aircraft, as in World War I
FLECK *n* small mark, streak, or speck ▷ *vb* speckle
FLECKED > FLECK
FLECKER *same as* > FLECK
FLECKERED > FLECKER
FLECKERS > FLECKER
FLECKIER > FLECKY
FLECKIEST > FLECKY
FLECKING > FLECK
FLECKLESS > FLECK
FLECKS > FLECK
FLECKY > FLECK
FLECTION *n* act of bending or the state of being bent
FLECTIONS > FLECTION
FLED > FLEE
FLEDGE *vb* feed and care for (a young bird) until it is able to fly

FLEDGED > FLEDGE
FLEDGES > FLEDGE
FLEDGIER > FLEDGY
FLEDGIEST > FLEDGY
FLEDGING > FLEDGE
FLEDGLING *n* young bird ▷ *adj* new or inexperienced
FLEDGY *adj* feathery or feathered
FLEE *vb* run away (from)
FLEECE *n* sheep's coat of wool ▷ *vb* defraud or overcharge
FLEECED > FLEECE
FLEECER > FLEECE
FLEECERS > FLEECE
FLEECES > FLEECE
FLEECH *vb* flatter
FLEECHED > FLEECH
FLEECHES > FLEECH
FLEECHING > FLEECH
FLEECIE *n* person who collects fleeces for baling
FLEECIER > FLEECY
FLEECIES > FLEECIE
FLEECIEST > FLEECY
FLEECILY > FLEECY
FLEECING > FLEECE
FLEECY *adj* made of or like fleece ▷ *n* person who collects fleeces after shearing and prepares them for baling
FLEEING > FLEE
FLEER *vb* grin or laugh at ▷ *n* derisory glance or grin
FLEERED > FLEER
FLEERER > FLEER
FLEERERS > FLEER
FLEERING > FLEER
FLEERINGS > FLEER
FLEERS > FLEER
FLEES > FLEE
FLEET *n* number of warships organized as a unit ▷ *adj* swift in movement ▷ *vb* move rapidly
FLEETED > FLEET
FLEETER > FLEET
FLEETEST > FLEET
FLEETING *adj* rapid and soon passing
FLEETLY > FLEET
FLEETNESS > FLEET
FLEETS > FLEET
FLEG *vb* scare
FLEGGED > FLEG
FLEGGING > FLEG
FLEGS > FLEG
FLEHMEN *vb* (of mammal) grimace
FLEHMENED > FLEHMEN
FLEHMENS > FLEHMEN
FLEISHIG *same as* > FLEISHIK
FLEISHIK *adj* (of food) containing or derived from meat or meat products and therefore to be prepared and eaten separately from dairy foods
FLEME *vb* drive out

FLEMED > FLEME
FLEMES > FLEME
FLEMING *n* inhabitant of Flanders or a Flemish-speaking Belgian
FLEMISH *vb* stow (a rope) in a Flemish coil
FLEMISHED > FLEMISH
FLEMISHES > FLEMISH
FLEMIT > FLEME
FLENCH *same as* > FLENSE
FLENCHED > FLENCH
FLENCHER > FLENCH
FLENCHERS > FLENCH
FLENCHES > FLENCH
FLENCHING > FLENCH
FLENSE *vb* strip (a whale, seal, etc) of (its blubber or skin)
FLENSED > FLENSE
FLENSER > FLENSE
FLENSERS > FLENSE
FLENSES > FLENSE
FLENSING > FLENSE
FLEROVIUM *n* transuranic element
FLESH *n* soft part of a human or animal body ▷ *vb* remove flesh from
FLESHED > FLESH
FLESHER *n* person or machine that fleshes hides or skins
FLESHERS > FLESHER
FLESHES > FLESH
FLESHHOOD *n* incarnation
FLESHIER > FLESHY
FLESHIEST > FLESHY
FLESHILY > FLESHY
FLESHING > FLESH
FLESHINGS *pl n* flesh-coloured tights
FLESHLESS > FLESH
FLESHLIER > FLESHLY
FLESHLING *n* voluptuary
FLESHLY *adj* carnal
FLESHMENT *n* act of fleshing
FLESHPOT *n* pot in which meat is cooked
FLESHPOTS *pl n* places, such as brothels and strip clubs, where sexual desires are catered to
FLESHWORM *n* flesh-eating worm
FLESHY *adj* plump
FLETCH *same as* > FLEDGE
FLETCHED > FLETCH
FLETCHER *n* person who makes arrows
FLETCHERS > FLETCHER
FLETCHES > FLETCH
FLETCHING > FLETCH
FLETTON *n* type of brick
FLETTONS > FLETTON
FLEUR *n* flower emblem used in heraldry
FLEURET *same as* > FLEURETTE
FLEURETS > FLEURET
FLEURETTE *n* ornament resembling a flower

FLEURON *n* decorative piece of pastry
FLEURONS > FLEURON
FLEURS > FLEUR
FLEURY *same as* > FLORY
FLEW > FLY
FLEWED *adj* having large flews
FLEWS *pl n* upper lip of a bloodhound or similar dog
FLEX *n* flexible insulated electric cable ▷ *vb* bend
FLEXAGON *n* hexagon made from a single pliable strip of triangles
FLEXAGONS > FLEXAGON
FLEXED > FLEX
FLEXES > FLEX
FLEXIBLE *adj* easily bent
FLEXIBLY > FLEXIBLE
FLEXILE *same as* > FLEXIBLE
FLEXING > FLEX
FLEXION *n* act of bending a joint or limb
FLEXIONAL > FLEXION
FLEXIONS > FLEXION
FLEXITIME *n* system permitting variation in starting and finishing times of work
FLEXO *n, adj, adv* flexography
FLEXOR *n* type of muscle
FLEXORS > FLEXOR
FLEXOS > FLEXO
FLEXTIME *same as* > FLEXITIME
FLEXTIMER > FLEXTIME
FLEXTIMES > FLEXTIME
FLEXUOSE *same as* > FLEXUOUS
FLEXUOUS *adj* full of bends or curves
FLEXURAL > FLEXURE
FLEXURE *n* act of flexing or the state of being flexed
FLEXURES > FLEXURE
FLEXWING *n* collapsible fabric wing used in hang gliding
FLEXWINGS > FLEXWING
FLEY *vb* be afraid or cause to be afraid
FLEYED > FLEY
FLEYING > FLEY
FLEYS > FLEY
FLIBBERT *n* small piece or bit
FLIBBERTS > FLIBBERT
FLIC *n* French police officer
FLICHTER *vb* flutter
FLICHTERS > FLICHTER
FLICK *vb* touch or move in a quick movement ▷ *n* tap or quick stroke
FLICKABLE > FLICK
FLICKED > FLICK
FLICKER *vb* shine unsteadily or intermittently ▷ *n* unsteady brief light
FLICKERED > FLICKER

FLICKERS > FLICKER
FLICKERY > FLICKER
FLICKING > FLICK
FLICKS > FLICK
FLICS > FLIC
FLIED > FLY
FLIER *same as* > FLY
FLIERS > FLY
FLIES > FLY
FLIEST > FLY
FLIGHT *n* journey by air ▷ *vb* cause (a ball, dart, etc) to float slowly or deceptively towards its target
FLIGHTED > FLIGHT
FLIGHTIER > FLIGHTY
FLIGHTILY > FLIGHTY
FLIGHTING > FLIGHT
FLIGHTS > FLIGHT
FLIGHTY *adj* frivolous and fickle
FLIM *n* five-pound note
FLIMFLAM *n* nonsense ▷ *vb* deceive
FLIMFLAMS > FLIMFLAM
FLIMP *vb* steal
FLIMPED > FLIMP
FLIMPING > FLIMP
FLIMPS > FLIMP
FLIMS > FLIM
FLIMSIER > FLIMSY
FLIMSIES > FLIMSY
FLIMSIEST > FLIMSY
FLIMSILY > FLIMSY
FLIMSY *adj* not strong or substantial ▷ *n* thin paper used for making carbon copies
FLINCH *same as* > FLENSE
FLINCHED > FLINCH
FLINCHER > FLINCH
FLINCHERS > FLINCH
FLINCHES > FLINCH
FLINCHING > FLINCH
FLINDER *n* fragment ▷ *vb* scamper about flutteringly
FLINDERED > FLINDER
FLINDERS > FLINDER
FLING *vb* throw, send, or move forcefully or hurriedly ▷ *n* spell of self-indulgent enjoyment
FLINGER > FLING
FLINGERS > FLING
FLINGING > FLING
FLINGS > FLING
FLINKITE *n* anhydrous phosphate
FLINKITES > FLINKITE
FLINT *n* hard grey stone ▷ *vb* fit or provide with a flint
FLINTED > FLINT
FLINTHEAD *n* American wading bird
FLINTIER > FLINTY
FLINTIEST > FLINTY
FLINTIFY *vb* turn to flint
FLINTILY > FLINTY
FLINTING > FLINT
FLINTLIKE > FLINT

FLINTLOCK *n* obsolete gun in which the powder was lit by a spark from a flint
FLINTS > FLINT
FLINTY *adj* cruel
FLIP *vb* throw (something small or light) carelessly ▷ *n* snap or tap ▷ *adj* flippant
FLIPBOARD *n* piece of office equipment consisting of a board to which a flipchart, etc can be attached
FLIPBOOK *n* book of drawings made to seem animated by flipping pages
FLIPBOOKS > FLIPBOOK
FLIPCHART *n* pad containing large sheets of paper, mounted on a stand and used to present reports, etc
FLIPFLOP *n* rubber sandal
FLIPFLOPS > FLIPFLOP
FLIPPANCY > FLIPPANT
FLIPPANT *adj* treating serious things lightly
FLIPPED > FLIP
FLIPPER *n* limb of a sea animal adapted for swimming
FLIPPERS > FLIPPER
FLIPPEST > FLIP
FLIPPIER > FLIPPY
FLIPPIEST > FLIPPY
FLIPPING *n* act or instance of flipping
FLIPPINGS > FLIPPING
FLIPPY *adj* (of clothes) moving to and fro as the wearer walks
FLIPS > FLIP
FLIPSIDE *n* reverse or opposite side
FLIPSIDES > FLIPSIDE
FLIR *n* forward looking infrared radar
FLIRS > FLIR
FLIRT *vb* behave as if sexually attracted to someone ▷ *n* person who flirts
FLIRTED > FLIRT
FLIRTER > FLIRT
FLIRTERS > FLIRT
FLIRTIER > FLIRT
FLIRTIEST > FLIRT
FLIRTING > FLIRT
FLIRTINGS > FLIRT
FLIRTISH > FLIRT
FLIRTS > FLIRT
FLIRTY > FLIRT
FLISK *vb* skip
FLISKED > FLISK
FLISKIER > FLISK
FLISKIEST > FLISK
FLISKING > FLISK
FLISKS > FLISK
FLISKY > FLISK
FLIT *vb* move lightly and rapidly ▷ *n* act of flitting

FLITCH *n* side of pork salted and cured ▷ *vb* cut (a tree trunk) into flitches
FLITCHED > FLITCH
FLITCHES > FLITCH
FLITCHING > FLITCH
FLITE *vb* scold or rail at ▷ *n* dispute or scolding
FLITED > FLITE
FLITES > FLITE
FLITING > FLITE
FLITS > FLIT
FLITT *adj* fleet ▷ *vb* to flit
FLITTED > FLIT
FLITTER > FLIT
FLITTERED > FLIT
FLITTERN *n* bark of young oak tree
FLITTERNS > FLITTERN
FLITTERS > FLIT
FLITTING > FLIT
FLITTINGS > FLIT
FLITTS > FLITT
FLIVVER *n* old, cheap, or battered car
FLIVVERS > FLIVVER
FLIX *n* fur ▷ *vb* have fur
FLIXED > FLIX
FLIXES > FLIX
FLIXING > FLIX
FLIXWEED *n* plant of the mustard family
FLIXWEEDS > FLIXWEED
FLOAT *vb* rest on the surface of a liquid ▷ *n* object used to help someone or something float
FLOATABLE > FLOAT
FLOATAGE *same as* > FLOTAGE
FLOATAGES > FLOATAGE
FLOATANT *n* substance used in fly-fishing, to help dry flies to float
FLOATANTS > FLOATANT
FLOATCUT *adj* as in *floatcut file* file with rows of parallel teeth
FLOATED > FLOAT
FLOATEL *same as* > FLOTEL
FLOATELS > FLOATEL
FLOATER *n* person or thing that floats
FLOATERS > FLOATER
FLOATIER > FLOATY
FLOATIEST > FLOATY
FLOATING *adj* moving about, changing
FLOATINGS > FLOATING
FLOATS *pl n* footlights
FLOATY *adj* filmy and light
FLOB *vb* spit
FLOBBED > FLOB
FLOBBING > FLOB
FLOBS > FLOB
FLOC *same as* > FLOCK
FLOCCED > FLOC
FLOCCI > FLOCCUS
FLOCCING > FLOC
FLOCCOSE *adj* consisting of or covered with woolly tufts or hairs

FLOCCULAR > FLOCCUS
FLOCCULE *n* small aggregate of flocculent material
FLOCCULES > FLOCCULE
FLOCCULI > FLOCCULUS
FLOCCULUS *same as* > FLOCCULE
FLOCCUS *n* downy or woolly covering ▷ *adj* (of a cloud) having the appearance of woolly tufts
FLOCK *n* number of animals of one kind together ▷ *vb* gather in a crowd ▷ *adj* (of wallpaper) with a velvety raised pattern
FLOCKED > FLOCK
FLOCKIER > FLOCK
FLOCKIEST > FLOCK
FLOCKING > FLOCK
FLOCKINGS > FLOCK
FLOCKLESS > FLOCK
FLOCKS > FLOCK
FLOCKY > FLOCK
FLOCS > FLOC
FLOE *n* sheet of floating ice
FLOES > FLOE
FLOG *vb* beat with a whip or stick
FLOGGABLE > FLOG
FLOGGED > FLOG
FLOGGER > FLOG
FLOGGERS > FLOG
FLOGGING > FLOG
FLOGGINGS > FLOG
FLOGS > FLOG
FLOKATI *n* Greek hand-woven shaggy woollen rug
FLOKATIS > FLOKATI
FLONG *n* material used for making moulds in stereotyping
FLONGS > FLONG
FLOOD *n* overflow of water onto a normally dry area ▷ *vb* cover or become covered with water
FLOODABLE > FLOOD
FLOODED > FLOOD
FLOODER > FLOOD
FLOODERS > FLOOD
FLOODGATE *n* gate used to control the flow of water
FLOODING *n* submerging of land under water, esp due to heavy rain, a lake or river overflowing, etc
FLOODINGS > FLOODING
FLOODLESS > FLOOD
FLOODLIT *adj* illuminated with a floodlight
FLOODMARK *n* high-water mark
FLOODS > FLOOD
FLOODTIDE *n* rising tide
FLOODWALL *n* wall built as a defence against floods
FLOODWAY *n* conduit for floodwater
FLOODWAYS > FLOODWAY

FLOOEY *adj* awry

FLOOIE *same as* > FLOOEY

FLOOR *n* lower surface of a room ▷ *vb* knock down

FLOORAGE *n* area of floor

FLOORAGES > FLOORAGE

FLOORED > FLOOR

FLOORER *n* coup de grâce

FLOORERS > FLOORER

FLOORHEAD *n* upper side of a floor timber

FLOORING > FLOOR

FLOORINGS > FLOOR

FLOORLESS > FLOOR

FLOORPAN *n* bottom part of a motor vehicle's interior

FLOORPANS > FLOORPAN

FLOORS > FLOOR

FLOORSHOW *n* entertainment on floor of nightclub

FLOOSIE *same as* > FLOOZY

FLOOSIES > FLOOSIE

FLOOSY *variant of* > FLOOSIE

FLOOZIE *same as* > FLOOZY

FLOOZIES > FLOOZY

FLOOZY *n* disreputable woman

FLOP *vb* bend, fall, or collapse loosely or carelessly ▷ *n* failure

FLOPHOUSE *n* cheap lodging house, esp one used by tramps

FLOPOVER *n* TV visual effect of page being turned

FLOPOVERS > FLOPOVER

FLOPPED > FLOP

FLOPPER > FLOP

FLOPPERS > FLOP

FLOPPIER > FLOPPY

FLOPPIES > FLOPPY

FLOPPIEST > FLOPPY

FLOPPILY > FLOPPY

FLOPPING > FLOP

FLOPPY *adj* hanging downwards, loose ▷ *n* floppy disk

FLOPS > FLOP

FLOPTICAL *n* type of floppy disk

FLOR *n* type of yeast

FLORA *n* plants of a given place or time

FLORAE > FLORA

FLORAL *adj* consisting of or decorated with flowers ▷ *n* class of perfume

FLORALLY > FLORAL

FLORALS > FLORAL

FLORAS > FLORA

FLOREANT > FLOREAT

FLOREAT *vb* may (a person, institution, etc) flourish

FLOREATED *same as* > FLORIATED

FLORENCE *n* type of fennel

FLORENCES > FLORENCE

FLORET *n* part of a composite flower head

FLORETS > FLORET

FLORIATED *adj* having ornamentation based on flowers and leaves

FLORICANE *n* fruiting stem of plant

FLORID *adj* with a red or flushed complexion

FLORIDEAN *n* member of the red seaweed family

FLORIDER > FLORID

FLORIDEST > FLORID

FLORIDITY > FLORID

FLORIDLY > FLORID

FLORIER > FLORY

FLORIEST > FLORY

FLORIFORM *adj* flower-shaped

FLORIGEN *n* hypothetical plant hormone that induces flowering, thought to be synthesized in the leaves as a photoperiodic response and transmitted to the flower buds

FLORIGENS > FLORIGEN

FLORIN *n* former British and Australian coin

FLORINS > FLORIN

FLORIST *n* seller of flowers

FLORISTIC *adj* of or relating to flowers or a flora

FLORISTRY > FLORIST

FLORISTS > FLORIST

FLORS > FLOR

FLORUIT *prep* (he or she) flourished in ▷ *n* such a period in a person's life

FLORUITS > FLORUIT

FLORULA *n* flora of a small single environment

FLORULAE > FLORULA

FLORULE *same as* > FLORULA

FLORULES > FLORULE

FLORY *adj* containing a fleur-de-lys

FLOSCULAR > FLOSCULE

FLOSCULE *n* floret

FLOSCULES > FLOSCULE

FLOSH *n* hopper-shaped box

FLOSHES > FLOSH

FLOSS *n* fine silky fibres ▷ *vb* clean (between the teeth) with dental floss

FLOSSED > FLOSS

FLOSSER > FLOSS

FLOSSERS > FLOSS

FLOSSES > FLOSS

FLOSSIE *variant of* > FLOSSY

FLOSSIER > FLOSSY

FLOSSIES > FLOSSY

FLOSSIEST > FLOSSY

FLOSSILY > FLOSSY

FLOSSING > FLOSS

FLOSSINGS > FLOSS

FLOSSY *adj* consisting of or resembling floss ▷ *n* floozy

FLOTA *n* formerly, Spanish commercial fleet

FLOTAGE *n* act or state of floating

FLOTAGES > FLOTAGE

FLOTANT *adj* in heraldry, flying in the air

FLOTAS > FLOTA

FLOTATION *n* launching or financing of a business enterprise

FLOTE *n* aquatic perennial grass ▷ *vb* skim (eg milk)

FLOTED > FLOTE

FLOTEL *n* (in the oil industry) a rig or boat used as accommodation

FLOTELS > FLOTEL

FLOTES > FLOTE

FLOTILLA *n* small fleet or fleet of small ships

FLOTILLAS > FLOTILLA

FLOTING > FLOTE

FLOTSAM *n* floating wreckage

FLOTSAMS > FLOTSAM

FLOUNCE *vb* go with emphatic movements ▷ *n* flouncing movement

FLOUNCED > FLOUNCE

FLOUNCES > FLOUNCE

FLOUNCIER > FLOUNCE

FLOUNCING *n* material, such as lace or embroidered fabric, used for making flounces

FLOUNCY > FLOUNCE

FLOUNDER *vb* move with difficulty, as in mud ▷ *n* edible flatfish

FLOUNDERS > FLOUNDER

FLOUR *n* powder made by grinding grain, esp wheat ▷ *vb* sprinkle with flour

FLOURED > FLOUR

FLOURIER > FLOUR

FLOURIEST > FLOUR

FLOURING > FLOUR

FLOURISH *vb* be active, successful, or widespread ▷ *n* dramatic waving motion

FLOURISHY > FLOURISH

FLOURLESS > FLOUR

FLOURS > FLOUR

FLOURY > FLOUR

FLOUSE *vb* splash

FLOUSED > FLOUSE

FLOUSES > FLOUSE

FLOUSH *variant of* > FLOUSE

FLOUSHED > FLOUSH

FLOUSHES > FLOUSH

FLOUSHING > FLOUSH

FLOUSING > FLOUSE

FLOUT *vb* deliberately disobey (a rule, law, etc)

FLOUTED > FLOUT

FLOUTER > FLOUT

FLOUTERS > FLOUT

FLOUTING > FLOUT

FLOUTS > FLOUT

FLOW *vb* (of liquid) move in a stream ▷ *n* act, rate, or manner of flowing

FLOWABLE *adj* capable of flowing

FLOWAGE *n* act of overflowing or the state of having overflowed

FLOWAGES > FLOWAGE

FLOWCHART *n* diagrammatic representation of the sequence of operations or equipment in an industrial process, computer program, etc

FLOWED > FLOW

FLOWER *n* part of a plant that produces seeds ▷ *vb* produce flowers, bloom

FLOWERAGE *n* mass of flowers

FLOWERBED *n* piece of ground for growing flowers

FLOWERED *adj* decorated with a floral design

FLOWERER *n* plant that flowers at a specified time or in a specified way

FLOWERERS > FLOWERER

FLOWERET *another name for* > FLORET

FLOWERETS > FLOWERET

FLOWERFUL *adj* having plentiful flowers

FLOWERIER > FLOWERY

FLOWERILY > FLOWERY

FLOWERING *adj* (of certain species of plants) capable of producing conspicuous flowers

FLOWERPOT *n* pot in which plants are grown

FLOWERS > FLOWER

FLOWERY *adj* decorated with a floral design

FLOWING > FLOW

FLOWINGLY > FLOW

FLOWMETER *n* instrument that measures the rate of flow of a liquid or gas within a pipe or tube

FLOWN > FLY

FLOWS > FLOW

FLOWSTONE *n* type of speleothem

FLOX *adj* as in *flox silk* type of silk

FLU *n* any of various viral infections

FLUATE *n* fluoride

FLUATES > FLUATE

FLUB *vb* bungle

FLUBBED > FLUB

FLUBBER > FLUB

FLUBBERS > FLUB

FLUBBING > FLUB

FLUBDUB *n* bunkum

FLUBDUBS > FLUBDUB

FLUBS > FLUB

FLUCTUANT *adj* inclined to vary or fluctuate

FLUCTUATE vb change frequently and erratically

FLUE n passage or pipe for smoke or hot air

FLUED adj having a flue

FLUELLEN n type of plant

FLUELLENS > FLUELLEN

FLUELLIN same as > FLUELLEN

FLUELLINS > FLUELLIN

FLUENCE > FLUENCY

FLUENCES > FLUENCY

FLUENCIES > FLUENCY

FLUENCY n quality of being fluent

FLUENT adj able to speak or write with ease ▷ n variable quantity in fluxions

FLUENTLY > FLUENT

FLUENTS > FLUENT

FLUERIC adj of or relating to fluidics

FLUERICS pl n fluidics

FLUES > FLUE

FLUEWORK n collectively, organ stops

FLUEWORKS > FLUEWORK

FLUEY adj involved in, caused by, or like influenza

FLUFF n soft fibres ▷ vb make or become soft and puffy

FLUFFED > FLUFF

FLUFFER n person employed on a pornographic film set

FLUFFERS n fluffer

FLUFFIER > FLUFFY

FLUFFIEST > FLUFFY

FLUFFILY > FLUFFY

FLUFFING > FLUFF

FLUFFS > FLUFF

FLUFFY adj of, resembling, or covered with fluff

FLUGEL n grand piano or harpsichord

FLUGELMAN variant of > FUGLEMAN

FLUGELMEN > FLUGELMAN

FLUGELS > FLUGEL

FLUID n substance able to flow and change its shape ▷ adj able to flow or change shape easily

FLUIDAL > FLUID

FLUIDALLY > FLUID

FLUIDIC > FLUIDICS

FLUIDICS n study and use of systems in which the flow of fluids in tubes simulates the flow of electricity in conductors. Such systems are used in place of electronics in certain applications, such as the control of apparatus

FLUIDIFY vb make fluid

FLUIDISE same as > FLUIDIZE

FLUIDISED > FLUIDISE

FLUIDISER > FLUIDISE

FLUIDISES > FLUIDISE

FLUIDITY n state of being fluid

FLUIDIZE vb make fluid, esp to make (solids) fluid by pulverizing them so that they can be transported in a stream of gas as if they were liquids

FLUIDIZED > FLUIDIZE

FLUIDIZER > FLUIDIZE

FLUIDIZES > FLUIDIZE

FLUIDLIKE > FLUID

FLUIDLY > FLUID

FLUIDNESS > FLUID

FLUIDRAM n British imperial measure

FLUIDRAMS > FLUIDRAM

FLUIDS > FLUID

FLUIER > FLUEY

FLUIEST > FLUEY

FLUISH > FLU

FLUKE n accidental stroke of luck ▷ vb gain, make, or hit by a fluke

FLUKED > FLUKE

FLUKES > FLUKE

FLUKEY same as > FLUKY

FLUKIER > FLUKY

FLUKIEST > FLUKY

FLUKILY > FLUKY

FLUKINESS > FLUKY

FLUKING > FLUKE

FLUKY adj done or gained by an accident

FLUME n narrow sloping channel for water ▷ vb transport (logs) in a flume

FLUMED > FLUME

FLUMES > FLUME

FLUMING > FLUME

FLUMMERY n silly or trivial talk

FLUMMOX vb puzzle or confuse

FLUMMOXED > FLUMMOX

FLUMMOXES > FLUMMOX

FLUMP vb move or fall heavily

FLUMPED > FLUMP

FLUMPING > FLUMP

FLUMPS > FLUMP

FLUNG > FLING

FLUNK vb fail ▷ n low grade below the pass standard

FLUNKED > FLUNK

FLUNKER > FLUNK

FLUNKERS > FLUNK

FLUNKEY same as > FLUNKY

FLUNKEYS > FLUNKEY

FLUNKIE same as > FLUNKY

FLUNKIES > FLUNKY

FLUNKING > FLUNK

FLUNKS > FLUNK

FLUNKY n servile person

FLUNKYISM > FLUNKY

FLUOR same as > FLUORSPAR

FLUORENE n white insoluble crystalline solid

FLUORENES > FLUORENE

FLUORESCE vb exhibit fluorescence

FLUORIC adj of, concerned with, or produced from fluorine or fluorspar

FLUORID same as > FLUORIDE

FLUORIDE n compound containing fluorine

FLUORIDES > FLUORIDE

FLUORIDS same as > FLUORID

FLUORIN same as > FLUORINE

FLUORINE n toxic yellow gas: most reactive of all the elements

FLUORINES > FLUORINE

FLUORINS > FLUORIN

FLUORITE same as > FLUORSPAR

FLUORITES > FLUORITE

FLUOROSES > FLUOROSIS

FLUOROSIS n fluoride poisoning, due to ingestion of too much fluoride in drinking water over a long period or to ingestion of pesticides containing fluoride salts. Chronic fluorosis results in mottling of the teeth of children

FLUOROTIC > FLUOROSIS

FLUORS > FLUOR

FLUORSPAR n white or colourless mineral, consisting of calcium fluoride in crystalline form: the chief ore of fluorine

FLURR vb scatter

FLURRED > FLURR

FLURRIED > FLURRY

FLURRIES > FLURRY

FLURRING > FLURR

FLURRS > FLURR

FLURRY n sudden commotion ▷ vb confuse

FLURRYING > FLURRY

FLUS > FLU

FLUSH vb blush or cause to blush ▷ n blush ▷ adj level with the surrounding surface ▷ adv so as to be level

FLUSHABLE > FLUSH

FLUSHED > FLUSH

FLUSHER > FLUSH

FLUSHERS > FLUSH

FLUSHES > FLUSH

FLUSHEST > FLUSH

FLUSHIER > FLUSHY

FLUSHIEST > FLUSHY

FLUSHING n extra feeding given to ewes before mating to increase the lambing percentage

FLUSHINGS > FLUSHING

FLUSHNESS > FLUSH

FLUSHWORK n decorative treatment of the surface of an outside wall with flints split to show their smooth black surface, combined with dressed stone to form patterns such as tracery or initials

FLUSHY adj ruddy

FLUSTER vb make nervous or upset ▷ n nervous or upset state

FLUSTERED > FLUSTER

FLUSTERS > FLUSTER

FLUSTERY > FLUSTER

FLUSTRATE vb fluster

FLUTE n wind instrument ▷ vb utter in a high-pitched tone

FLUTED adj having decorative grooves

FLUTELIKE > FLUTE

FLUTER n craftsman who makes flutes or fluting

FLUTERS > FLUTER

FLUTES > FLUTE

FLUTEY adj resembling a flute in sound

FLUTEYER > FLUTEY

FLUTEYEST > FLUTEY

FLUTIER > FLUTE

FLUTIEST > FLUTE

FLUTINA n type of accordion

FLUTINAS > FLUTINA

FLUTING n design of decorative grooves

FLUTINGS > FLUTING

FLUTIST same as > FLAUTIST

FLUTISTS > FLUTIST

FLUTTER vb wave rapidly ▷ n flapping movement

FLUTTERED > FLUTTER

FLUTTERER > FLUTTER

FLUTTERS > FLUTTER

FLUTTERY adj flapping rapidly

FLUTY > FLUTE

FLUVIAL adj of rivers

FLUVIATIC > FLUVIAL

FLUX n constant change or instability ▷ vb make or become fluid

FLUXED > FLUX

FLUXES > FLUX

FLUXGATE n type of magnetometer

FLUXGATES > FLUXGATE

FLUXING > FLUX

FLUXION n rate of change of a function

FLUXIONAL > FLUXION

FLUXIONS > FLUXION

FLUXIVE > FLUX

FLUXMETER n any instrument for measuring magnetic flux, usually by measuring the charge that flows through a coil when the flux changes

FLUYT n Dutch sailing ship

FLUYTS > FLUYT

FLY *vb* move through the air on wings or in an aircraft ▷ *n* fastening at the front of trousers ▷ *adj* sharp and cunning

FLYABLE > FLY

FLYAWAY *adj* (of hair) very fine and soft ▷ *n* person who is frivolous or flighty

FLYAWAYS > FLYAWAY

FLYBACK *n* item of electrical equipment

FLYBACKS > FLYBACK

FLYBANE *n* type of campion

FLYBANES > FLYBANE

FLYBELT *n* strip of tsetse-infested land

FLYBELTS > FLYBELT

FLYBLEW > FLYBLOW

FLYBLOW *vb* contaminate ▷ *n* egg or young larva of a blowfly

FLYBLOWN *adj* covered with blowfly eggs

FLYBLOWS > FLYBLOW

FLYBOAT *n* any small swift boat

FLYBOATS > FLYBOAT

FLYBOOK *n* small case or wallet for storing artificial flies

FLYBOOKS > FLYBOOK

FLYBOY *n* air force pilot

FLYBOYS > FLYBOY

FLYBRIDGE *n* highest navigational bridge on a ship

FLYBY *n* flight past a particular position or target

FLYBYS > FLYBY

FLYER > FLY

FLYERS > FLY

FLYEST > FLY

FLYHAND *n* device on a printing press

FLYHANDS > FLYHAND

FLYING > FLY

FLYINGS > FLY

FLYLEAF *n* blank leaf at the beginning or end of a book

FLYLEAVES > FLYLEAF

FLYLESS > FLY

FLYLINE *n* type of line used in fly fishing

FLYLINES > FLYLINE

FLYMAKER *n* person who makes fishing flies

FLYMAKERS > FLYMAKER

FLYMAN *n* stagehand

FLYMEN > FLYMAN

FLYOFF *n* all water transferred from the earth to the atmosphere

FLYOFFS > FLYOFF

FLYOVER *n* road passing over another by a bridge

FLYOVERS > FLYOVER

FLYPAPER *n* paper with a sticky poisonous coating, used to kill flies

FLYPAPERS > FLYPAPER

FLYPAST *n* ceremonial flight of aircraft over a given area

FLYPASTS > FLYPAST

FLYPE *vb* fold back

FLYPED > FLYPE

FLYPES > FLYPE

FLYPING > FLYPE

FLYPITCH *n* area for unlicensed stalls at markets

FLYPOSTER *n* person who puts up posters illegally

FLYRODDER *n* angler using artificial fly

FLYSCH *n* type of marine sedimentary facies

FLYSCHES > FLYSCH

FLYSCREEN *n* wire-mesh screen over a window to prevent flies from entering a room

FLYSHEET *n* part of tent

FLYSHEETS > FLYSHEET

FLYSPECK *n* small speck of the excrement of a fly ▷ *vb* mark with flyspecks

FLYSPECKS > FLYSPECK

FLYSPRAY *n* insecticide sprayed from an aerosol

FLYSPRAYS > FLYSPRAY

FLYSTRIKE *n* infestation of wounded sheep by blowflies or maggots

FLYTE *same as* > FLITE

FLYTED > FLYTE

FLYTES > FLYTE

FLYTIER *n* person who makes his own fishing flies

FLYTIERS > FLYTIER

FLYTING > FLYTE

FLYTINGS > FLYTE

FLYTRAP *n* any of various insectivorous plants

FLYTRAPS > FLYTRAP

FLYWAY *n* usual route used by birds when migrating

FLYWAYS > FLYWAY

FLYWEIGHT *n* boxer weighing up to 112lb (professional) or 51kg (amateur)

FLYWHEEL *n* heavy wheel regulating the speed of a machine

FLYWHEELS > FLYWHEEL

FOAL *n* young of a horse or related animal ▷ *vb* give birth to a foal

FOALED > FOAL

FOALFOOT *n* coltsfoot

FOALFOOTS > FOALFOOT

FOALING *n* act of flanging

FOALINGS > FOALING

FOALS > FOAL

FOAM *n* mass of small bubbles on a liquid ▷ *vb* produce foam

FOAMABLE > FOAM

FOAMED > FOAM

FOAMER *n* (possibly obsessive) enthusiast

FOAMERS > FOAMER

FOAMIER > FOAMY

FOAMIEST > FOAMY

FOAMILY > FOAMY

FOAMINESS > FOAMY

FOAMING > FOAM

FOAMINGLY > FOAM

FOAMINGS > FOAM

FOAMLESS > FOAM

FOAMLIKE > FOAM

FOAMS > FOAM

FOAMY *adj* of, resembling, consisting of, or covered with foam

FOB *n* short watch chain ▷ *vb* cheat

FOBBED > FOB

FOBBING > FOB

FOBS > FOB

FOCACCIA *n* flat Italian bread made with olive oil and yeast

FOCACCIAS > FOCACCIA

FOCAL *adj* of or at a focus

FOCALISE *same as* > FOCUS

FOCALISED > FOCUS

FOCALISES > FOCUS

FOCALIZE *less common word for* > FOCUS

FOCALIZED > FOCALIZE

FOCALIZES > FOCALIZE

FOCALLY > FOCAL

FOCI > FOCUS

FOCIMETER *n* photographic focusing device

FOCOMETER *n* instrument for measuring the focal length of a lens

FOCUS *n* point at which light or sound waves converge ▷ *vb* bring or come into focus

FOCUSABLE > FOCUS

FOCUSED > FOCUS

FOCUSER > FOCUS

FOCUSERS > FOCUS

FOCUSES > FOCUS

FOCUSING > FOCUS

FOCUSINGS > FOCUS

FOCUSLESS > FOCUS

FOCUSSED > FOCUS

FOCUSSES > FOCUS

FOCUSSING > FOCUS

FODDER *n* feed for livestock ▷ *vb* supply (livestock) with fodder

FODDERED > FODDER

FODDERER > FODDER

FODDERERS > FODDER

FODDERING > FODDER

FODDERS > FODDER

FODGEL *adj* buxom

FOE *n* enemy, opponent

FOEDARIE *variant of* > FEDARIE

FOEDARIES > FOEDARIE

FOEDERATI *pl n* (in ancient Rome) tribes bound by treaty to support the Roman Empire

FOEFIE *adj* as in *foefie slide* (in S Africa) rope along

which a person suspended on a pulley may traverse, esp across a river

FOEHN *same as* > FOHN

FOEHNS > FOEHN

FOEMAN *n* enemy in war

FOEMEN > FOEMAN

FOEN *same as* > FOE

FOES > FOE

FOETAL *same as* > FETAL

FOETATION *same as* > FETATION

FOETICIDE *same as* > FETICIDE

FOETID *same as* > FETID

FOETIDER > FOETID

FOETIDEST > FOETID

FOETIDLY > FOETID

FOETOR *same as* > FETOR

FOETORS > FOETOR

FOETUS *same as* > FETUS

FOETUSES > FOETUS

FOG *n* mass of condensed water vapour in the lower air ▷ *vb* cover with steam

FOGASH *n* type of Hungarian pike perch

FOGASHES > FOGASH

FOGBOUND *adj* prevented from operating by fog

FOGBOW *n* faint arc of light sometimes seen in a fog bank

FOGBOWS > FOGBOW

FOGDOG *n* spot sometimes seen in fog near the horizon

FOGDOGS > FOGDOG

FOGEY *n* old-fashioned person

FOGEYDOM > FOGEY

FOGEYDOMS > FOGEY

FOGEYISH > FOGEY

FOGEYISM > FOGEY

FOGEYISMS > FOGEY

FOGEYS > FOGEY

FOGFRUIT *n* wildflower of the verbena family

FOGFRUITS > FOGFRUIT

FOGGAGE *n* grass grown for winter grazing

FOGGAGES > FOGGAGE

FOGGED > FOG

FOGGER *n* device that generates a fog

FOGGERS > FOGGER

FOGGIER > FOG

FOGGIEST > FOG

FOGGILY > FOG

FOGGINESS > FOG

FOGGING *n* act of fogging

FOGGINGS > FOGGING

FOGGY *same as* > FOG

FOGHORN *n* large horn sounded to warn ships in fog

FOGHORNS > FOGHORN

FOGIE *variant of* > FOGEY

FOGIES > FOGIE

FOGLE *n* silk handkerchief

FOGLES > FOGLE

FOGLESS > FOG

FOGLIGHT *n* motor-vehicle light used in fog

FOGLIGHTS > FOGLIGHT
FOGMAN n person in charge of railway fog-signals
FOGMEN > FOGMAN
FOGOU n subterranean building found in Cornwall
FOGOUS > FOGOU
FOGRAM n fogey
FOGRAMITE > FOGRAM
FOGRAMITY > FOGRAM
FOGRAMS > FOGRAM
FOGS > FOG
FOGY same as > FOGEY
FOGYDOM > FOGY
FOGYDOMS > FOGY
FOGYISH > FOGY
FOGYISM > FOGY
FOGYISMS > FOGY
FOH interj expression of disgust
FOHN n type of warm dry wind
FOHNS > FOHN
FOIBLE n minor weakness or slight peculiarity
FOIBLES > FOIBLE
FOID n rock-forming mineral similar to feldspar
FOIDS > FOID
FOIL vb ruin (someone's plan) ▷ n metal in a thin sheet, esp for wrapping food
FOILABLE > FOIL
FOILBORNE adj moving by means of hydrofoils
FOILED > FOIL
FOILING > FOIL
FOILINGS > FOIL
FOILIST n person who fences with a foil
FOILISTS > FOILIST
FOILS > FOIL
FOILSMAN n person who uses or specializes in using a foil
FOILSMEN > FOILSMAN
FOIN n thrust or lunge with a weapon ▷ vb thrust with a weapon
FOINED > FOIN
FOINING > FOIN
FOININGLY > FOIN
FOINS > FOIN
FOISON n plentiful supply or yield
FOISONS > FOISON
FOIST vb force or impose on
FOISTED > FOIST
FOISTER > FOIST
FOISTERS > FOIST
FOISTING > FOIST
FOISTS > FOIST
FOLACIN n folic acid
FOLACINS > FOLACIN
FOLATE n folic acid
FOLATES > FOLIC
FOLD vb bend so that one part covers another ▷ n folded piece or part
FOLDABLE > FOLD

FOLDAWAY adj (of a bed) able to be folded and put away when not in use
FOLDAWAYS > FOLDAWAY
FOLDBACK n (in multitrack recording) a process for returning a signal to a performer instantly
FOLDBACKS > FOLDBACK
FOLDBOAT another name for > FALTBOAT
FOLDBOATS > FOLDBOAT
FOLDED > FOLD
FOLDER n piece of folded cardboard for holding loose papers
FOLDEROL same as > FALDERAL
FOLDEROLS > FOLDEROL
FOLDERS > FOLDER
FOLDING > FOLD
FOLDINGS > FOLDING
FOLDOUT another name for > GATEFOLD
FOLDOUTS > FOLDOUT
FOLDS > FOLD
FOLDUP n something that folds up
FOLDUPS > FOLDUP
FOLEY n footsteps editor
FOLEYS > FOLEY
FOLIA > FOLIUM
FOLIAGE n leaves
FOLIAGED adj having foliage
FOLIAGES > FOLIAGE
FOLIAR adj of or relating to a leaf or leaves
FOLIATE adj relating to, possessing, or resembling leaves ▷ vb ornament with foliage or with leaf forms such as foils
FOLIATED adj ornamented with or made up of foliage or foils
FOLIATES > FOLIATE
FOLIATING > FOLIATE
FOLIATION n process of producing leaves
FOLIATURE > FOLIATION
FOLIC adj as in folic acid any of a group of vitamins of the B complex
FOLIE n madness
FOLIES > FOLIE
FOLIO n sheet of paper folded in half to make two leaves of a book ▷ adj of or made in the largest book size, common esp in early centuries of European printing ▷ vb number the leaves of (a book) consecutively
FOLIOED > FOLIO
FOLIOING > FOLIO
FOLIOLATE adj possessing or relating to leaflets
FOLIOLE n part of a compound leaf

FOLIOLES > FOLIOLE
FOLIOLOSE > FOLIOLE
FOLIOS > FOLIO
FOLIOSE adj (of a tree) leaf-bearing
FOLIOUS adj foliose
FOLIUM n plane geometrical curve
FOLIUMS > FOLIUM
FOLK n people in general ▷ adj traditional to the common people of a country
FOLKIE n devotee of folk music ▷ adj of or relating to folk music
FOLKIER > FOLKIE
FOLKIES > FOLKIE
FOLKIEST > FOLKIE
FOLKISH > FOLK
FOLKLAND n former type of land tenure
FOLKLANDS > FOLKLAND
FOLKLIFE n traditional customs, arts, crafts, and other forms of cultural expression of a people
FOLKLIKE > FOLK
FOLKLIVES > FOLKLIFE
FOLKLORE n traditional beliefs and stories of a people
FOLKLORES > FOLKLORE
FOLKLORIC > FOLKLORE
FOLKMOOT n (in early medieval England) an assembly of the people of a district, town, or shire
FOLKMOOTS > FOLKMOOT
FOLKMOT same as > FOLKMOOT
FOLKMOTE same as > FOLKMOOT
FOLKMOTES > FOLKMOTE
FOLKMOTS > FOLKMOT
FOLKS > FOLK
FOLKSIER > FOLKSY
FOLKSIEST > FOLKSY
FOLKSILY > FOLKSY
FOLKSONG n traditional song
FOLKSONGS > FOLKSONG
FOLKSY adj simple and unpretentious
FOLKTALE n tale or legend originating among a people and typically becoming part of an oral tradition
FOLKTALES > FOLKTALE
FOLKWAY singular form of > FOLKWAYS
FOLKWAYS pl n traditional and customary ways of living
FOLKY same as > FOLKIE
FOLLES > FOLLIS
FOLLICLE n small cavity in the body, esp one from which a hair grows
FOLLICLES > FOLLICLE
FOLLIED > FOLLY
FOLLIES > FOLLY
FOLLIS n Roman coin

FOLLOW vb go or come after
FOLLOWED > FOLLOW
FOLLOWER n disciple or supporter
FOLLOWERS > FOLLOWER
FOLLOWING adj about to be mentioned ▷ n group of supporters ▷ prep as a result of
FOLLOWS > FOLLOW
FOLLOWUP n further action
FOLLOWUPS > FOLLOWUP
FOLLY n foolishness ▷ vb behave foolishly
FOLLYING > FOLLY
FOMENT vb encourage or stir up (trouble)
FOMENTED > FOMENT
FOMENTER > FOMENT
FOMENTERS > FOMENT
FOMENTING > FOMENT
FOMENTS > FOMENT
FOMES n any material that may harbour pathogens
FOMITE > FOMES
FOMITES > FOMES
FON vb compel
FOND adj tender, loving ▷ n background of a design, as in lace ▷ vb dote
FONDA n Spanish hotel
FONDANT n (sweet made from) flavoured paste of sugar and water ▷ adj (of a colour) soft
FONDANTS > FONDANT
FONDAS > FONDA
FONDED > FOND
FONDER > FOND
FONDEST > FOND
FONDING > FOND
FONDLE vb caress
FONDLED > FONDLE
FONDLER > FONDLE
FONDLERS > FONDLE
FONDLES > FONDLE
FONDLING > FONDLE
FONDLINGS > FONDLE
FONDLY > FOND
FONDNESS > FOND
FONDS > FOND
FONDU n ballet movement
FONDUE n Swiss dish ▷ vb cook and serve (food) as a fondue
FONDUED > FONDUE
FONDUEING > FONDUE
FONDUES > FONDUE
FONDUING > FONDUE
FONDUS > FONDU
FONE variant of > FOE
FONLY adv foolishly
FONNED > FON
FONNING > FON
FONS > FON
FONT n bowl in a church for baptismal water
FONTAL > FONT
FONTANEL n soft membraneous gap in an infant's skull

FONTANELS > FONTANEL

FONTANGE n type of tall headdress

FONTANGES > FONTANGE

FONTICULI pl n fontanelles

FONTINA n mild Italian cheese

FONTINAS > FONTINA

FONTLET > FONT

FONTLETS > FONT

FONTS > FONT

FOO n temporary computer variable or file

FOOBAR same as > FUBAR

FOOD n what one eats; solid nourishment

FOODBANK n charity which distributes food to the needy

FOODBANKS > FOODBANK

FOODERIES > FOODERY

FOODERY n restaurant

FOODFUL adj supplying abundant food

FOODIE n gourmet

FOODIES > FOODIE

FOODISM n enthusiasm for and interest in good food

FOODISMS > FOODISM

FOODLAND n land on which food is produced

FOODLANDS > FOODLAND

FOODLESS > FOOD

FOODOIR n book or blog that combines a personal memoir with recipes

FOODOIRS > FOODOIR

FOODS > FOOD

FOODSHED n the area through which food is transported from farm to consumer

FOODSHEDS > FOODSHED

FOODSTUFF n substance used as food

FOODWAYS pl n customs and traditions relating to food and its preparation

FOODY same as > FOODIE

FOOFARAW n vulgar ornamentation

FOOFARAWS > FOOFARAW

FOOL n person lacking sense or judgment ▷ vb deceive (someone)

FOOLED > FOOL

FOOLERIES > FOOLERY

FOOLERY n foolish behaviour

FOOLFISH n orange filefish or winter flounder

FOOLHARDY adj recklessly adventurous

FOOLING > FOOL

FOOLINGS > FOOL

FOOLISH adj unwise, silly, or absurd

FOOLISHER > FOOLISH

FOOLISHLY > FOOLISH

FOOLPROOF adj unable to fail

FOOLS > FOOL

FOOLSCAP n size of paper, 34.3 x 43.2 centimetres

FOOLSCAPS > FOOLSCAP

FOOS > FOO

FOOSBALL n US and Canadian name for table football

FOOSBALLS > FOOSBALL

FOOT n part of the leg below the ankle ▷ vb kick

FOOTAGE n amount of film used

FOOTAGES > FOOTAGE

FOOTBAG n type of sport

FOOTBAGS > FOOTBAG

FOOTBALL n game played by two teams of eleven players kicking a ball in an attempt to score goals

FOOTBALLS > FOOTBALL

FOOTBAR n any bar used by the foot

FOOTBARS > FOOTBAR

FOOTBATH n vessel for bathing the feet

FOOTBATHS > FOOTBATH

FOOTBED n insole in a boot or shoe

FOOTBEDS > FOOTBED

FOOTBOARD n treadle or foot-operated lever on a machine

FOOTBOY n boy servant

FOOTBOYS > FOOTBOY

FOOTBRAKE n brake operated with the foot

FOOTCLOTH obsolete word for > CAPARISON

FOOTED > FOOT

FOOTER n person who goes on foot ▷ vb potter

FOOTERED > FOOTER

FOOTERS > FOOTER

FOOTFALL n sound of a footstep

FOOTFALLS > FOOTFALL

FOOTFAULT n fault that occurs when the server fails to keep both feet behind the baseline until he/she has served

FOOTGEAR another name for > FOOTWEAR

FOOTGEARS > FOOTGEAR

FOOTHILL n lower slope of a mountain or a relatively low hill at the foot of a mountain

FOOTHILLS > FOOTHILL

FOOTHOLD n secure position from which progress may be made

FOOTHOLDS > FOOTHOLD

FOOTIE same as > FOOTY

FOOTIER > FOOTY

FOOTIES > FOOTIE

FOOTIEST > FOOTY

FOOTING n basis or foundation

FOOTINGS > FOOTING

FOOTLE vb loiter aimlessly ▷ n foolishness

FOOTLED > FOOTLE

FOOTLER > FOOTLE

FOOTLERS > FOOTLE

FOOTLES > FOOTLE

FOOTLESS > FOOT

FOOTLIGHT n light illuminating the front of a stage

FOOTLIKE > FOOT

FOOTLING adj trivial ▷ n trifle

FOOTLINGS > FOOTLING

FOOTLONG n type of extra-long frankfurter

FOOTLONGS > FOOTLONG

FOOTLOOSE adj free from ties

FOOTMAN n male servant in uniform

FOOTMARK n mark or trace of mud, wetness, etc, left by a person's foot on a surface

FOOTMARKS > FOOTMARK

FOOTMEN > FOOTMAN

FOOTMUFF n muff used to keep the feet warm

FOOTMUFFS > FOOTMUFF

FOOTNOTE n note printed at the foot of a page ▷ vb supply (a page, book, etc) with footnotes

FOOTNOTED > FOOTNOTE

FOOTNOTES > FOOTNOTE

FOOTPACE n normal or walking pace

FOOTPACES > FOOTPACE

FOOTPAD n highwayman, on foot rather than horseback

FOOTPADS > FOOTPAD

FOOTPAGE n errand-boy

FOOTPAGES > FOOTPAGE

FOOTPATH n narrow path for walkers only

FOOTPATHS > FOOTPATH

FOOTPLATE n platform in the cab of a locomotive for the driver

FOOTPOST n post delivered on foot

FOOTPOSTS > FOOTPOST

FOOTPRINT n mark left by a foot

FOOTPUMP n pump operated with the foot

FOOTPUMPS > FOOTPUMP

FOOTRA variant of > FOUTRA

FOOTRACE n race run on foot

FOOTRACES > FOOTRACE

FOOTRAS > FOOTRA

FOOTREST n something that provides a support for the feet, such as a low stool, rail, etc

FOOTRESTS > FOOTREST

FOOTROPE n part of a boltrope to which the foot of a sail is stitched

FOOTROPES > FOOTROPE

FOOTRULE n rigid measure, one foot in length

FOOTRULES > FOOTRULE

FOOTS pl n sediment that accumulates at the bottom of a vessel

FOOTSAL n type of indoor football with five players on each side

FOOTSALS > FOOTSAL

FOOTSIE n flirtation involving the touching together of feet

FOOTSIES > FOOTSIE

FOOTSLOG vb march

FOOTSLOGS > FOOTSLOG

FOOTSORE adj having sore or tired feet, esp from much walking

FOOTSTALK n small supporting stalk in animals and plants

FOOTSTALL n pedestal, plinth, or base of a column, pier, or statue

FOOTSTEP n step in walking

FOOTSTEPS > FOOTSTEP

FOOTSTOCK another name for > TAILSTOCK

FOOTSTONE n memorial stone at the foot of a grave

FOOTSTOOL n low stool used to rest the feet on while sitting

FOOTSY variant of > FOOTSIE

FOOTWALL n rocks on the lower side of an inclined fault plane or mineral vein

FOOTWALLS > FOOTWALL

FOOTWAY n way or path for pedestrians

FOOTWAYS > FOOTWAY

FOOTWEAR n anything worn to cover the feet

FOOTWEARS > FOOTWEAR

FOOTWEARY adj tired from walking

FOOTWELL n part of a car in which the foot pedals are located

FOOTWELLS > FOOTWELL

FOOTWORK n skilful use of the feet, as in sport or dancing

FOOTWORKS > FOOTWORK

FOOTWORN adj footsore

FOOTY n football ▷ adj mean

FOOZLE vb bungle (a shot) ▷ n bungled shot

FOOZLED > FOOZLE

FOOZLER > FOOZLE

FOOZLERS > FOOZLE

FOOZLES > FOOZLE

FOOZLING > FOOZLE

FOOZLINGS > FOOZLE

FOP n man excessively concerned with fashion ▷ vb act like a fop

FOPLING n vain affected dandy

FOPLINGS > FOPLING

FOPPED > FOP

FOPPERIES > FOPPERY

FOPPERY n clothes, affectations, etc, of or befitting a fop
FOPPING > FOP
FOPPISH > FOP
FOPPISHLY > FOP
FOPS > FOP
FOR prep indicating a person intended to benefit from or receive something, span of time or distance, person or thing represented by someone, etc
FORA > FORUM
FORAGE vb search about (for) ▷ n food for cattle or horses
FORAGED > FORAGE
FORAGER > FORAGE
FORAGERS > FORAGE
FORAGES > FORAGE
FORAGING > FORAGE
FORAM n marine protozoan
FORAMEN n natural hole
FORAMENS > FORAMEN
FORAMINA > FORAMEN
FORAMINAL > FORAMEN
FORAMS > FORAM
FORANE adj as in vicar forane type of Roman Catholic priest
FORASMUCH conj since
FORAY n brief raid or attack ▷ vb raid or ravage (a town, district, etc)
FORAYED > FORAY
FORAYER > FORAY
FORAYERS > FORAY
FORAYING > FORAY
FORAYS > FORAY
FORB n any herbaceous plant that is not a grass
FORBAD > FORBID
FORBADE > FORBID
FORBARE > FORBEAR
FORBEAR vb cease or refrain (from doing something)
FORBEARER > FORBEAR
FORBEARS > FORBEAR
FORBID vb prohibit, refuse to allow
FORBIDAL > FORBID
FORBIDALS > FORBIDAL
FORBIDDAL n prohibition
FORBIDDEN adj not permitted by order or law
FORBIDDER > FORBID
FORBIDS > FORBID
FORBODE vb obsolete word meaning forbid ▷ n obsolete word meaning forbidding
FORBODED > FORBODE
FORBODES > FORBODE
FORBODING > FORBODE
FORBORE past tense of > FORBEAR
FORBORNE > FORBEAR
FORBS > FORB
FORBY adv besides
FORBYE same as > FORBY

FORCAT n convict or galley slave
FORCATS > FORCAT
FORCE n strength or power ▷ vb compel, make (someone) do something
FORCEABLE > FORCE
FORCED adj compulsory
FORCEDLY > FORCED
FORCEFUL adj emphatic and confident
FORCELESS > FORCE
FORCEMEAT n mixture of chopped ingredients used for stuffing
FORCEOUT n play in baseball in which a runner is forced to run to next base and is put out
FORCEOUTS > FORCEOUT
FORCEPS pl n surgical pincers
FORCEPSES > FORCEPS
FORCER > FORCE
FORCERS > FORCE
FORCES > FORCE
FORCIBLE adj involving physical force or violence
FORCIBLY > FORCIBLE
FORCING > FORCE
FORCINGLY > FORCE
FORCIPATE > FORCEPS
FORCIPES > FORCEPS
FORD n shallow place where a river may be crossed ▷ vb cross (a river) at a ford
FORDABLE > FORD
FORDED > FORD
FORDID > FORDO
FORDING > FORD
FORDLESS > FORD
FORDO vb destroy
FORDOES > FORDO
FORDOING > FORDO
FORDONE > FORDO
FORDONNE vb as in from fordonne fordone
FORDS > FORD
FORE adj in, at, or towards the front ▷ n front part ▷ interj golfer's shouted warning
FOREANENT prep opposite
FOREARM n arm from the wrist to the elbow ▷ vb prepare beforehand
FOREARMED > FOREARM
FOREARMS > FOREARM
FOREBAY n reservoir or canal
FOREBAYS > FOREBAY
FOREBEAR n ancestor
FOREBEARS > FOREBEAR
FOREBITT n post at a ship's foremast for securing cables
FOREBITTS > FOREBITT
FOREBODE vb warn of or indicate (an event, result, etc) in advance
FOREBODED > FOREBODE
FOREBODER > FOREBODE

FOREBODES > FOREBODE
FOREBODY n part of a ship forward of the foremast
FOREBOOM n boom of a foremast
FOREBOOMS > FOREBOOM
FOREBRAIN n the part of the brain that develops from the anterior portion of the neural tube
FOREBY variant of > FORBY
FOREBYE variant of > FORBY
FORECABIN n forward cabin on a vessel
FORECADDY n caddy who goes ahead of the golfer to point out the ball's location
FORECAR n vehicle attached to a motorcycle
FORECARS > FORECAR
FORECAST vb predict (weather, events, etc) ▷ n prediction
FORECASTS > FORECAST
FORECHECK vb in ice-hockey, to try to gain control of the puck while at opponents' end of rink
FORECLOSE vb take possession of (property bought with borrowed money which has not been repaid)
FORECLOTH n cloth hung over the front of something, especially an altar
FORECOURT n courtyard or open space in front of a building
FOREDATE vb antedate
FOREDATED > FOREDATE
FOREDATES > FOREDATE
FOREDECK n deck between the bridge and the forecastle
FOREDECKS > FOREDECK
FOREDID > FOREDO
FOREDO same as > FORDO
FOREDOES > FOREDO
FOREDOING > FOREDO
FOREDONE > FOREDO
FOREDOOM vb doom or condemn beforehand
FOREDOOMS > FOREDOOM
FOREFACE n muzzle of an animal
FOREFACES > FOREFACE
FOREFEEL vb have a premonition of
FOREFEELS > FOREFEEL
FOREFEET > FOREFOOT
FOREFELT > FOREFEEL
FOREFEND same as > FORFEND
FOREFENDS > FOREFEND
FOREFOOT n either of the front feet of an animal
FOREFRONT n most active or prominent position
FOREGLEAM n early or premonitory inkling or indication

FOREGO same as > FORGO
FOREGOER > FOREGO
FOREGOERS > FOREGO
FOREGOES > FOREGO
FOREGOING adj going before, preceding
FOREGONE adj gone or completed
FOREGUT n anterior part of the digestive tract of vertebrates
FOREGUTS > FOREGUT
FOREHAND n stroke played with the palm of the hand facing forward ▷ adj (of a stroke) made so that the racket is held with the wrist facing the direction of play ▷ adv with a forehand stroke ▷ vb play (a shot) forehand
FOREHANDS > FOREHAND
FOREHEAD n part of the face above the eyebrows
FOREHEADS > FOREHEAD
FOREHENT vb seize in advance
FOREHENTS > FOREHENT
FOREHOCK n foreleg cut of bacon or pork
FOREHOCKS > FOREHOCK
FOREHOOF n front hoof
FOREHOOFS > FOREHOOF
FOREIGN adj not of, or in, one's own country
FOREIGNER n person from a foreign country
FOREIGNLY > FOREIGN
FOREJUDGE same as > FORJUDGE
FOREKING n previous king
FOREKINGS > FOREKING
FOREKNEW > FOREKNOW
FOREKNOW vb know in advance
FOREKNOWN > FOREKNOW
FOREKNOWS > FOREKNOW
FOREL n type of parchment
FORELADY n forewoman of a jury
FORELAID > FORELAY
FORELAIN > FORELIE
FORELAND n headland, cape, or coastal promontory
FORELANDS > FORELAND
FORELAY archaic word for > AMBUSH
FORELAYS > FORELAY
FORELEG n either of the front legs of an animal
FORELEGS > FORELEG
FORELEND vb give up
FORELENDS > FORELEND
FORELENT > FORELEND
FORELIE vb lie in front of
FORELIES > FORELIE
FORELIFT vb lift up in front
FORELIFTS > FORELIFT
FORELIMB n either of the front or anterior limbs of a

four-limbed vertebrate: a foreleg, flipper, or wing

FORELIMBS > FORELIMB

FORELOCK *n* lock of hair over the forehead ▷ *vb* secure (a bolt) by means of a forelock

FORELOCKS > FORELOCK

FORELS > FOREL

FORELYING > FORELIE

FOREMAN *n* person in charge of a group of workers

FOREMAST *n* mast nearest the bow of a ship

FOREMASTS > FOREMAST

FOREMEAN *vb* intend in advance

FOREMEANS > FOREMEAN

FOREMEANT > FOREMEAN

FOREMEN > FOREMAN

FOREMILK *n* first milk drawn from a cow's udder prior to milking

FOREMILKS > FOREMILK

FOREMOST *adv* first in time, place, or importance ▷ *adj* first in time, place, or importance

FORENAME *n* first name

FORENAMED *adj* named or mentioned previously

FORENAMES > FORENAME

FORENIGHT *n* evening

FORENOON *n* morning

FORENOONS > FORENOON

FORENSIC *adj* used in or connected with courts of law

FORENSICS *n* art or study of formal debating

FOREPART *n* first or front part in place, order, or time

FOREPARTS > FOREPART

FOREPAST *adj* bygone

FOREPAW *n* either of the front feet of a land mammal

FOREPAWS > FOREPAW

FOREPEAK *n* interior part of a vessel that is furthest forward

FOREPEAKS > FOREPEAK

FOREPLAN *vb* plan in advance

FOREPLANS > FOREPLAN

FOREPLAY *n* sexual stimulation before intercourse

FOREPLAYS > FOREPLAY

FOREPOINT *vb* predetermine or indicate in advance

FORERAN > FORERUN

FORERANK *n* first rank

FORERANKS > FORERANK

FOREREACH *vb* keep moving under momentum without engine or sails

FOREREAD *vb* foretell

FOREREADS > FOREREAD

FORERUN *vb* serve as a herald for

FORERUNS > FORERUN

FORES > FORE

FORESAID *less common word for* > AFORESAID

FORESAIL *n* main sail on the foremast of a ship

FORESAILS > FORESAIL

FORESAW > FORESEE

FORESAY *vb* foretell

FORESAYS > FORESAY

FORESEE *vb* see or know beforehand

FORESEEN > FORESEE

FORESEER > FORESEE

FORESEERS > FORESEE

FORESEES > FORESEE

FORESHANK *n* top of the front leg of an animal

FORESHEET *n* sheet of a foresail

FORESHEW *variant of* > FORESHOW

FORESHEWN > FORESHEW

FORESHEWS > FORESHEW

FORESHIP *n* fore part of a ship

FORESHIPS > FORESHIP

FORESHOCK *n* relatively small earthquake heralding the arrival of a much larger one. Some large earthquakes are preceded by a series of foreshocks

FORESHORE *n* part of the shore between high- and low-tide marks

FORESHOW *vb* indicate in advance

FORESHOWN > FORESHOW

FORESHOWS > FORESHOW

FORESIDE *n* front or upper side or part

FORESIDES > FORESIDE

FORESIGHT *n* ability to anticipate and provide for future needs

FORESKIN *n* fold of skin covering the tip of the penis

FORESKINS > FORESKIN

FORESKIRT *n* front skirt of a garment (as opposed to the train)

FORESLACK *variant of* > FORSLACK

FORESLOW *variant of* > FORSLOW

FORESLOWS > FORESLOW

FORESPAKE > FORESPEAK

FORESPEAK *vb* predict

FORESPEND *variant of* > FORSPEND

FORESPENT > FORSPEND

FORESPOKE > FORESPEAK

FOREST *n* large area with a thick growth of trees ▷ *vb* create a forest (in)

FORESTAGE *n* part of a stage in front of the curtain

FORESTAIR *n* external stair

FORESTAL > FOREST

FORESTALL *vb* prevent or guard against in advance

FORESTAY *n* adjustable stay leading from the truck of the foremast to the deck, stem, or bowsprit, for controlling the motion or bending of the mast

FORESTAYS > FORESTAY

FORESTEAL > FOREST

FORESTED > FOREST

FORESTER *n* person skilled in forestry

FORESTERS > FORESTER

FORESTIAL > FOREST

FORESTINE > FOREST

FORESTING > FOREST

FORESTRY *n* science of planting and caring for trees

FORESTS > FOREST

FORESWEAR *vb* forgo

FORESWORE > FORESWEAR

FORESWORN > FORESWEAR

FORETASTE *n* early limited experience of something to come ▷ *vb* have a foretaste of

FORETEACH *vb* teach beforehand

FORETEETH > FORETOOTH

FORETELL *vb* tell or indicate beforehand

FORETELLS > FORETELL

FORETHINK *vb* have prescience

FORETIME *n* time already gone

FORETIMES > FORETIME

FORETOKEN *n* sign of a future event ▷ *vb* foreshadow

FORETOLD > FORETELL

FORETOOTH *another word for an* > INCISOR

FORETOP *n* platform at the top of the foremast

FORETOPS > FORETOP

FOREVER *adv* without end

FOREVERS > FOREVER

FOREWARD *n* vanguard ▷ *vb* guard (something) in front

FOREWARDS > FOREWARD

FOREWARN *vb* warn beforehand

FOREWARNS > FOREWARN

FOREWEIGH *vb* assess in advance

FOREWENT *past tense of* > FOREGO

FOREWIND *n* favourable wind

FOREWINDS > FOREWIND

FOREWING *n* either wing of the anterior pair of an insect's two pairs of wings

FOREWINGS > FOREWING

FOREWOMAN *n* woman in charge of a group of workers

FOREWOMEN > FOREWOMAN

FOREWORD *n* introduction to a book

FOREWORDS > FOREWORD

FOREWORN *same as* > FORWORN

FOREX *n* foreign exchange

FOREXES > FOREX

FOREYARD *n* yard for supporting the foresail of a square-rigger

FOREYARDS > FOREYARD

FORFAIR *vb* perish

FORFAIRED > FORFAIR

FORFAIRN *adj* worn out

FORFAIRS > FORFAIR

FORFAITER *n* someone who purchases receivables from exporters

FORFAULT *variant of* > FORFEIT

FORFAULTS > FORFAULT

FORFEIT *n* thing lost or given up as a penalty for a fault or mistake ▷ *vb* lose as a forfeit ▷ *adj* lost as a forfeit

FORFEITED > FORFEIT

FORFEITER > FORFEIT

FORFEITS > FORFEIT

FORFEND *vb* protect or secure

FORFENDED > FORFEND

FORFENDS > FORFEND

FORFEX *n* pair of pincers, esp the paired terminal appendages of an earwig

FORFEXES > FORFEX

FORFICATE *adj* (esp of the tails of certain birds) deeply forked

FORFOCHEN *Scots word for* > EXHAUSTED

FORGAT *past tense of* > FORGET

FORGATHER *vb* gather together

FORGAVE > FORGIVE

FORGE *n* place where metal is worked, smithy ▷ *vb* make a fraudulent imitation of (something)

FORGEABLE > FORGE

FORGED > FORGE

FORGEMAN > FORGE

FORGEMEN > FORGE

FORGER > FORGE

FORGERIES > FORGERY

FORGERS > FORGE

FORGERY *n* illegal copy of something

FORGES > FORGE

FORGET *vb* fail to remember

FORGETFUL *adj* tending to forget

FORGETIVE *adj* imaginative and inventive

FORGETS > FORGET

FORGETTER > FORGET

FORGING *n* process of producing a metal component by hammering

FORGINGS > FORGING

FORGIVE *vb* cease to blame or hold resentment against, pardon

FORGIVEN > FORGIVE

FORGIVER > FORGIVE

FORGIVERS > FORGIVE

FORGIVES > FORGIVE

FORGIVING *adj* willing to forgive

FORGO *vb* do without or give up

FORGOER > FORGO

FORGOERS > FORGO

FORGOES > FORGO

FORGOING > FORGO

FORGONE > FORGO

FORGOT *past tense of* > FORGET

FORGOTTEN *past participle of* > FORGET

FORHAILE *vb* distress

FORHAILED > FORHAILE

FORHAILES > FORHAILE

FORHENT *variant of* > FOREHENT

FORHENTS > FORHENT

FORHOO *vb* forsake

FORHOOED > FORHOO

FORHOOIE *variant of* > FORHOO

FORHOOIED > FORHOOIE

FORHOOIES > FORHOOIE

FORHOOING > FORHOO

FORHOOS > FORHOO

FORHOW *variant of* > FORHOO

FORHOWED > FORHOW

FORHOWING > FORHOW

FORHOWS > FORHOW

FORINSEC *adj* foreign

FORINT *n* standard monetary unit of Hungary

FORINTS > FORINT

FORJASKIT *adj* exhausted

FORJESKIT *variant of* > FORJASKIT

FORJUDGE *vb* deprive of a right by the judgment of a court

FORJUDGED > FORJUDGE

FORJUDGES > FORJUDGE

FORK *n* tool for eating food ▷ *vb* pick up, dig, etc with a fork

FORKBALL *n* method of pitching in baseball

FORKBALLS > FORKBALL

FORKED *adj* having a fork or forklike parts

FORKEDLY > FORKED

FORKER > FORK

FORKERS > FORK

FORKFUL > FORK

FORKFULS > FORK

FORKHEAD *n* forked head of a rod

FORKHEADS > FORKHEAD

FORKIER > FORKY

FORKIEST > FORKY

FORKINESS > FORKY

FORKING > FORK

FORKLESS > FORK

FORKLIFT *n* vehicle having two power-operated horizontal prongs that can be raised and lowered for loading, transporting, and unloading goods, esp goods that are stacked on wooden pallets

FORKLIFTS > FORKLIFT

FORKLIKE > FORK

FORKS > FORK

FORKSFUL > FORK

FORKTAIL *n* bird belonging to the flycatcher family

FORKTAILS > FORKTAIL

FORKY *adj* forked

FORLANA *n* Venetian dance

FORLANAS > FORLANA

FORLEND *variant of* > FORELEND

FORLENDS > FORLEND

FORLENT > FORLEND

FORLESE *vb* lose, forsake

FORLESES > FORLESE

FORLESING > FORLESE

FORLORE > FORLESE

FORLORN *adj* lonely and unhappy ▷ *n* forsaken person

FORLORNER > FORLORN

FORLORNLY > FORLORN

FORLORNS > FORLORN

FORM *n* shape or appearance ▷ *vb* give a (particular) shape to or take a (particular) shape

FORMABLE > FORM

FORMABLY > FORM

FORMAL *adj* of or characterized by conventions of behaviour

FORMALIN *n* solution of formaldehyde in water, used as a disinfectant or a preservative for biological specimens

FORMALINE *n* forty per cent solution of formaldehyde in water, used as a disinfectant

FORMALINS > FORMALIN

FORMALISE *same as* > FORMALIZE

FORMALISM *n* concern with outward appearances and structure at the expense of content

FORMALIST > FORMALISM

FORMALITY *n* requirement of custom or etiquette

FORMALIZE *vb* make official or formal

FORMALLY > FORMAL

FORMALS > FORMAL

FORMAMIDE *n* amide derived from formic acid

FORMANT *n* any of several frequency ranges

FORMANTS > FORMANT

FORMAT *n* size and shape of a publication ▷ *vb* arrange in a format

FORMATE *n* type of salt or ester of formic acid ▷ *vb* fly aircraft in formation

FORMATED > FORMAT

FORMATES > FORMATE

FORMATING > FORMAT

FORMATION *n* forming

FORMATIVE *adj* of or relating to development ▷ *n* inflectional or derivational affix

FORMATS > FORMAT

FORMATTED > FORMAT

FORMATTER > FORMAT

FORME *n* type matter assembled and ready for printing

FORMED > FORM

FORMEE *n* type of heraldic cross

FORMEES > FORMEE

FORMER *adj* of an earlier time, previous ▷ *n* person or thing that forms or shapes

FORMERLY *adv* in the past

FORMERS > FORMER

FORMES > FORME

FORMFUL *adj* imaginative

FORMIATE *variant of* > FORMATE

FORMIATES > FORMIATE

FORMIC *adj* of, relating to, or derived from ants

FORMICA *n* tradename for any of various laminated plastic sheets

FORMICANT *adj* low-tension (of pulse)

FORMICARY *n* ant hill

FORMICAS > FORMICA

FORMICATE *vb* crawl around like ants

FORMING > FORM

FORMINGS > FORM

FORMLESS *adj* without a definite shape or form

FORMOL *same as* > FORMALIN

FORMOLS > FORMOL

FORMS > FORM

FORMULA *n* written form of a scientific or mathematical rule

FORMULAE > FORMULA

FORMULAIC > FORMULA

FORMULAR *adj* of or relating to formulas ▷ *n* model or set form

FORMULARS > FORMULAR

FORMULARY *n* book of prescribed formulas ▷ *adj* of, relating to, or of the nature of a formula

FORMULAS > FORMULA

FORMULATE *vb* plan or describe precisely and clearly

FORMULISE *vb* express in a formula

FORMULISM *n* adherence to or belief in formulas

FORMULIST > FORMULISM

FORMULIZE *variant of* > FORMULISE

FORMWORK *n* arrangement of wooden boards, bolts, etc, used to shape reinforced concrete while it is setting

FORMWORKS > FORMWORK

FORMYL *n* of, consisting of, or containing the monovalent group HCO-

FORMYLS > FORMYL

FORNENST *prep* situated against or facing towards

FORNENT *variant of* > FORNENST

FORNICAL > FORNIX

FORNICATE *vb* have sexual intercourse without being married ▷ *adj* arched or hoodlike in form

FORNICES > FORNIX

FORNIX *n* any archlike structure

FORPET *n* quarter of a peck (measure)

FORPETS > FORPET

FORPINE *vb* waste away

FORPINED > FORPINE

FORPINES > FORPINE

FORPINING > FORPINE

FORPIT *variant of* > FORPET

FORPITS > FORPIT

FORRAD *adv* forward ▷ *n* forward

FORRADER > FORRAD

FORRADS > FORRAD

FORRARDER *adv* further forward

FORRAY *archaic variant of* > FORAY

FORRAYED > FORRAY

FORRAYING > FORRAY

FORRAYS > FORRAY

FORREN *adj* foreign

FORRIT *adv* forward(s)

FORSAID > FORSAY

FORSAKE *vb* withdraw support or friendship from

FORSAKEN *adj* completely deserted or helpless

FORSAKER > FORSAKE

FORSAKERS > FORSAKE

FORSAKES > FORSAKE

FORSAKING > FORSAKE

FORSAY *vb* renounce

FORSAYING > FORSAY

FORSAYS > FORSAY

FORSLACK *vb* be neglectful

FORSLACKS > FORSLACK

FORSLOE *variant of* > FORSLOW

FORSLOED > FORSLOE

FORSLOES > FORSLOE

FORSLOW *vb* hinder

FORSLOWED > FORSLOW

FORSLOWS > FORSLOW
FORSOOK *past tense of* > FORSAKE
FORSOOTH *adv* indeed
FORSPEAK *vb* bewitch
FORSPEAKS > FORSPEAK
FORSPEND *vb* exhaust
FORSPENDS > FORSPEND
FORSPENT > FORSPEND
FORSPOKE > FORSPEAK
FORSPOKEN > FORSPEAK
FORSWATT *adj* sweat-covered
FORSWEAR *vb* renounce or reject
FORSWEARS > FORSWEAR
FORSWINK *vb* exhaust through toil
FORSWINKS > FORSWINK
FORSWONCK *variant of* > FORSWUNK
FORSWORE > FORSWEAR
FORSWORN *past participle of* > FORSWEAR
FORSWUNK *adj* overworked
FORSYTHIA *n* shrub with yellow flowers in spring
FORT *n* fortified building or place ▷ *vb* fortify
FORTALICE *n* small fort or outwork of a fortification
FORTE *n* thing at which a person excels ▷ *adv* loudly
FORTED > FORT
FORTES > FORTIS
FORTH *adv* forwards, out, or away ▷ *prep* out of
FORTHCAME > FORTHCOME
FORTHCOME *vb* come forth
FORTHINK *vb* regret
FORTHINKS > FORTHINK
FORTHWITH *adv* at once
FORTHY *adv* therefore
FORTIES > FORTY
FORTIETH *adj* being the ordinal number of *forty* in numbering or counting order, position, time, etc. Often written: 40th ▷ *n* one of 40 approximately equal parts of something
FORTIETHS > FORTIETH
FORTIFIED > FORTIFY
FORTIFIER > FORTIFY
FORTIFIES > FORTIFY
FORTIFY *vb* make (a place) defensible, as by building walls
FORTILAGE *n* small fort
FORTING > FORT
FORTIS *adj* (of a consonant) articulated with considerable muscular tension ▷ *n* type of consonantal pronunciation
FORTITUDE *n* courage in adversity or pain
FORTLET > FORT

FORTLETS > FORT
FORTNIGHT *n* two weeks
FORTRESS *n* large fort or fortified town ▷ *vb* protect with or as if with a fortress
FORTS > FORT
FORTUITY *n* chance or accidental occurrence
FORTUNATE *adj* having good luck
FORTUNE *n* luck, esp when favourable ▷ *vb* befall
FORTUNED > FORTUNE
FORTUNES > FORTUNE
FORTUNING > FORTUNE
FORTUNISE *same as* > FORTUNIZE
FORTUNIZE *vb* make happy
FORTY *n* four times ten ▷ *adj* amounting to forty ▷ *determiner* amounting to forty
FORTYISH > FORTY
FORUM *n* meeting or medium for open discussion or debate
FORUMS > FORUM
FORWANDER *vb* wander far
FORWARD *same as* > FORWARDS
FORWARDED > FORWARD
FORWARDER *n* person or thing that forwards
FORWARDLY > FORWARD
FORWARDS *adv* towards or at a place further ahead in space or time
FORWARN *archaic word for* > FORBID
FORWARNED > FORWARN
FORWARNS > FORWARN
FORWASTE *vb* lay waste
FORWASTED > FORWASTE
FORWASTES > FORWASTE
FORWEARY *vb* exhaust
FORWENT *past tense of* > FORGO
FORWHY *adv* for what reason
FORWORN *adj* weary
FORZA *n* force
FORZANDI > FORZANDO
FORZANDO *another word for* > SFORZANDO
FORZANDOS > FORZANDO
FORZATI > FORZATO
FORZATO *variant of* > FORZANDO
FORZATOS > FORZATO
FORZE > FORZA
FOSCARNET *n* drug used to treat AIDS
FOSS *same as* > FOSSE
FOSSA *n* anatomical depression, trench, or hollow area
FOSSAE > FOSSA
FOSSAS > FOSSA
FOSSATE *adj* having cavities or depressions
FOSSE *n* ditch or moat, esp one dug as a fortification

FOSSED *adj* having a ditch or moat
FOSSES > FOSSE
FOSSETTE *n* small depression or fossa, as in a bone
FOSSETTES > FOSSETTE
FOSSICK *vb* search, esp for gold or precious stones
FOSSICKED > FOSSICK
FOSSICKER > FOSSICK
FOSSICKS > FOSSICK
FOSSIL *n* hardened remains of an animal or plant preserved in rock ▷ *adj* of, like, or being a fossil
FOSSILISE *same as* > FOSSILIZE
FOSSILIZE *vb* turn into a fossil
FOSSILS > FOSSIL
FOSSOR *n* grave digger
FOSSORIAL *adj* (of the forelimbs and skeleton of burrowing animals) adapted for digging
FOSSORS > FOSSOR
FOSSULA *n* small fossa
FOSSULAE > FOSSULA
FOSSULATE *adj* hollowed
FOSTER *vb* promote the growth or development of ▷ *adj* of or involved in fostering a child
FOSTERAGE *n* act of caring for or bringing up a foster child
FOSTERED > FOSTER
FOSTERER > FOSTER
FOSTERERS > FOSTER
FOSTERING > FOSTER
FOSTERS > FOSTER
FOSTRESS *n* female fosterer
FOTHER *vb* stop a leak in a ship's hull
FOTHERED > FOTHER
FOTHERING > FOTHER
FOTHERS > FOTHER
FOU *adj* full ▷ *n* bushel
FOUAT *n* succulent pink-flowered plant
FOUATS > FOUAT
FOUD *n* sheriff in Orkney and Shetland
FOUDRIE *n* foud's district or office
FOUDRIES > FOUDRIE
FOUDS > FOUD
FOUER > FOU
FOUEST > FOU
FOUET *n* archaic word for a whip
FOUETS > FOUET
FOUETTE *n* step in ballet
FOUETTES > FOUETTE
FOUGADE *n* booby-trapped pit or type of mine
FOUGADES > FOUGADE
FOUGASSE *n* type of bread made with olive oil
FOUGASSES > FOUGASSE
FOUGHT > FIGHT

FOUGHTEN > FIGHT
FOUGHTIER > FOUGHTY
FOUGHTY *adj* musty
FOUL *adj* loathsome or offensive ▷ *vb* make dirty or polluted
FOULARD *n* soft light fabric
FOULARDS > FOULARD
FOULBROOD *n* disease of honeybees
FOULDER *vb* flash like lightning
FOULDERED > FOULDER
FOULDERS > FOULDER
FOULE *n* type of woollen cloth
FOULED > FOUL
FOULER > FOUL
FOULES > FOULE
FOULEST > FOUL
FOULIE *n* bad mood
FOULIES > FOULIE
FOULING > FOUL
FOULINGS > FOUL
FOULLY > FOUL
FOULMART *n* polecat
FOULMARTS > FOULMART
FOULNESS *n* state or quality of being foul
FOULS > FOUL
FOUMART *former name for the* > POLECAT
FOUMARTS > FOUMART
FOUND *vb* set up or establish (an institution, etc)
FOUNDED > FOUND
FOUNDER *vb* break down or fail ▷ *n* person who establishes an institution, etc
FOUNDERED > FOUNDER
FOUNDERS > FOUNDER
FOUNDING > FOUND
FOUNDINGS > FOUND
FOUNDLING *n* abandoned baby
FOUNDRESS > FOUNDER
FOUNDRIES > FOUNDRY
FOUNDRY *n* place where metal is melted and cast
FOUNDS > FOUND
FOUNT *same as* > FONT
FOUNTAIN *n* jet of water
FOUNTAINS > FOUNTAIN
FOUNTFUL *adj* full of springs
FOUNTS > FOUNT
FOUR *n* one more than three ▷ *adj* amounting to four ▷ *determiner* amounting to four
FOURBALL *n* in golf, match for two pairs in which each player uses his own ball, the better score of each pair being counted at every hole
FOURBALLS > FOURBALL
FOURCHEE *n* type of heraldic cross

FOURCHEES > FOURCHEE
FOUREYED adj wearing spectacles
FOURFOLD adj having four times as many or as much ▷ adv by four times as many or as much
FOURGON n long covered wagon
FOURGONS > FOURGON
FOURPENCE n former English silver coin then worth four pennies
FOURPENNY adj blow, esp with the fist
FOURPLAY n supply of television, internet, landline and mobile phone services by one provider
FOURPLAYS > FOURPLAY
FOURPLEX n building that contains four separate dwellings
FOURS > FOUR
FOURSCORE adj eighty
FOURSES n snack eaten at four o'clock
FOURSOME n group of four people
FOURSOMES > FOURSOME
FOURTEEN n four and ten ▷ adj amounting to fourteen ▷ determiner amounting to fourteen
FOURTEENS > FOURTEEN
FOURTH n (of) number four in a series ▷ adj of or being number four in a series ▷ adv after the third person, position, event, etc
FOURTHLY > FOURTH
FOURTHS > FOURTH
FOUS > FOU
FOUSSA n Madagascan civet-like animal
FOUSSAS > FOUSSA
FOUSTIER > FOUSTY
FOUSTIEST > FOUSTY
FOUSTY archaic variant of > FUSTY
FOUTER same as > FOOTER
FOUTERED > FOUTER
FOUTERING > FOUTER
FOUTERS > FOUTER
FOUTH n abundance
FOUTHS > FOUTH
FOUTRA n fig; expression of contempt
FOUTRAS > FOUTRA
FOUTRE vb footer
FOUTRED > FOUTRE
FOUTRES > FOUTRE
FOUTRING > FOUTRE
FOVEA n any small pit in the surface of a bodily organ or part
FOVEAE > FOVEA
FOVEAL > FOVEA
FOVEAS > FOVEA
FOVEATE > FOVEA
FOVEATED > FOVEA
FOVEIFORM adj shaped like small pit

FOVEOLA n small fovea
FOVEOLAE > FOVEOLA
FOVEOLAR > FOVEOLA
FOVEOLAS > FOVEOLA
FOVEOLATE > FOVEOLA
FOVEOLE same as > FOVEOLA
FOVEOLES > FOVEOLE
FOVEOLET same as > FOVEOLA
FOVEOLETS > FOVEOLET
FOWL n domestic cock or hen ▷ vb hunt or snare wild birds
FOWLED > FOWL
FOWLER > FOWLING
FOWLERS > FOWLING
FOWLING n shooting or trapping of birds for sport or as a livelihood
FOWLINGS > FOWLING
FOWLPOX n viral infection of poultry and other birds
FOWLPOXES > FOWLPOX
FOWLS > FOWL
FOWTH variant of > FOUTH
FOWTHS > FOWTH
FOX n reddish-brown bushy-tailed animal of the dog family ▷ vb perplex or deceive
FOXBERRY n lingonberry
FOXED > FOX
FOXES > FOX
FOXFIRE n glow emitted by certain fungi
FOXFIRES > FOXFIRE
FOXFISH n type of shark
FOXFISHES > FOXFISH
FOXGLOVE n tall plant with purple or white flowers
FOXGLOVES > FOXGLOVE
FOXHOLE n small pit dug for protection
FOXHOLES > FOXHOLE
FOXHOUND n dog bred for hunting foxes
FOXHOUNDS > FOXHOUND
FOXHUNT n hunting of foxes with hounds ▷ vb hunt foxes with hounds
FOXHUNTED > FOXHUNT
FOXHUNTER > FOXHUNT
FOXHUNTS > FOXHUNT
FOXIE n fox terrier
FOXIER > FOXY
FOXIES > FOXIE
FOXIEST > FOXY
FOXILY > FOXY
FOXINESS > FOXY
FOXING n piece of leather used on part of the upper of a shoe
FOXINGS > FOXING
FOXLIKE > FOX
FOXSHARK n thresher shark
FOXSHARKS > FOXSHARK
FOXSHIP n cunning
FOXSHIPS > FOXSHIP

FOXSKIN adj made from the skin of a fox ▷ n skin of a fox
FOXSKINS > FOXSKIN
FOXTAIL n type of grass
FOXTAILS > FOXTAIL
FOXTROT n ballroom dance with slow and quick steps ▷ vb perform this dance
FOXTROTS > FOXTROT
FOXY adj of or like a fox, esp in craftiness
FOY n loyalty
FOYBOAT n small rowing boat
FOYBOATS > FOYBOAT
FOYER n entrance hall in a theatre, cinema, or hotel
FOYERS > FOYER
FOYLE variant of > FOIL
FOYLED > FOYLE
FOYLES > FOYLE
FOYLING > FOYLE
FOYNE variant of > FOIN
FOYNED > FOYNE
FOYNES > FOYNE
FOYNING > FOYNE
FOYS > FOY
FOZIER > FOZY
FOZIEST > FOZY
FOZINESS > FOZY
FOZY adj spongy
FRA n brother: a title given to an Italian monk or friar
FRAB vb nag
FRABBED > FRAB
FRABBING > FRAB
FRABBIT adj peevish
FRABJOUS adj splendid
FRABS > FRAB
FRACAS n noisy quarrel
FRACASES > FRACAS
FRACK adj bold ▷ vb release oil or gas from rock by fracking
FRACKED > FRACK
FRACKER n individual or company which engages in fracking
FRACKERS > FRACKER
FRACKING n method of releasing oil or gas from rock
FRACKINGS > FRACKING
FRACKS > FRACK
FRACT vb break
FRACTAL n mathematically repeating structure ▷ adj of, relating to, or involving such a process
FRACTALS > FRACTAL
FRACTED > FRACT
FRACTI > FRACTUS
FRACTING > FRACT
FRACTION n numerical quantity that is not a whole number ▷ vb divide
FRACTIONS > FRACTION
FRACTIOUS adj easily upset and angered
FRACTS > FRACT

FRACTUR variant of > FRAKTUR
FRACTURAL > FRACTURE
FRACTURE n breaking, esp of a bone ▷ vb break
FRACTURED > FRACTURE
FRACTURER > FRACTURE
FRACTURES > FRACTURE
FRACTURS > FRACTUR
FRACTUS n ragged-shaped cloud formation
FRAE Scot word for > FROM
FRAENA > FRAENUM
FRAENUM n fold of membrane or skin that supports an organ
FRAENUMS > FRAENUM
FRAG vb kill or wound (a fellow soldier or superior officer) deliberately
FRAGGED > FRAG
FRAGGING > FRAG
FRAGGINGS > FRAG
FRAGILE adj easily broken or damaged
FRAGILELY > FRAGILE
FRAGILER > FRAGILE
FRAGILEST > FRAGILE
FRAGILITY > FRAGILE
FRAGMENT n piece broken off ▷ vb break into pieces
FRAGMENTS > FRAGMENT
FRAGOR n sudden sound
FRAGORS > FRAGOR
FRAGRANCE n pleasant smell
FRAGRANCY same as > FRAGRANCE
FRAGRANT adj sweet-smelling
FRAGS > FRAG
FRAICHEUR n freshness
FRAIL adj physically weak ▷ n rush basket for figs or raisins
FRAILER > FRAIL
FRAILEST > FRAIL
FRAILISH > FRAIL
FRAILLY > FRAIL
FRAILNESS > FRAIL
FRAILS > FRAIL
FRAILTEE variant of > FRAILTY
FRAILTEES > FRAILTEE
FRAILTIES > FRAILTY
FRAILTY n physical or moral weakness
FRAIM n stranger
FRAIMS > FRAIM
FRAISE n neck ruff worn during the 16th century ▷ vb provide a rampart with a palisade
FRAISED > FRAISE
FRAISES > FRAISE
FRAISING > FRAISE
FRAKTUR n style of typeface
FRAKTURS > FRAKTUR
FRAMABLE > FRAME
FRAMBESIA n infectious disease

FRAMBOISE n brandy distilled from raspberries in the Alsace-Lorraine region

FRAME n structure giving shape or support ▷ vb put together, construct

FRAMEABLE > FRAME

FRAMED > FRAME

FRAMELESS > FRAME

FRAMER > FRAME

FRAMERS > FRAME

FRAMES > FRAME

FRAMEWORK n supporting structure

FRAMING n frame, framework, or system of frames

FRAMINGS > FRAMING

FRAMPAL same as > FRAMPOLD

FRAMPLER n quarrelsome person

FRAMPLERS > FRAMPLER

FRAMPOLD adj peevish

FRANC n monetary unit

FRANCHISE n right to vote ▷ vb grant (a person, firm, etc) a franchise

FRANCISE same as > FRANCIZE

FRANCISED > FRANCISE

FRANCISES > FRANCISE

FRANCIUM n radioactive metallic element

FRANCIUMS > FRANCIUM

FRANCIZE vb make French

FRANCIZED > FRANCIZE

FRANCIZES > FRANCIZE

FRANCO adj post-free

FRANCOLIN n African or Asian partridge

FRANCS > FRANC

FRANGER n condom

FRANGERS > FRANGER

FRANGIBLE adj breakable or fragile

FRANGLAIS n informal French containing a high proportion of words of English origin

FRANION n lover, paramour

FRANIONS > FRANION

FRANK adj honest and straightforward in speech or attitude ▷ n official mark on a letter permitting delivery ▷ vb put such a mark on a (letter)

FRANKABLE > FRANK

FRANKED > FRANK

FRANKER > FRANK

FRANKERS > FRANK

FRANKEST > FRANK

FRANKFORT same as > FRANKFURT

FRANKFURT n light brown smoked sausage

FRANKING > FRANK

FRANKLIN n (in 14th- and 15th-century England)

a substantial landholder of free but not noble birth

FRANKLINS > FRANKLIN

FRANKLY adv in truth

FRANKNESS > FRANK

FRANKS > FRANK

FRANKUM n spruce resin

FRANKUMS > FRANKUM

FRANSERIA n American shrub

FRANTIC adj distracted with rage, grief, joy, etc

FRANTICLY > FRANTIC

FRANZIER > FRANZY

FRANZIEST > FRANZY

FRANZY adj irritable

FRAP vb lash down or together

FRAPE adj tightly bound ▷ vb alter information on a person's social networking profile

FRAPEAGE n act of altering information on a person's social networking profile

FRAPEAGES > FRAPEAGE

FRAPED > FRAPE

FRAPES > FRAPE

FRAPING > FRAPE

FRAPPANT adj striking, vivid

FRAPPE adj (of drinks) chilled ▷ n type of drink

FRAPPED > FRAP

FRAPPEE > FRAPPE

FRAPPES > FRAPPE

FRAPPING > FRAP

FRAPS > FRAP

FRAS > FRA

FRASCATI n dry or semisweet white wine from the Lazio region of Italy

FRASCATIS > FRASCATI

FRASS n refuse left by insects and insect larvae

FRASSES > FRASS

FRAT n member of a fraternity

FRATCH n quarrel

FRATCHES > FRATCH

FRATCHETY same as > FRATCHY

FRATCHIER > FRATCHY

FRATCHING > FRATCH

FRATCHY adj quarrelsome

FRATE n friar

FRATER n mendicant friar or a lay brother in a monastery or priory

FRATERIES > FRATER

FRATERNAL adj of a brother, brotherly

FRATERS > FRATER

FRATERY > FRATER

FRATI > FRATE

FRATRIES > FRATER

FRATRY > FRATER

FRATS > FRAT

FRAU n married German woman

FRAUD n (criminal) deception, swindle

FRAUDFUL > FRAUD

FRAUDS > FRAUD

FRAUDSMAN n practitioner of criminal fraud

FRAUDSMEN > FRAUDSMAN

FRAUDSTER n person who commits a fraud

FRAUGHAN n small shrub

FRAUGHANS > FRAUGHAN

FRAUGHT adj tense or anxious ▷ vb archaic word for load ▷ n archaic word for freight

FRAUGHTED > FRAUGHT

FRAUGHTER > FRAUGHT

FRAUGHTS > FRAUGHT

FRAULEIN n unmarried German woman

FRAULEINS > FRAULEIN

FRAUS > FRAU

FRAUTAGE n cargo

FRAUTAGES > FRAUTAGE

FRAWZEY n celebration

FRAWZEYS > FRAWZEY

FRAY n noisy quarrel or conflict ▷ vb make or become ragged at the edge

FRAYED > FRAY

FRAYING > FRAY

FRAYINGS > FRAY

FRAYS > FRAY

FRAZIL n small pieces of ice that form in turbulently moving water

FRAZILS > FRAZIL

FRAZZLE n exhausted state ▷ vb tire out

FRAZZLED > FRAZZLE

FRAZZLES > FRAZZLE

FRAZZLING > FRAZZLE

FREAK n abnormal person or thing ▷ adj abnormal ▷ vb streak with colour

FREAKED > FREAK

FREAKERY n as in control freakery obsessive need to be in control of events

FREAKFUL variant of > FREAKISH

FREAKIER > FREAKY

FREAKIEST > FREAKY

FREAKILY > FREAKY

FREAKING > FREAK

FREAKISH adj of, related to, or characteristic of a freak

FREAKOUT n heightened emotional state

FREAKOUTS > FREAKOUT

FREAKS > FREAK

FREAKY adj weird, peculiar

FRECKLE n small brown spot on the skin ▷ vb mark or become marked with freckles

FRECKLED > FRECKLE

FRECKLES > FRECKLE

FRECKLIER > FRECKLE

FRECKLING > FRECKLE

FRECKLY > FRECKLE

FREDAINE n escapade

FREDAINES > FREDAINE

FREE adj able to act at will, not compelled or restrained ▷ vb release, liberate

FREEBASE n cocaine that has been refined by heating it in ether or some other solvent ▷ vb refine (cocaine) in this way

FREEBASED > FREEBASE

FREEBASER > FREEBASE

FREEBASES > FREEBASE

FREEBEE variant of > FREEBIE

FREEBEES > FREEBEE

FREEBIE n something provided without charge ▷ adj without charge

FREEBIES > FREEBIE

FREEBOARD n space or distance between the deck of a vessel and the water line

FREEBOOT vb act as a freebooter

FREEBOOTS > FREEBOOT

FREEBOOTY > FREEBOOT

FREEBORN adj not born in slavery

FREECYCLE vb recycle an unwanted item by donating it

FREED > FREE

FREEDIVER n person who dives without breathing apparatus

FREEDMAN n man freed from slavery

FREEDMEN > FREEDMAN

FREEDOM n being free

FREEDOMS > FREEDOM

FREEFALL adj as in freefall parachuting parachuting in which the jumper manoeuvres in free fall before opening the parachute

FREEFORM n irregular flowing shape, often used in industrial or fabric design ▷ adj freely flowing, spontaneous

FREEGAN n person who avoids buying consumer goods

FREEGANS > FREEGAN

FREEHAND adj drawn without guiding instruments

FREEHOLD n tenure of land for life without restrictions ▷ adj of or held by freehold

FREEHOLDS > FREEHOLD

FREEING > FREE

FREELANCE n (of) a self-employed person doing specific pieces of work for various employers ▷ vb work as a freelance ▷ adv of or as a freelance

FREELOAD vb act as a freeloader

FREELOADS > FREELOAD

FREELY > FREE

FREEMAN n person who has been given the freedom of a city

FREEMASON n member of a guild of itinerant skilled stonemasons, who had a system of secret signs and passwords with which they recognized each other

FREEMEN > FREEMAN

FREENESS > FREE

FREEPHONE n system of telephone use in which the cost of calls in response to an advertisement is borne by the advertiser

FREER n liberator

FREERIDE n extreme form of skiing, snowboarding, or mountain biking

FREERIDES > FREERIDE

FREERS > FREER

FREES > FREE

FREESHEET n newspaper that is distributed free, paid for by its advertisers

FREESIA n plant with fragrant tubular flowers

FREESIAS > FREESIA

FREEST > FREE

FREESTONE n any fine-grained stone, esp sandstone or limestone, that can be cut and worked in any direction without breaking

FREESTYLE n competition, such as in swimming, in which each participant may use a style of his or her choice ▷ vb perform (music, a sport, etc) in a freestyle manner

FREET n omen or superstition

FREETIER > FREETY

FREETIEST > FREETY

FREETS > FREET

FREETY adj superstitious

FREEWARE n computer software that may be distributed and used without payment

FREEWARES
> FREEWARE

FREEWAY n motorway

FREEWAYS > FREEWAY

FREEWHEEL vb travel downhill on a bicycle without pedalling ▷ n device in the rear hub of a bicycle wheel that permits it to rotate freely while the pedals are stationary

FREEWILL n apparent human ability to make choices that are not externally determined

FREEWOMAN n woman who is free or at liberty

FREEWOMEN
> FREEWOMAN

FREEWRITE vb write freely without stopping or thinking

FREEWROTE
> FREEWRITE

FREEZABLE > FREEZE

FREEZE vb turn from liquid to solid by the reduction of temperature ▷ n period of very cold weather

FREEZER n insulated cabinet for cold-storage of perishable foods

FREEZERS > FREEZER

FREEZES > FREEZE

FREEZING > FREEZE

FREEZINGS > FREEZE

FREIGHT n commercial transport of goods ▷ vb send by freight

FREIGHTED > FREIGHT

FREIGHTER n ship or aircraft for transporting goods

FREIGHTS > FREIGHT

FREIT variant of > FREET

FREITIER > FREITY

FREITIEST > FREITY

FREITS > FREIT

FREITY adj superstitious

FREMD adj, n alien or strange (person or thing)

FREMDS > FREMD

FREMIT same as > FREMD

FREMITS > FREMIT

FREMITUS n vibration felt by the hand when placed on a part of the body, esp the chest, when the patient is speaking or coughing

FRENA > FRENUM

FRENCH vb (of food) cut into thin strips

FRENCHED > FRENCH

FRENCHES > FRENCH

FRENCHIFY vb make or become French in appearance, behaviour, etc

FRENCHING > FRENCH

FRENEMIES > FRENEMY

FRENEMY n supposed friend who behaves in a treacherous manner

FRENETIC adj uncontrolled, excited ▷ n madman

FRENETICS > FRENETIC

FRENNE variant of > FREMD

FRENNES > FRENNE

FRENULA > FRENULUM

FRENULAR > FRENULUM

FRENULUM n strong bristle or group of bristles on the hind wing of some moths and other insects, by which the forewing and hind wing are united during flight

FRENULUMS > FRENULUM

FRENUM same as > FRAENUM

FRENUMS > FRENUM

FRENZICAL > FRENZY

FRENZIED adj filled with or as if with frenzy

FRENZIES > FRENZY

FRENZILY > FRENZY

FRENZY n violent mental derangement ▷ vb make frantic

FRENZYING > FRENZY

FREON n tradename for an aerosol refrigerant

FREONS > FREON

FREQUENCE same as
> FREQUENCY

FREQUENCY n rate of occurrence

FREQUENT adj happening often ▷ vb visit habitually

FREQUENTS > FREQUENT

FRERE n friar

FRERES > FRERE

FRESCADE n shady place or cool walk

FRESCADES > FRESCADE

FRESCO n watercolour painting done on wet plaster ▷ vb paint a fresco

FRESCOED > FRESCO

FRESCOER > FRESCO

FRESCOERS > FRESCO

FRESCOES > FRESCO

FRESCOING > FRESCO

FRESCOIST > FRESCO

FRESCOS > FRESCO

FRESH adj newly made, acquired, etc ▷ adv recently ▷ vb freshen

FRESHED > FRESH

FRESHEN vb make or become fresh or fresher

FRESHENED > FRESHEN

FRESHENER > FRESHEN

FRESHENS > FRESHEN

FRESHER n first-year student

FRESHERS > FRESHER

FRESHES > FRESH

FRESHEST > FRESH

FRESHET n sudden overflowing of a river

FRESHETS > FRESHET

FRESHIE n new Indian immigrant to the UK

FRESHIES > FRESHIE

FRESHING > FRESH

FRESHISH > FRESH

FRESHLY > FRESH

FRESHMAN same as
> FRESHER

FRESHMEN > FRESHMAN

FRESHNESS > FRESH

FRESNEL n unit of frequency equivalent to 10^{12} hertz

FRESNELS > FRESNEL

FRET vb be worried ▷ n worried state

FRETBOARD n fingerboard with frets on a stringed musical instrument

FRETFUL adj irritable

FRETFULLY > FRETFUL

FRETLESS > FRET

FRETS > FRET

FRETSAW n fine saw with a narrow blade, used for fretwork

FRETSAWS > FRETSAW

FRETSOME adj vexing

FRETTED > FRET

FRETTER > FRET

FRETTERS > FRET

FRETTIER > FRETTY

FRETTIEST > FRETTY

FRETTING > FRET

FRETTINGS > FRET

FRETTY adj decorated with frets

FRETWORK n decorative carving in wood

FRETWORKS > FRETWORK

FRIABLE adj easily crumbled

FRIAND n small almond cake

FRIANDE variant of
> FRIAND

FRIANDES > FRIANDE

FRIANDS > FRIAND

FRIAR n member of a male Roman Catholic religious order

FRIARBIRD n Australian honeyeater with a naked head

FRIARIES > FRIARY

FRIARLY > FRIAR

FRIARS > FRIAR

FRIARY n house of friars

FRIB n piece of wool removed from a fleece during classing

FRIBBLE vb fritter away ▷ n wasteful or frivolous person or action ▷ adj frivolous

FRIBBLED > FRIBBLE

FRIBBLER > FRIBBLE

FRIBBLERS > FRIBBLE

FRIBBLES > FRIBBLE

FRIBBLING > FRIBBLE

FRIBBLISH adj trifling

FRIBS > FRIB

FRICADEL variant of
> FRIKKADEL

FRICADELS > FRICADEL

FRICANDO n larded and braised veal fillet

FRICASSEE n stewed meat served in a thick white sauce ▷ vb prepare (meat) as a fricassee

FRICATIVE n consonant produced by friction of the breath through a partially open mouth, such as (f) or (z) ▷ adj relating to or being a fricative

FRICHT vb frighten

FRICHTED > FRICHT

FRICHTING > FRICHT

FRICHTS > FRICHT

FRICKING adj slang word for absolute

FRICOT n Acadian stew of potatoes, meat or fish

FRICOTS > FRICOT

FRICTION n resistance met with by a body moving over another

FRICTIONS > FRICTION

FRIDGE n apparatus in which food and drinks are kept cool ▷ vb archaic word for chafe

FRIDGED > FRIDGE

FRIDGES > FRIDGE

FRIDGING > FRIDGE

FRIED > FRY

FRIEDCAKE n type of doughnut

FRIEND n person whom one knows well and likes ▷ vb befriend

FRIENDED > FRIEND

FRIENDING > FRIEND

FRIENDLY adj showing or expressing liking ▷ n match played for its own sake and not as part of a competition

FRIENDS > FRIEND

FRIER same as > FRYER

FRIERS > FRIER

FRIES > FRY

FRIEZE n ornamental band on a wall ▷ vb give a nap to (cloth)

FRIEZED > FRIEZE

FRIEZES > FRIEZE

FRIEZING > FRIEZE

FRIG vb taboo word meaning masturbate ▷ n fridge

FRIGATE n medium-sized fast warship

FRIGATES > FRIGATE

FRIGATOON n Venetian sailing ship

FRIGES > FRIG

FRIGGED > FRIG

FRIGGER > FRIG

FRIGGERS > FRIG

FRIGGING > FRIG

FRIGGINGS > FRIG

FRIGHT n sudden fear or alarm

FRIGHTED > FRIGHT

FRIGHTEN vb scare or terrify

FRIGHTENS > FRIGHTEN

FRIGHTFUL adj horrifying

FRIGHTING > FRIGHT

FRIGHTS > FRIGHT

FRIGID adj (of a woman) sexually unresponsive

FRIGIDER > FRIGID

FRIGIDEST > FRIGID

FRIGIDITY > FRIGID

FRIGIDLY > FRIGID

FRIGOT variant of > FRIGATE

FRIGOTS > FRIGOT

FRIGS > FRIG

FRIJOL n variety of bean

FRIJOLE variant of > FRIJOL

FRIJOLES > FRIJOL

FRIKKADEL n South African meatball

FRILL n gathered strip of fabric attached at one edge ▷ vb adorn or fit with a frill or frills

FRILLED > FRILL

FRILLER > FRILL

FRILLERS > FRILL

FRILLERY n fabric or clothing arranged in frills

FRILLIER > FRILLY

FRILLIES pl n flimsy women's underwear

FRILLIEST > FRILLY

FRILLING > FRILL

FRILLINGS > FRILL

FRILLS > FRILL

FRILLY adj with a frill or frills

FRINGE n hair cut short and hanging over the forehead ▷ vb decorate with a fringe ▷ adj (of theatre) unofficial or unconventional

FRINGED > FRINGE

FRINGES > FRINGE

FRINGIER > FRINGY

FRINGIEST > FRINGY

FRINGING n act of fringing

FRINGINGS > FRINGING

FRINGY adj having a fringe

FRIPON n rogue

FRIPONS > FRIPON

FRIPPER n dealer in old clothes

FRIPPERER same as > FRIPPER

FRIPPERS > FRIPPER

FRIPPERY n useless ornamentation

FRIPPET n frivolous or flamboyant young woman

FRIPPETS > FRIPPET

FRIS same as > FRISKA

FRISBEE n tradename of a light plastic disc

FRISBEES > FRISBEE

FRISE n fabric with a long normally uncut nap used for upholstery and rugs

FRISEE n endive

FRISEES > FRISEE

FRISES > FRIS

FRISETTE n curly or frizzed fringe, often an artificial hairpiece, worn by women on the forehead

FRISETTES > FRISETTE

FRISEUR n hairdresser

FRISEURS > FRISEUR

FRISK vb move or leap playfully ▷ n playful movement

FRISKA n (in Hungarian music) the fast movement of a piece

FRISKAS > FRISKA

FRISKED > FRISK

FRISKER > FRISK

FRISKERS > FRISK

FRISKET n part of a hand printing press

FRISKETS > FRISKET

FRISKFUL > FRISK

FRISKIER > FRISKY

FRISKIEST > FRISKY

FRISKILY > FRISKY

FRISKING > FRISK

FRISKINGS > FRISK

FRISKS > FRISK

FRISKY adj lively or high-spirited

FRISSON n shiver of fear or excitement

FRISSONS > FRISSON

FRIST archaic word for > POSTPONE

FRISTED > FRIST

FRISTING > FRIST

FRISTS > FRIST

FRISURE n styling the hair into curls

FRISURES > FRISURE

FRIT n basic materials for making glass, glazes for pottery, etc ▷ vb fuse (materials) in making frit

FRITES pl n chipped potatoes

FRITFLIES > FRITFLY

FRITFLY n type of small black fly

FRITH same as > FIRTH

FRITHBORH n type of pledge

FRITHS > FRITH

FRITS > FRIT

FRITT same as > FRIT

FRITTATA n Italian dish made with eggs and chopped vegetables or meat, resembling a flat thick omelette

FRITTATAS > FRITTATA

FRITTED > FRIT

FRITTER n piece of food fried in batter ▷ vb waste or squander

FRITTERED > FRITTER

FRITTERER > FRITTER

FRITTERS > FRITTER

FRITTING > FRIT

FRITTS > FRITT

FRITURE archaic word for > FRITTER

FRITURES > FRITURE

FRITZ n as in on the fritz in a state of disrepair ▷ vb (of an appliance, etc) become broken or start malfunctioning

FRITZED > FRITZ

FRITZES > FRITZ

FRITZING > FRITZ

FRIULANO n type of Italian cheese

FRIULANOS > FRIULANO

FRIVOL vb behave frivolously

FRIVOLED > FRIVOL

FRIVOLER > FRIVOL

FRIVOLERS > FRIVOL

FRIVOLING > FRIVOL

FRIVOLITY > FRIVOLOUS

FRIVOLLED > FRIVOL

FRIVOLLER > FRIVOL

FRIVOLOUS adj not serious or sensible

FRIVOLS > FRIVOL

FRIZ variant of > FRIZZ

FRIZADO n fine frieze-like fabric

FRIZADOS > FRIZADO

FRIZE n coarse woollen fabric ▷ vb freeze

FRIZED > FRIZE

FRIZER n person who gives nap to cloth

FRIZERS > FRIZER

FRIZES > FRIZE

FRIZETTE same as > FRISETTE

FRIZETTES > FRIZETTE

FRIZING > FRIZE

FRIZZ vb form (hair) into stiff wiry curls ▷ n hair that has been frizzed

FRIZZANTE adj (of wine) slightly effervescent

FRIZZED > FRIZZ

FRIZZER > FRIZZ

FRIZZERS > FRIZZ

FRIZZES > FRIZZ

FRIZZIER > FRIZZY

FRIZZIES n condition of having frizzy hair

FRIZZIEST > FRIZZY

FRIZZILY > FRIZZY

FRIZZING > FRIZZ

FRIZZLE vb cook or heat until crisp and shrivelled ▷ n tight curl

FRIZZLED > FRIZZLE

FRIZZLER > FRIZZLE

FRIZZLERS > FRIZZLE

FRIZZLES > FRIZZLE

FRIZZLIER > FRIZZLE

FRIZZLING > FRIZZLE

FRIZZLY > FRIZZLE

FRIZZY adj (of the hair) in tight crisp wiry curls

FRO adv away ▷ n afro

FROCK n dress ▷ vb invest (a person) with the office or status of a cleric

FROCKED > FROCK

FROCKING n coarse material suitable for making frocks or work clothes

FROCKINGS > FROCKING

FROCKLESS > FROCK

FROCKS > FROCK

FROE n cutting tool

FROES > FROE

FROG n type of amphibian

FROGBIT n floating aquatic Eurasian plant

FROGBITS > FROGBIT

FROGEYE n plant disease

FROGEYED adj affected by frogeye

FROGEYES > FROGEYE

FROGFISH n type of angler fish whose body is covered with fleshy processes, including a fleshy lure on top of the head

FROGGED adj decorated with frogging

FROGGERY n place where frogs are kept

FROGGIER > FROGGY

FROGGIEST > FROGGY

FROGGING n decorative fastening of looped braid on a coat

FROGGINGS > FROGGING

FROGGY adj like a frog

FROGLET n young frog

FROGLETS > FROGLET

FROGLIKE > FROG

FROGLING n young frog

FROGLINGS > FROGLING

FROGMAN n swimmer with equipment for working under water

FROGMARCH vb force (a resisting person) to move by holding his arms ▷ n method of carrying a resisting person in which each limb is held and the victim is face downwards

FROGMEN > FROGMAN

FROGMOUTH n type of nocturnal insectivorous bird of SE Asia and Australia

FROGS > FROG

FROGSPAWN n jelly-like substance containing frog's eggs

FROIDEUR n coldness

FROIDEURS > FROIDEUR

FROING n as in toing and froing going back and forth

FROINGS > FROING

FROISE n kind of pancake

FROISES > FROISE

FROLIC vb run and play in a lively way ▷ n lively and merry behaviour ▷ adj full of merriment or fun

FROLICKED > FROLIC

FROLICKER > FROLIC

FROLICKY adj frolicsome

FROLICS > FROLIC

FROM prep indicating the point of departure, source, etc

FROMAGE n as in fromage frais low-fat soft cheese

FROMAGES > FROMAGE

FROMENTY same as > FRUMENTY

FROND n long leaf or leaflike part of a fern, palm, or seaweed

FRONDAGE n fronds collectively

FRONDAGES > FRONDAGE

FRONDED adj having fronds

FRONDENT adj leafy

FRONDEUR n 17th-century French rebel

FRONDEURS > FRONDEUR

FRONDLESS > FROND

FRONDOSE adj leafy or like a leaf

FRONDOUS adj leafy or like a leaf

FRONDS > FROND

FRONS n plate on the head of some insects

FRONT n fore part ▷ adj of or at the front ▷ vb face (onto)

FRONTAGE n facade of a building

FRONTAGER n owner of a building or land on the front of a street

FRONTAGES > FRONTAGE

FRONTAL adj of, at, or in the front ▷ n decorative hanging for the front of an altar

FRONTALLY > FRONTAL

FRONTALS > FRONTAL

FRONTED > FRONT

FRONTENIS n racket used in Basque ball game

FRONTER n front side

FRONTERS > FRONTER

FRONTES > FRONS

FRONTEST > FRONT

FRONTIER n area of a country bordering on another

FRONTIERS > FRONTIER

FRONTING > FRONT

FRONTLESS > FRONT

FRONTLET n small decorative loop worn on a woman's forehead, projecting from under her headdress, in the 15th century

FRONTLETS > FRONTLET

FRONTLINE adj of, relating to, or suitable for the front line of a military formation

FRONTLIST n list of books about to be published

FRONTMAN n nominal leader of an organization, etc, who lacks real power or authority, esp one who lends respectability to some nefarious activity

FRONTMEN > FRONTMAN

FRONTON n wall against which pelota or jai alai is played

FRONTONS > FRONTON

FRONTOON variant of > FRONTON

FRONTOONS > FRONTOON

FRONTPAGE adj on or suitable for the front page of a newspaper ▷ vb place something on the front page of a newspaper

FRONTS > FRONT

FRONTWARD adv towards the front

FRONTWAYS adv with the front forward

FRONTWISE variant of > FRONTWAYS

FRORE adj very cold or frosty

FROREN variant of > FRORE

FRORN variant of > FRORE

FRORNE variant of > FRORE

FRORY adj frozen

FROS > FRO

FROSH n freshman

FROSHES > FROSH

FROST n white frozen dew or mist ▷ vb become covered with frost

FROSTBIT > FROSTBITE

FROSTBITE n destruction of tissue, esp of the fingers or ears, by cold ▷ vb affect with frostbite

FROSTED adj (of glass) having a rough surface to make it opaque ▷ n type of ice cream dish

FROSTEDS > FROSTED

FROSTFISH n American fish appearing in frosty weather

FROSTIER > FROSTY

FROSTIEST > FROSTY

FROSTILY > FROSTY

FROSTING n sugar icing

FROSTINGS > FROSTING

FROSTLESS > FROST

FROSTLIKE > FROST

FROSTLINE n depth to which ground freezes in winter

FROSTNIP n milder form of frostbite

FROSTNIPS > FROSTNIP

FROSTS > FROST

FROSTWORK n patterns made by frost on glass, metal, etc

FROSTY adj characterized or covered by frost

FROTH n mass of small bubbles ▷ vb foam

FROTHED > FROTH

FROTHER > FROTH

FROTHERS > FROTH

FROTHERY n anything insubstantial, like froth

FROTHIER > FROTH

FROTHIEST > FROTH

FROTHILY > FROTH

FROTHING n act of frothing

FROTHINGS > FROTHING

FROTHLESS > FROTH

FROTHS > FROTH

FROTHY > FROTH

FROTTAGE n act or process of taking a rubbing from a rough surface, such as wood, for a work of art

FROTTAGES > FROTTAGE

FROTTEUR n person who rubs against another person's body for a sexual thrill

FROTTEURS > FROTTEUR

FROUFROU n swishing sound, as made by a long silk dress

FROUFROUS > FROUFROU

FROUGHIER > FROUGHY

FROUGHY adj rancid

FROUNCE vb wrinkle

FROUNCED > FROUNCE

FROUNCES > FROUNCE

FROUNCING > FROUNCE

FROUZIER > FROUZY

FROUZIEST > FROUZY

FROUZY same as > FROWZY

FROW same as > FROE

FROWARD adj obstinate

FROWARDLY > FROWARD

FROWARDS > FROWARD

FROWIE variant of > FROUGHY

FROWIER > FROWIE

FROWIEST > FROWIE

FROWN vb wrinkle one's brows in worry, anger, or thought ▷ n frowning expression

FROWNED > FROWN

FROWNER > FROWN

FROWNERS > FROWN

FROWNING > FROWN

FROWNS > FROWN

FROWS > FROW

FROWSIER > FROWSY

FROWSIEST > FROWSY

FROWST n hot and stale atmosphere ▷ vb abandon oneself to such an atmosphere

FROWSTED > FROWST

FROWSTER > FROWST

FROWSTERS > FROWST

FROWSTIER > FROWSTY

FROWSTING > FROWST

FROWSTS > FROWST

FROWSTY adj stale or musty

FROWSY same as > FROWZY

FROWY variant of > FROUGHY

FROWZIER > FROWZY

FROWZIEST > FROWZY

FROWZILY > FROWZY

FROWZY adj dirty or unkempt

FROZE > FREEZE

FROZEN > FREEZE

FROZENLY > FREEZE

FRUCTAN n type of polymer of fructose

FRUCTANS > FRUCTAN

FRUCTED adj fruit-bearing

FRUCTIFY vb (cause to) bear fruit

FRUCTIVE adj fruitful

FRUCTOSE n crystalline sugar occurring in many fruits

FRUCTOSES > FRUCTOSE

FRUCTUARY n archaic word for a person who enjoys the fruits of something

FRUCTUATE vb bear fruit

FRUCTUOUS adj productive or fruitful

FRUG vb perform the frug, a 1960s dance

FRUGAL adj thrifty, sparing

FRUGALIST > FRUGAL
FRUGALITY > FRUGAL
FRUGALLY > FRUGAL
FRUGGED > FRUG
FRUGGING > FRUG
FRUGIVORE *adj* fruit-eating
FRUGS > FRUG
FRUICT *obsolete variant of* > FRUIT
FRUICTS > FRUICT
FRUIT *n* part of a plant containing seeds ▷ *vb* bear fruit
FRUITAGE *n* process, state, or season of producing fruit
FRUITAGES > FRUITAGE
FRUITCAKE *n* cake containing dried fruit
FRUITED > FRUIT
FRUITER *n* fruit grower
FRUITERER *n* person who sells fruit
FRUITERS > FRUITER
FRUITERY *n* fruitage
FRUITFUL *adj* useful or productive
FRUITIER > FRUITY
FRUITIEST > FRUITY
FRUITILY > FRUITY
FRUITING > FRUIT
FRUITINGS > FRUIT
FRUITION *n* fulfilment of something worked for or desired
FRUITIONS > FRUITION
FRUITIVE *adj* enjoying
FRUITLESS *adj* useless or unproductive
FRUITLET *n* small fruit
FRUITLETS > FRUITLET
FRUITLIKE > FRUIT
FRUITS > FRUIT
FRUITWOOD *n* wood of a fruit tree
FRUITY *adj* of or like fruit
FRUMENTY *n* kind of porridge made from hulled wheat boiled with milk, sweetened, and spiced
FRUMP *n* dowdy woman ▷ *vb* mock or taunt
FRUMPED > FRUMP
FRUMPIER > FRUMPY
FRUMPIEST > FRUMPY
FRUMPILY > FRUMPY
FRUMPING > FRUMP
FRUMPISH *same as* > FRUMPY
FRUMPLE *vb* wrinkle or crumple
FRUMPLED > FRUMPLE
FRUMPLES > FRUMPLE
FRUMPLING > FRUMPLE
FRUMPS > FRUMP
FRUMPY *adj* (of a woman, clothes, etc) dowdy or unattractive
FRUSEMIDE *n* diuretic used to relieve oedema, for example caused by heart or kidney disease

FRUSH *vb* break into pieces
FRUSHED > FRUSH
FRUSHES > FRUSH
FRUSHING > FRUSH
FRUST *n* fragment
FRUSTA > FRUSTUM
FRUSTRATE *vb* upset or anger ▷ *adj* frustrated or thwarted
FRUSTS > FRUST
FRUSTULE *n* hard siliceous cell wall of a diatom
FRUSTULES > FRUSTULE
FRUSTUM *n* part of a solid
FRUSTUMS > FRUSTUM
FRUTEX *n* shrub
FRUTICES > FRUTEX
FRUTICOSE *adj* shrubby
FRUTIFIED > FRUTIFY
FRUTIFIES > FRUTIFY
FRUTIFY *vb* malapropism for notify
FRY *vb* cook or be cooked in fat or oil ▷ *n* dish of fried food
FRYABLE > FRY
FRYBREAD *n* Native American fried bread
FRYBREADS > FRYBREAD
FRYER *n* person or thing that fries
FRYERS > FRYER
FRYING > FRY
FRYINGS > FRY
FRYPAN *n* long-handled shallow pan used for frying
FRYPANS > FRYPAN
FUB *vb* cheat
FUBAR *adj* irreparably damaged or bungled
FUBBED > FUB
FUBBERIES > FUBBERY
FUBBERY *n* cheating
FUBBIER > FUBBY
FUBBIEST > FUBBY
FUBBING > FUB
FUBBY *adj* chubby
FUBS > FUB
FUBSIER > FUBSY
FUBSIEST > FUBSY
FUBSY *adj* short and stout
FUCHSIA *n* ornamental shrub
FUCHSIAS > FUCHSIA
FUCHSIN *n* greenish crystalline substance
FUCHSINE *same as* > FUCHSIN
FUCHSINES > FUCHSINE
FUCHSINS > FUCHSIN
FUCHSITE *n* form of mica
FUCHSITES > FUCHSITE
FUCI > FUCUS
FUCK *vb* taboo word meaning to have sexual intercourse (with) ▷ *n* taboo word for an act of sexual intercourse
FUCKED > FUCK
FUCKER *n* taboo word for a despicable or obnoxious person

FUCKERS > FUCKER
FUCKFACE *n* stupid or contemptible person
FUCKFACES > FUCKFACE
FUCKHEAD *n* stupid or contemptible person
FUCKHEADS > FUCKHEAD
FUCKING > FUCK
FUCKINGS > FUCK
FUCKOFF *n* taboo word for an annoying or unpleasant person
FUCKOFFS > FUCKOFF
FUCKS > FUCK
FUCKUP *vb* taboo word meaning to damage or bungle ▷ *n* taboo word meaning an act or an instance of bungling
FUCKUPS > FUCKUP
FUCKWIT *n* taboo word for a fool or idiot
FUCKWITS > FUCKWIT
FUCOID *n* type of seaweed
FUCOIDAL *n* type of seaweed
FUCOIDS > FUCOID
FUCOSE *n* aldose
FUCOSES > FUCOSE
FUCOUS *same as* > FUCOIDAL
FUCUS *n* type of seaweed
FUCUSED *adj* archaic word meaning made up with cosmetics
FUCUSES > FUCUS
FUD *n* rabbit's tail
FUDDIER > FUDDY
FUDDIES > FUDDY
FUDDIEST > FUDDY
FUDDLE *vb* cause to be intoxicated or confused ▷ *n* confused state
FUDDLED > FUDDLE
FUDDLER > FUDDLE
FUDDLERS > FUDDLE
FUDDLES > FUDDLE
FUDDLING > FUDDLE
FUDDLINGS > FUDDLE
FUDDY *n* old-fashioned person ▷ *adj* old-fashioned
FUDGE *n* soft caramel-like sweet ▷ *vb* make (an issue) less clear deliberately ▷ *interj* mild exclamation of annoyance
FUDGED > FUDGE
FUDGES > FUDGE
FUDGIER > FUDGY
FUDGIEST > FUDGY
FUDGING > FUDGE
FUDGY *adj* resembling or containing fudge
FUDS > FUD
FUEHRER *n* leader: applied esp to Adolf Hitler
FUEHRERS > FUEHRER
FUEL *n* substance burned or treated to produce heat or power ▷ *vb* provide with fuel
FUELED > FUEL
FUELER > FUEL

FUELERS > FUEL
FUELING > FUEL
FUELLED > FUEL
FUELLER > FUEL
FUELLERS > FUEL
FUELLING > FUEL
FUELS > FUEL
FUELWOOD *n* any wood used as a fuel
FUELWOODS > FUELWOOD
FUERO *n* Spanish code of laws
FUEROS > FUERO
FUFF *vb* puff
FUFFED > FUFF
FUFFIER > FUFFY
FUFFIEST > FUFFY
FUFFING > FUFF
FUFFS > FUFF
FUFFY *adj* puffy
FUG *n* hot stale atmosphere ▷ *vb* sit in a fug
FUGACIOUS *adj* passing quickly away
FUGACITY *n* property of a gas that expresses its tendency to escape or expand
FUGAL *adj* of, relating to, or in the style of a fugue
FUGALLY > FUGAL
FUGATO *adj* in the manner or style of a fugue ▷ *n* movement, section, or piece in this style
FUGATOS > FUGATO
FUGGED > FUG
FUGGIER > FUG
FUGGIEST > FUG
FUGGILY > FUG
FUGGINESS *n* state or condition of being fuggy
FUGGING > FUG
FUGGY > FUG
FUGHETTA *n* short fugue
FUGHETTAS > FUGHETTA
FUGIE *n* runaway
FUGIES > FUGIE
FUGIO *n* former US copper coin
FUGIOS > FUGIO
FUGITIVE *n* person who flees, esp from arrest or pursuit ▷ *adj* fleeing
FUGITIVES > FUGITIVE
FUGLE *vb* act as a fugleman
FUGLED > FUGLE
FUGLEMAN *n* (formerly) a soldier used as an example for those learning drill
FUGLEMEN > FUGLEMAN
FUGLES > FUGLE
FUGLIER > FUGLY
FUGLIEST > FUGLY
FUGLING > FUGLE
FUGLY *adj* offensive word for very ugly
FUGS > FUG
FUGU *n* puffer fish

FUGUE *n* type of musical composition ▷ *vb* be in a dreamlike, altered state of consciousness

FUGUED > FUGUE

FUGUELIKE > FUGUE

FUGUES > FUGUE

FUGUING > FUGUE

FUGUIST *n* composer of fugues

FUGUISTS > FUGUIST

FUGUS > FUGU

FUHRER *same as* > FUEHRER

FUHRERS > FUHRER

FUJI *n* type of African music

FUJIS > FUJI

FULCRA > FULCRUM

FULCRATE > FULCRUM

FULCRUM *n* pivot about which a lever turns

FULCRUMS > FULCRUM

FULFIL *vb* achieve (a desire or promise)

FULFILL *same as* > FULFIL

FULFILLED > FULFILL

FULFILLER > FULFILL

FULFILLS > FULFILL

FULFILS > FULFIL

FULGENCY > FULGENT

FULGENT *adj* shining brilliantly

FULGENTLY > FULGENT

FULGID *same as* > FULGENT

FULGOR *n* brilliance

FULGOROUS > FULGOR

FULGORS > FULGOR

FULGOUR *variant of* > FULGOR

FULGOURS > FULGOUR

FULGURAL > FULGURATE

FULGURANT > FULGURATE

FULGURATE *vb* flash like lightning

FULGURITE *n* tube of glassy mineral matter found in sand and rock, formed by the action of lightning

FULGUROUS *adj* flashing like or resembling lightning

FULHAM *n* loaded die

FULHAMS > FULHAM

FULL *adj* containing as much or as many as possible ▷ *adv* completely ▷ *vb* clean, shrink, and press cloth

FULLAGE *n* price charged for fulling cloth

FULLAGES > FULLAGE

FULLAM *variant of* > FULHAM

FULLAMS > FULLAM

FULLAN *variant of* > FULHAM

FULLANS > FULLAN

FULLBACK *n* defensive player

FULLBACKS > FULLBACK

FULLBLOOD *n* person of unmixed race

FULLED > FULL

FULLER *n* person who fulls cloth for his living ▷ *vb* forge (a groove) or caulk (a riveted joint) with a fuller

FULLERED > FULLER

FULLERENE *n* any of various carbon molecules with a polyhedral structure similar to that of buckminsterfullerene, such as C_{70}, C_{76}, and C_{84}

FULLERIDE *n* compound of a fullerene in which atoms are trapped inside the cage of carbon atoms

FULLERIES > FULLERY

FULLERING > FULLER

FULLERITE *n* crystalline form of a fullerene

FULLERS > FULLER

FULLERY *n* place where fulling is carried out

FULLEST > FULL

FULLFACE *n* in printing, a letter that takes up full body size

FULLFACES > FULLFACE

FULLING > FULL

FULLISH > FULL

FULLNESS > FULL

FULLS > FULL

FULLY *adv* greatest degree or extent

FULMAR *n* Arctic sea bird

FULMARS > FULMAR

FULMINANT *adj* sudden and violent

FULMINATE *vb* criticize or denounce angrily ▷ *n* any salt or ester of fulminic acid, esp the mercury salt, which is used as a detonator

FULMINE *vb* fulminate

FULMINED > FULMINE

FULMINES > FULMINE

FULMINIC *adj* as in *fulminic acid*, unstable volatile acid known only in solution and in the form of its salts and esters

FULMINING > FULMINE

FULMINOUS *adj* harshly critical

FULNESS > FULL

FULNESSES > FULL

FULSOME *adj* distastefully excessive or insincere

FULSOMELY > FULSOME

FULSOMER > FULSOME

FULSOMEST > FULSOME

FULVID *variant of* > FULVOUS

FULVOUS *adj* of a dull brownish-yellow colour

FUM *n* phoenix, in Chinese mythology

FUMADO *n* salted, smoked fish

FUMADOES > FUMADO

FUMADOS > FUMADO

FUMAGE *n* hearth money

FUMAGES > FUMAGE

FUMARASE *n* enzyme

FUMARASES > FUMARASE

FUMARATE *n* salt of fumaric acid

FUMARATES > FUMARATE

FUMARIC *adj* as in *fumaric acid* colourless crystalline acid

FUMAROLE *n* vent in or near a volcano from which hot gases, esp steam, are emitted

FUMAROLES > FUMAROLE

FUMAROLIC > FUMAROLE

FUMATORIA *pl n* small airtight chambers for fumigating insects or fungi

FUMATORY *n* chamber where insects and fungi are destroyed by fumigation

FUMBLE *vb* handle awkwardly ▷ *n* act of fumbling

FUMBLED > FUMBLE

FUMBLER > FUMBLE

FUMBLERS > FUMBLE

FUMBLES > FUMBLE

FUMBLING > FUMBLE

FUME *vb* be very angry

FUMED *adj* (of wood) having been exposed to ammonia fumes

FUMELESS > FUME

FUMELIKE > FUME

FUMER > FUME

FUMEROLE *variant of* > FUMAROLE

FUMEROLES > FUMEROLE

FUMERS > FUME

FUMES > FUME

FUMET *n* liquor from cooking fish, meat, or game

FUMETS > FUMET

FUMETTE *variant of* > FUMET

FUMETTES > FUMETTE

FUMETTI > FUMETTO

FUMETTO *n* speech balloon in a comic or cartoon

FUMETTOS > FUMETTO

FUMIER > FUME

FUMIEST > FUME

FUMIGANT *n* substance used for fumigating

FUMIGANTS > FUMIGANT

FUMIGATE *vb* disinfect with fumes

FUMIGATED > FUMIGATE

FUMIGATES > FUMIGATE

FUMIGATOR > FUMIGATE

FUMING > FUME

FUMINGLY > FUME

FUMITORY *n* chiefly European plant with spurred flowers, formerly used medicinally

FUMOSITY > FUME

FUMOUS > FUME

FUMS > FUM

FUMULI > FUMULUS

FUMULUS *n* smokelike cloud

FUMY > FUME

FUN *n* enjoyment or amusement ▷ *vb* trick

FUNBOARD *n* type of surfboard

FUNBOARDS > FUNBOARD

FUNCKIA *n* type of plant resembling the lily

FUNCKIAS > FUNCKIA

FUNCTION *n* purpose something exists for ▷ *vb* operate or work

FUNCTIONS > FUNCTION

FUNCTOR *n* performer of a function

FUNCTORS > FUNCTOR

FUND *n* stock of money for a special purpose ▷ *vb* provide money to

FUNDABLE > FUND

FUNDAMENT *n* buttocks

FUNDED > FUND

FUNDER > FUND

FUNDERS > FUND

FUNDI *n* expert or boffin

FUNDIC > FUNDUS

FUNDIE *n* fundamentalist Christian

FUNDIES > FUNDIE

FUNDING > FUND

FUNDINGS > FUND

FUNDIS > FUNDI

FUNDLESS > FUND

FUNDRAISE *vb* raise money for a cause

FUNDS *pl n* money that is readily available

FUNDUS *n* base of an organ

FUNDY *n* fundamentalist

FUNEBRAL *variant of* > FUNEBRIAL

FUNEBRE *adj* funereal or mournful

FUNEBRIAL *same as* > FUNEREAL

FUNERAL *n* ceremony of burying or cremating a dead person

FUNERALS > FUNERAL

FUNERARY *adj* of or for a funeral

FUNEREAL *adj* gloomy or sombre

FUNEST *adj* lamentable

FUNFAIR *n* entertainment with machines to ride on and stalls

FUNFAIRS > FUNFAIR

FUNFEST *n* enjoyable time

FUNFESTS > FUNFEST

FUNG *same as* > FUNK

FUNGAL *adj* of, derived from, or caused by a fungus or fungi ▷ *n* fungus or fungal infection

FUNGALS > FUNGAL

FUNGI > FUNGUS

FUNGIBLE *n* moveable perishable goods of a sort that may be estimated by number or weight, such as grain, wine, etc ▷ *adj* having the nature or quality of fungibles
FUNGIBLES > FUNGIBLE
FUNGIC > FUNGUS
FUNGICIDE *n* substance that destroys fungi
FUNGIFORM *adj* shaped like a mushroom or similar fungus
FUNGISTAT *n* substance that inhibits the growth of fungi
FUNGO *n* in baseball, act of tossing and hitting the ball ▷ *vb* toss and hit a ball
FUNGOED > FUNGO
FUNGOES > FUNGO
FUNGOID *adj* resembling a fungus
FUNGOIDAL > FUNGOID
FUNGOIDS > FUNGOID
FUNGOING > FUNGO
FUNGOS > FUNGO
FUNGOSITY > FUNGOUS
FUNGOUS *adj* appearing and spreading quickly like a fungus
FUNGS > FUNG
FUNGUS *n* plant such as a mushroom or mould
FUNGUSES > FUNGUS
FUNHOUSE *n* amusing place at fairground
FUNHOUSES > FUNHOUSE
FUNICLE *n* stalk that attaches an ovule to the wall of the ovary
FUNICLES > FUNICLE
FUNICULAR *n* cable railway on a mountainside or cliff ▷ *adj* relating to or operated by a rope, cable, etc
FUNICULI > FUNICULUS
FUNICULUS *same as* > FUNICLE
FUNK *n* style of dance music with a strong beat ▷ *vb* avoid (doing something) through fear
FUNKED > FUNK
FUNKER > FUNK
FUNKERS > FUNK
FUNKHOLE *n* dugout
FUNKHOLES > FUNKHOLE
FUNKIA *n* hosta
FUNKIAS > FUNKIA
FUNKIER > FUNKY
FUNKIEST > FUNKY
FUNKILY > FUNKY
FUNKINESS > FUNKY
FUNKING > FUNK
FUNKS > FUNK
FUNKSTER *n* performer or fan of funk music
FUNKSTERS > FUNKSTER
FUNKY *adj* (of music) having a strong beat
FUNNED > FUN

FUNNEL *n* cone-shaped tube ▷ *vb* (cause to) move through or as if through a funnel
FUNNELED > FUNNEL
FUNNELING > FUNNEL
FUNNELLED > FUNNEL
FUNNELS > FUNNEL
FUNNER > FUN
FUNNEST > FUN
FUNNIER > FUNNY
FUNNIES *pl n* comic strips in a newspaper
FUNNIEST > FUNNY
FUNNILY > FUNNY
FUNNINESS > FUNNY
FUNNING > FUN
FUNNY *adj* comical, humorous ▷ *n* joke or witticism
FUNNYMAN *n* comedian
FUNNYMEN > FUNNYMAN
FUNPLEX *n* large amusement centre
FUNPLEXES > FUNPLEX
FUNS > FUN
FUNSTER *n* funnyman
FUNSTERS > FUNSTER
FUR *n* soft hair of a mammal ▷ *vb* cover or become covered with fur
FURACIOUS *adj* thievish
FURACITY > FURACIOUS
FURAL *n* furfural
FURALS > FURAL
FURAN *n* colourless flammable toxic liquid heterocyclic compound
FURANE *variant of* > FURAN
FURANES > FURANE
FURANOSE *n* simple sugar containing a furan ring
FURANOSES > FURANOSE
FURANS > FURAN
FURBALL *n* ball of fur regurgitated by an animal
FURBALLS > FURBALL
FURBEARER *n* mammal hunted for its pelt or fur
FURBELOW *n* flounce, ruffle, or other ornamental trim ▷ *vb* put a furbelow on (a garment)
FURBELOWS > FURBELOW
FURBISH *vb* smarten up
FURBISHED > FURBISH
FURBISHER > FURBISH
FURBISHES > FURBISH
FURCA *n* any forklike structure, esp in insects
FURCAE > FURCA
FURCAL > FURCA
FURCATE *vb* divide into two parts ▷ *adj* forked, branching
FURCATED > FURCATE
FURCATELY > FURCATE
FURCATES > FURCATE
FURCATING > FURCATE
FURCATION > FURCATE
FURCRAEA *n* plant belonging to the Agave family

FURCRAEAS > FURCRAEA
FURCULA *n* any forklike part or organ
FURCULAE > FURCULA
FURCULAR > FURCULA
FURCULUM *same as* > FURCULA
FURDER *same as* > FURTHER
FUREUR *n* rage or anger
FUREURS > FUREUR
FURFAIR *variant of* > FURFUR
FURFAIRS > FURFAIR
FURFUR *n* scurf or scaling of the skin
FURFURAL *n* colourless liquid used as a solvent
FURFURALS > FURFURAL
FURFURAN *same as* > FURAN
FURFURANS > FURFURAN
FURFURES > FURFUR
FURFUROL *variant of* > FURFURAL
FURFUROLE *variant of* > FURFURAL
FURFUROLS > FURFUROL
FURFUROUS > FURFUR
FURFURS > FURFUR
FURIBUND *adj* furious
FURIES > FURY
FURIOSITY > FURIOUS
FURIOSO *adv* in a frantically rushing manner ▷ *n* passage or piece to be performed in this way
FURIOSOS > FURIOSO
FURIOUS *adj* very angry
FURIOUSLY > FURIOUS
FURKID *n* companion animal
FURKIDS > FURKID
FURL *vb* roll up and fasten (a sail, umbrella, or flag) ▷ *n* act or an instance of furling
FURLABLE > FURL
FURLANA *variant of* > FORLANA
FURLANAS > FURLANA
FURLED > FURL
FURLER > FURL
FURLERS > FURL
FURLESS > FUR
FURLING > FURL
FURLONG *n* unit of length
FURLONGS > FURLONG
FURLOUGH *n* leave of absence ▷ *vb* grant a furlough to
FURLOUGHS > FURLOUGH
FURLS > FURL
FURMENTY *same as* > FRUMENTY
FURMETIES > FURMETY
FURMETY *same as* > FRUMENTY
FURMITIES > FURMITY
FURMITY *same as* > FRUMENTY
FURNACE *n* enclosed chamber containing a very

hot fire ▷ *vb* burn in a furnace
FURNACED > FURNACE
FURNACES > FURNACE
FURNACING > FURNACE
FURNIMENT *n* furniture
FURNISH *vb* provide with furniture
FURNISHED > FURNISH
FURNISHER > FURNISH
FURNISHES > FURNISH
FURNITURE *n* large movable articles such as chairs and wardrobes
FUROL *variant of* > FURFURAL
FUROLE *variant of* > FURFURAL
FUROLES > FUROLE
FUROLS > FUROL
FUROR *same as* > FURORE
FURORE *n* very excited or angry reaction
FURORES > FURORE
FURORS > FUROR
FURPHIES > FURPHY
FURPHY *n* rumour or fictitious story
FURPIECE *n* item of clothing made of or decorated with fur
FURPIECES > FURPIECE
FURR *vb* furrow
FURRED *same as* > FURRY
FURRIER *n* dealer in furs
FURRIERS > FURRIER
FURRIERY *n* occupation of a furrier
FURRIES > FURRY
FURRIEST > FURRY
FURRILY > FURRY
FURRINER *n* dialect rendering of foreigner
FURRINERS > FURRINER
FURRINESS > FURRY
FURRING > FUR
FURRINGS > FUR
FURROW *n* trench made by a plough ▷ *vb* make or become wrinkled
FURROWED > FURROW
FURROWER > FURROW
FURROWERS > FURROW
FURROWING > FURROW
FURROWS > FURROW
FURROWY > FURROW
FURRS > FURR
FURRY *adj* like or covered with fur or something furlike ▷ *n* child's fur-covered toy animal
FURS > FUR
FURTH *adv* out
FURTHER *adv* in addition ▷ *adj* more distant ▷ *vb* promote
FURTHERED > FURTHER
FURTHERER > FURTHER
FURTHERS > FURTHER
FURTHEST *adv* to the greatest degree ▷ *adj* most distant

f

FURTIVE adj sly and secretive
FURTIVELY > FURTIVE
FURUNCLE technical name for > BOIL
FURUNCLES > FURUNCLE
FURY n wild anger
FURZE n gorse
FURZES > FURZE
FURZIER > FURZE
FURZIEST > FURZE
FURZY > FURZE
FUSAIN n fine charcoal pencil
FUSAINS > FUSAIN
FUSARIA > FUSARIUM
FUSARIUM n type of fungus
FUSARIUMS > FUSARIUM
FUSAROL variant of > FUSAROLE
FUSAROLE n type of architectural moulding
FUSAROLES > FUSAROLE
FUSAROLS > FUSAROL
FUSBALL same as > FOOSBALL
FUSBALLS > FUSBALL
FUSC adj dark or dark-brown
FUSCOUS adj of a brownish-grey colour
FUSE n cord containing an explosive for detonating a bomb ▷ vb (cause to) fail as a result of a blown fuse
FUSED > FUSE
FUSEE n (in early clocks and watches) a spirally grooved spindle
FUSEES > FUSEE
FUSEL n mixture of amyl alcohols, propanol, and butanol
FUSELAGE n body of an aircraft
FUSELAGES > FUSELAGE
FUSELESS > FUSE
FUSELIKE > FUSE
FUSELS > FUSEL
FUSES > FUSE
FUSHION n spirit
FUSHIONS > FUSHION
FUSIBLE adj capable of being melted
FUSIBLY > FUSIBLE
FUSIDIC adj as in fusidic acid kind of acid
FUSIFORM adj elongated and tapering at both ends
FUSIL n light flintlock musket
FUSILE adj easily melted
FUSILEER same as > FUSILIER

FUSILEERS > FUSILEER
FUSILIER n soldier of certain regiments
FUSILIERS > FUSILIER
FUSILLADE n continuous discharge of firearms ▷ vb attack with a fusillade
FUSILLI n spiral-shaped pasta
FUSILLIS > FUSILLI
FUSILS > FUSIL
FUSING > FUSE
FUSION n melting ▷ adj of a style of cooking
FUSIONAL > FUSION
FUSIONISM n favouring of coalitions among political groups
FUSIONIST > FUSIONISM
FUSIONS > FUSION
FUSK vb obtain data from (a website) by using a fusker
FUSKED > FUSK
FUSKER n piece of software that generates obvious passwords and filenames in order to extract data held on free websites
FUSKERS > FUSKER
FUSKING > FUSK
FUSKS > FUSK
FUSS n needless activity or worry ▷ vb make a fuss
FUSSBALL same as > FOOSBALL
FUSSBALLS > FUSSBALL
FUSSED > FUSS
FUSSER > FUSS
FUSSERS > FUSS
FUSSES > FUSS
FUSSIER > FUSSY
FUSSIEST > FUSSY
FUSSILY > FUSSY
FUSSINESS > FUSSY
FUSSING > FUSS
FUSSPOT n person who is difficult to please and complains often
FUSSPOTS > FUSSPOT
FUSSY adj inclined to fuss
FUST vb become mouldy
FUSTED > FUST
FUSTET n wood of the Venetian sumach shrub
FUSTETS > FUSTET
FUSTIAN n (formerly) a hard-wearing fabric of cotton mixed with flax or wool ▷ adj cheap
FUSTIANS > FUSTIAN
FUSTIC n large tropical American tree

FUSTICS > FUSTIC
FUSTIER > FUSTY
FUSTIEST > FUSTY
FUSTIGATE vb beat
FUSTILUGS n fat person
FUSTILY > FUSTY
FUSTINESS > FUSTY
FUSTING > FUST
FUSTOC variant of > FUSTIC
FUSTOCS > FUSTOC
FUSTS > FUST
FUSTY adj stale-smelling
FUSULINID n any of various extinct foraminifers
FUSUMA n Japanese sliding door
FUTCHEL n timber support in a carriage
FUTCHELS > FUTCHEL
FUTHARC same as > FUTHARK
FUTHARCS > FUTHARC
FUTHARK n phonetic alphabet consisting of runes
FUTHARKS > FUTHARK
FUTHORC same as > FUTHARK
FUTHORCS > FUTHORC
FUTHORK same as > FUTHARK
FUTHORKS > FUTHORK
FUTILE adj unsuccessful or useless
FUTILELY > FUTILE
FUTILER > FUTILE
FUTILEST > FUTILE
FUTILITY n lack of effectiveness or success
FUTON n Japanese-style bed
FUTONS > FUTON
FUTSAL n form of association football
FUTSALS > FUTSAL
FUTTOCK n one of the ribs in the frame of a wooden vessel
FUTTOCKS > FUTTOCK
FUTURAL adj relating to the future
FUTURE n time to come ▷ adj yet to come or be
FUTURES pl n type of commodity trading
FUTURISM n early 20th-century artistic movement making use of the characteristics of the machine age
FUTURISMS > FUTURISM
FUTURIST > FUTURISM
FUTURISTS > FUTURISM

FUTURITY n future
FUTZ vb fritter time away
FUTZED > FUTZ
FUTZES > FUTZ
FUTZING > FUTZ
FUZE same as > FUSE
FUZED > FUZE
FUZEE same as > FUSEE
FUZEES > FUZEE
FUZELESS adj without a fuze
FUZES > FUZE
FUZIL variant of > FUSIL
FUZILS > FUZIL
FUZING > FUZE
FUZZ n mass of fine or curly hairs or fibres ▷ vb make or become fuzzy
FUZZBALL n ball of fuzz
FUZZBALLS > FUZZBALL
FUZZBOX n device that distorts sound
FUZZBOXES > FUZZBOX
FUZZED > FUZZ
FUZZES > FUZZ
FUZZIER > FUZZY
FUZZIEST > FUZZY
FUZZILY > FUZZY
FUZZINESS > FUZZY
FUZZING > FUZZ
FUZZLE vb make drunk
FUZZLED > FUZZLE
FUZZLES > FUZZLE
FUZZLING > FUZZLE
FUZZTONE n device distorting electric guitar sound
FUZZTONES > FUZZTONE
FUZZY adj of, like, or covered with fuzz
FY interj exclamation of disapproval
FYCE variant of > FICE
FYCES > FYCE
FYKE n fish trap ▷ vb catch fish in this manner
FYKED > FYKE
FYKES > FYKE
FYKING > FYKE
FYLE variant of > FILE
FYLES > FYLE
FYLFOT rare word for > SWASTIKA
FYLFOTS > FYLFOT
FYNBOS n area of low-growing, evergreen vegetation
FYNBOSES > FYNBOS
FYRD n militia of an Anglo-Saxon shire
FYRDS > FYRD
FYTTE n song
FYTTES > FYTTE

Gg

GAB vb talk or chatter ▷ n mechanical device
GABARDINE n strong twill cloth used esp for raincoats
GABBA n type of electronic dance music
GABBARD same as > GABBART
GABBARDS > GABBARD
GABBART n Scottish sailing barge
GABBARTS > GABBART
GABBAS > GABBA
GABBED > GAB
GABBER > GAB
GABBERS > GAB
GABBIER > GABBY
GABBIEST > GABBY
GABBINESS > GABBY
GABBING > GAB
GABBLE vb speak rapidly and indistinctly ▷ n rapid indistinct speech
GABBLED > GABBLE
GABBLER > GABBLE
GABBLERS > GABBLE
GABBLES > GABBLE
GABBLING > GABBLE
GABBLINGS > GABBLE
GABBRO n dark basic plutonic igneous rock
GABBROIC > GABBRO
GABBROID adj gabbro-like
GABBROS > GABBRO
GABBY adj talkative
GABELLE n salt tax levied until 1790
GABELLED > GABELLE
GABELLER n person who collects the gabelle
GABELLERS > GABELLER
GABELLES > GABELLE
GABERDINE same as > GABARDINE
GABFEST n prolonged gossiping or conversation
GABFESTS > GABFEST
GABIES > GABY
GABION n cylindrical metal container filled with stones
GABIONADE n row of gabions submerged in a waterway, stream, river, etc, to control the flow of water
GABIONAGE n structure composed of gabions
GABIONED > GABION

GABIONS > GABION
GABLE n triangular upper part of a wall between sloping roofs
GABLED > GABLE
GABLELIKE > GABLE
GABLES > GABLE
GABLET n small gable
GABLETS > GABLET
GABLING > GABLE
GABNASH n chatter
GABNASHES > GABNASH
GABOON n dark wood
GABOONS > GABOON
GABS > GAB
GABY n simpleton
GACH vb behave boastfully
GACHED > GACH
GACHER n person who gaches
GACHERS > GACHER
GACHES > GACH
GACHING > GACH
GAD vb go about in search of pleasure ▷ n carefree adventure
GADABOUT n pleasure-seeker
GADABOUTS > GADABOUT
GADARENE adj headlong
GADDED > GAD
GADDER > GAD
GADDERS > GAD
GADDI n cushion on an Indian prince's throne
GADDING > GAD
GADDIS > GADDI
GADE same as > GAD
GADES > GADE
GADFLIES > GADFLY
GADFLY n fly that bites cattle
GADGE n man
GADGES > GADGE
GADGET n small mechanical device or appliance
GADGETEER n person who delights in gadgetry
GADGETRY n gadgets
GADGETS > GADGET
GADGETY > GADGET
GADGIE n fellow
GADGIES > GADGIE
GADI n Indian throne
GADID n type of marine fish
GADIDS > GADID
GADIS > GADI

GADJE same as > GADGIE
GADJES > GADJE
GADJO same as > GORGIO
GADJOS > GADJO
GADLING n vagabond
GADLINGS > GADLING
GADMAN n person who drives horses at the plough
GADMEN > GADMAN
GADOID adj of the cod family of marine fishes ▷ n gadoid fish
GADOIDS > GADOID
GADOLINIC adj relating to gadolinium, a silvery white metallic element
GADROON n type of decorative moulding
GADROONED > GADROON
GADROONS > GADROON
GADS > GAD
GADSMAN n person who uses a gad when driving animals
GADSMEN > GADSMAN
GADSO n archaic expression of surprise
GADWALL n type of duck related to the mallard
GADWALLS > GADWALL
GADZOOKS interj mild oath
GAE Scot word for > GO
GAED > GAE
GAEING > GAE
GAELICISE vb adapt to conform to Gaelic spelling and pronunciation
GAELICISM > GAELICISE
GAELICIZE same as > GAELICISE
GAEN > GAE
GAES > GAE
GAFF n stick with an iron hook for landing large fish ▷ vb hook or land (a fish) with a gaff
GAFFE n social blunder
GAFFED > GAFF
GAFFER n foreman or boss
GAFFERS > GAFFER
GAFFES > GAFFE
GAFFING > GAFF
GAFFINGS > GAFF
GAFFS > GAFF
GAFFSAIL n quadrilateral fore-and-aft sail on a sailing vessel
GAFFSAILS > GAFFSAIL

GAG vb choke or retch ▷ n cloth etc put into or tied across the mouth
GAGA adj senile
GAGAKU n type of traditional Japanese music
GAGAKUS > GAGAKU
GAGE vb gauge ▷ n (formerly) an object thrown down as a challenge to fight
GAGEABLE > GAGE
GAGEABLY > GAGE
GAGED > GAGE
GAGER same as > GAUGER
GAGERS > GAGER
GAGES > GAGE
GAGGED > GAG
GAGGER n person or thing that gags
GAGGERIES > GAGGERY
GAGGERS > GAGGER
GAGGERY n practice of telling jokes
GAGGING > GAG
GAGGLE n disorderly crowd ▷ vb (of geese) to cackle
GAGGLED > GAGGLE
GAGGLES > GAGGLE
GAGGLING > GAGGLE
GAGGLINGS > GAGGLE
GAGING > GAGE
GAGMAN n person who writes gags for a comedian
GAGMEN > GAGMAN
GAGS > GAG
GAGSTER n standup comedian
GAGSTERS > GAGSTER
GAHNITE n dark green mineral
GAHNITES > GAHNITE
GAID same as > GAD
GAIDS > GAID
GAIETIES > GAIETY
GAIETY n cheerfulness
GAIJIN n (in Japan) a foreigner
GAILLARD same as > GALLIARD
GAILLARDE same as > GAILLARD
GAILY adv merrily
GAIN vb acquire or obtain ▷ n profit or advantage ▷ adj straight or near
GAINABLE > GAIN
GAINED > GAIN

GAINER n person or thing that gains
GAINERS > GAINER
GAINEST > GAIN
GAINFUL adj useful or profitable
GAINFULLY > GAINFUL
GAINING > GAIN
GAININGS pl n profits or earnings
GAINLESS > GAIN
GAINLIER > GAINLY
GAINLIEST > GAINLY
GAINLY adj graceful or well-formed ▷ adv conveniently or suitably
GAINS pl n profits or winnings
GAINSAID > GAINSAY
GAINSAY vb deny or contradict
GAINSAYER > GAINSAY
GAINSAYS > GAINSAY
GAINST short for > AGAINST
GAIR n strip of green grass on a hillside
GAIRFOWL same as > GAREFOWL
GAIRFOWLS > GAIRFOWL
GAIRS > GAIR
GAIT n manner of walking ▷ vb teach (a horse) a particular gait
GAITA n type of bagpipe
GAITAS > GAITA
GAITED > GAIT
GAITER n cloth or leather covering for the lower leg
GAITERED adj wearing gaiters
GAITERS > GAITER
GAITING > GAIT
GAITS > GAIT
GAITT Scots word for > GATE
GAITTS > GAITT
GAJO same as > GORGIO
GAJOS > GAJO
GAK n (slang) cocaine
GAKS > GAK
GAL n girl
GALA n festival
GALABEA same as > DJELLABA
GALABEAH same as > DJELLABA
GALABEAHS > GALABEAH
GALABEAS > GALABEA
GALABIA same as > DJELLABA
GALABIAH same as > DJELLABA
GALABIAHS > GALABIAH
GALABIAS > GALABIA
GALABIEH same as > DJELLABA
GALABIEHS > GALABIEH
GALABIYA same as > DJELLABA
GALABIYAH same as > DJELLABA

GALABIYAS > GALABIYA
GALACTIC adj of the Galaxy or other galaxies
GALACTICO n famous and highly paid footballer
GALACTOSE n white water-soluble monosaccharide found in lactose
GALAGE same as > GALOSH
GALAGES > GALAGE
GALAGO another name for > BUSHBABY
GALAGOS > GALAGO
GALAH n Australian cockatoo
GALAHS > GALAH
GALANGA same as > GALINGALE
GALANGAL same as > GALINGALE
GALANGALS > GALANGAL
GALANGAS > GALANGAL
GALANT n 18th-century style of music
GALANTINE n cold dish of meat or poultry, which is boned, cooked, stuffed, then pressed into a neat shape and glazed
GALANTY n as in galanty show pantomime shadow play
GALAPAGO n tortoise
GALAPAGOS > GALAPAGO
GALAS > GALA
GALATEA n strong twill-weave cotton fabric
GALATEAS > GALATEA
GALAVANT same as > GALLIVANT
GALAVANTS > GALAVANT
GALAX n coltsfoot
GALAXES > GALAX
GALAXIES > GALAXY
GALAXY n system of stars
GALBANUM n bitter aromatic gum resin extracted from various Asian plants, used in incense and medicinally
GALBANUMS > GALBANUM
GALDRAGON old Scots word for a > SORCERESS
GALE n strong wind ▷ vb be very stormy
GALEA n part or organ shaped like a helmet
GALEAE > GALEA
GALEAS > GALEA
GALEATE > GALEA
GALEATED > GALEA
GALED > GALE
GALEIFORM > GALEA
GALENA n soft bluish-grey mineral
GALENAS > GALENA
GALENGALE same as > GALINGALE
GALENIC > GALENA
GALENICAL n any drug prepared from plant or animal tissue, esp

vegetables, rather than being chemically synthesized ▷ adj denoting or belonging to this group of drugs
GALENITE same as > GALENA
GALENITES > GALENITE
GALENOID adj pertaining to galena
GALERE n group of people having a common interest
GALERES > GALERE
GALES > GALE
GALETTE n type of savoury pancake
GALETTES > GALETTE
GALILEE n type of porch or chapel
GALILEES > GALILEE
GALING > GALE
GALINGALE n European plant with rough-edged leaves, reddish spikelets of flowers, and aromatic roots
GALIONGEE n sailor
GALIOT n small swift galley
GALIOTS > GALIOT
GALIPOT n resin obtained from several species of pine
GALIPOTS > GALIPOT
GALIVANT same as > GALLIVANT
GALIVANTS > GALIVANT
GALL n impudence ▷ vb annoy
GALLABEA same as > DJELLABA
GALLABEAH same as > DJELLABA
GALLABEAS > GALLABEA
GALLABIA same as > DJELLABA
GALLABIAH same as > DJELLABA
GALLABIAS > GALLABIA
GALLABIEH same as > DJELLABA
GALLABIYA same as > DJELLABA
GALLAMINE n muscle relaxant used in anaesthesia
GALLANT adj brave and noble ▷ n man who tried to impress with fashionable clothes or daring acts ▷ vb court or flirt (with)
GALLANTED > GALLANT
GALLANTER > GALLANT
GALLANTLY > GALLANT
GALLANTRY n showy, attentive treatment of women
GALLANTS > GALLANT
GALLATE n salt of gallic acid
GALLATES > GALLATE
GALLEASS n three-masted lateen-rigged

galley used as a warship in the Mediterranean from the 15th to the 18th centuries
GALLED > GALL
GALLEIN n type of dyestuff
GALLEINS > GALLEIN
GALLEON n large three-masted sailing ship
GALLEONS > GALLEON
GALLERIA n central court through several storeys of a shopping centre or department store onto which shops or departments open at each level
GALLERIAS > GALLERIA
GALLERIED adj having a gallery or galleries
GALLERIES > GALLERY
GALLERIST n person who owns or runs an art gallery
GALLERY n room or building for displaying works of art ▷ vb tunnel; form an underground gallery
GALLET vb use mixture to support a roof-slate
GALLETA n low-growing, coarse grass
GALLETAS > GALLETA
GALLETED > GALLET
GALLETING > GALLET
GALLETS > GALLET
GALLEY n kitchen of a ship or aircraft
GALLEYS > GALLEY
GALLFLIES > GALLFLY
GALLFLY n any of several small insects
GALLIARD n spirited dance in triple time for two persons, popular in the 16th and 17th centuries ▷ adj lively
GALLIARDS > GALLIARD
GALLIASS same as > GALLEASS
GALLIC adj of or containing gallium in the trivalent state
GALLICA n variety of rose
GALLICAN adj of or relating to a movement favouring the restriction of papal control and greater autonomy for the French church
GALLICAS > GORGIO
GALLICISE same as > GALLICIZE
GALLICISM n word or idiom borrowed from French
GALLICIZE vb make or become French in attitude, language, etc
GALLIED > GALLY
GALLIER > GALLY
GALLIES > GALLY

GALLIEST > GALLY
GALLINAZO n black vulture
GALLING adj annoying or bitterly humiliating
GALLINGLY > GALLING
GALLINULE n moorhen
GALLIOT same as > GALIOT
GALLIOTS > GALLIOT
GALLIPOT same as > GALIPOT
GALLIPOTS > GALLIPOT
GALLISE vb use method to increase the quantity of wine produced
GALLISED > GALLISE
GALLISES > GALLISE
GALLISING > GALLISE
GALLISISE vb gallise
GALLISIZE same as > GALLISE
GALLIUM n soft grey metallic element
GALLIUMS > GALLIUM
GALLIVANT vb go about in search of pleasure
GALLIVAT n Oriental armed vessel
GALLIVATS > GALLIVAT
GALLIWASP n type of Central American lizard
GALLIZE same as > GALLISE
GALLIZED > GALLIZE
GALLIZES > GALLIZE
GALLIZING > GALLIZE
GALLNUT n type of plant gall that resembles a nut
GALLNUTS > GALLNUT
GALLOCK adj left-handed
GALLON n liquid measure of eight pints, equal to 4.55 litres
GALLONAGE n capacity measured in gallons
GALLONS > GALLON
GALLOON n narrow band of cord, gold braid, etc
GALLOONED > GALLOON
GALLOONS > GALLOON
GALLOOT same as > GALLOOT
GALLOOTS > GALLOOT
GALLOP n horse's fastest pace ▷ vb go or ride at a gallop
GALLOPADE n gallop ▷ vb perform a gallopade
GALLOPED > GALLOP
GALLOPER > GALLOP
GALLOPERS > GALLOP
GALLOPING adj progressing at or as if at a gallop
GALLOPS > GALLOP
GALLOUS adj of or containing gallium in the divalent state
GALLOW vb frighten
GALLOWAY n breed of hornless beef cattle
GALLOWAYS > GALLOWAY
GALLOWED > GALLOW

GALLOWING > GALLOW
GALLOWS n wooden structure used for hanging criminals
GALLOWSES > GALLOWS
GALLS > GALL
GALLSTONE n hard mass formed in the gall bladder or its ducts
GALLUMPH same as > GALUMPH
GALLUMPHS > GALLUMPH
GALLUS adj bold ▷ n suspender for trousers
GALLUSED adj held up by galluses
GALLUSES > GALLUS
GALLY vb frighten ▷ adj (of land) damp or barren
GALLYING > GALLY
GALOCHE same as > GALOSH
GALOCHED > GALOCHE
GALOCHES > GALOCHE
GALOCHING > GALOCHE
GALOOT n clumsy or uncouth person
GALOOTS > GALOOT
GALOP n 19th-century dance in quick duple time ▷ vb dance a galop
GALOPADE same as > GALOP
GALOPADES > GALOP
GALOPED > GALOP
GALOPIN n boy who ran errands for a cook
GALOPING > GALOP
GALOPINS > GALOPIN
GALOPPED > GALOP
GALOPPING > GALOP
GALOPS > GALOP
GALORE adv in abundance ▷ adj in abundance ▷ n abundance
GALORES > GALORE
GALOSH n waterproof overshoe ▷ vb cover with galoshes
GALOSHE same as > GALOSH
GALOSHED > GALOSH
GALOSHES > GALOSH
GALOSHING > GALOSH
GALOWSES Shakespearean plural for > GALLOWS
GALRAVAGE same as > GILRAVAGE
GALS > GAL
GALTONIA n type of bulbous plant with waxy white flowers and a fragrant scent
GALTONIAS > GALTONIA
GALUMPH vb leap or move about clumsily
GALUMPHED > GALUMPH
GALUMPHER > GALUMPH
GALUMPHS > GALUMPH
GALUT same as > GALUTH
GALUTH n exile of Jews from Palestine
GALUTHS > GALUTH
GALUTS > GALUT

GALVANIC adj of or producing an electric current generated by chemical means
GALVANISE same as > GALVANIZE
GALVANISM n electricity, esp when produced by chemical means as in a cell or battery
GALVANIST > GALVANISM
GALVANIZE vb stimulate into action ▷ n galvanized iron, usually in the form of corrugated sheets as used in roofing
GALVO n instrument for measuring electric current
GALVOS > GALVO
GALYAC same as > GALYAK
GALYACS > GALYAC
GALYAK n smooth glossy fur
GALYAKS > GALYAK
GAM n school of whales ▷ vb (of whales) form a school
GAMA n tall perennial grass
GAMAHUCHE vb practise cunnilingus or fellatio on ▷ n cunnilingus or fellatio
GAMARUCHE same as > GAMAHUCHE
GAMAS > GAMA
GAMASH n type of gaiter
GAMASHES > GAMASH
GAMAY n red grape variety, or the wine made from it
GAMAYS > GAMAY
GAMB n in heraldry, the whole foreleg of a beast
GAMBA n second-largest member of the viol family
GAMBADE same as > GAMBADO
GAMBADES > GAMBADE
GAMBADO n leap or gambol; caper ▷ vb perform a gambado
GAMBADOED > GAMBADO
GAMBADOES > GAMBADO
GAMBADOS > GAMBADO
GAMBAS > GAMBA
GAMBE same as > GAMB
GAMBES > GAMBE
GAMBESON n quilted and padded or stuffed leather or cloth garment worn under mail in the Middle Ages and later as a doublet by men and women
GAMBESONS > GAMBESON
GAMBET n tattler
GAMBETS > GAMBET
GAMBETTA n redshank
GAMBETTAS > GAMBETTA
GAMBIA same as > GAMBIER
GAMBIAS > GAMBIA
GAMBIER n astringent resinous substance

GAMBIERS > GAMBIER
GAMBIR same as > GAMBIER
GAMBIRS > GAMBIR
GAMBIST n person who plays the (viola da) gamba
GAMBISTS > GAMBIST
GAMBIT n opening move intended to secure an advantage ▷ vb sacrifice a chess piece to gain a better position
GAMBITED > GAMBIT
GAMBITING > GAMBIT
GAMBITS > GAMBIT
GAMBLE vb play games of chance to win money ▷ n risky undertaking
GAMBLED > GAMBLE
GAMBLER > GAMBLE
GAMBLERS > GAMBLE
GAMBLES > GAMBLE
GAMBLING > GAMBLE
GAMBLINGS > GAMBLE
GAMBO n farm cart
GAMBOES > GAMBO
GAMBOGE n gum resin
GAMBOGES > GAMBOGE
GAMBOGIAN > GAMBOGE
GAMBOGIC > GAMBOGE
GAMBOL vb jump about playfully, frolic ▷ n frolic
GAMBOLED > GAMBOL
GAMBOLING > GAMBOL
GAMBOLLED > GAMBOL
GAMBOLS > GAMBOL
GAMBOS > GAMBO
GAMBREL n hock of a horse or similar animal
GAMBRELS > GAMBREL
GAMBROON n type of linen cloth
GAMBROONS > GAMBROON
GAMBS > GAMB
GAMBUSIA n small fish that feeds on mosquito larvae
GAMBUSIAS > GAMBUSIA
GAME n amusement or pastime ▷ vb gamble ▷ adj brave
GAMEBAG n bag for carrying hunted game birds
GAMEBAGS > GAMEBAG
GAMEBOOK n book containing a range of possible strategies for a game
GAMEBOOKS > GAMEBOOK
GAMECOCK n cock bred and trained for fighting
GAMECOCKS > GAMECOCK
GAMED > GAME
GAMEFISH n fish caught for sport
GAMEFOWL n cock bred for cockfighting
GAMEFOWLS > GAMEFOWL
GAMELAN n type of percussion orchestra
GAMELANS > GAMELAN
GAMELIKE > GAME

GAMELY adv in a brave or sporting manner

GAMENESS n courage or bravery

GAMEPLAY n plot of a computer or video game or the way that it is played

GAMEPLAYS > GAMEPLAY

GAMER n person who plays computer games

GAMERS > GAMER

GAMES > GAME

GAMESIER > GAMESY

GAMESIEST > GAMESY

GAMESMAN n one who practises gamesmanship: the art of winning by cunning practices without actually cheating

GAMESMEN > GAMESMAN

GAMESOME adj full of merriment

GAMEST > GAME

GAMESTER n gambler

GAMESTERS > GAMESTER

GAMESY adj sporty

GAMETAL > GAMETE

GAMETE n reproductive cell

GAMETES > GAMETE

GAMETIC > GAMETE

GAMEY adj having the smell or flavour of game

GAMEYNESS n quality of being gamey

GAMGEE n as in gamgee tissue type of wound-dressing

GAMIC adj (esp of reproduction) requiring the fusion of gametes

GAMIER > GAMEY

GAMIEST > GAMEY

GAMIFIED > GAMIFY

GAMIFIES > GAMIFY

GAMIFY vb add gamelike elements to a task to encourage participation

GAMIFYING > GAMIFY

GAMILY > GAMEY

GAMIN n street urchin

GAMINE n slim boyish young woman

GAMINERIE n impish behaviour

GAMINES > GAMINE

GAMINESS > GAMEY

GAMING n gambling

GAMINGS > GAMING

GAMINS > GAMIN

GAMMA n third letter of the Greek alphabet

GAMMADIA > GAMMADION

GAMMADION n decorative figure composed of a number of Greek capital gammas, esp radiating from a centre, as in a swastika

GAMMAS > GAMMA

GAMMAT n derogatory term for a Cape Coloured person

GAMMATIA > GAMMATION

GAMMATION same as > GAMMADION

GAMMATS > GAMMAT

GAMME n musical scale

GAMMED > GAM

GAMMER n dialect word for an old woman: now chiefly humorous or contemptuous

GAMMERS > GAMMER

GAMMES > GAMME

GAMMIER > GAMMY

GAMMIEST > GAMMY

GAMMING > GAM

GAMMOCK vb clown around

GAMMOCKED > GAMMOCK

GAMMOCKS > GAMMOCK

GAMMON n cured or smoked ham ▷ vb score a double victory in backgammon over

GAMMONED > GAMMON

GAMMONER > GAMMON

GAMMONERS > GAMMON

GAMMONING > GAMMON

GAMMONS > GAMMON

GAMMY adj (of the leg) lame

GAMODEME n isolated breeding population

GAMODEMES > GAMODEME

GAMONE n chemical used by gametes during sexual reproduction

GAMONES > GAMONE

GAMP n umbrella

GAMPISH adj bulging

GAMPS > GAMP

GAMS > GAM

GAMUT n whole range or scale (of music, emotions, etc)

GAMUTS > GAMUT

GAMY same as > GAMEY

GAMYNESS > GAMY

GAN vb go

GANACHE n rich icing or filling

GANACHES > GANACHE

GANCH vb impale

GANCHED > GANCH

GANCHES > GANCH

GANCHING > GANCH

GANDER n male goose ▷ vb look

GANDERED > GANDER

GANDERING > GANDER

GANDERISM > GANDER

GANDERS > GANDER

GANDY adj as in gandy dancer railway track maintenance worker

GANE > GANGUE

GANEF n unscrupulous opportunist

GANEFS > GANEF

GANEV same as > GANEF

GANEVS > GANEV

GANG n (criminal) group ▷ vb become or act as a gang

GANGBANG n sexual intercourse between one woman and several men

one after the other, esp against her will ▷ vb force (a woman) to take part in a gangbang

GANGBANGS > GANGBANG

GANGBO n order restricting the activities of a gang member

GANGBOARD n gangway

GANGBOS > GANGBO

GANGED > GANG

GANGER n foreman of a gang of labourers

GANGERS > GANGER

GANGING > GANG

GANGINGS > GANG

GANGLAND n criminal underworld

GANGLANDS > GANGLAND

GANGLE vb move awkwardly

GANGLED > GANGLE

GANGLES > GANGLE

GANGLIA > GANGLION

GANGLIAL > GANGLION

GANGLIAR > GANGLION

GANGLIATE vb form a ganglion

GANGLIER > GANGLY

GANGLIEST > GANGLY

GANGLING adj lanky and awkward

GANGLION n group of nerve cells

GANGLIONS > GANGLION

GANGLY same as > GANGLING

GANGPLANK n portable bridge for boarding or leaving a ship

GANGPLOW n plough designed to produce parallel furrows

GANGPLOWS > GANGPLOW

GANGREL n wandering beggar

GANGRELS > GANGREL

GANGRENE n decay of body tissue as a result of disease or injury ▷ vb become or cause to become affected with gangrene

GANGRENED > GANGRENE

GANGRENES > GANGRENE

GANGS > GANG

GANGSHAG vb participate in group sex with

GANGSHAGS > GANGSHAG

GANGSMAN n foreman

GANGSMEN > GANGSMAN

GANGSTA n member of a street gang

GANGSTAS > GANGSTA

GANGSTER n member of a criminal gang

GANGSTERS > GANGSTER

GANGUE n valueless material in an ore

GANGUES > GANGUE

GANGWAY same as > GANGPLANK

GANGWAYS > GANGWAY

GANISTER n highly refractory siliceous sedimentary rock occurring beneath coal seams: used for lining furnaces

GANISTERS > GANISTER

GANJA n highly potent form of cannabis

GANJAH same as > GANJA

GANJAHS > GANJAH

GANJAS > GANJA

GANNED > GAN

GANNET n large sea bird

GANNETRY n gannets' breeding-place

GANNETS > GANNET

GANNING > GAN

GANNISTER same as > GANISTER

GANOF same as > GANEF

GANOFS > GANOF

GANOID adj of the scales of certain fishes ▷ n ganoid fish

GANOIDS > GANOID

GANOIN n the outer layer of fish scales

GANOINE same as > GANOIN

GANOINES > GANOINE

GANOINS > GANOIN

GANS > GAN

GANSEY n jersey or pullover

GANSEYS > GANSEY

GANT vb yawn

GANTED > GANT

GANTELOPE same as > GAUNTLET

GANTING > GANT

GANTLET n section of a railway where two tracks overlap ▷ vb make railway tracks form a gantlet

GANTLETED > GANTLET

GANTLETS > GANTLET

GANTLINE n line rove through a sheave for hoisting men or gear

GANTLINES > GANTLINE

GANTLOPE same as > GAUNTLET

GANTLOPES > GANTLOPE

GANTRIES > GANTRY

GANTRY n structure supporting something

GANTS > GANT

GANYMEDE n catamite

GANYMEDES > GANYMEDE

GANZFELD n type of experiment used in parapsychology

GANZFELDS > GANZFELD

GAOL same as > JAIL

GAOLBIRD n person who is or has been confined to gaol, esp repeatedly

GAOLBIRDS > GAOLBIRD

GAOLBREAK less common spelling of > JAILBREAK

GAOLBROKE > GAOLBREAK

GAOLED > GAOL

GAOLER > GAOL
GAOLERESS n female gaoler
GAOLERS > GAOL
GAOLING > GAOL
GAOLLESS adj without a gaol
GAOLS > GAOL
GAP n break or opening
GAPE vb stare in wonder ▷ n act of gaping
GAPED > GAPE
GAPER n person or thing that gapes
GAPERS > GAPER
GAPES n disease of young domestic fowl
GAPESEED n person who stares, mouth agape, at something
GAPESEEDS > GAPESEED
GAPEWORM n type of parasitic worm that lives in the trachea of birds
GAPEWORMS > GAPEWORM
GAPIER > GAPES
GAPIEST > GAPES
GAPING adj wide open ▷ n state of having a gaping mouth
GAPINGLY > GAPING
GAPINGS > GAPING
GAPLESS > GAP
GAPO n forest near a river, flooded in the rainy season
GAPOS > GAPO
GAPOSIS n gap between closed fastenings on a garment
GAPOSISES > GAPOSIS
GAPPED > GAP
GAPPER n person taking a year out of education
GAPPERS > GAPPER
GAPPIER > GAP
GAPPIEST > GAP
GAPPING n the act of taking a gap year
GAPPINGS > GAPPING
GAPPY > GAP
GAPS > GAP
GAPY > GAPES
GAR same as > GARPIKE
GARAGE n building used to house cars ▷ vb put or keep a car in a garage
GARAGED > GARAGE
GARAGEMAN n car mechanic
GARAGEMEN > GARAGEMAN
GARAGES > GARAGE
GARAGEY adj (of music) in a garage style
GARAGING n accommodation for housing a motor vehicle
GARAGINGS > GARAGING
GARAGIST n person who runs a garage
GARAGISTE n small-scale wine-maker
GARAGISTS > GARAGIST

GARB n clothes ▷ vb clothe
GARBAGE n rubbish
GARBAGES > GARBAGE
GARBAGEY > GARBAGE
GARBAGY > GARBAGE
GARBANZO another name for > CHICKPEA
GARBANZOS > GARBANZO
GARBE n in heraldry, a wheat-sheaf
GARBED > GARB
GARBES > GARBE
GARBING > GARB
GARBLE vb jumble (a story, quotation, etc), esp unintentionally ▷ n act of garbling
GARBLED adj (of a story etc) jumbled and confused
GARBLER > GARBLE
GARBLERS > GARBLE
GARBLES > GARBLE
GARBLESS > GARB
GARBLING > GARBLE
GARBLINGS > GARBLE
GARBO n dustman
GARBOARD n bottommost plank of a vessel's hull
GARBOARDS > GARBOARD
GARBOIL n confusion or disturbance
GARBOILS > GARBOIL
GARBOLOGY n study of the contents of domestic dustbins to analyse the consumption patterns of households
GARBOS > GARBO
GARBS > GARB
GARBURE n thick soup from Bearn in France
GARBURES > GARBURE
GARCINIA n tropical tree
GARCINIAS > GARCINIA
GARCON n waiter
GARCONS > GARCON
GARDA n member of the Irish police force
GARDAI > GARDA
GARDANT same as > GUARDANT
GARDANTS > GUARDANT
GARDEN n piece of land for growing flowers, fruit, or vegetables ▷ vb cultivate a garden
GARDENED > GARDEN
GARDENER n person who works in or takes care of a garden as an occupation or pastime
GARDENERS > GARDENER
GARDENFUL n quantity that will fill a garden
GARDENIA n large fragrant white waxy flower
GARDENIAS > GARDENIA
GARDENING n planning and cultivation of a garden
GARDENS > GARDEN
GARDEROBE n wardrobe or the contents of a wardrobe

GARDYLOO n act of throwing slops from a window
GARDYLOOS > GARDYLOO
GARE n filth ▷ adj greedy; covetous
GAREFOWL n great auk
GAREFOWLS > GAREFOWL
GARES > GARE
GARFISH same as > GARPIKE
GARFISHES > GARFISH
GARGANEY n small Eurasian duck, closely related to the mallard
GARGANEYS > GARGANEY
GARGANTUA n monster in Japanese film
GARGARISE vb gargle
GARGARISM n gargle
GARGARIZE same as > GARGARISE
GARGET n inflammation of the mammary gland
GARGETS > GARGET
GARGETY > GARGET
GARGLE vb wash the throat ▷ n liquid used for gargling
GARGLED > GARGLE
GARGLER > GARGLE
GARGLERS > GARGLE
GARGLES > GARGLE
GARGLING > GARGLE
GARGOYLE n waterspout carved in the form of a grotesque face, esp on a church ▷ vb provide with gargoyles
GARGOYLED > GARGOYLE
GARGOYLES > GARGOYLE
GARI n thinly sliced pickled ginger
GARIAL same as > GAVIAL
GARIALS > GARIAL
GARIBALDI n woman's loose blouse with long sleeves popular in the 1860s, copied from the red flannel shirt worn by Garibaldi's soldiers
GARIGUE n open shrubby vegetation of dry Mediterranean regions
GARIGUES > GARIGUE
GARIS > GARI
GARISH adj crudely bright or colourful ▷ vb heal
GARISHED > GARISH
GARISHES > GARISH
GARISHING > GARISH
GARISHLY > GARISH
GARJAN same as > GURJUN
GARJANS > GARJAN
GARLAND n wreath of flowers worn or hung as a decoration ▷ vb decorate with garlands
GARLANDED > GARLAND
GARLANDRY n collective term for garlands
GARLANDS > GARLAND
GARLIC n pungent bulb of a plant of the onion family

GARLICKED adj flavoured with garlic
GARLICKY adj containing or resembling the taste or odour of garlic
GARLICS > GARLIC
GARMENT n article of clothing ▷ vb cover or clothe
GARMENTED > GARMENT
GARMENTS > GARMENT
GARMS pl n clothing
GARNER vb collect or store ▷ n place for storage or safekeeping
GARNERED > GARNER
GARNERING > GARNER
GARNERS > GARNER
GARNET n red semiprecious stone
GARNETS > GARNET
GARNI adj garnished
GARNISH vb decorate (food) ▷ n decoration for food
GARNISHED > GARNISH
GARNISHEE n person upon whom a notice of warning has been served ▷ vb attach (a debt or other property) by a notice of warning
GARNISHER > GARNISH
GARNISHES > GARNISH
GARNISHOR n person who or thing that garnishes
GARNISHRY n decoration
GARNITURE n decoration or embellishment
GAROTE same as > GARROTTE
GAROTED > GAROTE
GAROTES > GAROTE
GAROTING > GAROTE
GAROTTE same as > GARROTTE
GAROTTED > GAROTTE
GAROTTER > GAROTTE
GAROTTERS > GAROTTE
GAROTTES > GAROTTE
GAROTTING > GAROTTE
GAROUPA in Chinese and SE Asian cookery, another name for > GROPER
GAROUPAS > GAROUPA
GARPIKE n primitive freshwater bony fish
GARPIKES > GARPIKE
GARRAN same as > GARRON
GARRANS > GARRAN
GARRE vb compel
GARRED > GAR
GARRES > GARRE
GARRET n attic in a house
GARRETED adj living in a garret
GARRETEER n person who lives in a garret
GARRETS > GARRET
GARRIGUE same as > GARIGUE
GARRIGUES > GARRIGUE
GARRING > GAR

g

GARRISON *n* troops stationed in a town or fort ▷ *vb* station troops in
GARRISONS > GARRISON
GARRON *n* small sturdy pony
GARRONS > GARRON
GARROT *n* goldeneye duck
GARROTE *same as* > GARROTTE
GARROTED > GARROTE
GARROTER > GARROTE
GARROTERS > GARROTE
GARROTES > GARROTE
GARROTING > GARROTE
GARROTS > GARROT
GARROTTE *n* Spanish method of execution by strangling ▷ *vb* kill by this method
GARROTTED > GARROTTE
GARROTTER > GARROTTE
GARROTTES > GARROTTE
GARRULITY > GARRULOUS
GARRULOUS *adj* talkative
GARRYA *n* catkin-bearing evergreen shrub
GARRYAS > GARRYA
GARRYOWEN *n* (in rugby union) high kick forwards followed by a charge to the place where the ball lands
GARS > GAR
GART *vb* compel
GARTER *n* band used to hold up a sock or stocking ▷ *vb* secure with a garter
GARTERED > GARTER
GARTERING > GARTER
GARTERS > GARTER
GARTH *n* courtyard surrounded by a cloister
GARTHS > GARTH
GARUDA *n* Hindu god
GARUDAS > GARUDA
GARUM *n* fermented fish sauce
GARUMS > GARUM
GARVEY *n* small flat-bottomed yacht
GARVEYS > GARVEY
GARVIE *n* sprat
GARVIES > GARVIE
GARVOCK *n* sprat
GARVOCKS > GARVOCK
GAS *n* airlike substance that is not liquid or solid ▷ *vb* poison or render unconscious with gas
GASAHOL *n* mixture of petrol and alcohol used as fuel
GASAHOLS > GASAHOL
GASALIER *same as* > GASOLIER
GASALIERS > GASALIER
GASBAG *n* person who talks too much ▷ *vb* talk in a voluble way
GASBAGGED > GASBAG
GASBAGS > GASBAG
GASCON *n* boaster

GASCONADE *n* boastful talk, bragging, or bluster ▷ *vb* boast, brag, or bluster
GASCONISM > GASCON
GASCONS > GASCON
GASEITIES > GASEITY
GASEITY *n* state of being gaseous
GASELIER *same as* > GASOLIER
GASELIERS > GASELIER
GASEOUS *adj* of or like gas
GASES > GAS
GASFIELD *n* area in which natural gas is found underground
GASFIELDS > GASFIELD
GASH *vb* make a long deep cut in ▷ *n* long deep cut ▷ *adj* surplus to requirements ▷ *adj* witty
GASHED > GASH
GASHER > GASH
GASHES > GASH
GASHEST > GASH
GASHFUL *adj* full of gashes
GASHING > GASH
GASHLIER > GASHLY
GASHLIEST > GASHLY
GASHLY *adv* wittily ▷ *adj* hideous; ghastly
GASHOLDER *n* large tank for storing gas
GASHOUSE *n* gasworks
GASHOUSES > GASHOUSE
GASIFIED > GASIFY
GASIFIER > GASIFY
GASIFIERS > GASIFY
GASIFIES > GASIFY
GASIFORM *adj* in a gaseous form
GASIFY *vb* change into a gas
GASIFYING > GASIFY
GASKET *n* type of seal
GASKETED *adj* having a gasket
GASKETS > GASKET
GASKIN *n* lower part of a horse's thigh
GASKING *same as* > GASKET
GASKINGS > GASKING
GASKINS > GASKIN
GASLESS > GAS
GASLIGHT *n* lamp in which light is produced by burning gas
GASLIGHTS > GASLIGHT
GASLIT *adj* lit by gas
GASMAN *n* man employed by a gas company
GASMEN > GASMAN
GASOGENE *n* siphon bottle
GASOGENES > GASOGENE
GASOHOL *n* mixture of petrol and ethyl alcohol
GASOHOLS > GASOHOL
GASOLENE *same as* > GASOLINE
GASOLENES > GASOLENE
GASOLIER *n* branched hanging fitting for gaslights

GASOLIERS > GASOLIER
GASOLINE *n* petrol
GASOLINES > GASOLINE
GASOLINIC > GASOLINE
GASOMETER *same as* > GASHOLDER
GASOMETRY *n* measurement of quantities of gases
GASP *vb* draw in breath sharply or with difficulty ▷ *n* convulsive intake of breath
GASPED > GASP
GASPER *n* person who gasps
GASPEREAU *another name for* > ALEWIFE
GASPERS > GASPER
GASPIER > GASP
GASPIEST > GASP
GASPINESS > GASP
GASPING > GASP
GASPINGLY > GASP
GASPINGS > GASP
GASPS > GASP
GASPY > GASP
GASSED > GAS
GASSER *n* drilling or well that yields natural gas
GASSERS > GASSER
GASSES > GAS
GASSIER > GASSY
GASSIEST > GASSY
GASSILY > GASSY
GASSINESS > GASSY
GASSING > GAS
GASSINGS > GAS
GASSY *adj* filled with gas
GAST *vb* frighten
GASTED > GAST
GASTER *vb* frighten
GASTERED > GASTER
GASTERING > GASTER
GASTERS > GASTER
GASTFULL *adj* dismal
GASTHAUS *n* guest house
GASTIGHT *adj* not allowing gas to enter or escape
GASTING > GAST
GASTNESS *n* dread
GASTNESSE *same as* > GASTNESS
GASTRAEA *n* hypothetical primeval form posited by Haeckel
GASTRAEAS > GASTRAEA
GASTRAEUM *n* underside of the body
GASTRAL *adj* relating to the stomach
GASTREA *same as* > GASTRAEA
GASTREAS > GASTREAS
GASTRIC *adj* of the stomach
GASTRIN *n* polypeptide hormone
GASTRINS > GASTRIN
GASTRITIC > GASTRITIS

GASTRITIS *n* inflammation of the stomach lining
GASTROPOD *n* type of mollusc, such as a snail, with a single flattened muscular foot
GASTROPUB *n* pub specializing in high-quality food
GASTRULA *n* saclike animal embryo consisting of three layers of cells (ectoderm, mesoderm, and endoderm) surrounding a central cavity (archenteron) with a small opening (blastopore) to the exterior
GASTRULAE > GASTRULA
GASTRULAR > GASTRULA
GASTRULAS > GASTRULA
GASTS > GAST
GASWORKS *n* plant where coal gas is made
GAT *n* pistol or revolver
GATCH *vb* behave boastfully
GATCHED > GATCH
GATCHER *n* person who gatches
GATCHERS > GATCHER
GATCHES > GATCH
GATCHING > GATCH
GATE *n* movable barrier, usu hinged, in a wall or fence ▷ *vb* provide with a gate or gates
GATEAU *n* rich elaborate cake
GATEAUS > GATEAU
GATEAUX > GATEAU
GATECRASH *vb* gain entry to (a party, concert, etc) without invitation or payment
GATED > GATE
GATEFOLD *n* oversize page in a book or magazine that is folded in
GATEFOLDS > GATEFOLD
GATEHOUSE *n* building at or above a gateway
GATELEG *n* table having hinged legs that swing out
GATELEGS > GATELEG
GATELESS > GATE
GATELIKE > GATE
GATEMAN *n* gatekeeper
GATEMEN > GATEMAN
GATEPOST *n* post on which a gate is hung
GATEPOSTS > GATEPOST
GATER *variant of* > GATOR
GATERS > GATER
GATES > GATE
GATEWAY *n* entrance with a gate
GATEWAYS > GATEWAY
GATH *n* (in Indian music) second section of a raga
GATHER *vb* assemble ▷ *n* act of gathering

GATHERED > GATHER
GATHERER > GATHER
GATHERERS > GATHER
GATHERING *n* assembly
GATHERS > GATHER
GATHS > GATH
GATING > GATE
GATINGS > GATE
GATLING *n* as in *gatling gun* kind of machinegun
GATOR *shortened form of* **>** ALLIGATOR
GATORS > GATOR
GATS > GAT
GATVOL *adj* in South African English, fed up
GAU *n* district set up by the Nazi Party
GAUCH *vb* behave boastfully
GAUCHE *adj* socially awkward ▷ *vb* make gauche
GAUCHED > GAUCHE
GAUCHELY > GAUCHE
GAUCHER *n* gauche person
GAUCHERIE *n* quality of being gauche
GAUCHERS > GAUCHER
GAUCHES > GAUCHE
GAUCHESCO *adj* relating to the folk traditions of the gauchos
GAUCHEST > GAUCHE
GAUCHING > GAUCHE
GAUCHO *n* S American cowboy
GAUCHOS > GAUCHO
GAUCIE *variant of* **>** GAUCY
GAUCIER > GAUCY
GAUCIEST > GAUCY
GAUCY *adj* plump or jolly
GAUD *n* article of cheap finery ▷ *vb* decorate gaudily
GAUDEAMUS *n* first word of a traditional graduation song, hence the song itself
GAUDED > GAUD
GAUDERIES > GAUDERY
GAUDERY *n* cheap finery or display
GAUDGIE *same as* **>** GADGIE
GAUDGIES > GADGIE
GAUDIER > GAUDY
GAUDIES > GAUDY
GAUDIEST > GAUDY
GAUDILY > GAUDY
GAUDINESS > GAUDY
GAUDING > GAUD
GAUDS > GAUD
GAUDY *adj* vulgarly bright or colourful ▷ *n* festival held at some schools and colleges
GAUFER *n* wafer
GAUFERS > GAUFER
GAUFFER *same as* **>** GOFFER
GAUFFERED > GAUFFER
GAUFFERS > GAUFFER
GAUFRE *same as* **>** GAUFER

GAUFRES > GAUFRE
GAUGE *vb* estimate or judge ▷ *n* measuring instrument ▷ *adj* of a pressure measurement
GAUGEABLE > GAUGE
GAUGEABLY > GAUGE
GAUGED > GAUGE
GAUGER *n* person or thing that gauges
GAUGERS > GAUGER
GAUGES > GAUGE
GAUGING > GAUGE
GAUGINGS > GAUGE
GAUJE *same as* **>** GADGIE
GAUJES > GAUJE
GAULEITER *n* person in a position of authority who behaves in an overbearing authoritarian manner
GAULT *n* stiff compact clay or thick heavy clayey soil
GAULTER *n* person who digs gault
GAULTERS > GAULTER
GAULTS > GAULT
GAUM *vb* understand
GAUMED > GAUM
GAUMIER > GAUMY
GAUMIEST > GAUMY
GAUMING > GAUM
GAUMLESS *variant spelling of* **>** GORMLESS
GAUMS > GAUM
GAUMY *adj* clogged
GAUN > GO
GAUNCH *same as* **>** GANCH
GAUNCHED > GAUNCH
GAUNCHES > GAUNCH
GAUNCHING > GAUNCH
GAUNT *adj* lean and haggard ▷ *vb* yawn
GAUNTED > GAUNT
GAUNTER > GAUNT
GAUNTEST > GAUNT
GAUNTING > GAUNT
GAUNTLET *n* heavy glove with a long cuff ▷ *vb* run (or cause to run) the gauntlet
GAUNTLETS > GAUNTLET
GAUNTLY > GAUNT
GAUNTNESS > GAUNT
GAUNTREE *same as* **>** GANTRY
GAUNTREES > GAUNTREE
GAUNTRIES > GAUNTRY
GAUNTRY *same as* **>** GANTRY
GAUNTS > GAUNT
GAUP *same as* **>** GAWP
GAUPED > GAUP
GAUPER > GAUP
GAUPERS > GAUP
GAUPING > GAUP
GAUPS > GAUP
GAUPUS *same as* **>** GAWPUS
GAUPUSES > GAUPUS
GAUR *n* large wild member of the cattle tribe
GAURS > GAUR
GAUS > GAU

GAUSS *n* cgs unit of magnetic flux density
GAUSSES > GAUSS
GAUSSIAN *adj* of or relating to the principles established by Karl Friedrich Gauss, the German mathematician
GAUZE *n* transparent loosely-woven fabric
GAUZELIKE > GAUZE
GAUZES > GAUZE
GAUZIER > GAUZY
GAUZIEST > GAUZY
GAUZILY > GAUZY
GAUZINESS > GAUZY
GAUZY *adj* resembling gauze
GAVAGE *n* forced feeding by means of a tube
GAVAGES > GAVAGE
GAVE > GIVE
GAVEL *n* small hammer banged on a table ▷ *vb* use a gavel to restore order
GAVELED > GAVEL
GAVELING > GAVEL
GAVELKIND *n* former system of land tenure peculiar to Kent based on the payment of rent to the lord instead of the performance of services by the tenant
GAVELLED > GAVEL
GAVELLING > GAVEL
GAVELMAN *n* gavelkind tenant
GAVELMEN > GAVELMAN
GAVELOCK *n* iron crowbar
GAVELOCKS > GAVELOCK
GAVELS > GAVEL
GAVIAL *n* as in *false gavial* small crocodile
GAVIALOID *adj* of or like gavials
GAVIALS > GAVIAL
GAVOT *same as* **>** GAVOTTE
GAVOTS > GAVOT
GAVOTTE *n* old formal dance ▷ *vb* dance a gavotte
GAVOTTED > GAVOTTE
GAVOTTES > GAVOTTE
GAVOTTING > GAVOTTE
GAW *n* as in *weather gaw* partial rainbow
GAWCIER > GAWCY
GAWCIEST > GAWCY
GAWCY *same as* **>** GAUCY
GAWD *same as* **>** GAUD
GAWDS > GAWD
GAWK *vb* stare stupidly ▷ *n* clumsy awkward person
GAWKED > GAWK
GAWKER > GAWK
GAWKERS > GAWK
GAWKIER > GAWKY
GAWKIES > GAWKY
GAWKIEST > GAWKY
GAWKIHOOD *n* state of being gawky

GAWKILY > GAWKY
GAWKINESS > GAWKY
GAWKING > GAWK
GAWKISH *same as* **>** GAWKY
GAWKISHLY > GAWKY
GAWKS > GAWK
GAWKY *adj* clumsy or awkward ▷ *n* simpleton
GAWMOGE *n* clownish person
GAWMOGES > GAWMOGE
GAWP *vb* stare stupidly
GAWPED > GAWP
GAWPER > GAWP
GAWPERS > GAWP
GAWPING > GAWP
GAWPS > GAWP
GAWPUS *n* silly person
GAWPUSES > GAWPUS
GAWS > GAW
GAWSIE *same as* **>** GAUCY
GAWSIER > GAWSIE
GAWSIEST > GAWSIE
GAWSY *same as* **>** GAUCY
GAY *adj* homosexual ▷ *n* homosexual
GAYAL *n* type of ox
GAYALS > GAYAL
GAYCATION *n* holiday designed for the gay market
GAYDAR *n* supposed ability of one homosexual person to know another
GAYDARS > GAYDAR
GAYER > GAY
GAYEST > GAY
GAYETIES > GAYETY
GAYETY *same as* **>** GAIETY
GAYLY > GAY
GAYNESS > GAY
GAYNESSES > GAY
GAYS > GAY
GAYSOME *adj* full of merriment
GAYWINGS *n* flowering wintergreen
GAZABO *n* fellow or companion
GAZABOES > GAZABO
GAZABOS > GAZABO
GAZAL *same as* **>** GHAZAL
GAZALS > GAZAL
GAZANG *vb* inconvenience a buyer by declining to sell a house just before the purchase is completed
GAZANGED > GAZANG
GAZANGING > GAZANG
GAZANGS > GAZANG
GAZANIA *n* S African plant
GAZANIAS > GAZANIA
GAZAR *n* type of silk cloth
GAZARS > GAZAR
GAZE *vb* look fixedly ▷ *n* fixed look
GAZEBO *n* summerhouse with a good view
GAZEBOES > GAZEBO
GAZEBOS > GAZEBO
GAZED > GAZE
GAZEFUL *adj* gazing

GAZEHOUND n hound such as a greyhound that hunts by sight rather than by scent

GAZELLE n small graceful antelope

GAZELLES > GAZELLE

GAZEMENT n view

GAZEMENTS > GAZEMENT

GAZER > GAZE

GAZERS > GAZE

GAZES > GAZE

GAZETTE n official publication containing announcements ▷ vb announce or report (facts or an event) in a gazette

GAZETTED > GAZETTE

GAZETTEER n (part of) a book that lists and describes places ▷ vb list in a gazetteer

GAZETTES > GAZETTE

GAZETTING > GAZETTE

GAZIER > GAZY

GAZIEST > GAZY

GAZILLION n in informal English, an extremely large but unspecified number, quantity, or amount

GAZING > GAZE

GAZINGS > GAZE

GAZOGENE same as > GASOGENE

GAZOGENES > GAZOGENE

GAZON n sod used to cover a parapet in a fortification

GAZONS > GAZON

GAZOO n kazoo

GAZOOKA same as > GAZOO

GAZOOKAS > GAZOOKA

GAZOON same as > GAZON

GAZOONS > GAZOON

GAZOOS > GAZOO

GAZPACHO n Spanish soup made from tomatoes, peppers, etc, and served cold

GAZPACHOS > GAZPACHO

GAZUMP vb raise the price of a property after verbally agreeing with (a prospective buyer) ▷ n act or an instance of gazumping

GAZUMPED > GAZUMP

GAZUMPER > GAZUMP

GAZUMPERS > GAZUMP

GAZUMPING n act of gazumping

GAZUMPS > GAZUMP

GAZUNDER vb reduce an offer on a property immediately before exchanging contracts having earlier agreed a higher price with the seller ▷ n act or instance of gazundering

GAZUNDERS > GAZUNDER

GAZY adj prone to gazing

GEAL vb congeal

GEALED > GEAL

GEALING > GEAL

GEALOUS Spenserian spelling of > JEALOUS

GEALOUSY Spenserian spelling of > JEALOUSY

GEALS > GEAL

GEAN n white-flowered tree

GEANS > GEAN

GEAR n set of toothed wheels used to change direction or speed ▷ vb prepare or organize for something

GEARBOX n case enclosing a set of gears in a motor vehicle

GEARBOXES > GEARBOX

GEARCASE n protective casing for gears

GEARCASES > GEARCASE

GEARE Spenserian spelling of > JEER

GEARED > GEAR

GEARES > GEARE

GEARHEAD n part in engine gear system

GEARHEADS > GEARHEAD

GEARING n system of gears designed to transmit motion

GEARINGS > GEARING

GEARLESS > GEAR

GEARS > GEAR

GEARSHIFT n lever used to move gearwheels relative to each other, esp in a motor vehicle

GEARSTICK n lever used to move gear wheels in a motor vehicle

GEARWHEEL n one of the toothed wheels in the gears of a motor vehicle

GEASON adj wonderful

GEAT n in casting, the channel which leads to a mould

GEATS > GEAT

GEBUR n tenant farmer

GEBURS > GEBUR

GECK vb beguile

GECKED > GECK

GECKING > GECK

GECKO n small tropical lizard

GECKOES > GECKO

GECKOS > GECKO

GECKS > GECK

GED Scots word for > PIKE

GEDACT n flutelike stopped metal diapason organ pipe

GEDACTS > GEDACT

GEDDIT interj exclamation meaning do you understand it?

GEDECKT same as > GEDACT

GEDECKTS > GEDECKT

GEDS > GED

GEE interj mild exclamation of surprise, admiration, etc ▷ vb move (an animal, esp a horse) ahead

GEEBAG n in Irish slang, a disagreeable woman

GEEBAGS > GEEBAG

GEEBUNG n Australian tree or shrub

GEEBUNGS > GEEBUNG

GEECHEE n Black person from the southern states of the US

GEECHEES > GEECHEE

GEED > GEE

GEEGAW same as > GEWGAW

GEEGAWS > GEEGAW

GEEING > GEE

GEEK n boring, unattractive person

GEEKDOM > GEEK

GEEKDOMS > GEEK

GEEKED adj highly excited

GEEKERIES > GEEKERY

GEEKERY n preoccupation with, or great knowledge about, a specialized subject

GEEKIER > GEEK

GEEKIEST > GEEK

GEEKINESS > GEEK

GEEKISH adj of or like a geek

GEEKISM n preoccupation with subjects generally considered unfashionable or boring

GEEKISMS > GEEKISM

GEEKS > GEEK

GEEKSPEAK n slang word for jargon used by geeks, esp computer enthusiasts

GEEKY adj of or like a geek

GEELBEK n edible marine fish

GEELBEKS > GEELBEK

GEEP n cross between a goat and a sheep

GEEPOUND another name for > SLUG

GEEPOUNDS > SLUG

GEEPS > GEEP

GEES > GEE

GEESE > GOOSE

GEEST n area of heathland in N Germany and adjacent areas

GEESTS > GEEST

GEEZ interj expression of surprise

GEEZAH variant spelling of > GEEZER

GEEZAHS > GEEZAH

GEEZER n man

GEEZERS > GEEZER

GEFILTE adj as in gefilte fish dish of fish stuffed with various ingredients

GEFUFFLE same as > KERFUFFLE

GEFUFFLED > GEFUFFLE

GEFUFFLES > GEFUFFLE

GEFULLTE adj as in gefullte fish dish of fish stuffed with various ingredients

GEGGIE Scottish, esp Glaswegian, slang word for the > MOUTH

GEGGIES > GEGGIE

GEHLENITE n green mineral consisting of calcium aluminium silicate in tetragonal crystalline form

GEISHA n (in Japan) professional female companion for men

GEISHAS > GEISHA

GEIST n spirit

GEISTS > GEIST

GEIT n border on clothing ▷ vb put a border on (an article of clothing)

GEITED > GEIT

GEITING > GEIT

GEITS > GEIT

GEL n jelly-like substance ▷ vb form a gel

GELABLE adj capable of forming a gel

GELADA n NE African baboon

GELADAS > GELADA

GELANDE adj as in gelande jump jump made in downhill skiing

GELANT same as > GELLANT

GELANTS > GELANT

GELASTIC adj relating to laughter

GELATE vb form a gel

GELATED > GELATE

GELATES > GELATE

GELATI n layered dessert

GELATIN same as > GELATINE

GELATINE n substance made by boiling animal bones

GELATINES > GELATINE

GELATING > GELATE

GELATINS > GELATIN

GELATION n act or process of freezing a liquid

GELATIONS > GELATION

GELATIS > GELATI

GELATO n Italian frozen dessert, similar to ice cream

GELATOS > GELATO

GELCAP n medicine enclosed in gelatine

GELCAPS > GELCAP

GELCOAT n thin layer of gel or resin applied to the surface

GELCOATS > GELCOAT

GELD vb castrate ▷ n tax on land in Anglo-Saxon and Norman England

GELDED > GELD

GELDER > GELD

GELDERS > GELD

GELDING > GELD

GELDINGS > GELD

GELDS > GELD

GELEE n jelly

GELEES > GELEE

GELID adj very cold, icy, or frosty

GELIDER > GELID**

g

GELIDEST > GELID
GELIDITY > GELID
GELIDLY > GELID
GELIDNESS > GELID
GELIGNITE n type of dynamite used for blasting
GELLANT n compound that forms a solid structure
GELLANTS > GELLANT
GELLED > GEL
GELLIES > GELLY
GELLING > GEL
GELLY same as > GELIGNITE
GELOSIES > GELOSY
GELOSY Spenserian spelling of > JEALOUSY
GELS > GEL
GELSEMIA > GELSEMIUM
GELSEMINE n alkaloid obtained from gelsemium
GELSEMIUM n type of climbing shrub of SE Asia and North America, esp the yellow jasmine
GELT > GELD
GELTS > GELD
GEM n precious stone or jewel ▷ vb set or ornament with gems
GEMATRIA n numerology of the Hebrew language and alphabet
GEMATRIAS > GEMATRIA
GEMCLIP n paperclip
GEMCLIPS > GEMCLIP
GEMEL n in heraldry, parallel bars
GEMELS > GEMEL
GEMFISH n Australian food fish with a delicate flavour
GEMFISHES > GEMFISH
GEMINAL adj occurring in pairs
GEMINALLY > GEMINAL
GEMINATE adj combined in pairs ▷ vb arrange or be arranged in pairs
GEMINATED > GEMINATE
GEMINATES > GEMINATE
GEMINI n expression of surprise
GEMINIES > GEMINY
GEMINOUS adj in pairs
GEMINY n pair
GEMLIKE > GEM
GEMMA n reproductive structure in liverworts, mosses, etc
GEMMAE > GEMMA
GEMMAN dialect form of > GENTLEMAN
GEMMATE adj (of some plants and animals) having gemmae ▷ vb produce or reproduce by gemmae
GEMMATED > GEMMATE
GEMMATES > GEMMATE
GEMMATING > GEMMATE
GEMMATION > GEMMATE

GEMMATIVE adj relating to gemmation
GEMMED > GEM
GEMMEN > GEMMAN
GEMMEOUS adj gem-like
GEMMERIES > GEMMERY
GEMMERY n gems collectively
GEMMIER > GEM
GEMMIEST > GEM
GEMMILY > GEM
GEMMINESS > GEM
GEMMING > GEM
GEMMOLOGY same as > GEMOLOGY
GEMMULE n result of asexual reproduction by sponges
GEMMULES > GEMMULE
GEMMY > GEM
GEMOLOGY n branch of mineralogy that is concerned with gems and gemstones
GEMONY same as > JIMINY
GEMOT n (in Anglo-Saxon England) a legal or administrative assembly
GEMOTE same as > GEMOT
GEMOTES > GEMOTE
GEMOTS > GEMOT
GEMS > GEM
GEMSBOK same as > ORYX
GEMSBOKS > GEMSBOK
GEMSBUCK same as > ORYX
GEMSBUCKS > GEMSBUCK
GEMSHORN n type of medieval flute
GEMSHORNS > GEMSHORN
GEMSTONE n precious or semiprecious stone, esp one which has been cut and polished
GEMSTONES > GEMSTONE
GEMUTLICH adj having a feeling or atmosphere of warmth and friendliness
GEN n information ▷ vb gain information
GENA n cheek
GENAL > GENA
GENAPPE n smooth worsted yarn used for braid, etc
GENAPPES > GENAPPE
GENAS > GENA
GENDARME n member of the French police force
GENDARMES > GENDARME
GENDER n state of being male or female ▷ vb have sex
GENDERED > GENDER
GENDERING > GENDER
GENDERISE same as > GENDERIZE
GENDERIZE vb make distinctions according to gender in or among
GENDERS > GENDER
GENE n part of a cell
GENEALOGY n (study of) the history and descent of a family or families

GENERA > GENUS
GENERABLE adj able to be generated
GENERAL adj common or widespread ▷ n very senior army officer ▷ vb act as a general
GENERALCY n rank of general
GENERALE singular form of > GENERALIA
GENERALIA n generalities
GENERALLY adv usually
GENERALS > GENERAL
GENERANT n something that generates
GENERANTS > GENERANT
GENERATE vb produce or bring into being
GENERATED > GENERATE
GENERATES > GENERATE
GENERATOR n machine for converting mechanical energy into electrical energy
GENERIC adj of a class, group, or genus ▷ n drug, food product, etc that does not have a trademark
GENERICAL same as > GENERIC
GENERICS > GENERIC
GENEROUS adj free in giving
GENES > GENE
GENESES > GENESIS
GENESIS n beginning or origin
GENET n type of agile catlike mammal
GENETIC adj of genes or genetics
GENETICAL same as > GENETIC
GENETICS n study of heredity and variation in organisms
GENETRIX n female progenitor
GENETS > GENET
GENETTE same as > GENET
GENETTES > GENETTE
GENEVA n gin
GENEVAS > GENEVA
GENIAL adj cheerful and friendly
GENIALISE vb make genial
GENIALITY > GENIAL
GENIALIZE same as > GENIALISE
GENIALLY > GENIAL
GENIC adj of or relating to a gene or genes
GENICALLY > GENIC
GENICULAR adj of or relating to the knee
GENIE n (in fairy tales) magical wish-granting servant
GENIES > GENIE
GENII > GENIUS
GENIP same as > GENIPAP

GENIPAP n evergreen Caribbean tree
GENIPAPO n tropical American tree
GENIPAPOS > GENIPAPO
GENIPAPS > GENIPAP
GENIPS > GENIP
GENISTA n any member of the broom family
GENISTAS > GENISTA
GENISTEIN n substance found in plants, thought to fight cancer
GENITAL adj of the sexual organs or reproduction
GENITALIA same as > GENITALS
GENITALIC > GENITALIA
GENITALLY > GENITAL
GENITALS pl n external sexual organs
GENITIVAL > GENITIVE
GENITIVE n grammatical case indicating possession or association ▷ adj denoting a case of nouns, pronouns, and adjectives in inflected languages used to indicate a relation of ownership or association, usually translated by English of
GENITIVES > GENITIVE
GENITOR n biological father
GENITORS > GENITOR
GENITRIX same as > GENETRIX
GENITURE n birth
GENITURES > GENITURE
GENIUS n (person with) an exceptional ability
GENIUSES > GENIUS
GENIZAH n repository for sacred objects which may not be destroyed
GENIZAHS > GENIZAH
GENIZOT > GENIZAH
GENIZOTH > GENIZAH
GENLOCK n generator locking device ▷ vb activate a genlock
GENLOCKED > GENLOCK
GENLOCKS > GENLOCK
GENNAKER n type of sail for boats
GENNAKERS > GENNAKER
GENNED > GEN
GENNEL same as > GINNEL
GENNELS > GENNEL
GENNET n female donkey or ass
GENNETS > GENNET
GENNIES > GENNY
GENNING > GEN
GENNY same as > GENOA
GENOA n large triangular jib sail
GENOAS > GENOA
GENOCIDAL > GENOCIDE
GENOCIDE n murder of a race of people
GENOCIDES > GENOCIDE

g

GENOGRAM n expanded family tree

GENOGRAMS > GENOGRAM

GENOISE n rich sponge cake

GENOISES > GENOISE

GENOM same as > GENOME

GENOME n all genetic material within an organism

GENOMES > GENOME

GENOMIC > GENOME

GENOMICS n branch of molecular genetics concerned with the study of genomes

GENOMS > GENOM

GENOTOXIC adj harmful to genetic material

GENOTYPE n genetic constitution of an organism

GENOTYPES > GENOTYPE

GENOTYPIC > GENOTYPE

GENRE n style of literary, musical, or artistic work

GENRES > GENRE

GENRO n group of Japanese statesmen

GENROS > GENRO

GENS n (in ancient Rome) a group of aristocratic families

GENSENG same as > GINSENG

GENSENGS > GENSENG

GENT n gentleman

GENTEEL adj affectedly proper and polite

GENTEELER > GENTEEL

GENTEELLY > GENTEEL

GENTES > GENS

GENTIAN n mountain plant with deep blue flowers

GENTIANS > GENTIAN

GENTIER > GENTY

GENTIEST > GENTY

GENTIL adj gentle

GENTILE n non-Jewish person ▷ adj used to designate a place or the inhabitants of a place

GENTILES > GENTILE

GENTILIC adj tribal

GENTILISE vb live like a gentile

GENTILISH adj heathenish

GENTILISM n heathenism

GENTILITY n noble birth or ancestry

GENTILIZE same as > GENTILISE

GENTLE adj mild or kindly ▷ vb tame or subdue (a horse) ▷ n maggot, esp when used as bait in fishing

GENTLED > GENTLE

GENTLEMAN n polite well-bred man

GENTLEMEN > GENTLEMAN

GENTLER > GENTLE

GENTLES > GENTLE

GENTLEST > GENTLE

GENTLING > GENTLE

GENTLY > GENTLE

GENTOO n grey-backed penguin

GENTOOS > GENTOO

GENTRICE n high birth

GENTRICES > GENTRICE

GENTRIES > GENTRY

GENTRIFY vb change the character of a neighbourhood by restoring property or introducing amenities that appeal to the middle classes

GENTRY n term for people just below the nobility in social rank

GENTS n men's public toilet

GENTY adj neat

GENU n any knee-like bend in a structure or part

GENUA > GENU

GENUFLECT vb bend the knee as a sign of reverence or deference

GENUINE adj not fake, authentic

GENUINELY > GENUINE

GENUS n group of animals or plants

GENUSES > GENUS

GEO n (esp in Shetland) a small fjord or gully

GEOBOTANY n study of plants in relation to their geological habitat

GEOCACHE vb search for hidden containers using GPS as a recreational activity

GEOCACHED > GEOCACHE

GEOCACHER n person who participates in geocaching

GEOCACHES > GEOCACHE

GEOCARPIC > GEOCARPY

GEOCARPY n ripening of fruits below ground, as occurs in the peanut

GEOCODE vb assign geographical coordinates to a physical location using a digital code

GEOCODED > GEOCODE

GEOCODES > GEOCODE

GEOCODING > GEOCODE

GEOCORONA n outer layer of earth's atmosphere

GEODATA n information about geographical location held in a digital format

GEODE n cavity within a rock mass or nodule

GEODES > GEODE

GEODESIC adj of the geometry of curved surfaces ▷ n shortest line between two points on a curve

GEODESICS > GEODESIC

GEODESIES > GEODESY

GEODESIST > GEODESY

GEODESY n study of the shape and size of the earth

GEODETIC same as > GEODESIC

GEODETICS same as > GEODETIC

GEODIC > GEODE

GEODUCK n king clam

GEODUCKS > GEODUCK

GEOFACT n rock shaped by natural forces

GEOFACTS > GEOFACT

GEOGENIES > GEOGENY

GEOGENY same as > GEOGONY

GEOGNOSES > GEOGNOSY

GEOGNOSIS same as > GEOGNOSY

GEOGNOST > GEOGNOSY

GEOGNOSTS > GEOGNOSY

GEOGNOSY n study of the origin and distribution of minerals and rocks in the earth's crust: superseded generally by the term 'geology'

GEOGONIC > GEOGONY

GEOGONIES > GEOGONY

GEOGONY n science of the earth's formation

GEOGRAPHY n study of the earth's physical features, climate, population, etc

GEOID n hypothetical surface

GEOIDAL > GEOID

GEOIDS > GEOID

GEOLATRY n worship of the earth

GEOLOGER > GEOLOGY

GEOLOGERS > GEOLOGY

GEOLOGIAN > GEOLOGY

GEOLOGIC > GEOLOGY

GEOLOGIES > GEOLOGY

GEOLOGISE same as > GEOLOGIZE

GEOLOGIST > GEOLOGY

GEOLOGIZE vb study the geological features of (an area)

GEOLOGY n study of the earth

GEOMANCER > GEOMANCY

GEOMANCY n prophecy from the pattern made when a handful of earth is cast down or dots are drawn at random and connected with lines

GEOMANT n geomancer

GEOMANTIC > GEOMANCY

GEOMANTS > GEOMANT

GEOMATICS n branch of science dealing with the collection, storage, and analysis of geographical data

GEOMETER n person who is practised in or who studies geometry

GEOMETERS > GEOMETER

GEOMETRIC adj of geometry

GEOMETRID n type of moth, the larvae of which are called measuring worms, inchworms, or loopers

GEOMETRY n branch of mathematics dealing with points, lines, curves, and surfaces

GEOMYOID adj relating to burrowing rodents of the genus Geomys

GEONOMICS n doctrine holding that those things found in nature belong to no one person but instead belong equally to all

GEOPHAGIA same as > GEOPHAGY

GEOPHAGY n practice of eating earth, clay, chalk, etc, found in some primitive tribes

GEOPHILIC adj soil-loving

GEOPHONE n device for recording seismic movement

GEOPHONES > GEOPHONE

GEOPHYTE n perennial plant that propagates by means of buds below the soil surface

GEOPHYTES > GEOPHYTE

GEOPHYTIC > GEOPHYTE

GEOPONIC adj of or relating to agriculture, esp as a science

GEOPONICS n science of agriculture

GEOPROBE n probing device used for sampling soil

GEOPROBES > GEOPROBE

GEORGETTE n fine silky fabric

GEORGIC adj agricultural ▷ n poem about rural or agricultural life

GEORGICAL same as > GEORGIC

GEORGICS > GEORGIC

GEOS > GEO

GEOSPHERE n the rigid outer layer of the earth

GEOSTATIC adj denoting or relating to the pressure exerted by a mass of rock or a similar substance

GEOTACTIC > GEOTAXIS

GEOTAG n geographical co-ordinates digitally applied to data ▷ vb apply a geotag to data

GEOTAGGED > GEOTAG

GEOTAGS > GEOTAG

GEOTAXES > GEOTAXIS

GEOTAXIS n movement of an organism in response to the stimulus of gravity

GEOTHERM n line or surface within or on the

earth connecting points of equal temperature

GEOTHERMS > GEOTHERM

GEOTROPIC *adj* of geotropism: the response of a plant to the stimulus of gravity

GER *n* portable Mongolian dwelling

GERAH *n* ancient Hebrew unit of weight

GERAHS > GERAH

GERANIAL *n* cis- isomer of citral

GERANIALS > GERANIAL

GERANIOL *n* colourless or pale yellow terpine alcohol with an odour of roses, found in many essential oils: used in perfumery

GERANIOLS > GERANIOL

GERANIUM *n* cultivated plant with red, pink, or white flowers

GERANIUMS > GERANIUM

GERARDIA *n* any plant of the genus Gerardia

GERARDIAS > GERARDIA

GERBE *same as* > GARBE

GERBERA *n* type of plant

GERBERAS > GERBERA

GERBES > GARBE

GERBIL *n* burrowing desert rodent of Asia and Africa

GERBILLE *same as* > GERBIL

GERBILLES > GERBILLE

GERBILS > GERBIL

GERE *Spenserian spelling of* > GEAR

GERENT *n* person who rules or manages

GERENTS > GERENT

GERENUK *n* slender antelope

GERENUKS > GERENUK

GERES > GEAR

GERFALCON *same as* > GYRFALCON

GERIATRIC *n* derogatory term for old person ▷ *adj* of geriatrics or old people

GERLE *Spenserian spelling of* > GIRL

GERLES > GERLE

GERM *n* microbe, esp one causing disease ▷ *vb* sprout

GERMAIN *same as* > GERMEN

GERMAINE *same as* > GERMEN

GERMAINES > GERMAINE

GERMAINS > GERMAIN

GERMAN *n* type of dance ▷ *adj* having the same parents as oneself

GERMANDER *n* type of plant

GERMANE *adj* relevant

GERMANELY > GERMANE

GERMANIC *adj* of or containing germanium in the tetravalent state

GERMANISE *same as* > GERMANIZE

GERMANITE *n* mineral consisting of a complex copper arsenic sulphide containing germanium, gallium, iron, zinc, and lead: an ore of germanium and gallium

GERMANIUM *n* brittle grey element that is a semiconductor

GERMANIZE *vb* adopt or cause to adopt German customs, speech, institutions, etc

GERMANOUS *adj* of or containing germanium in the divalent state

GERMANS > GERMAN

GERMED > GERM

GERMEN *n* cells that gives rise to the germ cells

GERMENS > GERMEN

GERMFREE > GERM

GERMICIDE *n* substance that kills germs

GERMIER > GERMY

GERMIEST > GERMY

GERMIN *same as* > GERMEN

GERMINA > GERMEN

GERMINAL *adj* of or in the earliest stage of development

GERMINANT *adj* in the process of germinating

GERMINATE *vb* (cause to) sprout or begin to grow

GERMINESS > GERMY

GERMING > GERM

GERMINS > GERMIN

GERMLIKE > GERM

GERMPLASM *n* plant genetic material

GERMPROOF *adj* protected against the penetration of germs

GERMS > GERM

GERMY *adj* full of germs

GERNE *vb* grin

GERNED > GERNE

GERNES > GERNE

GERNING > GERNE

GERONIMO *interj* shout given by US paratroopers as they jump into battle

GERONTIC *adj* of or relating to the senescence of an organism

GEROPIGA *n* grape syrup used to sweeten inferior port wines

GEROPIGAS > GEROPIGA

GERS > GER

GERT *adv* in dialect, great or very big

GERTCHA *interj* get out of here!

GERUND *n* noun formed from a verb

GERUNDIAL > GERUND

GERUNDIVE *n* (in Latin grammar) an adjective formed from a verb, expressing the desirability of the activity denoted by the verb ▷ *adj* of or relating to the gerund or gerundive

GERUNDS > GERUND

GESNERIA *n* S American plant grown as a greenhouse plant for its large leaves and showy brightly-coloured flowers

GESNERIAD > GESNERIA

GESNERIAS > GESNERIA

GESSAMINE *another word for* > JASMINE

GESSE *Spenserian spelling of* > GUESS

GESSED > GESSE

GESSES > GESSE

GESSING > GESSE

GESSO *n* plaster used for painting or in sculpture ▷ *vb* apply gesso to

GESSOED > GESSO

GESSOES > GESSO

GEST *n* notable deed or exploit

GESTALT *n* perceptual pattern or structure

GESTALTEN > GESTALT

GESTALTS > GESTALT

GESTANT *adj* laden

GESTAPO *n* any secret state police organization

GESTAPOS > GESTAPO

GESTATE *vb* carry (young) in the uterus during pregnancy

GESTATED > GESTATE

GESTATES > GESTATE

GESTATING > GESTATE

GESTATION *n* (period of) carrying of young in the womb between conception and birth

GESTATIVE > GESTATION

GESTATORY > GESTATION

GESTE *same as* > GEST

GESTES > GESTE

GESTIC *adj* consisting of gestures

GESTICAL > GESTIC

GESTS > GEST

GESTURAL > GESTURE

GESTURE *n* movement to convey meaning ▷ *vb* gesticulate

GESTURED > GESTURE

GESTURER > GESTURE

GESTURERS > GESTURE

GESTURES > GESTURE

GESTURING > GESTURE

GET *vb* obtain or receive

GETA *n* type of Japanese wooden sandal

GETABLE > GET

GETAS > GETA

GETATABLE *adj* accessible

GETAWAY *n* used in escape

GETAWAYS > GETAWAY

GETOUT *n* excuse to get out of doing something

GETOUTS > GETOUT

GETS > GET

GETTABLE > GET

GETTER *n* person or thing that gets ▷ *vb* remove (a gas) by the action of a getter

GETTERED > GETTER

GETTERING > GETTER

GETTERS > GETTER

GETTING > GET

GETTINGS > GET

GETUP *n* outfit

GETUPS > GETUP

GEUM *n* type of herbaceous plant

GEUMS > GEUM

GEWGAW *n* showy but valueless trinket ▷ *adj* showy and valueless

GEWGAWED *adj* decorated gaudily

GEWGAWS > GEWGAW

GEY *adv* extremely ▷ *adj* gallant

GEYAN *adv* somewhat

GEYER > GEY

GEYEST > GEY

GEYSER *n* spring that discharges steam and hot water ▷ *vb* erupt like a geyser

GEYSERED > GEYSER

GEYSERING > GEYSER

GEYSERITE *n* mineral form of hydrated silica resembling opal, deposited from the waters of geysers and hot springs

GEYSERS > GEYSER

GHARIAL *same as* > GAVIAL

GHARIALS > GHARIAL

GHARRI *same as* > GHARRY

GHARRIES > GHARRY

GHARRIS > GHARRI

GHARRY *n* (in India) horse-drawn vehicle

GHAST *vb* terrify

GHASTED > GHAST

GHASTFUL *adj* dismal

GHASTING > GHAST

GHASTLIER > GHASTLY

GHASTLY *adj* unpleasant ▷ *adv* unhealthily

GHASTNESS *n* dread

GHASTS > GHAST

GHAT *n* (in India) steps leading down to a river

GHATS > GHAT

GHAUT *n* small cleft in a hill

GHAUTS > GHAUT

GHAZAL *n* Arabic love poem

GHAZALS > GHAZAL

GHAZEL *same as* > GHAZAL

GHAZELS > GHAZEL

GHAZI *n* Muslim fighter against infidels

GHAZIES > GHAZI

GHAZIS > GHAZI

GHEE n (in Indian cookery) clarified butter
GHEES > GHEE
GHERAO n form of industrial action in India ▷ vb trap an employer in his office, to indicate the workforce's discontent
GHERAOED > GHERAO
GHERAOES > GHERAO
GHERAOING > GHERAO
GHERAOS > GHERAO
GHERKIN n small pickled cucumber
GHERKINS > GHERKIN
GHESSE Spenserian spelling of > GUESS
GHESSED > GHESSE
GHESSES > GHESSE
GHESSING > GHESSE
GHEST > GHESSE
GHETTO n slum area inhabited by a deprived minority ▷ vb ghettoize
GHETTOED > GHETTO
GHETTOES > GHETTO
GHETTOING > GHETTO
GHETTOISE same as > GHETTOIZE
GHETTOIZE vb confine (someone or something) to a particular area or category
GHETTOS > GHETTO
GHI same as > GHEE
GHIBLI n fiercely hot wind of North Africa
GHIBLIS > GHIBLI
GHILGAI same as > GILGAI
GHILGAIS > GHILGAI
GHILLIE n type of tongueless shoe ▷ vb act as a g(h)illie
GHILLIED > GHILLIE
GHILLIES > GHILLIE
GHILLYING > GHILLIE
GHIS > GHI
GHOST n disembodied spirit of a dead person ▷ vb ghostwrite
GHOSTED > GHOST
GHOSTIER > GHOSTY
GHOSTIEST > GHOSTY
GHOSTING > GHOST
GHOSTINGS > GHOST
GHOSTLIER > GHOSTLY
GHOSTLIKE > GHOST
GHOSTLY adj frightening in appearance or effect
GHOSTS > GHOST
GHOSTY adj pertaining to ghosts
GHOUL n person with morbid interests
GHOULIE n goblin
GHOULIES > GHOULIE
GHOULISH adj of or relating to ghouls
GHOULS > GHOUL
GHRELIN n hormone that stimulates appetite
GHRELINS > GHRELIN

GHUBAR adj as in ghubar numeral type of numeral
GHYLL same as > GILL
GHYLLS > GHYLL
GI n white suit worn in martial arts
GIAMBEUX n jambeaux; leg armour
GIANT n mythical being of superhuman size ▷ adj huge
GIANTESS same as > GIANT
GIANTHOOD n condition of being a giant
GIANTISM same as > GIGANTISM
GIANTISMS > GIANTISM
GIANTLIER > GIANTLY
GIANTLIKE > GIANT
GIANTLY adj giantlike
GIANTRIES > GIANTRY
GIANTRY n collective term for giants
GIANTS > GIANT
GIANTSHIP n style of address for a giant
GIAOUR n derogatory term for a non-Muslim, esp a Christian, used esp by the Turks
GIAOURS > GIAOUR
GIARDIA n species of parasite
GIARDIAS > GIARDIA
GIB n metal wedge, pad, or thrust bearing ▷ vb fasten or supply with a gib
GIBBED > GIB
GIBBER vb speak or utter rapidly and unintelligibly ▷ n boulder
GIBBERED > GIBBER
GIBBERING > GIBBER
GIBBERISH n rapid unintelligible talk
GIBBERS > GIBBER
GIBBET n gallows for displaying executed criminals ▷ vb put to death by hanging on a gibbet
GIBBETED > GIBBET
GIBBETING > GIBBET
GIBBETS > GIBBET
GIBBETTED > GIBBET
GIBBING > GIB
GIBBON n agile tree-dwelling ape of S Asia
GIBBONS > GIBBON
GIBBOSE same as > GIBBOUS
GIBBOSITY n state of being gibbous
GIBBOUS adj (of the moon) between half and fully illuminated
GIBBOUSLY > GIBBOUS
GIBBSITE n mineral consisting of hydrated aluminium oxide
GIBBSITES > GIBBSITE
GIBE vb make jeering or scoffing remarks (at)

▷ n derisive or provoking remark
GIBED > GIBE
GIBEL n Prussian carp
GIBELS > GIBEL
GIBER > GIBE
GIBERS > GIBE
GIBES > GIBE
GIBING > GIBE
GIBINGLY > GIBE
GIBLET > GIBLETS
GIBLETS pl n gizzard, liver, heart, and neck of a fowl
GIBLI same as > GHIBLI
GIBLIS > GIBLI
GIBS > GIB
GIBSON n martini garnished with onion
GIBSONS > GIBSON
GIBUS n collapsible top hat
GIBUSES > GIBUS
GID n disease of sheep
GIDDAP interj exclamation used to make a horse go faster
GIDDAY interj expression of greeting
GIDDIED > GIDDY
GIDDIER > GIDDY
GIDDIES > GIDDY
GIDDIEST > GIDDY
GIDDILY > GIDDY
GIDDINESS > GIDDY
GIDDUP same as > GIDDYUP
GIDDY adj having or causing a feeling of dizziness ▷ vb make giddy
GIDDYAP same as > GIDDYUP
GIDDYING > GIDDY
GIDDYUP interj exclamation used to make a horse go faster
GIDGEE n small acacia tree
GIDGEES > GIDGEE
GIDJEE same as > GIDGEE
GIDJEES > GIDJEE
GIDS > GID
GIE Scot word for > GIVE
GIED > GIVE
GIEING > GIVE
GIEN > GIVE
GIES > GIVE
GIF n file held in GIF format
GIFS > GIF
GIFT n present ▷ vb make a present of
GIFTABLE adj suitable as gift ▷ n something suitable as gift
GIFTABLES > GIFTABLE
GIFTED adj talented
GIFTEDLY > GIFTED
GIFTEE n person given a gift
GIFTEES > GIFTEE
GIFTING n act of gifting
GIFTINGS > GIFTING
GIFTLESS > GIFT

GIFTS > GIFT
GIFTSHOP n shop selling articles suitable for gifts
GIFTSHOPS > GIFTSHOP
GIFTWARE n anything that may be given as a present
GIFTWARES > GIFTWARE
GIFTWRAP vb wrap (a gift) in decorative wrapping paper
GIFTWRAPS > GIFTWRAP
GIG n single performance by pop or jazz musicians ▷ vb play a gig or gigs
GIGA same as > GIGUE
GIGABIT n unit of information in computing
GIGABITS > GIGABIT
GIGABYTE n one thousand and twenty-four megabytes
GIGABYTES > GIGABYTE
GIGACYCLE same as > GIGAHERTZ
GIGAFLOP n measure of processing speed, consisting of a thousand million floating-point operations a second
GIGAFLOPS > GIGAFLOP
GIGAHERTZ n unit of frequency equal to 10^9 hertz
GIGANTEAN adj gigantic
GIGANTIC adj enormous
GIGANTISM n excessive growth of the entire body, caused by overproduction of growth hormone by the pituitary gland during childhood or adolescence
GIGAS > GIGA
GIGATON n unit of explosive force
GIGATONS > GIGATON
GIGAWATT n unit of power equal to 1 billion watts
GIGAWATTS > GIGAWATT
GIGGED > GIG
GIGGING > GIG
GIGGIT vb move quickly
GIGGITED > GIGGIT
GIGGITING > GIGGIT
GIGGITS > GIGGIT
GIGGLE vb laugh nervously or foolishly ▷ n such a laugh
GIGGLED > GIGGLE
GIGGLER > GIGGLE
GIGGLERS > GIGGLE
GIGGLES > GIGGLE
GIGGLIER > GIGGLE
GIGGLIEST > GIGGLE
GIGGLING > GIGGLE
GIGGLINGS > GIGGLE
GIGGLY > GIGGLE
GIGHE > GIGA
GIGLET n flighty girl
GIGLETS > GIGLET
GIGLOT same as > GIGLET
GIGLOTS > GIGLOT
GIGMAN n one who places great importance on respectability
GIGMANITY > GIGMAN

GIGMEN > GIGMAN
GIGOLO n man paid by an older woman to be her escort or lover
GIGOLOS > GIGOLO
GIGOT n leg of lamb or mutton
GIGOTS > GIGOT
GIGS > GIG
GIGUE n piece of music incorporated into the classical suite
GIGUES > GIGUE
GILA n large venomous brightly coloured lizard
GILAS > GILA
GILBERT n unit of magnetomotive force
GILBERTS > GILBERT
GILCUP same as > GILTCUP
GILCUPS > GILCUP
GILD vb put a thin layer of gold on
GILDED > GILD
GILDEN adj gilded
GILDER > GILD
GILDERS > GILD
GILDHALL same as > GUILDHALL
GILDHALLS > GILDHALL
GILDING > GILD
GILDINGS > GILD
GILDS > GILD
GILDSMAN > GILD
GILDSMEN > GILD
GILET n waist- or hip-length garment
GILETS > GILET
GILGAI n natural water hole
GILGAIS > GILGAI
GILGIE n type of freshwater crayfish
GILGIES > GILGIE
GILL n radiating structure beneath the cap of a mushroom ▷ vb catch (fish) or (of fish) to be caught in a gill net
GILLAROO n type of brown trout
GILLAROOS > GILLAROO
GILLED > GILL
GILLER > GILL
GILLERS > GILL
GILLET n mare
GILLETS > GILLET
GILLFLIRT n flirtatious woman
GILLIE n (in Scotland) attendant for hunting or fishing ▷ vb act as a gillie
GILLIED > GILLIE
GILLIES > GILLY
GILLING > GILL
GILLION n (no longer in technical use) one thousand million
GILLIONS > GILLION
GILLNET n net designed to catch fish by the gills ▷ vb fish using a gillnet

GILLNETS > GILLNET
GILLS pl n breathing organs in fish and other water creatures
GILLY vb act as a gillie
GILLYING > GILLY
GILLYVOR n type of carnation
GILLYVORS > GILLYVOR
GILPEY n mischievous, frolicsome boy or girl
GILPEYS > GILPEY
GILPIES > GILPEY
GILPY same as > GILPEY
GILRAVAGE vb make merry, especially to excess
GILSONITE n very pure form of asphalt found in Utah and Colorado
GILT > GILD
GILTCUP n buttercup
GILTCUPS > GILTCUP
GILTHEAD n type of fish of Mediterranean and European Atlantic waters, with a gold-coloured band between the eyes
GILTHEADS > GILTHEAD
GILTS > GILD
GILTWOOD adj made of wood and gilded
GIMBAL vb support on gimbals
GIMBALED > GIMBAL
GIMBALING > GIMBAL
GIMBALLED > GIMBAL
GIMBALS pl n set of pivoted rings
GIMCRACK adj showy but cheap ▷ n cheap showy trifle or gadget
GIMCRACKS > GIMCRACK
GIMEL n third letter of the Hebrew alphabet
GIMELS > GIMEL
GIMLET n small tool ▷ adj penetrating or piercing ▷ vb make holes in (wood) using a gimlet
GIMLETED > GIMLET
GIMLETING > GIMLET
GIMLETS > GIMLET
GIMMAL n ring composed of interlocking rings ▷ vb provide with gimmals
GIMMALLED > GIMMAL
GIMMALS > GIMMAL
GIMME interj give me! ▷ n term used in shot putt
GIMMER n year-old ewe
GIMMERS > GIMMER
GIMMES > GIMME
GIMMICK n something designed to attract attention ▷ vb make gimmicky
GIMMICKED > GIMMICK
GIMMICKRY > GIMMICK
GIMMICKS > GIMMICK
GIMMICKY > GIMMICK
GIMMIE n very short putt in golf
GIMMIES > GIMMIE

GIMMOR n mechanical device
GIMMORS > GIMMOR
GIMP n tapelike trimming of silk, wool, or cotton, often stiffened with wire ▷ vb derogatory term for limp
GIMPED > GIMP
GIMPIER > GIMPY
GIMPIEST > GIMPY
GIMPING > GIMP
GIMPS > GIMP
GIMPY same as > GAMMY
GIN n spirit flavoured with juniper berries ▷ vb free (cotton) of seeds with an engine; begin
GINCH same as > GITCH
GINCHES > GINCH
GING n child's catapult
GINGAL n type of musket mounted on a swivel
GINGALL same as > GINGAL
GINGALLS > GINGALL
GINGALS > GINGAL
GINGE n person with ginger hair
GINGELEY same as > GINGILI
GINGELEYS > GINGELEY
GINGELI same as > GINGILI
GINGELIES > GINGELY
GINGELIS > GINGELI
GINGELLI same as > GINGILI
GINGELLIS > GINGILI
GINGELLY same as > GINGILI
GINGELY same as > GINGILI
GINGER n root of a tropical plant, used as a spice ▷ adj light reddish-brown ▷ vb add the spice ginger to (a dish)
GINGERADE n fizzy drink flavoured with ginger
GINGERED > GINGER
GINGERING > GINGER
GINGERLY adv cautiously ▷ adj cautious
GINGEROUS adj reddish
GINGERS > GINGER
GTNGERY adj like or tasting of ginger
GINGES > GINGE
GINGHAM n cotton cloth, usu checked or striped
GINGHAMS > GINGHAM
GINGILI n oil obtained from sesame seeds
GINGILIS > GINGILI
GINGILLI same as > GINGILI
GINGILLIS > GINGILLI
GINGIVA same as > GUM
GINGIVAE > GINGIVA
GINGIVAL > GINGIVA
GINGKO same as > GINKGO
GINGKOES > GINGKO
GINGKOS > GINGKO

GINGLE same as > JINGLE
GINGLES > GINGLE
GINGLYMI > GINGLYMUS
GINGLYMUS n hinge joint
GINGS > GING
GINHOUSE n building where cotton is ginned
GINHOUSES > GINHOUSE
GINK n man or boy
GINKGO n ornamental Chinese tree
GINKGOES > GINKGO
GINKGOS > GINKGO
GINKS > GINK
GINN same as > JINN
GINNED > GIN
GINNEL n narrow passageway between buildings
GINNELS > GINNEL
GINNER > GIN
GINNERIES > GINHOUSE
GINNERS > GIN
GINNERY another word for > GINHOUSE
GINNIER > GINNY
GINNIEST > GINNY
GINNING > GIN
GINNINGS > GIN
GINNY adj relating to the spirit gin
GINORMOUS adj very large
GINS > GIN
GINSENG n (root of) a plant
GINSENGS > GINSENG
GINSHOP n tavern
GINSHOPS > GINSHOP
GINZO n disparaging term for person of Italian descent
GINZOES > GINZO
GINZOS > GINZO
GIO same as > GEO
GIOCOSO adv (of music) to be expressed joyfully or playfully
GIOS > GIO
GIP same as > GYP
GIPON another word for > JUPON
GIPONS > GIPON
GIPPED > GIP
GIPPER > GIP
GIPPERS > GIP
GIPPIES > GIPPY
GIPPING > GIP
GIPPO same as > GIPPY
GIPPOES > GIPPO
GIPPOS > GIPPO
GIPPY n starling
GIPS > GIP
GIPSEN obsolete word for > GYPSY
GIPSENS > GIPSEN
GIPSIED > GIPSY
GIPSIES > GIPSY
GIPSY n member of a nomadic people ▷ vb live like a gypsy
GIPSYDOM > GIPSY
GIPSYDOMS > GIPSY
GIPSYHOOD > GIPSY

g

GIPSYING > GIPSY

GIPSYISH > GIPSY

GIPSYISM n gipsy custom

GIPSYISMS > GIPSYISM

GIPSYWORT n hairy Eurasian plant with two-lipped white flowers with purple dots on the lower lip

GIRAFFE n African ruminant mammal

GIRAFFES > GIRAFFE

GIRAFFID adj giraffe-like ▷ n member of the Giraffidae family

GIRAFFIDS > GIRAFFID

GIRAFFINE adj relating to a giraffe

GIRAFFISH > GIRAFFE

GIRAFFOID adj giraffe-like

GIRANDOLA same as > GIRANDOLE

GIRANDOLE n ornamental branched wall candleholder, usually incorporating a mirror

GIRASOL n type of opal

GIRASOLE same as > GIRASOL

GIRASOLES > GIRASOLE

GIRASOLS > GIRASOL

GIRD vb put a belt round ▷ n blow or stroke

GIRDED > GIRD

GIRDER n large metal beam

GIRDERS > GIRDER

GIRDING > GIRD

GIRDINGLY > GIRD

GIRDINGS > GIRD

GIRDLE n woman's elastic corset ▷ vb surround or encircle

GIRDLED > GIRDLE

GIRDLER n person or thing that girdles

GIRDLERS > GIRDLER

GIRDLES > GIRDLE

GIRDLING > GIRDLE

GIRDS > GIRD

GIRKIN same as > GHERKIN

GIRKINS > GIRKIN

GIRL n female child

GIRLHOOD n state or time of being a girl

GIRLHOODS > GIRLHOOD

GIRLIE adj (of a magazine, etc) featuring pictures of naked women ▷ n little girl

GIRLIER > GIRLY

GIRLIES > GIRLIE

GIRLIEST > GIRLY

GIRLISH adj of or like a girl in looks, behaviour, innocence, etc

GIRLISHLY > GIRLISH

GIRLOND obsolete word for > GARLAND

GIRLONDS > GIRLOND

GIRLS > GIRL

GIRLY same as > GIRLIE

GIRN vb snarl

GIRNED > GIRN

GIRNEL n large chest for storing meal

GIRNELS > GIRNEL

GIRNER > GIRN

GIRNIE adj peevish

GIRNIER > GIRNIE

GIRNIEST > GIRNIE

GIRNING > GIRN

GIRNS > GIRN

GIRO n system of transferring money

GIROLLE n chanterelle mushroom

GIROLLES > GIROLLE

GIRON n part of a heraldic shield

GIRONIC > GIRON

GIRONNY adj divided into segments from the fesse point

GIRONS > GIRON

GIROS > GIRO

GIROSOL same as > GIRASOL

GIROSOLS > GIROSOL

GIRR same as > GIRD

GIRRS > GIRR

GIRSH n currency unit of Saudi Arabia

GIRSHES > GIRSH

GIRT vb gird; bind

GIRTED > GIRT

GIRTH n measurement round something ▷ vb fasten a girth on (a horse)

GIRTHED > GIRTH

GIRTHING > GIRTH

GIRTHLINE same as > GIRTLINE

GIRTHS > GIRTH

GIRTING > GIRD

GIRTLINE n gantline

GIRTLINES > GIRTLINE

GIRTS > GIRT

GIS > GI

GISARME n long-shafted battle-axe

GISARMES > GISARME

GISM n semen

GISMO same as > GIZMO

GISMOLOGY same as > GIZMOLOGY

GISMOS > GISMO

GISMS > GISM

GIST n substance or main point of a matter

GISTS > GIST

GIT n contemptible person ▷ vb dialect version of get

GITANA n female gypsy

GITANAS > GITANA

GITANO n male gypsy

GITANOS > GITANO

GITCH n underwear

GITCHES > GITCH

GITE n self-catering holiday cottage for let in France

GITES > GITE

GITS > GIT

GITTARONE n acoustic bass guitar

GITTED > GIT

GITTERN n obsolete medieval instrument ▷ vb play the gittern

GITTERNED > GITTERN

GITTERNS > GITTERN

GITTIN n Jewish divorce

GITTING > GIT

GIUST same as > JOUST

GIUSTED > GIUST

GIUSTING > GIUST

GIUSTO adv as observed strictly

GIUSTS > GIUST

GIVABLE > GIVE

GIVE vb present (something) to another person ▷ n resilience or elasticity

GIVEABLE > GIVE

GIVEAWAY n something that reveals hidden feelings or intentions ▷ adj very cheap or free

GIVEAWAYS > GIVEAWAY

GIVEBACK n reduction in wages in return for some other benefit, in time of recession

GIVEBACKS > GIVEBACK

GIVED same as > GYVED

GIVEN n assumed fact

GIVENNESS n condition of being given

GIVENS > GIVEN

GIVER > GIVE

GIVERS > GIVE

GIVES > GIVE

GIVING > GIVE

GIVINGS > GIVE

GIZMO n device

GIZMOLOGY n study of gadgets

GIZMOS > GIZMO

GIZZ n wig

GIZZARD n part of a bird's stomach

GIZZARDS > GIZZARD

GIZZEN vb (of wood) to warp

GIZZENED > GIZZEN

GIZZENING > GIZZEN

GIZZENS > GIZZEN

GIZZES > GIZZ

GJETOST n type of Norwegian cheese

GJETOSTS > GJETOST

GJU n type of violin used in Shetland

GJUS > GJU

GLABELLA n smooth elevation of the frontal bone just above the bridge of the nose: a reference point in physical anthropology or craniometry

GLABELLAE > GLABELLA

GLABELLAR > GLABELLA

GLABRATE same as > GLABROUS

GLABROUS adj without hair or a similar growth

GLACE adj preserved in a thick sugary syrup ▷ vb ice or candy (cakes, fruits, etc)

GLACED > GLACE

GLACEED > GLACE

GLACEING > GLACE

GLACES > GLACE

GLACIAL adj of ice or glaciers ▷ n ice age

GLACIALLY > GLACIAL

GLACIALS > GLACIAL

GLACIATE vb cover or become covered with glaciers or masses of ice

GLACIATED > GLACIATE

GLACIATES > GLACIATE

GLACIER n slow-moving mass of ice

GLACIERED adj having a glacier or glaciers

GLACIERS > GLACIER

GLACIS n slight incline

GLACISES > GLACIS

GLAD adj pleased and happy ▷ vb become glad ▷ n gladiolus

GLADDED > GLAD

GLADDEN vb make glad

GLADDENED > GLADDEN

GLADDENER > GLADDEN

GLADDENS > GLADDEN

GLADDER > GLAD

GLADDEST > GLAD

GLADDIE same as > GLAD

GLADDIES > GLADDIE

GLADDING > GLAD

GLADDONS > GLADDON

GLADE n open space in a forest

GLADELIKE > GLADE

GLADES > GLADE

GLADFUL adj full of gladness

GLADIATE adj shaped like a sword

GLADIATOR n (in ancient Rome) man trained to fight in arenas to provide entertainment

GLADIER > GLADE

GLADIEST > GLADE

GLADIOLA same as > GLADIOLUS

GLADIOLAR > GLADIOLUS

GLADIOLAS > GLADIOLA

GLADIOLE same as > GLADIOLUS

GLADIOLES > GLADIOLE

GLADIOLI > GLADIOLUS

GLADIOLUS n garden plant with sword-shaped leaves

GLADIUS n short sword used by Roman legionaries

GLADIUSES > GLADIUS

GLADLIER > GLAD

GLADLIEST > GLAD

GLADLY > GLAD

GLADNESS > GLAD

GLADS > GLAD
GLADSOME adj joyous or cheerful
GLADSOMER > GLADSOME
GLADSTONE n light four-wheeled horse-drawn vehicle
GLADWRAP n in New Zealand English, thin film for wrapping food ▷ vb cover with gladwrap
GLADWRAPS > GLADWRAP
GLADY > GLADE
GLAIK n prank
GLAIKET same as > GLAIKIT
GLAIKIT adj foolish
GLAIKS > GLAIK
GLAIR n white of egg ▷ vb apply glair to (something)
GLAIRE same as > GLAIR
GLAIRED > GLAIR
GLAIREOUS > GLAIR
GLAIRES > GLAIRE
GLAIRIER > GLAIR
GLAIRIEST > GLAIR
GLAIRIN n viscous mineral deposit
GLAIRING > GLAIR
GLAIRINS > GLAIRIN
GLAIRS > GLAIR
GLAIRY > GLAIR
GLAIVE archaic word for > SWORD
GLAIVED adj armed with a sword
GLAIVES > GLAIVE
GLAM n magical illusion ▷ vb make oneself look glamorous ▷ adj glamorous
GLAMMED > GLAM
GLAMMER > GLAM
GLAMMEST > GLAM
GLAMMIER > GLAMMY
GLAMMIEST > GLAMMY
GLAMMING > GLAM
GLAMMY adj glamorous
GLAMOR same as > GLAMOUR
GLAMORED > GLAMOR
GLAMORING > GLAMOR
GLAMORISE same as > GLAMORIZE
GLAMORIZE vb cause to be or seem glamorous
GLAMOROUS adj alluring
GLAMORS > GLAMOR
GLAMOUR n alluring charm or fascination ▷ vb bewitch
GLAMOURED adj bewitched
GLAMOURS > GLAMOUR
GLAMPING n camping with luxurious physical comforts
GLAMPINGS > GLAMPING
GLAMS > GLAM
GLANCE vb look rapidly or briefly ▷ n brief look
GLANCED > GLANCE

GLANCER n log or pole used to protect trees from damage
GLANCERS > GLANCER
GLANCES > GLANCE
GLANCING > GLANCE
GLANCINGS > GLANCE
GLAND n organ that produces and secretes substances
GLANDERED > GLANDERS
GLANDERS n highly infectious bacterial disease of horses, sometimes transmitted to man
GLANDES > GLANS
GLANDLESS > GLAND
GLANDLIKE > GLAND
GLANDS > GLAND
GLANDULAR adj of or affecting a gland or glands
GLANDULE n small gland
GLANDULES > GLANDULE
GLANS n any small rounded body or glandlike mass
GLARE vb stare angrily ▷ n angry stare ▷ adj smooth and glassy
GLAREAL adj (of a plant) growing in cultivated land
GLARED > GLARE
GLARELESS > GLARE
GLAREOUS adj resembling the white of an egg
GLARES > GLARE
GLARIER > GLARE
GLARIEST > GLARE
GLARINESS > GLARE
GLARING adj conspicuous
GLARINGLY > GLARING
GLARY > GLARE
GLASNOST n policy of openness and accountability, esp, formerly, in the USSR
GLASNOSTS > GLASNOST
GLASS n hard brittle substance ▷ vb cover with, enclose in, or fit with glass
GLASSED > GLASS
GLASSEN adj glassy
GLASSES pl n pair of lenses for correcting faulty vision
GLASSFUL n amount held by a full glass
GLASSFULS > GLASSFUL
GLASSIE same as > GLASSY
GLASSIER > GLASSY
GLASSIES > GLASSY
GLASSIEST > GLASSY
GLASSIFY vb turn into glass
GLASSILY > GLASSY
GLASSINE n glazed translucent paper used for book jackets
GLASSINES > GLASSINE
GLASSING > GLASS
GLASSLESS > GLASS
GLASSLIKE > GLASS

GLASSMAN n man whose work is making or selling glassware
GLASSMEN > GLASSMAN
GLASSWARE n articles made of glass
GLASSWORK n production of glassware
GLASSWORM n larva of gnat
GLASSWORT n type of plant of salt marshes, with fleshy stems and scalelike leaves, formerly used in glass-making
GLASSY adj like glass ▷ n glass marble
GLAUCOMA n eye disease
GLAUCOMAS > GLAUCOMA
GLAUCOUS adj covered with a bluish waxy or powdery bloom
GLAUM vb snatch
GLAUMED > GLAUM
GLAUMING > GLAUM
GLAUMS > GLAUM
GLAUR n mud or mire
GLAURIER > GLAUR
GLAURIEST > GLAUR
GLAURS > GLAUR
GLAURY > GLAUR
GLAZE vb fit or cover with glass ▷ n transparent coating
GLAZED > GLAZE
GLAZEN adj glazed
GLAZER > GLAZE
GLAZERS > GLAZE
GLAZES > GLAZE
GLAZIER n person who fits windows with glass
GLAZIERS > GLAZIER
GLAZIERY > GLAZIER
GLAZIEST > GLAZE
GLAZILY > GLAZE
GLAZINESS > GLAZE
GLAZING n surface of a glazed object
GLAZINGS > GLAZING
GLAZY > GLAZE
GLEAM n small beam or glow of light ▷ vb emit a gleam
GLEAMED > GLEAM
GLEAMER n mirror used to cheat in card games
GLEAMERS > GLEAMER
GLEAMIER > GLEAM
GLEAMIEST > GLEAM
GLEAMING > GLEAM
GLEAMINGS > GLEAM
GLEAMS > GLEAM
GLEAMY > GLEAM
GLEAN vb gather (facts etc) bit by bit
GLEANABLE > GLEAN
GLEANED > GLEAN
GLEANER > GLEAN
GLEANERS > GLEAN
GLEANING > GLEAN
GLEANINGS pl n pieces of information that have been gleaned

GLEANS > GLEAN
GLEAVE same as > SWORD
GLEAVES > GLEAVE
GLEBA n mass of spores
GLEBAE > GLEBA
GLEBE n land granted to a member of the clergy
GLEBELESS > GLEBE
GLEBES > GLEBE
GLEBIER > GLEBY
GLEBIEST > GLEBY
GLEBOUS adj gleby
GLEBY adj relating to a glebe
GLED n kite
GLEDE same as > GLED
GLEDES > GLEDE
GLEDGE vb glance sideways
GLEDGED > GLEDGE
GLEDGES > GLEDGE
GLEDGING > GLEDGE
GLEDS > GLED
GLEE n triumph and delight ▷ vb be full of glee
GLEED n burning ember or hot coal
GLEEDS > GLEED
GLEEFUL adj merry or joyful
GLEEFULLY > GLEEFUL
GLEEING > GLEE
GLEEK vb jeer
GLEEKED > GLEEK
GLEEKING > GLEEK
GLEEKS > GLEEK
GLEEMAN n minstrel
GLEEMEN > GLEEMAN
GLEENIE n guinea fowl
GLEENIES > GLEENIE
GLEES > GLEE
GLEESOME adj full of glee
GLEET n stage of chronic gonorrhoea ▷ vb discharge pus
GLEETED > GLEET
GLEETIER > GLEET
GLEETIEST > GLEET
GLEETING > GLEET
GLEETS > GLEET
GLEETY > GLEET
GLEG adj quick
GLEGGER > GLEG
GLEGGEST > GLEG
GLEGLY > GLEG
GLEGNESS > GLEG
GLEI same as > GLEY
GLEIS > GLEI
GLEN n deep narrow valley, esp in Scotland
GLENGARRY n brimless Scottish cap with a crease down the crown
GLENLIKE > GLEN
GLENOID adj resembling or having a shallow cavity ▷ n shallow cavity
GLENOIDAL > GLENOID
GLENOIDS > GLENOID
GLENS > GLEN
GLENT same as > GLINT
GLENTED > GLENT
GLENTING > GLENT

g

GLENTS > GLENT
GLEY *n* bluish-grey compact sticky soil ▷ *vb* squint
GLEYED > GLEY
GLEYING > GLEY
GLEYINGS > GLEY
GLEYS > GLEY
GLIA *n* web of tissue that supports nerve cells
GLIADIN *n* protein of cereals with a high proline content
GLIADINE *same as* **>** GLIADIN
GLIADINES > GLIADINE
GLIADINS > GLIADIN
GLIAL > GLIA
GLIAS > GLIA
GLIB *adj* fluent but insincere or superficial ▷ *vb* castrate
GLIBBED > GLIB
GLIBBER > GLIB
GLIBBERY *adj* slippery
GLIBBEST > GLIB
GLIBBING > GLIB
GLIBLY > GLIB
GLIBNESS > GLIB
GLIBS > GLIB
GLID *adj* moving smoothly and easily
GLIDDER > GLID
GLIDDERY *adj* slippery
GLIDDEST > GLID
GLIDE *vb* move easily and smoothly ▷ *n* smooth easy movement
GLIDED > GLIDE
GLIDEPATH *n* path followed by aircraft coming in to land
GLIDER *n* flying phalanger
GLIDERS > GLIDER
GLIDES > GLIDE
GLIDING *n* sport of flying gliders
GLIDINGLY > GLIDE
GLIDINGS > GLIDING
GLIFF *n* slap
GLIFFING > GLIFF
GLIFFINGS > GLIFF
GLIFFS > GLIFF
GLIFT *n* moment
GLIFTS > GLIFT
GLIKE *same as* **>** GLEEK
GLIKES > GLIKE
GLIM *n* light or lamp
GLIME *vb* glance sideways
GLIMED > GLIME
GLIMES > GLIME
GLIMING > GLIME
GLIMMER *vb* shine faintly, flicker ▷ *n* faint gleam
GLIMMERED > GLIMMER
GLIMMERS > GLIMMER
GLIMMERY > GLIMMER
GLIMPSE *n* brief or incomplete view ▷ *vb* catch a glimpse of
GLIMPSED > GLIMPSE
GLIMPSER > GLIMPSE
GLIMPSERS > GLIMPSE

GLIMPSES > GLIMPSE
GLIMPSING > GLIMPSE
GLIMS > GLIM
GLINT *vb* gleam brightly ▷ *n* bright gleam
GLINTED > GLINT
GLINTIER > GLINT
GLINTIEST > GLINT
GLINTING > GLINT
GLINTS > GLINT
GLINTY > GLINT
GLIOMA *n* tumour of the brain and spinal cord
GLIOMAS > GLIOMA
GLIOMATA > GLIOMA
GLIOSES > GLIOSIS
GLIOSIS *n* process leading to scarring in the nervous system
GLISK *n* glimpse
GLISKS > GLISK
GLISSADE *n* gliding step in ballet ▷ *vb* perform a glissade
GLISSADED > GLISSADE
GLISSADER > GLISSADE
GLISSADES > GLISSADE
GLISSANDI **>** GLISSANDO
GLISSANDO *n* slide between two notes in which all intermediate notes are played
GLISSE *n* type of dance step
GLISSES > GLISSE
GLISTEN *vb* gleam by reflecting light ▷ *n* gleam or gloss
GLISTENED > GLISTEN
GLISTENS > GLISTEN
GLISTER *archaic word for* **>** GLITTER
GLISTERED > GLISTER
GLISTERS > GLISTER
GLIT *n* slimy matter
GLITCH *n* small problem that stops something from working
GLITCHES > GLITCH
GLITCHIER > GLITCH
GLITCHY > GLITCH
GLITS > GLIT
GLITTER *vb* shine with bright flashes ▷ *n* sparkle or brilliance
GLITTERED > GLITTER
GLITTERS > GLITTER
GLITTERY > GLITTER
GLITZ *n* ostentatious showiness ▷ *vb* make something more attractive
GLITZED > GLITZ
GLITZES > GLITZ
GLITZIER > GLITZY
GLITZIEST > GLITZY
GLITZILY > GLITZY
GLITZING > GLITZ
GLITZY *adj* showily attractive
GLOAM *n* dusk
GLOAMING *n* twilight

GLOAMINGS > GLOAMING
GLOAMS > GLOAM
GLOAT *vb* regard one's own good fortune with pleasure ▷ *n* act of gloating
GLOATED > GLOAT
GLOATER > GLOAT
GLOATERS > GLOAT
GLOATING *n* act of gloating
GLOATINGS > GLOATING
GLOATS > GLOAT
GLOB *n* rounded mass of thick fluid
GLOBAL *adj* worldwide
GLOBALISE *same as* **>** GLOBALIZE
GLOBALISM *n* policy which is worldwide in scope
GLOBALIST **>** GLOBALISM
GLOBALIZE *vb* put (something) into effect worldwide
GLOBALLY > GLOBAL
GLOBATE *adj* shaped like a globe
GLOBATED *same as* **>** GLOBATE
GLOBBIER > GLOBBY
GLOBBIEST > GLOBBY
GLOBBY *adj* thick and lumpy
GLOBE *n* sphere with a map of the earth on it ▷ *vb* form or cause to form into a globe
GLOBED > GLOBE
GLOBEFISH *another name for* **>** PUFFER
GLOBELIKE > GLOBE
GLOBES > GLOBE
GLOBESITY *n* informal word for obesity seen as a worldwide social problem
GLOBETROT *vb* regularly travel internationally
GLOBI > GLOBUS
GLOBIER > GLOBY
GLOBIEST > GLOBY
GLOBIN *n* protein component
GLOBING > GLOBE
GLOBINS > GLOBIN
GLOBOID *adj* shaped approximately like a globe ▷ *n* globoid body
GLOBOIDS > GLOBOID
GLOBOSE *adj* spherical or approximately spherical ▷ *n* globose object
GLOBOSELY > GLOBOSE
GLOBOSITY > GLOBOSE
GLOBOUS *same as* **>** GLOBOSE
GLOBS > GLOB
GLOBULAR *adj* shaped like a globe or globule ▷ *n* globular star cluster
GLOBULARS > GLOBULAR
GLOBULE *n* small round drop

GLOBULES > GLOBULE
GLOBULET *n* small globule
GLOBULETS > GLOBULET
GLOBULIN *n* simple protein found in living tissue
GLOBULINS > GLOBULIN
GLOBULITE *n* spherical form of crystallite
GLOBULOUS *same as* **>** GLOBULAR
GLOBUS *n* any spherelike structure
GLOBY *adj* round
GLOCHID *n* barbed spine on a plant
GLOCHIDIA *n* plural form of singular glochidium, a barbed hair on some plants
GLOCHIDS > GLOCHID
GLODE > GLIDE
GLOGG *n* hot alcoholic mixed drink
GLOGGS > GLOGG
GLOIRE *n* glory
GLOIRES > GLOIRE
GLOM *vb* attach oneself to or associate oneself with
GLOMERA > GLOMUS
GLOMERATE *adj* gathered into a compact rounded mass ▷ *vb* wind into a ball
GLOMERULE *n* cymose inflorescence in the form of a ball-like cluster of flowers
GLOMERULI *n* plural of singular glomerulus: a knot of blood vessels in the kidney
GLOMMED > GLOM
GLOMMING > GLOM
GLOMS > GLOM
GLOMUS *n* small anastomosis in an artery or vein
GLONOIN *n* nitroglycerin
GLONOINS > GLONOIN
GLOOM *n* melancholy or depression ▷ *vb* look sullen or depressed
GLOOMED > GLOOM
GLOOMFUL > GLOOM
GLOOMIER > GLOOMY
GLOOMIEST > GLOOMY
GLOOMILY > GLOOMY
GLOOMING > GLOOM
GLOOMINGS > GLOOM
GLOOMLESS > GLOOM
GLOOMS > GLOOM
GLOOMY *adj* despairing or sad
GLOOP *vb* cover with a viscous substance
GLOOPED > GLOOP
GLOOPIER > GLOOP
GLOOPIEST > GLOOP
GLOOPING > GLOOP
GLOOPS > GLOOP
GLOOPY > GLOOP
GLOP *vb* cover with a viscous substance
GLOPPED > GLOP

GLOPPIER > GLOP
GLOPPIEST > GLOP
GLOPPING > GLOP
GLOPPY > GLOP
GLOPS > GLOP
GLORIA n silk, wool, cotton, or nylon fabric
GLORIAS > GLORIA
GLORIED > GLORY
GLORIES > GLORY
GLORIFIED > GLORIFY
GLORIFIER > GLORIFY
GLORIFIES > GLORIFY
GLORIFY vb make (something) seem more worthy than it is
GLORIOLE another name for a > HALO
GLORIOLES > GLORIOLE
GLORIOSA n bulbous African tropical plant
GLORIOSAS > GLORIOSA
GLORIOUS adj brilliantly beautiful
GLORY n praise or honour ▷ vb triumph or exalt
GLORYING > GLORY
GLOSS n surface shine or lustre ▷ vb make glossy
GLOSSA n paired tonguelike lobe in the labium of an insect
GLOSSAE > GLOSSA
GLOSSAL > GLOSSA
GLOSSARY n list of special or technical words with definitions
GLOSSAS > GLOSSA
GLOSSATOR n writer of glosses and commentaries, esp (in the Middle Ages) an interpreter of Roman and Canon Law
GLOSSED > GLOSS
GLOSSEME n smallest meaningful unit of a language, such as stress, form, etc
GLOSSEMES > GLOSSEME
GLOSSER > GLOSS
GLOSSERS > GLOSS
GLOSSES > GLOSS
GLOSSIER > GLOSSY
GLOSSIES > GLOSSY
GLOSSIEST > GLOSSY
GLOSSILY > GLOSSY
GLOSSINA n tsetse fly
GLOSSINAS > GLOSSINA
GLOSSING > GLOSS
GLOSSIST same as > GLOSSATOR
GLOSSISTS > GLOSSIST
GLOSSITIC > GLOSSITIS
GLOSSITIS n inflammation of the tongue
GLOSSLESS > GLOSS
GLOSSY adj smooth and shiny ▷ n expensively produced magazine
GLOST n lead glaze used for pottery

GLOSTS > GLOST
GLOTTAL adj of the glottis
GLOTTIC adj of or relating to the tongue or the glottis
GLOTTIDES > GLOTTIS
GLOTTIS n vocal cords and the space between them
GLOTTISES > GLOTTIS
GLOUT vb look sullen
GLOUTED > GLOUT
GLOUTING > GLOUT
GLOUTS > GLOUT
GLOVE n covering for the hand
GLOVEBOX n small compartment in a car for miscellaneous articles
GLOVED > GLOVE
GLOVELESS > GLOVE
GLOVER n person who makes or sells gloves
GLOVERS > GLOVER
GLOVES > GLOVE
GLOVING > GLOVE
GLOVINGS > GLOVE
GLOW vb emit light and heat without flames ▷ n glowing light
GLOWED > GLOW
GLOWER n scowl ▷ vb stare angrily
GLOWERED > GLOWER
GLOWERING > GLOWER
GLOWERS > GLOWER
GLOWFLIES > GLOWFLY
GLOWFLY n firefly
GLOWING adj full of praise
GLOWINGLY > GLOWING
GLOWLAMP n small light consisting of two or more electrodes in an inert gas
GLOWLAMPS > GLOWLAMP
GLOWS > GLOW
GLOWSTICK n plastic tube containing a luminescent material, waved or held aloft esp at gigs, raves, etc
GLOWWORM n European beetle, the females and larvae of which bear luminescent organs producing a greenish light
GLOWWORMS > GLOWWORM
GLOXINIA n tropical plant with large bell-shaped flowers
GLOXINIAS > GLOXINIA
GLOZE vb explain away ▷ n flattery or deceit
GLOZED > GLOZE
GLOZES > GLOZE
GLOZINGS > GLOZE
GLOZINGS > GLOZE
GLUCAGON n polypeptide hormone, produced in the pancreas by the islets of Langerhans, that stimulates the release of glucose into the blood
GLUCAGONS > GLUCAGON
GLUCAN n any polysaccharide consisting of a polymer of glucose

GLUCANS > GLUCAN
GLUCINA n oxide of glucinum
GLUCINAS > GLUCINA
GLUCINIC > GLUCINIUM
GLUCINIUM former name of > BERYLLIUM
GLUCINUM same as > GLUCINIUM
GLUCINUMS > GLUCINIUM
GLUCONATE n compound formed when a mineral is bound to gluconic acid
GLUCONIC adj as in gluconic acid an acid that occurs naturally in fruit and wine
GLUCOSE n kind of sugar found in fruit
GLUCOSES > GLUCOSE
GLUCOSIC > GLUCOSE
GLUCOSIDE n any of a large group of glycosides that yield glucose on hydrolysis
GLUE n natural or synthetic sticky substance ▷ vb fasten with glue
GLUEBALL n hypothetical composite subatomic particle
GLUEBALLS > GLUEBALL
GLUED > GLUE
GLUEING > GLUE
GLUEISH > GLUISH
GLUELIKE > GLUE
GLUEPOT n container for holding glue
GLUEPOTS > GLUEPOT
GLUER > GLUE
GLUERS > GLUE
GLUES > GLUE
GLUEY > GLUE
GLUEYNESS > GLUE
GLUG n word representing a gurgling sound ▷ vb drink noisily, taking big gulps
GLUGGABLE adj (of wine) easy and pleasant to drink
GLUGGED > GLUG
GLUGGING > GLUG
GLUGS > GLUG
GLUHWEIN n mulled wine
GLUHWEINS > GLUHWEIN
GLUIER > GLUE
GLUIEST > GLUE
GLUILY > GLUE
GLUINESS > GLUE
GLUING > GLUE
GLUISH adj having the properties of glue
GLUM adj sullen or gloomy
GLUME n one of a pair of dry membranous bracts in grasses
GLUMELIKE > GLUME
GLUMELLA n palea
GLUMELLAS > GLUMELLA
GLUMES > GLUME
GLUMLY > GLUM
GLUMMER > GLUM
GLUMMEST > GLUM

GLUMNESS > GLUM
GLUMPIER > GLUMPY
GLUMPIEST > GLUMPY
GLUMPILY > GLUMPY
GLUMPISH > GLUMPY
GLUMPS n state of sulking
GLUMPY adj sullen
GLUMS n gloomy feelings
GLUNCH vb look sullen
GLUNCHED > GLUNCH
GLUNCHES > GLUNCH
GLUNCHING > GLUNCH
GLUON n hypothetical particle
GLUONS > GLUON
GLURGE n stories supposed to be true but often fabricated
GLURGES > GLURGE
GLUT n excessive supply ▷ vb oversupply
GLUTAEAL > GLUTAEUS
GLUTAEI > GLUTAEUS
GLUTAEUS same as > GLUTEUS
GLUTAMATE n any salt of glutamic acid, esp its sodium salt
GLUTAMIC adj as in glutamic acid nonessential amino acid that plays a part in nitrogen metabolism
GLUTAMINE n nonessential amino acid occurring in proteins: plays an important role in protein metabolism
GLUTCH vb swallow
GLUTCHED > GLUTCH
GLUTCHES > GLUTCH
GLUTCHING > GLUTCH
GLUTE same as > GLUTEUS
GLUTEAL > GLUTEUS
GLUTEI > GLUTEUS
GLUTELIN n any of a group of water-insoluble plant proteins found in cereals. They are precipitated by alcohol and are not coagulated by heat
GLUTELINS > GLUTELIN
GLUTEN n protein found in cereal grain
GLUTENIN n type of protein
GLUTENINS > GLUTENIN
GLUTENOUS > GLUTEN
GLUTENS > GLUTEN
GLUTES > GLUTE
GLUTEUS n any of the three muscles of the buttock
GLUTINOUS adj sticky or gluey
GLUTS > GLUT
GLUTTED > GLUT
GLUTTING > GLUT
GLUTTON n greedy person
GLUTTONS > GLUTTON
GLUTTONY n practice of eating too much

GLYCAEMIA n presence of glucose in blood
GLYCAEMIC > GLYCAEMIA
GLYCAN n polysaccharide
GLYCANS > GLYCAN
GLYCATION n the bonding of a sugar molecule to a protein or lipid
GLYCEMIA US spelling of > GLYCAEMIA
GLYCEMIAS > GLYCEMIA
GLYCEMIC > GLYCEMIA
GLYCERIA n manna grass
GLYCERIAS > GLYCERIA
GLYCERIC adj of, containing, or derived from glycerol
GLYCERIDE n any fatty-acid ester of glycerol
GLYCERIN same as > GLYCEROL
GLYCERINE same as > GLYCEROL
GLYCERINS > GLYCERIN
GLYCEROL n colourless odourless syrupy liquid obtained from animal and vegetable fats, used as a solvent, antifreeze, and sweetener, and in explosives
GLYCEROLS > GLYCEROL
GLYCERYL n (something) derived from glycerol by replacing or removing one or more of its hydroxyl groups
GLYCERYLS > GLYCERYL
GLYCIN same as > GLYCINE
GLYCINE n nonessential amino acid
GLYCINES > GLYCINE
GLYCINS > GLYCIN
GLYCOCOLL n glycine
GLYCOGEN n starchlike carbohydrate stored in the liver and muscles of humans and animals
GLYCOGENS > GLYCOGEN
GLYCOL n another name (not in technical usage) for a diol
GLYCOLIC > GLYCOL
GLYCOLLIC > GLYCOL
GLYCOLS > GLYCOL
GLYCONIC n verse consisting of a spondee, choriamb and pyrrhic
GLYCONICS > GLYCONIC
GLYCOSE n any of various monosaccharides
GLYCOSES > GLYCOSE
GLYCOSIDE n any of a group of substances, such as digitoxin, derived from monosaccharides by replacing the hydroxyl group by another group
GLYCOSYL n glucose-derived radical

GLYCOSYLS > GLYCOSYL
GLYCYL n radical of glycine
GLYCYLS > GLYCYL
GLYPH n carved channel or groove
GLYPHIC > GLYPH
GLYPHS > GLYPH
GLYPTAL n alkyd resin
GLYPTALS > GLYPTAL
GLYPTIC adj of or relating to engraving or carving
GLYPTICS n art of engraving precious stones
GMELINITE n zeolitic mineral
GNAMMA variant of > NAMMA
GNAR same as > GNARL
GNARL n any knotty protuberance or swelling on a tree ▷ vb knot or cause to knot
GNARLED adj rough, twisted, and knobbly
GNARLIER > GNARLY
GNARLIEST > GNARLY
GNARLING > GNARL
GNARLS > GNARL
GNARLY adj good
GNARR same as > GNARL
GNARRED > GNAR
GNARRING > GNAR
GNARRS > GNARR
GNARS > GNAR
GNASH vb grind (the teeth) together ▷ n act of gnashing the teeth
GNASHED > GNASH
GNASHER n tooth
GNASHERS pl n teeth, esp false ones
GNASHES > GNASH
GNASHING > GNASH
GNASHINGS > GNASHING
GNAT n small biting two-winged fly
GNATHAL same as > GNATHIC
GNATHIC adj of or relating to the jaw
GNATHION n lowest point of the midline of the lower jaw: a reference point in craniometry
GNATHIONS > GNATHION
GNATHITE n appendage of an arthropod that is specialized for grasping or chewing
GNATHITES > GNATHITE
GNATHONIC adj deceitfully flattering
GNATLIKE > GNAT
GNATLING n small gnat
GNATLINGS > GNATLING
GNATS > GNAT
GNATTIER > GNATTY
GNATTIEST > GNATTY
GNATTY adj infested with gnats
GNATWREN n small bird of the gnatcatcher family
GNATWRENS > GNATWREN

GNAW vb bite or chew steadily ▷ n act or an instance of gnawing
GNAWABLE > GNAW
GNAWED > GNAW
GNAWER > GNAW
GNAWERS > GNAW
GNAWING > GNAW
GNAWINGLY > GNAW
GNAWINGS > GNAW
GNAWN > GNAW
GNAWS > GNAW
GNEISS n coarse-grained metamorphic rock
GNEISSES > GNEISS
GNEISSIC > GNEISS
GNEISSOID > GNEISS
GNEISSOSE > GNEISS
GNOCCHI n dumplings
GNOMAE > GNOME
GNOME n imaginary creature like a little old man
GNOMELIKE > GNOME
GNOMES > GNOME
GNOMIC adj of pithy sayings
GNOMICAL same as > GNOMIC
GNOMISH > GNOME
GNOMIST n writer of pithy sayings
GNOMISTS > GNOMIST
GNOMON n stationary arm on a sundial
GNOMONIC > GNOMON
GNOMONICS > GNOMON
GNOMONS > GNOMON
GNOSES > GNOSIS
GNOSIS n supposedly revealed knowledge of spiritual truths
GNOSTIC adj of, relating to, or possessing knowledge ▷ n one who knows
GNOSTICAL same as > GNOSTIC
GNOSTICS > GNOSTIC
GNOW n Australian wild bird
GNOWS > GNOW
GNU n ox-like S African antelope
GNUS > GNU
GO vb move to or from a place ▷ n attempt
GOA n Tibetan gazelle
GOAD vb provoke (someone) to take some kind of action, usu in anger ▷ n spur or provocation
GOADED > GOAD
GOADING > GOAD
GOADLIKE > GOAD
GOADS > GOAD
GOADSMAN n person who uses a goad
GOADSMEN > GOADSMAN
GOADSTER n goadsman
GOADSTERS > GOADSTER
GOAF n waste left in old mine workings
GOAFS > GOAF

GOAL n posts through which the ball or puck has to move to score ▷ vb in rugby, to convert a try into a goal
GOALBALL n game played by two teams who compete to score goals by throwing a ball that emits audible sound when in motion. Players, who may be blind or sighted, are blindfolded during play
GOALBALLS > GOALBALL
GOALED > GOAL
GOALIE n goalkeeper
GOALIES > GOALIE
GOALING > GOAL
GOALLESS > GOAL
GOALMOUTH n area in front of the goal
GOALPOST n one of the two posts marking the limit of a goal
GOALPOSTS > GOALPOST
GOALS > GOAL
GOALWARD adv towards a goal
GOALWARDS same as > GOALWARD
GOANNA n large Australian lizard
GOANNAS > GOANNA
GOARY variant spelling of > GORY
GOAS > GOA
GOAT n sure-footed ruminant animal with horns
GOATEE n pointed tuft-like beard
GOATEED > GOATEE
GOATEES > GOATEE
GOATFISH n red mullet
GOATHERD n person who looks after a herd of goats
GOATHERDS > GOATHERD
GOATIER > GOATY
GOATIES > GOATY
GOATIEST > GOAT
GOATISH adj of, like, or relating to a goat
GOATISHLY > GOATISH
GOATLIKE > GOAT
GOATLING n young goat
GOATLINGS > GOATLING
GOATS > GOAT
GOATSE n deliberately offensive, usually pornographic, image placed maliciously into a website
GOATSES > GOATSE
GOATSKIN n leather made from the skin of a goat
GOATSKINS > GOATSKIN
GOATWEED n plant of the genus Capraria
GOATWEEDS > GOATWEED
GOATY n pointed tuft-like beard ▷ adj resembling a goat
GOB n lump of a soft substance ▷ vb spit

GOBAN n board on which go is played
GOBANG n Japanese board-game
GOBANGS > GOBANG
GOBANS > GOBAN
GOBAR adj as in gobar numeral kind of numeral
GOBBED > GOB
GOBBELINE same as > GOBLIN
GOBBET n lump, esp of food
GOBBETS > GOBBET
GOBBI > GOBBO
GOBBIER > GOBBY
GOBBIEST > GOBBY
GOBBING > GOB
GOBBLE vb eat hastily and greedily ▷ n rapid gurgling cry of the male turkey ▷ interj imitation of this sound
GOBBLED > GOBBLE
GOBBLER n turkey
GOBBLERS > GOBBLER
GOBBLES > GOBBLE
GOBBLING > GOBBLE
GOBBO n hunchback
GOBBY adj loudmouthed and offensive
GOBI n (in Indian cookery) cauliflower
GOBIES > GOBY
GOBIID n member of the genus Gobius
GOBIIDS > GOBIID
GOBIOID n type of spiny-finned fish
GOBIOIDS > GOBIOID
GOBIS > GOBI
GOBLET n drinking cup without handles
GOBLETS > GOBLET
GOBLIN n (in folklore) small malevolent creature
GOBLINS > GOBLIN
GOBO n shield placed around a microphone
GOBOES > GOBO
GOBONEE same as > GOBONY
GOBONY adj in heraldry, composed of a row of small, alternately-coloured, squares
GOBOS > GOBO
GOBS > GOB
GOBSHITE n stupid person
GOBSHITES > GOBSHITE
GOBURRA n kookaburra
GOBURRAS > GOBURRA
GOBY n small spiny-finned fish
GOD n spirit or being worshipped as having supernatural power ▷ vb deify
GODAWFUL adj very bad or unpleasant
GODCHILD n child for whom a person stands as godparent

GODDAM vb damn
GODDAMMED > GODDAM
GODDAMMIT interj an oath expressing anger, surprise, irritation, etc
GODDAMN interj oath expressing anger, surprise, etc ▷ adj extremely ▷ vb damn
GODDAMNED > GODDAMN
GODDAMNS > GODDAMN
GODDAMS > GODDAM
GODDED > GOD
GODDEN n evening greeting
GODDENS > GODDEN
GODDESS n female divinity
GODDESSES > GODDESS
GODDING > GOD
GODET n triangular piece of material inserted into a garment
GODETIA n plant with showy flowers
GODETIAS > GODETIA
GODETS > GODET
GODFATHER n male godparent ▷ vb be a godfather to
GODHEAD n essential nature and condition of being a god
GODHEADS > GODHEAD
GODHOOD n state of being divine
GODHOODS > GODHOOD
GODLESS adj wicked or unprincipled
GODLESSLY > GODLESS
GODLIER > GODLY
GODLIEST > GODLY
GODLIKE adj resembling or befitting a god or God
GODLILY > GODLY
GODLINESS > GODLY
GODLING n little god
GODLINGS > GODLING
GODLY adj devout or pious
GODMOTHER n female godparent
GODOWN n (in East Asia and India) warehouse
GODOWNS > GODOWN
GODPARENT n person who promises at a child's baptism to bring the child up as a Christian
GODROON same as > GADROON
GODROONED > GODROON
GODROONS > GODROON
GODS > GOD
GODSEND n something unexpected but welcome
GODSENDS > GODSEND
GODSHIP n divinity
GODSHIPS > GODSHIP
GODSLOT n time in a schedule for religious broadcasts
GODSLOTS > GODSLOT
GODSO same as > GADSO
GODSON n male godchild

GODSONS > GODSON
GODSPEED n expression of one's good wishes for a person's success and safety
GODSPEEDS > GODSPEED
GODSQUAD n informal, sometimes derogatory term for any group of evangelical Christians, members of which are regarded as intrusive and exuberantly pious
GODSQUADS > GODSQUAD
GODWARD adv towards God
GODWARDS same as > GODWARD
GODWIT n shore bird with long legs and an upturned bill
GODWITS > GODWIT
GOE same as > GO
GOEL n in Jewish law, blood-avenger
GOELS > GOEL
GOER n person who attends something regularly
GOERS > GOER
GOES > GO
GOEST vb archaic 2nd person sing present of go
GOETH vb archaic 3rd person sing present of go
GOETHITE n black, brown, or yellow mineral consisting of hydrated iron oxide in the form of orthorhombic crystals or fibrous masses
GOETHITES > GOETHITE
GOETIC > GOETY
GOETIES > GOETY
GOETY n witchcraft
GOEY adj go-ahead
GOFER n employee or assistant performing menial tasks
GOFERS > GOFER
GOFF obsolete variant of > GOLF
GOFFED > GOFF
GOFFER vb press pleats into (a frill) ▷ n ornamental frill made by pressing pleats
GOFFERED > GOFFER
GOFFERING > GOFFER
GOFFERS > GOFFER
GOFFING > GOFF
GOFFS > GOFF
GOGGA n any small insect
GOGGAS > GOGGA
GOGGLE vb (of the eyes) bulge ▷ n fixed or bulging stare
GOGGLEBOX n television set
GOGGLED > GOGGLE
GOGGLER n big-eyed scad
GOGGLERS > GOGGLER
GOGGLES > GOGGLE
GOGGLIER > GOGGLE

GOGGLIEST > GOGGLE
GOGGLING > GOGGLE
GOGGLINGS > GOGGLE
GOGGLY > GOGGLE
GOGLET n long-necked water-cooling vessel
GOGLETS > GOGLET
GOGO n disco
GOGOS > GOGO
GOHONZON n (in Nichiren Buddhism) paper scroll to which devotional chanting is directed
GOHONZONS > GOHONZON
GOIER > GOEY
GOIEST > GOEY
GOING > GO
GOINGS > GO
GOITER same as > GOITRE
GOITERED > GOITER
GOITERS > GOITER
GOITRE n swelling of the thyroid gland in the neck
GOITRED > GOITRE
GOITRES > GOITRE
GOITROGEN n substance that induces the formation of a goitre
GOITROUS > GOITRE
GOJI same as > WOLFBERRY
GOJIS > GOJI
GOLCONDA n source of wealth or riches, esp a mine
GOLCONDAS > GOLCONDA
GOLD n yellow precious metal ▷ adj made of gold
GOLDARN euphemistic variant of > GODDAMN
GOLDARNED > GOLDARN
GOLDARNS > GODDAMN
GOLDBRICK vb swindle
GOLDBUG n American beetle with a bright metallic lustre
GOLDBUGS > GOLDBUG
GOLDCREST n small bird with a yellow crown
GOLDEN adj made of gold ▷ vb gild
GOLDENED > GOLDEN
GOLDENER > GOLDEN
GOLDENEST > GOLDEN
GOLDENEYE n type of black-and-white diving duck of northern regions
GOLDENING > GOLDEN
GOLDENLY > GOLDEN
GOLDENROD n tall plant with spikes of small yellow flowers
GOLDENS > GOLDEN
GOLDER > GOLD
GOLDEST > GOLD
GOLDEYE n N American fish
GOLDEYES > GOLDEYE
GOLDFIELD n area in which there are gold deposits
GOLDFINCH n kind of finch, the male of which

g

has yellow-and-black wings

GOLDFINNY *same as* > GOLDSINNY

GOLDFISH *n* orange fish kept in ponds or aquariums

GOLDIER > GOLDY

GOLDIES > GOLDY

GOLDIEST > GOLDY

GOLDISH > GOLD

GOLDLESS > GOLD

GOLDMINER *n* miner who works in a gold mine

GOLDS > GOLD

GOLDSINNY *n* small European fish

GOLDSIZE *n* adhesive used to fix gold leaf to a surface

GOLDSIZES > GOLDSIZE

GOLDSMITH *n* dealer in or maker of gold articles

GOLDSPINK *n* goldfinch

GOLDSTICK *n* colonel in the Life Guards who carries out ceremonial duties

GOLDSTONE *n* dark-coloured glass, usually green or brown, spangled with fine particles of gold, copper, or some other metal

GOLDTAIL *n* as in *goldtail moth* European moth with white wings and a soft white furry body with a yellow tail tuft

GOLDTONE *adj* gold-coloured ▷ *n* photographic image printed on a glass-plate with a painted golden backing

GOLDTONES > GOLDTONE

GOLDURN *variant of* > GODDAMN

GOLDURNS > GOLDURN

GOLDWORK *n* gold objects collectively

GOLDWORKS > GOLDWORK

GOLDY *adj* gold-like ▷ *n* goldfinch

GOLE *obsolete spelling of* > GOAL

GOLEM *n* (in Jewish legend) artificially created human

GOLEMS > GOLEM

GOLES > GOLE

GOLF *n* outdoor sport ▷ *vb* play golf

GOLFED > GOLF

GOLFER *n* person who plays golf

GOLFERS > GOLFER

GOLFIANA *n* golfing collectibles

GOLFIANAS > GOLFIANA

GOLFING > GOLF

GOLFINGS > GOLF

GOLFS > GOLF

GOLGOTHA *n* place of burial

GOLGOTHAS > GOLGOTHA

GOLIARD *n* one of a number of wandering scholars

GOLIARDIC > GOLIARD

GOLIARDS > GOLIARD

GOLIARDY > GOLIARD

GOLIAS *vb* behave outrageously

GOLIASED > GOLIAS

GOLIASES > GOLIAS

GOLIASING > GOLIAS

GOLIATH *n* giant

GOLIATHS > GOLIATH

GOLLAN *n* yellow flower

GOLLAND *same as* > GOLLAN

GOLLANDS > GOLLAND

GOLLANS > GOLLAN

GOLLAR *same as* > GOLLER

GOLLARED > GOLLAR

GOLLARING > GOLLAR

GOLLARS > GOLLAR

GOLLER *vb* roar

GOLLERED > GOLLER

GOLLERING > GOLLER

GOLLERS > GOLLER

GOLLIED > GOLLY

GOLLIES > GOLLY

GOLLIWOG *n* soft black-faced doll

GOLLIWOGG *same as* > GOLLIWOG

GOLLIWOGS > GOLLIWOG

GOLLOP *vb* eat or drink (something) quickly or greedily

GOLLOPED > GOLLOP

GOLLOPER > GOLLOP

GOLLOPERS > GOLLOP

GOLLOPING > GOLLOP

GOLLOPS > GOLLOP

GOLLY *interj* exclamation of mild surprise ▷ *n* short for golliwog ▷ *vb* spit

GOLLYING > GOLLY

GOLLYWOG *same as* > GOLLIWOG

GOLLYWOGS > GOLLYWOG

GOLOMYNKA *n* oily fish found only in Lake Baikal

GOLOSH *same as* > GALOSH

GOLOSHE *same as* > GALOSH

GOLOSHED > GOLOSH

GOLOSHES > GOLOSH

GOLOSHING > GOLOSH

GOLOSHOES > GOLOSH

GOLP *same as* > GOLPE

GOLPE *n* in heraldry, a purple circle

GOLPES > GOLPE

GOLPS > GOLP

GOMBEEN *n* usury

GOMBEENS > GOMBEEN

GOMBO *same as* > GUMBO

GOMBOS > GOMBO

GOMBRO *same as* > GUMBO

GOMBROON *n* Persian and Chinese pottery and porcelain wares

GOMBROONS > GOMBROON

GOMBROS > GOMBRO

GOMER *n* unwanted hospital patient

GOMERAL *same as* > GOMERIL

GOMERALS > GOMERAL

GOMEREL *same as* > GOMERIL

GOMERELS > GOMEREL

GOMERIL *n* slow-witted or stupid person

GOMERILS > GOMERIL

GOMERS > GOMER

GOMOKU *another word for* > GOBANG

GOMOKUS > GOMOKU

GOMPA *n* Tibetan monastery

GOMPAS > GOMPA

GOMPHOSES > GOMPHOSIS

GOMPHOSIS *n* form of immovable articulation in which a peglike part fits into a cavity, as in the setting of a tooth in its socket

GOMUTI *n* E Indian feather palm

GOMUTIS > GOMUTI

GOMUTO *same as* > GOMUTI

GOMUTOS > GOMUTO

GON *n* geometrical grade

GONAD *n* organ producing reproductive cells

GONADAL > GONAD

GONADIAL > GONAD

GONADIC > GONAD

GONADS > GONAD

GONCH *same as* > GITCH

GONCHES > GONCH

GONDELAY *same as* > GONDOLA

GONDELAYS > GONDELAY

GONDOLA *n* long narrow boat used in Venice

GONDOLAS > GONDOLA

GONDOLIER *n* person who propels a gondola

GONE > GO

GONEF *same as* > GANEF

GONEFS > GONEF

GONENESS *n* faintness from hunger

GONER *n* person or thing beyond help or recovery

GONERS > GONER

GONFALON *n* banner hanging from a crossbar, used esp by certain medieval Italian republics or in ecclesiastical processions

GONFALONS > GONFALON

GONFANON *same as* > GONFALON

GONFANONS > GONFANON

GONG *n* rimmed metal disc ▷ *vb* sound a gong

GONGED > GONG

GONGING > GONG

GONGLIKE > GONG

GONGS > GONG

GONGSTER *n* person who strikes a gong

GONGSTERS > GONGSTER

GONGYO *n* Buddhist ceremony

GONGYOS > GONGYO

GONIA > GONION

GONIATITE *n* type of extinct cephalopod mollusc similar to an ammonite

GONIDIA > GONIDIUM

GONIDIAL > GONIDIUM

GONIDIC > GONIDIUM

GONIDIUM *n* green algal cell in the thallus of a lichen

GONIF *same as* > GANEF

GONIFF *same as* > GANEF

GONIFFS > GONIFF

GONIFS > GONIF

GONION *n* point or apex of the angle of the lower jaw

GONIUM *n* immature reproductive cell

GONK *n* stuffed toy, often used as a mascot

GONKS > GONK

GONNA *vb* going to

GONOCOCCI *n* plural of singular gonococcus: bacterium that causes gonorrhea

GONOCYTE *n* oocyte or spermatocyte

GONOCYTES > GONOCYTE

GONODUCT *n* duct leading from a gonad to the exterior, through which gametes pass

GONODUCTS > GONODUCT

GONOF *same as* > GANEF

GONOFS > GANOF

GONOPH *same as* > GANEF

GONOPHORE *n* polyp in certain coelenterates that bears gonads

GONOPHS > GONOPH

GONOPOD *n* either of the reproductive organs of insects

GONOPODS > GONOPOD

GONOPORE *n* external pore in insects, earthworms, etc, through which the gametes are extruded

GONOPORES > GONOPORE

GONORRHEA *n* infectious venereal disease

GONOSOME *n* individuals, collectively, in a colonial animal that are involved with reproduction

GONOSOMES > GONOSOME

GONS > GON

GONYS *n* lower outline of a bird's bill

GONYSES > GONYS

GONZO *adj* wild or crazy ▷ *n* wild or crazy person

GONZOS > GONZO

GOO *n* sticky substance

GOOBER *another name for* > PEANUT

GOOBERS > GOOBER

GOOBIES > GOOBY

GOOBY n spittle
GOOD adj giving pleasure ▷ n benefit
GOODBY same as > GOODBYE
GOODBYE n expression used on parting ▷ interj expression used on parting ▷ sentence substitute farewell
GOODBYES > GOODBYE
GOODBYS > GOODBY
GOODFACED adj with a handsome face
GOODFELLA n gangster, esp one in the Mafia
GOODIE same as > GOODY
GOODIER > GOODY
GOODIES > GOODY
GOODIEST > GOODY
GOODINESS > GOODY
GOODISH > GOOD
GOODLIER > GOODLY
GOODLIEST > GOODLY
GOODLY adj considerable
GOODMAN n husband
GOODMEN > GOODMAN
GOODNESS n quality of being good ▷ interj exclamation of surprise
GOODNIGHT n conventional expression of farewell used in the evening or at night
GOODS > GOOD
GOODSIRE n grandfather
GOODSIRES > GOODSIRE
GOODTIME adj wildly seeking pleasure
GOODWIFE n mistress of a household
GOODWILL n kindly feeling
GOODWILLS > GOODWILL
GOODWIVES > GOODWIFE
GOODY n hero in a book or film ▷ interj child's exclamation of pleasure ▷ adj smug and sanctimonious
GOODYEAR n euphemistic term for the Devil
GOODYEARS > GOODYEAR
GOOEY adj sticky and soft
GOOEYNESS > GOOEY
GOOF n mistake ▷ vb make a mistake
GOOFBALL n barbiturate sleeping pill
GOOFBALLS > GOOFBALL
GOOFED > GOOF
GOOFIER > GOOFY
GOOFIEST > GOOFY
GOOFILY > GOOFY
GOOFINESS > GOOFY
GOOFING > GOOF
GOOFS > GOOF
GOOFUS n slow-witted or stupid person
GOOFUSES > GOOFUS
GOOFY adj silly or ridiculous
GOOG n egg

GOOGLE vb search on the internet using a search engine
GOOGLED > GOOGLE
GOOGLES > GOOGLE
GOOGLIES > GOOGLY
GOOGLING > GOOGLE
GOOGLY n ball that spins unexpectedly on the bounce
GOOGOL n number shown as one followed by 100 zeros
GOOGOLS > GOOGOL
GOOGS > GOOG
GOOIER > GOOEY
GOOIEST > GOOEY
GOOILY > GOOEY
GOOINESS n quality of being gooey
GOOK n derogatory word for a person from a Far Eastern country
GOOKIER > GOOKY
GOOKIEST > GOOKY
GOOKS > GOOK
GOOKY adj sticky and messy
GOOL n corn marigold
GOOLD Scots word for > GOLD
GOOLDS > GOOLD
GOOLEY same as > GOOLIE
GOOLEYS > GOOLEY
GOOLIE n testicle
GOOLIES > GOOLIE
GOOLS > GOOL
GOOLY same as > GOOLIE
GOOMBAH n patron or mentor
GOOMBAHS > GOOMBAH
GOOMBAY n Bahamian soft drink
GOOMBAYS > GOOMBAY
GOON n stupid person
GOONDA n (in India) habitual criminal
GOONDAS > GOONDA
GOONERIES > GOONERY
GOONERY n behaviour typical of goons
GOONEY n albatross
GOONEYS > GOONEY
GOONIE Scots word for a > GOWN
GOONIER > GOON
GOONIES > GOONIE
GOONIEST > GOON
GOONS > GOON
GOONY > GOON
GOOP n rude or ill-mannered person
GOOPED adj as in gooped up sticky with goop
GOOPIER > GOOP
GOOPIEST > GOOP
GOOPINESS n quality of being goopy
GOOPS > GOOP
GOOPY > GOOP
GOOR same as > GUR
GOORAL same as > GORAL
GOORALS > GOORAL

GOORIE same as > KURI
GOORIES > GOORIE
GOOROO same as > GURU
GOOROOS > GOOROO
GOORS > GOOR
GOORY same as > GOOR
GOOS > GOO
GOOSANDER n type of duck
GOOSE n web-footed bird like a large duck ▷ vb prod (someone) playfully in the bottom
GOOSED > GOOSE
GOOSEFISH another name for > MONKFISH
GOOSEFOOT n type of usu weedy plant with small greenish flowers and leaves shaped like a goose's foot
GOOSEGOB n gooseberry
GOOSEGOBS > GOOSEGOB
GOOSEGOG n gooseberry
GOOSEGOGS > GOOSEGOG
GOOSEHERD n person who herds geese
GOOSENECK n pivot between the forward end of a boom and a mast, to allow the boom to swing freely
GOOSERIES > GOOSERY
GOOSERY n place for keeping geese
GOOSES > GOOSE
GOOSEY same as > GOOSY
GOOSEYS > GOOSEY
GOOSIER > GOOSY
GOOSIES > GOOSY
GOOSIEST > GOOSY
GOOSINESS > GOOSY
GOOSING > GOOSE
GOOSY adj of or like a goose
GOPAK n Russian peasant dance
GOPAKS > GOPAK
GOPHER n American burrowing rodent ▷ vb burrow
GOPHERED > GOPHER
GOPHERING > GOPHER
GOPHERS > GOPHER
GOPIK n money unit of Azerbaijan
GOPIKS > GOPIK
GOPURA n gateway tower of an Indian temple
GOPURAM same as > GOPURA
GOPURAMS > GOPURA
GOPURAS > GOPURA
GOR interj God! ▷ n seagull
GORA n (in Indian English) White or fair-skinned male
GORAL n small S Asian goat antelope
GORALS > GORAL
GORAMIES > GORAMY
GORAMY > GOURAMI
GORAS > GORA
GORBELLY n large belly

GORBLIMEY interj exclamation of surprise or annoyance ▷ n instance of having uttered this exclamation
GORBLIMY same as > GORBLIMEY
GORCOCK n male of the red grouse
GORCOCKS > GORCOCK
GORCROW n carrion crow
GORCROWS > GORCROW
GORDITA n small thick tortilla
GORDITAS > GORDITA
GORE n blood from a wound ▷ vb pierce with horns
GORED > GORE
GOREFEST n film featuring excessive depictions of bloodshed
GOREFESTS > GOREFEST
GOREHOUND n enthusiast of gory horror films
GORES > GORE
GORGE n deep narrow valley ▷ vb eat greedily
GORGEABLE > GORGE
GORGED > GORGE
GORGEDLY > GORGE
GORGEOUS adj strikingly beautiful or attractive
GORGER > GORGE
GORGERIN another name for > NECKING
GORGERINS > GORGERIN
GORGERS > GORGE
GORGES > GORGE
GORGET n collar-like piece of armour
GORGETED > GORGET
GORGETS > GORGET
GORGIA n improvised sung passage
GORGIAS > GORGIA
GORGING > GORGE
GORGIO n word used by gypsies for a non-gypsy
GORGIOS > GORGIO
GORGON n terrifying or repulsive woman
GORGONEIA n plural of gorgoneion: representation of a Gorgon's head
GORGONIAN n type of coral with a horny or chalky branching skeleton, such as the sea fan and red coral
GORGONISE vb turn to stone
GORGONIZE same as > GORGONISE
GORGONS > GORGON
GORHEN n female red grouse
GORHENS > GORHEN
GORI n (in Indian English) White or fair-skinned female
GORIER > GORY
GORIEST > GORY

GORILLA n largest of the apes, found in Africa
GORILLAS > GORILLA
GORILLIAN > GORILLA
GORILLINE > GORILLA
GORILLOID > GORILLA
GORILY > GORY
GORINESS > GORY
GORING > GORE
GORINGS > GORE
GORIS > GORI
GORM n foolish person ▷ vb understand
GORMAND same as > GOURMAND
GORMANDS > GOURMAND
GORMED > GORM
GORMIER > GORMY
GORMIEST > GORMY
GORMING > GORM
GORMLESS adj stupid
GORMS > GORM
GORMY adj gormless
GORP same as > GAWP
GORPED > GAWP
GORPING > GAWP
GORPS > GAWP
GORS > GOR
GORSE n prickly yellow-flowered shrub
GORSEDD n meeting held daily before an eisteddfod
GORSEDDS > GORSEDD
GORSES > GORSE
GORSIER > GORSE
GORSIEST > GORSE
GORSOON n young boy
GORSOONS > GORSOON
GORSY > GORSE
GORY adj horrific or bloodthirsty
GOS > GO
GOSH interj exclamation of mild surprise or wonder
GOSHAWK n large hawk
GOSHAWKS > GOSHAWK
GOSHT n Indian meat dish
GOSHTS > GOSHT
GOSLARITE n hydrated zinc sulphate
GOSLET n pygmy goose
GOSLETS > GOSLET
GOSLING n young goose
GOSLINGS > GOSLING
GOSPEL n any of the first four books of the New Testament ▷ adj denoting a kind of religious music ▷ vb teach the gospel
GOSPELER same as > GOSPELLER
GOSPELERS > GOSPELER
GOSPELISE vb evangelise
GOSPELIZE same as > GOSPELISE
GOSPELLED > GOSPEL
GOSPELLER n person who reads or chants the Gospel in a religious service
GOSPELLY > GOSPEL
GOSPELS > GOSPEL
GOSPODA > GOSPODIN

GOSPODAR n hospodar
GOSPODARS > GOSPODAR
GOSPODIN n Russian title of address, often indicating respect,
GOSPORT n aeroplane communication device
GOSPORTS > GOSPORT
GOSS vb spit
GOSSAMER n very fine fabric
GOSSAMERS > GOSSAMER
GOSSAMERY > GOSSAMER
GOSSAN n oxidised portion of a mineral vein in rock
GOSSANS > GOSSAN
GOSSE variant of > GORSE
GOSSED > GOSS
GOSSES > GOSSE
GOSSIB n gossip
GOSSIBS > GOSSIB
GOSSING > GOSS
GOSSIP n idle talk, esp about other people ▷ vb engage in gossip
GOSSIPED > GOSSIP
GOSSIPER > GOSSIP
GOSSIPERS > GOSSIP
GOSSIPING > GOSSIP
GOSSIPPED > GOSSIP
GOSSIPPER > GOSSIP
GOSSIPRY n idle talk
GOSSIPS > GOSSIP
GOSSIPY > GOSSIP
GOSSOON n boy, esp a servant boy
GOSSOONS > GOSSOON
GOSSYPINE adj cottony
GOSSYPOL n toxic crystalline pigment that is a constituent of cottonseed oil
GOSSYPOLS > GOSSYPOL
GOSTER vb laugh uncontrollably
GOSTERED > GOSTER
GOSTERING > GOSTER
GOSTERS > GOSTER
GOT > GET
GOTCH same as > GITCH
GOTCHA adj as in gotcha lizard Australian name for a crocodile
GOTCHAS > GOTCHA
GOTCHES > GOTCH
GOTCHIES pl n underwear
GOTH n aficionado of Goth music and fashion
GOTHIC adj of or relating to a literary style ▷ n family of heavy script typefaces
GOTHICISE same as > GOTHICIZE
GOTHICISM > GOTHIC
GOTHICIZE vb make gothic in style
GOTHICS > GOTHIC
GOTHIER > GOTHY
GOTHIEST > GOTHY
GOTHITE same as > GOETHITE
GOTHITES > GOTHITE

GOTHS > GOTH
GOTHY adj characteristic of Gothic clothing or music
GOTTA vb got to
GOTTEN past participle of > GET
GOUACHE n (painting using) watercolours mixed with glue
GOUACHES > GOUACHE
GOUCH vb become drowsy or lethargic under the influence of narcotics
GOUCHED > GOUCH
GOUCHES > GOUCH
GOUCHING > GOUCH
GOUGE vb scoop or force out ▷ n hole or groove
GOUGED > GOUGE
GOUGER n person or tool that gouges
GOUGERE n choux pastry flavoured with cheese
GOUGERES > GOUGERE
GOUGERS > GOUGER
GOUGES > GOUGE
GOUGING > GOUGE
GOUJEERS same as > GOODYEAR
GOUJON n small strip of food
GOUJONS > GOUJON
GOUK same as > GOWK
GOUKS > GOUK
GOULASH n rich stew seasoned with paprika
GOULASHES > GOULASH
GOURA n large, crested ground pigeon found in New Guinea
GOURAMI n large SE Asian labyrinth fish
GOURAMIES > GOURAMI
GOURAMIS > GOURAMI
GOURAS > GOURA
GOURD n fleshy fruit of a climbing plant
GOURDE n standard monetary unit of Haiti
GOURDES > GOURDE
GOURDFUL n as much as a gourd will hold
GOURDFULS > GOURDFUL
GOURDIER > GOURDY
GOURDIEST > GOURDY
GOURDLIKE > GOURD
GOURDS > GOURD
GOURDY adj (of horses) swollen-legged
GOURMAND n person who is very keen on food and drink
GOURMANDS > GOURMAND
GOURMET n connoisseur of food and drink
GOURMETS > GOURMET
GOUSTIER > GOUSTY
GOUSTIEST > GOUSTY
GOUSTROUS adj stormy
GOUSTY adj dismal
GOUT n drop or splash (of something)
GOUTFLIES > GOUTFLY

GOUTFLY n fly whose larvae infect crops
GOUTIER > GOUTY
GOUTIEST > GOUTY
GOUTILY > GOUTY
GOUTINESS > GOUTY
GOUTS > GOUT
GOUTTE n heraldic device
GOUTTES > GOUTTE
GOUTWEED n Eurasian plant with white flowers and creeping underground stems
GOUTWEEDS > GOUTWEED
GOUTWORT n bishop's weed
GOUTWORTS > GOUTWORT
GOUTY adj afflicted with the disease gout
GOV n boss
GOVERN vb rule, direct, or control ▷ n ability to be governed
GOVERNALL n government
GOVERNED > GOVERN
GOVERNESS n woman teacher in a private household ▷ vb act as a governess
GOVERNING > GOVERN
GOVERNOR n official governing a province or state
GOVERNORS > GOVERNOR
GOVERNS > GOVERN
GOVS > GOV
GOWAN n any of various flowers growing in fields
GOWANED > GOWAN
GOWANS > GOWAN
GOWANY > GOWAN
GOWD Scots word for > GOWD
GOWDER > GOWD
GOWDEST > GOWD
GOWDS > GOWD
GOWDSPINK n goldfinch
GOWF vb strike
GOWFED > GOWF
GOWFER > GOWF
GOWFERS > GOWF
GOWFING > GOWF
GOWFS > GOWF
GOWK n stupid person
GOWKS > GOWK
GOWL n substance in the corner of the eyes after sleep ▷ vb howl
GOWLAN same as > GOLLAN
GOWLAND same as > GOLLAN
GOWLANDS > GOWLAND
GOWLANS > GOWLAN
GOWLED > GOWL
GOWLING > GOWL
GOWLS > GOWL
GOWN n woman's long formal dress ▷ vb supply with or dress in a gown
GOWNBOY n foundationer schoolboy who wears a gown
GOWNBOYS > GOWNBOY

GOWNED > GOWN

GOWNING > GOWN

GOWNMAN n professional person who wears a gown

GOWNMEN > GOWNMAN

GOWNS > GOWN

GOWNSMAN same as **>** GOWNMAN

GOWNSMEN > GOWNSMAN

GOWPEN n pair of cupped hands

GOWPENFUL n amount that can be contained in cupped hands

GOWPENS > GOWPEN

GOX n gaseous oxygen

GOXES > GOX

GOY n Jewish word for a non-Jew

GOYIM > GOY

GOYISCH > GOY

GOYISH > GOY

GOYISHE adj like a goy

GOYLE n ravine

GOYLES > GOYLE

GOYS > GOY

GOZZAN same as **>** GOSSAN

GOZZANS > GOZZAN

GRAAL n holy grail

GRAALS > GRAAL

GRAB vb grasp suddenly, snatch **▷** n sudden snatch

GRABBABLE > GRAB

GRABBED > GRAB

GRABBER > GRAB

GRABBERS > GRAB

GRABBIER > GRABBY

GRABBIEST > GRABBY

GRABBING > GRAB

GRABBLE vb scratch or feel about with the hands

GRABBLED > GRABBLE

GRABBLER > GRABBLE

GRABBLERS > GRABBLE

GRABBLES > GRABBLE

GRABBLING > GRABBLE

GRABBY adj greedy or selfish

GRABEN n elongated trough of land

GRABENS > GRABEN

GRABS > GRAB

GRACE n beauty and elegance **▷** vb honour

GRACED > GRACE

GRACEFUL adj having beauty of movement, style, or form

GRACELESS adj lacking elegance

GRACES > GRACE

GRACILE adj gracefully thin or slender

GRACILES > GRACILIS

GRACILIS n thin muscle on the inner thigh

GRACILITY > GRACILE

GRACING > GRACE

GRACIOSO n clown in Spanish comedy

GRACIOSOS > GRACIOSO

GRACIOUS adj kind and courteous **▷** interj expression of mild surprise or wonder **▷** interj expression of surprise

GRACKLE n American songbird with a dark iridescent plumage

GRACKLES > GRACKLE

GRAD n graduate

GRADABLE adj capable of being graded **▷** n word of this kind

GRADABLES > GRADABLE

GRADATE vb change or cause to change imperceptibly

GRADATED > GRADATE

GRADATES > GRADATE

GRADATIM adv step by step

GRADATING > GRADATE

GRADATION n (stage in) a series of degrees or steps

GRADATORY adj moving step by step **▷** n flight of stairs

GRADDAN vb dress corn

GRADDANED > GRADDAN

GRADDANS > GRADDAN

GRADE n place on a scale of quality, rank, or size **▷** vb arrange in grades

GRADED > GRADE

GRADELESS > GRADE

GRADELIER > GRADELY

GRADELY adj fine

GRADER n person or thing that grades

GRADERS > GRADER

GRADES > GRADE

GRADIENT n (degree of) slope **▷** adj sloping uniformly

GRADIENTS > GRADIENT

GRADIN n ledge above or behind an altar

GRADINE same as **>** GRADIN

GRADINES > GRADINE

GRADING > GRADE

GRADINGS > GRADING

GRADINI > GRADINO

GRADINO n step above an altar

GRADINS > GRADIN

GRADS > GRAD

GRADUAL adj occurring or moving in small stages **▷** n antiphon or group of several antiphons

GRADUALLY > GRADUAL

GRADUALS > GRADUAL

GRADUAND n person who is about to graduate

GRADUANDS > GRADUAND

GRADUATE vb receive a degree or diploma **▷** n holder of a degree

GRADUATED > GRADUATE

GRADUATES > GRADUATE

GRADUATOR > GRADUATE

GRADUS n book of études or other musical exercises

GRADUSES > GRADUS

GRAECISE same as **>** GRAECIZE

GRAECISED > GRAECISE

GRAECISES > GRAECISE

GRAECIZE vb make or become like the ancient Greeks

GRAECIZED > GRAECIZE

GRAECIZES > GRAECIZE

GRAFF same as **>** GRAFT

GRAFFED > GRAFF

GRAFFING > GRAFF

GRAFFITI pl n words or drawings scribbled or sprayed on walls etc

GRAFFITIS > GRAFFITI

GRAFFITO n instance of graffiti

GRAFFS > GRAFF

GRAFT n surgical transplant of skin or tissue **▷** vb transplant (living tissue) surgically

GRAFTAGE n in horticulture, the art of grafting

GRAFTAGES > GRAFTAGE

GRAFTED > GRAFT

GRAFTER > GRAFT

GRAFTERS > GRAFT

GRAFTING > GRAFT

GRAFTINGS > GRAFT

GRAFTS > GRAFT

GRAHAM n made of graham flour

GRAHAMS > GRAHAM

GRAIL n any desired ambition or goal

GRAILE same as **>** GRAIL

GRAILES > GRAILE

GRAILS > GRAIL

GRAIN n seedlike fruit of a cereal plant **▷** vb paint in imitation of the grain of wood or leather

GRAINAGE n duty paid on grain

GRAINAGES > GRAINAGE

GRAINE n eggs of the silkworm

GRAINED > GRAIN

GRAINER > GRAIN

GRAINERS > GRAIN

GRAINES > GRAINE

GRAINIER > GRAINY

GRAINIEST > GRAINY

GRAINING n pattern or texture of the grain of wood, leather, etc

GRAININGS > GRAINING

GRAINLESS > GRAIN

GRAINS > GRAIN

GRAINY adj resembling, full of, or composed of grain

GRAIP n long-handled gardening fork

GRAIPS > GRAIP

GRAITH vb clothe

GRAITHED > GRAITH

GRAITHING > GRAITH

GRAITHLY > GRAITH

GRAITHS > GRAITH

GRAKLE same as **>** GRACKLE

GRAKLES > GRAKLE

GRALLOCH n entrails of a deer **▷** vb disembowel (a deer killed in a hunt)

GRALLOCHS > GRALLOCH

GRAM n metric unit of mass

GRAMA n type of grass

GRAMARIES > GRAMARY

GRAMARY same as **>** GRAMARYE

GRAMARYE n magic, necromancy, or occult learning

GRAMARYES > GRAMARYE

GRAMAS > GRAMA

GRAMASH n type of gaiter

GRAMASHES > GRAMASH

GRAME n sorrow

GRAMERCY interj many thanks

GRAMES > GRAME

GRAMMA n pasture grass of the South American plains

GRAMMAGE n weight of paper expressed as grams per square metre

GRAMMAGES > GRAMMAGE

GRAMMAR n branch of linguistics

GRAMMARS > GRAMMAR

GRAMMAS > GRAMMA

GRAMMATIC adj of or relating to grammar

GRAMME same as **>** GRAME

GRAMMES > GRAM

GRAMOCHE same as **>** GRAMASH

GRAMOCHES > GRAMOCHE

GRAMP n grandfather

GRAMPA variant of **>** GRANDPA

GRAMPAS > GRAMPA

GRAMPIES > GRAMPY

GRAMPS > GRAMP

GRAMPUS n dolphin-like mammal

GRAMPUSES > GRAMPUS

GRAMPY n grandfather

GRAMS > GRAM

GRAN n grandmother

GRANA > GRANUM

GRANARIES > GRANARY

GRANARY n storehouse for grain

GRAND adj large or impressive, imposing **▷** n thousand pounds or dollars

GRANDAD n grandfather

GRANDADDY same as **>** GRANDAD

GRANDADS > GRANDAD

GRANDAM n archaic word for grandmother

GRANDAME same as **>** GRANDAM

GRANDAMES > GRANDAME

GRANDAMS > GRANDAM

GRANDAUNT n great-aunt

GRANDBABY n very young grandchild

GRANDDAD same as **>** GRANDDAD

g

GRANDDADS > GRANDAD
GRANDDAM same as > GRANDAM
GRANDDAMS > GRANDDAM
GRANDE feminine form of > GRAND
GRANDEE n Spanish nobleman of the highest rank
GRANDEES > GRANDEE
GRANDER > GRAND
GRANDEST > GRAND
GRANDEUR n magnificence
GRANDEURS > GRANDEUR
GRANDIOSE adj imposing
GRANDIOSO adv (to be played) in a grand manner
GRANDKID n grandchild
GRANDKIDS > GRANDKID
GRANDLY > GRAND
GRANDMA n grandmother
GRANDMAMA same as > GRANDMA
GRANDMAS > GRANDMA
GRANDNESS > GRAND
GRANDPA n grandfather
GRANDPAPA same as > GRANDPA
GRANDPAS > GRANDPA
GRANDS > GRAND
GRANDSIR same as > GRANDSIRE
GRANDSIRE n grandfather
GRANDSIRS > GRANDSIR
GRANDSON n male grandchild
GRANDSONS > GRANDSON
GRANFER n grandfather
GRANFERS > GRANFER
GRANGE n country house with farm buildings
GRANGER n keeper or member of a grange
GRANGERS > GRANGER
GRANGES > GRANGE
GRANITA n Italian iced drink
GRANITAS > GRANITA
GRANITE n very hard igneous rock
GRANITES > GRANITE
GRANITIC > GRANITE
GRANITISE vb form granite
GRANITITE n any granite with a high content of biotite
GRANITIZE same as > GRANITISE
GRANITOID > GRANITE
GRANIVORE n animal that feeds on seeds and grain
GRANNAM n old woman
GRANNAMS > GRANNAM
GRANNIE vb defeat without conceding a single point
GRANNIED > GRANNY
GRANNIES pl n Granny Smith apples

GRANNOM n type of caddis fly esteemed as a bait by anglers
GRANNOMS > GRANNOM
GRANNY n grandmother ▷ vb defeat without conceding a single point
GRANNYING > GRANNY
GRANNYISH adj typical of or suitable for an elderly woman
GRANOLA n muesli-like breakfast cereal
GRANOLAS > GRANOLA
GRANOLITH n paving material consisting of a mixture of cement and crushed granite or granite chippings
GRANS > GRAN
GRANT vb consent to fulfil (a request) ▷ n money provided by a government for a specific purpose
GRANTABLE > GRANT
GRANTED > GRANT
GRANTEE n person to whom a grant is made
GRANTEES > GRANTEE
GRANTER > GRANT
GRANTERS > GRANT
GRANTING > GRANT
GRANTOR n person who makes a grant
GRANTORS > GRANTOR
GRANTS > GRANT
GRANTSMAN n student who specializes in obtaining grants
GRANTSMEN > GRANTSMAN
GRANULAR adj of or like grains
GRANULARY adj granular
GRANULATE vb make into grains
GRANULE n small grain
GRANULES > GRANULE
GRANULITE n granular foliated metamorphic rock in which the minerals form a mosaic of equal-sized granules
GRANULOMA n tumour composed of granulation tissue produced in response to chronic infection, inflammation, a foreign body, or to unknown causes
GRANULOSE less common word for > GRANULAR
GRANULOUS adj consisting of grains or granules
GRANUM n membrane layers in a chloroplast
GRAPE n small juicy green or purple berry ▷ vb grope
GRAPED > GRAPE
GRAPELESS > GRAPE
GRAPELICE pl n lice that are destructive to grape plants

GRAPELIKE > GRAPE
GRAPERIES > GRAPERY
GRAPERY n building where grapes are grown
GRAPES n abnormal growth on the fetlock of a horse
GRAPESEED n seed of the grape
GRAPESHOT n bullets which scatter when fired
GRAPETREE n sea grape, a shrubby plant resembling a grapevine
GRAPEVINE n grape-bearing vine
GRAPEY > GRAPE
GRAPH n type of graph ▷ vb draw or represent in a graph
GRAPHED > GRAPH
GRAPHEME n one of a set of letters or combinations of letters in a given language that serve to distinguish one word from another and usually correspond to or represent phonemes
GRAPHEMES > GRAPHEME
GRAPHEMIC > GRAPHEME
GRAPHENE n layer of graphite one atom thick
GRAPHENES > GRAPHENE
GRAPHIC adj vividly descriptive
GRAPHICAL same as > GRAPHIC
GRAPHICLY > GRAPHIC
GRAPHICS pl n diagrams, graphs, etc, esp as used on a television programme or computer screen
GRAPHING > GRAPH
GRAPHITE n soft black form of carbon, used in pencil leads
GRAPHITES > GRAPHITE
GRAPHITIC > GRAPHITE
GRAPHIUM n stylus (for writing)
GRAPHIUMS > GRAPHIUM
GRAPHS > GRAPH
GRAPIER > GRAPE
GRAPIEST > GRAPE
GRAPINESS > GRAPE
GRAPING > GRAPE
GRAPLE same as > GRAPPLE
GRAPLES > GRAPLE
GRAPLIN same as > GRAPNEL
GRAPLINE same as > GRAPNEL
GRAPLINES > GRAPLINE
GRAPLINS > GRAPLIN
GRAPNEL n device with several hooks
GRAPNELS > GRAPNEL
GRAPPA n type of spirit
GRAPPAS > GRAPPA
GRAPPLE vb try to cope with (something difficult) ▷ n grapnel

GRAPPLED > GRAPPLE
GRAPPLER > GRAPPLE
GRAPPLERS > GRAPPLE
GRAPPLES > GRAPPLE
GRAPPLING n act of gripping or seizing, as in wrestling
GRAPY same as > GRAPE
GRASP vb grip something firmly ▷ n grip or clasp
GRASPABLE > GRASP
GRASPED > GRASP
GRASPER > GRASP
GRASPERS > GRASP
GRASPING adj greedy or avaricious
GRASPLESS adj relaxed
GRASPS > GRASP
GRASS n common type of plant ▷ vb cover with grass
GRASSBIRD n type of warbler found in long grass and reed beds
GRASSED > GRASS
GRASSER n police informant
GRASSERS > GRASSER
GRASSES > GRASS
GRASSHOOK another name for > SICKLE
GRASSIER > GRASSY
GRASSIEST > GRASSY
GRASSILY > GRASSY
GRASSING > GRASS
GRASSINGS > GRASS
GRASSLAND n land covered with grass
GRASSLESS > GRASS
GRASSLIKE > GRASS
GRASSPLOT n plot of ground overgrown with grass
GRASSQUIT n tropical American finch
GRASSROOT adj relating to the ordinary people, especially as part of the electorate
GRASSUM n in Scots law, sum paid when taking a lease
GRASSUMS > GRASSUM
GRASSY adj covered with, containing, or resembling grass
GRASTE archaic past participle of > GRACE
GRAT > GREET
GRATE vb rub into small bits on a rough surface ▷ n framework of metal bars for holding fuel in a fireplace
GRATED > GRATE
GRATEFUL adj feeling or showing gratitude
GRATELESS > GRATE
GRATER n tool with a sharp surface for grating food
GRATERS > GRATER
GRATES > GRATE
GRATICULE n grid of intersecting lines, esp of

latitude and longitude on which a map is drawn

GRATIFIED > GRATIFY

GRATIFIER > GRATIFY

GRATIFIES > GRATIFY

GRATIFY vb satisfy or please ▷ adj giving one satisfaction or pleasure

GRATIN n crust of browned breadcrumbs

GRATINATE vb cook until the juice is absorbed and the surface crisps

GRATINE adj cooked au gratin

GRATINEE vb cook au gratin

GRATINEED > GRATINEE

GRATINEES > GRATINEE

GRATING adj harsh or rasping ▷ n framework of metal bars covering an opening

GRATINGLY > GRATING

GRATINGS > GRATING

GRATINS > GRATIN

GRATIS adj free, for nothing

GRATITUDE n feeling of being thankful for a favour or gift

GRATTOIR n scraper made of flint

GRATTOIRS > GRATTOIR

GRATUITY n money given for services rendered, tip

GRATULANT > GRATULATE

GRATULATE vb greet joyously

GRAUNCH vb crush or destroy

GRAUNCHED > GRAUNCH

GRAUNCHER > GRAUNCH

GRAUNCHES > GRAUNCH

GRAUPEL n soft hail or snow pellets

GRAUPELS > GRAUPEL

GRAV n unit of acceleration

GRAVADLAX same as > GRAVLAX

GRAVAMEN n that part of an accusation weighing most heavily against an accused

GRAVAMENS > GRAVAMEN

GRAVAMINA > GRAVAMEN

GRAVE n hole for burying a corpse ▷ adj causing concern ▷ vb cut, carve, sculpt, or engrave ▷ adv to be performed in a solemn manner

GRAVED > GRAVE

GRAVEL n mixture of small stones and coarse sand ▷ vb cover with gravel

GRAVELED > GRAVEL

GRAVELESS > GRAVE

GRAVELIKE > GRAVE

GRAVELING > GRAVEL

GRAVELISH > GRAVEL

GRAVELLED > GRAVEL

GRAVELLY adj covered with gravel

GRAVELS > GRAVEL

GRAVELY > GRAVE

GRAVEN > GRAVE

GRAVENESS > GRAVE

GRAVER n any of various tools

GRAVERS > GRAVER

GRAVES > GRAVE

GRAVESIDE n area surrounding a grave

GRAVESITE n site of grave

GRAVEST > GRAVE

GRAVEWARD adj moving towards grave

GRAVEYARD n cemetery

GRAVID adj pregnant

GRAVIDA n pregnant woman

GRAVIDAE > GRAVIDA

GRAVIDAS > GRAVIDA

GRAVIDITY > GRAVID

GRAVIDLY > GRAVID

GRAVIES > GRAVY

GRAVING > GRAVE

GRAVINGS > GRAVE

GRAVIS adj as in myasthenia gravis chronic muscle-weakening disease

GRAVITAS n seriousness or solemnity

GRAVITATE vb be influenced or drawn towards

GRAVITIES > GRAVITY

GRAVITINO n hypothetical subatomic particle

GRAVITON n postulated quantum of gravitational energy

GRAVITONS > GRAVITON

GRAVITY n force of attraction

GRAVLAKS same as > GRAVLAX

GRAVLAX n dry-cured salmon

GRAVLAXES > GRAVLAX

GRAVS > GRAV

GRAVURE n method of intaglio printing

GRAVURES > GRAVURE

GRAVY n juices from meat in cooking

GRAY same as > GREY

GRAYBACK same as > GREYBACK

GRAYBACKS > GRAYBACK

GRAYBEARD same as > GREYBEARD

GRAYED > GRAY

GRAYER > GRAY

GRAYEST > GRAY

GRAYFISH n dogfish

GRAYFLIES > GRAYFLY

GRAYFLY n trumpet fly

GRAYHEAD n one with grey hair

GRAYHEADS > GRAYHEAD

GRAYHEN n female of the black grouse

GRAYHENS > GRAYHEN

GRAYHOUND US spelling of > GREYHOUND

GRAYING > GRAY

GRAYISH > GRAY

GRAYLAG same as > GREYLAG

GRAYLAGS > GRAYLAG

GRAYLE n holy grail

GRAYLES > GRAYLE

GRAYLING n fish of the salmon family

GRAYLINGS > GRAYLING

GRAYLIST vb hold (someone) in suspicion, without actually excluding him or her from a particular activity

GRAYLISTS > GRAYLIST

GRAYLY > GRAY

GRAYMAIL n tactic to avoid prosecution in espionage case by threatening to expose state secrets during trial

GRAYMAILS > GRAYMAIL

GRAYNESS > GREY

GRAYOUT n impairment of vision due to lack of oxygen

GRAYOUTS > GRAYOUT

GRAYS > GRAY

GRAYSCALE adj in shades of grey

GRAYSTONE n grey igneous rock of volcanic origin

GRAYWACKE same as > GREYWACKE

GRAYWATER n water that has been used

GRAZABLE > GRAZE

GRAZE vb feed on grass ▷ n slight scratch or scrape

GRAZEABLE > GRAZE

GRAZED > GRAZE

GRAZER > GRAZE

GRAZERS > GRAZE

GRAZES > GRAZE

GRAZIER n person who feeds cattle for market

GRAZIERS > GRAZIER

GRAZING n land on which grass for livestock is grown

GRAZINGLY > GRAZE

GRAZINGS > GRAZING

GRAZIOSO adv (of music) to be played gracefully

GREASE n soft melted animal fat ▷ vb apply grease to

GREASED > GREASE

GREASER n mechanic, esp of motor vehicles

GREASERS > GREASER

GREASES > GREASE

GREASIER > GREASY

GREASIES > GREASY

GREASIEST > GREASY

GREASILY > GREASY

GREASING > GREASE

GREASY adj covered with or containing grease ▷ n shearer

GREAT adj large in size or number ▷ n distinguished person

GREATCOAT n heavy overcoat

GREATEN vb make or become great

GREATENED > GREATEN

GREATENS > GREATEN

GREATER > GREAT

GREATEST n most outstanding individual in a given field

GREATESTS > GREATEST

GREATLY > GREAT

GREATNESS > GREAT

GREATS > GREAT

GREAVE n piece of armour for the shin ▷ vb grieve

GREAVED > GREAVE

GREAVES pl n residue left after the rendering of tallow

GREAVING > GREAVE

GREBE n diving water bird

GREBES > GREBE

GREBO same as > GREEBO

GREBOS > GREBO

GRECE n flight of steps

GRECES > GRECE

GRECIAN same as > GRECE

GRECIANS > GRECIAN

GRECISE same as > GRAECIZE

GRECISED > GRECISE

GRECISES > GRECISE

GRECISING > GRECISE

GRECIZE same as > GRAECIZE

GRECIZED > GRECIZE

GRECIZES > GRECIZE

GRECIZING > GRECIZE

GRECQUE n ornament of Greek origin

GRECQUES > GRECQUE

GREE n superiority or victory ▷ vb come or cause to come to agreement or harmony

GREEBO n unkempt or dirty-looking young man

GREEBOES > GREEBO

GREECE same as > GRECE

GREECES > GREECE

GREED n excessive desire for food, wealth, etc

GREEDIER > GREEDY

GREEDIEST > GREEDY

GREEDILY > GREEDY

GREEDLESS > GREED

GREEDS > GREED

GREEDSOME same as > GREEDY

GREEDY adj having an excessive desire for something

GREEGREE same as > GRIGRI

GREEGREES > GREEGREE

GREEING > GREE

GREEK vb represent text as grey lines on a computer screen

GREEKED > GREEK

GREEKING > GREEK

GREEKINGS > GREEK

GREEN adj of a colour between blue and yellow ▷ n colour between blue and yellow ▷ vb make or become green

GREENBACK n inconvertible legal-tender US currency note originally issued during the Civil War in 1862

GREENBELT n zone of farmland, parks, and open country surrounding a town or city

GREENBONE n an eel-like food fish

GREENBUG n common name for Schizaphis graminum

GREENBUGS > GREENBUG

GREENED > GREEN

GREENER n recent immigrant

GREENERS > GREENER

GREENERY n vegetation

GREENEST > GREEN

GREENEYE n small slender fish with pale green eyes

GREENEYES > GREENEYE

GREENFLY n green aphid, a common garden pest

GREENGAGE n sweet green plum

GREENHAND n greenhorn

GREENHEAD n male mallard

GREENHORN n novice

GREENIE n conservationist

GREENIER > GREEN

GREENIES > GREENIE

GREENIEST > GREEN

GREENING n process of making or becoming more aware of environmental considerations

GREENINGS > GREENING

GREENISH > GREEN

GREENLET n type of insectivorous songbird

GREENLETS > GREENLET

GREENLING n type of food fish of the N Pacific Ocean

GREENLIT adj given permission to proceed

GREENLY > GREEN

GREENMAIL n practice of a company buying sufficient shares in another company to threaten takeover and making a quick profit as a result of the threatened company buying back its shares at a higher price ▷ vb carry out the practice of greenmail

GREENNESS > GREEN

GREENROOM n backstage room in a theatre where performers rest or receive visitors

GREENS > GREEN

GREENSAND n olive-green sandstone consisting mainly of quartz and glauconite

GREENSICK adj suffering from greensickness: same as chlorosis

GREENSOME n match for two pairs in which each of the four players tees off and after selecting the better drive the partners of each pair play that ball alternately

GREENTH n greenness

GREENTHS > GREENTH

GREENWASH n superficial or insincere display of concern for the environment that is shown by an organization ▷ vb adopt a 'greenwash' policy

GREENWAY n linear open space, with pedestrian and cycle paths

GREENWAYS > GREENWAY

GREENWEED n woodwaxen

GREENWING n teal

GREENWOOD n forest or wood when the leaves are green

GREENY > GREEN

GREES > GREE

GREESE same as > GRECE

GREESES > GREESE

GREESING > GREESE

GREESINGS > GREESE

GREET vb meet with expressions of welcome ▷ n weeping

GREETE same as > GREET

GREETED > GREET

GREETER n person who greets people

GREETERS > GREETER

GREETES > GREETE

GREETING n act or words of welcoming on meeting

GREETINGS > GREETING

GREETS > GREET

GREFFIER n registrar

GREFFIERS > GREFFIER

GREGALE n northeasterly wind occurring in the Mediterranean

GREGALES > GREGALE

GREGARIAN adj gregarious

GREGARINE n type of parasitic protozoan typically occurring in other invertebrates

GREGATIM adv in flocks or crowds

GREGE vb make heavy

GREGED > GREGE

GREGES > GREGE

GREGING > GREGE

GREGO n short, thick jacket

GREGOS > GREGO

GREIGE adj (of a fabric or material) not yet dyed ▷ n unbleached or undyed cloth or yarn

GREIGES > GREIGE

GREIN vb desire fervently

GREINED > GREIN

GREINING > GREIN

GREINS > GREIN

GREISEN n light-coloured metamorphic rock

GREISENS > GREISEN

GREISLY same as > GRISLY

GREMIAL n type of cloth used in Mass

GREMIALS > GREMIAL

GREMLIN n imaginary being

GREMLINS > GREMLIN

GREMMIE n young surfer

GREMMIES > GREMMIE

GREMMY same as > GREMMIE

GREMOLATA n garnish of finely chopped parsley, garlic and lemon

GREN same as > GRIN

GRENACHE n variety of grape used in wine-making

GRENACHES > GRENACHE

GRENADE n small bomb

GRENADES > GRENADE

GRENADIER n soldier of a regiment formerly trained to throw grenades

GRENADINE n syrup made from pomegranates

GRENNED > GREN

GRENNING > GREN

GRENS > GREN

GRESE same as > GRECE

GRESES > GRESE

GRESSING same as > GRECE

GRESSINGS > GRESSING

GREVE same as > GREAVE

GREVES > GREVE

GREVILLEA n any of various Australian evergreen trees and shrubs

GREW vb shudder

GREWED > GROW

GREWHOUND n greyhound

GREWING > GROW

GREWS > GROW

GREWSOME archaic or US spelling of > GRUESOME

GREWSOMER > GREWSOME

GREX n group of plants

GREXES > GREX

GREY adj of a colour between black and white ▷ n grey colour ▷ vb become or make grey

GREYBACK n any of various animals having a grey back, such as the grey

whale and the hooded crow

GREYBACKS > GREYBACK

GREYBEARD n old man, esp a sage

GREYED > GREY

GREYER > GREY

GREYEST > GREY

GREYHEAD n one having grey hair

GREYHEADS > GREYHEAD

GREYHEN n female of the black grouse

GREYHENS > GREYHEN

GREYHOUND n swift slender dog used in racing

GREYING > GREY

GREYINGS > GREY

GREYISH > GREY

GREYLAG n large grey goose

GREYLAGS > GREYLAG

GREYLIST vb hold (someone) in suspicion, without actually excluding him or her from a particular activity

GREYLISTS > GREYLIST

GREYLY > GREY

GREYNESS > GREY

GREYS > GREY

GREYSCALE n range of grey shades from white to black

GREYSTONE n type of grey rock

GREYWACKE n any dark sandstone or grit having a matrix of clay minerals

GRIBBLE n type of small marine crustacean

GRIBBLES > GRIBBLE

GRICE vb collect objects concerned with railways ▷ n object collected or place visited by a railway enthusiast

GRICED > GRICE

GRICER > GRICE

GRICERS > GRICE

GRICES > GRICE

GRICING > GRICE

GRICINGS > GRICE

GRID n network of horizontal and vertical lines, bars, etc ▷ vb form a grid pattern

GRIDDED > GRID

GRIDDER n American football player

GRIDDERS > GRIDDER

GRIDDING > GRID

GRIDDLE n flat iron plate for cooking ▷ vb cook (food) on a griddle

GRIDDLED > GRIDDLE

GRIDDLES > GRIDDLE

GRIDDLING > GRIDDLE

GRIDE vb grate or scrape harshly ▷ n harsh or piercing sound

GRIDED > GRIDE

GRIDELIN n greyish violet colour

GRIDELINS > GRIDELIN
GRIDES > GRIDE
GRIDING > GRIDE
GRIDIRON *n* frame of metal bars for grilling food ▷ *vb* cover with parallel lines
GRIDIRONS > GRIDIRON
GRIDLOCK *n* situation where traffic is not moving ▷ *vb* (of traffic) to obstruct (an area)
GRIDLOCKS > GRIDLOCK
GRIDS > GRID
GRIECE *same as* > GRECE
GRIECED > GRIECE
GRIECES > GRIECE
GRIEF *n* deep sadness
GRIEFER *n* online gamer who spoils the game for others on purpose
GRIEFERS > GRIEFER
GRIEFFUL *adj* stricken with grief
GRIEFLESS > GRIEF
GRIEFS > GRIEF
GRIESIE *same as* > GRISY
GRIESLY *same as* > GRISY
GRIESY *same as* > GRISY
GRIEVANCE *n* real or imaginary cause for complaint
GRIEVANT *n* any person with a grievance
GRIEVANTS > GRIEVANT
GRIEVE *vb* (cause to) feel grief ▷ *n* farm manager or overseer
GRIEVED > GRIEVE
GRIEVER > GRIEVE
GRIEVERS > GRIEVE
GRIEVES > GRIEVE
GRIEVING > GRIEVE
GRIEVINGS > GRIEVE
GRIEVOUS *adj* very severe or painful
GRIFF *n* information
GRIFFE *n* carved ornament at the base of a column
GRIFFES > GRIFFE
GRIFFIN *n* mythical monster
GRIFFINS > GRIFFIN
GRIFFON *same as* > GRIFFIN
GRIFFONS > GRIFFON
GRIFFS > GRIFF
GRIFT *vb* swindle
GRIFTED > GRIFT
GRIFTER > GRIFT
GRIFTERS > GRIFT
GRIFTING > GRIFT
GRIFTS > GRIFT
GRIG *n* lively person ▷ *vb* fish for grigs
GRIGGED > GRIG
GRIGGING > GRIG
GRIGRI *n* African talisman, amulet, or charm
GRIGRIS > GRIGRI
GRIGS > GRIG

GRIKE *n* fissure in rock
GRIKES > GRIKE
GRILL *n* device on a cooker ▷ *vb* cook under a grill
GRILLADE *n* grilled food
GRILLADES > GRILLADE
GRILLAGE *n* arrangement of beams and crossbeams used as a foundation on soft ground
GRILLAGES > GRILLAGE
GRILLE *n* grating over an opening
GRILLED *adj* cooked on a grill or gridiron
GRILLER > GRILL
GRILLERS > GRILL
GRILLERY *n* place where food is grilled
GRILLES > GRILLE
GRILLING > GRILL
GRILLINGS > GRILL
GRILLION *n* extremely large but unspecified number, quantity, or amount ▷ *determiner* amounting to a grillion
GRILLIONS > GRILLION
GRILLROOM *n* restaurant serving grilled foods
GRILLS > GRILL
GRILLWORK *same as* > GRILL
GRILSE *n* salmon on its first return from the sea to fresh water
GRILSES > GRILSE
GRIM *adj* stern
GRIMACE *n* ugly or distorted facial expression ▷ *vb* make a grimace
GRIMACED > GRIMACE
GRIMACER > GRIMACE
GRIMACERS > GRIMACE
GRIMACES > GRIMACE
GRIMACING > GRIMACE
GRIMALKIN *n* old cat, esp an old female cat
GRIME *n* ingrained dirt ▷ *vb* make very dirty
GRIMED > GRIME
GRIMES > GRIME
GRIMIER > GRIME
GRIMIEST > GRIME
GRIMILY > GRIME
GRIMINESS > GRIME
GRIMING > GRIME
GRIMLY > GRIM
GRIMMER > GRIM
GRIMMEST > GRIM
GRIMNESS > GRIM
GRIMOIRE *n* textbook of sorcery and magic
GRIMOIRES > GRIMOIRE
GRIMY > GRIME
GRIN *vb* smile broadly, showing the teeth ▷ *n* broad smile
GRINCH *n* person whose attitude has a depressing effect
GRINCHES > GRINCH

GRIND *vb* crush or rub to a powder ▷ *n* hard work
GRINDED *obsolete past participle of* > GRIND
GRINDELIA *n* type of coarse American plant with yellow daisy-like flower heads
GRINDER *n* device for grinding substances
GRINDERS > GRINDER
GRINDERY *n* place in which tools and cutlery are sharpened
GRINDING > GRIND
GRINDINGS > GRIND
GRINDS > GRIND
GRINGA *n* female gringo
GRINGAS > GRINGA
GRINGO *n* person from an English-speaking country: used as a derogatory term by Latin Americans
GRINGOS > GRINGO
GRINNED > GRIN
GRINNER > GRIN
GRINNERS > GRIN
GRINNING > GRIN
GRINNINGS > GRIN
GRINS > GRIN
GRIOT *n* (in W Africa) member of a caste recording tribal history
GRIOTS > GRIOT
GRIP *n* firm hold or grasp ▷ *vb* grasp or hold tightly
GRIPE *vb* complain persistently ▷ *n* complaint
GRIPED > GRIPE
GRIPER > GRIPE
GRIPERS > GRIPE
GRIPES > GRIPE
GRIPEY *adj* causing gripes
GRIPIER > GRIPEY
GRIPIEST > GRIPEY
GRIPING *n* act of griping
GRIPINGLY > GRIPE
GRIPINGS > GRIPING
GRIPLE *same as* > GRIPPLE
GRIPMAN *n* cable-car operator
GRIPMEN > GRIPMAN
GRIPPE *former name for* > INFLUENZA
GRIPPED > GRIP
GRIPPER > GRIP
GRIPPERS > GRIP
GRIPPES > GRIPPE
GRIPPIER > GRIPPY
GRIPPIEST > GRIPPY
GRIPPING > GRIP
GRIPPLE *adj* greedy ▷ *n* hook
GRIPPLES > GRIPPLE
GRIPPY *adj* having grip
GRIPS > GRIP
GRIPSACK *n* travel bag
GRIPSACKS > GRIPSACK
GRIPT *archaic variant of* > GRIPPED
GRIPTAPE *n* rough tape for sticking to a surface to

provide a greater grip
GRIPTAPES > GRIPTAPE
GRIPY *same as* > GRIPEY
GRIS *same as* > GRECE
GRISAILLE *n* technique of monochrome painting in shades of grey, as in an oil painting or a wall decoration, imitating the effect of relief
GRISE *vb* shudder
GRISED > GRISE
GRISELY *same as* > GRISLY
GRISEOUS *adj* streaked or mixed with grey
GRISES > GRISE
GRISETTE *n* (esp formerly) a French working-class girl, esp a pretty or flirtatious one
GRISETTES > GRISETTE
GRISGRIS *same as* > GRIGRI
GRISING > GRISE
GRISKIN *n* lean part of a loin of pork
GRISKINS > GRISKIN
GRISLED *another word for* > GRIZZLED
GRISLIER > GRISLY
GRISLIES > GRISLY
GRISLIEST > GRISLY
GRISLY *adj* horrifying or ghastly ▷ *n* large American bear
GRISON *n* type of mammal
GRISONS > GRISON
GRISSINI *pl n* thin crisp breadsticks
GRISSINO *n* Italian breadstick
GRIST *n* grain for grinding
GRISTER *n* device for grinding grain
GRISTERS > GRISTER
GRISTLE *n* tough stringy animal tissue found in meat
GRISTLES > GRISTLE
GRISTLIER > GRISTLE
GRISTLY > GRISTLE
GRISTMILL *n* mill, esp one equipped with large grinding stones for grinding grain
GRISTS > GRIST
GRISY *adj* grim
GRIT *n* rough particles of sand ▷ *vb* spread grit on (an icy road etc) ▷ *adj* great
GRITH *n* security or peace guaranteed for a period of time
GRITHS > GRITH
GRITLESS > GRIT
GRITS > GRIT
GRITSTONE *same as* > GRIT
GRITTED > GRIT
GRITTER *n* vehicle that spreads grit on the roads
GRITTERS > GRITTER

g

GRITTIER > GRIT

GRITTIER > GRITTY

GRITTIEST > GRITTY

GRITTILY > GRITTY

GRITTING n spreading grit on road surfaces

GRITTINGS > GRITTING

GRITTY adj courageous and tough

GRIVATION n (in navigation) grid variation

GRIVET n E African monkey

GRIVETS > GRIVET

GRIZ n grizzly bear

GRIZE same as > GRECE

GRIZES > GRIZE

GRIZZLE vb whine or complain ▷ n grey colour

GRIZZLED adj grey-haired

GRIZZLER > GRIZZLE

GRIZZLERS > GRIZZLE

GRIZZLES > GRIZZLE

GRIZZLIER > GRIZZLY

GRIZZLIES > GRIZZLY

GRIZZLING > GRIZZLY

GRIZZLY n large American bear ▷ adj somewhat grey

GROAN n deep sound of grief or pain ▷ vb utter a groan

GROANED > GROAN

GROANER n person or thing that groans

GROANERS > GROANER

GROANFUL adj sad

GROANING > GROAN

GROANINGS > GROAN

GROANS > GROAN

GROAT n fourpenny piece

GROATS pl n hulled and crushed grain of various cereals

GROCER n shopkeeper selling foodstuffs

GROCERIES pl n food and other household supplies

GROCERS > GROCER

GROCERY n business or premises of a grocer

GROCKED same as > GROKKED

GROCKING same as > GROKKING

GROCKLE n tourist in SW England

GROCKLES > GROCKLE

GRODIER > GRODY

GRODIEST > GRODY

GRODY adj unpleasant

GROG n spirit, usu rum, and water ▷ vb drink grog

GROGGED > GROG

GROGGERY n grogshop

GROGGIER > GROGGY

GROGGIEST > GROGGY

GROGGILY > GROGGY

GROGGING > GROG

GROGGY adj faint, shaky, or dizzy

GROGRAM n coarse fabric

GROGRAMS > GROGRAM

GROGS > GROG

GROGSHOP n drinking place, esp one of disreputable character

GROGSHOPS > GROGSHOP

GROIN n place where the legs join the abdomen ▷ vb provide or construct with groins

GROINED > GROIN

GROINING > GROIN

GROININGS > GROIN

GROINS > GROIN

GROK vb understand completely and intuitively

GROKED same as > GROKKED

GROKING same as > GROKKING

GROKKED > GROK

GROKKING > GROK

GROKS > GROK

GROMA n Roman surveying instrument

GROMAS > GROMA

GROMET same as > GROMMET

GROMETS > GROMET

GROMMET n ring or eyelet

GROMMETED adj having grommets

GROMMETS > GROMMET

GROMWELL n type of hairy plant with small greenish-white, yellow, or blue flowers, and smooth nutlike fruits

GROMWELLS > GROMWELL

GRONE obsolete word for > GROAN

GRONED > GRONE

GRONEFULL same as > GROANFUL

GRONES > GRONE

GRONING > GRONE

GROOF n face, or front of the body

GROOFS > GROOF

GROOLIER > GROOLY

GROOLIEST > GROOLY

GROOLY adj gruesome

GROOM n person who looks after horses ▷ vb make or keep one's clothes and appearance neat and tidy

GROOMED > GROOM

GROOMER > GROOM

GROOMERS > GROOM

GROOMING > GROOM

GROOMINGS > GROOM

GROOMS > GROOM

GROOMSMAN n man who attends the bridegroom at a wedding, usually the best man

GROOMSMEN > GROOMSMAN

GROOVE n long narrow channel in a surface

GROOVED > GROOVE

GROOVER n device that makes grooves

GROOVERS > GROOVER

GROOVES > GROOVE

GROOVIER > GROOVY

GROOVIEST > GROOVY

GROOVILY > GROOVY

GROOVING > GROOVE

GROOVY adj attractive or exciting

GROPE vb feel about or search uncertainly ▷ n instance of groping

GROPED > GROPE

GROPER n type of large fish of warm and tropical seas

GROPERS > GROPER

GROPES > GROPE

GROPING > GROPE

GROPINGLY > GROPE

GROSBEAK n finch with a large powerful bill

GROSBEAKS > GROSBEAK

GROSCHEN n former Austrian monetary unit worth one hundredth of a schilling

GROSCHENS > GROSCHEN

GROSER n gooseberry

GROSERS > GROSER

GROSERT another word for > GROSER

GROSERTS > GROSERT

GROSET another word for > GROSER

GROSETS > GROSET

GROSGRAIN n heavy ribbed silk or rayon fabric

GROSS adj flagrant ▷ n twelve dozen ▷ vb make as total revenue before deductions ▷ interj exclamation indicating disgust

GROSSART another word for > GROSER

GROSSARTS > GROSSART

GROSSED > GROSS

GROSSER > GROSS

GROSSERS > GROSS

GROSSES > GROSS

GROSSEST > GROSS

GROSSING > GROSS

GROSSLY > GROSS

GROSSNESS > GROSS

GROSSULAR n type of garnet

GROSZ n Polish monetary unit

GROSZE > GROSZ

GROSZY > GROSZ

GROT n rubbish

GROTESQUE adj strangely distorted ▷ n grotesque person or thing

GROTS > GROT

GROTTIER > GROTTY

GROTTIEST > GROTTY

GROTTO n small picturesque cave

GROTTOED adj having grotto

GROTTOES > GROTTO

GROTTOS > GROTTO

GROTTY adj nasty or in bad condition

GROUCH vb grumble or complain ▷ n person who is always complaining

GROUCHED > GROUCH

GROUCHES > GROUCH

GROUCHIER > GROUCHY

GROUCHILY > GROUCHY

GROUCHING > GROUCHY

GROUCHY adj bad-tempered

GROUF same as > GROOF

GROUFS > GROUF

GROUGH n natural channel or fissure in a peat moor

GROUGHS > GROUGH

GROUND n surface of the earth ▷ adj on or of the ground ▷ vb base or establish

GROUNDAGE n fee levied on a vessel entering a port or anchored off a shore

GROUNDED adj sensible and down-to-earth

GROUNDEN obsolete variant of > GROUND

GROUNDER n (in baseball) ball that travels along the ground

GROUNDERS > GROUNDER

GROUNDHOG another name for > WOODCHUCK

GROUNDING n basic knowledge of a subject

GROUNDMAN n groundsman

GROUNDMEN > GROUNDMAN

GROUNDNUT n peanut

GROUNDOUT n (in baseball) being put out after hitting a grounder that is fielded and thrown to first base

GROUNDS > GROUND

GROUNDSEL n yellow-flowered weed

GROUP n number of people or things regarded as a unit ▷ vb place or form into a group

GROUPABLE > GROUP

GROUPAGE n gathering people or objects into a group or groups

GROUPAGES > GROUPAGE

GROUPED > GROUP

GROUPER n large edible sea fish

GROUPERS > GROUPER

GROUPIE n ardent fan of a celebrity or of a sport or activity

GROUPIES > GROUPIE

GROUPING n set of people or organizations who act or work together to achieve a shared aim

GROUPINGS > GROUPING

GROUPIST n follower of a group

GROUPISTS > GROUPIST

GROUPLET n small group

GROUPLETS > GROUPLET

GROUPOID n magma
GROUPOIDS > GROUPOID
GROUPS > GROUP
GROUPWARE n software that enables computers within a group or organization to work together, allowing users to exchange electronic-mail messages, access shared files and databases, use video conferencing, etc
GROUPWORK n work done by a group acting together
GROUPY same as > GROUPIE
GROUSE n stocky game bird ▷ vb grumble or complain ▷ adj fine or excellent ▷ adj excellent
GROUSED > GROUSE
GROUSER > GROUSE
GROUSERS > GROUSE
GROUSES > GROUSE
GROUSEST > GROUSE
GROUSING > GROUSE
GROUT n thin mortar ▷ vb fill up with grout
GROUTED > GROUT
GROUTER > GROUT
GROUTERS > GROUT
GROUTIER > GROUTY
GROUTIEST > GROUTY
GROUTING > GROUT
GROUTINGS > GROUT
GROUTS pl n sediment or grounds
GROUTY adj sullen or surly
GROVE n small group of trees
GROVED > GROVE
GROVEL vb behave humbly in order to win a superior's favour
GROVELED > GROVEL
GROVELER > GROVEL
GROVELERS > GROVEL
GROVELESS > GROVE
GROVELING > GROVEL
GROVELLED > GROVEL
GROVELLER > GROVEL
GROVELS > GROVEL
GROVES > GROVE
GROVET n wrestling hold
GROVETS > GROVET
GROVIER > GROVY
GROVIEST > GROVY
GROVY adj like a grove
GROW vb develop physically
GROWABLE adj able to be cultivated
GROWER n person who grows plants
GROWERS > GROWER
GROWING > GROW
GROWINGLY > GROW
GROWINGS > GROW
GROWL vb make a low rumbling sound ▷ n growling sound
GROWLED > GROWL
GROWLER n person, animal, or thing that growls

GROWLERS > GROWLER
GROWLERY n place to retreat to, alone, when ill-humoured
GROWLIER > GROWL
GROWLIEST > GROWL
GROWLING > GROWL
GROWLINGS > GROWL
GROWLS > GROWL
GROWLY > GROWL
GROWN > GROW
GROWNUP n adult
GROWNUPS > GROWNUP
GROWS > GROW
GROWTH n growing ▷ adj of or relating to growth
GROWTHIER > GROWTHY
GROWTHIST n advocate of the importance of economic growth
GROWTHS > GROWTH
GROWTHY adj rapid-growing
GROYNE n wall built out from the shore to control erosion
GROYNES > GROYNE
GROZING adj as in grozing iron iron for smoothing joints between lead pipes
GRR interj expressing anger or annoyance
GRRL n as in riot grrl young woman who enjoys feminist punk rock
GRRLS > GRRL
GRRRL n as in riot grrrl young woman who enjoys feminist punk rock
GRRRLS > GRRRL
GRUB n legless insect larva ▷ vb search carefully for something
GRUBBED > GRUB
GRUBBER n person who grubs
GRUBBERS > GRUBBER
GRUBBIER > GRUBBY
GRUBBIEST > GRUBBY
GRUBBILY > GRUBBY
GRUBBING > GRUB
GRUBBLE same as > GRABBLE
GRUBBLED > GRUBBLE
GRUBBLES > GRUBBLE
GRUBBLING > GRUBBLE
GRUBBY adj dirty
GRUBS > GRUB
GRUBSTAKE n supplies provided for a prospector on the condition that the donor has a stake in any finds ▷ vb furnish with such supplies
GRUBWORM another word for > GRUB
GRUBWORMS > GRUBWORM
GRUDGE vb be unwilling to give or allow ▷ n resentment ▷ adj planned or carried out in order to settle a grudge
GRUDGED > GRUDGE

GRUDGEFUL adj envious
GRUDGER > GRUDGE
GRUDGERS > GRUDGE
GRUDGES > GRUDGE
GRUDGING > GRUDGE
GRUDGINGS > GRUDGE
GRUE n shiver or shudder ▷ vb shiver or shudder
GRUED > GRUE
GRUEING > GRUE
GRUEL n thin porridge ▷ vb subject to exhausting experiences
GRUELED > GRUEL
GRUELER > GRUEL
GRUELERS > GRUEL
GRUELING same as > GRUELLING
GRUELINGS > GRUELING
GRUELLED > GRUEL
GRUELLER > GRUEL
GRUELLERS > GRUEL
GRUELLING adj exhausting or severe ▷ n severe experience, esp punishment
GRUELS > GRUEL
GRUES > GRUE
GRUESOME adj causing horror and disgust
GRUESOMER > GRUESOME
GRUFE same as > GROOF
GRUFES > GRUFE
GRUFF adj rough or surly in manner or voice ▷ vb talk gruffly
GRUFFED > GRUFF
GRUFFER > GRUFF
GRUFFEST > GRUFF
GRUFFIER > GRUFFY
GRUFFIEST > GRUFFY
GRUFFILY > GRUFFY
GRUFFING > GRUFF
GRUFFISH > GRUFF
GRUFFLY > GRUFF
GRUFFNESS > GRUFF
GRUFFS > GRUFF
GRUFFY adj gruff
GRUFTED adj dirty
GRUGRU n tropical American palm
GRUGRUS > GRUGRU
GRUIFORM adj relating to an order of birds, including cranes and bustards
GRUING > GRUE
GRUM adj surly
GRUMBLE vb complain ▷ n complaint
GRUMBLED > GRUMBLE
GRUMBLER > GRUMBLE
GRUMBLERS > GRUMBLE
GRUMBLES > GRUMBLE
GRUMBLIER > GRUMBLE
GRUMBLING > GRUMBLE
GRUMBLY > GRUMBLE
GRUME n clot
GRUMES > GRUME
GRUMLY > GRUM
GRUMMER > GRUM
GRUMMEST > GRUM
GRUMMET same as > GROMMET

GRUMMETED adj having grummets
GRUMMETS > GRUMMET
GRUMNESS > GRUM
GRUMOSE same as > GRUMOUS
GRUMOUS adj (esp of plant parts) consisting of granular tissue
GRUMP n surly or bad-tempered person ▷ vb complain or grumble
GRUMPED > GRUMP
GRUMPH vb grunt
GRUMPHED > GRUMPH
GRUMPHIE n pig
GRUMPHIES > GRUMPHIE
GRUMPHING > GRUMPH
GRUMPHS > GRUMPH
GRUMPHY same as > GRUMPHIE
GRUMPIER > GRUMPY
GRUMPIES > GRUMPY
GRUMPIEST > GRUMPY
GRUMPILY > GRUMPY
GRUMPING > GRUMP
GRUMPISH same as > GRUMPY
GRUMPS > GRUMP
GRUMPY adj bad-tempered ▷ n bad-tempered person
GRUND n as in grund mail payment for right of burial
GRUNDIES pl n men's underpants
GRUNDLE n perineum
GRUNDLES > GRUNDLE
GRUNGE n style of rock music with a fuzzy guitar sound
GRUNGER n fan of grunge music
GRUNGERS > GRUNGER
GRUNGES > GRUNGE
GRUNGEY adj messy or dirty
GRUNGIER > GRUNGY
GRUNGIEST > GRUNGY
GRUNGY adj squalid or seedy
GRUNION n Californian marine fish that spawns on beaches
GRUNIONS > GRUNION
GRUNT vb make a low short gruff sound, like a pig ▷ n pig's sound
GRUNTED > GRUNT
GRUNTER n person or animal that grunts, esp a pig
GRUNTERS > GRUNTER
GRUNTING > GRUNT
GRUNTINGS > GRUNT
GRUNTLE vb grunt or groan
GRUNTLED > GRUNTLE
GRUNTLES > GRUNTLE
GRUNTLING > GRUNTLE
GRUNTS > GRUNT
GRUPPETTI > GRUPPETTO
GRUPPETTO n turn

GRUSHIE *adj* healthy and strong

GRUTCH *vb* grudge

GRUTCHED > GRUTCH

GRUTCHES > GRUTCH

GRUTCHING > GRUTCH

GRUTTEN > GREET

GRUYERE *n* hard flat whole-milk cheese with holes

GRUYERES > GRUYERE

GRYCE *same as* > GRICE

GRYCES > GRYCE

GRYDE *same as* > GRYDE

GRYDED > GRYDE

GRYDES > GRYDE

GRYDING > GRYDE

GRYESY *adj* grey

GRYFON *same as* > GRIFFIN

GRYFONS > GRYFON

GRYKE *same as* > GRIKE

GRYKES > GRYKE

GRYPE *same as* > GRIPE

GRYPES > GRIPE

GRYPHON *same as* > GRIFFIN

GRYPHONS > GRYPHON

GRYPT *archaic form of* > GRIPPED

GRYSBOK *n* small antelope

GRYSBOKS > GRYSBOK

GRYSELY *same as* > GRISLY

GRYSIE *same as* > GRISY

GU *same as* > GJU

GUACAMOLE *n* spread of mashed avocado, tomato pulp, mayonnaise, and seasoning

GUACHARO *another name for* > OILBIRD

GUACHAROS > GUACHARO

GUACO *n* any of several plants used as an antidote to snakebite

GUACOS > GUACO

GUAIAC *same as* > GUAIACUM

GUAIACOL *n* yellowish oily creosote-like liquid extracted from guaiacum resin and hardwood tar, used medicinally as an expectorant

GUAIACOLS > GUAIACOL

GUAIACS > GUAIACUM

GUAIACUM *n* tropical American evergreen tree

GUAIACUMS > GUAIACUM

GUAIOCUM *same as* > GUAIACUM

GUAIOCUMS > GUAIOCUM

GUAN *n* type of bird of Central and S America

GUANA *another word for* > IGUANA

GUANABANA *n* tropical tree or its fruit

GUANACO *n* S American animal related to the llama

GUANACOS > GUANACO

GUANAS > GUANA

GUANASE *n* type of enzyme

GUANASES > GUANASE

GUANAY *n* type of cormorant

GUANAYS > GUANAY

GUANAZOLO *n* form of guanine

GUANGO *n* rain tree

GUANGOS > GUANGO

GUANIDIN *same as* > GUANIDINE

GUANIDINE *n* strongly alkaline crystalline substance, soluble in water and found in plant and animal tissues

GUANIDINS > GUANIDIN

GUANIN *same as* > GUANINE

GUANINE *n* white almost insoluble compound

GUANINES > GUANINE

GUANINS > GUANINE

GUANO *n* dried sea-bird manure

GUANOS > GUANO

GUANOSINE *n* nucleoside consisting of guanine and ribose

GUANS > GUAN

GUANXI *n* Chinese social concept

GUANXIS > GUANXI

GUANYLIC *adj* as in *guanylic acid* nucleotide consisting of guanine, ribose or deoxyribose, and a phosphate group

GUAR *n* Indian plant

GUARACHA *same as* > HUARACHE

GUARACHAS > GUARACHA

GUARACHE *same as* > HUARACHE

GUARACHES > GUARACHE

GUARACHI *same as* > HUARACHE

GUARACHIS > GUARACHI

GUARANA *n* type of shrub native to Venezuela

GUARANAS > GUARANA

GUARANI *n* standard monetary unit of Paraguay

GUARANIES > GUARANI

GUARANIS > GUARANI

GUARANTEE *n* formal assurance, esp in writing, that a product will meet certain standards ▷ *vb* give a guarantee

GUARANTOR *n* person who gives or is bound by a guarantee

GUARANTY *n* pledge of responsibility for fulfilling another person's obligations in case of default

GUARD *vb* watch over to protect or to prevent escape ▷ *n* person or group that guards

GUARDABLE > GUARD

GUARDAGE *n* state of being in the care of a guardian

GUARDAGES > GUARDAGE

GUARDANT *adj* (of a beast) shown full face ▷ *n* guardian

GUARDANTS > GUARDANT

GUARDDOG *n* dog trained to protect premises

GUARDDOGS > GUARDDOG

GUARDED *adj* cautious or noncommittal

GUARDEDLY > GUARDED

GUARDEE *n* guardsman

GUARDEES > GUARDEE

GUARDER > GUARD

GUARDERS > GUARD

GUARDIAN *n* keeper or protector ▷ *adj* protecting or safeguarding

GUARDIANS > GUARDIAN

GUARDING > GUARD

GUARDLESS > GUARD

GUARDLIKE > GUARD

GUARDRAIL *n* railing at the side of a staircase, road, etc, as a safety barrier

GUARDROOM *n* room used by guards

GUARDS > GUARD

GUARDSHIP *n* warship responsible for the safety of other ships in its company

GUARDSMAN *n* member of the Guards

GUARDSMEN > GUARDSMAN

GUARISH *vb* heal

GUARISHED > GUARISH

GUARISHES > GUARISH

GUARS > GUAR

GUAVA *n* yellow-skinned tropical American fruit

GUAVAS > GUAVA

GUAYABERA *n* type of embroidered men's shirt

GUAYULE *n* bushy shrub of the southwestern US

GUAYULES > GUAYULE

GUB *n* white man ▷ *vb* hit or defeat

GUBBAH *same as* > GUB

GUBBAHS > GUBBAH

GUBBED > GUB

GUBBING > GUB

GUBBINS *n* object of little or no value

GUBBINSES > GUBBINS

GUBERNIYA *n* territorial division of imperial Russia

GUBS > GUB

GUCK *n* slimy matter

GUCKIER > GUCKY

GUCKIEST > GUCKY

GUCKS > GUCK

GUCKY *adj* slimy and mucky

GUDDLE *vb* catch (fish) with the hands ▷ *n* muddle

GUDDLED > GUDDLE

GUDDLES > GUDDLE

GUDDLING > GUDDLE

GUDE *Scots word for* > GOOD

GUDEMAN *n* male householder

GUDEMEN > GUDEMAN

GUDES *n* goods

GUDESIRE *n* grandfather

GUDESIRES > GUDESIRE

GUDEWIFE *n* female householder

GUDEWIVES > GUDEWIFE

GUDGEON *n* small freshwater fish ▷ *vb* trick or cheat

GUDGEONED > GUDGEON

GUDGEONS > GUDGEON

GUE *same as* > GJU

GUELDER *adj* as in *guelder rose* kind of shrub

GUENON *n* slender Old World monkey

GUENONS > GUENON

GUERDON *n* reward or payment ▷ *vb* give a guerdon to

GUERDONED > GUERDON

GUERDONER > GUERDON

GUERDONS > GUERDON

GUEREZA *n* handsome colobus monkey

GUEREZAS > GUEREZA

GUERIDON *n* small ornately-carved table

GUERIDONS > GUERIDON

GUERILLA *same as* > GUERRILLA

GUERILLAS > GUERILLA

GUERITE *n* turret used by a sentry

GUERITES > GUERITE

GUERNSEY *n* seaman's knitted woolen sweater

GUERNSEYS > GUERNSEY

GUERRILLA *n* member of an unofficial armed force fighting regular forces

GUES > GUE

GUESS *vb* estimate or draw a conclusion without proper knowledge ▷ *n* estimate or conclusion reached by guessing

GUESSABLE > GUESS

GUESSED > GUESS

GUESSER > GUESS

GUESSERS > GUESS

GUESSES > GUESS

GUESSING > GUESS

GUESSINGS > GUESS

GUESSWORK *n* process or results of guessing

GUEST *n* person entertained at another's expense ▷ *vb* appear as a visiting player or performer

GUESTBOOK *n* page on a website where users leave comments

GUESTED > GUEST

GUESTEN *vb* stay as a guest in someone's house

GUESTENED > GUESTEN

GUESTENS > GUESTEN
GUESTING > GUEST
GUESTS > GUEST
GUESTWISE adv as, or in the manner of, a guest
GUFF n nonsense
GUFFAW n crude noisy laugh ▷ vb laugh in this way
GUFFAWED > GUFFAW
GUFFAWING > GUFFAW
GUFFAWS > GUFFAW
GUFFIE Scots word for > PIG
GUFFIES > GUFFIE
GUFFS > GUFF
GUGA n gannet chick
GUGAS > GUGA
GUGGLE vb drink making a gurgling sound
GUGGLED > GUGGLE
GUGGLES > GUGGLE
GUGGLING > GUGGLE
GUGLET same as > GOGLET
GUGLETS > GUGLET
GUICHET n grating, hatch, or small opening in a wall
GUICHETS > GUICHET
GUID Scot word for > GOOD
GUIDABLE > GUIDE
GUIDAGE n guidance
GUIDAGES > GUIDAGE
GUIDANCE n leadership, instruction, or advice
GUIDANCES > GUIDANCE
GUIDE n person who conducts tour expeditions ▷ vb act as a guide for
GUIDEBOOK n handbook with information for visitors to a place
GUIDED > GUIDE
GUIDELESS > GUIDE
GUIDELINE n set principle for doing something
GUIDEPOST n sign on a post by a road indicating directions
GUIDER > GUIDE
GUIDERS > GUIDE
GUIDES > GUIDE
GUIDESHIP n supervision
GUIDEWAY n track controlling the motion of something
GUIDEWAYS > GUIDEWAY
GUIDEWORD n word at top of dictionary page indicating first entry on page
GUIDING > GUIDE
GUIDINGS > GUIDE
GUIDON n small pennant
GUIDONS > GUIDON
GUIDS n possessions
GUILD n organization or club
GUILDER n former monetary unit of the Netherlands
GUILDERS > GUILDER

GUILDHALL n hall where members of a guild meet
GUILDRIES > GUILDRY
GUILDRY n in Scotland, corporation of merchants
GUILDS > GUILD
GUILDSHIP n condition of being a member of a guild
GUILDSMAN n man who is a member of a guild
GUILDSMEN > GUILDSMAN
GUILE n cunning or deceit ▷ vb deceive
GUILED > GUILE
GUILEFUL > GUILE
GUILELESS adj free from guile
GUILER n deceiver
GUILERS > GUILER
GUILES > GUILE
GUILING > GUILE
GUILLEMET n (in printing) a duckfoot quote
GUILLEMOT n black-and-white diving sea bird of N hemisphere
GUILLOCHE n ornamental band or border with a repeating pattern of two or more interwoven wavy lines, as in architecture ▷ vb decorate with guilloches
GUILT n fact or state of having done wrong ▷ vb make (a person) feel guilty
GUILTED > GUILT
GUILTIER > GUILTY
GUILTIEST > GUILTY
GUILTILY > GUILTY
GUILTING > GUILT
GUILTLESS adj innocent
GUILTS > GUILT
GUILTY adj responsible for an offence or misdeed
GUIMBARD n Jew's harp
GUIMBARDS > GUIMBARD
GUIMP same as > GUIMPE
GUIMPE n short blouse worn under a pinafore dress ▷ vb make with gimp
GUIMPED > GUIMPE
GUIMPES > GUIMPE
GUIMPING > GUIMPE
GUIMPS > GUIMP
GUINEA n former British monetary unit
GUINEAS > GUINEA
GUINEP n type of tropical American tree
GUINEPS > GUINEP
GUIPURE n heavy lace
GUIPURES > GUIPURE
GUIRO n percussion instrument made from a hollow gourd
GUIROS > GUIRO
GUISARD n guiser
GUISARDS > GUISARD

GUISE n false appearance ▷ vb disguise or be disguised in fancy dress
GUISED > GUISE
GUISER n mummer, esp at Christmas or Halloween revels
GUISERS > GUISER
GUISES > GUISE
GUISING > GUISE
GUISINGS > GUISE
GUITAR n stringed instrument
GUITARIST > GUITAR
GUITARS > GUITAR
GUITGUIT n bird belonging to the family Coerebidae
GUITGUITS > GUITGUIT
GUIZER same as > GUISER
GUIZERS > GUIZER
GUL n design used in oriental carpets
GULA n gluttony
GULAG n forced-labour camp
GULAGS > GULAG
GULAR adj of or situated in the throat or oesophagus ▷ n throat or oesophagus
GULARS > GULAR
GULAS > GULA
GULCH n deep narrow valley ▷ vb swallow fast
GULCHED > GULCH
GULCHES > GULCH
GULCHING > GULCH
GULDEN same as > GUILDER
GULDENS > GULDEN
GULE Scots word for > MARIGOLD
GULES n red in heraldry
GULET n wooden Turkish sailing boat
GULETS > GULET
GULF n large deep bay ▷ vb swallow up
GULFED > GULF
GULFIER > GULF
GULFIEST > GULF
GULFING > GULF
GULFLIKE > GULF
GULFS > GULF
GULFWEED n type of brown seaweed
GULFWEEDS > GULFWEED
GULFY > GULF
GULL n long-winged sea bird ▷ vb cheat or deceive
GULLABLE same as > GULLIBLE
GULLABLY > GULLABLE
GULLED > GULL
GULLER n deceiver
GULLERIES > GULLERY
GULLERS > GULLER
GULLERY n breeding-place for gulls
GULLET n muscular tube from the mouth to the stomach
GULLETS > GULLET

GULLEY same as > GULLY
GULLEYED > GULLEY
GULLEYING > GULLEY
GULLEYS > GULLEY
GULLIBLE adj easily tricked
GULLIBLY > GULLIBLE
GULLIED > GULLY
GULLIES > GULLY
GULLING > GULL
GULLISH adj stupid
GULLS > GULL
GULLWING adj (of vehicle door) opening upwards
GULLY n channel cut by running water ▷ vb make (channels) in (the ground, sand, etc)
GULLYING > GULLY
GULOSITY n greed or gluttony
GULP vb swallow hastily ▷ n gulping
GULPED > GULP
GULPER > GULP
GULPERS > GULP
GULPH archaic word for > GULF
GULPHS > GULPH
GULPIER > GULP
GULPIEST > GULP
GULPING > GULP
GULPINGLY > GULP
GULPS > GULP
GULPY > GULP
GULS > GUL
GULY adj relating to gules
GUM n firm flesh in which the teeth are set ▷ vb stick with gum
GUMBALL n round piece of chewing gum
GUMBALLS > GUMBALL
GUMBO n mucilaginous pods of okra
GUMBOIL n abscess on the gum
GUMBOILS > GUMBOIL
GUMBOOT n rubber boot
GUMBOOTS pl n Wellington boots
GUMBOS > GUMBO
GUMBOTIL n sticky clay formed by the weathering of glacial drift
GUMBOTILS > GUMBOTIL
GUMDROP n hard jelly-like sweet
GUMDROPS > GUMDROP
GUMLANDS pl n infertile land from which the original kauri bush has been removed or burnt producing only kauri gum
GUMLESS > GUM
GUMLIKE > GUM
GUMLINE n line where gums meet teeth
GUMLINES > GUMLINE
GUMMA n rubbery tumour
GUMMAS > GUMMA
GUMMATA > GUMMA
GUMMATOUS > GUMMA

GUMMED > GUM
GUMMER n punch-cutting tool
GUMMERS > GUMMER
GUMMI n gelatin-based flavoured sweet
GUMMIER > GUMMY
GUMMIES > GUMMY
GUMMIEST > GUMMY
GUMMILY > GUMMY
GUMMINESS > GUMMY
GUMMING > GUM
GUMMINGS > GUM
GUMMIS > GUMMI
GUMMITE n orange or yellowish amorphous secondary mineral
GUMMITES > GUMMITE
GUMMOSE same as > GUMMOUS
GUMMOSES > GUMMOSE
GUMMOSIS n abnormal production of excessive gum in certain trees, esp fruit trees, as a result of wounding, infection, adverse weather conditions, pruning, etc
GUMMOSITY > GUMMOUS
GUMMOUS adj resembling or consisting of gum
GUMMY adj toothless ▷ n type of small crustacean-eating shark
GUMNUT n hardened seed container of the gumtree
GUMNUTS > GUMNUT
GUMP vb guddle
GUMPED > GUMP
GUMPHION n funeral banner
GUMPHIONS > GUMPHION
GUMPING > GUMP
GUMPS > GUMP
GUMPTION n resourcefulness
GUMPTIONS > GUMPTION
GUMPTIOUS > GUMPTION
GUMS > GUM
GUMSHIELD n plate or strip of soft waxy substance used by boxers to protect the teeth and gums
GUMSHOE n waterproof overshoe ▷ vb act stealthily
GUMSHOED > GUMSHOE
GUMSHOES > GUMSHOE
GUMSUCKER n native-born Australian
GUMTREE n any of various trees that yield gum
GUMTREES > GUMTREE
GUMWEED n any of several yellow-flowered plants
GUMWEEDS > GUMWEED
GUMWOOD same as > GUMTREE
GUMWOODS > GUMWOOD
GUN n weapon with a tube from which missiles are fired ▷ vb cause

(an engine) to run at high speed
GUNBOAT n small warship
GUNBOATS > GUNBOAT
GUNCOTTON n form of cellulose nitrate used as an explosive
GUNDIES > GUNDY
GUNDOG n dog trained to work with a hunter or gamekeeper
GUNDOGS > GUNDOG
GUNDY n toffee
GUNFIGHT n fight between persons using firearms ▷ vb fight with guns
GUNFIGHTS > GUNFIGHT
GUNFIRE n repeated firing of guns
GUNFIRES > GUNFIRE
GUNFLINT n piece of flint in a flintlock's hammer used to strike the spark that ignites the charge
GUNFLINTS > GUNFLINT
GUNFOUGHT > GUNFIGHT
GUNG adj as in gung ho extremely or excessively enthusiastic about something
GUNGE n sticky unpleasant substance ▷ vb block or encrust with gunge
GUNGED > GUNGE
GUNGES > GUNGE
GUNGIER > GUNGE
GUNGIEST > GUNGE
GUNGING > GUNGE
GUNGY > GUNGE
GUNHOUSE n on a warship, an armoured rotatable enclosure for guns
GUNHOUSES > GUNHOUSE
GUNITE n mortar sprayed in a very dense concrete layer
GUNITES > GUNITE
GUNK n slimy or filthy substance ▷ vb cover with gunk
GUNKED > GUNK
GUNKHOLE vb make a series of short boat excursions
GUNKHOLED > GUNKHOLE
GUNKHOLES > GUNKHOLE
GUNKIER > GUNK
GUNKIEST > GUNK
GUNKING > GUNK
GUNKS > GUNK
GUNKY > GUNK
GUNLAYER n person who aims a ship's gun
GUNLAYERS > GUNLAYER
GUNLESS > GUN
GUNLOCK n mechanism in some firearms
GUNLOCKS > GUNLOCK
GUNMAKER n person who makes guns
GUNMAKERS > GUNMAKER
GUNMAN n armed criminal

GUNMEN > GUNMAN
GUNMETAL n alloy of copper, tin, and zinc ▷ adj dark grey
GUNMETALS > GUNMETAL
GUNNAGE n number of guns carried by a warship
GUNNAGES > GUNNAGE
GUNNED > GUN
GUNNEL same as > GUNWALE
GUNNELS > GUNNEL
GUNNEN > GUN
GUNNER n artillery soldier
GUNNERA n type of herbaceous plant
GUNNERAS > GUNNERA
GUNNERIES > GUNNERY
GUNNERS > GUNNER
GUNNERY n use or science of large guns
GUNNIES > GUNNY
GUNNING > GUN
GUNNINGS > GUN
GUNNY n strong coarse fabric used for sacks
GUNNYBAG same as > GUNNYSACK
GUNNYBAGS > GUNNYBAG
GUNNYSACK n sack made from gunny
GUNPAPER n cellulose nitrate explosive made by treating paper with nitric acid
GUNPAPERS > GUNPAPER
GUNPLAY n use of firearms, as by criminals
GUNPLAYS > GUNPLAY
GUNPOINT n muzzle of a gun
GUNPOINTS > GUNPOINT
GUNPORT n porthole or other opening for a gun
GUNPORTS > GUNPORT
GUNPOWDER n explosive mixture of potassium nitrate, sulphur, and charcoal
GUNROOM n the mess allocated to junior officers
GUNROOMS > GUNROOM
GUNRUNNER n person who smuggles guns and ammunition
GUNS > GUN
GUNSEL n catamite
GUNSELS > GUNSEL
GUNSHIP n ship or helicopter armed with heavy guns
GUNSHIPS > GUNSHIP
GUNSHOT n shot or range of a gun
GUNSHOTS > GUNSHOT
GUNSIGHT n device on a gun which helps the user to aim
GUNSIGHTS > GUNSIGHT
GUNSMITH n person who manufactures or repairs firearms, esp portable guns
GUNSMITHS > GUNSMITH

GUNSTICK n ramrod
GUNSTICKS > GUNSTICK
GUNSTOCK n wooden handle to which the barrel of a rifle is attached
GUNSTOCKS > GUNSTOCK
GUNSTONE n cannonball
GUNSTONES > GUNSTONE
GUNTER n type of gaffing
GUNTERS > GUNTER
GUNWALE n top of a ship's side
GUNWALES > GUNWALE
GUNYAH n hut or shelter in the bush
GUNYAHS > GUNYAH
GUP n gossip
GUPPIES > GUPPY
GUPPY n small colourful aquarium fish
GUPS > GUP
GUQIN n type of Chinese zither
GUQINS > GUQIN
GUR n unrefined cane sugar
GURAMI same as > GOURAMI
GURAMIS > GURAMI
GURDIES > GURDY
GURDWARA n Sikh place of worship
GURDWARAS > GURDWARA
GURDY n winch on a fishing boat
GURGE vb swallow up
GURGED > GURGE
GURGES > GURGE
GURGING > GURGE
GURGLE n bubbling noise ▷ vb (of water) to make low bubbling noises when flowing
GURGLED > GURGLE
GURGLES > GURGLE
GURGLET same as > GOGLET
GURGLETS > GURGLET
GURGLIER > GURGLY
GURGLIEST > GURGLY
GURGLING > GURGLE
GURGLY adj making gurgling sounds
GURGOYLE same as > GARGOYLE
GURGOYLES > GURGOYLE
GURJUN n S or SE Asian tree that yields a resin
GURJUNS > GURJUN
GURL vb snarl
GURLED > GURL
GURLET n type of pickaxe
GURLETS > GURLET
GURLIER > GURLY
GURLIEST > GURLY
GURLING > GURL
GURLS > GURL
GURLY adj stormy
GURN variant spelling of > GIRN
GURNARD n spiny armour-headed sea fish
GURNARDS > GURNARD
GURNED > GURN

GURNET same as **>** GURNARD
GURNETS **>** GURNARD
GURNEY n wheeled stretcher for transporting hospital patients
GURNEYS **>** GURNEY
GURNING **>** GURN
GURNS **>** GURN
GURRAH n type of coarse muslin
GURRAHS **>** GURRAH
GURRIER n low-class tough ill-mannered person
GURRIERS **>** GURRIER
GURRIES **>** GURRY
GURRY n dog-fight
GURS **>** GUR
GURSH n unit of currency in Saudi Arabia
GURSHES **>** GURSH
GURU n Hindu or Sikh religious teacher or leader
GURUDOM n state of being a guru
GURUDOMS **>** GURUDOM
GURUISM **>** GURU
GURUISMS **>** GURU
GURUS **>** GURU
GURUSHIP **>** GURU
GURUSHIPS **>** GURU
GUS **>** GU
GUSH vb flow out suddenly and profusely **▷** n sudden copious flow
GUSHED **>** GUSH
GUSHER n spurting oil well
GUSHERS **>** GUSHER
GUSHES **>** GUSH
GUSHIER **>** GUSHY
GUSHIEST **>** GUSHY
GUSHILY **>** GUSHY
GUSHINESS **>** GUSHY
GUSHING **>** GUSH
GUSHINGLY **>** GUSH
GUSHY adj displaying excessive sentimentality
GUSLA n Balkan single-stringed musical instrument
GUSLAR n player of the gusla
GUSLARS **>** GUSLAR
GUSLAS **>** GUSLA
GUSLE same as **>** GUSLA
GUSLES **>** GUSLE
GUSLI n Russian harp-like musical instrument
GUSLIS **>** GUSLI
GUSSET n piece of material sewn into a garment to strengthen it **▷** vb put a gusset in (a garment)
GUSSETED **>** GUSSET
GUSSETING **>** GUSSET
GUSSETS **>** GUSSET
GUSSIE n young pig
GUSSIED **>** GUSSY
GUSSIES **>** GUSSY
GUSSY vb dress elaborately
GUSSYING **>** GUSSY
GUST n sudden blast of wind **▷** vb blow in gusts

GUSTABLE n anything that can be tasted
GUSTABLES **>** GUSTABLE
GUSTATION n act of tasting or the faculty of taste
GUSTATIVE **>** GUSTATION
GUSTATORY **>** GUSTATION
GUSTED **>** GUST
GUSTFUL adj tasty
GUSTIE adj tasty
GUSTIER **>** GUSTY
GUSTIEST **>** GUSTY
GUSTILY **>** GUSTY
GUSTINESS **>** GUSTY
GUSTING **>** GUST
GUSTLESS adj tasteless
GUSTO n enjoyment or zest
GUSTOES **>** GUSTO
GUSTOS **>** GUSTO
GUSTS **>** GUST
GUSTY adj blustery weather
GUT n intestine **▷** vb remove the guts from **▷** adj basic or instinctive
GUTBUCKET n highly emotional style of jazz playing
GUTCHER n grandfather
GUTCHERS **>** GUTCHER
GUTFUL n bellyful
GUTFULS **>** GUTFUL
GUTLESS adj cowardly
GUTLESSLY **>** GUTLESS
GUTLIKE **>** GUT
GUTROT n diarrhoea
GUTROTS **>** GUTROT
GUTS vb devour greedily
GUTSED **>** GUTS
GUTSER n as in come a gutser fall heavily to the ground
GUTSERS **>** GUTSER
GUTSES **>** GUTS
GUTSFUL n bellyful
GUTSFULS **>** GUTSFUL
GUTSIER **>** GUTSY
GUTSIEST **>** GUTSY
GUTSILY **>** GUTSY
GUTSINESS **>** GUTSY
GUTSING **>** GUTS
GUTSY adj courageous
GUTTA n small drop-like ornament
GUTTAE **>** GUTTA
GUTTAS **>** GUTTA
GUTTATE adj covered with small drops or drop-like markings **▷** vb exude droplets of liquid
GUTTATED same as **>** GUTTATE
GUTTATES **>** GUTTATE
GUTTATING **>** GUTTATE
GUTTATION **>** GUTTATE
GUTTED **>** GUT
GUTTER n shallow channel for carrying away water **▷** vb (of a candle) burn unsteadily

GUTTERED **>** GUTTER
GUTTERING n material for gutters
GUTTERS **>** GUTTER
GUTTERY **>** GUTTER
GUTTIER **>** GUTTY
GUTTIES **>** GUTTY
GUTTIEST **>** GUTTY
GUTTING **>** GUT
GUTTLE vb eat greedily
GUTTLED **>** GUTTLE
GUTTLER **>** GUTTLE
GUTTLERS **>** GUTTLE
GUTTLES **>** GUTTLE
GUTTLING **>** GUTTLE
GUTTURAL adj (of a sound) produced at the back of the throat **▷** n guttural consonant
GUTTURALS **>** GUTTURAL
GUTTY n urchin or delinquent **▷** adj courageous
GUTZER n bad fall
GUTZERS **>** GUTZER
GUV informal name for **>** GOVERNOR
GUVS **>** GUV
GUY n man or boy **▷** vb make fun of
GUYED **>** GUY
GUYING **>** GUY
GUYLE same as **>** GUILE
GUYLED **>** GUYLE
GUYLER **>** GUYLE
GUYLERS **>** GUYLE
GUYLES **>** GUYLE
GUYLINE n guy rope
GUYLINER n eyeliner worn by men
GUYLINERS **>** GUYLINER
GUYLINES **>** GUYLINE
GUYLING **>** GUYLE
GUYOT n flat-topped submarine mountain
GUYOTS **>** GUYOT
GUYS **>** GUY
GUYSE same as **>** GUISE
GUYSES **>** GUYSE
GUZZLE vb eat or drink greedily
GUZZLED **>** GUZZLE
GUZZLER n person or thing that guzzles
GUZZLERS **>** GUZZLER
GUZZLES **>** GUZZLE
GUZZLING **>** GUZZLE
GWEDUC same as **>** GEODUCK
GWEDUCK same as **>** GEODUCK
GWEDUCKS **>** GWEDUCK
GWEDUCS **>** GWEDUCK
GWINE dialect form of **>** GOING
GWINIAD n powan
GWINIADS **>** GWINIAD
GWYNIAD n type of freshwater white fish
GWYNIADS **>** GWYNIAD
GYAL same as **>** GAYAL
GYALS **>** GYAL

GYBE vb (of a sail) swing suddenly from one side to the other **▷** n instance of gybing
GYBED **>** GYBE
GYBES **>** GYBE
GYBING **>** GYBE
GYELD n guild
GYELDS **>** GYELD
GYLDEN adj golden
GYM n gymnasium
GYMBAL same as **>** GIMBAL
GYMBALS **>** GYMBAL
GYMKHANA n horse-riding competition
GYMKHANAS **>** GYMKHANA
GYMMAL same as **>** GIMMAL
GYMMALS **>** GYMMAL
GYMNASIA **>** GYMNASIUM
GYMNASIAL **>** GYMNASIUM
GYMNASIC **>** GYMNASIUM
GYMNASIEN **>** GYMNASIUM
GYMNASIUM n large room with equipment for physical training
GYMNAST n expert in gymnastics
GYMNASTIC adj of, relating to, like, or involving gymnastics
GYMNASTS **>** GYMNAST
GYMNIC adj gymnastic
GYMNOSOPH n adherent of gymnosophy: belief that food and clothing are detrimental to purity of thought
GYMP same as **>** GIMP
GYMPED **>** GYMP
GYMPIE n tall tree with stinging hairs on its leaves
GYMPIES **>** GYMPIE
GYMPING **>** GYMP
GYMPS **>** GYMP
GYMS **>** GYM
GYMSLIP n tunic or pinafore formerly worn by schoolgirls
GYMSLIPS **>** GYMSLIP
GYMSUIT n costume worn for gymnastics
GYMSUITS **>** GYMSUIT
GYNAE adj gynaecological **▷** n gynaecology
GYNAECEA **>** GYNAECIUM
GYNAECEUM same as **>** GYNAECIA
GYNAECIA **>** GYNAECIUM
GYNAECIUM same as **>** GYNOECIUM
GYNAECOID adj resembling, relating to, or like a woman
GYNAES **>** GYNAE
GYNANDRY n hermaphroditism
GYNARCHIC **>** GYNARCHY
GYNARCHY n government by women
GYNECIA **>** GYNECIUM
GYNECIC adj relating to the female sex

GYNECIUM *same as* > GYNOECIUM

GYNECOID *same as* > GYNAECOID

GYNIATRY *n* gynaecology: medicine concerned with diseases in women

GYNIE *n* gynaecology

GYNIES > GYNIE

GYNNEY *n* guinea hen

GYNNEYS > GYNNEY

GYNNIES > GYNNY

GYNNY *same as* > GYNNEY

GYNO *n* gynaecologist

GYNOCRACY *n* government by women

GYNOECIA > GYNOECIUM

GYNOECIUM *n* carpels of a flowering plant collectively

GYNOPHOBE *n* person who hates or fears women

GYNOPHORE *n* stalk in some plants that bears the gynoecium above the level of the other flower parts

GYNOS > GYNO

GYNY *n* gynaecology

GYOZA *n* Japanese fried dumpling

GYOZAS > GYOZA

GYP *vb* swindle, cheat, or defraud ▷ *n* act of cheating

GYPLURE *n* synthetic version of the gypsy moth sex pheromone

GYPLURES > GYPLURE

GYPO *n* small-scale independent logger

GYPOS > GYPO

GYPPED > GYP

GYPPER > GYP

GYPPERS > GYP

GYPPIE *same as* > GIPPY

GYPPIES > GYPPY

GYPPING > GYP

GYPPO *n* derogatory term for a gypsy

GYPPOS > GYPPO

GYPPY *same as* > GIPPY

GYPS > GYP

GYPSEIAN *adj* relating to gypsies

GYPSEOUS > GYPSUM

GYPSIED > GYPSY

GYPSIES > GYPSY

GYPSTER *n* swindler

GYPSTERS > GYPSTER

GYPSUM *n* chalklike mineral

GYPSUMS > GYPSUM

GYPSY *n* member of a nomadic people ▷ *vb* live like a gypsy

GYPSYDOM > GYPSY

GYPSYDOMS > GYPSYDOM

GYPSYHOOD > GYPSY

GYPSYING > GYPSY

GYPSYISH > GYPSY

GYPSYISM *n* state of being a gypsy

GYPSYISMS > GYPSYISM

GYPSYWORT *n* type of Eurasian herb with white flowers

GYRAL *adj* having a circular, spiral, or rotating motion

GYRALLY > GYRAL

GYRANT *adj* gyrating

GYRASE *n* topoisomerase enzyme

GYRASES > GYRASE

GYRATE *vb* rotate or spiral about a point or axis ▷ *adj* curved or coiled into a circle

GYRATED > GYRATE

GYRATES > GYRATE

GYRATING > GYRATE

GYRATION *n* act or process of gyrating

GYRATIONS > GYRATION

GYRATOR *n* electronic circuit that inverts the impedance

GYRATORS > GYRATOR

GYRATORY > GYRATE

GYRE *n* circular or spiral movement or path ▷ *vb* whirl

GYRED > GYRE

GYRENE *n* nickname for a member of the US Marine Corps

GYRENES > GYRENE

GYRES > GYRE

GYRFALCON *n* very large rare falcon of northern regions

GYRI > GYRUS

GYRING > GYRE

GYRO *n* gyrocompass

GYROCAR *n* two-wheeled car

GYROCARS > GYROCAR

GYRODYNE *n* aircraft that uses a powered rotor to take off and manoeuvre, but uses autorotation when cruising

GYRODYNES > GYRODYNE

GYROIDAL *adj* spiral

GYROLITE *n* silicate

GYROLITES > GYROLITE

GYROMANCY *n* divination by spinning in a circle, then falling on any of various letters that have been written on the ground

GYRON *same as* > GIRON

GYRONIC > GYRON

GYRONNY *same as* > GIRONNY

GYRONS > GYRON

GYROPILOT *n* type of automatic pilot

GYROPLANE *another name for* > AUTOGIRO

GYROS > GYRO

GYROSCOPE *n* disc rotating on an axis that can turn in any direction, so the disc maintains the same position regardless of the movement of the surrounding structure

GYROSE *adj* marked with sinuous lines

GYROSTAT *same as* > GYROSCOPE

GYROSTATS > GYROSTAT

GYROUS *adj* gyrose

GYROVAGUE *n* peripatetic monk

GYRUS *n* convolution

GYRUSES > GYRUS

GYTE *n* spoilt child

GYTES > GYTE

GYTRASH *n* spirit that haunts lonely roads

GYTRASHES > GYTRASH

GYTTJA *n* sediment on lake bottom

GYTTJAS > GYTTJA

GYVE *vb* shackle or fetter ▷ *n* fetters

GYVED > GYVE

GYVES > GYVE

GYVING > GYVE

Hh

HA *interj* exclamation of triumph, surprise, or scorn

HAAF *n* fishing ground off the Shetland and Orkney Islands

HAAFS > HAAF

HAANEPOOT *n* variety of grape

HAAR *n* cold sea mist or fog off the North Sea

HAARS > HAAR

HABANERA *n* slow Cuban dance in duple time

HABANERAS > HABANERA

HABANERO *n* variety of chilli pepper

HABANEROS > HABANERO

HABDABS *n* highly nervous state

HABDALAH *n* prayer at end of Jewish sabbath

HABDALAHS > HABDALAH

HABENDUM *n* part of a deed defining the limits of ownership

HABENDUMS > HABENDUM

HABERDINE *n* dried cod

HABERGEON *n* light sleeveless coat of mail worn in the 14th century under the plated hauberk

HABILABLE *adj* able to wear clothes

HABILE *adj* skilful

HABIT *n* established way of behaving ▷ *vb* clothe

HABITABLE *adj* fit to be lived in

HABITABLY > HABITABLE

HABITAN *same as* > HABITANT

HABITANS > HABITAN

HABITANT *n* early French settler in Canada or Louisiana or a descendant of one, esp a farmer

HABITANTS > HABITANT

HABITAT *n* natural home of an animal or plant

HABITATS > HABITAT

HABITED *adj* dressed in a habit

HABITING > HABIT

HABITS > HABIT

HABITUAL *adj* done regularly and repeatedly ▷ *n* person with a habit

HABITUALS > HABITUAL

HABITUATE *vb* accustom

HABITUDE *n* habit or tendency

HABITUDES > HABITUDE

HABITUE *n* frequent visitor to a place

HABITUES > HABITUE

HABITUS *n* general physical state

HABITUSES > HABITUS

HABLE *old form of* > ABLE

HABOOB *n* sandstorm

HABOOBS > HABOOB

HABU *n* large venomous snake

HABUS > HABU

HACEK *n* pronunciation symbol in Slavonic language

HACEKS > HACEK

HACENDADO *n* owner of hacienda

HACHIS *n* hash

HACHURE *n* shading drawn on a map to indicate steepness of a hill ▷ *n* mark or show by hachures

HACHURED > HACHURE

HACHURES > HACHURE

HACHURING > HACHURE

HACIENDA *n* ranch or large estate in Latin America

HACIENDAS > HACIENDA

HACK *vb* cut or chop violently ▷ *n* (inferior) writer or journalist ▷ *adj* unoriginal or of a low standard

HACKABLE > HACK

HACKAMORE *n* rope or rawhide halter used for unbroken foals

HACKBERRY *n* American tree or shrub with edible cherry-like fruits

HACKBOLT *n* shearwater

HACKBOLTS > HACKBOLT

HACKBUT *another word for* > ARQUEBUS

HACKBUTS > HACKBUT

HACKED > HACK

HACKEE *n* chipmunk

HACKEES > HACKEE

HACKER *n* computer enthusiast

HACKERIES > HACKERY

HACKERS > HACKER

HACKERY *n* journalism

HACKETTE *n* informal, derogatory term for female journalist

HACKETTES > HACKETTE

HACKIE *n* US word meaning cab driver

HACKIES > HACKIE

HACKING > HACK

HACKINGS > HACK

HACKLE *same as* > HECKLE

HACKLED > HACKLE

HACKLER > HACKLE

HACKLERS > HACKLE

HACKLES *pl n* hairs which rise in response to emotion

HACKLET *n* kittiwake

HACKLETS > HACKLET

HACKLIER > HACKLY

HACKLIEST > HACKLY

HACKLING > HACKLE

HACKLY *adj* rough or jagged

HACKMAN *n* taxi driver

HACKMEN > HACKMAN

HACKNEY *n* taxi ▷ *vb* make commonplace and banal by too frequent use

HACKNEYED *adj* (of a word or phrase) unoriginal and overused

HACKNEYS > HACKNEY

HACKS > HACK

HACKSAW *n* small saw for cutting metal ▷ *vb* cut with a hacksaw

HACKSAWED > HACKSAW

HACKSAWN > HACKSAW

HACKSAWS > HACKSAW

HACKWORK *n* dull repetitive work

HACKWORKS > HACKWORK

HACQUETON *n* padded jacket worn under chain mail

HAD *vb* Scots form of hold

HADAL *adj* denoting very deep zones of the oceans

HADARIM > HEDER

HADAWAY *sentence substitute* exclamation urging the hearer to refrain from delay

HADDEN > HAVE

HADDEST *same as* > HADST

HADDIE *n* finnan haddock

HADDIES > HADDIE

HADDING > HAVE

HADDOCK *n* edible sea fish of N Atlantic

HADDOCKS > HADDOCK

HADE *n* angle made to the vertical by the plane of a fault or vein ▷ *vb* incline from the vertical

HADED > HADE

HADEDAH *n* large grey-green S African ibis

HADEDAHS > HADEDAH

HADES > HADE

HADING > HADE

HADITH *n* body of legend about Mohammed and his followers

HADITHS > HADITH

HADJ *same as* > HAJJ

HADJEE *same as* > HADJI

HADJEES > HADJEE

HADJES > HADJ

HADJI *same as* > HAJJI

HADJIS > HADJI

HADROME *n* part of xylem

HADROMES > HADROME

HADRON *n* type of elementary particle

HADRONIC > HADRON

HADRONS > HADRON

HADROSAUR *n* any one of a large group of duck-billed partly aquatic bipedal dinosaurs

HADS > HAVE

HADST *singular form of the past tense (indicative mood) of* > HAVE

HAE *Scot variant of* > HAVE

HAECCEITY *n* property that uniquely identifies an object

HAED > HAE

HAEING > HAE

HAEM *n* red organic pigment containing ferrous iron

HAEMAL *adj* of the blood

HAEMATAL *same as* > HAEMAL

HAEMATEIN *n* dark purple water-insoluble crystalline substance obtained from logwood and used as an indicator and biological stain

HAEMATIC *n* agent that stimulates the production of red blood cells

HAEMATICS > HAEMATIC

HAEMATIN *n* dark bluish or brownish pigment containing iron in the

ferric state, obtained by
the oxidation of haem
HAEMATINS > HAEMATIN
HAEMATITE same as
> HEMATITE
HAEMATOID
adj resembling blood
HAEMATOMA n tumour of
clotted or partially clotted
blood
HAEMIC same as
> HAEMATIC
HAEMIN n haematin
chloride
HAEMINS > HAEMIN
HAEMOCOEL n body cavity
of many invertebrates,
including arthropods and
molluscs, developed from
part of the blood system
HAEMOCYTE n any blood
cell, esp a red blood cell
HAEMOID same as
> HAEMATOID
HAEMOLYSE same as
> HAEMOLYZE
HAEMOLYZE vb break
down red blood cells
HAEMONIES > HAEMONY
HAEMONY n plant
mentioned in Milton's
poetry
HAEMOSTAT n surgical
instrument that stops
bleeding by compression
of a blood vessel
HAEMS > HAEM
HAEN > HAE
HAEREDES > HAERES
HAEREMAI interj Māori
expression of welcome
▷ n act of saying 'haeremai'
HAEREMAIS > HAEREMAI
HAERES same as > HERES
HAES > HAE
HAET n whit
HAETS > HAET
HAFF n lagoon
HAFFET n side of head
HAFFETS > HAFFET
HAFFIT same as > HAFFET
HAFFITS > HAFFIT
HAFFLIN same as
> HALFLING
HAFFLINS > HAFFLIN
HAFFS > HAFF
HAFIZ n title for a person
who knows the Koran by
heart
HAFIZES > HAFIZ
HAFNIUM n metallic
element found in
zirconium ores
HAFNIUMS > HAFNIUM
HAFT n handle of an axe,
knife, or dagger ▷ vb
provide with a haft
HAFTARA same as
> HAFTARAH
HAFTARAH n (in Judaism)
short reading from the
Prophets which follows
the reading from the Torah
on Sabbaths and festivals

HAFTARAHS > HAFTARAH
HAFTARAS > HAFTARA
HAFTAROS > HAFTARAH
HAFTAROT > HAFTARAH
HAFTAROTH > HAFTARAH
HAFTED > HAFT
HAFTER > HAFT
HAFTERS > HAFT
HAFTING > HAFT
HAFTORAH same as
> HAFTARAH
HAFTORAHS > HAFTORAH
HAFTOROS > HAFTORAH
HAFTOROT > HAFTORAH
HAFTOROTH > HAFTORAH
HAFTS > HAFT
HAG n ugly old woman ▷ vb
hack
HAGADIC same as
> HAGGADIC
HAGADIST same as
> HAGGADIST
HAGADISTS > HAGADIST
HAGBERRY same as
> HACKBERRY
HAGBOLT same as
> HACKBOLT
HAGBOLTS > HAGBOLT
HAGBORN adj born of a
witch
HAGBUSH same as
> ARQUEBUS
HAGBUSHES > HAGBUSH
HAGBUT same as > HAGBUT
HAGBUTEER > HAGBUT
HAGBUTS > HAGBUT
HAGBUTTER > HAGBUT
HAGDEN same as
> HACKBOLT
HAGDENS > HAGDEN
HAGDON same as
> HACKBOLT
HAGDONS > HAGDON
HAGDOWN same as
> HACKBOLT
HAGDOWNS > HAGDOWN
HAGFISH n any of various
primitive eel-like
vertebrates
HAGFISHES > HAGFISH
HAGG n boggy place
HAGGADA same as
> HAGGADAH
HAGGADAH n book
containing the order of
service of the traditional
Jewish Passover meal
HAGGADAHS > HAGGADAH
HAGGADAS > HAGGADA
HAGGADIC > HAGGADAH
HAGGADIST n writer of
Aggadoth
HAGGADOT > HAGGADAH
HAGGADOTH > HAGGADAH
HAGGARD adj looking tired
and ill ▷ n hawk that has
reached maturity before
being caught
HAGGARDLY > HAGGARD
HAGGARDS > HAGGARD
HAGGED > HAG
HAGGING > HAG
HAGGIS n Scottish dish

HAGGISES > HAGGIS
HAGGISH > HAG
HAGGISHLY > HAG
HAGGLE vb bargain or
wrangle over a price
HAGGLED > HAGGLE
HAGGLER > HAGGLE
HAGGLERS > HAGGLE
HAGGLES > HAGGLE
HAGGLING n act of
haggling
HAGGLINGS > HAGGLING
HAGGS > HAGG
HAGIARCHY n
government by saints,
holy men, or men in holy
orders
HAGIOLOGY n literature
about the lives and
legends of saints
HAGLET same as
> HACKLET
HAGLETS > HAGLET
HAGLIKE > HAG
HAGRIDDEN > HAGRIDE
HAGRIDE vb torment or
obsess
HAGRIDER > HAGRIDE
HAGRIDERS > HAGRIDE
HAGRIDES > HAGRIDE
HAGRIDING > HAGRIDE
HAGRODE > HAGRIDE
HAGS > HAG
HAH same as > HA
HAHA n wall or other
boundary marker that is
set in a ditch
HAHAS > HAHA
HAHNIUM n transuranic
element
HAHNIUMS > HAHNIUM
HAHS > HAH
HAICK same as > HAIK
HAICKS > HAICK
HAIDUK n rural brigand
HAIDUKS > HAIDUK
HAIK n Arab's outer
garment
HAIKA > HAIK
HAIKAI same as > HAIKU
HAIKS > HAIK
HAIKU n Japanese verse
form in 17 syllables
HAIKUS > HAIKU
HAIL n (shower of) small
pellets of ice ▷ vb fall as or
like hail ▷ sentence
substitute exclamation of
greeting
HAILED > HAIL
HAILER > HAIL
HAILERS > HAIL
HAILIER > HAIL
HAILIEST > HAIL
HAILING > HAIL
HAILS > HAIL
HAILSHOT n small
scattering shot
HAILSHOTS > HAILSHOT
HAILSTONE n pellet of
hail
HAILSTORM n storm
during which hail falls

HAILY > HAIL
HAIMISH same as
> HEIMISH
HAIN vb Scots word
meaning save
HAINCH Scots form of
> HAUNCH
HAINCHED > HAINCH
HAINCHES > HAINCH
HAINCHING > HAINCH
HAINED > HAIN
HAINING > HAIN
HAININGS > HAIN
HAINS > HAIN
HAINT same as > HAUNT
HAINTS > HAINT
HAIQUE same as > HAIK
HAIQUES > HAIK
HAIR n threadlike growth
on the skin ▷ vb provide
with hair
HAIRBALL n compact
mass of hair that forms in
the stomach of cats,
calves, etc, as a result of
licking and swallowing the
fur, and causes vomiting,
coughing, bloat, weight
loss, and depression
HAIRBALLS > HAIRBALL
HAIRBAND n band worn
around head to control
hair
HAIRBANDS > HAIRBAND
HAIRBELL same as
> HAREBELL
HAIRBELLS > HAIRBELL
HAIRBRUSH n brush for
grooming the hair
HAIRCAP n type of moss
HAIRCAPS > HAIRCAP
HAIRCLOTH n cloth
woven from horsehair,
used in upholstery
HAIRCUT n act or an
instance of cutting the
hair
HAIRCUTS > HAIRCUT
HAIRDO n hairstyle
HAIRDOS > HAIRDO
HAIRDRIER same as
> HAIRDRYER
HAIRDRYER n hand-held
electric device that blows
out hot air and is used to
dry and, sometimes, assist
in styling the hair, as in
blow-drying
HAIRED adj with hair
HAIRGRIP n small bent
clasp used to fasten the
hair
HAIRGRIPS > HAIRGRIP
HAIRIER > HAIRY
HAIRIEST > HAIRY
HAIRIF another name for
> CLEAVERS
HAIRIFS > HAIRIF
HAIRILY adv in a hairy
manner
HAIRINESS > HAIRY
HAIRING > HAIR
HAIRLESS adj having
little or no hair ▷ n as in

Mexican hairless small breed of hairless dog

HAIRLIKE > HAIR

HAIRLINE *n* edge of hair at the top of the forehead ▷ *adj* very fine or narrow

HAIRLINES > HAIRLINE

HAIRLOCK *n* lock of hair

HAIRLOCKS > HAIRLOCK

HAIRNET *n* any of several kinds of light netting worn over the hair

HAIRNETS > HAIRNET

HAIRPIECE *n* section of false hair added to a person's real hair

HAIRPIN *n* U-shaped wire used to hold the hair in place

HAIRPINS > HAIRPIN

HAIRS > HAIR

HAIRSPRAY *n* fixative solution sprayed onto the hair to keep a hairstyle in shape

HAIRST *Scots form of* > HARVEST

HAIRSTED > HAIRST

HAIRSTING > HAIRST

HAIRSTS > HAIRST

HAIRSTYLE *n* cut and arrangement of a person's hair

HAIRTAIL *n* any of various marine spiny-finned fish having a long whiplike scaleless body and long sharp teeth

HAIRTAILS > HAIRTAIL

HAIRWING *n* fishing lure tied with hair

HAIRWINGS > HAIRWING

HAIRWORK *n* thing made from hair

HAIRWORKS > HAIRWORK

HAIRWORM *n* any of various hairlike nematode worms

HAIRWORMS > HAIRWORM

HAIRY *adj* covered with hair

HAIRYBACK *n* offensive word for an Afrikaner

HAITH *interj* Scots oath

HAJ *same as* > HADJ

HAJES > HAJ

HAJI *same as* > HAJJI

HAJIS > HAJI

HAJJ *n* pilgrimage a Muslim makes to Mecca

HAJJAH *n* Muslim woman who has made a pilgrimage to Mecca

HAJJAHS > HAJJAH

HAJJES > HAJJ

HAJJI *n* Muslim who has made a pilgrimage to Mecca

HAJJIS > HAJJI

HAKA *n* ceremonial Māori dance with chanting

HAKAM *n* text written by a rabbi

HAKAMS > HAKAM

HAKARI *n* Māori ritual feast

HAKARIS > HAKARI

HAKAS > HAKA

HAKE *n* edible sea fish of N hemisphere

HAKEA *n* Australian tree or shrub with hard woody fruit

HAKEAS > HAKEA

HAKEEM *same as* > HAKIM

HAKEEMS > HAKEEM

HAKES > HAKE

HAKIM *n* Muslim judge, ruler, or administrator

HAKIMS > HAKIM

HAKU *in New Zealand English, same as* > KINGFISH

HAKUS > HAKU

HALACHA *n* Jewish religious law

HALACHAS > HALACHA

HALACHIC > HALACHA

HALACHIST > HALACHA

HALACHOT > HALACHA

HALACHOTH > HALACHA

HALAKAH *same as* > HALACHA

HALAKAHS > HALAKAH

HALAKHA *same as* > HALACHA

HALAKHAH *same as* > HALACHA

HALAKHAHS > HALAKHAH

HALAKHAS > HALAKHA

HALAKHIC > HALAKHAH

HALAKHIST > HALAKHAH

HALAKHOT > HALAKHAH

HALAKHOTH > HALAKHAH

HALAKIC > HALAKHA

HALAKIST > HALAKHA

HALAKISTS > HALAKHA

HALAKOTH > HALAKHA

HALAL *n* meat from animals slaughtered according to Muslim law ▷ *adj* of or relating to such meat ▷ *vb* kill (animals) in this way

HALALA *n* money unit in Saudi Arabia

HALALAH *same as* > HALALA

HALALAHS > HALALAH

HALALAS > HALALA

HALALLED > HALAL

HALALLING > HALAL

HALALS > HALAL

HALATION *n* fogging usually seen as a bright ring surrounding a source of light: caused by reflection from the back of the film

HALATIONS > HALATION

HALAVAH *same as* > HALVAH

HALAVAHS > HALAVAH

HALAZONE *n* type of disinfectant

HALAZONES > HALAZONE

HALBERD *n* spear with an axe blade

HALBERDS > HALBERD

HALBERT *same as* > HALBERD

HALBERTS > HALBERT

HALCYON *adj* peaceful and happy ▷ *n* mythological bird

HALCYONIC *adj* peaceful and happy

HALCYONS > HALCYON

HALE *adj* healthy, robust ▷ *vb* pull or drag

HALED > HALE

HALENESS > HALE

HALER *same as* > HELLER

HALERS > HALER

HALERU > HALER

HALES > HALE

HALEST > HALE

HALF *n* either of two equal parts ▷ *adj* denoting one of two equal parts ▷ *adv* to the extent of half

HALFA *n* African grass

HALFAS > HALFA

HALFBACK *n* player positioned immediately behind the forwards

HALFBACKS > HALFBACK

HALFBEAK *n* type of fish with an elongated body, a short upper jaw, and a long protruding lower jaw

HALFBEAKS > HALFBEAK

HALFEN *same as* > HALF

HALFLIFE *n* time taken for half of the atoms in a radioactive material to undergo decay

HALFLIN *same as* > HALFLING

HALFLING *n* person only half-grown

HALFLINGS > HALFLING

HALFLINS > HALFLIN

HALFLIVES > HALFLIFE

HALFNESS > HALF

HALFPACE *n* landing on staircase

HALFPACES > HALFPACE

HALFPENCE > HALFPENNY

HALFPENNY *n* former British coin worth half an old penny

HALFPIPE *n* U-shaped object used in skateboarding stunts

HALFPIPES > HALFPIPE

HALFS > HALF

HALFTIME *n* rest period between the two halves of a game

HALFTIMES > HALFTIME

HALFTONE *n* illustration showing lights and shadows by means of very small dots ▷ *adj* relating to, used in, or made by halftone

HALFTONES > HALFTONE

HALFTRACK *n* vehicle with caterpillar tracks and wheels

HALFWAY *adj* at or to half the distance

HALFWIT *n* foolish or stupid person

HALFWITS > HALFWIT

HALIBUT *n* large edible flatfish of N Atlantic

HALIBUTS > HALIBUT

HALICORE *n* dugong

HALICORES > HALICORE

HALID *same as* > HALIDE

HALIDE *n* binary compound

HALIDES > HALIDE

HALIDOM *n* holy place or thing

HALIDOME *same as* > HALIDOM

HALIDOMES > HALIDOME

HALIDOMS > HALIDOME

HALIDS > HALID

HALIER *n* former currency unit of Slovakia

HALIEROV > HALIER

HALIERS > HALIER

HALIEUTIC *adj* of fishing

HALIMOT *n* court held by lord

HALIMOTE *same as* > HALIMOT

HALIMOTES > HALIMOTE

HALIMOTS > HALIMOT

HALING > HALE

HALIOTES > HALIOTIS

HALIOTIS *n* type of shellfish

HALITE *n* colourless or white mineral

HALITES > HALITE

HALITOSES > HALITOSIS

HALITOSIS *n* unpleasant-smelling breath

HALITOTIC > HALITUS

HALITOUS > HALITUS

HALITUS *n* vapour

HALITUSES > HALITUS

HALL *n* entrance passage

HALLAH *variant spelling of* > CHALLAH

HALLAHS > HALLAH

HALLAL *same as* > HALAL

HALLALI *n* bugle call

HALLALIS > HALLALI

HALLALLED > HALLAL

HALLALOO *same as* > HALLOO

HALLALOOS > HALLALOO

HALLALS > HALLAL

HALLAN *n* partition in cottage

HALLANS > HALLAN

HALLEL *n* (in Judaism) section of the liturgy

HALLELS > HALLEL

HALLIAN *same as* > HALLION

HALLIANS > HALLIAN

HALLIARD *same as* > HALYARD

HALLIARDS > HALLIARD**

HALLING n Norwegian country dance
HALLINGS > HALLING
HALLION n lout
HALLIONS > HALLION
HALLMARK n typical feature ▷ vb stamp with a hallmark
HALLMARKS > HALLMARK
HALLO same as > HALLOO
HALLOA same as > HALLOO
HALLOAED > HALLOA
HALLOAING > HALLOA
HALLOAS > HALLOA
HALLOED > HALLO
HALLOES > HALLO
HALLOING > HALLO
HALLOO interj shout used to call hounds at a hunt ▷ sentence substitute shout to attract attention, esp to call hounds at a hunt ▷ n shout of "halloo" ▷ vb shout (something) to (someone)
HALLOOED > HALLOO
HALLOOING > HALLOO
HALLOOS > HALLOO
HALLOS > HALLO
HALLOT > HALLAH
HALLOTH same as > CHALLAH
HALLOUMI n salty white sheep's cheese from Greece or Turkey, usually eaten grilled
HALLOUMIS > HALLOUMI
HALLOW vb consecrate or set apart as being holy
HALLOWED adj regarded as holy
HALLOWER > HALLOW
HALLOWERS > HALLOW
HALLOWING > HALLOW
HALLOWS > HALLOW
HALLS > HALL
HALLSTAND n piece of furniture on which are hung coats, hats, etc
HALLUCAL > HALLUX
HALLUCES > HALLUX
HALLUX n first digit on the hind foot of an animal
HALLWAY n entrance area
HALLWAYS > HALLWAY
HALLYON same as > HALLION
HALLYONS > HALLYON
HALM same as > HAULM
HALMA n board game
HALMAS > HALMA
HALMS > HALM
HALO n ring of light round the head of a sacred figure ▷ vb surround with a halo
HALOBIONT n plant or animal that lives in a salty environment such as the sea
HALOCLINE n gradient in salinity of sea
HALOED > HALO
HALOES > HALO
HALOGEN n any of a group of nonmetallic elements

HALOGENS > HALOGEN
HALOGETON n herbaceous plant
HALOID adj resembling or derived from a halogen ▷ n compound containing halogen atoms in its molecules
HALOIDS > HALOID
HALOING > HALO
HALOLIKE > HALO
HALON n any of a class of chemical compounds
HALONS > HALON
HALOPHILE n organism that thrives in an extremely salty environment, such as the Dead Sea
HALOPHILY n ability to live in salty environment
HALOPHOBE n plant unable to live in salty soil
HALOPHYTE n plant that grows in very salty soil, as in a salt marsh
HALOS > HALO
HALOSERE n plant community that originates and develops in conditions of high salinity
HALOSERES > HALOSERE
HALOTHANE n colourless volatile slightly soluble liquid with an odour resembling that of chloroform
HALOUMI same as > HALLOUMI
HALOUMIS > HALLOUMI
HALSE vb embrace
HALSED > HALSE
HALSER > HALSE
HALSERS > HALSE
HALSES > HALSE
HALSING > HALSE
HALT vb come or bring to a stop ▷ n temporary stop ▷ adj lame
HALTED > HALT
HALTER n strap round a horse's head with a rope to lead it with ▷ vb put a halter on (a horse)
HALTERE n one of a pair of modified hind wings in dipterous insects
HALTERED > HALTER
HALTERES > HALTERE
HALTERING > HALTER
HALTERS > HALTER
HALTING > HALT
HALTINGLY > HALT
HALTINGS > HALT
HALTLESS > HALT
HALTS > HALT
HALUTZ variant spelling of > CHALUTZ
HALUTZIM > HALUTZ
HALVA same as > HALVAH
HALVAH n E Mediterranean, Middle Eastern, or Indian sweetmeat

HALVAHS > HALVAH
HALVAS > HALVA
HALVE vb divide in half
HALVED > HALVE
HALVER > HALVE
HALVERS > HALVE
HALVES > HALVE
HALVING n act of halving
HALVINGS > HALVING
HALWA n type of sweet Indian dish
HALWAS > HALWA
HALYARD n rope for raising a ship's sail or flag
HALYARDS > HALYARD
HAM n smoked or salted meat from a pig's thigh ▷ vb overact
HAMADA n rocky plateau in desert
HAMADAS > HAMADA
HAMADRYAD n one of a class of nymphs, each of which inhabits a tree and dies with it
HAMADRYAS n type of baboon
HAMAL n (in Middle Eastern countries) a porter or servant
HAMALS > HAMAL
HAMAMELIS n any of several trees or shrubs native to E Asia and North America and cultivated as ornamentals
HAMARTIA n flaw in character which leads to the downfall of the protagonist in a tragedy
HAMARTIAS > HAMARTIA
HAMATE adj hook-shaped ▷ n small bone in the wrist
HAMATES > HAMATE
HAMATSA n Native Canadian dance
HAMATSAS > HAMATSA
HAMAUL same as > HAMAL
HAMAULS > HAMAUL
HAMBA interj usually offensive term for go away
HAMBLE vb mutilate
HAMBLED > HAMBLE
HAMBLES > HAMBLE
HAMBLING > HAMBLE
HAMBONE vb strike body to provide percussion
HAMBONED > HAMBONE
HAMBONES > HAMBONE
HAMBONING > HAMBONE
HAMBURG same as > HAMBURGER
HAMBURGER n minced beef shaped into a flat disc, cooked and usually served in a bread roll
HAMBURGS > HAMBURG
HAME n Scots word for home ▷ vb to home
HAMED > HAME
HAMES > HAME
HAMEWITH adv Scots word meaning homewards

HAMFAT n mediocre performer
HAMFATS > HAMFAT
HAMFATTER n inferior actor or musician
HAMING > HAME
HAMLET n small village
HAMLETS > HAMLET
HAMMADA same as > HAMADA
HAMMADAS > HAMMADA
HAMMAL same as > HAMAL
HAMMALS > HAMMAL
HAMMAM n bathing establishment
HAMMAMS > HAMMAM
HAMMED > HAM
HAMMER n tool ▷ vb hit (as if) with a hammer
HAMMERED > HAMMER
HAMMERER > HAMMER
HAMMERERS > HAMMER
HAMMERING > HAMMER
HAMMERKOP n shark with hammer-shaped head
HAMMERMAN n person working with hammer
HAMMERMEN > HAMMERMAN
HAMMERS > HAMMER
HAMMERTOE n condition in which the toe is permanently bent at the joint
HAMMIER > HAMMY
HAMMIEST > HAMMY
HAMMILY > HAMMY
HAMMINESS > HAMMY
HAMMING > HAM
HAMMOCK same as > HUMMOCK
HAMMOCKS > HAMMOCK
HAMMY adj (of an actor) overacting or tending to overact
HAMOSE adj shaped like a hook
HAMOUS same as > HAMOSE
HAMPER vb make it difficult for (someone or something) to move or progress ▷ n large basket with a lid
HAMPERED > HAMPER
HAMPERER > HAMPER
HAMPERERS > HAMPER
HAMPERING > HAMPER
HAMPERS > HAMPER
HAMPSTER same as > HAMSTER
HAMPSTERS > HAMPSTER
HAMS > HAM
HAMSTER n small rodent with a short tail and cheek pouches
HAMSTERS > HAMSTER
HAMSTRING n tendon at the back of the knee ▷ vb make it difficult for (someone) to take any action
HAMSTRUNG > HAMSTRING
HAMULAR > HAMULUS

HAMULATE > HAMULUS
HAMULI > HAMULUS
HAMULOSE > HAMULUS
HAMULOUS > HAMULUS
HAMULUS *n* biological attribute
HAMZA *n* sign used in Arabic to represent the glottal stop
HAMZAH *same as* > HAMZA
HAMZAHS > HAMZAH
HAMZAS > HAMZA
HAN *archaic inflected form of* > HAVE
HANAP *n* medieval drinking cup
HANAPER *n* small wickerwork basket
HANAPERS > HANAPER
HANAPS > HANAP
HANCE *same as* > HAUNCH
HANCES > HANCE
HANCH *vb* try to bite
HANCHED > HANCH
HANCHES > HANCH
HANCHING > HANCH
HAND *n* part of the body at the end of the arm ▷ *vb* pass, give
HANDAX *n* small axe held in one hand
HANDAXE *same as* > HANDAX
HANDAXES > HANDAX
HANDBAG *n* woman's small bag
HANDBAGS *pl n* incident in which people, esp sportsmen, fight or threaten to fight, but without real intent to inflict harm
HANDBALL *n* game in which two teams of seven players try to throw a ball into their opponent's goal ▷ *vb* pass (the ball) with a blow of the fist
HANDBALLS > HANDBALL
HANDBELL *n* bell rung by hand, esp one of a tuned set used in musical performance
HANDBELLS > HANDBELL
HANDBILL *n* small printed notice
HANDBILLS > HANDBILL
HANDBLOWN *adj* (of glass) made by hand
HANDBOOK *n* small reference or instruction book
HANDBOOKS > HANDBOOK
HANDBRAKE *n* brake in a motor vehicle operated by a hand lever
HANDCAR *n* small railway vehicle
HANDCARS > HANDCAR
HANDCART *n* simple cart pushed or pulled by hand, used for transporting goods
HANDCARTS > HANDCART

HANDCLAP *n* act of clapping hands
HANDCLAPS > HANDCLAP
HANDCLASP *another word for* > HANDSHAKE
HANDCRAFT *n* handicraft
HANDCUFF *n* one of a linked pair of metal rings designed to be locked round a prisoner's wrists by the police ▷ *vb* put handcuffs on
HANDCUFFS > HANDCUFF
HANDED > HAND
HANDER > HAND
HANDERS > HAND
HANDFAST *n* agreement, esp of marriage, confirmed by a handshake ▷ *vb* betroth or marry (two persons or another person) by joining the hands
HANDFASTS > HANDFAST
HANDFED > HANDFEED
HANDFEED *vb* feed (a person or an animal) by hand
HANDFEEDS > HANDFEED
HANDFUL *n* amount that can be held in the hand
HANDFULS > HANDFUL
HANDGRIP *n* covering, usually of towelling or rubber, that makes the handle of a racket or club easier to hold
HANDGRIPS > HANDGRIP
HANDGUN *n* firearm such as a pistol
HANDGUNS > HANDGUN
HANDHELD *adj* held in position by the hand ▷ *n* computer that can be held in the hand
HANDHELDS > HANDHELD
HANDHOLD *n* object, crevice, etc, that can be used as a grip or support, as in climbing
HANDHOLDS > HANDHOLD
HANDICAP *n* physical or mental disability ▷ *vb* make it difficult for (someone) to do something
HANDICAPS > HANDICAP
HANDIER > HANDY
HANDIEST > HANDY
HANDILY *adv* in a handy way or manner
HANDINESS > HANDY
HANDING > HAND
HANDISM *n* discrimination against left- or right-handed people
HANDISMS > HANDISM
HANDIWORK *n* result of someone's work or activity
HANDJAR *n* Persian dagger
HANDJARS > HANDJAR
HANDJOB *n* manual stimulation of another person's penis

HANDJOBS > HANDJOB
HANDKNIT *adj, n* (garment) knitted by hand
HANDKNITS > HANDKNIT
HANDLE *n* part of an object that is held so that it can be used ▷ *vb* hold, feel, or move with the hands
HANDLEBAR *adj* as in *handlebar moustache*: bushy extended moustache with curled ends that resembles the handlebars of a bicycle
HANDLED > HANDLE
HANDLER *n* person who controls an animal
HANDLERS > HANDLER
HANDLES > HANDLE
HANDLESS > HAND
HANDLIKE > HAND
HANDLINE *n* hand-operated fishing line
HANDLINES > HANDLINE
HANDLING *n* act or an instance of picking up, turning over, or touching something
HANDLINGS > HANDLING
HANDLIST *n* rough list
HANDLISTS > HANDLIST
HANDLOOM *n* weaving device operated by hand
HANDLOOMS > HANDLOOM
HANDMADE *adj* made by hand, not by machine
HANDMAID *n* person or thing that serves as a useful but subordinate purpose
HANDMAIDS > HANDMAID
HANDOFF *n* (in rugby) act of warding off an opposing player
HANDOFFS > HANDOFF
HANDOUT *n* clothing, food, or money given to a needy person
HANDOUTS > HANDOUT
HANDOVER *n* transfer or surrender
HANDOVERS > HANDOVER
HANDPASS *vb* (in Australian Rules football) pass the ball by holding it in one hand and striking it with the other
HANDPHONE *n* in SE Asian English, mobile phone
HANDPICK *vb* choose or select with great care, as for a special job or purpose
HANDPICKS > HANDPICK
HANDPLAY *n* fighting with fists
HANDPLAYS > HANDPLAY
HANDPRESS *n* printing press operated by hand
HANDPRINT *n* print of hand
HANDRAIL *n* rail alongside a stairway, to provide support
HANDRAILS > HANDRAIL

HANDROLL *n* large dried-seaweed cone filled with cold rice and other ingredients
HANDROLLS > HANDROLL
HANDS > HAND
HANDSAW *n* any saw for use in one hand only
HANDSAWS > HANDSAW
HANDSEL *n* gift for good luck ▷ *vb* give a handsel to (a person)
HANDSELED > HANDSEL
HANDSELS > HANDSEL
HANDSET *n* telephone mouth- and earpiece in a single unit
HANDSETS > HANDSET
HANDSEWN *adj* sewn by hand
HANDSFUL > HANDFUL
HANDSHAKE *n* act of grasping and shaking a person's hand, such as in greeting or when agreeing on a deal
HANDSOME *adj* (esp of a man) good-looking ▷ *n* term of endearment for a beloved person
HANDSOMER > HANDSOME
HANDSOMES > HANDSOME
HANDSPIKE *n* bar or length of pipe used as a lever
HANDSTAFF *n* staff held in hand
HANDSTAMP *vb* stamp by hand
HANDSTAND *n* act of supporting the body on the hands in an upside-down position
HANDSTURN *n* slightest amount of work
HANDTOWEL *n* towel for drying hands
HANDWHEEL *n* wheel operated by hand
HANDWORK *n* work done by hand rather than by machine
HANDWORKS > HANDWORK
HANDWOVEN *adj* woven by hand
HANDWRIT > HANDWRITE
HANDWRITE *vb* write by hand
HANDWROTE > HANDWRITE
HANDY *adj* convenient, useful
HANDYMAN *n* man who is good at making or repairing things
HANDYMEN > HANDYMAN
HANDYWORK *same as* > HANDIWORK
HANEPOOT *n* variety of muscat grape
HANEPOOTS > HANEPOOT
HANG *vb* attach or be attached at the top with the lower part free

HANGABLE adj suitable for hanging

HANGAR n large shed for storing aircraft ▷ vb put in a hangar

HANGARED > HANGAR

HANGARING > HANGAR

HANGARS > HANGAR

HANGBIRD n any bird, esp the Baltimore oriole, that builds a hanging nest

HANGBIRDS > HANGBIRD

HANGDOG adj guilty, ashamed ▷ n furtive or sneaky person

HANGDOGS > HANGDOG

HANGED > HANG

HANGER n curved piece of wood, wire, etc with a hook

HANGERS > HANGER

HANGFIRE n failure to fire

HANGFIRES > HANGFIRE

HANGI n Māori oven

HANGING > HANG

HANGINGS > HANG

HANGIS > HANGI

HANGMAN n man who executes people by hanging

HANGMEN > HANGMAN

HANGNAIL n piece of skin partly torn away from the base or side of a fingernail

HANGNAILS > HANGNAIL

HANGNEST same as > HANGBIRD

HANGNESTS > HANGNEST

HANGOUT n place where one lives or that one frequently visits

HANGOUTS > HANGOUT

HANGOVER n headache and nausea as a result of drinking too much alcohol

HANGOVERS > HANGOVER

HANGRIER > HANGRY

HANGRIEST > HANGRY

HANGRY adj irritable as a result of feeling hungry

HANGS > HANG

HANGTAG n attached label

HANGTAGS > HANGTAG

HANGUL n Korean language

HANGUP n emotional or psychological problem

HANGUPS > HANGUP

HANIWA n Japanese funeral offering

HANJAR same as > HANDJAR

HANJARS > HANJAR

HANK n coil, esp of yarn ▷ vb attach (a sail) to a stay by hanks

HANKED > HANK

HANKER vb desire intensely

HANKERED > HANKER

HANKERER > HANKER

HANKERERS > HANKER

HANKERING > HANKER

HANKERS > HANKER

HANKIE same as > HANKY

HANKIES > HANKY

HANKING > HANK

HANKS > HANK

HANKY n handkerchief

HANSA same as > HANSE

HANSAS > HANSA

HANSE n medieval guild of merchants

HANSEATIC > HANSA

HANSEL same as > HANDSEL

HANSELED > HANSEL

HANSELING > HANSEL

HANSELLED > HANSEL

HANSELS > HANSEL

HANSES > HANSE

HANSOM n two-wheeled one-horse carriage

HANSOMS > HANSOM

HANT same as > HAUNT

HANTED > HANT

HANTING > HANT

HANTLE n good deal

HANTLES > HANTLE

HANTS > HANT

HANUKIAH n candelabrum having nine branches that is lit during the festival of Hanukkah

HANUKIAHS > HANUKIAH

HANUMAN n type of monkey

HANUMANS > HANUMAN

HAO n monetary unit of Vietnam

HAOLE n Hawaiian word for white person

HAOLES > HAOLE

HAOMA n type of ritual drink

HAOMAS > HAOMA

HAOS > HAO

HAP n luck ▷ vb cover up

HAPAX n word that appears once in a work of literature

HAPAXES > HAPAX

HAPHAZARD adj not organized or planned ▷ n chance

HAPHTARA same as > HAFTARAH

HAPHTARAH same as > HAFTARAH

HAPHTARAS > HAPHTARA

HAPHTAROT > HAPHTARA

HAPKIDO n Korean martial art

HAPKIDOS > HAPKIDO

HAPLESS adj unlucky

HAPLESSLY > HAPLESS

HAPLITE variant of > APLITE

HAPLITES > HAPLITE

HAPLITIC > HAPLITE

HAPLOID adj denoting a cell or organism with unpaired chromosomes ▷ n haploid cell or organism

HAPLOIDIC adj denoting a cell or organism with unpaired chromosomes

HAPLOIDS > HAPLOID

HAPLOIDY > HAPLOID

HAPLOLOGY n omission of a repeated occurrence of a sound or syllable in fluent speech

HAPLONT n organism with a haploid number of chromosomes

HAPLONTIC > HAPLONT

HAPLONTS > HAPLONT

HAPLOPIA n normal single vision

HAPLOPIAS > HAPLOPIA

HAPLOSES > HAPLOSIS

HAPLOSIS n production of a haploid number of chromosomes during meiosis

HAPLOTYPE n collection of genetic markers usually inherited together

HAPLY archaic word for > PERHAPS

HAPPED > HAP

HAPPEN vb take place, occur

HAPPENED > HAPPEN

HAPPENING n event, occurrence ▷ adj fashionable and up-to-the-minute

HAPPENS > HAPPEN

HAPPI n type of loose Japanese coat

HAPPIED > HAPPY

HAPPIER > HAPPY

HAPPIES > HAPPY

HAPPIEST > HAPPY

HAPPILY > HAPPY

HAPPINESS > HAPPY

HAPPING > HAP

HAPPIS > HAPPI

HAPPOSHU n beer-like Japanese drink

HAPPOSHUS > HAPPOSHU

HAPPY adj feeling or causing joy ▷ vb make happy

HAPPYING > HAPPY

HAPS > HAP

HAPTEN n incomplete antigen

HAPTENE same as > HAPTEN

HAPTENES > HAPTENE

HAPTENIC > HAPTENE

HAPTENS > HAPTEN

HAPTERON n cell or group of cells that occurs in certain plants, esp seaweeds, and attaches the plant to its substratum

HAPTERONS > HAPTERON

HAPTIC adj relating to or based on the sense of touch

HAPTICAL same as > HAPTIC

HAPTICS n science of sense of touch

HAPU n subtribe

HAPUKA another name for > GROPER

HAPUKAS > HAPUKA

HAPUKU same as > HAPUKA

HAPUKUS > HAPUKU

HAPUS > HAPU

HAQUETON same as > HACQUETON

HAQUETONS > HAQUETON

HARAAM same as > HARAM

HARAKEKE in New Zealand English, another name for > FLAX

HARAKEKES > HARAKEKE

HARAM n anything that is forbidden by Islamic law

HARAMBEE n work chant used on the E African coast ▷ interj cry of harambee

HARAMBEES > HARAMBEE

HARAMDA same as > HARAMZADA

HARAMDAS > HARAMDA

HARAMDI same as > HARAMZADI

HARAMDIS > HARAMDI

HARAMS > HARAM

HARAMZADA n in Indian English, slang word for an illegitimate male

HARAMZADI n in Indian English, slang word for an illegitimate female

HARANGUE vb address angrily or forcefully ▷ n angry or forceful speech

HARANGUED > HARANGUE

HARANGUER > HARANGUE

HARANGUES > HARANGUE

HARASS vb annoy or trouble constantly

HARASSED > HARASS

HARASSER > HARASS

HARASSERS > HARASS

HARASSES > HARASS

HARASSING > HARASS

HARBINGER n someone or something that announces the approach of something ▷ vb announce the approach or arrival of

HARBOR same as > HARBOUR

HARBORAGE n shelter or refuge, as for a ship

HARBORED > HARBOR

HARBORER > HARBOR

HARBORERS > HARBOR

HARBORFUL n amount a harbour can hold

HARBORING > HARBOR

HARBOROUS adj hospitable

HARBORS > HARBOR

HARBOUR n sheltered port ▷ vb maintain secretly in the mind

HARBOURED > HARBOUR

HARBOURER > HARBOUR

HARBOURS > HARBOUR

HARD adj firm, solid, or rigid ▷ adv with great energy or effort

HARDASS n tough person

HARDASSES > HARDASS
HARDBACK n book with a stiff cover ▷ adj of or denoting a hardback
HARDBACKS > HARDBACK
HARDBAG n rigid container on a motorcycle
HARDBAGS > HARDBAG
HARDBAKE n almond toffee
HARDBAKES > HARDBAKE
HARDBALL n as in play hardball act in a ruthless or uncompromising way
HARDBALLS > HARDBALL
HARDBEAM same as > HORNBEAM
HARDBEAMS > HARDBEAM
HARDBOARD n thin stiff board made of compressed sawdust and wood chips
HARDBODY n attractive person with a muscular physique
HARDBOOT n type of skiing boot
HARDBOOTS > HARDBOOT
HARDBOUND same as > HARDBACK
HARDCASE n tough person ▷ adj relating to a container that has a rigid structure
HARDCASES > HARDCASE
HARDCORE n style of rock music with short fast songs and little melody
HARDCORES > HARDCORE
HARDCOURT adj (of tennis) played on hard surface
HARDCOVER same as > HARDBACK
HARDEDGE n style of painting in which vividly coloured subjects are clearly delineated ▷ adj of, relating to, or denoting this style of painting
HARDEDGES > HARDEDGE
HARDEN vb make or become hard ▷ n rough fabric made from hards
HARDENED adj toughened by experience
HARDENER n person or thing that hardens
HARDENERS > HARDENER
HARDENING n act or process of becoming or making hard
HARDENS > HARDEN
HARDER > HARD
HARDEST > HARD
HARDFACE n uncompromising person
HARDFACES > HARDFACE
HARDGOODS same as > HARDWARE
HARDGRASS n coarse grass
HARDHACK n woody North American rosaceous plant with downy leaves

and clusters of small pink or white flowers
HARDHACKS > HARDHACK
HARDHAT n hat made of a hard material for protection ▷ adj typical of construction workers
HARDHATS > HARDHAT
HARDHEAD same as > HARDHEADS
HARDHEADS n thistle-like plant
HARDIER > HARDY
HARDIES > HARDY
HARDIEST > HARDY
HARDIHEAD same as > HARDIHOOD
HARDIHOOD n courage or daring
HARDILY adv in a hardy manner
HARDIMENT same as > HARDIHOOD
HARDINESS n condition or quality of being hardy, robust, or bold
HARDISH > HARD
HARDLINE adj uncompromising
HARDLINER > HARDLINE
HARDLY adv scarcely or not at all
HARDMAN n tough, ruthless, or violent man
HARDMEN > HARDMAN
HARDNESS n quality or condition of being hard
HARDNOSE n tough person
HARDNOSED adj tough, shrewd, and practical
HARDNOSES > HARDNOSE
HARDOKE n burdock
HARDOKES > HARDOKE
HARDPACK n rigid backpack
HARDPACKS > HARDPACK
HARDPAN n hard impervious layer of clay below the soil
HARDPANS > HARDPAN
HARDPARTS n skeleton
HARDROCK adj (of mining) concerned with extracting minerals other than coal, usually from solid rock ▷ n tough uncompromising man
HARDROCKS > HARDROCK
HARDS pl n coarse fibres and other refuse from flax and hemp
HARDSCAPE n man-made features used in landscape architecture
HARDSET adj in difficulties
HARDSHELL adj having a shell or carapace that is thick, heavy, or hard
HARDSHIP n suffering
HARDSHIPS > HARDSHIP
HARDSTAND n hard surface on which vehicles may be parked

HARDTACK n kind of hard saltless biscuit, formerly eaten by sailors
HARDTACKS > HARDTACK
HARDTAIL n mountain bike with no rear suspension
HARDTAILS > HARDTAIL
HARDTOP n car equipped with a metal or plastic roof
HARDTOPS > HARDTOP
HARDWARE n metal tools or implements
HARDWARES > HARDWARE
HARDWIRE vb instal permanently in computer
HARDWIRED adj (of a circuit or instruction) permanently wired into a computer, replacing separate software
HARDWIRES > HARDWIRE
HARDWOOD n wood of a broad-leaved tree such as oak or ash
HARDWOODS > HARDWOOD
HARDY adj able to stand difficult conditions ▷ n any blacksmith's tool made with a square shank
HARE n animal like a large rabbit, with longer ears and legs ▷ vb run (away) quickly
HAREBELL n blue bell-shaped flower
HAREBELLS > HAREBELL
HARED > HARE
HAREEM same as > HAREM
HAREEMS > HAREEM
HARELD n long-tailed duck
HARELDS > HARELD
HARELIKE > HARE
HARELIP n slight split in the upper lip
HARELIPS > HARELIP
HAREM n Muslim man's wives and concubines
HAREMS > HAREM
HARES > HARE
HARESTAIL n species of cotton grass
HAREWOOD n sycamore wood that has been stained for use in furniture making
HAREWOODS > HAREWOOD
HARIANA n Indian breed of cattle
HARIANAS > HARIANA
HARICOT n variety of French bean
HARICOTS > HARICOT
HARIGALDS pl n intestines
HARIGALS same as > HARIGALDS
HARIJAN n member of an Indian caste
HARIJANS > HARIJAN
HARIM same as > HAREM
HARIMS > HARIM
HARING > HARE

HARIOLATE vb practise divination
HARIRA n Moroccan soup
HARIRAS > HARIRA
HARISH adj like hare
HARISSA n hot paste
HARISSAS > HARISSA
HARK vb listen
HARKED > HARK
HARKEN same as > HEARKEN
HARKENED > HARKEN
HARKENER > HARKEN
HARKENERS > HARKEN
HARKENING > HARKEN
HARKENS > HARKEN
HARKING > HARK
HARKS > HARK
HARL same as > HERL
HARLED > HARL
HARLEQUIN n stock comic character with a diamond-patterned costume and mask ▷ adj in many colours
HARLING > HARL
HARLINGS > HARL
HARLOT n prostitute ▷ adj of or like a harlot
HARLOTRY > HARLOT
HARLOTS > HARLOT
HARLS > HARL
HARM vb injure physically, mentally, or morally ▷ n physical, mental, or moral injury
HARMALA n African plant
HARMALAS > HARMALA
HARMALIN n chemical derived from harmala
HARMALINE same as > HARMALIN
HARMALINS > HARMALIN
HARMAN n constable
HARMANS > HARMAN
HARMATTAN n dry dusty wind from the Sahara blowing towards the W African coast, esp from November to March
HARMDOING n doing of harm
HARMED > HARM
HARMEL same as > HARMALA
HARMELS > HARMEL
HARMER > HARM
HARMERS > HARM
HARMFUL adj causing or tending to cause harm
HARMFULLY > HARMFUL
HARMIN same as > HARMALIN
HARMINE same as > HARMALIN
HARMINES > HARMINE
HARMING > HARM
HARMINS > HARMIN
HARMLESS adj safe to use, touch, or be near
HARMONIC adj of harmony ▷ n overtone of a musical note produced when that

HARMONICA n small wind instrument played by sucking and blowing

HARMONICS n science of musical sounds

HARMONIES > HARMONY

HARMONISE same as > HARMONIZE

HARMONIST n person skilled in the art and techniques of harmony

HARMONIUM n keyboard instrument like a small organ

HARMONIZE vb sing or play in harmony

HARMONY n peaceful agreement and cooperation

HARMOST n Spartan governor

HARMOSTS > HARMOST

HARMOSTY n office of a harmost

HARMOTOME n mineral of the zeolite group

HARMS > HARM

HARN n coarse linen

HARNESS n arrangement of straps for attaching a horse to a cart or plough ▷ vb put a harness on

HARNESSED > HARNESS

HARNESSER > HARNESS

HARNESSES > HARNESS

HARNS > HARN

HARO interj cry meaning alas

HAROS > HARO

HAROSET n Jewish dish eaten at Passover

HAROSETH same as > HAROSET

HAROSETHS > HAROSETH

HAROSETS > HAROSET

HARP n large triangular stringed instrument ▷ vb play the harp

HARPED > HARP

HARPER > HARP

HARPERS > HARP

HARPIES > HARPY

HARPIN n type of protein

HARPING > HARP

HARPINGS pl n wooden members used for strengthening the bow of a vessel

HARPINS same as > HARPINGS

HARPIST > HARP

HARPISTS > HARP

HARPOON n barbed spear attached to a rope for hunting whales ▷ vb spear with a harpoon

HARPOONED > HARPOON

HARPOONER > HARPOON

HARPOONS > HARPOON

HARPS > HARP

HARPY n nasty or bad-tempered woman

HARPYLIKE > HARPY

HARQUEBUS variant of > ARQUEBUS

HARRIDAN n nagging or vicious woman

HARRIDANS > HARRIDAN

HARRIED > HARRY

HARRIER n cross-country runner

HARRIERS > HARRIER

HARRIES > HARRY

HARROW n implement used to break up lumps of soil ▷ vb draw a harrow over

HARROWED > HARROW

HARROWER > HARROW

HARROWERS > HARROW

HARROWING > HARROW

HARROWS > HARROW

HARRUMPH vb clear or make the noise of clearing the throat

HARRUMPHS > HARRUMPH

HARRY vb keep asking (someone) to do something

HARRYING > HARRY

HARSH adj severe and difficult to cope with ▷ vb ruin or end a state of elation

HARSHED > HARSH

HARSHEN vb make harsh

HARSHENED > HARSHEN

HARSHENS > HARSHEN

HARSHER > HARSH

HARSHES > HARSH

HARSHEST > HARSH

HARSHING > HARSH

HARSHLY > HARSH

HARSHNESS > HARSH

HARSLET same as > HASLET

HARSLETS > HARSLET

HART n adult male deer

HARTAL n (in India) closing shops or suspending work

HARTALS > HARTAL

HARTBEES same as > HARTBEEST

HARTBEEST n African antelope

HARTELY archaic spelling of > HEARTILY

HARTEN same as > HEARTEN

HARTENED > HARTEN

HARTENING > HARTEN

HARTENS > HARTEN

HARTLESSE same as > HEARTLESS

HARTS > HART

HARTSHORN n sal volatile

HARUMPH same as > HARRUMPH

HARUMPHED > HARUMPH

HARUMPHS > HARUMPH

HARUSPEX n (in ancient Rome) a priest who practised divination, esp by examining the entrails of animals

HARUSPICY > HARUSPEX

HARVEST n (season for) the gathering of crops ▷ vb gather (a ripened crop)

HARVESTED > HARVEST

HARVESTER n harvesting machine, esp a combine harvester

HARVESTS > HARVEST

HAS > HAVE

HASBIAN n former lesbian

HASBIANS > HASBIAN

HASH n dish of diced cooked meat and vegetables reheated ▷ vb chop into small pieces

HASHED > HASH

HASHEESH same as > HASHISH

HASHES > HASH

HASHHEAD n regular marijuana user

HASHHEADS > HASHHEAD

HASHIER > HASH

HASHIEST > HASH

HASHING > HASH

HASHINGS > HASHING

HASHISH n drug made from the cannabis plant

HASHISHES > HASHISH

HASHMARK n character (#)

HASHMARKS > HASHMARK

HASHTAG n (on Twitter) word or phrase preceded by a hashmark, used to denote the topic of a post

HASHTAGS > HASHTAG

HASHY > HASH

HASK n archaic name for a basket for transporting fish

HASKS > HASK

HASLET n loaf of cooked minced pig's offal, eaten cold

HASLETS > HASLET

HASP n type of fastening ▷ vb secure (a door, window, etc) with a hasp

HASPED > HASP

HASPING > HASP

HASPS > HASP

HASS n as in white hass oatmeal pudding made with sheep's gullet

HASSAR n South American catfish

HASSARS > HASSAR

HASSEL variant of > HASSLE

HASSELS > HASSEL

HASSES > HASS

HASSIUM n chemical element

HASSIUMS > HASSIUM

HASSLE n trouble, bother ▷ vb bother or annoy

HASSLED > HASSLE

HASSLES > HASSLE

HASSLING > HASSLE

HASSOCK n cushion for kneeling on in church

HASSOCKS > HASSOCK

HASSOCKY > HASSOCK

HAST singular form of the present tense (indicative mood) of > HAVE

HASTA Spanish for > UNTIL

HASTATE adj shaped like a spear

HASTATED same as > HASTATE

HASTATELY > HASTATE

HASTE n (excessive) quickness ▷ vb hasten

HASTED > HASTE

HASTEFUL > HASTE

HASTEN vb (cause to) hurry

HASTENED > HASTEN

HASTENER > HASTEN

HASTENERS > HASTEN

HASTENING > HASTEN

HASTENS > HASTEN

HASTES > HASTE

HASTIER > HASTY

HASTIEST > HASTY

HASTILY > HASTY

HASTINESS > HASTY

HASTING > HASTE

HASTINGS > HASTE

HASTY adj (too) quick

HAT n covering for the head, often with a brim ▷ vb supply (a person) with a hat or put a hat on (someone)

HATABLE > HATE

HATBAND n band or ribbon around a hat

HATBANDS > HATBAND

HATBOX n box or case for a hat or hats

HATBOXES > HATBOX

HATBRUSH n brush for hats

HATCH vb (cause to) emerge from an egg ▷ n hinged door covering an opening in a floor or wall

HATCHABLE > HATCH

HATCHBACK n car with a lifting door at the back

HATCHECK n cloakroom

HATCHECKS > HATCHECK

HATCHED > HATCH

HATCHEL same as > HECKLE

HATCHELED > HATCHEL

HATCHELS > HATCHEL

HATCHER > HATCH

HATCHERS > HATCH

HATCHERY n place where eggs are hatched under artificial conditions

HATCHES > HATCH

HATCHET n small axe

HATCHETS > HATCHET

HATCHETY adj like a hatchet

HATCHING > HATCH

HATCHINGS > HATCH

HATCHLING n young animal that has newly hatched from an egg

HATCHMENT n diamond-shaped tablet displaying the coat of arms of a dead person

HATCHWAY n opening in the deck of a ship

HATCHWAYS > HATCHWAY

HATE vb dislike intensely ▷ n intense dislike

HATEABLE > HATE

HATED > HATE

HATEFUL adj causing or deserving hate

HATEFULLY > HATEFUL

HATELESS > HATE

HATER > HATE

HATERENT same as > HATRED

HATERENTS > HATERENT

HATERS > HATE

HATES > HATE

HATFUL n amount a hat will hold

HATFULS > HATFUL

HATGUARD n string to keep a hat from blowing off

HATGUARDS > HATGUARD

HATH form of the present tense (indicative mood) of > HAVE

HATHA n as in hatha yoga form of yoga

HATINATOR n small fancy hat

HATING > HATE

HATLESS > HAT

HATLIKE > HAT

HATMAKER n maker of hats

HATMAKERS > HATMAKER

HATPEG n peg to hang hat on

HATPEGS > HATPEG

HATPIN n pin used to secure a woman's hat to her hair

HATPINS > HATPIN

HATRACK n rack for hanging hats on

HATRACKS > HATRACK

HATRED n intense dislike

HATREDS > HATRED

HATS > HAT

HATSFUL > HATFUL

HATSTAND n frame or pole equipped with hooks or arms for hanging up hats, coats, etc

HATSTANDS > HATSTAND

HATTED > HAT

HATTER n person who makes and sells hats ▷ vb annoy

HATTERED > HATTER

HATTERIA n species of reptile

HATTERIAS > HATTERIA

HATTERING > HATTER

HATTERS > HATTER

HATTING > HAT

HATTINGS > HAT

HATTOCK n small hat

HATTOCKS > HATTOCK

HAUBERK n long sleeveless coat of mail

HAUBERKS > HAUBERK

HAUBOIS same as > HAUTBOY

HAUD Scot word for > HOLD

HAUDING > HAUD

HAUDS > HAUD

HAUF Scot word for > HALF

HAUFS > HAUF

HAUGH n low-lying often alluvial riverside meadow

HAUGHS > HAUGH

HAUGHT same as > HAUGHTY

HAUGHTIER > HAUGHTY

HAUGHTILY > HAUGHTY

HAUGHTY adj proud, arrogant

HAUL vb pull or drag with effort ▷ n hauling

HAULAGE n (charge for) transporting goods

HAULAGES > HAULAGE

HAULBACK n (in lumbering) line used to bring a cable back

HAULBACKS > HAULBACK

HAULD Scots word for > HOLD

HAULDS > HAULD

HAULED > HAUL

HAULER same as > HAULIER

HAULERS > HAULER

HAULIER n firm or person that transports goods by road

HAULIERS > HAULIER

HAULING n act of hauling

HAULINGS > HAULING

HAULM n stalks of beans, peas, or potatoes collectively

HAULMIER > HAULMY

HAULMIEST > HAULMY

HAULMS > HAULM

HAULMY adj having haulms

HAULOUT n act of hauling a boat out of water

HAULOUTS > HAULOUT

HAULS > HAUL

HAULST same as > HALSE

HAULT same as > HAUGHTY

HAULYARD same as > HALYARD

HAULYARDS > HAULYARD

HAUN n Scot word for hand

HAUNCH n human hip or fleshy hindquarter of an animal ▷ vb cause (an animal) to come down on its haunches

HAUNCHED > HAUNCH

HAUNCHES > HAUNCH

HAUNCHING > HAUNCH

HAUNS > HAUN

HAUNT vb visit in the form of a ghost ▷ n place visited frequently

HAUNTED adj frequented by ghosts

HAUNTER > HAUNT

HAUNTERS > HAUNT

HAUNTING adj memorably beautiful or sad

HAUNTINGS > HAUNT

HAUNTS > HAUNT

HAURIANT adj rising

HAURIENT same as > HAURIANT

HAUSE same as > HALSE

HAUSED > HAUSE

HAUSEN n variety of sturgeon

HAUSENS > HAUSEN

HAUSES > HAUSE

HAUSFRAU n German housewife

HAUSFRAUS > HAUSFRAU

HAUSING > HAUSE

HAUSTELLA n plural of haustellum: tip of the proboscis of an insect

HAUSTORIA n plural of haustorium: organ of a parasitic plant that absorbs food and water from host tissues

HAUT same as > HAUGHTY

HAUTBOIS same as > HAUTBOY

HAUTBOY n type of strawberry

HAUTBOYS > HAUTBOY

HAUTE adj French word meaning high

HAUTER > HAUT

HAUTEST > HAUT

HAUTEUR n haughtiness

HAUTEURS > HAUTEUR

HAUYNE n blue mineral containing calcium

HAUYNES > HAUYNE

HAVARTI n Danish cheese

HAVARTIS > HAVARTI

HAVDALAH n ceremony marking the end of the sabbath or of a festival, including the blessings over wine, candles, and spices

HAVDALAHS > HAVDALAH

HAVDOLOH same as > HAVDALAH

HAVDOLOHS > HAVDOLOH

HAVE vb possess, hold

HAVELOCK n light-coloured cover for a service cap with a flap extending over the back of the neck to protect the head and neck from the sun

HAVELOCKS > HAVELOCK

HAVEN n place of safety ▷ vb secure or shelter in or as if in a haven

HAVENED > HAVEN

HAVENING > HAVEN

HAVENLESS > HAVEN

HAVENS > HAVEN

HAVEOUR same as > HAVIOR

HAVEOURS > HAVEOUR

HAVER vb talk nonsense ▷ n nonsense

HAVERED > HAVER

HAVEREL n fool

HAVERELS > HAVEREL

HAVERING > HAVER

HAVERINGS > HAVER

HAVERS > HAVER

HAVERSACK n canvas bag carried on the back or shoulder

HAVERSINE n half the value of the versed sine

HAVES > HAVE

HAVILDAR n noncommissioned officer in the Indian army, equivalent in rank to sergeant

HAVILDARS > HAVILDAR

HAVING > HAVE

HAVINGS > HAVE

HAVIOR same as > HAVIOUR

HAVIORS > HAVIOR

HAVIOUR n possession

HAVIOURS > HAVIOUR

HAVOC n disorder and confusion ▷ vb lay waste

HAVOCKED > HAVOC

HAVOCKER > HAVOC

HAVOCKERS > HAVOC

HAVOCKING > HAVOC

HAVOCS > HAVOC

HAW n hawthorn berry ▷ vb make an inarticulate utterance

HAWALA n Middle Eastern system of money transfer

HAWALAS > HAWALA

HAWBUCK n bumpkin

HAWBUCKS > HAWBUCK

HAWEATER n resident of Manitoulin Island, Ontario

HAWEATERS > HAWEATER

HAWED > HAW

HAWFINCH n European finch with a stout bill and brown plumage with black-and-white wings

HAWING > HAW

HAWK n bird of prey ▷ vb offer (goods) for sale in the street or door-to-door

HAWKBELL n bell fitted to a hawk's leg

HAWKBELLS > HAWKBELL

HAWKBILL same as > HAWKSBILL

HAWKBILLS > HAWKBILL

HAWKBIT n any of three perennial plants

HAWKBITS > HAWKBIT

HAWKED > HAWK

HAWKER n travelling salesman

HAWKERS > HAWKER

HAWKEY same as > HOCKEY

HAWKEYED adj having extremely keen sight

HAWKEYS > HAWKEY

HAWKIE n cow with white stripe on face

HAWKIES > HAWKIE
HAWKING another name for > FALCONRY
HAWKINGS > HAWKING
HAWKISH adj favouring the use of force rather than diplomacy
HAWKISHLY > HAWKISH
HAWKIT adj having a white streak
HAWKLIKE > HAWK
HAWKMOTH n powerful narrow-winged moth with the ability to hover over flowers when feeding from the nectar
HAWKMOTHS > HAWKMOTH
HAWKNOSE n hooked nose
HAWKNOSES > HAWKNOSE
HAWKS > HAWK
HAWKSBILL n type of turtle
HAWKSHAW n private detective
HAWKSHAWS > HAWKSHAW
HAWKWEED n hairy plant with clusters of dandelion-like flowers
HAWKWEEDS > HAWKWEED
HAWM vb be idle and relaxed
HAWMED > HAWM
HAWMING > HAWM
HAWMS > HAWM
HAWS > HAW
HAWSE vb of boats, pitch violently when at anchor
HAWSED > HAWSE
HAWSEHOLE n one of the holes in the upper part of the bows of a vessel through which the anchor ropes pass
HAWSEPIPE n strong metal pipe through which an anchor rope passes
HAWSER n large rope used on a ship
HAWSERS > HAWSER
HAWSES > HAWSE
HAWSING > HAWSE
HAWTHORN n thorny shrub or tree
HAWTHORNS > HAWTHORN
HAWTHORN > HAWTHORN
HAY n grass cut and dried as fodder ▷ vb cut, dry, and store (grass, clover, etc) as fodder
HAYBAND n rope made by twisting hay together
HAYBANDS > HAYBAND
HAYBOX n airtight box used to keep partially cooked food warm
HAYBOXES > HAYBOX
HAYCATION n working holiday at a farm
HAYCOCK n pile of hay left until dry enough to move
HAYCOCKS > HAYCOCK
HAYED > HAY
HAYER n person who makes hay
HAYERS > HAYER

HAYEY > HAY
HAYFIELD n field of hay
HAYFIELDS > HAYFIELD
HAYFORK n long-handled fork
HAYFORKS > HAYFORK
HAYIER > HAYEY
HAYIEST > HAYEY
HAYING > HAY
HAYINGS > HAY
HAYLAGE n type of hay for animal fodder
HAYLAGES > HAYLAGE
HAYLE n welfare
HAYLES > HAYLE
HAYLOFT n loft for storing hay
HAYLOFTS > HAYLOFT
HAYMAKER n person who helps to cut, turn, toss, spread, or carry hay
HAYMAKERS > HAYMAKER
HAYMAKING > HAYMAKER
HAYMOW n part of a barn where hay is stored
HAYMOWS > HAYMOW
HAYRACK n rack for holding hay for feeding to animals
HAYRACKS > HAYRACK
HAYRAKE n large rake used to collect hay
HAYRAKES > HAYRAKE
HAYRICK same as > HAYSTACK
HAYRICKS > HAYRICK
HAYRIDE n pleasure trip in hay wagon
HAYRIDES > HAYRIDE
HAYS > HAY
HAYSEED n seeds or fragments of grass or straw
HAYSEEDS > HAYSEED
HAYSEL n season for making hay
HAYSELS > HAYSEL
HAYSTACK n large pile of stored hay
HAYSTACKS > HAYSTACK
HAYWARD n parish officer in charge of enclosures and fences
HAYWARDS > HAYWARD
HAYWIRE adj (of things) not functioning properly ▷ n wire for binding hay
HAYWIRES > HAYWIRE
HAZAN same as > CANTOR
HAZANIM > HAZAN
HAZANS > HAZAN
HAZARD n something that could be dangerous ▷ vb put in danger
HAZARDED > HAZARD
HAZARDER > HAZARD
HAZARDERS > HAZARD
HAZARDING > HAZARD
HAZARDIZE same as > HAZARD
HAZARDOUS adj involving great risk

HAZARDRY n taking of risks
HAZARDS > HAZARD
HAZE n mist, often caused by heat ▷ vb make or become hazy
HAZED > HAZE
HAZEL n small tree producing edible nuts ▷ adj (of eyes) greenish-brown
HAZELHEN n type of grouse
HAZELHENS > HAZELHEN
HAZELLY > HAZEL
HAZELNUT n nut of a hazel shrub, which has a smooth shiny hard shell
HAZELNUTS > HAZELNUT
HAZELS > HAZEL
HAZELWOOD n wood of the hazel
HAZER > HAZE
HAZERS > HAZE
HAZES > HAZE
HAZIER > HAZY
HAZIEST > HAZY
HAZILY > HAZY
HAZINESS > HAZY
HAZING > HAZE
HAZINGS > HAZE
HAZMAT n hazardous material
HAZMATS > HAZMAT
HAZY adj not clear, misty
HAZZAN same as > CANTOR
HAZZANIM > HAZZAN
HAZZANS > HAZZAN
HE pron male person or animal ▷ n male person or animal ▷ interj expression of amusement or derision
HEAD n upper or front part of the body ▷ adj chief, principal ▷ vb be at the top or front of
HEADACHE n continuous pain in the head
HEADACHES > HEADACHE
HEADACHEY same as > HEADACHY
HEADACHY adj suffering from, caused by, or likely to cause a headache
HEADAGE n payment to farmer based on animals owned
HEADAGES > HEADAGE
HEADBAND n ribbon or band worn around the head
HEADBANDS > HEADBAND
HEADBANG vb nod one's head violently to the beat of loud rock music
HEADBANGS > HEADBANG
HEADBOARD n vertical board at the top end of a bed
HEADCASE n insane person
HEADCASES > HEADCASE
HEADCHAIR n chair with support for the head

HEADCLOTH n kerchief worn on the head
HEADCOUNT n count of number of people present
HEADDRESS n decorative head covering
HEADED adj having a head or heads
HEADEND n facility from which cable television is transmitted
HEADENDS > HEADEND
HEADER n striking a ball with the head
HEADERS > HEADER
HEADFAST n mooring rope at the bows of a ship
HEADFASTS > HEADFAST
HEADFIRST adv with the head foremost
HEADFISH same as > SUNFISH
HEADFRAME n structure supporting winding machinery at mine
HEADFUCK n taboo slang for experience that is wildly exciting or impressive
HEADFUCKS > HEADFUCK
HEADFUL n amount head will hold
HEADFULS > HEADFUL
HEADGATE n gate used to control the flow of water at the upper end of a lock or conduit
HEADGATES > HEADGATE
HEADGEAR n hats collectively
HEADGEARS > HEADGEAR
HEADGUARD n padded helmet worn to protect the head in contact sports
HEADHUNT vb recruit employee from another company
HEADHUNTS > HEADHUNT
HEADIER > HEADY
HEADIEST > HEADY
HEADILY > HEADY
HEADINESS > HEADY
HEADING same as > HEAD
HEADINGS > HEADING
HEADLAMP same as > HEADLIGHT
HEADLAMPS > HEADLAMP
HEADLAND n area of land jutting out into the sea
HEADLANDS > HEADLAND
HEADLEASE n main lease often subdivided
HEADLESS adj without a head
HEADLIGHT n powerful light on the front of a vehicle
HEADLIKE > HEAD
HEADLINE n title at the top of a newspaper article, esp on the front page
HEADLINED > HEADLINE
HEADLINER n performer given prominent billing

HEADLINES > HEADLINE
HEADLOCK *n* wrestling hold in which a wrestler locks his opponent's head between the crook of his elbow and the side of his body
HEADLOCKS > HEADLOCK
HEADLONG *adj* with the head first ▷ *adv* with the head foremost
HEADMAN *n* chief or leader
HEADMARK *n* characteristic
HEADMARKS > HEADMARK
HEADMEN > HEADMAN
HEADMOST *less common word for >* FOREMOST
HEADNOTE *n* note at book chapter head
HEADNOTES > HEADNOTE
HEADPEACE *archaic form of >* HEADPIECE
HEADPHONE *n* small loudspeaker held against the ear
HEADPIECE *n* decorative band at the top of a page, chapter, etc
HEADPIN *another word for >* KINGPIN
HEADPINS > HEADPIN
HEADPOND *n* artificial pond behind a dam
HEADPONDS > HEADPOND
HEADRACE *n* channel that carries water to a water wheel, turbine, etc
HEADRACES > HEADRACE
HEADRAIL *n* end of the table from which play is started, nearest the baulkline
HEADRAILS > HEADRAIL
HEADREACH *n* distance made to windward while tacking ▷ *vb* gain distance over (another boat) when tacking
HEADREST *n* support for the head, as on a dentist's chair or car seat
HEADRESTS > HEADREST
HEADRIG *n* edge of ploughed field
HEADRIGS > HEADRIG
HEADRING *n* African head decoration
HEADRINGS > HEADRING
HEADROOM *n* space below a roof or bridge which allows an object to pass or stay underneath it without touching it
HEADROOMS > HEADROOM
HEADROPE *n* rope round an animal's head
HEADROPES > HEADROPE
HEADS *adv* with the side of a coin with a head on it uppermost
HEADSAIL *n* any sail set forward of the foremast
HEADSAILS > HEADSAIL

HEADSCARF *n* scarf for the head, often worn tied under the chin
HEADSET *n* pair of headphones
HEADSETS > HEADSET
HEADSHAKE *n* gesture of shaking head
HEADSHIP *n* position or state of being a leader, esp the head teacher of a school
HEADSHIPS > HEADSHIP
HEADSHOT *n* photo of person's head
HEADSHOTS > HEADSHOT
HEADSMAN *n* (formerly) an executioner who beheaded condemned persons
HEADSMEN > HEADSMAN
HEADSPACE *n* space between bolt and cartridge in a rifle
HEADSTALL *n* part of a bridle that fits round a horse's head
HEADSTAND *n* act or an instance of balancing on the head, usually with the hands as support
HEADSTAY *n* rope from mast to bow on ship
HEADSTAYS > HEADSTAY
HEADSTICK *n* piece of wood formerly used in typesetting
HEADSTOCK *n* part of a machine that supports and transmits the drive to the chuck
HEADSTONE *n* memorial stone on a grave
HEADWALL *n* steep slope at the head of a glacial cirque
HEADWALLS > HEADWALL
HEADWARD *same as >* HEADWARDS
HEADWARDS *adv* backwards beyond the original source
HEADWATER *n* highest part of river
HEADWAY *same as >* HEADROOM
HEADWAYS > HEADWAY
HEADWIND *n* wind blowing against the course of an aircraft or ship
HEADWINDS > HEADWIND
HEADWORD *n* key word placed at the beginning of a line, paragraph, etc, as in a dictionary entry
HEADWORDS > HEADWORD
HEADWORK *n* mental work
HEADWORKS > HEADWORK
HEADY *adj* intoxicating or exciting
HEAL *vb* make or become well
HEALABLE > HEAL

HEALD *same as >* HEDDLE
HEALDED > HEALD
HEALDING > HEALD
HEALDS > HEALD
HEALED > HEAL
HEALEE *n* person who is being healed
HEALEES > HEALEE
HEALER > HEAL
HEALERS > HEAL
HEALING > HEAL
HEALINGLY > HEAL
HEALINGS > HEAL
HEALS > HEAL
HEALSOME *Scots word for >* WHOLESOME
HEALTH *n* normal (good) condition of someone's body ▷ *interj* exclamation wishing someone good health as part of a toast
HEALTHFUL *same as >* HEALTHY
HEALTHIER > HEALTHY
HEALTHILY > HEALTHY
HEALTHISM *n* lifestyle that prioritizes health and fitness over anything else
HEALTHS > HEALTH
HEALTHY *adj* having good health
HEAME *old form of >* HOME
HEAP *n* pile of things one on top of another ▷ *vb* gather into a pile
HEAPED > HEAP
HEAPER > HEAP
HEAPERS > HEAP
HEAPIER > HEAPY
HEAPIEST > HEAPY
HEAPING *adj* (of a spoonful) heaped
HEAPS > HEAP
HEAPSTEAD *n* buildings at mine
HEAPY *adj* having many heaps
HEAR *vb* perceive (a sound) by ear
HEARABLE > HEAR
HEARD *same as >* HERD
HEARDS > HERD
HEARE *old form of >* HAIR
HEARER > HEAR
HEARERS > HEAR
HEARES > HEARE
HEARIE *old form of >* HAIRY
HEARING > HEAR
HEARINGS > HEAR
HEARKEN *vb* listen
HEARKENED > HEARKEN
HEARKENER > HEARKEN
HEARKENS > HEARKEN
HEARS > HEAR
HEARSAY *n* gossip, rumour
HEARSAYS > HEARSAY
HEARSE *n* funeral car used to carry a coffin ▷ *vb* put in hearse
HEARSED > HEARSE
HEARSES > HEARSE

HEARSIER > HEARSY
HEARSIEST > HEARSY
HEARSING > HEARSE
HEARSY *adj* like a hearse
HEART *n* organ that pumps blood round the body ▷ *vb* (of vegetables) form a heart
HEARTACHE *n* intense anguish
HEARTBEAT *n* one complete pulsation of the heart
HEARTBURN *n* burning sensation in the chest caused by indigestion
HEARTED > HEART
HEARTEN *vb* encourage, make cheerful
HEARTENED > HEARTEN
HEARTENER > HEARTEN
HEARTENS > HEARTEN
HEARTFELT *adj* felt sincerely or strongly
HEARTFREE *adj* not in love
HEARTH *n* floor of a fireplace
HEARTHRUG *n* rug laid before fireplace
HEARTHS > HEARTH
HEARTIER > HEARTY
HEARTIES > HEARTY
HEARTIEST > HEARTY
HEARTIKIN *n* little heart
HEARTILY *adv* thoroughly or vigorously
HEARTING > HEART
HEARTLAND *n* central region of a country or continent
HEARTLESS *adj* cruel, unkind
HEARTLET *n* little heart
HEARTLETS > HEART
HEARTLING *n* little heart
HEARTLY *adv* vigorously
HEARTPEA *same as >* HEARTSEED
HEARTPEAS > HEARTPEA
HEARTS *n* card game
HEARTSEED *n* type of vine
HEARTSICK *adj* deeply dejected or despondent
HEARTSINK *n* patient who visits a doctor with multiple non-specific symptoms that are impossible to treat
HEARTSOME *adj* cheering or encouraging
HEARTSORE *adj* greatly distressed ▷ *n* cause of pain in the heart or the pain itself
HEARTWOOD *n* central core of dark hard wood in tree trunks
HEARTWORM *n* parasitic nematode worm that lives in the heart and bloodstream of vertebrates

HEARTY adj substantial, nourishing ▷ n comrade, esp a sailor
HEAST same as > HEST
HEASTE same as > HEST
HEASTES > HEASTE
HEASTS > HEAST
HEAT vb make or become hot ▷ n state of being hot
HEATABLE > HEAT
HEATED adj angry and excited
HEATEDLY > HEATED
HEATER n device for supplying heat
HEATERS > HEATER
HEATH n area of open uncultivated land
HEATHBIRD n black grouse
HEATHCOCK same as > BLACKCOCK
HEATHEN n person who does not believe in an established religion ▷ adj of or relating to heathen peoples
HEATHENRY > HEATHEN
HEATHENS > HEATHEN
HEATHER n low-growing plant ▷ adj of a heather colour
HEATHERED > HEATHER
HEATHERS > HEATHER
HEATHERY > HEATHER
HEATHFOWL Compare > MOORFOWL
HEATHIER > HEATH
HEATHIEST > HEATH
HEATHLAND n area of heath
HEATHLESS > HEATH
HEATHLIKE > HEATH
HEATHS > HEATH
HEATHY > HEATH
HEATING n device or system for supplying heat
HEATINGS > HEATING
HEATLESS > HEAT
HEATPROOF > HEAT
HEATS > HEAT
HEATSPOT n spot on skin produced by heat
HEATSPOTS > HEATSPOT
HEATWAVE n prolonged period of unusually hot weather
HEATWAVES > HEATWAVE
HEAUME n large helmet reaching the shoulders
HEAUMES > HEAUME
HEAVE vb lift with effort ▷ n heaving
HEAVED > HEAVE
HEAVEN n place believed to be the home of God
HEAVENLY adj of or like heaven
HEAVENS > HEAVEN
HEAVER > HEAVE
HEAVERS > HEAVE
HEAVES > HEAVE
HEAVIER > HEAVY

HEAVIES > HEAVY
HEAVIEST > HEAVY
HEAVILY > HEAVY
HEAVINESS > HEAVY
HEAVING > HEAVE
HEAVINGS > HEAVE
HEAVY adj of great weight
HEAVYISH n rather heavy
HEAVYSET adj stockily built
HEBDOMAD n number seven or a group of seven
HEBDOMADS > HEBDOMAD
HEBE n any of various flowering shrubs
HEBEN old form of > EBONY
HEBENON n source of poison
HEBENONS > HEBENON
HEBENS > HEBEN
HEBES > HEBE
HEBETANT adj causing dullness
HEBETATE adj (of plant parts) having a blunt or soft point ▷ vb make or become blunted
HEBETATED > HEBETATE
HEBETATES > HEBETATE
HEBETIC adj of or relating to puberty
HEBETUDE n mental dullness or lethargy
HEBETUDES > HEBETUDE
HEBONA same as > HEBENON
HEBONAS > HEBONA
HEBRAISE same as > HEBRAIZE
HEBRAISED > HEBRAISE
HEBRAISES > HEBRAISE
HEBRAIZE vb become or cause to become Hebrew or Hebraic
HEBRAIZED > HEBRAIZE
HEBRAIZES > HEBRAIZE
HECATOMB n (in ancient Greece or Rome) any great public sacrifice and feast, originally one in which 100 oxen were sacrificed
HECATOMBS > HECATOMB
HECH interj expression of surprise
HECHT same as > HIGHT
HECHTING > HECHT
HECHTS > HECHT
HECK interj mild exclamation of surprise, irritation, etc ▷ n frame for obstructing the passage of fish in a river
HECKLE vb interrupt with comments, questions, or taunts ▷ n instrument for combing flax or hemp
HECKLED > HECKLE
HECKLER > HECKLE
HECKLERS > HECKLE
HECKLES > HECKLE
HECKLING > HECKLE
HECKLINGS > HECKLE
HECKS > HECK
HECKUVA adj heck of a

HECOGENIN n plant chemical used in drugs
HECTARE n one hundred ares
HECTARES > HECTARE
HECTIC adj rushed or busy ▷ n hectic fever or flush
HECTICAL same as > HECTIC
HECTICLY > HECTIC
HECTICS > HECTIC
HECTOGRAM n one hundred grams. 1 hectogram is equivalent to 3.527 ounces
HECTOR vb bully ▷ n blustering bully
HECTORED > HECTOR
HECTORER > HECTOR
HECTORERS > HECTOR
HECTORING > HECTOR
HECTORISM > HECTOR
HECTORLY > HECTOR
HECTORS > HECTOR
HEDARIM same as > HADARIM
HEDDLE n frame on a loom ▷ vb pass thread through a heddle
HEDDLED > HEDDLE
HEDDLES > HEDDLE
HEDDLING > HEDDLE
HEDER variant spelling of > CHEDER
HEDERA n ivy
HEDERAL > HEDERA
HEDERAS > HEDERA
HEDERATED adj honoured with crown of ivy
HEDERS > HEDER
HEDGE n row of bushes forming a barrier or boundary ▷ vb be evasive or noncommittal
HEDGEBILL n tool for pruning a hedge
HEDGED > HEDGE
HEDGEHOG n small mammal with a protective covering of spines
HEDGEHOGS > HEDGEHOG
HEDGEHOP vb (of an aircraft) to fly close to the ground, as in crop spraying
HEDGEHOPS > HEDGEHOP
HEDGEPIG same as > HEDGEHOG
HEDGEPIGS > HEDGEPIG
HEDGER > HEDGE
HEDGEROW n bushes forming a hedge
HEDGEROWS > HEDGEROW
HEDGERS > HEDGE
HEDGES > HEDGE
HEDGIER > HEDGE
HEDGIEST > HEDGE
HEDGING > HEDGE
HEDGINGLY > HEDGE
HEDGINGS > HEDGE
HEDGY > HEDGE
HEDONIC > HEDONISM
HEDONICS n branch of psychology concerned

with the study of pleasant and unpleasant sensations
HEDONISM n doctrine that pleasure is the most important thing in life
HEDONISMS > HEDONISM
HEDONIST > HEDONISM
HEDONISTS > HEDONISM
HEDYPHANE n variety of lead ore
HEED n careful attention ▷ vb pay careful attention to
HEEDED > HEED
HEEDER > HEED
HEEDERS > HEED
HEEDFUL > HEED
HEEDFULLY > HEED
HEEDIER > HEEDY
HEEDIEST > HEEDY
HEEDINESS > HEED
HEEDING > HEED
HEEDLESS adj taking no notice
HEEDS > HEED
HEEDY adj heedful; attentive
HEEHAW interj representation of the braying sound of a donkey ▷ vb make braying sound
HEEHAWED > HEEHAW
HEEHAWING > HEEHAW
HEEHAWS > HEEHAW
HEEL n back part of the foot ▷ vb repair the heel of (a shoe)
HEELBALL n mixture of beeswax and lampblack used by shoemakers
HEELBALLS > HEELBALL
HEELBAR n small shop where shoes are repaired
HEELBARS > HEELBAR
HEELED > HEEL
HEELER n dog that herds cattle by biting at their heels
HEELERS > HEELER
HEELING > HEEL
HEELINGS > HEEL
HEELLESS > HEEL
HEELPIECE n piece of a shoe, stocking, etc, designed to fit the heel
HEELPLATE n reinforcing piece of metal
HEELPOST n post for carrying the hinges of a door or gate
HEELPOSTS > HEELPOST
HEELS > HEEL
HEELTAP n layer of leather, etc, in the heel of a shoe
HEELTAPS > HEELTAP
HEEZE Scots word for > HOIST
HEEZED > HEEZE
HEEZES > HEEZE
HEEZIE n act of lifting
HEEZIES > HEEZIE
HEEZING > HEEZE

HEFT vb assess the weight of (something) by lifting ▷ n weight
HEFTE same as > HEAVE
HEFTED > HEFT
HEFTER > HEFT
HEFTERS > HEFT
HEFTIER > HEFTY
HEFTIEST > HEFTY
HEFTILY > HEFTY
HEFTINESS > HEFTY
HEFTING > HEFT
HEFTS > HEFT
HEFTY adj large, heavy, or strong
HEGARI n African sorghum
HEGARIS > HEGARI
HEGEMON n person in authority
HEGEMONIC > HEGEMONY
HEGEMONS > HEGEMON
HEGEMONY n political domination
HEGIRA n emigration escape or flight
HEGIRAS > HEGIRA
HEGUMEN n head of a monastery of the Eastern Church
HEGUMENE n head of Greek nunnery
HEGUMENES > HEGUMENE
HEGUMENOI > HEGUMENOS
HEGUMENOS same as > HEGUMEN
HEGUMENS > HEGUMEN
HEGUMENY n office of hegumen
HEH interj exclamation of surprise or inquiry
HEHS > HEH
HEID Scot word for > HEAD
HEIDS > HEID
HEIFER n young cow
HEIFERS > HEIFER
HEIGH same as > HEY
HEIGHT n distance from base to top
HEIGHTEN vb make or become higher or more intense
HEIGHTENS > HEIGHTEN
HEIGHTH obsolete form of > HEIGHT
HEIGHTHS > HEIGHTH
HEIGHTISM n discrimination based on people's heights
HEIGHTS > HEIGHT
HEIL vb give a German greeting
HEILED > HEIL
HEILING > HEIL
HEILS > HEIL
HEIMISH adj comfortable
HEINIE n buttocks
HEINIES > HEINIE
HEINOUS adj evil and shocking
HEINOUSLY > HEINOUS

HEIR n person entitled to inherit property or rank ▷ vb inherit
HEIRDOM n succession by right of blood
HEIRDOMS > HEIRDOM
HEIRED > HEIR
HEIRESS n woman who inherits or expects to inherit great wealth
HEIRESSES > HEIRESS
HEIRING > HEIR
HEIRLESS > HEIR
HEIRLOOM n object that has belonged to a family for generations
HEIRLOOMS > HEIRLOOM
HEIRS > HEIR
HEIRSHIP n state or condition of being an heir
HEIRSHIPS > HEIRSHIP
HEISHI n Native American shell jewellery
HEIST n robbery ▷ vb steal or burgle
HEISTED > HEIST
HEISTER > HEIST
HEISTERS > HEIST
HEISTING > HEIST
HEISTS > HEIST
HEITIKI n Māori neck ornament of greenstone
HEITIKIS > HEITIKI
HEJAB same as > HIJAB
HEJABS > HEJAB
HEJIRA same as > HEGIRA
HEJIRAS > HEJIRA
HEJRA same as > HEGIRA
HEJRAS > HEJRA
HEKETARA n small shrub that has flowers with white petals and yellow centres
HEKETARAS > HEKETARA
HEKTARE same as > HECTARE
HEKTARES > HEKTARE
HEKTOGRAM same as > HECTOGRAM
HELCOID adj having ulcers
HELD > HOLD
HELE vb as in hele in insert (cuttings, etc) into soil
HELED > HELE
HELENIUM n plant with daisy-like yellow or variegated flowers
HELENIUMS > HELENIUM
HELES > HELE
HELIAC same as > HELIACAL
HELIACAL adj as in heliacal rising rising of a celestial object at approximately the same time as the rising of the sun
HELIAST n ancient Greek juror
HELIASTS > HELIAST
HELIBORNE adj carried in helicopter
HELIBUS n helicopter carrying passengers

HELIBUSES > HELIBUS
HELICAL adj spiral
HELICALLY > HELICAL
HELICASE n enzyme vital to all living organisms
HELICASES > HELICASE
HELICES > HELIX
HELICITY n projection of the spin of an elementary particle on the direction of propagation
HELICLINE n spiral-shaped ramp
HELICOID adj shaped like a spiral ▷ n any surface resembling that of a screw thread
HELICOIDS > HELICOID
HELICON n bass tuba
HELICONIA n tropical flowering plant
HELICONS > HELICON
HELICOPT vb transport using a helicopter
HELICOPTS > HELICOPT
HELICTITE n twisted stalactite
HELIDECK n landing deck for helicopters on ships, oil platforms, etc
HELIDECKS > HELIDECK
HELIDROME n small airport for helicopters
HELILIFT vb transport by helicopter
HELILIFTS > HELILIFT
HELIMAN n helicopter pilot
HELIMEN > HELIMAN
HELING > HELE
HELIO n instrument for sending messages in Morse code
HELIODOR n clear yellow form of beryl used as a gemstone
HELIODORS > HELIODOR
HELIOGRAM n message sent by reflecting the sun's rays in a mirror
HELIOLOGY n study of sun
HELIOPSES > HELIOPSIS
HELIOPSIS n type of flowering plant
HELIOS > HELIO
HELIOSES > HELIOSIS
HELIOSIS n bad effect of overexposure to the sun
HELIOSTAT n astronomical instrument used to reflect the light of the sun in a constant direction
HELIOTYPE n printing process in which an impression is taken in ink from a gelatine surface that has been exposed under a negative and prepared for printing
HELIOTYPY same as > HELIOTYPE

HELIOZOAN n type of protozoan, typically having a siliceous shell and stiff radiating cytoplasmic projections
HELIOZOIC > HELIOZOAN
HELIPAD n place for helicopters to land and take off
HELIPADS > HELIPAD
HELIPILOT n helicopter pilot
HELIPORT n airport for helicopters
HELIPORTS > HELIPORT
HELISKI vb ski down a mountain after ascending it by helicopter
HELISKIED > HELISKI
HELISKIS > HELISKI
HELISTOP n landing place for helicopter
HELISTOPS > HELISTOP
HELITACK n use of helicopters to extinguish a forest fire
HELITACKS > HELITACK
HELIUM n very light colourless odourless gas
HELIUMS > HELIUM
HELIX n spiral
HELIXES > HELIX
HELL n believed to be where wicked people go when they die ▷ vb act wildly
HELLBENT adj intent
HELLBOX n (in printing) container for broken type
HELLBOXES > HELLBOX
HELLBROTH n evil concoction
HELLCAT n spiteful fierce-tempered woman
HELLCATS > HELLCAT
HELLDIVER n small greyish-brown North American grebe
HELLEBORE n plant with white flowers that bloom in winter
HELLED > HELL
HELLENISE same as > HELLENIZE
HELLENIZE vb make or become like the ancient Greeks
HELLER n monetary unit of the Czech Republic and Slovakia
HELLERI n Central American fish
HELLERIES > HELLERY
HELLERIS > HELLERI
HELLERS > HELLER
HELLERY n wild or mischievous behaviour
HELLFIRE n torment of hell, imagined as eternal fire
HELLFIRES > HELLFIRE
HELLHOLE n unpleasant or evil place

HELLHOLES > HELLHOLE
HELLHOUND n hound of hell
HELLICAT n evil creature
HELLICATS > HELLICAT
HELLIER n slater
HELLIERS > HELLIER
HELLING > HELL
HELLION n rough or rowdy person, esp a child
HELLIONS > HELLION
HELLISH adj very unpleasant
▷ adv (intensifier)
HELLISHLY > HELLISH
HELLKITE n bird of prey from hell
HELLKITES > HELLKITE
HELLO interj expression of greeting or surprise
▷ n act of saying 'hello'
▷ sentence substitute expression of greeting
▷ vb say hello
HELLOED > HELLO
HELLOES > HELLO
HELLOING > HELLO
HELLOS > HELLO
HELLOVA same as
> HELLUVA
HELLS > HELL
HELLUVA adj (intensifier)
HELLWARD adj towards hell
HELLWARDS adv towards hell
HELM n tiller or wheel for steering a ship ▷ vb direct or steer
HELMED > HELM
HELMER n film director
HELMERS > HELMER
HELMET n hard hat worn for protection
HELMETED > HELMET
HELMETING n wearing or provision of a helmet
HELMETS > HELMET
HELMING > HELM
HELMINTH n any parasitic worm, esp a nematode or fluke
HELMINTHS > HELMINTH
HELMLESS > HELM
HELMS > HELM
HELMSMAN n person at the helm who steers the ship
HELMSMEN > HELMSMAN
HELO n helicopter
HELOPHYTE n any perennial marsh plant that bears its overwintering buds in the mud below the surface
HELOS > HELO
HELOT n serf or slave
HELOTAGE same as
> HELOTISM
HELOTAGES
> HELOTAGE
HELOTISM n condition or quality of being a helot
HELOTISMS > HELOTISM
HELOTRIES > HELOTRY

HELOTRY n serfdom or slavery
HELOTS > HELOT
HELP vb make something easier, better, or quicker for (someone)
▷ n assistance or support
HELPABLE > HELP
HELPDESK n place where advice is given by telephone
HELPDESKS > HELPDESK
HELPED > HELP
HELPER > HELP
HELPERS > HELP
HELPFUL adj giving help
HELPFULLY > HELPFUL
HELPING n single portion of food
HELPINGS > HELPING
HELPLESS adj weak or incapable
HELPLINE n telephone line set aside for callers to contact an organization for help with a problem
HELPLINES > HELPLINE
HELPMATE n companion and helper, esp a husband or wife
HELPMATES > HELPMATE
HELPMEET less common word for > HELPMATE
HELPMEETS > HELPMEET
HELPS > HELP
HELVE n handle of a hand tool such as an axe or pick
▷ vb fit a helve to (a tool)
HELVED > HELVE
HELVES > HELVE
HELVETIUM same as
> ASTATINE
HELVING > HELVE
HEM n bottom edge of a garment ▷ vb provide with a hem
HEMAGOG same as
> HEMAGOGUE
HEMAGOGS > HEMAGOGUE
HEMAGOGUE n
haemagogue: drug that promotes the flow of blood
HEMAL same as > HAEMAL
HEMATAL same as > HEMAL
HEMATEIN same as
> HAEMATEIN
HEMATEINS > HEMATEIN
HEMATIC same as
> HAEMATIC
HEMATICS > HEMATIC
HEMATIN same as
> HAEMATIN
HEMATINE n red dye
HEMATINES > HEMATINE
HEMATINIC same as
> HAEMATIC
HEMATINS > HEMATIN
HEMATITE n red, grey, or black mineral
HEMATITES > HEMATITE
HEMATITIC > HEMATITE
HEMATOID same as
> HAEMATOID

HEMATOMA same as
> HAEMATOMA
HEMATOMAS > HEMATOMA
HEMATOSES
> HEMATOSIS
HEMATOSIS n
haematosis: oxygenation of venous blood in the lungs
HEMATOZOA n plural of hematozoon: protozoan that is parasitic in the blood
HEMATURIA n the presence of blood or red blood cells in the urine
HEMATURIC
> HEMATURIA
HEME same as > HAEM
HEMELYTRA n plural of hemelytron: forewing of plant bugs
HEMES > HEME
HEMIALGIA n pain limited to one side of the body
HEMIC same as
> HAEMATIC
HEMICYCLE n
semicircular structure, room, arena, wall, etc
HEMIHEDRA n plural of hemihedron, a solid hemihedrally derived
HEMIHEDRY n state of crystal having certain kind of symmetry
HEMIN same as > HAEMIN
HEMINA n old liquid measure
HEMINAS > HEMINA
HEMINS > HEMIN
HEMIOLA n rhythmic device
HEMIOLAS > HEMIOLA
HEMIOLIA same as
> HEMIOLA
HEMIOLIAS > HEMIOLIA
HEMIOLIC > HEMIOLA
HEMIONE same as
> HEMIONUS
HEMIONES > HEMIONE
HEMIONUS n Asian wild ass
HEMIOPIA n defective vision seeing only halves of things
HEMIOPIAS > HEMIOPIA
HEMIOPIC > HEMIOPIA
HEMIOPSIA same as
> HEMIOPIA
HEMIPOD same as
> HEMIPODE
HEMIPODE n button quail
HEMIPODES > HEMIPODE
HEMIPODS > HEMIPODE
HEMIPTER n insect with beaklike mouthparts
HEMIPTERS > HEMIPTER
HEMISPACE n area in brain
HEMISTICH n half line of verse

HEMITROPE another name for > TWIN
HEMITROPY n state of being a twin
HEMLINE n level to which the hem of a skirt hangs
HEMLINES > HEMLINE
HEMLOCK n poisonous plant
HEMLOCKS > HEMLOCK
HEMMED > HEM
HEMMER n attachment on a sewing machine for hemming
HEMMERS > HEMMER
HEMMING > HEM
HEMOCOEL same as
> HAEMOCOEL
HEMOCOELS
> HEMOCOEL
HEMOCONIA n the small particles of matter, thought to be particles of the structure of red blood cells, that are present in blood that is flowing around the body
HEMOCYTE same as
> HAEMOCYTE
HEMOCYTES > HEMOCYTE
HEMOID same as
> HAEMATOID
HEMOLYMPH n blood-like fluid in invertebrates
HEMOLYSE vb break down so that haemoglobulin is released
HEMOLYSED > HEMOLYSE
HEMOLYSES
> HEMOLYSIS
HEMOLYSIN n
haemolysin: substance that breaks down red blood cells
HEMOLYSIS n
haemolysis: disintegration of red blood cells
HEMOLYTIC adj
destroying red blood corpuscles
HEMOLYZE vb undergo or make undergo hemolysis
HEMOLYZED > HEMOLYZE
HEMOLYZES > HEMOLYZE
HEMOPHILE n
haemophile: person with haemophilia
HEMOSTAT same as
> HAEMOSTAT
HEMOSTATS > HEMOSTAT
HEMOTOXIC
> HEMOTOXIN
HEMOTOXIN n substance that destroys red blood cells
HEMP n Asian plant with tough fibres
HEMPEN > HEMP
HEMPIE variant of > HEMPY
HEMPIER > HEMPY
HEMPIES > HEMPY
HEMPIEST > HEMPY
HEMPLIKE > HEMP
HEMPS > HEMP

HEMPSEED n seed of hemp
HEMPSEEDS > HEMPSEED
HEMPWEED n climbing weed
HEMPWEEDS > HEMPWEED
HEMPY adj of or like hemp ▷ n rogue
HEMS > HEM
HEMSTITCH n decorative edging stitch, usually for a hem, in which the cross threads are stitched in groups ▷ vb decorate (a hem, etc) with hemstitches
HEN n female domestic fowl ▷ vb lose one's courage
HENBANE n poisonous plant with sticky hairy leaves
HENBANES > HENBANE
HENBIT n European plant with small dark red flowers
HENBITS > HENBIT
HENCE adv from this time ▷ interj begone! away!
HENCHMAN n person employed by someone powerful to carry out orders
HENCHMEN > HENCHMAN
HENCOOP n cage for poultry
HENCOOPS > HENCOOP
HEND vb seize
HENDED > HEND
HENDIADYS n rhetorical device by which two nouns joined by a conjunction are used instead of a noun and modifier
HENDING > HEND
HENDS > HEND
HENEQUEN n agave plant native to Yucatán
HENEQUENS > HENEQUEN
HENEQUIN same as > HENEQUEN
HENEQUINS > HENEQUIN
HENIQUEN same as > HENEQUEN
HENIQUENS > HENIQUEN
HENIQUIN same as > HENIQUEN
HENIQUINS > HENIQUIN
HENLEY n type of sweater
HENLEYS > HENLEY
HENLIKE > HEN
HENNA n reddish dye made from a shrub or tree ▷ vb dye (the hair) with henna
HENNAED > HENNA
HENNAING > HENNA

HENNAS > HENNA
HENNED > HEN
HENNER n challenge
HENNERIES > HENNERY
HENNERS > HENNER
HENNERY n place or farm for keeping poultry
HENNIER > HENNY
HENNIES > HENNY
HENNIEST > HENNY
HENNIN n former women's hat
HENNING > HEN
HENNINS > HENNIN
HENNISH > HEN
HENNISHLY > HEN
HENNY adj like hen ▷ n cock that looks like hen
HENOTIC adj acting to reconcile
HENPECK vb (of a woman) to harass or torment (a man)
HENPECKED adj (of a man) dominated by his wife
HENPECKS > HENPECK
HENRIES > HENRY
HENRY n unit of electrical inductance
HENRYS > HENRY
HENS > HEN
HENT vb seize ▷ n anything that has been grasped, esp by the mind
HENTED > HENT
HENTING > HENT
HENTS > HENT
HEP same as > HIP
HEPAR n compound containing sulphur
HEPARIN n polysaccharide present in most body tissues
HEPARINS > HEPARIN
HEPARS > HEPAR
HEPATIC adj of the liver ▷ n any of various drugs for use in treating diseases of the liver
HEPATICA n woodland plant with white, mauve, or pink flowers
HEPATICAE > HEPATICA
HEPATICAL same as > HEPATIC
HEPATICAS > HEPATICA
HEPATICS > HEPATIC
HEPATISE same as > HEPATIZE
HEPATISED > HEPATISE
HEPATISES > HEPATISE
HEPATITE n mineral containing sulphur
HEPATITES > HEPATITE
HEPATITIS n inflammation of the liver
HEPATIZE vb turn into liver
HEPATIZED > HEPATIZE
HEPATIZES > HEPATIZE
HEPATOMA n cancer of liver
HEPATOMAS > HEPATOMA

HEPCAT n person who is hep
HEPCATS > HEPCAT
HEPPER > HEP
HEPPEST > HEP
HEPS > HEP
HEPSTER same as > HIPSTER
HEPSTERS > HEPSTER
HEPT archaic spelling of > HEAPED
HEPTAD n group or series of seven
HEPTADS > HEPTAD
HEPTAGLOT n book written in seven languages
HEPTAGON n geometric figure with seven sides
HEPTAGONS > HEPTAGON
HEPTANE n alkane found in petroleum
HEPTANES > HEPTANE
HEPTAPODY n verse with seven beats in rhythm
HEPTARCH > HEPTARCHY
HEPTARCHS > HEPTARCHY
HEPTARCHY n government by seven rulers
HEPTOSE n any monosaccharide with seven carbon atoms per molecule
HEPTOSES > HEPTOSE
HER pron refers to anything personified as feminine ▷ adj belonging to her ▷ determiner of, belonging to, or associated with her
HERALD n person who announces important news ▷ vb signal the approach of
HERALDED > HERALD
HERALDIC adj of or relating to heraldry
HERALDING > HERALD
HERALDIST > HERALDRY
HERALDRY n study of coats of arms and family trees
HERALDS > HERALD
HERB n plant used for flavouring in cookery, and in medicine
HERBAGE n herbaceous plants collectively
HERBAGED adj with grass growing on it
HERBAGES > HERBAGE
HERBAL adj of or relating to herbs, usually culinary or medicinal herbs ▷ n book describing and listing the properties of plants
HERBALISM n use of herbal medicine
HERBALIST n person who grows or specializes in the use of medicinal herbs

HERBALS > HERBAL
HERBAR same as > HERBARY
HERBARIA > HERBARIUM
HERBARIAL > HERBARIUM
HERBARIAN same as > HERBALIST
HERBARIES > HERBARY
HERBARIUM n collection of dried plants that are mounted and classified systematically
HERBARS > HERBAR
HERBARY n herb garden
HERBED adj flavoured with herbs
HERBELET same as > HERBLET
HERBELETS > HERBELET
HERBICIDE n chemical used to destroy plants, esp weeds
HERBIER > HERBY
HERBIEST > HERBY
HERBIST same as > HERBALIST
HERBISTS > HERBIST
HERBIVORA n animals that eat grass
HERBIVORE n animal that eats only plants
HERBIVORY > HERBIVORE
HERBLESS > HERB
HERBLET n little herb
HERBLETS > HERBLET
HERBLIKE > HERB
HERBOLOGY n use or study of herbal medicine
HERBORISE same as > HERBORIZE
HERBORIST same as > HERBALIST
HERBORIZE vb collect herbs
HERBOSE same as > HERBOUS
HERBOUS adj with abundance of herbs
HERBS > HERB
HERBY adj abounding in herbs
HERCOGAMY n prevention of flower pollination
HERCULEAN adj requiring great strength or effort
HERCULES n as in hercules beetle very large tropical American beetle
HERCYNITE n mineral containing iron
HERD n group of animals feeding and living together ▷ vb collect into a herd
HERDBOY n boy who looks after herd
HERDBOYS > HERDBOY
HERDED > HERD
HERDEN n type of coarse cloth
HERDENS > HERDEN

HERDER same as
> HERDSMAN
HERDERS > HERDER
HERDESS n female herder
HERDESSES > HERDESS
HERDIC n small
horse-drawn carriage
HERDICS > HERDIC
HERDING n act of herding
HERDINGS > HERDING
HERDLIKE > HERD
HERDMAN same as
> HERDSMAN
HERDMEN > HERDMAN
HERDS > HERD
HERDSMAN n man who
looks after a herd of
animals
HERDSMEN > HERDSMAN
HERDWICK n hardy breed
of sheep
HERDWICKS > HERDWICK
HERE adv in, at, or to this
place or point ▷ n this
place
HEREABOUT adv
hereabouts
HEREAFTER adv after this
point or time ▷ n life after
death
HEREAT adv because of
this
HEREAWAY same as
> HEREABOUT
HEREAWAYS dialect form of
> HERE
HEREBY adv by means of
or as a result of this
HEREDES > HERES
HEREDITY n passing on of
characteristics from one
generation to another
HEREFROM adv from here
HEREIN adv in this place,
matter, or document
HEREINTO adv into this
place, circumstance, etc
HERENESS n state of
being here
HEREOF adv of or
concerning this
HEREON archaic word for
> HEREUPON
HERES > HERE
HERESIES > HERESY
HERESY n opinion
contrary to accepted
opinion or belief
HERETIC n person who
holds unorthodox
opinions
HERETICAL > HERETIC
HERETICS > HERETIC
HERETO adv this place,
matter, or document
HERETRIX n in Scots law,
female inheritor
HEREUNDER adv (in
documents, etc) below
this
HEREUNTO archaic word for
> HERETO
HEREUPON adv following
immediately after this

HEREWITH adv with this
HERIED > HERY
HERIES > HERY
HERIOT n (in medieval
England) a death duty paid
to the lord
HERIOTS > HERIOT
HERISSE adj with bristles
HERISSON n spiked beam
used as fortification
HERISSONS > HERISSON
HERITABLE adj capable
of being inherited
HERITABLY
> HERITABLE
HERITAGE n something
inherited
HERITAGES > HERITAGE
HERITOR n person who
inherits
HERITORS > HERITOR
HERITRESS > HERITOR
HERITRIX > HERITOR
HERKOGAMY same as
> HERCOGAMY
HERL n barb or barbs of a
feather
HERLING n Scots word for
a type of fish
HERLINGS > HERL
HERLS > HERL
HERM n (in ancient Greece)
a stone head of Hermes
HERMA same as > HERM
HERMAE > HERMA
HERMAEAN adj type of
statue
HERMAI > HERMA
HERMANDAD n
organization of middle
classes in Spain
HERMETIC adj sealed so as
to be airtight
HERMETICS n alchemy
HERMETISM n belief in
pagan mystical
knowledge
HERMETIST
> HERMETISM
HERMIT n person living in
solitude, esp for religious
reasons
HERMITAGE n home of a
hermit
HERMITESS n female
hermit
HERMITIC > HERMIT
HERMITISM n act of living
as hermit
HERMITRY n life as hermit
HERMITS > HERMIT
HERMS > HERM
HERN archaic or dialect word
for > HERON
HERNIA n medical
problem
HERNIAE > HERNIA
HERNIAL > HERNIA
HERNIAS > HERNIA
HERNIATE n form hernia
HERNIATED > HERNIA
HERNIATES > HERNIATE
HERNS > HERN

HERNSHAW same as
> HERONSHAW
HERNSHAWS > HERNSHAW
HERO n principal character
in a film, book, etc
HEROES > HERO
HEROIC adj courageous
HEROICAL same as
> HEROIC
HEROICISE same as
> HEROICIZE
HEROICIZE same as
> HEROIZE
HEROICLY > HEROIC
HEROICS pl n extravagant
behaviour
HEROIN n highly addictive
drug derived from
morphine
HEROINE n principal
female character in a
novel, play, etc
HEROINES > HEROINE
HEROINISM n addiction
to heroin
HEROINS > HEROIN
HEROISE same as
> HEROIZE
HEROISED > HEROISE
HEROISES > HEROISE
HEROISING > HEROISE
HEROISM n great courage
and bravery
HEROISMS > HEROISM
HEROIZE vb make into
hero
HEROIZED > HEROIZE
HEROIZES > HEROIZE
HEROIZING > HEROIZE
HERON n long-legged
wading bird
HERONRIES > HERONRY
HERONRY n colony of
breeding herons
HERONS > HERON
HERONSEW same as
> HERONSHAW
HERONSEWS > HERONSEW
HERONSHAW n young
heron
HEROON n temple or
monument dedicated to
hero
HEROONS > HEROON
HEROS > HERO
HEROSHIP > HERO
HEROSHIPS > HERO
HERPES n any of several
inflammatory skin
diseases
HERPESES > HERPES
HERPETIC adj of or
relating to any of the
herpes diseases ▷ n person
suffering from any of the
herpes diseases
HERPETICS > HERPETIC
HERPETOID adj like
reptile
HERPTILE adj denoting,
relating to, or
characterizing both
reptiles and amphibians
HERRIED > HERRY

HERRIES > HERRY
HERRIMENT n act of
plundering
HERRING n important
food fish of northern seas
HERRINGER n person or
boat catching herring
HERRINGS > HERRING
HERRY vb harry
HERRYING > HERRY
HERRYMENT same as
> HERRIMENT
HERS pron something
belonging to her
HERSALL n rehearsal
HERSALLS > HERSALL
HERSE n harrow
HERSED adj arranged like a
harrow
HERSELF pron feminine
singular reflexive form
HERSES > HERSE
HERSHIP n act of
plundering
HERSHIPS > HERSHIP
HERSTORY n history from
a female point of view or
as it relates to women
HERTZ n unit of frequency
HERTZES > HERTZ
HERY vb praise
HERYE same as > HERY
HERYED > HERYE
HERYES > HERYE
HERYING > HERY
HES > HE
HESITANCE > HESITANT
HESITANCY > HESITANT
HESITANT adj undecided
or wavering
HESITATE vb be slow or
uncertain in doing
something
HESITATED > HESITATE
HESITATER > HESITATE
HESITATES > HESITATE
HESITATOR > HESITATE
HESP same as > HASP
HESPED > HESP
HESPERID n species of
butterfly
HESPERIDS > HESPERID
HESPING > HESP
HESPS > HESP
HESSIAN n coarse jute
fabric
HESSIANS > HESSIAN
HESSITE n black or grey
metallic mineral
HESSITES > HESSITE
HESSONITE n orange-
brown variety of
grossularite garnet
HEST archaic word for
> BEHEST
HESTERNAL adj belonging
to yesterday
HESTS > HEST
HET n short for
heterosexual ▷ adj Scot
word for hot
HETAERA n (esp in ancient
Greece) a female prostitute

HETAERAE > HETAERA
HETAERAS > HETAERA
HETAERIC > HETAERA
HETAERISM n state of being a concubine
HETAERIST > HETAERISM
HETAIRA same as > HETAERA
HETAIRAI > HETAIRA
HETAIRAS > HETAIRA
HETAIRIA n society
HETAIRIAS > HETAIRIA
HETAIRIC > HETAERA
HETAIRISM same as > HETAERISM
HETAIRIST > HETAERIST
HETE same as > HIGHT
HETERO n short for heterosexual
HETERODOX adj differing from accepted doctrines or beliefs
HETERONYM n one of two or more words pronounced differently but spelt alike
HETEROPOD n marine invertebrate with a foot for swimming
HETEROS > HETERO
HETEROSES > HETEROSIS
HETEROSIS n increased size, strength, etc, of a hybrid as compared to either of its parents
HETEROTIC > HETEROSIS
HETES > HETE
HETH n eighth letter of the Hebrew alphabet
HETHER same as > HITHER
HETHS > HETH
HETING > HETE
HETMAN another word for > ATAMAN
HETMANATE > HETMAN
HETMANS > HETMAN
HETMEN > HETMAN
HETS > HET
HETTIE n slang term for a heterosexual
HETTIES > HETTIE
HEUCH Scots word for > CRAG
HEUCHERA n N American plant with heart-shaped leaves and mostly red flowers
HEUCHERAS > HEUCHERA
HEUCHS > HEUCH
HEUGH same as > HEUCH
HEUGHS > HEUGH
HEUREKA same as > EUREKA
HEUREKAS > HEUREKA
HEURETIC same as > HEURISTIC
HEURETICS n use of logic
HEURISM n use of logic
HEURISMS > HEURISM

HEURISTIC adj involving learning by investigation
  ▷ n science of heuristic procedure
HEVEA n rubber-producing South American tree
HEVEAS > HEVEA
HEW vb cut with an axe
HEWABLE > HEW
HEWED > HEW
HEWER > HEW
HEWERS > HEW
HEWGH interj sound made to imitate the flight of an arrow
HEWING > HEW
HEWINGS > HEW
HEWN > HEW
HEWS > HEW
HEX adj of or relating to hexadecimal notation
  ▷ n evil spell ▷ vb bewitch
HEXACHORD n (in medieval musical theory) any of three diatonic scales based upon C, F, and G, each consisting of six notes, from which solmization was developed
HEXACT n part of a sponge with six rays
HEXACTS > HEXACT
HEXAD n group or series of six
HEXADE same as > HEXAD
HEXADES > HEXADE
HEXADIC > HEXAD
HEXADS > HEXAD
HEXAFOIL n pattern with six lobes
HEXAFOILS > HEXAFOIL
HEXAGLOT n book written in six languages
HEXAGLOTS > HEXAGLOT
HEXAGON n geometrical figure with six sides
HEXAGONAL adj having six sides and six angles
HEXAGONS > HEXAGON
HEXAGRAM n star formed by extending the sides of a regular hexagon to meet at six points
HEXAGRAMS > HEXAGRAM
HEXAHEDRA n plural of hexahedron: solid figure with six plane faces
HEXAMERAL adj arranged in six groups
HEXAMETER n verse line consisting of six metrical feet
HEXAMINE n type of fuel produced in small solid blocks or tablets for use in miniature camping stoves
HEXAMINES > HEXAMINE
HEXANE n liquid alkane existing in five isomeric forms
HEXANES > HEXANE
HEXANOIC adj as in hexanoic acid insoluble oily

carboxylic acid found in coconut and palm oils and in milk
HEXAPLA n edition of the Old Testament
HEXAPLAR > HEXAPLA
HEXAPLAS > HEXAPLA
HEXAPLOID adj with six times the normal number of chromosomes
HEXAPOD n six-footed arthropod
HEXAPODAL adj relating to the Hexapoda, ie insects
HEXAPODIC > HEXAPODY
HEXAPODS > HEXAPOD
HEXAPODY n verse measure consisting of six metrical feet
HEXARCH adj (of plant) with six veins
HEXARCHY n alliance of six states
HEXASTICH n poem, stanza, or strophe that consists of six lines
HEXASTYLE n portico or façade with six columns
  ▷ adj having six columns
HEXATHLON n athletic contest comprising six events
HEXED > HEX
HEXENE same as > HEXYLENE
HEXENES > HEXENE
HEXER > HEX
HEXEREI n witchcraft
HEXEREIS > HEXEREI
HEXERS > HEX
HEXES > HEX
HEXING > HEX
HEXINGS > HEX
HEXONE n colourless insoluble liquid ketone
HEXONES > HEXONE
HEXOSAN n form of polysaccharide
HEXOSANS > HEXOSAN
HEXOSE n monosaccharide, such as glucose
HEXOSES > HEXOSE
HEXYL adj of or consisting of a specific group of atoms
HEXYLENE n chemical compound similar to ethylene
HEXYLENES > HEXYLENE
HEXYLIC > HEXYL
HEXYLS > HEXYL
HEY interj expression of surprise or for catching attention ▷ vb perform a country dance
HEYDAY n time of greatest success, prime
HEYDAYS > HEYDAY
HEYDEY variant of > HEYDAY
HEYDEYS > HEYDEY
HEYDUCK same as > HAIDUK

HEYDUCKS > HEYDUCK
HEYED > HEY
HEYING > HEY
HEYS > HEY
HI interj hello
HIANT adj gaping
HIATAL > HIATUS
HIATUS n pause or interruption in continuity
HIATUSES > HIATUS
HIBACHI n portable brazier for heating and cooking food
HIBACHIS > HIBACHI
HIBAKUSHA n survivor of either of the atomic-bomb attacks on Hiroshima and Nagasaki in 1945
HIBERNAL adj of or occurring in winter
HIBERNATE vb (of an animal) pass the winter as if in a deep sleep
HIBERNISE same as > HIBERNIZE
HIBERNIZE vb make Irish
HIBISCUS n tropical plant with large brightly coloured flowers
HIC interj representation of the sound of a hiccup
HICATEE same as > HICCATEE
HICATEES > HICATEE
HICCATEE n tortoise of West Indies
HICCATEES > HICCATEE
HICCOUGH same as > HICCUP
HICCOUGHS > HICCOUGH
HICCUP n spasm of the breathing organs ▷ vb make a hiccup
HICCUPED > HICCUP
HICCUPING > HICCUP
HICCUPPED > HICCUP
HICCUPS > HICCUP
HICCUPY > HICCUP
HICK n unsophisticated country person
  ▷ adj unsophisticated
HICKER > HICK
HICKEST > HICK
HICKEY n object or gadget
HICKEYS > HICKEY
HICKIE same as > HICKEY
HICKIES > HICKIE
HICKISH > HICK
HICKORIES > HICKORY
HICKORY n N American nut-bearing tree
HICKS > HICK
HICKWALL n green woodpecker
HICKWALLS > HICKWALL
HICKYMAL n titmouse
HICKYMALS > HICKYMAL
HID > HIDE
HIDABLE > HIDE
HIDAGE n former tax on land
HIDAGES > HIDAGE

HIDALGA n Spanish noblewoman
HIDALGAS > HIDALGA
HIDALGO n member of the lower nobility in Spain
HIDALGOS > HIDALGO
HIDDEN > HIDE
HIDDENITE n green transparent variety of the mineral spodumene, used as a gemstone
HIDDENLY > HIDE
HIDDER n young ram
HIDDERS > HIDDER
HIDE vb put (oneself or an object) somewhere difficult to see or find ▷ n place of concealment, esp for a bird-watcher
HIDEAWAY n private place
HIDEAWAYS > HIDEAWAY
HIDEBOUND adj unwilling to accept new ideas
HIDED > HIDE
HIDELESS > HIDE
HIDEOSITY > HIDEOUS
HIDEOUS adj ugly, revolting
HIDEOUSLY > HIDEOUS
HIDEOUT n hiding place
HIDEOUTS > HIDEOUT
HIDER > HIDE
HIDERS > HIDE
HIDES > HIDE
HIDING > HIDE
HIDINGS > HIDE
HIDLING n hiding place
HIDLINGS adv in secret
HIDLINS same as > HIDLINGS
HIDROSES > HIDROSIS
HIDROSIS n any skin disease affecting the sweat glands
HIDROTIC > HIDROSIS
HIDROTICS > HIDROSIS
HIE vb hurry
HIED > HIE
HIEING > HIE
HIELAMAN n Australian Aboriginal shield
HIELAMANS > HIELAMAN
HIELAND adj characteristic of Highlanders
HIEMAL less common word for > HIBERNAL
HIEMS n winter
HIERACIUM n plant of hawkweed family
HIERARCH n person in a position of high-priestly authority
HIERARCHS > HIERARCH
HIERARCHY n system of people or things arranged in a graded order
HIERATIC adj of or relating to priests ▷ n hieratic script of ancient Egypt
HIERATICA n type of papyrus
HIERATICS > HIERATIC

HIEROCRAT n person who believes in government by religious leaders
HIERODULE n (in ancient Greece) a temple slave, esp a sacral prostitute
HIEROGRAM n sacred symbol
HIEROLOGY n sacred literature
HIERURGY n performance of religious drama or music
HIES > HIE
HIFALUTIN adj pompous or pretentious
HIGGLE less common word for > HAGGLE
HIGGLED > HIGGLE
HIGGLER > HIGGLE
HIGGLERS > HIGGLE
HIGGLES > HIGGLE
HIGGLING > HIGGLE
HIGGLINGS > HIGGLE
HIGH adj being a relatively great distance from top to bottom; tall ▷ adv at or to a height ▷ n high place or level ▷ vb hie
HIGHBALL n tall drink of whiskey with soda water or ginger ale and ice ▷ vb move at great speed
HIGHBALLS > HIGHBALL
HIGHBORN adj of noble or aristocratic birth
HIGHBOY n tall chest of drawers in two sections
HIGHBOYS > HIGHBOY
HIGHBRED adj of noble breeding
HIGHBROW n intellectual and serious person ▷ adj concerned with serious, intellectual subjects
HIGHBROWS > HIGHBROW
HIGHBUSH adj (of bush) growing tall ▷ n tall-growing bush
HIGHCHAIR n long-legged chair with a tray attached, used by a very young child at mealtimes
HIGHED > HIGH
HIGHER n advanced level of the Scottish Certificate of Education ▷ vb raise up
HIGHERED > HIGHER
HIGHERING > HIGHER
HIGHERS > HIGHER
HIGHEST > HIGH
HIGHFLIER same as > HIGHFLYER
HIGHFLYER n person who is extreme in aims, ambition, etc
HIGHING > HIGH
HIGHISH > HIGH
HIGHJACK same as > HIJACK
HIGHJACKS > HIGHJACK

HIGHLAND n relatively high ground
HIGHLANDS > HIGHLAND
HIGHLIFE n style of music combining West African elements with US jazz forms, found esp in the cities of West Africa
HIGHLIFES > HIGHLIFE
HIGHLIGHT n outstanding part or feature ▷ vb give emphasis to
HIGHLY adv extremely
HIGHMAN n dice weighted to make it fall in particular way
HIGHMEN > HIGHMAN
HIGHMOST adj highest
HIGHNESS n condition of being high or lofty
HIGHRISE n tall building
HIGHRISES > HIGHRISE
HIGHROAD n main road
HIGHROADS > HIGHROAD
HIGHS > HIGH
HIGHSPOT n highlight
HIGHSPOTS > HIGHSPOT
HIGHT vb archaic word for name or call
HIGHTAIL vb go or move in a great hurry
HIGHTAILS > HIGHTAIL
HIGHTED > HIGHT
HIGHTH old form of > HEIGHT
HIGHTHS > HIGHTH
HIGHTING n oath
HIGHTINGS > HIGHTING
HIGHTOP n top of ship's mast
HIGHTOPS > HIGHTOP
HIGHTS > HIGHT
HIGHVELD n high-altitude grassland region of E South Africa
HIGHVELDS > HIGHVELD
HIGHWAY n main road
HIGHWAYS > HIGHWAY
HIJAB n covering for the head and face
HIJABS > HIJAB
HIJACK vb seize control of (an aircraft or other vehicle) while travelling ▷ n instance of hijacking
HIJACKED > HIJACK
HIJACKER > HIJACK
HIJACKERS > HIJACK
HIJACKING > HIJACK
HIJACKS > HIJACK
HIJINKS n lively enjoyment
HIJRA same as > HIJRAH
HIJRAH same as > HEGIRA
HIJRAHS > HIJRAH
HIJRAS > HIJRA
HIKE n long walk in the country, esp for pleasure ▷ vb go for a long walk
HIKED > HIKE
HIKER > HIKE
HIKERS > HIKE

HIKES > HIKE
HIKING > HIKE
HIKOI n walk or march, esp a Māori protest march ▷ vb take part in such a march
HIKOIED > HIKOI
HIKOIING > HIKOI
HIKOIS > HIKOI
HILA > HILUM
HILAR > HILUS
HILARIOUS adj very funny
HILARITY n mirth and merriment
HILCH vb hobble
HILCHED > HILCH
HILCHES > HILCH
HILCHING > HILCH
HILD same as > HOLD
HILDING n coward
HILDINGS > HILDING
HILI > HILUS
HILL n raised part of the earth's surface ▷ vb form into a hill or mound
HILLBILLY n usually disparaging term for an unsophisticated country person
HILLCREST n crest of hill
HILLED > HILL
HILLER > HILL
HILLERS > HILL
HILLFOLK n people living in the hills
HILLFORT n hilltop fortified with ramparts and ditches, dating from the second millennium BC
HILLFORTS > HILLFORT
HILLIER > HILL
HILLIEST > HILL
HILLINESS > HILL
HILLING > HILL
HILLINGS > HILLING
HILLMEN same as > HILLFOLK
HILLO same as > HELLO
HILLOA same as > HALLOA
HILLOAED > HILLOA
HILLOAING > HILLOA
HILLOAS > HILLOA
HILLOCK n small hill
HILLOCKED > HILLOCK
HILLOCKS > HILLOCK
HILLOCKY > HILLOCK
HILLOED > HILLO
HILLOES > HILLO
HILLOING > HILLO
HILLOS > HILLO
HILLS > HILL
HILLSIDE n side of a hill
HILLSIDES > HILLSIDE
HILLSLOPE same as > HILLSIDE
HILLTOP n top of hill
HILLTOPS > HILLTOP
HILLY > HILL
HILT n handle of a sword or knife ▷ vb supply with a hilt
HILTED > HILT

HILTING > HILT
HILTLESS > HILT
HILTS > HILT
HILUM n scar on a seed
HILUS rare word for > HILUM
HIM pron refers to a male person or animal ▷ n male person
HIMATIA > HIMATION
HIMATION n (in ancient Greece) a cloak draped around the body
HIMATIONS > HIMATION
HIMBO n slang, usually derogatory term for an attractive but empty-headed man
HIMBOS > HIMBO
HIMS > HIM
HIMSELF pron masculine singular reflexive form
HIN n Hebrew unit of capacity
HINAHINA same as > MAHOE
HINAHINAS > HINAHINA
HINAU n New Zealand tree
HINAUS > HINAU
HIND adj situated at the back ▷ n female deer
HINDBERRY n raspberry
HINDBRAIN n part of the brain comprising the cerebellum, pons and medulla oblongata
HINDCAST vb test (a mathematical model)
HINDCASTS > HINDCAST
HINDER vb get in the way of ▷ adj situated at the back
HINDERED > HINDER
HINDERER > HINDER
HINDERERS > HINDER
HINDERING > HINDER
HINDERS > HINDER
HINDFEET > HINDFOOT
HINDFOOT n back foot
HINDGUT n part of the vertebrate digestive tract
HINDGUTS > HINDGUT
HINDHEAD n back of head
HINDHEADS > HINDHEAD
HINDLEG n back leg
HINDLEGS > HINDLEG
HINDMILK n breast milk produced after the first part of feeding
HINDMILKS > HINDMILK
HINDMOST > HIND
HINDRANCE n obstruction or snag
HINDS > HIND
HINDSHANK n meat from animal's hind leg
HINDSIGHT n ability to understand, after something has happened, what should have been done
HINDWARD adj at back
HINDWING n back wing
HINDWINGS > HINDWING

HING n asafoetida
HINGE n device for holding two parts so one can swing freely ▷ vb depend (on)
HINGED > HINGE
HINGELESS > HINGE
HINGELIKE > HINGE
HINGER n tool for making hinges
HINGERS > HINGER
HINGES > HINGE
HINGING > HINGE
HINGS > HING
HINKIER > HINKY
HINKIEST > HINKY
HINKY adj strange
HINNIE n sweetheart
HINNIED > HINNY
HINNIES > HINNY
HINNY n offspring of a male horse and a female donkey ▷ vb whinny
HINNYING > HINNY
HINS > HIN
HINT n indirect suggestion ▷ vb suggest indirectly
HINTED > HINT
HINTER > HINT
HINTERS > HINT
HINTING > HINT
HINTINGLY > HINT
HINTINGS > HINT
HINTS > HINT
HIOI n New Zealand plant of the mint family
HIOIS > HIOI
HIP n either side of the body between the pelvis and the thigh ▷ adj aware of or following the latest trends ▷ interj exclamation used to introduce cheers
HIPBONE n either of the bones that form the sides of the pelvis
HIPBONES > HIPBONE
HIPHUGGER adj (of trousers) having a low waist
HIPLESS > HIP
HIPLIKE > HIP
HIPLINE n widest part of a person's hips
HIPLINES > HIPLINE
HIPLY > HIP
HIPNESS > HIP
HIPNESSES > HIP
HIPPARCH n (in ancient Greece) a cavalry commander
HIPPARCHS > HIPPARCH
HIPPED adj having a hip or hips
HIPPEN n baby's nappy
HIPPENS > HIPPEN
HIPPER > HIP
HIPPEST > HIP
HIPPIATRY n treatment of disease in horses
HIPPIC adj of horses
HIPPIE same as > HIPPY

HIPPIEDOM > HIPPIE
HIPPIEISH > HIPPIE
HIPPIER > HIPPY
HIPPIES > HIPPY
HIPPIEST > HIPPY
HIPPIN same as > HIPPEN
HIPPINESS > HIPPY
HIPPING same as > HIPPEN
HIPPINGS > HIPPING
HIPPINS > HIPPIN
HIPPISH adj in low spirits
HIPPO n hippopotamus
HIPPOCRAS n old English drink of wine flavoured with spices
HIPPODAME n sea horse
HIPPOLOGY n study of horses
HIPPOS > HIPPO
HIPPURIC adj as in hippuric acid crystalline solid excreted in the urine of mammals
HIPPURITE n type of fossil
HIPPUS n spasm of eye
HIPPUSES > HIPPUS
HIPPY n person whose behaviour implies a rejection of values ▷ adj having large hips
HIPPYDOM > HIPPY
HIPPYDOMS > HIPPY
HIPPYISH adj pertaining to or like a hippy
HIPS > HIP
HIPSHOT adj having a dislocated hip
HIPSTER n enthusiast of modern jazz
HIPSTERS pl n trousers cut so that the top encircles the hips
HIPT > HIP
HIRABLE > HIRE
HIRAGANA n one of the Japanese systems of syllabic writing based on Chinese cursive ideograms. The more widely used of the two current systems, it is employed in newspapers and general literature
HIRAGANAS > HIRAGANA
HIRAGE n fee for hiring
HIRAGES > HIRAGE
HIRCINE adj of or like a goat, esp in smell
HIRCOSITY n quality of being like a goat
HIRE vb pay to have temporary use of ▷ n hiring
HIREABLE > HIRE
HIREAGE same as > HIRAGE
HIREAGES > HIREAGE
HIRED > HIRE
HIREE n hired person
HIREES > HIREE
HIRELING n derogatory term for a person who works only for wages

HIRELINGS > HIRELING
HIRER > HIRE
HIRERS > HIRE
HIRES > HIRE
HIRING > HIRE
HIRINGS > HIRE
HIRLING n Scots word for a type of fish
HIRLINGS > HIRLING
HIRPLE vb limp ▷ n limping gait
HIRPLED > HIRPLE
HIRPLES > HIRPLE
HIRPLING > HIRPLE
HIRRIENT n trilled sound
HIRRIENTS > HIRRIENT
HIRSEL vb sort into groups
HIRSELED > HIRSEL
HIRSELING > HIRSEL
HIRSELLED > HIRSEL
HIRSELS > HIRSEL
HIRSLE vb wriggle or fidget
HIRSLED > HIRSLE
HIRSLES > HIRSLE
HIRSLING > HIRSLE
HIRSTIE adj dry
HIRSUTE adj hairy
HIRSUTISM > HIRSUTE
HIRUDIN n anticoagulant
HIRUDINS > HIRUDIN
HIRUNDINE adj of or resembling a swallow
HIS adj belonging to him
HISH same as > HISS
HISHED > HISH
HISHES > HISH
HISHING > HISH
HISN dialect form of > HIS
HISPANISM n Spanish turn of phrase
HISPID adj covered with stiff hairs or bristles
HISPIDITY > HISPID
HISS n sound like that of a long s (as an expression of contempt) ▷ vb utter a hiss ▷ interj exclamation of derision or disapproval
HISSED > HISS
HISSELF dialect form of > HIMSELF
HISSER > HISS
HISSERS > HISS
HISSES > HISS
HISSIER > HISSY
HISSIES > HISSY
HISSIEST > HISSY
HISSING > HISS
HISSINGLY > HISS
HISSINGS > HISS
HISSY n temper tantrum ▷ adj sound similar to a hiss
HIST interj exclamation used to attract attention ▷ vb make hist sound
HISTAMIN variant of > HISTAMINE
HISTAMINE n substance released by the body tissues in allergic reactions

HISTAMINS > HISTAMIN
HISTED > HIST
HISTIDIN variant of > HISTIDINE
HISTIDINE n nonessential amino acid that occurs in most proteins: a precursor of histamine
HISTIDINS > HISTIDIN
HISTIE same as > HIRSTIE
HISTING > HIST
HISTIOID same as > HISTOID
HISTOGEN n (formerly) any of three layers in an apical meristem that were thought to give rise to the different parts of the plant: the apical meristem is now regarded as comprising two layers
HISTOGENS > HISTOGEN
HISTOGENY > HISTOGEN
HISTOGRAM n statistical graph in which the frequency of values is represented by vertical bars of varying heights and widths
HISTOID adj (esp of a tumour)
HISTOLOGY n study of the tissues of an animal or plant
HISTONE n any of a group of proteins present in cell nuclei
HISTONES > HISTONE
HISTORIAN n writer of history
HISTORIC adj famous or significant in history
HISTORIED adj recorded in history
HISTORIES > HISTORY
HISTORIFY vb make part of history
HISTORISM n idea that history influences present
HISTORY n (record or account of) past events
HISTRIO n actor
HISTRION same as > HISTRIO
HISTRIONS > HISTRION
HISTRIOS > HISTRIO
HISTS > HIST
HIT vb strike, touch forcefully ▷ n hitting
HITCH n minor problem ▷ vb obtain (a lift) by hitchhiking
HITCHED > HITCH
HITCHER > HITCH
HITCHERS > HITCH
HITCHES > HITCH
HITCHHIKE vb travel by obtaining free lifts
HITCHIER > HITCH
HITCHIEST > HITCH
HITCHILY > HITCH
HITCHING > HITCH

HITCHY > HITCH
HITHE n small harbour
HITHER adv or towards this place ▷ vb come
HITHERED > HITHER
HITHERING > HITHER
HITHERS > HITHER
HITHERTO adv until this time
HITHES > HITHE
HITLESS > HIT
HITMAKER n successful performer or producer of popular music
HITMAKERS > HITMAKER
HITMAN n professional killer
HITMEN > HITMAN
HITS > HIT
HITTABLE > HIT
HITTER n boxer who has a hard punch rather than skill or finesse
HITTERS > HITTER
HITTING > HIT
HIVE n structure in which social bees live and rear their young ▷ vb cause (bees) to collect or (of bees) to collect inside a hive
HIVED > HIVE
HIVELESS > HIVE
HIVELIKE > HIVE
HIVER n person who keeps beehives
HIVERS > HIVER
HIVES n allergic reaction
HIVEWARD adj towards hive
HIVEWARDS adv towards hive
HIVING > HIVE
HIYA sentence substitute informal term of greeting
HIZEN n type of Japanese porcelain
HIZENS > HIZEN
HIZZ same as > HISS
HIZZED > HIZZ
HIZZES > HIZZ
HIZZING > HIZZ
HIZZONER n nickname for mayor
HIZZONERS > HIZZONER
HM interj sound made to express hesitation or doubt
HMM same as > HM
HMMM interj expressing thoughtful consideration
HO n derogatory term for a woman ▷ interj imitation or representation of the sound of a deep laugh ▷ vb halt
HOA same as > HO
HOACTZIN same as > HOATZIN
HOACTZINS > HOATZIN
HOAED > HOA
HOAGIE n sandwich made with long bread roll
HOAGIES > HOAGIE
HOAGY same as > HOAGIE

HOAING > HOA
HOAR adj covered with hoarfrost ▷ vb make hoary
HOARD n store hidden away for future use ▷ vb save or store
HOARDED > HOARD
HOARDER > HOARD
HOARDERS > HOARD
HOARDING n large board for displaying advertisements
HOARDINGS > HOARDING
HOARDS > HOARD
HOARED > HOAR
HOARFROST n white ground frost
HOARHEAD n person with white hair
HOARHEADS > HOARHEAD
HOARHOUND same as > HOREHOUND
HOARIER > HOARY
HOARIEST > HOARY
HOARILY > HOARY
HOARINESS > HOARY
HOARING > HOAR
HOARS > HOAR
HOARSE adj (of a voice) rough and unclear
HOARSELY > HOARSE
HOARSEN vb make or become hoarse
HOARSENED > HOARSEN
HOARSENS > HOARSEN
HOARSER > HOARSE
HOARSEST > HOARSE
HOARY adj grey or white(-haired)
HOAS > HOA
HOAST n cough ▷ vb cough
HOASTED > HOAST
HOASTING > HOAST
HOASTMAN n shipper of coal
HOASTMEN > HOASTMAN
HOASTS > HOAST
HOATCHING adj infested
HOATZIN n South American bird
HOATZINES > HOATZIN
HOATZINS > HOATZIN
HOAX n deception or trick ▷ vb deceive or play a trick upon
HOAXED > HOAX
HOAXER > HOAX
HOAXERS > HOAX
HOAXES > HOAX
HOAXING > HOAX
HOB n flat top part of a cooker ▷ vb cut or form with a hob
HOBBED > HOB
HOBBER n machine used in making gears
HOBBERS > HOBBER
HOBBIES > HOBBY
HOBBING > HOB
HOBBISH adj like a clown
HOBBIT n one of an imaginary race of half-size people

HOBBITRY > HOBBIT
HOBBITS > HOBBIT
HOBBLE vb walk lamely ▷ n strap, rope, etc, used to hobble a horse
HOBBLED > HOBBLE
HOBBLER > HOBBLE
HOBBLERS > HOBBLE
HOBBLES > HOBBLE
HOBBLING > HOBBLE
HOBBLINGS > HOBBLE
HOBBY n activity pursued in one's spare time
HOBBYISM > HOBBY
HOBBYISMS > HOBBY
HOBBYIST > HOBBY
HOBBYISTS > HOBBY
HOBBYLESS > HOBBY
HOBDAY vb alleviate a breathing problem in certain horses
HOBDAYED > HOBDAY
HOBDAYING > HOBDAY
HOBDAYS > HOBDAY
HOBGOBLIN n mischievous goblin
HOBJOB vb do odd jobs
HOBJOBBED > HOBJOB
HOBJOBBER > HOBJOB
HOBJOBS > HOBJOB
HOBLIKE > HOB
HOBNAIL n short nail with a large head for protecting soles ▷ vb provide with hobnails
HOBNAILED > HOBNAIL
HOBNAILS > HOBNAIL
HOBNOB vb be on friendly terms (with)
HOBNOBBED > HOBNOB
HOBNOBBER > HOBNOB
HOBNOBBY > HOBNOB
HOBNOBS > HOBNOB
HOBO n tramp or vagrant ▷ vb live as hobo
HOBODOM > HOBO
HOBODOMS > HOBO
HOBOED > HOBO
HOBOES > HOBO
HOBOING > HOBO
HOBOISM > HOBO
HOBOISMS > HOBO
HOBOS > HOBO
HOBS > HOB
HOC adj Latin for this
HOCK n joint in the leg of an animal corresponding to a human ankle ▷ vb pawn
HOCKED > HOCK
HOCKER > HOCK
HOCKERS > HOCK
HOCKEY n team sport
HOCKEYS > HOCKEY
HOCKING > HOCK
HOCKLE vb spit
HOCKLED > HOCKLE
HOCKLES > HOCKLE
HOCKLING > HOCKLE
HOCKS > HOCK
HOCKSHOP n pawnshop
HOCKSHOPS > HOCKSHOP
HOCUS vb take in
HOCUSED > HOCUS**

HOCUSES > HOCUS
HOCUSING > HOCUS
HOCUSSED > HOCUS
HOCUSSES > HOCUS
HOCUSSING > HOCUS
HOD n open wooden box attached to a pole ▷ vb bob up and down
HODAD n person who pretends to be a surfer
HODADDIES > HODADDY
HODADDY same as **>** HODAD
HODADS > HODAD
HODDED > HOD
HODDEN n coarse homespun cloth
HODDENS > HODDEN
HODDIN same as **>** HODDEN
HODDING > HOD
HODDINS > HODDIN
HODDLE vb waddle
HODDLED > HODDLE
HODDLES > HODDLE
HODDLING > HODDLE
HODIERNAL adj of the present day
HODJA n respectful Turkish form of address
HODJAS > HODJA
HODMAN n hod carrier
HODMANDOD n snail
HODMEN > HODMAN
HODOGRAPH n curve of which the radius vector represents the velocity of a moving particle
HODOMETER another name for **>** ODOMETER
HODOMETRY > HODOMETER
HODOSCOPE n any device for tracing the path of a charged particle, esp a particle found in cosmic rays
HODS > HOD
HOE n long-handled tool used for loosening soil or weeding ▷ vb scrape or weed with a hoe
HOECAKE n maize cake
HOECAKES > HOECAKE
HOED > HOE
HOEDOWN n boisterous square dance
HOEDOWNS > HOEDOWN
HOEING > HOE
HOELIKE > HOE
HOER > HOE
HOERS > HOE
HOES > HOE
HOG n castrated male pig ▷ vb take more than one's share of
HOGAN n wooden dwelling covered with earth
HOGANS > HOGAN
HOGBACK n narrow ridge of steeply inclined rock strata
HOGBACKS > HOGBACK
HOGEN n strong alcoholic drink

HOGENS > HOGEN
HOGFISH n type of fish
HOGFISHES > HOGFISH
HOGG same as **>** HOG
HOGGED > HOG
HOGGER > HOG
HOGGEREL n year-old sheep
HOGGERELS > HOGGEREL
HOGGERIES > HOGGERY
HOGGERS > HOG
HOGGERY n hogs collectively
HOGGET n young unsheared sheep
HOGGETS > HOGGET
HOGGIN n finely sifted gravel
HOGGING same as **>** HOGGIN
HOGGINGS > HOGGING
HOGGINS > HOGGIN
HOGGISH adj selfish, gluttonous, or dirty
HOGGISHLY > HOGGISH
HOGGS > HOGG
HOGH n ridge of land
HOGHOOD n condition of being hog
HOGHOODS > HOGHOOD
HOGHS > HOGH
HOGLIKE > HOG
HOGMANAY n New Year's Eve
HOGMANAYS > HOGMANAY
HOGMANE n short stiff mane
HOGMANES > HOGMANE
HOGMENAY variant of **>** HOGMANAY
HOGMENAYS > HOGMENAY
HOGNOSE n as in hognose snake puff adder
HOGNOSED adj as in hognosed skunk any of several American skunks having a broad snoutlike nose
HOGNOSES > HOGNOSE
HOGNUT another name for **>** PIGNUT
HOGNUTS > HOGNUT
HOGS > HOG
HOGSHEAD n large cask
HOGSHEADS > HOGSHEAD
HOGTIE vb tie together the legs or the arms and legs of
HOGTIED > HOGTIE
HOGTIEING > HOGTIE
HOGTIES > HOGTIE
HOGTYING > HOGTIE
HOGWARD n person looking after hogs
HOGWARDS > HOGWARD
HOGWASH n nonsense
HOGWASHES > HOGWASH
HOGWEED n any of several umbelliferous plants
HOGWEEDS > HOGWEED
HOH same as **>** HO
HOHA adj bored or annoyed
HOHED > HOH

HOHING > HOH
HOHS > HOH
HOI same as **>** HOY
HOICK vb raise abruptly and sharply
HOICKED > HOICK
HOICKING > HOICK
HOICKS interj cry used to encourage hounds to hunt ▷ vb shout hoicks
HOICKSED > HOICKS
HOICKSES > HOICKS
HOICKSING > HOICKS
HOIDEN same as **>** HOYDEN
HOIDENED > HOIDEN
HOIDENING > HOIDEN
HOIDENISH > HOIDEN
HOIDENS > HOIDEN
HOIED > HOI
HOIING > HOI
HOIK same as **>** HOICK
HOIKED > HOIK
HOIKING > HOIK
HOIKS > HOIK
HOING > HO
HOIS > HOI
HOISE same as **>** HOIST
HOISED > HOISE
HOISES > HOISE
HOISIN n Chinese sweet spicy sauce
HOISING > HOISE
HOISINS > HOISIN
HOIST vb raise or lift up ▷ n device for lifting things
HOISTED > HOIST
HOISTER > HOIST
HOISTERS > HOIST
HOISTING > HOIST
HOISTINGS > HOIST
HOISTMAN n person operating a hoist
HOISTMEN > HOISTMAN
HOISTS > HOIST
HOISTWAY n shaft for a hoist
HOISTWAYS > HOISTWAY
HOKA n red cod
HOKAS > HOKA
HOKE vb overplay (a part, etc)
HOKED > HOKE
HOKES > HOKE
HOKEY adj corny
HOKEYNESS > HOKEY
HOKI n fish of New Zealand waters
HOKIER > HOKEY
HOKIEST > HOKEY
HOKILY > HOKEY
HOKINESS > HOKEY
HOKING > HOKE
HOKIS > HOKI
HOKKU same as **>** HAIKU
HOKONUI n illicit whisky
HOKONUIS > HOKONUI
HOKUM n rubbish, nonsense
HOKUMS > HOKUM
HOKYPOKY n trickery
HOLANDRIC adj relating to Y-chromosomal genes

HOLARCHY n system composed of interacting holons
HOLARD n amount of water contained in soil
HOLARDS > HOLARD
HOLD vb keep or support in or with the hands or arms ▷ n act or way of holding
HOLDABLE > HOLD
HOLDALL n large strong travelling bag
HOLDALLS > HOLDALL
HOLDBACK n strap of the harness joining the breeching to the shaft, so that the horse can hold back the vehicle
HOLDBACKS > HOLDBACK
HOLDDOWN n control function in a computer
HOLDDOWNS > HOLDDOWN
HOLDEN past participle of **>** HOLD
HOLDER n person or thing that holds
HOLDERBAT n part of pipe used as fastening
HOLDERS > HOLDER
HOLDFAST n act of gripping strongly
HOLDFASTS > HOLDFAST
HOLDING > HOLD
HOLDINGS > HOLD
HOLDOUT n (in US English) someone or thing that refuses to change
HOLDOUTS > HOLDOUT
HOLDOVER n (in US and Canadian English) elected official who continues in office after his term has expired
HOLDOVERS > HOLDOVER
HOLDS > HOLD
HOLDUP n robbery, esp an armed one
HOLDUPS > HOLDUP
HOLE n area hollowed out in a solid ▷ vb make holes in
HOLED > HOLE
HOLELESS > HOLE
HOLES > HOLE
HOLESOM same as **>** HOLESOME
HOLESOME same as **>** WHOLESOME
HOLEY adj full of holes
HOLEYER > HOLEY
HOLEYEST > HOLEY
HOLIBUT same as **>** HALIBUT
HOLIBUTS > HOLIBUT
HOLIDAY n time spent away from home for rest or recreation ▷ vb spend a holiday
HOLIDAYED > HOLIDAY
HOLIDAYER > HOLIDAY
HOLIDAYS > HOLIDAY
HOLIER > HOLY
HOLIES > HOLY
HOLIEST > HOLY

HOLILY adv in a holy, devout, or sacred manner
HOLINESS n state of being holy
HOLING > HOLE
HOLINGS > HOLE
HOLISM n view that a whole is greater than the sum of its parts
HOLISMS > HOLISM
HOLIST > HOLISM
HOLISTIC adj considering the complete person, physically and mentally, in the treatment of an illness
HOLISTS > HOLISM
HOLK vb dig
HOLKED > HOLK
HOLKING > HOLK
HOLKS > HOLK
HOLLA same as > HOLLO
HOLLAED > HOLLA
HOLLAING > HOLLA
HOLLAND n coarse linen cloth, used esp for furnishing
HOLLANDS > HOLLAND
HOLLAS > HOLLA
HOLLER n shout, yell ▷ vb shout or yell
HOLLERED > HOLLER
HOLLERING > HOLLER
HOLLERS > HOLLER
HOLLIDAM same as > HALIDOM
HOLLIDAMS > HOLLIDAM
HOLLIES > HOLLY
HOLLO interj cry for attention, or of encouragement ▷ vb shout
HOLLOA same as > HOLLO
HOLLOAED > HOLLOA
HOLLOAING > HOLLOA
HOLLOAS > HOLLOA
HOLLOED > HOLLO
HOLLOES > HOLLO
HOLLOING > HOLLO
HOLLOO same as > HALLOO
HOLLOOED > HOLLOO
HOLLOOING > HOLLOO
HOLLOOS > HOLLOO
HOLLOS > HOLLO
HOLLOW adj having a hole or space inside ▷ n cavity or space ▷ vb form a hollow in
HOLLOWARE n hollow utensils such as cups
HOLLOWED > HOLLOW
HOLLOWER > HOLLOW
HOLLOWEST > HOLLOW
HOLLOWING > HOLLOW
HOLLOWLY > HOLLOW
HOLLOWS > HOLLOW
HOLLY n evergreen tree with prickly leaves and red berries
HOLLYHOCK n tall garden plant with spikes of colourful flowers
HOLM n island in a river, lake, or estuary

HOLME same as > HOLM
HOLMES > HOLME
HOLMIA n oxide of holmium
HOLMIAS > HOLMIA
HOLMIC adj of or containing holmium
HOLMIUM n silver-white metallic element
HOLMIUMS > HOLMIUM
HOLMS > HOLM
HOLO n short for hologram
HOLOCAUST n destruction or loss of life on a massive scale
HOLOCENE adj of, denoting, or formed in the second and most recent epoch of the Quaternary period, which began 10 000 years ago at the end of the Pleistocene
HOLOCRINE adj (of the secretion of glands) characterized by disintegration of the entire glandular cell in releasing its product, as in sebaceous glands
HOLOGAMY n condition of having gametes like ordinary cells
HOLOGRAM n three-dimensional photographic image
HOLOGRAMS > HOLOGRAM
HOLOGRAPH n document handwritten by the author
HOLOGYNIC adj passed down through females
HOLOGYNY n inheritance of genetic traits through females only
HOLOHEDRA n geometrical forms with particular symmetry
HOLON n autonomous self-reliant unit, esp in manufacturing
HOLONIC > HOLON
HOLONS > HOLON
HOLOPHOTE n device for directing light from lighthouse
HOLOPHYTE n plant capable of synthesizing food from inorganic molecules
HOLOPTIC adj with eyes meeting at the front
HOLOS > HOLO
HOLOTYPE n original specimen from which a description of a new species is made
HOLOTYPES > HOLOTYPE
HOLOTYPIC > HOLOTYPE
HOLOZOIC adj (of animals) obtaining nourishment by feeding on plants or other animals
HOLP past tense of > HELP
HOLPEN past participle of > HELP
HOLS pl n holidays

HOLSTEIN n breed of cattle
HOLSTEINS > HOLSTEIN
HOLSTER n leather case for a pistol, hung from a belt ▷ vb return (a pistol) to its holster
HOLSTERED > HOLSTER
HOLSTERS > HOLSTER
HOLT n otter's lair
HOLTS > HOLT
HOLUBTSI pl n cabbage rolls
HOLY adj of God or a god
HOLYDAM same as > HALIDOM
HOLYDAME same as > HALIDOM
HOLYDAMES > HOLYDAME
HOLYDAMS > HOLYDAM
HOLYDAY n day on which a religious festival is observed
HOLYDAYS > HOLYDAY
HOLYSTONE n soft sandstone used for scrubbing the decks of a vessel ▷ vb scrub (a vessel's decks) with a holystone
HOLYTIDE n time for special religious observance
HOLYTIDES > HOLYTIDE
HOM n sacred plant of the Parsees and ancient Persians
HOMA same as > HOM
HOMAGE n show of respect or honour towards someone or something ▷ vb render homage to
HOMAGED > HOMAGE
HOMAGER > HOMAGE
HOMAGERS > HOMAGE
HOMAGES > HOMAGE
HOMAGING > HOMAGE
HOMALOID n geometrical plane
HOMALOIDS > HOMALOID
HOMAS > HOMA
HOMBRE slang word for > MAN
HOMBRES > HOMBRE
HOMBURG n man's soft felt hat
HOMBURGS > HOMBURG
HOME n place where one lives ▷ adj of one's home, birthplace, or native country ▷ adv to or at home ▷ vb direct towards (a point or target)
HOMEBIRD n person who is reluctant to leave their home
HOMEBIRDS > HOMEBIRD
HOMEBIRTH n act of giving birth to a child in one's own home
HOMEBODY n person whose life and interests are centred on the home
HOMEBOUND adj heading for home

HOMEBOY n close friend
HOMEBOYS > HOMEBOY
HOMEBRED adj raised or bred at home ▷ n animal bred at home
HOMEBREDS > HOMEBRED
HOMEBREW n home-made beer
HOMEBREWS > HOMEBREW
HOMEBUILT adj built at home
HOMEBUYER n person buying a home
HOMECOMER n person coming home
HOMECRAFT n skills used in the home
HOMED > HOME
HOMEFELT adj felt personally
HOMEGIRL > HOMEBOY
HOMEGIRLS > HOMEBOY
HOMEGROWN adj (esp of fruit and vegetables) produced in one's own country, district, estate, or garden
HOMELAND n country from which a person's ancestors came
HOMELANDS > HOMELAND
HOMELESS adj having nowhere to live ▷ pl n people who have nowhere to live
HOMELIER > HOMELY
HOMELIEST > HOMELY
HOMELIKE > HOME
HOMELILY > HOMELY
HOMELY adj simple, ordinary, and comfortable
HOMELYN n species of ray
HOMELYNS > HOMELYN
HOMEMADE adj (esp of cakes, jam, and other foods) made at home or on the premises, esp of high-quality ingredients
HOMEMAKER n person, esp a housewife, who manages a home
HOMEOBOX adj of genes that regulate cell development
HOMEOMERY n condition of being made up of similar parts
HOMEOPATH n person who treats disease by the use of small amounts of a drug that produces symptoms like those of the disease being treated
HOMEOSES > HOMEOSIS
HOMEOSIS n process of one part coming to resemble another
HOMEOTIC > HOMEOSIS
HOMEOWNER n person who owns the home in which he or she lives
HOMEPAGE n main page of website
HOMEPAGES > HOMEPAGE

HOMEPLACE n person's home

HOMEPORT n port where vessel is registered

HOMEPORTS > HOMEPORT

HOMER n homing pigeon ▷ vb score a home run in baseball

HOMERED > HOMER

HOMERIC adj grand or heroic

HOMERING > HOMER

HOMEROOM n common room at school

HOMEROOMS > HOMEROOM

HOMERS > HOMER

HOMES > HOME

HOMESICK adj sad because missing one's home and family

HOMESITE n site for building house

HOMESITES > HOMESITE

HOMESPUN adj (of philosophies or opinions) plain and unsophisticated ▷ n cloth made at home or made of yarn spun at home

HOMESPUNS > HOMESPUN

HOMESTALL same as > HOMESTEAD

HOMESTAND n series of games played at a team's home ground

HOMESTAY n period spent living as a guest in someone's home

HOMESTAYS > HOMESTAY

HOMESTEAD n farmhouse plus the adjoining land

HOMETOWN n town where one lives or was born

HOMETOWNS > HOMETOWN

HOMEWARD adj going home ▷ adv towards home

HOMEWARDS adv towards home

HOMEWARE n crockery, furniture, and furnishings with which a house, room, etc, is furnished

HOMEWARES > HOMEWARE

HOMEWORK n school work done at home

HOMEWORKS > HOMEWORK

HOMEY same as > HOMY

HOMEYNESS > HOMEY

HOMEYS > HOMEY

HOMICIDAL adj of, involving, or characterized by homicide

HOMICIDE n killing of a human being

HOMICIDES > HOMICIDE

HOMIE short for > HOMEBOY

HOMIER > HOMY

HOMIES > HOMIE

HOMIEST > HOMY

HOMILETIC adj of or relating to a homily or sermon

HOMILIES > HOMILY

HOMILIST > HOMILY

HOMILISTS > HOMILY

HOMILY n speech telling people how they should behave

HOMINES > HOMO

HOMINESS > HOMY

HOMING adj relating to the ability to return home after travelling ▷ n ability to return home after travelling

HOMINGS > HOMING

HOMINIAN same as > HOMINID

HOMINIANS > HOMINIAN

HOMINID n man or any extinct forerunner of man ▷ adj of or belonging to this family

HOMINIDS > HOMINID

HOMINIES > HOMINY

HOMININ n member of a zoological family

HOMININE adj characteristic of humans

HOMININS > HOMININ

HOMINISE same as > HOMINIZE

HOMINISED > HOMINISE

HOMINISES > HOMINISE

HOMINIZE vb make suitable for humans

HOMINIZED > HOMINIZE

HOMINIZES > HOMINIZE

HOMINOID n manlike animal ▷ adj of or like man

HOMINOIDS > HOMINOID

HOMINY n coarsely ground maize

HOMME French word for > MAN

HOMMES > HOMME

HOMMOCK same as > HUMMOCK

HOMMOCKS > HOMMOCK

HOMMOS same as > HUMMUS

HOMMOSES > HOMMOS

HOMO n homogenized milk

HOMOCERCY n condition in fish of having a symmetrical tail

HOMODONT adj (of most nonmammalian vertebrates) having teeth that are all of the same type

HOMODYNE adj of strengthened radio waves

HOMOEOBOX same as > HOMEOBOX

HOMOEOSES > HOMOEOSIS

HOMOEOSIS n condition of controlling a system from within

HOMOEOTIC > HOMOEOSIS

HOMOGAMIC > HOMOGAMY

HOMOGAMY n condition in which all the flowers of an inflorescence are either of the same sex or hermaphrodite

HOMOGENY n similarity in structure of individuals or parts because of common ancestry

HOMOGONY n condition in a plant of having stamens and styles of the same length in all the flowers

HOMOGRAFT n tissue graft obtained from an organism of the same species as the recipient

HOMOGRAPH n word spelt the same as another, but with a different meaning

HOMOLOG same as > HOMOLOGUE

HOMOLOGIC adj having a related or similar position, structure, etc

HOMOLOGS > HOMOLOG

HOMOLOGUE n homologous part or organ

HOMOLOGY n condition of being homologous

HOMOLYSES > HOMOLYSIS

HOMOLYSIS n dissociation of a molecule into two neutral fragments

HOMOLYTIC > HOMOLYSIS

HOMOMORPH n thing same in form as something else

HOMONYM n word that is spelt the same as another

HOMONYMIC > HOMONYM

HOMONYMS > HOMONYM

HOMONYMY n the quality of being pronounced or spelt in the same way

HOMOPHILE n rare word for homosexual: person who is sexually attracted to members of the same sex

HOMOPHOBE n person who has an intense hatred of homosexuality

HOMOPHONE n word pronounced the same as another, but with a different meaning or spelling

HOMOPHONY n linguistic phenomenon whereby words of different origins become identical in pronunciation

HOMOPHYLY n resemblance due to common ancestry

HOMOPLASY n state of being derived from an individual of the same species as the recipient

HOMOPOLAR adj of uniform charge

HOMOS > HOMO

HOMOSEX n sexual activity between homosexuals

HOMOSEXES > HOMOSEX

HOMOSPORY n state of producing spores of one kind only

HOMOSTYLY n (in flowers) existence of styles of only one length

HOMOTAXES > HOMOTAXIS

HOMOTAXIC > HOMOTAXIS

HOMOTAXIS n similarity of composition and arrangement in rock strata of different ages or in different regions

HOMOTONIC adj of same tone

HOMOTONY > HOMOTONIC

HOMOTYPAL adj of normal type

HOMOTYPE n something with same structure as something else

HOMOTYPES > HOMOTYPE

HOMOTYPIC same as > HOMOTYPAL

HOMOTYPY > HOMOTYPE

HOMOUSIAN adj believing God the Son and God the Father to be of the same essence

HOMS > HOM

HOMUNCLE n homunculus

HOMUNCLES > HOMUNCLE

HOMUNCULE n homunculus

HOMUNCULI n plural of homunculus: miniature man

HOMY adj like a home

HON short for > HONEY

HONAN n silk fabric of rough weave

HONANS > HONAN

HONCHO n person in charge ▷ vb supervise or be in charge of

HONCHOED > HONCHO

HONCHOES > HONCHO

HONCHOING > HONCHO

HONCHOS > HONCHO

HOND old form of > HAND

HONDA n loop used to make a lasso

HONDAS > HONDA

HONDLE vb negotiate on price

HONDLED > HONDLE

HONDLES > HONDLE

HONDLING > HONDLE

HONDS > HOND

HONE vb sharpen ▷ n fine whetstone used for sharpening edged tools and knives

HONED > HONE

HONER > HONE

HONERS > HONE

HONES > HONE

HONEST adj truthful and moral

HONESTER > HONEST

HONESTEST > HONEST

HONESTIES > HONESTY

HONESTLY adv in an honest manner ▷ interj expression of disgust, surprise, etc

HONESTY n quality of being honest

HONEWORT n European plant that has clusters of small white flowers

HONEWORTS > HONEWORT

HONEY n edible substance made by bees; term of endearment ▷ vb sweeten with or as if with honey

HONEYBEE n bee widely domesticated as a source of honey and beeswax

HONEYBEES > HONEYBEE

HONEYBUN n term of endearment

HONEYBUNS > HONEYBUN

HONEYCOMB n waxy structure of six-sided cells in which honey is stored by bees in a beehive ▷ vb pierce or fill with holes, cavities, etc

HONEYDEW n sugary substance excreted by aphids and similar insects

HONEYDEWS > HONEYDEW

HONEYED > HONEY

HONEYEDLY > HONEY

HONEYFUL adj full of honey

HONEYING > HONEY

HONEYLESS > HONEY

HONEYMOON n holiday taken by a newly married couple ▷ vb take a honeymoon

HONEYPOT n container for honey

HONEYPOTS > HONEYPOT

HONEYS > HONEY

HONEYTRAP n scheme in which a victim is lured into a compromising sexual situation that provides the opportunity for blackmail

HONG n (in China) a factory, warehouse, etc ▷ vb archaic form of hang

HONGI n Māori greeting in which people touch noses ▷ vb touch noses

HONGIED > HONGI

HONGIES > HONGI

HONGIING > HONGI

HONGING > HONG

HONGIS > HONGI

HONGS > HONG

HONIED same as > HONEY

HONIEDLY > HONEY

HONING > HONE

HONK n sound made by a car horn ▷ vb (cause to) make this sound

HONKED > HONK

HONKER n person or thing that honks

HONKERS > HONKER

HONKEY same as > HONKY

HONKEYS > HONKEY

HONKIE same as > HONKY

HONKIES > HONKY

HONKING > HONK

HONKS > HONK

HONKY n derogatory slang for White man or White men collectively

HONOR same as > HONOUR

HONORABLE adj possessing high principles

HONORABLY adv in an honourable way

HONORAND n person being honoured

HONORANDS > HONORAND

HONORARIA n fee pain for a nominally free service

HONORARY adj held or given only as an honour

HONORED > HONOR

HONOREE same as > HONORAND

HONOREES > HONOREE

HONORER > HONOUR

HONORERS > HONOUR

HONORIFIC adj showing respect

HONORING > HONOR

HONORLESS > HONOUR

HONORS same as > HONOURS

HONOUR n sense of honesty and fairness ▷ vb give praise and attention to

HONOURARY less common spelling of > HONORARY

HONOURED > HONOUR

HONOUREE n person who is honoured

HONOUREES > HONOUREE

HONOURER > HONOUR

HONOURERS > HONOUR

HONOURING > HONOUR

HONOURS > HONOUR

HONS > HON

HOO interj expression of joy, excitement, etc

HOOCH n alcoholic drink, esp illicitly distilled spirits

HOOCHES > HOOCH

HOOCHIE n immoral woman

HOOCHIES > HOOCHIE

HOOD n head covering, often attached to a coat or jacket ▷ vb cover with or as if with a hood

HOODED adj (of a garment) having a hood

HOODIA n any of several southern African succulent plants

HOODIAS > HOODIA

HOODIE n hooded sweatshirt

HOODIER > HOOD

HOODIES > HOODIE

HOODIEST > HOOD

HOODING > HOOD

HOODLESS > HOOD

HOODLIKE > HOOD

HOODLUM n violent criminal, gangster

HOODLUMS > HOODLUM

HOODMAN n blindfolded person in blindman's buff

HOODMEN > HOODMAN

HOODMOLD n moulding over door or window

HOODMOLDS > HOODMOLD

HOODOO n (cause of) bad luck ▷ vb bring bad luck to

HOODOOED > HOODOO

HOODOOING > HOODOO

HOODOOISM > HOODOO

HOODOOS > HOODOO

HOODS > HOOD

HOODWINK vb trick, deceive

HOODWINKS > HOODWINK

HOODY > HOOD

HOOEY n nonsense ▷ interj nonsense

HOOEYS > HOOEY

HOOF n horny covering of the foot of a horse, deer, etc ▷ vb kick or trample with the hooves

HOOFBEAT n sound made by hoof on the ground

HOOFBEATS > HOOFBEAT

HOOFBOUND adj (of a horse) having dry contracted hooves, with resultant pain and lameness

HOOFED adj having a hoof or hoofs

HOOFER n professional dancer

HOOFERS > HOOFER

HOOFING > HOOF

HOOFLESS > HOOF

HOOFLIKE > HOOF

HOOFPRINT n mark made by hoof on ground

HOOFROT n disease of hoof

HOOFROTS > HOOFROT

HOOFS > HOOF

HOOK n curved object used to hang, hold, or pull something ▷ vb fasten or catch (as if) with a hook

HOOKA same as > HOOKAH

HOOKAH n oriental pipe

HOOKAHS > HOOKAH

HOOKAS > HOOKA

HOOKCHECK n in ice hockey, act of hooking an opposing player

HOOKED adj bent like a hook

HOOKER n prostitute

HOOKERS > HOOKER

HOOKEY same as > HOOKY

HOOKEYS > HOOKEY

HOOKIER > HOOKY

HOOKIES > HOOKY

HOOKIEST > HOOKY

HOOKING n act of hooking

HOOKINGS > HOOKING

HOOKLESS > HOOK

HOOKLET n little hook

HOOKLETS > HOOKLET

HOOKLIKE > HOOK

HOOKNOSE n nose with a pronounced outward and downward curve

HOOKNOSED > HOOKNOSE

HOOKNOSES > HOOKNOSE

HOOKS > HOOK

HOOKUP n contact of an aircraft with the hose of a tanker aircraft

HOOKUPS > HOOKUP

HOOKWORM n blood-sucking worm with hooked mouthparts

HOOKWORMS > HOOKWORM

HOOKY n truancy, usually from school ▷ adj hooklike

HOOLACHAN n Highland reel

HOOLEY n lively party

HOOLEYS > HOOLEY

HOOLICAN same as > HOOLACHAN

HOOLICANS > HOOLICAN

HOOLIE same as > HOOLEY

HOOLIER > HOOLY

HOOLIES > HOOLIE

HOOLIEST > HOOLY

HOOLIGAN n rowdy young person

HOOLIGANS > HOOLIGAN

HOOLOCK n Indian gibbon

HOOLOCKS > HOOLOCK

HOOLY adj careful or gentle

HOON n loutish youth who drives irresponsibly ▷ vb drive irresponsibly

HOONED > HOON

HOONING > HOON

HOONS > HOON

HOOP n rigid circular band ▷ vb surround with or as if with a hoop

HOOPED > HOOP

HOOPER rare word for > COOPER

HOOPERS > HOOPER

HOOPING > HOOP

HOOPLA n fairground game

HOOPLAS > HOOPLA

HOOPLESS > HOOP

HOOPLIKE > HOOP

HOOPOE n bird with a pinkish-brown plumage

HOOPOES > HOOPOE

HOOPOO same as > HOOPOE

HOOPOOS > HOOPOO

HOOPS > HOOP

HOOPSKIRT n skirt stiffened by hoops

HOOPSTER n basketball player

HOOPSTERS > HOOPSTER

HOOR n unpleasant or difficult thing

HOORAH same as > HURRAH

HOORAHED > HOORAH

HOORAHING > HOORAH

HOORAHS > HOORAH

HOORAY same as > HURRAH

HOORAYED > HOORAY

HOORAYING > HOORAY

HOORAYS > HOORAY

HOORD *same as* **>** HOARD

HOORDS > HOORD

HOOROO *same as* **>** HURRAH

HOORS > HOOR

HOOSEGOW *slang word for* **>** JAIL

HOOSEGOWS > HOOSEGOW

HOOSGOW *same as* **>** JAIL

HOOSGOWS > JAIL

HOOSH *vb* shoo away

HOOSHED > HOOSH

HOOSHES > HOOSH

HOOSHING > HOOSH

HOOT *n* sound of a car horn ▷ *vb* sound (a car horn) ▷ *interj* exclamation of impatience or dissatisfaction

HOOTCH *same as* **>** HOOCH

HOOTCHES > HOOTCH

HOOTED > HOOT

HOOTER *n* device that hoots

HOOTERS > HOOTER

HOOTIER > HOOT

HOOTIEST > HOOT

HOOTING > HOOT

HOOTNANNY *n* informal performance by folk singers

HOOTS *same as* **>** HOOT

HOOTY > HOOT

HOOVE *same as* **>** HEAVE

HOOVED > HOOVE

HOOVEN > HOOVE

HOOVER *vb* vacuum-clean (a carpet, furniture, etc)

HOOVERED > HOOVER

HOOVERING *n* act of hoovering

HOOVERS > HOOVER

HOOVES > HOOF

HOOVING > HOOVE

HOP *vb* jump on one foot ▷ *n* instance of hopping

HOPAK *n* type of Ukrainian dance

HOPAKS > HOPAK

HOPBIND *n* stalk of the hop

HOPBINDS > HOPBIND

HOPBINE *same as* **>** HOPBIND

HOPBINES > HOPBINE

HOPDOG *n* species of caterpillar

HOPDOGS > HOPDOG

HOPE *vb* want (something) to happen or be true ▷ *n* expectation of something desired

HOPED > HOPE

HOPEFUL *adj* having, expressing, or inspiring hope ▷ *n* person considered to be on the brink of success

HOPEFULLY *adv* in a hopeful manner

HOPEFULS > HOPEFUL

HOPELESS *adj* having or offering no hope

HOPER > HOPE

HOPERS > HOPE

HOPES > HOPE

HOPFIELD *n* field where hops are grown

HOPFIELDS > HOPFIELD

HOPHEAD *n* heroin or opium addict

HOPHEADS > HOPHEAD

HOPING > HOPE

HOPINGLY > HOPE

HOPLITE *n* (in ancient Greece) a heavily armed infantryman

HOPLITES > HOPLITE

HOPLITIC > HOPLITE

HOPLOLOGY *n* study of weapons or armour

HOPPED > HOP

HOPPER *n* container for storing substances

HOPPERCAR *same as* **>** HOPPER

HOPPERS > HOPPER

HOPPIER > HOPPY

HOPPIEST > HOPPY

HOPPING > HOP

HOPPINGS > HOP

HOPPLE *same as* **>** HOBBLE

HOPPLED > HOPPLE

HOPPLER > HOPPLE

HOPPLERS > HOPPLE

HOPPLES > HOPPLE

HOPPLING > HOPPLE

HOPPUS *adj* as in *hoppus foot* unit of volume for round timber

HOPPY *adj* tasting of hops

HOPS > HOP

HOPSACK *n* roughly woven fabric

HOPSACKS > HOPSACK

HOPSCOTCH *n* children's game of hopping in a pattern drawn on the ground

HOPTOAD *n* toad

HOPTOADS > HOPTOAD

HORA *n* traditional Israeli or Romanian circle dance

HORAH *same as* **>** HORA

HORAHS > HORAH

HORAL *less common word for* **>** HOURLY

HORARY *adj* relating to hours

HORAS > HORA

HORDE *n* large crowd ▷ *vb* form, move in, or live in a horde

HORDED > HORDE

HORDEIN *n* simple protein, rich in proline, that occurs in barley

HORDEINS > HORDEIN

HORDEOLA > HORDEOLUM

HORDEOLUM *n* (in medicine) stye

HORDES > HORDE

HORDING > HORDE

HORDOCK *same as* **>** HARDOKE

HORDOCKS > HORDOCK

HORE *same as* **>** HOAR

HOREHOUND *n* plant that produces a bitter juice formerly used as a cough medicine

HORI *n* derogatory term for Māori

HORIATIKI *n* traditional Greek salad consisting of tomatoes, cucumber, onion, olives, and feta cheese

HORIS > HORI

HORIZON *n* apparent line that divides the earth and the sky

HORIZONAL > HORIZON

HORIZONS > HORIZON

HORK *vb* spit

HORKED > HORK

HORKEY *same as* **>** HOCKEY

HORKEYS > HORKEY

HORKING > HORK

HORKS > HORK

HORLICKS *n* as in *make a horlicks* make a mistake or a mess

HORME *n* (in Jungian psychology) fundamental vital energy

HORMES > HORME

HORMESES > HORMES

HORMESIS *n* beneficial effect of exposure to a very small amount of a toxic substance

HORMETIC *adj* relating to hormesis

HORMIC > HORME

HORMONAL > HORMONE

HORMONE *n* substance secreted by certain glands

HORMONES > HORMONE

HORMONIC > HORMONE

HORN *n* one of a pair of bony growths ▷ *vb* provide with a horn or horns

HORNBAG *n* in Australian slang, a promiscuous woman

HORNBAGS > HORNBAG

HORNBEAK *n* garfish

HORNBEAKS > HORNBEAK

HORNBEAM *n* tree with smooth grey bark

HORNBEAMS > HORNBEAM

HORNBILL *n* bird with a bony growth on its large beak

HORNBILLS > HORNBILL

HORNBOOK *n* page bearing a religious text or the alphabet, held in a frame with a thin window of flattened cattle horn over it

HORNBOOKS > HORNBOOK

HORNBUG *n* stag beetle

HORNBUGS > HORNBUG

HORNDOG *n* sexually aggressive man

HORNDOGS > HORNDOG

HORNED *adj* having a horn, horns, or hornlike parts

HORNER *n* dealer in horn

HORNERS > HORNER

HORNET *n* large wasp with a severe sting

HORNETS > HORNET

HORNFELS *n* hard compact fine-grained metamorphic rock formed by the action of heat from a magmatic intrusion on neighbouring sedimentary rocks

HORNFUL *n* amount a horn will hold

HORNFULS > HORNFUL

HORNGELD *n* feudal rent based on number of cattle

HORNGELDS > HORNGELD

HORNIER > HORNY

HORNIEST > HORNY

HORNILY > HORNY

HORNINESS > HORNY

HORNING > HORN

HORNINGS > HORN

HORNISH *adj* like horn

HORNIST *n* horn player

HORNISTS > HORNIST

HORNITO *n* small vent in volcano

HORNITOS > HORNITO

HORNLESS > HORN

HORNLET *n* small horn

HORNLETS > HORNLET

HORNLIKE > HORN

HORNPIPE *n* (music for) a solo dance, traditionally performed by sailors

HORNPIPES > HORNPIPE

HORNPOUT *n* catfish

HORNPOUTS > HORNPOUT

HORNS > HORN

HORNSTONE *same as* **>** HORNFELS

HORNTAIL *n* wasplike insect

HORNTAILS > HORNTAIL

HORNWORK *n* bastion in fortifications

HORNWORKS > HORNWORK

HORNWORM *n* caterpillar of hawk moth

HORNWORMS > HORNWORM

HORNWORT *n* aquatic plant

HORNWORTS > HORNWORT

HORNWRACK *n* yellowish bryozoan or sea mat sometimes found on beaches after a storm

HORNY *adj* of or like horn

HORNYHEAD *n* species of fish

HORNYWINK *n* lapwing

HOROEKA *n* New Zealand tree

HOROEKAS > HOROEKA

HOROKAKA *n* low-growing New Zealand plant with fleshy leaves and pink or white flowers

HOROKAKAS > HOROKAKA

HOROLOGE *rare word for* **>** TIMEPIECE

HOROLOGER *n* an expert maker of timepieces

HOROLOGES > HOROLOGE
HOROLOGIA n plural of horologium: clocktower
HOROLOGIC > HOROLOGY
HOROLOGY n art of making clocks and watches or of measuring time
HOROMETRY n measurement of time
HOROPITO n New Zealand plant
HOROPITOS > HOROPITO
HOROPTER n locus of all points in space that stimulate points on each eye that yield the same visual direction as each other
HOROPTERS > HOROPTER
HOROSCOPE n prediction of a person's future based on the positions of the planets, sun, and moon at his or her birth
HOROSCOPY n casting and interpretation of horoscopes
HORRENT adj bristling
HORRIBLE adj disagreeable, unpleasant ▷ n horrible thing
HORRIBLES > HORRIBLE
HORRIBLY adv in a horrible manner
HORRID adj disagreeable, unpleasant
HORRIDER > HORRID
HORRIDEST > HORRID
HORRIDLY > HORRID
HORRIFIC adj causing horror
HORRIFIED adj terrified
HORRIFIES > HORRIFY
HORRIFY vb cause to feel horror or shock
HORROR n (thing or person causing) terror or hatred ▷ adj having a frightening subject
HORRORS pl n fit of depression or anxiety ▷ interj expression of dismay, sometimes facetious
HORS adv as in hors d'oeuvre appetizer
HORSE n large animal with hooves, a mane, and a tail ▷ vb provide with a horse
HORSEBACK n horse's back
HORSEBEAN n broad bean
HORSEBOX n trailer used for transporting horses
HORSECAR n streetcar drawn by horses
HORSECARS > HORSECAR
HORSED > HORSE
HORSEFLY n large bloodsucking fly
HORSEHAIR n hair from the tail or mane of a horse

HORSEHIDE n hide of a horse
HORSELESS > HORSE
HORSELIKE > HORSE
HORSEMAN n person skilled in riding
HORSEMEAT n flesh of the horse used as food
HORSEMEN > HORSEMAN
HORSEMINT n European mint plant
HORSEPLAY n rough or rowdy play
HORSEPOND n pond where horses drink
HORSEPOX n viral infection of horses
HORSERACE n race for horses
HORSES > HORSE
HORSESHIT n rubbish
HORSESHOD > HORSESHOE
HORSESHOE n protective U-shaped piece of iron nailed to a horse's hoof, regarded as a symbol of good luck ▷ vb fit with a horseshoe
HORSETAIL n plant with small dark toothlike leaves
HORSEWAY n road for horses
HORSEWAYS > HORSEWAY
HORSEWEED n US name for Canadian fleabane
HORSEWHIP n whip with a long thong, used for managing horses ▷ vb beat (a person or animal) with such a whip
HORSEY adj very keen on horses
HORSIE n child's word for a horse
HORSIER > HORSY
HORSIES > HORSIE
HORSIEST > HORSY
HORSILY > HORSEY
HORSINESS > HORSEY
HORSING > HORSE
HORSINGS > HORSE
HORSON same as > WHORESON
HORSONS > HORSON
HORST n ridge of land
HORSTE variant of > HORST
HORSTES > HORSTE
HORSTS > HORST
HORSY same as > HORSEY
HORTATION > HORTATORY
HORTATIVE same as > HORTATORY
HORTATORY adj encouraging
HOS > HO
HOSANNA interj exclamation of praise to God ▷ n act of crying "hosanna" ▷ vb cry hosanna
HOSANNAED > HOSANNA

HOSANNAH same as > HOSANNA
HOSANNAHS > HOSANNAH
HOSANNAS > HOSANNA
HOSE n flexible pipe for conveying liquid ▷ vb water with a hose
HOSED > HOSE
HOSEL n socket in head of golf club
HOSELIKE > HOSE
HOSELS > HOSEL
HOSEMAN n fireman in charge of hose
HOSEMEN > HOSEMAN
HOSEN > HOSE
HOSEPIPE n hose
HOSEPIPES > HOSEPIPE
HOSER n person who swindles or deceives others
HOSERS > HOSER
HOSES > HOSE
HOSEY vb claim possession
HOSEYED > HOSEY
HOSEYING > HOSEY
HOSEYS > HOSEY
HOSIER n person who sells stockings, etc
HOSIERIES > HOSIERY
HOSIERS > HOSIER
HOSIERY n stockings, socks, and tights collectively
HOSING > HOSE
HOSPICE n nursing home for the terminally ill
HOSPICES > HOSPICE
HOSPITAGE n behaviour of guest
HOSPITAL n place where people who are ill are looked after and treated
HOSPITALE n lodging
HOSPITALS > HOSPITAL
HOSPITIA > HOSPITIUM
HOSPITIUM same as > HOSPICE
HOSPODAR n (formerly) the governor or prince of Moldavia or Wallachia under Ottoman rule
HOSPODARS > HOSPODAR
HOSS n horse
HOSSES > HOSS
HOST n person who entertains guests ▷ vb be the host of
HOSTA n ornamental plant
HOSTAGE n person who is illegally held prisoner
HOSTAGES > HOSTAGE
HOSTAS > HOSTA
HOSTED > HOST
HOSTEL n building providing accommodation ▷ vb stay in hostels
HOSTELED > HOSTEL
HOSTELER same as > HOSTELLER
HOSTELERS > HOSTELER
HOSTELING n hostelling
HOSTELLED > HOSTEL

HOSTELLER n person who stays at youth hostels
HOSTELRY n inn, pub
HOSTELS > HOSTEL
HOSTESS n woman who receives and entertains guests ▷ vb act as hostess
HOSTESSED > HOSTESS
HOSTESSES > HOSTESS
HOSTIE n informal Australian word for an air hostess
HOSTIES > HOSTIE
HOSTILE adj unfriendly ▷ n hostile person
HOSTILELY > HOSTILE
HOSTILES > HOSTILE
HOSTILITY n unfriendly and aggressive feelings or behaviour
HOSTING > HOST
HOSTINGS > HOST
HOSTLER another name (esp Brit) for > OSTLER
HOSTLERS > HOSTLER
HOSTLESS adj lacking a host
HOSTLESSE adj inhospitable
HOSTLY > HOST
HOSTRIES > HOSTRY
HOSTRY n lodging
HOSTS > HOST
HOT adj having a high temperature
HOTBED n any place encouraging a particular activity
HOTBEDS > HOTBED
HOTBLOOD n type of horse
HOTBLOODS > HOTBLOOD
HOTBOX n closed room where marijuana is smoked ▷ vb smoke marijuana in a hotbox
HOTBOXED > HOTBOX
HOTBOXES > HOTBOX
HOTBOXING > HOTBOX
HOTCAKE n pancake
HOTCAKES > HOTCAKE
HOTCH vb jog
HOTCHED > HOTCH
HOTCHES > HOTCH
HOTCHING > HOTCH
HOTCHPOT n collecting of property so that it may be redistributed in equal shares, esp on the intestacy of a parent who has given property to his children in his lifetime
HOTCHPOTS > HOTCHPOT
HOTDOG vb perform a series of manoeuvres in skiing, etc
HOTDOGGED > HOTDOG
HOTDOGGER > HOTDOG
HOTDOGS > HOTDOG
HOTE > HIGHT
HOTEL n establishment providing lodging and meals
HOTELDOM n hotel business

HOTELDOMS > HOTELDOM
HOTELIER n owner or manager of a hotel
HOTELIERS > HOTELIER
HOTELING n office practice in which desk space is booked in advance by an employee as required
HOTELINGS > HOTELING
HOTELLING same as > HOTELING
HOTELMAN n hotel owner
HOTELMEN > HOTELMAN
HOTELS > HOTEL
HOTEN > HIGHT
HOTFOOT adv quickly and eagerly ▷ vb move quickly
HOTFOOTED > HOTFOOT
HOTFOOTS > HOTFOOT
HOTHEAD n excitable or fiery person
HOTHEADED adj impetuous, rash, or hot-tempered
HOTHEADS > HOTHEAD
HOTHOUSE n greenhouse
HOTHOUSED adj taught intensively
HOTHOUSES > HOTHOUSE
HOTLINE n direct telephone link for emergency use
HOTLINER n person running a phone-in radio programme
HOTLINERS > HOTLINER
HOTLINES > HOTLINE
HOTLINK n area on website connecting to another site
HOTLINKS > HOTLINK
HOTLY > HOT
HOTNESS > HOT
HOTNESSES > HOT
HOTPLATE n heated metal surface on an electric cooker
HOTPLATES > HOTPLATE
HOTPOT n casserole topped with potatoes
HOTPOTS > HOTPOT
HOTPRESS vb subject (paper, cloth, etc) to heat and pressure to give it a smooth surface or extract oil
HOTROD n car with a modified engine for increased power
HOTRODS > HOTROD
HOTS pl n as in the hots feeling of lust
HOTSHOT n important person or expert, esp when showy
HOTSHOTS > HOTSHOT
HOTSPOT n place where wireless broadband is provided
HOTSPOTS > HOTSPOT
HOTSPUR n impetuous or fiery person
HOTSPURS > HOTSPUR

HOTTED > HOT
HOTTENTOT n as in hottentot fig perennial plant with fleshy leaves, showy yellow or purple flowers, and edible fruits
HOTTER vb simmer
HOTTERED > HOTTER
HOTTERING > HOTTER
HOTTERS > HOTTER
HOTTEST > HOT
HOTTIE n sexually attractive person
HOTTIES > HOTTIE
HOTTING n stealing fast cars to put on a show of skilful driving
HOTTINGS > HOTTING
HOTTISH adj fairly hot
HOTTY same as > HOTTIE
HOUDAH same as > HOWDAH
HOUDAHS > HOUDAH
HOUDAN n breed of light domestic fowl
HOUDANS > HOUDAN
HOUF same as > HOWF
HOUFED > HOUF
HOUFF same as > HOWF
HOUFFED > HOUFF
HOUFFING > HOUFF
HOUFFS > HOUFF
HOUFING > HOUF
HOUFS > HOUF
HOUGH n in Scotland, a cut of meat corresponding to shin ▷ vb hamstring (cattle, horses, etc)
HOUGHED > HOUGH
HOUGHING > HOUGH
HOUGHS > HOUGH
HOUHERE n small evergreen New Zealand tree
HOUHERES > HOUHERE
HOUMMOS same as > HUMMUS
HOUMMOSES > HOUMMOS
HOUMOUS same as > HUMMUS
HOUMOUSES > HOUMOUS
HOUMUS same as > HUMMUS
HOUMUSES > HOUMUS
HOUND n hunting dog ▷ vb pursue relentlessly
HOUNDED > HOUND
HOUNDER > HOUND
HOUNDERS > HOUND
HOUNDFISH n name given to various small sharks or dogfish
HOUNDING > HOUND
HOUNDS > HOUND
HOUNGAN n voodoo priest
HOUNGANS > HOUNGAN
HOUR n twenty-fourth part of a day, sixty minutes
HOURGLASS n device with two glass compartments, containing a quantity of sand that takes an hour to trickle from the top section to the bottom one

HOURI n any of the nymphs of paradise
HOURIS > HOURI
HOURLIES > HOURLY
HOURLONG adj lasting an hour
HOURLY adv (happening) every hour ▷ adj of, occurring, or done once every hour ▷ n something that is done by the hour
HOURPLATE n dial of clock
HOURS pl n indefinite time
HOUSE n building used as a home ▷ vb give accommodation to ▷ adj (of wine) sold in a restaurant at a lower price than listed
HOUSEBOAT n stationary boat used as a home
HOUSEBOY n male domestic servant
HOUSEBOYS > HOUSEBOY
HOUSECARL n (in medieval Europe) a household warrior of Danish kings and noblemen
HOUSECOAT n woman's long loose coat-shaped garment for wearing at home
HOUSED > HOUSE
HOUSEFLY n common fly often found in houses
HOUSEFUL n full amount or number that can be accommodated in a particular house
HOUSEFULS > HOUSEFUL
HOUSEHOLD n all the people living in a house ▷ adj relating to the running of a household
HOUSEKEEP vb run household
HOUSEKEPT > HOUSEKEEP
HOUSEL vb give the Eucharist to (someone)
HOUSELED > HOUSEL
HOUSELEEK n plant that has a rosette of succulent leaves and pinkish flowers and grows on walls
HOUSELESS > HOUSE
HOUSELINE n tarred marline
HOUSELING > HOUSEL
HOUSELLED > HOUSEL
HOUSELS > HOUSEL
HOUSEMAID n female servant employed to do housework
HOUSEMAN n junior hospital doctor
HOUSEMATE n person who is not part of the same family, but with whom one shares a house
HOUSEMEN > HOUSEMAN
HOUSER > HOUSE

HOUSEROOM n room for storage or lodging
HOUSERS > HOUSE
HOUSES > HOUSE
HOUSESAT > HOUSESIT
HOUSESIT vb live in and look after a house during the absence of its owner or owners
HOUSESITS > HOUSESIT
HOUSETOP n rooftop
HOUSETOPS > HOUSETOP
HOUSEWIFE n woman who runs her own household and does not have a job
HOUSEWORK n work of running a home, such as cleaning, cooking, and shopping
HOUSEY adj of or like house music
HOUSIER > HOUSEY
HOUSIEST > HOUSEY
HOUSING n (providing of) houses
HOUSINGS > HOUSING
HOUSLING adj of sacrament ▷ n growing of the climbing stem of the hop into a dense mass at the top of the poles which support it
HOUSLINGS > HOUSLING
HOUSTONIA n small North American plant with blue, white or purple flowers
HOUT same as > HOOT
HOUTED > HOUT
HOUTING n type of fish
HOUTINGS > HOUTING
HOUTS > HOUT
HOVE > HEAVE
HOVEA n Australian plant with purple flowers
HOVEAS > HOVEA
HOVED > HEAVE
HOVEL n small dirty house or hut ▷ vb shelter or be sheltered in a hovel
HOVELED > HOVEL
HOVELING > HOVEL
HOVELLED > HOVEL
HOVELLER n man working on boat
HOVELLERS > HOVELLER
HOVELLING > HOVEL
HOVELS > HOVEL
HOVEN > HEAVE
HOVER vb (of a bird etc) remain suspended in one place in the air ▷ n act of hovering
HOVERED > HOVER
HOVERER > HOVER
HOVERERS > HOVER
HOVERFLY n hovering wasp-like fly
HOVERING > HOVER
HOVERPORT n port for hovercraft
HOVERS > HOVER
HOVES > HEAVE

h

HOVING > HEAVE
HOW *adv* in what way, by what means ▷ *n* the way a thing is done ▷ *sentence substitute* supposed American Indian greeting
HOWBE *same as* > HOWBEIT
HOWBEIT *adv* in archaic usage, however
HOWDAH *n* a canopied seat on an elephant's back
HOWDAHS > HOWDAH
HOWDIE *n* midwife
HOWDIED > HOWDY
HOWDIES > HOWDY
HOWDY *vb* greet someone
HOWDYING > HOWDY
HOWE *n* depression in the earth's surface
HOWES > HOWE
HOWEVER *adv* nevertheless
HOWF *n* haunt, esp a public house ▷ *vb* visit place frequently
HOWFED > HOWF
HOWFF *vb* visit place frequently
HOWFFED > HOWFF
HOWFFING > HOWFF
HOWFFS > HOWFF
HOWFING > HOWF
HOWFS > HOWF
HOWITZER *n* large gun firing shells at a steep angle
HOWITZERS > HOWITZER
HOWK *vb* dig (out or up)
HOWKED > HOWK
HOWKER > HOWK
HOWKERS > HOWK
HOWKING > HOWK
HOWKS > HOWK
HOWL *n* loud wailing cry ▷ *vb* utter a howl
HOWLBACK *same as* > HOWLROUND
HOWLBACKS > HOWLBACK
HOWLED > HOWL
HOWLER *n* stupid mistake
HOWLERS > HOWLER
HOWLET *another word for* > OWL
HOWLETS > HOWLET
HOWLING *adj* great
HOWLINGLY > HOWL
HOWLINGS > HOWL
HOWLROUND *n* condition, resulting in a howling noise, when sound from a loudspeaker is fed back into the microphone of a public-address or recording system
HOWLS > HOWL
HOWRE *same as* > HOUR
HOWRES > HOWRE
HOWS > HOW
HOWSO *same as* > HOWSOEVER
HOWSOEVER *less common word for* > HOWEVER
HOWTOWDIE *n* Scottish dish of boiled chicken with poached eggs and spinach

HOWZAT *interj* a cry in cricket appealing for dismissal of batsman
HOWZIT *informal word for* > HELLO
HOX *vb* hamstring
HOXED > HOX
HOXES > HOX
HOXING > HOX
HOY *interj* cry used to attract someone's attention ▷ *n* freight barge ▷ *vb* drive animal with cry
HOYA *n* any of various E Asian or Australian plants
HOYAS > HOYA
HOYDEN *n* wild or boisterous girl ▷ *vb* behave like a hoyden
HOYDENED > HOYDEN
HOYDENING > HOYDEN
HOYDENISH > HOYDEN
HOYDENISM > HOYDEN
HOYDENS > HOYDEN
HOYED > HOY
HOYING > HOY
HOYLE *n* archer's mark used as a target
HOYLES > HOYLE
HOYS > HOY
HRYVNA *n* standard monetary unit of Ukraine
HRYVNAS > HRYVNA
HRYVNIA *n* money unit of Ukraine
HRYVNIAS > HRYVNIA
HRYVNYA *same as* > HRYVNA
HRYVNYAS > HRYVNYA
HUANACO *same as* > GUANACO
HUANACOS > HUANACO
HUAQUERO *n* Central American tomb robber
HUAQUEROS > HUAQUERO
HUARACHE *n* Mexican sandal
HUARACHES > HUARACHE
HUARACHO *same as* > HUARACHE
HUARACHOS > HUARACHE
HUB *n* centre of a wheel, through which the axle passes
HUBBIES > HUBBY
HUBBLIER > HUBBLY
HUBBLIEST > HUBBLY
HUBBLY *adj* having an irregular surface
HUBBUB *n* confused noise of many voices
HUBBUBOO *same as* > HUBBUB
HUBBUBOOS > HUBBUBOO
HUBBUBS > HUBBUB
HUBBY *n* husband
HUBCAP *n* metal disc that protects the hub of a wheel
HUBCAPS > HUBCAP
HUBLESS *adj* without a hub
HUBRIS *n* pride, arrogance

HUBRISES > HUBRIS
HUBRISTIC > HUBRIS
HUBS > HUB
HUCK *same as* > HUCKABACK
HUCKABACK *n* coarse absorbent linen or cotton fabric used for towels and informal shirts, etc
HUCKED > HUCK
HUCKERY *adj* ugly
HUCKING > HUCK
HUCKLE *n* hip or haunch ▷ *vb* force out or arrest roughly
HUCKLED > HUCKLE
HUCKLES > HUCKLE
HUCKLING > HUCKLE
HUCKS > HUCK
HUCKSTER *n* person using aggressive methods of selling ▷ *vb* peddle
HUCKSTERS > HUCKSTER
HUCKSTERY > HUCKSTER
HUDDEN > HAUD
HUDDLE *vb* hunch (oneself) through cold or fear ▷ *n* small group
HUDDLED > HUDDLE
HUDDLER > HUDDLE
HUDDLERS > HUDDLE
HUDDLES > HUDDLE
HUDDLING > HUDDLE
HUDDUP *interj* get up
HUDNA *n* truce or ceasefire for a fixed duration
HUDNAS > HUDNA
HUDUD *n* set of laws and punishments in the Koran
HUDUDS > HUDUD
HUE *n* colour, shade
HUED *adj* having a hue or colour as specified
HUELESS > HUE
HUER *n* pilchard fisherman
HUERS > HUER
HUES > HUE
HUFF *n* passing mood of anger or resentment ▷ *vb* blow or puff heavily
HUFFED > HUFF
HUFFER > HUFFING
HUFFERS > HUFFING
HUFFIER > HUFF
HUFFIEST > HUFF
HUFFILY > HUFF
HUFFINESS > HUFF
HUFFING *n* practice of inhaling fumes for intoxicating effects
HUFFINGS > HUFFING
HUFFISH > HUFF
HUFFISHLY > HUFF
HUFFKIN *n* type of muffin
HUFFKINS > HUFFKIN
HUFFS > HUFF
HUFFY > HUFF
HUG *vb* clasp tightly in the arms, usu with affection ▷ *n* tight or fond embrace
HUGE *adj* very big
HUGELY *adv* very much
HUGENESS > HUGE

HUGEOUS *same as* > HUGE
HUGEOUSLY > HUGEOUS
HUGER > HUGE
HUGEST > HUGE
HUGGABLE > HUG
HUGGED > HUG
HUGGER > HUG
HUGGERS > HUG
HUGGIER > HUGGY
HUGGIEST > HUGGY
HUGGING > HUG
HUGGY *adj* sensitive and caring
HUGS > HUG
HUGY *same as* > HUGE
HUH *interj* exclamation of derision or inquiry
HUHU *n* type of hairy New Zealand beetle
HUHUS > HUHU
HUI *n* meeting of Māori people
HUIA *n* extinct bird of New Zealand
HUIAS > HUIA
HUIC *interj* in hunting, a call to hounds
HUIPIL *n* Mayan woman's blouse
HUIPILES > HUIPIL
HUIPILS > HUIPIL
HUIS > HUI
HUISACHE *n* American tree
HUISACHES > HUISACHE
HUISSIER *n* doorkeeper
HUISSIERS > HUISSIER
HUITAIN *n* verse of eighteen lines
HUITAINS > HUITAIN
HULA *n* swaying Hawaiian dance
HULAS > HULA
HULE *same as* > ULE
HULES > HULE
HULK *n* body of an abandoned ship ▷ *vb* move clumsily
HULKED > HULK
HULKIER > HULKY
HULKIEST > HULKY
HULKING *adj* bulky, unwieldy
HULKS > HULK
HULKY *same as* > HULKING
HULL *n* main body of a boat ▷ *vb* remove the hulls from
HULLED > HULL
HULLER > HULL
HULLERS > HULL
HULLIER > HULLY
HULLIEST > HULLY
HULLING > HULL
HULLO *same as* > HELLO
HULLOA *same as* > HALLOA
HULLOAED > HULLOA
HULLOAING > HULLOA
HULLOAS > HULLOA
HULLOED > HULLO
HULLOES > HULLO
HULLOING > HULLO
HULLOO *same as* > HALLOO
HULLOOED > HULLOO**

HULLOOING > HULLOO
HULLOOS > HULLOO
HULLOS > HULLO
HULLS > HULL
HULLY adj having husks
HUM vb make a low continuous vibrating sound ▷ n humming sound
HUMA n mythical bird
HUMAN adj of or typical of people ▷ n human being
HUMANE adj kind or merciful
HUMANELY > HUMANE
HUMANER > HUMANE
HUMANEST > HUMANE
HUMANHOOD n state of being human
HUMANISE same as > HUMANIZE
HUMANISED > HUMANISE
HUMANISER > HUMANISE
HUMANISES > HUMANISE
HUMANISM n belief in human effort rather than religion
HUMANISMS > HUMANISM
HUMANIST > HUMANISM
HUMANISTS > HUMANISM
HUMANITY n human race
HUMANIZE vb make human or humane
HUMANIZED > HUMANIZE
HUMANIZER > HUMANIZE
HUMANIZES > HUMANIZE
HUMANKIND n human race
HUMANLIKE > HUMAN
HUMANLY adv by human powers or means
HUMANNESS > HUMAN
HUMANOID adj resembling a human being in appearance ▷ n (in science fiction) a robot or creature resembling a human being
HUMANOIDS > HUMANOID
HUMANS > HUMAN
HUMAS > HUMA
HUMATE n decomposed plants used as fertilizer
HUMATES > HUMATE
HUMBLE adj conscious of one's failings ▷ vb cause to feel humble, humiliate
HUMBLEBEE another name for the > BUMBLEBEE
HUMBLED > HUMBLE
HUMBLER > HUMBLE
HUMBLERS > HUMBLE
HUMBLES > HUMBLE
HUMBLESSE n quality of being humble
HUMBLEST > HUMBLE
HUMBLING > HUMBLE
HUMBLINGS > HUMBLE
HUMBLY > HUMBLE
HUMBUCKER n twin-coil guitar pick-up
HUMBUG n hard striped peppermint sweet ▷ vb cheat or deceive (someone)

HUMBUGGED > HUMBUG
HUMBUGGER > HUMBUG
HUMBUGS > HUMBUG
HUMBUZZ n type of beetle
HUMBUZZES > HUMBUZZ
HUMDINGER n excellent person or thing
HUMDRUM adj ordinary, dull ▷ n monotonous routine, task, or person
HUMDRUMS > HUMDRUM
HUMECT vb make moist
HUMECTANT adj producing moisture ▷ n substance added to another substance to keep it moist
HUMECTATE vb produce moisture
HUMECTED > HUMECT
HUMECTING > HUMECT
HUMECTIVE > HUMECT
HUMECTS > HUMECT
HUMEFIED > HUMEFY
HUMEFIES > HUMEFY
HUMEFY same as > HUMIFY
HUMEFYING > HUMEFY
HUMERAL adj of or relating to the humerus ▷ n silk shawl worn by a priest at High Mass; humeral veil
HUMERALS > HUMERAL
HUMERI > HUMERUS
HUMERUS n bone from the shoulder to the elbow
HUMF same as > HUMPH
HUMFED > HUMF
HUMFING > HUMF
HUMFS > HUMF
HUMHUM n Indian cotton cloth
HUMHUMS > HUMHUM
HUMIC adj of, derived from, or resembling humus
HUMICOLE n any plant that thrives on humus
HUMICOLES > HUMICOLE
HUMID adj damp and hot
HUMIDER > HUMID
HUMIDEST > HUMID
HUMIDEX n system of measuring discomfort
HUMIDEXES > HUMIDEX
HUMIDICES > HUMIDEX
HUMIDIFY vb make the air in (a room) more humid or damp
HUMIDITY n dampness
HUMIDLY > HUMID
HUMIDNESS > HUMID
HUMIDOR n humid place for storing cigars, tobacco, etc
HUMIDORS > HUMIDOR
HUMIFIED > HUMIFY
HUMIFIES > HUMIFY
HUMIFY vb convert or be converted into humus
HUMIFYING > HUMIFY
HUMILIANT adj humiliating
HUMILIATE vb lower the dignity or hurt the pride of

HUMILITY n quality of being humble
HUMINT n human intelligence
HUMINTS > HUMINT
HUMITE n mineral containing magnesium
HUMITES > HUMITE
HUMITURE n measure of both humidity and temperature
HUMITURES > HUMITURE
HUMLIE n hornless cow
HUMLIES > HUMLIE
HUMMABLE > HUM
HUMMAUM same as > HAMMAM
HUMMAUMS > HUMMAUM
HUMMED > HUM
HUMMEL adj (of cattle) hornless ▷ vb remove horns from
HUMMELLED > HUMMEL
HUMMELLER > HUMMEL
HUMMELS > HUMMEL
HUMMER > HUM
HUMMERS > HUM
HUMMING > HUM
HUMMINGS > HUM
HUMMLE adj as in hummle bonnet type of Scottish cap
HUMMOCK n very small hill ▷ vb form into a hummock or hummocks
HUMMOCKED > HUMMOCK
HUMMOCKS > HUMMOCK
HUMMOCKY > HUMMOCK
HUMMUM same as > HAMMAM
HUMMUMS > HUMMUM
HUMMUS n creamy dip
HUMMUSES > HUMMUS
HUMOGEN n type of fertilizer
HUMOGENS > HUMOGEN
HUMONGOUS same as > HUMUNGOUS
HUMOR same as > HUMOUR
HUMORAL adj denoting or relating to a type of immunity
HUMORALLY > HUMORAL
HUMORED > HUMOR
HUMORESK n humorous musical composition
HUMORESKS > HUMORESK
HUMORFUL > HUMOR
HUMORING > HUMOR
HUMORIST n writer or entertainer who uses humour in his or her work
HUMORISTS > HUMORIST
HUMORLESS > HUMOR
HUMOROUS adj amusing, esp in a witty or clever way
HUMORS > HUMOR
HUMORSOME adj capricious
HUMOUR n ability to say or perceive things that are amusing ▷ vb be kind and indulgent to
HUMOURED > HUMOUR
HUMOURFUL > HUMOUR

HUMOURING > HUMOUR
HUMOURS > HUMOUR
HUMOUS same as > HUMUS
HUMOUSES > HUMOUS
HUMP n raised piece of ground ▷ vb carry or heave
HUMPBACK same as > HUNCHBACK
HUMPBACKS > HUMPBACK
HUMPED > HUMP
HUMPEN n old German drinking glass
HUMPENS > HUMPEN
HUMPER > HUMP
HUMPERS > HUMP
HUMPH interj exclamation of annoyance or scepticism ▷ vb exclaim humph
HUMPHED > HUMPH
HUMPHING > HUMPH
HUMPHS > HUMPH
HUMPIER > HUMPY
HUMPIES > HUMPY
HUMPIEST > HUMPY
HUMPINESS > HUMPY
HUMPING > HUMP
HUMPLESS > HUMP
HUMPLIKE > HUMP
HUMPS > HUMP
HUMPTIES > HUMPTY
HUMPTY n low padded seat
HUMPY adj full of humps ▷ n primitive hut
HUMS > HUM
HUMSTRUM n medieval musical instrument
HUMSTRUMS > HUMSTRUM
HUMUNGOUS adj very large
HUMUS n decomposing matter in the soil
HUMUSES > HUMUS
HUMUSY > HUMUS
HUMVEE n military vehicle
HUMVEES > HUMVEE
HUN n member of any of several nomadic peoples
HUNCH n feeling or suspicion not based on facts ▷ vb draw (one's shoulders) up or together
HUNCHBACK n person with an abnormal curvature of the spine
HUNCHED > HUNCH
HUNCHES > HUNCH
HUNCHING > HUNCH
HUNDRED n ten times ten ▷ adj amounting to a hundred
HUNDREDER n inhabitant of a hundred
HUNDREDOR same as > HUNDREDER
HUNDREDS > HUNDRED
HUNDREDTH adj being the ordinal number of 100 in numbering or counting order, position, time, etc ▷ n one of 100 approximately equal parts of something
HUNG > HANG

HUNGAN same as
> HOUNGAN
HUNGANS > HUNGAN
HUNGER n discomfort or
weakness from lack of
food ▷ vb want very much
HUNGERED > HUNGER
HUNGERFUL adj hungry
HUNGERING > HUNGER
HUNGERLY adj hungry
HUNGERS > HUNGER
HUNGOVER adj suffering
from hangover
HUNGRIER > HUNGRY
HUNGRIEST > HUNGRY
HUNGRILY > HUNGRY
HUNGRY adj desiring food
HUNH same as > HUH
HUNK n large piece
HUNKER vb squat
HUNKERED > HUNKER
HUNKERING > HUNKER
HUNKERS pl n haunches
HUNKEY n person of
Hungarian descent
HUNKEYS > HUNKEY
HUNKIE same as > HUNKEY
HUNKIER > HUNKY
HUNKIES > HUNKY
HUNKIEST > HUNKY
HUNKS n crotchety old
person
HUNKSES > HUNKS
HUNKY adj excellent
HUNNISH > HUN
HUNS > HUN
HUNT vb seek out and kill
(wild animals) for food or
sport ▷ n hunting
HUNTABLE > HUNT
HUNTAWAY n sheepdog
trained to drive sheep by
barking
HUNTAWAYS > HUNTAWAY
HUNTED adj harassed and
worn
HUNTEDLY > HUNT
HUNTER n person or animal
that hunts wild animals
HUNTERS > HUNTER
HUNTING n pursuit and
killing or capture of wild
animals
HUNTINGS > HUNTING
HUNTRESS same as
> HUNTER
HUNTS > HUNT
HUNTSMAN n man who
hunts wild animals, esp
foxes
HUNTSMEN > HUNTSMAN
HUP vb cry hup to get a
horse to move
HUPIRO in New Zealand
English, same as
> STINKWOOD
HUPIROS > HUPIRO
HUPPAH variant spelling of
> CHUPPAH
HUPPAHS > HUPPAH
HUPPED > HUP
HUPPING > HUP
HUPPOT > HUPPAH

HUPPOTH same as
> HUPPOT
HUPS > HUP
HURCHEON same as
> URCHIN
HURCHEONS > HURCHEON
HURDEN same as > HARDEN
HURDENS > HURDEN
HURDIES pl n buttocks or
haunches
HURDLE n light barrier for
jumping over in some
races ▷ vb jump over
(something)
HURDLED > HURDLE
HURDLER > HURDLE
HURDLERS > HURDLE
HURDLES > HURDLE
HURDLING > HURDLE
HURDLINGS > HURDLE
HURDS same as > HARDS
HURL vb throw or utter
forcefully ▷ n act or an
instance of hurling
HURLBAT same as
> WHIRLBAT
HURLBATS > HURLBAT
HURLED > HURL
HURLER > HURL
HURLERS > HURL
HURLEY n another word
for the game of hurling
HURLEYS > HURLEY
HURLIES > HURLY
HURLING n Irish game like
hockey
HURLINGS > HURLING
HURLS > HURL
HURLY n wheeled barrow
HURRA same as > HURRAH
HURRAED > HURRA
HURRAH interj exclamation
of joy or applause ▷ n
cheer of joy or victory
▷ vb shout "hurrah"
HURRAHED > HURRAH
HURRAHING > HURRAH
HURRAHS > HURRAH
HURRAING > HURRA
HURRAS > HURRA
HURRAY same as > HURRAH
HURRAYED > HURRAY
HURRAYING > HURRAY
HURRAYS > HURRAY
HURRICANE n very
strong, often destructive,
wind or storm
HURRICANO same as
> HURRICANE
HURRIED adj done quickly
or too quickly
HURRIEDLY > HURRIED
HURRIER > HURRY
HURRIERS > HURRY
HURRIES > HURRY
HURRY vb (cause to) move
or act very quickly
▷ n doing something or
the need to do something
quickly
HURRYING > HURRY
HURRYINGS > HURRY
HURST n wood

HURSTS > HURST
HURT vb cause physical or
mental pain to ▷ n physical
or mental pain ▷ adj injured
or pained
HURTER > HURT
HURTERS > HURT
HURTFUL adj unkind
HURTFULLY > HURTFUL
HURTING > HURT
HURTLE vb move quickly
or violently
HURTLED > HURTLE
HURTLES > HURTLE
HURTLESS adj uninjured
HURTLING > HURTLE
HURTS > HURT
HUSBAND n woman's
partner in marriage
▷ vb use economically
HUSBANDED > HUSBAND
HUSBANDER > HUSBAND
HUSBANDLY > HUSBAND
HUSBANDRY n farming
HUSBANDS > HUSBAND
HUSH vb make or be silent
▷ n stillness or silence
▷ interj plea or demand for
silence
HUSHABIED > HUSHABY
HUSHABIES > HUSHABY
HUSHABY interj used in
quietening a baby or child
to sleep ▷ n lullaby
▷ vb quieten to sleep
HUSHABYE same as
> HUSHABY
HUSHED > HUSH
HUSHEDLY > HUSH
HUSHER same as > USHER
HUSHERED > HUSHER
HUSHERING > HUSHER
HUSHERS > HUSHER
HUSHES > HUSH
HUSHFUL adj quiet
HUSHIER > HUSHY
HUSHIEST > HUSHY
HUSHING > HUSH
HUSHPUPPY n snack of
deep-fried dough
HUSHY adj secret
HUSK n outer covering of
certain seeds and fruits
▷ vb remove the husk from
HUSKED > HUSK
HUSKER > HUSK
HUSKERS > HUSK
HUSKIER > HUSKY
HUSKIES > HUSKY
HUSKIEST > HUSKY
HUSKILY > HUSKY
HUSKINESS > HUSKY
HUSKING > HUSK
HUSKINGS > HUSK
HUSKLIKE > HUSK
HUSKS > HUSK
HUSKY adj slightly hoarse
▷ n Arctic sledge dog with
thick hair and a curled tail
HUSO n sturgeon
HUSOS > HUSO
HUSS n flesh of the
European dogfish

HUSSAR n lightly armed
cavalry soldier
HUSSARS > HUSSAR
HUSSES > HUSS
HUSSIES > HUSSY
HUSSIF n sewing kit
HUSSIFS > HUSSIF
HUSSY n immodest or
promiscuous woman
HUSTINGS pl n political
campaigns and speeches
before an election
HUSTLE vb push about,
jostle ▷ n lively activity or
bustle.
HUSTLED > HUSTLE
HUSTLER > HUSTLE
HUSTLERS > HUSTLE
HUSTLES > HUSTLE
HUSTLING > HUSTLE
HUSTLINGS > HUSTLE
HUSWIFE same as
> HOUSEWIFE
HUSWIFES > HUSWIFE
HUSWIVES > HUSWIFE
HUT n small house, shelter,
or shed
HUTCH n cage for pet
rabbits etc ▷ vb store or
keep in or as if in a hutch
HUTCHED > HUTCH
HUTCHES > HUTCH
HUTCHIE n temporary
shelter
HUTCHIES > HUTCHIE
HUTCHING > HUTCH
HUTIA n rodent of West
Indies
HUTIAS > HUTIA
HUTLIKE > HUT
HUTMENT n number or
group of huts
HUTMENTS > HUTMENT
HUTS > HUT
HUTTED > HUT
HUTTING > HUT
HUTTINGS > HUT
HUTZPA same as
> HUTZPAH
HUTZPAH variant spelling of
> CHUTZPAH
HUTZPAHS > HUTZPAH
HUTZPAS > HUTZPA
HUZOOR n person of rank
in India
HUZOORS > HUZOOR
HUZZA same as > HUZZAH
HUZZAED > HUZZA
HUZZAH archaic word for
> HURRAH
HUZZAHED > HUZZAH
HUZZAHING > HUZZAH
HUZZAHS > HUZZAH
HUZZAING > HUZZA
HUZZAS > HUZZA
HUZZIES > HUZZY
HUZZY same as > HUSSY
HWAN another name for
> WON
HWYL n emotional fervour,
as in the recitation of
poetry
HWYLS > HWYL

HYACINE *same as*
> HYACINTH
HYACINES > HYACINE
HYACINTH *n* sweet-smelling spring flower that grows from a bulb
HYACINTHS > HYACINTH
HYAENA *same as* > HYENA
HYAENAS > HYAENA
HYAENIC > HYAENA
HYALIN *n* glassy translucent substance
HYALINE *adj* clear and translucent, with no fibres or granules ▷ *n* glassy transparent surface
HYALINES > HYALINE
HYALINISE *same as* > HYALINIZE
HYALINIZE *vb* give a glassy consistency to
HYALINS > HYALIN
HYALITE *n* clear and colourless variety of opal in globular form
HYALITES > HYALITE
HYALOGEN *n* insoluble substance in body structures
HYALOGENS > HYALOGEN
HYALOID *adj* clear and transparent ▷ *n* delicate transparent membrane
HYALOIDS > HYALOID
HYALONEMA *n* species of sponge
HYBRID *n* offspring of two plants or animals of different species ▷ *adj* of mixed origin
HYBRIDISE *same as* > HYBRIDIZE
HYBRIDISM > HYBRID
HYBRIDIST > HYBRID
HYBRIDITY > HYBRID
HYBRIDIZE *vb* produce or cause (species) to produce hybrids
HYBRIDOMA *n* hybrid cell formed by the fusion of two different types of cell, esp one capable of producing antibodies, but of limited lifespan, fused with an immortal tumour cell
HYBRIDOUS > HYBRID
HYBRIDS > HYBRID
HYBRIS *same as* > HUBRIS
HYBRISES > HYBRIS
HYBRISTIC > HYBRIS
HYDANTOIN *n* colourless odourless crystalline compound present in beet molasses and used in the manufacture of pharmaceuticals and synthetic resins
HYDATHODE *n* pore in plants, esp on the leaves, specialized for excreting water
HYDATID *n* cyst containing tapeworm larvae

HYDATIDS > HYDATID
HYDATOID *adj* watery
HYDRA *n* mythical many-headed water serpent
HYDRACID *n* acid, such as hydrochloric acid, that does not contain oxygen
HYDRACIDS > HYDRACID
HYDRAE > HYDRA
HYDRAEMIA *n* wateriness of blood
HYDRAGOG *n* drug that removes water
HYDRAGOGS > HYDRAGOG
HYDRANGEA *n* ornamental shrub with clusters of pink, blue, or white flowers
HYDRANT *n* outlet from a water main with a nozzle for a hose
HYDRANTH *n* polyp in a colony of hydrozoan coelenterates that is specialized for feeding rather than reproduction
HYDRANTHS > HYDRANTH
HYDRANTS > HYDRANT
HYDRAS > HYDRA
HYDRASE *n* enzyme that removes water
HYDRASES > HYDRASE
HYDRASTIS *n* any of various Japanese and E North American plants, such as goldenseal, having showy foliage and ornamental fruits
HYDRATE *n* chemical compound of water with another substance ▷ *vb* treat or impregnate with water
HYDRATED *adj* (of a compound) chemically bonded to water molecules
HYDRATES > HYDRATE
HYDRATING > HYDRATE
HYDRATION > HYDRATE
HYDRATOR > HYDRATE
HYDRATORS > HYDRATE
HYDRAULIC *adj* operated by pressure forced through a pipe by a liquid such as water or oil
HYDRAZIDE *n* any of a class of chemical compounds that result when hydrogen in hydrazine or any of its derivatives is replaced by an acid radical
HYDRAZINE *n* colourless basic liquid made from sodium hypochlorite and ammonia: a strong reducing agent, used chiefly as a rocket fuel
HYDRAZOIC *adj* as in *hydrazoic acid* colourless highly explosive liquid
HYDREMIA *same as* > HYDRAEMIA

HYDREMIAS
> HYDREMIA
HYDRIA *n* (in ancient Greece and Rome) a large water jar
HYDRIAE > HYDRIA
HYDRIC *adj* of or containing hydrogen
HYDRID *same as* > HYDROID
HYDRIDE *n* compound of hydrogen with another element
HYDRIDES > HYDRIDE
HYDRIDS > HYDRID
HYDRILLA *n* aquatic plant used as an oxygenator in aquaria and pools
HYDRILLAS > HYDRILLA
HYDRIODIC *adj* as in *hydriodic acid* colourless or pale yellow aqueous solution of hydrogen iodide: a strong acid
HYDRO *n* hotel offering facilities for hydropathy ▷ *adj* short for hydroelectric
HYDROCAST *n* gathering of water samples for analysis
HYDROCELE *n* abnormal collection of fluid in any saclike space, esp around the testicles
HYDROFOIL *n* fast light boat with its hull raised out of the water on one or more pairs of fins
HYDROGEL *n* gel in which the liquid constituent is water
HYDROGELS > HYDROGEL
HYDROGEN *n* light flammable colourless gas that combines with oxygen to form water
HYDROGENS
> HYDROGEN
HYDROID *adj* of an order of colonial hydrozoan coelenterates ▷ *n* hydroid colony or individual
HYDROIDS > HYDROID
HYDROLASE *n* enzyme, such as an esterase, that controls hydrolysis
HYDROLOGY *n* study of the distribution, conservation, and use of the water of the earth and its atmosphere
HYDROLYSE *vb* subject to or undergo hydrolysis
HYDROLYTE *n* substance subjected to hydrolysis
HYDROLYZE *same as* > HYDROLYSE
HYDROMA *same as* > HYGROMA
HYDROMAS > HYDROMA
HYDROMATA > HYDROMA
HYDROMEL *n* another word for 'mead' (the drink)
HYDROMELS > HYDROMEL

HYDRONAUT *n* person trained to operate deep submergence vessels
HYDRONIC *adj* using hot water in heating system
HYDRONIUM *n* as in *hydronium ion* positive ion, formed by the attachment of a proton to a water molecule: occurs in solutions of acids and behaves like a hydrogen ion
HYDROPATH *n* exponent of treating disease using large quantities of water
HYDROPIC > HYDROPSY
HYDROPS *n* anaemia in a fetus
HYDROPSES > HYDROPS
HYDROPSY *same as* > DROPSY
HYDROPTIC > HYDROPSY
HYDROPULT *n* type of water pump
HYDROS > HYDRO
HYDROSERE *n* sere that begins in an aquatic environment
HYDROSKI *n* hydrofoil used on some seaplanes to provide extra lift when taking off
HYDROSKIS > HYDROSKI
HYDROSOL *n* sol that has water as its liquid phase
HYDROSOLS > HYDROSOL
HYDROSOMA *same as* > HYDROSOME
HYDROSOME *n* body of a colonial hydrozoan
HYDROSTAT *n* device that detects the presence of water as a prevention against drying out, overflow, etc, esp one used as a warning in a steam boiler
HYDROUS *adj* containing water
HYDROVANE *n* vane on a seaplane conferring stability on water (a sponson) or facilitating take-off (a hydrofoil)
HYDROXIDE *n* compound containing a hydroxyl group or ion
HYDROXIUM *n* type of positive ion
HYDROXY *adj* of a type of chemical compound
HYDROXYL *adj* of or containing the monovalent group –OH or the ion OH⁻ ▷ *n* of, consisting of, or containing the monovalent group –OH or the ion OH⁻
HYDROXYLS > HYDROXYL
HYDROZOA > HYDROZOON
HYDROZOAN *n* type of invertebrate of the class which includes the hydra and Portuguese man-of-war

h

HYDROZOON same as > HYDROZOAN

HYDYNE n type of rocket fuel

HYDYNES > HYDYNE

HYE same as > HIE

HYED > HYE

HYEING > HYE

HYEN same as > HYENA

HYENA n scavenging doglike mammal of Africa and S Asia

HYENAS > HYENA

HYENIC > HYENA

HYENINE adj of hyenas

HYENOID adj of or like hyenas

HYENS > HYEN

HYES > HYE

HYETAL adj of or relating to rain, rainfall, or rainy regions

HYETOLOGY n study of rainfall

HYGEIST same as > HYGIENIST

HYGEISTS > HYGEIST

HYGIEIST same as > HYGIENIST

HYGIEISTS > HYGIEIST

HYGIENE n principles of health and cleanliness

HYGIÉNES > HYGIENE

HYGIENIC adj promoting health and cleanliness

HYGIENICS same as > HYGIENE

HYGIENIST n person skilled in the practice of hygiene

HYGRISTOR n electronic component the resistance of which varies with humidity

HYGRODEIK n type of thermometer

HYGROLOGY n study of humidity of air

HYGROMA n swelling soft tissue that occurs over a joint

HYGROMAS > HYGROMA

HYGROMATA > HYGROMA

HYGROPHIL adj moisture-loving

HYGROSTAT n device for maintaining constant humidity

HYING > HIE

HYKE same as > HAIK

HYKES > HYKE

HYLA n type of tropical American tree frog

HYLAS > HYLA

HYLDING same as > HILDING

HYLDINGS > HYLDING

HYLE n wood

HYLEG n dominant planet when someone is born

HYLEGS > HYLEG

HYLES > HYLE

HYLIC adj solid

HYLICISM n materialism

HYLICISMS > HYLICISM

HYLICIST > HYLICISM

HYLICISTS > HYLICISM

HYLISM same as > HYLICISM

HYLISMS > HYLISM

HYLIST > HYLISM

HYLISTS > HYLISM

HYLOBATE n gibbon

HYLOBATES > HYLOBATE

HYLOIST n materialist

HYLOISTS > HYLOIST

HYLOPHYTE n plant that grows in woods

HYLOZOIC > HYLOZOISM

HYLOZOISM n philosophical doctrine that life is one of the properties of matter

HYLOZOIST > HYLOZOISM

HYMEN n membrane partly covering a girl's vaginal opening

HYMENAEAL same as > HYMENEAL

HYMENAEAN n person who believes there will be no resurrection

HYMENAL > HYMEN

HYMENEAL adj of or relating to marriage ▷ n wedding song or poem

HYMENEALS > HYMENEAL

HYMENEAN n wedding song

HYMENEANS > HYMENEAN

HYMENIA > HYMENIUM

HYMENIAL > HYMENIUM

HYMENIUM n (in basidiomycetous and ascomycetous fungi) a layer of cells some of which produce the spores

HYMENIUMS > HYMENIUM

HYMENS > HYMEN

HYMN n Christian song of praise sung to God or a saint ▷ vb express (praises, thanks, etc) by singing hymns

HYMNAL n book of hymns ▷ adj of, relating to, or characteristic of hymns

HYMNALS > HYMNAL

HYMNARIES > HYMNARY

HYMNARY same as > HYMNAL

HYMNBOOK n book containing the words and music of hymns

HYMNBOOKS > HYMNBOOK

HYMNED > HYMN

HYMNIC > HYMN

HYMNING > HYMN

HYMNIST n person who composes hymns

HYMNISTS > HYMNIST

HYMNLESS > HYMN

HYMNLIKE > HYMN

HYMNODIES > HYMNODY

HYMNODIST same as > HYMNIST

HYMNODY n composition or singing of hymns

HYMNOLOGY same as > HYMNODY

HYMNS > HYMN

HYNDE same as > HIND

HYNDES > HYNDE

HYOID adj of or relating to the hyoid bone ▷ n horseshoe-shaped bone

HYOIDAL adj of or relating to the hyoid bone

HYOIDEAN same as > HYOIDAL

HYOIDS > HYOID

HYOSCINE n colourless viscous liquid alkaloid

HYOSCINES > HYOSCINE

HYP n short for hypotenuse

HYPALGIA n reduced ability to feel pain

HYPALGIAS > HYPALGIA

HYPALLAGE n figure of speech in which the natural relations of two words in a statement are interchanged, as in the fire spread the wind

HYPANTHIA n plural of hypanthium: cup-shaped receptacle of perigynous or epigynous flowers

HYPATE n string of lyre

HYPATES > HYPATE

HYPE n intensive or exaggerated publicity or sales promotion ▷ vb promote (a product) using intensive or exaggerated publicity

HYPED > HYPE

HYPER > HYPE

HYPERACID adj having excess acidity

HYPERARID adj extremely dry

HYPERBOLA n curve produced when a cone is cut by a plane at a steeper angle to its base than its side

HYPERBOLE n deliberate exaggeration for effect

HYPERCUBE n figure in a space of four or more dimensions having all its sides equal and all its angles right angles

HYPEREMIA n excessive blood in an organ or part

HYPEREMIC > HYPEREMIA

HYPERFINE adj as in hyperfine structure splitting of a spectral line of an atom or molecule into two or more closely spaced components as a result of interaction of the electrons with the magnetic moments of the nuclei

HYPERGAMY n custom that forbids a woman to marry a man of lower social status

HYPERGOL n type of fuel

HYPERGOLS > HYPERGOL

HYPERICIN n antidepressant and antiviral compound

HYPERICUM n herbaceous plant or shrub

HYPERLINK n link from a hypertext file that gives users instant access to related material in another file ▷ vb link (files) in this way

HYPERMART n very large supermarket

HYPERNOVA n exploding star that produces even more energy and light than a supernova

HYPERNYM n superordinate

HYPERNYMS > HYPERNYM

HYPERNYMY > HYPERNYM

HYPERON n any baryon that is not a nucleon

HYPERONS > HYPERON

HYPEROPE n person with hyperopia

HYPEROPES > HYPEROPE

HYPEROPIA n inability to see near objects clearly because the images received by the eye are focused behind the retina

HYPEROPIC > HYPEROPIA

HYPERPNEA n increase in breathing rate

HYPERPURE adj extremely pure

HYPERREAL adj involving or characterized by particularly realistic graphic representation ▷ n that which constitutes hyperreality

HYPERS > HYPE

HYPERTEXT n computer software and hardware that allows users to store and view text and move between related items easily

HYPES > HYPE

HYPESTER n person or organization that gives an idea or product intense publicity in order to promote it

HYPESTERS > HYPESTER

HYPETHRAL adj having no roof

HYPHA n any of the filaments in the mycelium of a fungus

HYPHAE > HYPHA

HYPHAL > HYPHA

HYPHEMIA n bleeding inside eye

HYPHEMIAS > HYPHEMIA

HYPHEN n punctuation mark (-) ▷ vb hyphenate

HYPHENATE *vb* separate (words) with a hyphen
HYPHENED > HYPHEN
HYPHENIC > HYPHEN
HYPHENING > HYPHEN
HYPHENISE *same as* > HYPHENIZE
HYPHENISM > HYPHEN
HYPHENIZE *same as* > HYPHENATE
HYPHENS > HYPHEN
HYPHIES > HYPHY
HYPHY *n* type of hip-hop music
HYPING > HYPE
HYPINGS > HYPE
HYPINOSES > HYPINOSIS
HYPINOSIS *n* protein deficiency in blood
HYPNIC *n* sleeping drug
HYPNICS > HYPNIC
HYPNOGENY *n* hypnosis
HYPNOID *adj* of or relating to a state resembling sleep
HYPNOIDAL *same as* > HYPNOID
HYPNOLOGY *n* study of sleep and hypnosis
HYPNONE *n* sleeping drug
HYPNONES > HYPNONE
HYPNOSES > HYPNOSIS
HYPNOSIS *n* artificially induced state of relaxation in which the mind is more than usually receptive to suggestion
HYPNOTEE *n* person being hypnotized
HYPNOTEES > HYPNOTEE
HYPNOTIC *adj* of or (as if) producing hypnosis ▷ *n* drug that induces sleep
HYPNOTICS > HYPNOTIC
HYPNOTISE *same as* > HYPNOTIZE
HYPNOTISM *n* inducing hypnosis in someone
HYPNOTIST *n* person skilled in the theory and practice of hypnosis
HYPNOTIZE *vb* induce hypnosis in (a person)
HYPNOTOID *adj* like hypnosis
HYPNUM *n* species of moss
HYPNUMS > HYPNUM
HYPO *vb* inject with a hypodermic syringe

HYPOACID *adj* abnormally acidic
HYPOBARIC *adj* below normal pressure
HYPOBLAST *n* inner layer of an embryo at an early stage of development that becomes the endoderm at gastrulation
HYPOBOLE *n* act of anticipating objection
HYPOBOLES > HYPOBOLE
HYPOCAUST *n* ancient Roman heating system in which hot air circulated under the floor and between double walls
HYPOCIST *n* type of juice
HYPOCISTS > HYPOCIST
HYPOCOTYL *n* part of an embryo plant between the cotyledons and the radicle
HYPOCRISY *n* (instance of) pretence of having standards or beliefs that are contrary to one's real character or actual behaviour
HYPOCRITE *n* person who pretends to be what he or she is not
HYPODERM *n* layer of thick-walled tissue in some plants
HYPODERMA *n* layer of skin tissue
HYPODERMS > HYPODERM
HYPOED > HYPO
HYPOGAEA > HYPOGAEUM
HYPOGAEAL > HYPOGAEUM
HYPOGAEAN > HYPOGAEUM
HYPOGAEUM *same as* > HYPOGEUM
HYPOGEA > HYPOGEUM
HYPOGEAL *adj* occurring or living below the surface of the ground
HYPOGEAN > HYPOGEUM
HYPOGENE *adj* formed, taking place, or originating beneath the surface of the earth
HYPOGENIC > HYPOGENE
HYPOGEOUS *same as* > HYPOGEAL
HYPOGEUM *n* underground

vault, esp one used for burials
HYPOGYNY *adj* having the gynoecium above the other floral parts
HYPOID *adj* as in *hypoid gear* type of gear ▷ *n* hypoid gear
HYPOIDS > HYPOID
HYPOING > HYPO
HYPOMANIA *n* abnormal condition of extreme excitement, milder than mania but characterized by great optimism and overactivity and often by reckless spending of money
HYPOMANIC > HYPOMANIA
HYPOMORPH *n* mutant gene
HYPONASTY *n* increased growth of the lower surface of a plant part, resulting in an upward bending of the part
HYPONEA *same as* > HYPOPNEA
HYPONEAS > HYPONEA
HYPONOIA *n* underlying meaning
HYPONOIAS > HYPONOIA
HYPONYM *n* word whose meaning is included as part of another
HYPONYMS > HYPONYM
HYPONYMY > HYPONYM
HYPOPHYGE *another name for* > APOPHYGE
HYPOPLOID *adj* having or designating a chromosome number that is less than a multiple of the haploid number
HYPOPNEA *same as* > HYPOPNOEA
HYPOPNEAS > HYPOPNEA
HYPOPNEIC > HYPOPNEA
HYPOPNOEA *n* abnormally shallow breathing, usually accompanied by a decrease in the breathing rate
HYPOPYON *n* pus in eye
HYPOPYONS > HYPOPYON
HYPOS > HYPO
HYPOSTOME *n* invertebrate body part

HYPOSTYLE *adj* having a roof supported by columns ▷ *n* building constructed in this way
HYPOTAXES > HYPOTAXIS
HYPOTAXIS *n* subordination of one clause to another by a conjunction
HYPOTHEC *n* charge on property in favour of a creditor
HYPOTHECA *n* inner and younger layer of the cell wall of a diatom
HYPOTHECS > HYPOTHEC
HYPOTONIA *n* state of being hypnotized
HYPOTONIC *adj* (of muscles) lacking normal tone or tension
HYPOXEMIA *n* lack of oxygen in blood
HYPOXEMIC > HYPOXEMIA
HYPOXIA *n* deficiency in oxygen delivery
HYPOXIAS > HYPOXIA
HYPOXIC > HYPOXIA
HYPPED > HYP
HYPPING > HYP
HYPS > HYP
HYPURAL *adj* below the tail
HYRACES > HYRAX
HYRACOID *n* hyrax
HYRACOIDS > HYRACOID
HYRAX *n* type of hoofed rodent-like animal of Africa and Asia
HYRAXES > HYRAX
HYSON *n* Chinese green tea
HYSONS > HYSON
HYSSOP *n* sweet-smelling herb used in folk medicine
HYSSOPS > HYSSOP
HYSTERIA *n* state of uncontrolled excitement, anger, or panic
HYSTERIAS > HYSTERIA
HYSTERIC *adj* of or suggesting hysteria
HYSTERICS *pl n* attack of hysteria
HYSTEROID *adj* resembling hysteria
HYTE *adj* insane
HYTHE *same as* > HITHE
HYTHES > HYTHE

h

I i

IAMB *n* metrical foot of two syllables
IAMBI > IAMBUS
IAMBIC *adj* written in a type of metrical unit ⊳ *n* iambic foot, line, or stanza
IAMBICS > IAMBIC
IAMBIST *n* one who writes iambs
IAMBISTS > IAMBIST
IAMBS > IAMB
IAMBUS *same as* > IAMB
IAMBUSES > IAMBUS
IANTHINE *adj* violet
IATRIC *adj* relating to medicine or physicians
IATRICAL *same as* > IATRIC
IATROGENY *n* disease caused by medical intervention
IBADAH *n* following of Islamic beliefs and practices
IBADAT > IBADAH
IBERIS *n* plant with white or purple flowers
IBERISES > IBERIS
IBEX *n* wild goat
IBEXES > IBEX
IBICES > IBEX
IBIDEM *adv* in the same place
IBIS *n* large wading bird with long legs
IBISES > IBIS
IBOGAINE *n* dopamine blocker
IBOGAINES > IBOGAINE
IBRIK *same as* > CEZVE
IBRIKS > IBRIK
IBUPROFEN *n* drug that relieves pain and reduces inflammation
ICE *n* water in the solid state, formed by freezing liquid water ⊳ *vb* form or cause to form ice
ICEBALL *n* ball of ice
ICEBALLS > ICEBALL
ICEBERG *n* large floating mass of ice
ICEBERGS > ICEBERG
ICEBLINK *n* yellowish-white reflected glare in the sky over an ice field
ICEBLINKS > ICEBLINK

ICEBOAT *n* boat that breaks up bodies of ice in water ⊳ *vb* pilot an iceboat
ICEBOATED > ICEBOAT
ICEBOATER > ICEBOAT
ICEBOATS > ICEBOAT
ICEBOUND *adj* covered or made immobile by ice
ICEBOX *n* refrigerator
ICEBOXES > ICEBOX
ICECAP *n* mass of ice permanently covering an area
ICECAPPED *adj* having an icecap
ICECAPS > ICECAP
ICED *adj* covered with icing
ICEFALL *n* part of a glacier
ICEFALLS > ICEFALL
ICEFIELD *n* very large flat expanse of ice floating in the sea, large ice floe
ICEFIELDS > ICEFIELD
ICEFISH *vb* fish through a hole in the ice on a lake
ICEFISHED > ICEFISH
ICEFISHES > ICEFISH
ICEHOUSE *n* building for storing ice
ICEHOUSES > ICEHOUSE
ICEKHANA *n* motor race on a frozen lake
ICEKHANAS > ICEKHANA
ICELESS > ICE
ICELIKE > ICE
ICEMAKER *n* device for making ice
ICEMAKERS > ICEMAKER
ICEMAN *n* person who sells or delivers ice
ICEMEN > ICEMAN
ICEPACK *n* bag or folded cloth containing ice
ICEPACKS > ICEPACK
ICER *n* person who ices cakes
ICERS > ICER
ICES > ICE
ICESCAPE *n* landscape covered in ice
ICESCAPES > ICESCAPE
ICESTONE *n* cryolite
ICESTONES > ICESTONE
ICEWINE *n* dessert wine made from grapes that have frozen before being harvested
ICEWINES > ICEWINE

ICEWORM *n* small worm found in glaciers
ICEWORMS > ICEWORM
ICH *archaic form of* > EKE
ICHABOD *interj* the glory has departed
ICHED > ICH
ICHES > ICH
ICHING > ICH
ICHNEUMON *n* greyish-brown mongoose
ICHNITE *n* trace fossil
ICHNITES > ICHNITE
ICHNOLITE *same as* > ICHNITE
ICHNOLOGY *n* study of trace fossils
ICHOR *n* fluid said to flow in the veins of the gods
ICHOROUS > ICHOR
ICHORS > ICHOR
ICHS > ICH
ICHTHIC *same as* > ICHTHYIC
ICHTHYIC *adj* of, relating to, or characteristic of fishes
ICHTHYOID *adj* resembling a fish ⊳ *n* fishlike vertebrate
ICHTHYS *n* early Christian emblem
ICHTHYSES > ICHTHYS
ICICLE *n* tapering spike of ice
ICICLED *adj* covered with icicles
ICICLES > ICICLE
ICIER > ICY
ICIEST > ICY
ICILY *adv* in an icy or reserved manner
ICINESS *n* condition of being icy or very cold
ICINESSES > ICINESS
ICING *n* mixture used to decorate cakes
ICINGS > ICING
ICK *interj* expression of disgust
ICKER *n* ear of corn
ICKERS > ICKER
ICKIER > ICKY
ICKIEST > ICKY
ICKILY > ICKY
ICKINESS > ICKY
ICKLE *ironically childish word for* > LITTLE
ICKLER > ICKLE
ICKLEST > ICKLE
ICKS > ICK

ICKY *adj* sticky
ICON *n* picture of Christ or another religious figure
ICONES > ICON
ICONIC *adj* relating to the character of an icon
ICONICAL *same as* > ICONIC
ICONICITY > ICONIC
ICONIFIED > ICONIFY
ICONIFIES > ICONIFY
ICONIFY *vb* render as an icon
ICONISE *same as* > ICONIZE
ICONISED > ICONISE
ICONISES > ICONISE
ICONISING > ICONISE
ICONIZE *vb* render as an icon
ICONIZED > ICONIZE
ICONIZES > ICONIZE
ICONIZING > ICONIZE
ICONOLOGY *n* study or field of art history concerning icons
ICONOSTAS *n* screen with doors and icons set in tiers, which separates the from the nave
ICONS > ICON
ICTAL > ICTUS
ICTERIC > ICTERUS
ICTERICAL > ICTERUS
ICTERICS > ICTERUS
ICTERID *n* bird of the oriole family
ICTERIDS > ICTERID
ICTERINE > ICTERID
ICTERUS *n* yellowing of plant leaves
ICTERUSES > ICTERUS
ICTIC > ICTUS
ICTUS *n* metrical or rhythmic stress in verse feet
ICTUSES > ICTUS
ICY *adj* very cold
ID *n* mind's instinctive unconscious energies
IDANT *n* chromosome
IDANTS > IDANT
IDE *n* silver orfe fish
IDEA *n* plan or thought formed in the mind ⊳ *vb* have or form an idea
IDEAED > IDEA
IDEAL *adj* most suitable ⊳ *n* conception of something that is perfect

IDEALESS > IDEA
IDEALISE *same as* > IDEALIZE
IDEALISED > IDEALISE
IDEALISER > IDEALISE
IDEALISES > IDEALISE
IDEALISM *n* tendency to seek perfection in everything
IDEALISMS > IDEALISM
IDEALIST > IDEALISM
IDEALISTS > IDEALISM
IDEALITY > IDEAL
IDEALIZE *vb* regard or portray as perfect or nearly perfect
IDEALIZED > IDEALIZE
IDEALIZER > IDEALIZE
IDEALIZES > IDEALIZE
IDEALIZES > IDEALIZE
IDEALLESS > IDEAL
IDEALLY > IDEAL
IDEALNESS > IDEAL
IDEALOGUE *corruption of* > IDEOLOGUE
IDEALOGY *corruption of* > IDEOLOGY
IDEALS > IDEAL
IDEAS > IDEA
IDEATA > IDEATUM
IDEATE *vb* form or have an idea of
IDEATED > IDEATE
IDEATES > IDEATE
IDEATING > IDEATE
IDEATION > IDEATE
IDEATIONS > IDEATE
IDEATIVE > IDEATE
IDEATUM *n* objective reality
IDEE *n* idea
IDEES > IDEE
IDEM *adj* same
IDENT *n* short visual image that works as a logo
IDENTIC *adj* having the same intention regarding another power
IDENTICAL *adj* exactly the same
IDENTIFY *vb* prove or recognize as being a certain person or thing
IDENTIKIT *n* trademark name for a set of transparencies of various typical facial characteristics that can be superimposed on one another to build up a picture of a person sought by the police
IDENTITY *n* state of being a specified person or thing
IDENTS > IDENT
IDEOGRAM *n* character or symbol that directly represents a concept or thing, rather than the sounds that form its name
IDEOGRAMS > IDEOGRAM
IDEOGRAPH *same as* > IDEOGRAM
IDEOLOGIC > IDEOLOGY

IDEOLOGUE *n* ideologist
IDEOLOGY *n* body of ideas and beliefs of a group, nation, etc
IDEOMOTOR *adj* designating automatic muscular movements stimulated by ideas
IDEOPHONE *n* sound that represents a complete idea
IDEOPOLIS *n* city whose economy mainly consists of intellectual enterprises
IDES *n* specific date of each month in the Roman calendar
IDIOBLAST *n* plant cell that differs from those around it in the same tissue
IDIOCIES > IDIOCY
IDIOCY *n* utter stupidity
IDIOGRAM *another name for* > KARYOGRAM
IDIOGRAMS > IDIOGRAM
IDIOGRAPH *n* trademark
IDIOLECT *n* variety or form of a language used by an individual
IDIOLECTS > IDIOLECT
IDIOM *n* group of words with special meaning
IDIOMATIC > IDIOM
IDIOMS > IDIOM
IDIOPATHY *n* any disease of unknown cause
IDIOPHONE *n* percussion instrument, such as a cymbal or xylophone, made of naturally sonorous material
IDIOPLASM *n* germ plasm
IDIOT *n* foolish or stupid person
IDIOTCIES > IDIOTCY
IDIOTCY *same as* > IDIOCY
IDIOTIC *adj* of or resembling an idiot
IDIOTICAL *same as* > IDIOTIC
IDIOTICON *n* dictionary of dialect
IDIOTISH *same as* > IDIOTIC
IDIOTISM *archaic word for* > IDIOCY
IDIOTISMS > IDIOTISM
IDIOTS > IDIOT
IDIOTYPE *n* unique part of antibody
IDIOTYPES > IDIOTYPE
IDIOTYPIC > IDIOTYPE
IDLE *adj* not doing anything ▷ *vb* spend (time) doing very little
IDLED > IDLE
IDLEHOOD > IDLE
IDLEHOODS > IDLE
IDLENESS > IDLE
IDLER *n* person who idles
IDLERS > IDLER

IDLES > IDLE
IDLESSE > IDLE
IDLESSES > IDLE
IDLEST > IDLE
IDLING > IDLE
IDLY > IDLE
IDOCRASE *n* green, brown, or yellow mineral
IDOCRASES > IDOCRASE
IDOL *n* object of excessive devotion
IDOLA > IDOLUM
IDOLATER > IDOLATRY
IDOLATERS > IDOLATRY
IDOLATOR *n* one who worships idols
IDOLATORS > IDOLATRY
IDOLATRY *n* worship of idols
IDOLISE *same as* > IDOLIZE
IDOLISED > IDOLISE
IDOLISER > IDOLISE
IDOLISERS > IDOLISE
IDOLISES > IDOLISE
IDOLISING > IDOLISE
IDOLISM > IDOLIZE
IDOLISMS > IDOL
IDOLIST > IDOLIZE
IDOLISTS > IDOLIZE
IDOLIZE *vb* love or admire excessively
IDOLIZED > IDOLIZE
IDOLIZER > IDOLIZE
IDOLIZERS > IDOLIZE
IDOLIZES > IDOLIZE
IDOLIZING > IDOLIZE
IDOLON *n* mental image
IDOLS > IDOL
IDOLUM *n* mental picture
IDONEITY > IDONEOUS
IDONEOUS *adj* appropriate
IDS > ID
IDYL *same as* > IDYLL
IDYLIST *same as* > IDYLLIST
IDYLISTS > IDYLIST
IDYLL *n* scene or time of great peace and happiness
IDYLLIAN *same as* > IDYLLIC
IDYLLIC *adj* of or relating to an idyll
IDYLLIST *n* writer of idylls
IDYLLISTS > IDYLLIST
IDYLLS > IDYLL
IDYLS > IDYL
IF *n* uncertainty or doubt
IFF *conj* in logic, a shortened form of if and only if
IFFIER > IFFY
IFFIEST > IFFY
IFFILY *adv* in an iffy manner
IFFINESS > IFFY
IFFY *adj* doubtful, uncertain
IFS > IF
IFTAR *n* meal eaten by Muslims
IFTARS > IFTAR

IGAD *same as* > EGAD
IGAPO *n* flooded forest
IGAPOS > IGAPO
IGARAPE *n* canoe route
IGARAPES > IGARAPE
IGG *vb* antagonize
IGGED > IGG
IGGING > IGG
IGGS > IGG
IGLOO *n* Inuit house
IGLOOS > IGLOO
IGLU *same as* > IGLOO
IGLUS > IGLU
IGNARO *n* ignoramus
IGNAROES > IGNARO
IGNAROS > IGNARO
IGNATIA *n* dried seed
IGNATIAS > IGNATIA
IGNEOUS *adj* (of rock) formed as molten rock cools
IGNESCENT *adj* giving off sparks when struck, as a flint ▷ *n* ignescent substance
IGNIFIED > IGNIFY
IGNIFIES > IGNIFY
IGNIFY *vb* turn into fire
IGNIFYING > IGNIFY
IGNITABLE > IGNITE
IGNITE *vb* catch fire or set fire to
IGNITED > IGNITE
IGNITER *n* person or thing that ignites
IGNITERS > IGNITER
IGNITES > IGNITE
IGNITIBLE > IGNITE
IGNITING > IGNITE
IGNITION *n* system that ignites the fuel-and-air mixture to start an engine
IGNITIONS > IGNITION
IGNITOR *same as* > IGNITER
IGNITORS > IGNITER
IGNITRON *n* mercury-arc rectifier controlled by a subsidiary electrode
IGNITRONS > IGNITRON
IGNOBLE *adj* dishonourable
IGNOBLER > IGNOBLE
IGNOBLEST > IGNOBLE
IGNOBLY > IGNOBLE
IGNOMIES > IGNOMY
IGNOMINY *n* humiliating disgrace
IGNOMY *Shakespearean variant of* > IGNOMINY
IGNORABLE > IGNORE
IGNORAMI > IGNORAMUS
IGNORAMUS *n* ignorant person
IGNORANCE *n* lack of knowledge or education
IGNORANT *adj* lacking knowledge ▷ *n* ignorant person
IGNORANTS > IGNORANT
IGNORE *vb* refuse to notice, disregard deliberately ▷ *n* disregard

IGNORED > IGNORE
IGNORER > IGNORE
IGNORERS > IGNORE
IGNORES > IGNORE
IGNORING > IGNORE
IGUANA *n* large tropical American lizard
IGUANAS > IGUANA
IGUANIAN > IGUANA
IGUANIANS > IGUANA
IGUANID *same as* > IGUANA
IGUANIDS > IGUANID
IGUANODON *n* massive herbivorous long-tailed bipedal dinosaur
IHRAM *n* white robes worn by Muslim pilgrims to Mecca
IHRAMS > IHRAM
IJTIHAD *n* effort of deriving a legal ruling from the Koran
IJTIHADS > IJTIHAD
IKAN *n* (in Malaysia) fish
IKANS > IKAN
IKAT *n* method of creating patterns in fabric
IKATS > IKAT
IKEBANA *n* Japanese art of flower arrangement
IKEBANAS > IKEBANA
IKON *same as* > ICON
IKONS > IKON
ILEA > ILEUM
ILEAC *adj* of or relating to the ileum
ILEAL *same as* > ILEAC
ILEITIDES > ILEITIS
ILEITIS *n* inflammation of the ileum
ILEITISES > ILEITIS
ILEOSTOMY *n* surgical formation of a permanent opening through the abdominal wall into the ileum
ILEUM *n* lowest part of the small intestine
ILEUS *n* obstruction of the intestine
ILEUSES > ILEUS
ILEX *n* any of a genus of trees or shrubs that includes holly
ILEXES > ILEX
ILIA > ILIUM
ILIAC *adj* of or relating to the ilium
ILIACUS *n* iliac
ILIACUSES > ILIACUS
ILIAD *n* epic poem
ILIADS > ILIAD
ILIAL > ILIUM
ILICES > ILEX
ILIUM *n* part of the hipbone
ILK *n* type *> determiner* each
ILKA *same as* > ILK
ILKADAY *n* every day
ILKADAYS > ILKADAY
ILKS > ILK

ILL *adj* not in good health *▷ n* evil, harm *▷ adv* badly
ILLAPSE *vb* slide in
ILLAPSED > ILLAPSE
ILLAPSES > ILLAPSE
ILLAPSING > ILLAPSE
ILLATION *rare word for* > INFERENCE
ILLATIONS > ILLATION
ILLATIVE *adj* of or relating to illation *▷ n* illative case
ILLATIVES > ILLATIVE
ILLAWARRA *n* Australian breed of shorthorn dairy cattle
ILLEGAL *adj* against the law *▷ n* person who entered or attempted to enter a country illegally
ILLEGALLY > ILLEGAL
ILLEGALS > ILLEGAL
ILLEGIBLE *adj* unable to be read or deciphered
ILLEGIBLY > ILLEGIBLE
ILLER > ILL
ILLEST > ILL
ILLIAD *n* wink
ILLIADS > ILLIAD
ILLIBERAL *adj* narrow-minded, intolerant
ILLICIT *adj* illegal
ILLICITLY > ILLICIT
ILLIMITED *adj* infinite
ILLINIUM *n* type of radioactive element
ILLINIUMS > ILLINIUM
ILLIPE *n* Asian tree
ILLIPES > ILLIPE
ILLIQUID *adj* (of an asset) not easily convertible into cash
ILLISION *n* act of striking against
ILLISIONS > ILLISION
ILLITE *n* clay mineral of the mica group
ILLITES > ILLITE
ILLITIC > ILLITE
ILLNESS *n* disease or indisposition
ILLNESSES > ILLNESS
ILLOGIC *n* reasoning characterized by lack of logic
ILLOGICAL *adj* unreasonable
ILLOGICS > ILLOGIC
ILLS > ILL
ILLTH *n* condition of poverty or misery
ILLTHS > ILLTH
ILLUDE *vb* trick or deceive
ILLUDED > ILLUDE
ILLUDES > ILLUDE
ILLUDING > ILLUDE
ILLUME *vb* illuminate
ILLUMED > ILLUME
ILLUMES > ILLUME
ILLUMINE *vb* throw light in or into
ILLUMINED > ILLUMINE

ILLUMINER *n* illuminator
ILLUMINES > ILLUMINE
ILLUMING > ILLUME
ILLUPI *same as* > ILLIPE
ILLUPIS > ILLUPI
ILLUSION *n* deceptive appearance or belief
ILLUSIONS > ILLUSION
ILLUSIVE *same as* > ILLUSORY
ILLUSORY *adj* seeming to be true, but actually false
ILLUVIA > ILLUVIUM
ILLUVIAL > ILLUVIUM
ILLUVIATE *vb* deposit illuvium
ILLUVIUM *n* material, which includes colloids and mineral salts, that is washed down from one layer of soil to a lower layer
ILLUVIUMS > ILLUVIUM
ILLY *adv* badly
ILMENITE *n* black mineral found in igneous rocks as layered deposits and in veins
ILMENITES > ILMENITE
IMAGE *n* mental picture of someone or something *▷ vb* picture in the mind
IMAGEABLE > IMAGE
IMAGED > IMAGE
IMAGELESS > IMAGE
IMAGER *n* device that produces images
IMAGERIES > IMAGERY
IMAGERS > IMAGER
IMAGERY *n* images collectively, esp in the arts
IMAGES > IMAGE
IMAGINAL *adj* of, relating to, or resembling an imago
IMAGINARY *adj* existing only in the imagination
IMAGINE *vb* form a mental image of *▷ sentence substitute* exclamation of surprise
IMAGINED > IMAGINE
IMAGINEER *n* person skilled in devising or implementing creative ideas *▷ vb* devise and implement (a creative idea)
IMAGINER > IMAGINE
IMAGINERS > IMAGINE
IMAGINES > IMAGO
IMAGING > IMAGE
IMAGINGS > IMAGE
IMAGINING > IMAGINE
IMAGINIST *n* imaginative person
IMAGISM *n* poetic movement
IMAGISMS > IMAGISM
IMAGIST > IMAGISM
IMAGISTIC > IMAGISM
IMAGISTS > IMAGISM
IMAGO *n* sexually mature adult insect
IMAGOES > IMAGO
IMAGOS > IMAGO

IMAM *n* leader of prayers in a mosque
IMAMATE *n* region or territory governed by an imam
IMAMATES > IMAMATE
IMAMS > IMAM
IMARET *n* (in Turkey) a hospice for pilgrims or travellers
IMARETS > IMARET
IMARI *n* Japanese porcelain
IMARIS > IMARI
IMAUM *same as* > IMAM
IMAUMS > IMAUM
IMBALANCE *n* lack of balance or proportion
IMBALM *same as* > EMBALM
IMBALMED > IMBALM
IMBALMER > IMBALM
IMBALMERS > IMBALM
IMBALMING > IMBALM
IMBALMS > IMBALM
IMBAR *vb* bar in
IMBARK *vb* cover in bark
IMBARKED > IMBARK
IMBARKING > IMBARK
IMBARKS > IMBARK
IMBARRED > IMBAR
IMBARRING > IMBAR
IMBARS > IMBAR
IMBASE *vb* degrade
IMBASED > IMBASE
IMBASES > IMBASE
IMBASING > IMBASE
IMBATHE *vb* bathe
IMBATHED > IMBATHE
IMBATHES > IMBATHE
IMBATHING > IMBATHE
IMBECILE *n* stupid person *▷ adj* stupid or senseless
IMBECILES > IMBECILE
IMBECILIC > IMBECILE
IMBED *same as* > EMBED
IMBEDDED > IMBED
IMBEDDING > IMBED
IMBEDS > IMBED
IMBIBE *vb* drink (alcoholic drinks)
IMBIBED > IMBIBE
IMBIBER > IMBIBE
IMBIBERS > IMBIBE
IMBIBES > IMBIBE
IMBIBING > IMBIBE
IMBITTER *same as* > EMBITTER
IMBITTERS > IMBITTER
IMBIZO *n* meeting in S Africa
IMBIZOS > IMBIZO
IMBLAZE *vb* depict heraldically
IMBLAZED > IMBLAZE
IMBLAZES > IMBLAZE
IMBLAZING > IMBLAZE
IMBODIED > IMBODY
IMBODIES > IMBODY
IMBODY *same as* > EMBODY
IMBODYING > IMBODY
IMBOLDEN *same as* > EMBOLDEN

IMBOLDENS > IMBOLDEN
IMBORDER vb enclose in a border
IMBORDERS > IMBORDER
IMBOSK vb conceal
IMBOSKED > IMBOSK
IMBOSKING > IMBOSK
IMBOSKS > IMBOSK
IMBOSOM vb hold in one's heart
IMBOSOMED > IMBOSOM
IMBOSOMS > IMBOSOM
IMBOSS same as > EMBOSS
IMBOSSED > IMBOSS
IMBOSSES > IMBOSS
IMBOSSING > IMBOSS
IMBOWER vb enclose in a bower
IMBOWERED > IMBOWER
IMBOWERS > IMBOWER
IMBRANGLE vb entangle
IMBRAST Spenserian past participle of > EMBRACE
IMBREX n curved tile
IMBRICATE adj having tiles or slates that overlap ▷ vb decorate with a repeating pattern resembling scales or overlapping tiles
IMBRICES > IMBREX
IMBROGLIO n confusing and complicated situation
IMBROWN vb make brown
IMBROWNED > IMBROWN
IMBROWNS > IMBROWN
IMBRUE vb stain, esp with blood
IMBRUED > IMBRUE
IMBRUES > IMBRUE
IMBRUING > IMBRUE
IMBRUTE vb reduce to a bestial state
IMBRUTED > IMBRUTE
IMBRUTES > IMBRUTE
IMBRUTING > IMBRUTE
IMBUE vb fill or inspire with (ideals or principles)
IMBUED > IMBUE
IMBUEMENT > IMBUE
IMBUES > IMBUE
IMBUING > IMBUE
IMBURSE vb pay
IMBURSED > IMBURSE
IMBURSES > IMBURSE
IMBURSING > IMBURSE
IMID n immunomodulatory drug
IMIDAZOLE n white crystalline basic heterocyclic compound
IMIDE n any of a class of organic compounds
IMIDES > IMIDE
IMIDIC > IMIDE
IMIDO > IMIDE
IMIDS > IMID
IMINAZOLE same as > IMIDAZOLE
IMINE n any of a class of organic compounds
IMINES > IMINE
IMINO > IMINE

IMINOUREA another name for > GUANIDINE
IMITABLE > IMITATE
IMITANCY n tendency to imitate
IMITANT same as > IMITATION
IMITANTS > IMITANT
IMITATE vb take as a model
IMITATED > IMITATE
IMITATES > IMITATE
IMITATING > IMITATE
IMITATION n copy of an original ▷ adj made to look like a material of superior quality
IMITATIVE adj imitating or tending to copy
IMITATOR > IMITATE
IMITATORS > IMITATE
IMMANACLE vb fetter
IMMANE adj monstrous
IMMANELY > IMMANE
IMMANENCE > IMMANENT
IMMANENCY > IMMANENT
IMMANENT adj present within and throughout something
IMMANITY > IMMANE
IMMANTLE vb cover with a mantle
IMMANTLED > IMMANTLE
IMMANTLES > IMMANTLE
IMMASK vb disguise
IMMASKED > IMMASK
IMMASKING > IMMASK
IMMASKS > IMMASK
IMMATURE n young animal ▷ adj not fully developed
IMMATURES > IMMATURE
IMMEDIACY > IMMEDIATE
IMMEDIATE adj occurring at once
IMMENSE adj extremely large
IMMENSELY > IMMENSE
IMMENSER > IMMENSE
IMMENSEST > IMMENSE
IMMENSITY n state or quality of being immense
IMMERGE archaic word for > IMMERSE
IMMERGED > IMMERGE
IMMERGES > IMMERGE
IMMERGING > IMMERGE
IMMERSE vb involve deeply, engross
IMMERSED adj sunk or submerged
IMMERSER > IMMERSE
IMMERSERS > IMMERSE
IMMERSES > IMMERSE
IMMERSING > IMMERSE
IMMERSION n form of baptism in which part or the whole of a person's body is submerged in the water
IMMERSIVE adj providing information or stimulation

for a number of senses, not only sight and sound
IMMESH variant of > ENMESH
IMMESHED > IMMESH
IMMESHES > IMMESH
IMMESHING > IMMESH
IMMEW vb confine
IMMEWED > IMMEW
IMMEWING > IMMEW
IMMEWS > IMMEW
IMMIES > IMMY
IMMIGRANT n person who comes to a foreign country in order to settle there
IMMIGRATE vb come to a place or country of which one is not a native in order to settle there
IMMINENCE > IMMINENT
IMMINENCY > IMMINENT
IMMINENT adj about to happen
IMMINGLE vb blend or mix together
IMMINGLED > IMMINGLE
IMMINGLES > IMMINGLE
IMMINUTE adj reduced
IMMISSION n insertion
IMMIT vb insert
IMMITS > IMMIT
IMMITTED > IMMIT
IMMITTING > IMMIT
IMMIX vb mix in
IMMIXED > IMMIX
IMMIXES > IMMIX
IMMIXING > IMMIX
IMMIXTURE > IMMIX
IMMOBILE adj not moving
IMMODEST adj behaving in an indecent or improper manner
IMMODESTY > IMMODEST
IMMOLATE vb kill as a sacrifice
IMMOLATED > IMMOLATE
IMMOLATES > IMMOLATE
IMMOLATOR > IMMOLATE
IMMOMENT adj of no value
IMMORAL adj morally wrong, corrupt
IMMORALLY > IMMORAL
IMMORTAL adj living forever ▷ n person whose fame will last for all time
IMMORTALS > IMMORTAL
IMMOTILE adj (esp of living organisms or their parts) not capable of moving spontaneously and independently
IMMOVABLE adj unable to be moved
IMMOVABLY > IMMOVABLE
IMMUNE adj protected against a specific disease ▷ n immune person or animal
IMMUNES > IMMUNE
IMMUNISE same as > IMMUNIZE
IMMUNISED > IMMUNISE

IMMUNISER > IMMUNISE
IMMUNISES > IMMUNISE
IMMUNITY n ability to resist disease
IMMUNIZE vb make immune to a disease
IMMUNIZED > IMMUNIZE
IMMUNIZER > IMMUNIZE
IMMUNIZES > IMMUNIZE
IMMUNOGEN n any substance that evokes an immune response
IMMURE vb imprison
IMMURED > IMMURE
IMMURES > IMMURE
IMMURING > IMMURE
IMMUTABLE adj unchangeable
IMMUTABLY > IMMUTABLE
IMMY n image-orthicon camera
IMP n (in folklore) creature with magical powers ▷ vb method of repairing the wing of a hawk or falcon
IMPACABLE adj incapable of being placated or pacified
IMPACT n strong effect ▷ vb have a strong effect on
IMPACTED > IMPACT
IMPACTER > IMPACT
IMPACTERS > IMPACT
IMPACTFUL > IMPACT
IMPACTING > IMPACT
IMPACTION > IMPACT
IMPACTITE n glassy rock formed in a meteor collision
IMPACTIVE adj of or relating to a physical impact
IMPACTOR > IMPACT
IMPACTORS > IMPACT
IMPACTS > IMPACT
IMPAINT vb paint
IMPAINTED > IMPAINT
IMPAINTS > IMPAINT
IMPAIR vb weaken or damage
IMPAIRED > IMPAIR
IMPAIRER > IMPAIR
IMPAIRERS > IMPAIR
IMPAIRING > IMPAIR
IMPAIRS > IMPAIR
IMPALA n southern African antelope
IMPALAS > IMPALA
IMPALE vb pierce with a sharp object
IMPALED > IMPALE
IMPALER > IMPALE
IMPALERS > IMPALE
IMPALES > IMPALE
IMPALING > IMPALE
IMPANATE adj embodied in bread
IMPANEL variant spelling (esp US) of > EMPANEL
IMPANELED > IMPANEL

IMPANELS > IMPANEL

IMPANNEL same as > IMPANEL

IMPANNELS > IMPANNEL

IMPARITY less common word for > DISPARITY

IMPARK vb make into a park

IMPARKED > IMPARK

IMPARKING > IMPARK

IMPARKS > IMPARK

IMPARL vb parley

IMPARLED > IMPARL

IMPARLING > IMPARL

IMPARLS > IMPARL

IMPART vb communicate (information)

IMPARTED > IMPART

IMPARTER > IMPART

IMPARTERS > IMPART

IMPARTIAL adj not favouring one side or the other

IMPARTING > IMPART

IMPARTS > IMPART

IMPASSE n situation in which progress is impossible

IMPASSES > IMPASSE

IMPASSION vb arouse the passions of

IMPASSIVE adj showing no emotion, calm

IMPASTE vb apply paint thickly to

IMPASTED > IMPASTE

IMPASTES > IMPASTE

IMPASTING > IMPASTE

IMPASTO n technique of applying paint thickly ▷ vb apply impasto

IMPASTOED > IMPASTO

IMPASTOS > IMPASTO

IMPATIENS n plant such as balsam, touch-me-not, busy Lizzie, and policeman's helmet

IMPATIENT adj irritable at any delay or difficulty

IMPAVE vb set in a pavement

IMPAVED > IMPAVE

IMPAVES > IMPAVE

IMPAVID adj fearless

IMPAVIDLY > IMPAVID

IMPAVING > IMPAVE

IMPAWN vb pawn

IMPAWNED > IMPAWN

IMPAWNING > IMPAWN

IMPAWNS > IMPAWN

IMPEACH vb charge with a serious crime against the state

IMPEACHED > IMPEACH

IMPEACHER > IMPEACH

IMPEACHES > IMPEACH

IMPEARL vb adorn with pearls

IMPEARLED > IMPEARL

IMPEARLS > IMPEARL

IMPECCANT adj not sinning

IMPED > IMP

IMPEDANCE n measure of the opposition to the flow of an alternating current

IMPEDE vb hinder in action or progress

IMPEDED > IMPEDE

IMPEDER > IMPEDE

IMPEDERS > IMPEDE

IMPEDES > IMPEDE

IMPEDING > IMPEDE

IMPEDOR n component that offers impedance

IMPEDORS > IMPEDOR

IMPEL vb push or force (someone) to do something

IMPELLED > IMPEL

IMPELLENT > IMPEL

IMPELLER n vaned rotating disc of a centrifugal pump, compressor, etc

IMPELLERS > IMPELLER

IMPELLING > IMPEL

IMPELLOR same as > IMPELLER

IMPELLORS > IMPELLOR

IMPELS > IMPEL

IMPEND vb be about to happen

IMPENDED > IMPEND

IMPENDENT adj impending; threatening

IMPENDING > IMPEND

IMPENDS > IMPEND

IMPENNATE adj (of birds) lacking true functional wings or feathers

IMPERATOR n (in imperial Rome) a title of the emperor

IMPERFECT adj having faults or mistakes ▷ n imperfect tense

IMPERIA > IMPERIUM

IMPERIAL adj of or like an empire or emperor ▷ n wine bottle holding the equivalent of eight normal bottles

IMPERIALS > IMPERIAL

IMPERIL vb put in danger

IMPERILED > IMPERIL

IMPERILS > IMPERIL

IMPERIOUS adj proud and domineering

IMPERIUM n (in ancient Rome) the supreme power, held esp by consuls and emperors, to command and administer in military, judicial, and civil affairs

IMPERIUMS > IMPERIUM

IMPETICOS vb put in a pocket

IMPETIGO n contagious skin disease

IMPETIGOS > IMPETIGO

IMPETRATE vb supplicate or entreat for, esp by prayer

IMPETUOUS adj done or acting without thought, rash

IMPETUS n incentive, impulse

IMPETUSES > IMPETUS

IMPHEE n African sugar cane

IMPHEES > IMPHEE

IMPI n group of Zulu warriors

IMPIES > IMPI

IMPIETIES > IMPIETY

IMPIETY n lack of respect or religious reverence

IMPING > IMP

IMPINGE vb affect or restrict

IMPINGED > IMPINGE

IMPINGENT adj striking against or upon

IMPINGER > IMPINGE

IMPINGERS > IMPINGE

IMPINGES > IMPINGE

IMPINGING > IMPINGE

IMPINGS > IMP

IMPIOUS adj showing a lack of respect or reverence

IMPIOUSLY > IMPIOUS

IMPIS > IMPI

IMPISH adj mischievous

IMPISHLY > IMPISH

IMPLANT n something put into someone's body ▷ vb put (something) into someone's body

IMPLANTED > IMPLANT

IMPLANTER > IMPLANT

IMPLANTS > IMPLANT

IMPLATE vb sheathe

IMPLATED > IMPLATE

IMPLATES > IMPLATE

IMPLATING > IMPLATE

IMPLEACH vb intertwine

IMPLEAD vb sue or prosecute

IMPLEADED > IMPLEAD

IMPLEADER > IMPLEAD

IMPLEADS > IMPLEAD

IMPLED > IMPLEAD

IMPLEDGE vb pledge

IMPLEDGED > IMPLEDGE

IMPLEDGES > IMPLEDGE

IMPLEMENT vb carry out (instructions etc) ▷ n tool, instrument

IMPLETE vb fill

IMPLETED > IMPLETE

IMPLETES > IMPLETE

IMPLETING > IMPLETE

IMPLETION > IMPLETE

IMPLEX n part of an arthropod

IMPLEXES > IMPLEX

IMPLEXION n complication

IMPLICATE vb show to be involved, esp in a crime

IMPLICIT adj expressed indirectly

IMPLICITY > IMPLICIT

IMPLIED adj hinted at or suggested

IMPLIEDLY > IMPLIED

IMPLIES > IMPLY

IMPLODE vb collapse inwards

IMPLODED > IMPLODE

IMPLODENT n sound of an implosion

IMPLODES > IMPLODE

IMPLODING > IMPLODE

IMPLORE vb beg earnestly

IMPLORED > IMPLORE

IMPLORER > IMPLORE

IMPLORERS > IMPLORE

IMPLORES > IMPLORE

IMPLORING > IMPLORE

IMPLOSION n act or process of imploding

IMPLOSIVE n consonant pronounced in a particular way

IMPLUNGE vb submerge

IMPLUNGED > IMPLUNGE

IMPLUNGES > IMPLUNGE

IMPLUVIA > IMPLUVIUM

IMPLUVIUM n rain-filled water tank

IMPLY vb indicate by hinting, suggest

IMPLYING > IMPLY

IMPOCKET vb put in a pocket

IMPOCKETS > IMPOCKET

IMPOLDER vb make into a polder

IMPOLDERS > IMPOLDER

IMPOLICY n act or an instance of being injudicious or impolitic

IMPOLITE adj showing bad manners

IMPOLITER > IMPOLITE

IMPOLITIC adj unwise or inadvisable

IMPONE vb impose

IMPONED > IMPONE

IMPONENT n person who imposes a duty, etc

IMPONENTS > IMPONENT

IMPONES > IMPONE

IMPONING > IMPONE

IMPOROUS adj not porous

IMPORT vb bring in (goods) from another country ▷ n something imported

IMPORTANT adj of great significance or value

IMPORTED > IMPORT

IMPORTER > IMPORT

IMPORTERS > IMPORT

IMPORTING > IMPORT

IMPORTS > IMPORT

IMPORTUNE vb harass with persistent requests

IMPOSABLE > IMPOSE

IMPOSE vb force the acceptance of

IMPOSED > IMPOSE

IMPOSER > IMPOSE

IMPOSERS > IMPOSE

IMPOSES > IMPOSE

IMPOSEX n acquisition by female organisms of male characteristics

IMPOSEXES > IMPOSEX

IMPOSING adj grand, impressive

IMPOST n tax, esp a customs duty ▷ vb classify (imported goods) according to the duty payable on them

IMPOSTED > IMPOST

IMPOSTER > IMPOST

IMPOSTERS > IMPOST

IMPOSTING > IMPOST

IMPOSTOR n person who cheats or swindles by pretending to be someone else

IMPOSTORS > IMPOSTOR

IMPOSTS > IMPOST

IMPOSTUME archaic word for > ABSCESS

IMPOSTURE n deception, esp by pretending to be someone else

IMPOT n slang term for the act of imposing

IMPOTENCE > IMPOTENT

IMPOTENCY > IMPOTENT

IMPOTENT n one who is impotent ▷ adj powerless

IMPOTENTS > IMPOTENT

IMPOTS > IMPOT

IMPOUND vb take legal possession of, confiscate

IMPOUNDED > IMPOUND

IMPOUNDER > IMPOUND

IMPOUNDS > IMPOUND

IMPOWER less common spelling of > EMPOWER

IMPOWERED > IMPOWER

IMPOWERS > IMPOWER

IMPRECATE vb swear, curse, or blaspheme

IMPRECISE adj inexact or inaccurate

IMPREGN vb impregnate

IMPREGNED > IMPREGN

IMPREGNS > IMPREGN

IMPRESA n heraldic device

IMPRESARI n impresarios

IMPRESAS > IMPRESA

IMPRESE same as > IMPRESA

IMPRESES > IMPRESE

IMPRESS vb affect strongly, usu favourably ▷ n impressing

IMPRESSE n heraldic device

IMPRESSED > IMPRESS

IMPRESSER > IMPRESS

IMPRESSES > IMPRESS

IMPREST n fund of cash used to pay incidental expenses

IMPRESTS > IMPREST

IMPRIMIS adv in the first place

IMPRINT n mark made by printing or stamping

▷ vb produce (a mark) by printing or stamping

IMPRINTED > IMPRINT

IMPRINTER > IMPRINT

IMPRINTS > IMPRINT

IMPRISON vb put in prison

IMPRISONS > IMPRISON

IMPRO n short for improvisation

IMPROBITY n dishonesty or wickedness

IMPROMPTU adj without planning or preparation ▷ adv in a spontaneous or improvised way ▷ n short piece of instrumental music resembling improvisation

IMPROPER adj indecent

IMPROS > IMPRO

IMPROV n improvisational comedy

IMPROVE vb make or become better

IMPROVED > IMPROVE

IMPROVER > IMPROVE

IMPROVERS > IMPROVE

IMPROVES > IMPROVE

IMPROVING > IMPROVE

IMPROVISE vb make use of whatever materials are available

IMPROVS > IMPROV

IMPRUDENT adj not sensible or wise

IMPS > IMP

IMPSONITE n asphaltite compound

IMPUDENCE n quality of being impudent

IMPUDENCY same as > IMPUDENCE

IMPUDENT adj cheeky, disrespectful

IMPUGN vb challenge the truth or validity of

IMPUGNED > IMPUGN

IMPUGNER > IMPUGN

IMPUGNERS > IMPUGN

IMPUGNING > IMPUGN

IMPUGNS > IMPUGN

IMPULSE vb give an impulse to ▷ n sudden urge to do something

IMPULSED > IMPULSE

IMPULSES > IMPULSE

IMPULSING > IMPULSE

IMPULSION n act of impelling or the state of being impelled

IMPULSIVE adj acting or done without careful consideration

IMPUNDULU n mythical bird associated with witchcraft, frequently manifested as the secretary bird

IMPUNITY n exemption or immunity from punishment or recrimination

IMPURE adj having dirty or unwanted substances mixed in

IMPURELY > IMPURE

IMPURER > IMPURE

IMPUREST > IMPURE

IMPURITY n impure element or thing

IMPURPLE vb colour purple

IMPURPLED > IMPURPLE

IMPURPLES > IMPURPLE

IMPUTABLE adj capable of being imputed

IMPUTABLY > IMPUTABLE

IMPUTE vb attribute responsibility to

IMPUTED > IMPUTE

IMPUTER > IMPUTE

IMPUTERS > IMPUTE

IMPUTES > IMPUTE

IMPUTING > IMPUTE

IMSHI interj go away!

IMSHY same as > IMSHI

IN prep indicating position inside, state or situation, etc ▷ adv indicating position inside, entry into, etc ▷ adj fashionable ▷ n way of approaching or befriending a person ▷ vb take in

INABILITY n lack of means or skill to do something

INACTION n act of doing nothing

INACTIONS > INACTION

INACTIVE adj idle

INAIDABLE adj beyond help

INAMORATA n woman with whom one is in love

INAMORATI > INAMORATO

INAMORATO n man with whom one is in love

INANE adj senseless, silly ▷ n something that is inane

INANELY > INANE

INANENESS > INANE

INANER > INANE

INANES > INANE

INANEST > INANE

INANGA n common type of New Zealand grass tree

INANGAS > INANGA

INANIMATE adj not living

INANITIES > INANITY

INANITION n exhaustion or weakness, as from lack of food

INANITY n lack of intelligence or imagination

INAPT adj not apt or fitting

INAPTLY > INAPT

INAPTNESS > INAPT

INARABLE adj not arable

INARCH vb graft (a plant)

INARCHED > INARCH

INARCHES > INARCH

INARCHING > INARCH

INARM vb embrace

INARMED > INARM

INARMING > INARM

INARMS > INARM

INASMUCH conj as in inasmuch as , in view of the fact that

INAUDIBLE adj not loud enough to be heard

INAUDIBLY > INAUDIBLE

INAUGURAL adj of or for an inauguration ▷ n speech made at an inauguration

INAURATE adj gilded ▷ vb cover in gold

INAURATED > INAURATE

INAURATES > INAURATE

INBEING n existence in something else

INBEINGS > INBEING

INBENT adj bent inwards

INBOARD adj (of a boat's engine) inside the hull ▷ adv within the sides of or towards the centre of a vessel or aircraft

INBOARDS same as > INBOARD

INBORN adj existing from birth, natural

INBOUND vb pass into the playing area from outside it ▷ adj coming in

INBOUNDED > INBOUND

INBOUNDS > INBOUND

INBOX n folder which stores in-coming email messages

INBOXES > INBOX

INBREAK n breaking in

INBREAKS > INBREAK

INBREATHE vb infuse or imbue

INBRED n inbred person or animal ▷ adj produced as a result of inbreeding

INBREDS > INBRED

INBREED vb breed from closely related individuals

INBREEDER > INBREED

INBREEDS > INBREED

INBRING vb bring in

INBRINGS > INBRING

INBROUGHT > INBRING

INBUILT adj present from the start

INBURNING adj burning within

INBURST n irruption ▷ vb burst in

INBURSTS > INBURST

INBY adv into the house or an inner room ▷ adj located near or nearest to the house

INBYE adv near the house

INCAGE vb confine in or as in a cage

INCAGED > INCAGE

INCAGES > INCAGE

INCAGING > INCAGE

INCANT vb chant (a spell)
INCANTED > INCANT
INCANTING > INCANT
INCANTS > INCANT
INCAPABLE adj unable (to do something)
INCAPABLY > INCAPABLE
INCARNATE adj in human form ▷ vb give a bodily or concrete form to
INCASE variant spelling of > ENCASE
INCASED > INCASE
INCASES > INCASE
INCASING > INCASE
INCAUTION n act of not being cautious
INCAVE vb hide
INCAVED > INCAVE
INCAVES > INCAVE
INCAVI > INCAVO
INCAVING > INCAVE
INCAVO n incised part of a carving
INCEDE vb advance
INCEDED > INCEDE
INCEDES > INCEDE
INCEDING > INCEDE
INCENSE vb make very angry ▷ n substance that gives off a perfume when burned
INCENSED > INCENSE
INCENSER n incense burner
INCENSERS > INCENSER
INCENSES > INCENSE
INCENSING > INCENSE
INCENSOR n incense burner
INCENSORS > INCENSOR
INCENSORY less common name for > CENSER
INCENT vb provide incentive
INCENTED > INCENT
INCENTER same as > INCENTRE
INCENTERS > INCENTER
INCENTING > INCENT
INCENTIVE n something that encourages effort or action ▷ adj encouraging greater effort
INCENTRE n centre of an inscribed circle
INCENTRES > INCENTRE
INCENTS > INCENT
INCEPT vb (of organisms) to ingest (food) ▷ n rudimentary organ
INCEPTED > INCEPT
INCEPTING > INCEPT
INCEPTION n beginning
INCEPTIVE adj beginning ▷ n type of verb
INCEPTOR > INCEPT
INCEPTORS > INCEPT
INCEPTS > INCEPT
INCERTAIN archaic form of > UNCERTAIN

INCESSANT adj never stopping
INCEST n sexual intercourse between two closely related people
INCESTS > INCEST
INCH n unit of length ▷ vb move slowly and gradually
INCHASE same as > ENCHASE
INCHASED > INCHASE
INCHASES > INCHASE
INCHASING > INCHASE
INCHED > INCH
INCHER n something measuring given amount of inches
INCHERS > INCHER
INCHES > INCH
INCHING > INCH
INCHMEAL adv gradually
INCHOATE adj just begun and not yet properly developed ▷ vb begin
INCHOATED > INCHOATE
INCHOATES > INCHOATE
INCHPIN n cervine sweetbread
INCHPINS > INCHPIN
INCHTAPE n measuring tape marked out in inches
INCHTAPES > INCHTAPE
INCHWORM n larva of a type of moth
INCHWORMS > INCHWORM
INCIDENCE n extent or frequency of occurrence
INCIDENT n something that happens ▷ adj related (to) or dependent (on)
INCIDENTS > INCIDENT
INCIPIENT adj just starting to appear or happen
INCIPIT n Latin introductory phrase
INCIPITS > INCIPIT
INCISAL adj relating to the cutting edge of incisors and cuspids
INCISE vb cut into with a sharp tool
INCISED > INCISE
INCISES > INCISE
INCISING > INCISE
INCISION n cut, esp one made during a surgical operation
INCISIONS > INCISION
INCISIVE adj direct and forceful
INCISOR n front tooth, used for biting into food
INCISORS > INCISOR
INCISORY > INCISOR
INCISURAL > INCISURE
INCISURE n incision or notch in an organ or part
INCISURES > INCISURE
INCITABLE > INCITE
INCITANT n something that incites
INCITANTS > INCITANT

INCITE vb stir up, provoke
INCITED > INCITE
INCITER > INCITE
INCITERS > INCITE
INCITES > INCITE
INCITING > INCITE
INCIVIL archaic form of > UNCIVIL
INCIVISM n neglect of a citizen's duties
INCIVISMS > INCIVISM
INCLASP vb clasp
INCLASPED > INCLASP
INCLASPS > INCLASP
INCLE same as > INKLE
INCLEMENT adj (of weather) stormy or severe
INCLES > INCLE
INCLINE vb lean, slope ▷ n slope
INCLINED adj having a disposition
INCLINER > INCLINE
INCLINERS > INCLINE
INCLINES > INCLINE
INCLINING > INCLINE
INCLIP vb embrace
INCLIPPED > INCLIP
INCLIPS > INCLIP
INCLOSE less common spelling of > ENCLOSE
INCLOSED > INCLOSE
INCLOSER > INCLOSE
INCLOSERS > INCLOSE
INCLOSES > INCLOSE
INCLOSING > INCLOSE
INCLOSURE > INCLOSE
INCLUDE vb have as part of the whole
INCLUDED adj (of the stamens or pistils of a flower) not protruding beyond the corolla
INCLUDES > INCLUDE
INCLUDING > INCLUDE
INCLUSION n including or being included
INCLUSIVE adj including everything (specified)
INCOG n incognito
INCOGNITA n female who is in disguise or unknown
INCOGNITO adv having adopted a false identity ▷ n false identity ▷ adj under an assumed name or appearance
INCOGS > INCOG
INCOME n amount of money earned
INCOMER n person who comes to a place in which they were not born
INCOMERS > INCOMER
INCOMES > INCOME
INCOMING adj coming in ▷ n act of coming in
INCOMINGS > INCOMING
INCOMMODE vb cause inconvenience to
INCOMPACT adj not compact

INCONDITE adj poorly constructed or composed
INCONIE adj fine or delicate
INCONNU n whitefish of Arctic waters
INCONNUE n unknown woman
INCONNUES > INCONNUE
INCONNUS > INCONNU
INCONY adj fine or delicate
INCORPSE vb incorporate
INCORPSED > INCORPSE
INCORPSES > INCORPSE
INCORRECT adj wrong
INCORRUPT adj free from corruption
INCREASE vb make or become greater in size, number, etc ▷ n rise in number, size, etc
INCREASED > INCREASE
INCREASER > INCREASE
INCREASES > INCREASE
INCREATE adj (esp of gods) never having been created
INCREMATE vb cremate
INCREMENT n increase in money or value, esp a regular salary increase
INCRETION n direct secretion into the bloodstream, esp of a hormone from an endocrine gland
INCRETORY > INCRETION
INCROSS n variation produced by inbreeding ▷ vb produce by inbreeding
INCROSSED > INCROSS
INCROSSES > INCROSS
INCRUST same as > ENCRUST
INCRUSTED > INCRUST
INCRUSTS > INCRUST
INCUBATE vb (of a bird) hatch (eggs) by sitting on them
INCUBATED > INCUBATE
INCUBATES > INCUBATE
INCUBATOR n heated enclosed apparatus for rearing premature babies
INCUBI > INCUBUS
INCUBOUS adj (of a liverwort) having the leaves arranged so that the upper margin of each leaf lies above the lower margin of the next leaf along
INCUBUS n (in folklore) type of demon
INCUBUSES > INCUBUS
INCUDAL > INCUS
INCUDATE > INCUS
INCUDES > INCUS
INCULCATE vb fix in someone's mind by constant repetition
INCULPATE vb cause (someone) to be blamed for a crime

INCULT adj (of land) uncultivated

INCUMBENT n person who holds a particular office or position ▷ adj morally binding as a duty

INCUMBER less common spelling of ENCUMBER

INCUMBERS > INCUMBER

INCUNABLE n early printed book

INCUR vb cause (something unpleasant) to happen

INCURABLE adj not able to be cured ▷ n person with an incurable disease

INCURABLY > INCURABLE

INCURIOUS adj showing no curiosity or interest

INCURRED > INCUR

INCURRENT adj (of anatomical ducts, tubes, channels, etc) having an inward flow

INCURRING > INCUR

INCURS > INCUR

INCURSION n sudden brief invasion

INCURSIVE > INCURSION

INCURVATE vb curve or cause to curve inwards ▷ adj curved inwards

INCURVE vb curve or cause to curve inwards

INCURVED > INCURVE

INCURVES > INCURVE

INCURVING > INCURVE

INCURVITY > INCURVE

INCUS n bone in the ear of mammals

INCUSE n design stamped or hammered onto a coin ▷ vb impress (a design) in a coin ▷ adj stamped or hammered onto a coin

INCUSED > INCUSE

INCUSES > INCUSE

INCUSING > INCUSE

INCUT adj cut or etched in ▷ n (in rock climbing) indent cut into the face of the rock, which can be used as a handhold or foothold

INCUTS > INCUT

INDABA n (among South Africans) a meeting to discuss a serious topic

INDABAS > INDABA

INDAGATE vb investigate

INDAGATED > INDAGATE

INDAGATES > INDAGATE

INDAGATOR > INDAGATE

INDAMIN same as > INDAMINE

INDAMINE n organic base used in the production of the dye safranine

INDAMINES > INDAMINE

INDAMINS > INDAMIN

INDART vb dart in

INDARTED > INDART

INDARTING > INDART

INDARTS > INDART

INDEBTED adj owing gratitude for help or favours

INDECENCY n state or quality of being indecent

INDECENT adj morally or sexually offensive

INDECORUM n indecorous behaviour or speech

INDEED adv really, certainly ▷ interj expression of indignation or surprise

INDEEDY interj indeed

INDELIBLE adj impossible to erase or remove

INDELIBLY > INDELIBLE

INDEMNIFY vb secure against loss, damage, or liability

INDEMNITY n insurance against loss or damage

INDENE n colourless liquid hydrocarbon

INDENES > INDENE

INDENT vb make a dent in

INDENTED > INDENT

INDENTER > INDENT

INDENTERS > INDENT

INDENTING > INDENT

INDENTION n space between a margin and the start of the line of text

INDENTOR > INDENT

INDENTORS > INDENT

INDENTS > INDENT

INDENTURE n contract, esp one binding an apprentice to his or her employer ▷ vb bind (an apprentice) by indenture

INDEVOUT adj not devout

INDEW same as > INDUE

INDEWED > INDEW

INDEWING > INDEW

INDEWS > INDEW

INDEX n alphabetical list of subjects dealt with in a book ▷ vb provide (a book) with an index

INDEXABLE > INDEX

INDEXAL > INDEX

INDEXED > INDEX

INDEXER > INDEX

INDEXERS > INDEX

INDEXES > INDEX

INDEXICAL adj arranged as or relating to an index or indexes ▷ n term whose reference depends on the context of utterance

INDEXING > INDEX

INDEXINGS > INDEX

INDEXLESS > INDEX

INDIA n code word for the letter I

INDIAS > INDIA

INDICAN n compound secreted in the urine

INDICANS > INDICAN

INDICANT n something that indicates

INDICANTS > INDICANT

INDICATE vb be a sign or symptom of

INDICATED > INDICATE

INDICATES > INDICATE

INDICATOR n something acting as a sign or indication

INDICES plural of > INDEX

INDICIA > INDICIUM

INDICIAL > INDICIUM

INDICIAS > INDICIUM

INDICIUM n notice

INDICIUMS > INDICIUM

INDICT vb formally charge with a crime

INDICTED > INDICT

INDICTEE > INDICT

INDICTEES > INDICT

INDICTER > INDICT

INDICTERS > INDICT

INDICTING > INDICT

INDICTION n recurring fiscal period of 15 years, often used as a unit for dating events

INDICTOR > INDICT

INDICTORS > INDICT

INDICTS > INDICT

INDIE adj (of rock music) released by an independent record label ▷ n independent record company

INDIES > INDIE

INDIGEN same as > INDIGENE

INDIGENCE > INDIGENT

INDIGENCY > INDIGENT

INDIGENE n indigenous person, animal, or thing

INDIGENES > INDIGENE

INDIGENS > INDIGEN

INDIGENT adj extremely poor ▷ n impoverished person

INDIGENTS > INDIGENT

INDIGEST n undigested mass ▷ vb suffer indigestion

INDIGESTS > INDIGEST

INDIGN adj undeserving

INDIGNANT adj feeling or showing indignation

INDIGNIFY vb treat in a humiliating manner

INDIGNITY n embarrassing or humiliating treatment

INDIGNLY > INDIGN

INDIGO adj deep violet-blue ▷ n dye of this colour

INDIGOES > INDIGO

INDIGOID adj of, concerned with, or resembling indigo or its blue colour ▷ n any of a number of synthetic dyes or pigments related in chemical structure to indigo

INDIGOIDS > INDIGOID

INDIGOS > INDIGO

INDIGOTIC > INDIGO

INDIGOTIN same as > INDIGO

INDINAVIR n drug used to treat AIDS

INDIRECT adj done or caused by someone or something else

INDIRUBIN n isomer of indigotin

INDISPOSE vb make unwilling or opposed

INDITE vb write

INDITED > INDITE

INDITER > INDITE

INDITERS > INDITE

INDITES > INDITE

INDITING > INDITE

INDIUM n soft silvery-white metallic element

INDIUMS > INDIUM

INDIVIDUA pl n indivisible entities

INDOCIBLE same as > INDOCILE

INDOCILE adj difficult to discipline or instruct

INDOL same as > INDOLE

INDOLE n crystalline heterocyclic compound

INDOLENCE > INDOLENT

INDOLENCY n laziness

INDOLENT adj lazy

INDOLES > INDOLE

INDOLS > INDOL

INDOOR adj inside a building

INDOORS adj inside or into a building

INDORSE variant spelling of > ENDORSE

INDORSED > INDORSE

INDORSEE n the person to whom a note or bill is indorsed

INDORSEES > INDORSE

INDORSER > INDORSE

INDORSERS > INDORSE

INDORSES > INDORSE

INDORSING > INDORSE

INDORSOR > INDORSE

INDORSORS > INDORSE

INDOW archaic variant of > INDOW

INDOWED > INDOW

INDOWING > INDOW

INDOWS > INDOW

INDOXYL n water-soluble crystalline compound

INDOXYLS > INDOXYL

INDRAFT same as > INDRAUGHT

INDRAFTS > INDRAFT

INDRAUGHT n act of drawing or pulling in

INDRAWN adj drawn or pulled in

INDRENCH vb submerge

INDRI same as > INDRIS

INDRIS n large lemuroid primate

INDRISES > INDRIS

INDUBIOUS adj certain

INDUCE vb persuade or influence

INDUCED > INDUCE

INDUCER > INDUCE

INDUCERS > INDUCE

INDUCES > INDUCE

INDUCIAE n time limit for a defendant to appear in court

INDUCIBLE > INDUCE

INDUCING > INDUCE

INDUCT vb formally install (someone) in office

INDUCTED > INDUCT

INDUCTEE n military conscript

INDUCTEES > INDUCTEE

INDUCTILE adj not ductile, pliant, or yielding

INDUCTING > INDUCT

INDUCTION n the act of inducing

INDUCTIVE adj of or using induction

INDUCTOR n device designed to create inductance in an electrical circuit

INDUCTORS > INDUCTOR

INDUCTS > INDUCT

INDUE variant spelling of > ENDUE

INDUED > INDUE

INDUES > INDUE

INDUING > INDUE

INDULGE vb allow oneself pleasure

INDULGED > INDULGE

INDULGENT adj kind or lenient, often to excess

INDULGER > INDULGE

INDULGERS > INDULGE

INDULGES > INDULGE

INDULGING > INDULGE

INDULIN same as > INDULINE

INDULINE n any of a class of blue dyes obtained from aniline and aminoazobenzene

INDULINES > INDULINE

INDULINS > INDULIN

INDULT n type of faculty granted by the Holy See

INDULTS > INDULT

INDUMENTA pl n outer coverings of feather, fur, etc

INDUNA n (in South Africa) a Black African overseer

INDUNAS > INDUNA

INDURATE vb make or become hard or callous ▷ adj hardened, callous, or unfeeling

INDURATED > INDURATE

INDURATES > INDURATE

INDUSIA > INDUSIUM

INDUSIAL > INDUSIUM

INDUSIATE adj covered in indusia

INDUSIUM n membranous outgrowth on the undersurface of fern leaves that covers and protects the developing sporangia

INDUSTRY n manufacture of goods

INDUVIAE pl n withered leaves

INDUVIAL > INDUVIAE

INDUVIATE > INDUVIAE

INDWELL vb (of a spirit, principle, etc) to inhabit

INDWELLER > INDWELL

INDWELLS > INDWELL

INDWELT > INDWELL

INEARTH poetic word for > BURY

INEARTHED > INEARTH

INEARTHS > INEARTH

INEBRIANT adj causing intoxication, esp drunkenness ▷ n something that inebriates

INEBRIATE adj (person who is) habitually drunk ▷ n person who is habitually drunk ▷ vb make drunk

INEBRIETY > INEBRIATE

INEBRIOUS adj drunk

INEDIBLE adj not fit to be eaten

INEDIBLY > INEDIBLE

INEDITA pl n unpublished writings

INEDITED adj not edited

INEFFABLE adj too great for words

INEFFABLY > INEFFABLE

INELASTIC adj not elastic

INELEGANT adj lacking elegance or refinement

INEPT adj clumsy, lacking skill

INEPTER > INEPT

INEPTEST > INEPT

INEPTLY > INEPT

INEPTNESS > INEPT

INEQUABLE adj unfair

INEQUITY n injustice or unfairness

INERM adj without thorns

INERMOUS same as > INERM

INERRABLE adj not liable to error ▷ n person or thing that is incapable of error

INERRABLY > INERRABLE

INERRANCY > INERRABLE

INERRANT same as > INERRABLE

INERT n inert thing ▷ adj without the power of motion or resistance

INERTER > INERT

INERTEST > INERT

INERTIA n feeling of unwillingness to do anything

INERTIAE > INERTIA

INERTIAL > INERTIA

INERTIAS > INERTIA

INERTLY > INERT

INERTNESS > INERT

INERTS > INERT

INERUDITE adj not erudite

INESSIVE n grammatical case in Finnish

INESSIVES > INESSIVE

INEXACT adj not exact or accurate

INEXACTLY > INEXACT

INEXPERT n unskilled person ▷ adj lacking skill

INEXPERTS > INEXPERT

INFALL vb move towards (something) under the influence of gravity

INFALLING > INFALL

INFALLS > INFALL

INFAME vb defame

INFAMED > INFAME

INFAMES > INFAME

INFAMIES > INFAMY

INFAMING > INFAME

INFAMISE same as > INFAMIZE

INFAMISED > INFAMISE

INFAMISES > INFAMISE

INFAMIZE vb make infamous

INFAMIZED > INFAMIZE

INFAMIZES > INFAMIZE

INFAMOUS adj well-known for something bad

INFAMY n state of being infamous

INFANCIES > INFANCY

INFANCY n early childhood

INFANT n very young child ▷ adj of, relating to, or designed for young children

INFANTA n (formerly) daughter of a king of Spain or Portugal

INFANTAS > INFANTA

INFANTE n (formerly) any son of a king of Spain or Portugal, except the heir to the throne

INFANTEER n solider belonging to the infantry

INFANTES > INFANTE

INFANTILE adj childish

INFANTINE adj infantile

INFANTRY n soldiers who , fight on foot

INFANTS > INFANT

INFARCT n localized area of dead tissue ▷ vb obstruct the blood supply to part of a body

INFARCTED > INFARCT

INFARCTS > INFARCT

INFARE vb enter

INFARES > INFARE

INFATUATE vb inspire or fill with an intense and unreasoning passion ▷ n person who is infatuated

INFAUNA n animals that live in ocean and river beds

INFAUNAE > INFAUNA

INFAUNAL > INFAUNA

INFAUNAS > INFAUNA

INFAUST adj unlucky

INFECT vb affect with a disease ▷ adj contaminated or polluted with or as if with a disease

INFECTANT adj causing infection ▷ n thing that infects or causes infection

INFECTED > INFECT

INFECTER > INFECT

INFECTERS > INFECT

INFECTING > INFECT

INFECTION n infectious disease

INFECTIVE adj capable of causing infection

INFECTOR > INFECT

INFECTORS > INFECT

INFECTS > INFECT

INFECUND less common word for > INFERTILE

INFEED n action of supplying a machine with a material

INFEEDS > INFEED

INFEFT vb give possession of heritable property

INFEFTED > INFEFT

INFEFTING > INFEFT

INFEFTS > INFEFT

INFELT adj heartfelt

INFEOFF same as > ENFEOFF

INFEOFFED > INFEOFF

INFEOFFS > INFEOFF

INFER vb work out from evidence

INFERABLE > INFER

INFERABLY > INFER

INFERE adv together

INFERENCE n act or process of reaching a conclusion by reasoning from evidence

INFERIAE pl n offerings made to the spirits of the dead

INFERIBLE > INFER

INFERIOR adj lower in quality, position, or status ▷ n person of lower position or status

INFERIORS > INFERIOR

INFERNAL adj of hell

INFERNO n intense raging fire

INFERNOS > INFERNO

INFERRED > INFER
INFERRER > INFER
INFERRERS > INFER
INFERRING > INFER
INFERS > INFER
INFERTILE adj unable to produce offspring
INFEST vb inhabit or overrun in unpleasantly large numbers
INFESTANT n parasite
INFESTED > INFEST
INFESTER > INFEST
INFESTERS > INFEST
INFESTING > INFEST
INFESTS > INFEST
INFICETE adj not witty
INFIDEL n person with no religion ▷ adj of unbelievers or unbelief
INFIDELIC > INFIDEL
INFIDELS > INFIDEL
INFIELD n area of the field near the pitch
INFIELDER n player positioned in the infield
INFIELDS > INFIELD
INFIGHT vb box at close quarters
INFIGHTER > INFIGHT
INFIGHTS > INFIGHT
INFILL vb fill in ▷ n act of filling or closing gaps in something
INFILLED > INFILL
INFILLING > INFILL
INFILLS > INFILL
INFIMA > INFIMUM
INFIMUM n greatest lower bound
INFIMUMS > INFIMUM
INFINITE adj without any limit or end ▷ n something without any limit or end
INFINITES > INFINITE
INFINITY n endless space, time, or number
INFIRM vb make infirm ▷ adj physically or mentally weak
INFIRMARY n hospital
INFIRMED > INFIRM
INFIRMER > INFIRM
INFIRMEST > INFIRM
INFIRMING > INFIRM
INFIRMITY n state of being infirm
INFIRMLY > INFIRM
INFIRMS > INFIRM
INFIX vb fix firmly in ▷ n affix inserted into the middle of a word
INFIXED > INFIX
INFIXES > INFIX
INFIXING > INFIX
INFIXION > INFIX
INFIXIONS > INFIX
INFLAME vb make angry or excited
INFLAMED > INFLAME
INFLAMER > INFLAME
INFLAMERS > INFLAME

INFLAMES > INFLAME
INFLAMING > INFLAME
INFLATE vb expand by filling with air or gas
INFLATED > INFLATE
INFLATER > INFLATE
INFLATERS > INFLATE
INFLATES > INFLATE
INFLATING > INFLATE
INFLATION n inflating
INFLATIVE adj causing inflation
INFLATOR > INFLATE
INFLATORS > INFLATE
INFLATUS n act of breathing in
INFLECT vb change (the voice) in tone or pitch
INFLECTED > INFLECT
INFLECTOR > INFLECT
INFLECTS > INFLECT
INFLEXED adj curved or bent inwards or downwards towards the axis
INFLEXION n modulation of the voice
INFLEXURE same as > INFLEXION
INFLICT vb impose (something unpleasant) on
INFLICTED > INFLICT
INFLICTER > INFLICT
INFLICTOR > INFLICT
INFLICTS > INFLICT
INFLIGHT adj provided during flight in an aircraft
INFLOW n something, such as liquid or gas, that flows in ▷ vb flow in
INFLOWING same as > INFLOW
INFLOWS > INFLOW
INFLUENCE n effect of one person or thing on another ▷ vb have an effect on
INFLUENT adj flowing in ▷ n something flowing in, esp a tributary
INFLUENTS > INFLUENT
INFLUENZA n contagious viral disease causing headaches, muscle pains, and fever
INFLUX n arrival or entry of many people or things
INFLUXES > INFLUX
INFLUXION same as > INFLUX
INFO n information
INFOBAHN same as > INTERNET
INFOBAHNS > INFOBAHN
INFOLD variant spelling of > ENFOLD
INFOLDED > INFOLD
INFOLDER > INFOLD
INFOLDERS > INFOLD
INFOLDING > INFOLD
INFOLDS > INFOLD
INFOMANIA n obsessive devotion to gathering information

INFORCE same as > ENFORCE
INFORCED > INFORCE
INFORCES > INFORCE
INFORCING > INFORCE
INFORM vb tell ▷ adj without shape
INFORMAL adj relaxed and friendly
INFORMANT n person who gives information
INFORMED > INFORM
INFORMER n person who informs to the police
INFORMERS > INFORMER
INFORMING > INFORM
INFORMS > INFORM
INFORTUNE n misfortune
INFOS > INFO
INFOTECH n information technology
INFOTECHS > INFOTECH
INFOUGHT > INFIGHT
INFRA adv (esp in textual annotation) below
INFRACT vb violate or break (a law, an agreement, etc)
INFRACTED > INFRACT
INFRACTOR > INFRACT
INFRACTS > INFRACT
INFRARED adj of or using rays below the red end of the visible spectrum ▷ n infrared part of the spectrum
INFRAREDS > INFRARED
INFRINGE vb break (a law or agreement)
INFRINGED > INFRINGE
INFRINGER > INFRINGE
INFRINGES > INFRINGE
INFRUGAL adj wasteful
INFULA same as > INFULAE
INFULAE pl n two ribbons hanging from a bishop's mitre
INFURIATE vb make very angry ▷ adj furious
INFUSCATE adj (esp of the wings of an insect) tinged with brown
INFUSE vb fill (with an emotion or quality)
INFUSED > INFUSE
INFUSER n any device used to make an infusion
INFUSERS > INFUSER
INFUSES > INFUSE
INFUSIBLE adj unable to be fused or melted
INFUSING > INFUSE
INFUSION n infusing
INFUSIONS > INFUSION
INFUSIVE > INFUSION
INFUSORIA pl n tiny water-dwelling animals
INFUSORY adj containing infusoria ▷ n infusorian, a tiny water-dwelling animal
ING n meadow near a river
INGAN Scots word for > ONION

INGANS > INGAN
INGATE n entrance
INGATES > INGATE
INGATHER vb gather together or in (a harvest)
INGATHERS > INGATHER
INGENER Shakespearean form of > ENGINEER
INGENERS > INGENER
INGENIOUS adj showing cleverness and originality
INGENIUM n genius
INGENIUMS > INGENIUM
INGENU n artless or inexperienced boy or young man
INGENUE n inexperienced girl or young woman
INGENUES > INGENUE
INGENUITY n cleverness at inventing things
INGENUOUS adj unsophisticated and trusting
INGENUS > INGENU
INGEST vb take (food or liquid) into the body
INGESTA pl n nourishment taken through the mouth
INGESTED > INGEST
INGESTING > INGEST
INGESTION > INGEST
INGESTIVE > INGEST
INGESTS > INGEST
INGINE n genius
INGINES > INGINE
INGLE n fire in a room or a fireplace
INGLENEUK same as > INGLENOOK
INGLENOOK n corner by a fireplace
INGLES > INGLE
INGLOBE vb shape as a sphere
INGLOBED > INGLOBE
INGLOBES > INGLOBE
INGLOBING > INGLOBE
INGLUVIAL > INGLUVIES
INGLUVIES n bird's craw
INGO n revelation
INGOES > INGO
INGOING same as > INGO
INGOINGS > INGO
INGOT n oblong block of cast metal ▷ vb shape (metal) into ingots
INGOTED > INGOT
INGOTING > INGOT
INGOTS > INGOT
INGRAFT variant spelling of > ENGRAFT
INGRAFTED > INGRAFT
INGRAFTS > INGRAFT
INGRAIN vb impress deeply on the mind or nature ▷ adj (of carpets) made of fibre that is dyed before being spun ▷ n carpet made from ingrained yarn
INGRAINED > INGRAIN

INGRAINER n person who ingrains

INGRAINS > INGRAIN

INGRAM adj ignorant ▷ n ignorant person

INGRAMS > INGRAM

INGRATE n ungrateful person ▷ adj ungrateful

INGRATELY > INGRATE

INGRATES > INGRATE

INGRESS n entrance

INGRESSES > INGRESS

INGROOVE vb cut a groove into

INGROOVED > INGROOVE

INGROOVES > INGROOVE

INGROSS archaic form of > ENGROSS

INGROSSED > INGROSS

INGROSSES > INGROSS

INGROUND adj sunk into ground ▷ vb fix (something) in the ground or in a foundation

INGROUNDS > INGROUND

INGROUP n highly cohesive and relatively closed social group

INGROUPS > INGROUP

INGROWING adj (of a toenail) growing abnormally into the flesh

INGROWN adj grown abnormally into the flesh

INGROWTH n act of growing inwards

INGROWTHS > INGROWTH

INGRUM adj ignorant ▷ n ignorant person

INGRUMS > INGRUM

INGS > ING

INGUINAL adj of or relating to the groin

INGULF variant spelling of > ENGULF

INGULFED > INGULF

INGULFING > INGULF

INGULFS > INGULF

INGULPH archaic form of > ENGULF

INGULPHED > INGULPH

INGULPHS > INGULPH

INHABIT vb live in

INHABITED > INHABIT

INHABITER n inhabitant

INHABITOR n inhabitant

INHABITS > INHABIT

INHALABLE adj that can be inhaled

INHALANT n medical preparation inhaled to help breathing problems ▷ adj inhaled for its soothing or therapeutic effect

INHALANTS > INHALANT

INHALATOR n device for converting drugs into a fine spray for inhaling

INHALE vb breathe in (air, smoke, etc)

INHALED > INHALE

INHALER n container for an inhalant

INHALERS > INHALER

INHALES > INHALE

INHALING > INHALE

INHARMONY n discord

INHAUL n line for hauling in a sail

INHAULER same as > INHAUL

INHAULERS > INHAULER

INHAULS > INHAUL

INHAUST vb drink in

INHAUSTED > INHAUST

INHAUSTS > INHAUST

INHEARSE vb bury

INHEARSED > INHEARSE

INHEARSES > INHEARSE

INHERCE same as > INHEARSE

INHERCED > INHERCE

INHERCES > INHERCE

INHERCING > INHERCE

INHERE vb be an inseparable part (of)

INHERED > INHERE

INHERENCE n state or condition of being inherent

INHERENCY same as > INHERENCE

INHERENT adj existing as an inseparable part

INHERES > INHERE

INHERING > INHERE

INHERIT vb receive (money etc) from someone who has died

INHERITED > INHERIT

INHERITOR > INHERIT

INHERITS > INHERIT

INHESION less common word for > INHERENCE

INHESIONS > INHESION

INHIBIN n peptide hormone

INHIBINS > INHIBIN

INHIBIT vb restrain (an impulse or desire)

INHIBITED > INHIBIT

INHIBITER same as > INHIBITOR

INHIBITOR n person or thing that inhibits

INHIBITS > INHIBIT

INHOLDER n inhabitant

INHOLDERS > INHOLDER

INHOLDING n privately owned land inside a federal reserve

INHOOP vb confine

INHOOPED > INHOOP

INHOOPING > INHOOP

INHOOPS > INHOOP

INHUMAN adj cruel or brutal

INHUMANE same as > INHUMAN

INHUMANLY > INHUMAN

INHUMATE vb bury

INHUMATED > INHUMATE

INHUMATES > INHUMATE

INHUME vb inter

INHUMED > INHUME

INHUMER > INHUME

INHUMERS > INHUME

INHUMES > INHUME

INHUMING > INHUME

INIA > INION

INIMICAL adj unfavourable or hostile

INION n most prominent point at the back of the head

INIONS > INION

INIQUITY n injustice or wickedness

INISLE vb put on or make into an island

INISLED > INISLE

INISLES > INISLE

INISLING > INISLE

INITIAL adj first, at the beginning ▷ n first letter, esp of a person's name ▷ vb sign with one's initials

INITIALED > INITIAL

INITIALER > INITIAL

INITIALLY > INITIAL

INITIALS > INITIAL

INITIATE vb begin or set going ▷ n recently initiated person ▷ adj initiated

INITIATED > INITIATE

INITIATES > INITIATE

INITIATOR n person or thing that initiates

INJECT vb put (a fluid) into the body with a syringe

INJECTANT n injected substance

INJECTED > INJECT

INJECTING > INJECT

INJECTION n fluid injected into the body, esp for medicinal purposes

INJECTIVE > INJECTION

INJECTOR same as > INJECT

INJECTORS > INJECT

INJECTS > INJECT

INJELLIED > INJELLY

INJELLIES > INJELLY

INJELLY vb place in jelly

INJERA n white Ethiopian flatbread, similar to a crepe

INJERAS > INJERA

INJOINT vb join

INJOINTED > INJOINT

INJOINTS > INJOINT

INJUNCT vb issue a legal injunction against (a person)

INJUNCTED > INJUNCT

INJUNCTS > INJUNCT

INJURABLE > INJURE

INJURE vb hurt physically or mentally

INJURED > INJURE

INJURER > INJURE

INJURERS > INJURE

INJURES > INJURE

INJURIES > INJURY

INJURING > INJURE

INJURIOUS adj causing harm

INJURY n physical hurt

INJUSTICE n unfairness

INK n coloured liquid used for writing or printing ▷ vb mark in ink (something already marked in pencil)

INKBERRY n North American holly tree

INKBLOT n abstract patch of ink

INKBLOTS > INKBLOT

INKED > INK

INKER > INK

INKERS > INK

INKHOLDER same as > INKHORN

INKHORN n (formerly) a small portable container for ink

INKHORNS > INKHORN

INKHOSI n Zulu clan chief

INKHOSIS > INKHOSI

INKIER > INKY

INKIEST > INKY

INKINESS > INKY

INKING > INK

INKJET adj of a method of printing ▷ n inkjet printer

INKJETS > INKJET

INKLE n kind of linen tape used for trimmings ▷ vb hint

INKLED > INKLE

INKLES > INKLE

INKLESS > INK

INKLIKE > INK

INKLING n slight idea or suspicion

INKLINGS > INKLING

INKOSI same as > INKHOSI

INKOSIS > INKOSI

INKPAD n pad used for rubber-stamping or fingerprinting

INKPADS > INKPAD

INKPOT n ink-bottle

INKPOTS > INKPOT

INKS > INK

INKSPOT n ink stain

INKSPOTS > INKSPOT

INKSTAIN n stain made by ink

INKSTAINS > INKSTAIN

INKSTAND n stand or tray for holding writing tools and containers for ink

INKSTANDS > INKSTAND

INKSTONE n stone used in making ink

INKSTONES > INKSTONE

INKWELL n small container for ink

INKWELLS > INKWELL

INKWOOD n type of tree

INKWOODS > INKWOOD

INKY adj dark or black

INLACE variant spelling of > ENLACE

INLACED > INLACE

INLACES > INLACE
INLACING > INLACE
INLAID > INLAY
INLAND adv in or towards the interior of a country ▷ adj of or in the interior of a country or region ▷ n interior of a country or region
INLANDER > INLAND
INLANDERS > INLAND
INLANDS > INLAND
INLAY n inlaid substance or pattern ▷ vb decorate by inserting wooden pieces
INLAYER > INLAY
INLAYERS > INLAY
INLAYING > INLAY
INLAYINGS > INLAY
INLAYS > INLAY
INLET n water extending from the sea into the land ▷ vb insert or inlay
INLETS > INLET
INLETTING > INLET
INLIER n outcrop of rocks surrounded by younger rocks
INLIERS > INLIER
INLOCK vb lock up
INLOCKED > INLOCK
INLOCKING > INLOCK
INLOCKS > INLOCK
INLY adv inwardly
INLYING adj situated within or inside
INMATE n person living in an institution such as a prison
INMATES > INMATE
INMESH variant spelling of > ENMESH
INMESHED > INMESH
INMESHES > INMESH
INMESHING > INMESH
INMIGRANT adj coming in from another area of the same country ▷ n inmigrant person or animal
INMOST adj innermost
INN n pub or small hotel, esp in the country ▷ vb stay at an inn
INNAGE n type of measurement
INNAGES > INNAGE
INNARDS pl n internal organs
INNATE adj being part of someone's nature, inborn
INNATELY > INNATE
INNATIVE adj native
INNED > INN
INNER adj happening or located inside ▷ n red innermost ring on a target
INNERLY > INNER
INNERMOST adj furthest inside
INNERNESS > INNER
INNERS > INNER
INNERSOLE same as > INSOLE

INNERVATE vb supply nerves to (a bodily organ or part)
INNERVE vb supply with nervous energy
INNERVED > INNERVE
INNERVES > INNERVE
INNERVING > INNERVE
INNERWEAR n underwear
INNING n division of baseball match
INNINGS > INNING
INNINGSES > INNINGS
INNIT interj isn't it
INNKEEPER n owner or manager of an inn
INNLESS adj without inns
INNOCENCE n quality or state of being innocent
INNOCENCY same as > INNOCENCE
INNOCENT adj not guilty of a crime ▷ n innocent person, esp a child
INNOCENTS > INNOCENT
INNOCUITY > INNOCUOUS
INNOCUOUS adj not harmful
INNOVATE vb introduce new ideas or methods
INNOVATED > INNOVATE
INNOVATES > INNOVATE
INNOVATOR > INNOVATE
INNOXIOUS adj not noxious
INNS > INN
INNUENDO n (remark making) an indirect reference to something rude or unpleasant
INNUENDOS > INNUENDO
INNYARD n courtyard of an inn
INNYARDS > INNYARD
INOCULA > INOCULUM
INOCULANT same as > INOCULUM
INOCULATE vb protect against disease by injecting with a vaccine
INOCULUM n substance used in giving an inoculation
INOCULUMS > INOCULUM
INODOROUS adj odourless
INOPINATE adj unexpected
INORB vb enclose in or as if in an orb
INORBED > INORB
INORBING > INORB
INORBS > INORB
INORGANIC adj not having the characteristics of living organisms
INORNATE adj simple
INOSINE n type of molecule making up cell
INOSINES > INOSINE
INOSITE same as > INOSITOL
INOSITES > INOSITE
INOSITOL n cyclic alcohol

INOSITOLS > INOSITOL
INOTROPE n drug for controlling muscular contractions
INOTROPES > INOTROPE
INOTROPIC adj affecting or controlling the contraction of muscles, esp those of the heart
INPATIENT n patient who stays in a hospital for treatment
INPAYMENT n money paid into a bank account
INPHASE adj in the same phase
INPOUR vb pour in
INPOURED > INPOUR
INPOURING > INPOUR
INPOURS > INPOUR
INPUT n resources put into a project etc ▷ vb enter (data) in a computer
INPUTS > INPUT
INPUTTED > INPUT
INPUTTER > INPUT
INPUTTERS > INPUT
INPUTTING > INPUT
INQILAB n (in India, Pakistan, etc) revolution
INQILABS > INQILAB
INQUERE Spenserian form of > INQUIRE
INQUERED > INQUERE
INQUERES > INQUERE
INQUERING > INQUERE
INQUEST n official inquiry into a sudden death
INQUESTS > INQUEST
INQUIET vb disturb
INQUIETED > INQUIET
INQUIETLY > INQUIET
INQUIETS > INQUIET
INQUILINE n animal that lives in close association with another animal without harming it ▷ adj of or living as an inquiline
INQUINATE vb corrupt
INQUIRE vb seek information or ask (about)
INQUIRED > INQUIRE
INQUIRER > INQUIRE
INQUIRERS > INQUIRE
INQUIRES > INQUIRE
INQUIRIES > INQUIRY
INQUIRING > INQUIRE
INQUIRY n question
INQUORATE adj without enough people present to make a quorum
INRO n Japanese seal-box
INROAD n invasion or hostile attack
INROADS > INROAD
INRUN n slope down which ski jumpers ski
INRUNS > INRUN
INRUSH n sudden and overwhelming inward flow
INRUSHES > INRUSH
INRUSHING same as > INRUSH

INS > IN
INSANE adj mentally ill
INSANELY > INSANE
INSANER > INSANE
INSANEST > INSANE
INSANIE n insanity
INSANIES > INSANIE
INSANITY n state of being insane
INSATIATE adj not able to be satisfied
INSATIETY n insatiability
INSCAPE n essential inner nature of a person, etc
INSCAPES > INSCAPE
INSCIENCE n ignorance
INSCIENT adj ignorant
INSCONCE vb fortify
INSCONCED > INSCONCE
INSCONCES > INSCONCE
INSCRIBE vb write or carve words on
INSCRIBED > INSCRIBE
INSCRIBER > INSCRIBE
INSCRIBES > INSCRIBE
INSCROLL vb write on a scroll
INSCROLLS > INSCROLL
INSCULP vb engrave
INSCULPED > INSCULP
INSCULPS > INSCULP
INSCULPT adj engraved
INSEAM vb contain
INSEAMED > INSEAM
INSEAMING > INSEAM
INSEAMS > INSEAM
INSECT n small animal with six legs
INSECTAN > INSECT
INSECTARY n place where insects are kept
INSECTEAN > INSECT
INSECTILE > INSECT
INSECTION n incision
INSECTS > INSECT
INSECURE adj anxious, not confident
INSEEM vb cover with grease
INSEEMED > INSEEM
INSEEMING > INSEEM
INSEEMS > INSEEM
INSELBERG n isolated rocky hill rising abruptly from a flat plain
INSENSATE adj without sensation, unconscious
INSERT vb put inside or include ▷ n something inserted
INSERTED adj (of a muscle) attached to the bone that it moves
INSERTER > INSERT
INSERTERS > INSERT
INSERTING > INSERT
INSERTION n act of inserting
INSERTS > INSERT
INSET n small picture inserted within a larger one ▷ vb place in or within

▷ *adj* decorated with something inserted
INSETS > INSET
INSETTED > INSET
INSETTER > INSET
INSETTERS > INSET
INSETTING > INSET
INSHALLAH *sentence substitute* if Allah wills it
INSHEATH *vb* sheathe
INSHEATHE *vb* sheathe
INSHEATHS > INSHEATH
INSHELL *vb* retreat, as into a shell
INSHELLED > INSHELL
INSHELLS > INSHELL
INSHELTER *vb* put in a shelter
INSHIP *vb* travel or send by ship
INSHIPPED > INSHIP
INSHIPS > INSHIP
INSHORE *adj* close to the shore ▷ *adv* towards the shore
INSHRINE *variant spelling of* > ENSHRINE
INSHRINED > INSHRINE
INSHRINES > INSHRINE
INSIDE *prep* in or to the interior of ▷ *adj* on or of the inside ▷ *adv* on, in, or to the inside, indoors ▷ *n* inner side, surface, or part
INSIDER *n* someone who has privileged knowledge
INSIDERS > INSIDER
INSIDES > INSIDE
INSIDIOUS *adj* subtle or unseen but dangerous
INSIGHT *n* deep understanding
INSIGHTS > INSIGHT
INSIGNE *same as* > INSIGNIA
INSIGNIA *n* badge or emblem of honour or office
INSIGNIAS > INSIGNIA
INSINCERE *adj* showing false feelings, not genuine
INSINEW *vb* connect or strengthen, as with sinews
INSINEWED > INSINEW
INSINEWS > INSINEW
INSINUATE *vb* suggest indirectly
INSIPID *adj* lacking interest, spirit, or flavour
INSIPIDLY > INSIPID
INSIPIENT *adj* lacking wisdom
INSIST *vb* demand or state firmly
INSISTED > INSIST
INSISTENT *adj* making persistent demands
INSISTER > INSIST
INSISTERS > INSIST
INSISTING > INSIST
INSISTS > INSIST

INSNARE *less common spelling of* > ENSNARE
INSNARED > INSNARE
INSNARER > INSNARE
INSNARERS > INSNARE
INSNARES > INSNARE
INSNARING > INSNARE
INSOFAR *adv* to the extent
INSOLATE *vb* expose to sunlight, as for bleaching
INSOLATED > INSOLATE
INSOLATES > INSOLATE
INSOLE *n* inner sole of a shoe or boot
INSOLENCE > INSOLENT
INSOLENT *n* insolent person ▷ *adj* rude and disrespectful
INSOLENTS > INSOLENT
INSOLES > INSOLE
INSOLUBLE *adj* incapable of being solved
INSOLUBLY > INSOLUBLE
INSOLVENT *adj* unable to pay one's debts ▷ *n* person who is insolvent
INSOMNIA *n* inability to sleep
INSOMNIAC *adj* exhibiting or causing insomnia ▷ *n* person experiencing insomnia
INSOMNIAS > INSOMNIA
INSOMUCH *adv* such an extent
INSOOTH *adv* indeed
INSOUL *variant of* > ENSOUL
INSOULED > INSOUL
INSOULING > INSOUL
INSOULS > INSOUL
INSOURCE *vb* subcontract work to a company under the same general ownership
INSOURCED > INSOURCE
INSOURCES > INSOURCE
INSPAN *vb* harness (animals) to (a vehicle)
INSPANNED > INSPAN
INSPANS > INSPAN
INSPECT *vb* check closely or officially
INSPECTED > INSPECT
INSPECTOR *n* person who inspects
INSPECTS > INSPECT
INSPHERE *variant spelling of* > ENSPHERE
INSPHERED > INSPHERE
INSPHERES > INSPHERE
INSPIRE *vb* fill with enthusiasm, stimulate
INSPIRED *adj* brilliantly creative
INSPIRER > INSPIRE
INSPIRERS > INSPIRE
INSPIRES > INSPIRE
INSPIRING > INSPIRE
INSPIRIT *vb* fill with vigour
INSPIRITS > INSPIRIT

INSTABLE *less common word for* > UNSTABLE
INSTAL *same as* > INSTALL
INSTALL *vb* put in and prepare (equipment) for use
INSTALLED > INSTALL
INSTALLER > INSTALL
INSTALLS > INSTALL
INSTALS > INSTAL
INSTANCE *n* particular example ▷ *vb* mention as an example
INSTANCED > INSTANCE
INSTANCES > INSTANCE
INSTANCY *n* quality of being urgent or imminent
INSTANT *n* very brief time ▷ *adj* happening at once
INSTANTER *adv* without delay
INSTANTLY *adv* immediately
INSTANTS > INSTANT
INSTAR *vb* decorate with stars ▷ *n* stage in the development of an insect
INSTARRED > INSTAR
INSTARS > INSTAR
INSTATE *vb* place in a position or office
INSTATED > INSTATE
INSTATES > INSTATE
INSTATING > INSTATE
INSTEAD *adv* as a replacement or substitute
INSTEP *n* part of the foot
INSTEPS > INSTEP
INSTIGATE *vb* cause to happen
INSTIL *vb* introduce (an idea etc) gradually into someone's mind
INSTILL *same as* > INSTIL
INSTILLED > INSTILL
INSTILLER > INSTIL
INSTILLS > INSTILL
INSTILS > INSTIL
INSTINCT *n* inborn tendency to behave in a certain way ▷ *adj* animated or impelled (by)
INSTINCTS > INSTINCT
INSTITUTE *n* organization set up for a specific purpose, esp research or teaching ▷ *vb* start or establish
INSTRESS *vb* create or sustain
INSTROKE *n* inward stroke
INSTROKES > INSTROKE
INSTRUCT *vb* order to do something
INSTRUCTS > INSTRUCT
INSUCKEN *adj* of a sucken
INSULA *n* pyramid-shaped area of the brain
INSULAE > INSULA
INSULANT *n* insulation
INSULANTS > INSULANT

INSULAR *adj* not open to new ideas, narrow-minded ▷ *n* islander
INSULARLY > INSULAR
INSULARS > INSULAR
INSULATE *vb* prevent or reduce the transfer of electricity, heat, or sound by surrounding or lining with a nonconducting material
INSULATED > INSULATE
INSULATES > INSULATE
INSULATOR *n* any material or device that insulates
INSULIN *n* hormone produced in the pancreas
INSULINS > INSULIN
INSULSE *adj* stupid
INSULSITY *n* stupidity
INSULT *vb* behave rudely to, offend ▷ *n* insulting remark or action
INSULTANT *adj* insulting
INSULTED > INSULT
INSULTER > INSULT
INSULTERS > INSULT
INSULTING > INSULT
INSULTS > INSULT
INSURABLE > INSURE
INSURANCE *n* agreement by which one makes regular payments to a company who pay an agreed sum if damage, loss, or death occurs
INSURANT *n* holder of an insurance policy
INSURANTS > INSURANT
INSURE *vb* protect by insurance
INSURED *adj* covered by insurance ▷ *n* those covered by an insurance policy
INSUREDS > INSURED
INSURER *n* person or company that sells insurance
INSURERS > INSURER
INSURES > INSURE
INSURGENT *adj* in revolt against an established authority ▷ *n* person who takes part in a rebellion
INSURING > INSURE
INSWATHE *vb* bind or wrap
INSWATHED > INSWATHE
INSWATHES > INSWATHE
INSWEPT *adj* narrowed towards the front
INSWING *n* movement of a bowled ball
INSWINGER *n* ball bowled so as to move from off to leg through the air
INSWINGS > INSWING
INTACT *adj* not changed or damaged in any way
INTACTLY > INTACT
INTAGLI > INTAGLIO
INTAGLIO *n* (gem carved with) an engraved design

INTAGLIOS > INTAGLIO
INTAKE n amount or number taken in
INTAKES > INTAKE
INTARSIA n decorative or pictorial mosaic of inlaid wood or sometimes ivory of a style developed in the Italian Renaissance and used esp on wooden wall panels
INTARSIAS > INTARSIA
INTEGER n positive or negative whole number or zero
INTEGERS > INTEGER
INTEGRAL adj being an essential part of a whole ▷ n sum of a large number of very small quantities
INTEGRALS > INTEGRAL
INTEGRAND n mathematical function to be integrated
INTEGRANT adj part of a whole ▷ n integrant thing or part
INTEGRATE vb combine into a whole ▷ adj made up of parts
INTEGRIN n protein that acts as a signal receptor between cells
INTEGRINS > INTEGRIN
INTEGRITY n quality of having high moral principles
INTEL n US military intelligence
INTELLECT n power of thinking and reasoning
INTELS > INTEL
INTENABLE adj untenable
INTEND vb propose or plan (to do something)
INTENDANT n provincial or colonial official of France, Spain, or Portugal
INTENDED adj planned or future ▷ n person whom one is to marry
INTENDEDS > INTENDED
INTENDER > INTEND
INTENDERS > INTEND
INTENDING > INTEND
INTENDS > INTEND
INTENIBLE adj incapable of holding
INTENSATE vb intensify
INTENSE adj of great strength or degree
INTENSELY > INTENSE
INTENSER > INTENSE
INTENSEST > INTENSE
INTENSIFY vb make or become more intense
INTENSION n set of characteristics or properties by which the referent or referents of a given word are determined
INTENSITY n state or quality of being intense

INTENSIVE adj using or needing concentrated effort or resources ▷ n intensifier or intensive pronoun or grammatical construction
INTENT n intention ▷ adj paying close attention
INTENTION n something intended
INTENTIVE adj intent
INTENTLY > INTENT
INTENTS > INTENT
INTER vb bury (a corpse)
INTERACT vb act on or in close relation with each other
INTERACTS > INTERACT
INTERAGE adj between different ages
INTERARCH vb have intersecting arches
INTERBANK adj conducted between or involving two or more banks
INTERBED vb lie between strata of different minerals
INTERBEDS > INTERBED
INTERBRED adj having been bred within a single family or strain so as to produce particular characteristics
INTERCEDE vb try to end a dispute between two people or groups
INTERCELL adj occurring between cells
INTERCEPT vb seize or stop in transit ▷ n point at which two figures intersect
INTERCITY adj (in Britain) denoting a fast train or passenger rail service, esp between main towns
INTERCLAN adj occurring between clans
INTERCLUB adj of, relating to, or conducted between two or more clubs
INTERCOM n internal communication system with loudspeakers
INTERCOMS > INTERCOM
INTERCROP n crop grown between the rows of another crop ▷ vb grow (one crop) between the rows of (another)
INTERCUT another word for > CROSSCUT
INTERCUTS > INTERCUT
INTERDASH vb dash between
INTERDEAL vb intrigue or plot
INTERDICT n official prohibition or restraint ▷ vb prohibit or forbid
INTERDINE vb eat together

INTERESS vb interest
INTERESSE vb interest
INTEREST n desire to know or hear more about something ▷ vb arouse the interest of
INTERESTS > INTEREST
INTERFACE n area where two things interact or link ▷ vb connect or be connected with by interface
INTERFERE vb try to influence other people's affairs where one is not involved or wanted
INTERFILE vb place (one or more items) among other items in a file or arrangement
INTERFIRM adj occurring between companies
INTERFLOW vb flow together
INTERFOLD vb fold together
INTERFUSE vb mix or become mixed
INTERGANG adj occurring between gangs
INTERGREW > INTERGROW
INTERGROW vb grow among
INTERIM adj temporary, provisional, or intervening ▷ n intervening time ▷ adv meantime
INTERIMS > INTERIM
INTERIOR n inside ▷ adj inside, inner
INTERIORS > INTERIOR
INTERJECT vb make (a remark) suddenly or as an interruption
INTERJOIN vb join together
INTERKNIT vb knit together
INTERKNOT vb knot together
INTERLACE vb join together as if by weaving
INTERLAID > INTERLAY
INTERLAP less common word for > OVERLAP
INTERLAPS > INTERLAP
INTERLARD vb insert in or occur throughout
INTERLAY vb insert (layers) between ▷ n material, such as paper, placed between a printing plate and its base
INTERLAYS > INTERLAY
INTERLEAF n extra leaf which is inserted
INTERLEND vb lend between libraries
INTERLENT > INTERLEND
INTERLINE vb write or print (matter) between the lines of (a text or book)

INTERLINK vb connect together
INTERLOAN n loan between one library and another
INTERLOCK vb join firmly together ▷ n device used to prevent a mechanism from operating independently or unsafely ▷ adj (of fabric) closely knitted
INTERLOOP vb loop together
INTERLOPE vb intrude
INTERLUDE n short rest or break in an activity or event
INTERMALE adj occurring between males
INTERMAT n patch of seabed devoid of vegetation
INTERMATS > INTERMAT
INTERMENT n burial
INTERMESH vb net together
INTERMIT vb suspend (activity) or (of activity) to be suspended temporarily or at intervals
INTERMITS > INTERMIT
INTERMIX vb mix together
INTERMONT adj located between mountains
INTERMURE vb wall in
INTERN vb imprison, esp during a war ▷ n trainee doctor in a hospital
INTERNAL adj of or on the inside ▷ n medical examination of the vagina, uterus, or rectum
INTERNALS > INTERNAL
INTERNE same as > INTERN
INTERNED > INTERN
INTERNEE n person who is interned
INTERNEES > INTERNEE
INTERNES > INTERNE
INTERNET n worldwide computer network
INTERNETS > INTERNET
INTERNING > INTERN
INTERNIST n physician who specializes in internal medicine
INTERNODE n part of a plant stem between two nodes
INTERNS > INTERN
INTERPAGE vb print (matter) on intervening pages
INTERPLAY n action and reaction of two things upon each other
INTERPLED adj having instituted a particular type of proceedings
INTERPONE vb interpose
INTERPOSE vb insert between or among things

INTERPRET vb explain the meaning of

INTERRACE adj between races

INTERRAIL vb travel on an international rail pass

INTERRED > INTER

INTERREX n person who governs during an interregnum

INTERRING > INTER

INTERROW adj occurring between rows

INTERRUPT vb break into (a conversation etc) ⊳ n signal to initiate the stopping of the running of one computer program in order to run another

INTERS > INTER

INTERSECT vb (of roads) meet and cross

INTERSERT vb insert between

INTERSEX n condition of having characteristics intermediate between those of a male and a female

INTERTERM adj occurring between terms ⊳ n intersession

INTERTEXT adj text seen as modifying another text in literary theory

INTERTIE n short roofing timber

INTERTIES > INTERTIE

INTERTILL vb cultivate between rows of crops

INTERUNIT adj occurring between units

INTERVAL n time between two particular moments or events

INTERVALE dialect form of > INTERVAL

INTERVALS > INTERVAL

INTERVEIN vb intersect

INTERVENE vb involve oneself in a situation, esp to prevent conflict

INTERVIEW n formal discussion, esp between a job-seeker and an employer ⊳ vb conduct an interview with

INTERWAR adj of or happening in the period between World War I and World War II

INTERWEB same as > INTERNET

INTERWEBS > INTERWEB

INTERWIND vb wind together

INTERWORK vb interweave

INTERWOVE adj having been woven together

INTERZONE n area between two occupied zones

INTESTACY > INTESTATE

INTESTATE adj not having made a will ⊳ n person who dies without having made a will

INTESTINE n lower part of the alimentary canal between the stomach and the anus

INTHRAL archaic form of > ENTHRAL

INTHRALL archaic form of > ENTHRAL

INTHRALLS > INTHRALL

INTHRALS > INTHRAL

INTHRONE archaic form of > ENTHRONE

INTHRONED > INTHRONE

INTHRONES > INTHRONE

INTI n former monetary unit of Peru

INTIFADA n Palestinian uprising against Israel in the West Bank and Gaza Strip

INTIFADAH same as > INTIFADA

INTIFADAS > INTIFADA

INTIFADEH same as > INTIFADA

INTIL Scot form of > INTO

INTIMA n innermost layer of an organ or part

INTIMACY n close or warm friendship

INTIMAE > INTIMA

INTIMAL > INTIMA

INTIMAS > INTIMA

INTIMATE adj having a close personal relationship ⊳ n close friend ⊳ vb hint at or suggest

INTIMATED > INTIMATE

INTIMATER > INTIMATE

INTIMATES > INTIMATE

INTIME adj intimate

INTIMISM n school of impressionist painting

INTIMISMS > INTIMISM

INTIMIST > INTIMISM

INTIMISTE > INTIMISM

INTIMISTS > INTIMISM

INTIMITY n intimacy

INTINE n inner wall of a pollen grain or a spore

INTINES > INTINE

INTIRE archaic form of > ENTIRE

INTIS > INTI

INTITLE archaic form of > ENTITLE

INTITLED > INTITLE

INTITLES > INTITLE

INTITLING > INTITLE

INTITULE vb (in Britain) to entitle (an act of parliament)

INTITULED > INTITULE

INTITULES > INTITULE

INTO prep indicating motion towards the centre, result of a change, etc

INTOED adj having inward-turning toes

INTOMB same as > ENTOMB

INTOMBED > INTOMB

INTOMBING > INTOMB

INTOMBS > INTOMB

INTONACO n wet plaster surface on which frescoes are painted

INTONACOS > INTONACO

INTONATE vb pronounce or articulate (continuous connected speech) with a characteristic rise and fall of the voice

INTONATED > INTONATE

INTONATES > INTONATE

INTONATOR > INTONATE

INTONE vb speak or recite in an unvarying tone of voice

INTONED > INTONE

INTONER > INTONE

INTONERS > INTONE

INTONES > INTONE

INTONING > INTONE

INTONINGS > INTONE

INTORSION n spiral twisting in plant stems or other parts

INTORT vb twist inward

INTORTED > INTORT

INTORTING > INTORT

INTORTION > INTORT

INTORTS > INTORT

INTOWN adj infield

INTRA prep within

INTRACITY same as > INTERCITY

INTRADA n prelude

INTRADAS > INTRADA

INTRADAY adj occurring within one day

INTRADOS n inner curve or surface of an arch or vault

INTRANET n internal network that makes use of Internet technology

INTRANETS > INTRANET

INTRANT n one who enters

INTRANTS > INTRANT

INTREAT archaic spelling of > ENTREAT

INTREATED > INTREAT

INTREATS > INTREAT

INTRENCH less common spelling of > ENTRENCH

INTREPID adj fearless, bold

INTRICACY > INTRICATE

INTRICATE adj involved or complicated

INTRIGANT n person who intrigues

INTRIGUE vb make interested or curious ⊳ n secret plotting

INTRIGUED > INTRIGUE

INTRIGUER > INTRIGUE

INTRIGUES > INTRIGUE

INTRINCE adj intricate

INTRINSIC adj essential to the basic nature of something

INTRO n introduction

INTRODUCE vb present (someone) by name (to another person)

INTROFIED > INTROFY

INTROFIES > INTROFY

INTROFY vb increase the wetting properties

INTROIT n short prayer said or sung

INTROITAL > INTROIT

INTROITS > INTROIT

INTROITUS n entrance to a body cavity

INTROJECT vb (esp of a child) to incorporate ideas of others, or (in fantasy) of objects

INTROLD variant of > ENTROLD

INTROMIT vb enter or insert or allow to enter or be inserted

INTROMITS > INTROMIT

INTRON n stretch of DNA

INTRONIC adj of or like an intron

INTRONS > INTRON

INTRORSE adj turned inwards or towards the axis

INTROS > INTRO

INTROVERT n person concerned more with his or her thoughts and feelings than with the outside world ⊳ adj shy and quiet ⊳ vb turn (a hollow organ or part) inside out

INTRUDE vb come in or join in without being invited

INTRUDED > INTRUDE

INTRUDER n person who enters a place without permission

INTRUDERS > INTRUDER

INTRUDES > INTRUDE

INTRUDING > INTRUDE

INTRUSION n act of intruding

INTRUSIVE adj characterized by intrusion or tending to intrude

INTRUST same as > ENTRUST

INTRUSTED > INTRUST

INTRUSTS > INTRUST

INTUBATE vb insert a tube or cannula into (a hollow organ)

INTUBATED > INTUBATE

INTUBATES > INTUBATE

INTUIT vb know or discover by intuition

INTUITED > INTUIT

INTUITING > INTUIT

INTUITION n instinctive knowledge or insight without conscious reasoning

INTUITIVE adj of, possessing, or resulting from intuition

INTUITS > INTUIT

INTUMESCE vb swell or become swollen

INTURN n inward turn

INTURNED adj turned inward

INTURNS > INTURN

INTUSE n contusion

INTUSES > INTUSE

INTWINE less common spelling of > ENTWINE

INTWINED > INTWINE

INTWINES > INTWINE

INTWINING > INTWINE

INTWIST vb twist together

INTWISTED > INTWIST

INTWISTS > INTWIST

INUKSHUIT > INUKSHUK

INUKSHUK n stone used by Inuit people to mark a location

INUKSHUKS > INUKSHUK

INUKSUIT > INUKSUK

INUKSUK same as > INUKSHUK

INUKSUKS > INUKSUK

INULA n plant of the elecampane genus

INULAS > INULA

INULASE n enzyme

INULASES > INULASE

INULIN n fructose polysaccharide

INULINS > INULIN

INUMBRATE vb shade

INUNCTION n application of an ointment to the skin, esp by rubbing

INUNDANT > INUNDATE

INUNDATE vb flood

INUNDATED > INUNDATE

INUNDATES > INUNDATE

INUNDATOR > INUNDATE

INURBANE adj not urbane

INURE vb cause to accept or become hardened to

INURED > INURE

INUREMENT > INURE

INURES > INURE

INURING > INURE

INURN vb place (esp cremated ashes) in an urn

INURNED > INURN

INURNING > INURN

INURNMENT > INURN

INURNS > INURN

INUSITATE adj out of use

INUST adj burnt in

INUSTION > INUST

INUSTIONS > INUST

INUTILE adj useless

INUTILELY > INUTILE

INUTILITY > INUTILE

INVADABLE > INVADE

INVADE vb enter (a country) by military force

INVADED > INVADE

INVADER > INVADE

INVADERS > INVADE

INVADES > INVADE

INVADING > INVADE

INVALID n disabled or chronically ill person ▷ vb dismiss from active service because of illness or injury ▷ adj having no legal force

INVALIDED > INVALID

INVALIDLY > INVALID

INVALIDS > INVALID

INVAR n alloy made from iron and nickel

INVARIANT n entity, quantity, etc, that is unaltered by a particular transformation of coordinates

INVARS > INVAR

INVASION n invading

INVASIONS > INVASION

INVASIVE adj of or relating to an invasion, intrusion, etc

INVEAGLE archaic form of > INVEIGLE

INVEAGLED > INVEAGLE

INVEAGLES > INVEAGLE

INVECKED same as > INVECTED

INVECTED adj bordered with small convex curves

INVECTIVE n abusive speech or writing ▷ adj characterized by or using abusive language, bitter sarcasm, etc

INVEIGH vb criticize strongly

INVEIGHED > INVEIGH

INVEIGHER > INVEIGH

INVEIGHS > INVEIGH

INVEIGLE vb coax by cunning or trickery

INVEIGLED > INVEIGLE

INVEIGLER > INVEIGLE

INVEIGLES > INVEIGLE

INVENIT sentence substitute (he or she) designed it

INVENT vb think up or create (something new)

INVENTED > INVENT

INVENTER same as > INVENTOR

INVENTERS > INVENTER

INVENTING > INVENT

INVENTION n something invented

INVENTIVE adj creative and resourceful

INVENTOR n person who invents, esp as a profession

INVENTORS > INVENTOR

INVENTORY n detailed list of goods or furnishings ▷ vb make a list of

INVENTS > INVENT

INVERITY n untruth

INVERNESS n type of cape

INVERSE vb make something opposite or contrary in effect ▷ adj reversed in effect, sequence, direction, etc ▷ n exact opposite

INVERSED > INVERSE

INVERSELY > INVERSE

INVERSES > INVERSE

INVERSING > INVERSE

INVERSION n act of inverting or state of being inverted

INVERSIVE > INVERSION

INVERT vb turn upside down or inside out ▷ n homosexual

INVERTASE n enzyme, occurring in the intestinal juice of animals and in yeasts

INVERTED > INVERT

INVERTER n any device for converting a direct current into an alternating current

INVERTERS > INVERTER

INVERTIN same as > INVERTASE

INVERTING > INVERT

INVERTINS > INVERTIN

INVERTOR same as > INVERTER

INVERTORS > INVERTOR

INVERTS > INVERT

INVEST vb spend (money, time, etc) with the expectation of profit

INVESTED > INVEST

INVESTING > INVEST

INVESTOR > INVEST

INVESTORS > INVEST

INVESTS > INVEST

INVEXED adj concave

INVIABLE adj not viable, esp financially

INVIABLY > INVIABLE

INVIDIOUS adj likely to cause resentment

INVIOLACY > INVIOLATE

INVIOLATE adj unharmed, unaffected

INVIOUS adj without paths or roads

INVIRILE adj unmanly

INVISCID adj not viscid

INVISIBLE adj not able to be seen ▷ n invisible item of trade

INVISIBLY > INVISIBLE

INVITAL adj not vital

INVITE vb request the company of ▷ n invitation

INVITED > INVITE

INVITEE n one who is invited

INVITEES > INVITEE

INVITER > INVITE

INVITERS > INVITE

INVITES > INVITE

INVITING adj tempting, attractive ▷ n old word for invitation

INVITINGS > INVITING

INVOCABLE > INVOKE

INVOCATE archaic word for > INVOKE

INVOCATED > INVOCATE

INVOCATES > INVOCATE

INVOCATOR > INVOCATE

INVOICE n bill for goods or services ▷ vb present (a customer) with an invoice

INVOICED > INVOICE

INVOICES > INVOICE

INVOICING n act of presenting an invoice for payment

INVOKE vb put (a law or penalty) into operation

INVOKED > INVOKE

INVOKER > INVOKE

INVOKERS > INVOKE

INVOKES > INVOKE

INVOKING > INVOKE

INVOLUCEL n ring of bracts at the base of the florets of a compound umbel

INVOLUCRA n involucres

INVOLUCRE n ring of bracts at the base of an inflorescence in such plants as the composites

INVOLUTE adj complex, intricate, or involved ▷ n curve described by the free end of a thread as it is wound around another curve on the same plane ▷ vb become involute

INVOLUTED > INVOLUTE

INVOLUTES > INVOLUTE

INVOLVE vb include as a necessary part

INVOLVED > INVOLVE

INVOLVER > INVOLVE

INVOLVERS > INVOLVE

INVOLVES > INVOLVE

INVOLVING > INVOLVE

INWALL vb surround with a wall

INWALLED > INWALL

INWALLING > INWALL

INWALLS > INWALL

INWARD adj directed towards the middle ▷ adv towards the inside or middle ▷ n inward part

INWARDLY adv within the private thoughts or feelings

INWARDS adv towards the inside or middle of something

INWEAVE vb weave together

INWEAVED > INWEAVE

INWEAVES > INWEAVE

INWEAVING > INWEAVE

INWICK vb perform a type of curling stroke

INWICKED > INWICK

INWICKING > INWICK

INWICKS > INWICK

INWIND vb wind or coil around

INWINDING > INWIND
INWINDS > INWIND
INWIT n conscience
INWITH adv within
INWITS > INWIT
INWORK vb work in
INWORKED > INWORK
INWORKING > INWORK
INWORKS > INWORK
INWORN adj worn in
INWOUND > INWIND
INWOVE > INWEAVE
INWOVEN > INWEAVE
INWRAP less common
spelling of > ENWRAP
INWRAPPED > INWRAP
INWRAPS > INWRAP
INWREATHE same as
> ENWREATHE
INWROUGHT adj worked
or woven into material,
esp decoratively
INYALA n antelope
INYALAS > INYALA
IO interj exclamation of
triumph ▷ n cry of "io"
IODATE same as > IODIZE
IODATED > IODATE
IODATES > IODATE
IODATING > IODATE
IODATION > IODATE
IODATIONS > IODATE
IODIC adj of or containing
iodine
IODID same as > IODIDE
IODIDE n chemical
compound
IODIDES > IODIDE
IODIDS > IODID
IODIN same as > IODINE
IODINATE vb cause to
combine with iodine
IODINATED > IODINATE
IODINATES > IODINATE
IODINE n bluish-black
element
IODINES > IODINE
IODINS > IODIN
IODISE same as > IODIZE
IODISED > IODISE
IODISER > IODISE
IODISERS > IODISE
IODISES > IODISE
IODISING > IODISE
IODISM n poisoning
caused by iodine or its
compounds
IODISMS > IODISM
IODIZE vb treat with
iodine
IODIZED > IODIZE
IODIZER > IODIZE
IODIZERS > IODIZE
IODIZES > IODIZE
IODIZING > IODIZE
IODOFORM n yellow
crystalline insoluble
volatile solid
IODOFORMS > IODOFORM
IODOMETRY n procedure
used in volumetric analysis
for determining the
quantity of substance

present that contains
iodine
IODOPHILE adj taking an
intense iodine stain
IODOPHOR n substance in
which iodine is combined
with an agent that renders
it soluble
IODOPHORS > IODOPHOR
IODOPSIN n violet
light-sensitive pigment in
the cones of the retina of
the eye that is responsible
for colour vision
IODOPSINS > IODOPSIN
IODOUS adj of or
containing iodine
IODURET n iodide
IODURETS > IODURET
IODYRITE n silver iodide
IODYRITES > IODYRITE
IOLITE n grey or
violet-blue dichroic
mineral
IOLITES > IOLITE
ION n electrically charged
atom
IONIC adj of or in the form
of ions
IONICITY n ionic
character
IONICS pl n study of ions
IONISABLE > IONISE
IONISE same as > IONIZE
IONISED > IONISE
IONISER same as
> IONIZER
IONISERS > IONISER
IONISES > IONISE
IONISING > IONISE
IONIUM n naturally
occurring radioisotope of
thorium
IONIUMS > IONIUM
IONIZABLE > IONIZE
IONIZE vb change into ions
IONIZED > IONIZE
IONIZER n person or
thing that ionizes
IONIZERS > IONIZER
IONIZES > IONIZE
IONIZING > IONIZE
IONOGEN n compound
that exists as ions when
dissolved
IONOGENIC adj forming
ions
IONOGENS > IONOGEN
IONOMER n type of
thermoplastic
IONOMERS > IONOMER
IONONE n yellowish liquid
mixture
IONONES > IONONE
IONOPAUSE n transitional
zone in the atmosphere
between the ionosphere
and the exosphere
IONOPHORE n chemical
compound capable of
forming a complex with an
ion and transporting it
through a biological
membrane

IONOSONDE n instrument
measuring ionization
IONOTROPY n reversible
interconversion of a pair of
organic isomers as a result
of the migration of an ionic
part of the molecule
IONS > ION
IOPANOIC adj as in
iopanoic acid type of acid
containing iodine
IOS > IO
IOTA n ninth letter in the
Greek alphabet
IOTACISM n
pronunciation tendency in
Modern Greek
IOTACISMS > IOTACISM
IOTAS > IOTA
IPECAC n type of S
American shrub
IPECACS > IPECAC
IPOMOEA n
convolvulaceous plant
IPOMOEAS > IPOMOEA
IPPON n winning point
awarded in a judo or
karate competition
IPPONS > IPPON
IPRINDOLE n
antidepressant
IRACUND adj easily
angered
IRADE n written edict of a
Muslim ruler
IRADES > IRADE
IRASCIBLE adj easily
angered
IRASCIBLY
> IRASCIBLE
IRATE adj very angry
IRATELY > IRATE
IRATENESS > IRATE
IRATER > IRATE
IRATEST > IRATE
IRE vb anger ▷ n anger
IRED > IRE
IREFUL > IRE
IREFULLY > IRE
IRELESS > IRE
IRENIC adj tending to
conciliate or promote
peace
IRENICAL same as
> IRENIC
IRENICISM > IRENICS
IRENICON variant spelling
of > EIRENICON
IRENICONS > IRENICON
IRENICS n branch of
theology
IRENOLOGY n study of
peace
IRES > IRE
IRID n type of iris
IRIDAL > IRID
IRIDEAL > IRID
IRIDES > IRIS
IRIDIAL > IRID
IRIDIAN > IRID
IRIDIC adj of or
containing iridium
IRIDISE vb make
iridescent

IRIDISED > IRIDISE
IRIDISES > IRIDISE
IRIDISING > IRIDISE
IRIDIUM n very hard
corrosion-resistant metal
IRIDIUMS > IRIDIUM
IRIDIZE vb make
iridescent
IRIDIZED > IRIDIZE
IRIDIZES > IRIDIZE
IRIDIZING > IRIDIZE
IRIDOCYTE n cell in the
skin of fish that gives them
iridescence
IRIDOLOGY n technique
used in complementary
medicine to diagnose
illness by studying a
patient's eyes
IRIDOTOMY n surgical
incision into the iris, esp to
create an artificial pupil
IRIDS > IRID
IRING > IRE
IRIS n part of the eye
▷ vb display iridescence
IRISATE vb make
iridescent
IRISATED > IRISATE
IRISATES > IRISATE
IRISATING > IRISATE
IRISATION > IRISATE
IRISCOPE n instrument
that displays the prismatic
colours
IRISCOPES > IRISCOPE
IRISED > IRIS
IRISES > IRIS
IRISING > IRIS
IRITIC > IRITIS
IRITIS n inflammation of
the iris of the eye
IRITISES > IRITIS
IRK vb irritate, annoy
IRKED > IRK
IRKING > IRK
IRKS > IRK
IRKSOME adj irritating,
annoying
IRKSOMELY > IRKSOME
IROKO n tropical African
hardwood tree
IROKOS > IROKO
IRON n strong
silvery-white metallic
element ▷ adj made of iron
▷ vb smooth (clothes or
fabric) with an iron
IRONBARK n Australian
eucalyptus with hard
rough bark
IRONBARKS > IRONBARK
IRONBOUND adj bound
with iron
IRONCLAD adj covered or
protected with iron
▷ n large wooden
19th-century warship with
armoured plating
IRONCLADS > IRONCLAD
IRONE n fragrant liquid
IRONED > IRON
IRONER > IRON
IRONERS > IRON

IRONES > IRONE
IRONIC adj using irony
IRONICAL same as > IRONIC
IRONIER > IRONY
IRONIES > IRONY
IRONIEST > IRONY
IRONING n clothes to be ironed
IRONINGS > IRONING
IRONISE same as > IRONIZE
IRONISED > IRONISE
IRONISES > IRONISE
IRONISING > IRONISE
IRONIST > IRONIZE
IRONISTS > IRONIZE
IRONIZE vb use or indulge in irony
IRONIZED > IRONIZE
IRONIZES > IRONIZE
IRONIZING > IRONIZE
IRONLESS > IRON
IRONLIKE > IRON
IRONMAN n very strong man
IRONMEN > IRONMAN
IRONNESS > IRON
IRONS > IRON
IRONSIDE n person with great stamina or resistance
IRONSIDES > IRONSIDE
IRONSMITH adj blacksmith
IRONSTONE n rock consisting mainly of iron ore
IRONWARE n domestic articles made of iron
IRONWARES > IRONWARE
IRONWEED n plant with purplish leaves
IRONWEEDS > IRONWEED
IRONWOMAN n very strong woman
IRONWOMEN > IRONWOMAN
IRONWOOD n any of various trees, such as hornbeam, with exceptionally hard wood
IRONWOODS > IRONWOOD
IRONWORK n work done in iron, esp decorative work
IRONWORKS n building in which iron is smelted, cast, or wrought
IRONY n grammatical device ▷ adj of, resembling, or containing iron
IRRADIANT adj radiating light
IRRADIATE vb subject to or treat with radiation
IRREAL adj unreal
IRREALITY n unreality
IRREDENTA same as > IRRIDENTA
IRREGULAR adj not regular or even ▷ n soldier not in a regular army
IRRELATED adj irrelevant

IRRIDENTA n region that is ethnically or historically tied to one country, but which is ruled by another
IRRIGABLE > IRRIGATE
IRRIGABLY > IRRIGATE
IRRIGATE vb supply (land) with water by artificial channels or pipes
IRRIGATED > IRRIGATE
IRRIGATES > IRRIGATE
IRRIGATOR > IRRIGATE
IRRIGUOUS adj well-watered
IRRISION n mockery
IRRISIONS > IRRISION
IRRISORY adj mocking
IRRITABLE adj easily annoyed
IRRITABLY > IRRITABLE
IRRITANCY > IRRITANT
IRRITANT adj causing irritation ▷ n something that annoys or irritates
IRRITANTS > IRRITANT
IRRITATE vb annoy, anger
IRRITATED > IRRITATE
IRRITATES > IRRITATE
IRRITATOR > IRRITATE
IRRUPT vb enter forcibly or suddenly
IRRUPTED > IRRUPT
IRRUPTING > IRRUPT
IRRUPTION > IRRUPT
IRRUPTIVE adj irrupting or tending to irrupt
IRRUPTS > IRRUPT
IRUKANDJI n tiny but highly venomous Australian jellyfish
IS third person singular present tense of > BE
ISABEL n brown yellow colour
ISABELLA same as > ISABEL
ISABELLAS > ISABELLA
ISABELS > ISABEL
ISAGOGE n academic introduction
ISAGOGES > ISAGOGE
ISAGOGIC > ISAGOGICS
ISAGOGICS n introductory studies, esp in the history of the Bible
ISALLOBAR n line on a map connecting places with equal pressure changes
ISARITHM n line on a map connecting places with the same population density
ISARITHMS > ISARITHM
ISATIN n yellowish-red crystalline compound
ISATINE same as > ISATIN
ISATINES > ISATINE
ISATINIC > ISATIN
ISATINS > ISATIN
ISBA n log hut

ISBAS > ISBA
ISCHAEMIA n inadequate supply of blood to an organ or part, as from an obstructed blood flow
ISCHAEMIC > ISCHAEMIA
ISCHEMIA same as > ISCHAEMIA
ISCHEMIAS > ISCHEMIA
ISCHEMIC > ISCHAEMIA
ISCHIA > ISCHIUM
ISCHIADIC > ISCHIUM
ISCHIAL > ISCHIUM
ISCHIATIC > ISCHIUM
ISCHIUM n part of the hipbone
ISCHURIA n retention of urine
ISCHURIAS > ISCHURIA
ISEIKONIA n seeing of same image in both eyes
ISEIKONIC > ISEIKONIA
ISENERGIC adj of equal energy
ISH n issue
ISHES > ISH
ISINGLASS n kind of gelatine obtained from some freshwater fish
ISIT sentence substitute expression used in response to a statement
ISLAND n piece of land surrounded by water ▷ vb cause to become an island
ISLANDED > ISLAND
ISLANDER n person who lives on an island
ISLANDERS > ISLANDER
ISLANDING > ISLAND
ISLANDS > ISLAND
ISLE vb make an isle of ▷ n island
ISLED > ISLE
ISLELESS adj without islands
ISLEMAN n islander
ISLEMEN > ISLEMAN
ISLES > ISLE
ISLESMAN same as > ISLEMAN
ISLESMEN > ISLESMAN
ISLET n small island
ISLETED adj having islets
ISLETS > ISLET
ISLING > ISLE
ISLOMANIA n obsessional enthusiasm or partiality for islands
ISM n doctrine, system, or practice
ISMATIC adj following fashionable doctrines
ISMATICAL same as > ISMATIC
ISMS > ISM
ISNA vb is not
ISNAE same as > ISNA
ISO n short segment of film that can be replayed easily

ISOAMYL n as in isoamyl acetate colourless volatile compound
ISOAMYLS > ISOAMYL
ISOBAR n line showing equal pressure
ISOBARE same as > ISOBAR
ISOBARES > ISOBARE
ISOBARIC adj having equal atmospheric pressure
ISOBARISM > ISOBAR
ISOBARS > ISOBAR
ISOBASE n line connecting points of equal land upheaval
ISOBASES > ISOBASE
ISOBATH n line showing equal depth of water
ISOBATHIC > ISOBATH
ISOBATHS > ISOBATH
ISOBRONT n line connecting points of simultaneous storm development
ISOBRONTS > ISOBRONT
ISOBUTANE n form of butane
ISOBUTENE n isomer of butene
ISOBUTYL n as in methyl isobutyl ketone colourless insoluble liquid ketone used as a solvent for organic compounds
ISOBUTYLS > ISOBUTYL
ISOCHASM n line connecting points of equal aurorae frequency
ISOCHASMS > ISOCHASM
ISOCHEIM n line on a map connecting places with the same mean winter temperature
ISOCHEIMS > ISOCHEIM
ISOCHIMAL > ISOCHIME
ISOCHIME same as > ISOCHEIM
ISOCHIMES > ISOCHIME
ISOCHOR n line showing equal pressure and temperature
ISOCHORE same as > ISOCHOR
ISOCHORES > ISOCHORE
ISOCHORIC > ISOCHOR
ISOCHORS > ISOCHOR
ISOCHRON n line on an isotope ratio diagram denoting a suite of rock or mineral samples all formed at the same time
ISOCHRONE n line on a map or diagram connecting places from which it takes the same time to travel to a certain point
ISOCHRONS > ISOCHRON
ISOCLINAL adj sloping in the same direction and at the same angle ▷ n imaginary line connecting

ISOCLINE *same as* > ISOCLINAL

points on the earth's surface having equal angles of dip

ISOCLINES > ISOCLINE

ISOCLINIC *same as* > ISOCLINAL

ISOCRACY *n* form of government in which all people have equal powers

ISOCRATIC > ISOCRACY

ISOCRYMAL *same as* > ISOCRYME

ISOCRYME *n* line connecting points of equal winter temperature

ISOCRYMES > ISOCRYME

ISOCYANIC *adj* as in *isocyanic acid*, hypothetical acid known only in the form of its compounds

ISOCYCLIC *adj* containing a closed ring of atoms of the same kind, esp carbon atoms

ISODICA > ISODICON

ISODICON *n* short anthem

ISODOMA > ISODOMON

ISODOMON *n* masonry formed of uniform blocks, with courses are of equal height

ISODOMOUS > ISODOMON

ISODOMUM *same as* > ISODOMON

ISODONT *n* animal in which the teeth are of similar size

ISODONTAL *same as* > ISODONT

ISODONTS > ISODONT

ISODOSE *n* dose of radiation applied in radiotherapy

ISODOSES > ISODOSE

ISOENZYME *same as* > ISOZYME

ISOETES *n* quillwort

ISOFORM *n* protein similar in function but not form to another

ISOFORMS > ISOFORM

ISOGAMETE *n* gamete that is similar in size and form to the one with which it unites in fertilization

ISOGAMIC > ISOGAMY

ISOGAMIES > ISOGAMY

ISOGAMOUS > ISOGAMY

ISOGAMY *n* fusion of similar gametes

ISOGENEIC *same as* > ISOGENIC

ISOGENIC *same as* > ISOGENOUS

ISOGENIES > ISOGENOUS

ISOGENOUS *adj* of similar origin, as parts derived from the same embryonic tissue

ISOGENY > ISOGENOUS

ISOGLOSS *n* line drawn on a map around the area in which a linguistic feature is to be found, such as a particular pronunciation of a given word

ISOGON *n* equiangular polygon

ISOGONAL *same as* > ISOGONIC

ISOGONALS > ISOGONAL

ISOGONE *same as* > ISOGONIC

ISOGONES > ISOGONE

ISOGONIC *adj* having, making, or involving equal angles ⊳ *n* imaginary line connecting points on the earth's surface having equal magnetic declination

ISOGONICS > ISOGONIC

ISOGONIES > ISOGONIC

ISOGONS > ISOGON

ISOGONY > ISOGONIC

ISOGRAFT *vb* grafting tissue from a donor genetically identical to the recipient

ISOGRAFTS > ISOGRAFT

ISOGRAM *same as* > ISOPLETH

ISOGRAMS > ISOGRAM

ISOGRAPH *n* line connecting points of the same linguistic usage

ISOGRAPHS > ISOGRAPH

ISOGRIV *n* line showing equal angular bearing

ISOGRIVS > ISOGRIV

ISOHEL *n* line showing equal sunshine

ISOHELS > ISOHEL

ISOHYDRIC *adj* having the same acidity or hydrogen-ion concentration

ISOHYET *n* line showing equal rainfall

ISOHYETAL *same as* > ISOHYET

ISOHYETS > ISOHYET

ISOKONT *same as* > ISOKONTAN

ISOKONTAN *n* alga whose zoophores have equal cilia

ISOKONTS > ISOKONT

ISOLABLE > ISOLATE

ISOLATE *vb* place apart or alone ⊳ *n* isolated person or group

ISOLATED > ISOLATE

ISOLATES > ISOLATE

ISOLATING > ISOLATE

ISOLATION > ISOLATE

ISOLATIVE *adj* concerned with isolation

ISOLATOR > ISOLATE

ISOLATORS > ISOLATE

ISOLEAD *n* line on a ballistic graph

ISOLEADS > ISOLEAD

ISOLEX *n* line on map showing where a particular word is used

ISOLEXES > ISOLEX

ISOLINE *same as* > ISOPLETH

ISOLINES > ISOLINE

ISOLOG > ISOLOGOUS

ISOLOGOUS *adj* (of two or more organic compounds) having a similar structure but containing different atoms of the same valency

ISOLOGS > ISOLOGOUS

ISOLOGUE > ISOLOGOUS

ISOLOGUES > ISOLOGOUS

ISOMER *n* compound that has the same molecular formula as another

ISOMERASE *n* any enzyme that catalyses the conversion of one isomeric form of a compound to another

ISOMERE *same as* > ISOMER

ISOMERES > ISOMERE

ISOMERIC > ISOMER

ISOMERISE *same as* > ISOMERIZE

ISOMERISM *n* existence of two or more compounds having the same molecular formula but a different arrangement of atoms within the molecule

ISOMERIZE *vb* change or cause to change from one isomer to another

ISOMEROUS *adj* having an equal number of parts or markings

ISOMERS > ISOMER

ISOMETRIC *adj* relating to muscular contraction without shortening of the muscle ⊳ *n* drawing made in this way

ISOMETRY *n* rigid motion of a plane or space such that the distance between any two points before and after this motion is unaltered

ISOMORPH *n* substance or organism that exhibits isomorphism

ISOMORPHS > ISOMORPH

ISONIAZID *n* soluble colourless crystalline compound used to treat tuberculosis

ISONOME *n* line on a map showing equal abundance of a species

ISONOMES > ISONOME

ISONOMIC > ISONOMY

ISONOMIES > ISONOMY

ISONOMOUS > ISONOMY

ISONOMY *n* equality before the law of the citizens of a state

ISOOCTANE *n* colourless liquid alkane hydrocarbon produced from petroleum and used in standardizing petrol

ISOPACH *n* line showing equal thickness

ISOPACHS > ISOPACH

ISOPHONE *n* isogloss marking off an area in which a particular feature of pronunciation is found

ISOPHONES > ISOPHONE

ISOPHOTAL > ISOPHOTE

ISOPHOTE *n* line on a diagram or image of a galaxy, nebula, or other celestial object joining points of equal surface brightness

ISOPHOTES > ISOPHOTE

ISOPLETH *n* line on a map connecting places registering the same amount or ratio of some geographical or meteorological phenomenon or phenomena

ISOPLETHS > ISOPLETH

ISOPOD *n* type of crustacean ⊳ *adj* of this type of crustacean

ISOPODAN > ISOPOD

ISOPODANS > ISOPOD

ISOPODOUS > ISOPOD

ISOPODS > ISOPOD

ISOPOLITY *n* equality of political rights

ISOPRENE *n* colourless volatile liquid with a penetrating odour

ISOPRENES > ISOPRENE

ISOPROPYL *n* group of atoms

ISOPTERAN *n* termite

ISOPYCNAL *n* line on a map connecting points of equal atmospheric density

ISOPYCNIC *same as* > ISOPYCNAL

ISOS > ISO

ISOSCELES *adj* (of a triangle) having two sides of equal length

ISOSMOTIC *same as* > ISOTONIC

ISOSPIN *n* number used to classify elementary particles

ISOSPINS > ISOSPIN

ISOSPORY *n* condition of having spores of only one kind

ISOSTACY *n* state of balance in earth's crust

ISOSTASY *same as* > ISOSTACY

ISOSTATIC > ISOSTASY

ISOSTERIC *adj* (of two different molecules) having the same number of atoms and the same number and configuration of valency electrons

ISOTACH n line showing equal wind speed
ISOTACHS > ISOTACH
ISOTACTIC adj (of a stereospecific polymer) having identical steric configurations of the groups on each asymmetric carbon atom on the chain
ISOTHERAL > ISOTHERE
ISOTHERE n line on a map linking places with the same mean summer temperature
ISOTHERES > ISOTHERE
ISOTHERM n line on a map connecting points of equal temperature
ISOTHERMS > ISOTHERM
ISOTONE n atom with same number of neutrons as another
ISOTONES > ISOTONE
ISOTONIC adj (of two or more muscles) having equal tension
ISOTOPE n atom with same atomic number as another
ISOTOPES > ISOTOPE
ISOTOPIC > ISOTOPE
ISOTOPIES > ISOTOPE
ISOTOPY > ISOTOPE
ISOTRON n device for separating small quantities of isotopes
ISOTRONS > ISOTRON
ISOTROPIC adj having uniform physical properties, such as elasticity or conduction in all directions
ISOTROPY > ISOTROPIC
ISOTYPE n pictorial presentation of statistical information
ISOTYPES > ISOTYPE
ISOTYPIC > ISOTYPE
ISOZYME n variant of an enzyme
ISOZYMES > ISOZYME
ISOZYMIC > ISOZYME
ISPAGHULA n dietary fibre derived from seed husks and used as a thickener or stabilizer in the food industry
ISSEI n first-generation Japanese immigrant
ISSEIS > ISSEI

ISSUABLE adj capable of issuing or being issued
ISSUABLY > ISSUABLE
ISSUANCE n act of issuing
ISSUANCES > ISSUANCE
ISSUANT adj emerging or issuing
ISSUE n topic of interest or discussion ▷ vb make (a statement etc) publicly
ISSUED > ISSUE
ISSUELESS > ISSUE
ISSUER > ISSUE
ISSUERS > ISSUE
ISSUES > ISSUE
ISSUING > ISSUE
ISTANA n (in Malaysia) a royal palace
ISTANAS > ISTANA
ISTHMI > ISTHMUS
ISTHMIAN n inhabitant of an isthmus ▷ adj relating to or situated in an isthmus
ISTHMIANS > ISTHMIAN
ISTHMIC > ISTHMUS
ISTHMOID > ISTHMUS
ISTHMUS n narrow strip of land connecting two areas of land
ISTHMUSES > ISTHMUS
ISTLE n fibre obtained from various agave and yucca trees
ISTLES > ISTLE
IT pron refers to a nonhuman, animal, plant, or inanimate object ▷ n player whose turn it is to catch the others in children's games
ITA n type of palm
ITACISM n pronunciation of the Greek letter eta
ITACISMS > ITACISM
ITACONIC adj as in itaconic acid, white colourless crystalline carboxylic acid
ITALIC adj (of printing type) sloping to the right ▷ n style of printing type
ITALICISE same as > ITALICIZE
ITALICIZE vb put in italics
ITALICS > ITALIC
ITAS > ITA
ITCH n skin irritation causing a desire to scratch ▷ vb have an itch

ITCHED > ITCH
ITCHES > ITCH
ITCHIER > ITCH
ITCHIEST > ITCH
ITCHILY > ITCH
ITCHINESS > ITCH
ITCHING > ITCH
ITCHINGS > ITCH
ITCHWEED n white hellebore
ITCHWEEDS > ITCHWEED
ITCHY > ITCH
ITEM n single thing in a list or collection ▷ adv likewise ▷ vb itemize
ITEMED > ITEM
ITEMING > ITEM
ITEMISE same as > ITEMIZE
ITEMISED > ITEMISE
ITEMISER > ITEMISE
ITEMISERS > ITEMISE
ITEMISES > ITEMISE
ITEMISING > ITEMISE
ITEMIZE vb make a list of
ITEMIZED > ITEMIZE
ITEMIZER > ITEMIZE
ITEMIZERS > ITEMIZE
ITEMIZES > ITEMIZE
ITEMIZING > ITEMIZE
ITEMS > ITEM
ITERANCE > ITERATE
ITERANCES > ITERATE
ITERANT > ITERATE
ITERATE vb repeat
ITERATED > ITERATE
ITERATES > ITERATE
ITERATING > ITERATE
ITERATION > ITERATE
ITERATIVE adj repetitious or frequent
ITERUM adv again
ITHER Scot word for > OTHER
ITINERACY n travelling from place to place
ITINERANT adj travelling from place to place ▷ n itinerant worker or other person
ITINERARY n detailed plan of a journey ▷ adj of or relating to travel or routes of travel
ITINERATE vb travel from place to place
ITS pron belonging to it ▷ adj of or belonging to it
ITSELF pron reflexive form of it

IURE adv by law
IVIED adj covered with ivy
IVIES > IVY
IVORIED > IVORY
IVORIES pl n keys of a piano
IVORIST n worker in ivory
IVORISTS > IVORIST
IVORY n bony substance forming the tusks of elephants ▷ adj yellowish-white
IVORYBILL n large American woodpecker
IVORYLIKE > IVORY
IVORYWOOD n yellowish-white wood of an Australian tree, used for engraving, inlaying, and turnery
IVRESSE n drunkenness
IVRESSES > IVRESSE
IVY n evergreen climbing plant
IVYLEAF adj as in ivyleaf geranium type of geranium plant
IVYLIKE > IVY
IWI n Māori tribe
IWIS archaic word for > CERTAINLY
IXIA n southern African plant
IXIAS > IXIA
IXNAY interj nix
IXODIASES > IXODIASIS
IXODIASIS n disease transmitted by ticks
IXODID n hard-bodied tick
IXODIDS > IXODID
IXORA n flowering shrub
IXORAS > IXORA
IXTLE same as > ISTLE
IXTLES > IXTLE
IZAR n long garment worn by Muslim women
IZARD n type of goat-antelope
IZARDS > IZARD
IZARS > IZAR
IZVESTIA > IZVESTIA
IZVESTIAS > IZVESTIA
IZVESTIYA same as > IZVESTIA
IZZARD n letter Z
IZZARDS > IZZARD
IZZAT n honour or prestige
IZZATS > IZZAT

Jj

JA *interj* yes ▷ *sentence substitute* yes

JAAP *n* S African offensive word for a simpleton or country bumpkin

JAAPS > JAAP

JAB *vb* poke sharply ▷ *n* quick punch or poke

JABBED > JAB

JABBER *vb* talk rapidly or incoherently ▷ *n* rapid or incoherent talk

JABBERED > JABBER

JABBERER > JABBER

JABBERERS > JABBER

JABBERING > JABBER

JABBERS > JABBER

JABBING > JAB

JABBINGLY > JAB

JABBLE *vb* ripple

JABBLED > JABBLE

JABBLES > JABBLE

JABBLING > JABBLE

JABERS *interj* Irish exclamation

JABIRU *n* large white-and-black Australian stork

JABIRUS > JABIRU

JABORANDI *n* any of several tropical American rutaceous shrubs

JABOT *n* frill or ruffle on the front of a blouse or shirt

JABOTS > JABOT

JABS > JAB

JACAL *n* Mexican daub hut

JACALES > JACAL

JACALS > JACAL

JACAMAR *n* tropical American bird with an iridescent plumage

JACAMARS > JACAMAR

JACANA *n* long-legged long-toed bird

JACANAS > JACANA

JACARANDA *n* tropical tree with sweet-smelling wood

JACARE *another name for* > CAYMAN

JACARES > JACARE

JACCHUS *n* small monkey

JACCHUSES > JACCHUS

JACENT *adj* lying

JACINTH *another name for* > HYACINTH

JACINTHE *n* hyacinth

JACINTHES > JACINTHE

JACINTHS > JACINTH

JACK *n* device for raising a motor vehicle or other heavy object ▷ *vb* lift or push (an object) with a jack

JACKAL *n* doglike wild animal of Africa and Asia ▷ *vb* behave like a jackal

JACKALLED > JACKAL

JACKALS > JACKAL

JACKAROO *same as* > JACKEROO

JACKAROOS > JACKAROO

JACKASS *n* fool

JACKASSES > JACKASS

JACKBOOT *n* high military boot ▷ *vb* oppress

JACKBOOTS > JACKBOOT

JACKDAW *n* Eurasian bird of the crow family

JACKDAWS > JACKDAW

JACKED > JACK

JACKEEN *n* slick self-assertive lower-class Dubliner

JACKEENS > JACKEEN

JACKER *n* labourer

JACKEROO *n* young male management trainee on a sheep or cattle station ▷ *vb* work as a jackeroo

JACKEROOS > JACKEROO

JACKERS > JACKER

JACKET *n* short coat ▷ *vb* put a jacket on (someone or something)

JACKETED > JACKET

JACKETING > JACKET

JACKETS > JACKET

JACKFISH *n* small pike fish

JACKFRUIT *n* tropical Asian tree

JACKIES > JACKY

JACKING > JACK

JACKINGS > JACK

JACKKNIFE *vb* (of an articulated truck) go out of control so that the trailer swings round at a sharp angle to the cab ▷ *n* large clasp knife

JACKLEG *n* unskilled worker

JACKLEGS > JACKLEG

JACKLIGHT *same as* > JACK

JACKLING *n* particular way of winning the ball in rugby

JACKLINGS > JACKLING

JACKMAN *n* retainer

JACKMEN > JACKMAN

JACKPLANE *n* large woodworking plane

JACKPOT *n* largest prize that may be won in a game ▷ *vb* accumulate stake money in a prize fund

JACKPOTS > JACKPOT

JACKROLL *vb* gang-rape

JACKROLLS > JACKROLL

JACKS *n* type of game

JACKSCREW *n* lifting device

JACKSHAFT *n* short length of shafting that transmits power from an engine or motor to a machine

JACKSIE *n* buttocks or anus

JACKSIES > JACKSIE

JACKSMELT *n* food fish of the North Pacific

JACKSMITH *n* smith who makes jacks

JACKSNIPE *n* small Eurasian short-billed snipe

JACKSTAY *n* metal rod, wire rope, or wooden batten to which an edge of a sail is fastened along a yard

JACKSTAYS > JACKSTAY

JACKSTONE *n* small round pebble

JACKSTRAW *n* straw mannequin

JACKSY *same as* > JACKSIE

JACKY *n* offensive word for a native Australian

JACOBIN *n* variety of fancy pigeon

JACOBINS > JACOBIN

JACOBUS *n* English gold coin

JACOBUSES > JACOBUS

JACONET *n* light cotton fabric

JACONETS > JACONET

JACQUARD *n* fabric in which the design is incorporated into the weave instead of being printed or dyed on

JACQUARDS > JACQUARD

JACQUERIE *n* peasant rising or revolt

JACTATION *n* act of boasting

JACULATE *vb* hurl

JACULATED > JACULATE

JACULATES > JACULATE

JACULATOR > JACULATE

JACUZZI *n* type of bath or pool

JACUZZIS > JACUZZI

JADE *n* semiprecious stone ▷ *adj* bluish-green ▷ *vb* exhaust or make exhausted from work or use

JADED *adj* tired and unenthusiastic

JADEDLY > JADED

JADEDNESS > JADED

JADEITE *n* usually green or white mineral

JADEITES > JADEITE

JADELIKE > JADE

JADERIES > JADERY

JADERY *n* shrewishness

JADES > JADE

JADING > JADE

JADISH > JADE

JADISHLY > JADE

JADITIC > JADE

JAEGER *n* German or Austrian marksman

JAEGERS > JAEGER

JAFA *n* offensive name for a person from Auckland

JAFAS > JAFA

JAFFA *n* (in cricket) well-bowled ball

JAFFAS > JAFFA

JAG *n* period of uncontrolled indulgence in an activity ▷ *vb* cut unevenly

JAGA *n* guard ▷ *vb* guard or watch

JAGAED > JAGA

JAGAING > JAGA

JAGAS > JAGA

JAGER *same as* > JAEGER

JAGERS > JAGER

JAGG *same as* > JAG

JAGGARIES > JAGGARY

JAGGARY *same as* > JAGGERY

JAGGED > JAG

JAGGEDER > JAG

JAGGEDEST > JAG

JAGGEDLY > JAG

JAGGER n pedlar
JAGGERIES > JAGGERY
JAGGERS > JAGGER
JAGGERY n coarse brown sugar
JAGGHERY same as **>** JAGGERY
JAGGIER > JAGGY
JAGGIES > JAGGY
JAGGIEST > JAGGY
JAGGING > JAG
JAGGS > JAGG
JAGGY adj prickly ▷ n jagged computer image
JAGHIR n Indian regional governance
JAGHIRDAR n Indian regional governor
JAGHIRE n Indian regional governance
JAGHIRES > JAGHIRE
JAGHIRS > JAGHIR
JAGIR n Indian regional governance
JAGIRS > JAGIR
JAGLESS > JAG
JAGRA n Hindu festival
JAGRAS > JAGRA
JAGS > JAG
JAGUAR n large S American spotted cat
JAGUARS > JAGUAR
JAI interj victory (to)
JAIL n prison ▷ vb send to prison
JAILABLE > JAIL
JAILBAIT n young woman, or young women collectively, considered sexually attractive but below the age of consent
JAILBAITS > JAILBAIT
JAILBIRD n person who has often been in prison
JAILBIRDS > JAILBIRD
JAILBREAK n escape from jail ▷ vb adapt an electronic device to use unauthorized software
JAILBROKE > JAILBREAK
JAILED > JAIL
JAILER n person in charge of a jail
JAILERESS > JAILER
JAILERS > JAILER
JAILHOUSE n jail
JAILING > JAIL
JAILLESS > JAIL
JAILOR same as **>** JAILER
JAILORESS > JAILOR
JAILORS > JAILOR
JAILS > JAIL
JAK same as **>** JACK
JAKE adj slang word meaning all right
JAKES n human excrement
JAKESES > JAKES
JAKEY n derogatory Scots word for a homeless alcoholic

JAKEYS > JAKEY
JAKFRUIT same as **>** JACKFRUIT
JAKFRUITS > JAKFRUIT
JAKS > JACK
JALABIB > JILBAB
JALAP n Mexican convolvulaceous plant
JALAPENO n very hot type of green chilli pepper, used esp in Mexican cookery
JALAPENOS > JALAPENO
JALAPIC > JALAP
JALAPIN n purgative resin
JALAPINS > JALAPIN
JALAPS > JALAP
JALEBI n type of Asian sweet fried snack
JALEBIS > JALEBI
JALFREZI adj (in Indian cookery) stir-fried with green peppers, onions, and green chillies ▷ n curry made with green peppers, onions, and green chillies
JALFREZIS > JALFREZI
JALLEBI same as **>** JALEBI
JALLEBIS > JALLEBI
JALOP same as **>** JALAP
JALOPIES > JALOPY
JALOPPIES > JALOPPY
JALOPPY same as **>** JALOPY
JALOPS > JALOP
JALOPY n old car
JALOUSE vb suspect
JALOUSED > JALOUSE
JALOUSES > JALOUSE
JALOUSIE n window blind or shutter constructed from angled slats of wood, plastic, etc
JALOUSIED > JALOUSIE
JALOUSIES > JALOUSIE
JALOUSING > JALOUSIE
JAM vb pack tightly into a place ▷ n fruit preserve or hold-up of traffic
JAMAAT n Islamic council
JAMAATS > JAMAAT
JAMADAR n Indian army officer
JAMADARS > JAMADAR
JAMB n side post of a door or window frame ▷ vb climb up a crack in rock
JAMBALAYA n Creole dish made of shrimps, ham, rice, onions, etc
JAMBART same as **>** GREAVE
JAMBARTS > JAMBART
JAMBE same as **>** JAMB
JAMBEAU another word for **>** GREAVE
JAMBEAUS > JAMBEAU
JAMBEAUX > JAMBEAU
JAMBED > JAMB
JAMBEE n light cane
JAMBEES > JAMBEE
JAMBER same as **>** GREAVE

JAMBERS > JAMBER
JAMBES > JAMBE
JAMBEUX > JAMBEAU
JAMBIER n greave
JAMBIERS > JAMBIER
JAMBING > JAMB
JAMBIYA n curved dagger
JAMBIYAH same as **>** JAMBIYA
JAMBIYAHS > JAMBIYAH
JAMBIYAS > JAMBIYA
JAMBO sentence substitute E African salutation
JAMBOK same as **>** SJAMBOK
JAMBOKKED > JAMBOK
JAMBOKS > JAMBOK
JAMBOLAN n Asian tree
JAMBOLANA same as **>** JAMBOLAN
JAMBOLANS > JAMBOLAN
JAMBONE n type of play in the card game euchre
JAMBONES > JAMBONE
JAMBOOL same as **>** JAMBOLAN
JAMBOOLS > JAMBOOL
JAMBOREE n large gathering or celebration
JAMBOREES > JAMBOREE
JAMBS > JAMB
JAMBU same as **>** JAMBOLAN
JAMBUL same as **>** JAMBOLAN
JAMBULS > JAMBUL
JAMBUS > JAMBU
JAMDANI n patterned muslin
JAMDANIS > JAMDANI
JAMES n jemmy
JAMESES > JAMES
JAMJAR n container for preserves
JAMJARS > JAMJAR
JAMLIKE > JAM
JAMMABLE > JAM
JAMMED > JAM
JAMMER > JAM
JAMMERS > JAM
JAMMIER > JAMMY
JAMMIES informal word for **>** PYJAMAS
JAMMIEST > JAMMY
JAMMING > JAM
JAMMINGS > JAM
JAMMY adj lucky
JAMON n as in jamon serrano cured ham from Spain
JAMPACKED adj very crowded
JAMPAN n type of sedan chair used in India
JAMPANEE n jampan bearer
JAMPANEES > JAMPANEE
JAMPANI same as **>** JAMPANEE
JAMPANIS > JAMPANI
JAMPANS > JAMPAN
JAMPOT n container for preserves
JAMPOTS > JAMPOT

JAMS > JAM
JANE n girl or woman
JANES > JANE
JANGLE vb (cause to) make a harsh ringing noise ▷ n harsh ringing noise
JANGLED > JANGLE
JANGLER > JANGLE
JANGLERS > JANGLE
JANGLES > JANGLE
JANGLIER > JANGLY
JANGLIEST > JANGLY
JANGLING > JANGLE
JANGLINGS > JANGLE
JANGLY adj making a jangling sound
JANIFORM adj with two faces
JANISARY same as **>** JANISSARY
JANISSARY n infantryman in the Turkish army, originally a member of the sovereign's personal guard, from the 14th to the early 19th century
JANITOR n caretaker of a school or other building
JANITORS > JANITOR
JANITRESS > JANITOR
JANITRIX > JANITOR
JANIZAR same as **>** JANISSARY
JANIZARS > JANIZAR
JANIZARY same as **>** JANISSARY
JANKER n device for transporting logs
JANKERS > JANKER
JANN n lesser jinn
JANNEY vb act as a disguised reveller at Christmas
JANNEYED > JANNEY
JANNEYING > JANNEY
JANNEYS > JANNEY
JANNIED > JANNY
JANNIES > JANNY
JANNOCK same as **>** JONNOCK
JANNOCKS > JANNOCK
JANNS > JANN
JANNY n janitor ▷ vb work as a janitor
JANNYING > JANNY
JANNYINGS > JANNYING
JANSKY n unit of flux density
JANSKYS > JANSKY
JANTEE archaic version of **>** JAUNTY
JANTIER > JANTY
JANTIES > JANTY
JANTIEST > JANTY
JANTY n petty officer ▷ adj (in archaic usage) jaunty
JAP vb splash
JAPAN n very hard varnish, usu black ▷ vb cover with this varnish ▷ adj relating to or varnished with japan

JAPANISE same as
> JAPANIZE
JAPANISED > JAPANISE
JAPANISES > JAPANISE
JAPANIZE vb make
Japanese
JAPANIZED > JAPANIZE
JAPANIZES > JAPANIZE
JAPANNED > JAPAN
JAPANNER > JAPAN
JAPANNERS > JAPAN
JAPANNING > JAPAN
JAPANS > JAPAN
JAPE n joke or prank
> vb joke or jest (about)
JAPED > JAPE
JAPER > JAPE
JAPERIES > JAPE
JAPERS > JAPE
JAPERY > JAPE
JAPES > JAPE
JAPING > JAPE
JAPINGLY > JAPE
JAPINGS > JAPE
JAPONICA n shrub with
red flowers
JAPONICAS > JAPONICA
JAPPED > JAP
JAPPING > JAP
JAPS > JAP
JAR n wide-mouthed
container > vb have a
disturbing or unpleasant
effect
JARARACA n South
American snake
JARARACAS
> JARARACA
JARARAKA same as
> JARARACA
JARARAKAS
> JARARACA
JARFUL same as > JAR
JARFULS > JARFUL
JARGON n specialized
technical language > vb
use or speak in jargon
JARGONED > JARGON
JARGONEER n user of
jargon
JARGONEL n pear
JARGONELS > JARGONEL
JARGONING > JARGON
JARGONISE same as
> JARGONIZE
JARGONISH > JARGON
JARGONIST > JARGON
JARGONIZE vb render
into jargon
JARGONS > JARGON
JARGONY > JARGON
JARGOON same as
> JARGON
JARGOONS > JARGON
JARHEAD n US Marine
JARHEADS > JARHEAD
JARINA n South American
palm tree
JARINAS > JARINA
JARK n seal or pass
JARKMAN n forger of
passes or licences
JARKMEN > JARKMAN

JARKS > JARK
JARL n Scandinavian
chieftain or noble
JARLDOM > JARL
JARLDOMS > JARL
JARLS > JARL
JARLSBERG n Norwegian
cheese
JAROOL n Indian tree
JAROOLS > JAROOL
JAROSITE n yellow to
brown mineral
JAROSITES > JAROSITE
JAROVISE same as
> JAROVIZE
JAROVISED > JAROVISE
JAROVISES > JAROVISE
JAROVIZE vb vernalize
JAROVIZED > JAROVIZE
JAROVIZES > JAROVIZE
JARP vb strike or smash
JARPED > JARP
JARPING > JARP
JARPS > JARP
JARRAH n Australian
eucalypt yielding valuable
timber
JARRAHS > JARRAH
JARRED > JAR
JARRING > JAR
JARRINGLY > JAR
JARRINGS > JAR
JARS > JAR
JARSFUL > JARFUL
JARTA n heart
JARTAS > JARTA
JARUL variant of > JAROOL
JARULS > JARUL
JARVEY n hackney
coachman
JARVEYS > JARVEY
JARVIE same as > JARVEY
JARVIES > JARVIE
JASEY n wig
JASEYS > JASEY
JASIES > JASEY
JASMIN same as
> JASMINE
JASMINE n shrub with
sweet-smelling yellow or
white flowers
JASMINES > JASMINE
JASMINS > JASMIN
JASMONATE n plant
hormone that regulates
growth
JASP another word for
> JASPER
JASPE adj resembling
jasper > n subtly striped
woven fabric
JASPER n variety of quartz
JASPERISE same as
> JASPERIZE
JASPERIZE vb turn into
jasper
JASPEROUS > JASPER
JASPERS > JASPER
JASPERY > JASPER
JASPES > JASPE
JASPIDEAN > JASPER
JASPILITE n rock like
jasper

JASPIS archaic word for
> JASPER
JASPISES > JASPIS
JASPS > JASP
JASS obsolete variant of
> JAZZ
JASSES > JASS
JASSID n leafhopper
JASSIDS > JASSID
JASY n wig
JATAKA n text describing
the birth of Buddha
JATAKAS > JATAKA
JATO n jet-assisted takeoff
JATOS > JATO
JATROPHA n poisonous
shrub of C America used
primarily as a biofuel
JATROPHAS > JATROPHA
JAUK vb dawdle
JAUKED > JAUK
JAUKING > JAUK
JAUKS > JAUK
JAUNCE vb prance
JAUNCED > JAUNCE
JAUNCES > JAUNCE
JAUNCING > JAUNCE
JAUNDICE n disease
marked by yellowness of
the skin > vb distort (the
judgment, etc) adversely
JAUNDICED > JAUNDICE
JAUNDICES > JAUNDICE
JAUNSE same as > JAUNCE
JAUNSED > JAUNSE
JAUNSES > JAUNSE
JAUNSING > JAUNSE
JAUNT n short journey for
pleasure > vb make such a
journey
JAUNTED > JAUNT
JAUNTEE old spelling of
> JAUNTY
JAUNTIE old spelling of
> JAUNTY
JAUNTIER > JAUNTY
JAUNTIES > JAUNTY
JAUNTIEST > JAUNTY
JAUNTILY > JAUNTY
JAUNTING > JAUNT
JAUNTS > JAUNT
JAUNTY adj sprightly and
cheerful > n master-at-
arms on a naval ship
JAUP same as > JARP
JAUPED > JAUP
JAUPING > JAUP
JAUPS > JAUP
JAVA n coffee or a variety
of it
JAVAS > JAVA
JAVEL adj as in javel water
bleach or disinfectant
JAVELIN n light spear
thrown in sports
competitions > vb spear
with a javelin
JAVELINA n collared
peccary
JAVELINAS > JAVELINA
JAVELINED > JAVELIN
JAVELINS > JAVELIN
JAVELS > JAVEL

JAW n one of the bones in
which the teeth are set
> vb talk lengthily
JAWAN n (in India) a soldier
JAWANS > JAWAN
JAWARI n variety of
sorghum
JAWARIS > JAWARI
JAWBATION n scolding
JAWBONE n lower jaw of a
person or animal > vb try
to persuade by virtue of
one's high office or
position
JAWBONED > JAWBONE
JAWBONER > JAWBONE
JAWBONERS > JAWBONE
JAWBONES > JAWBONE
JAWBONING > JAWBONE
JAWBOX n metal sink
JAWBOXES > JAWBOX
JAWED > JAW
JAWFALL n depression
JAWFALLS > JAWFALL
JAWHOLE n cesspit
JAWHOLES > JAWHOLE
JAWING > JAW
JAWINGS > JAW
JAWLESS > JAW
JAWLIKE > JAW
JAWLINE n outline of the
jaw
JAWLINES > JAWLINE
JAWS > JAW
JAXIE same as > JACKSIE
JAXIES > JAXIE
JAXY same as > JACKSIE
JAY n type of bird
JAYBIRD n jay
JAYBIRDS > JAYBIRD
JAYCEE n member of a
Junior Chamber of
Commerce
JAYCEES > JAYCEE
JAYGEE n lieutenant
junior grade in the US
army
JAYGEES > JAYGEE
JAYHAWKER n Unionist
guerrilla in US Civil War
JAYS > JAY
JAYVEE n junior varsity
sports team
JAYVEES > JAYVEE
JAYWALK vb cross or walk
in a street recklessly or
illegally
JAYWALKED > JAYWALK
JAYWALKER > JAYWALK
JAYWALKS > JAYWALK
JAZERANT n coat of metal
plates sewn onto cloth
JAZERANTS > JAZERANT
JAZIES > JAZY
JAZY n wig
JAZZ n kind of music
> vb play or dance to jazz
music
JAZZBO n jazz musician
or fan
JAZZBOS > JAZZBO
JAZZED > JAZZ
JAZZER > JAZZ

JAZZERS > JAZZ

JAZZES > JAZZ

JAZZIER > JAZZY

JAZZIEST > JAZZY

JAZZILY > JAZZY

JAZZINESS > JAZZY

JAZZING > JAZZ

JAZZLIKE > JAZZ

JAZZMAN > JAZZ

JAZZMEN > JAZZ

JAZZY *adj* flashy or showy

JEALOUS *adj* fearful of losing (something) to a rival

JEALOUSE *vb* be jealous of

JEALOUSED > JEALOUSE

JEALOUSES > JEALOUSE

JEALOUSLY > JEALOUS

JEALOUSY *n* state of or an instance of feeling jealous

JEAN *n* tough twill-weave cotton fabric

JEANED *adj* wearing jeans

JEANETTE *n* light jean cloth

JEANETTES > JEANETTE

JEANS *pl n* casual denim trousers

JEAT *n* jet

JEATS > JEAT

JEBEL *n* hill or mountain in an Arab country

JEBELS > JEBEL

JEDI *n* person claiming to live according to the Jedi philosophy

JEDIS > JEDI

JEE *variant of* > GEE

JEED > JEE

JEEING > JEE

JEEL *vb* make into jelly

JEELED > JEEL

JEELIE *same as* > JEELY

JEELIED > JEELY

JEELIEING > JEELIE

JEELIES > JEELY

JEELING > JEEL

JEELS > JEEL

JEELY *n* jelly ▷ *vb* make into jelly

JEELYING > JEELY

JEEP *n* small military four-wheel drive road vehicle ▷ *vb* travel in a jeep

JEEPED > JEEP

JEEPERS *interj* mild exclamation of surprise

JEEPING > JEEP

JEEPNEY *n* Filipino bus converted from a jeep

JEEPNEYS > JEEPNEY

JEEPS > JEEP

JEER *vb* scoff or deride ▷ *n* cry of derision

JEERED > JEER

JEERER > JEER

JEERERS > JEER

JEERING > JEER

JEERINGLY > JEER

JEERINGS > JEER

JEERS > JEER

JEES > JEE

JEESLY *same as* > JEEZLY

JEEZ *interj* expression of surprise or irritation

JEEZE *same as* > JEEZ

JEEZELY *same as* > JEEZLY

JEEZLY *adj* (intensifier)

JEFE *n* (in Spanish-speaking countries) a military or political leader

JEFES > JEFE

JEFF *vb* downsize or close down (an organization)

JEFFED > JEFF

JEFFING > JEFF

JEFFS > JEFF

JEGGINGS *pl n* women's leggings designed to look like tight denim jeans

JEHAD *same as* > JIHAD

JEHADEEN *same as* > JIHADEEN

JEHADI *same as* > JIHADI

JEHADIS > JEHADI

JEHADISM *same as* > JIHADISM

JEHADISMS > JEHADISM

JEHADIST > JEHADISM

JEHADISTS > JEHADISM

JEHADS > JEHAD

JEHU *n* fast driver

JEHUS > JEHU

JEJUNA > JEJUNUM

JEJUNAL > JEJUNUM

JEJUNE *adj* simple or naive

JEJUNELY > JEJUNE

JEJUNITY > JEJUNE

JEJUNUM *n* part of the small intestine

JEJUNUMS > JEJUNUM

JELAB *same as* > JELLABA

JELABS > JELAB

JELL *vb* form into a jelly-like substance

JELLABA *n* loose robe with a hood

JELLABAH *same as* > JELLABA

JELLABAHS > JELLABAH

JELLABAS > JELLABA

JELLED > JELL

JELLIED > JELLY

JELLIES > JELLY

JELLIFIED > JELLIFY

JELLIFIES > JELLIFY

JELLIFY *vb* make into or become jelly

JELLING > JELL

JELLO *n* (in US English) type of dessert

JELLOS > JELLO

JELLS > JELL

JELLY *n* fruit-flavoured clear dessert set with gelatine ▷ *vb* jellify

JELLYBEAN *n* bean-shaped sweet with a brightly coloured coating around a gelatinous filling

JELLYFISH *n* small jelly-like sea animal

JELLYING > JELLY

JELLYLIKE > JELLY

JELLYROLL *n* type of cake

JELUTONG *n* Malaysian tree

JELUTONGS > JELUTONG

JEMADAR *n* native officer serving as a mercenary in India

JEMADARS > JEMADAR

JEMBE *n* hoe

JEMBES > JEMBE

JEMIDAR *same as* > JEMADAR

JEMIDARS > JEMIDAR

JEMIMA *n* boot with elastic sides

JEMIMAS > JEMIMA

JEMMIED > JEMMY

JEMMIER > JEMMY

JEMMIES > JEMMY

JEMMIEST > JEMMY

JEMMINESS > JEMMY

JEMMY *n* short steel crowbar used by burglars ▷ *vb* prise (something) open with a jemmy ▷ *adj* neat

JEMMYING > JEMMY

JENNET *n* female donkey or ass

JENNETING *n* early-season apple

JENNETS > JENNET

JENNIES > JENNY

JENNY *same as* > JENNET

JEOFAIL *n* oversight in legal pleading

JEOFAILS > JEOFAIL

JEON *n* Korean pancake

JEONS > JEON

JEOPARD *vb* put in jeopardy

JEOPARDED > JEOPARD

JEOPARDER > JEOPARD

JEOPARDS > JEOPARD

JEOPARDY *n* danger ▷ *vb* put in jeopardy

JEQUERITY *same as* > JEQUIRITY

JEQUIRITY *n* seed of the Indian liquorice

JERBIL *variant spelling of* > GERBIL

JERBILS > JERBIL

JERBOA *n* small mouselike rodent with long hind legs

JERBOAS > JERBOA

JEREED *same as* > JERID

JEREEDS > JEREED

JEREMIAD *n* long mournful complaint

JEREMIADS > JEREMIAD

JEREPIGO *n* sweet fortified wine similar to port

JEREPIGOS > JEREPIGO

JERFALCON *variant of* > GYRFALCON

JERID *n* wooden javelin

JERIDS > JERID

JERK *vb* move or throw abruptly ▷ *n* sharp or abruptly stopped movement

JERKED > JERK

JERKER > JERK

JERKERS > JERK

JERKIER > JERKY

JERKIES > JERKY

JERKIEST > JERKY

JERKILY > JERKY

JERKIN *n* sleeveless jacket

JERKINESS > JERKY

JERKING > JERK

JERKINGLY > JERK

JERKINGS > JERK

JERKINS > JERKIN

JERKS > JERK

JERKWATER *adj* inferior and insignificant ▷ *n* railway locomotive

JERKY *adj* characterized by jerks ▷ *n* type of cured meat

JEROBOAM *n* wine bottle holding the equivalent of four normal bottles (approximately 104 ounces)

JEROBOAMS > JEROBOAM

JERQUE *vb* search for contraband

JERQUED > JERQUE

JERQUER > JERQUE

JERQUERS > JERQUE

JERQUES > JERQUE

JERQUING > JERQUE

JERQUINGS > JERQUE

JERREED *variant spelling of* > JERID

JERREEDS > JERREED

JERRICAN *n* five-gallon fuel can

JERRICANS > JERRICAN

JERRID *n* blunt javelin

JERRIDS > JERRID

JERRIES > JERRY

JERRY *short for* > JEROBOAM

JERRYCAN *n* flat-sided can used for storing or transporting liquids, esp motor fuel

JERRYCANS > JERRYCAN

JERSEY *n* knitted jumper

JERSEYED > JERSEY

JERSEYS > JERSEY

JESS *n* short leather strap used in falconry ▷ *vb* put jesses on (a hawk or falcon)

JESSAMIES > JESSAMY

JESSAMINE *same as* > JASMINE

JESSAMY *n* fop

JESSANT *adj* emerging

JESSE *same as* > JESS

JESSED > JESS

JESSERANT *n* coat of metal plates sewn onto cloth

JESSES > JESS

JESSIE *n* effeminate, weak, or cowardly boy or man

JESSIES > JESSIE

JESSING > JESS

JEST vb joke ▷ n something done or said for amusement

JESTBOOK n book of amusing stories

JESTBOOKS > JESTBOOK

JESTED > JEST

JESTEE n person about whom a joke is made

JESTEES > JESTEE

JESTER n professional clown at court

JESTERS > JESTER

JESTFUL > JEST

JESTING > JEST

JESTINGLY > JEST

JESTINGS > JEST

JESTS > JEST

JESUIT n offensive term for a person given to subtle and equivocating arguments

JESUITIC > JESUIT

JESUITISM > JESUIT

JESUITRY > JESUIT

JESUITS > JESUIT

JESUS n French paper size

JET n aircraft driven by jet propulsion ▷ vb fly by jet aircraft

JETBEAD n ornamental shrub

JETBEADS > JETBEAD

JETE n dance step

JETES > JETE

JETFOIL n type of hydrofoil that is propelled by water jets

JETFOILS > JETFOIL

JETLAG n tiredness caused by crossing timezones in jet flight

JETLAGS > JETLAG

JETLIKE > JET

JETLINER n commercial airliner powered by jet engines

JETLINERS > JETLINER

JETON n gambling chip

JETONS > JETON

JETPACK n wearable harness with jets, used for transport

JETPACKS > JETPACK

JETPORT n airport for jet planes

JETPORTS > JETPORT

JETS > JET

JETSAM n goods thrown overboard to lighten a ship

JETSAMS > JETSAM

JETSOM same as > JETSAM

JETSOMS > JETSOM

JETSON archaic form of > JETSAM

JETSONS > JETSON

JETSTREAM n narrow belt of high-altitude winds moving east at high speeds)

JETTATURA n evil eye

JETTED > JET

JETTIED > JETTY

JETTIER > JETTY

JETTIES > JETTY

JETTIEST > JETTY

JETTINESS > JETTY

JETTING > JET

JETTISON vb abandon

JETTISONS > JETTISON

JETTON n counter or token

JETTONS > JETTON

JETTY n small pier ▷ adj of or resembling jet, esp in colour or polish ▷ vb equip with a cantilevered floor

JETTYING > JETTY

JETWAY n tradename of device used in airports

JETWAYS > JETWAY

JEU n game

JEUNE adj young

JEUX > JEU

JEW vb obsolete offensive word for haggle ▷ n obsolete offensive word for a haggler

JEWED > JEW

JEWEL n precious or semiprecious stone ▷ vb fit or decorate with a jewel or jewels

JEWELED > JEWEL

JEWELER same as > JEWELLER

JEWELERS > JEWELER

JEWELFISH n beautifully coloured fish popular in aquaria

JEWELING > JEWEL

JEWELLED > JEWEL

JEWELLER n dealer in jewels

JEWELLERS > JEWELLER

JEWELLERY n objects decorated with precious stones

JEWELLIKE > JEWEL

JEWELLING > JEWEL

JEWELRIES > JEWELRY

JEWELRY same as > JEWELLERY

JEWELS > JEWEL

JEWELWEED n small bushy plant

JEWFISH n freshwater catfish

JEWFISHES > JEWFISH

JEWIE n jewfish

JEWIES > JEWIE

JEWING > JEW

JEWS > JEW

JEZAIL n Afghan musket

JEZAILS > JEZAIL

JEZEBEL n shameless or scheming woman

JEZEBELS > JEZEBEL

JHALA n Indian musical style

JHALAS > JHALA

JHATKA n slaughter of animals for food according to Sikh law

JHATKAS > JHATKA

JIAO n Chinese currency unit

JIAOS > JIAO

JIB same as > JIBE

JIBB same as > JIBE

JIBBA n long, loose coat worn by Muslim men

JIBBAH same as > JUBBAH

JIBBAHS > JIBBAH

JIBBAS > JIBBA

JIBBED > JIBB

JIBBER variant of > GIBBER

JIBBERED > JIBBER

JIBBERING > JIBBER

JIBBERS > JIBBER

JIBBING > JIBB

JIBBINGS > JIBB

JIBBONS pl n spring onions

JIBBOOM n spar forming an extension of the bowsprit

JIBBOOMS > JIBBOOM

JIBBS > JIBB

JIBE vb taunt or jeer ▷ n insulting or taunting remark

JIBED > JIBE

JIBER > JIBE

JIBERS > JIBE

JIBES > JIBE

JIBING > JIBE

JIBINGLY > JIBE

JIBS > JIB

JICAMA n pale brown turnip

JICAMAS > JICAMA

JICKAJOG vb engage in sexual intercourse

JICKAJOGS > JICKAJOG

JIFF same as > JIFFY

JIFFIES > JIFFY

JIFFS > JIFF

JIFFY n very short period of time

JIG n type of lively dance ▷ vb dance a jig

JIGABOO n offensive term for a Black person

JIGABOOS > JIGABOO

JIGAJIG vb engage in sexual intercourse

JIGAJIGS > JIGAJIG

JIGAJOG variant of > JIGAJIG

JIGAJOGS > JIGAJOG

JIGAMAREE n thing

JIGGED > JIG

JIGGER n small whisky glass ▷ vb interfere or alter

JIGGERED > JIGGER

JIGGERING > JIGGER

JIGGERS > JIGGER

JIGGIER > JIGGY

JIGGIEST > JIGGY

JIGGING > JIG

JIGGINGS > JIG

JIGGISH > JIG

JIGGLE vb move up and down with short jerky

movements ▷ n short jerky motion

JIGGLED > JIGGLE

JIGGLES > JIGGLE

JIGGLIER > JIGGLE

JIGGLIEST > JIGGLE

JIGGLING > JIGGLE

JIGGLY > JIGGLE

JIGGUMBOB n thing

JIGGY adj resembling a jig

JIGJIG variant of > JIGAJIG

JIGJIGGED > JIGJIG

JIGJIGS > JIGJIG

JIGLIKE > JIG

JIGOT same as > GIGOT

JIGOTS > JIGOT

JIGS > JIG

JIGSAW n type of game ▷ vb cut with a jigsaw

JIGSAWED > JIGSAW

JIGSAWING > JIGSAW

JIGSAWN > JIGSAW

JIGSAWS > JIGSAW

JIHAD n Islamic holy war against unbelievers

JIHADEEN pl n jihadists

JIHADI n person who takes part in a jihad

JIHADIS > JIHADI

JIHADISM n Islamic fundamentalist movement that favours the pursuit of jihads in defence of the Islamic faith

JIHADISMS > JIHADISM

JIHADIST > JIHADISM

JIHADISTS > JIHADISM

JIHADS > JIHAD

JILBAB n long robe worn by Muslim women

JILBABS > JILBAB

JILGIE n freshwater crayfish

JILGIES > JILGIE

JILL variant spelling of > GILL

JILLAROO n female jackeroo

JILLAROOS > JILLAROO

JILLET n wanton woman

JILLETS > JILLET

JILLFLIRT same as > JILLET

JILLION n extremely large number or amount

JILLIONS > JILLION

JILLIONTH > JILLION

JILLS > JILL

JILT vb leave or reject (one's lover) ▷ n woman who jilts a lover

JILTED > JILT

JILTER > JILT

JILTERS > JILT

JILTING > JILT

JILTS > JILT

JIMCRACK same as > GIMCRACK

JIMCRACKS > JIMCRACK

JIMINY interj expression of surprise

JIMJAM > JIMJAMS

JIMJAMS pl n state of nervous tension, excitement, or anxiety
JIMMIE same as > JIMMY
JIMMIED > JIMMY
JIMMIES > JIMMY
JIMMINY interj expression of surprise
JIMMY same as > JEMMY
JIMMYING > JIMMY
JIMP adj handsome
JIMPER > JIMP
JIMPEST > JIMP
JIMPIER > JIMPY
JIMPIEST > JIMPY
JIMPLY adv neatly
JIMPNESS > JIMP
JIMPSON same as > JIMSON
JIMPY adj neat and tidy
JIMSON n as in jimson weed type of poisonous plant
JIMSONS > JIMSON
JIN n Chinese unit of weight
JINGAL n swivel-mounted gun
JINGALL same as > JINGAL
JINGALLS > JINGALL
JINGALS > JINGAL
JINGBANG n entirety of something
JINGBANGS > JINGBANG
JINGKO same as > GINGKO
JINGKOES > JINGKO
JINGLE n catchy verse or song used in an advert ▷ vb (cause to) make a gentle ringing sound
JINGLED > JINGLE
JINGLER > JINGLE
JINGLERS > JINGLE
JINGLES > JINGLE
JINGLET n sleigh-bell clapper
JINGLETS > JINGLET
JINGLIER > JINGLE
JINGLIEST > JINGLE
JINGLING > JINGLE
JINGLY > JINGLE
JINGO n loud and bellicose patriot; chauvinism
JINGOES > JINGO
JINGOISH > JINGO
JINGOISM n aggressive nationalism
JINGOISMS > JINGOISM
JINGOIST > JINGOISM
JINGOISTS > JINGOISM
JINJILI n type of sesame
JINJILIS > JINJILI
JINK vb move quickly or jerkily in order to dodge someone ▷ n jinking movement
JINKED > JINK
JINKER n vehicle for transporting timber ▷ vb carry or transport in a jinker
JINKERED > JINKER
JINKERING > JINKER

JINKERS > JINKER
JINKING > JINK
JINKS > JINK
JINN > JINNI
JINNE interj South African exclamation
JINNEE same as > JINNI
JINNI n spirit in Muslim mythology
JINNIS > JINNI
JINNS > JINNI
JINRIKSHA same as > RICKSHAW
JINS > JIN
JINX n person or thing bringing bad luck ▷ vb be or put a jinx on
JINXED > JINX
JINXES > JINX
JINXING > JINX
JIPIJAPA n palmlike Central and South American plant whose fanlike leaves are bleached for making panama hats
JIPIJAPAS > JIPIJAPA
JIPYAPA same as > JIPIJAPA
JIPYAPAS > JIPYAPA
JIRBLE vb pour carelessly
JIRBLED > JIRBLE
JIRBLES > JIRBLE
JIRBLING > JIRBLE
JIRD n gerbil
JIRDS > JIRD
JIRGA n Afghan council
JIRGAS > JIRGA
JIRKINET n bodice
JIRKINETS > JIRKINET
JIRRE same as > JINNE
JISM slang word for > SEMEN
JISMS > JISM
JISSOM slang word for > SEMEN
JISSOMS > JISSOM
JITNEY n small cheap bus
JITNEYS > JITNEY
JITTER vb be anxious or nervous
JITTERBUG n fast jerky American dance that was popular in the 1940s ▷ vb dance the jitterbug
JITTERED > JITTER
JITTERIER > JITTERY
JITTERING > JITTER
JITTERS > JITTER
JITTERY adj nervous
JIUJITSU variant spelling of > JUJITSU
JIUJITSUS > JIUJITSU
JIUJUTSU same as > JUJITSU
JIUJUTSUS > JIUJUTSU
JIVE n lively dance of the 1940s and '50s ▷ vb dance the jive ▷ adj pertaining to or indicative of jive
JIVEASS adj misleading or phoney ▷ n person who loves fun and excitement
JIVEASSES > JIVEASS

JIVED > JIVE
JIVER > JIVE
JIVERS > JIVE
JIVES > JIVE
JIVEST > JIVE
JIVEY adj jazzy; lively
JIVIER > JIVEY
JIVIEST > JIVEY
JIVING > JIVE
JIVY same as > JIVEY
JIZ n wig
JIZZ n term for the characteristics that identify a particular species of bird or plant
JIZZES > JIZZ
JNANA n type of yoga
JNANAS > JNANA
JO n Scots word for sweetheart
JOANNA n piano
JOANNAS > JOANNA
JOANNES same as > JOHANNES
JOANNESES > JOANNES
JOB n occupation or paid employment ▷ vb work at casual jobs
JOBATION n scolding
JOBATIONS > JOBATION
JOBBED > JOB
JOBBER n person who jobs
JOBBERIES > JOBBERY
JOBBERS > JOBBER
JOBBERY n practice of making private profit out of a public office
JOBBIE n piece of excrement
JOBBIES > JOBBIE
JOBBING adj doing individual jobs for payment ▷ n act of seeking work
JOBBINGS > JOBBING
JOBCENTRE n office where unemployed people can find out about job vacancies
JOBE vb scold
JOBED > JOBE
JOBERNOWL n stupid person
JOBES > JOBE
JOBHOLDER n person who has a job
JOBING > JOBE
JOBLESS pl n as in the jobless unemployed people ▷ adj unemployed
JOBNAME n title of position
JOBNAMES > JOBNAME
JOBS > JOB
JOBSEEKER n person looking for employment
JOBSHARE n arrangement in which two or more people divide the duties and payment for one position between them, working at different times
JOBSHARES > JOBSHARE

JOBSWORTH n person in a position of minor authority who invokes the letter of the law in order to avoid any action requiring initiative, cooperation, etc
JOCK n athlete
JOCKDOM n world of male athletes
JOCKDOMS > JOCKDOM
JOCKETTE n female athlete
JOCKETTES > JOCKETTE
JOCKEY n person who rides horses in races ▷ vb ride (a horse) in a race
JOCKEYED > JOCKEY
JOCKEYING > JOCKEY
JOCKEYISH > JOCKEY
JOCKEYISM n skills and practices of jockeys
JOCKEYS > JOCKEY
JOCKIER > JOCKY
JOCKIEST > JOCKY
JOCKISH adj macho
JOCKNEY n the Scots dialect influenced by cockney speech patterns
JOCKNEYS > JOCKNEY
JOCKO n chimpanzee
JOCKOS > JOCKO
JOCKS > JOCK
JOCKSTRAP n belt with a pouch to support the genitals, worn by male athletes
JOCKTELEG n clasp knife
JOCKY adj indicating or appropriate to a male athlete
JOCO adj relaxed ▷ n joke
JOCOS > JOCO
JOCOSE adj playful or humorous
JOCOSELY > JOCOSE
JOCOSITY > JOCOSE
JOCULAR adj fond of joking
JOCULARLY > JOCULAR
JOCULATOR n joker
JOCUND adj merry or cheerful
JOCUNDITY > JOCUND
JOCUNDLY > JOCUND
JODEL same as > YODEL
JODELLED > JODEL
JODELLING > JODEL
JODELS > JODEL
JODHPUR n as in jodphur boots ankle-length leather riding boots
JODHPURS pl n riding breeches, loose-fitting around the hips and tight-fitting from the thighs to the ankles
JOE same as > JO
JOES > JOE
JOEY n young kangaroo
JOEYS > JOEY
JOG vb run at a gentle pace, esp for exercise ▷ n slow run
JOGGED > JOG

j

JOGGER n person who runs at a jog for exercise
JOGGERS > JOGGER
JOGGING > JOG
JOGGINGS > JOG
JOGGLE vb shake or move jerkily ▷ n act of joggling
JOGGLED > JOGGLE
JOGGLER > JOGGLE
JOGGLERS > JOGGLE
JOGGLES > JOGGLE
JOGGLING > JOGGLE
JOGPANTS pl n trousers worn for jogging
JOGS > JOG
JOGTROT n easy bouncy gait ▷ vb move at a jogtrot
JOGTROTS > JOGTROT
JOHANNES n Portuguese gold coin minted in the early 18th century
JOHN n toilet
JOHNBOAT n small flat-bottomed boat
JOHNBOATS > JOHNBOAT
JOHNNIE same as > JOHNNY
JOHNNIES > JOHNNY
JOHNNY n chap
JOHNS > JOHN
JOHNSON slang word for > PENIS
JOHNSONS > JOHNSON
JOIN vb become a member (of) ▷ n place where two things are joined
JOINABLE > JOIN
JOINDER n act of joining, esp in legal contexts
JOINDERS > JOINDER
JOINED > JOIN
JOINER n maker of finished woodwork
JOINERIES > JOINERY
JOINERS > JOINER
JOINERY n joiner's work
JOINING > JOIN
JOININGS > JOIN
JOINS > JOIN
JOINT adj shared by two or more ▷ n place where bones meet but can move ▷ vb divide meat into joints
JOINTED adj having a joint or joints
JOINTEDLY > JOINTED
JOINTER n tool for pointing mortar joints
JOINTERS > JOINTER
JOINTING > JOINT
JOINTINGS > JOINTING
JOINTLESS > JOINT
JOINTLY > JOINT
JOINTNESS > JOINT
JOINTRESS n woman entitled to a jointure
JOINTS > JOINT
JOINTURE n provision made by a husband for his wife by settling property upon her at marriage for her use after his death
JOINTURED > JOINTURE

JOINTURES > JOINTURE
JOINTWEED n American wild plant
JOINTWORM n larva of chalcid flies which form galls on the stems of cereal plants
JOIST n horizontal beam ▷ vb construct (a floor, roof, etc) with joists
JOISTED > JOIST
JOISTING > JOIST
JOISTS > JOIST
JOJOBA n shrub of SW North America
JOJOBAS > JOJOBA
JOKE n thing said or done to cause laughter ▷ vb make jokes
JOKED > JOKE
JOKER n person who jokes
JOKERS > JOKER
JOKES > JOKE
JOKESMITH n comedian
JOKESOME > JOKE
JOKESTER n person who makes jokes
JOKESTERS > JOKESTER
JOKEY adj intended as a joke
JOKIER > JOKEY
JOKIEST > JOKEY
JOKILY > JOKE
JOKINESS > JOKEY
JOKING n act of joking
JOKINGLY > JOKE
JOKINGS > JOKING
JOKOL Shetland word for > YES
JOKY same as > JOKEY
JOL n party ▷ vb have a good time
JOLE vb knock
JOLED > JOLE
JOLES > JOLE
JOLING > JOLE
JOLIOTIUM n former name proposed for dubnium
JOLL variant of > JOLE
JOLLED > JOL
JOLLER n person who has a good time
JOLLERS > JOLLER
JOLLEY same as > JOLLY
JOLLEYER > JOLLEY
JOLLEYERS > JOLLEY
JOLLEYING > JOLLEY
JOLLEYS > JOLLEY
JOLLIED > JOLLY
JOLLIER n joker
JOLLIERS > JOLLIER
JOLLIES > JOLLY
JOLLIEST > JOLLY
JOLLIFIED > JOLLIFY
JOLLIFIES > JOLLIFY
JOLLIFY vb be or cause to be jolly
JOLLILY > JOLLY
JOLLIMENT > JOLLY
JOLLINESS > JOLLY
JOLLING > JOL
JOLLITIES > JOLLITY

JOLLITY n condition of being jolly
JOLLOP n cream or unguent
JOLLOPS > JOLLOP
JOLLS > JOLL
JOLLY adj full of good humour ▷ adv extremely ▷ vb try to make or keep (someone) cheerful ▷ n festivity or celebration
JOLLYBOAT n small boat used as a utility tender for a vessel
JOLLYER > JOLLY
JOLLYERS > JOLLY
JOLLYHEAD same as > JOLLITY
JOLLYING > JOLLY
JOLLYINGS > JOLLY
JOLS > JOL
JOLT n unpleasant surprise or shock ▷ vb surprise or shock
JOLTED > JOLT
JOLTER > JOLT
JOLTERS > JOLT
JOLTHEAD n fool
JOLTHEADS > JOLTHEAD
JOLTIER > JOLT
JOLTIEST > JOLT
JOLTILY > JOLT
JOLTING n act of jolting
JOLTINGLY > JOLT
JOLTINGS > JOLTING
JOLTS > JOLT
JOLTY > JOLT
JOMO same as > ZO
JOMON n particular era in Japanese history
JOMONS > JOMON
JOMOS > JOMO
JONCANOE n Jamaican ceremony
JONCANOES > JONCANOE
JONES vb desire
JONESED > JONES
JONESES > JONES
JONESING > JONES
JONG n friend, often used in direct address
JONGLEUR n (in medieval France) an itinerant minstrel
JONGLEURS > JONGLEUR
JONGS > JONG
JONNOCK adj genuine ▷ adv honestly
JONNYCAKE n type of flat bread
JONQUIL n fragrant narcissus
JONQUILS > JONQUIL
JONTIES > JONTY
JONTY n petty officer
JOOK vb poke or puncture (the skin) ▷ n jab or the resulting wound
JOOKED > JOOK
JOOKERIES > JOOKERY
JOOKERY n mischief
JOOKING > JOOK
JOOKS > JOOK

JOR n movement in Indian music
JORAM same as > JORUM
JORAMS > JORAM
JORDAN n chamber pot
JORDANS > JORDAN
JORDELOO same as > GARDYLOO
JORDELOOS > JORDELOO
JORS > JOR
JORUM n large drinking bowl or vessel or its contents
JORUMS > JORUM
JOSEPH n woman's floor-length riding coat
JOSEPHS > JOSEPH
JOSH vb tease ▷ n teasing or bantering joke
JOSHED > JOSH
JOSHER > JOSH
JOSHERS > JOSH
JOSHES > JOSH
JOSHING n act of joshing
JOSHINGLY > JOSH
JOSHINGS > JOSHING
JOSKIN n bumpkin
JOSKINS > JOSKIN
JOSS n Chinese deity
JOSSER n simpleton
JOSSERS > JOSSER
JOSSES > JOSS
JOSTLE vb knock or push against ▷ n act of jostling
JOSTLED > JOSTLE
JOSTLER > JOSTLE
JOSTLERS > JOSTLE
JOSTLES > JOSTLE
JOSTLING > JOSTLE
JOSTLINGS > JOSTLE
JOT vb write briefly ▷ n very small amount
JOTA n Spanish dance
JOTAS > JOTA
JOTS > JOT
JOTTED > JOT
JOTTER n notebook
JOTTERS > JOTTER
JOTTIER > JOTTY
JOTTIEST > JOTTY
JOTTING > JOT
JOTTINGS > JOT
JOTTY > JOT
JOTUN n giant
JOTUNN same as > JOTUN
JOTUNNS > JOTUNN
JOTUNS > JOTUN
JOUAL n nonstandard variety of Canadian French
JOUALS > JOUAL
JOUGS pl n iron ring for restraining an offender
JOUISANCE n joy
JOUK vb duck or dodge ▷ n sudden evasive movement
JOUKED > JOUK
JOUKERIES > JOUKERY
JOUKERY same as > JOOKERY
JOUKING > JOUK
JOUKS > JOUK

JOULE n unit of work or energy ▷ vb knock
JOULED > JOULE
JOULES > JOULE
JOULING > JOULE
JOUNCE vb shake or jolt or cause to shake or jolt ▷ n jolting movement
JOUNCED > JOUNCE
JOUNCES > JOUNCE
JOUNCIER > JOUNCE
JOUNCIEST > JOUNCE
JOUNCING > JOUNCE
JOUNCY > JOUNCE
JOUR n day
JOURNAL n daily newspaper or magazine ▷ vb record in a journal
JOURNALED > JOURNAL
JOURNALS > JOURNAL
JOURNEY n act of travelling from one place to another ▷ vb travel
JOURNEYED > JOURNEY
JOURNEYER > JOURNEY
JOURNEYS > JOURNEY
JOURNO n journalist
JOURNOS > JOURNO
JOURS > JOUR
JOUST n combat between two knights ▷ vb fight on horseback using lances
JOUSTED > JOUST
JOUSTER > JOUST
JOUSTERS > JOUST
JOUSTING n act of jousting
JOUSTINGS > JOUSTING
JOUSTS > JOUST
JOVIAL adj happy and cheerful
JOVIALITY > JOVIAL
JOVIALLY > JOVIAL
JOVIALTY same as > JOVIAL
JOW vb ring (a bell)
JOWAR n variety of sorghum
JOWARI same as > JOWAR
JOWARIS > JOWAR
JOWARS > JOWAR
JOWED > JOW
JOWING > JOW
JOWL n lower jaw ▷ vb knock
JOWLED > JOWL
JOWLER n dog with prominent jowls
JOWLERS > JOWLER
JOWLIER > JOWL
JOWLIEST > JOWL
JOWLINESS > JOWL
JOWLING > JOWL
JOWLS > JOWL
JOWLY > JOWL
JOWS > JOW
JOY n feeling of great delight or pleasure ▷ vb feel joy
JOYANCE n joyous feeling or festivity
JOYANCES > JOYANCE
JOYED > JOY

JOYFUL adj feeling or bringing great joy
JOYFULLER > JOYFUL
JOYFULLY > JOYFUL
JOYING > JOY
JOYLESS adj feeling or bringing no joy
JOYLESSLY > JOYLESS
JOYOUS adj extremely happy and enthusiastic
JOYOUSLY > JOYOUS
JOYPAD n computer games console
JOYPADS > JOYPAD
JOYPOP vb take addictive drugs occasionally
JOYPOPPED > JOYPOP
JOYPOPPER > JOYPOP
JOYPOPS > JOYPOP
JOYRIDDEN > JOYRIDE
JOYRIDE n drive in a car one has stolen ▷ vb take such a ride
JOYRIDER > JOYRIDE
JOYRIDERS > JOYRIDE
JOYRIDES > JOYRIDE
JOYRIDING > JOYRIDE
JOYRODE > JOYRIDE
JOYS > JOY
JOYSTICK n control device for an aircraft or computer
JOYSTICKS > JOYSTICK
JUBA n lively African-American dance
JUBAS > JUBA
JUBATE adj possessing a mane
JUBBAH n long loose outer garment with wide sleeves
JUBBAHS > JUBBAH
JUBE n part of a church or cathedral
JUBES > JUBE
JUBHAH same as > JUBBAH
JUBHAHS > JUBHAH
JUBILANCE > JUBILANT
JUBILANCY > JUBILANT
JUBILANT adj feeling or expressing great joy
JUBILATE vb have or express great joy
JUBILATED > JUBILATE
JUBILATES > JUBILATE
JUBILE same as > JUBILEE
JUBILEE n special anniversary, esp 25th or 50th
JUBILEES > JUBILEE
JUBILES > JUBILE
JUCO n junior college in America
JUCOS > JUCO
JUD n large block of coal
JUDAS n peephole
JUDASES > JUDAS
JUDDER vb vibrate violently ▷ n violent vibration
JUDDERED > JUDDER
JUDDERING > JUDDER
JUDDERS > JUDDER

JUDDERY adj shaky
JUDGE n public official ▷ vb act as a judge
JUDGEABLE > JUDGE
JUDGED > JUDGE
JUDGELESS > JUDGE
JUDGELIKE > JUDGE
JUDGEMENT same as > JUDGMENT
JUDGER > JUDGE
JUDGERS > JUDGE
JUDGES > JUDGE
JUDGESHIP n position, office, or function of a judge
JUDGING n act of judging
JUDGINGLY > JUDGE
JUDGINGS > JUDGING
JUDGMATIC adj judicious
JUDGMENT n opinion reached after careful thought
JUDGMENTS > JUDGMENT
JUDICABLE adj capable of being judged, esp in a court of law
JUDICARE n (in Canada) state-paid legal services
JUDICARES > JUDICARE
JUDICATOR n person who acts as a judge
JUDICIAL adj of or by a court or judge
JUDICIARY n system of courts and judges ▷ adj of or relating to courts of law, judgment, or judges
JUDICIOUS adj well-judged and sensible
JUDIES > JUDY
JUDO n type of sport
JUDOGI n white two-piece cotton costume
JUDOGIS > JUDOGI
JUDOIST > JUDO
JUDOISTS > JUDO
JUDOKA n competitor or expert in judo
JUDOKAS > JUDOKA
JUDOS > JUDO
JUDS > JUD
JUDY n woman
JUG n container for liquids ▷ vb stew or boil (meat, esp hare) in an earthenware container
JUGA > JUGUM
JUGAL adj of or relating to the zygomatic bone ▷ n cheekbone
JUGALS > JUGAL
JUGATE adj having parts arranged in pairs
JUGFUL same as > JUG
JUGFULS > JUGFUL
JUGGED > JUG
JUGGING > JUG
JUGGINGS > JUG
JUGGINS n silly person
JUGGINSES > JUGGINS
JUGGLE vb throw and catch (objects) to keep them in the air ▷ n act of juggling

JUGGLED > JUGGLE
JUGGLER n person who juggles, esp a professional entertainer
JUGGLERS > JUGGLER
JUGGLERY > JUGGLE
JUGGLES > JUGGLE
JUGGLING > JUGGLE
JUGGLINGS > JUGGLE
JUGHEAD n clumsy person
JUGHEADS > JUGHEAD
JUGLET n small jug
JUGLETS > JUGLET
JUGS > JUG
JUGSFUL > JUGFUL
JUGULA > JUGULUM
JUGULAR n one of three large veins of the neck
JUGULARS > JUGULAR
JUGULATE vb check (a disease) by extreme measures or remedies
JUGULATED > JUGULATE
JUGULATES > JUGULATE
JUGULUM n lower throat
JUGUM n part of an insect's forewing
JUGUMS > JUGUM
JUICE n liquid part of vegetables, fruit, or meat ▷ vb extract juice from fruits and vegetables
JUICED > JUICE
JUICEHEAD n alcoholic
JUICELESS > JUICE
JUICER n kitchen appliance
JUICERS > JUICER
JUICES > JUICE
JUICIER > JUICY
JUICIEST > JUICY
JUICILY > JUICY
JUICINESS > JUICY
JUICING > JUICE
JUICY adj full of juice
JUJITSU n Japanese martial art
JUJITSUS > JUJITSU
JUJU n W African magic charm or fetish
JUJUBE n chewy sweet made of flavoured gelatine
JUJUBES > JUJUBE
JUJUISM > JUJU
JUJUISMS > JUJU
JUJUIST > JUJU
JUJUISTS > JUJU
JUJUS > JUJU
JUJUTSU same as > JUJITSU
JUJUTSUS > JUJUTSU
JUKE vb dance or play dance music
JUKEBOX n coin-operated music box
JUKEBOXES > JUKEBOX
JUKED > JUKE
JUKES > JUKE
JUKING > JUKE
JUKSKEI n type of game
JUKSKEIS > JUKE
JUKU n Japanese martial art

JUKUS > JUKU
JULEP *n* sweet alcoholic drink
JULEPS > JULEP
JULIENNE *adj* (of vegetables or meat) cut into thin shreds ▷ *n* clear soup containing thinly shredded vegetables ▷ *vb* cut into thin pieces
JULIENNED > JULIENNE
JULIENNES > JULIENNE
JULIET *n* code word for the letter J
JULIETS > JULIET
JUMAR *n* climbing tool ▷ *vb* climb (up a fixed rope) using jumars
JUMARED > JUMAR
JUMARING > JUMAR
JUMARRED > JUMAR
JUMARRING > JUMAR
JUMARS > JUMAR
JUMART *n* mythical offspring of a bull and a mare
JUMARTS > JUMART
JUMBAL *same as* **>** JUMBLE
JUMBALS > JUMBAL
JUMBIE *n* Caribbean ghost
JUMBIES > JUMBIE
JUMBLE *n* confused heap or state ▷ *vb* mix in a disordered way
JUMBLED > JUMBLE
JUMBLER > JUMBLE
JUMBLERS > JUMBLE
JUMBLES > JUMBLE
JUMBLIER > JUMBLE
JUMBLIEST > JUMBLE
JUMBLING > JUMBLE
JUMBLY > JUMBLE
JUMBO *adj* very large ▷ *n* large jet airliner
JUMBOISE *same as* **>** JUMBOIZE
JUMBOISED > JUMBOISE
JUMBOISES > JUMBOISE
JUMBOIZE *vb* extend (a ship, esp a tanker) by cutting out the middle part and inserting a new larger part between the original bow and stern
JUMBOIZED > JUMBOIZE
JUMBOIZES > JUMBOIZE
JUMBOS > JUMBO
JUMBUCK *n* sheep
JUMBUCKS > JUMBUCK
JUMBY *n* Caribbean ghost
JUMELLE *n* paired objects
JUMELLES > JUMELLE
JUMP *vb* leap or spring into the air using the leg muscles ▷ *n* act of jumping
JUMPABLE > JUMP
JUMPED > JUMP
JUMPER *n* sweater or pullover
JUMPERS > JUMPER
JUMPIER > JUMPY

JUMPIEST > JUMPY
JUMPILY > JUMPY
JUMPINESS > JUMPY
JUMPING > JUMP
JUMPINGLY > JUMP
JUMPINGS > JUMP
JUMPOFF *n* round in a showjumping contest
JUMPOFFS > JUMPOFF
JUMPROPE *n* rope held in the hands and jumped over
JUMPROPES > JUMPROPE
JUMPS > JUMP
JUMPSHOT *n* type of shot in basketball in which a player jumps to reach the basket
JUMPSHOTS > JUMPSHOT
JUMPSIES *pl n* game involving jumping over a straight rope
JUMPSUIT *n* one-piece garment of combined trousers and jacket or shirt
JUMPSUITS > JUMPSUIT
JUMPY *adj* nervous
JUN *variant of* **>** CHON
JUNCATE *same as* **>** JUNKET
JUNCATES > JUNCATE
JUNCO *n* North American bunting
JUNCOES > JUNCO
JUNCOS > JUNCO
JUNCTION *n* place where routes, railway lines, or roads meet
JUNCTIONS > JUNCTION
JUNCTURAL > JUNCTURE
JUNCTURE *n* point in time, esp a critical one
JUNCTURES > JUNCTURE
JUNCUS *n* type of rush
JUNCUSES > JUNCUS
JUNEATING *n* early-season apple
JUNGLE *n* tropical forest of dense tangled vegetation
JUNGLED *adj* covered with jungle
JUNGLEGYM *n* climbing frame for children
JUNGLES > JUNGLE
JUNGLI *n* uncultured person
JUNGLIER > JUNGLE
JUNGLIEST > JUNGLE
JUNGLIS > JUNGLI
JUNGLIST *n* jungle-music enthusiast
JUNGLISTS > JUNGLIST
JUNGLY > JUNGLE
JUNIOR *adj* of lower standing ▷ *n* junior person ▷ *vb* work as a junior
JUNIORATE *n* preparatory course for candidates for religious orders
JUNIORED > JUNIOR
JUNIORING > JUNIOR
JUNIORITY *n* condition of being junior

JUNIORS > JUNIOR
JUNIPER *n* evergreen shrub with purple berries
JUNIPERS > JUNIPER
JUNK *n* discarded or useless objects ▷ *vb* discard as junk
JUNKANOO *n* Bahamian ceremony
JUNKANOOS > JUNKANOO
JUNKED > JUNK
JUNKER *n* (formerly) young German nobleman
JUNKERS > JUNKER
JUNKET *n* excursion by public officials ▷ *vb* (of a public official, committee, etc) to go on a junket
JUNKETED > JUNKET
JUNKETEER > JUNKET
JUNKETER > JUNKET
JUNKETERS > JUNKET
JUNKETING > JUNKET
JUNKETS > JUNKET
JUNKETTED > JUNKET
JUNKETTER > JUNKET
JUNKIE *n* drug addict
JUNKIER > JUNKY
JUNKIES > JUNKY
JUNKIEST > JUNKY
JUNKINESS > JUNKY
JUNKING > JUNK
JUNKMAN *n* man who trades in discarded items
JUNKMEN > JUNKMAN
JUNKS > JUNK
JUNKY *n* drug addict ▷ *adj* of low quality
JUNKYARD *n* place where junk is stored or collected for sale
JUNKYARDS > JUNKYARD
JUNTA *n* military officers holding power in a country
JUNTAS > JUNTA
JUNTO *same as* **>** JUNTA
JUNTOS > JUNTO
JUPATI *n* type of palm tree
JUPATIS > JUPATI
JUPE *n* sleeveless jacket
JUPES > JUPE
JUPON *n* short sleeveless padded garment
JUPONS > JUPON
JURA > JUS
JURAL *adj* of or relating to law or to the administration of justice
JURALLY > JURAL
JURANT *n* person taking oath
JURANTS > JURANT
JURASSIC *adj* of, denoting, or formed in the second period of the Mesozoic era, between the Triassic and Cretaceous periods, lasting for 55 million years during which dinosaurs and ammonites flourished
JURAT *n* statement at the foot of an affidavit

JURATORY *adj* of, relating to, or expressed in an oath
JURATS > JURAT
JURE *adv* by legal right ▷ *n* legal right
JUREL *n* edible fish
JURELS > JUREL
JURES > JURE
JURIDIC *same as* **>** JURIDICAL
JURIDICAL *adj* of law or the administration of justice
JURIED > JURY
JURIES > JURY
JURIST *n* expert in law
JURISTIC *adj* of or relating to jurists
JURISTS > JURIST
JUROR *n* member of a jury
JURORS > JUROR
JURY *n* group of people sworn to deliver a verdict in a court of law ▷ *adj* makeshift ▷ *vb* evaluate by jury
JURYING > JURY
JURYLESS > JURY
JURYMAN *n* member of a jury, esp a man
JURYMAST *n* replacement mast
JURYMASTS > JURYMAST
JURYMEN > JURYMAN
JURYWOMAN *n* female member of a jury
JURYWOMEN > JURYWOMAN
JUS *n* right, power, or authority
JUSSIVE *n* mood of verbs used for giving orders; imperative
JUSSIVES > JUSSIVE
JUST *adv* very recently ▷ *adj* fair or impartial in action or judgment ▷ *vb* joust
JUSTED > JUST
JUSTER > JUST
JUSTERS > JUST
JUSTEST > JUST
JUSTICE *n* quality of being just
JUSTICER *n* magistrate
JUSTICERS > JUSTICER
JUSTICES > JUSTICE
JUSTICIAR *n* chief political and legal officer from the time of William I to that of Henry III, who deputized for the king in his absence and presided over the kings' courts
JUSTIFIED > JUSTIFY
JUSTIFIER > JUSTIFY
JUSTIFIES > JUSTIFY
JUSTIFY *vb* prove right or reasonable
JUSTING > JOUST
JUSTLE *less common word for* **>** JOSTLE
JUSTLED > JUSTLE
JUSTLES > JUSTLE

JUSTLING > JUSTLE
JUSTLY > JUST
JUSTNESS > JUST
JUSTS *same as* **>** JOUST
JUT *vb* project or stick out
▷ *n* something that juts
out
JUTE *n* plant fibre, used for
rope, canvas, etc
JUTELIKE > JUTE
JUTES > JUTE

JUTS > JUT
JUTTED > JUT
JUTTIED > JUTTY
JUTTIER > JUTTY
JUTTIES > JUTTY
JUTTIEST > JUTTY
JUTTING > JUT
JUTTINGLY > JUT
JUTTY *vb* project beyond
▷ *adj* characterized by
jutting

JUTTYING > JUTTY
JUVE *same as*
> JUVENILE
JUVENAL *variant spelling*
(esp US) of **>** JUVENILE
JUVENALS > JUVENAL
JUVENILE *adj* young
▷ *n* young person or child
JUVENILES > JUVENILE
JUVENILIA *pl n*
works produced in an

author's youth
JUVES > JUVE
JUVIE *n* juvenile
detention centre
JUVIES > JUVIE
JUXTAPOSE *vb* put side
by side
JYMOLD *adj* having a
hinge
JYNX *n* wryneck
JYNXES > JYNX

j

Kk

KA *n* (in ancient Egypt) type of spirit ▷ *vb* (in archaic usage) help
KAAL *adj* naked
KAAMA *n* large African antelope with lyre-shaped horns
KAAMAS > KAAMA
KAAS *n* Dutch cabinet or wardrobe
KAB *variant spelling of* > CAB
KABAB *same as* > KEBAB
KABABBED > KABAB
KABABBING > KABAB
KABABS > KABAB
KABADDI *n* type of game
KABADDIS > KABADDI
KABAKA *n* any of the former rulers of the Baganda people
KABAKAS > KABAKA
KABALA *same as* > KABBALAH
KABALAS > KABALA
KABALISM > KABALA
KABALISMS > KABALA
KABALIST > KABALA
KABALISTS > KABALA
KABAR *archaic form of* > CABER
KABARS > KABAR
KABAYA *n* tunic
KABAYAS > KABAYA
KABBALA *same as* > KABBALAH
KABBALAH *n* ancient Jewish mystical tradition
KABBALAHS > KABBALAH
KABBALAS > KABBALA
KABBALISM > KABBALAH
KABBALIST > KABBALAH
KABELE *same as* > KEBELE
KABELES > KABELE
KABELJOU *n* large fish that is an important food fish of South African waters
KABELJOUS > KABELJOU
KABELJOUW *same as* > KABELJOU
KABIKI *n* fruit tree found in India
KABIKIS > KABIKI
KABLOOEY *interj* expressing alarming or surprising abruptness
KABLOOIE *same as* > KABLOOEY

KABLOONA *n* (among Canadian Inuits) person who is not Inuit
KABLOONAS > KABLOONA
KABLOONAT > KABLOONA
KABOB *same as* > KEBAB
KABOBBED > KABOB
KABOBBING > KABOB
KABOBS > KABOB
KABOCHA *n* type of Japanese pumpkin
KABOCHAS > KABOCHA
KABOODLE *same as* > CABOODLE
KABOODLES > KABOODLE
KABOOM *n* loud echoing explosive sound
KABOOMS > KABOOM
KABS > KAB
KABUKI *n* form of Japanese drama
KABUKIS > KABUKI
KACCHA *n* trousers worn traditionally by Sikhs
KACCHAS > KACCHA
KACHA *adj* crude
KACHAHRI *n* Indian courthouse
KACHAHRIS > KACHAHRI
KACHCHA *same as* > KACHA
KACHERI *same as* > KACHAHRI
KACHERIS > KACHERI
KACHINA *n* type of supernatural being
KACHINAS > KACHINA
KACHORI *n* balls of fried dough with various fillings, eaten as a snack
KACHORIS > KACHORI
KACHUMBER *n* salad of onion, tomato, and cucumber
KACK *same as* > CACK
KACKS > KACK
KADAI *same as* > KARAHI
KADAIS > KADAI
KADAITCHA *n* (in certain Central Australian Aboriginal tribes) man with the mission of avenging the death of a tribesman
KADDISH *n* ancient Jewish liturgical prayer
KADDISHES > KADDISH
KADDISHIM > KADDISH
KADE *same as* > KED
KADES > KADE

KADI *variant spelling of* > CADI
KADIS > KADI
KAE *n* dialect word for jackdaw or jay ▷ *vb* (in archaic usage) help
KAED > KAE
KAEING > KAE
KAES > KAE
KAF *n* letter of the Hebrew alphabet
KAFFIR *n* Southern African variety of sorghum
KAFFIRS > KAFFIR
KAFFIYAH *same as* > KAFFIYEH
KAFFIYAHS > KAFFIYAH
KAFFIYEH *same as* > KEFFIYEH
KAFFIYEHS > KAFFIYEH
KAFILA *n* caravan
KAFILAS > KAFILA
KAFIR *same as* > KAFFIR
KAFIRS > KAFIR
KAFS > KAF
KAFTAN *n* long loose Eastern garment
KAFTANS > KAFTAN
KAFUFFLE *n* commotion or disorder
KAFUFFLES > KAFUFFLE
KAGO *n* Japanese sedan chair
KAGOOL *variant spelling of* > CAGOULE
KAGOOLS > KAGOOL
KAGOS > KAGO
KAGOUL *variant spelling of* > CAGOULE
KAGOULE *same as* > KAGOUL
KAGOULES > KAGOULE
KAGOULS > KAGOUL
KAGU *n* crested nocturnal bird
KAGUS > KAGU
KAHAL *n* Jewish community
KAHALS > KAHAL
KAHAWAI *n* food and game fish of New Zealand
KAHAWAIS > KAHAWAI
KAHIKATEA *n* tall New Zealand coniferous tree
KAHIKATOA *n* tall New Zealand coniferous tree
KAHUNA *n* Hawaiian priest, shaman, or expert
KAHUNAS > KAHUNA
KAI *n* food

KAIAK *same as* > KAYAK
KAIAKED > KAIAK
KAIAKING > KAIAK
KAIAKS > KAIAK
KAID *n* North African chieftain or leader
KAIDS > KAID
KAIE *archaic form of* > KEY
KAIES > KAIE
KAIF *same as* > KIF
KAIFS > KAIF
KAIK *same as* > KAINGA
KAIKA *same as* > KAINGA
KAIKAI *n* food
KAIKAIS > KAIKAI
KAIKAS > KAIKA
KAIKAWAKA *n* small pyramid-shaped New Zealand conifer
KAIKOMAKO *n* small New Zealand tree with white flowers and black fruit
KAIKS > KAIK
KAIL *same as* > KALE
KAILS > KAIL
KAILYAIRD *same as* > KALEYARD
KAILYARD *same as* > KALEYARD
KAILYARDS > KAILYARD
KAIM *same as* > KAME
KAIMAKAM *n* Turkish governor
KAIMAKAMS > KAIMAKAM
KAIMS > KAIM
KAIN *variant spelling of* > CAIN
KAING > KA
KAINGA *n* (in New Zealand) a Māori village or small settlement
KAINGAS > KAINGA
KAINIT *same as* > KAINITE
KAINITE *n* white mineral
KAINITES > KAINITE
KAINITS > KAINIT
KAINS > KAIN
KAIROMONE *n* substance secreted by animal
KAIS > KAI
KAISER *n* German or Austro-Hungarian emperor
KAISERDOM > KAISER
KAISERIN *n* empress
KAISERINS > KAISERIN
KAISERISM > KAISER
KAISERS > KAISER

KAIZEN n type of philosophy
KAIZENS > KAIZEN
KAJAWAH n type of seat or pannier used on a camel
KAJAWAHS > KAJAWAH
KAJEPUT n variety of Australian melaleuca
KAJEPUTS > KAJEPUT
KAK n South African slang word for faeces
KAKA n parrot of New Zealand
KAKAPO n nocturnal New Zealand parrot
KAKAPOS > KAKAPO
KAKARIKI n green-feathered New Zealand parrot
KAKARIKIS > KAKARIKI
KAKAS > KAKA
KAKEMONO n Japanese paper or silk wall hanging, usually long and narrow, with a picture or inscription on it and a roller at the bottom
KAKEMONOS > KAKEMONO
KAKI n Asian persimmon tree
KAKIEMON n type of 17th century Japanese porcelain
KAKIEMONS > KAKIEMON
KAKIS > KAKI
KAKIVAK n fish spear used by Inuit people
KAKIVAKS > KAKIVAK
KAKODYL variant spelling of > CACODYL
KAKODYLS > KAKODYL
KAKS > KAK
KAKURO n crossword-style puzzle with numbers
KAKUROS > KAKURO
KALAM n discussion and debate
KALAMATA n as in kalamata olive aubergine-coloured Greek olive
KALAMATAS > KALAMATA
KALAMDAN n Persian box in which to keep pens
KALAMDANS > KALAMDAN
KALAMKARI n Indian cloth printing and printed Indian cloth
KALAMS > KALAM
KALANCHOE n tropical succulent plant having small brightly coloured flowers and dark shiny leaves
KALE n cabbage with crinkled leaves
KALENDAR variant form of > CALENDAR
KALENDARS > KALENDAR
KALENDS same as > CALENDS
KALES > KALE

KALEWIFE n Scots word for a female vegetable or cabbage seller
KALEWIVES > KALEWIFE
KALEYARD n vegetable garden
KALEYARDS > KALEYARD
KALI another name for > SALTWORT
KALIAN another name for > HOOKAH
KALIANS > KALIAN
KALIF variant spelling of > CALIPH
KALIFATE same as > CALIPHATE
KALIFATES > KALIFATE
KALIFS > KALIF
KALIMBA n musical instrument
KALIMBAS > KALIMBA
KALINITE n alum
KALINITES > KALINITE
KALIPH variant spelling of > CALIPH
KALIPHATE same as > CALIPHATE
KALIPHS > KALIPH
KALIS > KALI
KALIUM n Latin for potassium
KALIUMS > KALIUM
KALLIDIN n type of peptide
KALLIDINS > KALLIDIN
KALLITYPE n old printing process
KALMIA n evergreen ericaceous shrub
KALMIAS > KALMIA
KALONG n fruit bat
KALONGS > KALONG
KALOOKI n card game
KALOOKIE same as > KALOOKI
KALOOKIES > KALOOKIE
KALOOKIS > KALOOKI
KALOTYPE variant spelling of > CALOTYPE
KALOTYPES > KALOTYPE
KALPA n period in Hindu cosmology
KALPAC same as > CALPAC
KALPACS > KALPAC
KALPAK variant spelling of > CALPAC
KALPAKS > KALPAK
KALPAS > KALPA
KALPIS n Greek water jar
KALPISES > KALPIS
KALSOMINE variant of > CALCIMINE
KALUKI same as > KALOOKI
KALUKIS > KALUKI
KALUMPIT n type of Filipino fruit tree or its fruit
KALUMPITS > KALUMPIT
KALYPTRA n Greek veil
KALYPTRAS > KALYPTRA
KAM Shakespearean word for > CROOKED

KAMA n large African antelope with lyre-shaped horns
KAMAAINA n Hawaiian local
KAMAAINAS > KAMAAINA
KAMACITE n alloy of iron and nickel, occurring in meteorites
KAMACITES > KAMACITE
KAMAHI n hardwood tree
KAMAHIS > KAMAHI
KAMALA n East Indian tree
KAMALAS > KAMALA
KAMAS > KAMA
KAME n irregular mound of gravel, sand, etc
KAMEES > KAMEEZ
KAMEESES > KAMEES
KAMEEZ n long tunic
KAMEEZES > KAMEEZ
KAMELA same as > KAMALA
KAMELAS > KAMELA
KAMERAD interj shout of surrender ▷ vb surrender
KAMERADED > KAMERAD
KAMERADS > KAMERAD
KAMES > KAME
KAMI n divine being or spiritual force in Shinto
KAMICHI n South American bird
KAMICHIS > KAMICHI
KAMIK n traditional Inuit boot
KAMIKAZE n (in World War II) Japanese pilot who performed a suicide mission ▷ adj (of an action) undertaken in the knowledge that it will kill or injure the person performing it
KAMIKAZES > KAMIKAZE
KAMIKS > KAMIK
KAMILA same as > KAMALA
KAMILAS > KAMILA
KAMIS same as > KAMEEZ
KAMISES > KAMIS
KAMME same as > KAM
KAMOKAMO n kind of marrow found in New Zealand
KAMOKAMOS > KAMOKAMO
KAMOTIK n type of Inuit sled
KAMOTIKS > KAMOTIK
KAMOTIQ same as > KAMOTIK
KAMOTIQS > KAMOTIQ
KAMPONG n (in Malaysia) village
KAMPONGS > KAMPONG
KAMSEEN same as > KHAMSIN
KAMSEENS > KAMSEEN
KAMSIN same as > KAMSEEN
KAMSINS > KAMSIN
KANA n Japanese syllabary
KANAE n grey mullet
KANAES > KANAE

KANAKA n Australian word for any native of the South Pacific
KANAKAS > KANAKA
KANAMYCIN n type of antibiotic
KANAS > KANA
KANBAN n just-in-time manufacturing process
KANBANS > KANBAN
KANDIES > KANDY
KANDY same as > CANDIE
KANE n Hawaiian man or boy
KANEH n 6-cubit Hebrew measure
KANEHS > KANEH
KANES > KANE
KANG n Chinese heatable platform
KANGA n piece of gaily decorated thin cotton cloth
KANGAROO n Australian marsupial which moves by jumping with its powerful hind legs ▷ vb (of a car) move forward or to cause (a car) to move forward with short sudden jerks, as a result of improper use of the clutch
KANGAROOS > KANGAROO
KANGAS > KANGA
KANGHA n comb traditionally worn by Sikhs
KANGHAS > KANGHA
KANGS > KANG
KANJI n Japanese writing system
KANJIS > KANJI
KANS n Indian wild sugar cane
KANSES > KANS
KANT archaic spelling of > CANT
KANTAR n unit of weight
KANTARS > KANTAR
KANTED > KANT
KANTELA same as > KANTELE
KANTELAS > KANTELA
KANTELE n Finnish stringed instrument
KANTELES > KANTELE
KANTEN same as > AGAR
KANTENS > KANTEN
KANTHA n Bengali embroidered quilt
KANTHAS > KANTHA
KANTIKOY vb dance ceremonially
KANTIKOYS > KANTIKOY
KANTING > KANT
KANTS > KANT
KANUKA n New Zealand myrtaceous tree
KANUKAS > KANUKA
KANZU n long garment
KANZUS > KANZU
KAOLIANG n any of various E Asian varieties of sorghum
KAOLIANGS > KAOLIANG

KAOLIN n fine white clay
KAOLINE same as > KAOLIN
KAOLINES > KAOLINE
KAOLINIC > KAOLIN
KAOLINISE same as > KAOLINIZE
KAOLINITE n white or grey clay mineral consisting of hydrated aluminium silicate in triclinic crystalline form, the main constituent of kaolin
KAOLINIZE vb change into kaolin
KAOLINS > KAOLIN
KAON n type of meson
KAONIC > KAON
KAONS > KAON
KAPA n Hawaiian cloth made from beaten mulberry bark
KAPAS > KAPA
KAPEEK > KAPEYKA
KAPEYKA n small currency unit of Belarus
KAPH n 11th letter of the Hebrew alphabet
KAPHS > KAPH
KAPOK n fluffy fibre
KAPOKS > KAPOK
KAPOW n sharp explosive sound
KAPOWS > KAPOW
KAPPA n tenth letter in the Greek alphabet
KAPPAS > KAPPA
KAPU n (in Hawaii) system of rules for daily life
KAPUKA same as > BROADLEAF
KAPUKAS > KAPUKA
KAPUS > KAPU
KAPUT adj ruined or broken
KAPUTT same as > KAPUT
KARA n steel bangle traditionally worn by Sikhs
KARABINER n metal clip with a spring for attaching to a piton, belay, etc
KARAHI n type of wok
KARAHIS > KARAHI
KARAISM n beliefs and doctrines of a Jewish sect
KARAISMS > KARAISM
KARAIT same as > KRAIT
KARAITS > KRAIT
KARAKA n New Zealand tree
KARAKAS > KARAKA
KARAKIA n prayer
KARAKIAS > KARAKIA
KARAKUL n sheep of central Asia
KARAKULS > KARAKUL
KARAMU n small New Zealand tree
KARAMUS > KARAMU
KARANGA n call or chant of welcome, sung by a female elder ▷ vb perform a karanga
KARANGAED > KARANGA

KARANGAS > KARANGA
KARAOKE n form of entertainment
KARAOKES > KARAOKE
KARAS > KARA
KARAT n measure of the proportion of gold in an alloy
KARATE n Japanese system of unarmed combat
KARATEIST same as > KARATEKA
KARATEKA n competitor or expert in karate
KARATEKAS > KARATEKA
KARATES > KARATE
KARATS > KARAT
KAREAREA n New Zealand falcon
KAREAREAS > KAREAREA
KARENGO n edible type of Pacific seaweed
KARENGOS > KARENGO
KARITE n shea tree
KARITES > KARITE
KARK variant spelling of > CARK
KARKED > KARK
KARKING > KARK
KARKS > KARK
KARMA n person's actions affecting his or her fate in the next reincarnation
KARMAS > KARMA
KARMIC > KARMA
KARN old word for > CAIRN
KARNS > KARN
KARO n small New Zealand tree or shrub
KAROO n high arid plateau
KAROOS > KAROO
KARORO n large seagull
KAROROS > KARORO
KAROS > KARO
KAROSHI n (in Japan) death caused by overwork
KAROSHIS > KAROSHI
KAROSS n type of blanket
KAROSSES > KAROSS
KARRI n Australian eucalypt
KARRIS > KARRI
KARROO same as > KAROO
KARROOS > KAROO
KARSEY variant spelling of > KHAZI
KARSEYS > KARSEY
KARSIES > KARSY
KARST n geological term
KARSTIC > KARST
KARSTIFY vb become karstic
KARSTS > KARST
KARSY variant spelling of > KHAZI
KART n light low-framed vehicle
KARTER > KART
KARTERS > KART
KARTING > KART
KARTINGS > KART
KARTS > KART

KARYOGAMY n fusion of two gametic nuclei during fertilization
KARYOGRAM n diagram or photograph of the chromosomes of a cell, arranged in homologous pairs and in a numbered sequence
KARYOLOGY n study of cell nuclei, esp with reference to the number and shape of the chromosomes
KARYON n nucleus of a cell
KARYONS > KARYON
KARYOSOME n any of the dense aggregates of chromatin in the nucleus of a cell
KARYOTIN less common word for > CHROMATIN
KARYOTINS > KARYOTIN
KARYOTYPE n appearance of the chromosomes in a somatic cell of an individual or species, with reference to their number, size, shape, etc ▷ vb determine the karyotype of (a cell)
KARZIES > KARZY
KARZY variant spelling of > KHAZI
KAS > KA
KASBAH n citadel of any of various North African cities
KASBAHS > KASBAH
KASHA n dish originating in Eastern Europe
KASHAS > KASHA
KASHER vb make fit for use
KASHERED > KASHER
KASHERING > KASHER
KASHERS > KASHER
KASHMIR variant spelling of > CASHMERE
KASHMIRS > KASHMIR
KASHRUS same as > KASHRUTH
KASHRUSES > KASHRUS
KASHRUT same as > KASHRUTH
KASHRUTH n condition of being fit for ritual use in general
KASHRUTHS > KASHRUTH
KASHRUTS > KASHRUT
KASME interj (in Indian English) I swear
KAT same as > KHAT
KATA n form of exercise
KATABASES > KATABASIS
KATABASIS n retreat of the Greek mercenaries of Cyrus the Younger, after his death at Cunaxa, from the Euphrates to the Black Sea in 401–400 BC under the leadership of Xenophon

KATABATIC adj (of winds) blowing downhill through having become denser with cooling, esp at night when heat is lost from the earth's surface
KATABOLIC same as > CATABOLIC
KATAKANA n one of the two systems of syllabic writing employed for the representation of Japanese, based on Chinese ideograms. It is used mainly for foreign or foreign-derived words
KATAKANAS > KATAKANA
KATAL n SI unit of catalytic activity
KATALS > KATAL
KATANA n Japanese samurai sword
KATANAS > KATANA
KATAS > KATA
KATCHINA variant spelling of > KACHINA
KATCHINAS > KATCHINA
KATCINA variant spelling of > KACHINA
KATCINAS > KATCINA
KATHAK n form of dancing
KATHAKALI n form of dance drama of S India using mime and based on Hindu literature
KATHAKS > KATHAK
KATHARSES > KATHARSIS
KATHARSIS variant spelling of > CATHARSIS
KATHODAL > KATHODE
KATHODE variant spelling of > CATHODE
KATHODES > KATHODE
KATHODIC > KATHODE
KATHUMP n sound of a dull heavy blow
KATHUMPS > KATHUMP
KATI variant spelling of > CATTY
KATION variant spelling of > CATION
KATIONS > KATION
KATIPO n small poisonous New Zealand spider
KATIPOS > KATIPO
KATIS > KATI
KATORGA n type of labour camp
KATORGAS > KATORGA
KATS > KAT
KATSINA n (among the Hopi) doll representing spirit messengers
KATSINAM > KATSINA
KATSINAS > KATSINA
KATSURA n Asian tree
KATSURAS > KATSURA
KATTI variant spelling of > CATTY
KATTIS > KATTI
KATYDID n large green grasshopper of N America
KATYDIDS > KATYDID

KAUGH same as > KIAUGH
KAUGHS > KAUGH
KAUMATUA n senior member of a tribe
KAUMATUAS > KAUMATUA
KAUPAPA n strategy, policy, or cause
KAUPAPAS > KAUPAPA
KAURI n large NZ conifer
KAURIES > KAURY
KAURIS > KAURI
KAURU n edible stem of the cabbage tree
KAURUS > KAURU
KAURY variant spelling of > KAURI
KAVA n Polynesian shrub
KAVAKAVA same as > KAVA
KAVAKAVAS > KAVAKAVA
KAVAL n type of flute played in the Balkans
KAVALS > KAVAL
KAVAS > KAVA
KAVASS n armed Turkish constable
KAVASSES > KAVASS
KAW variant spelling of > CAW
KAWA n protocol or etiquette
KAWAII n (in Japan) quality of being lovable or cute
KAWAIIS > KAWAII
KAWAKAWA n aromatic shrub or small tree of New Zealand
KAWAKAWAS > KAWAKAWA
KAWAS > KAWA
KAWAU n New Zealand name for black shag
KAWAUS > KAWAU
KAWED > KAW
KAWING > KAW
KAWS > KAW
KAY n name of the letter K
KAYAK n Inuit canoe ▷ vb travel by kayak
KAYAKED > KAYAK
KAYAKER > KAYAK
KAYAKERS > KAYAK
KAYAKING > KAYAK
KAYAKINGS > KAYAK
KAYAKS > KAYAK
KAYLE n one of a set of ninepins
KAYLES pl n ninepins
KAYLIED adj (in British slang) intoxicated or drunk
KAYO another term for > KNOCKOUT
KAYOED > KAYO
KAYOES > KAYO
KAYOING > KAYO
KAYOINGS > KAYO
KAYOS > KAYO
KAYS > KAY
KAZACHKI same as > KAZACHOK
KAZACHOC n Ukrainian folk dance
KAZACHOCS > KAZACHOC

KAZACHOK n Russian folk dance in which the performer executes high kicks from a squatting position
KAZACHOKS > KAZACHOK
KAZATSKI same as > KAZACHOK
KAZATSKY same as > KAZACHOK
KAZATZKA same as > KAZACHOK
KAZATZKAS > KAZACHOK
KAZI variant spelling of > KHAZI
KAZILLION same as > GAZILLION
KAZIS > KAZI
KAZOO n musical instrument
KAZOOS > KAZOO
KBAR n kilobar
KBARS > KBAR
KEA n large brownish-green parrot of NZ
KEAS > KEA
KEASAR archaic variant of > KAISER
KEASARS > KEASAR
KEAVIE n archaic or dialect word for a type of crab
KEAVIES > KEAVIE
KEB vb Scots word meaning miscarry or reject a lamb
KEBAB n food grilled on a skewer ▷ vb skewer
KEBABBED > KEBAB
KEBABBING > KEBAB
KEBABS > KEBAB
KEBAR n Scots word for beam or rafter
KEBARS > KEBAR
KEBBED > KEB
KEBBIE n Scots word for shepherd's crook
KEBBIES > KEBBIE
KEBBING > KEB
KEBBOCK n Scots word for a cheese
KEBBOCKS > CHEESE
KEBBUCK same as > KEBBOCK
KEBBUCKS > KEBBUCK
KEBELE n Ethiopian local council
KEBELES > KEBELE
KEBLAH same as > KIBLAH
KEBLAHS > KEBLAH
KEBOB same as > KEBAB
KEBOBBED > KEBOB
KEBOBBING > KEBOB
KEBOBS > KEBOB
KEBS > KEB
KECK vb retch or feel nausea
KECKED > KECK
KECKING > KECK
KECKLE Scots variant of > CACKLE
KECKLED > KECKLE
KECKLES > KECKLE

KECKLING > KECKLE
KECKLINGS > KECKLE
KECKS pl n trousers
KECKSES > KECKS
KECKSIES > KECKSY
KECKSY n dialect word meaning hollow plant stalk
KED n as in sheep ked sheep tick
KEDDAH same as > KHEDA
KEDDAHS > KEDDAH
KEDGE vb move (a ship) using cable attached to an anchor ▷ n light anchor used for kedging
KEDGED > KEDGE
KEDGER n small anchor
KEDGEREE n dish of fish with rice and eggs
KEDGEREES > KEDGEREE
KEDGERS > KEDGER
KEDGES > KEDGE
KEDGIER > KEDGY
KEDGIEST > KEDGY
KEDGING > KEDGE
KEDGY adj dialect word for happy or lively
KEDS > KED
KEECH n old word for lump of fat
KEECHES > KEECH
KEEF same as > KIF
KEEFS > KEEF
KEEK Scot word for > PEEP
KEEKED > KEEK
KEEKER > KEEK
KEEKERS > KEEK
KEEKING > KEEK
KEEKS > KEEK
KEEL n part of a ship ▷ vb mark with a stain
KEELAGE n fee charged by certain ports
KEELAGES > KEELAGE
KEELBOAT n river boat with a shallow draught and a keel, used for freight and moved by towing, punting, or rowing
KEELBOATS > KEELBOAT
KEELED > KEEL
KEELER n bargeman
KEELERS > KEELER
KEELHALE same as > KEELHAUL
KEELHALED > KEELHALE
KEELHALES > KEELHALE
KEELHAUL vb reprimand (someone) harshly
KEELHAULS > KEELHAUL
KEELIE n kestrel
KEELIES > KEELIE
KEELING > KEEL
KEELINGS > KEEL
KEELIVINE Scots word for > PENCIL
KEELLESS > KEEL
KEELMAN n bargeman
KEELMEN > KEELMAN
KEELS > KEEL
KEELSON n part of a ship
KEELSONS > KEELSON

KEELYVINE same as > KEELIVINE
KEEMA n (in Indian cookery) minced meat
KEEMAS > KEEMA
KEEN adj eager or enthusiastic ▷ vb wail over the dead ▷ n lament for the dead
KEENED > KEEN
KEENER > KEEN
KEENERS > KEEN
KEENEST > KEEN
KEENING > KEEN
KEENINGS > KEEN
KEENLY > KEEN
KEENNESS > KEEN
KEENO same as > KENO
KEENOS > KEENO
KEENS > KEEN
KEEP vb have or retain possession of ▷ n cost of food and everyday expenses
KEEPABLE > KEEP
KEEPER n person who looks after animals in a zoo
KEEPERS > KEEPER
KEEPING > KEEP
KEEPINGS > KEEP
KEEPNET n cylindrical net used to keep fish alive
KEEPNETS > KEEPNET
KEEPS > KEEP
KEEPSAKE n gift treasured for the sake of the giver
KEEPSAKES > KEEPSAKE
KEEPSAKY > KEEPSAKE
KEESHOND n breed of dog of the spitz type with a shaggy greyish coat and tightly curled tail, originating in Holland
KEESHONDS > KEESHOND
KEESTER same as > KEISTER
KEESTERS > KEESTER
KEET short for > PARAKEET
KEETS > KEET
KEEVE n tub or vat
KEEVES > KEEVE
KEF same as > KIF
KEFFEL dialect word for > HORSE
KEFFELS > KEFFEL
KEFFIYAH same as > KAFFIYEH
KEFFIYAHS > KEFFIYAH
KEFFIYEH n cotton headdress worn by Arabs
KEFFIYEHS > KEFFIYEH
KEFIR n effervescent drink
KEFIRS > KEFIR
KEFS > KEF
KEFTEDES n Greek dish of meatballs cooked with herbs and onions
KEFUFFLE same as > KERFUFFLE
KEFUFFLED > KEFUFFLE
KEFUFFLES > KEFUFFLE

k

KEG n small metal beer barrel ▷ vb put in kegs
KEGELER same as > KEGLER
KEGELERS > KEGELER
KEGGED > KEG
KEGGER > KEG
KEGGERS > KEG
KEGGING > KEG
KEGLER n participant in a game of tenpin bowling
KEGLERS > KEGLER
KEGLING n bowling
KEGLINGS > KEGLING
KEGS > KEG
KEHUA n ghost or spirit
KEHUAS > KEHUA
KEIGHT > KETCH
KEIR same as > KIER
KEIREN n type of track cycling event
KEIRENS > KEIREN
KEIRETSU n group of Japanese businesses
KEIRETSUS > KEIRETSU
KEIRIN n cycling race originating in Japan
KEIRINS > KEIRIN
KEIRS > KEIR
KEISTER n rump
KEISTERS > KEISTER
KEITLOA n type of rhinoceros
KEITLOAS > KEITLOA
KEKENO n New Zealand fur seal
KEKENOS > KEKENO
KEKERENGU n Māori bug
KEKS same as > KECKS
KEKSYE same as > KEX
KEKSYES > KEKSYE
KELEP n large ant found in Central and South America
KELEPS > KELEP
KELIM same as > KILIM
KELIMS > KELIM
KELL dialect word for > HAIRNET
KELLAUT same as > KHILAT
KELLAUTS > KELLAUT
KELLIES > KELLY
KELLS > KELL
KELLY n part of a drill system
KELOID n type of scar tissue
KELOIDAL > KELOID
KELOIDS > KELOID
KELP n large brown seaweed ▷ vb burn seaweed to make a type of ash
KELPED > KELP
KELPER n Falkland Islander
KELPERS > KELPER
KELPFISH n type of fish that lives among kelp
KELPIE n Australian sheepdog
KELPIES > KELPY
KELPING > KELP

KELPS > KELP
KELPY same as > KELPIE
KELSON same as > KEELSON
KELSONS > KELSON
KELT n salmon that has recently spawned
KELTER same as > KILTER
KELTERS > KELTER
KELTIE variant spelling of > KELTY
KELTIES > KELTY
KELTS > KELT
KELTY n old Scots word for a drink imposed on someone not thought to be drinking enough
KELVIN n SI unit of temperature
KELVINS > KELVIN
KEMB old word for > COMB
KEMBED > KEMB
KEMBING > KEMB
KEMBLA n small change
KEMBLAS > KEMBLA
KEMBO same as > KIMBO
KEMBOED > KEMBO
KEMBOING > KEMBO
KEMBOS > KEMBO
KEMBS > KEMB
KEMP n coarse hair or strand of hair ▷ vb dialect word meaning to compete or try to come first
KEMPED > KEMP
KEMPER > KEMP
KEMPERS > KEMP
KEMPIER > KEMPY
KEMPIEST > KEMPY
KEMPING > KEMP
KEMPINGS > KEMP
KEMPLE n variable Scottish measure for hay or straw
KEMPLES > KEMPLE
KEMPS > KEMP
KEMPT adj (of hair) tidy
KEMPY > KEMP
KEN vb know ▷ n range of knowledge or perception
KENAF another name for > AMBARY
KENAFS > KENAF
KENCH n bin for salting and preserving fish
KENCHES > KENCH
KENDO n Japanese sport of fencing using wooden staves
KENDOIST n person who practises kendo
KENDOISTS > KENDOIST
KENDOS > KENDO
KENNED > KEN
KENNEL n hutlike shelter for a dog ▷ vb put or go into a kennel
KENNELED > KENNEL
KENNELING > KENNEL
KENNELLED > KENNEL
KENNELMAN n man who works in a kennels

KENNELMEN > KENNELMAN
KENNELS > KENNEL
KENNER > KEN
KENNERS > KEN
KENNET n old word for a small hunting dog
KENNETS > KENNET
KENNETT vb spoil or destroy ruthlessly
KENNETTED > KENNETT
KENNETTS > KENNETT
KENNING > KEN
KENNINGS > KEN
KENO n game of chance similar to bingo
KENOS > KENO
KENOSES > KENOSIS
KENOSIS n Christ's renunciation of certain divine attributes
KENOSISES > KENOSIS
KENOTIC > KENOSIS
KENOTICS > KENOSIS
KENOTRON n signal-amplifying device
KENOTRONS > KENOTRON
KENS > KEN
KENSPECK adj Scots for easily seen or recognized
KENT dialect word for > PUNT
KENTE n brightly coloured handwoven cloth
KENTED > KENT
KENTES > KENTE
KENTIA n plant name
KENTIAS > KENTIA
KENTING > KENT
KENTLEDGE n scrap metal used as ballast in a vessel
KENTS > KENT
KEP vb catch
KEPHALIC variant spelling of > CEPHALIC
KEPHALICS > KEPHALIC
KEPHALIN same as > CEPHALIN
KEPHALINS > KEPHALIN
KEPHIR same as > KEFIR
KEPHIRS > KEPHIR
KEPI n French military cap with a flat top and a horizontal peak
KEPIS > KEPI
KEPPED > KEP
KEPPEN > KEP
KEPPING > KEP
KEPPIT > KEP
KEPS > KEP
KEPT > KEEP
KERAMIC rare variant of > CERAMIC
KERAMICS rare variant of > CERAMICS
KERATIN n fibrous protein found in the hair and nails
KERATINS > KERATIN
KERATITIS n inflammation of the cornea
KERATOID adj resembling horn

KERATOMA n horny growth on the skin
KERATOMAS > KERATOMA
KERATOSE adj (esp of certain sponges) having a horny skeleton
KERATOSES > KERATOSIS
KERATOSIC > KERATOSE
KERATOSIS n any skin condition marked by a horny growth, such as a wart
KERATOTIC > KERATOSIS
KERB n edging to a footpath ▷ vb provide with or enclose with a kerb
KERBAYA n blouse worn by Malay women
KERBAYAS > KERBAYA
KERBED > KERB
KERBING n material used for a kerb
KERBINGS > KERBING
KERBS > KERB
KERBSIDE n edge of a pavement where it drops to the level of the road
KERBSIDES > KERBSIDE
KERBSTONE n one of a series of stones that form a kerb
KERCHIEF n piece of cloth worn over the head or round the neck
KERCHIEFS > KERCHIEF
KERCHOO interj atishoo
KEREL n chap or fellow
KERELS > KEREL
KERERU n New Zealand pigeon
KERERUS > KERERU
KERF n cut made by a saw, an axe, etc ▷ vb cut
KERFED > KERF
KERFING > KERF
KERFLOOEY adv into state of destruction or malfunction
KERFS > KERF
KERFUFFLE n commotion or disorder ▷ vb put into disorder or disarray
KERKIER > KERKY
KERKIEST > KERKY
KERKY adj stupid
KERMA n quantity of radiation
KERMAS > KERMA
KERMES n dried bodies of female scale insects
KERMESES > KERMES
KERMESITE n red antimony
KERMESS same as > KERMIS
KERMESSE same as > KERMIS
KERMESSES > KERMESSE
KERMIS n (formerly) annual country festival or carnival

KERMISES > KERMIS
KERMODE n type of black bear found in Canada
KERMODES > KERMODE
KERN n projection of a printed character ▷ vb furnish (a typeface) with a kern
KERNE same as > KERN
KERNED > KERNE
KERNEL n seed of a nut, cereal, or fruit stone ▷ vb form kernels
KERNELED > KERNEL
KERNELING > KERNEL
KERNELLED > KERNEL
KERNELLY adj with or like kernels
KERNELS > KERNEL
KERNES > KERNE
KERNING n provision of kerns in printing
KERNINGS > KERNING
KERNISH adj resembling an armed foot soldier or peasant
KERNITE n light soft colourless or white mineral
KERNITES > KERNITE
KERNS > KERN
KERO short for > KEROSENE
KEROGEN n material that produces hydrocarbons when heated
KEROGENS > KEROGEN
KEROS > KERO
KEROSENE n liquid mixture distilled from petroleum and used as a fuel or solvent
KEROSENES > KEROSENE
KEROSINE same as > KEROSENE
KEROSINES > KEROSINE
KERPLUNK vb land noisily
KERPLUNKS > KERPLUNK
KERRIA n type of shrub with yellow flowers
KERRIAS > KERRIA
KERRIES > KERRY
KERRY n breed of dairy cattle
KERSEY n smooth woollen cloth
KERSEYS > KERSEY
KERVE dialect word for > CARVE
KERVED > KERVE
KERVES > KERVE
KERVING > KERVE
KERYGMA n Christian gospel
KERYGMAS > KERYGMA
KERYGMATA > KERYGMA
KESAR old variant of > KAISER
KESARS > KESAR
KESH n beard and uncut hair traditionally worn by Sikhs
KESHES > KESH
KEST old form of > CAST
KESTING > KEST

KESTREL n type of small falcon
KESTRELS > KESTREL
KESTS > KEST
KET n dialect word for carrion
KETA n type of salmon
KETAINE adj in poor taste
KETAMINE n drug, chemically related to PCP, that is used in medicine as a general anaesthetic, being administered by injection
KETAMINES > KETAMINE
KETAS > KETA
KETCH n two-masted sailing vessel ▷ vb (in archaic usage) catch
KETCHES > KETCH
KETCHING > KETCH
KETCHUP n thick cold sauce, usu made of tomatoes
KETCHUPS > KETCHUP
KETCHUPY adj like ketchup
KETE n basket woven from flax
KETENE n colourless irritating toxic gas
KETENES > KETENE
KETES > KETE
KETMIA n as in bladder ketmia plant with pale yellow flowers
KETMIAS > KETMIA
KETO adj as in keto form form of tautomeric compounds
KETOGENIC adj forming or able to stimulate the production of ketone bodies
KETOL n nitrogenous substance
KETOLS > KETOL
KETONE n type of organic solvent
KETONEMIA n excess of ketone bodies in the blood
KETONES > KETONE
KETONIC > KETONE
KETONURIA n presence of ketone bodies in the urine
KETOSE n any monosaccharide that contains a ketone group
KETOSES > KETOSIS
KETOSIS n high concentration of ketone bodies in the blood
KETOTIC > KETOSIS
KETOXIME n oxime formed by reaction between hydroxylamine and a ketone
KETOXIMES > KETOXIME
KETS > KET
KETTLE n container used for boiling water ▷ vb contain a public protest in an enclosed space

KETTLED > KETTLE
KETTLEFUL > KETTLE
KETTLES > KETTLE
KETTLING > KETTLE
KETUBAH n Jewish marriage contract
KETUBAHS > KETUBAH
KETUBOT > KETUBAH
KETUBOTH > KETUBAH
KEVEL n strong bitt or bollard for securing heavy hawsers
KEVELS > KEVEL
KEVIL old variant of > KEVEL
KEVILS > KEVIL
KEWL nonstandard variant spelling of > COOL
KEWLER > KEWL
KEWLEST > KEWL
KEWPIE n type of brightly coloured doll
KEWPIES > KEWPIE
KEX n any of several hollow-stemmed umbelliferous plants
KEXES > KEX
KEY n device for operating a lock by moving a bolt ▷ adj of great importance ▷ vb enter (text) using a keyboard
KEYBOARD n set of keys on a piano, computer, etc ▷ vb enter (text) using a keyboard
KEYBOARDS > KEYBOARD
KEYBUGLE n bugle with keys
KEYBUGLES > KEYBUGLE
KEYBUTTON n on a keyboard, an object which, when pressed, causes the letter, number, or symbol shown on it to be printed in a document
KEYCARD n electronic card used as a key
KEYCARDS > KEYCARD
KEYED > KEY
KEYER n device that keys signals or information into a device or computing system
KEYERS > KEYER
KEYFRAME n image used to show the start and end of animation sequence
KEYFRAMES > KEYFRAME
KEYHOLE n opening for inserting a key into a lock
KEYHOLES > KEYHOLE
KEYING > KEY
KEYINGS > KEY
KEYLESS > KEY
KEYLINE n outline image on artwork or plans to show where it is to be placed
KEYLINES > KEYLINE
KEYLOGGER n device or software application used for covertly recording and monitoring keystrokes

made on a remote computer
KEYNOTE adj central or dominating ▷ n dominant idea of a speech etc ▷ vb deliver a keynote address to (a political convention, etc)
KEYNOTED > KEYNOTE
KEYNOTER n person delivering a keynote address
KEYNOTERS > KEYNOTER
KEYNOTES > KEYNOTE
KEYNOTING > KEYNOTE
KEYPAD n small panel with a set of buttons
KEYPADS > KEYPAD
KEYPAL n person one regularly exchanges emails with for fun
KEYPALS > KEYPAL
KEYPRESS n single depression of a keyboard key
KEYPUNCH n device having a keyboard that is operated manually to transfer data onto punched cards, paper tape, etc ▷ vb transfer (data) onto punched cards, paper tape, etc, by using a key punch
KEYRING n metal ring for keeping keys together
KEYRINGS > KEYRING
KEYS interj children's cry for truce
KEYSET n set of computer keys used for a particular purpose
KEYSETS > KEYSET
KEYSTER same as > KEISTER
KEYSTERS > KEYSTER
KEYSTONE n most important part of a process, organization, etc ▷ vb project or provide with a distorted image
KEYSTONED > KEYSTONE
KEYSTONES > KEYSTONE
KEYSTROKE n single operation of the mechanism of a typewriter or keyboard-operated typesetting machine by the action of a key ▷ vb enter or cause to be recorded by pressing a key
KEYWAY n engineering device
KEYWAYS > KEYWAY
KEYWORD n word or phrase used to find something on a computer
KEYWORDS > KEYWORD
KEYWORKER n public sector worker regarded as providing an essential service
KGOTLA n (in South African English) meeting place

k

KGOTLAS > KGOTLA
KHADDAR *n* cotton cloth
KHADDARS > KHADDAR
KHADI *same as* > KHADDAR
KHADIS > KHADI
KHAF *n* letter of the Hebrew alphabet
KHAFS > KHAF
KHAKI *adj* dull yellowish-brown ▷ *n* fabric of this colour used for military uniforms
KHAKILIKE > KHAKI
KHAKIS > KHAKI
KHALAT *same as* > KHILAT
KHALATS > KHALAT
KHALIF *variant spelling of* > CALIPH
KHALIFA *same as* > CALIPH
KHALIFAH *same as* > CALIPH
KHALIFAHS > KHALIFAH
KHALIFAS > KHALIFA
KHALIFAT *same as* > CALIPHATE
KHALIFATE *same as* > CALIPHATE
KHALIFATS > KHALIFAT
KHALIFS > KHALIF
KHAMSEEN *same as* > KHAMSIN
KHAMSEENS > KHAMSEEN
KHAMSIN *n* hot southerly wind
KHAMSINS > KHAMSIN
KHAN *n* title of respect in Afghanistan and central Asia
KHANATE *n* territory ruled by a khan
KHANATES > KHANATE
KHANDA *n* double-edged sword
KHANDAS > KHANDA
KHANGA *same as* > KANGA
KHANGAS > KHANGA
KHANJAR *n* type of dagger
KHANJARS > KHANJAR
KHANS > KHAN
KHANSAMA *same as* > KHANSAMAH
KHANSAMAH *n* Indian cook or other male servant
KHANSAMAS > KHANSAMA
KHANUM *feminine form of* > KHAN
KHANUMS > KHANUM
KHAPH *n* letter of the Hebrew alphabet
KHAPHS > KHAPH
KHARIF *n* crop harvested at the beginning of winter
KHARIFS > KHARIF
KHAT *n* white-flowered evergreen shrub
KHATS > KHAT
KHAYA *n* type of African tree
KHAYAL *n* kind of Indian classical vocal music
KHAYALS > KHAYAL
KHAYAS > KHAYA

KHAZEN *same as* > CHAZAN
KHAZENIM > KHAZEN
KHAZENS > KHAZEN
KHAZI *n* lavatory
KHAZIS > KHAZI
KHEDA *n* enclosure used to capture wild elephants
KHEDAH *same as* > KHEDA
KHEDAHS > KHEDAH
KHEDAS > KHEDA
KHEDIVA *n* khedive's wife
KHEDIVAL > KHEDIVE
KHEDIVAS > KHEDIVA
KHEDIVATE > KHEDIVE
KHEDIVE *n* viceroy of Egypt under Ottoman suzerainty
KHEDIVES > KHEDIVE
KHEDIVIAL > KHEDIVE
KHET *n* Thai district
KHETH *same as* > HETH
KHETHS > KHETH
KHETS > KHET
KHI *n* letter of the Greek alphabet
KHILAFAT *same as* > CALIPHATE
KHILAFATS > KHILAFAT
KHILAT *n* (in the Middle East) gift given to someone as a mark of honour
KHILATS > KHILAT
KHILIM *same as* > KILIM
KHILIMS > KHILIM
KHIMAR *n* type of headscarf worn by Muslim women
KHIMARS > KHIMAR
KHIRKAH *n* dervish's woollen or cotton outer garment
KHIRKAHS > KHIRKAH
KHIS > KHI
KHODJA *same as* > KHOJA
KHODJAS > KHODJA
KHOJA *n* teacher in a Muslim school
KHOJAS > KHOJA
KHOR *n* watercourse
KHORS > KHOR
KHOTBAH *same as* > KHUTBAH
KHOTBAHS > KHOTBAH
KHOTBEH *same as* > KHUTBAH
KHOTBEHS > KHOTBEH
KHOUM *n* Mauritanian monetary unit
KHOUMS > KHOUM
KHUD *n* Indian ravine
KHUDS > KHUD
KHURTA *same as* > KURTA
KHURTAS > KHURTA
KHUSKHUS *n* aromatic perennial Indian grass whose roots are woven into mats, fans, and baskets
KHUTBAH *n* sermon in a Mosque, especially on a Friday
KHUTBAHS > KHUTBAH
KI *n* vital energy

KIAAT *n* tropical African leguminous tree
KIAATS > KIAAT
KIACK *n* N American fish of the herring family
KIACKS > KIACK
KIANG *n* variety of wild ass
KIANGS > KIANG
KIAUGH *n* (in Scots) anxiety
KIAUGHS > KIAUGH
KIBBE *n* Middle Eastern dish
KIBBEH *same as* > KIBBE
KIBBEHS > KIBBEH
KIBBES > KIBBE
KIBBI *same as* > KIBBE
KIBBIS > KIBBI
KIBBITZ *same as* > KIBITZ
KIBBITZED > KIBBITZ
KIBBITZER > KIBBITZ
KIBBITZES > KIBBITZ
KIBBLE *n* bucket used in wells or in mining for hoisting ▷ *vb* grind into small pieces
KIBBLED > KIBBLE
KIBBLES > KIBBLE
KIBBLING > KIBBLE
KIBBUTZ *n* communal farm or factory in Israel
KIBBUTZIM > KIBBUTZ
KIBE *n* chilblain
KIBEI *n* someone of Japanese ancestry born in the US and educated in Japan
KIBEIS > KIBEI
KIBES > KIBE
KIBITKA *n* (in Russia) covered sledge or wagon
KIBITKAS > KIBITKA
KIBITZ *vb* interfere or offer unwanted advice
KIBITZED > KIBITZ
KIBITZER > KIBITZ
KIBITZERS > KIBITZ
KIBITZES > KIBITZ
KIBITZING > KIBITZ
KIBLA *same as* > KIBLAH
KIBLAH *n* direction of Mecca
KIBLAHS > KIBLAH
KIBLAS > KIBLA
KIBOSH *vb* put a stop to
KIBOSHED > KIBOSH
KIBOSHES > KIBOSH
KIBOSHING > KIBOSH
KICK *vb* drive, push, or strike with the foot ▷ *n* thrust or blow with the foot
KICKABLE > KICK
KICKABOUT *n* informal game of soccer
KICKBACK *n* money paid illegally for favours done ▷ *vb* have a strong reaction
KICKBACKS > KICKBACK
KICKBALL *n* children's ball game or the large ball used in it
KICKBALLS > KICKBALL

KICKBOARD *n* type of float held on to by a swimmer when practising leg strokes
KICKBOX *vb* box with hands and feet
KICKBOXED > KICKBOX
KICKBOXER *n* someone who practises kickboxing, a martial art that resembles boxing but in which kicks are permitted
KICKBOXES > KICKBOX
KICKDOWN *n* method of changing gear in a car with automatic transmission, by fully depressing the accelerator
KICKDOWNS > KICKDOWN
KICKED > KICK
KICKER *n* person or thing that kicks
KICKERS > KICKER
KICKFLIP *n* type of skateboarding manoeuvre ▷ *vb* perform a kickflip in skateboarding
KICKFLIPS > KICKFLIP
KICKIER > KICKY
KICKIEST > KICKY
KICKING *n* act of kicking
KICKINGS > KICKING
KICKOFF *n* kick that starts a game of football
KICKOFFS > KICKOFF
KICKOUT *n* (in basketball) instance of kicking the ball
KICKOUTS > KICKOUT
KICKS > KICK
KICKSHAW *n* valueless trinket
KICKSHAWS *same as* > KICKSHAW
KICKSTAND *n* short metal bar on a motorcycle, which when kicked into a vertical position holds the cycle upright when stationary
KICKSTART *vb* start by kicking pedal
KICKUP *n* fuss
KICKUPS > KICKUP
KICKY *adj* excitingly unusual and different
KID *n* child ▷ *vb* tease or deceive (someone) ▷ *adj* younger
KIDDED > KID
KIDDER > KID
KIDDERS > KID
KIDDIE *same as* > KIDDY
KIDDIED > KIDDY
KIDDIER *n* old word for a market trader
KIDDIERS > KIDDIER
KIDDIES > KIDDY
KIDDING *n* act of kidding
KIDDINGLY > KID
KIDDINGS > KIDDING
KIDDISH > KID
KIDDLE *n* device for catching fish in a river or in the sea**

KIDDLES > KIDDLE

KIDDO *n* very informal term of address for a young person

KIDDOES > KIDDO

KIDDOS > KIDDO

KIDDUSH *n* (in Judaism) special blessing

KIDDUSHES > KIDDUSH

KIDDY *n* affectionate word for a child ▷ *vb* tease or deceive

KIDDYING > KIDDY

KIDDYWINK *n* humorous word for a child

KIDEL *same as* **>** KIDDLE

KIDELS > KIDEL

KIDGE *dialect word for* **>** LIVELY

KIDGIE *adj* dialect word for friendly and welcoming

KIDGIER > KIDGIE

KIDGIEST > KIDGIE

KIDGLOVE *adj* overdelicate or overrefined

KIDLET *n* humorous word for small child

KIDLETS > KIDLET

KIDLIKE > KID

KIDLING *n* young kid

KIDLINGS > KIDLING

KIDLIT *n* children's literature

KIDLITS > KIDLIT

KIDNAP *vb* seize and hold (a person) to ransom

KIDNAPED > KIDNAP

KIDNAPEE > KIDNAP

KIDNAPEES > KIDNAP

KIDNAPER > KIDNAP

KIDNAPERS > KIDNAP

KIDNAPING > KIDNAP

KIDNAPPED > KIDNAP

KIDNAPPEE > KIDNAP

KIDNAPPER > KIDNAP

KIDNAPS > KIDNAP

KIDNEY *n* either of the pair of organs that produce urine

KIDNEYS > KIDNEY

KIDOLOGY *n* practice of bluffing or deception in order to gain a psychological advantage over someone

KIDS > KID

KIDSKIN *n* soft smooth leather

KIDSKINS > KIDSKIN

KIDSTAKES *pl n* pretence

KIDULT *n* adult interested in entertainments intended for children ▷ *adj* aimed at or suitable for kidults, or both children and adults

KIDULTS > KIDULT

KIDVID *n* informal word for children's video or television

KIDVIDS > KIDVID

KIEF *same as* **>** KIF

KIEFS > KIEF

KIEKIE *n* climbing bush plant of New Zealand

KIEKIES > KIEKIE

KIELBASA *n* Polish sausage

KIELBASAS > KIELBASA

KIELBASI *same as* **>** KIELBASA

KIELBASY *same as* **>** KIELBASA

KIER *n* vat in which cloth is bleached

KIERIE *n* South African cudgel

KIERIES > KIERIE

KIERS > KIER

KIESELGUR *n* type of mineral

KIESERITE *n* white mineral consisting of hydrated magnesium sulphate

KIESTER *same as* **>** KEISTER

KIESTERS > KIESTER

KIEV *n* type of chicken dish

KIEVE *same as* **>** KEEVE

KIEVES > KIEVE

KIEVS > KIEV

KIF *n* type of drug

KIFF *adj* South African slang for excellent

KIFS > KIF

KIGHT *n* archaic spelling of kite, the bird of prey

KIGHTS > KIGHT

KIKE *n* offensive word for a Jewish person

KIKES > KIKE

KIKOI *n* piece of cotton cloth

KIKOIS > KIKOI

KIKUMON *n* emblem of the imperial family of Japan

KIKUMONS > KIKUMON

KIKUYU *n* type of grass

KIKUYUS > KIKUYU

KILD *old spelling of* **>** KILLED

KILDERKIN *n* obsolete unit of liquid capacity equal to 16 or 18 Imperial gallons or of dry capacity equal to 16 or 18 wine gallons

KILERG *n* 1000 ergs

KILERGS > KILERG

KILEY *same as* **>** KYLIE

KILEYS > KILEY

KILIM *n* pileless woven rug

KILIMS > KILIM

KILL *vb* cause the death of ▷ *n* act of killing

KILLABLE > KILL

KILLADAR *n* fort commander or governor

KILLADARS > KILLADAR

KILLAS *n* Cornish clay slate

KILLASES > KILLAS

KILLCOW *n* important person

KILLCOWS > KILLCOW

KILLCROP *n* ever-hungry baby, thought to be a fairy changeling

KILLCROPS > KILLCROP

KILLDEE *same as* **>** KILLDEER

KILLDEER *n* large brown-and-white North American plover with a noisy cry

KILLDEERS > KILLDEER

KILLDEES > KILLDEE

KILLED > KILL

KILLER *n* person or animal that kills, esp habitually

KILLERS > KILLER

KILLICK *n* small anchor, esp one made of a heavy stone

KILLICKS > KILLICK

KILLIE *same as* **>** KILLIFISH

KILLIES > KILLIE

KILLIFISH *n* any of various chiefly American minnow-like fishes

KILLING *adj* very tiring ▷ *n* sudden financial success

KILLINGLY > KILLING

KILLINGS > KILLING

KILLJOY *n* person who spoils others' pleasure

KILLJOYS > KILLJOY

KILLOCK *same as* **>** KILLICK

KILLOCKS > KILLOCK

KILLOGIE *n* sheltered place in front of a kiln

KILLOGIES > KILLOGIE

KILLS > KILL

KILLUT *same as* **>** KHILAT

KILLUTS > KILLUT

KILN *n* type of oven ▷ *vb* fire or process in a kiln

KILNED > KILN

KILNING > KILN

KILNS > KILN

KILO *n* code word for the letter k

KILOBAR *n* 1000 bars

KILOBARS > KILOBAR

KILOBASE *n* unit of measurement for DNA and RNA equal to 1000 base pairs

KILOBASES > KILOBASE

KILOBAUD *n* 1000 baud

KILOBAUDS > KILOBAUD

KILOBIT *n* 1024 bits

KILOBITS > KILOBIT

KILOBYTE *n* 1024 units of information

KILOBYTES > KILOBYTE

KILOCURIE *n* unit of thousand curies

KILOCYCLE *n* short for kilocycle per second: a former unit of frequency equal to 1 kilohertz

KILOGAUSS *n* 1000 gauss

KILOGRAM *n* one thousand grams

KILOGRAMS > KILOGRAM

KILOGRAY *n* 1000 gray

KILOGRAYS > KILOGRAY

KILOHERTZ *n* one thousand hertz

KILOJOULE *n* 1000 joules

KILOLITER *US spelling of* **>** KILOLITRE

KILOLITRE *n* 1000 litres

KILOMETER *same as* **>** KILOMETRE

KILOMETRE *n* one thousand metres

KILOMOLE *n* 1000 moles

KILOMOLES > KILOMOLE

KILOPOND *n* informal unit of gravitational force

KILOPONDS > KILOPOND

KILORAD *n* 1000 rads

KILORADS > KILORAD

KILOS > KILO

KILOTON *n* one thousand tons

KILOTONNE *same as* **>** KILOTON

KILOTONS > KILOTON

KILOVOLT *n* one thousand volts

KILOVOLTS > KILOVOLT

KILOWATT *n* one thousand watts

KILOWATTS > KILOWATT

KILP *dialect form of* **>** KELP

KILPS > KILP

KILT *n* knee-length pleated tartan skirt-like garment ▷ *vb* put pleats in (cloth)

KILTED > KILT

KILTER *n* working order or alignment

KILTERS > KILTER

KILTIE *n* someone wearing a kilt

KILTIES > KILTIE

KILTING > KILT

KILTINGS > KILT

KILTLIKE > KILT

KILTS > KILT

KILTY *same as* **>** KILTIE

KIMBO *vb* place akimbo

KIMBOED > KIMBO

KIMBOING > KIMBO

KIMBOS > KIMBO

KIMCHEE *same as* **>** KIMCHI

KIMCHEES > KIMCHEE

KIMCHI *n* Korean dish

KIMCHIS > KIMCHI

KIMMER *same as* **>** CUMMER

KIMMERS > KIMMER

KIMONO *n* loose wide-sleeved Japanese robe

KIMONOED > KIMONO

KIMONOS > KIMONO

KIN *n* person's relatives collectively ▷ *adj* related by blood

KINA *n* standard monetary unit of Papua New Guinea

KINAKINA *same as* **>** QUININE

k

KINAKINAS > KINAKINA
KINARA n African candle holder
KINARAS > KINARA
KINAS > KINA
KINASE n type of enzyme
KINASES > KINASE
KINCHIN old slang word for **>** CHILD
KINCHINS > KINCHIN
KINCOB n fine silk fabric
KINCOBS > KINCOB
KIND adj considerate, friendly, and helpful ▷ n class or group with common characteristics ▷ vb old word for beget or father
KINDA adv very informal shortening of kind of
KINDED > KIND
KINDER adj more kind ▷ n kindergarten or nursery school
KINDERS > KINDER
KINDEST > KIND
KINDIE same as **>** KINDY
KINDIES > KINDY
KINDING > KIND
KINDLE vb set (a fire) alight
KINDLED > KINDLE
KINDLER > KINDLE
KINDLERS > KINDLE
KINDLES > KINDLE
KINDLESS adj heartless
KINDLIER > KINDLY
KINDLIEST > KINDLY
KINDLILY > KINDLY
KINDLING n dry wood or straw for starting fires
KINDLINGS > KINDLING
KINDLY adj having a warm-hearted nature ▷ adv in a considerate way
KINDNESS n quality of being kind
KINDRED adj having similar qualities ▷ n blood relationship
KINDREDS > KINDRED
KINDS > KIND
KINDY n kindergarten
KINE pl n cows or cattle ▷ n Japanese pestle
KINEMA same as **>** CINEMA
KINEMAS > KINEMA
KINEMATIC adj of or relating to the study of the motion of bodies without reference to mass or force
KINES > KINE
KINESCOPE n US name for a television tube ▷ vb record on film
KINESES > KINESIS
KINESIC adj of or relating to kinesics
KINESICS n study of the role of body movements, such as winking, shrugging, etc, in communication
KINESIS n movement of an organism

KINESISES > KINESIS
KINETIC adj relating to or caused by motion
KINETICAL same as **>** KINETIC
KINETICS n branch of mechanics concerned with the study of bodies in motion
KINETIN n plant hormone
KINETINS > KINETIN
KINFOLK another word for **>** KINSFOLK
KINFOLKS > KINFOLK
KING n male ruler of a monarchy ▷ vb make king
KINGBIRD n any of several large American flycatchers
KINGBIRDS > KINGBIRD
KINGBOLT n pivot bolt that connects the body of a horse-drawn carriage to the front axle and provides the steering joint
KINGBOLTS > KINGBOLT
KINGCRAFT n art of ruling as a king, esp by diplomacy and cunning
KINGCUP n yellow-flowered plant
KINGCUPS > KINGCUP
KINGDOM n state ruled by a king or queen
KINGDOMED adj old word for with a kingdom
KINGDOMS > KINGDOM
KINGED > KING
KINGFISH n food and game fish occurring in warm American Atlantic coastal waters
KINGHOOD > KING
KINGHOODS > KING
KINGING > KING
KINGKLIP n edible eel-like marine fish of S Africa
KINGKLIPS > KINGKLIP
KINGLE n Scots word for a type of hard rock
KINGLES > KINGLE
KINGLESS > KING
KINGLET n king of a small or insignificant territory
KINGLETS > KINGLET
KINGLIER > KINGLY
KINGLIEST > KINGLY
KINGLIKE > KING
KINGLING n minor king
KINGLINGS > KINGLING
KINGLY adj appropriate to a king ▷ adv in a manner appropriate to a king
KINGMAKER n person who has control over appointments to positions of authority
KINGPIN n most important person in an organization
KINGPINS > KINGPIN

KINGPOST n vertical post connecting the apex of a triangular roof truss to the tie beam
KINGPOSTS > KINGPOST
KINGS > KING
KINGSHIP n position or authority of a king
KINGSHIPS > KINGSHIP
KINGSIDE n (in chess) side of the board on which a particular king is at the start of a game as opposed to the side the queen is on
KINGSIDES > KINGSIDE
KINGSNAKE n North American snake
KINGWOOD n hard fine-grained violet-tinted wood of a Brazilian leguminous tree
KINGWOODS > KINGWOOD
KININ n type of polypeptide
KININS > KININ
KINK n twist or bend in rope, wire, hair, etc ▷ vb form or cause to form a kink
KINKAJOU n arboreal fruit-eating mammal of Central and South America, with a long prehensile tail
KINKAJOUS > KINKAJOU
KINKED > KINK
KINKIER > KINKY
KINKIEST > KINKY
KINKILY > KINKY
KINKINESS > KINKY
KINKING > KINK
KINKLE n little kink
KINKLES > KINKLE
KINKS > KINK
KINKY adj given to unusual sexual practices
KINLESS adj without any relatives
KINO same as **>** KENO
KINONE n benzoquinone
KINONES > KINONE
KINOS > KINO
KINRED old form of **>** KINDRED
KINREDS > KINRED
KINS > KIN
KINSFOLK pl n one's family or relatives
KINSFOLKS > KINSFOLK
KINSHIP n blood relationship
KINSHIPS > KINSHIP
KINSMAN n relative
KINSMEN > KINSMAN
KINSWOMAN > KINSMAN
KINSWOMEN > KINSMAN
KINTLEDGE same as **>** KENTLEDGE
KIORE n small brown rat native to New Zealand
KIORES > KIORE
KIOSK n small booth
KIOSKS > KIOSK

KIP vb sleep ▷ n sleep or slumber
KIPE n dialect word for a basket for catching fish
KIPES > KIPE
KIPP uncommon variant of **>** KIP
KIPPA n skullcap worn by male Jews
KIPPAGE n Scots word for a state of anger or excitement
KIPPAGES > KIPPAGE
KIPPAH same as **>** KIPPA
KIPPAHS > KIPPAH
KIPPAS > KIPPA
KIPPED > KIP
KIPPEN > KEP
KIPPER n cleaned, salted, and smoked herring ▷ vb cure (a herring) by salting and smoking it
KIPPERED adj (of fish, esp herring) having been cleaned, salted, and smoked
KIPPERER > KIPPER
KIPPERERS > KIPPER
KIPPERING > KIPPER
KIPPERS > KIPPER
KIPPING > KIP
KIPPS > KIPP
KIPS > KIP
KIPSKIN same as **>** KIP
KIPSKINS > KIPSKIN
KIPUNJI n Tanzanian species of monkey
KIPUNJIS > KIPUNJI
KIR n drink made from dry white wine and cassis
KIRANA n small family-owned shop in India
KIRANAS > KIRANA
KIRBEH n leather bottle
KIRBEHS > KIRBEH
KIRBIGRIP n hairgrip
KIRBY n as in kirby grip type of hairgrip
KIRIGAMI n art, originally Japanese, of folding and cutting paper into decorative shapes
KIRIGAMIS > KIRIGAMI
KIRIMON n Japanese imperial crest
KIRIMONS > KIRIMON
KIRK Scot word for **>** CHURCH
KIRKED > KIRK
KIRKING > KIRK
KIRKINGS > KIRK
KIRKMAN n member or strong upholder of the Kirk
KIRKMEN > KIRKMAN
KIRKS > KIRK
KIRKTON n village or town with a parish church
KIRKTONS > KIRKTON
KIRKWARD adv towards the church
KIRKYAIRD same as **>** KIRKYARD
KIRKYARD n churchyard

k

KIRKYARDS > KIRKYARD
KIRMESS same as
> KERMIS
KIRMESSES > KIRMESS
KIRN dialect word for
> CHURN
KIRNED > KIRN
KIRNING > KIRN
KIRNS > KIRN
KIRPAN n short sword
traditionally carried by
Sikhs
KIRPANS > KIRPAN
KIRRI n Hottentot stick
KIRRIS > KIRRI
KIRS > KIR
KIRSCH n cherry brandy
KIRSCHES > KIRSCH
KIRTAN n devotional
singing
KIRTANS > KIRTAN
KIRTLE n woman's skirt
or dress ▷ vb dress with a
kirtle
KIRTLED > KIRTLE
KIRTLES > KIRTLE
KIS > KI
KISAN n peasant or farmer
KISANS > KISAN
KISH n graphite formed on
the surface of molten iron
KISHES > KISH
KISHKA same as > KISHKE
KISHKAS > KISHKA
KISHKE n stuffed beef or
fowl intestine, boiled and
roasted
KISHKES > KISHKE
KISKADEE n large
flycatcher of tropical
America
KISKADEES > KISKADEE
KISMAT same as > KISMET
KISMATS > KISMAT
KISMET n fate or destiny
KISMETIC > KISMET
KISMETS > KISMET
KISS vb touch with the lips
in affection or greeting
▷ n touch with the lips
KISSABLE > KISS
KISSABLY > KISS
KISSAGRAM n greetings
service in which a
messenger kisses the
person celebrating
KISSED > KISS
KISSEL n Russian dessert
KISSELS > KISSEL
KISSER n mouth or face
KISSERS > KISSER
KISSES > KISS
KISSIER > KISSY
KISSIEST > KISSY
KISSING > KISS
KISSINGS > KISSING
KISSOGRAM same as
> KISSAGRAM
KISSY adj showing
exaggerated affection
KIST n large wooden chest
▷ vb place in a coffin
KISTED > KIST

KISTFUL > KIST
KISTFULS > KIST
KISTING > KIST
KISTS > KIST
KISTVAEN n stone tomb
KISTVAENS > KISTVAEN
KIT n outfit or equipment
for a specific purpose
▷ vb fit or provide
KITBAG n bag for a
soldier's or traveller's
belongings
KITBAGS > KITBAG
KITCHEN n room used for
cooking ▷ vb (in archaic
usage) provide with food
KITCHENED > KITCHEN
KITCHENER n someone
employed in kitchen work
KITCHENET n small
kitchen or part of another
room equipped for use as a
kitchen
KITCHENS > KITCHEN
KITE n light frame covered
with a thin material
▷ vb soar and glide
KITEBOARD n board like a
windsurfing board, towed
by a large kite
KITED > KITE
KITELIKE > KITE
KITENGE n thick cotton
cloth
KITENGES > KITENGE
KITER > KITE
KITERS > KITE
KITES > KITE
KITH n one's friends and
acquaintances
KITHARA variant of
> CITHARA
KITHARAS > KITHARA
KITHE same as > KYTHE
KITHED > KITHE
KITHES > KITHE
KITHING > KITHE
KITHS > KITH
KITING > KITE
KITINGS > KITE
KITLING dialect word for
> KITTEN
KITLINGS > KITLING
KITS > KIT
KITSCH n art or literature
with popular sentimental
appeal ▷ n object or art
that is tawdry, vulgarized,
oversentimental or
pretentious
KITSCHES > KITSCH
KITSCHIER > KITSCH
KITSCHIFY vb make
kitsch
KITSCHILY > KITSCH
KITSCHY > KITSCH
KITSET n New Zealand
word for furniture supplied
in pieces
KITSETS > KITSET
KITTED > KIT
KITTEL n white garment
worn for certain Jewish
rituals or burial

KITTELS > KITTEL
KITTEN n young cat
▷ vb (of cats) give birth
KITTENED > KITTEN
KITTENING > KITTEN
KITTENISH adj lively and
flirtatious
KITTENS > KITTEN
KITTENY > KITTEN
KITTIES > KITTY
KITTING > KIT
KITTIWAKE n type of
seagull
KITTLE adj capricious and
unpredictable ▷ vb be
troublesome or puzzling
to (someone)
KITTLED > KITTLE
KITTLER > KITTLE
KITTLES > KITTLE
KITTLEST > KITTLE
KITTLIER > KITTLY
KITTLIEST > KITTLY
KITTLING > KITTLE
KITTLY Scots word for
> TICKLISH
KITTUL n type of palm
from which jaggery sugar
comes
KITTULS > KITTUL
KITTY n communal fund
KITUL same as > KITTUL
KITULS > KITUL
KIVA n large room in a
Pueblo Indian village
KIVAS > KIVA
KIWI n New Zealand
flightless bird with a long
beak and no tail
KIWIFRUIT n edible oval
fruit of the kiwi plant
KIWIS > KIWI
KLANG n (in music) kind of
tone
KLANGS > KLANG
KLAP vb slap or spank
KLAPPED > KLAP
KLAPPING > KLAP
KLAPS > KLAP
KLATCH n gathering,
especially over coffee
KLATCHES > KLATCH
KLATSCH same as
> KLATCH
KLATSCHES > KLATSCH
KLAVERN n local Ku Klux
Klan group
KLAVERNS > KLAVERN
KLAVIER same as
> CLAVIER
KLAVIERS > KLAVIER
KLAXON n loud horn used
on emergency vehicles
▷ vb hoot with a klaxon
KLAXONED > KLAXON
KLAXONING > KLAXON
KLAXONS > KLAXON
KLEAGLE n person with a
particular rank in the Ku
Klux Klan
KLEAGLES > KLEAGLE
KLEENEX n tradename for
a kind of tissue

KLEENEXES > KLEENEX
KLEFTIKO n type of Greek
lamb dish
KLEFTIKOS > KLEFTIKO
KLENDUSIC adj disease-
resistant
KLEPHT n group of
Greeks
KLEPHTIC > KLEPHT
KLEPHTISM > KLEPHT
KLEPHTS > KLEPHT
KLEPTO n compulsive
thief
KLEPTOS > KLEPTO
KLETT n lightweight
climbing boot
KLETTS > KLETT
KLEZMER n Jewish folk
musician
KLEZMERS > KLEZMER
KLEZMORIM > KLEZMER
KLICK n kilometre
KLICKS > KLICK
KLIEG n as in klieg light
intense carbon-arc light
KLIEGS > KLIEG
KLIK US military slang word
for > KILOMETRE
KLIKS > KLIK
KLINKER n type of brick
used in paving
KLINKERS > KLINKER
KLINOSTAT n rotating
and tilting plant holder for
studying and
experimenting with plant
growth
KLIPDAS n rock hyrax
KLIPDASES > KLIPDAS
KLISTER n type of ski
dressing for improving grip
on snow
KLISTERS > KLISTER
KLONDIKE n rich source of
something ▷ vb transfer
(bulk loads of fish) to
factory ships at sea for
processing
KLONDIKED > KLONDIKE
KLONDIKER same as
> KLONDYKER
KLONDIKES > KLONDIKE
KLONDYKE n rich source of
something ▷ vb transfer
(bulk loads of fish) to
factory ships at sea for
processing
KLONDYKED > KLONDYKE
KLONDYKER n East
European factory ship
KLONDYKES > KLONDYKE
KLONG n type of canal in
Thailand
KLONGS > KLONG
KLOOCH same as
> KLOOCHMAN
KLOOCHES > KLOOCH
KLOOCHMAN n North
American Indian woman
KLOOCHMEN
> KLOOCHMAN
KLOOF n mountain pass or
gorge
KLOOFS > KLOOF

k

KLOOTCH same as > KLOOCHMAN

KLOOTCHES > KLOOTCH

KLUDGE n untidy solution ▷ vb cobble something together

KLUDGED > KLUDGE

KLUDGES > KLUDGE

KLUDGEY > KLUDGE

KLUDGIER > KLUDGE

KLUDGIEST > KLUDGE

KLUDGING > KLUDGE

KLUDGY > KLUDGE

KLUGE same as > KLUDGE

KLUGED > KLUGE

KLUGES > KLUGE

KLUGING > KLUGE

KLUTZ n clumsy or stupid person

KLUTZES > KLUTZ

KLUTZIER > KLUTZ

KLUTZIEST > KLUTZ

KLUTZY > KLUTZ

KLYSTRON n electron tube for the amplification or generation of microwaves by means of velocity modulation

KLYSTRONS > KLYSTRON

KNACK n skilful way of doing something ▷ vb dialect word for crack or snap

KNACKED adj broken or worn out

KNACKER n buyer of old horses for killing ▷ vb exhaust

KNACKERED adj extremely tired

KNACKERS > KNACKER

KNACKERY n slaughterhouse for horses

KNACKIER > KNACKY

KNACKIEST > KNACKY

KNACKING > KNACK

KNACKISH adj old word meaning cunning or artful

KNACKS > KNACK

KNACKY adj old or dialect word for cunning or artful

KNAG n knot in wood

KNAGGIER > KNAGGY

KNAGGIEST > KNAGGY

KNAGGY adj knotty

KNAGS > KNAG

KNAIDEL same as > KNEIDEL

KNAIDELS > KNAIDEL

KNAIDLACH > KNAIDEL

KNAP n crest of a hill ▷ vb hit, hammer, or chip

KNAPPED > KNAP

KNAPPER > KNAP

KNAPPERS > KNAP

KNAPPING > KNAP

KNAPPLE old word for > NIBBLE

KNAPPLED > KNAPPLE

KNAPPLES > KNAPPLE

KNAPPLING > KNAPPLE

KNAPS > KNAP

KNAPSACK n soldier's or traveller's bag worn strapped on the back

KNAPSACKS > KNAPSACK

KNAPWEED n plant with purplish thistle-like flowers

KNAPWEEDS > KNAPWEED

KNAR old spelling of > GNAR

KNARL old spelling of > GNARL

KNARLIER > KNARLY

KNARLIEST > KNARLY

KNARLS > KNARL

KNARLY same as > GNARLY

KNARRED > KNAR

KNARRIER > KNAR

KNARRIEST > KNAR

KNARRING > KNAR

KNARRY > KNAR

KNARS > KNAR

KNAUR variant form of > KNUR

KNAURS > KNAUR

KNAVE n jack at cards

KNAVERIES > KNAVERY

KNAVERY n dishonest behaviour

KNAVES > KNAVE

KNAVESHIP n old Scottish legal term for the small proportion of milled grain due to the person doing the milling

KNAVISH > KNAVE

KNAVISHLY > KNAVE

KNAWE same as > KNAWEL

KNAWEL n type of Old World plant

KNAWELS > KNAWEL

KNAWES > KNAWE

KNEAD vb work (dough) into a smooth mixture with the hands

KNEADABLE > KNEAD

KNEADED > KNEAD

KNEADER > KNEAD

KNEADERS > KNEAD

KNEADING > KNEAD

KNEADS > KNEAD

KNEE n joint between thigh and lower leg ▷ vb strike or push with the knee

KNEECAP nontechnical name for > PATELLA

KNEECAPS > KNEECAP

KNEED > KNEE

KNEEHOLE n space for the knees, esp under a desk

KNEEHOLES > KNEEHOLE

KNEEING > KNEE

KNEEJERK adj (of a reply or reaction) automatic and predictable

KNEEL vb fall or rest on one's knees ▷ n act or position of kneeling

KNEELED > KNEEL

KNEELER > KNEEL

KNEELERS > KNEEL

KNEELING > KNEEL

KNEELS > KNEEL

KNEEPAD n protective covering for the knee

KNEEPADS > KNEEPAD

KNEEPAN another word for > PATELLA

KNEEPANS > KNEEPAN

KNEEPIECE n knee-shaped piece of timber in ship

KNEEROOM n space to put one's knees

KNEEROOMS > KNEEROOM

KNEES > KNEE

KNEESIES n flirtatious touching of knees under table

KNEESOCK n type of sock that comes up to the knee

KNEESOCKS > KNEESOCK

KNEIDEL n (in Jewish cookery) small dumpling

KNEIDELS > KNEIDEL

KNEIDLACH > KNEIDEL

KNELL n sound of a bell, esp at a funeral or death ▷ vb ring a knell

KNELLED > KNELL

KNELLING > KNELL

KNELLS > KNELL

KNELT > KNEEL

KNESSET n parliament or assembly

KNESSETS > KNESSET

KNEVELL vb old Scots word meaning beat

KNEVELLED > KNEVELL

KNEVELLS > KNEVELL

KNEW > KNOW

KNICKER n woman's or girl's undergarment

KNICKERED > KNICKER

KNICKERS pl n woman's or girl's undergarment covering the lower trunk and having legs or legholes

KNICKS pl n knickers

KNIFE n sharp-edged blade with a handle ▷ vb cut or stab with a knife

KNIFED > KNIFE

KNIFELESS > KNIFE

KNIFELIKE > KNIFE

KNIFEMAN n man who is armed with a knife

KNIFEMEN > KNIFEMAN

KNIFER > KNIFE

KNIFEREST n support on which a carving knife or carving fork is placed at the table

KNIFERS > KNIFE

KNIFES > KNIFE

KNIFING > KNIFE

KNIFINGS > KNIFE

KNIGHT n man who has been given a knighthood ▷ vb award a knighthood to

KNIGHTAGE n group of knights or knights collectively

KNIGHTED > KNIGHT

KNIGHTING > KNIGHT

KNIGHTLY adj of, resembling, or appropriate for a knight

KNIGHTS > KNIGHT

KNIPHOFIA n any of several perennial southern African flowering plants

KNISH n type of dish

KNISHES > KNISH

KNIT vb make (a garment) by interlocking a series of loops in wool or other yarn ▷ n fabric made by knitting

KNITBONE n comfrey

KNITBONES > KNITBONE

KNITCH dialect word for > BUNDLE

KNITCHES > KNITCH

KNITS > KNIT

KNITTABLE > KNIT

KNITTED > KNIT

KNITTER > KNIT

KNITTERS > KNIT

KNITTING > KNIT

KNITTINGS > KNIT

KNITTLE n old word for string or cord

KNITTLES > KNITTLE

KNITWEAR n knitted clothes, such as sweaters

KNITWEARS > KNITWEAR

KNIVE rare variant of > KNIFE

KNIVED > KNIVE

KNIVES > KNIFE

KNIVING > KNIVE

KNOB n rounded projection, such as a switch on a radio ▷ vb supply with knobs

KNOBBED > KNOB

KNOBBER n two-year-old male deer

KNOBBERS > KNOBBER

KNOBBIER > KNOB

KNOBBIEST > KNOB

KNOBBING > KNOB

KNOBBLE n small knob ▷ vb dialect word meaning strike

KNOBBLED same as > KNOBBLY

KNOBBLES > KNOBBLE

KNOBBLIER > KNOBBLY

KNOBBLING > KNOBBLE

KNOBBLY adj covered with small bumps

KNOBBY > KNOB

KNOBHEAD n stupid person

KNOBHEADS > KNOBHEAD

KNOBLIKE > KNOB

KNOBS > KNOB

KNOBSTICK n stick with a round knob at the end, used as a club or missile by South African tribesmen

KNOCK vb give a blow or push to ▷ n blow or rap

KNOCKBACK n rejection, esp of a job application or invitation to go on a date

KNOCKDOWN adj (of a price) very low

KNOCKED > KNOCK
KNOCKER *n* metal fitting for knocking on a door
KNOCKERS > KNOCKER
KNOCKING > KNOCK
KNOCKINGS > KNOCK
KNOCKLESS > KNOCK
KNOCKOFF *n* informal word for a cheap, often illegal, copy of something
KNOCKOFFS > KNOCKOFF
KNOCKOUT *n* blow that renders an opponent unconscious ▷ *vb* render (someone) unconscious
KNOCKOUTS > KNOCKOUT
KNOCKS > KNOCK
KNOLL *n* small rounded hill ▷ *vb* (in archaic or dialect usage) knell
KNOLLED > KNOLL
KNOLLER > KNOLL
KNOLLERS > KNOLL
KNOLLIER > KNOLL
KNOLLIEST > KNOLL
KNOLLING > KNOLL
KNOLLS > KNOLL
KNOLLY > KNOLL
KNOP *n* knob, esp an ornamental one
KNOPPED > KNOP
KNOPS > KNOP
KNOSP *n* budlike architectural feature
KNOSPS > KNOSP
KNOT *n* type of fastening ▷ *vb* tie with or into a knot
KNOTGRASS *n* polygonaceous weedy plant whose small green flowers produce numerous seeds
KNOTHEAD *n* stupid person
KNOTHEADS > KNOTHEAD
KNOTHOLE *n* hole in a piece of wood where a knot has been
KNOTHOLES > KNOTHOLE
KNOTLESS > KNOT
KNOTLIKE > KNOT
KNOTS > KNOT
KNOTTED > KNOT
KNOTTER > KNOT
KNOTTERS > KNOT
KNOTTIER > KNOTTY
KNOTTIEST > KNOTTY
KNOTTILY > KNOTTY
KNOTTING > KNOT
KNOTTINGS > KNOT
KNOTTY *adj* full of knots
KNOTWEED *n* type of plant with small flowers and jointed stems
KNOTWEEDS > KNOTWEED
KNOTWORK *n* ornamentation consisting of a mass of intertwined and knotted cords
KNOTWORKS > KNOTWORK
KNOUT *n* stout whip ▷ *vb* whip

KNOUTED > KNOUT
KNOUTING > KNOUT
KNOUTS > KNOUT
KNOW *vb* be or feel certain of the truth of (information etc)
KNOWABLE > KNOW
KNOWE *same as* > KNOLL
KNOWER > KNOW
KNOWERS > KNOW
KNOWES > KNOWE
KNOWHOW *n* ingenuity, knack, or skill
KNOWHOWS > KNOWHOW
KNOWING > KNOW
KNOWINGER > KNOW
KNOWINGLY > KNOW
KNOWINGS > KNOW
KNOWLEDGE *n* facts, feelings or experiences known by a person or group of people ▷ *vb* (in archaic usage) acknowledge
KNOWN > KNOW
KNOWNS > KNOW
KNOWS > KNOW
KNUB *dialect word for* > KNOB
KNUBBIER > KNUB
KNUBBIEST > KNUB
KNUBBLE *vb* dialect word for beat or pound using one's fists
KNUBBLED > KNUBBLE
KNUBBLES > KNUBBLE
KNUBBLIER > KNUBBLY
KNUBBLING > KNUBBLE
KNUBBLY *adj* having small lumps or protuberances
KNUBBY *adj* knub
KNUBS > KNUB
KNUCKLE *n* bone at the finger joint
KNUCKLED > KNUCKLE
KNUCKLER *n* type of throw in baseball
KNUCKLERS > KNUCKLER
KNUCKLES > KNUCKLE
KNUCKLIER > KNUCKLE
KNUCKLING > KNUCKLE
KNUCKLY > KNUCKLE
KNUR *n* knot or protuberance in a tree trunk or in wood
KNURL *n* small ridge, often one of a series ▷ *vb* impress with a series of fine ridges or serrations
KNURLED > KNURL
KNURLIER > KNURLY
KNURLIEST > KNURLY
KNURLING > KNURL
KNURLINGS > KNURL
KNURLS > KNURL
KNURLY *rare word for* > GNARLED
KNURR *same as* > KNUR
KNURRS > KNURR
KNURS > KNUR
KNUT *n* dandy
KNUTS > KNUT

KO *n* (in New Zealand) traditional digging tool
KOA *n* Hawaiian leguminous tree
KOALA *n* tree-dwelling Australian marsupial with dense grey fur
KOALAS > KOALA
KOAN *n* (in Zen Buddhism) problem that admits no logical solution
KOANS > KOAN
KOAP *n* (in Papua New Guinean slang) sexual intercourse
KOAPS > KOAP
KOAS > KOA
KOB *n* any of several species of antelope
KOBAN *n* old oval-shaped Japanese gold coin
KOBANG *same as* > KOBAN
KOBANGS > KOBANG
KOBANS > KOBAN
KOBO *n* Nigerian monetary unit
KOBOLD *n* mischievous household sprite
KOBOLDS > KOBOLD
KOBOS > KOBO
KOBS > KOB
KOCHIA *n* any of several plants whose foliage turns dark red
KOCHIAS > KOCHIA
KOEKOEA *n* long-tailed cuckoo of New Zealand
KOEKOEAS > KOEKOEA
KOEL *n* any of several parasitic cuckoos
KOELS > KOEL
KOFF *n* Dutch masted merchant vessel
KOFFS > KOFF
KOFTA *n* Indian dish
KOFTAS > KOFTA
KOFTGAR *n* (in India) person skilled at inlaying steel with gold
KOFTGARI *n* ornamental Indian metalwork
KOFTGARIS > KOFTGARI
KOFTGARS > KOFTGAR
KOFTWORK *same as* > KOFTGARI
KOFTWORKS > KOFTWORK
KOGAL *n* (in Japan) trendy teenage girl
KOGALS > KOGAL
KOHA *n* gift or donation, esp of cash
KOHANIM > KOHEN
KOHAS > KOHA
KOHEKOHE *n* New Zealand tree with large glossy leaves and reddish wood
KOHEKOHES > KOHEKOHE
KOHEN *n* member of the Jewish priestly caste
KOHL *n* cosmetic powder
KOHLRABI *n* type of cabbage with an edible stem
KOHLRABIS > KOHLRABI

KOHLS > KOHL
KOI *n* any of various ornamental forms of the common carp
KOINE *n* common language among speakers of different languages
KOINES > KOINE
KOIS > KOI
KOJI *n* Japanese steamed rice
KOJIS > KOJI
KOKA *n* former type of score in judo
KOKAKO *n* type of crow
KOKAKOS > KOKAKO
KOKAM *same as* > KOKUM
KOKAMS > KOKAM
KOKANEE *n* type of freshwater salmon
KOKANEES > KOKANEE
KOKAS > KOKA
KOKER *n* Guyanese sluice
KOKERS > KOKER
KOKIRI *n* type of rough-skinned New Zealand triggerfish
KOKIRIS > KOKIRI
KOKOBEH *adj* (of certain fruit) having a rough skin
KOKOPU *n* any of several small freshwater fish of New Zealand
KOKOPUS > KOKOPU
KOKOWAI *n* type of clay
KOKOWAIS > KOKOWAI
KOKRA *n* type of wood
KOKRAS > KOKRA
KOKUM *n* tropical tree
KOKUMS > KOKUM
KOLA *n* as in kola nut caffeine-containing seed used in medicine and soft drinks
KOLACKIES > KOLACKY
KOLACKY *n* sweet bun with a fruit, jam, or nut filling
KOLAS > KOLA
KOLBASI *same as* > KOLBASSI
KOLBASIS > KOLBASI
KOLBASSA *same as* > KIELBASA
KOLBASSAS > KOLBASSA
KOLBASSI *n* type of sausage
KOLBASSIS > KOLBASSI
KOLHOZ *same as* > KOLKHOZ
KOLHOZES > KOLKHOZ
KOLHOZY *same as* > KOLKHOZ
KOLINSKI *same as* > KOLINSKY
KOLINSKY *n* Asian mink
KOLKHOS *same as* > KOLKHOZ
KOLKHOSES > KOLKHOS
KOLKHOSY > KOLKHOS
KOLKHOZ *n* (formerly) collective farm in the Soviet Union
KOLKHOZES > KOLKHOZ

k

KOLKHOZY > KOLKHOZ
KOLKOZ same as
> KOLKHOZ
KOLKOZES > KOLKOZ
KOLKOZY > KOLKOZ
KOLO n Serbian folk dance
KOLOS > KOLO
KOMATIK n type of sledge
KOMATIKS > KOMATIK
KOMBU n dark brown
seaweed
KOMBUS > KOMBU
KOMISSAR same as
> COMMISSAR
KOMISSARS > KOMISSAR
KOMITAJI n rebel or
revolutionary
KOMITAJIS > KOMITAJI
KOMONDOR n large
powerful dog of an ancient
Hungarian breed,
originally used for sheep
herding
KOMONDORS > KOMONDOR
KON old word for > KNOW
KONAKI same as > KONEKE
KONAKIS > KONAKI
KONBU same as > KOMBU
KONBUS > KONBU
KOND > KON
KONDO n (in Uganda) thief
or armed robber
KONDOS > KONDO
KONEKE n type of farm
vehicle
KONEKES > KONEKE
KONFYT n South African
fruit preserve
KONFYTS > KONFYT
KONGONI n E African
hartebeest
KONIMETER n device for
measuring airborne dust
concentration in which
samples are obtained by
sucking the air through a
hole and allowing it to
pass over a glass plate
coated with grease on
which the particles collect
KONINI n edible dark
purple berry
KONINIS > KONINI
KONIOLOGY n study of
atmospheric dust and its
effects
KONISCOPE n device for
detecting and measuring
dust in the air
KONK same as > CONK
KONKED > KONK
KONKING > KONK
KONKS > KONK
KONNING > KON
KONS > KON
KOODOO same as > KUDU
KOODOOS > KOODOO
KOOK n eccentric person
▷ vb dialect word for
vanish
KOOKED > KOOK
KOOKIE same as > KOOKY
KOOKIER > KOOKY
KOOKIEST > KOOKY

KOOKILY > KOOKY
KOOKINESS > KOOKY
KOOKING > KOOK
KOOKS > KOOK
KOOKUM same as > KOKUM
KOOKUMS > KOOKUM
KOOKY adj crazy, eccentric,
or foolish
KOOLAH old form of
> KOALA
KOOLAHS > KOOLAH
KOORI n Australian
Aborigine
KOORIES > KOORI
KOORIS > KOORI
KOP n prominent isolated
hill or mountain in
southern Africa
KOPASETIC same as
> COPACETIC
KOPECK n former Russian
monetary unit
KOPECKS > KOPECK
KOPEK same as > KOPECK
KOPEKS > KOPEK
KOPH n 19th letter in the
Hebrew alphabet
KOPHS > KOPH
KOPIYKA n monetary unit
of Ukraine
KOPIYKAS > KOPIYKA
KOPIYOK > KOPIYKA
KOPJE n small hill
KOPJES > KOPJE
KOPPA n consonantal
letter in the Greek
alphabet
KOPPAS > KOPPA
KOPPIE same as > KOPJE
KOPPIES > KOPPIE
KOPS > KOP
KOR n ancient Hebrew unit
of capacity
KORA n West African
instrument
KORAI > KORE
KORARI n native New
Zealand flax plant
KORARIS > KORARI
KORAS > KORA
KORAT n as in korat cat rare
blue-grey breed of cat
KORATS > KORAT
KORE n ancient Greek
statue of a young woman
wearing clothes
KORERO n talk or
discussion ▷ vb speak or
converse
KOREROED > KORERO
KOREROING > KORERO
KOREROS > KORERO
KORES > KORE
KORFBALL n game similar
to basketball, in which
each team consists of six
men and six women
KORFBALLS > KORFBALL
KORIMAKO another name
for > BELLBIRD
KORIMAKOS > KORIMAKO
KORKIR n variety of lichen
used in dyeing

KORKIRS > KORKIR
KORMA n type of mild
Indian dish
KORMAS > KORMA
KORO n elderly Māori man
KOROMIKO n flowering
New Zealand shrub
KOROMIKOS > KOROMIKO
KORORA n small New
Zealand penguin
KORORAS > KORORA
KOROS > KORO
KOROWAI n decorative
woven cloak worn by a
Māori chief
KOROWAIS > KOROWAI
KORS > KOR
KORU n stylized curved
pattern used esp in
carving
KORUN > KORUNA
KORUNA n standard
monetary unit of the
Czech Republic and
Slovakia
KORUNAS > KORUNA
KORUNY > KORUNA
KORU > KORU
KOS n Indian unit of
distance
KOSES > KOS
KOSHER adj conforming to
Jewish religious law
▷ n kosher food ▷ vb
prepare in accordance
with Jewish dietary rules
KOSHERED > KOSHER
KOSHERING > KOSHER
KOSHERS > KOSHER
KOSMOS variant form of
> COSMOS
KOSMOSES > KOSMOS
KOSS same as > KOS
KOSSES > KOSS
KOTARE n small
greenish-blue kingfisher
KOTARES > KOTARE
KOTCH vb South African
slang for vomit
KOTCHED > KOTCH
KOTCHES > KOTCH
KOTCHING > KOTCH
KOTO n Japanese stringed
instrument
KOTOS > KOTO
KOTOW same as > KOWTOW
KOTOWED > KOTOW
KOTOWER > KOTOW
KOTOWERS > KOTOW
KOTOWING > KOTOW
KOTOWS > KOTOW
KOTTABOS > COTTABUS
KOTUKU n type of white
heron
KOTUKUS > KOTUKU
KOTWAL n senior police
officer or magistrate in an
Indian town
KOTWALS > KOTWAL
KOULAN same as > KULAN
KOULANS > KOULAN
KOUMIS same as > KUMISS
KOUMISES > KOUMIS

KOUMISS same as
> KUMISS
KOUMISSES > KOUMISS
KOUMYS same as > KUMISS
KOUMYSES > KOUMYS
KOUMYSS same as
> KUMISS
KOUMYSSES > KOUMYSS
KOUPREY n large wild SE
Asian ox
KOUPREYS > KOUPREY
KOURA n New Zealand
freshwater crayfish
KOURAS > KOURA
KOURBASH same as
> KURBASH
KOUROI > KOUROS
KOUROS n ancient Greek
statue of a young man
KOUSKOUS same as
> COUSCOUS
KOUSSO n Abyssinian tree
KOUSSOS > KOUSSO
KOW old variant of > COW
KOWHAI n New Zealand
tree
KOWHAIS > KOWHAI
KOWS > KOW
KOWTOW vb be servile
(towards) ▷ n act of
kowtowing
KOWTOWED > KOWTOW
KOWTOWER > KOWTOW
KOWTOWERS > KOWTOW
KOWTOWING > KOWTOW
KOWTOWS > KOWTOW
KRAAL n S African village
surrounded by a strong
fence ▷ adj denoting or
relating to the tribal
aspects of the Black
African way of life
▷ vb enclose (livestock)
in a kraal
KRAALED > KRAAL
KRAALING > KRAAL
KRAALS > KRAAL
KRAB same as
> KARABINER
KRABS > KRAB
KRAFT n strong wrapping
paper
KRAFTS > KRAFT
KRAI n administrative
division of Russia
KRAIS > KRAI
KRAIT n brightly coloured
venomous snake of S and
SE Asia
KRAITS > KRAIT
KRAKEN n legendary sea
monster
KRAKENS > KRAKEN
KRAKOWIAK n Polish
dance
KRAMERIA another name
for > RHATANY
KRAMERIAS > KRAMERIA
KRANG n dead whale from
which the blubber has
been removed
KRANGS > KRANG
KRANS n sheer rock face
KRANSES > KRANS

KRANTZ same as > KRANS
KRANTZES > KRANTZ
KRANZ same as > KRANS
KRANZES > KRANS
KRATER same as > CRATER
KRATERS > KRATER
KRAUT n sauerkraut
KRAUTS > KRAUT
KRAY same as > KRAI
KRAYS > KRAY
KREASOTE same as > CREOSOTE
KREASOTED > KREASOTE
KREASOTES > KREASOTE
KREATINE same as > CREATINE
KREATINES > KREATINE
KREEP n lunar substance
KREEPS > KREEP
KREESE same as > KRIS
KREESED > KREESE
KREESES > KREESE
KREESING > KREESE
KREMLIN n citadel of any Russian city
KREMLINS > KREMLIN
KRENG same as > KRANG
KRENGS > KRENG
KREOSOTE same as > CREOSOTE
KREOSOTED > KREOSOTE
KREOSOTES > KREOSOTE
KREPLACH pl n small filled dough casings usually served in soup
KREPLECH same as > KREPLACH
KREUTZER n any of various former copper and silver coins of Germany or Austria
KREUTZERS > KREUTZER
KREUZER same as > KREUTZER
KREUZERS > KREUZER
KREWE n club taking part in New Orleans carnival parade
KREWES > KREWE
KRILL n small shrimplike sea creature
KRILLS > KRILL
KRIMMER n tightly curled light grey fur
KRIMMERS > KRIMMER
KRIS n type of Malayan and Indonesian knife ⊳ vb stab or slash with a kris
KRISED > KRIS
KRISES > KRIS
KRISING > KRIS
KROMESKY n croquette consisting of a piece of bacon wrapped round minced meat or fish
KRONA n standard monetary unit of Sweden
KRONE n standard monetary unit of Norway and Denmark
KRONEN > KRONE
KRONER > KRONE

KRONOR > KRONA
KRONUR > KRONA
KROON n standard monetary unit of Estonia
KROONI > KROON
KROONS > KROON
KRUBI n aroid plant with an unpleasant smell
KRUBIS > KRUBI
KRUBUT same as > KRUBI
KRUBUTS > KRUBUT
KRULLER variant spelling of > CRULLER
KRULLERS > KRULLER
KRUMHORN variant spelling of > CRUMHORN
KRUMHORNS > KRUMHORN
KRUMKAKE n Scandinavian biscuit
KRUMKAKES > KRUMKAKE
KRUMMHOLZ n zone of stunted wind-blown trees growing at high altitudes just above the timberline on tropical mountains
KRUMMHORN variant spelling of > CRUMHORN
KRUMPER > KRUMPING
KRUMPERS > KRUMPER
KRUMPING n type of dance in which participants wear face-paint and compete aggressively in lieu of violent conflict
KRUMPINGS > KRUMPING
KRUNK n style of hip-hop music
KRUNKED same as > CRUNKED
KRUNKS > KRUNK
KRYOLITE variant spelling of > CRYOLITE
KRYOLITES > KRYOLITE
KRYOLITH same as > CRYOLITE
KRYOLITHS > KRYOLITH
KRYOMETER same as > CRYOMETER
KRYPSES > KRYPSIS
KRYPSIS n idea that Christ made secret use of his divine attributes
KRYPTON n colourless gas
KRYPTONS > KRYPTON
KRYTRON n type of fast electronic gas-discharge switch
KRYTRONS > KRYTRON
KSAR old form of > TSAR
KSARS > KSAR
KUBASA same as > KIELBASA
KUBASAS > KUBASA
KUBIE n Ukrainian roll filled with kielbasa
KUBIES > KUBIE
KUCCHA same as > KACCHA
KUCCHAS > KUCCHA
KUCHCHA same as > KACHA
KUCHEN n breadlike cake
KUCHENS > KUCHEN
KUDLIK n Inuit soapstone seal-oil lamp
KUDLIKS > KUDLIK

KUDO variant of > KUDOS
KUDOS n fame or credit
KUDOSES > KUDOS
KUDU n African antelope with spiral horns
KUDUS > KUDU
KUDZU n hairy leguminous climbing plant
KUDZUS > KUDZU
KUE n name of the letter Q
KUEH n (in Malaysia) any cake of Malay, Chinese, or Indian origin
KUES > KUE
KUFI n cap for Muslim man
KUFIS > KUFI
KUFIYAH same as > KEFFIYEH
KUFIYAHS > KUFIYAH
KUGEL n baked pudding in traditional Jewish cooking
KUGELS > KUGEL
KUIA n Māori female elder or elderly woman
KUIAS > KUIA
KUKRI n heavy, curved knife used by Gurkhas
KUKRIS > KUKRI
KUKU n mussel
KUKUS > KUKU
KULA n ceremonial gift exchange among islanders in the W Pacific
KULAK n (formerly) property-owning Russian peasant
KULAKI > KULAK
KULAKS > KULAK
KULAN n Asiatic wild ass
KULANS > KULAN
KULAS > KULA
KULBASA same as > KIELBASA
KULBASAS > KULBASA
KULFI n Indian dessert
KULFIS > KULFI
KULTUR n German civilization
KULTURS > KULTUR
KUMARA n tropical root vegetable with yellow flesh
KUMARAHOU n New Zealand shrub
KUMARAS > KUMARA
KUMARI n (in Indian English) maiden
KUMARIS > KUMARI
KUMBALOI pl n worry beads
KUMERA same as > KUMARA
KUMERAS > KUMERA
KUMIKUMI same as > KAMOKAMO
KUMIKUMIS > KUMIKUMI
KUMIS same as > KUMISS
KUMISES > KUMIS
KUMISS n drink made from fermented mare's or other milk
KUMISSES > KUMISS

KUMITE n freestyle sparring or fighting
KUMITES > KUMITE
KUMKUM n red pigment used by Hindu women to make a mark on the forehead
KUMKUMS > KUMKUM
KUMMEL n German liqueur
KUMMELS > KUMMEL
KUMQUAT n citrus fruit resembling a tiny orange
KUMQUATS > KUMQUAT
KUMYS same as > KUMISS
KUMYSES > KUMYS
KUNA n standard monetary unit of Croatia
KUNDALINI n (in yoga) life force that resides at the base of the spine
KUNE > KUNA
KUNEKUNE n feral pig
KUNEKUNES > KUNEKUNE
KUNJOOS adj (in Indian English) mean or stingy
KUNKAR n type of limestone
KUNKARS > KUNKAR
KUNKUR same as > KUNKAR
KUNKURS > KUNKUR
KUNZITE n variety of the mineral spodumene
KUNZITES > KUNZITE
KURBASH vb whip with a hide whip
KURBASHED > KURBASH
KURBASHES > KURBASH
KURFUFFLE same as > KERFUFFLE
KURGAN n Russian burial mound
KURGANS > KURGAN
KURI n mongrel dog
KURIS > KURI
KURRAJONG n Australian tree or shrub with tough fibrous bark
KURRE old variant of > CUR
KURRES > KURRE
KURSAAL n public room at a health resort
KURSAALS > KURSAAL
KURTA n long loose garment
KURTAS > KURTA
KURTOSES > KURTOSIS
KURTOSIS n measure of the concentration of a distribution around its mean
KURU n degenerative disease of the nervous system
KURUS > KURU
KURUSH n small currency unit of Turkey
KURUSHES > KURUSH
KURVEY vb (in old South African English) transport goods by ox cart
KURVEYED > KURVEY
KURVEYING > KURVEY
KURVEYOR > KURVEY
KURVEYORS > KURVEY

KURVEYS > KURVEY
KUSSO *variant spelling of* > KOUSSO
KUSSOS > KUSSO
KUTA *n* (in Indian English) male dog
KUTAS > KUTA
KUTCH *same as* > CATECHU
KUTCHA *adj* makeshift or not solid
KUTCHES > KUTCH
KUTI *n* (in Indian English) female dog or bitch
KUTIS > KUTI
KUTU *n* body louse
KUTUS > KUTU
KUVASZ *n* breed of dog from Hungary
KUVASZOK > KUVASZ
KUZU *same as* > KUDZU
KUZUS > KUZU
KVAS *same as* > KVASS
KVASES > KVAS
KVASS *n* alcoholic drink
KVASSES > KVASS
KVELL *vb* US word meaning be happy
KVELLED > KVELL
KVELLING > KVELL
KVELLS > KVELL
KVETCH *vb* complain or grumble
KVETCHED > KVETCH
KVETCHER > KVETCH
KVETCHERS > KVETCH
KVETCHES > KVETCH
KVETCHIER > KVETCHY
KVETCHILY > KVETCHY
KVETCHING > KVETCH

KVETCHY *adj* tending to grumble or complain
KWACHA *n* standard monetary unit of Zambia
KWACHAS > KWACHA
KWAITO *n* type of South African pop music
KWAITOS > KWAITO
KWANZA *n* standard monetary unit of Angola
KWANZAS > KWANZA
KWELA *n* type of pop music
KWELAS > KWELA
KY *pl n* Scots word for cows
KYACK *n* type of pannier
KYACKS > KYACK
KYAK *same as* > KAYAK
KYAKS > KYAK
KYANG *same as* > KIANG
KYANGS > KYANG
KYANISE *same as* > KYANIZE
KYANISED > KYANISE
KYANISES > KYANISE
KYANISING > KYANISE
KYANITE *n* grey, green, or blue mineral
KYANITES > KYANITE
KYANITIC > KYANITE
KYANIZE *vb* treat (timber) with corrosive sublimate
KYANIZED > KYANIZE
KYANIZES > KYANIZE
KYANIZING > KYANIZE
KYAR *same as* > COIR
KYARS > KYAR
KYAT *n* standard monetary unit of Myanmar
KYATS > KYAT

KYBO *n* temporary lavatory used when camping
KYBOS > KYBO
KYBOSH *same as* > KIBOSH
KYBOSHED > KYBOSH
KYBOSHES > KYBOSH
KYBOSHING > KYBOSH
KYDST > KYTHE
KYE *n* Korean fundraising meeting
KYES > KYE
KYLE *n* narrow strait or channel
KYLES > KYLE
KYLICES > KYLIX
KYLIE *n* type of boomerang
KYLIES > KYLIE
KYLIKES > KYLIX
KYLIN *n* (in Chinese art) mythical animal
KYLINS > KYLIN
KYLIX *n* drinking vessel used in ancient Greece
KYLIXES > KYLIX
KYLLOSES > KYLLOSIS
KYLLOSIS *n* club foot
KYLOE *n* breed of beef cattle
KYLOES > KYLOE
KYMOGRAM *n* image or other visual record created by a kymograph
KYMOGRAMS > KYMOGRAM
KYMOGRAPH *n* rotatable drum for holding paper on which a tracking stylus continuously records variations in blood

pressure, respiratory movements, etc
KYND *old variant of* > KIND
KYNDE *old variant of* > KIND
KYNDED > KYND
KYNDES > KYNDE
KYNDING > KYND
KYNDS > KYND
KYNE *pl n* archaic word for cows
KYOGEN *n* type of Japanese drama
KYOGENS > KYOGEN
KYPE *n* hook on the lower jaw of a mature male salmon
KYPES > KYPE
KYPHOSES > KYPHOSIS
KYPHOSIS *n* backward curvature of the thoracic spine
KYPHOTIC > KYPHOSIS
KYRIE *n* type of prayer
KYRIELLE *n* verse form of French origin characterized by repeated lines or words
KYRIELLES > KYRIELLE
KYRIES > KYRIE
KYTE *n* belly
KYTES > KYTE
KYTHE *vb* appear
KYTHED > KYTHE
KYTHES > KYTHE
KYTHING > KYTHE
KYU *n* (in judo) one of the five student grades
KYUS > KYU

LI

LA n exclamation of surprise or emphasis ▷ n the sixth note of the musical scale

LAAGER n (in Africa) a camp defended by a circular formation of wagons ▷ vb form (wagons) into a laager

LAAGERED > LAAGER

LAAGERING > LAAGER

LAAGERS > LAAGER

LAARI same as > LARI

LAARIS > LAARI

LAB n laboratory

LABARA > LABARUM

LABARUM n standard carried in Christian processions

LABARUMS > LABARUM

LABDA same as > LAMBDA

LABDACISM n excessive use or idiosyncratic pronunciation of (l)

LABDANUM n dark resinous juice obtained from various rockroses

LABDANUMS > LABDANUM

LABDAS > LABDA

LABEL n piece of card or other material fixed to an object to show its ownership, destination, etc ▷ vb give a label to

LABELABLE > LABEL

LABELED > LABEL

LABELER > LABEL

LABELERS > LABEL

LABELING > LABEL

LABELLA > LABELLUM

LABELLATE > LABELLUM

LABELLED > LABEL

LABELLER > LABEL

LABELLERS > LABEL

LABELLING > LABEL

LABELLIST n person who wears only clothes with fashionable brand names

LABELLOID > LABELLUM

LABELLUM n lip-like part of certain plants

LABELMATE n musician or singer who records for the same company as another

LABELS > LABEL

LABIA > LABIUM

LABIAL adj of the lips ▷ n speech sound that involves the lips

LABIALISE same as > LABIALIZE

LABIALISM > LABIALIZE

LABIALITY > LABIAL

LABIALIZE vb pronounce with articulation involving rounded lips

LABIALLY > LABIAL

LABIALS > LABIAL

LABIATE n plant with square stems, aromatic leaves, and a two-lipped flower ▷ adj of this family

LABIATED adj having a lip

LABIATES > LABIATE

LABILE adj (of a compound) prone to chemical change

LABILITY > LABILE

LABIS n cochlear

LABISES > LABIS

LABIUM n lip or liplike structure

LABLAB n twining leguminous plant

LABLABS > LABLAB

LABOR same as > LABOUR

LABORED same as > LABOURED

LABOREDLY > LABOURED

LABORER same as > LABOURER

LABORERS > LABORER

LABORING > LABOR

LABORIOUS adj involving great prolonged effort

LABORISM same as > LABOURISM

LABORISMS > LABORISM

LABORIST same as > LABOURIST

LABORISTS > LABORIST

LABORITE n adherent of the Labour party

LABORITES > LABORITE

LABORS > LABOR

LABORSOME adj requiring hard work

LABOUR n physical work or exertion ▷ vb work hard

LABOURED adj uttered or done with difficulty

LABOURER n person who labours, esp someone doing manual work for wages

LABOURERS > LABOURER

LABOURING > LABOUR

LABOURISM n dominance of the working classes

LABOURIST n person who supports workers' rights

LABOURITE n person who supports workers' rights

LABOURS > LABOUR

LABRA > LABRUM

LABRADOR n large retriever dog with a usu gold or black coat

LABRADORS > LABRADOR

LABRAL adj of or like a lip

LABRET n piece of bone or shell

LABRETS > LABRET

LABRID same as > LABROID

LABRIDS > LABRID

LABROID n type of fish ▷ adj of or relating to such fish

LABROIDS > LABROID

LABROSE adj thick-lipped

LABRUM n lip or liplike part

LABRUMS > LABRUM

LABRUSCA n grape variety

LABRUSCAS > LABRUSCA

LABRYS n type of axe

LABRYSES > LABRYS

LABS > LAB

LABURNUM n ornamental tree with yellow hanging flowers

LABURNUMS > LABURNUM

LABYRINTH n complicated network of passages

LAC same as > LAKH

LACCOLITE same as > LACCOLITH

LACCOLITH n dome-shaped body of igneous rock between two layers of older sedimentary rock

LACE n delicate fabric ▷ vb fasten with shoelaces, cords, etc

LACEBARK n small evergreen tree

LACEBARKS > LACEBARK

LACED > LACE

LACELESS > LACE

LACELIKE > LACE

LACEMAKER n one who makes lace

LACER > LACE

LACERABLE > LACERATE

LACERANT adj painfully distressing

LACERATE vb tear (flesh) ▷ adj having edges that are jagged or torn

LACERATED > LACERATE

LACERATES > LACERATE

LACERS > LACE

LACERTIAN n type of reptile

LACERTID n type of lizard

LACERTIDS > LACERTID

LACERTINE adj relating to lacertid

LACES > LACE

LACET n braidwork

LACETS > LACET

LACEWING n any of various neuropterous insects

LACEWINGS > LACEWING

LACEWOOD n wood of sycamore tree

LACEWOODS > LACEWOOD

LACEWORK n work made from lace

LACEWORKS > LACEWORK

LACEY same as > LACY

LACHES n unreasonable delay in pursuing a legal remedy

LACHESES > LACHES

LACHRYMAL same as > LACRIMAL

LACIER > LACY

LACIEST > LACY

LACILY > LACY

LACINESS > LACY

LACING > LACE

LACINGS > LACE

LACINIA n narrow fringe on petal

LACINIAE > LACINIA

LACINIATE adj jagged

LACK n shortage of something needed ▷ vb need

LACKADAY another word for > ALAS

LACKED > LACK

LACKER variant spelling of > LACQUER

LACKERED > LACKER

LACKERING > LACKER

LACKERS > LACKER

LACKEY n servile follower ▷ vb act as a lackey (to)

LACKEYED > LACKEY

LACKEYING > LACKEY

LACKEYS > LACKEY

LACKING > LACK
LACKLAND n fool
LACKLANDS > LACKLAND
LACKS > LACK
LACMUS n old form of litmus
LACMUSES > LACMUS
LACONIC adj using only a few words, terse
LACONICAL same as > LACONIC
LACONISM n economy of expression
LACONISMS > LACONISM
LACQUER n hard varnish for wood or metal ▷ vb apply lacquer to
LACQUERED > LACQUER
LACQUERER > LACQUER
LACQUERS > LACQUER
LACQUEY same as > LACKEY
LACQUEYED > LACQUEY
LACQUEYS > LACQUEY
LACRIMAL adj of tears or the glands which produce them ▷ n bone near tear gland
LACRIMALS > LACRIMAL
LACRIMARY adj of or relating to tears or to the glands that secrete tears
LACRIMOSO adj tearful
LACROSSE n sport in which teams catch and throw a ball using long sticks with a pouched net at the end, in an attempt to score goals
LACROSSES > LACROSSE
LACRYMAL same as > LACRIMAL
LACRYMALS > LACRYMAL
LACS > LAC
LACTAM n any of a group of inner amides
LACTAMS > LACTAM
LACTARIAN n vegetarian who eats dairy products
LACTARY adj relating to milk
LACTASE n any of a group of enzymes that hydrolyse lactose to glucose and galactose
LACTASES > LACTASE
LACTATE vb secrete milk ▷ n ester or salt of lactic acid
LACTATED > LACTATE
LACTATES > LACTATE
LACTATING > LACTATE
LACTATION n secretion of milk by female mammals to feed young
LACTEAL adj of or like milk ▷ n any of the lymphatic vessels that convey chyle from the small intestine to the blood
LACTEALLY > LACTEAL
LACTEALS > LACTEAL
LACTEAN another word for > LACTEOUS

LACTEOUS adj milky
LACTIC adj of or derived from milk
LACTIFIC adj yielding milk
LACTITOL n type of artificial sweetener
LACTITOLS > LACTITOL
LACTIVISM > LACTIVIST
LACTIVIST n person who advocates breast-feeding
LACTONE n any of a class of organic compounds
LACTONES > LACTONE
LACTONIC > LACTONE
LACTOSE n white crystalline sugar found in milk
LACTOSES > LACTOSE
LACUNA n gap or missing part, esp in a document or series
LACUNAE > LACUNA
LACUNAL > LACUNA
LACUNAR n ceiling, soffit, or vault having coffers ▷ adj having a lacuna
LACUNARIA > LACUNAR
LACUNARS > LACUNAR
LACUNARY > LACUNA
LACUNAS > LACUNA
LACUNATE > LACUNA
LACUNE n hiatus
LACUNES > LACUNE
LACUNOSE > LACUNA
LACY adj fine, like lace
LAD n boy or young man
LADANUM same as > LABDANUM
LADANUMS > LADANUM
LADDER n frame of two poles connected by horizontal steps for climbing ▷ vb cause to have a line of undone stitches
LADDERED > LADDER
LADDERING > LADDER
LADDERS > LADDER
LADDERY > LADDER
LADDIE n familiar term for a male, esp a young man
LADDIER > LADDY
LADDIES > LADDIE
LADDIEST > LADDY
LADDISH adj behaving in a macho or immature manner
LADDISM n laddish attitudes and behaviour
LADDISMS > LADDISM
LADDY adj laddish
LADE vb put cargo on board ▷ n watercourse
LADED > LADE
LADEN adj loaded ▷ vb load with cargo
LADENED > LADEN
LADENING > LADEN
LADENS > LADEN
LADER > LADE

LADERS > LADE
LADES > LADE
LADETTE n young woman who behaves like a young man
LADETTES > LADETTE
LADHOOD > LAD
LADHOODS > LAD
LADIES n women's public toilet
LADIFIED > LADIFY
LADIFIES > LADIFY
LADIFY same as > LADYFY
LADIFYING > LADIFY
LADING > LADE
LADINGS > LADE
LADINO n Italian variety of white clover
LADINOS > LADINO
LADLE n long-handled spoon with a large bowl ▷ vb serve out
LADLED > LADLE
LADLEFUL > LADLE
LADLEFULS > LADLE
LADLER n person who serves with a ladle
LADLERS > LADLER
LADLES > LADLE
LADLING > LADLE
LADRON same as > LADRONE
LADRONE n thief
LADRONES > LADRONE
LADRONS > LADRON
LADS > LAD
LADY n woman of good breeding or high rank ▷ adj female
LADYBIRD n small red beetle with black spots
LADYBIRDS > LADYBIRD
LADYBOY n transvestite or transsexual from the Far East
LADYBOYS > LADYBOY
LADYBUG same as > LADYBIRD
LADYBUGS > LADYBUG
LADYCOW another word for > LADYBIRD
LADYCOWS > LADYCOW
LADYFIED > LADYFY
LADYFIES > LADYFY
LADYFISH n type of game fish
LADYFLIES > LADYFLY
LADYFLY another word for > LADYBIRD
LADYFY vb make a lady of (someone)
LADYFYING > LADYFY
LADYHOOD > LADY
LADYHOODS > LADY
LADYISH > LADY
LADYISM > LADY
LADYISMS > LADY
LADYKIN n endearing form of lady
LADYKINS > LADYKIN
LADYLIKE adj polite and dignified

LADYLOVE n beloved woman
LADYLOVES > LADYLOVE
LADYNESS n state of being a lady
LADYPALM n small palm, grown indoors
LADYPALMS > LADYPALM
LADYSHIP n title of a peeress
LADYSHIPS > LADYSHIP
LAER another word for > LAAGER
LAERED > LAER
LAERING > LAER
LAERS > LAER
LAESIE old form of > LAZY
LAETARE n fourth Sunday of Lent
LAETARES > LAETARE
LAETRILE n drug used to treat cancer
LAETRILES > LAETRILE
LAEVIGATE same as > LEVIGATE
LAEVO adj on the left
LAEVULIN n polysaccharide occurring in the tubers of certain helianthus plants
LAEVULINS > LAEVULIN
LAEVULOSE n fructose
LAG vb go too slowly, fall behind ▷ n delay between events
LAGAN n goods or wreckage on the sea bed
LAGANS > LAGAN
LAGENA n bottle with a narrow neck
LAGENAS > LAGENA
LAGEND same as > LAGAN
LAGENDS > LAGEND
LAGER n light-bodied beer ▷ vb ferment into lager
LAGERED > LAGER
LAGERING > LAGER
LAGERS > LAGER
LAGGARD n person who lags behind ▷ adj sluggish, slow
LAGGARDLY > LAGGARD
LAGGARDS > LAGGARD
LAGGED > LAG
LAGGEN n spar of a barrel
LAGGENS > LAGGEN
LAGGER n person who lags pipes
LAGGERS > LAGGER
LAGGIN same as > LAGGEN
LAGGING > LAG
LAGGINGLY > LAG
LAGGINGS > LAG
LAGGINS > LAGGIN
LAGNAPPE same as > LAGNIAPPE
LAGNAPPES > LAGNAPPE
LAGNIAPPE n small gift, esp one given to a customer who makes a purchase
LAGOMORPH n type of placental mammal of the

order which includes
rabbits and hares

LAGOON n water cut off
from the sea by reefs or
sand bars

LAGOONAL > LAGOON

LAGOONS > LAGOON

LAGRIMOSO adj mournful

LAGS > LAG

LAGUNA n lagoon

LAGUNAS > LAGUNA

LAGUNE same as > LAGOON

LAGUNES > LAGUNE

LAH n (in tonic sol-fa) sixth
degree of any major scale

LAHAL n game played by
native peoples of the
Pacific Northwest

LAHALS > LAHAL

LAHAR n landslide of
volcanic debris and water

LAHARS > LAHAR

LAHS > LAH

LAIC adj laical ⊳ n layman

LAICAL adj secular

LAICALLY > LAIC

LAICH n low-lying piece of
land

LAICHS > LAICH

LAICISE same as
> LAICIZE

LAICISED > LAICISE

LAICISES > LAICISE

LAICISING > LAICISE

LAICISM > LAIC

LAICISMS > LAIC

LAICITIES > LAICITY

LAICITY n state of being
laical

LAICIZE vb remove
ecclesiastical status from

LAICIZED > LAICIZE

LAICIZES > LAICIZE

LAICIZING > LAICIZE

LAICS > LAIC

LAID Scots form of > LOAD

LAIDED > LAID

LAIDING > LAID

LAIDLIER > LAIDLY

LAIDLIEST > LAIDLY

LAIDLY adj very ugly

LAIDS > LAID

LAIGH adj low-lying ⊳ n
area of low-lying ground

LAIGHER > LAIGH

LAIGHEST > LAIGH

LAIGHS > LAIGH

LAIK vb play (a game, etc)

LAIKA n type of small dog

LAIKAS > LAIKA

LAIKED > LAIK

LAIKER > LAIK

LAIKERS > LAIK

LAIKING > LAIK

LAIKS > LAIK

LAIN > LIE

LAIPSE vb beat soundly

LAIPSED > LAIPSE

LAIPSES > LAIPSE

LAIPSING > LAIPSE

LAIR n resting place of an
animal ⊳ vb retreat to or
rest in a lair

LAIRAGE n
accommodation for farm
animals

LAIRAGES > LAIRAGE

LAIRD n Scottish
landowner

LAIRDLIER > LAIRDLY

LAIRDLY adj pertaining to
laird(s)

LAIRDS > LAIRD

LAIRDSHIP n state of
being laird

LAIRED > LAIR

LAIRIER > LAIRY

LAIRIEST > LAIRY

LAIRING > LAIR

LAIRISE same as
> LAIRIZE

LAIRISED > LAIRISE

LAIRISES > LAIRISE

LAIRISING > LAIRISE

LAIRIZE vb show off

LAIRIZED > LAIRIZE

LAIRIZES > LAIRIZE

LAIRIZING > LAIRIZE

LAIRS > LAIR

LAIRY adj gaudy or flashy

LAISSE n type of rhyme
scheme

LAISSES > LAISSE

LAITANCE n white film
forming on drying concrete

LAITANCES > LAITANCE

LAITH Scots form of
> LOATH

LAITHLY same as
> LAIDLY

LAITIES > LAITY

LAITY n non-clergy

LAKE n expanse of water
entirely surrounded by
land ⊳ vb take time away
from work

LAKEBED n bed of lake

LAKEBEDS > LAKEBED

LAKED > LAKE

LAKEFILL n area of land
on a filled lake

LAKEFILLS > LAKEFILL

LAKEFRONT n area at
edge of lake

LAKEHEAD n shore of a
lake farthest from the
outlet

LAKEHEADS > LAKEHEAD

LAKELAND n countryside
with a lot of lakes

LAKELANDS > LAKELAND

LAKELET n small lake

LAKELETS > LAKELET

LAKELIKE > LAKE

LAKEPORT n port on lake

LAKEPORTS > LAKEPORT

LAKER n lake cargo vessel

LAKERS > LAKER

LAKES > LAKE

LAKESHORE n area at
edge of lake

LAKESIDE n area at edge
of lake

LAKESIDES > LAKESIDE

LAKEVIEW adj having a
view of a lake

LAKEWARD same as
> LAKEWARDS

LAKEWARDS adj towards a
lake

LAKH n (in India) 100 000,
esp referring to this sum of
rupees

LAKHS > LAKH

LAKIER > LAKY

LAKIEST > LAKY

LAKIN short form of
> LADYKIN

LAKING > LAKE

LAKINGS > LAKE

LAKINS > LAKIN

LAKISH adj similar to
poetry of Lake poets

LAKSA n (in Malaysia)
Chinese dish of rice
noodles in curry or hot
soup

LAKSAS > LAKSA

LAKY adj of the reddish
colour of the pigment lake

LALANG n coarse weedy
Malaysian grass

LALANGS > LALANG

LALDIE n great gusto

LALDIES > LALDIE

LALDY same as > LALDIE

LALIQUE n ornamental
glass

LALIQUES > LALIQUE

LALL vb make bad 'l' or 'r'
sounds

LALLAN n literary version
of the English spoken in
Lowland Scotland

LALLAND same as
> LALLAN

LALLANDS > LALLAND

LALLANS > LALLAN

LALLATION n defect of
speech consisting of the
pronunciation of 'r' as 'l'

LALLED > LALL

LALLING > LALL

LALLINGS > LALL

LALLS > LALL

LALLYGAG vb loiter
aimlessly

LALLYGAGS > LALLYGAG

LAM vb attack vigorously

LAMA n Buddhist priest in
Tibet or Mongolia

LAMAISTIC adj relating
to the Mahayana form of
Buddhism

LAMANTIN another word for
> MANATEE

LAMANTINS > LAMANTIN

LAMAS > LAMA

LAMASERAI same as
> LAMASERY

LAMASERY n monastery
of lamas

LAMB n young sheep ⊳ vb
give birth to a lamb or
lambs

LAMBADA n erotic
Brazilian dance

LAMBADAS > LAMBADA

LAMBAST vb beat or
thrash

LAMBASTE same as
> LAMBAST

LAMBASTED > LAMBAST

LAMBASTES > LAMBASTE

LAMBASTS > LAMBAST

LAMBDA n 11th letter of the
Greek alphabet

LAMBDAS > LAMBDA

LAMBDOID adj having the
shape of the Greek letter
lambda

LAMBED > LAMB

LAMBENCY > LAMBENT

LAMBENT adj (of a flame)
flickering softly

LAMBENTLY > LAMBENT

LAMBER n person that
attends to lambing ewes

LAMBERS > LAMBER

LAMBERT n cgs unit of
illumination, equal to 1
lumen per square
centimetre

LAMBERTS > LAMBERT

LAMBIE same as
> LAMBKIN

LAMBIER > LAMBY

LAMBIES > LAMBIE

LAMBIEST > LAMBY

LAMBING n birth of lambs
at the end of winter

LAMBINGS > LAMBING

LAMBITIVE n medicine
taken by licking

LAMBKILL n N American
dwarf shrub

LAMBKILLS > LAMBKILL

LAMBKIN n young lamb

LAMBKINS > LAMBKIN

LAMBLIKE > LAMB

LAMBLING n small lamb

LAMBLINGS > LAMBLING

LAMBOYS n skirt-like piece
of armour made from
metal strips

LAMBRUSCO n Italian
sparkling wine

LAMBS > LAMB

LAMBSKIN n skin of a
lamb, usually with the
wool still on, used to make
coats, slippers, etc

LAMBSKINS > LAMBSKIN

LAMBSWOOL n wool from
a lamb's first shearing

LAMBY adj lamb-like

LAME adj having an injured
or disabled leg or foot
⊳ vb make lame ⊳ n fabric
interwoven with gold or
silver threads

LAMEBRAIN n stupid or
slow-witted person

LAMED n 12th letter in the
Hebrew alphabet

LAMEDH same as > LAMED

LAMEDHS > LAMEDH

LAMEDS > LAMED

LAMELLA n thin layer,
plate, etc, like the calcified
layers of which bone is
formed

LAMELLAE > LAMELLA

LAMELLAR > LAMELLA

LAMELLAS > LAMELLA
LAMELLATE > LAMELLA
LAMELLOID another word for > LAMELLA
LAMELLOSE > LAMELLA
LAMELY > LAME
LAMENESS > LAME
LAMENT vb feel or express sorrow (for) ▷ n passionate expression of grief
LAMENTED adj grieved for
LAMENTER > LAMENT
LAMENTERS > LAMENT
LAMENTING > LAMENT
LAMENTS > LAMENT
LAMER > LAME
LAMES > LAME
LAMEST > LAME
LAMETER Scots form of > LAMIGER
LAMETERS > LAMETER
LAMIA n female monster with a snake's body and a woman's head and breasts
LAMIAE > LAMIA
LAMIAS > LAMIA
LAMIGER n disabled person
LAMIGERS > LAMIGER
LAMINA n thin plate, esp of bone or mineral
LAMINABLE > LAMINATE
LAMINAE > LAMINA
LAMINAL n consonant articulated with blade of tongue
LAMINALS > LAMINAL
LAMINAR > LAMINA
LAMINARIA n type of brown seaweed
LAMINARIN n carbohydrate, consisting of repeated glucose units, that is the main storage product of brown algae
LAMINARY > LAMINA
LAMINAS > LAMINA
LAMINATE vb make (a sheet of material) by sticking together thin sheets ▷ n laminated sheet ▷ adj composed of lamina
LAMINATED adj composed of many layers stuck together
LAMINATES > LAMINATE
LAMINATOR > LAMINATE
LAMING > LAME
LAMINGTON n sponge cake coated with a sweet coating
LAMININ n type of protein
LAMININS > LAMININ
LAMINITIS n (in animals with hooves) inflammation of the tissue to which the hoof is attached
LAMINOSE > LAMINA
LAMINOUS > LAMINA
LAMISH adj rather lame
LAMISTER n fugitive

LAMISTERS > LAMISTER
LAMITER same as > LAMETER
LAMITERS > LAMITER
LAMMED > LAM
LAMMER Scots word for > AMBER
LAMMERS > LAMMER
LAMMIE same as > LAMMY
LAMMIES > LAMMY
LAMMIGER same as > LAMIGER
LAMMIGERS > LAMIGER
LAMMING > LAM
LAMMINGS > LAM
LAMMY n thick woollen jumper
LAMP n device which produces light from electricity, oil, or gas ▷ vb go quickly with long steps
LAMPAD n candlestick
LAMPADARY n person who lights the lamps in an Orthodox Greek Church
LAMPADIST n prizewinner in race run by young men with torches
LAMPADS > LAMPAD
LAMPAS n swelling of the mucous membrane of the hard palate of horses
LAMPASES > LAMPAS
LAMPASSE same as > LAMPAS
LAMPASSES > LAMPASSE
LAMPBLACK n fine black soot used as a pigment in paint and ink ▷ vb blacken with fine black soot
LAMPBRUSH n as in lampbrush chromosome type of chromosome
LAMPED > LAMP
LAMPER n lamprey
LAMPERN n migratory European lamprey
LAMPERNS > LAMPERN
LAMPERS > LAMPER
LAMPERSES > LAMPERS
LAMPHOLE n hole in ground for lowering lamp into sewer
LAMPHOLES > LAMPHOLE
LAMPING > LAMP
LAMPINGS > LAMP
LAMPION n oil-burning lamp
LAMPIONS > LAMPION
LAMPLESS adj without a lamp
LAMPLIGHT n light produced by lamp
LAMPLIT adj lit by lamps
LAMPOON n humorous satire ridiculing someone ▷ vb satirize or ridicule
LAMPOONED > LAMPOON
LAMPOONER > LAMPOON
LAMPOONS > LAMPOON
LAMPPOST n post supporting a lamp in the street

LAMPPOSTS > LAMPPOST
LAMPREY n eel-like fish with a round sucking mouth
LAMPREYS > LAMPREY
LAMPS > LAMP
LAMPSHADE n shade used to reduce light shed by light bulb
LAMPSHELL n brachiopod
LAMPSTAND n stand for a lamp
LAMPUKA same as > LAMPUKI
LAMPUKAS > LAMPUKA
LAMPUKI n type of fish
LAMPUKIS > LAMPUKI
LAMPYRID n firefly
LAMPYRIDS > LAMPYRID
LAMS > LAM
LAMSTER n fugitive
LAMSTERS > LAMSTER
LANA n wood from genipap tree
LANAI Hawaiian word for > VERANDA
LANAIS > LANAI
LANAS > LANA
LANATE adj having or consisting of a woolly covering of hairs
LANATED same as > LANATE
LANCE n long spear used by a mounted soldier ▷ vb pierce (a boil or abscess) with a lancet
LANCED > LANCE
LANCEGAY n kind of ancient spear
LANCEGAYS > LANCEGAY
LANCEJACK n lance corporal
LANCELET n type of marine invertebrate
LANCELETS > LANCELET
LANCEOLAR adj narrow and tapering to a point at each end
LANCER n formerly, cavalry soldier armed with a lance
LANCERS n quadrille for eight or sixteen couples
LANCES > LANCE
LANCET n pointed two-edged surgical knife
LANCETED adj having one or more lancet arches or windows
LANCETS > LANCET
LANCEWOOD n New Zealand tree with slender leaves
LANCH obsolete form of > LAUNCH
LANCHED > LANCH
LANCHES > LANCH
LANCHING > LANCH
LANCIERS pl n type of dance
LANCIFORM adj in the form of a lance

LANCINATE adj (esp of pain) sharp or cutting
LANCING > LANCE
LAND n solid part of the earth's surface ▷ vb come or bring to earth after a flight, jump, or fall
LANDAMMAN n chairman of the governing council in some Swiss cantons
LANDAU n four-wheeled carriage with two folding hoods
LANDAULET n small landau
LANDAUS > LANDAU
LANDBOARD n narrow board, with wheels larger than those on a skateboard, usually ridden while standing
LANDDAMNE vb Shakespearian word for make (a person's life) unbearable
LANDDROS n sheriff
LANDDROST n South African magistrate
LANDE n type of moorland in SW France
LANDED adj possessing or consisting of lands
LANDER n spacecraft which lands on a planet or other body
LANDERS > LANDER
LANDES > LANDE
LANDFALL n ship's first landing after a voyage
LANDFALLS > LANDFALL
LANDFAST adj (of ice) attached to the shore
LANDFILL n disposing of rubbish by covering it with earth
LANDFILLS > LANDFILL
LANDFORCE n body of people trained for land warfare
LANDFORM n any natural feature of the earth's surface, such as valleys and mountains
LANDFORMS > LANDFORM
LANDGRAB n sudden attempt to establish ownership of or copyright on something in advance of competitors
LANDGRABS > LANDGRAB
LANDGRAVE n (from the 13th century to 1806) a count who ruled over a specified territory
LANDING n floor area at the top of a flight of stairs
LANDINGS > LANDING
LANDLADY n woman who owns and leases property
LANDLER n Austrian country dance
LANDLERS > LANDLER
LANDLESS > LAND

LANDLINE n telecommunications cable laid over land

LANDLINES > LANDLINE

LANDLOPER n vagabond or vagrant

LANDLORD n person who rents out land, houses, etc

LANDLORDS > LANDLORD

LANDMAN n person who lives and works on land

LANDMARK n prominent object in or feature of a landscape

LANDMARKS > LANDMARK

LANDMASS n large continuous area of land

LANDMEN > LANDMAN

LANDMINE n type of bomb laid on or just under the surface of the ground ▷ vb lay (an area) with landmines

LANDMINED > LANDMINE

LANDMINES > LANDMINE

LANDOWNER n person who owns land

LANDRACE n white very long-bodied lop-eared breed of pork pig

LANDRACES > LANDRACE

LANDRAIL n type of bird

LANDRAILS > LANDRAIL

LANDS pl n holdings in land

LANDSCAPE n extensive piece of inland scenery seen from one place ▷ vb improve natural features of (a piece of land) ▷ adj (of a publication or an illustration in a publication) of greater width than height

LANDSHARK n person who makes inordinate profits by buying and selling land

LANDSIDE n part of an airport farthest from the aircraft

LANDSIDES > LANDSIDE

LANDSKIP another word for > LANDSCAPE

LANDSKIPS > LANDSKIP

LANDSLEIT > LANDSMAN

LANDSLID > LANDSLIDE

LANDSLIDE vb cause land or rock to fall from hillside

LANDSLIP same as > LANDSLIDE

LANDSLIPS > LANDSLIP

LANDSMAN n person who works or lives on land, as distinguished from a seaman

LANDSMEN > LANDSMAN

LANDWARD same as > LANDWARDS

LANDWARDS adv towards land

LANDWASH n part of the shore between the high-water mark and the sea

LANDWIND n wind that comes from the land

LANDWINDS > LANDWIND

LANE n narrow road

LANELY Scots form of > LONELY

LANES > LANE

LANEWAY n lane

LANEWAYS > LANEWAY

LANG Scot word for > LONG

LANGAHA n type of Madagascan snake

LANGAHAS > LANGAHA

LANGAR n dining hall in a gurdwara

LANGARS > LANGAR

LANGER informal Irish word for > PENIS

LANGERED adj drunk

LANGERS > LANGER

LANGEST > LANG

LANGLAUF n cross-country skiing

LANGLAUFS > LANGLAUF

LANGLEY n unit of solar radiation

LANGLEYS > LANGLEY

LANGOUSTE n spiny lobster

LANGRAGE n shot consisting of scrap iron packed into a case, formerly used in naval warfare

LANGRAGES > LANGRAGE

LANGREL same as > LANGRAGE

LANGRELS > LANGREL

LANGRIDGE same as > LANGRAGE

LANGSHAN n breed of chicken

LANGSHANS > LANGSHAN

LANGSPEL n type of Scandinavian stringed instrument

LANGSPELS > LANGSPEL

LANGSPIEL same as > LANGSPEL

LANGSPIL n type of Scandinavian stringed instrument

LANGSPILS > LANGSPIL

LANGSYNE adv long ago ▷ n times long past, esp those fondly remembered

LANGSYNES > LANGSYNE

LANGUAGE n system of sounds, symbols, etc for communicating thought ▷ vb express in language

LANGUAGED > LANGUAGE

LANGUAGES > LANGUAGE

LANGUE n language considered as an abstract system

LANGUED adj having a tongue

LANGUES > LANGUE

LANGUET n anything resembling a tongue

LANGUETS > LANGUET

LANGUETTE same as > LANGUET

LANGUID adj lacking energy

LANGUIDLY > LANGUID

LANGUISH vb suffer neglect or hardship

LANGUOR n dreamy relaxation

LANGUORS > LANGUOR

LANGUR n type of arboreal Old World monkey

LANGURS > LANGUR

LANIARD same as > LANYARD

LANIARDS > LANIARD

LANIARIES > LANIARY

LANIARY adj adapted for tearing ▷ n tooth adapted for tearing

LANITAL n fibre used in production of synthetic wool

LANITALS > LANITAL

LANK adj straight and limp ▷ vb become lank

LANKED > LANK

LANKER > LANK

LANKEST > LANK

LANKIER > LANKY

LANKIEST > LANKY

LANKILY > LANKY

LANKINESS > LANKY

LANKING > LANK

LANKLY > LANK

LANKNESS > LANK

LANKS > LANK

LANKY adj tall and thin

LANNER n large falcon

LANNERET n male or tercel of the lanner falcon

LANNERETS > LANNERET

LANNERS > LANNER

LANOLATED > LANOLIN

LANOLIN n grease from sheep's wool used in ointments etc

LANOLINE same as > LANOLIN

LANOLINES > LANOLINE

LANOLINS > LANOLIN

LANOSE same as > LANATE

LANOSITY > LANOSE

LANT n stale urine

LANTANA n shrub with orange or yellow flowers

LANTANAS > LANTANA

LANTERLOO n old card game

LANTERN n light in a transparent protective case ▷ vb supply with lantern

LANTERNED > LANTERN

LANTERNS > LANTERN

LANTHANON n one of a group of chemical elements

LANTHANUM n silvery-white metallic element

LANTHORN archaic word for > LANTERN

LANTHORNS > LANTHORN

LANTS > LANT

LANTSKIP another word for > LANDSCAPE

LANTSKIPS > LANTSKIP

LANUGO n layer of fine hairs, esp the covering of the human fetus before birth

LANUGOS > LANUGO

LANX n dish; plate

LANYARD n neck cord to hold a knife or whistle

LANYARDS > LANYARD

LAODICEAN adj indifferent, esp in religious matters ▷ n person having a lukewarm attitude towards religious matters

LAOGAI n forced labour camp in China

LAOGAIS > LAOGAI

LAP n part between the waist and knees when sitting ▷ vb overtake so as to be one or more circuits ahead

LAPBOARD n flat board that can be used on the lap as a makeshift table or desk

LAPBOARDS > LAPBOARD

LAPDOG n small pet dog

LAPDOGS > LAPDOG

LAPEL n part of the front of a coat or jacket folded back towards the shoulders

LAPELED > LAPEL

LAPELLED > LAPEL

LAPELS > LAPEL

LAPFUL same as > LAP

LAPFULS > LAPFUL

LAPHELD adj small enough to be used on one's lap

LAPIDARY adj of or relating to stones ▷ n person who cuts, polishes, sets, or deals in gemstones

LAPIDATE vb pelt with stones

LAPIDATED > LAPIDATE

LAPIDATES > LAPIDATE

LAPIDEOUS adj having appearance or texture of stone

LAPIDES > LAPIS

LAPIDIFIC adj transforming into stone

LAPIDIFY vb change into stone

LAPIDIST n cutter and engraver of precious stones

LAPIDISTS > LAPIDIST

LAPILLI > LAPILLUS

LAPILLUS n small piece of lava thrown from a volcano

LAPIN n castrated rabbit

LAPINS > LAPIN

LAPIS n as in lapis lazuli brilliant blue mineral gemstone
LAPISES > LAPIS
LAPJE same as > LAPPIE
LAPJES > LAPJE
LAPPED > LAP
LAPPEL same as > LAPEL
LAPPELS > LAPPEL
LAPPER n one that laps ▷ vb curdle
LAPPERED > LAPPER
LAPPERING > LAPPER
LAPPERS > LAPPER
LAPPET n small hanging flap
LAPPETED > LAPPET
LAPPETS > LAPPET
LAPPIE n rag
LAPPIES > LAPPIE
LAPPING > LAP
LAPPINGS > LAP
LAPS > LAP
LAPSABLE > LAPSE
LAPSANG n Chinese tea
LAPSANGS > LAPSANG
LAPSE n temporary drop in a standard ▷ vb drop in standard
LAPSED > LAPSE
LAPSER > LAPSE
LAPSERS > LAPSE
LAPSES > LAPSE
LAPSIBLE > LAPSE
LAPSING > LAPSE
LAPSTONE n device used by a cobbler on which leather is beaten
LAPSTONES > LAPSTONE
LAPSTRAKE n clinker-built boat
LAPSTREAK same as > LAPSTRAKE
LAPSUS n lapse or error
LAPTOP adj small enough to fit on a user's lap ▷ n small computer
LAPTOPS > LAPTOP
LAPTRAY n tray with a cushioned underside
LAPTRAYS > LAPTRAY
LAPWING n plover with a tuft of feathers on the head
LAPWINGS > LAPWING
LAPWORK n work with lapping edges
LAPWORKS > LAPWORK
LAQUEARIA n ceiling made of panels
LAR n boy or young man
LARBOARD n port (side of a ship)
LARBOARDS > LARBOARD
LARCENER > LARCENY
LARCENERS > LARCENY
LARCENIES > LARCENY
LARCENIST > LARCENY
LARCENOUS > LARCENY
LARCENY n theft
LARCH n deciduous coniferous tree
LARCHEN adj of larch

LARCHES > LARCH
LARD n soft white pig fat ▷ vb insert strips of bacon in before cooking
LARDALITE n type of mineral
LARDED > LARD
LARDER n storeroom for food
LARDERER n person in charge of larder
LARDERERS > LARDERER
LARDERS > LARDER
LARDIER > LARDY
LARDIEST > LARDY
LARDING > LARD
LARDLIKE > LARD
LARDON n strip or cube of fat or bacon used in larding meat
LARDONS > LARDON
LARDOON same as > LARDON
LARDOONS > LARDOON
LARDS > LARD
LARDY adj fat
LARE another word for > LORE
LAREE n Asian fish-hook
LAREES > LAREE
LARES > LARE
LARGANDO adv (music) growing slower and more marked
LARGE adj great in size, number ▷ n formerly, musical note
LARGELY adv principally
LARGEN another word for > ENLARGE
LARGENED > LARGEN
LARGENESS > LARGE
LARGENING > LARGEN
LARGENS > LARGEN
LARGER > LARGE
LARGES > LARGE
LARGESS same as > LARGESSE
LARGESSE n generous giving, esp of money
LARGESSES > LARGESSE
LARGEST > LARGE
LARGHETTO adv be performed moderately slowly ▷ n piece or passage to be performed in this way
LARGISH adj fairly large
LARGITION n act of being generous
LARGO adv in a slow and dignified manner ▷ n performance piece in a slow manner
LARGOS > LARGO
LARI n monetary unit of Georgia
LARIAT n lasso ▷ vb tether with lariat
LARIATED > LARIAT
LARIATING > LARIAT
LARIATS > LARIAT
LARIGAN n type of tanned moccasin boot

LARIGANS > LARIGAN
LARINE adj of, relating to, or resembling a gull
LARIS > LARI
LARK n small brown songbird ▷ vb frolic
LARKED > LARK
LARKER > LARK
LARKERS > LARK
LARKIER > LARKY
LARKIEST > LARKY
LARKINESS > LARKY
LARKING > LARK
LARKISH > LARK
LARKS > LARK
LARKSOME adj mischievous
LARKSPUR n plant with spikes of blue, pink, or white flowers with spurs
LARKSPURS > LARKSPUR
LARKY adj frolicsome
LARMIER n pouch under lower eyelid of deer
LARMIERS > LARMIER
LARN vb learn
LARNAKES > LARNAX
LARNAX n terracotta coffin
LARNED > LARN
LARNEY n white person ▷ adj (of clothes) smart
LARNEYS > LARNEY
LARNIER > LARNEY
LARNIEST > LARNEY
LARNING > LARN
LARNS > LARN
LARNT > LARN
LAROID adj relating to Larus genus of gull family
LARRIGAN n knee-high oiled leather moccasin boot worn by trappers, etc
LARRIGANS > LARRIGAN
LARRIKIN n mischievous or unruly person
LARRIKINS > LARRIKIN
LARRUP vb beat or flog
LARRUPED > LARRUP
LARRUPER > LARRUP
LARRUPERS > LARRUP
LARRUPING > LARRUP
LARRUPS > LARRUP
LARS > LAR
LARUM archaic word for > ALARM
LARUMS > LARUM
LARVA n immature insect
LARVAE > LARVA
LARVAL > LARVA
LARVAS > LARVA
LARVATE adj masked; concealed
LARVATED same as > LARVATE
LARVICIDE n chemical used for killing larvae
LARVIFORM adj in the form of a larva
LARVIKITE n type of mineral
LARYNGAL adj laryngeal ▷ n sound articulated in the larynx

LARYNGALS > LARYNGAL
LARYNGEAL adj of or relating to the larynx
LARYNGES > LARYNX
LARYNX n part of the throat containing the vocal cords
LARYNXES > LARYNX
LAS > LA
LASAGNA same as > LASAGNE
LASAGNAS > LASAGNA
LASAGNE n sheet pasta
LASAGNES > LASAGNE
LASCAR n East Indian seaman
LASCARS > LASCAR
LASE vb to be capable of acting as a laser
LASED > LASE
LASER n device producing a very narrow intense beam of light ▷ vb use a laser on (something), esp as part of medical treatment
LASERDISC n disk similar in size to a long-playing record, on which data is stored in pits in a similar way to data storage on a compact disk
LASERDISK same as > LASERDISC
LASERED > LASER
LASERING > LASER
LASERS > LASER
LASERWORT n type of plant
LASES > LASE
LASH n eyelash ▷ vb hit with a whip
LASHED > LASH
LASHER > LASH
LASHERS > LASH
LASHES > LASH
LASHING > LASH
LASHINGLY > LASH
LASHINGS pl n great amount of
LASHINS variant of > LASHINGS
LASHKAR n troop of Indian men with weapons
LASHKARS > LASHKAR
LASHLESS n (of a whip) without a lash
LASING > LASE
LASINGS > LASE
LASKET n loop at the foot of a sail onto which an extra sail may be fastened
LASKETS > LASKET
LASQUE n flat-cut diamond
LASQUES > LASQUE
LASS n girl
LASSES > LASS
LASSI n cold drink made of yoghurt or buttermilk, flavoured with sugar, salt, or spice
LASSIE n little lass
LASSIES > LASSIE

LASSIS > LASSI
LASSITUDE n physical or mental weariness
LASSLORN adj abandoned by a young girl
LASSO n rope with a noose ▷ vb catch with a lasso
LASSOCK another word for > LASS
LASSOCKS > LASSOCK
LASSOED > LASSO
LASSOER > LASSO
LASSOERS > LASSO
LASSOES > LASSO
LASSOING n act of lassoing
LASSOINGS > LASSOING
LASSOS > LASSO
LASSU n slow part of csárdás folk dance
LASSUS > LASSU
LASSY n short for molasses
LAST adv coming at the end or after all others ▷ adj only remaining ▷ n last person or thing ▷ vb continue
LASTAGE n space for storing goods in ship
LASTAGES > LASTAGE
LASTBORN n last child to be born
LASTBORNS > LASTBORN
LASTED > LAST
LASTER > LAST
LASTERS > LAST
LASTING adj remaining effective for a long time ▷ n strong durable fabric used for shoe uppers, etc
LASTINGLY > LASTING
LASTINGS > LASTING
LASTLY adv at the end or at the last point
LASTS > LAST
LAT n former coin of Latvia
LATAH n psychological condition
LATAHS > LATAH
LATAKIA n Turkish tobacco
LATAKIAS > LATAKIA
LATCH n fastening for a door with a bar and lever ▷ vb fasten with a latch
LATCHED > LATCH
LATCHES > LATCH
LATCHET n shoe fastening
LATCHETS > LATCHET
LATCHING > LATCH
LATCHKEY n key for an outside door or gate, esp one that lifts a latch
LATCHKEYS > LATCHKEY
LATE adj after the normal or expected time ▷ adv after the normal or expected time
LATECOMER n person or thing that comes late
LATED archaic word for > BELATED

LATEEN adj of a rig with a triangular sail bent to a yard hoisted to the head of a low mast
LATEENER n lateen-rigged ship
LATEENERS > LATEEN
LATEENS > LATEEN
LATELY adv in recent times
LATEN vb become or cause to become late
LATENCE > LATENT
LATENCES > LATENCE
LATENCIES > LATENT
LATENCY > LATENT
LATENED > LATEN
LATENESS > LATE
LATENING > LATEN
LATENS > LATEN
LATENT adj hidden and not yet developed ▷ n fingerprint that is not visible to the eye
LATENTLY > LATENT
LATENTS > LATENT
LATER adv afterwards
LATERAD adv towards the side
LATERAL adj of or relating to the side or sides ▷ n lateral object, part, passage, or movement ▷ vb pass laterally
LATERALED > LATERAL
LATERALLY > LATERAL
LATERALS > LATERAL
LATERBORN adj born later ▷ n one born later
LATERISE same as > LATERIZE
LATERISED > LATERISE
LATERISES > LATERISE
LATERITE n any of a group of deposits consisting of residual insoluble ferric and aluminium oxides
LATERITES > LATERITE
LATERITIC > LATERITE
LATERIZE vb develop into a laterite
LATERIZED > LATERIZE
LATERIZES > LATERIZE
LATESCENT n becoming latent
LATEST n the most recent news
LATESTS > LATEST
LATEWAKE n vigil held over corpse
LATEWAKES > LATEWAKE
LATEWOOD n wood formed later in tree's growing season
LATEWOODS > LATEWOOD
LATEX n milky fluid found in some plants
LATEXES > LATEX
LATH n thin strip of wood ▷ vb attach laths to
LATHE n machine for turning wood or metal while it is being shaped

▷ vb shape, bore, or cut a screw thread in or on (a workpiece) on a lathe
LATHED > LATHE
LATHEE same as > LATHI
LATHEES > LATHEE
LATHEN adj covered with laths
LATHER n froth of soap and water ▷ vb make frothy
LATHERED > LATHER
LATHERER > LATHER
LATHERERS > LATHER
LATHERIER > LATHER
LATHERING > LATHER
LATHERS > LATHER
LATHERY > LATHER
LATHES > LATHE
LATHI n long heavy wooden stick used as a weapon in India
LATHIER > LATHY
LATHIEST > LATHY
LATHING > LATHE
LATHINGS > LATHE
LATHIS > LATHI
LATHLIKE > LATH
LATHS > LATH
LATHWORK n work made of laths
LATHWORKS > LATHWORK
LATHY adj resembling a lath, esp in being tall and thin
LATHYRISM n neurological disease often resulting in weakness and paralysis of the legs
LATHYRUS n genus of climbing plant
LATI > LAT
LATICES > LATEX
LATICIFER n cell or group of cells in a plant that contains latex
LATICLAVE n broad stripe on Roman senator's tunic
LATIFONDI > LATIFONDO
LATIFONDO n large agricultural estate in ancient Rome
LATIGO n strap on horse's saddle
LATIGOES > LATIGO
LATIGOS > LATIGO
LATILLA n stick making up part of ceiling
LATILLAS > LATILLA
LATIMERIA n type of coelacanth fish
LATINA n US female of Latin American origin
LATINAS > LATINA
LATINISE same as > LATINIZE
LATINISED > LATINISE
LATINISES > LATINISE
LATINITY n facility in the use of Latin

LATINIZE vb translate into Latin
LATINIZED > LATINIZE
LATINIZES > LATINIZE
LATINO n US male of Latin American origin
LATINOS > LATINO
LATISH adv rather late ▷ adj rather late
LATITANCY > LATITANT
LATITANT adj concealed
LATITAT n writ presuming that person accused was hiding
LATITATS > LATITAT
LATITUDE n angular distance measured in degrees N or S of the equator
LATITUDES > LATITUDE
LATKE n crispy Jewish pancake
LATKES > LATKE
LATOSOL n type of deep, well-drained soil
LATOSOLIC > LATOSOL
LATOSOLS > LATOSOL
LATRANT adj barking
LATRATION n instance of barking
LATRIA n adoration that may be offered to God alone
LATRIAS > LATRIA
LATRINE n toilet in a barracks
LATRINES > LATRINE
LATROCINY n banditry
LATRON n bandit
LATRONS > LATRON
LATS > LAT
LATTE n coffee with hot milk
LATTEN n metal or alloy, esp brass, made in thin sheets
LATTENS > LATTEN
LATTER adj second of two ▷ n second of two people or things
LATTERLY adv recently
LATTERS > LATTER
LATTES > LATTE
LATTICE n framework of intersecting strips of wood ▷ vb adorn with a lattice
LATTICED > LATTICE
LATTICES > LATTICE
LATTICING > LATTICE
LATTICINI > LATTICINO
LATTICINO n type of Italian glass
LATTIN n brass alloy beaten into a thin sheet
LATTINS > LATTIN
LATU n type of edible Asian seaweed
LATUS > LATU
LAUAN n type of wood used in furniture-making
LAUANS > LAUAN
LAUCH Scots form of > LAUGH

LAUCHING > LAUCH

LAUCHS > LAUCH

LAUD *vb* praise or glorify ▷ *n* praise or glorification

LAUDABLE *adj* praiseworthy

LAUDABLY > LAUDABLE

LAUDANUM *n* opium-based sedative

LAUDANUMS > LAUDANUM

LAUDATION *formal word for* > PRAISE

LAUDATIVE *same as* > LAUDATORY

LAUDATOR *n* one who praises highly

LAUDATORS > LAUDATOR

LAUDATORY *adj* praising or glorifying

LAUDED > LAUD

LAUDER > LAUD

LAUDERS > LAUD

LAUDING > LAUD

LAUDS *n* traditional morning prayer of the Western Church

LAUF *n* run in bobsleighing

LAUFS > LAUF

LAUGH *vb* make sounds with the voice expressing amusement ▷ *n* act of laughing

LAUGHABLE *adj* ridiculously inadequate

LAUGHABLY > LAUGHABLE

LAUGHED > LAUGH

LAUGHER > LAUGH

LAUGHERS > LAUGH

LAUGHFUL > LAUGH

LAUGHIER > LAUGHY

LAUGHIEST > LAUGHY

LAUGHING > LAUGH

LAUGHINGS > LAUGH

LAUGHLINE *n* funny line in dialogue

LAUGHS > LAUGH

LAUGHSOME *adj* causing laughter

LAUGHTER *n* sound or action of laughing

LAUGHTERS > LAUGHTER

LAUGHY *adj* laughing a lot

LAUNCE *old form of* > LANCE

LAUNCED > LAUNCE

LAUNCES > LAUNCE

LAUNCH *vb* put into the water for the first time ▷ *n* launching

LAUNCHED > LAUNCH

LAUNCHER *n* any installation, vehicle, or other device for launching rockets, missiles, or other projectiles

LAUNCHERS > LAUNCHER

LAUNCHES > LAUNCH

LAUNCHING *n* act of launching

LAUNCHPAD *n* platform from which a spacecraft is launched

LAUNCING > LAUNCE

LAUND *n* open grassy space

LAUNDER *vb* wash and iron ▷ *n* water trough

LAUNDERED > LAUNDER

LAUNDERER > LAUNDER

LAUNDERS > LAUNDER

LAUNDRESS *n* woman who launders clothes, sheets, etc, for a living

LAUNDRIES > LAUNDRY

LAUNDRY *n* clothes for washing

LAUNDS > LAUND

LAURA *n* group of monastic cells

LAURAE > LAURA

LAURAS > LAURA

LAUREATE *adj* crowned with laurel leaves as a sign of honour ▷ *n* person honoured with an award for art or science ▷ *vb* crown with laurel

LAUREATED > LAUREATE

LAUREATES > LAUREATE

LAUREL *n* glossy-leaved shrub, bay tree ▷ *vb* crown with laurel

LAURELED > LAUREL

LAURELING > LAUREL

LAURELLED > LAUREL

LAURELS > LAUREL

LAURIC *adj* as in *lauric acid* dodecanoic acid

LAURYL *n* as in *lauryl alcohol* crystalline solid used to make detergents

LAURYLS > LAURYL

LAUWINE *n* avalanche

LAUWINES > LAUWINE

LAV *short for* > LAVATORY

LAVA *n* molten rock thrown out by volcanoes

LAVABO *n* ritual washing of priest's hands at Mass

LAVABOES > LAVABO

LAVABOS > LAVABO

LAVAFORM *n* in form of lava

LAVAGE *n* washing out of a hollow organ

LAVAGES > LAVAGE

LAVALAVA *n* draped skirtlike garment worn by Polynesians

LAVALAVAS > LAVALAVA

LAVALIER *n* decorative pendant worn on chain

LAVALIERE *same as* > LAVALIER

LAVALIERS > LAVALIER

LAVALIKE > LAVA

LAVANDIN *n* hybrid of two varieties of the lavender plant

LAVANDINS > LAVANDIN

LAVAS > LAVA

LAVASH *n* Armenian flat bread

LAVASHES > LAVASH

LAVATERA *n* type of plant closely resembling the mallow

LAVATERAS > LAVATERA

LAVATION *n* act or process of washing

LAVATIONS > LAVATION

LAVATORY *n* toilet

LAVE *archaic word for* > WASH

LAVED > LAVE

LAVEER *vb* (in sailing) tack

LAVEERED > LAVEER

LAVEERING > LAVEER

LAVEERS > LAVEER

LAVEMENT *n* washing with injections of water

LAVEMENTS > LAVEMENT

LAVENDER *n* shrub with fragrant flowers ▷ *adj* bluish-purple

LAVENDERS > LAVENDER

LAVER *n* priest's waterbasin for ritual ablutions

LAVEROCK *Scot and northern English dialect word for* > SKYLARK

LAVEROCKS > LAVEROCK

LAVERS > LAVER

LAVES > LAVE

LAVING > LAVE

LAVISH *adj* prolific ▷ *vb* give or spend generously

LAVISHED > LAVISH

LAVISHER > LAVISH

LAVISHERS > LAVISH

LAVISHES > LAVISH

LAVISHEST > LAVISH

LAVISHING > LAVISH

LAVISHLY > LAVISH

LAVOLT *same as* > LAVOLTA

LAVOLTA *n* old Italian dance ▷ *vb* dance the lavolta

LAVOLTAED > LAVOLTA

LAVOLTAS > LAVOLTA

LAVOLTED > LAVOLT

LAVOLTING > LAVOLT

LAVOLTS > LAVOLT

LAVRA *same as* > LAURA

LAVRAS > LAVRA

LAVROCK *same as* > LAVEROCK

LAVROCKS > LAVROCK

LAVS > LAV

LAVVIES > LAVVY

LAVVY *n* lavatory

LAW *n* rule binding on a community ▷ *vb* prosecute ▷ *adj* (in archaic usage) low

LAWBOOK *n* book on subject of law

LAWBOOKS > LAWBOOK

LAWCOURT *n* court of law

LAWCOURTS > LAWCOURT

LAWED > LAW

LAWER > LAW

LAWEST > LAW

LAWFARE *n* use of the law by a country against its enemies

LAWFARES > LAWFARE

LAWFUL *adj* allowed by law

LAWFULLY > LAWFUL

LAWGIVER *n* giver of a code of laws

LAWGIVERS > LAWGIVER

LAWGIVING > LAWGIVER

LAWIN *n* bill or reckoning

LAWINE *n* avalanche

LAWINES > LAWINE

LAWING *same as* > LAWIN

LAWINGS > LAWING

LAWINS > LAWIN

LAWK *interj* used to show surprise

LAWKS *same as* > LAWK

LAWLAND *same as* > LOWLAND

LAWLANDS > LAWLAND

LAWLESS *adj* breaking the law

LAWLESSLY > LAWLESS

LAWLIKE > LAW

LAWMAKER *same as* > LAWGIVER

LAWMAKERS > LAWMAKER

LAWMAKING *n* process of legislating

LAWMAN *n* officer of the law

LAWMEN > LAWMAN

LAWMONGER *n* inferior lawyer

LAWN *n* area of tended and mown grass ▷ *vb* create or make into a lawn

LAWNED *adj* having a lawn

LAWNIER > LAWN

LAWNIEST > LAWN

LAWNING > LAWN

LAWNMOWER *n* machine for cutting grass on lawns

LAWNS > LAWN

LAWNY > LAWN

LAWS > LAW

LAWSUIT *n* court case

LAWSUITS > LAWSUIT

LAWYER *n* professional legal expert ▷ *vb* act as lawyer

LAWYERED > LAWYER

LAWYERING > LAWYER

LAWYERLY > LAWYER

LAWYERS > LAWYER

LAX *adj* not strict ▷ *n* laxative

LAXATION *n* act of making lax or the state of being lax

LAXATIONS > LAXATION

LAXATIVE *adj* (medicine) inducing the emptying of the bowels ▷ *n* medicine that induces the emptying of the bowels

LAXATIVES > LAXATIVE

LAXATOR *n* muscle that loosens body part

LAXATORS > LAXATOR

LAXER > LAX

LAXES > LAX

LAXEST > LAX

LAXISM > LAXIST

LAXISMS > LAXIST

LAXIST n lenient or tolerant person
LAXISTS > LAXIST
LAXITIES > LAX
LAXITY > LAX
LAXLY > LAX
LAXNESS > LAX
LAXNESSES > LAX
LAY > LIE
LAYABOUT n lazy person ▷ vb hit it out with violent and repeated blows in all directions
LAYABOUTS > LAYABOUT
LAYAWAY n merchandise reserved for future delivery
LAYAWAYS > LAYAWAY
LAYBACK n technique for climbing cracks ▷ vb use layback technique
LAYBACKED > LAYBACK
LAYBACKS > LAYBACK
LAYDEEZ pl n jocular spelling of ladies
LAYED > LAY
LAYER n single thickness of some substance ▷ vb form a layer
LAYERAGE n covering stem or branch with soil to encourage new roots
LAYERAGES > LAYERAGE
LAYERED > LAYER
LAYERING n method of propagation that induces a shoot or branch to take root while it is still attached to the parent plant
LAYERINGS > LAYERING
LAYERS > LAYER
LAYETTE n clothes for a newborn baby
LAYETTES > LAYETTE
LAYIN n basketball score
LAYING > LAY
LAYINGS > LAY
LAYINS > LAYIN
LAYLOCK old form of > LILAC
LAYLOCKS > LAYLOCK
LAYMAN n person who is not a member of the clergy
LAYMANISE same as > LAYMANIZE
LAYMANIZE vb make (information) easier to understand
LAYMEN > LAYMAN
LAYOFF n act of suspending employees
LAYOFFS > LAYOFF
LAYOUT n arrangement, esp of printing matter
LAYOUTS > LAYOUT
LAYOVER n break in a journey
LAYOVERS > LAYOVER
LAYPEOPLE > LAYPERSON
LAYPERSON n person who is not a member of the clergy
LAYS > LIE

LAYSHAFT n auxiliary shaft in a gearbox
LAYSHAFTS > LAYSHAFT
LAYSTALL n place where waste is deposited
LAYSTALLS > LAYSTALL
LAYTIME n time allowed for loading cargo
LAYTIMES > LAYTIME
LAYUP n period of incapacity through illness
LAYUPS > LAYUP
LAYWOMAN n woman who is not a member of the clergy
LAYWOMEN > LAYWOMAN
LAZAR archaic word for > LEPER
LAZARET same as > LAZARETTO
LAZARETS > LAZARET
LAZARETTE same as > LAZARETTO
LAZARETTO n small locker at the stern of a boat or a storeroom between decks of a ship
LAZARS > LAZAR
LAZE vb be idle or lazy ▷ n time spent lazing
LAZED > LAZE
LAZES > LAZE
LAZIED > LAZY
LAZIER > LAZY
LAZIES > LAZY
LAZIEST > LAZY
LAZILY > LAZY
LAZINESS > LAZY
LAZING > LAZE
LAZO another word for > LASSO
LAZOED > LAZO
LAZOES > LAZO
LAZOING > LAZO
LAZOS > LAZO
LAZULI n lapis lazuli
LAZULIS > LAZULI
LAZULITE n blue mineral, consisting of hydrated magnesium iron phosphate, occurring in metamorphic rocks
LAZULITES > LAZULITE
LAZURITE n rare blue mineral consisting of a sodium-calcium-aluminium silicate
LAZURITES > LAZURITE
LAZY vb laze ▷ adj not inclined to work or exert oneself
LAZYBONES n lazy person
LAZYING > LAZY
LAZYISH > LAZY
LAZZARONE n Italian street beggar
LAZZARONI > LAZZARONE
LAZZI > LAZZO
LAZZO n comic routine in the commedia dell'arte
LEA n meadow
LEACH vb remove by passing a liquid through

▷ n act or process of leaching
LEACHABLE > LEACH
LEACHATE n water that carries salts dissolved out of materials through which it has percolated
LEACHATES > LEACHATE
LEACHED > LEACH
LEACHER > LEACH
LEACHERS > LEACH
LEACHES > LEACH
LEACHIER > LEACHY
LEACHIEST > LEACHY
LEACHING > LEACH
LEACHINGS > LEACH
LEACHOUR old form of > LECHER
LEACHOURS > LEACHOUR
LEACHY adj porous
LEAD vb guide or conduct ▷ n first or most prominent place ▷ adj acting as a leader or lead
LEADABLE n able to be led
LEADED adj (of windows) made from many small panes of glass held together by lead strips
LEADEN adj heavy or sluggish ▷ vb become or cause to become leaden
LEADENED > LEADEN
LEADENING > LEADEN
LEADENLY > LEADEN
LEADENS > LEADEN
LEADER n person who leads
LEADERENE n strong female leader
LEADERS > LEADER
LEADIER > LEADY
LEADIEST > LEADY
LEADING > LEAD
LEADINGLY > LEAD
LEADINGS > LEAD
LEADLESS adj without lead
LEADMAN n man who leads
LEADMEN > LEADMAN
LEADOFF n initial move
LEADOFFS > LEADOFF
LEADPLANT n N American shrub
LEADS > LEAD
LEADSCREW n threaded rod in a lathe
LEADSMAN n sailor who takes soundings with a lead line
LEADSMEN > LEADSMAN
LEADWORK n maintenance work involving lead pipes, etc
LEADWORKS > LEADWORK
LEADWORT n type of tropical or subtropical shrub with red, blue, or white flowers
LEADWORTS > LEADWORT
LEADY adj like lead
LEAF n flat usu green blade attached to the stem of a

plant ▷ vb turn (pages) cursorily
LEAFAGE n leaves of plants
LEAFAGES > LEAFAGE
LEAFBUD n bud producing leaves rather than flowers
LEAFBUDS > LEAFBUD
LEAFED > LEAF
LEAFERIES > LEAFERY
LEAFERY n foliage
LEAFIER > LEAFY
LEAFIEST > LEAFY
LEAFINESS > LEAFY
LEAFING > LEAF
LEAFLESS > LEAF
LEAFLET n sheet of printed matter for distribution ▷ vb distribute leaflets (to)
LEAFLETED > LEAFLET
LEAFLETER > LEAFLET
LEAFLETS > LEAFLET
LEAFLIKE > LEAF
LEAFMOLD n fungus on decayed leaves
LEAFMOLDS > LEAFMOLD
LEAFROLL n viral disease of potatoes
LEAFROLLS > LEAFROLL
LEAFS > LEAF
LEAFSTALK n stalk attaching a leaf to a stem or branch
LEAFWORM n cotton plant pest
LEAFWORMS > LEAFWORM
LEAFY adj covered with leaves
LEAGUE n association promoting the interests of its members
LEAGUED > LEAGUE
LEAGUER vb harass; beset ▷ n encampment, esp of besiegers
LEAGUERED > LEAGUER
LEAGUERS > LEAGUER
LEAGUES > LEAGUE
LEAGUING > LEAGUE
LEAK n hole or defect that allows the escape or entrance of liquid, gas, radiation, etc ▷ vb let liquid etc in or out
LEAKAGE n act or instance of leaking
LEAKAGES > LEAKAGE
LEAKED > LEAK
LEAKER > LEAK
LEAKERS > LEAK
LEAKIER > LEAKY
LEAKIEST > LEAKY
LEAKILY > LEAKY
LEAKINESS > LEAKY
LEAKING > LEAK
LEAKLESS > LEAK
LEAKPROOF adj not likely to leak
LEAKS > LEAK
LEAKY adj leaking
LEAL adj loyal
LEALER > LEAL

LEALEST > LEAL
LEALLY > LEAL
LEALTIES > LEAL
LEALTY > LEAL
LEAM vb shine
LEAMED > LEAM
LEAMING > LEAM
LEAMS > LEAM
LEAN vb rest (against) ▷ adj thin but healthy-looking ▷ n lean part of meat
LEANED > LEAN
LEANER > LEAN
LEANERS > LEAN
LEANEST > LEAN
LEANING > LEAN
LEANINGS > LEAN
LEANLY > LEAN
LEANNESS > LEAN
LEANS > LEAN
LEANT > LEAN
LEANY old form of > LEAN
LEAP vb make a sudden powerful jump ▷ n sudden powerful jump
LEAPED > LEAP
LEAPER > LEAP
LEAPEROUS old form of > LEPROUS
LEAPERS > LEAP
LEAPFROG n game in which a player vaults over another bending down ▷ vb play leapfrog
LEAPFROGS > LEAPFROG
LEAPING > LEAP
LEAPOROUS old form of > LEPROUS
LEAPROUS old form of > LEPROUS
LEAPS > LEAP
LEAPT > LEAP
LEAR vb instruct
LEARE same as > LEAR
LEARED > LEAR
LEARES > LEARE
LEARIER > LEARY
LEARIEST > LEARY
LEARINESS > LEARY
LEARING > LEAR
LEARN vb gain skill or knowledge by study, practice, or teaching
LEARNABLE > LEARN
LEARNED > LEARN
LEARNEDLY > LEARN
LEARNER n someone who is learning something
LEARNERS > LEARNER
LEARNING > LEARN
LEARNINGS > LEARN
LEARNS > LEARN
LEARNT > LEARN
LEARS > LEAR
LEARY same as > LEERY
LEAS > LEA
LEASABLE > LEASE
LEASE n contract by which land or property is rented for a stated time by the owner to a tenant ▷ vb let or rent by lease

LEASEBACK n property transaction in which the buyer leases the property to the seller
LEASED > LEASE
LEASEHOLD adj (land or property) held on lease ▷ n land or property held under a lease
LEASER > LEASE
LEASERS > LEASE
LEASES > LEASE
LEASH n lead for a dog ▷ vb control by a leash
LEASHED > LEASH
LEASHES > LEASH
LEASHING > LEASH
LEASING > LEASE
LEASINGS > LEASE
LEASOW vb pasture
LEASOWE same as > LEASOW
LEASOWED > LEASOW
LEASOWES > LEASOWE
LEASOWING > LEASOW
LEASOWS > LEASOW
LEAST n smallest amount ▷ adj smallest ▷ n smallest one ▷ adv in the smallest degree
LEASTS > LEAST
LEASTWAYS adv at least
LEASTWISE same as > LEASTWAYS
LEASURE old form of > LEISURE
LEASURES > LEASURE
LEAT n trench or ditch that conveys water to a mill wheel
LEATHER n material made from treated animal skins ▷ adj of leather ▷ vb beat or thrash
LEATHERED > LEATHER
LEATHERN adj made of or resembling leather
LEATHERS > LEATHER
LEATHERY adj like leather, tough
LEATS > LEAT
LEAVE vb go away from ▷ n permission to be absent
LEAVED adj with leaves
LEAVEN n substance that causes dough to rise ▷ vb raise with leaven
LEAVENED > LEAVEN
LEAVENER n person or thing that leavens
LEAVENERS > LEAVENER
LEAVENING > LEAVEN
LEAVENOUS adj containing leaven
LEAVENS > LEAVEN
LEAVER > LEAVE
LEAVERS > LEAVE
LEAVES > LEAF
LEAVIER > LEAVY
LEAVIEST > LEAVY
LEAVING > LEAVE
LEAVINGS pl n something remaining, such as refuse

LEAVY same as > LEAFY
LEAZE same as > LEASE
LEAZES > LEAZE
LEBBEK n type of timber tree
LEBBEKS > LEBBEK
LEBEN n semiliquid food made from curdled milk
LEBENS > LEBEN
LEBKUCHEN n biscuit, originating from Germany, usually containing honey, spices, etc
LECANORA n type of lichen
LECANORAS > LECANORA
LECCIES > LECCY
LECCY n electricity
LECH vb behave lecherously ▷ n lecherous act
LECHAIM interj drinking toast ▷ n drink for a toast
LECHAIMS > LECHAIM
LECHAYIM same as > LECHAIM
LECHAYIMS > LECHAYIM
LECHED > LECH
LECHER n man who has or shows excessive sexual desire ▷ vb behave lecherously
LECHERED > LECHER
LECHERIES > LECHERY
LECHERING > LECHER
LECHEROUS adj (of a man) having or showing excessive sexual desire
LECHERS > LECHER
LECHERY n unrestrained and promiscuous sexuality
LECHES > LECH
LECHING > LECH
LECHWE n African antelope
LECHWES > LECHWE
LECITHIN n yellow-brown compound found in plant and animal tissues
LECITHINS > LECITHIN
LECTERN n reading desk
LECTERNS > LECTERN
LECTIN n type of protein
LECTINS > LECTIN
LECTION n variant reading of a passage in a text
LECTIONS > LECTION
LECTOR n university lecturer
LECTORATE > LECTOR
LECTORS > LECTOR
LECTOTYPE n specimen designated by author after the publication of a species name
LECTRESS n female reader
LECTURE n informative talk ▷ vb give a talk
LECTURED > LECTURE
LECTURER n person who lectures, esp in a university or college
LECTURERS > LECTURER
LECTURES > LECTURE

LECTURING > LECTURE
LECTURN old form of > LECTERN
LECTURNS > LECTURN
LECYTHI > LECYTHUS
LECYTHIS n genus of very tall trees
LECYTHUS n (in ancient Greece) a vase with a narrow neck
LED > LEAD
LEDDEN n language; speech
LEDDENS > LEDDEN
LEDE n introductory part of a news story
LEDES > LEDE
LEDGE n narrow shelf
LEDGED > LEDGE
LEDGER n book of debit and credit accounts ▷ vb fish using a wire trace while the bait floats freely and the weight sinks
LEDGERED > LEDGER
LEDGERING > LEDGER
LEDGERS > LEDGER
LEDGES > LEDGE
LEDGIER > LEDGE
LEDGIEST > LEDGE
LEDGY > LEDGE
LEDUM n evergreen shrub
LEDUMS > LEDUM
LEE n sheltered side ▷ vb (Scots) lie
LEEAR Scots form of > LIAR
LEEARS > LEEAR
LEEBOARD n one of two paddle-like boards that can be lowered along the lee side of a vessel to reduce sideways drift
LEEBOARDS > LEEBOARD
LEECH n bloodsucking worm ▷ vb use leeches to suck the blood of
LEECHDOM n remedy
LEECHDOMS > LEECHDOM
LEECHED > LEECH
LEECHEE same as > LITCHI
LEECHEES > LEECHEE
LEECHES > LEECH
LEECHING > LEECH
LEECHLIKE > LEECH
LEED > LEE
LEEING > LEE
LEEK n vegetable with a long bulb and thick stem
LEEKS > LEEK
LEEP vb boil; scald
LEEPED > LEEP
LEEPING > LEEP
LEEPS > LEEP
LEER vb look or grin at in a sneering manner ▷ n sneering look or grin
LEERED > LEER
LEERIER > LEERY
LEERIEST > LEERY
LEERILY > LEERY
LEERINESS > LEERY
LEERING > LEER

LEERINGLY > LEER
LEERINGS > LEER
LEERS > LEER
LEERY adj suspicious or wary (of)
LEES pl n sediment of wine
LEESE old form of > LOOSE
LEESES > LEESE
LEESING > LEESE
LEET n shortlist
LEETLE form of > LITTLE
LEETS > LEET
LEETSPEAK n jargon used by some internet groups
LEEWARD n lee side ▷ adv towards this side ▷ adj towards where the wind blows
LEEWARDLY > LEEWARD
LEEWARDS adv towards the lee side
LEEWAY n room for free movement within limits
LEEWAYS > LEEWAY
LEEZE adj as in leeze me Scots for lief is me, an expression of affection
LEFT adj on the opposite side from right ▷ n left side
LEFTE old past tense of > LIFT
LEFTER > LEFT
LEFTEST > LEFT
LEFTIE same as > LEFTY
LEFTIES > LEFTY
LEFTISH > LEFT
LEFTISM > LEFTIST
LEFTISMS > LEFTIST
LEFTIST adj of the political left ▷ n supporter of the political left
LEFTISTS > LEFTIST
LEFTMOST > LEFT
LEFTMOSTS > LEFT
LEFTOVER n unused portion of food or material ▷ adj left as an unused portion
LEFTOVERS > LEFTOVER
LEFTS > LEFT
LEFTWARD same as > LEFTWARDS
LEFTWARDS adv towards or on the left
LEFTWING adj of or relating to the leftist faction of a party, etc
LEFTY n left-winger
LEG n limb on which a person or animal walks, runs, or stands
LEGACIES > LEGACY
LEGACY n thing left in a will
LEGAL adj established or permitted by law ▷ n legal expert
LEGALESE n conventional language in which legal documents are written
LEGALESES > LEGALESE
LEGALISE same as > LEGALIZE
LEGALISED > LEGALISE

LEGALISER > LEGALISE
LEGALISES > LEGALISE
LEGALISM n strict adherence to the letter of the law
LEGALISMS > LEGALISM
LEGALIST > LEGALISM
LEGALISTS > LEGALISM
LEGALITY n state or quality of being legal or lawful
LEGALIZE vb make legal
LEGALIZED > LEGALIZE
LEGALIZER > LEGALIZE
LEGALIZES > LEGALIZE
LEGALLY > LEGAL
LEGALS > LEGAL
LEGATARY n legatee
LEGATE n messenger or representative, esp from the Pope ▷ vb leave as legacy
LEGATED > LEGATE
LEGATEE n recipient of a legacy
LEGATEES > LEGATEE
LEGATES > LEGATE
LEGATINE > LEGATE
LEGATING > LEGATE
LEGATION n diplomatic minister and his staff
LEGATIONS > LEGATION
LEGATO adv smoothly ▷ n playing with no gaps between notes
LEGATOR n person who gives a legacy or makes a bequest
LEGATORS > LEGATOR
LEGATOS > LEGATO
LEGEND n traditional story
LEGENDARY adj famous
LEGENDISE same as > LEGENDIZE
LEGENDIST n writer of legends
LEGENDIZE vb make into legend
LEGENDRY > LEGEND
LEGENDS > LEGEND
LEGER variant of > LEDGER
LEGERING > LEGER
LEGERINGS > LEGER
LEGERITY n agility
LEGERS > LEGER
LEGES > LEX
LEGGE vb lighten or lessen
LEGGED > LEG
LEGGER n man who moves barge through tunnel using legs
LEGGERS > LEGGER
LEGGES > LEGGE
LEGGIE n leg spin bowler
LEGGIER > LEGGY
LEGGIERO adj light; delicate
LEGGIES > LEGGIE
LEGGIEST > LEGGY
LEGGIN same as > LEGGING
LEGGINESS > LEGGY

LEGGING n extra outer covering for the lower leg
LEGGINGED > LEGGING
LEGGINGS > LEGGING
LEGGINS > LEGGIN
LEGGISM n blacklegging
LEGGISMS > LEGGISM
LEGGO sentence substitute let go!
LEGGY adj having long legs
LEGHOLD n type of animal trap that clamps down on the animal's leg
LEGHOLDS > LEGHOLD
LEGHORN n Italian wheat straw woven into hats
LEGHORNS > LEGHORN
LEGIBLE adj easily read
LEGIBLY > LEGIBLE
LEGION n large military force ▷ adj very large or numerous
LEGIONARY adj of or relating to a legion ▷ n soldier belonging to a legion
LEGIONED adj arranged in legions
LEGIONS > LEGION
LEGISLATE vb make laws
LEGIST n legal mind
LEGISTS > LEGIST
LEGIT n legitimate drama ▷ adj legitimate
LEGITIM n inheritance due to children from father
LEGITIMS > LEGITIM
LEGITS > LEGIT
LEGLAN same as > LEGLIN
LEGLANS > LEGLAN
LEGLEN same as > LEGLIN
LEGLENS > LEGLEN
LEGLESS adj without legs
LEGLET n leg jewellery
LEGLETS > LEGLET
LEGLIKE > LEG
LEGLIN n milk-pail
LEGLINS > LEGLIN
LEGMAN n newsman who reports from the scene
LEGMEN > LEGMAN
LEGONG n Indonesian dance
LEGONGS > LEGONG
LEGROOM n space to put one's legs
LEGROOMS > LEGROOM
LEGS > LEG
LEGSIDE n part of a cricket field to the left of a right-handed batsman as he faces the bowler
LEGSIDES > LEGSIDE
LEGUAAN n S African lizard
LEGUAANS > LEGUAAN
LEGUAN same as > LEGUAAN
LEGUANS > LEGUAN
LEGUME n pod of a plant of the pea or bean family
LEGUMES > LEGUME
LEGUMIN n protein from leguminous plants

LEGUMINS > LEGUMIN
LEGWARMER n one of a pair of garments resembling stockings without feet
LEGWEAR n clothing for legs
LEGWEARS > LEGWEAR
LEGWORK n work that involves travelling on foot or as if on foot
LEGWORKS > LEGWORK
LEHAIM same as > LECHAIM
LEHAIMS > LEHAIM
LEHAYIM same as > LEHAIM
LEHAYIMS > LEHAYIM
LEHR n long tunnel-shaped oven used for annealing glass
LEHRJAHRE n apprenticeship
LEHRS > LEHR
LEHUA n flower of Hawaii
LEHUAS > LEHUA
LEI > LEU
LEIDGER same as > LEDGER
LEIDGERS > LEIDGER
LEIGER same as > LEDGER
LEIGERS > LEIGER
LEIOMYOMA same as > FIBROID
LEIPOA n Australian bird
LEIPOAS > LEIPOA
LEIR same as > LEAR
LEIRED > LEIR
LEIRING > LEIR
LEIRS > LEIR
LEIS > LEU
LEISH adj agile
LEISHER > LEISH
LEISHEST > LEISH
LEISLER n small bat
LEISLERS > LEISLER
LEISTER n pronged fishing spear ▷ vb spear with a leister
LEISTERED > LEISTER
LEISTERS > LEISTER
LEISURE n time for relaxation or hobbies ▷ vb have leisure
LEISURED > LEISURE
LEISURELY adj deliberate, unhurried ▷ adv slowly
LEISURES > LEISURE
LEISURING > LEISURE
LEITMOTIF n recurring theme associated with a person, situation, or thought
LEITMOTIV same as > LEITMOTIF
LEK n bird display area ▷ vb gather at lek
LEKE old form of > LEAK
LEKGOTLA n meeting place for village assemblies, court cases, and meetings of village leaders

LEKGOTLAS > LEKGOTLA
LEKKED > LEK
LEKKER adj attractive or nice
LEKKING > LEK
LEKKINGS > LEK
LEKS > LEK
LEKU > LEK
LEKVAR n prune or apricot pie filling
LEKVARS > LEKVAR
LEKYTHI > LEKYTHOS
LEKYTHOI > LEKYTHOS
LEKYTHOS n Greek flask
LEKYTHUS same as > LEKYTHOS
LEMAN n beloved
LEMANS > LEMAN
LEME same as > LEAM
LEMED > LEME
LEMEL n metal filings
LEMELS > LEMEL
LEMES > LEME
LEMING > LEME
LEMMA n word in its citation form
LEMMAS > LEMMA
LEMMATA > LEMMA
LEMMATISE same as > LEMMATIZE
LEMMATIZE vb group together the inflected forms of (a word) for analysis as a single item
LEMME vb (short for) let me
LEMMING n rodent of arctic regions
LEMMINGS > LEMMING
LEMNISCAL adj relating to a type of closed plane curve
LEMNISCI > LEMNISCUS
LEMNISCUS technical name for > FILLET
LEMON n yellow oval fruit ▷ adj pale-yellow ▷ vb flavour with lemon
LEMONADE n lemon-flavoured soft drink, often fizzy
LEMONADES > LEMONADE
LEMONED > LEMON
LEMONFISH n type of game fish
LEMONIER > LEMONY
LEMONIEST > LEMONY
LEMONING > LEMON
LEMONISH > LEMON
LEMONLIKE > LEMON
LEMONS > LEMON
LEMONWOOD n small tree of New Zealand
LEMONY adj like a lemon
LEMPIRA n monetary unit of Honduras
LEMPIRAS > LEMPIRA
LEMUR n animal like a small monkey
LEMURES pl n spirits of the dead
LEMURIAN same as > LEMUROID
LEMURIANS > LEMURIAN

LEMURINE same as > LEMUROID
LEMURINES > LEMURINE
LEMURLIKE > LEMUR
LEMUROID adj of, relating to, or belonging to the superfamily which includes the lemurs and indrises ▷ n animal that resembles or is closely related to a lemur
LEMUROIDS > LEMUROID
LEMURS > LEMUR
LEND vb give temporary use of
LENDABLE > LEND
LENDER > LEND
LENDERS > LEND
LENDING > LEND
LENDINGS > LEND
LENDS > LEND
LENES > LENIS
LENG vb linger ▷ adj long
LENGED > LENG
LENGER > LENG
LENGEST > LENG
LENGING > LENG
LENGS > LENG
LENGTH n extent or measurement from end to end
LENGTHEN vb make or become longer
LENGTHENS > LENGTHEN
LENGTHFUL > LENGTH
LENGTHIER > LENGTHY
LENGTHILY > LENGTHY
LENGTHMAN n person whose job it is to maintain a particular length of road or railway line
LENGTHMEN > LENGTHMAN
LENGTHS > LENGTH
LENGTHY adj very long
LENIENCE > LENIENT
LENIENCES > LENIENT
LENIENCY > LENIENT
LENIENT adj tolerant, not strict or severe ▷ n lenient person
LENIENTLY > LENIENT
LENIENTS > LENIENT
LENIFIED > LENIFY
LENIFIES > LENIFY
LENIFY vb make lenient
LENIFYING > LENIFY
LENIS adj pronounced with little muscular tension ▷ n consonant like this
LENITE vb undergo lenition
LENITED > LENITE
LENITES > LENITE
LENITIES > LENITY
LENITING > LENITE
LENITION n weakening of consonant sound
LENITIONS > LENITION
LENITIVE adj soothing or alleviating of pain or distress ▷ n lenitive drug

LENITIVES > LENITIVE
LENITY n mercy or clemency
LENO n weave in which the warp yarns are twisted in pairs between the weft
LENOS > LENO
LENS n piece of glass or similar material with one or both sides curved
LENSE same as > LENS
LENSED adj incorporating a lens
LENSES > LENS
LENSING n materials which colour and diffuse light
LENSINGS > LENSING
LENSLESS > LENS
LENSMAN n camera operator
LENSMEN > LENSMAN
LENT > LEND
LENTANDO adv slowing down
LENTEN adj of or relating to Lent
LENTI > LENTO
LENTIC adj of, relating to, or inhabiting still water
LENTICEL n any of numerous pores in the stem of a woody plant
LENTICELS > LENTICEL
LENTICLE n lens-shaped layer of mineral or rock embedded in a matrix of different constitution
LENTICLES > LENTICLE
LENTICULE n small lentil
LENTIFORM adj shaped like a biconvex lens
LENTIGO technical name for a > FRECKLE
LENTIL n edible seed
LENTILS > LENTIL
LENTISC same as > LENTISK
LENTISCS > LENTISC
LENTISK n mastic tree
LENTISKS > LENTISK
LENTO adv slowly ▷ n movement or passage performed slowly
LENTOID adj lentiform ▷ n lentiform object
LENTOIDS > LENTOID
LENTOR n lethargy
LENTORS > LENTOR
LENTOS > LENTO
LENTOUS adj lethargic
LENVOY another word for > ENVOY
LENVOYS > LENVOY
LEONE n monetary unit of Sierra Leone
LEONES > LEONE
LEONINE adj like a lion
LEOPARD n large spotted animal of the cat family
LEOPARDS > LEOPARD
LEOTARD n tight-fitting garment covering the upper body

LEOTARDED adj wearing a leotard
LEOTARDS > LEOTARD
LEP dialect word for > LEAP
LEPER n person with leprosy
LEPERS > LEPER
LEPID adj amusing
LEPIDOTE adj covered with scales, scaly leaves, or spots ▷ n lepidote person, creature, or thing
LEPIDOTES > LEPIDOTE
LEPORID adj of the family of mammals including rabbits and hares ▷ n any animal belonging to this family
LEPORIDAE > LEPORID
LEPORIDS > LEPORID
LEPORINE adj of, relating to, or resembling a hare
LEPPED > LEP
LEPPING > LEP
LEPRA n leprosy
LEPRAS > LEPRA
LEPROSE adj having or denoting a whitish scurfy surface
LEPROSERY n hospital for leprosy sufferers
LEPROSIES > LEPROSY
LEPROSITY n state of being leprous
LEPROSY n disease attacking the nerves and skin
LEPROTIC adj relating to leprosy
LEPROUS adj having leprosy
LEPROUSLY > LEPROUS
LEPS > LEP
LEPT > LEAP
LEPTA > LEPTON
LEPTIN n protein that regulates the amount of fat in the body
LEPTINS > LEPTIN
LEPTOME n tissue of plant conducting food
LEPTOMES > LEPTOME
LEPTON n any of a group of elementary particles with weak interactions
LEPTONIC > LEPTON
LEPTONS > LEPTON
LEPTOPHOS n type of pesticide
LEPTOSOME n person with a small bodily frame and a slender physique
LEPTOTENE n (in reproduction) early stage in cell division
LEQUEAR same as > LACUNAR
LEQUEARS > LEQUEAR
LERE same as > LEAR
LERED > LERE
LERES > LERE
LERING > LERE
LERNAEAN adj in Greek myth relating to Lerna, the

swamp or lake near Argos in which dwelt the Hydra which Hercules slew

LERP n crystallized honeydew

LERPS > LERP

LES short form of > LESBIAN

LESBIAN n homosexual woman ▷ adj of homosexual women

LESBIANS > LESBIAN

LESBIC adj relating to lesbians

LESBIGAY n characteristic of or intended for the lesbian, bisexual, and gay community

LESBIGAYS > LESBIGAY

LESBO n lesbian

LESBOS > LESBO

LESES > LES

LESION n change in an organ of the body caused by injury ▷ vb cause lesions

LESIONED > LESION

LESIONING > LESION

LESIONS > LESION

LESPEDEZA n bush clover

LESS n smaller amount ▷ adj smaller in extent, degree, or duration ▷ pron smaller part or quantity ▷ adv smaller extent or degree ▷ prep after deducting, minus

LESSEE n person to whom a lease is granted

LESSEES > LESSEE

LESSEN vb make or become smaller or not as much

LESSENED > LESSEN

LESSENING n act of lessening

LESSENS > LESSEN

LESSER adj not as great in quantity, size, or worth

LESSES > LESS

LESSON n class or single period of instruction in a subject ▷ vb censure or punish

LESSONED > LESSON

LESSONING > LESSON

LESSONS > LESSON

LESSOR n person who grants a lease of property

LESSORS > LESSOR

LEST conj so as to prevent any possibility that ▷ vb listen

LESTED > LEST

LESTING > LEST

LESTS > LEST

LESULA n a species of monkey inhabiting forests in DR Congo

LESULAS > LESULA

LET n act of letting property ▷ vb obstruct

LETCH same as > LECH

LETCHED > LETCH

LETCHES > LETCH

LETCHING > LETCH

LETCHINGS > LETCH

LETDOWN n disappointment

LETDOWNS > LETDOWN

LETHAL adj deadly ▷ n weapon, etc capable of causing death

LETHALITY > LETHAL

LETHALLY > LETHAL

LETHALS > LETHAL

LETHARGIC > LETHARGY

LETHARGY n sluggishness or dullness

LETHE n forgetfulness

LETHEAN > LETHE

LETHEE n life-blood

LETHEES > LETHEE

LETHES > LETHE

LETHIED adj forgetful

LETOUT n circumstance that serves as an excuse not to do something

LETOUTS > LETOUT

LETROZOLE n drug used to treat breast cancer

LETS > LET

LETTABLE > LET

LETTED > LET

LETTER n written message ▷ vb put letters on

LETTERBOX n slot through which letters are delivered into a building

LETTERED adj learned

LETTERER > LETTER

LETTERERS > LETTER

LETTERING n act, art, or technique of inscribing letters on to something

LETTERMAN n successful college sportsman

LETTERMEN > LETTERMAN

LETTERN another word for > LECTERN

LETTERNS > LETTERN

LETTERS pl n literary knowledge

LETTERSET n method of rotary printing in which ink is transferred from raised surfaces to paper via a rubber-covered cylinder

LETTING > LET

LETTINGS > LET

LETTRE n letter

LETTRES > LETTRE

LETTUCE n plant with large green leaves used in salads

LETTUCES > LETTUCE

LETUP n lessening or abatement

LETUPS > LETUP

LEU n monetary unit of Romania

LEUCAEMIA same as > LEUKAEMIA

LEUCAEMIC > LEUCAEMIA

LEUCEMIA same as > LEUKAEMIA

LEUCEMIAS > LEUCEMIA

LEUCEMIC adj of or like leucemia

LEUCH > LAUCH

LEUCHEN > LAUCH

LEUCIN same as > LEUCINE

LEUCINE n essential amino acid

LEUCINES > LEUCINE

LEUCINS > LEUCIN

LEUCISTIC adj having reduced pigmentation in the skin but normally-coloured eyes

LEUCITE n grey or white mineral

LEUCITES > LEUCITE

LEUCITIC > LEUCITE

LEUCO n as in leuco base colourless compound

LEUCOCYTE n white blood cell

LEUCOMA n white opaque scar of the cornea

LEUCOMAS > LEUCOMA

LEUCON n type of sponge

LEUCONS > LEUCON

LEUCOSES > LEUCOSIS

LEUCOSIN n albumin in cereal grains

LEUCOSINS > LEUCOSIN

LEUCOSIS same as > LEUKAEMIA

LEUCOTIC adj of or relating to leucosis

LEUCOTOME n needle used in leucotomy

LEUCOTOMY n surgical operation of cutting some of the nerve fibres in the frontal lobes of the brain

LEUD Scots word for > BREADTH

LEUDES > LEUD

LEUDS > LEUD

LEUGH > LAUCH

LEUGHEN > LAUCH

LEUKAEMIA n disease caused by uncontrolled overproduction of white blood cells

LEUKAEMIC adj of or relating to leukaemia

LEUKEMIA same as > LEUKAEMIA

LEUKEMIAS > LEUKEMIA

LEUKEMIC > LEUKEMIA

LEUKEMICS > LEUKEMIA

LEUKEMOID adj resembling leukaemia

LEUKOCYTE same as > LEUCOCYTE

LEUKOMA same as > LEUCOMA

LEUKOMAS > LEUKOMA

LEUKON n white blood cell count

LEUKONS > LEUKON

LEUKOSES > LEUKOSIS

LEUKOSIS n abnormal growth of white blood cells

LEUKOTIC > LEUKOSIS

LEUKOTOME same as > LEUCOTOME

LEUKOTOMY n lobotomy

LEV n monetary unit of Bulgaria

LEVA > LEV

LEVANT n leather made from the skins of goats, sheep, or seals ▷ vb bolt or abscond

LEVANTED > LEVANT

LEVANTER n easterly wind in the W Mediterranean area, esp in the late summer

LEVANTERS > LEVANTER

LEVANTINE n cloth of twilled silk

LEVANTING > LEVANT

LEVANTS > LEVANT

LEVAS > LEV

LEVATOR n muscle that raises a part of the body

LEVATORES > LEVATOR

LEVATORS > LEVATOR

LEVE adj darling ▷ adv gladly

LEVEE n natural or artificial river embankment ▷ vb go to the reception of

LEVEED > LEVEE

LEVEEING > LEVEE

LEVEES > LEVEE

LEVEL adj horizontal ▷ vb make even or horizontal ▷ n horizontal line or surface

LEVELED > LEVEL

LEVELER same as > LEVELLER

LEVELERS > LEVELER

LEVELING > LEVEL

LEVELLED > LEVEL

LEVELLER n person or thing that levels

LEVELLERS > LEVELLER

LEVELLEST > LEVEL

LEVELLING > LEVEL

LEVELLY > LEVEL

LEVELNESS > LEVEL

LEVELS > LEVEL

LEVER n handle used to operate machinery ▷ vb prise or move with a lever

LEVERAGE n action or power of a lever ▷ vb borrow capital required

LEVERAGED > LEVERAGE

LEVERAGES > LEVERAGE

LEVERED > LEVER

LEVERET n young hare

LEVERETS > LEVERET

LEVERING > LEVER

LEVERS > LEVER

LEVES > LEVE

LEVIABLE adj (of taxes, tariffs, etc) liable to be levied

LEVIATHAN n sea
monster
LEVIED > LEVY
LEVIER > LEVY
LEVIERS > LEVY
LEVIES > LEVY
LEVIGABLE > LEVIGATE
LEVIGATE vb grind into a
fine powder or a smooth
paste ▷ adj having a
smooth polished surface
LEVIGATED > LEVIGATE
LEVIGATES > LEVIGATE
LEVIGATOR > LEVIGATE
LEVIN archaic word for
> LIGHTNING
LEVINS > LEVIN
LEVIRATE n practice,
required by Old Testament
law, of marrying the
widow of one's brother
LEVIRATES > LEVIRATE
LEVIRATIC > LEVIRATE
LEVIS n jeans
LEVITATE vb rise or cause
to rise into the air
LEVITATED > LEVITATE
LEVITATES > LEVITATE
LEVITATOR > LEVITATE
LEVITE n Christian
clergyman
LEVITES > LEVITE
LEVITIC > LEVITE
LEVITICAL > LEVITE
LEVITIES > LEVITY
LEVITY n fickleness
LEVO adj anticlockwise
LEVODOPA n substance
occurring naturally in the
body and used to treat
Parkinson's disease
LEVODOPAS > LEVODOPA
LEVOGYRE n
counterclockwise spiral
LEVOGYRES > LEVOGYRE
LEVS > LEV
LEVULIN n substance
obtained from certain
bulbs
LEVULINS > LEVULIN
LEVULOSE n fructose
LEVULOSES > LEVULOSE
LEVY vb impose and collect
(a tax) ▷ n imposition or
collection of taxes
LEVYING > LEVY
LEW adj tepid
LEWD adj lustful or
indecent
LEWDER > LEWD
LEWDEST > LEWD
LEWDLY > LEWD
LEWDNESS > LEWD
LEWDSBIES > LEWDSBY
LEWDSBY another word for
> LEWDSTER
LEWDSTER n lewd person
LEWDSTERS > LEWDSTER
LEWIS n lifting device for
heavy stone or concrete
blocks
LEWISES > LEWIS
LEWISIA n type of herb

LEWISIAS > LEWISIA
LEWISITE n colourless
oily poisonous liquid
LEWISITES > LEWISITE
LEWISSON same as
> LEWIS
LEWISSONS > LEWISSON
LEX n system or body of
laws
LEXEME n minimal
meaningful unit of
language
LEXEMES > LEXEME
LEXEMIC > LEXEME
LEXES > LEX
LEXICA > LEXICON
LEXICAL adj relating to
the vocabulary of a
language
LEXICALLY > LEXICAL
LEXICON n dictionary
LEXICONS > LEXICON
LEXIGRAM n figure or
symbol that represents a
word
LEXIGRAMS > LEXIGRAM
LEXIS n totality of
vocabulary in a language
LEXISES > LEXIS
LEY n land under grass
LEYLANDI same as
> LEYLANDII
LEYLANDII n type of
fast-growing cypress tree
LEYLANDIS > LEYLANDI
LEYS > LEY
LEZ short form of
> LESBIAN
LEZES > LEZ
LEZZ short form of
> LESBIAN
LEZZA same as > LEZZIE
LEZZAS > LEZZA
LEZZES > LEZZ
LEZZIE n lesbian
LEZZIES > LEZZIE
LEZZY short form of
> LESBIAN
LI n Chinese measurement
of distance
LIABILITY n hindrance
or disadvantage
LIABLE adj legally obliged
or responsible
LIAISE vb establish and
maintain communication
LIAISED > LIAISE
LIAISES > LIAISE
LIAISING > LIAISE
LIAISON n
communication and
contact between groups
LIAISONS > LIAISON
LIANA n climbing plant
LIANAS > LIANA
LIANE same as > LIANA
LIANES > LIANE
LIANG n Chinese unit of
weight
LIANGS > LIANG
LIANOID > LIANA
LIAR n person who tells
lies

LIARD adj grey ▷ n former
small coin
LIARDS > LIARD
LIARS > LIAR
LIART Scots form of
> LIARD
LIAS n lowest series of
rocks of the Jurassic
system
LIASES > LIAS
LIASSIC adj relating to
the earliest epoch of the
Jurassic period
LIATRIS n North
American plant with white
flowers
LIATRISES > LIATRIS
LIB n informal word for
liberation ▷ vb geld
LIBANT adj touching
lightly
LIBATE vb offer as gift to
the gods
LIBATED > LIBATE
LIBATES > LIBATE
LIBATING > LIBATE
LIBATION n drink poured
as an offering to the gods
LIBATIONS > LIBATION
LIBATORY > LIBATE
LIBBARD another word for
> LEOPARD
LIBBARDS > LIBBARD
LIBBED > LIB
LIBBER n liberationist
LIBBERS > LIBBER
LIBBING > LIB
LIBECCHIO same as
> LIBECCIO
LIBECCIO n strong
westerly or southwesterly
wind blowing onto the W
coast of Corsica
LIBECCIOS > LIBECCIO
LIBEL n published
statement falsely
damaging a person's
reputation ▷ vb falsely
damage the reputation of
LIBELANT same as
> LIBELLANT
LIBELANTS > LIBELANT
LIBELED > LIBEL
LIBELEE same as
> LIBELLEE
LIBELEES > LIBELEE
LIBELER > LIBEL
LIBELERS > LIBEL
LIBELING > LIBEL
LIBELINGS > LIBEL
LIBELIST > LIBEL
LIBELISTS > LIBEL
LIBELLANT n party who
brings an action in the
ecclesiastical courts by
presenting a libel
LIBELLED > LIBEL
LIBELLEE n person
against whom a libel has
been filed in an
ecclesiastical court
LIBELLEES > LIBELLEE
LIBELLER > LIBEL
LIBELLERS > LIBEL

LIBELLING > LIBEL
LIBELLOUS > LIBEL
LIBELOUS > LIBEL
LIBELS > LIBEL
LIBER n tome or book
LIBERAL adj having social
and political views that
favour progress and
reform ▷ n person with
such views
LIBERALLY > LIBERAL
LIBERALS > LIBERAL
LIBERATE vb set free
LIBERATED adj not
bound by traditional
sexual and social roles
LIBERATES > LIBERATE
LIBERATOR > LIBERATE
LIBERO another name for
> SWEEPER
LIBEROS > LIBERO
LIBERS > LIBER
LIBERTIES > LIBERTY
LIBERTINE n morally
dissolute person ▷ adj
promiscuous and
unscrupulous
LIBERTY n freedom
LIBIDINAL > LIBIDO
LIBIDO n psychic energy
LIBIDOS > LIBIDO
LIBKEN n lodging
LIBKENS > LIBKEN
LIBLAB n 19th century
British liberal
LIBLABS > LIBLAB
LIBRA n ancient Roman
unit of weight
LIBRAE > LIBRA
LIBRAIRE n bookseller
LIBRAIRES > LIBRAIRE
LIBRAIRIE n bookshop
LIBRARIAN n keeper of or
worker in a library
LIBRARIES > LIBRARY
LIBRARY n room or
building where books are
kept
LIBRAS > LIBRA
LIBRATE vb oscillate or
waver
LIBRATED > LIBRATE
LIBRATES > LIBRATE
LIBRATING > LIBRATE
LIBRATION n act or an
instance of oscillating
LIBRATORY > LIBRATE
LIBRETTI > LIBRETTO
LIBRETTO n words of an
opera
LIBRETTOS > LIBRETTO
LIBRI > LIBER
LIBRIFORM adj (of a fibre
of woody tissue)
elongated and having a
pitted thickened cell wall
LIBS > LIB
LICE > LOUSE
LICENCE n document
giving official permission
▷ vb (in the US) give
permission to
LICENCED > LICENCE

LICENCEE same as
> LICENSEE
LICENCEES > LICENCEE
LICENCER > LICENCE
LICENCERS > LICENCE
LICENCES > LICENCE
LICENCING > LICENCE
LICENSE vb grant or give
a licence for
LICENSED > LICENSE
LICENSEE n holder of a
licence, esp to sell alcohol
LICENSEES > LICENSEE
LICENSER > LICENSE
LICENSERS > LICENSE
LICENSES > LICENSE
LICENSING > LICENSE
LICENSOR > LICENSE
LICENSORS > LICENSE
LICENSURE n act of
conferring licence
LICENTE adj permitted;
allowed
LICH n dead body
LICHANOS n note played
using forefinger
LICHEE same as > LITCHI
LICHEES > LICHEE
LICHEN n small flowerless
plant forming a crust on
rocks, trees, etc ⊳ vb cover
with lichen
LICHENED > LICHEN
LICHENIN n complex
polysaccharide occurring
in certain species of moss
LICHENING > LICHEN
LICHENINS > LICHENIN
LICHENISM n an
association of fungus and
alga as lichen
LICHENIST n person
who studies lichens
LICHENOID > LICHEN
LICHENOSE > LICHEN
LICHENOUS > LICHEN
LICHENS > LICHEN
LICHES > LICH
LICHGATE n roofed gate
to a churchyard
LICHGATES > LICHGATE
LICHI same as > LITCHI
LICHIS > LICHI
LICHT Scot word for
> LIGHT
LICHTED > LICHT
LICHTER > LICHT
LICHTEST > LICHT
LICHTING > LICHT
LICHTLIED > LICHTLY
LICHTLIES > LICHTLY
LICHTLY vb treat
discourteously
LICHTS > LICHT
LICHWAKE n night vigil
over a dead body
LICHWAKES > LICHWAKE
LICHWAY n path used to
carry coffin into church
LICHWAYS > LICHWAY
LICIT adj lawful,
permitted
LICITLY > LICIT

LICITNESS > LICIT
LICK vb pass the tongue
over ⊳ n licking
LICKED > LICK
LICKER > LICK
LICKERISH adj lecherous
or lustful
LICKERS > LICK
LICKING n beating
LICKINGS > LICKING
LICKPENNY n something
that uses up large
amounts of money
LICKS > LICK
LICKSPIT n flattering or
servile person
LICKSPITS > LICKSPIT
LICORICE same as
> LIQUORICE
LICORICES > LICORICE
LICTOR n one of a group
of ancient Roman officials
LICTORIAN > LICTOR
LICTORS > LICTOR
LID n movable cover
LIDAR n radar-type
instrument
LIDARS > LIDAR
LIDDED > LID
LIDDING n lids
LIDDINGS > LIDDING
LIDGER variant form of
> LEDGER
LIDGERS > LEDGER
LIDLESS adj having no lid
or top
LIDO n open-air centre for
swimming and water
sports
LIDOCAINE n powerful
local anaesthetic
administered by injection
LIDOS > LIDO
LIDS > LID
LIE vb make a false
statement ⊳ n falsehood
LIED n setting for solo
voice and piano of a poem
LIEDER > LIED
LIEF adv gladly ⊳ adj ready
⊳ n beloved person
LIEFER > LIEF
LIEFEST > LIEF
LIEFLY > LIEF
LIEFS > LIEF
LIEGE adj bound to give or
receive feudal service
⊳ n lord
LIEGEDOM > LIEGE
LIEGEDOMS > LIEGE
LIEGELESS > LIEGE
LIEGEMAN n (formerly)
the subject of a sovereign
or feudal lord
LIEGEMEN > LIEGEMAN
LIEGER same as > LEDGER
LIEGERS > LIEGER
LIEGES > LIEGE
LIEN n right to hold
another's property until a
debt is paid
LIENABLE adj that can be
subject of a lien

LIENAL adj of or relating
to the spleen
LIENEE n person against
whom a lien has been
placed
LIENEES > LIENEE
LIENOR n person who
holds a lien
LIENORS > LIENOR
LIENS > LIEN
LIENTERIC > LIENTERY
LIENTERY n passage of
undigested food in the
faeces
LIER n person who lies
down
LIERNE n short secondary
rib that connects
intersections of the
primary ribs
LIERNES > LIERNE
LIERS > LIER
LIES > LIE
LIEU n stead
LIEUS > LIEU
LIEVE same as > LEVE
LIEVER > LIEVE
LIEVES > LIEVE
LIEVEST > LIEVE
LIFE n state of living
beings
LIFEBELT n ring filled
with air, used to keep a
person afloat when in
danger of drowning
LIFEBELTS > LIFEBELT
LIFEBLOOD n blood vital
to life
LIFEBOAT n boat used for
rescuing people at sea
LIFEBOATS > LIFEBOAT
LIFEBUOY n any of
various kinds of buoyant
device for keeping people
afloat
LIFEBUOYS > LIFEBUOY
LIFECARE n care of
person's health and
welfare
LIFECARES > LIFECARE
LIFEFUL adj full of life
LIFEGUARD n person
who saves people from
drowning ⊳ vb work as
lifeguard
LIFEHACK n action that
simplifies a task or reduces
frustration in everyday life
⊳ vb perform a lifehack
LIFEHACKS > LIFEHACK
LIFEHOLD adj (of land)
held while one is alive
LIFELESS adj dead
LIFELIKE adj closely
resembling or
representing life
LIFELINE n means of
contact or support
LIFELINES > LIFELINE
LIFELONG adj lasting all
of a person's life
LIFER n prisoner
sentenced to
imprisonment for life

LIFERS > LIFER
LIFES pl n as in still lifes
paintings or drawings of
inanimate objects
LIFESAVER n saver of a
person's life
LIFESOME adj full of life
LIFESPAN n period of
time during which a
person or animal may be
expected to live
LIFESPANS > LIFESPAN
LIFESTYLE n particular
attitudes, habits, etc
⊳ adj suggestive of a
fashionable or desirable
lifestyle
LIFETIME n length of
time a person is alive
LIFETIMES > LIFETIME
LIFEWAY n way of life
LIFEWAYS > LIFEWAY
LIFEWORK n work to
which a person has
devoted their life
LIFEWORKS > LIFEWORK
LIFEWORLD n way
individual experiences
world
LIFT vb move upwards in
position, status, volume,
etc ⊳ n cage raised and
lowered in a vertical shaft
LIFTABLE > LIFT
LIFTBACK n hatchback
LIFTBACKS > LIFTBACK
LIFTBOY n person who
operates a lift
LIFTBOYS > LIFTBOY
LIFTED > LIFT
LIFTER > LIFT
LIFTERS > LIFT
LIFTGATE n rear opening
of hatchback
LIFTGATES > LIFTGATE
LIFTING > LIFT
LIFTMAN same as
> LIFTBOY
LIFTMEN > LIFTMAN
LIFTOFF n moment a
rocket leaves the ground
⊳ vb (of a rocket) to leave
its launch pad
LIFTOFFS > LIFTOFF
LIFTS > LIFT
LIFULL obsolete form of
> LIFEFUL
LIG n function with free
entertainment and
refreshments ⊳ vb attend
such a function
LIGAMENT n band of
tissue joining bones
LIGAMENTS > LIGAMENT
LIGAN same as > LAGAN
LIGAND n atom, molecule,
radical, or ion forming a
complex with a central
atom
LIGANDS > LIGAND
LIGANS > LIGAN
LIGASE n any of a class of
enzymes
LIGASES > LIGASE

LIGATE *vb* tie up or constrict (something) with a ligature
LIGATED > LIGATE
LIGATES > LIGATE
LIGATING > LIGATE
LIGATION > LIGATE
LIGATIONS > LIGATE
LIGATIVE > LIGATE
LIGATURE *n* link, bond, or tie ▷ *vb* bind with a ligature
LIGATURED > LIGATURE
LIGATURES > LIGATURE
LIGER *n* hybrid offspring of a female tiger and a male lion
LIGERS > LIGER
LIGGE *obsolete form of* > LIE
LIGGED > LIG
LIGGER > LIG
LIGGERS > LIG
LIGGES > LIGGE
LIGGING > LIG
LIGGINGS > LIG
LIGHT *n* electromagnetic radiation by which things are visible ▷ *adj* bright ▷ *vb* ignite ▷ *adv* with little luggage
LIGHTBULB *n* glass bulb containing gas that emits light when a current is passed through it
LIGHTED > LIGHT
LIGHTEN *vb* make less dark
LIGHTENED > LIGHTEN
LIGHTENER > LIGHTEN
LIGHTENS > LIGHTEN
LIGHTER *n* device for lighting cigarettes etc ▷ *vb* convey in a type of flat-bottomed barge
LIGHTERED > LIGHTER
LIGHTERS > LIGHTER
LIGHTEST > LIGHT
LIGHTFACE *n* weight of type in printing
LIGHTFAST *adj* (of a dye) unaffected by light
LIGHTFUL *adj* full of light
LIGHTING > LIGHT
LIGHTINGS > LIGHT
LIGHTISH > LIGHT
LIGHTLESS > LIGHT
LIGHTLIED > LIGHTLY
LIGHTLIES > LIGHTLY
LIGHTLY *adv* in a light way ▷ *vb* belittle
LIGHTNESS *n* quality of being light
LIGHTNING *n* visible discharge of electricity in the atmosphere ▷ *adj* fast and sudden
LIGHTS > LIGHT
LIGHTSHIP *n* moored ship used as a lighthouse
LIGHTSOME *adj* lighthearted
LIGHTWAVE *adj* using light waves

LIGHTWOOD *n* Australian acacia
LIGNAGE *another word for* > LINEAGE
LIGNAGES > LIGNAGE
LIGNALOES *another name for* > EAGLEWOOD
LIGNAN *n* beneficial substance found in plants
LIGNANS > LIGNAN
LIGNE *n* unit of measurement
LIGNEOUS *adj* of or like wood
LIGNES > LIGNE
LIGNICOLE *adj* growing or living in wood
LIGNIFIED > LIGNIFY
LIGNIFIES > LIGNIFY
LIGNIFORM *adj* having the appearance of wood
LIGNIFY *vb* become woody with the deposition of lignin in cell walls
LIGNIN *n* complex polymer occurring in certain plant cell walls making the plant rigid
LIGNINS > LIGNIN
LIGNITE *n* woody textured rock used as fuel
LIGNITES > LIGNITE
LIGNITIC > LIGNITE
LIGNOSE *n* explosive compound
LIGNOSES > LIGNOSE
LIGNUM *n* wood
LIGNUMS > LIGNUM
LIGROIN *n* volatile fraction of petroleum
LIGROINE *same as* > LIGROIN
LIGROINES > LIGROINE
LIGROINS > LIGROIN
LIGS > LIG
LIGULA *same as* > LIGULE
LIGULAE > LIGULA
LIGULAR > LIGULA
LIGULAS > LIGULA
LIGULATE *adj* having the shape of a strap
LIGULATED *same as* > LIGULATE
LIGULE *n* membranous outgrowth between the leaf blade and sheath
LIGULES > LIGULE
LIGULOID > LIGULA
LIGURE *n* any of the 12 precious stones used in the breastplates of high priests
LIGURES > LIGURE
LIKABLE *adj* easy to like
LIKABLY > LIKABLE
LIKE *adj* similar ▷ *vb* find enjoyable ▷ *n* favourable feeling, desire, or preference
LIKEABLE *same as* > LIKABLE
LIKEABLY *same as* > LIKABLY
LIKED > LIKE

LIKELIER > LIKELY
LIKELIEST > LIKELY
LIKELY *adj* tending or inclined ▷ *adv* probably
LIKEN *vb* compare
LIKENED > LIKEN
LIKENESS *n* resemblance
LIKENING > LIKEN
LIKENS > LIKEN
LIKER > LIKE
LIKERS > LIKE
LIKES > LIKE
LIKEST > LIKE
LIKEWAKE *same as* > LYKEWAKE
LIKEWAKES > LIKEWAKE
LIKEWALK *same as* > LYKEWAKE
LIKEWALKS > LIKEWALK
LIKEWISE *adv* similarly
LIKIN *n* historically, Chinese tax
LIKING *n* fondness
LIKINGS > LIKING
LIKINS > LIKIN
LIKUTA *n* coin in Zaïre
LILAC *n* shrub with pale mauve flowers ▷ *adj* light-purple
LILACS > LILAC
LILANGENI *n* standard monetary unit of Swaziland, divided into 100 cents
LILIED *adj* decorated with lilies
LILIES > LILY
LILL *obsolete form of* > LOLL
LILLED > LILL
LILLING > LILL
LILLIPUT *adj* tiny ▷ *n* tiny person or being
LILLIPUTS > LILLIPUT
LILLS > LILL
LILO *n* inflatable mattress
LILOS > LILO
LILT *n* musical quality in speech ▷ *vb* speak with a lilt
LILTED > LILT
LILTING > LILT
LILTINGLY > LILT
LILTS > LILT
LILY *n* plant which has large, often white, flowers
LILYLIKE *adj* resembling a lily
LIMA *n* type of edible bean
LIMACEL *n* small shell inside some kinds of slug
LIMACELS > LIMACEL
LIMACEOUS *adj* relating to the slug
LIMACES > LIMAX
LIMACINE *adj* relating to slugs
LIMACON *n* heart-shaped curve
LIMACONS > LIMACON
LIMAIL *same as* > LEMEL
LIMAILS > LIMAIL
LIMAN *n* lagoon

LIMANS > LIMAN
LIMAS > LIMA
LIMATION *n* polishing
LIMATIONS > LIMATION
LIMAX *n* slug
LIMB *n* arm, leg, or wing ▷ *vb* dismember
LIMBA *n* type of African tree
LIMBAS > LIMBA
LIMBATE *adj* having an edge or border of a different colour from the rest
LIMBEC *obsolete form of* > ALEMBIC
LIMBECK *obsolete form of* > ALEMBIC
LIMBECKS > LIMBECK
LIMBECS > LIMBEC
LIMBED > LIMB
LIMBER *vb* loosen stiff muscles by exercising ▷ *adj* pliant or supple ▷ *n* part of a gun carriage
LIMBERED > LIMBER
LIMBERER > LIMBER
LIMBEREST > LIMBER
LIMBERING > LIMBER
LIMBERLY > LIMBER
LIMBERS > LIMBER
LIMBI > LIMBUS
LIMBIC > LIMBUS
LIMBIER > LIMBY
LIMBIEST > LIMBY
LIMBING > LIMB
LIMBLESS > LIMB
LIMBMEAL *adv* piece by piece
LIMBO *n* region between Heaven and Hell for the unbaptized ▷ *vb* perform a Caribbean dance that entails passing under a bar while leaning backwards
LIMBOED > LIMBO
LIMBOES > LIMBO
LIMBOING > LIMBO
LIMBOS > LIMBO
LIMBOUS *adj* with overlapping edges
LIMBS > LIMB
LIMBUS *n* border
LIMBUSES > LIMBUS
LIMBY *adj* with long legs, stem, branches, etc
LIME *n* calcium compound used as a fertilizer or in making cement ▷ *vb* spread a calcium compound upon (land) ▷ *adj* having the flavour of lime fruit
LIMEADE *n* drink made from sweetened lime juice and plain or carbonated water
LIMEADES > LIMEADE
LIMED > LIME
LIMEKILN *n* kiln in which calcium carbonate is burned to produce quicklime
LIMEKILNS > LIMEKILN

LIMELESS > LIME
LIMELIGHT n glare of publicity ▷ vb illuminate with limelight
LIMELIT > LIMELIGHT
LIMEN another term for > THRESHOLD
LIMENS > LIMEN
LIMEPIT n pit containing lime in which hides are placed to remove the hair
LIMEPITS > LIMEPIT
LIMERENCE n psychological state resulting from romantic attraction
LIMERICK n humorous verse of five lines
LIMERICKS > LIMERICK
LIMES n fortified boundary of the Roman Empire
LIMESCALE n flaky deposit left in containers such as kettles by the action of heat on water containing calcium salts
LIMESTONE n sedimentary rock used in building
LIMEWASH n mixture of lime and water used to whitewash walls, ceilings, etc
LIMEWATER n clear colourless solution of calcium hydroxide in water
LIMEY n British person ▷ adj British
LIMEYS > LIMEY
LIMIER > LIMY
LIMIEST > LIMY
LIMINA > LIMEN
LIMINAL adj relating to the point (or threshold) beyond which a sensation becomes too faint to be experienced
LIMINESS > LIMY
LIMING > LIME
LIMINGS > LIME
LIMIT n ultimate extent, degree, or amount of something ▷ vb restrict or confine
LIMITABLE > LIMIT
LIMITARY adj of, involving, or serving as a limit
LIMITED adj having a limit ▷ n limited train, bus, etc
LIMITEDLY > LIMITED
LIMITEDS > LIMITED
LIMITER n electronic circuit whose amplitude is limited to some fixed value above which the peaks become flattened
LIMITERS > LIMITER
LIMITES > LIMES
LIMITING > LIMIT
LIMITINGS > LIMIT

LIMITLESS > LIMIT
LIMITS > LIMIT
LIMMA n semitone
LIMMAS > LIMMA
LIMMER n scoundrel
LIMMERS > LIMMER
LIMN vb represent in drawing or painting
LIMNAEID n type of snail
LIMNAEIDS > LIMNAEID
LIMNED > LIMN
LIMNER > LIMN
LIMNERS > LIMN
LIMNETIC adj of, relating to, or inhabiting the open water of lakes down to the depth of light penetration
LIMNIC adj relating to lakes
LIMNING > LIMN
LIMNOLOGY n study of bodies of fresh water with reference to their plant and animal life, physical properties, geographical features, etc
LIMNS > LIMN
LIMO short for > LIMOUSINE
LIMONENE n liquid optically active terpene with a lemon-like odour
LIMONENES > LIMONENE
LIMONITE n common brown, black, or yellow amorphous secondary mineral
LIMONITES > LIMONITE
LIMONITIC > LIMONITE
LIMONIUM n sea plant with funnel-shaped flowers
LIMONIUMS > LIMONIUM
LIMOS > LIMO
LIMOSES > LIMOSIS
LIMOSIS n excessive hunger
LIMOUS adj muddy
LIMOUSINE n large luxurious car
LIMP vb walk with an uneven step ▷ n limping walk ▷ adj without firmness or stiffness
LIMPA n type of rye bread
LIMPAS > LIMPA
LIMPED > LIMP
LIMPER > LIMP
LIMPERS > LIMP
LIMPEST > LIMP
LIMPET n shellfish which sticks to rocks ▷ adj denoting weapons that are magnetically attached to their targets
LIMPETS > LIMPET
LIMPID adj clear or transparent
LIMPIDITY > LIMPID
LIMPIDLY > LIMPID
LIMPING > LIMP
LIMPINGLY > LIMP
LIMPINGS > LIMP

LIMPKIN n rail-like wading bird
LIMPKINS > LIMPKIN
LIMPLY > LIMP
LIMPNESS > LIMP
LIMPS > LIMP
LIMPSEY same as > LIMPSY
LIMPSIER > LIMPSY
LIMPSIEST > LIMPSY
LIMPSY adj limp
LIMULI > LIMULUS
LIMULOID n type of crab
LIMULOIDS > LIMULOID
LIMULUS n horseshoe crab
LIMULUSES > LIMULUS
LIMY adj of, like, or smeared with birdlime
LIN vb cease
LINABLE > LINE
LINAC n linear accelerator
LINACS > LINAC
LINAGE n number of lines in written or printed matter
LINAGES > LINAGE
LINALOL same as > LINALOOL
LINALOLS > LINALOL
LINALOOL n optically active colourless fragrant liquid
LINALOOLS > LINALOOL
LINCH n ledge
LINCHES > LINCH
LINCHET another word for > LINCH
LINCHETS > LINCHET
LINCHPIN n pin to hold a wheel on its axle
LINCHPINS > LINCHPIN
LINCRUSTA n type of wallpaper having a hard embossed surface
LINCTURE n medicine taken by licking
LINCTURES > LINCTURE
LINCTUS n cough medicine
LINCTUSES > LINCTUS
LIND variant of > LINDEN
LINDANE n white poisonous crystalline powder
LINDANES > LINDANE
LINDEN n large tree with heart-shaped leaves and fragrant yellowish flowers
LINDENS > LINDEN
LINDIED > LINDY
LINDIES > LINDY
LINDS > LIND
LINDWORM n wingless serpent-like dragon
LINDWORMS > LINDWORM
LINDY n lively dance ▷ vb perform the lindy
LINDYING > LINDY
LINE n long narrow mark ▷ vb mark with lines
LINEABLE > LINE

LINEAGE n descent from an ancestor
LINEAGES > LINEAGE
LINEAL adj in direct line of descent
LINEALITY > LINEAL
LINEALLY > LINEAL
LINEAMENT n facial feature
LINEAR adj of or in lines
LINEARISE same as > LINEARIZE
LINEARITY > LINEAR
LINEARIZE vb make linear
LINEARLY > LINEAR
LINEATE adj marked with lines
LINEATED same as > LINEATE
LINEATION n act of marking with lines
LINEBRED adj having an ancestor that is common to sire and dam
LINECUT n method of relief printing
LINECUTS > LINECUT
LINED > LINE
LINELESS > LINE
LINELIKE > LINE
LINEMAN same as > LINESMAN
LINEMATE n ice hockey player on the same line as another
LINEMATES > LINEMATE
LINEMEN > LINEMAN
LINEN n cloth or thread made from flax
LINENS > LINEN
LINENY > LINEN
LINEOLATE adj marked with very fine parallel lines
LINER n large passenger ship
LINERLESS adj having no lining
LINERS > LINER
LINES > LINE
LINESMAN n (in some sports) an official who helps the referee or umpire
LINESMEN > LINESMAN
LINEUP n row or arrangement of people or things
LINEUPS > LINEUP
LINEY > LINE
LING n slender food fish
LINGA same as > LINGAM
LINGAM n (in Sanskrit) masculine gender
LINGAMS > LINGAM
LINGAS > LINGA
LINGBERRY same as > COWBERRY
LINGCOD n type of food fish
LINGCODS > LINGCOD
LINGEL n shoemaker's thread
LINGELS > LINGEL

LINGER vb delay or prolong departure
LINGERED > LINGER
LINGERER > LINGER
LINGERERS > LINGER
LINGERIE n women's underwear or nightwear
LINGERIES > LINGERIE
LINGERING > LINGER
LINGERS > LINGER
LINGIER > LINGY
LINGIEST > LINGY
LINGLE same as > LINGEL
LINGLES > LINGLE
LINGO n foreign or unfamiliar language or jargon
LINGOES > LINGO
LINGOS > LINGO
LINGOT n ingot
LINGOTS > LINGOT
LINGS > LING
LINGSTER n person able to communicate with aliens
LINGSTERS > LINGSTER
LINGUA n any tongue-like structure
LINGUAE > LINGUA
LINGUAL adj of the tongue ▷ n lingual consonant
LINGUALLY > LINGUAL
LINGUALS > LINGUAL
LINGUAS > LINGUA
LINGUICA n Portuguese sausage
LINGUICAS > LINGUICA
LINGUINE n kind of pasta in the shape of thin flat strands
LINGUINES > LINGUINE
LINGUINI same as > LINGUINE
LINGUINIS > LINGUINI
LINGUISA same as > LINGUICA
LINGUISAS > LINGUISA
LINGUIST n person skilled in foreign languages
LINGUISTS > LINGUIST
LINGULA n small tongue
LINGULAE > LINGULA
LINGULAR > LINGULA
LINGULAS > LINGULA
LINGULATE adj shaped like a tongue
LINGY adj heather-covered
LINHAY n farm building with an open front
LINHAYS > LINHAY
LINIER > LINE
LINIEST > LINE
LINIMENT n medicated liquid rubbed on the skin to relieve pain or stiffness
LINIMENTS > LINIMENT
LININ n network of viscous material in the nucleus of a cell that connects the chromatin granules

LINING n layer of cloth attached to the inside of a garment etc
LININGS > LINING
LININS > LININ
LINISH vb polish metal
LINISHED > LINISH
LINISHER > LINISH
LINISHERS > LINISH
LINISHES > LINISH
LINISHING > LINISH
LINK n any of the rings forming a chain ▷ vb connect with or as if with links
LINKABLE > LINK
LINKAGE n act of linking or the state of being linked
LINKAGES > LINKAGE
LINKBOY n (formerly) a boy who carried a torch for pedestrians in dark streets
LINKBOYS > LINKBOY
LINKED > LINK
LINKER n person or thing that links
LINKERS > LINKER
LINKIER > LINKY
LINKIEST > LINKY
LINKING > LINK
LINKMAN same as > LINKBOY
LINKMEN > LINKMAN
LINKROT n state of having expired hyperlinks on a website
LINKROTS > LINKROT
LINKS > LINK
LINKSLAND n land near sea used for golf
LINKSMAN same as > LINKBOY
LINKSMEN > LINKSMAN
LINKSPAN n hinged bridge on a quay, used to move vehicles on or off a vessel
LINKSPANS > LINKSPAN
LINKSTER n interpreter
LINKSTERS > LINKSTER
LINKUP n establishing of a union between objects, groups, organizations, etc
LINKUPS > LINKUP
LINKWORK n something made up of links
LINKWORKS > LINKWORK
LINKY adj (of countryside) consisting of links
LINN n waterfall or a pool at the foot of it
LINNED > LIN
LINNET n songbird of the finch family
LINNETS > LINNET
LINNEY same as > LINHAY
LINNEYS > LINNEY
LINNIES > LINNY
LINNING > LIN
LINNS > LINN
LINNY same as > LINHAY
LINO same as > LINOLEUM

LINOCUT n design cut in relief in lino mounted on a block of wood
LINOCUTS > LINOCUT
LINOLEATE n ester or salt of linoleic acid
LINOLEIC adj as in linoleic acid colourless oily essential fatty acid found in linseed
LINOLENIC adj as in linolenic acid colourless unsaturated essential fatty acid
LINOLEUM n type of floor covering
LINOLEUMS > LINOLEUM
LINOS > LINO
LINOTYPE n line of metal type produced by machine ▷ vb set as line of type
LINOTYPED > LINOTYPE
LINOTYPER > LINOTYPE
LINOTYPES > LINOTYPE
LINS > LIN
LINSANG n any of several forest-dwelling viverrine mammals
LINSANGS > LINSANG
LINSEED n seed of the flax plant
LINSEEDS > LINSEED
LINSEY n type of cloth
LINSEYS > LINSEY
LINSTOCK n long staff holding a lighted match, formerly used to fire a cannon
LINSTOCKS > LINSTOCK
LINT n shreds of fibre, etc ▷ vb shed or remove lint
LINTED adj having lint
LINTEL n horizontal beam at the top of a door or window
LINTELED adj (of a door or window) having a lintel
LINTELLED adj having a lintel
LINTELS > LINTEL
LINTER n machine for stripping the short fibres of ginned cotton seeds
LINTERS > LINTER
LINTIE Scot word for > LINNET
LINTIER > LINT
LINTIES > LINTIE
LINTIEST > LINT
LINTING n process of making lint
LINTINGS > LINTING
LINTLESS > LINT
LINTOL same as > LINTEL
LINTOLS > LINTOL
LINTS > LINT
LINTSEED same as > LINSEED
LINTSEEDS > LINTSEED
LINTSTOCK same as > LINSTOCK
LINTWHITE n linnet
LINTY > LINT

LINUM n type of plant of temperate regions
LINUMS > LINUM
LINURON n type of herbicide
LINURONS > LINURON
LINUX n nonproprietary computer operating system
LINUXES > LINUX
LINY > LINE
LION n large animal of the cat family
LIONCEL n (in heraldry) small lion
LIONCELLE same as > LIONCEL
LIONCELS > LIONCEL
LIONEL same as > LIONCEL
LIONELS > LIONEL
LIONESS n female lion
LIONESSES > LIONESS
LIONET n young lion
LIONETS > LIONET
LIONFISH n any of various scorpion fishes of the Pacific
LIONHEAD n small breed of rabbit with long fur around the face
LIONHEADS > LIONHEAD
LIONISE same as > LIONIZE
LIONISED > LIONISE
LIONISER > LIONISE
LIONISERS > LIONISE
LIONISES > LIONISE
LIONISING > LIONISE
LIONISM n lion-like appearance of leprosy
LIONISMS > LIONISM
LIONIZE vb treat as a celebrity
LIONIZED > LIONIZE
LIONIZER > LIONIZE
LIONIZERS > LIONIZE
LIONIZES > LIONIZE
LIONIZING > LIONIZE
LIONLIKE > LION
LIONLY > LION
LIONS > LION
LIP n either of the fleshy edges of the mouth ▷ vb touch with the lips
LIPA n monetary unit of Croatia
LIPAEMIA n abnormally large amount of fat in the blood
LIPAEMIAS > LIPAEMIA
LIPARITE n type of igneous rock
LIPARITES > LIPARITE
LIPAS > LIPA
LIPASE n any of a group of enzymes that digest fat
LIPASES > LIPASE
LIPE n lurching or jerking movement
LIPECTOMY n surgical operation to remove fat

LIPEMIA same as
> LIPAEMIA
LIPEMIAS > LIPEMIA
LIPES > LIPE
LIPGLOSS n cosmetic for
the lips to give a sheen
LIPID n any of a group of
organic compounds
including fats, oils, waxes,
and sterols
LIPIDE same as > LIPID
LIPIDES > LIPIDE
LIPIDIC > LIPID
LIPIDS > LIPID
LIPIN n family of nuclear
proteins
LIPINS > LIPIN
LIPLESS > LIP
LIPLIKE > LIP
LIPLINER n cosmetic
used to outline the lips
LIPLINERS > LIPLINER
LIPO n liposuction
LIPOCYTE n fat-storing
cell
LIPOCYTES > LIPOCYTE
LIPOGRAM n piece of
writing in which all words
containing a particular
letter have been
deliberately omitted
LIPOGRAMS
> LIPOGRAM
LIPOIC adj as in lipoic acid
sulphur-containing fatty
acid
LIPOID n fatlike
substance, such as wax
LIPOIDAL > LIPOID
LIPOIDS > LIPOID
LIPOLITIC same as
> LIPOLYTIC
LIPOLYSES
> LIPOLYSIS
LIPOLYSIS n hydrolysis
of fats resulting in the
production of carboxylic
acids and glycerol
LIPOLYTIC adj fat-
burning
LIPOMA n benign tumour
composed of fatty tissue
LIPOMAS > LIPOMA
LIPOMATA > LIPOMA
LIPOPLAST n small
particle in plant
cytoplasm, esp that of
seeds, in which fat is
stored
LIPOS > LIPO
LIPOSOMAL > LIPOSOME
LIPOSOME n particle
formed by lipids
LIPOSOMES > LIPOSOME
LIPOSUCK vb subject to
liposuction
LIPOSUCKS > LIPOSUCK
LIPOTROPY n breaking
down of fat in body
LIPPED > LIP
LIPPEN vb trust
LIPPENED > LIPPEN
LIPPENING > LIPPEN
LIPPENS > LIPPEN

LIPPER Scots word for
> RIPPLE
LIPPERED > LIPPER
LIPPERING > LIPPER
LIPPERS > LIPPER
LIPPIE variant of > LIPPY
LIPPIER > LIPPY
LIPPIES > LIPPIE
LIPPIEST > LIPPY
LIPPINESS > LIPPY
LIPPING > LIP
LIPPINGS > LIP
LIPPITUDE n state of
having bleary eyes
LIPPY adj insolent or
cheeky ▷ n lipstick
LIPREAD vb follow what
someone says by watching
their lips
LIPREADER > LIPREAD
LIPREADS > LIPREAD
LIPS > LIP
LIPSALVE n substance
used to prevent or relieve
chapped lips
LIPSALVES > LIPSALVE
LIPSTICK n cosmetic in
stick form, for colouring
the lips ▷ vb put lipstick
on
LIPSTICKS > LIPSTICK
LIPURIA n presence of fat
in the urine
LIPURIAS > LIPURIA
LIQUABLE adj that can be
melted
LIQUATE vb separate one
component of by heating
until the more fusible part
melts
LIQUATED > LIQUATE
LIQUATES > LIQUATE
LIQUATING > LIQUATE
LIQUATION > LIQUATE
LIQUEFIED > LIQUEFY
LIQUEFIER > LIQUEFY
LIQUEFIES > LIQUEFY
LIQUEFY vb become
liquid
LIQUESCE vb become
liquid
LIQUESCED > LIQUESCE
LIQUESCES > LIQUESCE
LIQUEUR n flavoured
and sweetened alcoholic
spirit ▷ vb flavour with
liqueur
LIQUEURED > LIQUEUR
LIQUEURS > LIQUEUR
LIQUID n substance in a
physical state which can
change shape but not size
▷ adj of or being a liquid
LIQUIDATE vb pay (a
debt)
LIQUIDISE same as
> LIQUIDIZE
LIQUIDITY n state of
being able to meet
financial obligations
LIQUIDIZE vb make or
become liquid
LIQUIDLY > LIQUID
LIQUIDS > LIQUID

LIQUIDUS n line on graph
above which a substance
is in liquid form
LIQUIDY adj having the
nature of liquid
LIQUIFIED > LIQUIFY
LIQUIFIER n something
that liquifies
LIQUIFIES > LIQUIFY
LIQUIFY same as
> LIQUEFY
LIQUITAB n soluble
plastic capsule containing
liquid detergent or
medicine
LIQUITABS > LIQUITAB
LIQUOR n alcoholic drink
▷ vb steep in warm water
to form wort in brewing
LIQUORED > LIQUOR
LIQUORICE n black
substance used in
medicine and as a sweet
LIQUORING > LIQUOR
LIQUORISH same as
> LICKERISH
LIQUORS > LIQUOR
LIRA n monetary unit of
Turkey, Malta, and
formerly of Italy
LIRAS > LIRA
LIRE > LIRA
LIRI > LIRA
LIRIOPE n grasslike plant
LIRIOPES > LIRIOPE
LIRIPIPE n tip of a
graduate's hood
LIRIPIPES > LIRIPIPE
LIRIPOOP same as
> LIRIPIPE
LIRIPOOPS > LIRIPOOP
LIRK vb wrinkle
LIRKED > LIRK
LIRKING > LIRK
LIRKS > LIRK
LIROT > LIRA
LIROTH > LIRA
LIS n fleur-de-lis
LISENTE > SENTE
LISK Yorkshire dialect for
> GROIN
LISKS > LISK
LISLE n strong fine cotton
thread or fabric
LISLES > LISLE
LISP n speech defect in
which s and z are
pronounced th ▷ vb speak
or utter with a lisp
LISPED > LISP
LISPER > LISP
LISPERS > LISP
LISPING > LISP
LISPINGLY > LISP
LISPINGS > LISP
LISPOUND n unit of
weight
LISPOUNDS > LISPOUND
LISPS > LISP
LISPUND same as
> LISPOUND
LISPUNDS > LISPUND
LISSES > LIS

LISSOM adj supple, agile
LISSOME same as > LISSOM
LISSOMELY > LISSOM
LISSOMLY > LISSOM
LIST n item-by-item
record of names or things,
usu written one below
another ▷ vb make a list of
LISTABLE > LIST
LISTBOX n small box on a
computer screen, showing
a list of options
LISTBOXES > LISTBOX
LISTED > LIST
LISTEE n person on list
LISTEES > LISTEE
LISTEL another name for
> FILLET
LISTELS > LISTEL
LISTEN vb concentrate on
hearing something
LISTENED > LISTEN
LISTENER > LISTEN
LISTENERS > LISTEN
LISTENING > LISTEN
LISTENS > LISTEN
LISTER n plough with a
double mouldboard to
throw soil to sides of a
central furrow
LISTERIA n type of
rodlike Gram-positive
bacterium
LISTERIAL > LISTERIA
LISTERIAS > LISTERIA
LISTERS > LISTER
LISTETH > LIST
LISTFUL adj paying
attention
LISTING n list or an entry
in a list
LISTINGS > LISTING
LISTLESS adj lacking
interest or energy
LISTS pl n field of combat
in a tournament
LISTSERV n service on
the internet that provides
an electronic mailing to
subscribers with similar
interests
LISTSERVS > LISTSERV
LIT n archaic word for dye
or colouring
LITAI > LITAS
LITANIES > LITANY
LITANY n prayer with
responses from the
congregation
LITAS n monetary unit of
Lithuania
LITCHI n Chinese tree
with round edible fruits
LITCHIS > LITCHI
LITE same as > LIGHT
LITED > LIGHT
LITENESS > LITE
LITER same as > LITRE
LITERACY n ability to
read and write
LITERAL adj according to
the explicit meaning of a
word or text ▷ n
misspelling in a text

LITERALLY adv in a literal manner
LITERALS > LITERAL
LITERARY adj of or knowledgeable about literature
LITERATE adj able to read and write ▷ n literate person
LITERATES > LITERATE
LITERATI pl n literary people
LITERATIM adv letter for letter
LITERATO > LITERATI
LITERATOR n professional writer
LITERATUS > LITERATI
LITEROSE adj affectedly literary
LITERS > LITER
LITES > LITE
LITEST > LITE
LITH n limb or joint
LITHARGE n lead monoxide
LITHARGES > LITHARGE
LITHATE n salt of uric acid
LITHATES > LITHATE
LITHE adj flexible or supple, pliant ▷ vb listen
LITHED > LITHE
LITHELY > LITHE
LITHEMIA n gout
LITHEMIAS > LITHEMIA
LITHEMIC > LITHEMIA
LITHENESS > LITHE
LITHER > LITHE
LITHERLY adj crafty; cunning
LITHES > LITHE
LITHESOME less common word for > LISSOM
LITHEST > LITHE
LITHIA n lithium present in mineral waters as lithium salts
LITHIAS > LITHIA
LITHIASES > LITHIASIS
LITHIASIS n formation of a calculus
LITHIC adj of stone
LITHIFIED > LITHIFY
LITHIFIES > LITHIFY
LITHIFY vb turn into rock
LITHING > LITHE
LITHISTID n type of sponge
LITHITE n part of cell with sensory element
LITHITES > LITHITE
LITHIUM n chemical element, the lightest known metal
LITHIUMS > LITHIUM
LITHO n lithography ▷ vb print using lithography
LITHOCYST n sac containing otoliths
LITHOED > LITHO
LITHOES > LITHO

LITHOID adj resembling rock
LITHOIDAL same as > LITHOID
LITHOING > LITHO
LITHOLOGY n physical characteristics of a rock
LITHOPONE n white pigment consisting of a mixture of zinc sulphide, zinc oxide, and barium sulphate
LITHOPS n fleshy-leaved plant
LITHOS > LITHO
LITHOSOL n type of azonal soil consisting chiefly of unweathered or partly weathered rock fragments
LITHOSOLS > LITHOSOL
LITHOTOME n instrument used in lithotomy operation
LITHOTOMY n surgical removal of a calculus, esp one in the urinary bladder
LITHS > LITH
LITIGABLE adj that may be the subject of litigation
LITIGANT n person involved in a lawsuit ▷ adj engaged in litigation
LITIGANTS > LITIGANT
LITIGATE vb bring or contest a law suit
LITIGATED > LITIGATE
LITIGATES > LITIGATE
LITIGATOR > LITIGATE
LITIGIOUS adj frequently going to law
LITING > LITE
LITMUS n soluble powder obtained from lichens
LITMUSES > LITMUS
LITTORAL same as > LITTORAL
LITOTES n ironical understatement used for effect
LITOTIC > LITOTES
LITRE n unit of liquid measure
LITREAGE n volume in litres
LITREAGES > LITREAGE
LITRES > LITRE
LITS > LIT
LITTEN adj lighted
LITTER n untidy rubbish ▷ vb strew with litter
LITTERBAG n bag for putting rubbish in
LITTERBUG n person who tends to drop rubbish in public places
LITTERED > LITTER
LITTERER n one who litters
LITTERERS > LITTERER
LITTERING > LITTER
LITTERS > LITTER
LITTERY adj covered in litter

LITTLE adj small ▷ adv not a lot ▷ n small amount, extent, or duration
LITTLER > LITTLE
LITTLES > LITTLE
LITTLEST > LITTLE
LITTLIE n young child
LITTLIES > LITTLIE
LITTLIN same as > LITTLING
LITTLING n child
LITTLINGS > LITTLING
LITTLINS > LITTLIN
LITTLISH adj rather small
LITTORAL adj of or by the seashore ▷ n coastal district
LITTORALS > LITTORAL
LITU > LITAS
LITURGIC > LITURGY
LITURGICS n study of liturgies
LITURGIES > LITURGY
LITURGISM > LITURGIST
LITURGIST n student or composer of liturgical forms
LITURGY n prescribed form of public worship
LITUUS n curved trumpet
LITUUSES > LITUUS
LIVABLE adj tolerable or pleasant to live (with)
LIVE vb be alive ▷ adj living, alive ▷ adv in the form of a live performance
LIVEABLE same as > LIVABLE
LIVEBLOG vb blog about (an event) as it happens
LIVEBLOGS > LIVEBLOG
LIVED > LIVE
LIVEDO n reddish discoloured patch on the skin
LIVEDOS > LIVEDO
LIVELIER > LIVELY
LIVELIEST > LIVELY
LIVELILY > LIVELY
LIVELOD n livelihood
LIVELODS > LIVELOD
LIVELONG adj long or seemingly long
LIVELONGS > LIVELONG
LIVELOOD n livelihood
LIVELOODS > LIVELOOD
LIVELY adj full of life or vigour
LIVEN vb make or become lively
LIVENED > LIVEN
LIVENER > LIVEN
LIVENERS > LIVEN
LIVENESS n state of being alive
LIVENING > LIVEN
LIVENS > LIVEN
LIVER n person who lives in a specified way

LIVERED adj having liver
LIVERIED adj wearing livery
LIVERIES > LIVERY
LIVERING n process of liquid becoming lumpy
LIVERINGS > LIVERING
LIVERISH adj having a disorder of the liver
LIVERLEAF n woodland plant
LIVERLESS > LIVER
LIVERS > LIVER
LIVERWORT n plant resembling seaweed or leafy moss
LIVERY n distinctive dress ▷ adj of or resembling liver
LIVERYMAN n member of a livery company
LIVERYMEN > LIVERYMAN
LIVES > LIFE
LIVEST > LIVE
LIVESTOCK n farm animals
LIVETRAP n box constructed to trap an animal without injuring it
LIVETRAPS > LIVETRAP
LIVEWARE n programmers, systems analysts, operating staff, and other personnel working in a computer system
LIVEWARES > LIVEWARE
LIVEWELL n container of water on a fishing boat used to store live fish
LIVEWELLS > LIVEWELL
LIVEYER n (in Newfoundland) a full-time resident
LIVEYERE same as > LIVEYER
LIVEYERES > LIVEYERE
LIVEYERS > LIVEYER
LIVID adj angry or furious
LIVIDER > LIVID
LIVIDEST > LIVID
LIVIDITY n state of being livid
LIVIDLY > LIVID
LIVIDNESS > LIVID
LIVIER same as > LIVEYER
LIVIERS > LIVIER
LIVING adj possessing life, not dead or inanimate ▷ n condition of being alive
LIVINGLY > LIVING
LIVINGS > LIVING
LIVOR another word for > LIVIDITY
LIVORS > LIVOR
LIVRAISON n one of the numbers of a book published in parts
LIVRE n former French unit of money of account
LIVRES > LIVRE
LIVYER same as > LIVEYER

LIVYERS > LIVYER
LIXIVIA > LIXIVIUM
LIXIVIAL > LIXIVIATE
LIXIVIATE *less common word for* > LEACH
LIXIVIOUS > LIXIVIUM
LIXIVIUM *n* alkaline solution obtained by leaching wood ash with water
LIXIVIUMS > LIXIVIUM
LIZARD *n* four-footed reptile with a long body and tail
LIZARDS > LIZARD
LIZZIE *n* as in *tin lizzie* old or decrepit car
LIZZIES > LIZZIE
LLAMA *n* woolly animal of the camel family
LLAMAS > LLAMA
LLANERO *n* native of llanos
LLANEROS > LLANERO
LLANO *n* extensive grassy treeless plain
LLANOS > LLANO
LO *interj* look!
LOACH *n* carplike fish
LOACHES > LOACH
LOAD *n* burden or weight ▷ *vb* put a load on or into
LOADABLE *adj* able to be loaded
LOADED *adj* containing a hidden trap
LOADEN *vb* load
LOADENED > LOADEN
LOADENING > LOADEN
LOADENS > LOADEN
LOADER *n* person who loads a gun or other firearm
LOADERS > LOADER
LOADING *n* load or burden
LOADINGS > LOADING
LOADS *pl n* lots or a lot
LOADSPACE *n* area in a motor vehicle where a load can be carried
LOADSTAR *same as* > LODESTAR
LOADSTARS > LOADSTAR
LOADSTONE *same as* > LODESTONE
LOAF *n* shaped mass of baked bread ▷ *vb* idle, loiter
LOAFED > LOAF
LOAFER *n* idler
LOAFERISH > LOAFER
LOAFERS > LOAFER
LOAFING > LOAF
LOAFINGS > LOAF
LOAFS > LOAF
LOAM *n* fertile soil ▷ *vb* cover, treat, or fill with loam
LOAMED > LOAM
LOAMIER > LOAM
LOAMIEST > LOAM
LOAMINESS > LOAM
LOAMING > LOAM

LOAMLESS > LOAM
LOAMS > LOAM
LOAMY > LOAM
LOAN *n* money lent at interest ▷ *vb* lend
LOANABLE > LOAN
LOANBACK *n* facility by which an individual can borrow from his or her pension fund ▷ *vb* make use of this facility
LOANBACKS > LOANBACK
LOANED > LOAN
LOANEE *n* sportsperson who is loaned out
LOANEES > LOANEE
LOANER > LOAN
LOANERS > LOAN
LOANING > LOAN
LOANINGS > LOANING
LOANS > LOAN
LOANSHIFT *n* adaptation of word from one language by another
LOANWORD *n* word adopted from one language into another
LOANWORDS > LOANWORD
LOAST > LOOSE
LOATH *adj* unwilling or reluctant (to)
LOATHE *vb* hate
LOATHED > LOATHE
LOATHER > LOATHE
LOATHERS > LOATHE
LOATHES > LOATHE
LOATHEST > LOATH
LOATHFUL *adj* causing loathing
LOATHING *n* strong disgust
LOATHINGS > LOATHING
LOATHLY *adv* with reluctance
LOATHNESS > LOATH
LOATHSOME *adj* causing loathing
LOATHY *obsolete form of* > LOATHSOME
LOAVE *vb* form a loaf
LOAVED > LOAVE
LOAVES > LOAF
LOAVING > LOAVE
LOB *n* ball struck in a high arc ▷ *vb* strike in a high arc
LOBAR *adj* of or affecting a lobe
LOBATE *adj* with or like lobes
LOBATED *same as* > LOBATE
LOBATELY > LOBATE
LOBATION *n* division into lobes
LOBATIONS > LOBATION
LOBBED > LOB
LOBBER *n* one who lobs
LOBBERS > LOBBER
LOBBIED > LOBBY
LOBBIES > LOBBY
LOBBING > LOB
LOBBY *n* corridor into which rooms open ▷ *vb* try

to influence (legislators) in the formulation of policy
LOBBYER > LOBBY
LOBBYERS > LOBBY
LOBBYGOW *n* errand boy
LOBBYGOWS > LOBBYGOW
LOBBYING > LOBBY
LOBBYINGS > LOBBY
LOBBYISM > LOBBYIST
LOBBYISMS > LOBBYIST
LOBBYIST *n* person who lobbies on behalf of a particular interest
LOBBYISTS > LOBBYIST
LOBE *n* rounded projection
LOBECTOMY *n* surgical removal of a lobe from any organ or gland in the body
LOBED > LOBE
LOBEFIN *n* type of fish
LOBEFINS > LOBEFIN
LOBELESS *adj* having no lobes
LOBELET *n* small lobe
LOBELETS > LOBELET
LOBELIA *n* garden plant
LOBELIAS > LOBELIA
LOBELINE *n* crystalline alkaloid extracted from the seeds of the Indian tobacco plant
LOBELINES > LOBELINE
LOBES > LOBE
LOBI > LOBUS
LOBING *n* formation of lobes
LOBINGS > LOBING
LOBIPED *adj* with lobed toes
LOBLOLLY *n* southern US pine tree
LOBO *n* timber wolf
LOBOLA *n* (in African custom) price paid by a bridegroom's family to his bride's family
LOBOLAS > LOBOLA
LOBOLO *same as* > LOBOLA
LOBOLOS > LOBOLO
LOBOS > LOBO
LOBOSE *another word for* > LOBATE
LOBOTOMY *n* surgical incision into a lobe of the brain to treat mental disorders
LOBS > LOB
LOBSCOUSE *n* sailor's stew of meat, vegetables, and hardtack
LOBSTER *n* shellfish ▷ *vb* fish for lobsters
LOBSTERED > LOBSTER
LOBSTERER *n* person who catches lobsters
LOBSTERS > LOBSTER
LOBSTICK *n* tree used as landmark
LOBSTICKS > LOBSTICK
LOBTAIL *vb* (of a whale) hit a surface of water with the tail
LOBTAILED > LOBTAIL
LOBTAILS > LOBTAIL

LOBULAR > LOBULE
LOBULARLY > LOBULE
LOBULATE > LOBULE
LOBULATED > LOBULE
LOBULE *n* small lobe or a subdivision of a lobe
LOBULES > LOBULE
LOBULI > LOBULUS
LOBULOSE > LOBULE
LOBULUS *n* small lobe
LOBUS *n* lobe
LOBWORM *same as* > LUGWORM
LOBWORMS > LOBWORM
LOCA > LOCUS
LOCAL *adj* of a particular place ▷ *n* person from a particular place
LOCALE *n* scene of an event
LOCALES > LOCALE
LOCALISE *same as* > LOCALIZE
LOCALISED > LOCALISE
LOCALISER > LOCALISE
LOCALISES > LOCALISE
LOCALISM *n* pronunciation, phrase, etc, peculiar to a particular locality
LOCALISMS > LOCALISM
LOCALIST > LOCALISM
LOCALISTS > LOCALISM
LOCALITE *n* resident of an area
LOCALITES > LOCALITE
LOCALITY *n* neighbourhood or area
LOCALIZE *vb* restrict to a particular place
LOCALIZED > LOCALIZE
LOCALIZER > LOCALIZE
LOCALIZES > LOCALIZE
LOCALLY *adv* within a particular area or place
LOCALNESS > LOCAL
LOCALS > LOCAL
LOCATABLE > LOCATE
LOCATE *vb* discover the whereabouts of
LOCATED > LOCATE
LOCATER > LOCATE
LOCATERS > LOCATE
LOCATES > LOCATE
LOCATING > LOCATE
LOCATION *n* site or position
LOCATIONS > LOCATION
LOCATIVE *adj* (of a word or phrase) indicating place or direction ▷ *n* locative case
LOCATIVES > LOCATIVE
LOCATOR *n* part of index that shows where to find information
LOCATORS > LOCATOR
LOCAVORE *n* person who prefers locally produced food
LOCAVORES > LOCAVORE
LOCELLATE *adj* split into secondary cells

LOCH n lake
LOCHAN n small inland loch
LOCHANS > LOCHAN
LOCHE n freshwater fish of the cod family
LOCHES > LOCHE
LOCHIA n vaginal discharge following childbirth
LOCHIAL > LOCHIA
LOCHIAS > LOCHIA
LOCHS > LOCH
LOCI > LOCUS
LOCIE n type of logging engine
LOCIES > LOCIE
LOCIS > LOCUS
LOCK n appliance for fastening a door, case, etc ▷ vb fasten or become fastened securely
LOCKABLE > LOCK
LOCKAGE n system of locks in a canal
LOCKAGES > LOCKAGE
LOCKAWAY n investment intended to be held for a relatively long time
LOCKAWAYS > LOCKAWAY
LOCKBOX n system of collecting funds from companies by banks
LOCKBOXES > LOCKBOX
LOCKDOWN n device used to secure equipment, etc
LOCKDOWNS > LOCKDOWN
LOCKED > LOCK
LOCKER n small cupboard with a lock
LOCKERS > LOCKER
LOCKET n small hinged pendant for a portrait etc
LOCKETS > LOCKET
LOCKFAST adj securely fastened with a lock
LOCKFUL n sufficient to fill a canal lock
LOCKFULS > LOCKFUL
LOCKHOUSE n house of lock-keeper
LOCKING > LOCK
LOCKINGS > LOCK
LOCKJAW n tetanus
LOCKJAWS > LOCKJAW
LOCKLESS adj having no lock
LOCKMAKER n maker of locks
LOCKMAN n lock-keeper
LOCKMEN > LOCKMAN
LOCKNUT n nut screwed down on a primary nut to stop it from loosening
LOCKNUTS > LOCKNUT
LOCKOUT n closing of a workplace by an employer to force workers to accept terms
LOCKOUTS > LOCKOUT
LOCKPICK another word for > PICKLOCK
LOCKPICKS > LOCKPICK

LOCKRAM n type of linen cloth
LOCKRAMS > LOCKRAM
LOCKS > LOCK
LOCKSET n hardware used to lock door
LOCKSETS > LOCKSET
LOCKSMAN same as > LOCKMAN
LOCKSMEN > LOCKSMAN
LOCKSMITH n person who makes and mends locks
LOCKSTEP n method of marching in step as closely as possible
LOCKSTEPS > LOCKSTEP
LOCKUP n prison
LOCKUPS > LOCKUP
LOCO n locomotive ▷ adj insane ▷ vb poison with locoweed
LOCOED > LOCO
LOCOES > LOCO
LOCOFOCO n match
LOCOFOCOS > LOCOFOCO
LOCOING > LOCO
LOCOISM n disease of cattle, sheep, and horses caused by eating locoweed
LOCOISMS > LOCOISM
LOCOMAN n railwayman
LOCOMEN > LOCOMAN
LOCOMOTE vb move from one place to another
LOCOMOTED > LOCOMOTE
LOCOMOTES > LOCOMOTE
LOCOMOTOR adj of or relating to locomotion
LOCOPLANT another word for > LOCOWEED
LOCOS > LOCO
LOCOWEED n any of several perennial leguminous plants
LOCOWEEDS > LOCOWEED
LOCULAR adj divided into compartments by septa
LOCULATE same as > LOCULAR
LOCULATED same as > LOCULATE
LOCULE n any of the chambers of an ovary or anther
LOCULED adj having locules
LOCULES > LOCULE
LOCULI > LOCULUS
LOCULUS same as > LOCULE
LOCUM n temporary stand-in for a doctor or clergyman
LOCUMS > LOCUM
LOCUPLETE adj well-stored
LOCUS n area or place where something happens
LOCUST n destructive insect ▷ vb ravage, as locusts
LOCUSTA n flower cluster unit in grasses

LOCUSTAE > LOCUSTA
LOCUSTAL > LOCUSTA
LOCUSTED > LOCUST
LOCUSTING > LOCUST
LOCUSTS > LOCUST
LOCUTION n manner or style of speech
LOCUTIONS > LOCUTION
LOCUTORY adj room intended for conversation
LOD n type of logarithm
LODE n vein of ore
LODEN n thick waterproof, woollen cloth
LODENS > LODEN
LODES > LODE
LODESMAN n pilot
LODESMEN > LODESMAN
LODESTAR n star used in navigation and astronomy as a point of reference
LODESTARS > LODESTAR
LODESTONE n magnetic iron ore
LODGE n gatekeeper's house ▷ vb live in another's house at a fixed charge
LODGEABLE > LODGE
LODGED > LODGE
LODGEMENT same as > LODGMENT
LODGEPOLE n type of pine tree
LODGER n tenant
LODGERS > LODGER
LODGES > LODGE
LODGING n temporary residence
LODGINGS pl n rented room or rooms in which to live, esp in another person's house
LODGMENT n act of lodging or the state of being lodged
LODGMENTS > LODGMENT
LODICULA n delicate scale in grass
LODICULAE > LODICULA
LODICULE n any of two or three minute scales at the base of the ovary in grass flowers that represent the corolla
LODICULES > LODICULE
LODS > LOD
LOERIE same as > LOURIE
LOERIES > LOERIE
LOESS n fine-grained soil
LOESSAL > LOESS
LOESSES > LOESS
LOESSIAL > LOESS
LOESSIC adj relating to or consisting of loess
LOFT n space between the top storey and roof of a building ▷ vb strike, throw, or kick (a ball) high into the air
LOFTED > LOFT
LOFTER n type of golf club
LOFTERS > LOFTER
LOFTIER > LOFTY

LOFTIEST > LOFTY
LOFTILY > LOFTY
LOFTINESS > LOFTY
LOFTING > LOFT
LOFTLESS > LOFT
LOFTLIKE > LOFT
LOFTS > LOFT
LOFTSMAN n person who reproduces in actual size a draughtsman's design for a ship or an aircraft
LOFTSMEN > LOFTSMAN
LOFTY adj of great height
LOG n portion of a felled tree stripped of branches ▷ vb saw logs from a tree
LOGAN another name for > BOGAN
LOGANIA n type of Australian plant
LOGANIAS > LOGANIA
LOGANS > LOGAN
LOGAOEDIC adj of or relating to verse in which mixed metres are combined within a single line to give the effect of prose ▷ n line or verse of this kind
LOGARITHM n one of a series of arithmetical functions used to make certain calculations easier
LOGBOARD n board used for logging a ship's records
LOGBOARDS > LOGBOARD
LOGBOOK n book recording the details about a car or a ship's journeys
LOGBOOKS > LOGBOOK
LOGE n small enclosure or box in a theatre or opera house
LOGES > LOGE
LOGGAT n small piece of wood
LOGGATS > LOGGAT
LOGGED > LOG
LOGGER n tractor or crane for handling logs
LOGGERS > LOGGER
LOGGETS n old-fashioned game played with sticks
LOGGIA n covered gallery at the side of a building
LOGGIAS > LOGGIA
LOGGIE > LOGGIA
LOGGIER > LOGGY
LOGGIEST > LOGGY
LOGGING > LOG
LOGGINGS > LOG
LOGGISH > LOG
LOGGY adj sluggish
LOGIA > LOGION
LOGIC n philosophy of reasoning
LOGICAL adj of logic
LOGICALLY > LOGICAL
LOGICIAN n person who specializes in or is skilled at logic
LOGICIANS > LOGICIAN

LOGICISE same as
> LOGICIZE
LOGICISED > LOGICISE
LOGICISES > LOGICISE
LOGICISM n
philosophical theory that
all of mathematics can be
deduced from logic
LOGICISMS > LOGICISM
LOGICIST > LOGICISM
LOGICISTS > LOGICISM
LOGICIZE vb present
reasons for or against
LOGICIZED > LOGICIZE
LOGICIZES > LOGICIZE
LOGICLESS > LOGIC
LOGICS > LOGIC
LOGIE n fire-place of a kiln
LOGIER > LOGY
LOGIES > LOGIE
LOGIEST > LOGY
LOGILY > LOGY
LOGIN n process by which
a computer user logs on
LOGINESS > LOGY
LOGINS > LOGIN
LOGION n saying of Christ
regarded as authentic
LOGIONS > LOGION
LOGISTIC n
uninterpreted calculus or
system of symbolic logic
▷ adj (of a curve) having a
particular form of
equation
LOGISTICS n detailed
planning and organization
of a large, esp military,
operation
LOGJAM n blockage of logs
in a river ▷ vb cause a
logjam
LOGJAMMED > LOGJAM
LOGJAMS > LOGJAM
LOGJUICE n poor quality
port wine
LOGJUICES > LOGJUICE
LOGLINE n synopsis of
screenplay
LOGLINES > LOGLINE
LOGLOG n logarithm of a
logarithm (in equations,
etc)
LOGLOGS > LOGLOG
LOGNORMAL adj (maths)
having a natural logarithm
with normal distribution
LOGO same as > LOGOTYPE
LOGOED adj having a logo
LOGOFF n process by
which a computer user
logs out
LOGOFFS > LOGOFF
LOGOGRAM n single
symbol representing an
entire morpheme, word,
or phrase
LOGOGRAMS > LOGOGRAM
LOGOGRAPH same as
> LOGOGRAM
LOGOGRIPH n word
puzzle, esp one based on
recombination of the
letters of a word

LOGOI > LOGOS
LOGOMACH n one who
argues over words
LOGOMACHS > LOGOMACH
LOGOMACHY n argument
about words or the
meaning of words
LOGON variant of > LOGIN
LOGONS > LOGON
LOGOPEDIC adj of or
relating to speech therapy
LOGOPHILE n one who
loves words
LOGORRHEA n excessive
or uncontrollable
talkativeness
LOGOS n reason expressed
in words and things,
argument, or justification
LOGOTHETE n officer of
Byzantine empire
LOGOTYPE n piece of type
with several uncombined
characters cast on it
LOGOTYPES > LOGOTYPE
LOGOTYPY > LOGOTYPE
LOGOUT variant of
> LOGOFF
LOGOUTS > LOGOUT
LOGROLL vb use logrolling
in order to procure the
passage of (legislation)
LOGROLLED > LOGROLL
LOGROLLER > LOGROLL
LOGROLLS > LOGROLL
LOGS > LOG
LOGWAY another name for
> GANGWAY
LOGWAYS > LOGWAY
LOGWOOD n tree of the
Caribbean and Central
America
LOGWOODS > LOGWOOD
LOGY adj dull or listless
LOHAN another word for
> ARHAT
LOHANS > LOHAN
LOIASES > LOIASIS
LOIASIS n disease caused
by a tropical eye worm
LOIASISES > LOIASIS
LOID vb open (a lock) using
a celluloid strip
LOIDED > LOID
LOIDING > LOID
LOIDS > LOID
LOIN n part of the body
between the ribs and the
hips
LOINCLOTH n piece of
cloth covering the loins
only
LOINS pl n hips and the
inner surface of the legs
LOIPE n cross-country
skiing track
LOIPEN > LOIPE
LOIR n large dormouse
LOIRS > LOIR
LOITER vb stand or wait
aimlessly or idly
LOITERED > LOITER
LOITERER > LOITER
LOITERERS > LOITER

LOITERING > LOITER
LOITERS > LOITER
LOKE n track
LOKES > LOKE
LOKSHEN pl n noodles
LOLIGO n type of squid
LOLIGOS > LOLIGO
LOLIUM n type of grass
LOLIUMS > LOLIUM
LOLL vb lounge lazily
▷ n act or instance of lolling
LOLLED > LOLL
LOLLER > LOLL
LOLLERS > LOLL
LOLLIES > LOLLY
LOLLING > LOLL
LOLLINGLY > LOLL
LOLLIPOP n boiled sweet
on a small wooden stick
LOLLIPOPS > LOLLIPOP
LOLLOP vb move clumsily
LOLLOPED > LOLLOP
LOLLOPING > LOLLOP
LOLLOPS > LOLLOP
LOLLOPY > LOLLOP
LOLLS > LOLL
LOLLY n lollipop or ice lolly
LOLLYGAG same as
> LALLYGAG
LOLLYGAGS > LOLLYGAG
LOLLYPOP same as
> LOLLIPOP
LOLLYPOPS > LOLLYPOP
LOLOG same as > LOGLOG
LOLOGS > LOLOG
LOLZ same as > LULZ
LOMA n lobe
LOMAS > LOMA
LOMATA > LOMA
LOME vb cover with fertile
soil
LOMED > LOME
LOMEIN n Chinese dish
LOMEINS > LOMEIN
LOMENT n pod of certain
leguminous plants
LOMENTA > LOMENTUM
LOMENTS > LOMENT
LOMENTUM same as
> LOMENT
LOMENTUMS > LOMENTUM
LOMES > LOME
LOMING > LOME
LOMPISH another word for
> LUMPISH
LONE adj solitary
LONELIER > LONELY
LONELIEST > LONELY
LONELILY > LONELY
LONELY adj sad because
alone
LONENESS > LONE
LONER n solitary person
LONERS > LONER
LONESOME adj lonely ▷ n
own
LONESOMES > LONESOME
LONG adj having length
▷ adv for a certain time
▷ vb have a strong desire
(for)
LONGA n long note
LONGAEVAL adj long-lived

LONGAN n sapindaceous
tree of tropical and
subtropical Asia
LONGANS > LONGAN
LONGAS > LONGA
LONGBOARD n type of
surfboard
LONGBOAT n largest boat
carried on a ship
LONGBOATS > LONGBOAT
LONGBOW n large powerful
bow
LONGBOWS > LONGBOW
LONGCASE n as in longcase
clock grandfather clock
LONGCLOTH n fine
plain-weave cotton cloth
made in long strips
LONGE n rope used in
training a horse ▷ vb train
using a longe
LONGED > LONG
LONGEING > LONGE
LONGER n line of barrels on
a ship
LONGERON n main
longitudinal structural
member of an aircraft
LONGERONS > LONGERON
LONGERS > LONGER
LONGES > LONGE
LONGEST > LONG
LONGEVAL another word for
> LONGAEVAL
LONGEVITY n long life
LONGEVOUS
> LONGEVITY
LONGHAIR n cat with long
hair
LONGHAIRS > LONGHAIR
LONGHAND n ordinary
writing, not shorthand or
typing
LONGHANDS > LONGHAND
LONGHEAD n person with
long head
LONGHEADS > LONGHEAD
LONGHORN n British breed
of beef cattle with long
curved horns
LONGHORNS > LONGHORN
LONGHOUSE n long
communal dwelling of
Native American peoples
LONGICORN n type of
beetle with long antennae
LONGIES n long johns
LONGING n yearning
▷ adj having or showing
desire
LONGINGLY > LONGING
LONGINGS > LONGING
LONGISH adj rather long
LONGITUDE n distance
east or west from a
standard meridian
LONGJUMP n jumping
contest decided by length
LONGJUMPS > LONGJUMP
LONGLEAF n North
American pine tree
LONGLINE n (tennis)
straight stroke played
down court

LONGLINES > LONGLINE

LONGLIST *n* initial list from which a shortlist is selected ▷ *vb* include (eg a candidate) on a longlist

LONGLISTS > LONGLIST

LONGLY > LONG

LONGNECK *n* US, Canadian and Australian word for a 330-ml beer bottle with a long narrow neck

LONGNECKS > LONGNECK

LONGNESS > LONG

LONGS *pl n* full-length trousers

LONGSHIP *n* narrow open boat with oars and a square sail, used by the Vikings

LONGSHIPS > LONGSHIP

LONGSHORE *adj* situated on, relating to, or along the shore

LONGSOME *adj* slow; boring

LONGSPUR *n* any of various Arctic and North American buntings

LONGSPURS > LONGSPUR

LONGTIME *adj* of long standing

LONGUEUR *n* period of boredom or dullness

LONGUEURS > LONGUEUR

LONGWALL *n* long face in coal mine

LONGWALLS > LONGWALL

LONGWAYS *adv* lengthways

LONGWISE *same as* > LONGWAYS

LONGWORM *n* as in *sea longworm* kind of marine worm

LONGWORMS > LONGWORM

LONICERA *n* honeysuckle

LONICERAS > LONICERA

LOO *n* toilet ▷ *vb* Scots word meaning love

LOOBIER > LOOBY

LOOBIES > LOOBY

LOOBIEST > LOOBY

LOOBILY > LOOBY

LOOBY *adj* foolish ▷ *n* foolish or stupid person

LOOED > LOO

LOOEY *n* lieutenant

LOOEYS > LOOEY

LOOF *n* part of ship's side

LOOFA *same as* > LOOFAH

LOOFAH *n* sponge made from the dried pod of a gourd

LOOFAHS > LOOFAH

LOOFAS > LOOFA

LOOFFUL *n* handful

LOOFFULS > LOOFFUL

LOOFS > LOOF

LOOIE *same as* > LOOEY

LOOIES > LOOIE

LOOING > LOO

LOOK *vb* direct the eyes or attention (towards) ▷ *n* instance of looking

LOOKALIKE *n* person who is the double of another

LOOKDOWN *n* way paper appears when looked at under reflected light

LOOKDOWNS > LOOKDOWN

LOOKED > LOOK

LOOKER *n* person who looks

LOOKERS > LOOKER

LOOKIE *interj* look (over here)

LOOKING > LOOK

LOOKISM *n* discrimination because of appearance

LOOKISMS > LOOKISM

LOOKIST > LOOKISM

LOOKISTS > LOOKISM

LOOKIT *interj* look at this

LOOKOUT *n* act of watching for danger or for an opportunity ▷ *vb* be careful

LOOKOUTS > LOOKOUT

LOOKOVER *n* inspection, esp a brief one

LOOKOVERS > LOOKOVER

LOOKS > LOOK

LOOKSISM *same as* > LOOKISM

LOOKSISMS > LOOKSISM

LOOKUP *n* act of looking up information

LOOKUPS > LOOKUP

LOOKY *same as* > LOOKIE

LOOM *n* machine for weaving cloth ▷ *vb* appear dimly

LOOMED > LOOM

LOOMING > LOOM

LOOMS > LOOM

LOON *n* diving bird

LOONEY *same as* > LOONY

LOONEYS > LOONY

LOONIE *n* Canadian dollar coin

LOONIER > LOONY

LOONIES > LOONY

LOONIEST > LOONY

LOONILY > LOONY

LOONINESS > LOONY

LOONING *n* cry of the loon

LOONINGS > LOONING

LOONS > LOON

LOONY *adj* foolish or insane ▷ *n* foolish or insane person

LOOP *n* round shape made by a curved line ▷ *vb* form with a loop

LOOPED > LOOP

LOOPER *n* person or thing that loops or makes loops

LOOPERS > LOOPER

LOOPHOLE *n* means of evading a rule without breaking it ▷ *vb* provide with loopholes

LOOPHOLED > LOOPHOLE

LOOPHOLES > LOOPHOLE

LOOPIER > LOOPY

LOOPIEST > LOOPY

LOOPILY > LOOPY

LOOPINESS > LOOPY

LOOPING > LOOP

LOOPINGS > LOOP

LOOPS > LOOP

LOOPY *adj* slightly mad or crazy

LOOR > LIEF

LOORD *obsolete word for* > LOUT

LOORDS > LOORD

LOOS > LOO

LOOSE *adj* not tight, fastened, fixed, or tense ▷ *adv* in a loose manner ▷ *vb* free

LOOSEBOX *n* enclosed stall with a door in which an animal can be kept

LOOSED > LOOSE

LOOSELY > LOOSE

LOOSEN *vb* make loose

LOOSENED > LOOSEN

LOOSENER > LOOSEN

LOOSENERS > LOOSEN

LOOSENESS > LOOSE

LOOSENING *n* act of loosening

LOOSENS > LOOSEN

LOOSER > LOOSE

LOOSES > LOOSE

LOOSEST > LOOSE

LOOSIE *n* informal word for loose forward

LOOSIES *pl n* cigarettes sold individually

LOOSING *n* celebration of one's 21st birthday

LOOSINGS > LOOSING

LOOT *vb* pillage ▷ *n* goods stolen during pillaging

LOOTED > LOOT

LOOTEN *Scots past form of* > LET

LOOTER > LOOT

LOOTERS > LOOT

LOOTING > LOOT

LOOTINGS > LOOT

LOOTS > LOOT

LOOVES > LOOF

LOP *vb* cut away ▷ *n* part(s) lopped off

LOPE *vb* run with long easy strides ▷ *n* loping stride

LOPED > LOPE

LOPER > LOPE

LOPERS > LOPE

LOPES > LOPE

LOPGRASS *n* smooth-bladed grass

LOPHODONT *adj* (of teeth) having elongated ridges

LOPING > LOPE

LOPINGLY *adv* in a loping manner

LOPOLITH *n* saucer- or lens-shaped body of intrusive igneous rock

LOPOLITHS > LOPOLITH

LOPPED > LOP

LOPPER *n* tool for lopping ▷ *vb* curdle

LOPPERED > LOPPER

LOPPERING > LOPPER

LOPPERS > LOPPER

LOPPET *n* long-distance cross-country ski race

LOPPETS > LOPPET

LOPPIER > LOPPY

LOPPIES > LOPPY

LOPPIEST > LOPPY

LOPPING > LOP

LOPPINGS > LOP

LOPPY *adj* floppy ▷ *n* ranch hand

LOPS > LOP

LOPSIDED *adj* greater in height, weight, or size on one side

LOPSTICK *variant of* > LOBSTICK

LOPSTICKS > LOPSTICK

LOQUACITY *n* tendency to talk a great deal

LOQUAT *n* ornamental evergreen rosaceous tree

LOQUATS > LOQUAT

LOQUITUR *n* stage direction meaning *he* or *she speaks*

LOR *interj* exclamation of surprise or dismay

LORAL *adj* of part of side of bird's head

LORAN *n* radio navigation system operating over long distances

LORANS > LORAN

LORATE *adj* like a strap

LORAZEPAM *n* type of tranquillizer

LORCHA *n* junk-rigged vessel

LORCHAS > LORCHA

LORD *n* person with power over others ▷ *vb* act in a superior way

LORDED > LORD

LORDING *n* gentleman

LORDINGS > LORDING

LORDKIN *n* little lord

LORDKINS > LORDKIN

LORDLESS > LORD

LORDLIER > LORDLY

LORDLIEST > LORDLY

LORDLIKE > LORD

LORDLING *n* young lord

LORDLINGS > LORDLING

LORDLY *adj* imperious, proud ▷ *adv* in the manner of a lord

LORDOMA *same as* > LORDOSIS

LORDOMAS > LORDOMA

LORDOSES > LORDOSIS

LORDOSIS *n* forward curvature of the lumbar spine

LORDOTIC > LORDOSIS

LORDS > LORD

LORDSHIP *n* position or authority of a lord

LORDSHIPS > LORDSHIP

LORDY *interj* exclamation of surprise or dismay

LORE *n* body of traditions

LOREAL *adj* concerning or relating to lore

LOREL *another word for* > LOSEL

LORELS > LOREL

LORES > LORE

LORETTE *n* concubine

LORETTES > LORETTE

LORGNETTE *n* pair of spectacles mounted on a long handle

LORGNON *n* monocle or pair of spectacles

LORGNONS > LORGNON

LORIC > LORICA

LORICA *n* hard outer covering of rotifers, ciliate protozoans, and similar organisms

LORICAE > LORICA

LORICAS > LORICA

LORICATE > LORICA

LORICATED > LORICA

LORICATES > LORICA

LORICS > LORICA

LORIES > LORY

LORIKEET *n* small brightly coloured Australian parrot

LORIKEETS > LORIKEET

LORIMER *n* (formerly) a person who made bits and spurs

LORIMERS > LORIMER

LORINER *same as* > LORIMER

LORINERS > LORINER

LORING *n* teaching

LORINGS > LORING

LORIOT *n* golden oriole (bird)

LORIOTS > LORIOT

LORIS *n* any of several prosimian primates

LORISES > LORIS

LORN *adj* forsaken or wretched

LORNNESS > LORN

LORRELL *obsolete word for* > LOSEL

LORRELLS > LORRELL

LORRIES > LORRY

LORRY *n* large vehicle for transporting loads by road

LORY *n* small parrot of Australia and Indonesia

LOS *n* approval

LOSABLE > LOOSE

LOSE *vb* part with

LOSED > LOSE

LOSEL *n* worthless person ▷ *adj* worthless

LOSELS > LOSEL

LOSEN > LOOSE

LOSER *n* person or thing that loses

LOSERS > LOSER

LOSES > LOOSE

LOSH *interj* lord

LOSING *adj* unprofitable; failing

LOSINGEST > LOSING

LOSINGLY > LOSE

LOSINGS *pl n* losses

LOSLYF *n* South African slang for a promiscuous female

LOSLYFS > LOSLYF

LOSS *n* losing

LOSSES > LOSS

LOSSIER > LOSSY

LOSSIEST > LOSSY

LOSSLESS > LOSS

LOSSMAKER *n* organization, industry, or enterprise that consistently fails to make a profit

LOSSY *adj* designed to have a high attenuation

LOST *adj* missing

LOSTNESS > LOST

LOT *pron* great number ▷ *n* collection of people or things ▷ *vb* draw lots for

LOTA *n* globular water container

LOTAH *same as* > LOTA

LOTAHS > LOTAH

LOTAS > LOTA

LOTE *another word for* > LOTUS

LOTES > LOTE

LOTH *same as* > LOATH

LOTHARIO *n* rake, libertine, or seducer

LOTHARIOS > LOTHARIO

LOTHEFULL *obsolete form of* > LOATHFUL

LOTHER > LOTH

LOTHEST > LOTH

LOTHFULL *obsolete form of* > LOATHFUL

LOTHNESS > LOTH

LOTHSOME *same as* > LOATHSOME

LOTI *n* monetary unit of Lesotho

LOTIC *adj* of communities living in rapidly flowing water

LOTION *n* medical or cosmetic liquid for use on the skin

LOTIONS > LOTION

LOTO *same as* > LOTTO

LOTOS *same as* > LOTUS

LOTOSES > LOTOS

LOTS > LOT

LOTSA *determiner* lots of

LOTTA *n* lot of

LOTTE *n* type of fish

LOTTED > LOT

LOTTER *n* someone who works at an allotment

LOTTERIES > LOTTERY

LOTTERS > LOTTER

LOTTERY *n* method of raising money by selling tickets that win prizes by chance

LOTTES > LOTTE

LOTTING > LOT

LOTTO *n* game of chance

LOTTOS > LOTTO

LOTUS *n* legendary plant whose fruit induces forgetfulness

LOTUSES > LOTUS

LOTUSLAND *n* idyllic place of contentment

LOU *Scot word for* > LOVE

LOUCHE *adj* shifty

LOUCHELY > LOUCHE

LOUCHER > LOUCHE

LOUCHEST > LOUCHE

LOUD *adj* noisy

LOUDEN *vb* make louder

LOUDENED > LOUDEN

LOUDENING > LOUDEN

LOUDENS > LOUDEN

LOUDER > LOUD

LOUDEST > LOUD

LOUDISH *adj* fairly loud

LOUDLIER > LOUD

LOUDLIEST > LOUD

LOUDLY > LOUD

LOUDMOUTH *n* person who talks too much, esp in a boastful or indiscreet way

LOUDNESS > LOUD

LOUED > LOU

LOUGH *n* loch

LOUGHS > LOUGH

LOUIE *same as* > LOOEY

LOUIES > LOUIE

LOUING > LOU

LOUIS *n* former French gold coin

LOUMA *n* market in developing countries

LOUMAS > LOUMA

LOUN *same as* > LOWN

LOUND *same as* > LOUN

LOUNDED > LOUND

LOUNDER *vb* beat severely

LOUNDERED > LOUNDER

LOUNDERS > LOUNDER

LOUNDING > LOUND

LOUNDS > LOUND

LOUNED > LOUN

LOUNGE *n* living room in a private house ▷ *vb* sit, lie, or stand in a relaxed manner

LOUNGED > LOUNGE

LOUNGER *n* comfortable sometimes adjustable couch or extending chair designed for someone to relax on

LOUNGERS > LOUNGER

LOUNGES > LOUNGE

LOUNGEY *n* suggestive of a lounge bar or easy-listening music

LOUNGIER > LOUNGEY

LOUNGIEST > LOUNGEY

LOUNGING > LOUNGE

LOUNGINGS > LOUNGE

LOUNGY *adj* casual; relaxed

LOUNING > LOUN

LOUNS > LOUN

LOUP *Scot word for* > LEAP

LOUPE *n* magnifying glass used by jewellers, horologists, etc

LOUPED > LOUP

LOUPEN > LOUP

LOUPES > LOUPE

LOUPING > LOUP

LOUPIT > LOUP

LOUPS > LOUP

LOUR *vb* be overcast ▷ *n* menacing scowl

LOURE *n* slow, former French dance

LOURED > LOUR

LOURES > LOURE

LOURIE *n* type of African bird

LOURIER > LOURY

LOURIES > LOURIE

LOURIEST > LOURY

LOURING > LOUR

LOURINGLY > LOUR

LOURINGS > LOUR

LOURS > LOUR

LOURY *adj* sombre

LOUS > LOU

LOUSE *n* wingless parasitic insect ▷ *vb* ruin or spoil

LOUSED > LOUSE

LOUSER *n* mean nasty person

LOUSERS > LOUSER

LOUSES > LOUSE

LOUSEWORT *n* any of various N temperate scrophulariaceous plants

LOUSIER > LOUSY

LOUSIEST > LOUSY

LOUSILY > LOUSY

LOUSINESS > LOUSY

LOUSING *n* act or instance of removing lice

LOUSINGS > LOUSING

LOUSY *adj* mean or unpleasant

LOUT *n* crude person ▷ *vb* bow or stoop

LOUTED > LOUT

LOUTERIES > LOUTERY

LOUTERY *n* crude or boorish behaviour

LOUTING > LOUT

LOUTISH *adj* of a lout

LOUTISHLY > LOUTISH

LOUTS > LOUT

LOUVAR *n* large silvery whalelike scombroid fish

LOUVARS > LOUVAR

LOUVER *same as* > LOUVRE

LOUVERED *same as* > LOUVRED

LOUVERS > LOUVER

LOUVRE *n* one of a set of parallel slats slanted to admit air but not rain

LOUVRED *adj* having louvres

LOUVRES > LOUVRE

LOVABLE *adj* attracting or deserving affection

LOVABLY > LOVABLE

LOVAGE *n* European plant used for flavouring food**

LOVAGES > LOVAGE
LOVAT n yellowish-or bluish-green mixture in tweeds
LOVATS > LOVAT
LOVE vb have a great affection for ▷ n great affection
LOVEABLE same as > LOVABLE
LOVEABLY > LOVABLE
LOVEBIRD n small parrot
LOVEBIRDS > LOVEBIRD
LOVEBITE n temporary red mark left on a person's skin by someone biting or sucking it
LOVEBITES > LOVEBITE
LOVEBUG n small US flying insect
LOVEBUGS > LOVEBUG
LOVED > LOVE
LOVEFEST n event when people talk about loving one another
LOVEFESTS > LOVEFEST
LOVELESS adj without love
LOVELIER > LOVELY
LOVELIES > LOVELY
LOVELIEST > LOVELY
LOVELIGHT n brightness of eyes of one in love
LOVELILY > LOVELY
LOVELOCK n long lock of hair worn on the forehead
LOVELOCKS > LOVELOCK
LOVELORN adj miserable because of unhappiness in love
LOVELY adj very attractive ▷ n attractive woman
LOVEMAKER n one involved in lovemaking
LOVER n person having a sexual relationship outside marriage
LOVERED adj having a lover
LOVERLESS > LOVER
LOVERLY adj loverlike
LOVERS > LOVER
LOVES > LOVE
LOVESEAT n armchair for two people
LOVESEATS > LOVESEAT
LOVESICK adj pining or languishing because of love
LOVESOME adj full of love
LOVEVINE n leafless parasitic vine
LOVEVINES > LOVEVINE
LOVEY adj loving; affectionate
LOVEYS > LOVEY
LOVIE n beloved person
LOVIER > LOVEY
LOVIES > LOVIE
LOVIEST > LOVEY
LOVING adj affectionate, tender
LOVINGLY > LOVING
LOVINGS > LOVING

LOW adj not high ▷ adv in a low position ▷ n low position ▷ vb moo
LOWAN n type of Australian bird
LOWANS > LOWAN
LOWBALL vb deliberately under-charge
LOWBALLED > LOWBALL
LOWBALLS > LOWBALL
LOWBORN adj of ignoble or common parentage
LOWBOY n table fitted with drawers
LOWBOYS > LOWBOY
LOWBRED same as > LOWBORN
LOWBROW adj with nonintellectual tastes and interests ▷ n person with nonintellectual tastes
LOWBROWED > LOWBROW
LOWBROWS > LOWBROW
LOWBUSH n type of blueberry bush
LOWBUSHES > LOWBUSH
LOWDOWN n inside info
LOWDOWNS > LOWDOWN
LOWE variant of > LOW
LOWED > LOW
LOWER adj below one or more other things ▷ vb cause or allow to move down
LOWERABLE > LOWER
LOWERCASE n small letters ▷ adj non-capitalized
LOWERED > LOWER
LOWERIER > LOWERY
LOWERIEST > LOWERY
LOWERING > LOWER
LOWERINGS > LOWER
LOWERMOST adj lowest
LOWERS > LOWER
LOWERY adj sombre
LOWES > LOWE
LOWEST > LOW
LOWING > LOW
LOWINGS > LOW
LOWISH > LOW
LOWLAND n low-lying country ▷ adj of a lowland or lowlands
LOWLANDER > LOWLAND
LOWLANDS > LOWLAND
LOWLIER > LOWLY
LOWLIEST > LOWLY
LOWLIFE n member or members of the underworld
LOWLIFER > LOWLIFE
LOWLIFERS > LOWLIFE
LOWLIFES > LOWLIFE
LOWLIGHT n unenjoyable or unpleasant part of an event
LOWLIGHTS > LOWLIGHT
LOWLIHEAD n state of being humble
LOWLILY > LOWLY
LOWLINESS > LOWLY
LOWLIVES > LOWLIFE

LOWLY adj modest, humble ▷ adv in a low or lowly manner
LOWN vb calm
LOWND same as > LOWN
LOWNDED > LOWND
LOWNDING > LOWND
LOWNDS > LOWND
LOWNE same as > LOON
LOWNED > LOWN
LOWNES > LOWNE
LOWNESS > LOW
LOWNESSES > LOW
LOWNING > LOWN
LOWNS > LOWN
LOWP same as > LOUP
LOWPASS adj (of a filter) transmitting frequencies below a certain value
LOWPED > LOWP
LOWPING > LOWP
LOWPS > LOWP
LOWRIDER n car with body close to ground
LOWRIDERS > LOWRIDER
LOWRIE another name for > LORY
LOWRIES > LOWRY
LOWRY another name for > LORY
LOWS > LOW
LOWSE vb release or loose ▷ adj loose
LOWSED > LOWSE
LOWSENING same as > LOOSING
LOWSER > LOWSE
LOWSES > LOWSE
LOWSEST > LOWSE
LOWSING > LOWSE
LOWSIT > LOWSE
LOWT same as > LOUT
LOWTED > LOWT
LOWTING > LOWT
LOWTS > LOWT
LOWVELD n low ground in S Africa
LOWVELDS > LOWVELD
LOX vb load fuel tanks of spacecraft with liquid oxygen ▷ n kind of smoked salmon
LOXED > LOX
LOXES > LOX
LOXING > LOX
LOXODROME n line on globe crossing all meridians at same angle
LOXODROMY n technique of navigating using rhumb lines
LOXYGEN n liquid oxygen
LOXYGENS > LOXYGEN
LOY n narrow spade with a single footrest
LOYAL adj faithful
LOYALER > LOYAL
LOYALEST > LOYAL
LOYALISM > LOYALIST
LOYALISMS > LOYALIST
LOYALIST n patriotic supporter of the sovereign or government

LOYALISTS > LOYALIST
LOYALLER > LOYAL
LOYALLEST > LOYAL
LOYALLY > LOYAL
LOYALNESS > LOYAL
LOYALTIES > LOYALTY
LOYALTY n quality of being loyal
LOYS > LOY
LOZELL obsolete form of > LOSEL
LOZELLS > LOZELL
LOZEN n window pane
LOZENGE n medicated tablet
LOZENGED adj decorated with lozenges
LOZENGES > LOZENGE
LOZENGY adj divided by diagonal lines to form a lattice
LOZENS > LOZEN
LUACH n Jewish calendar
LUAU n feast of Hawaiian food
LUAUS > LUAU
LUBBARD same as > LUBBER
LUBBARDS > LUBBARD
LUBBER n big, awkward, or stupid person
LUBBERLY > LUBBER
LUBBERS > LUBBER
LUBE n lubricating oil ▷ vb lubricate with oil
LUBED > LUBE
LUBES > LUBE
LUBFISH n type of fish
LUBFISHES > LUBFISH
LUBING > LUBE
LUBRA n Aboriginal woman
LUBRAS > LUBRA
LUBRIC adj slippery
LUBRICAL same as > LUBRIC
LUBRICANT n lubricating substance, such as oil ▷ adj serving to lubricate
LUBRICATE vb oil or grease to lessen friction
LUBRICITY n lewdness or salaciousness
LUBRICOUS adj lewd or lascivious
LUCARNE n type of dormer window
LUCARNES > LUCARNE
LUCE another name for > PIKE
LUCENCE > LUCENT
LUCENCES > LUCENT
LUCENCIES > LUCENT
LUCENCY > LUCENT
LUCENT adj brilliant
LUCENTLY > LUCENT
LUCERN same as > LUCERNE
LUCERNE n alfalfa
LUCERNES > LUCERNE
LUCERNS > LUCERN
LUCES > LUCE
LUCHOT > LUACH

LUCHOTH > LUACH
LUCID adj clear
LUCIDER > LUCID
LUCIDEST > LUCID
LUCIDITY > LUCID
LUCIDLY > LUCID
LUCIDNESS > LUCID
LUCIFER n friction match
LUCIFERIN n substance occurring in bioluminescent organisms, such as glow-worms and fireflies
LUCIFERS > LUCIFER
LUCIGEN n type of lamp
LUCIGENS > LUCIGEN
LUCITE n type of transparent acrylic-based plastic
LUCITES > LUCITE
LUCK n fortune, good or bad ▷ vb have good fortune
LUCKED > LUCK
LUCKEN adj shut
LUCKIE same as > LUCKY
LUCKIER > LUCKY
LUCKIES > LUCKIE
LUCKIEST > LUCKY
LUCKILY > LUCKY
LUCKINESS > LUCKY
LUCKING > LUCK
LUCKLESS adj having bad luck
LUCKPENNY n coin kept for luck
LUCKS > LUCK
LUCKY adj having or bringing good luck ▷ n old woman
LUCRATIVE adj very profitable
LUCRE n money or wealth
LUCRES > LUCRE
LUCTATION n effort; struggle
LUCUBRATE vb write or study, esp at night
LUCULENT adj easily understood
LUCUMA n S American tree
LUCUMAS > LUCUMA
LUCUMO n Etruscan king
LUCUMONES > LUCUMO
LUCUMOS > LUCUMO
LUD n lord ▷ interj exclamation of dismay or surprise
LUDE n slang word for drug for relieving anxiety
LUDERICK n Australian fish, usu black or dark brown in colour
LUDERICKS > LUDERICK
LUDES > LUDE
LUDIC adj playful
LUDICALLY > LUDIC
LUDICROUS adj absurd or ridiculous
LUDO n game played with dice and counters on a board
LUDOS > LUDO

LUDS > LUD
LUDSHIP > LUD
LUDSHIPS > LUD
LUES n any venereal disease
LUETIC > LUES
LUETICS > LUES
LUFF vb sail (a ship) towards the wind ▷ n leading edge of a fore-and-aft sail
LUFFA same as > LOOFAH
LUFFAS > LUFFA
LUFFED > LUFF
LUFFING > LUFF
LUFFS > LUFF
LUG vb carry with great effort ▷ n projection serving as a handle
LUGE n racing toboggan ▷ vb ride on a luge
LUGED > LUGE
LUGEING > LUGE
LUGEINGS > LUGE
LUGER n pistol
LUGERS > LUGER
LUGES > LUGE
LUGGABLE n unwieldy portable computer
LUGGABLES > LUGGABLE
LUGGAGE n suitcases, bags, etc
LUGGAGES > LUGGAGE
LUGGED > LUG
LUGGER n small working boat with an oblong sail
LUGGERS > LUGGER
LUGGIE n wooden bowl
LUGGIES > LUGGIE
LUGGING > LUG
LUGHOLE informal word for > EAR
LUGHOLES > LUGHOLE
LUGING > LUGE
LUGINGS > LUGE
LUGS > LUG
LUGSAIL n four-sided sail
LUGSAILS > LUGSAIL
LUGWORM n large worm used as bait
LUGWORMS > LUGWORM
LUIT Scots past form of > LET
LUITEN > LET
LUKE variant of > LUKEWARM
LUKEWARM adj moderately warm, tepid
LULIBUB obsolete form of > LOLLIPOP
LULIBUBS > LULIBUB
LULL vb soothe (someone) by soft sounds or motions ▷ n brief time of quiet in a storm etc
LULLABIED > LULLABY
LULLABIES > LULLABY
LULLABY n quiet song ▷ vb quiet with a lullaby
LULLED > LULL
LULLER > LULL
LULLERS > LULL
LULLING > LULL

LULLS > LULL
LULU n person or thing deemed to be outstanding
LULUS > LULU
LULZ pl n laughs at someone else's or one's own expense
LUM n chimney
LUMA n monetary unit of Armenia
LUMAS > LUMA
LUMBAGO n pain in the lower back
LUMBAGOS > LUMBAGO
LUMBANG n type of tree
LUMBANGS > LUMBANG
LUMBAR adj of the part of the body between the lowest ribs and the hipbones ▷ n old-fashioned kind of ship
LUMBARS > LUMBAR
LUMBER n unwanted disused household articles ▷ vb burden with something unpleasant
LUMBERED > LUMBER
LUMBERER > LUMBER
LUMBERERS > LUMBER
LUMBERING n business or trade of cutting, transporting, preparing, or selling timber ▷ adj awkward in movement
LUMBERLY adj heavy; clumsy
LUMBERMAN n person whose work involves felling trees
LUMBERMEN > LUMBERMAN
LUMBERS > LUMBER
LUMBI > LUMBUS
LUMBRICAL adj relating to any of the four wormlike muscles in the hand or foot
LUMBRICI > LUMBRICUS
LUMBRICUS n type of worm
LUMBUS n part of the lower back and sides between the pelvis and the ribs
LUMEN n derived SI unit of luminous flux
LUMENAL > LUMEN
LUMENS > LUMEN
LUMINA > LUMEN
LUMINAIRE n light fixture
LUMINAL > LUMEN
LUMINANCE n state or quality of radiating or reflecting light
LUMINANT n something used to give light
LUMINANTS > LUMINANT
LUMINARIA n type of candle
LUMINARY n famous person ▷ adj of, involving, or characterized by light or enlightenment

LUMINE vb illuminate
LUMINED > LUMINE
LUMINES > LUMINE
LUMINESCE vb exhibit luminescence
LUMINING > LUMINE
LUMINISM n US artistic movement
LUMINISMS > LUMINISM
LUMINIST > LUMINISM
LUMINISTS > LUMINISM
LUMINOUS adj reflecting or giving off light
LUMME interj exclamation of surprise or dismay
LUMMIER > LUMMY
LUMMIEST > LUMMY
LUMMOX n clumsy person
LUMMOXES > LUMMOX
LUMMY interj exclamation of surprise ▷ adj excellent
LUMP n shapeless mass ▷ vb consider as one group
LUMPED > LUMP
LUMPEN adj stupid or unthinking ▷ n member of underclass
LUMPENLY > LUMPEN
LUMPENS > LUMPEN
LUMPER n stevedore
LUMPERS > LUMPER
LUMPFISH n North Atlantic scorpaenoid fish
LUMPIA n type of Indonesian spring roll
LUMPIAS > LUMPIA
LUMPIER > LUMPY
LUMPIEST > LUMPY
LUMPILY > LUMPY
LUMPINESS > LUMPY
LUMPING > LUMP
LUMPINGLY > LUMP
LUMPISH adj stupid or clumsy
LUMPISHLY > LUMPISH
LUMPKIN n lout
LUMPKINS > LUMPKIN
LUMPS > LUMP
LUMPY adj full of lumps
LUMS > LUM
LUN n sheltered spot
LUNA n large American moth
LUNACIES > LUNACY
LUNACY n foolishness
LUNANAUT same as > LUNARNAUT
LUNANAUTS > LUNANAUT
LUNAR adj relating to the moon ▷ n lunar distance
LUNARIAN n inhabitant of the moon
LUNARIANS > LUNARIAN
LUNARIES > LUNARY
LUNARIST n one believing the moon influences weather
LUNARISTS > LUNARIST
LUNARNAUT n astronaut who travels to moon
LUNARS > LUNAR
LUNARY n moonwort herb
LUNAS > LUNA

LUNATE adj shaped like a crescent ▷ n crescent-shaped bone forming part of the wrist

LUNATED variant of > LUNATE

LUNATELY > LUNATE

LUNATES > LUNATE

LUNATIC adj foolish ▷ n foolish person

LUNATICAL variant of > LUNATIC

LUNATICS > LUNATIC

LUNATION See > MONTH

LUNATIONS > LUNATION

LUNCH n meal at midday ▷ vb eat lunch

LUNCHBOX n container for carrying a packed lunch

LUNCHED > LUNCH

LUNCHEON n formal lunch

LUNCHEONS > LUNCHEON

LUNCHER > LUNCH

LUNCHERS > LUNCH

LUNCHES > LUNCH

LUNCHING > LUNCH

LUNCHMEAT n mixture of meat and cereal

LUNCHPAIL n container for carrying a packed lunch

LUNCHROOM n room where lunch is served or people may eat lunches they bring

LUNCHTIME n time at which lunch is usually eaten

LUNE same as > LUNETTE

LUNES > LUNE

LUNET n small moon or satellite

LUNETS > LUNET

LUNETTE n anything that is shaped like a crescent

LUNETTES > LUNETTE

LUNG n organ that allows an animal or bird to breathe air

LUNGAN same as > LONGAN

LUNGANS > LUNGAN

LUNGE n sudden forward motion ▷ vb move with or make a lunge

LUNGED > LUNGE

LUNGEE same as > LUNGI

LUNGEES > LUNGEE

LUNGEING > LUNGE

LUNGER > LUNGE

LUNGERS > LUNGE

LUNGES > LUNGE

LUNGFISH n freshwater bony fish with an air-breathing lung

LUNGFUL > LUNG

LUNGFULS > LUNG

LUNGI n cotton cloth worn as a loincloth, sash, or turban

LUNGIE n guillemot

LUNGIES > LUNGIE

LUNGING > LUNGE

LUNGIS > LUNGI

LUNGLESS adj having no lungs

LUNGS > LUNG

LUNGWORM n type of parasitic worm occurring in the lungs of mammals

LUNGWORMS > LUNGWORM

LUNGWORT n Eurasian plant with spotted leaves and clusters of blue or purple flowers, formerly used to treat lung diseases

LUNGWORTS > LUNGWORT

LUNGYI same as > LUNGI

LUNGYIS > LUNGYI

LUNIER > LUNY

LUNIES > LUNY

LUNIEST > LUNY

LUNINESS > LUNY

LUNISOLAR adj resulting from or based on the combined gravitational attraction of the sun and moon

LUNITIDAL adj of or relating to tidal phenomena as produced by the moon

LUNK n awkward person

LUNKER n very large fish

LUNKERS > LUNKER

LUNKHEAD n stupid person

LUNKHEADS > LUNKHEAD

LUNKS > LUNK

LUNS > LUN

LUNT vb produce smoke

LUNTED > LUNT

LUNTING > LUNT

LUNTS > LUNT

LUNULA n white area at base of the fingernail

LUNULAE > LUNULA

LUNULAR same as > LUNULATE

LUNULATE adj having markings shaped like crescents

LUNULATED same as > LUNULATE

LUNULE same as > LUNULA

LUNULES > LUNULE

LUNY same as > LOONY

LUNYIE same as > LUNGIE

LUNYIES > LUNYIE

LUPANAR n brothel

LUPANARS > LUPANAR

LUPIN n garden plant

LUPINE adj like a wolf ▷ n lupin

LUPINES > LUPINE

LUPINS > LUPIN

LUPOID adj suffering from lupus

LUPOUS adj relating to lupus

LUPPEN Scots past form of > LEAP

LUPULIN n resinous powder extracted from the female flowers of the hop plant

LUPULINE adj relating to lupulin

LUPULINIC same as > LUPULINE

LUPULINS > LUPULIN

LUPUS n ulcerous skin disease

LUPUSES > LUPUS

LUR n large bronze musical horn

LURCH vb tilt suddenly ▷ n lurching movement

LURCHED > LURCH

LURCHER n crossbred dog trained to hunt silently

LURCHERS > LURCHER

LURCHES > LURCH

LURCHING > LURCH

LURDAN n stupid or dull person ▷ adj dull or stupid

LURDANE same as > LURDAN

LURDANES > LURDANE

LURDANS > LURDAN

LURDEN same as > LURDAN

LURDENS > LURDEN

LURE vb tempt by promise of reward ▷ n person that lures

LURED > LURE

LURER > LURE

LURERS > LURE

LURES > LURE

LUREX n thin glittery thread

LUREXES > LUREX

LURGI same as > LURGY

LURGIES > LURGY

LURGIS > LURGI

LURGY n any undetermined illness

LURID adj sensational

LURIDER > LURID

LURIDEST > LURID

LURIDLY > LURID

LURIDNESS > LURID

LURING > LURE

LURINGLY > LURE

LURINGS > LURING

LURK vb lie hidden

LURKED > LURK

LURKER > LURK

LURKERS > LURK

LURKING adj lingering

LURKINGLY > LURKING

LURKINGS > LURKING

LURKS > LURK

LURRIES > LURRY

LURRY n confused jumble

LURS > LUR

LURVE n love

LURVES > LURVE

LUSCIOUS adj extremely pleasurable to taste or smell

LUSER n humorous term for computer user

LUSERS > LUSER

LUSH adj growing thickly ▷ n alcoholic ▷ vb drink to excess

LUSHED > LUSH

LUSHER adj more lush ▷ n drunkard

LUSHERS > LUSHER

LUSHES > LUSH

LUSHEST > LUSH

LUSHIER > LUSHY

LUSHIES > LUSHY

LUSHIEST > LUSHY

LUSHING > LUSH

LUSHLY > LUSH

LUSHNESS > LUSH

LUSHY adj slightly intoxicated ▷ n drunkard

LUSK vb lounge around

LUSKED > LUSK

LUSKING > LUSK

LUSKISH adj lazy

LUSKS > LUSK

LUST n strong sexual desire ▷ vb have passionate desire (for)

LUSTED > LUST

LUSTER same as > LUSTRE

LUSTERED > LUSTER

LUSTERING > LUSTER

LUSTERS > LUSTER

LUSTFUL adj driven by lust

LUSTFULLY > LUSTFUL

LUSTICK obsolete word for > LUSTY

LUSTIER > LUSTY

LUSTIEST > LUSTY

LUSTIHEAD n vigour

LUSTIHOOD n vigour

LUSTILY > LUSTY

LUSTINESS > LUSTY

LUSTING > LUST

LUSTIQUE obsolete word for > LUSTY

LUSTLESS > LUST

LUSTRA > LUSTRUM

LUSTRAL adj of or relating to a ceremony of purification

LUSTRATE vb purify by means of religious rituals or ceremonies

LUSTRATED > LUSTRATE

LUSTRATES > LUSTRATE

LUSTRE n gloss, sheen ▷ vb make, be, or become lustrous

LUSTRED > LUSTRE

LUSTRES > LUSTRE

LUSTRINE same as > LUSTRING

LUSTRINES > LUSTRINE

LUSTRING n glossy silk cloth, formerly used for clothing, upholstery, etc

LUSTRINGS > LUSTRING

LUSTROUS > LUSTRE

LUSTRUM n period of five years

LUSTRUMS > LUSTRUM

LUSTS > LUST

LUSTY adj vigorous, healthy

LUSUS n freak, mutant

LUSUSES > LUSUS

LUTANIST same as > LUTENIST

LUTANISTS > LUTANIST

LUTE n musical instrument ▷ vb seal with cement and clay

LUTEA adj yellow

LUTEAL adj relating to the development of the corpus luteum

LUTECIUM same as > LUTETIUM

LUTECIUMS > LUTECIUM

LUTED > LUTE

LUTEFISK n Scandinavian fish dish

LUTEFISKS > LUTEFISK

LUTEIN n xanthophyll pigment

LUTEINISE same as > LUTEINIZE

LUTEINIZE vb develop into part of corpus luteum

LUTEINS > LUTEIN

LUTENIST n person who plays the lute

LUTENISTS > LUTENIST

LUTEOLIN n yellow crystalline compound found in many plants

LUTEOLINS > LUTEOLIN

LUTEOLOUS > LUTEOLIN

LUTEOUS adj of a greenish-yellow colour

LUTER n lute player

LUTERS > LUTER

LUTES > LUTE

LUTESCENT adj yellowish in colour

LUTETIUM n silvery-white metallic element

LUTETIUMS > LUTETIUM

LUTEUM adj yellow

LUTFISK same as > LUTEFISK

LUTFISKS > LUTFISK

LUTHERN another name for > DORMER

LUTHERNS > LUTHERN

LUTHIER n lute-maker

LUTHIERS > LUTHIER

LUTING n cement and clay

LUTINGS > LUTING

LUTIST same as > LUTENIST

LUTISTS > LUTIST

LUTITE another name for > PELITE

LUTITES > LUTITE

LUTTEN > LOOT

LUTZ n skating jump

LUTZES > LUTZ

LUV n love ▷ vb love

LUVS > LOVE

LUVVED > LUV

LUVVIE n person who is involved in acting or the theatre

LUVVIEDOM n theatrical world

LUVVIES > LUVVY

LUVVING > LUV

LUVVY same as > LUVVIE

LUX n unit of illumination ▷ vb clean with a vacuum cleaner

LUXATE vb put (a shoulder, knee, etc) out of joint

LUXATED > LUXATE

LUXATES > LUXATE

LUXATING > LUXATE

LUXATION > LUXATE

LUXATIONS > LUXATE

LUXE n as in de luxe luxuriousness ▷ adj luxury

LUXED > LUX

LUXER > LUXE

LUXES > LUXE

LUXEST > LUXE

LUXING > LUX

LUXMETER n device for measuring light

LUXMETERS > LUXMETER

LUXURIANT adj rich and abundant

LUXURIATE vb take self-indulgent pleasure (in)

LUXURIES > LUXURY

LUXURIOUS adj full of luxury, sumptuous

LUXURIST n lover of luxury

LUXURISTS > LUXURIST

LUXURY n enjoyment of rich, very comfortable living ▷ adj of or providing luxury

LUZ n supposedly indestructible bone of the human body

LUZERN n alfalfa

LUZERNS > LUZERN

LUZZES > LUZ

LWEI n Angolan monetary unit

LWEIS > LWEI

LYAM n leash

LYAMS > LYAM

LYARD same as > LIARD

LYART same as > LIARD

LYASE n any enzyme that catalyses the separation of two parts of a molecule

LYASES > LYASE

LYCAENID n type of butterfly

LYCAENIDS > LYCAENID

LYCEA > LYCEUM

LYCEE n secondary school

LYCEES > LYCEE

LYCEUM n public building for concerts

LYCEUMS > LYCEUM

LYCH same as > LICH

LYCHEE same as > LITCHI

LYCHEES > LYCHEE

LYCHES > LYCH

LYCHGATE same as > LICHGATE

LYCHGATES > LYCHGATE

LYCHNIS n plant with red, pink, or white flowers

LYCHNISES > LYCHNIS

LYCOPENE n red pigment

LYCOPENES > LYCOPENE

LYCOPOD n type of moss

LYCOPODS > LYCOPOD

LYCOPSID n type of club moss

LYCOPSIDS > LYCOPSID

LYCRA n type of elastic fabric used for tight-fitting garments

LYCRAS > LYCRA

LYDDITE n explosive consisting chiefly of fused picric acid

LYDDITES > LYDDITE

LYE n caustic solution

LYES > LYE

LYFULL obsolete form of > LIFEFUL

LYING > LIE

LYINGLY > LIE

LYINGS > LIE

LYKEWAKE n watch held over a dead person, often with festivities

LYKEWAKES > LYKEWAKE

LYKEWALK variant of > LYKEWAKE

LYKEWALKS > LYKEWALK

LYM obsolete form of > LYAM

LYME n as in lyme grass type of perennial dune grass

LYMES > LYME

LYMITER same as > LIMITER

LYMITERS > LIMITER

LYMPH n colourless bodily fluid

LYMPHAD n ancient rowing boat

LYMPHADS > LYMPHAD

LYMPHATIC adj of, relating to, or containing lymph ▷ n lymphatic vessel

LYMPHOID adj of or resembling lymph, or relating to the lymphatic system

LYMPHOMA n any form of cancer of the lymph nodes

LYMPHOMAS > LYMPHOMA

LYMPHOUS adj resembling lymph

LYMPHS n lymph

LYMS > LYM

LYNAGE obsolete form of > LINEAGE

LYNAGES > LYNAGE

LYNCEAN adj of a lynx

LYNCH vb put to death without a trial

LYNCHED > LYNCH

LYNCHER > LYNCH

LYNCHERS > LYNCH

LYNCHES > LYNCH

LYNCHET n ridge formed by ploughing a hillside

LYNCHETS > LYNCHET

LYNCHING > LYNCH

LYNCHINGS > LYNCH

LYNCHPIN same as > LINCHPIN

LYNCHPINS > LYNCHPIN

LYNE n flax

LYNES > LYNE

LYNX n animal of the cat family

LYNXES > LYNX

LYNXLIKE > LYNX

LYOLYSES > LYOLYSIS

LYOLYSIS n formation of an acid and a base from the interaction of a salt with a solvent

LYOMEROUS adj relating to Lyomeri fish

LYONNAISE adj (of food) cooked or garnished with onions, usually fried

LYOPHIL same as > LYOPHILIC

LYOPHILE same as > LYOPHILIC

LYOPHILED adj lyophilized

LYOPHILIC adj (of a colloid) having a dispersed phase with a high affinity for the continuous phase

LYOPHOBE same as > LYOPHOBIC

LYOPHOBIC adj (of a colloid) having a dispersed phase with little or no affinity for the continuous phase

LYRA n as in lyra viol lutelike musical instrument

LYRATE adj shaped like a lyre

LYRATED same as > LYRATE

LYRATELY > LYRATE

LYRE n ancient musical instrument

LYREBIRD n Australian bird, the male of which spreads its tail into the shape of a lyre

LYREBIRDS > LYREBIRD

LYRES > LYRE

LYRIC adj expressing emotion in songlike style ▷ n short poem in a songlike style

LYRICAL same as > LYRIC

LYRICALLY > LYRIC

LYRICISE same as > LYRICIZE

LYRICISED > LYRICISE

LYRICISES > LYRICISE

LYRICISM n quality or style of lyric poetry

LYRICISMS > LYRICISM

LYRICIST n person who writes the words of songs or musicals

LYRICISTS > LYRICIST

LYRICIZE vb write lyrics

LYRICIZED > LYRICIZE

LYRICIZES > LYRICIZE

LYRICON n wind synthesizer

LYRICONS > LYRICON

LYRICS > LYRIC

LYRIFORM adj lyre-shaped

LYRISM n art or technique of playing the lyre

LYRISMS > LYRISM

LYRIST same as > LYRICIST

LYRISTS > LYRIST

LYSATE n material formed by lysis

LYSATES > LYSATE

LYSE vb undergo lysis

LYSED > LYSE

LYSERGIC adj as in lysergic acid crystalline compound used in medical research

LYSERGIDE n LSD

LYSES > LYSIS

LYSIGENIC adj caused by breaking down of cells

LYSIMETER n instrument for determining solubility, esp the amount of water-soluble matter in soil

LYSIN n antibodies that dissolute cells against which they are directed

LYSINE n essential amino acid that occurs in proteins

LYSINES > LYSINE

LYSING > LYSE

LYSINS > LYSIN

LYSIS n destruction of cells by a lysin

LYSOGEN n lysis-inducing agent

LYSOGENIC > LYSOGEN

LYSOGENS > LYSOGEN

LYSOGENY > LYSOGEN

LYSOL n antiseptic solution

LYSOLS > LYSOL

LYSOSOMAL > LYSOSOME

LYSOSOME n any of numerous small particles that are present in the cytoplasm of most cells

LYSOSOMES > LYSOSOME

LYSOZYME n enzyme occurring in tears, certain body tissues, and egg white

LYSOZYMES > LYSOZYME

LYSSA less common word for > RABIES

LYSSAS > LYSSA

LYTE vb dismount

LYTED > LYTE

LYTES > LYTE

LYTHE n type of fish

LYTHES > LYTHE

LYTHRUM n genus of plants including loosestrife

LYTHRUMS > LYTHRUM

LYTIC adj relating to, causing, or resulting from lysis

LYTICALLY > LYTIC

LYTING > LYTE

LYTTA n mass of cartilage under the tongue in carnivores

LYTTAE > LYTTA

LYTTAS > LYTTA

Mm

MA *n* mother
MAA *vb* (of goats) bleat
MAAED > MAA
MAAING > MAA
MAAR *n* coneless volcanic crater
MAARE > MAAR
MAARS > MAAR
MAAS *n* thick soured milk
MAASES > MAAS
MAATJES *n* pickled herring
MABE *n* type of pearl
MABELA *n* ground kaffir corn
MABELAS > MABELAS
MABES > MABE
MAC *n* macintosh
MACABER *same as* > MACABRE
MACABRE *adj* strange and horrible, gruesome
MACABRELY > MACABRE
MACACO *n* type of lemur
MACACOS > MACACO
MACADAM *n* road surface
MACADAMED *adj* (of a road) paved with macadam
MACADAMIA *n* Australian tree with edible nuts
MACADAMS > MACADAM
MACAHUBA *n* South American palm tree
MACAHUBAS > MACAHUBA
MACALLUM *n* ice cream with raspberry sauce
MACALLUMS > MACALLUM
MACAQUE *n* monkey of Asia and Africa
MACAQUES > MACAQUE
MACARISE *vb* congratulate
MACARISED > MACARISE
MACARISES > MACARISE
MACARISM *n* blessing
MACARISMS > MACARISM
MACARIZE *same as* > MACARISE
MACARIZED > MACARIZE
MACARIZES > MACARIZE
MACARONI *n* pasta in short tube shapes
MACARONIC *adj* (of verse) characterized by a mixture of vernacular words jumbled together with Latin words or Latinized words or with words from one or more other foreign languages ▷ *n* macaronic verse

MACARONIS > MACARONI
MACAROON *n* small biscuit or cake made with ground almonds
MACAROONS > MACAROON
MACASSAR *n* oily preparation formerly put on the hair to make it smooth and shiny
MACASSARS > MACASSAR
MACAW *n* large tropical American parrot
MACAWS > MACAW
MACCABAW *same as* > MACCABOY
MACCABAWS > MACCABAW
MACCABOY *n* dark rose-scented snuff
MACCABOYS > MACCABOY
MACCARONI *same as* > MACARONI
MACCHIA *n* thicket in Italy
MACCHIATO *n* espresso coffee served with a dash of hot or cold milk
MACCHIE > MACCHIA
MACCOBOY *same as* > MACCABOY
MACCOBOYS > MACCOBOY
MACE *n* club ▷ *vb* use a mace
MACED > MACE
MACEDOINE *n* hot or cold mixture of diced vegetables
MACER *n* macebearer, esp (in Scotland) an official who acts as usher in a court of law
MACERAL *n* any of the organic units that constitute coal
MACERALS > MACERAL
MACERATE *vb* soften by soaking
MACERATED > MACERATE
MACERATER > MACERATE
MACERATES > MACERATE
MACERATOR > MACERATE
MACERS > MACER
MACES > MACE
MACH *n* ratio of the speed of a body in a particular medium to the speed of sound in that medium
MACHACA *n* Mexican dish of shredded dried beef
MACHACAS > MACHACA
MACHAIR *n* (in the western Highlands of

Scotland) a strip of sandy, grassy, land
MACHAIRS > MACHAIR
MACHAN *n* (in India) a raised platform used in tiger hunting
MACHANS > MACHAN
MACHE *n* papier-mâché
MACHER *n* important or influential person
MACHERS > MACHER
MACHES > MACHE
MACHETE *n* broad heavy knife used for cutting or as a weapon
MACHETES > MACHETE
MACHI *n* as in *machi chips* in Indian English, fish and chips
MACHINATE *vb* contrive, plan, or devise (schemes, plots, etc)
MACHINE *n* apparatus designed to perform a task ▷ *vb* make or produce by machine
MACHINED > MACHINE
MACHINERY *n* machines or machine parts collectively
MACHINES > MACHINE
MACHINIMA *n* use of real-time 3-D graphics to generate computer animation
MACHINING > MACHINE
MACHINIST *n* person who operates a machine
MACHISMO *n* exaggerated or strong masculinity
MACHISMOS > MACHISMO
MACHMETER *n* instrument for measuring the Mach number of an aircraft in flight
MACHO *adj* strongly masculine ▷ *n* strong masculinity
MACHOISM > MACHO
MACHOISMS > MACHO
MACHOS > MACHO
MACHREE *n* Irish form of address meaning my dear
MACHREES > MACHREE
MACHS > MACH
MACHZOR *n* Jewish prayer book
MACHZORIM > MACHZOR
MACHZORS > MACHZOR
MACING > MACE

MACINTOSH *n* waterproof raincoat
MACK *same as* > MAC
MACKEREL *n* edible sea fish
MACKERELS > MACKEREL
MACKINAW *n* thick short double-breasted plaid coat
MACKINAWS > MACKINAW
MACKLE *n* blurred impression ▷ *vb* mend hurriedly or in a makeshift way
MACKLED > MACKLE
MACKLES > MACKLE
MACKLING > MACKLE
MACKS > MACK
MACLE *n* crystal consisting of two parts
MACLED > MACLE
MACLES > MACLE
MACON *n* wine from the Mâcon area
MACONS > MACON
MACOYA *n* South American tree
MACOYAS > MACOYA
MACRAME *n* ornamental work of knotted cord
MACRAMES > MACRAME
MACRAMI *same as* > MACRAME
MACRAMIS > MACRAMI
MACRO *n* close-up lens
MACROBIAN *adj* long-lived
MACROCODE *n* computer instruction that triggers many other instructions
MACROCOPY *n* enlargement of printed material for easier reading
MACROCOSM *n* universe
MACROCYST *n* unusually large cyst
MACROCYTE *n* abnormally large red blood cell
MACRODOME *n* dome shape in crystal structure
MACRODONT *adj* having large teeth
MACROGLIA *n* one of the two types of non-nervous tissue (glia) found in the central nervous system: includes astrocytes
MACROLIDE *n* type of antibiotic drug
MACROLOGY *n* verbose but meaningless talk

MACROMERE *n* any of the large yolk-filled cells formed by unequal cleavage of a fertilized ovum

MACROMOLE *n* large chemistry mole

MACRON *n* mark placed over a letter to represent a long vowel

MACRONS > MACRON

MACROPOD *n* member of kangaroo family

MACROPODS > MACROPOD

MACROPSIA *n* condition of seeing everything in the field of view as larger than it really is, which can occur in diseases of the retina or in some brain disorders

MACROS > MACRO

MACROTOUS *adj* having large ears

MACRURAL *adj* long-tailed

MACRURAN *n* type of decapod crustacean of the group which includes the lobsters, prawns, and crayfish

MACRURANS > MACRURAN

MACRUROID *adj* long-tailed

MACRUROUS *adj* long-tailed

MACS > MAC

MACTATION *n* sacrificial killing

MACULA *n* small spot like a freckle

MACULAE > MACULA

MACULAR > MACULA

MACULAS > MACULA

MACULATE *vb* spot, stain, or pollute ▷ *adj* spotted or polluted

MACULATED > MACULATE

MACULATES > MACULATE

MACULE *same as* > MACKLE

MACULED > MACULE

MACULES > MACULE

MACULING > MACULE

MACULOSE *adj* having spots

MACUMBA *n* religious cult in Brazil

MACUMBAS > MACUMBA

MAD *adj* mentally deranged, insane ▷ *vb* make mad

MADAFU *n* coconut milk

MADAFUS > MADAFU

MADAM *n* polite term of address for a woman ▷ *vb* call someone madam

MADAME *n* French title equivalent to *Mrs*

MADAMED > MADAM

MADAMES > MADAME

MADAMING > MADAM

MADAMS > MADAM

MADAROSES > MADAROSIS

MADAROSIS *n* abnormal loss of eyebrows or eyelashes

MADBRAIN *adj* insane ▷ *n* rash or insane person

MADBRAINS > MADBRAIN

MADCAP *adj* foolish or reckless ▷ *n* impulsive or reckless person

MADCAPS > MADCAP

MADDED > MAD

MADDEN *vb* infuriate or irritate

MADDENED > MADDEN

MADDENING *adj* serving to send mad

MADDENS > MADDEN

MADDER *n* type of rose

MADDERS > MADAM

MADDEST > MAD

MADDING > MAD

MADDINGLY > MAD

MADDISH > MAD

MADDOCK *same as* > MATTOCK

MADDOCKS > MADDOCK

MADE > MAKE

MADEFIED > MADEFY

MADEFIES > MADEFY

MADEFY *vb* make moist

MADEFYING > MADEFY

MADEIRA *n* a kind of rich sponge cake

MADEIRAS > MADEIRA

MADELEINE *n* small fancy sponge cake

MADERISE *vb* become reddish

MADERISED > MADERISE

MADERISES > MADERISE

MADERIZE *same as* > MADERISE

MADERIZED > MADERIZE

MADERIZES > MADERIZE

MADEUPPY *adj* artificial or contrived in an obvious way

MADGE *n* type of hammer

MADGES > MADGE

MADHOUSE *n* place filled with uproar or confusion

MADHOUSES > MADHOUSE

MADID *adj* wet

MADISON *n* type of cycle relay race

MADISONS > MADISON

MADLING *n* insane person

MADLINGS > MADLING

MADLY *adv* with great speed and energy

MADMAN *n* person who is insane

MADMEN > MADMAN

MADNESS *n* insanity

MADNESSES > MADNESS

MADONNA *n* picture or statue of the Virgin Mary

MADONNAS > MADONNA

MADOQUA *n* Ethiopian antelope

MADOQUAS > MADOQUA

MADRAS *n* medium-hot curry

MADRASA *same as* > MADRASAH

MADRASAH *n* educational institution, particularly for Islamic religious instruction

MADRASAHS > MADRASAH

MADRASAS > MADRASA

MADRASES > MADRAS

MADRASSA *same as* > MADRASAH

MADRASSAH *same as* > MADRASAH

MADRASSAS > MADRASSA

MADRE *Spanish word for* > MOTHER

MADREPORE *n* type of coral which often occurs in tropical seas and forms large coral reefs

MADRES > MADRE

MADRIGAL *n* 16th–17th-century part song for unaccompanied voices

MADRIGALS > MADRIGAL

MADRILENE *n* cold consommé flavoured with tomato juice

MADRONA *n* N American evergreen tree or shrub

MADRONAS > MADRONA

MADRONE *same as* > MADRONA

MADRONES > MADRONE

MADRONO *same as* > MADRONA

MADRONOS > MADRONO

MADS > MAD

MADTOM *n* species of catfish

MADTOMS > MADTOM

MADURO *adj* (of cigars) dark and strong ▷ *n* cigar of this type

MADUROS > MADURO

MADWOMAN *n* woman who is insane, esp one who behaves violently

MADWOMEN > MADWOMAN

MADWORT *n* low-growing Eurasian plant with small blue flowers

MADWORTS > MADWORT

MADZOON *same as* > MATZOON

MADZOONS > MADZOON

MAE *adj* more

MAELID *n* mythical spirit of apple

MAELIDS > MAELID

MAELSTROM *n* great whirlpool

MAENAD *n* female disciple of Dionysus, the Greek god of wine

MAENADES > MAENAD

MAENADIC > MAENAD

MAENADISM > MAENAD

MAENADS > MAENAD

MAERL *n* type of red coralline algae

MAERLS > MAERL

MAES > MAE

MAESTOSO *adv* be performed majestically ▷ *n* piece or passage

directed to be played in this way

MAESTOSOS > MAESTOSO

MAESTRI > MAESTRO

MAESTRO *n* outstanding musician or conductor

MAESTROS > MAESTRO

MAFFIA *same as* > MAFIA

MAFFIAS > MAFFIA

MAFFICK *vb* celebrate extravagantly and publicly

MAFFICKED > MAFFICK

MAFFICKER > MAFFICK

MAFFICKS > MAFFICK

MAFFLED *adj* baffled

MAFFLIN *n* half-witted person

MAFFLING *same as* > MAFFLIN

MAFFLINGS > MAFFLING

MAFFLINS > MAFFLIN

MAFIA *n* international secret organization founded in Sicily

MAFIAS > MAFIA

MAFIC *n* minerals present in igneous rock

MAFICS > MAFIC

MAFIOSI > MAFIOSO

MAFIOSO *n* member of the Mafia

MAFIOSOS > MAFIOSO

MAFTED *adj* suffering under oppressive heat

MAFTIR *n* final section of the weekly Torah reading

MAFTIRS > MAFTIR

MAG *vb* talk ▷ *n* talk

MAGAININ *n* any of a series of related substances with antibacterial properties, derived from the skins of frogs

MAGAININS > MAGAININ

MAGALOG *same as* > MAGALOGUE

MAGALOGS > MAGALOG

MAGALOGUE *n* combination of a magazine and a catalogue

MAGAZINE *n* periodical publication with articles by different writers

MAGAZINES > MAGAZINE

MAGDALEN *n* reformed prostitute

MAGDALENE *same as* > MAGDALEN

MAGDALENS > MAGDALEN

MAGE *archaic word for* > MAGICIAN

MAGENTA *adj* deep purplish-red ▷ *n* deep purplish red

MAGENTAS > MAGENTA

MAGES > MAGE

MAGESHIP > MAGE

MAGESHIPS > MAGE

MAGG *same as* > MAG

MAGGED > MAG

MAGGIE *n* magpie

MAGGIES > MAGGIE

MAGGING > MAG

MAGGOT n larva of an insect
MAGGOTIER > MAGGOTY
MAGGOTS > MAGGOT
MAGGOTY adj relating to, resembling, or ridden with maggots
MAGGS > MAGG
MAGI > MAGUS
MAGIAN > MAGUS
MAGIANISM > MAGUS
MAGIANS > MAGUS
MAGIC n supposed art of invoking supernatural powers to influence events ▷ vb transform or produce by or as if by magic ▷ adj of, using, or like magic
MAGICAL > MAGIC
MAGICALLY > MAGIC
MAGICIAN n conjuror
MAGICIANS > MAGICIAN
MAGICKED > MAGIC
MAGICKING > MAGIC
MAGICS > MAGIC
MAGILP same as > MEGILP
MAGILPS > MAGILP
MAGISM > MAGUS
MAGISMS > MAGUS
MAGISTER n person entitled to teach in medieval university
MAGISTERS > MAGISTER
MAGISTERY n agency or substance, such as the philosopher's stone, believed to transmute other substances
MAGISTRAL adj of, relating to, or characteristic of a master ▷ n fortification in a determining position
MAGLEV n type of high-speed train
MAGLEVS > MAGLEV
MAGMA n molten rock inside the earth's crust
MAGMAS > MAGMA
MAGMATA > MAGMA
MAGMATIC > MAGMA
MAGMATISM > MAGMA
MAGNALIUM n alloy of magnesium and aluminium
MAGNATE n influential or wealthy person, esp in industry
MAGNATES > MAGNATE
MAGNES n magnetic iron ore
MAGNESES > MAGNES
MAGNESIA n white tasteless substance used as an antacid and a laxative
MAGNESIAL > MAGNESIA
MAGNESIAN > MAGNESIA
MAGNESIAS > MAGNESIA
MAGNESIC > MAGNESIA
MAGNESITE n white, colourless, or lightly tinted mineral

MAGNESIUM n silvery-white metallic element
MAGNET n piece of iron or steel capable of attracting iron and pointing north when suspended
MAGNETAR n type of neutron star that has a very intense magnetic field, over 1000 times greater than that of a pulsar
MAGNETARS > MAGNETAR
MAGNETIC adj having the properties of a magnet
MAGNETICS n branch of physics concerned with magnetism
MAGNETISE same as > MAGNETIZE
MAGNETISM n magnetic property
MAGNETIST > MAGNETISM
MAGNETITE n black magnetizable mineral that is an important source of iron
MAGNETIZE vb make into a magnet
MAGNETO n apparatus for ignition in an internal-combustion engine
MAGNETON n unit of magnetic moment
MAGNETONS > MAGNETON
MAGNETOS > MAGNETO
MAGNETRON n electronic valve used with a magnetic field to generate microwave oscillations, used esp in radar
MAGNETS > MAGNET
MAGNIFIC adj magnificent, grandiose, or pompous
MAGNIFICO n magnate
MAGNIFIED > MAGNIFY
MAGNIFIER > MAGNIFY
MAGNIFIES > MAGNIFY
MAGNIFY vb increase in apparent size, as with a lens
MAGNITUDE n relative importance or size
MAGNOLIA n shrub or tree with showy white or pink flowers
MAGNOLIAS > MAGNOLIA
MAGNON n short for Cro-Magnon
MAGNONS > MAGNON
MAGNOX n alloy used in fuel elements of some nuclear reactors
MAGNOXES > MAGNOX
MAGNUM n large wine bottle holding about 1.5 litres
MAGNUMS > MAGNUM
MAGNUS adj as in magnus hitch knot similar to a clove hitch but having one more turn

MAGOT n Chinese or Japanese figurine in a crouching position, usually grotesque
MAGOTS > MAGOT
MAGPIE n black-and-white bird
MAGPIES > MAGPIE
MAGS > MAG
MAGSMAN n raconteur
MAGSMEN > MAGSMAN
MAGUEY n tropical American agave plant
MAGUEYS > MAGUEY
MAGUS n Zoroastrian priest of the ancient Medes and Persians
MAGYAR adj of or relating to a style of sleeve
MAHA n as in maha yoga form of yoga
MAHANT n chief priest in a Hindu temple
MAHANTS > MAHANT
MAHARAJA same as > MAHARAJAH
MAHARAJAH n former title of some Indian princes
MAHARAJAS > MAHARAJA
MAHARANEE same as > MAHARANI
MAHARANI n wife of a maharaja
MAHARANIS > MAHARANI
MAHARISHI n Hindu religious teacher or mystic
MAHATMA n person revered for holiness and wisdom
MAHATMAS > MAHATMA
MAHEWU n (in South Africa) fermented liquid mealie-meal porridge
MAHEWUS > MAHEWU
MAHIMAHI n Pacific fish
MAHIMAHIS > MAHIMAHI
MAHJONG n game of Chinese origin, using tiles
MAHJONGG same as > MAHJONG
MAHJONGGS > MAHJONGG
MAHJONGS > MAHJONG
MAHLSTICK same as > MAULSTICK
MAHMAL n litter used in Muslim ceremony
MAHMALS > MAHMAL
MAHOE n New Zealand tree
MAHOES > MAHOE
MAHOGANY n hard reddish-brown wood of several tropical trees ▷ adj reddish-brown
MAHONIA n Asian and American evergreen shrub
MAHONIAS > MAHONIA
MAHOUT n (in India and the East Indies) elephant driver or keeper
MAHOUTS > MAHOUT
MAHSEER n large freshwater Indian fish
MAHSEERS > MAHSEER
MAHSIR same as > MAHSEER

MAHSIRS > MAHSIR
MAHUA n Indian tree
MAHUANG n herbal medicine from shrub
MAHUANGS > MAHUANG
MAHUAS > MAHUA
MAHWA same as > MAHUA
MAHWAS > MAHWA
MAHZOR same as > MACHZOR
MAHZORIM > MAHZOR
MAHZORS > MAHZOR
MAIASAUR same as > MAIASAURA
MAIASAURA n species of dinosaur
MAIASAURS > MAIASAURA
MAID n female servant ▷ vb work as maid
MAIDAN n (in Pakistan, India, etc) open area
MAIDANS > MAIDAN
MAIDED > MAID
MAIDEN n young unmarried woman ▷ adj unmarried
MAIDENISH > MAIDEN
MAIDENLY adj modest
MAIDENS > MAIDEN
MAIDHOOD > MAID
MAIDHOODS > MAID
MAIDING > MAID
MAIDISH > MAID
MAIDISM n pellagra
MAIDISMS > MAIDISM
MAIDLESS > MAID
MAIDS > MAID
MAIEUTIC adj of or relating to the Socratic method of eliciting knowledge by a series of questions and answers
MAIEUTICS n Socratic method
MAIGRE adj not containing meat ▷ n species of fish
MAIGRES > MAIGRE
MAIHEM same as > MAYHEM
MAIHEMS > MAIHEM
MAIK n old halfpenny
MAIKO n apprentice geisha
MAIKOS > MAIKO
MAIKS > MAIK
MAIL n letters and packages transported and delivered by the post office ▷ vb send by mail
MAILABLE > MAIL
MAILBAG n large bag for transporting or delivering mail
MAILBAGS > MAILBAG
MAILBOAT n boat that carries mail
MAILBOATS > MAILBOAT
MAILBOX n box into which letters and parcels are delivered
MAILBOXES > MAILBOX
MAILCAR same as > MAILCOACH
MAILCARS > MAILCAR

MAILCOACH n railway coach specially constructed for the transportation of mail

MAILE n halfpenny

MAILED > MAIL

MAILER n person who addresses or mails letters, etc

MAILERS > MAILER

MAILES > MAILE

MAILGRAM n telegram

MAILGRAMS > MAILGRAM

MAILING > MAIL

MAILINGS > MAILING

MAILL n Scots word meaning rent

MAILLESS > MAIL

MAILLOT n tights worn for ballet, gymnastics, etc

MAILLOTS > MAILLOT

MAILLS > MAILL

MAILMAN n postman

MAILMEN > MAILMAN

MAILMERGE n computer program for sending mass mailings

MAILPOUCH same as > MAILBAG

MAILROOM n room where mail to and from building is dealt with

MAILROOMS > MAILROOM

MAILS > MAIL

MAILSACK same as > MAILBAG

MAILSACKS > MAILSACK

MAILSHOT n posting of advertising material to many selected people at once

MAILSHOTS > MAILSHOT

MAILVAN n vehicle used to transport post

MAILVANS > MAILVAN

MAIM vb cripple or mutilate ▷ n injury or defect

MAIMED > MAIM

MAIMER > MAIM

MAIMERS > MAIM

MAIMING > MAIM

MAIMINGS > MAIM

MAIMS > MAIM

MAIN adj chief or principal ▷ n principal pipe or line carrying water, gas, or electricity ▷ vb lower sails

MAINBOOM n spar for mainsail

MAINBOOMS > MAINBOOM

MAINBRACE n brace attached to the mainyard

MAINDOOR n door from street into house

MAINDOORS > MAINDOOR

MAINED > MAIN

MAINER > MAIN

MAINEST > MAIN

MAINFRAME adj denoting a high-speed general-purpose computer ▷ n high-speed general-purpose computer, with a large store capacity

MAINING > MAIN

MAINLAND n stretch of land which forms the main part of a country

MAINLANDS > MAINLAND

MAINLINE n the trunk route between two points, usually fed by branch lines ▷ vb to inject a drug into a vein ▷ adj having an important position, esp having responsibility for the main areas of activity

MAINLINED > MAINLINE

MAINLINER > MAINLINE

MAINLINES > MAINLINE

MAINLY adv for the most part, chiefly

MAINMAST n chief mast of a ship

MAINMASTS > MAINMAST

MAINOR n act of doing something

MAINORS > MAINOR

MAINOUR same as > MAINOR

MAINOURS > MAINOUR

MAINPRISE n former legal surety ▷ vb allow a prisoner to go free based on a guarantee that he or she will appear in court on the designated day

MAINS > MAIN

MAINSAIL n largest sail on a mainmast

MAINSAILS > MAINSAIL

MAINSHEET n line used to control the angle of the mainsail to the wind

MAINSTAY n chief support

MAINSTAYS > MAINSTAY

MAINTAIN vb continue or keep in existence

MAINTAINS > MAINTAIN

MAINTOP n top or platform at the head of the mainmast

MAINTOPS > MAINTOP

MAINYARD n yard for a square mainsail

MAINYARDS > MAINYARD

MAIOLICA same as > MAJOLICA

MAIOLICAS > MAIOLICA

MAIR Scots form of > MORE

MAIRE n New Zealand tree

MAIREHAU n small aromatic shrub of New Zealand

MAIREHAUS > MAIREHAU

MAIRES > MAIRE

MAIRS > MAIR

MAISE n measure of herring

MAISES > MAISE

MAIST Scot word for > MOST

MAISTER Scots word for > MASTER

MAISTERED > MAISTER

MAISTERS > MAISTER

MAISTRIES > MAISTER

MAISTRING > MAISTER

MAISTRY > MAISTER

MAISTS > MAIST

MAIZE n type of corn with spikes of yellow grains

MAIZES > MAIZE

MAJAGUA same as > MAHOE

MAJAGUAS > MAJAGUA

MAJESTIC adj beautiful, dignified, and impressive

MAJESTIES > MAJESTY

MAJESTY n stateliness or grandeur

MAJLIS n (in Arab countries) an assembly

MAJLISES > MAJLIS

MAJOLICA n type of ornamented Italian pottery

MAJOLICAS > MAJOLICA

MAJOR adj greater in number, quality, or extent ▷ n middle-ranking army officer ▷ vb do one's principal study in (a particular subject)

MAJORAT n estate, the right to which is that of the first born child of a family

MAJORATS > MAJORAT

MAJORDOMO n chief steward or butler of a great household

MAJORED > MAJOR

MAJORETTE n one of a group of girls who practise formation marching and baton twirling

MAJORING > MAJOR

MAJORITY n greater number

MAJORLY adv very

MAJORS > MAJOR

MAJORSHIP > MAJOR

MAJUSCULE n large letter, either capital or uncial, used in printing or writing ▷ adj relating to, printed, or written in such letters

MAK Scot word for > MAKE

MAKABLE > MAKE

MAKAR same as > MAKER

MAKARS > MAKAR

MAKE vb create, construct, or establish ▷ n brand, type, or style

MAKEABLE > MAKE

MAKEBATE n troublemaker

MAKEBATES > MAKEBATE

MAKEFAST n strong support to which a vessel is secured

MAKEFASTS > MAKEFAST

MAKELESS > MAKE

MAKEOVER vb to transfer the title or possession of (property, etc) ▷ n series of alterations, including beauty treatments and new clothes, intended to make a noticeable improvement in a person's appearance

MAKEOVERS > MAKEOVER

MAKER n person or company that makes something

MAKEREADY n process of preparing the forme and the cylinder or platen packing to achieve the correct impression all over the forme

MAKERS > MAKER

MAKES > MAKE

MAKESHIFT adj serving as a temporary substitute ▷ n something serving in this capacity

MAKEUP n cosmetics applied to the face

MAKEUPS > MAKEUP

MAKHANI adj denoting an Indian dish made with butter or ghee

MAKI n in Japanese cuisine, rice and other ingredients wrapped in a short seaweed roll

MAKIMONO n Japanese scroll

MAKIMONOS > MAKIMONO

MAKING > MAKE

MAKINGS pl n potentials, qualities, or materials

MAKIS > MAKI

MAKO n powerful shark of the Atlantic and Pacific Oceans

MAKOS > MAKO

MAKS > MAK

MAKUTA plural of > LIKUTA

MAKUTU n Polynesian witchcraft ▷ vb cast a spell on

MAKUTUED > MAKUTU

MAKUTUING > MAKUTU

MAKUTUS > MAKUTU

MAL n illness

MALA n string of beads or knots, used in praying and meditating

MALACCA n stem of the rattan palm

MALACCAS > MALACCA

MALACHITE n green mineral

MALACIA n softening of an organ or tissue

MALACIAS > MALACIA

MALADIES > MALADY

MALADROIT adj clumsy or awkward

MALADY n disease or illness

MALAGUENA n Spanish dance similar to the fandango

MALAISE n something wrong which affects a section of society or area of activity

MALAISES > MALAISE

MALAM same as > MALLAM

MALAMS > MALAM

MALAMUTE n Alaskan sled dog of the spitz type,

having a dense usually greyish coat
MALAMUTES > MALAMUTE
MALANDER same as > MALANDERS
MALANDERS pl n disease of horses characterized by an eczematous inflammation behind the knee
MALANGA same as > COCOYAM
MALANGAS > MALANGA
MALAPERT adj saucy or impudent ▷ n saucy or impudent person
MALAPERTS > MALAPERT
MALAPROP n word unintentionally confused with one of similar sound, esp when creating a ridiculous effect
MALAPROPS > MALAPROP
MALAR n cheekbone ▷ adj of or relating to the cheek or cheekbone
MALARIA n infectious disease caused by mosquito bite
MALARIAL > MALARIA
MALARIAN > MALARIA
MALARIAS > MALARIA
MALARIOUS > MALARIA
MALARKEY n nonsense or rubbish
MALARKEYS > MALARKEY
MALARKIES > MALARKY
MALARKY same as > MALARKEY
MALAROMA n bad smell
MALAROMAS > MALAROMA
MALARS > MALAR
MALAS > MALA
MALATE n any salt or ester of malic acid
MALATES > MALATE
MALATHION n yellow organophosphorus insecticide used as a dust or mist for the control of house flies and garden pests
MALAX vb soften
MALAXAGE > MALAX
MALAXAGES > MALAX
MALAXATE same as > MALAX
MALAXATED > MALAXATE
MALAXATES > MALAXATE
MALAXATOR n machine for kneading or grinding
MALAXED > MALAX
MALAXES > MALAX
MALAXING > MALAX
MALE adj of the sex which can fertilize female reproductive cells ▷ n male person or animal
MALEATE n any salt or ester of maleic acid
MALEATES > MALEATE
MALEDICT vb utter a curse against ▷ adj cursed or detestable

MALEDICTS > MALEDICT
MALEFFECT n bad effect
MALEFIC adj causing evil
MALEFICE n wicked deed
MALEFICES > MALEFICE
MALEIC adj as in maleic acid colourless soluble crystalline substance
MALEMIUT same as > MALAMUTE
MALEMIUTS > MALEMIUT
MALEMUTE same as > MALAMUTE
MALEMUTES > MALEMUTE
MALENESS > MALE
MALENGINE n wicked plan
MALES > MALE
MALFED adj having malfunctioned
MALFORMED adj deformed
MALGRADO prep in spite of
MALGRE same as > MAUGRE
MALGRED > MALGRE
MALGRES > MALGRE
MALGRING > MALGRE
MALI n member of an Indian caste
MALIBU n as in malibu board lightweight surfboard
MALIC adj as in malic acid colourless crystalline compound occurring in apples
MALICE n desire to cause harm to others ▷ vb wish harm to
MALICED > MALICE
MALICES > MALICE
MALICHO n mischief
MALICHOS > MALICHO
MALICING > MALICE
MALICIOUS adj characterized by malice
MALIGN vb slander or defame ▷ adj evil in influence or effect
MALIGNANT adj seeking to harm others
MALIGNED > MALIGN
MALIGNER > MALIGN
MALIGNERS > MALIGN
MALIGNING > MALIGN
MALIGNITY n evil disposition
MALIGNLY > MALIGN
MALIGNS > MALIGN
MALIHINI n (in Hawaii) a foreigner or stranger
MALIHINIS > MALIHINI
MALIK n person of authority in India
MALIKS > MALIK
MALINE n stiff net
MALINES > MALINE
MALINGER vb feign illness to avoid work
MALINGERS > MALINGER
MALINGERY > MALINGER
MALIS > MALI

MALISM n belief that evil dominates world
MALISMS > MALISM
MALISON archaic or poetic word for > CURSE
MALISONS > MALISON
MALIST > MALISM
MALKIN archaic or dialect name for a > CAT
MALKINS > MALKIN
MALL n street or shopping area closed to vehicles ▷ vb maul
MALLAM n (in W Africa) expert in the Koran
MALLAMS > MALLAM
MALLANDER same as > MALANDERS
MALLARD n wild duck
MALLARDS > MALLARD
MALLCORE n type of rock music combining heavy metal and hip-hop
MALLCORES > MALLCORE
MALLEABLE adj capable of being hammered or pressed into shape
MALLEABLY > MALLEABLE
MALLEATE vb hammer
MALLEATED > MALLEATE
MALLEATES > MALLEATE
MALLECHO same as > MALICHO
MALLECHOS > MALLECHO
MALLED > MALL
MALLEE n low-growing eucalypt in dry regions
MALLEES > MALLEE
MALLEI > MALLEUS
MALLEMUCK n any of various sea birds, such as the albatross, fulmar, or shearwater
MALLENDER same as > MALANDERS
MALLEOLAR > MALLEOLUS
MALLEOLI > MALLEOLUS
MALLEOLUS n either of two rounded bony projections of the tibia and fibula on the sides of each ankle joint
MALLET n (wooden) hammer
MALLETS > MALLET
MALLEUS n small bone in the middle ear
MALLEUSES > MALLEUS
MALLING > MALL
MALLINGS > MALL
MALLOW n plant with pink or purple flowers
MALLOWS > MALLOW
MALLS > MALL
MALM n soft greyish limestone that crumbles easily
MALMAG n Asian monkey
MALMAGS > MALMAG
MALMIER > MALMY
MALMIEST > MALMY
MALMS > MALM

MALMSEY n sweet Madeira wine
MALMSEYS > MALMSEY
MALMSTONE same as > MALM
MALMY adj looking like malm
MALODOR same as > MALODOUR
MALODORS > MALODOR
MALODOUR n unpleasant smell
MALODOURS > MALODOUR
MALONATE n salt of malonic acid
MALONATES > MALONATE
MALONIC adj as in malonic acid colourless crystalline compound
MALOTI plural of > LOTI
MALPIGHIA n type of tropical shrub
MALPOSED adj in abnormal position
MALS > MAL
MALSTICK same as > MAULSTICK
MALSTICKS > MALSTICK
MALT n grain, such as barley, prepared for use in making beer or whisky ▷ vb make into or make with malt
MALTALENT n evil intention
MALTASE n enzyme that hydrolyses maltose to glucose
MALTASES > MALTASE
MALTED > MALT
MALTEDS > MALT
MALTESE adj as in maltese cross cross-shaped part of a film projector
MALTHA n any of various naturally occurring mixtures of hydrocarbons
MALTHAS > MALTHA
MALTIER > MALTY
MALTIEST > MALTY
MALTINESS > MALTY
MALTING n building in which malt is made or stored
MALTINGS > MALTING
MALTMAN same as > MALTSTER
MALTMEN > MALTMAN
MALTOL n food additive
MALTOLS > MALTOL
MALTOSE n sugar formed by the action of enzymes on starch
MALTOSES > MALTOSE
MALTREAT vb treat badly
MALTREATS > MALTREAT
MALTS > MALT
MALTSTER n person who makes or deals in malt
MALTSTERS > MALTSTER
MALTWORM n heavy drinker
MALTWORMS > MALTWORM

MALTY *adj* of, like, or containing malt

MALUS *n* financial penalty incurred by an investor

MALUSES > MALUS

MALVA *n* mallow plant

MALVAS > MALVA

MALVASIA *n* type of grape used to make malmsey

MALVASIAN > MALVASIA

MALVASIAS > MALVASIA

MALVESIE *same as* > MALMSEY

MALVESIES > MALVESIE

MALVOISIE *n* amber dessert wine made in France, similar to malmsey

MALWA *n* Ugandan drink brewed from millet

MALWARE *n* computer program designed to cause damage to a system

MALWARES > MALWARE

MALWAS > MALWA

MAM *same as* > MOTHER

MAMA *n* mother

MAMAGUY *vb* deceive or tease ▷ *n* deception or flattery

MAMAGUYED > MAMAGUY

MAMAGUYS > MAMAGUY

MAMAKAU *same as* > MAMAKU

MAMAKAUS > MAMAKAU

MAMAKO *same as* > MAMAKU

MAMAKOS > MAMAKO

MAMAKU *n* tall edible New Zealand tree fern

MAMAKUS > MAMAKU

MAMALIGA *same as* > POLENTA

MAMALIGAS > MAMALIGA

MAMAS > MAMA

MAMASAN *n* (in Japan) woman in a position of authority

MAMASANS > MAMASAN

MAMATEEK *n* type of wigwam

MAMATEEKS > MAMATEEK

MAMBA *n* deadly S African snake

MAMBAS > MAMBA

MAMBO *n* Latin American dance resembling the rumba ▷ *vb* perform this dance

MAMBOED > MAMBO

MAMBOES > MAMBO

MAMBOING > MAMBO

MAMBOS > MAMBO

MAMEE *same as* > MAMEY

MAMEES > MAMEE

MAMELON *n* small rounded hillock

MAMELONS > MAMELON

MAMELUCO *n* Brazilian of mixed European and South American descent

MAMELUCOS > MAMELUCO

MAMELUKE *n* member of a military class, originally of Turkish slaves, ruling in Egypt from about 1250 to 1517 and remaining powerful until crushed in 1811

MAMELUKES > MAMELUKE

MAMEY *n* tropical tree

MAMEYES > MAMEY

MAMEYS > MAMEY

MAMIE *n* tropical tree

MAMIES > MAMIE

MAMILLA *n* nipple or teat

MAMILLAE > MAMILLA

MAMILLAR *adj* of breast

MAMILLARY > MAMILLA

MAMILLATE *adj* having nipples or nipple-like protuberances

MAMLUK *same as* > MAMELUKE

MAMLUKS > MAMLUK

MAMMA *n* buxom and voluptuous woman

MAMMAE > MAMMA

MAMMAL *n* animal of the type that suckles its young

MAMMALIAN > MAMMAL

MAMMALITY > MAMMAL

MAMMALOGY *n* branch of zoology concerned with the study of mammals

MAMMALS > MAMMAL

MAMMARIES > MAMMARY

MAMMARY *adj* of the breasts or milk-producing glands ▷ *n* breast

MAMMAS > MAMMA

MAMMATE *adj* having breasts

MAMMATI > MAMMATUS

MAMMATUS *n* breast-shaped cloud

MAMMEE *same as* > MAMEY

MAMMEES > MAMMEE

MAMMER *vb* hesitate

MAMMERED > MAMMER

MAMMERING > MAMMER

MAMMERS > MAMMER

MAMMET *same as* > MAUMET

MAMMETRY *n* worship of idols

MAMMETS > MAMMET

MAMMEY *same as* > MAMEY

MAMMEYS > MAMMEY

MAMMIE *same as* > MAMMY

MAMMIES > MAMMY

MAMMIFER *same as* > MAMMAL

MAMMIFERS > MAMMIFER

MAMMIFORM *adj* in form of breast

MAMMILLA *same as* > MAMILLA

MAMMILLAE > MAMMILLA

MAMMILLAR *same as* > MAMILLAR

MAMMITIS *same as* > MASTITIS

MAMMOCK *n* fragment ▷ *vb* tear or shred

MAMMOCKED > MAMMOCK

MAMMOCKS > MAMMOCK

MAMMOGRAM *n* x-ray to examine the breasts in early detection of cancer

MAMMON *n* wealth regarded as a source of evil

MAMMONISH > MAMMON

MAMMONISM > MAMMON

MAMMONIST > MAMMON

MAMMONITE > MAMMON

MAMMONS > MAMMON

MAMMOTH *n* extinct elephant-like mammal ▷ *adj* colossal

MAMMOTHS > MAMMOTH

MAMMY *n* Black woman employed as a nurse or servant to a White family

MAMPARA *n* foolish person, idiot

MAMPARAS > MAMPARA

MAMPOER *n* home-distilled brandy

MAMPOERS > MAMPOER

MAMS > MAM

MAMSELLE *n* mademoiselle

MAMSELLES > MAMSELLE

MAMZER *n* child of an incestuous or adulterous union

MAMZERIM > MAMZER

MAMZERS > MAMZER

MAN *n* adult male ▷ *vb* supply with sufficient people for operation or defence

MANA *n* authority, influence

MANACLE *vb* handcuff or fetter ▷ *n* metal ring or chain put round the wrists or ankles

MANACLED > MANACLE

MANACLES > MANACLE

MANACLING > MANACLE

MANAGE *vb* succeed in doing

MANAGED > MANAGE

MANAGER *n* person in charge of a business, institution, actor, sports team, etc

MANAGERS > MANAGER

MANAGES > MANAGE

MANAGING *adj* having administrative control or authority

MANAIA *n* figure in Māori carving

MANAIAS > MANAIA

MANAKIN *same as* > MANIKIN

MANAKINS > MANAKIN

MANANA *n* tomorrow ▷ *adv* tomorrow

MANANAS > MANANA

MANAS > MANA

MANAT *n* standard monetary unit of Azerbaijan

MANATEE *n* large tropical plant-eating aquatic mammal

MANATEES > MANATEE

MANATI *same as* > MANATEE

MANATIS > MANATI

MANATOID > MANATEE

MANATS > MANAT

MANATU *n* large flowering deciduous New Zealand tree

MANATUS > MANATU

MANAWA *in New Zealand, same as* > MANGROVE

MANAWAS > MANAWA

MANBAG *n* small handbag with a shoulder strap, carried by men

MANBAGS > MANBAG

MANBAND *n* boy band whose members have reached maturity

MANBANDS > MANBAND

MANCALA *n* African and Asian board game

MANCALAS > MANCALA

MANCANDO *adv* musical direction meaning fading away

MANCHE *n* long sleeve

MANCHES > MANCHE

MANCHET *n* type of bread

MANCHETS > MANCHET

MANCIPATE *vb* make legal transfer in ancient Rome

MANCIPLE *n* steward who buys provisions, esp in a college, Inn of Court, or monastery

MANCIPLES > MANCIPLE

MANCUS *n* former English coin

MANCUSES > MANCUS

MAND > MAN

MANDALA *n* circular design symbolizing the universe

MANDALAS > MANDALA

MANDALIC > MANDALA

MANDAMUS *n* formerly a writ from, now an order of, a superior court commanding an inferior tribunal, public official, corporation, etc, to carry out a public duty

MANDARIN *n* high-ranking government official

MANDARINE *same as* > MANDARIN

MANDARINS > MANDARIN

MANDATARY *same as* > MANDATORY

MANDATE *n* official or authoritative command ▷ *vb* give authority to

MANDATED > MANDATE

MANDATES > MANDATE

MANDATING > MANDATE

MANDATOR > MANDATE

MANDATORS > MANDATE

MANDATORY *adj* compulsory ▷ *n* person or state holding a mandate

MANDI *n* (in India) a big market

MANDIBLE *n* lower jawbone or jawlike part

MANDIBLES > MANDIBLE

MANDILION *same as* > MANDYLION**

MANDIOC same as > MANIOC

MANDIOCA same as > MANIOC

MANDIOCAS > MANDIOCA

MANDIOCCA same as > MANIOC

MANDIOCS > MANDIOC

MANDIR n Hindu or Jain temple

MANDIRA same as > MANDIR

MANDIRAS > MANDIRA

MANDIRS > MANDIR

MANDIS > MANDI

MANDOLA n early type of mandolin

MANDOLAS > MANDOLA

MANDOLIN n musical instrument with four pairs of strings

MANDOLINE same as > MANDOLIN

MANDOLINS > MANDOLIN

MANDOM n mankind

MANDOMS > MANDOM

MANDORA n ancestor of mandolin

MANDORAS > MANDORA

MANDORLA n (in painting, sculpture, etc) an almond-shaped area of light, usually surrounding the resurrected Christ or the Virgin at the Assumption

MANDORLAS > MANDORLA

MANDRAKE n plant with a forked root, formerly used as a narcotic

MANDRAKES > MANDRAKE

MANDREL n shaft on which work is held in a lathe

MANDRELS > MANDREL

MANDRIL same as > MANDREL

MANDRILL n large blue-faced baboon

MANDRILLS > MANDRILL

MANDRILS > MANDRIL

MANDUCATE vb eat or chew

MANDYLION n loose garment formerly worn over armour

MANE n long hair on the neck of a horse, lion, etc

MANEB n powdered fungicide

MANEBS > MANEB

MANED > MANE

MANEGE n art of training horses and riders ▷ vb train horse

MANEGED > MANEGE

MANEGES > MANEGE

MANEGING > MANEGE

MANEH same as > MINA

MANEHS > MANEH

MANELESS > MANE

MANENT > MANET

MANES pl n spirits of the dead, often revered as minor deities

MANET vb theatre direction, remain on stage

MANEUVER same as > MANOEUVRE

MANEUVERS > MANEUVER

MANFUL adj determined and brave

MANFULLY > MANFUL

MANG vb speak

MANGA n type of Japanese comic book

MANGABEY n large Old World monkey of central Africa, with long limbs and tail and white upper eyelids

MANGABEYS > MANGABEY

MANGABIES > MANGABEY

MANGABY same as > MANGABEY

MANGAL n Turkish brazier

MANGALS > MANGAL

MANGANATE n salt of manganic acid

MANGANESE n brittle greyish-white metallic element

MANGANIC adj of or containing manganese in the trivalent state

MANGANIN n copper-based alloy

MANGANINS > MANGANIN

MANGANITE n blackish mineral

MANGANOUS adj of or containing manganese in the divalent state

MANGAS > MANGA

MANGE n skin disease of domestic animals

MANGEAO n small New Zealand tree with glossy leaves

MANGEAOS > MANGEAO

MANGED > MANG

MANGEL n Eurasian variety of the beet plant

MANGELS > MANGEL

MANGER n eating trough in a stable or barn

MANGERS > MANGER

MANGES > MANGE

MANGETOUT n variety of pea with an edible pod

MANGEY same as > MANGY

MANGIER > MANGY

MANGIEST > MANGY

MANGILY > MANGY

MANGINESS > MANGY

MANGING > MANG

MANGLE vb destroy by crushing and twisting ▷ n machine with rollers for squeezing water from washed clothes

MANGLED > MANGLE

MANGLER > MANGLE

MANGLERS > MANGLE

MANGLES > MANGLE

MANGLING > MANGLE

MANGO n tropical fruit with sweet juicy yellow flesh

MANGOES > MANGO

MANGOLD n type of root vegetable

MANGOLDS > MANGOLD

MANGONEL n war engine for hurling stones

MANGONELS > MANGONEL

MANGOS > MANGO

MANGOSTAN n East Indian tree with thick leathery leaves and edible fruit

MANGOUSTE same as > MONGOOSE

MANGROVE n tropical tree with exposed roots, which grows beside water

MANGROVES > MANGROVE

MANGS > MANG

MANGULATE vb bend or twist out of shape

MANGY adj having mange

MANHANDLE vb treat roughly

MANHATTAN n mixed drink consisting of four parts whisky, one part vermouth, and a dash of bitters

MANHOLE n hole with a cover, through which a person can enter a drain or sewer

MANHOLES > MANHOLE

MANHOOD n state or quality of being a man or being manly

MANHOODS > MANHOOD

MANHUNT n organized search, usu by police, for a wanted man

MANHUNTER > MANHUNT

MANHUNTS > MANHUNT

MANI n place to pray

MANIA n extreme enthusiasm

MANIAC n mad person

MANIACAL adj affected with or characteristic of mania

MANIACS > MANIAC

MANIAS > MANIA

MANIC adj extremely excited or energetic ▷ n person afflicted with mania

MANICALLY > MANIC

MANICOTTI pl n large tubular noodles, usually stuffed with ricotta cheese and baked in a tomato sauce

MANICS > MANIC

MANICURE n cosmetic care of the fingernails and hands ▷ vb care for (the fingernails and hands) in this way

MANICURED > MANICURE

MANICURES > MANICURE

MANIES > MANY

MANIFEST adj easily noticed, obvious ▷ vb show plainly ▷ n list of cargo or passengers for customs

MANIFESTO n declaration of policy as issued by a political party ▷ vb issued manifesto

MANIFESTS > MANIFEST

MANIFOLD adj numerous and varied ▷ n pipe with several outlets, esp in an internal-combustion engine ▷ vb duplicate (a page, book, etc)

MANIFOLDS > MANIFOLD

MANIFORM adj like hand

MANIHOC variation of > MANIOC

MANIHOCS > MANIHOC

MANIHOT n tropical American plant

MANIHOTS > MANIHOT

MANIKIN n little man or dwarf

MANIKINS > MANIKIN

MANILA n strong brown paper used for envelopes

MANILAS > MANILA

MANILLA n early currency in W Africa in the form of a small bracelet

MANILLAS > MANILLA

MANILLE n (in ombre and quadrille) the second best trump

MANILLES > MANILLE

MANIOC same as > CASSAVA

MANIOCA same as > MANIOC

MANIOCAS > MANIOCA

MANIOCS > MANIOC

MANIPLE n (in ancient Rome) a unit of 120 to 200 foot soldiers

MANIPLES > MANIPLE

MANIPLIES same as > MANYPLIES

MANIPULAR adj of or relating to an ancient Roman maniple

MANIS n pangolin

MANISES > MANIS

MANITO same as > MANITOU

MANITOS > MANITO

MANITOU n (among the Algonquian Indians) a deified spirit or force

MANITOUS > MANITOU

MANITU same as > MANITOU

MANITUS > MANITU

MANJACK n single individual

MANJACKS > MANJACK

MANKIER > MANKY

MANKIEST > MANKY

MANKIND n human beings collectively

MANKINDS > MANKIND

MANKINI n revealing man's swimming costume

MANKINIS > MANKINI

MANKY adj worthless, rotten, or in bad taste

MANLESS > MAN

MANLIER > MANLY
MANLIEST > MANLY
MANLIKE adj resembling or befitting a man
MANLIKELY > MANLIKE
MANLILY > MANLY
MANLINESS > MANLY
MANLY adj (possessing qualities) appropriate to a man
MANMADE adj made or produced by man
MANNA n miraculous food which sustained the Israelites in the wilderness
MANNAN n drug derived from mannose
MANNANS > MANNAN
MANNAS > MANNA
MANNED > MAN
MANNEQUIN n woman who models clothes at a fashion show
MANNER n way a thing happens or is done
MANNERED adj affected
MANNERISM n person's distinctive habit or trait
MANNERIST > MANNERISM
MANNERLY adj having good manners, polite ▷ adv with good manners
MANNERS pl n person's social conduct
MANNIKIN same as > MANIKIN
MANNIKINS > MANNIKIN
MANNING > MAN
MANNISH adj (of a woman) like a man
MANNISHLY > MANNISH
MANNITE same as > MANNITOL
MANNITES > MANNITE
MANNITIC > MANNITOL
MANNITOL n white crystalline water-soluble sweet-tasting alcohol
MANNITOLS > MANNITOL
MANNOSE n hexose sugar
MANNOSES > MANNOSE
MANO n stone for grinding grain
MANOAO n New Zealand shrub
MANOAOS > MANOAO
MANOES > MANO
MANOEUVRE n skilful movement ▷ vb manipulate or contrive skilfully or cunningly
MANOMETER n instrument for comparing pressures
MANOMETRY > MANOMETER
MANOR n large country house and its lands
MANORIAL > MANOR
MANORS > MANOR
MANOS > MANO
MANOSCOPY n measurement of the densities of gases

MANPACK n load carried by one person
MANPACKS > MANPACK
MANPOWER n available number of workers
MANPOWERS > MANPOWER
MANQUE adj would-be ▷ n section on a roulette table which includes the numbers 1 to 18 or a bet placed in this area
MANQUES > MANQUE
MANRED n homage
MANREDS > MANRED
MANRENT same as > MANRED
MANRENTS > MANRENT
MANRIDER n train carrying miners in coal mine
MANRIDERS > MANRIDER
MANRIDING adj carrying people rather than goods
MANROPE n rope railing
MANROPES > MANROPE
MANS > MAN
MANSARD n type of sloping roof
MANSARDED adj having mansard roof
MANSARDS > MANSARD
MANSCAPE vb groom a man's bodily hair for aesthetics
MANSCAPED > MANSCAPE
MANSCAPES > MANSCAPE
MANSE n house provided for a minister in some religious denominations
MANSES > MANSE
MANSHIFT n work done by one person in one shift
MANSHIFTS > MANSHIFT
MANSION n large house
MANSIONS > MANSION
MANSLAYER n person who kills man
MANSONRY n mansions collectively
MANSUETE adj gentle
MANSWORN adj perjured ▷ n someone who perjures
MANSWORNS > MANSWORN
MANTA n type of large ray with very wide winglike pectoral fins
MANTAS > MANTA
MANTEAU n cloak or mantle
MANTEAUS > MANTEAU
MANTEAUX > MANTEAU
MANTEEL n cloak
MANTEELS > MANTEEL
MANTEL n structure round a fireplace ▷ vb construct a mantel
MANTELET n woman's short mantle, often lace-trimmed, worn in the mid-19th century
MANTELETS > MANTELET
MANTELS > MANTEL
MANTES > MANTIS
MANTIC adj of or relating to divination and prophecy

MANTICORA same as > MANTICORE
MANTICORE n mythical monster with body of lion and human head
MANTID same as > MANTIS
MANTIDS > MANTID
MANTIES > MANTY
MANTILLA n (in Spain) a lace scarf covering a woman's head and shoulders
MANTILLAS > MANTILLA
MANTIS n carnivorous insect like a grasshopper
MANTISES > MANTIS
MANTISSA n part of a common logarithm consisting of the decimal point and the figures following it
MANTISSAS > MANTISSA
MANTLE same as > MANTEL
MANTLED > MANTLE
MANTLES > MANTLE
MANTLET same as > MANTELET
MANTLETS > MANTLET
MANTLING n drapery or scrollwork around a shield
MANTLINGS > MANTLING
MANTO same as > MANTEAU
MANTOES > MANTO
MANTOS > MANTO
MANTRA n any sacred word or syllable used as an object of concentration
MANTRAM same as > MANTRA
MANTRAMS > MANTRAM
MANTRAP n snare for catching people, esp trespassers
MANTRAPS > MANTRAP
MANTRAS > MANTRA
MANTRIC > MANTRA
MANTUA n loose gown of the 17th and 18th centuries
MANTUAS > MANTUA
MANTY Scots variant of > MANTUA
MANTYHOSE n tights that are worn by men
MANUAL adj of or done with the hands ▷ n handbook
MANUALLY > MANUAL
MANUALS > MANUAL
MANUARY same as > MANUAL
MANUBRIA > MANUBRIUM
MANUBRIAL > MANUBRIUM
MANUBRIUM n any handle-shaped part, esp the upper part of the sternum
MANUCODE n bird of Paradise with blue-black plumage
MANUCODES > MANUCODE
MANUHIRI n visitor to a Māori marae
MANUHIRIS > MANUHIRI

MANUKA n New Zealand tree
MANUKAS > MANUKA
MANUL n Asian wildcat
MANULS > MANUL
MANUMEA n pigeon of Samoa
MANUMEAS > MANUMEA
MANUMIT vb free from slavery
MANUMITS > MANUMIT
MANURANCE n cultivation of land
MANURE n animal excrement used as a fertilizer ▷ vb fertilize (land) with this
MANURED > MANURE
MANURER > MANURE
MANURERS > MANURE
MANURES > MANURE
MANURIAL > MANURE
MANURING > MANURE
MANURINGS > MANURE
MANUS n wrist and hand
MANWARD adv towards humankind
MANWARDS same as > MANWARD
MANWISE adv in human way
MANY adj numerous ▷ n large number
MANYATA same as > MANYATTA
MANYATAS > MANYATA
MANYATTA n settlement of Masai people
MANYATTAS > MANYATTA
MANYFOLD adj many in number
MANYPLIES n third component of the stomach of ruminants
MANZANITA n Californian plant
MANZELLO n instrument like saxophone
MANZELLOS > MANZELLO
MAOMAO n fish of New Zealand seas
MAOMAOS > MAOMAO
MAORMOR same as > MORMAOR
MAORMORS > MAORMOR
MAP n representation of the earth's surface or some part of it ▷ vb make a map of
MAPAU n small New Zealand tree
MAPAUS > MAPAU
MAPLE n tree with broad leaves, a variety of which yields sugar
MAPLELIKE > MAPLE
MAPLES > MAPLE
MAPLESS > MAP
MAPLIKE > MAP
MAPMAKER n person who draws maps
MAPMAKERS > MAPMAKER
MAPMAKING > MAPMAKER
MAPPABLE > MAP

MAPPED > MAP
MAPPEMOND n map of world
MAPPER > MAP
MAPPERIES > MAPPERY
MAPPERS > MAP
MAPPERY n making of maps
MAPPING > MAP
MAPPINGS > MAP
MAPPIST > MAP
MAPPISTS > MAP
MAPS > MAP
MAPSTICK same as > MOPSTICK
MAPSTICKS > MAPSTICK
MAPWISE adv like map
MAQUETTE n sculptor's small preliminary model or sketch
MAQUETTES > MAQUETTE
MAQUI n Chilean shrub
MAQUILA n US-owned factory in Mexico
MAQUILAS > MAQUILA
MAQUIS n French underground movement in World War II
MAQUISARD n member of French maquis
MAR vb spoil or impair ▷ n disfiguring mark
MARA n harelike S American rodent
MARABI n kind of music popular in S African townships in the 1930s
MARABIS > MARABI
MARABOU n large black-and-white African stork
MARABOUS > MARABOU
MARABOUT n Muslim holy man or hermit of North Africa
MARABOUTS > MARABOUT
MARABUNTA n any of several social wasps
MARACA n shaken percussion instrument
MARACAS > MARACA
MARAE n enclosed space in front of a Māori meeting house
MARAES > MARAE
MARAGING adj as in maraging steel strong low-carbon steel containing nickel and small amounts of titanium, aluminium, and niobium, produced by transforming to a martensitic structure and heating at 500°C
MARAGINGS > MARAGING
MARAH n bitterness
MARAHS > MARAH
MARANATHA n member of Christian sect
MARANTA n tropical American plant
MARANTAS > MARANTA

MARARI n eel-like blennioid food fish
MARARIS > MARARI
MARAS > MARA
MARASCA n European cherry tree with red acid-tasting fruit
MARASCAS > MARASCA
MARASMIC > MARASMUS
MARASMOID > MARASMUS
MARASMUS n general emaciation and wasting, esp of infants, thought to be associated with severe malnutrition or impaired utilization of nutrients
MARATHON n long-distance race of 26 miles 385 yards (42.195 kilometres) ▷ adj of or relating to a race on foot of 26 miles 385 yards (42.195 kilometres)
MARATHONS > MARATHON
MARAUD vb wander or raid in search of plunder
MARAUDED > MARAUD
MARAUDER > MARAUD
MARAUDERS > MARAUD
MARAUDING adj wandering or raiding in search of plunder
MARAUDS > MARAUD
MARAVEDI n any of various Spanish coins of copper or gold
MARAVEDIS > MARAVEDI
MARBELISE same as > MARBLEIZE
MARBELIZE same as > MARBLEIZE
MARBLE n kind of limestone with a mottled appearance ▷ vb mottle with variegated streaks in imitation of marble
MARBLED > MARBLE
MARBLEISE same as > MARBLEIZE
MARBLEIZE vb give a marble-like appearance to
MARBLER > MARBLE
MARBLERS > MARBLE
MARBLES n game in which marble balls are rolled at one another
MARBLIER > MARBLE
MARBLIEST > MARBLE
MARBLING n mottled effect or pattern resembling marble
MARBLINGS > MARBLING
MARBLY > MARBLE
MARC n remains of grapes or other fruit that have been pressed for wine-making
MARCASITE n crystals of iron pyrites, used in jewellery
MARCATO adj (of notes) heavily accented ▷ adv with each note heavily accented ▷ n heavily accented note

MARCATOS > MARCATO
MARCEL n hairstyle characterized by repeated regular waves ▷ vb make such waves in (the hair)
MARCELLA n type of fabric
MARCELLAS > MARCELLA
MARCELLED > MARCEL
MARCELLER > MARCEL
MARCELS > MARCEL
MARCH vb walk with a military step ▷ n action of marching
MARCHED > MARCH
MARCHEN n German story
MARCHER n person who marches
MARCHERS > MARCHER
MARCHES > MARCH
MARCHESA n (in Italy) the wife or widow of a marchese
MARCHESAS > MARCHESA
MARCHESE n (in Italy) a nobleman ranking below a prince and above a count
MARCHESI > MARCHESE
MARCHING > MARCH
MARCHLAND n border land
MARCHLIKE adj like march in rhythm
MARCHMAN n person living on border
MARCHMEN > MARCHMAN
MARCHPANE same as > MARZIPAN
MARCONI vb communicate by wireless
MARCONIED > MARCONI
MARCONIS > MARCONI
MARCS > MARC
MARD > MAR
MARDIED > MARDY
MARDIER > MARDY
MARDIES > MARDY
MARDIEST > MARDY
MARDY adj (of a child) spoilt ▷ vb behave in mardy way
MARDYING > MARDY
MARE n female horse or zebra
MAREMMA n marshy unhealthy region near the shore, esp in Italy
MAREMMAS > MAREMMA
MAREMME > MAREMMA
MARENGO adj browned in oil and cooked with tomatoes, mushrooms, garlic, wine, etc
MARERO n member of a C American organized criminal gang
MAREROS > MARERO
MARES > MARE
MARESCHAL same as > MARSHAL
MARG short for > MARGARINE
MARGARIC adj of or resembling pearl
MARGARIN n ester of margaric acid

MARGARINE n butter substitute made from animal or vegetable fats
MARGARINS > MARGARIN
MARGARITA n mixed drink consisting of tequila and lemon juice
MARGARITE n pink pearly micaceous mineral
MARGATE n greyish fish of W Atlantic
MARGATES > MARGATE
MARGAY n feline mammal of Central and S America
MARGAYS > MARGAY
MARGE n margarine
MARGENT same as > MARGIN
MARGENTED > MARGENT
MARGENTS > MARGENT
MARGES > MARGE
MARGIN n edge or border ▷ vb provide with a margin
MARGINAL adj insignificant, unimportant ▷ n marginal constituency
MARGINALS > MARGINAL
MARGINATE vb provide with a margin or margins ▷ adj having a margin of a distinct colour or form
MARGINED > MARGIN
MARGINING > MARGIN
MARGINS > MARGIN
MARGOSA n Indian tree
MARGOSAS > MARGOSA
MARGRAVE n (formerly) a German nobleman ranking above a count
MARGRAVES > MARGRAVE
MARGS > MARG
MARIA > MARE
MARIACHI n small ensemble of street musicians in Mexico
MARIACHIS > MARIACHI
MARIALITE n silicate mineral
MARID n spirit in Muslim mythology
MARIDS > MARID
MARIES > MARY
MARIGOLD n plant with yellow or orange flowers
MARIGOLDS > MARIGOLD
MARIGRAM n graphic record of the tide levels at a particular coastal station
MARIGRAMS > MARIGRAM
MARIGRAPH n gauge for recording the levels of the tides
MARIHUANA same as > MARIJUANA
MARIJUANA n dried flowers and leaves of the cannabis plant, used as a drug, esp in cigarettes
MARIMBA n Latin American percussion instrument
MARIMBAS > MARIMBA

MARIMBIST > MARIMBA
MARINA n harbour for yachts and other pleasure boats
MARINADE n seasoned liquid in which fish or meat is soaked before cooking
MARINADED > MARINADE
MARINADES > MARINADE
MARINARA n Italian pasta sauce
MARINARAS > MARINARA
MARINAS > MARINA
MARINATE vb soak in marinade
MARINATED > MARINATE
MARINATES > MARINATE
MARINE adj of the sea or shipping ▷ n (esp in Britain and the US) soldier trained for land and sea combat
MARINER n sailor
MARINERA n folk dance of Peru
MARINERAS > MARINERA
MARINERS > MARINER
MARINES > MARINE
MARINIERE adj served in white wine and onion sauce
MARIPOSA n type of plant of the southwestern US and Mexico, with brightly coloured tulip-like flowers
MARIPOSAS > MARIPOSA
MARISCHAL Scots variant of > MARSHAL
MARISH n marsh
MARISHES > MARISH
MARITAGE n right of a lord to choose the spouses of his wards
MARITAGES > MARITAGE
MARITAL adj relating to marriage
MARITALLY > MARITAL
MARITIME adj relating to shipping
MARJORAM n aromatic herb used for seasoning food and in salads
MARJORAMS > MARJORAM
MARK n line, dot, scar, etc visible on a surface ▷ vb make a mark on
MARKA n unit of currency introduced as an interim currency in Bosnia-Herzegovina
MARKAS > MARKA
MARKDOWN n price reduction ▷ vb reduce in price
MARKDOWNS > MARKDOWN
MARKED adj noticeable
MARKEDLY > MARKED
MARKER n object used to show the position of something
MARKERS > MARKER
MARKET n assembly or place for buying and selling ▷ vb offer or produce for sale

MARKETED > MARKET
MARKETEER n supporter of the European Union and of Britain's membership of it
MARKETER > MARKET
MARKETERS > MARKET
MARKETING n part of a business that controls the way that goods or services are sold
MARKETISE same as > MARKETIZE
MARKETIZE vb convert (a national economy) to a market economy
MARKETS > MARKET
MARKHOOR same as > MARKHOR
MARKHOORS > MARKHOOR
MARKHOR n large wild Himalayan goat
MARKHORS > MARKHOR
MARKING n arrangement of colours on an animal or plant
MARKINGS > MARKING
MARKKA n former standard monetary unit of Finland
MARKKAA > MARKKA
MARKKAS > MARKKA
MARKMAN n person owning land
MARKMEN > MARKMAN
MARKS > MARK
MARKSMAN n person skilled at shooting
MARKSMEN > MARKSMAN
MARKUP n percentage or amount added to the cost of a commodity to provide the seller with a profit and to cover overheads, costs, etc
MARKUPS > MARKUP
MARL n soil formed of clay and lime, used as fertilizer ▷ vb fertilize (land) with marl
MARLE same as > MARVEL
MARLED > MARL
MARLES > MARLE
MARLIER > MARLY
MARLIEST > MARLY
MARLIN same as > MARLINE
MARLINE n light rope, usually tarred, made of two strands laid left-handed
MARLINES > MARLINE
MARLING same as > MARLINE
MARLINGS > MARLING
MARLINS > MARLIN
MARLITE n type of marl that contains clay and calcium carbonate
MARLITES > MARLITE
MARLITIC > MARLITE
MARLS > MARL
MARLSTONE same as > MARLITE
MARLY adj marl-like

MARM same as > MADAM
MARMALADE n jam made from citrus fruits ▷ adj (of cats) streaked orange or yellow and brown
MARMALISE vb beat soundly or defeat utterly
MARMALIZE same as > MARMALISE
MARMARISE same as > MARMARIZE
MARMARIZE vb turn to marble
MARMELISE same as > MARMELIZE
MARMELIZE vb beat soundly
MARMEM n as in marmem alloy type of alloy
MARMITE n large cooking pot
MARMITES > MARMITE
MARMOREAL adj of or like marble
MARMOREAN same as > MARMOREAL
MARMOSE n South American opossum
MARMOSES > MARMOSE
MARMOSET n small bushy-tailed monkey
MARMOSETS > MARMOSET
MARMOT n burrowing rodent
MARMOTS > MARMOT
MARMS > MARM
MAROCAIN n fabric of ribbed crepe
MAROCAINS > MAROCAIN
MARON n freshwater crustacean
MARONS > MARON
MAROON adj reddish-purple ▷ vb abandon ashore, esp on an island ▷ n exploding firework or flare used as a warning signal
MAROONED > MAROON
MAROONER > MAROON
MAROONERS > MAROON
MAROONING > MAROON
MAROONS > MAROON
MAROQUIN n morocco leather
MAROQUINS > MAROQUIN
MAROR n Jewish ceremonial dish of bitter herbs
MARORS > MAROR
MARPLOT n person interfering with plot
MARPLOTS > MARPLOT
MARQUE n brand of product, esp of a car
MARQUEE n large tent used for a party or exhibition
MARQUEES > MARQUEE
MARQUES > MARQUE
MARQUESS n nobleman of the rank below a duke
MARQUETRY n ornamental inlaid work of wood

MARQUIS n (in some European countries) nobleman of the rank above a count
MARQUISE same as > MARQUEE
MARQUISES > MARQUISE
MARRA n (in N England) friend
MARRAM n as in marram grass any of several grasses that grow on sandy shores
MARRAMS > MARRAM
MARRANO n Spanish or Portuguese Jew of the late Middle Ages who was converted to Christianity
MARRANOS > MARRANO
MARRAS > MARRA
MARRED > MAR
MARRELS same as > MERILS
MARRER > MAR
MARRERS > MAR
MARRI n W Australian eucalyptus
MARRIAGE n state of being married
MARRIAGES > MARRIAGE
MARRIED > MARRY
MARRIEDS pl n married people
MARRIER > MARRY
MARRIERS > MARRY
MARRIES > MARRY
MARRING > MAR
MARRIS > MARRI
MARRON n large edible sweet chestnut
MARRONS > MARRON
MARROW n fatty substance inside bones ▷ vb be mate to
MARROWED > MARROW
MARROWFAT n variety of large pea
MARROWING > MARROW
MARROWISH > MARROW
MARROWS > MARROW
MARROWSKY n spoonerism
MARROWY > MARROW
MARRUM same as > MARRAM
MARRUMS > MARRUM
MARRY vb take as a husband or wife ▷ interj exclamation of surprise or anger
MARRYING > MARRY
MARRYINGS > MARRY
MARS > MAR
MARSALA n dark sweet dessert wine made in Sicily
MARSALAS > MARSALA
MARSE same as > MASTER
MARSEILLE n strong cotton fabric with a raised pattern, used for bedspreads, etc
MARSES > MARSE
MARSH n low-lying wet land
MARSHAL n officer of the highest rank ▷ vb arrange in order

MARSHALCY > MARSHAL
MARSHALED > MARSHAL
MARSHALER > MARSHAL
MARSHALL n shortened form of Marshall Plan, programme of US economic aid for the reconstruction of post-World War II Europe (1948–52)
MARSHALLS > MARSHALL
MARSHALS > MARSHAL
MARSHBUCK n antelope of the central African swamplands, with spreading hoofs adapted to boggy ground
MARSHED adj having a marsh
MARSHES > MARSH
MARSHIER > MARSHY
MARSHIEST > MARSHY
MARSHLAND n land consisting of marshes
MARSHLIKE > MARSH
MARSHWORT n type of creeping aquatic plant with small white flowers
MARSHY adj of, involving, or like a marsh
MARSPORT n spoilsport
MARSPORTS > MARSPORT
MARSQUAKE n Martian equivalent of earthquake
MARSUPIA > MARSUPIUM
MARSUPIAL n animal that carries its young in a pouch, such as a kangaroo ▷ adj of or like a marsupial
MARSUPIAN > MARSUPIAL
MARSUPIUM n external pouch in most female marsupials within which the newly born offspring are suckled and complete their development
MART n market ▷ vb sell or trade
MARTAGON n Eurasian lily plant cultivated for its mottled purplish-red flowers
MARTAGONS > MARTAGON
MARTED > MART
MARTEL n hammer-shaped weapon ▷ vb use such a weapon
MARTELLED > MARTEL
MARTELLO n small circular tower for coastal defence, formerly much used in Europe
MARTELLOS > MARTELLO
MARTELS > MARTEL
MARTEN n weasel-like animal
MARTENS > MARTEN
MARTEXT n preacher who makes many mistakes
MARTEXTS > MARTEXT
MARTIAL adj of war, warlike
MARTIALLY > MARTIAL

MARTIALS pl n as in court martials military courts that try people subject to military law
MARTIAN n inhabitant of Mars
MARTIANS > MARTIAN
MARTIN n bird with a slightly forked tail
MARTINET n person who maintains strict discipline
MARTINETS > MARTINET
MARTING > MART
MARTINGAL n strap of a horse's harness
MARTINI n cocktail of vermouth and gin
MARTINIS > MARTINI
MARTINS > MARTIN
MARTLET n footless bird often found in coats of arms
MARTLETS > MARTLET
MARTS > MART
MARTYR n person who dies or suffers for his or her beliefs ▷ vb make a martyr of
MARTYRDOM n sufferings or death of a martyr
MARTYRED > MARTYR
MARTYRIA > MARTYRIUM
MARTYRIES > MARTYRY
MARTYRING > MARTYR
MARTYRISE > MARTYR
MARTYRIUM same as > MARTYRY
MARTYRIZE > MARTYR
MARTYRLY > MARTYR
MARTYRS > MARTYR
MARTYRY n shrine or chapel erected in honour of a martyr
MARVEL vb be filled with wonder ▷ n wonderful thing
MARVELED > MARVEL
MARVELER n (US) person who marvels
MARVELERS > MARVELER
MARVELING > MARVEL
MARVELLED > MARVEL
MARVELOUS adj causing great wonder
MARVELS > MARVEL
MARVER vb roll molten glass on slab
MARVERED > MARVER
MARVERING > MARVER
MARVERS > MARVER
MARVIER > MARVY
MARVIEST > MARVY
MARVY shortened form of > MARVELOUS
MARXISANT adj sympathetic to Marxism
MARY n woman
MARYBUD n bud of marigold
MARYBUDS > MARYBUD
MARYJANE n slang for marijuana
MARYJANES > MARYJANE

MARZIPAN n paste of ground almonds, sugar, and egg whites ▷ vb cover with marzipan
MARZIPANS > MARZIPAN
MAS > MA
MASA n Mexican maize dough
MASALA n mixture of spices ground into a paste ▷ adj spicy
MASALAS > MASALA
MASAS > MASA
MASCARA n cosmetic for darkening the eyelashes
MASCARAED adj wearing mascara
MASCARAS > MASCARA
MASCARON n in architecture, a face carved in stone or metal
MASCARONS n grotesque face used as decoration
MASCLE n charge consisting of a lozenge with a lozenge-shaped hole in the middle
MASCLED > MASCLE
MASCLES > MASCLE
MASCON n any of several lunar regions of high gravity
MASCONS > MASCON
MASCOT n person, animal, or thing supposed to bring good luck
MASCOTS > MASCOT
MASCULINE adj relating to males
MASCULIST n advocate of rights of men)
MASCULY > MASCLE
MASE vb function as maser
MASED > MASE
MASER n device for amplifying microwaves
MASERS > MASER
MASES > MASE
MASH n soft pulpy mass ▷ vb crush into a soft mass
MASHALLAH interj what Allah wishes
MASHED > MASH
MASHER > MASH
MASHERS > MASH
MASHES > MASH
MASHGIACH n person who ensures adherence to kosher rules
MASHGIAH same as > MASHGIACH
MASHGIHIM > MASHGIACH
MASHIACH n messiah
MASHIACHS > MASHIACH
MASHIE n former golf club, used for approach shots
MASHIER > MASHY
MASHIES > MASHIE
MASHIEST > MASHY
MASHING > MASH
MASHINGS > MASH
MASHLAM same as > MASLIN

MASHLAMS > MASHLAM
MASHLIM same as > MASLIN
MASHLIMS > MASHLIM
MASHLIN same as > MASLIN
MASHLINS > MASHLIN
MASHLOCH same as > MASLIN
MASHLOCHS > MASHLOCH
MASHLUM same as > MASLIN
MASHLUMS > MASHLUM
MASHMAN n brewery worker
MASHMEN > MASHMAN
MASHUA n South American plant
MASHUAS > MASHUA
MASHUP n piece of music in which a producer or DJ blends together two or more tracks
MASHUPS > MASHUP
MASHY adj like mash
MASING > MASE
MASJID same as > MOSQUE
MASJIDS > MASJID
MASK n covering for the face, as a disguise or protection ▷ vb cover with a mask
MASKABLE > MASK
MASKED adj disguised or covered by or as if by a mask
MASKEG n North American bog
MASKEGS > MASKEG
MASKER n person who wears a mask or takes part in a masque
MASKERS > MASKER
MASKING n act or practice of masking
MASKINGS > MASKING
MASKLIKE > MASK
MASKS > MASK
MASLIN n mixture of wheat, rye or other grain
MASLINS > MASLIN
MASOCHISM n condition in which (sexual) pleasure is obtained from feeling pain or from being humiliated
MASOCHIST > MASOCHISM
MASON n person who works with stone ▷ vb construct or strengthen with masonry
MASONED > MASON
MASONIC adj of, characteristic of, or relating to Freemasons
MASONING > MASON
MASONITE n tradename for a kind of dark brown hardboard used for partitions, lining, etc
MASONITES > MASONITE
MASONRIED adj built of masonry

MASONRIES > MASONRY

MASONRY n stonework

MASONS > MASON

MASOOLAH n Indian boat used in surf

MASOOLAHS > MASOOLAH

MASQUE n 16th–17th-century form of dramatic entertainment

MASQUER same as > MASKER

MASQUERS > MASQUER

MASQUES > MASQUE

MASS n coherent body of matter ▷ adj large-scale ▷ vb form into a mass

MASSA old fashioned variant of > MASTER

MASSACRE n indiscriminate killing of large numbers of people ▷ vb kill in large numbers

MASSACRED > MASSACRE

MASSACRER > MASSACRE

MASSACRES > MASSACRE

MASSAGE n rubbing and kneading of parts of the body to reduce pain or stiffness ▷ vb give a massage to

MASSAGED > MASSAGE

MASSAGER > MASSAGE

MASSAGERS > MASSAGE

MASSAGES > MASSAGE

MASSAGING > MASSAGE

MASSAGIST > MASSAGE

MASSAS > MASSA

MASSCULT n culture of masses

MASSCULTS > MASSCULT

MASSE n billiard stroke that makes the ball move in a curve around another ball

MASSED > MASS

MASSEDLY > MASS

MASSES pl n body of common people

MASSETER n muscle of the cheek used in moving the jaw, esp in chewing

MASSETERS > MASSETER

MASSEUR n person who gives massages

MASSEURS > MASSEUR

MASSEUSE n woman who gives massages, esp as a profession

MASSEUSES > MASSEUSE

MASSICOT n yellow earthy secondary mineral

MASSICOTS > MASSICOT

MASSIER > MASSY

MASSIEST > MASSY

MASSIF n connected group of mountains

MASSIFS > MASSIF

MASSINESS > MASSY

MASSING > MASS

MASSIVE adj large and heavy ▷ n group of friends or associates

MASSIVELY > MASSIVE

MASSIVES > MASSIVE

MASSLESS > MASS

MASSOOLA same as > MASOOLAH

MASSOOLAS > MASSOOLA

MASSTIGE n impression of exclusivity in mass-produced goods

MASSTIGES > MASSTIGE

MASSY literary word for > MASSIVE

MASSYMORE n underground prison

MAST n tall pole for supporting something, esp a ship's sails

MASTABA n mud-brick superstructure above tombs in ancient Egypt

MASTABAH same as > MASTABA

MASTABAHS > MASTABAH

MASTABAS > MASTABA

MASTED > MAST

MASTER n person in control, such as an employer or an owner of slaves or animals ▷ vb acquire knowledge of or skill in

MASTERATE n status of master

MASTERDOM > MASTER

MASTERED > MASTER

MASTERFUL adj domineering

MASTERIES > MASTERY

MASTERING > MASTER

MASTERLY adj showing great skill

MASTERS > MASTER

MASTERY n expertise

MASTFUL > MAST

MASTHEAD n head of a mast ▷ vb send (a sailor) to the masthead as a punishment

MASTHEADS > MASTHEAD

MASTHOUSE n place for storing masts

MASTIC n gum obtained from certain trees

MASTICATE vb chew

MASTICH same as > MASTIC

MASTICHE same as > MASTIC

MASTICHES > MASTICHE

MASTICHS > MASTICH

MASTICOT same as > MASSICOT

MASTICOTS > MASTICOT

MASTICS > MASTIC

MASTIER > MAST

MASTIEST > MAST

MASTIFF n large dog

MASTIFFS > MASTIFF

MASTING > MAST

MASTITIC > MASTITIS

MASTITIS n inflammation of a breast or udder

MASTIX n type of gum

MASTIXES > MASTIX

MASTLESS > MAST

MASTLIKE > MAST

MASTODON n extinct elephant-like mammal

MASTODONS > MASTODON

MASTODONT same as > MASTODON

MASTOID n projection of the bone behind the ear ▷ adj shaped like a nipple or breast

MASTOIDAL > MASTOID

MASTOIDS > MASTOID

MASTOPEXY n cosmetic surgery of breasts

MASTS > MAST

MASTY > MAST

MASU n Japanese salmon

MASULA same as > MASOOLAH

MASULAS > MASULA

MASURIUM n silver-grey metallic element

MASURIUMS > MASURIUM

MASUS > MASU

MAT n piece of fabric used as a floor covering or to protect a surface ▷ vb tangle or become tangled into a dense mass ▷ adj having a dull, lustreless, or roughened surface

MATACHIN n dancer with sword

MATACHINA n female matachin

MATACHINI > MATACHIN

MATACHINS > MATACHIN

MATADOR n man who kills the bull in bullfights

MATADORA n female matador

MATADORAS > MATADORA

MATADORE n form of dominoes game

MATADORES > MATADORE

MATADORS > MATADOR

MATAGOURI n thorny bush of New Zealand that forms thickets in open country

MATAI n New Zealand tree, the wood of which is used for timber for building

MATAIS > MATAI

MATAMATA (in Malaysia) a former name for > POLICE

MATAMATAS > MATAMATA

MATAMBALA > TAMBALA

MATATA same as > FERNBIRD

MATATAS > MATATA

MATATU n type of shared taxi used in Kenya

MATATUS > MATATU

MATCH n contest in a game or sport ▷ vb be exactly like, equal to, or in harmony with

MATCHABLE > MATCH

MATCHBOOK n number of cardboard matches attached in folder

MATCHBOX n small box for holding matches

MATCHED > MATCH

MATCHER > MATCH

MATCHERS > MATCH

MATCHES > MATCH

MATCHET same as > MACHETE

MATCHETS > MATCHET

MATCHING > MATCH

MATCHLESS adj unequalled

MATCHLOCK n obsolete type of gunlock igniting the powder by means of a slow match

MATCHMADE > MATCHMAKE

MATCHMAKE vb bring suitable people together for marriage

MATCHMARK n mark made on mating components of an engine, machine, etc, to ensure that the components are assembled in the correct relative positions ▷ vb stamp (an object) with matchmarks

MATCHPLAY adj of a golf scoring system relating to holes won and lost ▷ n (in golf) scoring system in which a point is earned for each hole won

MATCHUP n sports match

MATCHUPS > MATCHUP

MATCHWOOD n small splinters

MATE n friend ▷ vb pair (animals) or (of animals) be paired for reproduction

MATED > MATE

MATELASSE adj (in textiles) having a raised design, as quilting

MATELESS > MATE

MATELOT n sailor

MATELOTE n fish served with a sauce of wine, onions, seasonings, and fish stock

MATELOTES > MATELOTE

MATELOTS > MATELOT

MATELOTTE same as > MATELOTE

MATER n mother: often used facetiously

MATERIAL n substance of which a thing is made ▷ adj of matter or substance

MATERIALS pl n equipment necessary for a particular activity

MATERIEL n materials and equipment of an organization, esp of a military force

MATERIELS > MATERIEL

MATERNAL adj of a mother

MATERNITY n motherhood ▷ adj of or for pregnant women

MATERS > MATER
MATES > MATE
MATESHIP n comradeship of friends, usually male, viewed as an institution
MATESHIPS > MATESHIP
MATEY adj friendly or intimate ▷ n friend or fellow: usually used in direct address
MATEYNESS > MATEY
MATEYS > MATEY
MATFELLON n knapweed
MATFELON n knapweed
MATFELONS > MATFELON
MATGRASS n widespread perennial European grass with dense tufts of bristly leaves, characteristic of peaty moors
MATH same as > MATHS
MATHESES > MATHESIS
MATHESIS n learning or wisdom
MATHS same as > MATH
MATICO n Peruvian shrub
MATICOS > MATICO
MATIER > MATY
MATIES > MATY
MATIEST > MATY
MATILDA n bushman's swag
MATILDAS > MATILDA
MATILY > MATY
MATIN adj of or relating to matins
MATINAL same as > MATIN
MATINEE n afternoon performance in a theatre or cinema
MATINEES > MATINEE
MATINESS > MATY
MATING > MATE
MATINGS > MATE
MATINS pl n early morning church service
MATIPO n New Zealand shrub
MATIPOS > MATIPO
MATJES same as > MAATJES
MATLESS > MAT
MATLO same as > MATELOT
MATLOS > MATLO
MATLOW same as > MATELOT
MATLOWS > MATLOW
MATOKE n (in Uganda) the flesh of bananas, boiled and mashed as a food
MATOKES > MATOKE
MATOOKE same as > MATOKE
MATOOKES > MATOOKE
MATRASS n long-necked glass flask
MATRASSES > MATRASS
MATRES > MATER
MATRIARCH n female head of a tribe or family
MATRIC n matriculation
MATRICE same as > MATRIX

MATRICES > MATRIX
MATRICIDE n crime of killing one's mother
MATRICS > MATRIC
MATRICULA n register
MATRILINY n attention to descent of kinship through the female line
MATRIMONY n marriage
MATRIX n substance or situation in which something originates, takes form, or is enclosed
MATRIXES > MATRIX
MATRON n staid or dignified married woman
MATRONAGE n state of being a matron
MATRONAL > MATRON
MATRONISE same as > MATRONIZE
MATRONIZE vb make matronly
MATRONLY adj (of a woman) middle-aged and plump
MATRONS > MATRON
MATROSS n gunner's assistant
MATROSSES > MATROSS
MATS > MAT
MATSAH same as > MATZO
MATSAHS > MATSAH
MATSURI n Japanese religious ceremony
MATSURIS > MATSURI
MATSUTAKE n Japanese mushroom
MATT adj dull, not shiny
MATTAMORE n subterranean storehouse or dwelling
MATTE same as > MATT
MATTED > MAT
MATTEDLY > MAT
MATTER n substance of which something is made ▷ vb be of importance
MATTERED > MATTER
MATTERFUL > MATTER
MATTERING > MATTER
MATTERS > MATTER
MATTERY adj discharging pus
MATTES > MATTE
MATTIE n young herring
MATTIES > MATTIE
MATTIFIED > MATTIFY
MATTIFIES > MATTIFY
MATTIFY vb make (the skin of the face) less oily or shiny using cosmetics
MATTIN same as > MATIN
MATTING > MAT
MATTINGS > MAT
MATTINS same as > MATINS
MATTOCK n large pick with one of its blade ends flattened for loosening soil
MATTOCKS > MATTOCK
MATTOID n person displaying eccentric

behaviour and mental characteristics
MATTOIDS > MATTOID
MATTRASS same as > MATRASS
MATTRESS n large stuffed flat case, often with springs, used on or as a bed
MATTS > MATT
MATURABLE > MATURE
MATURATE vb mature or bring to maturity
MATURATED > MATURATE
MATURATES > MATURATE
MATURE adj fully developed or grown-up ▷ vb make or become mature
MATURED > MATURE
MATURELY > MATURE
MATURER > MATURE
MATURERS > MATURE
MATURES > MATURE
MATUREST > MATURE
MATURING > MATURE
MATURITY n state of being mature
MATUTINAL adj of, occurring in, or during the morning
MATUTINE same as > MATUTINAL
MATWEED n grass found on moors
MATWEEDS > MATWEED
MATY same as > MATEY
MATZA same as > MATZO
MATZAH same as > MATZO
MATZAHS > MATZAH
MATZAS > MATZA
MATZO n large very thin biscuit of unleavened bread
MATZOH same as > MATZO
MATZOHS > MATZOH
MATZOON n fermented milk product similar to yogurt
MATZOONS > MATZOON
MATZOS > MATZO
MATZOT > MATZO
MATZOTH > MATZOH
MAUBIES > MAUBY
MAUBY n Caribbean bittersweet drink
MAUD n shawl or rug of grey wool plaid
MAUDLIN adj foolishly or tearfully sentimental
MAUDLINLY > MAUDLIN
MAUDS > MAUD
MAUGER same as > MAUGRE
MAUGRE prep in spite of ▷ vb behave spitefully towards
MAUGRED > MAUGRE
MAUGRES > MAUGRE
MAUGRING > MAUGRE
MAUL vb handle roughly ▷ n loose scrum
MAULED > MAUL
MAULER > MAUL

MAULERS pl n hands
MAULGRE same as > MAUGRE
MAULGRED > MAULGRE
MAULGRES > MAULGRE
MAULGRING > MAULGRE
MAULING n act of mauling
MAULINGS > MAULING
MAULS > MAUL
MAULSTICK n long stick used by artists to steady the hand holding the brush
MAULVI n expert in Islamic law
MAULVIS > MAULVI
MAUMET n false god
MAUMETRY > MAUMET
MAUMETS > MAUMET
MAUN dialect word for > MUST
MAUND n unit of weight used in Asia ▷ vb beg
MAUNDED > MAUND
MAUNDER vb talk or act aimlessly or idly
MAUNDERED > MAUNDER
MAUNDERER > MAUNDER
MAUNDERS > MAUNDER
MAUNDIES > MAUNDY
MAUNDING > MAUND
MAUNDS > MAUND
MAUNDY n ceremonial washing of the feet of poor people
MAUNGIER > MAUNGY
MAUNGIEST > MAUNGY
MAUNGY adj (esp of a child) sulky, bad-tempered, or peevish
MAUNNA vb Scots term meaning must not
MAURI n soul
MAURIS > MAURI
MAUSIER > MAUSY
MAUSIEST > MAUSY
MAUSOLEA > MAUSOLEUM
MAUSOLEAN > MAUSOLEUM
MAUSOLEUM n stately tomb
MAUSY adj foggy; misty
MAUT same as > MAHOUT
MAUTHER n girl
MAUTHERS > MAUTHER
MAUTS > MAUT
MAUVAIS adj bad
MAUVAISE feminine form of > MAUVAIS
MAUVE adj pale purple ▷ n any of various pale purple colours
MAUVEIN same as > MAUVEINE
MAUVEINE same as > MAUVE
MAUVEINES > MAUVEINE
MAUVEINS > MAUVEIN
MAUVER > MAUVE
MAUVES > MAUVE
MAUVEST > MAUVE
MAUVIN same as > MAUVEINE

MAUVINE same as
> MAUVEINE
MAUVINES > MAUVINE
MAUVINS > MAUVIN
MAUZIER > MAUZY
MAUZIEST > MAUZY
MAUZY adj foggy; misty
MAVEN n expert or
connoisseur
MAVENS > MAVEN
MAVERICK adj
independent and
unorthodox (person)
▷ n person of independent
or unorthodox views
▷ vb take illegally
MAVERICKS > MAVERICK
MAVIE n type of thrush
MAVIES > MAVIE
MAVIN same as > MAVEN
MAVINS > MAVIN
MAVIS n song thrush
MAVISES > MAVIS
MAVOURNIN n Irish form
of address meaning my
darling
MAW n animal's mouth,
throat, or stomach ▷ vb
eat or bite
MAWBOUND adj (of cattle)
constipated
MAWED > MAW
MAWGER adj (of persons or
animals) thin or lean
MAWING > MAW
MAWK n maggot
MAWKIER > MAWK
MAWKIEST > MAWK
MAWKIN n slovenly
woman
MAWKINS > MAWKIN
MAWKISH adj foolishly
sentimental
MAWKISHLY > MAWKISH
MAWKS > MAWK
MAWKY > MAWK
MAWMET same as > MAUMET
MAWMETRY > MAWMET
MAWMETS > MAWMET
MAWN n measure of
capacity
MAWNS > MAWN
MAWPUS same as > MOPUS
MAWPUSES > MAWPUS
MAWR same as > MAUTHER
MAWRS > MAWR
MAWS > MAW
MAWSEED n poppy seed
MAWSEEDS > MAWSEED
MAWTHER same as
> MAUTHER
MAWTHERS > MAWTHER
MAX vb reach the full extent
MAXED > MAX
MAXES > MAX
MAXI adj (of a garment)
very long ▷ n type of large
racing yacht
MAXIBOAT n large racing
yacht
MAXIBOATS > MAXIBOAT
MAXICOAT n long coat
MAXICOATS > MAXICOAT

MAXIDRESS n dress that
reaches the ankle
MAXILLA n upper
jawbone of a vertebrate
MAXILLAE > MAXILLA
MAXILLAR > MAXILLA
MAXILLARY > MAXILLA
MAXILLAS > MAXILLA
MAXILLULA n jaw in
crustacean
MAXIM n general truth or
principle
MAXIMA > MAXIMUM
MAXIMAL adj maximum
▷ n maximum
MAXIMALLY > MAXIMAL
MAXIMALS > MAXIMAL
MAXIMAND n something
that is to be maximized
MAXIMANDS > MAXIMAND
MAXIMIN n highest of a
set of minimum values
MAXIMINS > MAXIMIN
MAXIMISE same as
> MAXIMIZE
MAXIMISED > MAXIMISE
MAXIMISER > MAXIMIZE
MAXIMISES > MAXIMISE
MAXIMIST > MAXIM
MAXIMISTS > MAXIM
MAXIMITE n type of
explosive
MAXIMITES > MAXIMITE
MAXIMIZE vb increase to
a maximum
MAXIMIZED > MAXIMIZE
MAXIMIZER > MAXIMIZE
MAXIMIZES > MAXIMIZE
MAXIMS > MAXIM
MAXIMUM n greatest
possible (amount or
number) ▷ adj of, being, or
showing a maximum or
maximums
MAXIMUMLY > MAXIMUM
MAXIMUMS > MAXIMUM
MAXIMUS n method rung
on twelve bells
MAXIMUSES > MAXIMUS
MAXING > MAX
MAXIS > MAXI
MAXIXE n Brazilian dance
in duple time
MAXIXES > MAXIXE
MAXWELL n cgs unit of
magnetic flux
MAXWELLS > MAXWELL
MAY vb used as an auxiliary
to express possibility,
permission, opportunity,
etc ▷ vb gather may
MAYA n illusion, esp the
material world of the
senses regarded as illusory
MAYAN > MAYA
MAYAPPLE n American
plant
MAYAPPLES > MAYAPPLE
MAYAS > MAYA
MAYBE adv perhaps,
possibly ▷ sentence
substitute possibly
MAYBES > MAYBE

MAYBIRD n American
songbird
MAYBIRDS > MAYBIRD
MAYBUSH n flowering
shrub
MAYBUSHES > MAYBUSH
MAYDAY n international
radiotelephone distress
signal
MAYDAYS > MAYDAY
MAYED > MAY
MAYEST same as > MAYST
MAYFISH n type of N
American fish
MAYFISHES > MAYFISH
MAYFLIES > MAYFLY
MAYFLOWER n any of
various plants that bloom
in May
MAYFLY n short-lived
aquatic insect
MAYHAP archaic word for
> PERHAPS
MAYHAPPEN same as
> MAYHAP
MAYHEM n violent
destruction or confusion
MAYHEMS > MAYHEM
MAYING > MAY
MAYINGS > MAYING
MAYO n mayonnaise
MAYOR n head of a
municipality
MAYORAL > MAYOR
MAYORALTY n (term of)
office of a mayor
MAYORESS n mayor's wife
MAYORS > MAYOR
MAYORSHIP > MAYOR
MAYOS > MAYO
MAYPOLE n pole set up for
dancing round on the first
day of May to celebrate
spring
MAYPOLES > MAYPOLE
MAYPOP n American wild
flower
MAYPOPS > MAYPOP
MAYS > MAY
MAYST singular form of the
present tense of > MAY
MAYSTER same as
> MASTER
MAYSTERS > MAYSTER
MAYVIN same as > MAVEN
MAYVINS > MAYVIN
MAYWEED n widespread
Eurasian weedy plant
MAYWEEDS > MAYWEED
MAZAEDIA > MAZAEDIUM
MAZAEDIUM n part of
lichen
MAZARD same as > MAZER
MAZARDS > MAZARD
MAZARINE n blue colour
MAZARINES > MAZARINE
MAZE n complex network
of paths or lines
MAZED > MAZE
MAZEDLY adv in a
bewildered way
MAZEDNESS n
bewilderment

MAZEFUL > MAZE
MAZELIKE > MAZE
MAZELTOV interj
congratulations
MAZEMENT > MAZE
MAZEMENTS > MAZE
MAZER n large hardwood
drinking bowl
MAZERS > MAZER
MAZES > MAZE
MAZEY adj dizzy
MAZHBI n low-caste Sikh
MAZHBIS > MAZHBI
MAZIER > MAZY
MAZIEST > MAZY
MAZILY > MAZY
MAZINESS > MAZY
MAZING > MAZE
MAZOURKA same as
> MAZURKA
MAZOURKAS > MAZOURKA
MAZOUT same as > MAZUT
MAZOUTS > MAZOUT
MAZUMA n money
MAZUMAS > MAZUMA
MAZURKA n lively Polish
dance
MAZURKAS > MAZURKA
MAZUT n residue left after
distillation of petrol
MAZUTS > MAZUT
MAZY adj of or like a maze
MAZZARD same as
> MAZARD
MAZZARDS > MAZZARD
MBAQANGA n style of Black
popular music of urban
South Africa
MBAQANGAS > MBAQANGA
MBIRA n African musical
instrument
MBIRAS > MBIRA
ME n (in tonic sol-fa) third
degree of any major scale
▷ pron refers to the speaker
or writer
MEACOCK n timid person
MEACOCKS > MEACOCK
MEAD n alcoholic drink
made from honey
MEADOW n piece of
grassland
MEADOWS > MEADOW
MEADOWY > MEADOW
MEADS > MEAD
MEAGER same as > MEAGRE
MEAGERER > MEAGER
MEAGEREST > MEAGER
MEAGERLY > MEAGRE
MEAGRE adj scanty or
insufficient ▷ n
Mediterranean fish
MEAGRELY > MEAGRE
MEAGRER > MEAGRE
MEAGRES > MEAGRE
MEAGREST > MEAGRE
MEAL n occasion when
food is served and eaten
▷ vb cover with meal
MEALED > MEAL
MEALER n person eating
but not lodging at
boarding house

m

MEALERS > MEALER
MEALIE n maize
MEALIER > MEALY
MEALIES South African word for > MAIZE
MEALIEST > MEALY
MEALINESS > MEALY
MEALING > MEAL
MEALLESS > MEAL
MEALS > MEAL
MEALTIME n time for meal
MEALTIMES > MEALTIME
MEALWORM n larva of various beetles which feeds on meal, flour, and similar stored foods
MEALWORMS > MEALWORM
MEALY adj resembling meal
MEALYBUG n plant-eating homopterous insect
MEALYBUGS > MEALYBUG
MEAN vb intend to convey or express ▷ adj miserly, ungenerous, or petty ▷ n middle point between two extremes
MEANDER vb follow a winding course ▷ n winding course
MEANDERED > MEANDER
MEANDERER > MEANDER
MEANDERS > MEANDER
MEANDRIAN > MEANDER
MEANDROUS > MEANDER
MEANE vb moan
MEANED > MEANE
MEANER > MEAN
MEANERS > MEAN
MEANES > MEANE
MEANEST > MEAN
MEANIE n unkind or miserly person
MEANIES > MEANY
MEANING n what something means
MEANINGLY > MEAN
MEANINGS > MEANING
MEANLY > MEAN
MEANNESS > MEAN
MEANS > MEAN
MEANT > MEAN
MEANTIME n intervening period ▷ adv meanwhile
MEANTIMES > MEANTIME
MEANWHILE adv during the intervening period
MEANY same as > MEANIE
MEARE same as > MERE
MEARES > MEARE
MEARING adj forming boundary
MEASE vb assuage
MEASED > MEASE
MEASES > MEASE
MEASING > MEASE
MEASLE vb infect with measles
MEASLED adj (of cattle, sheep, or pigs) infested with tapeworm larvae
MEASLES n infectious disease producing red spots

MEASLIER > MEASLY
MEASLIEST > MEASLY
MEASLING > MEASLE
MEASLY adj meagre
MEASURE n size or quantity ▷ vb determine the size or quantity of
MEASURED adj slow and steady
MEASURER > MEASURE
MEASURERS > MEASURE
MEASURES pl n rock strata that contain a particular type of deposit
MEASURING adj used to measure quantities, esp in cooking
MEAT n animal flesh as food
MEATAL > MEATUS
MEATAXE n meat cleaver
MEATAXES > MEATAXE
MEATBALL n minced beef, shaped into a ball before cooking
MEATBALLS > MEATBALL
MEATED adj fattened
MEATH same as > MEAD
MEATHE same as > MEAD
MEATHEAD n stupid person
MEATHEADS > MEATHEAD
MEATHES > MEATHE
MEATHOOK n hook on which to hang meat
MEATHOOKS > MEATHOOK
MEATHS > MEATH
MEATIER > MEATY
MEATIEST > MEATY
MEATILY > MEATY
MEATINESS > MEATY
MEATLESS > MEAT
MEATLOAF n chopped meat served in loaf-shaped mass
MEATMAN n meat seller
MEATMEN > MEATMAN
MEATS > MEAT
MEATSPACE n real physical world, as contrasted with the world of cyberspace
MEATUS n natural opening or channel
MEATUSES > MEATUS
MEATY adj (tasting) of or like meat
MEAWES same as > MEWS
MEAZEL same as > MESEL
MEAZELS > MEAZEL
MEBOS n South African dish of dried apricots
MEBOSES > MEBOS
MECCA n place that attracts many visitors
MECCAS > MECCA
MECH n mechanic
MECHANIC n person skilled in repairing or operating machinery
MECHANICS n scientific study of motion and force

MECHANISE same as > MECHANIZE
MECHANISM n way a machine works
MECHANIST same as > MECHANIC
MECHANIZE vb equip with machinery
MECHITZA n screen in synagogue separating men and women
MECHITZAS > MECHITZA
MECHITZOT > MECHITZA
MECHOUI n Canadian dish of meat roasted on a spit
MECHOUIS > MECHOUI
MECHS > MECH
MECK same as > MAIK
MECKS > MECK
MECLIZINE n drug used to treat motion sickness
MECONATE n salt of meconic acid
MECONATES > MECONATE
MECONIC adj derived from poppies
MECONIN n substance found in opium
MECONINS > MECONIN
MECONIUM n dark green mucoid material that forms the first faeces of a newborn infant
MECONIUMS > MECONIUM
MED n doctor
MEDACCA n Japanese freshwater fish
MEDACCAS > MEDACCA
MEDAILLON n small round thin piece of food
MEDAKA same as > MEDACCA
MEDAKAS > MEDAKA
MEDAL n piece of metal with an inscription etc, given as a reward or memento ▷ vb honour with a medal
MEDALED > MEDAL
MEDALET n small medal
MEDALETS > MEDALET
MEDALING > MEDAL
MEDALIST same as > MEDALLIST
MEDALISTS > MEDALIST
MEDALLED > MEDAL
MEDALLIC > MEDAL
MEDALLING > MEDAL
MEDALLION n disc-shaped ornament worn on a chain round the neck
MEDALLIST n winner of a medal
MEDALPLAY n (in golf) scoring system in which the score is based on the total number of strokes taken
MEDALS > MEDAL
MEDCINAL same as > MEDICINAL
MEDDLE vb interfere annoyingly
MEDDLED > MEDDLE

MEDDLER > MEDDLE
MEDDLERS > MEDDLE
MEDDLES > MEDDLE
MEDDLING > MEDDLE
MEDDLINGS > MEDDLE
MEDEVAC n evacuation of casualties ▷ vb transport (a wounded or sick person) to hospital
MEDEVACED > MEDEVAC
MEDEVACS > MEDEVAC
MEDFLIES > MEDFLY
MEDFLY n Mediterranean fruit fly
MEDIA n medium of cultivation, conveyance, or expression
MEDIACIES > MEDIACY
MEDIACY n quality or state of being mediate
MEDIAD adj situated near the median line or plane of an organism
MEDIAE > MEDIUM
MEDIAEVAL adj of, relating to, or in the style of the Middle Ages ▷ n person living in medieval times
MEDIAL adj of or in the middle ▷ n speech sound between being fortis and lenis
MEDIALLY > MEDIAL
MEDIALS > MEDIAL
MEDIAN n middle (point or line) ▷ adj of, relating to, situated in, or directed towards the middle
MEDIANLY > MEDIAN
MEDIANS > MEDIAN
MEDIANT n third degree of a major or minor scale
MEDIANTS > MEDIANT
MEDIAS > MEDIUM
MEDIATE vb intervene in a dispute to bring about agreement ▷ adj occurring as a result of or dependent upon mediation
MEDIATED > MEDIATE
MEDIATELY > MEDIATE
MEDIATES > MEDIATE
MEDIATING > MEDIATE
MEDIATION n act of mediating
MEDIATISE same as > MEDIATIZE
MEDIATIVE > MEDIATE
MEDIATIZE vb annex (a state) to another state, allowing the former ruler to retain his title and some authority
MEDIATOR > MEDIATE
MEDIATORS > MEDIATE
MEDIATORY > MEDIATE
MEDIATRIX n female mediator
MEDIC n doctor or medical student
MEDICABLE adj potentially able to be treated or cured medically

MEDICABLY
>MEDICABLE
MEDICAID *n* health assistance programme financed by federal, state, and local taxes to help pay hospital and medical costs for persons of low income
MEDICAIDS >MEDICAID
MEDICAL *adj* of the science of medicine ▷ *n* medical examination
MEDICALLY >MEDICAL
MEDICALS >MEDICAL
MEDICANT *n* medicinal substance
MEDICANTS >MEDICANT
MEDICARE *n* (in the US) a federally sponsored health insurance programme for persons of 65 or older
MEDICARES >MEDICARE
MEDICATE *vb* treat with a medicinal substance
MEDICATED *adj* (of a patient) having been treated with a medicine or drug
MEDICATES >MEDICATE
MEDICIDE *n* suicide assisted by doctor
MEDICIDES >MEDICIDE
MEDICINAL *adj* having therapeutic properties ▷ *n* medicinal substance
MEDICINE *n* substance used to treat disease ▷ *vb* treat with medicine
MEDICINED >MEDICINE
MEDICINER *n* physician
MEDICINES >MEDICINE
MEDICK *n* type of small leguminous plant with yellow or purple flowers
MEDICKS >MEDICK
MEDICO *n* doctor or medical student
MEDICOS >MEDICO
MEDICS >MEDIC
MEDIEVAL *adj* of the Middle Ages ▷ *n* person living in medieval times
MEDIEVALS >MEDIEVAL
MEDIGAP *n* private health insurance
MEDIGAPS >MEDIGAP
MEDII >MEDIUS
MEDINA *n* ancient quarter of North African city
MEDINAS >MEDINA
MEDIOCRE *adj* average in quality
MEDITATE *vb* reflect deeply, esp on spiritual matters
MEDITATED >MEDITATE
MEDITATES >MEDITATE
MEDITATOR >MEDITATE
MEDIUM *adj* midway between extremes, average ▷ *n* middle state, degree, or condition
MEDIUMS *pl n* medium-dated gilt-edged securities

MEDIUS *n* middle finger
MEDIUSES >MEDIUS
MEDIVAC *variant spelling of* >MEDEVAC
MEDIVACED >MEDIVAC
MEDIVACS >MEDIVAC
MEDLAR *n* apple-like fruit of a small tree
MEDLARS >MEDLAR
MEDLE *same as* >MEDDLE
MEDLED >MEDLE
MEDLES >MEDLE
MEDLEY *n* miscellaneous mixture ▷ *adj* of, being, or relating to a mixture or variety
MEDLEYS >MEDLEY
MEDLING >MEDLE
MEDRESA *same as* >MADRASAH
MEDRESAS >MEDRESA
MEDRESE *same as* >MADRASAH
MEDRESES >MEDRESE
MEDRESSEH *same as* >MADRASAH
MEDS >MED
MEDULLA *n* marrow, pith, or inner tissue
MEDULLAE >MEDULLA
MEDULLAR >MEDULLA
MEDULLARY >MEDULLA
MEDULLAS >MEDULLA
MEDULLATE *adj* having medulla
MEDUSA *n* jellyfish
MEDUSAE >MEDUSA
MEDUSAL >MEDUSA
MEDUSAN >MEDUSA
MEDUSANS >MEDUSA
MEDUSAS >MEDUSA
MEDUSOID *same as* >MEDUSA
MEDUSOIDS >MEDUSOID
MEE *n* Malaysian noodle dish
MEED *n* recompense
MEEDS >MEED
MEEK *adj* submissive or humble
MEEKEN *vb* make meek
MEEKENED >MEEKEN
MEEKENING >MEEKEN
MEEKENS >MEEKEN
MEEKER >MEEK
MEEKEST >MEEK
MEEKLY >MEEK
MEEKNESS >MEEK
MEEMIE *n* hysterical person
MEEMIES >MEEMIE
MEER *same as* >MERE
MEERCAT *same as* >MEERKAT
MEERCATS >MEERCAT
MEERED >MEER
MEERING >MEER
MEERKAT *n* S African mongoose
MEERKATS >MEERKAT
MEERS >MEER
MEES >MEE

MEET *vb* come together (with) ▷ *n* meeting, esp a sports meeting ▷ *adj* fit or suitable
MEETER >MEET
MEETERS >MEET
MEETEST >MEET
MEETING >MEET
MEETINGS >MEET
MEETLY >MEET
MEETNESS *n* properness
MEETS >MEET
MEFF *dialect word for* >TRAMP
MEFFS >MEFF
MEG *short for* >MEGABYTE
MEGA *adj* extremely good, great, or successful
MEGABAR *n* unit of million bars
MEGABARS >MEGABAR
MEGABIT *n* one million bits
MEGABITS >MEGABIT
MEGABUCK *n* million dollars
MEGABUCKS >MEGABUCK
MEGABYTE *n* 2^{20} or 1 048 576 bytes
MEGABYTES >MEGABYTE
MEGACITY *n* city with over 10 million inhabitants
MEGACURIE *n* unit of million curies
MEGACYCLE *same as* >MEGAHERTZ
MEGADEAL *n* very good deal
MEGADEALS >MEGADEAL
MEGADEATH *n* death of a million people, esp in a nuclear war or attack
MEGADOSE *n* very large dose, as of a medicine, vitamin, etc
MEGADOSES >MEGADOSE
MEGADYNE *n* unit of million dynes
MEGADYNES >MEGADYNE
MEGAFARAD *n* unit of million farads
MEGAFAUNA *n* component of the fauna of a region or period that comprises the larger terrestrial animals
MEGAFLOP *n* measure of processing speed, consisting of a million floating-point operations a second
MEGAFLOPS >MEGAFLOP
MEGAFLORA *n* plants large enough to be seen by naked eye
MEGAFOG *n* amplified fog signal
MEGAFOGS >MEGAFOG
MEGAGAUSS *n* unit of million gauss
MEGAHERTZ *n* one million hertz
MEGAHIT *n* great success
MEGAHITS >MEGAHIT

MEGAJOULE *n* unit of million joules
MEGALITH *n* great stone, esp as part of a prehistoric monument
MEGALITHS >MEGALITH
MEGALITRE *n* one million litres
MEGALODON *n* an extinct giant shark of the Cenozoic era
MEGALOPIC *adj* having large eyes
MEGALOPS *n* crab in larval stage
MEGAMALL *n* very large shopping mall
MEGAMALLS >MEGAMALL
MEGAPHONE *n* cone-shaped instrument used to amplify the voice ▷ *vb* speak through megaphone
MEGAPHYLL *n* relatively large type of leaf produced by ferns and seed plants
MEGAPIXEL *n* one million pixels
MEGAPLEX *n* cinema complex containing a large number of separate screens, and usually a restaurant or bar
MEGAPOD *same as* >MEGAPODE
MEGAPODE *n* bird of Australia, New Guinea, and adjacent islands
MEGAPODES >MEGAPODE
MEGAPODS >MEGAPOD
MEGAQUAKE *n* very large earthquake
MEGARA >MEGARON
MEGARAD *n* unit of million rads
MEGARADS >MEGARAD
MEGARON *n* tripartite rectangular room, found in Bronze Age Greece and Asia Minor
MEGARONS >MEGARON
MEGASCOPE *n* type of image projector
MEGASPORE *n* larger of the two types of spore produced by some spore-bearing plants, which develops into the female gametophyte
MEGASS *another name for* >BAGASSE
MEGASSE *same as* >MEGASS
MEGASSES >MEGASS
MEGASTAR *n* very well-known personality in the entertainment business
MEGASTARS >MEGASTAR
MEGASTORE *n* very large store
MEGASTORM *n* very large storm
MEGATHERE *n* type of gigantic extinct American

sloth common in late Cenozoic times

MEGATON n explosive power equal to that of one million tons of TNT

MEGATONIC > MEGATON

MEGATONS > MEGATON

MEGAVOLT n one million volts

MEGAVOLTS > MEGAVOLT

MEGAWATT n one million watts

MEGAWATTS > MEGAWATT

MEGILLA same as > MEGILLAH

MEGILLAH n scroll of the Book of Esther, read on the festival of Purim

MEGILLAHS > MEGILLAH

MEGILLAS > MEGILLA

MEGILLOTH > MEGILLAH

MEGILP n oil-painting medium of linseed oil mixed with mastic varnish or turpentine

MEGILPH same as > MEGILP

MEGILPHS > MEGILPH

MEGILPS > MEGILP

MEGOHM n one million ohms

MEGOHMS > MEGOHM

MEGRIM n caprice

MEGRIMS n fit of depression

MEGS > MEG

MEH interj expression of indifference or boredom

MEHNDI n (esp in India) the practice of painting designs on the hands, feet, etc using henna

MEHNDIS > MEHNDI

MEIBOMIAN adj as in meibomian gland any of the small sebaceous glands in the eyelid, beneath the conjunctiva

MEIKLE adj Scots word meaning large

MEIN Scots word for > MOAN

MEINED > MEIN

MEINEY same as > MEINY

MEINEYS > MEINEY

MEINIE same as > MEINY

MEINIES > MEINY

MEINING > MEIN

MEINS > MEIN

MEINT same as > MING

MEINY n retinue or household

MEIOCYTE n cell that divides by meiosis to produce four haploid spores

MEIOCYTES > MEIOCYTE

MEIOFAUNA n component of the fauna of a sea or lake bed comprising small (but not microscopic) animals, such as tiny worms and crustaceans

MEIONITE n mineral containing silica

MEIONITES > MEIONITE

MEIOSES > MEIOSIS

MEIOSIS n type of cell division

MEIOSPORE n haploid spore

MEIOTIC > MEIOSIS

MEISHI n business card in Japan

MEISHIS > MEISHI

MEISTER n person who excels at a particular activity

MEISTERS > MEISTER

MEITH n landmark

MEITHS > MEITH

MEJLIS same as > MAJLIS

MEJLISES > MEJLIS

MEKKA same as > MECCA

MEKKAS > MEKKA

MEKOMETER n device for measuring distance

MEL n pure form of honey

MELA n Asian cultural or religious fair or festival

MELAENA n medical condition

MELAENAS > MELAENA

MELALEUCA n Australian shrub or tree with a white trunk and black branches

MELAMDIM > MELAMED

MELAMED n Hebrew teacher

MELAMINE n colourless crystalline compound used in making synthetic resins

MELAMINES > MELAMINE

MELAMPODE n poisonous plant

MELANGE n mixture

MELANGES > MELANGE

MELANIAN n freshwater mollusc

MELANIANS > MELANIAN

MELANIC adj relating to melanism or melanosis ▷ n darker form of creature

MELANICS > MELANIC

MELANIN n dark pigment found in the hair, skin, and eyes

MELANINS > MELANIN

MELANISE same as > MELANIZE

MELANISED > MELANISE

MELANISES > MELANISE

MELANISM same as > MELANOSIS

MELANISMS > MELANISM

MELANIST > MELANISM

MELANISTS > MELANISM

MELANITE n black variety of andradite garnet

MELANITES > MELANITE

MELANITIC > MELANITE

MELANIZE vb turn into melanin

MELANIZED > MELANIZE

MELANIZES > MELANIZE

MELANO n person with abnormally dark skin

MELANOID adj resembling melanin ▷ n dark substance formed in skin

MELANOIDS > MELANOID

MELANOMA n tumour composed of dark-coloured cells, occurring in some skin cancers

MELANOMAS > MELANOMA

MELANOS > MELANO

MELANOSES > MELANOSIS

MELANOSIS n skin condition characterized by excessive deposits of melanin

MELANOTIC > MELANOSIS

MELANOUS adj having a dark complexion and black hair

MELANURIA n presence of melanin in urine

MELANURIC > MELANURIA

MELAPHYRE n type of weathered amygdaloidal basalt or andesite

MELAS > MELA

MELASTOME n tropical flowering plant

MELATONIN n hormone-like secretion of the pineal gland, causing skin colour changes in some animals and thought to be involved in reproductive function

MELBA adj relating to a type of dessert sauce or toast

MELD vb merge or blend ▷ n act of melding

MELDED > MELD

MELDER > MELD

MELDERS > MELD

MELDING > MELD

MELDS > MELD

MELEE n noisy confused fight or crowd

MELEES > MELEE

MELENA n excrement or vomit stained by blood

MELENAS > MELENA

MELIC adj (of poetry, esp ancient Greek lyric poems) intended to be sung ▷ n type of grass

MELICK n either of two pale green perennial grasses

MELICKS > MELICK

MELICS > MELIC

MELIK same as > MALIK

MELIKS > MELIK

MELILITE n mineral containing calcium

MELILITES > MELILITE

MELILOT n plant with small white or yellow fragrant flowers

MELILOTS > MELILOT

MELINITE n high explosive made from picric acid

MELINITES > MELINITE

MELIORATE vb improve

MELIORISM n notion that the world can be improved by human effort

MELIORIST > MELIORISM

MELIORITY n improved state

MELISMA n expressive vocal phrase or passage consisting of several notes sung to one syllable

MELISMAS > MELISMA

MELISMATA > MELISMA

MELITTIN n main toxic component in bee venom

MELITTINS > MELITTIN

MELL vb mix

MELLAY same as > MELEE

MELLAYS > MELLAY

MELLED > MELL

MELLIFIC adj forming or producing honey

MELLING > MELL

MELLITE n soft yellow mineral

MELLITES > MELLITE

MELLITIC > MELLITE

MELLOTRON n musical synthesizer

MELLOW adj soft, not harsh ▷ vb make or become mellow

MELLOWED > MELLOW

MELLOWER > MELLOW

MELLOWEST > MELLOW

MELLOWING > MELLOW

MELLOWLY > MELLOW

MELLOWS > MELLOW

MELLOWY same as > MELLOW

MELLS > MELL

MELOCOTON n variety of peach

MELODEON n small accordion

MELODEONS > MELODEON

MELODIA same as > MELODICA

MELODIAS > MELODIA

MELODIC adj of melody

MELODICA n type of flute

MELODICAS > MELODICA

MELODICS n study of melody

MELODIES > MELODY

MELODION same as > MELODEON

MELODIONS > MELODION

MELODIOUS adj pleasing to the ear

MELODISE same as > MELODIZE

MELODISED > MELODISE

MELODISER > MELODISE

MELODISES > MELODISE

MELODIST n composer of melodies

MELODISTS > MELODIST

MELODIZE vb provide with a melody

MELODIZED > MELODIZE

MELODIZER > MELODIZE

MELODIZES > MELODIZE

MELODRAMA n play full of extravagant action and emotion

MELODRAME same as > MELODRAMA

MELODY n series of musical notes which make a tune

MELOID n type of long-legged beetle

MELOIDS > MELOID

MELOMANIA n great enthusiasm for music

MELOMANIC > MELOMANIA

MELON n large round juicy fruit with a hard rind

MELONGENE n aubergine

MELONS > MELON

MELONY adj like a melon

MELOXICAM n anti-inflammatory drug used to treat osteoarthritis

MELPHALAN n drug used to treat leukaemia

MELS > MEL

MELT vb (cause to) become liquid by heat ▷ n act or process of melting

MELTABLE > MELT

MELTAGE n process or result of melting or the amount melted

MELTAGES > MELTAGE

MELTDOWN n (in a nuclear reactor) melting of the fuel rods, with the possible release of radiation

MELTDOWNS > MELTDOWN

MELTED > MELT

MELTEMI n northerly wind in the northeast Mediterranean

MELTEMIS > MELTEMI

MELTER > MELT

MELTERS > MELT

MELTIER > MELTY

MELTIEST > MELTY

MELTING > MELT

MELTINGLY > MELT

MELTINGS > MELT

MELTITH n meal

MELTITHS > MELTITH

MELTON n heavy smooth woollen fabric with a short nap, used esp for overcoats

MELTONS > MELTON

MELTS > MELT

MELTWATER n melted snow or ice

MELTY adj tending to melt

MELUNGEON n any of a dark-skinned group of people of the Appalachians in E Tennessee, of mixed Indian, White, and Black ancestry

MEM n 13th letter in the Hebrew alphabet, transliterated as m

MEMBER n individual making up a body or society ▷ adj (of a country or group) belonging to an organization or alliance

MEMBERED adj having members

MEMBERS > MEMBER

MEMBRAL adj of limbs

MEMBRANAL > MEMBRANE

MEMBRANE n thin flexible tissue in a plant or animal body

MEMBRANED adj having membrane

MEMBRANES > MEMBRANE

MEME n idea or element of social behaviour

MEMENTO n thing serving to remind, souvenir

MEMENTOES > MEMENTO

MEMENTOS > MEMENTO

MEMES > MEME

MEMETIC adj of or relating to a meme

MEMETICS n study of genetic transmission of culture

MEMO n memorandum

MEMOIR n biography or historical account based on personal knowledge

MEMOIRISM n writing of memoirs

MEMOIRIST > MEMOIRISM

MEMOIRS pl n collection of reminiscences about a period or series of events

MEMORABLE adj worth remembering, noteworthy

MEMORABLY > MEMORABLE

MEMORANDA n plural of memorandum: written statement of communications

MEMORIAL n something serving to commemorate a person or thing ▷ adj serving as a memorial

MEMORIALS > MEMORIAL

MEMORIES > MEMORY

MEMORISE same as > MEMORIZE

MEMORISED > MEMORISE

MEMORISER > MEMORIZE

MEMORISES > MEMORISE

MEMORITER adv from memory

MEMORIZE vb commit to memory

MEMORIZED > MEMORIZE

MEMORIZER > MEMORIZE

MEMORIZES > MEMORIZE

MEMORY n ability to remember

MEMOS > MEMO

MEMS > MEM

MEMSAHIB n (formerly, in India) term of respect used for a European married woman

MEMSAHIBS > MEMSAHIB

MEN > MAN

MENACE n threat ▷ vb threaten, endanger

MENACED > MENACE

MENACER > MENACE

MENACERS > MENACE

MENACES > MENACE

MENACING > MENACE

MENAD same as > MAENAD

MENADIONE n yellow crystalline compound

MENADS > MENAD

MENAGE old form of > MANAGE

MENAGED > MENAGE

MENAGERIE n collection of wild animals for exhibition

MENAGES > MENAGE

MENAGING > MENAGE

MENARCHE n first occurrence of menstruation in a woman's life

MENARCHES > MENARCHE

MENAZON n type of insecticide

MENAZONS > MENAZON

MEND vb repair or patch ▷ n mended area

MENDABLE > MEND

MENDACITY n (tendency to) untruthfulness

MENDED > MEND

MENDER > MEND

MENDERS > MEND

MENDICANT adj begging ▷ n beggar

MENDICITY > MENDICANT

MENDIGO n Spanish beggar or vagrant

MENDIGOS > MENDIGO

MENDING n something to be mended, esp clothes

MENDINGS > MENDING

MENDS > MEND

MENE Scots form of > MOAN

MENED > MENE

MENEER n S African title of address

MENEERS > MENEER

MENES > MENE

MENFOLK pl n men collectively, esp the men of a particular family

MENFOLKS same as > MENFOLK

MENG vb mix

MENGE same as > MENG

MENGED > MENG

MENGES > MENGE

MENGING > MENG

MENGS > MENG

MENHADEN n marine N American fish, source of fishmeal, fertilizer, and oil

MENHADENS > MENHADEN

MENHIR n single upright prehistoric stone

MENHIRS > MENHIR

MENIAL adj involving boring work of low status ▷ n person with a menial job

MENIALLY > MENIAL

MENIALS > MENIAL

MENILITE n liver opal

MENILITES > MENILITE

MENING > MENE

MENINGEAL > MENINX

MENINGES > MENINX

MENINX n one of three membranes that envelop the brain and spinal cord

MENISCAL > MENISCUS

MENISCATE > MENISCUS

MENISCI > MENISCUS

MENISCOID > MENISCUS

MENISCUS n curved surface of a liquid

MENO adv musical instruction indicating 'less'

MENOLOGY n ecclesiastical calendar of the months

MENOMINEE n whitefish, found in N America and Siberia

MENOMINI same as > MENOMINEE

MENOMINIS > MENOMINI

MENOPAUSE n time when a woman's menstrual cycle ceases

MENOPOLIS n informal word for an area with a high proportion of single men

MENOPOME n American salamander

MENOPOMES > MENOPOME

MENORAH n seven-branched candelabrum used as an emblem of Judaism

MENORAHS > MENORAH

MENORRHEA n normal bleeding in menstruation

MENSA n faint constellation in the S hemisphere

MENSAE n star of the mensa constellation

MENSAL adj monthly

MENSAS > MENSA

MENSCH n decent person

MENSCHEN > MENSCH

MENSCHES > MENSCH

MENSCHIER > MENSCHY

MENSCHY adj decent

MENSE vb grace

MENSED > MENSE

MENSEFUL adj gracious

MENSELESS adj graceless

MENSES n menstruation

MENSH vb mention

MENSHED > MENSH

MENSHEN n Chinese door god

MENSHES > MENSH

MENSHING > MENSH

MENSING > MENSE

MENSTRUA > MENSTRUUM

MENSTRUAL adj of or relating to menstruation

MENSTRUUM *n* solvent, esp one used in the preparation of a drug
MENSUAL *same as* >MENSAL
MENSURAL *adj* of or involving measure
MENSWEAR *n* clothing for men
MENSWEARS >MENSWEAR
MENT *same as* >MING
MENTA >MENTUM
MENTAL *adj* of, in, or done by the mind
MENTALESE *n* picturing of concepts in mind without words
MENTALISM *n* doctrine that mind is the fundamental reality and that objects of knowledge exist only as aspects of the subject's consciousness
MENTALIST >MENTALISM
MENTALITY *n* way of thinking
MENTALLY >MENTAL
MENTATION *n* process or result of mental activity
MENTEE *n* person trained by mentor
MENTEES >MENTEE
MENTHENE *n* liquid obtained from menthol
MENTHENES >MENTHENE
MENTHOL *n* organic compound found in peppermint
MENTHOLS >MENTHOL
MENTICIDE *n* destruction of person's mental independence
MENTION *vb* refer to briefly ▷ *n* brief reference
MENTIONED >MENTION
MENTIONER >MENTION
MENTIONS >MENTION
MENTO *n* Jamaican song
MENTOR *n* adviser or guide ▷ *vb* act as a mentor to (someone) ▷ *vb* act as mentor for
MENTORED >MENTOR
MENTORIAL >MENTOR
MENTORING *n* (in business) the practice of assigning a junior member of staff to the care of a more experienced person who assists him in his career
MENTORS >MENTOR
MENTOS >MENTO
MENTUM *n* chin
MENU *n* list of dishes to be served, or from which to order
MENUDO *n* Mexican soup
MENUDOS >MENUDO
MENUISIER *n* joiner
MENUS >MENU
MENYIE *same as* >MEINIE
MENYIES >MENYIE

MEOU *same as* >MEOW
MEOUED >MEOU
MEOUING >MEOU
MEOUS >MEOU
MEOW *vb* (of a cat) to make a characteristic crying sound ▷ *interj* imitation of this sound
MEOWED >MEOW
MEOWING >MEOW
MEOWS >MEOW
MEPACRINE *n* drug formerly widely used to treat malaria
MEPHITIC *adj* poisonous
MEPHITIS *n* foul-smelling discharge
MEPHITISM *n* poisoning
MERANTI *n* wood from any of several Malaysian trees
MERANTIS >MERANTI
MERBROMIN *n* green iridescent crystalline compound
MERC *n* mercenary
MERCADO *n* market
MERCADOS >MERCADO
MERCAPTAN *another name (not in technical usage) for* >THIOL
MERCAPTO *adj* of a particular chemical group
MERCAT *Scots word for* >MARKET
MERCATS >MERCAT
MERCENARY *adj* influenced by greed ▷ *n* hired soldier
MERCER *n* dealer in textile fabrics and fine cloth
MERCERIES >MERCER
MERCERISE *same as* >MERCERIZE
MERCERIZE *vb* treat (cotton yarn) with an alkali to increase its strength and reception to dye and impart a lustrous silky appearance
MERCERS >MERCER
MERCERY >MERCER
MERCES >MERC
MERCH *n* merchandise
MERCHANT *n* person engaged in trade, wholesale trader ▷ *adj* of ships involved in commercial trade or their crews ▷ *vb* conduct trade in
MERCHANTS >MERCHANT
MERCHES >MERCH
MERCHET *n* (in feudal England) fine paid by tenant to his lord for allowing the marriage of his daughter
MERCHETS >MERCHET
MERCHILD *n* mythical creature with upper body of child and lower body of fish
MERCIABLE *adj* merciful

MERCIES >MERCY
MERCIFIDE >MERCIFY
MERCIFIED >MERCIFY
MERCIFIES >MERCIFY
MERCIFUL *adj* compassionate
MERCIFY *vb* show mercy to
MERCILESS *adj* without mercy
MERCS >MERC
MERCURATE *vb* treat or mix with mercury
MERCURIAL *adj* lively, changeable ▷ *n* any salt of mercury for use as a medicine
MERCURIC *adj* of or containing mercury in the divalent state
MERCURIES >MERCURY
MERCURISE *same as* >MERCURATE
MERCURIZE *same as* >MERCURISE
MERCUROUS *adj* of or containing mercury in the monovalent state
MERCURY *n* silvery liquid metal
MERCY *n* compassionate treatment
MERDE *French word for* >EXCREMENT
MERDES >MERDE
MERE *adj* nothing more than ▷ *n* lake ▷ *vb* old form of survey
MERED *adj* forming a boundary
MEREL *same as* >MERIL
MERELL *same as* >MERIL
MERELLS *same as* >MERILS
MERELS >MERILS
MERELY *adv* only
MERENGUE *n* type of lively dance music originating in the Dominican Republic, which combines African and Spanish elements
MERENGUES >MERENGUE
MEREOLOGY *n* formal study of the logical properties of the relation of part and whole
MERER >MERE
MERES >MERE
MERESMAN *n* man who decides on boundaries
MERESMEN >MERESMAN
MEREST >MERE
MERESTONE *n* stone marking boundary
MERFOLK *n* mermaids and mermen
MERFOLKS >MERFOLK
MERGANSER *n* large crested diving duck
MERGE *vb* combine or blend
MERGED >MERGE
MERGEE *n* business taken over by merger
MERGEES >MERGEE

MERGENCE >MERGE
MERGENCES >MERGE
MERGER *n* combination of business firms into one
MERGERS >MERGER
MERGES >MERGE
MERGING >MERGE
MERGINGS >MERGE
MERGUEZ *n* heavily spiced N African sausage
MERI *n* Māori war club
MERICARP *n* part of plant fruit
MERICARPS >MERICARP
MERIDIAN *n* imaginary circle of the earth passing through both poles ▷ *adj* along or relating to a meridian
MERIDIANS >MERIDIAN
MERIL *n* counter used in merils
MERILS *n* old board game
MERIMAKE *n* merrymaking
MERIMAKES >MERIMAKE
MERING >MERE
MERINGS >MERING
MERINGUE *n* baked mixture of egg whites and sugar
MERINGUES >MERINGUE
MERINO *n* breed of sheep with fine soft wool
MERINOS >MERINO
MERIS >MERI
MERISES >MERISIS
MERISIS *n* growth by division of cells
MERISM *n* duplication of biological parts
MERISMS >MERISM
MERISTEM *n* plant tissue responsible for growth, whose cells divide and differentiate to form the tissues and organs of the plant
MERISTEMS >MERISTEM
MERISTIC *adj* of or relating to the number of organs or parts in an animal or plant body
MERIT *n* excellence or worth ▷ *vb* deserve
MERITED >MERIT
MERITING >MERIT
MERITLESS >MERIT
MERITS >MERIT
MERK *n* old Scots coin
MERKIN *n* artificial hairpiece for the pudendum
MERKINS >MERKIN
MERKS >MERK
MERL *same as* >MERLE
MERLE *adj* (of a dog, esp a collie) having a bluish-grey coat with speckles or streaks of black
MERLES >MERLE
MERLIN *n* small falcon
MERLING *n* whiting
MERLINGS >MERLING

MERLINS > MERLIN

MERLON n solid upright section in a crenellated battlement

MERLONS > MERLON

MERLOT n type of black grape

MERLOTS > MERLOT

MERLS > MERL

MERMAID n imaginary sea creature with the upper part of a woman and the lower part of a fish

MERMAIDEN same as > MERMAID

MERMAIDS > MERMAID

MERMAN n male counterpart of the mermaid

MERMEN > MERMAN

MEROCRINE adj (of the secretion of glands) characterized by formation of the product without undergoing disintegration

MEROGONY n development of embryo from part of ovum

MEROISTIC adj producing yolk and ova

MEROME same as > MEROSOME

MEROMES > MEROME

MERONYM n part of something used to refer to the whole

MERONYMS > MERONYM

MERONYMY > MERONYM

MEROPIA n partial blindness

MEROPIAS > MEROPIA

MEROPIC > MEROPIA

MEROPIDAN n bird of bee-eater family

MEROSOME n segment in body of worm

MEROSOMES > MEROSOME

MEROZOITE n any of the cells formed by fission of a schizont during the life cycle of sporozoan protozoans, such as the malaria parasite

MERPEOPLE same as > MERFOLK

MERRIE adj (archaic) merry

MERRIER > MERRY

MERRIES > MERRY

MERRIEST > MERRY

MERRILY > MERRY

MERRIMENT n gaiety, fun, or mirth

MERRINESS > MERRY

MERRY adj cheerful or jolly ▷ n gean

MERRYMAN n jester

MERRYMEN > MERRYMAN

MERSALYL n salt of sodium

MERSALYLS > MERSALYL

MERSE n low level ground by a river or shore

MERSES > MERSE

MERSION n dipping in water

MERSIONS > MERSION

MERYCISM n rumination

MERYCISMS > MERYCISM

MES > ME

MESA n flat-topped hill found in arid regions

MESAIL n visor

MESAILS > MESAIL

MESAL same as > MESIAL

MESALLY > MESAL

MESARAIC adj of mesentery

MESARCH adj (of a xylem strand) having the first-formed xylem surrounded by that formed later, as in fern stems

MESAS > MESA

MESCAL n spineless globe-shaped cactus

MESCALIN same as > MESCALINE

MESCALINE n hallucinogenic drug obtained from the tops of mescals

MESCALINS > MESCALIN

MESCALISM n addiction to mescal

MESCALS > MESCAL

MESCLUM same as > MESCLUN

MESCLUMS > MESCLUM

MESCLUN n type of green salad

MESCLUNS > MESCLUN

MESDAMES > MADAM

MESE n middle string on lyre

MESEEMED > MESEEMS

MESEEMETH same as > MESEEMS

MESEEMS vb it seems to me

MESEL n leper

MESELED adj afflicted by leprosy

MESELS > MESEL

MESENTERA n plural of mesenteron, the midgut

MESENTERY n double layer of peritoneum that is attached to the back wall of the abdominal cavity and supports most of the small intestine

MESES > MESE

MESETA n plateau in Spain

MESETAS > MESETA

MESH n network or net ▷ vb (of gear teeth) engage ▷ adj made from mesh

MESHED > MESH

MESHES > MESH

MESHIER > MESH

MESHIEST > MESH

MESHING > MESH

MESHINGS > MESH

MESHUGA n crazy person

MESHUGAAS n madness

MESHUGAH same as > MESHUGA

MESHUGAS adj crazy

MESHUGGA same as > MESHUGA

MESHUGGAH same as > MESHUGA

MESHUGGE same as > MESHUGA

MESHWORK n network

MESHWORKS > MESHWORK

MESHY > MESH

MESIAD adj relating to or situated at the middle or centre

MESIAL another word for > MEDIAL

MESIALLY > MESIAL

MESIAN same as > MESIAL

MESIC > MESON

MESICALLY > MESON

MESMERIC adj holding (someone) as if spellbound

MESMERISE same as > MESMERIZE

MESMERISM n hypnotic state induced by the operator's imposition of his will on that of the patient

MESMERIST > MESMERISM

MESMERIZE vb hold spellbound

MESNALTY n lands of a mesne lord

MESNE adj (in law) intermediate or intervening

MESNES > MESNE

MESOBLAST another name for > MESODERM

MESOCARP n middle layer of the pericarp of a fruit, such as the flesh of a peach

MESOCARPS > MESOCARP

MESOCRANY n medium skull breadth

MESODERM n middle germ layer of an animal embryo, giving rise to muscle, blood, bone, connective tissue, etc

MESODERMS > MESODERM

MESOGLEA n gelatinous material between the outer and inner cellular layers of jellyfish and other coelenterates

MESOGLEAL > MESOGLEA

MESOGLEAS > MESOGLEA

MESOGLOEA same as > MESOGLEA

MESOLITE n type of mineral

MESOLITES > MESOLITE

MESOMERE n cell in fertilized ovum

MESOMERES > MESOMERE

MESOMORPH n person with a muscular body build: said to be correlated with somatotonia

MESON n elementary atomic particle

MESONIC > MESON

MESONS > MESON

MESOPAUSE n zone of minimum temperature between the mesosphere and the thermosphere

MESOPHILE n ideal growth temperature of 20-45 degrees

MESOPHYL same as > MESOPHYLL

MESOPHYLL n soft chlorophyll-containing tissue of a leaf between the upper and lower layers of epidermis: involved in photosynthesis

MESOPHYLS > MESOPHYL

MESOPHYTE n any plant that grows in surroundings receiving an average supply of water

MESOSAUR n extinct aquatic reptile

MESOSAURS > MESOSAUR

MESOSCALE adj of weather phenomena of medium duration

MESOSOME n part of bacterial cell

MESOSOMES > MESOSOME

MESOTRON same as > MESON

MESOTRONS > MESOTRON

MESOZOAN n type of parasite

MESOZOANS > MESOZOAN

MESOZOIC adj of, denoting, or relating to an era of geological time

MESPIL n type of N American tree

MESPILS > MESPIL

MESPRISE same as > MISPRISE

MESPRISES > MESPRISE

MESPRIZE same as > MISPRISE

MESPRIZES > MESPRIZE

MESQUIN adj mean

MESQUINE same as > MESQUIN

MESQUIT same as > MESQUITE

MESQUITE n small tree whose sugary pods are used as animal fodder

MESQUITES > MESQUITE

MESQUITS > MESQUIT

MESS n untidy or dirty confusion ▷ vb muddle or dirty

MESSAGE n communication sent ▷ vb send as a message

MESSAGED > MESSAGE

MESSAGES > MESSAGE

MESSAGING n sending and receiving of messages

MESSALINE n light lustrous twilled-silk fabric

MESSAN Scots word for > DOG

MESSANS > MESSAN

MESSED > MESS

MESSENGER n bearer of a message ▷ vb send by messenger

MESSES > MESS

MESSIAH n exceptional or hoped for liberator

MESSIAHS > MESSIAH

MESSIANIC adj of or relating to the Messiah, his awaited deliverance of the Jews, or the new age of peace expected to follow this

MESSIAS same as > MESSIAH

MESSIASES > MESSIAS

MESSIER > MESSY

MESSIEST > MESSY

MESSIEURS > MONSIEUR

MESSILY > MESSY

MESSINESS > MESSY

MESSING > MESS

MESSMAN n sailor working in ship's mess

MESSMATE n person with whom one shares meals in a mess, esp in the army

MESSMATES > MESSMATE

MESSMEN > MESSMAN

MESSUAGE n dwelling house together with its outbuildings, curtilage, and the adjacent land appropriated to its use

MESSUAGES > MESSUAGE

MESSY adj dirty, confused, or untidy

MESTEE same as > MUSTEE

MESTEES > MESTEE

MESTER n master: used as a term of address for a man who is the head of a house

MESTERS > MESTER

MESTESO n Spanish music genre

MESTESOES > MESTESO

MESTESOS > MESTESO

MESTINO n person of mixed race

MESTINOES > MESTINO

MESTINOS > MESTINO

MESTIZA > MESTIZO

MESTIZAS > MESTIZO

MESTIZO n person of mixed parentage

MESTIZOES > MESTIZO

MESTIZOS > MESTIZO

MESTO adj sad

MESTOM same as > MESTOME

MESTOME n conducting tissue associated with parenchyma

MESTOMES > MESTOME

MESTOMS > MESTOM

MESTRANOL n synthetic oestrogen

MET n meteorology

META adj in a self-parodying style

METABASES > METABASIS

METABASIS n change

METABATIC > METABASIS

METABOLIC adj of or related to the sum total of the chemical processes that occurs in living organisms, resulting in growth, production of energy, elimination of waste material, etc

METABOLY n ability of some cells, esp protozoans, to alter their shape

METACARPI n skeleton of the hand between the wrist and the fingers

METADATA n data which accompanies digital data and provides underlying information but is not visible to the end user

METADATAS > METADATA

METAFILE n (in computing) file format that can hold other types of file

METAFILES > METAFILE

METAGE n official measuring of weight or contents

METAGENIC adj of or relating to the production within the life cycle of an organism of alternating asexual and sexual reproductive forms

METAGES > METAGE

METAIRIE n area of land on which farmer pays rent in kind

METAIRIES > METAIRIE

METAL n chemical element, such as iron or copper, that is malleable and capable of conducting heat and electricity ▷ adj made of metal ▷ vb fit or cover with metal

METALED > METAL

METALHEAD n fan of heavy metal music

METALING > METAL

METALISE same as > METALLIZE

METALISED > METALISE

METALISES > METALISE

METALIST same as > METALLIST

METALISTS > METALIST

METALIZE same as > METALLIZE

METALIZED > METALIZE

METALIZES > METALIZE

METALLED > METAL

METALLIC adj of or consisting of metal ▷ n something metallic

METALLICS > METALLIC

METALLIKE > METAL

METALLINE adj of, resembling, or relating to metals

METALLING > METAL

METALLISE same as > METALLIZE

METALLIST n person who works with metals

METALLIZE vb make metallic or to coat or treat with metal

METALLOID n nonmetallic element, such as arsenic or silicon, that has some of the properties of a metal ▷ adj of or being a metalloid

METALLY adj like metal

METALMARK n variety of butterfly

METALS > METAL

METALWARE n items made of metal

METALWORK n craft of making objects from metal

METAMALE n sterile male organism, esp a fruit fly that has one X chromosome and three sets of autosomes

METAMALES > METAMALE

METAMER n any of two or more isomeric compounds exhibiting metamerism

METAMERAL > METAMERE

METAMERE n one of the similar body segments into which earthworms, crayfish, and similar animals are divided longitudinally

METAMERES > METAMERE

METAMERIC adj divided into or consisting of metameres

METAMERS > METAMER

METAMICT adj of or denoting the amorphous state of a substance that has lost its crystalline structure as a result of the radioactivity of uranium or thorium within it

METANOIA n repentance

METANOIAS > METANOIA

METAPELET n foster mother

METAPHASE n second stage of mitosis during which the condensed chromosomes attach to the centre of the spindle

METAPHOR n figure of speech in which a term is applied to something it does not literally denote in order to imply a resemblance

METAPHORS > METAPHOR

METAPLASM n nonliving constituents, such as starch and pigment granules, of the cytoplasm of a cell

METAPLOT > METAPELET

METARCHON n nontoxic substance, such as a chemical to mask pheromones, that reduces the persistence of a pest

METASOMA n posterior part of an arachnid's abdomen (opisthosoma) that never carries appendages

METASOMAS > METASOMA

METATAG n element of HTML code used by search engines to index pages

METATAGS > METATAG

METATARSI pl n skeleton of human foot between toes and tarsus

METATE n stone for grinding grain on

METATES > METATE

METAVERSE n virtual universe, eg one of a computer or role-playing game

METAXYLEM n xylem tissue that consists of rigid thick-walled cells and occurs in parts of the plant that have finished growing

METAYAGE n farming in which rent is paid in kind

METAYAGES > METAYAGE

METAYER n farmer who pays rent in kind

METAYERS > METAYER

METAZOA > METAZOAN

METAZOAL > METAZOAN

METAZOAN n any animal having a body composed of many cells: includes all animals except sponges and protozoans ▷ adj of the metazoans

METAZOANS > METAZOAN

METAZOIC adj relating to the group of multicellular animals that includes all animals except sponges

METAZOON same as > METAZOAN

METCAST n weather forecast

METCASTS > METCAST

METE vb deal out as punishment ▷ n (to) measure

METED > METE

METEOR n small fast-moving heavenly body

METEORIC adj of a meteor

METEORISM n distension of the abdomen

METEORIST n person who studies meteors

METEORITE n meteor that has fallen to earth

METEOROID n any of the small celestial bodies that are thought to orbit the sun. When they enter the earth's atmosphere, they become visible as meteors

METEOROUS > METEOR
METEORS > METEOR
METEPA n type of pesticide
METEPAS > METEPA
METER same as > METRE
METERAGE n act of measuring
METERAGES > METERAGE
METERED > METER
METERING > METER
METERS > METER
METES > METE
METESTICK n measuring rod
METESTRUS n period in the oestrous cycle following oestrus, characterized by lack of sexual activity
METEWAND same as > METESTICK
METEWANDS > METEWAND
METEYARD same as > METESTICK
METEYARDS > METEYARD
METFORMIN n drug used to treat diabetes
METH n variety of amphetamine
METHADON same as > METHADONE
METHADONE n drug similar to morphine, sometimes prescribed as a heroin substitute
METHADONS > METHADON
METHANAL n colourless poisonous irritating gas with a pungent characteristic odour, made by the oxidation of methanol and used as formalin and in the manufacture of synthetic resins
METHANALS > METHANAL
METHANE n colourless inflammable gas
METHANES > METHANE
METHANOIC adj as in methanoic acid systematic name for formic acid
METHANOL n colourless poisonous liquid used as a solvent and fuel
METHANOLS > METHANOL
METHEGLIN n (esp formerly) spiced or medicated mead
METHINK same as > METHINKS
METHINKS vb it seems to me
METHO n methylated spirits
METHOD n way or manner
METHODIC same as > METHOD
METHODISE same as > METHODIZE
METHODISM n system and practices of the Methodist Church, developed by the English

preacher John Wesley (1703–91) and his followers
METHODIST > METHODISM
METHODIZE vb organize according to a method
METHODS > METHOD
METHOS > METHO
METHOUGHT > METHINKS
METHOXIDE n saltlike compound in which the hydrogen atom in the hydroxyl group of methanol has been replaced by a metal atom, usually an alkali metal atom as in sodium methoxide, NaOCH$_3$
METHOXIES > METHOXY
METHOXY n steroid drug
METHOXYL n chemical compound of methyl and hydroxyl
METHOXYLS > METHOXYL
METHS n methylated spirits
METHYL n compound containing a saturated hydrocarbon group of atoms
METHYLAL n colourless volatile flammable liquid
METHYLALS > METHYLAL
METHYLASE n enzyme
METHYLATE vb mix with methanol
METHYLENE adj of, consisting of, or containing the divalent group of atoms =CH$_2$
METHYLIC > METHYL
METHYLS > METHYL
METHYSES > METHYSIS
METHYSIS n drunkenness
METHYSTIC adj intoxicating
METIC n (in ancient Greece) alien having some rights of citizenship
METICAIS > METICAL
METICAL n money unit in Mozambique
METICALS > METICAL
METICS > METIC
METIER n profession or trade
METIERS > METIER
METIF n person of mixed race
METIFS > METIF
METING > METE
METIS n person of mixed parentage
METISSE > METIS
METISSES > METIS
METOL n organic substance used as a photographic developer
METOLS > METOL
METONYM n word used in metonymy
METONYMIC > METONYMY
METONYMS > METONYM

METONYMY n figure of speech in which one thing is replaced by another associated with it
METOPAE > METOPE
METOPE n square space between two triglyphs in a Doric frieze
METOPES > METOPE
METOPIC adj of or relating to the forehead
METOPISM n congenital disfigurement of forehead
METOPISMS > METOPISM
METOPON n painkilling drug
METOPONS > METOPON
METOPRYL n type of anaesthetic
METOPRYLS > METOPRYL
METRALGIA n pain in the uterus
METRAZOL n drug used to improve blood circulation
METRAZOLS > METRAZOL
METRE n unit of length ▷ vb express in poetry
METRED > METRE
METRES > METRE
METRIC adj of the decimal system of weights and measures based on the metre
METRICAL adj of measurement
METRICATE vb convert a measuring system or instrument to metric units
METRICIAN n writer of metrical verse
METRICISE vb study metre of poetry
METRICISM > METRICISE
METRICIST same as > METRICIAN
METRICIZE same as > METRICISE
METRICS n art of using poetic metre
METRIFIED > METRIFY
METRIFIER > METRIFY
METRIFIES > METRIFY
METRIFY vb render into poetic metre
METRING > METRE
METRIST n person skilled in the use of poetic metre
METRISTS > METRIST
METRITIS n inflammation of the uterus
METRO n underground railway system, esp in Paris
METROLOGY n science of weights and measures
METRONOME n instrument which marks musical time by means of a ticking pendulum
METROPLEX n large urban area
METROS > METRO

METS > MET
METTLE n courage or spirit
METTLED adj spirited, courageous, or valiant
METTLES > METTLE
METUMP n band for carrying a load or burden
METUMPS > METUMP
MEU another name for > SPIGNEL
MEUNIERE adj (of fish) dredged with flour, fried in butter, and served with butter, lemon juice, and parsley
MEUS > MEU
MEUSE n gap through which an animal passed ▷ vb go through this gap
MEUSED > MEUSE
MEUSES > MEUSE
MEUSING > MEUSE
MEVE same as > MOVE
MEVED > MEVE
MEVES > MEVE
MEVING > MEVE
MEVROU n S African title of address
MEVROUS > MEVROU
MEW n cry of a cat ▷ vb utter this cry
MEWED > MEW
MEWING > MEW
MEWL vb (esp of a baby) to cry weakly ▷ n weak or whimpering cry
MEWLED > MEWL
MEWLER > MEWL
MEWLERS > MEWL
MEWLING > MEWL
MEWLS > MEWL
MEWS same as > MEUSE
MEWSED > MEWS
MEWSES > MEWS
MEWSING > MEWS
MEYNT > MING
MEZAIL same as > MESAIL
MEZAILS > MEZAIL
MEZCAL variant spelling of > MESCAL
MEZCALINE variant spelling of > MESCALINE
MEZCALS > MEZCAL
MEZE n type of hors d'oeuvre
MEZEREON same as > MEZEREUM
MEZEREONS > MEZEREON
MEZEREUM n dried bark of certain shrubs, formerly used to treat arthritis
MEZEREUMS > MEZEREUM
MEZES > MEZE
MEZQUIT same as > MESQUITE
MEZQUITE same as > MESQUITE
MEZQUITES > MEZQUITE
MEZQUITS > MEZQUIT
MEZUZA same as > MEZUZAH

MEZUZAH n piece of parchment inscribed with biblical passages

MEZUZAHS > MEZUZAH

MEZUZAS > MEZUZA

MEZUZOT > MEZUZAH

MEZUZOTH > MEZUZAH

MEZZ same as **>** MEZZANINE

MEZZALUNA n half-moon shaped kitchen chopper

MEZZANINE n intermediate storey, esp between the ground and first floor ▷ adj of or relating to an intermediate stage in a financial process

MEZZE same as **>** MEZE

MEZZES > MEZZE

MEZZO adv moderately

MEZZOS > MEZZO

MEZZOTINT n method of engraving by scraping the roughened surface of a metal plate ▷ vb engrave (a copper plate) in this fashion

MGANGA n witch doctor

MGANGAS > MGANGA

MHO former name for **>** SIEMENS

MHORR n African gazelle

MHORRS > MHORR

MHOS > MHO

MI n (in tonic sol-fa) the third degree of any major scale

MIAOU same as **>** MEOW

MIAOUED > MIAOU

MIAOUING > MIAOU

MIAOUS > MIAOU

MIAOW same as **>** MEOW

MIAOWED > MIAOW

MIAOWING > MIAOW

MIAOWS > MIAOW

MIASM same as **>** MIASMA

MIASMA n unwholesome or foreboding atmosphere

MIASMAL > MIASMA

MIASMAS > MIASMA

MIASMATA > MIASMA

MIASMATIC > MIASMA

MIASMIC > MIASMA

MIASMOUS > MIASMA

MIASMS > MIASM

MIAUL same as **>** MEOW

MIAULED > MIAUL

MIAULING > MIAUL

MIAULS > MIAUL

MIB n marble used in games

MIBS > MIB

MIBUNA n type of Japanese leafy vegetable

MIBUNAS > MIBUNA

MIC n microphone

MICA n glasslike mineral used as an electrical insulator

MICACEOUS > MICA

MICAS > MICA

MICATE vb add mica to

MICATED > MICATE

MICATES > MICATE

MICATING > MICATE

MICAWBER n person who idles and trusts to fortune

MICAWBERS > MICAWBER

MICE > MOUSE

MICELL same as **>** MICELLE

MICELLA same as **>** MICELLE

MICELLAE > MICELLA

MICELLAR > MICELLE

MICELLAS > MICELLA

MICELLE n charged aggregate of molecules of colloidal size in a solution

MICELLES > MICELLE

MICELLS > MICELL

MICH same as **>** MITCH

MICHAEL n as in take the michael teasing

MICHAELS > MICHAEL

MICHE same as **>** MICH

MICHED > MICH

MICHER > MICH

MICHERS > MICH

MICHES > MICH

MICHIGAN US name for **>** NEWMARKET

MICHIGANS > MICHIGAN

MICHING > MICH

MICHINGS > MICH

MICHT n Scots word for might

MICHTS > MICHT

MICK n derogatory term for an Irish person

MICKERIES > MICKERY

MICKERY n waterhole, esp in a dry riverbed

MICKEY n young bull ▷ vb drug person's drink

MICKEYED > MICKEY

MICKEYING > MICKEY

MICKEYS > MICKEY

MICKIES > MICKY

MICKLE adj large or abundant ▷ adv much ▷ n great amount

MICKLER > MICKLE

MICKLES > MICKLE

MICKLEST > MICKLE

MICKS > MICK

MICKY same as **>** MICKEY

MICO n marmoset

MICOS > MICO

MICRA > MICRON

MICRIFIED > MICRIFY

MICRIFIES > MICRIFY

MICRIFY vb make very small

MICRO n small computer

MICROBAR n millionth of bar of pressure

MICROBARS > MICROBAR

MICROBE n minute organism, esp one causing disease

MICROBEAM n X-ray machine with narrow focussed beam

MICROBES > MICROBE

MICROBIAL > MICROBE

MICROBIAN > MICROBE

MICROBIC > MICROBE

MICROBLOG vb contribute to a blog which limits the length of individual postings

MICROBREW n beer made in small brewery

MICROBUS n small bus

MICROCAP adj (of investments) involving very small amounts of capital

MICROCAR n small car

MICROCARD n card containing microprint

MICROCARS > MICROCAR

MICROCHIP n small wafer of silicon containing electronic circuits ▷ vb implant (an animal) with a microchip tag for purposes of identification

MICROCODE n set of computer instructions

MICROCOPY n greatly reduced photographic copy of a printed page, drawing, etc, on microfilm or microfiche

MICROCOSM n miniature representation of something

MICROCYTE n unusually small red blood cell

MICRODONT adj having unusually small teeth

MICRODOT n photographic copy of a document reduced to pinhead size

MICRODOTS > MICRODOT

MICROFILM n miniaturized recording of books or documents on a roll of film ▷ vb photograph a page or document on microfilm

MICROFORM n method of storing symbolic information by using photographic reduction techniques, such as microfilm, microfiche, etc

MICROGLIA n one of the two types of non-nervous tissue (glia) found in the central nervous system, having macrophage activity

MICROGRAM n photograph or drawing of an object as viewed through a microscope

MICROHM n millionth of ohm

MICROHMS > MICROHM

MICROINCH n millionth of inch

MICROJET n light jet-propelled aircraft

MICROJETS > MICROJET

MICROLITE n small private aircraft carrying no more than two people, with an empty weight of not more than 150 kg and a wing area not less than 10 square metres: used in pleasure flying and racing

MICROLITH n small Mesolithic flint tool which was made from a blade and formed part of hafted tools

MICROLOAN n very small loan

MICROLOGY n study of microscopic things

MICROLUX n millionth of a lux

MICROMERE n any of the small cells formed by unequal cleavage of a fertilized ovum

MICROMESH n very fine mesh

MICROMHO n millionth of mho

MICROMHOS > MICROMHO

MICROMINI n very short skirt

MICROMOLE n millionth of mole

MICROMORT n unit of risk

MICRON n unit of length equal to 10^{-6} metre

MICRONISE same as **>** MICRONIZE

MICRONIZE vb break down to very small particles

MICRONS > MICRON

MICROPORE n very small pore

MICROPSIA n defect of vision in which objects appear to be smaller than they appear to a person with normal vision

MICROPUMP n small pump inserted in skin to automatically deliver medicine

MICROPYLE n small opening in the integuments of a plant ovule through which the male gametes pass

MICROS > MICRO

MICROSITE n website that is intended for a specific limited purpose and is often temporary

MICROSOME n any of the small particles consisting of ribosomes and fragments of attached endoplasmic reticulum that can be isolated from cells by centrifugal action

MICROTOME n instrument used for cutting thin sections, esp of biological material, for microscopical examination

MICROTOMY n cutting of sections with a microtome

MICROTONE n any musical interval smaller than a semitone

MICROVOLT n millionth of volt

MICROWATT n millionth of watt

MICROWAVE n electromagnetic wave with a wavelength of a few centimetres, used in radar and cooking ▷ vb cook in a microwave oven

MICROWIRE n very fine wire

MICRURGY n manipulation and examination of single cells under a microscope

MICS > MIC

MICTION n urination

MICTIONS > MICTION

MICTURATE vb urinate

MID adj intermediate, middle ▷ n middle ▷ prep amid

MIDAIR n some point above ground level, in the air

MIDAIRS > MIDAIR

MIDBAND adj using a range of frequencies between narrowband and broadband

MIDBRAIN n part of the brain that develops from the middle portion of the embryonic neural tube

MIDBRAINS > MIDBRAIN

MIDCAP adj (of investments) involving medium-sized amounts of capital

MIDCOURSE adj in middle of course

MIDCULT n middlebrow culture

MIDCULTS > MIDCULT

MIDDAY n noon

MIDDAYS > MIDDAY

MIDDEN n dunghill or rubbish heap

MIDDENS > MIDDEN

MIDDEST adj in middle

MIDDIE n glass or bottle containing 285ml of beer

MIDDIES > MIDDY

MIDDLE adj equidistant from two extremes ▷ n middle point or part ▷ vb place in the middle

MIDDLED > MIDDLE

MIDDLEMAN n trader who buys from the producer and sells to the consumer

MIDDLEMEN > MIDDLEMAN

MIDDLER n pupil in middle years at school

MIDDLERS > MIDDLER

MIDDLES > MIDDLE

MIDDLING adj mediocre ▷ adv moderately

MIDDLINGS pl n poorer or coarser part of flour or other products

MIDDORSAL adj in middle or back

MIDDY n middle-sized glass of beer

MIDFIELD n area between the two opposing defences

MIDFIELDS > MIDFIELD

MIDGE n small mosquito-like insect

MIDGES > MIDGE

MIDGET n very small person or thing ▷ adj much smaller than normal

MIDGETS > MIDGET

MIDGIE n informal word for a small winged biting insect such as the midge or sandfly

MIDGIER > MIDGE

MIDGIES > MIDGIE

MIDGIEST > MIDGE

MIDGUT n middle part of the digestive tract

MIDGUTS > MIDGUT

MIDGY > MIDGE

MIDI adj (of a skirt, coat, etc) reaching to below the knee or midcalf ▷ n skirt, coat, etc reaching to below the knee or midcalf

MIDINETTE n Parisian seamstress or salesgirl in a clothes shop

MIDIRON n golf club used for medium-length approach shots

MIDIRONS > MIDIRON

MIDIS > MIDI

MIDISKIRT n skirt of medium length

MIDLAND n middle part of a country

MIDLANDER n person living in the midlands

MIDLANDS > MIDLAND

MIDLEG n middle of leg

MIDLEGS > MIDLEG

MIDLIFE n middle age

MIDLIFER n middle-aged person

MIDLIFERS > MIDLIFER

MIDLINE n line at middle of something

MIDLINES > MIDLINE

MIDLIST n books in publisher's range that sell reasonably well

MIDLISTS > MIDLIST

MIDLIVES > MIDLIFE

MIDMONTH n middle of month

MIDMONTHS > MIDMONTH

MIDMOST adv in the middle or midst ▷ n the middle or midst

MIDMOSTS > MIDMOST

MIDNIGHT n twelve o'clock at night

MIDNIGHTS > MIDNIGHT

MIDNOON n noon

MIDNOONS > MIDNOON

MIDPAY adj paying more than an unskilled job but less than a high-income one

MIDPOINT n point on a line equally distant from either end

MIDPOINTS > MIDPOINT

MIDRANGE n part of loudspeaker

MIDRANGES > MIDRANGE

MIDRASH n homily on a Jewish scriptural passage

MIDRASHIC > MIDRASH

MIDRASHIM > MIDRASH

MIDRASHOT > MIDRASH

MIDRIB n main vein of a leaf

MIDRIBS > MIDRIB

MIDRIFF n middle part of the body

MIDRIFFS > MIDRIFF

MIDS > MID

MIDSEASON adj taking place in the middle of the season

MIDSHIP adj in, of, or relating to the middle of a vessel ▷ n middle of a vessel

MIDSHIPS See > AMIDSHIPS

MIDSHORE adj between the inshore and the offshore

MIDSIZE adj medium-sized

MIDSIZED same as > MIDSIZE

MIDSOLE n layer between the inner and the outer sole of a shoe

MIDSOLES > MIDSOLE

MIDSPACE n area in middle of space

MIDSPACES > MIDSPACE

MIDST See > AMID

MIDSTORY n level of forest trees between smallest and tallest

MIDSTREAM n middle of a stream or river ▷ adj in or towards the middle of a stream or river

MIDSTS > MIDST

MIDSUMMER n middle of summer

MIDTERM n middle of a term in a school, university, etc

MIDTERMS > MIDTERM

MIDTOWN n centre of a town

MIDTOWNS > MIDTOWN

MIDWATCH n naval watch period beginning at midnight

MIDWATER n middle part of a body of water

MIDWATERS > MIDWATER

MIDWAY adv halfway ▷ adj in or at the middle of the distance ▷ n place in a fair, carnival, etc, where sideshows are located

MIDWAYS > MIDWAY

MIDWEEK n middle of the week

MIDWEEKLY > MIDWEEK

MIDWEEKS > MIDWEEK

MIDWIFE n trained person who assists at childbirth ▷ vb act as midwife

MIDWIFED > MIDWIFE

MIDWIFERY n art or practice of a midwife

MIDWIFES > MIDWIFE

MIDWIFING > MIDWIFE

MIDWINTER n middle or depth of winter

MIDWIVE vb act as midwife

MIDWIVED > MIDWIVE

MIDWIVES > MIDWIVE

MIDWIVING > MIDWIVE

MIDYEAR n middle of the year

MIDYEARS > MIDYEAR

MIELIE same as > MEALIE

MIELIES > MIELIE

MIEN n person's bearing, demeanour, or appearance

MIENS > MIEN

MIEVE same as > MOVE

MIEVED > MIEVE

MIEVES > MIEVE

MIEVING > MIEVE

MIFF vb take offence or offend ▷ n petulant mood

MIFFED > MIFF

MIFFIER > MIFFY

MIFFIEST > MIFFY

MIFFILY > MIFFY

MIFFINESS > MIFFY

MIFFING > MIFF

MIFFS > MIFF

MIFFY adj easily upset

MIFTY same as > MIFFY

MIG n marble used in games

MIGAWD interj interjection used to express surprise

MIGG same as > MIG

MIGGLE n US word for playing marble

MIGGLES > MIGGLE

MIGGS > MIGG

MIGHT > MAY

MIGHTEST > MAY

MIGHTFUL same as > MIGHTY

MIGHTIER > MIGHTY

MIGHTIEST > MIGHTY

MIGHTILY adv great extent, amount, or degree

MIGHTS > MAY

MIGHTST > MAY

MIGHTY adj powerful ▷ adv very

MIGMATITE n composite rock body containing two

types of rock (esp igneous and metamorphic rock) that have interacted with each other but are nevertheless still distinguishable

MIGNON adj small and pretty ▷ n tender boneless cut of meat

MIGNONNE > MIGNON

MIGNONNES > MIGNON

MIGNONS > MIGNON

MIGRAINE n severe headache, often with nausea and visual disturbances

MIGRAINES > MIGRAINE

MIGRANT n person or animal that moves from one place to another ▷ adj moving from one place to another

MIGRANTS > MIGRANT

MIGRATE vb move from one place to settle in another

MIGRATED > MIGRATE

MIGRATES > MIGRATE

MIGRATING > MIGRATE

MIGRATION n act or an instance of migrating

MIGRATOR > MIGRATE

MIGRATORS > MIGRATE

MIGRATORY adj (of an animal) migrating every year

MIGS > MIG

MIHA n young fern frond which has not yet opened

MIHAS > MIHA

MIHI n Māori ceremonial greeting ▷ vb greet

MIHIED > MIHI

MIHIING > MIHI

MIHIS > MIHI

MIHRAB n niche in a mosque showing the direction of Mecca

MIHRABS > MIHRAB

MIJNHEER same as > MYNHEER

MIJNHEERS > MIJNHEER

MIKADO n Japanese emperor

MIKADOS > MIKADO

MIKE n microphone ▷ vb supply with a microphone

MIKED > MIKE

MIKES > MIKE

MIKING > MIKE

MIKRA > MIKRON

MIKRON same as > MICRON

MIKRONS > MIKRON

MIKVA n place for ritual bathing by Orthodox Jews

MIKVAH n pool used for ritual purification

MIKVAHS > MIKVAH

MIKVAS > MIKVA

MIKVEH same as > MIKVAH

MIKVEHS > MIKVEH

MIKVOS > MIKVEH

MIKVOT > MIKVEH

MIKVOTH > MIKVAH

MIL n unit of length equal to one thousandth of an inch

MILADI same as > MILADY

MILADIES > MILADY

MILADIS > MILADI

MILADY n (formerly) a continental title for an English gentlewoman

MILAGE same as > MILEAGE

MILAGES > MILAGE

MILCH adj (of a cow) giving milk

MILCHIG same as > MILCHIK

MILCHIK adj containing or used in the preparation of milk products

MILD adj not strongly flavoured ▷ n dark beer flavoured with fewer hops than bitter ▷ vb become gentle

MILDED > MILD

MILDEN vb make or become mild or milder

MILDENED > MILDEN

MILDENING > MILDEN

MILDENS > MILDEN

MILDER > MILD

MILDEST > MILD

MILDEW same as > MOULD

MILDEWED > MILDEW

MILDEWING > MILDEW

MILDEWS > MILDEW

MILDEWY > MILDEW

MILDING > MILD

MILDISH adj rather mild

MILDLY > MILD

MILDNESS > MILD

MILDS > MILD

MILE n unit of length equal to 1760 yards or 1.609 kilometres

MILEAGE n distance travelled in miles

MILEAGES > MILEAGE

MILEPOST n signpost that shows the distance in miles to or from a place

MILEPOSTS > MILEPOST

MILER n athlete, horse, etc, that specializes in races of one mile

MILERS > MILER

MILES > MILE

MILESIAN adj Irish

MILESIMO n Spanish word meaning thousandth

MILESIMOS > MILESIMO

MILESTONE same as > MILEPOST

MILF n sexually attractive older woman

MILFOIL same as > YARROW

MILFOILS > MILFOIL

MILFS > MILF

MILIA > MILIUM

MILIARIA n acute itching eruption of the skin,

caused by blockage of the sweat glands

MILIARIAL > MILIARIA

MILIARIAS > MILIARIA

MILIARY adj resembling or relating to millet seeds

MILIEU n environment or surroundings

MILIEUS > MILIEU

MILIEUX > MILIEU

MILING n activity of running one mile

MILINGS > MILING

MILITANCE n the condition or fact of being militant, esp in pursuing a political or social end

MILITANCY > MILITANT

MILITANT adj aggressive or vigorous in support of a cause ▷ n militant person

MILITANTS > MILITANT

MILITAR same as > MILITARY

MILITARIA pl n items of military interest, such as weapons, uniforms, medals, etc, esp from the past

MILITARY adj of or for soldiers, armies, or war ▷ n armed services

MILITATE vb have a strong influence or effect

MILITATED > MILITATE

MILITATES > MILITATE

MILITIA n military force of trained citizens

MILITIAS > MILITIA

MILIUM n pimple

MILK n white fluid produced by female mammals to feed their young ▷ vb draw milk from

MILKED > MILK

MILKEN adj of or like milk

MILKER n cow, goat, etc, that yields milk

MILKERS > MILKER

MILKFISH n type of large silvery tropical food and game fish

MILKIER > MILKY

MILKIEST > MILKY

MILKILY > MILKY

MILKINESS > MILKY

MILKING > MILK

MILKINGS > MILKING

MILKLESS > MILK

MILKLIKE > MILK

MILKMAID n (esp in former times) woman who milks cows

MILKMAIDS > MILKMAID

MILKMAN n man who delivers milk to people's houses

MILKMEN > MILKMAN

MILKO informal name for > MILKMAN

MILKOS > MILKO

MILKS > MILK

MILKSHAKE n drink of flavoured milk

MILKSHED n area where milk is produced

MILKSHEDS > MILKSHED

MILKSOP n feeble man

MILKSOPPY > MILKSOP

MILKSOPS > MILKSOP

MILKTOAST n meek, submissive, or timid person

MILKWEED n monarch butterfly

MILKWEEDS > MILKWEED

MILKWOOD n tree producing latex

MILKWOODS > MILKWOOD

MILKWORT n type of plant with small blue, pink, or white flowers, formerly believed to increase milk production in cows

MILKWORTS > MILKWORT

MILKY adj of or like milk

MILL n factory ▷ vb grind, press, or process in or as if in a mill

MILLABLE > MILL

MILLAGE adj American tax rate calculated in thousandths per dollar

MILLAGES > MILLAGE

MILLBOARD n strong pasteboard, used esp in book covers

MILLCAKE n food for livestock

MILLCAKES > MILLCAKE

MILLDAM n dam built to raise the water level to turn a millwheel

MILLDAMS > MILLDAM

MILLE French word for > THOUSAND

MILLED adj crushed or ground in a mill

MILLENARY adj of or relating to a thousand or to a thousand years ▷ n adherent of millenarianism

MILLENNIA n plural of millennium: period or cycle of one thousand years

MILLEPED same as > MILLEPEDE

MILLEPEDE same as > MILLIPEDE

MILLEPEDS > MILLEPED

MILLEPORE n type of tropical colonial coral-like hydrozoan

MILLER n person who works in a mill

MILLERITE n yellow mineral consisting of nickel sulphide

MILLERS > MILLER

MILLES > MILLE

MILLET n type of cereal grass

MILLETS > MILLET

MILLHAND n person who works in a mill

MILLHANDS > MILLHAND

MILLHOUSE n house attached to mill

MILLIAMP n one thousandth of an ampere

MILLIAMPS > MILLIAMP

MILLIARD n one thousand millions

MILLIARDS > MILLIARD

MILLIARE n ancient Roman unit of distance

MILLIARES > MILLIARE

MILLIARY adj relating to or marking a distance equal to an ancient Roman mile of a thousand paces

MILLIBAR n unit of atmospheric pressure

MILLIBARS > MILLIBAR

MILLIE n derogatory name for a young working-class woman

MILLIEME n Tunisian monetary unit worth one thousandth of a dinar

MILLIEMES > MILLIEME

MILLIER n metric weight of million grams

MILLIERS > MILLIER

MILLIES > MILLIE

MILLIGAL n unit of gravity

MILLIGALS > MILLIGAL

MILLIGRAM n thousandth part of a gram

MILLILUX n thousandth of lux

MILLIME same as > MILLIEME

MILLIMES > MILLIME

MILLIMHO n thousandth of mho

MILLIMHOS > MILLIMHO

MILLIMOLE n thousandth of mole

MILLINE n measurement of advertising space

MILLINER n maker or seller of women's hats

MILLINERS > MILLINER

MILLINERY n hats, trimmings, etc, sold by a milliner

MILLINES > MILLINE

MILLING n act or process of grinding, cutting, pressing, or crushing in a mill

MILLINGS > MILLING

MILLIOHM n thousandth of ohm

MILLIOHMS > MILLIOHM

MILLION n one thousand thousands

MILLIONS > MILLION

MILLIONTH n one of 1 000 000 approximately equal parts of something ▷ adj being the ordinal number of 1 000 000 in numbering or counting order, etc

MILLIPED same as > MILLIPEDE

MILLIPEDE n small animal with a jointed body and many pairs of legs

MILLIPEDS > MILLIPED

MILLIREM n unit of radiation

MILLIREMS > MILLIREM

MILLIVOLT n thousandth of volt

MILLIWATT n thousandth of watt

MILLOCRAT n member of a government of millowners

MILLPOND n pool which provides water to turn a millwheel

MILLPONDS > MILLPOND

MILLRACE n current of water that turns a millwheel

MILLRACES > MILLRACE

MILLRIND n iron support fitted across an upper millstone

MILLRINDS > MILLRIND

MILLRUN same as > MILLRACE

MILLRUNS > MILLRUN

MILLS > MILL

MILLSCALE n scale on metal being heated

MILLSTONE n flat circular stone for grinding corn

MILLTAIL n channel carrying water away from mill

MILLTAILS > MILLTAIL

MILLWHEEL n waterwheel that drives a mill

MILLWORK n work done in a mill

MILLWORKS > MILLWORK

MILNEB n type of pesticide

MILNEBS > MILNEB

MILO n variety of sorghum with heads of yellow or pinkish seeds

MILOMETER n device that records the number of miles that a bicycle or motor vehicle has travelled

MILOR same as > MILORD

MILORD n (formerly) a continental title used for an English gentleman

MILORDS > MILORD

MILORS > MILOR

MILOS > MILO

MILPA n form of subsistence agriculture in Mexico

MILPAS > MILPA

MILREIS n former monetary unit of Portugal and Brazil

MILS > MIL

MILSEY n milk strainer

MILSEYS > MILSEY

MILT n sperm of fish ▷ vb fertilize (the roe of a female fish) with milt, esp artificially

MILTED > MILT

MILTER n male fish that is mature and ready to breed

MILTERS > MILTER

MILTIER > MILTY

MILTIEST > MILTY

MILTING > MILT

MILTONIA n tropical American orchid

MILTONIAS > MILTONIA

MILTS > MILT

MILTY adj full of milt

MILTZ same as > MILT

MILTZES > MILTZ

MILVINE adj of kites and related birds

MIM adj prim, modest, or demure

MIMBAR n pulpit in mosque

MIMBARS > MIMBAR

MIME n acting without the use of words ▷ vb act in mime

MIMED > MIME

MIMEO vb mimeograph

MIMEOED > MIMEO

MIMEOING > MIMEO

MIMEOS > MIMEO

MIMER > MIME

MIMERS > MIME

MIMES > MIME

MIMESES > MIMESIS

MIMESIS n imitative representation of nature or human behaviour

MIMESISES > MIMESIS

MIMESTER > MIME

MIMESTERS > MIME

MIMETIC adj imitating or representing something

MIMETICAL > MIMETIC

MIMETITE n rare secondary mineral

MIMETITES > MIMETITE

MIMIC vb imitate (a person or manner), esp for satirical effect ▷ n person or animal that is good at mimicking ▷ adj of, relating to, or using mimicry

MIMICAL > MIMIC

MIMICKED > MIMIC

MIMICKER > MIMIC

MIMICKERS > MIMIC

MIMICKING > MIMIC

MIMICRIES > MIMICRY

MIMICRY n act or art of copying or imitating closely

MIMICS > MIMIC

MIMING > MIME

MIMIVIRUS n type of large virus

MIMMER > MIM

MIMMEST > MIM

MIMMICK same as > MINNICK

MIMMICKED > MIMMICK

MIMMICKS > MIMMICK

MIMOSA n shrub with fluffy yellow flowers and sensitive leaves

MIMOSAE > MIMOSA

MIMOSAS > MIMOSA

MIMSEY same as > MIMSY

MIMSIER > MIMSY

MIMSIEST > MIMSY

MIMSY adj prim, underwhelming, and ineffectual

MIMULUS n plants cultivated for their yellow or red flowers

MIMULUSES > MIMULUS

MINA n ancient unit of weight and money, used in Asia Minor

MINABLE > MINE

MINACIOUS adj threatening

MINACITY > MINACIOUS

MINAE > MINA

MINAR n tower

MINARET n tall slender tower of a mosque

MINARETED > MINARET

MINARETS > MINARET

MINARS > MINAR

MINAS > MINA

MINATORY adj threatening or menacing

MINBAR same as > MIMBAR

MINBARS > MINBAR

MINCE vb cut or grind into very small pieces ▷ n minced meat

MINCED > MINCE

MINCEMEAT n sweet mixture of dried fruit and spices

MINCER n machine for mincing meat

MINCERS > MINCER

MINCES > MINCE

MINCEUR adj (of food) low-fat

MINCIER > MINCY

MINCIEST > MINCY

MINCING adj affected in manner

MINCINGLY > MINCING

MINCY adj effeminate

MIND n thinking faculties ▷ vb take offence at

MINDED adj having an inclination as specified

MINDEDLY adv in the manner of a person with the kind of mind specified

MINDER n aide or bodyguard

MINDERS > MINDER

MINDFUCK n taboo term for deliberate infliction of psychological damage

MINDFUCKS > MINDFUCK

MINDFUL adj heedful

MINDFULLY > MINDFUL

MINDING > MIND

MINDINGS > MIND

MINDLESS adj stupid
MINDS > MIND
MINDSET n ideas and attitudes with which a person approaches a situation
MINDSETS > MINDSET
MINDSHARE n level of awareness in the minds of consumers that a particular product commands
MINE pron belonging to me ▷ n deep hole for digging out coal, ores, etc ▷ vb dig for minerals
MINEABLE > MINE
MINED > MINE
MINEFIELD n area of land or water containing mines
MINELAYER n warship or aircraft for carrying and laying mines
MINEOLA same as > MINNEOLA
MINEOLAS > MINEOLA
MINER n person who works in a mine
MINERAL n naturally occurring inorganic substance, such as metal ▷ adj of, containing, or like minerals
MINERALS > MINERAL
MINERS > MINER
MINES > MINE
MINESHAFT n vertical entrance into mine
MINESTONE n ore
MINETTE n type of rock
MINETTES > MINETTE
MINEVER same as > MINIVER
MINEVERS > MINEVER
MING vb mix
MINGE n taboo word fore female genitals
MINGED > MING
MINGER n unattractive person
MINGERS > MINGER
MINGES > MINGE
MINGIER > MINGY
MINGIEST > MINGY
MINGILY adv in a miserly manner
MINGINESS > MINGY
MINGING adj unattractive or unpleasant
MINGLE vb mix or blend
MINGLED > MINGLE
MINGLER > MINGLE
MINGLERS > MINGLE
MINGLES > MINGLE
MINGLING > MINGLE
MINGLINGS > MINGLE
MINGS > MING
MINGY adj miserly
MINI same as > MINIDRESS
MINIATE vb paint with minium
MINIATED > MINIATE
MINIATES > MINIATE

MINIATING > MINIATE
MINIATION > MINIATE
MINIATURE n small portrait, model, or copy ▷ adj small-scale ▷ vb reproduce in miniature
MINIBAR n selection of drinks and confectionery provided in a hotel room
MINIBARS > MINIBAR
MINIBIKE n light motorcycle
MINIBIKER > MINIBIKE
MINIBIKES > MINIBIKE
MINIBREAK n short holiday
MINIBUS n small bus
MINIBUSES > MINIBUS
MINICAB n ordinary car used as a taxi
MINICABS > MINICAB
MINICAM n portable television camera
MINICAMP n period spent together in isolation by sports team
MINICAMPS > MINICAMP
MINICAMS > MINICAM
MINICAR n small car
MINICARS > MINICAR
MINICOM n device allowing typed telephone messages to be sent and received
MINICOMS > MINICOM
MINIDISC n small recordable compact disc
MINIDISCS > MINIDISC
MINIDISH n small parabolic aerial for reception or transmission to a communications satellite
MINIDISK same as > MINIDISC
MINIDISKS > MINIDISK
MINIDRESS n very short dress, at least four inches above the knee
MINIER > MINY
MINIEST > MINY
MINIFIED > MINIFY
MINIFIES > MINIFY
MINIFY vb minimize or lessen the size or importance of (something)
MINIFYING > MINIFY
MINIGOLF n putting game played via various obstacles
MINIGOLFS > MINIGOLF
MINIKIN n small, dainty, or affected person or thing ▷ adj dainty, prim, or affected
MINIKINS > MINIKIN
MINILAB n equipment for processing photographic film
MINILABS > MINILAB
MINIM n note half the length of a semibreve ▷ adj very small

MINIMA > MINIMUM
MINIMAL adj minimum ▷ n small surfboard
MINIMALLY > MINIMAL
MINIMALS > MINIMAL
MINIMART n convenience store
MINIMARTS > MINIMART
MINIMAX n lowest of a set of maximum values ▷ vb make maximum as low as possible
MINIMAXED > MINIMAX
MINIMAXES > MINIMAX
MINIMENT same as > MUNIMENT
MINIMENTS > MINIMENT
MINIMILL n small mill
MINIMILLS > MINIMILL
MINIMISE same as > MINIMIZE
MINIMISED > MINIMISE
MINIMISER > MINIMIZE
MINIMISES > MINIMISE
MINIMISM n desire to reduce to minimum
MINIMISMS > MINIMISM
MINIMIST > MINIMISM
MINIMISTS > MINIMISM
MINIMIZE vb reduce to a minimum
MINIMIZED > MINIMIZE
MINIMIZER > MINIMIZE
MINIMIZES > MINIMIZE
MINIMOTO n reduced-size replica motorcycle used for racing
MINIMOTOS > MINIMOTO
MINIMS > MINIM
MINIMUM n least possible (amount or number) ▷ adj of, being, or showing a minimum or minimums
MINIMUMS > MINIMUM
MINIMUS adj youngest: used after the surname of a schoolboy with elder brothers at the same school
MINIMUSES > MINIMUS
MINING n act, process, or industry of extracting coal or ores from the earth
MININGS > MINING
MINION n servile assistant ▷ adj dainty, pretty, or elegant
MINIONS > MINION
MINIPARK n small park
MINIPARKS > MINIPARK
MINIPILL n low-dose oral contraceptive containing a progestogen only
MINIPILLS > MINIPILL
MINIRUGBY n version of rugby with fewer players
MINIS > MINI
MINISCULE same as > MINUSCULE
MINISH vb diminish
MINISHED > MINISH
MINISHES > MINISH
MINISHING > MINISH

MINISKI n short ski
MINISKIRT n very short skirt
MINISKIS > MINISKI
MINISODE n episode of a television series shortened for broadcast on the internet
MINISODES > MINISODE
MINISTATE n small independent state
MINISTER n head of a government department ▷ vb attend to the needs of
MINISTERS > MINISTER
MINISTRY n profession or duties of a clergyman
MINITOWER n computer in small vertical cabinet
MINITRACK n satellite tracking system
MINIUM n bright red poisonous insoluble oxide of lead
MINIUMS > MINIUM
MINIVAN n small van, esp one with seats in the back for carrying passengers
MINIVANS > MINIVAN
MINIVER n white fur, used in ceremonial costumes
MINIVERS > MINIVER
MINIVET n brightly coloured tropical Asian cuckoo shrike
MINIVETS > MINIVET
MINK n stoatlike animal
MINKE n as in minke whale type of small whalebone whale or rorqual
MINKES > MINKE
MINKS > MINK
MINNEOLA n juicy citrus fruit that is a cross between a tangerine and a grapefruit
MINNEOLAS > MINNEOLA
MINNICK vb behave in fussy way
MINNICKED > MINNICK
MINNICKS > MINNICK
MINNIE n mother
MINNIES > MINNIE
MINNOCK same as > MINNICK
MINNOCKED > MINNOCK
MINNOCKS > MINNOCK
MINNOW n small freshwater fish
MINNOWS > MINNOW
MINNY same as > MINNIE
MINO same as > MYNAH
MINOR adj lesser ▷ n person regarded legally as a child ▷ vb take a minor
MINORCA n breed of light domestic fowl
MINORCAS > MINORCA
MINORED > MINOR
MINORING > MINOR
MINORITY n lesser number
MINORS > MINOR
MINORSHIP > MINOR

m

MINOS >MINO

MINOTAUR *n* as in *minotaur beetle* kind of dung-beetle

MINOXIDIL *n* drug used to counter baldness

MINSHUKU *n* guesthouse in Japan

MINSHUKUS >MINSHUKU

MINSTER *n* cathedral or large church

MINSTERS >MINSTER

MINSTREL *n* medieval singer or musician

MINSTRELS >MINSTREL

MINT *n* plant with aromatic leaves ▷ *vb* make (coins)

MINTAGE *n* process of minting

MINTAGES >MINTAGE

MINTED >MINT

MINTER >MINT

MINTERS >MINT

MINTIER >MINT

MINTIEST >MINT

MINTING >MINT

MINTS >MINT

MINTY >MINT

MINUEND *n* number from which another number is to be subtracted

MINUENDS >MINUEND

MINUET *n* stately dance ▷ *vb* dance the minuet

MINUETED >MINUET

MINUETING >MINUET

MINUETS >MINUET

MINUS *adj* indicating subtraction ▷ *n* sign (-) denoting subtraction or a number less than zero ▷ *prep* reduced by the subtraction of

MINUSCULE *adj* very small ▷ *n* lower-case letter

MINUSES >MINUS

MINUTE *n* 60th part of an hour or degree ▷ *vb* record in the minutes ▷ *adj* very small

MINUTED >MINUTE

MINUTELY *adv* in great detail ▷ *adj* occurring every minute

MINUTEMAN *n* (in the War of American Independence) colonial militiaman who promised to be ready to fight at one minute's notice

MINUTEMEN >MINUTEMAN

MINUTER >MINUTE

MINUTES *pl n* official record of the proceedings of a meeting or conference

MINUTEST >MINUTE

MINUTIA *singular noun of* >MINUTIAE

MINUTIAE *pl n* trifling or precise details

MINUTIAL >MINUTIAE

MINUTING >MINUTE

MINUTIOSE >MINUTIAE

MINX *n* bold or flirtatious girl

MINXES >MINX

MINXISH >MINX

MINY *adj* of or like mines

MINYAN *n* number of persons required by Jewish law to be present for a religious service

MINYANIM >MINYAN

MINYANS >MINYAN

MIOCENE *adj* of, denoting, or formed in the fourth epoch of the Tertiary period

MIOMBO *n* (in E Africa) a dry wooded area with sparse deciduous growth

MIOMBOS >MIOMBO

MIOSES >MIOSIS

MIOSIS *n* excessive contraction of the pupil of the eye, as in response to drugs

MIOSISES >MIOSIS

MIOTIC >MIOSIS

MIOTICS >MIOSIS

MIPS *n* unit used to express the speed of a computer's central processing unit

MIQUELET *n* type of lock on old firearm

MIQUELETS >MIQUELET

MIR *n* peasant commune in prerevolutionary Russia

MIRABELLE *n* small sweet yellow-orange fruit that is a variety of greengage

MIRABILIA *n* wonders

MIRABILIS *n* tropical American plant

MIRABLE *adj* wonderful

MIRACIDIA *n* plural form of singular miracidium: flat ciliated larva of flukes that hatches from the egg and gives rise asexually to other larval forms

MIRACLE *n* wonderful supernatural event

MIRACLES >MIRACLE

MIRADOR *n* window, balcony, or turret

MIRADORS >MIRADOR

MIRAGE *n* optical illusion, esp one caused by hot air

MIRAGES >MIRAGE

MIRANDISE *same as* >MIRANDIZE

MIRANDIZE *vb* (in USA) inform arrested person of rights

MIRBANE *n* substance used in perfumes

MIRBANES >MIRBANE

MIRCHI *Indian English word for* >HOT

MIRE *n* swampy ground ▷ *vb* sink or be stuck in a mire

MIRED >MIRE

MIREPOIX *n* mixture of sautéed root vegetables used as a base for braising meat or for various sauces

MIRES >MIRE

MIREX *n* type of insecticide

MIREXES >MIREX

MIRI >MIR

MIRID *n* variety of leaf bug

MIRIDS >MIRID

MIRIER >MIRE

MIRIEST >MIRE

MIRIFIC *adj* achieving wonderful things

MIRIFICAL *same as* >MIRIFIC

MIRIN *n* Japanese rice wine

MIRINESS >MIRE

MIRING >MIRE

MIRINS >MIRIN

MIRITI *n* South American palm

MIRITIS >MIRITI

MIRK *same as* >MURK

MIRKER >MIRK

MIRKEST >MIRK

MIRKIER >MIRK

MIRKIEST >MURKY

MIRKILY >MIRK

MIRKINESS >MIRK

MIRKS >MIRK

MIRKY >MIRK

MIRLIER >MIRLY

MIRLIEST >MIRLY

MIRLIGOES *n* dizzy feeling

MIRLITON *another name (chiefly US) for* >CHAYOTE

MIRLITONS >MIRLITON

MIRLY *same as* >MARLY

MIRO *n* tall New Zealand tree

MIROMIRO *n* small New Zealand bird

MIROMIROS >MIROMIRO

MIROS >MIRO

MIRROR *n* coated glass surface for reflecting images ▷ *vb* reflect in or as if in a mirror

MIRRORED >MIRROR

MIRRORING *n* act of mirroring

MIRRORS >MIRROR

MIRS >MIR

MIRTH *n* laughter, merriment, or gaiety

MIRTHFUL >MIRTH

MIRTHLESS >MIRTH

MIRTHS >MIRTH

MIRV *n* missile that has several warheads, each one being directed to different enemy targets ▷ *vb* arm with mirvs

MIRVED >MIRV

MIRVING >MIRV

MIRVS >MIRV

MIRY >MIRE

MIRZA *n* title of respect placed before the surname of a distinguished man

MIRZAS >MIRZA

MIS >MI

MISACT *vb* act wrongly

MISACTED >MISACT

MISACTING >MISACT

MISACTS >MISACT

MISADAPT *vb* adapt badly

MISADAPTS >MISADAPT

MISADD *vb* add badly

MISADDED >MISADD

MISADDING >MISADD

MISADDS >MISADD

MISADJUST *vb* adjust wrongly

MISADVICE *n* bad advice

MISADVISE *vb* give bad advice to

MISAGENT *n* bad agent

MISAGENTS >MISAGENT

MISAIM *vb* aim badly

MISAIMED >MISAIM

MISAIMING >MISAIM

MISAIMS >MISAIM

MISALIGN *vb* align badly

MISALIGNS >MISALIGN

MISALLEGE *vb* allege wrongly

MISALLIED >MISALLY

MISALLIES >MISALLY

MISALLOT *vb* allot wrongly

MISALLOTS >MISALLOT

MISALLY *vb* form unsuitable alliance

MISALTER *vb* alter wrongly

MISALTERS >MISALTER

MISANDRY *n* hatred of men

MISAPPLY *vb* use something for a purpose for which it is not intended or is not suited

MISARRAY *n* disarray

MISARRAYS >MISARRAY

MISASSAY *vb* assay wrongly

MISASSAYS >MISASSAY

MISASSIGN *vb* assign wrongly

MISATE >MISEAT

MISATONE *vb* atone wrongly

MISATONED >MISATONE

MISATONES >MISATONE

MISAUNTER *n* misadventure

MISAVER *vb* claim wrongly

MISAVERS >MISAVER

MISAVISED *adj* badly advised

MISAWARD *vb* award wrongly

MISAWARDS >MISAWARD

MISBECAME >MISBECOME

MISBECOME *vb* be unbecoming to or unsuitable for

MISBEGAN >MISBEGIN

MISBEGIN *vb* begin badly

MISBEGINS >MISBEGIN

MISBEGOT adj illegitimate
MISBEGUN > MISBEGIN
MISBEHAVE vb behave badly
MISBELIEF n false or unorthodox belief
MISBESEEM vb be unsuitable for
MISBESTOW vb bestow wrongly
MISBIAS vb prejudice wrongly
MISBIASED > MISBIAS
MISBIASES > MISBIAS
MISBILL vb present inaccurate bill
MISBILLED > MISBILL
MISBILLS > MISBILL
MISBIND vb bind wrongly
MISBINDS > MISBIND
MISBIRTH n abortion
MISBIRTHS > MISBIRTH
MISBORN adj abortive
MISBOUND > MISBIND
MISBRAND vb put misleading label on
MISBRANDS > MISBRAND
MISBUILD vb build badly
MISBUILDS > MISBUILD
MISBUILT > MISBUILD
MISBUTTON vb button wrongly
MISCALL vb call by the wrong name
MISCALLED > MISCALL
MISCALLER > MISCALL
MISCALLS > MISCALL
MISCARRY vb have a miscarriage
MISCAST vb cast (a role or actor) inappropriately
MISCASTS > MISCAST
MISCEGEN n person of mixed race
MISCEGENE same as > MISCEGEN
MISCEGENS > MISCEGEN
MISCEGINE same as > MISCEGEN
MISCH adj as in misch metal alloy of cerium and other rare earth metals
MISCHANCE n unlucky event
MISCHANCY adj unlucky
MISCHARGE vb charge wrongly
MISCHIEF n annoying but not malicious behaviour
MISCHIEFS > MISCHIEF
MISCHOICE n bad choice
MISCHOOSE vb make bad choice
MISCHOSE > MISCHOOSE
MISCHOSEN > MISCHOOSE
MISCIBLE adj able to be mixed
MISCITE vb cite wrongly
MISCITED > MISCITE
MISCITES > MISCITE
MISCITING > MISCITE

MISCLAIM vb claim wrongly
MISCLAIMS > MISCLAIM
MISCLASS adj class badly
MISCODE vb code wrongly
MISCODED > MISCODE
MISCODES > MISCODE
MISCODING > MISCODE
MISCOIN vb coin wrongly
MISCOINED > MISCOIN
MISCOINS > MISCOIN
MISCOLOR same as > MISCOLOUR
MISCOLORS > MISCOLOR
MISCOLOUR vb give wrong colour to
MISCOOK vb cook badly
MISCOOKED > MISCOOK
MISCOOKS > MISCOOK
MISCOPIED > MISCOPY
MISCOPIES > MISCOPY
MISCOPY vb copy badly
MISCOUNT vb count or calculate incorrectly ▷ n false count or calculation
MISCOUNTS > MISCOUNT
MISCREANT n wrongdoer ▷ adj evil or villainous
MISCREATE vb create (something) badly or incorrectly ▷ adj badly or unnaturally formed or made
MISCREDIT vb disbelieve
MISCREED n false creed
MISCREEDS > MISCREED
MISCUE n faulty stroke in snooker, etc ▷ vb make a miscue
MISCUED > MISCUE
MISCUEING > MISCUE
MISCUES > MISCUE
MISCUING > MISCUE
MISCUT n cut wrongly
MISCUTS > MISCUT
MISDATE vb date (a letter, event, etc) wrongly
MISDATED > MISDATE
MISDATES > MISDATE
MISDATING > MISDATE
MISDEAL vb deal out cards incorrectly ▷ n faulty deal
MISDEALER > MISDEAL
MISDEALS > MISDEAL
MISDEALT > MISDEAL
MISDEED n wrongful act
MISDEEDS > MISDEED
MISDEEM vb form bad opinion of
MISDEEMED > MISDEEM
MISDEEMS > MISDEEM
MISDEFINE vb define badly
MISDEMEAN rare word for > MISBEHAVE
MISDEMPT > MISDEEM
MISDESERT n quality of being undeserving
MISDIAL vb dial telephone number incorrectly

MISDIALED > MISDIAL
MISDIALS > MISDIAL
MISDID > MISDO
MISDIET n wrong diet ▷ vb diet or eat improperly
MISDIETED > MISDIET
MISDIETS > MISDIET
MISDIGHT adj done badly ▷ vb mismanage or treat badly
MISDIGHTS > MISDIGHT
MISDIRECT vb give (someone) wrong directions or instructions
MISDIVIDE vb divide wrongly
MISDO vb do badly or wrongly
MISDOER > MISDO
MISDOERS > MISDO
MISDOES > MISDO
MISDOING > MISDO
MISDOINGS > MISDO
MISDONE adj done badly
MISDONNE same as > MISDONE
MISDOUBT archaic word for > DOUBT
MISDOUBTS > MISDOUBT
MISDRAW vb draw poorly
MISDRAWN > MISDRAW
MISDRAWS > MISDRAW
MISDREAD n fear of approaching evil ▷ vb fear or dread
MISDREADS > MISDREAD
MISDREW > MISDRAW
MISDRIVE vb drive badly
MISDRIVEN > MISDRIVE
MISDRIVES > MISDRIVE
MISDROVE > MISDRIVE
MISE n issue in the obsolete writ of right
MISEASE n unease
MISEASES > MISEASE
MISEAT vb eat unhealthy food
MISEATEN > MISEAT
MISEATING > MISEAT
MISEATS > MISEAT
MISEDIT vb edit badly
MISEDITED > MISEDIT
MISEDITS > MISEDIT
MISEMPLOY vb employ badly
MISENROL vb enrol wrongly
MISENROLL same as > MISENROL
MISENROLS > MISENROL
MISENTER vb enter wrongly
MISENTERS > MISENTER
MISENTRY n wrong or mistaken entry
MISER n person who hoards money and hates spending it
MISERABLE adj very unhappy, wretched ▷ n wretched person
MISERABLY > MISERABLE

MISERE n call in solo whist and other card games declaring a hand that will win no tricks
MISERERE n type of psalm
MISERERES > MISERERE
MISERES > MISERE
MISERIES > MISERY
MISERLIER > MISERLY
MISERLY adj of or resembling a miser
MISERS > MISER
MISERY n great unhappiness
MISES > MISE
MISESTEEM n lack of respect
MISEVENT n mishap
MISEVENTS > MISEVENT
MISFAITH n distrust
MISFAITHS > MISFAITH
MISFALL vb happen as piece of bad luck
MISFALLEN > MISFALL
MISFALLS > MISFALL
MISFALNE > MISFALL
MISFARE vb get on badly
MISFARED > MISFARE
MISFARES > MISFARE
MISFARING > MISFARE
MISFEASOR n someone who carries out the improper performance of an act that is lawful in itself
MISFED > MISFEED
MISFEED vb feed wrongly
MISFEEDS > MISFEED
MISFEIGN vb feign with evil motive
MISFEIGNS > MISFEIGN
MISFELL > MISFALL
MISFIELD vb fail to field properly
MISFIELDS > MISFIELD
MISFILE vb file (papers, records, etc) wrongly
MISFILED > MISFILE
MISFILES > MISFILE
MISFILING > MISFILE
MISFIRE vb (of a firearm or engine) fail to fire correctly ▷ n act or an instance of misfiring
MISFIRED > MISFIRE
MISFIRES > MISFIRE
MISFIRING > MISFIRE
MISFIT n person not suited to his or her social environment ▷ vb fail to fit or be fitted
MISFITS > MISFIT
MISFITTED > MISFIT
MISFOCUS n wrong or poor focus
MISFORM vb form badly
MISFORMED > MISFORM
MISFORMS > MISFORM
MISFRAME vb frame wrongly
MISFRAMED > MISFRAME
MISFRAMES > MISFRAME

m

MISGAUGE vb gauge badly
MISGAUGED > MISGAUGE
MISGAUGES > MISGAUGE
MISGAVE > MISGIVE
MISGIVE vb make or be apprehensive or suspicious
MISGIVEN > MISGIVE
MISGIVES > MISGIVE
MISGIVING n feeling of fear or doubt
MISGO vb go wrong way
MISGOES > MISGO
MISGOING > MISGO
MISGONE > MISGO
MISGOTTEN adj obtained dishonestly
MISGOVERN vb govern badly
MISGRADE vb grade wrongly
MISGRADED > MISGRADE
MISGRADES > MISGRADE
MISGRAFF adj badly done
MISGRAFT vb graft wrongly
MISGRAFTS > MISGRAFT
MISGREW > MISGROW
MISGROW vb grow in unsuitable way
MISGROWN > MISGROW
MISGROWS > MISGROW
MISGROWTH > MISGROW
MISGUESS vb guess wrongly
MISGUGGLE vb handle incompetently
MISGUIDE vb guide or direct wrongly or badly
MISGUIDED adj mistaken or unwise
MISGUIDER > MISGUIDE
MISGUIDES > MISGUIDE
MISHANDLE vb handle badly or inefficiently
MISHANTER n misfortune
MISHAP n minor accident ▷ vb happen as bad luck
MISHAPPED > MISHAP
MISHAPPEN vb happen as bad luck
MISHAPS > MISHAP
MISHAPT same as > MISSHAPEN
MISHEAR vb hear (what someone says) wrongly
MISHEARD > MISHEAR
MISHEARS > MISHEAR
MISHEGAAS same as > MESHUGGAS
MISHEGOSS same as > MESHUGGAS
MISHIT n faulty shot, kick, or stroke ▷ vb hit or kick a ball with a faulty stroke
MISHITS > MISHIT
MISHMASH n confused collection or mixture
MISHMEE n root of Asian plant
MISHMEES > MISHMEE
MISHMI n evergreen perennial plant

MISHMIS > MISHMI
MISHMOSH same as > MISHMASH
MISHUGAS same as > MESHUGGAS
MISINFER vb infer wrongly
MISINFERS > MISINFER
MISINFORM vb give incorrect information to
MISINTEND vb intend to harm
MISINTER vb bury wrongly
MISINTERS > MISINTER
MISJOIN vb join badly
MISJOINED > MISJOIN
MISJOINS > MISJOIN
MISJUDGE vb judge wrongly or unfairly
MISJUDGED > MISJUDGE
MISJUDGER > MISJUDGE
MISJUDGES > MISJUDGE
MISKAL n unit of weight in Iran
MISKALS > MISKAL
MISKEEP vb keep wrongly
MISKEEPS > MISKEEP
MISKEN vb be unaware of
MISKENNED > MISKEN
MISKENS > MISKEN
MISKENT > MISKEN
MISKEPT > MISKEEP
MISKEY vb key wrongly
MISKEYED > MISKEY
MISKEYING > MISKEY
MISKEYS > MISKEY
MISKICK vb fail to kick properly
MISKICKED > MISKICK
MISKICKS > MISKICK
MISKNEW > MISKNOW
MISKNOW vb have wrong idea about
MISKNOWN > MISKNOW
MISKNOWS > MISKNOW
MISLABEL vb label badly
MISLABELS > MISLABEL
MISLABOR vb labour wrongly
MISLABORS > MISLABOR
MISLABOUR vb labour wrongly
MISLAID > MISLAY
MISLAIN > MISLAY
MISLAY vb lose (something) temporarily
MISLAYER > MISLAY
MISLAYERS > MISLAY
MISLAYING > MISLAY
MISLAYS > MISLAY
MISLEAD vb give false or confusing information to
MISLEADER > MISLEAD
MISLEADS > MISLEAD
MISLEARED adj badly brought up
MISLEARN vb learn wrongly
MISLEARNS > MISLEARN
MISLEARNT > MISLEARN
MISLED > MISLEAD

MISLEEKE same as > MISLIKE
MISLEEKED > MISLEEKE
MISLEEKES > MISLEEKE
MISLETOE same as > MISTLETOE
MISLETOES > MISLETOE
MISLIE vb lie wrongly
MISLIES > MISLIE
MISLIGHT vb use light to lead astray
MISLIGHTS > MISLIGHT
MISLIKE vb dislike ▷ n dislike or aversion
MISLIKED > MISLIKE
MISLIKER > MISLIKE
MISLIKERS > MISLIKE
MISLIKES > MISLIKE
MISLIKING > MISLIKE
MISLIPPEN vb distrust
MISLIT > MISLIGHT
MISLIVE vb live wickedly
MISLIVED > MISLIVE
MISLIVES > MISLIVE
MISLIVING > MISLIVE
MISLOCATE vb put in wrong place
MISLODGE vb lodge wrongly
MISLODGED > MISLODGE
MISLODGES > MISLODGE
MISLUCK vb have bad luck
MISLUCKED > MISLUCK
MISLUCKS > MISLUCK
MISLYING > MISLIE
MISMADE > MISMAKE
MISMAKE vb make badly
MISMAKES > MISMAKE
MISMAKING > MISMAKE
MISMANAGE vb organize or run (something) badly
MISMARK vb mark wrongly
MISMARKED > MISMARK
MISMARKS > MISMARK
MISMARRY vb make unsuitable marriage
MISMATCH vb form an unsuitable partner, opponent, or set ▷ n unsuitable match
MISMATE vb mate wrongly
MISMATED > MISMATE
MISMATES > MISMATE
MISMATING > MISMATE
MISMEET vb fail to meet
MISMEETS > MISMEET
MISMET > MISMEET
MISMETRE vb fail to follow the metre of a poem
MISMETRED > MISMETRE
MISMETRES > MISMETRE
MISMOVE vb move badly
MISMOVED > MISMOVE
MISMOVES > MISMOVE
MISMOVING > MISMOVE
MISNAME vb name badly
MISNAMED > MISNAME
MISNAMES > MISNAME
MISNAMING > MISNAME
MISNOMER n incorrect or unsuitable name ▷ vb apply a misnomer to

MISNOMERS > MISNOMER
MISNUMBER vb number wrongly
MISO n thick brown salty paste made from soya beans
MISOCLERE adj hostile to clergy
MISOGAMIC > MISOGAMY
MISOGAMY n hatred of marriage
MISOGYNIC adj hating women
MISOGYNY n hatred of women
MISOLOGY n hatred of reasoning or reasoned argument
MISONEISM n hatred of anything new
MISONEIST > MISONEISM
MISORDER vb order badly
MISORDERS > MISORDER
MISORIENT vb orient incorrectly
MISOS > MISO
MISPAGE vb page wrongly
MISPAGED > MISPAGE
MISPAGES > MISPAGE
MISPAGING > MISPAGE
MISPAINT vb paint badly or wrongly
MISPAINTS > MISPAINT
MISPARSE vb parse wrongly
MISPARSED > MISPARSE
MISPARSES > MISPARSE
MISPART vb part wrongly
MISPARTED > MISPART
MISPARTS > MISPART
MISPATCH vb patch wrongly
MISPEN vb write wrongly
MISPENNED > MISPEN
MISPENS > MISPEN
MISPHRASE vb phrase badly
MISPICKEL n white or grey metallic mineral consisting of a sulphide of iron and arsenic that forms monoclinic crystals with an orthorhombic shape: an ore of arsenic
MISPLACE vb mislay
MISPLACED adj (of an emotion or action) directed towards a person or thing that does not deserve it
MISPLACES > MISPLACE
MISPLAN vb plan badly or wrongly
MISPLANS > MISPLAN
MISPLANT vb plant badly or wrongly
MISPLANTS > MISPLANT
MISPLAY vb play badly or wrongly in games or sports ▷ n wrong or unskilful play
MISPLAYED > MISPLAY

MISPLAYS > MISPLAY
MISPLEAD vb plead incorrectly
MISPLEADS > MISPLEAD
MISPLEASE vb displease
MISPLED > MISPLEAD
MISPOINT vb punctuate badly
MISPOINTS > MISPOINT
MISPOISE n lack of poise ▷ vb lack poise
MISPOISED > MISPOISE
MISPOISES > MISPOISE
MISPRAISE vb fail to praise properly
MISPRICE vb give the wrong price to
MISPRICED > MISPRICE
MISPRICES > MISPRICE
MISPRINT n printing error ▷ vb print a letter incorrectly
MISPRINTS > MISPRINT
MISPRISE same as > MISPRIZE
MISPRISED > MISPRISE
MISPRISES > MISPRISE
MISPRIZE vb fail to appreciate the value of
MISPRIZED > MISPRIZE
MISPRIZER > MISPRIZE
MISPRIZES > MISPRIZE
MISPROUD adj undeservedly proud
MISQUOTE vb quote inaccurately
MISQUOTED > MISQUOTE
MISQUOTER > MISQUOTE
MISQUOTES > MISQUOTE
MISRAISE vb raise wrongly or excessively
MISRAISED > MISRAISE
MISRAISES > MISRAISE
MISRATE vb rate wrongly
MISRATED > MISRATE
MISRATES > MISRATE
MISRATING > MISRATE
MISREAD vb misinterpret (a situation etc)
MISREADS > MISREAD
MISRECKON vb reckon wrongly
MISRECORD vb record wrongly
MISREFER vb refer wrongly
MISREFERS > MISREFER
MISREGARD n lack of attention ▷ vb have no regard for; disregard
MISRELATE vb relate badly
MISRELIED > MISRELY
MISRELIES > MISRELY
MISRELY vb rely wrongly
MISRENDER vb render wrongly
MISREPORT vb report falsely or inaccurately ▷ n inaccurate or false report
MISRHYMED adj badly rhymed

MISROUTE vb send wrong way
MISROUTED > MISROUTE
MISROUTES > MISROUTE
MISRULE vb govern inefficiently or unjustly ▷ n inefficient or unjust government
MISRULED > MISRULE
MISRULES > MISRULE
MISRULING > MISRULE
MISS vb fail to notice, hear, hit, reach, find, or catch ▷ n fact or instance of missing
MISSA n Roman Catholic mass
MISSABLE > MISS
MISSAE > MISSA
MISSAID > MISSAY
MISSAL n book containing the prayers and rites of the Mass
MISSALS > MISSAL
MISSAW > MISSEE
MISSAY vb say wrongly
MISSAYING > MISSAY
MISSAYS > MISSAY
MISSEAT vb seat wrongly
MISSEATED > MISSEAT
MISSEATS > MISSEAT
MISSED > MISS
MISSEE vb see wrongly
MISSEEING > MISSEE
MISSEEM vb be unsuitable for
MISSEEMED > MISSEEM
MISSEEMS > MISSEEM
MISSEEN > MISSEE
MISSEES > MISSEE
MISSEL adj as in missel thrush large European thrush
MISSELL vb sell (a product, esp a financial one) misleadingly
MISSELLS > MISSELL
MISSELS > MISSEL
MISSEND vb send wrongly
MISSENDS > MISSEND
MISSENSE n type of genetic mutation ▷ vb give a wrong sense or meaning
MISSENSED > MISSENSE
MISSENSES > MISSENSE
MISSENT > MISSEND
MISSES > MISS
MISSET vb set wrongly
MISSETS > MISSET
MISSHAPE vb shape badly ▷ n something that is badly shaped
MISSHAPED > MISSHAPE
MISSHAPEN adj badly shaped, deformed
MISSHAPER > MISSHAPE
MISSHAPES > MISSHAPE
MISSHOD adj badly shod
MISSHOOD n state of being an unmarried woman
MISSHOODS > MISSHOOD

MISSIER > MISSY
MISSIES > MISSY
MISSIEST > MISSY
MISSILE n rocket with an exploding warhead
MISSILEER n serviceman or servicewoman who is responsible for firing missiles
MISSILERY n missiles collectively
MISSILES > MISSILE
MISSILRY same as > MISSILERY
MISSING adj lost or absent
MISSINGLY > MISSING
MISSION n specific task or duty ▷ vb direct a mission to or establish a mission in
MISSIONAL adj emphasizing preaching of gospel
MISSIONED > MISSION
MISSIONER n person heading a parochial mission in a Christian country
MISSIONS > MISSION
MISSIS same as > MISSUS
MISSISES > MISSIS
MISSISH adj like a schoolgirl
MISSIVE n letter ▷ adj sent or intended to be sent
MISSIVES > MISSIVE
MISSOLD > MISSELL
MISSORT vb sort wrongly
MISSORTED > MISSORT
MISSORTS > MISSORT
MISSOUND vb sound wrongly
MISSOUNDS > MISSOUND
MISSOUT n someone who has been overlooked
MISSOUTS > MISSOUT
MISSPACE vb space out wrongly
MISSPACED > MISSPACE
MISSPACES > MISSPACE
MISSPEAK vb speak wrongly
MISSPEAKS > MISSPEAK
MISSPELL vb spell (a word) wrongly
MISSPELLS > MISSPELL
MISSPELT > MISSPELL
MISSPEND vb waste or spend unwisely
MISSPENDS > MISSPEND
MISSPENT > MISSPEND
MISSPOKE > MISSPEAK
MISSPOKEN > MISSPEAK
MISSTAMP vb stamp badly
MISSTAMPS > MISSTAMP
MISSTART vb start wrongly
MISSTARTS > MISSTART
MISSTATE vb state incorrectly
MISSTATED > MISSTATE
MISSTATES > MISSTATE

MISSTEER vb steer badly
MISSTEERS > MISSTEER
MISSTEP n false step ▷ vb take a false step
MISSTEPS > MISSTEP
MISSTOP vb stop wrongly
MISSTOPS > MISSTOP
MISSTRIKE vb fail to strike properly
MISSTRUCK > MISSTRIKE
MISSTYLE vb call by the wrong name
MISSTYLED > MISSTYLE
MISSTYLES > MISSTYLE
MISSUIT vb be unsuitable for
MISSUITED > MISSUIT
MISSUITS > MISSUIT
MISSUS n one's wife or the wife of the person addressed or referred to
MISSUSES > MISSUS
MISSY n affectionate or disparaging form of address to a girl ▷ adj missish
MIST n thin fog ▷ vb cover or be covered with mist
MISTAKE n error or blunder ▷ vb misunderstand
MISTAKEN adj wrong in judgment or opinion
MISTAKER > MISTAKE
MISTAKERS > MISTAKE
MISTAKES > MISTAKE
MISTAKING > MISTAKE
MISTAL n cow shed
MISTALS > MISTAL
MISTAUGHT > MISTEACH
MISTBOW same as > FOGBOW
MISTBOWS > MISTBOW
MISTEACH vb teach badly
MISTED > MIST
MISTELL vb tell wrongly
MISTELLS > MISTELL
MISTEMPER vb make disordered
MISTEND vb tend wrongly
MISTENDED > MISTEND
MISTENDS > MISTEND
MISTER n informal form of address for a man ▷ vb call (someone) mister
MISTERED > MISTER
MISTERIES > MISTERY
MISTERING > MISTER
MISTERM vb term badly
MISTERMED > MISTERM
MISTERMS > MISTERM
MISTERS > MISTER
MISTERY same as > MYSTERY
MISTEUK Scots variant of > MISTOOK
MISTFUL > MIST
MISTHINK vb have poor opinion of
MISTHINKS > MISTHINK
MISTHREW > MISTHROW

MISTHROW vb fail to throw properly
MISTHROWN > MISTHROW
MISTHROWS > MISTHROW
MISTICO n small Mediterranean sailing ship
MISTICOS > MISTICO
MISTIER > MISTY
MISTIEST > MISTY
MISTIGRIS n joker or a blank card used as a wild card in a variety of draw poker
MISTILY > MISTY
MISTIME vb do (something) at the wrong time
MISTIMED > MISTIME
MISTIMES > MISTIME
MISTIMING n act of mistiming
MISTINESS > MISTY
MISTING n application of a fake suntan by spray
MISTINGS > MISTING
MISTITLE vb name badly
MISTITLED > MISTITLE
MISTITLES > MISTITLE
MISTLE same as > MIZZLE
MISTLED > MISTLE
MISTLES > MISTLE
MISTLETOE n evergreen plant with white berries growing as a parasite on trees
MISTLING > MISTLE
MISTOLD > MISTELL
MISTOOK past tense of > MISTAKE
MISTOUCH vb fail to touch properly
MISTRACE vb trace wrongly
MISTRACED > MISTRACE
MISTRACES > MISTRACE
MISTRAIN vb train wrongly
MISTRAINS > MISTRAIN
MISTRAL n strong dry northerly wind of S France
MISTRALS > MISTRAL
MISTREAT vb treat (a person or animal) badly
MISTREATS > MISTREAT
MISTRESS n woman who has a continuing sexual relationship with a married man ▷ vb make into mistress
MISTRIAL n trial made void because of some error
MISTRIALS > MISTRIAL
MISTRUST vb have doubts or suspicions about ▷ n lack of trust
MISTRUSTS > MISTRUST
MISTRUTH n something untrue
MISTRUTHS > MISTRUTH
MISTRYST vb fail to keep an appointment with
MISTRYSTS > MISTRYST
MISTS > MIST

MISTUNE vb fail to tune properly
MISTUNED > MISTUNE
MISTUNES > MISTUNE
MISTUNING > MISTUNE
MISTUTOR vb instruct badly
MISTUTORS > MISTUTOR
MISTY adj full of mist
MISTYPE vb type badly
MISTYPED > MISTYPE
MISTYPES > MISTYPE
MISTYPING > MISTYPE
MISUNION n wrong or bad union
MISUNIONS > MISUNION
MISUSAGE > MISUSE
MISUSAGES > MISUSE
MISUSE n incorrect, improper, or careless use ▷ vb use wrongly
MISUSED > MISUSE
MISUSER n abuse of some right, privilege, office, etc
MISUSERS > MISUSER
MISUSES > MISUSE
MISUSING > MISUSE
MISUST > MISUSE
MISVALUE vb value badly
MISVALUED > MISVALUE
MISVALUES > MISVALUE
MISWEEN vb assess wrongly
MISWEENED > MISWEEN
MISWEENS > MISWEEN
MISWEND vb become lost
MISWENDS > MISWEND
MISWENT > MISWEND
MISWORD vb word badly
MISWORDED > MISWORD
MISWORDS > MISWORD
MISWRIT > MISWRITE
MISWRITE vb write badly
MISWRITES > MISWRITE
MISWROTE > MISWRITE
MISYOKE vb join wrongly
MISYOKED > MISYOKE
MISYOKES > MISYOKE
MISYOKING > MISYOKE
MITCH vb play truant from school
MITCHED > MITCH
MITCHES > MITCH
MITCHING > MITCH
MITE n very small spider-like animal
MITER same as > MITRE
MITERED > MITER
MITERER > MITER
MITERERS > MITER
MITERING > MITER
MITERS > MITER
MITERWORT same as > MITREWORT
MITES > MITE
MITHER vb fuss over or moan about something
MITHERED > MITHER
MITHERING > MITHER
MITHERS > MITHER
MITICIDAL > MITICIDE
MITICIDE n any drug or agent that destroys mites

MITICIDES > MITICIDE
MITIER > MITY
MITIEST > MITY
MITIGABLE > MITIGATE
MITIGANT adj acting to mitigate ▷ n means of easing, lessening, or assuaging
MITIGANTS > MITIGANT
MITIGATE vb make less severe
MITIGATED > MITIGATE
MITIGATES > MITIGATE
MITIGATOR > MITIGATE
MITIS n malleable iron
MITISES > MITIS
MITOGEN n any agent that induces mitosis
MITOGENIC > MITOGEN
MITOGENS > MITOGEN
MITOMYCIN n kind of antibiotic
MITOSES > MITOSIS
MITOSIS n type of cell division
MITOTIC > MITOSIS
MITRAILLE n hail of bullets
MITRAL adj of or like a mitre
MITRE n bishop's pointed headdress ▷ vb join with a mitre joint
MITRED > MITRE
MITRES > MITRE
MITREWORT n Asian and N American plant with clusters of small white flowers and capsules resembling a bishop's mitre
MITRIFORM adj shaped like a mitre
MITRING > MITRE
MITSVAH same as > MITZVAH
MITSVAHS > MITSVAH
MITSVOTH > MITSVAH
MITT same as > MITTEN
MITTEN n glove with one section for the thumb and one for the four fingers together
MITTENED adj wearing mittens
MITTENS > MITTEN
MITTIMUS n warrant of commitment to prison or a command to a jailer directing him to hold someone in prison
MITTS > MITT
MITUMBA n used clothes imported for sale in African countries
MITUMBAS > MITUMBA
MITY adj having mites
MITZVAH n commandment or precept, esp one found in the Bible
MITZVAHS > MITZVAH
MITZVOTH > MITZVAH
MIURUS n type of rhythm in poetry

MIURUSES > MIURUS
MIX vb combine or blend into one mass ▷ n mixture
MIXABLE > MIX
MIXDOWN n (in sound recording) the transfer of a multitrack master mix to two-track stereo tape
MIXDOWNS > MIXDOWN
MIXED adj formed or blended together by mixing
MIXEDLY > MIXED
MIXEDNESS > MIXED
MIXEN n dunghill
MIXENS > MIXEN
MIXER n kitchen appliance used for mixing foods
MIXERS > MIXER
MIXES > MIX
MIXIBLE > MIX
MIXIER > MIX
MIXIEST > MIX
MIXING n act of mixing
MIXINGS > MIXING
MIXMASTER n disc jockey
MIXOLOGY n art of mixing cocktails
MIXT > MIX
MIXTAPE n compilation of songs from various sources
MIXTAPES > MIXTAPE
MIXTE adj of or denoting a type of bicycle frame in which angled twin lateral tubes run back to the rear axle
MIXTION n amber-based mixture used in making gold leaf
MIXTIONS > MIXTION
MIXTURE n something mixed
MIXTURES > MIXTURE
MIXUP n something that is mixed up
MIXUPS > MIXUP
MIXY adj mixed
MIZ shortened form of > MISERY
MIZEN same as > MIZZEN
MIZENMAST n (on a yawl, ketch, or dandy) the after mast
MIZENS > MIZEN
MIZMAZE n maze
MIZMAZES > MIZMAZE
MIZUNA n Japanese variety of lettuce
MIZUNAS > MIZUNA
MIZZ same as > MIZ
MIZZEN n sail set on a mizzenmast ▷ adj of or relating to any kind of gear used with a mizzenmast
MIZZENS > MIZZEN
MIZZES > MIZ
MIZZLE vb decamp
MIZZLED > MIZZLE
MIZZLES > MIZZLE
MIZZLIER > MIZZLE
MIZZLIEST > MIZZLE

MIZZLING > MIZZLE

MIZZLINGS > MIZZLE

MIZZLY > MIZZLE

MIZZONITE n mineral containing sodium

MIZZY adj as in mizzy maze dialect expression meaning state of confusion

MM interj expression of enjoyment of taste or smell

MMM interj interjection expressing agreement or enjoyment

MNA same as > MINA

MNAS > MNA

MNEME n ability to retain memory

MNEMES > MNEME

MNEMIC > MNEME

MNEMON n unit of memory

MNEMONIC adj intended to help the memory ▷ n something, for instance a verse, intended to help the memory

MNEMONICS n art or practice of improving or of aiding the memory

MNEMONIST > MNEMONICS

MNEMONS > MNEMON

MO n moment

MOA n large extinct flightless New Zealand bird

MOAI n any of the gigantic carved stone figures found on Easter Island (Rapa Nui)

MOAN n low cry of pain ▷ vb make or utter with a moan

MOANED > MOAN

MOANER > MOAN

MOANERS > MOAN

MOANFUL > MOAN

MOANFULLY > MOAN

MOANING > MOAN

MOANINGLY > MOAN

MOANINGS > MOAN

MOANS > MOAN

MOAS > MOA

MOAT n deep wide ditch, esp round a castle ▷ vb surround with or as if with a moat

MOATED > MOAT

MOATING > MOAT

MOATLIKE > MOAT

MOATS > MOAT

MOB n disorderly crowd ▷ vb surround in a mob

MOBBED > MOB

MOBBER > MOB

MOBBERS > MOB

MOBBIE same as > MOBBY

MOBBIES > MOBBY

MOBBING > MOB

MOBBINGS > MOB

MOBBISH > MOB

MOBBISHLY > MOB

MOBBISM n behaviour as mob

MOBBISMS > MOBBISM

MOBBLE same as > MOBLE

MOBBLED > MOBBLE

MOBBLES > MOBBLE

MOBBLING > MOBBLE

MOBBY n West Indian drink

MOBCAP n woman's 18th-century cotton cap

MOBCAPS > MOBCAP

MOBCAST vb create and upload a podcast directly from a mobile phone

MOBCASTED > MOBCAST

MOBCASTS > MOBCAST

MOBE n mobile phone

MOBES > MOBE

MOBEY same as > MOBY

MOBEYS > MOBEY

MOBIE n mobile phone

MOBIES > MOBY

MOBILE adj able to move ▷ n hanging structure designed to move in air currents

MOBILES > MOBILE

MOBILISE same as > MOBILIZE

MOBILISED > MOBILISE

MOBILISER > MOBILISE

MOBILISES > MOBILISE

MOBILITY n ability to move physically

MOBILIZE vb (of the armed services) prepare for active service

MOBILIZED > MOBILIZE

MOBILIZER > MOBILIZE

MOBILIZES > MOBILIZE

MOBISODE n episode of a TV show made for viewing on a mobile phone

MOBISODES > MOBISODE

MOBLE vb muffle

MOBLED > MOBLE

MOBLES > MOBLE

MOBLING > MOBLE

MOBLOG n blog recorded in the form of mobile phone calls, text messages, and photographs

MOBLOGGER > MOBLOG

MOBLOGS > MOBLOG

MOBOCRACY n rule or domination by a mob

MOBOCRAT > MOBOCRACY

MOBOCRATS > MOBOCRACY

MOBS > MOB

MOBSMAN n person in mob

MOBSMEN > MOBSMAN

MOBSTER n member of a criminal organization

MOBSTERS > MOBSTER

MOBY n mobile phone

MOC shortening of > MOCCASIN

MOCASSIN same as > MOCCASIN

MOCASSINS > MOCASSIN

MOCCASIN n soft leather shoe

MOCCASINS > MOCCASIN

MOCCIES pl n informal Australian word for moccasins

MOCH n spell of humid weather ▷ vb (of foods) become musty or spoiled

MOCHA n kind of strong dark coffee

MOCHAS > MOCHA

MOCHED > MOCH

MOCHELL same as > MUCH

MOCHELLS > MOCHELL

MOCHI n confection made with rice flour and sweetened bean paste

MOCHIE adj damp or humid

MOCHIER > MOCHIE

MOCHIEST > MOCHIE

MOCHILA n South American shoulder bag

MOCHILAS > MOCHILA

MOCHINESS > MOCHIE

MOCHING > MOCH

MOCHIS > MOCHI

MOCHS > MOCH

MOCHY same as > MOCHIE

MOCK vb make fun of ▷ adj sham or imitation ▷ n act of mocking

MOCKABLE > MOCK

MOCKADO n imitation velvet

MOCKADOES > MOCKADO

MOCKAGE same as > MOCKERY

MOCKAGES > MOCKAGE

MOCKED > MOCK

MOCKER vb dress up

MOCKERED > MOCKER

MOCKERIES > MOCKERY

MOCKERING > MOCKER

MOCKERNUT n type of smooth-barked hickory with fragrant foliage that turns bright yellow in autumn

MOCKERS > MOCKER

MOCKERY n derision

MOCKING > MOCK

MOCKINGLY > MOCK

MOCKINGS > MOCK

MOCKNEY n person who affects a cockney accent ▷ adj denoting an affected cockney accent or a person who has one

MOCKNEYS > MOCKNEY

MOCKS > MOCK

MOCKTAIL n cocktail without alcohol

MOCKTAILS > MOCKTAIL

MOCKUP n working full-scale model of a machine, apparatus, etc, for testing, research, etc

MOCKUPS > MOCKUP

MOCOCK n Native American birchbark container

MOCOCKS > MOCOCK

MOCS > MOC

MOCUCK same as > MOCOCK

MOCUCKS > MOCUCK

MOCUDDUM same as > MUQADDAM

MOCUDDUMS > MOCUDDUM

MOD n member of a group of fashionable young people, orig. in the 1960s ▷ vb modify (a piece of software or hardware)

MODAFINIL n type of drug used as a stimulant

MODAL adj of or relating to mode or manner ▷ n modal word

MODALISM n type of Christian doctrine

MODALISMS > MODALISM

MODALIST > MODALISM

MODALISTS > MODALISM

MODALITY n condition of being modal

MODALLY > MODAL

MODALS > MODAL

MODDED > MOD

MODDER n person who modifies a piece of hardware or software

MODDERS > MODDER

MODDING n practice of modifying a car to alter its appearance or performance

MODDINGS > MODDING

MODE n method or manner

MODEL n (miniature) representation ▷ adj excellent or perfect ▷ vb make a model of

MODELED > MODEL

MODELER > MODEL

MODELERS > MODEL

MODELING same as > MODELLING

MODELINGS > MODELING

MODELIST same as > MODELLIST

MODELISTS > MODELIST

MODELLED > MODEL

MODELLER > MODEL

MODELLERS > MODEL

MODELLI > MODELLO

MODELLING n act or an instance of making a model

MODELLIST n person who makes models

MODELLO n artist's preliminary sketch or model

MODELLOS > MODELLO

MODELS > MODEL

MODEM n device for connecting two computers by a telephone line ▷ vb send or receive by modem

MODEMED > MODEM

MODEMING > MODEM

MODEMS > MODEM

MODENA n popular variety of domestic fancy pigeon

MODENAS > MODENA

MODER n intermediate layer in humus

MODERATE adj not extreme ▷ n person of moderate views ▷ vb make or become less violent or extreme
MODERATED > MODERATE
MODERATES > MODERATE
MODERATO adv at a moderate speed ▷ n moderato piece
MODERATOR n (Presbyterian Church) minister appointed to preside over a Church court, general assembly, etc
MODERATOS > MODERATO
MODERN adj of present or recent times ▷ n contemporary person
MODERNE n style of architecture and design of the late 1920s and 1930s ▷ adj of or relating to this style of architecture and design
MODERNER > MODERN
MODERNES > MODERNE
MODERNEST > MODERN
MODERNISE same as > MODERNIZE
MODERNISM n (support of) modern tendencies, thoughts, or styles
MODERNIST > MODERNISM
MODERNITY n quality or state of being modern
MODERNIZE vb bring up to date
MODERNLY > MODERN
MODERNS > MODERN
MODERS > MODER
MODES > MODE
MODEST adj not vain or boastful
MODESTER > MODEST
MODESTEST > MODEST
MODESTIES > MODESTY
MODESTLY > MODEST
MODESTY n quality or condition of being modest
MODGE vb do shoddily
MODGED > MODGE
MODGES > MODGE
MODGING > MODGE
MODI > MODUS
MODICA > MODICUM
MODICUM n small quantity
MODICUMS > MODICUM
MODIFIED > MODIFY
MODIFIER n word that qualifies the sense of another
MODIFIERS > MODIFIER
MODIFIES > MODIFY
MODIFY vb change slightly
MODIFYING > MODIFY
MODII > MODIUS
MODILLION n one of a set of ornamental brackets under a cornice, esp as used in the Corinthian order

MODIOLAR > MODIOLUS
MODIOLI > MODIOLUS
MODIOLUS n central bony pillar of the cochlea
MODISH adj in fashion
MODISHLY > MODISH
MODIST n follower of fashion
MODISTE n fashionable dressmaker or milliner
MODISTES > MODISTE
MODISTS > MODIST
MODIUS n ancient Roman quantity measure
MODIWORT Scots variant of > MOULDWARP
MODIWORTS > MODIWORT
MODS > MOD
MODULAR adj of, consisting of, or resembling a module or modulus ▷ n thing comprised of modules
MODULARLY > MODULAR
MODULARS > MODULAR
MODULATE vb vary in tone
MODULATED > MODULATE
MODULATES > MODULATE
MODULATOR > MODULATE
MODULE n self-contained unit, section, or component with a specific function
MODULES > MODULE
MODULI > MODULUS
MODULO adv with reference to modulus
MODULUS n coefficient expressing a specified property
MODUS n way of doing something
MOE adv more ▷ n wry face
MOELLON n rubble
MOELLONS > MOELLON
MOER n in South Africa, slang word for the womb ▷ vb in South Africa, attack (someone or something) violently
MOERED > MOER
MOERING > MOER
MOERS > MOER
MOES > MOE
MOFETTE n opening in a region of nearly extinct volcanic activity, through which gases pass
MOFETTES > MOFETTE
MOFFETTE same as > MOFETTE
MOFFETTES > MOFFETTE
MOFFIE n homosexual ▷ adj homosexual
MOFFIES > MOFFIE
MOFO n offensive term, a shortened form of motherfucker
MOFOS > MOFO
MOFUSSIL n provincial area in India
MOFUSSILS > MOFUSSIL
MOG vb go away

MOGGAN n stocking without foot
MOGGANS > MOGGAN
MOGGED > MOG
MOGGIE same as > MOGGY
MOGGIES > MOGGY
MOGGING > MOG
MOGGY n cat
MOGHUL same as > MOGUL
MOGHULS > MOGHUL
MOGS > MOG
MOGUL n important or powerful person
MOGULED adj having moguls
MOGULS > MOGUL
MOHAIR n fine hair of the Angora goat
MOHAIRS > MOHAIR
MOHALIM same as > MOHELIM
MOHAWK n half turn from either edge of either skate to the corresponding edge of the other skate
MOHAWKS > MOHAWK
MOHEL n man qualified to conduct circumcisions
MOHELIM > MOHEL
MOHELS > MOHEL
MOHICAN n punk hairstyle
MOHICANS > MOHICAN
MOHO n boundary between the earth's crust and mantle
MOHOS > MOHO
MOHR same as > MHORR
MOHRS > MOHR
MOHUA n small New Zealand bird
MOHUAS > MOHUA
MOHUR n former Indian gold coin worth 15 rupees
MOHURS > MOHUR
MOI pron (used facetiously) me
MOIDER same as > MOITHER
MOIDERED > MOIDER
MOIDERING > MOIDER
MOIDERS > MOIDER
MOIDORE n former Portuguese gold coin
MOIDORES > MOIDORE
MOIETIES > MOIETY
MOIETY n half
MOIL vb moisten or soil or become moist, soiled, etc ▷ n toil
MOILE n type of rice pudding made with almond milk
MOILED > MOIL
MOILER > MOIL
MOILERS > MOIL
MOILES > MOILE
MOILING > MOIL
MOILINGLY > MOIL
MOILS > MOIL
MOINEAU n small fortification
MOINEAUS > MOINEAU
MOIRA n fate

MOIRAI > MOIRA
MOIRE adj having a watered or wavelike pattern ▷ n any fabric that has such a pattern
MOIRES > MOIRE
MOISER n informer
MOISERS > MOISER
MOIST adj slightly wet ▷ vb moisten
MOISTED > MOIST
MOISTEN vb make or become moist
MOISTENED > MOISTEN
MOISTENER > MOISTEN
MOISTENS > MOISTEN
MOISTER > MOIST
MOISTEST > MOIST
MOISTFUL adj full of moisture
MOISTIFY vb moisten
MOISTING > MOIST
MOISTLY > MOIST
MOISTNESS > MOIST
MOISTS > MOIST
MOISTURE n liquid diffused as vapour or condensed in drops
MOISTURES > MOISTURE
MOIT same as > MOTE
MOITHER vb bother or bewilder
MOITHERED > MOITHER
MOITHERS > MOITHER
MOITS > MOIT
MOJAHEDIN pl n fundamentalist Muslim guerrillas
MOJARRA n tropical American sea fish
MOJARRAS > MOJARRA
MOJITO n rum-based cocktail
MOJITOS > MOJITO
MOJO n charm or magic spell
MOJOES > MOJO
MOJOS > MOJO
MOKADDAM same as > MUQADDAM
MOKADDAMS > MOKADDAM
MOKE n donkey
MOKES > MOKE
MOKI n edible sea fish of New Zealand
MOKIHI n Māori raft
MOKIHIS > MOKIHI
MOKIS > MOKI
MOKO n Māori tattoo or tattoo pattern
MOKOMOKO n type of skink found in New Zealand
MOKOMOKOS > MOKOMOKO
MOKOPUNA n grandchild or young person
MOKOPUNAS > MOKOPUNA
MOKORO n (in Botswana) the traditional dugout canoe of the people of the Okavango Delta
MOKOROS > MOKORO
MOKOS > MOKO

MOKSHA n freedom from the endless cycle of transmigration into a state of bliss

MOKSHAS > MOKSHA

MOL n the SI unit mole

MOLA another name for > SUNFISH

MOLAL adj of or consisting of a solution containing one mole of solute per thousand grams of solvent

MOLALITY n (not in technical usage) a measure of concentration equal to the number of moles of solute in a thousand grams of solvent

MOLAR n large back tooth used for grinding ▷ adj of any of these teeth

MOLARITY n concentration

MOLARS > MOLAR

MOLAS > MOLA

MOLASSE n soft sediment produced by the erosion of mountain ranges after the final phase of mountain building

MOLASSES n dark syrup, a by-product of sugar refining

MOLD same as > MOULD

MOLDABLE > MOLD

MOLDAVITE n green tektite found in the Czech Republic, thought to be the product of an ancient meteorite impact in Germany

MOLDBOARD n curved blade of a plough

MOLDED > MOLD

MOLDER same as > MOULDER

MOLDERED > MOLDER

MOLDERING > MOLDER

MOLDERS > MOLDER

MOLDIER > MOLDY

MOLDIEST > MOLDY

MOLDINESS > MOLDY

MOLDING same as > MOULDING

MOLDINGS > MOLDING

MOLDS > MOLD

MOLDWARP same as > MOULDWARP

MOLDWARPS > MOLDWARP

MOLDY same as > MOULDY

MOLE n small dark raised spot on the skin ▷ vb as in mole out seek as if by burrowing

MOLECAST n molehill

MOLECASTS > MOLECAST

MOLECULAR adj of or relating to molecules

MOLECULE n simplest freely existing chemical unit, composed of two or more atoms

MOLECULES > MOLECULE

MOLED > MOLE

MOLEHILL n small mound of earth thrown up by a burrowing mole

MOLEHILLS > MOLEHILL

MOLEHUNT n hunt for a mole

MOLEHUNTS > MOLEHUNT

MOLES > MOLE

MOLESKIN n dark grey dense velvety pelt of a mole, used as a fur

MOLESKINS pl n clothing of moleskin

MOLEST vb interfere with sexually

MOLESTED > MOLEST

MOLESTER > MOLEST

MOLESTERS > MOLEST

MOLESTFUL adj molesting

MOLESTING > MOLEST

MOLESTS > MOLEST

MOLIES > MOLY

MOLIMEN n effort needed to perform bodily function

MOLIMENS > MOLIMEN

MOLINE adj (of a cross) having arms of equal length, forked and curved back at the ends ▷ n moline cross

MOLINES > MOLINE

MOLINET n stick for whipping chocolate

MOLINETS > MOLINET

MOLING > MOLE

MOLL n gangster's female accomplice

MOLLA same as > MOLLAH

MOLLAH same as > MULLAH

MOLLAHS > MOLLAH

MOLLAS > MOLLA

MOLLIE same as > MOLLY

MOLLIES > MOLLY

MOLLIFIED > MOLLIFY

MOLLIFIER > MOLLIFY

MOLLIFIES > MOLLIFY

MOLLIFY vb pacify or soothe

MOLLITIES n softness

MOLLS > MOLL

MOLLUSC n soft-bodied, usu hard-shelled, animal

MOLLUSCA n molluscs collectively

MOLLUSCAN > MOLLUSC

MOLLUSCS > MOLLUSC

MOLLUSCUM n viral skin infection

MOLLUSK same as > MOLLUSC

MOLLUSKAN > MOLLUSK

MOLLUSKS > MOLLUSK

MOLLY n American freshwater fish

MOLLYHAWK n juvenile of the southern black-backed gull

MOLLYMAWK informal name for > MALLEMUCK

MOLOCH n spiny Australian desert-living lizard

MOLOCHISE vb sacrifice to deity

MOLOCHIZE same as > MOLOCHISE

MOLOCHS > MOLOCH

MOLOSSI > MOLOSSUS

MOLOSSUS n division of metre in poetry

MOLS > MOL

MOLT same as > MOULT

MOLTED > MOLT

MOLTEN > MELT

MOLTENLY > MELT

MOLTER > MOLT

MOLTERS > MOLT

MOLTING > MOLT

MOLTO adv very

MOLTS > MOLT

MOLY n mythical magic herb

MOLYBDATE n salt or ester of a molybdic acid

MOLYBDIC adj of or containing molybdenum in the trivalent or hexavalent state

MOLYBDOUS adj of or containing molybdenum, esp in a low valence state

MOLYS > MOLY

MOM same as > MOTHER

MOME n fool

MOMENT n short space of time

MOMENTA > MOMENTUM

MOMENTANY same as > MOMENTARY

MOMENTARY adj lasting only a moment

MOMENTLY same as > MOMENT

MOMENTO same as > MEMENTO

MOMENTOES > MOMENTO

MOMENTOS > MOMENTO

MOMENTOUS adj of great significance

MOMENTS > MOMENT

MOMENTUM n impetus to go forward, develop, or get stronger

MOMENTUMS > MOMENTUM

MOMES > MOME

MOMI same as > MOM

MOMISM n excessive domination of a child by his or her mother

MOMISMS > MOMISM

MOMMA same as > MAMMA

MOMMAS > MOMMA

MOMMET same as > MAMMET

MOMMETS > MOMMET

MOMMIES > MOMMY

MOMMY same as > MOM

MOMOIR n memoir written by a woman about motherhood

MOMOIRS > MOMOIR

MOMS > MOM

MOMSER same as > MOMZER

MOMSERS > MOMSER

MOMUS n person who ridicules

MOMUSES > MOMUS

MOMZER same as > MAMZER

MOMZERIM > MOMZER

MOMZERS > MOMZER

MON dialect variant of > MAN

MONA n W African guenon monkey

MONACHAL less common word for > MONASTIC

MONACHISM > MONACHAL

MONACHIST > MONACHAL

MONACID same as > MONOACID

MONACIDIC same as > MONACID

MONACIDS > MONACID

MONACT adj (of sponge) with single-spiked structures in skeleton

MONACTINE n monactinal sponge spicule

MONACTS > MONACT

MONAD n any fundamental singular metaphysical entity

MONADAL > MONAD

MONADES > MONAS

MONADIC adj being or relating to a monad

MONADICAL > MONAD

MONADISM n (esp in the writings of Gottfried Leibnitz, the German rationalist philosopher and mathematician (1646–1716) the philosophical doctrine that monads are the ultimate units of reality

MONADISMS > MONADISM

MONADNOCK n residual hill that consists of hard rock in an otherwise eroded area

MONADS > MONAD

MONAL n S Asian pheasant

MONALS > MONAL

MONAMINE n type of amine

MONAMINES > MONAMINE

MONANDRY n preference of only one male sexual partner over a period of time

MONARCH n sovereign ruler of a state

MONARCHAL > MONARCH

MONARCHIC > MONARCH

MONARCHS > MONARCH

MONARCHY n government by or a state ruled by a sovereign

MONARDA n mintlike N American plant

MONARDAS > MONARDA

MONAS same as > MONAD

MONASES > MONAS

MONASTERY n residence of a community of monks

MONASTIC adj of monks, nuns, or monasteries ▷ n person who is committed to this way of life, esp a monk

MONASTICS > MONASTIC

MONATOMIC *adj* consisting of single atoms
MONAUL *same as* > MONAL
MONAULS > MONAUL
MONAURAL *adj* relating to, having, or hearing with only one ear
MONAXIAL *another word for* > UNIAXIAL
MONAXON *n* type of sponge
MONAXONIC > MONAXON
MONAXONS > MONAXON
MONAZITE *n* yellow to reddish-brown mineral consisting of a phosphate of thorium, cerium, and lanthanum in monoclinic crystalline form
MONAZITES > MONAZITE
MONDAIN *n* man who moves in fashionable society ▷ *adj* characteristic of fashionable society
MONDAINE *n* woman who moves in fashionable society ▷ *adj* characteristic of fashionable society
MONDAINES > MONDAINE
MONDAINS > MONDAIN
MONDE *n* French word meaning world or society
MONDES > MONDE
MONDIAL *adj* of or involving the whole world
MONDO *n* Buddhist questioning technique
MONDOS > MONDO
MONECIAN *same as* > MONOECIOUS
MONECIOUS *adj* (of some flowering plants) having the male and female reproductive organs in separate flowers on the same plant
MONELLIN *n* sweet protein
MONELLINS > MONELLIN
MONEME *less common word for* > MORPHEME
MONEMES > MONEME
MONER *n* hypothetical simple organism
MONERA > MONER
MONERAN *n* type of bacterium
MONERANS > MONERAN
MONERGISM *n* Christian doctrine on spiritual regeneration
MONERON *same as* > MONER
MONETARY *adj* of money or currency
MONETH *same as* > MONTH
MONETHS > MONETH
MONETISE *same as* > MONETIZE
MONETISED > MONETISE
MONETISES > MONETISE
MONETIZE *vb* establish as the legal tender of a country
MONETIZED > MONETIZE
MONETIZES > MONETIZE

MONEY *n* medium of exchange, coins or banknotes
MONEYBAG *n* bag for money
MONEYBAGS *n* very rich person
MONEYBOX *n* box for keeping money in
MONEYED *adj* rich
MONEYER *n* person who coins money
MONEYERS > MONEYER
MONEYLESS > MONEY
MONEYMAN *n* person supplying money
MONEYMEN > MONEY
MONEYS > MONEY
MONEYWORT *n* European and N American creeping plant with round leaves and yellow flowers
MONG *n* stupid or foolish person
MONGCORN *same as* > MASLIN
MONGCORNS > MONGCORN
MONGED *adj* under the influence of drugs
MONGEESE > MONGOOSE
MONGER *n* trader or dealer ▷ *vb* deal in
MONGERED > MONGER
MONGERIES > MONGER
MONGERING > MONGER
MONGERS > MONGER
MONGERY > MONGER
MONGO *same as* > MUNGO
MONGOE *same as* > MONGO
MONGOES > MONGOE
MONGOL *adj* offensive word for a person affected for Down's syndrome
MONGOLIAN *adj* offensive term meaning affected by Down's syndrome
MONGOLISM > MONGOL
MONGOLOID *adj* offensive term meaning characterized by Down's syndrome ▷ *n* offensive word for a person affected by Down's syndrome
MONGOLS > MONGOL
MONGOOSE *n* stoatlike mammal of Asia and Africa that kills snakes
MONGOOSES > MONGOOSE
MONGOS > MONGO
MONGREL *n* animal, esp a dog, of mixed breed ▷ *adj* of mixed breed or origin
MONGRELLY > MONGREL
MONGRELS > MONGREL
MONGS > MONG
MONGST *short for* > AMONGST
MONIAL *n* mullion
MONIALS > MONIAL
MONIC *adj* denoting a type of polynomial
MONICKER *same as* > MONIKER

MONICKERS > MONICKER
MONIE *Scots word for* > MANY
MONIED *same as* > MONEYED
MONIES > MONEY
MONIKER *n* person's name or nickname
MONIKERED *adj* having a moniker
MONIKERS > MONIKER
MONILIA *n* type of fungus
MONILIAE > MONILIA
MONILIAL *adj* denoting a thrush infection caused by a fungus
MONILIAS > MONILIA
MONIMENT *same as* > MONUMENT
MONIMENTS > MONIMENT
MONIPLIES *same as* > MANYPLIES
MONISH *same as* > ADMONISH
MONISHED > MONISH
MONISHES > MONISH
MONISHING > MONISH
MONISM *n* doctrine that reality consists of only one basic substance or element
MONISMS > MONISM
MONIST > MONISM
MONISTIC > MONISM
MONISTS > MONISM
MONITION *n* warning or caution
MONITIONS > MONITION
MONITIVE *adj* reproving
MONITOR *n* person or device that checks, controls, warns, or keeps a record of something ▷ *vb* watch and check on
MONITORED > MONITOR
MONITORS > MONITOR
MONITORY *adj* acting as or giving a warning ▷ *n* letter containing a monition
MONITRESS > MONITOR
MONK *n* member of an all-male religious community
MONKERIES > MONKERY
MONKERY *n* derogatory word for monastic life or practices
MONKEY *n* long-tailed primate ▷ *vb* meddle or fool
MONKEYED > MONKEY
MONKEYING > MONKEY
MONKEYISH > MONKEY
MONKEYISM *n* practice of behaving like monkey
MONKEYPOD *n* Central American tree
MONKEYPOT *n* type of tropical tree
MONKEYPOX *n* rare viral disease found in Africa
MONKEYS > MONKEY
MONKFISH *n* type of fish

MONKHOOD *n* condition of being a monk
MONKHOODS > MONKHOOD
MONKISH *adj* of, relating to, or resembling a monk or monks
MONKISHLY > MONKISH
MONKS > MONK
MONKSHOOD *n* poisonous plant with hooded flowers
MONO *n* monophonic sound
MONOACID *adj* a base which is capable of reacting with only one molecule of a monobasic acid
MONOACIDS > MONOACID
MONOAMINE *n* substance, such as adrenaline, noradrenaline, or serotonin, that contains a single amine group
MONOAO *n* New Zealand plant with rigid leaves
MONOAOS > MONOAO
MONOBASIC *adj* (of an acid, such as hydrogen chloride) having only one replaceable hydrogen atom per molecule
MONOBLOC *adj* made from a single piece of something
MONOBROW *n* appearance of a single eyebrow as a result of the eyebrows joining above a person's nose
MONOBROWS > MONOBROW
MONOCARP *n* plant that is monocarpic
MONOCARPS > MONOCARP
MONOCEROS *n* faint constellation on the celestial equator crossed by the Milky Way and lying close to Orion and Canis Major
MONOCHORD *n* instrument employed in acoustic analysis or investigation, consisting usually of one string stretched over a resonator of wood
MONOCLE *n* eyeglass for one eye only
MONOCLED > MONOCLE
MONOCLES > MONOCLE
MONOCLINE *n* fold in stratified rocks in which the strata are inclined in the same direction from the horizontal
MONOCOQUE *n* vehicle body moulded from a single piece of material with no separate load-bearing parts ▷ *adj* of or relating to the design characteristic of a monocoque
MONOCOT *n* type of flowering plant with a single embryonic seed leaf
MONOCOTS > MONOCOT

MONOCOTYL *same as* > MONOCOT

MONOCRACY *n* government by one person

MONOCRAT > MONOCRACY

MONOCRATS > MONOCRACY

MONOCROP *vb* plant the same crop in a field every year

MONOCROPS > MONOCROP

MONOCULAR *adj* having or for one eye only ▷ *n* device for use with one eye, such as a field glass

MONOCYCLE *another name for* > UNICYCLE

MONOCYTE *n* large phagocytic leucocyte with a spherical nucleus and clear cytoplasm

MONOCYTES > MONOCYTE

MONOCYTIC > MONOCYTE

MONODIC > MONODY

MONODICAL > MONODY

MONODIES > MONODY

MONODIST > MONODY

MONODISTS > MONODY

MONODONT *adj* (of certain animals, esp the male narwhal) having a single tooth throughout life

MONODRAMA *n* play or other dramatic piece for a single performer

MONODY *n* (in Greek tragedy) an ode sung by a single actor

MONOECIES > MONOECY

MONOECISM *n* being both male and female

MONOECY *same as* > MONOECISM

MONOESTER *n* type of ester

MONOFIL *n* synthetic thread or yarn composed of a single strand rather than twisted fibres

MONOFILS > MONOFIL

MONOFUEL *n* single type of fuel

MONOFUELS > MONOFUEL

MONOGAMIC > MONOGAMY

MONOGAMY *n* custom of being married to one person at a time

MONOGENIC *adj* of or relating to an inherited character difference that is controlled by a single gene

MONOGENY *n* the hypothetical descent of all organisms from a single cell or organism

MONOGERM *adj* containing single seed

MONOGLOT *n* person speaking only one language

MONOGLOTS > MONOGLOT

MONOGONY *n* asexual reproduction

MONOGRAM *n* design of combined letters, esp a person's initials ▷ *vb* decorate (clothing, stationery, etc) with a monogram

MONOGRAMS > MONOGRAM

MONOGRAPH *n* book or paper on a single subject ▷ *vb* write a monograph on

MONOGYNY *n* custom of having only one female sexual partner over a period of time

MONOHULL *n* sailing vessel with a single hull

MONOHULLS > MONOHULL

MONOICOUS *adj* (of some flowering plants) having the male and female reproductive organs in separate flowers on the same plant

MONOKINE *n* type of protein

MONOKINES > MONOKINE

MONOKINI *n* bottom half of a bikini

MONOKINIS > MONOKINI

MONOLATER > MONOLATRY

MONOLATRY *n* exclusive worship of one god without excluding the existence of others

MONOLAYER *n* single layer of atoms or molecules adsorbed on a surface

MONOLINE *adj* as in *monoline insurer* insurer who pays the principal and interest on a bond in the event of a default

MONOLITH *n* large upright block of stone

MONOLITHS > MONOLITH

MONOLOG *same as* > MONOLOGUE

MONOLOGIC > MONOLOGUE

MONOLOGS > MONOLOG

MONOLOGUE *n* long speech by one person

MONOLOGY > MONOLOGUE

MONOMACHY *n* combat between two individuals

MONOMANIA *n* obsession with one thing

MONOMARK *n* series of letters or figures to identify goods, personal articles, etc

MONOMARKS > MONOMARK

MONOMER *n* compound whose molecules can join together to form a polymer

MONOMERIC > MONOMER

MONOMERS > MONOMER

MONOMETER *n* line of verse consisting of one metrical foot

MONOMIAL *n* expression consisting of a single term, such as $5ax$ ▷ *adj* consisting of a single algebraic term

MONOMIALS > MONOMIAL

MONOMODE *adj* denoting or relating to a type of optical fibre with a core less than 10 micrometres in diameter

MONONYM *n* person who is famous enough to be known only by one name

MONONYMS > MONONYM

MONOPHAGY *n* feeding on only one type of food

MONOPHASE *adj* having single alternating electric current ▷ *n* type of matter that contains only one phase or a clear-cut and unattached type of matter

MONOPHONY > MONO

MONOPHYLY *n* group of ancestor and all descendants

MONOPITCH *adj* (of a roof) having only one slope ▷ *n* a monotone

MONOPLANE *n* aeroplane with one pair of wings

MONOPLOID *less common word for* > HAPLOID

MONOPOD *same as* > MONOPODE

MONOPODE *n* member of a legendary one-legged race of Africa

MONOPODES > MONOPODE

MONOPODIA *pl n* main axes of growth in the pine tree and similar plants

MONOPODS > MONOPOD

MONOPODY *n* single-foot measure in poetry

MONOPOLE *n* magnetic pole considered in isolation

MONOPOLES > MONOPOLE

MONOPOLY *n* exclusive possession of or right to do something

MONOPSONY *n* situation in which the entire market demand for a product or service consists of only one buyer

MONOPTERA *n* plural of monopteron: circular classical building, esp a temple, that has a single ring of columns surrounding it

MONOPTOTE *n* word with only one form

MONOPULSE *n* radar transmitting single pulse only

MONORAIL *n* single-rail railway

MONORAILS > MONORAIL

MONORCHID *adj* having only one testicle ▷ *n* animal or person with only one testicle

MONORHINE *adj* having single nostril ▷ *n* animal that has one nasal orifice

MONORHYME *n* poem in which all lines rhyme

MONOS > MONO

MONOSEMIC *adj* having only a single meaning

MONOSEMY *n* fact of having only a single meaning

MONOSES > MONOSIS

MONOSIES > MONOSY

MONOSIS *n* abnormal separation

MONOSKI *n* wide ski on which the skier stands with both feet ▷ *vb* ski on a monoski

MONOSKIED > MONOSKI

MONOSKIER > MONOSKI

MONOSKIS > MONOSKI

MONOSOME *n* unpaired chromosome, esp an X-chromosome in an otherwise diploid cell

MONOSOMES > MONOSOME

MONOSOMIC > MONOSOME

MONOSOMY *n* condition with a missing pair of chromosomes

MONOSTELE *n* type of plant tissue

MONOSTELY > MONOSTELE

MONOSTICH *n* poem of a single line

MONOSTOME *adj* having only one mouth, pore, or similar opening

MONOSTYLE *adj* having single shaft

MONOSY *same as* > MONOSIS

MONOTASK *vb* perform only one task at a time

MONOTASKS > MONOTASK

MONOTINT *n* black-and-white photograph or transparency

MONOTINTS > MONOTINT

MONOTONE *n* unvaried pitch in speech or sound ▷ *adj* unvarying ▷ *vb* speak in monotone

MONOTONED > MONOTONE

MONOTONES > MONOTONE

MONOTONIC *same as* > MONOTONE

MONOTONY *n* wearisome routine, dullness

MONOTREME *n* type of primitive egg-laying toothless mammal of Australia and New Guinea

MONOTROCH *n* wheelbarrow

MONOTYPE *n* single print made from a metal or glass plate on which a picture has been painted

MONOTYPES > MONOTYPE

MONOTYPIC *adj* (of a genus or species)

consisting of only one type of animal or plant

MONOVULAR adj of a single ovum

MONOXIDE n oxide that contains one oxygen atom per molecule

MONOXIDES > MONOXIDE

MONOXYLON n canoe made from one log

MONS > MON

MONSIEUR n French title of address equivalent to sir or Mr

MONSIGNOR n ecclesiastical title attached to certain offices or distinctions usually bestowed by the Pope

MONSOON n seasonal wind of SE Asia

MONSOONAL > MONSOON

MONSOONS > MONSOON

MONSTER n imaginary, usu frightening, beast ▷ adj huge ▷ vb criticize (a person or group) severely

MONSTERA n type of tropical climbing plant, sometimes grown as a greenhouse or pot plant for its unusual leathery perforated leaves

MONSTERAS > MONSTERA

MONSTERED > MONSTER

MONSTERS > MONSTER

MONSTROUS adj unnatural or ugly

MONTADALE n breed of sheep

MONTAGE n (making of) a picture composed from pieces of others ▷ vb make as a montage

MONTAGED > MONTAGE

MONTAGES > MONTAGE

MONTAGING > MONTAGE

MONTAN adj as in montan wax hard wax obtained from lignite and peat

MONTANE n area of mountain dominated by vegetation ▷ adj of or inhabiting mountainous regions

MONTANES > MONTANE

MONTANT n vertical part in woodwork

MONTANTO n rising blow

MONTANTOS > MONTANTO

MONTANTS > MONTANT

MONTARIA n Brazilian canoe

MONTARIAS > MONTARIA

MONTE n gambling card game of Spanish origin

MONTEITH n large ornamental bowl, usually of silver, for cooling wineglasses, which are suspended from the notched rim

MONTEITHS > MONTEITH

MONTEM n former money-raising practice at Eton school

MONTEMS > MONTEM

MONTERO n round cap with a flap at the back worn by hunters

MONTEROS > MONTERO

MONTES > MONTE

MONTH n one of the twelve divisions of the calendar year

MONTHLIES > MONTHLY

MONTHLING n month-old child

MONTHLONG adj lasting all month

MONTHLY adj happening or payable once a month ▷ adv once a month ▷ n monthly magazine

MONTHS > MONTH

MONTICLE same as **>** MONTICULE

MONTICLES > MONTICLE

MONTICULE n small hill or mound, such as a secondary volcanic cone

MONTIES > MONTY

MONTRE n pipes of organ

MONTRES > MONTRE

MONTURE n mount or frame

MONTURES > MONTURE

MONTY n complete form of something

MONUMENT n something, esp a building or statue, that commemorates something

MONUMENTS > MONUMENT

MONURON n type of weedkiller

MONURONS > MONURON

MONY Scot word for **>** MANY

MONYPLIES same as **>** MANYPLIES

MONZONITE n coarse-grained plutonic igneous rock consisting of equal amounts of plagioclase and orthoclase feldspar, with ferromagnesian minerals

MOO n long deep cry of a cow ▷ vb make this noise ▷ interj instance or imitation of this sound

MOOBIES pl n overdeveloped breasts on a man

MOOBS pl n overdeveloped breasts on a man

MOOCH vb loiter about aimlessly

MOOCHED > MOOCH

MOOCHER > MOOCH

MOOCHERS > MOOCH

MOOCHES > MOOCH

MOOCHING > MOOCH

MOOD n temporary (gloomy) state of mind

MOODIED > MOODY

MOODIER > MOODY

MOODIES > MOODY

MOODIEST > MOODY

MOODILY > MOODY

MOODINESS > MOODY

MOODS > MOOD

MOODY adj sullen or gloomy ▷ vb flatter

MOODYING > MOODY

MOOED > MOO

MOOI adj pleasing or nice

MOOING > MOO

MOOK n person regarded with contempt, esp a stupid person

MOOKS > MOOK

MOOKTAR same as **>** MUKHTAR

MOOKTARS > MOOKTAR

MOOL same as **>** MOULD

MOOLA same as **>** MOOLAH

MOOLAH slang word for **>** MONEY

MOOLAHS > MOOLAH

MOOLAS > MOOLA

MOOLED > MOOL

MOOLEY same as **>** MOOLY

MOOLEYS > MOOLEY

MOOLI n type of large white radish

MOOLIES > MOOLY

MOOLING > MOOL

MOOLIS > MOOLI

MOOLOO n person from the Waikato

MOOLOOS > MOOLOO

MOOLS > MOOL

MOOLVI same as **>** MOOLVIE

MOOLVIE n (esp in India) Muslim learned man

MOOLVIES > MOOLVIE

MOOLVIS > MOOLVIE

MOOLY same as **>** MULEY

MOON n natural satellite of the earth ▷ vb be idle in a listless or dreamy way

MOONBEAM n ray of moonlight

MOONBEAMS > MOONBEAM

MOONBLIND adj (of horses) having a disorder which causes inflammation of the eyes and sometimes blindness

MOONBOOTS pl n thickly padded boots

MOONBOW n rainbow made by moonlight

MOONBOWS > MOONBOW

MOONCAKE n type of round Chinese cake

MOONCAKES > MOONCAKE

MOONCALF n born fool

MOONCHILD n someone who is born under the Cancer star sign

MOONCRAFT n lunar module

MOONDOG n bright spot in the sky caused by moonlight

MOONDOGS > MOONDOG

MOONDUST n dust on surface of moon

MOONDUSTS > MOONDUST

MOONED adj decorated with a moon

MOONER > MOON

MOONERS > MOON

MOONEYE n N American large-eyed freshwater fish

MOONEYES > MOONEYE

MOONFACE n big round face ▷ vb have a moon face

MOONFACED > MOONFACE

MOONFACES > MOONFACE

MOONFISH n any of several deep-bodied silvery carangid fishes, occurring in warm and tropical American coastal waters

MOONG n as in moong bean kind of bean

MOONGATE n circular gateway in a wall

MOONGATES > MOONGATE

MOONIER > MOONY

MOONIES > MOONY

MOONIEST > MOONY

MOONILY > MOONY

MOONINESS > MOONY

MOONING > MOON

MOONISH > MOON

MOONISHLY > MOON

MOONLESS > MOON

MOONLET n small moon

MOONLETS > MOONLET

MOONLIGHT n light from the moon ▷ adj illuminated by the moon ▷ vb work at a secondary job, esp illegally

MOONLIKE > MOON

MOONLIT adj illuminated by the moon

MOONPHASE n phase of moon

MOONPORT n place from which flights leave for moon

MOONPORTS > MOONPORT

MOONQUAKE n light tremor of the moon, detected on the moon's surface

MOONRAKER n small square sail set above a skysail

MOONRISE n moment when the moon appears above the horizon

MOONRISES > MOONRISE

MOONROCK n rock from moon

MOONROCKS > MOONROCK

MOONROOF same as **>** SUNROOF

MOONROOFS > MOONROOF

MOONS > MOON

MOONSAIL n small sail high on a mast

MOONSAILS > MOONSAIL

MOONSCAPE n surface of the moon or a picture or model of it

MOONSEED *n* type of climbing plant with red or black fruits and crescent-shaped or ring-shaped seeds

MOONSEEDS > MOONSEED

MOONSET *n* moment when the moon disappears below the horizon

MOONSETS > MOONSET

MOONSHEE *same as* > MUNSHI

MOONSHEES > MOONSHEE

MOONSHINE *same as* > MOONLIGHT

MOONSHINY *adj* lacking substance

MOONSHIP *n* lunar module

MOONSHIPS > MOONSHIP

MOONSHOT *n* launching of a spacecraft to the moon

MOONSHOTS > MOONSHOT

MOONSTONE *n* translucent semiprecious stone

MOONWALK *n* instance of walking on the moon

MOONWALKS > MOONWALK

MOONWARD *adj* towards moon

MOONWARDS *adv* towards the moon

MOONWORT *n* type of fern with crescent-shaped leaflets

MOONWORTS > MOONWORT

MOONY *adj* dreamy or listless ▷ *n* crazy or foolish person

MOOP *same as* > MOUP

MOOPED > MOOP

MOOPING > MOOP

MOOPS > MOOP

MOOR *n* tract of open uncultivated ground covered with grass and heather ▷ *vb* secure (a ship) with ropes etc

MOORAGE *n* place for mooring a vessel

MOORAGES > MOORAGE

MOORBURN *n* practice of burning off old growth on a heather moor to encourage new growth for grazing

MOORBURNS > MOORBURN

MOORCOCK *n* male of the red grouse

MOORCOCKS > MOORCOCK

MOORED > MOOR

MOORFOWL *n* red grouse

MOORFOWLS > MOORFOWL

MOORHEN *n* small black water bird

MOORHENS > MOORHEN

MOORIER > MOOR

MOORIEST > MOOR

MOORILL *n* disease of cattle on moors

MOORILLS > MOORILL

MOORING *n* place for mooring a ship

MOORINGS *pl n* ropes and anchors used in mooring a vessel

MOORISH *adj* of or relating to the Moor people of North Africa

MOORLAND *n* area of moor

MOORLANDS > MOORLAND

MOORLOG *n* rotted wood below the surface of a moor

MOORLOGS > MOOR

MOORMAN *n* person living on a moor

MOORMEN > MOORMAN

MOORS > MOOR

MOORVA *same as* > MURVA

MOORVAS > MOORVA

MOORWORT *n* low-growing pink-flowered shrub that grows in peaty bogs

MOORWORTS > MOORWORT

MOORY > MOOR

MOOS > MOO

MOOSE *n* large N American deer

MOOSEBIRD *n* North American jay

MOOSEWOOD *n* North American tree

MOOSEYARD *n* place where moose spend winter

MOOT *adj* debatable ▷ *vb* bring up for discussion ▷ *n* (in Anglo-Saxon England) a local administrative assembly

MOOTABLE > MOOT

MOOTED > MOOT

MOOTER > MOOT

MOOTERS > MOOT

MOOTEST > MOOT

MOOTING > MOOT

MOOTINGS > MOOT

MOOTMAN *n* person taking part in a moot

MOOTMEN > MOOTMAN

MOOTNESS > MOOT

MOOTS > MOOT

MOOVE *same as* > MOVE

MOOVED > MOOVE

MOOVES > MOOVE

MOOVING > MOOVE

MOP *n* long stick with twists of cotton or a sponge on the end, used for cleaning ▷ *vb* clean or soak up with or as if with a mop

MOPANE *same as* > MOPANI

MOPANES > MOPANE

MOPANI *n* S African tree that is highly resistant to drought

MOPANIS > MOPANI

MOPBOARD *n* wooden border fixed round the base of an interior wall

MOPBOARDS > MOPBOARD

MOPE *vb* be gloomy and apathetic ▷ *n* gloomy person

MOPED *n* light motorized cycle

MOPEDS > MOPED

MOPEHAWK *same as* > MOPOKE

MOPEHAWKS > MOPEHAWK

MOPER > MOPE

MOPERIES > MOPERY

MOPERS > MOPE

MOPERY *n* gloominess

MOPES > MOPE

MOPEY > MOPE

MOPHEAD *n* person with shaggy hair

MOPHEADS > MOPHEAD

MOPIER > MOPE

MOPIEST > MOPE

MOPILY > MOPY

MOPINESS > MOPE

MOPING > MOPE

MOPINGLY > MOPE

MOPISH > MOPE

MOPISHLY > MOPE

MOPOKE *n* species of owl

MOPOKES > MOPOKE

MOPPED > MOP

MOPPER > MOP

MOPPERS > MOP

MOPPET *same as* > POPPET

MOPPETS > MOPPET

MOPPIER > MOPPY

MOPPIEST > MOPPY

MOPPING > MOP

MOPPY *adj* drunk

MOPS > MOP

MOPSIES > MOPSY

MOPSTICK *n* mop handle

MOPSTICKS > MOPSTICK

MOPSY *n* untidy or dowdy person

MOPUS *n* person who mopes

MOPUSES > MOPUS

MOPY > MOPE

MOQUETTE *n* thick velvety fabric used for carpets and upholstery

MOQUETTES > MOQUETTE

MOR *n* layer of acidic humus formed in cool moist areas

MORA *n* quantity of a short syllable in verse

MORACEOUS *adj* relating to a mostly tropical and subtropical family of trees and shrubs which includes the mulberry, fig, and breadfruit

MORAE > MORA

MORAINAL > MORAINE

MORAINE *n* accumulated mass of debris deposited by a glacier

MORAINES > MORAINE

MORAINIC > MORAINE

MORAL *adj* concerned with right and wrong conduct ▷ *n* lesson to be obtained from a story or event ▷ *vb* moralize

MORALE *n* degree of confidence or hope of a person or group

MORALES > MORALE

MORALISE *same as* > MORALIZE

MORALISED > MORALISE

MORALISER > MORALIZE

MORALISES > MORALISE

MORALISM *n* habit or practice of moralizing

MORALISMS > MORALISM

MORALIST *n* person with a strong sense of right and wrong

MORALISTS > MORALIST

MORALITY *n* good moral conduct

MORALIZE *vb* make moral pronouncements

MORALIZED > MORALIZE

MORALIZER > MORALIZE

MORALIZES > MORALIZE

MORALL *same as* > MURAL

MORALLED > MORALL

MORALLER > MORAL

MORALLERS > MORAL

MORALLING > MORALL

MORALLS > MORALL

MORALLY > MORAL

MORALS > MORAL

MORAS > MORA

MORASS *n* marsh

MORASSES > MORASS

MORASSY > MORASS

MORAT *n* drink containing mulberry juice

MORATORIA *pl n* legally authorized postponements of the fulfilment of an obligation

MORATORY > MORATORIA

MORATS > MORAT

MORAY *n* large voracious eel

MORAYS > MORAY

MORBID *adj* unduly interested in death or unpleasant events

MORBIDER > MORBID

MORBIDEST > MORBID

MORBIDITY *n* state of being morbid

MORBIDLY > MORBID

MORBIFIC *adj* causing disease

MORBILLI *same as* > MEASLES

MORBUS *n* disease

MORBUSES > MORBUS

MORCEAU *n* fragment or morsel

MORCEAUX > MORCEAU

MORCHA *n* (in India) hostile demonstration

MORCHAS > MORCHA

MORDACITY *n* quality of sarcasm

MORDANCY > MORDANT

MORDANT *adj* sarcastic or scathing ▷ *n* substance used to fix dyes ▷ *vb* treat (a fabric, yarn, etc) with a mordant

MORDANTED > MORDANT

MORDANTLY > MORDANT

MORDANTS > MORDANT

m

MORDENT n melodic ornament in music
MORDENTS > MORDENT
MORE adj greater in amount or degree ▷ adv greater extent ▷ pron greater or additional amount or number
MOREEN n heavy, usually watered, fabric of wool or wool and cotton
MOREENS > MOREEN
MOREISH adj (of food) causing a desire for more
MOREL n edible mushroom with a pitted cap
MORELLE n nightshade
MORELLES > MORELLE
MORELLO n variety of small very dark sour cherry
MORELLOS > MORELLO
MORELS > MOREL
MORENDO adv (in music) dying away ▷ n gentle decrescendo at the end of a musical strain
MORENDOS > MORENDO
MORENESS > MORE
MOREOVER adv in addition to what has already been said
MOREPORK same as > MOPOKE
MOREPORKS > MOREPORK
MORES pl n customs and conventions embodying the fundamental values of a community
MORESQUE adj (esp of decoration and architecture) of Moorish style ▷ n Moorish design or decoration
MORESQUES > MORESQUE
MORGAN n American breed of small compact saddle horse
MORGANITE n pink variety of beryl, used as a gemstone
MORGANS > MORGAN
MORGAY n small dogfish
MORGAYS > MORGAY
MORGEN n South African unit of area
MORGENS > MORGEN
MORGUE same as > MORTUARY
MORGUES > MORGUE
MORIA n folly
MORIAS > MORIA
MORIBUND adj without force or vitality
MORICHE same as > MIRITI
MORICHES > MORICHE
MORION n 16th-century helmet with a brim and wide comb
MORIONS > MORION
MORISCO n morris dance
MORISCOES > MORISCO
MORISCOS > MORISCO

MORISH same as > MOREISH
MORKIN n animal dying in accident
MORKINS > MORKIN
MORLING n sheep killed by disease
MORLINGS > MORLING
MORMAOR n former high-ranking Scottish nobleman
MORMAORS > MORMAOR
MORN n morning
MORNAY adj served with a cheese sauce
MORNAYS > MORNAY
MORNE same as > MOURN
MORNED > MORNE
MORNES > MORNE
MORNING n part of the day before noon
MORNINGS > MORNING
MORNS > MORN
MOROCCO n goatskin leather
MOROCCOS > MOROCCO
MORON n foolish or stupid person
MORONIC > MORON
MORONISM > MORON
MORONISMS > MORON
MORONITY > MORON
MORONS > MORON
MOROSE adj sullen or moody
MOROSELY > MOROSE
MOROSER > MOROSE
MOROSEST > MOROSE
MOROSITY > MOROSE
MORPH n phonological representation of a morpheme ▷ vb undergo or cause to undergo morphing
MORPHEAN adj of or relating to Morpheus, the god of sleep and dreams
MORPHED > MORPH
MORPHEME n speech element having a meaning or grammatical function that cannot be subdivided into further such elements
MORPHEMES > MORPHEME
MORPHEMIC > MORPHEME
MORPHETIC same as > MORPHEAN
MORPHEW n blemish on skin
MORPHEWS > MORPHEW
MORPHIA same as > MORPHINE
MORPHIAS > MORPHIA
MORPHIC adj as in morphic resonance idea that an event can lead to similar events in the future through a telepathic effect
MORPHIN variant form of > MORPHINE
MORPHINE n drug extracted from opium, used as an anaesthetic and sedative

MORPHINES > MORPHINE
MORPHING n computer technique used for graphics and in films, in which one image is gradually transformed into another image without individual changes being noticeable in the process
MORPHINGS > MORPHING
MORPHINIC > MORPHINE
MORPHINS > MORPHINE
MORPHO n type of butterfly
MORPHOGEN n chemical in body that influences growth
MORPHOS > MORPHO
MORPHOSES > MORPHOSIS
MORPHOSIS n development in an organism or its parts characterized by structural change
MORPHOTIC > MORPHOSIS
MORPHS > MORPH
MORRA same as > MORA
MORRAS > MORRA
MORRELL n tall SW Australian eucalyptus with pointed buds
MORRELLS > MORRELL
MORRHUA n cod
MORRHUAS > MORRHUA
MORRICE same as > MORRIS
MORRICES > MORRICE
MORRION same as > MORION
MORRIONS > MORRION
MORRIS vb perform morris dance
MORRISED > MORRIS
MORRISES > MORRIS
MORRISING > MORRIS
MORRO n rounded hill or promontory
MORROS > MORRO
MORROW n next day
MORROWS > MORROW
MORS > MOR
MORSAL same as > MORSEL
MORSALS > MORSAL
MORSE n clasp or fastening on a cope
MORSEL n small piece, esp of food ▷ vb divide into morsels
MORSELED > MORSEL
MORSELING > MORSEL
MORSELLED > MORSEL
MORSELS > MORSEL
MORSES > MORSE
MORSURE n bite
MORSURES > MORSURE
MORT n call blown on a hunting horn to signify the death of the animal hunted
MORTAL adj subject to death ▷ n human being

MORTALISE same as > MORTALIZE
MORTALITY n state of being mortal
MORTALIZE vb make mortal
MORTALLY > MORTAL
MORTALS > MORTAL
MORTAR n small cannon with a short range ▷ vb fire on with mortars
MORTARED > MORTAR
MORTARING > MORTAR
MORTARMAN n person firing mortar
MORTARMEN > MORTAR
MORTARS > MORTAR
MORTARY adj of or like mortar
MORTBELL n bell rung for funeral
MORTBELLS > MORTBELL
MORTCLOTH n cloth spread over coffin
MORTGAGE n conditional pledging of property, esp a house, as security for the repayment of a loan ▷ vb pledge (property) as security thus ▷ adj of or relating to a mortgage
MORTGAGED > MORTGAGE
MORTGAGEE n creditor in a mortgage
MORTGAGER same as > MORTGAGOR
MORTGAGES > MORTGAGE
MORTGAGOR n debtor in a mortgage
MORTICE same as > MORTISE
MORTICED > MORTICE
MORTICER > MORTICE
MORTICERS > MORTICE
MORTICES > MORTICE
MORTICIAN n undertaker
MORTICING > MORTICE
MORTIFIC adj causing death
MORTIFIED > MORTIFY
MORTIFIER > MORTIFY
MORTIFIES > MORTIFY
MORTIFY vb humiliate
MORTISE n slot cut into a piece of wood, stone, etc ▷ vb cut a slot in (a piece of wood, stone, etc)
MORTISED > MORTISE
MORTISER > MORTISE
MORTISERS > MORTISE
MORTISES > MORTISE
MORTISING > MORTISE
MORTLING n corpse
MORTLINGS > MORTLING
MORTMAIN n state or condition of lands, buildings, etc, held inalienably, as by an ecclesiastical or other corporation
MORTMAINS > MORTMAIN
MORTS > MORT
MORTSAFE n heavy iron cage or grille placed over

the grave of a newly deceased person during the 19th century in order to deter body snatchers

MORTSAFES > MORTSAFE

MORTUARY n building where corpses are kept before burial or cremation ▷ adj of or relating to death or burial

MORULA n solid ball of cells resulting from cleavage of a fertilized ovum

MORULAE > MORULA

MORULAR > MORULA

MORULAS > MORULA

MORWONG n food fish of Australasian coastal waters

MORWONGS > MORWONG

MORYAH interj exclamation of annoyance, disbelief, etc

MOS > MO

MOSAIC n design or decoration using small pieces of coloured stone or glass

MOSAICISM n occurrence of different types of tissue side by side

MOSAICIST > MOSAIC

MOSAICKED adj arranged in mosaic form

MOSAICS > MOSAIC

MOSASAUR n type of extinct Cretaceous giant marine lizard, typically with paddle-like limbs

MOSASAURI > MOSASAUR

MOSASAURS > MOSASAUR

MOSCATO n type of sweet dessert wine

MOSCATOS > MOSCATO

MOSCHATE n odour like musk

MOSCHATEL n small N temperate plant with greenish-white musk-scented flowers

MOSE vb have glanders

MOSED > MOSE

MOSELLE n German white wine from the Moselle valley

MOSELLES > MOSELLE

MOSES > MOSE

MOSEY vb walk in a leisurely manner

MOSEYED > MOSEY

MOSEYING > MOSEY

MOSEYS > MOSEY

MOSH n dance performed to loud rock music ▷ vb dance in this manner

MOSHAV n cooperative settlement in Israel

MOSHAVIM > MOSHAV

MOSHED > MOSH

MOSHER > MOSH

MOSHERS > MOSH

MOSHES > MOSH

MOSHING > MOSH

MOSHINGS > MOSH

MOSING > MOSE

MOSK same as > MOSQUE

MOSKONFYT n South African grape syrup

MOSKS > MOSK

MOSLINGS n shavings from animal skin being prepared

MOSQUE n Muslim temple

MOSQUES > MOSQUE

MOSQUITO n blood-sucking flying insect

MOSQUITOS > MOSQUITO

MOSS n small flowerless plant growing in masses on moist surfaces ▷ vb gather moss

MOSSBACK n old turtle, shellfish, etc, that has a growth of algae on its back

MOSSBACKS > MOSSBACK

MOSSED > MOSS

MOSSER > MOSS

MOSSERS > MOSS

MOSSES > MOSS

MOSSGROWN adj covered in moss

MOSSIE n common sparrow

MOSSIER > MOSS

MOSSIES > MOSSIE

MOSSIEST > MOSS

MOSSINESS > MOSS

MOSSING > MOSS

MOSSLAND n land covered in peat

MOSSLANDS > MOSSLAND

MOSSLIKE > MOSS

MOSSO adv to be performed with rapidity

MOSSPLANT n individual plant in moss

MOSSY > MOSS

MOST n greatest number or degree ▷ adj greatest in number or degree ▷ adv in the greatest degree

MOSTE > MOTE

MOSTEST > MOST

MOSTESTS > MOST

MOSTLY adv for the most part, generally

MOSTS > MOST

MOSTWHAT adv mostly

MOT n girl or young woman, esp one's girlfriend

MOTE n tiny speck ▷ vb may or might

MOTED adj containing motes

MOTEL n roadside hotel for motorists

MOTELIER n person running motel

MOTELIERS > MOTELIER

MOTELS > MOTEL

MOTEN > MOTE

MOTES > MOTE

MOTET n short sacred choral song

MOTETS > MOTET

MOTETT same as > MOTET

MOTETTIST > MOTET

MOTETTS > MOTET

MOTEY adj containing motes ▷ n pigment made from earth

MOTEYS > MOTEY

MOTH n nocturnal insect like a butterfly

MOTHBALL n small ball of camphor or naphthalene used to repel moths from stored clothes ▷ vb store (something operational) for future use

MOTHBALLS > MOTHBALL

MOTHED adj damaged by moths

MOTHER n female parent ▷ adj native or inborn ▷ vb look after as a mother

MOTHERED > MOTHER

MOTHERESE n simplified and repetitive type of speech, with exaggerated intonation and rhythm, often used by adults when speaking to babies

MOTHERING > MOTHER

MOTHERLY adj of or resembling a mother, esp in warmth, or protectiveness

MOTHERS > MOTHER

MOTHERY > MOTHER

MOTHIER > MOTHY

MOTHIEST > MOTHY

MOTHLIKE > MOTH

MOTHPROOF adj (esp of clothes) chemically treated so as to repel clothes moths ▷ vb make mothproof

MOTHS > MOTH

MOTHY adj ragged

MOTI n derogatory Indian English word for a fat woman or girl

MOTIER > MOTEY

MOTIEST > MOTEY

MOTIF n (recurring) theme or design

MOTIFIC adj causing motion

MOTIFS > MOTIF

MOTILE adj capable of independent movement ▷ n person whose mental imagery strongly reflects movement

MOTILES > MOTILE

MOTILITY > MOTILE

MOTION n process, action, or way of moving ▷ vb direct (someone) by gesture

MOTIONAL > MOTION

MOTIONED > MOTION

MOTIONER > MOTION

MOTIONERS > MOTION

MOTIONING > MOTION

MOTIONIST n person proposing many motions

MOTIONS > MOTION

MOTIS > MOTI

MOTIVATE vb give incentive to

MOTIVATED > MOTIVATE

MOTIVATES > MOTIVATE

MOTIVATOR > MOTIVATE

MOTIVE n reason for a course of action ▷ adj causing motion ▷ vb motivate

MOTIVED > MOTIVE

MOTIVES > MOTIVE

MOTIVIC adj of musical motif

MOTIVING > MOTIVE

MOTIVITY n power of moving or of initiating motion

MOTLEY adj miscellaneous ▷ n costume of a jester

MOTLEYER > MOTLEY

MOTLEYEST > MOTLEY

MOTLEYS > MOTLEY

MOTLIER > MOTLEY

MOTLIEST > MOTLEY

MOTMOT n tropical American bird with a long tail and blue and brownish-green plumage

MOTMOTS > MOTMOT

MOTOCROSS n motorcycle race over a rough course

MOTOR n engine, esp of a vehicle ▷ vb travel by car ▷ adj of or relating to cars and other vehicles powered by engines

MOTORABLE adj (of a road) suitable for use by motor vehicles

MOTORAIL n transport of cars by train

MOTORAILS > MOTORAIL

MOTORBIKE n motorcycle

MOTORBOAT n any boat powered by a motor

MOTORBUS n bus driven by an internal-combustion engine

MOTORCADE n procession of cars carrying important people

MOTORCAR n self-propelled electric railway car

MOTORCARS > MOTORCAR

MOTORDOM n world of motor cars

MOTORDOMS > MOTORDOM

MOTORED > MOTOR

MOTORHOME n large motor vehicle with living quarters behind the driver's compartment

MOTORIAL > MOTOR

MOTORIC > MOTOR

MOTORING > MOTOR

MOTORINGS > MOTOR

MOTORISE same as > MOTORIZE

MOTORISED > MOTORISE

MOTORISES > MOTORISE

MOTORIST n driver of a car

MOTORISTS > MOTORIST

MOTORIUM n area of nervous system involved in movement

MOTORIUMS > MOTORIUM

MOTORIZE vb equip with a motor

MOTORIZED > MOTORIZE

MOTORIZES > MOTORIZE

MOTORLESS > MOTOR

MOTORMAN n driver of an electric train

MOTORMEN > MOTORMAN

MOTORS > MOTOR

MOTORSHIP n ship with motor

MOTORWAY n main road for fast-moving traffic

MOTORWAYS > MOTORWAY

MOTORY > MOTOR

MOTOSCAFI > MOTOSCAFO

MOTOSCAFO n motorboat

MOTS > MOT

MOTSER n large sum of money, esp a gambling win

MOTSERS > MOTSER

MOTT n clump of trees

MOTTE n mound on which a castle was built

MOTTES > MOTTE

MOTTIER > MOTTY

MOTTIES > MOTTY

MOTTIEST > MOTTY

MOTTLE vb colour with streaks or blotches of different shades ▷ n mottled appearance, as of the surface of marble

MOTTLED > MOTTLE

MOTTLER n paintbrush for mottled effects

MOTTLERS > MOTTLER

MOTTLES > MOTTLE

MOTTLING > MOTTLE

MOTTLINGS > MOTTLE

MOTTO n saying expressing an ideal or rule of conduct

MOTTOED adj having motto

MOTTOES > MOTTO

MOTTOS > MOTTO

MOTTS > MOTT

MOTTY n target at which coins are aimed in pitch-and-toss ▷ adj containing motes

MOTU n derogatory Indian English word for a fat man or boy

MOTUCA n Brazilian fly

MOTUCAS > MOTUCA

MOTUS > MOTU

MOTZA same as > MOTSER

MOTZAS > MOTZA

MOU Scots word for > MOUTH

MOUCH same as > MOOCH

MOUCHARD n police informer

MOUCHARDS > MOUCHARD

MOUCHED > MOUCH

MOUCHER > MOUCH

MOUCHERS > MOUCH

MOUCHES > MOUCH

MOUCHING > MOUCH

MOUCHOIR n handkerchief

MOUCHOIRS > MOUCHOIR

MOUDIWART same as > MOULDWARP

MOUDIWORT same as > MOULDWARP

MOUE n disdainful or pouting look

MOUES > MOUE

MOUFFLON same as > MOUFLON

MOUFFLONS > MOUFFLON

MOUFLON n wild mountain sheep of Corsica and Sardinia

MOUFLONS > MOUFLON

MOUGHT > MOTE

MOUILLE adj palatalized, as in the sounds represented by Spanish ll or ñ

MOUJIK same as > MUZHIK

MOUJIKS > MOUJIK

MOULAGE n mould making

MOULAGES > MOULAGE

MOULD n hollow container in which metal etc is cast ▷ vb shape

MOULDABLE > MOULD

MOULDED > MOULD

MOULDER vb decay into dust ▷ n person who moulds or makes moulds

MOULDERED > MOULDER

MOULDERS > MOULDER

MOULDIER > MOULDY

MOULDIEST > MOULDY

MOULDING n moulded ornamental edging

MOULDINGS > MOULDING

MOULDS > MOULD

MOULDWARP archaic or dialect name for a > MOLE

MOULDY adj stale or musty

MOULIN n vertical shaft in a glacier

MOULINET n device for bending crossbow

MOULINETS > MOULINET

MOULINS > MOULIN

MOULS Scots word for > MOULD

MOULT vb shed feathers, hair, or skin to make way for new growth ▷ n process of moulting

MOULTED > MOULT

MOULTEN adj having moulted

MOULTER > MOULT

MOULTERS > MOULT

MOULTING > MOULT

MOULTINGS > MOULT

MOULTS > MOULT

MOUND n heap, esp of earth or stones ▷ vb gather into a mound

MOUNDBIRD n Australian bird laying eggs in mounds

MOUNDED > MOUND

MOUNDING > MOUND

MOUNDS > MOUND

MOUNSEER same as > MONSIEUR

MOUNSEERS > MOUNSEER

MOUNT vb climb or ascend ▷ n backing or support on which something is fixed

MOUNTABLE > MOUNT

MOUNTAIN n hill of great size ▷ adj of, found on, or for use on a mountain or mountains

MOUNTAINS > MOUNTAIN

MOUNTAINY > MOUNTAIN

MOUNTANT n adhesive for mounting pictures

MOUNTANTS > MOUNTANT

MOUNTED adj riding horses

MOUNTER > MOUNT

MOUNTERS > MOUNT

MOUNTING same as > MOUNT

MOUNTINGS > MOUNTING

MOUNTS > MOUNT

MOUP n nibble

MOUPED > MOUP

MOUPING > MOUP

MOUPS > MOUP

MOURN vb feel or express sorrow for (a dead person or lost thing)

MOURNED > MOURN

MOURNER n person attending a funeral

MOURNERS > MOURNER

MOURNFUL adj sad or dismal

MOURNING n grieving ▷ adj of or relating to mourning

MOURNINGS > MOURNING

MOURNIVAL n card game

MOURNS > MOURN

MOUS > MOU

MOUSAKA same as > MOUSSAKA

MOUSAKAS > MOUSAKA

MOUSE n small long-tailed rodent ▷ vb stalk and catch mice

MOUSEBIRD another name for > COLY

MOUSED > MOUSE

MOUSEKIN n little mouse

MOUSEKINS > MOUSEKIN

MOUSELIKE > MOUSE

MOUSEMAT n piece of material on which a computer mouse is moved

MOUSEMATS > MOUSEMAT

MOUSEOVER n on a web page, any item that changes or pops up when the pointer of a mouse moves over it

MOUSEPAD n pad for computer mouse

MOUSEPADS > MOUSEPAD

MOUSER n cat used to catch mice

MOUSERIES > MOUSERY

MOUSERS > MOUSER

MOUSERY n place infested with mice

MOUSES > MOUSE

MOUSETAIL n N temperate plant with tail-like flower spikes

MOUSETRAP n spring-loaded trap for killing mice

MOUSEY same as > MOUSY

MOUSIE n little mouse

MOUSIER > MOUSY

MOUSIES > MOUSIE

MOUSIEST > MOUSY

MOUSILY > MOUSY

MOUSINESS > MOUSY

MOUSING n device for closing off a hook

MOUSINGS > MOUSING

MOUSLE vb handle roughly

MOUSLED > MOUSLE

MOUSLES > MOUSLE

MOUSLING > MOUSLE

MOUSME n Japanese girl

MOUSMEE same as > MOUSME

MOUSMEES > MOUSMEE

MOUSMES > MOUSME

MOUSSAKA n dish made with meat, aubergines, and tomatoes, topped with cheese sauce

MOUSSAKAS > MOUSSAKA

MOUSSE n dish of flavoured cream whipped and set ▷ vb apply mousse to

MOUSSED > MOUSSE

MOUSSES > MOUSSE

MOUSSEUX n type of sparkling wine

MOUSSING > MOUSSE

MOUST same as > MUST

MOUSTACHE n hair on the upper lip

MOUSTED > MOUST

MOUSTING > MOUST

MOUSTS > MOUST

MOUSY adj like a mouse, esp in hair colour

MOUTAN n variety of peony

MOUTANS > MOUTAN

MOUTER same as > MULTURE

MOUTERED > MOUTER

MOUTERER > MOUTER

MOUTERERS > MOUTER

MOUTERING > MOUTER

MOUTERS > MOUTER

MOUTH n opening in the head for eating and issuing sounds ▷ vb form (words) with the lips without speaking

MOUTHABLE adj able to be recited

MOUTHED > MOUTH

MOUTHER > MOUTH

MOUTHERS > MOUTH

MOUTHFEEL n texture of a substance as it is perceived in the mouth

MOUTHFUL n amount of food or drink put into the mouth at any one time when eating or drinking

MOUTHFULS > MOUTHFUL
MOUTHIER > MOUTHY
MOUTHIEST > MOUTHY
MOUTHILY > MOUTHY
MOUTHING > MOUTH
MOUTHLESS > MOUTH
MOUTHLIKE > MOUTH
MOUTHPART *n* any of the paired appendages in arthropods that surround the mouth and are specialized for feeding
MOUTHS > MOUTH
MOUTHWASH *n* medicated liquid for gargling and cleansing the mouth
MOUTHY *adj* bombastic
MOUTON *n* sheepskin processed to resemble the fur of another animal
MOUTONNEE *adj* rounded by action of glacier
MOUTONS > MOUTON
MOVABLE *adj* able to be moved or rearranged ▷ *n* movable article, esp a piece of furniture
MOVABLES > MOVABLE
MOVABLY > MOVABLE
MOVANT *n* person who applies to a court of law
MOVANTS > MOVANT
MOVE *vb* change in place or position ▷ *n* moving
MOVEABLE *same as* > MOVABLE
MOVEABLES > MOVEABLE
MOVEABLY > MOVEABLE
MOVED > MOVE
MOVELESS *adj* immobile
MOVEMENT *n* action or process of moving
MOVEMENTS > MOVEMENT
MOVER *n* person or animal that moves in a particular way
MOVERS > MOVER
MOVES > MOVE
MOVIE *n* cinema film
MOVIEDOM *n* world of cinema
MOVIEDOMS > MOVIEDOM
MOVIEGOER *n* person who goes to cinema
MOVIELAND *same as* > MOVIEDOM
MOVIEOKE *n* entertainment in which people act out well-known scenes from movies that are silently playing in the background
MOVIEOKES > MOVIEOKE
MOVIEOLA *same as* > MOVIOLA
MOVIEOLAS > MOVIEOLA
MOVIES > MOVIE
MOVING *adj* arousing or touching the emotions
MOVINGLY > MOVING
MOVIOLA *n* viewing machine used in cutting and editing film
MOVIOLAS > MOVIOLA

MOW *vb* cut (grass or crops) ▷ *n* part of a barn where hay, straw, etc, is stored
MOWA *same as* > MAHUA
MOWAS > MOWA
MOWBURN *vb* heat up in mow
MOWBURNED > MOWBURN
MOWBURNS > MOWBURN
MOWBURNT *adj* (of hay, straw, etc) damaged by overheating in a mow
MOWDIE *Scot word for* > MOLE
MOWDIES > MOWDIE
MOWED > MOW
MOWER > MOW
MOWERS > MOW
MOWING > MOW
MOWINGS > MOW
MOWN > MOW
MOWRA *same as* > MAHUA
MOWRAS > MOWRA
MOWS > MOW
MOXA *n* downy material obtained from various plants
MOXAS > MOXA
MOXIE *n* courage, nerve, or vigour
MOXIES > MOXIE
MOY *n* coin
MOYA *n* mud emitted from a volcano
MOYAS > MOYA
MOYGASHEL *n* type of Irish linen
MOYITIES > MOIETY
MOYITY *same as* > MOIETY
MOYL *same as* > MOYLE
MOYLE *vb* toil
MOYLED > MOYLE
MOYLES > MOYLE
MOYLING > MOYLE
MOYLS > MOYL
MOYS > MOY
MOZ *n* hex
MOZE *vb* give nap to
MOZED > MOZE
MOZES > MOZ
MOZETTA *same as* > MOZZETTA
MOZETTAS > MOZETTA
MOZETTE > MOZETTA
MOZING > MOZE
MOZO *n* porter in southwest USA
MOZOS > MOZO
MOZZ *same as* > MOZ
MOZZES > MOZZ
MOZZETTA *n* short hooded cape worn by the pope, cardinals, etc
MOZZETTAS > MOZZETTA
MOZZETTE > MOZZETTA
MOZZIE *same as* > MOSSIE
MOZZIES > MOZZIE
MOZZLE *n* luck ▷ *vb* hamper or impede (someone)
MOZZLED > MOZZLE
MOZZLES > MOZZLE
MOZZLING > MOZZLE

MPRET *n* former Albanian ruler
MPRETS > MPRET
MRIDAMGAM *same as* > MRIDANG
MRIDANG *n* drum used in Indian music
MRIDANGA *same as* > MRIDANG
MRIDANGAM *same as* > MRIDANG
MRIDANGAS > MRIDANGA
MRIDANGS > MRIDANG
MU *n* 12th letter in the Greek alphabet
MUCATE *n* salt of mucic acid
MUCATES > MUCATE
MUCH *adj* large amount or degree of ▷ *n* large amount or degree ▷ *adv* great degree
MUCHACHA *n* (in Spain etc) young woman or female servant
MUCHACHAS > MUCHACHA
MUCHACHO *n* young man
MUCHACHOS > MUCHACHO
MUCHEL *same as* > MUCH
MUCHELL *same as* > MUCH
MUCHELLS > MUCHELL
MUCHELS > MUCHEL
MUCHES > MUCH
MUCHLY > MUCH
MUCHNESS *n* magnitude
MUCHO *adv* Spanish for very
MUCIC *adj* as in mucic acid colourless crystalline solid carboxylic acid
MUCID *adj* mouldy, musty, or slimy
MUCIDITY > MUCID
MUCIDNESS > MUCID
MUCIGEN *n* substance present in mucous cells that is converted into mucin
MUCIGENS > MUCIGEN
MUCILAGE *n* gum or glue
MUCILAGES > MUCILAGE
MUCIN *n* any of a group of nitrogenous mucoproteins occurring in saliva, skin, tendon, etc
MUCINOGEN *n* substance forming mucin
MUCINOID *adj* of or like mucin
MUCINOUS > MUCIN
MUCINS > MUCIN
MUCK *n* dirt, filth
MUCKAMUCK *n* food ▷ *vb* consume food
MUCKED > MUCK
MUCKENDER *n* handkerchief
MUCKER *n* person who shifts broken rock or waste ▷ *vb* hoard
MUCKERED > MUCKER
MUCKERING > MUCKER
MUCKERISH > MUCKER
MUCKERS > MUCKER
MUCKHEAP *n* dunghill

MUCKHEAPS > MUCKHEAP
MUCKIER > MUCKY
MUCKIEST > MUCKY
MUCKILY > MUCKY
MUCKINESS > MUCKY
MUCKING > MUCK
MUCKLE *same as* > MICKLE
MUCKLES > MUCKLE
MUCKLUCK *same as* > MUKLUK
MUCKLUCKS > MUCKLUCK
MUCKRAKE *n* agricultural rake for spreading manure ▷ *vb* seek out and expose scandal, esp concerning public figures
MUCKRAKED > MUCKRAKE
MUCKRAKER > MUCKRAKE
MUCKRAKES > MUCKRAKE
MUCKS > MUCK
MUCKSWEAT *n* profuse sweat
MUCKWORM *n* any larva or worm that lives in mud
MUCKWORMS > MUCKWORM
MUCKY *adj* dirty or muddy
MUCKYMUCK *n* person who is or appears to be very important
MUCLUC *same as* > MUKLUK
MUCLUCS > MUCLUC
MUCOID *adj* of the nature of or resembling mucin ▷ *n* substance like mucin
MUCOIDAL *same as* > MUCOID
MUCOIDS > MUCOID
MUCOLYTIC *adj* breaking down mucus ▷ *n* agent that is able to break down mucus
MUCOR *n* type of fungus
MUCORS > MUCOR
MUCOSA *n* mucus-secreting membrane that lines body cavities
MUCOSAE > MUCOSA
MUCOSAL > MUCOSA
MUCOSAS > MUCOSA
MUCOSE *same as* > MUCOUS
MUCOSITY > MUCOUS
MUCOUS *adj* of, resembling, or secreting mucus
MUCRO *n* short pointed projection from certain parts or organs
MUCRONATE *adj* terminating in a sharp point
MUCRONES > MUCRO
MUCROS > MUCRO
MUCULENT *adj* like mucus
MUCUS *n* slimy secretion of the mucous membranes
MUCUSES > MUCUS
MUD *n* wet soft earth ▷ *vb* cover in mud
MUDBANK *n* sloping area of mud beside a body of water
MUDBANKS > MUDBANK
MUDBATH *n* medicinal bath in heated mud
MUDBATHS > MUDBATH

m

MUDBUG n crayfish

MUDBUGS > MUDBUG

MUDCAP vb use explosive charge in blasting

MUDCAPPED > MUDCAP

MUDCAPS > MUDCAP

MUDCAT n any of several large North American catfish

MUDCATS > MUDCAT

MUDDED > MUD

MUDDER n horse that runs well in mud

MUDDERS > MUDDER

MUDDIED > MUDDY

MUDDIER > MUDDY

MUDDIES > MUDDY

MUDDIEST > MUDDY

MUDDILY > MUDDY

MUDDINESS > MUDDY

MUDDING > MUD

MUDDLE vb confuse ▷ n state of confusion

MUDDLED > MUDDLE

MUDDLER n person who muddles or muddles through

MUDDLERS > MUDDLER

MUDDLES > MUDDLE

MUDDLIER > MUDDLE

MUDDLIEST > MUDDLE

MUDDLING > MUDDLE

MUDDLINGS > MUDDLE

MUDDLY > MUDDLE

MUDDY adj covered or filled with mud ▷ vb make muddy

MUDDYING > MUDDY

MUDEJAR n Spanish Moor ▷ adj of or relating to a style of architecture

MUDEJARES > MUDEJAR

MUDEYE n larva of the dragonfly

MUDEYES > MUDEYE

MUDFISH n fish that lives at the muddy bottoms of rivers, lakes, etc

MUDFISHES > MUDFISH

MUDFLAP n flap above wheel to deflect mud

MUDFLAPS > MUDFLAP

MUDFLAT n tract of low muddy land

MUDFLATS > MUDFLAT

MUDFLOW n flow of soil mixed with water down a steep unstable slope

MUDFLOWS > MUDFLOW

MUDGE vb speak vaguely

MUDGED > MUDGE

MUDGER > MUDGE

MUDGERS > MUDGE

MUDGES > MUDGE

MUDGING > MUDGE

MUDGUARD n cover over a wheel to prevent mud or water being thrown up by it

MUDGUARDS > MUDGUARD

MUDHEN n water bird living in muddy place

MUDHENS > MUDHEN

MUDHOLE n hole with mud at bottom

MUDHOLES > MUDHOLE

MUDHOOK n anchor

MUDHOOKS > MUDHOOK

MUDHOPPER n type of amphibious fish found on mud flats and in mangrove swamps

MUDIR n local governor

MUDIRIA n province of mudir

MUDIRIAS > MUDIRIA

MUDIRIEH same as > MUDIRIA

MUDIRIEHS > MUDIRIEH

MUDIRS > MUDIR

MUDLARK n street urchin ▷ vb play in mud

MUDLARKED > MUDLARK

MUDLARKS > MUDLARK

MUDLOGGER n person checking mud for traces of oil

MUDPACK n cosmetic paste applied to the face

MUDPACKS > MUDPACK

MUDPIE n small mass of mud moulded into a pie shape

MUDPIES > MUDPIE

MUDPUPPY n aquatic North American salamander of the genus with red feathery external gills and other persistent larval features

MUDRA n hand movement in Hindu religious dancing

MUDRAS > MUDRA

MUDROCK n type of sedimentary rock

MUDROCKS > MUDROCK

MUDROOM n room where muddy shoes may be left

MUDROOMS > MUDROOM

MUDS > MUD

MUDSCOW n boat for travelling over mudflats

MUDSCOWS > MUDSCOW

MUDSILL n support for building at or below ground

MUDSILLS > MUDSILL

MUDSLIDE n landslide of mud

MUDSLIDES > MUDSLIDE

MUDSLING vb make accusations against a rival candidate

MUDSLINGS > MUDSLING

MUDSLUNG > MUDSLING

MUDSTONE n dark grey clay rock similar to shale but with the lamination less well developed

MUDSTONES > MUDSTONE

MUDWORT n plant growing in mud

MUDWORTS > MUDWORT

MUEDDIN same as > MUEZZIN

MUEDDINS > MUEDDIN

MUENSTER n whitish-yellow semihard whole milk cheese, often flavoured with caraway or aniseed

MUENSTERS > MUENSTER

MUESLI n mixture of grain, nuts, and dried fruit

MUESLIS > MUESLI

MUEZZIN n official who summons Muslims to prayer

MUEZZINS > MUEZZIN

MUFF n tube-shaped covering to keep the hands warm ▷ vb bungle (an action)

MUFFED > MUFF

MUFFETTEE n small muff worn over the wrist

MUFFIN n light round flat yeast cake

MUFFINEER n muffin dish

MUFFING > MUFF

MUFFINS > MUFFIN

MUFFISH > MUFF

MUFFLE vb wrap up for warmth or to deaden sound ▷ n something that muffles

MUFFLED > MUFFLE

MUFFLER n scarf

MUFFLERED adj with muffler

MUFFLERS > MUFFLER

MUFFLES > MUFFLE

MUFFLING > MUFFLE

MUFFS > MUFF

MUFLON same as > MOUFFLON

MUFLONS > MUFLON

MUFTI n civilian clothes worn by a person who usually wears a uniform

MUFTIS > MUFTI

MUG n large drinking cup ▷ vb attack in order to rob

MUGEARITE n crystalline rock

MUGFUL same as > MUG

MUGFULS > MUGFUL

MUGG same as > MUG

MUGGA n Australian eucalyptus tree

MUGGAR same as > MUGGER

MUGGARS > MUGGAR

MUGGAS > MUGGA

MUGGED > MUG

MUGGEE n mugged person

MUGGEES > MUGGEE

MUGGER n person who commits robbery with violence

MUGGERS > MUGGER

MUGGIER > MUGGY

MUGGIEST > MUGGY

MUGGILY > MUGGY

MUGGINESS > MUGGY

MUGGING > MUG

MUGGINGS > MUG

MUGGINS n stupid or gullible person

MUGGINSES > MUGGINS

MUGGISH same as > MUGGY

MUGGLE n person who does not possess supernatural powers

MUGGLES > MUGGLE

MUGGS > MUG

MUGGUR same as > MUGGER

MUGGURS > MUGGUR

MUGGY adj (of weather) damp and stifling

MUGHAL same as > MOGUL

MUGHALS > MUGHAL

MUGS > MUG

MUGSHOT n police photograph of person's face

MUGSHOTS > MUGSHOT

MUGWORT n N temperate herbaceous plant with aromatic leaves

MUGWORTS > MUGWORT

MUGWUMP n neutral or independent person

MUGWUMPS > MUGWUMP

MUHLIES > MUHLY

MUHLY n American grass

MUID n former French measure of capacity

MUIDS > MUID

MUIL same as > MULE

MUILS > MUIL

MUIR same as > MOOR

MUIRBURN same as > MOORBURN

MUIRBURNS > MUIRBURN

MUIRS > MUIR

MUIST same as > MUST

MUISTED > MUIST

MUISTING > MUIST

MUISTS > MUIST

MUJAHEDIN n Muslim guerrilla

MUJAHIDIN same as > MUJAHEDIN

MUJIK same as > MUZHIK

MUJIKS > MUJIK

MUKHTAR n lawyer in India

MUKHTARS > MUKHTAR

MUKLUK n soft boot, usually of sealskin

MUKLUKS > MUKLUK

MUKTUK n thin outer skin of the beluga, used as food

MUKTUKS > MUKTUK

MULATRESS n offensive term for a woman with one Black and one White parent

MULATTA n female mulatto

MULATTAS > MULATTA

MULATTO n offensive term for a child of one Black and one White parent ▷ adj of a light brown colour

MULATTOES > MULATTO

MULATTOS > MULATTO

MULBERRY n tree whose leaves are used to feed silkworms ▷ adj dark purple

MULCH n mixture of wet straw, leaves, etc

▷ *vb* cover (land) with mulch

MULCHED > MULCH

MULCHES > MULCH

MULCHING > MULCH

MULCT *vb* cheat or defraud ▷ *n* fine or penalty

MULCTED > MULCT

MULCTING > MULCT

MULCTS > MULCT

MULE *n* offspring of a horse and a donkey ▷ *vb* strike coin with different die on each side

MULED > MULE

MULES *vb* surgically remove folds of skin from a sheep

MULESED > MULES

MULESES > MULES

MULESING > MULES

MULESINGS > MULESING

MULETA *n* small cape attached to a stick used by a matador

MULETAS > MULETA

MULETEER *n* mule driver

MULETEERS > MULETEER

MULEY *adj* (of cattle) having no horns ▷ *n* any hornless cow

MULEYS > MULEY

MULGA *n* Australian acacia shrub growing in desert regions

MULGAS > MULGA

MULIE *n* type of N American deer

MULIES > MULIE

MULING > MULE

MULISH *adj* obstinate

MULISHLY > MULISH

MULL *vb* think (over) or ponder ▷ *n* promontory or headland

MULLA *same as* > MULLAH

MULLAH *n* Muslim scholar, teacher, or religious leader

MULLAHED *same as* > MULLERED

MULLAHING *same as* > MULLERING

MULLAHISM *n* rule by mullahs

MULLAHS > MULLAH

MULLARKY *same as* > MALARKEY

MULLAS > MULLA

MULLED > MULL

MULLEIN *n* type of European plant

MULLEINS > MULLEIN

MULLEN *same as* > MULLEIN

MULLENS > MULLEN

MULLER *n* flat heavy implement used to grind material ▷ *vb* beat up or defeat thoroughly

MULLERED *adj* drunk

MULLERING > MULLER

MULLERS > MULLER

MULLET *n* edible sea fish

MULLETS > MULLET

MULLEY *same as* > MULEY

MULLEYS > MULLEY

MULLIGAN *n* stew made from odds and ends of food

MULLIGANS > MULLIGAN

MULLING > MULL

MULLION *n* vertical dividing bar in a window ▷ *vb* furnish with mullions

MULLIONED > MULLION

MULLIONS > MULLION

MULLITE *n* colourless mineral

MULLITES > MULLITE

MULLOCK *n* waste material from a mine

MULLOCKS > MULLOCK

MULLOCKY > MULLOCK

MULLOWAY *n* large Australian sea fish, valued for sport and food

MULLOWAYS > MULLOWAY

MULLS > MULL

MULMUL *n* muslin

MULMULL *same as* > MULMUL

MULMULLS > MULMULL

MULMULS > MULMUL

MULSE *n* drink containing honey

MULSES > MULSE

MULSH *same as* > MULCH

MULSHED > MULSH

MULSHES > MULSH

MULSHING > MULSH

MULTEITY *n* manifoldness

MULTIAGE *adj* involving different age groups

MULTIATOM *adj* involving many atoms

MULTIBAND *adj* involving more than one waveband

MULTIBANK *adj* involving more than one bank

MULTICAR *adj* involving several cars

MULTICAST *n* broadcast from one source simultaneously to several receivers on a network

MULTICELL *adj* involving many cells

MULTICIDE *n* mass murder

MULTICITY *adj* involving more than one city

MULTICOPY *adj* involving many copies ▷ *n* any of several or many copies (of a book, document, record, etc)

MULTIDAY *adj* involving more than one day

MULTIDISC *adj* involving more than one disc

MULTIDRUG *adj* involving more than one drug

MULTIFID *adj* having or divided into many lobes or similar segments

MULTIFIL *n* fibre made up of many filaments

MULTIFILS > MULTIFIL

MULTIFOIL *n* ornamental design having a large number of foils

MULTIFOLD *adj* many times doubled

MULTIFORM *adj* having many shapes or forms

MULTIGERM *adj* (of plants) having the ability to multiply germinate

MULTIGRID *adj* involving several grids

MULTIGYM *n* exercise apparatus incorporating a variety of weights, used for toning the muscles

MULTIGYMS > MULTIGYM

MULTIHUED *adj* having many colours

MULTIHULL *n* sailing vessel with two or more hulls

MULTIJET *adj* involving more than one jet

MULTILANE *adj* having several lanes

MULTILINE *adj* involving several lines ▷ *n* variety of crop with several lines, each having different genes to improve disease resistance

MULTILOBE *adj* having more than one lobe

MULTIMODE *adj* involving several modes

MULTIPACK *n* form of packaging of foodstuffs, etc, that contains several units and is offered at a price below that of the equivalent number of units

MULTIPAGE *adj* involving many pages

MULTIPARA *n* woman who has given birth to more than one viable fetus or living child

MULTIPART *adj* involving many parts

MULTIPATH *adj* relating to television or radio signals that travel by more than one route from a transmitter and arrive at slightly different times, causing ghost images or audio distortion

MULTIPED *adj* having many feet ▷ *n* insect or animal having many feet

MULTIPEDE *same as* > MULTIPED

MULTIPEDS > MULTIPED

MULTIPION *adj* involving many pions

MULTIPLE *adj* having many parts ▷ *n* quantity which contains another an exact number of times

MULTIPLES > MULTIPLE

MULTIPLET *n* set of closely spaced lines in a spectrum, resulting from small differences between the energy levels of atoms or molecules

MULTIPLEX *n* purpose-built complex containing several cinemas and usu restaurants and bars ▷ *adj* having many elements, complex ▷ *vb* send (messages or signals) or (of messages or signals) be sent by multiplex

MULTIPLY *vb* increase in number or degree

MULTIPOLE *adj* involving more than one pole

MULTIPORT *adj* involving more than one port

MULTIRISK *adj* (of insurance) covering several risks

MULTIROLE *adj* having a number of roles, functions, etc

MULTIROOM *adj* having many rooms

MULTISITE *adj* involving more than one site

MULTISIZE *adj* involving more than size

MULTISTEP *adj* involving several steps

MULTITASK *vb* work at several different tasks simultaneously

MULTITON *adj* weighing several tons

MULTITONE *adj* involving more than one tone

MULTITOOL *n* device containing various tools attached to one handle

MULTITUDE *n* great number

MULTIUNIT *adj* involving more than one unit

MULTIUSE *adj* suitable for more than one use

MULTIUSER > MULTIUSE

MULTIWALL *adj* involving several layers

MULTIWAY *adj* having several paths or routes

MULTIYEAR *adj* involving more than one year

MULTUM *n* substance used in brewing

MULTUMS > MULTUM

MULTURE *n* fee formerly paid to a miller for grinding grain ▷ *vb* take multure

MULTURED > MULTURE

MULTURER > MULTURE

MULTURERS > MULTURE

MULTURES > MULTURE

MULTURING > MULTURE

MUM *n* mother ▷ *vb* act in a mummer's play

MUMBLE *vb* speak indistinctly, mutter ▷ *n* indistinct utterance

MUMBLED > MUMBLE

MUMBLER > MUMBLE

MUMBLERS > MUMBLE

MUMBLES > MUMBLE

MUMBLIER > MUMBLY

MUMBLIEST > MUMBLY

MUMBLING > MUMBLE

MUMBLINGS > MUMBLE

MUMBLY > MUMBLE

MUMCHANCE adj silent

MUMM same as > MUM

MUMMED > MUM

MUMMER n actor in a traditional English folk play ▷ vb perform as a mummer

MUMMERED > MUMMER

MUMMERIES > MUMMERY

MUMMERING n Christmas tradition of house-visiting in parts of Canada

MUMMERS > MUMMER

MUMMERY n performance by mummers

MUMMIA n mummified flesh used as medicine

MUMMIAS > MUMMIA

MUMMICHOG n small American fish

MUMMIED > MUMMY

MUMMIES > MUMMY

MUMMIFIED > MUMMIFY

MUMMIFIES > MUMMIFY

MUMMIFORM adj like a mummy ▷ n sarcophagus

MUMMIFY vb preserve a body as a mummy

MUMMING > MUM

MUMMINGS > MUM

MUMMOCK same as > MAMMOCK

MUMMOCKS > MUMMOCK

MUMMS > MUMM

MUMMY n body embalmed and wrapped for burial in ancient Egypt ▷ vb mummify

MUMMYING > MUMMY

MUMP vb be silent

MUMPED > MUMP

MUMPER > MUMP

MUMPERS > MUMP

MUMPING > MUMP

MUMPISH > MUMPS

MUMPISHLY > MUMPS

MUMPS n infectious disease with swelling in the glands of the neck

MUMPSIMUS n opinion held obstinately

MUMS > MUM

MUMSIER > MUMSY

MUMSIES > MUMSY

MUMSIEST > MUMSY

MUMSINESS n the state of being mumsy

MUMSY n woman whose clothes are out of fashion

MUMU n oven in Papua New Guinea

MUMUS > MUMU

MUN same as > MAUN

MUNCH vb chew noisily and steadily

MUNCHABLE > MUNCH

MUNCHED > MUNCH

MUNCHER > MUNCH

MUNCHERS > MUNCH

MUNCHES > MUNCH

MUNCHIE n small amount of food eaten between meals

MUNCHIER > MUNCHY

MUNCHIES pl n craving for food, induced by alcohol or drugs

MUNCHIEST > MUNCHY

MUNCHING > MUNCH

MUNCHKIN n undersized person or a child, esp an appealing one

MUNCHKINS > MUNCHKIN

MUNCHY adj suitable for snacking

MUNDANE adj everyday

MUNDANELY > MUNDANE

MUNDANER > MUNDANE

MUNDANEST > MUNDANE

MUNDANITY > MUNDANE

MUNDIC n iron pyrites

MUNDICS > MUNDIC

MUNDIFIED > MUNDIFY

MUNDIFIES > MUNDIFY

MUNDIFY vb cleanse

MUNDUNGO n tripe in Spain

MUNDUNGOS > MUNDUNGO

MUNDUNGUS n smelly tobacco

MUNG vb process (computer data)

MUNGA n army canteen

MUNGAS > MUNGA

MUNGCORN n maslin

MUNGCORNS > MUNGCORN

MUNGE vb modify a password into an unguessable state

MUNGED > MUNG

MUNGES > MUNG

MUNGING > MUNG

MUNGO n cheap felted fabric made from waste wool

MUNGOES > MUNGO

MUNGOOSE same as > MONGOOSE

MUNGOOSES > MUNGOOSE

MUNGOS > MUNGO

MUNGS > MUNG

MUNI n municipal radio broadcast

MUNICIPAL adj relating to a city or town

MUNIFIED > MUNIFY

MUNIFIES > MUNIFY

MUNIFY vb fortify

MUNIFYING > MUNIFY

MUNIMENT n means of defence

MUNIMENTS pl n title deeds or similar documents

MUNIS > MUNI

MUNITE vb strengthen

MUNITED > MUNITE

MUNITES > MUNITE

MUNITING > MUNITE

MUNITION vb supply with munitions

MUNITIONS pl n military stores

MUNNION archaic word for > MULLION

MUNNIONS > MUNNION

MUNS > MUN

MUNSHI n secretary in India

MUNSHIS > MUNSHI

MUNSTER variant of > MUENSTER

MUNSTERS > MUNSTER

MUNT n derogatory word for a Black African

MUNTED adj destroyed or ruined; drunk

MUNTER n unattractive person

MUNTERS > MUNTER

MUNTIN n supporting or strengthening bar

MUNTINED adj having a muntin

MUNTING same as > MUNTIN

MUNTINGS > MUNTING

MUNTINS > MUNTIN

MUNTJAC n small Asian deer

MUNTJACS > MUNTJAC

MUNTJAK same as > MUNTJAC

MUNTJAKS > MUNTJAK

MUNTRIE n Australian shrub with green-red edible berries

MUNTRIES > MUNTRIE

MUNTS > MUNT

MUNTU same as > MUNT

MUNTUS > MUNTU

MUON n elementary particle with a mass 207 times that of an electron

MUONIC > MUON

MUONIUM n form of hydrogen

MUONIUMS > MUONIUM

MUONS > MUON

MUPPET n stupid person

MUPPETS > MUPPET

MUQADDAM n person of authority in India

MUQADDAMS > MUQADDAM

MURA n group of people living together in Japanese countryside

MURAENA n moray eel

MURAENAS > MURAENA

MURAENID n eel of moray family

MURAENIDS > MURAENID

MURAGE n tax levied for the construction or maintenance of town walls

MURAGES > MURAGE

MURAL n painting on a wall ▷ adj of or relating to a wall

MURALED same as > MURALLED

MURALIST > MURAL

MURALISTS > MURAL

MURALLED adj decorated with mural

MURALS > MURAL

MURAS > MURA

MURDABAD interj down with

MURDER n unlawful intentional killing of a human being ▷ vb kill in this way

MURDERED > MURDER

MURDEREE n murder victim

MURDEREES > MURDEREE

MURDERER > MURDER

MURDERERS > MURDER

MURDERESS > MURDER

MURDERING > MURDER

MURDEROUS adj intending, capable of, or guilty of murder

MURDERS > MURDER

MURE archaic or literary word for > IMMURE

MURED > MURE

MUREIN n polymer found in cells

MUREINS > MUREIN

MURENA same as > MURAENA

MURENAS > MURENA

MURES > MURE

MUREX n marine gastropod formerly used as a source of purple dye

MUREXES > MUREX

MURGEON vb grimace at

MURGEONED > MURGEON

MURGEONS > MURGEON

MURIATE obsolete name for a > CHLORIDE

MURIATED > MURIATE

MURIATES > MURIATE

MURIATIC adj as in muriatic acid former name for a strong acid used in many industrial processes

MURICATE adj having a surface roughened by numerous short points

MURICATED same as > MURICATE

MURICES > MUREX

MURID n animal of mouse family

MURIDS > MURID

MURIFORM adj like mouse

MURINE n animal belonging to the family that includes rats and mice

MURINES > MURINE

MURING > MURE

MURK n thick darkness ▷ adj dark or gloomy ▷ vb murder (a person)

MURKED > MURK

MURKER > MURK

MURKEST > MURK

MURKIER > MURKY

MURKIEST > MURKY

MURKILY > MURKY

MURKINESS > MURKY

MURKING > MURK

MURKISH > MURK
MURKLY > MURK
MURKS > MURK
MURKSOME > MURK
MURKY *adj* dark or gloomy
MURL *vb* crumble
MURLAIN *n* type of basket
MURLAINS > MURLAIN
MURLAN *same as*
  > MURLAIN
MURLANS > MURLAN
MURLED > MURL
MURLIER > MURL
MURLIEST > MURL
MURLIN *same as*
  > MURLAIN
MURLING > MURL
MURLINS > MURLIN
MURLS > MURL
MURLY > MURL
MURMUR *vb* speak or say in
  a quiet indistinct way
  ▷ *n* continuous low
  indistinct sound
MURMURED > MURMUR
MURMURER > MURMUR
MURMURERS > MURMUR
MURMURING > MURMUR
MURMUROUS > MURMUR
MURMURS > MURMUR
MURPHIES > MURPHY
MURPHY *dialect or informal
  word for* **>** POTATO
MURR *n* former name for
  a cold
MURRA *same as*
  > MURRHINE
MURRAGH *n* type of large
  caddis fly
MURRAGHS > MURRAGH
MURRAIN *n* cattle plague
MURRAINED > MURRAIN
MURRAINS > MURRAIN
MURRAM *n* type of gravel
MURRAMS > MURRAM
MURRAS > MURRA
MURRAY *n* large Australian
  freshwater fish
MURRAYS > MURRAY
MURRE *n* type of guillemot
MURREE *n* native
  Australian
MURREES > MURREE
MURRELET *n* type of small
  diving bird related to the
  auks
MURRELETS > MURRELET
MURREN *same as*
  > MURRAIN
MURRENS > MURREN
MURRES > MURRE
MURREY *adj* mulberry
  colour
MURREYS > MURREY
MURRHA *same as* **>** MURRA
MURRHAS > MURRHA
MURRHINE *adj* of or
  relating to an unknown
  substance used in ancient
  Rome to make vases,
  cups, etc ▷ *n* substance
  so used
MURRHINES > MURRHINE

MURRI *same as* **>** MURREE
MURRIES > MURRY
MURRIN *same as*
  > MURRAIN
MURRINE *same as*
  > MURRHINE
MURRINES > MURRINE
MURRINS > MURRIN
MURRION *same as*
  > MURRAIN
MURRIONS > MURRION
MURRIS > MURRI
MURRS > MURR
MURRY *same as* **>** MORAY
MURTHER *same as*
  > MURDER
MURTHERED > MURTHER
MURTHERER > MURTHER
MURTHERS > MURTHER
MURTI *n* image of a deity,
  which itself is considered
  divine
MURTIS > MURTI
MURVA *n* type of hemp
MURVAS > MURVA
MUS > MU
MUSACEOUS *adj* of,
  relating to, a family of
  tropical flowering plants
  with large leaves and
  clusters of elongated berry
  fruits: includes the
  banana, edible plantain,
  and Manila hemp
MUSANG *n* catlike animal of
  Malaysia
MUSANGS > MUSANG
MUSAR *n* rabbinic literature
  concerned with ethics
MUSARS > MUSAR
MUSCA *n* small
  constellation in the S
  hemisphere
MUSCADEL *same as*
  > MUSCATEL
MUSCADELS > MUSCADEL
MUSCADET *n* white grape,
  grown esp in the Loire
  valley, used for making
  wine
MUSCADETS > MUSCADET
MUSCADIN *n* Parisian
  dandy
MUSCADINE *n* woody
  climbing plant of the
  southeastern US
MUSCADINS > MUSCADIN
MUSCAE > MUSCA
MUSCARINE *n* poisonous
  alkaloid occurring in
  certain mushrooms
MUSCAT *same as*
  > MUSCATEL
MUSCATEL *n* rich sweet
  wine made from muscat
  grapes
MUSCATELS > MUSCATEL
MUSCATS > MUSCAT
MUSCAVADO *same as*
  > MUSCOVADO
MUSCID *n* type of fly
MUSCIDS > MUSCID
MUSCLE *n* tissue in the
  body which produces

movement ▷ *vb* force
  one's way (in)
MUSCLED > MUSCLE
MUSCLEMAN *n* man with
  highly developed muscles
MUSCLEMEN
  > MUSCLEMAN
MUSCLES > MUSCLE
MUSCLEY *adj* of a
  muscular build
MUSCLIER > MUSCLE
MUSCLIEST > MUSCLE
MUSCLING > MUSCLE
MUSCLINGS > MUSCLE
MUSCLY > MUSCLE
MUSCOID *adj* moss-like
  ▷ *n* moss-like plant
MUSCOIDS > MUSCOID
MUSCOLOGY *n* branch of
  botany
MUSCONE *same as*
  > MUSKONE
MUSCONES > MUSCONE
MUSCOSE *adj* like moss
MUSCOVADO *n* raw sugar
  obtained from the juice of
  sugar cane by evaporating
  the molasses
MUSCOVITE *n* pale
  brown, or green, or
  colourless mineral of the
  mica group
MUSCOVY *adj* as in *muscovy
  duck* a kind of duck
MUSCULAR *adj* with
  well-developed muscles
MUSCULOUS *adj* muscular
MUSE *vb* ponder quietly
  ▷ *n* state of abstraction
MUSED > MUSE
MUSEFUL > MUSE
MUSEFULLY > MUSE
MUSEOLOGY *n* science of
  museum organization
MUSER > MUSE
MUSERS > MUSE
MUSES > MUSE
MUSET *same as* **>** MUSIT
MUSETS > MUSET
MUSETTE *n* type of
  bagpipe formerly popular
  in France
MUSETTES > MUSETTE
MUSEUM *n* building where
  objects are exhibited and
  preserved
MUSEUMS > MUSEUM
MUSH *n* soft pulpy mass
  ▷ *interj* order to dogs in a
  sled team to start up or go
  faster ▷ *vb* travel by or
  drive a dogsled
MUSHA *interj* Irish
  exclamation of surprise
MUSHED > MUSH
MUSHER > MUSH
MUSHERS > MUSH
MUSHES > MUSH
MUSHIER > MUSHY
MUSHIEST > MUSHY
MUSHILY > MUSHY
MUSHINESS > MUSHY
MUSHING *n* act of mushing
MUSHINGS > MUSHING

MUSHMOUTH *n* person
  speaking indistinctly
MUSHRAT *same as*
  > MUSKRAT
MUSHRATS *same as*
  > MUSHRAT
MUSHROOM *n* edible
  fungus with a stem and
  cap ▷ *vb* grow rapidly
MUSHROOMS > MUSHROOM
MUSHY *adj* soft and pulpy
MUSIC *n* art form using a
  melodious and
  harmonious combination
  of notes ▷ *vb* play music
MUSICAL *adj* of or like
  music ▷ *n* play or film with
  songs and dancing
MUSICALE *n* party or
  social evening with a
  musical programme
MUSICALES > MUSICALE
MUSICALLY > MUSICAL
MUSICALS > MUSICAL
MUSICIAN *n* person who
  plays or composes music,
  esp as a profession
MUSICIANS > MUSICIAN
MUSICK *same as* **>** MUSIC
MUSICKED > MUSIC
MUSICKER > MUSIC
MUSICKERS > MUSIC
MUSICKING > MUSIC
MUSICKS > MUSICK
MUSICLESS > MUSIC
MUSICS > MUSIC
MUSIMON *same as*
  > MOUFFLON
MUSIMONS > MUSIMON
MUSING > MUSE
MUSINGLY > MUSE
MUSINGS > MUSE
MUSIT *n* gap in fence
MUSITS > MUSIT
MUSIVE *adj* mosaic
MUSJID *same as* **>** MASJID
MUSJIDS > MUSJID
MUSK *n* scent obtained
  from a gland of the musk
  deer or produced
  synthetically ▷ *vb* perfume
  with musk
MUSKED > MUSK
MUSKEG *n* area of
  undrained boggy land
MUSKEGS > MUSKEG
MUSKET *n* long-barrelled
  gun
MUSKETEER *n* (formerly) a
  soldier armed with a
  musket
MUSKETOON *n* small
  musket
MUSKETRY *n* (use of)
  muskets
MUSKETS > MUSKET
MUSKIE *n* large North
  American freshwater
  game fish
MUSKIER > MUSKIE
MUSKIES > MUSKIE
MUSKIEST > MUSKIE
MUSKILY > MUSKY
MUSKINESS > MUSKY

m

MUSKING > MUSK
MUSKIT *same as*
> MESQUITE
MUSKITS > MUSKIT
MUSKLE *same as* **>** MUSSEL
MUSKLES > MUSKLE
MUSKMELON *n* any of
several varieties of melon,
such as the cantaloupe
and honeydew
MUSKONE *n* substance in
musk
MUSKONES > MUSKONE
MUSKOX *n* large Canadian
mammal
MUSKOXEN > MUSKOX
MUSKRAT *n* N American
beaver-like rodent
MUSKRATS > MUSKRAT
MUSKROOT *same as*
> MOSCHATEL
MUSKROOTS > MUSKROOT
MUSKS > MUSK
MUSKY *same as* **>** MUSKIE
MUSLIN *n* fine cotton
fabric
MUSLINED *adj* wearing
muslin
MUSLINET *n* coarse
muslin
MUSLINETS > MUSLINET
MUSLINS > MUSLIN
MUSMON *same as*
> MUSIMON
MUSMONS > MUSMON
MUSO *n* musician who is
concerned with technique
rather than content or
expression
MUSOS > MUSO
MUSPIKE *n* Canadian
freshwater fish
MUSPIKES > MUSPIKE
MUSQUASH *same as*
> MUSKRAT
MUSROL *n* part of bridle
MUSROLS > MUSROL
MUSS *vb* make untidy
▷ *n* state of disorder
MUSSE *same as* **>** MUSS
MUSSED > MUSS
MUSSEL *n* edible shellfish
with a dark hinged shell
MUSSELLED *adj* poisoned
through eating bad
mussels
MUSSELS > MUSSEL
MUSSES > MUSS
MUSSIER > MUSSY
MUSSIEST > MUSSY
MUSSILY > MUSSY
MUSSINESS > MUSSY
MUSSING > MUSS
MUSSITATE *vb* mutter
MUSSY *adj* untidy or
disordered
MUST *vb* used as an
auxiliary to express
obligation, certainty, or
resolution **▷** *n* essential or
necessary thing
MUSTACHE *same as*
> MOUSTACHE
MUSTACHED > MUSTACHE

MUSTACHES > MUSTACHE
MUSTACHIO *n*
moustache, esp a bushy
or elaborate one
MUSTANG *n* wild horse of
SW USA
MUSTANGS > MUSTANG
MUSTARD *n* paste made
from the powdered seeds
of a plant **▷** *adj* brownish-
yellow
MUSTARDS > MUSTARD
MUSTARDY > MUSTARD
MUSTED > MUST
MUSTEE *n* offspring of a
White and a quadroon
MUSTEES > MUSTEE
MUSTELID *n* member of
weasel family
MUSTELIDS > MUSTELID
MUSTELINE *n* type of
predatory mammal of the
family which includes
weasels, ferrets, polecats,
badgers, and otters
MUSTER *vb* summon up
▷ *n* assembly of military
personnel
MUSTERED > MUSTER
MUSTERER > MUSTER
MUSTERERS > MUSTER
MUSTERING > MUSTER
MUSTERS > MUSTER
MUSTH *n* state of frenzied
sexual excitement in the
males of certain large
mammals
MUSTHS > MUSTH
MUSTIER > MUSTY
MUSTIEST > MUSTY
MUSTILY > MUSTY
MUSTINESS > MUSTY
MUSTING > MUST
MUSTS > MUST
MUSTY *adj* smelling
mouldy and stale
MUT *another word for* **>** EM
MUTABLE *adj* liable to
change
MUTABLY > MUTABLE
MUTAGEN *n* any substance
that can induce genetic
mutation
MUTAGENIC > MUTAGEN
MUTAGENS > MUTAGEN
MUTANDA > MUTANDUM
MUTANDUM *n* something
to be changed
MUTANT *n* mutated
animal, plant, etc **▷** *adj*
of or resulting from
mutation
MUTANTS > MUTANT
MUTASE *n* type of enzyme
MUTASES > MUTASE
MUTATE *vb* (cause to)
undergo mutation
MUTATED > MUTATE
MUTATES > MUTATE
MUTATING > MUTATE
MUTATION *same as*
> MUTANT
MUTATIONS > MUTATION
MUTATIVE > MUTATE

MUTATOR *n* something
that causes a mutation
MUTATORS > MUTATOR
MUTATORY *adj* subject to
change
MUTCH *n* close-fitting linen
cap **▷** *vb* cadge
MUTCHED > MUTCH
MUTCHES > MUTCH
MUTCHING > MUTCH
MUTCHKIN *n* Scottish unit
of liquid measure equal to
slightly less than one pint
MUTCHKINS > MUTCHKIN
MUTE *adj* silent **▷** *n* person
who is unable to speak
▷ *vb* reduce the volume or
soften the tone of a
musical instrument
MUTED *adj* (of sound or
colour) softened
MUTEDLY > MUTED
MUTELY > MUTE
MUTENESS > MUTE
MUTER > MUTE
MUTES > MUTE
MUTEST > MUTE
MUTHA *n* taboo slang word
derived from
motherfucker
MUTHAS > MUTHA
MUTI *n* medicine, esp
herbal medicine
MUTICATE *same as*
> MUTICOUS
MUTICOUS *adj* lacking an
awn, spine, or point
MUTILATE *vb* deprive of a
limb or other part
MUTILATED > MUTILATE
MUTILATES > MUTILATE
MUTILATOR > MUTILATE
MUTINE *vb* mutiny
MUTINED > MUTINE
MUTINEER *n* person who
mutinies
MUTINEERS > MUTINEER
MUTINES > MUTINE
MUTING > MUTE
MUTINIED > MUTINY
MUTINIES > MUTINY
MUTINING > MUTINE
MUTINOUS *adj* openly
rebellious
MUTINY *n* rebellion
against authority, esp by
soldiers or sailors **▷** *vb*
commit mutiny
MUTINYING > MUTINY
MUTIS > MUTI
MUTISM *n* state of being
mute
MUTISMS > MUTISM
MUTON *n* part of gene
MUTONS > MUTON
MUTOSCOPE *n* early form
of cine camera
MUTS > MUT
MUTT *n* mongrel dog
MUTTER *vb* utter or speak
indistinctly **▷** *n* muttered
sound or grumble
MUTTERED > MUTTER

MUTTERER > MUTTER
MUTTERERS > MUTTER
MUTTERING > MUTTER
MUTTERS > MUTTER
MUTTON *n* flesh of sheep,
used as food
MUTTONS > MUTTON
MUTTONY > MUTTON
MUTTS > MUTT
MUTUAL *adj* felt or
expressed by each of two
people about the other
▷ *n* mutual company
MUTUALISE *same as*
> MUTUALIZE
MUTUALISM *another name
for* **>** SYMBIOSIS
MUTUALIST
> MUTUALISM
MUTUALITY > MUTUAL
MUTUALIZE *vb* make or
become mutual
MUTUALLY > MUTUAL
MUTUALS > MUTUAL
MUTUCA *same as* **>** MOTUCA
MUTUCAS > MUTUCA
MUTUEL *n* system of
betting
MUTUELS > MUTUEL
MUTULAR > MUTULE
MUTULE *n* flat block in a
Doric cornice
MUTULES > MUTULE
MUTUUM *n* contract for
loan of goods
MUTUUMS > MUTUUM
MUUMUU *n* loose
brightly-coloured dress
worn by women in Hawaii
MUUMUUS > MUUMUU
MUX *vb* spoil
MUXED > MUX
MUXES > MUX
MUXING > MUX
MUZAK *n* piped background
music
MUZAKS > MUZAK
MUZAKY *adj* having a bland
sound
MUZHIK *n* Russian
peasant, esp under the
tsars
MUZHIKS > MUZHIK
MUZJIK *same as* **>** MUZHIK
MUZJIKS > MUZJIK
MUZZ *vb* make (something)
muzzy
MUZZED > MUZZ
MUZZES > MUZZ
MUZZIER > MUZZY
MUZZIEST > MUZZY
MUZZILY > MUZZY
MUZZINESS > MUZZY
MUZZING > MUZZ
MUZZLE *n* animal's mouth
and nose **▷** *vb* prevent
from being heard or
noticed
MUZZLED > MUZZLE
MUZZLER > MUZZLE
MUZZLERS > MUZZLE
MUZZLES > MUZZLE
MUZZLING > MUZZLE

MUZZY *adj* confused or muddled

MVULE *n* tropical African tree

MVULES > MVULE

MWAH *interj* representation of the sound of a kiss

MWALIMU *n* teacher

MWALIMUS > MWALIMU

MY *adj* belonging to me ▷ *interj* exclamation of surprise or awe

MYAL > MYALISM

MYALGIA *n* pain in a muscle or a group of muscles

MYALGIAS > MYALGIA

MYALGIC > MYALGIA

MYALISM *n* kind of witchcraft

MYALISMS > MYALISM

MYALIST > MYALISM

MYALISTS > MYALISM

MYALL *n* Australian acacia with hard scented wood

MYALLS > MYALL

MYASES > MYASIS

MYASIS *same as* > MYIASIS

MYC *n* oncogene that aids the growth of tumorous cells

MYCELE *n* microscopic spike-like structure in mucus

MYCELES > MYCELE

MYCELIA > MYCELIUM

MYCELIAL > MYCELIUM

MYCELIAN > MYCELIUM

MYCELIUM *n* mass forming the body of a fungus

MYCELLA *n* blue-veined Danish cream cheese

MYCELLAS > MYCELLA

MYCELOID > MYCELIUM

MYCETES *n* fungus

MYCETOMA *n* chronic fungal infection, esp of the foot, characterized by swelling, usually resulting from a wound

MYCETOMAS > MYCETOMA

MYCOBIONT *n* fungal constituent of a lichen

MYCOFLORA *n* all fungus growing in particular place

MYCOLOGIC > MYCOLOGY

MYCOLOGY *n* study of fungi

MYCOPHAGY *n* eating of mushrooms

MYCOPHILE *n* person who likes eating mushrooms

MYCORHIZA *n* association of a fungus and a plant in which the fungus lives within or on the outside of the plant's roots forming a symbiotic or parasitic relationship

MYCOSES > MYCOSIS

MYCOSIS *n* any infection or disease caused by fungus

MYCOTIC > MYCOSIS

MYCOTOXIN *n* any of various toxic substances produced by fungi some of which may affect food and others of which are alleged to have been used in warfare

MYCOVIRUS *n* virus attacking fungi

MYCS > MYC

MYDRIASES > MYDRIASIS

MYDRIASIS *n* abnormal dilation of the pupil of the eye, produced by drugs, coma, etc

MYDRIATIC *adj* relating to or causing mydriasis ▷ *n* mydriatic drug

MYELIN *n* white tissue forming an insulating sheath around certain nerve fibres

MYELINE *same as* > MYELIN

MYELINES > MYELINE

MYELINIC > MYELINE

MYELINS > MYELIN

MYELITES > MYELITIS

MYELITIS *n* inflammation of the spinal cord or of the bone marrow

MYELOCYTE *n* immature granulocyte, normally occurring in the bone marrow but detected in the blood in certain diseases

MYELOGRAM *n* X-ray of the spinal cord, after injection with a radio-opaque medium

MYELOID *adj* of or relating to the spinal cord or the bone marrow

MYELOMA *n* tumour of the bone marrow

MYELOMAS > MYELOMA

MYELOMATA > MYELOMA

MYELON *n* spinal cord

MYELONS > MYELON

MYGALE *n* large American spider

MYGALES > MYGALE

MYIASES > MYIASIS

MYIASIS *n* infestation of the body by the larvae of flies

MYIOPHILY *same as* > MYOPHILY

MYLAR *n* tradename for a kind of strong polyester film

MYLARS > MYLAR

MYLODON *n* prehistoric giant sloth

MYLODONS > MYLODON

MYLODONT *same as* > MYLODON

MYLODONTS > MYLODONT

MYLOHYOID *n* muscle in neck

MYLONITE *n* fine-grained metamorphic rock, often showing banding and micaceous fracture, formed by the crushing, grinding, or rolling of the original structure

MYLONITES > MYLONITE

MYLONITIC > MYLONITE

MYNA *same as* > MYNAH

MYNAH *n* tropical Asian starling which can mimic human speech

MYNAHS > MYNAH

MYNAS > MYNA

MYNHEER *n* Dutch title of address

MYNHEERS > MYNHEER

MYOBLAST *n* cell from which muscle develops

MYOBLASTS > MYOBLAST

MYOCARDIA *pl n* muscular tissues of the heart

MYOCLONIC > MYOCLONUS

MYOCLONUS *n* sudden involuntary muscle contraction

MYOFIBRIL *n* type of cell in muscle

MYOGEN *n* albumin found in muscle

MYOGENIC *adj* originating in or forming muscle tissue

MYOGENS > MYOGEN

MYOGLOBIN *n* protein that is the main oxygen-carrier of muscle

MYOGRAM *n* tracings of muscular contractions

MYOGRAMS > MYOGRAM

MYOGRAPH *n* instrument for recording tracings of muscular contractions

MYOGRAPHS > MYOGRAPH

MYOGRAPHY > MYOGRAPH

MYOID *adj* like muscle ▷ *n* section of a retinal cone or rod which is sensitive to changes in light intensity

MYOIDS > MYOID

MYOLOGIC > MYOLOGY

MYOLOGIES > MYOLOGY

MYOLOGIST > MYOLOGY

MYOLOGY *n* study of the structure and diseases of muscles

MYOMA *n* benign tumour composed of muscle tissue

MYOMANCY *n* divination through observing mice

MYOMANTIC > MYOMANCY

MYOMAS > MYOMA

MYOMATA > MYOMA

MYOMATOUS > MYOMA

MYOMERE *n* part of a vertebrate embryo

MYOMERES > MYOMERE

MYONEURAL *adj* involving muscle and nerve

MYOPATHIC > MYOPATHY

MYOPATHY *n* any disease affecting muscles or muscle tissue

MYOPE *n* any person afflicted with myopia

MYOPES > MYOPE

MYOPHILY *n* pollination of plants by flies

MYOPIA *n* short-sightedness

MYOPIAS > MYOPIA

MYOPIC *n* shortsighted person

MYOPICS > MYOPIC

MYOPIES > MYOPY

MYOPS *same as* > MYOPE

MYOPSES > MYOPS

MYOPY *same as* > MYOPIA

MYOSCOPE *n* electrical instrument for stimulating muscles

MYOSCOPES > MYOSCOPE

MYOSES > MYOSIS

MYOSIN *n* protein found in muscle

MYOSINS > MYOSIN

MYOSIS *same as* > MIOSIS

MYOSISES > MYOSIS

MYOSITIS *n* inflammation of muscle

MYOSOTE *same as* > MYOSOTIS

MYOSOTES > MYOSOTE

MYOSOTIS *n* type of hairy-leaved flowering plant, such as the forget-me-not

MYOSTATIN *n* protein that inhibits muscle tissue growth

MYOTIC > MIOSIS

MYOTICS > MIOSIS

MYOTOME *n* any segment of embryonic mesoderm that develops into skeletal muscle

MYOTOMES > MYOTOME

MYOTONIA *n* lack of muscle tone, frequently including muscle spasm or rigidity

MYOTONIAS > MYOTONIA

MYOTONIC > MYOTONIA

MYOTUBE *n* cylindrical cell in muscle

MYOTUBES > MYOTUBE

MYRBANE *same as* > MIRBANE

MYRBANES > MYRBANE

MYRIAD *adj* innumerable ▷ *n* large indefinite number

MYRIADS > MYRIAD

MYRIADTH > MYRIAD

MYRIADTHS > MYRIADTH

MYRIAPOD *n* type of invertebrate with a long segmented body and many legs, such as a centipede

MYRIAPODS > MYRIAPOD

m

MYRICA n dried root bark of the wax myrtle, used as a tonic and to treat diarrhoea

MYRICAS > MYRICA

MYRINGA n eardrum

MYRINGAS > MYRINGA

MYRIOPOD same as > MYRIAPOD

MYRIOPODS > MYRIOPOD

MYRIORAMA n picture made up of different parts

MYRISTIC adj of nutmeg plant family

MYRMECOID adj ant-like

MYRMIDON n follower or henchman

MYRMIDONS > MYRMIDON

MYROBALAN n dried plumlike fruit of various tropical trees, used in dyeing, tanning, ink, and medicine

MYRRH n aromatic gum used in perfume, incense, and medicine

MYRRHIC > MYRRH

MYRRHINE > MURRA

MYRRHOL n oil of myrrh

MYRRHOLS > MYRRHOL

MYRRHS > MYRRH

MYRRHY adj of or like myrrh

MYRTLE n flowering evergreen shrub

MYRTLES > MYRTLE

MYSELF pron reflexive form of I or me

MYSID n small shrimplike crustacean

MYSIDS > MYSID

MYSOST n Norwegian cheese

MYSOSTS > MYSOST

MYSPACE vb search for (someone) on the MySpace website

MYSPACED > MYSPACE

MYSPACES > MYSPACE

MYSPACING > MYSPACE

MYSTAGOG n person instructing others in religious mysteries

MYSTAGOGS > MYSTAGOG

MYSTAGOGY n instruction of those who are preparing for initiation into the mysteries

MYSTERIES > MYSTERY

MYSTERY n strange or inexplicable thing

MYSTIC n person who seeks spiritual knowledge ▷ adj mystical

MYSTICAL adj having a spiritual or religious significance beyond human understanding

MYSTICETE n species of whale

MYSTICISM n belief in or experience of a reality beyond normal human understanding or experience

MYSTICLY > MYSTIC

MYSTICS > MYSTIC

MYSTIFIED > MYSTIFY

MYSTIFIER > MYSTIFY

MYSTIFIES > MYSTIFY

MYSTIFY vb bewilder or puzzle

MYSTIQUE n aura of mystery or power

MYSTIQUES > MYSTIQUE

MYTH n tale with supernatural characters

MYTHI > MYTHUS

MYTHIC same as > MYTHICAL

MYTHICAL adj of or relating to myth

MYTHICISE same as > MYTHICIZE

MYTHICISM n theory that explains miracles as myths

MYTHICIST > MYTHICIZE

MYTHICIZE vb make into or treat as a myth

MYTHIER > MYTHY

MYTHIEST > MYTHY

MYTHISE same as > MYTHIZE

MYTHISED > MYTHISE

MYTHISES > MYTHISE

MYTHISING > MYTHISE

MYTHISM same as > MYTHICISM

MYTHISMS > MYTHISM

MYTHIST > MYTHISM

MYTHISTS > MYTHISM

MYTHIZE same as > MYTHICIZE

MYTHIZED > MYTHIZE

MYTHIZES > MYTHIZE

MYTHIZING > MYTHIZE

MYTHMAKER n person who creates myth

MYTHOI > MYTHOS

MYTHOLOGY n myths collectively

MYTHOMANE n obsession with lying, exaggerating, or relating incredible imaginary adventures as if they had really happened

MYTHOPEIC adj of myths

MYTHOPOET n poet writing on mythical theme

MYTHOS n beliefs of a specific group or society

MYTHS > MYTH

MYTHUS same as > MYTHOS

MYTHY adj of or like myth

MYTILOID adj like mussel

MYXAMEBA same as > MYXAMOEBA

MYXAMEBAE > MYXAMEBA

MYXAMEBAS > MYXAMEBA

MYXAMOEBA n cell produced by spore

MYXEDEMA same as > MYXOEDEMA

MYXEDEMAS > MYXEDEMA

MYXEDEMIC > MYXOEDEMA

MYXO n viral disease of rabbits

MYXOCYTE n cell in mucous tissue

MYXOCYTES > MYXOCYTE

MYXOEDEMA n disease caused by an underactive thyroid gland, characterized by puffy eyes, face, and hands, and mental sluggishness

MYXOID adj containing mucus

MYXOMA n tumour composed of mucous connective tissue

MYXOMAS > MYXOMA

MYXOMATA > MYXOMA

MYXOS > MYXO

MYXOVIRAL > MYXOVIRUS

MYXOVIRUS n any of a group of viruses that cause influenza, mumps, and certain other diseases

MZEE n old person ▷ adj advanced in years

MZEES > MZEE

MZUNGU n White person

MZUNGUS > MZUNGU

Nn

NA *same as* > NAE
NAAM *same as* > NAM
NAAMS > NAAM
NAAN *n* slightly leavened flat Indian bread
NAANS > NAAN
NAARTJE *same as* > NAARTJIE
NAARTJES > NAARTJIE
NAARTJIE *n* tangerine
NAARTJIES > NAARTJIE
NAB *vb* arrest (someone)
NABBED > NAB
NABBER *n* thief
NABBERS > NABBER
NABBING > NAB
NABE *n* Japanese hotpot
NABES > NABE
NABIS *n* Parisian art movement
NABK *n* edible berry
NABKS > NABK
NABLA *another name for* > DEL
NABLAS > NABLA
NABOB *same as* > NAWAB
NABOBERY > NABOB
NABOBESS *n* rich, powerful, or important woman
NABOBISH > NABOB
NABOBISM > NABOB
NABOBISMS > NABOB
NABOBS > NABOB
NABS > NAB
NACARAT *n* red-orange colour
NACARATS > NACARAT
NACELLE *n* streamlined enclosure on an aircraft
NACELLES > NACELLE
NACH *n* Indian dance
NACHAS *n* pleasure
NACHE *n* rump
NACHES > NACHE
NACHO *n* snack of a piece of tortilla with a topping
NACHOS > NACHO
NACHTMAAL *same as* > NAGMAAL
NACKET *n* light lunch, snack
NACKETS > NACKET
NACRE *n* mother of pearl
NACRED > NACRE
NACREOUS *adj* relating to or consisting of mother-of-pearl
NACRES > NACRE
NACRITE *n* mineral

NACRITES > NACRITE
NACROUS > NACRE
NADA *n* nothing
NADAS > NADA
NADIR *n* point in the sky opposite the zenith
NADIRAL > NADIR
NADIRS > NADIR
NADORS *n* thirst brought on by excess of alcohol
NADS *pl n* testicles
NAE *Scot word for* > NO
NAEBODIES > NAEBODY
NAEBODY *Scots variant of* > NOBODY
NAES > NAE
NAETHING *Scots variant of* > NOTHING
NAETHINGS > NAETHING
NAEVE *n* birthmark
NAEVES > NAEVUS
NAEVI > NAEVUS
NAEVOID > NAEVUS
NAEVUS *n* birthmark or mole
NAFF *adj* lacking quality or taste ▷ *vb* go away
NAFFED > NAFF
NAFFER > NAFF
NAFFEST > NAFF
NAFFING > NAFF
NAFFLY > NAFF
NAFFNESS > NAFF
NAFFS > NAFF
NAG *vb* scold or find fault constantly ▷ *n* person who nags
NAGA *n* cobra
NAGANA *n* disease of all domesticated animals of central and southern Africa
NAGANAS > NAGANA
NAGAPIE *n* bushbaby
NAGAPIES > NAGAPIE
NAGARI *n* scripts for writing several languages of India
NAGARIS > NAGARI
NAGAS > NAGA
NAGGED > NAG
NAGGER > NAG
NAGGERS > NAG
NAGGIER > NAG
NAGGIEST > NAG
NAGGING > NAG
NAGGINGLY > NAG
NAGGINGS > NAGGING
NAGGY > NAG

NAGMAAL *n* Communion
NAGMAALS > NAGMAAL
NAGOR *another name for* > REEDBUCK
NAGORS > NAGOR
NAGS > NAG
NAGWARE *n* software that is initially free and then requires payment
NAGWARES > NAGWARE
NAH *same as* > NO
NAHAL *n* agricultural settlement run by an Israeli military youth organization
NAHALS > NAHAL
NAIAD *n* nymph living in a lake or river
NAIADES > NAIAD
NAIADS > NAIAD
NAIANT *adj* swimming
NAIF *less common word for* > NAIVE
NAIFER > NAIF
NAIFEST > NAIF
NAIFLY > NAIVE
NAIFNESS > NAIVE
NAIFS > NAIF
NAIK *n* chief
NAIKS > NAIK
NAIL *n* pointed piece of metal used to join two objects together ▷ *vb* attach (something) with nails
NAILBITER *n* person who bites his or her nails
NAILBRUSH *n* small stiff-bristled brush for cleaning the fingernails
NAILED > NAIL
NAILER > NAIL
NAILERIES > NAILERY
NAILERS > NAIL
NAILERY *n* nail factory
NAILFILE *n* small metal file used to shape and smooth the nails
NAILFILES > NAILFILE
NAILFOLD *n* skin at base of fingernail
NAILFOLDS > NAILFOLD
NAILHEAD *n* decorative device, as on tooled leather, resembling the round head of a nail
NAILHEADS > NAILHEAD
NAILING > NAIL
NAILINGS > NAIL
NAILLESS > NAIL

NAILS > NAIL
NAILSET *n* punch for driving down the head of a nail
NAILSETS > NAILSET
NAIN *adj* own
NAINSELL *n* own self
NAINSELLS > NAINSELL
NAINSOOK *n* light soft plain-weave cotton fabric, used esp for babies' wear
NAINSOOKS > NAINSOOK
NAIRA *n* standard monetary unit of Nigeria, divided into 100 kobo
NAIRAS > NAIRA
NAIRU *n* Non-Accelerating Inflation Rate of Unemployment
NAIRUS > NAIRU
NAISSANCE *French for* > BIRTH
NAISSANT *adj* (of a beast) having only the forepart shown above a horizontal division of a shield
NAIVE *adj* innocent and gullible ▷ *n* person who is naive, esp in artistic style
NAIVELY > NAIVE
NAIVENESS > NAIVE
NAIVER > NAIVE
NAIVES > NAIVE
NAIVEST > NAIVE
NAIVETE *variant of* > NAIVETY
NAIVETES > NAIVETE
NAIVETIES > NAIVETY
NAIVETY *n* state or quality of being naive
NAIVIST > NAIVE
NAKED *adj* without clothes
NAKEDER > NAKED
NAKEDEST > NAKED
NAKEDLY > NAKED
NAKEDNESS > NAKED
NAKER *n* small kettledrum used in medieval music
NAKERS > NAKER
NAKFA *n* standard currency unit of Eritrea
NAKFAS > NAKFA
NALA *n* ravine
NALAS > NALA
NALED *n* type of insecticide
NALEDS > NALED
NALIDIXIC *adj* as in nalidixic acid type of acid
NALLA *n* ravine
NALLAH *same as* > NALLA

NALLAHS > NALLAH
NALLAS > NALLA
NALOXONE n chemical substance that counteracts the effects of opiates by binding to opiate receptors on cells
NALOXONES > NALOXONE
NAM n distraint
NAMABLE > NAME
NAMASKAR n salutation used in India
NAMASKARS > NAMASKAR
NAMASTE n Indian greeting
NAMASTES > NAMASTE
NAMAYCUSH n North American freshwater fish
NAME n word by which a person or thing is known ▷ vb give a name to
NAMEABLE > NAME
NAMECHECK vb mention (someone) by name ▷ n mention of someone's name, for example on a radio programme
NAMED > NAME
NAMELESS adj without a name
NAMELY adv that is to say
NAMEPLATE n small sign on or by a door giving the occupant's name and, sometimes, profession
NAMER > NAME
NAMERS > NAME
NAMES > NAME
NAMESAKE n person with the same name as another
NAMESAKES > NAMESAKE
NAMETAG n identification badge
NAMETAGS > NAMETAG
NAMETAPE n narrow cloth tape bearing the owner's name and attached to an article
NAMETAPES > NAMETAPE
NAMING > NAME
NAMINGS > NAME
NAMMA adj as in namma hole Australian word for a natural well in rock
NAMS > NAM
NAMU n black New Zealand sandfly
NAMUS > NAMU
NAN n grandmother
NANA same as > NAN
NANAS > NANA
NANCE n homosexual man
NANCES >NANCE
NANCIES > NANCY
NANCIFIED adj effeminate
NANCY n effeminate or homosexual boy or man
NANDIN n type of shrub
NANDINA n type of shrub
NANDINAS > NANDINA
NANDINE n African palm civet
NANDINES > NANDINE

NANDINS > NANDIN
NANDOO > NANDU
NANDOOS > NANDOO
NANDU n type of ostrich
NANDUS > NANDU
NANE Scot word for > NONE
NANG adj excellent; cool
NANISM n dwarfism
NANISMS > NANISM
NANITE n microscopically small machine or robot
NANITES > NANITE
NANKEEN n hard-wearing buff-coloured cotton fabric
NANKEENS > NANKEEN
NANKIN same as > NANKEEN
NANKINS > NANKIN
NANNA same as > NAN
NANNAS > NANNA
NANNIE same as > NANNY
NANNIED > NANNY
NANNIES > NANNY
NANNY n woman whose job is looking after young children ▷ vb be too protective towards
NANNYGAI n edible sea fish of Australia which is red in colour and has large prominent eyes
NANNYGAIS > NANNYGAI
NANNYING n act of nannying
NANNYINGS > NANNYING
NANNYISH > NANNY
NANO n science concerned with materials on a molecular scale
NANOBE n microbe that is smaller than the smallest known bacterium
NANOBEE n artificial nanoparticle
NANOBEES > NANOBEE
NANOBES > NANOBE
NANOBOT n microscopically small robot
NANOBOTS > NANOBOT
NANODOT n microscopic cluster of atoms used to store data in a computer chip
NANODOTS > NANODOT
NANOGRAM n unit of measurement
NANOGRAMS > NANOGRAM
NANOGRASS n type of synthetic surface
NANOMETER same as > NANOMETRE
NANOMETRE n one thousand-millionth of a metre
NANOOK n polar bear
NANOOKS > NANOOK
NANOPORE n microscopically small pore in an electrically insulating membrane
NANOPORES > NANOPORE
NANOS > NANO

NANOSCALE adj on very small scale
NANOTECH n technology of very small objects
NANOTECHS > NANOTECH
NANOTESLA n unit of measurement
NANOTUBE n cylindrical molecule of carbon
NANOTUBES > NANOTUBE
NANOWATT n unit of measurement
NANOWATTS > NANOWATT
NANOWIRE n microscopically thin wire
NANOWIRES > NANOWIRE
NANOWORLD n world at a microscopic level, as dealt with by nanotechnology
NANS > NAN
NANUA same as > MOKI
NANUAS > NANUA
NAOI > NAOS
NAOS n ancient classical temple
NAOSES > NAOS
NAP n short sleep ▷ vb have a short sleep
NAPA n type of leather
NAPALM n highly inflammable jellied petrol, used in bombs ▷ vb attack (people or places) with napalm
NAPALMED > NAPALM
NAPALMING > NAPALM
NAPALMS > NAPALM
NAPAS > NAPA
NAPE n back of the neck ▷ vb attack with napalm
NAPED > NAPE
NAPERIES > NAPERY
NAPERY n household linen, esp table linen
NAPES > NAPE
NAPHTHA n liquid mixture used as a solvent and in petrol
NAPHTHAS > NAPHTHA
NAPHTHENE n any of a class of cycloalkanes found in petroleum
NAPHTHOL n white crystalline solid used in dyes
NAPHTHOLS > NAPHTHOL
NAPHTHOUS > NAPHTHA
NAPHTHYL n of, consisting of, or containing either of two forms of the monovalent group $C_{10}H_7-$
NAPHTHYLS > NAPHTHYL
NAPHTOL same as > NAPHTHOL
NAPHTOLS > NAPHTOL
NAPIFORM adj shaped like a turnip
NAPING > NAPE
NAPKIN same as > NAPPY
NAPKINS > NAPKIN
NAPLESS adj threadbare
NAPOLEON n former French gold coin worth 20 francs
NAPOLEONS > NAPOLEON
NAPOO vb kill

NAPOOED > NAPOO
NAPOOING > NAPOO
NAPOOS > NAPOO
NAPPA n soft leather
NAPPAS > NAPPA
NAPPE n mass of rock that has been thrust from its original position by earth movements
NAPPED > NAP
NAPPER n person or thing that raises the nap on cloth
NAPPERS > NAPPER
NAPPES > NAPPE
NAPPIE same as > NAPPY
NAPPIER > NAPPY
NAPPIES > NAPPY
NAPPIEST > NAPPY
NAPPINESS > NAPPY
NAPPING > NAP
NAPPY n piece of absorbent material fastened round a baby's lower torso ▷ adj having a nap
NAPRON same as > APRON
NAPRONS > NAPRON
NAPROXEN n pain-killing drug
NAPROXENS > NAPROXEN
NAPS > NAP
NARAS same as > NARRAS
NARASES > NARAS
NARC n narcotics agent
NARCEEN same as > NARCEINE
NARCEENS > NARCEEN
NARCEIN same as > NARCEINE
NARCEINE n narcotic alkaloid that occurs in opium
NARCEINES > NARCEINE
NARCEINS > NARCEIN
NARCISM n exceptional admiration for oneself
NARCISMS > NARCISM
NARCISSI > NARCISSUS
NARCISSUS n yellow, orange, or white flower related to the daffodil
NARCIST n narcissist
NARCISTIC adj excessively admiring of oneself
NARCISTS > NARCIST
NARCO n officer working in the area of anti-drug operations
NARCOMA n coma caused by intake of narcotic drugs
NARCOMAS > NARCOMA
NARCOMATA > NARCOMA
NARCOS n drug smugglers
NARCOSE same as > NARCOSIS
NARCOSES > NARCOSIS
NARCOSIS n effect of a narcotic
NARCOTIC adj of a drug, such as morphine or opium, which produces numbness and drowsiness, used medicinally but addictive ▷ n such a drug

NARCOTICS > NARCOTIC
NARCOTINE n type of drug
NARCOTISE same as > NARCOTIZE
NARCOTISM n stupor or addiction induced by narcotic drugs
NARCOTIST n person affected by narcotics
NARCOTIZE vb place under the influence of a narcotic drug
NARCS > NARC
NARD n any of several plants with aromatic roots ▷ vb anoint with nard oil
NARDED > NARD
NARDINE > NARD
NARDING > NARD
NARDOO n cloverlike fern which grows in swampy areas
NARDOOS > NARDOO
NARDS > NARD
NARE n nostril
NARES pl n nostrils
NARGHILE another name for > HOOKAH
NARGHILES > NARGHILE
NARGHILLY same as > NARGHILE
NARGHILY same as > NARGHILE
NARGILE same as > NARGHILE
NARGILEH same as > NARGHILE
NARGILEHS > NARGILEH
NARGILES > NARGILE
NARGILIES > NARGILE
NARGILY same as > NARGHILE
NARGUILEH n hookah
NARIAL adj of or relating to the nares
NARIC > NARE
NARICORN n bird's nostril
NARICORNS > NARICORN
NARINE same as > NARIAL
NARIS > NARES
NARK vb annoy ▷ n informer or spy
NARKED > NARK
NARKIER > NARKY
NARKIEST > NARKY
NARKING > NARK
NARKS > NARK
NARKY adj irritable or complaining
NARQUOIS adj malicious
NARRAS n type of shrub
NARRASES > NARRAS
NARRATE vb tell (a story)
NARRATED > NARRATE
NARRATER same as > NARRATOR
NARRATERS > NARRATER
NARRATES > NARRATE
NARRATING > NARRATE
NARRATION n narrating
NARRATIVE n account, story ▷ adj telling a story

NARRATOR n person who tells a story or gives an account of something
NARRATORS > NARRATOR
NARRATORY > NARRATIVE
NARRE adj nearer
NARROW adj small in breadth in comparison to length ▷ vb make or become narrow
NARROWED > NARROW
NARROWER > NARROW
NARROWEST > NARROW
NARROWING > NARROW
NARROWISH > NARROW
NARROWLY > NARROW
NARROWS pl n narrow part of a strait, river, or current
NARTHEX n portico at the west end of a basilica or church
NARTHEXES > NARTHEX
NARTJIE same as > NAARTJIE
NARTJIES > NARTJIE
NARWAL same as > NARWHAL
NARWALS > NARWAL
NARWHAL n arctic whale with a long spiral tusk
NARWHALE same as > NARWHAL
NARWHALES > NARWHALE
NARWHALS > NARWHAL
NARY adv not
NAS vb has not
NASAL adj of the nose ▷ n nasal speech sound, such as English m, n, or ng
NASALISE same as > NASALIZE
NASALISED > NASALISE
NASALISES > NASALISE
NASALISM n nasal pronunciation
NASALISMS > NASALISM
NASALITY > NASAL
NASALIZE vb pronounce nasally
NASALIZED > NASALIZE
NASALIZES > NASALIZE
NASALLY > NASAL
NASALS > NASAL
NASARD n organ stop
NASARDS > NASARD
NASCENCE > NASCENT
NASCENCES > NASCENT
NASCENCY > NASCENT
NASCENT adj starting to grow or develop
NASEBERRY another name for > SAPODILLA
NASHGAB n chatter
NASHGABS > NASHGAB
NASHI n fruit of the Japanese pear
NASHIS > NASHI
NASIAL > NASION
NASION n craniometric point where the top of the nose meets the ridge of the forehead

NASIONS > NASION
NASSELLA n as in nassella tussock type of tussock grass
NASTALIK n type of script
NASTALIKS > NASTALIK
NASTIC adj (of movement of plants) independent of the direction of the external stimulus
NASTIER > NASTY
NASTIES > NASTY
NASTIEST > NASTY
NASTILY > NASTY
NASTINESS > NASTY
NASTY adj unpleasant ▷ n something unpleasant
NASUTE n type of termite
NASUTES > NASUTE
NAT n supporter of nationalism
NATAL adj of or relating to birth
NATALITY n birth rate in a given place
NATANT adj (of aquatic plants) floating on the water
NATANTLY adv in a floating manner
NATATION n swimming
NATATIONS > NATATION
NATATORIA pl n indoor swimming pools
NATATORY adj of or relating to swimming
NATCH sentence substitute naturally ▷ n notch
NATCHES > NATCH
NATES pl n buttocks
NATHELESS prep notwithstanding
NATHEMO same as > NATHEMORE
NATHEMORE adv nevermore
NATHLESS same as > NATHELESS
NATIFORM adj resembling buttocks
NATION n people of one or more cultures or races organized as a single state
NATIONAL adj of or serving a nation as a whole ▷ n citizen of a nation
NATIONALS > NATIONAL
NATIONS > NATION
NATIS > NATES
NATIVE adj relating to a place where a person was born ▷ n person born in a place
NATIVELY > NATIVE
NATIVES > NATIVE
NATIVISM n policy of favouring the natives of a country over the immigrants
NATIVISMS > NATIVISM
NATIVIST > NATIVISM
NATIVISTS > NATIVISM
NATIVITY n birth or origin

NATRIUM obsolete name for > SODIUM
NATRIUMS > NATRIUM
NATROLITE n colourless, white, or yellow zeolite mineral
NATRON n whitish or yellow mineral
NATRONS > NATRON
NATS > NAT
NATTER vb talk idly or chatter ▷ n long idle chat
NATTERED > NATTER
NATTERER > NATTER
NATTERERS > NATTER
NATTERING > NATTER
NATTERS > NATTER
NATTERY adj irritable
NATTIER > NATTY
NATTIEST > NATTY
NATTILY > NATTY
NATTINESS > NATTY
NATTY adj smart and spruce
NATURA n nature
NATURAE > NATURA
NATURAL adj normal or to be expected ▷ n person with an inborn talent or skill
NATURALLY > NATURAL
NATURALS > NATURAL
NATURE n whole system of the physical world not controlled by human beings
NATURED adj having a certain disposition
NATURES > NATURE
NATURING adj creative
NATURISM n nudism
NATURISMS > NATURISM
NATURIST > NATURISM
NATURISTS > NATURISM
NAUCH same as > NAUTCH
NAUCHES > NAUCH
NAUGAHYDE n type of vinyl-coated fabric
NAUGHT n nothing ▷ adv not at all
NAUGHTIER > NAUGHTY
NAUGHTIES > NAUGHTY
NAUGHTILY > NAUGHTY
NAUGHTS > NAUGHT
NAUGHTY adj disobedient or mischievous ▷ n act of sexual intercourse
NAUMACHIA n mock sea fight performed as an entertainment
NAUMACHY same as > NAUMACHIA
NAUNT n aunt
NAUNTS > NAUNT
NAUPLIAL adj of or like a nauplius, the larval form of certain crustaceans
NAUPLII > NAUPLIUS
NAUPLIOID > NAUPLIUS
NAUPLIUS n larva of many crustaceans
NAUSEA n feeling of being about to vomit

n

NAUSEANT *n* substance inducing nausea
NAUSEANTS > NAUSEANT
NAUSEAS > NAUSEA
NAUSEATE *vb* make (someone) feel sick
NAUSEATED > NAUSEATE
NAUSEATES > NAUSEATE
NAUSEOUS *adj* as if about to vomit
NAUTCH *n* intricate traditional Indian dance
NAUTCHES > NAUTCH
NAUTIC *same as* > NAUTICAL
NAUTICAL *adj* of the sea or ships
NAUTICS > NAUTIC
NAUTILI > NAUTILUS
NAUTILOID *n* type of mollusc ▷ *adj* of this type of mollusc
NAUTILUS *n* shellfish with many tentacles
NAV *n* (short for) navigation
NAVAID *n* navigational aid
NAVAIDS > NAVAID
NAVAL *adj* of or relating to a navy or ships
NAVALISM *n* domination of naval interests
NAVALISMS > NAVALISM
NAVALLY > NAVAL
NAVAR *n* system of air navigation
NAVARCH *n* admiral
NAVARCHS > NAVARCH
NAVARCHY *n* navarch's term of office
NAVARHO *n* aircraft navigation system
NAVARHOS > NAVARHO
NAVARIN *n* stew of mutton or lamb with root vegetables
NAVARINS > NAVARIN
NAVARS > NAVAR
NAVE *n* long central part of a church
NAVEL *n* hollow in the middle of the abdomen
NAVELS > NAVEL
NAVELWORT *another name for* > PENNYWORT
NAVES > NAVE
NAVETTE *n* gem cut
NAVETTES > NAVETTE
NAVEW *another name for* > TURNIP
NAVEWS > NAVEW
NAVICERT *n* certificate specifying the contents of a neutral ship's cargo
NAVICERTS > NAVICERT
NAVICULA *n* incense holder
NAVICULAR *adj* shaped like a boat ▷ *n* small boat-shaped bone of the wrist or foot
NAVICULAS > NAVICULA
NAVIES > NAVY
NAVIGABLE *adj* wide, deep, or safe enough

to be sailed through
NAVIGABLY > NAVIGABLE
NAVIGATE *vb* direct or plot the path or position of a ship, aircraft, or car
NAVIGATED > NAVIGATE
NAVIGATES > NAVIGATE
NAVIGATOR *n* person who is skilled in or performs navigation, esp on a ship or aircraft
NAVS > NAV
NAVVIED > NAVVY
NAVVIES > NAVVY
NAVVY *n* labourer employed on a road or a building site ▷ *vb* work as a navvy
NAVVYING > NAVVY
NAVY *n* warships with their crews and organization ▷ *adj* navy-blue
NAW *same as* > NO
NAWAB *n* (formerly) a Muslim ruler or landowner in India
NAWABS > NAWAB
NAY *interj* no ▷ *n* person who votes against a motion ▷ *adv* used for emphasis ▷ *sentence substitute* no
NAYS > NAY
NAYSAID > NAYSAY
NAYSAY *vb* say no
NAYSAYER *n* refuser
NAYSAYERS > NAYSAYER
NAYSAYING > NAYSAY
NAYSAYS > NAYSAY
NAYTHLES *same as* > NATHELESS
NAYWARD *n* towards denial
NAYWARDS *same as* > NAYWARD
NAYWORD *n* proverb
NAYWORDS > NAYWORD
NAZE *n* flat marshy headland
NAZES > NAZE
NAZI *n* person who thinks or acts in a brutal or dictatorial way
NAZIFIED > NAZIFY
NAZIFIES > NAZIFY
NAZIFY *vb* make nazi in character
NAZIFYING > NAZIFY
NAZIR *n* Muslim official
NAZIRS > NAZIR
NAZIS > NAZI
NE *conj* nor
NEAFE *same as* > NIEVE
NEAFES > NEAFE
NEAFFE *same as* > NIEVE
NEAFFES > NEAFFE
NEAL *same as* > ANNEAL
NEALED > NEAL
NEALING > NEAL
NEALS > NEAL
NEANIC *adj* of or relating to the early stages in a life cycle

NEAP *adj* of, relating to, or constituting a neap tide ▷ *vb* be grounded by a neap tide
NEAPED > NEAP
NEAPING > NEAP
NEAPS > NEAP
NEAR *adj* indicating a place or time not far away ▷ *vb* draw close (to) ▷ *prep* at or to a place or time not far away from ▷ *adv* at or to a place or time not far away ▷ *n* left side of a horse or vehicle
NEARBY *adj* not far away ▷ *adv* close at hand
NEARED > NEAR
NEARER > NEAR
NEAREST > NEAR
NEARING > NEAR
NEARISH *adj* quite near
NEARLIER > NEARLY
NEARLIEST > NEARLY
NEARLY *adv* almost
NEARNESS > NEAR
NEARS > NEAR
NEARSHORE *n* area of coastline water ▷ *adj* situated close to a shore ▷ *vb* get business services carried out in a neighbouring country
NEARSIDE *n* side of a vehicle that is nearer the kerb
NEARSIDES > NEARSIDE
NEAT *adj* tidy and clean ▷ *n* domestic bovine animal
NEATEN *vb* make neat
NEATENED > NEATEN
NEATENING > NEATEN
NEATENS > NEATEN
NEATER > NEAT
NEATEST > NEAT
NEATH *short for* > BENEATH
NEATHERD *n* cowherd
NEATHERDS > NEATHERD
NEATLY > NEAT
NEATNESS > NEAT
NEATNIK *n* very neat and tidy person
NEATNIKS > NEATNIK
NEATS > NEAT
NEB *n* beak of a bird or the nose of an animal ▷ *vb* look around nosily
NEBBED > NEB
NEBBICH *same as* > NEBBISH
NEBBICHS > NEBBICH
NEBBING > NEB
NEBBISH *n* unfortunate simpleton
NEBBISHE *same as* > NEBBISH
NEBBISHER *same as* > NEBBISH
NEBBISHES > NEBBISH
NEBBISHY *adj* like a nebbish, wimpy
NEBBUK *n* type of shrub

NEBBUKS > NEBBUK
NEBECK *same as* > NEBBUK
NEBECKS > NEBECK
NEBEK *same as* > NEBBUK
NEBEKS > NEBEK
NEBEL *n* Hebrew musical instrument
NEBELS > NEBEL
NEBENKERN *n* component of insect sperm
NEBISH *same as* > NEBBISH
NEBISHES > NEBISH
NEBRIS *n* fawn-skin
NEBRISES > NEBRIS
NEBS > NEB
NEBULA *n* hazy cloud of particles and gases
NEBULAE > NEBULA
NEBULAR > NEBULA
NEBULAS > NEBULA
NEBULE *n* cloud
NEBULES > NEBULE
NEBULISE *same as* > NEBULIZE
NEBULISED > NEBULISE
NEBULISER *same as* > NEBULIZER
NEBULISES > NEBULISE
NEBULIUM *n* element
NEBULIUMS > NEBULIUM
NEBULIZE *vb* turn (a liquid) into a fine spray
NEBULIZED > NEBULIZE
NEBULIZER *n* device which turns a drug from a liquid into a fine spray which can be inhaled
NEBULIZES > NEBULIZE
NEBULOSE *same as* > NEBULOUS
NEBULOUS *adj* vague and unclear
NEBULY *adj* wavy
NECESSARY *adj* needed to obtain the desired result
NECESSITY *n* circumstances that inevitably require a certain result
NECK *n* part of the body joining the head to the shoulders ▷ *vb* kiss and cuddle
NECKATEE *n* piece of ornamental cloth worn around the neck
NECKATEES > NECKATEE
NECKBAND *n* band around the neck of a garment
NECKBANDS > NECKBAND
NECKBEEF *n* cheap cattle flesh
NECKBEEFS > NECKBEEF
NECKCLOTH *n* large ornamental usually white cravat worn formerly by men
NECKED > NECK
NECKER > NECK
NECKERS > NECK
NECKGEAR *n* any neck covering
NECKGEARS > NECKGEAR

NECKING n activity of kissing and embracing passionately

NECKINGS > NECKING

NECKLACE n decorative piece of jewellery worn around the neck ▷ vb kill (someone) by placing a burning tyre round his or her neck

NECKLACED > NECKLACE

NECKLACES > NECKLACE

NECKLESS > NECK

NECKLET n ornament worn round the neck

NECKLETS > NECKLET

NECKLIKE > NECK

NECKLINE n shape or position of the upper edge of a dress or top

NECKLINES > NECKLINE

NECKPIECE n piece of fur, cloth, etc, worn around the neck or neckline

NECKS > NECK

NECKSHOT n shot in the neck of an animal

NECKSHOTS > NECKSHOT

NECKTIE same as > TIE

NECKTIES > NECKTIE

NECKVERSE n verse read to prove clergy membership

NECKWEAR n articles of clothing, such as ties, scarves, etc, worn around the neck

NECKWEARS > NECKWEAR

NECKWEED n type of plant

NECKWEEDS > NECKWEED

NECROLOGY n list of people recently dead

NECROPHIL n person who is sexually attracted to dead bodies

NECROPOLI pl n burial sites or cemeteries

NECROPSY n postmortem examination ▷ vb carry out a necropsy

NECROSE vb cause or undergo necrosis

NECROSED > NECROSE

NECROSES > NECROSE

NECROSING > NECROSE

NECROSIS n death of cells in the body

NECROTIC > NECROSIS

NECROTISE same as > NECROTIZE

NECROTIZE vb undergo necrosis

NECROTOMY n dissection of a dead body

NECTAR n sweet liquid collected from flowers by bees

NECTAREAL adj of or like nectar

NECTAREAN adj of or like nectar

NECTARED adj filled with nectar

NECTARIAL > NECTARY

NECTARIED adj having nectaries

NECTARIES > NECTARY

NECTARINE n smooth-skinned peach

NECTAROUS > NECTAR

NECTARS > NECTAR

NECTARY n structure secreting nectar in a plant

NED n derogatory name for an adolescent hooligan

NEDDIER > NEDDY

NEDDIES > NEDDY

NEDDIEST > NEDDY

NEDDISH > NEDDY

NEDDY n donkey ▷ adj of or relating to neds

NEDETTE n derogatory name for a female adolescent hooligan

NEDETTES > NEDETTE

NEDS > NED

NEE prep indicating the maiden name of a married woman ▷ adj indicating the maiden name of a married woman

NEED vb require or be in want of ▷ n condition of lacking something

NEEDED > NEED

NEEDER > NEED

NEEDERS > NEED

NEEDFIRE n beacon

NEEDFIRES > NEEDFIRE

NEEDFUL adj necessary or required

NEEDFULLY > NEEDFUL

NEEDFULS n must-haves

NEEDIER > NEEDY

NEEDIEST > NEEDY

NEEDILY > NEEDY

NEEDINESS n state of being needy

NEEDING > NEED

NEEDLE n thin pointed piece of metal with an eye through which thread is passed for sewing ▷ vb goad or provoke

NEEDLED > NEEDLE

NEEDLEFUL n length of thread cut for use in a needle

NEEDLER n needle maker

NEEDLERS > NEEDLER

NEEDLES > NEEDLE

NEEDLESS adj unnecessary

NEEDLIER > NEEDLE

NEEDLIEST > NEEDLE

NEEDLING > NEEDLE

NEEDLINGS > NEEDLE

NEEDLY adj like or full of needles

NEEDMENT n a necessity

NEEDMENTS > NEED

NEEDS adv necessarily ▷ pl n what is required

NEEDY adj poor, in need of financial support

NEELD same as > NEEDLE

NEELDS > NEELD

NEELE same as > NEEDLE

NEELES > NEELE

NEEM n type of large Indian tree

NEEMB same as > NEEM

NEEMBS > NEEMB

NEEMS > NEEM

NEEP dialect name for > TURNIP

NEEPS > NEEP

NEESBERRY same as > NASEBERRY

NEESE same as > NEEZE

NEESED > NEESE

NEESES > NEESE

NEESING > NEESE

NEEZE vb sneeze

NEEZED > NEEZE

NEEZES > NEEZE

NEEZING > NEEZE

NEF n church nave

NEFANDOUS adj unmentionable

NEFARIOUS adj wicked

NEFAST adj wicked

NEFS > NEF

NEG n photographic negative

NEGATE vb invalidate

NEGATED > NEGATE

NEGATER > NEGATE

NEGATERS > NEGATE

NEGATES > NEGATE

NEGATING > NEGATE

NEGATION n opposite or absence of something

NEGATIONS > NEGATION

NEGATIVE adj expressing a denial or refusal ▷ n negative word or statement

NEGATIVED > NEGATIVE

NEGATIVES > NEGATIVE

NEGATON same as > NEGATRON

NEGATONS > NEGATON

NEGATOR > NEGATE

NEGATORS > NEGATE

NEGATORY adj relating to the act of negation

NEGATRON obsolete word for > ELECTRON

NEGATRONS > NEGATRON

NEGLECT vb take no care of ▷ n neglecting or being neglected

NEGLECTED > NEGLECT

NEGLECTER > NEGLECT

NEGLECTOR > NEGLECT

NEGLECTS > NEGLECT

NEGLIGE variant of > NEGLIGEE

NEGLIGEE n woman's lightweight usu lace-trimmed dressing gown

NEGLIGEES > NEGLIGEE

NEGLIGENT adj habitually neglecting duties, responsibilities, etc

NEGLIGES > NEGLIGE

NEGOCIANT n wine merchant

NEGOTIANT n person, nation, organization, etc, involved in a negotiation

NEGOTIATE vb discuss in order to reach (an agreement)

NEGRESS n old-fashioned offensive name for a Black woman

NEGRESSES > NEGRESS

NEGRITUDE n fact of being a Negro

NEGRO n old-fashioned offensive name for a Black man

NEGROES > NEGRO

NEGROHEAD n type of rubber

NEGROID n member of one of the major racial groups of mankind, which is characterized by brown-black skin and tightly-curled hair

NEGROIDAL same as > NEGROID

NEGROIDS > NEGROID

NEGROISM > NEGRO

NEGROISMS > NEGRO

NEGRONI n type of cocktail

NEGRONIS > NEGRONI

NEGROPHIL n person who admires Black people and their culture

NEGS > NEG

NEGUS n hot drink of port and lemon juice

NEGUSES > NEGUS

NEIF same as > NIEVE

NEIFS > NEIF

NEIGH n loud high-pitched sound made by a horse ▷ vb make this sound

NEIGHBOR same as > NEIGHBOUR

NEIGHBORS > NEIGHBOR

NEIGHBOUR n person who lives or is situated near another ▷ vb be or live close (to a person or thing)

NEIGHED > NEIGH

NEIGHING n act of neighing

NEIGHINGS > NEIGHING

NEIGHS > NEIGH

NEINEI n type of plant

NEINEIS > NEINEI

NEIST Scots variant of > NEXT

NEITHER pron not one nor the other ▷ adj not one nor the other (of two)

NEIVE same as > NIEVE

NEIVES > NEIVE

NEK n mountain pass

NEKS > NEK

NEKTON n free-swimming animals in the middle depths of a sea or lake

NEKTONIC > NEKTON

NEKTONS > NEKTON

NELIES same as > NELIS**

NELIS n type of pear
NELLIE n effeminate man
NELLIES > NELLIE
NELLY n as in *not on your nelly* not under any circumstances
NELSON n type of wrestling hold
NELSONS > NELSON
NELUMBIUM same as > NELUMBO
NELUMBO n type of aquatic plant
NELUMBOS > NELUMBO
NEMA n filament
NEMAS > NEMA
NEMATIC n substance having a mesomorphic state in which a linear orientation of the molecules causes anisotropic properties
NEMATICS > NEMATIC
NEMATODE n slender cylindrical unsegmented worm
NEMATODES > NEMATODE
NEMATOID > NEMATODE
NEMERTEAN n type of ribbon-like marine worm ▷ adj of this worm
NEMERTIAN same as > NEMERTEAN
NEMERTINE same as > NEMERTEAN
NEMESES > NEMESIS
NEMESIA n type of southern African plant
NEMESIAS > NEMESIA
NEMESIS n retribution or vengeance
NEMN vb name
NEMNED > NEMN
NEMNING > NEMN
NEMNS > NEMN
NEMOPHILA n any of a genus of low-growing hairy annual plants
NEMORAL adj of a wood
NEMOROUS adj woody
NEMPT adj named
NENE n rare black-and-grey short-winged Hawaiian goose
NENES > NENE
NENNIGAI same as > NANNYGAI
NENNIGAIS > NENNIGAI
NENUPHAR n type of water lily
NENUPHARS > NENUPHAR
NEOBLAST n worm cell
NEOBLASTS > NEOBLAST
NEOCON n supporter of conservative politics
NEOCONS > NEOCON
NEOCORTEX n part of the brain
NEODYMIUM n silvery-white metallic element of lanthanide series
NEOGENE adj of, denoting, or formed during the

Miocene and Pliocene epochs
NEOGOTHIC n style of architecture popular in Britain in the 18th and 19th centuries
NEOLITH n Neolithic stone implement
NEOLITHIC adj relating to the Neolithic period
NEOLITHS > NEOLITH
NEOLOGIAN > NEOLOGY
NEOLOGIC > NEOLOGISM
NEOLOGIES > NEOLOGY
NEOLOGISE same as > NEOLOGIZE
NEOLOGISM n newly-coined word or an established word used in a new sense
NEOLOGIST > NEOLOGISM
NEOLOGIZE vb invent or use neologisms
NEOLOGY same as > NEOLOGISM
NEOMORPH n genetic component
NEOMORPHS > NEOMORPH
NEOMYCIN n type of antibiotic obtained from a bacterium
NEOMYCINS > NEOMYCIN
NEON n element used in illuminated signs and lights ▷ adj of or illuminated by neon
NEONATAL adj relating to the first few weeks of a baby's life
NEONATE n newborn child
NEONATES > NEONATE
NEONED adj lit with neon
NEONOMIAN n Christian religious belief
NEONS > NEON
NEOPAGAN n advocate of the revival of paganism
NEOPAGANS > NEOPAGAN
NEOPHILE n person who welcomes new things
NEOPHILES > NEOPHILE
NEOPHILIA n tendency to like anything new
NEOPHOBE > NEOPHOBIA
NEOPHOBES > NEOPHOBIA
NEOPHOBIA n tendency to dislike anything new
NEOPHOBIC > NEOPHOBIA
NEOPHYTE n beginner or novice
NEOPHYTES > NEOPHYTE
NEOPHYTIC > NEOPHYTE
NEOPILINA n type of mollusc
NEOPLASIA n abnormal growth of tissue
NEOPLASM n any abnormal new growth of tissue
NEOPLASMS > NEOPLASM
NEOPLASTY n surgical formation of new tissue structures or repair of damaged structures

NEOPRENE n synthetic rubber used in waterproof products
NEOPRENES > NEOPRENE
NEOSOUL n soul music combined with other genres
NEOSOULS > NEOSOUL
NEOTEINIA n state of prolonged immaturity
NEOTENIC > NEOTENY
NEOTENIES > NEOTENY
NEOTENOUS > NEOTENY
NEOTENY n persistence of larval or fetal features in the adult form of an animal
NEOTERIC adj belonging to a new fashion or trend ▷ n new writer or philosopher
NEOTERICS > NEOTERIC
NEOTERISE same as > NEOTERIZE
NEOTERISM n the introduction of new things, especially words
NEOTERIST n one who introduces new words or phrases
NEOTERIZE vb introduce new things
NEOTOXIN n harmful agent
NEOTOXINS > NEOTOXIN
NEOTROPIC adj of tropical America
NEOTYPE n specimen selected to replace a type specimen that has been lost or destroyed
NEOTYPES > NEOTYPE
NEP n catmint
NEPENTHE n drug that ancient writers referred to as a means of forgetting grief or trouble
NEPENTHES > NEPENTHE
NEPER n unit expressing the ratio of two quantities
NEPERS > NEPER
NEPETA same as > CATMINT
NEPETAS > NEPETA
NEPHALISM n teetotalism
NEPHALIST n one who advocates or practices nephalism
NEPHELINE n whitish mineral
NEPHELITE same as > NEPHELINE
NEPHEW n son of one's sister or brother
NEPHEWS > NEPHEW
NEPHOGRAM n photograph of a cloud
NEPHOLOGY n study of clouds
NEPHRALGY n pain in a kidney
NEPHRIC adj renal
NEPHRIDIA pl n simple excretory organs of many invertebrates

NEPHRISM n chronic kidney disease
NEPHRISMS > NEPHRISM
NEPHRITE n tough fibrous amphibole mineral
NEPHRITES > NEPHRITE
NEPHRITIC adj of or relating to the kidneys
NEPHRITIS n inflammation of a kidney
NEPHROID adj kidney-shaped
NEPHRON n urine-secreting tubule in the kidney
NEPHRONS > NEPHRON
NEPHROSES > NEPHROSIS
NEPHROSIS n any noninflammatory degenerative kidney disease
NEPHROTIC > NEPHROSIS
NEPIONIC adj of or relating to the juvenile period in the life cycle of an organism
NEPIT n unit of information equal to 1.44 bits
NEPITS > NEPIT
NEPOTIC > NEPOTISM
NEPOTISM n favouritism in business shown to relatives and friends
NEPOTISMS > NEPOTISM
NEPOTIST > NEPOTISM
NEPOTISTS > NEPOTISM
NEPS > NEP
NEPTUNIUM n synthetic radioactive metallic element
NERAL n isomer of citral
NERALS > NERAL
NERD n boring person obsessed with a particular subject
NERDIC same as > GEEKSPEAK
NERDICS > NERDIC
NERDIER > NERD
NERDIEST > NERD
NERDINESS > NERD
NERDISH > NERD
NERDS > NERD
NERDY adj clumsy, socially inept
NEREID n sea nymph in Greek mythology
NEREIDES > NEREID
NEREIDS > NEREID
NEREIS n type of marine worm
NERINE n type of S African plant related to the amaryllis
NERINES > NERINE
NERITE n type of sea snail
NERITES > NERITE
NERITIC adj of or formed in shallow seas near a coastline
NERK n fool

NERKA n type of salmon

NERKAS > NERKA

NERKS > NERK

NEROL n scented liquid

NEROLI n brown oil used in perfumery

NEROLIS > NEROLI

NEROLS > NEROL

NERTS interj nuts

NERTZ same as > NERTS

NERVAL > NERVE

NERVATE adj (of leaves) with veins

NERVATION less common word for > VENATION

NERVATURE same as > NERVATION

NERVE n cordlike bundle of fibres that conducts impulses between the brain and other parts of the body ▷ vb give courage to oneself

NERVED > NERVE

NERVELESS adj numb, without feeling

NERVELET n small nerve

NERVELETS > NERVELET

NERVER n someone or something which nerves

NERVERS > NERVE

NERVES > NERVE

NERVIER > NERVY

NERVIEST > NERVY

NERVILY > NERVY

NERVINE adj having a soothing effect upon the nerves ▷ n nervine drug or agent

NERVINES > NERVINE

NERVINESS > NERVY

NERVING > NERVE

NERVINGS > NERVE

NERVOSITY n nervousness

NERVOUS adj apprehensive or worried

NERVOUSLY > NERVOUS

NERVULAR adj relating to a nervule

NERVULE n small vein

NERVULES > NERVULE

NERVURE n stiff rod in an insect's wing

NERVURES > NERVURE

NERVY adj excitable or nervous

NESCIENCE formal or literary word for > IGNORANCE

NESCIENT > NESCIENCE

NESCIENTS > NESCIENCE

NESH adj sensitive to the cold

NESHER > NESH

NESHEST > NESH

NESHNESS > NESH

NESS n headland, cape

NESSES > NESS

NEST n place or structure in which birds or certain animals lay eggs or give birth to young ▷ vb make or inhabit a nest

NESTABLE > NEST

NESTED > NEST

NESTER > NEST

NESTERS > NEST

NESTFUL n the contents of a nest

NESTFULS > NEST

NESTING > NEST

NESTINGS > NEST

NESTLE vb snuggle

NESTLED > NESTLE

NESTLER > NESTLE

NESTLERS > NESTLE

NESTLES > NESTLE

NESTLIKE > NEST

NESTLING n bird too young to leave the nest

NESTLINGS > NESTLING

NESTMATE n bird that shares a nest with another bird

NESTMATES > NESTMATE

NESTOR n wise old man

NESTORS > NESTOR

NESTS > NEST

NET n fabric of meshes of string, thread, or wire with many openings ▷ vb catch (a fish or animal) in a net ▷ adj left after all deductions

NETBALL n team game in which a ball has to be thrown through a high net

NETBALLER > NETBALL

NETBALLS > NETBALL

NETBOOK n type of small laptop computer

NETBOOKS > NETBOOK

NETE n lyre string

NETES > NETE

NETFUL n the contents of a net

NETFULS > NET

NETHEAD n expert on the internet

NETHEADS > NETHEAD

NETHELESS same as > NATHELESS

NETHER adj lower

NETIZEN n person who regularly uses the internet

NETIZENS > NETIZEN

NETLESS adj without a net

NETLIKE adj resembling a net

NETMINDER n goalkeeper

NETOP n friend

NETOPS > NETOP

NETROOT n activist who promotes a cause via the internet

NETROOTS > NETROOT

NETS > NET

NETSPEAK n jargon, abbreviations, and emoticons typically used by frequent internet users

NETSPEAKS > NETSPEAK

NETSUKE n (in Japan) a carved ornamental toggle

NETSUKES > NETSUKE

NETSURF vb browse the internet for information

NETSURFED > NETSURF

NETSURFER n person who surfs the internet

NETSURFS > NETSURF

NETT same as > NET

NETTABLE adj that can be netted

NETTED > NET

NETTER n person that makes nets

NETTERS > NETTER

NETTIE n enthusiastic user of the internet

NETTIER > NET

NETTIES > NETTY

NETTIEST > NET

NETTING > NET

NETTINGS > NET

NETTLE n plant with stinging hairs on the leaves ▷ vb bother or irritate

NETTLED > NETTLE

NETTLER n one that nettles

NETTLERS > NETTLE

NETTLES > NETTLE

NETTLIER > NETTLE

NETTLIEST > NETTLE

NETTLING > NETTLE

NETTLY adj like a nettle

NETTS > NETT

NETTY n lavatory, originally an earth closet

NETWORK n system of intersecting lines, roads, etc ▷ vb broadcast (a programme) over a network

NETWORKED > NETWORK

NETWORKER n person who forms business contacts through informal social meetings

NETWORKS > NETWORK

NEUK Scot word for > NOOK

NEUKS > NEUK

NEUM same as > NEUME

NEUMATIC adj relating to a neume

NEUME n notational symbol

NEUMES > NEUME

NEUMIC > NEUME

NEUMS > NEUM

NEURAL adj of a nerve or the nervous system

NEURALGIA n severe pain along a nerve

NEURALGIC > NEURALGIA

NEURALLY > NEURAL

NEURATION n arrangement of veins

NEURAXON n biological cell component

NEURAXONS > NEURAXON

NEURILITY n properties of the nerves

NEURINE n poisonous alkaloid

NEURINES > NEURINE

NEURISM n nerve force

NEURISMS > NEURISM

NEURITE n biological cell component

NEURITES > NEURITE

NEURITIC > NEURITIS

NEURITICS > NEURITIS

NEURITIS n inflammation of a nerve or nerves

NEUROCHIP n semiconductor chip designed for use in an electronic neural network

NEUROCOEL n cavity in brain

NEUROGLIA another name for > GLIA

NEUROGRAM same as > ENGRAM

NEUROID adj nervelike ▷ n either of the halves of a neural arch

NEUROIDS > NEUROID

NEUROLOGY n scientific study of the nervous system

NEUROMA n any tumour composed of nerve tissue

NEUROMAS > NEUROMA

NEUROMAST n sensory cell in fish

NEUROMATA > NEUROMA

NEURON same as > NEURONE

NEURONAL > NEURONE

NEURONE n cell specialized to conduct nerve impulses

NEURONES > NEURONE

NEURONIC > NEURONE

NEURONS > NEURON

NEUROPATH n person suffering from or predisposed to a disorder of the nervous system

NEUROPIL n dense network of neurons and glia in the central nervous system

NEUROPILS > NEUROPIL

NEUROSAL adj relating to neurosis

NEUROSES > NEUROSIS

NEUROSIS n mental disorder producing hysteria, anxiety, depression, or obsessive behaviour

NEUROTIC adj emotionally unstable ▷ n neurotic person

NEUROTICS > NEUROTIC

NEUROTOMY n surgical cutting of a nerve, esp to relieve intractable pain

NEURULA n stage of embryonic development

NEURULAE > NEURULA

NEURULAR > NEURULA

NEURULAS > NEURULA

NEUSTIC > NEUSTON

NEUSTON n organisms that float on the surface of open water

NEUSTONIC > NEUSTON
NEUSTONS > NEUSTON
NEUTER adj belonging to a particular class of grammatical inflections in some languages ▷ vb castrate (an animal) ▷ n neuter gender
NEUTERED > NEUTER
NEUTERING > NEUTER
NEUTERS > NEUTER
NEUTRAL adj taking neither side in a war or dispute ▷ n neutral person or nation
NEUTRALLY > NEUTRAL
NEUTRALS > NEUTRAL
NEUTRETTO n neutrino associated with the muon
NEUTRINO n elementary particle with no mass or electrical charge
NEUTRINOS > NEUTRINO
NEUTRON n electrically neutral elementary particle
NEUTRONIC > NEUTRON
NEUTRONS > NEUTRON
NEVE n mass of porous ice, formed from snow
NEVEL vb beat with the fists
NEVELLED > NEVEL
NEVELLING > NEVEL
NEVELS > NEVEL
NEVER adv at no time ▷ sentence substitute at no time ▷ interj surely not!
NEVERMIND n difference
NEVERMORE adv never again
NEVES > NEVE
NEVI > NEVUS
NEVOID > NAEVUS
NEVUS same as > NAEVUS
NEW adj not existing before ▷ adv recently ▷ vb make new
NEWB n newbie
NEWBIE n person new to a job, club, etc
NEWBIES > NEWBIE
NEWBORN adj recently or just born ▷ n newborn baby
NEWBORNS > NEWBORN
NEWBS > NEWB
NEWCOME > NEWCOMER
NEWCOMER n recent arrival or participant
NEWCOMERS > NEWCOMER
NEWED > NEW
NEWEL n post at the top or bottom of a flight of stairs
NEWELL n new thing
NEWELLED > NEWEL
NEWELLS > NEWELL
NEWELS > NEWEL
NEWER > NEW
NEWEST > NEW
NEWFANGLE adj newly come into existence or fashion ▷ n newfangled thing

NEWFOUND adj newly or recently discovered
NEWIE n fresh idea or thing
NEWIES > NEWIE
NEWING > NEW
NEWISH adj fairly new
NEWISHLY > NEWISH
NEWLY adv recently
NEWLYWED n recently married person
NEWLYWEDS > NEWLYWED
NEWMARKET n double-breasted waisted coat with a full skirt
NEWMOWN adj freshly cut
NEWNESS > NEW
NEWNESSES > NEW
NEWS n important or interesting new happenings ▷ vb report
NEWSAGENT n shopkeeper who sells newspapers and magazines
NEWSBEAT n particular area of news reporting
NEWSBEATS > NEWSBEAT
NEWSBOY n boy who sells or delivers newspapers
NEWSBOYS > NEWSBOY
NEWSBREAK n newsflash
NEWSCAST n radio or television broadcast of the news
NEWSCASTS > NEWSCAST
NEWSCLIP n brief extract from news broadcast
NEWSCLIPS > NEWSCLIP
NEWSDESK n news gathering and reporting department
NEWSDESKS > NEWSDESK
NEWSED > NEWS
NEWSES > NEWS
NEWSFEED n service that provides news articles for distribution
NEWSFEEDS > NEWSFEED
NEWSFLASH n brief important news item, which interrupts a radio or television programme
NEWSGIRL n female newsreader or reporter
NEWSGIRLS > NEWSGIRL
NEWSGROUP n forum where subscribers exchange information about a specific subject by e-mail
NEWSHAWK n newspaper reporter
NEWSHAWKS > NEWSHAWK
NEWSHOUND same as > NEWSHAWK
NEWSIE same as > NEWSY
NEWSIER > NEWSY
NEWSIES > NEWSIE
NEWSIEST > NEWSY
NEWSINESS > NEWSY
NEWSING > NEWS
NEWSLESS > NEWS
NEWSMAKER n person whose activities are reported in news

NEWSMAN n male newsreader or reporter
NEWSMEN > NEWSMAN
NEWSPAPER n weekly or daily publication containing news ▷ vb do newspaper related work
NEWSPEAK n language of politicians and officials regarded as deliberately ambiguous and misleading
NEWSPEAKS > NEWSPEAK
NEWSPRINT n inexpensive paper used for newspapers
NEWSREEL n short film giving news
NEWSREELS > NEWSREEL
NEWSROOM n room where news is received and prepared for publication or broadcasting
NEWSROOMS > NEWSROOM
NEWSSHEET n sheet giving news and information
NEWSSTAND n portable stand from which newspapers are sold
NEWSTRADE n newspaper retail
NEWSWIRE n electronic means of delivering up-to-the-minute news
NEWSWIRES > NEWSWIRE
NEWSWOMAN n female newsreader or reporter
NEWSWOMEN > NEWSWOMAN
NEWSY adj full of news ▷ n newsagent
NEWT n small amphibious creature
NEWTON n unit of force
NEWTONS > NEWTON
NEWTS > NEWT
NEWWAVER n member of new wave
NEWWAVERS > NEWWAVER
NEXT adv immediately following ▷ n next person or thing
NEXTDOOR adj in or at the adjacent house or building
NEXTLY > NEXT
NEXTNESS > NEXT
NEXTS > NEXT
NEXUS n connection or link
NEXUSES > NEXUS
NGAI n clan or tribe
NGAIO n small New Zealand tree
NGAIOS > NGAIO
NGANA same as > NAGANA
NGANAS > NGANA
NGARARA n lizard found in New Zealand
NGARARAS > NGARARA
NGATI n (occurring as part of the tribe name) a tribe or clan
NGATIS > NGATI
NGOMA n type of drum
NGOMAS > NGOMA

NGULTRUM n standard monetary unit of Bhutan, divided into 100 chetrum
NGULTRUMS > NGULTRUM
NGWEE n Zambian monetary unit
NGWEES > NGWEE
NHANDU n type of spider
NHANDUS > NHANDU
NIACIN n vitamin of the B complex
NIACINS > NIACIN
NIAGARA n deluge or outpouring
NIAGARAS > NIAGARA
NIAISERIE n simplicity
NIALAMIDE n type of drug
NIB n writing point of a pen ▷ vb provide with a nib
NIBBED > NIB
NIBBING > NIB
NIBBLE vb take little bites (of) ▷ n little bite
NIBBLED > NIBBLE
NIBBLER n person, animal, or thing that nibbles
NIBBLERS > NIBBLER
NIBBLES > NIBBLE
NIBBLIES > NIBBLY
NIBBLING > NIBBLE
NIBBLINGS > NIBBLE
NIBBLY n small item of food
NIBLET n very small piece of food
NIBLETS > NIBLET
NIBLICK n former golf club giving a great deal of lift
NIBLICKS > NIBLICK
NIBLIKE > NIB
NIBS > NIB
NICAD n rechargeable dry-cell battery
NICADS > NICAD
NICCOLITE n copper-coloured mineral
NICE adj pleasant
NICEISH > NICE
NICELY > NICE
NICENESS > NICE
NICER > NICE
NICEST > NICE
NICETIES > NICETY
NICETY n subtle point
NICHE n hollow area in a wall ▷ adj of or aimed at a specialist group or market ▷ vb place (a statue) in a niche
NICHED > NICHE
NICHER vb snigger
NICHERED > NICHER
NICHERING > NICHER
NICHERS > NICHER
NICHES > NICHE
NICHING > NICHE
NICHROME n (tradename) alloy of nickel and chrome
NICHROMES > NICHROME
NICHT Scot word for > NIGHT

NICHTS > NICHT

NICISH > NICE

NICK vb make a small cut in ▷ n small cut

NICKAR n hard seed

NICKARS > NICKAR

NICKED > NICK

NICKEL n silvery-white metal often used in alloys ▷ vb plate with nickel

NICKELED > NICKEL

NICKELIC adj of or containing metallic nickel

NICKELINE another name for > NICCOLITE

NICKELING > NICKEL

NICKELISE same as > NICKELIZE

NICKELIZE vb treat with nickel

NICKELLED > NICKEL

NICKELOUS adj of or containing nickel, esp in the divalent state

NICKELS > NICKEL

NICKER n pound sterling ▷ vb (of a horse) to neigh softly

NICKERED > NICKER

NICKERING > NICKER

NICKERS > NICKER

NICKING > NICK

NICKLE same as > NICKEL

NICKLED > NICKLE

NICKLES > NICKLE

NICKLING > NICKLE

NICKNACK n cheap ornament or trinket

NICKNACKS > NICKNACK

NICKNAME n familiar name given to a person or place ▷ vb call by a nickname

NICKNAMED > NICKNAME

NICKNAMER > NICKNAME

NICKNAMES > NICKNAME

NICKPOINT n break in the slope of a river caused by renewed erosion

NICKS > NICK

NICKSTICK n tally

NICKUM n mischievous person

NICKUMS > NICKUM

NICOISE adj prepared with tomatoes, black olives, garlic and anchovies

NICOL n device for producing plane-polarized light

NICOLS > NICOL

NICOMPOOP n stupid person

NICOTIAN n tobacco user

NICOTIANA n American and Australian plant such as tobacco, with white, yellow, or purple fragrant flowers

NICOTIANS > NICOTIAN

NICOTIN same as > NICOTINE

NICOTINE n poisonous substance found in tobacco

NICOTINED > NICOTINE

NICOTINES > NICOTINE

NICOTINIC > NICOTINE

NICOTINS same as > NICOTIN

NICTATE same as > NICTITATE

NICTATED > NICTATE

NICTATES > NICTATE

NICTATING > NICTATE

NICTATION n act of blinking

NICTITANT adj blinking

NICTITATE vb blink

NID same as > NIDE

NIDAL > NIDUS

NIDAMENTA pl n egg capsules

NIDATE vb undergo nidation

NIDATED > NIDATE

NIDATES > NIDATE

NIDATING > NIDATE

NIDATION n implantation

NIDATIONS > NIDATION

NIDDERING n coward ▷ adj cowardly

NIDDICK n nape of the neck

NIDDICKS > NIDDICK

NIDE vb nest

NIDED > NIDE

NIDERING same as > NIDDERING

NIDERINGS > NIDERING

NIDERLING same as > NIDDERING

NIDES > NIDE

NIDGET n fool ▷ vb assist a woman in labour

NIDGETED > NIDGET

NIDGETING > NIDGET

NIDGETS > NIDGET

NIDI > NIDUS

NIDIFIED > NIDIFY

NIDIFIES > NIDIFY

NIDIFY vb (of a bird) to make or build a nest

NIDIFYING > NIDIFY

NIDING n coward

NIDINGS > NIDING

NIDOR n cooking smell

NIDOROUS > NIDOR

NIDORS > NIDOR

NIDS > NID

NIDUS n nest in which insects or spiders deposit their eggs

NIDUSES > NIDUS

NIE archaic spelling of > NIGH

NIECE n daughter of one's sister or brother

NIECES > NIECE

NIED > NIE

NIEF same as > NIEVE

NIEFS > NIEF

NIELLATED > NIELLO

NIELLI > NIELLO

NIELLIST > NIELLO

NIELLISTS > NIELLO

NIELLO n black compound of sulphur and silver, lead, or copper ▷ vb decorate or treat with niello

NIELLOED > NIELLO

NIELLOING > NIELLO

NIELLOS > NIELLO

NIENTE adv softly fading away

NIES > NIE

NIEVE n closed hand

NIEVEFUL n a closed handful

NIEVEFULS > NIEVE

NIEVES > NIEVE

NIFE n earth's core

NIFES > NIFE

NIFF n stink ▷ vb stink

NIFFED > NIFF

NIFFER vb barter

NIFFERED > NIFFER

NIFFERING > NIFFER

NIFFERS > NIFFER

NIFFIER > NIFF

NIFFIEST > NIFF

NIFFING > NIFF

NIFFNAFF vb trifle

NIFFNAFFS > NIFFNAFF

NIFFS > NIFF

NIFFY > NIFF

NIFTIER > NIFTY

NIFTIES > NIFTY

NIFTIEST > NIFTY

NIFTILY > NIFTY

NIFTINESS > NIFTY

NIFTY adj neat or smart ▷ n nifty thing

NIGELLA n type of Mediterranean plant

NIGELLAS > NIGELLA

NIGER n obsolete offensive term for a Black person

NIGERS > NIGER

NIGGARD n stingy person ▷ adj miserly ▷ vb act in a niggardly way

NIGGARDED > NIGGARD

NIGGARDLY adj stingy ▷ adv stingily

NIGGARDS > NIGGARD

NIGGER n offensive name for a Black person ▷ vb burn

NIGGERDOM > NIGGER

NIGGERED > NIGGER

NIGGERING > NIGGER

NIGGERISH > NIGGER

NIGGERISM n offensive name for an idiom supposedly characteristic of Black people

NIGGERS > NIGGER

NIGGERY > NIGGER

NIGGLE vb worry slightly ▷ n small worry or doubt

NIGGLED > NIGGLE

NIGGLER > NIGGLE

NIGGLERS > NIGGLE

NIGGLES > NIGGLE

NIGGLIER > NIGGLE

NIGGLIEST > NIGGLE

NIGGLING adj petty ▷ n act or instance of niggling

NIGGLINGS > NIGGLING

NIGGLY > NIGGLE

NIGH prep near ▷ adv nearly ▷ adj near ▷ vb approach

NIGHED > NIGH

NIGHER > NIGH

NIGHEST > NIGH

NIGHING > NIGH

NIGHLY > NIGH

NIGHNESS > NIGH

NIGHS > NIGH

NIGHT n time of darkness between sunset and sunrise ▷ adj of, occurring, or working at night

NIGHTBIRD same as > NIGHTHAWK

NIGHTCAP n drink taken just before bedtime

NIGHTCAPS > NIGHTCAP

NIGHTCLUB n establishment for dancing, music, etc, open late at night ▷ vb go to nightclubs

NIGHTED adj darkened

NIGHTFALL n approach of darkness

NIGHTFIRE n fire burned at night

NIGHTGEAR n nightclothes

NIGHTGLOW n faint light from the upper atmosphere in the night sky, esp in low latitudes

NIGHTGOWN n loose dress worn in bed by women

NIGHTHAWK n type of American nightjar

NIGHTIE same as > NIGHTGOWN

NIGHTIES > NIGHTY

NIGHTJAR n nocturnal bird with a harsh cry

NIGHTJARS > NIGHTJAR

NIGHTLESS > NIGHT

NIGHTLIFE n entertainment and social activities available at night in a town or city

NIGHTLIKE > NIGHT

NIGHTLONG adv throughout the night

NIGHTLY adv (happening) each night ▷ adj happening each night

NIGHTMARE n very bad dream

NIGHTMARY > NIGHTMARE

NIGHTS adv at night or on most nights

NIGHTSIDE n dark side

NIGHTSPOT n nightclub

NIGHTTIDE same as > NIGHTTIME

NIGHTTIME n time from sunset to sunrise

NIGHTWARD > NIGHT

NIGHTWEAR n apparel worn in bed or before retiring to bed

n

NIGHTY same as
> NIGHTIE

NIGIRI n small oval block of cold rice, wasabi and fish

NIGIRIS > NIGIRI

NIGRICANT adj black

NIGRIFIED > NIGRIFY

NIGRIFIES > NIGRIFY

NIGRIFY vb blacken

NIGRITUDE n blackness

NIGROSIN same as
> NIGROSINE

NIGROSINE n type of black pigment and dye used in inks and shoe polishes

NIGROSINS > NIGROSIN

NIHIL n nil

NIHILISM n rejection of all established authority and institutions

NIHILISMS > NIHILISM

NIHILIST > NIHILISM

NIHILISTS > NIHILISM

NIHILITY n state or condition of being nothing

NIHILS > NIHIL

NIHONGA n Japanese form of painting

NIHONGAS > NIHONGA

NIKAB same as > NIQAB

NIKABS > NIKAB

NIKAH n Islamic marriage contract

NIKAHS > NIKAH

NIKAU n palm tree native to New Zealand

NIKAUS > NIKAU

NIL n nothing, zero

NILGAI n large Indian antelope

NILGAIS > NILGAI

NILGAU same as
> NILGHAU

NILGAUS > NILGAU

NILGHAI same as
> NILGAI

NILGHAIS > NILGHAI

NILGHAU same as
> NILGAI

NILGHAUS > NILGHAU

NILL vb be unwilling

NILLED > NILL

NILLING > NILL

NILLS > NILL

NILPOTENT n mathematical term

NILS > NIL

NIM n game involving removing one or more small items from several rows or piles ▷ vb steal

NIMB n halo

NIMBED > NIMB

NIMBI > NIMBUS

NIMBLE adj agile and quick

NIMBLER > NIMBLE

NIMBLESSE > NIMBLE

NIMBLEST > NIMBLE

NIMBLEWIT n alert, bright, and clever person

NIMBLY > NIMBLE

NIMBS > NIMB

NIMBUS n dark grey rain cloud

NIMBUSED > NIMBUS

NIMBUSES > NIMBUS

NIMBYISM n practice of objecting to something that will affect one or take place in one's locality

NIMBYISMS > NIMBYISM

NIMBYNESS same as
> NIMBYISM

NIMIETIES > NIMIETY

NIMIETY rare word for
> EXCESS

NIMIOUS > NIMIETY

NIMMED > NIM

NIMMER > NIM

NIMMERS > NIM

NIMMING > NIM

NIMONIC adj as in nimonic alloy type of nickel-based alloy

NIMPS adj easy

NIMROD n hunter

NIMRODS > NIMROD

NIMS > NIM

NINCOM same as
> NICOMPOOP

NINCOMS > NINCOM

NINCUM same as
> NICOMPOOP

NINCUMS > NINCUM

NINE n one more than eight

NINEBARK n North American shrub

NINEBARKS > NINEBARK

NINEFOLD adj having nine times as many or as much ▷ adv by nine times as much or as many

NINEHOLES n type of game

NINEPENCE n coin worth nine pennies

NINEPENNY same as
> NINEPENCE

NINEPIN n skittle used in ninepins

NINEPINS n game of skittles

NINER n (US) student in the ninth grade

NINERS > NINER

NINES > NINE

NINESCORE n product of nine times twenty

NINETEEN n ten and nine

NINETEENS > NINETEEN

NINETIES > NINETY

NINETIETH adj being the ordinal number of ninety in numbering order ▷ n one of 90 approximately equal parts of something

NINETY n ten times nine ▷ determiner amounting to ninety

NINHYDRIN n chemical reagent used for the detection and analysis of primary amines

NINJA n person skilled in ninjutsu

NINJAS > NINJA

NINJITSU same as
> NINJUTSU

NINJITSUS > NINJITSU

NINJUTSU n Japanese martial art

NINJUTSUS > NINJUTSU

NINNIES > NINNY

NINNY n stupid person

NINNYISH > NINNY

NINON n fine strong silky fabric

NINONS > NINON

NINTH n (of) number nine in a series ▷ adj coming after the eighth ▷ adv after the eighth

NINTHLY same as > NINTH

NINTHS > NINTH

NIOBATE n type of salt crystal

NIOBATES > NIOBATE

NIOBIC adj of or containing niobium in the pentavalent state

NIOBITE another name for
> COLUMBITE

NIOBITES > NIOBITE

NIOBIUM n white metallic element

NIOBIUMS > NIOBIUM

NIOBOUS adj of or containing niobium in the trivalent state

NIP vb hurry ▷ n pinch or light bite

NIPA n palm tree of S and SE Asia

NIPAS > NIPA

NIPCHEESE n ship's purser

NIPPED > NIP

NIPPER n small child ▷ vb secure with rope

NIPPERED > NIPPER

NIPPERING > NIPPER

NIPPERKIN n small quantity of alcohol

NIPPERS pl n instrument or tool for pinching or squeezing

NIPPIER > NIPPY

NIPPIEST > NIPPY

NIPPILY > NIPPY

NIPPINESS > NIPPY

NIPPING > NIP

NIPPINGLY > NIP

NIPPLE n projection in the centre of a breast ▷ vb provide with a nipple

NIPPLED > NIPPLE

NIPPLES > NIPPLE

NIPPLING > NIPPLE

NIPPY adj frosty or chilly

NIPS > NIP

NIPTER n type of religious ceremony

NIPTERS > NIPTER

NIQAAB n veil worn by some Muslim women

NIQAABS > NIQAAB

NIQAB n type of veil worn by some Muslim women

NIQABS > NIQAB

NIRAMIAI n sumo wrestling procedure

NIRAMIAIS > NIRAMIAI

NIRL vb shrivel

NIRLED > NIRL

NIRLIE variant of
> NIRLY

NIRLIER > NIRLY

NIRLIEST > NIRLY

NIRLING > NIRL

NIRLIT > NIRL

NIRLS > NIRL

NIRLY adj shrivelled

NIRVANA n absolute spiritual enlightenment and bliss

NIRVANAS > NIRVANA

NIRVANIC > NIRVANA

NIS n friendly goblin

NISBERRY same as
> NASEBERRY

NISEI n native-born citizen of the US or Canada whose parents were Japanese

NISEIS > NISEI

NISGUL n smallest and weakest bird in a brood of chickens

NISGULS > NISGUL

NISH n nothing

NISHES > NISH

NISI adj (of a court order) coming into effect on a specified date

NISSE same as > NIS

NISSES > NISSE

NISUS n impulse towards or striving after a goal

NIT n egg or larva of a louse

NITCHIE n offensive term for a Native American person

NITCHIES > NITCHIE

NITE variant of > NIGHT

NITER same as > NITRE

NITERIE n nightclub

NITERIES > NITERIE

NITERS > NITER

NITERY > NITER

NITES > NITE

NITHER vb shiver

NITHERED > NITHER

NITHERING > NITHER

NITHERS > NITHER

NITHING n coward

NITHINGS > NITHING

NITID adj bright

NITINOL n metal alloy

NITINOLS > NITINOL

NITON less common name for > RADON

NITONS > NITON

NITPICK vb criticize unnecessarily

NITPICKED > NITPICK

NITPICKER > NITPICK

NITPICKS > NITPICK

NITPICKY > NITPICK

NITRAMINE another name for > TETRYL

NITRATE n compound of nitric acid, used as a fertilizer ▷ vb treat with nitric acid or a nitrate
NITRATED > NITRATE
NITRATES > NITRATE
NITRATINE n type of mineral
NITRATING > NITRATE
NITRATION > NITRATE
NITRATOR > NITRATE
NITRATORS > NITRATE
NITRE n potassium nitrate
NITREOUS adj as in nitreous silica, another name for quartz glass
NITRES > NITRE
NITRIC adj of or containing nitrogen
NITRID same as > NITRIDE
NITRIDE n compound of nitrogen ▷ vb make into a nitride
NITRIDED > NITRIDE
NITRIDES > NITRIDE
NITRIDING > NITRIDE
NITRIDS > NITRID
NITRIFIED > NITRIFY
NITRIFIER > NITRIFY
NITRIFIES > NITRIFY
NITRIFY vb treat or cause to react with nitrogen
NITRIL same as > NITRILE
NITRILE n any one of a particular class of organic compounds
NITRILES > NITRILE
NITRILS > NITRIL
NITRITE n salt or ester of nitrous acid
NITRITES > NITRITE
NITRO n nitroglycerine
NITROGEN n colourless odourless gas that forms four fifths of the air
NITROGENS > NITROGEN
NITROLIC adj pertaining to a group of acids
NITROS > NITRO
NITROSO adj of a particular monovalent group
NITROSYL another word for > NITROSO
NITROSYLS > NITROSYL
NITROUS adj derived from or containing nitrogen in a low valency state
NITROX n mixture of nitrogen and oxygen used in diving
NITROXES > NITROX
NITROXYL n type of chemical
NITROXYLS > NITROXYL
NITRY adj nitrous
NITRYL n chemical compound
NITRYLS > NITRYL
NITS > NIT
NITTIER > NITTY
NITTIEST > NITTY

NITTY adj infested with nits
NITWIT n stupid person
NITWITS > NITWIT
NITWITTED > NITWIT
NIVAL adj of or growing in or under snow
NIVATION n weathering of rock around a patch of snow by alternate freezing and thawing
NIVATIONS > NIVATION
NIVEOUS adj resembling snow, esp in colour
NIX sentence substitute be careful! watch out! ▷ n rejection or refusal ▷ vb veto, deny, reject, or forbid (plans, suggestions, etc)
NIXE n water sprite
NIXED > NIX
NIXER n spare-time job
NIXERS > NIXER
NIXES > NIX
NIXIE n female water sprite, usually unfriendly to humans
NIXIES > NIXIE
NIXING > NIX
NIXY same as > NIXIE
NIZAM n (formerly) a Turkish regular soldier
NIZAMATE n territory of the nizam
NIZAMATES > NIZAMATE
NIZAMS > NIZAM
NKOSI n term of address to a superior
NKOSIS > NKOSI
NO interj expresses denial, disagreement, or refusal ▷ adj not any, not a ▷ adv not at all ▷ n answer or vote of 'no'
NOAH n shark
NOAHS > NOAH
NOB n person of wealth or social distinction
NOBBIER > NOB
NOBBIEST > NOB
NOBBILY > NOB
NOBBINESS > NOB
NOBBLE vb attract the attention of
NOBBLED > NOBBLE
NOBBLER > NOBBLE
NOBBLERS > NOBBLE
NOBBLES > NOBBLE
NOBBLING > NOBBLE
NOBBUT adv nothing but
NOBBY > NOB
NOBELIUM n artificially-produced radioactive element
NOBELIUMS > NOBELIUM
NOBILESSE same as > NOBLESSE
NOBILIARY adj of or relating to the nobility
NOBILITY n quality of being noble
NOBLE adj showing or having high moral

qualities ▷ n member of the nobility
NOBLEMAN n person of noble rank
NOBLEMEN > NOBLEMAN
NOBLENESS > NOBLE
NOBLER > NOBLE
NOBLES > NOBLE
NOBLESSE n noble birth or condition
NOBLESSES > NOBLESSE
NOBLEST > NOBLE
NOBLY > NOBLE
NOBODIES > NOBODY
NOBODY pron no person ▷ n person of no importance
NOBS > NOB
NOCAKE n Indian meal made from dried corn
NOCAKES > NOCAKE
NOCEBO n harmless substance that causes harmful effects in patients who expect it to be harmful
NOCEBOS > NOCEBO
NOCENT n guilty person
NOCENTLY > NOCENT
NOCENTS > NOCENT
NOCHEL same as > NOTCHEL
NOCHELED same as > NOTCHELED
NOCHELING n refusal to pay another person's debts
NOCHELLED > NOCHEL
NOCHELS > NOCHEL
NOCK n notch on an arrow or a bow for the bowstring ▷ vb fit (an arrow) on a bowstring
NOCKED > NOCK
NOCKET same as > NACKET
NOCKETS > NOCKET
NOCKING > NOCK
NOCKS > NOCK
NOCTILIO n type of bat
NOCTILIOS > NOCTILIO
NOCTILUCA n type of bioluminescent unicellular marine organism
NOCTUA n type of moth
NOCTUARY n nightly journal
NOCTUAS > NOCTUA
NOCTUID n type of nocturnal moth ▷ adj of or relating to this type of moth
NOCTUIDS > NOCTUID
NOCTULE n any of several large Old World insectivorous bats
NOCTULES > NOCTULE
NOCTUOID adj of or like a noctuid ▷ n member of the family of moths Noctuidae
NOCTUOIDS > NOCTUOID
NOCTURIA n excessive urination during the night
NOCTURIAS > NOCTURIA
NOCTURN n any of the main sections of the office of matins

NOCTURNAL adj of the night ▷ n something active at night
NOCTURNE n short dreamy piece of music
NOCTURNES > NOCTURNE
NOCTURNS > NOCTURN
NOCUOUS adj harmful
NOCUOUSLY > NOCUOUS
NOD vb lower and raise (one's head) briefly in agreement or greeting ▷ n act of nodding
NODAL adj of or like a node
NODALISE same as > NODALIZE
NODALISED same as > NODALISE
NODALISES same as > NODALISE
NODALITY > NODAL
NODALIZE vb make something nodal
NODALIZED > NODALIZE
NODALIZES > NODALIZE
NODALLY > NODAL
NODATED adj knotted
NODATION n knottiness
NODATIONS > NODATION
NODDED > NOD
NODDER > NOD
NODDERS > NOD
NODDIER > NODDY
NODDIES > NODDY
NODDIEST > NODDY
NODDING > NOD
NODDINGLY > NOD
NODDINGS > NOD
NODDLE n head ▷ vb nod (the head), as through drowsiness
NODDLED > NODDLE
NODDLES > NODDLE
NODDLING > NODDLE
NODDY n tropical tern with a dark plumage ▷ adj very easy to use or understand
NODE n point on a plant stem from which leaves grow
NODES > NODE
NODI > NODUS
NODICAL adj of or relating to the nodes of a celestial body
NODOSE adj having nodes or knotlike swellings
NODOSITY > NODOSE
NODOUS same as > NODOSE
NODS > NOD
NODULAR > NODULE
NODULATED > NODULE
NODULE n small knot or lump
NODULED > NODULE
NODULES > NODULE
NODULOSE > NODULE
NODULOUS > NODULE
NODUS n problematic idea, situation, etc
NOEL n Christmas
NOELS > NOEL
NOES > NO

n

NOESES > NOESIS

NOESIS *n* exercise of reason

NOESISES > NOESIS

NOETIC *adj* of or relating to the mind

NOG *same as* > NOGGING

NOGAKU *n* Japanese style of drama

NOGG *same as* > NOG

NOGGED *adj* built with timber and brick

NOGGIN *n* head

NOGGING *n* short horizontal timber member

NOGGINGS > NOGGING

NOGGINS > NOGGIN

NOGGS > NOGG

NOGS > NOG

NOH *n* stylized classic drama of Japan

NOHOW *adv* under any conditions

NOHOWISH > NOHOW

NOIL *n* short or knotted fibres that are separated from the long fibres by combing

NOILIER > NOILY

NOILIES > NOILY

NOILIEST > NOILY

NOILS > NOIL

NOILY *n* dry white vermouth drink from France

NOINT *vb* anoint

NOINTED > NOINT

NOINTER *n* mischievous child

NOINTERS > NOINTER

NOINTING > NOINT

NOINTS > NOINT

NOIR *adj* (of a film) showing characteristics of a *film noir*, in plot or style ▷ *n* film noir

NOIRISH > NOIR

NOIRS > NOIR

NOISE *n* sound, usu a loud or disturbing one

NOISED > NOISE

NOISEFUL > NOISE

NOISELESS *adj* making little or no sound

NOISENIK *n* rock musician who performs loud harsh music

NOISENIKS > NOISENIK

NOISES > NOISE

NOISETTE *n* hazelnut chocolate ▷ *adj* flavoured or made with hazelnuts

NOISETTES > NOISETTE

NOISIER > NOISY

NOISIEST > NOISY

NOISILY > NOISY

NOISINESS > NOISY

NOISING > NOISE

NOISOME *adj* (of smells) offensive

NOISOMELY > NOISOME

NOISY *adj* making a lot of noise

NOLE *same as* > NOLL

NOLES > NOLE

NOLITION *n* unwillingness

NOLITIONS > NOLITION

NOLL *n* head

NOLLS > NOLL

NOLO *vb* as in *nolo contendere* plea indicating that the defendant does not wish to contest the case

NOLOS > NOLO

NOM *n* name

NOMA *n* gangrenous inflammation of the mouth

NOMAD *n* member of a tribe with no fixed dwelling place

NOMADE *same as* > NOMAD

NOMADES > NOMADE

NOMADIC *adj* relating to or characteristic of nomads

NOMADIES > NOMADY

NOMADISE *same as* > NOMADIZE

NOMADISED > NOMADISE

NOMADISES > NOMADISE

NOMADISM > NOMAD

NOMADISMS > NOMAD

NOMADIZE *vb* live as nomads

NOMADIZED > NOMADIZE

NOMADIZES > NOMADIZE

NOMADS > NOMAD

NOMADY *n* practice of living like nomads

NOMARCH *n* head of an ancient Egyptian nome

NOMARCHS > NOMARCH

NOMARCHY *n* any of the provinces of modern Greece

NOMAS > NOMA

NOMBLES *variant spelling of* > NUMBLES

NOMBRIL *n* point on a shield

NOMBRILS > NOMBRIL

NOME *n* any of the former provinces of modern Greece

NOMEN *n* ancient Roman's second name

NOMENS > NOMEN

NOMES > NOME

NOMIC *adj* normal or habitual

NOMINA > NOMEN

NOMINABLE *adj* that can be nominated

NOMINAL *adj* in name only ▷ *n* nominal element

NOMINALLY > NOMINAL

NOMINALS > NOMINAL

NOMINATE *vb* suggest as a candidate ▷ *adj* having a particular name

NOMINATED > NOMINATE

NOMINATES > NOMINATE

NOMINATOR > NOMINATE

NOMINEE *n* candidate

NOMINEES > NOMINEE

NOMISM *n* adherence to laws as a primary exercise of religion

NOMISMS > NOMISM

NOMISTIC > NOMISM

NOMOCRACY *n* government based on the rule of law rather than arbitrary will, terror, etc

NOMOGENY *n* law of life originating as a natural process

NOMOGRAM *n* arrangement of two linear or logarithmic scales

NOMOGRAMS > NOMOGRAM

NOMOGRAPH *same as* > NOMOGRAM

NOMOI > NOMOS

NOMOLOGIC > NOMOLOGY

NOMOLOGY *n* science of law and law-making

NOMOS *n* convention

NOMOTHETE *n* legislator

NOMS > NOM

NON *adv* not

NONA *n* sleeping sickness

NONACID *adj* not acid ▷ *n* nonacid substance

NONACIDIC *adj* not acidic

NONACIDS > NONACID

NONACTING *adj* not acting ▷ *n* acting of poor quality

NONACTION *n* not action

NONACTIVE *adj* not active

NONACTOR *n* person who is not an actor

NONACTORS > NONACTOR

NONADDICT *n* person who is not an addict

NONADULT *n* person who is not an adult

NONADULTS > NONADULT

NONAGE *n* state of being under full legal age

NONAGED > NONAGE

NONAGES > NONAGE

NONAGON *n* geometric figure with nine sides

NONAGONAL > NONAGON

NONAGONS > NONAGON

NONANE *n* type of chemical compound

NONANES > NONANE

NONANIMAL *adj* not animal

NONANOIC *adj* as in *nonanoic acid* colourless oily fatty acid with a rancid odour

NONANSWER *n* unsatisfactory reply ▷ *vb* decline to answer

NONARABLE *adj* not arable

NONARIES > NONARY

NONART *n* something that does not constitute art

NONARTIST *n* person who is not an artist

NONARTS > NONART

NONARY *n* set or group of nine

NONAS > NONES

NONATOMIC *adj* not atomic

NONAUTHOR *n* person who is not the author

NONBANK *n* business or institution that is not a bank but provides similar services

NONBANKS > NONBANK

NONBASIC *adj* not basic

NONBEING *n* philosophical problem relating to the question of existence

NONBEINGS > NONBEING

NONBELIEF *n* state of not believing

NONBINARY *adj* not binary

NONBITING *adj* not biting

NONBLACK *n* person or thing that is not black

NONBLACKS > NONBLACK

NONBODIES > NONBODY

NONBODY *n* nonphysical nature of a person

NONBONDED *adj* not bonded

NONBOOK *n* book with little substance

NONBOOKS > NONBOOK

NONBRAND *adj* not produced by a well-known company

NONBUYING *adj* not buying

NONCAKING *adj* not liable to cake

NONCAMPUS *adj* not on campus

NONCAREER *adj* not career-related

NONCASH *adj* other than cash

NONCASUAL *adj* not casual

NONCAUSAL *adj* not causal

NONCE *n* present time or occasion

NONCEREAL *adj* not cereal

NONCES > NONCE

NONCHURCH *adj* not related to the church ▷ *vb* take away the status of a church

NONCLASS *n* lack of class

NONCLING *adj* not liable to stick

NONCODING *adj* (of DNA) not containing instructions for making protein

NONCOITAL *adj* not involving sexual intercourse

NONCOKING *adj* not liable to coke

NONCOLA *n* soft drink other than cola

NONCOLAS > NONCOLA

NONCOLOR *same as* > NONCOLOUR

NONCOLORS > NONCOLOR
NONCOLOUR n colour such as black or white
NONCOM n person not involved in combat
NONCOMBAT adj not involving combat
NONCOMS > NONCOM
NONCONCUR vb disagree
NONCORE adj not central or essential
NONCOUNT adj not capable of being counted
NONCOUNTY adj not controlled or run by a county
NONCREDIT adj relating to an educational course not providing a credit towards a degree
NONCRIME n incident that is not a crime
NONCRIMES > NONCRIME
NONCRISES > NONCRISIS
NONCRISIS n situation that is not a crisis
NONCYCLIC adj not cyclic
NONDAIRY adj not containing dairy products
NONDANCE n series of movements that do not constitute a dance
NONDANCER n person who is not a dancer
NONDANCES > NONDANCE
NONDEGREE adj not leading to a degree
NONDEMAND adj not involving demand
NONDESERT adj not belonging to the desert
NONDOCTOR n person who is not a doctor
NONDOLLAR adj not involving the dollar
NONDRIP adj (of paint) specially formulated to minimize dripping during application
NONDRIVER n person who does not drive
NONDRUG adj not involving the use of drugs
NONDRYING adj not drying
NONE pron not any
NONEDIBLE n not edible
NONEGO n everything that is outside one's conscious self
NONEGOS > NONEGO
NONELECT n person not chosen
NONELITE adj not elite
NONEMPTY adj mathematical term
NONENDING adj not ending
NONENERGY adj without energy
NONENTITY n insignificant person or thing

NONENTRY n failure to enter
NONEQUAL adj not equal ▷ n person who is not the equal of another person
NONEQUALS > NONEQUAL
NONEROTIC adj not erotic
NONES n (in the Roman calendar) the ninth day before the ides of each month
NONESUCH n matchless person or thing
NONET n piece of music composed for a group of nine instruments
NONETHNIC adj not ethnic
NONETS > NONET
NONETTE same as > NONET
NONETTES > NONETTE
NONETTI same as > NONET
NONETTO same as > NONET
NONETTOS > NONETTO
NONEVENT n disappointing or insignificant occurrence
NONEVENTS > NONEVENT
NONEXEMPT adj not exempt
NONEXOTIC adj not e xotic
NONEXPERT n person who is not an expert
NONEXTANT adj no longer in existence
NONFACT n event or thing not provable
NONFACTOR n something that is not a factor
NONFACTS > NONFACT
NONFADING adj colourfast
NONFAMILY n household that does not consist of a family
NONFAN n person who is not a fan
NONFANS > NONFAN
NONFARM adj not connected with a farm
NONFARMER n person who is not a farmer
NONFAT adj fat free
NONFATAL adj not resulting in or capable of causing death
NONFATTY adj not fatty
NONFEUDAL adj not feudal
NONFILIAL adj not involving parent-child relationship
NONFINAL adj not final
NONFINITE adj not finite
NONFISCAL adj not involving government funds
NONFLUID adj not fluid ▷ n something that is not a fluid
NONFLUIDS > NONFLUID
NONFLYING adj not capable of flying
NONFOCAL adj not focal

NONFOOD n item that is not food ▷ adj relating to items other than food
NONFOODS > NONFOOD
NONFORMAL adj not formal
NONFOSSIL adj not consisting of fossils
NONFROZEN adj not frozen
NONFUEL adj not relating to fuel ▷ n energy not used for generating heat, power, or electricity
NONFUELS > NONFUEL
NONFUNDED adj not receiving funding
NONG n stupid or incompetent person
NONGAME adj not pursued for competitive sport purposes
NONGAY n person who is not gay
NONGAYS > NONGAY
NONGHETTO adj not belonging to the ghetto
NONGLARE adj not causing glare ▷ n any of various nonglare materials
NONGLARES > NONGLARE
NONGLAZED adj not glazed
NONGLOSSY adj not glossy
NONGOLFER n person who is not a golfer
NONGRADED adj not graded
NONGREASY adj not greasy
NONGREEN adj not green
NONGROWTH n failure to grow ▷ adj characterized by a lack of growth
NONGS > NONG
NONGUEST n person who is not a guest
NONGUESTS > NONGUEST
NONGUILT n state of being innocent
NONGUILTS > NONGUILT
NONHARDY adj fragile
NONHEME adj of dietary iron, obtained from vegetable foods
NONHERO n person who is not a hero
NONHEROES > NONHERO
NONHEROIC adj not heroic
NONHOME adj not of the home
NONHUMAN n something not human
NONHUMANS > NONHUMAN
NONHUNTER n person or thing that does not hunt
NONI n tree of SE Asia and the Pacific islands
NONIDEAL adj not ideal
NONILLION n (in Britain, France, and Germany) the

number represented as one followed by 54 zeros
NONIMAGE n person who is not a celebrity
NONIMAGES > NONIMAGE
NONIMMUNE adj not immune
NONIMPACT adj not involving impact ▷ n lack of impact
NONINERT adj not inert
NONINJURY adj not involving injury
NONINSECT n animal that is not an insect
NONIONIC adj not ionic
NONIRON adj not requiring ironing
NONIS > NONI
NONISSUE n matter of little importance
NONISSUES > NONISSUE
NONJOINER n person who does not join (an organisation, etc)
NONJURIES > NONJURY
NONJURING adj refusing the oath of allegiance
NONJUROR n person who refuses to take an oath, as of allegiance
NONJURORS > NONJUROR
NONJURY n trial without a jury
NONKOSHER adj not kosher
NONLABOR same as > NONLABOUR
NONLABOUR adj not concerned with labour
NONLAWYER n person who is not a lawyer
NONLEADED adj not leaded
NONLEAFY adj not leafy
NONLEAGUE adj not belonging to a league
NONLEGAL adj not legal
NONLEGUME n not a pod of the pea or bean family
NONLETHAL adj not resulting in or capable of causing death
NONLEVEL adj not level
NONLIABLE adj not liable
NONLIFE n matter which is not living
NONLINEAL same as > NONLINEAR
NONLINEAR adj not of, in, along, or relating to a line
NONLIQUID n substance which is not liquid
NONLIVES > NONLIFE
NONLIVING adj not living
NONLOCAL adj not of, affecting, or confined to a limited area or part ▷ n person who is not local to an area
NONLOCALS > NONLOCAL
NONLOVING adj not loving
NONLOYAL adj not loyal
NONLYRIC adj without lyrics

n

NONMAJOR n student who is not majoring in a specified subject

NONMAJORS > NONMAJOR

NONMAN n being that is not a man

NONMANUAL adj not manual

NONMARKET adj not relating to markets

NONMATURE adj not mature

NONMEAT n substance that does not contain meat ▷ adj not containing meat

NONMEATS > NONMEAT

NONMEMBER n person who is not a member of a particular club or organization

NONMEN > NONMAN

NONMENTAL adj not mental

NONMETAL n chemical element that forms acidic oxides and is a poor conductor of heat and electricity

NONMETALS > NONMETAL

NONMETRIC adj not metric

NONMETRO adj not metropolitan

NONMOBILE adj not mobile

NONMODAL adj not modal

NONMODERN adj not modern

NONMONEY adj not involving money

NONMORAL adj not involving morality

NONMORTAL adj not fatal

NONMOTILE adj not capable of movement

NONMOVING adj not moving

NONMUSIC n (unpleasant) noise

NONMUSICS > NONMUSIC

NONMUTANT n person or thing that is not mutated

NONMUTUAL adj not mutual

NONNASAL adj not nasal

NONNATIVE adj not native ▷ n person who is not native to a place

NONNAVAL adj not belonging to the navy

NONNEURAL adj not neural

NONNEWS adj not concerned with news

NONNIES > NONNY

NONNOBLE adj not noble

NONNORMAL adj not normal

NONNOVEL n literary work that is not a novel

NONNOVELS > NONNOVEL

NONNY n meaningless word

NONOBESE adj not obese

NONOHMIC adj not having electrical resistance

NONOILY adj not oily

NONORAL adj not oral

NONORALLY > NONORAL

NONOWNER n person who is not an owner

NONOWNERS > NONOWNER

NONPAGAN n person who is not a pagan

NONPAGANS > NONPAGAN

NONPAID adj without payment

NONPAPAL adj not of the pope

NONPAPIST adj not papist

NONPAR adj nonparticipating

NONPAREIL n person or thing that is unsurpassed ▷ adj having no match or equal

NONPARENT n person who is not a parent

NONPARITY n state of not being equal

NONPAROUS adj never having given birth

NONPARTY adj not connected with a political party

NONPAST n grammatical term

NONPASTS > NONPAST

NONPAYING adj (of guests, customers, etc) not expected or requested to pay

NONPEAK n period of low demand

NONPEAKS > NONPEAK

NONPERSON n person regarded as nonexistent or unimportant

NONPLANAR adj not planar

NONPLAY n social behaviour that is not classed as play

NONPLAYER n person not playing

NONPLAYS > NONPLAY

NONPLIANT adj not pliant

NONPLUS vb put at a loss ▷ n state of utter perplexity prohibiting action or speech

NONPLUSED > NONPLUS

NONPLUSES > NONPLUS

NONPOETIC adj not poetic

NONPOINT adj without a specific site

NONPOLAR adj not polar

NONPOLICE adj not related to the police

NONPOOR adj not poor ▷ n person who is not poor

NONPOORS > NONPOOR

NONPOROUS adj not permeable to water, air, or other fluids

NONPOSTAL adj not postal

NONPRINT adj published in a format other than print on paper

NONPROFIT n organization that is not intended to make a profit

NONPROS vb enter a judgment of non prosequitur

NONPROVEN adj not tried and tested

NONPUBLIC adj not public

NONQUOTA adj not included in a quota

NONRACIAL adj not related to racial factors or discrimination

NONRANDOM adj not random

NONRATED adj not rated

NONREADER n person who does not or cannot read

NONRETURN adj denoting a mechanism that permits flow in a pipe in one direction only

NONRHOTIC adj denoting or speaking a dialect of English in which preconsonantal r s are not pronounced

NONRIGID adj not rigid

NONRIOTER n person who does not participate in a riot

NONRIVAL n person or thing not competing for success

NONRIVALS > NONRIVAL

NONROYAL adj not royal ▷ n person who is not a member of a royal family

NONROYALS > NONROYAL

NONRUBBER adj not containing rubber

NONRULING adj not ruling

NONRUN adj (of tights) not laddering

NONRUNNER n person who is not a runner

NONRURAL adj not rural

NONSACRED adj not sacred

NONSALINE adj not containing salt

NONSCHOOL adj not relating to school

NONSECRET adj not sacred

NONSECURE adj not secure

NONSELF n foreign molecule in the body

NONSELVES > NONSELF

NONSENSE n something that has or makes no sense ▷ interj exclamation of disagreement

NONSENSES > NONSENSE

NONSERIAL adj not serial

NONSEXIST adj not discriminating on the basis of sex, esp not against women

NONSEXUAL adj not of, relating to, or characterized by sex or sexuality

NONSHRINK adj not likely to shrink

NONSIGNER n person who cannot use sign language

NONSKATER n person who does not skate

NONSKED n non-scheduled aeroplane

NONSKEDS > NONSKED

NONSKID adj designed to reduce skidding

NONSKIER n person who does not ski

NONSKIERS > NONSKIER

NONSLIP adj designed to prevent slipping

NONSMOKER n person who does not smoke

NONSOCIAL adj not social

NONSOLAR adj not related to the sun

NONSOLID n substance that is not a solid

NONSOLIDS > NONSOLID

NONSPEECH adj not involving speech ▷ n absence of speech

NONSTAPLE adj not staple

NONSTATIC adj not static

NONSTEADY adj not steady

NONSTICK adj coated with a substance that food will not stick to when cooked

NONSTICKY adj not sticky

NONSTOP adv without a stop ▷ adj without a stop ▷ n nonstop flight

NONSTOPS > NONSTOP

NONSTORY n story of little substance or importance

NONSTYLE n style that cannot be identified

NONSTYLES > NONSTYLE

NONSUCH same as > NONESUCH

NONSUCHES > NONSUCH

NONSUGAR n substance that is not a sugar

NONSUGARS > NONSUGAR

NONSUIT n order of a judge dismissing a suit ▷ vb order the dismissal of the suit of (a person)

NONSUITED > NONSUIT

NONSUITS > NONSUIT

NONSYSTEM adj having no system

NONTALKER n person who does not talk

NONTARGET adj not being a target

NONTARIFF adj without tariff

NONTAX *n* tax that has little real effect

NONTAXES > NONTAX

NONTHEIST *n* person who believes the existence or non-existence of God is irrelevant

NONTIDAL *adj* not having a tide

NONTITLE *adj* without title

NONTONAL *adj* not written in a key

NONTONIC *adj* not tonic

NONTOXIC *adj* not poisonous

NONTRAGIC *adj* not tragic

NONTRIBAL *adj* not tribal

NONTRUMP *adj* not of the trump suit

NONTRUTH *same as* > UNTRUTH

NONTRUTHS > NONTRUTH

NONUNION *adj* (of a company) not employing trade union members ▷ *n* failure of broken bones or bone fragments to heal

NONUNIONS > NONUNION

NONUNIQUE *adj* not unique

NONUPLE *adj* ninefold ▷ *n* ninefold number

NONUPLES > NONUPLE

NONUPLET *n* child born in a multiple birth of nine siblings

NONUPLETS > NONUPLET

NONURBAN *adj* rural

NONURGENT *adj* not urgent

NONUSABLE *adj* not usable

NONUSE *n* failure to use

NONUSER > NONUSE

NONUSERS > NONUSE

NONUSES > NONUSE

NONUSING > NONUSE

NONVACANT *adj* not vacant

NONVALID *adj* not valid

NONVECTOR *n* quantity without size and direction

NONVENOUS *adj* not venous

NONVERBAL *adj* not involving the use of language

NONVESTED *adj* not vested

NONVIABLE *adj* not viable

NONVIEWER *n* person who does not watch (television)

NONVIRAL *adj* not caused by a virus

NONVIRGIN *n* person who is not a virgin

NONVIRILE *adj* not virile

NONVISUAL *adj* not visual

NONVITAL *adj* not vital

NONVOCAL *n* music track without singing

NONVOCALS > NONVOCAL

NONVOTER *n* person who does not vote

NONVOTERS > NONVOTER

NONVOTING *adj* (of shares in a company) not entitling the owner to vote at company meetings

NONWAGE *adj* not part of wages

NONWAR *n* state of nonviolence

NONWARS > NONWAR

NONWHITE *n* person who is not white

NONWHITES > NONWHITE

NONWINGED *adj* without wings

NONWOODY *adj* not woody

NONWOOL *adj* not wool

NONWORD *n* series of letters not recognised as a word

NONWORDS > NONWORD

NONWORK *adj* not involving work ▷ *n* part of life which does not involve work

NONWORKER *n* person who does not work

NONWORKS > NONWORK

NONWOVEN *n* material made by a method other than weaving

NONWOVENS > NONWOVEN

NONWRITER *n* person who is not a writer

NONYL *n* type of chemical

NONYLS > NONYL

NONZERO *adj* not equal to zero

NOO *n* type of Japanese musical drama

NOOB *same as* > NEWBIE

NOOBS > NOOB

NOODGE *vb* annoy persistently

NOODGED > NOODGE

NOODGES > NOODGE

NOODGING > NOODGE

NOODLE *n* simpleton ▷ *vb* improvise aimlessly on a musical instrument

NOODLED > NOODLE

NOODLEDOM *n* state of being a simpleton

NOODLES > NOODLE

NOODLING *n* aimless musical improvisation

NOODLINGS > NOODLING

NOOGIE *n* act of inflicting pain by rubbing head hard

NOOGIES > NOOGIE

NOOIT *interj* South African exclamation of surprise

NOOK *n* corner or recess

NOOKIE *same as* > NOOKY

NOOKIER > NOOKY

NOOKIES > NOOKIE

NOOKIEST > NOOKY

NOOKLIKE > NOOK

NOOKS > NOOK

NOOKY *n* sexual intercourse ▷ *adj* resembling a nook

NOOLOGIES > NOOLOGY

NOOLOGY *n* study of intuition

NOOMETRY *n* mind measurement

NOON *n* twelve o'clock midday ▷ *vb* take a rest at noon

NOONDAY *adj* happening at noon ▷ *n* middle of the day

NOONDAYS > NOONDAY

NOONED > NOON

NOONER *n* sexual encounter during a lunch hour

NOONERS > NOONER

NOONING *n* midday break for rest or food

NOONINGS > NOONING

NOONS > NOON

NOONTIDE *same as* > NOONTIME

NOONTIDES > NOONTIDE

NOONTIME *n* middle of the day

NOONTIMES > NOONTIME

NOOP *n* point of the elbow

NOOPS > NOOP

NOOSE *n* loop in the end of a rope, tied with a slipknot

NOOSED > NOOSE

NOOSER *n* person who uses a noose

NOOSERS > NOOSER

NOOSES > NOOSE

NOOSING > NOOSE

NOOSPHERE *n* sphere of human thought

NOOTROPIC *adj* acting on mind

NOPAL *n* type of cactus

NOPALES > NOPAL

NOPALITO *n* small cactus

NOPALITOS > NOPALITO

NOPALS > NOPAL

NOPE *interj* no

NOPLACE *same as* > NOWHERE

NOR *prep* and not

NORDIC *adj* of competitions in cross-country racing and ski-jumping

NORI *n* edible seaweed

NORIA *n* water wheel with buckets attached to its rim

NORIAS > NORIA

NORIMON *n* Japanese passenger vehicle

NORIMONS > NORIMON

NORIS > NORI

NORITE *n* variety of gabbro

NORITES > NORITE

NORITIC > NORITE

NORK *n* female breast

NORKS > NORK

NORLAND *n* north part of a country or the earth

NORLANDS > NORLAND

NORM *n* standard that is regarded as normal

NORMA *n* norm or standard

NORMAL *adj* usual, regular, or typical ▷ *n* usual or regular state, degree or form

NORMALCY > NORMAL

NORMALISE *same as* > NORMALIZE

NORMALITY > NORMAL

NORMALIZE *vb* make or become normal

NORMALLY *adv* as a rule

NORMALS > NORMAL

NORMAN *n* post used for winding on a ship

NORMANDE *n* type of cattle

NORMANDES > NORMANDE

NORMANS > NORMAN

NORMAS > NORMA

NORMATIVE *adj* of or setting a norm or standard

NORMED *n* mathematical term

NORMLESS *adj* without a norm

NORMS > NORM

NOROVIRUS *n* virus that causes gastroenteritis

NORSEL *vb* fit with short lines for fastening hooks

NORSELLED > NORSEL

NORSELLER > NORSEL

NORSELS > NORSEL

NORTENA *same as* > NORTENO

NORTENAS > NORTENA

NORTENO *n* type of Mexican music

NORTENOS > NORTENO

NORTH *n* direction towards the North Pole, opposite south ▷ *adj* or in the north ▷ *adv* in, to, or towards the north ▷ *vb* move north

NORTHEAST *adv* (in or to) direction between north and east ▷ *n* point of the compass or direction midway between north and east ▷ *adj* of or denoting the northeast part of a specified country, area, etc

NORTHED > NORTH

NORTHER *n* wind or storm from the north ▷ *vb* move north

NORTHERED > NORTHER

NORTHERLY *adj* of or in the north ▷ *adv* towards the north ▷ *n* wind from the north

NORTHERN *adj* situated in or towards the north ▷ *n* person from the north

NORTHERNS > NORTHERN

NORTHERS > NORTHER

NORTHING *n* movement or distance covered in a northerly direction

NORTHINGS > NORTHING

NORTHLAND *n* lands that are far to the north

NORTHMOST *adj* situated furthest north

n

NORTHS > NORTH

NORTHWARD *adv* towards the north

NORTHWEST *adv* (in or to) direction between north and west ▷ *n* point of the compass or direction midway between north and west ▷ *adj* of or denoting the northwestern part of a specified country, area, etc

NORWARD *same as* > NORTHWARD

NORWARDS *same as* > NORWARD

NOS > NO

NOSE *n* organ of smell, used also in breathing ▷ *vb* move forward slowly and carefully

NOSEAN *n* type of mineral

NOSEANS > NOSEAN

NOSEBAG *n* bag containing feed fastened round a horse's head

NOSEBAGS > NOSEBAG

NOSEBAND *n* part of a horse's bridle that goes around the nose

NOSEBANDS > NOSEBAND

NOSEBLEED *n* bleeding from the nose

NOSED > NOSE

NOSEDIVE *vb* (of an aircraft) plunge suddenly with the nose pointing downwards

NOSEDIVED > NOSEDIVE

NOSEDIVES > NOSEDIVE

NOSEDOVE > NOSEDIVE

NOSEGAY *n* small bunch of flowers

NOSEGAYS > NOSEGAY

NOSEGUARD *n* position in American football

NOSELESS > NOSE

NOSELIKE > NOSE

NOSELITE *same as* > NOSEAN

NOSELITES > NOSELITE

NOSEPIECE *same as* > NOSEBAND

NOSER *n* strong headwind

NOSERS > NOSER

NOSES > NOSE

NOSEWHEEL *n* wheel fitted under the nose of an aircraft

NOSEY *adj* prying or inquisitive ▷ *n* nosey person

NOSEYS > NOSEY

NOSH *n* food ▷ *vb* eat

NOSHED > NOSH

NOSHER > NOSH

NOSHERIE *same as* > NOSHERY

NOSHERIES > NOSHERIE

NOSHERS > NOSH

NOSHERY *n* restaurant or other place where food is served

NOSHES > NOSH

NOSHING > NOSH

NOSIER > NOSY

NOSIES > NOSY

NOSIEST > NOSY

NOSILY > NOSY

NOSINESS > NOSY

NOSING *n* edge of a step or stair tread

NOSINGS > NOSING

NOSODE *n* homeopathic remedy

NOSODES > NOSODE

NOSOLOGIC > NOSOLOGY

NOSOLOGY *n* branch of medicine concerned with the classification of diseases

NOSTALGIA *n* sentimental longing for the past

NOSTALGIC *adj* of or characterized by nostalgia ▷ *n* person who indulges in nostalgia

NOSTOC *n* type of bacterium occurring in moist places

NOSTOCS > NOSTOC

NOSTOI > NOSTOS

NOSTOLOGY *n* scientific study of ageing

NOSTOS *n* story of a return home

NOSTRIL *n* one of the two openings at the end of the nose

NOSTRILS > NOSTRIL

NOSTRO *adj* as in *nostro account* bank account conducted by a British bank with a foreign bank

NOSTRUM *n* quack medicine

NOSTRUMS > NOSTRUM

NOSY *adj* prying or inquisitive

NOT *adv* expressing negation, refusal, or denial

NOTA > NOTUM

NOTABILIA *n* things worthy of notice

NOTABLE *adj* worthy of being noted, remarkable ▷ *n* person of distinction

NOTABLES > NOTABLE

NOTABLY *adv* particularly or especially

NOTAEUM *n* back of a bird's body

NOTAEUMS > NOTAEUM

NOTAIRE *n* (in France) notary

NOTAIRES > NOTAIRE

NOTAL > NOTUM

NOTANDA > NOTANDUM

NOTANDUM *n* notable fact

NOTAPHILY *n* study of paper money

NOTARIAL > NOTARY

NOTARIES > NOTARY

NOTARISE *same as* > NOTARIZE

NOTARISED > NOTARISE

NOTARISES > NOTARISE

NOTARIZE *vb* attest to or authenticate (a document, contract, etc), as a notary

NOTARIZED > NOTARIZE

NOTARIZES > NOTARIZE

NOTARY *n* person authorized to witness legal documents

NOTATE *vb* write (esp music) in notation

NOTATED > NOTATE

NOTATES > NOTATE

NOTATING > NOTATE

NOTATION *n* representation of numbers or quantities in a system by a series of symbols

NOTATIONS > NOTATION

NOTATOR *n* person who notates

NOTATORS > NOTATOR

NOTCH *n* V-shaped cut ▷ *vb* make a notch in

NOTCHBACK *n* type of car

NOTCHED > NOTCH

NOTCHEL *vb* refuse to pay another person's debts

NOTCHELED > NOTCHEL

NOTCHELS > NOTCHEL

NOTCHER *n* person who cuts notches

NOTCHERS > NOTCHER

NOTCHES > NOTCH

NOTCHIER > NOTCHY

NOTCHIEST > NOTCHY

NOTCHING > NOTCH

NOTCHINGS > NOTCH

NOTCHY *adj* (of a motor vehicle gear mechanism) requiring careful gear-changing

NOTE *n* short letter ▷ *vb* notice, pay attention to

NOTEBOOK *n* book for writing in

NOTEBOOKS > NOTEBOOK

NOTECARD *n* greetings card with space to write note

NOTECARDS > NOTECARD

NOTECASE *same as* > WALLET

NOTECASES > NOTECASE

NOTED *adj* well-known

NOTEDLY > NOTED

NOTEDNESS > NOTED

NOTELESS > NOTE

NOTELET *n* small folded card with a design on the front

NOTELETS > NOTELET

NOTEPAD *n* number of sheets of paper fastened together

NOTEPADS > NOTEPAD

NOTEPAPER *n* paper used for writing letters

NOTER *n* person who takes notes

NOTERS > NOTER

NOTES *pl n* short descriptive or summarized jottings

NOTHER *same as* > OTHER

NOTHING *pron* not anything ▷ *adv* not at all ▷ *n* person or thing of no importance

NOTHINGS > NOTHING

NOTICE *n* observation or attention ▷ *vb* observe, become aware of

NOTICED > NOTICE

NOTICER *n* person who takes notice

NOTICERS > NOTICER

NOTICES > NOTICE

NOTICING > NOTICE

NOTIFIED > NOTIFY

NOTIFIER > NOTIFY

NOTIFIERS > NOTIFY

NOTIFIES > NOTIFY

NOTIFY *vb* inform

NOTIFYING > NOTIFY

NOTING > NOTE

NOTION *n* idea or opinion

NOTIONAL *adj* speculative, imaginary, or unreal

NOTIONIST *n* person whose opinions are merely notions

NOTIONS *pl n* pins, cotton, ribbon, and similar wares used for sewing

NOTITIA *n* register or list, esp of ecclesiastical districts

NOTITIAE > NOTITIA

NOTITIAS > NOTITIA

NOTOCHORD *n* fibrous longitudinal rod in all embryo and some adult chordate animals

NOTORIETY > NOTORIOUS

NOTORIOUS *adj* well known for something bad

NOTORNIS *n* rare flightless rail of New Zealand

NOTOUR *adj* notorious

NOTT *same as* > NOT

NOTTURNI > NOTTURNO

NOTTURNO *n* piece of music

NOTUM *n* cuticular plate on an insect

NOUGAT *n* chewy sweet containing nuts and fruit

NOUGATINE *n* type of brown nougat with a firm texture

NOUGATS > NOUGAT

NOUGHT *n* figure o

NOUGHTIES *pl n* decade from 2000 to 2009

NOUGHTS > NOUGHT

NOUL *same as* > NOLL

NOULD *vb* would not

NOULDE *same as* > NOULD

NOULE *same as* > NOLL

NOULES > NOULE

NOULS > NOUL

NOUMENA > NOUMENON

NOUMENAL > NOUMENON

NOUMENON n (in the philosophy of Kant) a thing as it is in itself, incapable of being known, but only inferred from the nature of experience

NOUN n word that refers to a person, place, or thing

NOUNAL > NOUN

NOUNALLY > NOUN

NOUNIER > NOUNY

NOUNIEST > NOUNY

NOUNLESS > NOUN

NOUNS > NOUN

NOUNY adj nounlike

NOUP n steep headland

NOUPS > NOUP

NOURICE n nurse

NOURICES > NOURICE

NOURISH vb feed

NOURISHED > NOURISH

NOURISHER > NOURISH

NOURISHES > NOURISH

NOURITURE n nourishment

NOURSLE vb nurse

NOURSLED > NOURSLE

NOURSLES > NOURSLE

NOURSLING > NOURSLE

NOUS n common sense

NOUSELL vb foster

NOUSELLED > NOUSELL

NOUSELLS > NOUSELL

NOUSES > NOUS

NOUSLE vb nuzzle

NOUSLED > NOUSLE

NOUSLES > NOUSLE

NOUSLING > NOUSLE

NOUT same as > NOUGHT

NOUVEAU adj having recently become the thing specified

NOUVEAUX same as > NOUVEAU

NOUVELLE n long short story

NOUVELLES > NOUVELLE

NOVA n type of star

NOVAE > NOVA

NOVALIA n newly reclaimed land

NOVALIKE adj resembling a nova

NOVAS > NOVA

NOVATE vb substitute one thing in place of another

NOVATED adj as in novated lease Australian system of employer-aided car purchase

NOVATES > NOVATE

NOVATING > NOVATE

NOVATION n substitution of a new obligation for an old one by mutual agreement between the parties

NOVATIONS > NOVATION

NOVEL n long fictitious story in book form ▷ adj fresh, new, or original

NOVELDOM n realm of fiction

NOVELDOMS > NOVELDOM

NOVELESE n style of writing characteristic of poor novels

NOVELESES > NOVELESE

NOVELETTE n short novel, esp one regarded as trivial or sentimental

NOVELISE same as > NOVELIZE

NOVELISED > NOVELISE

NOVELISER n person who novelizes

NOVELISES > NOVELISE

NOVELISH adj resembling a novel

NOVELISM n innovation

NOVELISMS > NOVELISM

NOVELIST n writer of novels

NOVELISTS > NOVELIST

NOVELIZE vb convert (a true story, film, etc) into a novel

NOVELIZED > NOVELIZE

NOVELIZER n person who novelizes

NOVELIZES > NOVELIZE

NOVELLA n short novel

NOVELLAE > NOVELLA

NOVELLAS > NOVELLA

NOVELLE > NOVELLA

NOVELLY > NOVEL

NOVELS > NOVEL

NOVELTIES > NOVELTY

NOVELTY n newness

NOVEMBER n code word for the letter N

NOVEMBERS > NOVEMBER

NOVENA n set of prayers or services on nine consecutive days

NOVENAE > NOVENA

NOVENARY n set of nine

NOVENAS > NOVENA

NOVENNIAL adj recurring every ninth year

NOVERCAL adj stepmotherly

NOVERINT n writ

NOVERINTS > NOVERINT

NOVICE n beginner

NOVICES > NOVICE

NOVICIATE same as > NOVITIATE

NOVITIATE n period of being a novice

NOVITIES > NOVITY

NOVITY n novelty

NOVOCAINE n tradename of a painkilling substance used as a local anaesthetic

NOVODAMUS n type of charter

NOVUM n game played with dice

NOVUMS > NOVUM

NOW adv at or for the present time ▷ n the present time

NOWADAYS adv in these times

NOWAY adv in no manner ▷ sentence substitute used to make an emphatic refusal, denial etc

NOWAYS same as > NOWAY

NOWCAST n report on current weather conditions

NOWCASTS > NOWCAST

NOWED adj knotted

NOWHENCE adv from no place

NOWHERE adv not anywhere ▷ n nonexistent or insignificant place

NOWHERES > NOWHERE

NOWHITHER adv no place

NOWISE another word for > NOWAY

NOWL n crown of the head

NOWLS > NOWL

NOWN same as > OWN

NOWNESS > NOWN

NOWNESSES > NOWN

NOWS > NOW

NOWT n nothing

NOWTIER > NOWTY

NOWTIEST > NOWTY

NOWTS > NOWT

NOWTY adj bad-tempered

NOWY adj having a small projection at the centre (of a cross)

NOX n nitrogen oxide

NOXAL adj relating to damage done by something belonging to another

NOXES > NOX

NOXIOUS adj poisonous or harmful

NOXIOUSLY > NOXIOUS

NOY vb harass

NOYADE n execution by drowning

NOYADES > NOYADE

NOYANCE n nuisance

NOYANCES > NOYANCE

NOYAU n brandy-based liqueur

NOYAUS > NOYAU

NOYAUX > NOYAU

NOYED > NOY

NOYES archaic form of > NOISE

NOYESES > NOYES

NOYING > NOY

NOYOUS > NOY

NOYS > NOY

NOYSOME > NOY

NOZZER n new recruit (in the Navy)

NOZZERS > NOZZER

NOZZLE n projecting spout through which fluid is discharged

NOZZLES > NOZZLE

NTH adj of an unspecified number

NU n 13th letter in the Greek alphabet

NUANCE n subtle difference in colour, meaning, or tone ▷ vb give subtle differences to

NUANCED > NUANCE

NUANCES > NUANCE

NUANCING > NUANCE

NUB n point or gist (of a story etc) ▷ vb hang from the gallows

NUBBED > NUB

NUBBIER > NUBBY

NUBBIEST > NUBBY

NUBBIN n something small or undeveloped, esp a fruit or ear of corn

NUBBINESS > NUBBY

NUBBING n act of hanging (a criminal)

NUBBINGS > NUBBING

NUBBINS > NUBBIN

NUBBLE n small lump

NUBBLED > NUBBLE

NUBBLES > NUBBLE

NUBBLIER > NUBBLE

NUBBLIEST > NUBBLE

NUBBLING > NUBBLE

NUBBLY > NUBBLE

NUBBY adj having small lumps or protuberances

NUBECULA n small irregular galaxy near the S celestial pole

NUBECULAE > NUBECULA

NUBIA n fleecy scarf for the head, worn by women

NUBIAS > NUBIA

NUBIFORM adj cloudlike

NUBILE adj sexually attractive

NUBILITY > NUBILE

NUBILOSE same as > NUBILOUS

NUBILOUS adj cloudy

NUBS > NUB

NUBUCK n type of leather with a velvety finish

NUBUCKS > NUBUCK

NUCELLAR > NUCELLUS

NUCELLI > NUCELLUS

NUCELLUS n central part of a plant ovule containing the embryo sac

NUCHA n back or nape of the neck

NUCHAE > NUCHA

NUCHAL n scale on a reptile's neck

NUCHALS > NUCHAL

NUCLEAL > NUCLEUS

NUCLEAR adj of nuclear weapons or energy

NUCLEASE n any of a group of enzymes that hydrolyse nucleic acids to simple nucleotides

NUCLEASES > NUCLEASE

NUCLEATE adj having a nucleus ▷ vb form a nucleus

NUCLEATED > NUCLEATE

NUCLEATES > NUCLEATE

NUCLEATOR > NUCLEATE

NUCLEI > NUCLEUS

NUCLEIC adj as in nucleic acid type of complex compound that is a vital constituent of living cells

NUCLEIDE same as > NUCLIDE

n

NUCLEIDES > NUCLEIDE

NUCLEIN n protein that occurs in the nuclei of living cells

NUCLEINIC > NUCLEIN

NUCLEINS > NUCLEIN

NUCLEOID n component of a bacterium

NUCLEOIDS > NUCLEOID

NUCLEOLAR > NUCLEOLUS

NUCLEOLE variant of > NUCLEOLUS

NUCLEOLES > NUCLEOLE

NUCLEOLI > NUCLEOLUS

NUCLEOLUS n small rounded body within a resting nucleus that contains RNA and proteins

NUCLEON n proton or neutron

NUCLEONIC adj relating to the branch of physics concerned with the applications of nuclear energy

NUCLEONS > NUCLEON

NUCLEUS n centre, esp of an atom or cell

NUCLEUSES > NUCLEUS

NUCLIDE n species of atom characterized by its atomic number and its mass number

NUCLIDES > NUCLIDE

NUCLIDIC > NUCLIDE

NUCULE n small seed

NUCULES > NUCULE

NUDATION n act of stripping

NUDATIONS > NUDATION

NUDDIES > NUDDY

NUDDY n as in in the nuddy in the nude

NUDE adj naked ▷ n naked figure in painting, sculpture, or photography

NUDELY > NUDE

NUDENESS > NUDE

NUDER > NUDE

NUDES > NUDE

NUDEST > NUDE

NUDGE vb push gently, esp with the elbow ▷ n gentle push or touch

NUDGED > NUDGE

NUDGER > NUDGE

NUDGERS > NUDGE

NUDGES > NUDGE

NUDGING > NUDGE

NUDICAUL adj (of plants) having stems without leaves

NUDIE n film, show, or magazine depicting nudity

NUDIES > NUDIE

NUDISM n practice of not wearing clothes

NUDISMS > NUDISM

NUDIST > NUDISM

NUDISTS > NUDISM

NUDITIES > NUDITY

NUDITY n state or fact of being nude

NUDNICK same as > NUDNIK

NUDNICKS > NUDNICK

NUDNIK n boring person

NUDNIKS > NUDNIK

NUDZH same as > NUDGE

NUDZHED > NUDZH

NUDZHES > NUDZH

NUDZHING > NUDZH

NUFF slang form of > ENOUGH

NUFFIN slang form of > NOTHING

NUFFINS > NUFFIN

NUFFS > NUFF

NUG n lump of wood sawn from a log

NUGAE n jests

NUGATORY adj of little value

NUGGAR n sailing boat used to carry cargo on the Nile

NUGGARS > NUGGAR

NUGGET n small lump of gold in its natural state ▷ vb polish footwear

NUGGETED > NUGGET

NUGGETING > NUGGET

NUGGETS > NUGGET

NUGGETTED > NUGGET

NUGGETY adj of or resembling a nugget

NUGS > NUG

NUISANCE n something or someone that causes annoyance or bother ▷ adj causing annoyance or bother

NUISANCER n person or thing causing a nuisance

NUISANCES > NUISANCE

NUKE vb attack with nuclear weapons ▷ n nuclear weapon

NUKED > NUKE

NUKES > NUKE

NUKING > NUKE

NULL adj without legal force ▷ vb make negative

NULLA same as > NULLAH

NULLAH n stream or drain

NULLAHS > NULLAH

NULLAS > NULLA

NULLED > NULL

NULLIFIED > NULLIFY

NULLIFIER > NULLIFY

NULLIFIES > NULLIFY

NULLIFY vb make ineffective

NULLING n knurling

NULLINGS > NULLING

NULLIPARA n woman who has never borne a child

NULLIPORE n any of several red seaweeds

NULLITIES > NULLITY

NULLITY n state of being null

NULLNESS > NULL

NULLS > NULL

NUMB adj without feeling, as through cold, shock, or fear ▷ vb make numb

NUMBAT n small Australian marsupial

NUMBATS > NUMBAT

NUMBED > NUMB

NUMBER n sum or quantity ▷ vb count

NUMBERED > NUMBER

NUMBERER n person who numbers

NUMBERERS > NUMBERER

NUMBERING > NUMBER

NUMBERS > NUMBER

NUMBEST > NUMB

NUMBFISH n any of several electric ray fish

NUMBHEAD n stupid person

NUMBHEADS > NUMBHEAD

NUMBING > NUMB

NUMBINGLY > NUMB

NUMBLES pl n animal organs, cooked for food

NUMBLY > NUMB

NUMBNESS > NUMB

NUMBNUT n idiot

NUMBNUTS n idiot

NUMBS > NUMB

NUMBSKULL n stupid person

NUMCHUCK same as > NUNCHAKU

NUMCHUCKS > NUMCHUCK

NUMDAH n coarse felt made esp in India

NUMDAHS > NUMDAH

NUMEN n deity or spirit presiding over a thing or place

NUMERABLE adj able to be numbered or counted

NUMERABLY > NUMERABLE

NUMERACY n ability to use numbers, esp in arithmetical operations

NUMERAIRE n unit in which prices are measured

NUMERAL n word or symbol used to express a sum or quantity ▷ adj of, consisting of, or denoting a number

NUMERALLY > NUMERAL

NUMERALS > NUMERAL

NUMERARY adj of or relating to numbers

NUMERATE adj able to do basic arithmetic ▷ vb read (a numerical expression)

NUMERATED > NUMERATE

NUMERATES > NUMERATE

NUMERATOR n number above the line in a fraction

NUMERIC n number or numeral

NUMERICAL adj measured or expressed in numbers

NUMERICS > NUMERIC

NUMEROUS adj existing or happening in large numbers

NUMINA plural of > NUMEN

NUMINOUS adj arousing religious or spiritual emotions ▷ n something that arouses religious or spiritual emotions

NUMMARY adj of or relating to coins

NUMMIER > NUMMY

NUMMIEST > NUMMY

NUMMULAR adj shaped like a coin

NUMMULARY > NUMMULAR

NUMMULINE > NUMMULAR

NUMMULITE n type of large fossil protozoan

NUMMY adj delicious

NUMNAH same as > NUMDAH

NUMNAHS > NUMNAH

NUMPKIN n stupid person

NUMPKINS > NUMPKIN

NUMPTIES > NUMPTY

NUMPTY n stupid person

NUMSKULL same as > NUMBSKULL

NUMSKULLS > NUMSKULL

NUN n female member of a religious order

NUNATAK n isolated mountain peak projecting through glacial ice

NUNATAKER > NUNATAK

NUNATAKS > NUNATAK

NUNCHAKU n rice flail used as a weapon

NUNCHAKUS > NUNCHAKU

NUNCHEON n light snack

NUNCHEONS > NUNCHEON

NUNCHUCKS same as > NUNCHAKU

NUNCHUK n type of weapon used in martial arts

NUNCHUKS > NUNCHUK

NUNCIO n pope's ambassador

NUNCIOS > NUNCIO

NUNCLE archaic or dialect word for > UNCLE

NUNCLES > NUNCLE

NUNCUPATE vb declare publicly

NUNDINAL > NUNDINE

NUNDINE n market day

NUNDINES > NUNDINE

NUNHOOD n condition, practice, or character of a nun

NUNHOODS > NUNHOOD

NUNLIKE > NUN

NUNNATION n pronunciation of n at the end of words

NUNNERIES > NUNNERY

NUNNERY n convent

NUNNISH > NUN

NUNNY n as in nunny bag small sealskin haversack used in Canada

NUNS > NUN

NUNSHIP > NUN

NUNSHIPS > NUN

NUPTIAL adj relating to marriage

NUPTIALLY > NUPTIAL
NUPTIALS pl n wedding
NUR n wooden ball
NURAGHE n Sardinian round tower
NURAGHI > NURAGHE
NURAGHIC > NURAGHE
NURD same as > NERD
NURDIER > NERD
NURDIEST > NERD
NURDISH > NERD
NURDLE vb score runs in cricket by soft deflections
NURDLED > NURDLE
NURDLES > NURDLE
NURDLING > NURDLE
NURDS > NURD
NURDY > NURD
NURHAG n Sardinian round tower
NURHAGS > NURHAG
NURL variant of > KNURL
NURLED > NURL
NURLING > NURL
NURLS > NURL
NURR n wooden ball
NURRS > NURR
NURS > NUR
NURSE n person employed to look after sick people ▷ vb look after (a sick person)
NURSED > NURSE
NURSELIKE > NURSE
NURSELING same as > NURSLING
NURSEMAID n woman employed to look after children
NURSER n person who treats something carefully
NURSERIES > NURSERY
NURSERS > NURSER
NURSERY n room where children sleep or play
NURSES > NURSE
NURSING n practice or profession of caring for the sick and injured
NURSINGS > NURSING
NURSLE vb nuzzle
NURSLED > NURSLE
NURSLES > NURSLE
NURSLING n child or young animal that is being suckled, nursed, or fostered
NURSLINGS > NURSLING
NURTURAL > NURTURE
NURTURANT > NURTURE
NURTURE n act or process of promoting development ▷ vb promote or encourage development
NURTURED > NURTURE
NURTURER > NURTURE
NURTURERS > NURTURE
NURTURES > NURTURE
NURTURING > NURTURE
NUS > NU
NUT n fruit consisting of a hard shell and a kernel

▷ vb gather nuts
NUTANT adj having the apex hanging down
NUTARIAN n person whose diet is based around nuts
NUTARIANS > NUTARIAN
NUTATE vb nod
NUTATED > NUTATE
NUTATES > NUTATE
NUTATING > NUTATE
NUTATION n periodic variation in the precession of the earth's axis
NUTATIONS > NUTATION
NUTBAR n bar made from chopped nuts
NUTBARS > NUTBAR
NUTBROWN adj of a brownish colour, esp a reddish-brown
NUTBUTTER n ground nuts blended with butter
NUTCASE n insane person
NUTCASES > NUTCASE
NUTGALL n nut-shaped gall caused by gall wasps on the oak and other trees
NUTGALLS > NUTGALL
NUTGRASS n type of plant
NUTHATCH n small songbird
NUTHIN n nothing
NUTHOUSE n mental hospital or asylum
NUTHOUSES > NUTHOUSE
NUTJOB n crazy person
NUTJOBBER n nuthatch
NUTJOBS > NUTJOB
NUTLET n portion of a fruit that fragments when mature
NUTLETS > NUTLET
NUTLIKE > NUT
NUTLOAF n savoury loaf made from nuts
NUTLOAVES > NUTLOAF
NUTMEAL n type of grain
NUTMEALS > NUTMEAL
NUTMEAT n kernel of a nut
NUTMEATS > NUTMEAT
NUTMEG n spice made from the seed of a tropical tree ▷ vb kick or hit the ball between the legs of (an opposing player)
NUTMEGGED > NUTMEG
NUTMEGGY adj of or similar to nutmeg
NUTMEGS > NUTMEG
NUTPECKER n nuthatch
NUTPICK n tool used to dig the meat from nuts
NUTPICKS > NUTPICK
NUTRIA n fur of the coypu
NUTRIAS > NUTRIA
NUTRIENT n substance that provides nourishment ▷ adj providing nourishment
NUTRIENTS > NUTRIENT
NUTRIMENT n food or

nourishment required by all living things to grow and stay healthy
NUTRITION n process of taking in and absorbing nutrients
NUTRITIVE adj of nutrition ▷ n nutritious food
NUTS > NUT
NUTSEDGE same as > NUTGRASS
NUTSEDGES > NUTSEDGE
NUTSHELL n shell around the kernel of a nut
NUTSHELLS > NUTSHELL
NUTSIER > NUTSY
NUTSIEST > NUTSY
NUTSO n insane person
NUTSOS > NUTSO
NUTSY adj lunatic
NUTTED > NUT
NUTTER n insane person
NUTTERIES > NUTTERY
NUTTERS > NUTTER
NUTTERY n place where nut trees grow
NUTTIER > NUTTY
NUTTIEST > NUTTY
NUTTILY > NUTTY
NUTTINESS > NUTTY
NUTTING n act of gathering nuts
NUTTINGS > NUTTING
NUTTY adj containing or resembling nuts
NUTWOOD n any of various nut-bearing trees, such as walnut
NUTWOODS > NUTWOOD
NUZZER n present given to a superior in India
NUZZERS > NUZZER
NUZZLE vb push or rub gently with the nose or snout
NUZZLED > NUZZLE
NUZZLER n person or thing that nuzzles
NUZZLERS > NUZZLER
NUZZLES > NUZZLE
NUZZLING > NUZZLE
NY same as > NIGH
NYAFF n small or contemptible person ▷ vb yelp like a small dog
NYAFFED > NYAFF
NYAFFING > NYAFF
NYAFFS > NYAFF
NYAH interj interjection used to express contempt
NYALA n spiral-horned southern African antelope
NYALAS > NYALA
NYANZA n (in E Africa) a lake
NYANZAS > NYANZA
NYAS n young hawk
NYASES > NYAS
NYBBLE n small byte
NYBBLES > NYBBLE
NYCTALOPE n person affected by nyctalopia

NYCTALOPS n person or thing with night-vision
NYE n flock of pheasants ▷ vb near
NYED > NYE
NYES > NYE
NYING > NYE
NYLGHAI same as > NILGAI
NYLGHAIS > NYLGHAI
NYLGHAU same as > NILGAI
NYLGHAUS > NYLGHAU
NYLON n synthetic material used for clothing etc
NYLONED adj wearing nylons
NYLONS pl n stockings made of nylon
NYM adj as in nym war dispute about publishing material online under a pseudonym
NYMPH n mythical spirit of nature, represented as a beautiful young woman ▷ vb fish with a particular type of fly on the hook
NYMPHA n either one of the labia minora
NYMPHAE > NYMPHA
NYMPHAEA n water lily
NYMPHAEAS > NYMPHAEA
NYMPHAEUM n shrine of the nymphs
NYMPHAL > NYMPH
NYMPHALID n butterfly of the family that includes the fritillaries and red admirals ▷ adj of this family of butterflies
NYMPHEAN > NYMPH
NYMPHED > NYMPH
NYMPHET n sexually precocious young girl
NYMPHETIC > NYMPHET
NYMPHETS > NYMPHET
NYMPHETTE same as > NYMPHET
NYMPHIC > NYMPH
NYMPHICAL > NYMPH
NYMPHING > NYMPH
NYMPHISH > NYMPH
NYMPHLIKE > NYMPH
NYMPHLY > NYMPH
NYMPHO n nymphomaniac
NYMPHOS > NYMPHO
NYMPHS > NYMPH
NYS > NY
NYSSA n type of tree
NYSSAS > NYSSA
NYSTAGMIC > NYSTAGMUS
NYSTAGMUS n involuntary movement of the eye comprising a smooth drift followed by a flick back
NYSTATIN n type of antibiotic obtained from a bacterium
NYSTATINS > NYSTATIN

n

Oo

OAF *n* stupid or clumsy person
OAFISH > OAF
OAFISHLY > OAF
OAFS > OAF
OAK *n* deciduous forest tree
OAKED *adj* relating to wine that is stored for a time in oak barrels prior to bottling
OAKEN *adj* made of the wood of the oak
OAKENSHAW *n* small forest of oaks
OAKER *same as* > OCHRE
OAKERS > OAKER
OAKIER > OAKY
OAKIES > OAKY
OAKIEST > OAKY
OAKINESS *n* quality of being oaky
OAKLEAF *n* the leaf of the oak
OAKLEAVES > OAKLEAF
OAKLIKE > OAK
OAKLING *n* young oak
OAKLINGS > OAKLING
OAKMOSS *n* type of lichen
OAKMOSSES > OAKMOSS
OAKS > OAK
OAKUM *n* fibre obtained by unravelling old rope
OAKUMS > OAKUM
OAKWOOD *n* the wood of the oak
OAKWOODS > OAKWOOD
OAKY *adj* hard like the wood of an oak ▷ *n* ice cream
OANSHAGH *n* foolish girl or woman
OANSHAGHS > OANSHAGH
OAR *n* pole with a broad blade, used for rowing a boat ▷ *vb* propel with oars
OARAGE *n* use or number of oars
OARAGES > OARAGE
OARED *adj* equipped with oars
OARFISH *n* very long ribbonfish with long slender ventral fins
OARFISHES > OARFISH
OARIER > OARY
OARIEST > OARY
OARING > OAR
OARLESS > OAR

OARLIKE > OAR
OARLOCK *n* swivelling device that holds an oar in place
OARLOCKS > OARLOCK
OARS > OAR
OARSMAN *n* person who rows
OARSMEN > OARSMAN
OARSWOMAN *n* female oarsman
OARSWOMEN > OARSWOMAN
OARWEED *n* type of brown seaweed
OARWEEDS > OARWEED
OARY *adj* of or like an oar
OASES > OASIS
OASIS *n* fertile area in a desert
OAST *n* oven for drying hops
OASTHOUSE *n* building with kilns for drying hops
OASTS > OAST
OAT *n* hard cereal grown as food
OATCAKE *n* thin flat biscuit of oatmeal
OATCAKES > OATCAKE
OATEN *adj* made of oats or oat straw
OATER *n* film about the American Wild West
OATERS > OATER
OATH *n* solemn promise, esp to be truthful in court
OATHABLE *adj* able to take an oath
OATHS > OATH
OATIER > OATY
OATIEST > OATY
OATLIKE > OAT
OATMEAL *n* coarse flour made from oats ▷ *adj* pale brownish-cream
OATMEALS > OATMEAL
OATS > OAT
OATY *adj* of, like, or containing oats
OAVES > OAF
OB *n* expression of opposition
OBA *n* (in W Africa) a Yoruba chief or ruler
OBANG *n* former Japanese coin
OBANGS > OBANG
OBAS > OBA
OBBLIGATI > OBBLIGATO

OBBLIGATO *n* essential part or accompaniment ▷ *adj* not to be omitted in performance
OBCONIC *adj* shaped like a cone and attached at the pointed end
OBCONICAL *same as* > OBCONIC
OBCORDATE *adj* heart-shaped and attached at the pointed end
OBDURACY > OBDURATE
OBDURATE *adj* hardhearted or stubborn ▷ *vb* make obdurate
OBDURATED > OBDURATE
OBDURATES > OBDURATE
OBDURE *vb* make obdurate
OBDURED > OBDURE
OBDURES > OBDURE
OBDURING > OBDURE
OBE *n* ancient Laconian village
OBEAH *vb* cast spell on
OBEAHED > OBEAH
OBEAHING > OBEAH
OBEAHISM > OBEAH
OBEAHISMS > OBEAH
OBEAHS > OBEAH
OBECHE *n* African tree
OBECHES > OBECHE
OBEDIENCE *n* condition or quality of being obedient
OBEDIENT *adj* obeying or willing to obey
OBEISANCE *n* attitude of respect
OBEISANT > OBEISANCE
OBEISM *n* belief in obeah
OBEISMS > OBEISM
OBELI > OBELUS
OBELIA *n* type of jellyfish
OBELIAS > OBELIA
OBELION *n* area of skull
OBELISCAL > OBELISK
OBELISE *same as* > OBELIZE
OBELISED > OBELISE
OBELISES > OBELISE
OBELISING > OBELISE
OBELISK *n* stone column tapering to a pyramid at the top
OBELISKS > OBELISK
OBELISM *n* practice of marking passages in text

OBELISMS > OBELISM
OBELIZE *vb* mark (a word or passage) with an obelus
OBELIZED > OBELIZE
OBELIZES > OBELIZE
OBELIZING > OBELIZE
OBELUS *n* mark used to indicate spurious words or passages
OBENTO *n* Japanese lunch box
OBENTOS > OBENTO
OBES > OBE
OBESE *adj* very fat
OBESELY > OBESE
OBESENESS > OBESE
OBESER > OBESE
OBESEST > OBESE
OBESITIES > OBESITY
OBESITY > OBESE
OBESOGEN *n* agent causing obesity
OBESOGENS > OBESOGEN
OBEY *vb* carry out instructions or orders
OBEYABLE > OBEY
OBEYED > OBEY
OBEYER > OBEY
OBEYERS > OBEY
OBEYING > OBEY
OBEYS > OBEY
OBFUSCATE *vb* make (something) confusing
OBI *n* broad sash tied in a large flat bow at the back ▷ *vb* bewitch
OBIA *same as* > OBEAH
OBIAS > OBIA
OBIED > OBI
OBIING > OBI
OBIISM > OBI
OBIISMS > OBI
OBIIT *vb* died
OBIS > OBI
OBIT *n* memorial service
OBITAL *adj* of obits
OBITER *adv* by the way
OBITS > OBIT
OBITUAL *adj* of obits
OBITUARY *n* announcement of someone's death, esp in a newspaper
OBJECT *n* physical thing ▷ *vb* express disapproval
OBJECTED > OBJECT
OBJECTIFY *vb* represent concretely
OBJECTING > OBJECT

OBJECTION n expression or feeling of opposition or disapproval

OBJECTIVE n aim or purpose ▷ adj not biased

OBJECTOR > OBJECT

OBJECTORS > OBJECT

OBJECTS > OBJECT

OBJET n object

OBJETS > OBJET

OBJURE vb put on oath

OBJURED > OBJURE

OBJURES > OBJURE

OBJURGATE vb scold or reprimand

OBJURING > OBJURE

OBLAST n administrative division of the constituent republics of Russia

OBLASTI > OBLAST

OBLASTS > OBLAST

OBLATE adj (of a sphere) flattened at the poles ▷ n person dedicated to a monastic or religious life

OBLATELY > OBLATE

OBLATES > OBLATE

OBLATION n religious offering

OBLATIONS > OBLATION

OBLATORY > OBLATION

OBLIGABLE > OBLIGATE

OBLIGANT n person promising to pay a sum

OBLIGANTS > OBLIGANT

OBLIGATE vb compel, constrain, or oblige morally or legally ▷ adj compelled, bound, or restricted

OBLIGATED > OBLIGATE

OBLIGATES > OBLIGATE

OBLIGATI > OBLIGATO

OBLIGATO same as > OBBLIGATO

OBLIGATOR > OBLIGATE

OBLIGATOS > OBLIGATO

OBLIGE vb compel (someone) morally or by law

OBLIGED > OBLIGE

OBLIGEE n person in whose favour an obligation, contract, or bond is created

OBLIGEES > OBLIGEE

OBLIGER > OBLIGE

OBLIGERS > OBLIGE

OBLIGES > OBLIGE

OBLIGING adj ready to help other people

OBLIGOR n person who binds himself by contract

OBLIGORS > OBLIGOR

OBLIQUE adj slanting ▷ n symbol (/) ▷ vb take or have an oblique direction

OBLIQUED > OBLIQUE

OBLIQUELY > OBLIQUE

OBLIQUER > OBLIQUE

OBLIQUES > OBLIQUE

OBLIQUEST > OBLIQUE

OBLIQUID adj oblique

OBLIQUING > OBLIQUE

OBLIQUITY n state or condition of being oblique

OBLIVION n state of being forgotten

OBLIVIONS > OBLIVION

OBLIVIOUS adj unaware

OBLONG adj having two long sides, two short sides, and four right angles ▷ n oblong figure

OBLONGLY > OBLONG

OBLONGS > OBLONG

OBLOQUIAL > OBLOQUY

OBLOQUIES > OBLOQUY

OBLOQUY n verbal abuse

OBNOXIOUS adj offensive

OBO n ship carrying oil and ore

OBOE n double-reeded woodwind instrument

OBOES > OBOE

OBOIST > OBOE

OBOISTS > OBOE

OBOL same as > OBOLUS

OBOLARY adj very poor

OBOLE n former weight unit in pharmacy

OBOLES > OBOLE

OBOLI > OBOLUS

OBOLS > OBOL

OBOLUS n Greek unit of weight

OBOS > OBO

OBOVATE adj (of a leaf) shaped like the longitudinal section of an egg with the narrower end at the base

OBOVATELY > OBOVATE

OBOVOID adj (of a fruit) egg-shaped with the narrower end at the base

OBREPTION n obtaining of something by giving false information

OBS > OB

OBSCENE adj portraying sex offensively

OBSCENELY > OBSCENE

OBSCENER > OBSCENE

OBSCENEST > OBSCENE

OBSCENITY n state or quality of being obscene

OBSCURANT n opposer of reform and enlightenment ▷ adj of or relating to an obscurant

OBSCURE adj not well known ▷ vb make (something) obscure

OBSCURED > OBSCURE

OBSCURELY > OBSCURE

OBSCURER > OBSCURE

OBSCURERS > OBSCURE

OBSCURES > OBSCURE

OBSCUREST > OBSCURE

OBSCURING > OBSCURE

OBSCURITY n state or quality of being obscure

OBSECRATE rare word for > BESEECH

OBSEQUENT adj (of a river) flowing into a subsequent

stream in the opposite direction to the original slope of the land

OBSEQUIAL > OBSEQUIES

OBSEQUIE same as > OBSEQUY

OBSEQUIES pl n funeral rites

OBSEQUY singular of > OBSEQUIES

OBSERVANT adj quick to notice things

OBSERVE vb see or notice

OBSERVED > OBSERVE

OBSERVER n person who observes, esp one who watches someone or something carefully

OBSERVERS > OBSERVER

OBSERVES > OBSERVE

OBSERVING > OBSERVE

OBSESS vb preoccupy (someone) compulsively

OBSESSED > OBSESS

OBSESSES > OBSESS

OBSESSING > OBSESS

OBSESSION n something that preoccupies a person to the exclusion of other things

OBSESSIVE adj motivated by a persistent overriding idea or impulse ▷ n person subject to obsession

OBSESSOR > OBSESS

OBSESSORS > OBSESS

OBSIDIAN n dark glassy volcanic rock

OBSIDIANS > OBSIDIAN

OBSIGN vb confirm

OBSIGNATE same as > OBSIGN

OBSIGNED > OBSIGN

OBSIGNING > OBSIGN

OBSIGNS > OBSIGN

OBSOLESCE vb become obsolete

OBSOLETE adj no longer in use ▷ vb make obsolete

OBSOLETED > OBSOLETE

OBSOLETES > OBSOLETE

OBSTACLE n something that makes progress difficult

OBSTACLES > OBSTACLE

OBSTETRIC adj of or relating to childbirth

OBSTINACY n state or quality of being obstinate

OBSTINATE adj stubborn

OBSTRUCT vb block with an obstacle

OBSTRUCTS > OBSTRUCT

OBSTRUENT adj causing obstruction, esp of the intestinal tract ▷ n anything that causes obstruction

OBTAIN vb acquire intentionally

OBTAINED > OBTAIN

OBTAINER > OBTAIN

OBTAINERS > OBTAIN

OBTAINING > OBTAIN

OBTAINS > OBTAIN

OBTECT adj (of a pupa) encased in a hardened secretion

OBTECTED same as > OBTECT

OBTEMPER vb comply (with)

OBTEMPERS > OBTEMPER

OBTEND vb put forward

OBTENDED > OBTEND

OBTENDING > OBTEND

OBTENDS > OBTEND

OBTENTION n act of obtaining

OBTEST vb beg (someone) earnestly

OBTESTED > OBTEST

OBTESTING > OBTEST

OBTESTS > OBTEST

OBTRUDE vb push oneself or one's ideas on others

OBTRUDED > OBTRUDE

OBTRUDER > OBTRUDE

OBTRUDERS > OBTRUDE

OBTRUDES > OBTRUDE

OBTRUDING > OBTRUDE

OBTRUSION > OBTRUDE

OBTRUSIVE adj unpleasantly noticeable

OBTUND vb deaden or dull

OBTUNDED > OBTUND

OBTUNDENT > OBTUND

OBTUNDING > OBTUND

OBTUNDITY n semi-conscious state

OBTUNDS > OBTUND

OBTURATE vb stop up (an opening, esp the breech of a gun)

OBTURATED > OBTURATE

OBTURATES > OBTURATE

OBTURATOR > OBTURATE

OBTUSE adj mentally slow

OBTUSELY > OBTUSE

OBTUSER > OBTUSE

OBTUSEST > OBTUSE

OBTUSITY > OBTUSE

OBUMBRATE vb overshadow

OBVENTION n incidental expense

OBVERSE n opposite way of looking at an idea ▷ adj facing or turned towards the observer

OBVERSELY > OBVERSE

OBVERSES > OBVERSE

OBVERSION > OBVERT

OBVERT vb deduce the obverse of (a proposition)

OBVERTED > OBVERT

OBVERTING > OBVERT

OBVERTS > OBVERT

OBVIABLE > OBVIATE

OBVIATE vb make unnecessary

OBVIATED > OBVIATE

OBVIATES > OBVIATE

OBVIATING > OBVIATE

OBVIATION > OBVIATE
OBVIATOR > OBVIATE
OBVIATORS > OBVIATE
OBVIOUS adj easy to see or understand, evident
OBVIOUSLY adv in a way that is easy to see or understand
OBVOLUTE adj (of leaves or petals in the bud) folded so that the margins overlap each other
OBVOLUTED same as > OBVOLUTE
OBVOLVENT adj curving around something
OBVS adv obviously
OCA n any of various South American herbaceous plants
OCARINA n small oval wind instrument
OCARINAS > OCARINA
OCAS > OCA
OCCAM n computer programming language
OCCAMIES > OCCAMY
OCCAMS > OCCAM
OCCAMY n type of alloy
OCCASION n time at which a particular thing happens ▷ vb cause
OCCASIONS pl n needs
OCCIDENT literary or formal word for > WEST
OCCIDENTS > OCCIDENT
OCCIES > OCCY
OCCIPITA > OCCIPUT
OCCIPITAL adj of or relating to the back of the head or skull
OCCIPUT n back of the head
OCCIPUTS > OCCIPUT
OCCLUDE vb obstruct
OCCLUDED > OCCLUDE
OCCLUDENT > OCCLUDE
OCCLUDER > OCCLUDE
OCCLUDERS > OCCLUDE
OCCLUDES > OCCLUDE
OCCLUDING > OCCLUDE
OCCLUSAL > OCCLUSION
OCCLUSION n act or process of occluding or the state of being occluded
OCCLUSIVE adj of or relating to the act of occlusion ▷ n occlusive speech sound
OCCLUSOR n muscle for closing opening
OCCLUSORS > OCCLUSOR
OCCULT adj relating to the supernatural ▷ vb (of a celestial body) to hide (another celestial body) from view
OCCULTED > OCCULT
OCCULTER n something that obscures
OCCULTERS > OCCULTER
OCCULTING > OCCULT
OCCULTISM n belief in and the study and practice of magic, astrology, etc

OCCULTIST > OCCULTISM
OCCULTLY > OCCULT
OCCULTS > OCCULT
OCCUPANCE same as > OCCUPANCY
OCCUPANCY n (length of) a person's stay in a specified place
OCCUPANT n person occupying a specified place
OCCUPANTS > OCCUPANT
OCCUPATE same as > OCCUPY
OCCUPATED > OCCUPATE
OCCUPATES > OCCUPATE
OCCUPIED > OCCUPY
OCCUPIER n person who lives in a particular house, whether as owner or tenant
OCCUPIERS > OCCUPIER
OCCUPIES > OCCUPY
OCCUPY vb live or work in (a building)
OCCUPYING > OCCUPY
OCCUR vb happen
OCCURRED > OCCUR
OCCURRENT adj (of a property) relating to some observable feature of its bearer
OCCURRING > OCCUR
OCCURS > OCCUR
OCCY n as in all over the occy dialect expression meaning in every direction
OCEAN n vast area of sea between continents
OCEANARIA pl n large saltwater aquaria for marine life
OCEANAUT n undersea explorer
OCEANAUTS > OCEANAUT
OCEANIC adj of or relating to the ocean
OCEANID n ocean nymph in Greek mythology
OCEANIDES > OCEANID
OCEANIDS > OCEANID
OCEANS > OCEAN
OCELLAR > OCELLUS
OCELLATE > OCELLUS
OCELLATED > OCELLUS
OCELLI > OCELLUS
OCELLUS n simple eye of insects and some other invertebrates
OCELOID adj of or like an ocelot
OCELOT n American wild cat with a spotted coat
OCELOTS > OCELOT
OCH interj expression of surprise, annoyance, or disagreement
OCHE n (in darts) mark behind which a player must stand
OCHER same as > OCHRE
OCHERED > OCHER
OCHERING > OCHER
OCHERISH adj (US) resembling ochre

OCHEROID adj (US) of or like ochre
OCHEROUS > OCHER
OCHERS > OCHER
OCHERY > OCHER
OCHES > OCHE
OCHIDORE n type of crab
OCHIDORES > OCHIDORE
OCHLOCRAT n supporter of rule by the mob
OCHONE interj expression of sorrow or regret
OCHRE n brownish-yellow earth ▷ adj moderate yellow-orange to orange ▷ vb colour with ochre
OCHREA n cup-shaped structure that sheathes the stems of certain plants
OCHREAE > OCHREA
OCHREAS > OCHREA
OCHREATE same as > OCREATE
OCHRED > OCHRE
OCHREOUS > OCHRE
OCHRES > OCHRE
OCHREY > OCHRE
OCHRING > OCHRE
OCHROID > OCHRE
OCHROUS > OCHRE
OCHRY > OCHRE
OCICAT n breed of cat with a spotted coat
OCICATS > OCICAT
OCKER n uncultivated or boorish Australian
OCKERISM n Australian boorishness
OCKERISMS > OCKERISM
OCKERS > OCKER
OCKODOLS pl n one's feet when wearing boots
OCOTILLO n cactus-like tree
OCOTILLOS > OCOTILLO
OCREA same as > OCHREA
OCREAE > OCREA
OCREAS > OCREA
OCREATE adj possessing an ocrea
OCTA same as > OKTA
OCTACHORD n eight-stringed musical instrument
OCTAD n group or series of eight
OCTADIC > OCTAD
OCTADS > OCTAD
OCTAGON n geometric figure with eight sides
OCTAGONAL adj having eight sides and eight angles
OCTAGONS > OCTAGON
OCTAHEDRA pl n solid eight-sided figures; octahedrons
OCTAL n number system with a base 8
OCTALS > OCTAL
OCTAMETER n verse line consisting of eight metrical feet

OCTAN n illness that occurs weekly
OCTANE n hydrocarbon found in petrol
OCTANES > OCTANE
OCTANGLE same as > OCTAGON
OCTANGLES > OCTANGLE
OCTANOL n alcohol containing eight carbon atoms
OCTANOLS > OCTANOL
OCTANS > OCTAN
OCTANT n any of the eight parts into which the three planes containing the Cartesian coordinate axes divide space
OCTANTAL > OCTANT
OCTANTS > OCTANT
OCTAPLA n book with eight texts
OCTAPLAS > OCTAPLA
OCTAPLOID adj having eight parts
OCTAPODIC > OCTAPODY
OCTAPODY n line of verse with eight metrical feet
OCTARCHY n government by eight rulers
OCTAROON same as > OCTOROON
OCTAROONS > OCTAROON
OCTAS > OCTA
OCTASTICH n verse of eight lines
OCTASTYLE adj (of building) having eight columns
OCTAVAL > OCTAVE
OCTAVE n (interval between the first and) eighth note of a scale ▷ adj consisting of eight parts
OCTAVES > OCTAVE
OCTAVO n book size in which the sheets are folded into eight leaves
OCTAVOS > OCTAVO
OCTENNIAL adj occurring every eight years
OCTET n group of eight performers
OCTETS > OCTET
OCTETT same as > OCTET
OCTETTE same as > OCTET
OCTETTES > OCTETTE
OCTETTS > OCTETT
OCTILLION n (in Britain and Germany) the number represented as one followed by 48 zeros
OCTOFID adj divided into eight
OCTOHEDRA same as > OCTAHEDRA
OCTONARII pl n lines with eight feet
OCTONARY adj relating to or based on the number eight ▷ n stanza of eight lines
OCTOPI > OCTOPUS

OCTOPLOID same as > OCTAPLOID

OCTOPOD n type of mollusc ▷ adj of these molluscs

OCTOPODAN > OCTOPOD

OCTOPODES > OCTOPOD

OCTOPODS > OCTOPOD

OCTOPOID adj of or like an octopus

OCTOPUS n sea creature with a soft body and eight tentacles

OCTOPUSES > OCTOPUS

OCTOPUSH n hockey-like game played underwater

OCTOROON n person having one quadroon and one White parent

OCTOROONS > OCTOROON

OCTOSTYLE same as > OCTASTYLE

OCTOTHORP n type of symbol in printing

OCTROI n duty on various goods brought into certain European towns

OCTROIS > OCTROI

OCTUOR n octet

OCTUORS > OCTUOR

OCTUPLE n quantity or number eight times as great as another ▷ adj eight times as much or as many ▷ vb multiply by eight

OCTUPLED > OCTUPLE

OCTUPLES > OCTUPLE

OCTUPLET n one of eight offspring from one birth

OCTUPLETS > OCTUPLET

OCTUPLEX n something made up of eight parts

OCTUPLING > OCTUPLE

OCTUPLY adv by eight times

OCTYL n group of atoms

OCTYLS > OCTYL

OCULAR adj relating to the eyes or sight ▷ n lens in an optical instrument

OCULARIST n person who makes artificial eyes

OCULARLY > OCULAR

OCULARS > OCULAR

OCULATE adj possessing eyes

OCULATED same as > OCULATE

OCULI > OCULUS

OCULIST n ophthalmologist

OCULISTS > OCULIST

OCULUS n round window

OD n hypothetical force

ODA n room in a harem

ODAH same as > ODA

ODAHS > ODAH

ODAL same as > UDAL

ODALIQUE same as > ODALISQUE

ODALIQUES > ODALIQUE

ODALISK same as > ODALISQUE

ODALISKS > ODALISK

ODALISQUE n female slave in a harem

ODALLER > ODAL

ODALLERS > ODAL

ODALS > ODAL

ODAS > ODA

ODD adj unusual

ODDBALL n eccentric person ▷ adj strange or peculiar

ODDBALLS > ODDBALL

ODDER > ODD

ODDEST > ODD

ODDISH > ODD

ODDITIES > ODDITY

ODDITY n odd person or thing

ODDLY > ODD

ODDMENT n odd piece or thing

ODDMENTS > ODDMENT

ODDNESS > ODD

ODDNESSES > ODD

ODDS pl n probability of something happening

ODDSMAKER n person setting odds in betting

ODDSMAN n umpire

ODDSMEN > ODDSMAN

ODE n lyric poem, usu addressed to a particular subject

ODEA > ODEUM

ODEON same as > ODEUM

ODEONS > ODEON

ODES > ODE

ODEUM n ancient building for musical performances

ODEUMS > ODEUM

ODIC > OD

ODIFEROUS adj having odour

ODIOUS adj offensive

ODIOUSLY > ODIOUS

ODISM > OD

ODISMS > OD

ODIST > OD

ODISTS > OD

ODIUM n widespread dislike

ODIUMS > ODIUM

ODOGRAPH same as > ODOMETER

ODOGRAPHS > ODOGRAPH

ODOMETER n device that records the number of miles that a bicycle or motor vehicle has travelled

ODOMETERS > ODOMETER

ODOMETRY > ODOMETER

ODONATA pl n insects of an order that includes dragonflies

ODONATE n dragonfly or related insect

ODONATES > ODONATE

ODONATIST n dragonfly expert

ODONTALGY n toothache

ODONTIC adj of teeth

ODONTIST n dentist

ODONTISTS > ODONTIST

ODONTOID adj toothlike ▷ n bone in the spine

ODONTOIDS > ODONTOID

ODONTOMA n tumour near teeth

ODONTOMAS > ODONTOMA

ODOR same as > ODOUR

ODORANT n something with a strong smell

ODORANTS > ODORANT

ODORATE adj having a strong smell

ODORED same as > ODOURED

ODORFUL same as > ODOURFUL

ODORISE same as > ODORIZE

ODORISED > ODORISE

ODORISER same as > ODORIZER

ODORISERS > ODORISER

ODORISES > ODORISE

ODORISING > ODORISE

ODORIZE vb give an odour to

ODORIZED > ODORIZE

ODORIZER n something that odorizes

ODORIZERS > ODORIZER

ODORIZES > ODORIZE

ODORIZING > ODORIZE

ODORLESS > ODOR

ODOROUS adj having or emitting a characteristic smell

ODOROUSLY > ODOROUS

ODORS > ODOR

ODOUR n particular smell

ODOURED adj having odour

ODOURFUL adj full of odour

ODOURLESS > ODOUR

ODOURS > ODOUR

ODS > OD

ODSO n cry of surprise

ODYL same as > OD

ODYLE same as > OD

ODYLES > ODYLE

ODYLISM > ODYL

ODYLISMS > ODYL

ODYLS > ODYL

ODYSSEAN adj of or like an odyssey

ODYSSEY n long eventful journey

ODYSSEYS > ODYSSEY

ODZOOKS interj cry of surprise

OE n grandchild

OECIST n colony founder

OECISTS > OECIST

OECOLOGIC same as > ECOLOGIC

OECOLOGY less common spelling of > ECOLOGY

OECUMENIC variant of > ECUMENIC

OEDEMA n abnormal swelling

OEDEMAS > OEDEMA

OEDEMATA > OEDEMA

OEDIPAL adj relating to a complex whereby a male child wants to replace his father

OEDIPALLY > OEDIPAL

OEDIPEAN same as > OEDIPAL

OEDOMETER n instrument for measuring the consolidation of a soil specimen under pressure

OEILLADE n amorous or suggestive glance

OEILLADES > OEILLADE

OENANTHIC adj smelling of or like wine

OENOLOGY n study of wine

OENOMANCY n divination by studying the colour of wine

OENOMANIA n craving for wine

OENOMEL n drink made of wine and honey

OENOMELS > OENOMEL

OENOMETER n device for measuring the strength of wine

OENOPHIL same as > OENOPHILE

OENOPHILE n lover or connoisseur of wines

OENOPHILS > OENOPHIL

OENOPHILY n love of wine

OENOTHERA n type of American plant with yellow flowers that open in the evening

OERLIKON n type of cannon

OERLIKONS > OERLIKON

OERSTED n cgs unit of magnetic field strength

OERSTEDS > OERSTED

OES > OE

OESOPHAGI pl n gullets

OESTRAL > OESTRUS

OESTRIN obsolete term for > OESTROGEN

OESTRINS > OESTRIN

OESTRIOL n weak oestrogenic hormone secreted by the mammalian ovary

OESTRIOLS > OESTRIOL

OESTROGEN n female hormone that controls the reproductive cycle

OESTRONE n weak oestrogenic hormone secreted by the mammalian ovary

OESTRONES > OESTRONE

OESTROUS > OESTRUS

OESTRUAL adj relating to oestrus

OESTRUM same as > OESTRUS

OESTRUMS > OESTRUM

OESTRUS n regularly occurring period of fertility in female mammals

OESTRUSES > OESTRUS

O

OEUVRE n work of art, literature, music, etc
OEUVRES > OEUVRE
OF prep belonging to
OFAY n derogatory term for a White person
OFAYS > OFAY
OFF prep away from ▷ adv away ▷ adj not operating ▷ n side of the field to which the batsman's feet point ▷ vb kill
OFFA prep off
OFFAL n edible organs of an animal, such as liver or kidneys
OFFALS > OFFAL
OFFBEAT adj unusual or eccentric ▷ n any of the normally unaccented beats in a bar
OFFBEATS > OFFBEAT
OFFCAST n cast-off
OFFCASTS > OFFCAST
OFFCUT n piece remaining after the required parts have been cut out
OFFCUTS > OFFCUT
OFFED > OFF
OFFENCE n (cause of) hurt feelings or annoyance
OFFENCES > OFFENCE
OFFEND vb hurt the feelings of, insult
OFFENDED > OFFEND
OFFENDER > OFFEND
OFFENDERS > OFFEND
OFFENDING > OFFEND
OFFENDS > OFFEND
OFFENSE same as > OFFENCE
OFFENSES > OFFENSE
OFFENSIVE adj disagreeable ▷ n position or action of attack
OFFER vb present (something) for acceptance or rejection ▷ n something offered
OFFERABLE > OFFER
OFFERED > OFFER
OFFEREE n person to whom an offer is made
OFFEREES > OFFEREE
OFFERER > OFFER
OFFERERS > OFFER
OFFERING n thing offered
OFFERINGS > OFFERING
OFFEROR > OFFER
OFFERORS > OFFER
OFFERS > OFFER
OFFERTORY n offering of the bread and wine for Communion
OFFHAND adj casual, curt ▷ adv without preparation
OFFHANDED adj without care oe consideration
OFFICE n room or building where people work at desks
OFFICER n person in authority in the armed services ▷ vb furnish with officers

OFFICERED > OFFICER
OFFICERS > OFFICER
OFFICES > OFFICE
OFFICIAL adj of a position of authority ▷ n person who holds a position of authority
OFFICIALS > OFFICIAL
OFFICIANT n person who presides and officiates at a religious ceremony
OFFICIARY n body of officials ▷ adj of, relating to, or derived from office
OFFICIATE vb act in an official role
OFFICINAL adj (of pharmaceutical products) available without prescription ▷ n officinal preparation or plant
OFFICIOUS adj interfering unnecessarily
OFFIE n off-licence
OFFIES > OFFIE
OFFING n area of the sea visible from the shore
OFFINGS > OFFING
OFFISH adj aloof or distant in manner
OFFISHLY > OFFISH
OFFKEY adj out of tune
OFFLINE adj disconnected from a computer or the internet
OFFLOAD vb pass responsibility to someone else
OFFLOADED > OFFLOAD
OFFLOADS > OFFLOAD
OFFPEAK adj relating to times outside periods of intensive use
OFFPRINT n separate reprint of an article that originally appeared in a larger publication ▷ vb reprint (an article taken from a larger publication) separately
OFFPRINTS > OFFPRINT
OFFPUT n act of putting off
OFFPUTS > OFFPUT
OFFRAMP n road allowing traffic to leave a motorway
OFFRAMPS > OFFRAMP
OFFS > OFF
OFFSADDLE vb unsaddle
OFFSCREEN adj unseen by film viewers
OFFSCUM n scum
OFFSCUMS > OFFSCUM
OFFSEASON n period of little trade in a business
OFFSET vb cancel out ▷ n printing method
OFFSETS > OFFSET
OFFSHOOT n something developed from something else
OFFSHOOTS > OFFSHOOT

OFFSHORE adv away from or at some distance from the shore ▷ adj sited or conducted at sea ▷ n company operating abroad where the tax system is more advantageous than at home ▷ vb transfer (work) to another country where wages are lower
OFFSHORED > OFFSHORE
OFFSHORES > OFFSHORE
OFFSIDE adv (positioned) illegally ahead of the ball ▷ n side of a vehicle nearest the centre of the road
OFFSIDER n partner or assistant
OFFSIDERS > OFFSIDER
OFFSIDES > OFFSIDE
OFFSPRING n child
OFFSTAGE adv out of the view of the audience ▷ n something that happens offstage
OFFSTAGES > OFFSTAGE
OFFTAKE n act of taking off
OFFTAKES > OFFTAKE
OFFTRACK adj not at a racetrack
OFFY same as > OFFIE
OFLAG n prisoner-of-war camp for officers in World War II
OFLAGS > OFLAG
OFT adv often
OFTEN adv frequently, much of the time
OFTENER > OFTEN
OFTENEST > OFTEN
OFTENNESS > OFTEN
OFTER > OFT
OFTEST > OFT
OFTTIMES same as > OFTEN
OGAM same as > OGHAM
OGAMIC > OGAM
OGAMS > OGAM
OGDOAD n group of eight
OGDOADS > OGDOAD
OGEE n moulding having a cross section in the form of a letter S
OGEED adj (of an arch or moulding) having an ogee
OGEES > OGEE
OGGIN n sea
OGGINS > OGGIN
OGHAM n ancient writing system used by the Celts
OGHAMIC > OGHAM
OGHAMIST > OGHAM
OGHAMISTS > OGHAM
OGHAMS > OGHAM
OGIVAL > OGIVE
OGIVE n diagonal rib or groin of a Gothic vault
OGIVES > OGIVE
OGLE vb stare at (someone) lustfully ▷ n flirtatious or lewd look

OGLED > OGLE
OGLER > OGLE
OGLERS > OGLE
OGLES > OGLE
OGLING > OGLE
OGLINGS > OGLE
OGMIC > OGAM
OGRE n giant that eats human flesh
OGREISH > OGRE
OGREISHLY > OGRE
OGREISM > OGRE
OGREISMS > OGRE
OGRES > OGRE
OGRESS > OGRE
OGRESSES > OGRE
OGRISH > OGRE
OGRISHLY > OGRE
OGRISM > OGRE
OGRISMS > OGRE
OH interj exclamation of surprise, pain, etc ▷ vb say oh
OHED > OH
OHIA n Hawaiian plant
OHIAS > OHIA
OHING > OH
OHM n unit of electrical resistance
OHMAGE n electrical resistance in ohms
OHMAGES > OHMAGE
OHMIC adj of or relating to a circuit element
OHMICALLY > OHMIC
OHMMETER n instrument for measuring electrical resistance
OHMMETERS > OHMMETER
OHMS > OHM
OHO n exclamation expressing surprise, exultation, or derision
OHONE same as > OCHONE
OHS > OH
OI interj shout to attract attention ▷ n grey-faced petrel
OIDIA > OIDIUM
OIDIOID > OIDIUM
OIDIUM n type of fungal spore
OIK n person regarded as inferior because ignorant or lower-class
OIKIST same as > OECIST
OIKISTS > OIKIST
OIKS > OIK
OIL n viscous liquid, insoluble in water and usu flammable ▷ vb lubricate (a machine) with oil
OILBIRD n type of nocturnal gregarious cave-dwelling bird
OILBIRDS > OILBIRD
OILCAMP n camp for oilworkers
OILCAMPS > OILCAMP
OILCAN n container with a long nozzle for applying oil to machinery
OILCANS > OILCAN

OILCLOTH n waterproof material

OILCLOTHS > OILCLOTH

OILCUP n cup-shaped oil reservoir in a machine providing continuous lubrication for a bearing

OILCUPS > OILCUP

OILED > OIL

OILER n person, device, etc, that lubricates or supplies oil

OILERIES > OILERY

OILERS > OILER

OILERY n oil business

OILFIELD n area containing oil reserves

OILFIELDS > OILFIELD

OILFIRED adj using oil as fuel

OILGAS n gaseous mixture of hydrocarbons used as a fuel

OILGASES > OILGAS

OILHOLE n hole for oil

OILHOLES > OILHOLE

OILIER > OILY

OILIEST > OILY

OILILY > OILY

OILINESS > OILY

OILING > OIL

OILLET same as > EYELET

OILLETS > OILLET

OILMAN n person who owns or operates oil wells

OILMEN > OILMAN

OILNUT n nut from which oil is extracted

OILNUTS > OILNUT

OILPAN n sump

OILPANS > OILPAN

OILPAPER n oiled paper

OILPAPERS > OILPAPER

OILPROOF adj resistant to oil

OILS > OIL

OILSEED n seed from which oil is extracted

OILSEEDS > OILSEED

OILSKIN n (garment made from) waterproof material

OILSKINS > OILSKIN

OILSTONE n stone with a fine grain lubricated with oil and used for sharpening cutting tools

OILSTONES > OILSTONE

OILTIGHT adj not allowing oil through

OILWAY n channel for oil

OILWAYS > OILWAY

OILY adj soaked or covered with oil

OINK n grunt of a pig or an imitation of this ▷ interj imitation or representation of the grunt of a pig ▷ vb make noise of pig

OINKED > OINK

OINKING > OINK

OINKS > OINK

OINOLOGY same as > OENOLOGY

OINOMEL same as > OENOMEL

OINOMELS > OINOMEL

OINT vb anoint

OINTED > OINT

OINTING > OINT

OINTMENT n greasy substance used for healing skin or as a cosmetic

OINTMENTS > OINTMENT

OINTS > OINT

OIS > OI

OITICICA n South American tree

OITICICAS > OITICICA

OJIME n Japanese bead used to secure cords

OJIMES > OJIME

OKA n unit of weight used in Turkey

OKAPI n African animal related to the giraffe but with a shorter neck

OKAPIS > OKAPI

OKAS > OKA

OKAY adj satisfactory ▷ vb approve or endorse ▷ n approval or agreement ▷ interj expression of approval

OKAYED > OKAY

OKAYING > OKAY

OKAYS > OKAY

OKE same as > OKA

OKEH variant of > OKAY

OKEHS > OKEH

OKES > OKE

OKEYDOKE variant of > OKAY

OKEYDOKEY variant of > OKAY

OKIMONO n Japanese ornamental item

OKIMONOS > OKIMONO

OKRA n tropical plant with edible green pods

OKRAS > OKRA

OKTA n unit used in meteorology to measure cloud cover

OKTAS > OKTA

OLD adj having lived or existed for a long time ▷ n earlier or past time

OLDE adj old-world or quaint, used facetiously

OLDEN adj old ▷ vb grow old

OLDENED > OLDEN

OLDENING > OLDEN

OLDENS > OLDEN

OLDER adj having lived or existed longer

OLDEST > OLD

OLDIE n old but popular song or film

OLDIES > OLDIE

OLDISH > OLD

OLDNESS > OLD

OLDNESSES > OLD

OLDS > OLD

OLDSQUAW n type of long-tailed sea duck

OLDSQUAWS > OLDSQUAW

OLDSTER n older person

OLDSTERS > OLDSTER

OLDSTYLE n printing type style

OLDSTYLES > OLDSTYLE

OLDWIFE n any of various fishes, esp the menhaden or the alewife

OLDWIVES > OLDWIFE

OLDY same as > OLDIE

OLE interj exclamation of approval or encouragement customary at bullfights ▷ n cry of olé

OLEA > OLEUM

OLEACEOUS adj relating to a family of trees and shrubs, including the ash, jasmine, and olive

OLEANDER n Mediterranean flowering evergreen shrub

OLEANDERS > OLEANDER

OLEARIA n daisy bush

OLEARIAS > OLEARIA

OLEASTER n type of shrub with silver-white twigs and yellow flowers

OLEASTERS > OLEASTER

OLEATE n any salt or ester of oleic acid

OLEATES > OLEATE

OLECRANAL > OLECRANON

OLECRANON n bony projection of the ulna behind the elbow joint

OLEFIANT adj forming oil

OLEFIN same as > OLEFINE

OLEFINE another name for > ALKENE

OLEFINES > OLEFINE

OLEFINIC > OLEFINE

OLEFINS > OLEFIN

OLEIC adj as in oleic acid colourless oily liquid used in making soap

OLEIN another name for > TRIOLEIN

OLEINE same as > OLEIN

OLEINES > OLEINE

OLEINS > OLEIN

OLENT adj having smell

OLEO n as in oleo oil oil extracted from beef fat

OLEOGRAPH n chromolithograph printed in oil colours to imitate the appearance of an oil painting

OLEORESIN n semisolid mixture of a resin and essential oil

OLEOS > OLEO

OLES > OLE

OLESTRA n trademark term for an artificial fat

OLESTRAS > OLESTRA

OLEUM n type of sulphuric acid

OLEUMS > OLEUM

OLFACT vb smell something

OLFACTED > OLFACT

OLFACTING > OLFACT

OLFACTION n sense of smell

OLFACTIVE adj of sense of smell

OLFACTORY adj relating to the sense of smell ▷ n organ or nerve concerned with the sense of smell

OLFACTS > OLFACT

OLIBANUM n frankincense

OLIBANUMS > OLIBANUM

OLICOOK n doughnut

OLICOOKS > OLICOOK

OLID adj foul-smelling

OLIGAEMIA n reduction in the volume of the blood, as occurs after haemorrhage

OLIGAEMIC > OLIGAEMIA

OLIGARCH n member of an oligarchy

OLIGARCHS > OLIGARCH

OLIGARCHY n government by a small group of people

OLIGEMIA same as > OLIGAEMIA

OLIGEMIAS > OLIGEMIA

OLIGEMIC > OLIGAEMIA

OLIGIST n type of iron ore

OLIGISTS > OLIGIST

OLIGOCENE adj belonging to geological time period

OLIGOGENE n type of gene

OLIGOMER n compound of relatively low molecular weight containing up to five monomer units

OLIGOMERS > OLIGOMER

OLIGOPOLY n market situation in which control over the supply of a commodity is held by a small number of producers

OLIGURIA n excretion of an abnormally small volume of urine

OLIGURIAS > OLIGURIA

OLIGURIC adj relating to oliguria

OLINGO n South American mammal

OLINGOS > OLINGO

OLINGUITO n type of small S American mammal

OLIO n dish of many different ingredients

OLIOS > OLIO

OLIPHANT archaic variant of > ELEPHANT

OLIPHANTS > OLIPHANT

OLITORIES > OLITORY

OLITORY n kitchen garden

OLIVARY adj shaped like an olive

O

OLIVE n small green or black fruit used as food or pressed for its oil ▷ adj greyish-green

OLIVENITE n green to black rare secondary mineral

OLIVER n as in Bath oliver type of unsweetened biscuit

OLIVERS > OLIVER

OLIVES > OLIVE

OLIVET n button shaped like olive

OLIVETS > OLIVET

OLIVEWOOD n the wood of the olive tree

OLIVINE n olive-green mineral of the olivine group

OLIVINES > OLIVINE

OLIVINIC adj containing olivine

OLLA n cooking pot

OLLAMH n old Irish term for a wise man

OLLAMHS > OLLAMH

OLLAS > OLLA

OLLAV same as > OLLAMH

OLLAVS > OLLAV

OLLER n waste ground

OLLERS > OLLER

OLLIE n type of skateboarding jump ▷ vb perform an ollie

OLLIED > OLLIE

OLLIEING > OLLIE

OLLIES > OLLIE

OLM n pale blind eel-like salamander

OLMS > OLM

OLOGIES > OLOGY

OLOGIST n scientist

OLOGISTS > OLOGIST

OLOGOAN vb complain loudly without reason

OLOGOANED > OLOGOAN

OLOGOANS > OLOGOAN

OLOGY n science or other branch of knowledge

OLOLIUQUI n medicinal plant used by the Aztecs

OLOROSO n golden-coloured sweet sherry

OLOROSOS > OLOROSO

OLPAE > OLPE

OLPE n ancient Greek jug

OLPES > OLPE

OLYCOOK same as > OLYKOEK

OLYCOOKS > OLYCOOK

OLYKOEK n American type of doughnut

OLYKOEKS > OLYKOEK

OLYMPIAD n staging of the modern Olympic Games

OLYMPIADS > OLYMPIAD

OLYMPICS pl n modern revival of the ancient Greek games, featuring sporting contests

OM n sacred syllable in Hinduism

OMA n grandmother

OMADHAUN n foolish man or boy

OMADHAUNS > OMADHAUN

OMAS > OMA

OMASA > OMASUM

OMASAL > OMASUM

OMASUM n compartment in the stomach of a ruminant animal

OMBER same as > OMBRE

OMBERS > OMBER

OMBRE n 18th-century card game

OMBRELLA old form of > UMBRELLA

OMBRELLAS > OMBRELLA

OMBRES > OMBRE

OMBROPHIL n plant flourishing in rainy conditions

OMBU n South American tree

OMBUDSMAN n official who investigates complaints against government organizations

OMBUDSMEN > OMBUDSMAN

OMBUS > OMBU

OMEGA n last letter in the Greek alphabet

OMEGAS > OMEGA

OMELET same as > OMELETTE

OMELETS > OMELET

OMELETTE n dish of eggs beaten and fried

OMELETTES > OMELETTE

OMEN n happening or object thought to foretell success or misfortune ▷ vb portend

OMENED > OMEN

OMENING > OMEN

OMENS > OMEN

OMENTA > OMENTUM

OMENTAL > OMENTUM

OMENTUM n double fold of the peritoneum

OMENTUMS > OMENTUM

OMER n ancient Hebrew unit of dry measure

OMERS > OMER

OMERTA n conspiracy of silence

OMERTAS > OMERTA

OMICRON n 15th letter in the Greek alphabet

OMICRONS > OMICRON

OMIGOD interj exclamation of surprise, pleasure, dismay, etc

OMIKRON same as > OMICRON

OMIKRONS > OMIKRON

OMINOUS adj worrying, seeming to foretell misfortune

OMINOUSLY > OMINOUS

OMISSIBLE > OMIT

OMISSION n something that has been left out or passed over

OMISSIONS > OMISSION

OMISSIVE > OMISSION

OMIT vb leave out

OMITS > OMIT

OMITTANCE n omission

OMITTED > OMIT

OMITTER > OMIT

OMITTERS > OMIT

OMITTING > OMIT

OMLAH n staff team in India

OMLAHS > OMLAH

OMMATEA > OMMATEUM

OMMATEUM n insect eye

OMMATIDIA pl n cone-shaped parts of the eyes of some arthropods

OMNEITIES > OMNEITY

OMNEITY n state of being all

OMNIANA n miscellaneous collection

OMNIARCH n ruler of everything

OMNIARCHS > OMNIARCH

OMNIBUS n several books or TV or radio programmes made into one ▷ adj consisting of or dealing with several different things at once

OMNIBUSES > OMNIBUS

OMNIETIES > OMNIETY

OMNIETY same as > OMNEITY

OMNIFIC adj creating all things

OMNIFIED > OMNIFY

OMNIFIES > OMNIFY

OMNIFORM adj of all forms

OMNIFY vb make something universal

OMNIFYING > OMNIFY

OMNIMODE adj of all functions

OMNIRANGE n very-high-frequency ground radio navigational system

OMNIUM n total value

OMNIUMS > OMNIUM

OMNIVORA n group of omnivorous mammals

OMNIVORE n omnivorous animal

OMNIVORES > OMNIVORE

OMNIVORY n state of being omnivorous

OMOHYOID n muscle in shoulder

OMOHYOIDS > OMOHYOID

OMOPHAGIA n eating of raw food, esp meat

OMOPHAGIC > OMOPHAGIA

OMOPHAGY same as > OMOPHAGIA

OMOPHORIA pl n stole-like bands worn by some bishops

OMOPLATE n shoulder blade

OMOPLATES > OMOPLATE

OMOV n voting system in which each voter has one vote to cast

OMOVS > OMOV

OMPHACITE n type of mineral

OMPHALI > OMPHALOS

OMPHALIC > OMPHALOS

OMPHALOI > OMPHALOS

OMPHALOID adj like navel

OMPHALOS n (in the ancient world) a sacred conical object, esp a stone

OMRAH n Muslim noble

OMRAHS > OMRAH

OMS > OM

ON prep indicating position above, attachment, closeness, etc ▷ adv in operation ▷ adj operating ▷ n side of the field on which the batsman stands ▷ vb go on

ONAGER n wild ass of Persia

ONAGERS > ONAGER

ONAGRI > ONAGER

ONANISM n withdrawal in sexual intercourse before ejaculation

ONANISMS > ONANISM

ONANIST > ONANISM

ONANISTIC > ONANISM

ONANISTS > ONANISM

ONBEAT n first and third beats in a bar of four-four time

ONBEATS > ONBEAT

ONBOARD adj on a ship or other craft

ONCE adv on one occasion ▷ n one occasion

ONCER n (formerly) a one-pound note

ONCERS > ONCER

ONCES > ONCE

ONCET dialect form of > ONCE

ONCIDIUM n American orchid

ONCIDIUMS > ONCIDIUM

ONCOGEN n substance causing tumours to form

ONCOGENE n gene that can cause cancer when abnormally activated

ONCOGENES > ONCOGENE

ONCOGENIC adj causing the formation of a tumour

ONCOGENS > ONCOGEN

ONCOLOGIC > ONCOLOGY

ONCOLOGY n branch of medicine concerned with the study, classification, and treatment of tumours

ONCOLYSES > ONCOLYSIS

ONCOLYSIS n destruction of tumours

ONCOLYTIC adj destroying tumours

ONCOME n act of coming on

ONCOMES > ONCOME

ONCOMETER n instrument for measuring body organs

ONCOMICE > ONCOMOUSE

ONCOMING *adj* approaching from the front ▷ *n* approach or onset

ONCOMINGS > ONCOMING

ONCOMOUSE *n* mouse bred for cancer treatment research

ONCOST *same as* > OVERHEADS

ONCOSTMAN *n* miner paid daily

ONCOSTMEN > ONCOSTMAN

ONCOSTS > ONCOST

ONCOTOMY *n* surgical cutting of a tumour

ONCOVIRUS *n* virus causing cancer

ONCUS *same as* > ONKUS

ONDATRA *same as* > MUSQUASH

ONDATRAS > ONDATRA

ONDINE *same as* > UNDINE

ONDINES > ONDINE

ONDING *Scots word for* > ONSET

ONDINGS > ONDING

ONDOGRAM *n* record made by ondograph

ONDOGRAMS > ONDOGRAM

ONDOGRAPH *n* instrument for producing a graphical recording of an alternating current

ONE *adj* single, lone ▷ *n* number or figure 1 ▷ *pron* any person

ONEFOLD *adj* simple

ONEIRIC *adj* of or relating to dreams

ONELY *same as* > ONLY

ONENESS *n* unity

ONENESSES > ONENESS

ONER *n* single continuous action

ONERIER > ONERY

ONERIEST > ONERY

ONEROUS *adj* (of a task) difficult to carry out

ONEROUSLY > ONEROUS

ONERS > ONER

ONERY *same as* > ORNERY

ONES > ONE

ONESELF *pron* reflexive form of *one*

ONESIE *n* one-piece garment combining a top with trousers

ONESIES > ONESIE

ONETIME *adj* at some time in the past

ONEYER *old form of* > ONE

ONEYERS > ONEYER

ONEYRE *same as* > ONEYER

ONEYRES > ONEYRE

ONFALL *n* attack or onset

ONFALLS > ONFALL

ONFLOW *n* flowing on

ONFLOWS > ONFLOW

ONGAONGA *n* New Zealand nettle with a severe or fatal sting

ONGAONGAS > ONGAONGA

ONGOING *adj* in progress, continuing

ONGOINGS *pl n* things that are happening

ONIE *variant spelling of* > ONY

ONION *n* strongly flavoured edible bulb ▷ *vb* add onion to

ONIONED > ONION

ONIONIER > ONION

ONIONIEST > ONION

ONIONING > ONION

ONIONS > ONION

ONIONSKIN *n* glazed translucent paper

ONIONY > ONION

ONIRIC *same as* > ONEIRIC

ONISCOID *adj* of or like woodlice

ONIUM *n* as in *onium compound* type of chemical salt

ONIUMS > ONIUM

ONKUS *adj* bad

ONLAY *n* artificial veneer for a tooth

ONLAYS > ONLAY

ONLIEST *same as* > ONLY

ONLINE *adj* connected to a computer or the internet

ONLINER *n* person who uses the internet regularly

ONLINERS > ONLINER

ONLOAD *vb* load files on to a computer

ONLOADED > ONLOAD

ONLOADING > ONLOAD

ONLOADS > ONLOAD

ONLOOKER *n* person who watches without taking part

ONLOOKERS > ONLOOKER

ONLOOKING > ONLOOKER

ONLY *adj* alone of its kind ▷ *adv* exclusively

ONNED > ON

ONNING > ON

ONO *n* Hawaiian fish

ONOMAST *n* person who studies proper names

ONOMASTIC *adj* of or relating to proper names

ONOMASTS > ONOMAST

ONOS > ONO

ONRUSH *n* forceful forward rush or flow

ONRUSHES > ONRUSH

ONRUSHING *adj* approaching quickly

ONS > ON

ONSCREEN *adj* appearing on screen

ONSET *n* beginning

ONSETS > ONSET

ONSETTER *n* attacker

ONSETTERS > ONSET

ONSETTING *n* attack

ONSHORE *adv* towards the land

ONSHORING *n* practice of employing white-collar workers from abroad

ONSIDE *adv* (of a player in various sports) in a legal position ▷ *adj* taking one's part or side ▷ *n* part of cricket field where a batsman stands

ONSIDES > ONSIDE

ONSLAUGHT *n* violent attack

ONST *same as* > ONCE

ONSTAGE *adj* visible by audience

ONSTEAD *Scots word for* > FARMSTEAD

ONSTEADS > ONSTEAD

ONSTREAM *adj* in operation

ONTIC *adj* having real existence

ONTICALLY > ONTIC

ONTO *prep* a position on

ONTOGENIC > ONTOGENY

ONTOGENY *n* entire sequence of events involved in the development of an individual organism

ONTOLOGIC > ONTOLOGY

ONTOLOGY *n* branch of philosophy concerned with existence

ONUS *n* responsibility or burden

ONUSES > ONUS

ONWARD *same as* > ONWARDS

ONWARDLY > ONWARD

ONWARDS *adv* at or towards a point or position ahead

ONY *Scots word for* > ANY

ONYCHA *n* part of mollusc

ONYCHAS > ONYCHA

ONYCHIA *n* inflammation of the nails or claws of animals

ONYCHIAS > ONYCHIA

ONYCHITE *n* type of stone

ONYCHITES > ONYCHITE

ONYCHITIS *n* inflammation of nails

ONYCHIUM *n* part of insect foot

ONYCHIUMS > ONYCHIUM

ONYMOUS *adj* (of a book) bearing its author's name

ONYX *n* type of quartz with coloured layers

ONYXES > ONYX

OO *Scots word for* > WOOL

OOBIT *n* hairy caterpillar

OOBITS > OOBIT

OOCYST *n* type of zygote

OOCYSTS > OOCYST

OOCYTE *n* immature female germ cell that gives rise to an ovum

OOCYTES > OOCYTE

OODLES *pl n* great quantities

OODLINS *same as* > OODLES

OOF *n* money

OOFIER > OOF

OOFIEST > OOF

OOFS > OOF

OOFTISH *n* money

OOFTISHES > OOFTISH

OOFY > OOF

OOGAMETE *n* female gamete

OOGAMETES > OOGAMETE

OOGAMIES > OOGAMY

OOGAMOUS > OOGAMY

OOGAMY *n* type of sexual reproduction

OOGENESES > OOGENESIS

OOGENESIS *n* formation and maturation of ova from undifferentiated cells in the ovary

OOGENETIC > OOGENESIS

OOGENIES > OOGENY

OOGENY *same as* > OOGENESIS

OOGONIA > OOGONIUM

OOGONIAL > OOGONIUM

OOGONIUM *n* immature female germ cell forming oocytes by repeated divisions

OOGONIUMS > OOGONIUM

OOH *interj* exclamation of surprise, pleasure, pain, etc ▷ *vb* say ooh

OOHED > OOH

OOHING *n* act of exclaiming 'ooh'

OOHINGS > OOHING

OOHS > OOH

OOIDAL *adj* shaped like egg

OOLACHAN *same as* > EULACHON

OOLACHANS > OOLACHAN

OOLAKAN *same as* > EULACHON

OOLAKANS > OOLAKAN

OOLICHAN *n* north Pacific candlefish

OOLICHANS > OOLICHAN

OOLITE *n* limestone made up of tiny grains of calcium carbonate

OOLITES > OOLITE

OOLITH *n* tiny spherical grain of sedimentary rock

OOLITHS > OOLITH

OOLITIC > OOLITE

OOLOGIC > OOLOGY

OOLOGICAL > OOLOGY

OOLOGIES > OOLOGY

OOLOGIST > OOLOGY

OOLOGISTS > OOLOGY

OOLOGY *n* study of birds' eggs

OOLONG *n* kind of dark tea

OOLONGS > OOLONG

OOM *n* title of respect used to refer to an elderly man

OOMIAC *same as* > UMIAK

OOMIACK *same as* > UMIAK

OOMIACKS > OOMIACK

OOMIACS > OOMIAC

OOMIAK *same as* > UMIAK

o

OOMIAKS > OOMIAK
OOMPAH *n* representation of the sound made by a deep brass instrument ▷ *vb* make the noise of a brass instrument
OOMPAHED > OOMPAH
OOMPAHING > OOMPAH
OOMPAHS > OOMPAH
OOMPH *n* enthusiasm, vigour, or energy
OOMPHS > OOMPH
OOMS > OOM
OOMYCETE *n* organism formerly classified as fungi
OOMYCETES > OOMYCETE
OON *Scots word for* **>** OVEN
OONS > OON
OONT *n* camel
OONTS > OONT
OOP *vb* Scots word meaning to bind
OOPED > OOP
OOPHORON *n* ovary
OOPHORONS > OOPHORON
OOPHYTE *n* gametophyte in mosses, liverworts, and ferns
OOPHYTES > OOPHYTE
OOPHYTIC > OOPHYTE
OOPING > OOP
OOPS *interj* exclamation of surprise or apology
OOR *Scots form of* **>** OUR
OORALI *n* member of Indian people
OORALIS > OORALI
OORIAL *n* Himalayan sheep
OORIALS > OORIAL
OORIE *adj* Scots word meaning shabby
OORIER > OORIE
OORIEST > OORIE
OOS > OO
OOSE *n* dust
OOSES > OOSE
OOSIER > OOSE
OOSIEST > OOSE
OOSPERM *n* fertilized ovum
OOSPERMS > OOSPERM
OOSPHERE *n* large female gamete produced in the oogonia of algae and fungi
OOSPHERES > OOSPHERE
OOSPORE *n* thick-walled sexual spore
OOSPORES > OOSPORE
OOSPORIC > OOSPORE
OOSPOROUS > OOSPORE
OOSY > OOSE
OOT *Scots word for* **>** OUT
OOTHECA *n* capsule containing eggs
OOTHECAE > OOTHECA
OOTHECAL > OOTHECA
OOTID *n* immature female gamete that develops into an ovum
OOTIDS > OOTID
OOTS > OOT
OOZE *vb* flow slowly ▷ *n* sluggish flow

OOZED > OOZE
OOZES > OOZE
OOZIER > OOZY
OOZIEST > OOZY
OOZILY > OOZY
OOZINESS > OOZY
OOZING > OOZE
OOZY *adj* moist or dripping
OP *n* operation
OPA *n* grandfather
OPACIFIED > OPACIFY
OPACIFIER > OPACIFY
OPACIFIES > OPACIFY
OPACIFY *vb* become or make opaque
OPACITIES > OPACITY
OPACITY *n* state or quality of being opaque
OPACOUS *same as* **>** OPAQUE
OPAH *n* large soft-finned deep-sea fish
OPAHS > OPAH
OPAL *n* iridescent precious stone
OPALED *adj* made like opal
OPALESCE *vb* exhibit a milky iridescence
OPALESCED > OPALESCE
OPALESCES > OPALESCE
OPALINE *adj* opalescent ▷ *n* opaque or semiopaque whitish glass
OPALINES > OPALINE
OPALISED *same as* **>** OPALIZED
OPALIZED *adj* made into opal
OPALS > OPAL
OPAQUE *adj* not able to be seen through, not transparent ▷ *n* opaque pigment used to block out particular areas on a negative ▷ *vb* make opaque
OPAQUED > OPAQUE
OPAQUELY > OPAQUE
OPAQUER > OPAQUE
OPAQUES > OPAQUE
OPAQUEST > OPAQUE
OPAQUING > OPAQUE
OPAS > OPA
OPCODE *n* computer code containing operating instructions
OPCODES > OPCODE
OPE *archaic or poetic word for* **>** OPEN
OPED > OPE
OPEN *adj* not closed ▷ *vb* (cause to) become open ▷ *n* competition which all may enter
OPENABLE > OPEN
OPENCAST *n* as in *opencast mining* mining by excavating from the surface
OPENED > OPEN
OPENER *n* tool for opening cans and bottles
OPENERS > OPENER
OPENEST > OPEN

OPENING *n* beginning ▷ *adj* first
OPENINGS > OPENING
OPENLY > OPEN
OPENNESS > OPEN
OPENS > OPEN
OPENSIDE *n* in rugby, flanker who plays on the open side of the scrum
OPENSIDES > OPENSIDE
OPENWORK *n* ornamental work, as of metal or embroidery, having a pattern of openings or holes
OPENWORKS > OPENWORK
OPEPE *n* African tree
OPEPES > OPEPE
OPERA *n* drama in which the text is sung to an orchestral accompaniment
OPERABLE *adj* capable of being treated by a surgical operation
OPERABLY > OPERABLE
OPERAGOER *n* person who goes to operas
OPERAND *n* quantity, variable, or function upon which an operation is performed
OPERANDS > OPERAND
OPERANT *adj* producing effects ▷ *n* person or thing that operates
OPERANTLY > OPERANT
OPERANTS > OPERANT
OPERAS > OPERA
OPERATE *vb* (cause to) work
OPERATED > OPERATE
OPERATES > OPERATE
OPERATIC *adj* of or relating to opera
OPERATICS *n* performance of operas
OPERATING > OPERATE
OPERATION *n* method or procedure of working
OPERATISE *same as* **>** OPERATIZE
OPERATIVE *adj* working ▷ *n* worker with a special skill
OPERATIZE *vb* turn (a play, novel, etc) into an opera
OPERATOR *n* person who operates a machine or instrument
OPERATORS > OPERATOR
OPERCELE *same as* **>** OPERCULE
OPERCELES > OPERCELE
OPERCULA > OPERCULUM
OPERCULAR **>** OPERCULUM
OPERCULE *n* gill cover
OPERCULES > OPERCULE
OPERCULUM *n* covering flap or lidlike structure in animals or plants
OPERETTA *n* light-hearted comic opera

OPERETTAS > OPERETTA
OPERON *n* group of adjacent genes in bacteria
OPERONS > OPERON
OPEROSE *adj* laborious
OPEROSELY > OPEROSE
OPEROSITY > OPEROSE
OPES > OPE
OPGEFOK *adj* South African taboo slang for damaged or bungled
OPHIDIAN *n* reptile of the suborder which comprises the snakes
OPHIDIANS > OPHIDIAN
OPHIOLITE *n* type of mineral
OPHIOLOGY *n* branch of zoology that is concerned with the study of snakes
OPHITE *n* any of several greenish mottled rocks
OPHITES > OPHITE
OPHITIC *adj* having small elongated feldspar crystals enclosed
OPHIURA *n* sea creature like a starfish
OPHIURAN *same as* **>** OPHIURA
OPHIURANS > OPHIURAN
OPHIURAS > OPHIURA
OPHIURID *same as* **>** OPHIURA
OPHIURIDS > OPHIURID
OPHIUROID *adj* of or like ophiura
OPIATE *n* narcotic drug containing opium ▷ *adj* containing or consisting of opium ▷ *vb* treat with an opiate
OPIATED > OPIATE
OPIATES > OPIATE
OPIATING > OPIATE
OPIFICER *n* craftsman
OPIFICERS > OPIFICER
OPINABLE *adj* thinkable
OPINE *vb* express an opinion
OPINED > OPINE
OPINES > OPINE
OPING > OPE
OPINICUS *n* mythical monster
OPINING > OPINE
OPINION *n* personal belief or judgment
OPINIONED *adj* having strong opinions
OPINIONS > OPINION
OPIOID *n* substance that resembles morphine
OPIOIDS > OPIOID
OPIUM *n* addictive narcotic drug made from poppy seeds
OPIUMISM *n* addiction to opium
OPIUMISMS > OPIUMISM
OPIUMS > OPIUM
OPOBALSAM *n* soothing ointment
OPODELDOC *n* medical ointment

OPOPANAX n medical resin from plant
OPORICE n former medicine made from fruit
OPORICES > OPORICE
OPOSSUM n small marsupial of America or Australasia
OPOSSUMS > OPOSSUM
OPPIDAN adj of a town ▷ n person living in a town
OPPIDANS > OPPIDAN
OPPILANT > OPPILATE
OPPILATE vb block (the pores, bowels, etc)
OPPILATED > OPPILATE
OPPILATES > OPPILATE
OPPO n counterpart in another organization
OPPONENCY > OPPONENT
OPPONENS n muscle of the thumb
OPPONENT n person one is working against in a contest, battle, or argument ▷ adj opposite, as in position
OPPONENTS > OPPONENT
OPPORTUNE adj happening at a suitable time
OPPOS > OPPO
OPPOSABLE adj (of the thumb) capable of touching the tip of all the other fingers
OPPOSABLY > OPPOSABLE
OPPOSE vb work against
OPPOSED > OPPOSE
OPPOSER > OPPOSE
OPPOSERS > OPPOSE
OPPOSES > OPPOSE
OPPOSING > OPPOSE
OPPOSITE adj situated on the other side ▷ n person or thing that is opposite ▷ prep facing ▷ adv on the other side
OPPOSITES > OPPOSITE
OPPRESS vb control by cruelty or force
OPPRESSED > OPPRESS
OPPRESSES > OPPRESS
OPPRESSOR > OPPRESS
OPPUGN vb call into question
OPPUGNANT adj combative, antagonistic, or contrary
OPPUGNED > OPPUGN
OPPUGNER > OPPUGN
OPPUGNERS > OPPUGN
OPPUGNING > OPPUGN
OPPUGNS > OPPUGN
OPS > OP
OPSIMATH n person who learns late in life
OPSIMATHS > OPSIMATH
OPSIMATHY > OPSIMATH
OPSIN n type of protein
OPSINS > OPSIN
OPSOMANIA n extreme enthusiasm for a particular food

OPSONIC > OPSONIN
OPSONIFY same as > OPSONIZE
OPSONIN n constituent of blood serum
OPSONINS > OPSONIN
OPSONISE same as > OPSONIZE
OPSONISED > OPSONISE
OPSONISES > OPSONISE
OPSONIUM n relish eaten with bread
OPSONIUMS > OPSONIUM
OPSONIZE vb subject (bacteria) to the action of opsonins
OPSONIZED > OPSONIZE
OPSONIZES > OPSONIZE
OPT vb show a preference, choose
OPTANT n person who opts
OPTANTS > OPTANT
OPTATIVE adj indicating or expressing choice, preference, or wish ▷ n optative mood
OPTATIVES > OPTATIVE
OPTED > OPT
OPTER > OPT
OPTERS > OPT
OPTIC adj relating to the eyes or sight
OPTICAL adj of or involving light or optics
OPTICALLY > OPTICAL
OPTICIAN n person qualified to prescribe glasses
OPTICIANS > OPTICIAN
OPTICIST n optics expert
OPTICISTS > OPTICIST
OPTICS n science of sight and light
OPTIMA > OPTIMUM
OPTIMAL adj best or most favourable
OPTIMALLY > OPTIMAL
OPTIMATE n Roman aristocrat
OPTIMATES > OPTIMATE
OPTIME n mathematics student at Cambridge University
OPTIMES > OPTIME
OPTIMISE same as > OPTIMIZE
OPTIMISED > OPTIMISE
OPTIMISER > OPTIMISE
OPTIMISES > OPTIMISE
OPTIMISM n tendency to take the most hopeful view
OPTIMISMS > OPTIMISM
OPTIMIST > OPTIMISM
OPTIMISTS > OPTIMISM
OPTIMIZE vb make the most of
OPTIMIZED > OPTIMIZE
OPTIMIZER > OPTIMIZE
OPTIMIZES > OPTIMIZE
OPTIMUM n best possible conditions ▷ adj most favourable

OPTIMUMS > OPTIMUM
OPTING > OPT
OPTION n choice ▷ vb obtain an option on
OPTIONAL adj possible but not compulsory ▷ n optional thing
OPTIONALS > OPTIONAL
OPTIONED > OPTION
OPTIONEE n holder of a financial option
OPTIONEES > OPTIONEE
OPTIONING > OPTION
OPTIONS > OPTION
OPTOLOGY n science of sight
OPTOMETER n any of various instruments for measuring the refractive power of the eye
OPTOMETRY n science or practice of testing visual acuity and prescribing corrective lenses
OPTOPHONE n device for blind people that converts printed words into sounds
OPTRONIC adj relating to optronics
OPTRONICS n science of electronic and light signals
OPTS > OPT
OPULENCE > OPULENT
OPULENCES > OPULENT
OPULENCY > OPULENT
OPULENT adj having or indicating wealth
OPULENTLY > OPULENT
OPULUS n flowering shrub
OPULUSES > OPULUS
OPUNTIA n type of cactus
OPUNTIAS > OPUNTIA
OPUS n artistic creation, esp a musical work
OPUSCLE same as > OPUSCULE
OPUSCLES > OPUSCLE
OPUSCULA > OPUSCULUM
OPUSCULAR > OPUSCULE
OPUSCULE n small or insignificant artistic work
OPUSCULES > OPUSCULE
OPUSCULUM same as > OPUSCULE
OPUSES > OPUS
OQUASSA n American trout
OQUASSAS > OQUASSA
OR prep before ▷ adj of the metal gold ▷ n gold
ORA > OS
ORACH same as > ORACHE
ORACHE n type of plant
ORACHES > ORACHE
ORACIES > ORACY
ORACLE n shrine of an ancient god ▷ vb utter as an oracle
ORACLED > ORACLE
ORACLES > ORACLE
ORACLING > ORACLE
ORACULAR adj of or like an oracle

ORACULOUS adj of an oracle
ORACY n capacity to use speech
ORAD adv towards the mouth
ORAGIOUS adj stormy
ORAL adj spoken ▷ n spoken examination
ORALISM n oral method of communicating with deaf people
ORALISMS > ORALISM
ORALIST > ORALISM
ORALISTS > ORALISM
ORALITIES > ORALITY
ORALITY n state of being oral
ORALLY > ORAL
ORALS > ORAL
ORANG n orangutan
ORANGE n reddish-yellow citrus fruit ▷ adj reddish-yellow
ORANGEADE n orange-flavoured, usu fizzy drink
ORANGER > ORANGE
ORANGERIE archaic variant of > ORANGERY
ORANGERY n greenhouse for growing orange trees
ORANGES > ORANGE
ORANGEST > ORANGE
ORANGEY > ORANGE
ORANGIER > ORANGE
ORANGIEST > ORANGE
ORANGISH > ORANGE
ORANGS > ORANG
ORANGUTAN n large ape with shaggy reddish-brown hair
ORANGY > ORANGE
ORANT n artistic representation of worshipper
ORANTS > ORANT
ORARIA > ORARIUM
ORARIAN n person who lives on the coast
ORARIANS > ORARIAN
ORARION n garment worn by Greek clergyman
ORARIONS > ORARION
ORARIUM n handkerchief
ORARIUMS > ORARIUM
ORATE vb make or give an oration
ORATED > ORATE
ORATES > ORATE
ORATING > ORATE
ORATION n formal speech
ORATIONS > ORATION
ORATOR n skilful public speaker
ORATORIAL adj of oratory
ORATORIAN n clergyman of a particular type of church
ORATORIES > ORATORY
ORATORIO n musical composition for choir and orchestra
ORATORIOS > ORATORIO

ORATORS > ORATOR
ORATORY n art of making speeches
ORATRESS n female orator
ORATRICES > ORATRIX
ORATRIX n female orator
ORATRIXES > ORATRIX
ORATURE n oral forms of literature
ORATURES > ORATURE
ORB n ceremonial decorated sphere ▷ vb make or become circular or spherical
ORBED > ORB
ORBICULAR adj circular or spherical
ORBIER > ORBY
ORBIEST > ORBY
ORBING > ORB
ORBIT n curved path ▷ vb move in an orbit around
ORBITA same as > ORBIT
ORBITAL adj of or denoting an orbit ▷ n region surrounding an atomic nucleus
ORBITALLY > ORBITAL
ORBITALS > ORBITAL
ORBITAS > ORBITA
ORBITED > ORBIT
ORBITER n spacecraft or satellite designed to orbit a planet without landing on it
ORBITERS > ORBITER
ORBITIES > ORBITY
ORBITING > ORBIT
ORBITS > ORBIT
ORBITY n bereavement
ORBLESS > ORB
ORBS > ORB
ORBY adj orb-shaped
ORC n any of various whales, such as the killer and grampus
ORCA n killer whale
ORCAS > ORCA
ORCEIN n brown crystalline material
ORCEINS > ORCEIN
ORCHARD n area where fruit trees are grown
ORCHARDS > ORCHARD
ORCHAT same as > ORCHARD
ORCHATS > ORCHAT
ORCHEL same as > ORCHIL
ORCHELLA same as > ORCHIL
ORCHELLAS > ORCHELLA
ORCHELS > ORCHEL
ORCHESES > ORCHESIS
ORCHESIS n art of dance
ORCHESTIC adj of dance
ORCHESTRA n large group of musicians, esp playing a variety of instruments
ORCHID n plant with flowers that have unusual lip-shaped petals

ORCHIDIST n orchid grower
ORCHIDS > ORCHID
ORCHIL n any of various lichens
ORCHILLA same as > ORCHIL
ORCHILLAS > ORCHILLA
ORCHILS > ORCHIL
ORCHIS n type of orchid
ORCHISES > ORCHIS
ORCHITIC > ORCHITIS
ORCHITIS n inflammation of one or both testicles
ORCIN same as > ORCINOL
ORCINE same as > ORCINOL
ORCINES > ORCINE
ORCINOL n colourless crystalline water-soluble solid
ORCINOLS > ORCINOL
ORCINS > ORCIN
ORCS > ORC
ORD n pointed weapon
ORDAIN vb make (someone) a member of the clergy
ORDAINED > ORDAIN
ORDAINER > ORDAIN
ORDAINERS > ORDAIN
ORDAINING > ORDAIN
ORDAINS > ORDAIN
ORDALIAN adj of an ordeal
ORDALIUM same as > ORDEAL
ORDALIUMS > ORDALIUM
ORDEAL n painful or difficult experience
ORDEALS > ORDEAL
ORDER n instruction to be carried out ▷ vb give an instruction to
ORDERABLE > ORDER
ORDERED > ORDER
ORDERER > ORDER
ORDERERS > ORDER
ORDERING > ORDER
ORDERINGS > ORDER
ORDERLESS > ORDER
ORDERLIES > ORDERLY
ORDERLY adj well-organized ▷ n hospital attendant ▷ adv according to custom or rule
ORDERS > ORDER
ORDINAIRE adj ordinary
ORDINAL adj denoting a certain position in a sequence of numbers ▷ n book containing the forms of services for the ordination of ministers
ORDINALLY > ORDINAL
ORDINALS > ORDINAL
ORDINANCE n official rule or order
ORDINAND n candidate for ordination
ORDINANDS > ORDINAND
ORDINANT n person who ordains
ORDINANTS > ORDINANT

ORDINAR Scots word for > ORDINARY
ORDINARS > ORDINAR
ORDINARY adj usual or normal
ORDINATE n vertical coordinate of a point in a two-dimensional system of coordinates ▷ vb ordain
ORDINATED > ORDINATE
ORDINATES > ORDINATE
ORDINEE n person being ordained
ORDINEES > ORDINEE
ORDINES > ORDO
ORDNANCE n weapons and military supplies
ORDNANCES > ORDNANCE
ORDO n religious order
ORDOS > ORDO
ORDS > ORD
ORDURE n excrement
ORDURES > ORDURE
ORDUROUS > ORDURE
ORE n (rock containing) a mineral which yields metal
OREAD n mountain nymph
OREADES > OREAD
OREADS > OREAD
OREBODIES > OREBODY
OREBODY n mass of ore in a mine
ORECTIC adj of or relating to the desires
ORECTIVE > OREXIS
OREGANO n sweet-smelling herb used in cooking
OREGANOS > OREGANO
OREIDE same as > OROIDE
OREIDES > OREIDE
OREODONT n extinct prehistoric mammal
OREODONTS > OREODONT
OREOLOGY same as > OROLOGY
OREPEARCH same as > OVERPERCH
ORES > ORE
ORESTUNCK > OVERSTINK
OREWEED n seaweed
OREWEEDS > OREWEED
OREXIN n hormone that promotes wakefulness and stimulates the appetite
OREXINS > OREXIN
OREXIS n appetite
OREXISES > OREXIS
ORF n infectious disease of sheep
ORFE n small slender European fish
ORFES > ORFE
ORFRAY same as > ORPHREY
ORFRAYS > ORFRAY
ORFS > ORF
ORG n organization
ORGAN n part of an animal or plant that has a particular function

ORGANA > ORGANON
ORGANDIE n fine cotton fabric
ORGANDIES > ORGANDY
ORGANDY same as > ORGANDIE
ORGANELLE n structural and functional unit in a cell
ORGANIC adj of or produced from animals or plants ▷ n substance that is derived from animal or vegetable matter
ORGANICAL same as > ORGANIC
ORGANICS > ORGANIC
ORGANISE same as > ORGANIZE
ORGANISED same as > ORGANIZED
ORGANISER same as > ORGANIZER
ORGANISES > ORGANISE
ORGANISM n any living animal or plant
ORGANISMS > ORGANISM
ORGANIST n organ player
ORGANISTS > ORGANIST
ORGANITY same as > ORGANISM
ORGANIZE vb make arrangements for
ORGANIZED > ORGANIZE
ORGANIZER n person who organizes or is capable of organizing
ORGANIZES > ORGANIZE
ORGANON n system of logical or scientific rules
ORGANONS > ORGANON
ORGANOSOL n resin-based coating
ORGANOTIN adj of an organic compound used as a pesticide
ORGANS > ORGAN
ORGANUM same as > ORGANON
ORGANUMS > ORGANUM
ORGANZA n thin stiff fabric of silk, cotton, or synthetic fibre
ORGANZAS > ORGANZA
ORGANZINE n strong thread made of twisted strands of raw silk
ORGASM n most intense point of sexual pleasure ▷ vb experience orgasm
ORGASMED > ORGASM
ORGASMIC > ORGASM
ORGASMING > ORGASM
ORGASMS > ORGASM
ORGASTIC > ORGASM
ORGEAT n drink made with orange flower water
ORGEATS > ORGEAT
ORGIA same as > ORGY
ORGIAC > ORGY
ORGIAS > ORGIA
ORGIAST n participant in orgy
ORGIASTIC > ORGY
ORGIASTS > ORGIAST

ORGIC > ORGY

ORGIES > ORGY

ORGILLOUS *same as* > ORGULOUS

ORGONE *n* substance claimed to be needed for sexual activity and mental health

ORGONES > ORGONE

ORGS > ORG

ORGUE *n* number of stakes lashed together

ORGUES > ORGUE

ORGULOUS *adj* proud

ORGY *n* party involving promiscuous sexual activity

ORIBATID *n* type of mite

ORIBATIDS > ORIBATID

ORIBI *n* small African antelope

ORIBIS > ORIBI

ORICALCHE *same as* > ORICHALC

ORICHALC *n* type of alloy

ORICHALCS > ORICHALC

ORIEL *n* type of bay window

ORIELLED *adj* having an oriel

ORIELS > ORIEL

ORIENCIES > ORIENCY

ORIENCY *n* state of being orient

ORIENT *vb* position (oneself) according to one's surroundings ▷ *n* eastern sky or the dawn ▷ *adj* eastern

ORIENTAL *adj* eastern ▷ *n* native of the orient

ORIENTALS > ORIENTAL

ORIENTATE *vb* position (oneself) according to one's surroundings

ORIENTED > ORIENT

ORIENTEER *vb* take part in orienteering ▷ *n* person who takes part in orienteering

ORIENTER > ORIENT

ORIENTERS > ORIENT

ORIENTING > ORIENT

ORIENTS > ORIENT

ORIFEX *same as* > ORIFICE

ORIFEXES > ORIFEX

ORIFICE *n* opening or hole

ORIFICES > ORIFICE

ORIFICIAL > ORIFICE

ORIFLAMME *n* scarlet flag adopted as the national banner of France in the Middle Ages

ORIGAMI *n* Japanese decorative art of paper folding

ORIGAMIS > ORIGAMI

ORIGAN *another name for* > MARJORAM

ORIGANE *same as* > ORIGAN

ORIGANES > ORIGANE

ORIGANS > ORIGAN

ORIGANUM *n* type of aromatic plant

ORIGANUMS > ORIGANUM

ORIGIN *n* point from which something develops

ORIGINAL *adj* first or earliest ▷ *n* first version, from which others are copied

ORIGINALS > ORIGINAL

ORIGINATE *vb* come or bring into existence

ORIGINS > ORIGIN

ORIHOU *n* small New Zealand tree

ORIHOUS > ORIHOU

ORILLION *n* part of bastion

ORILLIONS > ORILLION

ORINASAL *adj* pronounced with simultaneous oral and nasal articulation ▷ *n* orinasal speech sound

ORINASALS > ORINASAL

ORIOLE *n* tropical or American songbird

ORIOLES > ORIOLE

ORISHA *n* any of the minor gods or spirits of traditional Yoruba religion

ORISHAS > ORISHA

ORISON *another word for* > PRAYER

ORISONS > ORISON

ORIXA *same as* > ORISHA

ORIXAS > ORIXA

ORLE *n* border around a shield

ORLEANS *n* type of fabric

ORLEANSES > ORLEANS

ORLES > ORLE

ORLISTAT *n* drug used for slimming

ORLISTATS > ORLISTAT

ORLON *n* crease-resistant acrylic fibre or fabric

ORLONS > ORLON

ORLOP *n* (in a vessel with four or more decks) the lowest deck

ORLOPS > ORLOP

ORMER *n* edible marine mollusc

ORMERS > ORMER

ORMOLU *n* gold-coloured alloy used for decoration

ORMOLUS > ORMOLU

ORNAMENT *n* decorative object ▷ *vb* decorate

ORNAMENTS > ORNAMENT

ORNATE *adj* highly decorated, elaborate

ORNATELY > ORNATE

ORNATER > ORNATE

ORNATEST > ORNATE

ORNERIER > ORNERY

ORNERIEST > ORNERY

ORNERY *adj* stubborn or vile-tempered

ORNIS *less common word for* > AVIFAUNA

ORNISES > ORNIS

ORNITHES *n* birds in Greek myth

ORNITHIC *adj* of or relating to birds or a bird fauna

ORNITHINE *n* type of amino acid

ORNITHOID *adj* like bird

OROGEN *n* part of earth subject to orogeny

OROGENIC > OROGENY

OROGENIES > OROGENY

OROGENS > OROGEN

OROGENY *n* formation of mountain ranges

OROGRAPHY *n* study or mapping of relief, esp of mountains

OROIDE *n* alloy containing copper, tin, and other metals

OROIDES > OROIDE

OROLOGIES > OROLOGY

OROLOGIST > OROGRAPHY

OROLOGY *same as* > OROGRAPHY

OROMETER *n* aneroid barometer with an altitude scale

OROMETERS > OROMETER

ORONASAL *adj* of or relating to the mouth and nose

OROPESA *n* float used in minesweeping

OROPESAS > OROPESA

OROTUND *adj* (of the voice) resonant and booming

ORPHAN *n* child whose parents are dead ▷ *vb* deprive of parents

ORPHANAGE *n* children's home for orphans

ORPHANED > ORPHAN

ORPHANING > ORPHAN

ORPHANISM *n* state of being an orphan

ORPHANS > ORPHAN

ORPHARION *n* large lute in use during the 16th and 17th centuries

ORPHIC *adj* mystical or occult

ORPHICAL *same as* > ORPHIC

ORPHISM *n* style of abstract art

ORPHISMS > ORPHISM

ORPHREY *n* richly embroidered band or border

ORPHREYED *adj* embroidered with gold

ORPHREYS > ORPHREY

ORPIMENT *n* yellow mineral

ORPIMENTS > ORPIMENT

ORPIN *same as* > ORPINE

ORPINE *n* type of plant

ORPINES > ORPINE

ORPINS > ORPIN

ORRA *adj* odd or unmatched

ORRAMAN *n* man who does odd jobs

ORRAMEN > ORRAMAN

ORRERIES > ORRERY

ORRERY *n* mechanical model of the solar system

ORRICE *same as* > ORRIS

ORRICES > ORRICE

ORRIS *n* kind of iris

ORRISES > ORRIS

ORRISROOT *n* rhizome of a type of iris, used as perfume

ORS > OR

ORSEILLE *same as* > ORCHIL

ORSEILLES > ORSEILLE

ORSELLIC > ORSEILLE

ORT *n* fragment

ORTANIQUE *n* hybrid between an orange and a tangerine

ORTHIAN *adj* having high pitch

ORTHICON *n* type of television camera tube

ORTHICONS > ORTHICON

ORTHO *n* type of photographic plate

ORTHOAXES > ORTHOAXIS

ORTHOAXIS *n* axis in a crystal

ORTHODOX *adj* conforming to established views

ORTHODOXY *n* orthodox belief or practice

ORTHOEPIC > ORTHOEPY

ORTHOEPY *n* study of correct or standard pronunciation

ORTHOPEDY *n* treatment of deformity

ORTHOPOD *n* surgeon

ORTHOPODS > ORTHOPOD

ORTHOPTER *n* type of aircraft propelled by flapping wings

ORTHOPTIC *adj* relating to normal binocular vision

ORTHOS > ORTHO

ORTHOSES > ORTHOSIS

ORTHOSIS *n* artificial or mechanical aid to support a weak part of the body

ORTHOTIC > ORTHOTICS

ORTHOTICS *n* use of artificial or mechanical aids to assist movement of weak joints or muscles

ORTHOTIST *n* person who is qualified to practise orthotics

ORTHOTONE *adj* (of a word) having an independent accent ▷ *n* independently accented word

ORTHROS *n* canonical hour in the Greek Church

ORTHROSES > ORTHROS

ORTOLAN *n* small European songbird eaten as a delicacy

ORTOLANS > ORTOLAN
ORTS pl n scraps or leavings
ORVAL n plant of sage family
ORVALS > ORVAL
ORYX n large African antelope
ORYXES > ORYX
ORZO n pasta in small grain shapes
ORZOS > ORZO
OS n mouth or mouthlike part or opening
OSAR > OS
OSCAR n cash
OSCARS > OSCAR
OSCHEAL adj of scrotum
OSCILLATE vb swing back and forth
OSCINE n songbird ▷ adj of songbirds
OSCINES > OSCINE
OSCININE > OSCINE
OSCITANCE same as > OSCITANCY
OSCITANCY n state of being drowsy, lazy, or inattentive
OSCITANT > OSCITANCY
OSCITATE vb yawn
OSCITATED > OSCITATE
OSCITATES > OSCITATE
OSCULA > OSCULUM
OSCULANT adj possessing some of the characteristics of two different taxonomic groups
OSCULAR adj of or relating to an osculum
OSCULATE vb kiss
OSCULATED > OSCULATE
OSCULATES > OSCULATE
OSCULE n small mouth or opening
OSCULES > OSCULE
OSCULUM n mouthlike aperture
OSE same as > ESKER
OSES > OSE
OSETRA n type of caviar
OSETRAS > OSETRA
OSHAC n plant smelling of ammonia
OSHACS > OSHAC
OSIER n willow tree
OSIERED adj covered with osiers
OSIERIES > OSIERY
OSIERS > OSIER
OSIERY n work done with osiers
OSMATE n salt of osmic acid
OSMATES > OSMATE
OSMATIC adj relying on sense of smell
OSMETERIA pl n glands in some caterpillars that secrete foul-smelling substances to deter predators
OSMIATE same as > OSMATE

OSMIATES > OSMIATE
OSMIC adj of or containing osmium in a high valence state
OSMICALLY > OSMIC
OSMICS n science of smell
OSMIOUS same as > OSMOUS
OSMIUM n heaviest known metallic element
OSMIUMS > OSMIUM
OSMOL same as > OSMOLE
OSMOLAL > OSMOLE
OSMOLAR adj containing one osmole per litre
OSMOLE n unit of osmotic pressure
OSMOLES > OSMOLE
OSMOLS > OSMOL
OSMOMETER n instrument for measuring osmotic pressure
OSMOMETRY > OSMOMETER
OSMOSE vb undergo or cause to undergo osmosis
OSMOSED > OSMOSE
OSMOSES > OSMOSE
OSMOSING > OSMOSE
OSMOSIS n movement of a liquid through a membrane
OSMOTIC > OSMOSIS
OSMOUS adj of or containing osmium in a low valence state
OSMUND same as > OSMUNDA
OSMUNDA n type of fern
OSMUNDAS > OSMUNDA
OSMUNDINE n type of compost
OSMUNDS > OSMUND
OSNABURG n coarse plain-woven cotton used for sacks, furnishings, etc
OSNABURGS > OSNABURG
OSPREY n large fish-eating bird of prey
OSPREYS > OSPREY
OSSA > OS
OSSARIUM same as > OSSUARY
OSSARIUMS > OSSARIUM
OSSATURE n skeleton
OSSATURES > OSSATURE
OSSEIN n protein that forms the organic matrix of bone
OSSEINS > OSSEIN
OSSELET n growth on knee of horse
OSSELETS > OSSELET
OSSEOUS adj consisting of or like bone
OSSEOUSLY > OSSEOUS
OSSETER n sturgeon
OSSETERS > OSSETER
OSSETRA same as > OSETRA
OSSETRAS > OSSETRA
OSSIA n alternate version or passage ▷ conj or
OSSIAS > OSSIA

OSSICLE n small bone, esp one of those in the middle ear
OSSICLES > OSSICLE
OSSICULAR > OSSICLE
OSSIFIC adj making something turn to bone
OSSIFIED adj converted into bone
OSSIFIER > OSSIFY
OSSIFIERS > OSSIFY
OSSIFIES > OSSIFY
OSSIFRAGA n large sea bird
OSSIFRAGE n osprey
OSSIFY vb (cause to) become bone, harden
OSSIFYING > OSSIFY
OSSOBUCO n Italian dish of veal shank and vegetables stewed in wine
OSSOBUCOS > OSSOBUCO
OSSUARIES > OSSUARY
OSSUARY n any container for the burial of human bones, such as an urn or vault
OSTEAL adj of or relating to bone or to the skeleton
OSTEITIC > OSTEITIS
OSTEITIS n inflammation of a bone
OSTENSIVE adj directly showing or pointing out
OSTENSORY n (in the RC Church) receptacle for displaying the consecrated Host
OSTENT n appearance ▷ vb display boastfully
OSTENTED > OSTENT
OSTENTING > OSTENT
OSTENTS > OSTENT
OSTEOCYTE n bone cell
OSTEODERM n bony area in skin
OSTEOGEN n material from which bone forms
OSTEOGENS > OSTEOGEN
OSTEOGENY n forming of bone
OSTEOID adj of or resembling bone ▷ n bony deposit
OSTEOIDS > OSTEOID
OSTEOLOGY n study of the structure and function of bones
OSTEOMA n tumour composed of bone or bonelike tissue
OSTEOMAS > OSTEOMA
OSTEOMATA > OSTEOMA
OSTEOPATH n person who practises osteopathy
OSTEOSES > OSTEOSIS
OSTEOSIS n forming of bony tissue
OSTEOTOME n surgical instrument for cutting bone, usually a special chisel
OSTEOTOMY n surgical cutting or dividing of bone

OSTIA > OSTIUM
OSTIAL > OSTIUM
OSTIARIES > OSTIARY
OSTIARY another word for > PORTER
OSTIATE adj having ostium
OSTINATI > OSTINATO
OSTINATO n persistently repeated phrase or rhythm
OSTINATOS > OSTINATO
OSTIOLAR > OSTIOLE
OSTIOLATE > OSTIOLE
OSTIOLE n pore in the reproductive bodies of certain algae and fungi
OSTIOLES > OSTIOLE
OSTIUM n pore in sponges through which water enters the body
OSTLER n stableman at an inn
OSTLERESS n female ostler
OSTLERS > OSTLER
OSTMARK n currency of the former East Germany
OSTMARKS > OSTMARK
OSTOMATE n person with an ostomy
OSTOMATES > OSTOMATE
OSTOMIES > OSTOMY
OSTOMY n surgically made opening
OSTOSES > OSTOSIS
OSTOSIS n formation of bone
OSTOSISES > OSTOSIS
OSTRACA > OSTRACON
OSTRACEAN adj of oysters ▷ n type of bivalve
OSTRACISE same as > OSTRACIZE
OSTRACISM > OSTRACIZE
OSTRACIZE vb exclude (a person) from a group
OSTRACOD n type of minute crustacean
OSTRACODE adj of ostracods
OSTRACODS > OSTRACOD
OSTRACON n (in ancient Greece) a potsherd used for ostracizing
OSTRAKA > OSTRAKON
OSTRAKON same as > OSTRACON
OSTREGER n keeper of hawks
OSTREGERS > OSTREGER
OSTRICH n large African bird that runs fast but cannot fly
OSTRICHES > OSTRICH
OTAKU n Japanese computer geek
OTAKUS > OTAKU
OTALGIA technical name for > EARACHE
OTALGIAS > OTALGIA
OTALGIC > OTALGIA
OTALGIES > OTALGY
OTALGY same as > OTALGIA

OTARID adj of or like an otary, an eared seal
OTARIES > OTARY
OTARINE > OTARY
OTARY n seal with ears
OTHER adj remaining in a group of which one or some have been specified ▷ n other person or thing
OTHERNESS n quality of being different or distinct in appearance, character, etc
OTHERS > OTHER
OTHERWISE adv differently, in another way ▷ adj of an unexpected nature ▷ pron something different in outcome
OTIC adj of or relating to the ear
OTIOSE adj not useful
OTIOSELY > OTIOSE
OTIOSITY > OTIOSE
OTITIC > OTITIS
OTITIDES > OTITIS
OTITIS n inflammation of the ear
OTITISES > OTITIS
OTOCYST n embryonic structure in vertebrates that develops into the inner ear
OTOCYSTIC > OTOCYST
OTOCYSTS > OTOCYST
OTOLITH n granule of calcium carbonate in the inner ear of vertebrates
OTOLITHIC > OTOLITH
OTOLITHS > OTOLITH
OTOLOGIC adj relating to otology
OTOLOGIES > OTOLOGY
OTOLOGIST > OTOLOGY
OTOLOGY n branch of medicine concerned with the ear
OTOPLASTY n cosmetic surgery on ears
OTORRHOEA n discharge from the ears
OTOSCOPE another name for > AURISCOPE
OTOSCOPES > OTOSCOPE
OTOSCOPIC > OTOSCOPY
OTOSCOPY n examination of ear using otoscope
OTOTOXIC adj toxic to the ear
OTTAR variant of > ATTAR
OTTARS > OTTAR
OTTAVA n interval of an octave
OTTAVAS > OTTAVA
OTTAVINO n piccolo
OTTAVINOS > OTTAVINO
OTTER n small brown freshwater mammal that eats fish ▷ vb fish using an otter board
OTTERED > OTTER
OTTERING > OTTER
OTTERS > OTTER

OTTO another name for > ATTAR
OTTOMAN n storage chest with a padded lid for use as a seat
OTTOMANS > OTTOMAN
OTTOS > OTTO
OTTRELITE n type of mineral
OU interj expressing concession ▷ n man, bloke, or chap
OUABAIN n poisonous white crystalline glycoside
OUABAINS > OUABAIN
OUAKARI n South American monkey
OUAKARIS > OUAKARI
OUBAAS n man in authority
OUBAASES > OUBAAS
OUBIT n hairy caterpillar
OUBITS > OUBIT
OUBLIETTE n dungeon entered only by a trapdoor
OUCH interj exclamation of sudden pain ▷ n brooch or clasp set with gems ▷ vb say ouch
OUCHED > OUCH
OUCHES > OUCH
OUCHING > OUCH
OUCHT Scots word for > ANYTHING
OUCHTS > OUCHT
OUD n Arabic stringed musical instrument
OUDS > OUD
OUENS > OU
OUGHLIED > OUGHLY
OUGHLIES > OUGHLY
OUGHLY variant of > UGLY
OUGHLYING > OUGHLY
OUGHT vb have an obligation ▷ n zero
OUGHTED > OUGHT
OUGHTING > OUGHT
OUGHTNESS n state of being right
OUGHTS > OUGHT
OUGIYA n monetary unit of Mauretania
OUGIYAS > OUGIYA
OUGLIE variant of > UGLY
OUGLIED > OUGLIE
OUGLIEING > OUGLIE
OUGLIES > OUGLIE
OUGUIYA n standard monetary unit of Mauritania
OUGUIYAS > OUGUIYA
OUIJA n tradename for a board through which spirits supposedly answer questions
OUIJAS > OUIJA
OUISTITI n marmoset
OUISTITIS > OUISTITI
OUK Scots word for > WEEK
OUKS > OUK
OULACHON same as > EULACHON
OULACHONS > OULACHON

OULAKAN same as > EULACHON
OULAKANS > OULAKAN
OULD Scots or Irish form of > OLD
OULDER > OULD
OULDEST > OULD
OULK Scots form of > WEEK
OULKS > OULK
OULONG same as > OOLONG
OULONGS > OULONG
OUMA n grandmother, often as a title with a surname
OUMAS > OUMA
OUNCE n unit of weight equal to one sixteenth of a pound
OUNCES > OUNCE
OUNDIER > OUNDY
OUNDIEST > OUNDY
OUNDY adj wavy
OUP same as > OOP
OUPA n grandfather, often as a title with a surname
OUPAS > OUPA
OUPED > OUP
OUPH same as > OAF
OUPHE same as > OAF
OUPHES > OUPHE
OUPHS > OUPH
OUPING > OUP
OUPS > OUP
OUR adj belonging to us ▷ determiner of, belonging to, or associated in some way with us
OURALI n plant from which curare comes
OURALIS > OURALI
OURANG same as > ORANG
OURANGS > OURANG
OURARI same as > OURALI
OURARIS > OURARI
OUREBI same as > ORIBI
OUREBIS > OUREBI
OURIE same as > OORIE
OURIER > OURIE
OURIEST > OURIE
OURN dialect form of > OUR
OUROBOROS n mythical serpent
OUROLOGY same as > UROLOGY
OUROSCOPY same as > UROSCOPY
OURS pron thing(s) belonging to us
OURSELF pron formal word for myself used by monarchs
OURSELVES pron reflexive form of we or us
OUS > OU
OUSEL same as > OUZEL
OUSELS > OUSEL
OUST vb force (someone) out, expel
OUSTED > OUST
OUSTER n act of forcing someone out of a position
OUSTERS > OUSTER
OUSTING > OUST

OUSTITI n device for opening locked door
OUSTITIS > OUSTITI
OUSTS > OUST
OUT adj denoting movement or distance away from ▷ vb name (a public figure) as being homosexual
OUTA prep an informal contraction of out of
OUTACT vb surpass in acting
OUTACTED > OUTACT
OUTACTING > OUTACT
OUTACTS > OUTACT
OUTADD vb beat or surpass at adding
OUTADDED > OUTADD
OUTADDING > OUTADD
OUTADDS > OUTADD
OUTAGE n period of power failure
OUTAGES > OUTAGE
OUTARGUE vb defeat in argument
OUTARGUED > OUTARGUE
OUTARGUES > OUTARGUE
OUTASIGHT adj excellent or wonderful
OUTASITE adj amazing, excellent
OUTASK vb declare wedding banns
OUTASKED > OUTASK
OUTASKING > OUTASK
OUTASKS > OUTASK
OUTATE > OUTEAT
OUTBACK n remote bush country of Australia
OUTBACKER > OUTBACK
OUTBACKS > OUTBACK
OUTBAKE vb bake more or better than
OUTBAKED > OUTBAKE
OUTBAKES > OUTBAKE
OUTBAKING > OUTBAKE
OUTBAR vb keep out
OUTBARK vb bark more or louder than
OUTBARKED > OUTBARK
OUTBARKS > OUTBARK
OUTBARRED > OUTBAR
OUTBARS > OUTBAR
OUTBAWL vb bawl more or louder than
OUTBAWLED > OUTBAWL
OUTBAWLS > OUTBAWL
OUTBEAM vb beam more or brighter than
OUTBEAMED > OUTBEAM
OUTBEAMS > OUTBEAM
OUTBEG vb beg more or better than
OUTBEGGED > OUTBEG
OUTBEGS > OUTBEG
OUTBID vb offer a higher price than
OUTBIDDEN > OUTBID
OUTBIDDER > OUTBID
OUTBIDS > OUTBID
OUTBITCH vb bitch more or better than

OUTBLAZE vb blaze more or hotter than

OUTBLAZED > OUTBLAZE

OUTBLAZES > OUTBLAZE

OUTBLEAT vb bleat more or louder than

OUTBLEATS > OUTBLEAT

OUTBLESS vb bless more than

OUTBLOOM vb bloom more or better than

OUTBLOOMS > OUTBLOOM

OUTBLUFF vb surpass in bluffing

OUTBLUFFS > OUTBLUFF

OUTBLUSH vb blush more than

OUTBOARD adj (of a boat's engine) portable, with its own propeller ▷ adv away from the centre line of a vessel or aircraft ▷ n outboard motor

OUTBOARDS > OUTBOARD

OUTBOAST vb surpass in boasting

OUTBOASTS > OUTBOAST

OUTBOUGHT > OUTBUY

OUTBOUND adj going out

OUTBOUNDS n boundaries

OUTBOX vb surpass in boxing

OUTBOXED > OUTBOX

OUTBOXES > OUTBOX

OUTBOXING > OUTBOX

OUTBRAG vb brag more or better than

OUTBRAGS > OUTBRAG

OUTBRAVE vb surpass in bravery

OUTBRAVED > OUTBRAVE

OUTBRAVES > OUTBRAVE

OUTBRAWL vb defeat in a brawl

OUTBRAWLS > OUTBRAWL

OUTBRAZEN vb be more brazen than

OUTBREAK n sudden occurrence (of something unpleasant) ▷ vb break out

OUTBREAKS > OUTBREAK

OUTBRED > OUTBREED

OUTBREED vb produce offspring through sexual relations outside a particular family or tribe

OUTBREEDS > OUTBREED

OUTBRIBE vb bribe more than

OUTBRIBED > OUTBRIBE

OUTBRIBES > OUTBRIBE

OUTBROKE > OUTBREAK

OUTBROKEN > OUTBREAK

OUTBUILD vb exceed in building

OUTBUILDS > OUTBUILD

OUTBUILT > OUTBUILD

OUTBULGE vb bulge outwards

OUTBULGED > OUTBULGE

OUTBULGES > OUTBULGE

OUTBULK vb exceed in bulk

OUTBULKED > OUTBULK

OUTBULKS > OUTBULK

OUTBULLY vb exceed in bullying

OUTBURN vb burn longer or brighter than

OUTBURNED > OUTBURN

OUTBURNS > OUTBURN

OUTBURNT > OUTBURN

OUTBURST n sudden expression of emotion ▷ vb burst out

OUTBURSTS > OUTBURST

OUTBUY vb buy more than

OUTBUYING > OUTBUY

OUTBUYS > OUTBUY

OUTBY adv outside

OUTBYE same as > OUTBY

OUTCALL n visit to customer's home by professional ▷ vb bid higher than another player in a card game

OUTCALLED > OUTCALL

OUTCALLS > OUTCALL

OUTCAPER vb exceed in capering

OUTCAPERS > OUTCAPER

OUTCAST n person rejected by a particular group ▷ adj rejected, abandoned, or discarded

OUTCASTE n person who has been expelled from a caste ▷ vb cause (someone) to lose his caste

OUTCASTED > OUTCASTE

OUTCASTES > OUTCASTE

OUTCASTS > OUTCAST

OUTCATCH vb catch more than

OUTCAUGHT > OUTCATCH

OUTCAVIL vb exceed in cavilling

OUTCAVILS > OUTCAVIL

OUTCHARGE vb charge more than

OUTCHARM vb exceed in charming

OUTCHARMS > OUTCHARM

OUTCHEAT vb exceed in cheating

OUTCHEATS > OUTCHEAT

OUTCHIDE > OUTCHIDE

OUTCHIDE vb exceed in chiding

OUTCHIDED > OUTCHIDE

OUTCHIDES > OUTCHIDE

OUTCITIES > OUTCITY

OUTCITY n anywhere outside a city's confines

OUTCLASS vb surpass in quality

OUTCLIMB vb exceed in climbing

OUTCLIMBS > OUTCLIMB

OUTCLOMB > OUTCLIMB

OUTCOACH vb exceed in coaching

OUTCOME n result

OUTCOMES > OUTCOME

OUTCOOK vb cook more or better than

OUTCOOKED > OUTCOOK

OUTCOOKS > OUTCOOK

OUTCOUNT vb exceed in counting

OUTCOUNTS > OUTCOUNT

OUTCRAFTY vb be craftier than

OUTCRAWL vb crawl further or faster than

OUTCRAWLS > OUTCRAWL

OUTCRIED > OUTCRY

OUTCRIES > OUTCRY

OUTCROP n part of a rock formation that sticks out of the earth ▷ vb (of rock strata) to protrude through the surface of the earth

OUTCROPS > OUTCROP

OUTCROSS vb breed (animals or plants of the same breed but different strains) ▷ n animal or plant produced as a result of outcrossing

OUTCROW vb exceed in crowing

OUTCROWD vb have more crowd than

OUTCROWDS > OUTCROWD

OUTCROWED > OUTCROW

OUTCROWS > OUTCROW

OUTCRY n vehement or widespread protest ▷ vb cry louder or make more noise than (someone or something)

OUTCRYING > OUTCRY

OUTCURSE vb exceed in cursing

OUTCURSED > OUTCURSE

OUTCURSES > OUTCURSE

OUTCURVE n baseball thrown to curve away from batter

OUTCURVES > OUTCURVE

OUTDANCE vb surpass in dancing

OUTDANCED > OUTDANCE

OUTDANCES > OUTDANCE

OUTDARE vb be more brave than

OUTDARED > OUTDARE

OUTDARES > OUTDARE

OUTDARING > OUTDARE

OUTDATE vb make or become old-fashioned or obsolete

OUTDATED adj old-fashioned

OUTDATES > OUTDATE

OUTDATING > OUTDATE

OUTDAZZLE vb exceed in dazzling

OUTDEBATE vb exceed in debate

OUTDESIGN vb exceed in designing

OUTDID > OUTDO

OUTDO vb surpass in performance

OUTDODGE vb surpass in dodging

OUTDODGED > OUTDODGE

OUTDODGES > OUTDODGE

OUTDOER > OUTDO

OUTDOERS > OUTDO

OUTDOES > OUTDO

OUTDOING > OUTDO

OUTDONE > OUTDO

OUTDOOR adj taking place in the open air

OUTDOORS adv in(to) the open air ▷ n open air

OUTDOORSY adj taking part in activities relating to the outdoors

OUTDRAG vb beat in drag race

OUTDRAGS > OUTDRAG

OUTDRANK > OUTDRINK

OUTDRAW vb draw (a gun) faster than

OUTDRAWN > OUTDRAW

OUTDRAWS > OUTDRAW

OUTDREAM vb exceed in dreaming

OUTDREAMS > OUTDREAM

OUTDREAMT > OUTDREAM

OUTDRESS vb dress better than

OUTDREW > OUTDRAW

OUTDRINK vb drink more than

OUTDRINKS > OUTDRINK

OUTDRIVE vb exceed in driving

OUTDRIVEN > OUTDRIVE

OUTDRIVES > OUTDRIVE

OUTDROP same as > OUTCROP

OUTDROPS > OUTDROP

OUTDROVE > OUTDRIVE

OUTDRUNK > OUTDRINK

OUTDUEL vb defeat in duel

OUTDUELED > OUTDUEL

OUTDUELS > OUTDUEL

OUTDURE vb last longer than

OUTDURED > OUTDURE

OUTDURES > OUTDURE

OUTDURING > OUTDURE

OUTDWELL vb live outside something

OUTDWELLS > OUTDWELL

OUTDWELT > OUTDWELL

OUTEARN vb earn more than

OUTEARNED > OUTEARN

OUTEARNS > OUTEARN

OUTEAT vb eat more than

OUTEATEN > OUTEAT

OUTEATING > OUTEAT

OUTEATS > OUTEAT

OUTECHO vb echo more than

OUTECHOED > OUTECHO

OUTECHOES > OUTECHO

OUTED > OUT

OUTEDGE n furthest limit

OUTEDGES > OUTEDGE

OUTER adj on the outside ▷ n white outermost ring on a target

OUTERCOAT same as > OVERCOAT

OUTERMOST adj furthest out

OUTERS > OUTER

OUTERWEAR *n* clothes worn on top of other clothes

OUTFABLE *vb* exceed in creating fables

OUTFABLED > OUTFABLE

OUTFABLES > OUTFABLE

OUTFACE *vb* subdue or disconcert by staring

OUTFACED > OUTFACE

OUTFACES > OUTFACE

OUTFACING > OUTFACE

OUTFALL *n* mouth of a river or drain

OUTFALLS > OUTFALL

OUTFAST *vb* fast longer than

OUTFASTED > OUTFAST

OUTFASTS > OUTFAST

OUTFAWN *vb* exceed in fawning

OUTFAWNED > OUTFAWN

OUTFAWNS > OUTFAWN

OUTFEAST *vb* exceed in feasting

OUTFEASTS > OUTFEAST

OUTFEEL *vb* exceed in feeling

OUTFEELS > OUTFEEL

OUTFELT > OUTFEEL

OUTFENCE *vb* surpass at fencing

OUTFENCED > OUTFENCE

OUTFENCES > OUTFENCE

OUTFIELD *n* area far from the pitch

OUTFIELDS > OUTFIELD

OUTFIGHT *vb* surpass in fighting

OUTFIGHTS > OUTFIGHT

OUTFIGURE *same as* > OUTTHINK

OUTFIND *vb* exceed in finding

OUTFINDS > OUTFIND

OUTFIRE *vb* exceed in firing

OUTFIRED > OUTFIRE

OUTFIRES > OUTFIRE

OUTFIRING > OUTFIRE

OUTFISH *vb* catch more fish than

OUTFISHED > OUTFISH

OUTFISHES > OUTFISH

OUTFIT *n* matching set of clothes ▷ *vb* furnish or be furnished with an outfit

OUTFITS > OUTFIT

OUTFITTED > OUTFIT

OUTFITTER *n* supplier of men's clothes

OUTFLANK *vb* get round the side of (an enemy army)

OUTFLANKS > OUTFLANK

OUTFLASH *vb* be flashier than

OUTFLEW > OUTFLY

OUTFLIES > OUTFLY

OUTFLING *n* cutting remark ▷ *vb* whip out

OUTFLINGS > OUTFLING

OUTFLOAT *vb* surpass at floating

OUTFLOATS > OUTFLOAT

OUTFLOW *n* anything that flows out, such as liquid or money ▷ *vb* flow faster than

OUTFLOWED > OUTFLOW

OUTFLOWN > OUTFLY

OUTFLOWS > OUTFLOW

OUTFLUNG > OUTFLING

OUTFLUSH *n* burst of light

OUTFLY *vb* fly better or faster than

OUTFLYING > OUTFLY

OUTFOOL *vb* be more foolish than

OUTFOOLED > OUTFOOL

OUTFOOLS > OUTFOOL

OUTFOOT *vb* (of a boat) to go faster than (another boat)

OUTFOOTED > OUTFOOT

OUTFOOTS > OUTFOOT

OUTFOUGHT > OUTFIGHT

OUTFOUND > OUTFIND

OUTFOX *vb* defeat or foil by being more cunning

OUTFOXED > OUTFOX

OUTFOXES > OUTFOX

OUTFOXING > OUTFOX

OUTFROWN *vb* dominate by frowning more than

OUTFROWNS > OUTFROWN

OUTFUMBLE *vb* exceed in fumbling

OUTGAIN *vb* gain more than

OUTGAINED > OUTGAIN

OUTGAINS > OUTGAIN

OUTGALLOP *vb* gallop faster than

OUTGAMBLE *vb* defeat at gambling

OUTGAS *vb* undergo the removal of adsorbed or absorbed gas from solids

OUTGASES > OUTGAS

OUTGASSED > OUTGAS

OUTGASSES > OUTGAS

OUTGATE *n* way out

OUTGATES > OUTGATE

OUTGAVE > OUTGIVE

OUTGAZE *vb* gaze beyond

OUTGAZED > OUTGAZE

OUTGAZES > OUTGAZE

OUTGAZING > OUTGAZE

OUTGIVE *vb* exceed in giving

OUTGIVEN > OUTGIVE

OUTGIVES > OUTGIVE

OUTGIVING > OUTGIVE

OUTGLARE *vb* exceed in glaring

OUTGLARED > OUTGLARE

OUTGLARES > OUTGLARE

OUTGLEAM *vb* gleam more than

OUTGLEAMS > OUTGLEAM

OUTGLOW *vb* glow more than

OUTGLOWED > OUTGLOW

OUTGLOWS > OUTGLOW

OUTGNAW *vb* exceed in gnawing

OUTGNAWED > OUTGNAW

OUTGNAWN > OUTGNAW

OUTGNAWS > OUTGNAW

OUTGO *vb* exceed or outstrip ▷ *n* cost

OUTGOER > OUTGO

OUTGOERS > OUTGO

OUTGOES > OUTGO

OUTGOING *adj* leaving ▷ *n* act of going out

OUTGOINGS *pl n* expenses

OUTGONE > OUTGO

OUTGREW > OUTGROW

OUTGRIN *vb* exceed in grinning

OUTGRINS > OUTGRIN

OUTGROSS *vb* earn more than

OUTGROUP *n* group of people outside one's own group of people

OUTGROUPS > OUTGROUP

OUTGROW *vb* become too large or too old for

OUTGROWN > OUTGROW

OUTGROWS > OUTGROW

OUTGROWTH *n* natural development

OUTGUARD *n* guard furthest away from main party

OUTGUARDS > OUTGUARD

OUTGUESS *vb* surpass in guessing

OUTGUIDE *n* folder in filing system ▷ *vb* beat or surpass at guiding

OUTGUIDED > OUTGUIDE

OUTGUIDES > OUTGUIDE

OUTGUN *vb* surpass in fire power

OUTGUNNED > OUTGUN

OUTGUNS > OUTGUN

OUTGUSH *vb* gush out

OUTGUSHED > OUTGUSH

OUTGUSHES > OUTGUSH

OUTHANDLE *vb* handle better than

OUTHAUL *n* line or cable for tightening the foot of a sail

OUTHAULER *same as* > OUTHAUL

OUTHAULS > OUTHAUL

OUTHEAR *vb* exceed in hearing

OUTHEARD > OUTHEAR

OUTHEARS > OUTHEAR

OUTHER *same as* > OTHER

OUTHIRE *vb* hire out

OUTHIRED > OUTHIRE

OUTHIRES > OUTHIRE

OUTHIRING > OUTHIRE

OUTHIT *vb* hit something further than (someone else)

OUTHITS > OUTHIT

OUTHOMER *vb* score more home runs than

OUTHOMERS > OUTHOMER

OUTHOUSE *n* building near a main building

OUTHOUSES > OUTHOUSE

OUTHOWL *vb* exceed in howling

OUTHOWLED > OUTHOWL

OUTHOWLS > OUTHOWL

OUTHUMOR *same as* > OUTHUMOUR

OUTHUMORS > OUTHUMOR

OUTHUMOUR *vb* exceed in humouring

OUTHUNT *vb* exceed in hunting

OUTHUNTED > OUTHUNT

OUTHUNTS > OUTHUNT

OUTHUSTLE *vb* be more competitive than

OUTHYRE *same as* > OUTHIRE

OUTHYRED > OUTHYRE

OUTHYRES > OUTHYRE

OUTHYRING > OUTHYRE

OUTING *n* leisure trip

OUTINGS > OUTING

OUTJEST *vb* exceed in jesting

OUTJESTED > OUTJEST

OUTJESTS > OUTJEST

OUTJET *n* projecting part

OUTJETS > OUTJET

OUTJINX *vb* exceed in jinxing

OUTJINXED > OUTJINX

OUTJINXES > OUTJINX

OUTJOCKEY *vb* outwit by deception

OUTJUGGLE *vb* surpass at juggling

OUTJUMP *vb* jump higher or farther than

OUTJUMPED > OUTJUMP

OUTJUMPS > OUTJUMP

OUTJUT *vb* jut out ▷ *n* projecting part

OUTJUTS > OUTJUT

OUTJUTTED > OUTJUT

OUTKEEP *vb* beat or surpass at keeping

OUTKEEPS > OUTKEEP

OUTKEPT > OUTKEEP

OUTKICK *vb* exceed in kicking

OUTKICKED > OUTKICK

OUTKICKS > OUTKICK

OUTKILL *vb* exceed in killing

OUTKILLED > OUTKILL

OUTKILLS > OUTKILL

OUTKISS *vb* exceed in kissing

OUTKISSED > OUTKISS

OUTKISSES > OUTKISS

OUTLAID > OUTLAY

OUTLAIN > OUTLAY

OUTLAND *adj* outlying or distant ▷ *n* outlying areas of a country or region

OUTLANDER *n* foreigner or stranger

OUTLANDS > OUTLAND

OUTLASH *n* sudden attack ▷ *vb* shed tears

OUTLASHED > OUTLASH

OUTLASHES > OUTLASH

OUTLAST vb last longer than
OUTLASTED > OUTLAST
OUTLASTS > OUTLAST
OUTLAUGH vb laugh longer or louder than
OUTLAUGHS > OUTLAUGH
OUTLAUNCE same as **>** OUTLAUNCH
OUTLAUNCH vb send out
OUTLAW n criminal deprived of legal protection, bandit ▷ vb make illegal
OUTLAWED > OUTLAW
OUTLAWING > OUTLAW
OUTLAWRY n act of outlawing or the state of being outlawed
OUTLAWS > OUTLAW
OUTLAY n expenditure ▷ vb spend (money)
OUTLAYING > OUTLAY
OUTLAYS > OUTLAY
OUTLEAD vb be better leader than
OUTLEADS > OUTLEAD
OUTLEAP vb leap higher or farther than
OUTLEAPED > OUTLEAP
OUTLEAPS > OUTLEAP
OUTLEAPT > OUTLEAP
OUTLEARN vb exceed in learning
OUTLEARNS > OUTLEARN
OUTLEARNT > OUTLEARN
OUTLED > OUTLEAD
OUTLER n farm animal kept out of doors
OUTLERS > OUTLER
OUTLET n means of expressing emotion
OUTLETS > OUTLET
OUTLIE vb lie outside a particular place
OUTLIED > OUTLIE
OUTLIER n outcrop of rocks that is entirely surrounded by older rocks
OUTLIERS > OUTLIER
OUTLIES > OUTLIE
OUTLINE n short general explanation ▷ vb summarize
OUTLINEAR > OUTLINE
OUTLINED > OUTLINE
OUTLINER > OUTLINE
OUTLINERS > OUTLINE
OUTLINES > OUTLINE
OUTLINING > OUTLINE
OUTLIVE vb live longer than
OUTLIVED > OUTLIVE
OUTLIVER > OUTLIVE
OUTLIVERS > OUTLIVE
OUTLIVES > OUTLIVE
OUTLIVING > OUTLIVE
OUTLOOK n attitude ▷ vb look out
OUTLOOKED > OUTLOOK
OUTLOOKS > OUTLOOK
OUTLOVE vb exceed in loving
OUTLOVED > OUTLOVE

OUTLOVES > OUTLOVE
OUTLOVING > OUTLOVE
OUTLUSTRE vb outshine
OUTLYING adj distant from the main area
OUTMAN vb surpass in manpower
OUTMANNED > OUTMAN
OUTMANS > OUTMAN
OUTMANTLE vb be better dressed than
OUTMARCH vb exceed in marching
OUTMASTER vb surpass
OUTMATCH vb surpass or outdo (someone)
OUTMODE vb make unfashionable
OUTMODED adj no longer fashionable or accepted
OUTMODES > OUTMODE
OUTMODING > OUTMODE
OUTMOST another word for **>** OUTERMOST
OUTMOVE vb move faster or better than
OUTMOVED > OUTMOVE
OUTMOVES > OUTMOVE
OUTMOVING > OUTMOVE
OUTMUSCLE vb dominate by physical strength
OUTNAME vb be more notorious than
OUTNAMED > OUTNAME
OUTNAMES > OUTNAME
OUTNAMING > OUTNAME
OUTNESS n state or quality of being external
OUTNESSES > OUTNESS
OUTNIGHT vb refer to night more often than
OUTNIGHTS > OUTNIGHT
OUTNUMBER vb exceed in number
OUTOFFICE n outbuilding
OUTPACE vb go faster than (someone)
OUTPACED > OUTPACE
OUTPACES > OUTPACE
OUTPACING > OUTPACE
OUTPAINT vb exceed in painting
OUTPAINTS > OUTPAINT
OUTPART n remote region
OUTPARTS > OUTPART
OUTPASS vb exceed in passing
OUTPASSED > OUTPASS
OUTPASSES > OUTPASS
OUTPEEP vb peep out
OUTPEEPED > OUTPEEP
OUTPEEPS > OUTPEEP
OUTPEER vb surpass
OUTPEERED > OUTPEER
OUTPEERS > OUTPEER
OUTPEOPLE vb rid a country of its people
OUTPITCH vb exceed in pitching
OUTPITTIED > OUTPITY
OUTPITIES > OUTPITY
OUTPITY vb exceed in pitying

OUTPLACE vb find job for ex-employee
OUTPLACED > OUTPLACE
OUTPLACER > OUTPLACE
OUTPLACES > OUTPLACE
OUTPLAN vb exceed in planning
OUTPLANS > OUTPLAN
OUTPLAY vb perform better than one's opponent
OUTPLAYED > OUTPLAY
OUTPLAYS > OUTPLAY
OUTPLOD vb exceed in plodding
OUTPLODS > OUTPLOD
OUTPLOT vb exceed in plotting
OUTPLOTS > OUTPLOT
OUTPOINT vb score more points than
OUTPOINTS > OUTPOINT
OUTPOLL vb win more votes than
OUTPOLLED > OUTPOLL
OUTPOLLS > OUTPOLL
OUTPORT n isolated fishing village, esp in Newfoundland
OUTPORTER n inhabitant or native of a Newfoundland outport
OUTPORTS > OUTPORT
OUTPOST n outlying settlement
OUTPOSTS > OUTPOST
OUTPOUR n act of flowing or pouring out ▷ vb pour or cause to pour out freely or rapidly
OUTPOURED > OUTPOUR
OUTPOURER > OUTPOUR
OUTPOURS > OUTPOUR
OUTPOWER vb have more power than
OUTPOWERS > OUTPOWER
OUTPRAY vb exceed in praying
OUTPRAYED > OUTPRAY
OUTPRAYS > OUTPRAY
OUTPREACH vb outdo in preaching
OUTPREEN vb exceed in preening
OUTPREENS > OUTPREEN
OUTPRESS vb exceed in pressing
OUTPRICE vb sell at better price than
OUTPRICED > OUTPRICE
OUTPRICES > OUTPRICE
OUTPRIZE vb prize more highly than
OUTPRIZED > OUTPRIZE
OUTPRIZES > OUTPRIZE
OUTPSYCH vb defeat by psychological means
OUTPSYCHS > OUTPSYCH
OUTPULL vb exceed in pulling
OUTPULLED > OUTPULL
OUTPULLS > OUTPULL
OUTPUNCH vb punch better than

OUTPUPIL n student sent to a different school to the one he or she would normally attend
OUTPUPILS > OUTPUPIL
OUTPURSUE vb pursue farther than
OUTPUSH vb exceed in pushing
OUTPUSHED > OUTPUSH
OUTPUSHES > OUTPUSH
OUTPUT n amount produced ▷ vb produce (data) at the end of a process
OUTPUTS > OUTPUT
OUTPUTTED > OUTPUT
OUTQUOTE vb exceed in quoting
OUTQUOTED > OUTQUOTE
OUTQUOTES > OUTQUOTE
OUTRACE vb surpass in racing
OUTRACED > OUTRACE
OUTRACES > OUTRACE
OUTRACING > OUTRACE
OUTRAGE n great moral indignation ▷ vb offend morally
OUTRAGED > OUTRAGE
OUTRAGES > OUTRAGE
OUTRAGING > OUTRAGE
OUTRAISE vb raise more money than
OUTRAISED > OUTRAISE
OUTRAISES > OUTRAISE
OUTRAN > OUTRUN
OUTRANCE n furthest extreme
OUTRANCES > OUTRANCE
OUTRANG > OUTRING
OUTRANGE vb have a greater range than
OUTRANGED > OUTRANGE
OUTRANGES > OUTRANGE
OUTRANK vb be of higher rank than (someone)
OUTRANKED > OUTRANK
OUTRANKS > OUTRANK
OUTRATE vb offer better rate than
OUTRATED > OUTRATE
OUTRATES > OUTRATE
OUTRATING > OUTRATE
OUTRAVE vb outdo in raving
OUTRAVED > OUTRAVE
OUTRAVES > OUTRAVE
OUTRAVING > OUTRAVE
OUTRE adj shockingly eccentric
OUTREACH vb surpass in reach ▷ n act or process of reaching out
OUTREAD vb outdo in reading
OUTREADS > OUTREAD
OUTREASON vb surpass in reasoning
OUTRECKON vb surpass in reckoning
OUTRED vb be redder than
OUTREDDED > OUTRED

OUTREDDEN same as > OUTRED

OUTREDS > OUTRED

OUTREIGN vb reign for longer than

OUTREIGNS > OUTREIGN

OUTRELIEF n aid given outdoors

OUTREMER n land overseas

OUTREMERS > OUTREMER

OUTRIDDEN > OUTRIDE

OUTRIDE vb outdo by riding faster, farther, or better than ▷ n extra unstressed syllable within a metrical foot

OUTRIDER n motorcyclist acting as an escort

OUTRIDERS > OUTRIDER

OUTRIDES > OUTRIDE

OUTRIDING > OUTRIDE

OUTRIG vb supply with outfit

OUTRIGGED > OUTRIG

OUTRIGGER n stabilizing frame projecting from a boat

OUTRIGHT adv absolute(ly) ▷ adj complete

OUTRIGS > OUTRIG

OUTRING vb exceed in ringing

OUTRINGS > OUTRING

OUTRIVAL vb surpass

OUTRIVALS > OUTRIVAL

OUTRO n instrumental passage that concludes a piece of music

OUTROAR vb roar louder than

OUTROARED > OUTROAR

OUTROARS > OUTROAR

OUTROCK vb outdo in rocking

OUTROCKED > OUTROCK

OUTROCKS > OUTROCK

OUTRODE > OUTRIDE

OUTROLL vb exceed in rolling

OUTROLLED > OUTROLL

OUTROLLS > OUTROLL

OUTROOP n auction

OUTROOPER > OUTROOP

OUTROOPS > OUTROOP

OUTROOT vb root out

OUTROOTED > OUTROOT

OUTROOTS > OUTROOT

OUTROPE same as > OUTROOP

OUTROPER > OUTROPE

OUTROPERS > OUTROPE

OUTROPES > OUTROPE

OUTROS > OUTRO

OUTROW vb outdo in rowing

OUTROWED > OUTROW

OUTROWING > OUTROW

OUTROWS > OUTROW

OUTRUN vb run faster than

OUTRUNG > OUTRING

OUTRUNNER n attendant who runs in front of a carriage, etc

OUTRUNS > OUTRUN

OUTRUSH n flowing or rushing out ▷ vb rush out

OUTRUSHED > OUTRUSH

OUTRUSHES > OUTRUSH

OUTS > OUT

OUTSAID > OUTSAY

OUTSAIL vb sail better than

OUTSAILED > OUTSAIL

OUTSAILS > OUTSAIL

OUTSANG > OUTSING

OUTSAT > OUTSIT

OUTSAVOR same as > OUTSAVOR

OUTSAVORS > OUTSAVOR

OUTSAVOUR vb exceed in savouring

OUTSAW > OUTSEE

OUTSAY vb say something out loud

OUTSAYING > OUTSAY

OUTSAYS > OUTSAY

OUTSCHEME vb outdo in scheming

OUTSCOLD vb outdo in scolding

OUTSCOLDS > OUTSCOLD

OUTSCOOP vb outdo in achieving scoops

OUTSCOOPS > OUTSCOOP

OUTSCORE vb score more than

OUTSCORED > OUTSCORE

OUTSCORES > OUTSCORE

OUTSCORN vb defy with scorn

OUTSCORNS > OUTSCORN

OUTSCREAM vb scream louder than

OUTSEE vb exceed in seeing

OUTSEEING > OUTSEE

OUTSEEN > OUTSEE

OUTSEES > OUTSEE

OUTSELL vb be sold in greater quantities than

OUTSELLS > OUTSELL

OUTSERT another word for > WRAPROUND

OUTSERTS > OUTSERT

OUTSERVE vb serve better at tennis than

OUTSERVED > OUTSERVE

OUTSERVES > OUTSERVE

OUTSET n beginning

OUTSETS > OUTSET

OUTSHAME vb greatly shame

OUTSHAMED > OUTSHAME

OUTSHAMES > OUTSHAME

OUTSHINE vb surpass (someone) in excellence

OUTSHINED > OUTSHINE

OUTSHINES > OUTSHINE

OUTSHONE > OUTSHINE

OUTSHOOT vb surpass or excel in shooting ▷ n thing that projects or shoots out

OUTSHOOTS > OUTSHOOT

OUTSHOT n projecting part

OUTSHOTS > OUTSHOT

OUTSHOUT vb shout louder than

OUTSHOUTS > OUTSHOUT

OUTSIDE adv indicating movement to or position on the exterior ▷ adj unlikely ▷ n external area or surface

OUTSIDER n person outside a specific group

OUTSIDERS > OUTSIDER

OUTSIDES > OUTSIDE

OUTSIGHT n power of seeing

OUTSIGHTS > OUTSIGHT

OUTSIN vb sin more than

OUTSING vb sing better or louder than

OUTSINGS > OUTSING

OUTSINNED > OUTSIN

OUTSINS > OUTSIN

OUTSIT vb sit longer than

OUTSITS > OUTSIT

OUTSIZE adj larger than normal ▷ n outsize garment

OUTSIZED same as > OUTSIZE

OUTSIZES > OUTSIZE

OUTSKATE vb skate better than

OUTSKATED > OUTSKATE

OUTSKATES > OUTSKATE

OUTSKIRT singular of > OUTSKIRTS

OUTSKIRTS pl n outer areas, esp of a town

OUTSLEEP vb sleep longer than

OUTSLEEPS > OUTSLEEP

OUTSLEPT > OUTSLEEP

OUTSLICK vb outsmart

OUTSLICKS > OUTSLICK

OUTSMART vb outwit

OUTSMARTS > OUTSMART

OUTSMELL vb surpass in smelling

OUTSMELLS > OUTSMELL

OUTSMELT > OUTSMELL

OUTSMILE vb outdo in smiling

OUTSMILED > OUTSMILE

OUTSMILES > OUTSMILE

OUTSMOKE vb smoke more than

OUTSMOKED > OUTSMOKE

OUTSMOKES > OUTSMOKE

OUTSNORE vb outdo in snoring

OUTSNORED > OUTSNORE

OUTSNORES > OUTSNORE

OUTSOAR vb fly higher than

OUTSOARED > OUTSOAR

OUTSOARS > OUTSOAR

OUTSOLD > OUTSELL

OUTSOLE n outermost sole of a shoe

OUTSOLES > OUTSOLE

OUTSOURCE vb subcontract (work) to another company

OUTSPAN vb relax

OUTSPANS > OUTSPAN

OUTSPEAK vb speak better or louder than

OUTSPEAKS > OUTSPEAK

OUTSPED > OUTSPEED

OUTSPEED vb go faster than

OUTSPEEDS > OUTSPEED

OUTSPELL vb exceed at spelling

OUTSPELLS > OUTSPELL

OUTSPELT > OUTSPELL

OUTSPEND vb spend more than

OUTSPENDS > OUTSPEND

OUTSPENT > OUTSPEND

OUTSPOKE > OUTSPEAK

OUTSPOKEN adj tending to say what one thinks

OUTSPORT vb sport in excess of

OUTSPORTS > OUTSPORT

OUTSPRANG > OUTSPRING

OUTSPREAD adj spread or stretched out as far as possible ▷ vb spread out or cause to spread out ▷ n spreading out

OUTSPRING vb spring out

OUTSPRINT vb run faster than (someone)

OUTSPRUNG > OUTSPRING

OUTSTAND vb be outstanding or excel

OUTSTANDS > OUTSTAND

OUTSTARE vb stare longer than

OUTSTARED > OUTSTARE

OUTSTARES > OUTSTARE

OUTSTART vb jump out ▷ n outset

OUTSTARTS > OUTSTART

OUTSTATE vb surpass in stating

OUTSTATED > OUTSTATE

OUTSTATES > OUTSTATE

OUTSTAY vb overstay

OUTSTAYED > OUTSTAY

OUTSTAYS > OUTSTAY

OUTSTEER vb steer better than

OUTSTEERS > OUTSTEER

OUTSTEP vb step farther than

OUTSTEPS > OUTSTEP

OUTSTOOD > OUTSTAND

OUTSTRAIN vb strain too much

OUTSTRIDE vb surpass in striding

OUTSTRIKE vb exceed in striking

OUTSTRIP vb surpass

OUTSTRIPS > OUTSTRIP

OUTSTRIVE vb strive harder than

OUTSTRODE > OUTSTRIDE

OUTSTROKE n outward stroke

OUTSTROVE > OUTSTRIVE

O

OUTSTRUCK
> OUTSTRIKE
OUTSTUDY vb outdo in studying
OUTSTUNT vb outdo in performing stunts
OUTSTUNTS > OUTSTUNT
OUTSULK vb outdo in sulking
OUTSULKED > OUTSULK
OUTSULKS > OUTSULK
OUTSUM vb add up to more than
OUTSUMMED > OUTSUM
OUTSUMS > OUTSUM
OUTSUNG > OUTSING
OUTSWAM > OUTSWIM
OUTSWARE > OUTSWEAR
OUTSWEAR vb swear more than
OUTSWEARS > OUTSWEAR
OUTSWEEP n outward movement of arms in swimming breaststroke
OUTSWEEPS > OUTSWEEP
OUTSWELL vb exceed in swelling
OUTSWELLS > OUTSWELL
OUTSWEPT adj curving outwards
OUTSWIM vb outdo in swimming
OUTSWIMS > OUTSWIM
OUTSWING n (in cricket) movement of a ball from leg to off through the air
OUTSWINGS > OUTSWING
OUTSWORE > OUTSWEAR
OUTSWORN > OUTSWEAR
OUTSWUM > OUTSWIM
OUTSWUNG adj made to curve outwards
OUTTA prep an informal contraction of out of
OUTTAKE n unreleased take from a recording session, film, or TV programme ▷ vb take out
OUTTAKEN > OUTTAKE
OUTTAKES > OUTTAKE
OUTTAKING > OUTTAKE
OUTTALK vb talk more, longer, or louder than (someone)
OUTTALKED > OUTTALK
OUTTALKS > OUTTALK
OUTTASK vb assign task to staff outside organization
OUTTASKED > OUTTASK
OUTTASKS > OUTTASK
OUTTELL vb make known
OUTTELLS > OUTTELL
OUTTHANK vb outdo in thanking
OUTTHANKS > OUTTHANK
OUTTHIEVE vb surpass in stealing
OUTTHINK vb outdo in thinking
OUTTHINKS > OUTTHINK
OUTTHREW > OUTTHROW
OUTTHROB vb outdo in throbbing

OUTTHROBS > OUTTHROB
OUTTHROW vb throw better than
OUTTHROWN > OUTTHROW
OUTTHROWS > OUTTHROW
OUTTHRUST vb extend outwards
OUTTOLD > OUTTELL
OUTTONGUE vb speak louder than
OUTTOOK > OUTTAKE
OUTTOP vb rise higher than
OUTTOPPED > OUTTOP
OUTTOPS > OUTTOP
OUTTOWER vb tower over
OUTTOWERS > OUTTOWER
OUTTRADE vb surpass in trading
OUTTRADED > OUTTRADE
OUTTRADES > OUTTRADE
OUTTRAVEL vb outdo in travelling
OUTTRICK vb outdo in trickery
OUTTRICKS > OUTTRICK
OUTTROT vb exceed at trotting
OUTTROTS > OUTTROT
OUTTRUMP vb count for more than
OUTTRUMPS > OUTTRUMP
OUTTURN same as
> OUTPUT
OUTTURNS > OUTTURN
OUTVALUE vb surpass in value
OUTVALUED > OUTVALUE
OUTVALUES > OUTVALUE
OUTVAUNT vb outdo in boasting
OUTVAUNTS > OUTVAUNT
OUTVENOM vb surpass in venomousness
OUTVENOMS > OUTVENOM
OUTVIE vb outdo in competition
OUTVIED > OUTVIE
OUTVIES > OUTVIE
OUTVOICE vb surpass in noise
OUTVOICED > OUTVOICE
OUTVOICES > OUTVOICE
OUTVOTE vb defeat by getting more votes than
OUTVOTED > OUTVOTE
OUTVOTER > OUTVOTE
OUTVOTERS > OUTVOTE
OUTVOTES > OUTVOTE
OUTVOTING > OUTVOTE
OUTVYING > OUTVIE
OUTWAIT vb wait longer than
OUTWAITED > OUTWAIT
OUTWAITS > OUTWAIT
OUTWALK vb walk farther or longer than
OUTWALKED > OUTWALK
OUTWALKS > OUTWALK
OUTWAR vb surpass or exceed in warfare
OUTWARD same as
> OUTWARDS

OUTWARDLY adv in outward appearance
OUTWARDS adv towards the outside
OUTWARRED > OUTWAR
OUTWARS > OUTWAR
OUTWASH n gravel carried and deposited by water from melting glaciers
OUTWASHES > OUTWASH
OUTWASTE vb outdo in wasting
OUTWASTED > OUTWASTE
OUTWASTES > OUTWASTE
OUTWATCH vb surpass in watching
OUTWEAR vb use up or destroy by wearing
OUTWEARS > OUTWEAR
OUTWEARY vb exhaust
OUTWEED vb root out
OUTWEEDED > OUTWEED
OUTWEEDS > OUTWEED
OUTWEEP vb outdo in weeping
OUTWEEPS > OUTWEEP
OUTWEIGH vb be more important, significant, or influential than
OUTWEIGHS
> OUTWEIGH
OUTWELL vb pour out
OUTWELLED > OUTWELL
OUTWELLS > OUTWELL
OUTWENT > OUTGO
OUTWEPT > OUTWEEP
OUTWHIRL vb surpass at whirling
OUTWHIRLS > OUTWHIRL
OUTWICK vb move one curling stone by striking with another
OUTWICKED > OUTWICK
OUTWICKS > OUTWICK
OUTWILE vb surpass in cunning
OUTWILED > OUTWILE
OUTWILES > OUTWILE
OUTWILING > OUTWILE
OUTWILL vb demonstrate stronger will than
OUTWILLED > OUTWILL
OUTWILLS > OUTWILL
OUTWIN vb get out of
OUTWIND vb unwind
OUTWINDED > OUTWIND
OUTWINDS > OUTWIND
OUTWING vb surpass in flying
OUTWINGED > OUTWING
OUTWINGS > OUTWING
OUTWINS > OUTWIN
OUTWISH vb surpass in wishing
OUTWISHED > OUTWISH
OUTWISHES > OUTWISH
OUTWIT vb get the better of (someone) by cunning
OUTWITH prep outside
OUTWITS > OUTWIT
OUTWITTED > OUTWIT
OUTWON > OUTWIN
OUTWORE > OUTWEAR

OUTWORK n defences which lie outside main defensive works ▷ vb work better, harder, etc, than
OUTWORKED > OUTWORK
OUTWORKER > OUTWORK
OUTWORKS > OUTWORK
OUTWORN adj no longer in use
OUTWORTH vb be more valuable than
OUTWORTHS > OUTWORTH
OUTWOUND > OUTWIND
OUTWREST vb extort
OUTWRESTS > OUTWREST
OUTWRIT > OUTWRITE
OUTWRITE vb outdo in writing
OUTWRITES > OUTWRITE
OUTWROTE > OUTWRITE
OUTYELL vb outdo in yelling
OUTYELLED > OUTYELL
OUTYELLS > OUTYELL
OUTYELP vb outdo in yelping
OUTYELPED > OUTYELP
OUTYELPS > OUTYELP
OUTYIELD vb yield more than
OUTYIELDS > OUTYIELD
OUVERT adj open
OUVERTE feminine form of
> OUVERT
OUVRAGE n work
OUVRAGES > OUVRAGE
OUVRIER n worker
OUVRIERE feminine form of
> OUVRIER
OUVRIERES > OUVRIERE
OUVRIERS > OUVRIER
OUZEL n type of bird
OUZELS > OUZEL
OUZO n strong aniseed-flavoured spirit from Greece
OUZOS > OUZO
OVA > OVUM
OVAL adj egg-shaped ▷ n anything that is oval in shape
OVALBUMIN n albumin in egg whites
OVALITIES > OVAL
OVALITY > OVAL
OVALLY > OVAL
OVALNESS > OVAL
OVALS > OVAL
OVARIAL > OVARY
OVARIAN > OVARY
OVARIES > OVARY
OVARIOLE n tube in insect ovary
OVARIOLES
> OVARIOLE
OVARIOUS adj of eggs
OVARITIS n inflammation of an ovary
OVARY n female egg-producing organ
OVATE adj shaped like an egg ▷ vb give ovation
OVATED > OVATE

OVATELY > OVATE

OVATES > OVATE

OVATING > OVATE

OVATION n enthusiastic round of applause

OVATIONAL > OVATION

OVATIONS > OVATION

OVATOR > OVATE

OVATORS > OVATE

OVEL n mourner, esp during the first seven days after a death

OVELS > OVEL

OVEN n heated compartment or container for cooking ▷ vb cook in an oven

OVENABLE adj (of food) suitable for cooking in an oven

OVENBIRD n type of small brownish South American bird

OVENBIRDS > OVENBIRD

OVENED > OVEN

OVENING > OVEN

OVENLIKE > OVEN

OVENPROOF adj able to be used in an oven

OVENS > OVEN

OVENWARE n heat-resistant dishes in which food can be both cooked and served

OVENWARES > OVENWARE

OVENWOOD n pieces of wood for burning in an oven

OVENWOODS > OVENWOOD

OVER adv indicating position on the top of, amount greater than, etc ▷ adj finished ▷ n (in cricket) series of six balls bowled from one end ▷ vb jump over

OVERABLE adj too able

OVERACT vb act in an exaggerated way

OVERACTED > OVERACT

OVERACTS > OVERACT

OVERACUTE adj too acute

OVERAGE adj beyond a specified age ▷ n amount beyond given limit

OVERAGED adj very old

OVERAGES > OVERAGE

OVERALERT adj abnormally alert

OVERALL adv in total ▷ n coat-shaped protective garment ▷ adj from one end to the other

OVERALLED adj wearing overalls

OVERALLS > OVERALL

OVERAPT adj tending excessively

OVERARCH vb form an arch over

OVERARM adv with the arm above the shoulder ▷ adj bowled, thrown, or performed with the arm raised above the shoulder ▷ vb throw (a ball) overarm

OVERARMED > OVERARM

OVERARMS > OVERARM

OVERATE > OVEREAT

OVERAWE vb affect (someone) with an overpowering sense of awe

OVERAWED > OVERAWE

OVERAWES > OVERAWE

OVERAWING > OVERAWE

OVERBAKE vb bake too long

OVERBAKED > OVERBAKE

OVERBAKES > OVERBAKE

OVERBANK n sediment deposited on the flood plain of a river

OVERBANKS > OVERBANK

OVERBEAR vb dominate or overcome

OVERBEARS > OVERBEAR

OVERBEAT vb beat too much

OVERBEATS > OVERBEAT

OVERBED adj fitting over bed

OVERBET vb bet too much

OVERBETS > OVERBET

OVERBID vb bid for more tricks than one can expect to win ▷ n bid higher than someone else's bid

OVERBIDS > OVERBID

OVERBIG adj too big

OVERBILL vb charge too much money

OVERBILLS > OVERBILL

OVERBITE n extension of the upper front teeth over the lower front teeth when the mouth is closed

OVERBITES > OVERBITE

OVERBLEW > OVERBLOW

OVERBLOW vb blow into (a wind instrument) with greater force than normal

OVERBLOWN adj excessive

OVERBLOWS > OVERBLOW

OVERBOARD adv from a boat into the water

OVERBOIL vb boil too much

OVERBOILS > OVERBOIL

OVERBOLD adj too bold

OVERBOOK vb accept too many bookings

OVERBOOKS > OVERBOOK

OVERBOOT n protective boot worn over an ordinary boot or shoe

OVERBOOTS > OVERBOOT

OVERBORE > OVERBEAR

OVERBORN > OVERBEAR

OVERBORNE > OVERBEAR

OVERBOUND vb jump over

OVERBRAKE vb brake too much

OVERBRED adj produced by too much selective breeding

OVERBREED vb produce by too much selective breeding

OVERBRIEF adj too brief

OVERBRIM vb overflow

OVERBRIMS > OVERBRIM

OVERBROAD adj not specific enough

OVERBROW vb hang over

OVERBROWS > OVERBROW

OVERBUILD vb build over or on top of

OVERBUILT > OVERBUILD

OVERBULK vb loom large over

OVERBULKS > OVERBULK

OVERBURN vb copy information onto CD

OVERBURNS > OVERBURN

OVERBURNT > OVERBURN

OVERBUSY adj too busy ▷ vb make too busy

OVERBUY vb buy too much or too many

OVERBUYS > OVERBUY

OVERBY adv Scots expression meaning over the road or across the way

OVERCALL n bid higher than the preceding one ▷ vb bid higher than (an opponent)

OVERCALLS > OVERCALL

OVERCAME > OVERCOME

OVERCARRY vb carry too far or too many

OVERCAST adj (of the sky) covered by clouds ▷ vb make or become overclouded or gloomy ▷ n covering, as of clouds or mist

OVERCASTS > OVERCAST

OVERCATCH vb overtake

OVERCHEAP adj too cheap

OVERCHECK n thin leather strap attached to a horse's bit to keep its head up

OVERCHILL vb make too cold

OVERCIVIL adj too civil

OVERCLAD vb wearing too many clothes

OVERCLAIM vb claim too much

OVERCLASS n dominant group in society

OVERCLEAN adj too clean

OVERCLEAR adj too clear

OVERCLOCK vb modify a computer to run at greater speeds than originally intended

OVERCLOSE adj too close

OVERCLOUD vb make or become covered with clouds

OVERCLOY vb weary with excess

OVERCLOYS > OVERCLOY

OVERCLUB vb (in golf) use a club which causes the shot to go too far

OVERCLUBS > OVERCLUB

OVERCOACH vb coach too much

OVERCOAT n heavy coat

OVERCOATS > OVERCOAT

OVERCOLD adj too cold

OVERCOLOR vb colour too highly

OVERCOME vb gain control over after an effort

OVERCOMER > OVERCOME

OVERCOMES > OVERCOME

OVERCOOK vb spoil food by cooking it for too long

OVERCOOKS > OVERCOOK

OVERCOOL vb cool too much

OVERCOOLS > OVERCOOL

OVERCOUNT vb outnumber

OVERCOVER vb cover up

OVERCOY adj too modest

OVERCRAM vb fill too full

OVERCRAMS > OVERCRAM

OVERCRAW same as > OVERCROW

OVERCRAWS > OVERCRAW

OVERCROP vb exhaust (land) by excessive cultivation

OVERCROPS > OVERCROP

OVERCROW vb crow over

OVERCROWD vb fill with more people or things than is desirable

OVERCROWS > OVERCROW

OVERCURE vb take curing process too far

OVERCURED > OVERCURE

OVERCURES > OVERCURE

OVERCUT vb cut too much

OVERCUTS > OVERCUT

OVERDARE vb dare too much

OVERDARED > OVERDARE

OVERDARES > OVERDARE

OVERDATED adj outdated

OVERDEAR adj too dear

OVERDECK n upper deck

OVERDECKS > OVERDECK

OVERDID > OVERDO

OVERDIGHT adj covered up

OVERDO vb do to excess

OVERDOER > OVERDO

OVERDOERS > OVERDO

OVERDOES > OVERDO

OVERDOG n person or side in an advantageous position

OVERDOGS > OVERDOG

OVERDOING > OVERDO

OVERDONE > OVERDO

OVERDOSE n excessive dose of a drug ▷ vb take an overdose

OVERDOSED > OVERDOSE

OVERDOSES > OVERDOSE

OVERDRAFT n overdrawing

OVERDRANK > OVERDRINK

OVERDRAW vb withdraw more money than is in (one's bank account)

OVERDRAWN > OVERDRAW

OVERDRAWS > OVERDRAW

OVERDRESS vb dress (oneself or another) too elaborately or finely ⊳ n dress that may be worn over a jumper, blouse, etc

OVERDREW > OVERDRAW

OVERDRIED > OVERDRY

OVERDRIES > OVERDRY

OVERDRINK vb drink too much alcohol

OVERDRIVE n very high gear in a motor vehicle

OVERDROVE
> OVERDRIVE

OVERDRUNK
> OVERDRINK

OVERDRY vb dry too much

OVERDUB vb add (new sounds) to a tape so that the old and the new sounds can be heard ⊳ n sound or series of sounds added by this method

OVERDUBS > OVERDUB

OVERDUE adj still due after the time allowed

OVERDUST vb dust too much

OVERDUSTS
> OVERDUST

OVERDYE vb dye (a fabric, yarn, etc) excessively

OVERDYED > OVERDYE

OVERDYER > OVERDYE

OVERDYERS > OVERDYE

OVERDYES > OVERDYE

OVEREAGER adj excessively eager or keen

OVEREASY adj too easy

OVEREAT vb eat more than is necessary or healthy

OVEREATEN > OVEREAT

OVEREATER > OVEREAT

OVEREATS > OVEREAT

OVERED > OVER

OVEREDIT vb edit too much

OVEREDITS > OVEREDIT

OVEREGG vb exaggerate absurdly

OVEREGGED > OVEREGG

OVEREGGS > OVEREGG

OVEREMOTE vb emote too much

OVEREQUIP vb equip, furnish with, or supply excessively

OVEREXERT vb exhaust or injure (oneself) by doing too much

OVEREYE vb survey

OVEREYED > OVEREYE

OVEREYES > OVEREYE

OVEREYING > OVEREYE

OVERFALL n turbulent stretch of water caused by marine currents over an underwater ridge

OVERFALLS > OVERFALL

OVERFAR adv too far

OVERFAST adj too fast

OVERFAT adj too fat

OVERFAVOR vb favour too much

OVERFEAR vb fear too much

OVERFEARS > OVERFEAR

OVERFED > OVERFEED

OVERFEED vb give (a person, plant, or animal) more food than is necessary or healthy

OVERFEEDS > OVERFEED

OVERFELL > OVERFALL

OVERFILL vb put more into (something) than there is room for

OVERFILLS > OVERFILL

OVERFINE adj too fine

OVERFISH vb fish too much

OVERFIT adj too fit

OVERFLEW > OVERFLY

OVERFLIES > OVERFLY

OVERFLOOD vb flood excessively

OVERFLOW vb flow over ⊳ n something that overflows

OVERFLOWN > OVERFLY

OVERFLOWS > OVERFLOW

OVERFLUSH adj too flush

OVERFLY vb fly over (a territory) or past (a point)

OVERFOCUS vb focus too much

OVERFOLD n fold in which one or both limbs have been inclined more than 90° from their original orientation

OVERFOLDS > OVERFOLD

OVERFOND adj excessively keen (on)

OVERFOUL adj too foul

OVERFRANK adj too frank

OVERFREE adj too forward

OVERFULL adj excessively full

OVERFUND vb supply with too much money

OVERFUNDS > OVERFUND

OVERFUSSY adj too fussy

OVERGALL vb make sore all over

OVERGALLS > OVERGALL

OVERGANG vb dominate

OVERGANGS > OVERGANG

OVERGAVE > OVERGIVE

OVERGEAR vb cause (a company) to have too high a proportion of loan stock

OVERGEARS > OVERGEAR

OVERGET vb overtake

OVERGETS > OVERGET

OVERGILD vb gild too much

OVERGILDS > OVERGILD

OVERGILT > OVERGILD

OVERGIRD vb gird too tightly

OVERGIRDS > OVERGIRD

OVERGIRT > OVERGIRD

OVERGIVE vb give up

OVERGIVEN > OVERGIVE

OVERGIVES > OVERGIVE

OVERGLAD adj too glad

OVERGLAZE adj (of decoration or colours) applied to porcelain above the glaze

OVERGLOOM vb make gloomy

OVERGO vb go beyond

OVERGOAD vb goad too much

OVERGOADS
> OVERGOAD

OVERGOES > OVERGO

OVERGOING > OVERGO

OVERGONE > OVERGO

OVERGORGE vb overeat

OVERGOT > OVERGET

OVERGRADE vb grade too highly

OVERGRAIN vb apply grainy texture to

OVERGRASS vb grow grass on top of

OVERGRAZE vb graze (land) too intensively

OVERGREAT adj too great

OVERGREEN vb cover with vegetation

OVERGREW > OVERGROW

OVERGROW vb grow over or across (an area, path, lawn, etc)

OVERGROWN > OVERGROW

OVERGROWS > OVERGROW

OVERHAILE vb pull over

OVERHAIR n outer coat of animal

OVERHAIRS > OVERHAIR

OVERHALE same as > OVERHAILE

OVERHALED > OVERHALE

OVERHALES > OVERHALE

OVERHAND adj thrown or performed with the hand raised above the shoulder ⊳ adv with the hand above the shoulder ⊳ vb sew with the thread passing over two edges in one direction

OVERHANDS > OVERHAND

OVERHANG vb project beyond something ⊳ n overhanging part

OVERHANGS > OVERHANG

OVERHAPPY adj too happy

OVERHARD adj too hard

OVERHASTE n excessive haste

OVERHASTY
> OVERHASTE

OVERHATE vb hate too much

OVERHATED > OVERHATE

OVERHATES > OVERHATE

OVERHAUL vb examine and repair ⊳ n examination and repair

OVERHAULS > OVERHAUL

OVERHEAD adj above one's head ⊳ adv over or above head height ⊳ n stroke in

racket games played from above head height

OVERHEADS pl n general cost of maintaining a business

OVERHEAP vb supply too much

OVERHEAPS > OVERHEAP

OVERHEAR vb hear (a speaker or remark) unintentionally

OVERHEARD > OVERHEAR

OVERHEARS > OVERHEAR

OVERHEAT vb make or become excessively hot ⊳ n condition of being overheated

OVERHEATS > OVERHEAT

OVERHELD > OVERHOLD

OVERHENT vb overtake

OVERHENTS > OVERHENT

OVERHIGH adj too high

OVERHIT vb hit too strongly

OVERHITS > OVERHIT

OVERHOLD vb value too highly

OVERHOLDS > OVERHOLD

OVERHOLY adj too holy

OVERHONOR vb honour too highly

OVERHOPE vb hope too much

OVERHOPED > OVERHOPE

OVERHOPES > OVERHOPE

OVERHOT adj too hot

OVERHUNG > OVERHANG

OVERHUNT vb hunt too much

OVERHUNTS > OVERHUNT

OVERHYPE vb hype too much

OVERHYPED > OVERHYPE

OVERHYPES > OVERHYPE

OVERIDLE adj too idle

OVERING > OVER

OVERINKED adj printed using too much ink

OVERISSUE vb issue (shares, banknotes, etc) in excess of demand or ability to pay ⊳ n shares, banknotes, etc, thus issued

OVERJOY vb give great delight to

OVERJOYED adj extremely pleased

OVERJOYS > OVERJOY

OVERJUMP vb jump too far

OVERJUMPS > OVERJUMP

OVERJUST adj too just

OVERKEEN adj too keen

OVERKEEP vb keep too long

OVERKEEPS > OVERKEEP

OVERKEPT > OVERKEEP

OVERKEST same as > OVERCAST

OVERKILL n treatment that is greater than required

OVERKILLS > OVERKILL

OVERKIND adj too kind

OVERKING n supreme king
OVERKINGS > OVERKING
OVERKNEE adj reaching to above knee
OVERLABOR vb spend too much work on
OVERLADE vb overburden
OVERLADED > OVERLADE
OVERLADEN > OVERLADE
OVERLADES > OVERLADE
OVERLAID > OVERLAY
OVERLAIN > OVERLIE
OVERLAND adv by land ▷ vb drive (cattle or sheep) overland
OVERLANDS > OVERLAND
OVERLAP vb share part of the same space or period of time (as) ▷ n area overlapping
OVERLAPS > OVERLAP
OVERLARD vb cover with lard
OVERLARDS > OVERLARD
OVERLARGE adj excessively large
OVERLATE adj too late
OVERLAX adj too lax
OVERLAY vb cover with a thin layer ▷ n something that is laid over something else
OVERLAYS > OVERLAY
OVERLEAF adv on the back of the current page
OVERLEAP vb leap too far
OVERLEAPS > OVERLEAP
OVERLEAPT > OVERLEAP
OVERLEARN vb study too intensely
OVERLEND vb lend too much
OVERLENDS > OVERLEND
OVERLENT > OVERLEND
OVERLET vb let to too many
OVERLETS > OVERLET
OVERLEWD adj too lewd
OVERLIE vb lie on or cover (something or someone)
OVERLIER > OVERLIE
OVERLIERS > OVERLIE
OVERLIES > OVERLIE
OVERLIGHT vb illuminate too brightly
OVERLIT > OVERLIGHT
OVERLIVE vb live longer than (another person)
OVERLIVED > OVERLIVE
OVERLIVES > OVERLIVE
OVERLOAD vb put too large a load on or in ▷ n excessive load
OVERLOADS > OVERLOAD
OVERLOCK vb sew fabric with interlocking stitch
OVERLOCKS > OVERLOCK
OVERLONG adj too or excessively long
OVERLOOK vb fail to notice ▷ n high place affording a view
OVERLOOKS > OVERLOOK

OVERLORD n supreme lord or master
OVERLORDS > OVERLORD
OVERLOUD adj too loud
OVERLOVE vb love too much
OVERLOVED > OVERLOVE
OVERLOVES > OVERLOVE
OVERLUSH adj too lush
OVERLUSTY adj too lusty
OVERLY adv excessively
OVERLYING > OVERLIE
OVERMAN vb provide with too many staff ▷ n man who oversees others
OVERMANS > OVERMAN
OVERMANY adj too many ▷ n excess of people
OVERMAST vb provide mast that is too big
OVERMASTS > OVERMAST
OVERMATCH vb be more than a match for ▷ n person superior in ability
OVERMEEK adj too meek
OVERMELT vb melt too much
OVERMELTS > OVERMELT
OVERMEN > OVERMAN
OVERMERRY adj very merry
OVERMILD adj too mild
OVERMILK vb milk too much
OVERMILKS > OVERMILK
OVERMINE vb mine too much
OVERMINED > OVERMINE
OVERMINES > OVERMINE
OVERMIX vb mix too much
OVERMIXED > OVERMIX
OVERMIXES > OVERMIX
OVERMOUNT vb surmount
OVERMUCH adj too much ▷ n excessive amount
OVERNAME vb repeat (someone's) name
OVERNAMED > OVERNAME
OVERNAMES > OVERNAME
OVERNEAR adj too near
OVERNEAT adj too neat
OVERNET vb cover with net
OVERNETS > OVERNET
OVERNEW adj too new
OVERNICE adj too fastidious, precise, etc
OVERNIGHT adv (taking place) during one night ▷ adj done in, occurring in, or lasting the night ▷ vb stay the night
OVERPACK vb pack too much
OVERPACKS > OVERPACK
OVERPAGE same as > OVERLEAF
OVERPAID > OVERPAY
OVERPAINT vb apply too much paint
OVERPART vb give an actor too difficult a role

OVERPARTS > OVERPART
OVERPASS vb pass over, through, or across
OVERPAST > OVERPASS
OVERPAY vb pay (someone) at too high a rate
OVERPAYS > OVERPAY
OVERPEDAL vb use piano pedal too much
OVERPEER vb look down over
OVERPEERS > OVERPEER
OVERPERCH vb fly up to perch on
OVERPERT adj too insolent
OVERPITCH vb bowl (a cricket ball) so that it pitches too close to the stumps
OVERPLAID n plaid in double layer
OVERPLAN vb plan excessively
OVERPLANS > OVERPLAN
OVERPLANT vb plant more than is necessary
OVERPLAST adj put above
OVERPLAY same as > OVERACT
OVERPLAYS > OVERPLAY
OVERPLIED > OVERPLY
OVERPLIES > OVERPLY
OVERPLOT vb plot onto existing graph or map
OVERPLOTS > OVERPLOT
OVERPLUS n surplus or excess quantity
OVERPLY vb ply too much
OVERPOISE vb weigh more than
OVERPOST vb hurry over
OVERPOSTS > OVERPOST
OVERPOWER vb subdue or overcome (someone)
OVERPRESS vb oppress
OVERPRICE vb put too high a price on
OVERPRINT vb print (additional matter) onto (something already printed) ▷ n additional matter printed onto something already printed
OVERPRIZE vb prize too highly
OVERPROOF adj containing more alcohol than standard spirit ▷ n spirit with a higher content of alcohol than standard spirit
OVERPROUD adj too proud
OVERPUMP vb pump too much
OVERPUMPS > OVERPUMP
OVERQUICK adj too quick
OVERRACK vb strain too much
OVERRACKS > OVERRACK
OVERRAKE vb rake over
OVERRAKED > OVERRAKE
OVERRAKES > OVERRAKE

OVERRAN > OVERRUN
OVERRANK adj too rank ▷ vb assign an unnecessarily high rank to
OVERRANKS > OVERRANK
OVERRASH adj too rash
OVERRATE vb have too high an opinion of
OVERRATED > OVERRATE
OVERRATES > OVERRATE
OVERREACH vb defeat or thwart (oneself) by attempting to do or gain too much
OVERREACT vb react more strongly than is necessary
OVERREAD vb read over
OVERREADS > OVERREAD
OVERRED vb paint over in red
OVERREDS > OVERRED
OVERREN same as > OVERRUN
OVERRENS > OVERREN
OVERRICH adj (of food) excessively flavoursome or fatty
OVERRIDE vb overrule ▷ n device or system that can override an automatic control
OVERRIDER > OVERRIDE
OVERRIDES > OVERRIDE
OVERRIFE adj too rife
OVERRIGID adj too rigid
OVERRIPE adj (of a fruit or vegetable) so ripe that it has started to decay
OVERRIPEN vb become overripe
OVERROAST vb roast too long
OVERRODE > OVERRIDE
OVERRUDE adj very rude
OVERRUFF vb defeat trump card by playing higher trump
OVERRUFFS > OVERRUFF
OVERRULE vb reverse the decision of (a person with less power)
OVERRULED > OVERRULE
OVERRULER > OVERRULE
OVERRULES > OVERRULE
OVERRUN vb conquer rapidly ▷ n act or an instance of overrunning
OVERRUNS > OVERRUN
OVERS > OVER
OVERSAD adj too sad
OVERSAIL vb project beyond
OVERSAILS > OVERSAIL
OVERSALE n selling of more than is available
OVERSALES > OVERSALE
OVERSALT vb put too much salt in
OVERSALTS > OVERSALT
OVERSAUCE vb put too much sauce on
OVERSAVE vb put too much money in savings

OVERSAVED > OVERSAVE

OVERSAVES > OVERSAVE

OVERSAW > OVERSEE

OVERSCALE adj at higher scale than standard

OVERSCORE vb cancel by drawing a line or lines over or through

OVERSEA same as > OVERSEAS

OVERSEAS adj to, of, or from a distant country ▷ adv across the sea ▷ n foreign country or foreign countries collectively

OVERSEE vb watch over from a position of authority

OVERSEED vb plant too much seed in

OVERSEEDS > OVERSEED

OVERSEEN > OVERSEE

OVERSEER n person who oversees others, esp workmen

OVERSEERS > OVERSEER

OVERSEES > OVERSEE

OVERSELL vb exaggerate the merits or abilities of

OVERSELLS > OVERSELL

OVERSET vb disturb or upset

OVERSETS > OVERSET

OVERSEW vb sew (two edges) with stitches that pass over them both

OVERSEWED > OVERSEW

OVERSEWN > OVERSEW

OVERSEWS > OVERSEW

OVERSEXED adj more interested in sex than is thought decent

OVERSHADE vb appear more important than

OVERSHARP adj too sharp

OVERSHINE vb shine down on

OVERSHIRT n shirt worn over lighter clothes

OVERSHOE n protective shoe worn over an ordinary shoe

OVERSHOES > OVERSHOE

OVERSHONE > OVERSHINE

OVERSHOOT vb go beyond (a mark or target) ▷ n act or instance of overshooting

OVERSHOT adj (of a water wheel) driven by a flow of water that passes over the wheel ▷ n type of fishing rod

OVERSHOTS > OVERSHOT

OVERSICK adj too sick

OVERSIDE adv over the side (of a ship) ▷ n top side

OVERSIDES > OVERSIDE

OVERSIGHT n mistake caused by not noticing something

OVERSIZE adj larger than the usual size ▷ n size larger than the usual or proper size

OVERSIZED same as > OVERSIZE

OVERSIZES > OVERSIZE

OVERSKIP vb skip over

OVERSKIPS > OVERSKIP

OVERSKIRT n outer skirt, esp one that reveals a decorative underskirt

OVERSLEEP vb sleep beyond the intended time

OVERSLEPT > OVERSLEEP

OVERSLIP vb slip past

OVERSLIPS > OVERSLIP

OVERSLIPT > OVERSLIP

OVERSLOW adj too slow

OVERSMAN n overseer

OVERSMEN > OVERSMAN

OVERSMOKE vb smoke something too much

OVERSOAK vb soak too much

OVERSOAKS > OVERSOAK

OVERSOFT adj too soft

OVERSOLD > OVERSELL

OVERSOON adv too soon

OVERSOUL n universal divine essence

OVERSOULS > OVERSOUL

OVERSOW vb sow again after first sowing

OVERSOWED > OVERSOW

OVERSOWN > OVERSOW

OVERSOWS > OVERSOW

OVERSPEND vb spend more than one can afford ▷ n amount by which someone or something is overspent

OVERSPENT > OVERSPEND

OVERSPICE vb add too much spice to

OVERSPILL n rehousing of people from crowded cities in smaller towns ▷ vb overflow

OVERSPILT > OVERSPILL

OVERSPIN n forward spinning motion

OVERSPINS > OVERSPIN

OVERSTAFF vb provide an excessive number of staff for (a factory, hotel, etc)

OVERSTAIN vb stain too much

OVERSTAND vb remain longer than

OVERSTANK > OVERSTINK

OVERSTARE vb outstare

OVERSTATE vb state too strongly

OVERSTAY vb stay beyond the limit or duration of

OVERSTAYS > OVERSTAY

OVERSTEER vb (of a vehicle) to turn more sharply than is desirable or anticipated

OVERSTEP vb go beyond (a certain limit)

OVERSTEPS > OVERSTEP

OVERSTINK vb exceed in stinking

OVERSTIR vb stir too much

OVERSTIRS > OVERSTIR

OVERSTOCK vb hold or supply (a commodity) in excess of requirements

OVERSTOOD > OVERSTAND

OVERSTORY n highest level of trees in a rainforest

OVERSTREW vb scatter over

OVERSTUDY vb study too much

OVERSTUFF vb force too much into

OVERSTUNK > OVERSTINK

OVERSUDS vb produce too much lather

OVERSUP vb sup too much

OVERSUPS > OVERSUP

OVERSURE adj too sure

OVERSWAM > OVERSWIM

OVERSWAY vb overrule

OVERSWAYS > OVERSWAY

OVERSWEAR vb swear again

OVERSWEET adj too sweet

OVERSWELL vb overflow

OVERSWIM vb swim across

OVERSWIMS > OVERSWIM

OVERSWING vb swing too much or too far

OVERSWORE > OVERSWEAR

OVERSWORN > OVERSWEAR

OVERSWUM > OVERSWIM

OVERSWUNG > OVERSWING

OVERT adj open, not hidden

OVERTAKE vb move past (a vehicle or person) travelling in the same direction

OVERTAKEN > OVERTAKE

OVERTAKES > OVERTAKE

OVERTALK vb talk over

OVERTALKS > OVERTALK

OVERTAME adj too tame

OVERTART adj too bitter

OVERTASK vb impose too heavy a task upon

OVERTASKS > OVERTASK

OVERTAX vb put too great a strain on

OVERTAXED > OVERTAX

OVERTAXES > OVERTAX

OVERTEACH vb teach too much

OVERTEEM vb be too full of something

OVERTEEMS > OVERTEEM

OVERTHICK adj too thick

OVERTHIN adj too thin

OVERTHINK vb give too much thought to

OVERTHREW > OVERTHROW

OVERTHROW vb defeat and replace ▷ n downfall, destruction

OVERTIGHT adj too tight

OVERTIME adv in addition to one's normal working hours ▷ n work at a regular job done in addition to regular working hours ▷ vb exceed the required time for (a photographic exposure)

OVERTIMED > OVERTIME

OVERTIMER > OVERTIME

OVERTIMES > OVERTIME

OVERTIMID adj too timid

OVERTIP vb give too much money as a tip

OVERTIPS > OVERTIP

OVERTIRE vb make too tired

OVERTIRED > OVERTIRE

OVERTIRES > OVERTIRE

OVERTLY > OVERT

OVERTNESS > OVERT

OVERTOIL vb work too hard

OVERTOILS > OVERTOIL

OVERTONE n additional meaning

OVERTONES > OVERTONE

OVERTOOK > OVERTAKE

OVERTOP vb exceed in height

OVERTOPS > OVERTOP

OVERTOWER vb tower above

OVERTRADE vb (of an enterprise) to trade in excess of working capital

OVERTRAIN vb train too much

OVERTREAT vb give too much medical treatment to

OVERTRICK n trick by which a player exceeds his contract

OVERTRIM vb trim too much

OVERTRIMS > OVERTRIM

OVERTRIP vb tread lightly over

OVERTRIPS > OVERTRIP

OVERTRUMP vb (in cards) play a trump higher than (one previously played to the trick)

OVERTRUST vb trust too much

OVERTURE n orchestral introduction ▷ vb make or present an overture to

OVERTURED > OVERTURE

OVERTURES > OVERTURE

OVERTURN vb turn upside down ▷ n act of overturning or the state of being overturned

OVERTURNS > OVERTURN

OVERTYPE vb type over existing text

OVERTYPED > OVERTYPE
OVERTYPES > OVERTYPE
OVERURGE *vb* urge too strongly
OVERURGED > OVERURGE
OVERURGES > OVERURGE
OVERUSE *vb* use excessively ▷ *n* excessive use
OVERUSED > OVERUSE
OVERUSES > OVERUSE
OVERUSING > OVERUSE
OVERVALUE *vb* regard (someone or something) as much more important than is the case
OVERVEIL *vb* cover over
OVERVEILS > OVERVEIL
OVERVIEW *n* general survey
OVERVIEWS > OVERVIEW
OVERVIVID *adj* too vivid
OVERVOTE *vb* vote more times than is allowed
OVERVOTED > OVERVOTE
OVERVOTES > OVERVOTE
OVERWARM *vb* make too warm
OVERWARMS > OVERWARM
OVERWARY *adj* excessively wary
OVERWASH *n* act of washing over something
OVERWATCH *vb* watch over
OVERWATER *vb* give too much water to
OVERWEAK *adj* too weak
OVERWEAR *vb* wear out
OVERWEARS > OVERWEAR
OVERWEARY *vb* make too tired
OVERWEEN *vb* think too highly of
OVERWEENS > OVERWEEN
OVERWEIGH *vb* exceed in weight
OVERWENT > OVERGO
OVERWET *vb* make too wet
OVERWETS > OVERWET
OVERWHELM *vb* overpower, esp emotionally
OVERWIDE *adj* too wide
OVERWILY *adj* too crafty
OVERWIND *vb* wind (a watch) beyond the proper limit
OVERWINDS > OVERWIND
OVERWING *vb* fly above
OVERWINGS > OVERWING
OVERWISE *adj* too wise
OVERWORD *n* repeated word or phrase
OVERWORDS > OVERWORD
OVERWORE > OVERWEAR
OVERWORK *vb* work too much ▷ *n* excessive work
OVERWORKS > OVERWORK
OVERWORN > OVERWEAR
OVERWOUND > OVERWIND
OVERWRAP *vb* cover with a wrapping

OVERWRAPS > OVERWRAP
OVERWREST *vb* strain too much
OVERWRITE *vb* write (something) in an excessively ornate or prolix style
OVERWROTE > OVERWRITE
OVERYEAR *vb* keep for later year
OVERYEARS > OVERYEAR
OVERZEAL *n* excess of zeal
OVERZEALS > OVERZEAL
OVIBOS *n* type of ox
OVIBOSES > OVIBOS
OVIBOVINE > OVIBOS
OVICIDAL > OVICIDE
OVICIDE *n* killing of sheep
OVICIDES > OVICIDE
OVIDUCAL > OVIDUCT
OVIDUCT *n* tube through which eggs are conveyed
OVIDUCTAL > OVIDUCT
OVIDUCTS > OVIDUCT
OVIFEROUS *adj* carrying or producing eggs or ova
OVIFORM *adj* shaped like an egg
OVIGEROUS *same as* > OVIFEROUS
OVINE *adj* of or like a sheep ▷ *n* member of sheep family
OVINES > OVINE
OVIPARA *n* all oviparous animals
OVIPARITY > OVIPAROUS
OVIPAROUS *adj* producing eggs that hatch outside the body of the mother
OVIPOSIT *vb* (of insects and fishes) to deposit eggs through an ovipositor
OVIPOSITS > OVIPOSIT
OVIRAPTOR *n* egg-eating dinosaur
OVISAC *n* capsule or sac in which egg cells are produced
OVISACS > OVISAC
OVIST *n* person believing ovum contains all subsequent generations
OVISTS > OVIST
OVOID *adj* egg-shaped ▷ *n* something that is ovoid
OVOIDAL *adj* ovoid ▷ *n* something that is ovoid
OVOIDALS > OVOIDAL
OVOIDS > OVOID
OVOLI > OVOLO
OVOLO *n* type of convex moulding
OVOLOS > OVOLO
OVONIC *adj* using particular electronic storage batteries
OVONICS *n* science of ovonic equipment

OVOTESTES > OVOTESTIS
OVOTESTIS *n* reproductive organ of snails
OVULAR > OVULE
OVULARY > OVULE
OVULATE *vb* produce or release an egg cell from an ovary
OVULATED > OVULATE
OVULATES > OVULATE
OVULATING > OVULATE
OVULATION > OVULATE
OVULATORY > OVULATE
OVULE *n* plant part that contains the egg cell
OVULES > OVULE
OVUM *n* unfertilized egg cell
OW *interj* exclamation of pain
OWCHE *same as* > OUCH
OWCHES > OWCHE
OWE *vb* be obliged to pay (a sum of money) to (a person)
OWED > OWE
OWELTIES > OWELTY
OWELTY *n* equality, esp in financial transactions
OWER *Scots word for* > OVER
OWERBY *adv* over there
OWERLOUP *n* Scots word meaning encroachment
OWERLOUPS > OWERLOUP
OWES > OWE
OWING > OWE
OWL *n* night bird of prey ▷ *vb* act like an owl
OWLED > OWL
OWLER *vb* smuggler
OWLERIES > OWLERY
OWLERS > OWLER
OWLERY *n* place where owls live
OWLET *n* young or nestling owl
OWLETS > OWLET
OWLIER > OWLY
OWLIEST > OWLY
OWLING > OWL
OWLISH *adj* like an owl
OWLISHLY > OWLISH
OWLLIKE > OWL
OWLS > OWL
OWLY *same as* > OWLISH
OWN *adj* used to emphasize possession ▷ *pron* thing(s) belonging to a particular person ▷ *vb* possess
OWNABLE *adj* able to be owned
OWNED > OWN
OWNER *n* person who owns
OWNERLESS > OWNER
OWNERS > OWNER
OWNERSHIP *n* state or fact of being an owner
OWNING > OWN
OWNS > OWN
OWNSOME *n* solitary state
OWNSOMES > OWNSOME
OWRE *same as* > OWER
OWRECAME > OWRECOME

OWRECOME *n* chorus of song ▷ *vb* overcome
OWRECOMES > OWRECOME
OWRELAY *Scots form of* > OVERLAY
OWRELAYS > OWRELAY
OWRES > OWRE
OWREWORD *variant of* > OVERWORD
OWREWORDS > OWREWORD
OWRIE *same as* > OORIE
OWRIER > OWRIE
OWRIEST > OWRIE
OWSE *Scots form of* > OX
OWSEN *Scots word for* > OXEN
OWT *dialect word for* > ANYTHING
OWTS > OWT
OX *n* castrated bull
OXACILLIN *n* antibiotic drug
OXALATE *n* salt or ester of oxalic acid ▷ *vb* treat with oxalate
OXALATED > OXALATE
OXALATES > OXALATE
OXALATING > OXALATE
OXALIC *adj* as in *oxalic acid* poisonous acid found in many plants
OXALIS *n* type of plant
OXALISES > OXALIS
OXAZEPAM *n* drug used to relieve anxiety
OXAZEPAMS > OXAZEPAM
OXAZINE *n* type of chemical compound
OXAZINES > OXAZINE
OXAZOLE *n* type of liquid chemical compound
OXAZOLES > OXAZOLE
OXBLOOD *n* dark reddish-brown colour ▷ *adj* of this colour
OXBLOODS > OXBLOOD
OXBOW *n* piece of wood fitted around the neck of a harnessed ox
OXBOWS > OXBOW
OXCART *n* cart pulled by ox
OXCARTS > OXCART
OXEN > OX
OXER *n* high fence
OXERS > OXER
OXES > OX
OXEYE *n* daisy-like flower
OXEYES > OXEYE
OXFORD *n* type of stout laced shoe with a low heel
OXFORDS > OXFORD
OXGANG *n* old measure of farmland
OXGANGS > OXGANG
OXGATE *same as* > OXGANG
OXGATES > OXGATE
OXHEAD *n* head of an ox
OXHEADS > OXHEAD
OXHEART *n* heart-shaped cherry
OXHEARTS > OXHEART
OXHERD *n* person who tends oxen**

OXHERDS > OXHERD
OXHIDE *n* leather made from the hide of an ox
OXHIDES > OXHIDE
OXIC *adj* involving oxygen
OXID *same as* > OXIDE
OXIDABLE *adj* able to undergo oxidation
OXIDANT *n* substance that acts or is used as an oxidizing agent
OXIDANTS > OXIDANT
OXIDASE *n* enzyme that brings about oxidation
OXIDASES > OXIDASE
OXIDASIC > OXIDASE
OXIDATE *another word for* > OXIDIZE
OXIDATED > OXIDATE
OXIDATES > OXIDATE
OXIDATING > OXIDATE
OXIDATION *n* oxidizing
OXIDATIVE > OXIDATION
OXIDE *n* compound of oxygen and one other element
OXIDES > OXIDE
OXIDIC > OXIDE
OXIDISE *same as* > OXIDIZE
OXIDISED > OXIDISE
OXIDISER *same as* > OXIDIZER
OXIDISERS > OXIDISER
OXIDISES > OXIDISE
OXIDISING > OXIDISE
OXIDIZE *vb* combine chemically with oxygen
OXIDIZED > OXIDIZE
OXIDIZER *same as* > OXIDANT
OXIDIZERS > OXIDIZER
OXIDIZES > OXIDIZE
OXIDIZING > OXIDIZE
OXIDS > OXID
OXIES > OXY
OXIM *same as* > OXIME
OXIME *n* type of chemical compound
OXIMES > OXIME
OXIMETER *n* instrument for measuring oxygen in blood
OXIMETERS > OXIMETER
OXIMETRY > OXIMETER
OXIMS > OXIM

OXLAND *same as* > OXGANG
OXLANDS > OXLAND
OXLIKE > OX
OXLIP *n* type of woodland plant
OXLIPS > OXLIP
OXO *n* as in *oxo acid* acid that contains oxygen
OXONIUM *n* as in *oxonium compound* type of salt derived from an organic ether
OXONIUMS > OXONIUM
OXPECKER *n* type of African starling
OXPECKERS > OXPECKER
OXSLIP *same as* > OXLIP
OXSLIPS > OXSLIP
OXTAIL *n* tail of an ox, used in soups and stews
OXTAILS > OXTAIL
OXTER *n* armpit ▷ *vb* grip under arm
OXTERED > OXTER
OXTERING > OXTER
OXTERS > OXTER
OXTONGUE *n* type of plant
OXTONGUES > OXTONGUE
OXY > OX
OXYACID *n* any acid that contains oxygen
OXYACIDS > OXYACID
OXYCODONE *n* as in *oxycodone hydrochloride* opiate drug used as a painkiller
OXYGEN *n* gaseous element essential to life and combustion
OXYGENASE *n* enzyme
OXYGENATE *vb* add oxygen to
OXYGENIC > OXYGEN
OXYGENISE *variant of* > OXYGENIZE
OXYGENIZE *vb* add oxygen to
OXYGENOUS > OXYGEN
OXYGENS > OXYGEN
OXYMEL *n* mixture of vinegar and honey
OXYMELS > OXYMEL
OXYMORA > OXYMORON
OXYMORON *n* figure of speech that combines two apparently contradictory ideas

OXYMORONS > OXYMORON
OXYNTIC *adj* of or denoting stomach cells that secrete acid
OXYPHIL *n* type of cell found in glands
OXYPHILE *same as* > OXYPHIL
OXYPHILES > OXYPHILE
OXYPHILIC > OXYPHIL
OXYPHILS > OXYPHIL
OXYSALT *n* any salt of an oxyacid
OXYSALTS > OXYSALT
OXYSOME *n* group of molecules
OXYSOMES > OXYSOME
OXYTOCIC *adj* accelerating childbirth by stimulating uterine contractions ▷ *n* oxytocic drug or agent
OXYTOCICS > OXYTOCIC
OXYTOCIN *n* hormone that stimulates the ejection of milk in mammals
OXYTOCINS > OXYTOCIN
OXYTONE *adj* having an accent on the final syllable ▷ *n* oxytone word
OXYTONES > OXYTONE
OXYTONIC *adj* (of a word) having the stress or acute accent on the last syllable
OXYTROPE *n* type of flowering plant
OXYTROPES > OXYTROPE
OY *n* grandchild
OYE *same as* > OY
OYER *n* (in the 13th century) an assize
OYERS > OYER
OYES *same as* > OYEZ
OYESES > OYES
OYESSES > OYES
OYEZ *interj* shouted three times by a public crier calling for attention ▷ *n* such a cry
OYEZES > OYEZ
OYS > OY
OYSTER *n* edible shellfish ▷ *vb* dredge for, gather, or raise oysters
OYSTERED > OYSTER
OYSTERER *n* person fishing for oysters

OYSTERERS > OYSTERER
OYSTERING > OYSTER
OYSTERMAN *n* person who gathers, cultivates, or sells oysters
OYSTERMEN > OYSTERMAN
OYSTERS > OYSTER
OYSTRIGE *archaic variant of* > OSTRICH
OYSTRIGES > OYSTRIGE
OZAENA *n* inflammation of nasal mucous membrane
OZAENAS > OZAENA
OZALID *n* method of duplicating writing or illustrations
OZALIDS > OZALID
OZEKI *n* sumo wrestling champion
OZEKIS > OZEKI
OZOCERITE *n* brown or greyish wax
OZOKERITE *same as* > OZOCERITE
OZONATE *vb* add ozone to
OZONATED > OZONATE
OZONATES > OZONATE
OZONATING > OZONATE
OZONATION > OZONATE
OZONE *n* strong-smelling form of oxygen
OZONES > OZONE
OZONIC > OZONE
OZONIDE *n* type of unstable explosive compound
OZONIDES > OZONIDE
OZONISE *same as* > OZONIZE
OZONISED > OZONISE
OZONISER > OZONISE
OZONISERS > OZONISE
OZONISES > OZONISE
OZONISING > OZONISE
OZONIZE *vb* convert (oxygen) into ozone
OZONIZED > OZONIZE
OZONIZER > OZONIZE
OZONIZERS > OZONIZE
OZONIZES > OZONIZE
OZONIZING > OZONIZE
OZONOUS > OZONE
OZZIE *n* hospital
OZZIES > OZZIE

Pp

PA _n_ (formerly) fortified Māori settlement
PAAL _n_ stake driven into the ground
PAALS > PAAL
PAAN _n_ leaf of the betel tree
PAANS > PAAN
PABLUM _same as_ > PABULUM
PABLUMS > PABLUM
PABOUCHE _n_ soft shoe
PABOUCHES > PABOUCHE
PABULAR > PABULUM
PABULOUS > PABULUM
PABULUM _n_ food
PABULUMS > PABULUM
PAC _n_ soft shoe
PACA _n_ large burrowing rodent
PACABLE _adj_ easily appeased
PACAS > PACA
PACATION _n_ act of making peace
PACATIONS > PACATION
PACE _n_ single step in walking ▷ _vb_ walk up and down, esp in anxiety ▷ _prep_ with due respect to: used to express polite disagreement
PACED > PACE
PACEMAKER _n_ electronic device surgically implanted in a person with heart disease to regulate the heartbeat
PACEMAN _n_ (in cricket) fast bowler
PACEMEN > PACEMAN
PACER _n_ horse trained to move at a special gait, esp for racing
PACERS > PACER
PACES > PACE
PACEWAY _n_ racecourse for trotting and pacing
PACEWAYS > PACEWAY
PACEY _adj_ fast-moving, quick, lively
PACHA _same as_ > PASHA
PACHADOM _n_ rank of pacha
PACHADOMS > PACHADOM
PACHAK _n_ fragrant roots of Asian plant
PACHAKS > PACHAK
PACHALIC _n_ jurisdiction of pasha

PACHALICS > PACHALIC
PACHAS > PACHA
PACHINKO _n_ Japanese game similar to pinball
PACHINKOS > PACHINKO
PACHISI _n_ Indian game resembling backgammon
PACHISIS > PACHISI
PACHOULI _same as_ > PATCHOULI
PACHOULIS > PACHOULI
PACHUCO _n_ young Mexican living in the US
PACHUCOS > PACHUCO
PACHYDERM _n_ thick-skinned animal such as an elephant
PACHYTENE _n_ third stage of the prophase of meiosis during which the chromosomes become shorter and thicker and divide into chromatids
PACIER > PACY
PACIEST > PACY
PACIFIC _adj_ tending to bring peace
PACIFICAE _pl n_ medieval letters of introduction from the Church
PACIFICAL > PACIFIC
PACIFIED > PACIFY
PACIFIER _n_ baby's dummy
PACIFIERS > PACIFIER
PACIFIES > PACIFY
PACIFISM _n_ belief that violence of any kind is unjustifiable and that one should not participate in war
PACIFISMS > PACIFISM
PACIFIST _n_ person who refuses on principle to take part in war ▷ _adj_ advocating, relating to, or characterized by pacifism
PACIFISTS > PACIFIST
PACIFY _vb_ soothe, calm
PACIFYING > PACIFY
PACING _n_ act of pacing
PACINGS > PACING
PACK _vb_ put (clothes etc) together in a suitcase or bag ▷ _n_ bag carried on a person's or animal's back
PACKABLE > PACK
PACKAGE _same as_ > PACKET

PACKAGED > PACKAGE
PACKAGER _n_ independent firm specializing in design and production, as of illustrated books or television programmes which are sold to publishers or television companies as finished products
PACKAGERS > PACKAGER
PACKAGES > PACKAGE
PACKAGING _n_ box or wrapping in which a product is offered for sale
PACKBOARD _n_ frame for carrying goods
PACKCLOTH _n_ cloth used for packing
PACKED _adj_ completely filled
PACKER _n_ person or company who packs goods
PACKERS > PACKER
PACKET _n_ small container (and contents) ▷ _vb_ wrap up in a packet or as a packet
PACKETED > PACKET
PACKETING > PACKET
PACKETS > PACKET
PACKFONG _n_ Chinese alloy
PACKFONGS > PACKFONG
PACKFRAME _n_ light metal frame with shoulder straps, used for carrying heavy or awkward loads
PACKHORSE _n_ horse used for carrying goods
PACKING _n_ material, such as paper or plastic, used to protect packed goods
PACKINGS > PACKING
PACKLY > PACK
PACKMAN _n_ person carrying pack
PACKMEN > PACKMAN
PACKMULE _n_ mule used to carry burdens
PACKMULES > PACKMULE
PACKNESS > PACK
PACKS > PACK
PACKSACK _n_ bag carried strapped on the back or shoulder
PACKSACKS > PACKSACK
PACKSHEET _n_ cover for pack

PACKSTAFF _n_ staff for supporting pack
PACKWAX _n_ neck ligament
PACKWAXES > PACKWAX
PACKWAY _n_ path for pack animals
PACKWAYS > PACKWAY
PACO _n_ S American mammal
PACOS > PACO
PACS > PAC
PACT _n_ formal agreement
PACTA > PACTUM
PACTION _vb_ concur with
PACTIONAL > PACTION
PACTIONED > PACTION
PACTIONS > PACTION
PACTS > PACT
PACTUM _n_ pact
PACY _same as_ > PACEY
PACZKI _n_ round filled doughnut
PACZKIS > PACZKI
PAD _n_ piece of soft material used for protection, support, absorption of liquid, etc ▷ _vb_ protect or fill with soft material
PADANG _n_ (in Malaysia) playing field
PADANGS > PADANG
PADAUK _n_ tropical African or Asian tree
PADAUKS > PADAUK
PADDED > PAD
PADDER _n_ highwayman who robs on foot
PADDERS > PADDER
PADDIES > PADDY
PADDING > PAD
PADDINGS > PAD
PADDLE _n_ short oar with a broad blade at one or each end ▷ _vb_ move (a canoe etc) with a paddle
PADDLED > PADDLE
PADDLER > PADDLE
PADDLERS > PADDLE
PADDLES > PADDLE
PADDLING > PADDLE
PADDLINGS > PADDLE
PADDOCK _n_ small field or enclosure for horses ▷ _vb_ place (a horse) in a paddock
PADDOCKED > PADDOCK
PADDOCKS > PADDOCK
PADDY _n_ fit of temper
PADDYWACK _vb_ spank or smack

PADELLA n type of candle
PADELLAS > PADELLA
PADEMELON n small Australian wallaby
PADERERO same as > PATERERO
PADEREROS > PADERERO
PADI same as > PADDY
PADIS > PADI
PADISHAH n Iranian ruler
PADISHAHS > PADISHAH
PADKOS n snacks and provisions for a journey
PADLE another name for > LUMPFISH
PADLES > PADLE
PADLOCK n detachable lock with a hinged hoop ▷ vb fasten (something) with a padlock
PADLOCKED > PADLOCK
PADLOCKS > PADLOCK
PADMA n type of lotus
PADMAS > PADMA
PADNAG n ambling horse
PADNAGS > PADNAG
PADOUK same as > PADAUK
PADOUKS > PADOUK
PADRE n chaplain to the armed forces
PADRES > PADRE
PADRI > PADRE
PADRONA n female boss or employer
PADRONAS > PADRONA
PADRONE n owner or proprietor of an inn, esp in Italy
PADRONES > PADRONE
PADRONI > PADRONE
PADRONISM n system of work controlled by a padrone
PADS > PAD
PADSAW n small narrow saw used for cutting curves
PADSAWS > PADSAW
PADSHAH same as > PADISHAH
PADSHAHS > PADSHAH
PADUASOY n rich strong silk fabric used for hangings, vestments, etc
PADUASOYS > PADUASOY
PADYMELON same as > PADEMELON
PAEAN n song of triumph or thanksgiving
PAEANISM > PAEAN
PAEANISMS > PAEAN
PAEANS > PAEAN
PAEDERAST same as > PEDERAST
PAEDEUTIC adj of or relating to the study of teaching
PAEDIATRY n branch of medical science concerned with children and their diseases
PAEDO n paedophile
PAEDOLOGY n study of the character, growth, and development of children

PAEDOS > PAEDO
PAELLA n Spanish dish of rice, chicken, shellfish, and vegetables
PAELLAS > PAELLA
PAENULA n ancient Roman cloak
PAENULAE > PAENULA
PAENULAS > PAENULA
PAEON n metrical foot of four syllables
PAEONIC > PAEON
PAEONICS > PAEON
PAEONIES > PAEONY
PAEONS > PAEON
PAEONY same as > PEONY
PAESAN n fellow countryman
PAESANI > PAESANO
PAESANO n Italian-American man
PAESANOS > PAESANO
PAESANS > PAESAN
PAGAN adj not belonging to one of the world's main religions ▷ n pagan person
PAGANDOM > PAGAN
PAGANDOMS > PAGAN
PAGANISE same as > PAGANIZE
PAGANISED > PAGANISE
PAGANISER > PAGANISE
PAGANISES > PAGANISE
PAGANISH > PAGAN
PAGANISM > PAGAN
PAGANISMS > PAGAN
PAGANIST > PAGAN
PAGANISTS > PAGAN
PAGANIZE vb become pagan, render pagan, or convert to paganism
PAGANIZED > PAGANIZE
PAGANIZER > PAGANIZE
PAGANIZES > PAGANIZE
PAGANS > PAGAN
PAGE n (one side of) sheet of paper forming a book etc ▷ vb summon (someone) by bleeper or loudspeaker
PAGEANT n parade or display of people in costume
PAGEANTRY n spectacular display or ceremony
PAGEANTS > PAGEANT
PAGEBOY n type of hairstyle
PAGEBOYS > PAGEBOY
PAGED > PAGE
PAGEFUL n amount (of text, etc) that a page will hold
PAGEFULS > PAGEFUL
PAGEHOOD n state of being a page
PAGEHOODS > PAGEHOOD
PAGER n small electronic device, capable of receiving short messages
PAGERS > PAGER
PAGES > PAGE

PAGEVIEW n electronic page of information displayed at the request of a user
PAGEVIEWS > PAGEVIEW
PAGINAL adj page-for-page
PAGINATE vb number the pages of (a book, manuscript, etc) in sequence
PAGINATED > PAGINATE
PAGINATES > PAGINATE
PAGING > PAGE
PAGINGS > PAGE
PAGLE same as > PAIGLE
PAGLES > PAGLE
PAGOD n oriental idol
PAGODA n pyramid-shaped Asian temple or tower
PAGODAS > PAGODA
PAGODITE n type of soft mineral used for carving
PAGODITES > PAGODITE
PAGODS > PAGOD
PAGRI n type of turban
PAGRIS > PAGRI
PAGURIAN n type of decapod crustacean of the family which includes the hermit crabs
PAGURIANS > PAGURIAN
PAGURID same as > PAGURIAN
PAGURIDS > PAGURID
PAH same as > PA
PAHAUTEA same as > KAIKAWAKA
PAHAUTEAS > PAHAUTEA
PAHLAVI n Iranian coin
PAHLAVIS > PAHLAVI
PAHOEHOE n hardened lava
PAHOEHOES > PAHOEHOE
PAHS > PAH
PAID > PAY
PAIDEUTIC same as > PAEDEUTIC
PAIDLE Scots variant of > PADDLE
PAIDLES > PAIDLE
PAIGLE n cowslip
PAIGLES > PAIGLE
PAIK vb thump or whack
PAIKED > PAIK
PAIKING > PAIK
PAIKS > PAIK
PAIL n bucket
PAILFUL same as > PAIL
PAILFULS > PAILFUL
PAILLARD n thin slice of meat
PAILLARDS > PAILLARD
PAILLASSE same as > PALLIASSE
PAILLETTE n sequin or spangle sewn onto a costume
PAILLON n thin leaf of metal
PAILLONS > PAILLON
PAILS > PAIL
PAILSFUL > PAILFUL

PAIN n physical or mental suffering ▷ vb cause (someone) mental or physical suffering
PAINCH Scots variant of > PAUNCH
PAINCHES > PAINCH
PAINED adj having or suggesting pain or distress
PAINFUL adj causing pain or distress
PAINFULLY > PAINFUL
PAINIM n heathen or pagan
PAINIMS > PAINIM
PAINING > PAIN
PAINLESS adj not causing pain or distress
PAINS pl n care or trouble
PAINT n coloured substance, spread on a surface with a brush or roller ▷ vb colour or coat with paint
PAINTABLE > PAINT
PAINTBALL n game in which teams of players simulate a military skirmish, shooting each other with paint pellets
PAINTBOX n box containing a tray of dry watercolour paints
PAINTED > PAINT
PAINTER n rope at the front of a boat, for tying it up
PAINTERLY adj having qualities peculiar to painting, esp the depiction of shapes by means of solid masses of colour, rather than by lines
PAINTERS > PAINTER
PAINTIER > PAINT
PAINTIEST > PAINT
PAINTING n picture produced by using paint
PAINTINGS > PAINTING
PAINTPOT n pot for holding paint
PAINTPOTS > PAINTPOT
PAINTRESS n female painter
PAINTS > PAINT
PAINTURE n art of painting
PAINTURES > PAINTURE
PAINTWORK n covering of paint on parts of a vehicle, building, etc
PAINTY > PAINT
PAIOCK obsolete word for > PEACOCK
PAIOCKE obsolete word for > PEACOCK
PAIOCKES > PAIOCKE
PAIOCKS > PAIOCK
PAIR n set of two things matched for use together ▷ vb group or be grouped in twos
PAIRE obsolete spelling of > PAIR

PAIRED > PAIR

PAIRER > PAIR

PAIRES > PAIRE

PAIREST > PAIR

PAIRIAL *variant of* > PRIAL

PAIRIALS > PAIRIAL

PAIRING > PAIR

PAIRINGS > PAIR

PAIRS > PAIR

PAIRWISE *adv* in pairs

PAIS *n* country

PAISA *n* monetary unit of Bangladesh, Bhutan, India, Nepal, and Pakistan

PAISAN *n* fellow countryman

PAISANA *n* female peasant

PAISANAS > PAISANA

PAISANO *n* friend

PAISANOS > PAISANO

PAISANS > PAISAN

PAISAS > PAISA

PAISE > PAISA

PAISLEY *n* pattern of small curving shapes with intricate detailing

PAISLEYS > PAISLEY

PAITRICK *Scots word for* > PARTRIDGE

PAITRICKS > PAITRICK

PAJAMA *same as* > PYJAMA

PAJAMAED *adj* wearing pajamas

PAJAMAS > PAJAMA

PAJOCK *obsolete word for* > PEACOCK

PAJOCKE *obsolete word for* > PEACOCK

PAJOCKES > PAJOCKE

PAJOCKS > PAJOCK

PAK *n* pack

PAKAHI *n* acid land that is unsuitable for cultivation

PAKAHIS > PAKAHI

PAKAPOO *n* Chinese lottery

PAKAPOOS > PAKAPOO

PAKEHA *n* person of European descent, as distinct from a Māori

PAKEHAS > PAKEHA

PAKFONG *same as* > PACKFONG

PAKFONGS > PAKFONG

PAKIHI *n* area of swampy infertile land

PAKIHIS > PAKIHI

PAKKA *variant of* > PUKKA

PAKOKO *n* small freshwater fish

PAKOKOS > PAKOKO

PAKORA *n* fried battered pieces of vegetable, chicken, etc

PAKORAS > PAKORA

PAKS > PAK

PAKTHONG *n* white alloy containing copper, zinc, and nickel

PAKTHONGS > PAKTHONG

PAKTONG *same as* > PAKTHONG

PAKTONGS > PAKTONG

PAL *n* friend ⊳ *vb* associate as friends

PALABRA *n* word

PALABRAS > PALABRA

PALACE *n* residence of a king, bishop, etc

PALACED *adj* having palaces

PALACES > PALACE

PALADIN *n* knight who did battle for a monarch

PALADINS > PALADIN

PALAEOSOL *n* an ancient soil horizon

PALAESTRA *n* (in ancient Greece or Rome) public place devoted to the training of athletes

PALAFITTE *n* prehistoric dwelling

PALAGI *n* (in Samoa) European

PALAGIS > PALAGI

PALAIS *n* dance hall

PALAMA *n* webbing on bird's feet

PALAMAE > PALAMA

PALAMATE > PALAMA

PALAMINO *same as* > PALOMINO

PALAMINOS > PALAMINO

PALAMPORE *same as* > PALEMPORE

PALANKEEN *same as* > PALANQUIN

PALANQUIN *n* (formerly, in the Orient) covered bed in which someone could be carried on the shoulders of four men

PALAPA *n* open-sided tropical building

PALAPAS > PALAPA

PALAS *n* East Indian tree

PALASES > PALAS

PALATABLE *adj* pleasant to taste

PALATABLY > PALATABLE

PALATAL *adj* of or relating to the palate ⊳ *n* bony plate that forms the palate

PALATALLY > PALATAL

PALATALS > PALATAL

PALATE *n* roof of the mouth ⊳ *vb* perceive by taste

PALATED > PALATE

PALATES > PALATE

PALATIAL *adj* like a palace, magnificent

PALATINE *same as* > PALATAL

PALATINES > PALATINE

PALATING > PALATE

PALAVER *n* time-wasting fuss ⊳ *vb* (often used humorously) have a conference

PALAVERED > PALAVER

PALAVERER > PALAVER

PALAVERS > PALAVER

PALAY *n* type of rubber

PALAYS > PALAY

PALAZZI > PALAZZO

PALAZZO *n* Italian palace

PALAZZOS > PALAZZO

PALE *adj* light, whitish ⊳ *vb* become pale ⊳ *n* wooden or metal post used in fences

PALEA *n* bract in a grass spikelet

PALEAE > PALEA

PALEAL > PALEA

PALEATE *adj* having scales

PALEBUCK *n* small African antelope

PALEBUCKS > PALEBUCK

PALED > PALE

PALEFACE *n* offensive term for a White person, said to have been used by Native Americans of N America

PALEFACES > PALEFACE

PALELY > PALE

PALEMPORE *n* bed covering

PALENESS > PALE

PALEOCENE *adj* belonging to geological time period

PALEOCON *n* extremely right-wing conservative

PALEOCONS > PALEOCON

PALEOGENE *adj* of early geological time period

PALEOLITH *n* Stone Age artefact

PALEOLOGY *n* study of prehistory

PALEOSOL *n* ancient soil horizon

PALEOSOLS > PALEOSOL

PALEOZOIC *adj* belonging to geological time period

PALER > PALE

PALES > PALE

PALEST > PALE

PALESTRA *same as* > PALAESTRA

PALESTRAE > PALESTRA

PALESTRAL > PALESTRA

PALESTRAS > PALESTRA

PALET *n* perpendicular band on escutcheon

PALETOT *n* loose outer garment

PALETOTS > PALETOT

PALETS > PALET

PALETTE *n* artist's flat board for mixing colours on

PALETTES > PALETTE

PALEWAYS *same as* > PALEWISE

PALEWISE *adv* by perpendicular lines

PALFREY *n* light saddle horse, esp ridden by women

PALFREYED > PALFREY

PALFREYS > PALFREY

PALI *n* cliff in Hawaii

PALIER > PALY

PALIEST > PALY

PALIFORM *adj* resembling coral

PALIKAR *n* Greek soldier

PALIKARS > PALIKAR

PALILALIA *n* speech disorder in which a word or phrase is rapidly repeated

PALILLOGY *n* repetition of word or phrase

PALIMONY *n* alimony awarded to a nonmarried partner after the break-up of a long-term relationship

PALING *n* wooden or metal post used in fences

PALINGS > PALING

PALINKA *n* type of apricot brandy

PALINKAS > PALINKA

PALINODE *n* poem in which the poet recants something he has said in a former poem

PALINODES > PALINODE

PALINODY > PALINODE

PALINOPIA *n* visual disorder in which the patient perceives a prolonged afterimage

PALIS > PALI

PALISADE *n* fence made of wooden posts driven into the ground ⊳ *vb* enclose with a palisade

PALISADED > PALISADE

PALISADES > PALISADE

PALISADO *same as* > PALISADE

PALISH *adj* rather pale

PALKEE *n* covered Oriental litter

PALKEES > PALKEE

PALKI *same as* > PALKEE

PALKIS > PALKI

PALL *n* cloth spread over a coffin ⊳ *vb* become boring

PALLA *n* ancient Roman cloak

PALLADIA > PALLADIUM

PALLADIC *adj* of or containing palladium in the trivalent or tetravalent state

PALLADIUM *n* silvery-white element of the platinum metal group

PALLADOUS *adj* of or containing palladium in the divalent state

PALLAE > PALLA

PALLAH *n* S African antelope

PALLAHS > PALLAH

PALLED > PALL

PALLET *same as* > PALETTE

PALLETED > PALLET

PALLETING > PALLET

PALLETISE *same as* > PALLETIZE

PALLETIZE *vb* stack or transport on a pallet or pallets

p

PALLETS > PALLET
PALLETTE *n* armpit plate of a suit of armour
PALLETTES > PALLETTE
PALLIA > PALLIUM
PALLIAL *adj* relating to cerebral cortex
PALLIARD *n* person who begs
PALLIARDS > PALLIARD
PALLIASSE *n* straw-filled mattress
PALLIATE *vb* lessen the severity of (something) without curing it
PALLIATED > PALLIATE
PALLIATES > PALLIATE
PALLIATOR > PALLIATE
PALLID *adj* pale, esp because ill or weak
PALLIDER > PALLID
PALLIDEST > PALLID
PALLIDITY > PALLID
PALLIDLY > PALLID
PALLIED > PALLY
PALLIER > PALLY
PALLIES > PALLY
PALLIEST > PALLY
PALLING > PALL
PALLIUM *n* garment worn by men in ancient Greece or Rome
PALLIUMS > PALLIUM
PALLONE *n* Italian ball game
PALLONES > PALLONE
PALLOR *n* paleness of complexion
PALLORS > PALLOR
PALLS > PALL
PALLY *adj* on friendly terms ⊳ *vb* as in *pally up* become friends with
PALLYING > PALLY
PALM *n* inner surface of the hand ⊳ *vb* conceal in or about the hand, as in sleight-of-hand tricks
PALMAR *adj* of or relating to the palm of the hand
PALMARIAN *adj* pre-eminent
PALMARY *adj* worthy of praise
PALMATE *adj* shaped like an open hand
PALMATED *same as* > PALMATE
PALMATELY > PALMATE
PALMATION *n* state of being palmate
PALMBALL *n* baseball pitched from the palm and thumb
PALMBALLS > PALMBALL
PALMED > PALM
PALMER *n* medieval pilgrim
PALMERS > PALMER
PALMETTE *n* ornament or design resembling the palm leaf
PALMETTES > PALMETTE

PALMETTO *n* small palm tree with fan-shaped leaves
PALMETTOS > PALMETTO
PALMFUL *n* amount that can be held in the palm of a hand
PALMFULS > PALMFUL
PALMHOUSE *n* greenhouse for palms, etc
PALMIE *n* palmtop computer
PALMIER *n* type of French pastry
PALMIERS > PALMIER
PALMIES > PALMIE
PALMIEST > PALMY
PALMIET *n* South African rush
PALMIETS > PALMIET
PALMING > PALM
PALMIPED *n* web-footed bird
PALMIPEDE *same as* > PALMIPED
PALMIPEDS > PALMIPED
PALMIST > PALMISTRY
PALMISTER *n* person telling fortunes by reading palms
PALMISTRY *n* fortune-telling from lines on the palm of the hand
PALMISTS > PALMISTRY
PALMITATE *n* any salt or ester of palmitic acid
PALMITIC *adj* as in *palmitic acid* white crystalline solid that is a saturated fatty acid
PALMITIN *n* colourless glyceride of palmitic acid
PALMITINS > PALMITIN
PALMLIKE > PALM
PALMS > PALM
PALMTOP *adj* small enough to be held in the hand ⊳ *n* computer small enough to be held in the hand
PALMTOPS > PALMTOP
PALMY *adj* successful, prosperous and happy
PALMYRA *n* tall tropical Asian palm
PALMYRAS > PALMYRA
PALOLO *n* polychaete worm of the S Pacific Ocean
PALOLOS > PALOLO
PALOMINO *n* gold-coloured horse with a white mane and tail
PALOMINOS > PALOMINO
PALOOKA *n* stupid or clumsy boxer or other person
PALOOKAS > PALOOKA
PALOVERDE *n* thorny American shrub
PALP *n* sensory appendage in crustaceans and insects ⊳ *vb* feel

PALPABLE *adj* obvious
PALPABLY > PALPABLE
PALPAL > PALP
PALPATE *vb* examine (an area of the body) by touching ⊳ *adj* of, relating to, or possessing a palp or palps
PALPATED > PALPATE
PALPATES > PALPATE
PALPATING > PALPATE
PALPATION > PALPATE
PALPATOR *n* type of beetle
PALPATORS > PALPATOR
PALPATORY > PALPATE
PALPEBRA *n* eyelid
PALPEBRAE > PALPEBRA
PALPEBRAL *adj* of or relating to the eyelid
PALPEBRAS > PALPEBRA
PALPED > PALP
PALPI > PALPUS
PALPING > PALP
PALPITANT > PALPITATE
PALPITATE *vb* (of the heart) beat rapidly
PALPS > PALP
PALPUS *same as* > PALP
PALPUSES > PALPUS
PALS > PAL
PALSA *n* landform of subarctic regions
PALSAS > PALSA
PALSGRAVE *n* German count palatine
PALSHIP *n* state of being pals
PALSHIPS > PALSHIP
PALSIED > PALSY
PALSIER > PALSY
PALSIES > PALSY
PALSIEST > PALSY
PALSTAFF *variant of* > PALSTAVE
PALSTAFFS > PALSTAFF
PALSTAVE *n* kind of celt, usually of bronze, made to fit into a split wooden handle rather than having a socket for the handle
PALSTAVES > PALSTAVE
PALSY *n* paralysis ⊳ *vb* paralyse ⊳ *adj* friendly
PALSYING > PALSY
PALSYLIKE > PALSY
PALTER *vb* act or talk insincerely
PALTERED > PALTER
PALTERER > PALTER
PALTERERS > PALTER
PALTERING > PALTER
PALTERS > PALTER
PALTRIER > PALTRY
PALTRIEST > PALTRY
PALTRILY > PALTRY
PALTRY *adj* insignificant
PALUDAL *adj* of, relating to, or produced by marshes
PALUDIC *adj* of malaria
PALUDINAL *adj* inhabiting swamps

PALUDINE *adj* relating to marsh
PALUDISM *rare word for* > MALARIA
PALUDISMS > PALUDISM
PALUDOSE *adj* growing or living in marshes
PALUDOUS *adj* marshy
PALUSTRAL *adj* marshy
PALY *adj* vertically striped
PAM *n* knave of clubs
PAMPA *n* grassland area
PAMPAS *pl n* vast grassy plains in S America
PAMPASES > PAMPAS
PAMPEAN > PAMPAS
PAMPEANS > PAMPAS
PAMPER *vb* treat (someone) with great indulgence, spoil
PAMPERED > PAMPER
PAMPERER > PAMPER
PAMPERERS > PAMPER
PAMPERING > PAMPER
PAMPERO *n* dry cold wind in South America
PAMPEROS > PAMPERO
PAMPERS > PAMPER
PAMPHLET *n* thin paper-covered booklet ⊳ *vb* produce pamphlets
PAMPHLETS > PAMPHLET
PAMPHREY *n* cabbage
PAMPHREYS > PAMPHREY
PAMPOEN *n* pumpkin
PAMPOENS > PAMPOEN
PAMPOOTIE *n* rawhide slipper worn by men in the Aran Islands
PAMS > PAM
PAN *n* wide long-handled metal container used in cooking ⊳ *vb* sift gravel from (a river) in a pan to search for gold
PANACEA *n* remedy for all diseases or problems
PANACEAN > PANACEA
PANACEAS > PANACEA
PANACHAEA *variant of* > PANACEA
PANACHE *n* confident elegant style
PANACHES > PANACHE
PANADA *n* mixture used as a thickening in cookery
PANADAS > PANADA
PANAMA *n* hat made of plaited leaves
PANAMAS > PANAMA
PANARIES > PANARY
PANARY *n* storehouse for bread
PANATELA *same as* > PANATELLA
PANATELAS > PANATELA
PANATELLA *n* long slender cigar
PANAX *n* genus of perennial herbs
PANAXES > PANAX
PANBROIL *vb* broil in a pan

PANBROILS > PANBROIL
PANCAKE *n* thin flat circle of fried batter ▷ *vb* cause (an aircraft) to make a pancake landing
PANCAKED > PANCAKE
PANCAKES > PANCAKE
PANCAKING > PANCAKE
PANCE *n* pansy
PANCES > PANCE
PANCETTA *n* lightly spiced cured bacon from Italy
PANCETTAS > PANCETTA
PANCHAX *n* brightly coloured tropical Asian cyprinodont fish
PANCHAXES > PANCHAX
PANCHAYAT *n* village council in India
PANCHEON *n* shallow bowl
PANCHEONS > PANCHEON
PANCHION *same as* > PANCHEON
PANCHIONS > PANCHION
PANCOSMIC *adj* of every cosmos
PANCRATIA *n* wrestling and boxing contests
PANCRATIC > PANCRATIA
PANCREAS *n* large gland behind the stomach that produces insulin and helps digestion
PAND *n* valance
PANDA *n* large black-and-white bearlike mammal from China
PANDAN *n* type of palm of S E Asia
PANDANI *n* tropical tree
PANDANIS > PANDANI
PANDANS > PANDAN
PANDANUS *n* Old World tropical palmlike plant
PANDAR *vb* act as a pimp
PANDARED > PANDAR
PANDARING > PANDAR
PANDARS > PANDAR
PANDAS > PANDA
PANDATION *n* warping
PANDECT *n* treatise covering all aspects of a particular subject
PANDECTS > PANDECT
PANDEMIA *n* epidemic affecting everyone
PANDEMIAN *adj* sensual
PANDEMIAS > PANDEMIA
PANDEMIC *adj* (of a disease) occurring over a wide area ▷ *n* pandemic disease
PANDEMICS > PANDEMIC
PANDER *vb* indulge (a person his or her desires) ▷ *n* person who procures a sexual partner for someone
PANDERED > PANDER
PANDERER *n* person who procures a sexual partner for someone
PANDERERS > PANDERER

PANDERESS *n* female panderer
PANDERING > PANDER
PANDERISM > PANDER
PANDERLY > PANDER
PANDEROUS > PANDER
PANDERS > PANDER
PANDIED > PANDY
PANDIES > PANDY
PANDIT *same as* > PUNDIT
PANDITS > PANDIT
PANDOOR *same as* > PANDOUR
PANDOORS > PANDOOR
PANDORA *n* handsome red sea bream
PANDORAS > PANDORA
PANDORE *another word for* > BANDORE
PANDORES > PANDORE
PANDOUR *n* one of an 18th-century force of Croatian soldiers
PANDOURS > PANDOUR
PANDOWDY *n* deep-dish pie made from fruit, esp apples, with a cake topping
PANDROP *n* hard mint-flavoured sweet
PANDROPS > PANDROP
PANDS > PAND
PANDURA *n* ancient stringed instrument
PANDURAS > PANDURA
PANDURATE *adj* (of plant leaves) shaped like the body of a fiddle
PANDY *n* (in schools) stroke on the hand with a strap as a punishment ▷ *vb* punish with such strokes
PANDYING > PANDY
PANE *n* sheet of glass in a window or door ▷ *adj* (of fish, meat, etc) dipped or rolled in breadcrumbs before cooking
PANED > PANE
PANEER *n* soft white cheese, used in Indian cookery
PANEERS > PANEER
PANEGOISM *n* form of scepticism
PANEGYRIC *n* formal speech or piece of writing in praise of someone or something
PANEGYRY *n* panegyric
PANEITIES > PANEITY
PANEITY *n* state of being bread
PANEL *n* flat distinct section of a larger surface, for example in a door ▷ *vb* cover or decorate with panels ▷ *adj* of a group acting as a panel
PANELED > PANEL
PANELESS > PANE
PANELING *same as* > PANELLING
PANELINGS > PANELING

PANELISED *same as* > PANELIZED
PANELIST *same as* > PANELLIST
PANELISTS > PANELIST
PANELIZED *adj* made in sections for quick assembly
PANELLED > PANEL
PANELLING *n* panels collectively, esp on a wall
PANELLIST *n* member of a panel
PANELS > PANEL
PANES > PANE
PANETELA *same as* > PANATELA
PANETELAS > PANETELA
PANETELLA *n* long thin cigar
PANETTONE *n* kind of Italian spiced brioche containing sultanas
PANETTONI > PANETTONE
PANFISH *n* small food fish ▷ *vb* fish for panfish
PANFISHED > PANFISH
PANFISHES > PANFISH
PANFORTE *n* hard spicy cake
PANFORTES > PANFORTE
PANFRIED > PANFRY
PANFRIES > PANFRY
PANFRY *vb* fry in a pan
PANFRYING > PANFRY
PANFUL *n* the contents of a pan
PANFULS > PAN
PANG *n* sudden sharp feeling of pain or sadness ▷ *vb* cause pain
PANGA *n* broad heavy knife of E Africa, used as a tool or weapon
PANGAMIC *adj* relating to pangamy
PANGAMIES > PANGAMY
PANGAMY *n* unrestricted mating
PANGAS > PANGA
PANGED > PANG
PANGEN *same as* > PANGENE
PANGENE *n* hypothetical particle of protoplasm
PANGENES > PANGENE
PANGENS > PANGEN
PANGING > PANG
PANGLESS *adj* without pangs
PANGOLIN *n* animal of tropical countries with a scaly body and a long snout for eating ants and termites
PANGOLINS > PANGOLIN
PANGRAM *n* sentence incorporating all the letters of the alphabet
PANGRAMS > PANGRAM
PANGS > PANG
PANHANDLE *n* (in the US) narrow strip of land that

projects from one state into another ▷ *vb* accost and beg from (passers-by), esp on the street
PANHUMAN *adj* relating to all humanity
PANIC *n* sudden overwhelming fear ▷ *vb* feel or cause to feel panic ▷ *adj* of or resulting from such terror
PANICALLY > PANIC
PANICK *old word for* > PANIC
PANICKED > PANIC
PANICKIER > PANIC
PANICKING > PANIC
PANICKS > PANICK
PANICKY > PANIC
PANICLE *n* loose, irregularly branched cluster of flowers
PANICLED > PANICLE
PANICLES > PANICLE
PANICS > PANIC
PANICUM *n* type of grass
PANICUMS > PANICUM
PANIER *same as* > PANNIER
PANIERS > PANIER
PANIM *n* heathen or pagan
PANIMS > PANIM
PANING > PANE
PANINI > PANINO
PANINIS > PANINI
PANINO *n* Italian sandwich
PANISC *n* faun; attendant of Pan
PANISCS > PANISC
PANISK *same as* > PANISC
PANISKS > PANISK
PANISLAM *n* all of Islam or the Muslim world
PANISLAMS > PANISLAM
PANJANDRA *n* pompous self-important officials of people of rank
PANKO *n* flaky breadcrumbs used in Japanese cookery
PANKOS > PANKO
PANLIKE *adj* resembling a pan
PANLOGISM *n* metaphysics of Leibniz
PANMICTIC > PANMIXIA
PANMIXES > PANMIXIA
PANMIXIA *n* (in population genetics) random mating within an interbreeding population
PANMIXIAS > PANMIXIA
PANMIXIS *same as* > PANMIXIA
PANNAGE *n* pasturage for pigs, esp in a forest
PANNAGES > PANNAGE
PANNE *n* lightweight velvet fabric
PANNED > PAN
PANNELLED *adj* divided into panels
PANNER > PAN

PANNERS > PAN
PANNES > PANNE
PANNICK old spelling of the noun > PANIC
PANNICKS > PANNICK
PANNICLE n thin layer of body tissue
PANNICLES > PANNICLE
PANNIER n bag fixed on the back of a cycle
PANNIERED > PANNIER
PANNIERS > PANNIER
PANNIKEL n skull
PANNIKELL same as > PANNIKEL
PANNIKELS > PANNIKEL
PANNIKIN n small metal cup or pan
PANNIKINS > PANNIKIN
PANNING > PAN
PANNINGS > PAN
PANNIST n person who plays a steel drum
PANNISTS > PANNIST
PANNOSE adj like felt
PANNUS n inflammatory fleshy lesion on the surface of the eye
PANNUSES > PANNUS
PANOCHA n coarse grade of sugar made in Mexico
PANOCHAS > PANOCHA
PANOCHE n type of dark sugar
PANOCHES > PANOCHE
PANOISTIC adj producing ova
PANOPLIED > PANOPLY
PANOPLIES > PANOPLY
PANOPLY n magnificent array
PANOPTIC adj taking in all parts, aspects, etc, in a single view
PANORAMA n wide unbroken view of a scene
PANORAMAS > PANORAMA
PANORAMIC > PANORAMA
PANPIPE n wind instrument
PANPIPES > PANPIPE
PANS > PAN
PANSEXUAL n person open to any sexual activity
PANSIED adj covered with pansies
PANSIES > PANSY
PANSOPHIC > PANSOPHY
PANSOPHY n universal knowledge
PANSPERMY n 19th-century evolutionary theory
PANSTICK n type of cosmetic in stick form
PANSTICKS > PANSTICK
PANSY n small garden flower
PANT vb breathe quickly and noisily during or after exertion ▷ n act of panting
PANTABLE n soft shoe
PANTABLES > PANTABLE

PANTAGAMY n marriage to everyone
PANTALEON n percussion instrument
PANTALET same as > PANTALETS
PANTALETS pl n long drawers, usually trimmed with ruffles, extending below the skirts
PANTALON n keyboard instrument
PANTALONE n Italian comic character
PANTALONS > PANTALON
PANTALOON n (in pantomime) absurd old man, the butt of the clown's tricks
PANTDRESS n dress with divided skirt
PANTED > PANT
PANTER n person who pants
PANTERS > PANTER
PANTHEISM n belief that God is present in everything
PANTHEIST > PANTHEISM
PANTHENOL n pantothenyl alcohol
PANTHEON n (in ancient Greece and Rome) temple built to honour all the gods
PANTHEONS > PANTHEON
PANTHER n leopard, esp a black one
PANTHERS > PANTHER
PANTIE same as > PANTY
PANTIES pl n women's underpants
PANTIHOSE same as > PANTYHOSE
PANTILE n roofing tile with an S-shaped cross section ▷ vb tile roof with pantiles
PANTILED > PANTILE
PANTILES > PANTILE
PANTILING > PANTILE
PANTINE n pasteboard puppet
PANTINES > PANTINE
PANTING > PANT
PANTINGLY > PANT
PANTINGS > PANT
PANTLEG n leg part of a pair of trousers
PANTLEGS > PANTLEG
PANTLER n pantry servant
PANTLERS > PANTLER
PANTO same as > PANTOMIME
PANTOFFLE same as > PANTOFLE
PANTOFLE n kind of slipper
PANTOFLES > PANTOFLE
PANTOMIME n play based on a fairy tale, performed at Christmas time
PANTON n type of horseshoe

PANTONS > PANTON
PANTOS > PANTO
PANTOUFLE same as > PANTOFLE
PANTOUM n verse form
PANTOUMS > PANTOUM
PANTRIES > PANTRY
PANTROPIC adj found throughout tropics
PANTRY n small room or cupboard for storing food
PANTRYMAN n pantry servant
PANTRYMEN > PANTRYMAN
PANTS pl n undergarment for the lower part of the body
PANTSUIT n woman's suit of a jacket or top and trousers
PANTSUITS > PANTSUIT
PANTUN n Malayan poetry
PANTUNS > PANTUN
PANTY n woman's undergarment
PANTYHOSE pl n women's tights
PANZER n German tank
PANZERS > PANZER
PANZOOTIC n disease that affects all the animals in a geographical area
PAOLI > PAOLO
PAOLO n Italian silver coin
PAP n soft food for babies or invalids ▷ vb (of the paparazzi) to follow and photograph (a famous person) ▷ vb feed with pap
PAPA n father
PAPABLE adj suitable for papacy
PAPACIES > PAPACY
PAPACY n position or term of office of a pope
PAPADAM variant of > POPPADOM
PAPADAMS > PAPADAM
PAPADOM variant of > POPPADOM
PAPADOMS > PAPADOM
PAPADUM variant of > POPPADOM
PAPADUMS > PAPADUM
PAPAIN n enzyme in the unripe fruit of the papaya
PAPAINS > PAPAIN
PAPAL adj of the pope
PAPALISE same as > PAPALIZE
PAPALISED > PAPALISE
PAPALISES > PAPALISE
PAPALISM n papal system
PAPALISMS > PAPALISM
PAPALIST n supporter of a pope
PAPALISTS > PAPALIST
PAPALIZE vb make papal
PAPALIZED > PAPALIZE
PAPALIZES > PAPALIZE
PAPALLY > PAPAL
PAPARAZZI > PAPARAZZO

PAPARAZZO n photographer specializing in candid photographs of famous people
PAPAS > PAPA
PAPAUMA n New Zealand word for broadleaf
PAPAUMAS > PAPAUMA
PAPAVER n genus of poppies
PAPAVERS > PAPAVER
PAPAW same as > PAPAYA
PAPAWS > PAPAW
PAPAYA n large sweet West Indian fruit
PAPAYAN > PAPAYA
PAPAYAS > PAPAYA
PAPE n spiritual father
PAPER n material made in sheets from wood pulp or other fibres ▷ vb cover (walls) with wallpaper
PAPERBACK n book with covers made of flexible card ▷ adj of a paperback or publication of paperbacks ▷ vb publish in paperback
PAPERBARK n Australian tree of swampy regions, with spear-shaped leaves and papery bark
PAPERBOY n boy employed to deliver newspapers to people's homes
PAPERBOYS > PAPERBOY
PAPERCLIP n bent wire clip for holding sheets of paper together
PAPERED > PAPER
PAPERER > PAPER
PAPERERS > PAPER
PAPERGIRL n girl employed to deliver newspapers to people's homes
PAPERIER > PAPERY
PAPERIEST > PAPERY
PAPERING > PAPER
PAPERINGS > PAPER
PAPERLESS adj of, relating to, or denoting a means of communication, record keeping, etc, esp electronic, that does not use paper
PAPERS > PAPER
PAPERWARE n printed matter
PAPERWORK n clerical work, such as writing reports and letters
PAPERY adj like paper, esp in thinness, flimsiness, or dryness
PAPES > PAPE
PAPETERIE n box or case for papers and other writing materials
PAPHIAN n prostitute
PAPHIANS > PAPHIAN
PAPILIO n butterfly
PAPILIOS > PAPILIO

PAPILLA n small projection of tissue
PAPILLAE > PAPILLA
PAPILLAR > PAPILLA
PAPILLARY > PAPILLA
PAPILLATE > PAPILLA
PAPILLOMA n benign tumour derived from epithelial tissue and forming a rounded or lobulated mass
PAPILLON n breed of toy spaniel with large ears
PAPILLONS > PAPILLON
PAPILLOSE > PAPILLA
PAPILLOTE n paper frill around cutlets, etc
PAPILLOUS > PAPILLA
PAPILLULE n tubercle
PAPISH n Catholic
PAPISHER n derogatory term for a Roman Catholic
PAPISHERS > PAPISHER
PAPISHES > PAPISH
PAPISM n derogatory term for Roman Catholicism
PAPISMS > PAPISM
PAPIST n derogatory term for a Roman Catholic
PAPISTIC > PAPIST
PAPISTRY > PAPIST
PAPISTS > PAPIST
PAPOOSE n Native American child
PAPOOSES > PAPOOSE
PAPPADAM same as > POPPADOM
PAPPADAMS > PAPPADAM
PAPPADOM same as > POPPADOM
PAPPADOMS > PAPPADOM
PAPPADUM n thin circle of dough fried in oil until crisp
PAPPADUMS > PAPPADUM
PAPPED > PAP
PAPPI > PAPPUS
PAPPIER > PAPPY
PAPPIES > PAPPY
PAPPIEST > PAPPY
PAPPING > PAP
PAPPOOSE same as > PAPOOSE
PAPPOOSES > PAPPOOSE
PAPPOSE > PAPPUS
PAPPOUS > PAPPUS
PAPPUS n ring of hairs surrounding the fruit in composite plants
PAPPUSES > PAPPUS
PAPPY adj resembling pap
PAPRICA same as > PAPRIKA
PAPRICAS > PAPRICA
PAPRIKA n mild powdered seasoning
PAPRIKAS > PAPRIKA
PAPS > PAP
PAPULA same as > PAPULE
PAPULAE > PAPULA
PAPULAR > PAPULE
PAPULAS > PAPULA

PAPULE n small solid usually round elevation of the skin
PAPULES > PAPULE
PAPULOSE > PAPULE
PAPULOUS > PAPULE
PAPYRAL > PAPYRUS
PAPYRI > PAPYRUS
PAPYRIAN > PAPYRUS
PAPYRINE > PAPYRUS
PAPYRUS n tall water plant
PAPYRUSES > PAPYRUS
PAR n usual or average condition ▷ vb play (a golf hole) in par
PARA n paratrooper
PARABASES > PARABASIS
PARABASIS n (in classical Greek comedy) address from the chorus to the audience
PARABEMA n architectural feature
PARABEN n carcinogenic ester
PARABENS > PARABEN
PARABLAST n yolk of an egg, such as a hen's egg, that undergoes meroblastic cleavage
PARABLE n story that illustrates a religious teaching ▷ vb write parable
PARABLED > PARABLE
PARABLES > PARABLE
PARABLING > PARABLE
PARABOLA n regular curve resembling the course of an object thrown forward and up
PARABOLAE > PARABOLA
PARABOLAS > PARABOLA
PARABOLE n similitude
PARABOLES > PARABOLE
PARABOLIC adj of, relating to, or shaped like a parabola
PARABRAKE n parachute attached to the rear of a vehicle and opened to assist braking
PARACHOR n quantity constant over range of temperatures
PARACHORS > PARACHOR
PARACHUTE n large fabric canopy that slows the descent of a person or object from an aircraft ▷ vb land or drop by parachute
PARACLETE n mediator or advocate
PARACME n phase where fever lessens
PARACMES > PARACME
PARACRINE adj of signalling between biological cells
PARACUSES > PARACUSIS

PARACUSIS n hearing disorder
PARADE n procession or march ▷ vb display or flaunt
PARADED > PARADE
PARADER > PARADE
PARADERS > PARADE
PARADES > PARADE
PARADIGM n example or model
PARADIGMS > PARADIGM
PARADING > PARADE
PARADISAL adj of, relating to, or resembling paradise
PARADISE n heaven
PARADISES > PARADISE
PARADISIC > PARADISE
PARADOR n state-run hotel in Spain
PARADORES > PARADOR
PARADORS > PARADOR
PARADOS n bank behind a trench or other fortification
PARADOSES > PARADOS
PARADOX n person or thing made up of contradictory elements
PARADOXAL adj paradoxical
PARADOXER n proposer of paradox
PARADOXES > PARADOX
PARADOXY n state of being paradoxical
PARADROP n delivery of personnel or equipment from an aircraft by parachute
PARADROPS > PARADROP
PARAE n type of fish
PARAFFIN n liquid mixture distilled from petroleum and used as a fuel or solvent ▷ vb treat with paraffin or paraffin wax
PARAFFINE same as > PARAFFIN
PARAFFINS > PARAFFIN
PARAFFINY adj like paraffin
PARAFFLE n extravagant display
PARAFFLES > PARAFFLE
PARAFLE same as > PARAFFLE
PARAFLES > PARAFLE
PARAFOIL n airfoil used on a paraglider
PARAFOILS > PARAFOIL
PARAFORM n paraformaldehyde
PARAFORMS > PARAFORM
PARAGE n type of feudal land tenure
PARAGES > PARAGE
PARAGLIDE vb glide through the air on a special parachute
PARAGOGE n addition of a sound or a syllable to the

end of a word, such as st in amongst
PARAGOGES > PARAGOGE
PARAGOGIC > PARAGOGE
PARAGOGUE same as > PARAGOGE
PARAGON n model of perfection ▷ vb equal or surpass
PARAGONED > PARAGON
PARAGONS > PARAGON
PARAGRAM n pun
PARAGRAMS > PARAGRAM
PARAGRAPH n section of a piece of writing starting on a new line ▷ vb put (a piece of writing) into paragraphs
PARAKEET n small long-tailed parrot
PARAKEETS > PARAKEET
PARAKELIA n succulent herb with purple flowers that thrives in inland Australia
PARAKITE n series of linked kites
PARAKITES > PARAKITE
PARALALIA n any of various speech disorders, esp the production of a sound different from that intended
PARALEGAL n person trained to assist lawyers but not qualified to practise law ▷ adj of or designating such a person
PARALEXIA n disorder of the ability to read in which words and syllables are meaninglessly transposed
PARALEXIC > PARALEXIA
PARALLAX n apparent change in an object's position due to a change in the observer's position
PARALLEL adj separated by an equal distance at every point ▷ n line separated from another by an equal distance at every point ▷ vb correspond to
PARALLELS > PARALLEL
PARALOGIA n self-deception
PARALOGUE n either of a pair of genes derived from the same ancestral gene
PARALOGY n anatomical similarity
PARALYSE vb affect with paralysis
PARALYSED > PARALYSE
PARALYSER > PARALYSE
PARALYSES > PARALYSIS
PARALYSIS n inability to move or feel, because of damage to the nervous system
PARALYTIC adj affected with paralysis ▷ n person who is paralysed

PARALYZE *same as* > PARALYSE

PARALYZED > PARALYZE

PARALYZER > PARALYSE

PARALYZES > PARALYZE

PARAMATTA *n* lightweight twill-weave fabric of wool with silk or cotton

PARAMECIA *n* freshwater protozoans

PARAMEDIC *n* person working in support of the medical profession ▷ *adj* of or designating such a person

PARAMENT *n* ecclesiastical vestment or decorative hanging

PARAMENTA > PARAMENT

PARAMENTS > PARAMENT

PARAMESE *n* note in ancient Greek music

PARAMESES > PARAMESE

PARAMETER *n* limiting factor, boundary

PARAMO *n* high plateau in the Andes

PARAMORPH *n* mineral that has undergone paramorphism

PARAMOS > PARAMO

PARAMOUNT *adj* of the greatest importance ▷ *n* supreme ruler

PARAMOUR *n* lover, esp of a person married to someone else

PARAMOURS > PARAMOUR

PARAMYLUM *n* starch-like substance

PARANETE *n* note in ancient Greek music

PARANETES > PARANETE

PARANG *n* knife used by the Dyaks of Borneo

PARANGS > PARANG

PARANOEA *same as* > PARANOIA

PARANOEAS > PARANOEA

PARANOEIC *same as* > PARANOIAC

PARANOIA *n* mental illness causing delusions of grandeur or persecution

PARANOIAC > PARANOIA

PARANOIAS > PARANOIA

PARANOIC > PARANOIA

PARANOICS > PARANOIA

PARANOID *adj* of, characterized by, or resembling paranoia ▷ *n* person who shows the behaviour patterns associated with paranoia

PARANOIDS > PARANOID

PARANYM *n* euphemism

PARANYMPH *n* bridesmaid or best man

PARANYMS > PARANYM

PARAPARA *n* small carnivorous New Zealand tree

PARAPARAS > PARAPARA

PARAPENTE *n* sport of jumping off high mountains wearing skis and a light parachute

PARAPET *n* low wall or railing along the edge of a balcony or roof ▷ *vb* provide with a parapet

PARAPETED > PARAPET

PARAPETS > PARAPET

PARAPH *n* flourish after a signature ▷ *vb* embellish signature

PARAPHED > PARAPH

PARAPHING > PARAPH

PARAPHS > PARAPH

PARAPODIA *n* paired unjointed lateral appendages of polychaete worms

PARAQUAT *n* yellow extremely poisonous soluble solid used in solution as a weedkiller

PARAQUATS > PARAQUAT

PARAQUET *n* long-tailed parrot

PARAQUETS > PARAQUET

PARAQUITO *n* parakeet

PARARHYME *n* type of rhyme

PARAS > PARA

PARASAIL *vb* glide through air on parachute towed by boat

PARASAILS > PARASAIL

PARASANG *n* Persian unit of distance equal to about 5.5 km or 3.4 miles

PARASANGS > PARASANG

PARASCEVE *n* preparation

PARASHAH *n* section of the Torah read in the synagogue

PARASHAHS > PARASHAH

PARASHOT > PARASHAH

PARASHOTH > PARASHAH

PARASITE *n* animal or plant living in or on another

PARASITES > PARASITE

PARASITIC > PARASITE

PARASOL *n* umbrella-like sunshade

PARASOLED *adj* having a parasol

PARASOLS > PARASOL

PARATAXES > PARATAXIS

PARATAXIS *n* juxtaposition of clauses in a sentence without the use of a conjunction

PARATHA *n* (in Indian cookery) flat unleavened bread

PARATHAS > PARATHA

PARATHION *n* slightly water-soluble toxic oil, odourless and colourless when pure, used as an insecticide

PARATONIC *adj* (of a plant movement) occurring in response to an external stimulus

PARATROOP *n* paratrooper

PARAVAIL *adj* lowest

PARAVANE *n* torpedo-shaped device towed from the bow of a vessel so that the cables will cut the anchors of any moored mines

PARAVANES > PARAVANE

PARAVANT *adv* pre-eminently ▷ *n* pre-eminent person or thing

PARAVANTS > PARAVANT

PARAVAUNT *same as* > PARAVANT

PARAWING *n* paraglider

PARAWINGS > PARAWING

PARAXIAL *adj* (of a light ray) parallel to the axis of an optical system

PARAZOA > PARAZOAN

PARAZOAN *n* sea sponge

PARAZOANS > PARAZOAN

PARAZOON *n* parasitic animal

PARBAKE *vb* partially bake

PARBAKED > PARBAKE

PARBAKES > PARBAKE

PARBAKING > PARBAKE

PARBOIL *vb* boil until partly cooked

PARBOILED > PARBOIL

PARBOILS > PARBOIL

PARBREAK *vb* vomit

PARBREAKS > PARBREAK

PARBUCKLE *n* rope sling for lifting or lowering a heavy cylindrical object, such as a cask or tree trunk ▷ *vb* raise or lower (an object) with such a sling

PARCEL *n* something wrapped up, package ▷ *vb* wrap up

PARCELED > PARCEL

PARCELING > PARCEL

PARCELLED > PARCEL

PARCELS > PARCEL

PARCENARY *n* joint heirship

PARCENER *n* person who takes an equal share with another or others

PARCENERS > PARCENER

PARCH *vb* make very hot and dry

PARCHED > PARCH

PARCHEDLY > PARCH

PARCHEESI *n* modern board game derived from the ancient game of pachisi

PARCHES > PARCH

PARCHESI *same as* > PARCHEESI

PARCHESIS > PARCHESI

PARCHING > PARCH

PARCHISI *same as* > PARCHEESI

PARCHISIS > PARCHISI

PARCHMENT *n* thick smooth writing material made from animal skin

PARCIMONY *obsolete variant of* > PARSIMONY

PARCLOSE *n* screen or railing in a church separating off an altar, chapel, etc

PARCLOSES > PARCLOSE

PARD *n* leopard or panther

PARDAH *same as* > PURDAH

PARDAHS > PARDAH

PARDAL *variant spelling of* > PARDALE

PARDALE *n* leopard

PARDALES > PARDALE

PARDALIS *n* leopard

PARDALOTE *n* small Australian songbird

PARDALS > PARDAL

PARDED *adj* having spots

PARDEE *adv* certainly

PARDI *same as* > PARDEE

PARDIE *same as* > PARDEE

PARDINE *adj* spotted

PARDNER *n* friend or partner: used as a term of address

PARDNERS > PARDNER

PARDON *vb* forgive, excuse ▷ *n* forgiveness ▷ *interj* sorry ▷ *sentence substitute* sorry

PARDONED > PARDON

PARDONER *n* (before the Reformation) person licensed to sell ecclesiastical indulgences

PARDONERS > PARDONER

PARDONING > PARDON

PARDONS > PARDON

PARDS > PARD

PARDY *same as* > PARDEE

PARE *vb* cut off the skin or top layer of

PARECIOUS *adj* having the male and female reproductive organs at different levels on the same stem

PARECISM *n* state of having male and female organs close together

PARECISMS > PARECISM

PARED > PARE

PAREGORIC *n* medicine containing opium, benzoic acid, camphor or ammonia, and anise oil

PAREIRA *n* root of a South American climbing plant

PAREIRAS > PAREIRA

PARELLA *n* type of lichen

PARELLAS > PARELLA

PARELLE *same as* > PARELLA

PARELLES > PARELLE

PAREN *n* parenthesis

PARENESES > PARENESIS

PARENESIS *n* exhortation

PARENS > PAREN
PARENT n father or mother ▷ vb raise offspring
PARENTAGE n ancestry or family
PARENTAL adj of or relating to a parent or parenthood
PARENTED > PARENT
PARENTING n activity of bringing up children
PARENTS > PARENT
PAREO same as > PAREU
PAREOS > PAREU
PARER > PARE
PARERA n New Zealand duck
PARERAS > PARERA
PARERGA > PARERGON
PARERGON n work that is not one's main employment
PARERS > PARE
PARES > PARE
PARESES > PARESIS
PARESIS n incomplete or slight paralysis of motor functions
PARETIC > PARESIS
PARETICS > PARESIS
PAREU n Polynesian skirt or loincloth
PAREUS > PAREU
PAREV adj containing neither meat nor milk products
PAREVE same as > PAREV
PARFAIT n dessert consisting of layers of ice cream, fruit, and sauce
PARFAITS > PARFAIT
PARFLECHE n sheet of rawhide that has been dried after soaking in lye and water to remove the hair
PARFLESH same as > PARFLECHE
PARFOCAL adj with focal points in the same plane
PARGANA n Indian sub-district
PARGANAS > PARGANA
PARGASITE n dark green mineral
PARGE vb coat with plaster
PARGED > PARGE
PARGES > PARGE
PARGET n plaster, mortar, etc, used to line chimney flues or cover walls ▷ vb cover or decorate with parget
PARGETED > PARGET
PARGETER n one who pargets
PARGETERS > PARGET
PARGETING same as > PARGET
PARGETS > PARGET
PARGETTED > PARGET
PARGETTER n plasterer
PARGING > PARGE

PARGINGS > PARGE
PARGO n sea bream
PARGOES > PARGO
PARGOS > PARGO
PARGYLINE n monoamine oxidase inhibitor
PARHELIA > PARHELION
PARHELIC > PARHELION
PARHELION n one of several bright spots on the parhelic circle or solar halo
PARHYPATE n note in ancient Greek music
PARIAH n social outcast
PARIAHS > PARIAH
PARIAL n pair royal of playing cards
PARIALS > PARIAL
PARIAN n type of marble or porcelain
PARIANS > PARIAN
PARIES n wall of an organ or bodily cavity
PARIETAL adj of the walls of a body cavity such as the skull ▷ n parietal bone
PARIETALS > PARIETAL
PARIETES > PARIES
PARING n piece pared off
PARINGS > PARING
PARIS n type of herb
PARISCHAN variant of > PAROCHIN
PARISES > PARIS
PARISH n area that has its own church and a priest or pastor
PARISHAD n Indian assembly
PARISHADS > PARISHAD
PARISHEN n member of parish
PARISHENS > PARISHEN
PARISHES > PARISH
PARISON n unshaped mass of glass
PARISONS > PARISON
PARITIES > PARITY
PARITOR n official who summons witnesses
PARITORS > PARITOR
PARITY n equality or equivalence
PARK n area of open land for recreational use by the public ▷ vb stop and leave (a vehicle) temporarily
PARKA n large waterproof jacket with a hood
PARKADE n building used as a car park
PARKADES > PARKADE
PARKAS > PARKA
PARKED > PARK
PARKEE n Eskimo outer garment
PARKEES > PARKEE
PARKER > PARK
PARKERS > PARK
PARKETTE n small public car park
PARKETTES > PARKETTE

PARKI variant of > PARKA
PARKIE n park keeper
PARKIER > PARKY
PARKIES > PARKIE
PARKIEST > PARKY
PARKIN n moist spicy ginger cake
PARKING > PARK
PARKINGS > PARK
PARKINS > PARKIN
PARKIS > PARKI
PARKISH adj like a park
PARKLAND n grassland with scattered trees
PARKLANDS > PARKLAND
PARKLIKE > PARK
PARKLY adj having many parks or resembling a park
PARKOUR n sport of running in urban areas over obstacles
PARKOURS > PARKOUR
PARKS > PARK
PARKWARD adv towards a park
PARKWARDS adv towards a park
PARKWAY n wide road planted with trees, turf, etc
PARKWAYS > PARKWAY
PARKY adj (of the weather) chilly
PARLANCE n particular way of speaking, idiom
PARLANCES > PARLANCE
PARLANDO adv to be performed as though speaking
PARLANTE same as > PARLANDO
PARLAY vb stake (winnings from one bet) on a subsequent wager ▷ n bet in which winnings are parlayed
PARLAYED > PARLAY
PARLAYING > PARLAY
PARLAYS > PARLAY
PARLE vb speak
PARLED > PARLE
PARLEMENT n parliament
PARLES > PARLE
PARLEY n meeting between opponents to discuss terms ▷ vb have a parley
PARLEYED > PARLEY
PARLEYER > PARLEY
PARLEYERS > PARLEY
PARLEYING > PARLEY
PARLEYS > PARLEY
PARLEYVOO vb speak French ▷ n French language
PARLIES pl n small Scottish biscuits
PARLING > PARLE
PARLOR same as > PARLOUR
PARLORS > PARLOR
PARLOUR n living room for receiving visitors
PARLOURS > PARLOUR

PARLOUS adj dire ▷ adv extremely
PARLOUSLY > PARLOUS
PARLY n short form of parliament
PARMESAN n Italian hard cheese
PARMESANS > PARMESAN
PAROCHIAL adj narrow in outlook
PAROCHIN n old Scottish parish
PAROCHINE same as > PAROCHIN
PAROCHINS > PAROCHIN
PARODIC > PARODY
PARODICAL > PARODY
PARODIED > PARODY
PARODIES > PARODY
PARODIST > PARODY
PARODISTS > PARODY
PARODOI n path leading to Greek theatre
PARODOS n ode sung by Greek chorus
PARODY n exaggerated and amusing imitation of someone else's style ▷ vb make a parody of
PARODYING > PARODY
PAROECISM n state of being paroecious
PAROEMIA n proverb
PAROEMIAC adj of proverbs
PAROEMIAL adj of proverbs
PAROEMIAS > PAROEMIA
PAROICOUS same as > PARECIOUS
PAROL n (formerly) pleadings in an action when presented by word of mouth ▷ adj (of a contract, lease, etc) not made under seal
PAROLABLE > PAROLE
PAROLE n early freeing of a prisoner on condition that he or she behaves well ▷ vb put on parole
PAROLED > PAROLE
PAROLEE > PAROLE
PAROLEES > PAROLE
PAROLES > PAROLE
PAROLING > PAROLE
PAROLS > PAROL
PARONYM n cognate word
PARONYMIC > PARONYM
PARONYMS > PARONYM
PARONYMY > PARONYM
PAROQUET n small long-tailed parrot
PAROQUETS > PARROQUET
PARORE n type of fish found around Australia and New Zealand
PARORES > PARORE
PAROSMIA n any disorder of the sense of smell
PAROSMIAS > PAROSMIA
PAROTIC adj situated near the ear

PAROTID adj relating to or situated near the parotid gland ▷ n parotid gland
PAROTIDES > PAROTID
PAROTIDS > PAROTID
PAROTIS n parotid gland
PAROTISES > PAROTIS
PAROTITIC > PAROTITIS
PAROTITIS n inflammation of the parotid gland
PAROTOID n any of various warty poison glands on the head and back of certain toads and salamanders ▷ adj resembling a parotid gland
PAROTOIDS > PAROTOID
PAROUS adj having given birth
PAROUSIA n Second Coming
PAROUSIAS > PAROUSIA
PAROXYSM n uncontrollable outburst of rage, delight, etc
PAROXYSMS > PAROXYSM
PARP vb make a honking sound
PARPANE n parapet on bridge
PARPANES > PARPANE
PARPED > PARP
PARPEN same as > PARPEND
PARPEND same as > PERPEND
PARPENDS > PARPEND
PARPENS > PARPEN
PARPENT n parapet on bridge
PARPENTS > PARPENT
PARPING > PARP
PARPOINT n parapet on bridge
PARPOINTS > PARPOINT
PARPS > PARP
PARQUET n floor covering made of wooden blocks ▷ vb cover with parquet
PARQUETED > PARQUET
PARQUETRY n pieces of wood arranged in a geometric pattern, used to cover floors
PARQUETS > PARQUET
PARR n salmon up to two years of age
PARRA n tourist or non-resident on a beach
PARRAKEET same as > PARAKEET
PARRAL same as > PARREL
PARRALS > PARRAL
PARRAS > PARRA
PARRED > PAR
PARREL n ring that holds the jaws of a boom to the mast
PARRELS > PARREL
PARRHESIA n boldness of speech

PARRICIDE n crime of killing either of one's parents
PARRIDGE Scottish variant of > PORRIDGE
PARRIDGES > PARRIDGE
PARRIED > PARRY
PARRIER > PARRY
PARRIERS > PARRY
PARRIES > PARRY
PARRING > PAR
PARRITCH Scottish variant of > PORRIDGE
PARROCK vb put (an animal) in a small field
PARROCKED > PARROCK
PARROCKS > PARROCK
PARROKET n small long-tailed parrot
PARROKETS > PARROKET
PARROQUET n small long-tailed parrot
PARROT n tropical bird with a short hooked beak ▷ vb repeat (someone else's words) without thinking
PARROTED > PARROT
PARROTER n person who repeats what is said
PARROTERS > PARROTER
PARROTING > PARROT
PARROTRY > PARROT
PARROTS > PARROT
PARROTY adj like a parrot; chattering
PARRS > PARR
PARRY vb ward off (an attack) ▷ n parrying
PARRYING > PARRY
PARS > PAR
PARSABLE > PARSE
PARSE vb analyse (a sentence) in terms of grammar
PARSEC n unit of astronomical distance
PARSECS > PARSEC
PARSED > PARSE
PARSER n program that interprets input to a computer
PARSERS > PARSER
PARSES > PARSE
PARSIMONY n extreme caution in spending money
PARSING > PARSE
PARSINGS > PARSE
PARSLEY n herb used for seasoning and decorating food ▷ vb garnish with parsley
PARSLEYED > PARSLEY
PARSLEYS > PARSLEY
PARSLIED > PARSLEY
PARSNEP same as > PARSNIP
PARSNEPS > PARSNEP
PARSNIP n long tapering cream-coloured root vegetable
PARSNIPS > PARSNIP
PARSON n Anglican parish priest

PARSONAGE n parson's house
PARSONIC > PARSON
PARSONISH adj like a parson
PARSONS > PARSON
PART n one of the pieces that make up a whole ▷ vb divide or separate
PARTAKE vb take (food or drink)
PARTAKEN > PARTAKE
PARTAKER > PARTAKE
PARTAKERS > PARTAKE
PARTAKES > PARTAKE
PARTAKING > PARTAKE
PARTAN Scottish word for > CRAB
PARTANS > PARTAN
PARTED adj divided almost to the base
PARTER n thing that parts
PARTERRE n formally patterned flower garden
PARTERRES > PARTERRE
PARTERS > PARTER
PARTI n concept of architectural design
PARTIAL adj not complete ▷ n any of the component tones of a single musical sound ▷ vb remove (a factor) from a set of statistics
PARTIALLY > PARTIAL
PARTIALS > PARTIAL
PARTIBLE adj (esp of property or an inheritance) divisible
PARTICLE n extremely small piece or amount
PARTICLES > PARTICLE
PARTIED > PARTY
PARTIER n person who parties
PARTIERS > PARTIER
PARTIES > PARTY
PARTIM adv in part
PARTING same as > PART
PARTINGS > PARTING
PARTIS > PARTI
PARTISAN n strong supporter of a party or group ▷ adj prejudiced or one-sided
PARTISANS > PARTISAN
PARTITA n type of suite
PARTITAS > PARTITA
PARTITE adj composed of or divided into a specified number of parts
PARTITION n screen or thin wall that divides a room ▷ vb divide with a partition
PARTITIVE adj (of a noun) referring to part of something ▷ n partitive word
PARTITURA n music score for several parts
PARTIZAN same as > PARTISAN
PARTIZANS > PARTIZAN

PARTLET n woman's garment
PARTLETS > PARTLET
PARTLY adv not completely
PARTNER n either member of a couple in a relationship or activity ▷ vb be the partner of
PARTNERED > PARTNER
PARTNERS > PARTNER
PARTON n hypothetical elementary particle
PARTONS > PARTON
PARTOOK > PARTAKE
PARTRIDGE n game bird of the grouse family
PARTS pl n abilities or talents
PARTURE n departure
PARTURES > PARTURE
PARTWAY adv some of the way
PARTWORK n series of magazines issued at weekly or monthly intervals, which are designed to be bound together to form a complete course or book
PARTWORKS > PARTWORK
PARTY n social gathering for pleasure ▷ vb celebrate, have fun ▷ adj (of a shield) divided vertically into two
PARTYER n person who parties
PARTYERS > PARTYER
PARTYGOER n person who goes to party
PARTYING n act of partying
PARTYINGS > PARTYING
PARTYISM n devotion to political party
PARTYISMS > PARTYISM
PARULIDES > PARULIS
PARULIS another name for > GUMBOIL
PARULISES > PARULIS
PARURA same as > PARURE
PARURAS > PARURA
PARURE n set of jewels or other ornaments
PARURES > PARURE
PARURESES > PARURES
PARURESIS n phobia in which the sufferer cannot urinate in the presence of others
PARVE same as > PAREV
PARVENU n person newly risen to a position of power or wealth ▷ adj of or characteristic of a parvenu
PARVENUE n woman who, having risen socially or economically, is considered to be an upstart or to lack the appropriate refinement for her new position

▷ *adj* of or characteristic of a parvenue

PARVENUES > PARVENUE

PARVENUS > PARVENU

PARVIS *n* court or portico in front of a building, esp a church

PARVISE *same as* **>** PARVIS

PARVISES > PARVISE

PARVO *n* disease of cattle and dogs

PARVOLIN *n* substance resulting from the putrefaction of flesh

PARVOLINE *n* liquid derived from coal tar

PARVOLINS > PARVOLIN

PARVOS > PARVO

PAS *n* dance step or movement, esp in ballet

PASCAL *n* unit of pressure

PASCALS > PASCAL

PASCHAL *adj* of the Passover or Easter ▷ *n* Passover or Easter

PASCHALS > PASCHAL

PASCUAL *adj* relating to pasture ▷ *n* plant that grows in pasture

PASCUALS > PASCUAL

PASE *n* movement of the cape or muleta by a matador

PASEAR *vb* go for a rambling walk

PASEARED > PASEAR

PASEARING > PASEAR

PASEARS > PASEAR

PASELA *same as* **>** BONSELA

PASELAS > PASELA

PASEO *n* bullfighters' procession

PASEOS > PASEO

PASES > PASE

PASH *n* infatuation ▷ *vb* throw or be thrown and break or be broken to bits

PASHA *n* high official of the Ottoman Empire

PASHADOM *n* territory of a pasha

PASHADOMS **>** PASHADOM

PASHALIC *same as* **>** PASHALIK

PASHALICS > PASHALIC

PASHALIK *n* province or jurisdiction of a pasha

PASHALIKS > PASHALIK

PASHAS > PASHA

PASHED > PASH

PASHES > PASH

PASHIM *same as* **>** PASHM

PASHIMS > PASHM

PASHING > PASH

PASHKA *n* rich Russian dessert

PASHKAS > PASHKA

PASHM *n* underfur of various Tibetan animals, esp goats, used for cashmere shawls

PASHMINA *n* type of cashmere scarf or shawl made from the underfur of Tibetan goats

PASHMINAS > PASHMINA

PASHMS > PASHM

PASKA *same as* **>** PASKHA

PASKAS > PASKA

PASKHA *n* Russian dessert eaten at Easter

PASKHAS > PASKHA

PASODOBLE *n* fast modern ballroom dance

PASPALUM *n* type of grass with wide leaves

PASPALUMS > PASPALUM

PASPIES > PASPY

PASPY *n* piece of music in triple time

PASQUIL *n* abusive lampoon or satire ▷ *vb* ridicule with pasquil

PASQUILER *n* person who lampoons

PASQUILS > PASQUIL

PASS *vb* go by, past, or through ▷ *n* successful result in a test or examination

PASSABLE *adj* (just) acceptable

PASSABLY *adv* fairly

PASSADE *n* act of moving back and forth in the same place

PASSADES > PASSADE

PASSADO *n* forward thrust with sword

PASSADOES > PASSADO

PASSADOS > PASSADO

PASSAGE *n* channel or opening providing a way through ▷ *vb* move or cause to move at a passage

PASSAGED > PASSAGE

PASSAGER *n* as in *passager hawk* young hawk or falcon caught while on migration

PASSAGES > PASSAGE

PASSAGING > PASSAGE

PASSALONG *adj* (of plants) easily propagated and given to others

PASSAMENT *vb* sew border on garment

PASSANT *adj* (of a heraldic beast) walking

PASSATA *n* sauce made from sieved tomatoes

PASSATAS > PASSATA

PASSBAND *n* band of frequencies that is transmitted with maximum efficiency through a circuit, filter, etc

PASSBANDS > PASSBAND

PASSBOOK *n* book issued by a bank or building society for keeping a record of deposits and withdrawals

PASSBOOKS > PASSBOOK

PASSE *adj* out-of-date

PASSED > PASS

PASSEE *adj* out of fashion

PASSEL *n* group or quantity of no fixed number

PASSELS > PASSEL

PASSEMENT *vb* sew border on garment

PASSENGER *n* person travelling in a vehicle driven by someone else

PASSEPIED *n* lively minuet of Breton origin

PASSER *n* person or thing that passes

PASSERBY *n* person that is passing or going by, esp on foot

PASSERINE *adj* belonging to the order of perching birds ▷ *n* any bird of this order

PASSERS > PASSER

PASSERSBY > PASSERBY

PASSES > PASS

PASSIBLE *adj* susceptible to emotion or suffering

PASSIBLY > PASSIBLE

PASSIM *adv* everywhere, throughout

PASSING *adj* brief or transitory ▷ *n* death

PASSINGLY > PASSING

PASSINGS > PASSING

PASSION *n* intense sexual love ▷ *vb* give passionate character to

PASSIONAL *adj* of, relating to, or due to passion or the passions ▷ *n* book recounting the sufferings of Christian martyrs or saints

PASSIONED > PASSION

PASSIONS > PASSION

PASSIVATE *vb* render (a metal) less susceptible to corrosion by coating the surface with a substance, such as an oxide

PASSIVE *adj* not playing an active part ▷ *n* passive form of a verb

PASSIVELY > PASSIVE

PASSIVES > PASSIVE

PASSIVISM *n* theory, belief, or practice of passive resistance

PASSIVIST **>** PASSIVISM

PASSIVITY > PASSIVE

PASSKEY *n* private key

PASSKEYS > PASSKEY

PASSLESS *adj* having no pass

PASSMAN *n* student who passes without honours

PASSMEN > PASSMAN

PASSMENT *same as* **>** PASSEMENT

PASSMENTS > PASSMENT

PASSOUT *n* (in ice hockey) pass by an attacking

player from behind the opposition goal line

PASSOUTS > PASSOUT

PASSOVER *n* lamb eaten during Passover

PASSOVERS > PASSOVER

PASSPORT *n* official document of nationality granting permission to travel abroad

PASSPORTS > PASSPORT

PASSUS *n* division or section of a poem, story, etc

PASSUSES > PASSUS

PASSWORD *n* secret word or phrase that ensures admission

PASSWORDS > PASSWORD

PAST *adj* of the time before the present ▷ *n* period of time before the present ▷ *adv* ago ▷ *prep* beyond

PASTA *n* type of food that is made from flour and water

PASTALIKE > PASTA

PASTANCE *n* activity that passes time

PASTANCES > PASTANCE

PASTAS > PASTA

PASTE *n* moist soft mixture, such as toothpaste ▷ *vb* fasten with paste

PASTED > PASTE

PASTEDOWN *n* portion of endpaper pasted to cover of book

PASTEL *n* coloured chalk crayon for drawing ▷ *adj* pale and delicate in colour

PASTELIST > PASTEL

PASTELS > PASTEL

PASTER *n* person or thing that pastes

PASTERN *n* part of a horse's foot

PASTERNS > PASTERN

PASTERS > PASTER

PASTES > PASTE

PASTEUP *n* material pasted on a sheet of paper or board

PASTEUPS > PASTEUP

PASTICCI **>** PASTICCIO

PASTICCIO *n* art work borrowing various styles

PASTICHE *n* work of art that mixes styles or copies the style of another artist

PASTICHES > PASTICHE

PASTIE *n* decorative cover for nipple

PASTIER > PASTY

PASTIES > PASTY

PASTIEST > PASTY

PASTIL *same as* **>** PASTILLE

PASTILLE *n* small fruit-flavoured and sometimes medicated sweet

PASTILLES > PASTILLE
PASTILS > PASTIL
PASTILY > PASTY
PASTIME n activity that makes time pass pleasantly
PASTIMES > PASTIME
PASTINA n small pieces of pasta
PASTINAS > PASTINA
PASTINESS > PASTY
PASTING n heavy defeat
PASTINGS > PASTING
PASTIS n anise-flavoured alcoholic drink
PASTISES > PASTIS
PASTITSIO n Greek dish consisting of minced meat and macaroni topped with bechamel sauce
PASTITSO n Greek dish of baked pasta
PASTITSOS > PASTITSO
PASTLESS adj having no past
PASTNESS n quality of being past
PASTOR n member of the clergy in charge of a congregation ▷ vb act as a pastor
PASTORAL adj of or depicting country life ▷ n poem or picture portraying country life
PASTORALE n musical composition that suggests country life
PASTORALI > PASTORALE
PASTORALS > PASTORAL
PASTORATE n office or term of office of a pastor
PASTORED > PASTOR
PASTORING > PASTOR
PASTORIUM n residence of pastor
PASTORLY > PASTOR
PASTORS > PASTOR
PASTRAMI n highly seasoned smoked beef
PASTRAMIS > PASTRAMI
PASTRIES > PASTRY
PASTROMI same as
> PASTRAMI
PASTROMIS > PASTROMI
PASTRY n baking dough made of flour, fat, and water
PASTS > PAST
PASTURAGE n business of grazing cattle
PASTURAL adj of pasture
PASTURE n grassy land for farm animals to graze on ▷ vb cause (livestock) to graze
PASTURED > PASTURE
PASTURER n person who tends cattle
PASTURERS > PASTURER
PASTURES > PASTURE
PASTURING > PASTURE

PASTY adj (of a complexion) pale and unhealthy ▷ n round of pastry folded over a savoury filling
PAT vb tap lightly ▷ n gentle tap or stroke ▷ adj quick, ready, or glib
PATACA n monetary unit of Macao
PATACAS > PATACA
PATAGIA > PATAGIUM
PATAGIAL > PATAGIUM
PATAGIUM n web of skin between the neck, limbs, and tail in bats and gliding mammals that functions as a wing
PATAKA n building on stilts, used for storing provisions
PATAKAS > PATAKA
PATAMAR n type of boat
PATAMARS > PATAMAR
PATBALL n game like squash but using hands
PATBALLS > PATBALL
PATCH n piece of material sewn on a garment ▷ vb mend with a patch
PATCHABLE > PATCH
PATCHED > PATCH
PATCHER > PATCH
PATCHERS > PATCH
PATCHERY n bungling work
PATCHES > PATCH
PATCHIER > PATCHY
PATCHIEST > PATCHY
PATCHILY > PATCHY
PATCHING > PATCH
PATCHINGS > PATCH
PATCHOCKE Spenserian word for > CLOWN
PATCHOULI n Asiatic tree, the leaves of which yield a heavy fragrant oil
PATCHOULY same as
> PATCHOULI
PATCHWORK n needlework made of pieces of different materials sewn together
PATCHY adj of uneven quality or intensity
PATE n head
PATED > PATE
PATELLA n kneecap
PATELLAE > PATELLA
PATELLAR > PATELLA
PATELLAS > PATELLA
PATELLATE adj having the shape of a patella
PATEN n plate used for the bread at Communion
PATENCIES > PATENCY
PATENCY n condition of being obvious
PATENS > PATEN
PATENT n document giving the exclusive right to make or sell an invention ▷ adj open to public inspection ▷ vb obtain a patent for

PATENTED > PATENT
PATENTEE n person, group, company, etc, that has been granted a patent
PATENTEES > PATENTEE
PATENTING > PATENT
PATENTLY adv obviously
PATENTOR n person who or official body that grants a patent or patents
PATENTORS > PATENTOR
PATENTS > PATENT
PATER n father
PATERA n shallow ancient Roman bowl
PATERAE > PATERA
PATERCOVE n fraudulent priest
PATERERO n type of cannon
PATEREROS > PATERERO
PATERNAL adj fatherly
PATERNITY n fact or state of being a father
PATERS > PATER
PATES > PATE
PATH n surfaced walk or track ▷ vb make a path
PATHED > PATH
PATHETIC adj causing feelings of pity or sadness ▷ pl n pathetic sentiments ▷ n pathetic person
PATHETICS > PATHETIC
PATHIC n catamite ▷ adj of or relating to a catamite
PATHICS > PATHIC
PATHING > PATH
PATHLESS > PATH
PATHNAME n name of a file or directory together with its position in relation to other directories traced back in a line to the root
PATHNAMES > PATHNAME
PATHOGEN n thing that causes disease
PATHOGENE same as
> PATHOGEN
PATHOGENS > PATHOGEN
PATHOGENY n origin, development, and resultant effects of a disease
PATHOLOGY n scientific study of diseases
PATHOS n power of arousing pity or sadness
PATHOSES > PATHOS
PATHS > PATH
PATHWAY n path
PATHWAYS > PATHWAY
PATIBLE adj endurable
PATIENCE n quality of being patient
PATIENCES > PATIENCE
PATIENT adj enduring difficulties or delays calmly ▷ n person receiving medical treatment ▷ vb make calm
PATIENTED > PATIENT
PATIENTER > PATIENT

PATIENTLY > PATIENT
PATIENTS > PATIENT
PATIKI n New Zealand sand flounder or dab
PATIKIS > PATIKI
PATIN same as > PATEN
PATINA n fine layer on a surface
PATINAE > PATINA
PATINAED adj having a patina
PATINAS > PATINA
PATINATE vb coat with patina
PATINATED > PATINATE
PATINATES > PATINATE
PATINE vb cover with patina
PATINED > PATINE
PATINES > PATINE
PATINING > PATINE
PATINISE same as
> PATINIZE
PATINISED > PATINISE
PATINISES > PATINISE
PATINIZE vb coat with patina
PATINIZED > PATINIZE
PATINIZES > PATINIZE
PATINS > PATIN
PATIO n paved area adjoining a house
PATIOS > PATIO
PATISSIER n pastry chef
PATKA n head covering worn by Sikh men
PATKAS > PATKA
PATLY adv fitly
PATNESS n appropriateness
PATNESSES > PATNESS
PATOIS n regional dialect, esp of French
PATONCE adj (of cross) with limbs which broaden from centre
PATOOT same as
> PATOOTIE
PATOOTIE n person's bottom
PATOOTIES > PATOOTIE
PATOOTS > PATOOT
PATRIAL n (in Britain, formerly) person with a right to live in the United Kingdom
PATRIALS > PATRIAL
PATRIARCH n male head of a family or tribe
PATRIATE vb bring under the authority of an autonomous country
PATRIATED > PATRIATE
PATRIATES > PATRIATE
PATRICIAN n member of the nobility ▷ adj of noble birth
PATRICIDE n crime of killing one's father
PATRICK n former Irish coin
PATRICKS > PATRICK
PATRICO n fraudulent priest

PATRICOES > PATRICO
PATRICOS > PATRICO
PATRILINY n tracing of family descent through males
PATRIMONY n property inherited from ancestors
PATRIOT n person who loves his or her country
PATRIOTIC > PATRIOT
PATRIOTS > PATRIOT
PATRISTIC adj of or relating to the Fathers of the Church, their writings, or the study of these
PATROL n regular circuit by a guard ▷ vb go round on guard, or reconnoitring
PATROLLED > PATROL
PATROLLER > PATROL
PATROLMAN n man, esp a policeman, who patrols a certain area
PATROLMEN > PATROLMAN
PATROLOGY n study of the writings of the Fathers of the Church
PATROLS > PATROL
PATRON n person who gives financial support
PATRONAGE n support given by a patron
PATRONAL > PATRONESS
PATRONESS n woman who sponsors or aids artists, charities, etc
PATRONISE same as > PATRONIZE
PATRONIZE vb treat in a condescending way
PATRONLY > PATRONESS
PATRONNE n woman who owns or manages a hotel, restaurant, or bar
PATRONNES > PATRONNE
PATRONS > PATRON
PATROON n Dutch land-holder in New Netherland and New York
PATROONS > PATROON
PATS > PAT
PATSIES > PATSY
PATSY n person who is easily cheated, victimized, etc
PATTAMAR n Indian courier
PATTAMARS > PATTAMAR
PATTE n band keeping belt in place
PATTED > PAT
PATTEE adj (of a cross) having triangular arms widening outwards
PATTEN n wooden clog or sandal ▷ vb wear pattens
PATTENED > PATTEN
PATTENING > PATTEN
PATTENS > PATTEN
PATTER vb make repeated soft tapping sounds ▷ n quick succession of taps

PATTERED > PATTER
PATTERER > PATTER
PATTERERS > PATTER
PATTERING > PATTER
PATTERN n arrangement of repeated parts or decorative designs ▷ vb model
PATTERNED > PATTERN
PATTERNS > PATTERN
PATTERS > PATTER
PATTES > PATTE
PATTEST > PAT
PATTIE same as > PATTY
PATTIES > PATTY
PATTING > PAT
PATTLE dialect for > PADDLE
PATTLES > PATTLE
PATTRESS n box for the space behind electrical sockets and switches
PATTY n small flattened cake of minced food
PATTYPAN n small round flattish squash
PATTYPANS > PATTYPAN
PATU n short Māori club, now used ceremonially
PATULENT adj spreading widely
PATULIN n toxic antibiotic
PATULINS > PATULIN
PATULOUS adj spreading widely or expanded
PATUS > PATU
PATUTUKI n blue cod
PATUTUKIS > PATUTUKI
PATY adj (of cross) having arms of equal length
PATZER n novice chess player
PATZERS > PATZER
PAUA n edible shellfish of New Zealand
PAUAS > PAUA
PAUCAL n grammatical number for words in contexts where a few of their referents are described ▷ adj relating to or inflected for this number
PAUCALS > PAUCAL
PAUCITIES > PAUCITY
PAUCITY n scarcity
PAUGHTIER > PAUGHTY
PAUGHTY Scots word for > HAUGHTY
PAUL same as > PAWL
PAULDRON n either of two metal plates worn with armour to protect the shoulders
PAULDRONS > PAULDRON
PAULIN n tarpaulin
PAULINS > PAULIN
PAULOWNIA n Japanese tree with large heart-shaped leaves and clusters of purplish or white flowers
PAULS > PAUL

PAUNCE n pansy
PAUNCES > PAUNCE
PAUNCH n protruding belly ▷ vb stab in the stomach
PAUNCHED > PAUNCH
PAUNCHES > PAUNCH
PAUNCHIER > PAUNCHY
PAUNCHING > PAUNCH
PAUNCHY adj having a protruding belly or abdomen
PAUPER n very poor person ▷ vb reduce to beggary
PAUPERDOM n state of being a pauper
PAUPERED > PAUPER
PAUPERESS n female pauper
PAUPERING > PAUPER
PAUPERISE same as > PAUPERIZE
PAUPERISM > PAUPER
PAUPERIZE vb make a pauper of
PAUPERS > PAUPER
PAUPIETTE n rolled stuffed fish or meat
PAURAQUE n type of long-tailed nocturnal bird
PAURAQUES > PAURAQUE
PAUROPOD n minute myriapod
PAUROPODS > PAUROPOD
PAUSAL > PAUSE
PAUSE vb stop for a time ▷ n stop or rest in speech or action
PAUSED > PAUSE
PAUSEFUL adj taking pauses
PAUSELESS adj without pauses
PAUSER > PAUSE
PAUSERS > PAUSE
PAUSES > PAUSE
PAUSING > PAUSE
PAUSINGLY adv with pauses
PAUSINGS > PAUSE
PAV short for > PAVLOVA
PAVAGE n tax towards paving streets
PAVAGES > PAVAGE
PAVAN same as > PAVANE
PAVANE n slow and stately dance
PAVANES > PAVANE
PAVANS > PAVAN
PAVE vb form (a surface) with stone or brick ▷ n paved surface, esp an uneven one
PAVED > PAVE
PAVEED adj (of jewels) set close together
PAVEMENT n paved path for pedestrians ▷ vb provide with pavement
PAVEMENTS > PAVEMENT
PAVEN same as > PAVANE
PAVENS > PAVEN
PAVER > PAVE

PAVERS > PAVE
PAVES > PAVE
PAVID adj fearful
PAVILION n building on a playing field etc ▷ vb place or set in or as if in a pavilion
PAVILIONS > PAVILION
PAVILLON n bell of wind instrument
PAVILLONS > PAVILLON
PAVIN same as > PAVANE
PAVING n paved surface ▷ adj of or for a paved surface or pavement
PAVINGS > PAVING
PAVINS > PAVIN
PAVIOR same as > PAVIOUR
PAVIORS > PAVIOR
PAVIOUR n person who lays paving
PAVIOURS > PAVIOUR
PAVIS n large square shield
PAVISE same as > PAVIS
PAVISER n soldier holding pavise
PAVISERS > PAVISER
PAVISES > PAVISE
PAVISSE same as > PAVIS
PAVISSES > PAVISSE
PAVLOVA n meringue cake topped with whipped cream and fruit
PAVLOVAS > PAVLOVA
PAVONAZZO n white Italian marble
PAVONE n peacock
PAVONES > PAVONE
PAVONIAN same as > PAVONINE
PAVONINE adj of or resembling a peacock or the colours, design, or iridescence of a peacock's tail
PAVS > PAV
PAW n animal's foot with claws and pads ▷ vb scrape with the paw or hoof
PAWA old word for > PEACOCK
PAWAS > PAWA
PAWAW vb recite N American incantation
PAWAWED > PAWAW
PAWAWING > PAWAW
PAWAWS > PAWAW
PAWED > PAW
PAWER n person or animal that paws
PAWERS > PAWER
PAWING > PAW
PAWK Scots word for > TRICK
PAWKIER > PAWKY
PAWKIEST > PAWKY
PAWKILY > PAWKY
PAWKINESS > PAWKY
PAWKS > PAWK
PAWKY adj having or characterized by a dry wit

PAWL n pivoted lever shaped to engage with a ratchet
PAWLS > PAWL
PAWN vb deposit (an article) as security for money borrowed ▷ n chessman of the lowest value
PAWNABLE > PAWN
PAWNAGE > PAWN
PAWNAGES > PAWN
PAWNCE old word for > PANSY
PAWNCES > PAWNCE
PAWNED > PAWN
PAWNEE n one who accepts goods in pawn
PAWNEES > PAWNEE
PAWNER n one who pawns his or her possessions
PAWNERS > PAWNER
PAWNING > PAWN
PAWNOR same as > PAWNER
PAWNORS > PAWNOR
PAWNS > PAWN
PAWNSHOP n premises of a pawnbroker
PAWNSHOPS > PAWNSHOP
PAWPAW same as > PAPAW
PAWPAWS > PAWPAW
PAWS > PAW
PAX n peace ▷ interj call signalling a desire to end hostilities
PAXES > PAX
PAXIUBA n tropical tree
PAXIUBAS > PAXIUBA
PAXWAX n strong ligament in the neck of many mammals
PAXWAXES > PAXWAX
PAY vb give money etc in return for goods or services ▷ n wages or salary
PAYABLE adj due to be paid
PAYABLES n debts to be paid
PAYABLY > PAYABLE
PAYBACK n return on an investment
PAYBACKS > PAYBACK
PAYCHECK n payment for work done
PAYCHECKS > PAYCHECK
PAYCHEQUE n payment for work done
PAYDAY n day on which wages or salaries are paid
PAYDAYS > PAYDAY
PAYDOWN n reduction of debt through repayment
PAYDOWNS > PAYDOWN
PAYED > PAY
PAYEE n person to whom money is paid or due
PAYEES > PAYEE
PAYER n person who pays
PAYERS > PAYER
PAYESS pl n uncut sideburns worn by some Jewish men

PAYFONE US spelling of > PAYPHONE
PAYFONES > PAYFONE
PAYGRADE n military rank
PAYGRADES > PAYGRADE
PAYING > PAY
PAYINGS > PAY
PAYLIST n list of people to be paid
PAYLISTS > PAYLIST
PAYLOAD n passengers or cargo of an aircraft
PAYLOADS > PAYLOAD
PAYMASTER n official responsible for the payment of wages and salaries
PAYMENT n act of paying
PAYMENTS > PAYMENT
PAYNIM n heathen or pagan
PAYNIMRY n state of being heathen
PAYNIMS > PAYNIM
PAYOFF n final settlement, esp in retribution
PAYOFFS > PAYOFF
PAYOLA n bribe to promote a commercial product
PAYOLAS > PAYOLA
PAYOR same as > PAYER
PAYORS > PAYOR
PAYOUT n sum of money paid out
PAYOUTS > PAYOUT
PAYPHONE n coin-operated telephone
PAYPHONES > PAYPHONE
PAYROLL n list of employees who receive regular pay
PAYROLLS > PAYROLL
PAYS > PAY
PAYSAGE n landscape
PAYSAGES > PAYSAGE
PAYSAGIST n painter of landscapes
PAYSD Spenserian form of > POISED
PAYSLIP n note of payment given to employee
PAYSLIPS > PAYSLIP
PAYWALL n system that denies access to a website unless a payment is made
PAYWALLS > PAYWALL
PAZAZZ same as > PIZZAZZ
PAZAZZES > PAZAZZ
PAZZAZZ same as > PIZZAZZ
PAZZAZZES > PAZZAZZ
PE n 17th letter of the Hebrew alphabet, transliterated as p
PEA n climbing plant with seeds growing in pods
PEABERRY n coffee berry containing one seed
PEABRAIN n stupid person

PEABRAINS > PEABRAIN
PEACE n calm, quietness
PEACEABLE adj inclined towards peace
PEACEABLY > PEACEABLE
PEACED > PEACE
PEACEFUL adj not in a state of war or disagreement
PEACELESS adj without peace
PEACENIK n activist who opposes war
PEACENIKS > PEACENIK
PEACES > PEACE
PEACETIME n period without war
PEACH n soft juicy fruit ▷ adj pinkish-orange ▷ vb inform against an accomplice
PEACHBLOW n type of glaze on porcelain
PEACHED > PEACH
PEACHER > PEACH
PEACHERS > PEACH
PEACHES > PEACH
PEACHICK n young peafowl
PEACHICKS > PEACHICK
PEACHIER > PEACHY
PEACHIEST > PEACHY
PEACHILY > PEACHY
PEACHING > PEACH
PEACHY adj of or like a peach, esp in colour or texture
PEACING > PEACE
PEACOAT n woollen jacket
PEACOATS > PEACOAT
PEACOCK n large male bird with a brilliantly coloured fanlike tail ▷ vb display (oneself) proudly
PEACOCKED > PEACOCK
PEACOCKS > PEACOCK
PEACOCKY > PEACOCK
PEACOD same as > PEACOD
PEACODS > PEACOD
PEAFOWL n peacock or peahen
PEAFOWLS > PEAFOWL
PEAG n (formerly) money used by North American Indians
PEAGE same as > PEAG
PEAGES > PEAGE
PEAGS > PEAG
PEAHEN > PEACOCK
PEAHENS > PEACOCK
PEAK n pointed top, esp of a mountain ▷ vb form or reach a peak ▷ adj of or at the point of greatest demand
PEAKED adj having a peak
PEAKIER > PEAK
PEAKIEST > PEAK
PEAKING n act of peaking
PEAKINGS > PEAKING
PEAKISH adj sickly

PEAKLESS adj without a peak
PEAKLIKE > PEAK
PEAKS > PEAK
PEAKY > PEAK
PEAL n long loud echoing sound, esp of bells or thunder ▷ vb sound with a peal or peals
PEALED > PEAL
PEALIKE > PEA
PEALING > PEAL
PEALS > PEAL
PEAN same as > PEEN
PEANED > PEAN
PEANING > PEAN
PEANS > PEAN
PEANUT n pea-shaped nut that ripens underground
PEANUTS > PEANUT
PEANUTTY adj having the taste of peanuts
PEAPOD n pod of the pea plant
PEAPODS > PEAPOD
PEAR n sweet juicy fruit with a narrow top and rounded base
PEARCE old spelling of > PIERCE
PEARCED > PEARCE
PEARCES > PEARCE
PEARCING > PEARCE
PEARE obsolete spelling of > PEAR
PEARES > PEARE
PEARL same as > PURL
PEARLASH n granular crystalline form of potassium carbonate
PEARLED > PEARL
PEARLER n person who dives for or trades in pearls ▷ adj excellent
PEARLERS > PEARLER
PEARLIER > PEARLY
PEARLIES > PEARLY
PEARLIEST > PEARLY
PEARLIN n type of lace used to trim clothes
PEARLING > PEARL
PEARLINGS > PEARL
PEARLINS n type of lace
PEARLISED same as > PEARLIZED
PEARLITE same as > PERLITE
PEARLITES > PEARLITE
PEARLITIC > PEARLITE
PEARLIZED adj having or given a pearly lustre
PEARLS > PEARL
PEARLWORT n plant with small white flowers that are spherical in bud
PEARLY adj resembling a pearl, esp in lustre ▷ n London costermonger who wears pearl buttons
PEARMAIN n any of several varieties of apple having a red skin
PEARMAINS > PEARMAIN
PEARS > PEAR

PEARST archaic variant of > PIERCED
PEART adj lively
PEARTER > PEART
PEARTEST > PEART
PEARTLY > PEART
PEARTNESS > PEART
PEARWOOD n wood from pear tree
PEARWOODS > PEARWOOD
PEAS > PEA
PEASANT n person working on the land
PEASANTRY n peasants collectively
PEASANTS > PEASANT
PEASANTY adj having qualities ascribed to traditional country life or people
PEASCOD same as > COD
PEASCODS > PEASCOD
PEASE n archaic or dialect word for pea ▷ vb appease
PEASECOD n pod of a pea plant
PEASECODS > PEASECOD
PEASED > PEASE
PEASEN obsolete plural of > PEASE
PEASES > PEASE
PEASING > PEASE
PEASON obsolete plural of > PEASE
PEASOUPER n thick fog
PEAT n decayed vegetable material found in bogs
PEATARIES > PEATARY
PEATARY n area covered with peat
PEATERIES > PEATERY
PEATERY same as > PEATARY
PEATIER > PEAT
PEATIEST > PEAT
PEATLAND n area of land consisting of peat bogs, usually containing many species of flora and fauna
PEATLANDS > PEATLAND
PEATMAN n person who collects peat
PEATMEN > PEATMAN
PEATS > PEAT
PEATSHIP n ship carrying peat
PEATSHIPS > PEATSHIP
PEATY > PEAT
PEAVEY n wooden lever used for handling logs
PEAVEYS > PEAVEY
PEAVIES > PEAVY
PEAVY same as > PEAVEY
PEAZE same as > PEASE
PEAZED > PEAZE
PEAZES > PEAZE
PEAZING > PEAZE
PEBA n type of armadillo
PEBAS > PEBA
PEBBLE n small roundish stone ▷ vb cover with pebbles
PEBBLED > PEBBLE

PEBBLES > PEBBLE
PEBBLIER > PEBBLE
PEBBLIEST > PEBBLE
PEBBLING n (in curling) act of spraying the rink with drops of hot water to slow down the stone
PEBBLINGS > PEBBLING
PEBBLY > PEBBLE
PEBRINE n disease of silkworms
PEBRINES > PEBRINE
PEC n pectoral muscle
PECAN n edible nut of a N American tree
PECANS > PECAN
PECCABLE adj liable to sin
PECCANCY > PECCANT
PECCANT adj guilty of an offence
PECCANTLY > PECCANT
PECCARIES > PECCARY
PECCARY n piglike animal of American forests
PECCAVI n confession of guilt
PECCAVIS > PECCAVI
PECH Scottish word for > PANT
PECHAN Scots word for > STOMACH
PECHANS > PECHAN
PECHED > PECH
PECHING > PECH
PECHS > PECH
PECK vb strike or pick up with the beak ▷ n pecking movement
PECKE n quarter of bushel
PECKED > PECK
PECKER n slang word for penis
PECKERS > PECKER
PECKES > PECKE
PECKIER > PECKY
PECKIEST > PECKY
PECKING > PECK
PECKINGS > PECK
PECKISH adj slightly hungry
PECKISHLY > PECKISH
PECKS > PECK
PECKY adj discoloured
PECORINI > PECORINO
PECORINO n Italian cheese made from ewes' milk
PECORINOS > PECORINO
PECS pl n pectoral muscles
PECTASE n enzyme occurring in certain ripening fruits
PECTASES > PECTASE
PECTATE n salt or ester of pectic acid
PECTATES > PECTATE
PECTEN n comblike structure in the eye of birds and reptiles
PECTENS > PECTEN
PECTIC > PECTIN
PECTIN n substance in fruit that makes jam set

PECTINAL adj resembling a comb ▷ n fish with bones or a spine resembling a comb
PECTINALS > PECTINAL
PECTINATE adj shaped like a comb
PECTINEAL adj relating to pubic bone
PECTINES > PECTEN
PECTINOUS > PECTIN
PECTINS > PECTIN
PECTISE same as > PECTIZE
PECTISED > PECTISE
PECTISES > PECTISE
PECTISING > PECTISE
PECTIZE vb change into a jelly
PECTIZED > PECTIZE
PECTIZES > PECTIZE
PECTIZING > PECTIZE
PECTOLITE n silicate of lime and soda
PECTORAL adj of the chest or thorax ▷ n pectoral muscle or fin
PECTORALS > PECTORAL
PECTOSE n insoluble carbohydrate found in unripe fruit
PECTOSES > PECTOSE
PECULATE vb embezzle (public money)
PECULATED > PECULATE
PECULATES > PECULATE
PECULATOR > PECULATE
PECULIA > PECULIUM
PECULIAR adj strange ▷ n special sort, esp an accented letter
PECULIARS > PECULIAR
PECULIUM n property that a father or master allowed his child or slave to hold as his own
PECUNIARY adj relating to, or consisting of, money
PECUNIOUS adj having lots of money
PED n pannier
PEDAGOG same as > PEDAGOGUE
PEDAGOGIC > PEDAGOGUE
PEDAGOGS > PEDAGOG
PEDAGOGUE n schoolteacher, esp a pedantic one
PEDAGOGY n principles, practice, or profession of teaching
PEDAL n foot-operated lever ▷ vb propel (a bicycle) by using its pedals ▷ adj of or relating to the foot or the feet
PEDALBOAT n boat that is propelled by operating the pedals
PEDALCAR n child's vehicle that is operated by pedals
PEDALCARS > PEDALCAR

PEDALED > PEDAL
PEDALER > PEDAL
PEDALERS > PEDAL
PEDALFER n type of zonal soil deficient in lime but containing deposits of aluminium and iron
PEDALFERS > PEDALFER
PEDALIER n pedal piano
PEDALIERS > PEDALIER
PEDALING > PEDAL
PEDALLED > PEDAL
PEDALLER n person who pedals
PEDALLERS > PEDALLER
PEDALLING > PEDAL
PEDALO n pedal-operated pleasure craft
PEDALOES > PEDALO
PEDALOS > PEDALO
PEDALS > PEDAL
PEDANT n person who is excessively concerned with details and rules
PEDANTIC adj of, relating to, or characterized by pedantry
PEDANTISE same as > PEDANTIZE
PEDANTISM > PEDANT
PEDANTIZE vb make pedantic comments
PEDANTRY n practice of being a pedant, esp in the minute observance of petty rules or details
PEDANTS > PEDANT
PEDATE adj (of a plant leaf) divided into several lobes arising at a common point
PEDATELY > PEDATE
PEDATIFID adj (of a plant leaf) pedately divided, with the divisions less deep than in a pedate leaf
PEDDER old form of > PEDLAR
PEDDERS > PEDDER
PEDDLE vb sell (goods) from door to door
PEDDLED > PEDDLE
PEDDLER same as > PEDLAR
PEDDLERS > PEDDLER
PEDDLERY n business of peddler
PEDDLES > PEDDLE
PEDDLING > PEDDLE
PEDDLINGS > PEDDLE
PEDERAST n man who has homosexual relations with boys
PEDERASTS > PEDERAST
PEDERASTY n homosexual relations between men and boys
PEDERERO n type of cannon
PEDEREROS > PEDERERO
PEDES > PES
PEDESES > PEDESIS
PEDESIS n random motion of small particles

PEDESTAL n base supporting a column, statue, etc

PEDESTALS > PEDESTAL

PEDETIC adj of feet

PEDIATRIC adj of or relating to the medical science of children and their diseases

PEDICAB n pedal-operated tricycle, available for hire

PEDICABS > PEDICAB

PEDICEL n stalk bearing a single flower of an inflorescence

PEDICELS > PEDICEL

PEDICLE n any small stalk

PEDICLED > PEDICLE

PEDICLES > PEDICLE

PEDICULAR adj relating to, infested with, or caused by lice

PEDICULI > PEDICULUS

PEDICULUS n wingless parasite

PEDICURE n medical or cosmetic treatment of the feet ▷ vb give a pedicure

PEDICURED > PEDICURE

PEDICURES > PEDICURE

PEDIFORM adj shaped like a foot

PEDIGREE n register of ancestors, esp of a purebred animal

PEDIGREED > PEDIGREE

PEDIGREES > PEDIGREE

PEDIMENT n triangular part over a door etc

PEDIMENTS > PEDIMENT

PEDIPALP n either member of the second pair of head appendages of arachnids

PEDIPALPI > PEDIPALP

PEDIPALPS > PEDIPALP

PEDLAR n person who sells goods from door to door

PEDLARIES > PEDLARY

PEDLARS > PEDLAR

PEDLARY same as > PEDLERY

PEDLER same as > PEDLAR

PEDLERIES > PEDLERY

PEDLERS > PEDLER

PEDLERY n business of pedler

PEDOCAL n type of soil that is rich in lime

PEDOCALIC > PEDOCAL

PEDOCALS > PEDOCAL

PEDOGENIC adj relating to soil

PEDOLOGIC > PEDOLOGY

PEDOLOGY same as > PAEDOLOGY

PEDOMETER n instrument which measures the distance walked

PEDOPHILE n person who is sexually attracted to children

PEDORTHIC adj (of footwear) designed to alleviate foot problems

PEDRAIL n device replacing wheel on rough surfaces

PEDRAILS > PEDRAIL

PEDRERO n type of cannon

PEDREROES > PEDRERO

PEDREROS > PEDRERO

PEDRO n card game

PEDROS > PEDRO

PEDS > PED

PEDUNCLE same as > PEDICEL

PEDUNCLED > PEDUNCLE

PEDUNCLES > PEDUNCLE

PEDWAY n walkway for pedestrians only

PEDWAYS > PEDWAY

PEE vb urinate ▷ n urine

PEEBEEN n type of large evergreen

PEEBEENS > PEEBEEN

PEECE obsolete variant of > PIECE

PEECES > PEECE

PEED > PEE

PEEING > PEE

PEEK n peep or glance ▷ vb glance quickly or secretly

PEEKABO same as > PEEKABOO

PEEKABOO n game for young children, in which one person hides his face and suddenly reveals it and cries 'peekaboo' ▷ adj (of a garment) made of fabric that is almost transparent or patterned with small holes

PEEKABOOS > PEEKABOO

PEEKABOS > PEEKABO

PEEKAPOO n dog which is cross between Pekingese and poodle

PEEKAPOOS > PEEKAPOO

PEEKED > PEEK

PEEKING > PEEK

PEEKS > PEEK

PEEL vb remove the skin or rind of (a vegetable or fruit) ▷ n rind or skin

PEELABLE > PEEL

PEELED > PEEL

PEELER n device for peeling vegetables, fruit, etc

PEELERS > PEELER

PEELING n strip that has been peeled off

PEELINGS > PEELING

PEELS > PEEL

PEEN n end of a hammer head opposite the striking face ▷ vb strike with the peen of a hammer

PEENED > PEEN

PEENGE vb complain

PEENGED > PEENGE

PEENGEING > PEENGE

PEENGES > PEENGE

PEENGING > PEENGE

PEENING n act of peening

PEENINGS > PEENING

PEENS > PEEN

PEEOY n homemade firework

PEEOYS > PEEOY

PEEP vb look slyly or quickly ▷ n peeping look

PEEPBO n game of peekaboo

PEEPBOS > PEEPBO

PEEPE old spelling of > PIP

PEEPED > PEEP

PEEPER n person who peeps

PEEPERS > PEEPER

PEEPES archaic spelling of > PEEPS

PEEPHOLE n small aperture, such as one in the door of a flat for observing callers before opening

PEEPHOLES > PEEPHOLE

PEEPING > PEEP

PEEPS > PEEP

PEEPSHOW n box containing a series of pictures that can be seen through a small hole

PEEPSHOWS > PEEPSHOW

PEEPTOE adj of a shoe in which the toe is not covered

PEEPUL n Indian moraceous tree

PEEPULS > PEEPUL

PEER n (in Britain) member of the nobility ▷ vb look closely and intently

PEERAGE n whole body of peers

PEERAGES > PEERAGE

PEERED > PEER

PEERESS n (in Britain) woman holding the rank of a peer

PEERESSES > PEERESS

PEERIE n spinning top ▷ adj small

PEERIER > PEERIE

PEERIES > PEERIE

PEERIEST > PEERIE

PEERING > PEER

PEERLESS adj unequalled, unsurpassed

PEERS > PEER

PEERY n child's spinning top

PEES > PEE

PEESWEEP n early spring storm

PEESWEEPS > PEESWEEP

PEETWEET n spotted sandpiper

PEETWEETS > PEETWEET

PEEVE vb irritate or annoy ▷ n something that irritates

PEEVED > PEEVE

PEEVER n hopscotch

PEEVERS > PEEVER

PEEVES > PEEVE

PEEVING > PEEVE

PEEVISH adj fretful or irritable

PEEVISHLY > PEEVISH

PEEWEE same as > PEWEE

PEEWEES > PEEWEE

PEEWIT same as > LAPWING

PEEWITS > PEEWIT

PEG n pin or clip for joining, fastening, marking, etc ▷ vb fasten with pegs

PEGASUS n winged horse

PEGASUSES > PEGASUS

PEGBOARD n board with a pattern of holes into which small pegs can be fitted, used for playing certain games or keeping a score

PEGBOARDS > PEGBOARD

PEGBOX n part of stringed instrument that holds tuning pegs

PEGBOXES > PEGBOX

PEGGED > PEG

PEGGIER > PEGGY

PEGGIES > PEGGY

PEGGIEST > PEGGY

PEGGING > PEG

PEGGINGS > PEG

PEGGY n type of small warbler ▷ adj resembling a peg

PEGH variant of > PECH

PEGHED > PEGH

PEGHING > PEGH

PEGHS > PEGH

PEGLEGGED adj having wooden leg

PEGLESS > PEG

PEGLIKE > PEG

PEGMATITE n exceptionally coarse-grained intrusive igneous rock

PEGS > PEG

PEGTOP n type of spinning top

PEGTOPS > PEGTOP

PEH same as > PE

PEHS > PEH

PEIGNOIR n woman's light dressing gown

PEIGNOIRS > PEIGNOIR

PEIN same as > PEEN

PEINCT vb paint

PEINCTED > PEINCT

PEINCTING > PEINCT

PEINCTS > PEINCT

PEINED > PEIN

PEINING > PEIN

PEINS > PEIN

PEIRASTIC adj experimental

PEISE same as > PEIZE

PEISED > PEISE

PEISES > PEISE

PEISHWA n Indian leader

PEISHWAH same as > PEISHWA

PEISHWAHS > PEISHWAH

PEISHWAS > PEISHWA
PEISING > PEISE
PEIZE *vb* weight or poise
PEIZED > PEIZE
PEIZES > PEIZE
PEIZING > PEIZE
PEJORATE *vb* change for the worse
PEJORATED > PEJORATE
PEJORATES > PEJORATE
PEKAN *n* large North American marten
PEKANS > PEKAN
PEKE *n* Pekingese dog
PEKEPOO *same as* > PEEKAPOO
PEKEPOOS > PEKEPOO
PEKES > PEKE
PEKIN *n* silk fabric
PEKINS > PEKIN
PEKOE *n* high-quality tea
PEKOES > PEKOE
PEL *n* pixel
PELA *n* insect living on wax
PELAGE *n* coat of a mammal, consisting of hair, wool, fur, etc
PELAGES > PELAGE
PELAGIAL *adj* of the open sea ▷ *n* open body of water such as a lake or the sea
PELAGIALS > PELAGIAL
PELAGIAN *adj* of or inhabiting the open sea ▷ *n* pelagic creature
PELAGIANS > PELAGIAN
PELAGIC *adj* of or relating to the open sea ▷ *n* any pelagic creature
PELAGICS > PELAGIC
PELAS > PELA
PELAU *n* dish made with meat, rice, and pigeon peas
PELAUS > PELAU
PELE *Spenserian variant of* > PEAL
PELECYPOD *another word for* > BIVALVE
PELERINE *n* woman's narrow cape with long pointed ends in front
PELERINES > PELERINE
PELES > PELE
PELF *n* money or wealth
PELFS > PELF
PELHAM *n* horse's bit for a double bridle
PELHAMS > PELHAM
PELICAN *n* large water bird with a pouch beneath its bill
PELICANS > PELICAN
PELISSE *n* cloak or loose coat which is usually fur-trimmed
PELISSES > PELISSE
PELITE *n* any argillaceous rock such as shale
PELITES > PELITE
PELITIC > PELITE
PELL *n* hide of an animal ▷ *vb* hit violently

PELLACH *same as* > PELLACK
PELLACHS > PELLACH
PELLACK *n* porpoise
PELLACKS > PELLACK
PELLAGRA *n* disease caused by lack of vitamin B
PELLAGRAS > PELLAGRA
PELLAGRIN *n* person who suffers from pellagra
PELLED > PELL
PELLET *n* small ball of something ▷ *vb* strike with pellets
PELLETAL > PELLET
PELLETED > PELLET
PELLETIFY *vb* shape into pellets
PELLETING > PELLET
PELLETISE *vb* shape into pellets
PELLETIZE *vb* shape into pellets
PELLETS > PELLET
PELLICLE *n* thin skin or film
PELLICLES > PELLICLE
PELLING > PELL
PELLITORY *n* urticaceous plant
PELLMELL *n* disorder
PELLMELLS > PELLMELL
PELLOCK *n* porpoise
PELLOCKS > PELLOCK
PELLS > PELL
PELLUCID *adj* very clear
PELLUM *n* dust
PELLUMS > PELLUM
PELMA *n* sole of the foot
PELMANISM *n* memory card game
PELMAS > PELMA
PELMATIC > PELMA
PELMET *n* ornamental drapery or board, concealing a curtain rail
PELMETS > PELMET
PELOID *n* mud used therapeutically
PELOIDS > PELOID
PELOLOGY *n* study of therapeutic uses of mud
PELON *adj* hairless ▷ *n* hairless person or animal
PELONS > PELON
PELORIA *n* abnormal production of flowers in a plant
PELORIAN > PELORIA
PELORIAS > PELORIA
PELORIC > PELORIA
PELORIES > PELORY
PELORISED *adj* affected by peloria
PELORISM *n* floral mutation
PELORISMS > PELORISM
PELORIZED *same as* > PELORISED
PELORUS *n* sighting device
PELORUSES > PELORUS

PELORY *n* floral mutation
PELOTA *n* game where players propel a ball against a wall
PELOTAS > PELOTA
PELOTON *n* main field of riders in a road race
PELOTONS > PELOTON
PELS > PEL
PELT *vb* throw missiles at ▷ *n* skin of a fur-bearing animal
PELTA *n* small ancient shield
PELTAE > PELTA
PELTAS > PELTA
PELTAST *n* (in ancient Greece) lightly armed foot soldier
PELTASTS > PELTAST
PELTATE *adj* (of leaves) having the stalk attached to the centre of the lower surface
PELTATELY > PELTATE
PELTATION > PELTATE
PELTED > PELT
PELTER *vb* rain heavily
PELTERED > PELT
PELTERING > PELT
PELTERS > PELT
PELTING > PELT
PELTINGLY > PELT
PELTINGS > PELT
PELTLESS > PELT
PELTRIES > PELTRY
PELTRY *n* pelts of animals collectively
PELTS > PELT
PELVES > PELVIS
PELVIC *adj* of, near, or relating to the pelvis ▷ *n* pelvic bone
PELVICS > PELVIC
PELVIFORM *adj* shaped like pelvis
PELVIS *n* framework of bones at the base of the spine
PELVISES > PELVIS
PEMBINA *n* type of cranberry
PEMBINAS > PEMBINA
PEMBROKE *n* small table
PEMBROKES > PEMBROKE
PEMICAN *same as* > PEMMICAN
PEMICANS > PEMICAN
PEMMICAN *n* small pressed cake of shredded dried meat, pounded into paste with fat and berries or dried fruits
PEMMICANS > PEMMICAN
PEMOLINE *n* mild stimulant
PEMOLINES > PEMOLINE
PEMPHIGI > PEMPHIGUS
PEMPHIGUS *n* any of a group of blistering skin diseases
PEMPHIX *n* type of crustacean
PEMPHIXES > PEMPHIX

PEN *n* instrument for writing in ink ▷ *vb* write or compose
PENAL *adj* of or used in punishment
PENALISE *same as* > PENALIZE
PENALISED > PENALISE
PENALISES > PENALISE
PENALITY > PENAL
PENALIZE *vb* impose a penalty on
PENALIZED > PENALIZE
PENALIZES > PENALIZE
PENALLY > PENAL
PENALTIES > PENALTY
PENALTY *n* punishment for a crime or offence
PENANCE *n* voluntary self-punishment ▷ *vb* impose a penance upon (a sinner)
PENANCED > PENANCE
PENANCES > PENANCE
PENANCING > PENANCE
PENANG *variant of* > PINANG
PENANGS > PENANG
PENATES *pl n* household gods
PENCE > PENNY
PENCEL *n* small pennon
PENCELS > PENCEL
PENCES > PENNY
PENCHANT *n* inclination or liking
PENCHANTS > PENCHANT
PENCIL *n* thin cylindrical instrument for writing or drawing ▷ *vb* draw, write, or mark with a pencil
PENCILED > PENCIL
PENCILER > PENCIL
PENCILERS > PENCIL
PENCILING > PENCIL
PENCILLED > PENCIL
PENCILLER > PENCIL
PENCILS > PENCIL
PENCRAFT *n* skill in writing
PENCRAFTS > PENCRAFT
PEND *vb* await judgment or settlement ▷ *n* archway or vaulted passage
PENDANT *n* ornament worn on a chain round the neck
PENDANTLY > PENDANT
PENDANTS > PENDANT
PENDED > PEND
PENDENCY > PENDENT
PENDENT *adj* hanging ▷ *n* pendant
PENDENTLY > PENDENT
PENDENTS > PENDENT
PENDICLE *n* something dependent on another
PENDICLER *n* person who rents a croft
PENDICLES > PENDICLE
PENDING *prep* while waiting for ▷ *adj* not yet decided or settled

PENDRAGON n supreme war chief or leader of the ancient Britons

PENDS > PEND

PENDU adj in informal Indian English, culturally backward

PENDULAR adj pendulous

PENDULATE vb swing as pendulum

PENDULE n type of climbing manoeuvre

PENDULES > PENDULE

PENDULINE adj building nests that hang down

PENDULOUS adj hanging, swinging

PENDULUM same as > PENDULE

PENDULUMS > PENDULUM

PENE variant of > PEEN

PENED variant of > PENE

PENEPLAIN n relatively flat land surface produced by a long period of erosion

PENEPLANE same as > PENEPLAIN

PENES > PENIS

PENETRANT adj sharp ▷ n substance that lowers the surface tension of a liquid and thus causes it to penetrate or be absorbed more easily

PENETRATE vb find or force a way into or through

PENFOLD same as > PINFOLD

PENFOLDS > PENFOLD

PENFUL n contents of pen

PENFULS > PENFUL

PENGO n former monetary unit of Hungary

PENGOS > PENGO

PENGUIN n flightless black-and-white sea bird

PENGUINRY n breeding place of penguins

PENGUINS > PENGUIN

PENHOLDER n container for pens

PENI old spelling of > PENNY

PENIAL > PENIS

PENICIL n small pad for wounds

PENICILLI n plural of penicillus, small pad for wounds

PENICILS > PENICIL

PENIE old spelling of > PENNY

PENIES > PENIE

PENILE adj of or relating to the penis

PENILL > PENILLION

PENILLION pl n Welsh art or practice of singing poetry in counterpoint to a traditional melody played on the harp

PENING > PENE

PENINSULA n strip of land nearly surrounded by water

PENIS n organ of copulation and urination in male mammals

PENISES > PENIS

PENISTONE n coarse woollen cloth

PENITENCE > PENITENT

PENITENCY > PENITENT

PENITENT adj feeling sorry for having done wrong ▷ n someone who is penitent

PENITENTS > PENITENT

PENK n small fish

PENKNIFE n small knife with blade(s) that fold into the handle

PENKNIVES > PENKNIFE

PENKS > PENK

PENLIGHT n small thin flashlight

PENLIGHTS > PENLIGHT

PENLITE same as > PENLIGHT

PENLITES > PENLITE

PENMAN n person skilled in handwriting

PENMEN > PENMAN

PENNA n large feather

PENNAE > PENNA

PENNAL n first-year student of Protestant university

PENNALISM n menial choring at college

PENNALS > PENNAL

PENNAME n author's pseudonym

PENNAMES > PENNAME

PENNANT same as > PENDANT

PENNANTS > PENNANT

PENNATE adj having feathers, wings, or winglike structures

PENNATED same as > PENNATE

PENNATULA n sea pen

PENNE n pasta in the form of short tubes

PENNED > PEN

PENNEECH n card game

PENNEECHS > PENNEECH

PENNEECK same as > PENNEECH

PENNEECKS > PENNEECK

PENNER n person who writes

PENNERS > PENNER

PENNES > PENNE

PENNI n former Finnish monetary unit

PENNIA > PENNI

PENNIED adj having money

PENNIES > PENNY

PENNIFORM adj shaped like a feather

PENNILESS adj very poor

PENNILL n stanza in a Welsh poem

PENNINE n mineral found in the Pennine Alps

PENNINES > PENNINE

PENNING > PEN

PENNINITE n bluish-green variety of chlorite occurring in the form of thick crystals

PENNIS > PENNI

PENNON n triangular or tapering flag

PENNONCEL n small narrow flag

PENNONED n equipped with a pennon

PENNONS > PENNON

PENNY n coin worth one hundredth of a pound

PENNYBOY n employee whose duties include menial tasks, such as running errands

PENNYBOYS > PENNYBOY

PENNYFEE n small payment

PENNYFEES > PENNYFEE

PENNYLAND n old Scottish division of land

PENNYWISE adj careful with small amounts of money

PENNYWORT n Eurasian rock plant with whitish-green tubular flowers and rounded leaves

PENOCHE n type of fudge

PENOCHES > PENOCHE

PENOLOGY n study of punishment and prison management

PENONCEL n small narrow flag

PENONCELS > PENONCEL

PENPOINT n tip of pen

PENPOINTS > PENPOINT

PENPUSHER n person whose work involves a lot of boring paperwork

PENS > PEN

PENSEE n thought put down on paper

PENSEES > PENSEE

PENSEL same as > PENCEL

PENSELS > PENSEL

PENSEROSO n pensive person

PENSIL same as > PENCEL

PENSILE adj designating or building a hanging nest

PENSILITY > PENSILE

PENSILS > PENSIL

PENSION n regular payment to people above a certain age, etc ▷ vb grant a pension to

PENSIONE n Italian boarding house

PENSIONED > PENSION

PENSIONER n person receiving a pension

PENSIONES > PENSIONE

PENSIONI > PENSIONE

PENSIONS > PENSION

PENSIVE adj deeply thoughtful, often with a tinge of sadness

PENSIVELY > PENSIVE

PENSTEMON n North American flowering plant with five stamens

PENSTER n writer

PENSTERS > PENSTER

PENSTOCK n conduit that supplies water to a hydroelectric power plant

PENSTOCKS > PENSTOCK

PENSUM n school exercise

PENSUMS > PENSUM

PENT n penthouse

PENTACLE same as > PENTAGRAM

PENTACLES > PENTACLE

PENTACT n sponge spicule with five rays

PENTACTS > PENTACT

PENTAD n group or series of five

PENTADIC > PENTAD

PENTADS > PENTAD

PENTAGON n geometric figure with five sides

PENTAGONS > PENTAGON

PENTAGRAM n five-pointed star

PENTALOGY n combination of five closely related symptoms

PENTALPHA n five-pointed star

PENTAMERY n state of consisting of five parts

PENTANE n alkane hydrocarbon with three isomers

PENTANES > PENTANE

PENTANGLE same as > PENTAGRAM

PENTANOIC adj as in pentanoic acid colourless liquid carboxylic acid

PENTANOL n colourless oily liquid

PENTANOLS > PENTANOL

PENTAPODY n series or measure of five feet

PENTARCH n member of pentarchy

PENTARCHS > PENTARCH

PENTARCHY n government by five rulers

PENTATHLA n pentathlons

PENTENE n colourless flammable liquid alkene

PENTENES > PENTENE

PENTHIA n child born fifth

PENTHIAS > PENTHIA

PENTHOUSE n flat built on the roof or top floor of a building

PENTICE vb accommodate in a penthouse

PENTICED > PENTICE

PENTICES > PENTICE

PENTICING > PENTICE

PENTISE same as > PENTICE

PENTISED > PENTISE

PENTISES > PENTISE
PENTISING > PENTISE
PENTITI > PENTITO
PENTITO *n* criminal who offers information to the police
PENTODE *n* electronic valve having five electrodes
PENTODES > PENTODE
PENTOMIC *adj* denoting or relating to the subdivision of an army division into five battle groups, esp for nuclear warfare
PENTOSAN *n* polysaccharide occurring in plants, humus, etc
PENTOSANE *same as* > PENTOSAN
PENTOSANS > PENTOSAN
PENTOSE *n* monosaccharide containing five atoms of carbon per molecule
PENTOSES > PENTOSE
PENTOSIDE *n* compound containing sugar
PENTOXIDE *n* oxide of an element with five atoms of oxygen per molecule
PENTROOF *n* lean-to
PENTROOFS > PENTROOF
PENTS > PENT
PENTYL *n* one of a particular chemical group
PENTYLENE *n* type of chemical
PENTYLS > PENTYL
PENUCHE *same as* > PANOCHA
PENUCHES > PENUCHE
PENUCHI *same as* > PANOCHA
PENUCHIS > PENUCHI
PENUCHLE *same as* > PINOCHLE
PENUCHLES > PENUCHLE
PENUCKLE *same as* > PINOCHLE
PENUCKLES > PENUCKLE
PENULT *n* last syllable but one in a word
PENULTIMA *same as* > PENULT
PENULTS > PENULT
PENUMBRA *n* (in an eclipse) partially shadowed region which surrounds the full shadow
PENUMBRAE > PENUMBRA
PENUMBRAL > PENUMBRA
PENUMBRAS > PENUMBRA
PENURIES > PENURY
PENURIOUS *adj* niggardly with money
PENURY *n* extreme poverty
PENWIPER *n* something for cleaning the ink from a pen
PENWIPERS > PENWIPER

PENWOMAN *n* female writer
PENWOMEN > PENWOMAN
PEON *n* Spanish-American farm labourer or unskilled worker
PEONAGE *n* state of being a peon
PEONAGES > PEONAGE
PEONES > PEON
PEONIES > PEONY
PEONISM *same as* > PEONAGE
PEONISMS > PEONISM
PEONS > PEON
PEONY *n* garden plant
PEOPLE *pl n* persons generally ▷ *vb* provide with inhabitants
PEOPLED > PEOPLE
PEOPLER *n* settler
PEOPLERS > PEOPLER
PEOPLES > PEOPLE
PEOPLING > PEOPLE
PEP *n* high spirits, energy, or enthusiasm ▷ *vb* liven by imbuing with new vigour
PEPERINO *n* type of volcanic rock
PEPERINOS > PEPERINO
PEPEROMIA *n* plant from tropical and subtropical America with slightly fleshy ornamental leaves
PEPERONI *same as* > PEPPERONI
PEPERONIS > PEPPERONI
PEPFUL *adj* full of vitality
PEPINO *n* purple-striped yellow fruit
PEPINOS > PEPINO
PEPITA *n* edible dried seed of a squash
PEPITAS > PEPITA
PEPLA > PEPLUM
PEPLOS *n* part of a woman's attire in ancient Greece
PEPLOSES > PEPLOS
PEPLUM *same as* > PEPLOS
PEPLUMED > PEPLUM
PEPLUMS > PEPLUM
PEPLUS *same as* > PEPLOS
PEPLUSES > PEPLUS
PEPO *n* fruit such as the melon, squash, cucumber, or pumpkin
PEPONIDA *variant of* > PEPO
PEPONIDAS > PEPO
PEPONIUM *variant of* > PEPO
PEPONIUMS > PEPONIUM
PEPOS > PEPO
PEPPED > PEP
PEPPER *n* sharp hot condiment ▷ *vb* season with pepper
PEPPERBOX *n* container for pepper
PEPPERED > PEPPER
PEPPERER > PEPPER

PEPPERERS > PEPPER
PEPPERIER > PEPPERY
PEPPERING > PEPPER
PEPPERONI *n* dry sausage of pork and beef spiced with pepper
PEPPERS > PEPPER
PEPPERY *adj* tasting of pepper
PEPPIER > PEPPY
PEPPIEST > PEPPY
PEPPILY > PEPPY
PEPPINESS > PEPPY
PEPPING > PEP
PEPPY *adj* full of vitality
PEPS > PEP
PEPSI *n* (tradename) brand of soft drink
PEPSIN *n* enzyme produced in the stomach
PEPSINATE *vb* treat (a patient) with pepsin
PEPSINE *same as* > PEPSIN
PEPSINES > PEPSINE
PEPSINS > PEPSIN
PEPSIS > PEPSI
PEPTALK *n* talk meant to inspire ▷ *vb* give a peptalk to
PEPTALKED > PEPTALK
PEPTALKS > PEPTALK
PEPTIC *adj* relating to digestion or the digestive juices ▷ *n* substance that aids digestion
PEPTICITY > PEPTIC
PEPTICS > PEPTIC
PEPTID *variant of* > PEPTIDE
PEPTIDASE *n* any of a group of proteolytic enzymes that hydrolyse peptides to amino acids
PEPTIDE *n* organic chemical compound
PEPTIDES > PEPTIDE
PEPTIDIC *adj* of peptides
PEPTIDS > PEPTID
PEPTISE *same as* > PEPTIZE
PEPTISED > PEPTISE
PEPTISER > PEPTISE
PEPTISERS > PEPTISE
PEPTISES > PEPTISE
PEPTISING > PEPTISE
PEPTIZE *vb* disperse into a colloidal state
PEPTIZED > PEPTIZE
PEPTIZER > PEPTIZE
PEPTIZERS > PEPTIZE
PEPTIZES > PEPTIZE
PEPTIZING > PEPTIZE
PEPTONE *n* any of a group of organic compounds
PEPTONES > PEPTONE
PEPTONIC > PEPTONE
PEPTONISE *same as* > PEPTONIZE
PEPTONIZE *vb* hydrolyse (a protein) to peptones by enzymic action, esp by

pepsin or pancreatic extract
PEQUISTE *n* in Canada, member or supporter of the Parti Québécois
PEQUISTES > PEQUISTE
PER *prep* for each
PERACID *n* acid in which the element forming the acid radical exhibits its highest valency
PERACIDS > PERACID
PERACUTE *adj* very acute
PERAEA > PERAEON
PERAEON *same as* > PEREION
PERAEONS > PERAEON
PERAEOPOD *same as* > PEREIOPOD
PERAI *another name for* > PIRANHA
PERAIS > PERAI
PERBORATE *n* salt derived, or apparently derived, from perboric acid
PERC *n* perchloride
PERCALE *n* close-textured woven cotton fabric
PERCALES > PERCALE
PERCALINE *n* fine light cotton fabric, used esp for linings
PERCASE *adv* perchance
PERCE *obsolete word for* > PIERCE
PERCEABLE *adj* pierceable
PERCEANT *adj* piercing
PERCED > PERCE
PERCEIVE *vb* become aware of (something) through the senses
PERCEIVED > PERCEIVE
PERCEIVER > PERCEIVE
PERCEIVES > PERCEIVE
PERCEN > PERCE
PERCENT *n* percentage or proportion
PERCENTAL > PERCENT
PERCENTS > PERCENT
PERCEPT *n* concept that depends on recognition of some external object or phenomenon
PERCEPTS > PERCEPT
PERCES > PERCE
PERCH *n* resting place for a bird ▷ *vb* alight, rest, or place on or as if on a perch
PERCHANCE *adv* perhaps
PERCHED > PERCH
PERCHER > PERCH
PERCHERON *n* compact heavy breed of carthorse
PERCHERS > PERCH
PERCHERY *n* barn in which hens are allowed to move without restriction
PERCHES > PERCH
PERCHING > PERCH
PERCHINGS > PERCH
PERCID *n* type of freshwater fish
PERCIDS > PERCID

PERCIFORM *n* perch-like fish ▷ *adj* of perch-like fish

PERCINE *adj* of perches ▷ *n* type of perch-like fish

PERCINES > PERCINE

PERCING > PERCE

PERCOCT *adj* well-cooked ▷ *vb* cook thoroughly

PERCOCTED > PERCOCT

PERCOCTS > PERCOCT

PERCOID *n* type of spiny-finned teleost fish

PERCOIDS > PERCOID

PERCOLATE *vb* pass or filter through small holes ▷ *n* product of percolation

PERCOLIN *n* pain-relieving drug

PERCOLINS > PERCOLIN

PERCS > PERC

PERCUSS *vb* strike sharply, rapidly, or suddenly

PERCUSSED > PERCUSS

PERCUSSES > PERCUSS

PERCUSSOR > PERCUSS

PERDENDO *adj* (of music) getting gradually quieter and slower

PERDIE *adv* certainly

PERDITION *n* spiritual ruin

PERDU *adj* (of a soldier) placed on hazardous sentry duty ▷ *n* soldier placed on hazardous sentry duty

PERDUE *same as* > PERDU

PERDUES > PERDUE

PERDURE *vb* last for long time

PERDURED > PERDURE

PERDURES > PERDURE

PERDURING > PERDURE

PERDUS > PERDU

PERDY *adv* certainly

PERE *n* addition to a French surname to specify the father

PEREA > PEREON

PEREGAL *adj* equal ▷ *n* equal

PEREGALS > PEREGAL

PEREGRIN *variant spelling of* > PEREGRINE

PEREGRINE *adj* coming from abroad

PEREGRINS > PEREGRIN

PEREIA > PEREION

PEREION *n* thorax of some crustaceans

PEREIONS > PEREION

PEREIOPOD *n* appendage of the pereion

PEREIRA *n* bark of a South American apocynaceous tree

PEREIRAS > PEREIRA

PERENNATE *vb* (of plants) live from one growing season to another

PERENNIAL *adj* lasting through many years ▷ *n* plant lasting more than two years

PERENNITY *n* state of being perennial

PERENTIE *n* large dark-coloured Australian monitor lizard

PERENTIES > PERENTY

PERENTY *same as* > PERENTIE

PEREON *same as* > PEREION

PEREONS > PEREON

PEREOPOD *same as* > PEREIOPOD

PEREOPODS > PEREOPOD

PERES > PERE

PERFAY *interj* by my faith

PERFECT *adj* having all the essential elements ▷ *n* perfect tense ▷ *vb* improve

PERFECTA *n* bet on the order of the first and second in a race

PERFECTAS > PERFECTA

PERFECTED > PERFECT

PERFECTER *same as* > PERFECTOR

PERFECTI *n* ascetic group of elite Cathars

PERFECTLY *adv* completely, utterly, or absolutely

PERFECTO *n* large cigar that is tapered from both ends

PERFECTOR *n* person who completes or makes something perfect

PERFECTOS > PERFECTO

PERFECTS > PERFECT

PERFERVID *adj* extremely ardent, enthusiastic, or zealous

PERFERVOR *n* zealous person

PERFET *obsolete variant of* > PERFECT

PERFIDIES > PERFIDY

PERFIDY *n* perfidious act

PERFIN *former name for* > SPIF

PERFING *n* practice of taking early retirement from the police force

PERFINGS > PERFING

PERFINS > PERFIN

PERFORANS *adj* perforating or penetrating

PERFORANT *adj* perforating

PERFORATE *vb* make holes in ▷ *adj* pierced by small holes

PERFORCE *adv* of necessity

PERFORM *vb* carry out (an action)

PERFORMED > PERFORM

PERFORMER > PERFORM

PERFORMS > PERFORM

PERFUME *n* liquid cosmetic worn for its pleasant smell ▷ *vb* give a pleasant smell to

PERFUMED > PERFUME

PERFUMER *n* person who makes or sells perfume

PERFUMERS > PERFUMER

PERFUMERY *n* perfumes in general

PERFUMES > PERFUME

PERFUMIER *same as* > PERFUMER

PERFUMING > PERFUME

PERFUMY *adj* like perfume

PERFUSATE *n* fluid flowing through tissue or organ

PERFUSE *vb* permeate through or over

PERFUSED > PERFUSE

PERFUSES > PERFUSE

PERFUSING > PERFUSE

PERFUSION > PERFUSE

PERFUSIVE > PERFUSE

PERGOLA *n* framework of trellis supporting climbing plants

PERGOLAS > PERGOLA

PERGUNNAH *same as* > PARGANA

PERHAPS *adv* possibly, maybe ▷ *sentence substitute* it may happen, be so, etc ▷ *n* something that might have happened

PERHAPSES > PERHAPS

PERI *n* (in Persian folklore) one of a race of beautiful supernatural beings

PERIAGUA *n* dugout canoe

PERIAGUAS > PERIAGUA

PERIAKTOI > PERIAKTOS

PERIAKTOS *n* ancient device for changing theatre scenery

PERIANTH *n* outer part of a flower

PERIANTHS > PERIANTH

PERIAPSES > PERIAPSIS

PERIAPSIS *n* closest point to a central body reached by a body in orbit

PERIAPT *n* charm or amulet

PERIAPTS > PERIAPT

PERIBLAST *n* tissue surrounding blastoderm in meroblastic eggs

PERIBLEM *n* layer of meristematic tissue in stems and roots that gives rise to the cortex

PERIBLEMS > PERIBLEM

PERIBOLI > PERIBOLOS

PERIBOLOI > PERIBOLOS

PERIBOLOS *n* enclosed court surrounding ancient temple

PERIBOLUS *same as* > PERIBOLOS

PERICARP *n* part of a fruit enclosing the seed that develops from the wall of the ovary

PERICARPS > PERICARP

PERICLASE *n* mineral consisting of magnesium oxide in the form of isometric crystals or grains

PERICLINE *n* white translucent variety of albite in the form of elongated crystals

PERICON *n* Argentinian dance

PERICONES > PERICON

PERICOPAE > PERICOPE

PERICOPAL > PERICOPE

PERICOPE *n* selection from a book, esp a passage from the Bible read at religious services

PERICOPES > PERICOPE

PERICOPIC > PERICOPE

PERICYCLE *n* layer of plant tissue beneath the endodermis

PERIDERM *n* outer corky protective layer of woody stems and roots

PERIDERMS > PERIDERM

PERIDIA > PERIDIUM

PERIDIAL > PERIDIUM

PERIDINIA *n* genus of flagellate organisms

PERIDIUM *n* distinct outer layer of the spore-bearing organ in many fungi

PERIDIUMS > PERIDIUM

PERIDOT *n* pale green transparent gemstone

PERIDOTE *same as* > PERIDOT

PERIDOTES > PERIDOTE

PERIDOTIC > PERIDOT

PERIDOTS > PERIDOT

PERIDROME *n* space between the columns and inner room of a classical temple

PERIGEAL > PERIGEE

PERIGEAN > PERIGEE

PERIGEE *n* point in the orbit of the moon or a satellite that is nearest the earth

PERIGEES > PERIGEE

PERIGON *n* angle of 360°

PERIGONE *n* part enclosing the essential organs of a flower

PERIGONES > PERIGONE

PERIGONIA *n* perigones

PERIGONS > PERIGON

PERIGYNY *n* (of a flower) condition of having a concave or flat receptacle with the gynoecium and other floral parts at the same level

PERIHELIA *n* points in the orbits of planets at which they are nearest the sun

PERIKARYA *n* parts of nerve cells that contain the nuclei
PERIL *n* great danger ▷ *vb* expose to danger
PERILED > PERIL
PERILING > PERIL
PERILLA *n* type of mint
PERILLAS > PERILLA
PERILLED > PERIL
PERILLING > PERIL
PERILOUS *adj* very hazardous or dangerous
PERILS > PERIL
PERILUNE *n* point in a lunar orbit when a spacecraft launched from the moon is nearest the moon
PERILUNES > PERILUNE
PERILYMPH *n* fluid filling the space between the membranous and bony labyrinths of the internal ear
PERIMETER *n* outer edge of an area
PERIMETRY > PERIMETER
PERIMORPH *n* mineral that encloses another mineral of a different type
PERIMYSIA *n* sheaths of fibrous connective tissue surrounding the primary bundles of muscle fibres
PERINAEUM *same as* > PERINEUM
PERINATAL *adj* of or in the weeks shortly before or after birth
PERINEA > PERINEUM
PERINEAL > PERINEUM
PERINEUM *n* region of the body between the anus and the genitals
PERINEUMS > PERINEUM
PERIOD *n* particular portion of time ▷ *adj* (of furniture, dress, a play, etc) dating from or in the style of an earlier time ▷ *vb* divide into periods
PERIODATE *n* any salt or ester of a periodic acid
PERIODED > PERIOD
PERIODIC *adj* recurring at intervals
PERIODID *n* kind of iodide
PERIODIDE *variant of* > PERIODID
PERIODIDS > PERIODID
PERIODING > PERIOD
PERIODISE *same as* > PERIODIZE
PERIODIZE *vb* divide (a portion of time) into periods
PERIODS > PERIOD
PERIOST *n* thick fibrous two-layered membrane covering the surface of bones
PERIOSTEA > PERIOSTS

PERIOSTS > PERIOST
PERIOTIC *adj* of or relating to the structures situated around the internal ear ▷ *n* periotic bone
PERIOTICS > PERIOTIC
PERIPATUS *n* wormlike arthropod with a segmented body and short unjointed limbs
PERIPETIA *n* abrupt turn of events or reversal of circumstances
PERIPETY *n* an abrupt turn of events or reversal of circumstances
PERIPHERY *n* boundary or edge
PERIPLASM *n* region inside wall of biological cell
PERIPLAST *n* nutritive and supporting tissue in animal organ
PERIPLUS *n* circumnavigation
PERIPROCT *n* tough membrane surrounding anus in echinoderms
PERIPTER *n* type of ancient temple
PERIPTERS > PERIPTER
PERIPTERY *n* region surrounding moving body
PERIQUE *n* strong highly-flavoured tobacco
PERIQUES > PERIQUE
PERIS > PERI
PERISARC *n* outer chitinous layer secreted by colonial hydrozoan coelenterates
PERISARCS > PERISARC
PERISCIAN *adj* person whose shadow moves round every point of compass during day
PERISCOPE *n* instrument used, esp in submarines, to give a view of objects on a different level
PERISH *vb* be destroyed or die
PERISHED *adj* (of a person, part of the body, etc) extremely cold
PERISHER *n* mischievous person
PERISHERS > PERISHER
PERISHES > PERISH
PERISHING *adj* very cold
PERISPERM *n* nutritive tissue surrounding the embryo in certain seeds, and developing from the nucellus of the ovule
PERISTOME *n* fringe of pointed teeth surrounding the opening of a moss capsule
PERISTYLE *n* colonnade that surrounds a court or building
PERITI > PERITUS

PERITONEA *n* thin translucent serous sacs that line the walls of abdominal cavities and cover the viscera
PERITRACK *another name for* > TAXIWAY
PERITRICH *n* ciliate protozoan in which the cilia are restricted to a spiral around the mouth
PERITUS *n* Catholic theology consultant
PERIWIG *same as* > PERUKE
PERIWIGS > PERIWIG
PERJINK *adj* prim or finicky
PERJURE *vb* render (oneself) guilty of perjury
PERJURED *adj* having sworn falsely
PERJURER > PERJURE
PERJURERS > PERJURE
PERJURES > PERJURE
PERJURIES > PERJURY
PERJURING > PERJURE
PERJUROUS > PERJURY
PERJURY *n* act or crime of lying while under oath in a court
PERK *n* incidental benefit gained from a job, such as a company car ▷ *adj* pert ▷ *vb* (of coffee) percolate
PERKED > PERK
PERKIER > PERKY
PERKIEST > PERKY
PERKILY > PERKY
PERKIN *same as* > PARKIN
PERKINESS > PERKY
PERKING > PERK
PERKINS > PERKIN
PERKISH *adj* perky
PERKS > PERK
PERKY *adj* lively or cheerful
PERLEMOEN *n* edible sea creature with a shell lined with mother of pearl
PERLITE *n* variety of obsidian
PERLITES > PERLITE
PERLITIC > PERLITE
PERLOUS *same as* > PERILOUS
PERM *n* long-lasting curly hairstyle ▷ *vb* give (hair) a perm
PERMABEAR *n* an investor who consistently acts in the expectation that the value of stocks and shares will fall
PERMABULL *n* an investor who consistently acts in the expectation that the value of stocks and shares will rise
PERMALINK *n* permanent internet hyperlink
PERMALLOY *n* any of various alloys containing iron and nickel

PERMANENT *adj* lasting forever
PERMATAN *n* permanent tan, esp artificial
PERMATANS > PERMATAN
PERMEABLE *adj* able to be permeated, esp by liquid
PERMEABLY > PERMEABLE
PERMEANCE *n* act of permeating
PERMEANT > PERMEANCE
PERMEANTS > PERMEANCE
PERMEASE *n* carrier protein
PERMEASES > PERMEASE
PERMEATE *vb* pervade or pass through the whole of (something)
PERMEATED > PERMEATE
PERMEATES > PERMEATE
PERMEATOR > PERMEATE
PERMED > PERM
PERMIAN *adj* of, denoting, or formed in the last period of the Palaeozoic era
PERMIE *n* person, esp an office worker, employed by a firm on a permanent basis
PERMIES > PERMIE
PERMING > PERM
PERMIT *vb* give permission, allow ▷ *n* document giving permission to do something
PERMITS > PERMIT
PERMITTED > PERMIT
PERMITTEE *n* person given a permit
PERMITTER > PERMIT
PERMS > PERM
PERMUTATE *vb* alter the sequence or arrangement (of)
PERMUTE *vb* change the sequence of
PERMUTED > PERMUTE
PERMUTES > PERMUTE
PERMUTING > PERMUTE
PERN *n* type of buzzard ▷ *vb* spin
PERNANCY *n* receiving of rents
PERNED > PERN
PERNING > PERN
PERNIO *n* chilblain
PERNIONES > PERNIO
PERNOD *n* aniseed-flavoured aperitif from France
PERNODS > PERNOD
PERNS > PERN
PEROG *same as* > PIROG
PEROGI *n* type of Polish dumpling
PEROGIE *same as* > PEROGI
PEROGIES > PEROGI
PEROGIS > PEROGI
PEROGS > PEROG
PEROGY *same as* > PEROGI

PERONE *n* fibula

PERONEAL *adj* of or relating to the fibula or the outer side of the leg

PERONES > PERONE

PERONEUS *n* lateral muscle of the leg

PERORAL *adj* administered through mouth

PERORALLY > PERORAL

PERORATE *vb* speak at length, esp in a formal manner

PERORATED > PERORATE

PERORATES > PERORATE

PERORATOR > PERORATE

PEROVSKIA *n* Russian sage

PEROXID *variant of* > PEROXIDE

PEROXIDE *n* hydrogen peroxide used as a hair bleach ▷ *adj* bleached with or resembling peroxide ▷ *vb* bleach (the hair) with peroxide

PEROXIDED > PEROXIDE

PEROXIDES > PEROXIDE

PEROXIDIC > PEROXIDE

PEROXIDS > PEROXID

PEROXO *n* type of acid

PEROXY *adj* containing the peroxide group

PERP *n* someone who has committed a crime

PERPEND *n* large stone that passes through a wall from one side to the other ▷ *vb* ponder

PERPENDED > PERPEND

PERPENDS > PERPEND

PERPENT *same as* > PERPEND

PERPENTS > PERPENT

PERPETUAL *adj* lasting forever ▷ *n* (of a crop plant) continually producing edible parts

PERPLEX *vb* puzzle, bewilder

PERPLEXED > PERPLEX

PERPLEXER > PERPLEX

PERPLEXES > PERPLEX

PERPS > PERP

PERRADIAL *adj* situated around radii of radiate

PERRADII > PERRADIUS

PERRADIUS *n* primary tentacle of a polyp

PERRIER *n* short mortar

PERRIERS > PERRIER

PERRIES > PERRY

PERRON *n* external flight of steps

PERRONS > PERRON

PERRUQUE *old spelling of* > PERUKE

PERRUQUES > PERRUQUE

PERRY *n* alcoholic drink made from fermented pears

PERSALT *n* any salt of a peracid

PERSALTS > PERSALT

PERSANT *adj* piercing

PERSAUNT *adj* piercing

PERSE *old variant of* > PIERCE

PERSECUTE *vb* treat cruelly because of race, religion, etc

PERSEITY *n* quality of having substance independently of real objects

PERSELINE *same as* > PURSLANE

PERSES > PERSE

PERSEVERE *vb* keep making an effort despite difficulties

PERSICO *same as* > PERSICOT

PERSICOS > PERSICO

PERSICOT *n* cordial made from apricots

PERSICOTS > PERSICOT

PERSIENNE *n* printed calico

PERSIMMON *n* sweet red tropical fruit

PERSING > PERSE

PERSIST *vb* continue to be or happen, last

PERSISTED > PERSIST

PERSISTER > PERSIST

PERSISTS > PERSIST

PERSON *n* human being

PERSONA *n* someone's personality as presented to others

PERSONAE > PERSONA

PERSONAGE *n* important person

PERSONAL *adj* individual or private ▷ *n* item of movable property

PERSONALS > PERSONAL

PERSONAS > PERSONA

PERSONATE *vb* assume the identity of (another person) with intent to deceive ▷ *adj* (of the corollas of certain flowers) having two lips in the form of a face

PERSONIFY *vb* give human characteristics to

PERSONISE *same as* > PERSONIZE

PERSONIZE *vb* personify

PERSONNED *adj* manned

PERSONNEL *n* people employed in an organization

PERSONS > PERSON

PERSPEX *n* any of various clear acrylic resins

PERSPEXES > PERSPEX

PERSPIRE *vb* sweat

PERSPIRED > PERSPIRE

PERSPIRES > PERSPIRE

PERSPIRY *adj* perspiring

PERST *adj* perished

PERSUADE *vb* make (someone) do something by argument, charm, etc

PERSUADED > PERSUADE

PERSUADER > PERSUADE

PERSUADES > PERSUADE

PERSUE *obsolete form of* > PURSUE

PERSUED > PERSUE

PERSUES > PERSUE

PERSUING > PERSUE

PERSWADE *obsolete form of* > PERSUADE

PERSWADED > PERSWADE

PERSWADES > PERSWADE

PERT *adj* saucy and cheeky ▷ *n* pert person

PERTAIN *vb* belong or be relevant (to)

PERTAINED > PERTAIN

PERTAINS > PERTAIN

PERTAKE *obsolete form of* > PARTAKE

PERTAKEN > PERTAKE

PERTAKES > PERTAKE

PERTAKING > PERTAKE

PERTER > PERT

PERTEST > PERT

PERTHITE *n* type of feldspar

PERTHITES > PERTHITE

PERTHITIC > PERTHITE

PERTINENT *adj* relevant

PERTLY > PERT

PERTNESS > PERT

PERTOOK > PERTAKE

PERTS > PERT

PERTURB *vb* disturb greatly

PERTURBED > PERTURB

PERTURBER > PERTURB

PERTURBS > PERTURB

PERTUSATE *adj* pierced at apex

PERTUSE *adj* having holes

PERTUSED *adj* having holes

PERTUSION *n* punched hole

PERTUSSAL > PERTUSSIS

PERTUSSES > PERTUSSIS

PERTUSSIS *n* whooping cough

PERUKE *n* wig for men worn in the 17th and 18th centuries

PERUKED *adj* wearing wig

PERUKES > PERUKE

PERUSABLE > PERUSE

PERUSAL > PERUSE

PERUSALS > PERUSE

PERUSE *vb* read in a careful or leisurely manner

PERUSED > PERUSE

PERUSER > PERUSE

PERUSERS > PERUSE

PERUSES > PERUSE

PERUSING > PERUSE

PERV *n* pervert ▷ *vb* give a person an erotic look

PERVADE *vb* spread right through (something)

PERVADED > PERVADE

PERVADER > PERVADE

PERVADERS > PERVADE

PERVADES > PERVADE

PERVADING > PERVADE

PERVASION > PERVADE

PERVASIVE *adj* pervading or tending to pervade

PERVE *same as* > PERV

PERVED > PERV

PERVERSE *adj* deliberately doing something different from what is thought normal or proper

PERVERSER > PERVERSE

PERVERT *vb* use or alter for a wrong purpose ▷ *n* person who practises sexual perversion

PERVERTED *adj* deviating greatly from what is regarded as normal or right

PERVERTER > PERVERT

PERVERTS > PERVERT

PERVES > PERV

PERVIATE *vb* perforate or burrow

PERVIATED > PERVIATE

PERVIATES > PERVIATE

PERVICACY *n* obstinacy

PERVIER > PERVY

PERVIEST > PERVY

PERVING > PERV

PERVIOUS *adj* able to be penetrated, permeable

PERVO *n* pervert

PERVOS > PERVO

PERVS > PERV

PERVY *adj* perverted

PES *n* animal part corresponding to the foot

PESADE *n* position in which the horse stands on the hind legs with the forelegs in the air

PESADES > PESADE

PESANT *obsolete spelling of* > PEASANT

PESANTE *adv* to be performed clumsily

PESANTS > PESANT

PESAUNT *obsolete spelling of* > PEASANT

PESAUNTS > PESAUNT

PESETA *n* former monetary unit of Spain

PESETAS > PESETA

PESEWA *n* Ghanaian monetary unit

PESEWAS > PESEWA

PESHWA *same as* > PEISHWA

PESHWAS > PESHWA

PESKIER > PESKY

PESKIEST > PESKY

PESKILY > PESKY

PESKINESS > PESKY

PESKY *adj* troublesome

PESO *n* monetary unit of Argentina, Mexico, etc

PESOS > PESO

PESSARIES > PESSARY

PESSARY n appliance worn in the vagina
PESSIMA n lowest point
PESSIMAL adj (of animal's environment) least favourable for survival
PESSIMISM n tendency to expect the worst in all things
PESSIMIST > PESSIMISM
PESSIMUM same as > PESSIMAL
PEST n annoying person
PESTER vb annoy or nag continually
PESTERED > PESTER
PESTERER > PESTER
PESTERERS > PESTER
PESTERING > PESTER
PESTEROUS adj inclined to annoy
PESTERS > PESTER
PESTFUL adj causing annoyance
PESTHOLE n breeding ground for disease
PESTHOLES > PESTHOLE
PESTHOUSE n hospital for treating persons with infectious diseases
PESTICIDE n chemical for killing insect pests
PESTIER > PESTY
PESTIEST > PESTY
PESTILENT adj annoying, troublesome
PESTLE n club-shaped implement for grinding ▷ vb pound with or as if with a pestle
PESTLED > PESTLE
PESTLES > PESTLE
PESTLING > PESTLE
PESTO n sauce for pasta
PESTOLOGY n study of pests
PESTOS > PESTO
PESTS > PEST
PESTY adj persistently annoying
PET n animal kept for pleasure and companionship ▷ adj kept as a pet ▷ vb treat as a pet
PETABYTE n in computing, 10^{15} or 2^{50} bytes
PETABYTES > PETABYTE
PETAFLOP n (in computing) unit of processing speed
PETAFLOPS > PETAFLOP
PETAHERTZ n very large unit of electrical frequency
PETAL n one of the brightly coloured outer parts of a flower
PETALED > PETAL
PETALINE > PETAL
PETALISM n ostracism in ancient Syracuse
PETALISMS > PETALISM
PETALLED > PETAL
PETALLIKE adj like a petal

PETALODIC > PETALODY
PETALODY n condition in certain plants in which stamens or other parts of the flower assume the form and function of petals
PETALOID adj resembling a petal, esp in shape
PETALOUS adj bearing or having petals
PETALS > PETAL
PETANQUE n game, popular in France, in which metal bowls are thrown to land as near as possible to a target ball
PETANQUES > PETANQUE
PETAR obsolete variant of > PETARD
PETARA n clothes basket
PETARAS > PETARA
PETARD n device containing explosives
PETARDS > PETARD
PETARIES > PETARY
PETARS > PETAR
PETARY n weapon for hurling stones
PETASOS same as > PETASUS
PETASOSES > PETASOS
PETASUS n broad-brimmed hat worn by the ancient Greeks
PETASUSES > PETASUS
PETAURINE adj similar to a flying phalanger ▷ n a flying phalanger
PETAURIST n flying phalanger
PETCHARY n type of kingbird
PETCOCK n small valve
PETCOCKS > PETCOCK
PETECHIA n minute discoloured spot on the surface of the skin or mucous membrane, caused by an underlying ruptured blood vessel
PETECHIAE > PETECHIA
PETECHIAL > PETECHIA
PETER vb fall (off) in volume, intensity, etc, and finally cease ▷ n act of petering
PETERED > PETER
PETERING > PETER
PETERMAN n burglar skilled in safe-breaking
PETERMEN > PETERMAN
PETERS > PETER
PETERSHAM n thick corded ribbon used to stiffen belts, button bands, etc
PETHER old variant of > PEDLAR
PETHERS > PETHER
PETHIDINE n white crystalline water-soluble drug used to relieve pain
PETILLANT adj (of wine) slightly effervescent

PETIOLAR > PETIOLE
PETIOLATE adj (of a plant or leaf) having a leafstalk
PETIOLE n stalk which attaches a leaf to a plant
PETIOLED > PETIOLE
PETIOLES > PETIOLE
PETIOLULE n stalk of any of the leaflets making up a compound leaf
PETIT adj of little or lesser importance
PETITE adj (of a woman) small and dainty ▷ n clothing size for small women
PETITES > PETITE
PETITION n formal request, esp one signed by many people and presented to parliament ▷ vb present a petition to
PETITIONS > PETITION
PETITORY adj soliciting
PETNAP vb steal pet
PETNAPER > PETNAP
PETNAPERS > PETNAP
PETNAPING > PETNAP
PETNAPPED > PETNAP
PETNAPPER > PETNAP
PETNAPS > PETNAP
PETRALE n type of sole
PETRALES > PETRALE
PETRARIES > PETRARY
PETRARY n weapon for hurling stones
PETRE same as > SALTPETRE
PETREL n sea bird with a hooked bill and tubular nostrils
PETRELS > PETREL
PETRES > PETRE
PETRI n as in petri dish shallow glass dish used for cultures of bacteria
PETRICHOR n sweet smell caused by rain falling on parched earth
PETRIFIC adj petrifying
PETRIFIED > PETRIFY
PETRIFIER > PETRIFY
PETRIFIES > PETRIFY
PETRIFY vb frighten severely
PETROGENY n origin of rocks
PETROGRAM n prehistoric rock painting
PETROL n flammable liquid obtained from petroleum ▷ vb supply with petrol
PETROLAGE n addition of petrol (to a body of water) to get rid of mosquitoes
PETROLEUM n thick dark oil found underground
PETROLEUR n person using petrol to cause explosions
PETROLIC adj of, relating to, containing, or obtained from petroleum

PETROLLED > PETROL
PETROLOGY n study of the composition, origin, structure, and formation of rocks
PETROLS > PETROL
PETRONEL n firearm of large calibre used in the 16th and early 17th centuries, esp by cavalry soldiers
PETRONELS > PETRONEL
PETROSAL adj of, relating to, or situated near the dense part of the temporal bone that surrounds the inner ear ▷ n petrosal bone
PETROSALS > PETROSAL
PETROUS adj denoting the dense part of the temporal bone around the inner ear
PETS > PET
PETSAI n Chinese cabbage
PETSAIS > PETSAI
PETTABLE > PET
PETTED > PET
PETTEDLY > PET
PETTER > PET
PETTERS > PET
PETTI > PETTO
PETTICOAT n woman's skirt-shaped undergarment
PETTIER > PETTY
PETTIES > PETTI
PETTIEST > PETTY
PETTIFOG vb quibble or fuss over details
PETTIFOGS > PETTIFOG
PETTILY > PETTY
PETTINESS > PETTY
PETTING > PET
PETTINGS > PET
PETTISH adj peevish or fretful
PETTISHLY > PETTISH
PETTITOES pl n pig's trotters, esp when used as food
PETTLE vb pat animal
PETTLED > PETTLE
PETTLES > PETTLE
PETTLING > PETTLE
PETTO n breast of animal
PETTY adj unimportant, trivial
PETULANCE > PETULANT
PETULANCY > PETULANT
PETULANT adj childishly irritable or peevish
PETUNIA n garden plant with funnel-shaped flowers
PETUNIAS > PETUNIA
PETUNTSE n fusible feldspathic mineral used in hard-paste porcelain
PETUNTSES > PETUNTSE
PETUNTZE same as > PETUNTSE
PETUNTZES > PETUNTZE

PEW n fixed benchlike seat in a church
PEWEE n small N American flycatcher
PEWEES > PEWEE
PEWHOLDER n renter of pew
PEWIT another name for > LAPWING
PEWITS > PEWIT
PEWS > PEW
PEWTER n greyish metal made of tin and lead
PEWTERER > PEWTER
PEWTERERS > PEWTER
PEWTERS > PEWTER
PEWTERY adj of or like pewter
PEYOTE another name for > MESCAL
PEYOTES > PEYOTE
PEYOTISM n ritual use of peyote
PEYOTISMS > PEYOTISM
PEYOTIST n person who uses peyote
PEYOTISTS > PEYOTIST
PEYOTL same as > PEYOTE
PEYOTLS > PEYOTL
PEYSE vb weight or poise
PEYSED > PEYSE
PEYSES > PEYSE
PEYSING > PEYSE
PEYTRAL same as > PEYTREL
PEYTRALS > PEYTRAL
PEYTREL n breastplate of horse's armour
PEYTRELS > PEYTREL
PEZANT obsolete spelling of > PEASANT
PEZANTS > PEZANT
PEZIZOID adj having cup-like form
PFENNIG n former German monetary unit
PFENNIGE > PFENNIG
PFENNIGS > PFENNIG
PFENNING old variant of > PFENNIG
PFENNINGS > PFENNING
PFFT interj sound indicating sudden disappearance of something
PFUI interj phooey
PHABLET n type of handheld personal computer
PHABLETS > PHABLET
PHACELIA n plant grown for its large, deep blue bell flowers
PHACELIAS > PHACELIA
PHACOID adj lentil- or lens-shaped
PHACOIDAL same as > PHACOID
PHACOLITE n colourless variety of chabazite
PHACOLITH n lens-shaped igneous rock structure
PHAEIC adj (of animals) having dusky coloration

PHAEISM > PHAEIC
PHAEISMS > PHAEIC
PHAENOGAM n seed-bearing plant
PHAETON n light four-wheeled horse-drawn carriage
PHAETONS > PHAETON
PHAGE n parasitic virus that destroys its host
PHAGEDENA n rapidly spreading ulcer that destroys tissues as it increases in size
PHAGES > PHAGE
PHAGOCYTE n cell or protozoan that engulfs particles, such as microorganisms
PHAGOSOME n part of biological cell
PHALANGAL > PHALANGE
PHALANGE another name for > PHALANX
PHALANGER same as > POSSUM
PHALANGES > PHALANX
PHALANGID n type of arachnid
PHALANX n closely grouped mass of people
PHALANXES > PHALANX
PHALAROPE n aquatic shore bird of northern oceans and lakes
PHALLI > PHALLUS
PHALLIC adj of or resembling a phallus
PHALLIN n poisonous substance from mushroom
PHALLINS > PHALLIN
PHALLISM n worship or veneration of the phallus
PHALLISMS > PHALLISM
PHALLIST n worshipper or venerator of the phallus
PHALLISTS > PHALLIST
PHALLOID adj resembling penis
PHALLUS n penis, esp as a symbol of reproductive power
PHALLUSES > PHALLUS
PHANG old variant spelling of > FANG
PHANGED > PHANG
PHANGING > PHANG
PHANGS > PHANG
PHANSIGAR n Indian assassin
PHANTASIM same as > PHANTASM
PHANTASM n unreal vision, illusion
PHANTASMA same as > PHANTASM
PHANTASMS > PHANTASM
PHANTAST same as > FANTAST
PHANTASTS > PHANTAST
PHANTASY same as > FANTASY

PHANTOM n ghost ▷ adj deceptive or unreal
PHANTOMS > PHANTOM
PHANTOMY adj of phantoms
PHANTOSME old spelling of > PHANTASM
PHARAOH n ancient Egyptian king
PHARAOHS > PHARAOH
PHARAONIC adj of or relating to the Pharaohs
PHARE n beacon tower
PHARES > PHARE
PHARISAIC n righteously hypocritical
PHARISEE n self-righteous or hypocritical person
PHARISEES > PHARISEE
PHARM vb redirect (a website user) to another, bogus website
PHARMA n pharmaceutical companies considered together as an industry
PHARMACY n preparation and dispensing of drugs and medicines
PHARMAS > PHARMA
PHARMED > PHARM
PHARMER n person who pharms
PHARMERS > PHARMER
PHARMING n practice of rearing or growing genetically-modified animals or plants in order to develop pharmaceutical products
PHARMINGS > PHARMING
PHARMS > PHARM
PHAROS n lighthouse
PHAROSES > PHAROS
PHARYNGAL adj of, relating to, or situated in or near the pharynx
PHARYNGES > PHARYNX
PHARYNX n cavity forming the back part of the mouth
PHARYNXES > PHARYNX
PHASE n distinct or characteristic stage in a development or chain of events ▷ vb arrange or carry out in stages
PHASEAL > PHASE
PHASED > PHASE
PHASEDOWN n gradual reduction
PHASELESS > PHASE
PHASEOLIN n anti-fungal substance from kidney bean
PHASEOUT n gradual reduction
PHASEOUTS > PHASEOUT
PHASER n type of science-fiction weapon
PHASERS > PHASER
PHASES > PHASE
PHASIC > PHASE
PHASING n effect achieved by varying the

phase relationship of two similar audio signals
PHASINGS > PHASING
PHASIS another word for > PHASE
PHASMID n stick insect or leaf insect
PHASMIDS > PHASMID
PHASOR n rotating vector representing a quantity that varies sinusoidally
PHASORS > PHASOR
PHAT adj terrific
PHATIC adj (of speech) used to express sociability rather than specific meaning
PHATTER > PHAT
PHATTEST > PHAT
PHEASANT n game bird with bright plumage
PHEASANTS > PHEASANT
PHEAZAR old variant of > VIZIER
PHEAZARS > PHEAZAR
PHEER same as > FERE
PHEERE same as > FERE
PHEERES > PHEERE
PHEERS > PHEER
PHEESE vb worry
PHEESED > PHEESE
PHEESES > PHEESE
PHEESING > PHEESE
PHEEZE same as > PHEESE
PHEEZED > PHEEZE
PHEEZES > PHEEZE
PHEEZING > PHEEZE
PHELLEM technical name for > CORK
PHELLEMS > PHELLEM
PHELLOGEN n cork cambium
PHELLOID adj like cork
PHELONIA > PHELONION
PHELONION n vestment for an Orthodox priest
PHENACITE n colourless or white glassy mineral
PHENAKISM n deception
PHENAKITE same as > PHENACITE
PHENATE n ester or salt of phenol
PHENATES > PHENATE
PHENAZIN same as > PHENAZINE
PHENAZINE n yellow crystalline tricyclic compound
PHENAZINS > PHENAZIN
PHENE n genetically determined characteristic of organism
PHENES > PHENE
PHENETIC > PHENETICS
PHENETICS n system of classification based on similarities between organisms without regard to their evolutionary relationships
PHENETOL same as > PHENETOLE

PHENETOLE n colourless oily compound
PHENETOLS > PHENETOL
PHENGITE n type of alabaster
PHENGITES > PHENGITE
PHENIC adj of phenol
PHENIX same as **>** PHOENIX
PHENIXES > PHENIX
PHENOCOPY n noninheritable change in an organism that is caused by environmental influence during development but resembles the effects of a genetic mutation
PHENOGAM same as **>** PHAENOGAM
PHENOGAMS > PHENOGAM
PHENOL n chemical used in disinfectants and antiseptics
PHENOLATE vb treat or disinfect with phenol
PHENOLIC adj of, containing, or derived from phenol **▷** n derivative of phenol
PHENOLICS > PHENOLIC
PHENOLOGY n study of recurring phenomena, such as animal migration, esp as influenced by climatic conditions
PHENOLS > PHENOL
PHENOM n person or thing of outstanding abilities
PHENOME n full complement of phenotypical traits of an organism, species, etc
PHENOMENA n phenomenons
PHENOMES > PHENOME
PHENOMS > PHENOM
PHENOTYPE n physical form of an organism as determined by the interaction of its genetic make-up and its environment
PHENOXIDE n any of a class of salts of phenol
PHENOXY modifier as in phenoxy resin any of a class of resins derived from polyhydroxy ethers
PHENYL n chemical substance
PHENYLENE n compound derived from benzene
PHENYLIC > PHENYL
PHENYLS > PHENYL
PHENYTOIN n anticonvulsant drug
PHEON n barbed iron head of dart
PHEONS > PHEON
PHERESES > PHERESIS
PHERESIS n specialized form of blood donation

PHEROMONE n chemical substance, secreted externally by certain animals, such as insects, affecting the behaviour or physiology of other animals of the same species
PHESE same as **>** PHEESE
PHESED > PHESE
PHESES > PHESE
PHESING > PHESE
PHEW interj exclamation of relief, surprise, etc
PHI n 21st letter in the Greek alphabet
PHIAL n small bottle for medicine etc **▷** vb put in phial
PHIALLED > PHIAL
PHIALLING > PHIAL
PHIALS > PHIAL
PHILABEG same as **>** FILIBEG
PHILABEGS > PHILABEG
PHILAMOT variant of **>** FILEMOT
PHILAMOTS > PHILAMOT
PHILANDER vb (of a man) flirt or have many casual love affairs with women
PHILATELY n stamp collecting
PHILAVERY n collection of rare and obscure words
PHILHORSE n last horse in a team
PHILIBEG variant spelling of **>** FILIBEG
PHILIBEGS > PHILIBEG
PHILIPPIC n bitter or impassioned speech of denunciation, invective
PHILISTIA n domain of cultural philistine
PHILLABEG same as **>** FILIBEG
PHILLIBEG same as **>** FILIBEG
PHILOGYNY n fondness for women
PHILOLOGY n science of the structure and development of languages
PHILOMATH n lover of learning
PHILOMEL n nightingale
PHILOMELA same as **>** PHILOMEL
PHILOMELS > PHILOMEL
PHILOMOT n colour of dead leaf
PHILOMOTS > PHILOMOT
PHILOPENA n gift made as forfeit in game
PHILTER vb drink supposed to arouse love, desire, etc **▷** vb arouse sexual or romantic feelings by means of a philter
PHILTERED > PHILTER
PHILTERS > PHILTER
PHILTRA > PHILTRUM

PHILTRE n magic drink supposed to arouse love in the person who drinks it **▷** vb mix with love potion
PHILTRED > PHILTRE
PHILTRES > PHILTRE
PHILTRING > PHILTRE
PHILTRUM n indentation above the upper lip
PHIMOSES > PHIMOSIS
PHIMOSIS n abnormal tightness of the foreskin, preventing its being retracted over the tip of the penis
PHIMOTIC > PHIMOSIS
PHINNOCK variant spelling of **>** FINNOCK
PHINNOCKS > PHINNOCK
PHIS > PHI
PHISH vb engage in phishing
PHISHED > PHISH
PHISHER n person who phishes
PHISHERS > PHISHER
PHISHES > PHISH
PHISHING n use of fraudulent e-mails and lookalike websites to extract personal and financial details for criminal purposes
PHISHINGS > PHISHING
PHISNOMY n physiognomy
PHIZ n face or a facial expression
PHIZES > PHIZ
PHIZOG same as **>** PHIZ
PHIZOGS > PHIZOG
PHIZZ n face
PHIZZES > PHIZ
PHLEBITIC > PHLEBITIS
PHLEBITIS n inflammation of a vein
PHLEGM n thick yellowish substance formed in the nose and throat during a cold
PHLEGMIER > PHLEGM
PHLEGMON n inflammatory mass that may progress to abscess
PHLEGMONS > PHLEGMON
PHLEGMS > PHLEGM
PHLEGMY > PHLEGM
PHLOEM n plant tissue that acts as a path for the distribution of food
PHLOEMS > PHLOEM
PHLOMIS n plant of Phlomis genus
PHLOMISES > PHLOMIS
PHLORIZIN n chemical found in root bark of fruit trees
PHLOX n flowering garden plant
PHLOXES > PHLOX
PHLYCTENA n small blister, vesicle, or pustule

PHO n Vietnamese noodle soup
PHOBIA n intense and unreasoning fear or dislike
PHOBIAS > PHOBIA
PHOBIC adj of, relating to, or arising from a phobia **▷** n person suffering from a phobia
PHOBICS > PHOBIC
PHOBISM n phobia
PHOBISMS > PHOBISM
PHOBIST > PHOBISM
PHOBISTS > PHOBISM
PHOCA n genus of seals
PHOCAE > PHOCA
PHOCAS > PHOCA
PHOCINE adj of, relating to, or resembling a seal
PHOCOMELY n congenital deformity resulting from prenatal interference with the development of the fetal limbs, characterized esp by short stubby hands or feet attached close to the body
PHOEBE n greyish-brown North American flycatcher
PHOEBES > PHOEBE
PHOEBUS n sun
PHOEBUSES > PHOEBUS
PHOENIX n legendary bird said to set fire to itself and rise anew from its ashes
PHOENIXES > PHOENIX
PHOH variant of **>** FOH
PHOLADES > PHOLAS
PHOLAS n type of bivalve mollusc
PHON n unit of loudness
PHONAL adj relating to voice
PHONATE vb articulate speech sounds
PHONATED > PHONATE
PHONATES > PHONATE
PHONATHON n telephone-based fund-raising campaign
PHONATING > PHONATE
PHONATION > PHONATE
PHONATORY > PHONATE
PHONE vb telephone **▷** n single uncomplicated speech sound
PHONECAM n digital camera incorporated in a mobile phone
PHONECAMS > PHONECAM
PHONECARD n card used to operate certain public telephones
PHONED > PHONE
PHONEME n one of the set of speech sounds in a language
PHONEMES > PHONEME
PHONEMIC adj of or relating to the phoneme
PHONEMICS n classification and analysis of the phonemes of a language

P

PHONER n person making a telephone call
PHONERS > PHONER
PHONES > PHONE
PHONETIC adj of speech sounds
PHONETICS n science of speech sounds
PHONETISE same as > PHONETIZE
PHONETISM n phonetic writing
PHONETIST n person who advocates or uses a system of phonetic spelling
PHONETIZE vb represent by phonetic signs
PHONEY adj not genuine ▷ n phoney person or thing ▷ vb fake
PHONEYED > PHONEY
PHONEYING > PHONEY
PHONEYS > PHONEY
PHONIC > PHONICS
PHONICS n method of teaching people to read
PHONIED > PHONY
PHONIER > PHONY
PHONIES > PHONY
PHONIEST > PHONY
PHONILY > PHONY
PHONINESS > PHONY
PHONING > PHONE
PHONMETER n instrument measuring sound levels
PHONO n phonograph
PHONOGRAM n any written symbol standing for a sound, syllable, morpheme, or word
PHONOLITE n fine-grained volcanic igneous rock consisting of alkaline feldspars and nepheline
PHONOLOGY n study of the speech sounds in a language
PHONON n quantum of vibrational energy
PHONONS > PHONON
PHONOPORE n device for conveying sound
PHONOS > PHONO
PHONOTYPE n letter or symbol representing a sound
PHONOTYPY n transcription of speech into phonetic symbols
PHONS > PHON
PHONY vb fake
PHONYING > PHONY
PHOOEY interj exclamation of scorn or contempt
PHORATE n type of insecticide
PHORATES > PHORATE
PHORESIES > PHORESY
PHORESY n association in which one animal clings to another to ensure movement from place to place

PHORETIC adj relating to phoresy
PHORMINX n ancient Greek stringed instrument
PHORMIUM n New Zealand plant with leathery evergreen leaves and red or yellow flowers in panicles
PHORMIUMS > PHORMIUM
PHORONID n small wormlike marine animal
PHORONIDS > PHORONID
PHOS > PHO
PHOSGENE n poisonous gas used in warfare
PHOSGENES > PHOSGENE
PHOSPHATE n compound of phosphorus
PHOSPHENE n sensation of light caused by pressure on the eyelid of a closed eye or by other mechanical or electrical interference with the visual system
PHOSPHID same as > PHOSPHIDE
PHOSPHIDE n any compound of phosphorus with another element, esp a more electropositive element
PHOSPHIDS > PHOSPHID
PHOSPHIN same as > PHOSPHINE
PHOSPHINE n colourless flammable gas that is slightly soluble in water and has a strong fishy odour
PHOSPHINS > PHOSPHIN
PHOSPHITE n any salt or ester of phosphorous acid
PHOSPHOR n substance capable of emitting light when irradiated with particles of electromagnetic radiation
PHOSPHORE same as > PHOSPHOR
PHOSPHORI n plural of phosphorus
PHOSPHORS > PHOSPHOR
PHOSSY adj as in phossy jaw gangrenous condition of the lower jawbone
PHOT n unit of illumination
PHOTIC adj of or concerned with light
PHOTICS n science of light
PHOTINIA n genus of garden plants
PHOTINIAS > PHOTINIA
PHOTINO n hypothetical elementary particle
PHOTINOS > PHOTINO
PHOTISM n sensation of light or colour caused by stimulus of another sense
PHOTISMS > PHOTISM
PHOTO n photograph ▷ vb take a photograph of
PHOTOBLOG n blog in which the main content

consists of photographs ▷ vb keep a photoblog
PHOTOBOMB vb intrude into the background of a photograph without the subject's knowledge
PHOTOCALL n occasion when people have their photograph taken together
PHOTOCARD n identity card containing a photograph of the bearer
PHOTOCELL n cell which produces a current or voltage when exposed to light or other electromagnetic radiation
PHOTOCOPY n photographic reproduction ▷ vb make a photocopy of
PHOTODISK n computer disk that contains photographs
PHOTOED > PHOTO
PHOTOFIT n method of combining photographs of facial features, hair, etc, into a composite picture of a face
PHOTOFITS > PHOTOFIT
PHOTOG n photograph
PHOTOGEN same as > PHOTOGENE
PHOTOGENE n afterimage
PHOTOGENS > PHOTOGEN
PHOTOGENY n photography
PHOTOGRAM n picture, usually abstract, produced on a photographic material without the use of a camera, as by placing an object on the material and exposing to light
PHOTOGS > PHOTOG
PHOTOING > PHOTO
PHOTOLYSE vb cause to undergo photolysis
PHOTOLYZE same as > PHOTOLYZE
PHOTOMAP n map constructed by adding grid lines, place names, etc, to one or more aerial photographs ▷ vb map (an area) using aerial photography
PHOTOMAPS > PHOTOMAP
PHOTOMASK n material on which etching pattern for integrated circuit is drawn
PHOTON n quantum of electromagnetic radiation energy
PHOTONIC > PHOTON
PHOTONICS n study and design of devices and systems, such as optical fibres, that depend on the transmission, modulation, or amplification of streams of photons
PHOTONS > PHOTON

PHOTOPHIL n light-seeking organism
PHOTOPIA n normal adaptation of the eye to light
PHOTOPIAS > PHOTOPIA
PHOTOPIC > PHOTOPIA
PHOTOPLAY n play filmed as movie
PHOTOPSIA n appearance of flashes due to retinal irritation
PHOTOPSY same as > PHOTOPSIA
PHOTOS > PHOTO
PHOTOSCAN n photographic scan
PHOTOSET vb set (type matter) by photosetting
PHOTOSETS > PHOTOSET
PHOTOSHOP vb edit or alter a picture digitally, usu with Adobe Photoshop
PHOTOSTAT n copy made by photocopying machine ▷ vb make a photostat copy (of)
PHOTOTAXY n movement of an entire organism in response to light
PHOTOTUBE n type of photocell in which radiation falling on a photocathode causes electrons to flow to an anode and thus produce an electric current
PHOTOTYPE n printing plate produced by photography ▷ vb reproduce (an illustration) using a phototype
PHOTOTYPY n process of producing phototypes
PHOTS > PHOT
PHPHT interj expressing irritation or reluctance
PHRASAL adj of, relating to, or composed of phrases
PHRASALLY > PHRASAL
PHRASE n group of words forming a unit of meaning, esp within a sentence ▷ vb express in words
PHRASED > PHRASE
PHRASEMAN n coiner of phrases
PHRASEMEN > PHRASEMAN
PHRASER > PHRASE
PHRASERS > PHRASE
PHRASES > PHRASE
PHRASIER > PHRASY
PHRASIEST > PHRASY
PHRASING n exact words used to say or write something
PHRASINGS > PHRASING
PHRASY adj containing phrases
PHRATRAL > PHRATRY
PHRATRIC > PHRATRY

PHRATRIES > PHRATRY

PHRATRY *n* group of people within a tribe who have a common ancestor

PHREAK *vb* hack into a telecommunications system

PHREAKED > PHREAK

PHREAKER > PHREAK

PHREAKERS > PHREAK

PHREAKING > PHREAK

PHREAKS > PHREAK

PHREATIC *adj* of or relating to ground water occurring below the water table

PHRENESES > PHRENESIS

PHRENESIS *n* mental confusion

PHRENETIC *obsolete spelling of* > FRENETIC

PHRENIC *adj* of or relating to the diaphragm ▷ *n* (a nerve, blood vessel, etc) located in the diaphragm

PHRENICS > PHRENIC

PHRENISM *n* belief in non-physical life force

PHRENISMS > PHRENISM

PHRENITIC > PHRENITIS

PHRENITIS *n* state of frenzy

PHRENSIED > PHRENSY

PHRENSIES > PHRENSY

PHRENSY *obsolete spelling of* > FRENZY

PHRENTICK *obsolete spelling of* > PHRENETIC

PHRYGANA *another name for* > GARIGUE

PHRYGANAS > PHRYGANA

PHT *same as* > PHPHT

PHTHALATE *n* salt or ester of phthalic acid

PHTHALEIN *n* any of a class of organic compounds obtained by the reaction of phthalic anhydride with a phenol and used in dyes

PHTHALIC *adj* as in *phthalic anhydride* white crystalline substance used mainly in producing dyestuffs

PHTHALIN *n* colourless compound formed by reduction of phthalein

PHTHALINS > PHTHALIN

PHTHISES > PHTHISIS

PHTHISIC *adj* relating to or affected with phthisis ▷ *n* person suffering from phthisis

PHTHISICS > PHTHISIC

PHTHISIS *n* any disease that causes wasting of the body, esp pulmonary tuberculosis

PHUT *vb* make muffled explosive sound

PHUTS > PHUT

PHUTTED > PHUT

PHUTTING > PHUT

PHWOAH *same as* > PHWOAR

PHWOAR *interj* expression of sexual interest or attraction

PHYCOCYAN *n* type of protein found in some algae

PHYCOLOGY *n* study of algae

PHYLA > PHYLUM

PHYLACTIC *adj* defending or protecting against disease

PHYLAE > PHYLE

PHYLAR > PHYLUM

PHYLARCH *n* chief of tribe

PHYLARCHS > PHYLARCH

PHYLARCHY > PHYLARCH

PHYLAXIS *n* protection against infection

PHYLE *n* tribe or clan of an ancient Greek people

PHYLESES > PHYLESIS

PHYLESIS *n* evolutionary events that modify taxon without causing speciation

PHYLETIC *adj* of or relating to the evolution of a species or group of organisms

PHYLETICS *n* study of the evolution of species

PHYLIC > PHYLE

PHYLLARY *n* bract subtending flower head of composite plant

PHYLLID *n* leaf of a liverwort or moss

PHYLLIDS > PHYLLID

PHYLLITE *n* compact lustrous metamorphic rock, rich in mica, derived from a shale or other clay-rich rock

PHYLLITES > PHYLLITE

PHYLLITIC > PHYLLITE

PHYLLO *variant of* > FILO

PHYLLODE *n* flattened leafstalk that resembles and functions as a leaf

PHYLLODES > PHYLLODE

PHYLLODIA > PHYLLODE

PHYLLODY *n* abnormal development of leaves from parts of flower

PHYLLOID *adj* resembling a leaf ▷ *n* leaf-like organ

PHYLLOIDS > PHYLLOID

PHYLLOME *n* leaf or a leaflike organ

PHYLLOMES > PHYLLOME

PHYLLOMIC > PHYLLOME

PHYLLOPOD *n* crustacean with leaf-like appendages

PHYLLOS > PHYLLO

PHYLOGENY *n* sequence of events involved in the evolution of a species, genus, etc

PHYLON *n* tribe

PHYLUM *n* major taxonomic division of animals and plants

PHYSALIA *n* Portuguese man-of-war

PHYSALIAS > PHYSALIA

PHYSALIS *n* strawberry tomato

PHYSED *n* physical education

PHYSEDS > PHYSED

PHYSES > PHYSIS

PHYSETER *n* creature such as the sperm whale

PHYSETERS > PHYSETER

PHYSIATRY *n* treatment of injury by physical means

PHYSIC *n* medicine or drug, esp a cathartic or purge ▷ *vb* treat (a patient) with medicine

PHYSICAL *adj* of the body, as contrasted with the mind or spirit

PHYSICALS *pl n* commodities that can be purchased and used, as opposed to those bought and sold in a futures market

PHYSICIAN *n* doctor of medicine

PHYSICISM *n* belief in the physical as opposed to the spiritual

PHYSICIST *n* person skilled in or studying physics

PHYSICKED > PHYSIC

PHYSICKY > PHYSIC

PHYSICS *n* science of the properties of matter and energy

PHYSIO *n* physiotherapy

PHYSIOS > PHYSIO

PHYSIQUE *n* person's bodily build and muscular development

PHYSIQUED *adj* having particular physique

PHYSIQUES > PHYSIQUE

PHYSIS *n* part of bone responsible for lengthening

PHYTANE *n* hydrocarbon found in fossilised plant remains

PHYTANES > PHYTANE

PHYTIN *n* substance from plants used as an energy supplement

PHYTINS > PHYTIN

PHYTOGENY *n* branch of botany that is concerned with the detailed description of plants

PHYTOID *adj* resembling plant

PHYTOL *n* alcohol used to synthesize some vitamins

PHYTOLITH *n* microscopic particle in plants

PHYTOLOGY *rare name for* > BOTANY

PHYTOLS > PHYTOL

PHYTON *n* unit of plant structure

PHYTONIC > PHYTON

PHYTONS > PHYTON

PHYTOSES > PHYTOSIS

PHYTOSIS *n* disease caused by vegetable parasite

PHYTOTOMY *n* dissection of plants

PHYTOTRON *n* building in which plants can be grown on a large scale, under controlled conditions

PI *n* sixteenth letter in the Greek alphabet ▷ *vb* spill and mix (set type) indiscriminately

PIA *n* innermost of the three membranes that cover the brain and the spinal cord

PIACEVOLE *adv* to be performed in playful manner

PIACULAR *adj* making expiation for a sacrilege

PIAFFE *n* passage done on the spot ▷ *vb* strut on the spot

PIAFFED > PIAFFE

PIAFFER > PIAFFE

PIAFFERS > PIAFFE

PIAFFES > PIAFFE

PIAFFING > PIAFFE

PIAL *adj* relating to pia mater

PIAN *n* contagious tropical skin disease

PIANETTE *n* small piano

PIANETTES > PIANETTE

PIANI > PIANO

PIANIC *adj* of piano

PIANINO *n* small upright piano

PIANINOS > PIANINO

PIANISM *n* technique, skill, or artistry in playing the piano

PIANISMS > PIANISM

PIANIST *n* person who plays the piano

PIANISTE *variant of* > PIANIST

PIANISTES > PIANISTE

PIANISTIC > PIANISM

PIANISTS > PIANIST

PIANO *n* musical instrument with strings which are struck by hammers worked by a keyboard ▷ *adv* quietly

PIANOLA *n* type of player piano

PIANOLAS > PIANOLA

PIANOLIST *n* person who plays the Pianola

PIANOS > PIANO

PIANS > PIAN

PIARIST *n* member of a Roman religious order

PIARISTS > PIARIST
PIAS > PIA
PIASABA same as > PTASSAVA
PIASABAS > PIASABA
PIASAVA same as > PIASSAVA
PIASAVAS > PIASAVA
PIASSABA same as > PIASSAVA
PIASSABAS > PIASSABA
PIASSAVA n South American palm tree
PIASSAVAS > PIASSAVA
PIASTER same as > PIASTRE
PIASTERS > PIASTER
PIASTRE n standard monetary unit of South Vietnam
PIASTRES > PIASTRE
PIAZZA n square or marketplace, esp in Italy
PIAZZAS > PIAZZA
PIAZZE > PIAZZA
PIAZZIAN > PIAZZA
PIBAL n method of measuring wind
PIBALS > PIBAL
PIBROCH n form of bagpipe music
PIBROCHS > PIBROCH
PIC n photograph or illustration
PICA n abnormal craving to ingest substances
PICACHO n pointed solitary mountain
PICACHOS > PICACHO
PICADILLO n Mexican dish
PICADOR n mounted bullfighter with a lance
PICADORES > PICADOR
PICADORS > PICADOR
PICAL adj relating to pica
PICAMAR n hydrocarbon extract of beechwood tar
PICAMARS > PICAMAR
PICANINNY n offensive term for a small Black or Aboriginal child
PICANTE adj spicy
PICARA n female adventurer
PICARAS > PICARA
PICARIAN n tree-haunting bird
PICARIANS > PICARIAN
PICARO n roguish adventurer
PICAROON n adventurer or rogue
PICAROONS > PICAROON
PICAROS > PICARO
PICAS > PICA
PICAYUNE adj of small value or importance ▷ n any coin of little value, such as a five-cent piece
PICAYUNES > PICAYUNE
PICCADILL n high stiff collar

PICCANIN n offensive word for a Black African child
PICCANINS > PICCANIN
PICCATA adj sautéed and served in a lemon sauce ▷ n dish of food sautéed and served in a lemon sauce
PICCATAS > PICCATA
PICCIES > PICCY
PICCOLO n small flute
PICCOLOS > PICCOLO
PICCY n picture or photograph
PICE n former Indian coin worth one sixty-fourth of a rupee
PICENE n type of hydrocarbon
PICENES > PICENE
PICEOUS adj of, relating to, or resembling pitch
PICHOLINE n variety of olive
PICHURIM n S American laurel tree
PICHURIMS > PICHURIM
PICIFORM adj relating to certain tree-haunting birds
PICINE adj relating to woodpeckers
PICK vb choose ▷ n choice
PICKABACK same as > PIGGYBACK
PICKABLE > PICK
PICKADIL same as > PICCADILL
PICKADILL same as > PICCADILL
PICKADILS > PICKADIL
PICKAPACK same as > PICKABACK
PICKAROON same as > PICAROON
PICKAX same as > PICKAXE
PICKAXE n large pick ▷ vb use a pickaxe on (earth, rocks, etc)
PICKAXED > PICKAXE
PICKAXES > PICKAXE
PICKAXING > PICKAXE
PICKBACK vb carry by piggyback
PICKBACKS > PICKBACK
PICKED > PICK
PICKEER vb make raid for booty
PICKEERED > PICKEER
PICKEERER > PICKEER
PICKEERS > PICKEER
PICKER n person or thing that picks
PICKEREL n North American freshwater game fish
PICKERELS > PICKEREL
PICKERIES > PICKERY
PICKERS > PICKER
PICKERY n petty theft
PICKET n person or group standing outside a

workplace during a strike ▷ vb form a picket outside (a workplace)
PICKETED > PICKET
PICKETER > PICKET
PICKETERS > PICKET
PICKETING > PICKET
PICKETS > PICKET
PICKIER > PICKY
PICKIEST > PICKY
PICKILY > PICKY
PICKIN n small child
PICKINESS > PICKY
PICKING > PICK
PICKINGS pl n money easily acquired
PICKINS > PICKIN
PICKLE n food preserved in vinegar or salt water ▷ vb preserve in vinegar or salt water
PICKLED adj (of food) preserved
PICKLER > PICKLE
PICKLERS > PICKLE
PICKLES > PICKLE
PICKLING > PICKLE
PICKLOCK n person who picks locks, esp one who gains unlawful access to premises by this means
PICKLOCKS > PICKLOCK
PICKMAW n type of gull
PICKMAWS > PICKMAW
PICKNEY n (in Jamaica) child
PICKNEYS > PICKNEY
PICKOFF n baseball play
PICKOFFS > PICKOFF
PICKPROOF adj (of a lock) unable to be picked
PICKS > PICK
PICKTHANK n flatterer
PICKUP n small truck with an open body and low sides
PICKUPS > PICKUP
PICKWICK n tool for raising the short wick of an oil lamp
PICKWICKS > PICKWICK
PICKY adj fussy
PICLORAM n type of herbicide
PICLORAMS > PICLORAM
PICNIC n informal meal out of doors ▷ vb have a picnic
PICNICKED > PICNIC
PICNICKER > PICNIC
PICNICKY > PICNIC
PICNICS > PICNIC
PICOCURIE n unit of radioactivity
PICOFARAD n unit of capacitance
PICOGRAM n trillionth of gram
PICOGRAMS > PICOGRAM
PICOLIN variant of > PICOLINE
PICOLINE n liquid derivative of pyridine

found in bone oil and coal tar
PICOLINES > PICOLINE
PICOLINIC > PICOLINE
PICOLINS > PICOLIN
PICOMETER same as > PICOMETRE
PICOMETRE n trillionth fraction of metre
PICOMOLE n trillionth of a mole
PICOMOLES > PICOMOLE
PICONG n any teasing or satirical banter
PICONGS > PICONG
PICOT n any of pattern of small loops, as on lace ▷ vb decorate material with small loops
PICOTE adj (of material) picoted
PICOTED > PICOT
PICOTEE n type of carnation
PICOTEES > PICOTEE
PICOTING > PICOT
PICOTITE n dark-brown mineral
PICOTITES > PICOTITE
PICOTS > PICOT
PICOWAVE vb treat food with gamma waves
PICOWAVED > PICOWAVE
PICOWAVES > PICOWAVE
PICQUET vb provide early warning of attack
PICQUETED > PICQUET
PICQUETS > PICQUET
PICRA n powder of aloes and canella
PICRAS > PICRA
PICRATE n any salt or ester of picric acid
PICRATED adj containing picrate
PICRATES > PICRATE
PICRIC adj as in picric acid toxic sparingly soluble crystalline yellow acid
PICRITE n coarse-grained ultrabasic igneous rock
PICRITES > PICRITE
PICRITIC > PICRITE
PICS > PIC
PICTARNIE Scots word for > TERN
PICTOGRAM n picture or symbol standing for a word or group of words, as in written Chinese
PICTORIAL adj of or in painting or pictures ▷ n newspaper etc with many pictures
PICTURAL n picture
PICTURALS > PICTURAL
PICTURE n drawing or painting ▷ vb visualize, imagine
PICTURED > PICTURE
PICTURES > PICTURE
PICTURING > PICTURE

PICTURISE *same as*
> PICTURIZE
PICTURIZE *vb* adorn
with pictures
PICUL *n* unit of weight,
used in China, Japan, and
SE Asia
PICULET *n* small tropical
woodpecker with a short
tail
PICULETS > PICULET
PICULS > PICUL
PIDDLE *vb* urinate
PIDDLED > PIDDLE
PIDDLER > PIDDLE
PIDDLERS > PIDDLE
PIDDLES > PIDDLE
PIDDLIER > PIDDLY
PIDDLIEST > PIDDLY
PIDDLING *adj* small or
unimportant
PIDDLY *adj* trivial
PIDDOCK *n* marine bivalve
that bores into rock, clay,
or wood
PIDDOCKS > PIDDOCK
PIDGEON *variant of*
> PIDGIN
PIDGEONS > PIDGEON
PIDGIN *n* language made
up of elements of other
languages
PIDGINISE *same as*
> PIDGINIZE
PIDGINIZE *vb* create
pidgin language
PIDGINS > PIDGIN
PIE *n* dish of meat, fruit,
etc baked in pastry
PIEBALD *adj* (horse) with
irregular black-and-white
markings ▷ *n* black-and-
white horse
PIEBALDS > PIEBALD
PIECE *n* separate bit or
part
PIECED > PIECE
PIECELESS > PIECE
PIECEMEAL *adv* bit by bit
▷ *adj* fragmentary or
unsystematic
PIECEN *vb* join broken
threads
PIECENED > PIECEN
PIECENER > PIECEN
PIECENERS > PIECEN
PIECENING > PIECEN
PIECENS > PIECEN
PIECER *n* person who
mends, repairs, or joins
something
PIECERS > PIECER
PIECES > PIECE
PIECEWISE *adv* with
respect to number of
discrete pieces
PIECEWORK *n* work paid
for according to the
quantity produced
PIECING > PIECE
PIECINGS > PIECE
PIECRUST *n* pastry used
for making pies
PIECRUSTS > PIECRUST

PIED > PI
PIEDFORT *n* coin thicker
than normal
PIEDFORTS > PIEDFORT
PIEDISH *n* container for
baking pies
PIEDISHES > PIEDISH
PIEDMONT *adj* (of glaciers,
plains, etc) formed or
situated at the foot of a
mountain or mountain
range ▷ *n* gentle slope
leading from mountains to
flat land
PIEDMONTS > PIEDMONT
PIEDNESS *n* state of
being pied
PIEFORT *same as*
> PIEDFORT
PIEFORTS > PIEFORT
PIEHOLE *n* person's
mouth
PIEHOLES > PIEHOLE
PIEING *n* act of pushing a
pie into a person's face
PIEINGS > PIEING
PIEMAN *n* seller of pies
PIEMEN > PIEMAN
PIEND *n* salient angle
PIENDS > PIEND
PIEPLANT *n* rhubarb
PIEPLANTS > PIEPLANT
PIEPOWDER *n* former
court for dealing with
certain disputes
PIER *n* platform on stilts
sticking out into the sea
PIERAGE *n*
accommodation for ships
at piers
PIERAGES > PIERAGE
PIERCE *vb* make a hole in
or through with a sharp
instrument
PIERCED > PIERCE
PIERCER > PIERCE
PIERCERS > PIERCE
PIERCES > PIERCE
PIERCING *adj* (of a sound)
shrill and high-pitched
▷ *n* art or practice of
piercing body parts for the
insertion of jewellery
PIERCINGS > PIERCING
PIERHEAD *n* end of a pier
farthest from the shore
PIERHEADS > PIERHEAD
PIERID *n* type of butterfly
PIERIDINE *adj* relating
to the family Pieridae of
butterflies, that includes
the whites, brimstones,
and sulphurs
PIERIDS > PIERID
PIERIS *n* American or
Asiatic shrub
PIERISES > PIERIS
PIEROG *same as* > PIROG
PIEROGI *n* Polish
dumpling
PIEROGIES > PIEROGI
PIEROGS > PIEROG
PIERRETTE *n* female
pierrot

PIERROT *n* clown or
masquerader with a
whitened face
PIERROTS > PIERROT
PIERS > PIER
PIERST *archaic spelling of*
> PIERCED
PIERT *n* small plant with
small greenish flowers
PIERTS > PIERT
PIES > PIE
PIET *n* magpie
PIETA *n* sculpture,
painting, or drawing of the
dead Christ, supported by
the Virgin Mary
PIETAS > PIETA
PIETIES > PIETY
PIETISM *n* exaggerated
piety
PIETISMS > PIETISM
PIETIST > PIETISM
PIETISTIC > PIETISM
PIETISTS > PIETISM
PIETS > PIET
PIETY *n* deep devotion to
God and religion
PIEZO *adj* piezoelectric
PIFFERARI
> PIFFERARO
PIFFERARO *n* player of
piffero
PIFFERO *n* small rustic
flute
PIFFEROS > PIFFERO
PIFFLE *n* nonsense
▷ *vb* talk or behave feebly
PIFFLED > PIFFLE
PIFFLER *n* talker of
nonsense
PIFFLERS > PIFFLER
PIFFLES > PIFFLE
PIFFLING *adj* worthless
PIG *n* animal kept and
killed for pork, ham, and
bacon ▷ *vb* eat greedily
PIGBOAT *n* submarine
PIGBOATS > PIGBOAT
PIGEON *n* bird with a
heavy body and short legs
▷ *vb* pigeonhole
PIGEONED > PIGEON
PIGEONING > PIGEON
PIGEONITE *n* brownish
mineral
PIGEONRY *n* loft for
keeping pigeons
PIGEONS > PIGEON
PIGFACE *n* creeping
succulent plant
PIGFACES > PIGFACE
PIGFEED *n* food for pigs
PIGFEEDS > PIGFEED
PIGFISH *n* grunting fish
of the North American
Atlantic coast
PIGFISHES > PIGFISH
PIGGED > PIG
PIGGERIES > PIGGERY
PIGGERY *n* place for
keeping and breeding pigs
PIGGIE *same as* > PIGGY
PIGGIER > PIGGY

PIGGIES > PIGGY
PIGGIEST > PIGGY
PIGGIN *n* small wooden
bucket or tub
PIGGINESS > PIGGY
PIGGING > PIG
PIGGINGS > PIG
PIGGINS > PIGGIN
PIGGISH *adj* like a pig, esp
in appetite or manners
PIGGISHLY > PIGGISH
PIGGY *n* child's word for a
pig ▷ *adj* like a pig
PIGGYBACK *n* ride on
someone's shoulders ▷ *adv*
carried on someone's
shoulders ▷ *adj* on the
back and shoulders of
another person ▷ *vb* give
(a person) a piggyback on
one's back and shoulders
PIGHEADED *adj* stupidly
stubborn
PIGHT *vb* pierce
PIGHTED > PIGHT
PIGHTING > PIGHT
PIGHTLE *n* small
enclosure
PIGHTLES > PIGHTLE
PIGHTS > PIGHT
PIGLET *n* young pig
PIGLETS > PIGLET
PIGLIKE > PIG
PIGLING *n* young pig
PIGLINGS > PIGLING
PIGMAEAN *same as*
> PYGMAEAN
PIGMAN *n* male pig farmer
PIGMEAN *same as*
> PYGMAEAN
PIGMEAT *less common*
name for > PORK
PIGMEATS > PIGMEAT
PIGMEN > PIGMAN
PIGMENT *n* colouring
matter, paint or dye
▷ *vb* colour with pigment
PIGMENTAL > PIGMENT
PIGMENTED > PIGMENT
PIGMENTS > PIGMENT
PIGMIES > PIGMY
PIGMOID *adj* of pygmies
▷ *n* pigmy
PIGMOIDS > PIGMOID
PIGMY *same as* > PYGMY
PIGNERATE *vb* pledge or
pawn
PIGNOLI *same as*
> PIGNOLIA
PIGNOLIA *n* edible seed
of nut pine
PIGNOLIAS > PIGNOLIA
PIGNOLIS > PIGNOLI
PIGNORA > PIGNUS
PIGNORATE *same as*
> PIGNERATE
PIGNUS *n* pawn or pledge
PIGNUT *n* bitter nut of
hickory trees
PIGNUTS > PIGNUT
PIGOUT *n* binge
PIGOUTS > PIGOUT
PIGPEN *same as* > PIGSTY

p

PIGPENS > PIGPEN

PIGS > PIG

PIGSCONCE *n* foolish person

PIGSKIN *n* skin of the domestic pig ▷ *adj* made of pigskin

PIGSKINS > PIGSKIN

PIGSNEY same as **>** PIGSNY

PIGSNEYS > PIGSNEY

PIGSNIE same as **>** PIGSNY

PIGSNIES > PIGSNIE

PIGSNY *n* former pet name for girl

PIGSTICK *vb* (esp in India) hunt and spear wild boar, esp from horseback

PIGSTICKS > PIGSTICK

PIGSTIES > PIGSTY

PIGSTUCK > PIGSTICK

PIGSTY same as **>** PIGPEN

PIGSWILL *n* waste food or other edible matter fed to pigs

PIGSWILLS > PIGSWILL

PIGTAIL *n* plait of hair hanging from the back or either side of the head

PIGTAILED > PIGTAIL

PIGTAILS > PIGTAIL

PIGWASH *n* wet feed for pigs

PIGWASHES > PIGWASH

PIGWEED *n* coarse North American weed

PIGWEEDS > PIGWEED

PIHOIHOI *n* variety of New Zealand pipit

PIHOIHOIS > PIHOIHOI

PIING > PI

PIKA *n* burrowing mammal

PIKAKE *n* type of Asian vine

PIKAKES > PIKAKE

PIKAS > PIKA

PIKAU *n* pack, knapsack, or rucksack

PIKAUS > PIKAU

PIKE *n* large predatory freshwater fish ▷ *vb* stab or pierce using a pike ▷ *adj* (of the body position of a diver) bent at the hips but with the legs straight

PIKED > PIKE

PIKELET *n* small thick pancake

PIKELETS > PIKELET

PIKEMAN *n* (formerly) soldier armed with a pike

PIKEMEN > PIKEMAN

PIKEPERCH *n* pikelike freshwater teleost fish

PIKER *n* shirker

PIKERS > PIKER

PIKES > PIKE

PIKESTAFF *n* wooden handle of a pike

PIKEY *n* in British English, derogatory word for gypsy or vagrant

PIKEYS > PIKEY

PIKI *n* bread made from blue cornmeal

PIKING > PIKE

PIKINGS > PIKE

PIKIS > PIKI

PIKUL same as **>** PICUL

PIKULS > PIKUL

PILA *n* pillar-like anatomical structure

PILAE > PILA

PILAF same as **>** PILAU

PILAFF same as **>** PILAFF

PILAFFS > PILAFF

PILAFS > PILAF

PILAO same as **>** PILAU

PILAOS > PILAO

PILAR *adj* relating to hair

PILASTER *n* square column, usu set in a wall

PILASTERS > PILASTER

PILAU *n* Middle Eastern dish

PILAUS > PILAU

PILAW same as **>** PILAU

PILAWS > PILAW

PILCH *n* outer garment, originally one made of skin

PILCHARD *n* small edible sea fish of the herring family

PILCHARDS > PILCHARD

PILCHER *n* scabbard for sword

PILCHERS > PILCHER

PILCHES > PILCH

PILCORN *n* type if oat

PILCORNS > PILCORN

PILCROW *n* paragraph mark

PILCROWS > PILCROW

PILE *n* number of things lying on top of each other ▷ *vb* collect into a pile

PILEA *n* plant which releases a cloud of pollen when shaken

PILEAS > PILEA

PILEATE *adj* (of birds) having a crest

PILEATED same as **>** PILEATE

PILED > PILE

PILEI > PILEUS

PILELESS > PILE

PILEOUS *adj* hairy

PILER *n* placer of things on pile

PILERS > PILER

PILES *pl n* swollen veins in the rectum, haemorrhoids

PILEUM *n* top of a bird's head

PILEUP *n* multiple collision of vehicles

PILEUPS > PILEUP

PILEUS *n* upper cap-shaped part of a mushroom

PILEWORK *n* construction built from heavy stakes or cylinders

PILEWORKS > PILEWORK

PILEWORT *n* any of several plants, such as lesser celandine, thought to be effective in treating piles

PILEWORTS > PILEWORT

PILFER *vb* steal in small quantities

PILFERAGE *n* act or practice of stealing small quantities or articles

PILFERED > PILFER

PILFERER > PILFER

PILFERERS > PILFER

PILFERIES > PILFERY

PILFERING > PILFER

PILFERS > PILFER

PILFERY *n* theft

PILGARLIC *n* bald head or a man with a bald head

PILGRIM *n* person who journeys to a holy place ▷ *vb* travel as a pilgrim

PILGRIMED > PILGRIM

PILGRIMER *n* one who undertakes a pilgrimage

PILGRIMS > PILGRIM

PILI *n* Philippine tree with edible seeds resembling almonds

PILIFORM *adj* resembling a long hair

PILING *n* act of driving piles

PILINGS > PILING

PILINUT *n* type of nut found in the Philippines

PILINUTS > PILINUT

PILIS > PILI

PILL *n* small ball of medicine swallowed whole ▷ *vb* peel or skin (something)

PILLAGE *vb* steal property by violence in war ▷ *n* violent seizure of goods, esp in war

PILLAGED > PILLAGE

PILLAGER > PILLAGE

PILLAGERS > PILLAGE

PILLAGES > PILLAGE

PILLAGING *n* act of pillaging

PILLAR *n* upright post, usu supporting a roof ▷ *vb* provide or support with pillars

PILLARED > PILLAR

PILLARING > PILLAR

PILLARIST *n* recluse who sat on high pillar

PILLARS > PILLAR

PILLAU same as **>** PILAU

PILLAUS > PILLAU

PILLBOX *n* small box for pills

PILLBOXES > PILLBOX

PILLBUG *n* type of woodlouse

PILLBUGS > PILLBUG

PILLED > PILL

PILLHEAD *n* person addicted to pills

PILLHEADS > PILLHEAD

PILLICOCK *n* penis

PILLIE *n* pilchard

PILLIES > PILLIE

PILLING > PILL

PILLINGS > PILL

PILLION *n* seat for a passenger behind the rider of a motorcycle ▷ *adv* on a pillion ▷ *vb* ride pillion

PILLIONED > PILLION

PILLIONS > PILLION

PILLOCK *n* stupid or annoying person

PILLOCKS > PILLOCK

PILLORIED > PILLORY

PILLORIES > PILLORY

PILLORISE same as **>** PILLORIZE

PILLORIZE *vb* put in pillory

PILLORY *n* frame in which an offender was locked and exposed to public abuse ▷ *vb* ridicule publicly

PILLOW *n* stuffed cloth bag for supporting the head in bed ▷ *vb* rest as if on a pillow

PILLOWED > PILLOW

PILLOWING > PILLOW

PILLOWS > PILLOW

PILLOWY > PILLOW

PILLS > PILL

PILLWORM *n* worm that rolls up spirally

PILLWORMS > PILLWORM

PILLWORT *n* small Eurasian water fern

PILLWORTS > PILLWORT

PILOMOTOR *adj* causing movement of hairs

PILONIDAL *adj* of crease above buttocks

PILOSE *adj* covered with fine soft hairs

PILOSITY > PILOSE

PILOT *n* person qualified to fly an aircraft or spacecraft ▷ *adj* experimental and preliminary ▷ *vb* act as the pilot of

PILOTAGE *n* act of piloting an aircraft or ship

PILOTAGES > PILOTAGE

PILOTED > PILOT

PILOTFISH *n* fish that accompanies sharks

PILOTING *n* navigational handling of a ship near land using buoys, soundings, landmarks, etc, or the finding of a ship's position by such means

PILOTINGS > PILOTING

PILOTIS *pl n* posts raising a building up from the ground

PILOTLESS > PILOT

PILOTMAN *n* railway worker who directs trains through hazardous stretches of track

PILOTMEN > PILOTMAN
PILOTS > PILOT
PILOUS same as > PILOSE
PILOW same as > PILAU
PILOWS > PILOW
PILSENER same as > PILSNER
PILSENERS > PILSENER
PILSNER n type of pale beer with a strong flavour of hops
PILSNERS > PILSNER
PILULA n pill
PILULAE > PILULA
PILULAR > PILULE
PILULAS > PILULA
PILULE n small pill
PILULES > PILULE
PILUM n ancient Roman javelin
PILUS > PILI
PILY adj like wool or pile
PIMA n type of cotton
PIMAS > PIMA
PIMENT n wine flavoured with spices
PIMENTO same as > PIMIENTO
PIMENTON n smoked chilli powder
PIMENTONS > PIMENTON
PIMENTOS > PIMENTO
PIMENTS > PIMENT
PIMIENTO n Spanish pepper with a red fruit used as a vegetable
PIMIENTOS > PIMIENTO
PIMP n man who gets customers for a prostitute ▷ vb act as a pimp
PIMPED > PIMP
PIMPERNEL n wild plant with small star-shaped flowers
PIMPING > PIMP
PIMPINGS > PIMPING
PIMPLE n small pus-filled spot on the skin
PIMPLED > PIMPLE
PIMPLES > PIMPLE
PIMPLIER > PIMPLE
PIMPLIEST > PIMPLE
PIMPLY > PIMPLE
PIMPS > PIMP
PIN n short thin piece of stiff wire with a point and head, for fastening things ▷ vb fasten with a pin
PINA n cone of silver amalgam
PINACEOUS adj relating to a family of conifers with needle-like leaves which includes the pine, spruce, fir, larch, and cedar
PINACOID n pair of opposite parallel faces of crystal
PINACOIDS > PINACOID
PINAFORE n apron
PINAFORED > PINAFORE
PINAFORES > PINAFORE

PINAKOID same as > PINACOID
PINAKOIDS > PINAKOID
PINANG n areca tree
PINANGS > PINANG
PINAS > PINA
PINASTER n Mediterranean pine tree
PINASTERS > PINASTER
PINATA n papier-mâché party decoration filled with sweets
PINATAS > PINATA
PINBALL vb ricochet
PINBALLED > PINBALL
PINBALLS > PINBALL
PINBOARD n cork board for pinning notices, messages etc on
PINBOARDS > PINBOARD
PINBONE n part of sirloin
PINBONES > PINBONE
PINCASE n case for holding pins
PINCASES > PINCASE
PINCER vb grip with pincers
PINCERED > PINCER
PINCERING > PINCER
PINCERS pl n tool consisting of two hinged arms, for gripping
PINCH vb squeeze between finger and thumb ▷ n act of pinching
PINCHBECK n alloy of zinc and copper, used as imitation gold ▷ adj sham or cheap
PINCHBUG n type of crab
PINCHBUGS > PINCHBUG
PINCHCOCK n clamp used to compress a flexible tube to control the flow of fluid through it
PINCHECK n small check woven into fabric
PINCHECKS > PINCHECK
PINCHED > PINCH
PINCHER > PINCH
PINCHERS > PINCH
PINCHES > PINCH
PINCHFIST n mean person
PINCHGUT n miserly person
PINCHGUTS > PINCHGUT
PINCHING > PINCH
PINCHINGS > PINCH
PINCURL n curl secured by a hairpin
PINCURLS > PINCURL
PINDAN n desert region of Western Australia
PINDANS > PINDAN
PINDAREE same as > PINDARI
PINDAREES > PINDAREE
PINDARI n former irregular Indian horseman
PINDARIS > PINDARI
PINDER n person who impounds
PINDERS > PINDER

PINDLING adj peevish or fractious
PINDOWN n wrestling manoeuvre
PINDOWNS > PINDOWN
PINE n evergreen coniferous tree ▷ vb feel great longing (for)
PINEAL adj resembling a pine cone ▷ n pineal gland
PINEALS > PINEAL
PINEAPPLE n large tropical fruit with juicy yellow flesh and a hard skin
PINECONE n seed-producing structure of a pine tree
PINECONES > PINECONE
PINED > PINE
PINEDROPS n parasitic herb of pine trees
PINELAND n area covered with pine forest
PINELANDS > PINELAND
PINELIKE > PINE
PINENE n isomeric terpene found in many essential oils
PINENES > PINENE
PINERIES > PINERY
PINERY n place, esp a hothouse, where pineapples are grown
PINES > PINE
PINESAP n red herb of N America
PINESAPS > PINESAP
PINETA > PINETUM
PINETUM n area of land where pine trees are grown
PINEWOOD n wood of pine trees
PINEWOODS > PINEWOOD
PINEY > PINE
PINFALL another name for > FALL
PINFALLS > PINFALL
PINFISH n small porgy of the Atlantic
PINFISHES > PINFISH
PINFOLD n pound for stray cattle ▷ vb gather or confine in or as if in a pinfold
PINFOLDED > PINFOLD
PINFOLDS > PINFOLD
PING n short high-pitched sound ▷ vb make such a noise
PINGED > PING
PINGER n device, esp a timer, that makes a pinging sound
PINGERS > PINGER
PINGING > PING
PINGLE vb enclose small area of ground
PINGLED > PINGLE
PINGLER > PINGLE
PINGLERS > PINGLE
PINGLES > PINGLE
PINGLING > PINGLE

PINGO n mound of earth or gravel formed in Arctic regions
PINGOES > PINGO
PINGOS > PINGO
PINGPONG n Australian football
PINGPONGS > PINGPONG
PINGRASS n weed with fernlike leaves
PINGS > PING
PINGUEFY vb become greasy or fat
PINGUID adj fatty, oily, or greasy
PINGUIN same as > PENGUIN
PINGUINS > PINGUIN
PINHEAD n head of a pin
PINHEADED adj stupid or silly
PINHEADS > PINHEAD
PINHOLE n small hole made with or as if with a pin
PINHOLES > PINHOLE
PINHOOKER n trader of young thoroughbred horses
PINIER > PINY
PINIES > PINY
PINIEST > PINY
PINING > PINE
PINION n bird's wing ▷ vb immobilize (someone) by tying or holding his or her arms
PINIONED > PINION
PINIONING > PINION
PINIONS > PINION
PINITE n greyish-green or brown mineral
PINITES > PINITE
PINITOL n compound found in pinewood
PINITOLS > PINITOL
PINK n pale reddish colour ▷ adj of the colour pink ▷ vb (of an engine) make a metallic noise because not working properly
PINKED > PINK
PINKEN vb turn pink
PINKENED > PINKEN
PINKENING > PINKEN
PINKENS > PINKEN
PINKER n something that pinks
PINKERS > PINKER
PINKERTON n private detective
PINKEST > PINK
PINKEY n type of ship
PINKEYE n acute inflammation of the conjunctiva of the eye
PINKEYES > PINKEYE
PINKEYS > PINKEY
PINKIE n little finger
PINKIER > PINKY
PINKIES > PINKIE
PINKIEST > PINKY
PINKINESS n quality of being pink

PINKING > PINK
PINKINGS > PINK
PINKISH > PINK
PINKLY > PINK
PINKNESS > PINK
PINKO n person regarded as mildly left-wing
PINKOES > PINKO
PINKOS > PINKO
PINKROOT n plant with red-and-yellow flowers and pink roots
PINKROOTS > PINKROOT
PINKS > PINK
PINKY adj of a pink colour
PINLESS adj without a pin
PINNA n external part of the ear
PINNACE n ship's boat
PINNACES > PINNACE
PINNACLE n highest point of fame or success ▷ vb set on or as if on a pinnacle
PINNACLED > PINNACLE
PINNACLES > PINNACLE
PINNAE > PINNA
PINNAL > PINNA
PINNAS > PINNA
PINNATE adj (of compound leaves) having leaflets growing opposite each other in pairs
PINNATED same as > PINNATE
PINNATELY > PINNATE
PINNATION > PINNATE
PINNED > PIN
PINNER n person or thing that pins
PINNERS > PINNER
PINNET n pinnacle
PINNETS > PINNET
PINNIE same as > PINNY
PINNIES > PINNIE
PINNING > PIN
PINNINGS > PIN
PINNIPED n aquatic placental mammal such as the seal, sea lion, walrus, etc
PTNNIPEDE same as > PINNIPED
PINNIPEDS > PINNIPED
PINNOCK n small bird
PINNOCKS > PINNOCK
PINNOED adj held or bound by the arms
PINNULA same as > PINNULE
PINNULAE > PINNULA
PINNULAR > PINNULE
PINNULAS > PINNULA
PINNULATE > PINNULE
PINNULE n lobe of a leaflet of a pinnate compound leaf
PINNULES > PINNULE
PINNY informal or child's name for > PINAFORE
PINOCHLE n card game for two to four players similar to bezique

PINOCHLES > PINOCHLE
PINOCLE same as > PINOCHLE
PINOCLES > PINOCLE
PINOCYTIC adj of process of pinocytosis
PINOLE n flour made in the southwestern United States
PINOLES > PINOLE
PINON n low-growing pine
PINONES > PINON
PINONS > PINON
PINOT n any of several grape varieties
PINOTAGE n variety of red wine grape
PINOTAGES > PINOTAGE
PINOTS > PINOT
PINPOINT vb locate or identify exactly ▷ adj exact ▷ n insignificant or trifling thing
PINPOINTS > PINPOINT
PINPRICK n small irritation or annoyance ▷ vb puncture with or as if with a pin
PINPRICKS > PINPRICK
PINS > PIN
PINSCHER n breed of dog
PINSCHERS > PINSCHER
PINSETTER n device that sets pins in bowling alley
PINSPOT vb illuminate with a small spotlight
PINSPOTS > PINSPOT
PINSTRIPE n very narrow stripe in fabric
PINSWELL n small boil
PINSWELLS > PINSWELL
PINT n liquid measure, 1/8 gallon (.568 litre)
PINTA n pint of milk
PINTABLE n pinball machine
PINTABLES > PINTABLE
PINTADA same as > PINTADO
PINTADAS > PINTADA
PINTADERA n decorative stamp, usually made of clay, found in the Neolithic of the E Mediterranean and in many American cultures
PINTADO n species of seagoing petrel
PINTADOES > PINTADO
PINTADOS > PINTADO
PINTAIL n greyish-brown duck with a pointed tail
PINTAILED adj having tapered tail
PINTAILS > PINTAIL
PINTANO n tropical reef fish
PINTANOS > PINTANO
PINTAS > PINTA
PINTLE n pin or bolt forming the pivot of a hinge
PINTLES > PINTLE

PINTO adj marked with patches of white ▷ n pinto horse
PINTOES > PINTO
PINTOS > PINTO
PINTS > PINT
PINTSIZE same as > PINTSIZED
PINTSIZED adj very small
PINTUCK vb tuck with a narrow fold of fabric
PINTUCKED > PINTUCK
PINTUCKS > PINTUCK
PINUP n picture of a sexually attractive person
PINUPS > PINUP
PINWALE n fabric with narrow ridges
PINWALES > PINWALE
PINWEED n herb with tiny flowers
PINWEEDS > PINWEED
PINWHEEL n cogwheel whose teeth are formed by small pins projecting either axially or radially from the rim of the wheel
PINWHEELS > PINWHEEL
PINWORK n (in needlepoint lace) fine raised stitches
PINWORKS > PINWORK
PINWORM n parasitic nematode worm
PINWORMS > PINWORM
PINWRENCH n wrench with a projection to fit a hole
PINXIT vb (he or she) painted (it)
PINY variant of > PEONY
PINYIN n system of romanized spelling for the Chinese language
PINYINS > PINYIN
PINYON n low-growing pine
PINYONS > PINYON
PIOLET n type of ice axe
PIOLETS > PIOLET
PION n type of subatomic particle
PIONED adj abounding in marsh marigolds
PIONEER n explorer or early settler of a new country ▷ vb be the pioneer or leader of
PIONEERED > PIONEER
PIONEERS > PIONEER
PIONER obsolete spelling of > PIONEER
PIONERS > PIONER
PIONEY same as > PEONY
PIONEYS > PIONEY
PIONIC > PION
PIONIES > PIONY
PIONING n work of pioneers
PIONINGS > PIONING
PIONS > PION
PIONY same as > PEONY

PIOPIO n New Zealand thrush, thought to be extinct
PIOPIOS > PIOPIO
PIOSITIES > PIOSITY
PIOSITY n grandiose display of piety
PIOTED adj pied
PIOUS adj deeply religious, devout
PIOUSLY > PIOUS
PIOUSNESS > PIOUS
PIOY variant of > PEEOY
PIOYE variant of > PEEOY
PIOYES > PIOYE
PIOYS > PIOY
PIP n small seed in a fruit ▷ vb chirp
PIPA n tongueless S American toad
PIPAGE n pipes collectively
PIPAGES > PIPAGE
PIPAL same as > PEEPUL
PIPALS > PIPAL
PIPAS > PIPA
PIPE n tube for conveying liquid or gas ▷ vb play on a pipe
PIPEAGE same as > PIPAGE
PIPEAGES > PIPEAGE
PIPECLAY n fine white pure clay, used in tobacco pipes and pottery and to whiten leather and similar materials ▷ vb whiten with pipeclay
PIPECLAYS > PIPECLAY
PIPED > PIPE
PIPEFISH n teleost fish with a long tubelike snout and an elongated body covered with bony plates
PIPEFUL n as much tobacco, etc as will fill a pipe
PIPEFULS > PIPE
PIPELESS > PIPE
PIPELIKE > PIPE
PIPELINE n long pipe for transporting oil, water, etc
PIPELINED > PIPELINE
PIPELINES > PIPELINE
PIPER n player on a pipe or bagpipes
PIPERIC > PIPERINE
PIPERINE n crystalline insoluble alkaloid that is the active ingredient of pepper
PIPERINES > PIPERINE
PIPERONAL n white fragrant aldehyde used in flavourings, perfumery, and suntan lotions
PIPERS > PIPER
PIPES > PIPE
PIPESTEM n hollow stem of pipe
PIPESTEMS > PIPESTEM
PIPESTONE n variety of consolidated red clay used by American Indians to make tobacco pipes

PIPET same as
> PIPETTE

PIPETS > PIPET

PIPETTE n slender glass
tube used to transfer or
measure fluids ▷ vb
transfer or measure out
(a liquid) using a pipette

PIPETTED > PIPETTE

PIPETTES > PIPETTE

PIPETTING > PIPETTE

PIPEWORK n stops and
flues on pipe organ

PIPEWORKS > PIPEWORK

PIPEWORT n perennial
plant with a twisted
flower stalk and a
greenish-grey scaly flower
head

PIPEWORTS > PIPEWORT

PIPI n edible mollusc
often used as bait

PIPIER > PIPE

PIPIEST > PIPE

PIPINESS n material's
suitability for use as pipe

PIPING n system of pipes

PIPINGLY > PIPING

PIPINGS > PIPING

PIPIS > PIPI

PIPISTREL n species of
bat

PIPIT n small brownish
songbird

PIPITS > PIPIT

PIPKIN same as > PIGGIN

PIPKINS > PIPKIN

PIPLESS > PIP

PIPPED > PIP

PIPPIER > PIPPY

PIPPIEST > PIPPY

PIPPIN n type of eating
apple

PIPPING > PIP

PIPPINS > PIPPIN

PIPPY adj containing
many pips

PIPS > PIP

PIPSQUEAK n
insignificant or
contemptible person

PIPUL n Indian fig tree

PIPULS > PIPUL

PIPY > PIPE

PIQUANCE same as
> PIQUANT

PIQUANCES > PIQUANT

PIQUANCY > PIQUANT

PIQUANT adj having a
pleasant spicy taste

PIQUANTLY > PIQUANT

PIQUE n feeling of hurt
pride, baffled curiosity, or
resentment ▷ vb hurt the
pride of

PIQUED > PIQUE

PIQUES > PIQUE

PIQUET n card game for
two ▷ vb play game of
piquet

PIQUETED > PIQUET

PIQUETING > PIQUET

PIQUETS > PIQUET

PIQUILLO n variety of
sweet red pepper

PIQUILLOS > PIQUILLO

PIQUING > PIQUE

PIR n Sufi master

PIRACETAM n drug used
to treat muscle spasm

PIRACIES > PIRACY

PIRACY n robbery on the
seas

PIRAGUA same as
> PIROGUE

PIRAGUAS > PIRAGUA

PIRAI n large S American
fish

PIRAIS > PIRAI

PIRANA same as
> PIRANHA

PIRANAS > PIRANA

PIRANHA n fierce fish of
tropical America

PIRANHAS > PIRANHA

PIRARUCU n large S
American food fish

PIRARUCUS > PIRARUCU

PIRATE n sea robber
▷ vb sell or reproduce
(artistic work etc)
illegally

PIRATED > PIRATE

PIRATES > PIRATE

PIRATIC > PIRATE

PIRATICAL > PIRATE

PIRATING n act of
pirating

PIRATINGS > PIRATING

PIRAYA same as > PIRAI

PIRAYAS > PIRAYA

PIRIFORM adj shaped like
pear

PIRL n ripple in water

PIRLICUE same as
> PURLICUE

PIRLICUED > PIRLICUE

PIRLICUES > PIRLICUE

PIRLS > PIRL

PIRN n reel or bobbin

PIRNIE n stripy nightcap

PIRNIES > PIRNIE

PIRNIT adj striped

PIRNS > PIRN

PIROG n type of large
Russian pie

PIROGEN n turnovers
made from kneaded
dough

PIROGHI > PIROG

PIROGI > PIROG

PIROGIES > PIROG

PIROGUE n any of various
kinds of dugout canoes

PIROGUES > PIROGUE

PIROJKI same as
> PIROSHKI

PIROPLASM n parasite of
red blood cells

PIROQUE same as
> PIROGUE

PIROQUES > PIROQUE

PIROSHKI same as
> PIROZHKI

PIROUETTE n spinning
turn balanced on the toes

of one foot ▷ vb perform a
pirouette

PIROZHKI > PIROZHOK

PIROZHOK n small
triangular pastry filled
with meat, vegetables, etc

PIRS > PIR

PIS > PI

PISCARIES > PISCARY

PISCARY n place where
fishing takes place

PISCATOR n fisherman

PISCATORS > PISCATOR

PISCATORY adj of or
relating to fish, fishing, or
fishermen

PISCATRIX n female
angler

PISCIFORM adj having
form of fish

PISCINA n stone basin
where water used at Mass
is poured away

PISCINAE > PISCINA

PISCINAL > PISCINA

PISCINAS > PISCINA

PISCINE n pond or pool

PISCINES > PISCINE

PISCIVORE n eater of fish

PISCO n S American
brandy

PISCOS > PISCO

PISE n rammed earth or
clay used to make floors or
walls

PISES > PISE

PISH interj exclamation of
impatience or contempt
▷ vb make this
exclamation at (someone
or something)

PISHED > PISH

PISHEOG same as
> PISHOGUE

PISHEOGS > PISHEOG

PISHER n Yiddish term for
small boy

PISHERS > PISHER

PISHES > PISH

PISHING > PISH

PISHOGE same as
> PISHOGUE

PISHOGES > PISHOGE

PISHOGUE n sorcery

PISHOGUES > PISHOGUE

PISIFORM adj resembling
a pea ▷ n small pealike
bone on the ulnar side of
the carpus

PISIFORMS > PISIFORM

PISKIES > PISKY

PISKY n Cornish fairy

PISMIRE archaic or dialect
word for > ANT

PISMIRES > PISMIRE

PISO n peso of the
Philippines

PISOLITE n sedimentary
rock

PISOLITES > PISOLITE

PISOLITH same as
> PISOLITE

PISOLITHS > PISOLITH

PISOLITIC > PISOLITE

PISOS > PISO

PISS vb urinate ▷ n act of
urinating

PISSANT n insignificant
person

PISSANTS > PISSANT

PISSED adj drunk

PISSER n someone or
something that pisses

PISSERS > PISSER

PISSES > PISS

PISSHEAD n drunkard

PISSHEADS > PISSHEAD

PISSHOLE n hole made in
soluble matter by
urinating

PISSHOLES > PISSHOLE

PISSIER > PISSY

PISSIEST > PISSY

PISSING > PISS

PISSOIR n public urinal,
usu enclosed by a wall or
screen

PISSOIRS > PISSOIR

PISSY adj soiled with
urine

PISTACHE n tree yielding
pistachio nut

PISTACHES > PISTACHE

PISTACHIO n edible nut
of a Mediterranean tree
▷ adj of a yellowish-green
colour

PISTAREEN n Spanish
coin, used in the US and
the West Indies until the
18th century

PISTE n ski slope

PISTED adj marked off
into pistes

PISTES > PISTE

PISTIL n seed-bearing
part of a flower

PISTILLAR adj relating
to a pistil

PISTILS > PISTIL

PISTOL n short-barrelled
handgun ▷ vb shoot with
a pistol

PISTOLE n gold coin
formerly used in Europe

PISTOLED > PISTOL

PISTOLEER n person, esp
a soldier, who is armed
with or fires a pistol

PISTOLERO n shooter of
pistols

PISTOLES > PISTOLE

PISTOLET n small pistol

PISTOLETS > PISTOLET

PISTOLIER n shooter of
pistols

PISTOLING > PISTOL

PISTOLLED > PISTOL

PISTOLS > PISTOL

PISTON n cylindrical part
in an engine that slides to
and fro in a cylinder

PISTONS > PISTON

PISTOU n French sauce

PISTOUS > PISTOU

PIT n deep hole in the
ground ▷ vb mark with
small dents or scars

PITA n any of several agave plants yielding a strong fibre

PITAHAYA n any giant cactus of Central America and the SW United States

PITAHAYAS > PITAHAYA

PITAPAT adv with quick light taps ▷ n such taps ▷ vb make quick light taps or beats

PITAPATS > PITAPAT

PITARA variant of **>** PETARA

PITARAH variant of **>** PETARA

PITARAHS > PITARAH

PITARAS > PITARA

PITAS > PITA

PITAYA same as **>** PITAHAYA

PITAYAS > PITAYA

PITCH vb throw, hurl ▷ n area marked out for playing sport

PITCHBEND n electronic device that enables a player to bend the pitch of a note being sounded on a synthesizer, usually with a pitch wheel, strip, or lever

PITCHED > PITCH

PITCHER n large jug with a narrow neck

PITCHERS > PITCHER

PITCHES > PITCH

PITCHFORK n large long-handled fork for lifting hay ▷ vb thrust abruptly or violently

PITCHIER > PITCHY

PITCHIEST > PITCHY

PITCHILY > PITCHY

PITCHING > PITCH

PITCHINGS > PITCH

PITCHMAN n itinerant pedlar of small merchandise who operates from a stand at a fair, etc

PITCHMEN > PITCHMAN

PITCHOUT n type of baseball pitch

PITCHOUTS > PITCHOUT

PITCHPINE n large N American pine tree

PITCHPIPE n small one-note pipe used for tuning instruments

PITCHPOLE vb turn end over end

PITCHY adj full of or covered with pitch

PITEOUS adj arousing pity

PITEOUSLY > PITEOUS

PITFALL n hidden difficulty or danger

PITFALLS > PITFALL

PITH n soft white lining of the rind of oranges etc ▷ vb destroy the brain and spinal cord of a laboratory animal

PITHBALL n type of conductor

PITHBALLS > PITHBALL

PITHEAD n top of a mine shaft and the buildings and hoisting gear around it

PITHEADS > PITHEAD

PITHECOID adj relating to apes ▷ n ape, esp an anthropoid ape

PITHED > PITH

PITHFUL > PITH

PITHIER > PITHY

PITHIEST > PITHY

PITHILY > PITHY

PITHINESS > PITHY

PITHING > PITH

PITHLESS > PITH

PITHLIKE > PITH

PITHOI > PITHOS

PITHOS n large ceramic container for oil or grain

PITHS > PITH

PITHY adj short and full of meaning

PITIABLE adj arousing or deserving pity or contempt

PITIABLY > PITIABLE

PITIED > PITY

PITIER > PITY

PITIERS > PITY

PITIES > PITY

PITIETH vb as in it pitieth me archaic inflection of 'pity'

PITIFUL adj arousing pity

PITIFULLY > PITIFUL

PITIKINS n as in ods pitikins mild oath

PITILESS adj feeling no pity or mercy

PITMAN n coal miner ▷ n connecting rod (in a machine)

PITMANS > PITMAN

PITMEN > PITMAN

PITON n metal spike used in climbing to secure a rope

PITONS > PITON

PITOT n tube used to measure the pressure of a liquid stream

PITOTS > PITOT

PITPROP n support beam in mine shaft

PITPROPS > PITPROP

PITS > PIT

PITSAW n large saw formerly used for cutting logs into planks

PITSAWS > PITSAW

PITTA n small brightly coloured ground-dwelling tropical bird

PITTANCE n very small amount of money

PITTANCES > PITTANCE

PITTAS > PITTA

PITTED > PIT

PITTEN adj having been put

PITTER vb make pattering sound

PITTERED > PITTER

PITTERING > PITTER

PITTERS > PITTER

PITTING > PIT

PITTINGS > PIT

PITTITE n occupant of a theatre pit

PITTITES > PITTITE

PITUITA n thick nasal secretion

PITUITARY n gland at the base of the brain, that helps to control growth ▷ adj of or relating to the pituitary gland

PITUITAS > PITUITA

PITUITE n mucus

PITUITES > PITUITE

PITUITRIN n extract from pituitary gland

PITURI n Australian solanaceous shrub

PITURIS > PITURI

PITY n sympathy or sorrow for others' suffering ▷ vb feel pity for

PITYING > PITY

PITYINGLY > PITY

PITYROID adj resembling bran

PIU adv more (quickly, softly, etc)

PIUM n stinging insect

PIUMS > PIUM

PIUPIU n skirt worn by Māoris on ceremonial occasions

PIUPIUS > PIUPIU

PIVOT n central shaft on which something turns ▷ vb provide with or turn on a pivot

PIVOTABLE > PIVOT

PIVOTAL adj of crucial importance

PIVOTALLY > PIVOTAL

PIVOTED > PIVOT

PIVOTER > PIVOT

PIVOTERS > PIVOT

PIVOTING > PIVOT

PIVOTINGS > PIVOT

PIVOTMAN n person in rank around whom others wheel

PIVOTMEN > PIVOTMAN

PIVOTS > PIVOT

PIX less common spelling of **>** PYX

PIXEL n any of a number of very small picture elements

PIXELATE vb divide an image into pixels

PIXELATED > PIXELATE

PIXELATES > PIXELATE

PIXELLATE same as **>** PIXELATE

PIXELS > PIXEL

PIXES > PIX

PIXIE n (in folklore) fairy

PIXIEISH > PIXIE

PIXIES > PIXIE

PIXILATE same as **>** PIXELATE

PIXILATED adj eccentric or whimsical

PIXILATES > PIXILATE

PIXILLATE same as **>** PIXELATE

PIXINESS > PIXIE

PIXY same as **>** PIXIE

PIXYISH > PIXY

PIZAZZ same as **>** PIZZAZZ

PIZAZZES > PIZAZZ

PIZAZZY > PIZAZZ

PIZE vb strike (someone a blow)

PIZED > PIZE

PIZES > PIZE

PIZING > PIZE

PIZZA n flat disc of dough covered with a wide variety of savoury toppings and baked

PIZZAIOLA adj having a type of tomato sauce

PIZZALIKE > PIZZA

PIZZAS > PIZZA

PIZZAZ same as **>** PZAZZ

PIZZAZES > PIZZAZ

PIZZAZZ n attractive combination of energy and style

PIZZAZZES > PIZZAZZ

PIZZAZZY > PIZZAZZ

PIZZELLE n Italian sweet wafer

PIZZELLES > PIZZELLE

PIZZERIA n place where pizzas are made, sold, or eaten

PIZZERIAS > PIZZERIA

PIZZICATI **>** PIZZICATO

PIZZICATO adj played by plucking the string of a violin etc with the finger ▷ adv (in music for the violin family) to be plucked with the finger ▷ n style or technique of playing a normally bowed stringed instrument in this manner

PIZZLE n penis of an animal, esp a bull

PIZZLES > PIZZLE

PLAAS n farm

PLAASES > PLAAS

PLACABLE adj easily placated or appeased

PLACABLY > PLACABLE

PLACARD n notice that is carried or displayed in public ▷ vb attach placards to

PLACARDED > PLACARD

PLACARDS > PLACARD

PLACATE vb make (someone) stop feeling angry or upset

PLACATED > PLACATE

PLACATER > PLACATE

PLACATERS > PLACATE

PLACATES > PLACATE

PLACATING > PLACATE
PLACATION > PLACATE
PLACATIVE *same as*
> PLACATORY
PLACATORY *adj* placating
or intended to placate
PLACCAT *variant of*
> PLACKET
PLACCATE *variant of*
> PLACKET
PLACCATES > PLACCATE
PLACCATS > PLACCAT
PLACE *n* particular part of
an area or space ▷ *vb* put
in a particular place
PLACEABLE > PLACE
PLACEBO *n* pill given to a
patient instead of an
active drug
PLACEBOES > PLACEBO
PLACEBOS > PLACEBO
PLACED > PLACE
PLACEKICK *n* (in football)
kick in which the ball is
placed in position before it
is kicked ▷ *vb* take a
placekick
PLACELESS *adj* not
rooted in a specific place or
community
PLACEMAN *n* person who
holds a public office, esp
for private profit and as a
reward for political
support
PLACEMAT *n* table mat
for a person to put their
plate on
PLACEMATS
> PLACEMAT
PLACEMEN > PLACEMAN
PLACEMENT *n*
arrangement
PLACENTA *n* organ
formed in the womb
during pregnancy,
providing nutrients for
the fetus
PLACENTAE > PLACENTA
PLACENTAL *adj* (esp of
animals) having a placenta
PLACENTAS > PLACENTA
PLACER *n* surface
sediment containing
particles of gold or some
other valuable mineral
PLACERS > PLACER
PLACES > PLACE
PLACET *n* vote or
expression of assent
PLACETS > PLACET
PLACID *adj* not easily
excited or upset, calm
PLACIDER > PLACID
PLACIDEST > PLACID
PLACIDITY > PLACID
PLACIDLY > PLACID
PLACING *n* method of
issuing securities to the
public using an
intermediary
PLACINGS > PLACING
PLACIT *n* decree or
dictum

PLACITA > PLACITUM
PLACITORY > PLACIT
PLACITS > PLACIT
PLACITUM *n* court or
assembly in Middle Ages
PLACK *n* small former
Scottish coin
PLACKET *n* opening at the
waist of a dress or skirt for
buttons or zips or for
access to a pocket
PLACKETS > PLACKET
PLACKLESS *adj* lacking
money
PLACKS > PLACK
PLACODERM *n* extinct
bony-plated fishlike
vertebrate
PLACOID *adj* platelike or
flattened ▷ *n* fish with
placoid scales
PLACOIDS > PLACOID
PLAFOND *n* ceiling, esp
one having
ornamentation
PLAFONDS > PLAFOND
PLAGAL *adj* (of a cadence)
progressing from the
subdominant to the tonic
chord
PLAGE *n* bright patch in
the sun's chromosphere
PLAGES > PLAGE
PLAGIARY *n* person who
plagiarizes or a piece of
plagiarism
PLAGIUM *n* crime of
kidnapping
PLAGIUMS > PLAGIUM
PLAGUE *n* fast-spreading
fatal disease ▷ *vb* trouble
or annoy continually
PLAGUED > PLAGUE
PLAGUER > PLAGUE
PLAGUERS > PLAGUE
PLAGUES > PLAGUE
PLAGUEY *same as*
> PLAGUY
PLAGUIER > PLAGUEY
PLAGUIEST > PLAGUEY
PLAGUILY > PLAGUY
PLAGUING > PLAGUE
PLAGUY *adj* disagreeable
or vexing ▷ *adv*
disagreeably or annoyingly
PLAICE *n* edible European
flatfish
PLAICES > PLAICE
PLAID *n* long piece of
tartan cloth worn as part
of Highland dress ▷ *vb*
weave cloth into plaid
PLAIDED > PLAID
PLAIDING > PLAID
PLAIDINGS > PLAID
PLAIDMAN *n* wearer of
plaid
PLAIDMEN > PLAIDMAN
PLAIDS > PLAID
PLAIN *adj* easy to see or
understand ▷ *n* large
stretch of level country
▷ *adv* clearly or simply
▷ *vb* complain

PLAINANT *n* plaintiff
PLAINANTS > PLAINANT
PLAINED > PLAIN
PLAINER > PLAIN
PLAINEST > PLAIN
PLAINFUL *adj* apt to
complain
PLAINING > PLAIN
PLAININGS > PLAIN
PLAINISH > PLAIN
PLAINLY > PLAIN
PLAINNESS > PLAIN
PLAINS *pl n* extensive
tracts of flat treeless
countryside
PLAINSMAN *n* person
who lives in a plains
region, esp in the Great
Plains of North America
PLAINSMEN
> PLAINSMAN
PLAINSONG *n*
unaccompanied singing,
esp in a medieval church
PLAINT *n* complaint or
lamentation
PLAINTEXT *n* (in
telecommunications)
message set in a directly
readable form rather than
in coded groups
PLAINTFUL *adj*
complaining
PLAINTIFF *n* person
who sues in a court of law
PLAINTIVE *adj* sad,
mournful
PLAINTS > PLAINT
PLAINWORK *n* weaving
PLAISTER *n* plaster
PLAISTERS > PLAISTER
PLAIT *n* intertwined
length of hair ▷ *vb*
intertwine separate
strands in a pattern
PLAITED > PLAIT
PLAITER > PLAIT
PLAITERS > PLAIT
PLAITING > PLAIT
PLAITINGS > PLAIT
PLAITS > PLAIT
PLAN *n* way thought out
to do or achieve
something ▷ *vb* arrange
beforehand
PLANAR *adj* of or relating
to a plane
PLANARIA *n* type of
flatworm
PLANARIAN *n* type of
flatworm
PLANARIAS > PLANARIA
PLANARITY > PLANAR
PLANATE *adj* having been
flattened
PLANATION *n* erosion of a
land surface until it is
basically flat
PLANCH *vb* cover with
planks
PLANCHE *same as*
> PLANCH
PLANCHED > PLANCH
PLANCHES > PLANCH

PLANCHET *n* piece of
metal ready to be stamped
as a coin, medal, etc
PLANCHETS > PLANCHET
PLANCHING > PLANCH
PLANE *n* aeroplane ▷ *adj*
perfectly flat or level ▷ *vb*
glide or skim
PLANED > PLANE
PLANELOAD *n* amount or
number carried by plane
PLANENESS > PLANE
PLANER *n* machine with a
cutting tool that makes
repeated horizontal
strokes
PLANERS > PLANER
PLANES > PLANE
PLANESIDE *n* area next
to aeroplane
PLANET *n* large body in
space that revolves round
the sun or another star
PLANETARY *adj* of or
relating to a planet
▷ *n* train of planetary gears
PLANETIC > PLANET
PLANETOID *See*
> ASTEROID
PLANETS > PLANET
PLANFORM *n* outline or
silhouette of an object, esp
an aircraft, as seen from
above
PLANFORMS > PLANFORM
PLANGENCY > PLANGENT
PLANGENT *adj* (of sounds)
mournful and resounding
PLANIGRAM *n* x-ray
photograph of a plane
section of something
PLANING > PLANE
PLANISH *vb* give a smooth
surface to (a metal)
PLANISHED > PLANISH
PLANISHER > PLANISH
PLANISHES > PLANISH
PLANK *n* long flat piece of
sawn timber ▷ *vb* cover or
provide (an area) with
planks
PLANKED > PLANK
PLANKING *n* number of
planks
PLANKINGS > PLANKING
PLANKS > PLANK
PLANKTER *n* organism in
plankton
PLANKTERS > PLANKTER
PLANKTIC *adj* relating to
plankton
PLANKTON *n* minute
animals and plants
floating in the surface
water of a sea or lake
PLANKTONS > PLANKTON
PLANLESS *adj* having no
plan
PLANNED > PLAN
PLANNER *n* person who
makes plans
PLANNERS > PLANNER
PLANNING > PLAN
PLANNINGS > PLAN

p

PLANOGRAM n type of schematic plan for displaying merchandise in a shop
PLANOSOL n type of intrazonal soil of humid or subhumid uplands having a strongly leached upper layer overlying a clay hardpan
PLANOSOLS > PLANOSOL
PLANS > PLAN
PLANT n living organism that grows in the ground and has no power to move ▷ vb put in the ground to grow
PLANTA n sole of foot
PLANTABLE > PLANT
PLANTAE > PLANTA
PLANTAGE n plants
PLANTAGES > PLANTAGE
PLANTAIN n low-growing wild plant with broad leaves
PLANTAINS > PLANTAIN
PLANTAR adj of, relating to, or occurring on the sole of the foot
PLANTAS > PLANTA
PLANTED > PLANT
PLANTER n owner of a plantation
PLANTERS > PLANTER
PLANTING > PLANT
PLANTINGS > PLANT
PLANTLESS > PLANT
PLANTLET n small plant
PLANTLETS > PLANTLET
PLANTLIKE > PLANT
PLANTLING n young plant
PLANTS > PLANT
PLANTSMAN n experienced gardener who specializes in collecting rare or interesting plants
PLANTSMEN > PLANTSMAN
PLANTULE n embryo in act of germination
PLANTULES > PLANTULE
PLANULA n free-swimming larva of hydrozoan coelenterates
PLANULAE > PLANULA
PLANULAR > PLANULA
PLANULATE adj flat
PLANULOID adj of planula
PLANURIA n expulsion of urine from abnormal opening
PLANURIAS > PLANURIA
PLANURIES > PLANURY
PLANURY another name for > PLANURY
PLANXTIES > PLANXTY
PLANXTY n Celtic melody for harp
PLAP same as > PLOP
PLAPPED > PLAP
PLAPPING > PLAP
PLAPS > PLAP

PLAQUE n inscribed commemorative stone or metal plate
PLAQUES > PLAQUE
PLAQUETTE n small plaque
PLASH same as > PLEACH
PLASHED > PLASH
PLASHER n type of farm tool
PLASHERS > PLASHER
PLASHES > PLASH
PLASHET n small pond
PLASHETS > PLASHET
PLASHIER > PLASHY
PLASHIEST > PLASHY
PLASHING > PLASH
PLASHINGS > PLASH
PLASHY adj wet or marshy
PLASM same as > PLASMA
PLASMA n clear liquid part of blood
PLASMAGEL another name for > ECTOPLASM
PLASMAS > PLASMA
PLASMASOL another name for > ENDOPLASM
PLASMATIC > PLASMA
PLASMIC > PLASMA
PLASMID n small circle of bacterial DNA
PLASMIDS > PLASMID
PLASMIN n proteolytic enzyme that causes fibrinolysis in blood clots
PLASMINS > PLASMIN
PLASMODIA n amoeboid masses of protoplasm, each containing many nuclei
PLASMOID n section of a plasma having a characteristic shape
PLASMOIDS > PLASMOID
PLASMON n sum total of plasmagenes in a cell
PLASMONS > PLASMON
PLASMS > PLASM
PLAST archaic past participle of > PLACE
PLASTE archaic past participle of > PLACE
PLASTER n mixture of lime, sand, etc for coating walls ▷ vb cover with plaster
PLASTERED adj drunk
PLASTERER n PLASTER
PLASTERS > PLASTER
PLASTERY > PLASTER
PLASTIC n synthetic material that can be moulded when soft but sets in a hard long-lasting shape ▷ adj made of plastic
PLASTICKY adj made of or resembling plastic
PLASTICLY > PLASTIC
PLASTICS > PLASTIC
PLASTID n small particle in the cells of plants and some animals
PLASTIDS > PLASTID

PLASTIQUE n easily-moulded plastic explosive
PLASTISOL n suspension of resin particles convertible into solid plastic
PLASTRAL > PLASTRON
PLASTRON n bony plate forming the ventral part of the shell of a tortoise or turtle
PLASTRONS > PLASTRON
PLASTRUM variant of > PLASTRON
PLASTRUMS > PLASTRUM
PLAT n small area of ground
PLATAN n plane tree
PLATANE same as > PLATAN
PLATANES > PLATANE
PLATANNA n S African frog
PLATANNAS > PLATANNA
PLATANS > PLATAN
PLATBAND n border of flowers in garden
PLATBANDS > PLATBAND
PLATE n shallow dish for holding food ▷ vb cover with a thin coating of gold, silver, or other metal
PLATEASM n talking with mouth open too wide
PLATEASMS > PLATEASM
PLATEAU n area of level high land ▷ vb remain stable for a long period
PLATEAUED > PLATEAU
PLATEAUS > PLATEAU
PLATEAUX > PLATEAU
PLATED adj coated with a layer of metal
PLATEFUL same as > PLATE
PLATEFULS > PLATEFUL
PLATELESS adj having no plate
PLATELET n minute particle occurring in blood of vertebrates and involved in clotting of blood
PLATELETS > PLATELET
PLATELIKE > PLATE
PLATEMAN n one of crew of steam train
PLATEMARK another name for > HALLMARK
PLATEMEN > PLATEMAN
PLATEN n roller of a typewriter, against which the paper is held
PLATENS > PLATEN
PLATER n person or thing that plates
PLATERS > PLATER
PLATES > PLATE
PLATESFUL > PLATEFUL
PLATFORM n raised floor
PLATFORMS > PLATFORM
PLATIER > PLATY
PLATIES > PLATY
PLATIEST > PLATY

PLATINA n alloy of platinum and several other metals
PLATINAS > PLATINA
PLATING n coating of metal
PLATINGS > PLATING
PLATINIC adj of or containing platinum, esp in the tetravalent state
PLATINISE same as > PLATINIZE
PLATINIZE vb coat with platinum
PLATINOID adj containing or resembling platinum
PLATINOUS adj of or containing platinum, esp in the divalent state
PLATINUM n valuable silvery-white metal
PLATINUMS > PLATINUM
PLATITUDE n remark that is true but not interesting or original
PLATONIC adj (of a relationship) friendly or affectionate but not sexual ▷ n platonic friend
PLATONICS > PLATONIC
PLATONISM n philosophy of Plato
PLATOON n smaller unit within a company of soldiers ▷ vb organise into platoons
PLATOONED > PLATOON
PLATOONS > PLATOON
PLATS > PLAT
PLATT adj as in scale and platt denoting a modern straight staircase with landings as opposed to a spiral staircase
PLATTED > PLAT
PLATTER n large dish
PLATTERS > PLATTER
PLATTING > PLAT
PLATTINGS > PLAT
PLATY adj of, relating to, or designating rocks the constituents of which occur in flaky layers ▷ n brightly coloured freshwater fish
PLATYFISH same as > PLATY
PLATYPI > PLATYPUS
PLATYPUS n Australian egg-laying amphibious mammal, with dense fur, webbed feet, and a ducklike bill
PLATYS > PLATY
PLATYSMA n muscle located on side of neck
PLATYSMAS > PLATYSMA
PLAUDIT n expression of enthusiastic approval
PLAUDITE interj give a round of applause!
PLAUDITS > PLAUDIT

PLAUSIBLE *adj* apparently true or reasonable

PLAUSIBLY > PLAUSIBLE

PLAUSIVE *adj* expressing praise or approval

PLAUSTRAL *adj* relating to wagons

PLAY *vb* occupy oneself in (a game or recreation) ▷ *n* story performed on stage or broadcast

PLAYA *n* (in the US) temporary lake in a desert basin

PLAYABLE > PLAY

PLAYACT *vb* pretend or make believe

PLAYACTED > PLAYACT

PLAYACTOR > PLAYACT

PLAYACTS > PLAYACT

PLAYAS > PLAYA

PLAYBACK *n* playing of a recording on magnetic tape ▷ *vb* listen to or watch (something recorded)

PLAYBACKS > PLAYBACK

PLAYBILL *n* poster or bill advertising a play

PLAYBILLS > PLAYBILL

PLAYBOOK *n* book containing a range of possible set plays

PLAYBOOKS > PLAYBOOK

PLAYBOY *n* rich man who lives only for pleasure

PLAYBOYS > PLAYBOY

PLAYBUS *n* mobile playground in a bus

PLAYBUSES > PLAYBUS

PLAYDATE *n* gathering of children at house for play

PLAYDATES > PLAYDATE

PLAYDAY *n* day given to play

PLAYDAYS > PLAYDAY

PLAYDOUGH *n* soft modelling material used by children

PLAYDOWN *same as* > PLAYOFF

PLAYDOWNS > PLAYDOWN

PLAYED > PLAY

PLAYER *n* person who plays a game or sport

PLAYERS > PLAYER

PLAYFIELD *n* field for sports

PLAYFUL *adj* lively

PLAYFULLY > PLAYFUL

PLAYGIRL *n* rich woman devoted to pleasure

PLAYGIRLS > PLAYGIRL

PLAYGOER *n* person who goes often to the theatre

PLAYGOERS > PLAYGOER

PLAYGOING > PLAYGOER

PLAYGROUP *n* playschool

PLAYHOUSE *n* theatre

PLAYING *n* act of playing

PLAYINGS > PLAYING

PLAYLAND *n* playground

PLAYLANDS > PLAYLAND

PLAYLESS > PLAY

PLAYLET *n* short play

PLAYLETS > PLAYLET

PLAYLIKE > PLAY

PLAYLIST *n* list of records chosen for playing, such as on a radio station ▷ *vb* put (a song or record) on a playlist

PLAYLISTS > PLAYLIST

PLAYMAKER *n* player who creates scoring opportunities for his or her team-mates

PLAYMATE *n* companion in play

PLAYMATES > PLAYMATE

PLAYOFF *n* extra contest to decide the winner when two or more competitors are tied

PLAYOFFS > PLAYOFF

PLAYPEN *n* small portable enclosure in which a young child can safely be left to play

PLAYPENS > PLAYPEN

PLAYROOM *n* recreation room, esp for children

PLAYROOMS > PLAYROOM

PLAYS > PLAY

PLAYSET *n* outdoor equipment for children to play on

PLAYSETS > PLAYSET

PLAYSLIP *n* form used to select numbers in a lottery draw

PLAYSLIPS > PLAYSLIP

PLAYSOME *adj* playful

PLAYSUIT *n* woman's or child's outfit, usually comprising shorts and a top

PLAYSUITS > PLAYSUIT

PLAYTHING *n* toy

PLAYTIME *n* time for play or recreation, such as a school break

PLAYTIMES > PLAYTIME

PLAYWEAR *n* clothes suitable for playing in

PLAYWEARS > PLAYWEAR

PLAZA *n* open space or square

PLAZAS > PLAZA

PLEA *n* serious or urgent request, entreaty ▷ *vb* entreat

PLEACH *vb* interlace the stems or boughs of (a tree or hedge)

PLEACHED > PLEACH

PLEACHES > PLEACH

PLEACHING > PLEACH

PLEAD *vb* ask urgently or with deep feeling

PLEADABLE > PLEAD

PLEADED > PLEAD

PLEADER > PLEAD

PLEADERS > PLEAD

PLEADING > PLEAD

PLEADINGS > PLEAD

PLEADS > PLEAD

PLEAED > PLEA

PLEAING > PLEA

PLEAS > PLEA

PLEASABLE > PLEASE

PLEASANCE *n* secluded part of a garden laid out with trees, walks, etc

PLEASANT *adj* pleasing, enjoyable

PLEASE *vb* give pleasure or satisfaction to ▷ *adv* polite word of request

PLEASED > PLEASE

PLEASEDLY > PLEASE

PLEASEMAN *n* person who courts favour

PLEASEMEN > PLEASEMAN

PLEASER > PLEASE

PLEASERS > PLEASE

PLEASES > PLEASE

PLEASETH *obsolete inflection of* > PLEASE

PLEASING *adj* giving pleasure or satisfaction ▷ *n* act of giving pleasure

PLEASINGS > PLEASING

PLEASURE *n* feeling of happiness and satisfaction ▷ *vb* give pleasure to or take pleasure (in)

PLEASURED > PLEASURE

PLEASURER > PLEASURE

PLEASURES > PLEASURE

PLEAT *n* fold made by doubling material back on itself ▷ *vb* arrange (material) in pleats

PLEATED > PLEAT

PLEATER *n* attachment on a sewing machine that makes pleats

PLEATERS > PLEATER

PLEATHER *n* synthetic leather

PLEATHERS > PLEATHER

PLEATING *n* act of pleating

PLEATINGS > PLEATING

PLEATLESS > PLEAT

PLEATS > PLEAT

PLEB *n* common vulgar person

PLEBBIER > PLEBBY

PLEBBIEST > PLEBBY

PLEBBY *adj* common or vulgar

PLEBE *n* member of the lowest class at the US Naval Academy or Military Academy

PLEBEAN *old variant of* > PLEBEIAN

PLEBEIAN *adj* of the lower social classes ▷ *n* member of the lower social classes

PLEBEIANS > PLEBEIAN

PLEBES > PLEBE

PLEBIFIED > PLEBIFY

PLEBIFIES > PLEBIFY

PLEBIFY *vb* make plebeian

PLEBS *n* common people

PLECTRA > PLECTRUM

PLECTRE *variant of* > PLECTRUM

PLECTRES > PLECTRE

PLECTRON *same as* > PLECTRUM

PLECTRONS > PLECTRON

PLECTRUM *n* small implement for plucking the strings of a guitar etc

PLECTRUMS > PLECTRUM

PLED > PLEAD

PLEDGABLE > PLEDGE

PLEDGE *n* solemn promise ▷ *vb* promise solemnly

PLEDGED > PLEDGE

PLEDGEE *n* person to whom a pledge is given

PLEDGEES > PLEDGEE

PLEDGEOR *same as* > PLEDGOR

PLEDGEORS > PLEDGEOR

PLEDGER *same as* > PLEDGOR

PLEDGERS > PLEDGER

PLEDGES > PLEDGE

PLEDGET *n* small flattened pad of wool, cotton, etc

PLEDGETS > PLEDGET

PLEDGING > PLEDGE

PLEDGOR *n* person who gives or makes a pledge

PLEDGORS > PLEDGOR

PLEIAD *n* brilliant or talented group, esp one with seven members

PLEIADES > PLEIAD

PLEIADS > PLEIAD

PLEIOCENE *variant spelling of* > PLIOCENE

PLEIOMERY *n* state of having more than normal number

PLEIOTAXY *n* increase in whorls in flower

PLENA > PLENUM

PLENARIES > PLENARY

PLENARILY > PLENARY

PLENARTY *n* state of endowed church office when occupied

PLENARY *adj* (of a meeting) attended by all members ▷ *n* book read at the Eucharist

PLENCH *n* tool combining wrench and pliers

PLENCHES > PLENCH

PLENILUNE *n* full moon

PLENIPO *n* plenipotentiary diplomat

PLENIPOES > PLENIPO

PLENIPOS > PLENIPO

PLENISH *vb* fill, stock, or resupply

PLENISHED > PLENISH

PLENISHER > PLENISH

PLENISHES > PLENISH

PLENISM *n* philosophical theory

PLENISMS > PLENISM

PLENIST > PLENISM

PLENISTS > PLENISM

PLENITUDE *n* completeness, abundance

PLENTEOUS *adj* plentiful

PLENTIES > PLENTY

PLENTIFUL *adj* existing in large amounts or numbers

PLENTY *n* large amount or number ▷ *adj* very many ▷ *adv* more than adequately

PLENUM *n* enclosure containing gas at a high pressure

PLENUMS > PLENUM

PLEON *n* abdomen of crustacean

PLEONAL *adj* of the abdomen of a crustacean

PLEONASM *n* use of more words than necessary

PLEONASMS > PLEONASM

PLEONAST *n* person using more words than necessary

PLEONASTE *n* type of black mineral

PLEONASTS > PLEONAST

PLEONEXIA *n* greed

PLEONIC > PLEON

PLEONS > PLEON

PLEOPOD *another name for* > SWIMMERET

PLEOPODS > PLEOPOD

PLERION *n* filled-centre supernova remnant

PLERIONS > PLERION

PLEROMA *n* abundance

PLEROMAS > PLEROMA

PLEROME *n* central column in growing stem or root

PLEROMES > PLEROME

PLESH *n* small pool

PLESHES > PLESH

PLESSOR *same as* > PLEXOR

PLESSORS > PLESSOR

PLETHORA *n* excess

PLETHORAS > PLETHORA

PLETHORIC > PLETHORA

PLEUCH *same as* > PLEUGH

PLEUCHED > PLEUCH

PLEUCHING > PLEUCH

PLEUCHS > PLEUCH

PLEUGH *Scottish word for* > PLOUGH

PLEUGHED > PLEUGH

PLEUGHING > PLEUGH

PLEUGHS > PLEUGH

PLEURA > PLEURON

PLEURAE > PLEURON

PLEURAL > PLEURON

PLEURAS > PLEURON

PLEURISY *n* inflammation of the membrane covering the lungs

PLEURITIC > PLEURISY

PLEURITIS *n* pleurisy

PLEURON *n* part of the cuticle of arthropods

PLEURONIA *n* combined disorder of pleurisy and pneumonia

PLEUSTON *n* mass of small organisms, esp algae, floating at the surface of shallow pools

PLEUSTONS > PLEUSTON

PLEW *n* (formerly in Canada) beaver skin used as a standard unit of value in the fur trade

PLEWS > PLEW

PLEX *n* shortening of multiplex ▷ *vb* make a plexus

PLEXAL > PLEXUS

PLEXED > PLEX

PLEXES > PLEX

PLEXIFORM *adj* like or having the form of a network or plexus

PLEXING > PLEX

PLEXOR *n* small hammer with a rubber head

PLEXORS > PLEXOR

PLEXURE *n* act of weaving together

PLEXURES > PLEXURE

PLEXUS *n* complex network of nerves or blood vessels

PLEXUSES > PLEXUS

PLIABLE *adj* easily bent

PLIABLY > PLIABLE

PLIANCIES > PLIANT

PLIANCY > PLIANT

PLIANT *adj* pliable

PLIANTLY > PLIANT

PLICA *n* folding over of parts, such as a fold of skin, muscle, peritoneum, etc

PLICAE > PLICA

PLICAL > PLICA

PLICAS > PLICA

PLICATE *adj* having or arranged in parallel folds or ridges ▷ *vb* arrange into parallel folds

PLICATED > PLICATE

PLICATELY > PLICATE

PLICATES > PLICATE

PLICATING > PLICATE

PLICATION *n* act of folding or the condition of being folded or plicate

PLICATURE *same as* > PLICATION

PLIE *n* classic ballet practice posture with back erect and knees bent

PLIED > PLY

PLIER *n* person who plies a trade

PLIERS *pl n* tool with hinged arms and jaws for gripping

PLIES > PLY

PLIGHT *n* difficult or dangerous situation

PLIGHTED > PLIGHT

PLIGHTER > PLIGHT

PLIGHTERS > PLIGHT

PLIGHTFUL > PLIGHT

PLIGHTING > PLIGHT

PLIGHTS > PLIGHT

PLIM *vb* swell with water

PLIMMED > PLIM

PLIMMING > PLIM

PLIMS > PLIM

PLIMSOL *same as* > PLIMSOLE

PLIMSOLE *same as* > PLIMSOLL

PLIMSOLES > PLIMSOLE

PLIMSOLL *n* light rubber-soled canvas shoe worn for various sports

PLIMSOLLS > PLIMSOLL

PLIMSOLS > PLIMSOL

PLING *n* (in computer jargon) an exclamation mark ▷ *vb* beg from

PLINGED > PLING

PLINGING > PLING

PLINGS > PLING

PLINK *n* short sharp often metallic sound ▷ *vb* make such a noise

PLINKED > PLINK

PLINKER > PLINK

PLINKERS > PLINK

PLINKIER > PLINKY

PLINKIEST > PLINKY

PLINKING > PLINK

PLINKINGS > PLINK

PLINKS > PLINK

PLINKY *adj* (of a sound) short, sharp, and often metallic

PLINTH *n* slab forming the base of a statue, column, etc

PLINTHS > PLINTH

PLIOCENE *adj* of the Pliocene geological time period

PLIOFILM *n* transparent plastic material

PLIOFILMS > PLIOFILM

PLIOSAUR *n* type of dinosaur

PLIOSAURS > PLIOSAUR

PLIOTRON *n* type of vacuum tube

PLIOTRONS > PLIOTRON

PLISKIE *n* practical joke ▷ *adj* tricky or mischievous

PLISKIER > PLISKIE

PLISKIES > PLISKIE

PLISKIEST > PLISKIE

PLISKY *same as* > PLISKIE

PLISSE *n* fabric with a wrinkled finish, achieved by treatment involving caustic soda

PLISSES > PLISSE

PLOAT *vb* thrash

PLOATED > PLOAT

PLOATING > PLOAT

PLOATS > PLOAT

PLOD *vb* walk with slow heavy steps ▷ *n* act of plodding

PLODDED > PLOD

PLODDER *n* person who plods

PLODDERS > PLODDER

PLODDING > PLOD

PLODDINGS > PLOD

PLODGE *vb* wade in water, esp the sea ▷ *n* act of wading

PLODGED > PLODGE

PLODGES > PLODGE

PLODGING > PLODGE

PLODS > PLOD

PLOIDIES > PLOIDY

PLOIDY *n* number of copies of set of chromosomes in cell

PLONG *obsolete variant of* > PLUNGE

PLONGD > PLONG

PLONGE *same as* > PLUNGE

PLONGED > PLONGE

PLONGES > PLONGE

PLONGING > PLONGE

PLONGS > PLONG

PLONK *vb* put (something) down heavily and carelessly ▷ *n* cheap inferior wine ▷ *interj* exclamation imitative of this sound

PLONKED > PLONK

PLONKER *n* stupid person

PLONKERS > PLONKER

PLONKIER > PLONK

PLONKIEST > PLONK

PLONKING > PLONK

PLONKINGS > PLONK

PLONKO *n* alcoholic, esp one who drinks wine

PLONKOS > PLONKO

PLONKS > PLONK

PLONKY > PLONK

PLOOK *same as* > PLOUK

PLOOKIE *same as* > PLOUKY

PLOOKIER > PLOUK

PLOOKIEST > PLOUK

PLOOKS > PLOOK

PLOOKY > PLOOK

PLOP *n* sound of an object falling into water without a splash ▷ *vb* make this sound ▷ *interj* exclamation imitative of this sound

PLOPPED > PLOP

PLOPPING > PLOP

PLOPS > PLOP

PLOSION *n* sound of an abrupt break or closure, esp the audible release of a stop

PLOSIONS > PLOSION

PLOSIVE *adj* pronounced with a sudden release of breath ▷ *n* plosive consonant

PLOSIVES > PLOSIVE

PLOT *n* secret plan to do something illegal or wrong ▷ *vb* plan secretly, conspire

PLOTFUL > PLOT
PLOTLESS > PLOT
PLOTLINE *n* literary or dramatic plot
PLOTLINES > PLOTLINE
PLOTS > PLOT
PLOTTAGE *n* land that makes up plot
PLOTTAGES > PLOTTAGE
PLOTTED > PLOT
PLOTTER *same as* > PLOUTER
PLOTTERED > PLOTTER
PLOTTERS > PLOTTER
PLOTTIE *n* hot spiced drink
PLOTTIER > PLOTTY
PLOTTIES > PLOTTIE
PLOTTIEST > PLOTTY
PLOTTING > PLOT
PLOTTINGS > PLOT
PLOTTY *adj* intricately plotted
PLOTZ *vb* faint or collapse
PLOTZED > PLOTZ
PLOTZES > PLOTZ
PLOTZING > PLOTZ
PLOUGH *n* agricultural tool for turning over soil ▷ *vb* turn over (earth) with a plough
PLOUGHBOY *n* boy who guides the animals drawing a plough
PLOUGHED > PLOUGH
PLOUGHER > PLOUGH
PLOUGHERS > PLOUGH
PLOUGHING *n* act of ploughing
PLOUGHMAN *n* man who ploughs
PLOUGHMEN > PLOUGHMAN
PLOUGHS > PLOUGH
PLOUK *n* pimple
PLOUKIE > PLOUK
PLOUKIER > PLOUK
PLOUKIEST > PLOUK
PLOUKS > PLOUK
PLOUKY > PLOUK
PLOUTER *same as* > PLOWTER
PLOUTERED > PLOUTER
PLOUTERS > PLOUTER
PLOVER *n* shore bird with a straight bill and long pointed wings
PLOVERS > PLOVER
PLOVERY > PLOVER
PLOW *same as* > PLOUGH
PLOWABLE > PLOW
PLOWBACK *n* reinvestment of profits
PLOWBACKS > PLOWBACK
PLOWBOY *same as* > PLOUGHBOY
PLOWBOYS > PLOWBOY
PLOWED > PLOW
PLOWER > PLOW
PLOWERS > PLOW
PLOWHEAD *n* draught iron of plow
PLOWHEADS > PLOWHEAD

PLOWING > PLOUGHING
PLOWINGS > PLOWING
PLOWLAND *n* land plowed
PLOWLANDS > PLOWLAND
PLOWMAN *same as* > PLOUGHMAN
PLOWMEN > PLOWMAN
PLOWS > PLOW
PLOWSHARE *n* horizontal pointed cutting blade of a mouldboard plow
PLOWSTAFF *n* one of the handles of a plow
PLOWTAIL *n* the end of a plough where the handles are
PLOWTAILS > PLOWTAIL
PLOWTER *vb* work or play in water or mud ▷ *n* act of plowtering
PLOWTERED > PLOWTER
PLOWTERS > PLOWTER
PLOWWISE *adv* as in ploughing
PLOY *n* manoeuvre designed to gain an advantage ▷ *vb* form a column from a line of troops
PLOYE *n* buckwheat pancake
PLOYED > PLOY
PLOYES > PLOYE
PLOYING > PLOY
PLOYS > PLOY
PLU *same as* > PLEW
PLUCK *vb* pull or pick off ▷ *n* courage
PLUCKED > PLUCK
PLUCKER > PLUCK
PLUCKERS > PLUCK
PLUCKIER > PLUCKY
PLUCKIEST > PLUCKY
PLUCKILY > PLUCKY
PLUCKING > PLUCK
PLUCKS > PLUCK
PLUCKY *adj* brave
PLUE *same as* > PLEW
PLUES > PLUE
PLUFF *vb* expel in puffs
PLUFFED > PLUFF
PLUFFIER > PLUFF
PLUFFIEST > PLUFF
PLUFFING > PLUFF
PLUFFS > PLUFF
PLUFFY > PLUFF
PLUG *n* thing fitting into and filling a hole ▷ *vb* block or seal (a hole or gap) with a plug
PLUGBOARD *n* device with a large number of sockets in which electrical plugs can be inserted to form many different temporary circuits
PLUGGED > PLUG
PLUGGER > PLUG
PLUGGERS > PLUG
PLUGGING > PLUG
PLUGGINGS > PLUG
PLUGHOLE *n* hole, esp in a bath, basin, or sink,

through which waste water drains and which can be closed with a plug
PLUGHOLES > PLUGHOLE
PLUGLESS > PLUG
PLUGOLA *n* plugging of products on television
PLUGOLAS > PLUGOLA
PLUGS > PLUG
PLUGUGLY *n* city tough; ruffian
PLUM *n* oval usu dark red fruit with a stone in the middle ▷ *adj* dark purplish-red
PLUMAGE *n* bird's feathers
PLUMAGED > PLUMAGE
PLUMAGES > PLUMAGE
PLUMATE *adj* of, relating to, or possessing one or more feathers or plumes
PLUMB *vb* understand (something obscure) ▷ *adv* exactly ▷ *n* weight suspended at the end of a line
PLUMBABLE > PLUMB
PLUMBAGO *n* plant of warm regions with clusters of blue, white, or red flowers
PLUMBAGOS > PLUMBAGO
PLUMBATE *n* compound formed from lead oxide
PLUMBATES > PLUMBATE
PLUMBED > PLUMB
PLUMBEOUS *adj* made of or relating to lead or resembling lead in colour
PLUMBER *n* person who fits and repairs pipes and fixtures for water and drainage systems
PLUMBERS > PLUMBER
PLUMBERY *same as* > PLUMBING
PLUMBIC *adj* of or containing lead in the tetravalent state
PLUMBING *n* pipes and fixtures used in water and drainage systems
PLUMBINGS > PLUMBING
PLUMBISM *n* chronic lead poisoning
PLUMBISMS > PLUMBISM
PLUMBITE *n* substance containing lead oxide
PLUMBITES > PLUMBITE
PLUMBLESS *adj* incapable of being sounded
PLUMBNESS > PLUMB
PLUMBOUS *adj* of or containing lead in the divalent state
PLUMBS > PLUMB
PLUMBUM *n* obsolete name for lead (the metal)
PLUMBUMS > PLUMBUM
PLUMCAKE *n* cake with raisins in it
PLUMCAKES > PLUMCAKE
PLUMCOT *n* hybrid of apricot and plum

PLUMCOTS > PLUMCOT
PLUMDAMAS *n* prune
PLUME *n* feather, esp one worn as an ornament ▷ *vb* adorn or decorate with feathers or plumes
PLUMED > PLUME
PLUMELESS > PLUME
PLUMELET *n* small plume
PLUMELETS > PLUMELET
PLUMELIKE > PLUME
PLUMERIA *n* tropical tree with candelabra-like branches
PLUMERIAS > PLUMERIA
PLUMERIES > PLUMERY
PLUMERY *n* plumes collectively
PLUMES > PLUME
PLUMIER > PLUMY
PLUMIEST > PLUMY
PLUMING > PLUME
PLUMIPED *n* bird with feathered feet
PLUMIPEDS > PLUMIPED
PLUMIST *n* person who makes plumes
PLUMISTS > PLUMIST
PLUMLIKE > PLUM
PLUMMER > PLUM
PLUMMEST > PLUM
PLUMMET *vb* plunge downward ▷ *n* weight on a plumb line or fishing line
PLUMMETED > PLUMMET
PLUMMETS > PLUMMET
PLUMMIER > PLUMMY
PLUMMIEST > PLUMMY
PLUMMY *adj* of, full of, or like plums
PLUMOSE *same as* > PLUMATE
PLUMOSELY > PLUMOSE
PLUMOSITY > PLUMOSE
PLUMOUS *adj* having plumes or feathers
PLUMP *adj* moderately or attractively fat ▷ *vb* sit or fall heavily and suddenly ▷ *n* heavy abrupt fall or the sound of this ▷ *adv* suddenly or heavily
PLUMPED > PLUMP
PLUMPEN *vb* make or become plump
PLUMPENED > PLUMPEN
PLUMPENS > PLUMPEN
PLUMPER *n* pad carried in the mouth by actors to round out the cheeks
PLUMPERS > PLUMPER
PLUMPEST > PLUMP
PLUMPIE *same as* > PLUMPY
PLUMPIER > PLUMPY
PLUMPIEST > PLUMPY
PLUMPING > PLUMP
PLUMPISH *adj* on the plump side
PLUMPLY > PLUMP
PLUMPNESS > PLUMP
PLUMPS > PLUMP
PLUMPY *adj* plump

PLUMS > PLUM
PLUMULA n down feather
PLUMULAE > PLUMULA
PLUMULAR > PLUMULE
PLUMULATE adj covered with soft fine feathers
PLUMULE n embryonic shoot of seed-bearing plants
PLUMULES > PLUMULE
PLUMULOSE adj having hairs branching out like feathers
PLUMY adj like a feather
PLUNDER vb take by force, esp in time of war ▷ n things plundered, spoils
PLUNDERED > PLUNDER
PLUNDERER > PLUNDER
PLUNDERS > PLUNDER
PLUNGE vb put or throw forcibly or suddenly (into) ▷ n plunging dive
PLUNGED > PLUNGE
PLUNGER n rubber suction cup used to clear blocked pipes
PLUNGERS > PLUNGER
PLUNGES > PLUNGE
PLUNGING > PLUNGE
PLUNGINGS > PLUNGE
PLUNK vb pluck the strings of (a banjo etc) to produce a twanging sound ▷ n act or sound of plunking ▷ interj exclamation imitative of the sound of something plunking ▷ adv exactly
PLUNKED > PLUNK
PLUNKER > PLUNK
PLUNKERS > PLUNK
PLUNKIER > PLUNKY
PLUNKIEST > PLUNKY
PLUNKING > PLUNK
PLUNKS > PLUNK
PLUNKY adj sounding like plucked banjo string
PLUOT n hybrid fruit of the plum and apricot
PLUOTS > PLUOT
PLURAL adj of or consisting of more than one ▷ n word indicating more than one
PLURALISE same as > PLURALIZE
PLURALISM n existence and toleration of a variety of peoples, opinions, etc in a society
PLURALIST > PLURALISM
PLURALITY n state of being plural
PLURALIZE vb make or become plural
PLURALLY > PLURAL
PLURALS > PLURAL
PLURIPARA n woman who has borne more than one child
PLURISIE same as > PLEURISY

PLURISIES > PLURISIE
PLURRY euphemism for > BLOODY
PLUS vb make or become greater in value
PLUSAGE same as > PLUSSAGE
PLUSAGES > PLUSAGE
PLUSED > PLUS
PLUSES > PLUS
PLUSH n fabric with long velvety pile ▷ adj luxurious
PLUSHED adj showily luxurious
PLUSHER > PLUSH
PLUSHES > PLUSH
PLUSHEST > PLUSH
PLUSHIER > PLUSHY
PLUSHIEST > PLUSHY
PLUSHILY > PLUSHY
PLUSHLY > PLUSH
PLUSHNESS > PLUSH
PLUSHY same as > PLUSH
PLUSING > PLUS
PLUSSAGE n amount over and above another amount
PLUSSAGES > PLUSSAGE
PLUSSED > PLUS
PLUSSES > PLUS
PLUSSING > PLUS
PLUTEAL > PLUTEUS
PLUTEI > PLUTEUS
PLUTEUS n larva of sea urchin
PLUTEUSES > PLUTEUS
PLUTOCRAT n person who is powerful because of being very rich
PLUTOID n dwarf planet whose orbit is beyond Neptune's
PLUTOIDS > PLUTOID
PLUTOLOGY n study of wealth
PLUTON n any mass of igneous rock that has solidified below the surface of the earth
PLUTONIAN adj of or relating to the underworld
PLUTONIC adj (of igneous rocks) formed from molten rock that has cooled and solidified below the earth's surface
PLUTONISM n theory that the earth's crust was formed by volcanoes
PLUTONIUM n radioactive metallic element used esp in nuclear reactors and weapons
PLUTONOMY n economics
PLUTONS > PLUTON
PLUVIAL adj of or caused by the action of rain ▷ n of or relating to rainfall or precipitation
PLUVIALS > PLUVIAL
PLUVIAN n crocodile bird
PLUVIANS > PLUVIAN
PLUVIOSE same as > PLUVIOUS

PLUVIOUS adj of or relating to rain
PLUVIUS adj as in pluvius insurance insurance against rain
PLY vb work at (a job or trade) ▷ n thickness of wool, fabric, etc
PLYER n person who plies trade
PLYERS > PLYER
PLYING > PLY
PLYINGLY > PLY
PLYWOOD n board made of thin layers of wood glued together
PLYWOODS > PLYWOOD
PNEUMA n person's vital spirit, soul, or creative energy
PNEUMAS > PNEUMA
PNEUMATIC adj worked by or inflated with wind or air
PNEUMONIA n inflammation of the lungs
PNEUMONIC adj of, relating to, or affecting the lungs
PO n chamber pot
POA n type of grass
POACEOUS adj relating to the plant family which comprises grasses
POACH vb catch (animals) illegally on someone else's land
POACHABLE > POACH
POACHED > POACH
POACHER n person who catches animals illegally on someone else's land
POACHERS > POACHER
POACHES > POACH
POACHIER > POACHY
POACHIEST > POACHY
POACHING > POACH
POACHINGS > POACH
POACHY adj (of land) wet and soft
POAKA n type of stilt (bird) native to New Zealand
POAKAS > POAKA
POAKE n waste matter from tanning of hides
POAKES > POAKE
POAS > POA
POBLANO n variety of chilli pepper
POBLANOS > POBLANO
POBOY n New Orleans sandwich
POBOYS > POBOY
POCHARD n European diving duck
POCHARDS > POCHARD
POCHAY n closed horse-drawn four-wheeled coach ▷ vb transport by pochay
POCHAYED > POCHAY
POCHAYING > POCHAY
POCHAYS > POCHAY

POCHETTE n envelope-shaped handbag used by women and men
POCHETTES > POCHETTE
POCHOIR n print made from stencils
POCHOIRS > POCHOIR
POCK n pus-filled blister resulting from smallpox ▷ vb mark with scars
POCKARD variant of > POCHARD
POCKARDS > POCKARD
POCKED > POCK
POCKET n small bag sewn into clothing for carrying things ▷ vb put into one's pocket ▷ adj small
POCKETED > POCKET
POCKETER > POCKET
POCKETERS > POCKET
POCKETFUL n as much as a pocket will hold
POCKETING > POCKET
POCKETS > POCKET
POCKIER > POCK
POCKIES pl n woollen mittens
POCKIEST > POCK
POCKILY > POCK
POCKING > POCK
POCKMANKY n portmanteau
POCKMARK n pitted scar left on the skin after the healing of a smallpox or similar pustule ▷ vb scar or pit (a surface) with pockmarks
POCKMARKS > POCKMARK
POCKPIT n mark left on skin after a pock has gone
POCKPITS > POCKPIT
POCKS > POCK
POCKY > POCK
POCO adv little
POCOSEN same as > POCOSIN
POCOSENS > POCOSEN
POCOSIN n swamp in US upland coastal region
POCOSINS > POCOSIN
POCOSON same as > POCOSIN
POCOSONS > POCOSON
POD n long narrow seed case of peas, beans, etc ▷ vb remove the pod from
PODAGRA n gout of the foot or big toe
PODAGRAL > PODAGRA
PODAGRAS > PODAGRA
PODAGRIC > PODAGRA
PODAGROUS > PODAGRA
PODAL adj relating to feet
PODALIC adj relating to feet
PODARGUS n bird of SE Asia and Australia
PODCAST n audio file able to be downloaded and listened to on a computer or MP3 player ▷ vb make available in this format

PODCASTED > PODCAST
PODCASTER > PODCAST
PODCASTS > PODCAST
PODDED > POD
PODDIE n user of or enthusiast for the iPod, a portable digital music player
PODDIER > PODDY
PODDIES > PODDY
PODDIEST > PODDY
PODDING > POD
PODDLE vb move or travel in a leisurely manner
PODDLED > PODDLE
PODDLES > PODDLE
PODDLING > PODDLE
PODDY n handfed calf or lamb ▷ adj fat
PODESTA n (in modern Italy) subordinate magistrate in some towns
PODESTAS > PODESTA
PODEX n posterior
PODEXES > PODEX
PODGE n short chubby person
PODGES > PODGE
PODGIER > PODGY
PODGIEST > PODGY
PODGILY > PODGY
PODGINESS > PODGY
PODGY adj short and fat
PODIA > PODIUM
PODIAL > PODIUM
PODIATRIC > PODIATRY
PODIATRY another word for > CHIROPODY
PODITE n crustacean leg
PODITES > PODITE
PODITIC adj similar to the limb segment of an arthropod
PODIUM n small raised platform for a conductor or speaker ▷ vb finish in the top three places in a sporting competition
PODIUMED > PODIUM
PODIUMING > PODIUM
PODIUMS > PODIUM
PODLEY n young coalfish
PODLEYS > PODLEY
PODLIKE > POD
PODOCARP n stem supporting fruit
PODOCARPS > PODOCARP
PODOLOGY n study of feet
PODOMERE n segment of limb of arthropod
PODOMERES > PODOMERE
PODS > POD
PODSOL same as > PODZOL
PODSOLIC > PODZOL
PODSOLISE same as > PODZOLIZE
PODSOLIZE same as > PODZOLIZE
PODSOLS > PODSOL
PODUNK adj small or unimportant ▷ n small or unimportant thing
PODUNKS > PODUNK

PODZOL n type of soil characteristic of coniferous forest regions
PODZOLIC > PODZOL
PODZOLISE same as > PODZOLIZE
PODZOLIZE vb make into or form a podzol
PODZOLS > PODZOL
POECHORE n dry region
POECHORES > POECHORE
POEM n imaginative piece of writing in rhythmic lines
POEMATIC adj of poetry
POEMS > POEM
POENOLOGY same as > PENOLOGY
POEP n emission of gas from the anus ▷ vb break wind
POEPED > POEP
POEPING > POEP
POEPOL n South African slang for anus
POEPOLS > POEPOL
POEPS > POEP
POESIED > POESY
POESIES > POESY
POESY n poetry ▷ vb write poems
POESYING > POESY
POET n writer of poems
POETASTER n writer of inferior verse
POETASTRY > POETASTER
POETESS n female poet
POETESSES > POETESS
POETIC adj of or like poetry
POETICAL n poet
POETICALS > POETICAL
POETICISE same as > POETICIZE
POETICISM > POETICIZE
POETICIZE vb put into poetry or make poetic
POETICS n principles and forms of poetry or the study of these
POETICULE n inferior poet
POETISE same as > POETICIZE
POETISED > POETISE
POETISER > POETISE
POETISERS > POETISE
POETISES > POETISE
POETISING > POETISE
POETIZE same as > POETICIZE
POETIZED > POETIZE
POETIZER > POETIZE
POETIZERS > POETIZE
POETIZES > POETIZE
POETIZING > POETIZE
POETLESS > POET
POETLIKE > POET
POETRESSE old variant of > POETESS
POETRIES > POETRY
POETRY n poems

POETS > POET
POETSHIP n state of being poet
POETSHIPS > POETSHIP
POFFLE n small piece of land
POFFLES > POFFLE
POGEY n financial or other relief given to the unemployed by the government
POGEYS > POGEY
POGGE n European marine scorpaenoid fish
POGGES > POGGE
POGIES > POGY
POGO vb jump up and down in one spot
POGOED > POGO
POGOER > POGO
POGOERS > POGO
POGOES > POGO
POGOING > POGO
POGONIA n orchid with pink or white fragrant flowers
POGONIAS > POGONIA
POGONIP n icy winter fog
POGONIPS > POGONIP
POGOS > POGO
POGROM n organized persecution and massacre ▷ vb carry out a pogrom
POGROMED > POGROM
POGROMING > POGROM
POGROMIST > POGROM
POGROMS > POGROM
POGY same as > POGEY
POH interj exclamation expressing contempt or disgust ▷ vb reject contemptuously
POHED > POH
POHING > POH
POHIRI variant spelling of > POWHIRI
POHIRIS > POHIRI
POHS > POH
POI n ball of woven flax swung rhythmically by Māori women during poi dances
POIGNADO old variant of > PONIARD
POIGNANCE > POIGNANT
POIGNANCY > POIGNANT
POIGNANT adj sharply painful to the feelings
POILU n infantryman in the French Army
POILUS > POILU
POINADO old variant of > PONIARD
POINADOES > POINADO
POINCIANA n tropical leguminous tree with large orange or red flowers
POIND vb take (property of a debtor) in execution or by way of distress
POINDED > POIND
POINDER > POIND
POINDERS > POIND
POINDING > POIND

POINDINGS > POIND
POINDS > POIND
POINT n main idea in a discussion, argument, etc ▷ vb show the direction or position of something or draw attention to it by extending a finger or other pointed object towards it
POINTABLE > POINT
POINTE n tip of the toe
POINTED adj having a sharp end
POINTEDLY > POINTED
POINTEL n engraver's tool
POINTELLE n fabric design in form of chevrons
POINTELS > POINTEL
POINTER n helpful hint
POINTERS > POINTER
POINTES > POINTE
POINTIER > POINTY
POINTIEST > POINTY
POINTILLE n dotted lines and curves impressed on cover of book
POINTING n insertion of mortar between the joints in brickwork
POINTINGS > POINTING
POINTLESS adj meaningless, irrelevant
POINTMAN n soldier who walks at the front of an infantry patrol in combat
POINTMEN > POINTMAN
POINTS > POINT
POINTSMAN n person who operates railway points
POINTSMEN > POINTSMAN
POINTY adj having a sharp point or points
POIS > POI
POISE n calm dignified manner ▷ vb be balanced or suspended
POISED adj absolutely ready
POISER n balancing organ of some insects
POISERS > POISER
POISES > POISE
POISHA n monetary unit of Bangladesh
POISHAS > POISHA
POISING > POISE
POISON n substance that kills or injures when swallowed or absorbed ▷ vb give poison to
POISONED > POISON
POISONER > POISON
POISONERS > POISON
POISONING n the act of giving poison to someone
POISONOUS adj of or like a poison
POISONS > POISON
POISSON n fish
POISSONS > POISSON

POITTIN variant spelling of
> POTEEN

POITTINS > POITTIN

POITREL n breastplate of
horse's armour

POITRELS > POITREL

POITRINE n woman's
bosom

POITRINES > POITRINE

POKABLE > POKE

POKAL n tall drinking cup

POKALS > POKAL

POKE vb jab or prod with
one's finger, a stick, etc
▷ n poking

POKEBERRY same as
> POKEWEED

POKED > POKE

POKEFUL n contents of
small bag

POKEFULS > POKEFUL

POKELOGAN another name
for > BOGAN

POKER n metal rod for
stirring a fire

POKERISH adj stiff like
poker

POKEROOT same as
> POKEWEED

POKEROOTS > POKEROOT

POKERS > POKER

POKERWORK n art of
producing pictures or
designs on wood by
burning it with a heated
metal point

POKES > POKE

POKEWEED n tall North
American plant that has
small white flowers, juicy
purple berries, and a
poisonous purple root
used medicinally

POKEWEEDS > POKEWEED

POKEY same as > POKIE

POKEYS > POKEY

POKIE n poker machine

POKIER > POKY

POKIES > POKY

POKIEST > POKY

POKILY > POKY

POKINESS > POKY

POKING > POKE

POKY adj small and
cramped

POL n political campaigner

POLACCA same as
> POLACRE

POLACCAS > POLACCA

POLACK n person of Polish
birth or descent

POLACKS > POLACK

POLACRE n three-masted
sailing vessel

POLACRES > POLACRE

POLAR adj of or near either
of the earth's poles
▷ n type of line in
geometry

POLARISE same as
> POLARIZE

POLARISED > POLARISE

POLARISER same as
> POLARIZER

POLARISES > POLARISE

POLARITY n state of
having two directly
opposite tendencies or
opinions

POLARIZE vb form or
cause to form into groups
with directly opposite
views

POLARIZED > POLARIZE

POLARIZER n person or a
device that causes
polarization

POLARIZES > POLARIZE

POLARON n kind of
electron

POLARONS > POLARON

POLARS > POLAR

POLDER n land reclaimed
from the sea, esp in the
Netherlands ▷ vb reclaim
land from the sea

POLDERED > POLDER

POLDERING > POLDER

POLDERS > POLDER

POLE n long rounded piece
of wood etc ▷ vb strike or
push with a pole

POLEAX same as
> POLEAXE

POLEAXE vb hit or stun
with a heavy blow ▷ n axe
formerly used in battle or
used by a butcher

POLEAXED > POLEAXE

POLEAXES > POLEAXE

POLEAXING > POLEAXE

POLECAT n small animal
of the weasel family

POLECATS > POLECAT

POLED > POLE

POLEIS > POLIS

POLELESS > POLE

POLEMARCH n (in ancient
Greece) civilian official,
originally a supreme
general

POLEMIC n fierce attack
on or defence of a
particular opinion, belief,
etc ▷ adj of or involving
dispute or controversy

POLEMICAL adj related to
polemics, debate

POLEMICS n art of
dispute

POLEMISE same as
> POLEMIZE

POLEMISED > POLEMISE

POLEMISES > POLEMISE

POLEMIST > POLEMIC

POLEMISTS > POLEMIC

POLEMIZE vb engage in
controversy

POLEMIZED > POLEMIZE

POLEMIZES > POLEMIZE

POLENTA n thick porridge
made in Italy, usually from
maize

POLENTAS > POLENTA

POLER n person or thing
that poles, esp a punter

POLERS > POLER

POLES > POLE

POLESTAR n guiding
principle, rule, standard,
etc

POLESTARS
> POLESTAR

POLEWARD adv towards a
pole

POLEY adj (of cattle)
hornless or polled
▷ n animal with horns
removed

POLEYN n piece of armour
for protecting the knee

POLEYNS > POLEYN

POLEYS > POLEY

POLIANITE n manganese
dioxide occurring as hard
crystals

POLICE n organized force
in a state which keeps law
and order ▷ vb control or
watch over with police or a
similar body

POLICED > POLICE

POLICEMAN n member of
a police force

POLICEMEN
> POLICEMAN

POLICER n computer
device controlling use

POLICERS > POLICER

POLICES > POLICE

POLICIER n film
featuring police
investigating crimes

POLICIERS > POLICIER

POLICIES > POLICY

POLICING > POLICE

POLICINGS > POLICE

POLICY n plan of action
adopted by a person,
group, or state

POLIES > POLY

POLING > POLE

POLINGS > POLE

POLIO n acute viral
disease

POLIOS > POLIO

POLIS n ancient Greek
city-state

POLISES > POLIS

POLISH vb make smooth
and shiny by rubbing
▷ n substance used for
polishing

POLISHED adj
accomplished

POLISHER > POLISH

POLISHERS > POLISH

POLISHES > POLISH

POLISHING > POLISH

POLITBURO n supreme
policy-making authority in
most communist
countries

POLITE adj showing
consideration for others
in one's manners, speech,
etc

POLITELY > POLITE

POLITER > POLITE

POLITESSE n formal or
genteel politeness

POLITEST > POLITE

POLITIC adj wise and
likely to prove
advantageous

POLITICAL adj of the
state, government, or
public administration

POLITICK vb engage in
politics

POLITICKS > POLITICK

POLITICLY > POLITIC

POLITICO n politician

POLITICOS > POLITICO

POLITICS n winning and
using of power to govern
society

POLITIES > POLITY

POLITIQUE n 16th-
century French moderate

POLITY n politically
organized state, church, or
society

POLJE n large elliptical
depression in karst regions

POLJES > POLJE

POLK vb dance a polka

POLKA n lively
19th-century dance
▷ vb dance a polka

POLKAED > POLKA

POLKAING > POLKA

POLKAS > POLKA

POLKED > POLK

POLKING > POLK

POLKS > POLK

POLL n questioning of a
random sample of people
to find out general opinion
▷ vb receive (votes)

POLLACK n food fish
related to the cod, found in
northern seas

POLLACKS > POLLACK

POLLAN n whitefish that
occurs in lakes in Northern
Ireland

POLLANS > POLLAN

POLLARD n animal that
has shed its horns or has
had them removed
▷ vb cut off the top of (a
tree) to make it grow
bushy

POLLARDED > POLLARD

POLLARDS > POLLARD

POLLAXE same as
> POLEAXE

POLLAXED > POLLAXE

POLLAXES > POLLAXE

POLLAXING > POLLAXE

POLLED adj (of animals,
esp cattle) having the
horns cut off or being
naturally hornless

POLLEE > POLL

POLLEES > POLL

POLLEN n fine dust
produced by flowers to
fertilize other flowers
▷ vb collect pollen

POLLENATE same as
> POLLINATE

POLLENED > POLLEN

POLLENING > POLLEN

POLLENS > POLLEN

POLLENT *adj* strong
POLLER > POLL
POLLERS > POLL
POLLEX *n* first digit of the forelimb of amphibians, reptiles, birds, and mammals
POLLICAL > POLLEX
POLLICES > POLLEX
POLLICIE *obsolete spelling of* > POLICY
POLLICIES > POLLICIE
POLLICY *obsolete spelling of* > POLICY
POLLIES > POLLY
POLLINATE *vb* fertilize with pollen
POLLING *n* casting or registering of votes at an election
POLLINGS > POLLING
POLLINIA > POLLINIUM
POLLINIC > POLLEN
POLLINISE *same as* > POLLINIZE
POLLINIUM *n* mass of cohering pollen grains, produced by plants such as orchids and transported as a whole during pollination
POLLINIZE *same as* > POLLINATE
POLLIST *n* one advocating the use of polls
POLLISTS > POLLIST
POLLIWIG *same as* > POLLIWOG
POLLIWIGS > POLLIWOG
POLLIWOG *n* sailor who has not crossed the equator
POLLIWOGS > POLLIWOG
POLLMAN *n* one passing a degree without honours
POLLMEN > POLLMAN
POLLOCK *same as* > POLLACK
POLLOCKS > POLLOCK
POLLS > POLL
POLLSTER *n* person who conducts opinion polls
POLLSTERS > POLLSTER
POLLTAKER *n* person conducting poll
POLLUCITE *n* colourless rare mineral consisting of a hydrated caesium aluminium silicate
POLLUSION *n* comic Shakespearian character's version of "allusion"
POLLUTANT *n* something that pollutes
POLLUTE *vb* contaminate with something poisonous or harmful
POLLUTED *adj* made unclean or impure
POLLUTER > POLLUTE
POLLUTERS > POLLUTE
POLLUTES > POLLUTE
POLLUTING > POLLUTE
POLLUTION *n* act of

polluting or the state of being polluted
POLLUTIVE *adj* causing pollution
POLLY *n* politician
POLLYANNA *n* person who is constantly or excessively optimistic
POLLYWIG *same as* > POLLIWOG
POLLYWIGS > POLLYWIG
POLLYWOG *same as* > POLLIWOG
POLLYWOGS > POLLYWOG
POLO *n* game like hockey played by teams of players on horseback
POLOIDAL *adj* relating to a type of magnetic field
POLOIST *n* devotee of polo
POLOISTS > POLOIST
POLONAISE *n* old stately dance
POLONIE *same as* > POLONY
POLONIES > POLONY
POLONISE *same as* > POLONIZE
POLONISED > POLONISE
POLONISES > POLONISE
POLONISM > POLONISE
POLONISMS > POLONISE
POLONIUM *n* radioactive element that occurs in trace amounts in uranium ores
POLONIUMS > POLONIUM
POLONIZE *vb* make Polish
POLONIZED > POLONIZE
POLONIZES > POLONIZE
POLONY *n* bologna sausage
POLOS > POLO
POLS > POL
POLT *n* thump or blow ▷ *vb* strike
POLTED > POLT
POLTFEET > POLTFOOT
POLTFOOT *adj* having a club foot ▷ *n* club foot
POLTING > POLT
POLTROON *n* utter coward
POLTROONS > POLTROON
POLTS > POLT
POLVERINE *n* glassmakers' potash
POLY *n* polytechnic
POLYACID *adj* having two or more hydroxyl groups ▷ *n* compound made up of two or more hydroxyl groups
POLYACIDS > POLYACID
POLYACT *adj* (of a sea creature) having many tentacles or limb-like protrusions
POLYADIC *adj* (of a relation, operation, etc) having several argument places
POLYAMIDE *n* synthetic polymeric material

POLYAMINE *n* compound containing two or more amine groups
POLYAMORY *n* practice of openly having more than one intimate relationship at a time
POLYANDRY *n* practice of having more than one husband at the same time
POLYANTHA *n* type of flower
POLYANTHI *n* hybrid garden primroses
POLYARCH *n* member of polyarchy
POLYARCHY *n* political system in which power is dispersed
POLYAXIAL *n* joint in which movement occurs in more than one axis
POLYAXON *n* nerve cell with multiple branches
POLYAXONS > POLYAXON
POLYBAG *vb* put into a polythene bag
POLYBAGS > POLYBAG
POLYBASIC *adj* (of an acid) having two or more replaceable hydrogen atoms per molecule
POLYBRID *n* hybrid plant with more than two parental groups
POLYBRIDS > POLYBRID
POLYCARPY *n* condition of being able to produce flowers and fruit several times in successive years or seasons
POLYCHETE *n* variety of worm
POLYCONIC *adj* as in *polyconic projection* type of projection used in making maps of large areas
POLYCOT *n* plant that has or appears to have more than two cotyledons
POLYCOTS > POLYCOT
POLYDEMIC *adj* growing in or inhabiting more than two regions
POLYDRUG *adj* relating to using several drugs together
POLYENE *n* organic chemical compound
POLYENES > POLYENE
POLYENIC > POLYENE
POLYESTER *n* synthetic material used to make plastics and textile fibres
POLYGALA *n* herbaceous plant or small shrub
POLYGALAS > POLYGALA
POLYGAM *n* plant of the Polygamia class
POLYGAMIC > POLYGAMY
POLYGAMS > POLYGAM
POLYGAMY *n* practice of having more than one husband or wife at the same time

POLYGENE *n* any of a group of genes that each produce a small quantitative effect on a particular characteristic of the phenotype, such as height
POLYGENES > POLYGENE
POLYGENIC *adj* of, relating to, or controlled by polygenes
POLYGENY > POLYGENIC
POLYGLOT *adj* (person) able to speak or write several languages ▷ *n* person who can speak many languages
POLYGLOTS > POLYGLOT
POLYGLOTT *variant of* > POLYGLOT
POLYGON *n* geometrical figure with three or more angles and sides
POLYGONAL > POLYGON
POLYGONS > POLYGON
POLYGONUM *n* plant with stems with knotlike joints and spikes of small white, green, or pink flowers
POLYGONY > POLYGON
POLYGRAPH *n* instrument for recording pulse rate and perspiration, used esp as a lie detector
POLYGYNE *adj* (of a colony of insects) having more than one egg-laying queen
POLYGYNY *n* practice of having more than one wife at the same time
POLYHEDRA *n* solid figures, each consisting of four or more plane faces
POLYIMIDE *n* type of polymer
POLYLEMMA *n* debate forcing choice between contradictory positions
POLYMASTY *n* condition in which more than two breasts are present
POLYMATH *n* person of great and varied learning
POLYMATHS > POLYMATH
POLYMATHY > POLYMATH
POLYMER *n* chemical compound with large molecules made of simple molecules of the same kind
POLYMERIC *adj* of or being a polymer
POLYMERS > POLYMER
POLYMERY > POLYMER
POLYMORPH *n* species of animal or plant that exhibits polymorphism
POLYMYXIN *n* polypeptide antibiotic
POLYNIA *same as* > POLYNYA
POLYNIAS > POLYNIA
POLYNYA *n* stretch of open water surrounded by ice

P

POLYNYAS > POLYNYA
POLYNYI > POLYNYA
POLYOL *n* type of alcohol
POLYOLS > POLYOL
POLYOMA *n* type of tumour caused by virus
POLYOMAS > POLYOMA
POLYOMINO *n* polygon made from joining identical squares at their edges
POLYONYM *n* object with many names
POLYONYMS > POLYONYM
POLYONYMY > POLYONYM
POLYP *n* small simple sea creature with a hollow cylindrical body
POLYPARIA *n* polyparies
POLYPARY *n* common base and connecting tissue of a colony of coelenterate polyps, esp coral
POLYPE *variant of* > POLYP
POLYPED *same as* > POLYPOD
POLYPEDS > POLYPED
POLYPES > POLYPE
POLYPHAGY *n* insatiable appetite
POLYPHASE *adj* (of an electrical system, circuit, or device) having, generating, or using two or more alternating voltages of the same frequency, the phases of which are cyclically displaced by fractions of a period
POLYPHON *n* musical instrument resembling a lute
POLYPHONE *n* letter or character with more than one phonetic value
POLYPHONS > POLYPHON
POLYPHONY *n* polyphonic style of composition or a piece of music using it
POLYPI > POLYPUS
POLYPIDE *n* polyp forming part of a colonial animal
POLYPIDES > POLYPIDE
POLYPIDOM *same as* > POLYPARY
POLYPILL *n* proposed combined medication intended to reduce the likelihood of heart attacks and strokes
POLYPILLS > POLYPILL
POLYPINE *adj* of or relating to polyps
POLYPITE *same as* > POLYPIDE
POLYPITES > POLYPITE
POLYPLOID *adj* (of cells, organisms, etc) having more than twice the basic (haploid) number of chromosomes ▷ *n* individual or cell of this type

POLYPNEA *n* rapid breathing
POLYPNEAS > POLYPNEA
POLYPNEIC > POLYPNEA
POLYPOD *adj* (esp of insect larvae) having many legs or similar appendages ▷ *n* animal of this type
POLYPODS > POLYPOD
POLYPODY *n* fern with deeply divided leaves and round naked sori
POLYPOID > POLYP
POLYPORE *n* type of fungi
POLYPORES > POLYPORE
POLYPOSES > POLYPOSIS
POLYPOSIS *n* formation of many polyps
POLYPOUS > POLYP
POLYPS > POLYP
POLYPTYCH *n* altarpiece consisting of more than three panels, set with paintings or carvings, and usually hinged for folding
POLYPUS *same as* > POLYP
POLYPUSES > POLYPUS
POLYS > POLY
POLYSEME *n* word with many meanings
POLYSEMES > POLYSEME
POLYSEMIC > POLYSEME
POLYSEMY *n* existence of several meanings in a single word
POLYSOME *n* assemblage of ribosomes associated with a messenger RNA molecule
POLYSOMES > POLYSOME
POLYSOMIC *adj* of, relating to, or designating a basically diploid chromosome complement, in which some but not all the chromosomes are represented more than twice
POLYSOMY > POLYSOME
POLYSTYLE *adj* with many columns ▷ *n* building with many columns
POLYTENE *adj* denoting a type of giant-size chromosome
POLYTENY > POLYTENE
POLYTHENE *n* light plastic used for bags etc
POLYTONAL *adj* using more than two different tones or keys simultaneously
POLYTYPE *n* crystal occurring in more than one form ▷ *vb* produce by use of a polytype
POLYTYPED > POLYTYPE
POLYTYPES > POLYTYPE
POLYTYPIC *adj* existing in, consisting of, or incorporating several different types or forms

POLYURIA *n* state or condition of discharging abnormally large quantities of urine, often accompanied by a need to urinate frequently
POLYURIAS > POLYURIA
POLYURIC > POLYURIA
POLYVINYL *n* designating a plastic or resin formed by polymerization of a vinyl derivative
POLYWATER *n* liquid formerly supposed to be polymeric form of water
POLYZOA *n* small mosslike aquatic creatures
POLYZOAN *another word for* > BRYOZOAN
POLYZOANS > POLYZOAN
POLYZOARY *n* colony of bryozoan animals
POLYZOIC *adj* (of certain colonial animals) having many zooids or similar polyps
POLYZONAL *adj* having many zones
POLYZOOID *adj* resembling a polyzoon
POLYZOON *n* individual zooid within polyzoan
POM *same as* > POMMY
POMACE *n* apple pulp left after pressing for juice
POMACEOUS *adj* of, relating to, or bearing pomes, such as the apple, pear, and quince trees
POMACES > POMACE
POMADE *n* perfumed oil put on the hair to make it smooth and shiny ▷ *vb* put pomade on
POMADED > POMADE
POMADES > POMADE
POMADING > POMADE
POMANDER *n* mixture of sweet-smelling petals, herbs, etc
POMANDERS > POMANDER
POMATO *n* hybrid of tomato and potato
POMATOES > POMATO
POMATUM *same as* > POMADE
POMATUMS > POMATUM
POMBE *n* any alcoholic drink
POMBES > POMBE
POME *n* fleshy fruit of the apple and related plants
POMELO *n* edible yellow fruit, like a grapefruit
POMELOS > POMELO
POMEROY *n* bullet used to down airships
POMEROYS > POMEROY
POMES > POME
POMFRET *n* small black rounded liquorice sweet
POMFRETS > POMFRET

POMMEE *adj* (of cross) having end of each arm ending in disk
POMMEL *same as* > PUMMEL
POMMELE *adj* having a pommel
POMMELED > POMMEL
POMMELING > POMMEL
POMMELLED > POMMEL
POMMELS > POMMEL
POMMETTY *adj* having a pommel
POMMIE *same as* > POMMY
POMMIES > POMMY
POMMY *n* word used by Australians and New Zealanders for a British person
POMO *n* postmodernism
POMOERIUM *n* space around town within city walls
POMOLOGY *n* branch of horticulture that is concerned with the study and cultivation of fruit
POMOS > POMO
POMP *n* stately display or ceremony
POMPADOUR *n* early 18th-century hairstyle for women, having the front hair arranged over a pad to give it greater height and bulk
POMPANO *n* deep-bodied carangid food fish
POMPANOS > POMPANO
POMPELO *n* large Asian citrus fruit
POMPELOS > POMPELO
POMPEY *vb* mollycoddle
POMPEYED > POMPEY
POMPEYING > POMPEY
POMPEYS > POMPEY
POMPHOLYX *n* type of eczema
POMPIER *adj* slavishly conventional ▷ *n* conventional or imitative artist
POMPIERS > POMPIER
POMPILID *n* spider-hunting wasp
POMPILIDS > POMPILID
POMPION *n* pumpkin
POMPIONS > POMPION
POMPOM *n* decorative ball of tufted wool, silk, etc
POMPOMS > POMPOM
POMPON *same as* > POMPOM
POMPONS > POMPON
POMPOON *variant of* > POMPOM
POMPOONS > POMPOON
POMPOSITY *n* vain or ostentatious display of dignity or importance
POMPOSO *adj* (of music) to be played in a ceremonial manner
POMPOUS *adj* foolishly serious and grand, self-important

POMPOUSLY > POMPOUS
POMPS > POMP
POMROY variant of > POMEROY
POMROYS > POMROY
POMS > POM
POMWATER n kind of apple
POMWATERS > POMWATER
PONCE n derogatory word for an effeminate man ▷ vb act stupidly or waste time
PONCEAU n scarlet red
PONCEAUS > PONCEAU
PONCEAUX > PONCEAU
PONCED > PONCE
PONCES > PONCE
PONCEY adj ostentatious, pretentious, or effeminate
PONCHO n loose circular cloak with a hole for the head
PONCHOED adj wearing poncho
PONCHOS > PONCHO
PONCIER > PONCEY
PONCIEST > PONCEY
PONCING > PONCE
PONCY same as > PONCEY
POND n small area of still water ▷ vb hold back (flowing water)
PONDAGE n water held in reservoir
PONDAGES > PONDAGE
PONDED > POND
PONDER vb think thoroughly or deeply (about)
PONDERAL adj relating to weight
PONDERATE vb consider
PONDERED > PONDER
PONDERER > PONDER
PONDERERS > PONDER
PONDERING > PONDER
PONDEROSA n N American pine tree
PONDEROUS adj serious and dull
PONDERS > PONDER
PONDING > POND
PONDOK n (in southern Africa) crudely made house or shack
PONDOKKIE same as > PONDOK
PONDOKS > PONDOK
PONDS > POND
PONDWEED n plant that grows in ponds
PONDWEEDS > PONDWEED
PONE n bread made of maize
PONENT adj westerly ▷ n the west
PONENTS > PONENT
PONES > PONE
PONEY same as > PONY
PONEYS > PONEY
PONG n strong unpleasant smell ▷ vb give off a strong unpleasant smell

PONGA n tall New Zealand tree fern
PONGAL n Indian dish of cooked rice
PONGALS > PONGAL
PONGAS > PONGA
PONGED > PONG
PONGEE n thin plain-weave silk fabric
PONGEES > PONGEE
PONGID n primate of the family which includes the gibbons and the great apes
PONGIDS > PONGID
PONGIER > PONG
PONGIEST > PONG
PONGING > PONG
PONGO n anthropoid ape, esp an orang-utan or (formerly) a gorilla
PONGOES > PONGO
PONGOS > PONGO
PONGS > PONG
PONGY > PONG
PONIARD n small slender dagger ▷ vb stab with a poniard
PONIARDED > PONIARD
PONIARDS > PONIARD
PONIED > PONY
PONIES > PONY
PONK n evil spirit ▷ vb stink
PONKED > PONK
PONKING > PONK
PONKS > PONK
PONS n bridge of connecting tissue
PONT n (in South Africa) river ferry
PONTAGE n tax paid for repairing bridge
PONTAGES > PONTAGE
PONTAL adj of or relating to the pons
PONTES > PONS
PONTIANAC same as > PONTIANAK
PONTIANAK n (in Malay folklore) female vampire
PONTIC adj of or relating to the pons
PONTIE same as > PONTY
PONTIES > PONTY
PONTIFEX n (in ancient Rome) any of the senior members of the Pontifical College
PONTIFF n Pope
PONTIFFS > PONTIFF
PONTIFIC > PONTIFF
PONTIFICE n structure of bridge
PONTIFIED > PONTIFY
PONTIFIES > PONTIFY
PONTIFY vb speak or behave in a pompous or dogmatic manner
PONTIL same as > PUNTY
PONTILE adj relating to pons ▷ n metal bar used in glass-making
PONTILES > PONTILE

PONTILS > PONTIL
PONTINE adj of or relating to bridges
PONTLEVIS n horse rearing repeatedly
PONTON variant of > PONTOON
PONTONEER same as > PONTONIER
PONTONIER n person in charge of or involved in building a pontoon bridge
PONTONS > PONTON
PONTOON n floating platform supporting a temporary bridge ▷ vb cross a river using pontoons
PONTOONED > PONTOON
PONTOONER > PONTOON
PONTOONS > PONTOON
PONTS > PONT
PONTY n rod used for shaping molten glass
PONY n small horse ▷ vb settle bill or debt
PONYING > PONY
PONYSKIN n leather from pony hide
PONYSKINS > PONYSKIN
PONYTAIL n long hair tied in one bunch at the back of the head
PONYTAILS > PONYTAIL
PONZU n type of Japanese dipping sauce
PONZUS > PONZU
POO vb defecate
POOBAH n influential person
POOBAHS > POOBAH
POOCH n slang word for dog ▷ vb bulge or protrude
POOCHED > POOCH
POOCHES > POOCH
POOCHING > POOCH
POOD n unit of weight, used in Russia
POODLE n dog with curly hair often clipped fancifully
POODLES > POODLE
POODS > POOD
POOED > POO
POOF n derogatory word for a homosexual man
POOFIER > POOF
POOFIEST > POOF
POOFS > POOF
POOFTAH same as > POOFTER
POOFTAHS > POOFTAH
POOFTER n derogatory word for a man who is considered effeminate or homosexual
POOFTERS > POOFTER
POOFY > POOF
POOGYE n Hindu nose-flute
POOGYES > POOGYE
POOH interj exclamation of disdain, contempt, or

disgust ▷ vb make such an exclamation
POOHED > POOH
POOHING > POOH
POOHS > POOH
POOING > POO
POOJA variant of > PUJA
POOJAH variant of > PUJA
POOJAHS > POOJAH
POOJAS > POOJA
POOK vb pluck
POOKA n malevolent Irish spirit
POOKAS > POOKA
POOKING > POOK
POOKIT > POOK
POOKS > POOK
POOL n small body of still water ▷ vb put in a common fund
POOLED > POOL
POOLER n person taking part in pool
POOLERS > POOLER
POOLHALL n room containing pool tables
POOLHALLS > POOLHALL
POOLING > POOL
POOLROOM n hall or establishment where pool, billiards, etc, are played
POOLROOMS > POOLROOM
POOLS pl n organized nationwide gambling pool
POOLSIDE n area surrounding swimming pool
POOLSIDES > POOLSIDE
POON n SE Asian tree
POONAC n coconut residue
POONACS > POONAC
POONCE n derogatory word for a homosexual man ▷ vb behave effeminately
POONCED > POONCE
POONCES > POONCE
POONCING > POONCE
POONS > POON
POONTANG n taboo word for the female pudenda
POONTANGS > POONTANG
POOP n raised part at the back of a sailing ship ▷ vb (of a wave or sea) break over the stern of (a vessel)
POOPED > POOP
POOPER n as in party pooper person who spoils other people's enjoyment
POOPERS > POOPER
POOPIER > POOPY
POOPIEST > POOPY
POOPING > POOP
POOPS > POOP
POOPY adj stupid or ineffectual
POOR adj having little money and few possessions
POORBOX n box used for the collection of money for the poor

POORBOXES > POORBOX
POORER > POOR
POOREST > POOR
POORHOUSE n (formerly) publicly maintained institution offering accommodation to the poor
POORI n unleavened Indian bread
POORIS > POORI
POORISH > POOR
POORLIER > POORLY
POORLIEST > POORLY
POORLY adv in a poor manner ⊳ adj not in good health
POORMOUTH vb complain about being poor
POORNESS > POOR
POORT n (in South Africa) steep narrow mountain pass
POORTITH same as > PUIRTITH
POORTITHS > POORTITH
POORTS > POORT
POORWILL n bird of N America
POORWILLS > POORWILL
POOS > POO
POOT vb break wind
POOTED > POOT
POOTER > POOT
POOTERS > POOT
POOTING > POOT
POOTLE vb travel or go in a relaxed or leisurely manner
POOTLED > POOTLE
POOTLES > POOTLE
POOTLING > POOTLE
POOTS > POOT
POOVE same as > POOF
POOVERIES > POOVERY
POOVERY n derogatory word for homosexuality
POOVES > POOVE
POOVIER > POOVE
POOVIEST > POOVE
POOVY > POOVE
POP vb make or cause to make a small explosive sound ⊳ n small explosive sound ⊳ adj popular
POPADUM same as > POPPADOM
POPADUMS > POPADUM
POPCORN n grains of maize heated until they puff up and burst
POPCORNS > POPCORN
POPE n bishop of Rome as head of the Roman Catholic Church
POPEDOM n office or dignity of a pope
POPEDOMS > POPEDOM
POPEHOOD > POPE
POPEHOODS > POPE
POPELESS > POPE
POPELIKE > POPE

POPELING n deputy or supporter of pope
POPELINGS > POPELING
POPERA n music drawing on opera or classical music and aiming for popular appeal
POPERAS > POPERA
POPERIES > POPERY
POPERIN n kind of pear
POPERINS > POPERIN
POPERY n derogatory word for Roman Catholicism
POPES > POPE
POPESEYE adj denoting a cut of steak
POPESHIP > POPE
POPESHIPS > POPE
POPETTE n young female fan or performer of pop music
POPETTES > POPETTE
POPEYED adj staring in astonishment
POPGUN n toy gun that fires a pellet or cork by means of compressed air
POPGUNS > POPGUN
POPINAC n type of thorny shrub
POPINACK same as > POPINAC
POPINACKS > POPINACK
POPINACS > POPINAC
POPINJAY n conceited, foppish, or overly talkative person
POPINJAYS > POPINJAY
POPISH adj derogatory word for Roman Catholic
POPISHLY > POPISH
POPJOY vb amuse oneself
POPJOYED > POPJOY
POPJOYING > POPJOY
POPJOYS > POPJOY
POPLAR n tall slender tree
POPLARS > POPLAR
POPLIN n ribbed cotton material
POPLINS > POPLIN
POPLITEAL adj of, relating to, or near the part of the leg behind the knee
POPLITEI > POPLITEUS
POPLITEUS n muscle in leg
POPLITIC same as > POPLITEAL
POPOUT n type of out in baseball
POPOUTS > POPOUT
POPOVER n individual Yorkshire pudding, often served with roast beef
POPOVERS > POPOVER
POPPA same as > PAPA
POPPADOM n thin round crisp Indian bread
POPPADOMS > POPPADOM
POPPADUM same as > POPPADOM
POPPADUMS > POPPADUM

POPPAS > POPPA
POPPED > POP
POPPER n press stud
POPPERING n method of fishing
POPPERS > POPPER
POPPET n term of affection for a small child or sweetheart
POPPETS > POPPET
POPPIED adj covered with poppies
POPPIER > POPPY
POPPIES > POPPY
POPPIEST > POPPY
POPPING > POP
POPPISH adj like pop music
POPPIT n bead used to form necklace
POPPITS > POPPIT
POPPLE vb (of boiling water or a choppy sea) to heave or toss
POPPLED > POPPLE
POPPLES > POPPLE
POPPLIER > POPPLY
POPPLIEST > POPPLY
POPPLING > POPPLE
POPPLY adj covered in small bumps
POPPY n plant with a large red flower ⊳ adj reddish-orange
POPPYCOCK n nonsense
POPPYHEAD n hard dry seed-containing capsule of a poppy
POPRIN same as > POPERIN
POPS > POP
POPSICLE n tradename for a kind of ice lolly
POPSICLES > POPSICLE
POPSIE same as > POPSY
POPSIES > POPSY
POPSOCK n women's knee-length nylon stocking
POPSOCKS > POPSOCK
POPSTER n pop star
POPSTERS > POPSTER
POPSTREL n young, attractive female pop star
POPSTRELS > POPSTREL
POPSY n attractive young woman
POPULACE n ordinary people
POPULACES > POPULACE
POPULAR adj widely liked and admired ⊳ n cheap newspapers with mass circulation
POPULARLY adv by the public as a whole
POPULARS > POPULAR
POPULATE vb live in, inhabit
POPULATED > POPULATE
POPULATES > POPULATE
POPULISM n political strategy based on a calculated appeal to the

interests or prejudices of ordinary people
POPULISMS > POPULISM
POPULIST adj (person) appealing to the interests or prejudices of ordinary people ⊳ n person, esp a politician, who appeals to the interests or prejudices of ordinary people
POPULISTS > POPULIST
POPULOUS adj densely populated
PORAE n large edible sea fish of New Zealand waters
PORAES > PORAE
PORAL adj relating to pores
PORANGI adj crazy
PORBEAGLE n kind of shark
PORCELAIN n fine china
PORCH n covered approach to the entrance of a building
PORCHED adj having a porch
PORCHES > PORCH
PORCHETTA n Italian boneless stuffed pork cut from a whole roast pig
PORCINE adj of or like a pig
PORCINI > PORCINO
PORCINIS > PORCINO
PORCINO n edible woodland fungus
PORCUPINE n animal covered with long pointed quills
PORCUPINY > PORCUPINE
PORE n tiny opening in the skin or in the surface of a plant ⊳ vb make a close intent examination or study
PORED > PORE
PORER n person who pores
PORERS > PORE
PORES > PORE
PORGE vb cleanse (slaughtered animal) ceremonially
PORGED > PORGE
PORGES > PORGE
PORGIE same as > PORGY
PORGIES > PORGY
PORGING > PORGE
PORGY n any of various sparid fishes
PORIER > PORY
PORIEST > PORY
PORIFER n type of invertebrate
PORIFERAL > PORIFERAN
PORIFERAN n invertebrate of the phylum which comprises the sponges
PORIFERS > PORIFER
PORIN n protein through which molecules can pass

PORINA n larva of a moth which causes damage to grassland

PORINAS > PORINA

PORINESS > PORY

PORING > PORE

PORINS > PORIN

PORISM n type of mathematical proposition

PORISMS > PORISM

PORISTIC > PORISM

PORK vb eat ravenously ▷ n the flesh of pigs used as food

PORKED > PORK

PORKER n pig raised for food

PORKERS > PORKER

PORKIER > PORKY

PORKIES > PORKY

PORKIEST > PORKY

PORKINESS > PORKY

PORKING > PORK

PORKLING n pig

PORKLINGS > PORKLING

PORKPIE n hat with a round flat crown and a brim that can be turned up or down

PORKPIES > PORKPIE

PORKS > PORK

PORKWOOD n wood of small American tree

PORKWOODS > PORKWOOD

PORKY adj of or like pork ▷ n lie

PORLOCK vb interrupt or intrude at an awkward moment

PORLOCKED > PORLOCK

PORLOCKS > PORLOCK

PORN n pornography

PORNIER > PORNY

PORNIEST > PORNY

PORNO same as > PORN

PORNOMAG n pornographic magazine

PORNOMAGS > PORNOMAG

PORNOS > PORNO

PORNS > PORN

PORNY adj pornographic

POROGAMIC > POROGAMY

POROGAMY n fertilization of seed plants

POROMERIC adj (of a plastic) permeable to water vapour ▷ n substance having this characteristic, esp one based on polyurethane and used in place of leather in making shoe uppers

POROSCOPE n instrument for assessing porosity

POROSCOPY > POROSCOPE

POROSE adj pierced with small pores

POROSES > POROSIS

POROSIS n porous condition of bones

POROSITY n state or condition of being porous

POROUS adj allowing liquid to pass through gradually

POROUSLY > POROUS

PORPESS n type of fish

PORPESSE same as > PORPOISE

PORPESSES > PORPESS

PORPHYRIA n hereditary disease of body metabolism, producing abdominal pain, mental confusion, etc

PORPHYRIC > PORPHYRIA

PORPHYRIN n any of a group of pigments occurring widely in animal and plant tissues and having a heterocyclic structure formed from four pyrrole rings linked by four methylene groups

PORPHYRIO n aquatic bird

PORPHYRY n reddish rock with large crystals in it

PORPOISE n fishlike sea mammal ▷ vb (of an aeroplane) nose-dive during landing

PORPOISED > PORPOISE

PORPOISES > PORPOISE

PORPORATE adj wearing purple

PORRECT adj extended forwards ▷ vb stretch forward

PORRECTED > PORRECT

PORRECTS > PORRECT

PORRENGER same as > PORRINGER

PORRIDGE n breakfast food made of oatmeal cooked in water or milk

PORRIDGES > PORRIDGE

PORRIDGY > PORRIDGE

PORRIGO n disease of the scalp

PORRIGOS > PORRIGO

PORRINGER n small dish, often with a handle, used esp formerly for soup or porridge

PORT same as > PORTHOLE

PORTA n aperture in an organ

PORTABLE adj easily carried ▷ n article designed to be easily carried, such as a television or typewriter

PORTABLES > PORTABLE

PORTABLY > PORTABLE

PORTAGE n (route for) transporting boats overland ▷ vb transport (boats) in this way

PORTAGED > PORTAGE

PORTAGES > PORTAGE

PORTAGING > PORTAGE

PORTAGUE n Portuguese gold coin

PORTAGUES > PORTAGUE

PORTAL n large imposing doorway or gate

PORTALED > PORTAL

PORTALS > PORTAL

PORTANCE n person's bearing

PORTANCES > PORTANCE

PORTAPACK n combined videotape recorder and camera

PORTAPAK same as > PORTAPACK

PORTAPAKS > PORTAPAK

PORTAS > PORTA

PORTASES variant of > PORTESSE

PORTATE adj diagonally athwart escutcheon

PORTATILE adj portable

PORTATIVE adj concerned with the act of carrying

PORTED > PORT

PORTEND vb be a sign of

PORTENDED > PORTEND

PORTENDS > PORTEND

PORTENT n sign of a future event

PORTENTS > PORTENT

PORTEOUS variant of > PORTESSE

PORTER n man who carries luggage ▷ vb carry luggage

PORTERAGE n work of carrying supplies, goods, etc, done by porters

PORTERED > PORTER

PORTERESS n female porter

PORTERING > PORTER

PORTERLY adj like a porter

PORTERS > PORTER

PORTESS variant of > PORTESSE

PORTESSE n prayer book

PORTESSES > PORTESSE

PORTFIRE n (formerly) slow-burning fuse used for firing rockets and fireworks and, in mining, for igniting explosives

PORTFIRES > PORTFIRE

PORTFOLIO n (flat case for carrying) examples of an artist's work

PORTHOLE n small round window in a ship or aircraft

PORTHOLES > PORTHOLE

PORTHORS same as > PORTESSE

PORTHOS same as > PORTESSE

PORTHOSES > PORTHOS

PORTHOUSE n company producing port

PORTICO n porch or covered walkway with columns supporting the roof

PORTICOED > PORTICO

PORTICOES > PORTICO

PORTICOS > PORTICO

PORTIER > PORT

PORTIERE n curtain hung in a doorway

PORTIERED adj having a portiere, a curtain hanging across a doorway

PORTIERES > PORTIERE

PORTIEST > PORT

PORTIGUE same as > PORTAGUE

PORTIGUES > PORTIGUE

PORTING > PORT

PORTION n part or share ▷ vb divide (something) into shares

PORTIONED > PORTION

PORTIONER > PORTION

PORTIONS > PORTION

PORTLAND n type of rose

PORTLANDS > PORTLAND

PORTLAST n gunwale of ship

PORTLASTS > PORTLAST

PORTLESS > PORT

PORTLIER > PORTLY

PORTLIEST > PORTLY

PORTLY adj rather fat

PORTMAN n inhabitant of port

PORTMEN > PORTMAN

PORTOISE same as > PORTLAST

PORTOISES > PORTOISE

PORTOLAN n book of sailing charts

PORTOLANI > PORTOLANO

PORTOLANO variant of > PORTOLAN

PORTOLANS > PORTOLAN

PORTOUS variant of > PORTESSE

PORTOUSES > PORTOUS

PORTRAIT n picture of a person ▷ adj (of a publication or an illustration in a publication) of greater height than width

PORTRAITS > PORTRAIT

PORTRAY vb describe or represent by artistic means, as in writing or film

PORTRAYAL > PORTRAY

PORTRAYED > PORTRAY

PORTRAYER > PORTRAY

PORTRAYS > PORTRAY

PORTREEVE n Saxon magistrate

PORTRESS n female porter, esp a doorkeeper

PORTS > PORT

PORTSIDE adj beside port

PORTULACA n tropical American plant with yellow, pink, or purple showy flowers

PORTULAN same as > PORTOLAN

PORTULANS > PORTULAN

PORTY adj like port

PORWIGGLE n tadpole

PORY adj containing pores
POS > PO
POSABLE > POSE
POSADA n inn in a Spanish-speaking country
POSADAS > POSADA
POSAUNE n organ chorus reed
POSAUNES > POSAUNE
POSE vb place in or take up a particular position to be photographed or drawn ▷ n position while posing
POSEABLE adj able to be manipulated into poses
POSED > POSE
POSER n puzzling question
POSERISH same as > POSEY
POSERS > POSER
POSES > POSE
POSEUR n person who behaves in an affected way to impress others
POSEURS > POSEUR
POSEUSE n female poseur
POSEUSES > POSEUSE
POSEY adj (of a place) for, characteristic of, or full of posers
POSH adj smart, luxurious ▷ adv in a manner associated with the upper class ▷ vb make posh
POSHED > POSH
POSHER > POSH
POSHES > POSH
POSHEST > POSH
POSHING > POSH
POSHLY > POSH
POSHNESS > POSH
POSHO n corn meal
POSHOS > POSHO
POSHTEEN same as > POSTEEN
POSHTEENS > POSHTEEN
POSIDRIVE adj having a patent screwhead that allows greater torque
POSIER > POSY
POSIES > POSY
POSIEST > POSY
POSIGRADE adj producing positive thrust
POSING > POSE
POSINGLY > POSE
POSINGS > POSE
POSIT vb lay down as a basis for argument ▷ n fact, idea, etc, that is posited
POSITED > POSIT
POSITIF n (on older organs) manual controlling soft stops
POSITIFS > POSITIF
POSITING > POSIT
POSITION n place ▷ vb place
POSITIONS > POSITION
POSITIVE same as > PLUS
POSITIVER > POSITIVE

POSITIVES > POSITIVE
POSITON n part of chromosome
POSITONS > POSITON
POSITRON n particle with same mass as electron but positive charge
POSITRONS > POSITRON
POSITS > POSIT
POSNET n small basin or dish
POSNETS > POSNET
POSOLE n hominy
POSOLES > POSOLE
POSOLOGIC > POSOLOGY
POSOLOGY n branch of medicine concerned with the determination of appropriate doses of drugs or agents
POSS vb wash (clothes) by agitating them with a long rod, pole, etc
POSSE n group of men organized to maintain law and order
POSSED > POSS
POSSER n short stick used for stirring clothes in a washtub
POSSERS > POSSER
POSSES > POSSE
POSSESS vb have as one's property
POSSESSED adj owning or having
POSSESSES > POSSESS
POSSESSOR > POSSESS
POSSET n drink of hot milk curdled with ale, beer, etc, flavoured with spices ▷ vb treat with a posset
POSSETED > POSSET
POSSETING > POSSET
POSSETS > POSSET
POSSIBLE adj able to exist, happen, or be done ▷ n person or thing that might be suitable or chosen
POSSIBLER > POSSIBLE
POSSIBLES > POSSIBLE
POSSIBLY adv perhaps, not necessarily
POSSIE n place
POSSIES > POSSIE
POSSING > POSS
POSSUM vb pretend to be dead, asleep, ignorant, etc
POSSUMED > POSSUM
POSSUMING > POSSUM
POSSUMS > POSSUM
POST n official system of delivering letters and parcels ▷ vb send by post
POSTAGE n charge for sending a letter or parcel by post
POSTAGES > POSTAGE
POSTAL adj of a Post Office or the mail-delivery service ▷ n postcard
POSTALLY > POSTAL
POSTALS > POSTAL

POSTANAL adj behind the anus
POSTAXIAL adj situated or occurring behind the axis of the body
POSTBAG n postman's bag
POSTBAGS > POSTBAG
POSTBASE n morpheme used as a suffix on a root word
POSTBASES > POSTBASE
POSTBOX n box into which mail is put for collection by the postal service
POSTBOXES > POSTBOX
POSTBOY n man or boy who brings the post round to offices
POSTBOYS > POSTBOY
POSTBURN adj after injury from burns
POSTBUS n vehicle carrying the mail that also carries passengers
POSTBUSES > POSTBUS
POSTCARD n card for sending a message by post without an envelope
POSTCARDS > POSTCARD
POSTCAVA n inferior vena cava
POSTCAVAE > POSTCAVA
POSTCAVAL > POSTCAVA
POSTCAVAS > POSTCAVA
POSTCODE n system of letters and numbers used to aid the sorting of mail ▷ vb put a postcode on a letter
POSTCODED > POSTCODE
POSTCODES > POSTCODE
POSTCOUP adj after coup
POSTCRASH adj after a crash
POSTDATE vb write a date on (a cheque) that is later than the actual date
POSTDATED > POSTDATE
POSTDATES > POSTDATE
POSTDIVE adj following a dive
POSTDOC n postdoctoral degree
POSTDOCS > POSTDOC
POSTDRUG adj of time after drug has been taken
POSTED > POST
POSTEEN n Afghan leather jacket
POSTEENS > POSTEEN
POSTER n large picture or notice stuck on a wall ▷ vb cover with posters
POSTERED > POSTER
POSTERING > POSTER
POSTERIOR n buttocks ▷ adj behind, at the back of
POSTERISE same as > POSTERIZE
POSTERITY n future generations, descendants
POSTERIZE vb humiliate (a sporting opponent) by

performing a dramatic feat against them
POSTERN n small back door or gate ▷ adj situated at the rear or the side
POSTERNS > POSTERN
POSTERS > POSTER
POSTFACE n note added to the end of a text
POSTFACES > POSTFACE
POSTFAULT adj after a fault
POSTFIRE adj of the period after a fire
POSTFIX vb add or append at the end of something
POSTFIXAL > POSTFIX
POSTFIXED > POSTFIX
POSTFIXES > POSTFIX
POSTFORM vb mould or shape (plastic) while it hot from reheating
POSTFORMS > POSTFORM
POSTGAME adj of period after sports match
POSTGRAD n graduate taking further degree
POSTGRADS > POSTGRAD
POSTHASTE adv with great speed ▷ n great haste
POSTHEAT n industrial heating process ▷ vb heat a material after welding to relieve stresses
POSTHEATS > POSTHEAT
POSTHOLE n hole dug in ground to hold fence post
POSTHOLES > POSTHOLE
POSTHORSE n horse kept at an inn or posthouse for use by postriders or for hire to travellers
POSTHOUSE n house or inn where horses were kept for postriders or for hire to travellers
POSTICAL adj (of the position of plant parts) behind another part
POSTICHE adj (of architectural ornament) inappropriately applied ▷ n imitation, counterfeit, or substitute
POSTICHES > POSTICHE
POSTICOUS same as > POSTICAL
POSTIE n postman
POSTIES > POSTIE
POSTIL n commentary or marginal note, as in a Bible ▷ vb annotate (a biblical passage)
POSTILED > POSTIL
POSTILING > POSTIL
POSTILION n person riding one of a pair of horses drawing a carriage
POSTILLED > POSTIL
POSTILLER > POSTIL
POSTILS > POSTIL

POSTIN variant of
> POSTEEN
POSTING n job to which
someone is assigned
POSTINGS > POSTING
POSTINS > POSTIN
POSTIQUE variant of
> POSTICHE
POSTIQUES > POSTIQUE
POSTLUDE n final or
concluding piece or
movement
POSTLUDES > POSTLUDE
POSTMAN n person who
collects and delivers post
POSTMARK n official mark
stamped on letters
showing place and date of
posting ▷ vb put such a
mark on (mail)
POSTMARKS > POSTMARK
POSTMEN > POSTMAN
POSTNASAL adj situated
at the back of the nose
POSTNATAL adj occurring
after childbirth
POSTNATI pl n those born
in Scotland after its union
with England
POSTOP n person
recovering from surgery
POSTOPS > POSTOP
POSTORAL adj situated at
the back of the mouth
POSTPAID adj with the
postage prepaid
POSTPONE vb put off to a
later time
POSTPONED > POSTPONE
POSTPONER > POSTPONE
POSTPONES > POSTPONE
POSTPOSE vb place (word
or phrase) after other
constituents in sentence
POSTPOSED > POSTPOSE
POSTPOSES > POSTPOSE
POSTPUNK adj (of pop
music) belonging to a style
that followed punk rock
▷ n musician of the
musical trend after punk
POSTPUNKS > POSTPUNK
POSTRACE adj of the
period after a race
POSTRIDER n (formerly)
person who delivered post
on horseback
POSTRIOT adj of the
period after a riot
POSTS > POST
POSTSHOW adj of the
period after a show
POSTSYNC vb add a sound
recording to (and
synchronize with) an
existing video or film
recording
POSTSYNCS > POSTSYNC
POSTTAX adj of the period
after tax is paid
POSTTEEN n young adult
POSTTEENS > POSTTEEN
POSTTEST n test taken
after a lesson

POSTTESTS > POSTTEST
POSTTRIAL adj of the
period after a trial
POSTULANT n candidate
for admission to a religious
order
POSTULATA pl n things
postulated
POSTULATE vb assume to
be true as the basis of an
argument or theory
▷ n something postulated
POSTURAL > POSTURE
POSTURE n position or
way in which someone
stands, walks, etc
▷ vb behave in an
exaggerated way to get
attention
POSTURED > POSTURE
POSTURER > POSTURE
POSTURERS > POSTURE
POSTURES > POSTURE
POSTURING n act of
posturing
POSTURISE same as
> POSTURIZE
POSTURIST > POSTURE
POSTURIZE less common
word for > POSTURE
POSTVIRAL adj as in
postviral syndrome
debilitating condition
occurring as a sequel to
viral illness
POSTWAR adj occurring or
existing after a war
POSTWOMAN n woman
who carries and delivers
mail as a profession
POSTWOMEN
> POSTWOMAN
POSY n small bunch of
flowers
POT n round deep
container ▷ vb plant in a
pot
POTABLE adj drinkable
▷ n something fit to drink
POTABLES > POTABLE
POTAE n hat
POTAES > POTAE
POTAGE n thick soup
POTAGER n small kitchen
garden
POTAGERS > POTAGER
POTAGES > POTAGE
POTALE n residue from a
grain distillery, used as
animal feed
POTALES > POTALE
POTAMIC adj of or relating
to rivers
POTASH n white powdery
substance obtained from
ashes and used as fertilizer
▷ vb treat with potash
POTASHED > POTASH
POTASHES > POTASH
POTASHING > POTASH
POTASS abbreviated form of
> POTASSIUM
POTASSA n potassium
oxide

POTASSAS > POTASSA
POTASSES > POTASS
POTASSIC > POTASSIUM
POTASSIUM n silvery
metallic element
POTATION n act of
drinking
POTATIONS > POTATION
POTATO n roundish
starchy vegetable that
grows underground
POTATOBUG n Colorado
beetle
POTATOES > POTATO
POTATORY adj of, relating
to, or given to drinking
POTBELLY n bulging belly
POTBOIL vb boil in a pot
POTBOILED > POTBOIL
POTBOILER n inferior
work of art produced
quickly to make money
POTBOILS > POTBOIL
POTBOUND adj (of plant)
unable to grow because
pot is too small
POTBOY n (esp formerly)
youth or man employed at
a public house to serve
beer, etc
POTBOYS > POTBOY
POTCH n inferior quality
opal used in jewellery for
mounting precious opals
POTCHE vb stab
POTCHED > POTCHE
POTCHER > POTCHE
POTCHERS > POTCHE
POTCHES > POTCH
POTCHING > POTCHE
POTE vb push
POTED > POTE
POTEEN n (in Ireland)
illegally made alcoholic
drink
POTEENS > POTEEN
POTENCE same as
> POTENCY
POTENCES > POTENCE
POTENCIES > POTENCY
POTENCY n state or
quality of being potent
POTENT adj having great
power or influence
▷ n potentate or ruler
POTENTATE n ruler or
monarch
POTENTIAL adj possible
but not yet actual ▷ n
ability or talent not yet
fully used
POTENTISE same as
> POTENTIZE
POTENTIZE vb make
more potent
POTENTLY > POTENT
POTENTS > POTENT
POTES > POTE
POTFUL n amount held by
a pot
POTFULS > POTFUL
POTGUN n pot-shaped
mortar
POTGUNS > POTGUN

POTHEAD n habitual user
of cannabis
POTHEADS > POTHEAD
POTHECARY n pharmacist
POTHEEN rare variant of
> POTEEN
POTHEENS > POTHEEN
POTHER n fuss or
commotion ▷ vb make or
be troubled or upset
POTHERB n plant whose
leaves, flowers, or stems
are used in cooking
POTHERBS > POTHERB
POTHERED > POTHER
POTHERING > POTHER
POTHERS > POTHER
POTHERY adj stuffy
POTHOLDER n piece of
material used to protect
hands while lifting pot
from oven
POTHOLE n hole in the
surface of a road
POTHOLED > POTHOLE
POTHOLER > POTHOLING
POTHOLERS
> POTHOLING
POTHOLES > POTHOLE
POTHOLING n sport of
exploring underground
caves
POTHOOK n S-shaped hook
for suspending a pot over
a fire
POTHOOKS > POTHOOK
POTHOS n climbing plant
POTHOUSE n (formerly)
small tavern or pub
POTHOUSES > POTHOUSE
POTHUNTER n person
who hunts for food or for
profit without regard to
the rules of sport
POTICARY obsolete spelling
of > POTHECARY
POTICHE n tall vase or jar
that narrows towards the
neck
POTICHES > POTICHE
POTIN n bronze alloy with
high tin content
POTING > POTE
POTINS > POTIN
POTION n dose of
medicine or poison
POTIONS > POTION
POTJIE n three-legged
iron pot used for cooking
POTJIES > POTJIE
POTLACH same as
> POTLATCH
POTLACHE same as
> POTLATCH
POTLACHES > POTLACHE
POTLATCH n competitive
ceremonial activity among
certain North American
Indians
POTLIKE > POT
POTLINE n row of
electrolytic cells for
reducing metals
POTLINES > POTLINE

POTLUCK n whatever food happens to be available without special preparation

POTLUCKS > POTLUCK

POTMAN same as > POTBOY

POTMEN > POTMAN

POTOMETER n apparatus that measures the rate of water uptake by a plant or plant part

POTOO n nocturnal tropical bird

POTOOS > POTOO

POTOROO n Australian leaping rodent

POTOROOS > POTOROO

POTPIE n meat and vegetable stew with a pie crust on top

POTPIES > POTPIE

POTPOURRI n fragrant mixture of dried flower petals

POTS > POT

POTSHARD same as > POTSHERD

POTSHARDS > POTSHARD

POTSHARE same as > POTSHERD

POTSHARES > POTSHARE

POTSHERD n broken fragment of pottery

POTSHERDS > POTSHERD

POTSHOP n public house

POTSHOPS > POTSHOP

POTSHOT n shot taken without careful aim

POTSHOTS > POTSHOT

POTSIE same as > POTSY

POTSIES > POTSY

POTSTONE n impure massive variety of soapstone, formerly used for making cooking vessels

POTSTONES > POTSTONE

POTSY n hopscotch

POTT old variant of > POT

POTTABLE adj (esp of a snooker ball) easily potted

POTTAGE n thick soup or stew

POTTAGES > POTTAGE

POTTED > POT

POTTEEN same as > POTEEN

POTTEENS > POTTEEN

POTTER same as > PUTTER

POTTERED > POTTER

POTTERER > POTTER

POTTERERS > POTTER

POTTERIES > POTTERY

POTTERING > POTTER

POTTERS > POTTER

POTTERY n articles made from baked clay

POTTIER > POTTY

POTTIES > POTTY

POTTIEST > POTTY

POTTINESS > POTTY

POTTING > POT

POTTINGAR same as > POTTINGER

POTTINGER n apothecary

POTTLE n liquid measure equal to half a gallon

POTTLES > POTTLE

POTTO n short-tailed prosimian primate

POTTOS > POTTO

POTTS > POTT

POTTY adj crazy or silly ▷ n bowl used by a small child as a toilet

POTWALLER n man entitled to the franchise before 1832 by virtue of possession of his own fireplace

POTZER same as > PATZER

POTZERS > POTZER

POUCH n small bag ▷ vb place in or as if in a pouch

POUCHED > POUCH

POUCHES > POUCH

POUCHFUL n amount a pouch will hold

POUCHFULS > POUCHFUL

POUCHIER > POUCH

POUCHIEST > POUCH

POUCHING > POUCH

POUCHY > POUCH

POUDER obsolete spelling of > POWDER

POUDERS > POUDER

POUDRE old spelling of > POWDER

POUDRES > POUDRE

POUF n large solid cushion used as a seat ▷ vb pile up hair into rolled puffs

POUFED > POUF

POUFF same as > POUF

POUFFE same as > POUF

POUFFED > POUFFE

POUFFES > POUFFE

POUFFIER > POUFFY

POUFFIEST > POUFFY

POUFFING > POUFFE

POUFFS > POUFF

POUFFY same as > POOFY

POUFING > POUF

POUFS > POUF

POUFTAH same as > POOFTER

POUFTAHS > POUFTAH

POUFTER same as > POOFTER

POUFTERS > POUFTER

POUK Scots variant of > POKE

POUKE n mischievous spirit

POUKES > POUKE

POUKING > POUK

POUKIT > POUK

POUKS > POUK

POULAINE n tapering toe of shoe

POULAINES > POULAINE

POULARD n hen that has been spayed for fattening

POULARDE same as > POULARD

POULARDES > POULARDE

POULARDS > POULARD

POULDER obsolete spelling of > POWDER

POULDERS > POULDER

POULDRE archaic spelling of > POWDER

POULDRES > POULDRE

POULDRON same as > PAULDRON

POULDRONS > POULDRON

POULE n fowl suitable for slow stewing

POULES > POULE

POULP n octopus

POULPE variant of > POULP

POULPES > POULPE

POULPS > POULP

POULT n young of a gallinaceous bird

POULTER n poultry dealer

POULTERER same as > POULTER

POULTERS > POULTER

POULTICE n moist dressing, often heated, applied to inflamed skin ▷ vb apply poultice to

POULTICED > POULTICE

POULTICES > POULTICE

POULTRIES > POULTRY

POULTRY n domestic fowls

POULTS > POULT

POUNCE vb spring upon suddenly to attack or capture ▷ n pouncing

POUNCED > POUNCE

POUNCER > POUNCE

POUNCERS > POUNCE

POUNCES > POUNCE

POUNCET n box with a perforated top used for perfume

POUNCETS > POUNCET

POUNCHING old variant of > PUNCHING

POUNCING > POUNCE

POUND n monetary unit of Britain and some other countries ▷ vb hit heavily and repeatedly

POUNDAGE n charge of so much per pound of weight or sterling

POUNDAGES > POUNDAGE

POUNDAL n fps unit of force

POUNDALS > POUNDAL

POUNDCAKE n cake containing a pound of each ingredient

POUNDED > POUND

POUNDER > POUND

POUNDERS > POUND

POUNDING > POUND

POUNDINGS > POUNDING

POUNDS > POUND

POUPE vb make sudden blowing sound

POUPED > POUPE

POUPES > POUPE

POUPING > POUPE

POUPT > POUPE

POUR vb flow or cause to flow out in a stream

POURABLE > POUR

POURBOIRE n tip or gratuity

POURED > POUR

POURER > POUR

POURERS > POUR

POURIE n jug

POURIES > POURIE

POURING > POUR

POURINGLY > POUR

POURINGS > POUR

POURPOINT n man's stuffed quilted doublet of a kind worn between the Middle Ages and the 17th century

POURS > POUR

POURSEW obsolete spelling of > PURSUE

POURSEWED > POURSEW

POURSEWS > POURSEW

POURSUE obsolete spelling of > PURSUE

POURSUED > PURSUE

POURSUES > PURSUE

POURSUING > PURSUE

POURSUIT same as > PURSUIT

POURSUITS > POURSUIT

POURTRAY obsolete spelling of > PORTRAY

POURTRAYD > POURTRAY

POURTRAYS > POURTRAY

POUSADA n traditional Portuguese hotel

POUSADAS > POUSADA

POUSOWDIE n Scottish stew made from sheep's head

POUSSE same as > PEASE

POUSSES > POUSSE

POUSSETTE n figure in country dancing in which couples hold hands and move up or down the set to change positions ▷ vb perform such a figure

POUSSIE old variant of > PUSSY

POUSSIES > POUSSIE

POUSSIN n young chicken reared for eating

POUSSINS > POUSSIN

POUT vb thrust out one's lips, look sulky ▷ n pouting look

POUTASSOU n another name for the blue whiting

POUTED > POUT

POUTER n pigeon that can puff out its crop

POUTERS > POUTER

POUTFUL adj tending to pout

POUTHER Scots variant of > POWDER

POUTHERED > POUTHER

POUTHERS > POUTHER

POUTIER > POUT

POUTIEST > POUT

POUTINE n dish of chipped potatoes topped with cheese and sauce

POUTINES > POUTINE
POUTING > POUT
POUTINGLY > POUT
POUTINGS > POUT
POUTS > POUT
POUTY > POUT
POVERTIES > POVERTY
POVERTY *n* state of being without enough food or money
POW *interj* exclamation to indicate that a collision or explosion has taken place ▷ *n* head or a head of hair
POWAN *n* type of freshwater whitefish occurring in some Scottish lakes
POWANS > POWAN
POWDER *n* substance in the form of tiny loose particles ▷ *vb* apply powder to
POWDERED > POWDER
POWDERER > POWDER
POWDERERS > POWDER
POWDERIER > POWDER
POWDERING *n* sprinkling of something on a surface
POWDERS > POWDER
POWDERY > POWDER
POWELLISE *same as* > POWELLIZE
POWELLITE *n* type of mineral
POWELLIZE *vb* treat wood with a sugar solution
POWER *n* ability to do or act ▷ *vb* give or provide power to
POWERBOAT *n* fast powerful motorboat
POWERED > POWER
POWERFUL *adj* having great power or influence ▷ *adv* extremely
POWERING > POWER
POWERLESS *adj* without power or authority
POWERPLAY *n* behaviour intended to maximise person's power
POWERS > POWER
POWFAGGED *adj* exhausted
POWHIRI *n* Māori ceremony of welcome, esp to a marae
POWHIRIS > POWHIRI
POWIN *n* peacock
POWINS > POWIN
POWN *variant of* > POWIN
POWND *obsolete spelling of* > POUND
POWNDED > POWND
POWNDING > POWND
POWNDS > POWND
POWNEY *old Scots spelling of* > PONY
POWNEYS > POWNEY
POWNIE *old Scots spelling of* > PONY
POWNIES > POWNIE
POWNS > POWN

POWNY *old Scots spelling of* > PONY
POWRE *obsolete spelling of* > POWER
POWRED > POWRE
POWRES > POWRE
POWRING > POWRE
POWS > POW
POWSOWDY *same as* > POUSOWDIE
POWTER *vb* scrabble about
POWTERED > POWTER
POWTERING > POWTER
POWTERS > POWTER
POWWAW *interj* expression of disbelief or contempt
POWWOW *n* talk or conference ▷ *vb* hold a powwow
POWWOWED > POWWOW
POWWOWING > POWWOW
POWWOWS > POWWOW
POX *n* disease in which skin pustules form ▷ *vb* infect with pox
POXED > POX
POXES > POX
POXIER > POXY
POXIEST > POXY
POXING > POX
POXVIRUS *n* virus such as smallpox
POXY *adj* having or having had syphilis
POYNANT *old variant of* > POIGNANT
POYNT *obsolete spelling of* > POINT
POYNTED > POYNT
POYNTING > POYNT
POYNTS > POYNT
POYOU *n* type of armadillo
POYOUS > POYOU
POYSE *obsolete variant of* > POISE
POYSED > POYSE
POYSES > POYSE
POYSING > POYSE
POYSON *obsolete spelling of* > POISON
POYSONED > POYSON
POYSONING > POYSON
POYSONS > POYSON
POZ *adj* positive
POZIDRIVE *same as* > POSIDRIVE
POZOLE *same as* > POSOLE
POZOLES > POZOLE
POZZ *adj* positive
POZZIES > POZZY
POZZOLAN *same as* > POZZOLANA
POZZOLANA *n* type of porous volcanic ash
POZZOLANS > POZZOLAN
POZZY *same as* > POSSIE
PRAAM *same as* > PRAM
PRAAMS > PRAAM
PRABBLE *variant of* > BRABBLE
PRABBLES > PRABBLE
PRACHARAK *n* (in India) person appointed to

propagate a cause through personal contact, meetings, public lectures, etc
PRACTIC *adj* practical ▷ *n* practice ▷ *vb* put (a theory) into practice
PRACTICAL *adj* involving experience or actual use rather than theory ▷ *n* examination in which something has to be done or made
PRACTICE *same as* > PRACTISE
PRACTICED > PRACTICE
PRACTICER > PRACTICE
PRACTICES > PRACTICE
PRACTICK *obsolete word for* > PRACTICE
PRACTICKS > PRACTICK
PRACTICS > PRACTIC
PRACTICUM *n* course in which theory is put into practice
PRACTIQUE *variant of* > PRACTIC
PRACTISE *vb* do repeatedly so as to gain skill
PRACTISED > PRACTISE
PRACTISER > PRACTISE
PRACTISES > PRACTISE
PRACTIVE *obsolete word for* > ACTIVE
PRACTOLOL *n* type of drug
PRAD *n* horse
PRADS > PRAD
PRAEAMBLE *same as* > PREAMBLE
PRAECIPE *n* written request addressed to court
PRAECIPES > PRAECIPE
PRAECOCES *n* division of birds whose young are able to run when first hatched
PRAEDIAL *adj* of or relating to land, farming, etc ▷ *n* slave attached to a farm
PRAEDIALS > PRAEDIAL
PRAEFECT *same as* > PREFECT
PRAEFECTS > PRAEFECT
PRAELECT *same as* > PRAELECT
PRAELECTS > PRAELECT
PRAELUDIA *n* musical preludes
PRAENOMEN *n* ancient Roman's first or given name
PRAESES *n* Roman governor
PRAESIDIA *n* presidiums
PRAETOR *n* (in ancient Rome) senior magistrate ranking just below the consuls
PRAETORS > PRAETOR
PRAGMATIC *adj* concerned with practical

consequences rather than theory
PRAHU *same as* > PROA
PRAHUS > PRAHU
PRAIRIE *n* large treeless area of grassland
PRAIRIED > PRAIRIE
PRAIRIES > PRAIRIE
PRAISE *vb* express approval of (someone or something) ▷ *n* something said or written to show approval
PRAISEACH *n* type of porridge
PRAISED > PRAISE
PRAISEFUL > PRAISE
PRAISER > PRAISE
PRAISERS > PRAISE
PRAISES > PRAISE
PRAISING > PRAISE
PRAISINGS > PRAISE
PRAJNA *n* wisdom or understanding
PRAJNAS > PRAJNA
PRALINE *n* sweet made of nuts and caramelized sugar
PRALINES > PRALINE
PRAM *n* four-wheeled carriage for a baby, pushed by hand
PRAMS > PRAM
PRANA *n* cosmic energy believed to come from the sun
PRANAS > PRANA
PRANAYAMA *n* breath control in yoga
PRANCE *vb* walk with exaggerated bouncing steps ▷ *n* act of prancing
PRANCED > PRANCE
PRANCER > PRANCE
PRANCERS > PRANCE
PRANCES > PRANCE
PRANCING > PRANCE
PRANCINGS > PRANCE
PRANCK *obsolete variant of* > PRANK
PRANCKE *obsolete variant of* > PRANK
PRANCKED > PRANCK
PRANCKES > PRANCKE
PRANCKING > PRANCK
PRANCKS > PRANCK
PRANDIAL *adj* of or relating to a meal
PRANG *n* crash in a car or aircraft ▷ *vb* crash or damage (an aircraft or car)
PRANGED > PRANG
PRANGING > PRANG
PRANGS > PRANG
PRANK *n* mischievous trick ▷ *vb* dress or decorate showily or gaudily
PRANKED > PRANK
PRANKFUL > PRANK
PRANKIER > PRANK
PRANKIEST > PRANK
PRANKING > PRANK
PRANKINGS > PRANK

PRANKISH > PRANK
PRANKLE *obsolete variant of* > PRANCE
PRANKLED > PRANKLE
PRANKLES > PRANKLE
PRANKLING > PRANKLE
PRANKS > PRANK
PRANKSOME > PRANK
PRANKSTER *n* practical joker
PRANKY > PRANK
PRAO *same as* > PROA
PRAOS > PRAO
PRASE *n* light green translucent variety of chalcedony
PRASES > PRASE
PRAT *n* stupid person
PRATE *vb* talk idly and at length ▷ *n* chatter
PRATED > PRATE
PRATER > PRATE
PRATERS > PRATE
PRATES > PRATE
PRATFALL *vb* fall upon one's buttocks
PRATFALLS > PRATFALL
PRATFELL > PRATFALL
PRATIE *n* potato
PRATIES > PRATIE
PRATING > PRATE
PRATINGLY > PRATE
PRATINGS > PRATE
PRATIQUE *n* formal permission given to a vessel to use a foreign port upon satisfying the requirements of local health authorities
PRATIQUES > PRATIQUE
PRATS > PRAT
PRATT *n* buttocks ▷ *vb* hit on the buttocks
PRATTED > PRATT
PRATTING > PRATT
PRATTLE *vb* chatter in a childish or foolish way ▷ *n* childish or foolish talk
PRATTLED > PRATTLE
PRATTLER > PRATTLE
PRATTLERS > PRATTLE
PRATTLES > PRATTLE
PRATTLING > PRATTLE
PRATTS > PRATT
PRATY *obsolete variant of* > PRETTY
PRAU *same as* > PROA
PRAUNCE *obsolete variant of* > PRANCE
PRAUNCED > PRAUNCE
PRAUNCES > PRAUNCE
PRAUNCING > PRAUNCE
PRAUS > PRAU
PRAVITIES > PRAVITY
PRAVITY *n* moral degeneracy
PRAWLE *n* Shakespearian spelling of "brawl"
PRAWLES > PRAWLE
PRAWLIN *variant of* > PRALINE
PRAWLINS > PRAWLIN

PRAWN *n* edible shellfish like a large shrimp ▷ *vb* catch prawns
PRAWNED > PRAWN
PRAWNER > PRAWN
PRAWNERS > PRAWN
PRAWNING > PRAWN
PRAWNS > PRAWN
PRAXES > PRAXIS
PRAXIS *n* practice as opposed to theory
PRAXISES > PRAXIS
PRAY *vb* say prayers ▷ *adv* I beg you ▷ *interj* I beg you
PRAYED > PRAY
PRAYER *n* thanks or appeal addressed to one's God
PRAYERFUL *adj* inclined to or characterized by prayer
PRAYERS > PRAYER
PRAYING > PRAY
PRAYINGLY > PRAY
PRAYINGS > PRAY
PRAYS > PRAY
PRE *prep* before
PREABSORB *vb* absorb beforehand
PREACCUSE *vb* accuse beforehand
PREACE *obsolete variant of* > PRESS
PREACED > PREACE
PREACES > PREACE
PREACH *vb* give a talk on a religious theme as part of a church service
PREACHED > PREACH
PREACHER *n* person who preaches, esp in church
PREACHERS > PREACHER
PREACHES > PREACH
PREACHIER > PREACHY
PREACHIFY *vb* preach or moralize in a tedious manner
PREACHILY > PREACHY
PREACHING > PREACH
PREACHY *adj* inclined to or marked by preaching
PREACING > PREACE
PREACT *vb* act beforehand
PREACTED > PREACT
PREACTING > PREACT
PREACTS > PREACT
PREADAMIC *adj* of or relating to the belief that there were people on earth before Adam
PREADAPT *vb* adapt beforehand
PREADAPTS > PREADAPT
PREADJUST *vb* adjust beforehand
PREADMIT *vb* prepare patient prior to treatment
PREADMITS > PREADMIT
PREADOPT *vb* adopt in advance
PREADOPTS > PREADOPT
PREADULT *n* animal or person who has not reached adulthood

PREADULTS > PREADULT
PREAGED *adj* treated to appear older
PREALLOT *vb* allot beforehand
PREALLOTS > PREALLOT
PREALTER *vb* alter beforehand
PREALTERS > PREALTER
PREAMBLE *n* introductory part to something said or written ▷ *vb* write a preamble
PREAMBLED > PREAMBLE
PREAMBLES > PREAMBLE
PREAMP *n* electronic amplifier
PREAMPS > PREAMP
PREANAL *adj* situated in front of anus
PREAPPLY *vb* apply beforehand
PREARM *vb* arm beforehand
PREARMED > PREARM
PREARMING > PREARM
PREARMS > PREARM
PREASE *vb* crowd or press
PREASED > PREASE
PREASES > PREASE
PREASING > PREASE
PREASSE *obsolete spelling of* > PRESS
PREASSED > PREASSE
PREASSES > PREASSE
PREASSIGN *vb* assign beforehand
PREASSING > PREASSE
PREASSURE *vb* assure beforehand
PREATOMIC *adj* before the atomic age
PREATTUNE *vb* attune beforehand
PREAUDIT *n* examination of contracts before a transaction
PREAUDITS > PREAUDIT
PREAVER *vb* aver in advance
PREAVERS > PREAVER
PREAXIAL *adj* situated or occurring in front of the axis of the body
PREBADE > PREBID
PREBAKE *vb* bake before further cooking
PREBAKED > PREBAKE
PREBAKES > PREBAKE
PREBAKING > PREBAKE
PREBASAL *adj* in front of a base
PREBATTLE *adj* of the period before a battle
PREBEND *n* allowance paid to a canon or member of the cathedral chapter
PREBENDAL > PREBEND
PREBENDS > PREBEND
PREBID *vb* bid beforehand
PREBIDDEN > PREBID
PREBIDS > PREBID

PREBILL *vb* issue an invoice before the service has been provided
PREBILLED > PREBILL
PREBILLS > PREBILL
PREBIND *vb* bind a book in a hard-wearing binding
PREBINDS > PREBIND
PREBIOTIC *adj* of the period before the existence of life on earth
PREBIRTH *n* period of life before birth
PREBIRTHS > PREBIRTH
PREBLESS *vb* bless a couple before they marry
PREBOARD *vb* board an aircraft before other passengers
PREBOARDS > PREBOARD
PREBOIL *vb* boil beforehand
PREBOILED > PREBOIL
PREBOILS > PREBOIL
PREBOOK *vb* book well in advance
PREBOOKED > PREBOOK
PREBOOKS > PREBOOK
PREBOOM *adj* of the period before an economic boom
PREBORN *adj* unborn
PREBOUGHT > PREBUY
PREBOUND > PREBIND
PREBUDGET *adj* before budget
PREBUILD *vb* build beforehand
PREBUILDS > PREBUILD
PREBUILT > PREBUILD
PREBUTTAL *n* prepared response to an anticipated criticism
PREBUY *vb* buy in advance
PREBUYING > PREBUY
PREBUYS > PREBUY
PRECANCEL *vb* cancel (postage stamps) before placing them on mail ▷ *n* precancelled stamp
PRECANCER *n* condition that may develop into cancer
PRECAST *adj* cast in a particular form before being used ▷ *vb* cast (concrete) in a particular form before use
PRECASTS > PRECAST
PRECATIVE *same as* > PRECATORY
PRECATORY *adj* of, involving, or expressing entreaty
PRECAUDAL *adj* in front of the caudal fin
PRECAVA *n* superior vena cava
PRECAVAE > PRECAVA
PRECAVAL > PRECAVA
PRECEDE *vb* go or be before
PRECEDED > PRECEDE
PRECEDENT *n* previous case or occurrence

regarded as an example to be followed ▷ *adj* preceding

PRECEDES > PRECEDE

PRECEDING *adj* going or coming before

PRECEESE *Scots variant of* > PRECISE

PRECENSOR *vb* censor (a film, play, book, etc) before its publication

PRECENT *vb* issue a command or law

PRECENTED > PRECENT

PRECENTOR *n* person who leads the singing in a church

PRECENTS > PRECENT

PRECEPIT *old word for* > PRECIPICE

PRECEPITS > PRECEPIT

PRECEPT *n* rule of behaviour

PRECEPTOR *n* instructor

PRECEPTS > PRECEPT

PRECES *pl n* prayers

PRECESS *vb* undergo or cause to undergo precession

PRECESSED > PRECESS

PRECESSES > PRECESS

PRECHARGE *vb* charge beforehand

PRECHECK *vb* check beforehand

PRECHECKS > PRECHECK

PRECHILL *vb* chill beforehand

PRECHILLS > PRECHILL

PRECHOOSE *vb* choose in advance

PRECHOSE > PRECHOOSE

PRECHOSEN > PRECHOOSE

PRECIEUSE *n* pretentious female

PRECIEUX *n* pretentious male

PRECINCT *n* area in a town closed to traffic

PRECINCTS *pl n* surrounding region

PRECIOUS *adj* of great value and importance ▷ *adv* very

PRECIP *n* precipitation

PRECIPE *n* type of legal document

PRECIPES > PRECIPE

PRECIPICE *n* very steep face of a cliff

PRECIPS > PRECIP

PRECIS *n* short written summary of a longer piece ▷ *vb* make a precis of

PRECISE *adj* exact, accurate in every detail

PRECISED > PRECIS

PRECISELY *adv* in a precise manner

PRECISER > PRECISE

PRECISES > PRECIS

PRECISEST > PRECISE

PRECISIAN *n* punctilious observer of rules or forms, esp in the field of religion

PRECISING > PRECIS

PRECISION *n* quality of being precise ▷ *adj* accurate

PRECISIVE *adj* limiting by cutting off all that is unnecessary

PRECITED *adj* cited previously

PRECLEAN *vb* clean beforehand

PRECLEANS > PRECLEAN

PRECLEAR *vb* approve in advance

PRECLEARS > PRECLEAR

PRECLUDE *vb* make impossible to happen

PRECLUDED > PRECLUDE

PRECLUDES > PRECLUDE

PRECOCIAL *adj* (of the young of some species of birds after hatching) covered with down, having open eyes, and capable of leaving the nest within a few days of hatching ▷ *n* precocial bird

PRECOCITY *n* early maturing or development

PRECODE *vb* code beforehand

PRECODED > PRECODE

PRECODES > PRECODE

PRECODING > PRECODE

PRECOITAL *adj* before sex

PRECONISE *same as* > PRECONIZE

PRECONIZE *vb* announce or commend publicly

PRECOOK *vb* cook (food) beforehand

PRECOOKED > PRECOOK

PRECOOKER *n* device for preparing food before cooking

PRECOOKS > PRECOOK

PRECOOL *vb* cool in advance

PRECOOLED > PRECOOL

PRECOOLS > PRECOOL

PRECOUP *adj* of the period before a coup

PRECRASH *adj* of the period before a crash

PRECREASE *vb* provide with a crease in advance

PRECRISIS *adj* occurring before a crisis

PRECURE *vb* cure in advance

PRECURED > PRECURE

PRECURES > PRECURE

PRECURING > PRECURE

PRECURRER > PRECURE

PRECURSE *n* forerunning ▷ *vb* be a precursor of

PRECURSED > PRECURSE

PRECURSES > PRECURSE

PRECURSOR *n* something that precedes and is a

signal of something else, forerunner

PRECUT *vb* cut in advance

PRECUTS > PRECUT

PRECYCLE *vb* preemptive approach to waste reduction involving minimal use of packaging

PRECYCLED > PRECYCLE

PRECYCLES > PRECYCLE

PREDACITY *n* predatory nature

PREDATE *vb* occur at an earlier date than

PREDATED > PREDATE

PREDATES > PREDATE

PREDATING > PREDATE

PREDATION *n* relationship between two species of animal in a community, in which one (the predator) hunts, kills, and eats the other (the prey)

PREDATISM *n* state of preying on other animals

PREDATIVE > PREDATE

PREDATOR *n* predatory animal

PREDATORS > PREDATOR

PREDATORY *adj* habitually hunting and killing other animals for food

PREDAWN *n* period before dawn

PREDAWNS > PREDAWN

PREDEATH *n* period immediately before death

PREDEATHS > PREDEATH

PREDEBATE *adj* before a debate

PREDEDUCT *vb* deduct beforehand

PREDEFINE *vb* define in advance

PREDELLA *n* painting or sculpture or a series of small paintings or sculptures in a long narrow strip forming the lower edge of an altarpiece or the face of an altar step or platform

PREDELLAS > PREDELLA

PREDELLE > PREDELLA

PREDESIGN *vb* design beforehand

PREDEVOTE *adj* preordained ▷ *vb* devote or dedicate beforehand

PREDIAL *same as* > PRAEDIAL

PREDIALS > PREDIAL

PREDICANT *same as* > PREDIKANT

PREDICATE *n* part of a sentence in which something is said about the subject ▷ *vb* declare or assert ▷ *adj* of or relating to something that has been predicated

PREDICT *vb* tell about in advance, prophesy

PREDICTED > PREDICT

PREDICTER > PREDICT

PREDICTOR *n* person or thing that predicts

PREDICTS > PREDICT

PREDIED > PREDY

PREDIES > PREDY

PREDIGEST *vb* treat (food) artificially to aid subsequent digestion in the body

PREDIKANT *n* minister in the Dutch Reformed Church in South Africa

PREDILECT *adj* chosen or preferred

PREDINNER *adj* of the period before dinner

PREDIVE *adj* happening before a dive

PREDOOM *vb* pronounce (someone or something's) doom beforehand

PREDOOMED > PREDOOM

PREDOOMS > PREDOOM

PREDRAFT *adj* before a draft ▷ *n* preliminary draft prior to an official draft

PREDRAFTS > PREDRAFT

PREDRIED > PREDRY

PREDRIES > PREDRY

PREDRILL *vb* drill in advance

PREDRILLS > PREDRILL

PREDRY *vb* dry beforehand

PREDRYING > PREDRY

PREDUSK *n* period before dawn

PREDUSKS > PREDUSK

PREDY *vb* prepare for action

PREDYING > PREDY

PREE *vb* try or taste

PREED > PREE

PREEDIT *vb* edit beforehand

PREEDITED > PREEDIT

PREEDITS > PREEDIT

PREEING > PREE

PREELECT *vb* elect beforehand

PREELECTS > PREELECT

PREEMIE *n* premature infant

PREEMIES > PREEMIE

PREEMPT *vb* acquire in advance of or to the exclusion of others

PREEMPTED > PREEMPT

PREEMPTOR *n* one who preempts

PREEMPTS > PREEMPT

PREEN *vb* (of a bird) clean or trim (feathers) with the beak ▷ *n* pin, esp a decorative one

PREENACT *vb* enact beforehand

PREENACTS > PREENACT

PREENED > PREEN

PREENER > PREEN

PREENERS > PREEN

p

PREENING > PREEN

PREENS > PREEN

PREERECT *vb* erect beforehand

PREERECTS > PREERECT

PREES > PREE

PREEVE *old form of* > PROVE

PREEVED > PREEVE

PREEVES > PREEVE

PREEVING > PREEVE

PREEXCITE *vb* stimulate in preparation

PREEXEMPT *vb* exempt beforehand

PREEXILIC *adj* prior to the Babylonian exile of the Jews

PREEXIST *vb* exist beforehand

PREEXISTS > PREEXIST

PREEXPOSE *vb* expose beforehand

PREFAB *n* prefabricated house ▷ *vb* manufacture sections of (building) in factory

PREFABBED > PREFAB

PREFABS > PREFAB

PREFACE *n* introduction to a book ▷ *vb* serve as an introduction to (a book, speech, etc)

PREFACED > PREFACE

PREFACER > PREFACE

PREFACERS > PREFACE

PREFACES > PREFACE

PREFACIAL *adj* anterior to face

PREFACING > PREFACE

PREFADE *vb* fade beforehand

PREFADED > PREFADE

PREFADES > PREFADE

PREFADING > PREFADE

PREFARD *vb* old form of preferred

PREFATORY *adj* concerning a preface

PREFECT *n* senior pupil in a school, with limited power over others

PREFECTS > PREFECT

PREFER *vb* like better

PREFERRED > PREFER

PREFERRER > PREFER

PREFERS > PREFER

PREFEUDAL *adj* of the period before the feudal era

PREFIGHT *adj* of the period before a boxing match

PREFIGURE *vb* represent or suggest in advance

PREFILE *vb* file beforehand

PREFILED > PREFILE

PREFILES > PREFILE

PREFILING > PREFILE

PREFILLED *adj* having been filled beforehand

PREFIRE *vb* fire beforehand

PREFIRED > PREFIRE

PREFIRES > PREFIRE

PREFIRING > PREFIRE

PREFIX *n* letters put at the beginning of a word to make a new word ▷ *vb* put as an introduction or prefix (to)

PREFIXAL > PREFIX

PREFIXED > PREFIX

PREFIXES > PREFIX

PREFIXING > PREFIX

PREFIXION > PREFIX

PREFLAME *adj* of the period before combustion

PREFLIGHT *adj* of or relating to the period just prior to a plane taking off

PREFOCUS *vb* focus in advance

PREFORM *vb* form beforehand

PREFORMAT *vb* format in advance

PREFORMED > PREFORM

PREFORMS > PREFORM

PREFRANK *vb* frank in advance

PREFRANKS > PREFRANK

PREFREEZE *vb* freeze beforehand

PREFROZE > PREFREEZE

PREFROZEN > PREFREEZE

PREFUND *vb* pay for in advance

PREFUNDED > PREFUND

PREFUNDS > PREFUND

PREGAME *adj* of the period before a sports match ▷ *n* such a period

PREGAMES > PREGAME

PREGGERS *informal word for* > PREGNANT

PREGGIER > PREGGY

PREGGIEST > PREGGY

PREGGY *informal word for* > PREGNANT

PREGNABLE *adj* capable of being assailed or captured

PREGNANCE *obsolete word for* > PREGNANCY

PREGNANCY *n* state or condition of being pregnant

PREGNANT *adj* carrying a fetus in the womb

PREGROWTH *n* period before something begins to grow

PREGUIDE *vb* give guidance in advance

PREGUIDED > PREGUIDE

PREGUIDES > PREGUIDE

PREHAB *n* any programme of training designed to prevent sports injury

PREHABS > PREHAB

PREHALLUX *n* extra first toe

PREHANDLE *vb* handle beforehand

PREHARDEN *vb* harden beforehand

PREHEAT *vb* heat (an oven, grill, pan, etc) beforehand

PREHEATED > PREHEAT

PREHEATER > PREHEAT

PREHEATS > PREHEAT

PREHEND *vb* take hold of

PREHENDED > PREHEND

PREHENDS > PREHEND

PREHENSOR *n* part that grasps

PREHIRING *adj* relating to early hiring

PREHNITE *n* green mineral

PREHNITES > PREHNITE

PREHUMAN *n* hominid that predates man

PREHUMANS > PREHUMAN

PREIF *old form of* > PROOF

PREIFE *old form of* > PROOF

PREIFES > PREIFE

PREIFS > PREIF

PREIMPOSE *vb* impose beforehand

PREINFORM *vb* inform beforehand

PREINSERT *vb* insert beforehand

PREINVITE *vb* invite before others

PREJINK *variant of* > PERJINK

PREJUDGE *vb* judge beforehand without sufficient evidence

PREJUDGED > PREJUDGE

PREJUDGER > PREJUDGE

PREJUDGES > PREJUDGE

PREJUDICE *n* unreasonable or unfair dislike or preference ▷ *vb* cause (someone) to have a prejudice

PREJUDIZE *old form of* > PREJUDICE

PRELACIES > PRELACY

PRELACY *n* office or status of a prelate

PRELATE *n* bishop or other churchman of high rank

PRELATES > PRELATE

PRELATESS *n* female prelate

PRELATIAL > PRELATE

PRELATIC > PRELATE

PRELATIES > PRELATY

PRELATION *n* setting of one above another

PRELATISE *same as* > PRELATIZE

PRELATISH *adj* like a prelate

PRELATISM *same as* > PRELACY

PRELATIST > PRELATISM

PRELATIZE *vb* exercise prelatical power

PRELATURE *same as* > PRELACY

PRELATY *n* prelacy

PRELAUNCH *adj* of the period before a launch

PRELAW *adj* before taking up study of law

PRELECT *vb* lecture or discourse in public

PRELECTED > PRELECT

PRELECTOR > PRELECT

PRELECTS > PRELECT

PRELEGAL *adj* of the period before the start of a law course

PRELIFE *n* life lived before one's life on earth

PRELIM *n* event which precedes another

PRELIMIT *vb* limit beforehand

PRELIMITS > PRELIMIT

PRELIMS *pl n* pages of a book which come before the main text

PRELIVES > PRELIFE

PRELOAD *vb* load beforehand

PRELOADED > PRELOAD

PRELOADS > PRELOAD

PRELOCATE *vb* locate beforehand

PRELOVED *adj* previously owned or used

PRELUDE *n* introductory movement in music ▷ *vb* act as a prelude to (something)

PRELUDED > PRELUDE

PRELUDER > PRELUDE

PRELUDERS > PRELUDE

PRELUDES > PRELUDE

PRELUDI > PRELUDIO

PRELUDIAL > PRELUDE

PRELUDING > PRELUDE

PRELUDIO *n* musical prelude

PRELUNCH *adj* of the period before lunch

PRELUSION > PRELUDE

PRELUSIVE > PRELUDE

PRELUSORY > PRELUDE

PREM *n* informal word for a premature infant

PREMADE *adj* made in advance

PREMAN *n* hominid

PREMARKET *adj* of the period before a product is available

PREMATURE *adj* happening or done before the normal or expected time

PREMEAL *adj* of the period before a meal

PREMED *n* premedical student

PREMEDIC *same as* > PREMED

PREMEDICS > PREMEDIC

PREMEDS > PREMED

PREMEET *adj* happening before a meet

PREMEN > PREMAN
PREMERGER adj of the period prior to a merger
PREMIA > PREMIUM
PREMIE same as > PREEMIE
PREMIER n prime minister ▷ adj chief, leading
PREMIERE n first performance of a play, film, etc ▷ vb give, or (of a film, play, or opera) be, a premiere
PREMIERED > PREMIERE
PREMIERES > PREMIERE
PREMIERS > PREMIER
PREMIES > PREMIE
PREMISE n statement used as the basis of reasoning ▷ vb state or assume (a proposition) as a premise
PREMISED > PREMISE
PREMISES > PREMISE
PREMISING > PREMISE
PREMISS same as > PREMISE
PREMISSED > PREMISS
PREMISSES > PREMISS
PREMIUM n additional sum of money, as on a wage or charge
PREMIUMS > PREMIUM
PREMIX vb mix beforehand
PREMIXED > PREMIX
PREMIXES > PREMIX
PREMIXING > PREMIX
PREMIXT > PREMIX
PREMODERN adj of the period before a modern era
PREMODIFY vb modify in advance
PREMOLAR n tooth between the canine and first molar in adult humans ▷ adj situated before a molar tooth
PREMOLARS > PREMOLAR
PREMOLD same as > PREMOULD
PREMOLDED > PREMOLD
PREMOLDS > PREMOLD
PREMOLT same as > PREMOULT
PREMONISH vb admonish beforehand
PREMORAL adj not governed by sense of right and wrong
PREMORSE adj appearing as though the end had been bitten off
PREMOSAIC adj of the period before Moses
PREMOTION n previous motion
PREMOTOR adj relating to a part of the frontal lobe of the brain
PREMOULD vb mould in advance
PREMOULDS > PREMOULD

PREMOULT adj happening in the period before an animal molts
PREMOVE vb prompt to action
PREMOVED > PREMOVE
PREMOVES > PREMOVE
PREMOVING > PREMOVE
PREMS > PREM
PREMUNE adj having immunity to a disease as a result of latent infection
PREMY variant of > PREEMIE
PRENAME n forename
PRENAMES > PRENAME
PRENASAL n bone in the front of the nose
PRENASALS > PRENASAL
PRENATAL adj before birth, during pregnancy ▷ n prenatal examination
PRENATALS > PRENATAL
PRENEED adj arranged in advance of eventual requirements
PRENOMEN less common spelling of > PRAENOMEN
PRENOMENS > PRENOMEN
PRENOMINA > PRENOMEN
PRENOON adj of the period before noon
PRENOTIFY vb notify in advance
PRENOTION n preconception
PRENT Scots variant of > PRINT
PRENTED > PRENT
PRENTICE vb bind as an apprentice
PRENTICED > PRENTICE
PRENTICES > PRENTICE
PRENTING > PRENT
PRENTS > PRENT
PRENUBILE adj of the period from birth to puberty
PRENUMBER vb number in advance
PRENUP n prenuptial agreement
PRENUPS > PRENUP
PRENZIE adj Shakespearian word supposed by some to mean "princely"
PREOBTAIN vb obtain in advance
PREOCCUPY vb fill the thoughts or attention of (someone) to the exclusion of other things
PREOCULAR adj relating to the scale in front of the eye of a reptile or fish ▷ n scale in front of the eye of a reptile or fish
PREON n (in particle physics) hypothetical subcomponent of a quark
PREONS > PREON
PREOP n patient being prepared for surgery

PREOPS > PREOP
PREOPTION n right of first choice
PREORAL adj situated in front of mouth
PREORDAIN vb ordain, decree, or appoint beforehand
PREORDER vb order in advance
PREORDERS > PREORDER
PREOWNED adj second-hand
PREP vb prepare
PREPACK vb pack in advance of sale
PREPACKED adj sold already wrapped
PREPACKS > PREPACK
PREPAID > PREPAY
PREPARE vb make or get ready
PREPARED > PREPARE
PREPARER > PREPARE
PREPARERS > PREPARE
PREPARES > PREPARE
PREPARING > PREPARE
PREPASTE vb paste in advance
PREPASTED > PREPASTE
PREPASTES > PREPASTE
PREPAVE vb pave beforehand
PREPAVED > PREPAVE
PREPAVES > PREPAVE
PREPAVING > PREPAVE
PREPAY vb pay for in advance
PREPAYING > PREPAY
PREPAYS > PREPAY
PREPENSE adj (usually in legal contexts) arranged in advance ▷ vb consider beforehand
PREPENSED > PREPENSE
PREPENSES > PREPENSE
PREPILL adj of the period before the contraceptive pill became available
PREPLACE vb place in advance
PREPLACED > PREPLACE
PREPLACES > PREPLACE
PREPLAN vb plan beforehand
PREPLANS > PREPLAN
PREPLANT adj planted in advance
PREPOLLEX n additional digit on thumb of some animals
PREPONE vb bring forward to an earlier time
PREPONED > PREPONE
PREPONES > PREPONE
PREPONING > PREPONE
PREPOSE vb place before
PREPOSED > PREPOSE
PREPOSES > PREPOSE
PREPOSING > PREPOSE
PREPOSTOR n prefect in certain public schools

PREPOTENT adj greater in power, force, or influence
PREPPED > PREP
PREPPIE same as > PREPPY
PREPPIER > PREPPY
PREPPIES > PREPPY
PREPPIEST > PREPPY
PREPPILY > PREPPY
PREPPING > PREP
PREPPY adj denoting a fashion style of neat, understated clothes ▷ n person exhibiting such style
PREPREG n material already impregnated with synthetic resin
PREPREGS > PREPREG
PREPRESS adj before printing
PREPRICE vb price in advance
PREPRICED > PREPRICE
PREPRICES > PREPRICE
PREPRINT vb print in advance
PREPRINTS > PREPRINT
PREPS > PREP
PREPUBES > PREPUBIS
PREPUBIS n animal hip bone
PREPUCE n foreskin
PREPUCES > PREPUCE
PREPUEBLO adj belonging to the period before the Pueblo Indians
PREPUNCH vb pierce with holes in advance
PREPUPA n insect in stage of life before pupa
PREPUPAE > PREPUPA
PREPUPAL adj of the period between the larval and pupal stages
PREPUPAS > PREPUPA
PREPUTIAL > PREPUCE
PREQUEL n film or book about an earlier stage of a story
PREQUELS > PREQUEL
PRERACE adj of the period before a race
PRERADIO adj before the invention of radio
PRERECORD vb record (music or a programme) in advance so that it can be played or broadcast later
PRERECTAL adj in front of the rectum
PREREFORM adj before reform
PRERENAL adj anterior to kidney
PRERETURN adj of the period before return
PREREVIEW adj of the period before review
PRERINSE vb treat before rinsing
PRERINSED > PRERINSE
PRERINSES > PRERINSE
PRERIOT adj of the period before a riot

PREROCK *adj* of the era before rock music

PRERUPT *adj* abrupt

PRESA *n* musical sign or symbol to indicate the entry of a part

PRESAGE *vb* be a sign or warning of ▷ *n* omen

PRESAGED > PRESAGE

PRESAGER > PRESAGE

PRESAGERS > PRESAGE

PRESAGES > PRESAGE

PRESAGING > PRESAGE

PRESALE *n* practice of arranging the sale of a product before it is available

PRESALES > PRESALE

PRESBYOPE *n* person with presbyopy

PRESBYOPY *n* diminishing ability of the eye to focus

PRESBYTE *n* person with presbyopy

PRESBYTER *n* (in some episcopal Churches) official with administrative and priestly duties

PRESBYTES > PRESBYTE

PRESBYTIC > PRESBYTE

PRESCHOOL *adj* of or for children below the age of five

PRESCIENT *adj* having knowledge of events before they take place

PRESCIND *vb* withdraw attention (from something)

PRESCINDS > PRESCIND

PRESCIOUS *adj* prescient

PRESCORE *vb* record (the score of a film) before shooting

PRESCORED > PRESCORE

PRESCORES > PRESCORE

PRESCREEN *vb* screen in advance

PRESCRIBE *vb* recommend the use of (a medicine)

PRESCRIPT *n* something laid down or prescribed ▷ *adj* prescribed as a rule

PRESCUTA > PRESCUTUM

PRESCUTUM *n* part of an insect's thorax

PRESE > PRESA

PRESEASON *n* period before the start of a sport season

PRESELECT *vb* select beforehand

PRESELL *vb* promote in advance of appearance

PRESELLS > PRESELL

PRESENCE *n* fact of being in a specified place

PRESENCES > PRESENCE

PRESENILE *adj* occurring before the onset of old age

PRESENT *adj* being in a specified place ▷ *n* present time or tense ▷ *vb* introduce formally or publicly

PRESENTED > PRESENT

PRESENTEE *n* person who is presented, as at court

PRESENTER *n* person introducing a TV or radio show

PRESENTLY *adv* soon

PRESENTS *pl n* used in a deed or document to refer to itself

PRESERVE *vb* keep from being damaged, changed, or ended ▷ *n* area of interest restricted to a particular person or group

PRESERVED > PRESERVE

PRESERVER > PRESERVE

PRESERVES > PRESERVE

PRESES *variant of* > PRAESES

PRESET *vb* set a timer so that equipment starts to work at a specific time ▷ *adj* (of equipment) with the controls set in advance ▷ *n* control that is used to set initial conditions

PRESETS > PRESET

PRESETTLE *vb* settle beforehand

PRESHAPE *vb* shape beforehand

PRESHAPED > PRESHAPE

PRESHAPES > PRESHAPE

PRESHIP *vb* ship in advance

PRESHIPS > PRESHIP

PRESHOW *vb* show in advance

PRESHOWED > PRESHOW

PRESHOWN > PRESHOW

PRESHOWS > PRESHOW

PRESHRANK > PRESHRINK

PRESHRINK *vb* subject to a shrinking process so that further shrinkage will not occur

PRESHRUNK > PRESHRINK

PRESIDE *vb* be in charge, esp of a meeting

PRESIDED > PRESIDE

PRESIDENT *n* head of state in many countries

PRESIDER > PRESIDE

PRESIDERS > PRESIDE

PRESIDES > PRESIDE

PRESIDIA > PRESIDIUM

PRESIDIAL *adj* presidential

PRESIDING > PRESIDE

PRESIDIO *n* military post or establishment, esp in countries under Spanish control

PRESIDIOS > PRESIDIO

PRESIDIUM *n* (in Communist countries) permanent administrative committee

PRESIFT *vb* sift beforehand

PRESIFTED > PRESIFT

PRESIFTS > PRESIFT

PRESIGNAL *vb* signal in advance

PRESLEEP *adj* of the period before sleep

PRESLICE *vb* slice in advance

PRESLICED > PRESLICE

PRESLICES > PRESLICE

PRESOAK *vb* soak beforehand

PRESOAKED > PRESOAK

PRESOAKS > PRESOAK

PRESOLD > PRESELL

PRESOLVE *vb* solve beforehand

PRESOLVED > PRESOLVE

PRESOLVES > PRESOLVE

PRESONG *adj* of the period before a song is sung

PRESORT *vb* sort in advance

PRESORTED > PRESORT

PRESORTS > PRESORT

PRESPLIT *adj* of the period prior to a split

PRESS *vb* apply force or weight to ▷ *n* printing machine

PRESSED > PRESS

PRESSER > PRESS

PRESSERS > PRESS

PRESSES > PRESS

PRESSFAT *n* wine vat

PRESSFATS > PRESSFAT

PRESSFUL > PRESS

PRESSFULS > PRESS

PRESSGANG *n* squad of sailors forcing others into navy

PRESSIE *informal word for* > PRESENT

PRESSIES > PRESSIE

PRESSING *adj* urgent ▷ *n* large number of gramophone records produced at one time

PRESSINGS > PRESSING

PRESSION *n* act of pressing

PRESSIONS > PRESSION

PRESSMAN *n* person who works for the press

PRESSMARK *n* location mark on a book indicating a specific bookcase

PRESSMEN > PRESSMAN

PRESSOR *n* something that produces an increase in blood pressure

PRESSORS > PRESSOR

PRESSROOM *n* room in a printing establishment that houses the printing presses

PRESSRUN *n* number of books printed at one time

PRESSRUNS > PRESSRUN

PRESSURE *n* force produced by pressing ▷ *vb* persuade forcefully

PRESSURED > PRESSURE

PRESSURES > PRESSURE

PRESSWORK *n* operation of a printing press

PRESSY *same as* > PRESSIE

PREST *adj* prepared for action or use ▷ *n* loan of money ▷ *vb* give as a loan

PRESTAMP *vb* stamp in advance

PRESTAMPS > PRESTAMP

PRESTED > PREST

PRESTER > PREST

PRESTERNA *adj* anterior to sternum

PRESTERS > PREST

PRESTIGE *n* high status or respect resulting from success or achievements

PRESTIGES > PRESTIGE

PRESTING > PREST

PRESTO *adv* very quickly ▷ *n* passage to be played very quickly

PRESTORE *vb* store in advance

PRESTORED > PRESTORE

PRESTORES > PRESTORE

PRESTOS > PRESTO

PRESTRESS *vb* apply tensile stress to (the steel cables, wires, etc, of a precast concrete part) before the load is applied

PRESTRIKE *adj* of the period before a strike

PRESTS > PREST

PRESUME *vb* suppose to be the case

PRESUMED > PRESUME

PRESUMER > PRESUME

PRESUMERS > PRESUME

PRESUMES > PRESUME

PRESUMING > PRESUME

PRESUMMIT *n* meeting held prior to a summit

PRESURVEY *vb* survey in advance

PRETAPE *vb* tape in advance

PRETAPED > PRETAPE

PRETAPES > PRETAPE

PRETAPING > PRETAPE

PRETASTE *vb* taste in advance

PRETASTED > PRETASTE

PRETASTES > PRETASTE

PRETAX *adj* before tax

PRETEEN *n* boy or girl approaching his or her teens

PRETEENS > PRETEEN

PRETELL *vb* predict

PRETELLS > PRETELL

PRETENCE *n* behaviour intended to deceive, pretending

PRETENCES > PRETENCE

PRETEND vb claim (something untrue) ▷ adj fanciful

PRETENDED > PRETEND

PRETENDER n person who makes a false or disputed claim to a position of power

PRETENDS > PRETEND

PRETENSE same as > PRETENCE

PRETENSES > PRETENSE

PRETERIST n person interested in past

PRETERIT same as > PRETERITE

PRETERITE n past tense of verbs, such as jumped, swam ▷ adj expressing such a past tense

PRETERITS > PRETERIT

PRETERM n premature baby

PRETERMIT vb overlook intentionally

PRETERMS > PRETERM

PRETEST vb test (something) before presenting it to its intended public or client ▷ n act or instance of pretesting

PRETESTED > PRETEST

PRETESTS > PRETEST

PRETEXT n false reason given to hide the real one ▷ vb get personal information under false pretences

PRETEXTED > PRETEXT

PRETEXTS > PRETEXT

PRETOLD > PRETELL

PRETONIC adj denoting or relating to the syllable before the one bearing the primary stress in a word

PRETOR same as > PRAETOR

PRETORIAL > PRETOR

PRETORIAN n person with the rank of praetor

PRETORS > PRETOR

PRETRAIN vb train in advance

PRETRAINS > PRETRAIN

PRETRAVEL adj of the period before travel

PRETREAT vb treat in advance

PRETREATS > PRETREAT

PRETRIAL n hearing prior to a trial

PRETRIALS > PRETRIAL

PRETRIM vb trim in advance

PRETRIMS > PRETRIM

PRETTIED > PRETTY

PRETTIER > PRETTY

PRETTIES > PRETTY

PRETTIEST > PRETTY

PRETTIFY vb make pretty

PRETTILY > PRETTY

PRETTY adj pleasing to look at ▷ adv fairly, moderately ▷ vb pretty

PRETTYING > PRETTY

PRETTYISH adj quite pretty

PRETTYISM n affectedly pretty style

PRETYPE vb type in advance

PRETYPED > PRETYPE

PRETYPES > PRETYPE

PRETYPING > PRETYPE

PRETZEL n brittle salted biscuit ▷ vb bend or twist

PRETZELS > PRETZEL

PREUNION n early form of trade union

PREUNIONS > PREUNION

PREUNITE vb unite in advance

PREUNITED > PREUNITE

PREUNITES > PREUNITE

PREVAIL vb gain mastery

PREVAILED > PREVAIL

PREVAILER > PREVAIL

PREVAILS > PREVAIL

PREVALENT adj widespread, common

PREVALUE vb value beforehand

PREVALUED > PREVALUE

PREVALUES > PREVALUE

PREVE vb prove

PREVED > PREVE

PREVENE vb come before

PREVENED > PREVENE

PREVENES > PREVENE

PREVENING > PREVENE

PREVENT vb keep from happening or doing

PREVENTED > PREVENT

PREVENTER n person or thing that prevents

PREVENTS > PREVENT

PREVERB n particle preceding root of verb

PREVERBAL > PREVERB

PREVERBS > PREVERB

PREVES > PREVE

PREVIABLE adj not yet viable

PREVIEW n advance showing of a film or exhibition before it is shown to the public ▷ vb view in advance

PREVIEWED > PREVIEW

PREVIEWER > PREVIEW

PREVIEWS > PREVIEW

PREVING > PREVE

PREVIOUS adj coming or happening before

PREVISE vb predict or foresee

PREVISED > PREVISE

PREVISES > PREVISE

PREVISING > PREVISE

PREVISION n act or power of foreseeing

PREVISIT vb visit beforehand

PREVISITS > PREVISIT

PREVISOR > PREVISE

PREVISORS > PREVISE

PREVUE same as > PREVIEW

PREVUED > PREVUE

PREVUES > PREVUE

PREVUING > PREVUE

PREWAR adj relating to the period before a war, esp before World War I or II

PREWARM vb warm beforehand

PREWARMED > PREWARM

PREWARMS > PREWARM

PREWARN vb warn in advance

PREWARNED > PREWARN

PREWARNS > PREWARN

PREWASH vb give a preliminary wash to (clothes) ▷ n preliminary wash

PREWASHED > PREWASH

PREWASHES > PREWASH

PREWEIGH vb weigh beforehand

PREWEIGHS > PREWEIGH

PREWIRE vb wire beforehand

PREWIRED > PREWIRE

PREWIRES > PREWIRE

PREWIRING > PREWIRE

PREWORK vb work in advance

PREWORKED > PREWORK

PREWORKS > PREWORK

PREWORN adj (of clothes) second-hand

PREWRAP vb wrap in advance

PREWRAPS > PREWRAP

PREWYN obsolete spelling of > PRUNE

PREWYNS > PREWYN

PREX same as > PREXY

PREXES > PREX

PREXIE same as > PREXY

PREXIES > PREXY

PREXY n US college president

PREY n animal hunted and killed for food by another animal ▷ vb hunt or seize food by killing other animals

PREYED > PREY

PREYER > PREY

PREYERS > PREY

PREYFUL adj rich in prey

PREYING > PREY

PREYS > PREY

PREZ n president

PREZES > PREZ

PREZZIE same as > PRESSIE

PREZZIES > PREZZIE

PRIAL n pair royal of cards

PRIALS > PRIAL

PRIAPEAN same as > PRIAPIC

PRIAPI > PRIAPUS

PRIAPIC adj phallic

PRIAPISM n prolonged painful erection of the penis, caused by neurological disorders, obstruction of the penile blood vessels, etc

PRIAPISMS > PRIAPISM

PRIAPUS n representation of the penis

PRIAPUSES > PRIAPUS

PRIBBLE variant of > PRABBLE

PRIBBLES > PRIBBLE

PRICE n amount of money for which a thing is bought or sold ▷ vb fix or ask the price of

PRICEABLE > PRICE

PRICED > PRICE

PRICELESS adj very valuable

PRICER > PRICE

PRICERS > PRICE

PRICES > PRICE

PRICEY adj expensive

PRICIER > PRICY

PRICIEST > PRICY

PRICILY > PRICY

PRICINESS > PRICEY

PRICING > PRICE

PRICINGS > PRICE

PRICK vb pierce lightly with a sharp point ▷ n sudden sharp pain caused by pricking

PRICKED > PRICK

PRICKER n person or thing that pricks

PRICKERS > PRICKER

PRICKET n male deer in the second year of life

PRICKETS > PRICKET

PRICKIER > PRICKY

PRICKIEST > PRICKY

PRICKING > PRICK

PRICKINGS > PRICK

PRICKLE n thorn or spike on a plant ▷ vb have a tingling or pricking sensation

PRICKLED > PRICKLE

PRICKLES > PRICKLE

PRICKLIER > PRICKLY

PRICKLING > PRICKLE

PRICKLY adj having prickles

PRICKS > PRICK

PRICKWOOD n shrub with wood used for skewers

PRICKY adj covered with pricks

PRICY same as > PRICEY

PRIDE n feeling of pleasure and satisfaction when one has done well

PRIDED > PRIDE

PRIDEFUL > PRIDE

PRIDELESS > PRIDE

PRIDES > PRIDE

PRIDIAN adj relating to yesterday

PRIDING > PRIDE

PRIED > PRY

PRIEDIEU n piece of furniture consisting of a low surface for kneeling upon and a narrow front surmounted by a rest for the elbows or for books, for use when praying

PRIEDIEUS > PRIEDIEU

PRIEDIEUX > PRIEDIEU

PRIEF *obsolete variant of* > PROOF

PRIEFE *obsolete variant of* > PROOF

PRIEFES > PRIEFE

PRIEFS > PRIEF

PRIER *n* person who pries

PRIERS > PRIER

PRIES > PRY

PRIEST *n* (in the Christian church) person who can administer the sacraments and preach ▷ *vb* make a priest

PRIESTED > PRIEST

PRIESTESS *n* female official who offers sacrifice on behalf of the people and performs various other religious ceremonies

PRIESTING > PRIEST

PRIESTLY *adj* of, relating to, characteristic of, or befitting a priest

PRIESTS > PRIEST

PRIEVE *obsolete variant of* > PROOF

PRIEVED > PRIEVE

PRIEVES > PRIEVE

PRIEVING > PRIEVE

PRIG *n* self-righteous person who acts as if superior to others

PRIGGED > PRIG

PRIGGER *n* thief

PRIGGERS > PRIGGER

PRIGGERY > PRIG

PRIGGING > PRIG

PRIGGINGS > PRIG

PRIGGISH > PRIG

PRIGGISM > PRIG

PRIGGISMS > PRIG

PRIGS > PRIG

PRILL *vb* convert (a material) into a granular free-flowing form ▷ *n* prilled material

PRILLED > PRILL

PRILLING > PRILL

PRILLS > PRILL

PRIM *adj* formal, proper, and rather prudish ▷ *vb* make prim

PRIMA *same as* > PRIMO

PRIMACIES > PRIMACY

PRIMACY *n* state of being first in rank, grade, etc

PRIMAEVAL *same as* > PRIMEVAL

PRIMAGE *n* tax added to customs duty

PRIMAGES > PRIMAGE

PRIMAL *adj* of basic causes or origins

PRIMALITY *n* state of being prime

PRIMALLY > PRIMAL

PRIMARIES > PRIMARY

PRIMARILY *adv* chiefly or mainly

PRIMARY *adj* chief, most important ▷ *n* person or thing that is first in position, time, or importance

PRIMAS > PRIMA

PRIMATAL *n* primate

PRIMATALS > PRIMATAL

PRIMATE *n* member of an order of mammals including monkeys and humans

PRIMATES > PRIMATE

PRIMATIAL > PRIMATE

PRIMATIC > PRIMATE

PRIMAVERA *n* springtime

PRIME *adj* main, most important ▷ *n* time when someone is most vigorous ▷ *vb* give (someone) information in advance

PRIMED > PRIME

PRIMELY > PRIME

PRIMENESS > PRIME

PRIMER *n* special paint applied to bare wood etc before the main paint

PRIMERO *n* 16th- and 17th-century card game

PRIMEROS > PRIMERO

PRIMERS > PRIMER

PRIMES > PRIME

PRIMETIME *adj* occurring during or designed for prime time

PRIMEUR *n* anything (esp fruit) produced early

PRIMEURS > PRIMEUR

PRIMEVAL *adj* of the earliest age of the world

PRIMI > PRIMO

PRIMINE *n* integument surrounding an ovule or the outer of two such integuments

PRIMINES > PRIMINE

PRIMING *same as* > PRIMER

PRIMINGS > PRIMING

PRIMIPARA *n* woman who has borne only one child

PRIMITIAE *pl n* first fruits of the season

PRIMITIAL > PRIMITIAE

PRIMITIAS > PRIMITIAE

PRIMITIVE *adj* of an early simple stage of development ▷ *n* primitive person or thing

PRIMLY > PRIM

PRIMMED > PRIM

PRIMMER > PRIM

PRIMMERS > PRIM

PRIMMEST > PRIM

PRIMMING > PRIM

PRIMNESS > PRIM

PRIMO *n* upper or right-hand part in a piano duet

PRIMORDIA *pl n* organs or parts in the earliest stage of development

PRIMOS > PRIMO

PRIMP *vb* tidy (one's hair or clothes) fussily

PRIMPED > PRIMP

PRIMPING > PRIMP

PRIMPS > PRIMP

PRIMROSE *n* pale yellow spring flower ▷ *adj* pale yellow

PRIMROSED > PRIMROSE

PRIMROSES > PRIMROSE

PRIMROSY > PRIMROSE

PRIMS > PRIM

PRIMSIE *Scots variant of* > PRIM

PRIMSIER > PRIMSIE

PRIMSIEST > PRIMSIE

PRIMULA *n* type of primrose with brightly coloured flowers

PRIMULAS > PRIMULA

PRIMULINE *n* type of dye

PRIMUS *n* presiding bishop in the Synod

PRIMUSES > PRIMUS

PRIMY *adj* prime

PRINCE *vb* act the prince

PRINCED > PRINCE

PRINCEDOM *n* dignity, rank, or position of a prince

PRINCEKIN *n* young prince

PRINCELET *n* petty or minor prince

PRINCELY *adj* of or like a prince ▷ *adv* in a princely manner

PRINCES > PRINCE

PRINCESS *n* female member of a royal family, esp the daughter of the king or queen

PRINCESSE *same as* > PRINCESS

PRINCING > PRINCE

PRINCIPAL *adj* main, most important ▷ *n* head of a school or college

PRINCIPE *n* prince

PRINCIPI > PRINCIPE

PRINCIPIA *n* principles

PRINCIPLE *n* moral rule guiding behaviour

PRINCOCK *same as* > PRINCOX

PRINCOCKS > PRINCOCK

PRINCOX *n* pert youth

PRINCOXES > PRINCOX

PRINK *vb* dress (oneself) finely

PRINKED > PRINK

PRINKER > PRINK

PRINKERS > PRINK

PRINKING > PRINK

PRINKS > PRINK

PRINT *vb* reproduce (a newspaper, book, etc) in large quantities by mechanical or electronic

means ▷ *n* printed words etc

PRINTABLE *adj* capable of being printed or of producing a print

PRINTED > PRINT

PRINTER *n* person or company engaged in printing

PRINTERS > PRINTER

PRINTERY *n* establishment in which printing is carried out

PRINTHEAD *n* component in a printer that forms a printed character

PRINTING *n* process of producing printed matter

PRINTINGS > PRINTING

PRINTLESS > PRINT

PRINTOUT *n* printed information produced by a computer output device

PRINTOUTS > PRINTOUT

PRINTS > PRINT

PRION *n* dovelike petrel with a serrated bill

PRIONS > PRION

PRIOR *adj* earlier ▷ *n* head monk in a priory

PRIORATE *n* office, status, or term of office of a prior

PRIORATES > PRIORATE

PRIORESS *n* deputy head nun in a convent

PRIORIES > PRIORY

PRIORITY *n* most important thing that must be dealt with first

PRIORLY > PRIOR

PRIORS > PRIOR

PRIORSHIP *n* office of prior

PRIORY *n* place where certain orders of monks or nuns live

PRISAGE *n* customs duty levied until 1809 upon wine imported into England

PRISAGES > PRISAGE

PRISE *same as* > PRY

PRISED > PRISE

PRISER > PRISE

PRISERE *n* primary sere or succession from bare ground to the community climax

PRISERES > PRISERE

PRISERS > PRISE

PRISES > PRISE

PRISING > PRISE

PRISM *n* transparent block used to disperse light into a spectrum

PRISMATIC *adj* of or shaped like a prism

PRISMOID *n* prismatoid having an equal number of vertices in each of the two parallel planes and whose sides are trapeziums or parallelograms

PRISMOIDS > PRISMOID
PRISMS > PRISM
PRISMY > PRISM
PRISON n building where criminals and accused people are held ▷ vb imprison
PRISONED > PRISON
PRISONER n person held captive
PRISONERS > PRISONER
PRISONING > PRISON
PRISONOUS > PRISON
PRISONS > PRISON
PRISS n prissy person ▷ vb act prissily
PRISSED > PRISS
PRISSES > PRISS
PRISSIER > PRISSY
PRISSIES > PRISSY
PRISSIEST > PRISSY
PRISSILY > PRISSY
PRISSING > PRISS
PRISSY adj prim, correct, and easily shocked ▷ n prissy person
PRISTANE n colourless combustible liquid
PRISTANES > PRISTANE
PRISTINE adj clean, new, and unused
PRITHEE interj pray thee
PRIVACIES > PRIVACY
PRIVACY n condition of being private
PRIVADO n close friend
PRIVADOES > PRIVADO
PRIVADOS > PRIVADO
PRIVATE adj for the use of one person or group only ▷ n soldier of the lowest rank
PRIVATEER n privately owned armed vessel authorized by the government to take part in a war ▷ vb competitor, esp in motor racing, who is privately financed rather than sponsored by a manufacturer
PRIVATELY > PRIVATE
PRIVATER > PRIVATE
PRIVATES > PRIVATE
PRIVATEST > PRIVATE
PRIVATION n loss or lack of the necessities of life
PRIVATISE same as > PRIVATIZE
PRIVATISM n lack of concern for public life
PRIVATIST > PRIVATISM
PRIVATIVE adj causing privation
PRIVATIZE vb sell (a publicly owned company) to individuals or a private company
PRIVET n bushy evergreen shrub used for hedges
PRIVETS > PRIVET
PRIVIER > PRIVY

PRIVIES > PRIVY
PRIVIEST > PRIVY
PRIVILEGE n advantage or favour that only some people have ▷ vb bestow a privilege or privileges upon
PRIVILY adv in a secret way
PRIVITIES > PRIVITY
PRIVITY n legally recognized relationship between two parties
PRIVY adj sharing knowledge of something secret ▷ n toilet, esp an outside one
PRIZABLE adj of worth
PRIZE n reward given for success in a competition etc ▷ adj winning or likely to win a prize ▷ vb value highly
PRIZED > PRIZE
PRIZEMAN n winner of prize
PRIZEMEN > PRIZEMAN
PRIZER n contender for prize
PRIZERS > PRIZER
PRIZES > PRIZE
PRIZING > PRIZE
PRO prep in favour of ▷ n professional ▷ adv in favour of a motion etc
PROA n canoe-like boat used in the South Pacific
PROACTION n action that initiates change as opposed to reaction to events
PROACTIVE adj tending to initiate change rather than reacting to events
PROAS > PROA
PROB n problem
PROBABLE adj likely to happen or be true ▷ n person who is likely to be chosen for a team, event, etc
PROBABLES > PROBABLE
PROBABLY adv in all likelihood ▷ sentence substitute I believe such a thing or situation may be the case
PROBALL adj believable
PROBAND n first patient to be investigated in a family study
PROBANDS > PROBAND
PROBANG n long flexible rod used to apply medication
PROBANGS > PROBANG
PROBATE n process of proving the validity of a will ▷ vb establish officially the authenticity and validity of (a will)
PROBATED > PROBATE
PROBATES > PROBATE
PROBATING > PROBATE

PROBATION n system of dealing with law-breakers, esp juvenile ones, by placing them under supervision
PROBATIVE adj serving to test or designed for testing
PROBATORY same as > PROBATIVE
PROBE vb search into or examine closely ▷ n surgical instrument used to examine a wound, cavity, etc
PROBEABLE > PROBE
PROBED > PROBE
PROBER > PROBE
PROBERS > PROBE
PROBES > PROBE
PROBING n act of making a thorough enquiry
PROBINGLY > PROBE
PROBINGS > PROBING
PROBIOTIC n bacterium that protects the body from harmful bacteria
PROBIT n statistical measurement
PROBITIES > PROBITY
PROBITS > PROBIT
PROBITY n honesty, integrity
PROBLEM n something difficult to deal with or solve ▷ adj of a literary work that deals with difficult moral questions
PROBLEMS > PROBLEM
PROBOSCIS n long trunk or snout
PROBS > PROB
PROCACITY n insolence
PROCAINE n colourless or white crystalline water-soluble substance
PROCAINES > PROCAINE
PROCAMBIA n plant part in stem and root
PROCARP n female reproductive organ in red algae
PROCARPS > PROCARP
PROCARYON same as > PROKARYON
PROCEDURE n way of doing something, esp the correct or usual one
PROCEED vb start or continue doing
PROCEEDED > PROCEED
PROCEEDER > PROCEED
PROCEEDS pl n money obtained from an event or activity
PROCERITY n tallness
PROCESS n series of actions or changes ▷ vb handle or prepare by a special method of manufacture
PROCESSED > PROCESS
PROCESSER same as > PROCESSOR
PROCESSES > PROCESS

PROCESSOR n person or thing that carries out a process
PROCHAIN variant of > PROCHEIN
PROCHEIN adj next or nearest
PROCHOICE adj in favour of women's right to abortion
PROCHURCH adj favourable to church
PROCIDENT adj relating to prolapsus
PROCINCT n state of preparedness
PROCINCTS > PROCINCT
PROCLAIM vb declare publicly
PROCLAIMS > PROCLAIM
PROCLISES > PROCLITIC
PROCLISIS > PROCLITIC
PROCLITIC adj relating to or denoting a monosyllabic word or form having no stress or accent and pronounced as a prefix of the following word, as in English 't for it in 'twas ▷ n proclitic word or form
PROCLIVE adj prone
PROCONSUL n administrator or governor of a colony, occupied territory, or other dependency
PROCREANT > PROCREATE
PROCREATE vb produce offspring
PROCTAL adj relating to the rectum
PROCTITIS n inflammation of the rectum
PROCTODEA pl n parts of the anus
PROCTOR n university worker who enforces discipline ▷ vb invigilate (an examination)
PROCTORED > PROCTOR
PROCTORS > PROCTOR
PROCURACY n office of a procurator
PROCURAL > PROCURE
PROCURALS > PROCURE
PROCURE vb get, provide
PROCURED > PROCURE
PROCURER n person who obtains people to act as prostitutes
PROCURERS > PROCURER
PROCURES > PROCURE
PROCURESS same as > PROCURER
PROCUREUR n law officer in Guernsey
PROCURING > PROCURE
PROCYONID n animal of the raccoon family

P

PROD vb poke with something pointed ▷ n prodding
PRODDED > PROD
PRODDER > PROD
PRODDERS > PROD
PRODDING n act of prodding
PRODDINGS > PRODDING
PRODIGAL adj recklessly extravagant, wasteful ▷ n person who spends lavishly or squanders money
PRODIGALS > PRODIGAL
PRODIGIES > PRODIGY
PRODIGY n person with some marvellous talent
PRODITOR n traitor
PRODITORS > PRODITOR
PRODITORY > PRODITOR
PRODNOSE vb make uninvited inquiries (about someone else's business, for example)
PRODNOSED > PRODNOSE
PRODNOSES > PRODNOSE
PRODROMA n symptom that signals the onset of a disease
PRODROMAL > PRODROME
PRODROME n any symptom that signals the impending onset of a disease
PRODROMES > PRODROME
PRODROMI > PRODROME
PRODROMIC > PRODROME
PRODROMUS same as > PRODROME
PRODRUG n compound that is metabolized in the body to produce an active drug
PRODRUGS > PRODRUG
PRODS > PROD
PRODUCE vb bring into existence ▷ n food grown for sale
PRODUCED > PRODUCE
PRODUCER n person with control over the making of a film, record, etc
PRODUCERS > PRODUCER
PRODUCES > PRODUCE
PRODUCING > PRODUCE
PRODUCT n something produced
PRODUCTS > PRODUCT
PROEM n introduction or preface
PROEMBRYO n stage prior to embryo in plants
PROEMIAL > PROEM
PROEMS > PROEM
PROENZYME n inactive form of an enzyme
PROESTRUS n period in the estrous cycle that immediately precedes estrus
PROETTE n female golfing professional

PROETTES > PROETTE
PROF short for > PROFESSOR
PREFACE interj much good may it do you
PROFAMILY adj in favour of family
PROFANE adj showing disrespect for religion or holy things ▷ vb treat (something sacred) irreverently, desecrate
PROFANED > PROFANE
PROFANELY > PROFANE
PROFANER > PROFANE
PROFANERS > PROFANE
PROFANES > PROFANE
PROFANING > PROFANE
PROFANITY n profane talk or behaviour, blasphemy
PROFESS vb state or claim (something as true), sometimes falsely
PROFESSED adj supposed
PROFESSES > PROFESS
PROFESSOR n teacher of the highest rank in a university
PROFFER vb offer ▷ n act of proffering
PROFFERED > PROFFER
PROFFERER > PROFFER
PROFFERS > PROFFER
PROFILE n outline, esp of the face, as seen from the side ▷ vb draw, write, or make a profile of
PROFILED > PROFILE
PROFILER n person or device that creates a profile, esp someone with psychological training who assists police investigations by identifying the likely characteristics of the perpetrator of a particular crime
PROFILERS > PROFILER
PROFILES > PROFILE
PROFILING > PROFILE
PROFILIST > PROFILE
PROFIT n money gained ▷ vb gain or benefit
PROFITED > PROFIT
PROFITEER n person who makes excessive profits at the expense of the public ▷ vb make excessive profits
PROFITER > PROFIT
PROFITERS > PROFIT
PROFITING > PROFIT
PROFITS > PROFIT
PROFLUENT adj flowing smoothly or abundantly
PROFORMA n invoice issued before an order is placed or before the goods are delivered giving all the details and the cost of the goods

PROFOUND adj showing or needing great knowledge ▷ n great depth
PROFOUNDS > PROFOUND
PROFS > PROF
PROFUSE adj plentiful
PROFUSELY > PROFUSE
PROFUSER > PROFUSE
PROFUSERS > PROFUSE
PROFUSION > PROFUSE
PROFUSIVE same as > PROFUSE
PROG vb prowl about for or as if for food or plunder ▷ n food obtained by begging
PROGENIES > PROGENY
PROGENY n children
PROGERIA n premature old age, a rare condition occurring in children and characterized by small stature, absent or greying hair, wrinkled skin, and other signs of old age
PROGERIAS > PROGERIA
PROGESTIN n type of steroid hormone
PROGGED > PROG
PROGGER n fan of progressive rock
PROGGERS > PROGGER
PROGGING > PROG
PROGGINS n proctor
PROGNOSE vb predict course of disease
PROGNOSED > PROGNOSE
PROGNOSES > PROGNOSIS
PROGNOSIS n doctor's forecast about the progress of an illness
PROGRADE vb (of beach) advance towards sea
PROGRADED > PROGRADE
PROGRADES > PROGRADE
PROGRAM same as > PROGRAMME
PROGRAMED > PROGRAM
PROGRAMER n US spelling of programmer
PROGRAMME same as > PROGRAM
PROGRAMS > PROGRAM
PROGRESS n improvement, development ▷ vb become more advanced or skilful
PROGS > PROG
PROGUN adj in favour of public owning firearms
PROHIBIT vb forbid or prevent from happening
PROHIBITS > PROHIBIT
PROIGN same as > PROIN
PROIGNED > PROIGN
PROIGNING > PROIGN
PROIGNS > PROIGN
PROIN vb trim or prune
PROINE same as > PROIN
PROINED > PROIN
PROINES > PROINE
PROINING > PROIN
PROINS > PROIN

PROJECT n planned scheme to do or examine something over a period ▷ vb make a forecast based on known data
PROJECTED > PROJECT
PROJECTOR n apparatus for projecting photographic images, films, or slides on a screen
PROJECTS > PROJECT
PROJET n draft of a proposed treaty
PROJETS > PROJET
PROKARYON n nucleus of a prokaryote
PROKARYOT n any organism having cells in each of which the genetic material is in a single DNA chain, not enclosed in a nucleus
PROKE vb thrust or poke
PROKED > PROKE
PROKER > PROKE
PROKERS > PROKE
PROKES > PROKE
PROKING > PROKE
PROLABOR adj favouring the Labor party
PROLABOUR adj favouring an organized labour movement
PROLACTIN n gonadotrophic hormone secreted by the anterior lobe of the pituitary gland
PROLAMIN same as > PROLAMINE
PROLAMINE n any of a group of simple plant proteins, including gliadin, hordein, and zein
PROLAMINS > PROLAMIN
PROLAN n constituent of human pregnancy urine
PROLANS > PROLAN
PROLAPSE n slipping down of an internal organ of the body from its normal position ▷ vb (of an internal organ) slip from its normal position
PROLAPSED > PROLAPSE
PROLAPSES > PROLAPSE
PROLAPSUS same as > PROLAPSE
PROLATE adj having a polar diameter which is longer than the equatorial diameter ▷ vb pronounce or utter
PROLATED > PROLATE
PROLATELY > PROLATE
PROLATES > PROLATE
PROLATING > PROLATE
PROLATION > PROLATE
PROLATIVE > PROLATE
PROLE old form of > PROWL
PROLED > PROLE
PROLEG n appendage on abdominal segment of a caterpillar

PROLEGS > PROLEG
PROLEPSES
> PROLEPSIS
PROLEPSIS *n* rhetorical device by which objections are anticipated and answered in advance
PROLEPTIC
> PROLEPSIS
PROLER *n* prowler
PROLERS > PROLER
PROLES > PROLE
PROLETARY *n* member of the proletariat
PROLICIDE *n* killing of one's child
PROLIFIC *adj* very productive
PROLINE *n* nonessential amino acid that occurs in protein
PROLINES > PROLINE
PROLING > PROLE
PROLIX *adj* (of speech or a piece of writing) overlong and boring
PROLIXITY > PROLIX
PROLIXLY > PROLIX
PROLL *vb* prowl or search
PROLLED > PROLL
PROLLER > PROLL
PROLLERS > PROLL
PROLLING > PROLL
PROLLS > PROLL
PROLLY *adv* probably
PROLOG *same as*
> PROLOGUE
PROLOGED > PROLOG
PROLOGING > PROLOG
PROLOGISE *same as*
> PROLOGIZE
PROLOGIST *n* prologue writer
PROLOGIZE *vb* write a prologue
PROLOGS > PROLOG
PROLOGUE *n* introduction to a play or book ▷ *vb* introduce or preface with or as if with a prologue
PROLOGUED > PROLOGUE
PROLOGUES > PROLOGUE
PROLONG *vb* make (something) last longer
PROLONGE *n* (formerly) specially fitted rope used as part of the towing equipment of a gun carriage
PROLONGED > PROLONG
PROLONGER > PROLONG
PROLONGES
> PROLONGE
PROLONGS > PROLONG
PROLUSION *n* preliminary written exercise
PROLUSORY
> PROLUSION
PROM *n* formal dance held at a high school or college
PROMACHOS *n* defender or champion
PROMENADE *n* paved walkway along the

seafront at a holiday resort ▷ *vb* take a leisurely walk
PROMETAL *n* type of cast iron
PROMETALS > PROMETAL
PROMETRIC *adj* in favour of the metric system
PROMINE *n* substance promoting cell growth
PROMINENT *adj* very noticeable
PROMINES > PROMINE
PROMISE *vb* say that one will definitely do or not do something ▷ *n* undertaking to do or not to do something
PROMISED > PROMISE
PROMISEE *n* person to whom a promise is made
PROMISEES > PROMISEE
PROMISER > PROMISE
PROMISES > PROMISE
PROMISING *adj* likely to succeed or turn out well
PROMISOR *n* person who makes a promise
PROMISORS > PROMISOR
PROMISSOR *n* (in law) person who makes a promise
PROMMER *n* spectator at promenade concert
PROMMERS > PROMMER
PROMO *vb* promote (something)
PROMODERN *adj* in favour of the modern
PROMOED > PROMO
PROMOING > PROMO
PROMOS > PROMO
PROMOTE *vb* help to make (something) happen or increase
PROMOTED > PROMOTE
PROMOTER *n* person who organizes or finances an event etc
PROMOTERS > PROMOTER
PROMOTES > PROMOTE
PROMOTING > PROMOTE
PROMOTION > PROMOTE
PROMOTIVE *adj* tending to promote
PROMOTOR *variant of*
> PROMOTER
PROMOTORS > PROMOTOR
PROMPT *vb* cause (an action) ▷ *adj* done without delay ▷ *adv* exactly ▷ *n* anything that serves to remind
PROMPTED > PROMPT
PROMPTER *n* person offstage who prompts actors
PROMPTERS > PROMPTER
PROMPTEST > PROMPT
PROMPTING > PROMPT
PROMPTLY > PROMPT
PROMPTS > PROMPT
PROMPTURE *n* prompting
PROMS > PROM

PROMULGE *vb* bring to public knowledge
PROMULGED > PROMULGE
PROMULGES > PROMULGE
PROMUSCES > PROMUSCIS
PROMUSCIS *n* proboscis of certain insects
PRONAOI > PRONAOS
PRONAOS *n* inner area of the portico of a classical temple
PRONATE *vb* turn (a limb, hand, or foot) so that the palm or sole is directed downwards
PRONATED > PRONATE
PRONATES > PRONATE
PRONATING > PRONATE
PRONATION > PRONATE
PRONATOR *n* any muscle whose contractions produce or affect pronation
PRONATORS > PRONATOR
PRONE *n* sermon ▷ *adj* sloping downwards
PRONELY > PRONE
PRONENESS > PRONE
PRONEPHRA *n* parts of the kidneys of lower vertebrates
PRONER > PRONE
PRONES > PRONE
PRONEST > PRONE
PRONEUR *n* flatterer
PRONEURS > PRONEUR
PRONG *n* one spike of a fork or similar instrument ▷ *vb* prick or spear with or as if with a prong
PRONGBUCK *n* horned N American ruminant
PRONGED > PRONG
PRONGHORN *n* ruminant mammal inhabiting rocky deserts of North America and having small branched horns
PRONGING > PRONG
PRONGS > PRONG
PRONK *vb* jump straight up
PRONKED > PRONK
PRONKING > PRONK
PRONKINGS > PRONKING
PRONKS > PRONK
PRONOTA > PRONOTUM
PRONOTAL > PRONOTUM
PRONOTUM *n* notum of the prothorax of an insect
PRONOUN *n* word, such as *she* or *it*, used to replace a noun
PRONOUNCE *vb* form the sounds of (words or letters), esp clearly or in a particular way
PRONOUNS > PRONOUN
PRONTO *adv* at once
PRONUCLEI *pl n* nuclei of mature ova or spermatozoa before fertilization
PRONUNCIO *n* papal ambassador

PROO *interj* (to a horse) stop!
PROOEMION *n* preface
PROOEMIUM *n* preface
PROOF *n* evidence that shows that something is true or has happened ▷ *adj* able to withstand ▷ *vb* take a proof from (type matter)
PROOFED > PROOF
PROOFER *n* reader of proofs
PROOFERS > PROOFER
PROOFING > PROOF
PROOFINGS > PROOF
PROOFLESS > PROOF
PROOFREAD *vb* read and correct (printer's proofs)
PROOFROOM *n* room for proofreading
PROOFS > PROOF
PROOTIC *n* bone in front of ear
PROOTICS > PROOTIC
PROP *vb* support (something) so that it stays upright or in place ▷ *n* pole, beam, etc used as a support
PROPAGATE *vb* spread (information and ideas)
PROPAGE *vb* propagate
PROPAGED > PROPAGE
PROPAGES > PROPAGE
PROPAGING > PROPAGE
PROPAGULA
> PROPAGULE
PROPAGULE *n* plant part, such as a bud, that becomes detached from the rest of the plant and grows into a new plant
PROPALE *vb* publish (something)
PROPALED > PROPALE
PROPALES > PROPALE
PROPALING > PROPALE
PROPANE *n* flammable gas found in petroleum and used as a fuel
PROPANES > PROPANE
PROPANOIC *adj* as in *propanoic acid* colourless liquid carboxylic acid
PROPANOL *n* colourless alcohol
PROPANOLS
> PROPANOL
PROPANONE *n* systematic name of acetone
PROPEL *vb* cause to move forward
PROPELLED > PROPEL
PROPELLER *n* revolving shaft with blades for driving a ship or aircraft
PROPELLOR *same as*
> PROPELLER
PROPELS > PROPEL
PROPENAL *n* type of aldehyde used as a herbicide and tear gas
PROPENALS > PROPENAL

PROPEND vb be inclined or disposed

PROPENDED > PROPEND

PROPENDS > PROPEND

PROPENE n colourless gaseous alkene obtained by cracking petroleum

PROPENES > PROPENE

PROPENOIC adj as in propenoic acid systematic name of acrylic acid

PROPENOL n liquid used to make allylic alcohol

PROPENOLS > PROPENOL

PROPENSE adj inclining forward

PROPENYL n three-carbon radical

PROPENYLS > PROPENYL

PROPER adj real or genuine ▷ n service or psalm regarded as appropriate to a specific day, season, etc

PROPERDIN n protein present in blood serum that, acting with complement, is involved in the destruction of alien cells, such as bacteria

PROPERER > PROPER

PROPEREST > PROPER

PROPERLY > PROPER

PROPERS > PROPER

PROPERTY same as > PROPRIUM

PROPHAGE n virus that exists in a bacterial cell and undergoes division with its host without destroying it

PROPHAGES > PROPHAGE

PROPHASE n first stage of mitosis, during which the nuclear membrane disappears and the nuclear material resolves itself into chromosomes

PROPHASES > PROPHASE

PROPHASIC > PROPHASE

PROPHECY n prediction

PROPHESY vb foretell

PROPHET n person supposedly chosen by God to spread His word

PROPHETIC adj foretelling what will happen

PROPHETS > PROPHET

PROPHYLL n leaf-shaped plant structure

PROPHYLLS > PROPHYLL

PROPINE vb drink a toast to

PROPINED > PROPINE

PROPINES > PROPINE

PROPINING > PROPINE

PROPIONIC adj as in propionic acid former name for propanoic acid

PROPJET another name for > TURBOPROP

PROPJETS > PROPJET

PROPMAN n member of the stage crew in charge of the stage props

PROPMEN > PROPMAN

PROPODEON n part of an insect's thorax

PROPODEUM variant of > PROPODEON

PROPOLIS n greenish-brown resinous aromatic substance collected by bees from the buds of trees for use in the construction of hives

PROPONE vb propose or put forward, esp before a court

PROPONED > PROPONE

PROPONENT n person who argues in favour of something

PROPONES > PROPONE

PROPONING > PROPONE

PROPOSAL n act of proposing

PROPOSALS > PROPOSAL

PROPOSE vb put forward for consideration

PROPOSED > PROPOSE

PROPOSER > PROPOSE

PROPOSERS > PROPOSE

PROPOSES > PROPOSE

PROPOSING > PROPOSE

PROPOSITA n woman from whom a line of descent is traced

PROPOSITI n people from whom lines of descent are traced

PROPOUND vb put forward for consideration

PROPOUNDS > PROPOUND

PROPPANT n material used in the oil extraction process

PROPPANTS > PROPPANT

PROPPED > PROP

PROPPING > PROP

PROPRETOR n (in ancient Rome) citizen, esp an ex-praetor, granted a praetor's imperium, to be exercised outside Rome

PROPRIA > PROPRIUM

PROPRIETY n quality of being appropriate or fitting

PROPRIUM n attribute that is not essential to a species but is common and peculiar to it

PROPS > PROP

PROPTOSES > PROPTOSIS

PROPTOSIS n forward displacement of an organ or part, such as the eyeball

PROPULSOR n propeller

PROPYL n of, consisting of, or containing the monovalent group of atoms C_3H_7-

PROPYLA > PROPYLON

PROPYLAEA n porticos, esp those that form the entrances to temples

PROPYLENE n gas found in petroleum and used to produce many organic compounds

PROPYLIC > PROPYL

PROPYLITE n altered andesite or similar rock containing calcite, chlorite, etc, produced by the action of hot water

PROPYLON n portico, esp one that forms the entrance to a temple

PROPYLONS > PROPYLON

PROPYLS > PROPYL

PROPYNE n type of gaseous methyl acetylene

PROPYNES > PROPYNE

PRORATE vb divide, assess, or distribute (something) proportionately

PRORATED > PRORATE

PRORATES > PRORATE

PRORATING > PRORATE

PRORATION > PRORATE

PRORE n forward part of ship

PRORECTOR n official in German academia

PROREFORM adj in favour of or supporting reform, esp within politics

PRORES > PRORE

PROROGATE vb discontinue legislative meetings

PROROGUE vb suspend (parliament) without dissolving it

PROROGUED > PROROGUE

PROROGUES > PROROGUE

PROS > PRO

PROSAIC adj lacking imagination, dull

PROSAICAL same as > PROSAIC

PROSAISM n prosaic quality or style

PROSAISMS > PROSAISM

PROSAIST > PROSATSM

PROSAISTS > PROSAISM

PROSATEUR n writer of prose

PROSCENIA pl n arches or openings separating stages from auditoria together with the areas immediately in front of the arches

PROSCRIBE vb prohibit, outlaw

PROSCRIPT n proscription or prohibition

PROSE n ordinary speech or writing in contrast to poetry ▷ vb speak or write in a tedious style

PROSECCO n Italian sparkling white wine

PROSECCOS > PROSECCO

PROSECT vb dissect a cadaver for a public demonstration

PROSECTED > PROSECT

PROSECTOR n person who prepares or dissects anatomical subjects for demonstration

PROSECTS > PROSECT

PROSECUTE vb bring a criminal charge against

PROSED > PROSE

PROSELIKE > PROSE

PROSELYTE n recent convert

PROSEMAN n writer of prose

PROSEMEN > PROSEMAN

PROSER n writer of prose

PROSERS > PROSER

PROSES > PROSE

PROSEUCHA n place of prayer

PROSEUCHE n prayer

PROSIER > PROSY

PROSIEST > PROSY

PROSIFIED > PROSIFY

PROSIFIES > PROSIFY

PROSIFY vb write prose

PROSILY > PROSY

PROSIMIAN n primate of the primitive suborder which includes lemurs, lorises, and tarsiers

PROSINESS > PROSY

PROSING > PROSE

PROSINGS > PROSE

PROSIT interj good health! cheers!

PROSO n millet

PROSOCIAL adj acting to the benefit of society

PROSODIAL adj of prosody

PROSODIAN n writer of prose

PROSODIC > PROSODY

PROSODIES > PROSODY

PROSODIST > PROSODY

PROSODY n study of poetic metre and techniques

PROSOMA n head and thorax of an arachnid

PROSOMAL > PROSOMA

PROSOMAS > PROSOMA

PROSOMATA > PROSOMA

PROSOPON n (in Christianity) manifestation of any of the persons of the Trinity

PROSOPONS > PROSOPON

PROSOS > PROSO

PROSPECT n something anticipated ▷ vb explore, esp for gold

PROSPECTS > PROSPECT

PROSPER vb be successful

PROSPERED > PROSPER

PROSPERS > PROSPER

PROSS n prostitute

PROSSES > PROSS

PROSSIE n prostitute

PROSSIES > PROSSIE
PROST same as > PROSIT
PROSTATE n gland in male mammals that surrounds the neck of the bladder ▷ adj of or relating to the prostate gland
PROSTATES > PROSTATE
PROSTATIC same as > PROSTATE
PROSTERNA n sternums or thoraces of insects
PROSTIE n prostitute
PROSTIES > PROSTIE
PROSTOMIA pl n lobes at the head ends of earthworms and other annelids
PROSTRATE adj lying face downwards ▷ vb lie face downwards
PROSTYLE adj (of a building) having a row of columns in front, esp as in the portico of a Greek temple ▷ n prostyle building, portico, etc
PROSTYLES > PROSTYLE
PROSUMER n amateur user of electronic equipment suitable for professionals
PROSUMERS > PROSUMER
PROSY adj dull and long-winded
PROTAMIN same as > PROTAMINE
PROTAMINE n any of a group of basic simple proteins that occur, in association with nucleic acids, in the sperm of some fish
PROTAMINS > PROTAMIN
PROTANDRY n condition (in hermaphrodite plants) of maturing the anthers before the stigma
PROTANOPE n person with type of colour blindness
PROTASES > PROTASIS
PROTASIS n antecedent of a conditional statement
PROTATIC > PROTASIS
PROTEA n African shrub with showy flowers
PROTEAN adj constantly changing ▷ n creature that can change shape
PROTEANS > PROTEAN
PROTEAS > PROTEA
PROTEASE n any enzyme involved in proteolysis
PROTEASES > PROTEASE
PROTECT vb defend from trouble, harm, or loss
PROTECTED > PROTECT
PROTECTER same as > PROTECTOR
PROTECTOR n person or thing that protects
PROTECTS > PROTECT

PROTEGE n person who is protected and helped by another
PROTEGEE n woman or girl who is protected and helped by another
PROTEGEES > PROTEGEE
PROTEGES > PROTEGE
PROTEI > PROTEUS
PROTEID n protein
PROTEIDE variant of > PROTEID
PROTEIDES > PROTEIDE
PROTEIDS > PROTEID
PROTEIN n any of a group of complex organic compounds that are essential for life
PROTEINIC > PROTEIN
PROTEINS > PROTEIN
PROTEND vb hold out or stretch
PROTENDED > PROTEND
PROTENDS > PROTEND
PROTENSE n extension
PROTENSES > PROTENSE
PROTEOME n full complement of proteins that occur within a cell, tissue, or organism
PROTEOMES > PROTEOME
PROTEOMIC > PROTEOME
PROTEOSE n compound formed during proteolysis that is less complex than metaproteins but more so than peptones
PROTEOSES > PROTEOSE
PROTEST n declaration or demonstration of objection ▷ vb object, disagree
PROTESTED > PROTEST
PROTESTER > PROTEST
PROTESTOR > PROTEST
PROTESTS > PROTEST
PROTEUS n aerobic bacterium
PROTEUSES > PROTEUS
PROTHALLI n small flat free-living gametophytes in ferns, club mosses etc
PROTHESES > PROTHESIS
PROTHESIS n process in the development of a language by which a phoneme or syllable is prefixed to a word to facilitate pronunciation
PROTHETIC > PROTHESIS
PROTHORAX n first segment of the thorax of an insect, which bears the first pair of walking legs
PROTHYL variant of > PROTYLE
PROTHYLS > PROTHYL
PROTIST n organism belonging to the protozoans, unicellular algae, and simple fungi
PROTISTAN > PROTIST

PROTISTIC > PROTIST
PROTISTS > PROTIST
PROTIUM n most common isotope of hydrogen
PROTIUMS > PROTIUM
PROTO n as in proto team relating to a team of people trained to deal with underground rescues, etc
PROTOAVIS n bird-like fossil
PROTOCOL n rules of behaviour for formal occasions
PROTOCOLS > PROTOCOL
PROTODERM n outer primary meristem of a plant
PROTOGINE n type of granite
PROTOGYNY n (in hermaphrodite plants and animals) condition of producing female gametes before male ones
PROTON n positively charged particle in the nucleus of an atom
PROTONATE vb provide atom with proton
PROTONEMA n branched threadlike structure that grows from a moss spore and eventually develops into the moss plant
PROTONIC adj (of a solvent, such as water) able to donate hydrogen ions to solute molecules
PROTONS > PROTON
PROTOPOD n part of crustacean's leg
PROTOPODS > PROTOPOD
PROTORE n primary mineral deposit
PROTORES > PROTORE
PROTOSTAR n cloud of interstellar gas and dust that gradually collapses, forming a hot dense core, and evolves into a star once nuclear fusion can occur in the core
PROTOTYPE n original or model to be copied or developed
PROTOXID variant of > PROTOXIDE
PROTOXIDE n oxide of an element that contains the smallest amount of oxygen of any of its oxides
PROTOXIDS > PROTOXID
PROTOZOA > PROTOZOAN
PROTOZOAL > PROTOZOAN
PROTOZOAN n microscopic one-celled creature ▷ adj of or relating to protozoans
PROTOZOIC adj of or pertaining to the protozoa
PROTOZOON same as > PROTOZOAN

PROTRACT vb lengthen or extend (a situation etc)
PROTRACTS > PROTRACT
PROTRADE adj in favour of trade
PROTRUDE vb stick out, project
PROTRUDED > PROTRUDE
PROTRUDES > PROTRUDE
PROTURAN n any of an order of white wingless insects
PROTURANS > PROTURAN
PROTYL same as > PROTYLE
PROTYLE n hypothetical primitive substance
PROTYLES > PROTYLE
PROTYLS > PROTYL
PROUD adj feeling pleasure and satisfaction
PROUDER > PROUD
PROUDEST > PROUD
PROUDFUL adj full of pride
PROUDISH adj rather proud
PROUDLY > PROUD
PROUDNESS > PROUD
PROUL variant of > PROWL
PROULED > PROUL
PROULER Scots variant of > PROWLER
PROULERS > PROULER
PROULING > PROUL
PROULS > PROUL
PROUNION adj in favour of or supporting the constitutional union between two or more countries
PROUSTITE n red mineral consisting of silver arsenic sulphide in hexagonal crystalline form
PROVABLE > PROVE
PROVABLY > PROVE
PROVAND n food
PROVANDS > PROVAND
PROVANT adj supplied with provisions ▷ vb supply with provisions
PROVANTED > PROVANT
PROVANTS > PROVANT
PROVE vb establish the validity of
PROVEABLE adj able to be proved
PROVEABLY > PROVEABLE
PROVED > PROVE
PROVEDOR variant of > PROVEDORE
PROVEDORE n purveyor
PROVEDORS > PROVEDOR
PROVEN > PROVE
PROVEND same as > PROVAND
PROVENDER n fodder
PROVENDS > PROVEND
PROVENLY > PROVE
PROVER > PROVE
PROVERB n short saying that expresses a truth or

p

gives a warning ▷ *vb* utter or describe (something) in the form of a proverb

PROVERBED > PROVERB

PROVERBS > PROVERB

PROVERS > PROVE

PROVES > PROVE

PROVIANT *variant of* > PROVAND

PROVIANTS > PROVIANT

PROVIDE *vb* make available

PROVIDED > PROVIDE

PROVIDENT *adj* thrifty

PROVIDER > PROVIDE

PROVIDERS > PROVIDE

PROVIDES > PROVIDE

PROVIDING > PROVIDE

PROVIDOR *variant of* > PROVEDORE

PROVIDORS > PROVIDOR

PROVINCE *n* area governed as a unit of a country or empire

PROVINCES > PROVINCE

PROVINE *vb* plant branch of vine in ground for propagation

PROVINED > PROVINE

PROVINES > PROVINE

PROVING > PROVE

PROVINGS > PROVE

PROVINING > PROVINE

PROVIRAL > PROVIRUS

PROVIRUS *n* inactive form of a virus in a host cell

PROVISION *n* act of supplying something ▷ *vb* supply with food

PROVISO *n* condition, stipulation

PROVISOES > PROVISO

PROVISOR *n* person who receives provision

PROVISORS > PROVISOR

PROVISORY *adj* containing a proviso

PROVISOS > PROVISO

PROVOCANT *n* provocateur; one who deliberately behaves controversially to provoke argument or other strong reactions

PROVOKE *vb* deliberately anger

PROVOKED > PROVOKE

PROVOKER > PROVOKE

PROVOKERS > PROVOKE

PROVOKES > PROVOKE

PROVOKING > PROVOKE

PROVOLONE *n* mellow, pale yellow, soft, and sometimes smoked cheese, made of cow's milk: usually moulded in the shape of a pear

PROVOST *n* head of certain university colleges in Britain

PROVOSTRY *n* office of provost

PROVOSTS > PROVOST

PROW *n* bow of a vessel ▷ *adj* gallant

PROWAR *adj* in favour of or supporting war

PROWER > PROW

PROWESS *n* superior skill or ability

PROWESSED *adj* brave or skilful

PROWESSES > PROWESS

PROWEST > PROW

PROWL *vb* move stealthily around a place as if in search of prey or plunder ▷ *n* prowling

PROWLED > PROWL

PROWLER > PROWL

PROWLERS > PROWL

PROWLING > PROWL

PROWLINGS > PROWL

PROWLS > PROWL

PROWS > PROW

PROXEMIC > PROXEMICS

PROXEMICS *n* study of spatial interrelationships in humans or in populations of animals of the same species

PROXIES > PROXY

PROXIMAL *same as* > PROXIMATE

PROXIMATE *adj* next or nearest in space or time

PROXIMITY *n* nearness in space or time

PROXIMO *adv* in or during the next or coming month

PROXY *n* person authorized to act on behalf of someone else

PROYN *obsolete spelling of* > PRUNE

PROYNE *obsolete spelling of* > PRUNE

PROYNED > PROYN

PROYNES > PROYNE

PROYNING > PROYN

PROYNS > PROYN

PROZYMITE *n* Christian using leavened bread for the Eucharist

PRUDE *n* person who is excessively modest, prim, or proper

PRUDENCE *n* caution in practical affairs

PRUDENCES > PRUDENCE

PRUDENT *adj* cautious, discreet, and sensible

PRUDENTLY > PRUDENT

PRUDERIES > PRUDE

PRUDERY > PRUDE

PRUDES > PRUDE

PRUDISH > PRUDE

PRUDISHLY > PRUDE

PRUH *variant of* > PROO

PRUINA *n* woolly white covering on some lichens

PRUINAS > PRUINA

PRUINE *obsolete spelling of* > PRUNE

PRUINES > PRUINE

PRUINOSE *adj* coated with a powdery or waxy bloom

PRUNABLE > PRUNE

PRUNE *n* dried plum ▷ *vb* cut off dead parts or excessive branches from (a tree or plant)

PRUNED > PRUNE

PRUNELLA *n* strong fabric, esp a twill-weave worsted, used for gowns and the uppers of some shoes

PRUNELLAS > PRUNELLA

PRUNELLE *same as* > PRUNELLA

PRUNELLES > PRUNELLE

PRUNELLO *same as* > PRUNELLA

PRUNELLOS > PRUNELLO

PRUNER > PRUNE

PRUNERS > PRUNE

PRUNES > PRUNE

PRUNEY *adj* resembling a prune

PRUNIER > PRUNEY

PRUNIEST > PRUNEY

PRUNING > PRUNE

PRUNINGS > PRUNE

PRUNT *n* glass ornamentation

PRUNTED > PRUNT

PRUNTS > PRUNT

PRUNUS *n* type of ornamental tree or shrub

PRUNUSES > PRUNUS

PRURIENCE > PRURIENT

PRURIENCY *n* sexual desire

PRURIENT *adj* excessively interested in sexual matters

PRURIGO *n* chronic inflammatory disease of the skin

PRURIGOS > PRURIGO

PRURITIC > PRURITUS

PRURITUS *n* any intense sensation of itching

PRUSIK *n* sliding knot used in climbing ▷ *vb* climb (up a rope) using prusiks

PRUSIKED > PRUSIK

PRUSIKING > PRUSIK

PRUSIKS > PRUSIK

PRUSSIAN *adj* as in prussian blue colour pigment, discovered in Berlin

PRUSSIATE *n* any cyanide, ferrocyanide, or ferricyanide

PRUSSIC *adj* as in prussic acid weakly acidic extremely poisonous aqueous solution of hydrogen cyanide

PRUTA *same as* > PRUTAH

PRUTAH *n* former Israeli coin

PRUTOT > PRUTAH

PRUTOTH > PRUTAH

PRY *vb* make an impertinent or uninvited inquiry into a private matter ▷ *n* act of prying

PRYER *same as* > PRIER

PRYERS > PRYER

PRYING > PRY

PRYINGLY > PRY

PRYINGS > PRY

PRYS *old variant of* > PRICE

PRYSE *old variant of* > PRICE

PRYSED > PRYSE

PRYSES > PRYSE

PRYSING > PRYSE

PRYTANEA > PRYTANEUM

PRYTANEUM *n* public hall of a city in ancient Greece

PRYTHEE *same as* > PRITHEE

PSALM *n* sacred song ▷ *vb* sing a psalm

PSALMBOOK *n* book of psalms

PSALMED > PSALM

PSALMIC > PSALM

PSALMING > PSALM

PSALMIST *n* writer of psalms

PSALMISTS > PSALMIST

PSALMODIC > PSALMODY

PSALMODY *n* singing of sacred music

PSALMS > PSALM

PSALTER *n* book containing a version of Psalms

PSALTERIA *n* omasa

PSALTERS > PSALTER

PSALTERY *n* ancient instrument played by plucking strings

PSALTRESS *n* woman who sings psalms

PSALTRIES > PSALTRY

PSALTRY *same as* > PSALTERY

PSAMMITE *rare name for* > SANDSTONE

PSAMMITES > PSAMMITE

PSAMMITIC > PSAMMITE

PSAMMON *n* microscopic life forms living between grains of sand

PSAMMONS > PSAMMON

PSCHENT *n* ancient Egyptian crown

PSCHENTS > PSCHENT

PSELLISM *n* stammering

PSELLISMS > PSELLISM

PSEPHISM *n* proposition adopted by a majority vote

PSEPHISMS > PSEPHISM

PSEPHITE *n* any rock, such as a breccia, that consists of large fragments embedded in a finer matrix

PSEPHITES > PSEPHITE

PSEPHITIC > PSEPHITE

PSEUD *n* pretentious person

PSEUDAXES > PSEUDAXIS

PSEUDAXIS *another name for* > SYMPODIUM

PSEUDERY *n* pretentious talk

PSEUDISH > PSEUD
PSEUDO n pretentious person
PSEUDONYM n fictitious name adopted esp by an author
PSEUDOPOD n temporary projection from the body of a single-celled animal
PSEUDOS > PSEUDO
PSEUDS > PSEUD
PSHAW n exclamation of disgust, impatience, disbelief, etc ▷ vb make this exclamation
PSHAWED > PSHAW
PSHAWING > PSHAW
PSHAWS > PSHAW
PSI n 23rd letter of the Greek alphabet
PSILOCIN n hallucinogenic substance
PSILOCINS > PSILOCIN
PSILOSES > PSILOSIS
PSILOSIS n disease of the small intestine
PSILOTIC > PSILOSIS
PSION n type of elementary particle
PSIONIC > PSIONICS
PSIONICS n study of the practical use of psychic powers
PSIONS > PSION
PSIS > PSI
PSOAE > PSOAS
PSOAI > PSOAS
PSOAS n either of two muscles of the loins that aid in flexing and rotating the thigh
PSOASES > PSOAS
PSOATIC > PSOAS
PSOCID n tiny wingless insect
PSOCIDS > PSOCID
PSORA n itching skin complaint
PSORALEA n type of tropical and subtropical plant with curly leaves and white or purple flowers
PSORALEAS > PSORALEA
PSORALEN n treatment for some skin diseases
PSORALENS > PSORALEN
PSORAS > PSORA
PSORIASES > PSORIASIS
PSORIASIS n skin disease with reddish spots and patches covered with silvery scales
PSORIATIC > PSORIASIS
PSORIC > PSORA
PSST interj sound made to attract someone's attention, esp without others noticing
PST interj sound made to attract someone's attention

PSYCH vb psychoanalyse
PSYCHE same as > PSYCH
PSYCHED > PSYCH
PSYCHES > PSYCH
PSYCHIC adj having mental powers which cannot be explained by natural laws ▷ n person with psychic powers
PSYCHICAL > PSYCHIC
PSYCHICS > PSYCHIC
PSYCHING > PSYCH
PSYCHISM n belief in a universal soul
PSYCHISMS > PSYCHISM
PSYCHIST > PSYCHISM
PSYCHISTS > PSYCHISM
PSYCHO n psychopath
PSYCHOGAS n gas with a mind-altering effect
PSYCHOID n name for an animal's innate impetus to perform actions
PSYCHOIDS > PSYCHOID
PSYCHOS > PSYCHO
PSYCHOSES > PSYCHOSIS
PSYCHOSIS n severe mental disorder in which the sufferer's contact with reality becomes distorted
PSYCHOTIC adj of, relating to, or characterized by psychosis ▷ n person suffering from psychosis
PSYCHS > PSYCH
PSYLLA same as > PSYLLID
PSYLLAS > PSYLLA
PSYLLID n type of insect of the family which comprises the jumping plant lice
PSYLLIDS > PSYLLID
PSYLLIUM n grain, the husks of which are used medicinally as a laxative and to reduce blood cholesterol levels
PSYLLIUMS > PSYLLIUM
PSYOP n psychological operation
PSYOPS > PSYOP
PSYWAR n psychological warfare
PSYWARS > PSYWAR
PTARMIC n material that causes sneezing
PTARMICS > PTARMIC
PTARMIGAN n bird of the grouse family which turns white in winter
PTERIA > PTERION
PTERIDINE n yellow crystalline base
PTERIN n compound such as folic acid
PTERINS > PTERIN
PTERION n point on the side of the skull where a number of bones meet

PTEROIC adj as in pteroic acid a kind of acid found in spinach
PTEROPOD n small marine gastropod mollusc in which the foot is expanded into two winglike lobes for swimming and the shell is absent or thin-walled
PTEROPODS > PTEROPOD
PTEROSAUR n extinct flying reptile
PTERYGIA > PTERYGIUM
PTERYGIAL adj of or relating to a fin or wing
PTERYGIUM n abnormal tissue over corner of eye
PTERYGOID n either of two bony plates extending downwards from each side of the sphenoid bone within the skull
PTERYLA n any of the tracts of skin that bear contour feathers
PTERYLAE > PTERYLA
PTILOSES > PTILOSIS
PTILOSIS n falling out of eye lashes
PTISAN n grape juice drained off without pressure
PTISANS > PTISAN
PTOMAIN same as > PTOMAINE
PTOMAINE n any of a group of poisonous alkaloids found in decaying matter
PTOMAINES > PTOMAINE
PTOMAINIC > PTOMAINE
PTOMAINS > PTOMAIN
PTOOEY interj imitation of the sound of spitting
PTOSES > PTOSIS
PTOSIS n prolapse or drooping of a part, esp the eyelid
PTOTIC > PTOSIS
PTUI same as > PTOOEY
PTYALIN n amylase secreted in the saliva of man and other animals
PTYALINS > PTYALIN
PTYALISE same as > PTYALIZE
PTYALISED > PTYALISE
PTYALISES > PTYALISE
PTYALISM n excessive secretion of saliva
PTYALISMS > PTYALISM
PTYALIZE vb expel saliva from the mouth
PTYALIZED > PTYALIZE
PTYALIZES > PTYALIZE
PTYXES > PTYXIS
PTYXIS n folding of a leaf in a bud
PTYXISES > PTYXIS
PUB n building with a bar licensed to sell alcoholic drinks ▷ vb visit a pub or pubs

PUBBED > PUB
PUBBING > PUB
PUBBINGS > PUBBING
PUBCO n company operating a chain of pubs
PUBCOS > PUBCO
PUBE n pubic hair
PUBERAL adj relating to puberty
PUBERTAL > PUBERTY
PUBERTIES > PUBERTY
PUBERTY n beginning of sexual maturity
PUBES > PUBE
PUBESCENT adj reaching or having reached puberty
PUBIC adj of the lower abdomen
PUBIS n one of the three sections of the hipbone that forms part of the pelvis
PUBISES > PUBIS
PUBLIC adj of or concerning the people as a whole ▷ n community, people in general
PUBLICAN n person who owns or runs a pub
PUBLICANS > PUBLICAN
PUBLICISE same as > PUBLICIZE
PUBLICIST n person, esp a press agent or journalist, who publicizes something
PUBLICITY n process or information used to arouse public attention
PUBLICIZE vb bring to public attention
PUBLICLY adv in a public manner
PUBLICS > PUBLIC
PUBLISH vb produce and issue (printed matter) for sale
PUBLISHED > PUBLISH
PUBLISHER n company or person that publishes books, periodicals, music, etc
PUBLISHES > PUBLISH
PUBS > PUB
PUCAN n traditional Connemara open sailing boat
PUCANS > PUCAN
PUCCOON n N American plant that yields a red dye
PUCCOONS > PUCCOON
PUCE adj purplish-brown ▷ n colour varying from deep red to dark purplish-brown
PUCELAGE n virginity
PUCELAGES > PUCELAGE
PUCELLE n maid or virgin
PUCELLES > PUCELLE
PUCER > PUCE
PUCES > PUCE
PUCEST > PUCE
PUCK n mischievous or evil spirit ▷ vb strike (the ball) in hurling

PUCKA *same as* > PUKKA
PUCKED > PUCK
PUCKER *vb* gather into wrinkles ▷ *n* wrinkle or crease
PUCKERED > PUCKER
PUCKERER > PUCKER
PUCKERERS > PUCKER
PUCKERIER > PUCKERY
PUCKERIES > PUCKERY
PUCKERING > PUCKER
PUCKEROOD *adj* (NZ informal) ruined; exhausted
PUCKERS > PUCKER
PUCKERY *adj* (of wine) high in tannins ▷ *n* puckishness
PUCKFIST *n* puffball
PUCKFISTS > PUCKFIST
PUCKING > PUCK
PUCKISH > PUCK
PUCKISHLY > PUCK
PUCKLE *n* early type of machine gun
PUCKLES > PUCKLE
PUCKOUT *n* (in hurling) free hit made by the goalkeeper
PUCKOUTS > PUCKOUT
PUCKS > PUCK
PUCKSTER *n* hockey player
PUCKSTERS > PUCKSTER
PUD *short for* > PUDDING
PUDDEN *dialect spelling of* > PUDDING
PUDDENING *n* rope fender on boat
PUDDENS > PUDDEN
PUDDER *vb* make bother or fuss
PUDDERED > PUDDER
PUDDERING > PUDDER
PUDDERS > PUDDER
PUDDIER > PUDDY
PUDDIES > PUDDY
PUDDIEST > PUDDY
PUDDING *n* dessert, esp a cooked one served hot
PUDDINGS > PUDDING
PUDDINGY > PUDDING
PUDDLE *n* small pool of water, esp of rain ▷ *vb* make (clay etc) into puddle
PUDDLED > PUDDLE
PUDDLER > PUDDLE
PUDDLERS > PUDDLE
PUDDLES > PUDDLE
PUDDLIER > PUDDLE
PUDDLIEST > PUDDLE
PUDDLING *n* process for converting pig iron into wrought iron by heating it with ferric oxide in a furnace to oxidize the carbon
PUDDLINGS > PUDDLING
PUDDLY > PUDDLE
PUDDOCK *same as* > PADDOCK
PUDDOCKS > PUDDOCK

PUDDY *n* paw ▷ *adj* short and podgy
PUDENCIES > PUDENCY
PUDENCY *n* modesty, shame, or prudishness
PUDENDA > PUDENDUM
PUDENDAL > PUDENDUM
PUDENDOUS *adj* shameful
PUDENDUM *n* human external genital organs collectively, esp of a female
PUDENT *adj* lacking in ostentation; humble
PUDEUR *n* sense of shame or embarrassment
PUDEURS > PUDEUR
PUDGE *same as* > PODGE
PUDGES > PUDGE
PUDGIER > PUDGY
PUDGIEST > PUDGY
PUDGILY > PUDGY
PUDGINESS > PUDGY
PUDGY *adj* podgy
PUDIBUND *adj* prudish
PUDIC > PUDENDUM
PUDICITY *n* modesty
PUDOR *n* sense of shame
PUDORS > PUDOR
PUDS > PUD
PUDSEY *variant of* > PUDSY
PUDSIER > PUDSY
PUDSIES > PUDSY
PUDSIEST > PUDSY
PUDSY *adj* plump ▷ *n* plump person
PUDU *n* diminutive Andean antelope
PUDUS > PUDU
PUEBLO *n* communal village of flat-roofed houses
PUEBLOS > PUEBLO
PUER *vb* steep hides in an alkaline substance from the dung of dogs
PUERED > PUER
PUERILE *adj* silly and childish
PUERILELY > PUERILE
PUERILISM *n* immature or childish behaviour by an adult
PUERILITY > PUERILE
PUERING > PUER
PUERPERA *n* woman who has recently given birth
PUERPERAE > PUERPERA
PUERPERAL *adj* concerning the period following childbirth
PUERPERIA *n* periods of around six weeks following childbirth when uteruses return to their normal size and shape
PUERS > PUER
PUFF *n* (sound of) short blast of breath, wind, etc ▷ *vb* blow or breathe in short quick draughts
PUFFA *adj* type of quilted and padded jacket

PUFFBACK *n* type of small African bird
PUFFBACKS > PUFFBACK
PUFFBALL *n* ball-shaped fungus
PUFFBALLS > PUFFBALL
PUFFBIRD *n* brownish tropical American bird with a large head
PUFFBIRDS > PUFFBIRD
PUFFED > PUFF
PUFFER *n* person or thing that puffs
PUFFERIES > PUFFERY
PUFFERS > PUFFER
PUFFERY *n* exaggerated praise, esp in publicity or advertising
PUFFIER > PUFFY
PUFFIEST > PUFFY
PUFFILY > PUFFY
PUFFIN *n* sea bird with a brightly-coloured beak
PUFFINESS > PUFFY
PUFFING > PUFF
PUFFINGLY > PUFF
PUFFINGS > PUFF
PUFFINS > PUFFIN
PUFFS > PUFF
PUFFY *adj* short of breath
PUFTALOON *n* Australian fried scone
PUG *n* small snub-nosed dog ▷ *vb* mix or knead (clay) with water to form a malleable mass or paste
PUGAREE *same as* > PUGGREE
PUGAREES > PUGAREE
PUGGAREE *same as* > PUGGREE
PUGGAREES > PUGGAREE
PUGGED > PUG
PUGGERIES > PUGGERY
PUGGERY *same as* > PUGGREE
PUGGIE *n* Scottish word for fruit machine
PUGGIER > PUGGY
PUGGIES > PUGGIE
PUGGIEST > PUGGY
PUGGINESS > PUGGY
PUGGING > PUG
PUGGINGS > PUG
PUGGISH > PUG
PUGGLE *vb* stir up by poking
PUGGLED > PUGGLE
PUGGLES > PUGGLE
PUGGLING > PUGGLE
PUGGREE *n* scarf, usually pleated, around the crown of some hats, esp sun helmets
PUGGREES > PUGGREE
PUGGRIES > PUGGRY
PUGGRY *same as* > PUGGREE
PUGGY *adj* sticky, claylike ▷ *n* term of endearment
PUGH *interj* exclamation of disgust

PUGIL *n* pinch or small handful
PUGILISM *n* art, practice, or profession of fighting with the fists
PUGILISMS > PUGILISM
PUGILIST > PUGILISM
PUGILISTS > PUGILISM
PUGILS > PUGIL
PUGMARK *n* trail of an animal
PUGMARKS > PUGMARK
PUGNACITY *n* readiness to fight
PUGREE *same as* > PUGGREE
PUGREES > PUGREE
PUGS > PUG
PUH *interj* exclamation expressing contempt or disgust
PUHA *n* sow thistle
PUHAS > PUHA
PUIR *Scottish word for* > POOR
PUIRER > PUIR
PUIREST > PUIR
PUIRTITH *n* poverty
PUIRTITHS > PUIRTITH
PUISNE *adj* (esp of a subordinate judge) of lower rank ▷ *n* judge of lower rank
PUISNES > PUISNE
PUISNY *adj* younger or inferior
PUISSANCE *n* showjumping competition that tests a horse's ability to jump large obstacles
PUISSANT *adj* powerful
PUISSAUNT *same as* > PUISSANT
PUJA *n* ritual in honour of the gods, performed either at home or in the mandir (temple)
PUJAH *same as* > PUJA
PUJAHS > PUJAH
PUJARI *n* Hindu priest
PUJARIS > PUJARI
PUJAS > PUJA
PUKA *in New Zealand English, same as* > BROADLEAF
PUKAS > PUKA
PUKATEA *n* aromatic New Zealand tree
PUKATEAS > PUKATEA
PUKE *vb* vomit ▷ *n* act of vomiting
PUKED > PUKE
PUKEKO *n* brightly coloured New Zealand wading bird
PUKEKOS > PUKEKO
PUKER *n* person who vomits
PUKERS > PUKER
PUKES > PUKE
PUKEY *adj* of or like vomit
PUKIER > PUKEY
PUKIEST > PUKEY

PUKING > PUKE

PUKKA adj properly done, constructed, etc

PUKKAH adj genuine

PUKU n belly or stomach

PUKUS > PUKU

PUKY same as > PUKEY

PUL n Afghan monetary unit

PULA n standard monetary unit of Botswana

PULAO same as > PILAU

PULAOS > PULAO

PULAS > PULA

PULDRON same as > PAULDRON

PULDRONS > PULDRON

PULE vb whine or whimper

PULED > PULE

PULER > PULE

PULERS > PULE

PULES > PULE

PULI > PUL

PULICENE adj flea-ridden

PULICIDE n flea-killing substance

PULICIDES > PULICIDE

PULIER > PULY

PULIEST > PULY

PULIK > PUL

PULING > PULE

PULINGLY > PULE

PULINGS > PULE

PULIS > PUL

PULK same as > PULKA

PULKA n reindeer-drawn sleigh

PULKAS > PULKA

PULKHA same as > PULKA

PULKHAS > PULKHA

PULKS > PULK

PULL vb exert force on (an object) to move it towards the source of the force ▷ n act of pulling

PULLBACK n act of pulling back

PULLBACKS > PULLBACK

PULLED > PULL

PULLER > PULL

PULLERS > PULL

PULLET n young hen

PULLETS > PULLET

PULLEY n device for lifting weights by a downward pull ▷ vb lift with a pulley

PULLEYED > PULLEY

PULLEYING > PULLEY

PULLEYS > PULLEY

PULLI > PULLUS

PULLIES > PULLY

PULLING > PULL

PULLMAN n luxurious railway coach, esp a sleeping car

PULLMANS > PULLMAN

PULLORUM n as in pullorum disease acute serious bacterial disease of very young birds

PULLOUT n removable section of a magazine, etc

PULLOUTS > PULLOUT

PULLOVER n sweater that is pulled on over the head

PULLOVERS > PULLOVER

PULLS > PULL

PULLULATE vb (of animals, etc) breed rapidly or abundantly

PULLUP n exercise in which the body is raised by the arms pulling on a horizontal bar

PULLUPS > PULLUP

PULLUS n technical term for a chick or young bird

PULLY n pullover

PULMO n lung

PULMONARY adj of the lungs

PULMONATE adj having lungs or lung-like organs ▷ n any pulmonate mollusc

PULMONES > PULMO

PULMONIC adj of or relating to the lungs ▷ n person with lung disease

PULMONICS > PULMONIC

PULMOTOR n apparatus for pumping oxygen into the lungs during artificial respiration

PULMOTORS > PULMOTOR

PULP n soft wet substance made from crushed or beaten matter ▷ vb reduce to pulp

PULPAL > PULP

PULPALLY > PULP

PULPBOARD n board made from wood pulp

PULPED > PULP

PULPER > PULP

PULPERS > PULP

PULPIER > PULPY

PULPIEST > PULPY

PULPIFIED > PULPIFY

PULPIFIES > PULPIFY

PULPIFY vb reduce to pulp

PULPILY > PULPY

PULPINESS > PULPY

PULPING n act of pulping

PULPINGS > PULPING

PULPIT n raised platform for a preacher

PULPITAL > PULPIT

PULPITED > PULPIT

PULPITEER n deliverer of sermon ▷ vb preach from a pulpit

PULPITER n preacher

PULPITERS > PULPITER

PULPITRY n art of delivering sermons

PULPITS > PULPIT

PULPITUM n stone screen dividing nave and choir

PULPITUMS > PULPITUM

PULPLESS > PULP

PULPMILL n mill making raw material for paper

PULPMILLS > PULPMILL

PULPOUS n soft and yielding

PULPS > PULP

PULPSTONE n calcified mass in a tooth cavity

PULPWOOD n pine, spruce, or any other soft wood used to make paper

PULPWOODS > PULPWOOD

PULPY adj having a soft or soggy consistency

PULQUE n light alcoholic drink from Mexico

PULQUES > PULQUE

PULS > PUL

PULSANT adj vibrant

PULSAR n small dense star which emits regular bursts of radio waves

PULSARS > PULSAR

PULSATE vb throb, quiver

PULSATED > PULSATE

PULSATES > PULSATE

PULSATILE adj beating rhythmically

PULSATING > PULSATE

PULSATION n act of pulsating

PULSATIVE > PULSATE

PULSATOR n device that stimulates rhythmic motion of a body

PULSATORS > PULSATOR

PULSATORY adj of or relating to pulsation

PULSE n regular beating of blood through the arteries at each heartbeat ▷ vb beat, throb, or vibrate

PULSEBEAT n the pulse

PULSED > PULSE

PULSEJET n type of ramjet engine

PULSEJETS > PULSEJET

PULSELESS > PULSE

PULSER n thing that pulses

PULSERS > PULSER

PULSES > PULSE

PULSIDGE archaic word for > PULSE

PULSIDGES > PULSIDGE

PULSIFIC adj causing the pulse to increase

PULSING > PULSE

PULSION n act of driving forward

PULSIONS > PULSION

PULSOJET same as > PULSEJET

PULSOJETS > PULSOJET

PULTAN n native Indian regiment

PULTANS > PULTAN

PULTON same as > PULTAN

PULTONS > PULTON

PULTOON same as > PULTAN

PULTOONS > PULTOON

PULTRUDE vb produce reinforced plastic process by pultrusion

PULTRUDED > PULTRUDE

PULTRUDES > PULTRUDE

PULTUN same as > PULTAN

PULTUNS > PULTUN

PULTURE n food and drink claimed by foresters

PULTURES > PULTURE

PULU n substance used for stuffing cushions

PULUS > PULU

PULVER vb make into powder

PULVERED > PULVER

PULVERINE n ashes of the barilla plant

PULVERING > PULVER

PULVERISE same as > PULVERIZE

PULVERIZE vb reduce to fine pieces

PULVEROUS adj consisting of tiny particles

PULVERS > PULVER

PULVIL vb apply perfumed powder

PULVILIO n perfumed powder

PULVILIOS > PULVILIO

PULVILLAR adj like cushion

PULVILLE same as > PULVIL

PULVILLED > PULVIL

PULVILLES > PULVILLE

PULVILLI > PULVILLUS

PULVILLIO same as > PULVILIO

PULVILLUS n small pad between the claws at the end of an insect's leg

PULVILS > PULVIL

PULVINAR n part of the thalamus

PULVINARS > PULVINAR

PULVINATE adj (of a frieze) curved convexly

PULVINI > PULVINUS

PULVINULE n part of a leaf

PULVINUS n swelling at the base of a leafstalk

PULWAR n light Indian river boat

PULWARS > PULWAR

PULY adj whiny

PUMA n large American wild cat with a greyish-brown coat

PUMAS > PUMA

PUMELO same as > POMELO

PUMELOS > PUMELO

PUMICATE vb pound fruit with pumice to make juice

PUMICATED > PUMICATE

PUMICATES > PUMICATE

PUMICE n light porous stone used for scouring ▷ vb rub or polish with pumice

PUMICED > PUMICE

PUMICEOUS > PUMICE

PUMICER > PUMICE

PUMICERS > PUMICE

PUMICES > PUMICE

PUMICING > PUMICE

PUMICITE n fine-grained variety of pumice
PUMICITES > PUMICITE
PUMIE n small stone
PUMIES > PUMIE
PUMMEL vb strike repeatedly with or as if with the fists
PUMMELED > PUMMEL
PUMMELING > PUMMEL
PUMMELLED > PUMMEL
PUMMELO same as > POMELO
PUMMELOS > PUMMELO
PUMMELS > PUMMEL
PUMP n machine used to force a liquid or gas to move in a particular direction ▷ vb raise or drive with a pump
PUMPABLE adj capable of being pumped
PUMPED > PUMP
PUMPER > PUMP
PUMPERS > PUMP
PUMPHOOD n cover for the upper wheel of a chain pump
PUMPHOODS > PUMPHOOD
PUMPING > PUMP
PUMPINGS > PUMPING
PUMPION archaic word for > PUMPKIN
PUMPIONS > PUMPION
PUMPJACK n pumping apparatus at an oil well
PUMPJACKS > PUMPJACK
PUMPKIN n large round fruit with an orange rind
PUMPKING n person involved in a web-based project who has temporary but exclusive authority to make changes to the master source code
PUMPKINGS > PUMPKING
PUMPKINS > PUMPKIN
PUMPLESS > PUMP
PUMPLIKE > PUMP
PUMPS > PUMP
PUMY adj large and round
PUN n use of words to exploit double meanings for humorous effect ▷ vb make puns
PUNA n high cold dry plateau, esp in the Andes
PUNAANI same as > PUNANI
PUNAANY same as > PUNANI
PUNALUA n marriage between the sisters of one family to the brothers of another
PUNALUAN > PUNALUA
PUNALUAS > PUNALUA
PUNANI n vagina
PUNANY same as > PUNANI
PUNAS > PUNA
PUNCE n kick ▷ vb kick
PUNCED > PUNCE
PUNCES > PUNCE

PUNCH vb strike at with a clenched fist ▷ n blow with a clenched fist
PUNCHBAG n stuffed or inflated bag suspended by a flexible rod, that is punched for exercise, esp boxing training
PUNCHBAGS > PUNCHBAG
PUNCHBALL n stuffed or inflated ball supported by a flexible rod, that is punched for exercise, esp boxing training
PUNCHBOWL n large bowl for serving punch
PUNCHED > PUNCH
PUNCHEON n large cask of variable capacity, usually between 70 and 120 gallons
PUNCHEONS > PUNCHEON
PUNCHER > PUNCH
PUNCHERS > PUNCH
PUNCHES > PUNCH
PUNCHIER > PUNCHY
PUNCHIEST > PUNCHY
PUNCHILY > PUNCHY
PUNCHING > PUNCH
PUNCHLESS > PUNCH
PUNCHLINE n funny ending of a joke
PUNCHOUT n fist fight
PUNCHOUTS > PUNCHOUT
PUNCHY adj forceful
PUNCING > PUNCE
PUNCTA > PUNCTUM
PUNCTATE adj having or marked with minute spots, holes, or depressions
PUNCTATED same as > PUNCTATE
PUNCTATOR n marker of points
PUNCTILIO n strict attention to minute points of etiquette
PUNCTO n tip of a fencing sword
PUNCTOS > PUNCTO
PUNCTUAL adj arriving or taking place at the correct time
PUNCTUATE vb put punctuation marks in
PUNCTULE n very small opening
PUNCTULES > PUNCTULE
PUNCTUM n tip or small point
PUNCTURE n small hole made by a sharp object, esp in a tyre ▷ vb pierce a hole in
PUNCTURED > PUNCTURE
PUNCTURER > PUNCTURE
PUNCTURES > PUNCTURE
PUNDIT n expert who speaks publicly on a subject
PUNDITIC adj of or relating to pundits

PUNDITRY n expressing of expert opinions
PUNDITS > PUNDIT
PUNDONOR n point of honour
PUNG n horse-drawn sleigh with a boxlike body on runners
PUNGA variant spelling of > PONGA
PUNGAS > PUNGA
PUNGENCE n pungency
PUNGENCES > PUNGENCE
PUNGENCY > PUNGENT
PUNGENT adj having a strong sharp bitter flavour
PUNGENTLY > PUNGENT
PUNGLE vb make payment
PUNGLED > PUNGLE
PUNGLES > PUNGLE
PUNGLING > PUNGLE
PUNGS > PUNG
PUNIER > PUNY
PUNIEST > PUNY
PUNILY > PUNY
PUNINESS > PUNY
PUNISH vb cause (someone) to suffer or undergo a penalty for some wrongdoing
PUNISHED > PUNISH
PUNISHER > PUNISH
PUNISHERS > PUNISH
PUNISHES > PUNISH
PUNISHING > PUNISH
PUNITION n punishment
PUNITIONS > PUNITION
PUNITIVE adj relating to punishment
PUNITORY same as > PUNITIVE
PUNJI n sharpened bamboo stick ▷ vb fortify with punjis
PUNJIED > PUNJI
PUNJIES > PUNJI
PUNJIING > PUNJI
PUNJIS > PUNJI
PUNK n style of rock music of the late 1970s ▷ adj relating to the punk movement
PUNKA n fan made of a palm leaf or leaves
PUNKAH same as > PUNKA
PUNKAHS > PUNKAH
PUNKAS > PUNKA
PUNKER > PUNK
PUNKERS > PUNK
PUNKEST > PUNK
PUNKETTE n female follower of punk music
PUNKETTES > PUNKETTE
PUNKEY n small winged insect
PUNKEYS > PUNKEY
PUNKIE same as > PUNKEY
PUNKIER > PUNKY
PUNKIES > PUNKIE
PUNKIEST > PUNKY
PUNKIN same as > PUMPKIN
PUNKINESS > PUNKY

PUNKINS > PUNKIN
PUNKISH > PUNK
PUNKS > PUNK
PUNKY adj of punk music
PUNNED > PUN
PUNNER > PUN
PUNNERS > PUN
PUNNET n small basket for fruit
PUNNETS > PUNNET
PUNNIER > PUNNY
PUNNIEST > PUNNY
PUNNING > PUN
PUNNINGLY > PUN
PUNNINGS > PUN
PUNNY adj of puns
PUNS > PUN
PUNSTER n person who is fond of making puns
PUNSTERS > PUNSTER
PUNT n open flat-bottomed boat propelled by a pole ▷ vb travel in a punt
PUNTED > PUNT
PUNTEE same as > PUNTY
PUNTEES > PUNTEE
PUNTER n person who bets
PUNTERS > PUNTER
PUNTIES > PUNTY
PUNTING > PUNT
PUNTO n hit in fencing
PUNTOS > PUNTO
PUNTS > PUNT
PUNTSMAN n man in charge of a river punt
PUNTSMEN > PUNTSMAN
PUNTY n long iron rod used in the finishing process of glass-blowing
PUNY adj small and feeble
PUP n young of certain animals, such as dogs and seals ▷ vb (of dogs, seals, etc) to give birth to pups
PUPA n insect at the stage of development between a larva and an adult
PUPAE > PUPA
PUPAL > PUPA
PUPARIA > PUPARIUM
PUPARIAL > PUPARIUM
PUPARIUM n hard barrel-shaped case enclosing the pupae of the housefly and other dipterous insects
PUPAS > PUPA
PUPATE vb (of an insect larva) to develop into a pupa
PUPATED > PUPATE
PUPATES > PUPATE
PUPATING > PUPATE
PUPATION > PUPATE
PUPATIONS > PUPATE
PUPFISH n type of small fish
PUPFISHES > PUPFISH
PUPIL n person who is taught by a teacher

PUPILAGE same as
> PUPILLAGE
PUPILAGES > PUPILAGE
PUPILAR > PUPIL
PUPILARY same as
> PUPILLARY
PUPILLAGE n condition of being a pupil or duration for which one is a pupil
PUPILLAR > PUPIL
PUPILLARY adj of or relating to a pupil or a legal ward
PUPILLATE adj with a spot of a different colour in the middle ⊳ vb cry in the manner of a peacock
PUPILS > PUPIL
PUPILSHIP n state of being a pupil
PUPPED > PUP
PUPPET n small doll or figure moved by strings or by the operator's hand
PUPPETEER n person who operates puppets
PUPPETRY n art of making and manipulating puppets and presenting puppet shows
PUPPETS > PUPPET
PUPPIED > PUPPY
PUPPIES > PUPPY
PUPPING > PUP
PUPPODUM same as
> POPPADOM
PUPPODUMS > PUPPODUM
PUPPY n young dog ⊳ vb have puppies
PUPPYDOM n state of being a puppy
PUPPYDOMS > PUPPYDOM
PUPPYHOOD > PUPPY
PUPPYING > PUPPY
PUPPYISH > PUPPY
PUPPYISM n impudence
PUPPYISMS > PUPPYISM
PUPPYLIKE > PUPPY
PUPS > PUP
PUPU n Hawaiian dish
PUPUNHA n fruit of a type of palm tree
PUPUNHAS > PUPUNHA
PUPUS > PUPU
PUR same as > PURR
PURANA n type of Sanskrit sacred writing
PURANAS > PURANA
PURANIC > PURANA
PURBLIND adj partly or nearly blind
PURCHASE vb obtain by payment ⊳ n thing that is bought
PURCHASED > PURCHASE
PURCHASER > PURCHASE
PURCHASES > PURCHASE
PURDA same as > PURDAH
PURDAH n Muslim and Hindu custom of keeping women in seclusion
PURDAHED > PURDAH
PURDAHS > PURDAH
PURDAS > PURDA

PURDONIUM n type of coal scuttle having a slanted cover that is raised to open it, and an inner removable metal container for the coal
PURE adj unmixed, untainted ⊳ vb make pure
PUREBLOOD n purebred animal
PUREBRED adj denoting a pure strain obtained through many generations of controlled breeding ⊳ n purebred animal
PUREBREDS > PUREBRED
PURED > PURE
PUREE n smooth thick pulp of cooked and sieved fruit, vegetables, meat, or fish ⊳ vb make (cooked foods) into a puree
PUREED > PUREE
PUREEING > PUREE
PUREES > PUREE
PURELY adv in a pure manner
PURENESS > PURE
PURER > PURE
PURES > PURE
PUREST > PURE
PURFLE n ruffled or curved ornamental band ⊳ vb decorate with such a band or bands
PURFLED > PURFLE
PURFLER > PURFLE
PURFLERS > PURFLE
PURFLES > PURFLE
PURFLING same as
> PURFLE
PURFLINGS > PURFLING
PURFLY > PURFLE
PURGATION n act of purging or state of being purged
PURGATIVE adj (medicine) designed to cause defecation ⊳ n medicine for emptying the bowels
PURGATORY n place or state of temporary suffering
PURGE vb rid (a thing or place) of (unwanted things or people) ⊳ n purging
PURGEABLE > PURGE
PURGED > PURGE
PURGER > PURGE
PURGERS > PURGE
PURGES > PURGE
PURGING > PURGE
PURGINGS > PURGE
PURI n unleavened flaky Indian bread, that is deep-fried in ghee and served hot
PURIFIED > PURIFY
PURIFIER n device or substance that frees something of extraneous,

contaminating, or debasing matter
PURIFIERS > PURIFIER
PURIFIES > PURIFY
PURIFY vb make or become pure
PURIFYING > PURIFY
PURIN same as > PURINE
PURINE n colourless crystalline solid that can be prepared from uric acid
PURINES > PURINE
PURING > PURE
PURINS > PURIN
PURIRI n forest tree of New Zealand
PURIRIS > PURIRI
PURIS > PURI
PURISM n strict insistence on the correct usage or style
PURISMS > PURISM
PURIST > PURISM
PURISTIC > PURISM
PURISTS > PURISM
PURITAN n person who follows strict moral or religious principles ⊳ adj of or like a puritan
PURITANIC adj of or like a puritan
PURITANS > PURITAN
PURITIES > PURITY
PURITY n state or quality of being pure
PURL n stitch made by knitting a plain stitch backwards ⊳ vb knit in purl
PURLED > PURL
PURLER n headlong or spectacular fall
PURLERS > PURLER
PURLICUE vb finish a pen stroke with a flourish
PURLICUED > PURLICUE
PURLICUES > PURLICUE
PURLIEU n land on the edge of a royal forest
PURLIEUS > PURLIEU
PURLIEUX > PURLIEU
PURLIN n horizontal beam that supports the rafters of a roof
PURLINE same as
> PURLIN
PURLINES > PURLINE
PURLING > PURL
PURLINGS > PURL
PURLINS > PURLIN
PURLOIN vb steal
PURLOINED > PURLOIN
PURLOINER > PURLOIN
PURLOINS > PURLOIN
PURLS > PURL
PUROMYCIN n type of antibiotic
PURPIE old Scots word for
> PURSLANE
PURPIES > PURPIE
PURPLE n colour between red and blue ⊳ adj of a colour between red and blue ⊳ vb make purple

PURPLED > PURPLE
PURPLER > PURPLE
PURPLES > PURPLE
PURPLEST > PURPLE
PURPLIER > PURPLE
PURPLIEST > PURPLE
PURPLING > PURPLE
PURPLISH > PURPLE
PURPLY > PURPLE
PURPORT vb claim (to be or do something) ⊳ n apparent meaning, significance
PURPORTED adj alleged
PURPORTS > PURPORT
PURPOSE n reason for which something is done or exists
PURPOSED > PURPOSE
PURPOSELY adv intentionally
PURPOSES > PURPOSE
PURPOSING > PURPOSE
PURPOSIVE adj having or showing a definite intention
PURPURA n blood disease causing purplish spots
PURPURAS > PURPURA
PURPURE n purple
PURPUREAL adj having a purple colour
PURPURES > PURPURE
PURPURIC > PURPURA
PURPURIN n red crystalline compound used as a stain for biological specimens
PURPURINS > PURPURIN
PURPY variant of
> PURPIE
PURR vb (of cats) make low vibrant sound, usu when pleased ⊳ n this sound
PURRED > PURR
PURRING > PURR
PURRINGLY > PURR
PURRINGS > PURR
PURRS > PURR
PURS > PUR
PURSE n small bag for money ⊳ vb draw (one's lips) together into a small round shape
PURSED > PURSE
PURSEFUL n that which can be contained in purse
PURSEFULS > PURSEFUL
PURSELIKE > PURSE
PURSER n ship's officer who keeps the accounts
PURSERS > PURSER
PURSES > PURSE
PURSEW archaic spelling of
> PURSUE
PURSEWED > PURSEW
PURSEWING > PURSEW
PURSEWS > PURSEW
PURSIER > PURSY
PURSIEST > PURSY
PURSILY > PURSY
PURSINESS > PURSY
PURSING > PURSE

p

PURSLAIN same as
> PURSLANE
PURSLAINS > PURSLAIN
PURSLANE n type of
weedy plant with small
yellow flowers and fleshy
leaves, used in salads and
as a potherb
PURSLANES > PURSLANE
PURSUABLE > PURSUE
PURSUAL n act of pursuit
PURSUALS > PURSUAL
PURSUANCE n carrying
out of an action or plan
PURSUANT adj in
agreement or conformity
PURSUE vb chase
PURSUED > PURSUE
PURSUER > PURSUE
PURSUERS > PURSUE
PURSUES > PURSUE
PURSUING > PURSUE
PURSUINGS > PURSUE
PURSUIT n pursuing
PURSUITS > PURSUIT
PURSY adj short-winded
PURTIER > PURTY
PURTIEST > PURTY
PURTRAID > PURTRAYD
PURTRAYD adj archaic
spelling of portrayed
PURTY adj pretty
PURULENCE > PURULENT
PURULENCY > PURULENT
PURULENT adj of or
containing pus
PURVEY vb supply
(provisions) ▷ n food and
drink laid on at a wedding
reception, etc
PURVEYED > PURVEY
PURVEYING > PURVEY
PURVEYOR n person,
organization, etc, that
supplies food and
provisions
PURVEYORS > PURVEYOR
PURVEYS > PURVEY
PURVIEW n scope or range
of activity or outlook
PURVIEWS > PURVIEW
PUS n yellowish matter
produced by infected
tissue
PUSES > PUS
PUSH vb move or try to
move by steady force
▷ n act of pushing
PUSHBACK n negative or
unfavourable response
PUSHBACKS > PUSHBACK
PUSHBALL n game in
which two teams try to
push a heavy ball towards
opposite goals
PUSHBALLS > PUSHBALL
PUSHBIKE n pedal-driven
bicycle
PUSHBIKES > PUSHBIKE
PUSHCART n handcart,
typically having two
wheels and a canvas roof,
used esp by street vendors
PUSHCARTS > PUSHCART

PUSHCHAIR n folding
chair on wheels for a baby
PUSHDOWN n list in which
the last item added is at
the top
PUSHDOWNS > PUSHDOWN
PUSHED adj short of
PUSHER n person who
sells illegal drugs
PUSHERS > PUSHER
PUSHES > PUSH
PUSHFUL > PUSH
PUSHFULLY > PUSH
PUSHIER > PUSHY
PUSHIEST > PUSHY
PUSHILY > PUSHY
PUSHINESS > PUSHY
PUSHING prep almost or
nearly (a certain age,
speed, etc) ▷ adj
aggressively ambitious
▷ adv almost or nearly (a
certain age, speed, etc)
PUSHINGLY > PUSHING
PUSHOVER n something
easily achieved
PUSHOVERS > PUSHOVER
PUSHPIN n pin with a
small ball-shaped head
PUSHPINS > PUSHPIN
PUSHPIT n safety rail at
the stern of a boat
PUSHPITS > PUSHPIT
PUSHROD n metal rod
transmitting motion in an
engine
PUSHRODS > PUSHROD
PUSHUP n exercise in
which the body is
alternately raised from
and lowered to the floor by
the arms
PUSHUPS > PUSHUP
PUSHY adj too assertive or
ambitious
PUSLE old spelling of
> PUZZLE
PUSLED > PUSLE
PUSLES > PUSLE
PUSLEY same as
> PURSLANE
PUSLEYS > PUSLEY
PUSLIKE > PUS
PUSLING > PUSLE
PUSS same as > PUSSY
PUSSEL n slatternly
woman
PUSSELS > PUSSEL
PUSSER n naval purser
PUSSERS > PUSSER
PUSSES > PUSS
PUSSIER > PUSSY
PUSSIES > PUSSY
PUSSIEST > PUSSY
PUSSLEY n weedy trailing
herb
PUSSLEYS > PUSSLEY
PUSSLIES > PUSSLY
PUSSLIKE > PUSS
PUSSLY variant of
> PUSSLEY
PUSSY n cat ▷ adj
containing or full of pus

PUSSYCAT same as
> PUSSY
PUSSYCATS > PUSSYCAT
PUSSYFOOT vb behave
too cautiously ▷ n person
who pussyfoots
PUSSYTOES n type of
low-growing plant
PUSTULANT adj causing
the formation of pustules
▷ n agent causing such
formation
PUSTULAR > PUSTULE
PUSTULATE vb form into
pustules ▷ adj covered
with pustules
PUSTULE n pimple
containing pus
PUSTULED > PUSTULE
PUSTULES > PUSTULE
PUSTULOUS > PUSTULE
PUT vb cause to be (in a
position, state, or place)
▷ n throw in putting
the shot
PUTAMEN n hard endocarp
or stone of fruit
PUTAMENS > PUTAMEN
PUTAMINA > PUTAMEN
PUTATIVE adj reputed,
supposed
PUTCHEON n trap for
catching salmon
PUTCHEONS > PUTCHEON
PUTCHER n trap for
catching salmon
PUTCHERS > PUTCHER
PUTCHOCK same as
> PACHAK
PUTCHOCKS > PUTCHOCK
PUTCHUK same as
> PACHAK
PUTCHUKS > PUTCHUK
PUTDOWN n snub or insult
PUTDOWNS > PUTDOWN
PUTEAL n enclosure
around a well
PUTEALS > PUTEAL
PUTELI n (in India) type of
boat
PUTELIS > PUTELI
PUTID adj having an
unpleasant odour
PUTLOCK same as
> PUTLOG
PUTLOCKS > PUTLOCK
PUTLOG n short horizontal
beam that with others
supports the floor planks
of a scaffold
PUTLOGS > PUTLOG
PUTOFF n pretext or delay
PUTOFFS > PUTOFF
PUTOIS n brush to paint
pottery
PUTON n hoax or piece of
mockery
PUTONGHUA n Chinese
language
PUTONS > PUTON
PUTOUT n baseball play in
which the batter or runner
is put out
PUTOUTS > PUTOUT

PUTREFIED > PUTREFY
PUTREFIER > PUTREFY
PUTREFIES > PUTREFY
PUTREFY vb rot and
produce an offensive smell
PUTRID adj rotten and
foul-smelling
PUTRIDER > PUTRID
PUTRIDEST > PUTRID
PUTRIDITY > PUTRID
PUTRIDLY > PUTRID
PUTS > PUT
PUTSCH n sudden violent
attempt to remove a
government from power
PUTSCHES > PUTSCH
PUTSCHIST n person
taking part in putsch
PUTT n stroke on the
putting green to roll the
ball into or near the hole
▷ vb strike (the ball) in this
way
PUTTED > PUTT
PUTTEE n strip of cloth
worn wound around the
leg
PUTTEES > PUTTEE
PUTTEN old Scots past
participle of > PUT
PUTTER n golf club for
putting ▷ vb busy oneself
in a desultory though
agreeable manner
PUTTERED > PUTTER
PUTTERER > PUTTER
PUTTERERS > PUTTER
PUTTERING > PUTTER
PUTTERS > PUTTER
PUTTI > PUTTO
PUTTIE same as > PUTTEE
PUTTIED > PUTTY
PUTTIER n glazier
PUTTIERS > PUTTIER
PUTTIES > PUTTY
PUTTING > PUT
PUTTINGS > PUT
PUTTO n representation of
a small boy
PUTTOCK n type of bird of
prey
PUTTOCKS > PUTTOCK
PUTTS > PUTT
PUTTY n stiff paste of
whiting and linseed oil
▷ vb fill, fix, or coat with
putty
PUTTYING > PUTTY
PUTTYLESS > PUTTY
PUTTYLIKE > PUTTY
PUTTYROOT n North
American orchid
PUTURE n claim of
foresters for food
PUTURES > PUTURE
PUTZ n despicable or
stupid person ▷ vb waste
time
PUTZED > PUTZ
PUTZES > PUTZ
PUTZING > PUTZ
PUY n small volcanic cone
PUYS > PUY

PUZEL *same as* > PUCELLE
PUZELS > PUZEL
PUZZEL *n* prostitute
PUZZELS > PUZZEL
PUZZLE *vb* perplex and confuse or be perplexed or confused ▷ *n* problem that cannot be easily solved
PUZZLED > PUZZLE
PUZZLEDLY > PUZZLE
PUZZLEDOM > PUZZLE
PUZZLER *n* person or thing that puzzles
PUZZLERS > PUZZLER
PUZZLES > PUZZLE
PUZZLING > PUZZLE
PUZZOLANA *same as* > POZZOLANA
PWN *vb* defeat (an opponent) in conclusive and humiliating fashion
PWNED > PWN
PWNING > PWN
PWNS > PWN
PYA *n* monetary unit of Myanmar worth one hundredth of a kyat
PYAEMIA *n* blood poisoning with pus-forming microorganisms in the blood
PYAEMIAS > PYAEMIA
PYAEMIC > PYAEMIA
PYAS > PYA
PYAT *n* magpie ▷ *adj* pied
PYATS > PYAT
PYCNIC *same as* > PYKNIC
PYCNIDIA > PYCNIDIUM
PYCNIDIAL > PYCNIDIUM
PYCNIDIUM *n* small flask-shaped structure containing spores that occurs in ascomycetes and certain other fungi
PYCNITE *n* variety of topaz
PYCNITES > PYCNITE
PYCNON *old word for* > SEMITONE
PYCNONS > PYCNON
PYCNOSES > PYCNOSIS
PYCNOSIS *n* process of shrinking in a cell nucleus
PYCNOSOME *n* stocky body type
PYCNOTIC > PYCNOSIS
PYE *same as* > PIE
PYEBALD *same as* > PIEBALD
PYEBALDS > PYEBALD
PYEING > PYE
PYELITIC > PYELITIS
PYELITIS *n* inflammation of the pelvis of the kidney
PYELOGRAM *n* film produced by pyelography
PYEMIA *same as* > PYAEMIA
PYEMIAS > PYEMIA
PYEMIC > PYAEMIA
PYENGADU *variant of* > PYINKADO

PYENGADUS > PYENGADU
PYES > PYE
PYET *same as* > PYAT
PYETS > PYET
PYGAL *n* rear part
PYGALS > PYGAL
PYGARG *n* type of horned mammal
PYGARGS > PYGARG
PYGARGUS *n* white-tailed bird of prey
PYGIDIA > PYGIDIUM
PYGIDIAL > PYGIDIUM
PYGIDIUM *n* terminal segment, division, or other structure in certain annelids, arthropods, and other invertebrates
PYGIDIUMS > PYGIDIUM
PYGMAEAN > PYGMY
PYGMEAN > PYGMY
PYGMIES > PYGMY
PYGMOID *adj* of or like pygmies ▷ *n* pygmy
PYGMOIDS > PYGMOID
PYGMY *n* something that is a very small example of its type ▷ *adj* very small
PYGMYISH > PYGMY
PYGMYISM > PYGMY
PYGMYISMS > PYGMY
PYGOSTYLE *n* vertebral bone in birds
PYIC *adj* relating to pus
PYIN *n* constituent of pus
PYINKADO *n* leguminous tree native to India and Myanmar
PYINKADOS > PYINKADO
PYINS > PYIN
PYJAMA *same as* > PYJAMAS
PYJAMAED > PYJAMAS
PYJAMAS *pl n* loose-fitting trousers and top worn in bed
PYKNIC *adj* (of a physical type) characterized by a broad squat fleshy physique with a large chest and abdomen ▷ *n* person with this physical type
PYKNICS > PYKNIC
PYKNOSES > PYKNOSIS
PYKNOSIS *n* thickening of a cell
PYKNOSOME *n* stocky body type
PYKNOTIC > PYKNOSIS
PYLON *n* steel tower-like structure supporting electrical cables
PYLONS > PYLON
PYLORI > PYLORUS
PYLORIC > PYLORUS
PYLORUS *n* small circular opening at the base of the stomach
PYLORUSES > PYLORUS
PYNE *archaic variant of* > PINE
PYNED > PYNE
PYNES > PYNE

PYNING > PYNE
PYODERMA *n* any skin eruption characterized by pustules or the formation of pus
PYODERMAS > PYODERMA
PYODERMIC > PYODERMA
PYOGENIC *adj* of or relating to the formation of pus
PYOID *adj* resembling pus
PYONER *old variant of* > PIONEER
PYONERS > PYONER
PYONINGS *n* old term for the work of pioneers
PYORRHEA *same as* > PYORRHOEA
PYORRHEAL > PYORRHOEA
PYORRHEAS > PYORRHEA
PYORRHEIC > PYORRHOEA
PYORRHOEA *n* disease of the gums and tooth sockets which causes bleeding of the gums and the formation of pus
PYOSES > PYOSIS
PYOSIS *n* formation of pus
PYOT *same as* > PYAT
PYOTS > PYOT
PYRACANTH *n* type of thorny shrub
PYRAL > PYRE
PYRALID *n* tropical moth
PYRALIDID *same as* > PYRALID
PYRALIDS > PYRALID
PYRALIS *same as* > PYRALID
PYRALISES > PYRALIS
PYRAMID *n* solid figure with a flat base and triangular sides sloping upwards to a point ▷ *vb* build up or be arranged in the form of a pyramid
PYRAMIDAL > PYRAMID
PYRAMIDED > PYRAMID
PYRAMIDES > PYRAMIS
PYRAMIDIA *n* plural of pyramidion, small pyramid on top of obelisk
PYRAMIDIC > PYRAMID
PYRAMIDON *n* type of pipe for an organ
PYRAMIDS > PYRAMID
PYRAMIS *n* pyramid-shaped structure
PYRAMISES > PYRAMIS
PYRAN *n* unsaturated heterocyclic organic compound
PYRANOID > PYRAN
PYRANOSE *n* structure in many sugars
PYRANOSES > PYRANOSE
PYRANS > PYRAN
PYRAZOLE *n* crystalline soluble basic heterocyclic compound

PYRAZOLES > PYRAZOLE
PYRE *n* pile of wood for burning a corpse on
PYRENE *n* solid polynuclear aromatic hydrocarbon extracted from coal tar
PYRENEITE *n* dark mineral found in the Pyrenees
PYRENES > PYRENE
PYRENOID *n* any of various small protein granules that occur in certain algae, mosses, and protozoans and are involved in the synthesis of starch
PYRENOIDS > PYRENOID
PYRES > PYRE
PYRETHRIN *n* oily water-insoluble compound used as an insecticide
PYRETHRUM *n* Eurasian chrysanthemum with white, pink, red, or purple flowers
PYRETIC *adj* of, relating to, or characterized by fever
PYREX *n* tradename for glass used in cookery and chemical apparatus
PYREXES > PYREX
PYREXIA *technical name for* > FEVER
PYREXIAL > PYREXIA
PYREXIAS > PYREXIA
PYREXIC > PYREXIA
PYRIC *adj* of or relating to burning
PYRIDIC > PYRIDINE
PYRIDINE *n* colourless hygroscopic liquid with a characteristic odour
PYRIDINES > PYRIDINE
PYRIDOXAL *n* naturally occurring derivative of pyridoxine that is a precursor of a coenzyme involved in several enzymic reactions
PYRIDOXIN *n* derivative of pyridine
PYRIFORM *adj* (esp of organs of the body) pear-shaped
PYRITE *n* yellow mineral consisting of iron sulphide in cubic crystalline form
PYRITES *same as* > PYRITE
PYRITIC > PYRITE
PYRITICAL > PYRITE
PYRITISE *same as* > PYRITIZE
PYRITISED > PYRITISE
PYRITISES > PYRITISE
PYRITIZE *vb* convert into pyrites
PYRITIZED > PYRITIZE
PYRITIZES > PYRITIZE
PYRITOUS > PYRITE

PYRO n pyromaniac
PYROCERAM n transparent ceramic material
PYROCLAST n piece of lava ejected from a volcano
PYROGEN n any of a group of substances that cause a rise in temperature in an animal body
PYROGENIC adj produced by or producing heat
PYROGENS > PYROGEN
PYROGIES > PYROGY
PYROGY same as > PIEROGI
PYROHIES > PYROHY
PYROHY same as > PEROGI
PYROLA n evergreen perennial
PYROLAS > PYROLA
PYROLATER n worshipper of fire
PYROLATRY > PYROLATER
PYROLISE same as > PYROLIZE
PYROLISED > PYROLISE
PYROLISES > PYROLISE
PYROLIZE vb subject to pyrolysis
PYROLIZED > PYROLIZE
PYROLIZES > PYROLIZE
PYROLOGY n study of heat
PYROLYSE vb subject to pyrolysis
PYROLYSED > PYROLYSE
PYROLYSER > PYROLYSE
PYROLYSES > PYROLYSE
PYROLYSIS n application of heat to chemical

compounds in order to cause decomposition
PYROLYTIC > PYROLYSIS
PYROLYZE same as > PYROLYSE
PYROLYZED > PYROLYZE
PYROLYZER > PYROLYSE
PYROLYZES > PYROLYZE
PYROMANCY n divination by fire or flames
PYROMANIA n uncontrollable urge to set things on fire
PYROMETER n instrument for measuring high temperatures
PYROMETRY > PYROMETER
PYRONE n type of heterocyclic compound
PYRONES > PYRONE
PYRONIN n red dye used as a biological stain
PYRONINE same as > PYRONIN
PYRONINES > PYRONINE
PYRONINS > PYRONIN
PYROPE n deep yellowish-red garnet used as a gemstone
PYROPES > PYROPE
PYROPHONE n musical instrument using hydrogen flames
PYROPUS variant of > PYROPE
PYROPUSES > PYROPUS
PYROS > PYRO
PYROSCOPE n instrument for measuring intensity of heat

PYROSES > PYROSIS
PYROSIS technical name for > HEARTBURN
PYROSISES > PYROSIS
PYROSOME n tube-shaped glowing marine creature
PYROSOMES > PYROSOME
PYROSTAT n device that activates an alarm or extinguisher in the event of a fire
PYROSTATS > PYROSTAT
PYROXENE n silicate mineral
PYROXENES > PYROXENE
PYROXENIC > PYROXENE
PYROXYLE same as > PYROXYLIN
PYROXYLES > PYROXYLE
PYROXYLIC > PYROXYLIN
PYROXYLIN n yellow substance obtained by nitrating cellulose with a mixture of nitric and sulphuric acids
PYRRHIC n metrical foot of two short or unstressed syllables ▷ adj of or relating to such a metrical foot
PYRRHICS > PYRRHIC
PYRRHOUS adj ruddy or reddish
PYRROL same as > PYRROLE
PYRROLE n colourless insoluble toxic liquid
PYRROLES > PYRROLE
PYRROLIC > PYRROLE
PYRROLS > PYRROL
PYRUVATE n ester or salt of pyruvic acid

PYRUVATES > PYRUVATE
PYRUVIC adj as in pyruvic acid colourless pleasant-smelling liquid
PYSANKA n hand-painted Ukrainian Easter egg
PYSANKY > PYSANKA
PYTHIUM n type of fungi
PYTHIUMS > PYTHIUM
PYTHON n large nonpoisonous snake that crushes its prey
PYTHONESS n woman, such as Apollo's priestess at Delphi, believed to be possessed by an oracular spirit
PYTHONIC > PYTHON
PYTHONS > PYTHON
PYURIA n any condition characterized by the presence of pus in the urine
PYURIAS > PYURIA
PYX n any receptacle for the Eucharistic Host ▷ vb put (something) in a pyx
PYXED > PYX
PYXES > PYX
PYXIDES > PYXIS
PYXIDIA > PYXIDIUM
PYXIDIUM n dry fruit of such plants as the plantain
PYXIE n creeping evergreen shrub of the eastern US
PYXIES > PYXIE
PYXING > PYX
PYXIS same as > PYXIDIUM
PZAZZ same as > PIZZAZZ
PZAZZES > PZAZZ

Qq

QABALA *same as*
> KABBALAH
QABALAH *same as*
> KABBALAH
QABALAHS > QABALAH
QABALAS > QABALA
QABALISM > QABALAH
QABALISMS > QABALAH
QABALIST > QABALAH
QABALISTS > QABALAH
QADI *variant spelling of*
> CADI
QADIS > QADI
QAID *n* chief
QAIDS > QAID
QAIMAQAM *n* Turkish
officer or official
QAIMAQAMS > QAIMAQAM
QAJAQ *n* kayak
QAJAQS > QAJAQ
QALAMDAN *n* writing case
QALAMDANS > QALAMDAN
QAMUTIK *n* sled with
wooden runners
QAMUTIKS > QAMUTIK
QANAT *n* underground
irrigation channel
QANATS > QANAT
QASIDA *n* Arabic verse
form
QASIDAS > QASIDA
QAT *variant spelling of*
> KHAT
QATS > QAT
QAWWAL *n* qawwali singer
QAWWALI *n* Islamic
religious song, esp in Asia
QAWWALIS > QAWWALI
QAWWALS > QAWWAL
QI *variant of* > CHI
QIBLA *variant of* > KIBLAH
QIBLAS > QIBLA
QIGONG *n* system of
breathing and exercise
QIGONGS > QIGONG
QIN *n* Chinese stringed
instrument related to the
zither
QINDAR *n* Albanian
monetary unit
QINDARKA > QINDAR
QINDARS > QINDAR
QINGHAOSU *n* Chinese
herb
QINS > QIN
QINTAR *same as* > QINDAR
QINTARKA > QINTAR
QINTARS > QINTAR
QIS > QI

QIVIUT *n* soft muskox
wool
QIVIUTS > QIVIUT
QOPH *variant of* > KOPH
QOPHS > QOPH
QORMA *variant spelling of*
> KORMA
QORMAS > QORMA
QUA *prep* in the capacity of
QUAALUDE *n*
methaqualone
QUAALUDES > QUAALUDE
QUACK *vb* (of a duck) utter
a harsh guttural sound
▷ *n* unqualified person
who claims medical
knowledge
QUACKED > QUACK
QUACKER > QUACK
QUACKERS > QUACK
QUACKERY *n* activities or
methods of a quack
QUACKIER > QUACK
QUACKIEST > QUACK
QUACKING > QUACK
QUACKISH > QUACK
QUACKISM *same as*
> QUACKERY
QUACKISMS > QUACKISM
QUACKLE *same as* > QUACK
QUACKLED > QUACKLE
QUACKLES > QUACKLE
QUACKLING > QUACKLE
QUACKS > QUACK
QUACKY > QUACK
QUAD *n* quadrangle
QUADDED *adj* formed of
multiple quads
QUADDING *n*
birdwatching in a specified
area
QUADDINGS > QUADDING
QUADPLAY *same as*
> FOURPLAY
QUADPLAYS > QUADPLAY
QUADPLEX *n* apartment
on four floors
QUADRANS *n* Roman coin
QUADRANT *n* quarter of a
circle
QUADRANTS > QUADRANT
QUADRAT *n* area marked
out for study of the plants
in the surrounding area
QUADRATE *n* cube or
square, or a square or
cubelike object ▷ *vb* make
square or rectangular
▷ *adj* of or relating to this
bone

QUADRATED > QUADRATE
QUADRATES > QUADRATE
QUADRATI > QUADRATUS
QUADRATIC *n* equation in
which the variable is raised
to the power of two, but
nowhere raised to a higher
power ▷ *adj* of the second
power
QUADRATS > QUADRAT
QUADRATUS *n* type of
muscle
QUADRELLA *n* four
nominated horseraces in
which the punter bets on
selecting the four winners
QUADRIC *adj* having or
characterized by an
equation of the second
degree ▷ *n* quadric curve,
surface, or function
QUADRICEP *n* muscle in
thigh
QUADRICS > QUADRIC
QUADRIFID *adj* divided
into four lobes or other
parts
QUADRIGA *n* (in the
classical world) a
two-wheeled chariot
drawn by four horses
abreast
QUADRIGAE > QUADRIGA
QUADRIGAS > QUADRIGA
QUADRILLE *n* square
dance for four couples
QUADRIVIA *n* higher
divisions of the seven
liberal arts
QUADROON *n* an offensive
term for the offspring of a
mulatto and a white
person
QUADROONS
> QUADROON
QUADRUMAN *n* nonhuman
primate
QUADRUPED *n* any animal
with four legs ▷ *adj* having
four feet
QUADRUPLE *vb* multiply
by four ▷ *adj* four times as
much or as many ▷ *n*
quantity or number four
times as great as another
QUADRUPLY
> QUADRUPLE
QUADS > QUAD
QUAERE *n* query or
question ▷ *interj* ask or
inquire ▷ *vb* ask

QUAERED > QUAERE
QUAEREING > QUAERE
QUAERES > QUAERE
QUAERITUR *sentence
substitute* question is
asked
QUAESITUM *n* object
sought
QUAESTOR *n* any of
several magistrates of
ancient Rome, usually a
financial administrator
QUAESTORS > QUAESTOR
QUAFF *vb* drink heartily or
in one draught
QUAFFABLE > QUAFF
QUAFFED > QUAFF
QUAFFER > QUAFF
QUAFFERS > QUAFF
QUAFFING > QUAFF
QUAFFS > QUAFF
QUAG *another word for*
> QUAGMIRE
QUAGGA *n* recently extinct
zebra
QUAGGAS > QUAGGA
QUAGGIER > QUAGGY
QUAGGIEST > QUAGGY
QUAGGY *adj* resembling a
marsh or quagmire
QUAGMIRE *n* soft wet area
of land ▷ *vb* bog down
QUAGMIRED > QUAGMIRE
QUAGMIRES > QUAGMIRE
QUAGMIRY > QUAGMIRE
QUAGS > QUAG
QUAHAUG *same as*
> QUAHOG
QUAHAUGS > QUAHAUG
QUAHOG *n* edible clam
QUAHOGS > QUAHOG
QUAI *same as* > QUAY
QUAICH *n* small shallow
drinking cup
QUAICHES > QUAICH
QUAICHS > QUAICH
QUAIGH *same as* > QUAICH
QUAIGHS > QUAIGH
QUAIL *n* small game bird
of the partridge family
▷ *vb* shrink back with fear
QUAILED > QUAIL
QUAILING > QUAIL
QUAILINGS > QUAIL
QUAILS > QUAIL
QUAINT *adj* attractively
unusual, esp in an
old-fashioned style
QUAINTER > QUAINT
QUAINTEST > QUAINT

QUAINTLY > QUAINT
QUAIR n book
QUAIRS > QUAIR
QUAIS > QUAI
QUAKE vb shake or tremble with or as if with fear ▷ n earthquake
QUAKED > QUAKE
QUAKER > QUAKE
QUAKERS > QUAKE
QUAKES > QUAKE
QUAKIER > QUAKY
QUAKIEST > QUAKY
QUAKILY > QUAKY
QUAKINESS > QUAKY
QUAKING > QUAKE
QUAKINGLY > QUAKE
QUAKINGS > QUAKE
QUAKY adj inclined to quake
QUALE n essential property or quality
QUALIA > QUALE
QUALIFIED > QUALIFY
QUALIFIER n person or thing that qualifies, esp a contestant in a competition who wins a preliminary heat or contest and so earns the right to take part in the next round
QUALIFIES > QUALIFY
QUALIFY vb provide or be provided with the abilities necessary
QUALITIED adj possessing qualities
QUALITIES > QUALITY
QUALITY n degree or standard of excellence ▷ adj excellent or superior
QUALM n pang of conscience
QUALMIER > QUALM
QUALMIEST > QUALM
QUALMING adj having a qualm ▷ n state of having a qualm
QUALMINGS > QUALMING
QUALMISH > QUALM
QUALMLESS > QUALM
QUALMS > QUALM
QUALMY > QUALM
QUAMASH another name for > CAMASS
QUAMASHES > QUAMASH
QUANDANG same as > QUANDONG
QUANDANGS > QUANDANG
QUANDARY n difficult situation or dilemma
QUANDONG n small Australian tree with edible fruit and nuts used in preserves
QUANDONGS > QUANDONG
QUANGO n partly independent official body set up by a government
QUANGOS > QUANGO
QUANNET n flat file with handle at one end
QUANNETS > QUANNET

QUANT n long pole for propelling a boat ▷ vb propel (a boat) with a quant
QUANTA > QUANTUM
QUANTAL adj of or relating to a quantum or an entity that is quantized
QUANTALLY > QUANTAL
QUANTED > QUANT
QUANTIC n mathematical function
QUANTICAL > QUANTIC
QUANTICS > QUANTIC
QUANTIFY vb discover or express the quantity of
QUANTILE n element of a division
QUANTILES > QUANTILE
QUANTING > QUANT
QUANTISE same as > QUANTIZE
QUANTISED > QUANTISE
QUANTISER > QUANTISE
QUANTISES > QUANTISE
QUANTITY n specified or definite amount or number
QUANTIZE vb restrict (a physical quantity) to one of a set of values characterized by quantum numbers
QUANTIZED > QUANTIZE
QUANTIZER > QUANTIZE
QUANTIZES > QUANTIZE
QUANTONG same as > QUANDONG
QUANTONGS > QUANTONG
QUANTS > QUANT
QUANTUM n desired or required amount ▷ adj of or designating a major breakthrough
QUANTUMS > QUANTUM
QUARE adj remarkable or strange
QUARENDEN n dark-red apple
QUARENDER same as > QUARENDEN
QUARER > QUARE
QUAREST > QUARE
QUARK n subatomic particle thought to be the fundamental unit of matter
QUARKS > QUARK
QUARREL n angry disagreement ▷ vb have a disagreement or dispute
QUARRELED > QUARREL
QUARRELER > QUARREL
QUARRELS > QUARREL
QUARRIAN n cockatiel of scrub and woodland regions of inland Australia
QUARRIANS > QUARRIAN
QUARRIED > QUARRY
QUARRIER another word for > QUARRYMAN
QUARRIERS > QUARRIER
QUARRIES > QUARRY
QUARRION same as > QUARRIAN

QUARRIONS > QUARRION
QUARRY n place where stone is dug from the surface of the earth ▷ vb extract (stone) from a quarry
QUARRYING > QUARRY
QUARRYMAN n man who works in or manages a quarry
QUARRYMEN > QUARRYMAN
QUART n unit of liquid measure equal to two pints (1.136 litres)
QUARTAN adj (esp of a malarial fever) occurring every third day ▷ n quartan malaria
QUARTANS > QUARTAN
QUARTE n fourth of eight basic positions from which a parry or attack can be made in fencing
QUARTER n one of four equal parts of something ▷ vb divide into four equal parts ▷ adj being or consisting of one of four equal parts
QUARTERED adj (of a shield) divided into four sections, each having contrasting arms or having two sets of arms, each repeated in diagonally opposite corners
QUARTERER > QUARTER
QUARTERLY adj occurring, due, or issued at intervals of three months ▷ n magazine issued every three months ▷ adv once every three months
QUARTERN n fourth part of certain weights or measures, such as a peck or a pound
QUARTERNS > QUARTERN
QUARTERS pl n accommodation, esp as provided for military personnel
QUARTES > QUARTE
QUARTET n group of four performers
QUARTETS > QUARTET
QUARTETT same as > QUARTET
QUARTETTE same as > QUARTET
QUARTETTI > QUARTETTO
QUARTETTO same as > QUARTET
QUARTETTS > QUARTETT
QUARTIC n biquadratic equation
QUARTICS > QUARTIC
QUARTIER n city district
QUARTIERS > QUARTIER
QUARTILE n one of three values of a variable

dividing its distribution into four groups with equal frequencies ▷ adj of a quartile
QUARTILES > QUARTILE
QUARTO n book size in which the sheets are folded into four leaves
QUARTOS > QUARTO
QUARTS > QUART
QUARTZ n hard glossy mineral
QUARTZES > QUARTZ
QUARTZIER > QUARTZ
QUARTZITE n very hard metamorphic rock consisting of a mosaic of intergrown quartz crystals
QUARTZOSE > QUARTZ
QUARTZOUS > QUARTZ
QUARTZY > QUARTZ
QUASAR n extremely distant starlike object that emits powerful radio waves
QUASARS > QUASAR
QUASH vb annul or make void
QUASHED > QUASH
QUASHEE same as > QUASHIE
QUASHEES > QUASHEE
QUASHER > QUASH
QUASHERS > QUASH
QUASHES > QUASH
QUASHIE n in the Caribbean, an unsophisticated or gullible male Black peasant
QUASHIES > QUASHIE
QUASHING > QUASH
QUASI adv as if
QUASS variant of > KVASS
QUASSES > QUASS
QUASSIA n tropical American tree
QUASSIAS > QUASSIA
QUASSIN n bitter crystalline substance
QUASSINS > QUASSIN
QUAT n spot ▷ vb beat down or squash
QUATCH vb move
QUATCHED > QUATCH
QUATCHES > QUATCH
QUATCHING > QUATCH
QUATE n fortune
QUATES > QUATE
QUATORZE n cards worth 14 points in piquet
QUATORZES > QUATORZE
QUATRAIN n stanza or poem of four lines
QUATRAINS > QUATRAIN
QUATRE n playing card with four pips
QUATRES > QUATRE
QUATS > QUAT
QUATTED > QUAT
QUATTING > QUAT
QUAVER vb (of a voice) quiver or tremble ▷ n note half the length of a crotchet

QUAVERED > QUAVER
QUAVERER > QUAVER
QUAVERERS > QUAVER
QUAVERIER > QUAVER
QUAVERING > QUAVER
QUAVERS > QUAVER
QUAVERY > QUAVER
QUAY n wharf built parallel to the shore
QUAYAGE n system of quays
QUAYAGES > QUAYAGE
QUAYD archaic past participle of > QUAIL
QUAYLIKE > QUAY
QUAYS > QUAY
QUAYSIDE n edge of a quay along the water
QUAYSIDES > QUAYSIDE
QUAZZIER > QUAZZY
QUAZZIEST > QUAZZY
QUAZZY adj unwell
QUBIT n quantum bit
QUBITS > QUBIT
QUBYTE n unit of eight qubits
QUBYTES > QUBYTE
QUEACH n thicket
QUEACHES > QUEACH
QUEACHIER > QUEACHY
QUEACHY adj unwell
QUEAN n boisterous, impudent, or disreputable woman
QUEANS > QUEAN
QUEASIER > QUEASY
QUEASIEST > QUEASY
QUEASILY > QUEASY
QUEASY adj having the feeling that one is about to vomit
QUEAZIER > QUEAZY
QUEAZIEST > QUEAZY
QUEAZY same as > QUEASY
QUEBEC n code word for the letter Q
QUEBECS > QUEBEC
QUEBRACHO n anacardiaceous South American tree
QUEECHIER > QUEECHY
QUEECHY same as > QUEACHY
QUEEN n female sovereign who is the official ruler or head of state ▷ vb flaunt one's homosexuality
QUEENCAKE n small light cake containing currants
QUEENCUP n type of flowering plant
QUEENCUPS > QUEENCUP
QUEENDOM n territory, state, people, or community ruled over by a queen
QUEENDOMS > QUEENDOM
QUEENED > QUEEN
QUEENFISH n type of Californian marine fish
QUEENHOOD > QUEEN
QUEENIE n scallop
QUEENIER > QUEENY

QUEENIES > QUEENIE
QUEENIEST > QUEENY
QUEENING > QUEEN
QUEENINGS > QUEEN
QUEENITE n supporter of a queen
QUEENITES > QUEENITE
QUEENLESS > QUEEN
QUEENLET n queen of a small realm
QUEENLETS > QUEENLET
QUEENLIER > QUEENLY
QUEENLY adj resembling or appropriate to a queen ▷ adv in a manner appropriate to a queen
QUEENS > QUEEN
QUEENSHIP > QUEEN
QUEENSIDE n half of a chessboard in which the queen starts
QUEENY adj effeminate
QUEER adj not normal or usual ▷ n derogatory name for a homosexual person ▷ vb spoil or thwart
QUEERCORE n type of gay-oriented punk music
QUEERDOM n gay culture
QUEERDOMS > QUEERDOM
QUEERED > QUEER
QUEERER > QUEER
QUEEREST > QUEER
QUEERING > QUEER
QUEERISH > QUEER
QUEERITY > QUEER
QUEERLY > QUEER
QUEERNESS > QUEER
QUEERS > QUEER
QUEEST n wood pigeon
QUEESTS > QUEEST
QUEINT same as > QUAINT
QUELCH same as > SQUELCH
QUELCHED > QUELCH
QUELCHES > QUELCH
QUELCHING > QUELCH
QUELEA n East African weaver bird
QUELEAS > QUELEA
QUELL vb suppress
QUELLABLE > QUELL
QUELLED > QUELL
QUELLER > QUELL
QUELLERS > QUELL
QUELLING > QUELL
QUELLS > QUELL
QUEME vb please
QUEMED > QUEME
QUEMES > QUEME
QUEMING > QUEME
QUENA n Andean flute
QUENAS > QUENA
QUENCH vb satisfy (one's thirst)
QUENCHED > QUENCH
QUENCHER > QUENCH
QUENCHERS > QUENCH
QUENCHES > QUENCH
QUENCHING > QUENCH
QUENELLE n finely sieved mixture of cooked meat or

fish, shaped into various forms and cooked in stock or fried as croquettes
QUENELLES > QUENELLE
QUEP interj expression of derision
QUERCETIC > QUERCETIN
QUERCETIN n yellow crystalline pigment found naturally in the rind and bark of many plants
QUERCETUM n group of oak trees
QUERCINE adj of or relating to oak trees
QUERCITIN same as > QUERCETIN
QUERIDA n sweetheart
QUERIDAS > QUERIDA
QUERIED > QUERY
QUERIER > QUERY
QUERIERS > QUERY
QUERIES > QUERY
QUERIMONY n complaint
QUERIST n person who makes inquiries or queries
QUERISTS > QUERIST
QUERN n stone hand mill for grinding corn
QUERNS > QUERN
QUERULOUS adj complaining or whining
QUERY n question, esp one raising doubt ▷ vb express uncertainty, doubt, or an objection
QUERYING > QUERY
QUERYINGS > QUERY
QUEST n long and difficult search ▷ vb go in search of
QUESTANT n one who quests
QUESTANTS > QUEST
QUESTED > QUEST
QUESTER > QUEST
QUESTERS > QUEST
QUESTING > QUEST
QUESTINGS > QUEST
QUESTION n form of words addressed to a person in order to obtain an answer ▷ vb put a question or questions to (a person)
QUESTIONS > QUESTION
QUESTOR same as > QUAESTOR
QUESTORS > QUESTOR
QUESTRIST n one who quests
QUESTS > QUEST
QUETCH vb move
QUETCHED > QUETCH
QUETCHES > QUETCH
QUETCHING > QUETCH
QUETHE vb say
QUETHES > QUETHE
QUETHING > QUETHE
QUETSCH n plum brandy
QUETSCHES > QUETSCH
QUETZAL n crested bird of Central and N South America

QUETZALES > QUETZAL
QUETZALS > QUETZAL
QUEUE n line of people or vehicles waiting for something ▷ vb form or remain in a line while waiting
QUEUED > QUEUE
QUEUEING > QUEUE
QUEUEINGS > QUEUE
QUEUER > QUEUE
QUEUERS > QUEUE
QUEUES > QUEUE
QUEUING > QUEUE
QUEUINGS > QUEUE
QUEY n young cow
QUEYN n girl
QUEYNIE same as > QUEYN
QUEYNIES > QUEYNIE
QUEYNS > QUEYN
QUEYS > QUEY
QUEZAL same as > QUETZAL
QUEZALES > QUEZAL
QUEZALS > QUEZAL
QUIBBLE vb make trivial objections ▷ n trivial objection
QUIBBLED > QUIBBLE
QUIBBLER > QUIBBLE
QUIBBLERS > QUIBBLE
QUIBBLES > QUIBBLE
QUIBBLING > QUIBBLE
QUIBLIN same as > QUIBBLE
QUIBLINS > QUIBLIN
QUICH vb move
QUICHE n savoury flan with an egg custard filling
QUICHED > QUICH
QUICHES > QUICHE
QUICHING > QUICH
QUICK adj speedy, fast ▷ n area of sensitive flesh under a nail ▷ adv in a rapid manner
QUICKBEAM n rowan tree
QUICKEN vb make or become faster ▷ n rowan tree
QUICKENED > QUICKEN
QUICKENER > QUICKEN
QUICKENS > QUICKEN
QUICKER > QUICK
QUICKEST > QUICK
QUICKFIRE adj designed for rapid continuous gunfire
QUICKIE n anything done or made hurriedly ▷ adj made or done rapidly
QUICKIES > QUICKIE
QUICKLIME n white solid used in the manufacture of glass and steel
QUICKLY > QUICK
QUICKNESS > QUICK
QUICKS > QUICK
QUICKSAND n deep mass of loose wet sand that sucks anything on top of it into it

q

QUICKSET adj (of plants or-cuttings) planted so as to form a hedge ▷ n hedge composed of such plants

QUICKSETS > QUICKSET

QUICKSTEP n fast modern ballroom dance ▷ vb perform this dance

QUICKY n hastily arranged divorce

QUID n pound (sterling)

QUIDAM n specified person

QUIDAMS > QUIDAM

QUIDDANY n quince jelly ▷ vb make into quince jelly

QUIDDIT same as > QUIDDITY

QUIDDITCH n imaginary game in which players fly on broomsticks

QUIDDITS > QUIDDIT

QUIDDITY n essential nature of something

QUIDDLE vb waste time

QUIDDLED > QUIDDLE

QUIDDLER > QUIDDLE

QUIDDLERS > QUIDDLE

QUIDDLES > QUIDDLE

QUIDDLING > QUIDDLE

QUIDNUNC n person eager to learn news and scandal

QUIDNUNCS > QUIDNUNC

QUIDS > QUID

QUIESCE vb quieten

QUIESCED > QUIETEN

QUIESCENT adj quiet, inactive, or dormant

QUIESCES > QUIESCE

QUIESCING > QUIESCE

QUIET adj with little noise ▷ n quietness ▷ vb make or become quiet

QUIETED > QUIET

QUIETEN vb make or become quiet

QUIETENED > QUIETEN

QUIETENER > QUIETEN

QUIETENS > QUIETEN

QUIETER > QUIET

QUIETERS > QUIET

QUIETEST > QUIET

QUIETING > QUIET

QUIETINGS > QUIET

QUIETISM n passivity and calmness of mind towards external events

QUIETISMS > QUIETISM

QUIETIST > QUIETISM

QUIETISTS > QUIETISM

QUIETIVE n sedative drug

QUIETIVES > QUIETIVE

QUIETLY > QUIET

QUIETNESS > QUIET

QUIETS > QUIET

QUIETSOME > QUIET

QUIETUDE n quietness, peace, or tranquillity

QUIETUDES > QUIETUDE

QUIETUS n release from life

QUIETUSES > QUIETUS

QUIFF n tuft of hair brushed up above the forehead

QUIFFED adj having a quiff

QUIFFS > QUIFF

QUIGHT vb quit

QUIGHTED > QUIGHT

QUIGHTING > QUIGHT

QUIGHTS > QUIGHT

QUILL n pen made from the feather of a bird's wing or tail ▷ vb wind (thread, yarn, etc) onto a spool or bobbin

QUILLAI another name for > SOAPBARK

QUILLAIA same as > QUILLAI

QUILLAIAS > QUILLAIA

QUILLAIS > QUILLAI

QUILLAJA same as > QUILLAI

QUILLAJAS > QUILLAJA

QUILLBACK n freshwater fish

QUILLED > QUILL

QUILLET n quibble or subtlety

QUILLETS > QUILLET

QUILLING n decorative craftwork in which material such as glass, fabric or paper is formed into small bands or rolls that form the basis of a design

QUILLINGS > QUILLING

QUILLMAN n clerk

QUILLMEN > QUILLMAN

QUILLON n either half of the extended crosspiece of a sword or dagger

QUILLONS > QUILLON

QUILLOW n quilt folded to make a pillow

QUILLOWS > QUILLOW

QUILLS > QUILL

QUILLWORK n embroidery using porcupine quills

QUILLWORT n aquatic tracheophyte plant with quill-like leaves

QUILT n padded covering for a bed ▷ vb stitch together two layers of (fabric) with padding between them

QUILTED > QUILT

QUILTER > QUILT

QUILTERS > QUILT

QUILTING n material used for making a quilt

QUILTINGS > QUILTING

QUILTS > QUILT

QUIM n taboo word for the female genitals

QUIMS > QUIM

QUIN short for quintuplet

QUINA n quinine

QUINARIES > QUINARY

QUINARY adj consisting of fives or by fives ▷ n set of five

QUINAS > QUINA

QUINATE adj arranged in or composed of five parts

QUINCE n acid-tasting pear-shaped fruit

QUINCES > QUINCE

QUINCHE vb move

QUINCHED > QUINCHE

QUINCHES > QUINCHE

QUINCHING > QUINCHE

QUINCUNX n group of five objects arranged in the shape of a rectangle with one at each corner and the fifth in the centre

QUINE variant of > QUEAN

QUINELA same as > QUINELLA

QUINELAS > QUINELA

QUINELLA n form of betting on a horse race in which the punter bets on selecting the first and second place-winners in any order

QUINELLAS > QUINELLA

QUINES > QUINE

QUINIC adj as in quinic acid white crystalline soluble optically active carboxylic acid

QUINIDINE n crystalline alkaloid drug

QUINIE n girl

QUINIELA same as > QUINELLA

QUINIELAS > QUINIELA

QUINIES > QUINIE

QUININ same as > QUININE

QUININA same as > QUININE

QUININAS > QUININA

QUININE n bitter drug used as a tonic and formerly to treat malaria

QUININES > QUININE

QUININS > QUININ

QUINNAT n Pacific salmon

QUINNATS > QUINNAT

QUINO same as > KENO

QUINOA n type of grain high in nutrients

QUINOAS > QUINOA

QUINOID same as > QUINONOID

QUINOIDAL > QUINOID

QUINOIDS > QUINOID

QUINOL n white crystalline soluble phenol used as a photographic developer

QUINOLIN same as > QUINOLINE

QUINOLINE n oily colourless insoluble basic heterocyclic compound

QUINOLINS > QUINOLINE

QUINOLONE n any of a group of synthetic antibiotics

QUINOLS > QUINOL

QUINAS > QUINA

QUINONE n yellow crystalline water-soluble unsaturated ketone

QUINONES > QUINONE

QUINONOID adj of, resembling, or derived from quinone

QUINOS > QUINO

QUINQUINA same as > QUININE

QUINS > QUIN

QUINSIED > QUINSY

QUINSIES > QUINSY

QUINSY n inflammation of the throat or tonsils

QUINT same as > QUIN

QUINTA n Portuguese vineyard where grapes for wine or port are grown

QUINTAIN n post or target set up for tilting exercises for mounted knights or foot soldiers

QUINTAINS > QUINTAIN

QUINTAL n unit of weight

QUINTALS > QUINTAL

QUINTAN adj (of a fever) occurring every fourth day ▷ n quintan fever

QUINTANS > QUINTAN

QUINTAR n Albanian unit of currency

QUINTARS > QUINTAR

QUINTAS > QUINTA

QUINTE n fifth of eight basic positions from which a parry or attack can be made in fencing

QUINTES > QUINTE

QUINTET n group of five performers

QUINTETS > QUINTET

QUINTETT same as > QUINTET

QUINTETTE same as > QUINTET

QUINTETTI > QUINTETTO

QUINTETTO same as > QUINTET

QUINTETTS > QUINTETT

QUINTIC adj of or relating to the fifth degree ▷ n mathematical function

QUINTICS > QUINTIC

QUINTILE n aspect of 72° between two heavenly bodies

QUINTILES > QUINTILE

QUINTIN same as > QUINTAIN

QUINTINS > QUINTIN

QUINTROON n person with one Black great-great-grandparent

QUINTS > QUINT

QUINTUPLE vb multiply by five ▷ adj five times as much or as many ▷ n quantity or number five times as great as another

QUINTUPLY > QUINTUPLE

QUINZE n card game where players aim to score 15
QUINZES > QUINZE
QUINZHEE n shelter made from hollowed-out snow
QUINZHEES > QUINZHEE
QUINZIE same as > QUINZHEE
QUINZIES > QUINZIE
QUIP n witty saying ▷ vb make a quip
QUIPO same as > QUIPU
QUIPOS > QUIPO
QUIPPED > QUIP
QUIPPER > QUIP
QUIPPERS > QUIP
QUIPPIER > QUIP
QUIPPIEST > QUIP
QUIPPING > QUIP
QUIPPISH > QUIP
QUIPPU same as > QUIPU
QUIPPUS > QUIPPU
QUIPPY > QUIP
QUIPS > QUIP
QUIPSTER n person inclined to make sarcastic or witty remarks
QUIPSTERS > QUIPSTER
QUIPU n device of the Incas used to record information using knotted cords
QUIPUS > QUIPU
QUIRE n set of 24 or 25 sheets of paper ▷ vb arrange in quires
QUIRED > QUIRE
QUIRES > QUIRE
QUIRING > QUIRE
QUIRISTER same as > CHORISTER
QUIRK n peculiarity of character ▷ vb quip
QUIRKED > QUIRK
QUIRKIER > QUIRK
QUIRKIEST > QUIRK
QUIRKILY > QUIRK
QUIRKING > QUIRK
QUIRKISH > QUIRK
QUIRKS > QUIRK
QUIRKY > QUIRK
QUIRT n whip with a leather thong at one end ▷ vb strike with a quirt
QUIRTED > QUIRT
QUIRTING > QUIRT
QUIRTS > QUIRT
QUISLING n traitor who aids an occupying enemy force
QUISLINGS > QUISLING
QUIST n wood pigeon
QUISTS > QUIST
QUIT vb stop (doing something) ▷ adj free (from)

QUITCH vb move
QUITCHED > QUITCH
QUITCHES > QUITCH
QUITCHING > QUITCH
QUITCLAIM n formal renunciation of any claim against a person or of a right to land ▷ vb renounce (a claim) formally
QUITE archaic form of > QUIT
QUITED > QUITE
QUITES > QUITE
QUITING > QUITE
QUITRENT n (formerly) a rent payable by a freeholder or copyholder to his lord that released him from liability to perform services
QUITRENTS > QUITRENT
QUITS > QUIT
QUITTAL n repayment of an action with a similar action
QUITTALS > QUITTAL
QUITTANCE n release from debt or other obligation
QUITTED > QUIT
QUITTER n person who lacks perseverance
QUITTERS > QUITTER
QUITTING > QUIT
QUITTOR n infection of the cartilages on the side of a horse's foot
QUITTORS > QUITTOR
QUIVER vb shake with a tremulous movement ▷ n shaking or trembling
QUIVERED > QUIVER
QUIVERER > QUIVER
QUIVERERS > QUIVER
QUIVERFUL n amount that a quiver can hold
QUIVERIER > QUIVER
QUIVERING > QUIVER
QUIVERISH > QUIVER
QUIVERS > QUIVER
QUIVERY > QUIVER
QUIXOTE n impractical idealist
QUIXOTES > QUIXOTE
QUIXOTIC adj romantic and unrealistic
QUIXOTISM > QUIXOTIC
QUIXOTRY > QUIXOTE
QUIZ n entertainment in which the knowledge of the players is tested by a series of questions ▷ vb investigate by close questioning
QUIZZED > QUIZ
QUIZZER > QUIZ

QUIZZERS > QUIZ
QUIZZERY > QUIZ
QUIZZES > QUIZ
QUIZZICAL adj questioning and mocking
QUIZZIFY > QUIZ
QUIZZING > QUIZ
QUIZZINGS > QUIZ
QULLIQ n type of oil lamp used by Inuit people
QULLIQS > QULLIQ
QUOAD adv as far as
QUOD n jail ▷ vb say
QUODDED > QUOD
QUODDING > QUOD
QUODLIBET n light piece of music based on two or more popular tunes
QUODLIN n cooking apple
QUODLINS > QUODLIN
QUODS > QUOD
QUOHOG n edible clam
QUOHOGS > QUOHOG
QUOIF vb arrange (the hair)
QUOIFED > QUOIF
QUOIFING > QUOIF
QUOIFS > QUOIF
QUOIN n external corner of a building ▷ vb wedge
QUOINED > QUOIN
QUOINING > QUOIN
QUOININGS > QUOINING
QUOINS > QUOIN
QUOIST n wood pigeon
QUOISTS > QUOIST
QUOIT n large ring used in the game of quoits ▷ vb throw as a quoit
QUOITED > QUOIT
QUOITER > QUOIT
QUOITERS > QUOIT
QUOITING > QUOIT
QUOITS n game in which quoits are tossed at a stake in the ground
QUOKKA n small Australian wallaby
QUOKKAS > QUOKKA
QUOLL n Australian catlike carnivorous marsupial
QUOLLS > QUOLL
QUOMODO n manner
QUOMODOS > QUOMODO
QUONDAM adj of an earlier time
QUONK vb make an accidental noise while broadcasting
QUONKED > QUONK
QUONKING > QUONK
QUONKS > QUONK
QUOOKE archaic past participle of > QUAKE
QUOP vb pulsate or throb
QUOPPED > QUOP

QUOPPING > QUOP
QUOPS > QUOP
QUORATE adj having or being a quorum
QUORUM n minimum number of people required to be present at a meeting
QUORUMS > QUORUM
QUOTA n share that is due from, due to, or allocated to a group or person
QUOTABLE adj apt or suitable for quotation
QUOTABLY > QUOTABLE
QUOTAS > QUOTA
QUOTATION n written or spoken passage repeated exactly in a later work, speech, or conversation
QUOTATIVE n word indicating quotation ▷ adj introducing quoted words
QUOTE vb repeat (words) exactly ▷ n quotation ▷ interj expression used to indicate that the words that follow form a quotation
QUOTED > QUOTE
QUOTER > QUOTE
QUOTERS > QUOTE
QUOTES > QUOTE
QUOTH vb said
QUOTHA interj expression of mild sarcasm, used in picking up a word or phrase used by someone else
QUOTIDIAN adj daily ▷ n malarial fever characterized by attacks that recur daily
QUOTIENT n result of the division of one number or quantity by another
QUOTIENTS > QUOTIENT
QUOTING > QUOTE
QUOTITION n division by repeated subtraction
QUOTUM same as > QUOTA
QUOTUMS > QUOTUM
QURSH same as > QURUSH
QURSHES > QURUSH
QURUSH n Saudi Arabian currency unit
QURUSHES > QURUSH
QUYTE same as > QUIT
QUYTED > QUYTE
QUYTES > QUYTE
QUYTING > QUYTE
QWERTIES > QWERTY
QWERTY n standard English-language typewriter or computer keyboard
QWERTYS > QWERTY

q

Rr

RABANNA *n* Madagascan woven raffia
RABANNAS > RABANNA
RABASKA *n* large canoe
RABASKAS > RABASKA
RABAT *vb* rotate so that the plane rotated coincides with another
RABATINE *n* type of collar
RABATINES > RABATINE
RABATMENT > RABAT
RABATO *n* wired or starched collar
RABATOES > RABATO
RABATOS > RABATO
RABATS > RABAT
RABATTE *same as* > RABAT
RABATTED > RABAT
RABATTES > RABATTE
RABATTING > RABAT
RABBET *n* recess cut into a surface ▷ *vb* cut or form a rabbet in (timber)
RABBETED > RABBET
RABBETING > RABBET
RABBETS > RABBET
RABBI *n* Jewish spiritual leader
RABBIES > RABBI
RABBIN *same as* > RABBI
RABBINATE *n* position, function, or tenure of office of a rabbi
RABBINIC *adj* of or relating to the rabbis, their teachings, writings, views, language, etc
RABBINICS *n* study of rabbinic literature of the post-Talmudic period
RABBINISM *n* teachings and traditions of the rabbis of the Talmudic period
RABBINIST > RABBINISM
RABBINITE > RABBINISM
RABBINS > RABBIN
RABBIS > RABBI
RABBIT *n* small burrowing mammal with long ears ▷ *vb* talk too much
RABBITED > RABBIT
RABBITER *n* person who traps and sells rabbits
RABBITERS > RABBITER
RABBITING *n* activity of hunting rabbits
RABBITO *same as* > RABBITOH

RABBITOH *n* (formerly) an itinerant seller of rabbits for eating
RABBITOHS > RABBITOH
RABBITOS > RABBITO
RABBITRY *n* place where tame rabbits are kept and bred
RABBITS > RABBIT
RABBITY *adj* rabbitlike
RABBLE *n* disorderly crowd of noisy people ▷ *vb* stir, mix, or skim (the molten charge) in a roasting furnace
RABBLED > RABBLE
RABBLER *n* device for stirring, mixing, or skimming a molten charge in a furnace
RABBLERS > RABBLER
RABBLES > RABBLE
RABBLING > RABBLE
RABBLINGS > RABBLE
RABBONI *n* very respectful Jewish title or form of address
RABBONIS > RABBONI
RABI *n* (in Pakistan, India, etc) a crop that is harvested at the end of winter
RABIC > RABIES
RABID *adj* fanatical
RABIDER > RABID
RABIDEST > RABID
RABIDITY > RABID
RABIDLY > RABID
RABIDNESS > RABID
RABIES *n* usu fatal viral disease transmitted by dogs and certain other animals
RABIETIC > RABIES
RABIS > RABI
RACA *adj* biblical word meaning worthless or empty-headed
RACAHOUT *n* acorn flour or drink made from it
RACAHOUTS > RACAHOUT
RACCAHOUT *same as* > RACAHOUT
RACCOON *n* small N American mammal with a long striped tail
RACCOONS > RACCOON
RACE *n* contest of speed ▷ *vb* compete with in a race

RACEABLE *adj* fit for racing
RACECARD *n* card or booklet at a race meeting with the times of the races, names of the runners, etc, printed on it
RACECARDS > RACECARD
RACED > RACE
RACEGOER *n* one who attends a race meeting, esp a habitual frequenter of race meetings
RACEGOERS > RACEGOER
RACEGOING > RACEGOER
RACEHORSE *n* horse specially bred for racing
RACEMATE *n* racemic compound
RACEMATES > RACEMATE
RACEME *n* cluster of flowers along a central stem, as in the foxglove
RACEMED *adj* with or in racemes
RACEMES > RACEME
RACEMIC *adj* being a mixture of equal amounts of enantiomers
RACEMISE *same as* > RACEMIZE
RACEMISED > RACEMISE
RACEMISES > RACEMISE
RACEMISM > RACEMIC
RACEMISMS > RACEMIC
RACEMIZE *vb* change or cause to change into a racemic mixture
RACEMIZED > RACEMIZE
RACEMIZES > RACEMIZE
RACEMOID *adj* resembling a raceme
RACEMOSE *adj* being or resembling a raceme
RACEMOUS *same as* > RACEMOSE
RACEPATH *same as* > RACETRACK
RACEPATHS > RACEPATH
RACER *n* person, animal, or machine that races
RACERS > RACER
RACES > RACE
RACETRACK *n* track for racing
RACEWALK *vb* race by walking fast rather than running
RACEWALKS > RACEWALK

RACEWAY *n* racetrack, esp one for banger racing
RACEWAYS > RACEWAY
RACH *n* scent hound
RACHE *same as* > RACH
RACHES > RACH
RACHET *same as* > RATCHET
RACHETED > RACHET
RACHETING > RACHET
RACHETS > RACHET
RACHIAL > RACHIS
RACHIDES > RACHIS
RACHIDIAL > RACHIS
RACHIDIAN > RACHIS
RACHILLA *n* (in grasses) the short stem of a spikelet that bears the florets
RACHILLAE > RACHILLA
RACHILLAS > RACHILLA
RACHIS *n* main axis or stem of an inflorescence or compound leaf
RACHISES > RACHIS
RACHITIC > RACHITIS
RACHITIS *another name for* > RICKETS
RACIAL *adj* relating to the division of the human species into races
RACIALISE *same as* > RACIALIZE
RACIALISM *same as* > RACISM
RACIALIST > RACIALISM
RACIALIZE *vb* render racial in tone or content
RACIALLY > RACIAL
RACIATION *n* evolutionary development of races
RACIER > RACY
RACIEST > RACY
RACILY > RACY
RACINESS > RACY
RACING *adj* denoting or associated with horse races ▷ *n* practice of engaging in contests of speed
RACINGS > RACING
RACINO *n* combined racetrack and casino
RACINOS > RACINO
RACISM *n* hostile attitude or behaviour to members of other races
RACISMS > RACISM

RACIST > RACISM

RACISTS > RACISM

RACK n framework for holding particular articles, such as coats or luggage ▷ vb cause great suffering to

RACKED > RACK

RACKER > RACK

RACKERS > RACK

RACKET n bat with strings stretched in an oval frame, used in tennis etc ▷ vb strike with a racket

RACKETED > RACKET

RACKETEER n person making illegal profits ▷ vb operate a racket

RACKETER n someone making a racket

RACKETERS > RACKETEER

RACKETIER > RACKETY

RACKETING > RACKET

RACKETRY n noise and commotion

RACKETS n ball game played in a paved walled court

RACKETT n early double-reeded wind instrument

RACKETTS > RACKETT

RACKETY adj involving noise, commotion and excitement

RACKFUL > RACK

RACKFULS > RACK

RACKING > RACK

RACKINGLY > RACK

RACKINGS > RACK

RACKLE n (Scot) chain

RACKLES > RACKLE

RACKS > RACK

RACKWORK n mechanism with a rack and pinion

RACKWORKS > RACKWORK

RACLETTE n Swiss dish of melted cheese served on boiled potatoes

RACLETTES > RACLETTE

RACLOIR n scraper

RACLOIRS > RACLOIR

RACON n radar beacon

RACONS > RACON

RACONTEUR n skilled storyteller

RACOON same as > RACCOON

RACOONS > RACOON

RACQUET same as > RACKET

RACQUETED > RACQUET

RACQUETS > RACQUET

RACY adj slightly shocking

RAD n former unit of absorbed ionizing radiation dose ▷ vb fear ▷ adj slang term for great

RADAR n device for tracking distant objects

RADARS > RADAR

RADDED > RAD

RADDER > RAD

RADDEST > RAD

RADDING > RAD

RADDLE same as > RUDDLE

RADDLED adj (of a person) unkempt or run-down in appearance

RADDLEMAN same as > RUDDLEMAN

RADDLEMEN > RADDLEMAN

RADDLES > RADDLE

RADDLING > RADDLE

RADDOCKE same as > RUDDOCK

RADDOCKES > RADDOCKE

RADE (in Scots dialect) past tense of > RIDE

RADGE adj angry or uncontrollable ▷ n person acting in such a way

RADGER > RADGE

RADGES > RADGE

RADGEST > RADGE

RADIABLE adj able to be x-rayed

RADIAL adj spreading out from a common central point ▷ n radial-ply tyre

RADIALE n bone in the wrist

RADIALIA > RADIALE

RADIALISE same as > RADIALIZE

RADIALITY > RADIAL

RADIALIZE vb arrange in a pattern of radii

RADIALLY > RADIAL

RADIALS > RADIAL

RADIAN n unit for measuring angles, equal to 57.296°

RADIANCE n quality or state of being radiant

RADIANCES > RADIANCE

RADIANCY same as > RADIANCE

RADIANS > RADIAN

RADIANT adj looking happy ▷ n point or object that emits radiation

RADIANTLY > RADIANT

RADIANTS > RADIANT

RADIATA adj as in radiata pine type of pine tree

RADIATAS > RADIATA

RADIATE vb spread out from a centre ▷ adj having rays or a radial structure

RADIATED > RADIATE

RADIATELY > RADIATE

RADIATES > RADIATE

RADIATING > RADIATE

RADIATION n transmission of energy from one body to another

RADIATIVE adj emitting or causing the emission of radiation

RADIATOR n arrangement of pipes containing hot water or steam to heat a room

RADIATORS > RADIATOR

RADIATORY same as > RADIATIVE

RADICAL adj fundamental ▷ n person advocating fundamental (political) change

RADICALLY adv thoroughly

RADICALS > RADICAL

RADICAND n number or quantity from which a root is to be extracted, usually preceded by a radical sign

RADICANDS > RADICAND

RADICANT adj forming roots from the stem

RADICATE vb root or cause to take root

RADICATED > RADICATE

RADICATES > RADICATE

RADICCHIO n Italian variety of chicory, with purple leaves streaked with white that are eaten raw in salads

RADICEL n very small root

RADICELS > RADICEL

RADICES > RADIX

RADICLE n small or developing root

RADICLES > RADICLE

RADICULAR adj root-related

RADICULE same as > RADICLE

RADICULES > RADICULE

RADII > RADIUS

RADIO n use of electromagnetic waves for broadcasting, communication, etc ▷ vb transmit (a message) by radio ▷ adj of, relating to, or using radio

RADIOED > RADIO

RADIOES less common spelling of > RADIOS

RADIOGOLD n radioactive isotope of gold

RADIOGRAM n image produced on a specially sensitized photographic film or plate by radiation, usually by X-rays or gamma rays

RADIOING > RADIO

RADIOLOGY n science of using x-rays in medicine

RADIOMAN n radio operator

RADIOMEN > RADIOMAN

RADIONICS n dowsing technique using a pendulum to detect the energy fields that are emitted by all forms of matter

RADIOS > RADIO

RADIOTHON n lengthy radio programme to raise charity funds, etc

RADISH n small hot-flavoured root vegetable eaten raw in salads

RADISHES > RADISH

RADIUM n radioactive metallic element

RADIUMS > RADIUM

RADIUS n (length of) a straight line from the centre to the circumference of a circle ▷ vb give a round shape

RADIUSED > RADIUS

RADIUSES > RADIUS

RADIUSING > RADIUS

RADIX n any number that is the base of a number system or of a system of logarithms

RADIXES > RADIX

RADOME n protective housing for a radar antenna

RADOMES > RADOME

RADON n radioactive gaseous element

RADONS > RADON

RADS > RAD

RADULA n horny tooth-bearing strip on the tongue of molluscs

RADULAE > RADULA

RADULAR > RADULA

RADULAS > RADULA

RADULATE > RADULA

RADWASTE n radioactive wast

RADWASTES > RADWASTE

RAFALE n burst of artillery fire

RAFALES > RAFALE

RAFF n rubbish

RAFFIA n prepared palm fibre for weaving mats etc

RAFFIAS > RAFFIA

RAFFINATE n liquid left after a solute has been extracted by solvent extraction

RAFFINOSE n trisaccharide of fructose, glucose, and galactose that occurs in sugar beet, cotton seed, certain cereals, etc

RAFFISH adj slightly disreputable

RAFFISHLY > RAFFISH

RAFFLE n lottery with goods as prizes ▷ vb offer as a prize in a raffle

RAFFLED > RAFFLE

RAFFLER > RAFFLE

RAFFLERS > RAFFLE

RAFFLES > RAFFLE

RAFFLESIA n any of various tropical Asian parasitic leafless plants whose flowers smell of putrid meat and are pollinated by carrion flies

RAFFLING > RAFFLE

RAFFS > RAFF

RAFT n floating platform of logs, planks, etc ▷ vb convey on or travel by raft, or make a raft from

RAFTED > RAFT

RAFTER *n* one of the main beams of a roof ▷ *vb* fit with rafters
RAFTERED > RAFTER
RAFTERING > RAFTER
RAFTERS > RAFTER
RAFTING > RAFT
RAFTINGS > RAFT
RAFTMAN *same as* > RAFTSMAN
RAFTMEN > RAFTMAN
RAFTS > RAFT
RAFTSMAN *n* someone who does rafting
RAFTSMEN > RAFTSMAN
RAG *n* fragment of cloth ▷ *vb* tease ▷ *adj* (in British universities and colleges) of various events organized to raise money for charity
RAGA *n* pattern of melody and rhythm in Indian music
RAGAS > RAGA
RAGBAG *n* confused assortment, jumble
RAGBAGS > RAGBAG
RAGBOLT *n* bolt that has angled projections on it
RAGBOLTS > RAGBOLT
RAGDE *archaic past form of* > RAGE
RAGE *n* violent anger or passion ▷ *vb* speak or act with fury
RAGED > RAGE
RAGEE *same as* > RAGI
RAGEES > RAGEE
RAGEFUL > RAGE
RAGER > RAGE
RAGERS > RAGE
RAGES > RAGE
RAGG *same as* > RAGSTONE
RAGGA *n* dance-oriented style of reggae
RAGGAS > RAGGA
RAGGED > RAG
RAGGEDER > RAG
RAGGEDEST > RAG
RAGGEDIER > RAGGEDY
RAGGEDLY > RAG
RAGGEDY *adj* somewhat ragged
RAGGEE *same as* > RAGI
RAGGEES > RAGGEE
RAGGERIES > RAGGERY
RAGGERY *n* rags
RAGGIER > RAGGY
RAGGIES > RAGGY
RAGGIEST > RAGGY
RAGGING > RAG
RAGGINGS > RAG
RAGGLE *n* thin groove cut in stone or brickwork ▷ *vb* cut a raggle in
RAGGLED > RAGGLE
RAGGLES > RAGGLE
RAGGLING > RAGGLE
RAGGS > RAGG
RAGGY *adj* raglike ▷ *n* cereal grass cultivated in Africa and Asia for its edible grain

RAGHEAD *n* offensive term for an Arab person
RAGHEADS > RAGHEAD
RAGI *n* cereal grass cultivated in Africa and Asia for its edible grain
RAGING > RAGE
RAGINGLY > RAGE
RAGINGS > RAGE
RAGINI *n* Indian musical form related to a raga
RAGINIS > RAGINI
RAGIS > RAGI
RAGLAN *adj* (of a sleeve) joined to a garment from the neck to the underarm ▷ *n* coat with sleeves that continue to the collar
RAGLANS > RAGLAN
RAGMAN *n* rag-and-bone man
RAGMANS > RAGMAN
RAGMEN > RAGMAN
RAGMENT *n* statute, roll, or list
RAGMENTS > RAGMENT
RAGOUT *n* richly seasoned stew of meat and vegetables ▷ *vb* make into a ragout
RAGOUTED > RAGOUT
RAGOUTING > RAGOUT
RAGOUTS > RAGOUT
RAGPICKER *n* rag-and-bone man
RAGS > RAG
RAGSTONE *n* hard sandstone or limestone, esp when used for building
RAGSTONES > RAGSTONE
RAGTAG *n* disparaging term for common people
RAGTAGS > RAGTAG
RAGTAIL *adj* ragged; shabby
RAGTIME *n* style of jazz piano music
RAGTIMER > RAGTIME
RAGTIMERS > RAGTIME
RAGTIMES > RAGTIME
RAGTOP *n* informal word for a car with a folding or removable roof
RAGTOPS > RAGTOP
RAGU *n* Italian meat and tomato sauce
RAGULED *same as* > RAGULY
RAGULY *adj* (in heraldry) having toothlike or stublike projections
RAGUS > RAGU
RAGWEED *n* any of several plants
RAGWEEDS > RAGWEED
RAGWHEEL *n* toothed wheel
RAGWHEELS > RAGWHEEL
RAGWORK *n* weaving or needlework using rags
RAGWORKS > RAGWORK
RAGWORM *n* type of worm that lives chiefly in burrows in sand or mud

RAGWORMS > RAGWORM
RAGWORT *n* plant with ragged leaves and yellow flowers
RAGWORTS > RAGWORT
RAH *informal US word for* > CHEER
RAHED > RAH
RAHING > RAH
RAHS > RAH
RAHUI *n* Māori prohibition
RAHUIS > RAHUI
RAI *n* type of Algerian popular music
RAIA *same as* > RAYAH
RAIAS > RAIA
RAID *n* sudden surprise attack or search ▷ *vb* make a raid on
RAIDED > RAID
RAIDER > RAID
RAIDERS > RAID
RAIDING > RAID
RAIDINGS > RAID
RAIDS > RAID
RAIK *n* wander ▷ *vb* wander
RAIKED > RAIK
RAIKING > RAIK
RAIKS > RAIK
RAIL *n* horizontal bar, esp as part of a fence or track ▷ *vb* complain bitterly or loudly
RAILAGE *n* cost of transporting goods by rail
RAILAGES > RAILAGE
RAILBED *n* ballast layer supporting the sleepers of a railway track
RAILBEDS > RAILBED
RAILBIRD *n* racing aficionado
RAILBIRDS > RAILBIRD
RAILBUS *n* buslike vehicle for use on railway lines
RAILBUSES > RAILBUS
RAILCAR *n* passenger-carrying railway vehicle consisting of a single coach
RAILCARD *n* card which pensioners, young people, etc can buy, entitling them to cheaper rail travel
RAILCARDS > RAILCARD
RAILCARS > RAILCAR
RAILE *archaic spelling of* > RAIL
RAILED > RAIL
RAILER > RAIL
RAILERS > RAIL
RAILES > RAILE
RAILHEAD *n* terminal of a railway
RAILHEADS > RAILHEAD
RAILING *n* fence made of rails supported by posts
RAILINGLY > RAIL
RAILINGS > RAILING
RAILLERY *n* teasing or joking
RAILLESS > RAIL

RAILLIES > RAILLY
RAILLY *old word for* > MOCK
RAILMAN *n* railway employee
RAILMEN > RAILMAN
RAILROAD *same as* > RAILWAY
RAILROADS > RAILROAD
RAILS > RAIL
RAILWAY *n* track of iron rails on which trains run
RAILWAYS > RAILWAY
RAILWOMAN *n* female railway employee
RAILWOMEN > RAILWOMAN
RAIMENT *n* clothing
RAIMENTS > RAIMENT
RAIN *n* water falling in drops from the clouds ▷ *vb* fall or pour down as rain
RAINBAND *n* dark band in the solar spectrum caused by water in the atmosphere
RAINBANDS > RAINBAND
RAINBIRD *n* bird whose call is believed to be a sign of impending rain
RAINBIRDS > RAINBIRD
RAINBOW *n* arch of colours in the sky
RAINBOWED *adj* resembling or involving a rainbow
RAINBOWS > RAINBOW
RAINBOWY > RAINBOW
RAINCHECK *n* ticket stub allowing readmission to a game on a later date should bad weather prevent play
RAINCOAT *n* water-resistant overcoat
RAINCOATS > RAINCOAT
RAINDATE *n* US term for an alternative date in case of rain
RAINDATES > RAINDATE
RAINDROP *n* water droplet that falls from the sky when it is raining
RAINDROPS > RAINDROP
RAINE *archaic spelling of* > REIGN
RAINED > RAIN
RAINES > RAINE
RAINFALL *n* amount of rain
RAINFALLS > RAINFALL
RAINIER > RAINY
RAINIEST > RAINY
RAINILY > RAINY
RAININESS > RAINY
RAINING > RAIN
RAINLESS > RAIN
RAINMAKER *n* (among American Indians) a professional practitioner of ritual incantations or other actions intended to cause rain to fall

RAINOUT *n* radioactive fallout or atmospheric pollution carried to the earth by rain
RAINOUTS > RAINOUT
RAINPROOF *adj* (of garments, materials, buildings, etc) impermeable to rainwater ▷ *vb* make rainproof
RAINS > RAIN
RAINSPOUT *n* waterspout
RAINSTICK *n* musical instrument consisting of a tube filled with sand or pebbles
RAINSTORM *n* storm with heavy rain
RAINSUIT *n* waterproof jacket and trousers
RAINSUITS > RAINSUIT
RAINSWEPT *adj* (of a place) characterized by frequent heavy rain
RAINTIGHT *same as* > RAINPROOF
RAINWASH *n* action of rain ▷ *vb* erode or wet as a result of rain
RAINWATER *n* water from rain
RAINWEAR *n* protective garments intended for use in wet weather
RAINWEARS > RAINWEAR
RAINY *adj* characterized by a large rainfall
RAIRD *same as* > REIRD
RAIRDS > RAIRD
RAIS > RAI
RAISABLE > RAISE
RAISE *vb* lift up ▷ *n* increase in pay
RAISEABLE > RAISE
RAISED > RAISE
RAISER > RAISE
RAISERS > RAISE
RAISES > RAISE
RAISIN *n* dried grape
RAISING *n* rule that moves a constituent from an embedded clause into the main clause
RAISINGS > RAISING
RAISINS > RAISIN
RAISINY > RAISIN
RAISONNE *adj* carefully thought out
RAIT *same as* > RET
RAITA *n* Indian dish of chopped cucumber, mint, etc, in yogurt
RAITAS > RAITA
RAITED > RAIT
RAITING > RAIT
RAITS > RAIT
RAIYAT *same as* > RYOT
RAIYATS > RAIYAT
RAJ *n* (in India) government
RAJA *same as* > RAJAH
RAJAH *n* (in India, formerly) a ruler or

landlord: sometimes used as a form of address or as a title preceding a name
RAJAHS > RAJAH
RAJAHSHIP > RAJAH
RAJAS > RAJA
RAJASHIP > RAJA
RAJASHIPS > RAJA
RAJES > RAJ
RAKE *n* tool used for smoothing earth or gathering leaves, hay, etc ▷ *vb* gather or smooth with a rake
RAKED > RAKE
RAKEE *same as* > RAKI
RAKEES > RAKEE
RAKEHELL *n* dissolute man ▷ *adj* profligate
RAKEHELLS > RAKEHELL
RAKEHELLY *adj* profligate
RAKEOFF *n* share of profits, esp one that is illegal or given as a bribe
RAKEOFFS > RAKEOFF
RAKER *n* person who rakes
RAKERIES > RAKERY
RAKERS > RAKER
RAKERY *n* rakish behaviour
RAKES > RAKE
RAKESHAME *n* old word for someone shamefully dissolute
RAKI *n* strong spirit distilled from grain
RAKIA *n* strong fruit-based alcoholic drink popular in the Balkans
RAKIAS > RAKIA
RAKIJA *same as* > RAKIA
RAKIJAS > RAKIJA
RAKING *n* (in rugby) offence of scraping an opponent with the studs
RAKINGS > RAKING
RAKIS > RAKI
RAKISH *adj* dashing or jaunty
RAKISHLY > RAKISH
RAKSHAS *same as* > RAKSHASA
RAKSHASA *n* Hindu demon
RAKSHASAS > RAKSHASA
RAKSHASES > RAKSHAS
RAKU *n* type of Japanese pottery
RAKUS > RAKU
RALE *n* abnormal coarse crackling sound heard on auscultation of the chest
RALES > RALE
RALLIED > RALLY
RALLIER > RALLY
RALLIERS > RALLY
RALLIES > RALLY
RALLIFORM *adj* of rail family of birds
RALLINE *adj* relating to a family of birds that includes the rails, crakes, and coots

RALLY *n* large gathering of people for a meeting ▷ *vb* bring or come together after dispersal or for a common cause
RALLYE *US variant of* > RALLY
RALLYES > RALLYE
RALLYING > RALLY
RALLYINGS > RALLY
RALLYIST > RALLY
RALLYISTS > RALLY
RALPH *vb* slang word meaning vomit
RALPHED > RALPH
RALPHING > RALPH
RALPHS > RALPH
RAM *n* male sheep ▷ *vb* strike against with force
RAMADA *n* outdoor eating area with roof but open sides
RAMADAS > RAMADA
RAMAKIN *same as* > RAMEKIN
RAMAKINS > RAMAKIN
RAMAL *adj* relating to a branch or branches
RAMATE *adj* with branches
RAMBLA *n* dried-up riverbed
RAMBLAS > RAMBLA
RAMBLE *vb* walk without a definite route ▷ *n* walk, esp in the country
RAMBLED > RAMBLE
RAMBLER *n* person who rambles
RAMBLERS > RAMBLER
RAMBLES > RAMBLE
RAMBLING *adj* large and irregularly shaped ▷ *n* activity of going for long walks in the country
RAMBLINGS > RAMBLING
RAMBUTAN *n* SE Asian tree that has bright red edible fruit
RAMBUTANS > RAMBUTAN
RAMCAT *n* dialect word for a male cat
RAMCATS > RAMCAT
RAMEAL *same as* > RAMAL
RAMEE *same as* > RAMIE
RAMEES > RAMEE
RAMEKIN *n* small ovenproof dish for a single serving of food
RAMEKINS > RAMEKIN
RAMEN *n* Japanese dish consisting of a clear broth containing thin white noodles
RAMENS > RAMEN
RAMENTA > RAMENTUM
RAMENTUM *n* any of the thin brown scales that cover the stems and leaves of young ferns
RAMEOUS *same as* > RAMAL
RAMEQUIN *same as* > RAMEKIN
RAMEQUINS > RAMEQUIN

RAMET *n* any of the individuals in a group of clones
RAMETS > RAMET
RAMI *same as* > RAMIE
RAMIE *n* woody Asian shrub with broad leaves
RAMIES > RAMIE
RAMIFIED > RAMIFY
RAMIFIES > RAMIFY
RAMIFORM *adj* having a branchlike shape
RAMIFY *vb* become complex
RAMIFYING > RAMIFY
RAMILIE *same as* > RAMILLIE
RAMILIES > RAMILIE
RAMILLIE *n* wig with a plait at the back fashionable in the 18th century
RAMILLIES > RAMILLIE
RAMIN *n* swamp-growing tree found in Malaysia and Indonesia
RAMINS > RAMIN
RAMIS > RAMI
RAMJET *n* type of jet engine
RAMJETS > RAMJET
RAMMED > RAM
RAMMEL *n* discarded or waste matter
RAMMELS > RAMMEL
RAMMER > RAM
RAMMERS > RAM
RAMMIER > RAMMISH
RAMMIES > RAMMISH
RAMMIEST > RAMMISH
RAMMING > RAM
RAMMISH *adj* like a ram, esp in being lustful or foul-smelling
RAMMISHLY > RAMMISH
RAMMLE *n* collection of items saved in case they become useful
RAMMLES > RAMMLE
RAMMY *n* noisy disturbance or free-for-all ▷ *vb* make a rammy
RAMONA *same as* > SAGEBRUSH
RAMONAS > RAMONA
RAMOSE *adj* having branches
RAMOSELY > RAMOSE
RAMOSITY > RAMOSE
RAMOUS *same as* > RAMOSE
RAMOUSLY > RAMOSE
RAMP *n* slope joining two level surfaces ▷ *vb* (esp of animals) to rush around in a wild excited manner
RAMPAGE *vb* dash about violently
RAMPAGED > RAMPAGE
RAMPAGER > RAMPAGE
RAMPAGERS > RAMPAGE
RAMPAGES > RAMPAGE
RAMPAGING > RAMPAGE
RAMPANCY > RAMPANT

RAMPANT adj growing or spreading uncontrollably
RAMPANTLY > RAMPANT
RAMPART n mound or wall for defence ▷ vb provide with a rampart
RAMPARTED > RAMPART
RAMPARTS > RAMPART
RAMPAUGE Scots variant of **>** RAMPAGE
RAMPAUGED > RAMPAUGE
RAMPAUGES > RAMPAUGE
RAMPED > RAMP
RAMPER > RAMP
RAMPERS > RAMP
RAMPICK same as **>** RAMPIKE
RAMPICKED > RAMPICK
RAMPICKS > RAMPICK
RAMPIKE n US or dialect word for a dead tree
RAMPIKES > RAMPIKE
RAMPING > RAMP
RAMPINGS > RAMP
RAMPION n European and Asian plant
RAMPIONS > RAMPION
RAMPIRE archaic variant of **>** RAMPART
RAMPIRED > RAMPIRE
RAMPIRES > RAMPIRE
RAMPOLE same as **>** RAMPIKE
RAMPOLES > RAMPOLE
RAMPS > RAMP
RAMPSMAN n mugger
RAMPSMEN > RAMPSMAN
RAMROD n long thin rod used for cleaning the barrel of a gun ▷ adj (of someone's posture) very straight and upright ▷ vb drive
RAMRODDED > RAMROD
RAMRODS > RAMROD
RAMS > RAM
RAMSHORN n as in ramshorn snail any of various freshwater snails
RAMSHORNS > RAMSHORN
RAMSON n type of garlic
RAMSONS > RAMSON
RAMSTAM adv headlong ▷ adj headlong
RAMTIL n African plant grown in India esp for its oil
RAMTILLA same as **>** RAMTIL
RAMTILLAS > RAMTILLA
RAMTILS > RAMTIL
RAMULAR adj relating to a branch or branches
RAMULI > RAMULUS
RAMULOSE adj (of the parts or organs of animals and plants) having many small branches
RAMULOUS same as **>** RAMULOSE
RAMULUS n small branch
RAMUS n barb of a bird's feather
RAN > RUN

RANA n genus of frogs
RANARIAN adj of or relating to frogs
RANARIUM n place for keeping frogs
RANARIUMS > RANARIUM
RANAS > RANA
RANCE Scots word for **>** PROP
RANCED > RANCE
RANCEL vb (in Shetland and Orkney) carry out a search
RANCELS > RANCEL
RANCES > RANCE
RANCH n large cattle farm in the American West ▷ vb run a ranch
RANCHED > RANCH
RANCHER n person who owns, manages, or works on a ranch
RANCHERA n type of Mexican country music
RANCHERAS > RANCHERA
RANCHERIA n native American settlement or home of a rancher
RANCHERIE n (in British Columbia, Canada) a settlement of North American Indians, esp on a reserve
RANCHERO another word for **>** RANCHER
RANCHEROS > RANCHERO
RANCHERS > RANCHER
RANCHES > RANCH
RANCHING > RANCH
RANCHINGS > RANCH
RANCHLESS > RANCH
RANCHLIKE > RANCH
RANCHMAN n man who owns, manages, or works on a ranch
RANCHMEN > RANCHMAN
RANCHO n hut or group of huts for housing ranch workers
RANCHOS > RANCHO
RANCID adj (of butter, bacon, etc) stale and having an offensive smell
RANCIDER > RANCID
RANCIDEST > RANCID
RANCIDITY > RANCID
RANCIDLY > RANCID
RANCING > RANCE
RANCOR same as **>** RANCOUR
RANCORED > RANCOR
RANCOROUS > RANCOUR
RANCORS > RANCOR
RANCOUR n deep bitter hate
RANCOURED > RANCOUR
RANCOURS > RANCOUR
RAND n leather strip on the heel of a shoe ▷ vb cut into rands
RANDAN n boat rowed by three people
RANDANS > RANDAN
RANDED > RAND

RANDEM adv with three horses harnessed together as a team ▷ n carriage or team of horses so driven
RANDEMS > RANDEM
RANDIE same as **>** RANDY
RANDIER > RANDY
RANDIES > RANDY
RANDIEST > RANDY
RANDILY > RANDY
RANDINESS > RANDY
RANDING > RAND
RANDLORD n mining magnate during the 19th-century gold boom in Johannesburg
RANDLORDS > RANDLORD
RANDOM adj made or done by chance or without plan ▷ n (in mining) the course of a vein of ore
RANDOMISE same as **>** RANDOMIZE
RANDOMIZE vb set up (a selection process, sample, etc) in a deliberately random way in order to enhance the statistical validity of any results obtained
RANDOMLY > RANDOM
RANDOMS > RANDOM
RANDON old variant of **>** RANDOM
RANDONS > RANDON
RANDS > RAND
RANDY adj sexually aroused ▷ n rude or reckless person
RANEE same as **>** RANI
RANEES > RANEE
RANG n (Scot) rank
RANGA n person with red hair
RANGAS > RANGA
RANGATIRA n Māori chief of either sex
RANGE n limits of effectiveness or variation ▷ vb vary between one point and another
RANGED > RANGE
RANGELAND n land that naturally produces forage plants suitable for grazing but where rainfall is too low or erratic for growing crops
RANGER n official in charge of a nature reserve etc
RANGERS > RANGER
RANGES > RANGE
RANGI n sky
RANGIER > RANGY
RANGIEST > RANGY
RANGILY > RANGY
RANGINESS > RANGY
RANGING > RANGE
RANGIORA n evergreen New Zealand shrub or small tree with large ovate leaves and small greenish-white flowers

RANGIORAS > RANGIORA
RANGIS > RANGI
RANGOLI n traditional Indian ground decoration
RANGOLIS > RANGOLI
RANGS > RANG
RANGY adj having long slender limbs
RANI n wife or widow of a rajah
RANID n frog
RANIDS > RANID
RANIFORM n froglike
RANINE adj relating to frogs
RANIS > RANI
RANK n relative place or position ▷ vb have a specific rank or position ▷ adj complete or absolute
RANKE archaic variant of **>** RANK
RANKED > RANK
RANKER n soldier in the ranks
RANKERS > RANKER
RANKES > RANKE
RANKEST > RANK
RANKING adj prominent ▷ n position on a scale
RANKINGS > RANKING
RANKISH adj old word meaning rather rank
RANKISM n discrimination against people on the grounds of rank
RANKISMS > RANKISM
RANKIST n person who discriminates on the grounds of rank
RANKISTS > RANKIST
RANKLE vb continue to cause resentment or bitterness
RANKLED > RANKLE
RANKLES > RANKLE
RANKLESS > RANK
RANKLING > RANKLE
RANKLY > RANK
RANKNESS > RANK
RANKS > RANK
RANKSHIFT n phenomenon in which a unit at one rank in the grammar has the function of a unit at a lower rank, as for example in the phrase the house on the corner, where the words on the corner shift down from the rank of group to the rank of word ▷ vb shift or be shifted from (one linguistic rank to another)
RANPIKE same as **>** RAMPIKE
RANPIKES > RANPIKE
RANSACK vb search thoroughly
RANSACKED > RANSACK
RANSACKER > RANSACK
RANSACKS > RANSACK
RANSEL same as **>** RANCEL
RANSELS > RANSEL

RANSHAKLE Scots word for
> RANSACK
RANSOM n money
demanded for the release
of a kidnapped person
▷ vb pay money to obtain
the release of a captive
RANSOMED > RANSOM
RANSOMER > RANSOM
RANSOMERS > RANSOM
RANSOMING > RANSOM
RANSOMS > RANSOM
RANT vb talk in a loud and
excited way ▷ n loud
excited speech
RANTED > RANT
RANTER > RANT
RANTERISM > RANT
RANTERS > RANT
RANTING > RANT
RANTINGLY > RANT
RANTINGS > RANT
RANTIPOLE n reckless
person ▷ vb behave like a
rantipole
RANTS > RANT
RANULA n saliva-filled cyst
that develops under the
tongue
RANULAR adj of a cyst
under the tongue
RANULAS > RANULA
RANUNCULI pl n plants of
the genus that includes
the buttercup, crowfoot,
spearwort, and lesser
celandine
RANZEL same as > RANCEL
RANZELMAN n (in
Shetland and Orkney) type
of constable
RANZELMEN
> RANZELMAN
RANZELS > RANZEL
RAOULIA n flowering
plant of New Zealand
RAOULIAS > RAOULIA
RAP vb hit with a sharp
quick blow ▷ n quick sharp
blow
RAPACIOUS adj greedy or
grasping
RAPACITY > RAPACIOUS
RAPE vb force to submit to
sexual intercourse ▷ n act
of raping
RAPED > RAPE
RAPER > RAPE
RAPERS > RAPE
RAPES > RAPE
RAPESEED n seed of the
oilseed rape plant
RAPESEEDS > RAPESEED
RAPHAE > RAPHE
RAPHANIA n type of
ergotism possibly resulting
from consumption of
radish seeds
RAPHANIAS > RAPHANIA
RAPHE n elongated ridge
of conducting tissue along
the side of certain seeds
RAPHES > RAPHE
RAPHIA same as > RAFFIA

RAPHIAS > RAPHIA
RAPHIDE n needle-shaped
crystal that occurs in
many plant cells
RAPHIDES > RAPHIDE
RAPHIS same as
> RAPHIDE
RAPID adj quick, swift
RAPIDER > RAPID
RAPIDEST > RAPID
RAPIDITY > RAPID
RAPIDLY > RAPID
RAPIDNESS > RAPID
RAPIDS pl n part of a river
with a fast turbulent
current
RAPIER n fine-bladed
sword
RAPIERED adj carrying a
rapier
RAPIERS > RAPIER
RAPINE n pillage or
plundering
RAPINES > RAPINE
RAPING > RAPE
RAPINI n type of leafy
vegetable
RAPINIS > RAPINI
RAPIST n person who
commits rape
RAPISTS > RAPIST
RAPLOCH n Scots word for
homespun woollen
material ▷ adj Scots word
meaning coarse or
homemade
RAPLOCHS > RAPLOCH
RAPPAREE n Irish
irregular soldier of the late
17th century
RAPPAREES > RAPPAREE
RAPPE n Arcadian dish of
grated potatoes and pork
or chicken
RAPPED > RAP
RAPPEE n moist English
snuff of the 18th and 19th
centuries
RAPPEES > RAPPEE
RAPPEL n (formerly) a
drumbeat to call soldiers
to arms ▷ vb abseil
RAPPELED > RAPPEL
RAPPELING > RAPPEL
RAPPELLED > RAPPEL
RAPPELS > RAPPEL
RAPPEN n Swiss coin equal
to one hundredth of a
franc
RAPPER n something used
for rapping, such as a
knocker on a door
RAPPERS > RAPPER
RAPPES > RAPPE
RAPPING > RAP
RAPPINGS > RAP
RAPPINI same as
> RAPINI
RAPPORT n harmony or
agreement
RAPPORTS > RAPPORT
RAPS > RAP
RAPT adj engrossed or
spellbound

RAPTLY > RAPT
RAPTNESS > RAPT
RAPTOR n any bird of prey
RAPTORIAL adj (of the
feet of birds) adapted for
seizing prey
RAPTORS > RAPTOR
RAPTURE n ecstasy
▷ vb entrance
RAPTURED > RAPTURE
RAPTURES > RAPTURE
RAPTURING > RAPTURE
RAPTURISE same as
> RAPTURIZE
RAPTURIST > RAPTURE
RAPTURIZE vb go into
ecstasies
RAPTUROUS adj
experiencing or
manifesting ecstatic joy
or delight
RARE adj uncommon
▷ vb rear
RAREBIT n as in Welsh
rarebit dish made from
melted cheese served on
toast
RAREBITS > RAREBIT
RARED > RARE
RAREE n as in raree show
street show or carnival
RAREFIED adj highly
specialized, exalted
RAREFIER > RAREFY
RAREFIERS > RAREFY
RAREFIES > RAREFY
RAREFY vb make or
become rarer or less dense
RAREFYING > RAREFY
RARELY adv seldom
RARENESS > RARE
RARER > RARE
RARERIPE adj ripening
early ▷ n fruit or vegetable
that ripens early
RARERIPES > RARERIPE
RARES > RARE
RAREST > RARE
RARIFIED same as
> RAREFIED
RARIFIES > RARIFY
RARIFY same as > RAREFY
RARIFYING > RARIFY
RARING adj ready
RARITIES > RARITY
RARITY n something that
is valuable because it is
unusual
RARK vb as in rark up
informal New Zealand
expression meaning
reprimand severely
RARKED > RARK
RARKING > RARK
RARKS > RARK
RAS n headland
RASBORA n often brightly
coloured tropical fish
RASBORAS > RASBORA
RASCAILLE n rabble
RASCAL n rogue ▷ adj
belonging to the mob or
rabble
RASCALDOM > RASCAL

RASCALISM > RASCAL
RASCALITY n
mischievous, disreputable,
or dishonest character,
behaviour, or action
RASCALLY adj dishonest
or mean ▷ adv in a
dishonest or mean fashion
RASCALS > RASCAL
RASCASSE n any of
various fishes with
venomous spines on the
dorsal and anal fins
RASCASSES
> RASCASSE
RASCHEL n type of loosely
knitted fabric
RASCHELS > RASCHEL
RASE same as > RAZE
RASED > RASE
RASER > RASE
RASERS > RASE
RASES > RASE
RASH adj hasty, reckless, or
incautious ▷ n eruption of
spots or patches on the
skin ▷ vb (in old usage) cut
RASHED > RASH
RASHER n thin slice of
bacon
RASHERS > RASHER
RASHES > RASH
RASHEST > RASH
RASHIE n protective shirt
worn by surfers
RASHIES > RASHIE
RASHING > RASH
RASHLIKE > RASH
RASHLY > RASH
RASHNESS > RASH
RASING > RASE
RASMALAI n Indian
dessert made from cheese,
milk, and almonds
RASMALAIS > RASMALAI
RASORIAL adj (of birds
such as domestic poultry)
adapted for scratching the
ground for food
RASP n harsh grating noise
▷ vb speak in a grating
voice
RASPATORY n surgical
instrument for abrading
RASPBERRY n red juicy
edible berry
RASPED > RASP
RASPER > RASP
RASPERS > RASP
RASPIER > RASPY
RASPIEST > RASPY
RASPINESS > RASPY
RASPING adj (esp of a
noise) harsh or grating
RASPINGLY > RASPING
RASPINGS pl n browned
breadcrumbs for coating
fish and other foods before
frying, baking, etc
RASPISH > RASP
RASPS > RASP
RASPY same as > RASPING
RASSE n small S Asian civet
RASSES > RASSE

RASSLE *dialect variant of* > WRESTLE

RASSLED > RASSLE

RASSLER *n* wrestler

RASSLERS > RASSLER

RASSLES > RASSLE

RASSLING > RASSLE

RAST *archaic past form of* > RACE

RASTA *adj* of a member of a particular Black religious movement

RASTAFARI *n* Black religious movement ▷ *adj* of or relating to the Rastafarian religious movement

RASTER *n* image consisting of rows of pixel information ▷ *vb* turn a digital image into a large picture

RASTERED > RASTER

RASTERING > RASTER

RASTERISE *same as* > RASTERIZE

RASTERIZE *vb* (in computing) convert into pixels for screen output

RASTERS > RASTER

RASTRUM *n* pen for drawing the five lines of a musical stave simultaneously

RASTRUMS > RASTRUM

RASURE *n* scraping

RASURES > RASURE

RAT *n* small rodent ▷ *vb* inform (on)

RATA *n* New Zealand hard-wood forest tree

RATABLE *adj* able to be rated or evaluated ▷ *n* something that can be rated or evaluated

RATABLES *pl n* property that is liable to rates

RATABLY > RATABLE

RATAFEE *same as* > RATAFIA

RATAFEES > RATAFEE

RATAFIA *n* liqueur made from fruit

RATAFIAS > RATAFIA

RATAL *n* amount on which rates are assessed ▷ *adj* of or relating to rates (local taxation)

RATALS > RATAL

RATAN *same as* > RATTAN

RATANIES > RATANY

RATANS > RATAN

RATANY *n* flowering desert shrub

RATAPLAN *n* drumming sound ▷ *vb* drum

RATAPLANS > RATAPLAN

RATAS > RATA

RATATAT *n* sound of knocking on a door

RATATATS > RATATAT

RATBAG *n* eccentric, stupid, or unreliable person

RATBAGS > RATBAG

RATBITE *n* as in *ratbite fever* acute infectious disease that can be caught from rats

RATCH *same as* > RATCHET

RATCHED > RATCH

RATCHES > RATCH

RATCHET *n* set of teeth on a bar or wheel allowing motion in one direction only ▷ *vb* move using or as if using a ratchet system

RATCHETED > RATCHET

RATCHETS > RATCHET

RATCHING > RATCH

RATE *n* degree of speed or progress ▷ *vb* consider or value

RATEABLE *same as* > RATABLE

RATEABLES > RATEABLE

RATEABLY > RATEABLE

RATED > RATE

RATEEN *same as* > RATINE

RATEENS > RATEEN

RATEL *n* large African and S Asian musteline mammal

RATELS > RATEL

RATEMETER *n* device for counting and averaging the number of events in a given time

RATEPAYER *n* person who pays local rates on a building

RATER > RATE

RATERS > RATE

RATES *pl n* (in some countries) a tax on property levied by a local authority

RATFINK *n* contemptible or undesirable person

RATFINKS > RATFINK

RATFISH *n* deep-sea fish with a whiplike tail

RATFISHES > RATFISH

RATH *same as* > RATHE

RATHA *n* (in India) a four-wheeled carriage drawn by horses or bullocks

RATHAS > RATHA

RATHE *adj* blossoming or ripening early in the season

RATHER *adv* some extent ▷ *interj* expression of strong affirmation ▷ *sentence substitute* expression of strong affirmation, often in answer to a question

RATHEREST *adv* archaic word equivalent to soonest

RATHERIPE *same as* > RATHRIPE

RATHERISH *adv* (in informal English) quite or fairly

RATHEST *adv* dialect or archaic word meaning soonest

RATHOLE *n* rat's hiding place or burrow

RATHOLES > RATHOLE

RATHOUSE *n* psychiatric hospital or asylum

RATHOUSES > RATHOUSE

RATHRIPE *adj* dialect word meaning mature or ripe ahead of time ▷ *n* variety of apple or other fruit that is quick to ripen

RATHRIPES > RATHRIPE

RATHS > RATH

RATICIDE *n* rat poison

RATICIDES > RATICIDE

RATIFIED > RATIFY

RATIFIER > RATIFY

RATIFIERS > RATIFY

RATIFIES > RATIFY

RATIFY *vb* give formal approval to

RATIFYING > RATIFY

RATINE *n* coarse loosely woven cloth

RATINES > RATINE

RATING *n* valuation or assessment

RATINGS > RATING

RATIO *n* relationship between two numbers or amounts expressed as a proportion

RATION *n* fixed allowance of food etc ▷ *vb* limit to a certain amount per person

RATIONAL *adj* reasonable, sensible ▷ *n* rational number

RATIONALE *n* reason for an action or decision

RATIONALS > RATIONAL

RATIONED > RATION

RATIONING *n* act of restricting the use or consumption of certain things

RATIONS *pl n* fixed daily allowance of food

RATIOS > RATIO

RATITE *adj* (of flightless birds) having a breastbone that lacks a keel ▷ *n* bird that belongs to this group

RATITES > RATITE

RATLIKE > RAT

RATLIN *same as* > RATLINE

RATLINE *n* light line tied across the shrouds of a sailing vessel

RATLINES > RATLINE

RATLING *n* young rat

RATLINGS > RATLING

RATLINS > RATLIN

RATO *n* rocket-assisted take-off

RATOO *same as* > RATU

RATOON *n* new shoot that grows from near the root or crown of crop plants

▷ *vb* propagate by such a growth

RATOONED > RATOON

RATOONER *n* plant that spreads by ratooning

RATOONERS > RATOONER

RATOONING > RATOON

RATOONS > RATOON

RATOOS > RATOO

RATOS > RATO

RATPACK *n* members of the press who pursue celebrities

RATPACKS > RATPACK

RATPROOF *adj* impenetrable by rats

RATS > RAT

RATSBANE *n* rat poison, esp arsenic oxide

RATSBANES > RATSBANE

RATTAIL *n* type of fish

RATTAILED *adj* having tail like rat

RATTAILS > RATTAIL

RATTAN *n* climbing palm with jointed stems used for canes

RATTANS > RATTAN

RATTED > RAT

RATTEEN *same as* > RATINE

RATTEENS > RATTEEN

RATTEN *vb* sabotage or steal tools in order to disrupt the work of

RATTENED > RATTEN

RATTENER > RATTEN

RATTENERS > RATTEN

RATTENING > RATTEN

RATTENS > RATTEN

RATTER *n* dog or cat that catches and kills rats

RATTERIES > RATTERY

RATTERS > RATTER

RATTERY *n* rats' dwelling area

RATTIER > RATTY

RATTIEST > RATTY

RATTILY > RATTY

RATTINESS > RATTY

RATTING > RAT

RATTINGS > RAT

RATTISH *adj* of, resembling, or infested with rats

RATTLE *vb* give out a succession of short sharp sounds ▷ *n* short sharp sound

RATTLEBAG *n* rattle made out of a bag containing a variety of different things

RATTLEBOX *n* any of various tropical and subtropical leguminous plants that have inflated pods within which the seeds rattle

RATTLED > RATTLE

RATTLER *n* something that rattles

RATTLERS > RATTLER

RATTLES > RATTLE

RATTLIER > RATTLY

RATTLIEST > RATTLY
RATTLIN *same as*
> RATLINE
RATTLINE *same as*
> RATLINE
RATTLINES > RATTLINE
RATTLING *adv*
exceptionally, very ▷ *n*
succession of short sharp
sounds
RATTLINGS > RATTLING
RATTLINS > RATTLIN
RATTLY *adj* having a
rattle
RATTON *n* dialect word for
a little rat
RATTONS > RATTON
RATTOON *same as*
> RATOON
RATTOONED > RATTOON
RATTOONS > RATTOON
RATTRAP *n* device for
catching rats
RATTRAPS > RATTRAP
RATTY *adj* bad-tempered,
irritable
RATU *n* title used by Fijian
chiefs or nobles
RATUS > RATU
RAUCID *adj* raucous
RAUCITIES > RAUCOUS
RAUCITY > RAUCOUS
RAUCLE *adj* Scots word for
rough or tough
RAUCLER > RAUCLE
RAUCLEST > RAUCLE
RAUCOUS *adj* hoarse or
harsh
RAUCOUSLY > RAUCOUS
RAUGHT *archaic past form of*
> REACH
RAUN *n* fish roe or spawn
RAUNCH *n* lack of polish or
refinement ▷ *vb* behave in
a raunchy manner
RAUNCHED > RAUNCH
RAUNCHES > RAUNCH
RAUNCHIER > RAUNCHY
RAUNCHILY > RAUNCHY
RAUNCHING > RAUNCH
RAUNCHY *adj* earthy, sexy
RAUNGE *archaic word for*
> RANGE
RAUNGED > RAUNGE
RAUNGES > RAUNGE
RAUNGING > RAUNGE
RAUNS > RAUN
RAUPATU *n* confiscation
or seizure of land
RAUPATUS > RAUPATU
RAUPO *n* New Zealand
bulrush
RAUPOS > RAUPO
RAURIKI *n* any of various
plants with prickly leaves
RAURIKIS > RAURIKI
RAUWOLFIA *n* tropical
tree or shrub
RAV *n* Hebrew word for
rabbi
RAVAGE *vb* cause
extensive damage to
▷ *n* destructive action

RAVAGED > RAVAGE
RAVAGER > RAVAGE
RAVAGERS > RAVAGE
RAVAGES > RAVAGE
RAVAGING > RAVAGE
RAVE *vb* talk wildly or with
enthusiasm ▷ *n*
enthusiastically good
review
RAVED > RAVE
RAVEL *vb* tangle or
become entangled
▷ *n* tangle or complication
RAVELED > RAVEL
RAVELER > RAVEL
RAVELERS > RAVEL
RAVELIN *n* outwork
having two embankments
at a salient angle
RAVELING > RAVEL
RAVELINGS > RAVEL
RAVELINS > RAVELIN
RAVELLED > RAVEL
RAVELLER > RAVEL
RAVELLERS > RAVEL
RAVELLING > RAVEL
RAVELLY > RAVEL
RAVELMENT *n* ravel or
tangle
RAVELS > RAVEL
RAVEN *n* black bird like a
large crow ▷ *adj* (of hair)
shiny black ▷ *vb* seize or
seek (plunder, prey, etc)
RAVENED > RAVEN
RAVENER > RAVEN
RAVENERS > RAVEN
RAVENING *adj* (of
animals) hungrily
searching for prey
RAVENINGS *pl n*
rapacious behaviour
and activities
RAVENLIKE > RAVEN
RAVENOUS *adj* very
hungry
RAVENS > RAVEN
RAVER *n* person who
leads a wild or uninhibited
social life
RAVERS > RAVER
RAVES > RAVE
RAVEY *adj* characteristic of
a rave
RAVIER > RAVEY
RAVIEST > RAVEY
RAVIGOTE *n* rich white
sauce with herbs and
shallots
RAVIGOTES > RAVIGOTE
RAVIGOTTE *n* French
salad sauce
RAVIN *archaic spelling of*
> RAVEN
RAVINE *n* narrow
steep-sided valley worn by
a stream
RAVINED > RAVIN
RAVINES > RAVINE
RAVING *adj* delirious
▷ *n* frenzied, irrational, or
wildly extravagant talk or
utterances
RAVINGLY > RAVING

RAVINGS > RAVING
RAVINING > RAVIN
RAVINS > RAVIN
RAVIOLI *n* small squares
of pasta with a savoury
filling
RAVIOLIS > RAVIOLI
RAVISH *vb* enrapture
RAVISHED > RAVISH
RAVISHER > RAVISH
RAVISHERS > RAVISH
RAVISHES > RAVISH
RAVISHING *adj* lovely or
entrancing
RAVS > RAV
RAW *n* as in *in the raw*
without clothes
▷ *adj* uncooked
RAWARU *n* New Zealand
name for blue cod
RAWARUS > RAWARU
RAWBONE *archaic variant of*
> RAWBONED
RAWBONED *adj* having a
lean bony physique
RAWER > RAW
RAWEST > RAW
RAWHEAD *n* bogeyman
RAWHEADS > RAWHEAD
RAWHIDE *n* untanned hide
▷ *vb* whip
RAWHIDED > RAWHIDE
RAWHIDES > RAWHIDE
RAWHIDING > RAWHIDE
RAWIN *n* monitoring of
winds in the upper
atmosphere using radar
and a balloon
RAWING *(in dialect) same as*
> ROWEN
RAWINGS > RAWING
RAWINS > RAWIN
RAWISH > RAW
RAWLY > RAW
RAWMAISH *n* Irish word for
foolish or exaggerated talk
RAWN *(in dialect) same as*
> ROWEN
RAWNESS > RAW
RAWNESSES > RAW
RAWNS > RAWN
RAWS > RAW
RAX *vb* stretch or extend
▷ *n* act of stretching or
straining
RAXED > RAX
RAXES > RAX
RAXING > RAX
RAY *n* single line or narrow
beam of light ▷ *vb* (of an
object) to emit (light) in
rays or (of light) to issue in
the form of rays
RAYA *same as* > RAYAH
RAYAH *n* (formerly) a
non-Muslim subject of the
Ottoman Empire
RAYAHS > RAYAH
RAYAS > RAYA
RAYED > RAY
RAYGRASS *same as*
> RYEGRASS
RAYING > RAY

RAYLE *archaic spelling of*
> RAIL
RAYLED > RAYLE
RAYLES > RAYLE
RAYLESS *adj* dark
RAYLESSLY > RAYLESS
RAYLET *n* small ray
RAYLETS > RAYLET
RAYLIKE *adj* resembling
a ray
RAYLING > RAYLE
RAYNE *archaic spelling of*
> REIGN
RAYNES > RAYNE
RAYON *n* (fabric made of) a
synthetic fibre
RAYONS > RAYON
RAYS > RAY
RAZE *vb* destroy (buildings
or a town) completely
RAZED > RAZE
RAZEE *n* sailing ship that
has had its upper deck or
decks removed ▷ *vb*
remove the upper deck or
decks of (a sailing ship)
RAZEED > RAZEE
RAZEEING > RAZEE
RAZEES > RAZEE
RAZER > RAZE
RAZERS > RAZE
RAZES > RAZE
RAZING > RAZE
RAZMATAZ *n* noisy or
showy fuss or activity
RAZOO *n* imaginary coin
RAZOOS > RAZOO
RAZOR *n* sharp instrument
for shaving ▷ *vb* cut or
shave with a razor
RAZORABLE *adj* able to be
shaved
RAZORBACK *n* another
name for the common
rorqual
RAZORBILL *n* sea bird of
the North Atlantic with a
stout sideways flattened
bill
RAZORCLAM *n* type of
mollusc with a long,
narrow shell
RAZORED > RAZOR
RAZORFISH *n* type of
mollusc with a long,
narrow shell
RAZORING > RAZOR
RAZORS > RAZOR
RAZURE *same as* > RASURE
RAZURES > RAZURE
RAZZ *vb* make fun of
RAZZBERRY *US variant of*
> RASPBERRY
RAZZED > RAZZ
RAZZES > RAZZ
RAZZIA *n* raid for plunder
or slaves
RAZZIAS > RAZZIA
RAZZING *n* act of making
fun of someone
RAZZINGS > RAZZING
RAZZLE *n* as in *on the razzle*
out enjoying oneself or
celebrating

r

RAZZLES > RAZZLE
RE prep concerning ▷ n the second note of the musical scale
REABSORB vb absorb again
REABSORBS > REABSORB
REACCEDE vb accede again
REACCEDED > REACCEDE
REACCEDES > REACCEDE
REACCENT vb accent again
REACCENTS > REACCENT
REACCEPT vb accept again
REACCEPTS > REACCEPT
REACCLAIM vb acclaim again
REACCUSE vb accuse again
REACCUSED > REACCUSE
REACCUSES > REACCUSE
REACH vb arrive at ▷ n distance that one can reach
REACHABLE > REACH
REACHED > REACH
REACHER > REACH
REACHERS > REACH
REACHES > REACH
REACHING > REACH
REACHLESS adj unreachable or unattainable
REACQUIRE vb get or gain (something) again which one has owned
REACT vb act in response (to)
REACTANCE n resistance to the flow of an alternating current caused by the inductance or capacitance of the circuit
REACTANT n substance that participates in a chemical reaction
REACTANTS > REACTANT
REACTED > REACT
REACTING > REACT
REACTION n physical or emotional response to a stimulus
REACTIONS > REACTION
REACTIVE adj chemically active
REACTOR n apparatus in which a nuclear reaction is controlled to produce energy
REACTORS > REACTOR
REACTS > REACT
REACTUATE vb activate again
READ vb look at and understand or take in (written or printed matter) ▷ n matter suitable for reading
READABLE adj enjoyable to read
READABLY > READABLE
READAPT vb adapt again

READAPTED > READAPT
READAPTS > READAPT
READD vb add again
READDED > READD
READDICT vb cause to become addicted again
READDICTS > READDICT
READDING > READD
READDRESS vb look at or discuss (an issue, situation, etc) from a new or different point of view
READDS > READD
READER n person who reads
READERLY adj pertaining to or suitable for a reader
READERS > READER
READIED > READY
READIER > READY
READIES pl n ready money
READIEST > READY
READILY adv promptly
READINESS n state of being ready or prepared
READING > READ
READINGS > READ
READJUST vb adapt to a new situation
READJUSTS > READJUST
README n document which accompanies computer files or software
READMIT vb let (a person, country, etc) back in to a place or organization
READMITS > READMIT
READOPT vb adopt again
READOPTED > READOPT
READOPTS > READOPT
READORN vb adorn again
READORNED > READORN
READORNS > READORN
READOUT n act of retrieving information from a computer memory or storage device
READOUTS > READOUT
READS > READ
READVANCE vb advance again
READVISE vb advise again
READVISED > READVISE
READVISES > READVISE
READY adj prepared for use or action ▷ vb prepare
READYING > READY
READYMADE adj made for purchase and immediate use by any customer
REAEDIFY vb rebuild
REAEDIFYE same as > REAEDIFY
REAFFIRM vb state again, confirm
REAFFIRMS > REAFFIRM
REAFFIX vb affix again
REAFFIXED > REAFFIX
REAFFIXES > REAFFIX
REAGENCY > REAGENT

REAGENT n chemical substance that reacts with another
REAGENTS > REAGENT
REAGIN n type of antibody that is formed against an allergen
REAGINIC > REAGIN
REAGINS > REAGIN
REAK same as > RECK
REAKED > REAK
REAKING > REAK
REAKS > REAK
REAL adj existing in fact ▷ n standard monetary unit of Brazil
REALER > REAL
REALES > REAL
REALEST > REAL
REALGAR n rare orange-red soft mineral
REALGARS > REALGAR
REALIA pl n real-life facts and material used in teaching
REALIGN vb change or put back to a new or former place or position
REALIGNED > REALIGN
REALIGNS > REALIGN
REALISE same as > REALIZE
REALISED > REALISE
REALISER > REALISE
REALISERS > REALISE
REALISES > REALISE
REALISING > REALISE
REALISM n awareness or acceptance of things as they are
REALISMS > REALISM
REALIST n person who accepts events, etc, as they are
REALISTIC adj seeing and accepting things as they really are, practical
REALISTS > REALIST
REALITIES > REALITY
REALITY n state of things as they are
REALIZE vb become aware of or grasp the significance of
REALIZED > REALIZE
REALIZER > REALIZE
REALIZERS > REALIZE
REALIZES > REALIZE
REALIZING > REALIZE
REALLIE old or dialect variant of > REALLY
REALLIED > REALLY
REALLIES > REALLY
REALLOT vb allot again
REALLOTS > REALLOT
REALLY adv very ▷ interj exclamation of dismay, doubt, or surprise ▷ vb (in archaic usage) rally
REALLYING > REALLY
REALM n kingdom
REALMLESS > REALM
REALMS > REALM

REALNESS > REAL
REALO n member of the German Green party with moderate views
REALOS > REALO
REALS > REAL
REALTER vb alter again
REALTERED > REALTER
REALTERS > REALTER
REALTIE n archaic word meaning sincerity
REALTIES > REALTY
REALTIME adj (of a data-processing system) constantly updating to reflect the latest changes in data
REALTONE n audio clip of an original recording, used as a mobile phone ringtone
REALTONES > REALTONE
REALTOR n estate agent
REALTORS > REALTOR
REALTY n immovable property
REAM n twenty quires of paper, generally 500 sheets ▷ vb enlarge (a hole) by use of a reamer
REAME archaic variant of > REALM
REAMED > REAM
REAMEND vb amend again
REAMENDED > REAMEND
REAMENDS > REAMEND
REAMER n tool used for smoothing the bores of holes accurately to size
REAMERS > REAMER
REAMES > REAME
REAMIER > REAMY
REAMIEST > REAMY
REAMING > REAM
REAMS > REAM
REAMY Scots for > CREAMY
REAN same as > REEN
REANALYSE vb analyse again
REANALYZE US spelling of > REANALYSE
REANIMATE vb refresh or enliven (something) again
REANNEX vb annex again
REANNEXED > REANNEX
REANNEXES > REANNEX
REANOINT vb anoint again
REANOINTS > REANOINT
REANS > REAN
REANSWER vb answer again
REANSWERS > REANSWER
REAP vb cut and gather (a harvest)
REAPABLE > REAP
REAPED > REAP
REAPER n person who reaps or machine for reaping
REAPERS > REAPER
REAPHOOK n sickle
REAPHOOKS > REAPHOOK

REAPING n act of reaping
REAPINGS > REAPING
REAPPAREL vb clothe again
REAPPEAR vb appear again
REAPPEARS > REAPPEAR
REAPPLIED > REAPPLY
REAPPLIES > REAPPLY
REAPPLY vb put or spread (something) on again
REAPPOINT vb assign (a person, committee, etc) to a post or role again
REAPPROVE vb approve again
REAPS > REAP
REAR n back part ▷ vb care for and educate (children)
REARED > REAR
REARER > REAR
REARERS > REAR
REARGUARD n troops protecting the rear of an army
REARGUE vb argue again
REARGUED > REARGUE
REARGUES > REARGUE
REARGUING > REARGUE
REARHORSE n mantis
REARING n act of rearing
REARINGS > REARING
REARISE vb arise again
REARISEN > REARISE
REARISES > REARISE
REARISING > REARISE
REARLY old word for > EARLY
REARM vb arm again
REARMED > REARM
REARMICE > REARMOUSE
REARMING > REARM
REARMOST adj nearest the back
REARMOUSE same as > REREMOUSE
REARMS > REARM
REAROSE > REARISE
REAROUSAL > REAROUSE
REAROUSE vb arouse again
REAROUSED > REAROUSE
REAROUSES > REAROUSE
REARRANGE vb organize differently, alter
REARREST vb arrest again
REARRESTS > REARREST
REARS > REAR
REARWARD adj in the rear ▷ adv towards the rear ▷ n position in the rear, esp the rear division of a military formation
REARWARDS same as > REARWARD
REASCEND vb ascend again
REASCENDS > REASCEND
REASCENT n new ascent
REASCENTS > REASCENT
REASON n cause or motive ▷ vb think logically in forming conclusions

REASONED adj well thought out or well presented
REASONER > REASON
REASONERS > REASON
REASONING n process of drawing conclusions from facts or evidence
REASONS > REASON
REASSAIL vb assail again
REASSAILS > REASSAIL
REASSERT vb assert (rights, claims, etc) again
REASSERTS > REASSERT
REASSESS vb reconsider the value or importance of
REASSIGN vb move (personnel, resources, etc) to a new post, department, location, etc
REASSIGNS > REASSIGN
REASSORT vb assort again
REASSORTS > REASSORT
REASSUME vb assume again
REASSUMED > REASSUME
REASSUMES > REASSUME
REASSURE vb restore confidence to
REASSURED > REASSURE
REASSURER > REASSURE
REASSURES > REASSURE
REAST same as > REEST
REASTED > REAST
REASTIER > REASTY
REASTIEST > REASTY
REASTING > REAST
REASTS > REAST
REASTY adj (in dialect) rancid
REATA n lasso
REATAS > REATA
REATE n type of crowfoot
REATES > REATE
REATTACH vb attach again
REATTACK vb attack again
REATTACKS > REATTACK
REATTAIN vb attain again
REATTAINS > REATTAIN
REATTEMPT vb attempt again
REAVAIL vb avail again
REAVAILED > REAVAIL
REAVAILS > REAVAIL
REAVE vb carry off (property, prisoners, etc) by force
REAVED > REAVE
REAVER > REAVE
REAVERS > REAVE
REAVES > REAVE
REAVING > REAVE
REAVOW vb avow again
REAVOWED > REAVOW
REAVOWING > REAVOW
REAVOWS > REAVOW
REAWAKE vb awake again
REAWAKED > REAWAKE
REAWAKEN vb emerge or rouse from sleep
REAWAKENS > REAWAKEN

REAWAKES > REAWAKE
REAWAKING > REAWAKE
REAWOKE > REAWAKE
REAWOKEN > REAWAKE
REB n Confederate soldier in the American Civil War
REBACK vb provide with a new back, backing, or lining
REBACKED > REBACK
REBACKING > REBACK
REBACKS > REBACK
REBADGE vb relaunch (a product) under a new name, brand, or logo
REBADGED > REBADGE
REBADGES > REBADGE
REBADGING > REBADGE
REBAIT vb bait again
REBAITED > REBAIT
REBAITING > REBAIT
REBAITS > REBAIT
REBALANCE vb balance again
REBAPTISE same as > REBAPTIZE
REBAPTISM n new baptism
REBAPTIZE vb baptize again
REBAR n rod providing reinforcement in concrete structures
REBARS > REBAR
REBASE vb set on a new foundation
REBASED > REBASE
REBASES > REBASE
REBASING > REBASE
REBATABLE > REBATE
REBATE n discount or refund ▷ vb cut a rabbet in
REBATED > REBATE
REBATER > REBATE
REBATERS > REBATE
REBATES > REBATE
REBATING > REBATE
REBATO same as > RABATO
REBATOES > REBATO
REBATOS > REBATO
REBBE n individual's chosen spiritual mentor
REBBES > REBBE
REBBETZIN n wife of a rabbi
REBEC n medieval stringed instrument resembling the violin
REBECK same as > REBEC
REBECKS > REBECK
REBECS > REBEC
REBEGAN > REBEGIN
REBEGIN vb begin again
REBEGINS > REBEGIN
REBEGUN > REBEGIN
REBEL vb revolt against the ruling power ▷ n person who rebels ▷ adj rebelling
REBELDOM > REBEL
REBELDOMS > REBEL
REBELLED > REBEL
REBELLER > REBEL

REBELLERS > REBEL
REBELLING > REBEL
REBELLION n organized open resistance to authority
REBELLOW vb re-echo loudly
REBELLOWS > REBELLOW
REBELS > REBEL
REBID vb bid again
REBIDDEN > REBID
REBIDDING > REBID
REBIDS > REBID
REBILL vb bill again
REBILLED > REBILL
REBILLING > REBILL
REBILLS > REBILL
REBIND vb bind again
REBINDING > REBIND
REBINDS > REBIND
REBIRTH n revival or renaissance
REBIRTHER n person who has undergone rebirthing therapy
REBIRTHS > REBIRTH
REBIT > REBITE
REBITE vb (in printing) to give another application of acid
REBITES > REBITE
REBITING > REBITE
REBITTEN > REBITE
REBLEND vb blend again
REBLENDED > REBLEND
REBLENDS > REBLEND
REBLENT same as > REBLEND
REBLOCHON n type of soft French cheese
REBLOOM vb bloom again
REBLOOMED > REBLOOM
REBLOOMS > REBLOOM
REBLOSSOM vb blossom again
REBOANT adj resounding or reverberating
REBOARD vb board again
REBOARDED > REBOARD
REBOARDS > REBOARD
REBOATION n repeated bellow
REBODIED > REBODY
REBODIES > REBODY
REBODY vb give a new body to
REBODYING > REBODY
REBOIL vb boil again
REBOILED > REBOIL
REBOILING > REBOIL
REBOILS > REBOIL
REBOOK vb book again
REBOOKED > REBOOK
REBOOKING > REBOOK
REBOOKS > REBOOK
REBOOT vb shut down and then restart (a computer system)
REBOOTED > REBOOT
REBOOTING > REBOOT
REBOOTS > REBOOT
REBOP same as > BEBOP
REBOPS > REBOP

r

REBORE n boring of a cylinder to restore its true shape ▷ vb carry out this process

REBORED > REBORE

REBORES > REBORE

REBORING > REBORE

REBORN adj active again after a period of inactivity

REBORROW vb borrow again

REBORROWS > REBORROW

REBOTTLE vb bottle again

REBOTTLED > REBOTTLE

REBOTTLES > REBOTTLE

REBOUGHT > REBUY

REBOUND vb spring back ▷ n act of rebounding

REBOUNDED > REBOUND

REBOUNDER > REBOUND

REBOUNDS > REBOUND

REBOZO n long scarf covering the shoulders and head

REBOZOS > REBOZO

REBRACE vb brace again

REBRACED > REBRACE

REBRACES > REBRACE

REBRACING > REBRACE

REBRANCH vb branch again

REBRAND vb change or update the image of (an organization or product)

REBRANDED > REBRAND

REBRANDS > REBRAND

REBRED > REBREED

REBREED vb breed again

REBREEDS > REBREED

REBS > REB

REBUFF vb reject or snub ▷ n blunt refusal, snub

REBUFFED > REBUFF

REBUFFING > REBUFF

REBUFFS > REBUFF

REBUILD vb build (a building or town) again, after severe damage

REBUILDED archaic past form of > REBUILD

REBUILDS > REBUILD

REBUILT > REBUILD

REBUKABLE > REBUKE

REBUKE vb scold sternly ▷ n stern scolding

REBUKED > REBUKE

REBUKEFUL > REBUKE

REBUKER > REBUKE

REBUKERS > REBUKE

REBUKES > REBUKE

REBUKING > REBUKE

REBURIAL > REBURY

REBURIALS > REBURY

REBURIED > REBURY

REBURIES > REBURY

REBURY vb bury again

REBURYING > REBURY

REBUS n puzzle consisting of pictures and symbols representing words or syllables

REBUSES > REBUS

REBUT vb prove that (a claim) is untrue

REBUTMENT > REBUT

REBUTS > REBUT

REBUTTAL > REBUT

REBUTTALS > REBUT

REBUTTED > REBUT

REBUTTER n defendant's pleading in reply to a claimant's surrejoinder

REBUTTERS > REBUTTER

REBUTTING > REBUT

REBUTTON vb button again

REBUTTONS > REBUTTON

REBUY vb buy again

REBUYING > REBUY

REBUYS > REBUY

REC n short for recreation

RECAL same as > RECALL

RECALESCE vb glow again

RECALL vb recollect or remember ▷ n ability to remember

RECALLED > RECALL

RECALLER > RECALL

RECALLERS > RECALL

RECALLING > RECALL

RECALLS > RECALL

RECALMENT > RECAL

RECALS > RECAL

RECAMIER n shade of pink

RECAMIERS > RECAMIER

RECANE vb cane again

RECANED > RECANE

RECANES > RECANE

RECANING > RECANE

RECANT vb withdraw (a statement or belief) publicly

RECANTED > RECANT

RECANTER > RECANT

RECANTERS > RECANT

RECANTING > RECANT

RECANTS > RECANT

RECAP vb recapitulate ▷ n recapitulation

RECAPPED > RECAP

RECAPPING > RECAP

RECAPS > RECAP

RECAPTION n process of taking back one's own wife, child, property, etc, without causing a breach of the peace

RECAPTOR > RECAPTURE

RECAPTORS > RECAPTURE

RECAPTURE vb experience again ▷ n act of recapturing

RECARPET vb replace one carpet with another

RECARPETS > RECARPET

RECARRIED > RECARRY

RECARRIES > RECARRY

RECARRY vb carry again

RECAST vb organize or set out in a different way

RECASTING > RECAST

RECASTS > RECAST

RECATALOG vb catalogue again

RECATCH vb catch again

RECATCHES > RECATCH

RECAUGHT > RECATCH

RECAUTION vb caution again

RECCE vb reconnoitre ▷ n reconnaissance

RECCED > RECCE

RECCEED > RECCE

RECCEING > RECCE

RECCES > RECCE

RECCIED > RECCY

RECCIES > RECCY

RECCO same as > RECCE

RECCOS > RECCO

RECCY same as > RECCE

RECCYING > RECCY

RECEDE vb move to a more distant place

RECEDED > RECEDE

RECEDES > RECEDE

RECEDING > RECEDE

RECEIPT n written acknowledgment of money or goods received ▷ vb acknowledge payment of (a bill), as by marking it

RECEIPTED > RECEIPT

RECEIPTOR n person who receipts

RECEIPTS > RECEIPT

RECEIVAL n act of receiving or state of being received

RECEIVALS > RECEIVAL

RECEIVE vb take, accept, or get

RECEIVED adj generally accepted

RECEIVER n part of telephone that is held to the ear

RECEIVERS > RECEIVER

RECEIVES > RECEIVE

RECEIVING > RECEIVE

RECEMENT vb cement again

RECEMENTS > RECEMENT

RECENCIES > RECENT

RECENCY > RECENT

RECENSE vb revise

RECENSED > RECENSE

RECENSES > RECENSE

RECENSING > RECENSE

RECENSION n critical revision of a literary work

RECENSOR vb censor again

RECENSORS > RECENSOR

RECENT adj having happened lately

RECENTER > RECENT

RECENTEST > RECENT

RECENTLY > RECENT

RECENTRE vb centre again

RECENTRED > RECENTRE

RECENTRES > RECENTRE

RECEPT n idea or image formed in the mind by repeated experience

RECEPTION n area for receiving guests, clients, etc

RECEPTIVE adj willing to accept new ideas, suggestions, etc

RECEPTOR n sensory nerve ending that changes specific stimuli into nerve impulses

RECEPTORS > RECEPTOR

RECEIPTS > RECEIPT

RECERTIFY vb certify again

RECESS n niche or alcove ▷ vb place or set (something) in a recess

RECESSED > RECESS

RECESSES > RECESS

RECESSING > RECESS

RECESSION n period of economic difficulty when little is being bought or sold

RECESSIVE adj receding ▷ n recessive gene or character

RECHANGE vb change again

RECHANGED > RECHANGE

RECHANGES > RECHANGE

RECHANNEL vb channel again

RECHARGE vb cause (a battery etc) to take in and store electricity again

RECHARGED > RECHARGE

RECHARGER > RECHARGE

RECHARGES > RECHARGE

RECHART vb chart again

RECHARTED > RECHART

RECHARTER vb charter again

RECHARTS > RECHART

RECHATE same as > RECHEAT

RECHATES > RECHATE

RECHAUFFE n warmed-up leftover food

RECHEAT n (in a hunt) sounding of the horn to call back the hounds ▷ vb sound the horn to call back the hounds

RECHEATED > RECHEAT

RECHEATS > RECHEAT

RECHECK vb check again

RECHECKED > RECHECK

RECHECKS > RECHECK

RECHERCHE adj refined or elegant

RECHEW vb chew again

RECHEWED > RECHEW

RECHEWING > RECHEW

RECHEWS > RECHEW

RECHIE adj smoky

RECHIP vb put a new chip into (a stolen mobile phone) so it can be reused

RECHIPPED > RECHIP

RECHIPS > RECHIP

RECHLESSE archaic form of > RECKLESS

RECHOOSE *vb* choose again

RECHOOSES > RECHOOSE

RECHOSE > RECHOOSE

RECHOSEN > RECHOOSE

RECIPE *n* directions for cooking a dish

RECIPES > RECIPE

RECIPIENT *n* person who receives something

RECIRCLE *vb* circle again

RECIRCLED > RECIRCLE

RECIRCLES > RECIRCLE

RECISION *n* act of cancelling or rescinding

RECISIONS > RECISION

RECIT *n* narrative

RECITABLE > RECITE

RECITAL *n* musical performance by a soloist or soloists

RECITALS > RECITAL

RECITE *vb* repeat (a poem, story, etc) aloud to an audience

RECITED > RECITE

RECITER > RECITE

RECITERS > RECITE

RECITES > RECITE

RECITING > RECITE

RECITS > RECIT

RECK *vb* mind or care about (something)

RECKAN *adj* strained, tormented, or twisted ▷ *n* chain or hook for hanging a pot over a fire

RECKANS > RECKAN

RECKED > RECK

RECKING > RECK

RECKLESS *adj* heedless of danger

RECKLING *dialect word for* > RUNT

RECKLINGS > RECKLING

RECKON *vb* consider or think

RECKONED > RECKON

RECKONER *n* any of various devices or tables used to facilitate reckoning, esp a ready reckoner

RECKONERS > RECKONER

RECKONING *n* counting or calculating

RECKONS > RECKON

RECKS > RECK

RECLAD *vb* cover in a different substance

RECLADDED > RECLAD

RECLADS > RECLAD

RECLAIM *vb* regain possession of ▷ *n* act of reclaiming or state of being reclaimed

RECLAIMED > RECLAIM

RECLAIMER > RECLAIM

RECLAIMS > RECLAIM

RECLAME *n* public acclaim or attention

RECLAMES > RECLAME

RECLASP *vb* clasp again

RECLASPED > RECLASP

RECLASPS > RECLASP

RECLEAN *vb* clean again

RECLEANED > RECLEAN

RECLEANS > RECLEAN

RECLIMB *vb* climb again

RECLIMBED > RECLIMB

RECLIMBS > RECLIMB

RECLINATE *adj* (esp of a leaf or stem) naturally curved or bent backwards so that the upper part rests on the ground

RECLINE *vb* rest in a leaning position

RECLINED > RECLINE

RECLINER *n* type of armchair having a back that can be adjusted to slope at various angles and, usually, a leg rest

RECLINERS > RECLINER

RECLINES > RECLINE

RECLINING > RECLINE

RECLOSE *vb* close again

RECLOSED > RECLOSE

RECLOSES > RECLOSE

RECLOSING > RECLOSE

RECLOTHE *vb* clothe again

RECLOTHED > RECLOTHE

RECLOTHES > RECLOTHE

RECLUSE *n* person who avoids other people ▷ *adj* solitary

RECLUSELY > RECLUSE

RECLUSES > RECLUSE

RECLUSION > RECLUSE

RECLUSIVE > RECLUSE

RECLUSORY *n* recluse's dwelling or cell

RECOAL *vb* supply or be supplied with fresh coal

RECOALED > RECOAL

RECOALING > RECOAL

RECOALS > RECOAL

RECOAT *vb* coat again

RECOATED > RECOAT

RECOATING > RECOAT

RECOATS > RECOAT

RECOCK *vb* cock again

RECOCKED > RECOCK

RECOCKING > RECOCK

RECOCKS > RECOCK

RECODE *vb* put into a new code

RECODED > RECODE

RECODES > RECODE

RECODIFY *vb* codify again

RECODING > RECODE

RECOGNISE *same as* > RECOGNIZE

RECOGNIZE *vb* identify as (a person or thing) already known

RECOIL *vb* jerk or spring back ▷ *n* backward jerk

RECOILED > RECOIL

RECOILER > RECOIL

RECOILERS > RECOIL

RECOILING > RECOIL

RECOILS > RECOIL

RECOIN *vb* coin again

RECOINAGE *n* new coinage

RECOINED > RECOIN

RECOINING > RECOIN

RECOINS > RECOIN

RECOLLECT *vb* call back to mind, remember

RECOLLET *n* member of a particular Franciscan order

RECOLLETS > RECOLLET

RECOLOR *same as* > RECOLOUR

RECOLORED > RECOLOR

RECOLORS > RECOLOR

RECOLOUR *vb* give a new colour to

RECOLOURS > RECOLOUR

RECOMB *vb* comb again

RECOMBED > RECOMB

RECOMBINE *vb* join together again

RECOMBING > RECOMB

RECOMBS > RECOMB

RECOMFORT *archaic word for* > COMFORT

RECOMMEND *vb* advise or counsel

RECOMMIT *vb* send (a bill) back to a committee for further consideration

RECOMMITS > RECOMMIT

RECOMPACT *vb* compact again

RECOMPILE *vb* compile again

RECOMPOSE *vb* restore to composure or calmness

RECOMPUTE *vb* compute again

RECON *vb* make a preliminary survey

RECONCILE *vb* harmonize (conflicting beliefs etc)

RECONDITE *adj* difficult to understand

RECONDUCT *vb* conduct again

RECONFER *vb* confer again

RECONFERS > RECONFER

RECONFINE *vb* confine again

RECONFIRM *vb* confirm (an arrangement, agreement, etc) again

RECONNECT *vb* link or be linked together again

RECONNED > RECON

RECONNING > RECON

RECONQUER *vb* conquer again

RECONS > RECON

RECONSIGN *vb* consign again

RECONSOLE *vb* console again

RECONSULT *vb* consult again

RECONTACT *vb* contact again

RECONTOUR *vb* contour again

RECONVENE *vb* gather together again after an interval

RECONVERT *vb* change (something) back to a previous state or form

RECONVEY *vb* convey again

RECONVEYS > RECONVEY

RECONVICT *vb* convict again

RECOOK *vb* cook again

RECOOKED > RECOOK

RECOOKING > RECOOK

RECOOKS > RECOOK

RECOPIED > RECOPY

RECOPIES > RECOPY

RECOPY *vb* copy again

RECOPYING > RECOPY

RECORD *n* document or other thing that preserves information ▷ *vb* put in writing

RECORDED > RECORD

RECORDER *n* person or machine that records, esp a video, cassette, or tape recorder

RECORDERS > RECORDER

RECORDING *n* something, esp music, that has been recorded

RECORDIST *n* person that records

RECORDS > RECORD

RECORK *vb* cork again

RECORKED > RECORK

RECORKING > RECORK

RECORKS > RECORK

RECOUNT *vb* tell in detail

RECOUNTAL > RECOUNT

RECOUNTED > RECOUNT

RECOUNTER *n* narrator of a story

RECOUNTS > RECOUNT

RECOUP *vb* regain or make good (a loss)

RECOUPE *vb* (in law) keep back or withhold

RECOUPED > RECOUP

RECOUPES > RECOUPE

RECOUPING > RECOUP

RECOUPLE *vb* couple again

RECOUPLED > RECOUPLE

RECOUPLES > RECOUPLE

RECOUPS > RECOUP

RECOURE *archaic variant of* > RECOVER

RECOURED > RECOURE

RECOURES > RECOURE

RECOURING > RECOURE

RECOURSE *archaic word for* > RETURN

RECOURSED > RECOURSE

RECOURSES > RECOURSE

RECOVER *vb* become healthy again

RECOVERED > RECOVER

RECOVEREE *n* (in law) person found against in a recovery case

RECOVERER > RECOVER

r

RECOVEROR *n* (in law) person successfully demanding a right in a recovery case

RECOVERS > RECOVER

RECOVERY *n* act of recovering from sickness, a shock, or a setback

RECOWER *archaic variant of* **>** RECOVER

RECOWERED > RECOWER

RECOWERS > RECOWER

RECOYLE *archaic spelling of* **>** RECOIL

RECOYLED > RECOYLE

RECOYLES > RECOYLE

RECOYLING > RECOYLE

RECRATE *vb* crate again

RECRATED > RECRATE

RECRATES > RECRATE

RECRATING > RECRATE

RECREANCE > RECREANT

RECREANCY > RECREANT

RECREANT *n* disloyal or cowardly person ▷ *adj* cowardly

RECREANTS **>** RECREANT

RECREATE *vb* amuse (oneself or someone else)

RECREATED > RECREATE

RECREATES > RECREATE

RECREATOR > RECREATE

RECREMENT *n* any substance, such as bile, that is secreted from a part of the body and later reabsorbed instead of being excreted

RECROSS *vb* move or go across (something) again

RECROSSED > RECROSS

RECROSSES > RECROSS

RECROWN *vb* crown again

RECROWNED > RECROWN

RECROWNS > RECROWN

RECRUIT *vb* enlist (new soldiers, members, etc) ▷ *n* newly enlisted soldier

RECRUITAL *n* act of recruiting

RECRUITED > RECRUIT

RECRUITER > RECRUIT

RECRUITS > RECRUIT

RECS > REC

RECTA > RECTUM

RECTAL *adj* of the rectum

RECTALLY > RECTAL

RECTANGLE *n* oblong four-sided figure with four right angles

RECTI > RECTUS

RECTIFIED > RECTIFY

RECTIFIER *n* electronic device, such as a semiconductor diode or valve, that converts an alternating current to a direct current by suppression or inversion of alternate half cycles

RECTIFIES > RECTIFY

RECTIFY *vb* put right, correct

RECTION *n* (in grammar) the determination of the form of one word by another word

RECTIONS > RECTION

RECTITIC > RECTITIS

RECTITIS *n* inflammation of the rectum

RECTITUDE *n* moral correctness

RECTO *n* right-hand page of a book

RECTOCELE *n* protrusion or herniation of the rectum into the vagina

RECTOR *n* clergyman in charge of a parish

RECTORAL *adj* of or relating to God's rule or to a rector

RECTORATE > RECTOR

RECTORESS *n* female rector or the wife or widow of a rector

RECTORIAL *adj* of or relating to a rector ▷ *n* election of a rector

RECTORIES > RECTORY

RECTORS > RECTOR

RECTORY *n* rector's house

RECTOS > RECTO

RECTRESS *same as* **>** RECTORESS

RECTRICES > RECTRIX

RECTRIX *n* any of the large stiff feathers of a bird's tail

RECTUM *n* final section of the large intestine

RECTUMS > RECTUM

RECTUS *n* straight muscle

RECUILE *archaic variant of* **>** RECOIL

RECUILED > RECUILE

RECUILES > RECUILE

RECUILING > RECUILE

RECULE *archaic variant of* **>** RECOIL

RECULED > RECULE

RECULES > RECULE

RECULING > RECULE

RECUMBENT *adj* lying down

RECUR *vb* happen again

RECURE *vb* archaic word for cure or recover

RECURED > RECURE

RECURES > RECURE

RECURING > RECURE

RECURRED > RECUR

RECURRENT *adj* happening or tending to happen again or repeatedly

RECURRING > RECUR

RECURS > RECUR

RECURSION *n* act or process of returning or running back

RECURSIVE **>** RECURSION

RECURVATE *adj* bent back

RECURVE *vb* curve or bend (something) back or down

RECURVED > RECURVE

RECURVES > RECURVE

RECURVING > RECURVE

RECUSAL *n* withdrawal of a judge from a case

RECUSALS > RECUSAL

RECUSANCE > RECUSANT

RECUSANCY > RECUSANT

RECUSANT *n* Roman Catholic who did not attend the services of the Church of England ▷ *adj* (formerly, of Catholics) refusing to attend services of the Church of England

RECUSANTS > RECUSANT

RECUSE *vb* (in law) object to or withdraw (a judge)

RECUSED > RECUSE

RECUSES > RECUSE

RECUSING > RECUSE

RECUT *vb* cut again

RECUTS > RECUT

RECUTTING > RECUT

RECYCLATE *n* recyclable material

RECYCLE *vb* reprocess (used materials) for further use ▷ *n* repetition of a fixed sequence of events

RECYCLED > RECYCLE

RECYCLER > RECYCLE

RECYCLERS > RECYCLE

RECYCLES > RECYCLE

RECYCLING *n* act of recycling

RECYCLIST > RECYCLE

RED *adj* of a colour varying from crimson to orange and seen in blood, fire, etc ▷ *n* red colour

REDACT *vb* compose or draft (an edict, proclamation, etc)

REDACTED > REDACT

REDACTING > REDACT

REDACTION > REDACT

REDACTOR > REDACT

REDACTORS > REDACT

REDACTS > REDACT

REDAMAGE *vb* damage again

REDAMAGED > REDAMAGE

REDAMAGES > REDAMAGE

REDAN *n* fortification of two parapets at a salient angle

REDANS > REDAN

REDARGUE *vb* archaic word for disprove or refute

REDARGUED > REDARGUE

REDARGUES > REDARGUE

REDATE *vb* change date of

REDATED > REDATE

REDATES > REDATE

REDATING > REDATE

REDBACK *n* small venomous Australian spider

REDBACKS > REDBACK

REDBAIT *vb* harass those with leftwing leanings

REDBAITED > REDBAIT

REDBAITER *n* person who deliberately antagonizes communists

REDBAITS > REDBAIT

REDBAY *n* type of tree

REDBAYS > REDBAY

REDBELLY *n* any of various animals having red underparts, especially the char or the redbelly turtle

REDBIRD *n* type of bird, the male of which has bright red plumage

REDBIRDS > REDBIRD

REDBONE *n* type of American dog

REDBONES > REDBONE

REDBREAST *n* robin

REDBRICK *adj* (of a university in Britain) founded in the late 19th or early 20th century ▷ *n* denoting, relating to, or characteristic of a provincial British university of relatively recent foundation, esp as distinguished from Oxford and Cambridge

REDBRICKS > REDBRICK

REDBUD *n* American tree with heart-shaped leaves

REDBUDS > REDBUD

REDBUG *another name for* **>** CHIGGER

REDBUGS > REDBUG

REDCAP *n* military policeman

REDCAPS > REDCAP

REDCOAT *n* British soldier

REDCOATS > REDCOAT

REDD *vb* bring order to ▷ *n* act or an instance of redding

REDDED > REDD

REDDEN *vb* make or become red

REDDENDA > REDDENDUM

REDDENDO *n* (in Scotland) legal clause specifying what payment or duties are required in exchange for something

REDDENDOS > REDDENDO

REDDENDUM *n* legal clause specifying what shall be given in return for the granting of a lease

REDDENED > REDDEN

REDDENING > REDDEN

REDDENS > REDDEN

REDDER > REDD

REDDERS > REDD

REDDEST > RED

REDDIER > REDDY

REDDIEST > REDDY

REDDING > REDD

REDDINGS > REDD

REDDISH *adj* somewhat red

REDDISHLY > REDDISH

REDDLE *same as* **>** RUDDLE

REDDLED > REDDLE

REDDLEMAN same as
> RUDDLEMAN
REDDLEMEN
> REDDLEMAN
REDDLES > REDDLE
REDDLING > REDDLE
REDDS > REDD
REDDY adj reddish
REDE n advice or counsel
▷ vb advise
REDEAL vb deal again
REDEALING > REDEAL
REDEALS > REDEAL
REDEALT > REDEAL
REDEAR n variety of
sunfish with a red flash
above the gills
REDEARS > REDEAR
REDECIDE vb decide
again
REDECIDED > REDECIDE
REDECIDES > REDECIDE
REDECRAFT n logic
REDED > REDE
REDEEM vb make up for
REDEEMED > REDEEM
REDEEMER > REDEEM
REDEEMERS > REDEEM
REDEEMING adj making
up for faults or deficiencies
REDEEMS > REDEEM
REDEFEAT vb defeat
again
REDEFEATS > REDEFEAT
REDEFECT vb defect back
or again
REDEFECTS > REDEFECT
REDEFIED > REDEFY
REDEFIES > REDEFY
REDEFINE vb define
(something) again or
differently
REDEFINED > REDEFINE
REDEFINES > REDEFINE
REDEFY vb defy again
REDEFYING > REDEFY
REDELESS > REDE
REDELIVER vb deliver
again
REDEMAND vb demand
again
REDEMANDS > REDEMAND
REDENIED > REDENY
REDENIES > REDENY
REDENY vb deny again
REDENYING > REDENY
REDEPLOY vb assign to a
new position or task
REDEPLOYS > REDEPLOY
REDEPOSIT vb deposit
again
REDES > REDE
REDESCEND vb descend
again
REDESIGN vb change the
design of (something)
▷ n something that has
been redesigned
REDESIGNS > REDESIGN
REDEVELOP vb rebuild or
renovate (an area or
building)
REDEYE n inferior whiskey

REDEYES > REDEYE
REDFIN n any of various
small fishes with reddish
fins that are popular
aquarium fishes
REDFINS > REDFIN
REDFISH n male salmon
that has recently
spawned
REDFISHES > REDFISH
REDFOOT n fatal disease of
newborn lambs
REDFOOTS > REDFOOT
REDHANDED adj in the act
of doing something
criminal, wrong, or
shameful
REDHEAD n person with
reddish hair
REDHEADED, > REDHEAD
REDHEADS > REDHEAD
REDHORSE n type of fish
REDHORSES > REDHORSE
REDIA n parasitic larva of
flukes
REDIAE > REDIA
REDIAL vb dial (a
telephone number) again
REDIALED > REDIAL
REDIALING > REDIAL
REDIALLED > REDIAL
REDIALS > REDIAL
REDIAS > REDIA
REDICTATE vb dictate
again
REDID > REDO
REDIGEST vb digest again
REDIGESTS > REDIGEST
REDIGRESS vb digress
again
REDING > REDE
REDINGOTE n woman's
coat with a close-fitting
top and a full skirt
REDIP vb dip again
REDIPPED > REDIP
REDIPPING > REDIP
REDIPS > REDIP
REDIPT archaic past form of
> REDIP
REDIRECT vb send in a
new direction or course
REDIRECTS > REDIRECT
REDISCUSS vb discuss
again
REDISPLAY vb display
again
REDISPOSE vb dispose
again
REDISTIL vb distil again
REDISTILL US spelling of
> REDISTIL
REDISTILS > REDISTIL
REDIVIDE vb divide again
REDIVIDED > REDIVIDE
REDIVIDES > REDIVIDE
REDIVIVUS adj returned
to life
REDIVORCE vb divorce
again
REDLEG n derogatory
term for poor White
REDLEGS > REDLEG

REDLINE vb refuse a loan
to (a person or country)
because of the presumed
risks involved
REDLINED > REDLINE
REDLINER > REDLINE
REDLINERS > REDLINE
REDLINES > REDLINE
REDLINING > REDLINE
REDLY > RED
REDNECK n (in the
southwestern US)
derogatory term for a poor
uneducated White farm
worker ▷ adj reactionary
and bigoted
REDNECKED adj with a red
neck
REDNECKS > REDNECK
REDNESS > RED
REDNESSES > RED
REDO vb do over again in
order to improve ▷ n
instance of redoing
something
REDOCK vb dock again
REDOCKED > REDOCK
REDOCKING > REDOCK
REDOCKS > REDOCK
REDOES > REDO
REDOING > REDO
REDOLENCE > REDOLENT
REDOLENCY > REDOLENT
REDOLENT adj
reminiscent (of)
REDON vb don again
REDONE > REDO
REDONNED > REDON
REDONNING > REDON
REDONS > REDON
REDOS > REDO
REDOUBLE vb increase,
multiply, or intensify
▷ n act of redoubling
REDOUBLED > REDOUBLE
REDOUBLER > REDOUBLE
REDOUBLES > REDOUBLE
REDOUBT n small fort
defending a hilltop or pass
▷ vb fear
REDOUBTED > REDOUBT
REDOUBTS > REDOUBT
REDOUND vb cause
advantage or
disadvantage (to)
REDOUNDED > REDOUND
REDOUNDS > REDOUND
REDOUT n reddened vision
caused by a rush of blood
to the head
REDOUTS > REDOUT
REDOWA n Bohemian folk
dance similar to the waltz
REDOWAS > REDOWA
REDOX n chemical reaction
in which one substance is
reduced and the other is
oxidized
REDOXES > REDOX
REDPOLL n mostly
grey-brown finch with a
red crown and pink
breast
REDPOLLS > REDPOLL

REDRAFT vb write a
second copy of (a letter,
proposal, essay, etc)
▷ n second draft
REDRAFTED > REDRAFT
REDRAFTS > REDRAFT
REDRAW vb draw or draw
up (something) again or
differently
REDRAWER > REDRAW
REDRAWERS > REDRAW
REDRAWING > REDRAW
REDRAWN > REDRAW
REDRAWS > REDRAW
REDREAM vb dream again
REDREAMED > REDREAM
REDREAMS > REDREAM
REDREAMT > REDREAM
REDRESS vb make
amends for ▷ n
compensation or amends
REDRESSAL n act of
redressing
REDRESSED > REDRESS
REDRESSER > REDRESS
REDRESSES > REDRESS
REDRESSOR > REDRESS
REDREW > REDRAW
REDRIED > REDRY
REDRIES > REDRY
REDRILL vb drill again
REDRILLED > REDRILL
REDRILLS > REDRILL
REDRIVE vb drive again
REDRIVEN > REDRIVE
REDRIVES > REDRIVE
REDRIVING > REDRIVE
REDROOT n yellow-
flowered bog plant whose
roots yield a red dye
REDROOTS > REDROOT
REDROVE > REDRIVE
REDRY vb dry again
REDRYING > REDRY
REDS > RED
REDSEAR same as
> REDSHORT
REDSHANK n large
Eurasian sandpiper with
red legs
REDSHANKS > REDSHANK
REDSHARE n red algae
REDSHIFT n shift in the
lines of the spectrum of an
astronomical object
REDSHIFTS > REDSHIFT
REDSHIRE same as
> REDSHARE
REDSHIRT vb take a year
out of a sports team
REDSHIRTS > REDSHIRT
REDSHORT vb become
brittle at red-hot
temperatures
REDSKIN n offensive term
for Native American
REDSKINS > REDSKIN
REDSTART n European
bird of the thrush family,
the male of which has an
orange-brown tail and
breast
REDSTARTS > REDSTART

REDSTREAK n variety of apple

REDTAIL n variety of bird with red colouring on its tail

REDTAILS > REDTAIL

REDTOP n sensationalist tabloid newspaper

REDTOPS > REDTOP

REDUB vb fix or repair

REDUBBED > REDUB

REDUBBING > REDUB

REDUBS > REDUB

REDUCE vb bring down, lower

REDUCED > REDUCE

REDUCER n chemical solution used to lessen the density of a negative or print

REDUCERS > REDUCER

REDUCES > REDUCE

REDUCIBLE > REDUCE

REDUCIBLY > REDUCE

REDUCING > REDUCE

REDUCTANT n reducing agent

REDUCTASE n any enzyme that catalyses a biochemical reduction reaction

REDUCTION n act of reducing

REDUCTIVE n relating to chemical reduction

REDUCTOR n apparatus in which substances can be reduced

REDUCTORS > REDUCTOR

REDUIT n fortified part from which a garrison may fight on once an enemy has taken outworks

REDUITS > REDUIT

REDUNDANT adj (of a worker) no longer needed

REDUVIID n type of bug of the family which includes the assassin bug and the wheel bug

REDUVIIDS > REDUVIID

REDUX adj brought back or returned

REDWARE another name for > KELP

REDWARES > REDWARE

REDWATER n tick-borne disease of cattle

REDWATERS > REDWATER

REDWING n small European thrush

REDWINGS > REDWING

REDWOOD n giant Californian conifer with reddish bark

REDWOODS > REDWOOD

REDYE vb dye again

REDYED > REDYE

REDYEING > REDYE

REDYES > REDYE

REE n Scots word for walled enclosure

REEARN vb earn again

REEARNED > REEARN

REEARNING > REEARN

REEARNS > REEARN

REEBOK same as > RHEBOK

REEBOKS > REEBOK

REECH vb (in dialect) smoke

REECHED > REECH

REECHES > REECH

REECHIE same as > REECHY

REECHIER > REECHY

REECHIEST > REECHY

REECHING > REECH

REECHO vb echo again

REECHOED > REECHO

REECHOES > REECHO

REECHOING > REECHO

REECHY adj (in dialect) smoky

REED n tall grass that grows in swamps and shallow water

REEDBED n area of wetland with reeds growing in it

REEDBEDS > REEDBED

REEDBIRD n any of several birds that frequent reed beds, esp (in the US and Canada) the bobolink

REEDBIRDS > REEDBIRD

REEDBUCK n buff-coloured African antelope with inward-curving horns

REEDBUCKS > REEDBUCK

REEDE obsolete variant of > RED

REEDED > REED

REEDEN adj of or consisting of reeds

REEDER n thatcher

REEDERS > REEDER

REEDES > REEDE

REEDIER > REEDY

REEDIEST > REEDY

REEDIFIED > REEDIFY

REEDIFIES > REEDIFY

REEDIFY vb edify again or rebuild

REEDILY > REEDY

REEDINESS > REEDY

REEDING n set of small semicircular architectural mouldings

REEDINGS > REEDING

REEDIT vb edit again

REEDITED > REEDIT

REEDITING > REEDIT

REEDITION n new edition

REEDITS > REEDIT

REEDLIKE adj resembling a reed

REEDLING n tawny titlike Eurasian songbird common in reed beds

REEDLINGS > REEDLING

REEDMAN n musician who plays a wind instrument that has a reed

REEDMEN > REEDMAN

REEDS > REED

REEDSTOP n organ stop that controls a rank of reed pipes

REEDSTOPS > REEDSTOP

REEDUCATE vb educate again

REEDY adj harsh and thin in tone

REEF n ridge of rock or coral near the surface of the sea ▷ vb roll up part of a sail

REEFABLE > REEF

REEFED > REEF

REEFER n short thick jacket worn esp by sailors

REEFERS > REEFER

REEFIER > REEFY

REEFIEST > REEFY

REEFING > REEF

REEFINGS > REEF

REEFS > REEF

REEFY adj with reefs

REEJECT vb eject again

REEJECTED > REEJECT

REEJECTS > REEJECT

REEK vb smell strongly ▷ n strong unpleasant smell

REEKED > REEK

REEKER > REEK

REEKERS > REEK

REEKIE same as > REEKY

REEKIER > REEK

REEKIEST > REEK

REEKING > REEK

REEKINGLY > REEK

REEKS > REEK

REEKY adj steamy or smoky

REEL n cylindrical object on which film, tape, thread, or wire is wound ▷ vb stagger, sway, or whirl

REELABLE > REEL

REELECT vb elect again

REELECTED > REELECT

REELECTS > REELECT

REELED > REEL

REELER > REEL

REELERS > REEL

REELEVATE vb elevate again

REELING > REEL

REELINGLY > REEL

REELINGS > REEL

REELMAN n (formerly) member of a beach life-saving team operating a winch

REELMEN > REELMAN

REELS > REEL

REEMBARK vb embark again

REEMBARKS > REEMBARK

REEMBODY vb embody again

REEMBRACE vb embrace again

REEMERGE vb emerge again

REEMERGED > REEMERGE

REEMERGES > REEMERGE

REEMIT vb emit again

REEMITS > REEMIT

REEMITTED > REEMIT

REEMPLOY vb employ again

REEMPLOYS > REEMPLOY

REEN n ditch, esp a drainage channel

REENACT vb enact again

REENACTED > REENACT

REENACTOR > REENACT

REENACTS > REENACT

REENDOW vb endow again

REENDOWED > REENDOW

REENDOWS > REENDOW

REENFORCE vb enforce again

REENGAGE vb engage again

REENGAGED > REENGAGE

REENGAGES > REENGAGE

REENGRAVE vb engrave again

REENJOY vb enjoy again

REENJOYED > REENJOY

REENJOYS > REENJOY

REENLARGE vb enlarge again

REENLIST vb enlist again

REENLISTS > REENLIST

REENROLL vb enrol again

REENROLLS > REENROLL

REENS > REEN

REENSLAVE vb enslave again

REENTER vb enter again

REENTERED > REENTER

REENTERS > REENTER

REENTRANT n reentering angle ▷ adj (of an angle) pointing inwards

REENTRIES > REENTRY

REENTRY n return of a spacecraft into the earth's atmosphere

REEQUIP vb equip again

REEQUIPS > REEQUIP

REERECT vb erect again

REERECTED > REERECT

REERECTS > REERECT

REES > REE

REEST vb (esp of horses) to be noisily uncooperative

REESTED > REEST

REESTIER > REESTY

REESTIEST > REESTY

REESTING > REEST

REESTS > REEST

REESTY same as > REASTY

REEVE n local representative of the king in a shire until the early 11th century ▷ vb pass (a rope or cable) through an eye or other narrow opening

REEVED > REEVE

REEVES > REEVE

REEVING > REEVE

REEVOKE vb evoke again

REEVOKED > REEVOKE

REEVOKES > REEVOKE

REEVOKING > REEVOKE
REEXAMINE *vb* examine again
REEXECUTE *vb* execute again
REEXHIBIT *vb* exhibit again
REEXPEL *vb* expel again
REEXPELS > REEXPEL
REEXPLAIN *vb* explain again
REEXPLORE *vb* explore again
REEXPORT *vb* export again
REEXPORTS > REEXPORT
REEXPOSE *vb* expose again
REEXPOSED > REEXPOSE
REEXPOSES > REEXPOSE
REEXPRESS *vb* express again
REF *n* referee in sport ▷ *vb* referee
REFACE *vb* repair or renew the facing of (a wall)
REFACED > REFACE
REFACES > REFACE
REFACING > REFACE
REFALL *vb* fall again
REFALLEN > REFALL
REFALLING > REFALL
REFALLS > REFALL
REFASHION *vb* give a new form to (something)
REFASTEN *vb* fasten again
REFASTENS > REFASTEN
REFECT *vb* archaic word for restore or refresh with food and drink
REFECTED > REFECT
REFECTING > REFECT
REFECTION *n* refreshment with food and drink
REFECTIVE > REFECT
REFECTORY *n* room for meals in a college etc
REFECTS > REFECT
REFED > REFEED
REFEED *vb* feed again
REFEEDING > REFEED
REFEEDS > REFEED
REFEEL *vb* feel again
REFEELING > REFEEL
REFEELS > REFEEL
REFEL *vb* refute
REFELL > REFALL
REFELLED > REFEL
REFELLING > REFEL
REFELS > REFEL
REFELT > REFEEL
REFENCE *vb* fence again
REFENCED > REFENCE
REFENCES > REFENCE
REFENCING > REFENCE
REFER *vb* allude (to)
REFERABLE > REFER
REFEREE *n* umpire in sports, esp soccer or boxing ▷ *vb* act as referee of

REFEREED > REFEREE
REFEREES > REFEREE
REFERENCE *n* act of referring
REFERENDA *pl n* polls to determine the view of the electorate on something; referendums
REFERENT *n* object or idea to which a word or phrase refers
REFERENTS > REFERENT
REFERRAL > REFER
REFERRALS > REFER
REFERRED > REFER
REFERRER > REFER
REFERRERS > REFER
REFERRING > REFER
REFERS > REFER
REFFED > REF
REFFING *n* act or instance of refereeing a sports match
REFFINGS > REFFING
REFFO *n* offensive name for a European refugee after World War II
REFFOS > REFFO
REFI *n* refinancing of a debt
REFIGHT *vb* fight again ▷ *n* second or new fight
REFIGHTS > REFIGHT
REFIGURE *vb* figure again
REFIGURED > REFIGURE
REFIGURES > REFIGURE
REFILE *vb* file again
REFILED > REFILE
REFILES > REFILE
REFILING > REFILE
REFILL *vb* fill again ▷ *n* second or subsequent filling
REFILLED > REFILL
REFILLING > REFILL
REFILLS > REFILL
REFILM *vb* film again
REFILMED > REFILM
REFILMING > REFILM
REFILMS > REFILM
REFILTER *vb* filter again
REFILTERS > REFILTER
REFINABLE > REFINE
REFINANCE *vb* finance again
REFIND *vb* find again
REFINDING > REFIND
REFINDS > REFIND
REFINE *vb* purify
REFINED *adj* cultured or polite
REFINEDLY > REFINED
REFINER *n* person, device, or substance that removes impurities, etc
REFINERS > REFINER
REFINERY *n* place where sugar, oil, etc is refined
REFINES > REFINE
REFINING > REFINE
REFININGS > REFINE
REFINISH *vb* finish again
REFIRE *vb* fire again

REFIRED > REFIRE
REFIRES > REFIRE
REFIRING > REFIRE
REFIS > REFI
REFIT *vb* make ready for use again by repairing or re-equipping ▷ *n* repair or re-equipping for further use
REFITMENT > REFIT
REFITS > REFIT
REFITTED > REFIT
REFITTING > REFIT
REFIX *vb* fix again
REFIXED > REFIX
REFIXES > REFIX
REFIXING > REFIX
REFLAG *vb* flag again
REFLAGGED > REFLAG
REFLAGS > REFLAG
REFLATE *vb* inflate or be inflated again
REFLATED > REFLATE
REFLATES > REFLATE
**REFLATING
>** REFLATE
REFLATION *n* increase in the supply of money and credit designed to encourage economic activity
REFLECT *vb* throw back, esp rays of light, heat, etc
REFLECTED > REFLECT
REFLECTER *n* archaic word for a critic
REFLECTOR *n* polished surface for reflecting light etc
REFLECTS > REFLECT
REFLET *n* iridescent glow or lustre, as on ceramic ware
REFLETS > REFLET
REFLEW > REFLY
REFLEX *n* involuntary response to a stimulus or situation ▷ *adj* (of a muscular action) involuntary ▷ *vb* bend, turn, or reflect backwards
REFLEXED > REFLEX
REFLEXES > REFLEX
REFLEXING > REFLEX
REFLEXION *n* act of reflecting or the state of being reflected
REFLEXIVE *adj* denoting a pronoun that refers back to the subject of a sentence or clause ▷ *n* reflexive pronoun or verb
REFLEXLY > REFLEX
REFLIES > REFLY
REFLOAT *vb* float again
REFLOATED > REFLOAT
REFLOATS > REFLOAT
REFLOOD *vb* flood again
REFLOODED > REFLOOD
REFLOODS > REFLOOD
REFLOW *vb* flow again
REFLOWED > REFLOW
REFLOWER *vb* flower again

REFLOWERS > REFLOWER
REFLOWING > REFLOW
REFLOWN > REFLY
REFLOWS > REFLOW
REFLUENCE > REFLUENT
REFLUENT *adj* flowing back
REFLUX *vb* boil in a vessel attached to a condenser, so that the vapour condenses and flows back in ▷ *n* act of refluxing
REFLUXED > REFLUX
REFLUXES > REFLUX
REFLUXING > REFLUX
REFLY *vb* fly again
REFLYING > REFLY
REFOCUS *vb* focus again or anew
REFOCUSED > REFOCUS
REFOCUSES > REFOCUS
REFOLD *vb* fold again
REFOLDED > REFOLD
REFOLDING > REFOLD
REFOLDS > REFOLD
REFOOT *vb* foot again
REFOOTED > REFOOT
REFOOTING > REFOOT
REFOOTS > REFOOT
REFOREST *vb* replant (an area that was formerly forested) with trees
REFORESTS > REFOREST
REFORGE *vb* forge again
REFORGED > REFORGE
REFORGES > REFORGE
REFORGING > REFORGE
REFORM *n* improvement ▷ *vb* improve
REFORMADE *archaic variant of* REFORMADO
REFORMADO *n* formerly, an officer whose men have been disbanded
REFORMAT *vb* format again
REFORMATE *n* gas formed in certain processes
REFORMATS > REFORMAT
REFORMED > REFORM
REFORMER > REFORM
REFORMERS > REFORM
REFORMING > REFORM
REFORMISM *n* doctrine or movement advocating reform, esp political or religious reform, rather than abolition
**REFORMIST
>** REFORMISM
REFORMS > REFORM
REFORTIFY *vb* fortify again or further
REFOUGHT > REFIGHT
REFOUND *vb* found again
REFOUNDED > REFOUND
REFOUNDER > REFOUND
REFOUNDS > REFOUND
REFRACT *vb* change the course of (light etc) passing from one medium to another
REFRACTED > REFRACT

REFRACTOR *n* object or material that refracts
REFRACTS > REFRACT
REFRAIN *n* frequently repeated part of a song ▷ *vb* abstain (from action)
REFRAINED > REFRAIN
REFRAINER > REFRAIN
REFRAINS > REFRAIN
REFRAME *vb* support or enclose (a picture, photograph, etc) in a new or different frame
REFRAMED > REFRAME
REFRAMES > REFRAME
REFRAMING > REFRAME
REFREEZE *vb* freeze or be frozen again after having defrosted
REFREEZES > REFREEZE
REFRESH *vb* revive or reinvigorate, as through food, drink, or rest
REFRESHED > REFRESH
REFRESHEN *vb* freshen again
REFRESHER *n* something that refreshes, such as a cold drink
REFRESHES > REFRESH
REFRIED > REFRY
REFRIES > REFRY
REFRINGE *formerly used to mean* > REFRACT
REFRINGED > REFRINGE
REFRINGES > REFRINGE
REFRONT *vb* put a new front on
REFRONTED > REFRONT
REFRONTS > REFRONT
REFROZE > REFREEZE
REFROZEN > REFREEZE
REFRY *vb* fry again
REFRYING > REFRY
REFS > REF
REFT > REAVE
REFUEL *vb* supply or be supplied with fresh fuel
REFUELED > REFUEL
REFUELING *n* act of refueling
REFUELLED > REFUEL
REFUELS > REFUEL
REFUGE *n* (source of) shelter or protection ▷ *vb* take refuge or give refuge to
REFUGED > REFUGE
REFUGEE *n* person who seeks refuge, esp in a foreign country
REFUGEES > REFUGEE
REFUGES > REFUGE
REFUGIA > REFUGIUM
REFUGING > REFUGE
REFUGIUM *n* geographical region that has remained unaltered by a climatic change affecting surrounding regions and that therefore forms a haven for relict fauna and flora

REFULGENT *adj* shining, radiant
REFUND *vb* pay back ▷ *n* return of money
REFUNDED > REFUND
REFUNDER > REFUND
REFUNDERS > REFUND
REFUNDING > REFUND
REFUNDS > REFUND
REFURB *vb* refurbish ▷ *n* (act or instance of) refurbishment
REFURBED > REFURB
REFURBING > REFURB
REFURBISH *vb* renovate and brighten up
REFURBS > REFURB
REFURNISH *vb* furnish again
REFUSABLE > REFUSE
REFUSAL *n* denial of anything demanded or offered
REFUSALS > REFUSAL
REFUSE *vb* decline, deny, or reject ▷ *n* rubbish or useless matter
REFUSED > REFUSE
REFUSENIK *n* person who refuses to obey a law or cooperate with the government because of strong beliefs
REFUSER > REFUSE
REFUSERS > REFUSE
REFUSES > REFUSE
REFUSING > REFUSE
REFUSION *n* new or further fusion
REFUSIONS > REFUSION
REFUSNIK *same as* > REFUSENIK
REFUSNIKS > REFUSNIK
REFUTABLE > REFUTE
REFUTABLY > REFUTE
REFUTAL *n* act or process of refuting
REFUTALS > REFUTAL
REFUTE *vb* disprove
REFUTED > REFUTE
REFUTER > REFUTE
REFUTERS > REFUTE
REFUTES > REFUTE
REFUTING > REFUTE
REG *n* large expanse of stony desert terrain
REGAIN *vb* get back or recover ▷ *n* process of getting something back, esp lost weight
REGAINED > REGAIN
REGAINER > REGAIN
REGAINERS > REGAIN
REGAINING > REGAIN
REGAINS > REGAIN
REGAL *adj* of or like a king or queen ▷ *n* portable organ equipped only with small reed pipes
REGALE *vb* entertain (someone) with stories etc ▷ *n* feast
REGALED > REGALE
REGALER > REGALE

REGALERS > REGALE
REGALES > REGALE
REGALIA *pl n* ceremonial emblems of royalty or high office
REGALIAN *adj* royal
REGALIAS > REGALIA
REGALING > REGALE
REGALISM *n* principle that the sovereign has supremacy in church affairs
REGALISMS > REGALISM
REGALIST > REGALISM
REGALISTS > REGALISM
REGALITY *n* state or condition of being royal
REGALLY > REGAL
REGALNESS > REGAL
REGALS > REGAL
REGAR *same as* > REGUR
REGARD *vb* consider ▷ *n* respect or esteem
REGARDANT *adj* (of a beast) shown looking backwards over its shoulder
REGARDED > REGARD
REGARDER > REGARD
REGARDERS > REGARD
REGARDFUL *adj* showing regard (for)
REGARDING *prep* on the subject of
REGARDS > REGARD
REGARS > REGAR
REGATHER *vb* gather again
REGATHERS > REGATHER
REGATTA *n* meeting for yacht or boat races
REGATTAS > REGATTA
REGAUGE *vb* gauge again
REGAUGED > REGAUGE
REGAUGES > REGAUGE
REGAUGING > REGAUGE
REGAVE > REGIVE
REGEAR *vb* readjust
REGEARED > REGEAR
REGEARING > REGEAR
REGEARS > REGEAR
REGELATE *vb* undergo or cause to undergo regelation
REGELATED > REGELATE
REGELATES > REGELATE
REGENCE *old variant of* > REGENCY
REGENCES > REGENCE
REGENCIES > REGENCY
REGENCY *n* status or period of office of a regent
REGENT *n* ruler of a kingdom during the absence, childhood, or illness of its monarch ▷ *adj* ruling as a regent
REGENTAL > REGENT
REGENTS > REGENT
REGES > REX
REGEST *n* archaic word for register ▷ *vb* register
REGESTED > REGEST

REGESTING > REGEST
REGESTS > REGEST
REGGAE *n* style of Jamaican popular music with a strong beat
REGGAES > REGGAE
REGGAETON *n* popular music genre from Puerto Rico
REGGO *same as* > REGO
REGGOS > REGGO
REGICIDAL > REGICIDE
REGICIDE *n* killing of a king
REGICIDES > REGICIDE
REGIE *n* government-directed management or government monopoly
REGIES > REGIE
REGIFT *vb* give (a previously received gift) to someone else
REGIFTED > REGIFT
REGIFTER *n* person who regifts something
REGIFTERS > REGIFTER
REGIFTING > REGIFT
REGIFTS > REGIFT
REGILD *vb* gild again
REGILDED > REGILD
REGILDING > REGILD
REGILDS > REGILD
REGILT *archaic past form of* > REGILD
REGIME *n* system of government
REGIMEN *n* prescribed system of diet etc
REGIMENS > REGIMEN
REGIMENT *n* organized body of troops as a unit of the army ▷ *vb* force discipline or order on, esp in a domineering manner
REGIMENTS > REGIMENT
REGIMES > REGIME
REGIMINAL *adj* regimen-related
REGINA *n* queen
REGINAE > REGINA
REGINAL *adj* queenly
REGINAS > REGINA
REGION *n* administrative division of a country
REGIONAL *adj* of, characteristic of, or limited to a region ▷ *n* regional heat of a competition
REGIONALS > REGIONAL
REGIONARY *same as* > REGIONAL
REGIONS > REGION
REGISSEUR *n* official in a dance company with varying duties, usually including directing productions
REGISTER *n* (book containing) an official list or record of things ▷ *vb* enter in a register or set down in writing
REGISTERS > REGISTER

REGISTRAR n keeper of official records
REGISTRY n place where official records are kept
REGIUS adj as in regius professor Crown-appointed holder of a university chair
REGIVE vb give again or back
REGIVEN > REGIVE
REGIVES > REGIVE
REGIVING > REGIVE
REGLAZE vb glaze again
REGLAZED > REGLAZE
REGLAZES > REGLAZE
REGLAZING > REGLAZE
REGLET n flat narrow architectural moulding
REGLETS > REGLET
REGLORIFY vb glorify again
REGLOSS vb gloss again or give a new gloss to
REGLOSSED > REGLOSS
REGLOSSES > REGLOSS
REGLOW vb glow again
REGLOWED > REGLOW
REGLOWING > REGLOW
REGLOWS > REGLOW
REGLUE vb glue again
REGLUED > REGLUE
REGLUES > REGLUE
REGLUING > REGLUE
REGMA n type of fruit with cells that break open and break away when ripe
REGMAKER n drink taken to relieve the symptoms of a hangover
REGMAKERS > REGMAKER
REGMATA > REGMA
REGNA > REGNUM
REGNAL adj of a sovereign, reign, or kingdom
REGNANCY > REGNANT
REGNANT adj reigning
REGNUM n reign or rule
REGO n registration of a motor vehicle
REGOLITH n layer of loose material covering the bedrock of the earth and moon, etc, comprising soil, sand, rock fragments, volcanic ash, glacial drift, etc
REGOLITHS > REGOLITH
REGORGE vb vomit up
REGORGED > REGORGE
REGORGES > REGORGE
REGORGING > REGORGE
REGOS > REGO
REGOSOL n type of azonal soil
REGOSOLS > REGOSOL
REGRADE vb grade again
REGRADED > REGRADE
REGRADES > REGRADE
REGRADING > REGRADE
REGRAFT vb graft again
REGRAFTED > REGRAFT
REGRAFTS > REGRAFT
REGRANT vb grant again

REGRANTED > REGRANT
REGRANTS > REGRANT
REGRATE vb buy up (commodities) in advance so as to raise their price for resale
REGRATED > REGRATE
REGRATER > REGRATE
REGRATERS > REGRATE
REGRATES > REGRATE
REGRATING > REGRATE
REGRATOR > REGRATE
REGRATORS > REGRATE
REGREDE vb go back
REGREDED > REGREDE
REGREDES > REGREDE
REGREDING > REGREDE
REGREEN vb green again
REGREENED > REGREEN
REGREENS > REGREEN
REGREET vb greet again or return greetings of
REGREETED > REGREET
REGREETS > REGREET
REGRESS vb revert to a former worse condition ▷ n return to a former and worse condition
REGRESSED > REGRESS
REGRESSES > REGRESS
REGRESSOR > REGRESS
REGRET vb feel sorry about ▷ n feeling of repentance, guilt, or sorrow
REGRETFUL > REGRET
REGRETS > REGRET
REGRETTED > REGRET
REGRETTER > REGRET
REGREW > REGROW
REGRIND vb grind again
REGRINDS > REGRIND
REGROOM vb groom again
REGROOMED > REGROOM
REGROOMS > REGROOM
REGROOVE vb groove again
REGROOVED > REGROOVE
REGROOVES > REGROOVE
REGROUND > REGRIND
REGROUP vb reorganize (military forces) after an attack or a defeat
REGROUPED > REGROUP
REGROUPS > REGROUP
REGROW vb grow or be grown again after having been cut or having died or withered
REGROWING > REGROW
REGROWN > REGROW
REGROWS > REGROW
REGROWTH n growing back of hair, plants, etc
REGROWTHS > REGROWTH
REGS > REG
REGUERDON vb reward
REGULA n rule
REGULABLE adj able to be regulated
REGULAE > REGULA
REGULAR adj normal, customary, or usual ▷ n regular soldier

REGULARLY > REGULAR
REGULARS > REGULAR
REGULATE vb control, esp by rules
REGULATED > REGULATE
REGULATES > REGULATE
REGULATOR n device that automatically controls pressure, temperature, etc
REGULI > REGULUS
REGULINE > REGULUS
REGULISE variant spelling of > REGULIZE
REGULISED > REGULISE
REGULISES > REGULISE
REGULIZE vb turn into regulus
REGULIZED > REGULIZE
REGULIZES > REGULIZE
REGULO n any of a number of temperatures to which a gas oven may be set
REGULOS > REGULO
REGULUS n impure metal forming beneath the slag during the smelting of ores
REGULUSES > REGULUS
REGUR n black loamy Indian soil
REGURS > REGUR
REH n (in India) salty surface crust on the soil
REHAB vb help (a person) to readapt to society or a new job ▷ n treatment or help given to an addict, etc
REHABBED > REHAB
REHABBER > REHAB
REHABBERS > REHAB
REHABBING > REHAB
REHABS > REHAB
REHAMMER vb hammer again
REHAMMERS > REHAMMER
REHANDLE vb handle again
REHANDLED > REHANDLE
REHANDLES > REHANDLE
REHANG vb hang again
REHANGED > REHANG
REHANGING > REHANG
REHANGS > REHANG
REHARDEN vb harden again
REHARDENS > REHARDEN
REHASH vb rework or reuse ▷ n old ideas presented in a new form
REHASHED > REHASH
REHASHES > REHASH
REHASHING > REHASH
REHEAR vb hear again
REHEARD > REHEAR
REHEARING > REHEAR
REHEARS > REHEAR
REHEARSAL n preparatory practice session
REHEARSE vb practise (a play, concert, etc)
REHEARSED > REHEARSE
REHEARSER > REHEARSE
REHEARSES > REHEARSE

REHEAT vb heat or be heated again
REHEATED > REHEAT
REHEATER > REHEAT
REHEATERS > REHEAT
REHEATING > REHEAT
REHEATS > REHEAT
REHEEL vb put a new heel or new heels on
REHEELED > REHEEL
REHEELING > REHEEL
REHEELS > REHEEL
REHEM vb hem again
REHEMMED > REHEM
REHEMMING > REHEM
REHEMS > REHEM
REHINGE vb put a new hinge or new hinges on
REHINGED > REHINGE
REHINGES > REHINGE
REHINGING > REHINGE
REHIRE vb hire again
REHIRED > REHIRE
REHIRES > REHIRE
REHIRING > REHIRE
REHOBOAM n wine bottle holding the equivalent of six normal bottles (approximately 156 ounces)
REHOBOAMS > REHOBOAM
REHOME vb find a new home for (esp a pet)
REHOMED > REHOME
REHOMES > REHOME
REHOMING n act of rehoming
REHOMINGS > REHOMING
REHOUSE vb provide with a new (and better) home
REHOUSED > REHOUSE
REHOUSES > REHOUSE
REHOUSING > REHOUSE
REHS > REH
REHUNG > REHANG
REHYDRATE vb hydrate again
REI n name for a former Portuguese coin
REIF n Scots word meaning robbery or plunder
REIFIED > REIFY
REIFIER > REIFY
REIFIERS > REIFY
REIFIES > REIFY
REIFS > REIF
REIFY vb consider or make (an abstract idea or concept) real or concrete
REIFYING > REIFY
REIGN n period of a sovereign's rule ▷ vb rule (a country)
REIGNED > REIGN
REIGNING > REIGN
REIGNITE vb catch fire or cause to catch fire again
REIGNITED > REIGNITE
REIGNITES > REIGNITE
REIGNS > REIGN
REIK Scots word for > SMOKE

REIKI n form of therapy to encourage healing or restore wellbeing
REIKIS > REIKI
REIKS > REIK
REILLUME vb relight
REILLUMED > REILLUME
REILLUMES > REILLUME
REIMAGE vb image again
REIMAGED > REIMAGE
REIMAGES > REIMAGE
REIMAGINE vb imagine again
REIMAGING > REIMAGE
REIMBURSE vb refund, pay back
REIMMERSE vb immerse again
REIMPLANT vb implant again
REIMPORT vb import (goods manufactured from exported raw materials) ▷ n act of reimporting
REIMPORTS > REIMPORT
REIMPOSE vb establish previously imposed laws, controls, etc, again
REIMPOSED > REIMPOSE
REIMPOSES > REIMPOSE
REIN vb check or manage with reins
REINCITE vb incite again
REINCITED > REINCITE
REINCITES > REINCITE
REINCUR vb incur again
REINCURS > REINCUR
REINDEER n deer of arctic regions with large branched antlers
REINDEERS > REINDEER
REINDEX vb index again
REINDEXED > REINDEX
REINDEXES > REINDEX
REINDICT vb indict again
REINDICTS > REINDICT
REINDUCE vb induce again
REINDUCED > REINDUCE
REINDUCES > REINDUCE
REINDUCT vb induct again
REINDUCTS > REINDUCT
REINED > REIN
REINETTE n variety of apple
REINETTES > REINETTE
REINFECT vb infect or contaminate again
REINFECTS > REINFECT
REINFLAME vb inflame again
REINFLATE vb inflate again
REINFORCE vb give added emphasis to
REINFORM vb inform again
REINFORMS > REINFORM
REINFUND vb archaic word for pour in again
REINFUNDS > REINFUND

REINFUSE vb infuse again
REINFUSED > REINFUSE
REINFUSES > REINFUSE
REINHABIT vb inhabit again
REINING > REIN
REINJECT vb inject again
REINJECTS > REINJECT
REINJURE vb injure again
REINJURED > REINJURE
REINJURES > REINJURE
REINJURY n further injury
REINK vb ink again
REINKED > REINK
REINKING > REINK
REINKS > REINK
REINLESS > REIN
REINS pl n narrow straps attached to a bit to guide a horse
REINSERT vb insert again
REINSERTS > REINSERT
REINSMAN n driver in a trotting race
REINSMEN > REINSMAN
REINSPECT vb inspect again
REINSPIRE vb inspire again
REINSTAL same as > REINSTALL
REINSTALL vb put in place and connect (machinery, equipment, etc) again
REINSTALS > REINSTAL
REINSTATE vb restore to a former position
REINSURE vb insure again
REINSURED > REINSURE
REINSURER > REINSURE
REINSURES > REINSURE
REINTER vb inter again
REINTERS > REINTER
REINVADE vb invade again
REINVADED > REINVADE
REINVADES > REINVADE
REINVENT vb replace (a product, etc) with an entirely new version
REINVENTS > REINVENT
REINVEST vb put back profits from a previous investment into the same enterprise
REINVESTS > REINVEST
REINVITE vb invite again
REINVITED > REINVITE
REINVITES > REINVITE
REINVOKE vb invoke again
REINVOKED > REINVOKE
REINVOKES > REINVOKE
REINVOLVE vb involve again
REIRD Scots word for > DIN
REIRDS > REIRD
REIS > REI
REISES > REI

REISHI n type of mushroom with a shiny cap
REISHIS > REISHI
REISSUE n book, record, etc, that is released again after being unavailable ▷ vb release (a book, record, etc) again after a period of unavailability
REISSUED > REISSUE
REISSUER > REISSUE
REISSUERS > REISSUE
REISSUES > REISSUE
REISSUING > REISSUE
REIST same as > REEST
REISTAFEL same as > RIJSTAFEL
REISTED > REIST
REISTING > REIST
REISTS > REIST
REITBOK same as > REEDBUCK
REITBOKS > REITBOK
REITER n soldier in the German cavalry ▷ vb repeat something
REITERANT > REITERATE
REITERATE vb repeat again and again
REITERED > REITER
REITERING > REITER
REITERS > REITER
REIVE vb go on a plundering raid
REIVED > REIVE
REIVER > REIVE
REIVERS > REIVE
REIVES > REIVE
REIVING n act of going on a plundering raid
REIVINGS > REIVING
REJACKET n put a new jacket on
REJACKETS > REJACKET
REJECT vb refuse to accept or believe ▷ n person or thing rejected as not up to standard
REJECTED > REJECT
REJECTEE n someone who has been rejected
REJECTEES > REJECTEE
REJECTER > REJECT
REJECTERS > REJECT
REJECTING > REJECT
REJECTION > REJECT
REJECTIVE > REJECT
REJECTOR > REJECT
REJECTORS > REJECT
REJECTS > REJECT
REJIG vb re-equip (a factory or plant) ▷ n act or process of rejigging
REJIGGED > REJIG
REJIGGER > REJIG
REJIGGERS > REJIG
REJIGGING > REJIG
REJIGS > REJIG
REJOICE vb feel or express great happiness

REJOICED > REJOICE
REJOICER > REJOICE
REJOICERS > REJOICE
REJOICES > REJOICE
REJOICING > REJOICE
REJOIN vb join again
REJOINDER n answer, retort
REJOINED > REJOIN
REJOINING > REJOIN
REJOINS > REJOIN
REJON n bullfighting lance
REJONEO n bullfighting activity in which a mounted bullfighter spears the bull with lances
REJONEOS > REJONEO
REJONES > REJON
REJOURN vb archaic word meaning postpone or adjourn
REJOURNED > REJOURN
REJOURNS > REJOURN
REJUDGE vb judge again
REJUDGED > REJUDGE
REJUDGES > REJUDGE
REJUDGING > REJUDGE
REJUGGLE vb juggle again
REJUGGLED > REJUGGLE
REJUGGLES > REJUGGLE
REJUSTIFY vb justify again
REKE same as > RECK
REKED > REKE
REKES > REKE
REKEY vb key again
REKEYED > REKEY
REKEYING > REKEY
REKEYS > REKEY
REKINDLE vb arouse former emotions or interests
REKINDLED > REKINDLE
REKINDLES > REKINDLE
REKING > REKE
REKNIT vb knit again
REKNITS > REKNIT
REKNITTED > REKNIT
REKNOT vb knot again
REKNOTS > REKNOT
REKNOTTED > REKNOT
RELABEL vb label again
RELABELED > RELABEL
RELABELS > RELABEL
RELACE vb lace again
RELACED > RELACE
RELACES > RELACE
RELACHE n break
RELACHES > RELACHE
RELACING > RELACE
RELACQUER vb apply a new coat of lacquer to
RELAID > RELAY
RELAND vb land again
RELANDED > RELAND
RELANDING > RELAND
RELANDS > RELAND
RELAPSE vb fall back into bad habits, illness, etc ▷ n return of bad habits, illness, etc
RELAPSED > RELAPSE
RELAPSER > RELAPSE

RELAPSERS > RELAPSE
RELAPSES > RELAPSE
RELAPSING > RELAPSE
RELATA > RELATUM
RELATABLE > RELATE
RELATE vb establish a relation between
RELATED adj linked by kinship or marriage
RELATEDLY > RELATED
RELATER > RELATE
RELATERS > RELATE
RELATES > RELATE
RELATING > RELATE
RELATION n connection between things
RELATIONS pl n social or political dealings between individuals or groups
RELATIVAL adj of or relating to a relative
RELATIVE adj true to a certain degree or extent ▷ n person connected by blood or marriage
RELATIVES > RELATIVE
RELATOR n person who relates a story
RELATORS > RELATOR
RELATUM n one of the objects between which a relation is said to hold
RELAUNCH vb launch again ▷ n another launching, or something that is relaunched
RELAUNDER vb launder again
RELAX vb make or become looser, less tense, or less rigid
RELAXABLE > RELAX
RELAXANT n drug or agent that relaxes, esp one that relaxes tense muscles ▷ adj of, relating to, or tending to produce relaxation
RELAXANTS > RELAXANT
RELAXED > RELAX
RELAXEDLY > RELAX
RELAXER n person or thing that relaxes
RELAXERS > RELAXER
RELAXES > RELAX
RELAXIN n hormone secreted during pregnancy
RELAXING > RELAX
RELAXINS > RELAXIN
RELAY n fresh set of people or animals relieving others ▷ vb pass on (a message)
RELAYED > RELAY
RELAYING > RELAY
RELAYS > RELAY
RELEARN vb learn (something previously known) again
RELEARNED > RELEARN
RELEARNS > RELEARN
RELEARNT > RELEARN
RELEASE vb set free ▷ n setting free
RELEASED > RELEASE

RELEASEE n someone to whom an estate is released or someone released from captivity
RELEASEES > RELEASEE
RELEASER > RELEASE
RELEASERS > RELEASE
RELEASING > RELEASE
RELEASOR n someone releasing an estate to someone else
RELEASORS > RELEASOR
RELEGABLE adj able to be relegated
RELEGATE vb put in a less important position
RELEGATED > RELEGATE
RELEGATES > RELEGATE
RELEND vb lend again
RELENDING > RELEND
RELENDS > RELEND
RELENT vb give up a harsh intention, become less severe
RELENTED > RELENT
RELENTING > RELENT
RELENTS > RELENT
RELET vb let again
RELETS > RELET
RELETTER vb redo lettering of
RELETTERS > RELETTER
RELETTING > RELET
RELEVANCE > RELEVANT
RELEVANCY > RELEVANT
RELEVANT adj do with the matter in hand
RELEVE n dance move in which heels are off the ground
RELEVES > RELEVE
RELIABLE adj able to be trusted, dependable ▷ n something or someone believed to be reliable
RELIABLES > RELIABLE
RELIABLY > RELIABLE
RELIANCE n dependence, confidence, or trust
RELIANCES > RELIANCE
RELIANT > RELIANCE
RELIANTLY > RELIANCE
RELIC n something that has survived from the past
RELICENSE vb license again
RELICS > RELIC
RELICT n relic
RELICTION n process by which sea water or fresh water recedes over time, changing the waterline and leaving land exposed
RELICTS > RELICT
RELIDE archaic past form of > RELY
RELIE archaic spelling of > RELY
RELIED > RELY
RELIEF n gladness at the end or removal of pain, distress, etc
RELIEFS > RELIEF

RELIER > RELY
RELIERS > RELY
RELIES > RELY
RELIEVE vb bring relief to
RELIEVED adj experiencing relief, esp from worry or anxiety
RELIEVER n person or thing that relieves
RELIEVERS > RELIEVER
RELIEVES > RELIEVE
RELIEVING > RELIEVE
RELIEVO same as > RELIEF
RELIEVOS > RELIEVO
RELIGHT vb ignite or cause to ignite again
RELIGHTED > RELIGHT
RELIGHTS > RELIGHT
RELIGIEUX n member of a monastic order or clerical body
RELIGION n system of belief in and worship of a supernatural power or god
RELIGIONS > RELIGION
RELIGIOSE adj affectedly or extremely pious
RELIGIOSO adj religious ▷ adv in a religious manner ▷ n musical piece meant to be played devotionally
RELIGIOUS adj of religion ▷ n monk or nun
RELINE vb line again or anew
RELINED > RELINE
RELINES > RELINE
RELINING > RELINE
RELINK vb link again
RELINKED > RELINK
RELINKING > RELINK
RELINKS > RELINK
RELIQUARY n case or shrine for holy relics
RELIQUE archaic spelling of > RELIC
RELIQUEFY vb liquefy again
RELIQUES > RELIQUE
RELIQUIAE pl n fossil remains of animals or plants
RELISH vb enjoy, like very much ▷ n liking or enjoyment
RELISHED > RELISH
RELISHES > RELISH
RELISHING > RELISH
RELIST vb list again
RELISTED > RELIST
RELISTING > RELIST
RELISTS > RELIST
RELIT > RELIGHT
RELIVABLE > RELIVE
RELIVE vb experience (a sensation etc) again, esp in the imagination
RELIVED > RELIVE
RELIVER vb deliver up again
RELIVERED > RELIVER
RELIVERS > RELIVER

RELIVES > RELIVE
RELIVING > RELIVE
RELLENO n Mexican dish of stuffed vegetable
RELLENOS > RELLENO
RELLIE n relative
RELLIES pl n relatives or relations
RELLISH (in music) variant of > RELISH
RELLISHED > RELLISH
RELLISHES > RELLISH
RELOAD vb put fresh ammunition into (a firearm)
RELOADED > RELOAD
RELOADER > RELOAD
RELOADERS > RELOAD
RELOADING > RELOAD
RELOADS > RELOAD
RELOAN vb loan again
RELOANED > RELOAN
RELOANING > RELOAN
RELOANS > RELOAN
RELOCATE vb move to a new place to live or work
RELOCATED > RELOCATE
RELOCATEE n someone who is relocated
RELOCATES > RELOCATE
RELOCATOR n program designed to transfer files from one computer to another
RELOCK vb lock again
RELOCKED > RELOCK
RELOCKING > RELOCK
RELOCKS > RELOCK
RELOOK vb look again
RELOOKED > RELOOK
RELOOKING > RELOOK
RELOOKS > RELOOK
RELUCENT adj bright
RELUCT vb struggle or rebel
RELUCTANT adj unwilling or disinclined
RELUCTATE vb be or appear reluctant
RELUCTED > RELUCT
RELUCTING > RELUCT
RELUCTS > RELUCT
RELUME vb light or brighten again
RELUMED > RELUME
RELUMES > RELUME
RELUMINE same as > RELUME
RELUMINED > RELUMINE
RELUMINES > RELUMINE
RELUMING > RELUME
RELY vb depend (on)
RELYING > RELY
REM n dose of ionizing radiation
REMADE n object that has been reconstructed from original materials
REMADES > REMADE
REMAIL vb mail again
REMAILED > REMAIL
REMAILER n internet service that forwards emails anonymously

r

REMAILERS > REMAILER

REMAILING > REMAIL

REMAILS > REMAIL

REMAIN vb continue

REMAINDER n part which is left ▷ vb offer (copies of a poorly selling book) at reduced prices

REMAINED > REMAIN

REMAINING > REMAIN

REMAINS pl n relics, esp of ancient buildings

REMAKE vb make again in a different way ▷ n new version of an old film

REMAKER > REMAKE

REMAKERS > REMAKE

REMAKES > REMAKE

REMAKING > REMAKE

REMAN vb man again or afresh

REMAND vb send back into custody or put on bail before trial

REMANDED > REMAND

REMANDING > REMAND

REMANDS > REMAND

REMANENCE n ability of a material to retain magnetization, equal to the magnetic flux density of the material after the removal of the magnetizing field

REMANENCY archaic variant of > REMANENCE

REMANENT adj remaining or left over ▷ n archaic word meaning remainder

REMANET n something left over

REMANETS > REMANET

REMANIE n fragments and fossils of older origin found in a more recent deposit

REMANIES > REMANIE

REMANNED > REMAN

REMANNING > REMAN

REMANS > REMAN

REMAP vb map again

REMAPPED > REMAP

REMAPPING > REMAP

REMAPS > REMAP

REMARK vb make a casual comment (on) ▷ n observation or comment

REMARKED > REMARK

REMARKER > REMARK

REMARKERS > REMARK

REMARKET vb market again

REMARKETS > REMARKET

REMARKING > REMARK

REMARKS > REMARK

REMARQUE n printing mark in the margin of a plate

REMARQUED adj having had a remarque put on

REMARQUES > REMARQUE

REMARRIED > REMARRY

REMARRIES > REMARRY

REMARRY vb marry again

REMASTER vb make a new master audio recording, now usually digital, from (an earlier recording), to produce compact discs or stereo records with improved sound reproduction

REMASTERS > REMASTER

REMATCH n second or return game or contest between two players ▷ vb match (two contestants) again

REMATCHED > REMATCH

REMATCHES > REMATCH

REMATE vb mate again ▷ n finishing pass in bullfighting

REMATED > REMATE

REMATES > REMATE

REMATING > REMATE

REMBLAI n earth used for an embankment or rampart

REMBLAIS > REMBLAI

REMBLE dialect word for > REMOVE

REMBLED > REMBLE

REMBLES > REMBLE

REMBLING > REMBLE

REMEAD archaic or dialect word for > REMEDY

REMEADED > REMEAD

REMEADING > REMEAD

REMEADS > REMEAD

REMEASURE vb measure again

REMEDE archaic or dialect word for > REMEDY

REMEDED > REMEDE

REMEDES > REMEDE

REMEDIAL adj intended to correct a specific disability, handicap, etc

REMEDIAT archaic word for > REMEDIAL

REMEDIATE archaic word for > REMEDIAL

REMEDIED > REMEDY

REMEDIES > REMEDY

REMEDING > REMEDE

REMEDY n means of curing pain or disease ▷ vb put right

REMEDYING > REMEDY

REMEET vb meet again

REMEETING > REMEET

REMEETS > REMEET

REMEID archaic or dialect word for > REMEDY

REMEIDED > REMEID

REMEIDING > REMEID

REMEIDS > REMEID

REMELT vb melt again

REMELTED > REMELT

REMELTING > REMELT

REMELTS > REMELT

REMEMBER vb retain in or recall to one's memory

REMEMBERS > REMEMBER

REMEN n ancient Egyptian measurement unit

REMEND vb mend again

REMENDED > REMEND

REMENDING > REMEND

REMENDS > REMEND

REMENS > REMEN

REMERCIED > REMERCY

REMERCIES > REMERCY

REMERCY vb archaic word for thank

REMERGE vb merge again

REMERGED > REMERGE

REMERGES > REMERGE

REMERGING > REMERGE

REMET > REMEET

REMEX n any of the large flight feathers of a bird's wing

REMIGATE vb row

REMIGATED > REMIGATE

REMIGATES > REMIGATE

REMIGES > REMEX

REMIGIAL > REMEX

REMIGRATE vb migrate again

REMIND vb cause to remember

REMINDED > REMIND

REMINDER n something that recalls the past

REMINDERS > REMINDER

REMINDFUL adj serving to remind

REMINDING > REMIND

REMINDS > REMIND

REMINISCE vb talk or write of past times, experiences, etc

REMINT vb mint again

REMINTED > REMINT

REMINTING > REMINT

REMINTS > REMINT

REMISE vb give up or relinquish (a right, claim, etc) ▷ n second thrust made on the same lunge after the first has missed

REMISED > REMISE

REMISES > REMISE

REMISING > REMISE

REMISS adj negligent or careless

REMISSION n reduction in the length of a prison term

REMISSIVE > REMISSION

REMISSLY > REMISS

REMISSORY adj liable to or intended to gain remission

REMIT vb send (money) for goods, services, etc, esp by post ▷ n area of competence or authority

REMITMENT n archaic word for remittance or remission

REMITS > REMIT

REMITTAL > REMIT

REMITTALS > REMIT

REMITTED > REMIT

REMITTEE n recipient of a remittance

REMITTEES > REMITTEE

REMITTENT adj (of a disease) periodically less severe

REMITTER n person who remits

REMITTERS > REMITTER

REMITTING > REMIT

REMITTOR same as > REMITTER

REMITTORS > REMITTOR

REMIX vb change the relative prominence of each performer's part of (a recording) ▷ n remixed version of a recording

REMIXED > REMIX

REMIXER n person who remixes a recording

REMIXERS > REMIXER

REMIXES > REMIX

REMIXING > REMIX

REMIXT informal past form of > REMIX

REMIXTURE > REMIX

REMNANT n small piece, esp of fabric, left over ▷ adj remaining

REMNANTAL adj existing as remnant

REMNANTS > REMNANT

REMODEL vb give a different shape or form to ▷ n something that has been remodelled

REMODELED > REMODEL

REMODELER n person who remodels

REMODELS > REMODEL

REMODIFY vb modify again

REMOISTEN vb moisten again

REMOLADE same as > REMOULADE

REMOLADES > REMOLADE

REMOLD US spelling of > REMOULD

REMOLDED > REMOLD

REMOLDING > REMOLD

REMOLDS > REMOLD

REMONTANT adj (esp of cultivated roses) flowering more than once in a single season ▷ n rose having such a growth

REMONTOIR n any of various devices used in watches, clocks, etc, to compensate for errors arising from the changes in the force driving the escapement

REMORA n spiny-finned fish

REMORAS > REMORA

REMORID > REMORA

REMORSE n feeling of sorrow and regret for something one did

REMORSES > REMORSE

REMOTE adj far away, distant ▷ n (in informal usage) remote control

REMOTELY > REMOTE

REMOTER > REMOTE

REMOTES > REMOTE

REMOTEST > REMOTE

REMOTION n removal

REMOTIONS > REMOTION

REMOUD Spenserian variant of > REMOVED

REMOULADE n mayonnaise sauce flavoured with herbs, mustard, and capers, served with salads, cold meat, etc

REMOULD vb change completely ▷ n renovated tyre

REMOULDED > REMOULD

REMOULDS > REMOULD

REMOUNT vb get on (a horse, bicycle, etc) again ▷ n fresh horse

REMOUNTED > REMOUNT

REMOUNTS > REMOUNT

REMOVABLE > REMOVE

REMOVABLY > REMOVE

REMOVAL n removing, esp changing residence

REMOVALS > REMOVAL

REMOVE vb take away or off ▷ n degree of difference

REMOVED adj very different or distant

REMOVEDLY adv at a distance

REMOVER > REMOVE

REMOVERS > REMOVE

REMOVES > REMOVE

REMOVING > REMOVE

REMS > REM

REMUAGE n process of turning wine bottles to let the sediment out

REMUAGES > REMUAGE

REMUDA n stock of horses enabling riders to change mounts

REMUDAS > REMUDA

REMUEUR n person carrying out remuage

REMUEURS > REMUEUR

REMURMUR vb murmur again or murmur in reply

REMURMURS > REMURMUR

REN archaic variant of > RUN

RENAGUE same as > RENEGE

RENAGUED > RENAGUE

RENAGUES > RENAGUE

RENAGUING > RENAGUE

RENAIL vb nail again

RENAILED > RENAIL

RENAILING > RENAIL

RENAILS > RENAIL

RENAL adj of the kidneys

RENAME vb change the name of (someone or something)

RENAMED > RENAME

RENAMES > RENAME

RENAMING > RENAME

RENASCENT adj becoming active or vigorous again

RENATURE vb return to natural state

RENATURED > RENATURE

RENATURES > RENATURE

RENAY vb archaic word meaning renounce

RENAYED > RENAY

RENAYING > RENAY

RENAYS > RENAY

RENCONTRE n unexpected meeting ▷ vb meet, esp under negative circumstances

REND vb tear or wrench apart

RENDED > REND

RENDER vb cause to become ▷ n first thin coat of plaster applied to a surface

RENDERED > RENDER

RENDERER > RENDER

RENDERERS > RENDER

RENDERING n act or an instance of performing a play, piece of music, etc

RENDERS > RENDER

RENDIBLE > REND

RENDING > REND

RENDITION n performance ▷ vb subject someone to an extra-judiciary trial

RENDS > REND

RENDZINA n dark interzonal type of soil found in grassy or formerly grassy areas of moderate rainfall, esp on chalklands

RENDZINAS > RENDZINA

RENEAGUE same as > RENEGE

RENEAGUED > RENEAGUE

RENEAGUES > RENEAGUE

RENEGADE n person who deserts a cause ▷ vb become a renegade

RENEGADED > RENEGADE

RENEGADES > RENEGADE

RENEGADO archaic word for > RENEGADE

RENEGADOS > RENEGADO

RENEGATE old variant of > RENEGADE

RENEGATES > RENEGATE

RENEGE vb go back (on a promise etc)

RENEGED > RENEGE

RENEGER > RENEGE

RENEGERS > RENEGE

RENEGES > RENEGE

RENEGING > RENEGE

RENEGUE same as > RENEGE

RENEGUED > RENEGUE

RENEGUER > RENEGUE

RENEGUERS > RENEGUE

RENEGUES > RENEGUE

RENEGUING > RENEGUE

RENEST vb nest again or form a new nest

RENESTED > RENEST

RENESTING > RENEST

RENESTS > RENEST

RENEW vb begin again

RENEWABLE > RENEW

RENEWABLY > RENEW

RENEWAL n act of renewing or state of being renewed

RENEWALS > RENEWAL

RENEWED > RENEW

RENEWEDLY > RENEW

RENEWER > RENEW

RENEWERS > RENEW

RENEWING > RENEW

RENEWINGS > RENEW

RENEWS > RENEW

RENEY same as > RENAY

RENEYED > RENEY

RENEYING > RENEY

RENEYS > RENEY

RENFIERST adj archaic word for turned fierce

RENFORCE vb archaic word for reinforce

RENFORCED > RENFORCE

RENFORCES > RENFORCE

RENFORST > RENFORCE

RENGA n type of collaborative poetry found in Japan

RENGAS > RENGA

RENIED > RENY

RENIES > RENY

RENIFORM adj having the shape or profile of a kidney

RENIG same as > RENEGE

RENIGGED > RENIG

RENIGGING > RENIG

RENIGS > RENIG

RENIN n enzyme secreted by the kidneys

RENINS > RENIN

RENITENCE > RENITENT

RENITENCY > RENITENT

RENITENT adj reluctant

RENK adj unpleasant

RENKER > RENK

RENKEST > RENK

RENMINBI same as > YUAN

RENMINBIS > RENMINBI

RENNASE same as > RENNIN

RENNASES > RENNASE

RENNE archaic variant of > RUN

RENNED > REN

RENNES > RENNE

RENNET n substance for curdling milk to make cheese

RENNETS > RENNET

RENNIN n enzyme that occurs in gastric juice

RENNING > REN

RENNINGS > REN

RENNINS > RENNIN

RENO n renovated house

RENOGRAM n X-ray kidney image

RENOGRAMS > RENOGRAM

RENOS > RENO

RENOTIFY vb notify again

RENOUNCE vb give up (a belief, habit, etc)

voluntarily ▷ n failure to follow suit in a card game

RENOUNCED > RENOUNCE

RENOUNCER > RENOUNCE

RENOUNCES > RENOUNCE

RENOVATE vb restore to good condition

RENOVATED > RENOVATE

RENOVATES > RENOVATE

RENOVATOR > RENOVATE

RENOWN n widespread good reputation ▷ vb make famous

RENOWNED adj famous

RENOWNER n renown giver

RENOWNERS > RENOWNER

RENOWNING > RENOWN

RENOWNS > RENOWN

RENS > REN

RENT n payment made by a tenant to a landlord or owner of a property ▷ vb grant the right to use one's property for payment

RENTABLE > REND

RENTAL n sum payable as rent ▷ adj of or relating to rent

RENTALLER n (in Scots law) tenant with very favourable terms

RENTALS > RENTAL

RENTE n annual income from capital investment

RENTED > RENT

RENTER n person who lets his property in return for rent

RENTERS > RENTER

RENTES > RENTE

RENTIER n person who lives off unearned income such as rents or interest

RENTIERS > RENTIER

RENTING > RENT

RENTINGS > RENT

RENTS > RENT

RENUMBER vb number again or afresh

RENUMBERS > RENUMBER

RENVERSE vb archaic word meaning overturn

RENVERSED > RENVERSE

RENVERSES > RENVERSE

RENVERST > RENVERSE

RENVOI n referring of a dispute to a jurisdiction other than that in which it arose

RENVOIS > RENVOI

RENVOY old variant of > RENVOI

RENVOYS > RENVOY

RENY same as > RENAY

RENYING > RENY

REO n New Zealand language

REOBJECT vb object again

REOBJECTS > REOBJECT

REOBSERVE vb observe again

REOBTAIN vb obtain again

REOBTAINS > REOBTAIN
REOCCUPY vb occupy (a building, area, etc) again
REOCCUR vb happen, take place, or come about again
REOCCURS > REOCCUR
REOFFEND vb commit another offence
REOFFENDS > REOFFEND
REOFFER vb offer again
REOFFERED > REOFFER
REOFFERS > REOFFER
REOIL vb oil again
REOILED > REOIL
REOILING > REOIL
REOILS > REOIL
REOPEN vb open again after a period of being closed or suspended
REOPENED > REOPEN
REOPENER n clause in a legal document allowing for an issue to be revisited at a subsequent date
REOPENERS > REOPENER
REOPENING n act of reopening
REOPENS > REOPEN
REOPERATE vb operate again
REOPPOSE vb oppose again
REOPPOSED > REOPPOSE
REOPPOSES > REOPPOSE
REORDAIN vb ordain again
REORDAINS > REORDAIN
REORDER vb change the order of
REORDERED > REORDER
REORDERS > REORDER
REORG vb reorganize
REORGED > REORG
REORGING > REORG
REORGS > REORG
REORIENT vb adjust or align (something) in a new or different way
REORIENTS > REORIENT
REOS > REO
REOUTFIT vb outfit again
REOUTFITS > REOUTFIT
REOVIRUS n type of virus
REOXIDISE same as > REOXIDIZE
REOXIDIZE vb oxidize again
REP n sales representative ▷ vb work as a representative
REPACIFY vb pacify again
REPACK vb place or arrange (articles) in (a container) again or in a different way
REPACKAGE vb wrap or put (something) in a package again
REPACKED > REPACK
REPACKING > REPACK
REPACKS > REPACK
REPAID > REPAY

REPAINT vb apply a new or fresh coat of paint
REPAINTED > REPAINT
REPAINTS > REPAINT
REPAIR vb restore to good condition, mend ▷ n act of repairing
REPAIRED > REPAIR
REPAIRER > REPAIR
REPAIRERS > REPAIR
REPAIRING > REPAIR
REPAIRMAN n man whose job it is to repair machines, appliances, etc
REPAIRMEN > REPAIRMAN
REPAIRS > REPAIR
REPAND adj having a wavy margin
REPANDLY > REPAND
REPANEL vb panel again or anew
REPANELED > REPANEL
REPANELS > REPANEL
REPAPER vb paper again or afresh
REPAPERED > REPAPER
REPAPERS > REPAPER
REPARABLE adj able to be repaired or remedied
REPARABLY > REPARABLE
REPARK vb park again
REPARKED > REPARK
REPARKING > REPARK
REPARKS > REPARK
REPARTEE n interchange of witty retorts ▷ vb retort
REPARTEED > REPARTEE
REPARTEES > REPARTEE
REPASS vb pass again
REPASSAGE n passage back or return
REPASSED > REPASS
REPASSES > REPASS
REPASSING > REPASS
REPAST n meal ▷ vb feed (on)
REPASTED > REPAST
REPASTING > REPAST
REPASTS > REPAST
REPASTURE old word for > FOOD
REPATCH vb patch again
REPATCHED > REPATCH
REPATCHES > REPATCH
REPATTERN vb pattern again
REPAVE vb pave again
REPAVED > REPAVE
REPAVES > REPAVE
REPAVING > REPAVE
REPAY vb pay back, refund
REPAYABLE > REPAY
REPAYING > REPAY
REPAYMENT > REPAY
REPAYS > REPAY
REPEAL vb cancel (a law) officially ▷ n act of repealing
REPEALED > REPEAL
REPEALER > REPEAL
REPEALERS > REPEAL

REPEALING > REPEAL
REPEALS > REPEAL
REPEAT vb say or do again ▷ n act or instance of repeating
REPEATED adj done, made, or said again and again
REPEATER n firearm that may be discharged many times without reloading
REPEATERS > REPEATER
REPEATING > REPEAT
REPEATS > REPEAT
REPECHAGE n extra heat or test providing second chance to previous losers or failing candidates
REPEG vb peg again
REPEGGED > REPEG
REPEGGING > REPEG
REPEGS > REPEG
REPEL vb be disgusting to
REPELLANT same as > REPELLENT
REPELLED > REPEL
REPELLENT adj distasteful ▷ n something that repels, esp a chemical to repel insects
REPELLER > REPEL
REPELLERS > REPEL
REPELLING > REPEL
REPELS > REPEL
REPENT vb feel regret for (a deed or omission) ▷ adj lying or creeping along the ground
REPENTANT adj reproaching oneself for one's past actions or sins
REPENTED > REPENT
REPENTER > REPENT
REPENTERS > REPENT
REPENTING > REPENT
REPENTS > REPENT
REPEOPLE vb people again
REPEOPLED > REPEOPLE
REPEOPLES > REPEOPLE
REPERCUSS vb have repercussions
REPEREPE n New Zealand word for the elephant fish, a large fish of the southwest Pacific with a trunk-like snout
REPEREPES > REPEREPE
REPERK vb perk again
REPERKED > REPERK
REPERKING > REPERK
REPERKS > REPERK
REPERTORY n repertoire
REPERUSAL n fresh perusal
REPERUSE vb peruse again
REPERUSED > REPERUSE
REPERUSES > REPERUSE
REPETEND n digit or series of digits in a recurring decimal that repeats itself
REPETENDS > REPETEND

REPHRASE vb express in different words
REPHRASED > REPHRASE
REPHRASES > REPHRASE
REPIGMENT vb pigment again
REPIN vb pin again
REPINE vb fret or complain
REPINED > REPINE
REPINER > REPINE
REPINERS > REPINE
REPINES > REPINE
REPINING > REPINE
REPININGS > REPINE
REPINNED > REPIN
REPINNING > REPIN
REPINS > REPIN
REPIQUE n score of 30 in the card-game piquet ▷ vb score a repique against (someone)
REPIQUED > REPIQUE
REPIQUES > REPIQUE
REPIQUING > REPIQUE
REPLA > REPLUM
REPLACE vb substitute for
REPLACED > REPLACE
REPLACER > REPLACE
REPLACERS > REPLACE
REPLACES > REPLACE
REPLACING > REPLACE
REPLAN vb plan again
REPLANNED > REPLAN
REPLANS > REPLAN
REPLANT vb plant again
REPLANTED > REPLANT
REPLANTS > REPLANT
REPLASTER vb plaster again
REPLATE vb plate again
REPLATED > REPLATE
REPLATES > REPLATE
REPLATING > REPLATE
REPLAY n immediate reshowing on TV of an incident in sport ▷ vb play (a match, recording, etc) again
REPLAYED > REPLAY
REPLAYING > REPLAY
REPLAYS > REPLAY
REPLEAD vb plead again
REPLEADED > REPLEAD
REPLEADER n right to plead again
REPLEADS > REPLEAD
REPLED > REPLEAD
REPLEDGE vb pledge again
REPLEDGED > REPLEDGE
REPLEDGES > REPLEDGE
REPLENISH vb fill up again, resupply
REPLETE adj filled or gorged ▷ vb fill again
REPLETED > REPLETE
REPLETELY > REPLETE
REPLETES > REPLETE
REPLETING > REPLETE
REPLETION n state or condition of being replete
REPLEVIED > REPLEVY

REPLEVIES > REPLEVY

REPLEVIN *n* recovery of goods unlawfully taken, made subject to establishing the validity of the recovery in a legal action and returning the goods if the decision is adverse

REPLEVINS > REPLEVIN

REPLEVY *vb* recover possession of (goods) by replevin

REPLICA *n* exact copy

REPLICANT *n* (in science fiction) android indistinguishable from a human being

REPLICAS > REPLICA

REPLICASE *n* type of enzyme

REPLICATE *vb* make or be a copy of ▷ *adj* folded back on itself

REPLICON *n* region of a DNA molecule that is replicated from a single origin

REPLICONS > REPLICON

REPLIED > REPLY

REPLIER > REPLY

REPLIERS > REPLY

REPLIES > REPLY

REPLOT *vb* plot again

REPLOTS > REPLOT

REPLOTTED > REPLOT

REPLOUGH *vb* plough again

REPLOUGHS > REPLOUGH

REPLOW *vb* plow again

REPLOWED > REPLOW

REPLOWING > REPLOW

REPLOWS > REPLOW

REPLUM *n* internal separating wall in some fruits

REPLUMB *vb* plumb again

REPLUMBED > REPLUMB

REPLUMBS > REPLUMB

REPLUNGE *vb* plunge again

REPLUNGED > REPLUNGE

REPLUNGES > REPLUNGE

REPLY *vb* answer or respond ▷ *n* answer or response

REPLYING > REPLY

REPO *n* act of repossessing

REPOINT *vb* repair the joints of (brickwork, masonry, etc) with mortar or cement

REPOINTED > REPOINT

REPOINTS > REPOINT

REPOLISH *vb* polish again

REPOLL *vb* poll again

REPOLLED > REPOLL

REPOLLING > REPOLL

REPOLLS > REPOLL

REPOMAN *n* man employed to repossess goods in cases of non-payment

REPOMEN > REPOMAN

REPONE *vb* restore (someone) to his former status, office, etc

REPONED > REPONE

REPONES > REPONE

REPONING > REPONE

REPORT *vb* give an account of ▷ *n* account or statement

REPORTAGE *n* act or process of reporting news or other events of general interest

REPORTED > REPORT

REPORTER *n* person who gathers news for a newspaper, TV, etc

REPORTERS > REPORTER

REPORTING > REPORT

REPORTS > REPORT

REPOS > REPO

REPOSAL *n* repose

REPOSALL *archaic spelling of* > REPOSAL

REPOSALLS > REPOSALL

REPOSALS > REPOSE

REPOSE *n* peace ▷ *vb* lie or lay at rest

REPOSED > REPOSE

REPOSEDLY > REPOSE

REPOSEFUL > REPOSE

REPOSER > REPOSE

REPOSERS > REPOSE

REPOSES > REPOSE

REPOSING > REPOSE

REPOSIT *vb* put away, deposit, or store up

REPOSITED > REPOSIT

REPOSITOR *n* any instrument used for correcting the position of displaced organs or bones

REPOSITS > REPOSIT

REPOSSESS *vb* (of a lender) take back property from a customer who is behind with payments

REPOST *vb* post again

REPOSTED > REPOST

REPOSTING > REPOST

REPOSTS > REPOST

REPOSURE *old word for* > REPOSE

REPOSURES > REPOSURE

REPOT *vb* put (a house plant) into a new usually larger pot

REPOTS > REPOT

REPOTTED > REPOT

REPOTTING > REPOT

REPOUR *vb* pour back or again

REPOURED > REPOUR

REPOURING > REPOUR

REPOURS > REPOUR

REPOUSSE *adj* raised in relief, as a design on a thin piece of metal hammered through from the underside ▷ *n* design or surface made in this way

REPOUSSES > REPOUSSE

REPOWER *vb* put new engine in

REPOWERED > REPOWER

REPOWERS > REPOWER

REPP *same as* > REP

REPPED > REP

REPPING > REP

REPPINGS > REP

REPPS > REPP

REPREEVE *archaic spelling of* > REPRIEVE

REPREEVED > REPREEVE

REPREEVES > REPREEVE

REPREHEND *vb* find fault with

REPRESENT *vb* act as a delegate or substitute for

REPRESS *vb* keep (feelings) in check

REPRESSED *adj* (of a person) repressing feelings, instincts, desires, etc

REPRESSER > REPRESS

REPRESSES > REPRESS

REPRESSOR *n* protein synthesized under the control of a repressor gene, which has the capacity to bind to the operator gene and thereby shut off the expression of the structural genes of an operon

REPRICE *vb* price again

REPRICED > REPRICE

REPRICES > REPRICE

REPRICING > REPRICE

REPRIEFE *n* (in archaic usage) reproof

REPRIEFES > REPRIEFE

REPRIEVAL *old word for* > REPRIEVE

REPRIEVE *vb* postpone the execution of (a condemned person) ▷ *n* (document granting) postponement or cancellation of a punishment

REPRIEVED > REPRIEVE

REPRIEVER > REPRIEVE

REPRIEVES > REPRIEVE

REPRIMAND *vb* blame (someone) officially for a fault ▷ *n* official blame

REPRIME *vb* prime again

REPRIMED > REPRIME

REPRIMES > REPRIME

REPRIMING > REPRIME

REPRINT *vb* print further copies of (a book) ▷ *n* reprinted copy

REPRINTED > REPRINT

REPRINTER > REPRINT

REPRINTS > REPRINT

REPRISAL *n* retaliation

REPRISALS > REPRISAL

REPRISE *n* repeating of an earlier theme ▷ *vb* repeat an earlier theme

REPRISED > REPRISE

REPRISES > REPRISE

REPRISING > REPRISE

REPRIVE *archaic spelling of* > REPRIEVE

REPRIVED > REPRIVE

REPRIVES > REPRIVE

REPRIVING > REPRIVE

REPRIZE *archaic spelling of* > REPRISE

REPRIZED > REPRIZE

REPRIZES > REPRIZE

REPRIZING > REPRIZE

REPRO *n* imitation or facsimile of a work of art; reproduction

REPROACH *vb* blame, rebuke

REPROBACY > REPROBATE

REPROBATE *n* depraved or disreputable (person) ▷ *adj* morally unprincipled ▷ *vb* disapprove of

REPROBE *vb* probe again

REPROBED > REPROBE

REPROBES > REPROBE

REPROBING > REPROBE

REPROCESS *vb* treat or prepare (something) by a special method again

REPRODUCE *vb* produce a copy of

REPROGRAM *vb* program again

REPROOF *n* severe blaming of someone for a fault ▷ *vb* treat (a coat, jacket, etc) so as to renew its texture, etc

REPROOFED > REPROOF

REPROOFS > REPROOF

REPROS > REPRO

REPROVAL *same as* > REPROOF

REPROVALS > REPROVAL

REPROVE *vb* speak severely to (someone) about a fault

REPROVED > REPROVE

REPROVER > REPROVE

REPROVERS > REPROVE

REPROVES > REPROVE

REPROVING > REPROVE

REPRYVE *archaic spelling of* > REPRIEVE

REPRYVED > REPRYVE

REPRYVES > REPRYVE

REPRYVING > REPRYVE

REPS > REP

REPTANT *adj* creeping, crawling, or lying along the ground

REPTATION *n* creeping action

REPTILE *n* cold-blooded egg-laying vertebrate with horny scales or plates ▷ *adj* creeping, crawling, or squirming

REPTILES > REPTILE

REPTILIA > REPTILIUM

REPTILIAN *adj* of, relating to, resembling, or characteristic of reptiles

REPTILIUM *n* place where live reptiles are kept for show

REPTILOID *n* reptile or organism resembling a reptile

REPUBLIC n form of government in which the people or their elected representatives possess the supreme power

REPUBLICS > REPUBLIC

REPUBLISH vb publish again

REPUDIATE vb reject the authority or validity of

REPUGN vb oppose or conflict (with)

REPUGNANT adj offensive or distasteful

REPUGNED > REPUGN

REPUGNING > REPUGN

REPUGNS > REPUGN

REPULP vb pulp again

REPULPED > REPULP

REPULPING > REPULP

REPULPS > REPULP

REPULSE vb be disgusting to ▷ n driving back

REPULSED > REPULSE

REPULSER > REPULSE

REPULSERS > REPULSE

REPULSES > REPULSE

REPULSING > REPULSE

REPULSION n distaste or aversion

REPULSIVE adj loathsome, disgusting

REPUMP vb pump again

REPUMPED > REPUMP

REPUMPING > REPUMP

REPUMPS > REPUMP

REPUNIT n any number that consists entirely of the same repeated digits

REPUNITS > REPUNIT

REPURE vb archaic word meaning make pure again

REPURED > REPURE

REPURES > REPURE

REPURIFY vb purify again

REPURING > REPURE

REPURPOSE vb find new purpose for

REPURSUE vb pursue again

REPURSUED > REPURSUE

REPURSUES > REPURSUE

REPUTABLE adj of good reputation, respectable

REPUTABLY > REPUTABLE

REPUTE n reputation ▷ vb consider (a person or thing) to be as specified

REPUTED adj supposed

REPUTEDLY adv according to general belief or supposition

REPUTES > REPUTE

REPUTING > REPUTE

REPUTINGS > REPUTE

REQUALIFY vb qualify again

REQUERE archaic variant of > REQUIRE

REQUERED > REQUERE

REQUERES > REQUERE

REQUERING > REQUERE

REQUEST vb ask ▷ n asking

REQUESTED > REQUEST

REQUESTER > REQUEST

REQUESTOR > REQUEST

REQUESTS > REQUEST

REQUICKEN vb quicken again

REQUIEM n Mass celebrated for the dead

REQUIEMS > REQUIEM

REQUIGHT archaic spelling of > REQUITE

REQUIGHTS > REQUIGHT

REQUIN vb type of shark

REQUINS > REQUIN

REQUINTO n type of small guitar

REQUINTOS > REQUINTO

REQUIRE vb want or need

REQUIRED > REQUIRE

REQUIRER > REQUIRE

REQUIRERS > REQUIRE

REQUIRES > REQUIRE

REQUIRING > REQUIRE

REQUISITE adj necessary, essential ▷ n essential thing

REQUIT vb quit again

REQUITAL n act or an instance of requiting

REQUITALS > REQUITAL

REQUITE vb return to someone (the same treatment or feeling as received)

REQUITED > REQUITE

REQUITER > REQUITE

REQUITERS > REQUITE

REQUITES > REQUITE

REQUITING > REQUITE

REQUITS > REQUIT

REQUITTED > REQUIT

REQUOTE vb quote again

REQUOTED > REQUOTE

REQUOTES > REQUOTE

REQUOTING > REQUOTE

REQUOYLE archaic spelling of > RECOIL

REQUOYLED > REQUOYLE

REQUOYLES > REQUOYLE

RERACK vb rack again

RERACKED > RERACK

RERACKING > RERACK

RERACKS > RERACK

RERADIATE vb radiate again

RERAIL vb put back on a railway line

RERAILED > RERAIL

RERAILING n replacement of existing rails on a railway line

RERAILS > RERAIL

RERAISE vb raise again

RERAISED > RERAISE

RERAISES > RERAISE

RERAISING > RERAISE

RERAN > RERUN

REREAD vb read (something) again

REREADING > REREAD

REREADS > REREAD

REREBRACE n armour worn on the upper arm

RERECORD vb record again

RERECORDS > RERECORD

REREDOS n ornamental screen behind an altar

REREDOSES > REREDOS

REREDOSSE same as > REREDOS

RERELEASE vb release again

REREMAI n New Zealand word for the basking shark

REREMAIS > REREMAI

REREMICE > REREMOUSE

REREMIND vb remind again

REREMINDS > REREMIND

REREMOUSE n archaic or dialect word for 'bat' (the animal)

RERENT vb rent again

RERENTED > RERENT

RERENTING > RERENT

RERENTS > RERENT

REREPEAT vb repeat again

REREPEATS > REREPEAT

REREVIEW vb review again

REREVIEWS > REREVIEW

REREVISE vb revise again

REREVISED > REREVISE

REREVISES > REREVISE

REREWARD archaic spelling of > REARWARD

REREWARDS archaic spelling of > REARWARDS

RERIG vb rig again

RERIGGED > RERIG

RERIGGING > RERIG

RERIGS > RERIG

RERISE vb rise again

RERISEN > RERISE

RERISES > RERISE

RERISING > RERISE

REROLL vb roll again

REROLLED > REROLL

REROLLER > REROLL

REROLLERS > REROLL

REROLLING > REROLL

REROLLS > REROLL

REROOF vb put a new roof or roofs on

REROOFED > REROOF

REROOFING > REROOF

REROOFS > REROOF

REROSE > RERISE

REROUTE vb send or direct by a different route

REROUTED > REROUTE

REROUTES > REROUTE

REROUTING > REROUTE

RERUN n film or programme that is broadcast again, repeat ▷ vb put on (a film or programme) again

RERUNNING > RERUN

RERUNS > RERUN

RES informal word for > RESIDENCE

RESADDLE vb saddle again

RESADDLED > RESADDLE

RESADDLES > RESADDLE

RESAID > RESAY

RESAIL vb sail again

RESAILED > RESAIL

RESAILING > RESAIL

RESAILS > RESAIL

RESALABLE > RESALE

RESALE n selling of something purchased earlier

RESALES > RESALE

RESALGAR archaic variant of > REALGAR

RESALGARS > RESALGAR

RESALUTE vb salute back or again

RESALUTED > RESALUTE

RESALUTES > RESALUTE

RESAMPLE vb (in graphics or digital photography) change the size or resolution of

RESAMPLED > RESAMPLE

RESAMPLES > RESAMPLE

RESAT > RESIT

RESAW vb saw again

RESAWED > RESAW

RESAWING > RESAW

RESAWN > RESAW

RESAWS > RESAW

RESAY vb say again or in response

RESAYING > RESAY

RESAYS > RESAY

RESCALE vb resize

RESCALED > RESCALE

RESCALES > RESCALE

RESCALING > RESCALE

RESCHOOL vb retrain

RESCHOOLS > RESCHOOL

RESCIND vb annul or repeal

RESCINDED > RESCIND

RESCINDER > RESCIND

RESCINDS > RESCIND

RESCORE vb score afresh

RESCORED > RESCORE

RESCORES > RESCORE

RESCORING > RESCORE

RESCREEN vb screen again

RESCREENS > RESCREEN

RESCRIPT n (in ancient Rome) an ordinance taking the form of a reply by the emperor to a question on a point of law

RESCRIPTS > RESCRIPT

RESCUABLE > RESCUE

RESCUE vb deliver from danger or trouble, save ▷ n rescuing

RESCUED > RESCUE

RESCUEE n person who is rescued

RESCUEES > RESCUEE

RESCUER > RESCUE

RESCUERS > RESCUE

RESCUES > RESCUE

RESCUING > RESCUE

RESCULPT *vb* sculpt again
RESCULPTS > RESCULPT
RESEAL *vb* close or secure tightly again
RESEALED > RESEAL
RESEALING > RESEAL
RESEALS > RESEAL
RESEARCH *n* systematic investigation to discover facts or collect information ▷ *vb* carry out investigations
RESEASON *vb* season again
RESEASONS > RESEASON
RESEAT *vb* show (a person) to a new seat
RESEATED > RESEAT
RESEATING > RESEAT
RESEATS > RESEAT
RESEAU *n* mesh background to a lace or other pattern
RESEAUS > RESEAU
RESEAUX > RESEAU
RESECT *vb* cut out part of (a bone, an organ, or other structure or part)
RESECTED > RESECT
RESECTING > RESECT
RESECTION *n* excision of part of a bone, organ, or other part
RESECTS > RESECT
RESECURE *vb* secure again
RESECURED > RESECURE
RESECURES > RESECURE
RESEDA *n* plant that has small spikes of grey-green flowers ▷ *adj* of a greyish-green colour
RESEDAS > RESEDA
RESEE *vb* see again
RESEED *vb* form seed and reproduce naturally, forming a constant plant population
RESEEDED > RESEED
RESEEDING > RESEED
RESEEDS > RESEED
RESEEING > RESEE
RESEEK *vb* seek again
RESEEKING > RESEEK
RESEEKS > RESEEK
RESEEN > RESEE
RESEES > RESEE
RESEIZE *vb* seize again
RESEIZED > RESEIZE
RESEIZES > RESEIZE
RESEIZING > RESEIZE
RESEIZURE > RESEIZE
RESELECT *vb* choose (someone or something) again, esp to choose an existing office-holder as candidate for re-election
RESELECTS > RESELECT
RESELL *vb* sell (something) one has previously bought
RESELLER > RESELL
RESELLERS > RESELL
RESELLING > RESELL

RESELLS > RESELL
RESEMBLE *vb* be or look like
RESEMBLED > RESEMBLE
RESEMBLER > RESEMBLE
RESEMBLES > RESEMBLE
RESEND *vb* send again
RESENDING > RESEND
RESENDS > RESEND
RESENT *vb* feel bitter about
RESENTED > RESENT
RESENTER > RESENT
RESENTERS > RESENT
RESENTFUL *adj* feeling or characterized by resentment
RESENTING > RESENT
RESENTIVE *archaic word for* > RESENTFUL
RESENTS > RESENT
RESERPINE *n* insoluble alkaloid used medicinally to lower blood pressure and as a sedative
RESERVE *vb* set aside, keep for future use ▷ *n* something, esp money or troops, kept for emergencies
RESERVED *adj* not showing one's feelings, lacking friendliness
RESERVER > RESERVE
RESERVERS > RESERVE
RESERVES > RESERVE
RESERVICE *vb* service again
RESERVING > RESERVE
RESERVIST *n* member of a military reserve
RESERVOIR *n* natural or artificial lake storing water for community supplies
RESES > RES
RESET *vb* set again (a broken bone, matter in type, a gemstone, etc) ▷ *n* act or an instance of setting again
RESETS > RESET
RESETTED *same as* > RESET
RESETTER > RESET
RESETTERS > RESET
RESETTING > RESET
RESETTLE *vb* settle to live in a different place
RESETTLED > RESETTLE
RESETTLES > RESETTLE
RESEW *vb* sew again
RESEWED > RESEW
RESEWING > RESEW
RESEWN > RESEW
RESEWS > RESEW
RESH *n* 20th letter of the Hebrew alphabet
RESHAPE *vb* shape (something) again or differently
RESHAPED > RESHAPE
RESHAPER > RESHAPE
RESHAPERS > RESHAPE

RESHAPES > RESHAPE
RESHAPING *n* act of reshaping
RESHARPEN *vb* sharpen again
RESHAVE *vb* shave again
RESHAVED > RESHAVE
RESHAVEN > RESHAVE
RESHAVES > RESHAVE
RESHAVING > RESHAVE
RESHES > RESH
RESHINE *vb* shine again
RESHINED > RESHINE
RESHINES > RESHINE
RESHINING > RESHINE
RESHIP *vb* ship again
RESHIPPED > RESHIP
RESHIPPER > RESHIP
RESHIPS > RESHIP
RESHOD > RESHOE
RESHOE *vb* put a new shoe or shoes on
RESHOED > RESHOE
RESHOEING > RESHOE
RESHOES > RESHOE
RESHONE > RESHINE
RESHOOT *vb* shoot again
RESHOOTS > RESHOOT
RESHOT > RESHOOT
RESHOW *vb* show again
RESHOWED > RESHOW
RESHOWER *vb* have another shower
RESHOWERS > RESHOWER
RESHOWING > RESHOW
RESHOWN > RESHOW
RESHOWS > RESHOW
RESHUFFLE *n* reorganization ▷ *vb* reorganize
RESIANCE *archaic word for* > RESIDENCE
RESIANCES > RESIANCE
RESIANT *archaic word for* > RESIDENT
RESIANTS > RESIANT
RESID *n* residual oil left over from the petroleum distillation process
RESIDE *vb* dwell permanently
RESIDED > RESIDE
RESIDENCE *n* home or house
RESIDENCY *n* regular series of concerts by a band or singer at one venue
RESIDENT *n* person who lives in a place ▷ *adj* living in a place
RESIDENTS > RESIDENT
RESIDER > RESIDE
RESIDERS > RESIDE
RESIDES > RESIDE
RESIDING > RESIDE
RESIDS > RESID
RESIDUA > RESIDUUM
RESIDUAL *adj* of or being a remainder ▷ *n* something left over as a residue

RESIDUALS > RESIDUAL
RESIDUARY *adj* of, relating to, or constituting a residue
RESIDUE *n* what is left, remainder
RESIDUES > RESIDUE
RESIDUOUS *adj* residual
RESIDUUM *n* residue
RESIDUUMS > RESIDUUM
RESIFT *vb* sift again
RESIFTED > RESIFT
RESIFTING > RESIFT
RESIFTS > RESIFT
RESIGHT *vb* sight again
RESIGHTED > RESIGHT
RESIGHTS > RESIGHT
RESIGN *vb* give up office, a job, etc
RESIGNED *adj* content to endure
RESIGNER > RESIGN
RESIGNERS > RESIGN
RESIGNING > RESIGN
RESIGNS > RESIGN
RESILE *vb* spring or shrink back
RESILED > RESILE
RESILES > RESILE
RESILIENT *adj* (of a person) recovering quickly from a shock etc
RESILIN *n* substance found in insect bodies
RESILING > RESILE
RESILINS > RESILIN
RESILVER *vb* silver again
RESILVERS > RESILVER
RESIN *n* sticky substance from plants, esp pines ▷ *vb* treat or coat with resin
RESINATA *n* type of wine
RESINATAS > RESINATA
RESINATE *vb* impregnate with resin
RESINATED > RESINATE
RESINATES > RESINATE
RESINED > RESIN
RESINER *n* applier or collector of resin
RESINERS > RESINER
RESINIFY *vb* become or cause to be resinous
RESINING > RESIN
RESINISE *variant spelling of* > RESINIZE
RESINISED > RESINISE
RESINISES > RESINISE
RESINIZE *vb* apply resin to
RESINIZED > RESINIZE
RESINIZES > RESINIZE
RESINLIKE > RESIN
RESINOID *adj* resembling, characteristic of, or containing resin ▷ *n* any resinoid substance, esp a synthetic compound
RESINOIDS > RESINOID
RESINOSES > RESINOSIS

RESINOSIS n excessive resin loss in diseased or damaged conifers
RESINOUS > RESIN
RESINS > RESIN
RESINY adj resembling, containing or covered with resin
RESIST vb withstand or oppose ▷ n substance used to protect something
RESISTANT adj characterized by or showing resistance ▷ n person or thing that resists
RESISTED > RESIST
RESISTENT same as > RESISTANT
RESISTER > RESIST
RESISTERS > RESIST
RESISTING > RESIST
RESISTIVE adj exhibiting electrical resistance
RESISTOR n component of an electrical circuit producing resistance
RESISTORS > RESISTOR
RESISTS > RESIST
RESIT vb take (an exam) again ▷ n exam that has to be taken again
RESITE vb move to a different site
RESITED > RESITE
RESITES > RESITE
RESITING > RESITE
RESITS > RESIT
RESITTING > RESIT
RESITUATE vb situate elsewhere
RESIZE vb change size of
RESIZED > RESIZE
RESIZES > RESIZE
RESIZING > RESIZE
RESKETCH vb sketch again
RESKEW archaic spelling of > RESCUE
RESKEWED > RESKEW
RESKEWING > RESKEW
RESKEWS > RESKEW
RESKILL vb train (workers) to acquire new skills
RESKILLED > RESKILL
RESKILLS > RESKILL
RESKIN vb replace the outermost layer of an aircraft
RESKINNED > RESKIN
RESKINS > RESKIN
RESKUE archaic spelling of > RESCUE
RESKUED > RESKUE
RESKUES > RESKUE
RESKUING > RESKUE
RESLATE vb slate again
RESLATED > RESLATE
RESLATES > RESLATE
RESLATING > RESLATE
RESMELT vb smelt again
RESMELTED > RESMELT

RESMELTS > RESMELT
RESMOOTH vb smooth again
RESMOOTHS > RESMOOTH
RESNATRON n tetrode used to generate high power at high frequencies
RESOAK vb soak again
RESOAKED > RESOAK
RESOAKING > RESOAK
RESOAKS > RESOAK
RESOD vb returf
RESODDED > RESOD
RESODDING > RESOD
RESODS > RESOD
RESOFTEN vb soften again
RESOFTENS > RESOFTEN
RESOJET n type of jet engine
RESOJETS > RESOJET
RESOLD > RESELL
RESOLDER vb solder again
RESOLDERS > RESOLDER
RESOLE vb put a new sole or new soles on
RESOLED > RESOLE
RESOLES > RESOLE
RESOLING > RESOLE
RESOLUBLE adj able to be resolved
RESOLUTE adj firm in purpose ▷ n someone resolute
RESOLUTER > RESOLUTE
RESOLUTES > RESOLUTE
RESOLVE vb decide with an effort of will ▷ n absolute determination
RESOLVED adj determined
RESOLVENT adj serving to dissolve or separate something into its elements ▷ n something that resolves
RESOLVER > RESOLVE
RESOLVERS > RESOLVE
RESOLVES > RESOLVE
RESOLVING > RESOLVE
RESONANCE n echoing, esp with a deep sound
RESONANT adj resounding or re-echoing ▷ n type of unobstructed speech sound
RESONANTS > RESONANT
RESONATE vb resound or cause to resound
RESONATED > RESONATE
RESONATES > RESONATE
RESONATOR n any body or system that displays resonance, esp a tuned electrical circuit or a conducting cavity in which microwaves are generated by a resonant current
RESORB vb absorb again
RESORBED > RESORB
RESORBENT > RESORB
RESORBING > RESORB
RESORBS > RESORB
RESORCIN n substance used principally in dyeing

RESORCINS > RESORCIN
RESORT vb have recourse (to) for help etc ▷ n place for holidays
RESORTED > RESORT
RESORTER > RESORT
RESORTERS > RESORT
RESORTING > RESORT
RESORTS > RESORT
RESOUGHT > RESEEK
RESOUND vb echo or ring with sound
RESOUNDED > RESOUND
RESOUNDS > RESOUND
RESOURCE n thing resorted to for support ▷ vb provide funding or other resources for
RESOURCED > RESOURCE
RESOURCES > RESOURCE
RESOW vb sow again
RESOWED > RESOW
RESOWING > RESOW
RESOWN > RESOW
RESOWS > RESOW
RESPACE vb change the spacing of
RESPACED > RESPACE
RESPACES > RESPACE
RESPACING > RESPACE
RESPADE vb dig over
RESPADED > RESPADE
RESPADES > RESPADE
RESPADING > RESPADE
RESPEAK vb speak further
RESPEAKS > RESPEAK
RESPECIFY vb specify again
RESPECT n consideration ▷ vb treat with esteem
RESPECTED > RESPECT
RESPECTER n person who respects someone or something
RESPECTS > RESPECT
RESPELL vb spell again
RESPELLED > RESPELL
RESPELLS > RESPELL
RESPELT > RESPELL
RESPIRE vb breathe
RESPIRED > RESPIRE
RESPIRES > RESPIRE
RESPIRING > RESPIRE
RESPITE n pause, interval of rest ▷ vb grant a respite to
RESPITED > RESPITE
RESPITES > RESPITE
RESPITING > RESPITE
RESPLEND vb be resplendent
RESPLENDS > RESPLEND
RESPLICE vb splice again
RESPLICED > RESPLICE
RESPLICES > RESPLICE
RESPLIT vb split again
RESPLITS > RESPLIT
RESPOKE > RESPEAK
RESPOKEN > RESPEAK
RESPOND vb answer ▷ n pilaster or an engaged column that supports an arch or a lintel

RESPONDED > RESPOND
RESPONDER > RESPOND
RESPONDS > RESPOND
RESPONSA n that part of rabbinic literature concerned with written rulings in answer to questions
RESPONSE n answer
RESPONSER n radio or radar receiver used in conjunction with an interrogator to receive and display signals from a transponder
RESPONSES > RESPONSE
RESPONSOR same as > RESPONSER
RESPONSUM n written answer from a rabbinic authority to a question submitted
RESPOOL vb rewind onto spool
RESPOOLED > RESPOOL
RESPOOLS > RESPOOL
RESPOT vb (in billiards) replace on one of the spots
RESPOTS > RESPOT
RESPOTTED > RESPOT
RESPRANG > RESPRING
RESPRAY n new coat of paint applied to a car, van, etc ▷ vb spray (a car, wheels, etc) with a new coat of paint
RESPRAYED > RESPRAY
RESPRAYS > RESPRAY
RESPREAD vb spread again
RESPREADS > RESPREAD
RESPRING vb put new springs in
RESPRINGS > RESPRING
RESPROUT vb sprout again
RESPROUTS > RESPROUT
RESPRUNG > RESPRING
RESSALDAR n native cavalry commander in mixed Anglo-Indian army
REST n freedom from exertion etc ▷ vb take a rest
RESTABLE vb put in stable again or elsewhere
RESTABLED > RESTABLE
RESTABLES > RESTABLE
RESTACK vb stack again
RESTACKED > RESTACK
RESTACKS > RESTACK
RESTAFF vb staff again
RESTAFFED > RESTAFF
RESTAFFS > RESTAFF
RESTAGE vb produce or perform a new production of (a play)
RESTAGED > RESTAGE
RESTAGES > RESTAGE
RESTAGING > RESTAGE
RESTAMP vb stamp again
RESTAMPED > RESTAMP
RESTAMPS > RESTAMP

RESTART vb commence (something) or set (something) in motion again ▷ n act or an instance of starting again
RESTARTED > RESTART
RESTARTER > RESTART
RESTARTS > RESTART
RESTATE vb state or affirm (something) again or in a different way
RESTATED > RESTATE
RESTATES > RESTATE
RESTATING > RESTATE
RESTATION vb station elsewhere
RESTED > REST
RESTEM vb stem again
RESTEMMED > RESTEM
RESTEMS > RESTEM
RESTER > REST
RESTERS > REST
RESTFUL adj relaxing or soothing
RESTFULLY > RESTFUL
RESTIER > RESTY
RESTIEST > RESTY
RESTIFF same as > RESTIVE
RESTIFORM adj (esp of bundles of nerve fibres) shaped like a cord or rope
RESTING > REST
RESTINGS > REST
RESTITCH vb stitch again
RESTITUTE vb restore
RESTIVE adj restless or impatient
RESTIVELY > RESTIVE
RESTLESS adj bored or dissatisfied
RESTO n restored antique, vintage car, etc
RESTOCK vb replenish stores or supplies
RESTOCKED > RESTOCK
RESTOCKS > RESTOCK
RESTOKE vb stoke again
RESTOKED > RESTOKE
RESTOKES > RESTOKE
RESTOKING > RESTOKE
RESTORAL n restoration
RESTORALS > RESTORAL
RESTORE vb return (a building, painting, etc) to its original condition
RESTORED > RESTORE
RESTORER > RESTORE
RESTORERS > RESTORE
RESTORES > RESTORE
RESTORING > RESTORE
RESTOS > RESTO
RESTRAIN vb hold (someone) back from action
RESTRAINS > RESTRAIN
RESTRAINT n something that restrains
RESTRESS vb stress again or differently
RESTRETCH vb stretch again

RESTRICT vb confine to certain limits
RESTRICTS > RESTRICT
RESTRIKE vb strike again
RESTRIKES > RESTRIKE
RESTRING vb string again or anew
RESTRINGE vb restrict
RESTRINGS > RESTRING
RESTRIVE vb strive again
RESTRIVEN > RESTRIVE
RESTRIVES > RESTRIVE
RESTROOM n room in a public building having lavatories, washing facilities, and sometimes couches
RESTROOMS > RESTROOM
RESTROVE > RESTRIVE
RESTRUCK > RESTRIKE
RESTRUNG > RESTRING
RESTS > REST
RESTUDIED > RESTUDY
RESTUDIES > RESTUDY
RESTUDY vb study again
RESTUFF vb put new stuffing in
RESTUFFED > RESTUFF
RESTUFFS > RESTUFF
RESTUMP vb provide with new stumps
RESTUMPED > RESTUMP
RESTUMPS > RESTUMP
RESTY adj restive
RESTYLE vb style again
RESTYLED > RESTYLE
RESTYLES > RESTYLE
RESTYLING > RESTYLE
RESUBJECT vb subject again
RESUBMIT vb submit again
RESUBMITS > RESUBMIT
RESULT n outcome or consequence ▷ vb be the outcome or consequence (of)
RESULTANT adj arising as a result ▷ n sum of two or more vectors, such as the force resulting from two or more forces acting on a single point
RESULTED > RESULT
RESULTFUL > RESULT
RESULTING > RESULT
RESULTS > RESULT
RESUMABLE > RESUME
RESUME vb begin again ▷ n summary
RESUMED > RESUME
RESUMER > RESUME
RESUMERS > RESUME
RESUMES > RESUME
RESUMING > RESUME
RESUMMON vb summon again
RESUMMONS > RESUMMON
RESUPINE adj lying on the back
RESUPPLY vb provide (with something) again
RESURFACE vb arise or occur again

RESURGE vb rise again from or as if from the dead
RESURGED > RESURGE
RESURGENT adj rising again, as to new life, vigour, etc
RESURGES > RESURGE
RESURGING > RESURGE
RESURRECT vb restore to life
RESURVEY vb survey again
RESURVEYS > RESURVEY
RESUS n (short for) resuscitation room
RESUSES > RESUS
RESUSPEND vb put back into suspension
RESUSSES > RESUS
RESWALLOW vb swallow again
RET vb moisten or soak (flax, hemp, jute, etc) to facilitate separation of fibres
RETABLE n ornamental screenlike structure above and behind an altar
RETABLES > RETABLE
RETABLO n shelf for panels behind an altar
RETABLOS > RETABLO
RETACK vb tack again
RETACKED > RETACK
RETACKING > RETACK
RETACKLE vb tackle again
RETACKLED > RETACKLE
RETACKLES > RETACKLE
RETACKS > RETACK
RETAG vb tag again
RETAGGED > RETAG
RETAGGING > RETAG
RETAGS > RETAG
RETAIL n selling of goods individually or in small amounts to the public ▷ adj of or engaged in such selling ▷ adv by retail ▷ vb sell or be sold retail
RETAILED > RETAIL
RETAILER > RETAIL
RETAILERS > RETAIL
RETAILING > RETAIL
RETAILOR vb tailor afresh
RETAILORS > RETAILOR
RETAILS > RETAIL
RETAIN vb keep in one's possession
RETAINED > RETAIN
RETAINER n fee to retain someone's services
RETAINERS > RETAINER
RETAINING > RETAIN
RETAINS > RETAIN
RETAKE vb recapture ▷ n act of rephotographing a scene
RETAKEN > RETAKE
RETAKER > RETAKE
RETAKERS > RETAKE
RETAKES > RETAKE
RETAKING > RETAKE
RETAKINGS > RETAKE

RETALIATE vb repay an injury or wrong in kind
RETALLIED > RETALLY
RETALLIES > RETALLY
RETALLY vb count up again
RETAMA n type of shrub
RETAMAS > RETAMA
RETAPE vb tape again
RETAPED > RETAPE
RETAPES > RETAPE
RETAPING > RETAPE
RETARD vb delay or slow (progress or development) ▷ n offensive term for a retarded person
RETARDANT n substance that reduces the rate of a chemical reaction ▷ adj having a slowing effect
RETARDATE n person who is retarded
RETARDED adj underdeveloped, esp mentally
RETARDER n person or thing that retards
RETARDERS > RETARDER
RETARDING > RETARD
RETARDS > RETARD
RETARGET vb target afresh or differently
RETARGETS > RETARGET
RETASTE vb taste again
RETASTED > RETASTE
RETASTES > RETASTE
RETASTING > RETASTE
RETAUGHT > RETEACH
RETAX vb tax again
RETAXED > RETAX
RETAXES > RETAX
RETAXING > RETAX
RETCH vb try to vomit ▷ n involuntary spasm of the stomach
RETCHED > RETCH
RETCHES > RETCH
RETCHING n act of retching
RETCHINGS > RETCHING
RETCHLESS archaic variant of > RECKLESS
RETE n any network of nerves or blood vessels
RETEACH vb teach again
RETEACHES > RETEACH
RETEAM vb team up again
RETEAMED > RETEAM
RETEAMING > RETEAM
RETEAMS > RETEAM
RETEAR vb tear again
RETEARING > RETEAR
RETEARS > RETEAR
RETELL vb relate (a story, etc) again or differently
RETELLER > RETELL
RETELLERS > RETELL
RETELLING > RETELL
RETELLS > RETELL
RETEM n type of shrub
RETEMPER vb temper again
RETEMPERS > RETEMPER

RETEMS > RETEM
RETENE n yellow crystalline hydrocarbon found in tar oils
RETENES > RETENE
RETENTION n retaining
RETENTIVE adj capable of retaining or remembering
RETEST vb test (something) again or differently
RETESTED > RETEST
RETESTIFY vb testify again
RETESTING > RETEST
RETESTS > RETEST
RETEXTURE vb restore natural texture to
RETHINK vb consider again, esp with a view to changing one's tactics ▷ n act or an instance of thinking again
RETHINKER > RETHINK
RETHINKS > RETHINK
RETHOUGHT > RETHINK
RETHREAD vb thread again
RETHREADS > RETHREAD
RETIA > RETE
RETIAL > RETE
RETIARII > RETIARIUS
RETIARIUS n (in ancient Rome) a gladiator armed with a net and trident
RETIARY adj of, relating to, or resembling a net or web
RETICELLA n form of lace
RETICENCE > RETICENT
RETICENCY > RETICENT
RETICENT adj uncommunicative, reserved
RETICLE n network of fine lines, wires, etc, used in optical instruments
RETICLES > RETICLE
RETICULA > RETICULUM
RETICULAR adj in the form of a network or having a network of parts
RETICULE same as > RETICLE
RETICULES > RETICULE
RETICULUM n any fine network, esp one in the body composed of cells, fibres, etc
RETIE vb tie again
RETIED > RETIE
RETIEING > RETIE
RETIES > RETIE
RETIFORM adj netlike
RETIGHTEN vb tighten again
RETILE vb put new tiles in or on
RETILED > RETILE
RETILES > RETILE
RETILING > RETILE
RETIME vb time again or alter time of

RETIMED > RETIME
RETIMES > RETIME
RETIMING > RETIME
RETINA n light-sensitive membrane at the back of the eye
RETINAE > RETINA
RETINAL adj of or relating to the retina ▷ n aldehyde form of the polyene retinol
RETINALS > RETINAL
RETINAS > RETINA
RETINE n chemical found in body cells that slows cell growth and division
RETINENE n aldehyde form of the polyene retinol (vitamin A) that associates with the protein opsin to form the visual purple pigment rhodopsin
RETINENES > RETINENE
RETINES > RETINE
RETINITE n any of various resins of fossil origin, esp one derived from lignite
RETINITES > RETINITE
RETINITIS n inflammation of the retina
RETINOIC adj containing or derived from retinoid
RETINOID adj resinlike ▷ n derivative of vitamin A
RETINOIDS > RETINOID
RETINOL n another name for vitamin A and rosin oil
RETINOLS > RETINOL
RETINT vb tint again or change tint of
RETINTED > RETINT
RETINTING > RETINT
RETINTS > RETINT
RETINUE n band of attendants
RETINUED > RETINUE
RETINUES > RETINUE
RETINULA n part of the compound eye in certain arthropods
RETINULAE > RETINULA
RETINULAR > RETINULA
RETINULAS > RETINULA
RETIRACY n (in US English) retirement
RETIRAL n act of retiring from office, one's work, etc
RETIRALS > RETIRAL
RETIRANT n (in US English) retired person
RETIRANTS > RETIRANT
RETIRE vb (cause to) give up office or work, esp through age
RETIRED adj having retired from work etc
RETIREDLY > RETIRED
RETIREE n person who has retired from work
RETIREES > RETIREE
RETIRER > RETIRE
RETIRERS > RETIRE
RETIRES > RETIRE

RETIRING adj shy
RETITLE vb give a new title to
RETITLED > RETITLE
RETITLES > RETITLE
RETITLING > RETITLE
RETOLD > RETELL
RETOOK > RETAKE
RETOOL vb replace, re-equip, or rearrange the tools in (a factory, etc)
RETOOLED > RETOOL
RETOOLING > RETOOL
RETOOLS > RETOOL
RETORE > RETEAR
RETORN > RETEAR
RETORSION n retaliatory action taken by a state whose citizens have been mistreated by a foreign power by treating the subjects of that power similarly
RETORT vb reply quickly, wittily, or angrily ▷ n quick, witty, or angry reply
RETORTED > RETORT
RETORTER > RETORT
RETORTERS > RETORT
RETORTING > RETORT
RETORTION n act of retorting
RETORTIVE > RETORT
RETORTS > RETORT
RETOTAL vb add up again
RETOTALED > RETOTAL
RETOTALS > RETOTAL
RETOUCH vb restore or improve by new touches, esp of paint ▷ n art or practice of retouching
RETOUCHED > RETOUCH
RETOUCHER > RETOUCH
RETOUCHES > RETOUCH
RETOUR vb (in Scottish law) to return as heir
RETOURED > RETOUR
RETOURING > RETOUR
RETOURS > RETOUR
RETOX vb embark on a binge of something unhealthy after a period of abstinence
RETOXED > RETOX
RETOXES > RETOX
RETOXING > RETOX
RETRACE vb go back over (a route etc) again
RETRACED > RETRACE
RETRACER > RETRACE
RETRACERS > RETRACE
RETRACES > RETRACE
RETRACING > RETRACE
RETRACK vb track again
RETRACKED > RETRACK
RETRACKS > RETRACK
RETRACT vb withdraw (a statement etc)
RETRACTED > RETRACT
RETRACTOR n any of various muscles that retract an organ or part
RETRACTS > RETRACT

RETRAICT archaic form of > RETREAT
RETRAICTS > RETRAICT
RETRAIN vb train to do a new or different job
RETRAINED > RETRAIN
RETRAINEE > RETRAIN
RETRAINS > RETRAIN
RETRAIT archaic form of > RETREAT
RETRAITE archaic form of > RETREAT
RETRAITES > RETRAITE
RETRAITS > RETRAIT
RETRAITT n archaic word meaning portrait
RETRAITTS > RETRAITT
RETRAL adj at, near, or towards the back
RETRALLY > RETRAL
RETRATE archaic form of > RETREAT
RETRATED > RETRATE
RETRATES > RETRATE
RETRATING > RETRATE
RETREAD n remould ▷ vb remould
RETREADED > RETREAD
RETREADS > RETREAD
RETREAT vb move back from a position, withdraw ▷ n act of or military signal for retiring or withdrawal
RETREATED > RETREAT
RETREATER > RETREAT
RETREATS > RETREAT
RETREE n imperfectly made paper
RETREES > RETREE
RETRENCH vb reduce expenditure, cut back
RETRIAL n second trial of a case or defendant in a court of law
RETRIALS > RETRIAL
RETRIBUTE vb give back
RETRIED > RETRY
RETRIES > RETRY
RETRIEVAL n act or process of retrieving
RETRIEVE vb fetch back again ▷ n chance of being retrieved
RETRIEVED > RETRIEVE
RETRIEVER n dog trained to retrieve shot game
RETRIEVES > RETRIEVE
RETRIM vb trim again
RETRIMMED > RETRIM
RETRIMS > RETRIM
RETRO adj associated with or revived from the past ▷ n a retro style of art
RETROACT vb act in opposition
RETROACTS > RETROACT
RETROCEDE vb give back
RETROD > RETREAD
RETRODDEN > RETREAD
RETRODICT vb make surmises about the past using information from the present

RETROFIRE n act of firing a retrorocket
RETROFIT vb equip (a vehicle, piece of equipment, etc) with new parts, safety devices, etc, after manufacture
RETROFITS > RETROFIT
RETROFLEX adj bent or curved backwards ▷ vb bend or turn backwards
RETROJECT vb throw backwards
RETRONYM n word coined for existing thing to distinguish it from new thing
RETRONYMS > RETRONYM
RETROPACK n system of retrorockets on a spacecraft
RETRORSE adj (esp of plant parts) pointing backwards or in a direction opposite to normal
RETROS > RETRO
RETROUSSE adj (of a nose) turned upwards
RETROVERT vb turn back
RETRY vb try again (a case already determined)
RETRYING > RETRY
RETS > RET
RETSINA n Greek wine flavoured with resin
RETSINAS > RETSINA
RETTED > RET
RETTERIES > RETTERY
RETTERY n flax-retting place
RETTING > RET
RETUND vb weaken or blunt
RETUNDED > RETUND
RETUNDING > RETUND
RETUNDS > RETUND
RETUNE vb tune (a musical instrument) differently or again
RETUNED > RETUNE
RETUNES > RETUNE
RETUNING > RETUNE
RETURF vb turf again
RETURFED > RETURF
RETURFING > RETURF
RETURFS > RETURF
RETURN vb go or come back ▷ n returning ▷ adj of or being a return
RETURNED > RETURN
RETURNEE n person who returns to his native country, esp after war service
RETURNEES > RETURNEE
RETURNER n person or thing that returns
RETURNERS > RETURNER
RETURNIK n someone returning or intending to return to their native land, especially when this is in the former Soviet Union

RETURNIKS > RETURNIK
RETURNING > RETURN
RETURNS > RETURN
RETUSE adj having a rounded apex and a central depression
RETWEET vb post (another user's post) on the Twitter website for one's own followers
RETWEETED > RETWEET
RETWEETS > RETWEET
RETWIST vb twist again
RETWISTED > RETWIST
RETWISTS > RETWIST
RETYING > RETIE
RETYPE vb type again
RETYPED > RETYPE
RETYPES > RETYPE
RETYPING > RETYPE
REUNIFIED > REUNIFY
REUNIFIES > REUNIFY
REUNIFY vb bring together again something previously divided
REUNION n meeting of people who have been apart
REUNIONS > REUNION
REUNITE vb bring or come together again after a separation
REUNITED > REUNITE
REUNITER > REUNITE
REUNITERS > REUNITE
REUNITES > REUNITE
REUNITING > REUNITE
REUPTAKE vb absorb again ▷ n act of reabsorbing
REUPTAKEN > REUPTAKE
REUPTAKES > REUPTAKE
REUPTOOK > REUPTAKE
REURGE vb urge again
REURGED > REURGE
REURGES > REURGE
REURGING > REURGE
REUSABLE adj able to be used more than once
REUSABLES pl n products which can be used more than once
REUSE vb use again ▷ n act of using something again
REUSED > REUSE
REUSES > REUSE
REUSING > REUSE
REUTILISE same as > REUTILIZE
REUTILIZE vb utilize again
REUTTER vb utter again
REUTTERED > REUTTER
REUTTERS > REUTTER
REV n revolution (of an engine) ▷ vb increase the speed of revolution of (an engine)
REVALENTA n lentil flour
REVALUATE same as > REVALUE
REVALUE vb adjust the exchange value of (a currency) upwards

REVALUED > REVALUE
REVALUES > REVALUE
REVALUING > REVALUE
REVAMP vb renovate or restore ▷ n something that has been renovated or revamped
REVAMPED > REVAMP
REVAMPER > REVAMP
REVAMPERS > REVAMP
REVAMPING > REVAMP
REVAMPS > REVAMP
REVANCHE n revenge
REVANCHES > REVANCHE
REVARNISH vb varnish again
REVEAL vb make known ▷ n vertical side of an opening in a wall
REVEALED > REVEAL
REVEALER > REVEAL
REVEALERS > REVEAL
REVEALING adj disclosing information that one did not know
REVEALS > REVEAL
REVEHENT adj (in anatomy) carrying back
REVEILLE n morning bugle call to waken soldiers
REVEILLES > REVEILLE
REVEL vb take pleasure (in) ▷ n occasion of noisy merrymaking
REVELATOR n revealer
REVELED > REVEL
REVELER > REVEL
REVELERS > REVEL
REVELING > REVEL
REVELLED > REVEL
REVELLER > REVEL
REVELLERS > REVEL
REVELLING > REVEL
REVELMENT > REVEL
REVELRIES > REVELRY
REVELROUS > REVELRY
REVELRY n festivity
REVELS > REVEL
REVENANT n something, esp a ghost, that returns
REVENANTS > REVENANT
REVENGE n retaliation for wrong done ▷ vb make retaliation for
REVENGED > REVENGE
REVENGER > REVENGE
REVENGERS > REVENGE
REVENGES > REVENGE
REVENGING > REVENGE
REVENGIVE > REVENGE
REVENUAL > REVENUE
REVENUE n income, esp of a state
REVENUED > REVENUE
REVENUER n revenue officer or cutter
REVENUERS > REVENUER
REVENUES > REVENUE
REVERABLE > REVERE
REVERB n electronic device that creates

artificial acoustics ▷ vb reverberate
REVERBED > REVERB
REVERBING > REVERB
REVERBS > REVERB
REVERE vb be in awe of and respect greatly
REVERED > REVERE
REVERENCE n awe mingled with respect and esteem
REVEREND adj worthy of reverence ▷ n clergyman
REVERENDS > REVEREND
REVERENT adj showing reverence
REVERER > REVERE
REVERERS > REVERE
REVERES > REVERE
REVERIE n absent-minded daydream
REVERIES > REVERIE
REVERIFY vb verify again
REVERING > REVERE
REVERIST n someone given to reveries
REVERISTS > REVERIST
REVERS n turned back part of a garment, such as the lapel
REVERSAL n act or an instance of reversing
REVERSALS > REVERSAL
REVERSE vb turn upside down or the other way round ▷ n opposite ▷ adj opposite or contrary
REVERSED > REVERSE
REVERSELY > REVERSE
REVERSER > REVERSE
REVERSERS > REVERSE
REVERSES > REVERSE
REVERSI n game played on a draughtboard
REVERSING > REVERSE
REVERSION n return to a former state, practice, or belief
REVERSIS n type of card game
REVERSO another name for > VERSO
REVERSOS > REVERSO
REVERT vb return to a former state
REVERTANT n mutant that has reverted to an earlier form ▷ adj having mutated to an earlier form
REVERTED > REVERT
REVERTER > REVERT
REVERTERS > REVERT
REVERTING > REVERT
REVERTIVE > REVERT
REVERTS > REVERT
REVERY same as > REVERIE
REVEST vb restore (former power, authority, status, etc, to a person)
REVESTED > REVEST
REVESTING > REVEST
REVESTRY same as > VESTRY

REVESTS > REVEST
REVET *vb* face (a wall or embankment) with stones
REVETMENT *n* facing of stones, sandbags, etc, to protect a wall, embankment, or earthworks
REVETS > REVET
REVETTED > REVET
REVETTING > REVET
REVEUR *n* daydreamer
REVEURS > REVEUR
REVEUSE *n* female daydreamer
REVEUSES > REVEUSE
REVIBRATE *vb* vibrate again
REVICTUAL *vb* victual again
REVIE *vb* archaic cards term meaning challenge by placing a larger stake
REVIED > REVIE
REVIES > REVIE
REVIEW *n* critical assessment of a book, concert, etc ▷ *vb* hold or write a review of
REVIEWAL *same as* **>** REVIEW
REVIEWALS > REVIEWAL
REVIEWED > REVIEW
REVIEWER > REVIEW
REVIEWERS > REVIEW
REVIEWING > REVIEW
REVIEWS > REVIEW
REVILE *vb* be abusively scornful of
REVILED > REVILE
REVILER > REVILE
REVILERS > REVILE
REVILES > REVILE
REVILING > REVILE
REVILINGS > REVILE
REVIOLATE *vb* violate again
REVISABLE > REVISE
REVISAL > REVISE
REVISALS > REVISE
REVISE *vb* change or alter ▷ *n* act, process, or result of revising
REVISED > REVISE
REVISER > REVISE
REVISERS > REVISE
REVISES > REVISE
REVISING > REVISE
REVISION *n* act of revising
REVISIONS > REVISION
REVISIT *vb* visit again
REVISITED > REVISIT
REVISITS > REVISIT
REVISOR > REVISE
REVISORS > REVISE
REVISORY *adj* of or having the power of revision
REVIVABLE > REVIVE
REVIVABLY > REVIVE
REVIVAL *n* reviving or renewal

REVIVALS > REVIVAL
REVIVE *vb* bring or come back to life, vigour, use, etc
REVIVED > REVIVE
REVIVER > REVIVE
REVIVERS > REVIVE
REVIVES > REVIVE
REVIVIFY *vb* give new life to
REVIVING > REVIVE
REVIVINGS > REVIVE
REVIVOR *n* means of reviving a lawsuit that has been suspended
REVIVORS > REVIVOR
REVOCABLE *adj* capable of being revoked
REVOCABLY **>** REVOCABLE
REVOICE *vb* utter again
REVOICED > REVOICE
REVOICES > REVOICE
REVOICING > REVOICE
REVOKABLE *same as* **>** REVOCABLE
REVOKABLY **>** REVOCABLE
REVOKE *vb* cancel (a will, agreement, etc) ▷ *n* act of revoking
REVOKED > REVOKE
REVOKER > REVOKE
REVOKERS > REVOKE
REVOKES > REVOKE
REVOKING > REVOKE
REVOLT *n* uprising against authority ▷ *vb* rise in rebellion
REVOLTED > REVOLT
REVOLTER > REVOLT
REVOLTERS > REVOLT
REVOLTING *adj* disgusting, horrible
REVOLTS > REVOLT
REVOLUTE *adj* (esp of the margins of a leaf) rolled backwards and downwards
REVOLVE *vb* turn round, rotate ▷ *n* circular section of a stage that can be rotated
REVOLVED > REVOLVE
REVOLVER *n* repeating pistol
REVOLVERS > REVOLVER
REVOLVES > REVOLVE
REVOLVING *adj* denoting or relating to an engine, such as a radial aero engine, in which the cylinders revolve about a fixed shaft
REVOTE *vb* decide or grant again by a new vote
REVOTED > REVOTE
REVOTES > REVOTE
REVOTING > REVOTE
REVS > REV
REVUE *n* theatrical entertainment with topical sketches and songs
REVUES > REVUE
REVUIST > REVUE

REVUISTS > REVUE
REVULSED *adj* filled with disgust
REVULSION *n* strong disgust
REVULSIVE *adj* of or causing revulsion ▷ *n* counterirritant
REVVED > REV
REVVING > REV
REVYING > REVIE
REW *archaic spelling of* **>** RUE
REWAKE *vb* awaken again
REWAKED > REWAKE
REWAKEN *vb* awaken again
REWAKENED > REWAKEN
REWAKENS > REWAKEN
REWAKES > REWAKE
REWAKING > REWAKE
REWAN *archaic past form of* **>** REWIN
REWARD *n* something given in return for a service ▷ *vb* pay or give something to (someone) for a service, information, etc
REWARDED > REWARD
REWARDER > REWARD
REWARDERS > REWARD
REWARDFUL > REWARD
REWARDING *adj* giving personal satisfaction, worthwhile
REWARDS > REWARD
REWAREWA *n* New Zealand tree
REWAREWAS > REWAREWA
REWARM *vb* warm again
REWARMED > REWARM
REWARMING > REWARM
REWARMS > REWARM
REWASH *vb* wash again
REWASHED > REWASH
REWASHES > REWASH
REWASHING > REWASH
REWATER *vb* water again
REWATERED > REWATER
REWATERS > REWATER
REWAX *vb* wax again
REWAXED > REWAX
REWAXES > REWAX
REWAXING > REWAX
REWEAR *vb* wear again
REWEARING > REWEAR
REWEARS > REWEAR
REWEAVE *vb* weave again
REWEAVED > REWEAVE
REWEAVES > REWEAVE
REWEAVING > REWEAVE
REWED *vb* wed again
REWEDDED > REWED
REWEDDING > REWED
REWEDS > REWED
REWEIGH *vb* weigh again
REWEIGHED > REWEIGH
REWEIGHS > REWEIGH
REWELD *vb* weld again
REWELDED > REWELD
REWELDING > REWELD
REWELDS > REWELD
REWET *vb* wet again
REWETS > REWET

REWETTED > REWET
REWETTING > REWET
REWIDEN *vb* widen again
REWIDENED > REWIDEN
REWIDENS > REWIDEN
REWILD *vb* return areas of land to a wild state
REWILDED > REWILD
REWILDING *n* returning land areas to a wild state
REWILDS > REWILD
REWIN *vb* win again
REWIND *vb* wind again
REWINDED > REWIND
REWINDER > REWIND
REWINDERS > REWIND
REWINDING *n* act of rewinding
REWINDS > REWIND
REWINNING > REWIN
REWINS > REWIN
REWIRABLE > REWIRE
REWIRE *vb* provide (a house, engine, etc) with new wiring
REWIRED > REWIRE
REWIRES > REWIRE
REWIRING *n* act of rewiring
REWIRINGS > REWIRING
REWOKE > REWAKE
REWOKEN > REWAKE
REWON > REWIN
REWORD *vb* alter the wording of
REWORDED > REWORD
REWORDING > REWORD
REWORDS > REWORD
REWORE > REWEAR
REWORK *vb* improve or bring up to date
REWORKED > REWORK
REWORKING > REWORK
REWORKS > REWORK
REWORN > REWEAR
REWOUND > REWIND
REWOVE > REWEAVE
REWOVEN > REWEAVE
REWRAP *vb* wrap again
REWRAPPED > REWRAP
REWRAPS > REWRAP
REWRAPT > REWRAP
REWRITE *vb* write again in a different way ▷ *n* something rewritten
REWRITER > REWRITE
REWRITERS > REWRITE
REWRITES > REWRITE
REWRITING > REWRITE
REWRITTEN > REWRITE
REWROTE > REWRITE
REWROUGHT > REWORK
REWS > REW
REWTH *archaic variant of* **>** RUTH
REWTHS > REWTH
REX *n* king
REXES > REX
REXINE *n* tradename for a form of artificial leather
REXINES > REXINE
REYNARD *n* fox
REYNARDS > REYNARD

REZ *n* informal word for an instance of reserving; reservation

REZERO *vb* reset to zero

REZEROED > REZERO

REZEROES > REZERO

REZEROING > REZERO

REZEROS > REZERO

REZES > REZ

REZONE *vb* zone again

REZONED > REZONE

REZONES > REZONE

REZONING > REZONE

REZZES > REZ

RHABDOID *adj* rod-shaped ▷ *n* rod-shaped structure found in cells of some plants and animals

RHABDOIDS > RHABDOID

RHABDOM *n* rodlike structures found in the eye of insects

RHABDOMAL > RHABDOM

RHABDOME *same as* > RHABDOM

RHABDOMES > RHABDOME

RHABDOMS > RHABDOM

RHABDUS *n* sponge spicule

RHABDUSES > RHABDUS

RHACHIAL > RACHIS

RHACHIDES > RHACHIS

RHACHILLA *same as* > RACHILLA

RHACHIS *same as* > RACHIS

RHACHISES > RHACHIS

RHACHITIS *same as* > RACHITIS

RHAGADES *pl n* cracks found in the skin

RHAMNOSE *n* type of plant sugar

RHAMNOSES > RHAMNOSE

RHAMNUS *n* buckthorn

RHAMNUSES > RHAMNUS

RHAMPHOID *adj* beaklike

RHANJA *n* Indian English word for a male lover

RHANJAS > RHANJA

RHAPHAE > RHAPHE

RHAPHE *same as* > RAPHE

RHAPHES > RHAPHE

RHAPHIDE *same as* > RAPHIDE

RHAPHIDES > RHAPHIDE

RHAPHIS *same as* > RAPHIDE

RHAPONTIC *n* rhubarb

RHAPSODE *n* (in ancient Greece) professional reciter of poetry

RHAPSODES > RHAPSODE

RHAPSODIC *adj* of or like a rhapsody

RHAPSODY *n* freely structured emotional piece of music

RHATANIES > RHATANY

RHATANY *n* South American leguminous shrub

RHEA *n* S American three-toed ostrich

RHEAS > RHEA

RHEBOK *n* woolly brownish-grey southern African antelope

RHEBOKS > RHEBOK

RHEMATIC *adj* of or relating to word formation

RHEME *n* constituent of a sentence that adds most new information

RHEMES > RHEME

RHENIUM *n* silvery-white metallic element with a high melting point

RHENIUMS > RHENIUM

RHEOBASE *n* minimum nerve impulse required to elicit a response from a tissue

RHEOBASES > RHEOBASE

RHEOBASIC > RHEOBASE

RHEOCHORD *n* wire inserted into an electrical circuit to vary or regulate the current

RHEOCORD *same as* > RHEOCHORD

RHEOCORDS > RHEOCORD

RHEOLOGIC > RHEOLOGY

RHEOLOGY *n* branch of physics concerned with the flow and change of shape of matter

RHEOMETER *n* instrument for measuring the velocity of the blood flow

RHEOMETRY > RHEOMETER

RHEOPHIL *adj* liking flowing water

RHEOPHILE *n* something that likes flowing water

RHEOSTAT *n* instrument for varying the resistance of an electrical circuit

RHEOSTATS > RHEOSTAT

RHEOTAXES > RHEOTAXIS

RHEOTAXIS *n* movement of an organism towards or away from a current of water

RHEOTOME *n* interrupter

RHEOTOMES > RHEOTOME

RHEOTROPE *n* electric-current-reversing device

RHESUS *n* macaque monkey

RHESUSES > RHESUS

RHETOR *n* teacher of rhetoric

RHETORIC *n* art of effective speaking or writing

RHETORICS > RHETORIC

RHETORISE *same as* > RHETORIZE

RHETORIZE *vb* make use of rhetoric

RHETORS > RHETOR

RHEUM *n* watery discharge from the eyes or nose

RHEUMATIC *adj* (person) affected by rheumatism ▷ *n* person suffering from rheumatism

RHEUMATIZ *n* dialect word meaning rheumatism, any painful disorder of joints, muscles, or connective tissue

RHEUMED *adj* rheumy

RHEUMIC *adj* of or relating to rheum

RHEUMIER > RHEUMY

RHEUMIEST > RHEUMY

RHEUMS > RHEUM

RHEUMY *adj* of the nature of rheum

RHEXES > RHEXIS

RHEXIS *n* rupture

RHEXISES > RHEXIS

RHIES > RHY

RHIGOLENE *n* volatile liquid obtained from petroleum and used as a local anaesthetic

RHIME *old spelling of* > RHYME

RHIMES > RHIME

RHINAL *adj* of or relating to the nose

RHINE *n* dialect word for a ditch

RHINES > RHINE

RHINITIC > RHINITIS

RHINITIS *n* inflammation of the mucous membrane that lines the nose

RHINO *n* rhinoceros

RHINOCERI *n* rhinoceroses

RHINOLITH *n* calculus formed in the nose

RHINOLOGY *n* branch of medical science concerned with the nose and its diseases

RHINOS > RHINO

RHIPIDATE *adj* shaped like a fan

RHIPIDION *n* fan found in Greek Orthodox churches

RHIPIDIUM *n* on a plant, a fan-shaped arrangement of flowers

RHIZIC *adj* of or relating to the root of an equation

RHIZINE *same as* > RHIZOID

RHIZINES > RHIZINE

RHIZOBIA > RHIZOBIUM

RHIZOBIAL > RHIZOBIUM

RHIZOBIUM *n* type of rod-shaped bacterium typically occurring in the root nodules of leguminous plants

RHIZOCARP *n* plant that fruits underground or whose root remains intact while the leaves die off annually

RHIZOCAUL *n* rootlike stem

RHIZOID *n* hairlike structure in mosses, ferns, and related plants

RHIZOIDAL > RHIZOID

RHIZOIDS > RHIZOID

RHIZOMA *same as* > RHIZOME

RHIZOMATA > RHIZOMA

RHIZOME *n* thick underground stem producing new plants

RHIZOMES > RHIZOME

RHIZOMIC > RHIZOME

RHIZOPI > RHIZOPUS

RHIZOPOD *n* type of protozoan of the phylum which includes the amoebas

RHIZOPODS > RHIZOPOD

RHIZOPUS *n* type of fungus

RHIZOTOMY *n* surgical incision into the roots of spinal nerves, esp for the relief of pain

RHO *n* 17th letter in the Greek alphabet

RHODAMIN *same as* > RHODAMINE

RHODAMINE *n* any one of a group of synthetic red or pink basic dyestuffs used for wool and silk. They are made from phthalic anhydride and aminophenols

RHODAMINS > RHODAMIN

RHODANATE *n* sulphocyanate

RHODANIC *adj* of or relating to sulphocyanic acid

RHODANISE *same as* > RHODANIZE

RHODANIZE *vb* plate with rhodium

RHODIC *adj* of or containing rhodium, esp in the tetravalent state

RHODIE *same as* > RHODY

RHODIES > RHODY

RHODINAL *n* substance with a lemon-like smell found esp in citronella and certain eucalyptus oils

RHODINALS > RHODINAL

RHODIUM *n* hard metallic element

RHODIUMS > RHODIUM

RHODOLITE *n* pale violet or red variety of garnet, used as a gemstone

RHODONITE *n* brownish translucent mineral

RHODOPSIN *n* red pigment in the rods of the retina in vertebrates. It is dissociated by light into retinene, the light energy being converted into nerve signals, and is re-formed in the dark

RHODORA *n* type of shrub

RHODORAS > RHODORA

RHODOUS adj of or containing rhodium (but proportionally more than a rhodic compound)

RHODY n rhododendron

RHOEADINE n alkaloid found in the poppy

RHOMB same as > RHOMBUS

RHOMBI > RHOMBUS

RHOMBIC adj relating to or having the shape of a rhombus

RHOMBICAL same as > RHOMBIC

RHOMBOI > RHOMBOS

RHOMBOID n parallelogram with adjacent sides of unequal length ▷ adj having such a shape

RHOMBOIDS > RHOMBOID

RHOMBOS n wooden slat attached to a thong that makes a roaring sound when the thong is whirled

RHOMBS > RHOMB

RHOMBUS n diamond-shaped figure

RHOMBUSES > RHOMBUS

RHONCHAL > RHONCHUS

RHONCHI > RHONCHUS

RHONCHIAL > RHONCHUS

RHONCHUS n rattling or whistling respiratory sound resembling snoring, caused by secretions in the trachea or bronchi

RHONCUS n rattling or whistling respiratory sound resembling snoring

RHONCUSES > RHONCUS

RHONE same as > RONE

RHONES > RHONE

RHOPALIC adj describes verse in which each successive word has one more syllable than the word before

RHOPALISM > RHOPALIC

RHOS > RHO

RHOTACISE same as > RHOTACIZE

RHOTACISM n excessive use or idiosyncratic pronunciation of r

RHOTACIST > RHOTACISM

RHOTACIZE vb pronounce r excessively or idiosyncratically

RHOTIC adj denoting or speaking a dialect of English in which postvocalic r s are pronounced

RHOTICITY > RHOTIC

RHUBARB n garden plant with fleshy stalks ▷ interj noise made by actors to simulate conversation ▷ vb simulate conversation in this way

RHUBARBED > RHUBARB

RHUBARBS > RHUBARB

RHUBARBY > RHUBARB

RHUMB n as in rhumb line imaginary line on the surface of a sphere that intersects all meridians at the same angle

RHUMBA same as > RUMBA

RHUMBAED > RHUMBA

RHUMBAING > RHUMBA

RHUMBAS > RHUMBA

RHUMBS > RHUMB

RHUS n genus of shrubs and small trees

RHUSES > RHUS

RHY archaic spelling of > RYE

RHYME n sameness of the final sounds at the ends of lines of verse, or in words ▷ vb make a rhyme

RHYMED > RHYME

RHYMELESS > RHYME

RHYMER same as > RHYMESTER

RHYMERS > RHYMER

RHYMES > RHYME

RHYMESTER n mediocre poet

RHYMING > RHYME

RHYMIST > RHYME

RHYMISTS > RHYME

RHYNE same as > RHINE

RHYNES > RHYNE

RHYOLITE n fine-grained igneous rock consisting of quartz, feldspars, and mica or amphibole. It is the volcanic equivalent of granite

RHYOLITES > RHYOLITE

RHYOLITIC > RHYOLITE

RHYTA > RHYTON

RHYTHM n any regular movement or beat

RHYTHMAL adj rhythmic

RHYTHMED > RHYTHM

RHYTHMI > RHYTHMUS

RHYTHMIC adj of, relating to, or characterized by rhythm, as in movement or sound

RHYTHMICS n study of rhythmic movement

RHYTHMISE same as > RHYTHMIZE

RHYTHMIST n person who has a good sense of rhythm

RHYTHMIZE vb make rhythmic

RHYTHMS > RHYTHM

RHYTHMUS n rhythm

RHYTIDOME n bark

RHYTINA n type of sea cow

RHYTINAS > RHYTINA

RHYTON n (in ancient Greece) horn-shaped drinking vessel

RHYTONS > RHYTON

RIA n long narrow inlet of the seacoast

RIAD n traditional Moroccan house with an interior garden

RIADS > RIAD

RIAL n standard monetary unit of Iran

RIALS > RIAL

RIALTO n market or exchange

RIALTOS > RIALTO

RIANCIES > RIANT

RIANCY > RIANT

RIANT adj laughing

RIANTLY > RIANT

RIAS > RIA

RIATA same as > REATA

RIATAS > RIATA

RIB n one of the curved bones forming the framework of the upper part of the body ▷ vb provide or mark with ribs

RIBA n (in Islam) interest or usury

RIBALD adj humorously or mockingly rude or obscene ▷ n ribald person

RIBALDER > RIBALD

RIBALDEST > RIBALD

RIBALDLY > RIBALD

RIBALDRY n ribald language or behaviour

RIBALDS > RIBALD

RIBAND n ribbon awarded for some achievement

RIBANDS > RIBAND

RIBAS > RIBA

RIBATTUTA n (in music) type of trill

RIBAUD archaic variant of > RIBALD

RIBAUDRED archaic variant of > RIBALD

RIBAUDRY archaic variant of > RIBALDRY

RIBAUDS > RIBAUD

RIBAVIRIN n type of antiviral drug

RIBBAND same as > RIBAND

RIBBANDS > RIBBAND

RIBBED > RIB

RIBBER n someone who ribs

RIBBERS > RIBBER

RIBBIE n baseball run batted in

RIBBIER > RIBBY

RIBBIES > RIBBIE

RIBBIEST > RIBBY

RIBBING > RIB

RIBBINGS > RIB

RIBBIT n sound a frog makes

RIBBITS > RIBBIT

RIBBON n narrow band of fabric used for trimming, tying, etc ▷ vb adorn with a ribbon or ribbons

RIBBONED > RIBBON

RIBBONING > RIBBON

RIBBONRY n ribbons or ribbon work

RIBBONS > RIBBON

RIBBONY > RIBBON

RIBBY adj with noticeable ribs

RIBCAGE n bony structure of ribs enclosing the lungs

RIBCAGES > RIBCAGE

RIBES n genus of shrubs that includes currants

RIBEYE n beefsteak cut from the outer side of the rib section

RIBEYES > RIBEYE

RIBGRASS same as > RIBWORT

RIBIBE n rebeck

RIBIBES > RIBIBE

RIBIBLE same as > RIBIBE

RIBIBLES > RIBIBLE

RIBIER n variety of grape

RIBIERS > RIBIER

RIBLESS > RIB

RIBLET n small rib

RIBLETS > RIBLET

RIBLIKE > RIB

RIBOSE n pentose sugar that occurs in RNA and riboflavin

RIBOSES > RIBOSE

RIBOSOMAL > RIBOSOME

RIBOSOME n any of numerous minute particles in the cytoplasm of cells, either free or attached to the endoplasmic reticulum, that contain RNA and protein and are the site of protein synthesis

RIBOSOMES > RIBOSOME

RIBOZYMAL > RIBOZYME

RIBOZYME n RNA molecule capable of catalysing a chemical reaction, usually the cleavage of another RNA molecule

RIBOZYMES > RIBOZYME

RIBS > RIB

RIBSTON n variety of apple

RIBSTONE same as > RIBSTON

RIBSTONES > RIBSTONE

RIBSTONS > RIBSTON

RIBULOSE n type of sugar

RIBULOSES > RIBULOSE

RIBWORK n work or structure involving ribs

RIBWORKS > RIBWORK

RIBWORT n Eurasian plant with lancelike ribbed leaves

RIBWORTS > RIBWORT

RICE n cereal plant grown on wet ground in warm countries ▷ vb sieve (vegetables) to a coarse mashed consistency

RICEBIRD n any of various birds frequenting rice fields, esp the Java sparrow

RICEBIRDS > RICEBIRD

RICED > RICE

RICEFIELD n field used for growing rice

RICER *n* kitchen utensil through which soft foods are pressed to form a coarse mash

RICERCAR *same as* > RICERCARE

RICERCARE *n* elaborate polyphonic composition making extensive use of contrapuntal imitation and usually very slow in tempo

RICERCARI > RICERCARE

RICERCARS > RICERCAR

RICERCATA *same as* > RICERCARE

RICERS > RICER

RICES > RICE

RICEY *adj* resembling or containing rice

RICH *adj* owning a lot of money or property, wealthy ▷ *vb* (in archaic usage) enrich

RICHED > RICH

RICHEN *vb* enrich

RICHENED > RICHEN

RICHENING > RICHEN

RICHENS > RICHEN

RICHER > RICH

RICHES *pl n* wealth

RICHESSE *n* wealth or richness

RICHESSES > RICHESSE

RICHEST > RICH

RICHING > RICH

RICHLY *adv* elaborately

RICHNESS *n* state or quality of being rich

RICHT *adj, adv, n, vb* right

RICHTED > RICHT

RICHTER > RICHT

RICHTEST > RICHT

RICHTING > RICHT

RICHTS > RICHT

RICHWEED *n* type of plant

RICHWEEDS > RICHWEED

RICIER > RICY

RICIEST > RICY

RICIN *n* highly toxic protein, a lectin, derived from castor-oil seeds

RICING > RICE

RICINS > RICIN

RICINUS *n* genus of plants

RICINUSES > RICINUS

RICK *n* stack of hay etc ▷ *vb* wrench or sprain (a joint)

RICKED > RICK

RICKER *n* young kauri tree of New Zealand

RICKERS > RICKER

RICKET *n* mistake

RICKETIER > RICKETY

RICKETILY > RICKETY

RICKETS *n* disease of children marked by softening of the bones, bow legs, etc

RICKETTY *same as* > RICKETY

RICKETY *adj* shaky or unstable

RICKEY *n* cocktail consisting of gin or vodka, lime juice, and soda water, served iced

RICKEYS > RICKEY

RICKING > RICK

RICKLE *n* unsteady or shaky structure

RICKLES > RICKLE

RICKLIER > RICKLY

RICKLIEST > RICKLY

RICKLY *adj* archaic word for run-down or rickety

RICKRACK *n* zigzag braid used for trimming

RICKRACKS > RICKRACK

RICKS > RICK

RICKSHA *same as* > RICKSHAW

RICKSHAS > RICKSHA

RICKSHAW *n* light two-wheeled man-drawn Asian vehicle

RICKSHAWS > RICKSHAW

RICKSTAND *n* platform on which to put a rick

RICKSTICK *n* tool used when making hayricks

RICKYARD *n* place where hayricks are put

RICKYARDS > RICKYARD

RICOCHET *vb* (of a bullet) rebound from a solid surface ▷ *n* such a rebound

RICOCHETS > RICOCHET

RICOTTA *n* soft white unsalted Italian cheese made from sheep's milk

RICOTTAS > RICOTTA

RICRAC *same as* > RICKRACK

RICRACS > RICRAC

RICTAL > RICTUS

RICTUS *n* gape or cleft of an open mouth or beak

RICTUSES > RICTUS

RICY *same as* > RICEY

RID *vb* clear or relieve (of)

RIDABLE > RIDE

RIDDANCE *n* act of getting rid of something undesirable or unpleasant

RIDDANCES > RIDDANCE

RIDDED > RID

RIDDEN > RIDE

RIDDER > RID

RIDDERS > RID

RIDDING > RID

RIDDLE *n* question made puzzling to test one's ingenuity ▷ *vb* speak in riddles

RIDDLED > RIDDLE

RIDDLER > RIDDLE

RIDDLERS > RIDDLE

RIDDLES > RIDDLE

RIDDLING > RIDDLE

RIDDLINGS > RIDDLE

RIDE *vb* sit on and control or propel (a horse, bicycle, etc) ▷ *n* journey on a horse etc

RIDEABLE > RIDE

RIDENT *adj* laughing, smiling, or gay

RIDER *n* person who rides

RIDERED > RIDER

RIDERLESS > RIDER

RIDERS > RIDER

RIDERSHIP > RIDER

RIDES > RIDE

RIDGE *n* long narrow hill ▷ *vb* form into a ridge or ridges

RIDGEBACK *n* as in *Rhodesian ridgeback* large short-haired breed of dog characterized by a ridge of hair growing along the back in the opposite direction to the rest of the coat

RIDGED > RIDGE

RIDGEL *same as* > RIDGELING

RIDGELIKE > RIDGE

RIDGELINE *n* ridge

RIDGELING *n* domestic male animal with one or both testicles undescended, esp a horse

RIDGELS > RIDGEL

RIDGEPOLE *n* timber along the ridge of a roof, to which the rafters are attached

RIDGER *n* plough used to form furrows and ridges

RIDGERS > RIDGER

RIDGES > RIDGE

RIDGETOP *n* summit of ridge

RIDGETOPS > RIDGETOP

RIDGETREE *another name for* > RIDGEPOLE

RIDGEWAY *n* road or track along a ridge, esp one of great antiquity

RIDGEWAYS > RIDGEWAY

RIDGIER > RIDGE

RIDGIEST > RIDGE

RIDGIL *same as* > RIDGELING

RIDGILS > RIDGIL

RIDGING > RIDGE

RIDGINGS > RIDGE

RIDGLING *same as* > RIDGELING

RIDGLINGS > RIDGLING

RIDGY > RIDGE

RIDIC *adj* ridiculous

RIDICULE *n* treatment of a person or thing as ridiculous ▷ *vb* laugh at, make fun of

RIDICULED > RIDICULE

RIDICULER > RIDICULE

RIDICULES > RIDICULE

RIDING > RIDE

RIDINGS > RIDE

RIDLEY *n* marine turtle

RIDLEYS > RIDLEY

RIDOTTO *n* entertainment with music and dancing, often in masquerade

RIDOTTOS > RIDOTTO

RIDS > RID

RIEL *n* standard monetary unit of Cambodia

RIELS > RIEL

RIEM *n* strip of hide

RIEMPIE *n* leather thong or lace used mainly to make chair seats

RIEMPIES > RIEMPIE

RIEMS > RIEM

RIESLING *n* type of white wine

RIESLINGS > RIESLING

RIEVE *n* archaic word for rob or plunder

RIEVER *n* archaic word for robber or plunderer

RIEVERS > RIEVER

RIEVES > RIEVE

RIEVING > RIEVE

RIF *vb* lay off

RIFAMPIN *n* drug used in the treatment of tuberculosis, meningitis, and leprosy

RIFAMPINS > RIFAMPIN

RIFAMYCIN *n* antibiotic

RIFE *adj* widespread or common

RIFELY > RIFE

RIFENESS > RIFE

RIFER > RIFE

RIFEST > RIFE

RIFF *n* short repeated melodic figure ▷ *vb* play or perform riffs in jazz or rock music

RIFFAGE *n* (in jazz or rock music) act or an instance of playing a short series of chords

RIFFAGES > RIFFAGE

RIFFED > RIFF

RIFFING > RIFF

RIFFLE *vb* flick through (pages etc) quickly ▷ *n* rapid in a stream

RIFFLED > RIFFLE

RIFFLER *n* file with a curved face for filing concave surfaces

RIFFLERS > RIFFLER

RIFFLES > RIFFLE

RIFFLING > RIFFLE

RIFFOLA *n* use of an abundance of dominant riffs

RIFFOLAS > RIFFOLA

RIFFRAFF *n* rabble, disreputable people

RIFFRAFFS > RIFFRAFF

RIFFS > RIFF

RIFLE *n* firearm with a long barrel ▷ *vb* cut spiral grooves inside the barrel of a gun

RIFLEBIRD *n* any of various birds of paradise

RIFLED > RIFLE

RIFLEMAN *n* person skilled in the use of a rifle, esp a soldier

RIFLEMEN > RIFLEMAN

RIFLER > RIFLE

r

RIFLERIES > RIFLERY
RIFLERS > RIFLE
RIFLERY n rifle shots
RIFLES > RIFLE
RIFLING n cutting of spiral grooves on the inside of a firearm's barrel
RIFLINGS > RIFLING
RIFLIP n genetic difference between two individuals
RIFLIPS > RIFLIP
RIFS > RIF
RIFT n break in friendly relations ▷ vb burst or cause to burst open
RIFTE archaic word for > RIFT
RIFTED > RIFT
RIFTIER > RIFT
RIFTIEST > RIFT
RIFTING > RIFT
RIFTLESS > RIFT
RIFTS > RIFT
RIFTY > RIFT
RIG vb arrange in a dishonest way ▷ n apparatus for drilling for oil and gas
RIGADOON n old Provençal couple dance, light and graceful, in lively duple time
RIGADOONS > RIGADOON
RIGATONI n macaroni in the form of short ridged often slightly curved pieces
RIGATONIS > RIGATONI
RIGAUDON same as > RIGADOON
RIGAUDONS > RIGAUDON
RIGG n type of fish
RIGGALD same as > RIDGELING
RIGGALDS > RIGGALD
RIGGED > RIG
RIGGER n workman who rigs vessels, etc
RIGGERS > RIGGER
RIGGING > RIG
RIGGINGS > RIG
RIGGISH adj dialect word meaning wanton
RIGGS > RIGG
RIGHT adj just ▷ adv correctly ▷ n claim, title, etc allowed or due ▷ vb bring or come back to a normal or correct state
RIGHTABLE adj capable of being righted
RIGHTABLY > RIGHTABLE
RIGHTED > RIGHT
RIGHTEN vb set right
RIGHTENED > RIGHTEN
RIGHTENS > RIGHTEN
RIGHTEOUS adj upright, godly, or virtuous
RIGHTER > RIGHT
RIGHTERS > RIGHT
RIGHTEST > RIGHT

RIGHTFUL adj in accordance with what is right
RIGHTIER > RIGHTY
RIGHTIES > RIGHTY
RIGHTIEST > RIGHTY
RIGHTING > RIGHT
RIGHTINGS > RIGHT
RIGHTISH adj somewhat right, esp politically
RIGHTISM > RIGHTIST
RIGHTISMS > RIGHTIST
RIGHTIST adj (person) on the political right ▷ n supporter of the political right
RIGHTISTS > RIGHTIST
RIGHTLESS > RIGHT
RIGHTLY adv in accordance with the true facts or justice
RIGHTMOST > RIGHT
RIGHTNESS n state or quality of being right
RIGHTO interj expression of agreement or compliance
RIGHTS > RIGHT
RIGHTSIZE vb restructure (an organization) to cut costs and improve effectiveness without ruthlessly downsizing
RIGHTWARD adj situated on or directed towards the right ▷ adv towards or on the right
RIGHTY n right-handed person ▷ adj right-handed
RIGID adj inflexible or strict ▷ adv completely or excessively ▷ n strict and unbending person
RIGIDER > RIGID
RIGIDEST > RIGID
RIGIDIFY vb make or become rigid
RIGIDISE same as > RIGIDIZE
RIGIDISED > RIGIDISE
RIGIDISES > RIGIDISE
RIGIDITY > RIGID
RIGIDIZE vb make or become rigid
RIGIDIZED > RIGIDIZE
RIGIDIZES > RIGIDIZE
RIGIDLY > RIGID
RIGIDNESS > RIGID
RIGIDS > RIGID
RIGLIN same as > RIDGELING
RIGLING same as > RIDGELING
RIGLINGS > RIGLING
RIGLINS > RIGLIN
RIGMAROLE n long complicated procedure
RIGOL n (in dialect) ditch or gutter
RIGOLL same as > RIGOL
RIGOLLS > RIGOLL
RIGOLS > RIGOL
RIGOR same as > RIGOUR

RIGORISM n strictness in judgment or conduct
RIGORISMS > RIGORISM
RIGORIST > RIGORISM
RIGORISTS > RIGORISM
RIGOROUS adj harsh, severe, or stern
RIGORS > RIGOR
RIGOUR n harshness, severity, or strictness
RIGOURS > RIGOUR
RIGOUT n person's clothing
RIGOUTS > RIGOUT
RIGS > RIG
RIGSDALER n any of various former Scandinavian or Dutch small silver coins
RIGWIDDIE n part of the carthorse's harness to which the shafts of the cart attach
RIGWOODIE same as > RIGWIDDIE
RIJSTAFEL n assortment of Indonesian rice dishes
RIKISHA same as > RICKSHAW
RIKISHAS > RIKISHA
RIKISHI n sumo wrestler
RIKSHAW same as > RICKSHAW
RIKSHAWS > RIKSHAW
RILE vb anger or annoy
RILED > RILE
RILES > RILE
RILEY adj cross or irritable
RILIER > RILEY
RILIEST > RILEY
RILIEVI > RILIEVO
RILIEVO same as > RELIEF
RILING > RILE
RILL n small stream ▷ vb trickle
RILLE same as > RILL
RILLED > RILL
RILLES > RILLE
RILLET n little rill
RILLETS > RILLET
RILLETTES pl n potted meat
RILLING > RILL
RILLMARK n mark left by the trickle of a rill
RILLMARKS > RILLMARK
RILLS > RILL
RIM n edge or border ▷ vb put a rim on (a pot, cup, wheel, etc)
RIMA n long narrow opening
RIMAE > RIMA
RIMAYE n crevasse at the head of a glacier
RIMAYES > RIMAYE
RIME same as > RHYME
RIMED > RIME
RIMELESS > RHYME
RIMER same as > RHYMESTER
RIMERS > RIMER

RIMES > RIME
RIMESTER same as > RHYMESTER
RIMESTERS > RIMESTER
RIMFIRE adj (of a cartridge) having the primer in the rim of the base ▷ n cartridge of this type
RIMFIRES > RIMFIRE
RIMIER > RIMY
RIMIEST > RIMY
RIMINESS > RIMY
RIMING > RIME
RIMLAND n area situated on the outer edges of a region
RIMLANDS > RIMLAND
RIMLESS > RIM
RIMMED > RIM
RIMMER n tool for shaping the edge of something
RIMMERS > RIMMER
RIMMING > RIM
RIMMINGS > RIM
RIMOSE adj (esp of plant parts) having the surface marked by a network of intersecting cracks
RIMOSELY > RIMOSE
RIMOSITY > RIMOSE
RIMOUS same as > RIMOSE
RIMPLE vb crease or wrinkle
RIMPLED > RIMPLE
RIMPLES > RIMPLE
RIMPLING > RIMPLE
RIMROCK n rock forming the boundaries of a sandy or gravelly alluvial deposit
RIMROCKS > RIMROCK
RIMS > RIM
RIMSHOT n deliberate simultaneous striking of skin and rim of drum
RIMSHOTS > RIMSHOT
RIMU n New Zealand tree
RIMUS > RIMU
RIMY adj coated with rime
RIN Scots variant of > RUN
RIND n tough outer coating of fruits, cheese, or bacon ▷ vb take the bark off
RINDED > RIND
RINDIER > RINDY
RINDIEST > RINDY
RINDING > RIND
RINDLESS > RIND
RINDS > RIND
RINDY adj with a rind or rindlike skin
RINE archaic variant of > RIND
RINES > RINE
RING vb give out a clear resonant sound, as a bell ▷ n ringing
RINGBARK same as > RING
RINGBARKS > RINGBARK
RINGBIT n type of bit worn by a horse

RINGBITS > RINGBIT
RINGBOLT n bolt with a ring fitted through an eye attached to the bolt head
RINGBOLTS > RINGBOLT
RINGBONE n abnormal bony growth affecting the pastern of a horse, often causing lameness
RINGBONES > RINGBONE
RINGDOVE n large Eurasian pigeon with white patches on the wings and neck
RINGDOVES > RINGDOVE
RINGED > RING
RINGENT adj (of the corolla of plants) consisting of two gaping lips
RINGER n person or thing apparently identical to another
RINGERS > RINGER
RINGETTE n team sport played on ice, using straight sticks to control a rubber ring
RINGETTES > RINGETTE
RINGGIT n standard monetary unit of Malaysia
RINGGITS > RINGGIT
RINGHALS n variety of cobra
RINGING > RING
RINGINGLY > RING
RINGINGS > RING
RINGLESS > RING
RINGLET n curly lock of hair
RINGLETED > RINGLET
RINGLETS > RINGLET
RINGLETY adj resembling a ringlet
RINGLIKE > RING
RINGMAN n (in dialect) ring finger
RINGMEN > RINGMAN
RINGNECK n any bird that has ringlike markings round its neck
RINGNECKS > RINGNECK
RINGS > RING
RINGSIDE n row of seats nearest a boxing or circus ring ▷ adj providing a close uninterrupted view
RINGSIDER n someone with a ringside seat or position
RINGSIDES > RINGSIDER
RINGSTAND n stand for laboratory equipment
RINGSTER n member of a ring controlling a market in antiques, art treasures, etc
RINGSTERS > RINGSTER
RINGTAIL n possum with a curling tail used to grip branches while climbing
RINGTAILS > RINGTAIL
RINGTAW n game in which the aim is to knock marbles out of a ring

RINGTAWS > RINGTAW
RINGTONE n musical tune played by a mobile phone when a call is received
RINGTONES > RINGTONE
RINGTOSS n game in which participants try to throw hoops onto an upright stick
RINGWAY n bypass
RINGWAYS > RINGWAY
RINGWISE adj used to being in the ring and able to respond appropriately
RINGWOMB n complication at lambing resulting from failure of the cervix to open
RINGWOMBS > RINGWOMB
RINGWORK n circular earthwork
RINGWORKS > RINGWORK
RINGWORM n fungal skin disease in circular patches
RINGWORMS > RINGWORM
RINK n sheet of ice for skating or curling ▷ vb skate on a rink
RINKED > RINK
RINKHALS n S African cobra that can spit venom
RINKING > RINK
RINKS > RINK
RINKSIDE n area at the side of a rink
RINKSIDES > RINKSIDE
RINNING > RIN
RINS > RIN
RINSABLE > RINSE
RINSE vb remove soap from (washed clothes, hair, etc) by applying clean water ▷ n rinsing
RINSEABLE > RINSE
RINSED > RINSE
RINSER > RINSE
RINSERS > RINSE
RINSES > RINSE
RINSIBLE > RINSE
RINSING > RINSE
RINSINGS > RINSE
RIOJA n red or white Spanish wine with a vanilla bouquet and flavour
RIOJAS > RIOJA
RIOT n disorderly unruly disturbance ▷ vb take part in a riot
RIOTED > RIOT
RIOTER > RIOT
RIOTERS > RIOT
RIOTING > RIOT
RIOTINGS > RIOT
RIOTISE n archaic word for riotous behaviour and excess
RIOTISES > RIOTISE
RIOTIZE same as
> RIOTISE
RIOTIZES > RIOTIZE
RIOTOUS adj unrestrained
RIOTOUSLY > RIOTOUS

RIOTRIES > RIOTRY
RIOTRY n riotous behaviour
RIOTS > RIOT
RIP vb tear violently ▷ n split or tear
RIPARIAL adj riparian
RIPARIAN adj of or on the banks of a river ▷ n person who owns land on a river bank
RIPARIANS > RIPARIAN
RIPCORD n cord pulled to open a parachute
RIPCORDS > RIPCORD
RIPE adj ready to be reaped, eaten, etc ▷ vb ripen
RIPECK same as
> RYEPECK
RIPECKS > RIPECK
RIPED > RIPE
RIPELY > RIPE
RIPEN vb grow ripe
RIPENED > RIPEN
RIPENER > RIPEN
RIPENERS > RIPEN
RIPENESS > RIPE
RIPENING > RIPEN
RIPENS > RIPEN
RIPER adj more ripe ▷ n old Scots word meaning plunderer
RIPERS > RIPER
RIPES > RIPE
RIPEST > RIPE
RIPIENI > RIPIENO
RIPIENIST n orchestral member who is there to swell the sound rather than play solo
RIPIENO n (in baroque concertos and concerti grossi) the full orchestra
RIPIENOS > RIPIENO
RIPING > RIPE
RIPOFF n grossly overpriced article
RIPOFFS > RIPOFF
RIPOST same as
> RIPOSTE
RIPOSTE n verbal retort ▷ vb make a riposte
RIPOSTED > RIPOSTE
RIPOSTES > RIPOSTE
RIPOSTING > RIPOSTE
RIPOSTS > RIPOST
RIPP n old Scots word for a handful of grain
RIPPABLE > RIP
RIPPED > RIP
RIPPER n person who rips
RIPPERS > RIPPER
RIPPIER n archaic word for fish seller
RIPPIERS > RIPPIER
RIPPING > RIP
RIPPINGLY > RIP
RIPPINGS > RIPPING
RIPPLE n slight wave or ruffling of a surface ▷ vb flow or form into little waves (on)

RIPPLED > RIPPLE
RIPPLER > RIPPLE
RIPPLERS > RIPPLE
RIPPLES > RIPPLE
RIPPLET n tiny ripple
RIPPLETS > RIPPLET
RIPPLIER > RIPPLE
RIPPLIEST > RIPPLE
RIPPLING > RIPPLE
RIPPLINGS > RIPPLE
RIPPLY > RIPPLE
RIPPS > RIPP
RIPRAP vb deposit broken stones in or on
RIPRAPPED > RIPRAP
RIPRAPS > RIPRAP
RIPS > RIP
RIPSAW n handsaw for cutting along the grain of timber ▷ vb saw with a ripsaw
RIPSAWED > RIPSAW
RIPSAWING > RIPSAW
RIPSAWN > RIPSAW
RIPSAWS > RIPSAW
RIPSTOP n tear-resistant cloth
RIPSTOPS > RIPSTOP
RIPT archaic past form of
> RIP
RIPTIDE n stretch of turbulent water in the sea
RIPTIDES > RIPTIDE
RIRORIRO n small NZ bush bird that hatches the eggs of the shining cuckoo
RIRORIROS > RIRORIRO
RISALDAR n Indian cavalry officer
RISALDARS > RISALDAR
RISE vb get up from a lying, sitting, or kneeling position ▷ n rising
RISEN > RISE
RISER n person who rises, esp from bed
RISERS > RISER
RISES > RISE
RISHI n Indian seer or sage
RISHIS > RISHI
RISIBLE adj causing laughter, ridiculous
RISIBLES pl n sense of humour
RISIBLY > RISIBLE
RISING > RISE
RISINGS > RISE
RISK n chance of disaster or loss ▷ vb act in spite of the possibility of (injury or loss)
RISKED > RISK
RISKER > RISK
RISKERS > RISK
RISKFUL > RISK
RISKIER > RISKY
RISKIEST > RISKY
RISKILY > RISKY
RISKINESS > RISKY
RISKING > RISK
RISKLESS > RISK
RISKS > RISK

r

RISKY *adj* full of risk, dangerous

RISOLUTO *adj* musical term meaning firm and decisive ▷ *adv* firmly and decisively

RISORII > RISORIUS

RISORIUS *n* facial muscle responsible for smiling

RISOTTO *n* dish of rice cooked in stock with vegetables, meat, etc

RISOTTOS > RISOTTO

RISP *vb* Scots word meaning rasp

RISPED > RISP

RISPETTI > RISPETTO

RISPETTO *n* kind of folk song

RISPING > RISP

RISPINGS > RISP

RISPS > RISP

RISQUE *same as* > RISK

RISQUES > RISQUE

RISSOLE *n* cake of minced meat, coated with breadcrumbs and fried

RISSOLES > RISSOLE

RISTRA *n* string of dried chilli peppers

RISTRAS > RISTRA

RISUS *n* involuntary grinning expression

RISUSES > RISUS

RIT *vb* Scots word for cut or slit

RITARD *n* (in music) a slowing down

RITARDS > RITARD

RITE *n* formal practice or custom, esp religious

RITELESS > RITE

RITENUTO *adv* held back momentarily ▷ *n* (in music) a slowing down

RITENUTOS > RITENUTO

RITES > RITE

RITONAVIR *n* drug used to treat HIV

RITORNEL *n* (in music) orchestral passage

RITORNELL *same as* > RITORNEL

RITORNELS > RITORNEL

RITTS > RIT

RITT *same as* > RIT

RITTED > RIT

RITTER *n* knight or horseman

RITTERS > RITTER

RITTING > RIT

RITTS > RITT

RITUAL *n* prescribed order of rites ▷ *adj* concerning rites

RITUALISE *same as* > RITUALIZE

RITUALISM *n* exaggerated emphasis on the importance of rites and ceremonies

RITUALIST > RITUALISM

RITUALIZE *vb* engage in ritualism or devise rituals

RITUALLY > RITUAL

RITUALS > RITUAL

RITUXIMAB *n* drug used to treat non-Hodgkin's lymphoma

RITZ *modifier* as in *put on the ritz* assume a superior air or make an ostentatious display

RITZES > RITZ

RITZIER > RITZY

RITZIEST > RITZY

RITZILY > RITZY

RITZINESS > RITZY

RITZY *adj* luxurious or elegant

RIVA *n* rock cleft

RIVAGE *n* bank, shore, or coast

RIVAGES > RIVAGE

RIVAL *n* person or thing that competes with another ▷ *adj* in the position of a rival ▷ *vb* (try to) equal

RIVALED > RIVAL

RIVALESS *n* female rival

RIVALING > RIVAL

RIVALISE *same as* > RIVALIZE

RIVALISED > RIVALISE

RIVALISES > RIVALISE

RIVALITY > RIVAL

RIVALIZE *vb* become a rival

RIVALIZED > RIVALIZE

RIVALIZES > RIVALIZE

RIVALLED > RIVAL

RIVALLESS > RIVAL

RIVALLING > RIVAL

RIVALRIES > RIVALRY

RIVALROUS > RIVALRY

RIVALRY *n* keen competition

RIVALS > RIVAL

RIVALSHIP > RIVAL

RIVAS > RIVA

RIVE *vb* split asunder

RIVED > RIVE

RIVEL *vb* archaic word meaning wrinkle

RIVELLED > RIVEL

RIVELLING > RIVEL

RIVELS > RIVEL

RIVEN > RIVE

RIVER *n* large natural stream of water

RIVERAIN *same as* > RIPARIAN

RIVERAINS > RIVERAIN

RIVERBANK *n* bank of a river

RIVERBED *n* bed of a river

RIVERBEDS > RIVERBOAT

RIVERBOAT *n* boat, especially a barge, designed for use on rivers

RIVERED *adj* with a river or rivers

RIVERET *n* archaic word for rivulet or stream

RIVERETS > RIVERET

RIVERHEAD *n* source of river

RIVERINE *same as* > RIPARIAN

RIVERLESS > RIVER

RIVERLIKE *adj* resembling a river

RIVERMAN *n* boatman or man earning his living working on a river

RIVERMEN > RIVERMAN

RIVERS > RIVER

RIVERSIDE *n* area beside a river

RIVERWALK *n* paved walkway along the side of a river

RIVERWARD *adj* towards the river ▷ *adv* towards the river

RIVERWAY *n* river serving as a waterway

RIVERWAYS > RIVERWAY

RIVERWEED *n* type of plant found growing near rivers

RIVERY *adj* riverlike

RIVES > RIVE

RIVET *n* bolt for fastening metal plates ▷ *vb* fasten with rivets

RIVETED > RIVET

RIVETER > RIVET

RIVETERS > RIVET

RIVETING > RIVET

RIVETINGS > RIVET

RIVETS > RIVET

RIVETTED > RIVET

RIVETTING > RIVET

RIVIERA *n* coastline resembling the Mediterranean Riviera

RIVIERAS > RIVIERA

RIVIERE *n* necklace of diamonds which gradually increase in size

RIVIERES > RIVIERE

RIVING > RIVE

RIVLIN *n* Scots word for rawhide shoe

RIVLINS > RIVLIN

RIVO *interj* (in the past) an informal toast

RIVULET *n* small stream

RIVULETS > RIVULET

RIVULOSE *adj* having meandering lines

RIVULUS *n* type of small tropical American fish

RIVULUSES > RIVULUS

RIYAL *n* standard monetary unit of Qatar, divided into 100 dirhams

RIYALS > RIYAL

RIZ (*in some dialects*) past form of > RISE

RIZA *n* partial icon cover made from precious metal

RIZARD *n* redcurrant

RIZARDS > RIZARD

RIZAS > RIZA

RIZZAR *n* Scots word for red currant ▷ *vb* Scots word for sun-dry

RIZZARED > RIZZAR

RIZZARING > RIZZAR

RIZZARS > RIZZAR

RIZZART *n* Scots word for red currant

RIZZARTS > RIZZART

RIZZER *same as* > RIZZAR

RIZZERED > RIZZER

RIZZERING > RIZZER

RIZZERS > RIZZER

RIZZOR *vb* dry

RIZZORED > RIZZOR

RIZZORING > RIZZOR

RIZZORS > RIZZOR

ROACH *n* Eurasian freshwater fish ▷ *vb* clip (mane) short so that it stands upright

ROACHED *adj* arched convexly, as the back of certain breeds of dog, such as the whippet

ROACHES > ROACH

ROACHING > ROACH

ROAD *n* way prepared for passengers, vehicles, etc

ROADBED *n* material used to make a road

ROADBEDS > ROADBED

ROADBLOCK *n* barricade across a road to stop traffic for inspection etc

ROADCRAFT *n* skills and knowledge of a road user

ROADEO *n* competition testing driving skills

ROADEOS > ROADEO

ROADHOG *n* selfish or aggressive driver

ROADHOGS > ROADHOG

ROADHOUSE *n* pub or restaurant on a country road

ROADIE *n* person who transports and sets up equipment for a band

ROADIES > ROADIE

ROADING *n* road building

ROADINGS > ROADING

ROADKILL *n* remains of an animal or animals killed on the road by motor vehicles

ROADKILLS > ROADKILL

ROADLESS > ROAD

ROADMAN *n* someone involved in road repair or construction

ROADMEN > ROADMAN

ROADS > ROAD

ROADSHOW *n* radio show broadcast live from one of a number of places being visited by a touring disc jockey

ROADSHOWS > ROADSHOW

ROADSIDE *n* side of a road ▷ *adj* situated beside a road

ROADSIDES > ROADSIDE

ROADSMAN *same as* > ROADMAN

ROADSMEN > ROADSMAN
ROADSTEAD same as > ROAD
ROADSTER n open car with only two seats
ROADSTERS > ROADSTER
ROADWAY n part of a road used by vehicles
ROADWAYS > ROADWAY
ROADWORK n sports training by running along roads
ROADWORKS pl n repairs to a road, esp blocking part of the road
ROAM vb wander about ▷ n act of roaming
ROAMED > ROAM
ROAMER > ROAM
ROAMERS > ROAM
ROAMING > ROAM
ROAMINGS > ROAM
ROAMS > ROAM
ROAN adj (of a horse) having a brown or black coat sprinkled with white hairs ▷ n roan horse
ROANPIPE n drainpipe leading down from a gutter
ROANPIPES > ROANPIPE
ROANS > ROAN
ROAR vb make or utter a loud deep hoarse sound like that of a lion ▷ n such a sound
ROARED > ROAR
ROARER > ROAR
ROARERS > ROAR
ROARIE Scots word for > NOISY
ROARIER > ROARY
ROARIEST > ROARY
ROARING > ROAR
ROARINGLY > ROARING
ROARINGS > ROAR
ROARMING adj severe
ROARS > ROAR
ROARY adj roarlike or tending to roar
ROAST vb cook by dry heat, as in an oven ▷ n roasted joint of meat ▷ adj roasted
ROASTED > ROAST
ROASTER n person or thing that roasts
ROASTERS > ROASTER
ROASTIE n roast potato
ROASTIES > ROASTIE
ROASTING adj extremely hot ▷ n severe criticism or scolding
ROASTINGS > ROASTING
ROASTS > ROAST
ROATE archaic form of > ROTE
ROATED > ROATE
ROATES > ROATE
ROATING > ROATE
ROB vb steal from
ROBALO n tropical fish
ROBALOS > ROBALO

ROBAND n piece of marline used for fastening a sail to a spar
ROBANDS > ROBAND
ROBATA n grill used for Japanese cooking
ROBATAS > ROBATA
ROBBED > ROB
ROBBER > ROB
ROBBERIES > ROBBERY
ROBBERS > ROB
ROBBERY n stealing of property from a person by using or threatening to use force
ROBBIN same as > ROBAND
ROBBING > ROB
ROBBINS > ROBBIN
ROBE n long loose outer garment ▷ vb put a robe on
ROBED > ROBE
ROBES > ROBE
ROBIN n small brown bird with a red breast
ROBING > ROBE
ROBINGS > ROBE
ROBINIA n type of leguminous tree
ROBINIAS > ROBINIA
ROBINS > ROBIN
ROBLE n oak tree
ROBLES > ROBLE
ROBOCALL n automated telephone call that delivers a message to a large number of people
ROBOCALLS > ROBOCALL
ROBORANT adj tending to fortify or increase strength ▷ n drug or agent that increases strength
ROBORANTS > ROBORANT
ROBOT n automated machine, esp one performing functions in a human manner
ROBOTIC > ROBOT
ROBOTICS n science of designing and using robots
ROBOTISE same as > ROBOTIZE
ROBOTISED > ROBOTISE
ROBOTISES > ROBOTISE
ROBOTISM > ROBOT
ROBOTISMS > ROBOT
ROBOTIZE vb automate
ROBOTIZED > ROBOTIZE
ROBOTIZES > ROBOTIZE
ROBOTRIES > ROBOT
ROBOTRY > ROBOT
ROBOTS > ROBOT
ROBS > ROB
ROBURITE n flameless explosive
ROBURITES > ROBURITE
ROBUST adj very strong and healthy
ROBUSTA n species of coffee tree
ROBUSTAS > ROBUSTA
ROBUSTER > ROBUST

ROBUSTEST > ROBUST
ROBUSTLY > ROBUST
ROC n monstrous bird of Arabian mythology
ROCAILLE n decorative rock or shell work, esp as ornamentation in a rococo fountain, grotto, or interior
ROCAILLES > ROCAILLE
ROCAMBOLE n variety of sand leek whose garlic-like bulb is used for seasoning
ROCH same as > ROTCH
ROCHES > ROTCH
ROCHET n white surplice with tight sleeves, worn by Church dignitaries
ROCHETS > ROCHET
ROCK n hard mineral substance that makes up part of the earth's crust, stone ▷ vb (cause to) sway to and fro ▷ adj of or relating to rock music
ROCKABIES > ROCKABY
ROCKABLE > ROCK
ROCKABY same as > ROCKABYE
ROCKABYE n lullaby or rocking motion used with a baby during lullabies
ROCKABYES > ROCKABYE
ROCKAWAY n four-wheeled horse-drawn carriage, usually with two seats and a hard top
ROCKAWAYS > ROCKAWAY
ROCKBOUND adj hemmed in or encircled by rocks
ROCKCRESS n any plant of the annual or perennial genus Arabis
ROCKED > ROCK
ROCKER n rocking chair
ROCKERIES > ROCKERY
ROCKERS > ROCKER
ROCKERY n mound of stones in a garden for rock plants
ROCKET n self-propelling device powered by the burning of explosive contents ▷ vb move fast, esp upwards
ROCKETED > ROCKET
ROCKETEER n engineer or scientist concerned with the design, operation, or launching of rockets
ROCKETER n bird that launches itself into the air like a rocket when flushed
ROCKETERS > ROCKETER
ROCKETING > ROCKET
ROCKETRY n science and technology of the design and operation of rockets
ROCKETS > ROCKET
ROCKFALL n instance of rocks breaking away and falling from an outcrop
ROCKFALLS > ROCKFALL

ROCKFISH n any of various fishes that live among rocks
ROCKHOUND n person interested in rocks and minerals
ROCKIER n archaic or dialect word for rock pigeon
ROCKIERS > ROCKY
ROCKIEST > ROCKY
ROCKILY > ROCKY
ROCKINESS > ROCKY
ROCKING > ROCK
ROCKINGLY > ROCKING
ROCKINGS > ROCK
ROCKLAY same as > ROKELAY
ROCKLAYS > ROCKLAY
ROCKLESS > ROCK
ROCKLIKE > ROCK
ROCKLING n any of various small sea fishes having an elongated body and barbels around the mouth
ROCKLINGS > ROCKLING
ROCKOON n rocket fired from a balloon at high altitude
ROCKOONS > ROCKOON
ROCKROSE n any of various shrubs or herbaceous plants cultivated for their roselike flowers
ROCKROSES > ROCKROSE
ROCKS > ROCK
ROCKSHAFT n shaft that rotates backwards and forwards rather than continuously, esp one used in the valve gear of a steam engine
ROCKSLIDE n fall of rocks down hillside
ROCKWATER n water that comes out of rock
ROCKWEED n any of various seaweeds that grow on rocks exposed at low tide
ROCKWEEDS > ROCKWEED
ROCKWOOL n mineral wool used for insulation
ROCKWOOLS > ROCKWOOL
ROCKWORK n structure made of rock
ROCKWORKS > ROCKWORK
ROCKY adj having many rocks
ROCOCO adj (of furniture, architecture, etc) having much elaborate decoration ▷ n style of architecture and decoration characterized by elaborate ornamentation
ROCOCOS > ROCOCO
ROCQUET n another name for the salad plant rocket
ROCQUETS > ROCQUET
ROCS > ROC

r

ROD n slender straight bar, stick ▷ vb clear with a rod
RODDED > ROD
RODDING > ROD
RODDINGS > ROD
RODE vb (of the male woodcock) to perform a display flight
RODED > RODE
RODENT n animal with teeth specialized for gnawing
RODENTS > RODENT
RODEO n display of skill by cowboys, such as bareback riding ▷ vb take part in a rodeo
RODEOED > RODEO
RODEOING > RODEO
RODEOS > RODEO
RODES > RODE
RODEWAY archaic spelling of > ROADWAY
RODEWAYS > RODEWAY
RODFISHER n angler
RODGERSIA n flowering plant
RODING > RODE
RODINGS > RODE
RODLESS > ROD
RODLIKE > ROD
RODMAN n someone who uses or fishes with a rod
RODMEN > RODMAN
RODNEY n type of small fishing boat used in Canada
RODNEYS > RODNEY
RODS > ROD
RODSMAN same as > RODMAN
RODSMEN > RODSMAN
RODSTER n angler
RODSTERS > RODSTER
ROE n mass of eggs in a fish, sometimes eaten as food
ROEBUCK n male of the roe deer
ROEBUCKS > ROEBUCK
ROED adj with roe inside
ROEMER n drinking glass, typically having an ovoid bowl on a short stem
ROEMERS > ROEMER
ROENTGEN n unit measuring a radiation dose
ROENTGENS > ROENTGEN
ROES > ROE
ROESTI same as > ROSTI
ROESTIS > ROESTI
ROESTONE same as > OOLITE
ROESTONES > ROESTONE
ROGALLO n flexible fabric delta wing
ROGALLOS > ROGALLO
ROGATION n solemn supplication, esp in a form of ceremony prescribed by the Church
ROGATIONS > ROGATION
ROGATORY adj (esp in legal contexts) seeking or

authorized to seek information
ROGER interj (used in signalling) message received ▷ vb (of a man) to copulate (with)
ROGERED > ROGER
ROGERING > ROGER
ROGERINGS > ROGER
ROGERS > ROGER
ROGNON n isolated rock outcrop on a glacier
ROGNONS > ROGNON
ROGUE n dishonest or unprincipled person ▷ adj (of a wild beast) living apart from the herd ▷ vb rid (a field or crop) of inferior or unwanted plants
ROGUED > ROGUE
ROGUEING > ROGUE
ROGUER n rogue
ROGUERIES > ROGUERY
ROGUERS > ROGUER
ROGUERY n dishonest or immoral behaviour
ROGUES > ROGUE
ROGUESHIP n being a rogue
ROGUING > ROGUE
ROGUISH adj dishonest or unprincipled
ROGUISHLY > ROGUISH
ROGUY same as > ROGUISH
ROID adj as in roid rage, angry and aggressive behaviour caused by the use of anabolic steroids
ROIL vb make (a liquid) cloudy or turbid by stirring up dregs or sediment
ROILED > ROIL
ROILIER > ROILY
ROILIEST > ROILY
ROILING > ROIL
ROILS > ROIL
ROILY adj cloudy or muddy
ROIN same as > ROYNE
ROINED > ROIN
ROINING > ROIN
ROINISH same as > ROYNISH
ROINS > ROIN
ROIST archaic variant of > ROISTER
ROISTED > ROIST
ROISTER vb make merry noisily or boisterously
ROISTERED > ROISTER
ROISTERER > ROISTER
ROISTERS > ROISTER
ROISTING > ROIST
ROISTS > ROIST
ROJAK n (in Malaysia) a salad dish served in chilli sauce
ROJAKS > ROJAK
ROJI n Japanese tea garden or its path of stones
ROJIS > ROJI
ROK same as > ROC

ROKE vb (in dialect) steam or smoke
ROKED > ROKE
ROKELAY n type of cloak
ROKELAYS > ROKELAY
ROKER n variety of ray
ROKERS > ROKER
ROKES > ROKE
ROKIER > ROKY
ROKIEST > ROKY
ROKING > ROKE
ROKKAKU n hexagonal Japanese kite
ROKS > ROK
ROKY adj (in dialect) steamy or smoky
ROLAG n roll of carded wool ready for spinning
ROLAGS > ROLAG
ROLAMITE n type of bearing using two rollers and a moving flexible band
ROLAMITES > ROLAMITE
ROLE n task or function
ROLES > ROLE
ROLF vb massage following a particular technique
ROLFED > ROLF
ROLFER > ROLF
ROLFERS > ROLF
ROLFING > ROLF
ROLFINGS > ROLF
ROLFS > ROLF
ROLL vb move by turning over and over ▷ n act of rolling over or from side to side
ROLLABLE > ROLL
ROLLAWAY n mounted on rollers so as to be easily moved, esp to be stored away after use
ROLLAWAYS > ROLLAWAY
ROLLBACK n reduction to a previous price
ROLLBACKS > ROLLBACK
ROLLBAR n bar that reinforces the frame of a car
ROLLBARS > ROLLBAR
ROLLED > ROLL
ROLLER n rotating cylinder
ROLLERS > ROLLER
ROLLICK vb behave in a boisterous manner ▷ n boisterous or carefree escapade
ROLLICKED > ROLLICK
ROLLICKS > ROLLICK
ROLLICKY adj rollicking
ROLLIE n hand-rolled cigarette
ROLLIES > ROLLIE
ROLLING > ROLL
ROLLINGS > ROLL
ROLLMOP n herring fillet rolled round onion slices and pickled
ROLLMOPS > ROLLMOP
ROLLNECK adj (of a garment) having a high neck that is worn rolled

over ▷ n rollneck sweater or other garment
ROLLNECKS > ROLLNECK
ROLLOCK same as > ROWLOCK
ROLLOCKS > ROLLOCK
ROLLOUT n presentation to the public of a new aircraft, product, etc; launch
ROLLOUTS > ROLLOUT
ROLLOVER n instance of a prize continuing in force for an additional period
ROLLOVERS > ROLLOVER
ROLLS > ROLL
ROLLTOP n as in rolltop desk desk having a slatted wooden panel that can be pulled down over the writing surface
ROLLUP n something rolled into a tube shape
ROLLUPS > ROLLUP
ROLLWAY n incline down which logs are rolled
ROLLWAYS > ROLLWAY
ROM n male gypsy
ROMA n gypsy
ROMAGE archaic variant of > RUMMAGE
ROMAGES > ROMAGE
ROMAIKA n Greek dance
ROMAIKAS > ROMAIKA
ROMAINE n usual US and Canadian name for 'cos' (lettuce)
ROMAINES > ROMAINE
ROMAJI n Roman alphabet as used to write Japanese
ROMAJIS > ROMAJI
ROMAL same as > RUMAL
ROMALS > ROMAL
ROMAN adj in or relating to the vertical style of printing type used for most printed matter ▷ n roman type
ROMANCE n love affair ▷ vb exaggerate or fantasize
ROMANCED > ROMANCE
ROMANCER > ROMANCE
ROMANCERS > ROMANCE
ROMANCES > ROMANCE
ROMANCING > ROMANCE
ROMANESCO n type of green cauliflower
ROMANISE same as > ROMANIZE
ROMANISED > ROMANISE
ROMANISES > ROMANISE
ROMANIZE vb impart a Roman Catholic character to (a ceremony, practice, etc)
ROMANIZED > ROMANIZE
ROMANIZES > ROMANIZE
ROMANO n hard light-coloured sharp-tasting cheese
ROMANOS > ROMANO
ROMANS > ROMAN

ROMANTIC *adj* of or dealing with love ▷ *n* romantic person or artist
ROMANTICS > ROMANTIC
ROMANZA *n* short instrumental piece of song-like character
ROMANZAS > ROMANZA
ROMAUNT *n* verse romance
ROMAUNTS > ROMAUNT
ROMCOM *n* comedy based around the romantic relationships of the characters
ROMCOMS > ROMCOM
ROMELDALE *n* type of sheep
ROMEO *n* ardent male lover
ROMEOS > ROMEO
ROMNEYA *n* bushy type of poppy
ROMNEYAS > ROMNEYA
ROMP *vb* play wildly and joyfully ▷ *n* boisterous activity
ROMPED > ROMP
ROMPER *n* playful or boisterous child
ROMPERS *pl n* child's overalls
ROMPING > ROMP
ROMPINGLY > ROMP
ROMPISH *adj* inclined to romp
ROMPISHLY > ROMP
ROMPS > ROMP
ROMS > ROM
RONCADOR *n* any of several types of fish
RONCADORS > RONCADOR
RONDACHE *n* round shield
RONDACHES > RONDACHE
RONDAVEL *n* circular building, often thatched
RONDAVELS > RONDAVEL
RONDE *n* round dance
RONDEAU *n* poem with the opening words of the first line used as a refrain
RONDEAUX > RONDEAU
RONDEL *n* rondeau with a two-line refrain appearing twice or three times
RONDELET *n* brief rondeau, having five or seven lines and a refrain taken from the first line
RONDELETS > RONDELET
RONDELLE *n* type of bead
RONDELLES > RONDELLE
RONDELS > RONDEL
RONDES > RONDE
RONDINO *n* short rondo
RONDINOS > RONDINO
RONDO *n* piece of music with a leading theme continually returned to
RONDOS > RONDO
RONDURE *n* circle or curve
RONDURES > RONDURE
RONE *n* drainpipe or gutter for carrying rainwater from a roof

RONEO *vb* duplicate (a document) from a stencil ▷ *n* document reproduced by this process
RONEOED > RONEO
RONEOING > RONEO
RONEOS > RONEO
RONEPIPE *same as* > RONE
RONEPIPES > RONEPIPE
RONES > RONE
RONG *archaic past participle of* > RING
RONGGENG *n* Malay traditional dance
RONGGENGS > RONGGENG
RONIN *n* lordless samurai, esp one whose feudal lord had been deprived of his territory
RONINS > RONIN
RONION *same as* > RUNNION
RONIONS > RONION
RONNE *archaic form of* > RUN
RONNEL *n* type of pesticide
RONNELS > RONNEL
RONNIE *n* Dublin slang word for moustache
RONNIES > RONNIE
RONNING > RONNE
RONT *archaic variant of* > RUNT
RONTE *archaic variant of* > RUNT
RONTES > RONTE
RONTGEN *variant spelling of* > ROENTGEN
RONTGENS > RONTGEN
RONTS > RONT
RONYON *same as* > RUNNION
RONYONS > RUNNION
RONZ *n* rest of New Zealand
RONZER *n* New Zealand word for a New Zealander not from Auckland
RONZERS > RONZER
ROO *n* kangaroo
ROOD *n* Cross
ROODS > ROOD
ROOF *n* outside upper covering of a building, car, etc ▷ *vb* put a roof on
ROOFED > ROOF
ROOFER > ROOF
ROOFERS > ROOF
ROOFIE *n* tablet of sedative drug
ROOFIER > ROOFY
ROOFIES > ROOFIE
ROOFIEST > ROOFY
ROOFING *n* material used to build a roof
ROOFINGS > ROOFING
ROOFLESS > ROOF
ROOFLIKE > ROOF
ROOFLINE *n* uppermost edge of a roof
ROOFLINES > ROOFLINE
ROOFS > ROOF

ROOFSCAPE *n* view of the rooftops of a town, city, etc
ROOFTOP *n* outside part of the roof of a building
ROOFTOPS > ROOFTOP
ROOFTREE *same as* > RIDGEPOLE
ROOFTREES > ROOFTREE
ROOFY *adj* with roofs
ROOIBOS *n* tea prepared from the dried leaves of an African plant
ROOIBOSES > ROOIBOS
ROOIKAT *n* South African lynx
ROOIKATS > ROOIKAT
ROOINEK *n* contemptuous name for an Englishman
ROOINEKS > ROOINEK
ROOK *n* Eurasian bird of the crow family ▷ *vb* swindle
ROOKED > ROOK
ROOKERIES > ROOKERY
ROOKERY *n* colony of rooks, penguins, or seals
ROOKIE *n* new recruit
ROOKIER > ROOKY
ROOKIES > ROOKIE
ROOKIEST > ROOKY
ROOKING > ROOK
ROOKISH > ROOK
ROOKS > ROOK
ROOKY *adj* abounding in rooks
ROOM *n* enclosed area in a building ▷ *vb* occupy or share a room
ROOMED > ROOM
ROOMER > ROOM
ROOMERS > ROOM
ROOMETTE *n* self-contained compartment in a railway sleeping car
ROOMETTES > ROOMETTE
ROOMFUL *n* number or quantity sufficient to fill a room
ROOMFULS > ROOMFUL
ROOMIE *n* roommate
ROOMIER > ROOMY
ROOMIES > ROOMIE
ROOMIEST > ROOMY
ROOMILY > ROOMY
ROOMINESS > ROOMY
ROOMING > ROOM
ROOMMATE *n* person with whom one shares a room or apartment
ROOMMATES > ROOMMATE
ROOMS > ROOM
ROOMSFUL > ROOMFUL
ROOMSOME *adj* archaic word meaning roomy
ROOMY *adj* spacious
ROON *n* Scots word for shred or strip
ROONS > ROON
ROOP *same as* > ROUP
ROOPED > ROOP
ROOPIER > ROOPY
ROOPIEST > ROOPY
ROOPING > ROOP

ROOPIT *same as* > ROOPY
ROOPS > ROOP
ROOPY *adj* (in dialect) hoarse
ROORBACK *same as* > ROORBACK
ROORBACHS > ROORBACK
ROORBACK *n* false or distorted report or account, used to obtain political advantage
ROORBACKS > ROORBACK
ROOS > ROO
ROOSA *n* type of grass
ROOSAS > ROOSA
ROOSE *vb* flatter
ROOSED > ROOSE
ROOSER > ROOSE
ROOSERS > ROOSE
ROOSES > ROOSE
ROOSING > ROOSE
ROOST *n* perch for fowls ▷ *vb* perch
ROOSTED > ROOST
ROOSTER *n* domestic cock
ROOSTERS > ROOSTER
ROOSTING > ROOST
ROOSTS > ROOST
ROOT *n* part of a plant that grows down into the earth obtaining nourishment ▷ *vb* establish a root and start to grow
ROOTAGE *n* root system
ROOTAGES > ROOTAGE
ROOTBALL *n* mass of the roots of a plant
ROOTBALLS > ROOTBALL
ROOTBOUND *adj* (of a pot plant) having outgrown its pot, so that the roots are cramped and tangled
ROOTCAP *n* layer of cells at root tip
ROOTCAPS > ROOTCAP
ROOTED > ROOT
ROOTEDLY > ROOT
ROOTER > ROOT
ROOTERS > ROOT
ROOTHOLD > ROOT
ROOTHOLDS > ROOT
ROOTIER > ROOTY
ROOTIES > ROOTY
ROOTIEST > ROOT
ROOTINESS > ROOT
ROOTING > ROOT
ROOTINGS > ROOT
ROOTKIT *n* set of programs used to gain unauthorized access to a computer system
ROOTKITS > ROOTKIT
ROOTLE *same as* > ROOT
ROOTLED > ROOTLE
ROOTLES > ROOTLE
ROOTLESS *adj* having no sense of belonging
ROOTLET *n* small root or branch of a root
ROOTLETS > ROOTLET
ROOTLIKE > ROOT
ROOTLING > ROOTLE

r

ROOTS adj (of popular music) going back to the origins of a style
ROOTSIER > ROOTS
ROOTSIEST > ROOTS
ROOTSTALK same as > RHIZOME
ROOTSTOCK same as > RHIZOME
ROOTSY > ROOTS
ROOTWORM n beetle larva feeding on roots
ROOTWORMS > ROOTWORM
ROOTY adj rootlike ▷ n (in military slang) bread
ROPABLE adj capable of being roped
ROPE n thick cord
ROPEABLE same as > ROPABLE
ROPED > ROPE
ROPELIKE > ROPE
ROPER n someone who makes ropes
ROPERIES > ROPERY
ROPERS > ROPER
ROPERY n place where ropes are made
ROPES > ROPE
ROPEWALK n long narrow usually covered path or shed where ropes are made
ROPEWALKS > ROPEWALK
ROPEWAY n type of aerial lift
ROPEWAYS > ROPEWAY
ROPEWORK n making, mending, or tying ropes
ROPEWORKS > ROPEWORK
ROPEY adj inferior or inadequate
ROPIER > ROPY
ROPIEST > ROPY
ROPILY > ROPEY
ROPINESS > ROPEY
ROPING > ROPE
ROPINGS > ROPE
ROPY same as > ROPEY
ROQUE n game developed from croquet
ROQUES > ROQUE
ROQUET vb drive one's ball against (another person's ball) in croquet ▷ n act of roqueting
ROQUETED > ROQUET
ROQUETING > ROQUET
ROQUETS > ROQUET
ROQUETTE n another name for the salad plant rocket
ROQUETTES > ROQUETTE
RORAL archaic word for > DEWY
RORE archaic spelling of > ROAR
RORES > RORE
RORIC same as > RORAL
RORID same as > RORAL
RORIE same as > ROARY
RORIER > RORY
RORIEST > RORY

RORQUAL n toothless whale with a dorsal fin
RORQUALS > RORQUAL
RORT n dishonest scheme ▷ vb take unfair advantage of something
RORTED > RORT
RORTER n small-scale confidence trickster
RORTERS > RORTER
RORTIER > RORT
RORTIEST > RORT
RORTING > RORT
RORTINGS > RORTING
RORTS > RORT
RORTY > RORT
RORY adj dewy
ROSACE another name for > ROSETTE
ROSACEA n chronic inflammatory disease affecting the skin of the face
ROSACEAS > ROSACEA
ROSACEOUS adj of or belonging to a family of plants typically having five-petalled flowers, which includes the rose, strawberry, and many fruit trees
ROSACES > ROSACE
ROSAKER archaic word for > REALGAR
ROSAKERS > ROSAKER
ROSALIA n melody which is repeated but at a higher pitch each time
ROSALIAS > ROSALIA
ROSANILIN n reddish-brown crystalline insoluble derivative of aniline used as a red dye
ROSARIA > ROSARIUM
ROSARIAN n person who cultivates roses, esp professionally
ROSARIANS > ROSARIAN
ROSARIES > ROSARY
ROSARIUM n rose garden
ROSARIUMS > ROSARIUM
ROSARY n series of prayers
ROSBIF n term used in France for an English person
ROSBIFS > ROSBIF
ROSCID adj dewy
ROSCOE slang word for > GUN
ROSCOES > ROSCOE
ROSE > RISE
ROSEAL adj rosy or roselike
ROSEATE adj rose-coloured
ROSEATELY > ROSEATE
ROSEBAY n as in rosebay willowherb perennial plant with spikes of deep pink flowers
ROSEBAYS > ROSEBAY
ROSEBED n part of a garden where roses grow
ROSEBEDS > ROSEBED

ROSEBOWL n bowl for displaying roses or other flowers
ROSEBOWLS > ROSEBOWL
ROSEBUD n rose which has not yet fully opened
ROSEBUDS > ROSEBUD
ROSEBUSH n flowering shrub
ROSED > RISE
ROSEFINCH n any of various finches with pink patches
ROSEFISH n red food fish of North Atlantic coastal waters
ROSEHIP n berry-like fruit of a rose plant
ROSEHIPS > ROSEHIP
ROSELESS > RISE
ROSELIKE > RISE
ROSELLA n type of Australian parrot
ROSELLAS > ROSELLA
ROSELLE n Indian flowering plant
ROSELLES > ROSELLE
ROSEMARY n fragrant flowering shrub
ROSEOLA n feverish condition of young children caused by the human herpes virus
ROSEOLAR > ROSEOLA
ROSEOLAS > ROSEOLA
ROSERIES > ROSERY
ROSEROOT n Eurasian mountain plant
ROSEROOTS > ROSEROOT
ROSERY n bed or garden of roses
ROSES > RISE
ROSESLUG n one of various types of pest that feed on roses
ROSESLUGS > ROSESLUG
ROSET n Scots word meaning rosin ▷ vb rub rosin on
ROSETED > ROSET
ROSETING > ROSET
ROSETS > ROSET
ROSETTE n rose-shaped ornament
ROSETTED > ROSET
ROSETTES > ROSETTE
ROSETTING n abnormal leaf formation in a plant due to disease
ROSETTY > ROSET
ROSETY > ROSET
ROSEWATER n scented water used as a perfume and in cooking, made by the distillation of rose petals or by impregnation with oil of roses
ROSEWOOD n fragrant wood used to make furniture
ROSEWOODS > ROSEWOOD
ROSHAMBO n the game of rock-paper-scissors
ROSHAMBOS > ROSHAMBO

ROSHI n teacher of Zen Buddhism
ROSHIS > ROSHI
ROSIED > ROSY
ROSIER archaic word for > ROSEBUSH
ROSIERE archaic word for > ROSEBUSH
ROSIERES > ROSIERE
ROSIERS > ROSIER
ROSIES > ROSY
ROSIEST > ROSY
ROSILY > ROSY
ROSIN n resin used for treating the bows of violins etc ▷ vb apply rosin to
ROSINATE n chemical compound
ROSINATES > ROSINATE
ROSINED > ROSIN
ROSINER n strong alcoholic drink
ROSINERS > ROSINER
ROSINESS > ROSY
ROSING > RISE
ROSINING > ROSIN
ROSINOL n yellowish fluorescent oily liquid obtained from certain resins
ROSINOLS > ROSINOL
ROSINOUS adj rosiny
ROSINS > ROSIN
ROSINWEED n N American plant with resinous juice, sticky foliage, and a strong smell
ROSINY > ROSIN
ROSIT same as > ROSET
ROSITED > ROSIT
ROSITING > ROSIT
ROSITS > ROSIT
ROSMARINE archaic form of > ROSEMARY
ROSOGLIO same as > ROSOLIO
ROSOGLIOS > ROSOGLIO
ROSOLIO n type of cordial
ROSOLIOS > ROSOLIO
ROSSER n bark-removing machine
ROSSERS > ROSSER
ROST archaic spelling of > ROAST
ROSTED > ROST
ROSTELLA > ROSTELLUM
ROSTELLAR > ROSTELLUM
ROSTELLUM n small beaklike process, such as the hooked projection from the top of the head in tapeworms or the outgrowth from the stigma of an orchid
ROSTER n list of people and their turns of duty ▷ vb place on a roster
ROSTERED > ROSTER
ROSTERING > ROSTER
ROSTERS > ROSTER
ROSTI n cheese-topped fried Swiss dish of grated potato

ROSTING > ROST

ROSTIS > ROSTI

ROSTRA > ROSTRUM

ROSTRAL *adj* of or like a beak or snout

ROSTRALLY > ROSTRAL

ROSTRATE *adj* having a beak or beaklike process

ROSTRATED *same as* > ROSTRATE

ROSTRUM *n* platform or stage

ROSTRUMS > ROSTRUM

ROSTS > ROST

ROSULA *n* rosette

ROSULAS > ROSULA

ROSULATE *adj* in the form of a rose

ROSY *adj* pink-coloured ▷ *vb* redden or make pink

ROSYING > ROSY

ROT *vb* decompose or decay ▷ *n* decay

ROTA *n* list of people who take it in turn to do a particular task

ROTACHUTE *n* device serving the same purpose as a parachute, in which the canopy is replaced by freely revolving rotor blades, used for the delivery of stores or recovery of missiles

ROTAL *adj* of or relating to wheels or rotation

ROTAMETER *n* device for measuring the flow of a liquid

ROTAN *another name for* > RATTAN

ROTANS > ROTAN

ROTAPLANE *n* aircraft that derives its lift from freely revolving rotor blades

ROTARIES > ROTARY

ROTARY *adj* revolving ▷ *n* traffic roundabout

ROTAS > ROTA

ROTATABLE > ROTATE

ROTATE *vb* (cause to) move round a centre or on a pivot ▷ *adj* designating a corolla the united petals of which radiate from a central point

ROTATED > ROTATE

ROTATES > ROTATE

ROTATING *adj* revolving around a central axis, line, or point

ROTATION *n* act of rotating

ROTATIONS > ROTATION

ROTATIVE *same as* > ROTATORY

ROTATOR *n* person, device, or part that rotates or causes rotation

ROTATORES > ROTATOR

ROTATORS > ROTATOR

ROTATORY *adj* of, relating to, possessing, or causing rotation

ROTAVATE *same as* > ROTOVATE

ROTAVATED > ROTAVATE

ROTAVATES > ROTAVATE

ROTAVATOR *n* type of machine with rotating blades that will break up soil

ROTAVIRUS *n* any member of a genus of viruses that cause worldwide endemic infections. They occur in birds and mammals, cause diarrhoea in children, and are usually transmitted in food prepared with unwashed hands

ROTCH *n* little auk

ROTCHE *same as* > ROTCH

ROTCHES > ROTCH

ROTCHIE *same as* > ROTCH

ROTCHIES > ROTCHIE

ROTE *n* mechanical repetition ▷ *vb* learn by rote

ROTED > ROTE

ROTENONE *n* white odourless crystalline substance extracted from the roots of derris: a powerful insecticide

ROTENONES > ROTENONE

ROTES > ROTE

ROTGRASS *n* type of grass blamed for sheeprot

ROTGUT *n* alcoholic drink of inferior quality

ROTGUTS > ROTGUT

ROTHER *dialect word for* > OX

ROTHERS > ROTHER

ROTI *n* (in India and the Caribbean) a type of unleavened bread

ROTIFER *n* minute aquatic multicellular invertebrate

ROTIFERAL > ROTIFER

ROTIFERAN > ROTIFER

ROTIFERS > ROTIFER

ROTIFORM *adj* in the shape of a wheel

ROTING > ROTE

ROTINI *n* type of small spiral-shaped pasta

ROTINIS > ROTINI

ROTIS > ROTI

ROTL *n* unit of weight used in Muslim countries

ROTLS > ROTL

ROTO *n* printing process using a cylinder etched with many small recesses in a rotary press

ROTOGRAPH *n* photograph made using a particular method ▷ *vb* photograph using this method

ROTOLO *n* (in Italian cuisine) a roll

ROTOLOS > ROTOLO

ROTON *n* quantum of vortex motion

ROTONS > ROTON

ROTOR *n* revolving portion of a dynamo, motor, or turbine

ROTORS > ROTOR

ROTOS > ROTO

ROTOSCOPE *n* projection device used for creating animated images out of live-action ones ▷ *vb* create animated images using a rotoscope

ROTOTILL *vb* break up the soil using a rototiller

ROTOTILLS > ROTOTILL

ROTOVATE *vb* break up (the surface of the earth, or an area of ground) using a rotavator

ROTOVATED > ROTOVATE

ROTOVATES > ROTOVATE

ROTOVATOR *same as* > ROTAVATOR

ROTPROOF *adj* proof against rot

ROTS > ROT

ROTTAN *n* (in dialect) a rat

ROTTANS > ROTTAN

ROTTE *n* ancient stringed instrument

ROTTED > ROT

ROTTEN *adj* decaying ▷ *adv* extremely ▷ *n* (in dialect) a rat

ROTTENER > ROTTEN

ROTTENEST > ROTTEN

ROTTENLY > ROTTEN

ROTTENS > ROTTEN

ROTTER *n* despicable person

ROTTERS > ROTTER

ROTTES > ROTTE

ROTTING > ROT

ROTULA *n* kneecap

ROTULAE > ROTULA

ROTULAS > ROTULA

ROTUND *adj* round and plump ▷ *vb* make round

ROTUNDA *n* circular building or room, esp with a dome

ROTUNDAS > ROTUNDA

ROTUNDATE *adj* rounded

ROTUNDED > ROTUND

ROTUNDER > ROTUND

ROTUNDEST > ROTUND

ROTUNDING > ROTUND

ROTUNDITY > ROTUND

ROTUNDLY > ROTUND

ROTUNDS > ROTUND

ROTURIER *n* freeholder or ordinary person

ROTURIERS > ROTURIER

ROUBLE *n* monetary unit of Russia, Belarus, and Tajikistan

ROUBLES > ROUBLE

ROUCHE *same as* > RUCHE

ROUCHED *adj* trimmed with a rouche

ROUCHES > ROUCHE

ROUCHING *n* lace trimming

ROUCHINGS > ROUCHING

ROUCOU *another name for* > ANNATTO

ROUCOUS > ROUCOU

ROUE *n* man given to immoral living

ROUEN *n* breed of duck

ROUENS > ROUEN

ROUES > ROUE

ROUGE *n* red cosmetic used to colour the cheeks ▷ *vb* apply rouge to

ROUGED > ROUGE

ROUGES > ROUGE

ROUGH *adj* uneven or irregular ▷ *vb* make rough ▷ *n* rough state or area

ROUGHAGE *n* indigestible constituents of food which aid digestion

ROUGHAGES > ROUGHAGE

ROUGHBACK *n* rough-skinned flatfish

ROUGHCAST *n* mixture of plaster and small stones for outside walls ▷ *vb* coat with this ▷ *adj* covered with or denoting roughcast

ROUGHDRY *vb* dry (clothes or linen) without smoothing

ROUGHED > ROUGH

ROUGHEN *vb* make or become rough

ROUGHENED > ROUGHEN

ROUGHENS > ROUGHEN

ROUGHER *n* person that does the rough preparatory work on something ▷ *adj* more rough

ROUGHERS > ROUGHER

ROUGHEST > ROUGH

ROUGHHEW *vb* cut or hew (timber, stone, etc) roughly without finishing the surface

ROUGHHEWN > ROUGHHEW

ROUGHHEWS > ROUGHHEW

ROUGHIE *n* small food fish found in Australian waters

ROUGHIES > ROUGHIE

ROUGHING *n* (in ice hockey) excessive use of force

ROUGHINGS > ROUGHING

ROUGHISH *adj* somewhat rough

ROUGHLEG *n* any of several kinds of large hawk with feathered legs

ROUGHLEGS > ROUGHLEG

ROUGHLY *adv* without being exact or fully authenticated

ROUGHNECK *n* violent person

ROUGHNESS > ROUGH

ROUGHOUT *n* unfinished roughly-shaped artifact

ROUGHOUTS > ROUGHOUT

r

ROUGHS > ROUGH
ROUGHSHOD *adj* (of a horse) shod with rough-bottomed shoes to prevent sliding
ROUGHT *archaic past form of* > REACH
ROUGHY *spelling variant of* > ROUGHIE
ROUGING > ROUGE
ROUILLE *n* kind of sauce
ROUILLES > ROUILLE
ROUL *archaic form of* > ROLL
ROULADE *n* slice of meat rolled and cooked
ROULADES > ROULADE
ROULE *archaic form of* > ROLL
ROULEAU *n* roll of paper containing coins
ROULEAUS > ROULEAU
ROULEAUX > ROULEAU
ROULES > ROULE
ROULETTE *n* gambling game played with a revolving wheel and a ball ▷ *vb* use a toothed wheel on (something), as in engraving, making stationery, etc
ROULETTED > ROULETTE
ROULETTES > ROULETTE
ROULS > ROUL
ROUM *archaic spelling of* > ROOM
ROUMING *n* pasture given for an animal
ROUMINGS > ROUMING
ROUMS > ROUM
ROUNCE *n* handle that is turned to move paper and plates on a printing press
ROUNCES > ROUNCE
ROUNCEVAL *n* giant or monster
ROUNCIES > ROUNCY
ROUNCY *archaic word for* > HORSE
ROUND *adj* spherical, cylindrical, circular, or curved ▷ *prep* indicating an encircling movement, presence on all sides, etc ▷ *vb* move round ▷ *n* round shape
ROUNDARCH *adj* with rounded arches
ROUNDBALL *n* form of basketball
ROUNDED *adj* round or curved
ROUNDEDLY > ROUNDED
ROUNDEL *same as* > ROUNDELAY
ROUNDELAY *n* simple song with a refrain
ROUNDELS > ROUNDEL
ROUNDER *n* run round all four bases after one hit in rounders
ROUNDERS *n* bat-and-ball team game
ROUNDEST > ROUND

ROUNDHAND *n* style of handwriting with large rounded curves
ROUNDHEEL *n* immoral woman
ROUNDING *n* process in which a number is approximated as the closest number that can be expressed using the number of bits or digits available
ROUNDINGS > ROUNDING
ROUNDISH *adj* somewhat round
ROUNDLE *same as* > ROUNDEL
ROUNDLES > ROUNDLE
ROUNDLET *n* small circle
ROUNDLETS > ROUNDLET
ROUNDLY *adv* thoroughly
ROUNDNESS > ROUND
ROUNDS > ROUND
ROUNDSMAN *n* person who makes rounds, as for inspection or to deliver goods
ROUNDSMEN > ROUNDSMAN
ROUNDTRIP *n* US term for return trip
ROUNDUP *n* act of gathering together
ROUNDUPS > ROUNDUP
ROUNDURE *n* archaic word meaning roundness
ROUNDURES > ROUNDURE
ROUNDWOOD *n* small pieces of timber (about 5–15 cm, or 2–6 in.) in diameter
ROUNDWORM *n* worm that is a common intestinal parasite of man
ROUP *n* any of various chronic respiratory diseases of birds, esp poultry ▷ *vb* sell by auction
ROUPED > ROUP
ROUPET *adj* Scots word meaning hoarse or croaky
ROUPIER > ROUP
ROUPIEST > ROUP
ROUPILY > ROUP
ROUPING > ROUP
ROUPIT *same as* > ROUPET
ROUPS > ROUP
ROUPY > ROUP
ROUSABLE *adj* capable of being roused
ROUSANT *adj* (in heraldry) rising
ROUSE *same as* > REVEILLE
ROUSED > ROUSE
ROUSEMENT *n* stirring up
ROUSER *n* person or thing that rouses people
ROUSERS > ROUSER
ROUSES > ROUSE
ROUSING *adj* lively, vigorous
ROUSINGLY > ROUSING

ROUSSEAU *n* pemmican fried in its own fat
ROUSSEAUS > ROUSSEAU
ROUSSETTE *n* dogfish
ROUST *vb* rout or stir, as out of bed
ROUSTED > ROUST
ROUSTER *n* unskilled labourer on an oil rig
ROUSTERS > ROUSTER
ROUSTING > ROUST
ROUSTS > ROUST
ROUT *n* overwhelming defeat ▷ *vb* defeat and put to flight
ROUTE *n* roads taken to reach a destination ▷ *vb* send by a particular route
ROUTED > ROUTE
ROUTEING > ROUTE
ROUTEMAN *n* (in US English) delivery man or salesman doing a particular round
ROUTEMEN > ROUTEMAN
ROUTER *n* device that allows data to be moved between points on a network
ROUTERS > ROUTER
ROUTES > ROUTE
ROUTEWAY *n* track, road, or waterway, etc, used as a route to somewhere
ROUTEWAYS > ROUTEWAY
ROUTH *n* abundance ▷ *adj* abundant
ROUTHIE *adj* abundant, plentiful, or well filled
ROUTHIER > ROUTHIE
ROUTHIEST > ROUTHIE
ROUTHS > ROUTH
ROUTINE *n* usual or regular method of procedure ▷ *adj* ordinary or regular
ROUTINEER *n* someone who believes in routine
ROUTINELY > ROUTINE
ROUTINES > ROUTINE
ROUTING > ROUT
ROUTINGS > ROUT
ROUTINISE *same as* > ROUTINIZE
ROUTINISM > ROUTINE
ROUTINIST > ROUTINE
ROUTINIZE *vb* make routine
ROUTOUS > ROUT
ROUTOUSLY > ROUT
ROUTS > ROUT
ROUX *n* fat and flour cooked together as a basis for sauces
ROVE > REEVE
ROVED > REEVE
ROVEN > REEVE
ROVER *n* wanderer, traveller
ROVERS > ROVER
ROVES > REEVE
ROVING > ROVE
ROVINGLY > ROVING
ROVINGS > ROVE

ROW *n* straight line of people or things ▷ *vb* propel (a boat) by oars
ROWABLE > ROW
ROWAN *n* tree producing bright red berries, mountain ash
ROWANS > ROWAN
ROWBOAT *n* small boat propelled by one or more pairs of oars
ROWBOATS > ROWBOAT
ROWDEDOW *same as* > ROWDYDOW
ROWDEDOWS > ROWDEDOW
ROWDIER > ROWDY
ROWDIES > ROWDY
ROWDIEST > ROWDY
ROWDILY > ROWDY
ROWDINESS > ROWDY
ROWDY *adj* disorderly, noisy, and rough ▷ *n* person like this
ROWDYDOW *n* hullabaloo ▷ *vb* make noise
ROWDYDOWS > ROWDYDOW
ROWDYISH > ROWDY
ROWDYISM *n* rowdy behaviour or tendencies or a habitual pattern of rowdy behaviour
ROWDYISMS > ROWDYISM
ROWED > ROW
ROWEL *n* small spiked wheel on a spur ▷ *vb* goad (a horse) using a rowel
ROWELED > ROWEL
ROWELING > ROWEL
ROWELLED > ROWEL
ROWELLING > ROWEL
ROWELS > ROWEL
ROWEN *another word for* > AFTERMATH
ROWENS > ROWEN
ROWER > ROW
ROWERS > ROW
ROWIE *n* Scottish bread roll made with butter and fat
ROWIES > ROWIE
ROWING > ROW
ROWINGS > ROW
ROWLOCK *n* device on a boat that holds an oar in place
ROWLOCKS > ROWLOCK
ROWME *archaic variant of* > ROOM
ROWMES > ROWME
ROWND *archaic variant of* > ROUND
ROWNDED > ROWND
ROWNDELL *archaic variant of* > ROUNDEL
ROWNDELLS > ROWNDELL
ROWNDING > ROWND
ROWNDS > ROWND
ROWOVER *n* act of winning a rowing race unopposed
ROWOVERS > ROWOVER
ROWS > ROW
ROWT *archaic variant of* > ROUT
ROWTED > ROWT

ROWTH same as > ROUTH

ROWTHS > ROWTH

ROWTING > ROWT

ROWTS > ROWT

ROYAL adj of, befitting, or supported by a king or queen ▷ n member of a royal family

ROYALET n minor king

ROYALETS > ROYALET

ROYALISE same as > ROYALIZE

ROYALISED > ROYALISE

ROYALISES > ROYALISE

ROYALISM > ROYALIST

ROYALISMS > ROYALIST

ROYALIST n supporter of monarchy ▷ adj of or relating to royalists

ROYALISTS > ROYALIST

ROYALIZE vb make royal

ROYALIZED > ROYALIZE

ROYALIZES > ROYALIZE

ROYALLER > ROYAL

ROYALLEST > ROYAL

ROYALLY > ROYAL

ROYALMAST n highest part of mast

ROYALS > ROYAL

ROYALTIES > ROYALTY

ROYALTY n royal people

ROYNE archaic word for > GNAW

ROYNED > ROYNE

ROYNES > ROYNE

ROYNING > ROYNE

ROYNISH archaic word for > MANGY

ROYST same as > ROIST

ROYSTED > ROYST

ROYSTER same as > ROISTER

ROYSTERED > ROYSTER

ROYSTERER > ROYSTER

ROYSTERS > ROISTER

ROYSTING > ROYST

ROYSTS > ROYST

ROZELLE same as > ROSELLE

ROZELLES > ROZELLE

ROZET same as > ROSET

ROZETED > ROZET

ROZETING > ROZET

ROZETS > ROZET

ROZIT same as > ROSET

ROZITED > ROZIT

ROZITING > ROZIT

ROZITS > ROZIT

ROZZER n policeman

ROZZERS > ROZZER

RUANA n woollen wrap resembling a poncho

RUANAS > RUANA

RUB vb apply pressure with a circular or backwards-and-forwards movement ▷ n act of rubbing

RUBABOO n soup or stew made by boiling pemmican with, if available, flour and vegetables

RUBABOOS > RUBABOO

RUBACE same as > RUBASSE

RUBACES > RUBACE

RUBAI n verse form of Persian origin consisting of four-line stanzas

RUBAIS > RUBAI

RUBAIYAT n (in Persian poetry) a verse form consisting of four-line stanzas

RUBASSE n type of quartz containing red haematite

RUBASSES > RUBASSE

RUBATI > RUBATO

RUBATO n (with) expressive flexibility of tempo ▷ adv be played with a flexible tempo

RUBATOS > RUBATO

RUBBABOO same as > RUBABOO

RUBBABOOS > RUBABOO

RUBBED > RUB

RUBBER n strong waterproof elastic material ▷ adj made of or producing rubber ▷ vb provide with rubber coating

RUBBERED > RUBBER

RUBBERIER > RUBBERY

RUBBERING > RUBBERY

RUBBERISE same as > RUBBERIZE

RUBBERIZE vb coat or treat with rubber

RUBBERS > RUBBER

RUBBERY adj having the texture of or resembling rubber, esp in flexibility or toughness

RUBBET old Scots past form of > ROB

RUBBIDIES > RUBBIDY

RUBBIDY same as > RUBBITY

RUBBIES > RUBBY

RUBBING > RUB

RUBBINGS > RUB

RUBBISH n waste matter ▷ vb criticize

RUBBISHED > RUBBISH

RUBBISHES > RUBBISH

RUBBISHLY variant of > RUBBISHY

RUBBISHY adj worthless, of poor quality, or useless

RUBBIT old Scots past form of > ROB

RUBBITIES > RUBBITY

RUBBITY n pub

RUBBLE n fragments of broken stone, brick, etc ▷ vb turn into rubble

RUBBLED > RUBBLE

RUBBLES > RUBBLE

RUBBLIER > RUBBLE

RUBBLIEST > RUBBLE

RUBBLING > RUBBLE

RUBBLY > RUBBLE

RUBBOARD n board for scrubbing clothes on

RUBBOARDS > RUBBOARD

RUBBY n rubbing alcohol, esp when mixed with cheap wine for drinking

RUBBYDUB n alcoholic willing to drink anything that contains any alcohol

RUBBYDUBS > RUBBYDUB

RUBDOWN n act of drying or cleaning vigorously

RUBDOWNS > RUBDOWN

RUBE n unsophisticated countryman

RUBEFIED > RUBEFY

RUBEFIES > RUBEFY

RUBEFY vb make red

RUBEFYING > RUBEFY

RUBEL n currency unit of Belarus

RUBELLA n mild contagious viral disease

RUBELLAN n red-coloured mineral

RUBELLANS > RUBELLAN

RUBELLAS > RUBELLA

RUBELLITE n red transparent variety of tourmaline, used as a gemstone

RUBELS > RUBEL

RUBEOLA technical name for > MEASLES

RUBEOLAR > RUBEOLA

RUBEOLAS > RUBEOLA

RUBES > RUBE

RUBESCENT adj reddening

RUBICELLE n variety of spinel that is orange or yellow in colour

RUBICON n point of no return ▷ vb (in bezique) to beat before the loser has managed to gain as many as 1000 points

RUBICONED > RUBICON

RUBICONS > RUBICON

RUBICUND adj ruddy

RUBIDIC > RUBIDIUM

RUBIDIUM n soft highly reactive radioactive element

RUBIDIUMS > RUBIDIUM

RUBIED > RUBY

RUBIER > RUBY

RUBIES > RUBY

RUBIEST > RUBY

RUBIFIED > RUBIFY

RUBIFIES > RUBIFY

RUBIFY same as > RUBEFY

RUBIFYING > RUBIFY

RUBIGO old Scots word for > PENIS

RUBIGOS > RUBIGO

RUBIN archaic word for > RUBY

RUBINE archaic word for > RUBY

RUBINEOUS same as > RUBIOUS

RUBINES > RUBINE

RUBINS > RUBIN

RUBIOUS adj of the colour ruby

RUBLE same as > ROUBLE

RUBLES > RUBLE

RUBLI > RUBLE

RUBOFF n resulting effect on something else; consequences

RUBOFFS > RUBOFF

RUBOUT n killing or elimination

RUBOUTS > RUBOUT

RUBRIC n set of rules for behaviour ▷ adj written, printed, or marked in red

RUBRICAL > RUBRIC

RUBRICATE vb print (a book or manuscript) with red titles, headings, etc

RUBRICIAN n authority on liturgical rubrics

RUBRICS > RUBRIC

RUBS > RUB

RUBSTONE n stone used for sharpening or smoothing, esp a whetstone

RUBSTONES > RUBSTONE

RUBUS n fruit-bearing genus of shrubs

RUBUSES > RUBUS

RUBY n red precious gemstone ▷ adj deep red ▷ vb redden

RUBYING > RUBY

RUBYLIKE > RUBY

RUC same as > ROC

RUCHE n pleat or frill of lace etc as a decoration ▷ vb put a ruche on

RUCHED > RUCHE

RUCHES > RUCHE

RUCHING n material used for a ruche

RUCHINGS > RUCHING

RUCK n rough crowd of common people ▷ vb wrinkle or crease

RUCKED > RUCK

RUCKING > RUCK

RUCKLE another word for > RUCK

RUCKLED > RUCKLE

RUCKLES > RUCKLE

RUCKLING > RUCKLE

RUCKMAN n person who plays in the ruck

RUCKMEN > RUCKMAN

RUCKS > RUCK

RUCKSACK n large pack carried on the back

RUCKSACKS > RUCKSACK

RUCKSEAT n seat fixed to or forming part of a rucksack

RUCKSEATS > RUCKSEAT

RUCKUS n uproar

RUCKUSES > RUCKUS

RUCOLA n another name for the salad plant rocket

RUCOLAS > RUCOLA

RUCS > RUC

RUCTATION n archaic word meaning eructation or belch

RUCTION n uproar

RUCTIONS > RUCTION

r

RUCTIOUS adj tending or likely to cause ructions

RUD n red or redness ▷ vb redden

RUDACEOUS adj (of conglomerate, breccia, and similar rocks) composed of coarse-grained material

RUDAS n Scots word for a coarse, rude old woman

RUDASES > RUDAS

RUDBECKIA n N American plant cultivated for its showy flowers

RUDD n European freshwater fish

RUDDED > RUD

RUDDER n vertical hinged piece at the stern of a boat or at the rear of an aircraft, for steering

RUDDERS > RUDDER

RUDDIED > RUDDY

RUDDIER > RUDDY

RUDDIES > RUDDY

RUDDIEST > RUDDY

RUDDILY > RUDDY

RUDDINESS > RUDDY

RUDDING > RUD

RUDDLE n red ochre, used esp to mark sheep ▷ vb mark (sheep) with ruddle

RUDDLED > RUDDLE

RUDDLEMAN n ruddle dealer

RUDDLEMEN > RUDDLEMAN

RUDDLES > RUDDLE

RUDDLING > RUDDLE

RUDDOCK dialect name for the > ROBIN

RUDDOCKS > RUDDOCK

RUDDS > RUDD

RUDDY adj of a fresh healthy red colour ▷ adv bloody ▷ vb redden

RUDDYING > RUDDY

RUDE archaic spelling of > ROOD

RUDELY > RUDE

RUDENESS > RUDE

RUDER > RUDE

RUDERAL n plant that grows on waste ground ▷ adj growing in waste places

RUDERALS > RUDERAL

RUDERIES > RUDE

RUDERY > RUDE

RUDES > RUDE

RUDESBIES > RUDESBY

RUDESBY n archaic word for rude person

RUDEST > RUDE

RUDI same as > RUDIE

RUDIE n member of a youth movement originating in the 1960s

RUDIES > RUDIE

RUDIMENT n first principles or elementary stages of a subject

RUDIMENTS > RUDIMENT

RUDIS > RUDI

RUDISH adj somewhat rude

RUDIST n cone-shaped extinct mollusc

RUDISTID same as > RUDIST

RUDISTIDS > RUDISTID

RUDISTS > RUDIST

RUDS > RUD

RUDY same as > RUDIE

RUE vb feel regret for ▷ n plant with evergreen bitter leaves

RUED > RUE

RUEDA n type of Cuban round dance

RUEDAS > RUEDA

RUEFUL adj regretful or sorry

RUEFULLY > RUEFUL

RUEING > RUE

RUEINGS > RUE

RUELLE n area between bed and wall

RUELLES > RUELLE

RUELLIA n genus of plants

RUELLIAS > RUELLIA

RUER > RUE

RUERS > RUE

RUES > RUE

RUFESCENT adj tinged with red or becoming red

RUFF n circular pleated, gathered, or fluted collar ▷ vb trump

RUFFE n European freshwater fish

RUFFED > RUFF

RUFFES > RUFFE

RUFFIAN n violent lawless person ▷ vb act like a ruffian

RUFFIANED > RUFFIAN

RUFFIANLY > RUFFIAN

RUFFIANS > RUFFIAN

RUFFIN archaic name for > RUFFE

RUFFING > RUFF

RUFFINS > RUFFIN

RUFFLE vb disturb the calm of ▷ n frill or pleat

RUFFLED > RUFFLE

RUFFLER n person or thing that ruffles

RUFFLERS > RUFFLER

RUFFLES > RUFFLE

RUFFLIER > RUFFLY

RUFFLIEST > RUFFLY

RUFFLIKE > RUFF

RUFFLING > RUFFLE

RUFFLINGS > RUFFLE

RUFFLY adj ruffled

RUFFS > RUFF

RUFIYAA n standard monetary unit of the Maldives

RUFIYAAS > RUFIYAA

RUFOUS n reddish-brown colour

RUFOUSES > RUFOUS

RUG n small carpet ▷ vb (in dialect) tug

RUGA n fold, wrinkle, or crease

RUGAE > RUGA

RUGAL adj (in anatomy) with ridges or folds

RUGALACH same as > RUGELACH

RUGATE same as > RUGOSE

RUGBIES > RUGBY

RUGBY n form of football played with an oval ball which may be handled by the players

RUGELACH n fruit and nut pastry shaped like a croissant

RUGELACHS > RUGELACH

RUGGED adj rocky or steep

RUGGEDER > RUGGED

RUGGEDEST > RUGGED

RUGGEDISE same as > RUGGEDIZE

RUGGEDIZE vb make durable, as for military use

RUGGEDLY > RUGGED

RUGGELACH same as > RUGELACH

RUGGER same as > RUGBY

RUGGERS > RUGGER

RUGGIER > RUGGY

RUGGIEST > RUGGY

RUGGING > RUG

RUGGINGS > RUG

RUGGY adj (in dialect) rough or rugged

RUGLIKE > RUG

RUGOLA n another name for the salad plant rocket

RUGOLAS > RUGOLA

RUGOSA n any of various shrubs descended from a particular type of wild rose

RUGOSAS > RUGOSA

RUGOSE adj wrinkled

RUGOSELY > RUGOSE

RUGOSITY > RUGOSE

RUGOUS same as > RUGOSE

RUGRAT n young child

RUGRATS > RUGRAT

RUGS > RUG

RUGULOSE adj with little wrinkles

RUIN vb destroy or spoil completely ▷ n destruction or decay

RUINABLE > RUIN

RUINATE vb archaic word for bring or come to ruin

RUINATED > RUINATE

RUINATES > RUINATE

RUINATING > RUINATE

RUINATION n act of ruining

RUINED > RUIN

RUINER > RUIN

RUINERS > RUIN

RUING > RUE

RUINGS > RUE

RUINING > RUIN

RUININGS > RUIN

RUINOUS adj causing ruin

RUINOUSLY > RUINOUS

RUINS > RUIN

RUKH same as > ROC

RUKHS > RUKH

RULABLE > RULE

RULE n statement of what is allowed, for example in a game or procedure ▷ vb govern

RULED > RULE

RULELESS > RULE

RULER n person who governs ▷ vb punish by hitting with a ruler

RULERED > RULER

RULERING > RULER

RULERS > RULER

RULERSHIP > RULER

RULES > RULE

RULESSE adj archaic word meaning ruleless or without rules

RULIER > RULY

RULIEST > RULY

RULING n formal decision ▷ adj controlling or exercising authority

RULINGS > RULING

RULLION n Scots word for rawhide shoe

RULLIONS > RULLION

RULLOCK same as > ROWLOCK

RULLOCKS > RULLOCK

RULY adj orderly

RUM n alcoholic drink distilled from sugar cane ▷ adj odd, strange

RUMAKI n savoury of chicken liver and sliced water chestnut wrapped in bacon

RUMAKIS > RUMAKI

RUMAL n handkerchief or type of cloth

RUMALS > RUMAL

RUMBA n lively ballroom dance of Cuban origin ▷ vb dance the rumba

RUMBAED > RUMBA

RUMBAING > RUMBA

RUMBAS > RUMBA

RUMBELOW n nonsense word used in the refrain of certain sea shanties

RUMBELOWS > RUMBELOW

RUMBLE vb make a low continuous noise ▷ n deep resonant sound

RUMBLED > RUMBLE

RUMBLER > RUMBLE

RUMBLERS > RUMBLE

RUMBLES > RUMBLE

RUMBLIER > RUMBLY

RUMBLIEST > RUMBLY

RUMBLING > RUMBLE

RUMBLINGS > RUMBLE

RUMBLY adj rumbling or liable to rumble

RUMBO n rum-based cocktail

RUMBOS > RUMBO

RUMDUM n alcoholic

RUMDUMS > RUMDUM
RUME archaic form of
> RHEUM
RUMEN n first
compartment of the
stomach of ruminants
RUMENS > RUMEN
RUMES > RUME
RUMINA > RUMEN
RUMINAL > RUMEN
RUMINANT n cud-chewing
(animal, such as a cow,
sheep, or deer) ▷ adj of
ruminants
RUMINANTS > RUMINANT
RUMINATE vb chew the
cud
RUMINATED > RUMINATE
RUMINATES > RUMINATE
RUMINATOR > RUMINATE
RUMKIN n archaic term for
a drinking vessel
RUMKINS > RUMKIN
RUMLY > RUM
RUMMAGE vb search
untidily and at length
▷ n untidy search through
a collection of things
RUMMAGED > RUMMAGE
RUMMAGER > RUMMAGE
RUMMAGERS > RUMMAGE
RUMMAGES > RUMMAGE
RUMMAGING > RUMMAGE
RUMMER > RUM
RUMMERS > RUM
RUMMEST > RUM
RUMMIER > RUMMY
RUMMIES > RUMMY
RUMMIEST > RUMMY
RUMMILY > RUMMY
RUMMINESS > RUMMY
RUMMISH adj rather
strange, peculiar, or odd
▷ vb roar or protest
RUMMISHED > RUMMISH
RUMMISHES > RUMMISH
RUMMY n card game in
which players try to collect
sets or sequences ▷ adj of
or like rum in taste or smell
RUMNESS > RUM
RUMNESSES > RUM
RUMOR same as > RUMOUR
RUMORED > RUMOR
RUMORER n person given
to spreading rumours
RUMORERS > RUMORER
RUMORING > RUMOR
RUMOROUS adj involving
or containing rumours
RUMORS > RUMOR
RUMOUR n unproved
statement ▷ vb pass
around or circulate in the
form of a rumour
RUMOURED > RUMOUR
RUMOURER n someone
given to spreading rumours
RUMOURERS > RUMOURER
RUMOURING > RUMOUR
RUMOURS > RUMOUR
RUMP n buttocks ▷ vb turn
back on

RUMPED > RUMP
RUMPIES > RUMPY
RUMPING > RUMP
RUMPLE vb make untidy,
crumpled, or dishevelled
▷ n wrinkle, fold, or crease
RUMPLED > RUMPLE
RUMPLES > RUMPLE
RUMPLESS > RUMP
RUMPLIER > RUMPLE
RUMPLIEST > RUMPLE
RUMPLING > RUMPLE
RUMPLY > RUMPLE
RUMPO n slang word for
sexual intercourse
RUMPOS > RUMPO
RUMPOT n alcoholic
RUMPOTS > RUMPOT
RUMPS > RUMP
RUMPUS n noisy
commotion
RUMPUSES > RUMPUS
RUMPY n tailless Manx cat
▷ adj with a large or
noticeable rump
RUMRUNNER n alcohol
smuggler
RUMS > RUM
RUN vb move with a more
rapid gait than walking
▷ n act or spell of running
RUNABOUT n small car
used for short journeys
▷ vb move busily from
place to place
RUNABOUTS > RUNABOUT
RUNAGATE n vagabond,
fugitive, or renegade
RUNAGATES > RUNAGATE
RUNANGA n Māori
assembly or council
RUNANGAS > RUNANGA
RUNAROUND n deceitful or
evasive treatment of a
person
RUNAWAY n person or
animal that runs away
RUNAWAYS > RUNAWAY
RUNBACK n (in tennis) the
areas behind the baselines
of the court
RUNBACKS > RUNBACK
RUNCH n another name for
white charlock
RUNCHES > RUNCH
RUNCIBLE adj as in
runcible spoon forklike
utensil with two prongs
and one sharp curved
prong
RUNCINATE adj (of a leaf)
having a saw-toothed
margin with the teeth or
lobes pointing backwards
RUND same as > ROON
RUNDALE n system of land
tenure in Ireland
RUNDALES > RUNDALE
RUNDLE n rung of a ladder
RUNDLED adj rounded
RUNDLES > RUNDLE
RUNDLET n liquid
measure, generally about
15 gallons

RUNDLETS > RUNDLET
RUNDOWN adj tired;
exhausted ▷ n brief
review, résumé, or
summary
RUNDOWNS > RUNDOWN
RUNDS > RUND
RUNE n any character of
the earliest Germanic
alphabet
RUNECRAFT n
understanding of and
skill working with runes
RUNED n with runes on
RUNELIKE adj resembling
a rune or runes
RUNES > RUNE
RUNFLAT adj having a
safety feature that
prevents tyres becoming
dangerous when flat
RUNFLATS > RUNFLAT
RUNG > RING
RUNGED adj having rungs
RUNGLESS > RING
RUNGS > RING
RUNIC > RUNE
RUNKLE vb (in dialect)
crease or wrinkle
RUNKLED > RUNKLE
RUNKLES > RUNKLE
RUNKLING > RUNKLE
RUNLESS > RUN
RUNLET n cask for wine,
beer, etc
RUNLETS > RUNLET
RUNNABLE > RUN
RUNNEL n small brook
RUNNELS > RUNNEL
RUNNER n competitor in a
race
RUNNERS > RUNNER
RUNNET dialect word for
> RENNET
RUNNETS > RUNNET
RUNNIER > RUNNY
RUNNIEST > RUNNY
RUNNINESS > RUNNY
RUNNING > RUN
RUNNINGLY > RUN
RUNNINGS > RUN
RUNNION n archaic
pejorative term for a
woman
RUNNIONS > RUNNION
RUNNY adj tending to flow
RUNOFF n extra race to
decide the winner after
a tie
RUNOFFS > RUNOFF
RUNOUT n dismissal of a
batsman by running him
out
RUNOUTS > RUNOUT
RUNOVER n incident in
which someone is run over
by a vehicle
RUNOVERS > RUNOVER
RUNPROOF adj (of
stockings or tights)
designed to be especially
resistant to being ripped
RUNRIG same as
> RUNDALE

RUNRIGS > RUNRIG
RUNROUND same as
> RUNAROUND
RUNROUNDS > RUNROUND
RUNS > RUN
RUNT n smallest animal in
a litter
RUNTED adj stunted
RUNTIER > RUNT
RUNTIEST > RUNT
RUNTINESS > RUNT
RUNTISH > RUNT
RUNTISHLY > RUNT
RUNTS > RUNT
RUNTY > RUNT
RUNWAY n hard level
roadway where aircraft
take off and land
RUNWAYS > RUNWAY
RUPEE n monetary unit of
India and Pakistan
RUPEES > RUPEE
RUPIA n type of skin
eruption
RUPIAH n standard
monetary unit of
Indonesia
RUPIAHS > RUPIAH
RUPIAS > RUPIA
RUPTURE n breaking,
breach ▷ vb break, burst,
or sever
RUPTURED > RUPTURE
RUPTURES > RUPTURE
RUPTURING > RUPTURE
RURAL adj in or of the
countryside ▷ n country
dweller
RURALISE same as
> RURALIZE
RURALISED > RURALISE
RURALISES > RURALISE
RURALISM > RURAL
RURALISMS > RURAL
RURALIST > RURAL
RURALISTS > RURAL
RURALITE > RURAL
RURALITES > RURAL
RURALITY > RURAL
RURALIZE vb make rural
in character, appearance,
etc
RURALIZED > RURALIZE
RURALIZES > RURALIZE
RURALLY > RURAL
RURALNESS > RURAL
RURALS > RURAL
RURBAN adj part country,
part urban
RURP n very small piton
RURPS > RURP
RURU another name for
> MOPOKE
RURUS > RURU
RUSA n type of deer with a
mane
RUSALKA n water nymph
or spirit
RUSALKAS > RUSALKA
RUSAS > RUSA
RUSCUS n type of shrub
RUSCUSES > RUSCUS
RUSE n stratagem or trick

r

RUSES > RUSE

RUSH vb move or do very quickly ▷ n sudden quick or violent movement ▷ adj done with speed, hasty

RUSHED > RUSH

RUSHEE n someone interested in gaining fraternity or sorority membership

RUSHEES > RUSHEE

RUSHEN adj made of rushes

RUSHER > RUSH

RUSHERS > RUSH

RUSHES pl n (in film-making) the initial prints of a scene or scenes before editing

RUSHIER > RUSHY

RUSHIEST > RUSHY

RUSHINESS > RUSHY

RUSHING > RUSH

RUSHINGS > RUSH

RUSHLIGHT n narrow candle, formerly in use, made of the pith of various types of rush dipped in tallow

RUSHLIKE > RUSH

RUSHY adj full of rushes

RUSINE adj of or relating to rusa deer

RUSK n hard brown crisp biscuit, used esp for feeding babies

RUSKS > RUSK

RUSMA n Turkish depilatory

RUSMAS > RUSMA

RUSSE adj as in charlotte russe cold dessert made from cream, etc, surrounded by sponge fingers

RUSSEL n type of woollen fabric

RUSSELS > RUSSEL

RUSSET adj reddish-brown ▷ n apple with rough reddish-brown skin ▷ vb become russet-coloured

RUSSETED > RUSSET

RUSSETING > RUSSET

RUSSETS > RUSSET

RUSSETY > RUSSET

RUSSIA n Russia leather

RUSSIAS > RUSSIA

RUSSIFIED > RUSSIFY

RUSSIFIES > RUSSIFY

RUSSIFY vb cause to become Russian in character

RUSSULA n type of fungus, typically of toadstool shape

RUSSULAE > RUSSULA

RUSSULAS > RUSSULA

RUST n reddish-brown coating formed on iron etc that has been exposed to moisture ▷ adj reddish-brown ▷ vb become coated with rust

RUSTABLE adj liable to rust

RUSTED > RUST

RUSTIC adj of or resembling country people ▷ n person from the country

RUSTICAL n rustic

RUSTICALS > RUSTICAL

RUSTICANA pl n objects, such as agricultural implements, garden furniture, etc, relating to the countryside or made in imitation of rustic styles

RUSTICATE vb banish temporarily from university as a punishment

RUSTICIAL made-up variant of > RUSTIC

RUSTICISE same as > RUSTICIZE

RUSTICISM > RUSTIC

RUSTICITY > RUSTIC

RUSTICIZE vb make rustic

RUSTICLY > RUSTIC

RUSTICS > RUSTIC

RUSTIER > RUSTY

RUSTIEST > RUSTY

RUSTILY > RUSTY

RUSTINESS > RUSTY

RUSTING > RUST

RUSTINGS > RUST

RUSTLE n (make) a low whispering sound ▷ vb steal (cattle)

RUSTLED > RUSTLE

RUSTLER n cattle thief

RUSTLERS > RUSTLER

RUSTLES > RUSTLE

RUSTLESS > RUST

RUSTLING > RUSTLE

RUSTLINGS > RUSTLE

RUSTPROOF adj treated against rusting

RUSTRE n (in heraldry) lozenge with a round hole in the middle showing the background colour

RUSTRED > RUSTRE

RUSTRES > RUSTRE

RUSTS > RUST

RUSTY adj coated with rust

RUT n furrow made by wheels ▷ vb be in a period of sexual excitability

RUTABAGA n Eurasian plant with a bulbous edible root which is used as a vegetable and as cattle fodder

RUTABAGAS > RUTABAGA

RUTACEOUS adj relating to a family of tropical and temperate flowering plants which includes rue and citrus trees

RUTH n pity

RUTHENIC adj of or containing ruthenium, esp in a high valency state

RUTHENIUM n rare hard brittle white element

RUTHER adv rather

RUTHFUL adj full of or causing sorrow or pity

RUTHFULLY > RUTHFUL

RUTHLESS adj pitiless, merciless

RUTHS > RUTH

RUTILANT adj of a reddish colour or glow

RUTILATED adj (of minerals, esp quartz) containing needles of rutile

RUTILE n black, yellowish, or reddish-brown mineral

RUTILES > RUTILE

RUTIN n bioflavonoid found in various plants including rue

RUTINS > RUTIN

RUTS > RUT

RUTTED > RUT

RUTTER n (in history) type of cavalry soldier

RUTTERS > RUTTER

RUTTIER > RUTTY

RUTTIEST > RUTTY

RUTTILY > RUTTY

RUTTINESS > RUTTY

RUTTING > RUT

RUTTINGS > RUT

RUTTISH adj (of an animal) in a condition of rut

RUTTISHLY > RUTTISH

RUTTY adj full of ruts or holes

RYA n type of rug originating in Scandinavia

RYAL n one of several old coins

RYALS > RYAL

RYAS > RYA

RYBAT n polished stone piece forming the side of a window or door

RYBATS > RYBAT

RYBAUDRYE archaic variant of > RIBALDRY

RYE n kind of grain used for fodder and bread

RYEBREAD n any of various breads made entirely or partly from rye flour, often with caraway seeds

RYEBREADS > RYEBREAD

RYEFLOUR n flour made from rye

RYEFLOURS > RYEFLOUR

RYEGRASS n type of grass native to Europe, N Africa, and Asia, widely cultivated as a forage crop

RYEPECK n punt-mooring pole

RYEPECKS > RYEPECK

RYES > RYE

RYFE archaic variant of > RIFE

RYKE Scots variant of > REACH

RYKED > RYKE

RYKES > RYKE

RYKING > RYKE

RYMME same as > RIM

RYMMED > RYMME

RYMMES > RYMME

RYMMING > RYMME

RYND n (in milling) crossbar piece forming part of the support structure of the upper millstone

RYNDS > RYND

RYOKAN n traditional Japanese inn

RYOKANS > RYOKAN

RYOT n (in India) a peasant or tenant farmer

RYOTS > RYOT

RYOTWARI n (in India) system of land tenure in which land taxes are paid to the state

RYOTWARIS > RYOTWARI

RYPE n ptarmigan

RYPECK same as > RYEPECK

RYPECKS > RYEPECK

RYPER > RYPE

RYU n school of Japanese martial arts

RYUS > RYU

Ss

SAAG n (in Indian cookery) spinach

SAAGS > SAAG

SAB n person engaged in direct action to prevent a targeted activity taking place ▷ vb take part in such action

SABADILLA n tropical American liliaceous plant

SABAL n variety of palm tree

SABALS > SABAL

SABATON n foot covering in suit of armour

SABATONS > SABATON

SABAYON n dessert or sweet sauce made with egg yolks, sugar, and wine

SABAYONS > SABAYON

SABBAT n midnight meeting of witches

SABBATH n period of rest

SABBATHS > SABBATH

SABBATIC n period of leave granted to university staff

SABBATICS > SABBATIC

SABBATINE adj of Saturday

SABBATISE same as > SABBATIZE

SABBATISM n sabbath observance

SABBATIZE vb observe as sabbath

SABBATS > SABBAT

SABBED > SAB

SABBING > SAB

SABBINGS > SABBING

SABE n very informal word meaning sense or savvy ▷ vb very informal word meaning know or savvy

SABED > SABE

SABEING > SABE

SABELLA n marine worm

SABELLAS > SABELLA

SABER same as > SABRE

SABERED > SABER

SABERING > SABER

SABERLIKE > SABER

SABERS > SABER

SABES > SABE

SABHA n set of Muslim prayer beads

SABHAS > SABHA

SABICU n type of Caribbean tree

SABICUS > SABICU

SABIN n unit of acoustic absorption

SABINE variant of > SAVIN

SABINES > SABINE

SABINS > SABIN

SABIR n member of ancient Turkic people

SABIRS > SABIR

SABKHA n flat coastal plain with a salt crust, common in Arabia

SABKHAH n sabkha

SABKHAHS > SABKHAH

SABKHAS > SABKHA

SABKHAT n sabkha

SABKHATS > SABKHAT

SABLE n dark fur from a small weasel-like Arctic animal ▷ adj black

SABLED > SABLE

SABLEFISH n North American fish

SABLES > SABLE

SABLING > SABLE

SABOT n wooden shoe traditionally worn by peasants in France

SABOTAGE n intentional damage done to machinery, systems, etc ▷ vb damage intentionally

SABOTAGED > SABOTAGE

SABOTAGES > SABOTAGE

SABOTED adj wearing sabots

SABOTEUR n person who commits sabotage

SABOTEURS > SABOTEUR

SABOTIER n wearer of wooden clogs

SABOTIERS > SABOTIER

SABOTS > SABOT

SABRA n native-born Israeli Jew

SABRAS > SABRA

SABRE n curved cavalry sword ▷ vb injure or kill with a sabre

SABRED > SABRE

SABRELIKE > SABERLIKE

SABRES > SABRE

SABREUR n person wielding sabre

SABREURS > SABREUR

SABREWING n large type of hummingbird with long curved wings

SABRING > SABRE

SABS > SAB

SABULINE same as > SABULOUS

SABULOSE same as > SABULOUS

SABULOUS adj like sand in texture

SABURRA n granular deposit

SABURRAL > SABURRA

SABURRAS > SABURRA

SAC n pouchlike structure in an animal or plant

SACATON n coarse grass of the southwestern US and Mexico

SACATONS > SACATON

SACBUT n medieval trombone

SACBUTS > SACBUT

SACCADE n movement of the eye when it makes a sudden change of fixation, as in reading

SACCADES > SACCADE

SACCADIC > SACCADE

SACCATE adj in the form of a sac

SACCHARIC adj as in saccharic acid white soluble solid acid

SACCHARIN n artificial sweetener

SACCHARUM n cane sugar

SACCIFORM adj like a sac

SACCOI > SACCOS

SACCOS n bishop's garment in the Orthodox Church

SACCOSES > SACCOS

SACCULAR adj of or resembling a sac

SACCULATE adj of, relating to, or possessing a saccule, saccules, or a sacculus

SACCULE n small sac

SACCULES > SACCULE

SACCULI > SACCULUS

SACCULUS same as > SACCULE

SACELLA > SACELLUM

SACELLUM n tomb within a church

SACHEM same as > SAGAMORE

SACHEMDOM > SACHEM

SACHEMIC > SACHEM

SACHEMS > SACHEM

SACHET n small envelope or bag containing a single portion

SACHETED adj contained in a sachet

SACHETS > SACHET

SACK n large bag made of coarse material ▷ vb dismiss

SACKABLE adj of or denoting an offence, infraction of rules, etc, that is sufficiently serious to warrant dismissal from an employment

SACKAGE n act of sacking a place ▷ vb sack or plunder

SACKAGED > SACKAGE

SACKAGES > SACKAGE

SACKAGING > SACKAGE

SACKBUT n medieval form of trombone

SACKBUTS > SACKBUT

SACKCLOTH n coarse fabric used for sacks, formerly worn as a penance

SACKED > SACK

SACKER > SACK

SACKERS > SACK

SACKFUL > SACK

SACKFULS > SACKFUL

SACKING n rough woven material used for sacks

SACKINGS > SACKING

SACKLESS adj old word meaning innocent

SACKLIKE > SACK

SACKLOAD n amount of something that a sack contains

SACKLOADS > SACKLOAD

SACKS > SACK

SACKSFUL > SACKFUL

SACLESS adj old word meaning unchallengeable

SACLIKE > SAC

SACQUE same as > SACK

SACQUES > SACQUE

SACRA > SACRUM

SACRAL adj of or associated with sacred rites ▷ n sacral vertebra

SACRALGIA n pain in sacrum

SACRALISE same as > SACRALIZE

SACRALITY n sacredness

SACRALIZE vb make sacred

SACRALS > SACRAL

SACRAMENT n ceremony of the Christian Church, esp Communion

SACRARIA > SACRARIUM

SACRARIAL > SACRARIUM

SACRARIUM n sanctuary of a church

SACRED adj holy

SACREDER > SACRED

SACREDEST > SACRED

SACREDLY > SACRED

SACRIFICE n giving something up ▷ vb offer as a sacrifice

SACRIFIDE vb old form of sacrifice

SACRIFIED > SACRIFY

SACRIFIES > SACRIFY

SACRIFY vb old form of sacrifice

SACRILEGE n misuse or desecration of something sacred

SACRING n act or ritual of consecration

SACRINGS > SACRING

SACRIST same as > SACRISTAN

SACRISTAN n person in charge of the contents of a church

SACRISTS > SACRIST

SACRISTY n room in a church where sacred objects are kept

SACRUM n wedge-shaped bone at the base of the spine

SACRUMS > SACRUM

SACS > SAC

SAD adj sorrowful, unhappy ▷ vb New Zealand word meaning express sadness or displeasure strongly

SADDED > SAD

SADDEN vb make (someone) sad

SADDENED > SADDEN

SADDENING > SADDEN

SADDENS > SADDEN

SADDER > SAD

SADDEST > SAD

SADDHU same as > SADHU

SADDHUS > SADDHU

SADDIE same as > SADDO

SADDIES > SADDIE

SADDING > SAD

SADDISH > SAD

SADDLE n rider's seat on a horse or bicycle ▷ vb put a saddle on (a horse)

SADDLEBAG n pouch or small bag attached to the saddle of a horse, bicycle, or motorcycle

SADDLEBOW n pommel of a saddle

SADDLED > SADDLE

SADDLER n maker or seller of saddles

SADDLERS > SADDLER

SADDLERY n saddles and harness for horses collectively

SADDLES > SADDLE

SADDLING > SADDLE

SADDO vb make sad ▷ n socially inadequate or pathetic person

SADDOES > SADDO

SADDOS > SADDO

SADE same as > SADHE

SADES > SADE

SADHANA n one of a number of spiritual practices which lead to perfection

SADHANAS > SADHANA

SADHE n 18th letter in the Hebrew alphabet

SADHES > SADHE

SADHU n Hindu wandering holy man

SADHUS > SADHU

SADI variant of > SADHE

SADIRON n heavy iron pointed at both ends, for pressing clothes

SADIRONS > SADIRON

SADIS > SADI

SADISM n gaining of (sexual) pleasure from inflicting pain

SADISMS > SADISM

SADIST > SADISM

SADISTIC > SADISM

SADISTS > SADISM

SADLY > SAD

SADNESS > SAD

SADNESSES > SAD

SADO variant of > CHADO

SADOS > SADO

SADS > SAD

SADZA n southern African porridge

SADZAS > SADZA

SAE Scot word for > SO

SAECULA > SAECULUM

SAECULUM n age in astronomy

SAECULUMS > SAECULUM

SAETER n upland pasture in Norway

SAETERS > SAETER

SAFARI n expedition to hunt or observe wild animals, esp in Africa ▷ vb go on safari

SAFARIED > SAFARI

SAFARIING > SAFARI

SAFARIS > SAFARI

SAFARIST n person on safari

SAFARISTS > SAFARIST

SAFE adj secure, protected ▷ n strong lockable container ▷ vb make safe

SAFED > SAFE

SAFEGUARD vb protect ▷ n protection

SAFELIGHT n light that can be used in a room in which photographic material is handled, transmitting only those colours to which a particular type of film, plate, or paper is relatively insensitive

SAFELY > SAFE

SAFENESS > SAFE

SAFER > SAFE

SAFES > SAFE

SAFEST > SAFE

SAFETIED > SAFETY

SAFETIES > SAFETY

SAFETY n state of being safe ▷ vb make safe

SAFETYING > SAFETY

SAFETYMAN n defensive player in American football

SAFETYMEN > SAFETYMAN

SAFFIAN n leather tanned with sumach and usually dyed a bright colour

SAFFIANS > SAFFIAN

SAFFLOWER n thistle-like plant with flowers used for dye and oil

SAFFRON n orange-coloured flavouring obtained from a crocus ▷ adj orange

SAFFRONED adj containing saffron

SAFFRONS > SAFFRON

SAFFRONY adj like saffron

SAFING > SAFE

SAFRANIN same as > SAFRANINE

SAFRANINE n any of a class of azine dyes, used for textiles and biological stains

SAFRANINS > SAFRANIN

SAFROL n oily liquid obtained from sassafras

SAFROLE n colourless or yellowish oily water-insoluble liquid

SAFROLES > SAFROLE

SAFROLS > SAFROL

SAFRONAL n oily liquid derived from saffron

SAFRONALS > SAFRONAL

SAFT Scot word for > SOFT

SAFTER > SAFT

SAFTEST > SAFT

SAG vb sink in the middle ▷ n droop

SAGA n legend of Norse heroes

SAGACIOUS adj wise

SAGACITY n foresight, discernment, or keen perception

SAGAMAN n person reciting Norse sagas

SAGAMEN > SAGAMAN

SAGAMORE n (among some Native Americans) a chief or eminent man

SAGAMORES > SAGAMORE

SAGANASH n Algonquian term for an Englishman

SAGAPENUM n resin formerly used as drug

SAGAS > SAGA

SAGATHIES > SAGATHY

SAGATHY n type of light fabric

SAGBUT n medieval trombone

SAGBUTS > SAGBUT

SAGE n very wise man ▷ adj wise

SAGEBRUSH n aromatic plant of West N America

SAGEHOOD n state of being wise

SAGEHOODS > SAGEHOOD

SAGELY > SAGE

SAGENE n fishing net

SAGENES > SAGENE

SAGENESS > SAGE

SAGENITE n mineral found in crystal form

SAGENITES > SAGENITE

SAGENITIC > SAGENITE

SAGER > SAGE

SAGES > SAGE

SAGEST > SAGE

SAGGAR n box in which fragile ceramic wares are placed for protection ▷ vb put in a saggar

SAGGARD n saggar

SAGGARDS > SAGGARD

SAGGARED > SAGGAR

SAGGARING > SAGGAR

SAGGARS > SAGGAR

SAGGED > SAG

SAGGER same as > SAGGAR

SAGGERED > SAGGER

SAGGERING > SAGGER

SAGGERS > SAGGER

SAGGIER > SAGGY

SAGGIEST > SAGGY

SAGGING > SAG

SAGGINGS > SAG

SAGGY adj tending to sag

SAGIER > SAGY

SAGIEST > SAGY

SAGINATE vb fatten livestock

SAGINATED > SAGINATE

SAGINATES > SAGINATE

SAGITTA n sine of an arc

SAGITTAL adj resembling an arrow

SAGITTARY n centaur

SAGITTAS > SAGITTA

SAGITTATE adj (esp of leaves) shaped like the head of an arrow

SAGO n starchy cereal from the powdered pith of the sago palm tree

SAGOIN n South American monkey

SAGOINS > SAGOIN

SAGOS > SAGO

SAGOUIN n South American monkey

SAGOUINS > SAGOUIN

SAGRADA adj as in cascara sagrada dried bark of the cascara buckthorn

SAGS > SAG

SAGUARO n giant cactus of desert regions

SAGUIN n South American monkey

SAGUINS > SAGUIN

SAGUM n Roman soldier's cloak

SAGY adj like or containing sage

SAHEB same as > SAHIB

SAHEBS > SAHEB

SAHIB n Indian term of address placed after a man's name as a mark of respect

SAHIBA n respectful Indian term of address for woman

SAHIBAH n sahiba

SAHIBAHS > SAHIBAH

SAHIBAS > SAHIBA

SAHIBS > SAHIB

SAHIWAL n breed of cattle in India

SAHIWALS > SAHIWAL

SAHUARO same as > SAGUARO

SAHUAROS > SAHUARO

SAI n South American monkey

SAIBLING n freshwater fish

SAIBLINGS > SAIBLING

SAIC n boat of eastern Mediterranean

SAICE same as > SYCE

SAICES > SAICE

SAICK n boat of eastern Mediterranean

SAICKS > SAICK

SAICS > SAIC

SAID same as > SAYYID

SAIDEST > SAY

SAIDS > SAID

SAIDST > SAY

SAIGA n either of two antelopes of the plains of central Asia

SAIGAS > SAIGA

SAIKEI n Japanese ornamental miniature landscape

SAIKEIS > SAIKEI

SAIKLESS old Scots word for > INNOCENT

SAIL n sheet of fabric stretched to catch the wind for propelling a sailing boat ▷ vb travel by water

SAILABLE > SAIL

SAILBOARD n board with a mast and single sail, used for windsurfing

SAILBOAT n boat propelled chiefly by sail

SAILBOATS > SAILBOAT

SAILCLOTH n fabric for making sails

SAILED > SAIL

SAILER n vessel, esp one equipped with sails, with specified sailing characteristics

SAILERS > SAILER

SAILFISH n large tropical game fish, with a long sail-like fin on its back

SAILING n practice, art, or technique of sailing a vessel

SAILINGS > SAILING

SAILLESS > SAIL

SAILMAKER n person who makes sails

SAILOR n member of a ship's crew

SAILORING n activity of working as sailor

SAILORLY > SAILOR

SAILORS > SAILOR

SAILPAST n sailing of ships past a particular place

SAILPASTS > SAILPAST

SAILPLANE n high-performance glider

SAILROOM n space on ship for storing sails

SAILROOMS > SAILROOM

SAILS > SAIL

SAIM Scots word for > LARD

SAIMIN n Hawaiian dish of noodles

SAIMINS > SAIMIN

SAIMIRI n South American monkey

SAIMIRIS > SAIMIRI

SAIMS > SAIM

SAIN vb make the sign of the cross over so as to bless or protect from evil or sin

SAINE vb old form of say

SAINED > SAIN

SAINFOIN n Eurasian plant with pink flowers, widely grown as feed for grazing farm animals

SAINFOINS > SAINFOIN

SAINING > SAIN

SAINS > SAIN

SAINT n person venerated after death as specially holy ▷ vb canonize

SAINTDOM > SAINT

SAINTDOMS > SAINT

SAINTED adj formally recognized by a Christian Church as a saint

SAINTESS n female saint

SAINTFOIN n sainfoin

SAINTHOOD n state or character of being a saint

SAINTING > SAINT

SAINTISH > SAINT

SAINTISM n quality of being saint

SAINTISMS > SAINTISM

SAINTLESS > SAINT

SAINTLIER > SAINTLY

SAINTLIKE > SAINT

SAINTLILY > SAINTLY

SAINTLING n little saint

SAINTLY adj behaving in a very good, patient, or holy way

SAINTS > SAINT

SAINTSHIP > SAINT

SAIQUE n boat in eastern Mediterranean

SAIQUES > SAIQUE

SAIR Scot word for > SORE

SAIRED > SAIR

SAIRER > SAIR

SAIREST > SAIR

SAIRING > SAIR

SAIRS > SAIR

SAIS > SAI

SAIST > SAY

SAITH form of the present tense (indicative mood) of > SAY

SAITHE n dark-coloured food fish found in northern seas

SAITHES > SAITHE

SAITHS > SAITH

SAIYID n Muslim descended from Mohammed's grandson

SAIYIDS > SAIYID

SAJOU n South American monkey

SAJOUS > SAJOU

SAKAI n Malaysian aborigine

SAKAIS > SAKAI

SAKE n benefit

SAKER n large falcon of E Europe and central Asia

SAKERET n male saker

SAKERETS > SAKERET

SAKERS > SAKER

SAKES > SAKE

SAKI same as > SAKE

SAKIA n water wheel in Middle East

SAKIAS > SAKIA

SAKIEH n water wheel in Middle East

SAKIEHS > SAKIEH

SAKIS > SAKI

SAKIYEH n water wheel in Middle East

SAKIYEHS > SAKIYEH

SAKKOI > SAKKOS

SAKKOS n bishop's garment in Orthodox Church

SAKKOSES > SAKKOS

SAKSAUL n Asian tree

SAKSAULS > SAKSAUL

SAKTI n wife of a Hindu god

SAKTIS > SAKTI

SAL pharmacological term for > SALT

SALAAM n low bow of greeting among Muslims ▷ vb make a salaam

SALAAMED > SALAAM

SALAAMING > SALAAM

SALAAMS > SALAAM

SALABLE same as > SALEABLE

SALABLY > SALEABLY

SALACIOUS adj excessively concerned with sex

SALACITY n excessive interest in sex

SALAD n dish of raw vegetables, eaten as a meal or part of a meal

SALADANG n variety of ox

SALADANGS > SALADANG

SALADE same as > SALLET

SALADES > SALADE

SALADING n ingredients for salad

SALADINGS > SALADING

SALADS > SALAD

SALAL n North American shrub

SALALS > SALAL

SALAMI n highly spiced sausage

SALAMIS > SALAMI

SALAMON n word used in old oaths

SALAMONS > SALAMON

SALANGANE n Asian swift

SALARIAT n salary-earning class

SALARIATS > SALARIAT

SALARIED adj earning or providing a salary

SALARIES > SALARY

SALARY n fixed regular payment, usu monthly, to an employee ▷ vb pay a salary to

SALARYING > SALARY

SALARYMAN n (in Japan) an office worker

SALARYMEN > SALARYMAN

SALAT n obligatory series of Islamic prayers facing towards Mecca

SALATS > SALAT

SALBAND n coating of mineral

SALBANDS > SALBAND

SALCHOW n type of figure-skating jump

SALCHOWS > SALCHOW

SALE n exchange of goods for money

SALEABLE adj fit or likely to be sold

SALEABLY > SALEABLE

SALEP n dried ground starchy tubers of various orchids

SALEPS > SALEP

SALERATUS n sodium bicarbonate when used in baking powder

SALERING n enclosed area for livestock at market

SALERINGS > SALERING

SALEROOM n place where goods are sold by auction

SALEROOMS > SALEROOM

SALES > SALE

SALESGIRL n person who sells goods

SALESLADY n person who sells goods

SALESMAN n person who sells goods

SALESMEN > SALESMAN

SALESROOM n room in which merchandise on sale is displayed

SALET same as > SALLET

SALETS > SALET

SALEWD > SALUE

SALEYARD n area with pens for holding animals before auction

SALEYARDS > SALEYARD

SALFERN n plant of borage family

SALFERNS > SALFERN

SALIAUNCE n old word meaning onslaught

SALIC adj (of rocks and minerals) having a high content of silica and alumina

SALICES > SALIX

SALICET n soft-toned organ stop

SALICETA > SALICETUM

SALICETS > SALICET

SALICETUM n plantation of willows

SALICIN n colourless or white crystalline water-soluble glucoside

SALICINE same as > SALICIN

SALICINES > SALICINE

SALICINS > SALICIN

SALICYLIC adj as in salicylic acid white crystalline substance with a sweet taste and a bitter aftertaste

SALIENCE > SALIENT

SALIENCES > SALIENT

SALIENCY n quality of being prominent

SALIENT adj prominent, noticeable ▷ n projecting part of a front line

SALIENTLY > SALIENT

SALIENTS > SALIENT

SALIFIED > SALIFY

SALIFIES > SALIFY

SALIFY vb treat, mix with, or cause to combine with a salt

SALIFYING > SALIFY

SALIGOT n water chestnut

SALIGOTS > SALIGOT

SALIMETER n hydrometer for measuring salt in a solution

SALIMETRY > SALIMETER

SALINA n salt marsh, lake, or spring

SALINAS > SALINA

SALINE adj containing salt ▷ n solution of sodium chloride and water

SALINES > SALINE

SALINISE same as > SALINIZE

SALINISED > SALINISE

SALINISES > SALINISE

SALINITY > SALINE

SALINIZE vb treat with salt

SALINIZED > SALINIZE

SALINIZES > SALINIZE

SALIVA n liquid that forms in the mouth, spittle

SALIVAL > SALIVA

SALIVARY > SALIVA

SALIVAS > SALIVA

SALIVATE vb produce saliva

SALIVATED > SALIVATE

SALIVATES > SALIVATE

SALIVATOR > SALIVATE

SALIX n plant or tree of willow family

SALL archaic form of > SHALL

SALLAD old spelling of > SALAD

SALLADS > SALLAD

SALLAL n North American shrub

SALLALS > SALLAL

SALLE n hall

SALLEE n SE Australian eucalyptus

SALLEES > SALLEE

SALLES > SALLE

SALLET n light round helmet

SALLETS > SALLET

SALLIED > SALLY

SALLIER > SALLY

SALLIERS > SALLY

SALLIES > SALLY

SALLOW adj of an unhealthy pale or yellowish colour ▷ vb make sallow ▷ n any of several small willow trees

SALLOWED > SALLOW

SALLOWER > SALLOW

SALLOWEST > SALLOW

SALLOWING > SALLOW

SALLOWISH > SALLOW

SALLOWLY > SALLOW

SALLOWS > SALLOW

SALLOWY > SALLOW

SALLY n violent excursion ▷ vb set or rush out

SALLYING > SALLY

SALLYPORT n opening in a fortified place from which troops may make a sally

SALMI n ragout of game stewed in a rich brown sauce

SALMIS same as > SALMI

SALMON n large fish with orange-pink flesh valued as food ▷ adj orange-pink

SALMONET n young salmon

SALMONETS > SALMONET

SALMONID n type of soft-finned fish of the family which includes the salmon

SALMONIDS > SALMONID

SALMONOID adj belonging to the order of soft-finned teleost fishes that includes the salmon, whitefish, grayling, and char ▷ n any of these fish

SALMONS > SALMON

SALMONY adj of or like a salmon

SALOL n white sparingly soluble crystalline compound

SALOLS > SALOL

SALOMETER n instrument for measuring salt in solution

SALON n commercial premises of a hairdresser, beautician, etc

SALONS > SALON

SALOON n closed car with four or more seats

SALOONS > SALOON

SALOOP n infusion of aromatic herbs or other plant parts formerly used as a tonic or cure

SALOOPS > SALOOP

SALOP variant of > SALOOP

SALOPIAN > SALOOP

SALOPS > SALOP

SALP n minute animal floating in sea

SALPA n any of various minute floating animals of warm oceans

SALPAE > SALPA

SALPAS > SALPA

SALPIAN n minute animal floating in sea

SALPIANS > SALPIAN

SALPICON n mixture of chopped fish, meat, or vegetables in a sauce

SALPICONS > SALPICON

SALPID n minute animal floating in sea

SALPIDS > SALPID

SALPIFORM > SALPA

SALPINGES > SALPINX

SALPINX n Fallopian tube or Eustachian tube

SALPINXES > SALPINX

SALPS > SALP

SALS > SAL

SALSA n lively Puerto Rican dance ▷ vb dance the salsa

SALSAED > SALSA

SALSAING > SALSA

SALSAS > SALSA

SALSE n volcano expelling mud

SALSES > SALSE

SALSIFIES > SALSIFY

SALSIFY n Mediterranean plant with a long white edible root

SALSILLA n tropical American vine

SALSILLAS > SALSILLA

SALT n white crystalline substance used to season food ▷ vb season or preserve with salt

SALTANDO n staccato piece of violin playing

SALTANDOS > SALTANDO

SALTANT adj (of an organism) differing from others of its species because of a saltation ▷ n saltant organism

SALTANTS > SALTANT

SALTATE vb go through saltation

SALTATED > SALTATE

SALTATES > SALTATE

SALTATING > SALTATE

SALTATION n abrupt variation in the appearance of an organism, usu caused by genetic mutation

SALTATO n saltando

SALTATORY adj specialized for jumping

SALTATOS > SALTATO

SALTBOX n box for salt with a sloping lid

SALTBOXES > SALTBOX

SALTBUSH n shrub that grows in alkaline desert regions

SALTCAT n salty medicine for pigeons

SALTCATS > SALTCAT

SALTCHUCK n any body of salt water

SALTED adj seasoned, preserved, or treated with salt

SALTER n person who deals in or manufactures salt

SALTERIES > SALTERY

SALTERN n place where salt is obtained from pools of evaporated sea water

SALTERNS > SALTERN

SALTERS > SALTER

SALTERY n factory where fish is salted for storage

SALTEST > SALT

SALTFISH n salted cod

SALTIE n saltwater crocodile

SALTIER > SALTIRE

SALTIERS > SALTIER

SALTIES > SALTIE

SALTIEST > SALTY

SALTILY > SALTY

SALTINE n salty biscuit

SALTINES > SALTINE

SALTINESS > SALTY

SALTING n area of low ground regularly inundated with salt water

SALTINGS > SALTING

SALTIRE n diagonal cross on a shield

SALTIRES > SALTIRE

SALTISH > SALT

SALTISHLY > SALT

SALTLESS > SALT
SALTLIKE > SALT
SALTLY > SALT
SALTNESS > SALT
SALTO n daring jump ▷ vb perform a daring jump
SALTOED > SALTO
SALTOING > SALTO
SALTOS > SALTO
SALTPAN n shallow basin containing salt from an evaporated salt lake
SALTPANS > SALTPAN
SALTPETER same as > SALTPETRE
SALTPETRE n compound used in gunpowder and as a preservative
SALTS > SALT
SALTUS n break in the continuity of a sequence
SALTUSES > SALTUS
SALTWATER adj living in the sea
SALTWORK n place where salt is refined
SALTWORKS n place, building, or factory where salt is produced
SALTWORT n any of several chenopodiaceous plants with prickly leaves, striped stems, and small green flowers
SALTWORTS > SALTWORT
SALTY adj of, tasting of, or containing salt
SALUBRITY n quality of being favourable to health or wholesome
SALUE vb old word meaning salute
SALUED > SALUE
SALUES > SALUE
SALUING > SALUE
SALUKI n type of tall hound with a smooth coat
SALUKIS > SALUKI
SALURETIC n drug that increases secretion of salt in urine
SALUT interj cheers!
SALUTARY adj producing a beneficial result
SALUTE n motion of the arm as a formal military sign of respect ▷ vb greet with a salute
SALUTED > SALUTE
SALUTER > SALUTE
SALUTERS > SALUTE
SALUTES > SALUTE
SALUTING > SALUTE
SALVABLE adj capable of or suitable for being saved or salvaged
SALVABLY > SALVABLE
SALVAGE n saving of a ship or other property from destruction ▷ vb save from destruction or waste
SALVAGED > SALVAGE
SALVAGEE n rope on sailing ship

SALVAGEES > SALVAGEE
SALVAGER > SALVAGE
SALVAGERS > SALVAGE
SALVAGES > SALVAGE
SALVAGING > SALVAGE
SALVARSAN n old medicine containing arsenic
SALVATION n fact or state of being saved from harm or the consequences of sin
SALVATORY n place for storing something safely
SALVE n healing or soothing ointment ▷ vb soothe or appease
SALVED > SALVE
SALVER same as > SALVOR
SALVERS > SALVER
SALVES > SALVE
SALVETE n Latin greeting
SALVETES > SALVETE
SALVIA n plant with blue or red flowers
SALVIAS > SALVIA
SALVIFIC adj acting to salve
SALVING > SALVE
SALVINGS > SALVE
SALVO n simultaneous discharge of guns etc ▷ vb attack with a salvo
SALVOED > SALVO
SALVOES > SALVO
SALVOING > SALVO
SALVOR n person instrumental in salvaging a vessel or its cargo
SALVORS > SALVOR
SALVOS > SALVO
SALWAR n as in salwar kameez long tunic worn over a pair of baggy trousers
SALWARS > SALWAR
SAM vb collect
SAMA n Japanese title of respect
SAMAAN n South American tree
SAMAANS > SAMAAN
SAMADHI n state of deep meditative contemplation
SAMADHIS > SAMADHI
SAMAN n South American tree
SAMANS > SAMAN
SAMARA n dry indehiscent one-seeded fruit
SAMARAS > SAMARA
SAMARITAN n kindly person who helps another in distress
SAMARIUM n silvery metallic element
SAMARIUMS > SAMARIUM
SAMAS > SAMA
SAMBA n lively Brazilian dance ▷ vb perform such a dance
SAMBAED > SAMBA
SAMBAING > SAMBA
SAMBAL n Malaysian dish

SAMBALS > SAMBAL
SAMBAR n S Asian deer with three-tined antlers
SAMBARS > SAMBAR
SAMBAS > SAMBA
SAMBHAR n Indian dish
SAMBHARS > SAMBHAR
SAMBHUR n Asian deer
SAMBHURS > SAMBHUR
SAMBO n offensive word for a Black person
SAMBOES > SAMBO
SAMBOS > SAMBO
SAMBUCA n Italian liqueur
SAMBUCAS > SAMBUCA
SAMBUKE n ancient Greek stringed instrument
SAMBUKES > SAMBUKE
SAMBUR same as > SAMBAR
SAMBURS > SAMBUR
SAME adj identical, not different, unchanged ▷ n something identical
SAMECH n letter in Hebrew alphabet
SAMECHS > SAMECH
SAMEK variant of > SAMEKH
SAMEKH n 15th letter in the Hebrew alphabet
SAMEKHS > SAMEKH
SAMEKS > SAMEK
SAMEL adj of brick, not sufficiently fired
SAMELY adj the same
SAMEN old Scots form of > SAME
SAMENESS n state or quality of being the same
SAMES > SAME
SAMEY adj monotonous
SAMEYNESS n quality of being samey
SAMFOO n style of casual dress worn by Chinese women
SAMFOOS > SAMFOO
SAMFU n Chinese female outfit
SAMFUS > SAMFU
SAMIEL same as > SIMOOM
SAMIELS > SAMIEL
SAMIER > SAMEY
SAMIEST > SAMEY
SAMISEN n Japanese plucked stringed instrument with a long neck
SAMISENS > SAMISEN
SAMITE n heavy fabric of silk used in the Middle Ages
SAMITES > SAMITE
SAMITHI same as > SAMITI
SAMITHIS > SAMITHI
SAMITI n (in India) an association, esp one formed to organize political activity
SAMITIS > SAMITI
SAMIZDAT n (in the former Soviet Union) a system of secret printing

and distribution of banned literature
SAMIZDATS > SAMIZDAT
SAMLET n young salmon
SAMLETS > SAMLET
SAMLOR n motor vehicle in Thailand
SAMLORS > SAMLOR
SAMMED > SAM
SAMMIES > SAMMY
SAMMING > SAM
SAMMY n (in South Africa) an Indian fruit and vegetable vendor
SAMNITIS n poisonous plant mentioned by Spenser
SAMOSA n (in Indian cookery) a small fried triangular spiced meat or vegetable pasty
SAMOSAS > SAMOSA
SAMOVAR n Russian tea urn
SAMOVARS > SAMOVAR
SAMOYED n Siberian breed of dog with a tightly curled tail
SAMOYEDS > SAMOYED
SAMP n crushed maize used for porridge
SAMPAN n small boat with oars used in China
SAMPANS > SAMPAN
SAMPHIRE n plant found on rocks by the seashore
SAMPHIRES > SAMPHIRE
SAMPI n old Greek number character
SAMPIRE n samphire
SAMPIRES > SAMPIRE
SAMPIS > SAMPI
SAMPLE n part taken as representative of a whole ▷ vb take and test a sample of
SAMPLED > SAMPLE
SAMPLER n piece of embroidery showing the embroiderer's skill
SAMPLERS > SAMPLER
SAMPLERY n making of samplers
SAMPLES > SAMPLE
SAMPLING n process of selecting a random sample
SAMPLINGS > SAMPLING
SAMPS > SAMP
SAMS > SAM
SAMSARA n endless cycle of birth, death, and rebirth
SAMSARAS > SAMSARA
SAMSARIC adj relating to the eternal cycle of birth, suffering, death and rebirth in Indian religions
SAMSHOO n Chinese alcoholic drink
SAMSHOOS > SAMSHOO
SAMSHU n alcoholic drink made from fermented rice
SAMSHUS > SAMSHU
SAMSKARA n Hindu purification ceremony

S

SAMSKARAS > SAMSKARA
SAMURAI n member of an ancient Japanese warrior caste
SAMURAIS > SAMURAI
SAN n sanatorium
SANATIVE less common word for > CURATIVE
SANATORIA pl n institutions for the care of chronically ill people
SANATORY adj healing
SANBENITO n yellow garment bearing a red cross, worn by penitent heretics in the Inquisition
SANCAI n glaze in Chinese pottery
SANCAIS > SANCAI
SANCHO n African stringed instrument
SANCHOS > SANCHO
SANCTA > SANCTUM
SANCTIFY vb make holy
SANCTION n permission, authorization ▷ vb allow, authorize
SANCTIONS > SANCTION
SANCTITY n sacredness, inviolability
SANCTUARY n holy place
SANCTUM n sacred place
SANCTUMS > SANCTUM
SAND n substance consisting of small grains of rock, esp on a beach or in a desert ▷ vb smooth with sandpaper
SANDABLE > SAND
SANDAL n light shoe consisting of a sole attached by straps ▷ vb put sandals on
SANDALED > SANDAL
SANDALING > SANDAL
SANDALLED > SANDAL
SANDALS > SANDAL
SANDARAC n either of two coniferous trees having hard fragrant dark wood
SANDARACH same as > SANDARAC
SANDARACS > SANDARAC
SANDBAG n bag filled with sand, used as protection against flood water ▷ vb protect with sandbags
SANDBAGS > SANDBAG
SANDBANK n bank of sand below the surface of a river or sea
SANDBANKS > SANDBANK
SANDBAR n ridge of sand in a river or sea, often exposed at low tide
SANDBARS > SANDBAR
SANDBLAST n (clean with) a jet of sand blown from a nozzle under pressure ▷ vb clean or decorate (a surface) with a sandblast

SANDBOX n container on a locomotive from which sand is released onto the rails
SANDBOXES > SANDBOX
SANDBOY n as in happy as a sandboy very happy or high-spirited
SANDBOYS > SANDBOY
SANDBUR n variety of wild grass
SANDBURR n variety of wild grass
SANDBURRS > SANDBURR
SANDBURS > SANDBUR
SANDCRACK n crack in horse's hoof
SANDDAB n type of small Pacific flatfish
SANDDABS > SANDDAB
SANDED > SAND
SANDEK n man who holds a baby being circumcised
SANDEKS > SANDEK
SANDER n power tool for smoothing surfaces
SANDERS > SANDER
SANDERSES > SANDER
SANDFISH n burrowing Pacific fish
SANDFLIES > SANDFLY
SANDFLY n any of various small mothlike flies
SANDGLASS less common word for > HOURGLASS
SANDHEAP n heap of sand
SANDHEAPS > SANDHEAP
SANDHI n modification of a word under the influence of an adjacent word
SANDHILL n hill of sand
SANDHILLS > SANDHILL
SANDHIS > SANDHI
SANDHOG n person who works in underground or underwater construction projects
SANDHOGS > SANDHOG
SANDIER > SANDY
SANDIEST > SANDY
SANDINESS > SANDY
SANDING > SAND
SANDINGS > SAND
SANDIVER n scum forming on molten glass
SANDIVERS > SANDIVER
SANDLESS > SAND
SANDLIKE > SAND
SANDLING n sand eel
SANDLINGS > SANDLING
SANDLOT n area of vacant ground used for children's games
SANDLOTS > SANDLOT
SANDMAN n (in folklore) a magical person supposed to put children to sleep
SANDMEN > SANDMAN
SANDPAPER n paper coated with sand for smoothing a surface ▷ vb smooth with sandpaper

SANDPEEP n small sandpiper
SANDPEEPS > SANDPEEP
SANDPILE n pile of sand
SANDPILES > SANDPILE
SANDPIPER n shore bird with a long bill and slender legs
SANDPIT n shallow pit or container holding sand for children to play in
SANDPITS > SANDPIT
SANDPUMP n pump for wet sand
SANDPUMPS > SANDPUMP
SANDS > SAND
SANDSHOE n light canvas shoe with a rubber sole
SANDSHOES > SANDSHOE
SANDSOAP n gritty general-purpose soap
SANDSOAPS > SANDSOAP
SANDSPIT n small point of land created by sand dunes
SANDSPITS > SANDSPIT
SANDSPOUT n sand sucked into air by whirlwind
SANDSPUR n American wild grass
SANDSPURS > SANDSPUR
SANDSTONE n rock composed of sand
SANDSTORM n desert wind that whips up clouds of sand
SANDWICH n two slices of bread with a layer of food between ▷ vb insert between two other things
SANDWORM n any of various polychaete worms that live in burrows on sandy shores, esp the lugworm
SANDWORMS > SANDWORM
SANDWORT n any of numerous caryophyllaceous plants which grow in dense tufts on sandy soil and have white or pink solitary flowers
SANDWORTS > SANDWORT
SANDY adj covered with sand
SANDYISH adj somewhat sandy or covered with sand
SANE adj of sound mind ▷ vb heal
SANED > SANE
SANELY > SANE
SANENESS > SANE
SANER > SANE
SANES > SANE
SANEST > SANE
SANG Scots word for > SONG
SANGA n Ethiopian ox
SANGAR n breastwork of stone or sods
SANGAREE n spiced drink similar to sangria

SANGAREES > SANGAREE
SANGARS > SANGAR
SANGAS > SANGA
SANGEET n Indian pre-wedding celebration
SANGEETS > SANGEET
SANGER n sandwich
SANGERS > SANGER
SANGFROID n composure or self-possession
SANGH n Indian union or association
SANGHA n Buddhist monastic order or community
SANGHAS > SANGHA
SANGHAT n local Sikh community or congregation
SANGHATS > SANGHAT
SANGHS > SANGH
SANGLIER n wild boar
SANGLIERS > SANGLIER
SANGO same as > SANGER
SANGOMA n witch doctor or herbalist
SANGOMAS > SANGOMA
SANGOS > SANGO
SANGRAIL n legendary cup used by Christ at the Last Supper
SANGRAILS > SANGRAIL
SANGREAL same as > SANGRAIL
SANGREALS > SANGREAL
SANGRIA n Spanish drink of red wine and fruit
SANGRIAS > SANGRIA
SANGS > SANG
SANGUIFY vb turn into blood
SANGUINE adj cheerful, optimistic ▷ n red pencil containing ferric oxide, used in drawing
SANGUINED > SANGUINE
SANGUINES > SANGUINE
SANICLE n type of plant with clusters of small white flowers
SANICLES > SANICLE
SANIDINE n alkali feldspar that is found in lavas
SANIDINES > SANIDINE
SANIES n thin greenish foul-smelling discharge from a wound, etc
SANIFIED > SANIFY
SANIFIES > SANIFY
SANIFY vb make healthy
SANIFYING > SANIFY
SANING > SANE
SANIOUS > SANIES
SANITARIA variant of > SANATORIA
SANITARY adj promoting health by getting rid of dirt and germs
SANITATE vb make sanitary
SANITATED > SANITATE
SANITATES > SANITATE
SANITIES > SANITY

SANITISE same as
> SANITIZE
SANITISED > SANITISE
SANITISER > SANITISE
SANITISES > SANITISE
SANITIZE vb omit
unpleasant details to
make (news) more
acceptable
SANITIZED > SANITIZE
SANITIZER > SANITIZE
SANITIZES > SANITIZE
SANITORIA variant of
> SANATORIA
SANITY n state of having a
normal healthy mind
SANJAK n (in the Turkish
Empire) a subdivision of a
vilayet
SANJAKS > SANJAK
SANK > SINK
SANKO n African stringed
instrument
SANKOS > SANKO
SANNIE Scots word for
> SANDSHOE
SANNIES > SANNIE
SANNOP n Native
American married man
SANNOPS > SANNOP
SANNUP n Native
American married man
SANNUPS > SANNUP
SANNYASI n Brahman
who having attained the
fourth and last stage of life
as a beggar will not be
reborn, but will instead be
absorbed into the
Universal Soul
SANNYASIN same as
> SANNYASI
SANNYASIS > SANNYASI
SANPAN n sampan
SANPANS > SANPAN
SANPRO n sanitary-
protection products,
collectively
SANPROS > SANPRO
SANS archaic word for
> WITHOUT
SANSA n African musical
instrument
SANSAR n name of a wind
that blows in Iran
SANSARS > SANSAR
SANSAS > SANSA
SANSEI n American
whose parents were
Japanese immigrants
SANSEIS > SANSEI
SANSERIF n style of
printer's typeface
SANSERIFS
> SANSERIF
SANT n devout person in
India
SANTAL n sandalwood
SANTALIC adj of
sandalwood
SANTALIN n substance
giving sandalwood its
colour
SANTALINS > SANTALIN

SANTALOL n liquid from
sandalwood used in
perfume
SANTALOLS > SANTALOL
SANTALS > SANTAL
SANTERA n priestess of
santeria
SANTERAS > SANTERA
SANTERIA n Caribbean
religious cult
SANTERIAS > SANTERIA
SANTERO n priest of
santeria
SANTEROS > SANTERO
SANTIM n coin formerly
used in Latvia
SANTIMI > SANTIMS
SANTIMS n money unit in
Latvia
SANTIMU same as
> SANTIMS
SANTIR n Middle Eastern
stringed instrument
SANTIRS > SANTIR
SANTO n saint or
representation of one
SANTOL n fruit from
Southeast Asia
SANTOLINA n any plant of
an evergreen
Mediterranean genus
grown for its silvery-grey
felted foliage
SANTOLS > SANTOL
SANTON n French figurine
SANTONICA n oriental
wormwood plant
SANTONIN n white
crystalline soluble
substance extracted from
the dried flower heads of
santonica
SANTONINS > SANTONIN
SANTONS > SANTON
SANTOOR same as
> SANTIR
SANTOORS > SANTOOR
SANTOS > SANTO
SANTOUR n Middle
Eastern stringed
instrument
SANTOURS > SANTOUR
SANTS > SANT
SANTUR n Middle Eastern
stringed instrument
SANTURS > SANTUR
SANYASI same as
> SANNYASI
SANYASIS > SANNYASI
SAOLA n small, very rare
bovine mammal of
Vietnam and Laos
SAOLAS > SAOLA
SAOUARI n tropical
American tree
SAOUARIS > SAOUARI
SAP n moisture that
circulates in plants ▷ vb
undermine
SAPAJOU n capuchin
monkey
SAPAJOUS > SAPAJOU
SAPAN n tropical tree
SAPANS > SAPAN

SAPANWOOD n small
S Asian tree
SAPEGO n skin disease
SAPEGOES > SAPEGO
SAPELE n type of W
African tree
SAPELES > SAPELE
SAPFUL adj full of sap
SAPHEAD n simpleton,
idiot, or fool
SAPHEADED > SAPHEAD
SAPHEADS > SAPHEAD
SAPHENA n either of two
large superficial veins of
the legs
SAPHENAE > SAPHENA
SAPHENAS > SAPHENA
SAPHENOUS > SAPHENA
SAPID adj having a
pleasant taste
SAPIDITY > SAPID
SAPIDLESS adj lacking
flavour
SAPIDNESS > SAPID
SAPIENCE > SAPIENT
SAPIENCES > SAPIENT
SAPIENCY > SAPIENT
SAPIENS adj relating to or
like modern human beings
SAPIENT adj wise, shrewd
▷ n wise person
SAPIENTLY > SAPIENT
SAPIENTS > SAPIENT
SAPLESS > SAP
SAPLING n young tree
SAPLINGS > SAPLING
SAPODILLA n large
tropical American
evergreen tree
SAPOGENIN n substance
derived from saponin
SAPONARIA See
> SOAPWORT
SAPONATED adj treated or
combined with soap
SAPONIFY vb convert
(a fat) into a soap by
treatment with alkali
SAPONIN n any of a group
of plant glycosides
SAPONINE n saponin
SAPONINES > SAPONINE
SAPONINS > SAPONIN
SAPONITE n type of clay
mineral
SAPONITES > SAPONITE
SAPOR n quality in a
substance that is
perceived by the sense of
taste
SAPORIFIC > SAPOR
SAPOROUS > SAPOR
SAPORS > SAPOR
SAPOTA same as
> SAPODILLA
SAPOTAS > SAPOTA
SAPOTE n Central
American tree
SAPOTES > SAPOTE
SAPOUR variant of > SAPOR
SAPOURS > SAPOUR
SAPPAN n tropical tree
SAPPANS > SAPPAN

SAPPED > SAP
SAPPER n soldier in an
engineering unit
SAPPERS > SAPPER
SAPPHIC adj lesbian
▷ n verse written in a
particular form
SAPPHICS > SAPPHIC
SAPPHIRE n blue precious
stone ▷ adj deep blue
SAPPHIRED adj blue-
coloured
SAPPHIRES > SAPPHIRE
SAPPHISM n lesbianism
SAPPHISMS > SAPPHISM
SAPPHIST n lesbian
SAPPHISTS > SAPPHIST
SAPPIER > SAPPY
SAPPIEST > SAPPY
SAPPILY > SAPPY
SAPPINESS > SAPPY
SAPPING n act of sapping
SAPPINGS > SAPPING
SAPPLE vb Scots word
meaning wash in water
SAPPLED > SAPPLE
SAPPLES > SAPPLE
SAPPLING > SAPPLE
SAPPY adj (of plants) full
of sap
SAPRAEMIA n blood
poisoning caused by toxins
of putrefactive bacteria
SAPRAEMIC
> SAPRAEMIA
SAPREMIA American
spelling of > SAPRAEMIA
SAPREMIAS > SAPREMIA
SAPREMIC > SAPREMIA
SAPROBE n organism that
lives on decaying
organisms
SAPROBES > SAPROBE
SAPROBIAL > SAPROBE
SAPROBIC > SAPROBE
SAPROLITE n deposit of
earth, etc, formed by
decomposition of rocks
that has remained in its
original site
SAPROPEL n
unconsolidated sludge
consisting of the
decomposed remains of
aquatic organisms at the
bottoms of lakes and
oceans
SAPROPELS > SAPROPEL
SAPROZOIC adj (of
animals or plants) feeding
on dead organic matter
SAPS > SAP
SAPSAGO n hard greenish
Swiss cheese
SAPSAGOS > SAPSAGO
SAPSUCKER n either of
two North American
woodpeckers
SAPUCAIA n Brazilian tree
SAPUCAIAS > SAPUCAIA
SAPWOOD n soft wood, just
beneath the bark in tree
trunks, that consists of
living tissue

S

SAPWOODS > SAPWOOD
SAR *n* marine fish ▷ *vb* Scots word meaning savour
SARABAND *same as* > SARABANDE
SARABANDE *n* slow stately Spanish dance
SARABANDS > SARABAND
SARAFAN *n* Russian woman's cloak
SARAFANS > SARAFAN
SARAN *n* any one of a class of thermoplastic resins
SARANGI *n* stringed instrument of India played with a bow
SARANGIS > SARANGI
SARANS > SARAN
SARAPE *n* serape
SARAPES > SARAPE
SARBACANE *n* type of blowpipe
SARCASM *n* (use of) bitter or wounding ironic language
SARCASMS > SARCASM
SARCASTIC *adj* full of or showing sarcasm
SARCENET *n* fine soft silk fabric formerly from Italy and used for clothing, ribbons, etc
SARCENETS > SARCENET
SARCINA *n* type of bacterium
SARCINAE > SARCINA
SARCINAS > SARCINA
SARCOCARP *n* fleshy mesocarp of such fruits as the peach or plum
SARCODE *n* material making up living cell
SARCODES > SARCODE
SARCODIC > SARCODE
SARCOID *adj* of, relating to, or resembling flesh ▷ *n* tumour resembling a sarcoma
SARCOIDS > SARCOID
SARCOLOGY *n* study of flesh
SARCOMA *n* malignant tumour beginning in connective tissue
SARCOMAS > SARCOMA
SARCOMATA > SARCOMA
SARCOMERE *n* any of the units that together comprise skeletal muscle
SARCONET *n* type of silk
SARCONETS > SARCONET
SARCOPTIC *adj* relating to mange
SARCOSOME *n* energy-producing tissue in muscle
SARCOUS *adj* (of tissue) muscular or fleshy
SARD *n* orange, red, or brown variety of chalcedony
SARDANA *n* Catalan dance
SARDANAS > SARDANA

SARDAR *n* title used before the name of Sikh men
SARDARS > SARDAR
SARDEL *n* small fish
SARDELLE *n* small fish
SARDELLES > SARDELLE
SARDELS > SARDEL
SARDINE *n* small fish of the herring family ▷ *vb* cram together
SARDINED > SARDINE
SARDINES > SARDINE
SARDINING > SARDINE
SARDIUS *same as* > SARD
SARDIUSES > SARDIUS
SARDONIAN *adj* sardonic ▷ *n* person who flatters with harmful intent
SARDONIC *adj* mocking or scornful
SARDONYX *n* brown-and-white gemstone
SARDS > SARD
SARED > SAR
SAREE *same as* > SARI
SAREES > SAREE
SARGASSA > SARGASSUM
SARGASSO *same as* > SARGASSUM
SARGASSOS > SARGASSO
SARGASSUM *n* type of floating seaweed
SARGE *n* sergeant
SARGES > SARGE
SARGO *same as* > SARGUS
SARGOS *variant of* > SARGUS
SARGOSES > SARGOS
SARGUS *n* species of sea fish
SARGUSES > SARGUS
SARI *n* long piece of cloth draped around the body and over one shoulder
SARIN *n* chemical used in warfare as a lethal nerve gas producing asphyxia
SARING > SAR
SARINS > SARIN
SARIS > SARI
SARK *n* shirt or (formerly) chemise
SARKIER > SARKY
SARKIEST > SARKY
SARKILY > SARKY
SARKINESS *n* quality of being sarcastic
SARKING *n* flat planking supporting the roof cladding of a building
SARKINGS > SARKING
SARKS > SARK
SARKY *adj* sarcastic
SARMENT *n* thin twig
SARMENTA > SARMENTUM
SARMENTS > SARMENT
SARMENTUM *n* runner or plant
SARMIE *n* sandwich
SARMIES > SARMIE
SARNEY *n* sandwich
SARNEYS > SARNEY
SARNIE *n* sandwich

SARNIES > SARNIE
SAROD *n* Indian stringed musical instrument
SARODE *n* Indian stringed instrument
SARODES > SARODE
SARODIST *n* sarod player
SARODISTS > SARODIST
SARODS > SAROD
SARONG *n* long piece of cloth tucked around the waist or under the armpits
SARONGS > SARONG
SARONIC > SAROS
SAROS *n* cycle in which eclipses of the sun and moon occur in the same sequence
SAROSES > SAROS
SARPANCH *n* head of a panchayat
SARRASIN *n* buckwheat
SARRASINS > SARRASIN
SARRAZIN *n* buckwheat
SARRAZINS > SARRAZIN
SARS > SAR
SARSAR *same as* > SANSAR
SARSARS > SARSAR
SARSDEN *n* sarsen
SARSDENS > SARSDEN
SARSEN *n* boulder of silicified sandstone
SARSENET *same as* > SARCENET
SARSENETS > SARSENET
SARSENS > SARSEN
SARSNET *n* type of silk
SARSNETS > SARSNET
SARTOR *humorous or literary word for* > TAILOR
SARTORIAL *adj* of men's clothes or tailoring
SARTORIAN *adj* of tailoring
SARTORII > SARTORIUS
SARTORIUS *n* long ribbon-shaped muscle that aids in flexing the knee
SARTORS > SARTOR
SARUS *n* Indian bird of crane family
SARUSES > SARUS
SASANQUA *n* type of camellia
SASANQUAS > SASANQUA
SASARARA *n* scolding
SASARARAS > SASARARA
SASER *n* device for amplifying ultrasound
SASERS > SASER
SASH *n* decorative strip of cloth worn round the waist or over one shoulder ▷ *vb* furnish with a sash, sashes, or sash windows
SASHAY *vb* move or walk in a casual or a showy manner
SASHAYED > SASHAY
SASHAYING > SASHAY
SASHAYS > SASHAY
SASHED > SASH

SASHES > SASH
SASHIMI *n* Japanese dish of thin fillets of raw fish
SASHIMIS > SASHIMI
SASHING > SASH
SASHLESS > SASH
SASIN *another name for* > BLACKBUCK
SASINE *n* granting of legal possession of feudal property
SASINES > SASINE
SASINS > SASIN
SASKATOON *n* species of serviceberry of W Canada
SASQUATCH *n* (in Canadian folklore) hairy beast or manlike monster said to leave huge footprints
SASS *n* insolent or impudent talk or behaviour ▷ *vb* talk or answer back in such a way
SASSABIES > SASSABY
SASSABY *n* African antelope of grasslands and semideserts
SASSAFRAS *n* American tree with aromatic bark used medicinally
SASSARARA *n* scolding
SASSE *n* old word meaning canal lock
SASSED > SASS
SASSES > SASS
SASSIER > SASSY
SASSIES > SASSY
SASSIEST > SASSY
SASSILY > SASSY
SASSINESS > SASSY
SASSING > SASS
SASSOLIN *n* boric acid
SASSOLINS > SASSOLIN
SASSOLITE *n* boric acid
SASSWOOD *same as* > SASSY
SASSWOODS > SASSWOOD
SASSY *adj* insolent, impertinent ▷ *n* W African leguminous tree with poisonous bark
SASSYWOOD *n* trial by ordeal in Liberia
SASTRA *same as* > SHASTRA
SASTRAS > SASTRA
SASTRUGA *n* one of a series of ridges on snow-covered plains, caused by the action of wind laden with ice particles
SASTRUGI > SASTRUGA
SAT > SIT
SATAI *same as* > SATAY
SATAIS > SATAI
SATANG *n* monetary unit of Thailand worth one hundredth of a baht
SATANGS > SATANG
SATANIC *adj* of Satan
SATANICAL *same as* > SATANIC

SATANISM *n* worship of the devil

SATANISMS > SATANISM

SATANIST > SATANISM

SATANISTS > SATANISM

SATANITY *n* quality of being satanic

SATARA *n* type of cloth

SATARAS > SATARA

SATAY *n* Indonesian and Malaysian dish

SATAYS > SATAY

SATCHEL *n* bag, usu with a shoulder strap, for carrying books

SATCHELED *adj* carrying a satchel

SATCHELS > SATCHEL

SATCOM *n* satellite communications

SATCOMS > SATCOM

SATE *vb* satisfy (a desire or appetite) fully

SATED > SATE

SATEDNESS > SATE

SATEEN *n* glossy linen or cotton fabric, woven in such a way that it resembles satin

SATEENS > SATEEN

SATELESS *adj* old word meaning insatiable

SATELLES *n* species of bacteria

SATELLITE *n* man-made device orbiting in space ▷ *adj* of or used in the transmission of television signals from a satellite to the home ▷ *vb* transmit by communications satellite

SATEM *adj* denoting or belonging to a particular group of Indo-European languages

SATES > SATE

SATI *n* Indian widow suicide

SATIABLE *adj* capable of being satiated

SATIABLY > SATIABLE

SATIATE *vb* provide with more than enough, so as to disgust

SATIATED > SATIATE

SATIATES > SATIATE

SATIATING > SATIATE

SATIATION > SATIATE

SATIETIES > SATIETY

SATIETY *n* feeling of having had too much

SATIN *n* silky fabric with a glossy surface on one side ▷ *adj* like satin in texture ▷ *vb* cover with satin

SATINED > SATIN

SATINET *n* thin or imitation satin

SATINETS > SATINET

SATINETTA *n* thin satin

SATINETTE *same as* > SATINET

SATING > SATE

SATINING > SATIN

SATINPOD *n* honesty (the plant)

SATINPODS > SATINPOD

SATINS > SATIN

SATINWOOD *n* tropical tree yielding hard wood

SATINY > SATIN

SATIRE *n* use of ridicule to expose vice or folly

SATIRES > SATIRE

SATIRIC *same as* > SATIRICAL

SATIRICAL *adj* of, relating to, or containing satire

SATIRISE *same as* > SATIRIZE

SATIRISED > SATIRISE

SATIRISER > SATIRISE

SATIRISES > SATIRISE

SATIRIST *n* writer of satire

SATIRISTS > SATIRIST

SATIRIZE *vb* ridicule by means of satire

SATIRIZED > SATIRIZE

SATIRIZER > SATIRIZE

SATIRIZES > SATIRIZE

SATIS > SATI

SATISFICE *vb* act in such a way as to satisfy the minimum requirements for achieving a particular result

SATISFIED > SATISFY

SATISFIER > SATISFY

SATISFIES > SATISFY

SATISFY *vb* please, content

SATIVE *adj* old word meaning cultivated

SATNAV *n* satellite navigation system

SATNAVS > SATNAV

SATORI *n* state of sudden indescribable intuitive enlightenment

SATORIS > SATORI

SATRAP *n* (in ancient Persia) a provincial governor or subordinate ruler

SATRAPAL > SATRAP

SATRAPIES > SATRAPY

SATRAPS > SATRAP

SATRAPY *n* province, office, or period of rule of a satrap

SATSANG *n* sacred gathering in Hinduism

SATSANGS > SATSANG

SATSUMA *n* kind of small orange

SATSUMAS > SATSUMA

SATURABLE *adj* capable of being saturated

SATURANT *n* substance that causes a solution, etc, to be saturated ▷ *adj* (of a substance) causing saturation

SATURANTS > SATURANT

SATURATE *vb* soak thoroughly

SATURATED *adj* (of a solution or solvent) containing the maximum amount of solute that can normally be dissolved at a given temperature and pressure

SATURATER > SATURATE

SATURATES > SATURATE

SATURATOR > SATURATE

SATURNIC *adj* poisoned by lead

SATURNIID *n* type of mainly tropical moth, usu with large brightly coloured wings

SATURNINE *adj* gloomy in temperament or appearance

SATURNISM *n* lead poisoning

SATURNIST *n* old word meaning glum person

SATYR *n* woodland god, part man, part goat

SATYRA *n* female satyr

SATYRAL *n* mythical beast in heraldry

SATYRALS > SATYRAL

SATYRAS > SATYRA

SATYRE *n* as in *sea satyre* sea creature mentioned in Spenser's poetry

SATYRES > SATYRE

SATYRESS *n* female satyr

SATYRIC > SATYR

SATYRICAL > SATYR

SATYRID *n* butterfly with typically brown or dark wings with paler markings

SATYRIDS > SATYRID

SATYRISK *n* small satyr

SATYRISKS > SATYRISK

SATYRLIKE > SATYR

SATYRS > SATYR

SAU *archaic past tense of* > SEE

SAUBA *n* South American ant

SAUBAS > SAUBA

SAUCE *n* liquid added to food to enhance flavour ▷ *vb* prepare (food) with sauce

SAUCEBOAT *n* gravy boat

SAUCEBOX *n* saucy person

SAUCED > SAUCE

SAUCELESS > SAUCE

SAUCEPAN *n* cooking pot with a long handle

SAUCEPANS > SAUCEPAN

SAUCEPOT *n* cooking pot with lid

SAUCEPOTS > SAUCEPOT

SAUCER *n* small round dish put under a cup

SAUCERFUL > SAUCER

SAUCERS > SAUCER

SAUCES > SAUCE

SAUCH *n* sallow or willow

SAUCHS > SAUCH

SAUCIER *n* chef who makes sauces

SAUCIERS > SAUCIER

SAUCIEST > SAUCY

SAUCILY > SAUCY

SAUCINESS > SAUCY

SAUCING > SAUCE

SAUCISSE *n* type of explosive fuse

SAUCISSES > SAUCISSE

SAUCISSON *n* type of explosive fuse

SAUCY *adj* impudent

SAUFGARD *old form of* > SAFEGUARD

SAUFGARDS > SAUFGARD

SAUGER *n* small North American pikeperch

SAUGERS > SAUGER

SAUGH *same as* > SAUCH

SAUGHS > SAUGH

SAUGHY *adj* Scots word meaning made of willow

SAUL *Scots word for* > SOUL

SAULGE *n* old word for sage plant

SAULGES > SAULGE

SAULIE *n* Scots word meaning professional mourner

SAULIES > SAULIE

SAULS > SAUL

SAULT *n* waterfall in Canada

SAULTS > SAULT

SAUNA *n* Finnish-style steam bath ▷ *vb* have a sauna

SAUNAED > SAUNA

SAUNAING > SAUNA

SAUNAS > SAUNA

SAUNT *Scots form of* > SAINT

SAUNTED > SAUNT

SAUNTER *vb* walk in a leisurely manner, stroll ▷ *n* leisurely walk

SAUNTERED > SAUNTER

SAUNTERER > SAUNTER

SAUNTERS > SAUNTER

SAUNTING > SAUNT

SAUNTS > SAUNT

SAUREL *n* type of mackerel

SAURELS > SAUREL

SAURIAN *n* lizard

SAURIANS > SAURIAN

SAURIES > SAURY

SAUROID *adj* like a lizard ▷ *n* type of fish

SAUROIDS > SAUROID

SAUROPOD *n* type of herbivorous dinosaur including the brontosaurus and the diplodocus

SAUROPODS > SAUROPOD

SAURY *n* type of fish of tropical and temperate seas

SAUSAGE *n* minced meat in an edible tube-shaped skin

SAUSAGES > SAUSAGE

SAUT *Scot word for* > SALT

SAUTE vb fry quickly in a little fat ▷ n dish of sautéed food ▷ adj sautéed until lightly brown
SAUTED > SAUT
SAUTEED > SAUTE
SAUTEEING > SAUTE
SAUTEING > SAUTE
SAUTERNE n sauternes
SAUTERNES n sweet white French wine
SAUTES > SAUTE
SAUTING > SAUT
SAUTOIR n long necklace or pendant
SAUTOIRE variant of > SAUTOIR
SAUTOIRES > SAUTOIRE
SAUTOIRS > SAUTOIR
SAUTS > SAUT
SAV short for > SAVELOY
SAVABLE > SAVE
SAVAGE adj wild, untamed ▷ n uncivilized person ▷ vb attack ferociously
SAVAGED > SAVAGE
SAVAGEDOM > SAVAGE
SAVAGELY > SAVAGE
SAVAGER > SAVAGE
SAVAGERY n viciousness and cruelty
SAVAGES > SAVAGE
SAVAGEST > SAVAGE
SAVAGING > SAVAGE
SAVAGISM > SAVAGE
SAVAGISMS > SAVAGE
SAVANNA n open grasslands of tropical Africa
SAVANNAH same as > SAVANNA
SAVANNAHS > SAVANNAH
SAVANNAS > SAVANNA
SAVANT n learned person
SAVANTE > SAVANT
SAVANTES > SAVANT
SAVANTS > SAVANT
SAVARIN n type of cake
SAVARINS > SAVARIN
SAVATE n form of boxing in which blows may be delivered with the feet
SAVATES > SAVATE
SAVE vb rescue or preserve from harm, protect ▷ n act of preventing a goal ▷ prep except
SAVEABLE > SAVE
SAVED > SAVE
SAVEGARD vb old word meaning protect
SAVEGARDS > SAVEGARD
SAVELOY n spicy smoked sausage
SAVELOYS > SAVELOY
SAVER > SAVE
SAVERS > SAVE
SAVES > SAVE
SAVEY vb understand
SAVEYED > SAVEY
SAVEYING > SAVEY
SAVEYS > SAVEY

SAVIN n small spreading juniper bush of Europe, N Asia, and North America
SAVINE same as > SAVIN
SAVINES > SAVINE
SAVING n economy ▷ prep except ▷ adj tending to save or preserve
SAVINGLY > SAVING
SAVINGS > SAVING
SAVINS > SAVIN
SAVIOR same as > SAVIOUR
SAVIORS > SAVIOR
SAVIOUR n person who rescues another
SAVIOURS > SAVIOUR
SAVOR same as > SAVOUR
SAVORED > SAVOR
SAVORER > SAVOR
SAVORERS > SAVOR
SAVORIER > SAVORY
SAVORIES > SAVORY
SAVORIEST > SAVORY
SAVORILY > SAVORY
SAVORING > SAVOR
SAVORLESS > SAVOUR
SAVOROUS > SAVOUR
SAVORS > SAVOR
SAVORY same as > SAVOURY
SAVOUR vb enjoy, relish ▷ n characteristic taste or odour
SAVOURED > SAVOUR
SAVOURER > SAVOUR
SAVOURERS > SAVOUR
SAVOURIER > SAVOURY
SAVOURIES > SAVOURY
SAVOURILY > SAVOURY
SAVOURING > SAVOUR
SAVOURLY adv old word meaning refreshingly
SAVOURS > SAVOUR
SAVOURY adj salty or spicy ▷ n savoury dish served before or after a meal
SAVOY n variety of cabbage
SAVOYARD n person keenly interested in the operettas of Gilbert and Sullivan
SAVOYARDS > SAVOYARD
SAVOYS > SAVOY
SAVS > SAV
SAVVEY vb understand
SAVVEYED > SAVVEY
SAVVEYING > SAVVEY
SAVVEYS > SAVVEY
SAVVIED > SAVVY
SAVVIER > SAVVY
SAVVIES > SAVVY
SAVVIEST > SAVVY
SAVVILY > SAVVY
SAVVINESS > SAVVY
SAVVY vb understand ▷ n understanding, intelligence ▷ adj shrewd
SAVVYING > SAVVY
SAW n hand tool for cutting wood and metal ▷ vb cut with a saw

SAWAH n paddyfield
SAWAHS > SAWAH
SAWBILL n type of hummingbird
SAWBILLS > SAWBILL
SAWBLADE n blade of a saw
SAWBLADES > SAWBLADE
SAWBONES n surgeon or doctor
SAWBUCK n sawhorse, esp one having an X-shaped supporting structure
SAWBUCKS > SAWBUCK
SAWDER n flattery ▷ vb flatter
SAWDERED > SAWDER
SAWDERING > SAWDER
SAWDERS > SAWDER
SAWDUST n fine wood fragments made in sawing ▷ vb cover with sawdust
SAWDUSTED > SAWDUST
SAWDUSTS > SAWDUST
SAWDUSTY > SAWDUST
SAWED > SAW
SAWER > SAW
SAWERS > SAW
SAWFISH n fish with a long toothed snout
SAWFISHES > SAWFISH
SAWFLIES > SAWFLY
SAWFLY n any of various hymenopterous insects
SAWGRASS n type of sedge with serrated leaves
SAWHORSE n structure for supporting wood that is being sawn
SAWHORSES > SAWHORSE
SAWING > SAW
SAWINGS > SAW
SAWLIKE > SAW
SAWLOG n log suitable for sawing
SAWLOGS > SAWLOG
SAWMILL n mill where timber is sawn into planks
SAWMILLS > SAWMILL
SAWN past participle of > SAW
SAWNEY n derogatory word for a fool
SAWNEYS > SAWNEY
SAWPIT n pit above which a log is sawn into planks
SAWPITS > SAWPIT
SAWS > SAW
SAWSHARK n shark with long sawlike snout
SAWSHARKS > SAWSHARK
SAWTEETH > SAWTOOTH
SAWTIMBER n wood for sawing
SAWTOOTH adj (of a waveform) having an amplitude that varies linearly with time between two values
SAWYER n person who saws timber for a living
SAWYERS > SAWYER
SAX same as > SAXOPHONE

SAXATILE adj living among rocks
SAXAUL n Asian tree
SAXAULS > SAXAUL
SAXE adj as in saxe blue light greyish-blue colour
SAXES > SAX
SAXHORN n valved brass instrument used chiefly in brass and military bands
SAXHORNS > SAXHORN
SAXICOLE variant of > SAXATILE
SAXIFRAGE n alpine rock plant with small flowers
SAXIST n saxophone player
SAXISTS > SAXIST
SAXITOXIN n poison extracted from mollusc
SAXMAN n saxophone player
SAXMEN > SAXMAN
SAXONIES > SAXONY
SAXONITE n igneous rock
SAXONITES > SAXONITE
SAXONY n fine 3-ply yarn used for knitting and weaving
SAXOPHONE n brass wind instrument with keys and a curved body
SAXTUBA n bass saxhorn
SAXTUBAS > SAXTUBA
SAY vb speak or utter ▷ n right or chance to speak
SAYABLE > SAY
SAYED same as > SAYYID
SAYEDS > SAYED
SAYER > SAY
SAYERS > SAY
SAYEST > SAY
SAYID same as > SAYYID
SAYIDS > SAYID
SAYING > SAY
SAYINGS > SAY
SAYNE > SAY
SAYON n type of tunic
SAYONARA n Japanese farewell
SAYONARAS > SAYONARA
SAYONS > SAYON
SAYS > SAY
SAYST > SAY
SAYYID n Muslim claiming descent from Mohammed's grandson Husain
SAYYIDS > SAYYID
SAZ n Middle Eastern stringed instrument
SAZERAC n mixed drink of whisky, Pernod, syrup, bitters, and lemon
SAZERACS > SAZERAC
SAZES > SAZ
SAZHEN n Russian measure of length
SAZHENS > SAZHEN
SAZZES > SAZ
SBIRRI > SBIRRO

SBIRRO n Italian police officer

SCAB n crust formed over a wound ▷ vb become covered with a scab

SCABBARD n sheath for a sword or dagger

SCABBARDS > SCABBARD

SCABBED > SCAB

SCABBIER > SCABBY

SCABBIEST > SCABBY

SCABBILY > SCABBY

SCABBING > SCAB

SCABBLE vb shape (stone) roughly

SCABBLED > SCABBLE

SCABBLES > SCABBLE

SCABBLING > SCABBLE

SCABBY adj covered with scabs

SCABIES n itchy skin disease

SCABIETIC > SCABIES

SCABIOSA n flowering plant

SCABIOSAS > SCABIOSA

SCABIOUS n plant with showy blue, red, or whitish dome-shaped flower heads ▷ adj having or covered with scabs

SCABLAND n barren rocky land

SCABLANDS pl n type of terrain consisting of bare rock surfaces, with little or no soil cover and scanty vegetation

SCABLIKE > SCAB

SCABRID adj having a rough or scaly surface

SCABROUS adj rough and scaly

SCABS > SCAB

SCAD n any of various carangid fishes

SCADS pl n large amount or number

SCAFF n Scots word meaning food ▷ vb ask for (food) in a mean or rude manner

SCAFFED > SCAFF

SCAFFIE n Scots word meaning street cleaner

SCAFFIER > SCAFFY

SCAFFIES > SCAFFIE

SCAFFIEST > SCAFFY

SCAFFING > SCAFF

SCAFFOLD n temporary platform for workmen ▷ vb provide with a scaffold

SCAFFOLDS > SCAFFOLD

SCAFFS > SCAFF

SCAFFY adj having little value, cheap

SCAG n tear in a garment or piece of cloth ▷ vb make a tear in (cloth)

SCAGGED > SCAG

SCAGGING > SCAG

SCAGLIA n type of limestone

SCAGLIAS > SCAGLIA

SCAGLIOLA n type of imitation marble made of glued gypsum

SCAGS > SCAG

SCAIL vb Scots word meaning disperse

SCAILED > SCAIL

SCAILING > SCAIL

SCAILS > SCAIL

SCAITH vb old word meaning injure

SCAITHED > SCAITH

SCAITHING > SCAITH

SCAITHS > SCAITH

SCALA n passage inside the cochlea

SCALABLE adj capable of being scaled or climbed

SCALABLY > SCALABLE

SCALADE short for > ESCALADE

SCALADES > SCALADE

SCALADO same as > SCALADE

SCALADOS > SCALADO

SCALAE > SCALA

SCALAGE n percentage deducted from the price of goods liable to shrink or leak

SCALAGES > SCALAGE

SCALAR adj having magnitude but no direction ▷ n quantity that has magnitude but not direction

SCALARE another name for > ANGELFISH

SCALARES > SCALARE

SCALARS > SCALAR

SCALATION n way scales are arranged

SCALAWAG same as > SCALLYWAG

SCALAWAGS > SCALAWAG

SCALD same as > SKALD

SCALDED > SCALD

SCALDER > SCALD

SCALDERS > SCALD

SCALDFISH n small European flatfish

SCALDHEAD n diseased scalp

SCALDIC > SKALD

SCALDING > SCALD

SCALDINGS > SCALD

SCALDINI > SCALDINO

SCALDINO n Italian brazier

SCALDS > SCALD

SCALDSHIP n position of being Scandinavian poet

SCALE n one of the thin overlapping plates covering fishes and reptiles ▷ vb remove scales from

SCALEABLE same as > SCALABLE

SCALEABLY same as > SCALABLY

SCALED > SCALE

SCALELESS > SCALE

SCALELIKE > SCALE

SCALENE n triangle with three unequal sides

SCALENES > SCALENE

SCALENI > SCALENUS

SCALENUS n any one of the three muscles situated on each side of the neck

SCALEPAN n part of scales holding weighed object

SCALEPANS > SCALEPAN

SCALER n person or thing that scales

SCALERS > SCALER

SCALES > SCALE

SCALETAIL n type of squirrel

SCALEUP n increase

SCALEUPS > SCALEUP

SCALEWORK n artistic representation of scales

SCALIER > SCALY

SCALIEST > SCALY

SCALINESS > SCALY

SCALING > SCALING

SCALINGS > SCALE

SCALL n disease of the scalp characterized by itching and scab formation

SCALLAWAG same as > SCALLYWAG

SCALLED > SCALL

SCALLIES > SCALLY

SCALLION same as > SHALLOT

SCALLIONS > SCALLION

SCALLOP n edible shellfish with two fan-shaped shells ▷ vb decorate (an edge) with scallops

SCALLOPED > SCALLOP

SCALLOPER > SCALLOP

SCALLOPS > SCALLOP

SCALLS > SCALL

SCALLY n rascal

SCALLYWAG n scamp, rascal

SCALOGRAM n scale for measuring opinion

SCALP n skin and hair on top of the head ▷ vb cut off the scalp of

SCALPED > SCALP

SCALPEL n small surgical knife

SCALPELS > SCALPEL

SCALPER > SCALP

SCALPERS > SCALP

SCALPING n process in which the top portion of a metal ingot is machined away before use

SCALPINGS > SCALPING

SCALPINS n small stones

SCALPLESS > SCALP

SCALPRUM n large scalpel

SCALPRUMS > SCALPRUM

SCALPS > SCALP

SCALY adj resembling or covered in scales

SCAM n dishonest scheme ▷ vb swindle (someone) by means of a trick

SCAMBLE vb scramble

SCAMBLED > SCAMBLE

SCAMBLER > SCAMBLE

SCAMBLERS > SCAMBLE

SCAMBLES > SCAMBLE

SCAMBLING > SCAMBLE

SCAMEL n Shakespearian word of uncertain meaning

SCAMELS > SCAMEL

SCAMMED > SCAM

SCAMMER n person who perpetrates a scam

SCAMMERS > SCAMMER

SCAMMING > SCAM

SCAMMONY n twining Asian convolvulus plant

SCAMP n mischievous child ▷ vb perform without care

SCAMPED > SCAMP

SCAMPER vb run about hurriedly or in play ▷ n scampering

SCAMPERED > SCAMP

SCAMPERER > SCAMPER

SCAMPERS > SCAMP

SCAMPI pl n large prawns

SCAMPIES > SCAMPI

SCAMPING > SCAMP

SCAMPINGS > SCAMP

SCAMPIS > SCAMPI

SCAMPISH > SCAMP

SCAMPS > SCAMP

SCAMS > SCAM

SCAMSTER same as > SCAMMER

SCAMSTERS > SCAMSTER

SCAMTO n argot of urban South African Blacks

SCAMTOS > SCAMTO

SCAN vb scrutinize carefully ▷ n scanning

SCAND > SCAN

SCANDAL n disgraceful action or event ▷ vb disgrace

SCANDALED > SCANDAL

SCANDALS > SCANDAL

SCANDENT adj (of plants) having a climbing habit

SCANDIA n scandium oxide

SCANDIAS > SCANDIA

SCANDIC adj of or containing scandium

SCANDIUM n rare silvery-white metallic element

SCANDIUMS > SCANDIUM

SCANNABLE > SCAN

SCANNED > SCAN

SCANNER n electronic device used for scanning

SCANNERS > SCANNER

SCANNING > SCAN

SCANNINGS > SCAN

SCANS > SCAN

SCANSION n metrical scanning of verse

SCANSIONS > SCANSION

SCANT adj barely sufficient, meagre ▷ vb limit in size or quantity ▷ adv scarcely

S

SCANTED > SCANT
SCANTER > SCANT
SCANTEST > SCANT
SCANTIER > SCANTY
SCANTIES n women's underwear
SCANTIEST > SCANTY
SCANTILY > SCANTY
SCANTING > SCANT
SCANTITY n quality of being scant
SCANTLE vb stint
SCANTLED > SCANTLE
SCANTLES > SCANTLE
SCANTLING n piece of sawn timber, such as a rafter, that has a small cross section
SCANTLY > SCANT
SCANTNESS > SCANT
SCANTS > SCANT
SCANTY adj barely sufficient or not sufficient
SCAPA variant of > SCARPER
SCAPAED > SCAPA
SCAPAING > SCAPA
SCAPAS > SCAPA
SCAPE n leafless stalk in plants ▷ vb archaic word for escape
SCAPED > SCAPE
SCAPEGOAT n person made to bear the blame for others ▷ vb make a scapegoat of
SCAPELESS adj allowing no escape
SCAPEMENT n escapement
SCAPES > SCAPE
SCAPHOID obsolete word for > NAVICULAR
SCAPHOIDS > SCAPHOID
SCAPHOPOD n type of marine mollusc of the class which includes tusk (or tooth) shells
SCAPI > SCAPUS
SCAPING > SCAPE
SCAPOLITE n any of a group of colourless, white, grey, or violet fluorescent minerals
SCAPOSE > SCAPE
SCAPPLE vb shape roughly
SCAPPLED > SCAPPLE
SCAPPLES > SCAPPLE
SCAPPLING > SCAPPLE
SCAPULA n shoulder blade
SCAPULAE > SCAPULA
SCAPULAR adj of the scapula ▷ n loose sleeveless garment worn by monks over their habits
SCAPULARS > SCAPULAR
SCAPULARY same as > SCAPULAR
SCAPULAS > SCAPULA
SCAPUS n flower stalk
SCAR n mark left by a healed wound ▷ vb mark

or become marked with a scar
SCARAB n sacred beetle of ancient Egypt
SCARABAEI pl n scarabs
SCARABEE n old word for scarab beetle
SCARABEES > SCARABEE
SCARABOID adj resembling a scarab beetle ▷ n beetle that resembles a scarab
SCARABS > SCARAB
SCARCE adj insufficient to meet demand
SCARCELY adv hardly at all
SCARCER > SCARCE
SCARCEST > SCARCE
SCARCITY n inadequate supply
SCARE vb frighten or be frightened ▷ n fright, sudden panic ▷ adj causing (needless) fear or alarm
SCARECROW n figure dressed in old clothes, set up to scare birds away from crops
SCARED > SCARE
SCAREDER > SCARE
SCAREDEST > SCARE
SCAREDIES > SCAREDY
SCAREDY n someone who is easily frightened
SCAREHEAD n newspaper headline intended to shock
SCARER > SCARE
SCARERS > SCARE
SCARES > SCARE
SCAREWARE n type of malware which tricks the user into downloading it
SCAREY adj frightening
SCARF n piece of material worn round the neck, head, or shoulders ▷ vb join in this way
SCARFED > SCARF
SCARFER > SCARF
SCARFERS > SCARF
SCARFING > SCARF
SCARFINGS > SCARF
SCARFISH n type of fish
SCARFPIN n decorative pin securing scarf
SCARFPINS > SCARFPIN
SCARFS > SCARF
SCARFSKIN n outermost layer of the skin
SCARFWISE adv like scarf
SCARIER > SCARY
SCARIEST > SCARY
SCARIFIED > SCARIFY
SCARIFIER > SCARIFY
SCARIFIES > SCARIFY
SCARIFY vb scratch or cut slightly all over
SCARILY > SCARY
SCARINESS > SCARY
SCARING > SCARE

SCARIOSE same as > SCARIOUS
SCARIOUS adj (of plant parts) membranous, dry, and brownish in colour
SCARLESS > SCAR
SCARLET n brilliant red ▷ adj bright red ▷ vb make scarlet
SCARLETED > SCARLET
SCARLETS > SCARLET
SCARMOGE n old form of skirmish
SCARMOGES > SCARMOGE
SCARP n steep slope ▷ vb wear or cut so as to form a steep slope
SCARPA vb run away
SCARPAED > SCARPA
SCARPAING > SCARPA
SCARPAS > SCARPA
SCARPED > SCARP
SCARPER vb run away ▷ n hasty departure
SCARPERED > SCARPER
SCARPERS > SCARPER
SCARPETTI > SCARPETTO
SCARPETTO n type of shoe
SCARPH vb join with scarf joint
SCARPHED > SCARPH
SCARPHING > SCARPH
SCARPHS > SCARPH
SCARPINES n device for torturing feet
SCARPING > SCARP
SCARPINGS > SCARP
SCARPS > SCARP
SCARRE n Shakespearian word of unknown meaning
SCARRED > SCAR
SCARRES > SCARRE
SCARRIER > SCAR
SCARRIEST > SCAR
SCARRING > SCAR
SCARRINGS > SCAR
SCARRY > SCAR
SCARS > SCAR
SCART vb scratch or scrape ▷ n scratch or scrape
SCARTED > SCART
SCARTH Scots word for > CORMORANT
SCARTHS > SCARTH
SCARTING > SCART
SCARTS > SCART
SCARVED adj wearing a scarf
SCARVES > SCARF
SCARY adj frightening
SCAT vb go away ▷ n jazz singing using improvised vocal sounds instead of words
SCATBACK n American football player
SCATBACKS > SCATBACK
SCATCH same as > STILT
SCATCHES > SCATCH

SCATH vb old word meaning injure
SCATHE vb attack with severe criticism ▷ n harm
SCATHED > SCATHE
SCATHEFUL adj old word meaning harmful
SCATHES > SCATHE
SCATHING adj harshly critical
SCATHS > SCATH
SCATOLE n substance found in coal
SCATOLES > SCATOLE
SCATOLOGY n preoccupation with obscenity, esp with references to excrement
SCATS > SCAT
SCATT n old word meaning tax ▷ vb tax
SCATTED > SCAT
SCATTER vb throw about in various directions ▷ n scattering
SCATTERED > SCATTER
SCATTERER > SCATTER
SCATTERS > SCATTER
SCATTERY adj dispersed
SCATTIER > SCATTY
SCATTIEST > SCATTY
SCATTILY > SCATTY
SCATTING > SCAT
SCATTINGS > SCAT
SCATTS > SCATT
SCATTY adj empty-headed
SCAUD Scot word for > SCALD
SCAUDED > SCAUD
SCAUDING > SCAUD
SCAUDS > SCAUD
SCAUP variant of > SCALP
SCAUPED > SCAUP
SCAUPER same as > SCORPER
SCAUPERS > SCAUPER
SCAUPING > SCAUP
SCAUPS > SCAUP
SCAUR same as > SCAR
SCAURED > SCAUR
SCAURIES > SCAURY
SCAURING > SCAUR
SCAURS > SCAUR
SCAURY n young seagull
SCAVAGE n old word meaning toll ▷ vb scavenge
SCAVAGED > SCAVAGE
SCAVAGER > SCAVAGE
SCAVAGERS > SCAVAGER
SCAVAGES > SCAVAGE
SCAVAGING > SCAVAGE
SCAVENGE vb search for (anything usable) among discarded material
SCAVENGED > SCAVENGE
SCAVENGER n person who scavenges
SCAVENGES > SCAVENGE
SCAW n headland
SCAWS > SCAW
SCAWTITE n mineral containing calcium

SCAWTITES > SCAWTITE

SCAZON n metre in poetry

SCAZONES > SCAZON

SCAZONTES > SCAZON

SCAZONTIC > SCAZON

SCEAT n Anglo-Saxon coin

SCEATT n Anglo-Saxon coin

SCEATTAS > SCEAT

SCEDULE old spelling of > SCHEDULE

SCEDULED > SCEDULE

SCEDULES > SCEDULE

SCEDULING > SCEDULE

SCELERAT n villain

SCELERATE n villain

SCELERATS > SCELERAT

SCENA n scene in an opera, usually longer than a single aria

SCENARIES > SCENARY

SCENARIO n summary of the plot of a play or film

SCENARIOS > SCENARIO

SCENARISE same as > SCENARIZE

SCENARIST > SCENARIO

SCENARIZE vb create scenario

SCENARY n scenery

SCENAS > SCENA

SCEND vb (of a vessel) to surge upwards in a heavy sea ▷ n upward heaving of a vessel pitching

SCENDED > SCEND

SCENDING > SCEND

SCENDS > SCEND

SCENE n place of action of a real or imaginary event ▷ vb set in a scene

SCENED > SCENE

SCENEMAN n person shifting stage scenery

SCENEMEN > SCENEMAN

SCENERIES > SCENERY

SCENERY n natural features of a landscape

SCENES > SCENE

SCENESTER n person who tries to fit into a particular cultural scene

SCENIC adj picturesque ▷ n something scenic

SCENICAL > SCENE

SCENICS > SCENIC

SCENING > SCENE

SCENT n pleasant smell ▷ vb detect by smell

SCENTED > SCENT

SCENTFUL adj old word meaning having scent

SCENTING > SCENT

SCENTINGS > SCENT

SCENTLESS > SCENT

SCENTS > SCENT

SCEPSIS n doubt

SCEPSISES > SCEPSIS

SCEPTER same as > SCEPTRE

SCEPTERED > SCEPTER

SCEPTERS > SCEPTER

SCEPTIC n person who habitually doubts generally accepted beliefs ▷ adj of or relating to sceptics

SCEPTICAL adj not convinced that something is true

SCEPTICS > SCEPTIC

SCEPTRAL adj royal

SCEPTRE n ornamental rod symbolizing royal power ▷ vb invest with authority

SCEPTRED > SCEPTRE

SCEPTRES > SCEPTRE

SCEPTRING > SCEPTRE

SCEPTRY adj having sceptre

SCERNE vb old word meaning discern

SCERNED > SCERNE

SCERNES > SCERNE

SCERNING > SCERNE

SCHANSE n stones heaped to shelter soldier in battle

SCHANSES > SCHANSE

SCHANTZE n stones heaped to shelter soldier in battle

SCHANTZES > SCHANTZE

SCHANZE n stones heaped to shelter soldier in battle

SCHANZES > SCHANZE

SCHAPPE n yarn or fabric made from waste silk

SCHAPPED > SCHAPPE

SCHAPPES > SCHAPPE

SCHAPSKA n cap worn by lancer

SCHAPSKAS > SCHAPSKA

SCHATCHEN same as > SHADCHAN

SCHAV n Polish soup

SCHAVS > SCHAV

SCHECHITA n slaughter of animals according to Jewish law

SCHEDULAR > SCHEDULE

SCHEDULE n plan of procedure for a project ▷ vb plan to occur at a certain time

SCHEDULED adj arranged or planned according to a programme, timetable, etc

SCHEDULER > SCHEDULE

SCHEDULES > SCHEDULE

SCHEELITE n white, brownish, or greenish mineral

SCHELLIES > SCHELLY

SCHELLUM n Scots word meaning rascal

SCHELLUMS > SCHELLUM

SCHELLY n freshwater whitefish of the English Lake District

SCHELM n South African word meaning rascal

SCHELMS > SCHELM

SCHEMA n overall plan or diagram

SCHEMAS > SCHEMA

SCHEMATA > SCHEMA

SCHEMATIC adj presented as a plan or diagram ▷ n schematic diagram, esp of an electrical circuit

SCHEME n systematic plan ▷ vb plan in an underhand manner

SCHEMED > SCHEME

SCHEMER > SCHEME

SCHEMERS > SCHEME

SCHEMES > SCHEME

SCHEMIE n Scots derogatory word for a resident of a housing scheme

SCHEMIES > SCHEMIE

SCHEMING adj given to making plots ▷ n intrigues

SCHEMINGS > SCHEMING

SCHERZI > SCHERZO

SCHERZO n brisk lively piece of music

SCHERZOS > SCHERZO

SCHIAVONE n type of sword

SCHIEDAM n type of gin produced in the Netherlands

SCHIEDAMS > SCHIEDAM

SCHILLER n unusual iridescent or metallic lustre in some minerals

SCHILLERS > SCHILLER

SCHILLING n former monetary unit of Austria

SCHIMMEL n roan horse

SCHIMMELS > SCHIMMEL

SCHISM n (group resulting from) division in an organization

SCHISMA n musical term

SCHISMAS > SCHISMA

SCHISMS > SCHISM

SCHIST n crystalline rock which splits into layers

SCHISTOSE > SCHIST

SCHISTOUS > SCHIST

SCHISTS > SCHIST

SCHIZIER > SCHIZY

SCHIZIEST > SCHIZY

SCHIZO n derogatory term for a schizophrenic (person) ▷ adj schizophrenic

SCHIZOID adj abnormally introverted ▷ n schizoid person

SCHIZOIDS > SCHIZOID

SCHIZONT n cell formed from a trophozoite during the asexual stage of the life cycle of sporozoan protozoans

SCHIZONTS > SCHIZONT

SCHIZOPOD n any of various shrimplike crustaceans

SCHIZOS > SCHIZO

SCHIZY adj slang term meaning schizophrenic

SCHIZZIER > SCHIZZY

SCHIZZY adj slang term meaning schizophrenic

SCHLAGER n German duelling sword

SCHLAGERS > SCHLAGER

SCHLEMIEL n awkward or unlucky person whose endeavours usually fail

SCHLEMIHL same as > SCHLEMIEL

SCHLEP vb drag or lug (oneself or an object) with difficulty ▷ n stupid or clumsy person

SCHLEPP vb schlep

SCHLEPPED > SCHLEP

SCHLEPPER n incompetent person

SCHLEPPS > SCHLEPP

SCHLEPPY same as > SHLEPPY

SCHLEPS > SCHLEP

SCHLICH n finely crushed ore

SCHLICHS > SCHLICH

SCHLIERE n (in physics or geology) streak of different density or composition from surroundings

SCHLIEREN > SCHLIERE

SCHLIERIC > SCHLIERE

SCHLOCK n goods or produce of cheap or inferior quality ▷ adj cheap, inferior, or trashy

SCHLOCKER n thing of poor quality

SCHLOCKS > SCHLOCK

SCHLOCKY adj of poor quality

SCHLONG slang word for > PENIS

SCHLONGS > SCHLONG

SCHLOSS n castle

SCHLOSSES > SCHLOSS

SCHLUB n coarse or contemptible person

SCHLUBS > SCHLUB

SCHLUMP vb move in lazy way

SCHLUMPED > SCHLUMP

SCHLUMPS > SCHLUMP

SCHLUMPY > SCHLUMP

SCHMALTZ n excessive sentimentality

SCHMALTZY adj excessively sentimental

SCHMALZ same as > SCHMALTZ

SCHMALZES > SCHMALZ

SCHMALZY adj schmaltzy

SCHMATTE same as > SCHMUTTER

SCHMATTES > SCHMATTE

SCHMEAR n situation, matter, or affair ▷ vb spread or smear

SCHMEARED > SCHMEAR

SCHMEARS > SCHMEAR

SCHMECK n taste ▷ vb taste good

SCHMECKED > SCHMECK

SCHMECKER n heroin user

SCHMECKS > SCHMECK

SCHMEER *same as* > SCHMEAR

SCHMEERED > SCHMEER

SCHMEERS > SCHMEER

SCHMELZ *n* ornamental glass

SCHMELZE *variant of* > SCHMELZ

SCHMELZES > SCHMELZ

SCHMICK *adj* (in Australia) excellent, elegant, or stylish

SCHMICKER > SCHMICK

SCHMO *n* dull, stupid, or boring person

SCHMOCK *n* stupid person

SCHMOCKS > SCHMOCK

SCHMOE *n* stupid person

SCHMOES > SCHMO

SCHMOOS *variant of* > SCHMOOSE

SCHMOOSE *vb* chat

SCHMOOSED > SCHMOOSE

SCHMOOSES > SCHMOOSE

SCHMOOZ *n* chat

SCHMOOZE *vb* chat or gossip ▷ *n* trivial conversation

SCHMOOZED > SCHMOOZE

SCHMOOZER > SCHMOOZE

SCHMOOZES > SCHMOOZE

SCHMOOZY > SCHMOOZE

SCHMOS > SCHMO

SCHMUCK *n* stupid or contemptible person ▷ *vb* act as a schmuck

SCHMUCKED > SCHMUCK

SCHMUCKS > SCHMUCK

SCHMUCKY *adj* foolish

SCHMUTTER *n* cloth or clothing

SCHMUTZ *n* dirt; grime

SCHMUTZES > SCHMUTZ

SCHNAPPER *same as* > SNAPPER

SCHNAPPS *n* strong alcoholic spirit

SCHNAPS *same as* > SCHNAPPS

SCHNAPSES > SCHNAPS

SCHNAUZER *n* wire-haired breed of dog of the terrier type, originally from Germany

SCHNECKE > SCHNECKEN

SCHNECKEN *pl n* sweet spiral-shaped bread roll flavoured with cinnamon and nuts

SCHNELL *adj* German word meaning quick

SCHNITZEL *n* thin slice of meat, esp veal

SCHNOOK *n* stupid or gullible person

SCHNOOKS > SCHNOOK

SCHNORKEL *less common variant of* > SNORKEL

SCHNORR *vb* beg

SCHNORRED > SCHNORR

SCHNORRER *n* person who lives off the charity of others

SCHNORRS > SCHNORR

SCHNOZ *n* nose

SCHNOZES > SCHNOZ

SCHNOZZ *n* nose

SCHNOZZES > SCHNOZZ

SCHNOZZLE *slang word for* > NOSE

SCHOLAR *n* learned person

SCHOLARCH *n* head of school

SCHOLARLY > SCHOLAR

SCHOLARS > SCHOLAR

SCHOLIA > SCHOLIUM

SCHOLIAST *n* medieval annotator, esp of classical texts

SCHOLION *n* scholarly annotation

SCHOLIUM *n* commentary or annotation, esp on a classical text

SCHOLIUMS > SCHOLIUM

SCHOOL *n* place where children are taught or instruction is given in a subject ▷ *vb* educate or train

SCHOOLBAG *n* school pupil's bag

SCHOOLBOY *n* child attending school

SCHOOLDAY *n* day for going to school

SCHOOLE *n* old form of shoal

SCHOOLED > SCHOOL

SCHOOLER *n* pupil at a school of a certain kind

SCHOOLERS > SCHOOLER

SCHOOLERY *n* old word meaning something taught

SCHOOLES > SCHOOLE

SCHOOLIE *n* schoolteacher or a high-school student

SCHOOLIES > SCHOOLIE

SCHOOLING *n* education

SCHOOLKID *n* child who goes to school

SCHOOLMAN *n* scholar versed in the learning of the Schoolmen

SCHOOLMEN > SCHOOLMAN

SCHOOLS > SCHOOL

SCHOONER *n* sailing ship rigged fore-and-aft

SCHOONERS > SCHOONER

SCHORL *n* type of black tourmaline

SCHORLS > SCHORL

SCHOUT *n* council officer in Netherlands

SCHOUTS > SCHOUT

SCHRIK *variant of* > SKRIK

SCHRIKS > SCHRIK

SCHROD *n* young cod

SCHRODS > SCHROD

SCHTICK *same as* > SHTICK

SCHTICKS > SCHTICK

SCHTIK *n* schtick

SCHTIKS > SCHTIK

SCHTOOK *n* trouble

SCHTOOKS > SCHTOOK

SCHTOOM *adj* silent

SCHTUCK *n* trouble

SCHTUCKS > SCHTUCK

SCHTUM *adj* silent or dumb

SCHTUP *same as* > SHTUP

SCHTUPPED > SCHTUP

SCHTUPS > SCHTUP

SCHUIT *n* Dutch boat with flat bottom

SCHUITS > SCHUIT

SCHUL *same as* > SHUL

SCHULN > SCHUL

SCHULS > SCHUL

SCHUSS *n* straight high-speed downhill run ▷ *vb* perform a schuss

SCHUSSED > SCHUSS

SCHUSSER > SCHUSS

SCHUSSERS > SCHUSS

SCHUSSES > SCHUSS

SCHUSSING > SCHUSS

SCHUYT *n* Dutch boat with flat bottom

SCHUYTS > SCHUYT

SCHVARTZE *n* Yiddish word for black person

SCHVITZ *same as* > SHVITZ

SCHVITZED > SCHVITZ

SCHVITZES > SCHVITZ

SCHWA *n* vowel representing the sound in unstressed syllables

SCHWAG *n* promotional material given away for free

SCHWAGS > SCHWAG

SCHWARTZE *same as* > SCHVARTZE

SCHWAS > SCHWA

SCIAENID *adj* of or relating to a family of mainly tropical and subtropical marine percoid fishes ▷ *n* any of these fish

SCIAENIDS > SCIAENID

SCIAENOID *same as* > SCIAENID

SCIAMACHY *n* fight with an imaginary enemy

SCIARID *n* small fly

SCIARIDS > SCIARID

SCIATIC *adj* of the hip ▷ *n* sciatic part of the body

SCIATICA *n* severe pain in the large nerve in the back of the leg

SCIATICAL > SCIATICA

SCIATICAS > SCIATICA

SCIATICS > SCIATIC

SCIENCE *n* systematic study and knowledge of natural or physical phenomena

SCIENCED *adj* old word meaning learned

SCIENCES > SCIENCE

SCIENT *adj* old word meaning scientific

SCIENTER *adv* knowingly

SCIENTIAL *adj* of or relating to science

SCIENTISE *same as* > SCIENTIZE

SCIENTISM *n* application of, or belief in, the scientific method

SCIENTIST *n* person who studies or practises a science

SCIENTIZE *vb* treat scientifically

SCILICET *adv* namely

SCILLA *n* plant with small bell-shaped flowers

SCILLAS > SCILLA

SCIMETAR *n* scimitar

SCIMETARS > SCIMETAR

SCIMITAR *n* curved oriental sword

SCIMITARS > SCIMITAR

SCIMITER *n* scimitar

SCIMITERS > SCIMITER

SCINCOID *adj* of, relating to, or resembling a skink ▷ *n* any animal, esp a lizard, resembling a skink

SCINCOIDS > SCINCOID

SCINTILLA *n* very small amount

SCIOLISM *n* practice of opinionating on subjects of which one has only superficial knowledge

SCIOLISMS > SCIOLISM

SCIOLIST > SCIOLISM

SCIOLISTS > SCIOLISM

SCIOLOUS > SCIOLISM

SCIOLTO *adv* musical direction meaning freely

SCIOMACHY *same as* > SCIAMACHY

SCIOMANCY *n* divination with the help of ghosts

SCION *n* descendant or heir

SCIONS > SCION

SCIOPHYTE *n* any plant that grows best in the shade

SCIOSOPHY *n* unscientific system of knowledge

SCIROC *n* hot Mediterranean wind

SCIROCCO *n* hot Mediterranean wind

SCIROCCOS > SCIROCCO

SCIROCS > SCIROC

SCIRRHI > SCIRRHUS

SCIRRHOID > SCIRRHUS

SCIRRHOUS *adj* of or resembling a scirrhus

SCIRRHUS *n* hard cancerous growth composed of fibrous tissues

SCISSEL *n* waste metal left over from sheet metal after discs have been punched out of it

SCISSELS > SCISSEL

SCISSIL *n* scissel

SCISSILE *adj* capable of being cut or divided

SCISSILS > SCISSIL

SCISSION *n* act or an instance of cutting, splitting, or dividing
SCISSIONS > SCISSION
SCISSOR *vb* cut (an object) with scissors
SCISSORED > SCISSOR
SCISSORER > SCISSOR
SCISSORS *pl n* cutting instrument with two crossed pivoted blades
SCISSURE *n* longitudinal cleft
SCISSURES > SCISSURE
SCIURID *n* squirrel or related rodent
SCIURIDS > SCIURID
SCIURINE *adj* relating to a family of rodents that includes squirrels, marmots, and chipmunks ▷ *n* any sciurine animal
SCIURINES > SCIURINE
SCIUROID *adj* (of an animal) resembling a squirrel
SCLAFF *vb* cause (the club) to hit (the ground behind the ball) when making a stroke ▷ *n* sclaffing stroke or shot
SCLAFFED > SCLAFF
SCLAFFER > SCLAFF
SCLAFFERS > SCLAFF
SCLAFFING > SCLAFF
SCLAFFS > SCLAFF
SCLATE *vb* (Scots) slate ▷ *n* (Scots) slate
SCLATED > SCLATE
SCLATES > SCLATE
SCLATING > SCLATE
SCLAUNDER *n* old form of slander
SCLAVE *n* old form of slave
SCLAVES > SCLAVE
SCLERA *n* tough white substance that forms the outer covering of the eyeball
SCLERAE > SCLERA
SCLERAL > SCLERA
SCLERAS > SCLERA
SCLERE *n* supporting anatomical structure
SCLEREID *n* type of biological cell
SCLEREIDE *n* type of biological cell
SCLEREIDS > SCLEREID
SCLEREMA *n* condition in which body tissues harden
SCLEREMAS > SCLEREMA
SCLERES > SCLERE
SCLERITE *n* any of the hard chitinous plates that make up the exoskeleton of an arthropod
SCLERITES > SCLERITE
SCLERITIC > SCLERITE
SCLERITIS *n* inflammation of the sclera
SCLEROID *adj* (of organisms and their parts) hard or hardened

SCLEROMA *n* any small area of abnormally hard tissue, esp in a mucous membrane
SCLEROMAS > SCLEROMA
SCLEROSAL > SCLEROSIS
SCLEROSE *vb* affect with sclerosis
SCLEROSED *adj* hardened
SCLEROSES > SCLEROSIS
SCLEROSIS *n* abnormal hardening of body tissues
SCLEROTAL *n* bony area in sclerotic
SCLEROTIA *pl n* masses of hyphae formed in certain fungi
SCLEROTIC *same as* > SCLERA
SCLEROTIN *n* protein in the cuticle of insects that becomes hard and dark
SCLEROUS *adj* hard
SCLIFF *n* Scots word for small piece
SCLIFFS > SCLIFF
SCLIM *vb* Scots word meaning climb
SCLIMMED > SCLIM
SCLIMMING > SCLIM
SCLIMS > SCLIM
SCODIER > SCODY
SCODIEST > SCODY
SCODY *adj* unkempt
SCOFF *vb* express derision ▷ *n* mocking expression
SCOFFED > SCOFF
SCOFFER > SCOFF
SCOFFERS > SCOFF
SCOFFING > SCOFF
SCOFFINGS > SCOFF
SCOFFLAW *n* person who habitually flouts or violates the law
SCOFFLAWS > SCOFFLAW
SCOFFS > SCOFF
SCOG *vb* shelter
SCOGGED > SCOG
SCOGGING > SCOG
SCOGS > SCOG
SCOINSON *n* part of door or window frame
SCOINSONS > SCOINSON
SCOLD *vb* find fault with, reprimand ▷ *n* person who scolds
SCOLDABLE > SCOLD
SCOLDED > SCOLD
SCOLDER > SCOLD
SCOLDERS > SCOLD
SCOLDING > SCOLD
SCOLDINGS > SCOLD
SCOLDS > SCOLD
SCOLECES > SCOLEX
SCOLECID *n* variety of worm
SCOLECIDS > SCOLECID
SCOLECITE *n* white zeolite mineral
SCOLECOID *adj* like scolex
SCOLEX *n* headlike part of a tapeworm

SCOLIA > SCOLION
SCOLICES > SCOLEX
SCOLIOMA *n* condition with abnormal curvature of spine
SCOLIOMAS > SCOLIOMA
SCOLION *n* ancient Greek drinking song
SCOLIOSES > SCOLIOSIS
SCOLIOSIS *n* abnormal lateral curvature of the spine
SCOLIOTIC > SCOLIOSIS
SCOLLOP *variant of* > SCALLOP
SCOLLOPED > SCOLLOP
SCOLLOPS > SCOLLOP
SCOLYTID *n* type of beetle
SCOLYTIDS > SCOLYTID
SCOLYTOID *n* type of beetle
SCOMBRID *n* fish of mackerel family
SCOMBRIDS > SCOMBRID
SCOMBROID *adj* relating to a suborder of marine spiny-finned fishes ▷ *n* any fish belonging to this suborder
SCOMFISH *vb* Scots word meaning stifle
SCONCE *n* bracket on a wall for holding candles or lights ▷ *vb* challenge (a fellow student) to drink a large quantity of beer
SCONCED > SCONCE
SCONCES > SCONCE
SCONCHEON *n* part of door or window frame
SCONCING > SCONCE
SCONE *n* small plain cake baked in an oven or on a griddle
SCONES > SCONE
SCONTION *n* part of door or window frame
SCONTIONS > SCONTION
SCOOBIES > SCOOBY
SCOOBY *n* clue; notion
SCOOCH *vb* compress one's body into smaller space
SCOOCHED > SCOOCH
SCOOCHES > SCOOCH
SCOOCHING > SCOOCH
SCOOG *vb* shelter
SCOOGED > SCOOG
SCOOGING > SCOOG
SCOOGS > SCOOG
SCOOP *n* shovel-like tool for ladling or hollowing out ▷ *vb* take up or hollow out with or as if with a scoop
SCOOPABLE > SCOOP
SCOOPED > SCOOP
SCOOPER > SCOOP
SCOOPERS > SCOOP
SCOOPFUL > SCOOP
SCOOPFULS > SCOOP
SCOOPING > SCOOP

SCOOPINGS > SCOOP
SCOOPS > SCOOP
SCOOPSFUL > SCOOP
SCOOSH *vb* squirt ▷ *n* squirt or rush of liquid
SCOOSHED > SCOOSH
SCOOSHES > SCOOSH
SCOOSHING > SCOOSH
SCOOT *vb* leave or move quickly ▷ *n* act of scooting
SCOOTCH *same as* > SCOOCH
SCOOTCHED > SCOOTCH
SCOOTCHES > SCOOTCH
SCOOTED > SCOOT
SCOOTER *n* child's vehicle propelled by pushing on the ground with one foot ▷ *vb* go on a scooter
SCOOTERED > SCOOTER
SCOOTERS > SCOOTER
SCOOTING > SCOOT
SCOOTS > SCOOT
SCOP *n* (in Anglo-Saxon England) a bard or minstrel
SCOPA *n* tuft of hairs on the abdomen or hind legs of bees
SCOPAE > SCOPA
SCOPAS > SCOP
SCOPATE *adj* having tuft
SCOPE *n* opportunity for using abilities ▷ *vb* look at or examine carefully
SCOPED > SCOPE
SCOPELID *n* deep-sea fish
SCOPELIDS > SCOPELID
SCOPELOID *n* deep-sea fish
SCOPES > SCOPE
SCOPING > SCOPE
SCOPOLINE *n* soluble crystalline alkaloid
SCOPS > SCOP
SCOPULA *n* small tuft of dense hairs on the legs and chelicerae of some spiders
SCOPULAE > SCOPULA
SCOPULAS > SCOPULA
SCOPULATE > SCOPULA
SCORBUTIC *adj* of or having scurvy
SCORCH *vb* burn on the surface ▷ *n* slight burn
SCORCHED > SCORCH
SCORCHER *n* very hot day
SCORCHERS > SCORCHER
SCORCHES > SCORCH
SCORCHING > SCORCH
SCORDATO *adj* musical term meaning out of tune
SCORE *n* points gained in a game or competition ▷ *vb* gain (points) in a game
SCORECARD *n* card on which scores are recorded in games such as golf
SCORED > SCORE
SCORELESS *adj* without anyone scoring
SCORELINE *n* final score in game

SCOREPAD n pad for recording score in game
SCOREPADS > SCOREPAD
SCORER > SCORE
SCORERS > SCORE
SCORES > SCORE
SCORIA n mass of solidified lava containing many cavities
SCORIAC > SCORIA
SCORIAE > SCORIA
SCORIFIED > SCORIFY
SCORIFIER > SCORIFY
SCORIFIES > SCORIFY
SCORIFY vb remove (impurities) from metals by forming scoria
SCORING n act or practice of scoring
SCORINGS > SCORING
SCORIOUS > SCORIA
SCORN n open contempt ▷ vb despise
SCORNED > SCORN
SCORNER > SCORN
SCORNERS > SCORN
SCORNFUL > SCORN
SCORNING > SCORN
SCORNINGS > SCORN
SCORNS > SCORN
SCORODITE n mineral containing iron and aluminium
SCORPER n kind of fine chisel with a square or curved tip
SCORPERS > SCORPER
SCORPIOID adj of, relating to, or resembling scorpions
SCORPION n small lobster-shaped animal with a sting at the end of a jointed tail
SCORPIONS > SCORPION
SCORRENDO adj musical term meaning gliding
SCORSE vb exchange
SCORSED > SCORSE
SCORSER > SCORSE
SCORSERS > SCORSE
SCORSES > SCORSE
SCORSING > SCORSE
SCOT n payment or tax
SCOTCH vb put an end to ▷ n gash
SCOTCHED > SCOTCH
SCOTCHES > SCOTCH
SCOTCHING > SCOTCH
SCOTER n type of sea duck
SCOTERS > SCOTER
SCOTIA n deep concave moulding
SCOTIAS > SCOTIA
SCOTOMA n blind spot
SCOTOMAS > SCOTOMA
SCOTOMATA > SCOTOMA
SCOTOMIA n dizziness
SCOTOMIAS > SCOTOMIA
SCOTOMIES > SCOTOMY
SCOTOMY n dizziness
SCOTOPHIL adj liking darkness

SCOTOPIA n ability of the eye to adjust for night vision
SCOTOPIAS > SCOTOPIA
SCOTOPIC > SCOTOPIA
SCOTS > SCOT
SCOTTIE n type of small sturdy terrier
SCOTTIES > SCOTTIE
SCOUG vb shelter
SCOUGED > SCOUG
SCOUGING > SCOUG
SCOUGS > SCOUG
SCOUNDREL n cheat or deceiver
SCOUP vb Scots word meaning jump
SCOUPED > SCOUP
SCOUPING > SCOUP
SCOUPS > SCOUP
SCOUR vb clean or polish by rubbing with something rough ▷ n scouring
SCOURED > SCOUR
SCOURER > SCOUR
SCOURERS > SCOUR
SCOURGE n person or thing causing severe suffering ▷ vb cause severe suffering to
SCOURGED > SCOURGE
SCOURGER > SCOURGE
SCOURGERS > SCOURGE
SCOURGES > SCOURGE
SCOURING n act of scouring
SCOURIE n young seagull
SCOURIES > SCOURIE
SCOURING > SCOUR
SCOURINGS pl n residue left after cleaning grain
SCOURS > SCOUR
SCOURSE vb exchange
SCOURSED > SCOURSE
SCOURSES > SCOURSE
SCOURSING > SCOURSE
SCOUSE n stew made from left-over meat
SCOUSER n inhabitant of Liverpool
SCOUSERS > SCOUSER
SCOUSES > SCOUSE
SCOUT n person sent out to reconnoitre ▷ vb act as a scout
SCOUTED > SCOUT
SCOUTER > SCOUT
SCOUTERS > SCOUT
SCOUTH n Scots word meaning plenty of scope
SCOUTHER vb Scots word meaning scorch
SCOUTHERS > SCOUTHER
SCOUTHERY > SCOUTHER
SCOUTHS > SCOUTH
SCOUTING > SCOUT
SCOUTINGS > SCOUT
SCOUTS > SCOUT
SCOW n unpowered barge used for carrying freight ▷ vb transport by scow
SCOWDER vb Scots word meaning scorch

SCOWDERED > SCOWDER
SCOWDERS > SCOWDER
SCOWED > SCOW
SCOWING > SCOW
SCOWL n, vb (have an) angry or sullen expression
SCOWLED > SCOWL
SCOWLER n person who scowls
SCOWLERS > SCOWLER
SCOWLING > SCOWL
SCOWLS > SCOWL
SCOWP vb Scots word meaning jump
SCOWPED > SCOWP
SCOWPING > SCOWP
SCOWPS > SCOWP
SCOWRER n old word meaning hooligan
SCOWRERS > SCOWRER
SCOWRIE n young seagull
SCOWRIES > SCOWRIE
SCOWS > SCOW
SCOWTH n Scots word meaning plenty of scope
SCOWTHER vb Scots word meaning scorch
SCOWTHERS > SCOWTHER
SCOWTHS > SCOWTH
SCOZZA n rowdy person, esp one who drinks a lot of alcohol
SCOZZAS > SCOZZA
SCRAB vb scratch
SCRABBED > SCRAB
SCRABBING > SCRAB
SCRABBLE vb scrape at with the hands, feet, or claws ▷ n board game in which words are formed by letter tiles
SCRABBLED > SCRABBLE
SCRABBLER > SCRABBLE
SCRABBLES > SCRABBLE
SCRABBLY adj covered with stunted trees
SCRABS > SCRAB
SCRAE Scots word for > SCREE
SCRAES > SCRAE
SCRAG n thin end of a neck of mutton ▷ vb wring the neck of
SCRAGGED > SCRAG
SCRAGGIER > SCRAGGY
SCRAGGILY > SCRAGGY
SCRAGGING > SCRAG
SCRAGGLY adj untidy or irregular
SCRAGGY adj thin, bony
SCRAGS > SCRAG
SCRAICH vb Scots word meaning scream
SCRAICHED > SCRAICH
SCRAICHS > SCRAICH
SCRAIGH vb Scots word meaning scream
SCRAIGHED > SCRAIGH
SCRAIGHS > SCRAIGH
SCRAM vb go away quickly ▷ n emergency shutdown of a nuclear reactor

SCRAMB vb scratch with nails or claws
SCRAMBED > SCRAMB
SCRAMBING > SCRAMB
SCRAMBLE vb climb or crawl hastily or awkwardly ▷ n scrambling
SCRAMBLED > SCRAMBLE
SCRAMBLER n electronic device that makes transmitted speech unintelligible
SCRAMBLES > SCRAMBLE
SCRAMBS > SCRAMB
SCRAMJET n type of jet engine
SCRAMJETS > SCRAMJET
SCRAMMED > SCRAM
SCRAMMING > SCRAM
SCRAMS > SCRAM
SCRAN n food
SCRANCH vb crunch
SCRANCHED > SCRANCH
SCRANCHES > SCRANCH
SCRANNEL adj thin ▷ n thin person or thing
SCRANNELS > SCRANNEL
SCRANNIER > SCRANNY
SCRANNY adj scrawny
SCRANS > SCRAN
SCRAP n small piece ▷ vb discard as useless
SCRAPABLE > SCRAPE
SCRAPBOOK n book with blank pages in which newspaper cuttings or pictures are stuck ▷ vb keep (cuttings etc) in a scrapbook
SCRAPE vb rub with something rough or sharp ▷ n act or sound of scraping
SCRAPED > SCRAPE
SCRAPEGUT n old word for fiddle player
SCRAPER > SCRAPE
SCRAPERS > SCRAPE
SCRAPES > SCRAPE
SCRAPHEAP n pile of discarded material
SCRAPIE n disease of sheep and goats
SCRAPIES > SCRAPIE
SCRAPING n act of scraping
SCRAPINGS > SCRAPING
SCRAPPAGE n act of scrapping
SCRAPPED > SCRAP
SCRAPPER n person who scraps
SCRAPPERS > SCRAPPER
SCRAPPIER > SCRAPPY
SCRAPPILY > SCRAPPY
SCRAPPING n act of scrapping
SCRAPPLE n scraps of pork cooked with cornmeal and formed into a loaf
SCRAPPLES > SCRAPPLE
SCRAPPY adj fragmentary, disjointed

SCRAPS > SCRAP
SCRAPYARD n place for scrap metal
SCRAT vb scratch
SCRATCH vb mark or cut with anything rough or sharp ▷ n wound, mark, or sound made by scratching ▷ adj put together at short notice
SCRATCHED > SCRATCH
SCRATCHER n person, animal, or thing that scratches
SCRATCHES n disease of horses characterized by dermatitis in the region of the fetlock
SCRATCHIE n scratchcard
SCRATCHY > SCRATCH
SCRATS > SCRAT
SCRATTED > SCRAT
SCRATTING > SCRAT
SCRATTLE vb dialect word meaning scratch
SCRATTLED > SCRATTLE
SCRATTLES > SCRATTLE
SCRAUCH vb squawk
SCRAUCHED > SCRAUCH
SCRAUCHS > SCRAUCH
SCRAUGH vb squawk
SCRAUGHED > SCRAUGH
SCRAUGHS > SCRAUGH
SCRAVEL vb move quickly
SCRAVELED > SCRAVEL
SCRAVELS > SCRAVEL
SCRAW n sod from the surface of a peat bog or from a field
SCRAWB same as > SCROB
SCRAWBED > SCRAWB
SCRAWBING > SCRAWB
SCRAWBS > SCRAWB
SCRAWL vb write carelessly or hastily ▷ n scribbled writing
SCRAWLED > SCRAWL
SCRAWLER > SCRAWL
SCRAWLERS > SCRAWL
SCRAWLIER > SCRAWL
SCRAWLING > SCRAWL
SCRAWLS > SCRAWL
SCRAWLY > SCRAWL
SCRAWM vb dialect word meaning scratch
SCRAWMED > SCRAWM
SCRAWMING > SCRAWM
SCRAWMS > SCRAWM
SCRAWNIER > SCRAWNY
SCRAWNILY > SCRAWNY
SCRAWNY adj thin and bony
SCRAWP vb scratch (the skin) to relieve itching
SCRAWPED > SCRAWP
SCRAWPING > SCRAWP
SCRAWPS > SCRAWP
SCRAWS > SCRAW
SCRAY n tern
SCRAYE n tern
SCRAYES > SCRAYE
SCRAYS > SCRAY

SCREAK vb screech or creak ▷ n screech or creak
SCREAKED > SCREAK
SCREAKIER > SCREAK
SCREAKING > SCREAK
SCREAKS > SCREAK
SCREAKY > SCREAK
SCREAM vb utter a piercing cry, esp of fear or pain ▷ n shrill piercing cry
SCREAMED > SCREAM
SCREAMER n person or thing that screams
SCREAMERS > SCREAMER
SCREAMING n act or instance of screaming
SCREAMO n type of emo music featuring screaming vocals
SCREAMOS > SCREAMO
SCREAMS > SCREAM
SCREE n slope of loose shifting stones
SCREECH n (utter) a shrill cry ▷ vb utter a shrill cry
SCREECHED > SCREECH
SCREECHER > SCREECH
SCREECHES > SCREECH
SCREECHY adj loud and shrill
SCREED n long tedious piece of writing ▷ vb rip
SCREEDED > SCREED
SCREEDER > SCREED
SCREEDERS > SCREED
SCREEDING > SCREED
SCREEDS > SCREED
SCREEN n surface of a television set, VDU, etc ▷ vb shelter or conceal with or as if with a screen
SCREENED > SCREEN
SCREENER > SCREEN
SCREENERS > SCREEN
SCREENFUL > SCREEN
SCREENIE n informal Australian word for screensaver
SCREENIES > SCREENIE
SCREENING > SCREEN
SCREENS > SCREEN
SCREES > SCREE
SCREET vb shed tears ▷ n act or sound of crying
SCREETED > SCREET
SCREETING > SCREET
SCREETS > SCREET
SCREEVE vb write
SCREEVED > SCREEVE
SCREEVER > SCREEVE
SCREEVERS > SCREEVE
SCREEVES > SCREEVE
SCREEVING > SCREEVE
SCREICH same as > SCREIGH
SCREICHED > SCREICH
SCREICHS > SCREICH
SCREIGH Scot word for > SCREECH
SCREIGHED > SCREIGH
SCREIGHS > SCREIGH

SCREW n metal pin with a spiral ridge along its length ▷ vb turn (a screw)
SCREWABLE > SCREW
SCREWBALL n odd or eccentric person ▷ adj crazy or eccentric
SCREWBEAN n variety of mesquite
SCREWED adj fastened by a screw or screws
SCREWER > SCREW
SCREWERS > SCREW
SCREWIER > SCREWY
SCREWIEST > SCREWY
SCREWING > SCREW
SCREWINGS > SCREW
SCREWLIKE > SCREW
SCREWS > SCREW
SCREWTOP n lid with a threaded rim that is turned to close it securely
SCREWTOPS > SCREWTOP
SCREWUP n something done badly
SCREWUPS > SCREWUP
SCREWWORM n larva of a fly that develops beneath the skin of living mammals often causing illness or death
SCREWY adj crazy or eccentric
SCRIBABLE > SCRIBE
SCRIBAL > SCRIBE
SCRIBBLE vb write hastily or illegibly ▷ n something scribbled
SCRIBBLED > SCRIBBLE
SCRIBBLER n often derogatory term for a writer of poetry, novels, journalism, etc
SCRIBBLES > SCRIBBLE
SCRIBBLY > SCRIBBLE
SCRIBE n person who copies documents ▷ vb score a line with a pointed instrument
SCRIBED > SCRIBE
SCRIBER n pointed steel tool used to score materials as a guide to cutting, etc
SCRIBERS > SCRIBER
SCRIBES > SCRIBE
SCRIBING > SCRIBE
SCRIBINGS > SCRIBE
SCRIBISM > SCRIBE
SCRIBISMS > SCRIBE
SCRIECH vb Scots word meaning screech
SCRIECHED > SCRIECH
SCRIECHS > SCRIECH
SCRIED > SCRY
SCRIENE n old form of screen
SCRIENES > SCRIENE
SCRIES > SCRY
SCRIEVE vb Scots word meaning write
SCRIEVED > SCRIEVE
SCRIEVES > SCRIEVE
SCRIEVING > SCRIEVE

SCRIGGLE vb wriggle
SCRIGGLED > SCRIGGLE
SCRIGGLES > SCRIGGLE
SCRIGGLY > SCRIGGLE
SCRIKE vb old word meaning shriek
SCRIKED > SCRIKE
SCRIKES > SCRIKE
SCRIKING > SCRIKE
SCRIM n open-weave muslin or hessian fabric
SCRIMMAGE n rough or disorderly struggle ▷ vb engage in a scrimmage
SCRIMP vb be very economical
SCRIMPED > SCRIMP
SCRIMPER > SCRIMP
SCRIMPERS > SCRIMP
SCRIMPIER > SCRIMP
SCRIMPILY > SCRIMP
SCRIMPING n act of scrimping
SCRIMPIT adj Scots word meaning ungenerous
SCRIMPLY adv sparingly
SCRIMPS > SCRIMP
SCRIMPY > SCRIMP
SCRIMS > SCRIM
SCRIMSHAW n art of decorating or carving shells, etc, done by sailors as a leisure activity ▷ vb produce scrimshaw (from)
SCRIMURE old word for > FENCER
SCRIMURES > SCRIMURE
SCRINE n old form of shrine
SCRINES > SCRINE
SCRIP n certificate representing a claim to stocks or shares
SCRIPPAGE n contents of scrip
SCRIPS > SCRIP
SCRIPT n text of a film, play, or TV programme ▷ vb write a script for
SCRIPTED > SCRIPT
SCRIPTER n person who writes scripts for films, play, or television dramas
SCRIPTERS > SCRIPTER
SCRIPTING > SCRIPT
SCRIPTORY adj of writing
SCRIPTS > SCRIPT
SCRIPTURE n sacred writings of a religion
SCRITCH vb screech
SCRITCHED > SCRITCH
SCRITCHES > SCRITCH
SCRIVE Scots word for > WRITE
SCRIVED > SCRIVE
SCRIVENER n person who writes out deeds, letters, etc
SCRIVES > SCRIVE
SCRIVING > SCRIVE
SCROB vb scrape with claws

S

SCROBBED > SCROB
SCROBBING > SCROB
SCROBBLE vb record a person's music preferences in order to recommend similar music
SCROBBLED > SCROBBLE
SCROBBLES > SCROBBLE
SCROBE n groove
SCROBES > SCROBE
SCROBS > SCROB
SCROD n young cod or haddock
SCRODDLED adj made of scraps of pottery
SCRODS > SCROD
SCROFULA n tuberculosis of the lymphatic glands
SCROFULAS > SCROFULA
SCROG n Scots word meaning small tree
SCROGGIE adj having scrogs upon it
SCROGGIER > SCROGGIE
SCROGGIN n mixture of nuts and dried fruits
SCROGGINS > SCROGGIN
SCROGGY variant of > SCROGGIE
SCROGS > SCROG
SCROLL n roll of parchment or paper ▷ vb move (text) up or down on a VDU screen
SCROLLED > SCROLL
SCROLLER n person or thing that scrolls
SCROLLERS > SCROLLER
SCROLLING > SCROLL
SCROLLS > SCROLL
SCROME vb crawl or climb
SCROMED > SCROME
SCROMES > SCROME
SCROMING > SCROME
SCROOCH vb scratch (the skin) to relieve itching
SCROOCHED > SCROOCH
SCROOCHES > SCROOCH
SCROOGE variant of > SCROUGE
SCROOGED > SCROOGE
SCROOGES > SCROOGE
SCROOGING > SCROOGE
SCROOP vb emit a grating or creaking sound ▷ n such a sound
SCROOPED > SCROOP
SCROOPING > SCROOP
SCROOPS > SCROOP
SCROOTCH vb hunch up
SCRORP n deep scratch or weal
SCRORPS > SCRORP
SCROTA > SCROTUM
SCROTAL > SCROTUM
SCROTE n slang derogatory word meaning a worthless fellow
SCROTES > SCROTE
SCROTUM n pouch of skin containing the testicles
SCROTUMS > SCROTUM

SCROUGE vb crowd or press
SCROUGED > SCROUGE
SCROUGER n American word meaning whopper
SCROUGERS > SCROUGER
SCROUGES > SCROUGE
SCROUGING > SCROUGE
SCROUNGE vb get by cadging or begging
SCROUNGED > SCROUNGE
SCROUNGER > SCROUNGE
SCROUNGES > SCROUNGE
SCROUNGY adj shabby
SCROW n scroll
SCROWDGE vb squeeze
SCROWDGED > SCROWDGE
SCROWDGES > SCROWDGE
SCROWL vb old form of scroll
SCROWLE vb old form of scroll
SCROWLED > SCROWL
SCROWLES > SCROWLE
SCROWLING > SCROWL
SCROWLS > SCROWL
SCROWS > SCROW
SCROYLE n old word meaning wretch
SCROYLES > SCROYLE
SCRUB vb clean by rubbing, often with a hard brush and water ▷ n scrubbing ▷ adj stunted or inferior
SCRUBBED > SCRUB
SCRUBBER n woman who has many sexual partners
SCRUBBERS > SCRUBBER
SCRUBBIER > SCRUBBY
SCRUBBILY > SCRUBBY
SCRUBBING > SCRUB
SCRUBBY adj covered with scrub
SCRUBLAND n area of scrub vegetation
SCRUBS > SCRUB
SCRUFF same as > SCUM
SCRUFFED > SCRUFF
SCRUFFIER > SCRUFFY
SCRUFFILY > SCRUFFY
SCRUFFING > SCRUFF
SCRUFFS > SCRUFF
SCRUFFY adj unkempt or shabby
SCRUM n restarting of play in rugby ▷ vb form a scrum
SCRUMDOWN n forming of scrum in rugby
SCRUMMAGE same as > SCRUM
SCRUMMED > SCRUM
SCRUMMIE n informal word for a scrum half
SCRUMMIER > SCRUMMY
SCRUMMIES > SCRUMMIE
SCRUMMING > SCRUM
SCRUMMY adj delicious
SCRUMP vb steal (apples) from an orchard or garden
SCRUMPED > SCRUMP
SCRUMPIES > SCRUMPY
SCRUMPING > SCRUMP

SCRUMPLE vb crumple or crush
SCRUMPLED > SCRUMPLE
SCRUMPLES > SCRUMPLE
SCRUMPOX n skin infection spread among players in scrum
SCRUMPS > SCRUMP
SCRUMPY n rough dry cider
SCRUMS > SCRUM
SCRUNCH vb crumple or crunch or be crumpled or crunched ▷ n act or sound of scrunching
SCRUNCHED > SCRUNCH
SCRUNCHES > SCRUNCH
SCRUNCHIE n loop of elastic covered loosely with fabric, used to hold the hair in a ponytail
SCRUNCHY adj crunchy
SCRUNT n Scots word meaning stunted thing
SCRUNTIER > SCRUNT
SCRUNTS > SCRUNT
SCRUNTY > SCRUNT
SCRUPLE n doubt produced by one's conscience or morals ▷ vb have doubts on moral grounds
SCRUPLED > SCRUPLE
SCRUPLER > SCRUPLE
SCRUPLERS > SCRUPLE
SCRUPLES > SCRUPLE
SCRUPLING > SCRUPLE
SCRUTABLE adj open to or able to be understood by scrutiny
SCRUTATOR n person who examines or scrutinizes
SCRUTINY n close examination
SCRUTO n trapdoor on stage
SCRUTOIRE n writing desk
SCRUTOS > SCRUTO
SCRUZE vb old word meaning squeeze
SCRUZED > SCRUZE
SCRUZES > SCRUZE
SCRUZING > SCRUZE
SCRY vb divine, esp by crystal gazing
SCRYDE > SCRY
SCRYER > SCRY
SCRYERS > SCRY
SCRYING > SCRY
SCRYINGS > SCRY
SCRYNE n old form of shrine
SCRYNES > SCRYNE
SCUBA n apparatus used in diving ▷ vb dive using scuba equipment
SCUBAED > SCUBA
SCUBAING > SCUBA
SCUBAS > SCUBA
SCUCHIN n old form of scutcheon
SCUCHINS > SCUCHIN

SCUD vb move along swiftly ▷ n act of scudding
SCUDDALER n Scots word meaning leader of festivities
SCUDDED > SCUD
SCUDDER > SCUD
SCUDDERS > SCUD
SCUDDING > SCUD
SCUDDLE vb scuttle
SCUDDLED > SCUDDLE
SCUDDLES > SCUDDLE
SCUDDLING > SCUDDLE
SCUDI > SCUDO
SCUDLER n Scots word meaning leader of festivities
SCUDLERS > SCUDLER
SCUDO n any of several former Italian coins
SCUDS > SCUDO
SCUFF vb drag (the feet) while walking ▷ n mark caused by scuffing
SCUFFED > SCUFF
SCUFFER n type of sandal
SCUFFERS > SCUFFER
SCUFFING > SCUFF
SCUFFLE vb fight in a disorderly manner ▷ n disorderly struggle
SCUFFLED > SCUFFLE
SCUFFLER > SCUFFLE
SCUFFLERS > SCUFFLE
SCUFFLES > SCUFFLE
SCUFFLING n act of scuffling
SCUFFS > SCUFF
SCUFT n dialect word meaning nape of neck
SCUFTS > SCUFT
SCUG vb shelter
SCUGGED > SCUG
SCUGGING > SCUG
SCUGS > SCUG
SCUL n old form of school
SCULCH n rubbish
SCULCHES > SCULCH
SCULK vb old form of skulk
SCULKED > SCULK
SCULKER > SCULK
SCULKERS > SCULK
SCULKING > SCULK
SCULKS > SCULK
SCULL n small oar ▷ vb row (a boat) using sculls
SCULLE n old form of school
SCULLED > SCULL
SCULLER > SCULL
SCULLERS > SCULL
SCULLERY n small room where washing-up and other kitchen work is done
SCULLES > SCULLE
SCULLING > SCULL
SCULLINGS > SCULL
SCULLION n servant employed to do the hard work in a kitchen
SCULLIONS > SCULLION

SCULLS > SCULL
SCULP *variant of* > SCULPTURE
SCULPED > SCULP
SCULPIN *n* type of fish of the family which includes bullheads and sea scorpions
SCULPING > SCULP
SCULPINS > SCULPIN
SCULPS > SCULP
SCULPSIT *vb* (he or she) sculptured it: used formerly on sculptures next to a sculptor's name
SCULPT *same as* > SCULPTURE
SCULPTED > SCULPT
SCULPTING > SCULPT
SCULPTOR *n* person who makes sculptures
SCULPTORS > SCULPTOR
SCULPTS > SCULPT
SCULPTURE *n* art of making figures or designs in wood, stone, etc ▷ *vb* represent in sculpture
SCULS > SCUL
SCULTCH *same as* > SCULCH
SCULTCHES > SCULTCH
SCUM *n* impure or waste matter on the surface of a liquid ▷ *vb* remove scum from
SCUMBAG *n* offensive or despicable person
SCUMBAGS > SCUMBAG
SCUMBALL *n* contemptible person
SCUMBALLS > SCUMBALL
SCUMBER *vb* old word meaning defecate
SCUMBERED > SCUMBER
SCUMBERS > SCUMBER
SCUMBLE *vb* soften or blend (an outline or colour) with a thin upper coat of opaque colour ▷ *n* upper layer of colour applied in this way
SCUMBLED > SCUMBLE
SCUMBLES > SCUMBLE
SCUMBLING > SCUMBLE
SCUMFISH *vb* Scots word meaning disgust
SCUMLESS > SCUM
SCUMLIKE > SCUM
SCUMMED > SCUM
SCUMMER > SCUM
SCUMMERS > SCUM
SCUMMIER > SCUMMY
SCUMMIEST > SCUMMY
SCUMMILY > SCUMMY
SCUMMING > SCUM
SCUMMINGS > SCUM
SCUMMY *adj* of, resembling, consisting of, or covered with scum
SCUMS > SCUM
SCUNCHEON *n* inner part of a door jamb or window frame

SCUNDERED *adj* Irish dialect word for embarrassed
SCUNGE *vb* borrow ▷ *n* dirty or worthless person
SCUNGED > SCUNGE
SCUNGES > SCUNGE
SCUNGIER > SCUNGY
SCUNGIEST > SCUNGY
SCUNGILE *same as* > SCUNGILLE
SCUNGILI *same as* > SCUNGILLI
SCUNGILLE *n* meat of a conch, eaten as a delicacy
SCUNGILLI *n* seafood dish of conch
SCUNGING > SCUNGE
SCUNGY *adj* sordid or dirty
SCUNNER *vb* feel aversion ▷ *n* strong aversion
SCUNNERED *adj* annoyed, discontented, or bored
SCUNNERS > SCUNNER
SCUP *n* common sparid fish of American coastal regions of the Atlantic
SCUPPAUG *n* sea fish
SCUPPAUGS > SCUPPAUG
SCUPPER *vb* defeat or ruin ▷ *n* drain in the side of a ship
SCUPPERED > SCUPPER
SCUPPERS > SCUPPER
SCUPS > SCUP
SCUR *n* small unattached growth of horn at the site of a normal horn in cattle
SCURF *n* flaky skin on the scalp
SCURFIER > SCURF
SCURFIEST > SCURF
SCURFS > SCURF
SCURFY > SCURF
SCURRED > SCUR
SCURRIED > SCURRY
SCURRIER *n* old word meaning scout
SCURRIERS > SCURRIER
SCURRIES > SCURRY
SCURRIL *adj* old word meaning vulgar
SCURRILE *adj* old word meaning vulgar
SCURRING > SCUR
SCURRIOUR *n* old word meaning scout
SCURRY *vb* move hastily ▷ *n* act or sound of scurrying
SCURRYING > SCURRY
SCURS > SCUR
SCURVIER > SCURVY
SCURVIES > SCURVY
SCURVIEST > SCURVY
SCURVILY > SCURVY
SCURVY *n* disease caused by lack of vitamin C ▷ *adj* mean and despicable
SCUSE *shortened form of* > EXCUSE
SCUSED > SCUSE
SCUSES > SCUSE

SCUSING > SCUSE
SCUT *n* short tail of the hare, rabbit, or deer
SCUTA > SCUTUM
SCUTAGE *n* payment to a lord from his vassal in lieu of military service
SCUTAGES > SCUTAGE
SCUTAL > SCUTE
SCUTATE *adj* (of animals) having or covered with large bony or horny plates
SCUTATION > SCUTATE
SCUTCH *vb* separate the fibres from the woody part of (flax) by pounding ▷ *n* tool used for this
SCUTCHED > SCUTCH
SCUTCHEON *same as* > SHIELD
SCUTCHER *same as* > SCUTCH
SCUTCHERS > SCUTCHER
SCUTCHES > SCUTCH
SCUTCHING > SCUTCH
SCUTE *n* horny or chitinous plate that makes up part of the exoskeleton in armadillos, etc
SCUTELLA > SCUTELLUM
SCUTELLAR > SCUTELLUM
SCUTELLUM *n* last of three plates into which the notum of an insect's thorax is divided
SCUTES > SCUTE
SCUTIFORM *adj* (esp of plant parts) shaped like a shield
SCUTIGER *n* species of centipede
SCUTIGERS > SCUTIGER
SCUTS > SCUT
SCUTTER *informal word for* > SCURRY
SCUTTERED > SCUTTER
SCUTTERS > SCUTTER
SCUTTLE *n* fireside container for coal ▷ *vb* run with short quick steps
SCUTTLED > SCUTTLE
SCUTTLER > SCUTTLE
SCUTTLERS > SCUTTLE
SCUTTLES > SCUTTLE
SCUTTLING *n* act of scuttling
SCUTUM *n* middle of three plates into which the notum of an insect's thorax is divided
SCUTWORK *n* menial or dull work
SCUTWORKS > SCUTWORK
SCUZZ *n* dirt
SCUZZBAG *n* disagreeable or disgusting person
SCUZZBAGS > SCUZZBAG
SCUZZBALL *n* despicable person
SCUZZES > SCUZZ
SCUZZIER > SCUZZY
SCUZZIEST > SCUZZY

SCUZZY *adj* unkempt, dirty, or squalid
SCYBALA > SCYBALUM
SCYBALOUS > SCYBALUM
SCYBALUM *n* hard faeces in stomach
SCYE *n* Scots word meaning sleeve-hole
SCYES > SCYE
SCYPHATE *adj* shaped like cup
SCYPHI > SCYPHUS
SCYPHUS *n* ancient Greek two-handled drinking cup
SCYTALE *n* coded message in ancient Sparta
SCYTALES > SCYTALE
SCYTHE *n* long-handled tool with a curved blade for cutting grass ▷ *vb* cut with a scythe
SCYTHED > SCYTHE
SCYTHEMAN *n* scythe user
SCYTHEMEN > SCYTHEMAN
SCYTHER > SCYTHE
SCYTHERS > SCYTHE
SCYTHES > SCYTHE
SCYTHING > SCYTHE
SDAINE *vb* old form of disdain
SDAINED > SDAINE
SDAINES > SDAINE
SDAYN *vb* old form of disdain
SDAYNED > SDAYN
SDAYNING > SDAYN
SDAYNS > SDAYN
SDEIGN *vb* old form of disdain
SDEIGNE *vb* old form of disdain
SDEIGNED > SDEIGN
SDEIGNES > SDEIGNE
SDEIGNING > SDEIGN
SDEIGNS > SDEIGN
SDEIN *vb* old form of disdain
SDEINED > SDEIN
SDEINING > SDEIN
SDEINS > SDEIN
SEA *n* mass of salt water covering three quarters of the earth's surface
SEABAG *n* canvas bag for holding a sailor's belongings
SEABAGS > SEABAG
SEABANK *n* sea shore
SEABANKS > SEABANK
SEABEACH *n* beach at seaside
SEABED *n* bottom of sea
SEABEDS > SEABED
SEABIRD *n* bird that lives on the sea
SEABIRDS > SEABIRD
SEABLITE *n* prostrate annual plant of the goosefoot family
SEABLITES > SEABLITE
SEABOARD *n* coast

S

SEABOARDS > SEABOARD
SEABOOT n sailor's waterproof boot
SEABOOTS > SEABOOT
SEABORNE adj carried on or by the sea
SEABOTTLE n type of seaweed
SEACOAST n land bordering on the sea
SEACOASTS > SEACOAST
SEACOCK n valve in the hull of a vessel below the water line
SEACOCKS > SEACOCK
SEACRAFT n skill as sailor
SEACRAFTS > SEACRAFT
SEACUNNY n quartermaster on Indian ship
SEADOG another word for > FOGBOW
SEADOGS > SEADOG
SEADROME n aerodrome floating on sea
SEADROMES > SEADROME
SEAFARER n traveller who goes by sea
SEAFARERS > SEAFARER
SEAFARING adj working or travelling by sea ▷ n act of travelling by sea
SEAFLOOR n bottom of the sea
SEAFLOORS > SEAFLOOR
SEAFOAM n foam formed on the sea
SEAFOAMS > SEAFOAM
SEAFOLK n people who sail sea
SEAFOLKS > SEAFOLK
SEAFOOD n edible saltwater fish or shellfish
SEAFOODS > SEAFOOD
SEAFOWL n seabird
SEAFOWLS > SEAFOWL
SEAFRONT n built-up area facing the sea
SEAFRONTS > SEAFRONT
SEAGIRT adj surrounded by the sea
SEAGOING adj built for travelling on the sea
SEAGRASS n grass which grows by or in the sea
SEAGULL n gull
SEAGULLS > SEAGULL
SEAHAWK n skua
SEAHAWKS > SEAHAWK
SEAHOG n porpoise
SEAHOGS > SEAHOG
SEAHORSE n marine fish with a horselike head that swims upright
SEAHORSES > SEAHORSE
SEAHOUND n dogfish
SEAHOUNDS > SEAHOUND
SEAKALE n European coastal plant
SEAKALES > SEAKALE
SEAL n piece of wax, etc attached to a document as a mark of authentication

▷ vb close with or as if with a seal
SEALABLE > SEAL
SEALANT n any substance used for sealing
SEALANTS > SEALANT
SEALCH Scots word for > SEAL
SEALCHS > SEALCH
SEALED adj (of a road) having a hard surface
SEALER n person or thing that seals
SEALERIES > SEALERY
SEALERS > SEALER
SEALERY n occupation of hunting seals
SEALGH Scots word for > SEAL
SEALGHS > SEALGH
SEALIFT vb transport by ship
SEALIFTED > SEALIFT
SEALIFTS > SEALIFT
SEALINE n company running regular sailings
SEALINES > SEALINE
SEALING > SEAL
SEALINGS > SEAL
SEALLIKE adj resembling a seal
SEALPOINT n popular variety of Siamese cat
SEALS > SEAL
SEALSKIN n skin or prepared fur of a seal, used to make coats
SEALSKINS > SEALSKIN
SEALWAX n sealing wax
SEALWAXES > SEALWAX
SEALYHAM n type of short-legged terrier
SEALYHAMS > SEALYHAM
SEAM n line where two edges are joined, as by stitching ▷ vb mark with furrows or wrinkles
SEAMAID n mermaid
SEAMAIDS > SEAMAID
SEAMAN n sailor
SEAMANLY > SEAMAN
SEAMARK n conspicuous object on a shore used as a guide
SEAMARKS > SEAMARK
SEAME n old word meaning grease
SEAMED > SEAM
SEAMEN > SEAMAN
SEAMER n bowler who makes the ball bounce on its seam
SEAMERS > SEAMER
SEAMES > SEAME
SEAMFREE adj having no seam
SEAMIER > SEAMY
SEAMIEST > SEAMY
SEAMINESS > SEAMY
SEAMING > SEAM
SEAMINGS > SEAMING
SEAMLESS adj (of a garment) without seams

SEAMLIKE > SEAM
SEAMOUNT n submarine mountain rising more than 1000 metres above the surrounding ocean floor
SEAMOUNTS > SEAMOUNT
SEAMS > SEAM
SEAMSET n tool for flattening seams in metal
SEAMSETS > SEAMSET
SEAMSTER n person who sews
SEAMSTERS > SEAMSTER
SEAMY adj sordid
SEAN vb fish with seine net
SEANCE n meeting at which spiritualists attempt to communicate with the dead
SEANCES > SEANCE
SEANED > SEAN
SEANING > SEAN
SEANNACHY n Highland genealogist, chronicler, or bard
SEANS > SEAN
SEAPIECE n artwork depicting sea
SEAPIECES > SEAPIECE
SEAPLANE n aircraft designed to take off from and land on water
SEAPLANES > SEAPLANE
SEAPORT n town or city with a harbour for boats and ships
SEAPORTS > SEAPORT
SEAQUAKE n agitation and disturbance of the sea caused by an earthquake at the sea bed
SEAQUAKES > SEAQUAKE
SEAQUARIA pl n areas of salt water where sea animals are kept
SEAR vb scorch, burn the surface of ▷ n mark caused by searing ▷ adj dried up
SEARAT n pirate
SEARATS > SEARAT
SEARCE vb sift
SEARCED > SEARCE
SEARCES > SEARCE
SEARCH vb examine closely in order to find something ▷ n searching
SEARCHED > SEARCH
SEARCHER > SEARCH
SEARCHERS > SEARCH
SEARCHES > SEARCH
SEARCHING n act of searching
SEARCING > SEARCE
SEARE adj old word meaning dry and withered
SEARED > SEAR
SEARER > SEAR
SEAREST > SEAR
SEARING > SEAR
SEARINGLY > SEAR
SEARINGS > SEAR
SEARNESS > SEAR

SEAROBIN n type of American gurnard
SEAROBINS > SEAROBIN
SEARS > SEAR
SEAS > SEA
SEASCAPE n picture of a scene at sea
SEASCAPES > SEASCAPE
SEASCOUT n member of seagoing scouts
SEASCOUTS > SEASCOUT
SEASE vb old form of seize
SEASED > SEASE
SEASES > SEASE
SEASHELL n empty shell of a mollusc
SEASHELLS > SEASHELL
SEASHORE n land bordering on the sea
SEASHORES > SEASHORE
SEASICK adj suffering from nausea caused by the motion of a ship
SEASICKER > SEASICK
SEASIDE n area, esp a holiday resort, on the coast
SEASIDES > SEASIDE
SEASING > SEASE
SEASON n one of four divisions of the year ▷ vb flavour with salt, herbs, etc
SEASONAL adj depending on or varying with the seasons ▷ n seasonal thing
SEASONALS > SEASONAL
SEASONED > SEASON
SEASONER > SEASON
SEASONERS > SEASON
SEASONING n salt, herbs, etc added to food to enhance flavour
SEASONS > SEASON
SEASPEAK n language used by sailors
SEASPEAKS > SEASPEAK
SEASTRAND n seashore
SEASURE n old form of seizure
SEASURES > SEASURE
SEAT n thing designed or used for sitting on ▷ vb cause to sit
SEATBACK n back of seat
SEATBACKS > SEATBACK
SEATBELT n safety belt in vehicle
SEATBELTS > SEATBELT
SEATED > SEAT
SEATER n person or thing that seats
SEATERS > SEATER
SEATING n supply or arrangement of seats ▷ adj of or relating to the provision of places to sit
SEATINGS > SEATING
SEATLESS > SEAT
SEATMATE n person sitting in next seat
SEATMATES > SEATMATE

SEATRAIN n ship that can carry a train
SEATRAINS > SEATRAIN
SEATROUT n trout living in the sea
SEATROUTS > SEATROUT
SEATS > SEAT
SEATWORK n school work done at pupils' desks
SEATWORKS > SEATWORK
SEAWALL n wall built to prevent encroachment or erosion by the sea
SEAWALLED adj having a seawall
SEAWALLS > SEAWALL
SEAWAN n shell beads used by certain North American Indians as money
SEAWANS > SEAWAN
SEAWANT n Native American name for silver coins
SEAWANTS > SEAWANT
SEAWARD same as > SEAWARDS
SEAWARDLY > SEAWARD
SEAWARDS adv towards the sea
SEAWARE n any of numerous large coarse seaweeds
SEAWARES > SEAWARE
SEAWATER n water from sea
SEAWATERS > SEAWATER
SEAWAY n waterway giving access to an inland port
SEAWAYS > SEAWAY
SEAWEED n plant growing in the sea
SEAWEEDS > SEAWEED
SEAWEEDY adj full of seaweed
SEAWIFE n variety of sea fish
SEAWIVES > SEAWIFE
SEAWOMAN n mermaid
SEAWOMEN > SEAWOMAN
SEAWORM n marine worm
SEAWORMS > SEAWORM
SEAWORTHY adj (of a ship) in fit condition for a sea voyage
SEAZE vb old form of seize
SEAZED > SEAZE
SEAZES > SEAZE
SEAZING > SEAZE
SEBACEOUS adj of, like, or secreting fat or oil
SEBACIC adj derived from sebacic acid, a white crystalline acid
SEBASIC same as > SEBACIC
SEBATE n salt of sebacic acid
SEBATES > SEBATE
SEBESTEN n Asian tree
SEBESTENS > SEBESTEN
SEBIFIC adj producing fat

SEBORRHEA n skin disease in which excessive oil is secreted
SEBUM n oily substance secreted by the sebaceous glands
SEBUMS > SEBUM
SEBUNDIES > SEBUNDY
SEBUNDY n irregular soldier in India
SEC same as > SECANT
SECALOSE n type of sugar
SECALOSES > SECALOSE
SECANT n (in trigonometry) the ratio of the length of the hypotenuse to the length of the adjacent side
SECANTLY > SECANT
SECANTS > SECANT
SECATEUR n secateurs
SECATEURS pl n small pruning shears
SECCO n wall painting done on dried plaster with tempera
SECCOS > SECCO
SECEDE vb withdraw formally from a political alliance or federation
SECEDED > SECEDE
SECEDER > SECEDE
SECEDERS > SECEDE
SECEDES > SECEDE
SECEDING > SECEDE
SECERN vb (of a gland or follicle) to secrete
SECERNED > SECERN
SECERNENT > SECERN
SECERNING > SECERN
SECERNS > SECERN
SECESH n secessionist in US Civil War
SECESHER n secessionist in US Civil War
SECESHERS > SECESHER
SECESHES > SECESH
SECESSION n act of seceding
SECH n hyperbolic secant
SECHS > SECH
SECKEL variant of > SECKLE
SECKELS > SECKEL
SECKLE n type of pear
SECKLES > SECKLE
SECLUDE vb keep (a person) from contact with others
SECLUDED adj private, sheltered
SECLUDES > SECLUDE
SECLUDING > SECLUDE
SECLUSION n state of being secluded
SECLUSIVE adj tending to seclude
SECO adj (of wine) dry
SECODONT n animal with cutting back teeth
SECODONTS > SECODONT
SECONAL n tradename for secobarbital
SECONALS > SECONAL

SECOND adj coming directly after the first ▷ n person or thing coming second ▷ vb express formal support for (a motion proposed in a meeting)
SECONDARY adj of less importance ▷ n person or thing that is secondary
SECONDE n second of eight positions from which a parry or attack can be made in fencing
SECONDED > SECOND
SECONDEE n person who is seconded
SECONDEES > SECONDEE
SECONDER > SECOND
SECONDERS > SECOND
SECONDES > SECONDE
SECONDI > SECONDO
SECONDING n act of seconding
SECONDLY same as > SECOND
SECONDO n left-hand part in a piano duet
SECONDS > SECOND
SECPAR n distance unit in astronomy
SECPARS > SECPAR
SECRECIES > SECRECY
SECRECY n state of being secret
SECRET adj kept from the knowledge of others ▷ n something kept secret
SECRETA n secretions
SECRETAGE n use of mercury in treating furs
SECRETARY n person who deals with correspondence and general clerical work
SECRETE vb (of an organ, gland, etc) produce and release (a substance)
SECRETED > SECRETE
SECRETER > SECRET
SECRETES > SECRETE
SECRETEST > SECRET
SECRETIN n peptic hormone secreted by the mucosae of the duodenum and jejunum
SECRETING > SECRETE
SECRETINS > SECRETIN
SECRETION n substance that is released from a cell, organ, or gland
SECRETIVE adj inclined to keep things secret
SECRETLY > SECRET
SECRETOR > SECRETE
SECRETORS > SECRETE
SECRETORY adj of, relating to, or producing a secretion
SECRETS > SECRET
SECS > SEC
SECT n subdivision of a religious or political group
SECTARIAL > SECT

SECTARIAN adj of a sect ▷ n member of a sect
SECTARIES > SECTARY
SECTARY n member of a sect
SECTATOR n member of sect
SECTATORS > SECTATOR
SECTILE adj able to be cut smoothly
SECTILITY > SECTILE
SECTION n part cut off ▷ vb cut or divide into sections
SECTIONAL adj concerned with a particular area or group within a country or community
SECTIONED > SECTION
SECTIONS > SECTION
SECTOR n part or subdivision ▷ vb divide into sectors
SECTORAL > SECTOR
SECTORED > SECTOR
SECTORIAL adj of or relating to a sector
SECTORING > SECTOR
SECTORISE same as > SECTORIZE
SECTORIZE vb split into sectors
SECTORS > SECTOR
SECTS > SECT
SECULA > SECULUM
SECULAR adj worldly, as opposed to sacred ▷ n member of the secular clergy
SECULARLY > SECULAR
SECULARS > SECULAR
SECULUM n age in astronomy
SECULUMS > SECULUM
SECUND adj having or designating parts arranged on or turned to one side of the axis
SECUNDINE n one of the two integuments surrounding the ovule of a plant
SECUNDLY > SECUND
SECUNDUM adj according to
SECURABLE > SECURE
SECURANCE > SECURE
SECURE adj free from danger ▷ vb obtain
SECURED > SECURE
SECURELY > SECURE
SECURER > SECURE
SECURERS > SECURE
SECURES > SECURE
SECUREST > SECURE
SECURING > SECURE
SECURITAN n person believing they are secure
SECURITY n precautions against theft, espionage, or other danger
SED old spelling of > SAID
SEDAN same as > SALOON

SEDANS > SEDAN
SEDARIM > SEDER
SEDATE adj calm and dignified ▷ vb give a sedative drug to
SEDATED > SEDATE
SEDATELY > SEDATE
SEDATER > SEDATE
SEDATES > SEDATE
SEDATEST > SEDATE
SEDATING > SEDATE
SEDATION n state of calm, esp when brought about by sedatives
SEDATIONS > SEDATION
SEDATIVE adj having a soothing or calming effect ▷ n sedative drug
SEDATIVES > SEDATIVE
SEDENT adj seated
SEDENTARY adj done sitting down, involving little exercise
SEDER n Jewish ceremonial meal held on the first night or first two nights of Passover
SEDERS > SEDER
SEDERUNT n sitting of an ecclesiastical assembly, court, etc
SEDERUNTS > SEDERUNT
SEDES Latin word for > SEAT
SEDGE n coarse grasslike plant growing on wet ground
SEDGED adj having sedge
SEDGELAND n land covered with sedge
SEDGES > SEDGE
SEDGIER > SEDGE
SEDGIEST > SEDGE
SEDGY > SEDGE
SEDILE n seat for clergy in church
SEDILIA n group of three seats where the celebrant and ministers sit during High Mass
SEDILIUM n seat for clergy in church
SEDIMENT n matter which settles to the bottom of a liquid
SEDIMENTS > SEDIMENT
SEDITION n speech or action encouraging rebellion against the government
SEDITIONS > SEDITION
SEDITIOUS adj of, like, or causing sedition
SEDUCE vb persuade into sexual intercourse
SEDUCED > SEDUCE
SEDUCER n person who entices, allures, or seduces
SEDUCERS > SEDUCER
SEDUCES > SEDUCE
SEDUCIBLE > SEDUCE
SEDUCING > SEDUCE
SEDUCINGS > SEDUCE
SEDUCIVE adj seductive

SEDUCTION n act of seducing or the state of being seduced
SEDUCTIVE adj (of a woman) sexually attractive
SEDUCTOR n person who seduces
SEDUCTORS > SEDUCTOR
SEDULITY > SEDULOUS
SEDULOUS adj diligent or persevering
SEDUM n rock plant
SEDUMS > SEDUM
SEE vb perceive with the eyes or mind ▷ n diocese of a bishop
SEEABLE > SEE
SEECATCH n male seal in Aleutians
SEED n mature fertilized grain of a plant ▷ vb sow with seed
SEEDBED n area of soil prepared for the growing of seedlings before they are transplanted
SEEDBEDS > SEEDBED
SEEDBOX n part of plant that contains seeds
SEEDBOXES > SEEDBED
SEEDCAKE n sweet cake flavoured with caraway seeds and lemon rind or essence
SEEDCAKES > SEEDCAKE
SEEDCASE n part of a fruit enclosing the seeds
SEEDCASES > SEEDCASE
SEEDEATER n bird feeding on seeds
SEEDED > SEED
SEEDER n person or thing that seeds
SEEDERS > SEEDER
SEEDHEAD n flowerhead in a seed
SEEDHEADS > SEEDHEAD
SEEDIER > SEEDY
SEEDIEST > SEEDY
SEEDILY > SEEDY
SEEDINESS > SEEDY
SEEDING > SEED
SEEDINGS > SEED
SEEDLESS > SEED
SEEDLIKE > SEED
SEEDLING n young plant raised from a seed
SEEDLINGS > SEEDLING
SEEDLIP n basket holding seeds to be sown
SEEDLIPS > SEEDLIP
SEEDMAN n seller of seeds
SEEDMEN > SEEDMAN
SEEDNESS n old word meaning sowing of seeds
SEEDPOD n carpel enclosing the seeds of a flowering plant
SEEDPODS > SEEDPOD
SEEDS > SEED
SEEDSMAN n seller of seeds
SEEDSMEN > SEEDSMAN

SEEDSTOCK n livestock used for breeding
SEEDTIME n season when seeds are sown
SEEDTIMES > SEEDTIME
SEEDY adj shabby
SEEING > SEE
SEEINGS > SEE
SEEK vb try to find or obtain
SEEKER > SEEK
SEEKERS > SEEK
SEEKING > SEEK
SEEKS > SEEK
SEEL vb sew up the eyelids of (a hawk or falcon) so as to render it quiet and tame
SEELD adj old word meaning rare
SEELED > SEEL
SEELIE pl n good benevolent fairies
SEELIER > SEELY
SEELIEST > SEELY
SEELING > SEEL
SEELINGS > SEEL
SEELS > SEEL
SEELY adj old word meaning happy
SEEM vb appear to be
SEEMED > SEEM
SEEMER > SEEM
SEEMERS > SEEM
SEEMING adj apparent but not real ▷ n outward or false appearance
SEEMINGLY adv in appearance but not necessarily in actuality
SEEMINGS > SEEMING
SEEMLESS adj old word meaning unseemly
SEEMLIER > SEEMLY
SEEMLIEST > SEEMLY
SEEMLIHED n old word meaning seemliness
SEEMLY adj proper or fitting ▷ adv properly or decorously
SEEMLYHED n old word meaning seemliness
SEEMS > SEEM
SEEN > SEE
SEEP vb trickle through slowly, ooze ▷ n small spring or place where water, oil, etc, has oozed through the ground
SEEPAGE n act or process of seeping
SEEPAGES > SEEPAGE
SEEPED > SEEP
SEEPIER > SEEPY
SEEPIEST > SEEPY
SEEPING > SEEP
SEEPS > SEEP
SEEPY adj tending to seep
SEER n person who sees
SEERESS > SEER
SEERESSES > SEER
SEERS > SEER
SEES > SEE

SEESAW n plank balanced in the middle so that two people seated on either end ride up and down alternately ▷ vb move up and down
SEESAWED > SEESAW
SEESAWING > SEESAW
SEESAWS > SEESAW
SEETHE vb be very agitated ▷ n act or state of seething
SEETHED > SEETHE
SEETHER > SEETHE
SEETHERS > SEETHE
SEETHES > SEETHE
SEETHING adj boiling or foaming as if boiling
SEETHINGS > SEETHING
SEEWING n suing
SEEWINGS > SEEWING
SEFER n scrolls of the Law
SEG n metal stud on shoe sole
SEGAR n cigar
SEGARS > SEGAR
SEGETAL adj (of weeds) growing amongst crops
SEGGAR n box in which pottery is baked
SEGGARS > SEGGAR
SEGHOL n pronunciation mark in Hebrew
SEGHOLATE n vowel sound in Hebrew
SEGHOLS > SEGHOL
SEGMENT n one of several sections into which something may be divided ▷ vb divide into segments
SEGMENTAL adj of, like, or having the form of a segment
SEGMENTED > SEGMENT
SEGMENTS > SEGMENT
SEGNI > SEGNO
SEGNO n sign at the beginning or end of a section directed to be repeated
SEGNOS > SEGNO
SEGO n American variety of lily
SEGOL variant of > SEGHOL
SEGOLATE variant of > SEGHOLATE
SEGOLATES > SEGOLATE
SEGOLS > SEGOL
SEGOS > SEGO
SEGREANT adj having raised wings in heraldry
SEGREGANT n organism different because of segregation
SEGREGATE vb set apart
SEGS > SEG
SEGUE vb proceed from one section or piece of music to another without a break ▷ n practice or an instance of playing music in this way
SEGUED > SEGUE
SEGUEING > SEGUE

S

SEGUES > SEGUE
SEGUGIO *n* an Italian breed of dog
SEGUGIOS > SEGUGIO
SEHRI *n* meal eaten before sunrise by Muslims fasting during Ramadan
SEHRIS > SEHRI
SEI *n* type of rorqual
SEICENTO *n* 17th century with reference to Italian art and literature
SEICENTOS > SEICENTO
SEICHE *n* periodic oscillation of the surface of an enclosed or semienclosed body of water
SEICHES > SEICHE
SEIDEL *n* vessel for drinking beer
SEIDELS > SEIDEL
SEIF *n* long ridge of blown sand in a desert
SEIFS > SEIF
SEIGNEUR *n* feudal lord
SEIGNEURS > SEIGNEUR
SEIGNEURY *n* estate of a seigneur
SEIGNIOR *n* (in England) the lord of a seigniory
SEIGNIORS > SEIGNIOR
SEIGNIORY *n* (in England) the fee or manor of a seignior
SEIGNORAL *adj* relating to the quality of being a lord
SEIGNORY *n* lordship
SEIK *Scot word for* > SICK
SEIKER > SEIK
SEIKEST > SEIK
SEIL *vb* dialect word meaning strain
SEILED > SEIL
SEILING > SEIL
SEILS > SEIL
SEINE *n* large fishing net that hangs vertically from floats ▷ *vb* catch (fish) using this net
SEINED > SEINE
SEINER > SEINE
SEINERS > SEINE
SEINES > SEINE
SEINING > SEINE
SEININGS > SEINE
SEIR *n* fish of Indian seas
SEIRS > SEIR
SEIS > SEI
SEISABLE > SEISE
SEISE *vb* put into legal possession of (property, etc)
SEISED > SEISE
SEISER > SEISE
SEISERS > SEISE
SEISES > SEISE
SEISIN *n* feudal possession of an estate in land
SEISING > SEISE
SEISINGS > SEISE

SEISINS > SEISIN
SEISM *n* earthquake
SEISMAL *adj* of earthquakes
SEISMIC *adj* relating to earthquakes
SEISMICAL *same as* > SEISMIC
SEISMISM *n* occurrence of earthquakes
SEISMISMS > SEISMISM
SEISMS > SEISM
SEISOR *n* person who takes seisin
SEISORS > SEISOR
SEISURE *n* act of seisin
SEISURES > SEISURE
SEITAN *same as* > SEITEN
SEITANS > SEITAN
SEITEN *n* gluten from wheat
SEITENS > SEITEN
SEITIES > SEITY
SEITY *n* selfhood
SEIZA *n* traditional Japanese kneeling position
SEIZABLE > SEIZE
SEIZAS > SEIZA
SEIZE *vb* take hold of forcibly or quickly
SEIZED > SEIZE
SEIZER > SEIZE
SEIZERS > SEIZE
SEIZES > SEIZE
SEIZIN *same as* > SEISIN
SEIZING *n* binding used for holding together two ropes, two spars, etc
SEIZINGS > SEIZING
SEIZINS > SEIZIN
SEIZOR *n* person who takes seisin
SEIZORS > SEIZOR
SEIZURE *n* sudden violent attack of an illness
SEIZURES > SEIZURE
SEJANT *adj* (of a beast) shown seated
SEJEANT *same as* > SEJANT
SEKOS *n* holy place
SEKOSES > SEKOS
SEKT *n* German sparkling wine
SEKTS > SEKT
SEL *Scot word for* > SELF
SELACHIAN *adj* relating to a large subclass of cartilaginous fishes including the sharks, rays, dogfish, and skates ▷ *n* any fish belonging to this subclass
SELADANG *n* Malaysian tapir
SELADANGS > SELADANG
SELAH *n* Hebrew word of unknown meaning occurring in the Old Testament psalms
SELAHS > SELAH
SELAMLIK *n* men's quarters in Turkish house
SELAMLIKS > SELAMLIK

SELCOUTH *adj* old word meaning strange
SELD *adj* old word meaning rare
SELDOM *adv* not often, rarely
SELDOMLY > SELDOM
SELDSEEN *adj* old word meaning seldom seen
SELDSHOWN *adj* old word meaning seldom shown
SELE *n* old word meaning happiness
SELECT *vb* pick out or choose ▷ *adj* chosen in preference to others
SELECTA *n* disc jockey
SELECTAS > SELECTA
SELECTED > SELECT
SELECTEE *n* person who is selected, esp for military service
SELECTEES > SELECTEE
SELECTING > SELECT
SELECTION *n* selecting
SELECTIVE *adj* chosen or choosing carefully
SELECTLY > SELECT
SELECTMAN *n* any of the members of the local boards of most New England towns
SELECTMEN > SELECTMAN
SELECTOR *n* person or thing that selects
SELECTORS > SELECTOR
SELECTS > SELECT
SELENATE *n* any salt or ester formed by replacing one or both of the hydrogens of selenic acid with metal ions or organic groups
SELENATES > SELENATE
SELENIAN *adj* of the moon
SELENIC *adj* of or containing selenium, esp in the hexavalent state
SELENIDE *n* compound containing selenium
SELENIDES > SELENIDE
SELENIOUS *adj* of or containing selenium in the divalent or tetravalent state
SELENITE *n* colourless glassy variety of gypsum
SELENITES > SELENITE
SELENITIC > SELENITE
SELENIUM *n* nonmetallic element with photoelectric properties
SELENIUMS > SELENIUM
SELENOSES > SELENOSIS
SELENOSIS *n* poisoned condition caused by selenium
SELENOUS *same as* > SELENIOUS
SELES > SELE

SELF *n* distinct individuality or identity of a person or thing ▷ *pron* myself, yourself, himself, or herself ▷ *vb* reproduce by oneself
SELFDOM *n* selfhood
SELFDOMS > SELFDOM
SELFED > SELF
SELFHEAL *n* low-growing European herbaceous plant
SELFHEALS > SELFHEAL
SELFHOOD *n* state of having a distinct identity
SELFHOODS > SELFHOOD
SELFIE *n* photograph taken by pointing a camera at oneself
SELFIES > SELFIE
SELFING > SELF
SELFINGS > SELF
SELFISH *adj* caring too much about oneself and not enough about others
SELFISHLY > SELFISH
SELFISM *n* emphasis on self
SELFISMS > SELFISM
SELFIST > SELFISM
SELFISTS > SELFISM
SELFLESS *adj* unselfish
SELFNESS *n* egotism
SELFS > SELF
SELFSAME *adj* very same
SELFWARD *adj* toward self
SELFWARDS *adv* towards self
SELICTAR *n* Turkish sword-bearer
SELICTARS > SELICTAR
SELKIE *same as* > SILKIE
SELKIES > SELKIE
SELL *vb* exchange (something) for money ▷ *n* manner of selling
SELLA *n* area of bone in body
SELLABLE > SELL
SELLAE > SELLA
SELLAS > SELLA
SELLE *n* old word meaning seat
SELLER *n* person who sells
SELLERS > SELLER
SELLES > SELLE
SELLING *n* providing goods or services to customers in exchange for money
SELLINGS > SELLING
SELLOFF *n* act of selling cheaply
SELLOFFS > SELLOFF
SELLOTAPE *n* tradename for a type of transparent adhesive tape
SELLOUT *n* performance of a show etc for which all the tickets are sold
SELLOUTS > SELLOUT
SELLS > SELL
SELS > SEL

S

SELSYN same as
> SYNCHRO
SELSYNS > SELSYN
SELTZER n natural
effervescent water
containing minerals
SELTZERS > SELTZER
SELVA n dense equatorial
forest
SELVAGE n edge of cloth,
woven so as to prevent
unravelling ▷ vb edge or
border
SELVAGED > SELVAGE
SELVAGEE n rope used as
strap
SELVAGEES > SELVAGEE
SELVAGES > SELVAGE
SELVAGING > SELVAGE
SELVAS > SELVA
SELVEDGE same as
> SELVAGE
SELVEDGED > SELVEDGE
SELVEDGES > SELVEDGE
SELVES > SELF
SEMAINIER n chest of
drawers
SEMANTEME same as
> SEMEME
SEMANTIC adj relating to
the meaning of words
SEMANTICS n study of
linguistic meaning
SEMANTIDE n type of
molecule
SEMANTRA > SEMANTRON
SEMANTRON n bar struck
instead of bell in Orthodox
church
SEMAPHORE n system of
signalling by holding two
flags in different positions
to represent letters of the
alphabet ▷ vb signal
(information) by
semaphore
SEMATIC adj acting as a
warning, esp to potential
predators
SEMBLABLE adj
resembling or similar
▷ n something that
resembles another thing
SEMBLABLY
> SEMBLABLE
SEMBLANCE n outward or
superficial appearance
SEMBLANT n semblance
SEMBLANTS > SEMBLANT
SEMBLE vb seem
SEMBLED > SEMBLE
SEMBLES > SEMBLE
SEMBLING > SEMBLE
SEME adj dotted (with)
SEMEE variant of > SEME
SEMEED adj seme
SEMEIA > SEMEION
SEMEION n unit of metre
in ancient poetry
SEMEIOTIC same as
> SEMIOTIC
SEMEME n meaning of a
morpheme
SEMEMES > SEMEME

SEMEMIC > SEMEME
SEMEN n sperm-carrying
fluid produced by male
animals
SEMENS > SEMEN
SEMES > SEME
SEMESTER n either of two
divisions of the academic
year
SEMESTERS > SEMESTER
SEMESTRAL > SEMESTER
SEMI n semidetached
house
SEMIANGLE n half angle
SEMIARID adj denoting
land that lies on the edges
of a desert but has a
slightly higher rainfall
SEMIBALD adj partly bald
SEMIBOLD adj denoting a
weight of typeface
between medium and
bold face ▷ n semibold
type
SEMIBOLDS > SEMIBOLD
SEMIBREVE n musical
note four beats long
SEMIBULL n papal bull
issued before coronation
SEMIBULLS > SEMIBULL
SEMICOLON n
punctuation mark (;)
SEMICOMA n condition
similar to a coma
SEMICOMAS > SEMICOMA
SEMICURED adj partly
cured
SEMIDEAF adj partly deaf
SEMIDEIFY vb treat
almost as god
SEMIDOME n half-dome,
esp one used to cover a
semicircular apse
SEMIDOMED adj having
semidome
SEMIDOMES > SEMIDOME
SEMIDRIER > SEMIDRY
SEMIDRY adj partly dry
SEMIDWARF adj smaller
than standard variety
SEMIE n historical name
for a student in second
year at a Scottish
university
SEMIERECT adj partly
erect
SEMIES > SEMIE
SEMIFINAL n match or
round before the final
SEMIFIT adj not fully fit
SEMIFLUID adj having
properties between those
of a liquid and those of a
solid ▷ n substance that
has such properties
because of high viscosity
SEMIGALA adj
characterized by quite a
lot of celebration and fun
▷ n occasion that is festive
but not to the degree of a
gala
SEMIGALAS > SEMIGALA
SEMIGLOBE n half globe

SEMIGLOSS adj (of paint)
giving finish between matt
and gloss
SEMIGROUP n type of set
in mathematics
SEMIHARD adj partly hard
SEMIHIGH adj moderately
high
SEMIHOBO n person
looking almost like hobo
SEMIHOBOS > SEMIHOBO
SEMILLON n grape used
to make wine
SEMILLONS > SEMILLON
SEMILOG adj
semilogarithmic
SEMILUNAR adj shaped
like a crescent or
half-moon
SEMILUNE n half-moon
shape
SEMILUNES > SEMILUNE
SEMIMAT adj semimatt
SEMIMATT adj with
surface midway between
matt and gloss
SEMIMATTE adj semimatt
SEMIMETAL n metal not
fully malleable
SEMIMICRO adj using
microwaves
SEMIMILD adj somewhat
mild
SEMIMOIST adj slightly
wet
SEMIMUTE adj having
speech impairment
through hearing loss
▷ n person who is
semimute
SEMIMUTES > SEMIMUTE
SEMINA > SEMEN
SEMINAL adj original and
influential
SEMINALLY > SEMINAL
SEMINAR n meeting of a
group of students for
discussion
SEMINARS > SEMINAR
SEMINARY n college for
priests
SEMINATE vb sow
SEMINATED > SEMINATE
SEMINATES > SEMINATE
SEMINOMA n malignant
tumour of the testicle
SEMINOMAD n person
living partly nomadic life
SEMINOMAS > SEMINOMA
SEMINUDE adj partly nude
SEMIOLOGY same as
> SEMIOTICS
SEMIOPEN adj half-open
SEMIOSES > SEMIOSIS
SEMIOSIS n action
involving establishing
relationship between
signs
SEMIOTIC adj relating to
signs and symbols, esp
spoken or written signs
SEMIOTICS n study of
human communications,
esp signs and symbols

SEMIOVAL adj shaped like
half of oval
SEMIPED n measure in
poetic metre
SEMIPEDS > SEMIPED
SEMIPIOUS adj quite
pious
SEMIPLUME n type of bird
feather
SEMIPOLAR adj as in
semipolar bond type of
chemical bond
SEMIPRO n
semiprofessional
SEMIPROS > SEMIPRO
SEMIRAW adj not fully
cooked or processed
SEMIRIGID adj (of an
airship) maintaining shape
by means of a main
supporting keel and
internal gas pressure
SEMIROUND adj with one
flat side and one round
side ▷ n something
semiround
SEMIRURAL adj partly
rural
SEMIS > SEMI
SEMISES > SEMI
SEMISOFT adj partly soft
SEMISOLID adj having a
viscosity and rigidity
intermediate between
that of a solid and a liquid
▷ n substance in this state
SEMISOLUS n
advertisement that
appears on the same page
as another advertisement
but not adjacent to it
SEMISTIFF adj partly
stiff
SEMISWEET adj partly
sweet
SEMITAR old spelling of
> SCIMITAR
SEMITARS > SEMITAR
SEMITAUR old spelling of
> SCIMITAR
SEMITAURS > SEMITAR
SEMITIST n student of
Semitic languages and
culture
SEMITISTS > SEMITIST
SEMITONAL > SEMITONE
SEMITONE n smallest
interval between two
notes in Western music
SEMITONES > SEMITONE
SEMITONIC > SEMITONE
SEMITRUCK n articulated
lorry
SEMIURBAN adj
suburban
SEMIVOCAL adj of or
relating to a semivowel
SEMIVOWEL n vowel-like
sound that acts like a
consonant, such as the
sound w in well
SEMIWATER adj as in
semiwater gas a mixed gas
of steam and air

S

SEMIWILD *adj* not fully domesticated

SEMIWORKS *adj* equipped to manufacture but not in great numbers

SEMMIT *n* vest

SEMMITS > SEMMIT

SEMOLINA *n* hard grains of wheat left after the milling of flour, used to make puddings and pasta

SEMOLINAS > SEMOLINA

SEMPER *adv* Latin word meaning always

SEMPLE *adj* Scots word meaning simple

SEMPLER > SEMPLE

SEMPLEST > SEMPLE

SEMPLICE *adv* be performed in a simple manner

SEMPRE *adv* (preceding a tempo or dynamic marking) always

SEMPSTER *n* person who sews

SEMPSTERS > SEMPSTER

SEMSEM *n* sesame

SEMSEMS > SEMSEM

SEMUNCIA *n* ancient Roman coin

SEMUNCIAE > SEMUNCIA

SEMUNCIAL > SEMUNCIA

SEMUNCIAS > SEMUNCIA

SEN *n* monetary unit of Brunei, Cambodia, Indonesia, Malaysia, and formerly of Japan

SENA *n* (in India) the army

SENARIES > SENARY

SENARII > SENARIUS

SENARIUS *n* type of poem

SENARY *adj* of or relating to the number six

SENAS > SENA

SENATE *n* main governing body at some universities

SENATES > SENATE

SENATOR *n* member of a senate

SENATORS > SENATOR

SEND *vb* cause (a person or thing) to go to or be taken or transmitted to a place

SENDABLE > SEND

SENDAL *n* fine silk fabric used for ceremonial clothing, etc

SENDALS > SENDAL

SENDED *vb* old word meaning sent

SENDER > SEND

SENDERS > SEND

SENDING > SEND

SENDINGS > SEND

SENDOFF *n* demonstration of good wishes at a person's departure ▷ *vb* dispatch (something, such as a letter)

SENDOFFS > SENDOFF

SENDS > SEND

SENDUP *n* parody or imitation

SENDUPS > SENDUP

SENE *n* money unit in Samoa

SENECA *variant of* > SENEGA

SENECAS > SENECA

SENECIO *n* type of plant of the genus which includes groundsels and ragworts

SENECIOS > SENECIO

SENEGA *n* milkwort plant of the eastern US

SENEGAS > SENEGA

SENES > SENE

SENESCE *vb* grow old

SENESCED > SENESCE

SENESCENT *adj* growing old

SENESCES > SENESCE

SENESCHAL *n* steward of the household of a medieval prince or nobleman

SENESCING > SENESCE

SENGI *n* African shrew

SENGIS > SENGI

SENGREEN *n* house leek

SENGREENS > SENGREEN

SENHOR *n* Portuguese term of address for man

SENHORA *n* Portuguese term of address for woman

SENHORAS > SENHORA

SENHORES > SENHOR

SENHORITA *n* Portuguese term of address for girl

SENHORS > SENHOR

SENILE *adj* mentally or physically weak because of old age ▷ *n* senile person

SENILELY > SENILE

SENILES > SENILE

SENILITY > SENILE

SENIOR *adj* superior in rank or standing ▷ *n* senior person

SENIORITY *n* state of being senior

SENIORS > SENIOR

SENITI *n* money unit in Tonga

SENITIS > SENITI

SENNA *n* tropical plant

SENNACHIE *n* Gaelic storyteller

SENNAS > SENNA

SENNET *n* fanfare: used as a stage direction in Elizabethan drama

SENNETS > SENNET

SENNIGHT *archaic word for* > WEEK

SENNIGHTS > SENNIGHT

SENNIT *n* flat braided cordage used on ships

SENNITS > SENNIT

SENOPIA *n* short-sightedness in old age

SENOPIAS > SENOPIA

SENOR *n* Spanish term of address equivalent to *sir* or *Mr*

SENORA *n* Spanish term of address equivalent to *madam* or *Mrs*

SENORAS > SENORA

SENORES > SENOR

SENORITA *n* Spanish term of address equivalent to *madam* or *Miss*

SENORITAS > SENORITA

SENORS > SENOR

SENRYU *n* Japanese short poem

SENS > SEN

SENSA > SENSUM

SENSATE *adj* perceived by the senses ▷ *vb* make sensate

SENSATED > SENSATE

SENSATELY > SENSATE

SENSATES > SENSATE

SENSATING > SENSATE

SENSATION *n* ability to feel things physically

SENSE *n* any of the faculties of perception or feeling ▷ *vb* perceive

SENSED > SENSE

SENSEFUL *adj* full of sense

SENSEI *n* martial arts teacher

SENSEIS > SENSEI

SENSELESS *adj* foolish

SENSES > SENSE

SENSI *same as* > SENSEI

SENSIBLE *adj* having or showing good sense ▷ *n* sensible thing or person

SENSIBLER > SENSIBLE

SENSIBLES > SENSIBLE

SENSIBLY > SENSIBLE

SENSILE *adj* capable of feeling

SENSILLA > SENSILLUM

SENSILLAE > SENSILLUM

SENSILLUM *n* sense organ in insects

SENSING > SENSE

SENSINGS > SENSE

SENSIS > SENSI

SENSISM *n* theory that ideas spring from senses

SENSISMS > SENSISM

SENSIST > SENSISM

SENSISTS > SENSISM

SENSITISE *same as* > SENSITIZE

SENSITIVE *adj* easily hurt or offended

SENSITIZE *vb* make sensitive

SENSOR *n* device that detects or measures the presence of something, such as radiation

SENSORIA > SENSORIUM

SENSORIAL *same as* > SENSORY

SENSORILY > SENSORY

SENSORIUM *n* area of the brain considered responsible for receiving and integrating sensations from the outside world

SENSORS > SENSOR

SENSORY *adj* of the senses or sensation

SENSUAL *adj* giving pleasure to the body and senses rather than the mind

SENSUALLY > SENSUAL

SENSUM *n* sensation detached from the information it conveys

SENSUOUS *adj* pleasing to the senses

SENT *n* former monetary unit of Estonia

SENTE *n* money unit in Lesotho

SENTED > SEND

SENTENCE *n* sequence of words capable of standing alone as a statement, question, or command ▷ *vb* pass sentence on (a convicted person)

SENTENCED > SENTENCE

SENTENCER > SENTENCE

SENTENCES > SENTENCE

SENTENTIA *n* opinion

SENTI > SENT

SENTIENCE *n* state or quality of being sentient

SENTIENCY *same as* > SENTIENCE

SENTIENT *adj* capable of feeling ▷ *n* sentient person or thing

SENTIENTS > SENTIENT

SENTIMENT *n* thought, opinion, or attitude

SENTIMO *n* money unit in Philippines

SENTIMOS > SENTIMO

SENTINEL *n* sentry ▷ *vb* guard as a sentinel

SENTINELS > SENTINEL

SENTING > SEND

SENTRIES > SENTRY

SENTRY *n* soldier on watch

SENTS > SENT

SENVIES > SENVY

SENVY *n* mustard

SENZA *prep* without

SEPAD *vb* suppose

SEPADDED > SEPAD

SEPADDING > SEPAD

SEPADS > SEPAD

SEPAL *n* leaflike division of the calyx of a flower

SEPALED > SEPAL

SEPALINE *same as* > SEPALOID

SEPALLED > SEPAL

SEPALODY *n* changing of flower part into sepal

SEPALOID *adj* (esp of petals) resembling a sepal in structure and function

SEPALOUS *adj* with sepals

SEPALS > SEPAL

SEPARABLE adj able to be separated

SEPARABLY > SEPARABLE

SEPARATA > SEPARATUM

SEPARATE vb act as a barrier between ▷ adj not the same, different ▷ n item of clothing that only covers half the body

SEPARATED > SEPARATE

SEPARATES > SEPARATE

SEPARATOR n person or thing that separates

SEPARATUM n separate printing of article from magazine

SEPHEN n stingray

SEPHENS > SEPHEN

SEPIA n reddish-brown pigment ▷ adj dark reddish-brown

SEPIAS > SEPIA

SEPIC adj of sepia

SEPIMENT n hedge

SEPIMENTS > SEPIMENT

SEPIOLITE n meerschaum

SEPIOST n cuttlefish bone

SEPIOSTS > SEPIOST

SEPIUM n cuttlefish bone

SEPIUMS > SEPIUM

SEPMAG adj designating a film, etc for which the sound is recorded on separate magnetic material

SEPOY n (formerly) Indian soldier in the service of the British

SEPOYS > SEPOY

SEPPUKU n Japanese ritual suicide

SEPPUKUS > SEPPUKU

SEPS n species of lizard

SEPSES > SEPSIS

SEPSIS n poisoning caused by pus-forming bacteria

SEPT n clan, esp in Ireland or Scotland

SEPTA > SEPTUM

SEPTAGE n waste removed from septic tank

SEPTAGES > SEPTAGE

SEPTAL adj of or relating to a septum

SEPTARIA > SEPTARIUM

SEPTARIAN > SEPTARIUM

SEPTARIUM n mass of mineral substance having cracks filled with another mineral

SEPTATE adj divided by septa

SEPTATION n division by partitions

SEPTEMFID adj divided into seven

SEPTEMVIR n member of government of seven men

SEPTENARY adj of or relating to the number seven ▷ n number seven

SEPTENNIA pl n cycles of seven years

SEPTET n group of seven performers

SEPTETS > SEPTET

SEPTETTE same as > SEPTET

SEPTETTES > SEPTETTE

SEPTIC adj (of a wound) infected ▷ n infected wound

SEPTICAL > SEPTIC

SEPTICITY > SEPTIC

SEPTICS > SEPTIC

SEPTIFORM adj acting as partition

SEPTIMAL adj of number seven

SEPTIME n seventh of eight basic positions from which a parry can be made in fencing

SEPTIMES > SEPTIME

SEPTIMOLE n group of seven musical notes

SEPTLEVA n gambling term from old card game

SEPTLEVAS > SEPTLEVA

SEPTORIA n any of various parasitic fungi

SEPTORIAS > SEPTORIA

SEPTS > SEPT

SEPTUM n dividing partition between two cavities in the body

SEPTUMS > SEPTUM

SEPTUOR n group of seven musicians

SEPTUORS > SEPTUOR

SEPTUPLE vb multiply by seven ▷ adj seven times as much or as many ▷ n quantity or number seven times as great as another

SEPTUPLED > SEPTUPLE

SEPTUPLES > SEPTUPLE

SEPTUPLET n group of seven notes played in a time value of six, eight, etc

SEPULCHER same as > SEPULCHRE

SEPULCHRE n tomb or burial vault ▷ vb bury in a sepulchre

SEPULTURE n act of placing in a sepulchre

SEQUACITY n quality of being pliant or controllable

SEQUEL n novel, play, or film that continues the story of an earlier one

SEQUELA n disease related to or arising from a pre-existing disease

SEQUELAE > SEQUELA

SEQUELISE same as > SEQUELIZE

SEQUELIZE vb create sequel to

SEQUELS > SEQUEL

SEQUENCE n arrangement of two or more things in successive order ▷ vb arrange in a sequence

SEQUENCED > SEQUENCE

SEQUENCER n electronic device that determines the order in which a number of operations occur

SEQUENCES > SEQUENCE

SEQUENCY n number of changes in mathematical list

SEQUENT adj following in order or succession ▷ n something that follows

SEQUENTLY > SEQUENT

SEQUENTS > SEQUENT

SEQUESTER vb seclude

SEQUESTRA pl n detached pieces of necrotic bone that often migrate to wounds

SEQUIN n small ornamental metal disc on a garment ▷ vb apply sequins

SEQUINED > SEQUIN

SEQUINING > SEQUIN

SEQUINNED > SEQUIN

SEQUINS > SEQUIN

SEQUITUR n conclusion that follows from the premises

SEQUITURS > SEQUITUR

SEQUOIA n giant Californian coniferous tree

SEQUOIAS > SEQUOIA

SER n unit of weight used in India

SERA > SERUM

SERAC n pinnacle of ice among crevasses on a glacier, usually on a steep slope

SERACS > SERAC

SERAFILE n line of soldiers

SERAFILES > SERAFILE

SERAFIN n old silver coin of Goa

SERAFINS > SERAFIN

SERAGLIO n harem of a Muslim palace

SERAGLIOS > SERAGLIO

SERAI n (in the East) a caravanserai or inn

SERAIL same as > SERAGLIO

SERAILS > SERAIL

SERAIS > SERAI

SERAL > SERE

SERANG n native captain of a crew of sailors in the East Indies

SERANGS > SERANG

SERAPE n blanket-like shawl often of brightly-coloured wool

SERAPES > SERAPE

SERAPH n member of the highest order of angels

SERAPHIC adj of or resembling a seraph

SERAPHIM > SERAPH

SERAPHIMS > SERAPH

SERAPHIN n angel

SERAPHINE n old keyboard instrument

SERAPHINS > SERAPHIN

SERAPHS > SERAPH

SERASKIER n Turkish military leader

SERDAB n secret chamber in an ancient Egyptian tomb

SERDABS > SERDAB

SERE adj dried up or withered ▷ n series of changes occurring in the ecological succession of a particular community ▷ vb sear

SERED > SERE

SEREIN n fine rain falling from a clear sky after sunset

SEREINS > SEREIN

SERENADE n music played or sung to a woman by a lover ▷ vb sing or play a serenade to (someone)

SERENADED > SERENADE

SERENADER > SERENADE

SERENADES > SERENADE

SERENATA n 18th-century cantata, often dramatic in form

SERENATAS > SERENATA

SERENATE n old form of serenade ▷ vb make serene

SERENATED > SERENATE

SERENATES > SERENATE

SERENE adj calm, peaceful ▷ vb make serene

SERENED > SERENE

SERENELY > SERENE

SERENER > SERENE

SERENES > SERENE

SERENEST > SERENE

SERENING > SERENE

SERENITY n state or quality of being serene

SERER > SERE

SERES > SERE

SEREST > SERE

SERF n medieval farm labourer who could not leave the land he worked on

SERFAGE > SERF

SERFAGES > SERF

SERFDOM > SERF

SERFDOMS > SERF

SERFHOOD > SERF

SERFHOODS > SERF

SERFISH > SERF

SERFLIKE > SERF

SERFS > SERF

SERFSHIP > SERF

SERFSHIPS > SERF

SERGE n strong woollen fabric

SERGEANCY > SERGEANT**

SERGEANT n noncommissioned officer in the army
SERGEANTS > SERGEANT
SERGEANTY n form of feudal tenure
SERGED adj with sewn seam
SERGER n sewing machine attachment for finishing seams
SERGERS > SERGER
SERGES > SERGE
SERGING n type of sewing
SERGINGS > SERGING
SERIAL n story or play produced in successive instalments ▷ adj of or forming a series
SERIALISE same as > SERIALIZE
SERIALISM n musical technique using a sequence of notes in a definite order
SERIALIST n writer of serials
SERIALITY > SERIAL
SERIALIZE vb publish or present as a serial
SERIALLY > SERIAL
SERIALS > SERIAL
SERIATE adj forming a series ▷ vb form into a series
SERIATED > SERIATE
SERIATELY > SERIATE
SERIATES > SERIATE
SERIATIM adv in a series
SERIATING > SERIATE
SERIATION > SERIATE
SERIC adj of silk
SERICEOUS adj covered with a layer of small silky hairs
SERICIN n gelatinous protein found on the fibres of raw silk
SERICINS > SERICIN
SERICITE n type of mica
SERICITES > SERICITE
SERICITIC > SERICITE
SERICON n solution used in alchemy
SERICONS > SERICON
SERIEMA n either of two cranelike South American birds
SERIEMAS > SERIEMA
SERIES n group or succession of related things, usu arranged in order
SERIF n small line at the extremities of a main stroke in a type character
SERIFED adj having serifs
SERIFFED adj having serifs
SERIFS > SERIF
SERIGRAPH n colour print made by an adaptation of the silk-screen process

SERIN n any of various small yellow-and-brown finches
SERINE n sweet-tasting amino acid
SERINES > SERINE
SERINETTE n barrel organ
SERING > SERE
SERINGA n any of several trees that yield rubber
SERINGAS > SERINGA
SERINS > SERIN
SERIOUS adj giving cause for concern
SERIOUSLY adv in a serious manner or to a serious degree
SERIPH same as > SERIF
SERIPHS > SERIPH
SERJEANCY n rank of sergeant
SERJEANT same as > SERGEANT
SERJEANTS > SERJEANT
SERJEANTY n type of feudal tenure
SERK Scots word for > SHIRT
SERKALI n government in Africa
SERKALIS > SERKALI
SERKS > SERK
SERMON n speech on a religious or moral subject ▷ vb deliver a sermon
SERMONED > SERMON
SERMONEER n preacher
SERMONER variant of > SERMONEER
SERMONERS > SERMONER
SERMONET n short sermon
SERMONETS > SERMONET
SERMONIC > SERMON
SERMONING n preaching a sermon
SERMONISE same as > SERMONIZE
SERMONIZE vb make a long moralizing speech
SERMONS > SERMON
SEROGROUP n group of bacteria with a common antigen
SEROLOGIC > SEROLOGY
SEROLOGY n science concerned with serums
SERON n crate
SERONS > SERON
SEROON n crate
SEROONS > SEROON
SEROPUS n liquid consisting of serum and pus
SEROPUSES > SEROPUS
SEROSA n one of the thin membranes surrounding the embryo in an insect's egg
SEROSAE > SEROSA
SEROSAL > SEROSA
SEROSAS > SEROSA
SEROSITY > SEROUS

SEROTINAL same as > SEROTINE
SEROTINE adj produced, flowering, or developing late in the season ▷ n either of two insectivorous bats
SEROTINES > SEROTINE
SEROTINY n state of being serotinous
SEROTONIN n compound that occurs in the brain, intestines, and blood platelets and acts as a neurotransmitter
SEROTYPE n category into which material, usually a bacterium, is placed based on its serological activity ▷ vb class according to serotype
SEROTYPED > SEROTYPE
SEROTYPES > SEROTYPE
SEROTYPIC adj relating to a serotype
SEROUS adj of, containing, or like serum
SEROVAR n subdivision of species
SEROVARS > SEROVAR
SEROW n either of two antelopes of mountainous regions of S and SE Asia
SEROWS > SEROW
SERPENT n snake
SERPENTRY n serpents
SERPENTS > SERPENT
SERPIGO n any progressive skin eruption
SERPIGOES > SERPIGO
SERPIGOS > SERPIGO
SERPULA n type of marine mollusc
SERPULAE > SERPULA
SERPULAS > SERPULA
SERPULID n marine polychaete worm
SERPULIDS > SERPULID
SERPULITE n variety of fossil
SERR vb press close together
SERRA n sawlike part or organ
SERRAE > SERRA
SERRAN n species of fish
SERRANID n type of marine fish of the family which includes the sea bass and sea perch
SERRANIDS > SERRANID
SERRANO n type of Spanish ham
SERRANOID same as > SERRANID
SERRANOS > SERRANO
SERRANS > SERRAN
SERRAS > SERRA
SERRATE adj (of leaves) having a margin of forward pointing teeth ▷ vb make serrate
SERRATED adj having a notched or sawlike edge

SERRATES > SERRATE
SERRATI > SERRATUS
SERRATING > SERRATE
SERRATION n state or condition of being serrated
SERRATURE same as > SERRATION
SERRATUS n muscle in thorax
SERRE vb press close together
SERRED > SERRE
SERREFILE n file of soldiers
SERRES > SERRE
SERRICORN n beetle with serrate antennae ▷ adj (of a beetle) with serrate antennae
SERRIED adj in close formation
SERRIEDLY > SERRIED
SERRIES > SERRY
SERRIFORM adj resembling a notched or sawlike edge
SERRING > SERRE
SERRS > SERR
SERRULATE adj (esp of leaves) minutely serrate
SERRY vb close together
SERRYING > SERRY
SERS > SER
SERUEWE vb old word meaning survey
SERUEWED > SERUEWE
SERUEWES > SERUEWE
SERUEWING > SERUEWE
SERUM n watery fluid left after blood has clotted
SERUMAL > SERUM
SERUMS > SERUM
SERVABLE > SERVE
SERVAL n feline African mammal
SERVALS > SERVAL
SERVANT n person employed to do household work for another ▷ vb work as a servant
SERVANTED > SERVANT
SERVANTRY n servants
SERVANTS > SERVANT
SERVE vb work for (a person, community, or cause) ▷ n act of serving the ball
SERVEABLE > SERVE
SERVED > SERVE
SERVER n player who serves in racket games
SERVERIES > SERVERY
SERVERS > SERVER
SERVERY n room from which food is served
SERVES > SERVE
SERVEWE vb old word meaning survey
SERVEWED > SERVEWE
SERVEWES > SERVEWE
SERVEWING > SERVEWE
SERVICE n serving ▷ adj serving the public

S

rather than producing goods ▷ vb provide a service or services to

SERVICED > SERVICE

SERVICER > SERVICE

SERVICERS > SERVICE

SERVICES > SERVICE

SERVICING n act of servicing

SERVIENT adj subordinate

SERVIETTE n table napkin

SERVILE adj too eager to obey people, fawning ▷ n servile person

SERVILELY > SERVILE

SERVILES > SERVILE

SERVILISM n condition of being servile

SERVILITY > SERVILE

SERVING n portion of food

SERVINGS > SERVING

SERVITOR n servant or attendant

SERVITORS > SERVITOR

SERVITUDE n bondage or slavery

SERVLET n small program that runs on a web server

SERVLETS > SERVLET

SERVO n servomechanism ▷ adj of a servomechanism

SERVOS > SERVO

SERVQUAL n provision of high-quality products by an organization backed by a high level of service for consumers

SERVQUALS > SERVQUAL

SESAME n plant cultivated for its seeds and oil

SESAMES > SESAME

SESAMOID adj of or relating to various small bones formed in tendons ▷ n sesamoid bone

SESAMOIDS > SESAMOID

SESE interj exclamation found in Shakespeare

SESELI n garden plant

SESELIS > SESELI

SESEY interj exclamation found in Shakespeare

SESH short for > SESSION

SESHES > SESH

SESS n old word meaning tax ▷ vb to assess or impose (a tax)

SESSA interj exclamation found in Shakespeare

SESSED > SESS

SESSES > SESS

SESSILE adj (of flowers or leaves) having no stalk

SESSILITY > SESSILE

SESSING > SESS

SESSION n period spent in an activity

SESSIONAL > SESSION

SESSIONS pl n sittings or a sitting of justice in court

SESSPOOL n cesspool

SESSPOOLS > SESSPOOL

SESTERCE n silver or, later, bronze coin of ancient Rome worth a quarter of a denarius

SESTERCES > SESTERCE

SESTERTIA pl n ancient Roman money accounts

SESTERTII pl n sesterces

SESTET n last six lines of a sonnet

SESTETS > SESTET

SESTETT n group of six

SESTETTE n group of six

SESTETTES > SESTETTE

SESTETTO n composition for six musicians

SESTETTOS > SESTETTO

SESTETTS > SESTETT

SESTINA n elaborate verse form of Italian origin

SESTINAS > SESTINA

SESTINE n poem of six lines

SESTINES > SESTINE

SESTON n type of plankton

SESTONS > SESTON

SET vb put in a specified position or state ▷ n setting or being set ▷ adj fixed or established beforehand

SETA n bristle or bristle-like appendage

SETACEOUS > SETA

SETAE > SETA

SETAL > SETA

SETBACK n anything that delays progress

SETBACKS > SETBACK

SETENANT n pair of postage stamps of different values joined together

SETENANTS > SETENANT

SETIFORM adj shaped like a seta

SETLINE n any of various types of fishing line

SETLINES > SETLINE

SETNESS > SET

SETNESSES > SET

SETOFF n counterbalance

SETOFFS > SETOFF

SETON n surgical thread inserted below the skin

SETONS > SETON

SETOSE adj covered with setae

SETOUS > SETA

SETOUT n beginning or outset

SETOUTS > SETOUT

SETS > SET

SETSCREW n screw that fits into the boss or hub of a wheel, and prevents motion of the part relative to the shaft on which it is mounted

SETSCREWS > SETSCREW

SETT n badger's burrow

SETTEE n couch

SETTEES > SETTEE

SETTER n long-haired gun dog ▷ vb treat with a piece of setterwort

SETTERED > SETTER

SETTERING > SETTER

SETTERS > SETTER

SETTING > SET

SETTINGS > SET

SETTLE vb arrange or put in order ▷ n long wooden bench with high back and arms

SETTLED > SETTLE

SETTLER n colonist

SETTLERS > SETTLER

SETTLES > SETTLE

SETTLING > SETTLE

SETTLINGS pl n any matter or substance that has settled at the bottom of a liquid

SETTLOR n person who settles property on someone

SETTLORS > SETTLOR

SETTS > SETT

SETUALE n valerian

SETUALES > SETUALE

SETULE n small bristle

SETULES > SETULE

SETULOSE > SETULE

SETULOUS > SETULE

SETUP n way in which anything is organized or arranged

SETUPS > SETUP

SETWALL n valerian

SETWALLS > SETWALL

SEV n Indian snack of deep-fried noodles

SEVEN n one more than six ▷ adj amounting to seven ▷ determiner amounting to seven

SEVENFOLD adj having seven times as many or as much ▷ adv by seven times as many or as much

SEVENS n Rugby Union match or series of matches played with seven players on each side

SEVENTEEN n ten and seven ▷ adj amounting to seventeen ▷ determiner amounting to seventeen

SEVENTH n (of) number seven in a series ▷ adj coming after the sixth and before the eighth ▷ adv after the sixth person, position, event, etc

SEVENTHLY same as > SEVENTH

SEVENTHS > SEVENTH

SEVENTIES > SEVENTY

SEVENTY n ten times seven ▷ adj amounting to seventy ▷ determiner amounting to seventy

SEVER vb cut through or off

SEVERABLE adj able to be severed

SEVERAL adj some, a few ▷ n individual person

SEVERALLY adv separately

SEVERALS > SEVERAL

SEVERALTY n state of being several or separate

SEVERANCE n act of severing or state of being severed

SEVERE adj strict or harsh

SEVERED > SEVER

SEVERELY > SEVERE

SEVERER > SEVERE

SEVEREST > SEVERE

SEVERIES > SEVERY

SEVERING > SEVER

SEVERITY > SEVERE

SEVERS > SEVER

SEVERY n part of vaulted ceiling

SEVICHE n Mexican fish dish

SEVICHES > SEVICHE

SEVRUGA n species of sturgeon

SEVRUGAS > SEVRUGA

SEVS > SEV

SEW vb join with thread repeatedly passed through with a needle

SEWABLE > SEW

SEWAGE n waste matter or excrement carried away in sewers

SEWAGES > SEWAGE

SEWAN same as > SEAWAN

SEWANS > SEWAN

SEWAR n Asian dagger

SEWARS > SEWAR

SEWED > SEW

SEWEL n scarecrow

SEWELLEL n mountain beaver

SEWELLELS > SEWELLEL

SEWELS > SEWEL

SEWEN same as > SEWIN

SEWENS > SEWEN

SEWER n drain to remove waste water and sewage ▷ vb provide with sewers

SEWERAGE n system of sewers

SEWERAGES > SEWERAGE

SEWERED > SEWER

SEWERING > SEWER

SEWERINGS > SEWER

SEWERLESS > SEWER

SEWERLIKE > SEWER

SEWERS > SEWER

SEWIN n sea trout

SEWING > SEW

SEWINGS > SEW

SEWINS > SEWIN

SEWN > SEW

SEWS > SEW

SEX n state of being male or female ▷ vb find out the sex of ▷ adj of sexual matters

SEXAHOLIC n person who is addicted to sex

SEXED *adj* having a specified degree of sexuality

SEXENNIAL *adj* occurring once every six years or over a period of six years ▷ *n* sixth anniversary

SEXER *n* person checking sex of chickens

SEXERCISE *n* sexual activity, regarded as a way of keeping fit

SEXERS > SEXER

SEXES > SEX

SEXFID *adj* split into six

SEXFOIL *n* flower with six petals or leaves

SEXFOILS > SEXFOIL

SEXIER > SEXY

SEXIEST > SEXY

SEXILY > SEXY

SEXINESS > SEXY

SEXING > SEX

SEXINGS > SEXING

SEXISM *n* discrimination on the basis of a person's sex

SEXISMS > SEXISM

SEXIST > SEXISM

SEXISTS > SEXISM

SEXLESS *adj* neither male nor female

SEXLESSLY > SEXLESS

SEXLINKED *adj* (of a gene) found on a sex chromosome

SEXOLOGIC > SEXOLOGY

SEXOLOGY *n* study of sexual behaviour in human beings

SEXPERT *n* person who professes a knowledge of sexual matters

SEXPERTS > SEXPERT

SEXPOT *n* person considered as sexually very attractive

SEXPOTS > SEXPOT

SEXT *n* sexually explicit text message ▷ *vb* send a sexually explicit text message

SEXTAIN *same as* > SESTINA

SEXTAINS > SEXTAIN

SEXTAN *adj* (of a fever) marked by paroxysms that recur after an interval of five days

SEXTANS *n* Roman coin

SEXTANSES > SEXTANS

SEXTANT *n* navigator's instrument for measuring angles

SEXTANTAL > SEXTANT

SEXTANTS > SEXTANT

SEXTARII > SEXTARIUS

SEXTARIUS *n* ancient Roman quantity measure

SEXTED > SEXT

SEXTET *n* group of six performers

SEXTETS > SEXTET

SEXTETT *n* sextet

SEXTETTE *same as* > SEXTET

SEXTETTES > SEXTETTE

SEXTETTS > SEXTETT

SEXTILE *n* value of a variable dividing its distribution into six groups with equal frequencies

SEXTILES > SEXTILE

SEXTING *n* practice of sending sexually explicit text messages

SEXTINGS > SEXTING

SEXTO *same as* > SIXMO

SEXTOLET *n* group of six musical notes

SEXTOLETS > SEXTOLET

SEXTON *n* official in charge of a church and churchyard

SEXTONESS *n* female sexton

SEXTONS > SEXTON

SEXTOS > SEXTO

SEXTS > SEXT

SEXTUOR *n* sextet

SEXTUORS > SEXTUOR

SEXTUPLE *vb* multiply by six ▷ *adj* six times as much or as many ▷ *n* quantity or number six times as great as another

SEXTUPLED > SEXTUPLE

SEXTUPLES > SEXTUPLE

SEXTUPLET *n* one of six children born at one birth

SEXTUPLY > SEXTUPLE

SEXUAL *adj* of or characterized by sex

SEXUALISE *same as* > SEXUALIZE

SEXUALISM *n* emphasising of sexuality

SEXUALIST > SEXUALISM

SEXUALITY *n* state or quality of being sexual

SEXUALIZE *vb* make or become sexual or sexually aware

SEXUALLY > SEXUAL

SEXVALENT *adj* with valency of six

SEXY *adj* sexually exciting or attractive

SEY *n* Scots word meaning part of cow carcase

SEYEN *n* old form of scion

SEYENS > SEYEN

SEYS > SEY

SEYSURE *n* old form of seizure

SEYSURES > SEYSURE

SEZ *vb* informal spelling of 'says'

SFERICS *same as* > SPHERICS

SFORZANDI > SFORZANDO

SFORZANDO *adv* to be played with strong initial attack ▷ *n* symbol written above a note, indicating this

SFORZATI > SFORZATO

SFORZATO *same as* > SFORZANDO

SFORZATOS > SFORZATO

SFUMATO *n* gradual transition between areas of different colour in painting

SFUMATOS > SFUMATO

SGRAFFITI > SGRAFFITO

SGRAFFITO *n* technique in mural or ceramic decoration in which the top layer of glaze is incised with a design to reveal parts of the ground

SH *interj* hush

SHA *interj* be quiet

SHABASH *interj* (in Indian English) bravo or well done

SHABBATOT *pl n* Jewish sabbaths

SHABBIER > SHABBY

SHABBIEST > SHABBY

SHABBILY > SHABBY

SHABBLE *n* Scots word meaning old sword

SHABBLES > SHABBLE

SHABBY *adj* worn or dilapidated in appearance

SHABRACK *n* cavalryman's saddle cloth

SHABRACKS > SHABRACK

SHACK *n* rough hut ▷ *vb* evade (work or responsibility)

SHACKED > SHACK

SHACKIER > SHACKY

SHACKIEST > SHACKY

SHACKING > SHACK

SHACKLE *n* metal ring for securing a person's wrists or ankles ▷ *vb* fasten with shackles

SHACKLED > SHACKLE

SHACKLER > SHACKLE

SHACKLERS > SHACKLE

SHACKLES > SHACKLE

SHACKLING > SHACKLE

SHACKO *same as* > SHAKO

SHACKOES > SHACKO

SHACKOS > SHACKO

SHACKS > SHACK

SHACKY *adj* resembling a shack; dilapidated

SHAD *n* herring-like fish

SHADBERRY *n* edible purplish berry of the shadbush

SHADBLOW *n* type of shrub

SHADBLOWS > SHADBLOW

SHADBUSH *n* type of N American tree or shrub

SHADCHAN *n* Jewish marriage broker

SHADCHANS > SHADCHAN

SHADDOCK *another name for* > POMELO

SHADDOCKS > SHADDOCK

SHADDUP *interj* shut up

SHADE *n* relative darkness ▷ *vb* screen from light

SHADED > SHADE

SHADELESS > SHADE

SHADER > SHADE

SHADERS > SHADE

SHADES *pl n* gathering darkness at nightfall

SHADFLIES > SHADFLY

SHADFLY American name for > MAYFLY

SHADIER > SHADY

SHADIEST > SHADY

SHADILY > SHADY

SHADINESS > SHADY

SHADING *n* graded areas of tone indicating light and dark in a painting or drawing

SHADINGS > SHADING

SHADKHAN *same as* > SHADCHAN

SHADKHANS > SHADKHAN

SHADOOF *n* mechanism for raising water

SHADOOFS > SHADOOF

SHADOW *n* dark shape cast on a surface when something stands between a light and the surface ▷ *vb* cast a shadow over

SHADOWBOX *vb* practise boxing against an imaginary opponent

SHADOWED > SHADOW

SHADOWER > SHADOW

SHADOWERS > SHADOW

SHADOWIER > SHADOWY

SHADOWILY > SHADOWY

SHADOWING > SHADOW

SHADOWS > SHADOW

SHADOWY *adj* (of a place) full of shadows

SHADRACH *n* lump of iron that has not been melted in the furnace

SHADRACHS > SHADRACH

SHADS > SHAD

SHADUF *same as* > SHADOOF

SHADUFS > SHADUF

SHADY *adj* situated in or giving shade

SHAFT *n* long narrow straight handle of a tool or weapon ▷ *vb* treat badly

SHAFTED > SHAFT

SHAFTER > SHAFT

SHAFTERS > SHAFT

SHAFTING *n* assembly of rotating shafts for transmitting power

SHAFTINGS > SHAFTING

SHAFTLESS > SHAFT

SHAFTS > SHAFT

SHAG *n* coarse shredded tobacco ▷ *adj* (of a carpet) having a long pile ▷ *vb* have sexual intercourse with (a person)

SHAGBARK *n* North American hickory tree

SHAGBARKS > SHAGBARK
SHAGGABLE *adj* sexually attractive
SHAGGED > SHAG
SHAGGER *n* person who has sexual intercourse
SHAGGERS > SHAGGER
SHAGGIER > SHAGGY
SHAGGIEST > SHAGGY
SHAGGILY > SHAGGY
SHAGGING > SHAG
SHAGGY *adj* covered with rough hair or wool
SHAGPILE *adj* (of carpet) having long fibres
SHAGREEN *n* sharkskin
SHAGREENS > SHAGREEN
SHAGROON *n* nineteenth-century Australian settler in Canterbury
SHAGROONS > SHAGROON
SHAGS > SHAG
SHAH *n* formerly, ruler of Iran
SHAHADA *n* Islamic declaration of faith
SHAHADAH *same as* > SHAHADA
SHAHADAHS > SHAHADAH
SHAHADAS > SHAHADA
SHAHDOM > SHAH
SHAHDOMS > SHAH
SHAHEED *same as* > SHAHID
SHAHEEDS > SHAHEED
SHAHID *n* Muslim martyr
SHAHIDS > SHAHID
SHAHS > SHAH
SHAHTOOSH *n* soft wool that comes from the protected Tibetan antelope
SHAIKH *n* sheikh
SHAIKHS > SHAIKH
SHAIRD *n* Scots word meaning shred
SHAIRDS > SHAIRD
SHAIRN *Scots word for* > DUNG
SHAIRNS > SHAIRN
SHAITAN *n* (in Muslim countries) an evil spirit
SHAITANS > SHAITAN
SHAKABLE > SHAKE
SHAKE *vb* move quickly up and down or back and forth ▷ *n* shaking
SHAKEABLE > SHAKE
SHAKED *vb* old form of shook
SHAKEDOWN *n* act of extortion
SHAKEN > SHAKE
SHAKEOUT *n* process of reducing the number of people in a workforce
SHAKEOUTS > SHAKEOUT
SHAKER *n* container in which drinks are mixed or from which powder is shaken
SHAKERS > SHAKER
SHAKES > SHAKE

SHAKEUP *n* radical reorganization
SHAKEUPS > SHAKEUP
SHAKIER > SHAKY
SHAKIEST > SHAKY
SHAKILY > SHAKY
SHAKINESS > SHAKY
SHAKING > SHAKE
SHAKINGS > SHAKE
SHAKO *n* tall cylindrical peaked military hat with a plume
SHAKOES > SHAKO
SHAKOS > SHAKO
SHAKT *vb* old form of shook
SHAKUDO *n* Japanese alloy of copper and gold
SHAKUDOS > SHAKUDO
SHAKY *adj* unsteady
SHALE *n* flaky sedimentary rock
SHALED > SHALE
SHALELIKE > SHALE
SHALES > SHALE
SHALEY > SHALE
SHALIER > SHALE
SHALIEST > SHALE
SHALING > SHALE
SHALL *vb* used as an auxiliary to make the future tense
SHALLI *n* type of fabric
SHALLIS > SHALLI
SHALLON *n* American shrub
SHALLONS > SHALLON
SHALLOON *n* light twill-weave woollen fabric used chiefly for coat linings, etc
SHALLOONS > SHALLOON
SHALLOP *n* light boat used for rowing in shallow water
SHALLOPS > SHALLOP
SHALLOT *n* kind of small onion
SHALLOTS > SHALLOT
SHALLOW *adj* not deep ▷ *n* shallow place in a body of water ▷ *vb* make or become shallow
SHALLOWED > SHALLOW
SHALLOWER > SHALLOW
SHALLOWLY > SHALLOW
SHALLOWS > SHALLOW
SHALM *n* old woodwind instrument
SHALMS > SHALM
SHALOM *n* Jewish greeting meaning 'peace be with you'
SHALOMS > SHALOM
SHALOT *n* shallot
SHALOTS > SHALOT
SHALT *singular form of the present tense (indicative mood) of* > SHALL
SHALWAR *n* pair of loose-fitting trousers tapering to a narrow fit around the ankles
SHALWARS > SHALWAR

SHALY > SHALE
SHAM *n* thing or person that is not genuine ▷ *adj* not genuine ▷ *vb* fake, feign
SHAMA *n* Indian songbird
SHAMABLE > SHAME
SHAMABLY > SHAME
SHAMAL *n* hot northwesterly wind
SHAMALS > SHAMAL
SHAMAN *n* priest of shamanism
SHAMANIC > SHAMAN
SHAMANISM *n* religion of northern Asia, based on a belief in good and evil spirits
SHAMANIST > SHAMANISM
SHAMANS > SHAMAN
SHAMAS > SHAMA
SHAMATEUR *n* sportsperson who is officially an amateur but accepts payment
SHAMBA *n* (in E Africa) any field used for growing crops
SHAMBAS > SHAMBA
SHAMBLE *vb* walk in a shuffling awkward way ▷ *n* awkward or shuffling walk
SHAMBLED > SHAMBLE
SHAMBLES *n* disorderly event or place
SHAMBLIER > SHAMBLE
SHAMBLING > SHAMBLE
SHAMBLY > SHAMBLE
SHAMBOLIC *adj* completely disorganized
SHAME *n* painful emotion caused by awareness of having done something foolish ▷ *vb* cause to feel shame
SHAMEABLE > SHAME
SHAMEABLY > SHAME
SHAMED > SHAME
SHAMEFAST *adj* old form of shamefaced
SHAMEFUL *adj* causing or deserving shame
SHAMELESS *adj* with no sense of shame
SHAMER *n* cause of shame
SHAMERS > SHAME
SHAMES > SHAME
SHAMIANA *n* tent in India
SHAMIANAH *n* tent in India
SHAMIANAS > SHAMIANA
SHAMINA *n* wool blend of pashm and shahtoosh
SHAMINAS > SHAMINA
SHAMING > SHAME
SHAMISEN *n* Japanese stringed instrument
SHAMISENS > SHAMISEN
SHAMMAS *same as* > SHAMMES
SHAMMASH *same as* > SHAMMES

SHAMMASIM > SHAMMES
SHAMMED > SHAM
SHAMMER > SHAM
SHAMMERS > SHAM
SHAMMES *n* official acting as the beadle, sexton, and caretaker of a synagogue
SHAMMIED > SHAMMY
SHAMMIES > SHAMMY
SHAMMING > SHAM
SHAMMOS *same as* > SHAMMES
SHAMMOSIM > SHAMMES
SHAMMY *n* piece of chamois leather ▷ *vb* rub with a shammy
SHAMMYING > SHAMMY
SHAMOIS *n* chamois ▷ *vb* to clean with shamois
SHAMOISED > SHAMOIS
SHAMOISES > SHAMOIS
SHAMOS *same as* > SHAMMES
SHAMOSIM > SHAMMES
SHAMOY *n* chamois ▷ *vb* rub with a shamoy
SHAMOYED > SHAMOY
SHAMOYING > SHAMOY
SHAMOYS > SHAMOY
SHAMPOO *n* liquid soap for washing hair, carpets, or upholstery ▷ *vb* wash with shampoo
SHAMPOOED > SHAMPOO
SHAMPOOER > SHAMPOO
SHAMPOOS > SHAMPOO
SHAMROCK *n* clover leaf, esp as the Irish emblem
SHAMROCKS > SHAMROCK
SHAMS > SHAM
SHAMUS *n* police or private detective
SHAMUSES > SHAMUS
SHAN *variant of* > SHAND
SHANACHIE *n* Gaelic storyteller
SHAND *n* old word meaning fake coin
SHANDIES > SHANDY
SHANDRIES > SHANDRY
SHANDRY *n* light horse-drawn cart
SHANDS > SHAND
SHANDY *n* drink made of beer and lemonade
SHANGHAI *vb* force or trick (someone) into doing something ▷ *n* catapult
SHANGHAIS > SHANGHAI
SHANK *n* lower leg ▷ *vb* (of fruits, roots, etc) to show disease symptoms
SHANKBONE *n* bone in lower leg
SHANKED > SHANK
SHANKING > SHANK
SHANKS > SHANK
SHANNIES > SHANNY
SHANNY *n* European blenny of rocky coastal waters
SHANS > SHAN

SHANTEY same as
> SHANTY
SHANTEYS > SHANTEY
SHANTI n peace
SHANTIES > SHANTY
SHANTIH same as
> SHANTI
SHANTIHS > SHANTIH
SHANTIS > SHANTI
SHANTUNG n soft Chinese silk with a knobbly surface
SHANTUNGS > SHANTUNG
SHANTY n shack or crude dwelling
SHANTYMAN n man living in shanty
SHANTYMEN
> SHANTYMAN
SHAPABLE > SHAPE
SHAPE n outward form of an object ▷ vb form or mould
SHAPEABLE > SHAPE
SHAPED > SHAPE
SHAPELESS adj (of a person or object) lacking a pleasing shape
SHAPELIER > SHAPELY
SHAPELY adj having an attractive shape
SHAPEN vb shape
SHAPENED > SHAPEN
SHAPENING > SHAPEN
SHAPENS > SHAPEN
SHAPER > SHAPE
SHAPERS > SHAPE
SHAPES > SHAPE
SHAPEUP n system of hiring dockers for a day's work
SHAPEUPS > SHAPEUP
SHAPEWEAR n underwear that shapes body
SHAPING > SHAPE
SHAPINGS > SHAPE
SHAPS n leather over-trousers worn by cowboys
SHARABLE > SHARE
SHARD n broken piece of pottery or glass
SHARDED adj old word meaning hidden under dung
SHARDS > SHARD
SHARE n part of something that belongs to or is contributed by a person ▷ vb give or take a share of (something)
SHAREABLE adj that can be shared
SHARECROP vb cultivate (farmland) as a sharecropper
SHARED > SHARE
SHAREMAN n member of fishing-boat crew who shares profits
SHAREMEN > SHAREMAN
SHARER > SHARE
SHARERS > SHARE
SHARES > SHARE

SHARESMAN n member of fishing-boat crew who shares profits
SHARESMEN
> SHARESMAN
SHAREWARE n software available to all users without the need for a licence
SHARIA n body of doctrines that regulate the lives of Muslims
SHARIAH same as
> SHARIA
SHARIAHS > SHARIAH
SHARIAS > SHARIA
SHARIAT n Islamic religious law
SHARIATS > SHARIAT
SHARIF same as > SHERIF
SHARIFIAN > SHARIF
SHARIFS > SHARIF
SHARING > SHARE
SHARINGS > SHARE
SHARK n large usu predatory sea fish ▷ vb obtain (something) by cheating or deception
SHARKED > SHARK
SHARKER n shark hunter
SHARKERS > SHARKER
SHARKING > SHARK
SHARKINGS > SHARK
SHARKISH adj resembling or behaving like a shark
SHARKLIKE > SHARK
SHARKS > SHARK
SHARKSKIN n stiff glossy fabric
SHARN Scots word for
> DUNG
SHARNIER > SHARN
SHARNIES > SHARNY
SHARNIEST > SHARN
SHARNS > SHARN
SHARNY n (Scot) person who cleans a cow-house ▷ adj (Scot) covered in dung
SHARON n as in sharon fruit persimmon
SHARP adj having a keen cutting edge or fine point ▷ adv promptly ▷ n symbol raising a note one semitone above natural pitch ▷ vb make sharp
SHARPED > SHARP
SHARPEN vb make or become sharp or sharper
SHARPENED > SHARPEN
SHARPENER > SHARPEN
SHARPENS > SHARPEN
SHARPER n person who cheats
SHARPERS > SHARPER
SHARPEST > SHARP
SHARPIE n member of a teenage group having short hair and distinctive clothes
SHARPIES > SHARPIE
SHARPING > SHARP
SHARPINGS > SHARP

SHARPISH adj fairly sharp ▷ adv promptly
SHARPLY > SHARP
SHARPNESS > SHARP
SHARPS > SHARP
SHARPY n swindler
SHASH vb old form of sash
SHASHED > SHASH
SHASHES > SHASH
SHASHING > SHASH
SHASHLICK same as
> SHASHLIK
SHASHLIK n type of kebab
SHASHLIKS > SHASHLIK
SHASLIK n type of kebab
SHASLIKS > SHASLIK
SHASTA n plant of the daisy family
SHASTAS > SHASTA
SHASTER same as
> SHASTRA
SHASTERS > SHASTER
SHASTRA n any of the sacred writings of Hinduism
SHASTRAS > SHASTRA
SHAT past tense and past participle of > SHIT
SHATOOSH same as
> SHAHTOOSH
SHATTER vb break into pieces ▷ n fragment
SHATTERED adj completely exhausted
SHATTERER > SHATTER
SHATTERS > SHATTER
SHATTERY adj liable to shatter
SHAUCHLE vb Scots word meaning shuffle
SHAUCHLED > SHAUCHLE
SHAUCHLES > SHAUCHLE
SHAUCHLY > SHAUCHLE
SHAUGH n old word meaning small wood
SHAUGHS > SHAUGH
SHAUL vb old form of shawl
SHAULED > SHAUL
SHAULING > SHAUL
SHAULS > SHAUL
SHAVABLE > SHAVE
SHAVE vb remove (hair) from (the face, head, or body) with a razor or shaver ▷ n shaving
SHAVEABLE > SHAVE
SHAVED > SHAVE
SHAVELING n derogatory term for a priest or clergyman with a shaven head
SHAVEN adj closely shaved or tonsured
SHAVER n electric razor
SHAVERS > SHAVER
SHAVES > SHAUL
SHAVETAIL n American slang for second lieutenant
SHAVIE n Scots word meaning trick

SHAVIES > SHAVIE
SHAVING > SHAVE
SHAVINGS > SHAVE
SHAW n small wood ▷ vb show
SHAWARMA n strips of lamb, usu served in a pitta
SHAWARMAS > SHAWARMA
SHAWED > SHAW
SHAWING > SHAW
SHAWL n piece of cloth worn over a woman's shoulders or wrapped around a baby ▷ vb cover with a shawl
SHAWLED > SHAWL
SHAWLEY n Irish word for woman wearing shawl
SHAWLEYS > SHAWLEY
SHAWLIE n disparaging term for a working-class woman who wears a shawl
SHAWLIES > SHAWLIE
SHAWLING > SHAWL
SHAWLINGS > SHAWL
SHAWLLESS > SHAWL
SHAWLS > SHAWL
SHAWM n medieval form of the oboe with a conical bore and flaring bell
SHAWMS > SHAWM
SHAWN variant of > SHAWM
SHAWS > SHAW
SHAY dialect word for
> CHAISE
SHAYA n Indian plant
SHAYAS > SHAYA
SHAYKH same as > SHEIKH
SHAYKHS > SHAYKH
SHAYS > SHAY
SHAZAM interj magic slogan
SHCHI n Russian cabbage soup
SHCHIS > SHCHI
SHE pron female person or animal previously mentioned ▷ n female person or animal
SHEA n tropical African tree
SHEADING n any of the six subdivisions of the Isle of Man
SHEADINGS > SHEADING
SHEAF n bundle of papers ▷ vb tie into a sheaf
SHEAFED > SHEAF
SHEAFIER > SHEAF
SHEAFIEST > SHEAF
SHEAFING > SHEAF
SHEAFLIKE > SHEAF
SHEAFS > SHEAF
SHEAFY > SHEAF
SHEAL vb old word meaning shell
SHEALED > SHEAL
SHEALING > SHEAL
SHEALINGS > SHEAL
SHEALS > SHEAL
SHEAR vb clip hair or wool from ▷ n breakage caused through strain or twisting

SHEARED > SHEAR

SHEARER > SHEAR

SHEARERS > SHEAR

SHEARING > SHEAR

SHEARINGS > SHEAR

SHEARLEG *n* one spar of shearlegs

SHEARLEGS *same as* **>** SHEERLEGS

SHEARLING *n* young sheep after its first shearing

SHEARMAN *n* person who trims cloth

SHEARMEN > SHEARMAN

SHEARS > SHEAR

SHEAS > SHEA

SHEATFISH *n* European catfish

SHEATH *n* close-fitting cover, esp for a knife or sword

SHEATHE *vb* put into a sheath

SHEATHED > SHEATHE

SHEATHER > SHEATHE

SHEATHERS > SHEATHE

SHEATHES > SHEATHE

SHEATHIER > SHEATHE

SHEATHING *n* any material used as an outer layer

SHEATHS > SHEATH

SHEATHY > SHEATHE

SHEAVE *vb* gather or bind into sheaves ▷ *n* wheel with a grooved rim

SHEAVED > SHEAVE

SHEAVES > SHEAF

SHEAVING > SHEAVE

SHEBANG *n* situation, matter, or affair

SHEBANGS > SHEBANG

SHEBEAN *same as* **>** SHEBEEN

SHEBEANS > SHEBEAN

SHEBEEN *n* place where alcohol is sold illegally ▷ *vb* run a shebeen

SHEBEENED > SHEBEEN

SHEBEENER > SHEBEEN

SHEBEENS > SHEBEEN

SHECHITA *n* Jewish method of killing animals for food

SHECHITAH *same as* **>** SHECHITA

SHECHITAS > SHECHITA

SHED *n* building used for storage or shelter or as a workshop ▷ *vb* get rid of

SHEDABLE > SHED

SHEDDABLE > SHED

SHEDDED > SHED

SHEDDER *n* person or thing that sheds

SHEDDERS > SHEDDER

SHEDDING > SHED

SHEDDINGS > SHED

SHEDFUL *n* quantity or amount contained in a shed

SHEDFULS > SHEDFUL

SHEDHAND *n* labourer working in a shearing shed

SHEDHANDS > SHEDHAND

SHEDLIKE > SHED

SHEDLOAD *n* very large amount or number

SHEDLOADS > SHEDLOAD

SHEDS > SHED

SHEEL *vb* old word meaning shell

SHEELED > SHEEL

SHEELING > SHEEL

SHEELS > SHEEL

SHEEN *n* glistening brightness on the surface of something ▷ *adj* shining and beautiful ▷ *vb* give a sheen to

SHEENED > SHEEN

SHEENEY *n* offensive word for Jew

SHEENEYS > SHEENEY

SHEENFUL > SHEEN

SHEENIE *n* offensive word for Jew

SHEENIER > SHEEN

SHEENIES > SHEENIE

SHEENIEST > SHEEN

SHEENING > SHEEN

SHEENS > SHEEN

SHEENY > SHEEN

SHEEP *n* ruminant animal bred for wool and meat

SHEEPCOT *n* sheepcote

SHEEPCOTE *another word for* **>** SHEEPFOLD

SHEEPCOTS > SHEEPCOT

SHEEPDOG *n* dog used for herding sheep

SHEEPDOGS > SHEEPDOG

SHEEPFOLD *n* pen or enclosure for sheep

SHEEPHEAD *n* species of fish

SHEEPIER > SHEEP

SHEEPIEST > SHEEP

SHEEPISH *adj* embarrassed because of feeling foolish

SHEEPLE *pl n* people who follow the majority in matters of opinion, taste, etc

SHEEPLIKE > SHEEP

SHEEPMAN *n* person who keeps sheep

SHEEPMEN > SHEEPMAN

SHEEPO *n* person employed to bring sheep to the catching pen in a shearing shed

SHEEPOS > SHEEPO

SHEEPSKIN *n* skin of a sheep with the fleece still on, used for clothing or rugs

SHEEPWALK *n* tract of land for grazing sheep

SHEEPY > SHEEP

SHEER *adj* absolute, complete ▷ *adv* steeply ▷ *vb* change course suddenly ▷ *n* any transparent fabric used for making garments

SHEERED > SHEER

SHEERER > SHEER

SHEEREST > SHEER

SHEERING > SHEER

SHEERLEG *n* one spar of sheerlegs

SHEERLEGS *n* device for lifting heavy weights

SHEERLY > SHEER

SHEERNESS > SHEER

SHEERS > SHEER

SHEESH *interj* exclamation of surprise or annoyance

SHEESHA *n* Oriental water-pipe for smoking tobacco

SHEESHAS > SHEESHA

SHEET *n* large piece of cloth used as an inner bed cover ▷ *vb* provide with, cover, or wrap in a sheet

SHEETED > SHEET

SHEETER > SHEET

SHEETERS > SHEET

SHEETFED *adj* printing on separate sheets of paper

SHEETIER > SHEET

SHEETIEST > SHEET

SHEETING *n* material from which sheets are made

SHEETINGS > SHEETING

SHEETLESS > SHEET

SHEETLIKE > SHEET

SHEETROCK *n* brand name for plasterboard

SHEETS > SHEET

SHEETY > SHEET

SHEEVE *n* part of mine winding gear

SHEEVES > SHEEVE

SHEGETZ *n* offensive word for non-Jew

SHEHITA *n* slaughter of animal according to Jewish religious law

SHEHITAH *n* slaughter of animal according to Jewish religious law

SHEHITAHS > SHEHITAH

SHEHITAS > SHEHITA

SHEHNAI *n* Indian wind instrument

SHEHNAIS > SHEHNAI

SHEIK *same as* **>** SHEIKH

SHEIKDOM *same as* **>** SHEIKHDOM

SHEIKDOMS > SHEIKDOM

SHEIKH *n* Arab chief

SHEIKHA *n* chief wife of sheikh

SHEIKHAS > SHEIKHA

SHEIKHDOM *n* territory ruled by a sheikh

SHEIKHS > SHEIKH

SHEIKS > SHEIK

SHEILA *n* girl or woman

SHEILAS > SHEILA

SHEILING *n* hut used by shepherds

SHEILINGS > SHEILING

SHEITAN *n* Muslim demon

SHEITANS > SHEITAN

SHEITEL *n* traditional wig worn by Orthodox Jewish women

SHEITELS > SHEITEL

SHEKALIM > SHEKEL

SHEKEL *n* monetary unit of Israel

SHEKELIM > SHEKEL

SHEKELS > SHEKEL

SHELDDUCK *n* species of large duck

SHELDRAKE *same as* **>** SHELDUCK

SHELDUCK *n* large brightly coloured wild duck of Europe and Asia

SHELDUCKS > SHELDUCK

SHELF *n* board fixed horizontally for holding things ▷ *vb* put on a shelf

SHELFED > SHELF

SHELFFUL > SHELF

SHELFFULS > SHELF

SHELFIER > SHELF

SHELFIEST > SHELF

SHELFING > SHELF

SHELFLIKE > SHELF

SHELFROOM *n* space on shelf

SHELFS > SHELF

SHELFY > SHELF

SHELL *n* hard outer covering of an egg, nut, or certain animals ▷ *vb* take the shell from

SHELLAC *n* resin used in varnishes ▷ *vb* coat with shellac

SHELLACK *vb* shellac

SHELLACKS > SHELLAC

SHELLACS > SHELLAC

SHELLBACK *n* sailor who has crossed the equator

SHELLBARK *same as* **>** SHAGBARK

SHELLDUCK *n* shelduck

SHELLED > SHELL

SHELLER > SHELL

SHELLERS > SHELL

SHELLFIRE *n* firing of artillery shells

SHELLFISH *n* sea-living animal, esp one that can be eaten, with a shell

SHELLFUL > SHELL

SHELLFULS > SHELL

SHELLIER > SHELL

SHELLIEST > SHELL

SHELLING > SHELL

SHELLINGS > SHELL

SHELLS > SHELL

SHELLWORK *n* decoration with shells

SHELLY > SHELL

SHELTA *n* secret language used by some traveling people in Britain and Ireland

SHELTAS > SHELTA

SHELTER *n* structure providing protection from danger or the weather ▷ *vb* give shelter to

SHELTERED adj protected from wind and rain
SHELTERER > SHELTER
SHELTERS > SHELTER
SHELTERY > SHELTER
SHELTIE n small dog similar to a collie
SHELTIES > SHELTY
SHELTY same as **>** SHELTIE
SHELVE vb put aside or postpone
SHELVED > SHELVE
SHELVER > SHELVE
SHELVERS > SHELVE
SHELVES > SHELF
SHELVIER > SHELVY
SHELVIEST > SHELVY
SHELVING n (material for) shelves
SHELVINGS > SHELVING
SHELVY adj having shelves
SHEMALE n male who has acquired female physical characteristics through surgery
SHEMALES > SHEMALE
SHEMOZZLE n noisy confusion or dispute
SHEN n (in Chinese thought) spiritual element of the psyche
SHENAI same as **>** SHEHNAI
SHENAIS > SHENAI
SHEND vb put to shame
SHENDING > SHEND
SHENDS > SHEND
SHENT > SHEND
SHEOL n hell
SHEOLS > SHEOL
SHEPHERD n person who tends sheep **>** vb guide or watch over (people)
SHEPHERDS > SHEPHERD
SHEQALIM n plural of sheqel
SHEQEL same as **>** SHEKEL
SHEQELS > SHEQEL
SHERANG n person in charge
SHERANGS > SHERANG
SHERBERT same as **>** SHERBET
SHERBERTS > SHERBET
SHERBET n fruit-flavoured fizzy powder
SHERBETS > SHERBET
SHERD same as **>** SHARD
SHERDS > SHERD
SHERE old spelling of **>** SHEER
SHEREEF same as **>** SHERIF
SHEREEFS > SHEREEF
SHERIA same as **>** SHARIA
SHERIAS > SHERIA
SHERIAT n Muslim religious law
SHERIATS > SHERIAT
SHERIF n descendant of Mohammed through his daughter Fatima

SHERIFF n (in the US) chief law enforcement officer of a county
SHERIFFS > SHERIFF
SHERIFIAN > SHERIF
SHERIFS > SHERIF
SHERLOCK n detective **>** vb investigate (something)
SHERLOCKS > SHERLOCK
SHERO n woman considered a hero
SHEROES > SHERO
SHEROOT n cheroot
SHEROOTS > SHEROOT
SHERPA n official who assists at a summit meeting
SHERPAS > SHERPA
SHERRIED adj flavoured with sherry
SHERRIES > SHERRY
SHERRIS n old form of sherry
SHERRISES > SHERRIS
SHERRY n pale or dark brown fortified wine
SHERWANI n long coat closed up to the neck, worn by men in India
SHERWANIS > SHERWANI
SHES > SHE
SHET vb old form of shut
SHETLAND n type of wool spun in the Shetland islands
SHETLANDS > SHETLAND
SHETS > SHET
SHETTING > SHET
SHEUCH n ditch or trough **>** vb dig
SHEUCHED > SHEUCH
SHEUCHING > SHEUCH
SHEUCHS > SHEUCH
SHEUGH same as **>** SHEUCH
SHEUGHED > SHEUGH
SHEUGHING > SHEUGH
SHEUGHS > SHEUGH
SHEVA n mark in Hebrew writing
SHEVAS > SHEVA
SHEW archaic spelling of **>** SHOW
SHEWBREAD n loaves of bread placed every Sabbath on the table beside the altar of incense in the tabernacle of ancient Israel
SHEWED > SHEW
SHEWEL n old word meaning scarecrow
SHEWELS > SHEWEL
SHEWER > SHEW
SHEWERS > SHEW
SHEWING > SHEW
SHEWN > SHEW
SHEWS > SHEW
SHH interj sound made to ask for silence
SHHH interj an interjection requesting quietness
SHIAI n judo contest

SHIAIS > SHIAI
SHIATSU n type of massage
SHIATSUS > SHIATSU
SHIATZU n shiatzu
SHIATZUS > SHIATZU
SHIBAH n Jewish period of mourning
SHIBAHS > SHIBAH
SHIBUICHI n Japanese alloy of copper and silver
SHICKER n alcoholic drink
SHICKERED adj drunk
SHICKERS > SHICKER
SHICKSA n non-Jewish girl
SHICKSAS > SHICKSA
SHIDDER n old word meaning female animal
SHIDDERS > SHIDDER
SHIDDUCH n arranged marriage
SHIED > SHY
SHIEL vb sheal
SHIELD n piece of armour carried on the arm to protect the body from blows or missiles **>** vb protect
SHIELDED > SHIELD
SHIELDER > SHIELD
SHIELDERS > SHIELD
SHIELDING > SHIELD
SHIELDS > SHIELD
SHIELED > SHIEL
SHIELING n rough hut or shelter used by people tending cattle on high or remote ground
SHIELINGS > SHIELING
SHIELS > SHIEL
SHIER n horse that shies habitually
SHIERS > SHIER
SHIES > SHY
SHIEST > SHY
SHIFT vb move **>** n shifting
SHIFTABLE > SHIFT
SHIFTED > SHIFT
SHIFTER > SHIFT
SHIFTERS > SHIFT
SHIFTIER > SHIFTY
SHIFTIEST > SHIFTY
SHIFTILY > SHIFTY
SHIFTING > SHIFT
SHIFTINGS > SHIFT
SHIFTLESS adj lacking in ambition or initiative
SHIFTS > SHIFT
SHIFTWORK n system of employment where an individual's normal hours of work are outside the period of normal day working
SHIFTY adj evasive or untrustworthy
SHIGELLA n type of rod-shaped Gram-negative bacterium
SHIGELLAE > SHIGELLA
SHIGELLAS > SHIGELLA

SHIITAKE n kind of mushroom widely used in Oriental cookery
SHIITAKES > SHIITAKE
SHIKAR n hunting, esp big-game hunting **>** vb hunt (game, esp big game)
SHIKARA n (in Kashmir) light, flat-bottomed boat
SHIKARAS > SHIKARA
SHIKAREE same as **>** SHIKARI
SHIKAREES > SHIKAREE
SHIKARI n (in India) a hunter
SHIKARIS > SHIKARI
SHIKARRED > SHIKAR
SHIKARS > SHIKAR
SHIKKER n Yiddish term for drunk person
SHIKKERED same as **>** SHICKERED
SHIKKERS > SHIKKER
SHIKRA n small Asian sparrowhawk
SHIKRAS > SHIKRA
SHIKSA n often derogatory term for a non-Jewish girl
SHIKSAS > SHIKSA
SHIKSE n non-Jewish girl
SHIKSEH same as **>** SHIKSE
SHIKSEHS > SHIKSEH
SHIKSES > SHIKSE
SHILINGI n money unit in Tanzania
SHILINGIS > SHILINGI
SHILL n confidence trickster's assistant **>** vb act as a shill
SHILLABER n keen customer
SHILLALA n short Irish club or cudgel
SHILLALAH same as **>** SHILLALA
SHILLALAS > SHILLALA
SHILLED > SHILL
SHILLELAH same as **>** SHILLALA
SHILLING n former British coin
SHILLINGS > SHILLING
SHILLS > SHILL
SHILPIT adj puny
SHILY > SHY
SHIM n thin strip of material placed between two close surfaces to fill a gap **>** vb fit or fill up with a shim
SHIMAAL n hot Middle Eastern wind
SHIMAALS > SHIMAAL
SHIMMED > SHIM
SHIMMER n (shine with) a faint unsteady light **>** vb shine with a faint unsteady light
SHIMMERED > SHIMMER
SHIMMERS > SHIMMER
SHIMMERY adj shining with a glistening or tremulous light

SHIMMEY n chemise

SHIMMEYS > SHIMMEY

SHIMMIED > SHIMMY

SHIMMIES > SHIMMY

SHIMMING > SHIM

SHIMMY n American ragtime dance ▷ vb dance the shimmy

SHIMMYING > SHIMMY

SHIMOZZLE n predicament

SHIMS > SHIM

SHIN n front of the lower leg ▷ vb climb by using the hands or arms and legs

SHINBONE n tibia

SHINBONES > SHINBONE

SHINDIES > SHINDY

SHINDIG n noisy party

SHINDIGS > SHINDIG

SHINDY n quarrel or commotion

SHINDYS > SHINDY

SHINE vb give out or reflect light; cause to gleam ▷ n brightness or lustre

SHINED > SHINE

SHINELESS > SHINE

SHINER n black eye

SHINERS > SHINER

SHINES > SHINE

SHINESSES > SHY

SHINESS > SHY

SHINGLE n wooden roof tile ▷ vb cover (a roof) with shingles

SHINGLED > SHINGLE

SHINGLER > SHINGLE

SHINGLERS > SHINGLE

SHINGLES n disease causing a rash of small blisters along a nerve

SHINGLIER > SHINGLE

SHINGLING > SHINGLE

SHINGLY > SHINGLE

SHINGUARD n rigid piece of plastic to protect footballer's shin

SHINIER > SHINY

SHINIES > SHINY

SHINIEST > SHINY

SHINILY > SHINY

SHININESS > SHINY

SHINING > SHINE

SHININGLY > SHINE

SHINJU n (formerly, in Japan) a ritual double suicide of lovers

SHINJUS > SHINJU

SHINKIN n worthless person

SHINKINS > SHINKIN

SHINLEAF n wintergreen

SHINLEAFS > SHINLEAF

SHINNE n old form of chin

SHINNED > SHIN

SHINNERY n American oak tree

SHINNES > SHINNE

SHINNEY vb climb with hands and legs

SHINNEYED > SHINNEY

SHINNEYS > SHINNEY

SHINNIED > SHINNEY

SHINNIES > SHINNEY

SHINNING > SHIN

SHINNY same as > SHINTY

SHINNYING > SHINNY

SHINOLA n tradename of a kind of boot polish

SHINOLAS > SHINOLA

SHINS > SHIN

SHINTIED > SHINTY

SHINTIES > SHINTY

SHINTY n game like hockey ▷ vb play shinty

SHINTYING > SHINTY

SHINY adj bright and polished

SHIP n large seagoing vessel ▷ vb send or transport by carrier, esp a ship

SHIPBOARD adj taking place or used aboard a ship

SHIPBORNE adj carried on ship

SHIPFUL n amount carried by ship

SHIPFULS > SHIPFUL

SHIPLAP n method of constructing ship hull

SHIPLAPS > SHIPLAP

SHIPLESS > SHIP

SHIPLOAD n quantity carried by a ship

SHIPLOADS > SHIPLOAD

SHIPMAN n master or captain of a ship

SHIPMATE n sailor serving on the same ship as another

SHIPMATES > SHIPMATE

SHIPMEN > SHIPMAN

SHIPMENT n act of shipping cargo

SHIPMENTS > SHIPMENT

SHIPOWNER n person who owns or has shares in a ship or ships

SHIPPABLE > SHIP

SHIPPED > SHIP

SHIPPEN n dialect word for cattle shed

SHIPPENS > SHIPPEN

SHIPPER n person or company that ships

SHIPPERS > SHIPPER

SHIPPIE n prostitute who solicits at a port

SHIPPIES > SHIPPIE

SHIPPING > SHIP

SHIPPINGS > SHIP

SHIPPO n Japanese enamel work

SHIPPON n dialect word for cattle shed

SHIPPONS > SHIPPON

SHIPPOS > SHIPPO

SHIPPOUND n Baltic weight measure

SHIPS > SHIP

SHIPSHAPE adj orderly or neat ▷ adv in a neat and orderly manner

SHIPSIDE n part of wharf next to ship

SHIPSIDES > SHIPSIDE

SHIPTIME n arrival time of a supply ship

SHIPTIMES > SHIPTIME

SHIPWAY n structure on which a vessel is built, then launched

SHIPWAYS > SHIPWAY

SHIPWORM n type of wormlike marine bivalve mollusc

SHIPWORMS > SHIPWORM

SHIPWRECK n destruction of a ship through storm or collision ▷ vb cause to undergo shipwreck

SHIPYARD n place where ships are built

SHIPYARDS > SHIPYARD

SHIR n gathering in material

SHIRALEE n swag

SHIRALEES > SHIRALEE

SHIRAZ n variety of black grape used for wine

SHIRAZES > SHIRAZ

SHIRE n county ▷ vb refresh or rest

SHIRED > SHIRE

SHIREMAN n sheriff

SHIREMEN > SHIREMAN

SHIRES > SHIRE

SHIRING > SHIRE

SHIRK vb avoid (duty or work) ▷ n person who shirks

SHIRKED > SHIRK

SHIRKER > SHIRK

SHIRKERS > SHIRK

SHIRKING > SHIRK

SHIRKS > SHIRK

SHIRR vb gather (fabric) into parallel rows to decorate a dress, etc ▷ n series of gathered rows decorating a dress, etc

SHIRRA old Scots word for > SHERIFF

SHIRRALEE n swagman's bundle of possessions

SHIRRAS > SHIRRA

SHIRRED > SHIRR

SHIRRING > SHIRR

SHIRRINGS > SHIRR

SHIRRS > SHIRR

SHIRS > SHIR

SHIRT n garment for the upper part of the body ▷ vb put a shirt on

SHIRTBAND n neckband on shirt

SHIRTED > SHIRT

SHIRTIER > SHIRTY

SHIRTIEST > SHIRTY

SHIRTILY > SHIRTY

SHIRTING n fabric used in making men's shirts

SHIRTINGS > SHIRTING

SHIRTLESS > SHIRT

SHIRTS > SHIRT

SHIRTTAIL n part of a shirt that extends below the waist

SHIRTY adj bad-tempered or annoyed

SHISH adj as in shish kebab dish of meat and vegetables grilled on skewers

SHISHA same as > HOOKAH

SHISHAS > SHISHA

SHISO n Asian plant with aromatic leaves

SHISOS > SHISO

SHIST n schist

SHISTS > SHIST

SHIT vb defecate ▷ n excrement ▷ interj exclamation of anger or disgust

SHITAKE same as > SHIITAKE

SHITAKES > SHITAKE

SHITBAG n contemptible person

SHITBAGS > SHITBAG

SHITCAN vb discard or reject

SHITCANS > SHITCAN

SHITE same as > SHIT

SHITED > SHITE

SHITES > SHITE

SHITFACE n despicable person

SHITFACED adj drunk

SHITFACES > SHITFACE

SHITHEAD n fool

SHITHEADS > SHITHEAD

SHITHEEL n contemptible person

SHITHEELS > SHITHEEL

SHITHOLE n dirty place

SHITHOLES > SHITHOLE

SHITHOUSE n lavatory

SHITING > SHITE

SHITLESS adj very frightened

SHITLIST n list of hated things

SHITLISTS > SHITLIST

SHITLOAD n taboo slang for a lot

SHITLOADS > SHITLOAD

SHITS > SHIT

SHITTAH n tree mentioned in the Old Testament

SHITTAHS > SHITTAH

SHITTED > SHIT

SHITTER n toilet

SHITTERS > SHITTER

SHITTIER > SHIT

SHITTIEST > SHIT

SHITTILY > SHIT

SHITTIM > SHITTAH

SHITTIMS > SHITTAH

SHITTING > SHIT

SHITTY > SHIT

SHITWORK n work considered to be menial or routine

SHITWORKS > SHITWORK

SHITZU n breed of small dog with long, silky fur
SHITZUS > SHITZU
SHIUR n lesson in which a passage of the Talmud is studied
SHIURIM > SHIUR
SHIV variant spelling of **>** CHIV
SHIVA variant of **>** SHIVAH
SHIVAH n Jewish period of formal mourning
SHIVAHS > SHIVAH
SHIVAREE n discordant mock serenade to newlyweds, made with pans, kettles, etc
SHIVAREED > SHIVAREE
SHIVAREES > SHIVAREE
SHIVAS > SHIVA
SHIVE n flat cork or bung for wide-mouthed bottles
SHIVER vb tremble, as from cold or fear ▷ n shivering
SHIVERED > SHIVER
SHIVERER > SHIVER
SHIVERERS > SHIVER
SHIVERIER > SHIVERY
SHIVERING > SHIVER
SHIVERS > SHIVER
SHIVERY adj inclined to shiver or tremble
SHIVES > SHIVE
SHIVITI n Jewish decorative plaque with religious message
SHIVITIS > SHIVITI
SHIVOO n Australian word meaning rowdy party
SHIVOOS > SHIVOO
SHIVS > SHIV
SHIVVED > SHIV
SHIVVING > SHIV
SHIZZLE n form of US rap slang
SHIZZLES > SHIZZLE
SHKOTZIM n plural of shegetz
SHLEMIEHL Yiddish word for **>** FOOL
SHLEMIEL same as **>** SCHLEMIEL
SHLEMIELS > SHLEMIEL
SHLEP vb schlep
SHLEPP vb schlep
SHLEPPED > SHLEP
SHLEPPER > SHLEP
SHLEPPERS > SHLEP
SHLEPPIER > SHLEPPY
SHLEPPING > SHLEP
SHLEPPS > SHLEPP
SHLEPPY adj dingy, shabby, or rundown
SHLEPS > SHLEP
SHLIMAZEL n unlucky person
SHLOCK n something of poor quality
SHLOCKIER > SHLOCK
SHLOCKS > SHLOCK
SHLOCKY > SHLOCK

SHLONG same as **>** SCHLONG
SHLONGS > SHLONG
SHLOSHIM n period of thirty days' deep mourning following a death
SHLOSHIMS > SHLOSHIM
SHLUB same as **>** SCHLUB
SHLUBS > SHLUB
SHLUMP vb move in lazy way
SHLUMPED > SHLUMP
SHLUMPIER > SHLUMPY
SHLUMPING > SHLUMP
SHLUMPS > SHLUMP
SHLUMPY > SHLUMP
SHMALTZ n schmaltz
SHMALTZES > SHMALTZ
SHMALTZY > SHMALTZ
SHMATTE n rag
SHMATTES > SHMATTE
SHMEAR same as **>** SCHMEAR
SHMEARED > SHMEAR
SHMEARING > SHMEAR
SHMEARS > SHMEAR
SHMEER same as **>** SCHMEAR
SHMEERED > SHMEER
SHMEERING > SHMEER
SHMEERS > SHMEER
SHMEK n smell
SHMEKS > SHMEK
SHMO same as **>** SCHMO
SHMOCK n despicable person
SHMOCKS > SHMOCK
SHMOE same as **>** SCHMOE
SHMOES > SHMO
SHMOOSE variant of **>** SCHMOOZE
SHMOOSED > SHMOOSE
SHMOOSES > SHMOOSE
SHMOOSING > SHMOOSE
SHMOOZE variant of **>** SCHMOOZE
SHMOOZED > SHMOOZE
SHMOOZER same as **>** SCHMOOZER
SHMOOZERS > SHMOOZER
SHMOOZES > SHMOOZE
SHMOOZIER > SHMOOZY
SHMOOZING > SHMOOZE
SHMOOZY adj talking casually, gossipy
SHMUCK n despicable person
SHMUCKIER > SHMUCKY
SHMUCKS > SCHMUCK
SHMUCKY same as **>** SCHMUCKY
SHNAPPS same as **>** SCHNAPPS
SHNAPS n schnaps
SHNOOK n stupid person
SHNOOKS > SHNOOK
SHNORRER same as **>** SCHNORRER
SHNORRERS > SCHNORRER
SHO adj sure, as pronounced in southern US

SHOAL n large number of fish swimming together ▷ vb make or become shallow ▷ adj (of the draught of a vessel) drawing little water
SHOALED > SHOAL
SHOALER > SHOAL
SHOALEST > SHOAL
SHOALIER > SHOALY
SHOALIEST > SHOALY
SHOALING > SHOAL
SHOALINGS > SHOAL
SHOALNESS > SHOAL
SHOALS > SHOAL
SHOALWISE adv in a large group or in large groups
SHOALY adj shallow
SHOAT n piglet that has recently been weaned
SHOATS > SHOAT
SHOCHET n (in Judaism) a person licensed to slaughter animals and birds
SHOCHETIM > SHOCHET
SHOCHETS > SHOCHET
SHOCHU n type of Japanese alcoholic spirit
SHOCHUS > SHOCHU
SHOCK vb horrify, disgust, or astonish ▷ n sudden violent emotional disturbance ▷ adj bushy
SHOCKABLE > SHOCK
SHOCKED > SHOCK
SHOCKER n person or thing that shocks or horrifies
SHOCKERS > SHOCKER
SHOCKING adj causing horror, disgust, or astonishment
SHOCKS > SHOCK
SHOD > SHOE
SHODDEN vb old form of shod
SHODDIER > SHODDY
SHODDIES > SHODDY
SHODDIEST > SHODDY
SHODDILY > SHODDY
SHODDY adj made or done badly ▷ n yarn or fabric made from wool waste or clippings
SHODER n skins used in making gold leaf
SHODERS > SHODER
SHOE n outer covering for the foot, ending below the ankle ▷ vb fit with a shoe or shoes
SHOEBILL n large wading bird of tropical E African swamps
SHOEBILLS > SHOEBILL
SHOEBLACK n (esp formerly) a person who shines boots and shoes
SHOEBOX n cardboard box for shoes
SHOEBOXES > SHOEBOX
SHOEBRUSH n brush for cleaning shoes

SHOED > SHOE
SHOEHORN n smooth curved implement inserted at the heel of a shoe to ease the foot into it ▷ vb cram (people or things) into a very small space
SHOEHORNS > SHOEHORN
SHOEING > SHOE
SHOEINGS > SHOE
SHOELACE n cord for fastening shoes
SHOELACES > SHOELACE
SHOELESS > SHOE
SHOEMAKER n person who makes or repairs shoes or boots
SHOEPAC n waterproof boot
SHOEPACK n waterproof boot
SHOEPACKS > SHOEPACK
SHOEPACS > SHOEPAC
SHOER n person who shoes horses
SHOERS > SHOER
SHOES > SHOE
SHOESHINE n act or an instance of polishing a pair of shoes
SHOETREE n piece of metal, wood, or plastic inserted in a shoe to keep its shape
SHOETREES > SHOETREE
SHOFAR n ram's horn sounded in Jewish synagogue
SHOFARS > SHOFAR
SHOFROTH > SHOFAR
SHOG vb shake
SHOGGED > SHOG
SHOGGING > SHOG
SHOGGLE vb shake
SHOGGLED > SHOGGLE
SHOGGLES > SHOGGLE
SHOGGLIER > SHOGGLE
SHOGGLING > SHOGGLE
SHOGGLY > SHOGGLE
SHOGI n Japanese chess
SHOGIS > SHOGI
SHOGS > SHOG
SHOGUN n Japanese chief military commander
SHOGUNAL > SHOGUN
SHOGUNATE n office or rule of a shogun
SHOGUNS > SHOGUN
SHOJI n Japanese rice-paper screen in a sliding wooden frame
SHOJIS > SHOJI
SHOJO n genre of Japanese comics intended for girls
SHOLA n Indian plant
SHOLAS > SHOLA
SHOLOM n Hebrew greeting
SHOLOMS > SHOLOM
SHONE > SHINE
SHONEEN n Irishman who imitates English ways
SHONEENS > SHONEEN**

SHONKIER > SHONKY
SHONKIEST > SHONKY
SHONKY adj unreliable or unsound
SHOO interj go away! ▷ vb drive away as by saying 'shoo'
SHOOED > SHOO
SHOOFLIES > SHOOFLY
SHOOFLY n as in shoofly pie US dessert similar to treacle tart
SHOOGIE vb Scots word meaning swing
SHOOGIED > SHOOGIE
SHOOGIES > SHOOGIE
SHOOGLE vb shake, sway, or rock back and forth ▷ n rocking motion
SHOOGLED > SHOOGLE
SHOOGLES > SHOOGLE
SHOOGLIER > SHOOGLE
SHOOGLING > SHOOGLE
SHOOGLY > SHOOGLE
SHOOING > SHOO
SHOOK n set of parts ready for assembly
SHOOKS > SHOOK
SHOOL dialect word for > SHOVEL
SHOOLE dialect word for > SHOVEL
SHOOLED > SHOOL
SHOOLES > SHOOLE
SHOOLING > SHOOL
SHOOLS > SHOOL
SHOON plural of > SHOE
SHOORA same as > SHURA
SHOORAS > SHOORA
SHOOS > SHOO
SHOOSH vb make a rushing sound when moving
SHOOSHED > SHOOSH
SHOOSHES > SHOOSH
SHOOSHING > SHOOSH
SHOOT vb hit, wound, or kill with a missile fired from a weapon ▷ n new branch or sprout of a plant
SHOOTABLE > SHOOT
SHOOTDOWN n act of shooting down aircraft
SHOOTER n person or thing that shoots
SHOOTERS > SHOOTER
SHOOTIE n type of shoe that covers the ankle
SHOOTIES > SHOOTIE
SHOOTING > SHOOT
SHOOTINGS > SHOOT
SHOOTIST n person who shoots
SHOOTISTS > SHOOTIST
SHOOTOUT n conclusive gunfight
SHOOTOUTS > SHOOTOUT
SHOOTS > SHOOT
SHOP n place for sale of goods and services ▷ vb visit a shop or shops to buy goods
SHOPBOARD n shop counter

SHOPBOT n price-comparison website
SHOPBOTS > SHOPBOT
SHOPBOY n boy working in shop
SHOPBOYS > SHOPBOY
SHOPE n old form of shape
SHOPFRONT n area of shop facing street
SHOPFUL n amount stored in shop
SHOPFULS > SHOPFUL
SHOPGIRL n girl working in shop
SHOPGIRLS > SHOPGIRL
SHOPHAR same as > SHOFAR
SHOPHARS > SHOPHAR
SHOPHROTH > SHOPHAR
SHOPLESS adj (of an area) having no shops
SHOPLIFT vb steal from shop
SHOPLIFTS > SHOPLIFT
SHOPMAN n man working in shop
SHOPMEN > SHOPMAN
SHOPPE old-fashioned spelling of > SHOP
SHOPPED > SHOP
SHOPPER n person who buys goods in a shop
SHOPPERS > SHOPPER
SHOPPES > SHOPPE
SHOPPIER > SHOPPY
SHOPPIES > SHOPPY
SHOPPIEST > SHOPPY
SHOPPING > SHOP
SHOPPINGS > SHOP
SHOPPY adj of a shop ▷ n shop assistant
SHOPS > SHOP
SHOPTALK n conversation about one's work, carried on outside working hours
SHOPTALKS > SHOPTALK
SHOPWOMAN n woman working in a shop
SHOPWOMEN > SHOPWOMAN
SHOPWORN adj worn or faded from being displayed in a shop
SHORAN n short-range radar system
SHORANS > SHORAN
SHORE n edge of a sea or lake ▷ vb prop or support
SHOREBIRD n bird that lives close to the water
SHORED > SHORE
SHORELESS adj without a shore suitable for landing
SHORELINE n edge of a sea, lake, or wide river
SHOREMAN n person who lives on shore
SHOREMEN > SHOREMAN
SHORER > SHORE
SHORERS > SHORE
SHORES > SHORE
SHORESIDE n area at shore

SHORESMAN n fishing industry worker on shore
SHORESMEN > SHORESMAN
SHOREWARD adj near or facing the shore ▷ adv towards the shore
SHOREWEED n tufty aquatic perennial plant
SHORING > SHORE
SHORINGS > SHORE
SHORL n black mineral
SHORLS > SHORL
SHORN past participle of > SHEAR
SHORT adj not long ▷ adv abruptly ▷ n drink of spirits ▷ vb short-circuit
SHORTAGE n deficiency
SHORTAGES > SHORTAGE
SHORTARM adj (of a punch) with the arm bent
SHORTARSE n short person
SHORTCAKE n shortbread
SHORTCUT n route that is shorter than the usual one
SHORTCUTS > SHORTCUT
SHORTED > SHORT
SHORTEN vb make or become shorter
SHORTENED > SHORTEN
SHORTENER > SHORTEN
SHORTENS > SHORTEN
SHORTER > SHORT
SHORTEST > SHORT
SHORTFALL n deficit
SHORTGOWN n old Scots word meaning woman's jacket
SHORTHAIR n cat with short fur
SHORTHAND n system of rapid writing using symbols to represent words
SHORTHEAD n species of fish
SHORTHOLD n as in shorthold tenancy letting of a dwelling for between one and five years at a fair rent
SHORTHORN n member of a breed of cattle with short horns
SHORTIA n American flowering plant
SHORTIAS > SHORTIA
SHORTIE n person or thing that is extremely short
SHORTIES > SHORTY
SHORTING > SHORT
SHORTISH > SHORT
SHORTLIST n list of suitable applicants for a job, etc
SHORTLY adv soon
SHORTNESS > SHORT
SHORTS pl n trousers reaching the top of the thigh or partway to the knee

SHORTSTOP n fielding position to the left of second base viewed from home plate
SHORTWAVE n radio wave with a wavelength in the range 10–100 metres
SHORTY same as > SHORTIE
SHOT vb load with shot
SHOTE same as > SHOAT
SHOTES > SHOTE
SHOTFIRER n person detonating blasting charge
SHOTGUN n gun for firing a charge of shot at short range ▷ adj involving coercion or duress ▷ vb shoot or threaten with or as if with a shotgun
SHOTGUNS > SHOTGUN
SHOTHOLE n drilled hole in to which explosive is put for blasting
SHOTHOLES > SHOTHOLE
SHOTMAKER n sport player making good shots
SHOTPROOF adj able to withstand shot
SHOTS > SHOT
SHOTT n shallow temporary salt lake or marsh in the North African desert
SHOTTE n old form of shoat
SHOTTED > SHOT
SHOTTEN adj (of fish, esp herring) having recently spawned
SHOTTES > SHOTTE
SHOTTING > SHOT
SHOTTLE n small drawer
SHOTTLES > SHOTTLE
SHOTTS > SHOTT
SHOUGH n old word meaning lapdog
SHOUGHS > SHOUGH
SHOULD > SHALL
SHOULDER n part of the body to which an arm, foreleg, or wing is attached ▷ vb bear (a burden or responsibility)
SHOULDERS > SHOULDER
SHOULDEST same as > SHOULDST
SHOULDST form of the past tense of > SHALL
SHOUSE n toilet ▷ adj unwell or in poor spirits
SHOUSES > SHOUSE
SHOUT n loud cry ▷ vb cry out loudly
SHOUTED > SHOUT
SHOUTER > SHOUT
SHOUTERS > SHOUT
SHOUTHER Scots form of > SHOULDER
SHOUTHERS > SHOUTHER
SHOUTIER > SHOUTY
SHOUTIEST > SHOUTY

SHOUTING > SHOUT

SHOUTINGS > SHOUT

SHOUTLINE n line in advertisement made prominent to catch attention

SHOUTOUT n public greeting, esp one broadcast via television or radio

SHOUTOUTS > SHOUTOUT

SHOUTS > SHOUT

SHOUTY adj characterized by or involving shouting

SHOVE vb push roughly ▷ n rough push

SHOVED > SHOVE

SHOVEL n tool for lifting or moving loose material ▷ vb lift or move as with a shovel

SHOVELED > SHOVEL

SHOVELER n type of duck

SHOVELERS > SHOVELER

SHOVELFUL > SHOVEL

SHOVELING > SHOVEL

SHOVELLED > SHOVEL

SHOVELLER > SHOVEL

SHOVELS > SHOVEL

SHOVER > SHOVE

SHOVERS > SHOVE

SHOVES > SHOVE

SHOVING n act of pushing hard

SHOVINGS > SHOVING

SHOW vb make, be, or become noticeable or visible ▷ n public exhibition

SHOWABLE > SHOW

SHOWBIZ n entertainment industry including theatre, films, and TV

SHOWBIZZY > SHOWBIZ

SHOWBOAT n paddle-wheel river steamer with a theatre and a repertory company ▷ vb perform or behave in a showy and flamboyant way

SHOWBOATS > SHOWBOAT

SHOWBOX n box containing showman's material

SHOWBOXES > SHOWBOX

SHOWBREAD same as > SHEWBREAD

SHOWCASE n situation in which something is displayed to best advantage ▷ vb exhibit or display ▷ adj displayed or meriting display as in a showcase

SHOWCASED > SHOWCASE

SHOWCASES > SHOWCASE

SHOWD vb rock or sway to and fro ▷ n rocking motion

SHOWDED > SHOWD

SHOWDING > SHOWD

SHOWDOWN n confrontation that settles a dispute

SHOWDOWNS > SHOWDOWN

SHOWDS > SHOWD

SHOWED > SHOW

SHOWER n kind of bath in which a person stands while being sprayed with water ▷ vb wash in a shower

SHOWERED > SHOWER

SHOWERER > SHOWER

SHOWERERS > SHOWER

SHOWERFUL > SHOWER

SHOWERIER > SHOWER

SHOWERING > SHOWER

SHOWERS > SHOWER

SHOWERY > SHOWER

SHOWGHE n old word meaning lapdog

SHOWGHES > SHOWGHE

SHOWGIRL n girl who appears in shows, etc, esp as a singer or dancer

SHOWGIRLS > SHOWGIRL

SHOWGOER n member of the audience of a play, film, or show

SHOWGOERS > SHOWGOER

SHOWIER > SHOWY

SHOWIEST > SHOWY

SHOWILY > SHOWY

SHOWINESS > SHOWY

SHOWING > SHOW

SHOWINGS > SHOW

SHOWJUMP vb take part in a showjumping competition

SHOWJUMPS > SHOWJUMP

SHOWMAN n man skilled at presenting anything spectacularly

SHOWMANCE n romance between two stars that lasts only for the run of the show they are in

SHOWMANLY > SHOWMAN

SHOWMEN > SHOWMAN

SHOWN > SHOW

SHOWOFF n person who makes a vain display of himself or herself

SHOWOFFS > SHOWOFF

SHOWPIECE n excellent specimen shown for display or as an example

SHOWPLACE n place visited for its beauty or interest

SHOWRING n area where animals are displayed for sale or competition

SHOWRINGS > SHOWRING

SHOWROOM n room in which goods for sale are on display

SHOWROOMS > SHOWROOM

SHOWS > SHOW

SHOWTIME n time when show begins

SHOWTIMES > SHOWTIME

SHOWY adj gaudy

SHOWYARD n yard where cattle are displayed

SHOWYARDS > SHOWYARD

SHOYU n Japanese variety of soy sauce

SHOYUS > SHOYU

SHRADDHA n Hindu offering to an ancestor

SHRADDHAS > SHRADDHA

SHRANK > SHRINK

SHRAPNEL n artillery shell filled with pellets which scatter on explosion

SHRAPNELS > SHRAPNEL

SHRED n long narrow strip torn from something ▷ vb tear to shreds

SHREDDED > SHRED

SHREDDER > SHRED

SHREDDERS > SHRED

SHREDDIER > SHRED

SHREDDING > SHRED

SHREDDY > SHRED

SHREDLESS > SHRED

SHREDS > SHRED

SHREEK old spelling of > SHRIEK

SHREEKED > SHREEK

SHREEKING > SHREEK

SHREEKS > SHREEK

SHREIK old spelling of > SHRIEK

SHREIKED > SHREIK

SHREIKING > SHREIK

SHREIKS > SHREIK

SHREW n small mouselike animal ▷ vb curse or damn

SHREWD adj clever and perceptive

SHREWDER > SHREWD

SHREWDEST > SHREWD

SHREWDIE n shrewd person

SHREWDIES > SHREWDIE

SHREWDLY > SHREWD

SHREWED > SHREW

SHREWING > SHREW

SHREWISH adj (esp of a woman) bad-tempered and nagging

SHREWLIKE > SHREW

SHREWMICE pl n shrews

SHREWS > SHREW

SHRI n Indian title of respect

SHRIECH old spelling of > SHRIEK

SHRIECHED > SHRIECH

SHRIECHES > SHRIECH

SHRIEK n shrill cry ▷ vb utter (with) a shriek

SHRIEKED > SHRIEK

SHRIEKER > SHRIEK

SHRIEKERS > SHRIEK

SHRIEKIER > SHRIEK

SHRIEKING > SHRIEK

SHRIEKS > SHRIEK

SHRIEKY > SHRIEK

SHRIEVAL adj of or relating to a sheriff

SHRIEVE archaic word for > SHERIFF

SHRIEVED > SHRIEVE

SHRIEVES > SHRIEVE

SHRIEVING > SHRIEVE

SHRIFT n act or an instance of shriving or being shriven

SHRIFTS > SHRIFT

SHRIGHT n old word meaning shriek

SHRIGHTS > SHRIGHT

SHRIKE n songbird with a heavy hooked bill ▷ vb archaic word for shriek

SHRIKED > SHRIKE

SHRIKES > SHRIKE

SHRIKING > SHRIKE

SHRILL adj (of a sound) sharp and high-pitched ▷ vb utter shrilly

SHRILLED > SHRILL

SHRILLER > SHRILL

SHRILLEST > SHRILL

SHRILLIER > SHRILL

SHRILLING > SHRILL

SHRILLS > SHRILL

SHRILLY > SHRILL

SHRIMP n small edible shellfish ▷ vb fish for shrimps

SHRIMPED > SHRIMP

SHRIMPER > SHRIMP

SHRIMPERS > SHRIMP

SHRIMPIER > SHRIMP

SHRIMPING > SHRIMP

SHRIMPS > SHRIMP

SHRIMPY > SHRIMP

SHRINAL > SHRINE

SHRINE n place of worship associated with a sacred person or object ▷ vb enshrine

SHRINED > SHRINE

SHRINES > SHRINE

SHRINING > SHRINE

SHRINK vb become or make smaller ▷ n psychiatrist

SHRINKAGE n decrease in size, value, or weight

SHRINKER > SHRINK

SHRINKERS > SHRINK

SHRINKING > SHRINK

SHRINKS > SHRINK

SHRIS > SHRI

SHRITCH vb old word meaning shriek

SHRITCHED > SHRITCH

SHRITCHES > SHRITCH

SHRIVE vb hear the confession of (a penitent)

SHRIVED > SHRIVE

SHRIVEL vb shrink and wither

SHRIVELED > SHRIVEL

SHRIVELS > SHRIVEL

SHRIVEN > SHRIVE

SHRIVER > SHRIVE

SHRIVERS > SHRIVE

SHRIVES > SHRIVE

SHRIVING > SHRIVE

SHRIVINGS > SHRIVE

SHROFF n (in China and Japan) expert employed to identify counterfeit money ▷ vb test (money) and separate out the counterfeit and base

SHROFFAGE > SHROFF

SHROFFED > SHROFF

S

SHROFFING > SHROFF

SHROFFS > SHROFF

SHROOM n slang for magic mushroom ▷ vb take magic mushrooms

SHROOMED > SHROOM

SHROOMER > SHROOM

SHROOMERS > SHROOM

SHROOMING > SHROOM

SHROOMS > SHROOM

SHROUD n piece of cloth used to wrap a dead body ▷ vb conceal

SHROUDED > SHROUD

SHROUDIER > SHROUD

SHROUDING > SHROUD

SHROUDS > SHROUD

SHROUDY > SHROUD

SHROVE vb dialect word meaning to observe Shrove-tide

SHROVED > SHROVE

SHROVES > SHROVE

SHROVING > SHROVE

SHROW vb old form of shrew

SHROWD adj old form of shrewd

SHROWED > SHROW

SHROWING > SHROW

SHROWS > SHROW

SHRUB n woody plant smaller than a tree ▷ vb plant shrubs

SHRUBBED > SHRUB

SHRUBBERY n area planted with shrubs

SHRUBBIER > SHRUBBY

SHRUBBING > SHRUB

SHRUBBY adj consisting of, planted with, or abounding in shrubs

SHRUBLAND n land covered by shrubs

SHRUBLESS > SHRUB

SHRUBLIKE > SHRUB

SHRUBS > SHRUB

SHRUG vb raise and then drop (the shoulders) as a sign of indifference or doubt ▷ n shrugging

SHRUGGED > SHRUG

SHRUGGING > SHRUG

SHRUGS > SHRUG

SHRUNK > SHRINK

SHRUNKEN adj reduced in size

SHTCHI n Russian cabbage soup

SHTCHIS > SHTCHI

SHTETEL n Jewish community in Eastern Europe

SHTETELS > SHTETEL

SHTETL n Jewish community in Eastern Europe

SHTETLACH > SHTETL

SHTETLS > SHTETL

SHTICK n comedian's routine

SHTICKIER > SHTICK

SHTICKS > SHTICK

SHTICKY > SHTICK

SHTIK n shtick

SHTIKS > SHTIK

SHTOOK n trouble

SHTOOKS > SHTOOK

SHTOOM adj silent

SHTUCK n trouble

SHTUCKS > SHTUCK

SHTUM adj silent

SHTUMM adj silent

SHTUP vb have sex (with)

SHTUPPED > SHTUP

SHTUPPING > SHTUP

SHTUPS > SHTUP

SHUBUNKIN n type of goldfish

SHUCK n outer covering of something ▷ vb remove the shucks from

SHUCKED > SHUCK

SHUCKER > SHUCK

SHUCKERS > SHUCK

SHUCKING > SHUCK

SHUCKINGS > SHUCK

SHUCKS pl n something of little value ▷ interj exclamation of disappointment, annoyance, etc

SHUDDER vb shake or tremble violently, esp with horror ▷ n shaking or trembling

SHUDDERED > SHUDDER

SHUDDERS > SHUDDER

SHUDDERY > SHUDDER

SHUFFLE vb walk without lifting the feet ▷ n shuffling

SHUFFLED > SHUFFLE

SHUFFLER > SHUFFLE

SHUFFLERS > SHUFFLE

SHUFFLES > SHUFFLE

SHUFFLING > SHUFFLE

SHUFTI same as > SHUFTY

SHUFTIES > SHUFTY

SHUFTIS > SHUFTI

SHUFTY n look

SHUGGIES > SHUGGY

SHUGGY n swing, as at a fairground

SHUL Yiddish word for > SYNAGOGUE

SHULE vb saunter

SHULED > SHULE

SHULES > SHULE

SHULING > SHULE

SHULN > SHUL

SHULS > SHUL

SHUMAI pl n (in Japan) small stuffed dumplings

SHUN vb avoid

SHUNLESS adj old word meaning not to be shunned

SHUNNABLE > SHUN

SHUNNED > SHUN

SHUNNER > SHUN

SHUNNERS > SHUN

SHUNNING > SHUN

SHUNPIKE vb take side road to avoid toll at turnpike

SHUNPIKED > SHUNPIKE

SHUNPIKER > SHUNPIKE

SHUNPIKES > SHUNPIKE

SHUNS > SHUN

SHUNT vb move (objects or people) to a different position ▷ n shunting

SHUNTED > SHUNT

SHUNTER n small railway locomotive used for manoeuvring coaches

SHUNTERS > SHUNTER

SHUNTING > SHUNT

SHUNTINGS > SHUNT

SHUNTS > SHUNT

SHURA n consultative council or assembly

SHURAS > SHURA

SHURIKEN n Japanese weapon with blades or points, thrown by hand

SHURIKENS > SHURIKEN

SHUSH interj be quiet! ▷ vb quiet by saying 'shush'

SHUSHED > SHUSH

SHUSHER > SHUSH

SHUSHERS > SHUSH

SHUSHES > SHUSH

SHUSHING > SHUSH

SHUT vb bring together or fold, close

SHUTDOWN n closing of a factory, shop, or other business ▷ vb discontinue operations permanently

SHUTDOWNS > SHUTDOWN

SHUTE variant of > CHUTE

SHUTED > SHUTE

SHUTES > SHUTE

SHUTEYE n sleep

SHUTEYES > SHUTEYE

SHUTING > SHUTE

SHUTOFF n device that shuts something off

SHUTOFFS > SHUTOFF

SHUTOUT n game in which the opposing team does not score

SHUTOUTS > SHUTOUT

SHUTS > SHUT

SHUTTER n hinged doorlike cover for closing off a window ▷ vb close or equip with a shutter

SHUTTERED > SHUTTER

SHUTTERS > SHUTTER

SHUTTING > SHUT

SHUTTLE n bobbin-like device used in weaving ▷ vb move by or as if by a shuttle

SHUTTLED > SHUTTLE

SHUTTLER > SHUTTLE

SHUTTLERS > SHUTTLE

SHUTTLES > SHUTTLE

SHUTTLING > SHUTTLE

SHVARTZE same as > SCHVARTZE

SHVARTZES > SHVARTZE

SHVITZ vb sweat

SHVITZED > SHVITZ

SHVITZES > SHVITZ

SHVITZING > SHVITZ

SHWA same as > SCHWA

SHWANPAN same as > SWANPAN

SHWANPANS > SHWANPAN

SHWAS > SHWA

SHWESHWE n African cotton print fabric

SHWESHWES > SHWESHWE

SHY adj not at ease in company ▷ vb start back in fear ▷ n throw

SHYER > SHY

SHYERS > SHY

SHYEST > SHY

SHYING > SHY

SHYISH > SHY

SHYLOCK vb lend money at an exorbitant rate of interest

SHYLOCKED > SHYLOCK

SHYLOCKS > SHYLOCK

SHYLY > SHY

SHYNESS > SHY

SHYNESSES > SHY

SHYPOO n liquor of poor quality

SHYPOOS > SHYPOO

SHYSTER n person who uses discreditable or unethical methods

SHYSTERS > SHYSTER

SI same as > TE

SIAL n silicon-rich and aluminium-rich rocks of the earth's continental upper crust

SIALIC > SIAL

SIALID n species of fly

SIALIDAN > SIALID

SIALIDANS > SIALID

SIALIDS > SIALID

SIALOGRAM n X-ray of salivary gland

SIALOID adj resembling saliva

SIALOLITH n hard deposit formed in salivary gland

SIALON n type of ceramic

SIALONS > SIALON

SIALS > SIAL

SIAMANG n large black gibbon

SIAMANGS > SIAMANG

SIAMESE variant of > SIAMEZE

SIAMESED > SIAMESE

SIAMESES > SIAMESE

SIAMESING > SIAMESE

SIAMEZE vb join together

SIAMEZED > SIAMEZE

SIAMEZES > SIAMEZE

SIAMEZING > SIAMEZE

SIB n blood relative

SIBB n sib

SIBBS > SIBB

SIBILANCE > SIBILANT

SIBILANCY > SIBILANT

SIBILANT adj hissing ▷ n consonant pronounced with a hissing sound

SIBILANTS > SIBILANT

SIBILATE vb pronounce or utter (words or speech) with a hissing sound

SIBILATED > SIBILATE

SIBILATES > SIBILATE

SIBILATOR > SIBILATE

SIBILOUS > SIBILANT

SIBLING n brother or sister

SIBLINGS > SIBLING

SIBS > SIB

SIBSHIP n group of children of the same parents

SIBSHIPS > SIBSHIP

SIBYL n (in ancient Greece and Rome) prophetess

SIBYLIC > SIBYL

SIBYLLIC > SIBYL

SIBYLLINE > SIBYL

SIBYLS > SIBYL

SIC adv thus ▷ vb attack

SICARIO n hired gunman, esp in Latin America

SICARIOS > SICARIO

SICCAN adj Scots word meaning such

SICCAR adj sure

SICCATIVE n substance added to a liquid to promote drying

SICCED > SIC

SICCING > SIC

SICCITIES > SICCITY

SICCITY n dryness

SICE same as > SYCE

SICES > SICE

SICH adj old form of such

SICHT Scot word for > SIGHT

SICHTED > SICHT

SICHTING > SICHT

SICHTS > SICHT

SICILIANA n Sicilian dance

SICILIANE > SICILIANA

SICILIANO n old dance in six-beat or twelve-beat time

SICK adj vomiting or likely to vomit ▷ n vomit ▷ vb vomit

SICKBAY n room for the treatment of sick people

SICKBAYS > SICKBAY

SICKBED n bed where sick person lies

SICKBEDS > SICKBED

SICKED > SICK

SICKEE n person off work through illness

SICKEES > SICKEE

SICKEN vb make nauseated or disgusted

SICKENED > SICKEN

SICKENER n something that induces sickness or nausea

SICKENERS > SICKENER

SICKENING adj causing horror or disgust

SICKENS > SICKEN

SICKER > SICK

SICKERLY adv Scots word meaning surely

SICKEST > SICK

SICKIE n day of sick leave from work

SICKIES > SICKIE

SICKING > SICK

SICKISH > SICK

SICKISHLY > SICK

SICKLE n tool with a curved blade for cutting grass or grain ▷ vb cut with a sickle

SICKLED > SICKLE

SICKLEMAN n person reaping with sickle

SICKLEMEN > SICKLEMAN

SICKLEMIA n form of anaemia

SICKLEMIC > SICKLEMIA

SICKLES > SICKLE

SICKLIED > SICKLY

SICKLIER > SICKLY

SICKLIES > SICKLY

SICKLIEST > SICKLY

SICKLILY > SICKLY

SICKLING > SICKLE

SICKLY adj unhealthy, weak ▷ adv suggesting sickness ▷ vb make sickly

SICKLYING > SICKLY

SICKNESS n particular illness or disease

SICKNURSE n person nursing sick person ▷ vb act as a sicknurse

SICKO n person who is mentally disturbed or perverted ▷ adj perverted or in bad taste

SICKOS > SICKO

SICKOUT n industrial action in which all workers report sick simultaneously

SICKOUTS > SICKOUT

SICKROOM n room to which a person who is ill is confined

SICKROOMS > SICKROOM

SICKS > SICK

SICKY n day off work due to illness

SICLIKE adj Scots word meaning suchlike

SICS > SIC

SIDA n Australian hemp plant

SIDALCEA n type of perennial N American plant

SIDALCEAS > SIDALCEA

SIDAS > SIDA

SIDDHA n (in Hinduism) person who has achieved perfection

SIDDHAS > SIDDHA

SIDDHI n (in Hinduism) power attained with perfection

SIDDHIS > SIDDHI

SIDDHUISM n (in Indian English) any contrived metaphor or simile

SIDDUR n Jewish prayer book

SIDDURIM > SIDDUR

SIDDURS > SIDDUR

SIDE n line or surface that borders anything ▷ adj at or on the side

SIDEARM n weapon worn on belt ▷ vb provide with a sidearm

SIDEARMED > SIDEARM

SIDEARMS > SIDEARM

SIDEBAND n frequency band either above or below the carrier frequency

SIDEBANDS > SIDEBAND

SIDEBAR n small newspaper article beside larger one

SIDEBARS > SIDEBAR

SIDEBOARD n piece of furniture for holding plates, cutlery, etc in a dining room

SIDEBONE n damage to the cartilage in a horse's hoof

SIDEBONES n part of horse's hoof

SIDEBURN n strip of whiskers down one side of a man's face

SIDEBURNS > SIDEBURN

SIDECAR n small passenger car on the side of a motorcycle

SIDECARS > SIDECAR

SIDECHECK n part of horse's harness

SIDED > SIDE

SIDEDLY adv pertaining to given number of sides

SIDEDNESS > SIDE

SIDEDRESS vb place fertilizer in the soil near the roots of a plant

SIDEHILL n side of hill

SIDEHILLS > SIDEHILL

SIDEKICK n close friend or associate

SIDEKICKS > SIDEKICK

SIDELESS adj without sides

SIDELIGHT n either of two small lights on the front of a vehicle

SIDELINE n subsidiary interest or source of income ▷ vb prevent (a player) from taking part in a game

SIDELINED > SIDELINE

SIDELINER > SIDELINE

SIDELINES pl n area immediately outside the playing area, where substitute players sit

SIDELING adj to one side ▷ adv sideways ▷ n slope, esp on the side of a road

SIDELINGS > SIDELING

SIDELOCK n long lock of hair on side of head

SIDELOCKS > SIDELOCK

SIDELONG adj sideways ▷ adv obliquely

SIDEMAN n member of a dance band or a jazz group other than the leader

SIDEMEAT n meat from the side of a pig

SIDEMEATS > SIDEMEAT

SIDEMEN > SIDEMAN

SIDENOTE n note written in margin

SIDENOTES > SIDENOTE

SIDEPATH n minor path

SIDEPATHS > SIDEPATH

SIDEPIECE n part forming side of something

SIDER n one who sides with another

SIDERAL adj from the stars

SIDERATE vb strike violently

SIDERATED > SIDERATE

SIDERATES > SIDERATE

SIDEREAL adj of or determined with reference to the stars

SIDERITE n pale yellow to brownish-black mineral

SIDERITES > SIDERITE

SIDERITIC > SIDERITE

SIDEROAD n (esp in Ontario) a road going at right angles to concession roads

SIDEROADS > SIDEROAD

SIDEROSES > SIDEROSIS

SIDEROSIS n lung disease caused by breathing in fine particles of iron or other metallic dust

SIDEROTIC > SIDEROSIS

SIDERS > SIDER

SIDES > SIDE

SIDESHOOT n minor shoot growing on plant

SIDESHOW n entertainment offered along with the main show

SIDESHOWS > SIDESHOW

SIDESLIP same as > SLIP

SIDESLIPS > SIDESLIP

SIDESMAN n man elected to help the parish church warden

SIDESMEN > SIDESMAN

SIDESPIN n horizontal spin put on ball

SIDESPINS > SIDESPIN

SIDESTEP vb dodge (an issue) ▷ n movement to one side, such as in dancing or boxing

SIDESTEPS > SIDESTEP

SIDESWIPE n unexpected criticism of someone or

something while discussing another subject ▷ vb make a sideswipe
SIDETABLE n small table at the side of a room
SIDETRACK vb divert from the main topic ▷ n railway siding
SIDEWALK n paved path for pedestrians, at the side of a road
SIDEWALKS > SIDEWALK
SIDEWALL n either of the sides of a pneumatic tyre between the tread and the rim
SIDEWALLS > SIDEWALL
SIDEWARD adj directed or moving towards one side ▷ adv towards one side
SIDEWARDS adv towards one side
SIDEWAY variant of > SIDEWAYS
SIDEWAYS adv or from the side ▷ adj moving or directed to or from one side
SIDEWHEEL n one of the paddle wheels of a sidewheeler
SIDEWISE adv sideways
SIDH pl n fairy people
SIDHA n (in Hinduism) person who has achieved perfection
SIDHAS > SIDHA
SIDHE pl n inhabitants of fairyland
SIDING n short stretch of railway track on which trains are shunted from the main line
SIDINGS > SIDING
SIDLE vb walk in a furtive manner ▷ n sideways movement
SIDLED > SIDLE
SIDLER > SIDLE
SIDLERS > SIDLE
SIDLES > SIDLE
SIDLING > SIDLE
SIDLINGLY > SIDLE
SIECLE n century, period, or era
SIECLES > SIECLE
SIEGE n surrounding and blockading of a place ▷ vb lay siege to
SIEGED > SIEGE
SIEGER n person who besieges
SIEGERS > SIEGER
SIEGES > SIEGE
SIEGING > SIEGE
SIELD adj (archaic) provided with a ceiling
SIEMENS n SI unit of electrical conductance
SIEMENSES > SIEMENS
SIEN n old word meaning scion
SIENITE n type of igneous rock

SIENITES > SIENITE
SIENNA n reddish- or yellowish-brown pigment made from natural earth
SIENNAS > SIENNA
SIENS > SIEN
SIENT n old word meaning scion
SIENTS > SIENT
SIEROZEM n type of soil
SIEROZEMS > SIEROZEM
SIERRA n range of mountains in Spain or America with jagged peaks
SIERRAN > SIERRA
SIERRAS > SIERRA
SIES interj in South Africa, an exclamation of disgust
SIESTA n afternoon nap, taken in hot countries
SIESTAS > SIESTA
SIETH n old form of scythe
SIETHS > SIETH
SIEUR n French word meaning lord
SIEURS > SIEUR
SIEVE n utensil with mesh through which a substance is sifted or strained ▷ vb sift or strain through a sieve
SIEVED > SIEVE
SIEVELIKE > SIEVE
SIEVERT n derived SI unit of dose equivalent, equal to 1 joule per kilogram
SIEVERTS > SIEVERT
SIEVES > SIEVE
SIEVING > SIEVE
SIF adj South African slang for disgusting
SIFAKA n either of two large rare arboreal lemuroid primates
SIFAKAS > SIFAKA
SIFFLE vb whistle
SIFFLED > SIFFLE
SIFFLES > SIFFLE
SIFFLEUR n male professional whistler
SIFFLEURS > SIFFLEUR
SIFFLEUSE n female professional whistler
SIFFLING > SIFFLE
SIFREI > SEFER
SIFT vb remove the coarser particles from a substance with a sieve
SIFTED > SIFT
SIFTER > SIFT
SIFTERS > SIFT
SIFTING > SIFT
SIFTINGLY > SIFT
SIFTINGS pl n material or particles separated out by or as if by a sieve
SIFTS > SIFT
SIG n short for signature
SIGANID n tropical fish
SIGANIDS > SIGANID
SIGH n long audible breath expressing sadness, tiredness, relief, or longing ▷ vb utter a sigh

SIGHED > SIGH
SIGHER > SIGH
SIGHERS > SIGH
SIGHFUL > SIGH
SIGHING n act of sighing
SIGHINGLY > SIGH
SIGHINGS > SIGHING
SIGHLESS > SIGH
SIGHLIKE > SIGH
SIGHS > SIGH
SIGHT n ability to see ▷ vb catch sight of
SIGHTABLE > SIGHT
SIGHTED adj not blind
SIGHTER n any of six practice shots allowed to each competitor in a tournament
SIGHTERS > SIGHTER
SIGHTING > SIGHT
SIGHTINGS > SIGHT
SIGHTLESS adj blind
SIGHTLIER > SIGHTLY
SIGHTLINE n uninterrupted line of vision
SIGHTLY adj pleasing or attractive to see
SIGHTS > SIGHT
SIGHTSAW > SIGHTSEE
SIGHTSEE vb visit the famous or interesting sights of (a place)
SIGHTSEEN > SIGHTSEE
SIGHTSEER > SIGHTSEE
SIGHTSEES > SIGHTSEE
SIGHTSMAN n tourist guide
SIGHTSMEN > SIGHTSMAN
SIGIL n seal or signet
SIGILLARY > SIGIL
SIGILLATE adj closed with seal
SIGILS > SIGIL
SIGISBEI > SIGISBEO
SIGISBEO n male escort for a married woman
SIGLA n list of symbols used in a book
SIGLAS > SIGLA
SIGLOI > SIGLOS
SIGLOS n silver coin of ancient Persia
SIGLUM n symbol used in book
SIGMA n 18th letter in the Greek alphabet
SIGMAS > SIGMA
SIGMATE adj shaped like the Greek letter sigma or the Roman S ▷ n sigmate thing ▷ vb add a sigma
SIGMATED > SIGMATE
SIGMATES > SIGMATE
SIGMATIC > SIGMATE
SIGMATING > SIGMATE
SIGMATION > SIGMATE
SIGMATISM n repetition of letter s
SIGMATRON n machine for generating X-rays

SIGMOID adj shaped like the letter S ▷ n S-shaped bend in the final portion of the large intestine
SIGMOIDAL variant of > SIGMOID
SIGMOIDS > SIGMOID
SIGN n indication of something not immediately or outwardly observable ▷ vb write (one's name) on (a document or letter) to show its authenticity
SIGNA pl n symbols
SIGNABLE > SIGN
SIGNAGE n signs collectively
SIGNAGES > SIGNAGE
SIGNAL n sign or gesture to convey information ▷ adj very important ▷ vb convey (information) by signal
SIGNALED > SIGNAL
SIGNALER > SIGNAL
SIGNALERS > SIGNAL
SIGNALING > SIGNAL
SIGNALISE same as > SIGNALIZE
SIGNALIZE vb make noteworthy or conspicuous
SIGNALLED > SIGNAL
SIGNALLER > SIGNAL
SIGNALLY adv conspicuously or especially
SIGNALMAN n railwayman in charge of signals and points
SIGNALMEN > SIGNALMAN
SIGNALS > SIGNAL
SIGNARIES > SIGNARY
SIGNARY n set of symbols
SIGNATORY n one of the parties who sign a document ▷ adj having signed a document or treaty
SIGNATURE n person's name written by himself or herself in signing something
SIGNBOARD n board carrying a sign or notice, often to advertise a business or product
SIGNED > SIGN
SIGNEE n person signing document
SIGNEES > SIGNEE
SIGNER n person who signs something
SIGNERS > SIGNER
SIGNET n small seal used to authenticate documents ▷ vb stamp or authenticate with a signet
SIGNETED > SIGNET
SIGNETING > SIGNET
SIGNETS > SIGNET

SIGNEUR old spelling of > SENIOR
SIGNEURIE n old word meaning seniority
SIGNIEUR n old word meaning lord
SIGNIEURS > SIGNIEUR
SIGNIFICS n study of meaning
SIGNIFIED > SIGNIFY
SIGNIFIER > SIGNIFY
SIGNIFIES > SIGNIFY
SIGNIFY vb indicate or suggest
SIGNING n system of communication using hand and arm movements
SIGNINGS > SIGNING
SIGNIOR same as > SIGNOR
SIGNIORI > SIGNIOR
SIGNIORS > SIGNIOR
SIGNIORY n old word meaning lordship
SIGNLESS > SIGN
SIGNOR n Italian term of address equivalent to sir or Mr
SIGNORA n Italian term of address equivalent to madam or Mrs
SIGNORAS > SIGNORA
SIGNORE n Italian man: a title of respect equivalent to sir
SIGNORES > SIGNORE
SIGNORI > SIGNORE
SIGNORIA n government of Italian city
SIGNORIAL > SIGNORIA
SIGNORIAS > SIGNORIA
SIGNORIES > SIGNORY
SIGNORINA n Italian term of address equivalent to madam or Miss
SIGNORINE > SIGNORINA
SIGNORINI > SIGNORINO
SIGNORINO n young gentleman
SIGNORS > SIGNOR
SIGNORY same as > SEIGNIORY
SIGNPOST n post bearing a sign that shows the way ▷ vb mark with signposts
SIGNPOSTS > SIGNPOST
SIGNS > SIGN
SIGS > SIG
SIJO n Korean poem
SIJOS > SIJO
SIK adj excellent
SIKA n Japanese forest-dwelling deer
SIKAS > SIKA
SIKE n small stream
SIKER adj old spelling of sicker
SIKES > SIKE
SIKORSKY n type of helicopter
SIKSIK n Arctic ground squirrel

SIKSIKS > SIKSIK
SILAGE n fodder crop harvested while green and partially fermented in a silo ▷ vb make silage
SILAGED > SILAGE
SILAGEING > SILAGE
SILAGES > SILAGE
SILAGING > SILAGE
SILANE n gas containing silicon
SILANES > SILANE
SILASTIC n tradename for a type of flexible silicone rubber
SILASTICS > SILASTIC
SILD n any of various small young herrings
SILDS > SILD
SILE vb pour with rain
SILED > SILE
SILEN n god of woodland
SILENCE n absence of noise or speech ▷ vb make silent
SILENCED adj (of a clergyman) forbidden to preach or perform his clerical functions
SILENCER n device to reduce the noise of an engine exhaust or gun
SILENCERS > SILENCER
SILENCES > SILENCE
SILENCING > SILENCE
SILENE n type of plant with mostly red or pink flowers, often grown as a garden plant
SILENES > SILENE
SILENI > SILENUS
SILENS > SILEN
SILENT adj tending to speak very little ▷ n silent film
SILENTER > SILENT
SILENTEST > SILENT
SILENTLY > SILENT
SILENTS > SILENT
SILENUS n woodland deity
SILER n strainer
SILERS > SILER
SILES > SILE
SILESIA n twill-weave fabric of cotton or other fibre
SILESIAS > SILESIA
SILEX n type of heat-resistant glass made from fused quartz
SILEXES > SILEX
SILICA n hard glossy mineral found as quartz and in sandstone
SILICAS > SILICA
SILICATE n compound of silicon, oxygen, and a metal
SILICATED > SILICATE
SILICATES > SILICATE
SILICEOUS adj of, relating to, or containing abundant silica

SILICIC adj of, concerned with, or containing silicon or an acid obtained from silicon
SILICIDE n any one of a class of binary compounds formed between silicon and certain metals
SILICIDES > SILICIDE
SILICIFY vb convert or be converted into silica
SILICIOUS same as > SILICEOUS
SILICIUM rare name for > SILICON
SILICIUMS > SILICIUM
SILICLE same as > SILICULA
SILICLES > SILICLE
SILICON n brittle nonmetallic element ▷ adj denoting an area that contains much high-technology industry
SILICONE n tough synthetic substance made from silicon and used in lubricants
SILICONES > SILICONE
SILICONS > SILICON
SILICOSES > SILICOSIS
SILICOSIS n lung disease caused by inhaling silica dust
SILICOTIC n person suffering from silicosis
SILICULA n short broad siliqua, occurring in such cruciferous plants as honesty and shepherd's-purse
SILICULAE > SILICULA
SILICULAS > SILICULA
SILICULE same as > SILICULA
SILICULES > SILICULE
SILING > SILE
SILIQUA n long dry dehiscent fruit of cruciferous plants such as the wallflower
SILIQUAE > SILIQUA
SILIQUAS > SILIQUA
SILIQUE same as > SILIQUA
SILIQUES > SILIQUE
SILIQUOSE > SILIQUA
SILIQUOUS > SILIQUA
SILK n fibre made by the larva of a certain moth ▷ vb (of maize) develop long hairlike styles
SILKALENE same as > SILKALINE
SILKALINE n fine smooth cotton fabric used for linings, etc
SILKED > SILK
SILKEN adj made of silk ▷ vb make like silk
SILKENED > SILKEN
SILKENING > SILKEN
SILKENS > SILKEN

SILKIE n Scots word for a seal
SILKIER > SILKY
SILKIES > SILKIE
SILKIEST > SILKY
SILKILY > SILKY
SILKINESS > SILKY
SILKING > SILK
SILKLIKE > SILK
SILKOLINE n material like silk
SILKS > SILK
SILKTAIL n waxwing
SILKTAILS > SILKTAIL
SILKWEED another name for > MILKWEED
SILKWEEDS > SILKWEED
SILKWORM n caterpillar that spins a cocoon of silk
SILKWORMS > SILKWORM
SILKY adj of or like silk
SILL n ledge at the bottom of a window or door
SILLABUB same as > SYLLABUB
SILLABUBS > SILLABUB
SILLADAR n Indian irregular cavalryman
SILLADARS > SILLADAR
SILLER n silver ▷ adj silver
SILLERS > SILLER
SILLIBUB n syllabub
SILLIBUBS > SILLIBUB
SILLIER > SILLY
SILLIES > SILLY
SILLIEST > SILLY
SILLILY > SILLY
SILLINESS > SILLY
SILLOCK n young coalfish
SILLOCKS > SILLOCK
SILLS > SILL
SILLY adj foolish ▷ n foolish person
SILO n pit or airtight tower for storing silage or grains ▷ vb put in a silo
SILOED > SILO
SILOING > SILO
SILOS > SILO
SILOXANE n any of a class of compounds containing alternate silicon and oxygen atoms
SILOXANES > SILOXANE
SILPHIA > SILPHIUM
SILPHIUM n American flowering wild plant
SILPHIUMS > SILPHIUM
SILT n mud deposited by moving water ▷ vb fill or be choked with silt
SILTATION > SILT
SILTED > SILT
SILTIER > SILT
SILTIEST > SILT
SILTING > SILT
SILTS > SILT
SILTSTONE n variety of fine sandstone formed from consolidated silt
SILTY > SILT

SILURIAN adj formed in the third period of the Palaeozoic

SILURID n type of freshwater fish of the family which includes catfish

SILURIDS > SILURID

SILURIST n member of ancient Silurian tribe

SILURISTS > SILURIST

SILUROID n freshwater fish

SILUROIDS > SILUROID

SILVA same as **>** SYLVA

SILVAE > SILVA

SILVAN same as **>** SYLVAN

SILVAS > SILVA

SILVATIC adj wild, not domestic

SILVER n white precious metal ▷ adj made of or of the colour of silver ▷ vb coat with silver

SILVERED > SILVER

SILVERER > SILVER

SILVERERS > SILVER

SILVEREYE n greenish-coloured songbird of Africa, Australia, New Zealand, and Asia

SILVERIER > SILVERY

SILVERING > SILVER

SILVERISE same as **>** SILVERIZE

SILVERIZE vb coat with silver

SILVERLY adv like silver

SILVERN adj silver

SILVERS > SILVER

SILVERTIP n mature grizzly bear

SILVERY adj like silver

SILVEX n type of weedkiller

SILVEXES > SILVEX

SILVICAL adj of trees

SILVICS n study of trees

SILYMARIN n antioxidant found in milk thistle

SIM n computer game that simulates an activity

SIMA n silicon-rich and magnesium-rich rocks of the earth's oceanic crust

SIMAR variant spelling of **>** CYMAR

SIMAROUBA n tropical American tree with divided leaves and fleshy fruits

SIMARRE n woman's loose gown

SIMARRES > SIMARRE

SIMARS > SIMAR

SIMARUBA same as **>** SIMAROUBA

SIMARUBAS > SIMARUBA

SIMAS > SIMA

SIMATIC > SIMA

SIMAZINE n organic weedkiller

SIMAZINES > SIMAZINE

SIMBA E African word for **>** LION

SIMBAS > SIMBA

SIMCHA n Jewish celebration or festival

SIMCHAS > SIMCHA

SIMI n East African sword

SIMIAL adj of apes

SIMIAN n monkey or ape ▷ adj of or resembling a monkey or ape

SIMIANS > SIMIAN

SIMILAR adj alike but not identical

SIMILARLY > SIMILAR

SIMILE n figure of speech comparing one thing to another, using 'as' or 'like'

SIMILES > SIMILE

SIMILISE same as **>** SIMILIZE

SIMILISED > SIMILISE

SIMILISES > SIMILISE

SIMILIZE vb use similes

SIMILIZED > SIMILIZE

SIMILIZES > SIMILIZE

SIMILOR n alloy used in cheap jewellery

SIMILORS > SIMILOR

SIMIOID adj of apes

SIMIOUS adj of apes

SIMIS > SIMI

SIMITAR same as **>** SCIMITAR

SIMITARS > SIMITAR

SIMKIN word used in India for **>** CHAMPAGNE

SIMKINS > SIMKIN

SIMLIN n American variety of squash plant

SIMLINS > SIMLIN

SIMMER vb cook gently at just below boiling point ▷ n state of simmering

SIMMERED > SIMMER

SIMMERING > SIMMER

SIMMERS > SIMMER

SIMNEL n as in simnel cake fruit cake with marzipan eaten at Easter

SIMNELS > SIMNEL

SIMOLEON n American slang for dollar

SIMOLEONS > SIMOLEON

SIMONIAC n person who is guilty of practising simony

SIMONIACS > SIMONIAC

SIMONIES > SIMONY

SIMONIOUS > SIMONY

SIMONISE same as **>** SIMONIZE

SIMONISED > SIMONISE

SIMONISES > SIMONISE

SIMONIST > SIMONY

SIMONISTS > SIMONY

SIMONIZE vb polish with wax

SIMONIZED > SIMONIZE

SIMONIZES > SIMONIZE

SIMONY n practice of buying or selling Church benefits

SIMOOM n hot suffocating sand-laden desert wind

SIMOOMS > SIMOOM

SIMOON same as **>** SIMOOM

SIMOONS > SIMOON

SIMORG n bird in Persian myth

SIMORGS > SIMORG

SIMP short for **>** SIMPLETON

SIMPAI n Indonesian monkey

SIMPAIS > SIMPAI

SIMPATICO adj pleasant or congenial

SIMPER vb smile in a silly or affected way ▷ n simpering smile

SIMPERED > SIMPER

SIMPERER > SIMPER

SIMPERERS > SIMPER

SIMPERING > SIMPER

SIMPERS > SIMPER

SIMPKIN word used in India for **>** CHAMPAGNE

SIMPKINS > SIMPKIN

SIMPLE adj easy to understand or do ▷ n simpleton ▷ vb archaic word meaning to look for medicinal herbs

SIMPLED > SIMPLE

SIMPLER > SIMPLE

SIMPLERS > SIMPLE

SIMPLES > SIMPLE

SIMPLESSE n old word meaning simplicity

SIMPLEST > SIMPLE

SIMPLETON n foolish or half-witted person

SIMPLEX adj permitting the transmission of signals in only one direction in a radio circuit ▷ n simple not a compound word

SIMPLEXES > SIMPLEX

SIMPLICES > SIMPLEX

SIMPLICIA n species of moth

SIMPLIFY vb make less complicated

SIMPLING > SIMPLE

SIMPLINGS > SIMPLE

SIMPLISM n quality of being extremely naive

SIMPLISMS > SIMPLISM

SIMPLIST n old word meaning expert in herbal medicine

SIMPLISTE adj simplistic ▷ n person who tends to oversimplify

SIMPLISTS > SIMPLIST

SIMPLY adv in a simple manner

SIMPS > SIMP

SIMS > SIM

SIMUL adj simultaneous ▷ n simultaneous broadcast

SIMULACRA pl n representations of things

SIMULACRE n resemblance

SIMULANT adj simulating ▷ n simulant thing

SIMULANTS > SIMULANT

SIMULAR n person or thing that simulates or imitates ▷ adj fake

SIMULARS > SIMULAR

SIMULATE vb make a pretence of ▷ adj assumed or simulated

SIMULATED adj being an imitation of the genuine article, usually made from cheaper material

SIMULATES > SIMULATE

SIMULATOR n device that simulates specific conditions for the purposes of research or training

SIMULCAST vb broadcast (a programme) simultaneously on radio and television ▷ n programme broadcast in this way

SIMULIUM n tropical fly

SIMULIUMS > SIMULIUM

SIMULS > SIMUL

SIMURG n bird in Persian myth

SIMURGH n bird in Persian myth

SIMURGHS > SIMURGH

SIMURGS > SIMURG

SIN n offence or transgression ▷ vb commit a sin

SINAPISM n mixture of black mustard seeds and an adhesive, applied to the skin

SINAPISMS > SINAPISM

SINCE prep during the period of time after ▷ adv from that time

SINCERE adj without pretence or deceit

SINCERELY > SINCERE

SINCERER > SINCERE

SINCEREST > SINCERE

SINCERITY > SINCERE

SINCIPITA > SINCIPUT

SINCIPUT n forward upper part of the skull

SINCIPUTS > SINCIPUT

SIND variant of **>** SYNE

SINDED > SIND

SINDING > SIND

SINDINGS > SIND

SINDON n type of cloth

SINDONS > SINDON

SINDS > SIND

SINE same as **>** SYNE

SINECURE n paid job with minimal duties

SINECURES > SINECURE

SINED > SINE

SINES > SINE

SINEW n tough fibrous tissue joining muscle to bone ▷ vb make strong

SINEWED adj having sinews

SINEWIER > SINEWY
SINEWIEST > SINEWY
SINEWING > SINEW
SINEWLESS > SINEW
SINEWS > SINEW
SINEWY adj lean and muscular
SINFONIA n symphony orchestra
SINFONIAS > SINFONIA
SINFONIE > SINFONIA
SINFUL adj guilty of sin
SINFULLY > SINFUL
SING vb make musical sounds with the voice ▷ n act or performance of singing
SINGABLE > SING
SINGALONG n act of singing along with a performer
SINGE vb burn the surface of ▷ n superficial burn
SINGED > SINGE
SINGEING > SINGE
SINGER n person who sings, esp professionally
SINGERS > SINGER
SINGES > SINGE
SINGING > SING
SINGINGLY > SING
SINGINGS > SING
SINGLE adj one only ▷ n single thing ▷ vb pick out from others
SINGLED > SINGLE
SINGLEDOM n state of being unmarried or not involved in a long-term relationship
SINGLES pl n match played with one person on each side
SINGLET n sleeveless vest
SINGLETON n only card of a particular suit held by a player
SINGLETS > SINGLET
SINGLING > SINGLE
SINGLINGS > SINGLE
SINGLY adv one at a time
SINGS > SING
SINGSONG n informal singing session ▷ adj (of the voice) repeatedly rising and falling in pitch
SINGSONGS > SINGSONG
SINGSONGY > SINGSONG
SINGSPIEL n type of German comic opera with spoken dialogue
SINGULAR adj (of a word or form) denoting one person or thing ▷ n singular form of a word
SINGULARS > SINGULAR
SINGULARY adj (of an operator) monadic
SINGULT n old word meaning sob
SINGULTS > SINGULT
SINGULTUS technical name for > HICCUP
SINH n hyperbolic sine

SINHS > SINH
SINICAL > SINE
SINICISE same as > SINICIZE
SINICISED > SINICISE
SINICISES > SINICISE
SINICIZE vb make Chinese
SINICIZED > SINICIZE
SINICIZES > SINICIZE
SINING > SINE
SINISTER adj threatening or suggesting evil or harm
SINISTRAL adj of, relating to, or located on the left side, esp the left side of the body
SINK vb submerge (in liquid) ▷ n fixed basin with a water supply and drainage pipe
SINKABLE > SINK
SINKAGE n act of sinking or degree to which something sinks or has sunk
SINKAGES > SINKAGE
SINKER n weight for a fishing line
SINKERS > SINKER
SINKFUL n amount that can be held in a sink
SINKFULS > SINKFUL
SINKHOLE n depression in the ground surface, esp in limestone, where a surface stream disappears underground
SINKHOLES > SINKHOLE
SINKIER > SINKY
SINKIEST > SINKY
SINKING > SINK
SINKINGS > SINK
SINKS > SINK
SINKY adj giving underfoot
SINLESS adj free from sin or guilt
SINLESSLY > SINLESS
SINNED > SIN
SINNER n person that sins ▷ vb behave like a sinner
SINNERED > SINNER
SINNERING > SINNER
SINNERS > SIN
SINNET n braided rope
SINNETS > SINNET
SINNING > SIN
SINNINGIA n tropical flowering plant
SINOLOGUE > SINOLOGY
SINOLOGY n study of Chinese culture, etc
SINOPIA n pigment made from iron ore
SINOPIAS > SINOPIA
SINOPIE > SINOPIA
SINOPIS n pigment made from iron ore
SINOPISES > SINOPIS
SINOPITE n iron ore
SINOPITES > SINOPITE
SINS > SIN

SINSYNE adv Scots word meaning since
SINTER n whitish porous incrustation deposited from hot springs ▷ vb form large particles from (powders) by heating or pressure
SINTERED > SINTER
SINTERING > SINTER
SINTERS > SINTER
SINTERY > SINTER
SINUATE vb wind
SINUATED same as > SINUATE
SINUATELY > SINUATE
SINUATES > SINUATE
SINUATING > SINUATE
SINUATION same as > SINUOSITY
SINUITIS variant of > SINUSITIS
SINUOSE adj sinuous
SINUOSITY n quality of being sinuous
SINUOUS adj full of turns or curves
SINUOUSLY > SINUOUS
SINUS n hollow space in a bone, esp an air passage opening into the nose
SINUSES > SINUS
SINUSITIS n inflammation of a sinus membrane
SINUSLIKE > SINUS
SINUSOID n any of the irregular terminal blood vessels that replace capillaries in certain organs ▷ adj resembling a sinus
SINUSOIDS > SINUSOID
SIP vb drink in small mouthfuls ▷ n amount sipped
SIPE vb soak
SIPED > SIPE
SIPES > SIPE
SIPHON n bent tube which uses air pressure to draw liquid from a container ▷ vb draw off thus
SIPHONAGE > SIPHON
SIPHONAL adj like a siphon
SIPHONATE adj having a syphon
SIPHONED > SIPHON
SIPHONET n sucking tube on an aphid
SIPHONETS > SIPHONET
SIPHONIC same as > SIPHONAL
SIPHONING > SIPHON
SIPHONS > SIPHON
SIPHUNCLE n tube inside shellfish
SIPING > SIPE
SIPPABLE adj able to be sipped
SIPPED > SIP
SIPPER > SIP
SIPPERS > SIP

SIPPET n small piece of toast eaten with soup or gravy
SIPPETS > SIPPET
SIPPING > SIP
SIPPLE vb sip
SIPPLED > SIPPLE
SIPPLES > SIPPLE
SIPPLING > SIPPLE
SIPPY adj as in sippy cup infant's drinking cup with a tight-fitting lid and perforated spout
SIPS > SIP
SIR n polite term of address for a man ▷ vb call someone 'sir'
SIRCAR n government in India
SIRCARS > SIRCAR
SIRDAR same as > SARDAR
SIRDARS > SIRDAR
SIRE n male parent of a horse or other domestic animal ▷ vb father
SIRED > SIRE
SIREE emphasized form of > SIR
SIREES > SIREE
SIREN n device making a loud wailing noise as a warning
SIRENIAN n animal belonging to the order of aquatic herbivorous mammals that includes the dugong and manatee
SIRENIANS > SIRENIAN
SIRENIC > SIREN
SIRENISE variant of > SIRENIZE
SIRENISED > SIRENISE
SIRENISES > SIRENISE
SIRENIZE vb bewitch
SIRENIZED > SIRENIZE
SIRENIZES > SIRENIZE
SIRENS > SIREN
SIRES > SIRE
SIRGANG n Asian bird
SIRGANGS > SIRGANG
SIRI n betel
SIRIASES > SIRIASIS
SIRIASIS n sunstroke
SIRIH n betel
SIRIHS > SIRIH
SIRING > SIRE
SIRINGS > SIRING
SIRIS > SIRI
SIRKAR n government in India
SIRKARS > SIRKAR
SIRLOIN n prime cut of loin of beef
SIRLOINS > SIRLOIN
SIRNAME vb old form of surname
SIRNAMED > SIRNAME
SIRNAMES > SIRNAME
SIRNAMING > SIRNAME
SIROC n sirocco
SIROCCO n hot wind blowing from N Africa into S Europe

SIROCCOS > SIROCCO
SIROCS > SIROC
SIRONISE same as > SIRONIZE
SIRONISED > SIRONISE
SIRONISES > SIRONISE
SIRONIZE vb treat (a woollen fabric) chemically to prevent it wrinkling after being washed
SIRONIZED > SIRONIZE
SIRONIZES > SIRONIZE
SIROSET adj of the chemical treatment of woollen fabrics to give a permanent-press effect
SIRRA disrespectful form of > SIR
SIRRAH n contemptuous term used in addressing a man or boy
SIRRAHS > SIRRAH
SIRRAS > SIRRA
SIRRED > SIR
SIRREE n form of 'sir' used for emphasis
SIRREES > SIRREE
SIRRING > SIR
SIRS > SIR
SIRTUIN n protein that regulates cell metabolism and ageing
SIRTUINS > SIRTUIN
SIRUP same as > SYRUP
SIRUPED > SIRUP
SIRUPIER > SIRUP
SIRUPIEST > SIRUP
SIRUPING > SIRUP
SIRUPS > SIRUP
SIRUPY > SIRUP
SIRVENTE n verse form employed by the troubadours of Provence to satirize political themes
SIRVENTES > SIRVENTE
SIS n sister
SISAL n (fibre of) plant used in making ropes
SISALS > SISAL
SISERARY n scolding
SISES > SIS
SISKIN n yellow-and-black finch
SISKINS > SISKIN
SISS shortening of > SISTER
SISSES > SISS
SISSIER > SISSY
SISSIES > SISSY
SISSIEST > SISSY
SISSIFIED > SISSY
SISSINESS > SISSY
SISSOO n Indian tree
SISSOOS > SISSOO
SISSY n weak or cowardly (person) ▷ adj effeminate, weak, or cowardly
SISSYISH > SISSY
SISSYNESS > SISSY
SIST vb Scottish law term meaning stop

SISTA n informal term for an African-American woman
SISTAS > SISTA
SISTED > SIST
SISTER n girl or woman with the same parents as another person ▷ adj closely related, similar ▷ vb be or be like a sister
SISTERED > SISTER
SISTERING > SISTER
SISTERLY adj of or like a sister
SISTERS > SISTER
SISTING > SIST
SISTRA > SISTRUM
SISTROID adj contained between the convex sides of two intersecting curves
SISTRUM n musical instrument of ancient Egypt consisting of a metal rattle
SISTRUMS > SISTRUM
SISTS > SIST
SIT vb rest one's body upright on the buttocks
SITAR n Indian stringed musical instrument
SITARIST > SITAR
SITARISTS > SITAR
SITARS > SITAR
SITATUNGA another name for > MARSHBUCK
SITCOM n situation comedy
SITCOMS > SITCOM
SITE n place where something is, was, or is intended to be located ▷ vb provide with a site
SITED > SITE
SITELLA n type of small generally black-and-white bird
SITELLAS > SITELLA
SITES > SITE
SITFAST n sore on a horse's back caused by rubbing of the saddle
SITFASTS > SITFAST
SITH archaic word for > SINCE
SITHE vb old form of scythe
SITHED > SITHE
SITHEE interj look here! listen!
SITHEN adv old word meaning since
SITHENCE adv old word meaning since
SITHENS adv old word meaning since
SITHES > SITHE
SITHING > SITHE
SITING n act of siting
SITINGS > SITING
SITIOLOGY n study of diet and nutrition
SITKA modifier as in sitka spruce tall North American spruce tree

SITKAMER n sitting room
SITKAMERS > SITKAMER
SITOLOGY n scientific study of food, diet, and nutrition
SITREP n military situation report
SITREPS > SITREP
SITS > SIT
SITTAR n sitar
SITTARS > SITTAR
SITTELLA variant spelling of > SITELLA
SITTELLAS > SITTELLA
SITTEN adj dialect word for in the saddle
SITTER n baby-sitter
SITTERS > SITTER
SITTINE adj of nuthatch bird family ▷ n type of nuthatch
SITTINES > SITTINE
SITTING > SIT
SITTINGS > SIT
SITUATE vb place ▷ adj (now used esp in legal contexts) situated
SITUATED > SITUATE
SITUATES > SITUATE
SITUATING > SITUATE
SITUATION n state of affairs
SITULA n bucket-shaped container
SITULAE > SITULA
SITUP n exercise in which the body is brought into a sitting position
SITUPS > SITUP
SITUS n position or location
SITUSES > SITUS
SITUTUNGA n African antelope
SITZ n as in sitz bath bath in which the buttocks and hips are immersed in hot water
SITZKRIEG n period during a war in which both sides change positions very slowly or not at all
SITZMARK n depression in the snow where a skier has fallen
SITZMARKS > SITZMARK
SIVER same as > SYVER
SIVERS > SIVER
SIWASH vb (in the Pacific Northwest) to camp out with only natural shelter
SIWASHED > SIWASH
SIWASHES > SIWASH
SIWASHING > SIWASH
SIX n one more than five
SIXAIN n stanza or poem of six lines
SIXAINE n six-line stanza of poetry
SIXAINES > SIXAINE
SIXAINS > SIXAIN
SIXER same as > SIX
SIXERS > SIXER
SIXES > SIX

SIXFOLD adj having six times as many or as much ▷ adv by six times as many or as much
SIXISH adj around six years of age
SIXMO n book size resulting from folding a sheet of paper into six leaves
SIXMOS > SIXMO
SIXPENCE n former British and Australian coin worth six pennies
SIXPENCES > SIXPENCE
SIXPENNY adj (of a nail) two inches in length
SIXSCORE n hundred and twenty
SIXSCORES > SIXSCORE
SIXTE n sixth of eight basic positions from which a parry or attack can be made in fencing
SIXTEEN n six and ten ▷ adj amounting to sixteen ▷ determiner amounting to sixteen
SIXTEENER n poem verse with sixteen syllables
SIXTEENMO n book size resulting from folding a sheet of paper into 16 leaves or 32 pages
SIXTEENS > SIXTEEN
SIXTEENTH adj coming after the fifteenth in numbering order ▷ n one of 16 equal or nearly equal parts of something
SIXTES > SIXTE
SIXTH n (of) number six in a series ▷ adj coming after the fifth and before the seventh in numbering order ▷ adv after the fifth person, position, etc
SIXTHLY same as > SIXTH
SIXTHS > SIXTH
SIXTIES > SIXTY
SIXTIETH adj being the ordinal number of sixty in numbering order ▷ n one of 60 approximately equal parts of something
SIXTIETHS > SIXTIETH
SIXTY n six times ten ▷ adj amounting to sixty
SIXTYISH > SIXTY
SIZABLE adj quite large
SIZABLY > SIZABLE
SIZAR n undergraduate receiving a maintenance grant from the college
SIZARS > SIZAR
SIZARSHIP > SIZAR
SIZE n dimensions, bigness ▷ vb arrange according to size
SIZEABLE same as > SIZABLE
SIZEABLY > SIZABLE
SIZED adj of a specified size

SIZEISM n discrimination on the basis of a person's size
SIZEISMS > SIZEISM
SIZEIST > SIZEISM
SIZEISTS > SIZEISM
SIZEL n scrap metal clippings
SIZELS > SIZEL
SIZER > SIZE
SIZERS > SIZE
SIZES > SIZE
SIZIER > SIZE
SIZIEST > SIZE
SIZINESS > SIZE
SIZING > SIZE
SIZINGS > SIZE
SIZISM n discrimination against people because of weight
SIZISMS > SIZISM
SIZIST > SIZISM
SIZISTS > SIZISM
SIZY > SIZE
SIZZLE vb make a hissing sound like frying fat ▷ n hissing sound
SIZZLED > SIZZLE
SIZZLER n something that sizzles
SIZZLERS > SIZZLER
SIZZLES > SIZZLE
SIZZLING adj extremely hot
SIZZLINGS > SIZZLING
SJAMBOK n whip or riding crop made of hide ▷ vb beat with a sjambok
SJAMBOKED > SJAMBOK
SJAMBOKS > SJAMBOK
SJOE interj South African exclamation of surprise, admiration, exhaustion, etc
SKA n type of West Indian pop music of the 1960s
SKAG same as > SCAG
SKAGS > SKAG
SKAIL vb Scots word meaning disperse
SKAILED > SKAIL
SKAILING > SKAIL
SKAILS > SKAIL
SKAITH vb Scots word meaning injure
SKAITHED > SKAITH
SKAITHING > SKAITH
SKAITHS > SKAITH
SKALD n (in ancient Scandinavia) a bard or minstrel
SKALDIC > SKALD
SKALDS > SKALD
SKALDSHIP > SKALD
SKANGER n Irish derogatory slang for a young working-class person who wears casual sports clothes
SKANGERS > SKANGER
SKANK n fast dance to reggae music ▷ vb perform this dance

SKANKED > SKANK
SKANKER > SKANK
SKANKERS > SKANK
SKANKIER > SKANKY
SKANKIEST > SKANKY
SKANKING > SKANK
SKANKINGS > SKANK
SKANKS > SKANK
SKANKY adj dirty or unattractive
SKART Scots word for > CORMORANT
SKARTH Scots word for > CORMORANT
SKARTHS > SKARTH
SKARTS > SKART
SKAS > SKA
SKAT n three-handed card game using 32 cards
SKATE n boot with a steel blade or sets of wheels attached to the sole ▷ vb glide on or as if on skates
SKATED > SKATE
SKATEPARK n place for skateboarding
SKATER n person who skates
SKATERS > SKATER
SKATES > SKATE
SKATING > SKATE
SKATINGS > SKATE
SKATOL n skatole
SKATOLE n white or brownish crystalline solid
SKATOLES > SKATOLE
SKATOLS > SKATOL
SKATS > SKAT
SKATT n dialect word meaning throw
SKATTS > SKATT
SKAW variant of > SCAW
SKAWS > SKAW
SKEAN n kind of double-edged dagger
SKEANE same as > SKEIN
SKEANES > SKEANE
SKEANS > SKEAN
SKEAR dialect form of > SCARE
SKEARED > SKEAR
SKEARIER > SKEARY
SKEARIEST > SKEARY
SKEARING > SKEAR
SKEARS > SKEAR
SKEARY dialect form of > SCARY
SKED vb short for schedule
SKEDADDLE vb run off ▷ n hasty retreat
SKEDDED > SKED
SKEDDING > SKED
SKEDS > SKED
SKEE variant spelling of > SKI
SKEECHAN n old Scots type of beer
SKEECHANS > SKEECHAN
SKEED > SKEE
SKEEF adj, adv South African slang for at an oblique angle
SKEEING > SKEE

SKEELIER > SKEELY
SKEELIEST > SKEELY
SKEELY adj Scots word meaning skilful
SKEEN n type of ibex
SKEENS > SKEEN
SKEER dialect form of > SCARE
SKEERED > SKEER
SKEERIER > SKEERY
SKEERIEST > SKEERY
SKEERING > SKEER
SKEERS > SKEER
SKEERY dialect form of > SCARY
SKEES > SKEE
SKEESICKS American word meaning > ROGUE
SKEET n form of clay-pigeon shooting
SKEETER informal word for > MOSQUITO
SKEETERS > SKEETER
SKEETS > SKEET
SKEEVIER > SKEEVY
SKEEVIEST > SKEEVY
SKEEVY adj repulsive
SKEG n reinforcing brace between the after end of a keel and the rudderpost
SKEGG n skeg
SKEGGER n young salmon
SKEGGERS > SKEGGER
SKEGGS > SKEGG
SKEGS > SKEG
SKEIGH adj Scots word meaning shy
SKEIGHER > SKEIGH
SKEIGHEST > SKEIGH
SKEIN n yarn wound in a loose coil ▷ vb wind into a skein
SKEINED > SKEIN
SKEINING > SKEIN
SKEINS > SKEIN
SKELDER vb beg
SKELDERED > SKELDER
SKELDERS > SKELDER
SKELETAL > SKELETON
SKELETON n framework of bones inside a person's or animal's body ▷ adj reduced to a minimum
SKELETONS > SKELETON
SKELF n splinter of wood, esp when embedded accidentally in the skin
SKELFS > SKELF
SKELL n homeless person
SKELLIE adj skelly
SKELLIED > SKELLY
SKELLIER > SKELLY
SKELLIES > SKELLY
SKELLIEST > SKELLY
SKELLOCH n Scots word meaning scream
SKELLOCHS > SKELLOCH
SKELLS > SKELL
SKELLUM n rogue
SKELLUMS > SKELLUM
SKELLY n whitefish of certain lakes in the Lake

District ▷ vb look sideways or squint ▷ adj cross-eyed
SKELLYING > SKELLY
SKELM n villain or crook
SKELMS > SKELM
SKELP vb slap ▷ n slap
SKELPED > SKELP
SKELPING > SKELP
SKELPINGS > SKELP
SKELPIT vb Scots word meaning skelped
SKELPS > SKELP
SKELTER vb scurry
SKELTERED > SKELTER
SKELTERS > SKELTER
SKELUM n Scots word meaning rascal
SKELUMS > SKELUM
SKEN vb squint or stare
SKENE n Scots word meaning dagger
SKENES > SKENE
SKENNED > SKEN
SKENNING > SKEN
SKENS > SKEN
SKEO n Scots dialect word meaning hut
SKEOES > SKEO
SKEOS > SKEO
SKEP n beehive, esp one constructed of straw ▷ vb gather into a hive
SKEPFUL n amount skep will hold
SKEPFULS > SKEP
SKEPPED > SKEP
SKEPPING > SKEP
SKEPS > SKEP
SKEPSIS n doubt
SKEPSISES > SKEPSIS
SKEPTIC same as > SCEPTIC
SKEPTICAL > SKEPTIC
SKEPTICS > SKEPTIC
SKER vb scour
SKERRED > SKER
SKERRICK n small fragment or amount
SKERRICKS > SKERRICK
SKERRIES > SKERRY
SKERRING > SKER
SKERRY n rocky island or reef
SKERS > SKER
SKET vb splash (water)
SKETCH n rough drawing ▷ vb make a sketch (of)
SKETCHED > SKETCH
SKETCHER > SKETCH
SKETCHERS > SKETCH
SKETCHES > SKETCH
SKETCHIER > SKETCHY
SKETCHILY > SKETCHY
SKETCHING > SKETCH
SKETCHPAD n pad of paper for sketching
SKETCHY adj incomplete or inadequate
SKETS > SKET
SKETTED > SKET
SKETTING > SKET
SKEW vb make slanting or crooked ▷ adj slanting or

crooked ▷ *n* slanting
position
SKEWBACK *n* sloping
surface on both sides of a
segmental arch that takes
the thrust
SKEWBACKS > SKEWBACK
SKEWBALD *adj* (horse)
marked with patches of
white and another colour
▷ *n* horse with this
marking
SKEWBALDS > SKEWBALD
SKEWED > SKEW
SKEWER *n* pin to hold meat
together during cooking
▷ *vb* fasten with a skewer
SKEWERED > SKEWER
SKEWERING > SKEWER
SKEWERS > SKEWER
SKEWEST > SKEW
SKEWING > SKEW
SKEWNESS *n* quality or
condition of being skew
SKEWS > SKEW
SKEWWHIFF *adj* crooked
or slanting
SKI *n* one of a pair of long
runners fastened to boots
for gliding over snow or
water ▷ *vb* travel on skis
SKIABLE > SKI
SKIAGRAM *n* picture made
from shadows
SKIAGRAMS > SKIAGRAM
SKIAGRAPH *n* skiagram
SKIAMACHY *same as*
> SCIAMACHY
SKIASCOPE *n* medical
instrument for examining
the eye to detect errors of
refraction
SKIASCOPY
n retinoscopy
SKIATRON *n* type of
cathode ray tube
SKIATRONS > SKIATRON
SKIBOB *n* vehicle made of
two short skis for gliding
down snow slopes
SKIBOBBED > SKIBOB
SKIBOBBER > SKIBOB
SKIBOBS > SKIBOB
SKID *vb* (of a moving
vehicle) slide sideways
uncontrollably
▷ *n* skidding
SKIDDED > SKID
SKIDDER > SKID
SKIDDERS > SKID
SKIDDIER > SKID
SKIDDIEST > SKID
SKIDDING *n* act of
skidding
SKIDDINGS > SKIDDING
SKIDDOO *vb* go away
quickly
SKIDDOOED > SKIDDOO
SKIDDOOS > SKIDDOO
SKIDDY > SKID
SKIDLID *n* crash helmet
SKIDLIDS > SKIDLID
SKIDMARK *n* mark left by
a skid

SKIDMARKS > SKIDMARK
SKIDOO *n* snowmobile
▷ *vb* travel on a skidoo
SKIDOOED > SKIDOO
SKIDOOER *n* person who
rides a skidoo
SKIDOOERS > SKIDOOER
SKIDOOING > SKIDOO
SKIDOOS > SKIDOO
SKIDPAD *n* area of road
used to test skidding
SKIDPADS > SKIDPAD
SKIDPAN *n* area made
slippery so that vehicle
drivers can practise
controlling skids
SKIDPANS > SKIDPAN
SKIDPROOF *adj* (of a road
surface, tyre, etc)
preventing or resistant to
skidding
SKIDS > SKID
SKIDWAY *n* platform on
which logs ready for
sawing are piled
SKIDWAYS > SKIDWAY
SKIED > SKY
SKIER > SKI
SKIES > SKY
SKIEY *adj* of the sky
SKIEYER > SKIEY
SKIEYEST > SKIEY
SKIFF *n* small boat
▷ *vb* travel in a skiff
SKIFFED > SKIFF
SKIFFING > SKIFF
SKIFFLE *n* style of
popular music of the 1950s
▷ *vb* play this style of music
SKIFFLED > SKIFFLE
SKIFFLES > SKIFFLE
SKIFFLESS > SKIFF
SKIFFLING > SKIFFLE
SKIFFS > SKIFF
SKIING > SKI
SKIINGS > SKI
SKIJORER > SKIJORING
SKIJORERS
> SKIJORING
SKIJORING *n* sport in
which a skier is pulled over
snow or ice, usually by a
horse
SKIJUMPER *n* one who
engages in the sport of
skijumping
SKIKJORER *n* one who
engages in the sport of
skijoring
SKILFUL *adj* having or
showing skill
SKILFULL *less common
spelling of* > SKILFUL
SKILFULLY > SKILFUL
SKILL *n* special ability or
expertise
SKILLED *adj* possessing
or demonstrating skill, or
special training
SKILLESS > SKILL
SKILLET *n* small frying
pan or shallow cooking
pot

SKILLETS > SKILLET
SKILLFUL *same as*
> SKILFUL
SKILLIER > SKILLY
SKILLIES > SKILLY
SKILLIEST > SKILLY
SKILLING *n* former
Scandinavian coin of low
denomination
SKILLINGS > SKILLING
SKILLION *n* part of a
building having a lower,
esp sloping, roof
SKILLIONS > SKILLION
SKILLS > SKILL
SKILLY *n* thin soup or
gruel ▷ *adj* skilled
SKIM *vb* remove floating
matter from the surface of
(a liquid) ▷ *n* act or process
of skimming
SKIMBOARD *n* type of
surfboard, shorter than
standard and rounded at
both ends ▷ *vb* surf on a
skimboard
SKIMMED > SKIM
SKIMMER *n* person or
thing that skims
SKIMMERS > SKIMMER
SKIMMIA *n* shrub of S and
SE Asia
SKIMMIAS > SKIMMIA
SKIMMING > SKIM
SKIMMINGS *pl n* material
that is skimmed off a liquid
SKIMO *n* informal and
offensive word for an Inuit
SKIMOBILE *n* motor
vehicle with skis for
travelling on snow
SKIMOS > SKIMO
SKIMP *vb* not invest
enough time, money,
material, etc
SKIMPED > SKIMP
SKIMPIER > SKIMPY
SKIMPIEST > SKIMPY
SKIMPILY > SKIMPY
SKIMPING > SKIMP
SKIMPS > SKIMP
SKIMPY *adj* scanty or
insufficient
SKIMS > SKIM
SKIN *n* outer covering of
the body ▷ *vb* remove the
skin of
SKINCARE *n* use of
cosmetics in taking care of
skin
SKINCARES > SKINCARE
SKINFLICK *n* film
containing much nudity
and sex
SKINFLINT *n* miser
SKINFOOD *n* cosmetic
cream for the skin
SKINFOODS > SKINFOOD
SKINFUL *n* sufficient
alcoholic drink to make
one drunk
SKINFULS > SKINFUL
SKINHEAD *n* youth with
very short hair

SKINHEADS > SKINHEAD
SKINK *n* type of lizard with
reduced limbs and smooth
scales ▷ *vb* serve a drink
SKINKED > SKINK
SKINKER > SKINK
SKINKERS > SKINK
SKINKING > SKINK
SKINKS > SKINK
SKINLESS > SKIN
SKINLIKE > SKIN
SKINNED > SKIN
SKINNER *n* person who
prepares or deals in animal
skins
SKINNERS > SKINNER
SKINNIER > SKINNY
SKINNIES > SKINNY
SKINNIEST > SKINNY
SKINNING > SKIN
SKINNY *adj* thin
▷ *n* information
SKINS > SKIN
SKINSUIT *n* skintight
one-piece garment worn
by cyclists to reduce
friction
SKINSUITS > SKINSUIT
SKINT *adj* having no
money
SKINTER > SKINT
SKINTEST > SKINT
SKINTIGHT *adj* fitting
tightly over the body
SKIO *n* Scots dialect word
meaning hut
SKIOES > SKIO
SKIORER *n* one who
engages in the sport of
skijoring
SKIORERS > SKIORER
SKIORING *n* sport of
being towed on skis by
horse
SKIORINGS > SKIORING
SKIOS > SKIO
SKIP *vb* leap lightly from
one foot to the other
▷ *n* skipping
SKIPJACK *n* important
food fish of tropical seas
SKIPJACKS > SKIPJACK
SKIPLANE *n* aircraft fitted
with skis to enable it to
land on and take off from
snow
SKIPLANES > SKIPLANE
SKIPPABLE > SKIP
SKIPPED > SKIP
SKIPPER *vb* captain
▷ *n* captain of a ship or
aircraft
SKIPPERED > SKIPPER
SKIPPERS > SKIPPER
SKIPPET *n* small round
box for preserving a
document or seal
SKIPPETS > SKIPPET
SKIPPIER > SKIPPY
SKIPPIEST > SKIPPY
SKIPPING > SKIP
SKIPPINGS > SKIP
SKIPPY *adj* in high spirits

SKIPS > SKIP
SKIRL n sound of bagpipes ▷ vb (of bagpipes) to give out a shrill sound
SKIRLED > SKIRL
SKIRLING > SKIRL
SKIRLINGS > SKIRL
SKIRLS > SKIRL
SKIRMISH n brief or minor fight or argument ▷ vb take part in a skirmish
SKIRR vb move, run, or fly rapidly ▷ n whirring or grating sound, as of the wings of birds in flight
SKIRRED > SKIRR
SKIRRET n umbelliferous Old World plant
SKIRRETS > SKIRRET
SKIRRING > SKIRR
SKIRRS > SKIRR
SKIRT n woman's garment hanging from the waist ▷ vb border
SKIRTED > SKIRT
SKIRTER n man who skirts fleeces
SKIRTERS > SKIRTER
SKIRTING n border fixed round the base of an interior wall to protect it from kicks, dirt, etc
SKIRTINGS pl n ragged edges trimmed from the fleece of a sheep
SKIRTLESS > SKIRT
SKIRTLIKE > SKIRT
SKIRTS > SKIRT
SKIS > SKI
SKIT n brief satirical sketch
SKITCH vb (of a dog) to attack
SKITCHED > SKITCH
SKITCHES > SKITCH
SKITCHING > SKITCH
SKITE n, vb boast
SKITED > SKITE
SKITES > SKITE
SKITING > SKITE
SKITS > SKIT
SKITTER vb move or run rapidly or lightly
SKITTERED > SKITTER
SKITTERS > SKITTER
SKITTERY adj moving lightly and rapidly
SKITTISH adj playful or lively
SKITTLE n bottle-shaped object used as a target in some games ▷ vb play skittles
SKITTLED > SKITTLE
SKITTLES > SKITTLE
SKITTLING > SKITTLE
SKIVE vb evade work or responsibility
SKIVED > SKIVE
SKIVER n tanned outer layer split from a skin ▷ vb cut leather
SKIVERED > SKIVER

SKIVERING > SKIVER
SKIVERS > SKIVER
SKIVES > SKIVE
SKIVIE adj old Scots word meaning disarranged
SKIVIER > SKIVIE
SKIVIEST > SKIVIE
SKIVING > SKIVE
SKIVINGS > SKIVE
SKIVVIED > SKIVVY
SKIVVIES > SKIVVY
SKIVVY n female servant who does menial work ▷ vb work as a skivvy
SKIVVYING > SKIVVY
SKIVY > SKIVE
SKIWEAR n clothes for skiing in
SKLATE Scots word for > SLATE
SKLATED > SKLATE
SKLATES > SKLATE
SKLATING > SKLATE
SKLENT Scots word for > SLANT
SKLENTED > SKLENT
SKLENTING > SKLENT
SKLENTS > SKLENT
SKLIFF n Scots word meaning little piece ▷ vb shuffle (the feet)
SKLIFFED > SKLIFF
SKLIFFING > SKLIFF
SKLIFFS > SKLIFF
SKLIM vb Scots word meaning climb
SKLIMMED > SKLIM
SKLIMMING > SKLIM
SKLIMS > SKLIM
SKOAL same as > SKOL
SKOALED > SKOAL
SKOALING > SKOAL
SKOALS > SKOAL
SKOFF vb eat greedily
SKOFFED > SKOFF
SKOFFING > SKOFF
SKOFFS > SKOFF
SKOG same as > SCOG
SKOGGED > SKOG
SKOGGING > SKOG
SKOGS > SKOG
SKOKIAAN n (in South Africa) a potent alcoholic beverage
SKOKIAANS > SKOKIAAN
SKOL sentence substitute good health! (a drinking toast) ▷ vb down (an alcoholic drink) in one go
SKOLED > SKOL
SKOLIA > SKOLION
SKOLING > SKOL
SKOLION n ancient Greek drinking song
SKOLLED > SKOL
SKOLLIE same as > SKOLLY
SKOLLIES > SKOLLY
SKOLLING > SKOL
SKOLLY n hooligan, usually one of a gang
SKOLS > SKOL

SKOOKUM adj strong or brave ▷ n strong or brave person
SKOOKUMS > SKOOKUM
SKOOL ironically illiterate or childish spelling of > SCHOOL
SKOOLS > SKOOL
SKOOSH vb Scots word meaning squirt
SKOOSHED > SKOOSH
SKOOSHES > SKOOSH
SKOOSHING > SKOOSH
SKORT n pair of shorts with a front panel which gives the appearance of a skirt
SKORTS > SKORT
SKOSH n little bit
SKOSHES > SKOSH
SKRAN n food
SKRANS > SKRAN
SKREEGH vb Scots word meaning screech
SKREEGHED > SKREEGH
SKREEGHS > SKREEGH
SKREEN n screen
SKREENS > SKREEN
SKREIGH vb Scots word meaning screech
SKREIGHED > SKREIGH
SKREIGHS > SKREIGH
SKRIECH vb Scots word meaning screech
SKRIECHED > SKRIECH
SKRIECHS > SKRIECH
SKRIED > SKRY
SKRIEGH Scots word meaning screech
SKRIEGHED > SKRIEGH
SKRIEGHS > SKRIEGH
SKRIES > SKRY
SKRIK n South African word meaning fright
SKRIKE vb cry
SKRIKED > SKRIKE
SKRIKES > SKRIKE
SKRIKING > SKRIKE
SKRIKS > SKRIK
SKRIMMAGE vb scrimmage
SKRIMP vb steal apples
SKRIMPED > SKRIMP
SKRIMPING > SKRIMP
SKRIMPS > SKRIMP
SKRONK n type of dissonant, grating popular music
SKRONKS > SKRONK
SKRUMP vb steal apples
SKRUMPED > SKRUMP
SKRUMPING > SKRUMP
SKRUMPS > SKRUMP
SKRY vb try to tell future
SKRYER > SKRY
SKRYERS > SKRY
SKRYING > SKRY
SKUA n large predatory gull
SKUAS > SKUA
SKUDLER n Scots word meaning leader of festivities
SKUDLERS > SKUDLER

SKUG vb shelter
SKUGGED > SKUG
SKUGGING > SKUG
SKUGS > SKUG
SKULK vb move stealthily ▷ n person who skulks
SKULKED > SKULK
SKULKER > SKULK
SKULKERS > SKULK
SKULKING > SKULK
SKULKINGS > SKULK
SKULKS > SKULK
SKULL n bony framework of the head ▷ vb strike on the head
SKULLCAP n close-fitting brimless cap
SKULLCAPS > SKULLCAP
SKULLED > SKULL
SKULLING > SKULL
SKULLS > SKULL
SKULPIN n North American fish
SKULPINS > SKULPIN
SKUMMER vb defecate
SKUMMERED > SKUMMER
SKUMMERS > SKUMMER
SKUNK n small mammal which emits a foul-smelling fluid when attacked ▷ vb defeat overwhelmingly in a game
SKUNKBIRD n North American songbird
SKUNKED > SKUNK
SKUNKIER > SKUNK
SKUNKIEST > SKUNK
SKUNKING > SKUNK
SKUNKS > SKUNK
SKUNKWEED n low-growing fetid swamp plant of N America
SKUNKY > SKUNK
SKURRIED > SKURRY
SKURRIES > SKURRY
SKURRY vb scurry
SKURRYING > SKURRY
SKUTTLE vb scuttle
SKUTTLED > SKUTTLE
SKUTTLES > SKUTTLE
SKUTTLING > SKUTTLE
SKY n upper atmosphere as seen from the earth ▷ vb hit high in the air
SKYBOARD n small board used for skysurfing
SKYBOARDS > SKYBOARD
SKYBORN adj born in heaven
SKYBORNE adj flying through sky
SKYBOX n luxurious suite high up in the stand of a sports stadium
SKYBOXES > SKYBOX
SKYBRIDGE n covered, elevated bridge connecting two buildings
SKYCAP n luggage porter at American airport
SKYCAPS > SKYCAP
SKYCLAD adj naked

S

SKYDIVE vb take part in skydiving
SKYDIVED > SKYDIVE
SKYDIVER > SKYDIVE
SKYDIVERS > SKYDIVE
SKYDIVES > SKYDIVE
SKYDIVING n sport of jumping from an aircraft and performing manoeuvres before opening one's parachute
SKYDOVE > SKYDIVE
SKYED > SKY
SKYER n cricket ball hit up into air
SKYERS > SKYER
SKYEY adj of the sky
SKYF n South African slang for a cigarette or substance for smoking ▷ vb smoke a cigarette
SKYFED > SKYF
SKYFING > SKYF
SKYFS > SKYF
SKYGLOW n glow in the night sky caused by urban lights
SKYGLOWS > SKYGLOW
SKYHOME n Australian slang for a sub-penthouse flat in a tall building
SKYHOMES > SKYHOME
SKYHOOK n hook hung from helicopter
SKYHOOKS > SKYHOOK
SKYIER > SKYEY
SKYIEST > SKYEY
SKYING > SKY
SKYISH > SKY
SKYJACK vb hijack (an aircraft)
SKYJACKED > SKYJACK
SKYJACKER > SKYJACK
SKYJACKS > SKYJACK
SKYLAB n orbiting space station
SKYLABS > SKYLAB
SKYLARK n lark that sings while soaring at a great height ▷ vb play or frolic
SKYLARKED > SKYLARK
SKYLARKER > SKYLARK
SKYLARKS > SKYLARK
SKYLESS adj having no sky
SKYLIGHT n window in a roof or ceiling
SKYLIGHTS > SKYLIGHT
SKYLIKE > SKY
SKYLINE n outline of buildings, trees, etc against the sky
SKYLINES > SKYLINE
SKYLIT adj having skylight
SKYMAN n paratrooper
SKYMEN > SKYMAN
SKYPHOI > SKYPHOS
SKYPHOS n ancient Greek drinking cup
SKYR n Scandinavian cheese
SKYRE vb Scots word meaning shine

SKYRED > SKYRE
SKYRES > SKYRE
SKYRING > SKYRE
SKYRMION n (in theoretical physics) mathematical model used to model baryons
SKYRMIONS > SKYRMION
SKYROCKET vb rise very quickly
SKYRS > SKYR
SKYSAIL n square sail set above the royal on a square-rigger
SKYSAILS > SKYSAIL
SKYSCAPE n painting, drawing, photograph, etc, representing or depicting the sky
SKYSCAPES > SKYSCAPE
SKYSURF vb perform freefall aerobatics
SKYSURFED > SKYSURF
SKYSURFER n someone who performs stunts with a small board attached to his or her feet while in free fall
SKYSURFS > SKYSURF
SKYTE vb Scots word meaning slide
SKYTED > SKYTE
SKYTES > SKYTE
SKYTING > SKYTE
SKYWALK n tightrope walk at great height
SKYWALKS > SKYWALK
SKYWARD adj towards the sky ▷ adv towards the sky
SKYWARDS same as **>** SKYWARD
SKYWATCH vb watch the sky in search of celestial bodies or aircraft
SKYWAY n air route
SKYWAYS > SKYWAY
SKYWRITE vb write message in sky with smoke from aircraft
SKYWRITER > SKYWRITE
SKYWRITES > SKYWRITE
SKYWROTE > SKYWRITE
SLAB n broad flat piece ▷ vb cut or make into a slab or slabs
SLABBED > SLAB
SLABBER vb dribble from the mouth
SLABBERED > SLABBER
SLABBERER > SLABBER
SLABBERS > SLABBER
SLABBERY > SLABBER
SLABBIER > SLAB
SLABBIEST > SLAB
SLABBING n act of slabbing
SLABBINGS > SLABBING
SLABBY > SLAB
SLABLIKE > SLAB
SLABS > SLAB
SLABSTONE n flagstone
SLACK same as **>** SLAKE
SLACKED > SLACK

SLACKEN vb make or become slack
SLACKENED > SLACKEN
SLACKENER > SLACKEN
SLACKENS > SLACKEN
SLACKER n person who evades work or duty
SLACKERS > SLACKER
SLACKEST > SLACK
SLACKING > SLACK
SLACKLY > SLACK
SLACKNESS > SLACK
SLACKS pl n casual trousers
SLADANG n Malayan tapir
SLADANGS > SLADANG
SLADE n little valley
SLADES > SLADE
SLAE Scots word for **>** SLOE
SLAES > SLAE
SLAG n waste left after metal is smelted ▷ vb criticize
SLAGGED > SLAG
SLAGGIER > SLAG
SLAGGIEST > SLAG
SLAGGING > SLAG
SLAGGINGS > SLAG
SLAGGY > SLAG
SLAGS > SLAG
SLAHAL same as **>** LAHAL
SLAHALS > SLAHAL
SLAID vb (Scot) sledge
SLAIDS > SLAID
SLAIN > SLAY
SLAINTE interj cheers!
SLAIRG Scots word for **>** SPREAD
SLAIRGED > SLAIRG
SLAIRGING > SLAIRG
SLAIRGS > SLAIRG
SLAISTER vb cover with a sloppy mess ▷ n sloppy mess
SLAISTERS > SLAISTER
SLAISTERY > SLAISTER
SLAKABLE > SLAKE
SLAKE vb satisfy (thirst or desire)
SLAKEABLE > SLAKE
SLAKED > SLAKE
SLAKELESS adj impossible to slake
SLAKER > SLAKE
SLAKERS > SLAKE
SLAKES > SLAKE
SLAKING > SLAKE
SLALOM n skiing or canoeing race over a winding course ▷ vb take part in a slalom
SLALOMED > SLALOM
SLALOMER > SLALOM
SLALOMERS > SLALOM
SLALOMING > SLALOM
SLALOMIST > SLALOM
SLALOMS > SLALOM
SLAM vb shut, put down, or hit violently and noisily ▷ n act or sound of slamming
SLAMDANCE vb dance aggressively, bumping into others

SLAMMAKIN n woman's loose dress
SLAMMED > SLAM
SLAMMER n prison
SLAMMERS > SLAMMER
SLAMMING > SLAM
SLAMMINGS > SLAM
SLAMS > SLAM
SLANDER n false and malicious statement about a person ▷ vb utter slander about
SLANDERED > SLANDER
SLANDERER > SLANDER
SLANDERS > SLANDER
SLANE n spade for cutting turf
SLANES > SLANE
SLANG n very informal language ▷ vb use insulting language to (someone)
SLANGED > SLANG
SLANGER n street vendor
SLANGERS > SLANGER
SLANGIER > SLANG
SLANGIEST > SLANG
SLANGILY > SLANG
SLANGING > SLANG
SLANGINGS > SLANG
SLANGISH > SLANG
SLANGS > SLANG
SLANGUAGE n language using slang
SLANGULAR adj of or using slang
SLANGY > SLANG
SLANK dialect word for **>** LANK
SLANT vb lean at an angle, slope ▷ n slope
SLANTED > SLANT
SLANTER same as **>** SLINTER
SLANTERS > SLANTER
SLANTIER > SLANTY
SLANTIEST > SLANTY
SLANTING > SLANT
SLANTLY > SLANT
SLANTS > SLANT
SLANTWAYS same as **>** SLANTWISE
SLANTWISE adj in a slanting or oblique direction
SLANTY adj slanting
SLAP n blow with the open hand or a flat object ▷ vb strike with the open hand or a flat object
SLAPDASH adj careless and hasty ▷ adv carelessly or hastily ▷ n slapdash activity or work ▷ vb do in a hurried and careless manner
SLAPHAPPY adj cheerfully irresponsible or careless
SLAPHEAD n derogatory term for a bald person
SLAPHEADS > SLAPHEAD
SLAPJACK n simple card game
SLAPJACKS > SLAPJACK

SLAPPED > SLAP
SLAPPER > SLAP
SLAPPERS > SLAP
SLAPPING n as in happy slapping filming random acts of violence as a source of amusement
SLAPPINGS > SLAPPING
SLAPS > SLAP
SLAPSHOT n hard, fast, often wild, shot executed with a powerful downward swing
SLAPSHOTS > SLAPSHOT
SLAPSTICK n boisterous knockabout comedy
SLART vb spill (something)
SLARTED > SLART
SLARTING > SLART
SLARTS > SLART
SLASH vb cut with a sweeping stroke ▷ n sweeping stroke
SLASHED > SLASH
SLASHER n machine used for cutting scrub or undergrowth in the bush
SLASHERS > SLASHER
SLASHES > SLASH
SLASHFEST n film or computer game that features bloody killings involving blades
SLASHING adj aggressively critical ▷ n act of slashing
SLASHINGS > SLASHING
SLAT n narrow strip of wood or metal ▷ vb provide with slats
SLATCH n slack part of rope
SLATCHES > SLATCH
SLATE n rock which splits easily into thin layers ▷ vb cover with slates ▷ adj dark grey
SLATED > SLATE
SLATELIKE > SLATE
SLATER n person trained in laying roof slates
SLATERS > SLATER
SLATES > SLATE
SLATEY adj slightly mad
SLATHER vb spread quickly or lavishly
SLATHERED > SLATHER
SLATHERS > SLATHER
SLATIER > SLATY
SLATIEST > SLATY
SLATINESS > SLATY
SLATING n act or process of laying slates
SLATINGS > SLATING
SLATS > SLAT
SLATTED > SLAT
SLATTER vb be slovenly
SLATTERED > SLATTER
SLATTERN n slovenly woman
SLATTERNS > SLATTERN
SLATTERS > SLATTER
SLATTERY adj slovenly
SLATTING > SLAT

SLATTINGS > SLAT
SLATY adj consisting of or resembling slate
SLAUGHTER vb kill (animals) for food ▷ n slaughtering
SLAVE n person owned by another for whom he or she has to work ▷ vb work like a slave
SLAVED > SLAVE
SLAVER n person or ship engaged in the slave trade ▷ vb dribble saliva from the mouth
SLAVERED > SLAVER
SLAVERER > SLAVER
SLAVERERS > SLAVER
SLAVERIES > SLAVERY
SLAVERING > SLAVER
SLAVERS > SLAVER
SLAVERY n state or condition of being a slave
SLAVES > SLAVE
SLAVEY n female general servant
SLAVEYS > SLAVEY
SLAVING > SLAVE
SLAVISH adj of or like a slave
SLAVISHLY > SLAVISH
SLAVOCRAT n US slaveholder before the Civil War
SLAVOPHIL n person who admires the Slavs or their cultures
SLAW short for > COLESLAW
SLAWS > SLAW
SLAY vb kill
SLAYABLE > SLAY
SLAYED > SLAY
SLAYER > SLAY
SLAYERS > SLAY
SLAYING n act of slaying
SLAYINGS > SLAYING
SLAYS > SLAY
SLEAVE n tangled thread ▷ vb disentangle (twisted thread, etc)
SLEAVED > SLEAVE
SLEAVES > SLEAVE
SLEAVING > SLEAVE
SLEAZE n behaviour considered dishonest or disreputable ▷ vb behave in a sleazy manner
SLEAZEBAG n disgusting person
SLEAZED > SLEAZE
SLEAZES > SLEAZE
SLEAZIER > SLEAZY
SLEAZIEST > SLEAZY
SLEAZILY > SLEAZY
SLEAZING > SLEAZE
SLEAZO n sleazy person
SLEAZOID n sleazy person
SLEAZOIDS > SLEAZOID
SLEAZOS > SLEAZO
SLEAZY adj run-down or sordid
SLEB n celebrity

SLEBS > SLEB
SLED same as > SLEDGE
SLEDDED > SLED
SLEDDER > SLED
SLEDDERS > SLED
SLEDDING > SLED
SLEDDINGS > SLED
SLEDED > SLED
SLEDGE n carriage on runners for sliding on snow ▷ vb travel by sledge
SLEDGED > SLEDGE
SLEDGER > SLEDGE
SLEDGERS > SLEDGE
SLEDGES > SLEDGE
SLEDGING > SLEDGE
SLEDGINGS > SLEDGE
SLEDS > SLED
SLEE Scots word for > SLY
SLEECH n slippery mud
SLEECHES > SLEECH
SLEECHIER > SLEECH
SLEECHY > SLEECH
SLEEK adj glossy, smooth, and shiny ▷ vb make smooth and glossy, as by grooming, etc
SLEEKED > SLEEK
SLEEKEN vb make sleek
SLEEKENED > SLEEKEN
SLEEKENS > SLEEKEN
SLEEKER > SLEEK
SLEEKERS > SLEEK
SLEEKEST > SLEEK
SLEEKIER > SLEEK
SLEEKIEST > SLEEK
SLEEKING > SLEEK
SLEEKINGS > SLEEK
SLEEKIT adj smooth
SLEEKLY > SLEEK
SLEEKNESS > SLEEK
SLEEKS > SLEEK
SLEEKY > SLEEK
SLEEP n state of rest characterized by unconsciousness ▷ vb be in or as if in a state of sleep
SLEEPAWAY adj describing a type of camp for teenagers
SLEEPER n railway car fitted for sleeping in
SLEEPERS > SLEEPER
SLEEPERY Scots word for > SLEEPY
SLEEPIER > SLEEPY
SLEEPIEST > SLEEPY
SLEEPILY > SLEEPY
SLEEPING > SLEEP
SLEEPINGS > SLEEP
SLEEPLESS adj (of a night) one during which one does not sleep
SLEEPLIKE > SLEEP
SLEEPOUT n small building for sleeping in
SLEEPOUTS > SLEEPOUT
SLEEPOVER n occasion when a person stays overnight at a friend's house
SLEEPRY Scots word for > SLEEPY

SLEEPS > SLEEP
SLEEPSUIT n baby's sleeping garment
SLEEPWALK vb walk while asleep
SLEEPWEAR n clothes for sleeping in
SLEEPY adj needing sleep
SLEER > SLEE
SLEEST > SLEE
SLEET n rain and snow or hail falling together ▷ vb fall as sleet
SLEETED > SLEET
SLEETIER > SLEET
SLEETIEST > SLEET
SLEETING > SLEET
SLEETS > SLEET
SLEETY > SLEET
SLEEVE n part of a garment which covers the arm
SLEEVED > SLEEVE
SLEEVEEN n sly obsequious smooth-tongued person
SLEEVEENS > SLEEVEEN
SLEEVELET n protective covering for forearm
SLEEVER n old beer measure
SLEEVERS > SLEEVER
SLEEVES > SLEEVE
SLEEVING n tubular flexible insulation into which bare wire can be inserted
SLEEVINGS > SLEEVING
SLEEZIER > SLEEZY
SLEEZIEST > SLEEZY
SLEEZY adj sleazy
SLEIDED adj old word meaning separated
SLEIGH same as > SLEDGE
SLEIGHED > SLEIGH
SLEIGHER > SLEIGH
SLEIGHERS > SLEIGH
SLEIGHING > SLEIGH
SLEIGHS > SLEIGH
SLEIGHT n skill or cunning
SLEIGHTS > SLEIGHT
SLENDER adj slim
SLENDERER > SLENDER
SLENDERLY > SLENDER
SLENTER same as > SLINTER
SLENTERS > SLENTER
SLEPT > SLEEP
SLEUTH n detective ▷ vb track or follow
SLEUTHED > SLEUTH
SLEUTHING > SLEUTH
SLEUTHS > SLEUTH
SLEW vb twist sideways, esp awkwardly
SLEWED > SLEW
SLEWING > SLEW
SLEWS > SLEW
SLEY n weaver's tool for separating threads
SLEYS > SLEY

S

SLICE *n* thin flat piece cut from something ▷ *vb* cut into slices
SLICEABLE > SLICE
SLICED > SLICE
SLICER > SLICE
SLICERS > SLICE
SLICES > SLICE
SLICING > SLICE
SLICINGS > SLICE
SLICK *adj* persuasive and glib ▷ *n* patch of oil on water ▷ *vb* make smooth or sleek
SLICKED > SLICK
SLICKEN *vb* make smooth
SLICKENED > SLICKEN
SLICKENER > SLICKEN
SLICKENS > SLICKEN
SLICKER *n* sly or untrustworthy person
SLICKERED *adj* wearing a waterproof jacket
SLICKERS > SLICKER
SLICKEST > SLICK
SLICKING > SLICK
SLICKINGS > SLICK
SLICKLY > SLICK
SLICKNESS > SLICK
SLICKROCK *n* weathered and smooth sandstone or other rock
SLICKS > SLICK
SLICKSTER *n* dishonest person
SLID > SLIDE
SLIDABLE > SLIDE
SLIDDEN > SLIDE
SLIDDER *vb* slip
SLIDDERED > SLIDDER
SLIDDERS > SLIDDER
SLIDDERY *adj* slippery
SLIDE *vb* slip smoothly along (a surface) ▷ *n* sliding
SLIDED > SLIDE
SLIDER > SLIDE
SLIDERS > SLIDE
SLIDES > SLIDE
SLIDEWAY *n* sloping channel down which things are slid
SLIDEWAYS > SLIDEWAY
SLIDING > SLIDE
SLIDINGLY > SLIDE
SLIDINGS > SLIDE
SLIER > SLY
SLIEST > SLY
SLIEVE *n* Irish mountain
SLIEVES > SLIEVE
SLIGHT *adj* small in quantity or extent ▷ *n* snub ▷ *vb* insult (someone) by behaving rudely
SLIGHTED > SLIGHT
SLIGHTER > SLIGHT
SLIGHTERS > SLIGHT
SLIGHTEST > SLIGHT
SLIGHTING *adj* characteristic of a slight
SLIGHTISH > SLIGHT
SLIGHTLY *adv* in small measure or degree

SLIGHTS > SLIGHT
SLILY > SLY
SLIM *adj* not heavy or stout, thin ▷ *vb* make or become slim by diet and exercise
SLIMDOWN *n* instance of an organization cutting staff
SLIMDOWNS > SLIMDOWN
SLIME *n* unpleasant thick slippery substance ▷ *vb* cover with slime
SLIMEBAG *n* odious and contemptible person
SLIMEBAGS > SLIMEBAG
SLIMEBALL *n* odious and contemptible person
SLIMED > SLIME
SLIMES > SLIME
SLIMIER > SLIMY
SLIMIEST > SLIMY
SLIMILY > SLIMY
SLIMING > SLIME
SLIMLINE *adj* slim
SLIMLY > SLIM
SLIMMED > SLIM
SLIMMER > SLIM
SLIMMERS > SLIM
SLIMMEST > SLIM
SLIMMING > SLIM
SLIMMINGS > SLIM
SLIMMISH > SLIM
SLIMNESS > SLIM
SLIMPSIER > SLIMPSY
SLIMPSY *adj* thin and flimsy
SLIMS > SLIM
SLIMSIER > SLIMSY
SLIMSIEST > SLIMSY
SLIMSY *adj* frail
SLIMY *adj* of, like, or covered with slime
SLING *n* bandage hung from the neck to support an injured hand or arm ▷ *vb* throw
SLINGBACK *n* shoe with a strap that goes around the back of the heel
SLINGER > SLING
SLINGERS > SLING
SLINGING > SLING
SLINGS > SLING
SLINGSHOT *n* Y-shaped implement with a loop of elastic fastened to the ends of the two prongs, used for shooting small stones, etc
SLINK *vb* move furtively or guiltily ▷ *n* animal, esp a calf, born prematurely
SLINKED > SLINK
SLINKER > SLINK
SLINKERS > SLINK
SLINKIER > SLINKY
SLINKIEST > SLINKY
SLINKILY > SLINKY
SLINKING > SLINK
SLINKS > SLINK

SLINKSKIN *n* skin of premature calf
SLINKWEED *n* plant believed to make cow give birth prematurely
SLINKY *adj* (of clothes) figure-hugging
SLINTER *n* dodge, trick, or stratagem
SLINTERS > SLINTER
SLIOTAR *n* ball used in hurling
SLIOTARS > SLIOTAR
SLIP *vb* lose balance by sliding ▷ *n* slipping
SLIPCASE *n* protective case for a book that is open at one end so that only the spine of the book is visible
SLIPCASED *adj* having a slipcase
SLIPCASES > SLIPCASE
SLIPCOVER *n* fitted but easily removable cloth cover for a chair, sofa, etc
SLIPDRESS *n* silky sleeveless dress
SLIPE *n* wool removed from the pelt of a slaughtered sheep ▷ *vb* remove skin
SLIPED > SLIPE
SLIPES > SLIPE
SLIPFORM *n* mould used in building
SLIPFORMS > SLIPFORM
SLIPING > SLIPE
SLIPKNOT *n* knot tied so that it will slip along the rope round which it is made
SLIPKNOTS > SLIPKNOT
SLIPLESS > SLIP
SLIPNOOSE *n* noose made with a slipknot, so that it tightens when pulled
SLIPOUT *n* instance of slipping out
SLIPOUTS > SLIPOUT
SLIPOVER *adj* of or denoting a garment that can be put on easily over the head ▷ *n* such a garment, esp a sleeveless pullover
SLIPOVERS > SLIPOVER
SLIPPAGE *n* act or an instance of slipping
SLIPPAGES > SLIPPAGE
SLIPPED > SLIP
SLIPPER *n* light shoe for indoor wear ▷ *vb* hit or beat with a slipper
SLIPPERED > SLIPPER
SLIPPERS > SLIPPER
SLIPPERY *adj* so smooth or wet as to cause slipping or be difficult to hold
SLIPPIER > SLIPPY
SLIPPIEST > SLIPPY
SLIPPILY > SLIPPY
SLIPPING > SLIP

SLIPPY *adj* slippery
SLIPRAIL *n* rail in a fence that can be slipped out of place to make an opening
SLIPRAILS > SLIPRAIL
SLIPS > SLIP
SLIPSHEET *n* sheet of paper that is interleaved between freshly printed sheets
SLIPSHOD *adj* (of an action) careless
SLIPSLOP *n* weak or unappetizing food or drink
SLIPSLOPS > SLIPSLOP
SLIPSOLE *n* separate sole on shoe
SLIPSOLES > SLIPSOLE
SLIPT *vb* old form of slipped
SLIPUP *n* mistake or mishap
SLIPUPS > SLIPUP
SLIPWARE *n* pottery that has been decorated with slip
SLIPWARES > SLIPWARE
SLIPWAY *n* launching slope on which ships are built or repaired
SLIPWAYS > SLIPWAY
SLISH *n* old word meaning cut
SLISHES > SLISH
SLIT *n* long narrow cut or opening ▷ *vb* make a long straight cut in
SLITHER *vb* slide unsteadily ▷ *n* slithering movement
SLITHERED > SLITHER
SLITHERS > SLITHER
SLITHERY *adj* moving with a slithering motion
SLITLESS > SLIT
SLITLIKE > SLIT
SLITS > SLIT
SLITTED > SLIT
SLITTER > SLIT
SLITTERS > SLIT
SLITTIER > SLIT
SLITTIEST > SLIT
SLITTING > SLIT
SLITTY > SLIT
SLIVE *vb* slip
SLIVED > SLIVE
SLIVEN > SLIVE
SLIVER *n* small thin piece ▷ *vb* cut into slivers
SLIVERED > SLIVER
SLIVERER > SLIVER
SLIVERERS > SLIVER
SLIVERING > SLIVER
SLIVERS > SLIVER
SLIVES > SLIVE
SLIVING > SLIVE
SLIVOVIC *n* plum brandy
SLIVOVICA *n* plum brandy
SLIVOVITZ *n* plum brandy from E Europe
SLIVOWITZ *n* plum brandy

SLOAN n severe telling-off
SLOANS > SLOAN
SLOB n lazy and untidy person ▷ vb behave like a slob
SLOBBED > SLOB
SLOBBER vb dribble or drool ▷ n liquid or saliva spilt from the mouth
SLOBBERED > SLOBBER
SLOBBERER > SLOBBER
SLOBBERS > SLOBBER
SLOBBERY > SLOBBER
SLOBBIER > SLOB
SLOBBIEST > SLOB
SLOBBING > SLOB
SLOBBISH > SLOB
SLOBBY > SLOB
SLOBLAND n muddy ground
SLOBLANDS > SLOBLAND
SLOBS > SLOB
SLOCKEN vb Scots word meaning slake
SLOCKENED > SLOCKEN
SLOCKENS > SLOCKEN
SLOE n sour blue-black fruit
SLOEBUSH n bush on which sloes grow
SLOES > SLOE
SLOETHORN n sloe plant
SLOETREE n sloe plant
SLOETREES > SLOETREE
SLOG vb work hard and steadily ▷ n long and exhausting work or walk
SLOGAN n catchword or phrase used in politics or advertising
SLOGANED adj having a slogan
SLOGANEER n person who coins or employs slogans frequently ▷ vb coin or employ slogans so as to sway opinion
SLOGANISE same as > SLOGANIZE
SLOGANIZE vb use slogans
SLOGANS > SLOGAN
SLOGGED > SLOG
SLOGGER > SLOG
SLOGGERS > SLOG
SLOGGING > SLOG
SLOGS > SLOG
SLOID n Swedish woodwork
SLOIDS > SLOID
SLOJD n Swedish woodwork
SLOJDS > SLOJD
SLOKEN vb Scots word meaning slake
SLOKENED > SLOKEN
SLOKENING > SLOKEN
SLOKENS > SLOKEN
SLOMMOCK vb walk assertively with a hip-rolling gait
SLOMMOCKS > SLOMMOCK

SLOMO n slow-motion sequence in a film
SLOMOS > SLOMO
SLOOM vb slumber
SLOOMED > SLOOM
SLOOMIER > SLOOM
SLOOMIEST > SLOOM
SLOOMING > SLOOM
SLOOMS > SLOOM
SLOOMY > SLOOM
SLOOP n small single-masted ship
SLOOPS > SLOOP
SLOOSH vb wash with water
SLOOSHED > SLOOSH
SLOOSHES > SLOOSH
SLOOSHING > SLOOSH
SLOOT n ditch for irrigation or drainage
SLOOTS > SLOOT
SLOP vb splash or spill ▷ n spilt liquid
SLOPE vb slant ▷ n sloping surface
SLOPED > SLOPE
SLOPER > SLOPE
SLOPERS > SLOPE
SLOPES > SLOPE
SLOPEWISE > SLOPE
SLOPIER > SLOPE
SLOPIEST > SLOPE
SLOPING > SLOPE
SLOPINGLY > SLOPE
SLOPPED > SLOP
SLOPPIER > SLOPPY
SLOPPIEST > SLOPPY
SLOPPILY > SLOPPY
SLOPPING > SLOP
SLOPPY adj careless or untidy
SLOPS > SLOP
SLOPWORK n manufacture of cheap shoddy clothing or the clothes so produced
SLOPWORKS > SLOPWORK
SLOPY > SLOPE
SLORM vb wipe carelessly
SLORMED > SLORM
SLORMING > SLORM
SLORMS > SLORM
SLOSH vb pour carelessly ▷ n splashing sound
SLOSHED > SLOSH
SLOSHES > SLOSH
SLOSHIER > SLOSH
SLOSHIEST > SLOSH
SLOSHING > SLOSH
SLOSHINGS > SLOSH
SLOSHY > SLOSH
SLOT n narrow opening for inserting something ▷ vb make a slot or slots in
SLOTBACK n American football player
SLOTBACKS > SLOTBACK
SLOTH n slow-moving animal of tropical America ▷ vb be lazy
SLOTHED > SLOTH
SLOTHFUL adj lazy or idle
SLOTHING > SLOTH
SLOTHS > SLOTH

SLOTS > SLOT
SLOTTED > SLOT
SLOTTER > SLOT
SLOTTERS > SLOT
SLOTTING > SLOT
SLOUCH vb sit, stand, or move with a drooping posture ▷ n drooping posture
SLOUCHED > SLOUCH
SLOUCHER > SLOUCH
SLOUCHERS > SLOUCH
SLOUCHES > SLOUCH
SLOUCHIER > SLOUCHY
SLOUCHILY > SLOUCHY
SLOUCHING > SLOUCH
SLOUCHY adj slouching
SLOUGH n bog ▷ vb (of a snake) shed (its skin)
SLOUGHED > SLOUGH
SLOUGHI n N African breed of dog resembling a greyhound
SLOUGHIER > SLOUGH
SLOUGHING > SLOUGH
SLOUGHIS > SLOUGHI
SLOUGHS > SLOUGH
SLOUGHY > SLOUGH
SLOVE > SLIVE
SLOVEN n habitually dirty or untidy person
SLOVENLY adj dirty or untidy ▷ adv in a slovenly manner
SLOVENRY n quality of being slovenly
SLOVENS > SLOVEN
SLOW adj taking a longer time than is usual or expected ▷ adv slowly ▷ vb reduce the speed (of)
SLOWBACK n lazy person
SLOWBACKS > SLOWBACK
SLOWCOACH n person who moves or works slowly
SLOWDOWN n any slackening of pace
SLOWDOWNS > SLOWDOWN
SLOWED > SLOW
SLOWER > SLOW
SLOWEST > SLOW
SLOWING > SLOW
SLOWINGS > SLOW
SLOWISH > SLOW
SLOWLY > SLOW
SLOWNESS > SLOW
SLOWPOKE same as > SLOWCOACH
SLOWPOKES > SLOWPOKE
SLOWS > SLOW
SLOWWORM n small legless lizard
SLOWWORMS > SLOWWORM
SLOYD n Swedish woodwork
SLOYDS > SLOYD
SLUB n lump in yarn or fabric ▷ vb draw out and twist (a sliver of fibre) before spinning ▷ adj (of material) having an irregular appearance

SLUBB same as > SLUB
SLUBBED > SLUB
SLUBBER vb smear
SLUBBERED > SLUBBER
SLUBBERS > SLUBBER
SLUBBIER > SLUB
SLUBBIEST > SLUB
SLUBBING > SLUB
SLUBBINGS > SLUB
SLUBBS > SLUBB
SLUBBY > SLUB
SLUBS > SLUB
SLUDGE n thick mud ▷ vb convert into sludge
SLUDGED > SLUDGE
SLUDGES > SLUDGE
SLUDGIER > SLUDGY
SLUDGIEST > SLUDGY
SLUDGING > SLUDGE
SLUDGY adj consisting of, containing, or like sludge
SLUE same as > SLEW
SLUED > SLUE
SLUEING > SLUE
SLUES > SLUE
SLUFF same as > SLOUGH
SLUFFED > SLUFF
SLUFFING > SLUFF
SLUFFS > SLUFF
SLUG n land snail with no shell ▷ vb hit hard
SLUGABED n person who remains in bed through laziness
SLUGABEDS > SLUGABED
SLUGFEST n fist fight
SLUGFESTS > SLUGFEST
SLUGGABED same as > SLUGABED
SLUGGARD n lazy person ▷ adj lazy
SLUGGARDS > SLUGGARD
SLUGGED > SLUG
SLUGGER n (esp in boxing, baseball, etc) a person who strikes hard
SLUGGERS > SLUGGER
SLUGGING > SLUG
SLUGGISH adj slow-moving, lacking energy
SLUGHORN same as > SLOGAN
SLUGHORNE same as > SLOGAN
SLUGHORNS > SLUGHORN
SLUGS > SLUG
SLUICE n channel that carries a rapid current of water ▷ vb drain water by means of a sluice
SLUICED > SLUICE
SLUICES > SLUICE
SLUICEWAY same as > SLUICE
SLUICIER > SLUICE
SLUICIEST > SLUICE
SLUICING > SLUICE
SLUICY > SLUICE
SLUING > SLUE
SLUIT n water channel in South Africa
SLUITS > SLUIT

SLUM n squalid overcrowded house or area ▷ vb experience poorer places or conditions than usual

SLUMBER n sleep ▷ vb sleep

SLUMBERED > SLUMBER

SLUMBERER > SLUMBER

SLUMBERS > SLUMBER

SLUMBERY adj sleepy

SLUMBROUS adj sleepy

SLUMBRY same as > SLUMBERY

SLUMGUM n material left after wax is extracted from honeycomb

SLUMGUMS > SLUMGUM

SLUMISM n existence of slums

SLUMISMS > SLUMISM

SLUMLORD n absentee landlord of slum property, esp one who profiteers

SLUMLORDS > SLUMLORD

SLUMMED > SLUM

SLUMMER > SLUM

SLUMMERS > SLUM

SLUMMIER > SLUM

SLUMMIEST > SLUM

SLUMMING > SLUM

SLUMMINGS > SLUM

SLUMMOCK vb move slowly and heavily

SLUMMOCKS > SLUMMOCK

SLUMMY > SLUM

SLUMP vb (of prices or demand) decline suddenly ▷ n sudden decline in prices or demand

SLUMPED > SLUMP

SLUMPIER > SLUMPY

SLUMPIEST > SLUMPY

SLUMPING > SLUMP

SLUMPS > SLUMP

SLUMPY adj boggy

SLUMS > SLUM

SLUNG > SLING

SLUNGSHOT n weight attached to the end of a cord and used as a weapon

SLUNK > SLINK

SLUR vb pronounce or utter (words) indistinctly ▷ n slurring of words

SLURB n suburban slum

SLURBAN > SLURB

SLURBS > SLURB

SLURP vb eat or drink noisily ▷ n slurping sound

SLURPED > SLURP

SLURPER > SLURP

SLURPERS > SLURP

SLURPIER > SLURPY

SLURPIEST > SLURPY

SLURPING > SLURP

SLURPS > SLURP

SLURPY adj making a slurping noise

SLURRED > SLUR

SLURRIED > SLURRY

SLURRIES > SLURRY

SLURRING > SLUR

SLURRY n muddy liquid mixture ▷ vb spread slurry

SLURRYING > SLURRY

SLURS > SLUR

SLURVE n pitch in baseball combining elements of the slider and the curveball

SLURVES > SLURVE

SLUSE same as > SLUICE

SLUSES > SLUICE

SLUSH n watery muddy substance ▷ vb make one's way through or as if through slush

SLUSHED > SLUSH

SLUSHES > SLUSH

SLUSHIER > SLUSHY

SLUSHIES > SLUSHY

SLUSHIEST > SLUSHY

SLUSHILY > SLUSHY

SLUSHING > SLUSH

SLUSHY adj of, resembling, or consisting of slush ▷ n unskilled kitchen assistant

SLUT n derogatory term for a dirty or immoral woman

SLUTCH n mud

SLUTCHES > SLUTCH

SLUTCHIER > SLUTCH

SLUTCHY > SLUTCH

SLUTS > SLUT

SLUTTERY n state of being slut

SLUTTIER > SLUT

SLUTTIEST > SLUT

SLUTTILY > SLUTTY

SLUTTISH > SLUT

SLUTTY > SLUT

SLY adj crafty

SLYBOOTS pl n person who is sly

SLYER > SLY

SLYEST > SLY

SLYISH > SLY

SLYLY > SLY

SLYNESS > SLY

SLYNESSES > SLY

SLYPE n covered passageway in a church

SLYPES > SLYPE

SMA Scots word for > SMALL

SMAAK vb South African slang for like or love

SMAAKED > SMAAK

SMAAKING > SMAAK

SMAAKS > SMAAK

SMACK vb slap sharply ▷ n sharp slap ▷ adv squarely or directly

SMACKDOWN n severe beating or defeat

SMACKED > SMACK

SMACKER n loud kiss

SMACKERS > SMACKER

SMACKHEAD n person who is addicted to heroin

SMACKING adj brisk

SMACKINGS > SMACKING

SMACKS > SMACK

SMAIK n Scots word meaning rascal

SMAIKS > SMAIK

SMALL adj not large in size, number, or amount ▷ n narrow part of the lower back ▷ adv into small pieces ▷ vb make small

SMALLAGE n wild celery

SMALLAGES > SMALLAGE

SMALLBOY n steward's assistant or deputy steward in European households in W Africa

SMALLBOYS > SMALLBOY

SMALLED > SMALL

SMALLER > SMALL

SMALLEST > SMALL

SMALLING > SMALL

SMALLISH > SMALL

SMALLNESS > SMALL

SMALLPOX n contagious disease with blisters that leave scars

SMALLS > SMALL

SMALLSAT n small communications satellite

SMALLSATS > SMALLSAT

SMALLTIME adj unimportant

SMALM same as > SMARM

SMALMED > SMALM

SMALMIER > SMALMY

SMALMIEST > SMALMY

SMALMILY > SMALMY

SMALMING > SMALM

SMALMS > SMALM

SMALMY same as > SMARMY

SMALT n type of silica glass coloured deep blue with cobalt oxide

SMALTI > SMALTO

SMALTINE n mineral containing cobalt

SMALTINES > SMALTINE

SMALTITE n silver-white to greyish mineral

SMALTITES > SMALTITE

SMALTO n coloured glass, etc, used in mosaics

SMALTOS > SMALTO

SMALTS > SMALT

SMARAGD n any green gemstone, such as the emerald

SMARAGDE same as > SMARAGD

SMARAGDES > SMARAGDE

SMARAGDS > SMARAGD

SMARM vb bring (oneself) into favour (with) ▷ n obsequious flattery

SMARMED > SMARM

SMARMIER > SMARMY

SMARMIEST > SMARMY

SMARMILY > SMARMY

SMARMING > SMARM

SMARMS > SMARM

SMARMY adj unpleasantly suave or flattering

SMART adj well-kept and neat ▷ vb feel or cause stinging pain ▷ n stinging pain ▷ adv in a smart manner

SMARTARSE n derogatory term for a clever person, esp one who parades his knowledge offensively

SMARTASS same as > SMARTARSE

SMARTED > SMART

SMARTEN vb make or become smart

SMARTENED > SMARTEN

SMARTENS > SMARTEN

SMARTER > SMART

SMARTEST > SMART

SMARTIE same as > SMARTY

SMARTIES > SMARTY

SMARTING > SMART

SMARTISH > SMART

SMARTLY > SMART

SMARTNESS > SMART

SMARTS pl n know-how, intelligence, or wits

SMARTWEED n grass with acrid smell

SMARTY n would-be clever person

SMASH vb break violently and noisily ▷ n act or sound of smashing ▷ adv with a smash

SMASHABLE > SMASH

SMASHED adj completely intoxicated with alcohol

SMASHER n attractive person or thing

SMASHEROO n excellent person or thing

SMASHERS > SMASHER

SMASHES > SMASH

SMASHING adj excellent

SMASHINGS > SMASHING

SMASHUP n bad collision of cars

SMASHUPS > SMASHUP

SMATCH less common word for > SMACK

SMATCHED > SMATCH

SMATCHES > SMATCH

SMATCHING > SMATCH

SMATTER n smattering ▷ vb prattle

SMATTERED > SMATTER

SMATTERER > SMATTER

SMATTERS > SMATTER

SMAZE n smoky haze, less damp than fog

SMAZES > SMAZE

SMEAR vb spread with a greasy or sticky substance ▷ n dirty mark or smudge

SMEARCASE n American type of cottage cheese

SMEARED > SMEAR

SMEARER > SMEAR

SMEARERS > SMEAR

SMEARIER > SMEARY

SMEARIEST > SMEARY

SMEARILY > SMEARY

SMEARING > SMEAR

SMEARS > SMEAR

SMEARY adj smeared, dirty

SMEATH n duck

SMEATHS > SMEATH

SMECTIC *adj* (of a substance) existing in state in which the molecules are oriented in layers
SMECTITE *n* type of clay mineral
SMECTITES > SMECTITE
SMECTITIC > SMECTITE
SMEDDUM *n* any fine powder
SMEDDUMS > SMEDDUM
SMEE *n* duck
SMEECH *Southwest English dialect form of* > SMOKE
SMEECHED > SMEECH
SMEECHES > SMEECH
SMEECHING > SMEECH
SMEEK *vb* smoke
SMEEKED > SMEEK
SMEEKING > SMEECH
SMEEKS > SMEECH
SMEES > SMEE
SMEETH *n* duck ⊳ *vb* make smooth
SMEETHED > SMEETH
SMEETHING > SMEETH
SMEETHS > SMEETH
SMEGMA *n* whitish sebaceous secretion that accumulates beneath the prepuce
SMEGMAS > SMEGMA
SMEIK *same as* > SMEKE
SMEIKED > SMEKED
SMEIKING *same as* > SMEKING
SMEIKS > SMEIK
SMEKE *n* smoke ⊳ *vb* smoke
SMEKED > SMEKE
SMEKES > SMEKE
SMEKING > SMEKE
SMELL *vb* perceive (a scent or odour) by means of the nose ⊳ *n* ability to perceive odours by the nose
SMELLABLE *adj* capable of being smelled
SMELLED > SMELL
SMELLER > SMELL
SMELLERS > SMELL
SMELLIER > SMELLY
SMELLIES *pl n* pleasant-smelling products such as perfumes, body lotions, bath salts, etc
SMELLIEST > SMELLY
SMELLING > SMELL
SMELLINGS > SMELL
SMELLS > SMELL
SMELLY *adj* having a nasty smell
SMELT *vb* extract metal from an ore
SMELTED > SMELT
SMELTER *n* industrial plant where smelting is carried out
SMELTERS > SMELTER
SMELTERY *variant of* > SMELTER
SMELTING > SMELL

SMELTINGS > SMELL
SMELTS > SMELL
SMERK *same as* > SMIRK
SMERKED > SMERK
SMERKING > SMERK
SMERKS > SMERK
SMEUSE *n* way through hedge
SMEUSES > SMEUSE
SMEW *n* duck of N Europe and Asia
SMEWS > SMEW
SMICKER *vb* look at someone amorously
SMICKERED > SMICKER
SMICKERS > SMICKER
SMICKET *n* smock
SMICKETS > SMICKET
SMICKLY *adv* amorously
SMIDDIED > SMIDDY
SMIDDIES > SMIDDY
SMIDDY *Scots word for* > SMITHY
SMIDDYING > SMIDDY
SMIDGE *n* very small amount or part
SMIDGEN *n* very small amount or part
SMIDGENS > SMIDGEN
SMIDGEON *same as* > SMIDGEN
SMIDGEONS > SMIDGEON
SMIDGES > SMIDGE
SMIDGIN *same as* > SMIDGEN
SMIDGINS > SMIDGIN
SMIERCASE *same as* > SMEARCASE
SMIGHT *same as* > SMITE
SMIGHTING > SMIGHT
SMIGHTS > SMIGHT
SMILAX *n* type of climbing shrub
SMILAXES > SMILAX
SMILE *n* turning up of the corners of the mouth to show pleasure or friendliness ⊳ *vb* give a smile
SMILED > SMILE
SMILEFUL *adj* full of smiles
SMILELESS > SMILE
SMILER > SMILE
SMILERS > SMILE
SMILES > SMILE
SMILET *n* little smile
SMILETS > SMILET
SMILEY *n* symbol depicting a smile or other facial expression, used in e-mail ⊳ *adj* cheerful
SMILEYS > SMILEY
SMILIER > SMILEY
SMILIES > SMILEY
SMILIEST > SMILEY
SMILING > SMILE
SMILINGLY > SMILE
SMILINGS > SMILE
SMILODON *n* extinct sabre-toothed tiger
SMILODONS > SMILODON

SMIR *n* drizzly rain ⊳ *vb* drizzle lightly
SMIRCH *n* stain ⊳ *vb* disgrace
SMIRCHED > SMIRCH
SMIRCHER > SMIRCH
SMIRCHERS > SMIRCH
SMIRCHES > SMIRCH
SMIRCHING > SMIRCH
SMIRK *n* smug smile ⊳ *vb* give a smirk
SMIRKED > SMIRK
SMIRKER > SMIRK
SMIRKERS > SMIRK
SMIRKIER > SMIRK
SMIRKIEST > SMIRK
SMIRKILY > SMIRK
SMIRKING > SMIRK
SMIRKS > SMIRK
SMIRKY > SMIRK
SMIRR *same as* > SMIR
SMIRRED > SMIRR
SMIRRIER > SMIRR
SMIRRIEST > SMIRR
SMIRRING > SMIRR
SMIRRS > SMIRR
SMIRRY > SMIRR
SMIRS > SMIR
SMIRTING *n* flirting amongst those smoking outside a non-smoking office, pub, etc
SMIRTINGS > SMIRTING
SMIT > SMITE
SMITE *vb* strike hard
SMITER > SMITE
SMITERS > SMITE
SMITES > SMITE
SMITH *n* worker in metal ⊳ *vb* work in metal
SMITHED > SMITH
SMITHERS *pl n* little shattered pieces
SMITHERY *n* trade or craft of a blacksmith
SMITHIED > SMITHY
SMITHIES > SMITHY
SMITHING *n* act of working as a smith
SMITHINGS > SMITHING
SMITHS > SMITH
SMITHY *n* blacksmith's workshop ⊳ *vb* work as a smith
SMITHYING > SMITHY
SMITING > SMITE
SMITS > SMIT
SMITTED > SMIT
SMITTEN > SMITE
SMITTING > SMIT
SMITTLE *adj* infectious
SMOCK *n* loose overall ⊳ *vb* gather (material) by sewing in a honeycomb pattern
SMOCKED > SMOCK
SMOCKING *n* ornamental needlework used to gather material
SMOCKINGS > SMOCKING
SMOCKLIKE > SMOCK
SMOCKS > SMOCK

SMOG *n* mixture of smoke and fog
SMOGGIER > SMOG
SMOGGIEST > SMOG
SMOGGY > SMOG
SMOGLESS > SMOG
SMOGS > SMOG
SMOILE *same as* > SMILE
SMOILED > SMOILE
SMOILES > SMOILE
SMOILING > SMOILE
SMOKABLE > SMOKE
SMOKE *n* cloudy mass that rises from something burning ⊳ *vb* give off smoke or treat with smoke
SMOKEABLE > SMOKE
SMOKEBOX *n* part of a steam engine or boiler
SMOKEBUSH *n* plant with purple leaves and small flowers that turn grey-white
SMOKED > SMOKE
SMOKEHO *same as* > SMOKO
SMOKEHOOD *n* hood worn to keep out smoke
SMOKEHOS > SMOKEHO
SMOKEJACK *n* device formerly used for turning a roasting spit, operated by the movement of ascending gases in a chimney
SMOKELESS *adj* having or producing little or no smoke
SMOKELIKE > SMOKE
SMOKEPOT *n* device for producing smoke
SMOKEPOTS > SMOKEPOT
SMOKER *n* person who habitually smokes tobacco
SMOKERS > SMOKER
SMOKES > SMOKE
SMOKEY > SMOKY
SMOKEYS > SMOKEY
SMOKIE *n* smoked haddock
SMOKIER > SMOKY
SMOKIES > SMOKY
SMOKIEST > SMOKY
SMOKILY > SMOKY
SMOKINESS > SMOKY
SMOKING > SMOKE
SMOKINGS > SMOKING
SMOKO *n* short break from work for tea or a cigarette
SMOKOS > SMOKO
SMOKY *adj* filled with or giving off smoke, sometimes excessively ⊳ *n* haddock that has been smoked
SMOLDER *same as* > SMOULDER
SMOLDERED > SMOLDER
SMOLDERS > SMOLDER
SMOLT *n* young salmon at the stage when it migrates to the sea
SMOLTS > SMOLT
SMOOCH *vb* kiss and cuddle ⊳ *n* smooching

SMOOCHED > SMOOCH
SMOOCHER > SMOOCH
SMOOCHERS > SMOOCH
SMOOCHES > SMOOCH
SMOOCHIER > SMOOCHY
SMOOCHING > SMOOCH
SMOOCHY adj romantic
SMOODGE same as
> SMOOCH
SMOODGED > SMOODGE
SMOODGES > SMOODGE
SMOODGING > SMOODGE
SMOOGE same as > SMOOCH
SMOOGED > SMOOGE
SMOOGES > SMOOGE
SMOOGING > SMOOGE
SMOOR vb Scots word
meaning put out fire
SMOORED > SMOOR
SMOORING > SMOOR
SMOORS > SMOOR
SMOOSH vb paint to give
softened look
SMOOSHED > SMOOSH
SMOOSHES > SMOOSH
SMOOSHING > SMOOSH
SMOOT vb work as printer
SMOOTED > SMOOT
SMOOTH adj even in
surface, texture, or
consistency ▷ vb make
smooth ▷ adv in a smooth
manner ▷ n smooth part
of something
SMOOTHE same as
> SMOOTH
SMOOTHED > SMOOTH
SMOOTHEN vb make or
become smooth
SMOOTHENS > SMOOTHEN
SMOOTHER > SMOOTH
SMOOTHERS > SMOOTH
SMOOTHES > SMOOTH
SMOOTHEST > SMOOTH
SMOOTHIE n slang, usu
derogatory term for a
charming but possibly
insincere man
SMOOTHIES > SMOOTHIE
SMOOTHING > SMOOTH
SMOOTHISH > SMOOTH
SMOOTHLY > SMOOTH
SMOOTHS > SMOOTH
SMOOTHY same as
> SMOOTHIE
SMOOTING > SMOOT
SMOOTS > SMOOT
SMORBROD n Danish hors
d'oeuvre
SMORBRODS > SMORBROD
SMORE same as > SMOOR
SMORED > SMORE
SMORES > SMORE
SMORG n short for
smorgasbord
SMORGS > SMORG
SMORING > SMORE
SMORZANDO adv musical
instruction meaning
fading away gradually
SMORZATO same as
> SMORZANDO
SMOTE > SMITE

SMOTHER vb suffocate or
stifle ▷ n anything, such as
a cloud of smoke, that
stifles
SMOTHERED > SMOTHER
SMOTHERER > SMOTHER
SMOTHERS > SMOTHER
SMOTHERY > SMOTHER
SMOUCH vb kiss
SMOUCHED > SMOUCH
SMOUCHES > SMOUCH
SMOUCHING > SMOUCH
SMOULDER vb burn slowly
with smoke but no flame
▷ n dense smoke, as from a
smouldering fire
SMOULDERS > SMOULDER
SMOULDRY adj
smouldering
SMOUSE vb South African
word meaning peddle
SMOUSED > SMOUSE
SMOUSER > SMOUSE
SMOUSERS > SMOUSE
SMOUSES > SMOUSE
SMOUSING > SMOUSE
SMOUT n child or
undersized person
▷ vb creep or sneak
SMOUTED > SMOUT
SMOUTING > SMOUT
SMOUTS > SMOUT
SMOWT same as > SMOUT
SMOWTS > SMOWT
SMOYLE same as > SMILE
SMOYLED > SMOYLE
SMOYLES > SMOYLE
SMOYLING > SMOYLE
SMRITI n class of Hindu
sacred literature
SMRITIS > SMRITI
SMUDGE vb make or
become smeared or soiled
▷ n dirty mark
SMUDGED > SMUDGE
SMUDGEDLY > SMUDGE
SMUDGER > SMUDGE
SMUDGERS > SMUDGE
SMUDGES > SMUDGE
SMUDGIER > SMUDGY
SMUDGIEST > SMUDGY
SMUDGILY > SMUDGE
SMUDGING > SMUDGE
SMUDGINGS > SMUDGE
SMUDGY adj smeared,
blurred, or soiled, or likely
to become so
SMUG adj self-satisfied
▷ vb make neat
SMUGGED > SMUG
SMUGGER > SMUG
SMUGGERY n condition or
an instance of being smug
SMUGGEST > SMUG
SMUGGING > SMUG
SMUGGLE vb import or
export (goods) secretly
and illegally
SMUGGLED > SMUGGLE
SMUGGLER > SMUGGLE
SMUGGLERS > SMUGGLE
SMUGGLES > SMUGGLE
SMUGGLING > SMUGGLE

SMUGLY > SMUG
SMUGNESS > SMUG
SMUGS > SMUG
SMUR same as > SMIR
SMURFING n intentionally
flooding and overwhelming
a computer network with
messages by means of a
program
SMURFINGS > SMURFING
SMURRED > SMUR
SMURRIER > SMUR
SMURRIEST > SMUR
SMURRING > SMUR
SMURRY > SMUR
SMURS > SMUR
SMUSH vb crush
SMUSHED > SMUSH
SMUSHES > SMUSH
SMUSHING > SMUSH
SMUT n obscene jokes,
pictures, etc ▷ vb mark or
become marked or
smudged
SMUTCH vb smudge ▷ n
mark
SMUTCHED > SMUTCH
SMUTCHES > SMUTCH
SMUTCHIER > SMUTCH
SMUTCHING > SMUTCH
SMUTCHY > SMUTCH
SMUTS > SMUT
SMUTTED > SMUT
SMUTTIER > SMUT
SMUTTIEST > SMUT
SMUTTILY > SMUT
SMUTTING > SMUT
SMUTTY > SMUT
SMYTRIE n Scots word
meaning collection
SMYTRIES > SMYTRIE
SNAB same as > SNOB
SNABBLE same as
> SNAFFLE
SNABBLED > SNABBLE
SNABBLES > SNABBLE
SNABBLING > SNABBLE
SNABS > SNAB
SNACK n light quick meal
▷ vb eat a snack
SNACKED > SNACK
SNACKER > SNACK
SNACKERS > SNACK
SNACKETTE n snack bar
SNACKIER > SNACKY
SNACKIEST > SNACKY
SNACKING > SNACK
SNACKS > SNACK
SNACKY adj of the nature
of a snack
SNAFFLE n jointed bit for
a horse ▷ vb steal
SNAFFLED > SNAFFLE
SNAFFLES > SNAFFLE
SNAFFLING > SNAFFLE
SNAFU n confusion or chaos
regarded as the normal
state ▷ adj confused or
muddled up, as usual
▷ vb throw into chaos
SNAFUED > SNAFU
SNAFUING > SNAFU
SNAFUS > SNAFU

SNAG n difficulty or
disadvantage ▷ vb catch
or tear on a point
SNAGGED > SNAG
SNAGGER n type of fishing
hook
SNAGGERS > SNAGGER
SNAGGIER > SNAGGY
SNAGGIEST > SNAGGY
SNAGGING > SNAG
SNAGGLE n tangled mass
SNAGGLES > SNAGGLE
SNAGGY adj having sharp
protuberances
SNAGLIKE > SNAG
SNAGS > SNAG
SNAIL n slow-moving
mollusc with a spiral shell
▷ vb move slowly
SNAILED > SNAIL
SNAILERY n place where
snails are bred
SNAILFISH n sea snail
SNAILIER > SNAIL
SNAILIEST > SNAIL
SNAILING > SNAIL
SNAILLIKE adj
resembling a snail
SNAILS > SNAIL
SNAILY > SNAIL
SNAKE n long thin scaly
limbless reptile ▷ vb move
in a winding course like a
snake
SNAKEBIRD n darter bird
SNAKEBIT adj bitten by
snake
SNAKEBITE n bite of a
snake
SNAKED > SNAKE
SNAKEFISH n fish
resembling snake
SNAKEHEAD n Chinese
criminal involved in the
illegal transport of
Chinese citizens to other
parts of the world
SNAKELIKE > SNAKE
SNAKEPIT n pit filled with
snakes
SNAKEPITS > SNAKEPIT
SNAKEROOT n any of
various North American
plants
SNAKES > SNAKE
SNAKESKIN n skin of a
snake, esp when made
into a leather valued for
handbags, shoes, etc
SNAKEWEED same as
> SNAKEROOT
SNAKEWISE adv in
snakelike way
SNAKEWOOD n South
American tree
SNAKEY same as > SNAKY
SNAKIER > SNAKY
SNAKIEST > SNAKY
SNAKILY > SNAKY
SNAKINESS > SNAKY
SNAKING > SNAKE
SNAKISH > SNAKE
SNAKY adj twisted or
winding

SNAP *vb* break suddenly ▷ *n* act or sound of snapping ▷ *adj* made on the spur of the moment ▷ *adv* with a snap
SNAPBACK *n* sudden rebound or change in direction
SNAPBACKS > SNAPBACK
SNAPHANCE *n* flintlock gun
SNAPLESS > SNAP
SNAPLINK *n* metal link used in mountaineering
SNAPLINKS > SNAPLINK
SNAPPABLE > SNAP
SNAPPED > SNAP
SNAPPER *n* food fish of Australia and New Zealand ▷ *vb* stumble
SNAPPERED > SNAPPER
SNAPPERS > SNAPPER
SNAPPIER > SNAPPY
SNAPPIEST > SNAPPY
SNAPPILY > SNAPPY
SNAPPING > SNAP
SNAPPINGS > SNAP
SNAPPISH *same as* > SNAPPY
SNAPPY *adj* irritable
SNAPS > SNAP
SNAPSHOT *n* informal photograph
SNAPSHOTS > SNAPSHOT
SNAPTIN *n* container for food
SNAPTINS > SNAPTIN
SNAPWEED *n* impatiens
SNAPWEEDS > SNAPWEED
SNAR *same as* > SNARL
SNARE *n* trap with a noose ▷ *vb* catch in or as if in a snare
SNARED > SNARE
SNARELESS > SNARE
SNARER > SNARE
SNARERS > SNARE
SNARES > SNARE
SNARF *vb* eat or drink greedily
SNARFED > SNARF
SNARFING > SNARF
SNARFLE *vb* (of an animal) grunt and snort while rooting for food
SNARFLED > SNARFLE
SNARFLES > SNARFLE
SNARFLING > SNARFLE
SNARFS > SNARF
SNARIER > SNARE
SNARIEST > SNARE
SNARING > SNARE
SNARINGS > SNARE
SNARK *n* imaginary creature in Lewis Carroll's poetry
SNARKIER > SNARKY
SNARKIEST > SNARKY
SNARKILY > SNARKY
SNARKS > SNARK
SNARKY *adj* unpleasant and scornful

SNARL *vb* (of an animal) growl with bared teeth ▷ *n* act or sound of snarling
SNARLED > SNARL
SNARLER > SNARL
SNARLERS > SNARL
SNARLIER > SNARL
SNARLIEST > SNARL
SNARLING > SNARL
SNARLINGS > SNARL
SNARLS > SNARL
SNARLY > SNARL
SNARRED > SNAR
SNARRING > SNAR
SNARS > SNAR
SNARY > SNARE
SNASH *vb* Scots word meaning speak cheekily
SNASHED > SNASH
SNASHES > SNASH
SNASHING > SNASH
SNASTE *n* candle wick
SNASTES > SNASTE
SNATCH *vb* seize or try to seize suddenly ▷ *n* snatching
SNATCHED > SNATCH
SNATCHER > SNATCH
SNATCHERS > SNATCH
SNATCHES > SNATCH
SNATCHIER > SNATCHY
SNATCHILY > SNATCHY
SNATCHING > SNATCH
SNATCHY *adj* disconnected or spasmodic
SNATH *n* handle of a scythe
SNATHE *same as* > SNATH
SNATHES > SNATHE
SNATHS > SNATH
SNAW *Scots variant of* > SNOW
SNAWED > SNAW
SNAWING > SNAW
SNAWS > SNAW
SNAZZIER > SNAZZY
SNAZZIEST > SNAZZY
SNAZZILY > SNAZZY
SNAZZY *adj* stylish and flashy
SNEAD *n* scythe handle
SNEADS > SNEAD
SNEAK *vb* move furtively ▷ *n* cowardly or underhand person ▷ *adj* without warning
SNEAKBOX *n* small camouflaged boat, used for wildfowl hunting
SNEAKED > SNEAK
SNEAKER *n* soft shoe
SNEAKERED *adj* wearing sneakers
SNEAKERS *pl n* canvas shoes with rubber soles
SNEAKEUP *n* sneaky person
SNEAKEUPS > SNEAKEUP
SNEAKIER > SNEAK
SNEAKIEST > SNEAK
SNEAKILY > SNEAK
SNEAKING *adj* slight but persistent

SNEAKISH *adj* typical of sneak
SNEAKS > SNEAK
SNEAKSBY *n* sneak
SNEAKY > SNEAK
SNEAP *vb* nip
SNEAPED > SNEAP
SNEAPING > SNEAP
SNEAPS > SNEAP
SNEATH *same as* > SNATH
SNEATHS > SNEATH
SNEB *same as* > SNIB
SNEBBE *same as* > SNUB
SNEBBED > SNEB
SNEBBES > SNEBBE
SNEBBING > SNEB
SNEBS > SNEB
SNECK *n* small squared stone used in a rubble wall to fill spaces between stones ▷ *vb* fasten (a latch)
SNECKED > SNECK
SNECKING > SNECK
SNECKS > SNECK
SNED *vb* prune or trim
SNEDDED > SNED
SNEDDING > SNED
SNEDS > SNED
SNEE *vb* cut
SNEED > SNEE
SNEEING > SNEE
SNEER *n* contemptuous expression or remark ▷ *vb* show contempt by a sneer
SNEERED > SNEER
SNEERER > SNEER
SNEERERS > SNEER
SNEERFUL > SNEER
SNEERIER > SNEERY
SNEERIEST > SNEERY
SNEERING > SNEER
SNEERINGS > SNEER
SNEERS > SNEER
SNEERY *adj* contemptuous or scornful
SNEES > SNEE
SNEESH *n* Scots word meaning pinch of snuff ▷ *vb* take snuff
SNEESHAN *n* Scots word meaning pinch of snuff
SNEESHANS > SNEESHAN
SNEESHED > SNEESH
SNEESHES > SNEESH
SNEESHIN *same as* > SNEESHAN
SNEESHING *same as* > SNEESHAN
SNEESHINS > SNEESHIN
SNEEZE *vb* expel air from the nose suddenly, involuntarily, and noisily ▷ *n* act or sound of sneezing
SNEEZED > SNEEZE
SNEEZER > SNEEZE
SNEEZERS > SNEEZE
SNEEZIER > SNEEZE
SNEEZIEST > SNEEZE
SNEEZING > SNEEZE

SNEEZINGS > SNEEZE
SNEEZY > SNEEZE
SNELL *adj* biting ▷ *vb* attach hook to fishing line
SNELLED > SNELL
SNELLER > SNELL
SNELLEST > SNELL
SNELLING > SNELL
SNELLS > SNELL
SNELLY > SNELL
SNIB *n* catch of a door or window ▷ *vb* bolt or fasten (a door)
SNIBBED > SNIB
SNIBBING > SNIB
SNIBS > SNIB
SNICK *n* (make) a small cut or notch ▷ *vb* make a small cut or notch in (something)
SNICKED > SNICK
SNICKER *same as* > SNIGGER
SNICKERED > SNICKER
SNICKERER > SNICKER
SNICKERS > SNICKER
SNICKERY > SNICKER
SNICKET *n* passageway between walls or fences
SNICKETS > SNICKET
SNICKING > SNICK
SNICKS > SNICK
SNIDE *adj* critical in an unfair and nasty way ▷ *n* sham jewellery ▷ *vb* fill or load
SNIDED > SNIDE
SNIDELY > SNIDE
SNIDENESS > SNIDE
SNIDER > SNIDE
SNIDES > SNIDE
SNIDEST > SNIDE
SNIDEY *same as* > SNIDE
SNIDIER > SNIDEY
SNIDIEST > SNIDEY
SNIDING > SNIDE
SNIES > SNY
SNIFF *vb* inhale through the nose in short audible breaths ▷ *n* act or sound of sniffing
SNIFFABLE > SNIFF
SNIFFED > SNIFF
SNIFFER *n* device for detecting hidden substances such as drugs
SNIFFERS > SNIFFER
SNIFFIER > SNIFFY
SNIFFIEST > SNIFFY
SNIFFILY > SNIFFY
SNIFFING > SNIFF
SNIFFINGS > SNIFF
SNIFFISH *adj* disdainful
SNIFFLE *vb* sniff repeatedly, as when suffering from a cold ▷ *n* slight cold
SNIFFLED > SNIFFLE
SNIFFLER > SNIFFLE
SNIFFLERS > SNIFFLE
SNIFFLES > SNIFFLE
SNIFFLIER > SNIFFLE
SNIFFLING > SNIFFLE

S

SNIFFLY > SNIFFLE

SNIFFS > SNIFF

SNIFFY adj
contemptuous or scornful

SNIFT same as > SNIFF

SNIFTED > SNIFT

SNIFTER n small quantity of alcoholic drink ▷ vb sniff

SNIFTERED > SNIFTER

SNIFTERS > SNIFTER

SNIFTIER > SNIFTY

SNIFTIEST > SNIFTY

SNIFTING > SNIFT

SNIFTS > SNIFT

SNIFTY adj slang word meaning excellent

SNIG vb drag (a felled log) by a chain or cable

SNIGGED > SNIG

SNIGGER n sly laugh ▷ vb laugh slyly

SNIGGERED > SNIGGER

SNIGGERER > SNIGGER

SNIGGERS > SNIGGER

SNIGGING > SNIG

SNIGGLE vb fish for eels by dangling or thrusting a baited hook into cavities ▷ n baited hook used for sniggling eels

SNIGGLED > SNIGGLE

SNIGGLER > SNIGGLE

SNIGGLERS > SNIGGLE

SNIGGLES > SNIGGLE

SNIGGLING > SNIGGLE

SNIGLET n invented word

SNIGLETS > SNIGLET

SNIGS > SNIG

SNIP vb cut in small quick strokes with scissors or shears ▷ n bargain ▷ interj representation of the sound of scissors or shears closing

SNIPED > SNIPE

SNIPEFISH n type of fish of tropical and temperate seas, with a long snout and a single dorsal fin

SNIPELIKE > SNIPE

SNIPER n person who shoots at someone from cover

SNIPERS > SNIPER

SNIPES > SNIPE

SNIPIER > SNIPY

SNIPIEST > SNIPY

SNIPING > SNIPE

SNIPINGS > SNIPE

SNIPPED > SNIP

SNIPPER > SNIP

SNIPPERS > SNIP

SNIPPET n small piece

SNIPPETS > SNIPPET

SNIPPETY > SNIPPET

SNIPPIER > SNIPPY

SNIPPIEST > SNIPPY

SNIPPILY > SNIPPY

SNIPPING > SNIP

SNIPPINGS > SNIP

SNIPPY adj scrappy

SNIPS > SNIP

SNIPY adj like a snipe

SNIRT n Scots word meaning suppressed laugh ▷ vb to snigger

SNIRTED > SNIRT

SNIRTING > SNIRT

SNIRTLE vb Scots word meaning snicker

SNIRTLED > SNIRTLE

SNIRTLES > SNIRTLE

SNIRTLING > SNIRTLE

SNIRTS > SNIRT

SNIT n fit of temper

SNITCH vb act as an informer ▷ n informer

SNITCHED > SNITCH

SNITCHER > SNITCH

SNITCHERS > SNITCH

SNITCHES > SNITCH

SNITCHIER > SNITCHY

SNITCHING > SNITCH

SNITCHY adj bad-tempered or irritable

SNITS > SNIT

SNITTIER > SNITTY

SNITTIEST > SNITTY

SNITTY adj cross or irritable

SNIVEL vb cry in a whining way ▷ n act of snivelling

SNIVELED > SNIVEL

SNIVELER > SNIVEL

SNIVELERS > SNIVEL

SNIVELING > SNIVEL

SNIVELLED > SNIVEL

SNIVELLER > SNIVEL

SNIVELLY > SNIVEL

SNIVELS > SNIVEL

SNIVELY same as > SNIVELLY

SNOB n person who judges others by social rank

SNOBBERY > SNOB

SNOBBIER > SNOB

SNOBBIEST > SNOB

SNOBBILY > SNOB

SNOBBISH > SNOB

SNOBBISM > SNOB

SNOBBISMS > SNOB

SNOBBY > SNOB

SNOBLING n little snob

SNOBLINGS > SNOBLING

SNOBS > SNOB

SNOCOACH n bus-like vehicle for travelling on snow

SNOD vb Scots word meaning make tidy

SNODDED > SNOD

SNODDER > SNOD

SNODDEST > SNOD

SNODDING > SNOD

SNODDIT > SNOD

SNODS > SNOD

SNOEK n edible marine fish

SNOEKS > SNOEK

SNOEP adj mean or tight-fisted

SNOG vb kiss and cuddle ▷ n act of kissing and cuddling

SNOGGED > SNOG

SNOGGER n person who snogs

SNOGGERS > SNOGGER

SNOGGING > SNOG

SNOGS > SNOG

SNOKE same as > SNOOK

SNOKED > SNOKE

SNOKES > SNOKE

SNOKING > SNOKE

SNOOD n pouch loosely holding a woman's hair at the back ▷ vb hold (the hair) in a snood

SNOODED > SNOOD

SNOODING > SNOOD

SNOODS > SNOOD

SNOOK n any of several large game fishes ▷ vb lurk

SNOOKED > SNOOK

SNOOKER n game played on a billiard table ▷ vb leave (a snooker opponent) unable to hit the target ball

SNOOKERED > SNOOKER

SNOOKERS > SNOOKER

SNOOKING > SNOOK

SNOOKS > SNOOK

SNOOL vb Scots word meaning dominate

SNOOLED > SNOOL

SNOOLING > SNOOL

SNOOLS > SNOOL

SNOOP vb pry ▷ n snooping

SNOOPED > SNOOP

SNOOPER n person who snoops

SNOOPERS > SNOOPER

SNOOPIER > SNOOP

SNOOPIEST > SNOOP

SNOOPILY > SNOOP

SNOOPING > SNOOP

SNOOPS > SNOOP

SNOOPY > SNOOP

SNOOSE n snuff

SNOOSES > SNOOSE

SNOOT n nose ▷ vb look contemptuously at

SNOOTED > SNOOT

SNOOTFUL n enough alcohol to make someone drunk

SNOOTFULS > SNOOTFUL

SNOOTIER > SNOOTY

SNOOTIEST > SNOOTY

SNOOTILY > SNOOTY

SNOOTING > SNOOT

SNOOTS > SNOOT

SNOOTY adj haughty

SNOOZE vb take a brief light sleep ▷ n brief light sleep

SNOOZED > SNOOZE

SNOOZER > SNOOZE

SNOOZERS > SNOOZE

SNOOZES > SNOOZE

SNOOZIER > SNOOZE

SNOOZIEST > SNOOZE

SNOOZING > SNOOZE

SNOOZLE vb cuddle and sleep

SNOOZLED > SNOOZLE

SNOOZLES > SNOOZLE

SNOOZLING > SNOOZLE

SNOOZY > SNOOZE

SNORE vb make snoring sounds while sleeping ▷ n sound of snoring

SNORED > SNORE

SNORER > SNORE

SNORERS > SNORE

SNORES > SNORE

SNORING > SNORE

SNORINGS > SNORE

SNORKEL n tube allowing a swimmer to breathe ▷ vb swim using a snorkel

SNORKELED > SNORKEL

SNORKELER > SNORKEL

SNORKELS > SNORKEL

SNORT vb exhale noisily through the nostrils ▷ n act or sound of snorting

SNORTED > SNORT

SNORTER n person or animal that snorts

SNORTERS > SNORTER

SNORTIER > SNORT

SNORTIEST > SNORT

SNORTING > SNORT

SNORTINGS > SNORT

SNORTS > SNORT

SNORTY > SNORT

SNOT n mucus from the nose ▷ vb blow one's nose

SNOTRAG n handkerchief

SNOTRAGS > SNOTRAG

SNOTS > SNOT

SNOTTED > SNOT

SNOTTER vb breathe through obstructed nostrils

SNOTTERED > SNOTTER

SNOTTERS > SNOTTER

SNOTTERY n snot

SNOTTIE n midshipman

SNOTTIER > SNOTTY

SNOTTIES > SNOTTY

SNOTTIEST > SNOTTY

SNOTTILY > SNOTTY

SNOTTING > SNOT

SNOTTY adj covered with mucus from the nose

SNOUT n animal's projecting nose and jaws ▷ vb have or give a snout

SNOUTED > SNOUT

SNOUTIER > SNOUT

SNOUTIEST > SNOUT

SNOUTING > SNOUT

SNOUTISH > SNOUT

SNOUTLESS > SNOUT

SNOUTLIKE > SNOUT

SNOUTS > SNOUT

SNOUTY > SNOUT

SNOW n frozen vapour falling from the sky in flakes ▷ vb fall as or like snow

SNOWBALL n snow pressed into a ball for

throwing ▷ *vb* increase rapidly
SNOWBALLS > SNOWBALL
SNOWBANK *n* bank of snow
SNOWBANKS > SNOWBANK
SNOWBELL *n* Asian shrub
SNOWBELLS > SNOWBELL
SNOWBELT *n* northern states of USA
SNOWBELTS > SNOWBELT
SNOWBERRY *n* shrub grown for its white berries
SNOWBIRD *n* person addicted to cocaine, or sometimes heroin
SNOWBIRDS > SNOWBIRD
SNOWBLINK *n* whitish glare in the sky reflected from snow
SNOWBOARD *n* board on which a person stands to slide across the snow
SNOWBOOT *n* boot for walking in snow
SNOWBOOTS > SNOWBOOT
SNOWBOUND *adj* shut in by snow
SNOWBRUSH *n* brush for clearing snow
SNOWBUSH *n* North American plant
SNOWCAP *n* cap of snow on top of a mountain
SNOWCAPS > SNOWCAP
SNOWCAT *n* tracked vehicle for travelling over snow
SNOWCATS > SNOWCAT
SNOWCLONE *n* reusable verbal formula
SNOWDOME *n* leisure centre with facilities for skiing, skating, etc
SNOWDOMES > SNOWDOME
SNOWDRIFT *n* bank of deep snow
SNOWDROP *n* small white bell-shaped spring flower
SNOWDROPS > SNOWDROP
SNOWED *adj* under the influence of narcotic drugs
SNOWFALL *n* fall of snow
SNOWFALLS > SNOWFALL
SNOWFIELD *n* large area of permanent snow
SNOWFLAKE *n* single crystal of snow
SNOWFLEA *n* wingless insect that lives on or in snow
SNOWFLEAS > SNOWFLEA
SNOWFLECK *n* snow bunting
SNOWFLICK *same as* > SNOWFLECK
SNOWGLOBE *n* transparent sphere filled with water and white particles which resemble snow falling when shaken
SNOWIER > SNOWY
SNOWIEST > SNOWY
SNOWILY > SNOWY
SNOWINESS > SNOWY

SNOWING > SNOW
SNOWISH *adj* like snow
SNOWK *same as* > SNOOK
SNOWKED > SNOWK
SNOWKING > SNOWK
SNOWKS > SNOWK
SNOWLAND *n* area where snow lies
SNOWLANDS > SNOWLAND
SNOWLESS > SNOW
SNOWLIKE > SNOW
SNOWLINE *n* limit of permanent snow
SNOWLINES > SNOWLINE
SNOWMAKER *n* machine making artificial snow
SNOWMAN *n* figure shaped out of snow
SNOWMELT *n* melting of snow in spring
SNOWMELTS > SNOWMELT
SNOWMEN > SNOWMAN
SNOWMOLD *same as* > SNOWMOULD
SNOWMOLDS > SNOWMOLD
SNOWMOULD *n* fungus growing on grass under snow
SNOWPACK *n* body of hard-packed snow
SNOWPACKS > SNOWPACK
SNOWPLOW *n* implement or vehicle for clearing snow away
SNOWPLOWS > SNOWPLOW
SNOWS > SNOW
SNOWSCAPE *n* snow-covered landscape
SNOWSHED *n* shelter built over an exposed section of railway track to prevent its blockage by snow
SNOWSHEDS > SNOWSHED
SNOWSHOE *n* racket-shaped frame with a network of thongs stretched across it, worn on the feet to make walking on snow less difficult ▷ *vb* walk or go using snowshoes
SNOWSHOED > SNOWSHOE
SNOWSHOER > SNOWSHOE
SNOWSHOES > SNOWSHOE
SNOWSLIDE *n* snow avalanche
SNOWSLIP *n* small snow avalanche
SNOWSLIPS > SNOWSLIP
SNOWSTORM *n* storm with heavy snow
SNOWSUIT *n* one-piece winter outer garment for child
SNOWSUITS > SNOWSUIT
SNOWY *adj* covered with or abounding in snow
SNUB *vb* insult deliberately ▷ *n* deliberate insult ▷ *adj* (of a nose) short and blunt
SNUBBE *n* stub
SNUBBED > SNUB
SNUBBER > SNUB

SNUBBERS > SNUB
SNUBBES > SNUBBE
SNUBBIER > SNUB
SNUBBIEST > SNUB
SNUBBING > SNUB
SNUBBINGS > SNUB
SNUBBISH > SNUB
SNUBBY > SNUB
SNUBFIN *adj* as in *snubfin dolphin* Australian dolphin with a small dorsal fin
SNUBNESS > SNUB
SNUBS > SNUB
SNUCK *past tense and past participle of* > SNEAK
SNUDGE *vb* be miserly
SNUDGED > SNUDGE
SNUDGES > SNUDGE
SNUDGING > SNUDGE
SNUFF *n* powdered tobacco for sniffing up the nostrils ▷ *vb* extinguish (a candle)
SNUFFBOX *n* small container for holding snuff
SNUFFED > SNUFF
SNUFFER > SNUFF
SNUFFERS > SNUFF
SNUFFIER > SNUFFY
SNUFFIEST > SNUFFY
SNUFFILY > SNUFFY
SNUFFING > SNUFF
SNUFFINGS > SNUFF
SNUFFLE *vb* breathe noisily or with difficulty ▷ *n* act or the sound of snuffling
SNUFFLED > SNUFFLE
SNUFFLER > SNUFFLE
SNUFFLERS > SNUFFLE
SNUFFLES *same as* > SNIFFLES
SNUFFLIER > SNUFFLE
SNUFFLING > SNUFFLE
SNUFFLY > SNUFFLE
SNUFFS > SNUFF
SNUFFY *adj* of, relating to, or resembling snuff
SNUG *adj* warm and comfortable ▷ *n* (in Britain and Ireland) small room in a pub ▷ *vb* make or become comfortable and warm
SNUGGED > SNUG
SNUGGER > SNUG
SNUGGERIE *n* small bar in pub
SNUGGERY *n* cosy and comfortable place or room
SNUGGEST > SNUG
SNUGGIES *pl n* specially warm underwear
SNUGGING > SNUG
SNUGGLE *vb* nestle into a person or thing for warmth or from affection ▷ *n* act of snuggling
SNUGGLED > SNUGGLE
SNUGGLES > SNUGGLE
SNUGGLIER > SNUGGLY
SNUGGLING > SNUGGLE

SNUGGLY *adj* comfortably warm and suitable for snuggling
SNUGLY > SNUG
SNUGNESS > SNUG
SNUGS > SNUG
SNUSH *vb* take snuff
SNUSHED > SNUSH
SNUSHES > SNUSH
SNUSHING > SNUSH
SNUZZLE *vb* root in ground
SNUZZLED > SNUZZLE
SNUZZLES > SNUZZLE
SNUZZLING > SNUZZLE
SNY *same as* > SNYE
SNYE *n* side channel of a river
SNYES > SNYE
SO *adv* such an extent ▷ *interj* exclamation of surprise, triumph, or realization ▷ *n* the fifth note of the musical scale
SOAK *vb* make wet ▷ *n* soaking
SOAKAGE *n* process or a period in which a permeable substance is soaked in a liquid
SOAKAGES > SOAKAGE
SOAKAWAY *n* pit filled with rubble, etc, into which rain or waste water drains
SOAKAWAYS > SOAKAWAY
SOAKED > SOAK
SOAKEN > SOAK
SOAKER > SOAK
SOAKERS > SOAK
SOAKING > SOAK
SOAKINGLY > SOAK
SOAKINGS > SOAK
SOAKS > SOAK
SOAP *n* compound of alkali and fat, used with water as a cleaning agent ▷ *vb* apply soap to
SOAPBARK *n* W South American rosaceous tree
SOAPBARKS > SOAPBARK
SOAPBERRY *n* any of various chiefly tropical American sapindaceous trees
SOAPBOX *n* crate used as a platform for speech-making ▷ *vb* deliver a speech from a soapbox
SOAPBOXED > SOAPBOX
SOAPBOXES > SOAPBOX
SOAPDISH *n* dish for holding soap
SOAPED > SOAP
SOAPER *n* soap opera
SOAPERS > SOAPER
SOAPFISH *n* tropical fish with toxic mucus
SOAPIE *n* soap opera
SOAPIER > SOAPY
SOAPIES > SOAPIE
SOAPIEST > SOAPY
SOAPILY > SOAPY
SOAPINESS > SOAPY
SOAPING > SOAP

S

SOAPLAND n Japanese massage parlour and brothel

SOAPLANDS > SOAPLAND

SOAPLESS > SOAP

SOAPLIKE > SOAP

SOAPROOT n plant with roots used as soap substitute

SOAPROOTS > SOAPROOT

SOAPS > SOAP

SOAPSTONE n soft mineral used for making table tops and ornaments

SOAPSUDS pl n foam or lather produced when soap is mixed with water

SOAPSUDSY > SOAPSUDS

SOAPWORT n Eurasian plant with clusters of fragrant pink or white flowers

SOAPWORTS > SOAPWORT

SOAPY adj covered with soap

SOAR vb rise or fly upwards ▷ n act of soaring

SOARAWAY adj exceedingly successful

SOARE n young hawk

SOARED > SOAR

SOARER > SOAR

SOARERS > SOAR

SOARES > SOARE

SOARING > SOAR

SOARINGLY > SOAR

SOARINGS > SOAR

SOARS > SOAR

SOAVE n dry white Italian wine

SOAVES > SOAVE

SOB vb weep with convulsive gasps ▷ n act or sound of sobbing

SOBA n (in Japanese cookery) noodles made from buckwheat flour

SOBAS > SOBA

SOBBED > SOB

SOBBER > SOB

SOBBERS > SOB

SOBBING > SOB

SOBBINGLY > SOB

SOBBINGS > SOB

SOBEIT conj provided that

SOBER adj not drunk ▷ vb make or become sober

SOBERED > SOBER

SOBERER > SOBER

SOBEREST > SOBER

SOBERING > SOBER

SOBERISE same as > SOBERIZE

SOBERISED > SOBERISE

SOBERISES > SOBERISE

SOBERIZE vb make sober

SOBERIZED > SOBERIZE

SOBERIZES > SOBERIZE

SOBERLY > SOBER

SOBERNESS > SOBER

SOBERS > SOBER

SOBFUL adj tearful

SOBOLE n creeping underground stem that produces roots and buds

SOBOLES > SOBOLE

SOBRIETY n state of being sober

SOBRIQUET n nickname

SOBS > SOB

SOC n feudal right to hold court

SOCA n mixture of soul and calypso music

SOCAGE n tenure of land by certain services

SOCAGER > SOCAGE

SOCAGERS > SOCAGE

SOCAGES > SOCAGE

SOCAS > SOCA

SOCCAGE same as > SOCAGE

SOCCAGES > SOCCAGE

SOCCER n football played by two teams of eleven kicking a spherical ball

SOCCERS > SOCCER

SOCES > SOC

SOCIABLE adj friendly or companionable ▷ n type of open carriage with two seats facing each other

SOCIABLES > SOCIABLE

SOCIABLY > SOCIABLE

SOCIAL adj living in a community ▷ n informal gathering

SOCIALISE same as > SOCIALIZE

SOCIALISM n political system which advocates public ownership of industries, resources, and transport

SOCIALIST n supporter or advocate of socialism ▷ adj of or relating to socialism

SOCIALITE n member of fashionable society

SOCIALITY n tendency of groups and persons to develop social links and live in communities

SOCIALIZE vb meet others socially

SOCIALLY > SOCIAL

SOCIALS > SOCIAL

SOCIATE n associate

SOCIATES > SOCIATE

SOCIATION n plant community

SOCIATIVE adj of association

SOCIETAL adj of or relating to society, esp human society or social relations

SOCIETIES > SOCIETY

SOCIETY n human beings considered as a group

SOCIOGRAM n chart showing social relationships

SOCIOLECT n language spoken by particular social class

SOCIOLOGY n study of human societies

SOCIOPATH n person with a personality disorder characterized by a tendency to commit antisocial acts without any feelings of guilt

SOCK n knitted covering for the foot ▷ vb hit hard

SOCKED > SOCK

SOCKET n hole or recess into which something fits ▷ vb furnish with or place into a socket

SOCKETED > SOCKET

SOCKETING > SOCKET

SOCKETS > SOCKET

SOCKETTE n sock not covering ankle

SOCKETTES > SOCKETTE

SOCKEYE n Pacific salmon with red flesh

SOCKEYES > SOCKEYE

SOCKING > SOCK

SOCKLESS > SOCK

SOCKMAN same as > SOCMAN

SOCKMEN > SOCKMAN

SOCKO adj excellent

SOCKS > SOCK

SOCLE another name for > PLINTH

SOCLES > SOCLE

SOCMAN n tenant holding land by socage

SOCMEN > SOCMAN

SOCS > SOC

SOD n (piece of) turf ▷ vb cover with sods

SODA n compound of sodium

SODAIC adj containing soda

SODAIN same as > SUDDEN

SODAINE same as > SUDDEN

SODALESS > SODA

SODALIST n member of sodality

SODALISTS > SODALIST

SODALITE n blue, grey, yellow, or colourless mineral

SODALITES > SODALITE

SODALITY n religious or charitable society

SODAMIDE n white crystalline compound used as a dehydrating agent

SODAMIDES > SODAMIDE

SODAS > SODA

SODBUSTER n farmer who grows crops

SODDED > SOD

SODDEN adj soaked ▷ vb make or become sodden

SODDENED > SODDEN

SODDENING > SODDEN

SODDENLY > SODDEN

SODDENS > SODDEN

SODDIE n house made of sod

SODDIER > SODDY

SODDIES > SODDY

SODDIEST > SODDY

SODDING > SOD

SODDY adj covered with turf

SODGER dialect variant of > SOLDIER

SODGERED > SODGER

SODGERING > SODGER

SODGERS > SODGER

SODIC adj containing sodium

SODICITY > SODIC

SODIUM n silvery-white metallic element

SODIUMS > SODIUM

SODOM n person who performs sodomy

SODOMIES > SODOMY

SODOMISE same as > SODOMIZE

SODOMISED > SODOMISE

SODOMISES > SODOMISE

SODOMIST > SODOMY

SODOMISTS > SODOMY

SODOMITE n person who practises sodomy

SODOMITES > SODOMITE

SODOMITIC > SODOMY

SODOMIZE vb be the active partner in anal intercourse

SODOMIZED > SODOMIZE

SODOMIZES > SODOMIZE

SODOMS > SODOM

SODOMY n anal intercourse

SODS > SOD

SOEVER adv in any way at all

SOFA n couch

SOFABED n sofa that converts into a bed

SOFABEDS > SOFABED

SOFAR n system for determining a position at sea

SOFARS > SOFAR

SOFAS > SOFA

SOFFIONI n holes in volcano that emit steam

SOFFIT n underside of a part of a building or a structural component

SOFFITS > SOFFIT

SOFT adj easy to shape or cut ▷ adv softly ▷ vb soften

SOFTA n Muslim student of divinity and jurisprudence

SOFTAS > SOFTA

SOFTBACK n paperback

SOFTBACKS > SOFTBACK

SOFTBALL n game similar to baseball, played using a larger softer ball

SOFTBALLS > SOFTBALL

SOFTBOUND adj having paperback binding

SOFTCORE adj describing pornography that is not explicit

SOFTCOVER n book with paper covers

SOFTED > SOFT

SOFTEN vb make or become soft or softer

SOFTENED > SOFTEN

SOFTENER n substance added to another substance to increase its softness

SOFTENERS > SOFTENER

SOFTENING > SOFTEN

SOFTENS > SOFTEN

SOFTER > SOFT

SOFTEST > SOFT

SOFTGOODS n clothing and soft furniture

SOFTHEAD n half-witted person

SOFTHEADS > SOFTHEAD

SOFTIE n person who is easily upset

SOFTIES > SOFTY

SOFTING > SOFT

SOFTISH > SOFT

SOFTLING n weakling

SOFTLINGS > SOFTLING

SOFTLY > SOFT

SOFTNESS n quality or an instance of being soft

SOFTS > SOFT

SOFTSCAPE n vegetation featuring in a landscape

SOFTSHELL n crab or turtle with a soft shell

SOFTWARE n computer programs

SOFTWARES > SOFTWARE

SOFTWOOD n wood of a coniferous tree

SOFTWOODS > SOFTWOOD

SOFTY same as > SOFTIE

SOG vb soak

SOGER same as > SODGER

SOGERS > SOGER

SOGGED > SOG

SOGGIER > SOGGY

SOGGIEST > SOGGY

SOGGILY > SOGGY

SOGGINESS > SOGGY

SOGGING > SOG

SOGGINGS > SOG

SOGGY adj soaked

SOGS > SOG

SOH n (in tonic sol-fa) fifth degree of any major scale

SOHO interj exclamation announcing the sighting of a hare

SOHS > SOH

SOHUR same as > SUHUR

SOHURS > SOHUR

SOIGNE adj well-groomed, elegant

SOIGNEE variant of > SOIGNE

SOIL n top layer of earth ▷ vb make or become dirty

SOILAGE n green fodder

SOILAGES > SOILAGE

SOILBORNE adj carried in soil

SOILED > SOIL

SOILIER > SOIL

SOILIEST > SOIL

SOILINESS > SOIL

SOILING > SOIL

SOILINGS > SOIL

SOILLESS > SOIL

SOILS > SOIL

SOILURE n act of soiling or the state of being soiled

SOILURES > SOILURE

SOILY > SOIL

SOIREE n evening party or gathering

SOIREES > SOIREE

SOJA same as > SOYA

SOJAS > SOJA

SOJOURN n temporary stay ▷ vb stay temporarily

SOJOURNED > SOJOURN

SOJOURNER > SOJOURN

SOJOURNS > SOJOURN

SOJU n type of Korean vodka

SOJUS > SOJU

SOKAH same as > SOCA

SOKAHS > SOKAH

SOKAIYA n Japanese extortionist

SOKE n right to hold a local court

SOKEMAN same as > SOCMAN

SOKEMANRY n feudal tenure by socage

SOKEMEN > SOKEMAN

SOKEN n feudal district

SOKENS > SOKEN

SOKES > SOKE

SOKOL n Czech gymnastic association

SOKOLS > SOKOL

SOL n liquid colloidal solution

SOLA > SOLUM

SOLACE vb comfort in distress ▷ n comfort in misery or disappointment

SOLACED > SOLACE

SOLACER > SOLACE

SOLACERS > SOLACE

SOLACES > SOLACE

SOLACING > SOLACE

SOLACIOUS adj providing solace

SOLAH n Indian plant

SOLAHS > SOLAH

SOLAN archaic name for > GANNET

SOLAND n solan goose

SOLANDER n box for botanical specimens, maps, etc, made in the form of a book, the front cover being the lid

SOLANDERS > SOLANDER

SOLANDS > SOLAND

SOLANIN same as > SOLANINE

SOLANINE n poisonous alkaloid found in various solanaceous plants

SOLANINES > SOLANINE

SOLANINS > SOLANIN

SOLANO n hot wind in Spain

SOLANOS > SOLANO

SOLANS > SOLAN

SOLANUM n any plant of the genus that includes the potato

SOLANUMS > SOLANUM

SOLAR adj of the sun

SOLARIA > SOLARIUM

SOLARISE same as > SOLARIZE

SOLARISED > SOLARISE

SOLARISES > SOLARISE

SOLARISM n explanation of myths in terms of the movements and influence of the sun

SOLARISMS > SOLARISM

SOLARIST > SOLARISM

SOLARISTS > SOLARISM

SOLARIUM n place with beds and ultraviolet lights used for acquiring an artificial suntan

SOLARIUMS > SOLARIUM

SOLARIZE vb treat by exposure to the sun's rays

SOLARIZED > SOLARIZE

SOLARIZES > SOLARIZE

SOLARS > SOLUM

SOLAS > SOLUM

SOLATE vb change from gel to liquid

SOLATED > SOLATE

SOLATES > SOLATE

SOLATIA > SOLATIUM

SOLATING > SOLATE

SOLATION n liquefaction of a gel

SOLATIONS > SOLATION

SOLATIUM n compensation awarded for injury to the feelings

SOLD n obsolete word for salary

SOLDADO n soldier

SOLDADOES > SOLDADO

SOLDADOS > SOLDADO

SOLDAN archaic word for > SULTAN

SOLDANS > SOLDAN

SOLDE n wages

SOLDER n soft alloy used to join two metal surfaces ▷ vb join with solder

SOLDERED > SOLDER

SOLDERER > SOLDER

SOLDERERS > SOLDER

SOLDERING > SOLDER

SOLDERS > SOLDER

SOLDES > SOLDE

SOLDI > SOLDO

SOLDIER n member of an army ▷ vb serve in an army

SOLDIERED > SOLDIER

SOLDIERLY adj of or befitting a good soldier

SOLDIERS > SOLDIER

SOLDIERY n soldiers collectively

SOLDO n former Italian copper coin

SOLDS > SOLD

SOLE adj one and only ▷ n underside of the foot ▷ vb provide (a shoe) with a sole

SOLECISE variant of > SOLECIZE

SOLECISED > SOLECISE

SOLECISES > SOLECISE

SOLECISM n minor grammatical mistake

SOLECISMS > SOLECISM

SOLECIST > SOLECISM

SOLECISTS > SOLECISM

SOLECIZE vb commit a solecism

SOLECIZED > SOLECIZE

SOLECIZES > SOLECIZE

SOLED > SOLE

SOLEI > SOLEUS

SOLEIN same as > SULLEN

SOLELESS > SOLE

SOLELY adv only, completely

SOLEMN adj serious, deeply sincere

SOLEMNER > SOLEMN

SOLEMNESS > SOLEMN

SOLEMNEST > SOLEMN

SOLEMNIFY vb make serious or grave

SOLEMNISE same as > SOLEMNIZE

SOLEMNITY n state or quality of being solemn

SOLEMNIZE vb celebrate or perform (a ceremony)

SOLEMNLY > SOLEMN

SOLENESS > SOLE

SOLENETTE n small European sole

SOLENODON n either of two rare shrewlike nocturnal mammals of the Caribbean

SOLENOID n coil of wire magnetized by passing a current through it

SOLENOIDS > SOLENOID

SOLEPLATE n joist forming the lowest member of a timber frame

SOLEPRINT n print of sole of foot

SOLER same as > SOLE

SOLERA n system for aging sherry and other fortified wines

SOLERAS > SOLERA

SOLERET n armour for foot

SOLERETS > SOLERET

SOLERS > SOLER

SOLES > SOLE

SOLEUS n muscle in calf of leg

SOLEUSES > SOLEUS

SOLFATARA n volcanic vent emitting only

sulphurous gases and water vapour or sometimes hot mud

SOLFEGE *variant of* > SOLFEGGIO

SOLFEGES > SOLFEGE

SOLFEGGI > SOLFEGGIO

SOLFEGGIO *n* voice exercise in which runs, scales, etc, are sung to the same syllable or syllables

SOLFERINO *n* moderate purplish-red colour

SOLGEL *adj* changing between sol and gel

SOLI *adv* to be performed by or with soloists

SOLICIT *vb* request

SOLICITED > SOLICIT

SOLICITOR *n* lawyer who advises clients and prepares documents and cases

SOLICITS > SOLICIT

SOLICITY *n* act of making a request

SOLID *adj* (of a substance) keeping its shape ▷ *n* three-dimensional shape

SOLIDAGO *n* chiefly American plant of the genus which includes the goldenrods

SOLIDAGOS > SOLIDAGO

SOLIDARE *n* old coin

SOLIDARES > SOLIDARE

SOLIDARY *adj* marked by unity of interests, responsibilities, etc

SOLIDATE *vb* consolidate

SOLIDATED > SOLIDATE

SOLIDATES > SOLIDATE

SOLIDER > SOLID

SOLIDEST > SOLID

SOLIDI > SOLIDUS

SOLIDIFY *vb* make or become solid or firm

SOLIDISH > SOLID

SOLIDISM *n* belief that diseases spring from damage to solid parts of body

SOLIDISMS > SOLIDISM

SOLIDIST > SOLIDISM

SOLIDISTS > SOLIDISM

SOLIDITY > SOLID

SOLIDLY > SOLID

SOLIDNESS > SOLID

SOLIDS > SOLID

SOLIDUM *n* part of pedestal

SOLIDUMS > SOLIDUM

SOLIDUS *same as* > SLASH

SOLILOQUY *n* speech made by a person while alone, esp in a play

SOLING > SOLE

SOLION *n* amplifier used in chemistry

SOLIONS > SOLION

SOLIPED *n* animal whose hooves are not cloven

SOLIPEDS > SOLIPED

SOLIPSISM *n* doctrine that the self is the only thing known to exist

SOLIPSIST > SOLIPSISM

SOLIQUID *n* semi-solid, semi-liquid solution

SOLIQUIDS > SOLIQUID

SOLITAIRE *n* game for one person played with pegs set in a board

SOLITARY *adj* alone, single ▷ *n* hermit

SOLITO *adv* musical instruction meaning play in usual manner

SOLITON *n* type of isolated particle-like wave

SOLITONS > SOLITON

SOLITUDE *n* state of being alone

SOLITUDES > SOLITUDE

SOLIVE *n* type of joist

SOLIVES > SOLIVE

SOLLAR *n* archaic word meaning attic ▷ *vb* put in a sollar

SOLLARED > SOLLAR

SOLLARING > SOLLAR

SOLLARS > SOLLAR

SOLLER *same as* > SOLLAR

SOLLERET *n* protective covering for the foot consisting of riveted plates of armour

SOLLERETS > SOLLERET

SOLLERS > SOLLER

SOLLICKER *n* something very large

SOLO *n* music for one performer ▷ *adj* done alone ▷ *adv* by oneself, alone ▷ *vb* undertake a venture alone

SOLOED > SOLO

SOLOES > SOLO

SOLOING > SOLO

SOLOIST *n* person who performs a solo

SOLOISTIC > SOLOIST

SOLOISTS > SOLOIST

SOLON *n* US congressman

SOLONCHAK *n* type of intrazonal soil of arid regions with a greyish surface crust

SOLONETS *same as* > SOLONETZ

SOLONETZ *n* type of intrazonal soil with a high saline content characterized by leaching

SOLONS > SOLON

SOLOS > SOLO

SOLPUGID *n* venomous arachnid

SOLPUGIDS > SOLPUGID

SOLS > SOL

SOLSTICE *n* either the shortest (in winter) or longest (in summer) day of the year

SOLSTICES > SOLSTICE

SOLUBLE *adj* able to be dissolved ▷ *n* soluble substance

SOLUBLES > SOLUBLE

SOLUBLY > SOLUBLE

SOLUM *n* upper layers of the soil profile

SOLUMS > SOLUM

SOLUNAR *adj* relating to sun and moon

SOLUS *n* advert printed or published separately from others

SOLUSES > SOLUS

SOLUTAL *adj* relating to a solute

SOLUTE *n* substance in a solution that is dissolved ▷ *adj* loose or unattached

SOLUTES > SOLUTE

SOLUTION *n* answer to a problem

SOLUTIONS > SOLUTION

SOLUTIVE *adj* dissolving ▷ *n* solvent or laxative

SOLUTIVES > SOLUTIVE

SOLVABLE *adj* capable of being solved

SOLVATE *vb* undergo, cause to undergo, or partake in solvation

SOLVATED > SOLVATE

SOLVATES > SOLVATE

SOLVATING > SOLVATE

SOLVATION *n* type of chemical process

SOLVE *vb* find the answer to (a problem)

SOLVED > SOLVE

SOLVENCY *n* ability to pay all debts

SOLVENT *adj* having enough money to pay one's debts ▷ *n* liquid capable of dissolving other substances

SOLVENTLY > SOLVENT

SOLVENTS > SOLVENT

SOLVER > SOLVE

SOLVERS > SOLVE

SOLVES > SOLVE

SOLVING > SOLVE

SOM *n* currency of Kyrgyzstan and Uzbekistan

SOMA *n* body of an organism as distinct from the germ cells

SOMAN *n* compound developed as a nerve gas

SOMANS > SOMAN

SOMAS > SOMA

SOMASCOPE *n* instrument for inspecting internal organs

SOMATA > SOMA

SOMATIC *adj* of the body, as distinct from the mind

SOMATISM *n* materialism

SOMATISMS > SOMATISM

SOMATIST > SOMATISM

SOMATISTS > SOMATISM

SOMBER *adj* (in the US) sombre ▷ *vb* (in the US) make sombre

SOMBERED > SOMBER

SOMBERER > SOMBER

SOMBEREST > SOMBER

SOMBERING > SOMBER

SOMBERLY > SOMBER

SOMBERS > SOMBER

SOMBRE *adj* dark, gloomy ▷ *vb* make sombre

SOMBRED > SOMBRE

SOMBRELY > SOMBRE

SOMBRER > SOMBRE

SOMBRERO *n* wide-brimmed Mexican hat

SOMBREROS > SOMBRERO

SOMBRES > SOMBRE

SOMBREST > SOMBRE

SOMBRING > SOMBRE

SOMBROUS > SOMBRE

SOME *adj* unknown or unspecified ▷ *pron* certain unknown or unspecified people or things ▷ *adv* approximately ▷ *determiner* (a) certain unknown or unspecified

SOMEBODY *pron* some person ▷ *n* important person

SOMEDAY *adv* at some unspecified time in the future

SOMEDEAL *adv* to some extent ▷ *n* some part of something

SOMEDEALS > SOMEDEAL

SOMEDELE *same as* > SOMEDEAL

SOMEGATE *adv* Scots word meaning somehow

SOMEHOW *adv* in some unspecified way

SOMEONE *pron* somebody ▷ *n* significant or important person

SOMEONES > SOMEONE

SOMEPLACE *adv* in, at, or to some unspecified place or region

SOMERSET *n* somersault

SOMERSETS > SOMERSET

SOMETHING *pron* unknown or unspecified thing or amount ▷ *n* impressive or important person or thing

SOMETIME *adv* at some unspecified time ▷ *adj* former

SOMETIMES *adv* from time to time, now and then

SOMEWAY *adv* in some unspecified manner

SOMEWAYS *same as* > SOMEWAY

SOMEWHAT *adv* some extent, rather ▷ *n* vague amount

SOMEWHATS > SOMEWHAT

SOMEWHEN *adv* at some time

SOMEWHERE adv in, to, or at some unspecified or unknown place
SOMEWHILE adv sometimes
SOMEWHY adv for some reason
SOMEWISE adv in some way or to some degree
SOMITAL > SOMITE
SOMITE n segment of mesoderm in vertebrate embryos
SOMITES > SOMITE
SOMITIC > SOMITE
SOMMELIER n wine steward in a restaurant or hotel
SOMNIAL adj of dreams
SOMNIATE vb dream
SOMNIATED > SOMNIATE
SOMNIATES > SOMNIATE
SOMNIFIC adj inducing sleep
SOMNOLENT adj drowsy
SOMONI n monetary unit of Tajikistan
SOMONIS > SOMONI
SOMS > SOM
SOMY > SOM
SON n male offspring
SONANCE > SONANT
SONANCES > SONANT
SONANCIES > SONANT
SONANCY > SONANT
SONANT n voiced sound able to form a syllable or syllable nucleus ▷ adj denoting a voiced sound like this
SONANTAL > SONANT
SONANTIC > SONANT
SONANTS > SONANT
SONAR n device for detecting underwater objects by the reflection of sound waves
SONARMAN n sonar operator
SONARMEN > SONARMAN
SONARS > SONAR
SONATA n piece of music in several movements for one instrument
SONATAS > SONATA
SONATINA n short sonata
SONATINAS > SONATINA
SONATINE same as > SONATINA
SONCE n Scots word meaning good luck
SONCES > SONCE
SONDAGE n deep trial trench for inspecting stratigraphy
SONDAGES > SONDAGE
SONDE n rocket, balloon, or probe used for observing in the upper atmosphere
SONDELI n Indian shrew
SONDELIS > SONDELI
SONDER n yacht category
SONDERS > SONDER

SONDES > SONDE
SONE n subjective unit of loudness
SONERI n Indian cloth of gold
SONERIS > SONERI
SONES > SONE
SONG n music for the voice
SONGBIRD n any bird with a musical call
SONGBIRDS > SONGBIRD
SONGBOOK n book of songs
SONGBOOKS > SONGBOOK
SONGCRAFT n art of songwriting
SONGFEST n event with many songs
SONGFESTS > SONGFEST
SONGFUL adj tuneful
SONGFULLY > SONGFUL
SONGKOK n (in Malaysia and Indonesia) a kind of oval brimless hat, resembling a skull
SONGKOKS > SONGKOK
SONGLESS > SONG
SONGLIKE > SONG
SONGMAN n singer
SONGMEN > SONGMAN
SONGOLOLO n kind of millipede
SONGS > SONG
SONGSHEET n piece of paper with the words to a song on it
SONGSMITH n person who writes songs
SONGSTER n singer
SONGSTERS > SONGSTER
SONHOOD > SON
SONHOODS > SON
SONIC adj of or producing sound
SONICALLY > SONIC
SONICATE vb subject to sound waves
SONICATED > SONICATE
SONICATES > SONICATE
SONICATOR > SONICATE
SONICS n study of mechanical vibrations in matter
SONLESS > SON
SONLIKE > SON
SONLY adj like a son
SONNE same as > SON
SONNES > SONNE
SONNET n fourteen-line poem ▷ vb compose sonnets
SONNETARY > SONNET
SONNETED > SONNET
SONNETEER n writer of sonnets
SONNETING > SONNET
SONNETISE same as > SONNETIZE
SONNETIZE vb write sonnets
SONNETS > SONNET
SONNETTED > SONNET
SONNIES > SONNY

SONNY n term of address to a boy
SONOBUOY n buoy equipped to detect underwater noises and transmit them by radio
SONOBUOYS > SONOBUOY
SONOGRAM n three-dimensional representation of a sound signal
SONOGRAMS > SONOGRAM
SONOGRAPH n device for scanning sound
SONOMETER same as > MONOCHORD
SONORANT n type of frictionless continuant or nasal
SONORANTS > SONORANT
SONORITY > SONOROUS
SONOROUS adj (of sound) deep or resonant
SONOVOX n device used to alter sound of human voice in music recordings
SONOVOXES > SONOVOX
SONS > SON
SONSE same as > SONCE
SONSES > SONSE
SONSHIP > SON
SONSHIPS > SON
SONSIE same as > SONSY
SONSIER > SONSY
SONSIEST > SONSY
SONSY adj plump
SONTAG n type of knitted women's cape
SONTAGS > SONTAG
SONTIES n Shakespearian oath
SOOCHONG same as > SOUCHONG
SOOCHONGS > SOOCHONG
SOOEY interj call used to summon pigs
SOOGEE vb clean ship using a special solution
SOOGEED > SOOGEE
SOOGEEING > SOOGEE
SOOGEES > SOOGEE
SOOGIE same as > SOOGEE
SOOGIED > SOOGIE
SOOGIEING > SOOGIE
SOOGIES > SOOGIE
SOOJEY same as > SOOGEE
SOOJEYS > SOOJEY
SOOK n baby ▷ vb suck
SOOKED > SOOK
SOOKING > SOOK
SOOKS > SOOK
SOOL vb incite (a dog) to attack
SOOLE same as > SOOL
SOOLED > SOOL
SOOLER n person who incites a dog to attack
SOOLERS > SOOLER
SOOLES > SOOLE
SOOLING > SOOL
SOOLS > SOOL
SOOM Scots word for > SWIM
SOOMED > SOOM

SOOMING > SOOM
SOOMS > SOOM
SOON adv in a short time
SOONER adv rather ▷ n idler or shirker
SOONERS > SOONER
SOONEST adv as soon as possible
SOONISH adj somewhat soon
SOOP Scots word for > SWEEP
SOOPED > SOOP
SOOPING > SOOP
SOOPINGS > SOOP
SOOPS > SOOP
SOOPSTAKE adv sweeping up all stakes
SOOT n black powder formed by the incomplete burning of an organic substance ▷ vb cover with soot
SOOTE n sweet
SOOTED > SOOT
SOOTERKIN n mythical black afterbirth of Dutch women that was believed to result from their warming themselves on stoves
SOOTES > SOOT
SOOTFLAKE n speck of soot
SOOTH n truth or reality ▷ adj true or real
SOOTHE vb make calm
SOOTHED > SOOTHE
SOOTHER vb flatter
SOOTHERED > SOOTHE
SOOTHERS > SOOTHE
SOOTHES > SOOTHE
SOOTHEST > SOOTHE
SOOTHFAST adj truthful
SOOTHFUL adj truthful
SOOTHING adj having a calming, assuaging, or relieving effect
SOOTHINGS > SOOTHING
SOOTHLICH adv truly
SOOTHLY > SOOTH
SOOTHS > SOOTH
SOOTHSAID > SOOTHSAY
SOOTHSAY vb predict the future
SOOTHSAYS > SOOTHSAY
SOOTIER > SOOTY
SOOTIEST > SOOTY
SOOTILY > SOOTY
SOOTINESS > SOOTY
SOOTING n state of becoming covered with soot
SOOTINGS > SOOTING
SOOTLESS > SOOT
SOOTS > SOOT
SOOTY adj covered with soot
SOP n concession to pacify someone ▷ vb mop up or absorb (liquid)
SOPAPILLA n Mexican deep-fried pastry

S

SOPH *shortened form of*
> SOPHOMORE
SOPHERIC > SOPHERIM
SOPHERIM *n* Jewish
scribes
SOPHIES > SOPHY
SOPHISM *n* argument that
seems reasonable but is
actually false and
misleading
SOPHISMS > SOPHISM
SOPHIST *n* person who
uses clever but invalid
arguments
SOPHISTER *n* (esp
formerly) a second-year
undergraduate at certain
British universities
SOPHISTIC *adj* of or
relating to sophists or
sophistry
SOPHISTRY *n* clever but
invalid argument
SOPHISTS > SOPHIST
SOPHOMORE *n* student in
second year at college
SOPHS > SOPH
SOPHY *n* title of the Persian
monarchs
SOPITE *vb* lull to sleep
SOPITED > SOPITE
SOPITES > SOPITE
SOPITING > SOPITE
SOPOR *n* abnormally deep
sleep
SOPORIFIC *adj* causing
sleep ▷ *n* drug that causes
sleep
SOPOROSE *adj* sleepy
SOPOROUS *same as*
> SOPOROSE
SOPORS > SOPOR
SOPPED > SOP
SOPPIER > SOPPY
SOPPIEST > SOPPY
SOPPILY > SOPPY
SOPPINESS > SOPPY
SOPPING > SOP
SOPPINGS > SOP
SOPPY *adj* over-
sentimental
SOPRA *adv* musical
instruction meaning
above
SOPRANI > SOPRANO
SOPRANINI
> SOPRANINO
SOPRANINO *n* instrument
with the highest possible
pitch in a family of
instruments
SOPRANIST *n* soprano
SOPRANO *n* singer with
the highest female or boy's
voice ▷ *adj* of a musical
instrument that is the
highest or second highest
pitched in its family
SOPRANOS > SOPRANO
SOPS > SOP
SORA *n* North American
rail with a yellow bill
SORAGE *n* first year in
hawk's life

SORAGES > SORAGE
SORAL > SORUS
SORAS > SORA
SORB *n* any of various
related trees, esp the
mountain ash ▷ *vb* absorb
or adsorb
SORBABLE > SORB
SORBARIA *n* Asian shrub
SORBARIAS > SORBARIA
SORBATE *n* salt of sorbic
acid
SORBATES > SORBATE
SORBED > SORB
SORBENT > SORB
SORBENTS > SORB
SORBET *same as*
> SHERBET
SORBETS > SORBET
SORBIC > SORB
SORBING > SORB
SORBITAN *n* any of a
group of compounds
derived from sorbitol
SORBITANS > SORBITAN
SORBITE *n* mineral found
in steel
SORBITES > SORBITE
SORBITIC > SORBITE
SORBITISE *same as*
> SORBITIZE
SORBITIZE *vb* turn metal
into form containing
sorbite
SORBITOL *n* white
water-soluble crystalline
alcohol with a sweet taste
SORBITOLS > SORBITOL
SORBO *n* as in *sorbo rubber*
spongy form of rubber
SORBOSE *n* sugar derived
from the berries of the
mountain ash
SORBOSES > SORBOSE
SORBS > SORB
SORBUS *n* rowan or
related tree
SORBUSES > SORBUS
SORCERER *n* magician
SORCERERS > SORCERER
SORCERESS *same as*
> SORCERER
SORCERIES > SORCERY
SORCEROUS > SORCERY
SORCERY *n* witchcraft or
magic
SORD *n* flock of mallard
ducks ▷ *vb* ascend in flight
SORDA *n* deaf woman
SORDED > SORD
SORDES *pl n* dark
incrustations on the lips
and teeth of patients with
prolonged fever
SORDID *adj* dirty, squalid
SORDIDER > SORDID
SORDIDEST > SORDID
SORDIDLY > SORDID
SORDINE *same as*
> SORDINO
SORDINES > SORDINE
SORDING > SORD
SORDINI > SORDINO

SORDINO *n* mute for a
stringed or brass musical
instrument
SORDO *n* deaf man
SORDOR *n* sordidness
SORDORS > SORDOR
SORDS > SORD
SORE *adj* painful
▷ *n* painful area on the
body ▷ *adv* greatly
▷ *vb* make sore
SORED > SORE
SOREDIA > SOREDIUM
SOREDIAL > SOREDIUM
SOREDIATE > SOREDIUM
SOREDIUM *n* organ of
vegetative reproduction in
lichens
SOREE *same as* > SORA
SOREES > SOREE
SOREHEAD *n* peevish or
disgruntled person
SOREHEADS > SOREHEAD
SOREHON *n* old Irish feudal
right
SOREHONS > SOREHON
SOREL *variant of* > SORREL
SORELL *same as* > SORREL
SORELLS > SORELL
SORELS > SOREL
SORELY *adv* greatly
SORENESS > SORE
SORER > SORE
SORES > SORE
SOREST > SORE
SOREX *n* shrew or related
animal
SOREXES > SOREX
SORGHO *same as* > SORGO
SORGHOS > SORGHO
SORGHUM *n* kind of grass
cultivated for grain
SORGHUMS > SORGHUM
SORGO *n* any of several
varieties of sorghum that
have watery sweet juice
SORGOS > SORGO
SORI > SORUS
SORICINE *adj* of or
resembling a shrew
SORICOID *same as*
> SORICINE
SORING > SORE
SORINGS > SORE
SORITES *n* type of
syllogism in which only
the final conclusion is
stated
SORITIC > SORITES
SORITICAL > SORITES
SORN *vb* obtain food, etc,
from another person by
presuming on his or her
generosity
SORNED > SORN
SORNER > SORN
SORNERS > SORE
SORNING > SORN
SORNINGS > SORN
SORNS > SORN
SOROBAN *n* Japanese
abacus
SOROBANS > SOROBAN

SOROCHE *n* altitude
sickness
SOROCHES > SOROCHE
SORORAL *adj* of sister
SORORALLY > SORORAL
SORORATE *n* custom in
some societies of a
widower marrying his
deceased wife's younger
sister
SORORATES > SORORATE
SORORIAL *same as*
> SORORAL
SORORISE *same as*
> SORORIZE
SORORISED > SORORISE
SORORISES > SORORISE
SORORITY *n* society for
female students
SORORIZE *vb* socialize in
sisterly way
SORORIZED > SORORIZE
SORORIZES > SORORIZE
SOROSES > SOROSIS
SOROSIS *n* fleshy multiple
fruit
SOROSISES > SOROSIS
SORPTION *n* process in
which one substance takes
up or holds another
SORPTIONS > SORPTION
SORPTIVE > SORPTION
SORRA *Irish word for*
> SORROW
SORRAS > SORRA
SORREL *n* bitter-tasting
plant
SORRELS > SORREL
SORRIER > SORRY
SORRIEST > SORRY
SORRILY > SORRY
SORRINESS > SORRY
SORROW *n* grief or sadness
▷ *vb* grieve
SORROWED > SORROW
SORROWER > SORROW
SORROWERS > SORROW
SORROWFUL > SORROW
SORROWING > SORROW
SORROWS > SORROW
SORRY *adj* feeling pity or
regret ▷ *interj* exclamation
expressing apology or
asking someone to repeat
what he or she has said
SORRYISH > SORRY
SORT *n* group all sharing
certain qualities or
characteristics ▷ *vb*
arrange according
to kind
SORTA *adv* phonetic
representation of 'sort of'
SORTABLE > SORT
SORTABLY > SORT
SORTAL *n* type of logical or
linguistic concept
SORTALS > SORTAL
SORTANCE *n* suitableness
SORTANCES > SORTANCE
SORTATION *n* act of
sorting
SORTED *interj* exclamation
of satisfaction, approval,

etc ▷ *adj* possessing the desired recreational drugs
SORTER > SORT
SORTERS > SORT
SORTES *n* divination by opening book at random
SORTIE *n* relatively short return trip ▷ *vb* make a sortie
SORTIED > SORTIE
SORTIEING > SORTIE
SORTIES > SORTIE
SORTILEGE *n* act or practice of divination by drawing lots
SORTILEGY *same as* > SORTILEGE
SORTING > SORT
SORTINGS > SORT
SORTITION *n* act of casting lots
SORTMENT *n* assortment
SORTMENTS > SORTMENT
SORTS > SORT
SORUS *n* cluster of sporangia on the undersurface of certain fern leaves
SOS > SO
SOSATIE *n* skewer of curried meat pieces
SOSATIES > SOSATIE
SOSS *vb* make dirty or muddy
SOSSED > SOSS
SOSSES > SOSS
SOSSING > SOSS
SOSSINGS > SOSS
SOSTENUTI > SOSTENUTO
SOSTENUTO *adv* to be performed in a smooth sustained manner
SOT *n* habitual drunkard ▷ *adv* indeed: used to contradict a negative statement ▷ *vb* be a drunkard
SOTERIAL *adj* of salvation
SOTH *archaic variant of* > SOOTH
SOTHS > SOTH
SOTOL *n* American plant related to agave
SOTOLS > SOTOL
SOTS > SOT
SOTTED > SOT
SOTTEDLY > SOT
SOTTING > SOT
SOTTINGS > SOT
SOTTISH > SOT
SOTTISHLY > SOT
SOTTISIER *n* collection of jokes
SOU *n* former French coin
SOUARI *n* tree of tropical America
SOUARIS > SOUARI
SOUBISE *n* purée of onions mixed into a thick white sauce and served over eggs, fish, etc
SOUBISES > SOUBISE

SOUBRETTE *n* minor female role in comedy, often that of a pert maid
SOUCAR *n* Indian banker
SOUCARS > SOUCAR
SOUCE *same as* > SOUSE
SOUCED > SOUCE
SOUCES > SOUCE
SOUCHONG *n* black tea with large leaves
SOUCHONGS > SOUCHONG
SOUCING > SOUCE
SOUCT > SOUCE
SOUDAN *obsolete variant of* > SULTAN
SOUDANS > SOUDAN
SOUFFLE *n* light fluffy dish made with beaten egg whites ▷ *adj* made light and puffy
SOUFFLED > SOUFFLE
SOUFFLEED > SOUFFLE
SOUFFLES > SOUFFLE
SOUGH *vb* (of the wind) make a sighing sound ▷ *n* soft continuous murmuring sound
SOUGHED > SOUGH
SOUGHING > SOUGH
SOUGHS > SOUGH
SOUGHT > SEEK
SOUK *same as* > SOOK
SOUKED > SOUK
SOUKING > SOUK
SOUKOUS *n* style of African popular music
SOUKOUSES > SOUKOUS
SOUKS > SOUK
SOUL *n* spiritual and immortal part of a human being
SOULDAN *same as* > SOLDAN
SOULDANS > SOULDAN
SOULDIER *same as* > SOLDIER
SOULDIERS > SOULDIER
SOULED *adj* having soul
SOULFUL *adj* full of emotion
SOULFULLY > SOULFUL
SOULLESS *adj* lacking human qualities, mechanical
SOULLIKE *adj* resembling a soul
SOULMATE *n* person with whom one has most affinity
SOULMATES > SOULMATE
SOULS > SOUL
SOULSTER *n* soul music singer
SOULSTERS > SOULSTER
SOUM *vb* decide how many animals can graze particular pasture
SOUMED > SOUM
SOUMING > SOUM
SOUMINGS > SOUM
SOUMS > SOUM
SOUND *n* something heard, noise ▷ *vb* make or cause

to make a sound ▷ *adj* in good condition ▷ *adv* soundly
SOUNDABLE > SOUND
SOUNDBITE *n* short pithy sentence or phrase extracted from a longer speech
SOUNDBOX *n* resonating chamber of the hollow body of a violin, guitar, etc
SOUNDCARD *n* component giving computer sound effects
SOUNDED > SOUND
SOUNDER *n* device formerly used to convert electric signals into sounds
SOUNDERS > SOUNDER
SOUNDEST > SOUND
SOUNDING *adj* resounding
SOUNDINGS > SOUNDING
SOUNDLESS *adj* extremely still or silent
SOUNDLY > SOUND
SOUNDMAN *n* sound recorder in television crew
SOUNDMEN > SOUNDMAN
SOUNDNESS > SOUND
SOUNDPOST *n* small post on guitars, violins, etc, that joins the front surface to the back and allows the whole body of the instrument to vibrate
SOUNDS > SOUND
SOUP *n* liquid food made from meat, vegetables, etc ▷ *vb* give soup to
SOUPCON *n* small amount
SOUPCONS > SOUPCON
SOUPED > SOUP
SOUPER *n* person dispensing soup
SOUPERS > SOUPER
SOUPFIN *n* Pacific requiem shark valued for its fins
SOUPFINS > SOUPFIN
SOUPIER > SOUPY
SOUPIEST > SOUPY
SOUPILY *adv* in a soupy manner
SOUPING > SOUP
SOUPLE *same as* > SUPPLE
SOUPLED > SOUPLE
SOUPLES > SOUPLE
SOUPLESS > SOUP
SOUPLIKE > SOUP
SOUPLING > SOUPLE
SOUPS > SOUP
SOUPSPOON *n* spoon for eating soup
SOUPY *adj* having the appearance or consistency of soup
SOUR *adj* sharp-tasting ▷ *vb* make or become sour
SOURBALL *n* tart-flavoured boiled sweet
SOURBALLS > SOURBALL
SOURCE *n* origin or starting point

▷ *vb* establish a supplier of (a product, etc)
SOURCED > SOURCE
SOURCEFUL *adj* offering useful things
SOURCES > SOURCE
SOURCING > SOURCE
SOURCINGS > SOURCE
SOURDINE *n* soft stop on an organ or harmonium
SOURDINES > SOURDINE
SOURDOUGH *adj* (of bread) made with fermented dough used as a leaven ▷ *n* (in Western US, Canada, and Alaska) an old-time prospector or pioneer
SOURED > SOUR
SOURER > SOUR
SOUREST > SOUR
SOURGUM *n* tree of eastern N America
SOURGUMS > SOURGUM
SOURING > SOUR
SOURINGS > SOUR
SOURISH > SOUR
SOURISHLY > SOUR
SOURLY > SOUR
SOURNESS > SOUR
SOUROCK *n* Scots word for sorrel plant
SOUROCKS > SOUROCK
SOURPUSS *n* person who is always gloomy, pessimistic, or bitter
SOURS > SOUR
SOURSE *same as* > SOURCE
SOURSES > SOURSE
SOURSOP *n* small West Indian tree
SOURSOPS > SOURSOP
SOURVELD *n* grazing field with long coarse grass
SOURVELDS > SOURVELD
SOURWOOD *n* sorrel tree
SOURWOODS > SOURWOOD
SOUS > SOU
SOUSE *vb* plunge (something) into liquid ▷ *n* liquid used in pickling
SOUSED > SOUSE
SOUSER *n* person who frequently gets drunk
SOUSERS > SOUSER
SOUSES > SOUSE
SOUSING > SOUSE
SOUSINGS > SOUSE
SOUSLIK *same as* > SUSLIK
SOUSLIKS > SOUSLIK
SOUT *same as* > SOOT
SOUTACHE *n* narrow braid used as a decorative trimming
SOUTACHES > SOUTACHE
SOUTANE *n* Roman Catholic priest's cassock
SOUTANES > SOUTANE
SOUTAR *same as* > SOUTER
SOUTARS > SOUTAR
SOUTENEUR *n* pimp

SOUTER n shoemaker or cobbler
SOUTERLY > SOUTER
SOUTERS > SOUTER
SOUTH n direction towards the South Pole, opposite north ▷ adj or in the south ▷ adv in, to, or towards the south ▷ vb turn south
SOUTHEAST adv (in or to) direction between south and east ▷ n point of the compass or the direction midway between south and east ▷ adj of or denoting the southeastern part of a specified country, area, etc
SOUTHED > SOUTH
SOUTHER n strong wind or storm from the south ▷ vb turn south
SOUTHERED > SOUTHER
SOUTHERLY adj of or in the south ▷ adv towards the south ▷ n wind from the south
SOUTHERN adj situated in or towards the south ▷ n southerner
SOUTHERNS > SOUTHERN
SOUTHERS > SOUTHER
SOUTHING n movement, deviation, or distance covered in a southerly direction
SOUTHINGS > SOUTHING
SOUTHLAND n southern part of country
SOUTHMOST adj situated or occurring farthest south
SOUTHPAW n left-handed person, esp a boxer ▷ adj left-handed
SOUTHPAWS > SOUTHPAW
SOUTHRON n southerner
SOUTHRONS > SOUTHRON
SOUTHS > SOUTH
SOUTHSAID > SOUTHSAY
SOUTHSAY same as **>** SOOTHSAY
SOUTHSAYS > SOUTHSAY
SOUTHWARD adv towards the south
SOUTHWEST adv (in or to) direction between south and west ▷ n point of the compass or the direction midway between west and south ▷ adj of or denoting the southwestern part of a specified country, area, etc
SOUTIE same as **>** SOUTPIEL
SOUTIES > SOUTIE
SOUTPIEL n South African derogatory slang for an English-speaking South African
SOUTPIELS > SOUTPIEL
SOUTS > SOUT
SOUVENIR n keepsake, memento ▷ vb steal or

keep (something, esp a small article) for one's own use
SOUVENIRS > SOUVENIR
SOUVLAKI same as **>** SOUVLAKIA
SOUVLAKIA n Greek dish of kebabs, esp made with lamb
SOUVLAKIS > SOUVLAKI
SOV shortening of **>** SOVEREIGN
SOVENANCE n memory
SOVEREIGN n king or queen ▷ adj (of a state) independent
SOVIET n formerly, elected council in the USSR ▷ adj of the former USSR
SOVIETIC > SOVIET
SOVIETISE same as **>** SOVIETIZE
SOVIETISM n principle or practice of government through soviets
SOVIETIST > SOVIETISM
SOVIETIZE vb bring (a country, person, etc) under Soviet control or influence
SOVIETS > SOVIET
SOVKHOZ n large mechanized farm in former USSR
SOVKHOZES > SOVKHOZ
SOVKHOZY > SOVKHOZ
SOVRAN literary word for **>** SOVEREIGN
SOVRANLY > SOVRAN
SOVRANS > SOVRAN
SOVRANTY > SOVRAN
SOVS > SOV
SOW vb scatter or plant (seed) in or on (the ground) ▷ n female adult pig
SOWABLE > SOW
SOWANS same as **>** SOWENS
SOWAR n Indian cavalryman
SOWARREE n Indian mounted escort
SOWARREES > SOWARREE
SOWARRIES > SOWARRY
SOWARRY same as **>** SOWARREE
SOWARS > SOWAR
SOWBACK another name for **>** HOGBACK
SOWBACKS > SOWBACK
SOWBELLY n salt pork from pig's belly
SOWBREAD n S European primulaceous plant
SOWBREADS > SOWBREAD
SOWBUG n (in N America) woodlouse
SOWBUGS > SOWBUG
SOWCAR same as **>** SOUCAR
SOWCARS > SOWCAR
SOWCE same as **>** SOUSE
SOWCED > SOWCE
SOWCES > SOWCE

SOWCING > SOWCE
SOWDER same as **>** SAWDER
SOWDERS > SOWDER
SOWED > SOW
SOWENS n pudding made from oatmeal husks steeped and boiled
SOWER > SOW
SOWERS > SOW
SOWF same as **>** SOWTH
SOWFED > SOWF
SOWFF same as **>** SOWTH
SOWFFED > SOWFF
SOWFFING > SOWFF
SOWFFS > SOWFF
SOWFING > SOWF
SOWFS > SOWF
SOWING > SOW
SOWINGS > SOW
SOWL same as **>** SOLE
SOWLE same as **>** SOLE
SOWLED > SOWL
SOWLES > SOWLE
SOWLING > SOWL
SOWLS > SOWL
SOWM same as **>** SOUM
SOWMED > SOWM
SOWMING > SOWM
SOWMS > SOWM
SOWN > SOW
SOWND vb wield
SOWNDED > SOWND
SOWNDING > SOWND
SOWNDS > SOWND
SOWNE same as **>** SOUND
SOWNES > SOWNE
SOWP n spoonful ▷ vb soak
SOWPED > SOWP
SOWPING > SOWP
SOWPS > SOWP
SOWS > SOW
SOWSE same as **>** SOUSE
SOWSED > SOWSE
SOWSES > SOWSE
SOWSING > SOWSE
SOWSSE same as **>** SOUSE
SOWSSED > SOWSSE
SOWSSES > SOWSSE
SOWSSING > SOWSSE
SOWTER same as **>** SOUTER
SOWTERS > SOWTER
SOWTH vb Scots word meaning whistle
SOWTHED > SOWTH
SOWTHING > SOWTH
SOWTHS > SOWTH
SOX pl n informal spelling of 'socks'
SOY n as in soy sauce salty dark brown sauce made from soya beans
SOYA n plant whose edible bean is used for food and as a source of oil
SOYAS > SOYA
SOYBEAN n soya bean
SOYBEANS > SOYBEAN
SOYLE n body ▷ vb elucidate
SOYLED > SOYLE
SOYLES > SOYLE
SOYLING > SOYLE

SOYMEAL n foodstuff made from soybeans
SOYMEALS > SOYMEAL
SOYMILK n milk substitute made from soya
SOYMILKS > SOYMILK
SOYS > SOY
SOYUZ n Russian spacecraft
SOYUZES > SOYUZ
SOZ interj (slang) sorry
SOZIN n form of protein
SOZINE same as **>** SOZIN
SOZINES > SOZINE
SOZINS > SOZIN
SOZZLE vb make wet
SOZZLED adj drunk
SOZZLES > SOZZLE
SOZZLIER > SOZZLY
SOZZLIEST > SOZZLY
SOZZLING > SOZZLE
SOZZLY adj wet
SPA n resort with a mineral-water spring ▷ vb visit a spa
SPACE n unlimited expanse in which all objects exist and move ▷ vb place at intervals
SPACEBAND n device on a linecaster for evening up the spaces between words
SPACED > SPACE
SPACELAB n laboratory in space where scientific experiments are performed
SPACELABS > SPACELAB
SPACELESS adj having no limits in space
SPACEMAN n person who travels in space
SPACEMEN > SPACEMAN
SPACEPORT n base equipped to launch, maintain, and test spacecraft
SPACER n piece of material used to create or maintain a space between two things
SPACERS > SPACER
SPACES > SPACE
SPACESHIP n (in science fiction) a spacecraft used for travel between planets and galaxies
SPACESUIT n sealed pressurized suit worn by an astronaut
SPACEWALK n instance of floating and manoeuvring in space, outside but attached by a lifeline to a spacecraft ▷ vb float and manoeuvre in space while outside but attached to a spacecraft
SPACEWARD adv into space
SPACEY adj vague and dreamy, as if under the influence of drugs

SPACIAL same as
> SPATIAL
SPACIALLY > SPACIAL
SPACIER > SPACEY
SPACIEST > SPACEY
SPACINESS > SPACEY
SPACING n arrangement
of letters, words, etc, on a
page in order to achieve
legibility
SPACINGS > SPACING
SPACIOUS adj having a
large capacity or area
SPACKLE vb fill holes in
plaster
SPACKLED > SPACKLE
SPACKLES > SPACKLE
SPACKLING > SPACKLE
SPACY same as > SPACEY
SPADASSIN n
swordsman
SPADE n tool for digging
SPADED > SPADE
SPADEFISH n type of
spiny-finned food fish
SPADEFUL n amount
spade will hold
SPADEFULS > SPADEFUL
SPADELIKE > SPADE
SPADEMAN n man who
works with spade
SPADEMEN > SPADEMAN
SPADER > SPADE
SPADERS > SPADE
SPADES > SPADE
SPADESMAN same as
> SPADEMAN
SPADESMEN > SPADEMAN
SPADEWORK n hard
preparatory work
SPADGER n sparrow
SPADGERS > SPADGER
SPADICES > SPADIX
SPADILLE n (in ombre
and quadrille) the ace of
spades
SPADILLES > SPADILLE
SPADILLIO same as
> SPADILLE
SPADILLO same as
> SPADILLE
SPADILLOS > SPADILLO
SPADING > SPADE
SPADIX n spike of small
flowers on a fleshy stem
SPADIXES > SPADIX
SPADO n neutered animal
SPADOES > SPADO
SPADONES > SPADO
SPADOS > SPADO
SPADROON n type of
sword
SPADROONS > SPADROON
SPAE vb foretell (the
future)
SPAED > SPAE
SPAEING > SPAE
SPAEINGS > SPAE
SPAEMAN n man who
foretells future
SPAEMEN > SPAEMAN
SPAER > SPAE
SPAERS > SPAE

SPAES > SPAE
SPAETZLE n German
noodle dish
SPAETZLES > SPAETZLE
SPAEWIFE n woman who
can supposedly foretell the
future
SPAEWIVES > SPAEWIFE
SPAG vb (of a cat) to
scratch (a person) with the
claws ▷ n Australian
offensive slang for an
Italian
SPAGERIC same as
> SPAGYRIC
SPAGGED > SPAG
SPAGGING > SPAG
SPAGHETTI n pasta in the
form of long strings
SPAGIRIC same as
> SPAGYRIC
SPAGIRIST n an
alchemist
SPAGS > SPAG
SPAGYRIC adj of or
relating to alchemy ▷ n
alchemist
SPAGYRICS > SPAGYRIC
SPAGYRIST > SPAGYRIC
SPAHEE same as > SPAHI
SPAHEES > SPAHEE
SPAHI n (formerly) an
irregular cavalryman in
the Turkish armed forces
SPAHIS > SPAHI
SPAIL Scots word for
> SPALL
SPAILS > SPAIL
SPAIN variant of > SPANE
SPAINED > SPAIN
SPAING > SPA
SPAINGS > SPA
SPAINING > SPAIN
SPAINS > SPAIN
SPAIRGE Scots word for
> SPARGE
SPAIRGED > SPAIRGE
SPAIRGES > SPAIRGE
SPAIRGING > SPAIRGE
SPAIT same as > SPATE
SPAITS > SPAIT
SPAKE past tense of
> SPEAK
SPALD same as > SPAULD
SPALDEEN n ball used in
street game
SPALDEENS > SPALDEEN
SPALDS > SPALD
SPALE Scots word for
> SPALL
SPALES > SPALE
SPALL n splinter or chip of
ore, rock, or stone ▷ vb
split or cause to split into
such fragments
SPALLABLE > SPALL
SPALLE same as > SPAULD
SPALLED > SPALL
SPALLER > SPALL
SPALLERS > SPALL
SPALLES > SPALLE
SPALLING > SPALL
SPALLINGS > SPALL

SPALLS > SPALL
SPALPEEN n itinerant
seasonal labourer
SPALPEENS > SPALPEEN
SPALT vb split
SPALTED > SPALT
SPALTING > SPALT
SPALTS > SPALT
SPAM vb send unsolicited
e-mail simultaneously to
a number of newsgroups
on the internet ▷ n
unsolicited electronic mail
or text messages sent in
this way
SPAMBOT n computer
program that sends spam
SPAMBOTS > SPAMBOT
SPAMMED > SPAM
SPAMMER > SPAM
SPAMMERS > SPAM
SPAMMIE n love bite
SPAMMIER > SPAMMY
SPAMMIES > SPAMMIE
SPAMMIEST > SPAMMY
SPAMMING > SPAM
SPAMMINGS > SPAM
SPAMMY adj bland
SPAMS > SPAM
SPAN n space between two
points ▷ vb stretch or
extend across
SPANAEMIA n lack of red
corpuscles in blood
SPANAEMIC
> SPANAEMIA
SPANCEL n length of rope
for hobbling an animal
▷ vb hobble (an animal)
with a loose rope
SPANCELED > SPANCEL
SPANCELS > SPANCEL
SPANDEX n type of
synthetic stretch fabric
made from polyurethane
fibre
SPANDEXED adj wearing
spandex
SPANDEXES > SPANDEX
SPANDREL n triangular
surface bounded by the
outer curve of an arch and
the adjacent wall
SPANDRELS > SPANDREL
SPANDRIL same as
> SPANDREL
SPANDRILS > SPANDRIL
SPANE vb Scots word
meaning wean
SPANED > SPANE
SPANES > SPANE
SPANG adv exactly, firmly,
or straight ▷ vb dash
SPANGED > SPANG
SPANGHEW vb throw in air
SPANGHEWS > SPANGHEW
SPANGING > SPANG
SPANGLE n small shiny
metallic ornament
▷ vb decorate with
spangles
SPANGLED > SPANGLE
SPANGLER > SPANGLE
SPANGLERS > SPANGLE

SPANGLES > SPANGLE
SPANGLET n little spangle
SPANGLETS > SPANGLET
SPANGLIER > SPANGLE
SPANGLING > SPANGLE
SPANGLY > SPANGLE
SPANGS > SPANG
SPANIEL n dog with long
ears and silky hair
SPANIELS > SPANIEL
SPANING > SPANE
SPANK vb slap with the
open hand, on the
buttocks or legs ▷ n such
a slap
SPANKED > SPANK
SPANKER n fore-and-aft
sail or a mast that is
aftermost in a sailing
vessel
SPANKERS > SPANKER
SPANKING adj
outstandingly fine or
smart ▷ n series of spanks,
usually as a punishment
for children
SPANKINGS > SPANKING
SPANKS > SPANK
SPANLESS adj impossible
to span
SPANNED > SPAN
SPANNER n tool for
gripping and turning a nut
or bolt
SPANNERS > SPANNER
SPANNING > SPAN
SPANS > SPAN
SPANSPEK n cantaloupe
melon
SPANSPEKS > SPANSPEK
SPANSULE n modified-
release capsule of a drug
SPANSULES > SPANSULE
SPANWORM n larva of a
type of moth
SPANWORMS > SPANWORM
SPAR n pole used as a ship's
mast, boom, or yard
▷ vb box or fight using light
blows for practice
SPARABLE n small nail
with no head, used for
fixing the soles and heels
of shoes
SPARABLES > SPARABLE
SPARAXIS n type of plant
with dainty spikes of
star-shaped purple, red, or
orange flowers
SPARD > SPARE
SPARE adj extra ▷ n
duplicate kept in case
of damage or loss
▷ vb refrain from
punishing or harming
SPAREABLE > SPARE
SPARED > SPARE
SPARELESS adj merciless
SPARELY > SPARE
SPARENESS > SPARE
SPARER > SPARE
SPARERIB n cut of pork
ribs with most of the meat
trimmed off

S

SPARERIBS > SPARERIB
SPARERS > SPARE
SPARES > SPARE
SPAREST > SPARE
SPARGE vb sprinkle or scatter (something)
SPARGED > SPARGE
SPARGER > SPARGE
SPARGERS > SPARGE
SPARGES > SPARGE
SPARGING > SPARGE
SPARID n type of marine percoid fish ▷ adj of or belonging to this family of fish
SPARIDS > SPARID
SPARING adj economical
SPARINGLY > SPARING
SPARK n fiery particle thrown out from a fire or caused by friction ▷ vb give off sparks
SPARKE n weapon
SPARKED > SPARK
SPARKER > SPARK
SPARKERS > SPARK
SPARKES > SPARKE
SPARKIE n electrician
SPARKIER > SPARKY
SPARKIES > SPARKIE
SPARKIEST > SPARKY
SPARKILY > SPARKY
SPARKING > SPARK
SPARKISH > SPARK
SPARKLE vb glitter with many points of light ▷ n sparkling points of light
SPARKLED > SPARKLE
SPARKLER n hand-held firework that emits sparks
SPARKLERS > SPARKLER
SPARKLES > SPARKLE
SPARKLESS > SPARK
SPARKLET n little spark
SPARKLETS > SPARKLET
SPARKLIER > SPARKLY
SPARKLIES > SPARKLY
SPARKLING adj (of wine or mineral water) slightly fizzy
SPARKLY adj sparkling ▷ n sparkling thing
SPARKPLUG n device in an engine that ignites the fuel
SPARKS n electrician
SPARKY adj lively
SPARLIKE > SPAR
SPARLING n European smelt
SPARLINGS > SPARLING
SPAROID same as > SPARID
SPAROIDS > SPAROID
SPARRE same as > SPAR
SPARRED > SPAR
SPARRER > SPAR
SPARRERS > SPAR
SPARRES > SPARRE
SPARRIER > SPARRY
SPARRIEST > SPARRY
SPARRING > SPAR
SPARRINGS > SPAR

SPARROW n small brownish bird
SPARROWS > SPARROW
SPARRY adj (of minerals) containing, relating to, or resembling spar
SPARS > SPAR
SPARSE adj thinly scattered
SPARSEDLY > SPARSE
SPARSELY > SPARSE
SPARSER > SPARSE
SPARSEST > SPARSE
SPARSITY > SPARSE
SPART n esparto
SPARTAN adj strict and austere ▷ n disciplined or brave person
SPARTANS > SPARTAN
SPARTEINE n viscous oily alkaloid extracted from the broom plant and lupin seeds
SPARTERIE n things made from esparto
SPARTH n type of battle-axe
SPARTHE same as > SPARTH
SPARTHES > SPARTHE
SPARTHS > SPARTH
SPARTICLE n hypothetical elementary particle thought to have been produced in the Big Bang
SPARTINA n grass growing in salt marshes
SPARTINAS > SPARTINA
SPARTS > SPART
SPAS > SPA
SPASM n involuntary muscular contraction ▷ vb go into spasm
SPASMATIC > SPASM
SPASMED > SPASM
SPASMIC > SPASM
SPASMING > SPASM
SPASMODIC adj occurring in spasms
SPASMS > SPASM
SPASTIC n offensive slang for a person with cerebral palsy ▷ adj suffering from cerebral palsy
SPASTICS > SPASTIC
SPAT vb have a quarrel
SPATE n large number of things happening within a period of time
SPATES > SPATE
SPATFALL n mass of larvae on sea bed
SPATFALLS > SPATFALL
SPATHAL > SPATHE
SPATHE n large sheathlike leaf enclosing a flower cluster
SPATHED > SPATHE
SPATHES > SPATHE
SPATHIC adj (of minerals) resembling spar
SPATHOSE same as > SPATHIC

SPATIAL adj of or in space
SPATIALLY > SPATIAL
SPATLESE n type of German wine, usu white
SPATLESEN > SPATLESE
SPATLESES > SPATLESE
SPATS > SPAT
SPATTED > SPAT
SPATTEE n type of gaiter
SPATTEES > SPATTEE
SPATTER vb scatter or be scattered in drops over (something) ▷ n spattering sound
SPATTERED > SPATTER
SPATTERS > SPATTER
SPATTING > SPIT
SPATULA n utensil with a broad flat blade for spreading or stirring
SPATULAR > SPATULA
SPATULAS > SPATULA
SPATULATE adj shaped like a spatula
SPATULE n spatula
SPATULES > SPATULE
SPATZLE same as > SPAETZLE
SPATZLES > SPATZLE
SPAUL same as > SPAULD
SPAULD n shoulder
SPAULDS > SPAULD
SPAULS > SPAUL
SPAVIE Scots variant of > SPAVIN
SPAVIES > SPAVIE
SPAVIET adj Scots word meaning spavined
SPAVIN n enlargement of the hock of a horse by a bony growth
SPAVINED adj affected with spavin
SPAVINS > SPAVIN
SPAW same as > SPA
SPAWL vb spit
SPAWLED > SPAWL
SPAWLING > SPAWL
SPAWLS > SPAWL
SPAWN n jelly-like mass of eggs of fish, frogs, or molluscs ▷ vb (of fish, frogs, or molluscs) lay eggs
SPAWNED > SPAWN
SPAWNER > SPAWN
SPAWNERS > SPAWN
SPAWNIER > SPAWNY
SPAWNIEST > SPAWNY
SPAWNING > SPAWN
SPAWNINGS > SPAWN
SPAWNS > SPAWN
SPAWNY adj like spawn
SPAWS > SPAW
SPAY vb remove the ovaries from (a female animal)
SPAYAD n male deer
SPAYADS > SPAYAD
SPAYD same as > SPAYAD
SPAYDS > SPAYD
SPAYED > SPAY
SPAYING > SPAY
SPAYS > SPAY

SPAZ vb offensive slang meaning lose self-control
SPAZA adj as in spaza shop South African slang for a small shop in a township
SPAZZ same as > SPAZ
SPAZZED > SPAZ
SPAZZES > SPAZ
SPAZZING > SPAZ
SPEAK vb say words, talk
SPEAKABLE > SPEAK
SPEAKEASY n place where alcoholic drink was sold illegally during Prohibition
SPEAKER n person who speaks, esp at a formal occasion
SPEAKERS > SPEAKER
SPEAKING > SPEAK
SPEAKINGS > SPEAK
SPEAKOUT n firm or brave statement of one's beliefs
SPEAKOUTS > SPEAKOUT
SPEAKS > SPEAK
SPEAL same as > SPULE
SPEALS > SPEAL
SPEAN same as > SPANE
SPEANED > SPEAN
SPEANING > SPEAN
SPEANS > SPEAN
SPEAR n weapon consisting of a long shaft with a sharp point ▷ vb pierce with or as if with a spear
SPEARED > SPEAR
SPEARER > SPEAR
SPEARERS > SPEAR
SPEARFISH another name for > MARLIN
SPEARGUN n device for shooting spears underwater
SPEARGUNS > SPEARGUN
SPEARHEAD vb lead (an attack or campaign) ▷ n leading force in an attack or campaign
SPEARIER > SPEAR
SPEARIEST > SPEAR
SPEARING n act of spearing
SPEARINGS > SPEARING
SPEARLIKE > SPEAR
SPEARMAN n soldier armed with a spear
SPEARMEN > SPEARMAN
SPEARMINT n type of mint
SPEARS > SPEAR
SPEARWORT n any of several Eurasian ranunculaceous plants
SPEARY > SPEAR
SPEAT same as > SPATE
SPEATS > SPEAT
SPEC vb set specifications
SPECCED > SPEC
SPECCIER > SPECCY
SPECCIES > SPECCY
SPECCIEST > SPECCY
SPECCING > SPEC

SPECCY n person wearing spectacles ▷ adj wearing spectacles

SPECIAL adj distinguished from others of its kind ▷ n product, programme, etc which is only available at a certain time ▷ vb advertise and sell (an item) at a reduced price

SPECIALER > SPECIAL

SPECIALLY > SPECIAL

SPECIALS > SPECIAL

SPECIALTY n special interest or skill

SPECIATE vb form or develop into a new biological species

SPECIATED > SPECIATE

SPECIATES > SPECIATE

SPECIE n coins as distinct from paper money

SPECIES n group of plants or animals that are related closely enough to interbreed naturally

SPECIFIC adj particular, definite ▷ n drug used to treat a particular disease

SPECIFICS > SPECIFIC

SPECIFIED > SPECIFY

SPECIFIER > SPECIFY

SPECIFIES > SPECIFY

SPECIFY vb refer to or state specifically

SPECIMEN n individual or part typifying a whole

SPECIMENS > SPECIMEN

SPECIOUS adj apparently true, but actually false

SPECK n small spot or particle ▷ vb mark with specks or spots

SPECKED > SPECK

SPECKIER > SPECKY

SPECKIES > SPECKY

SPECKIEST > SPECKY

SPECKING > SPECK

SPECKLE n small spot ▷ vb mark with speckles

SPECKLED > SPECKLE

SPECKLES > SPECKLE

SPECKLESS > SPECK

SPECKLING > SPECKLE

SPECKS > SPECK

SPECKY same as > SPECCY

SPECS pl n spectacles

SPECT vb expect

SPECTACLE n strange, interesting, or ridiculous sight

SPECTATE vb watch

SPECTATED > SPECTATE

SPECTATES > SPECTATE

SPECTATOR n person viewing anything, onlooker

SPECTED > SPECT

SPECTER same as > SPECTRE

SPECTERS > SPECTER

SPECTING > SPECT

SPECTRA > SPECTRUM

SPECTRAL adj of or like a spectre

SPECTRE n ghost

SPECTRES > SPECTRE

SPECTRIN n any one of a class of fibrous proteins found in the membranes of red blood cells

SPECTRINS > SPECTRIN

SPECTRUM n range of different colours, radio waves, etc in order of their wavelengths

SPECTRUMS > SPECTRUM

SPECTS > SPECT

SPECULA > SPECULUM

SPECULAR adj of, relating to, or having the properties of a mirror

SPECULATE vb guess, conjecture

SPECULUM n medical instrument for examining body cavities

SPECULUMS > SPECULUM

SPED > SPEED

SPEECH n act, power, or manner of speaking ▷ vb make a speech

SPEECHED > SPEECH

SPEECHES > SPEECH

SPEECHFUL > SPEECH

SPEECHIFY vb make speeches, esp boringly

SPEECHING > SPEECH

SPEED n swiftness ▷ vb go quickly

SPEEDBALL n mixture of heroin with amphetamine or cocaine

SPEEDBOAT n light fast motorboat

SPEEDED > SPEED

SPEEDER > SPEED

SPEEDERS > SPEED

SPEEDFUL > SPEED

SPEEDIER > SPEEDY

SPEEDIEST > SPEEDY

SPEEDILY > SPEEDY

SPEEDING > SPEED

SPEEDINGS > SPEED

SPEEDLESS > SPEED

SPEEDO n speedometer

SPEEDOS > SPEEDO

SPEEDREAD vb read very quickly

SPEEDS > SPEED

SPEEDSTER n fast car, esp a sports model

SPEEDUP n acceleration

SPEEDUPS > SPEEDUP

SPEEDWALK n an endless conveyor belt or moving walkway used to transport standing persons from place to place

SPEEDWAY n track for motorcycle racing

SPEEDWAYS > SPEEDWAY

SPEEDWELL n plant with small blue flowers

SPEEDY adj prompt

SPEEL n splinter of wood ▷ vb Scots word meaning climb

SPEELED > SPEEL

SPEELER > SPEEL

SPEELERS > SPEEL

SPEELING > SPEEL

SPEELS > SPEEL

SPEER same as > SPEIR

SPEERED > SPEER

SPEERING > SPEER

SPEERINGS > SPEER

SPEERS > SPEER

SPEIL dialect word for > CLIMB

SPEILED > SPEIL

SPEILING > SPEIL

SPEILS > SPEIL

SPEIR vb ask

SPEIRED > SPEIR

SPEIRING > SPEIR

SPEIRINGS > SPEIR

SPEIRS > SPEIR

SPEISE same as > SPEISS

SPEISES > SPEISE

SPEISS n compounds formed when ores containing arsenic or antimony are smelted

SPEISSES > SPEISS

SPEK n bacon, fat, or fatty pork used for larding venison or other game

SPEKBOOM n South African shrub

SPEKBOOMS > SPEKBOOM

SPEKS > SPEK

SPELAEAN adj of, found in, or inhabiting caves

SPELD vb Scots word meaning spread

SPELDED > SPELD

SPELDER same as > SPELD

SPELDERED > SPELDER

SPELDERS > SPELDER

SPELDIN n fish split and dried

SPELDING same as > SPELDIN

SPELDINGS > SPELDING

SPELDINS > SPELDIN

SPELDRIN same as > SPELDIN

SPELDRING same as > SPELDIN

SPELDRINS > SPELDRIN

SPELDS > SPELD

SPELEAN same as > SPELAEAN

SPELK n splinter of wood

SPELKS > SPELK

SPELL vb give in correct order the letters that form (a word) ▷ n formula of words supposed to have magic power

SPELLABLE > SPELL

SPELLBIND vb cause to be spellbound

SPELLDOWN n spelling competition

SPELLED > SPELL

SPELLER n person who spells words in the manner specified

SPELLERS > SPELLER

SPELLFUL adj magical

SPELLICAN same as > SPILLIKIN

SPELLING > SPELL

SPELLINGS > SPELL

SPELLS > SPELL

SPELT > SPELL

SPELTER n impure zinc, usually containing about 3 per cent of lead and other impurities

SPELTERS > SPELTER

SPELTS > SPELT

SPELTZ n wheat variety

SPELTZES > SPELTZ

SPELUNK vb explore caves

SPELUNKED > SPELUNK

SPELUNKER n person whose hobby is the exploration and study of caves

SPELUNKS > SPELUNK

SPENCE n larder or pantry

SPENCER n short fitted coat or jacket

SPENCERS > SPENCER

SPENCES > SPENCE

SPEND vb pay out (money)

SPENDABLE > SPEND

SPENDALL n spendthrift

SPENDALLS > SPENDALL

SPENDER n person who spends money in a manner specified

SPENDERS > SPENDER

SPENDIER > SPENDY

SPENDIEST > SPENDY

SPENDING > SPEND

SPENDINGS > SPEND

SPENDS > SPEND

SPENDY adj expensive

SPENSE same as > SPENCE

SPENSES > SPENSE

SPENT > SPEND

SPEOS n (esp in ancient Egypt) a temple or tomb cut into a rock face

SPEOSES > SPEOS

SPERLING same as > SPARLING

SPERLINGS > SPERLING

SPERM n male reproductive cell released in semen during ejaculation

SPERMARIA pl n spermaries

SPERMARY n any organ in which spermatozoa are produced, esp a testis

SPERMATIA pl n male reproductive cells in red algae and some fungi

SPERMATIC adj of or relating to spermatozoa

SPERMATID n any of four immature male gametes that are formed from a spermatocyte

S

SPERMIC same as
> SPERMATIC
SPERMINE n colourless
basic water-soluble amine
that is found in semen,
sputum, and animal
tissues
SPERMINES > SPERMINE
SPERMOUS same as
> SPERMATIC
SPERMS > SPERM
SPERRE vb bolt
SPERRED > SPERRE
SPERRES > SPERRE
SPERRING > SPERRE
SPERSE vb disperse
SPERSED > SPERSE
SPERSES > SPERSE
SPERSING > SPERSE
SPERST > SPERSE
SPERTHE same as
> SPARTH
SPERTHES > SPERTHE
SPET same as > SPIT
SPETCH n piece of animal
skin
SPETCHED > SPETCH
SPETCHES > SPETCH
SPETCHING > SPETCH
SPETS > SPET
SPETSNAZ n Soviet
intelligence force
SPETTING > SPET
SPETZNAZ same as
· > SPETSNAZ
SPEUG n sparrow
SPEUGS > SPEUG
SPEW vb vomit ▷ n
something ejected from
the mouth
SPEWED > SPEW
SPEWER > SPEW
SPEWERS > SPEW
SPEWIER > SPEWY
SPEWIEST > SPEWY
SPEWINESS > SPEWY
SPEWING > SPEW
SPEWS > SPEW
SPEWY adj marshy
SPHACELUS n death of
living tissue
SPHAER same as > SPHERE
SPHAERE same as
> SPHERE
SPHAERES > SPHAERE
SPHAERITE n aluminium
phosphate
SPHAERS > SPHAERE
SPHAGNOUS > SPHAGNUM
SPHAGNUM n moss found
in bogs
SPHAGNUMS > SPHAGNUM
SPHAIREE n game
resembling tennis played
with wooden bats and a
perforated plastic ball
SPHAIREES > SPHAIREE
SPHEAR same as
> SPHERE
SPHEARE same as
> SPHERE
SPHEARES > SPHEARE
SPHEARS > SPHEAR

SPHENDONE n ancient
Greek headband
SPHENE n brown, yellow,
green, or grey lustrous
mineral
SPHENES > SPHENE
SPHENIC adj having the
shape of a wedge
SPHENODON technical
name for the > TUATARA
SPHENOID adj wedge-
shaped ▷ n wedge-shaped
thing
SPHENOIDS > SPHENOID
SPHERAL adj of or shaped
like a sphere
SPHERE n perfectly round
solid object ▷ vb surround
or encircle
SPHERED > SPHERE
SPHERES > SPHERE
SPHERIC same as
> SPHERICAL
SPHERICAL adj shaped
like a sphere
SPHERICS n geometry
and trigonometry of figures
on the surface of a sphere
SPHERIER > SPHERY
SPHERIEST > SPHERY
SPHERING > SPHERE
SPHEROID n solid figure
that is almost but not
exactly a sphere
SPHEROIDS > SPHEROID
SPHERULAR > SPHERULE
SPHERULE n very small
sphere or globule
SPHERULES > SPHERULE
SPHERY adj resembling a
sphere
SPHINCTER n ring of
muscle which controls the
opening and closing of a
hollow organ
SPHINGES > SPHINX
SPHINGID n hawk moth
SPHINGIDS > SPHINGID
SPHINX n huge statue
built by the ancient
Egyptians
SPHINXES > SPHINX
SPHYGMIC adj of or
relating to the pulse
SPHYGMOID adj
resembling the pulse
SPHYGMUS n person's
pulse
SPHYNX n breed of cat
SPHYNXES > SPHYNX
SPIAL n observation
SPIALS > SPIAL
SPIC n derogatory word
for a Spanish-speaking
person
SPICA n spiral bandage
formed by a series of
overlapping figure-of-
eight turns
SPICAE > SPICA
SPICAS > SPICA
SPICATE adj having,
arranged in, or relating to
spikes

SPICATED same as
> SPICATE
SPICCATO n style of
playing a bowed stringed
instrument in which the
bow bounces lightly off
the strings ▷ adv be played
in this manner
SPICCATOS > SPICCATO
SPICE n aromatic
substance used as
flavouring ▷ vb flavour
with spices
SPICEBUSH n North
American lauraceous shrub
SPICED > SPICE
SPICELESS > SPICE
SPICER > SPICE
SPICERIES > SPICERY
SPICERS > SPICE
SPICERY n spices
collectively
SPICES > SPICE
SPICEY same as > SPICY
SPICIER > SPICY
SPICIEST > SPICY
SPICILEGE n anthology
SPICILY > SPICY
SPICINESS > SPICY
SPICING > SPICE
SPICK adj neat and clean
▷ n spic
SPICKER > SPICK
SPICKEST > SPICK
SPICKNEL same as
> SPIGNEL
SPICKNELS > SPICKNEL
SPICKS > SPICK
SPICS > SPIC
SPICULA > SPICULUM
SPICULAE > SPICULUM
SPICULAR > SPICULUM
SPICULATE > SPICULE
SPICULE n small slender
pointed structure or
crystal
SPICULES > SPICULE
SPICULUM same as
> SPICULE
SPICY adj flavoured with
spices
SPIDE n Irish derogatory
slang for a young
working-class man who
dresses in casual sports
clothes
SPIDER n small
eight-legged creature
which spins a web to catch
insects for food ▷ vb follow
internet links to gather
information
SPIDERED > SPIDER
SPIDERIER > SPIDERY
SPIDERING > SPIDER
SPIDERISH > SPIDER
SPIDERMAN n person
who erects the steel
structure of a building
SPIDERMEN
> SPIDERMAN
SPIDERS > SPIDER
SPIDERWEB n spider's
web

SPIDERY adj thin and
angular like a spider's legs
SPIDES > SPIDE
SPIE same as > SPY
SPIED > SPY
SPIEGEL n manganese-
rich pig iron
SPIEGELS > SPIEGEL
SPIEL n speech made to
persuade someone to do
something ▷ vb deliver a
prepared spiel
SPIELED > SPIEL
SPIELER > SPIEL
SPIELERS > SPIEL
SPIELING > SPIEL
SPIELS > SPIEL
SPIER variant of > SPEIR
SPIERED > SPIER
SPIERING > SPIER
SPIERS > SPIER
SPIES > SPY
SPIF n postage stamp
perforated with the initials
of a firm to avoid theft by
employees
SPIFF vb make smart
SPIFFED > SPIFF
SPIFFIED > SPIFFY
SPIFFIER > SPIFFY
SPIFFIES > SPIFFY
SPIFFIEST > SPIFFY
SPIFFILY > SPIFFY
SPIFFING adj excellent
SPIFFS > SPIFF
SPIFFY adj smart ▷ n
smart thing or person
▷ vb smarten
SPIFFYING > SPIFFY
SPIFS > SPIF
SPIGHT same as > SPITE
SPIGHTED > SPIGHT
SPIGHTING > SPIGHT
SPIGHTS > SPIGHT
SPIGNEL n European
umbelliferous plant
SPIGNELS > SPIGNEL
SPIGOT n stopper for, or
tap fitted to, a cask
SPIGOTS > SPIGOT
SPIK same as > SPIC
SPIKE n sharp point
▷ vb put spikes on
SPIKED > SPIKE
SPIKEFISH n large sea
fish
SPIKELET n unit of a
grass inflorescence
SPIKELETS > SPIKELET
SPIKELIKE > SPIKE
SPIKENARD n fragrant
Indian plant with
rose-purple flowers
SPIKER > SPIKE
SPIKERIES > SPIKERY
SPIKERS > SPIKE
SPIKERY n High-Church
Anglicanism
SPIKES > SPIKE
SPIKEY same as > SPIKY
SPIKIER > SPIKY
SPIKIEST > SPIKY
SPIKILY > SPIKY

SPIKINESS > SPIKY
SPIKING > SPIKE
SPIKS > SPIK
SPIKY *adj* resembling a spike
SPILE *n* heavy timber stake or pile ▷ *vb* provide or support with a spile
SPILED > SPILE
SPILES > SPILE
SPILIKIN *same as* > SPILLIKIN
SPILIKINS > SPILIKIN
SPILING > SPILE
SPILINGS > SPILE
SPILITE *n* type of igneous rock
SPILITES > SPILITE
SPILITIC > SPILITE
SPILL *vb* pour from or as if from a container ▷ *n* fall
SPILLABLE > SPILL
SPILLAGE *n* instance or the process of spilling
SPILLAGES > SPILLAGE
SPILLED > SPILL
SPILLER > SPILL
SPILLERS > SPILL
SPILLIKIN *n* thin strip of wood, cardboard, or plastic used in spillikins
SPILLING > SPILL
SPILLINGS > SPILL
SPILLOVER *n* act of spilling over
SPILLS > SPILL
SPILLWAY *n* channel that carries away surplus water, as from a dam
SPILLWAYS > SPILLWAY
SPILOSITE *n* form of slate
SPILT > SPILL
SPILTH *n* something spilled
SPILTHS > SPILTH
SPIM *n* unsolicited communications received via an instant-messaging system
SPIMMER *n* person who sends spam via an instant-messaging system
SPIMMERS > SPIMMER
SPIMMING *n* the activity of sending unsolicited commercial communications via an instant-messaging system
SPIMMINGS > SPIMMING
SPIMS > SPIM
SPIN *vb* revolve or cause to revolve rapidly ▷ *n* revolving motion
SPINA *n* spine
SPINACENE *n* type of vaccine
SPINACH *n* dark green leafy vegetable
SPINACHES > SPINACH
SPINACHY > SPINACH
SPINAE > SPINA
SPINAGE *same as* > SPINACH

SPINAGES > SPINAGE
SPINAL *adj* of the spine ▷ *n* anaesthetic administered in the spine
SPINALLY > SPINAL
SPINALS > SPINAL
SPINAR *n* fast-spinning star
SPINARS > SPINAR
SPINAS > SPINA
SPINATE *adj* having a spine
SPINDLE *n* rotating rod that acts as an axle ▷ *vb* form into a spindle or equip with spindles
SPINDLED > SPINDLE
SPINDLER > SPINDLE
SPINDLERS > SPINDLE
SPINDLES > SPINDLE
SPINDLIER > SPINDLY
SPINDLING *adj* long and slender, esp disproportionately so ▷ *n* spindling person or thing
SPINDLY *adj* long, slender, and frail
SPINDRIFT *n* spray blown up from the sea
SPINE *n* backbone
SPINED > SPINE
SPINEL *n* any of a group of hard glassy minerals of variable colour
SPINELESS *adj* lacking courage
SPINELIKE > SPINE
SPINELLE *same as* > SPINEL
SPINELLES > SPINELLE
SPINELS > SPINEL
SPINES > SPINE
SPINET *n* small harpsichord
SPINETS > SPINET
SPINETTE *same as* > SPINET
SPINETTES > SPINETTE
SPINIER > SPINY
SPINIEST > SPINY
SPINIFEX *n* coarse spiny Australian grass
SPINIFORM *adj* like a thorn
SPININESS > SPINY
SPINK *n* finch ▷ *vb* (of a finch) chirp
SPINKED > SPINK
SPINKING > SPINK
SPINKS > SPINK
SPINLESS > SPIN
SPINNAKER *n* large sail on a racing yacht
SPINNER *n* bowler who makes the ball change direction when it bounces
SPINNERET *n* organ through which silk threads come out of a spider
SPINNERS > SPINNER
SPINNERY *n* spinning mill
SPINNET *same as* > SPINET

SPINNETS > SPINNET
SPINNEY *n* small wood
SPINNEYS > SPINNEY
SPINNIER > SPINNY
SPINNIES > SPINNY
SPINNIEST > SPINNY
SPINNING > SPIN
SPINNINGS > SPIN
SPINNY *adj* crazy
SPINODE *another name for* > CUSP
SPINODES > SPINODE
SPINOFF *n* development derived incidentally from an existing enterprise
SPINOFFS > SPINOFF
SPINONE *n* as in Italian *spinone* wiry-coated gun dog
SPINONI > SPINONE
SPINOR *n* type of mathematical object
SPINORS > SPINOR
SPINOSE *adj* (esp of plants) bearing many spines
SPINOSELY > SPINOSE
SPINOSITY > SPINOSE
SPINOUS *adj* resembling a spine or thorn
SPINOUT *n* spinning skid that causes a car to run off the road
SPINOUTS > SPINOUT
SPINS > SPIN
SPINSTER *n* unmarried woman
SPINSTERS > SPINSTER
SPINTEXT *n* preacher
SPINTEXTS > SPINTEXT
SPINTO *n* lyrical singing voice
SPINTOS > SPINTO
SPINULA *n* small spine
SPINULAE > SPINULA
SPINULATE *adj* like a spine
SPINULE *n* very small spine, thorn, or prickle
SPINULES > SPINULE
SPINULOSE > SPINULE
SPINULOUS > SPINULE
SPINY *adj* covered with spines
SPIRACLE *n* small blowhole for breathing through, such as that of a whale
SPIRACLES > SPIRACLE
SPIRACULA *pl n* spiracles
SPIRAEA *n* plant with small white or pink flowers
SPIRAEAS > SPIRAEA
SPIRAL *n* continuous curve formed by a point winding about a central axis ▷ *vb* move in a spiral ▷ *adj* having the form of a spiral
SPIRALED > SPIRAL
SPIRALING > SPIRAL
SPIRALISM *n* ascent in spiral structure
SPIRALIST > SPIRALISM

SPIRALITY > SPIRAL
SPIRALLED > SPIRAL
SPIRALLY > SPIRAL
SPIRALS > SPIRAL
SPIRANT *n* fricative consonant
SPIRANTS > SPIRANT
SPIRASTER *n* part of living sponge
SPIRATED *adj* twisted in spiral
SPIRATION *n* breathing
SPIRE *n* pointed part of a steeple ▷ *vb* assume the shape of a spire
SPIREA *same as* > SPIRAEA
SPIREAS > SPIREA
SPIRED > SPIRE
SPIRELESS > SPIRE
SPIRELET *another name for* > FLECHE
SPIRELETS > SPIRELET
SPIREM *same as* > SPIREME
SPIREME *n* tangled mass of chromatin threads
SPIREMES > SPIREME
SPIREMS > SPIREM
SPIRES > SPIRE
SPIREWISE > SPIRE
SPIRIC *n* type of curve
SPIRICS > SPIRIC
SPIRIER > SPIRE
SPIRIEST > SPIRE
SPIRILLA > SPIRILLUM
SPIRILLAR > SPIRILLUM
SPIRILLUM *n* any bacterium having a curved or spirally twisted rodlike body
SPIRING > SPIRE
SPIRIT *n* nonphysical aspect of a person concerned with profound thoughts ▷ *vb* carry away mysteriously
SPIRITED *adj* lively
SPIRITFUL > SPIRIT
SPIRITING > SPIRIT
SPIRITISM *n* belief that the spirits of the dead can communicate with the living
SPIRITIST > SPIRITISM
SPIRITOSO *adv* to be played in a spirited or animated manner
SPIRITOUS *adj* high-spirited
SPIRITS > SPIRIT
SPIRITUAL *adj* relating to the spirit ▷ *n* type of religious folk song originating among Black slaves in America
SPIRITUEL *adj* having a refined and lively mind or wit
SPIRITUS *n* spirit
SPIRITY *adj* spirited

S

SPIRLING same as
> SPARLING
SPIRLINGS > SPIRLING
SPIROGRAM n record
made by spirograph
SPIROGYRA n green
freshwater plant that
floats on the surface of
ponds and ditches
SPIROID adj resembling a
spiral or displaying a spiral
form
SPIRT same as > SPURT
SPIRTED > SPIRT
SPIRTING > SPIRT
SPIRTLE same as
> SPURTLE
SPIRTLES > SPIRTLE
SPIRTS > SPIRT
SPIRULA n tropical
cephalopod mollusc
SPIRULAE > SPIRULA
SPIRULAS > SPIRULA
SPIRULINA n type of
cyanobacterium
processed as a source of
nutrients
SPIRY > SPIRE
SPIT vb eject (saliva or
food) from the mouth
▷ n saliva
SPITAL n hospital, esp for
the needy sick
SPITALS > SPITAL
SPITBALL n small missile
made from chewed paper
▷ vb make suggestions
SPITBALLS > SPITBALL
SPITCHER adj doomed
▷ vb be doomed
SPITCHERS > SPITCHER
SPITE n deliberate
nastiness ▷ vb annoy or
hurt from spite
SPITED > SPITE
SPITEFUL adj full of or
motivated by spite
SPITES > SPITE
SPITFIRE n person with
a fiery temper
SPITFIRES > SPITFIRE
SPITING > SPITE
SPITS > SPIT
SPITTED > SPIT
SPITTEN > SPIT
SPITTER > SPIT
SPITTERS > SPIT
SPITTIER > SPITTY
SPITTIEST > SPITTY
SPITTING > SPIT
SPITTINGS > SPIT
SPITTLE n fluid produced
in the mouth, saliva
SPITTLES > SPITTLE
SPITTLIER > SPITTLY
SPITTLY adj covered with
spittle
SPITTOON n bowl to spit
into
SPITTOONS > SPITTOON
SPITTY adj covered with
saliva
SPITZ n stockily built dog
with a tightly curled tail

SPITZES > SPITZ
SPIV n smartly dressed
man who makes a living by
shady dealings
SPIVS > SPIV
SPIVVERY n behaviour of
spivs
SPIVVIER > SPIV
SPIVVIEST > SPIV
SPIVVISH adj
characteristic of a spiv
SPIVVY > SPIV
SPLAKE n type of hybrid
trout bred by Canadian
zoologists
SPLAKES > SPLAKE
SPLASH vb scatter liquid
on (something)
▷ n splashing sound
SPLASHED > SPLASH
SPLASHER n anything
used for protection
against splashes
SPLASHERS > SPLASHER
SPLASHES > SPLASH
SPLASHIER > SPLASHY
SPLASHILY > SPLASHY
SPLASHING > SPLASH
SPLASHY adj having
irregular marks
SPLAT n wet slapping
sound ▷ vb make wet
slapping sound
SPLATCH vb splash
SPLATCHED > SPLATCH
SPLATCHES > SPLATCH
SPLATS > SPLAT
SPLATTED > SPLAT
SPLATTER n splash
▷ vb splash (something or
someone) with small blobs
SPLATTERS > SPLATTER
SPLATTING > SPLAT
SPLAY vb spread out, with
ends spreading in different
directions ▷ adj spread out
▷ n surface of a wall that
forms an oblique angle to
the main flat surfaces
SPLAYED > SPLAY
SPLAYFEET
> SPLAYFOOT
SPLAYFOOT n foot of
which the toes are spread
out
SPLAYING > SPLAY
SPLAYS > SPLAY
SPLEEN n abdominal
organ which filters
bacteria from the blood
SPLEENFUL adj bad-
tempered or irritable
SPLEENIER > SPLEEN
SPLEENISH > SPLEEN
SPLEENS > SPLEEN
SPLEENY > SPLEEN
SPLENDENT adj shining
brightly
SPLENDID adj excellent
SPLENDOR same as
> SPLENDOUR
SPLENDORS > SPLENDOR
SPLENDOUR n state or
quality of being splendid

SPLENETIC adj spiteful or
irritable ▷ n spiteful or
irritable person
SPLENIA > SPLENIUM
SPLENIAL > SPLENIUS
SPLENIC adj of, relating
to, or in the spleen
SPLENII > SPLENIUS
SPLENITIS n
inflammation of the
spleen
SPLENIUM n structure in
brain
SPLENIUMS > SPLENIUM
SPLENIUS n either of two
flat muscles situated at
the back of the neck
SPLENT same as > SPLINT
SPLENTS > SPLENT
SPLEUCHAN n pouch for
tobacco
SPLICE vb join by
interweaving or
overlapping ends
SPLICED > SPLICE
SPLICER > SPLICE
SPLICERS > SPLICE
SPLICES > SPLICE
SPLICING > SPLICE
SPLICINGS > SPLICING
SPLIFF n cannabis, used
as a drug
SPLIFFS > SPLIFF
SPLINE n type of narrow
key around a shaft that fits
into a corresponding
groove ▷ vb provide (a
shaft, part, etc) with
splines
SPLINED > SPLINE
SPLINES > SPLINE
SPLINING > SPLINE
SPLINT n rigid support for
a broken bone ▷ vb apply a
splint to (a broken arm,
etc)
SPLINTED > SPLINT
SPLINTER n thin sharp
piece broken off, esp from
wood ▷ vb break into
fragments
SPLINTERS > SPLINTER
SPLINTERY adj liable to
produce or break into
splinters
SPLINTING > SPLINT
SPLINTS > SPLINT
SPLISH vb splash
SPLISHED > SPLISH
SPLISHES > SPLISH
SPLISHING > SPLISH
SPLIT vb break into
separate pieces
▷ n splitting
SPLITS > SPLIT
SPLITTED > SPLIT
SPLITTER > SPLIT
SPLITTERS > SPLIT
SPLITTING n Freudian
psychological defence
mechanism
SPLITTISM n advocation
of separatism from a larger
body

SPLITTIST n person who
advocates separatism
from a larger body
SPLODGE n large uneven
spot or stain ▷ vb mark
(something) with a
splodge or splodges
SPLODGED > SPLODGE
SPLODGES > SPLODGE
SPLODGIER > SPLODGE
SPLODGILY > SPLODGE
SPLODGING > SPLODGE
SPLODGY > SPLODGE
SPLOG n spam blog
SPLOGS > SPLOG
SPLOOSH vb splash or
cause to splash about
uncontrollably ▷ n
instance or sound of
splooshing
SPLOOSHED > SPLOOSH
SPLOOSHES > SPLOOSH
SPLORE n revel
SPLORES > SPLORE
SPLOSH vb scatter (liquid)
vigorously about in blobs
▷ n instance or sound of
sploshing
SPLOSHED > SPLOSH
SPLOSHES > SPLOSH
SPLOSHING > SPLOSH
SPLOTCH vb splash, daub
SPLOTCHED > SPLOTCH
SPLOTCHES > SPLOTCH
SPLOTCHY > SPLOTCH
SPLURGE vb spend money
extravagantly ▷ n bout of
extravagance
SPLURGED > SPLURGE
SPLURGER > SPLURGE
SPLURGERS > SPLURGE
SPLURGES > SPLURGE
SPLURGIER > SPLURGE
SPLURGING > SPLURGE
SPLURGY > SPLURGE
SPLURT vb gush out
SPLURTED > SPLURT
SPLURTING > SPLURT
SPLURTS > SPLURT
SPLUTTER vb utter with
spitting or choking sounds
▷ n spluttering
SPLUTTERS > SPLUTTER
SPLUTTERY > SPLUTTER
SPOD adj boring,
unattractive, or overly
studious
SPODDIER > SPOD
SPODDIEST > SPOD
SPODDY > SPOD
SPODE n type of English
china or porcelain
SPODES > SPODE
SPODIUM n black powder
SPODIUMS > SPODIUM
SPODOGRAM n ash from
plant used in studying it
SPODOSOL n ashy soil
SPODOSOLS > SPODOSOL
SPODS > SPOD
SPODUMENE n greyish-
white, green, or lilac
pyroxene mineral

SPOFFISH *adj* officious
SPOFFY *same as*
> SPOFFISH
SPOIL *vb* damage
SPOILABLE > SPOIL
SPOILAGE *n* amount of material that has been spoilt
SPOILAGES > SPOILAGE
SPOILED > SPOIL
SPOILER *n* device on an aircraft or car to increase drag
SPOILERS > SPOILER
SPOILFIVE *n* card game for two or more players with five cards each
SPOILFUL *adj* taking spoils
SPOILING > SPOIL
SPOILS > SPOIL
SPOILSMAN *n* person who shares in the spoils of office or advocates the spoils system
SPOILSMEN
> SPOILSMAN
SPOILT > SPOIL
SPOKE *n* radial member of a wheel ▷ *vb* equip with spokes
SPOKED > SPOKE
SPOKEN > SPEAK
SPOKES > SPOKE
SPOKESMAN *n* person chosen to speak on behalf of a group
SPOKESMEN
> SPOKESMAN
SPOKEWISE > SPEAK
SPOKING > SPOKE
SPOLIATE *less common word for* > DESPOIL
SPOLIATED > SPOLIATE
SPOLIATES > SPOLIATE
SPOLIATOR > SPOLIATE
SPONDAIC *adj* of, relating to, or consisting of spondees ▷ *n* spondaic line
SPONDAICS > SPONDAIC
SPONDEE *n* metrical foot of two long syllables
SPONDEES > SPONDEE
SPONDULIX *n* money
SPONDYL *n* vertebra
SPONDYLS > SPONDYL
SPONGE *n* sea animal with a porous absorbent skeleton ▷ *vb* wipe with a sponge
SPONGEBAG *n* small bag for holding toiletries when travelling
SPONGED > SPONGE
SPONGEING *same as*
> SPONGING
SPONGEOUS *adj* spongy
SPONGER *n* person who sponges on others
SPONGERS > SPONGER
SPONGES > SPONGE
SPONGIER > SPONGY
SPONGIEST > SPONGY

SPONGILY > SPONGY
SPONGIN *n* fibrous horny protein in sponges
SPONGING > SPONGE
SPONGINS > SPONGIN
SPONGIOSE > SPONGE
SPONGIOUS > SPONGE
SPONGOID > SPONGE
SPONGY *adj* of or resembling a sponge
SPONSAL *n* marriage
SPONSALIA *n* marriage ceremony
SPONSIBLE *adj* responsible
SPONSING *same as*
> SPONSON
SPONSINGS > SPONSING
SPONSION *n* act or process of becoming surety
SPONSIONS > SPONSION
SPONSON *n* outboard support for a gun enabling it to fire fore and aft
SPONSONS > SPONSON
SPONSOR *n* person who promotes something ▷ *vb* act as a sponsor for
SPONSORED > SPONSOR
SPONSORS > SPONSOR
SPONTOON *n* form of halberd carried by some junior infantry officers in the 18th and 19th centuries
SPONTOONS > SPONTOON
SPOOF *n* mildly satirical parody ▷ *vb* fool (a person) with a trick or deception
SPOOFED > SPOOF
SPOOFER > SPOOF
SPOOFERS > SPOOF
SPOOFERY > SPOOF
SPOOFIER > SPOOFY
SPOOFIEST > SPOOFY
SPOOFING > SPOOF
SPOOFINGS > SPOOF
SPOOFS > SPOOF
SPOOFY > SPOOF
SPOOK *n* ghost ▷ *vb* frighten
SPOOKED > SPOOK
SPOOKERY *n* spooky events
SPOOKIER > SPOOKY
SPOOKIEST > SPOOKY
SPOOKILY > SPOOKY
SPOOKING > SPOOK
SPOOKISH > SPOOK
SPOOKS > SPOOK
SPOOKY *adj* ghostly or eerie
SPOOL *n* cylinder round which something can be wound ▷ *vb* wind or be wound onto a spool or reel
SPOOLED > SPOOL
SPOOLER > SPOOL
SPOOLERS > SPOOL
SPOOLING > SPOOL
SPOOLINGS > SPOOL
SPOOLS > SPOOL
SPOOM *vb* sail fast before wind

SPOOMED > SPOOM
SPOOMING > SPOOM
SPOOMS > SPOOM
SPOON *n* shallow bowl attached to a handle for eating, stirring, or serving food ▷ *vb* lift with a spoon
SPOONBAIT *n* type of lure used in angling
SPOONBILL *n* wading bird of warm regions with a long flat bill
SPOONED > SPOON
SPOONER *n* person who engages in spooning
SPOONERS > SPOONER
SPOONEY *same as*
> SPOONY
SPOONEYS > SPOONEY
SPOONFED *adj* having been given someone else's opinions
SPOONFUL *n* amount that a spoon is able to hold
SPOONFULS > SPOONFUL
SPOONHOOK *n* type of fishing lure
SPOONIER > SPOONY
SPOONIES > SPOONY
SPOONIEST > SPOONY
SPOONILY > SPOONY
SPOONING > SPOON
SPOONS > SPOON
SPOONSFUL > SPOONFUL
SPOONWAYS *adv* like spoons
SPOONWISE *same as*
> SPOONWAYS
SPOONWORM *n* type of small marine worm with a spoonlike proboscis
SPOONY *adj* foolishly or stupidly amorous ▷ *n* fool or silly person, esp one in love
SPOOR *n* trail of an animal ▷ *vb* track (an animal) by following its trail
SPOORED > SPOOR
SPOORER > SPOOR
SPOORERS > SPOOR
SPOORING > SPOOR
SPOORS > SPOOR
SPOOT *n* razor shell
SPOOTS > SPOOT
SPORADIC *adj* intermittent, scattered
SPORAL > SPORE
SPORANGIA *pl n* organs in fungi in which asexual spores are produced
SPORE *n* minute reproductive body of some plants ▷ *vb* produce, carry, or release spores
SPORED > SPORE
SPORES > SPORE
SPORICIDE *n* substance killing spores
SPORIDESM *n* group of spores
SPORIDIA > SPORIDIUM
SPORIDIAL
> SPORIDIUM

SPORIDIUM *n* type of spore
SPORING > SPORE
SPORK *n* spoon-shaped piece of cutlery with tines like a fork
SPORKS > SPORK
SPOROCARP *n* specialized leaf branch in certain aquatic ferns that encloses the sori
SPOROCYST *n* thick-walled rounded structure produced by sporozoan protozoans
SPOROCYTE *n* diploid cell that divides by meiosis to produce four haploid spores
SPOROGENY *n* process of spore formation in plants and animals
SPOROGONY *n* process in sporozoans by which sporozoites are formed
SPOROID *adj* of or like a spore
SPOROPHYL *n* leaf in ferns that bears the sporangia
SPOROZOA *n* class of microscopic creature
SPOROZOAL > SPOROZOA
SPOROZOAN *n* type of parasitic protozoan
SPOROZOIC > SPOROZOA
SPOROZOON *same as*
> SPOROZOAN
SPORRAN *n* pouch worn in front of a kilt
SPORRANS > SPORRAN
SPORT *n* activity for pleasure, competition, or exercise ▷ *vb* wear proudly
SPORTABLE *adj* playful
SPORTANCE *n* playing
SPORTBIKE *n* type of high-performance motorcycle
SPORTED > SPORT
SPORTER > SPORT
SPORTERS > SPORT
SPORTFUL > SPORT
SPORTIER > SPORTY
SPORTIES > SPORTY
SPORTIEST > SPORTY
SPORTIF *adj* sporty ▷ *n* sporty person
SPORTIFS > SPORTIF
SPORTILY > SPORTY
SPORTING *adj* of sport
SPORTIVE *adj* playful
SPORTLESS > SPORT
SPORTS *adj* of or used in sports ▷ *n* meeting held at a school or college for competitions in athletic events
SPORTSMAN *n* person who plays sports
SPORTSMEN
> SPORTSMAN
SPORTY *adj* (of a person) interested in sport ▷ *n* young person who takes

S

an interest in sport and fitness

SPORULAR > SPORULE

SPORULATE *vb* produce spores, esp by multiple fission

SPORULE *n* spore, esp a very small spore

SPORULES > SPORULE

SPOSH *n* slush

SPOSHES > SPOSH

SPOSHIER > SPOSH

SPOSHIEST > SPOSH

SPOSHY > SPOSH

SPOT *n* small mark on a surface ▷ *vb* notice

SPOTLESS *adj* absolutely clean

SPOTLIGHT *n* powerful light illuminating a small area ▷ *vb* draw attention to

SPOTLIT > SPOTLIGHT

SPOTS > SPOT

SPOTTABLE > SPOT

SPOTTED > SPOT

SPOTTER *n* person who notes numbers or types of trains or planes

SPOTTERS > SPOTTER

SPOTTIE *n* young deer of up to three months of age

SPOTTIER > SPOTTY

SPOTTIES > SPOTTIE

SPOTTIEST > SPOTTY

SPOTTILY > SPOTTY

SPOTTING > SPOT

SPOTTINGS > SPOT

SPOTTY *adj* with spots

SPOUSAGE *n* marriage

SPOUSAGES
> SPOUSAGE

SPOUSAL *n* marriage ceremony ▷ *adj* of or relating to marriage

SPOUSALLY > SPOUSAL

SPOUSALS > SPOUSAL

SPOUSE *n* husband or wife ▷ *vb* marry

SPOUSED > SPOUSE

SPOUSES > SPOUSE

SPOUSING > SPOUSE

SPOUT *vb* pour out in a stream or jet ▷ *n* projecting tube or lip for pouring liquids

SPOUTED > SPOUT

SPOUTER > SPOUT

SPOUTERS > SPOUT

SPOUTIER > SPOUT

SPOUTIEST > SPOUT

SPOUTING *n* rainwater downpipe on the outside of a building

SPOUTINGS > SPOUTING

SPOUTLESS > SPOUT

SPOUTS > SPOUT

SPOUTY > SPOUT

SPRACK *adj* vigorous

SPRACKLE *vb* clamber

SPRACKLED > SPRACKLE

SPRACKLES > SPRACKLE

SPRAD > SPREAD

SPRADDLE *n* disease of fowl preventing them from standing

SPRADDLED *adj* affected by spraddle

SPRADDLES > SPRADDLE

SPRAG *n* device used to prevent a vehicle from running backwards on an incline ▷ *vb* use sprag to prevent vehicle from moving

SPRAGGED > SPRAG

SPRAGGING > SPRAG

SPRAGS > SPRAG

SPRAID *vb* chapped

SPRAIN *vb* injure (a joint) by a sudden twist ▷ *n* such an injury

SPRAINED > SPRAIN

SPRAINING > SPRAIN

SPRAINS > SPRAIN

SPRAINT *n* piece of otter's dung

SPRAINTS > SPRAINT

SPRANG *n* branch

SPRANGLE *vb* sprawl

SPRANGLED > SPRANGLE

SPRANGLES > SPRANGLE

SPRANGS > SPRANG

SPRAT *n* small sea fish

SPRATS > SPRAT

SPRATTLE *vb* scramble

SPRATTLED > SPRATTLE

SPRATTLES > SPRATTLE

SPRAUCHLE *same as*
> SPRACKLE

SPRAUNCY *adj* smart

SPRAWL *vb* lie or sit with the limbs spread out ▷ *n* part of a city that has spread untidily over a large area

SPRAWLED > SPRAWL

SPRAWLER > SPRAWL

SPRAWLERS > SPRAWL

SPRAWLIER > SPRAWL

SPRAWLING > SPRAWL

SPRAWLS > SPRAWL

SPRAWLY > SPRAWL

SPRAY *n* (device for producing) fine drops of liquid ▷ *vb* scatter in fine drops

SPRAYED > SPRAY

SPRAYER > SPRAY

SPRAYERS > SPRAY

SPRAYEY > SPRAY

SPRAYIER > SPRAY

SPRAYIEST > SPRAY

SPRAYING > SPRAY

SPRAYINGS > SPRAY

SPRAYS > SPRAY

SPREAD *vb* open out or be displayed to the fullest extent ▷ *n* spreading ▷ *adj* extended or stretched out, esp to the fullest extent

SPREADER *n* machine or device used for scattering bulk materials over a relatively wide area

SPREADERS > SPREADER

SPREADING > SPREAD

SPREADS > SPREAD

SPREAGH *n* cattle raid

SPREAGHS > SPREAGH

SPREATHE *vb* chap

SPREATHED *adj* sore

SPREATHES > SPREATHE

SPREAZE *same as*
> SPREATHE

SPREAZED *same as*
> SPREATHED

SPREAZES > SPREAZE

SPREAZING > SPREAZE

SPRECHERY *n* theft of cattle

SPRECKLED *adj* speckled

SPRED *same as* > SPREAD

SPREDD *same as*
> SPREAD

SPREDDE *same as*
> SPREAD

SPREDDEN > SPREDDE

SPREDDES > SPREDDE

SPREDDING > SPREDDE

SPREDDS > SPREDD

SPREDS > SPRED

SPREE *n* session of overindulgence, usu in drinking or spending money ▷ *vb* go on a spree

SPREED > SPREE

SPREEING > SPREE

SPREES > SPREE

SPREETHE *same as*
> SPREATHE

SPREETHED > SPREETHE

SPREETHES > SPREETHE

SPREEZE *same as*
> SPREATHE

SPREEZED > SPREEZE

SPREEZES > SPREEZE

SPREEZING > SPREEZE

SPREKELIA *n* bulbous plant grown for its striking crimson or white pendent flowers

SPRENT *adj* sprinkled ▷ *vb* leap forward in an agile manner

SPRENTED > SPRENT

SPRENTING > SPRENT

SPRENTS > SPRENT

SPREW *same as* > SPRUE

SPREWS > SPREW

SPRIER > SPRY

SPRIEST > SPRY

SPRIG *n* twig or shoot ▷ *vb* fasten or secure with sprigs

SPRIGGED > SPRIG

SPRIGGER > SPRIG

SPRIGGERS > SPRIG

SPRIGGIER > SPRIG

SPRIGGING > SPRIG

SPRIGGY > SPRIG

SPRIGHT *same as*
> SPRITE

SPRIGHTED > SPRIGHT

SPRIGHTLY *adj* lively and brisk ▷ *adv* in a lively manner

SPRIGHTS > SPRIGHT

SPRIGS > SPRIG

SPRIGTAIL *n* species of duck

SPRING *vb* move suddenly upwards or forwards in a single motion, jump ▷ *n* season between winter and summer

SPRINGAL *n* young man

SPRINGALD *same as*
> SPRINGAL

SPRINGALS > SPRINGAL

SPRINGBOK *n* S African antelope

SPRINGE *n* type of snare for catching small wild animals or birds ▷ *vb* set such a snare

SPRINGED > SPRINGE

SPRINGER *n* small spaniel

SPRINGERS > SPRINGER

SPRINGES > SPRINGE

SPRINGIER > SPRINGY

SPRINGILY > SPRINGY

SPRINGING > SPRING

SPRINGLE *same as*
> SPRINGE

SPRINGLES > SPRINGE

SPRINGLET *n* small spring

SPRINGS > SPRING

SPRINGY *adj* elastic

SPRINKLE *vb* scatter (liquid or powder) in tiny drops or particles over (something) ▷ *n* act or an instance of sprinkling or a quantity that is sprinkled

SPRINKLED > SPRINKLE

SPRINKLER *n* device with small holes that is attached to a garden hose or watering can and used to spray water

SPRINKLES > SPRINKLE

SPRINT *n* short race run at top speed ▷ *vb* run a short distance at top speed

SPRINTED > SPRINT

SPRINTER > SPRINT

SPRINTERS > SPRINT

SPRINTING > SPRINT

SPRINTS > SPRINT

SPRIT *n* small spar set diagonally across a sail to extend it

SPRITE *n* elf

SPRITEFUL *adj* lively

SPRITELY *same as*
> SPRIGHTLY

SPRITES > SPRITE

SPRITS > SPRIT

SPRITSAIL *n* sail extended by a sprit

SPRITZ *vb* spray liquid

SPRITZED > SPRITZ

SPRITZER *n* tall drink of wine and soda water

SPRITZERS > SPRITZER

SPRITZES > SPRITZ

SPRITZIER > SPRITZY

SPRITZIG *adj* (of wine) sparkling ▷ *n* sparkling wine

SPRITZIGS > SPRITZIG

SPRITZING > SPRITZ
SPRITZY *adj* fizzy
SPROCKET *n* wheel with teeth on the rim, that drives or is driven by a chain
SPROCKETS > SPROCKET
SPROD *n* young salmon
SPRODS > SPROD
SPROG *n* child
SPROGLET *n* small child
SPROGLETS > SPROGLET
SPROGS > SPROG
SPRONG > SPRING
SPROUT *vb* put forth shoots ▷ *n* shoot
SPROUTED > SPROUT
SPROUTING > SPROUT
SPROUTS > SPROUT
SPRUCE *n* kind of fir ▷ *adj* neat and smart
SPRUCED > SPRUCE
SPRUCELY > SPRUCE
SPRUCER > SPRUCE
SPRUCES > SPRUCE
SPRUCEST > SPRUCE
SPRUCIER > SPRUCE
SPRUCIEST > SPRUCE
SPRUCING > SPRUCE
SPRUCY > SPRUCE
SPRUE *n* vertical channel in a mould
SPRUES > SPRUE
SPRUG *n* sparrow
SPRUGS > SPRUG
SPRUIK *vb* speak in public (used esp of a showman or salesman)
SPRUIKED > SPRUIK
SPRUIKER > SPRUIK
SPRUIKERS > SPRUIK
SPRUIKING > SPRUIK
SPRUIKS > SPRUIK
SPRUIT *n* small tributary stream or watercourse
SPRUITS > SPRUIT
SPRUNG > SPRING
SPRUSH *Scots form of* > SPRUCE
SPRUSHED > SPRUSH
SPRUSHES > SPRUSH
SPRUSHING > SPRUSH
SPRY *adj* active or nimble
SPRYER > SPRY
SPRYEST > SPRY
SPRYLY > SPRY
SPRYNESS > SPRY
SPUD *n* potato ▷ *vb* remove (bark) or eradicate (weeds) with a spud
SPUDDED > SPUD
SPUDDER *same as* > SPUD
SPUDDERS > SPUDDER
SPUDDIER > SPUDDY
SPUDDIEST > SPUDDY
SPUDDING > SPUD
SPUDDINGS > SPUD
SPUDDLE *n* feeble movement
SPUDDLES > SPUDDLE
SPUDDY *adj* short and fat
SPUDGEL *n* bucket on a long handle
SPUDGELS > SPUDGEL

SPUDS > SPUD
SPUE *same as* > SPEW
SPUED > SPUE
SPUEING > SPUE
SPUER > SPUE
SPUERS > SPUE
SPUES > SPUE
SPUG *same as* > SPUGGY
SPUGGIES > SPUGGY
SPUGGY *n* house sparrow
SPUGS > SPUG
SPUILZIE *vb* plunder
SPUILZIED > SPUILZIE
SPUILZIES > SPUILZIE
SPUING > SPUE
SPULE *Scots word for* > SHOULDER
SPULES > SPULE
SPULYE *same as* > SPUILZIE
SPULYED > SPULYE
SPULYEING > SPULYE
SPULYES > SPULYE
SPULYIE *same as* > SPUILZIE
SPULYIED > SPULYIE
SPULYIES > SPULYIE
SPULZIE *same as* > SPUILZIE
SPULZIED > SPULZIE
SPULZIES > SPULZIE
SPUMANTE *n* Italian sparkling wine
SPUMANTES > SPUMANTE
SPUME *vb* froth ▷ *n* foam or froth on the sea
SPUMED > SPUME
SPUMES > SPUME
SPUMIER > SPUMY
SPUMIEST > SPUMY
SPUMING > SPUME
SPUMONE *n* creamy Italian ice cream
SPUMONES > SPUMONE
SPUMONI *same as* > SPUMONE
SPUMONIS > SPUMONI
SPUMOUS > SPUME
SPUMY > SPUME
SPUN > SPIN
SPUNGE *same as* > SPONGE
SPUNGES > SPUNGE
SPUNK *n* courage, spirit ▷ *vb* catch fire
SPUNKED > SPUNK
SPUNKIE *n* will-o'-the-wisp
SPUNKIER > SPUNK
SPUNKIES > SPUNKIE
SPUNKIEST > SPUNK
SPUNKILY > SPUNK
SPUNKING > SPUNK
SPUNKS > SPUNK
SPUNKY > SPUNK
SPUNYARN *n* small stuff made from rope yarns twisted together
SPUNYARNS > SPUNYARN
SPUR *n* stimulus or incentive ▷ *vb* urge on, incite (someone)
SPURDOG *n* the dogfish
SPURDOGS > SPURDOG

SPURGALL *vb* prod with spur
SPURGALLS > SPURGALL
SPURGE *n* plant with milky sap
SPURGES > SPURGE
SPURIAE *n* type of bird feathers
SPURIOUS *adj* not genuine
SPURLESS > SPUR
SPURLING *same as* > SPARLING
SPURLINGS > SPURLING
SPURN *vb* reject with scorn ▷ *n* instance of spurning
SPURNE *vb* spur
SPURNED > SPURN
SPURNER > SPURN
SPURNERS > SPURN
SPURNES > SPURNE
SPURNING > SPURN
SPURNINGS > SPURN
SPURNS > SPURN
SPURRED > SPUR
SPURRER > SPUR
SPURRERS > SPUR
SPURREY *n* any of several low-growing European plants
SPURREYS > SPURREY
SPURRIER *n* maker of spurs
SPURRIERS > SPURRIER
SPURRIES > SPURRY
SPURRIEST > SPURRY
SPURRING > SPUR
SPURRINGS > SPUR
SPURRY *n* spurrey ▷ *adj* resembling a spur
SPURS > SPUR
SPURT *vb* gush or cause to gush out in a jet ▷ *n* short sudden burst of activity or speed
SPURTED > SPURT
SPURTER > SPURT
SPURTERS > SPURT
SPURTING > SPURT
SPURTLE *n* wooden spoon for stirring porridge
SPURTLES > SPURTLE
SPURTS > SPURT
SPURWAY *n* path used by riders
SPURWAYS > SPURWAY
SPUTA > SPUTUM
SPUTNIK *n* early Soviet artificial satellite
SPUTNIKS > SPUTNIK
SPUTTER *n* splutter ▷ *vb* splutter
SPUTTERED > SPUTTER
SPUTTERER > SPUTTER
SPUTTERS > SPUTTER
SPUTTERY > SPUTTER
SPUTUM *n* spittle, usu mixed with mucus
SPY *n* person employed to obtain secret information ▷ *vb* act as a spy
SPYAL *n* spy
SPYALS > SPYAL

SPYCAM *n* camera used for covert surveillance
SPYCAMS > SPYCAM
SPYGLASS *n* small telescope
SPYHOLE *n* small hole in a door, etc through which one may watch secretly
SPYHOLES > SPYHOLE
SPYING > SPY
SPYINGS > SPY
SPYMASTER *n* person who controls spy network
SPYPLANE *n* military aeroplane used to spy on enemy
SPYPLANES > SPYPLANE
SPYRE *same as* > SPIRE
SPYRES > SPYRE
SPYWARE *n* software used to gain information about a computer user
SPYWARES > SPYWARE
SQUAB *n* young bird yet to leave the nest ▷ *adj* (of birds) recently hatched and still unfledged ▷ *vb* fall
SQUABASH *vb* crush
SQUABBED > SQUAB
SQUABBER > SQUAB
SQUABBEST > SQUAB
SQUABBIER > SQUAB
SQUABBING > SQUAB
SQUABBISH > SQUAB
SQUABBLE *n* (engage in) a petty or noisy quarrel ▷ *vb* quarrel over a small matter
SQUABBLED > SQUABBLE
SQUABBLER > SQUABBLE
SQUABBLES > SQUABBLE
SQUABBY > SQUAB
SQUABS > SQUAB
SQUACCO *n* S European heron
SQUACCOS > SQUACCO
SQUAD *n* small group of people working or training together ▷ *vb* set up squads
SQUADDED > SQUAD
SQUADDIE *n* private soldier
SQUADDIES > SQUADDY
SQUADDING > SQUAD
SQUADDY *same as* > SQUADDIE
SQUADOOSH *n* (US slang) nothing
SQUADRON *n* division of an air force, fleet, or cavalry regiment ▷ *vb* assign to squadrons
SQUADRONE *n* former Scottish political party
SQUADRONS > SQUADRON
SQUADS > SQUAD
SQUAIL *vb* throw sticks at
SQUAILED > SQUAIL
SQUAILER > SQUAIL
SQUAILERS > SQUAIL
SQUAILING > SQUAIL
SQUAILS > SQUAIL

S

SQUALENE n terpene first found in the liver of sharks
SQUALENES > SQUALENE
SQUALID adj dirty and unpleasant
SQUALIDER > SQUALID
SQUALIDLY > SQUALID
SQUALL n sudden strong wind ▷ vb cry noisily, yell
SQUALLED > SQUALL
SQUALLER > SQUALL
SQUALLERS > SQUALL
SQUALLIER > SQUALL
SQUALLING > SQUALL
SQUALLISH > SQUALL
SQUALLS > SQUALL
SQUALLY > SQUALL
SQUALOID adj of or like a shark
SQUALOR n disgusting dirt and filth
SQUALORS > SQUALOR
SQUAMA n scale or scalelike structure
SQUAMAE > SQUAMA
SQUAMATE > SQUAMA
SQUAMATES > SQUAMA
SQUAME same as > SQUAMA
SQUAMELLA n small scale
SQUAMES > SQUAME
SQUAMOSAL n thin platelike paired bone in the skull of vertebrates ▷ adj of or relating to this bone
SQUAMOSE same as > SQUAMOUS
SQUAMOUS adj (of epithelium) consisting of one or more layers of flat platelike cells
SQUAMULA same as > SQUAMELLA
SQUAMULAS > SQUAMULA
SQUAMULE same as > SQUAMELLA
SQUAMULES > SQUAMULE
SQUANDER vb waste (money or resources) ▷ n extravagance or dissipation
SQUANDERS > SQUANDER
SQUARE n geometric figure with four equal sides and four right angles ▷ adj square in shape ▷ vb multiply (a number) by itself ▷ adv squarely, directly
SQUARED > SQUARE
SQUARELY adv in a direct way
SQUARER > SQUARE
SQUARERS > SQUARE
SQUARES > SQUARE
SQUAREST > SQUARE
SQUARIAL n type of square dish for receiving satellite television
SQUARIALS > SQUARIAL
SQUARING > SQUARE
SQUARINGS > SQUARE
SQUARISH > SQUARE

SQUARK n hypothetical boson partner of a quark
SQUARKS > SQUARK
SQUARROSE adj having a rough surface
SQUARSON n clergyman who is also landowner
SQUARSONS > SQUARSON
SQUASH vb crush flat ▷ n sweet fruit drink diluted with water
SQUASHED > SQUASH
SQUASHER > SQUASH
SQUASHERS > SQUASH
SQUASHES > SQUASH
SQUASHIER > SQUASHY
SQUASHILY > SQUASHY
SQUASHING > SQUASH
SQUASHY adj soft and easily squashed
SQUAT vb crouch with the knees bent and the weight on the feet ▷ n place where squatters live ▷ adj short and broad
SQUATLY > SQUAT
SQUATNESS > SQUAT
SQUATS > SQUAT
SQUATTED > SQUAT
SQUATTER n illegal occupier of unused premises ▷ vb to splash along
SQUATTERS > SQUATTER
SQUATTEST > SQUAT
SQUATTIER > SQUATTY
SQUATTILY > SQUATTY
SQUATTING n act of squatting
SQUATTLE vb squat
SQUATTLED > SQUATTLE
SQUATTLES > SQUATTLE
SQUATTY adj short and broad
SQUAW n offensive term for a Native American woman
SQUAWBUSH n American shrub
SQUAWFISH n North American minnow
SQUAWK n loud harsh cry ▷ vb utter a squawk
SQUAWKED > SQUAWK
SQUAWKER > SQUAWK
SQUAWKERS > SQUAWK
SQUAWKIER > SQUAWK
SQUAWKING > SQUAWK
SQUAWKS > SQUAWK
SQUAWKY > SQUAWK
SQUAWMAN n offensive term for a White man married to a Native American woman
SQUAWMEN > SQUAWMAN
SQUAWROOT n North American parasitic plant
SQUAWS > SQUAW
SQUEAK n short shrill cry or sound ▷ vb make or utter a squeak
SQUEAKED > SQUEAK
SQUEAKER > SQUEAK
SQUEAKERS > SQUEAK

SQUEAKERY > SQUEAK
SQUEAKIER > SQUEAK
SQUEAKILY > SQUEAK
SQUEAKING > SQUEAK
SQUEAKS > SQUEAK
SQUEAKY > SQUEAK
SQUEAL n long shrill cry or sound ▷ vb make or utter a squeal
SQUEALED > SQUEAL
SQUEALER > SQUEAL
SQUEALERS > SQUEAL
SQUEALING > SQUEAL
SQUEALS > SQUEAL
SQUEAMISH adj easily sickened or shocked
SQUEEGEE n tool with a rubber blade for clearing water from a surface ▷ vb remove (water or other liquid) from (something) by use of a squeegee
SQUEEGEED > SQUEEGEE
SQUEEGEES > SQUEEGEE
SQUEEZE vb grip or press firmly ▷ n squeezing
SQUEEZED > SQUEEZE
SQUEEZER > SQUEEZE
SQUEEZERS > SQUEEZE
SQUEEZES > SQUEEZE
SQUEEZIER > SQUEEZE
SQUEEZING > SQUEEZE
SQUEEZY > SQUEEZE
SQUEG vb oscillate
SQUEGGED > SQUEG
SQUEGGER > SQUEG
SQUEGGERS > SQUEG
SQUEGGING > SQUEG
SQUEGS > SQUEG
SQUELCH vb make a wet sucking sound, as by walking through mud ▷ n squelching sound
SQUELCHED > SQUELCH
SQUELCHER > SQUELCH
SQUELCHES > SQUELCH
SQUELCHY > SQUELCH
SQUIB n small firework that hisses before exploding
SQUIBBED > SQUIB
SQUIBBER n (in baseball) ground ball that becomes a base hit
SQUIBBERS > SQUIBBER
SQUIBBING > SQUIB
SQUIBS > SQUIB
SQUID n sea creature with tentacles ▷ vb (of a parachute) to assume an elongated shape
SQUIDDED > SQUID
SQUIDDING > SQUID
SQUIDGE vb squash
SQUIDGED > SQUIDGE
SQUIDGES > SQUIDGE
SQUIDGIER > SQUIDGY
SQUIDGING > SQUIDGE
SQUIDGY adj soft, moist, and squashy
SQUIDS > SQUID
SQUIER same as > SQUIRE

SQUIERS > SQUIER
SQUIFF same as > SQUIFFY
SQUIFFED same as > SQUIFFY
SQUIFFER n concertina
SQUIFFERS > SQUIFFER
SQUIFFIER > SQUIFFY
SQUIFFY adj slightly drunk
SQUIGGLE n wavy line ▷ vb wriggle
SQUIGGLED > SQUIGGLE
SQUIGGLER > SQUIGGLE
SQUIGGLES > SQUIGGLE
SQUIGGLY > SQUIGGLE
SQUILGEE same as > SQUEEGEE
SQUILGEED > SQUILGEE
SQUILGEES > SQUILGEE
SQUILL n Mediterranean plant of the lily family
SQUILLA n type of mantis shrimp
SQUILLAE > SQUILLA
SQUILLAS > SQUILLA
SQUILLION n extremely large but unspecified number, quantity, or amount
SQUILLS > SQUILL
SQUINANCY same as > QUINSY
SQUINCH n small arch across an internal corner of a tower ▷ vb squeeze
SQUINCHED > SQUINCH
SQUINCHES > SQUINCH
SQUINIED > SQUINY
SQUINIES > SQUINY
SQUINNIED > SQUINNY
SQUINNIER > SQUINNY
SQUINNIES > SQUINNY
SQUINNY vb squint ▷ adj squint
SQUINT vb have eyes which face in different directions ▷ n squinting condition of the eye ▷ adj crooked
SQUINTED > SQUINT
SQUINTER > SQUINT
SQUINTERS > SQUINT
SQUINTEST > SQUINT
SQUINTIER > SQUINT
SQUINTING > SQUINT
SQUINTS > SQUINT
SQUINTY > SQUINT
SQUINY same as > SQUINNY
SQUINYING > SQUINY
SQUIRAGE n body of squires
SQUIRAGES > SQUIRAGE
SQUIRALTY same as > SQUIRAGE
SQUIRARCH n person who believes in government by squires
SQUIRE n country gentleman, usu the main landowner in a community ▷ vb (of a man) escort (a woman)

SQUIREAGE *same as* > SQUIRAGE

SQUIRED > SQUIRE

SQUIREDOM > SQUIRE

SQUIREEN *n* petty squire

SQUIREENS > SQUIREEN

SQUIRELY > SQUIRE

SQUIRES > SQUIRE

SQUIRESS *n* wife of squire

SQUIRING > SQUIRE

SQUIRISH > SQUIRE

SQUIRL *n* decorative flourish in handwriting

SQUIRLS > SQUIRL

SQUIRM *vb* wriggle, writhe ▷ *n* wriggling movement

SQUIRMED > SQUIRM

SQUIRMER > SQUIRM

SQUIRMERS > SQUIRM

SQUIRMIER > SQUIRMY

SQUIRMING > SQUIRM

SQUIRMS > SQUIRM

SQUIRMY *adj* moving with a wriggling motion

SQUIRR *same as* > SKIRR

SQUIRRED > SQUIRR

SQUIRREL *n* small bushy-tailed tree-living animal ▷ *vb* store for future use

SQUIRRELS > SQUIRREL

SQUIRRELY > SQUIRREL

SQUIRRING > SQUIRR

SQUIRRS > SQUIRR

SQUIRT *vb* force (a liquid) or (of a liquid) be forced out of a narrow opening ▷ *n* jet of liquid

SQUIRTED > SQUIRT

SQUIRTER > SQUIRT

SQUIRTERS > SQUIRT

SQUIRTING > SQUIRT

SQUIRTS > SQUIRT

SQUISH *n* a soft squelching sound ▷ *vb* crush (something) with a soft squelching sound

SQUISHED > SQUISH

SQUISHES > SQUISH

SQUISHIER > SQUISH

SQUISHING > SQUISH

SQUISHY *adj* soft and yielding to the touch

SQUIT *n* insignificant person

SQUITCH *n* couch grass

SQUITCHES > SQUITCH

SQUITS > SQUIT

SQUITTERS *pl n* diarrhoea

SQUIZ *n* look or glance, esp an inquisitive one

SQUIZZES > SQUIZ

SQUOOSH *vb* squash

SQUOOSHED > SQUOOSH

SQUOOSHES > SQUOOSH

SQUOOSHY > SQUOOSH

SQUUSH *same as* > SQUOOSH

SQUUSHED > SQUUSH

SQUUSHES > SQUUSH

SQUUSHING > SQUUSH

SRADDHA *n* Hindu offering to ancestor

SRADDHAS > SRADDHA

SRADHA *same as* > SRADDHA

SRADHAS > SRADHA

SRI *n* title of respect used when addressing a Hindu

SRIS > SRI

ST *interj* exclamation to attract attention

STAB *vb* pierce with something pointed ▷ *n* stabbing

STABBED > STAB

STABBER > STAB

STABBERS > STAB

STABBING > STAB

STABBINGS > STAB

STABILATE *n* preserved collection of tiny animals

STABILE *n* stationary abstract construction, usually of wire, metal, wood, etc ▷ *adj* fixed

STABILES > STABILE

STABILISE *same as* > STABILIZE

STABILITY *n* quality of being stable

STABILIZE *vb* make or become stable

STABLE *n* building in which horses are kept ▷ *vb* put or keep (a horse) in a stable ▷ *adj* firmly fixed or established

STABLEBOY *n* boy or man who works in a stable

STABLED > STABLE

STABLEMAN *same as* > STABLEBOY

STABLEMEN > STABLEMAN

STABLER *n* stable owner

STABLERS > STABLER

STABLES > STABLE

STABLEST > STABLE

STABLING *n* stable buildings or accommodation

STABLINGS > STABLING

STABLISH *archaic variant of* > ESTABLISH

STABLY > STABLE

STABS > STAB

STACATION *n* holiday spent at home, rather than travelling

STACCATI > STACCATO

STACCATO *adv* with the notes sharply separated ▷ *adj* consisting of short abrupt sounds ▷ *n* staccato note

STACCATOS > STACCATO

STACHYS *n* type of plant of the genus which includes lamb's ears and betony

STACHYSES > STACHYS

STACK *n* ordered pile ▷ *vb* pile in a stack

STACKABLE > STACK

STACKED > STACK

STACKER > STACK

STACKERS > STACK

STACKET *n* fence of wooden posts

STACKETS > STACKET

STACKING *n* arrangement of aircraft traffic in busy flight lanes

STACKINGS > STACKING

STACKLESS > STACK

STACKROOM *n* area of library where books are not on open shelves

STACKS > STACK

STACKUP *n* number of aircraft waiting to land

STACKUPS > STACKUP

STACKYARD *n* place where livestock are kept

STACTE *n* one of several sweet-smelling spices used in incense

STACTES > STACTE

STADDA *n* type of saw

STADDAS > STADDA

STADDLE *n* type of support or prop

STADDLES > STADDLE

STADE *same as* > STADIUM

STADES > STADE

STADIA *n* instrument used in surveying

STADIAL *n* stage in development of glacier

STADIALS > STADIAL

STADIAS > STADIA

STADIUM *n* sports arena with tiered seats for spectators

STADIUMS > STADIUM

STAFF *n* people employed in an organization ▷ *vb* supply with personnel

STAFFAGE *n* ornamentation in work of art

STAFFAGES > STAFFAGE

STAFFED > STAFF

STAFFER *n* member of staff, esp, in journalism, of editorial staff

STAFFERS > STAFFER

STAFFING *n* act of hiring employees

STAFFINGS > STAFFING

STAFFMAN *n* person who holds the levelling staff when a survey is being made

STAFFMEN > STAFFMAN

STAFFROOM *n* common room for teachers

STAFFS > STAFF

STAG *n* adult male deer ▷ *adv* without a female escort ▷ *vb* apply for (shares) with the intention of selling them for quick profit

STAGE *n* step or period of development ▷ *vb* put (a play) on stage

STAGEABLE > STAGE

STAGED > STAGE

STAGEFUL *n* amount that can appear on stage

STAGEFULS > STAGEFUL

STAGEHAND *n* person who moves props and scenery on a stage

STAGELIKE > STAGE

STAGER *n* person of experience

STAGERIES > STAGERY

STAGERS > STAGER

STAGERY *n* theatrical effects or techniques

STAGES > STAGE

STAGETTE *n* young unmarried professional woman

STAGETTES > STAGETTE

STAGEY *same as* > STAGY

STAGGARD *n* male red deer in the fourth year of life

STAGGARDS > STAGGARD

STAGGART *same as* > STAGGARD

STAGGARTS > STAGGART

STAGGED > STAG

STAGGER *vb* walk unsteadily ▷ *n* staggering

STAGGERED > STAGGER

STAGGERER > STAGGER

STAGGERS *n* disease of horses and other domestic animals that causes staggering

STAGGERY > STAGGER

STAGGIE *n* little stag

STAGGIER > STAG

STAGGIES > STAGGIE

STAGGIEST > STAG

STAGGING > STAG

STAGGY > STAG

STAGHORN *n* as in *staghorn fern* type of fern with fronds that resemble antlers

STAGHORNS > STAGHORN

STAGHOUND *n* breed of hound similar in appearance to the foxhound but larger

STAGIER > STAGY

STAGIEST > STAGY

STAGILY > STAGY

STAGINESS > STAGY

STAGING *n* temporary support used in building

STAGINGS > STAGING

STAGNANCE > STAGNANT

STAGNANCY > STAGNANT

STAGNANT *adj* (of water or air) stale from not moving

STAGNATE *vb* be stagnant

STAGNATED > STAGNATE

STAGNATES > STAGNATE

STAGS > STAG

STAGY *adj* too theatrical or dramatic

STAID *adj* sedate, serious, and rather dull

STAIDER > STAID

STAIDEST > STAID

STAIDLY > STAID

STAIDNESS > STAID
STAIG *Scots variant of* > STAG
STAIGS > STAIG
STAIN *vb* discolour, mark ▷ *n* discoloration or mark
STAINABLE > STAIN
STAINED > STAIN
STAINER > STAIN
STAINERS > STAIN
STAINING > STAIN
STAININGS > STAIN
STAINLESS *adj* resistant to discoloration, esp discoloration resulting from corrosion ▷ *n* stainless steel
STAINS > STAIN
STAIR *n* one step in a flight of stairs
STAIRCASE *n* flight of stairs with a handrail or banisters ▷ *vb* buy other houses in same building
STAIRED *adj* having stairs
STAIRFOOT *n* place at foot of stairs
STAIRHEAD *n* top of a flight of stairs
STAIRLESS > STAIR
STAIRLIFT *n* wall-mounted lifting device to carry person up stairs
STAIRLIKE > STAIR
STAIRS *pl n* flight of steps between floors, usu indoors
STAIRSTEP *n* one of the steps in a staircase
STAIRWAY *n* staircase
STAIRWAYS > STAIRWAY
STAIRWELL *n* vertical shaft in a building that contains a staircase
STAIRWISE *adv* by steps
STAIRWORK *n* unseen plotting
STAITH *same as* > STAITHE
STAITHE *n* wharf
STAITHES > STAITHE
STAITHS > STAITH
STAKE *n* pointed stick or post driven into the ground as a support or marker ▷ *vb* support or mark out with stakes
STAKED > STAKE
STAKEOUT *n* police surveillance of an area or house ▷ *vb* keep an area or house under surveillance
STAKEOUTS > STAKEOUT
STAKER *n* person who marks off an area with stakes
STAKERS > STAKER
STAKES > STAKE
STAKING > STAKE
STALACTIC *adj* relating to the masses of calcium carbonate hanging from the roofs of limestone caves

STALAG *n* German prisoner-of-war camp
STALAGMA *n* stalagmite
STALAGMAS > STALAGMA
STALAGS > STALAG
STALE *adj* not fresh ▷ *vb* make or become stale ▷ *n* urine of horses or cattle
STALED > STALE
STALELY > STALE
STALEMATE *n* (in chess) position in which any of a player's moves would put his king in check, resulting in a draw ▷ *vb* subject to a stalemate
STALENESS > STALE
STALER > STALE
STALES > STALE
STALEST > STALE
STALING > STALE
STALK *n* plant's stem ▷ *vb* follow or approach stealthily
STALKED > STALK
STALKER > STALK
STALKERS > STALK
STALKIER > STALKY
STALKIEST > STALKY
STALKILY > STALKY
STALKING > STALK
STALKINGS > STALK
STALKLESS > STALK
STALKLIKE > STALK
STALKO *n* idle gentleman
STALKOES > STALKO
STALKOS > STALKO
STALKS > STALK
STALKY *adj* like a stalk
STALL *n* small stand for the display and sale of goods ▷ *vb* (of a motor vehicle or engine) stop accidentally
STALLAGE *n* rent paid for market stall
STALLAGES > STALLAGE
STALLED > STALL
STALLING > STALL
STALLINGS > STALL
STALLION *n* uncastrated male horse
STALLIONS > STALLION
STALLMAN *n* keeper of a stall
STALLMEN > STALLMAN
STALLS > STALL
STALWART *adj* strong and sturdy ▷ *n* stalwart person
STALWARTS > STALWART
STALWORTH *n* stalwart person
STAMEN *n* pollen-producing part of a flower
STAMENED *adj* having stamen
STAMENS > STAMEN
STAMINA *n* enduring energy and strength
STAMINAL > STAMINA
STAMINAS > STAMINA

STAMINATE *adj* (of plants) having stamens, esp having stamens but no carpels
STAMINEAL *adj* having a stamen
STAMINODE *n* stamen that produces no pollen
STAMINODY *n* development of any of various plant organs into stamens
STAMINOID *adj* like a stamen
STAMMEL *n* coarse woollen cloth in former use for undergarments
STAMMELS > STAMMEL
STAMMER *vb* speak or say with involuntary pauses or repetition of syllables ▷ *n* tendency to stammer
STAMMERED > STAMMER
STAMMERER > STAMMER
STAMMERS > STAMMER
STAMNOI > STAMNOS
STAMNOS *n* ancient Greek jar
STAMP *n* piece of gummed paper stuck to an envelope or parcel ▷ *vb* bring (one's foot) down forcefully
STAMPED > STAMP
STAMPEDE *n* sudden rush of frightened animals or of a crowd ▷ *vb* (cause to) take part in a stampede
STAMPEDED > STAMPEDE
STAMPEDER > STAMPEDE
STAMPEDES > STAMPEDE
STAMPEDO *same as* > STAMPEDE
STAMPEDOS > STAMPEDO
STAMPER > STAMP
STAMPERS > STAMP
STAMPING > STAMP
STAMPINGS > STAMP
STAMPLESS > STAMP
STAMPS > STAMP
STANCE *n* attitude
STANCES > STANCE
STANCH *vb* stem the flow of (a liquid, esp blood) ▷ *adj* loyal and dependable
STANCHED > STANCH
STANCHEL *same as* > STANCHION
STANCHELS > STANCHEL
STANCHER > STANCH
STANCHERS > STANCH
STANCHES > STANCH
STANCHEST > STANCH
STANCHING > STANCH
STANCHION *n* upright bar used as a support ▷ *vb* provide or support with a stanchion or stanchions
STANCHLY > STANCH
STANCK *adj* faint
STAND *vb* be in, rise to, or place in an upright position ▷ *n* stall for the sale of goods

STANDARD *n* level of quality ▷ *adj* usual, regular, or average
STANDARDS > STANDARD
STANDAWAY *adj* erect
STANDBY *n* person or thing that is ready for use
STANDBYS > STANDBY
STANDDOWN *n* return to normal after alert
STANDEE *n* person who stands
STANDEES > STANDEE
STANDEN > STAND
STANDER > STAND
STANDERS > STAND
STANDFAST *n* reliable person or thing
STANDGALE *same as* > STANIEL
STANDING > STAND
STANDINGS > STAND
STANDISH *n* stand, usually of metal, for pens, ink bottles, etc
STANDOFF *n* act or an instance of standing off or apart ▷ *vb* stay at a distance
STANDOFFS > STANDOFF
STANDOUT *n* distinctive or outstanding person or thing
STANDOUTS > STANDOUT
STANDOVER *n* threatening or intimidating act
STANDPAT *n* (in poker) refusal to change one's card
STANDPIPE *n* tap attached to a water main to provide a public water supply
STANDS > STAND
STANDUP *n* comedian who performs solo
STANDUPS > STANDUP
STANE *Scot word for* > STONE
STANED > STANE
STANES > STANE
STANG *vb* sting
STANGED > STANG
STANGING > STANG
STANGS > STANG
STANHOPE *n* light one-seater carriage with two or four wheels
STANHOPES > STANHOPE
STANIEL *n* kestrel
STANIELS > STANIEL
STANINE *n* scale of nine levels
STANINES > STANINE
STANING > STANE
STANK *vb* dam
STANKED > STINK
STANKING > STINK
STANKS > STINK
STANNARY *n* place or region where tin is mined or worked

STANNATE n salt of stannic acid

STANNATES > STANNATE

STANNATOR n member of old Cornish parliament

STANNEL same as > STANIEL

STANNELS > STANNEL

STANNIC adj of or containing tin, esp in the tetravalent state

STANNITE n grey metallic mineral

STANNITES > STANNITE

STANNOUS adj of or containing tin, esp in the divalent state

STANNUM n tin (the metal)

STANNUMS > STANNUM

STANOL n drug taken to prevent heart disease

STANOLS > STANOL

STANYEL same as > STANIEL

STANYELS > STANYEL

STANZA n verse of a poem

STANZAED > STANZA

STANZAIC > STANZA

STANZAS > STANZA

STANZE same as > STANZA

STANZES > STANZE

STANZO same as > STANZA

STANZOES > STANZO

STANZOS > STANZO

STAP same as > STOP

STAPEDES > STAPES

STAPEDIAL > STAPES

STAPEDII > STAPEDIUS

STAPEDIUS n muscle in stapes

STAPELIA n fleshy cactus-like leafless African plant

STAPELIAS > STAPELIA

STAPES n stirrup-shaped bone in the middle ear of mammals

STAPH n staphylococcus

STAPHS > STAPH

STAPLE n U-shaped piece of metal used to fasten papers ▷ vb fasten with staples ▷ adj of prime importance

STAPLED > STAPLE

STAPLER n small device for fastening papers together

STAPLERS > STAPLER

STAPLES > STAPLE

STAPLING n as in stomach stapling surgical treatment for obesity

STAPLINGS > STAPLING

STAPPED > STAP

STAPPING > STAP

STAPPLE same as > STOPPLE

STAPPLES > STAPPLE

STAPS > STAP

STAR n hot gaseous mass in space, visible in the night sky as a point of light ▷ vb feature or be featured as a star ▷ adj leading, famous

STARAGEN n tarragon

STARAGENS > STARAGEN

STARBOARD n right-hand side of a ship, when facing forward ▷ adj of or on this side ▷ vb turn or be turned towards the starboard

STARBURST n pattern of rays or lines radiating from a light source

STARCH n carbohydrate forming the main food element in bread, potatoes, etc ▷ vb stiffen (fabric) with starch ▷ adj (of a person) formal

STARCHED > STARCH

STARCHER > STARCH

STARCHERS > STARCH

STARCHES > STARCH

STARCHIER > STARCHY

STARCHILY > STARCHY

STARCHING > STARCH

STARCHY adj containing starch

STARDOM n status of a star in the entertainment or sports world

STARDOMS > STARDOM

STARDRIFT n regular movement of stars

STARDUST n dusty material found between the stars

STARDUSTS > STARDUST

STARE vb look or gaze fixedly (at) ▷ n fixed gaze

STARED > STARE

STARER > STARE

STARERS > STARE

STARES > STARE

STARETS n Russian holy man

STARETSES > STARETS

STARETZ same as > STARETZ

STARETZES > STARETZ

STARFISH n star-shaped sea creature

STARFRUIT n tree with edible yellow fruit which is star-shaped on cross section

STARGAZE vb observe the stars

STARGAZED > STARGAZE

STARGAZER > STARGAZE

STARGAZES > STARGAZE

STARGAZEY adj as in stargazey pie Cornish fish pie

STARING > STARE

STARINGLY > STARE

STARINGS > STARE

STARK adj harsh, unpleasant, and plain ▷ adv completely ▷ vb stiffen

STARKED > STARK

STARKEN vb become or make stark

STARKENED > STARKEN

STARKENS > STARKEN

STARKER > STARK

STARKERS adj completely naked

STARKEST > STARK

STARKING > STARK

STARKLY > STARK

STARKNESS > STARK

STARKS > STARK

STARLESS > STAR

STARLET n young actress presented as a future star

STARLETS > STARLET

STARLIGHT n light that comes from the stars ▷ adj of or like starlight

STARLIKE > STAR

STARLING n songbird with glossy black speckled feathers

STARLINGS > STARLING

STARLIT same as > STARLIGHT

STARN same as > STERN

STARNED > STARN

STARNIE n Scots word for little star

STARNIES > STARNIE

STARNING > STARN

STARNOSE n American mole with starlike nose

STARNOSES > STARNOSE

STARNS > STARN

STAROSTA n headman of Russian village

STAROSTAS > STAROSTA

STAROSTY n estate of Polish nobleman

STARR n (in Judaism) release from a debt

STARRED > STAR

STARRIER > STARRY

STARRIEST > STARRY

STARRILY > STARRY

STARRING > STAR

STARRINGS > STARE

STARRS > STARR

STARRY adj full of or like stars

STARS > STAR

STARSHINE n starlight

STARSHIP n spacecraft in science fiction

STARSHIPS > STARSHIP

STARSPOT n dark patch on surface of star

STARSPOTS > STARSPOT

STARSTONE n precious stone reflecting light in starlike pattern

START vb take the first step, begin ▷ n first part of something

STARTED > START

STARTER n first course of a meal

STARTERS > STARTER

STARTFUL adj tending to start

STARTING > START

STARTINGS > START

STARTISH same as > STARTFUL

STARTLE vb slightly surprise or frighten

STARTLED > STARTLE

STARTLER > STARTLE

STARTLERS > STARTLE

STARTLES > STARTLE

STARTLING adj causing surprise or fear

STARTLISH adj easily startled

STARTLY same as > STARTLISH

STARTS > START

STARTSY > STARETS

STARTUP n business enterprise that has been launched recently

STARTUPS > STARTUP

STARVE vb die or suffer or cause to die or suffer from hunger

STARVED > STARVE

STARVER > STARVE

STARVERS > STARVE

STARVES > STARVE

STARVING > STARVE

STARVINGS > STARVE

STARWORT n plant with star-shaped flowers

STARWORTS > STARWORT

STASES > STASIS

STASH vb store in a secret place ▷ n secret store

STASHED > STASH

STASHES > STASH

STASHIE same as > STUSHIE

STASHIES > STASHIE

STASHING > STASH

STASIDION n stall in Greek church

STASIMA > STASIMON

STASIMON n ode sung in Greek tragedy

STASIS n stagnation in the normal flow of bodily fluids

STAT n statistic

STATABLE > STATE

STATAL adj of a federal state

STATANT adj (of an animal) in profile with all four feet on the ground

STATE n condition of a person or thing ▷ adj of or concerning the State ▷ vb express in words

STATEABLE > STATE

STATED adj (esp of a sum) determined by agreement

STATEDLY > STATED

STATEHOOD > STATE

STATELESS adj not belonging to any country

STATELET n small state

STATELETS > STATELET

STATELIER > STATELY

STATELILY > STATELY

STATELY adj dignified or grand ▷ adv in a stately manner

STATEMENT n something stated ▷ vb assess (a pupil)

S

with regard to his or her special educational needs

STATER n any of various usually silver coins of ancient Greece

STATEROOM n private cabin on a ship

STATERS > STATER

STATES > STATE

STATESIDE adv of, in, to, or towards the US

STATESMAN n experienced and respected political leader

STATESMEN > STATESMAN

STATEWIDE adj throughout a state

STATIC adj stationary or inactive ▷ n crackling sound or speckled picture caused by interference in radio or television reception

STATICAL > STATIC

STATICE n plant name formerly used for both thrift and sea lavender

STATICES > STATICE

STATICKY > STATIC

STATICS n study of the forces producing a state of equilibrium

STATIM adv right away

STATIN n type of drug that lowers the levels of low-density lipoproteins in the blood

STATING > STATE

STATINS > STATIN

STATION n place where trains stop for passengers ▷ vb assign (someone) to a particular place

STATIONAL > STATION

STATIONED > STATION

STATIONER n dealer in stationery

STATIONS > STATION

STATISM n theory or practice of concentrating economic and political power in the state

STATISMS > STATISM

STATIST n advocate of statism ▷ adj of, characteristic of, advocating, or relating to statism

STATISTIC n numerical fact collected and classified systematically

STATISTS > STATIST

STATIVE adj denoting a verb describing a state rather than an activity, act, or event ▷ n stative verb

STATIVES > STATIVE

STATOCYST n organ of balance in some invertebrates

STATOLITH n any of the granules of calcium carbonate occurring in a statocyst

STATOR n stationary part of a rotary machine or device

STATORS > STATOR

STATS > STAT

STATTO n person preoccupied with the facts and figures of a subject

STATTOS > STATTO

STATUA same as > STATUE

STATUARY n statues collectively ▷ adj of, relating to, or suitable for statues

STATUAS > STATUA

STATUE n large sculpture of a human or animal figure

STATUED adj decorated with or portrayed in a statue or statues

STATUES > STATUE

STATUETTE n small statue

STATURE n person's height

STATURED adj having stature

STATURES > STATURE

STATUS n social position

STATUSES > STATUS

STATUSY adj conferring or having status

STATUTE n written law

STATUTES > STATUTE

STATUTORY adj required or authorized by law

STAUMREL n stupid person

STAUMRELS > STAUMREL

STAUN Scot word for > STAND

STAUNCH same as > STANCH

STAUNCHED > STAUNCH

STAUNCHER > STAUNCH

STAUNCHES > STAUNCH

STAUNCHLY > STAUNCH

STAUNING > STAUN

STAUNS > STAUN

STAVE same as > STAFF

STAVED > STAVE

STAVES > STAVE

STAVING > STAVE

STAVUDINE n drug used to treat HIV

STAW Scots form of > STALL

STAWED > STAW

STAWING > STAW

STAWS > STAW

STAY vb remain in a place or condition ▷ n period of staying in a place

STAYAWAY n strike in South Africa

STAYAWAYS > STAYAWAY

STAYED > STAY

STAYER n person or thing that stays

STAYERS > STAYER

STAYING > STAY

STAYLESS adj with no stays or support

STAYMAKER n corset maker

STAYNE same as > STAIN

STAYNED > STAYNE

STAYNES > STAYNE

STAYNING > STAYNE

STAYRE same as > STAIR

STAYRES > STAYRE

STAYS pl n old-fashioned corsets with bones in them

STAYSAIL n sail fastened on a stay

STAYSAILS > STAYSAIL

STEAD n place or function that should be taken by another ▷ vb help or benefit

STEADED > STEAD

STEADFAST adj firm, determined

STEADIED > STEADY

STEADIER > STEADY

STEADIERS > STEADY

STEADIES > STEADY

STEADIEST > STEADY

STEADILY > STEADY

STEADING n farmstead

STEADINGS > STEADING

STEADS > STEAD

STEADY adj not shaky or wavering ▷ vb make steady ▷ adv in a steady manner

STEADYING > STEADY

STEAK n thick slice of meat, esp beef

STEAKS > STEAK

STEAL vb take unlawfully or without permission

STEALABLE > STEAL

STEALAGE n theft

STEALAGES > STEALAGE

STEALE n handle

STEALED > STEAL

STEALER n person who steals something

STEALERS > STEALER

STEALES > STEALE

STEALING > STEAL

STEALINGS > STEAL

STEALS > STEAL

STEALT > STEAL

STEALTH n moving carefully and quietly ▷ adj (of technology) able to render an aircraft almost invisible to radar ▷ vb approach undetected

STEALTHED > STEALTH

STEALTHS > STEALTH

STEALTHY adj characterized by great caution, secrecy, etc

STEAM n vapour into which water changes when boiled ▷ vb give off steam

STEAMBOAT n boat powered by a steam engine

STEAMED > STEAM

STEAMER n steam-propelled ship ▷ vb travel by steamer

STEAMERED > STEAMER

STEAMERS > STEAMER

STEAMIE n public wash house

STEAMIER > STEAMY

STEAMIES > STEAMIE

STEAMIEST > STEAMY

STEAMILY > STEAMY

STEAMING adj very hot ▷ n robbery, esp of passengers in a railway carriage or bus, by a large gang of armed youths

STEAMINGS > STEAMING

STEAMPUNK n subgenre of science fiction set in Victorian times

STEAMROLL vb crush (opposition) by overpowering force

STEAMS > STEAM

STEAMSHIP n ship powered by steam engines

STEAMY adj full of steam

STEAN n earthenware vessel

STEANE same as > STEEN

STEANED > STEANE

STEANES > STEANE

STEANING > STEANE

STEANINGS > STEANE

STEANS > STEAN

STEAPSIN n pancreatic lipase

STEAPSINS > STEAPSIN

STEAR same as > STEER

STEARAGE same as > STEERAGE

STEARAGES > STEARAGE

STEARATE n any salt or ester of stearic acid

STEARATES > STEARATE

STEARD > STEAR

STEARE same as > STEER

STEARED > STEARE

STEARES > STEARE

STEARIC adj of or relating to suet or fat

STEARIN n colourless crystalline ester of glycerol and stearic acid

STEARINE same as > STEARIN

STEARINES > STEARINE

STEARING > STEAR

STEARINS > STEARIN

STEARS > STEAR

STEARSMAN same as > STEERSMAN

STEARSMEN > STEARSMAN

STEATITE same as > SOAPSTONE

STEATITES > STEATITE

STEATITIC > STEATITE

STEATOMA n tumour of sebaceous gland

STEATOMAS > STEATOMA

STEATOSES > STEATOSIS

STEATOSIS n abnormal accumulation of fat

STED same as > STEAD

STEDD same as > STEAD
STEDDE same as > STEAD
STEDDED > STED
STEDDES > STEDDE
STEDDIED > STEDDY
STEDDIES > STEDDY
STEDDING > STED
STEDDS > STED
STEDDY same as > STEADY
STEDDYING > STEDDY
STEDE same as > STEAD
STEDED > STEDE
STEDES > STEDE
STEDFAST same as
> STEADFAST
STEDING > STEDE
STEDS > STED
STEED same as > STEAD
STEEDED > STEED
STEEDIED > STEEDY
STEEDIES > STEEDY
STEEDING > STEEDY
STEEDLIKE > STEED
STEEDS > STEED
STEEDY same as > STEADY
STEEDYING > STEEDY
STEEK vb Scots word
meaning shut
STEEKED > STEEK
STEEKING > STEEK
STEEKIT > STEEK
STEEKS > STEEK
STEEL n hard malleable
alloy of iron and carbon
▷ vb prepare (oneself) for
something unpleasant
STEELBOW n material lent
to tenant by landlord
STEELBOWS
> STEELBOW
STEELD > STEEL
STEELED > STEEL
STEELHEAD n silvery
North Pacific variety of the
rainbow trout
STEELIE n steel ball
bearing used as marble
STEELIER > STEELY
STEELIES > STEELIE
STEELIEST > STEELIE
STEELING > STEEL
STEELINGS > STEEL
STEELMAN n person
working in steel industry
STEELMEN > STEELMAN
STEELS pl n shares and
bonds of steel companies
STEELWARE n things
made of steel
STEELWORK n frame,
foundation, building, or
article made of steel
STEELY > STEEL
STEELYARD n portable
balance consisting of a
pivoted bar with two
unequal arms
STEEM variant of
> ESTEEM
STEEMED > STEEM
STEEMING > STEEM
STEEMS > STEEM
STEEN vb line with stone

STEENBOK n small
antelope of central and
southern Africa
STEENBOKS > STEENBOK
STEENBRAS n variety of
sea bream
STEENBUCK same as
> STEENBOK
STEENED > STEEN
STEENING > STEEN
STEENINGS > STEEN
STEENKIRK n type of
cravat
STEENS > STEEN
STEEP adj sloping sharply
▷ vb soak or be soaked in
liquid ▷ n instance or the
process of steeping
STEEPED > STEEP
STEEPEN vb become steep
or steeper
STEEPENED > STEEPEN
STEEPENS > STEEPEN
STEEPER > STEEP
STEEPERS > STEEP
STEEPEST > STEEP
STEEPEUP adj very steep
STEEPIER > STEEPY
STEEPIEST > STEEPY
STEEPING > STEEP
STEEPISH > STEEP
STEEPLE same as > SPIRE
STEEPLED > STEEPLE
STEEPLES > STEEPLE
STEEPLING adj going up
on a steep trajectory
STEEPLY > STEEP
STEEPNESS > STEEP
STEEPS > STEEP
STEEPUP adj very steep
STEEPY same as > STEEP
STEER vb direct the course
of (a vehicle or ship) ▷ n
castrated male ox
STEERABLE > STEER
STEERAGE n cheapest
accommodation on a
passenger ship
STEERAGES > STEERAGE
STEERED > STEER
STEERER > STEER
STEERERS > STEER
STEERIER > STEERY
STEERIES > STEERY
STEERIEST > STEERY
STEERING > STEER
STEERINGS > STEER
STEERLING n young
steer
STEERS > STEER
STEERSMAN n person
who steers a vessel
STEERSMEN
> STEERSMAN
STEERY n commotion
▷ adj busy or bustling
STEEVE n spar having a
pulley block at one end
▷ vb stow (cargo) securely
in the hold of a ship
STEEVED > STEEVE
STEEVELY > STEEVE
STEEVER > STEEVE

STEEVES > STEEVE
STEEVEST > STEEVE
STEEVING > STEEVE
STEEVINGS > STEEVE
STEGNOSES
> STEGNOSIS
STEGNOSIS n
constriction of bodily
pores
STEGNOTIC n medicine
that stops bleeding
STEGODON n mammal of
Pliocene to Pleistocene
times, similar to the
mastodon
STEGODONS
> STEGODON
STEGODONT same as
> STEGODON
STEGOMYIA former name
for > AEDES
STEGOSAUR n
quadrupedal herbivorous
dinosaur
STEIL same as > STEAL
STEILS > STEIL
STEIN same as > STEEN
STEINBOCK another name
for > IBEX
STEINBOK same as
> STEENBOK
STEINBOKS > STEINBOK
STEINED > STEIN
STEINING > STEIN
STEININGS > STEIN
STEINKIRK same as
> STEENKIRK
STEINS > STEIN
STELA same as > STELE
STELAE > STELE
STELAI > STELE
STELAR > STELE
STELE n upright stone slab
or column decorated with
figures or inscriptions
STELENE > STELE
STELES > STELE
STELIC > STELE
STELL n shelter for cattle
or sheep built on moorland
or hillsides ▷ vb position or
place
STELLA n star or
something star-shaped
STELLAR adj of stars
STELLAS > STELLA
STELLATE adj resembling
a star in shape
STELLATED same as
> STELLATE
STELLED > STELL
STELLERID n starfish
STELLIFY vb change or
be changed into a star
STELLING > STELL
STELLIO n as in stellio
lizard denoting type of
lizard
STELLION n
Mediterranean lizard
STELLIONS
> STELLION
STELLITE n tradename
for any of various alloys

containing cobalt,
chromium, carbon,
tungsten, and
molybdenum
STELLITES > STELLITE
STELLS > STELL
STELLULAR adj
displaying or abounding in
small stars
STEM vb stop (the flow of
something) ▷ n main axis
of a plant, which bears the
leaves, axillary buds, and
flowers
STEMBOK same as
> STEENBOK
STEMBOKS > STEMBOK
STEMBUCK same as
> STEENBOK
STEMBUCKS > STEMBUCK
STEME same as > STEAM
STEMED > STEME
STEMES > STEME
STEMHEAD n head of the
stem of a vessel
STEMHEADS > STEMHEAD
STEMING > STEME
STEMLESS > STEM
STEMLET n little stem
STEMLETS > STEMLET
STEMLIKE > STEM
STEMMA n family tree
STEMMAS > STEMMA
STEMMATA > STEMMA
STEMMATIC > STEMMA
STEMME archaic variant of
> STEM
STEMMED > STEM
STEMMER > STEM
STEMMERS > STEM
STEMMERY n tobacco
factory
STEMMES > STEMME
STEMMIER > STEMMY
STEMMIEST > STEMMY
STEMMING > STEM
STEMMINGS > STEM
STEMMY adj (of wine)
young and raw
STEMPEL n timber
support
STEMPELS > STEMPEL
STEMPLE same as
> STEMPEL
STEMPLES > STEMPLE
STEMS > STEM
STEMSON n curved timber
at the bow of a wooden
vessel
STEMSONS > STEMSON
STEMWARE n collective
term for glasses, goblets,
etc, with stems
STEMWARES > STEMWARE
STEN vb stride
STENCH n foul smell
▷ vb cause to smell
STENCHED > STENCH
STENCHES > STENCH
STENCHFUL > STENCH
STENCHIER > STENCH
STENCHING > STENCH
STENCHY > STENCH

STENCIL n thin sheet through which ink passes to form a pattern on the surface below ▷ vb make (a pattern) with a stencil
STENCILED > STENCIL
STENCILER > STENCIL
STENCILS > STENCIL
STEND vb Scots word meaning bound
STENDED > STEND
STENDING > STEND
STENDS > STEND
STENGAH same as > STINGER
STENGAHS > STENGAH
STENLOCK n fish of northern seas
STENLOCKS > STENLOCK
STENNED > STEN
STENNING > STEN
STENO n stenographer
STENOBATH n stenobathic organism
STENOKIES > STENOKY
STENOKOUS adj able to live in narrow range of environments
STENOKY n survival dependent on conditions remaining within a narrow range of variables
STENOPAIC adj having narrow opening
STENOS > STENO
STENOSED adj abnormally contracted
STENOSES > STENOSIS
STENOSING adj causing or characterized by stenosis
STENOSIS n abnormal narrowing of a bodily canal or passage
STENOTIC > STENOSIS
STENOTYPE n machine with a keyboard for recording speeches in a phonetic shorthand
STENOTYPY n form of shorthand in which alphabetic combinations are used to represent groups of sounds or short common words
STENS > STEN
STENT n surgical implant used to keep an artery open ▷ vb assess
STENTED > STENT
STENTING > STENT
STENTOR n person with an unusually loud voice
STENTORS > STENTOR
STENTOUR n tax assessor
STENTOURS > STENTOUR
STENTS > STENT
STEP vb move and set down the foot, as when walking ▷ n stepping
STEPBAIRN Scots word for > STEPCHILD
STEPCHILD n stepson or stepdaughter

STEPDAD n stepfather
STEPDADS > STEPDAD
STEPDAME n woman married to one's father
STEPDAMES > STEPDAME
STEPHANE n ancient Greek headdress
STEPHANES > STEPHANE
STEPLESS adj without steps
STEPLIKE > STEP
STEPMOM n stepmother
STEPMOMS > STEPMOM
STEPNEY n spare wheel
STEPNEYS > STEPNEY
STEPOVER n (in football) instance of raising the foot over the ball as a feint
STEPOVERS > STEPOVER
STEPPE n extensive grassy plain usually without trees
STEPPED > STEP
STEPPER n person who or animal that steps, esp a horse or a dancer
STEPPERS > STEPPER
STEPPES > STEPPE
STEPPING > STEP
STEPS > STEP
STEPSON n son of one's husband or wife by an earlier relationship
STEPSONS > STEPSON
STEPSTOOL n stool able to be used as step
STEPT > STEP
STEPWISE adj arranged in the manner of or resembling steps ▷ adv with the form or appearance of steps
STERADIAN n SI unit of solid angle
STERANE n any of a class of hydrocarbons found in crude oils
STERANES > STERANE
STERCORAL adj relating to excrement
STERCULIA n dietary fibre used as a food stabilizer and denture adhesive
STERE n unit used to measure volumes of stacked timber
STEREO n stereophonic record player ▷ adj feeding two loudspeakers through separate channels ▷ vb make stereophonic
STEREOED > STEREO
STEREOING > STEREO
STEREOME n tissue of a plant that provides mechanical support
STEREOMES > STEREOME
STEREOS > STEREO
STERES > STERE
STERIC adj of or caused by the spatial arrangement of atoms in a molecule
STERICAL same as > STERIC

STERIGMA n minute stalk bearing a spore or chain of spores in certain fungi
STERIGMAS > STERIGMA
STERILANT n any substance or agent used in sterilization
STERILE adj free from germs
STERILELY > STERILE
STERILISE same as > STERILIZE
STERILITY > STERILE
STERILIZE vb make sterile
STERLET n small sturgeon of N Asia and E Europe
STERLETS > STERLET
STERLING n British money system ▷ adj genuine and reliable
STERLINGS > STERLING
STERN adj severe, strict ▷ n rear part of a ship ▷ vb row boat backward
STERNA > STERNUM
STERNAGE n sterns
STERNAGES > STERNAGE
STERNAL > STERNUM
STERNEBRA n part of breastbone
STERNED > STERN
STERNER > STERN
STERNEST > STERN
STERNFAST n rope for securing boat at stern
STERNING > STERN
STERNITE n part of arthropod
STERNITES > STERNITE
STERNITIC > STERNITE
STERNLY > STERN
STERNMOST adj farthest to the stern
STERNNESS > STERN
STERNPORT n opening in stern of ship
STERNPOST n main upright timber or structure at the stern of a vessel
STERNS > STERN
STERNSON n timber scarfed into or bolted to the sternpost and keelson at the stern of a wooden vessel
STERNSÓNS > STERNSON
STERNUM n long flat bone to which most of the ribs are attached
STERNUMS > STERNUM
STERNWARD adv towards the stern
STERNWAY n movement of a vessel sternforemost
STERNWAYS > STERNWAY
STEROID n organic compound containing a carbon ring system
STEROIDAL > STEROID
STEROIDS > STEROID
STEROL n natural insoluble alcohol such as cholesterol and ergosterol

STEROLS > STEROL
STERTOR n laborious or noisy breathing
STERTORS > STERTOR
STERVE same as > STARVE
STERVED > STERVE
STERVES > STERVE
STERVING > STERVE
STET interj instruction to ignore an alteration previously made ▷ vb indicate to a printer that deleted matter is to be kept ▷ n mark indicating that deleted matter is to be kept
STETS > STET
STETSON n cowboy hat
STETSONS > STETSON
STETTED > STET
STETTING > STET
STEVEDORE n person who loads and unloads ships ▷ vb load or unload (a ship, ship's cargo, etc)
STEVEN n voice
STEVENS > STEVEN
STEVIA n any of a genus of plant with sweet leaves
STEVIAS > STEVIA
STEW n food cooked slowly in a closed pot ▷ vb cook slowly in a closed pot
STEWABLE > STEW
STEWARD n person who looks after passengers on a ship or aircraft ▷ vb act as a steward (of)
STEWARDED > STEWARD
STEWARDRY n office of steward
STEWARDS > STEWARD
STEWARTRY variant of > STEWARDRY
STEWBUM n drunkard
STEWBUMS > STEWBUM
STEWED adj (of food) cooked by stewing
STEWER > STEW
STEWERS > STEW
STEWIER > STEW
STEWIEST > STEW
STEWING > STEW
STEWINGS > STEW
STEWPAN n pan used for making stew
STEWPANS > STEWPAN
STEWPOND n fishpond
STEWPONDS > STEWPOND
STEWPOT n pot used for making stew
STEWPOTS > STEWPOT
STEWS > STEW
STEWY > STEW
STEY adj (Scots) steep ▷ n ladder
STEYER > STEY
STEYEST > STEY
STEYS > STEY
STHENIA n abnormal strength
STHENIAS > STHENIA

STHENIC adj abounding in energy or bodily strength

STIBBLE Scots form of > STUBBLE

STIBBLER n horse allowed to eat stubble

STIBBLERS > STIBBLE

STIBBLES > STIBBLE

STIBIAL > STIBIUM

STIBINE n colourless slightly soluble poisonous gas

STIBINES > STIBINE

STIBIUM obsolete name for > ANTIMONY

STIBIUMS > STIBIUM

STIBNITE n soft greyish mineral

STIBNITES > STIBNITE

STICCADO n type of xylophone

STICCADOS > STICCADO

STICCATO same as > STICCADO

STICCATOS > STICCATO

STICH n line of poetry

STICHARIA pl n priest's robes of the Greek Church

STICHERA > STICHERON

STICHERON n short hymn in Greek Church

STICHIC > STICH

STICHIDIA pl n seaweed branches

STICHOI > STICHOS

STICHOS n line of poem

STICHS > STICH

STICK n long thin piece of wood ▷ vb push (a pointed object) into (something)

STICKABLE > STICK

STICKBALL n form of baseball played in street

STICKED > STICK

STICKER n adhesive label or sign ▷ vb put stickers on

STICKERED > STICKER

STICKERS > STICKER

STICKFUL > STICK

STICKFULS > STICK

STICKIE n notepaper with an adhesive strip

STICKIED > STICKY

STICKIER > STICKY

STICKIES > STICKY

STICKIEST > STICKY

STICKILY > STICKY

STICKING > STICK

STICKINGS > STICK

STICKIT Scots form of > STUCK

STICKJAW n stodgy food

STICKJAWS > STICKJAW

STICKLE vb dispute stubbornly, esp about minor points

STICKLED > STICKLE

STICKLER n person who insists on something

STICKLERS > STICKLER

STICKLES > STICKLE

STICKLIKE > STICK

STICKLING n act of making insistent demands

STICKMAN n human figure drawn in thin strokes

STICKMEN > STICKMAN

STICKOUT n conspicuous person or thing

STICKOUTS > STICKOUT

STICKPIN n tiepin

STICKPINS > STICKPIN

STICKS > STICK

STICKSEED n type of Eurasian and North American plant

STICKUM n adhesive

STICKUMS > STICKUM

STICKUP n robbery at gun-point

STICKUPS > STICKUP

STICKWEED n any of several plants that have clinging fruits or seeds, esp the ragweed

STICKWORK n use of stick in hockey

STICKY adj covered with an adhesive substance ▷ vb make sticky ▷ n inquisitive look or stare

STICKYING > STICKY

STICTION n frictional force to be overcome to set one object in motion when it is in contact with another

STICTIONS > STICTION

STIDDIE same as > STITHY

STIDDIED > STIDDIE

STIDDIES > STIDDIE

STIE same as > STY

STIED > STY

STIES > STY

STIEVE same as > STEEVE

STIEVELY > STIEVE

STIEVER > STIEVE

STIEVEST > STIEVE

STIFF adj not easily bent or moved ▷ n corpse ▷ adv completely or utterly ▷ vb fail completely

STIFFED > STIFF

STIFFEN vb make or become stiff

STIFFENED > STIFFEN

STIFFENER > STIFFEN

STIFFENS > STIFFEN

STIFFER > STIFF

STIFFEST > STIFF

STIFFIE n erection of the penis

STIFFIES > STIFFIE

STIFFING > STIFF

STIFFISH > STIFF

STIFFLY > STIFF

STIFFNESS > STIFF

STIFFS > STIFF

STIFFWARE n computer software that is hard to modify

STIFFY n erection of the penis

STIFLE vb suppress ▷ n joint in the hind leg of a horse, dog, etc

STIFLED > STIFLE

STIFLER > STIFLE

STIFLERS > STIFLE

STIFLES > STIFLE

STIFLING adj uncomfortably hot and stuffy

STIFLINGS > STIFLING

STIGMA n mark of social disgrace

STIGMAL adj of part of insect wing

STIGMAS > STIGMA

STIGMATA > STIGMA

STIGMATIC adj relating to or having a stigma or stigmata ▷ n person marked with the stigmata

STIGME n dot in Greek punctuation

STIGMES > STIGME

STILB n unit of luminance

STILBENE n colourless or slightly yellow crystalline hydrocarbon used in the manufacture of dyes

STILBENES > STILBENE

STILBITE n white or yellow zeolite mineral

STILBITES > STILBITE

STILBS > STILB

STILE same as > STYLE

STILED > STILE

STILES > STILE

STILET same as > STYLET

STILETS > STILET

STILETTO n high narrow heel on a woman's shoe ▷ vb stab with a stiletto

STILETTOS > STILETTO

STILING > STILE

STILL adv now or in the future as before ▷ adj motionless ▷ n calmness; apparatus for distillation ▷ vb make still

STILLAGE n frame or stand for keeping things off the ground, such as casks in a brewery

STILLAGES > STILLAGE

STILLBORN adj born dead ▷ n stillborn fetus or baby

STILLED > STILL

STILLER > STILL

STILLERS > STILL

STILLEST > STILL

STILLIER > STILLY

STILLIEST > STILLY

STILLING > STILL

STILLINGS > STILL

STILLION n stand for cask

STILLIONS > STILLION

STILLMAN n someone involved in the operation of a still

STILLMEN > STILLMAN

STILLNESS > STILL

STILLROOM n room in which distilling is carried out

STILLS > STILL

STILLSON n type of wrench

STILLSONS > STILLSON

STILLY adv quietly or calmly ▷ adj still, quiet, or calm

STILT n either of a pair of long poles with footrests for walking raised from the ground ▷ vb raise or place on or as if on stilts

STILTBIRD n long-legged wading bird

STILTED adj stiff and formal in manner

STILTEDLY > STILTED

STILTER > STILT

STILTERS > STILT

STILTIER > STILT

STILTIEST > STILT

STILTING > STILT

STILTINGS > STILT

STILTISH > STILT

STILTS > STILT

STILTY > STILT

STIM n very small amount

STIME same as > STYME

STIMED > STIME

STIMES > STIME

STIMIE same as > STYMIE

STIMIED > STIMIE

STIMIES > STIMIE

STIMING > STIME

STIMS > STIM

STIMULANT n something, such as a drug, that acts as a stimulus ▷ adj stimulating

STIMULATE vb act as a stimulus (on)

STIMULI > STIMULUS

STIMULUS n something that rouses a person or thing to activity

STIMY same as > STYMIE

STIMYING > STIMY

STING vb (of certain animals or plants) wound by injecting with poison ▷ n wound or pain caused by or as if by stinging

STINGAREE popular name for > STINGRAY

STINGBULL n spiny fish

STINGE n stingy or miserly person

STINGED > STING

STINGER n person, plant, animal, etc, that stings or hurts

STINGERS > STINGER

STINGES > STINGE

STINGFISH same as > STINGBULL

STINGIER > STINGY

STINGIES > STINGY

STINGIEST > STINGY

STINGILY > STINGY

STINGING > STING

STINGINGS > STING

STINGLESS > STING
STINGO n strong alcohol
STINGOS > STINGO
STINGRAY n flatfish capable of inflicting painful wounds
STINGRAYS > STINGRAY
STINGS > STING
STINGY adj mean or miserly ▷ n stinging nettle
STINK n strong unpleasant smell ▷ vb give off a strong unpleasant smell
STINKARD n smelly person
STINKARDS > STINKARD
STINKBIRD same as > HOATZIN
STINKBUG n type of insect that releases an unpleasant odour
STINKBUGS > STINKBUG
STINKER n difficult or unpleasant person or thing
STINKEROO n bad or contemptible person or thing
STINKERS > STINKER
STINKHORN n type of fungus with an offensive odour
STINKIER > STINKY
STINKIEST > STINKY
STINKING > STINK
STINKO adj drunk
STINKPOT n person or thing that stinks
STINKPOTS > STINKPOT
STINKS > STINK
STINKWEED n plant that has a disagreeable smell when bruised
STINKWOOD n any of various trees having offensive-smelling wood
STINKY adj having a foul smell
STINT vb be miserly with (something) ▷ n allotted amount of work
STINTED > STINT
STINTEDLY > STINT
STINTER > STINT
STINTERS > STINT
STINTIER > STINT
STINTIEST > STINT
STINTING > STINT
STINTINGS > STINT
STINTLESS > STINT
STINTS > STINT
STINTY > STINT
STIPA n variety of grass
STIPAS > STIPA
STIPE n stalk in plants that bears reproductive structures
STIPED same as > STIPITATE
STIPEL n small paired leaflike structure at the base of certain leaflets
STIPELS > STIPEL

STIPEND n regular allowance or salary
STIPENDS > STIPEND
STIPES n second maxillary segment in insects and crustaceans
STIPIFORM > STIPES
STIPITATE adj possessing or borne on the end of a stipe
STIPITES > STIPES
STIPPLE vb paint, draw, or engrave using dots ▷ n technique of stippling
STIPPLED > STIPPLE
STIPPLER > STIPPLE
STIPPLERS > STIPPLE
STIPPLES > STIPPLE
STIPPLING > STIPPLE
STIPULAR > STIPULE
STIPULARY > STIPULE
STIPULATE vb specify as a condition of an agreement ▷ adj (of a plant) having stipules
STIPULE n small paired usually leaflike outgrowth occurring at the base of a leaf or its stalk
STIPULED > STIPULE
STIPULES > STIPULE
STIR vb mix up (a liquid) by moving a spoon etc around in it ▷ n stirring
STIRABOUT n kind of porridge originally made in Ireland
STIRE same as > STEER
STIRED > STIRE
STIRES > STIRE
STIRING > STIRE
STIRK n heifer of 6 to 12 months old
STIRKS > STIRK
STIRLESS > STIR
STIRP same as > STIRPS
STIRPES > STIRPS
STIRPS n line of descendants from an ancestor
STIRRA same as > SIRRA
STIRRABLE > STIR
STIRRAH same as > SIRRAH
STIRRAHS > STIRRAH
STIRRAS > STIRRA
STIRRE same as > STEER
STIRRED > STIR
STIRRER n person who deliberately causes trouble
STIRRERS > STIRRER
STIRRES > STIRRE
STIRRING > STIR
STIRRINGS > STIR
STIRRUP n metal loop attached to a saddle for supporting a rider's foot
STIRRUPS > STIRRUP
STIRS > STIR
STISHIE same as > STUSHIE
STISHIES > STISHIE
STITCH n link made by drawing thread through

material with a needle ▷ vb sew
STITCHED > STITCH
STITCHER > STITCH
STITCHERS > STITCH
STITCHERY n needlework, esp modern embroidery
STITCHES > STITCH
STITCHING > STITCH
STITHIED > STITHY
STITHIES > STITHY
STITHY n forge or anvil ▷ vb forge on an anvil
STITHYING > STITHY
STIVE vb stifle
STIVED > STIVE
STIVER n former Dutch coin worth
STIVERS > STIVER
STIVES > STIVE
STIVIER > STIVY
STIVIEST > STIVY
STIVING > STIVE
STIVY adj stuffy
STOA n covered walk that has a colonnade on one or both sides
STOAE > STOA
STOAI > STOA
STOAS > STOA
STOAT n small mammal of the weasel family
STOATS > STOAT
STOB same as > STAB
STOBBED > STOB
STOBBING > STOB
STOBIE adj as in stobie pole steel and concrete pole for supporting electricity wires
STOBS > STOB
STOCCADO n fencing thrust
STOCCADOS > STOCCADO
STOCCATA same as > STOCCADO
STOCCATAS > STOCCATA
STOCIOUS same as > STOTIOUS
STOCK n total amount of goods available for sale in a shop ▷ adj kept in stock, standard ▷ vb keep for sale or future use
STOCKADE n enclosure or barrier made of stakes ▷ vb surround with a stockade
STOCKADED > STOCKADE
STOCKADES > STOCKADE
STOCKAGE n livestock put to graze on crops
STOCKAGES > STOCKAGE
STOCKCAR n car that has been strengthened for a form of racing in which the cars often collide
STOCKCARS > STOCKCAR
STOCKED > STOCK
STOCKER > STOCK
STOCKERS > STOCK
STOCKFISH n fish, such as cod or haddock, cured

by splitting and drying in the air
STOCKHORN n type of obsolete woodwind instrument made from an animal horn
STOCKIER > STOCKY
STOCKIEST > STOCKY
STOCKILY > STOCKY
STOCKINET n machine-knitted elastic fabric
STOCKING n close-fitting covering for the foot and leg
STOCKINGS > STOCKING
STOCKISH adj stupid or dull
STOCKIST n dealer who stocks a particular product
STOCKISTS > STOCKIST
STOCKLESS > STOCK
STOCKLIST n list of items in stock
STOCKLOCK n lock that is enclosed in a wooden case
STOCKMAN n man engaged in the rearing or care of farm livestock, esp cattle
STOCKMEN > STOCKMAN
STOCKPILE vb store a large quantity of (something) for future use ▷ n accumulated store
STOCKPOT n pot in which stock for soup is made
STOCKPOTS > STOCKPOT
STOCKROOM n room in which a stock of goods is kept in a shop or factory
STOCKS pl n instrument of punishment in which an offender was locked
STOCKTAKE vb take stock
STOCKTOOK > STOCKTAKE
STOCKWORK n group of veins in mine
STOCKY adj (of a person) broad and sturdy
STOCKYARD n yard where farm animals are sold
STODGE n heavy starchy food ▷ vb stuff (oneself or another) with food
STODGED > STODGE
STODGER n dull person
STODGERS > STODGER
STODGES > STODGE
STODGIER > STODGY
STODGIEST > STODGY
STODGILY > STODGY
STODGING > STODGE
STODGY adj (of food) heavy and starchy
STOEP n verandah
STOEPS > STOEP
STOGEY same as > STOGY
STOGEYS > STOGEY
STOGIE same as > STOGY
STOGIES > STOGY
STOGY n any long cylindrical inexpensive cigar

STOIC n person who suffers hardship without showing his or her feelings ▷ adj suffering hardship without showing one's feelings

STOICAL adj suffering great difficulties without showing one's feelings

STOICALLY > STOICAL

STOICISM n indifference to pleasure and pain

STOICISMS > STOICISM

STOICS > STOIC

STOIT vb bounce

STOITED > STOIT

STOITER vb stagger

STOITERED > STOITER

STOITERS > STOITER

STOITING > STOIT

STOITS > STOIT

STOKE vb feed and tend (a fire or furnace)

STOKED adj very pleased

STOKEHOLD n hold for a ship's boilers

STOKEHOLE n hole in a furnace through which it is stoked

STOKER n person employed to tend a furnace on a ship or train powered by steam

STOKERS > STOKER

STOKES n cgs unit of kinematic viscosity

STOKESIA n American flowering plant

STOKESIAS > STOKESIA

STOKING > STOKE

STOKVEL n (in S Africa) informal savings pool or syndicate

STOKVELS > STOKVEL

STOLE n long scarf or shawl

STOLED adj wearing a stole

STOLEN > STEAL

STOLES > STOLE

STOLID adj showing little emotion or interest

STOLIDER > STOLID

STOLIDEST > STOLID

STOLIDITY > STOLID

STOLIDLY > STOLID

STOLLEN n rich sweet bread containing nuts, raisins, etc

STOLLENS > STOLLEN

STOLN > STEAL

STOLON n long horizontal stem that grows along the surface of the soil

STOLONIC > STOLON

STOLONS > STOLON

STOLPORT n airport for short take-off aircraft

STOLPORTS > STOLPORT

STOMA n pore in a plant leaf that controls the passage of gases

STOMACH n organ in the body which digests food ▷ vb put up with

STOMACHAL > STOMACH

STOMACHED > STOMACH

STOMACHER n decorative V-shaped panel of stiff material worn over the chest and stomach

STOMACHIC adj stimulating gastric activity ▷ n stomachic medicine

STOMACHS > STOMACH

STOMACHY adj having a large belly

STOMACK n as in have a stomack (in E Africa) be pregnant

STOMACKS > STOMACK

STOMAL > STOMA

STOMAS > STOMA

STOMATA > STOMA

STOMATAL adj of, relating to, or possessing stomata or a stoma

STOMATE n opening on leaf through which water evaporates

STOMATES > STOMATE

STOMATIC adj of or relating to a mouth or mouthlike part

STOMATOUS same as > STOMATAL

STOMIA > STOMIUM

STOMIUM n part of the sporangium of ferns that ruptures to release the spores

STOMIUMS > STOMIUM

STOMODAEA > STOMODEUM

STOMODEA > STOMODEUM

STOMODEAL > STOMODEUM

STOMODEUM n oral cavity of a vertebrate embryo

STOMP vb tread heavily ▷ n rhythmic stamping jazz dance

STOMPED > STOMP

STOMPER n song with a strong beat

STOMPERS > STOMPER

STOMPIE n cigarette butt

STOMPIER > STOMPY

STOMPIES > STOMPIE

STOMPIEST > STOMPY

STOMPING > STOMP

STOMPS > STOMP

STOMPY adj (of music) encouraging stomping of the feet

STONABLE > STONE

STOND same as > STAND

STONDS > STOND

STONE n material of which rocks are made ▷ vb throw stones at

STONEABLE > STONE

STONEBOAT n type of sleigh used for moving rocks from fields

STONECAST n short distance

STONECHAT n songbird that has black feathers and a reddish-brown breast

STONECROP n type of plant with fleshy leaves and red, yellow, or white flowers

STONECUT n (print made from) a carved block of stone

STONECUTS > STONECUT

STONED adj under the influence of alcohol or drugs

STONEFISH n venomous tropical marine scorpaenid fish

STONEFLY n type of insect whose larvae are aquatic

STONEHAND n type of compositor

STONELESS > STONE

STONELIKE > STONE

STONEN adj of stone

STONER n device for removing stones from fruit

STONERAG n type of lichen

STONERAGS > STONERAG

STONERAW same as > STONERAG

STONERAWS > STONERAW

STONERN same as > STONEN

STONERS > STONER

STONES > STONE

STONESHOT n stone's throw

STONEWALL vb obstruct or hinder discussion

STONEWARE n hard kind of pottery fired at a very high temperature ▷ adj made of stoneware

STONEWASH vb wash with stones to give worn appearance

STONEWORK n part of a building made of stone

STONEWORT n any of various green algae which grow in brackish or fresh water

STONEY same as > STONY

STONG > STING

STONIED > STONY

STONIER > STONY

STONIES > STONY

STONIEST > STONY

STONILY > STONY

STONINESS > STONY

STONING > STONE

STONINGS > STONE

STONISH same as > ASTONISH

STONISHED > STONISH

STONISHES > STONISH

STONK vb bombard (soldiers, buildings, etc) with artillery ▷ n concentrated bombardment

STONKED > STONK

STONKER vb destroy

STONKERED adj completely exhausted or beaten

STONKERS > STONKER

STONKING > STONK

STONKS > STONK

STONN same as > STUN

STONNE same as > STUN

STONNED > STONNE

STONNES > STONNE

STONNING > STONN

STONNS > STONN

STONY adj of or like stone ▷ vb astonish

STONYING > STONY

STOOD > STAND

STOODEN > STAND

STOOGE n actor who feeds lines to a comedian ▷ vb act as a stooge

STOOGED > STOOGE

STOOGES > STOOGE

STOOGING > STOOGE

STOOK n number of sheaves set upright in a field to dry ▷ vb set up (sheaves) in stooks

STOOKED > STOOK

STOOKER > STOOK

STOOKERS > STOOK

STOOKIE n stucco

STOOKIES > STOOKIE

STOOKING n act of stooking

STOOKINGS > STOOKING

STOOKS > STOOK

STOOL n chair without arms or back ▷ vb (of a plant) send up shoots from the base of the stem

STOOLBALL n game resembling cricket played by girls

STOOLED > STOOL

STOOLIE n police informer

STOOLIES > STOOLIE

STOOLING > STOOL

STOOLS > STOOL

STOOLY n (US) informant for the police

STOOP vb bend forward and downward

STOOPBALL n American street game

STOOPE same as > STOUP

STOOPED > STOOP

STOOPER > STOOP

STOOPERS > STOOP

STOOPES > STOOPE

STOOPING > STOOP

STOOPS > STOOP

STOOR same as > STOUR

STOORS > STOOR

STOOSHIE same as > STUSHIE

STOOSHIES > STOOSHIE

STOOZE vb borrow money cheaply and invest it to make a profit

STOOZED > STOOZE

STOOZER n person who stoozes

STOOZERS > STOOZER

STOOZES > STOOZE

STOOZING > STOOZE

STOOZINGS > STOOZING

STOP vb cease or cause to cease from doing (something) ▷ n stopping or being stopped

STOPBAND n band of frequencies stopped by a filter

STOPBANDS > STOPBAND

STOPBANK n embankment to prevent flooding

STOPBANKS > STOPBANK

STOPCOCK n valve to control or stop the flow of fluid in a pipe

STOPCOCKS > STOPCOCK

STOPE n steplike excavation made in a mine to extract ore ▷ vb mine (ore, etc) by cutting stopes

STOPED > STOPE

STOPER n drill used in mining

STOPERS > STOPER

STOPES > STOPE

STOPGAP n temporary substitute

STOPGAPS > STOPGAP

STOPING n process by which country rock is broken up and engulfed by magma

STOPINGS > STOPING

STOPLESS > STOP

STOPLIGHT n red light on a traffic signal indicating that vehicles coming towards it should stop

STOPOFF n break in a journey

STOPOFFS > STOPOFF

STOPOVER n short break in a journey ▷ vb make a stopover

STOPOVERS > STOPOVER

STOPPABLE > STOP

STOPPAGE n act of stopping something or the state of being stopped

STOPPAGES > STOPPAGE

STOPPED > STOP

STOPPER n plug for closing a bottle etc ▷ vb close or fit with a stopper

STOPPERED > STOPPER

STOPPERS > STOPPER

STOPPING > STOP

STOPPINGS > STOP

STOPPLE same as > STOPPER

STOPPLED > STOPPLE

STOPPLES > STOPPLE

STOPPLING > STOPPLE

STOPS > STOP

STOPT > STOP

STOPWATCH n watch which can be stopped

instantly for exact timing of a sporting event

STOPWORD n common word not used in computer search engines

STOPWORDS > STOPWORD

STORABLE > STORE

STORABLES > STORE

STORAGE n storing

STORAGES > STORAGE

STORAX n type of tree or shrub with white flowers

STORAXES > STORAX

STORE vb collect and keep (things) for future use ▷ n shop

STORECARD n charge card specific to one chain of shops

STORED > STORE

STOREMAN n man looking after storeroom

STOREMEN > STOREMAN

STORER > STORE

STOREROOM n room in which things are stored

STORERS > STORE

STORES pl n supply of food and essentials for a journey

STORESHIP n ship carrying naval stores

STOREWIDE adj throughout stores

STOREY n floor or level of a building

STOREYED adj having a storey or storeys

STOREYS > STOREY

STORGE n affection

STORGES > STORGE

STORIATED adj decorated with flowers or animals

STORIED > STORY

STORIES > STORY

STORIETTE n short story

STORING > STORE

STORK n large wading bird

STORKS > STORK

STORM n violent weather with wind, rain, or snow ▷ vb attack or capture (a place) suddenly

STORMBIRD n petrel

STORMCOCK n mistle thrush

STORMED > STORM

STORMER n outstanding example of its kind

STORMERS > STORMER

STORMFUL > STORM

STORMIER > STORMY

STORMIEST > STORMY

STORMILY > STORMY

STORMING adj characterized by or displaying dynamism, speed, and energy

STORMINGS > STORM

STORMLESS > STORM

STORMLIKE > STORM

STORMS > STORM

STORMY adj characterized by storms

STORNELLI > STORNELLO

STORNELLO n type of Italian poem

STORY n narration of a chain of events ▷ vb decorate with scenes from history

STORYBOOK n book containing stories for children ▷ adj better or happier than in real life

STORYETTE n short story

STORYING > STORY

STORYINGS > STORY

STORYLINE n plot of a book, film, play, etc

STOSS adj (of the side of a hill) facing the onward flow of a glacier ▷ n hillside facing glacier flow

STOSSES > STOSS

STOT n bullock ▷ vb bounce or cause to bounce

STOTIN n monetary unit of Slovenia

STOTINKA n monetary unit of Bulgaria, worth one hundredth of a lev

STOTINKI > STOTINKA

STOTINOV > STOTIN

STOTINS > STOTIN

STOTIOUS adj drunk

STOTS > STOT

STOTT same as > STOT

STOTTED > STOT

STOTTER same as > STOT

STOTTERED > STOTTER

STOTTERS > STOTTER

STOTTIE n wedge of bread cut from a flat round loaf

STOTTIES > STOTTIE

STOTTING > STOT

STOTTS > STOTT

STOTTY n type of flat, round loaf made in NE England

STOUN same as > STUN

STOUND n short while ▷ vb ache

STOUNDED > STOUND

STOUNDING > STOUND

STOUNDS > STOUND

STOUNING > STOUN

STOUNS > STOUN

STOUP n small basin for holy water

STOUPS > STOUP

STOUR n turmoil or conflict

STOURE same as > STOUR

STOURES > STOURE

STOURIE same as > STOURY

STOURIER > STOURY

STOURIEST > STOURY

STOURS > STOUR

STOURY adj dusty

STOUSH vb hit or punch (someone) ▷ n fighting or violence

STOUSHED > STOUSH

STOUSHES > STOUSH

STOUSHIE same as > STUSHIE

STOUSHIES > STOUSHIE

STOUSHING > STOUSH

STOUT adj fat ▷ n strong dark beer

STOUTEN vb make or become stout

STOUTENED > STOUTEN

STOUTENS > STOUTEN

STOUTER > STOUT

STOUTEST > STOUT

STOUTH n Scots word meaning theft

STOUTHS > STOUTH

STOUTISH > STOUT

STOUTLY > STOUT

STOUTNESS > STOUT

STOUTS > STOUT

STOVAINE n anaesthetic drug

STOVAINES > STOVAINE

STOVE n apparatus for cooking or heating ▷ vb process (ceramics, metalwork, etc) by heating in a stove

STOVED > STOVE

STOVEPIPE n pipe that takes fumes and smoke away from a stove

STOVER n fodder

STOVERS > STOVER

STOVES > STOVE

STOVETOP US word for > HOB

STOVETOPS > STOVETOP

STOVIES pl n potatoes stewed with onions

STOVING > STOVE

STOVINGS > STOVE

STOW vb pack or store

STOWABLE > STOW

STOWAGE n space or charge for stowing goods

STOWAGES > STOWAGE

STOWAWAY n person who hides on a ship or aircraft in order to travel free ▷ vb travel in such a way

STOWAWAYS > STOWAWAY

STOWDOWN n packing of ship's hold

STOWDOWNS > STOWDOWN

STOWED > STOW

STOWER > STOW

STOWERS > STOW

STOWING > STOW

STOWINGS > STOW

STOWLINS adv stealthily

STOWN > STEAL

STOWND same as > STOUND

STOWNDED > STOWND

STOWNDING > STOWND

STOWNDS > STOWND

STOWNLINS same as > STOWLINS

STOWP same as > STOUP

STOWPS > STOWP

STOWRE same as > STOUR

STOWRES > STOWRE

STOWS > STOW
STRABISM n abnormal alignment of one or both eyes
STRABISMS > STRABISM
STRACK vb archaic past tense form of strike
STRAD n violin made by Stradivarius
STRADDLE vb have one leg or part on each side of (something) ▷ n act or position of straddling
STRADDLED > STRADDLE
STRADDLER > STRADDLE
STRADDLES > STRADDLE
STRADIOT n Venetian cavalryman
STRADIOTS > STRADIOT
STRADS > STRAD
STRAE Scots form of > STRAW
STRAES > STRAE
STRAFE vb attack (an enemy) with machine guns from the air ▷ n act or instance of strafing
STRAFED > STRAFE
STRAFER > STRAFE
STRAFERS > STRAFE
STRAFES > STRAFE
STRAFF same as > STRAFE
STRAFFED > STRAFF
STRAFFING > STRAFF
STRAFFS > STRAFF
STRAFING n act of strafing
STRAFINGS > STRAFING
STRAG n straggler
STRAGGLE vb go or spread in a rambling or irregular way
STRAGGLED > STRAGGLE
STRAGGLER > STRAGGLE
STRAGGLES > STRAGGLE
STRAGGLY > STRAGGLE
STRAGS > STRAG
STRAICHT Scots word for > STRAIGHT
STRAIGHT adj not curved or crooked ▷ adv in a straight line ▷ n straight part, esp of a racetrack ▷ vb tighten
STRAIGHTS > STRAIGHT
STRAIK Scots word for > STROKE
STRAIKED > STRAIK
STRAIKING > STRAIK
STRAIKS > STRAIK
STRAIN vb subject to mental tension ▷ n tension or tiredness
STRAINED adj not natural, forced
STRAINER n sieve
STRAINERS > STRAINER
STRAINING > STRAIN
STRAINS > STRAIN
STRAINT n pressure
STRAINTS > STRAINT
STRAIT n narrow channel connecting two areas of sea ▷ adj (of spaces, etc)

affording little room
▷ vb tighten
STRAITED > STRAIT
STRAITEN vb embarrass or distress, esp financially
STRAITENS > STRAITEN
STRAITER > STRAIT
STRAITEST > STRAIT
STRAITING > STRAIT
STRAITLY > STRAIT
STRAITS > STRAIT
STRAK vb archaic past tense form of strike
STRAKE n curved metal plate forming part of the metal rim on a wooden wheel
STRAKED adj having a strake
STRAKES > STRAKE
STRAMACON same as > STRAMAZON
STRAMASH n uproar ▷ vb destroy
STRAMAZON n downward fencing stroke
STRAMMEL same as > STRUMMEL
STRAMMELS > STRAMMEL
STRAMONY n former asthma medicine made from the dried leaves and flowers of the thorn apple
STRAMP Scots variant of > TRAMP
STRAMPED > STRAMP
STRAMPING > STRAMP
STRAMPS > STRAMP
STRAND vb run aground ▷ n shore
STRANDED > STRAND
STRANDER > STRAND
STRANDERS > STRAND
STRANDING > STRAND
STRANDS > STRAND
STRANG dialect variant of > STRONG
STRANGE adj odd or unusual ▷ n odd or unfamiliar person or thing
STRANGELY > STRANGE
STRANGER n person who is not known or is new to a place or experience
STRANGERS > STRANGER
STRANGES > STRANGE
STRANGEST > STRANGE
STRANGLE vb kill by squeezing the throat
STRANGLED > STRANGLE
STRANGLER n person or thing that strangles
STRANGLES n acute bacterial disease of horses
STRANGURY n painful excretion of urine caused by muscular spasms of the urinary tract
STRAP n strip of flexible material for lifting or holding in place ▷ vb fasten with a strap or straps

STRAPHANG vb travel standing on public transport
STRAPHUNG > STRAPHANG
STRAPLESS adj (of women's clothes) without straps over the shoulders
STRAPLINE n subheading in a newspaper or magazine article or in an advertisement
STRAPPADO n system of torture in which a victim was hoisted by a rope tied to his wrists and then allowed to drop until his fall was suddenly checked by the rope ▷ vb subject to strappado
STRAPPED > STRAP
STRAPPER n strapping person
STRAPPERS > STRAPPER
STRAPPIER > STRAPPY
STRAPPING > STRAP
STRAPPY adj having straps
STRAPS > STRAP
STRAPWORT n plant with leaves like straps
STRASS another word for > PASTE
STRASSES > STRASS
STRATA > STRATUM
STRATAGEM n clever plan, trick
STRATAL > STRATUM
STRATAS > STRATUM
STRATEGIC adj advantageous
STRATEGY n overall plan
STRATH n flat river valley
STRATHS > STRATH
STRATI > STRATUS
STRATIFY vb form or be formed in layers or strata
STRATONIC adj of army
STRATOSE adj formed in strata
STRATOUS adj of stratus
STRATUM n layer, esp of rock
STRATUMS > STRATUM
STRATUS n grey layer cloud
STRATUSES > STRATUS
STRAUCHT Scots word for > STRETCH
STRAUCHTS > STRAUCHT
STRAUGHT same as > STRAUCHT
STRAUGHTS > STRAUGHT
STRAUNGE same as > STRANGE
STRAVAGE same as > STRAVAIG
STRAVAGED > STRAVAGE
STRAVAGES > STRAVAGE
STRAVAIG vb wander aimlessly
STRAVAIGS > STRAVAIG
STRAW n dried stalks of grain ▷ vb spread around

STRAWED > STRAW
STRAWEN adj of straw
STRAWHAT adj of summer dramatic performance
STRAWIER > STRAWY
STRAWIEST > STRAWY
STRAWING > STRAW
STRAWLESS > STRAW
STRAWLIKE > STRAW
STRAWN > STREW
STRAWS > STRAW
STRAWWORM n aquatic larva of a caddis fly
STRAWY adj containing straw, or like straw in colour or texture
STRAY vb wander ▷ adj having strayed ▷ n stray animal
STRAYED > STRAY
STRAYER > STRAY
STRAYERS > STRAY
STRAYING > STRAY
STRAYINGS > STRAY
STRAYLING n stray
STRAYS > STRAY
STRAYVE vb wander aimlessly
STRAYVED > STRAYVE
STRAYVES > STRAYVE
STRAYVING > STRAYVE
STREAK n long band of contrasting colour or substance ▷ vb mark with streaks
STREAKED > STREAK
STREAKER > STREAK
STREAKERS > STREAK
STREAKIER > STREAKY
STREAKILY > STREAKY
STREAKING > STREAK
STREAKS > STREAK
STREAKY adj marked with streaks
STREAM n small river ▷ vb flow steadily
STREAMBED n bottom of stream
STREAMED > STREAM
STREAMER n strip of coloured paper that unrolls when tossed
STREAMERS > STREAMER
STREAMIER > STREAMY
STREAMING > STREAM
STREAMLET > STREAM
STREAMS > STREAM
STREAMY adj (of an area, land, etc) having many streams
STREEK Scots word for > STRETCH
STREEKED > STREEK
STREEKER > STREEK
STREEKERS > STREEK
STREEKING > STREEK
STREEKS > STREEK
STREEL n slovenly woman ▷ vb trail
STREELED > STREEL
STREELING > STREEL
STREELS > STREEL

S

STREET n public road, usu lined with buildings ▷ vb lay out a street or streets

STREETAGE n toll charged for using a street

STREETBOY n boy living on the street

STREETCAR n tram

STREETED > STREET

STREETFUL n amount of people or things street can hold

STREETIER > STREETY

STREETING > STREET

STREETS > STREET

STREETY adj of streets

STREIGHT same as > STRAIT

STREIGHTS > STREIGHT

STREIGNE same as > STRAIN

STREIGNED > STREIGNE

STREIGNES > STREIGNE

STRELITZ n former Russian soldier

STRELITZI > STRELITZ

STRENE same as > STRAIN

STRENES > STRENE

STRENGTH n quality of being strong

STRENGTHS > STRENGTH

STRENUITY > STRENUOUS

STRENUOUS adj requiring great energy or effort

STREP n streptococcus

STREPENT adj noisy

STREPS > STREP

STRESS n tension or strain ▷ vb emphasize

STRESSED > STRESS

STRESSES > STRESS

STRESSFUL > STRESS

STRESSIER > STRESSY

STRESSING > STRESS

STRESSOR n event, experience, etc, that causes stress

STRESSORS > STRESSOR

STRESSY adj characterized by stress

STRETCH vb extend or be extended ▷ n stretching

STRETCHED > STRETCH

STRETCHER n frame covered with canvas, on which an injured person is carried ▷ vb transport (a sick or injured person) on a stretcher

STRETCHES > STRETCH

STRETCHY adj characterized by elasticity

STRETTA same as > STRETTO

STRETTAS > STRETTA

STRETTE > STRETTA

STRETTI > STRETTO

STRETTO n (in a fugue) the close overlapping of two parts or voices

STRETTOS > STRETTO

STREUSEL n crumbly topping for rich pastries

STREUSELS > STREUSEL

STREW vb scatter (things) over a surface

STREWAGE > STREW

STREWAGES > STREW

STREWED > STREW

STREWER > STREW

STREWERS > STREW

STREWING > STREW

STREWINGS > STREW

STREWMENT n strewing

STREWN > STREW

STREWS > STREW

STREWTH interj expression of surprise or alarm

STRIA n scratch or groove on the surface of a rock crystal

STRIAE > STRIA

STRIATA > STRIATUM

STRIATAL adj relating to the corpus striatum in the brain

STRIATE adj marked with striae ▷ vb mark with striae

STRIATED adj having a pattern of scratches or grooves

STRIATES > STRIATE

STRIATING > STRIATE

STRIATION same as > STRIA

STRIATUM n part of brain

STRIATUMS > STRIATUM

STRIATURE n way something is striated

STRICH n screech owl

STRICHES > STRICH

STRICK n any bast fibres preparatory to being made into slivers

STRICKEN adj seriously affected by disease, grief, pain, etc

STRICKLE n board used for sweeping off excess material in a container ▷ vb level, form, or sharpen with a strickle

STRICKLED > STRICKLE

STRICKLES > STRICKLE

STRICKS > STRICK

STRICT adj stern or severe

STRICTER > STRICT

STRICTEST > STRICT

STRICTION n act of restricting

STRICTISH > STRICT

STRICTLY > STRICT

STRICTURE n severe criticism

STRIDDEN > STRIDE

STRIDDLE same as > STRADDLE

STRIDDLED > STRIDDLE

STRIDDLES > STRIDDLE

STRIDE vb walk with long steps ▷ n long step

STRIDENCE > STRIDENT

STRIDENCY > STRIDENT

STRIDENT adj loud and harsh

STRIDER > STRIDE

STRIDERS > STRIDE

STRIDES > STRIDE

STRIDING > STRIDE

STRIDLING adv astride

STRIDOR n high-pitched whistling sound made during respiration

STRIDORS > STRIDOR

STRIFE n conflict, quarrelling

STRIFEFUL > STRIFE

STRIFES > STRIFE

STRIFT n struggle

STRIFTS > STRIFT

STRIG vb remove stalk from

STRIGA same as > STRIA

STRIGAE > STRIGA

STRIGATE adj streaked

STRIGGED > STRIG

STRIGGING > STRIG

STRIGIL n curved blade used to scrape the body after bathing

STRIGILS > STRIGIL

STRIGINE adj of or like owl

STRIGOSE adj bearing stiff hairs or bristles

STRIGS > STRIG

STRIKE vb cease work as a protest ▷ n stoppage of work as a protest

STRIKEOUT n dismissal in baseball due to three successive failures to hit the ball

STRIKER n striking worker

STRIKERS > STRIKER

STRIKES > STRIKE

STRIKING > STRIKE

STRIKINGS > STRIKE

STRIM vb cut (grass) using an electric trimmer

STRIMMED > STRIM

STRIMMING > STRIM

STRIMS > STRIM

STRINE n informal name for Australian English

STRINES > STRINE

STRING n thin cord used for tying ▷ vb provide with a string or strings

STRINGED adj (of a musical instrument) having strings that are plucked or played with a bow

STRINGENT adj strictly controlled or enforced

STRINGER n journalist retained by a newspaper to cover a particular town or area

STRINGERS > STRINGER

STRINGIER > STRINGY

STRINGILY > STRINGY

STRINGING > STRING

STRINGS > STRING

STRINGY adj like string

STRINKLE Scots variant of > SPRINKLE

STRINKLED > STRINKLE

STRINKLES > STRINKLE

STRIP vb take (the covering or clothes) off ▷ n act of stripping

STRIPE n long narrow band of contrasting colour or substance ▷ vb mark (something) with stripes

STRIPED adj marked or decorated with stripes

STRIPER n officer who has a stripe or stripes on his uniform

STRIPERS > STRIPER

STRIPES > STRIPE

STRIPEY same as > STRIPY

STRIPIER > STRIPY

STRIPIEST > STRIPY

STRIPING > STRIPE

STRIPINGS > STRIPE

STRIPLING n youth

STRIPPED > STRIP

STRIPPER n person who performs a striptease

STRIPPERS > STRIPPER

STRIPPING > STRIP

STRIPS > STRIP

STRIPT > STRIP

STRIPY adj marked by or with stripes

STRIVE vb make a great effort

STRIVED > STRIVE

STRIVEN > STRIVE

STRIVER > STRIVE

STRIVERS > STRIVE

STRIVES > STRIVE

STRIVING > STRIVE

STRIVINGS > STRIVE

STROAM vb wander

STROAMED > STROAM

STROAMING > STROAM

STROAMS > STROAM

STROBE n high intensity flashing beam of light ▷ vb give the appearance of slow motion by using a strobe

STROBED > STROBE

STROBES > STROBE

STROBIC adj spinning or appearing to spin

STROBIL n scaly multiple fruit

STROBILA n body of a tapeworm, consisting of a string of similar segments

STROBILAE > STROBILA

STROBILAR > STROBILA

STROBILE same as > STROBILUS

STROBILES > STROBILE

STROBILI > STROBILUS

STROBILS > STROBIL

STROBILUS technical name for > CONE

STROBING > STROBE

STROBINGS > STROBE

STRODDLE same as > STRADDLE

STRODDLED > STRODDLE

STRODDLES > STRODDLE

STRODE > STRIDE

STRODLE same as > STRADDLE

STRODLED > STRODLE

STRODLES > STRODLE

STRODLING > STRODLE

STROKABLE adj appearing pleasant to stroke

STROKE vb touch or caress lightly with the hand ▷ n light touch or caress with the hand

STROKED > STROKE

STROKEN > STRIKE

STROKER > STROKE

STROKERS > STROKE

STROKES > STROKE

STROKING > STROKE

STROKINGS > STROKE

STROLL vb walk in a leisurely manner ▷ n leisurely walk

STROLLED > STROLL

STROLLER n chair-shaped carriage for a baby

STROLLERS > STROLLER

STROLLING > STROLL

STROLLS > STROLL

STROMA n gel-like matrix of chloroplasts and certain cells

STROMAL > STROMA

STROMATA > STROMA

STROMATIC > STROMA

STROMB n shellfish like a whelk

STROMBS > STROMB

STROMBUS same as > STROMB

STROND same as > STRAND

STRONDS > STROND

STRONG adj having physical power

STRONGARM adj involving physical force

STRONGBOX n box in which valuables are locked for safety

STRONGER > STRONG

STRONGEST > STRONG

STRONGISH > STRONG

STRONGLY > STRONG

STRONGMAN n performer, esp one in a circus, who performs feats of strength

STRONGMEN > STRONGMAN

STRONGYL same as > STRONGYLE

STRONGYLE n type of parasitic worm chiefly occurring in the intestines of horses

STRONGYLS > STRONGYL

STRONTIA > STRONTIAN

STRONTIAN n type of white mineral

STRONTIAS > STRONTIA

STRONTIC > STRONTIUM

STRONTIUM n silvery-white metallic element

STROOK > STRIKE

STROOKE n stroke

STROOKEN same as > STRICKEN

STROOKES > STROOKE

STROP n leather strap for sharpening razors ▷ vb sharpen (a razor, etc) on a strop

STROPHE n movement made by chorus during a choral ode

STROPHES > STROPHE

STROPHIC adj of, relating to, or employing a strophe or strophes

STROPHOID n type of curve on graph

STROPHULI pl n skin inflammations seen primarily on small children

STROPPED > STROP

STROPPER > STROP

STROPPERS > STROP

STROPPIER > STROPPY

STROPPILY > STROPPY

STROPPING > STROP

STROPPY adj angry or awkward

STROPS > STROP

STROSSERS same as > TROUSERS

STROUD n coarse woollen fabric

STROUDING n woolly material for making strouds

STROUDS > STROUD

STROUP Scots word for > SPOUT

STROUPACH n cup of tea

STROUPAN same as > STROUPACH

STROUPANS > STROUPAN

STROUPS > STROUP

STROUT vb bulge

STROUTED > STROUT

STROUTING > STROUT

STROUTS > STROUT

STROVE > STRIVE

STROW archaic variant of > STREW

STROWED > STROW

STROWER > STROW

STROWERS > STROW

STROWING > STROW

STROWINGS > STROW

STROWN > STROW

STROWS > STROW

STROY archaic variant of > DESTROY

STROYED > STROY

STROYER > STROY

STROYERS > STROY

STROYING > STROY

STROYS > STROY

STRUCK > STRIKE

STRUCKEN same as > STRICKEN

STRUCTURE n complex construction ▷ vb give a structure to

STRUDEL n thin sheet of filled dough rolled up and baked

STRUDELS > STRUDEL

STRUGGLE vb work, strive, or make one's way with difficulty ▷ n striving

STRUGGLED > STRUGGLE

STRUGGLER > STRUGGLE

STRUGGLES > STRUGGLE

STRUM vb play (a guitar, etc) by sweeping the thumb across the strings

STRUMA n abnormal enlargement of the thyroid gland

STRUMAE > STRUMA

STRUMAS > STRUMA

STRUMATIC > STRUMA

STRUMITIS n inflammation of thyroid gland

STRUMMED > STRUM

STRUMMEL n straw

STRUMMELS > STRUMMEL

STRUMMER > STRUM

STRUMMERS > STRUM

STRUMMING > STRUM

STRUMOSE > STRUMA

STRUMOUS > STRUMA

STRUMPET n prostitute ▷ vb turn into a strumpet

STRUMPETS > STRUMPET

STRUMS > STRUM

STRUNG > STRING

STRUNT Scots word for > STRUT

STRUNTED > STRUNT

STRUNTING > STRUNT

STRUNTS > STRUNT

STRUT vb walk pompously, swagger ▷ n bar supporting a structure

STRUTS > STRUT

STRUTTED > STRUT

STRUTTER > STRUT

STRUTTERS > STRUT

STRUTTING > STRUT

STRYCHNIA n strychnine

STRYCHNIC adj of, relating to, or derived from strychnine

STUB n short piece left after use ▷ vb strike (the toe) painfully against an object

STUBBED > STUB

STUBBIE same as > STUBBY

STUBBIER > STUBBY

STUBBIES > STUBBY

STUBBIEST > STUBBY

STUBBILY > STUBBY

STUBBING > STUB

STUBBLE n short stalks of grain left in a field after reaping

STUBBLED adj having the stubs of stalks left after a crop has been cut and harvested

STUBBLES > STUBBLE

STUBBLIER > STUBBLE

STUBBLY > STUBBLE

STUBBORN adj refusing to agree or give in ▷ vb make stubborn

STUBBORNS > STUBBORN

STUBBY adj short and broad ▷ n small bottle of beer

STUBS > STUB

STUCCO n plaster used for coating or decorating walls ▷ vb apply stucco to (a building)

STUCCOED > STUCCO

STUCCOER > STUCCO

STUCCOERS > STUCCO

STUCCOES > STUCCO

STUCCOING > STUCCO

STUCCOS > STUCCO

STUCK n thrust

STUCKS > STUCK

STUD n small piece of metal attached to a surface for decoration ▷ vb set with studs

STUDBOOK n written record of the pedigree of a purebred stock, esp of racehorses

STUDBOOKS > STUDBOOK

STUDDED > STUD

STUDDEN > STAND

STUDDIE Scots word for > ANVIL

STUDDIES > STUDDIE

STUDDING > STUD

STUDDINGS > STUD

STUDDLE n post

STUDDLES > STUDDLE

STUDE vb past tense and past participle of staun (Scots form of stand)

STUDENT n person who studies a subject, esp at university

STUDENTRY n body of students

STUDENTS > STUDENT

STUDENTY adj informal, sometimes derogatory term denoting the characteristics believed typical of an undergraduate student

STUDFARM n farm where horses are bred

STUDFARMS > STUDFARM

STUDFISH n American minnow

STUDHORSE another word for > STALLION

STUDIED adj carefully practised

STUDIEDLY > STUDIED

STUDIER > STUDY

STUDIERS > STUDY

STUDIES > STUDY

STUDIO n workroom of an artist or photographer

STUDIOS > STUDIO

STUDIOUS adj fond of study

STUDLIER > STUDLY

STUDLIEST > STUDLY

STUDLY adj strong and virile

STUDS > STUD

STUDWORK n work decorated with studs

STUDWORKS > STUDWORK

STUDY vb be engaged in learning (a subject) ▷ n act or process of studying

STUDYING > STUDY

STUFF n substance or material ▷ vb pack, cram, or fill completely

STUFFED > STUFF

STUFFER > STUFF

STUFFERS > STUFF

STUFFIER > STUFFY

STUFFIEST > STUFFY

STUFFILY > STUFFY

STUFFING n seasoned mixture with which food is stuffed

STUFFINGS > STUFFING

STUFFLESS > STUFF

STUFFS > STUFF

STUFFY adj lacking fresh air

STUGGIER > STUGGY

STUGGIEST > STUGGY

STUGGY adj stout

STUIVER same as > STIVER

STUIVERS > STUIVER

STUKKEND adj South African slang for broken or wrecked

STULL n timber prop or platform in a stope

STULLS > STULL

STULM n shaft

STULMS > STULM

STULTIFY vb dull (the mind) by boring routine

STUM n partly fermented wine added to fermented wine as a preservative ▷ vb preserve (wine) by adding stum

STUMBLE vb trip and nearly fall ▷ n stumbling

STUMBLED > STUMBLE

STUMBLER > STUMBLE

STUMBLERS > STUMBLE

STUMBLES > STUMBLE

STUMBLIER > STUMBLY

STUMBLING > STUMBLE

STUMBLY adj tending to stumble

STUMER n forgery or cheat

STUMERS > STUMER

STUMM same as > SHTOOM

STUMMED > STUM

STUMMEL n bowl of pipe

STUMMELS > STUMMEL

STUMMING > STUM

STUMP n base of a tree left when the main trunk has been cut away ▷ vb baffle

STUMPAGE n standing timber or its value

STUMPAGES > STUMPAGE

STUMPED > STUMP

STUMPER > STUMP

STUMPERS > STUMP

STUMPIER > STUMPY

STUMPIES > STUMPY

STUMPIEST > STUMPY

STUMPILY > STUMPY

STUMPING > STUMP

STUMPINGS > STUMPING

STUMPS > STUMP

STUMPWORK n type of embroidery featuring raised figures, padded with cotton wool or hair

STUMPY adj short and thick ▷ n stumpy thing

STUMS > STUM

STUN vb shock or overwhelm ▷ n state or effect of being stunned

STUNG > STING

STUNK > STINK

STUNKARD adj sulky

STUNNED > STUN

STUNNER n beautiful person or thing

STUNNERS > STUNNER

STUNNING > STUN

STUNNINGS > STUN

STUNS > STUN

STUNSAIL n type of light auxiliary sail

STUNSAILS > STUNSAIL

STUNT vb prevent or impede the growth of ▷ n acrobatic or dangerous action

STUNTED > STUNT

STUNTING > STUNT

STUNTMAN n person who performs dangerous acts in a film, etc in place of an actor

STUNTMEN > STUNTMAN

STUNTS > STUNT

STUPA n domed edifice housing Buddhist or Jain relics

STUPAS > STUPA

STUPE n hot damp cloth applied to the body to relieve pain ▷ vb treat with a stupe

STUPED > STUPE

STUPEFIED > STUPEFY

STUPEFIER > STUPEFY

STUPEFIES > STUPEFY

STUPEFY vb make insensitive or lethargic

STUPENT adj astonished

STUPES > STUPE

STUPID adj lacking intelligence ▷ n stupid person

STUPIDER > STUPID

STUPIDEST > STUPID

STUPIDITY n quality or state of being stupid

STUPIDLY > STUPID

STUPIDS > STUPID

STUPING > STUPE

STUPOR n dazed or unconscious state

STUPOROUS > STUPOR

STUPORS > STUPOR

STUPRATE vb ravish

STUPRATED > STUPRATE

STUPRATES > STUPRATE

STURDIED > STURDY

STURDIER > STURDY

STURDIES > STURDY

STURDIEST > STURDY

STURDILY > STURDY

STURDY adj healthy and robust ▷ n disease of sheep

STURE same as > STOOR

STURGEON n fish from which caviar is obtained

STURGEONS > STURGEON

STURMER n type of eating apple with pale green skin

STURMERS > STURMER

STURNINE > STURNUS

STURNOID > STURNUS

STURNUS n bird of starling family

STURNUSES > STURNUS

STURT vb bother

STURTED > STURT

STURTING > STURT

STURTS > STURT

STUSHIE n commotion, rumpus, or row

STUSHIES > STUSHIE

STUTTER vb speak with repetition of initial consonants ▷ n tendency to stutter

STUTTERED > STUTTER

STUTTERER > STUTTER

STUTTERS > STUTTER

STY vb climb

STYE n inflammation at the base of an eyelash

STYED > STYE

STYES > STY

STYGIAN adj dark, gloomy, or hellish

STYING > STY

STYLAR > STYLUS

STYLATE adj having style

STYLE n shape or design ▷ vb shape or design

STYLEBOOK n book containing rules of punctuation, etc, for the use of writers, editors, and printers

STYLED > STYLE

STYLEE same as > STYLE

STYLEES > STYLEE

STYLELESS > STYLE

STYLER > STYLE

STYLERS > STYLE

STYLES > STYLE

STYLET n wire to stiffen a flexible cannula or catheter

STYLETS > STYLET

STYLI > STYLUS

STYLIE adj fashion-conscious

STYLIER > STYLIE

STYLIEST > STYLIE

STYLIFORM adj shaped like a stylus or bristle

STYLING > STYLE

STYLINGS > STYLE

STYLISE same as > STYLIZE

STYLISED > STYLISE

STYLISER > STYLISE

STYLISERS > STYLISE

STYLISES > STYLISE

STYLISH adj smart, elegant, and fashionable

STYLISHLY > STYLISH

STYLISING > STYLISE

STYLIST n hairdresser

STYLISTIC adj of literary or artistic style

STYLISTS > STYLIST

STYLITE n one of a class of recluses who in ancient times lived on the top of high pillars

STYLITES > STYLITE

STYLITIC > STYLITE

STYLITISM > STYLITE

STYLIZE vb cause to conform to an established stylistic form

STYLIZED > STYLIZE

STYLIZER > STYLIZE

STYLIZERS > STYLIZE

STYLIZES > STYLIZE

STYLIZING > STYLIZE

STYLO n type of fountain pen

STYLOBATE n continuous horizontal course of masonry that supports a colonnade

STYLOID adj resembling a stylus ▷ n spiny growth

STYLOIDS > STYLOID

STYLOLITE n any of the small striated columnar or irregular structures within the strata of some limestones

STYLOPES > STYLOPS

STYLOPID n type of parasitic insect

STYLOPIDS > STYLOPID

STYLOPISE same as > STYLOPIZE

STYLOPIZE vb (of a stylops) to parasitize (a host)

STYLOPS n type of insect that lives as a parasite in other insects

STYLOS > STYLO

STYLUS n needle-like device on a record player

STYLUSES > STYLUS

STYME vb peer

STYMED > STYME

STYMES > STYME

STYMIE vb hinder or thwart

STYMIED > STYMY

STYMIEING > STYMIE

STYMIES > STYMY

STYMING > STYME

STYMY same as > STYMIE

STYMYING > STYMY

STYPSIS n action, application, or use of a styptic

STYPSISES > STYPSIS
STYPTIC adj (drug) used to stop bleeding ▷ n styptic drug
STYPTICAL > STYPTIC
STYPTICS > STYPTIC
STYRAX n type of tropical or subtropical tree
STYRAXES > STYRAX
STYRE same as > STIR
STYRED > STYRE
STYRENE n colourless oily volatile flammable water-insoluble liquid
STYRENES > STYRENE
STYRES > STYRE
STYRING > STYRE
STYROFOAM n tradename for a light expanded polystyrene plastic
STYTE vb bounce
STYTED > STYTE
STYTES > STYTE
STYTING > STYTE
SUABILITY > SUABLE
SUABLE adj liable to be sued in a court
SUABLY > SUABLE
SUASIBLE > SUASION
SUASION n persuasion
SUASIONS > SUASION
SUASIVE > SUASION
SUASIVELY > SUASION
SUASORY > SUASION
SUAVE adj smooth and sophisticated in manner
SUAVELY > SUAVE
SUAVENESS > SUAVE
SUAVER > SUAVE
SUAVEST > SUAVE
SUAVITIES > SUAVE
SUAVITY > SUAVE
SUB n subeditor ▷ vb act as a substitute
SUBA n shepherd's cloak
SUBABBOT n abbot who is subordinate to another abbot
SUBABBOTS > SUBABBOT
SUBACID adj (esp of some fruits) moderately acid or sour
SUBACIDLY > SUBACID
SUBACRID adj slightly acrid
SUBACT vb subdue
SUBACTED > SUBACT
SUBACTING > SUBACT
SUBACTION > SUBACT
SUBACTS > SUBACT
SUBACUTE adj intermediate between acute and chronic
SUBADAR n chief native officer of a company of Indian soldiers in the British service
SUBADARS > SUBADAR
SUBADULT n animal not quite at adult stage
SUBADULTS > SUBADULT
SUBAERIAL adj in open air

SUBAGENCY n agency employed by larger agency
SUBAGENT n agent who is subordinate to another agent
SUBAGENTS > SUBAGENT
SUBAH same as > SUBADAR
SUBAHDAR same as > SUBADAR
SUBAHDARS > SUBAHDAR
SUBAHDARY n office of subahdar
SUBAHS > SUBAH
SUBAHSHIP > SUBAH
SUBALAR adj below a wing
SUBALPINE adj situated in or relating to the regions at the foot of mountains
SUBALTERN n British army officer below the rank of captain ▷ adj of inferior position or rank
SUBAPICAL adj below an apex
SUBAQUA adj of or relating to underwater sport
SUBARCTIC adj of or relating to latitudes immediately south of the Arctic Circle
SUBAREA n area within a larger area
SUBAREAS > SUBAREA
SUBARID adj receiving slightly more rainfall than arid regions
SUBAS > SUBA
SUBASTRAL adj terrestrial
SUBATOM n part of an atom
SUBATOMIC adj of or being one of the particles which make up an atom
SUBATOMS > SUBATOM
SUBAUDIO adj (of sound) low frequency
SUBAURAL adj below the ear
SUBAXIAL adj below an axis of the body
SUBBASAL > SUBBASE
SUBBASE same as > SUBBASS
SUBBASES > SUBBASE
SUBBASIN n geographical basin within larger basin
SUBBASINS > SUBBASIN
SUBBASS another name for > BOURDON
SUBBASSES > SUBBASS
SUBBED > SUB
SUBBIE n subcontractor
SUBBIES > SUBBIE
SUBBING > SUB
SUBBINGS > SUB
SUBBLOCK n part of mathematical matrix
SUBBLOCKS > SUBBLOCK
SUBBRANCH n branch within another branch
SUBBREED n breed within a larger breed
SUBBREEDS > SUBBREED

SUBBUREAU n bureau subordinate to the main bureau
SUBBY same as > SUBBIE
SUBCANTOR n deputy to a cantor
SUBCASTE n subdivision of a caste
SUBCASTES > SUBCASTE
SUBCAUDAL adj below a tail
SUBCAUSE n factor less important than a cause
SUBCAUSES > SUBCAUSE
SUBCAVITY n cavity within a larger cavity
SUBCELL n cell within a larger cell
SUBCELLAR n cellar below another cellar
SUBCELLS > SUBCELL
SUBCENTER n secondary center
SUBCENTRE same as > SUBCENTER
SUBCHASER n anti-submarine warship
SUBCHIEF n chief below the main chief
SUBCHIEFS > SUBCHIEF
SUBCHORD n part of a curve
SUBCHORDS > SUBCHORD
SUBCLAIM n claim that is part of a larger claim
SUBCLAIMS > SUBCLAIM
SUBCLAN n clan within a larger clan
SUBCLANS > SUBCLAN
SUBCLASS n principal subdivision of a class ▷ vb assign to a subclass
SUBCLAUSE n subordinate section of a larger clause in a document
SUBCLERK n clerk who is subordinate to another clerk
SUBCLERKS > SUBCLERK
SUBCLIMAX n community in which development has been arrested before climax has been attained
SUBCODE n computer tag identifying data
SUBCODES > SUBCODE
SUBCOLONY n colony established by existing colony
SUBCONSUL n assistant to a consul
SUBCOOL vb make colder
SUBCOOLED > SUBCOOL
SUBCOOLS > SUBCOOL
SUBCORTEX n matter of the brain situated beneath the cerebral cortex
SUBCOSTA n vein in insect wing
SUBCOSTAE > SUBCOSTA
SUBCOSTAL adj below the rib

SUBCOUNTY n division of a county
SUBCRUST n secondary crust below main crust
SUBCRUSTS > SUBCRUST
SUBCULT n cult within larger cult
SUBCULTS > SUBCULT
SUBCUTES > SUBCUTIS
SUBCUTIS n layer of tissue beneath outer skin
SUBDEACON n cleric who assists at High Mass
SUBDEALER n dealer who buys from other dealer
SUBDEAN n deputy of dean
SUBDEANS > SUBDEAN
SUBDEB n young woman who is not yet a debutante
SUBDEBS > SUBDEB
SUBDEPOT n depot within a larger depot
SUBDEPOTS > SUBDEPOT
SUBDEPUTY n assistant to a deputy
SUBDERMAL adj below the skin
SUBDEW same as > SUBDUE
SUBDEWED > SUBDUE
SUBDEWING > SUBDUE
SUBDEWS > SUBDUE
SUBDIVIDE vb divide (a part of something) into smaller parts
SUBDOLOUS adj clever
SUBDORSAL adj situated close to the back
SUBDUABLE > SUBDUE
SUBDUABLY > SUBDUE
SUBDUAL > SUBDUE
SUBDUALS > SUBDUE
SUBDUCE vb withdraw
SUBDUCED > SUBDUCE
SUBDUCES > SUBDUCE
SUBDUCING > SUBDUCE
SUBDUCT vb draw or turn (the eye, etc) downwards
SUBDUCTED > SUBDUCT
SUBDUCTS > SUBDUCT
SUBDUE vb overcome
SUBDUED adj cowed, passive, or shy
SUBDUEDLY > SUBDUED
SUBDUER > SUBDUE
SUBDUERS > SUBDUE
SUBDUES > SUBDUE
SUBDUING > SUBDUE
SUBDUPLE adj in proportion of one to two
SUBDURAL adj between the dura mater and the arachnoid
SUBDWARF n star smaller than a dwarf star
SUBDWARFS > SUBDWARF
SUBECHO n echo resonating more quietly than another echo
SUBECHOES > SUBECHO
SUBEDAR same as > SUBADAR
SUBEDARS > SUBEDAR

SUBEDIT vb edit and correct (written or printed material)
SUBEDITED > SUBEDIT
SUBEDITOR n person who checks and edits text for a newspaper or magazine
SUBEDITS > SUBEDIT
SUBENTIRE adj slightly indented
SUBENTRY n entry within another entry
SUBEPOCH n epoch within another epoch
SUBEPOCHS > SUBEPOCH
SUBEQUAL adj not quite equal
SUBER n cork
SUBERATE n salt of suberic acid
SUBERATES > SUBERATE
SUBERECT adj not quite erect
SUBEREOUS same as > SUBEROSE
SUBERIC same as > SUBEROSE
SUBERIN n fatty or waxy substance that is present in the walls of cork cells
SUBERINS > SUBERIN
SUBERISE same as > SUBERIZE
SUBERISED > SUBERISE
SUBERISES > SUBERISE
SUBERIZE vb impregnate (cell walls) with suberin during the formation of corky tissue
SUBERIZED > SUBERIZE
SUBERIZES > SUBERIZE
SUBEROSE adj relating to, resembling, or consisting of cork
SUBEROUS same as > SUBEROSE
SUBERS > SUBER
SUBFAMILY n taxonomic group that is a subdivision of a family
SUBFEU vb grant feu to vassal
SUBFEUED > SUBFEU
SUBFEUING > SUBFEU
SUBFEUS > SUBFEU
SUBFIELD n subdivision of a field
SUBFIELDS > SUBFIELD
SUBFILE n file within another file
SUBFILES > SUBFILE
SUBFIX n suffix
SUBFIXES > SUBFIX
SUBFLOOR n rough floor that forms a base for a finished floor
SUBFLOORS > SUBFLOOR
SUBFLUID adj viscous
SUBFOSSIL n something partly fossilized
SUBFRAME n frame on which car body is built
SUBFRAMES > SUBFRAME

SUBFUSC adj devoid of brightness or appeal ▷ n (at Oxford University) formal academic dress
SUBFUSCS > SUBFUSC
SUBFUSK same as > SUBFUSC
SUBFUSKS > SUBFUSK
SUBGENERA > SUBGENUS
SUBGENRE n genre within a larger genre
SUBGENRES > SUBGENRE
SUBGENUS n taxonomic group that is a subdivision of a genus but of higher rank than a species
SUBGOAL n secondary goal
SUBGOALS > SUBGOAL
SUBGRADE n ground beneath a roadway or pavement
SUBGRADES > SUBGRADE
SUBGRAPH n graph sharing vertices of other graph
SUBGRAPHS > SUBGRAPH
SUBGROUP n small group that is part of a larger group
SUBGROUPS > SUBGROUP
SUBGUM n Chinese dish
SUBGUMS > SUBGUM
SUBHA n string of beads used in praying and meditating
SUBHAS > SUBHA
SUBHEAD n heading of a subsection in a printed work
SUBHEADS > SUBHEAD
SUBHEDRAL adj with some characteristics of crystal
SUBHUMAN adj less than human
SUBHUMANS > SUBHUMAN
SUBHUMID adj not wet enough for trees to grow
SUBIDEA n secondary idea
SUBIDEAS > SUBIDEA
SUBIMAGO n first winged stage of the mayfly
SUBIMAGOS > SUBIMAGO
SUBINCISE vb perform subincision
SUBINDEX same as > SUBSCRIPT
SUBINFEUD vb grant by feudal tenant to further tenant
SUBITEM n item that is less important than another item
SUBITEMS > SUBITEM
SUBITISE same as > SUBITIZE
SUBITISED > SUBITISE
SUBITISES > SUBITISE
SUBITIZE vb perceive the number of (a group of items) at a glance and without counting

SUBITIZED > SUBITIZE
SUBITIZES > SUBITIZE
SUBITO adv (preceding or following a dynamic marking, etc) suddenly
SUBJACENT adj forming a foundation
SUBJECT n person or thing being dealt with or studied ▷ adj being under the rule of a monarch or government ▷ vb cause to undergo
SUBJECTED > SUBJECT
SUBJECTS > SUBJECT
SUBJOIN vb add or attach at the end of something spoken, written, etc
SUBJOINED > SUBJOIN
SUBJOINS > SUBJOIN
SUBJUGATE vb bring (a group of people) under one's control
SUBLATE vb deny
SUBLATED > SUBLATE
SUBLATES > SUBLATE
SUBLATING > SUBLATE
SUBLATION > SUBLATE
SUBLEASE n lease of property made by a person who is himself or herself a lessee or tenant of that property ▷ vb grant a sublease of (property)
SUBLEASED > SUBLEASE
SUBLEASES > SUBLEASE
SUBLESSEE > SUBLEASE
SUBLESSOR > SUBLEASE
SUBLET vb rent out (property rented from someone else) ▷ n sublease
SUBLETHAL adj not strong enough to kill
SUBLETS > SUBLET
SUBLETTER > SUBLET
SUBLEVEL n subdivision of a level
SUBLEVELS > SUBLEVEL
SUBLIMATE vb direct the energy of (a strong desire, esp a sexual one) into socially acceptable activities ▷ n material obtained when a substance is sublimed ▷ adj exalted or purified
SUBLIME adj of high moral, intellectual, or spiritual value ▷ vb change from a solid to a vapour without first melting
SUBLIMED > SUBLIME
SUBLIMELY > SUBLIME
SUBLIMER > SUBLIME
SUBLIMERS > SUBLIME
SUBLIMES > SUBLIME
SUBLIMEST > SUBLIME
SUBLIMING > SUBLIME
SUBLIMISE same as > SUBLIMIZE
SUBLIMIT n limit on a subcategory
SUBLIMITS > SUBLIMIT

SUBLIMITY > SUBLIME
SUBLIMIZE vb make sublime
SUBLINE n secondary headline
SUBLINEAR adj beneath a line
SUBLINES > SUBLINE
SUBLOT n subdivision of a lot
SUBLOTS > SUBLOT
SUBLUNAR same as > SUBLUNARY
SUBLUNARY adj situated between the moon and the earth
SUBLUNATE adj almost crescent-shaped
SUBLUXATE vb partially dislocate
SUBMAN n primitive form of human
SUBMARINE n vessel which can operate below the surface of the sea ▷ adj below the surface of the sea ▷ vb slide beneath seatbelt in car crash
SUBMARKET n specialized market within larger market
SUBMATRIX n part of matrix
SUBMEN > SUBMAN
SUBMENTA > SUBMENTUM
SUBMENTAL adj situated beneath the chin
SUBMENTUM n base of insect lip
SUBMENU n further list of options within computer menu
SUBMENUS > SUBMENU
SUBMERGE vb put or go below the surface of water or other liquid
SUBMERGED adj (of plants or plant parts) growing beneath the surface of the water
SUBMERGES > SUBMERGE
SUBMERSE same as > SUBMERGE
SUBMERSED same as > SUBMERGED
SUBMERSES > SUBMERSE
SUBMICRON n object only visible through powerful microscope
SUBMISS adj docile
SUBMISSLY adv submissively
SUBMIT vb surrender
SUBMITS > SUBMIT
SUBMITTAL > SUBMIT
SUBMITTED > SUBMIT
SUBMITTER > SUBMIT
SUBMUCOSA n connective tissue beneath a mucous membrane
SUBMUCOUS > SUBMUCOSA
SUBNASAL adj beneath nose

SUBNET n part of network
SUBNETS > SUBNET
SUBNEURAL adj beneath a nerve centre
SUBNICHE n subdivision of a niche
SUBNICHES > SUBNICHE
SUBNIVEAL adj beneath the snow
SUBNIVEAN same as **>** SUBNIVEAL
SUBNODAL adj below the level of a node
SUBNORMAL adj less than normal, esp in intelligence ▷ n subnormal person
SUBNUCLEI pl n plural of subnucleus, secondary nucleus
SUBOCEAN adj beneath the ocean
SUBOCTAVE n octave below another
SUBOCULAR adj below the eye
SUBOFFICE n office that is subordinate to another office
SUBOPTIC adj below the eye
SUBORAL adj not quite oral
SUBORDER n taxonomic group that is a subdivision of an order
SUBORDERS > SUBORDER
SUBORN vb bribe or incite (a person) to commit a wrongful act
SUBORNED > SUBORN
SUBORNER > SUBORN
SUBORNERS > SUBORN
SUBORNING > SUBORN
SUBORNS > SUBORN
SUBOSCINE adj belonging to a subfamily of birds
SUBOVAL adj not quite oval
SUBOVATE adj almost egg-shaped
SUBOXIDE n oxide of an element containing less oxygen than the common oxide formed by the element
SUBOXIDES > SUBOXIDE
SUBPANEL n panel that is part of larger panel
SUBPANELS > SUBPANEL
SUBPAR adj not up to standard
SUBPART n part within another part
SUBPARTS > SUBPART
SUBPENA same as **>** SUBPOENA
SUBPENAED > SUBPENA
SUBPENAS > SUBPENA
SUBPERIOD n subdivision of time period
SUBPHASE n subdivision of phase
SUBPHASES > SUBPHASE
SUBPHYLA > SUBPHYLUM

SUBPHYLAR > SUBPHYLUM
SUBPHYLUM n taxonomic group that is a subdivision of a phylum
SUBPLOT n secondary plot in a novel, play, or film
SUBPLOTS > SUBPLOT
SUBPOENA n writ requiring a person to appear before a lawcourt ▷ vb summon (someone) with a subpoena
SUBPOENAS > SUBPOENA
SUBPOLAR adj not quite polar
SUBPOTENT adj not at full strength
SUBPRIME n loan made to a borrower with a poor credit rating
SUBPRIMES > SUBPRIME
SUBPRIOR n monk junior to a prior
SUBPRIORS > SUBPRIOR
SUBPUBIC adj beneath the pubic bone
SUBRACE n race of people considered to be inferior
SUBRACES > SUBRACE
SUBREGION n subdivision of a region, esp a zoogeographical or ecological region
SUBRENT n rent paid to renter who rents to another ▷ vb rent out (a property that is already rented)
SUBRENTED > SUBRENT
SUBRENTS > SUBRENT
SUBRING n mathematical ring that is a subset of another ring
SUBRINGS > SUBRING
SUBROGATE vb put (one person or thing) in the place of another in respect of a right or claim
SUBRULE n rule within another rule
SUBRULES > SUBRULE
SUBS > SUB
SUBSACRAL adj below the sacrum
SUBSALE n sale carried out within the process of a larger sale
SUBSALES > SUBSALE
SUBSAMPLE vb take further sample from existing sample
SUBSCALE n scale within a scale
SUBSCALES > SUBSCALE
SUBSCHEMA n part of computer database used by an individual
SUBSCRIBE vb pay (a subscription)
SUBSCRIPT adj (character) printed below the line ▷ n subscript character

SUBSEA adj undersea
SUBSECIVE adj left over
SUBSECT n sect within a larger sect
SUBSECTOR n subdivision of sector
SUBSECTS > SUBSECT
SUBSELLIA pl n ledges underneath the hinged seats in a church
SUBSENSE n definition that is division of wider definition
SUBSENSES > SUBSENSE
SUBSERE n secondary sere arising when the progress of a sere has been interrupted
SUBSERES > SUBSERE
SUBSERIES n series within a larger series
SUBSERVE vb be helpful or useful to
SUBSERVED > SUBSERVE
SUBSERVES > SUBSERVE
SUBSET n mathematical set contained within a larger set
SUBSETS > SUBSET
SUBSHAFT n secondary shaft in mine
SUBSHAFTS > SUBSHAFT
SUBSHELL n part of a shell of an atom
SUBSHELLS > SUBSHELL
SUBSHRUB n small bushy plant that is woody except for the tips of the branches
SUBSHRUBS > SUBSHRUB
SUBSIDE vb become less intense
SUBSIDED > SUBSIDE
SUBSIDER > SUBSIDE
SUBSIDERS > SUBSIDE
SUBSIDES > SUBSIDE
SUBSIDIES > SUBSIDY
SUBSIDING > SUBSIDE
SUBSIDISE same as **>** SUBSIDIZE
SUBSIDIZE vb help financially
SUBSIDY n financial aid
SUBSIST vb manage to live
SUBSISTED > SUBSIST
SUBSISTER > SUBSIST
SUBSISTS > SUBSIST
SUBSITE n location within a website
SUBSITES > SUBSITE
SUBSIZAR n type of undergraduate at Cambridge
SUBSIZARS > SUBSIZAR
SUBSKILL n element of a wider skill
SUBSKILLS > SUBSKILL
SUBSOCIAL adj lacking a complex or definite social structure
SUBSOIL n earth just below the surface soil ▷ vb plough (land) to a

depth below the normal ploughing level
SUBSOILED > SUBSOIL
SUBSOILER > SUBSOIL
SUBSOILS > SUBSOIL
SUBSOLAR adj (of a point on the earth) directly below the sun
SUBSONG n subdued form of birdsong modified from the full territorial song
SUBSONGS > SUBSONG
SUBSONIC adj moving at a speed less than that of sound
SUBSPACE n part of a mathematical matrix
SUBSPACES > SUBSPACE
SUBSTAGE n part of a microscope below the stage
SUBSTAGES > SUBSTAGE
SUBSTANCE n physical composition of something
SUBSTATE n subdivision of state
SUBSTATES > SUBSTATE
SUBSTRACT same as **>** SUBTRACT
SUBSTRATA pl n layers lying underneath other layers
SUBSTRATE n substance upon which an enzyme acts
SUBSTRUCT vb build as a foundation
SUBSTYLAR > SUBSTYLE
SUBSTYLE n line on a dial
SUBSTYLES > SUBSTYLE
SUBSULTUS n abnormal twitching
SUBSUME vb include (an idea, case, etc) under a larger classification or group
SUBSUMED > SUBSUME
SUBSUMES > SUBSUME
SUBSUMING > SUBSUME
SUBSYSTEM n system operating within a larger system
SUBTACK Scots word for **>** SUBLEASE
SUBTACKS > SUBTACK
SUBTALAR adj beneath the ankle-bone
SUBTASK n task that is part of a larger task
SUBTASKS > SUBTASK
SUBTAXA > SUBTAXON
SUBTAXON n supplementary piece of identifying information in plant or animal scientific name
SUBTAXONS > SUBTAXON
SUBTEEN n young person who has not yet become a teenager
SUBTEENS > SUBTEEN
SUBTENANT n person who rents property from a tenant

S

SUBTEND vb be opposite (an angle or side)

SUBTENDED > SUBTEND

SUBTENDS > SUBTEND

SUBTENSE n line that subtends

SUBTENSES > SUBTENSE

SUBTENURE n tenancy given by other tenant

SUBTEST n test that is part of larger test

SUBTESTS > SUBTEST

SUBTEXT n underlying theme in a piece of writing

SUBTEXTS > SUBTEXT

SUBTHEME n secondary theme

SUBTHEMES > SUBTHEME

SUBTIDAL adj below the level of low tide

SUBTIL same as > SUBTLE

SUBTITLE rare spelling of > SUBTLE

SUBTILELY > SUBTILE

SUBTILER > SUBTILE

SUBTILEST > SUBTILE

SUBTILIN n antibiotic drug

SUBTILINS > SUBTILIN

SUBTILISE same as > SUBTILIZE

SUBTILITY > SUBTILE

SUBTILIZE vb bring to a purer state

SUBTILTY > SUBTILE

SUBTITLE n secondary title of a book ▷ vb provide with a subtitle or subtitles

SUBTITLED > SUBTITLE

SUBTITLES > SUBTITLE

SUBTLE adj not immediately obvious

SUBTLER > SUBTLE

SUBTLEST > SUBTLE

SUBTLETY n fine distinction

SUBTLY > SUBTLE

SUBTONE n subdivision of a tone

SUBTONES > SUBTONE

SUBTONIC n seventh degree of a major or minor scale

SUBTONICS > SUBTONIC

SUBTOPIA n suburban development that encroaches on rural areas yet appears to offer the attractions of country life to suburban dwellers

SUBTOPIAN > SUBTOPIA

SUBTOPIAS > SUBTOPIA

SUBTOPIC n topic within a larger topic

SUBTOPICS > SUBTOPIC

SUBTORRID same as > SUBTROPIC

SUBTOTAL n total made up by a column of figures, forming part of the total made up by a larger column or group ▷ vb establish or work out a

subtotal for (a column, group, etc)

SUBTOTALS > SUBTOTAL

SUBTRACT vb take (one number or quantity) from another

SUBTRACTS > SUBTRACT

SUBTRADE n (in N America) specialist hired by a building contractor

SUBTRADES > SUBTRADE

SUBTREND n minor trend

SUBTRENDS > SUBTREND

SUBTRIBE n tribe within a larger tribe

SUBTRIBES > SUBTRIBE

SUBTRIST adj slightly sad

SUBTROPIC adj relating to the region lying between the tropics and the temperate lands

SUBTRUDE vb intrude stealthily

SUBTRUDED > SUBTRUDE

SUBTRUDES > SUBTRUDE

SUBTUNIC adj below membrane ▷ n garment worn under a tunic

SUBTUNICS > SUBTUNIC

SUBTYPE n secondary or subordinate type or genre

SUBTYPES > SUBTYPE

SUBUCULA n ancient Roman man's undergarment

SUBUCULAS > SUBUCULA

SUBULATE adj (esp of plant parts) tapering to a point

SUBUNIT n distinct part or component of something larger

SUBUNITS > SUBUNIT

SUBURB n residential area on the outskirts of a city

SUBURBAN adj mildly derogatory term for inhabiting a suburb ▷ n mildly derogatory term for a person who lives in a suburb

SUBURBANS > SUBURBAN

SUBURBED > SUBURB

SUBURBIA n suburbs and their inhabitants

SUBURBIAS > SUBURBIA

SUBURBS > SUBURB

SUBURSINE adj of a bear subspecies

SUBVASSAL n vassal of a vassal

SUBVENE vb happen in such a way as to be of assistance

SUBVENED > SUBVENE

SUBVENES > SUBVENE

SUBVENING > SUBVENE

SUBVERSAL > SUBVERT

SUBVERSE same as > SUBVERT

SUBVERSED > SUBVERSE

SUBVERSES > SUBVERSE

SUBVERST > SUBVERSE

SUBVERT vb overthrow the authority of

SUBVERTED > SUBVERT

SUBVERTER > SUBVERT

SUBVERTS > SUBVERT

SUBVICAR n assistant to a vicar

SUBVICARS > SUBVICAR

SUBVIRAL adj of, caused by, or denoting a part of the structure of a virus

SUBVIRUS n organism smaller than a virus

SUBVISUAL adj not visible to the naked eye

SUBVOCAL adj formed in mind without being spoken aloud

SUBWARDEN n assistant to a warden

SUBWAY n passage under a road or railway ▷ vb travel by subway

SUBWAYED > SUBWAY

SUBWAYING > SUBWAY

SUBWAYS > SUBWAY

SUBWOOFER n loudspeaker for very low tones

SUBWORLD n underworld

SUBWORLDS > SUBWORLD

SUBWRITER n person carrying out writing tasks for other writer

SUBZERO adj lower than zero

SUBZONAL > SUBZONE

SUBZONE n subdivision of a zone

SUBZONES > SUBZONE

SUCCADE n piece of candied fruit

SUCCADES > SUCCADE

SUCCAH same as > SUKKAH

SUCCAHS > SUCCAH

SUCCEDENT adj following ▷ n successor

SUCCEED vb accomplish an aim

SUCCEEDED > SUCCEED

SUCCEEDER > SUCCEED

SUCCEEDS > SUCCEED

SUCCENTOR n deputy of the precentor of a cathedral that has retained its statutes from pre-Reformation days

SUCCES French word for > SUCCESS

SUCCESS n achievement of something attempted

SUCCESSES > SUCCESS

SUCCESSOR n person who succeeds someone in a position

SUCCI > SUCCUS

SUCCINATE n any salt or ester of succinic acid

SUCCINCT adj brief and clear

SUCCINIC adj of, relating to, or obtained from amber

SUCCINITE n type of amber

SUCCINYL n constituent of succinic acid

SUCCINYLS > SUCCINYL

SUCCISE adj ending abruptly, as if cut off

SUCCOR same as > SUCCOUR

SUCCORED > SUCCOR

SUCCORER > SUCCOR

SUCCORERS > SUCCOR

SUCCORIES > SUCCORY

SUCCORING > SUCCORY

SUCCORS > SUCCOR

SUCCORY another name for > CHICORY

SUCCOS same as > SUKKOTH

SUCCOSE > SUCCUS

SUCCOT same as > SUKKOTH

SUCCOTASH n mixture of cooked sweet corn kernels and lima beans, served as a vegetable

SUCCOTH variant of > SUKKOTH

SUCCOUR n help in distress ▷ vb give aid to (someone in time of difficulty)

SUCCOURED > SUCCOUR

SUCCOURER > SUCCOUR

SUCCOURS > SUCCOUR

SUCCOUS > SUCCUS

SUCCUBA same as > SUCCUBUS

SUCCUBAE > SUCCUBA

SUCCUBAS > SUCCUBA

SUCCUBI > SUCCUBUS

SUCCUBINE > SUCCUBUS

SUCCUBOUS adj having the leaves arranged so that the upper margin of each leaf is covered by the lower margin of the next leaf along

SUCCUBUS n female demon believed to have sex with sleeping men

SUCCULENT adj juicy and delicious ▷ n succulent plant

SUCCUMB vb give way (to something overpowering)

SUCCUMBED > SUCCUMB

SUCCUMBER > SUCCUMB

SUCCUMBS > SUCCUMB

SUCCURSAL adj (esp of a religious establishment) subsidiary ▷ n subsidiary establishment

SUCCUS n fluid

SUCCUSS vb shake (a patient) to detect the sound of fluid in a cavity

SUCCUSSED > SUCCUSS

SUCCUSSES > SUCCUSS

SUCH adj of the kind specified ▷ pron such things

SUCHLIKE pron such or similar things ▷ n such or similar things ▷ adj of such a kind

SUCHNESS > SUCH
SUCHWISE > SUCH
SUCK vb draw (liquid or air) into the mouth ▷ n sucking
SUCKED > SUCK
SUCKEN Scots word for > DISTRICT
SUCKENER n tenant
SUCKENERS > SUCKENER
SUCKENS > SUCKEN
SUCKER n person who is easily deceived or swindled ▷ vb strip off the suckers from (a plant)
SUCKERED > SUCKER
SUCKERING > SUCKER
SUCKERS > SUCKER
SUCKET same as > SUCCADE
SUCKETS > SUCKET
SUCKFISH n type of spiny-finned marine fish
SUCKHOLE n sycophant ▷ vb behave in a sycophantic manner
SUCKHOLED > SUCKHOLE
SUCKHOLES > SUCKHOLE
SUCKIER > SUCKY
SUCKIEST > SUCKY
SUCKING adj not yet weaned
SUCKINGS > SUCKING
SUCKLE vb feed at the breast
SUCKLED > SUCKLE
SUCKLER > SUCKLE
SUCKLERS > SUCKLE
SUCKLES > SUCKLE
SUCKLESS > SUCK
SUCKLING n unweaned baby or young animal
SUCKLINGS > SUCKLING
SUCKS interj expression of disappointment
SUCKY adj despicable
SUCRALOSE n artificial sweetener
SUCRASE another name for > INVERTASE
SUCRASES > SUCRASE
SUCRE n former standard monetary unit of Ecuador
SUCRES > SUCRE
SUCRIER n small container for sugar at table
SUCRIERS > SUCRIER
SUCROSE same as > SUGAR
SUCROSES > SUCROSE
SUCTION n sucking ▷ vb subject to suction
SUCTIONAL > SUCTION
SUCTIONED > SUCTION
SUCTIONS > SUCTION
SUCTORIAL adj specialized for sucking or adhering
SUCTORIAN n microscopic creature
SUCURUJU n anaconda
SUCURUJUS > SUCURUJU
SUD singular of > SUDS

SUDAMEN n small cavity in the skin
SUDAMENS > SUDAMEN
SUDAMINA > SUDAMEN
SUDAMINAL > SUDAMEN
SUDARIA > SUDARIUM
SUDARIES > SUDARY
SUDARIUM n room in a Roman bathhouse where sweating is induced by heat
SUDARY same as > SUDARIUM
SUDATE vb sweat
SUDATED > SUDATE
SUDATES > SUDATE
SUDATING > SUDATE
SUDATION > SUDATE
SUDATIONS > SUDATE
SUDATORIA same as > SUDARIA
SUDATORY > SUDATE
SUDD n floating masses of reeds and weeds on the White Nile
SUDDEN adj done or occurring quickly and unexpectedly
SUDDENLY adv quickly and without warning
SUDDENS > SUDDEN
SUDDENTY n suddenness
SUDDER n supreme court in India
SUDDERS > SUDDER
SUDDS > SUDD
SUDOKU n type of puzzle in which numbers must be arranged in a grid according to certain rules
SUDOKUS > SUDOKU
SUDOR technical name for > SWEAT
SUDORAL > SUDOR
SUDORIFIC adj (drug) causing sweating ▷ n drug that causes sweating
SUDOROUS > SUDOR
SUDORS > SUDOR
SUDS pl n froth of soap and water, lather ▷ vb wash in suds
SUDSED > SUDS
SUDSER n soap opera
SUDSERS > SUDSER
SUDSES > SUDS
SUDSIER > SUDS
SUDSIEST > SUDS
SUDSING > SUDS
SUDSLESS > SUDS
SUDSY > SUDS
SUE vb start legal proceedings against
SUEABLE > SUE
SUED > SUE
SUEDE n leather with a velvety finish on one side ▷ vb give a suede finish to
SUEDED > SUEDE
SUEDES > SUEDE
SUEDETTE n imitation suede fabric
SUEDETTES > SUEDETTE

SUEDING > SUEDE
SUENT adj smooth
SUER > SUE
SUERS > SUE
SUES > SUE
SUET n hard fat obtained from sheep and cattle
SUETE n southeasterly wind in Cape Breton Island
SUETES > SUETE
SUETIER > SUET
SUETIEST > SUET
SUETS > SUET
SUETTIER > SUET
SUETTIEST > SUET
SUETTY > SUET
SUETY > SUET
SUFFARI same as > SAFARI
SUFFARIS > SUFFARI
SUFFECT adj additional ▷ n additional consul in ancient Rome
SUFFECTS > SUFFECT
SUFFER vb undergo or be subjected to
SUFFERED > SUFFER
SUFFERER > SUFFER
SUFFERERS > SUFFER
SUFFERING n pain, misery, or loss experienced by a person who suffers
SUFFERS > SUFFER
SUFFETE n official in ancient Carthage
SUFFETES > SUFFETE
SUFFICE vb be enough for a purpose
SUFFICED > SUFFICE
SUFFICER > SUFFICE
SUFFICERS > SUFFICE
SUFFICES > SUFFICE
SUFFICING > SUFFICE
SUFFIX n letters added to the end of a word to form another word ▷ vb add (letters) to the end of a word to form another word
SUFFIXAL > SUFFIX
SUFFIXED > SUFFIX
SUFFIXES > SUFFIX
SUFFIXING > SUFFIX
SUFFIXION > SUFFIX
SUFFLATE archaic word for > INFLATE
SUFFLATED > SUFFLATE
SUFFLATES > SUFFLATE
SUFFOCATE vb kill or be killed by deprivation of oxygen
SUFFRAGAN n bishop appointed to assist an archbishop ▷ adj (of any bishop of a diocese) subordinate to and assisting his superior archbishop
SUFFRAGE n right to vote in public elections
SUFFRAGES > SUFFRAGE
SUFFUSE vb spread through or over (something)

SUFFUSED > SUFFUSE
SUFFUSES > SUFFUSE
SUFFUSING > SUFFUSE
SUFFUSION > SUFFUSE
SUFFUSIVE > SUFFUSE
SUG vb sell a product while pretending to conduct market research
SUGAN n straw rope
SUGANS > SUGAN
SUGAR n carbohydrate used to sweeten food and drinks ▷ vb sweeten or cover with sugar
SUGARALLY n liquorice
SUGARBUSH n area covered in sugar maple trees
SUGARCANE n coarse grass that yields sugar
SUGARCOAT vb cover with sugar
SUGARED adj made sweeter or more appealing with or as with sugar
SUGARER > SUGAR
SUGARERS > SUGAR
SUGARIER > SUGARY
SUGARIEST > SUGARY
SUGARING n method of removing unwanted body hair
SUGARINGS > SUGARING
SUGARLESS > SUGAR
SUGARLIKE > SUGAR
SUGARLOAF n large conical mass of unrefined sugar
SUGARPLUM n crystallized plum
SUGARS > SUGAR
SUGARY adj of, like, or containing sugar
SUGGED > SUG
SUGGEST vb put forward (an idea) for consideration
SUGGESTED > SUGGEST
SUGGESTER > SUGGEST
SUGGESTS > SUGGEST
SUGGING n practice of selling products under the pretence of conducting market research
SUGGINGS > SUGGING
SUGH same as > SOUGH
SUGHED > SUGH
SUGHING > SUGH
SUGHS > SUGH
SUGO n Italian pasta sauce
SUGOS > SUGO
SUGS > SUG
SUHUR n meal eaten before sunrise by Muslims fasting during Ramadan
SUHURS > SUHUR
SUI adj of itself
SUICIDAL adj liable to commit suicide
SUICIDE n killing oneself intentionally ▷ vb commit suicide
SUICIDED > SUICIDE
SUICIDES > SUICIDE
SUICIDING > SUICIDE

SUID *n* pig or related animal
SUIDIAN > SUID
SUIDIANS > SUID
SUIDS > SUID
SUILLINE *adj* of or like a pig
SUING > SUE
SUINGS > SUE
SUINT *n* water-soluble substance found in the fleece of sheep
SUINTS > SUINT
SUIPLAP *n* South African slang for a drunkard
SUIPLAPS > SUIPLAP
SUIT *n* set of clothes designed to be worn together ▷ *vb* be appropriate for
SUITABLE *adj* appropriate or proper
SUITABLY > SUITABLE
SUITCASE *n* portable travelling case for clothing
SUITCASES > SUITCASE
SUITE *n* set of connected rooms in a hotel
SUITED > SUIT
SUITER *n* piece of luggage for carrying suits and dresses
SUITERS > SUITER
SUITES > SUITE
SUITING *n* fabric used for suits
SUITINGS > SUITING
SUITLIKE > SUIT
SUITOR *n* man who is courting a woman ▷ *vb* act as a suitor
SUITORED > SUITOR
SUITORING > SUITOR
SUITORS > SUITOR
SUITRESS *n* female suitor
SUITS > SUIT
SUIVANTE *n* lady's maid
SUIVANTES > SUIVANTE
SUIVEZ *vb* musical direction meaning follow
SUJEE *same as* > SOOGEE
SUJEES > SUJEE
SUK *same as* > SOUK
SUKH *same as* > SOUK
SUKHS > SUKH
SUKIYAKI *n* Japanese dish consisting of very thinly sliced beef, vegetables, and seasonings cooked together quickly
SUKIYAKIS > SUKIYAKI
SUKKAH *n* structure in which orthodox Jews eat and sleep during Sukkoth
SUKKAHS > SUKKAH
SUKKOS *same as* > SUKKOTH
SUKKOT *same as* > SUKKOTH
SUKKOTH *n* eight-day Jewish harvest festival
SUKS > SUK

SUKUK *n* financial certificate conforming to Islam lending principles
SUKUKS > SUKUK
SULCAL > SULCUS
SULCALISE *same as* > SULCALIZE
SULCALIZE *vb* furrow
SULCATE *adj* marked with longitudinal parallel grooves
SULCATED *same as* > SULCATE
SULCATION > SULCATE
SULCI > SULCUS
SULCUS *n* linear groove, furrow, or slight depression
SULDAN *same as* > SULTAN
SULDANS > SULDAN
SULFA *same as* > SULPHA
SULFAS > SULFA
SULFATASE *n* type of enzyme
SULFATE *same as* > SULPHATE
SULFATED > SULFATE
SULFATES > SULFATE
SULFATIC *adj* relating to sulphate
SULFATING > SULFATE
SULFATION > SULFATE
SULFID *same as* > SULPHIDE
SULFIDE *same as* > SULPHIDE
SULFIDES > SULFIDE
SULFIDS > SULFID
SULFINYL *same as* > SULPHINYL
SULFINYLS > SULFINYL
SULFITE *same as* > SULPHITE
SULFITES > SULFITE
SULFITIC > SULFITE
SULFO *same as* > SULPHONIC
SULFONATE *n* salt or ester of sulphonic acid
SULFONE *same as* > SULPHONE
SULFONES > SULFONE
SULFONIC > SULFONE
SULFONIUM *n* one of a type of salts
SULFONYL *same as* > SULPHURYL
SULFONYLS > SULFONYL
SULFOXIDE *n* compound containing sulphur
SULFUR *variant of* > SULPHUR
SULFURATE *vb* treat with sulphur
SULFURED > SULFUR
SULFURET *same as* > SULPHURET
SULFURETS > SULFURET
SULFURIC > SULFUR
SULFURING > SULFUR
SULFURISE *variant of* > SULFURIZE
SULFURIZE *vb* combine or treat with sulphur

SULFUROUS *adj* resembling sulphur
SULFURS > SULFUR
SULFURY > SULFUR
SULFURYL *same as* > SULPHURYL
SULFURYLS > SULFURYL
SULK *vb* be silent and sullen because of resentment or bad temper ▷ *n* resentful or sullen mood
SULKED > SULK
SULKER *same as* > SULK
SULKERS > SULKER
SULKIER > SULKY
SULKIES > SULKY
SULKIEST > SULKY
SULKILY > SULKY
SULKINESS > SULKY
SULKING > SULK
SULKS > SULK
SULKY *adj* moody or silent because of anger or resentment ▷ *n* light two-wheeled vehicle for one person
SULLAGE *n* filth or waste, esp sewage
SULLAGES > SULLAGE
SULLEN *adj* unwilling to talk or be sociable ▷ *n* sullen mood
SULLENER > SULLEN
SULLENEST > SULLEN
SULLENLY > SULLEN
SULLENS > SULLEN
SULLIABLE > SULLY
SULLIED > SULLY
SULLIES > SULLY
SULLY *vb* ruin (someone's reputation) ▷ *n* stain
SULLYING > SULLY
SULPH *n* amphetamine sulphate
SULPHA *n* any of a group of sulphonamides that prevent the growth of bacteria
SULPHAS > SULPHA
SULPHATE *n* salt or ester of sulphuric acid ▷ *vb* treat with a sulphate or convert into a sulphate
SULPHATED > SULPHATE
SULPHATES > SULPHATE
SULPHATIC > SULPHATE
SULPHID *same as* > SULPHIDE
SULPHIDE *n* compound of sulphur with another element
SULPHIDES > SULPHIDE
SULPHIDS > SULPHID
SULPHINYL *another term for* > THIONYL
SULPHITE *n* salt or ester of sulphurous acid
SULPHITES > SULPHITE
SULPHITIC > SULPHITE
SULPHONE *n* type of organic compound
SULPHONES > SULPHONE

SULPHONIC *adj* as in sulphonic acid type of strong organic acid
SULPHONYL *same as* > SULPHURYL
SULPHS > SULPH
SULPHUR *n* pale yellow nonmetallic element ▷ *vb* treat with sulphur
SULPHURED > SULPHUR
SULPHURET *vb* treat or combine with sulphur
SULPHURIC > SULPHUR
SULPHURS > SULPHUR
SULPHURY > SULPHUR
SULPHURYL *n* particular chemical divalent group
SULTAN *n* sovereign of a Muslim country
SULTANA *n* kind of raisin
SULTANAS > SULTANA
SULTANATE *n* territory of a sultan
SULTANESS *same as* > SULTANA
SULTANIC > SULTAN
SULTANS > SULTAN
SULTRIER > SULTRY
SULTRIEST > SULTRY
SULTRILY > SULTRY
SULTRY *adj* (of weather or climate) hot and humid
SULU *n* type of sarong worn in Fiji
SULUS > SULU
SUM *n* result of addition, total ▷ *vb* add or form a total of (something)
SUMAC *same as* > SUMACH
SUMACH *n* type of temperate or subtropical shrub or small tree
SUMACHS > SUMACH
SUMACS > SUMAC
SUMATRA *n* violent storm blowing from the direction of Sumatra
SUMATRAS > SUMATRA
SUMBITCH *n* son of a bitch
SUMI *n* type of black ink used in Japan
SUMIS > SUMI
SUMLESS *adj* uncountable
SUMMA *n* compendium of theology, philosophy, or canon law
SUMMABLE > SUM
SUMMAE > SUMMA
SUMMAND *n* number or quantity forming part of a sum
SUMMANDS > SUMMAND
SUMMAR *Scots variant of* > SUMMER
SUMMARIES > SUMMARY
SUMMARILY > SUMMARY
SUMMARISE *same as* > SUMMARIZE
SUMMARIST > SUMMARIZE
SUMMARIZE *vb* make or be a summary of (something)

SUMMARY n brief account giving the main points of something ▷ adj done quickly, without formalities
SUMMAS > SUMMA
SUMMAT pron something ▷ n impressive or important person or thing
SUMMATE vb add up
SUMMATED > SUMMATE
SUMMATES > SUMMATE
SUMMATING > SUMMATE
SUMMATION n summary
SUMMATIVE > SUMMATION
SUMMATS > SUMMAT
SUMMED > SUM
SUMMER n warmest season of the year ▷ vb spend the summer (at a place)
SUMMERED > SUMMER
SUMMERIER > SUMMER
SUMMERING > SUMMER
SUMMERLY > SUMMER
SUMMERS > SUMMER
SUMMERSET n somersault
SUMMERY > SUMMER
SUMMING > SUM
SUMMINGS > SUM
SUMMIST n writer of summae
SUMMISTS > SUMMIST
SUMMIT n top of a mountain or hill ▷ vb reach summit
SUMMITAL > SUMMIT
SUMMITED > SUMMIT
SUMMITEER n person who participates in a summit conference
SUMMITING > SUMMIT
SUMMITRY n practice of conducting international negotiations by summit conferences
SUMMITS > SUMMIT
SUMMON vb order (someone) to come
SUMMONED > SUMMON
SUMMONER > SUMMON
SUMMONERS > SUMMON
SUMMONING > SUMMON
SUMMONS n command summoning someone ▷ vb order (someone) to appear in court
SUMMONSED > SUMMONS
SUMMONSES > SUMMONS
SUMO n Japanese style of wrestling
SUMOIST > SUMO
SUMOISTS > SUMO
SUMOS > SUMO
SUMOTORI n sumo wrestler
SUMOTORIS > SUMOTORI
SUMP n container in an internal-combustion engine into which oil can drain
SUMPH n stupid person
SUMPHISH > SUMPH
SUMPHS > SUMPH

SUMPIT n Malay blowpipe
SUMPITAN same as > SUMPIT
SUMPITANS > SUMPITAN
SUMPITS > SUMPIT
SUMPS > SUMP
SUMPSIMUS n correct form of expression
SUMPTER n packhorse, mule, or other beast of burden
SUMPTERS > SUMPTER
SUMPTUARY adj controlling expenditure or extravagant use of resources
SUMPTUOUS adj lavish, magnificent
SUMPWEED n American weed
SUMPWEEDS > SUMPWEED
SUMS > SUM
SUMY pl n the monetary units of Uzbekistan
SUN n star around which the earth and other planets revolve ▷ vb expose (oneself) to the sun's rays
SUNBACK adj (of dress) cut low at back
SUNBAKE vb sunbathe, esp in order to become tanned ▷ n period of sunbaking
SUNBAKED adj (esp of roads, etc) dried or cracked by the sun's heat
SUNBAKES > SUNBAKE
SUNBAKING > SUNBAKE
SUNBATH n exposure of the body to the sun to get a suntan
SUNBATHE vb lie in the sunshine in order to get a suntan
SUNBATHED > SUNBATHE
SUNBATHER > SUNBATHE
SUNBATHES > SUNBATHE
SUNBATHS > SUNBATH
SUNBEAM n ray of sun
SUNBEAMED > SUNBEAM
SUNBEAMS > SUNBEAM
SUNBEAMY > SUNBEAM
SUNBEAT adj exposed to sun
SUNBEATEN same as > SUNBEAT
SUNBED n machine for giving an artificial tan
SUNBEDS > SUNBED
SUNBELT n southern states of the US
SUNBELTS > SUNBELT
SUNBERRY n red fruit like the blackberry
SUNBIRD n type of small songbird with a bright plumage in the males
SUNBIRDS > SUNBIRD
SUNBLIND n blind that shades a room from the sun's glare

SUNBLINDS > SUNBLIND
SUNBLOCK n cream applied to the skin to protect it from the sun's rays
SUNBLOCKS > SUNBLOCK
SUNBONNET n hat that shades the face and neck from the sun
SUNBOW n bow of colours produced when sunlight shines through spray
SUNBOWS > SUNBOW
SUNBRIGHT adj bright as the sun
SUNBURN n painful reddening of the skin caused by overexposure to the sun ▷ vb become sunburnt
SUNBURNED > SUNBURN
SUNBURNS > SUNBURN
SUNBURNT > SUNBURN
SUNBURST n burst of sunshine, as through a break in the clouds
SUNBURSTS > SUNBURST
SUNCARE n use of products in protecting skin from the sun
SUNCARES > SUNCARE
SUNCHOKE n Jerusalem artichoke
SUNCHOKES > SUNCHOKE
SUNDAE n ice cream topped with fruit etc
SUNDAES > SUNDAE
SUNDARI n Indian tree
SUNDARIS > SUNDARI
SUNDECK n upper open deck on a passenger ship
SUNDECKS > SUNDECK
SUNDER vb break apart
SUNDERED > SUNDER
SUNDERER > SUNDER
SUNDERERS > SUNDER
SUNDERING > SUNDER
SUNDERS > SUNDER
SUNDEW n type of bog plant with leaves covered in sticky hairs
SUNDEWS > SUNDEW
SUNDIAL n device showing the time by means of a pointer that casts a shadow
SUNDIALS > SUNDIAL
SUNDOG n small rainbow or halo near the horizon
SUNDOGS > SUNDOG
SUNDOWN same as > SUNSET
SUNDOWNED > SUNDOWN
SUNDOWNER n tramp, esp one who seeks food and lodging at sundown when it is too late to work
SUNDOWNS > SUNDOWN
SUNDRA same as > SUNDARI
SUNDRAS > SUNDRA
SUNDRESS n dress for hot weather that exposes the shoulders, arms, and back,

esp one with straps over the shoulders
SUNDRI same as > SUNDARI
SUNDRIES > SUNDRY
SUNDRILY > SUNDRY
SUNDRIS > SUNDRI
SUNDROPS n American primrose
SUNDRY adj several, various
SUNFAST adj not fading in sunlight
SUNFISH n large sea fish with a rounded body
SUNFISHES > SUNFISH
SUNFLOWER n tall plant with large golden flowers
SUNG > SING
SUNGAR same as > SANGAR
SUNGARS > SUNGAR
SUNGAZER n person who practices sungazing
SUNGAZERS > SUNGAZER
SUNGAZING n staring directly at the sun
SUNGLASS n convex lens used to focus the sun's rays and thus produce heat or ignition
SUNGLOW n pinkish glow often seen in the sky before sunrise or after sunset
SUNGLOWS > SUNGLOW
SUNGREBE another name for > FINFOOT
SUNGREBES > SUNGREBE
SUNHAT n hat that shades the face and neck from the sun
SUNHATS > SUNHAT
SUNI n S African dwarf antelope
SUNIS > SUNI
SUNK n bank or pad
SUNKEN adj unhealthily hollow
SUNKER n rock (partially) submerged in shallow water
SUNKERS > SUNKER
SUNKET n something good to eat
SUNKETS > SUNKET
SUNKIE n little stool
SUNKIES > SUNKIE
SUNKS > SUNK
SUNLAMP n lamp that generates ultraviolet rays
SUNLAMPS > SUNLAMP
SUNLAND n sunny area
SUNLANDS > SUNLAND
SUNLESS adj without sun or sunshine
SUNLESSLY > SUNLESS
SUNLIGHT n light that comes from the sun
SUNLIGHTS > SUNLIGHT
SUNLIKE > SUN
SUNLIT > SUNLIGHT
SUNN n leguminous plant of the East Indies

SUNNA n body of traditional Islamic law

SUNNAH same as > SUNNA

SUNNAHS > SUNNAH

SUNNAS > SUNNA

SUNNED > SUN

SUNNIER > SUNNY

SUNNIES pl n pair of sunglasses

SUNNIEST > SUNNY

SUNNILY > SUNNY

SUNNINESS > SUNNY

SUNNING > SUN

SUNNS > SUNN

SUNNY adj full of or exposed to sunlight

SUNPORCH n porch for sunbathing on

SUNPROOF > SUN

SUNRAY n ray of light from the sun

SUNRAYS > SUNRAY

SUNRISE n daily appearance of the sun above the horizon

SUNRISES > SUNRISE

SUNRISING same as > SUNRISE

SUNROOF n panel in the roof of a car that opens to let in air

SUNROOFS > SUNROOF

SUNROOM n room or glass-enclosed porch designed to display beautiful views

SUNROOMS > SUNROOM

SUNS > SUN

SUNSCALD n sun damage on tomato plants

SUNSCALDS > SUNSCALD

SUNSCREEN n cream or lotion applied to exposed skin to protect it from the ultraviolet rays of the sun

SUNSEEKER n person looking for sunny weather

SUNSET n daily disappearance of the sun below the horizon

SUNSETS > SUNSET

SUNSHADE n anything used to protect people from the sun, such as a parasol or awning

SUNSHADES > SUNSHADE

SUNSHINE n light and warmth from the sun

SUNSHINES > SUNSHINE

SUNSHINY > SUNSHINE

SUNSPECS pl n sunglasses

SUNSPOT n dark patch appearing temporarily on the sun's surface

SUNSPOTS > SUNSPOT

SUNSTAR n type of starfish with up to 13 arms

SUNSTARS > SUNSTAR

SUNSTONE n type of translucent feldspar with reddish-gold speckles

SUNSTONES > SUNSTONE

SUNSTROKE n illness caused by prolonged exposure to intensely hot sunlight

SUNSTRUCK adj suffering from sunstroke

SUNSUIT n child's outfit consisting of a brief top and shorts or a short skirt

SUNSUITS > SUNSUIT

SUNTAN n browning of the skin caused by exposure to the sun

SUNTANNED > SUNTAN

SUNTANS > SUNTAN

SUNTRAP n very sunny sheltered place

SUNTRAPS > SUNTRAP

SUNUP same as > SUNRISE

SUNUPS > SUNUP

SUNWARD same as > SUNWARDS

SUNWARDS adv towards the sun

SUNWISE adv moving in the same direction as the sun

SUP same as > SUPINE

SUPAWN same as > SUPPAWN

SUPAWNS > SUPAWN

SUPE n superintendent

SUPER adj excellent ▷ n superannuation ▷ interj enthusiastic expression of approval or assent ▷ vb work as superintendent

SUPERABLE adj able to be surmounted or overcome

SUPERABLY > SUPERABLE

SUPERADD vb add (something) to something that has already been added

SUPERADDS > SUPERADD

SUPERATE vb overcome

SUPERATED > SUPERATE

SUPERATES > SUPERATE

SUPERATOM n cluster of atoms behaving like a single atom

SUPERB adj excellent, impressive, or splendid

SUPERBAD adj exceptionally bad

SUPERBANK n bank that owns other banks

SUPERBER > SUPERB

SUPERBEST > SUPERB

SUPERBIKE n high-performance motorcycle

SUPERBITY > SUPERB

SUPERBLY > SUPERB

SUPERBOLD adj exceptionally bold

SUPERBOMB n large bomb

SUPERBRAT n exceptionally unpleasant child

SUPERBUG n bacterium resistant to antibiotics

SUPERBUGS > SUPERBUG

SUPERCAR n very expensive fast or powerful car with a centrally located engine

SUPERCARS > SUPERCAR

SUPERCEDE former variant of > SUPERSEDE

SUPERCELL n unusually large storm cell

SUPERCHIC adj highly chic

SUPERCITY n very large city

SUPERCLUB n large and important club

SUPERCOIL vb form a complex coil

SUPERCOLD adj very cold

SUPERCOOL vb cool or be cooled to a temperature below that at which freezing or crystallization should occur

SUPERCOP n high-ranking police officer

SUPERCOPS > SUPERCOP

SUPERCOW n dairy cow that produces a very high milk yield

SUPERCOWS > SUPERCOW

SUPERCUTE adj very cute

SUPERED > SUPER

SUPEREGO n that part of the unconscious mind that governs ideas about what is right and wrong

SUPEREGOS > SUPEREGO

SUPERETTE n small store or dairy laid out along the lines of a supermarket

SUPERFAN n very devoted fan

SUPERFANS > SUPERFAN

SUPERFARM n very large farm

SUPERFAST adj very fast

SUPERFINE adj of exceptional fineness or quality

SUPERFIRM adj very firm

SUPERFIT adj highly fit

SUPERFIX n linguistic feature distinguishing the meaning of one word from that of another

SUPERFLUX n superfluity

SUPERFLY adj pretentiously flamboyant

SUPERFOOD n food thought to be beneficial to health

SUPERFUND n large fund

SUPERFUSE vb pour or be poured so as to cover something

SUPERGENE n cluster of genes

SUPERGLUE n extremely strong and quick-drying glue ▷ vb fix with superglue

SUPERGOOD adj very good

SUPERGUN n large powerful gun

SUPERGUNS > SUPERGUN

SUPERHEAT vb heat (a vapour, esp steam) to a temperature above its saturation point for a given pressure

SUPERHERO n any of various comic-strip characters with superhuman abilities or magical powers

SUPERHET n type of radio receiver

SUPERHETS > SUPERHET

SUPERHIGH adj extremely high

SUPERHIT n very popular hit

SUPERHITS > SUPERHIT

SUPERHIVE n upper part of beehive

SUPERHOT adj very hot

SUPERHYPE n exaggerated hype

SUPERING > SUPER

SUPERIOR adj greater in quality, quantity, or merit ▷ n person of greater rank or status

SUPERIORS > SUPERIOR

SUPERJET n supersonic aircraft

SUPERJETS > SUPERJET

SUPERJOCK n very athletic person

SUPERLAIN > SUPERLIE

SUPERLAY > SUPERLIE

SUPERLIE vb lie above

SUPERLIES > SUPERLIE

SUPERLOAD n variable weight on a structure

SUPERLONG adj very long

SUPERLOO n automated public toilet

SUPERLOOS > SUPERLOO

SUPERMALE former name for > METAMALE

SUPERMAN n man with great physical or mental powers

SUPERMART n large self-service store selling food and household supplies

SUPERMAX n jail or other facility having the very highest levels of security

SUPERMEN > SUPERMAN

SUPERMIND n very powerful brain

SUPERMINI n small car, usually a hatchback, that is economical to run but has a high level of performance

SUPERMOM n very capable and busy mother

SUPERMOMS > SUPERMOM

SUPERMOTO n form of motorcycle racing over part-tarmac and part-dirt circuits

SUPERNAL adj of or from the world of the divine

SUPERNATE n liquid lying above a sediment ▷ vb float on (a surface)
SUPERNOVA n star that explodes and briefly becomes exceptionally bright
SUPERPIMP n pimp controlling many prostitutes
SUPERPLUS n surplus
SUPERPORT n large port
SUPERPOSE vb transpose (the coordinates of one geometric figure) to coincide with those of another
SUPERPRO n person regarded as a real professional
SUPERPROS > SUPERPRO
SUPERRACE n important race
SUPERREAL adj surreal
SUPERRICH adj exceptionally wealthy
SUPERROAD n very large road
SUPERS > SUPER
SUPERSAFE adj very safe
SUPERSALE n large sale
SUPERSALT n acid salt
SUPERSAUR n very large dinosaur
SUPERSEDE vb replace, supplant
SUPERSELL vb sell in very large numbers
SUPERSEX n sterile organism in which the ratio between the sex chromosomes is disturbed
SUPERSHOW n very impressive show
SUPERSIZE vb make larger
SUPERSOFT adj very soft
SUPERSOLD > SUPERSELL
SUPERSPY n highly accomplished spy
SUPERSTAR n very famous entertainer or sportsperson
SUPERSTUD n highly virile man
SUPERTAX n extra tax on incomes above a certain level
SUPERTHIN adj very thin
SUPERTRAM n type of tram with greater capacity and speed than conventional trams
SUPERUSER n type of administration-level account in a computing system
SUPERVENE vb occur as an unexpected development
SUPERVISE vb watch over to direct or check

SUPERWAIF n very young and very thin supermodel
SUPERWAVE n large wave
SUPERWEED n hybrid plant that contains genes for herbicide resistance
SUPERWIDE n very wide lens
SUPERWIFE n highly accomplished wife
SUPES > SUPE
SUPINATE vb turn (the hand and forearm) so that the palm faces up or forwards
SUPINATED > SUPINATE
SUPINATES > SUPINATE
SUPINATOR n muscle of the forearm that can produce the motion of supination
SUPINE adj lying flat on one's back ▷ n noun form derived from a verb in Latin
SUPINELY > SUPINE
SUPINES > SUPINE
SUPLEX n type of wrestling hold
SUPLEXES > SUPLEX
SUPPAWN n kind of porridge
SUPPAWNS > SUPPAWN
SUPPEAGO same as > SERPIGO
SUPPED > SUP
SUPPER n light evening meal ▷ vb eat supper
SUPPERED > SUPPER
SUPPERING > SUPPER
SUPPERS > SUPPER
SUPPING > SUP
SUPPLANT vb take the place of, oust
SUPPLANTS > SUPPLANT
SUPPLE adj (of a person) moving and bending easily and gracefully ▷ vb make or become supple
SUPPLED > SUPPLE
SUPPLELY same as > SUPPLY
SUPPLER > SUPPLE
SUPPLES > SUPPLE
SUPPLEST > SUPPLE
SUPPLIAL n instance of supplying
SUPPLIALS > SUPPLIAL
SUPPLIANT n person who requests humbly
SUPPLICAT n university petition
SUPPLIED > SUPPLY
SUPPLIER > SUPPLY
SUPPLIERS > SUPPLY
SUPPLIES > SUPPLY
SUPPLING > SUPPLE
SUPPLY vb provide with something required ▷ n supplying ▷ adj acting as a temporary substitute ▷ adv in a supple manner
SUPPLYING > SUPPLY
SUPPORT vb bear the weight of ▷ n supporting

SUPPORTED > SUPPORT
SUPPORTER n person who supports a team, principle, etc
SUPPORTS > SUPPORT
SUPPOSAL n supposition
SUPPOSALS > SUPPOSAL
SUPPOSE vb presume to be true
SUPPOSED adj presumed to be true without proof, doubtful
SUPPOSER > SUPPOSE
SUPPOSERS > SUPPOSE
SUPPOSES > SUPPOSE
SUPPOSING > SUPPOSE
SUPPRESS vb put an end to
SUPPURATE vb (of a wound etc) produce pus
SUPRA adv above, esp referring to earlier parts of a book etc
SUPREMA > SUPREMUM
SUPREMACY n supreme power
SUPREME adj highest in authority, rank, or degree ▷ n rich sauce made with a base of veal or chicken stock
SUPREMELY > SUPREME
SUPREMER > SUPREME
SUPREMES > SUPREME
SUPREMEST > SUPREME
SUPREMITY n supremeness
SUPREMO n person in overall authority
SUPREMOS > SUPREMO
SUPREMUM n (in maths) smallest quantity greater than or equal to each of a set or subset
SUPREMUMS > SUPREMUM
SUPS > SUP
SUQ same as > SOUK
SUQS > SUQ
SUR prep above
SURA n any of the 114 chapters of the Koran
SURAH n twill-weave fabric of silk or rayon, used for dresses, blouses, etc
SURAHS > SURAH
SURAL adj of or relating to the calf of the leg
SURAMIN n drug used in treating sleeping sickness
SURAMINS > SURAMIN
SURANCE same as > ASSURANCE
SURANCES > SURANCE
SURAS > SURA
SURAT n cotton fabric from Surat in India
SURATS > SURAT
SURBAHAR n Indian string instrument
SURBAHARS > SURBAHAR
SURBASE n uppermost part, such as a moulding, of a pedestal, base, or skirting

SURBASED adj having a surbase
SURBASES > SURBASE
SURBATE vb make feet sore through walking
SURBATED > SURBATE
SURBATES > SURBATE
SURBATING > SURBATE
SURBED vb put something on its edge
SURBEDDED > SURBED
SURBEDS > SURBED
SURBET > SURBATE
SURCEASE n cessation or intermission ▷ vb desist from (some action)
SURCEASED > SURCEASE
SURCEASES > SURCEASE
SURCHARGE n additional charge ▷ vb charge (someone) an additional sum or tax
SURCINGLE n girth for a horse which goes around the body, used esp with a racing saddle ▷ vb put a surcingle on or over (a horse)
SURCOAT n tunic worn by a knight over his armour
SURCOATS > SURCOAT
SURCULI > SURCULUS
SURCULOSE adj (of a plant) bearing suckers
SURCULUS n sucker on plant
SURD n number that cannot be expressed in whole numbers ▷ adj of or relating to a surd
SURDITIES > SURDITY
SURDITY n deafness
SURDS > SURD
SURE adj free from uncertainty or doubt ▷ interj certainly ▷ vb archaic form of sewer
SURED > SURE
SUREFIRE adj certain to succeed
SURELY adv it must be true that
SURENESS > SURE
SURER > SURE
SURES > SURE
SUREST > SURE
SURETIED > SURETY
SURETIES > SURETY
SURETY n person who takes responsibility for the fulfilment of another's obligation ▷ vb be surety for
SURETYING > SURETY
SURF n foam caused by waves breaking on the shore ▷ vb take part in surfing
SURFABLE > SURF
SURFACE n outside or top of an object ▷ vb become apparent
SURFACED > SURFACE
SURFACER > SURFACE

S

SURFACERS > SURFACE
SURFACES > SURFACE
SURFACING > SURFACE
SURFBIRD n American shore bird
SURFBIRDS > SURFBIRD
SURFBOARD n long smooth board used in surfing
SURFBOAT n boat with a high bow and stern and flotation chambers
SURFBOATS > SURFBOAT
SURFED > SURF
SURFEIT n excessive amount ▷ vb supply or feed excessively
SURFEITED > SURFEIT
SURFEITER > SURFEIT
SURFEITS > SURFEIT
SURFER > SURFING
SURFERS > SURFING
SURFFISH n fish of American coastal seas
SURFICIAL adj superficial
SURFIE n young person whose main interest is in surfing
SURFIER > SURFIE
SURFIES > SURFIE
SURFIEST > SURF
SURFING n sport of riding on a board on the crest of a wave
SURFINGS > SURFING
SURFLIKE > SURF
SURFMAN n sailor skilled in sailing through surf
SURFMEN > SURFMAN
SURFPERCH n type of marine fish of North American Pacific coastal waters
SURFRIDE vb ride on surf
SURFRIDER > SURFRIDE
SURFRIDES > SURFRIDE
SURFRODE > SURFRIDE
SURFS > SURF
SURFSIDE adj next to the sea
SURFY > SURF
SURGE n sudden powerful increase ▷ vb increase suddenly
SURGED > SURGE
SURGEFUL > SURGE
SURGELESS > SURGE
SURGENT > SURGE
SURGEON n doctor who specializes in surgery
SURGEONCY n office, duties, or position of a surgeon, esp in the army or navy
SURGEONS > SURGEON
SURGER > SURGE
SURGERIES > SURGERY
SURGERS > SURGE
SURGERY n treatment in which the patient's body is cut open in order to treat the affected part
SURGES > SURGE

SURGICAL adj involving or used in surgery
SURGIER > SURGE
SURGIEST > SURGE
SURGING > SURGE
SURGINGS > SURGE
SURGY > SURGE
SURICATE n type of meerkat
SURICATES > SURICATE
SURIMI n blended seafood product made from precooked fish
SURIMIS > SURIMI
SURING > SURE
SURLIER > SURLY
SURLIEST > SURLY
SURLILY > SURLY
SURLINESS > SURLY
SURLOIN same as > SIRLOIN
SURLOINS > SURLOIN
SURLY adj ill-tempered and rude
SURMASTER n deputy headmaster
SURMISAL > SURMISE
SURMISALS > SURMISE
SURMISE n guess, conjecture ▷ vb guess (something) from incomplete or uncertain evidence
SURMISED > SURMISE
SURMISER > SURMISE
SURMISERS > SURMISE
SURMISES > SURMISE
SURMISING > SURMISE
SURMOUNT vb overcome (a problem)
SURMOUNTS > SURMOUNT
SURMULLET n red mullet
SURNAME n family name ▷ vb furnish with or call by a surname
SURNAMED > SURNAME
SURNAMER > SURNAME
SURNAMERS > SURNAME
SURNAMES > SURNAME
SURNAMING > SURNAME
SURPASS vb be greater than or superior to
SURPASSED > SURPASS
SURPASSER > SURPASS
SURPASSES > SURPASS
SURPLICE n loose white robe worn by clergymen and choristers
SURPLICED > SURPLICE
SURPLICES > SURPLICE
SURPLUS n amount left over in excess of what is required ▷ adj extra ▷ vb be left over in excess of what is required
SURPLUSED > SURPLUS
SURPLUSES > SURPLUS
SURPRINT vb print (additional matter) over something already printed ▷ n marks, printed matter, etc, that have been surprinted
SURPRINTS > SURPRINT

SURPRISAL > SURPRISE
SURPRISE n unexpected event ▷ vb cause to feel amazement or wonder
SURPRISED > SURPRISE
SURPRISER > SURPRISE
SURPRISES > SURPRISE
SURPRIZE same as > SURPRISE
SURPRIZED > SURPRIZE
SURPRIZES > SURPRIZE
SURQUEDRY n arrogance
SURQUEDY same as > SURQUEDRY
SURRA n tropical febrile disease of animals
SURRAS > SURRA
SURREAL adj bizarre ▷ n atmosphere or qualities evoked by surrealism
SURREALLY > SURREAL
SURREALS > SURREAL
SURREBUT vb give evidence to support the surrebutter
SURREBUTS > SURREBUT
SURREINED adj (of horse) ridden too much
SURREJOIN vb reply to legal rejoinder
SURRENDER vb give oneself up ▷ n surrendering
SURRENDRY same as > SURRENDER
SURREY n light four-wheeled horse-drawn carriage
SURREYS > SURREY
SURROGACY > SURROGATE
SURROGATE n substitute ▷ adj acting as a substitute ▷ vb put in another's position as a deputy, substitute, etc
SURROUND vb be, come, or place all around (a person or thing) ▷ n border or edging
SURROUNDS > SURROUND
SURROYAL n high point on stag's horns
SURROYALS > SURROYAL
SURTAX n extra tax on incomes above a certain level ▷ vb assess for liability to surtax
SURTAXED > SURTAX
SURTAXES > SURTAX
SURTAXING > SURTAX
SURTITLE n printed translation of the libretto of an opera in a language foreign to the audience
SURTITLES pl n brief translations of the text of an opera or play projected above the stage
SURTOUT n man's overcoat resembling a frock coat
SURTOUTS > SURTOUT

SURUCUCU n South American snake
SURUCUCUS > SURUCUCU
SURVEIL same as > SURVEILLE
SURVEILED > SURVEIL
SURVEILLE vb observe closely
SURVEILS > SURVEIL
SURVEY vb view or consider in a general way ▷ n surveying
SURVEYAL > SURVEY
SURVEYALS > SURVEY
SURVEYED > SURVEY
SURVEYING n practice of measuring altitudes, angles, and distances on the land surface so that they can be accurately plotted on a map
SURVEYOR n person whose occupation is to survey land or buildings
SURVEYORS > SURVEYOR
SURVEYS > SURVEY
SURVIEW vb survey
SURVIEWED > SURVIEW
SURVIEWS > SURVIEW
SURVIVAL n condition of having survived ▷ adj of, relating to, or assisting the act of surviving
SURVIVALS > SURVIVAL
SURVIVE vb continue to live or exist after (a difficult experience)
SURVIVED > SURVIVE
SURVIVER same as > SURVIVOR
SURVIVERS > SURVIVER
SURVIVES > SURVIVE
SURVIVING > SURVIVE
SURVIVOR n person or thing that survives
SURVIVORS > SURVIVOR
SUS same as > SUSS
SUSCEPTOR n sponsor
SUSCITATE vb excite
SUSED > SUS
SUSES > SUS
SUSHI n Japanese dish of small cakes of cold rice with a topping of raw fish
SUSHIS > SUSHI
SUSING > SUS
SUSLIK n central Eurasian ground squirrel
SUSLIKS > SUSLIK
SUSPECT vb believe (someone) to be guilty without having any proof ▷ adj not to be trusted ▷ n person who is suspected
SUSPECTED > SUSPECT
SUSPECTER > SUSPECT
SUSPECTS > SUSPECT
SUSPENCE same as > SUSPENSE
SUSPEND vb hang from a high place
SUSPENDED > SUSPEND

SUSPENDER n elastic strap for holding up women's stockings
SUSPENDS > SUSPEND
SUSPENS same as > SUSPENSE
SUSPENSE n state of uncertainty while awaiting news, an event, etc
SUSPENSER n film that creates a feeling of suspense
SUSPENSES > SUSPENSE
SUSPENSOR n ligament or muscle that holds a part in position
SUSPICION n feeling of not trusting a person or thing
SUSPIRE vb sigh or utter with a sigh
SUSPIRED > SUSPIRE
SUSPIRES > SUSPIRE
SUSPIRING > SUSPIRE
SUSS vb attempt to work out (a situation, etc), using one's intuition ▷ n sharpness of mind
SUSSED > SUSS
SUSSES > SUSS
SUSSING > SUSS
SUSTAIN vb maintain or prolong ▷ n prolongation of a note, by playing technique or electronics
SUSTAINED > SUSTAIN
SUSTAINER n rocket engine that maintains the velocity of a space vehicle after the booster has been jettisoned
SUSTAINS > SUSTAIN
SUSTINENT adj sustaining
SUSU n (in the Caribbean) savings fund shared by friends
SUSURRANT > SUSURRATE
SUSURRATE vb make a soft rustling sound
SUSURROUS adj full of murmuring sounds
SUSURRUS > SUSURRATE
SUSUS > SUSU
SUTILE adj involving sewing
SUTLER n merchant who accompanied an army in order to sell provisions
SUTLERIES > SUTLER
SUTLERS > SUTLER
SUTLERY > SUTLER
SUTOR n cobbler
SUTORIAL > SUTOR
SUTORIAN > SUTOR
SUTORS > SUTOR
SUTRA n Sanskrit sayings or collections of sayings
SUTRAS > SUTRA
SUTTA n Buddhist scripture
SUTTAS > SUTTA

SUTTEE n custom whereby a widow burnt herself on her husband's funeral pyre
SUTTEEISM > SUTTEE
SUTTEES > SUTTEE
SUTTLE vb work as sutler
SUTTLED > SUTTLE
SUTTLES > SUTTLE
SUTTLETIE same as > SUBTLETY
SUTTLING > SUTTLE
SUTTLY > SUBTLE
SUTURAL > SUTURE
SUTURALLY > SUTURE
SUTURE n stitch joining the edges of a wound ▷ vb join (the edges of a wound, etc) by means of sutures
SUTURED > SUTURE
SUTURES > SUTURE
SUTURING > SUTURE
SUZERAIN n state or sovereign with limited authority over another self-governing state
SUZERAINS > SUZERAIN
SVARAJ same as > SWARAJ
SVARAJES > SVARAJ
SVASTIKA same as > SWASTIKA
SVASTIKAS > SVASTIKA
SVEDBERG n unit used in physics
SVEDBERGS > SVEDBERG
SVELTE adj attractively or gracefully slim
SVELTELY > SVELTE
SVELTER > SVELTE
SVELTEST > SVELTE
SWAB n small piece of cotton wool used to apply medication, clean a wound, etc ▷ vb clean (a wound) with a swab
SWABBED > SWAB
SWABBER n person who uses a swab
SWABBERS > SWABBER
SWABBIE same as > SWABBY
SWABBIES > SWABBY
SWABBING > SWAB
SWABBY n seaman
SWABS > SWAB
SWACK adj flexible ▷ vb strike
SWACKED adj in a state of intoxication, stupor, or euphoria induced by drugs or alcohol
SWACKING > SWACK
SWACKS > SWACK
SWAD n loutish person
SWADDIE same as > SWADDY
SWADDIES > SWADDY
SWADDLE vb wrap (a baby) in swaddling clothes ▷ n swaddling clothes
SWADDLED > SWADDLE
SWADDLER > SWADDLE
SWADDLERS > SWADDLE

SWADDLES > SWADDLE
SWADDLING > SWADDLE
SWADDY n private soldier
SWADS > SWADDLE
SWAG n stolen property ▷ vb sway from side to side
SWAGE n shaped tool or die used in forming cold metal by hammering ▷ vb form (metal) with a swage
SWAGED > SWAGE
SWAGER > SWAGE
SWAGERS > SWAGE
SWAGES > SWAGE
SWAGGED > SWAG
SWAGGER vb walk or behave arrogantly ▷ n arrogant walk or manner ▷ adj elegantly fashionable
SWAGGERED > SWAGGER
SWAGGERER > SWAGGER
SWAGGERS > SWAGGER
SWAGGIE same as > SWAGGER
SWAGGIES > SWAGGIE
SWAGGING > SWAG
SWAGING > SWAGE
SWAGMAN n tramp who carries his belongings in a bundle on his back
SWAGMEN > SWAGMAN
SWAGS > SWAG
SWAGSHOP n shop selling cheap goods
SWAGSHOPS > SWAGSHOP
SWAGSMAN same as > SWAGMAN
SWAGSMEN > SWAGSMAN
SWAIL same as > SWALE
SWAILS > SWAIL
SWAIN n suitor
SWAINING n acting as suitor
SWAININGS > SWAINING
SWAINISH > SWAIN
SWAINS > SWAIN
SWALE n moist depression in a tract of land ▷ vb sway
SWALED > SWALE
SWALES > SWALE
SWALIER > SWALE
SWALIEST > SWALE
SWALING > SWALE
SWALINGS > SWALE
SWALLET n hole where water goes underground
SWALLETS > SWALLET
SWALLIES > SWALLY
SWALLOW vb cause to pass down one's throat ▷ n swallowing
SWALLOWED > SWALLOW
SWALLOWER > SWALLOW
SWALLOWS > SWALLOW
SWALLY n alcoholic drink
SWALY > SWALE
SWAM > SWIM
SWAMI n Hindu religious teacher
SWAMIES > SWAMI
SWAMIS > SWAMI

SWAMP n watery area of land, bog ▷ vb cause (a boat) to fill with water and sink
SWAMPED > SWAMP
SWAMPER n person who lives or works in a swampy region
SWAMPERS > SWAMPER
SWAMPIER > SWAMP
SWAMPIEST > SWAMP
SWAMPING > SWAMP
SWAMPISH > SWAMP
SWAMPLAND n permanently waterlogged area
SWAMPLESS > SWAMP
SWAMPS > SWAMP
SWAMPY > SWAMP
SWAMY same as > SWAMI
SWAN n large usu white water bird with a long graceful neck ▷ vb wander about idly
SWANG > SWING
SWANHERD n person who herds swans
SWANHERDS > SWANHERD
SWANK vb show off or boast ▷ n showing off or boasting
SWANKED > SWANK
SWANKER > SWANK
SWANKERS > SWANK
SWANKEST > SWANK
SWANKEY same as > SWANKY
SWANKEYS > SWANKY
SWANKIE same as > SWANKY
SWANKIER > SWANKY
SWANKIES > SWANKY
SWANKIEST > SWANKY
SWANKILY > SWANKY
SWANKING > SWANK
SWANKPOT same as > SWANK
SWANKPOTS > SWANKPOT
SWANKS > SWANK
SWANKY adj expensive and showy, stylish ▷ n lively person
SWANLIKE > SWAN
SWANNED > SWAN
SWANNERY n place where swans are kept and bred
SWANNIE n (in NZ) type of all-weather heavy woollen shirt
SWANNIER > SWANNY
SWANNIES > SWANNIE
SWANNIEST > SWANNY
SWANNING > SWAN
SWANNINGS > SWAN
SWANNY adj swanlike
SWANPAN n Chinese abacus
SWANPANS > SWANPAN
SWANS > SWAN
SWANSDOWN n fine soft feathers of a swan
SWANSKIN n skin of a swan with the feathers attached

S

SWANSKINS > SWANSKIN

SWANSONG n beautiful song fabled to be sung by a swan before it dies

SWANSONGS > SWANSONG

SWAP vb exchange (something) for something else ▷ n exchange

SWAPFILE n computer file which provides space for transferred programs

SWAPFILES > SWAPFILE

SWAPPED > SWAP

SWAPPER > SWAP

SWAPPERS > SWAP

SWAPPING > SWAP

SWAPPINGS > SWAP

SWAPS > SWAP

SWAPT > SWAP

SWAPTION another name for > SWAP

SWAPTIONS > SWAPTION

SWARAJ n (in British India) self-government

SWARAJES > SWARAJ

SWARAJISM > SWARAJ

SWARAJIST > SWARAJ

SWARD n stretch of short grass ▷ vb cover or become covered with grass

SWARDED > SWARD

SWARDIER > SWARDY

SWARDIEST > SWARDY

SWARDING > SWARD

SWARDS > SWARD

SWARDY adj covered with sward

SWARE > SWEAR

SWARF n material removed by cutting tools in the machining of metals, stone, etc ▷ vb faint

SWARFED > SWARF

SWARFING > SWARF

SWARFS > SWARF

SWARM n large group of bees or other insects ▷ vb move in a swarm

SWARMED > SWARM

SWARMER > SWARM

SWARMERS > SWARM

SWARMING > SWARM

SWARMINGS > SWARM

SWARMS > SWARM

SWART adj swarthy

SWARTH same as > SWART

SWARTHIER > SWARTHY

SWARTHILY > SWARTHY

SWARTHS > SWARTH

SWARTHY adj dark-complexioned

SWARTNESS > SWART

SWARTY > SWART

SWARVE same as > SWARF

SWARVED > SWARF

SWARVES > SWARF

SWARVING > SWARF

SWASH n rush of water up a beach following each break of the waves ▷ vb wash or move with noisy splashing

SWASHED > SWASH

SWASHER n braggart

SWASHERS > SWASHER

SWASHES > SWASH

SWASHIER > SWASHY

SWASHIEST > SWASHY

SWASHING > SWASH

SWASHINGS > SWASH

SWASHWORK n type of work done on lathe

SWASHY adj slushy

SWASTICA same as > SWASTIKA

SWASTICAS > SWASTICA

SWASTIKA n symbol in the shape of a cross with the arms bent at right angles, used as the emblem of Nazi Germany

SWASTIKAS > SWASTIKA

SWAT vb strike or hit sharply ▷ n swatter

SWATCH n sample of cloth

SWATCHES > SWATCH

SWATH n width of one sweep of a scythe or of the blade of a mowing machine

SWATHABLE > SWATHE

SWATHE vb bandage or wrap completely ▷ n bandage or wrapping

SWATHED > SWATHE

SWATHER > SWATHE

SWATHERS > SWATHE

SWATHES > SWATHE

SWATHIER > SWATH

SWATHIEST > SWATH

SWATHING > SWATHE

SWATHS > SWATH

SWATHY > SWATH

SWATS > SWAT

SWATTED > SWAT

SWATTER n device for killing insects ▷ vb splash

SWATTERED > SWATTER

SWATTERS > SWATTER

SWATTIER same as > SWOTTIER

SWATTIEST same as > SWOTTIEST

SWATTING > SWAT

SWATTINGS > SWAT

SWATTY same as > SWOTTY

SWAY vb swing to and fro or from side to side ▷ n power or influence

SWAYABLE > SWAY

SWAYBACK n abnormal sagging in the spine of older horses

SWAYBACKS > SWAYBACK

SWAYED > SWAY

SWAYER > SWAY

SWAYERS > SWAY

SWAYFUL > SWAY

SWAYING > SWAY

SWAYINGS > SWAY

SWAYL same as > SWEAL

SWAYLED > SWAYL

SWAYLING > SWAYL

SWAYLINGS > SWAYL

SWAYLS > SWAYL

SWAYS > SWAY

SWAZZLE n small metal instrument used to produce a shrill voice

SWAZZLES > SWAZZLE

SWEAL vb scorch

SWEALED > SWEAL

SWEALING > SWEAL

SWEALINGS > SWEAL

SWEALS > SWEAL

SWEAR vb use obscene or blasphemous language

SWEARD same as > SWORD

SWEARDS > SWEARD

SWEARER > SWEAR

SWEARERS > SWEAR

SWEARIER > SWEARY

SWEARIEST > SWEARY

SWEARING > SWEAR

SWEARINGS > SWEAR

SWEARS > SWEAR

SWEARWORD n word considered obscene or blasphemous

SWEARY adj using swear-words

SWEAT n salty liquid given off through the pores of the skin ▷ vb have sweat coming through the pores

SWEATBAND n strip of cloth tied around the forehead or wrist to absorb sweat

SWEATBOX n device for causing tobacco leaves, fruit, or hides to sweat

SWEATED adj made by exploited labour

SWEATER n (woollen) garment for the upper part of the body

SWEATERED adj wearing a sweater

SWEATERS > SWEATER

SWEATIER > SWEATY

SWEATIEST > SWEATY

SWEATILY > SWEATY

SWEATING > SWEAT

SWEATINGS > SWEAT

SWEATLESS > SWEAT

SWEATS > SWEAT

SWEATSHOP n place where employees work long hours in poor conditions for low pay

SWEATSUIT n knitted suit worn by athletes for training

SWEATY adj covered with sweat

SWEDE n kind of turnip

SWEDES > SWEDE

SWEDGER n Scots dialect word for sweet

SWEDGERS > SWEDGER

SWEE vb sway

SWEED > SWEE

SWEEING > SWEE

SWEEL same as > SWEAL

SWEELED > SWEEL

SWEELING > SWEEL

SWEELS > SWEEL

SWEENEY n police flying squad

SWEENEYS > SWEENEY

SWEENIES > SWEENY

SWEENY n wasting of the shoulder muscles of a horse

SWEEP vb remove dirt from (a floor) with a broom ▷ n sweeping

SWEEPBACK n rearward inclination of a component or surface

SWEEPER n device used to sweep carpets

SWEEPERS > SWEEPER

SWEEPIER > SWEEP

SWEEPIEST > SWEEP

SWEEPING > SWEEP

SWEEPINGS pl n debris, litter, or refuse

SWEEPS > SWEEP

SWEEPY > SWEEP

SWEER variant of > SWEIR

SWEERED > SWEER

SWEERING > SWEER

SWEERS > SWEER

SWEERT > SWEER

SWEES > SWEE

SWEET adj tasting of or like sugar ▷ n shaped piece of food consisting mainly of sugar ▷ vb sweeten

SWEETCORN n variety of maize, the kernels of which are eaten when young

SWEETED > SWEET

SWEETEN vb make (food or drink) sweet or sweeter

SWEETENED > SWEETEN

SWEETENER n sweetening agent that does not contain sugar

SWEETENS > SWEETEN

SWEETER > SWEET

SWEETEST > SWEET

SWEETFISH n small Japanese fish

SWEETIE n lovable person

SWEETIES > SWEETIE

SWEETING n variety of sweet apple

SWEETINGS > SWEETING

SWEETISH > SWEET

SWEETLIP n type of Australian fish with big lips

SWEETLIPS > SWEETLIP

SWEETLY > SWEET

SWEETMAN n (in the Caribbean) a man kept by a woman

SWEETMEAL adj (of biscuits) sweet and wholemeal

SWEETMEAT n sweet delicacy such as a small cake

SWEETMEN > SWEETMAN

SWEETNESS > SWEET

SWEETS > SWEET

SWEETSHOP n shop selling confectionery

SWEETSOP n small West Indian tree
SWEETSOPS > SWEETSOP
SWEETVELD n grazing field with high-quality grass
SWEETWOOD n tropical tree
SWEETY same as > SWEETIE
SWEIR vb swear ▷ adj lazy
SWEIRED > SWEIR
SWEIRER > SWEIR
SWEIREST > SWEIR
SWEIRING > SWEIR
SWEIRNESS > SWEIR
SWEIRS > SWEIR
SWEIRT > SWEIR
SWELCHIE n whirlpool in Orkney
SWELCHIES > SWELCHIE
SWELL vb expand or increase ▷ n swelling or being swollen ▷ adj excellent or fine
SWELLDOM n fashionable society
SWELLDOMS > SWELLDOM
SWELLED > SWELL
SWELLER > SWELL
SWELLERS > SWELL
SWELLEST > SWELL
SWELLFISH popular name for > PUFFER
SWELLHEAD n conceited person
SWELLING > SWELL
SWELLINGS > SWELL
SWELLISH > SWELL
SWELLS > SWELL
SWELT vb die
SWELTED > SWELT
SWELTER vb feel uncomfortably hot ▷ n hot and uncomfortable condition
SWELTERED > SWELTER
SWELTERS > SWELTER
SWELTING > SWELT
SWELTRIER > SWELTRY
SWELTRY adj sultry
SWELTS > SWELT
SWEPT > SWEEP
SWEPTBACK adj (of an aircraft wing) having the leading edge inclined backwards towards the rear
SWEPTWING adj (of an aircraft) having wings swept backwards
SWERF same as > SWARF
SWERFED > SWERF
SWERFING > SWERF
SWERFS > SWERF
SWERVABLE > SWERVE
SWERVE vb turn aside from a course sharply or suddenly ▷ n swerving
SWERVED > SWERVE
SWERVER > SWERVE
SWERVERS > SWERVE
SWERVES > SWERVE

SWERVING > SWERVE
SWERVINGS > SWERVE
SWEVEN n vision or dream
SWEVENS > SWEVEN
SWEY same as > SWEE
SWEYED > SWEY
SWEYING > SWEY
SWEYS > SWEY
SWIDDEN n area of land where slash-and-burn techniques have been used
SWIDDENS > SWIDDEN
SWIES > SWY
SWIFT adj moving or able to move quickly ▷ n fast-flying bird with pointed wings ▷ adv swiftly or quickly ▷ vb make tight
SWIFTED > SWIFT
SWIFTER n line run around the ends of capstan bars
SWIFTERS > SWIFTER
SWIFTEST > SWIFT
SWIFTIE n trick, ruse, or deception
SWIFTIES > SWIFTY
SWIFTING > SWIFT
SWIFTLET n type of small Asian swift
SWIFTLETS > SWIFTLET
SWIFTLY > SWIFT
SWIFTNESS > SWIFT
SWIFTS > SWIFT
SWIFTY same as > SWIFTIE
SWIG n large mouthful of drink ▷ vb drink in large mouthfuls
SWIGGED > SWIG
SWIGGER > SWIG
SWIGGERS > SWIG
SWIGGING > SWIG
SWIGS > SWIG
SWILE n seal (the marine animal)
SWILER n (in Newfoundland) a seal hunter
SWILERS > SWILER
SWILES > SWILE
SWILING n practice of hunting seals
SWILINGS > SWILING
SWILL vb drink greedily ▷ n sloppy mixture containing waste food, fed to pigs
SWILLED > SWILL
SWILLER > SWILL
SWILLERS > SWILL
SWILLING > SWILL
SWILLINGS > SWILL
SWILLS > SWILL
SWIM vb move along in water by movements of the limbs ▷ n act or period of swimming
SWIMMABLE > SWIM
SWIMMER > SWIM
SWIMMERET n any of the small paired appendages

on the abdomen of crustaceans
SWIMMERS pl n swimming costume
SWIMMIER > SWIMMY
SWIMMIEST > SWIMMY
SWIMMILY > SWIMMY
SWIMMING > SWIM
SWIMMINGS > SWIM
SWIMMY adj dizzy
SWIMS > SWIM
SWIMSUIT n woman's swimming garment that leaves the arms and legs bare
SWIMSUITS > SWIMSUIT
SWIMWEAR n swimming costumes
SWIMWEARS > SWIMWEAR
SWINDGE same as > SWINGE
SWINDGED > SWINDGE
SWINDGES > SWINDGE
SWINDGING > SWINDGE
SWINDLE vb cheat (someone) out of money ▷ n instance of swindling
SWINDLED > SWINDLE
SWINDLER > SWINDLE
SWINDLERS > SWINDLE
SWINDLES > SWINDLE
SWINDLING > SWINDLE
SWINE n contemptible person
SWINEHERD n person who looks after pigs
SWINEHOOD > SWINE
SWINELIKE > SWINE
SWINEPOX n acute infectious viral disease of pigs
SWINERIES > SWINERY
SWINERY n pig farm
SWINES > SWINE
SWING vb move to and fro, sway ▷ n swinging
SWINGARM n main part of the rear suspension on a motorcycle
SWINGARMS > SWINGARM
SWINGBEAT n type of modern dance music that combines soul, rhythm and blues, and hip-hop
SWINGBIN n rubbish bin with a lid that swings shut after being opened
SWINGBINS > SWINGBIN
SWINGBOAT n piece of fairground equipment consisting of a boat-shaped carriage for swinging in
SWINGBY n act of spacecraft passing close to planet
SWINGBYS > SWINGBY
SWINGE vb beat, flog, or punish
SWINGED > SWINGE
SWINGEING > SWINGE
SWINGER n person regarded as being modern and lively

SWINGERS > SWINGER
SWINGES > SWINGE
SWINGIER > SWINGY
SWINGIEST > SWINGY
SWINGING > SWING
SWINGINGS > SWING
SWINGISM n former resistance to use of agricultural machines
SWINGISMS > SWINGISM
SWINGLE n flat-bladed wooden instrument used for beating and scraping flax ▷ vb use a swingle on
SWINGLED > SWINGLE
SWINGLES > SWINGLE
SWINGLING > SWINGLE
SWINGMAN n musician specializing in swing music
SWINGMEN > SWINGMAN
SWINGS > SWING
SWINGTAIL n as in swingtail cargo aircraft kind of cargo aircraft
SWINGTREE n crossbar in a horse's harness
SWINGY adj lively and modern
SWINISH > SWINE
SWINISHLY > SWINE
SWINK vb toil or drudge ▷ n toil or drudgery
SWINKED > SWINK
SWINKER > SWINK
SWINKERS > SWINK
SWINKING > SWINK
SWINKS > SWINK
SWINNEY variant of > SWEENY
SWINNEYS > SWINNEY
SWIPE vb strike (at) with a sweeping blow ▷ n hard blow
SWIPED > SWIPE
SWIPER > SWIPE
SWIPERS > SWIPE
SWIPES pl n beer, esp when poor or weak
SWIPEY adj drunk
SWIPIER > SWIPEY
SWIPIEST > SWIPEY
SWIPING > SWIPE
SWIPLE same as > SWIPPLE
SWIPLES > SWIPLE
SWIPPLE n part of a flail that strikes the grain
SWIPPLES > SWIPPLE
SWIRE n neck
SWIRES > SWIRE
SWIRL vb turn with a whirling motion ▷ n whirling motion
SWIRLED > SWIRL
SWIRLIER > SWIRL
SWIRLIEST > SWIRL
SWIRLING > SWIRL
SWIRLS > SWIRL
SWIRLY > SWIRL
SWISH vb move with a whistling or hissing sound ▷ n whistling or hissing

S

sound ▷ adj fashionable, smart
SWISHED > SWISH
SWISHER > SWISH
SWISHERS > SWISH
SWISHES > SWISH
SWISHEST > SWISH
SWISHIER > SWISHY
SWISHIEST > SWISHY
SWISHING > SWISH
SWISHINGS > SWISH
SWISHY adj moving with a swishing sound
SWISS n type of muslin
SWISSES > SWISS
SWISSING n method of treating cloth
SWISSINGS > SWISSING
SWITCH n device for opening and closing an electric circuit ▷ vb change abruptly
SWITCHED > SWITCH
SWITCHEL n type of beer
SWITCHELS > SWITCHEL
SWITCHER > SWITCH
SWITCHERS > SWITCH
SWITCHES > SWITCH
SWITCHIER > SWITCH
SWITCHING > SWITCH
SWITCHMAN n person who operates railway points
**SWITCHMEN
>** SWITCHMAN
SWITCHY > SWITCH
SWITH adv swiftly
SWITHE same as **>** SWITH
SWITHER vb hesitate or be indecisive ▷ n state of hesitation or uncertainty
SWITHERED > SWITHER
SWITHERS > SWITHER
SWITHLY > SWITH
SWITS same as **>** SWITCH
SWITSES > SWITS
SWIVE vb have sexual intercourse with (a person)
SWIVED > SWIVE
SWIVEL vb turn on a central point ▷ n coupling device that allows an attached object to turn freely
SWIVELED > SWIVEL
SWIVELING > SWIVEL
SWIVELLED > SWIVEL
SWIVELS > SWIVEL
SWIVES > SWIVE
SWIVET n nervous state
SWIVETS > SWIVET
SWIVING > SWIVE
SWIZ n swindle or disappointment
SWIZZ same as **>** SWIZ
SWIZZED > SWIZZ
SWIZZES > SWIZZ
SWIZZING > SWIZZ
SWIZZLE n unshaken cocktail ▷ vb stir a swizzle stick in (a drink)
SWIZZLED > SWIZZLE

SWIZZLER > SWIZZLE
SWIZZLERS > SWIZZLE
SWIZZLES > SWIZZLE
SWIZZLING > SWIZZLE
SWOB less common word for **>** SWAB
SWOBBED > SWOB
SWOBBER > SWOB
SWOBBERS > SWOB
SWOBBING > SWOB
SWOBS > SWOB
SWOFFER > SWOFFING
SWOFFERS > SWOFFING
SWOFFING n sport of saltwater fly-fishing
SWOFFINGS > SWOFFING
SWOLLEN > SWELL
SWOLLENLY > SWELL
SWOLN > SWELL
SWOON n faint ▷ vb faint because of shock or strong emotion
SWOONED > SWOON
SWOONER > SWOON
SWOONERS > SWOON
SWOONIER > SWOONY
SWOONIEST > SWOONY
SWOONING > SWOON
SWOONINGS > SWOON
SWOONS > SWOON
SWOONY adj romantic or sexy
SWOOP vb sweep down or pounce on suddenly ▷ n swooping
SWOOPED > SWOOP
SWOOPER > SWOOP
SWOOPERS > SWOOP
SWOOPIER > SWOOP
SWOOPIEST > SWOOP
SWOOPING > SWOOP
SWOOPS > SWOOP
SWOOPY > SWOOP
SWOOSH vb make a swirling or rustling sound when moving or pouring out ▷ n swirling or rustling sound or movement
SWOOSHED > SWOOSH
SWOOSHES > SWOOSH
SWOOSHING > SWOOSH
SWOP same as **>** SWAP
SWOPPED > SWOP
SWOPPER > SWOP
SWOPPERS > SWOP
SWOPPING > SWOP
SWOPPINGS > SWOP
SWOPS > SWOP
SWOPT > SWOP
SWORD n weapon with a long sharp blade ▷ vb bear a sword
SWORDBILL n South American hummingbird
SWORDED > SWORD
SWORDER n fighter with sword
SWORDERS > SWORDER
SWORDFISH n large fish with a very long upper jaw
SWORDING > SWORD
SWORDLESS > SWORD

SWORDLIKE > SWORD
SWORDMAN same as **>** SWORDSMAN
SWORDMEN > SWORDMAN
SWORDPLAY n action or art of fighting with a sword
SWORDS > SWORD
SWORDSMAN n person skilled in the use of a sword
**SWORDSMEN
>** SWORDSMAN
SWORDTAIL n type of small freshwater fish of Central America
SWORE > SWEAR
SWORN > SWEAR
SWOT vb study (a subject) intensively ▷ n person who studies hard
SWOTS > SWOT
SWOTTED > SWOT
SWOTTER same as **>** SWOT
SWOTTERS > SWOT
SWOTTIER > SWOTTY
SWOTTIEST > SWOTTY
SWOTTING > SWOT
SWOTTINGS > SWOT
SWOTTY adj given to studying hard, esp to the exclusion of other activities
SWOUN same as **>** SWOON
SWOUND same as **>** SWOON
SWOUNDED > SWOUND
SWOUNDING > SWOUND
SWOUNDS less common spelling of **>** ZOUNDS
SWOUNE same as **>** SWOON
SWOUNES > SWOUNE
SWOUNING > SWOUNE
SWOUNS > SWOUN
SWOWND same as **>** SWOON
SWOWNDS > SWOWND
SWOWNE same as **>** SWOON
SWOWNES > SWOWNE
SWOZZLE same as **>** SWAZZLE
SWOZZLES > SWOZZLE
SWUM > SWIM
SWUNG > SWING
SWY n Australian gambling game involving two coins
SYBARITE n lover of luxury ▷ adj luxurious or sensuous
SYBARITES > SYBARITE
SYBARITIC > SYBARITE
SYBBE same as **>** SIB
SYBBES > SYBBE
SYBIL same as **>** SIBYL
SYBILS > SYBIL
SYBO n spring onion
SYBOE same as **>** SYBO
SYBOES > SYBOE
SYBOTIC adj of a swineherd
SYBOTISM > SYBOTIC
SYBOTISMS > SYBOTIC
SYBOW same as **>** SYBO
SYBOWS > SYBOW

SYCAMINE n mulberry tree mentioned in the Bible, thought to be the black mulberry
**SYCAMINES
>** SYCAMINE
SYCAMORE n tree with five-pointed leaves and two-winged fruits
SYCAMORES > SYCAMORE
SYCE n (formerly, in India) a servant employed to look after horses, etc
SYCEE n silver ingots formerly used as a medium of exchange in China
SYCEES > SYCEE
SYCES > SYCE
SYCOMORE same as **>** SYCAMORE
**SYCOMORES
>** SYCOMORE
SYCON n type of sponge
SYCONIA > SYCONIUM
SYCONIUM n fleshy fruit of the fig
SYCONOID adj of or like a sycon
SYCONS > SYCON
SYCOPHANT n person who uses flattery to win favour from people with power or influence
SYCOSES > SYCOSIS
SYCOSIS n chronic inflammation of the hair follicles
SYE vb strain
SYED > SYE
SYEING > SYE
SYEN same as **>** SCION
SYENITE n light-coloured coarse-grained plutonic igneous rock
SYENITES > SYENITE
SYENITIC > SYENITE
SYENS > SYEN
SYES > SYE
SYKE same as **>** SIKE
SYKER adv surely
SYKES > SYKE
SYLI n Finnish unit of volume
SYLIS > SYLI
SYLLABARY n table or list of syllables
SYLLABI > SYLLABUS
SYLLABIC adj of or relating to syllables ▷ n syllabic consonant
SYLLABICS > SYLLABIC
SYLLABIFY vb divide (a word) into syllables
SYLLABISE same as **>** SYLLABIZE
SYLLABISM n use of a writing system consisting of characters for syllables
SYLLABIZE vb divide into syllables
SYLLABLE n part of a word pronounced as a unit
SYLLABLED > SYLLABLE
SYLLABLES > SYLLABLE

SYLLABUB n dessert of beaten cream, sugar, and wine

SYLLABUBS > SYLLABUB

SYLLABUS n list of subjects for a course of study

SYLLEPSES > SYLLEPSIS

SYLLEPSIS n (in grammar or rhetoric) the use of a single sentence construction in which a verb, adjective, etc is made to cover two syntactical functions

SYLLEPTIC > SYLLEPSIS

SYLLOGE n collection or summary

SYLLOGES > SYLLOGE

SYLLOGISE same as > SYLLOGIZE

SYLLOGISM n form of logical reasoning consisting of two premises and a conclusion

SYLLOGIST > SYLLOGISM

SYLLOGIZE vb reason or infer by using syllogisms

SYLPH n slender graceful girl or woman

SYLPHIC > SYLPH

SYLPHID n little sylph

SYLPHIDE same as > SYLPHID

SYLPHIDES > SYLPHIDE

SYLPHIDS > SYLPHID

SYLPHIER > SYLPH

SYLPHIEST > SYLPH

SYLPHINE > SYLPH

SYLPHISH > SYLPH

SYLPHLIKE > SYLPH

SYLPHS > SYLPH

SYLPHY > SYLPH

SYLVA n trees growing in a particular region

SYLVAE > SYLVA

SYLVAN adj relating to woods and trees ▷ n inhabitant of the woods, esp a spirit

SYLVANER n German variety of grape

SYLVANERS > SYLVANER

SYLVANITE n silver-white mineral

SYLVANS > SYLVAN

SYLVAS > SYLVA

SYLVATIC adj growing, living, or occurring in a wood or beneath a tree

SYLVIA n songbird

SYLVIAS > SYLVIA

SYLVIINE > SYLVIA

SYLVIN same as > SYLVITE

SYLVINE same as > SYLVITE

SYLVINES > SYLVINE

SYLVINITE n rock containing sylvine

SYLVINS > SYLVIN

SYLVITE n soluble colourless, white, or coloured mineral

SYLVITES > SYLVITE

SYMAR same as > CYMAR

SYMARS > SYMAR

SYMBION same as > SYMBIONT

SYMBIONS > SYMBION

SYMBIONT n organism living in a state of symbiosis

SYMBIONTS > SYMBIONT

SYMBIOSES > SYMBIOSIS

SYMBIOSIS n close association of two species living together to their mutual benefit

SYMBIOT same as > SYMBIONT

SYMBIOTE same as > SYMBIONT

SYMBIOTES > SYMBIOTE

SYMBIOTIC > SYMBIOSIS

SYMBIOTS > SYMBIOT

SYMBOL n sign or thing that stands for something else ▷ vb be a symbol

SYMBOLE same as > CYMBAL

SYMBOLED > SYMBOL

SYMBOLES > SYMBOLE

SYMBOLIC adj of or relating to a symbol or symbols

SYMBOLICS n study of beliefs

SYMBOLING > SYMBOL

SYMBOLISE same as > SYMBOLIZE

SYMBOLISM n representation of something by symbols

SYMBOLIST n person who uses or can interpret symbols ▷ adj of, relating to, or characterizing symbolism or symbolists

SYMBOLIZE vb be a symbol of

SYMBOLLED > SYMBOL

SYMBOLOGY n use, study, or interpretation of symbols

SYMBOLS > SYMBOL

SYMITAR same as > SCIMITAR

SYMITARE same as > SCIMITAR

SYMITARES > SYMITARE

SYMITARS > SYMITAR

SYMMETRAL > SYMMETRY

SYMMETRIC adj (of a disease) affecting both sides of the body

SYMMETRY n state of having two halves that are mirror images of each other

SYMPATHIN n substance released at certain sympathetic nerve endings

SYMPATHY n compassion for someone's pain or distress

SYMPATICO adj nice

SYMPATRIC adj (of biological speciation or species) existing in the same geographical areas

SYMPATRY n existing of organisms together without interbreeding

SYMPETALY n quality of having petals that are united

SYMPHILE n insect that lives in the nests of social insects and is fed and reared by the inmates

SYMPHILES > SYMPHILE

SYMPHILY n presence of different kinds of animal in ants' nests

SYMPHONIC > SYMPHONY

SYMPHONY n composition for orchestra, with several movements

SYMPHYSES > SYMPHYSIS

SYMPHYSIS n growing together of parts or structures

SYMPHYTIC > SYMPHYSIS

SYMPLAST n continuous system of protoplasts, linked by plasmodesmata and bounded by the cell wall

SYMPLASTS > SYMPLAST

SYMPLOCE n word repetition in successive clauses

SYMPLOCES > SYMPLOCE

SYMPODIA > SYMPODIUM

SYMPODIAL > SYMPODIUM

SYMPODIUM n main axis of growth in the grapevine and similar plants

SYMPOSIA > SYMPOSIUM

SYMPOSIAC adj of, suitable for, or occurring at a symposium

SYMPOSIAL > SYMPOSIUM

SYMPOSIUM n conference for discussion of a particular topic

SYMPTOM n sign indicating the presence of an illness

SYMPTOMS > SYMPTOM

SYMPTOSES > SYMPTOSIS

SYMPTOSIS n wasting condition

SYMPTOTIC > SYMPTOSIS

SYN Scots word for > SINCE

SYNAGOG same as > SYNAGOGUE

SYNAGOGAL > SYNAGOGUE

SYNAGOGS > SYNAGOG

SYNAGOGUE n Jewish place of worship and religious instruction

SYNALEPHA n elision of vowels in speech

SYNANDRIA pl n peculiar bunchings of stamens

SYNANGIA > SYNANGIUM

SYNANGIUM n junction between arteries

SYNANON n type of therapy given to drug addicts

SYNANONS > SYNANON

SYNANTHIC > SYNANTHY

SYNANTHY n abnormal joining between flowers

SYNAPHEA n continuity in metre of verses of poem

SYNAPHEAS > SYNAPHEA

SYNAPHEIA same as > SYNAPHEA

SYNAPSE n gap where nerve impulses pass between two nerve cells ▷ vb create a synapse

SYNAPSED > SYNAPSE

SYNAPSES > SYNAPSIS

SYNAPSID n prehistoric mammal-like reptile

SYNAPSIDS > SYNAPSID

SYNAPSING > SYNAPSE

SYNAPSIS n association in pairs of homologous chromosomes at the start of meiosis

SYNAPTASE n type of enzyme

SYNAPTE n litany in Greek Orthodox Church

SYNAPTES > SYNAPTE

SYNAPTIC adj of or relating to a synapse

SYNARCHY n joint rule

SYNASTRY n coincidence of astrological influences

SYNAXARIA pl n readings in the Greek Orthodox Church

SYNAXES > SYNAXIS

SYNAXIS n early Christian meeting

SYNBIOTIC n synthesis of prebiotic bacteria and one or more probiotics, used in food products

SYNC n synchronization ▷ vb synchronize

SYNCARP n fleshy multiple fruit

SYNCARPS > SYNCARP

SYNCARPY n quality of consisting of united carpels

SYNCED > SYNC

SYNCH same as > SYNC

SYNCHED > SYNCH

SYNCHING > SYNCH

SYNCHRO n type of electrical device

SYNCHRONY n state of being synchronous

SYNCHROS > SYNCHRO

SYNCHS > SYNCH

SYNCHYSES
> SYNCHYSIS

SYNCHYSIS n muddled meaning

SYNCING > SYNC

SYNCLINAL > SYNCLINE

SYNCLINE n downward slope of stratified rock in which the layers dip towards each other from either side

SYNCLINES > SYNCLINE

SYNCOM n communications satellite in stationary orbit

SYNCOMS > SYNCOM

SYNCOPAL > SYNCOPE

SYNCOPATE vb stress the weak beats in (a rhythm) instead of the strong ones

SYNCOPE n omission of one or more sounds or letters from the middle of a word

SYNCOPES > SYNCOPE

SYNCOPIC > SYNCOPE

SYNCOPTIC > SYNCOPE

SYNCRETIC adj of the tendency of languages to reduce their use of inflection

SYNCS > SYNC

SYNCYTIA > SYNCYTIUM

SYNCYTIAL
> SYNCYTIUM

SYNCYTIUM n mass of cytoplasm containing many nuclei and enclosed in a cell membrane

SYND same as > SYNE

SYNDACTYL adj (of certain animals) having two or more digits growing fused together ▷ n animal with this arrangement of digits

SYNDED > SYND

SYNDESES > SYNDESIS

SYNDESIS n use of syndetic constructions

SYNDET n synthetic detergent

SYNDETIC adj denoting a grammatical construction in which two clauses are connected by a conjunction

SYNDETON n syndetic construction

SYNDETONS > SYNDETON

SYNDETS > SYNDET

SYNDIC n business or legal agent of some institutions

SYNDICAL adj relating to the theory that syndicates of workers should seize the means of production

SYNDICATE n group of people or firms undertaking a joint business project ▷ vb publish (material) in several newspapers

SYNDICS > SYNDIC

SYNDING > SYND

SYNDINGS > SYND

SYNDROME n combination of symptoms indicating a particular disease

SYNDROMES > SYNDROME

SYNDROMIC > SYNDROME

SYNDS > SYND

SYNE vb rinse ▷ n rinse ▷ adv since

SYNECHIA n abnormality of the eye

SYNECHIAS > SYNECHIA

SYNECIOUS adj having male and female organs together on a branch

SYNECTIC > SYNECTICS

SYNECTICS n method of identifying and solving problems that depends on creative thinking

SYNED > SYNE

SYNEDRIA > SYNEDRION

SYNEDRIAL
> SYNEDRION

SYNEDRION n assembly of judges

SYNEDRIUM same as > SYNEDRION

SYNERESES
> SYNERESIS

SYNERESIS n process in which a gel contracts on standing and exudes liquid

SYNERGIA same as > SYNERGY

SYNERGIAS > SYNERGIA

SYNERGIC > SYNERGY

SYNERGID n type of cell in embryo

SYNERGIDS > SYNERGID

SYNERGIES > SYNERGY

SYNERGISE same as > SYNERGIZE

SYNERGISM same as > SYNERGY

SYNERGIST n drug, muscle, etc, that increases the action of another ▷ adj of or relating to synergism

SYNERGIZE vb act in synergy

SYNERGY n collective effect that is greater than the sum of individual effects

SYNES > SYNE

SYNESES > SYNESIS

SYNESIS n grammatical construction in which the form of a word is conditioned by the meaning

SYNESISES > SYNESIS

SYNFUEL n synthetic fuel

SYNFUELS > SYNFUEL

SYNGAMIC > SYNGAMY

SYNGAMIES > SYNGAMY

SYNGAMOUS > SYNGAMY

SYNGAMY n sexual reproduction

SYNGAS n mixture of carbon monoxide and hydrogen

SYNGASES > SYNGAS

SYNGASSES > SYNGAS

SYNGENEIC adj with identical genes

SYNGENIC same as > SYNGENEIC

SYNGRAPH n document signed by several parties

SYNGRAPHS > SYNGRAPH

SYNING > SYNE

SYNIZESES
> SYNIZESIS

SYNIZESIS n contraction of two vowels originally belonging to separate syllables into a single syllable

SYNKARYA > SYNKARYON

SYNKARYON n nucleus of a fertilized egg

SYNOD n church council

SYNODAL adj of or relating to a synod ▷ n money paid to a bishop by less senior members of the clergy at a synod

SYNODALS > SYNOD

SYNODIC adj involving conjunction of the same star, planet, or satellite

SYNODICAL > SYNOD

SYNODS > SYNOD

SYNODSMAN n layman at synod

SYNODSMEN
> SYNODSMAN

SYNOECETE same as > SYNOEKETE

SYNOECISE same as > SYNOECIZE

SYNOECISM n union

SYNOECIZE vb unite

SYNOEKETE n insect that lives in the nests of social insects without receiving any attentions from the inmates

SYNOICOUS variant of > SYNECIOUS

SYNONYM n word with the same meaning as another

SYNONYME same as > SYNONYM

SYNONYMES > SYNONYME

SYNONYMIC > SYNONYM

SYNONYMS > SYNONYM

SYNONYMY n study of synonyms

SYNOPSES > SYNOPSIS

SYNOPSIS n summary or outline

SYNOPSISE same as > SYNOPSIZE

SYNOPSIZE vb make a synopsis of

SYNOPTIC adj of or relating to a synopsis ▷ n any of the three synoptic Gospels

SYNOPTICS > SYNOPTIC

SYNOPTIST > SYNOPTIC

SYNOVIA n clear thick fluid that lubricates the body joints

SYNOVIAL adj of or relating to the synovia

SYNOVIAS > SYNOVIA

SYNOVITIC
> SYNOVITIS

SYNOVITIS n inflammation of the membrane surrounding a joint

SYNROC n titanium-ceramic substance that can incorporate nuclear waste in its crystals

SYNROCS > SYNROC

SYNTACTIC adj relating to or determined by syntax

SYNTAGM same as > SYNTAGMA

SYNTAGMA n syntactic unit or a word or phrase forming a syntactic unit

SYNTAGMAS > SYNTAGMA

SYNTAGMIC > SYNTAGMA

SYNTAGMS > SYNTAGM

SYNTAN n synthetic tanning substance

SYNTANS > SYNTAN

SYNTAX n way in which words are arranged to form phrases and sentences

SYNTAXES > SYNTAX

SYNTECTIC > SYNTEXIS

SYNTENIC > SYNTENY

SYNTENIES > SYNTENY

SYNTENY n presence of two or more genes on the same chromosome

SYNTEXIS n liquefaction

SYNTH n type of electrophonic musical instrument operated by a keyboard and pedals

SYNTHASE n enzyme that catalyses a synthesis process

SYNTHASES > SYNTHASE

SYNTHESES
> SYNTHESIS

SYNTHESIS n combination of objects or ideas into a whole

SYNTHETIC adj (of a substance) made artificially ▷ n synthetic substance or material

SYNTHON n molecule used in synthesis

SYNTHONS > SYNTHON

SYNTHPOP n pop music using synthesizers

SYNTHPOPS > SYNTHPOP

SYNTHRONI pl n combined thrones for bishops and their subordinates

SYNTHS > SYNTH

SYNTONE n person who is syntonic

SYNTONES > SYNTONE

SYNTONIC adj emotionally in harmony with one's environment

SYNTONIES > SYNTONY

SYNTONIN *n* substance in muscle

SYNTONINS > SYNTONIN

SYNTONISE *same as* > SYNTONIZE

SYNTONIZE *vb* make frequencies match

SYNTONOUS *same as* > SYNTONIC

SYNTONY *n* matching of frequencies

SYNTYPE *n* an original specimen by which a new species is described

SYNTYPES > SYNTYPE

SYNURA *n* variety of microbe

SYNURAE > SYNURA

SYPE *same as* > SIPE

SYPED > SYPE

SYPES > SYPE

SYPH *shortening of* > SYPHILIS

SYPHER *vb* lap (a chamfered edge) in order to form a flush surface

SYPHERED > SYPHER

SYPHERING > SYPHER

SYPHERS > SYPHER

SYPHILIS *n* serious sexually transmitted disease

SYPHILISE *same as* > SYPHILIZE

SYPHILIZE *vb* infect

with syphilis

SYPHILOID > SYPHILIS

SYPHILOMA *n* tumour or gumma caused by infection with syphilis

SYPHON *same as* > SIPHON

SYPHONAL *same as* > SIPHONAL

SYPHONED > SYPHON

SYPHONIC *same as* > SIPHONIC

SYPHONING > SYPHON

SYPHONS > SYPHON

SYPHS > SYPH

SYPING > SYPE

SYRAH *n* type of French red wine

SYRAHS > SYRAH

SYREN *same as* > SIREN

SYRENS > SYREN

SYRETTE *n* small disposable syringe

SYRETTES > SYRETTE

SYRINGA *n* mock orange or lilac

SYRINGAS > SYRINGA

SYRINGE *n* device for withdrawing or injecting fluids ▷ *vb* wash out or inject with a syringe

SYRINGEAL > SYRINX

SYRINGED > SYRINGE

SYRINGES > SYRINX

SYRINGING > SYRINGE

SYRINX *n* vocal organ of a bird

SYRINXES > SYRINX

SYRPHIAN *same as* > SYRPHID

SYRPHIANS > SYRPHIAN

SYRPHID *n* type of fly

SYRPHIDS > SYRPHID

SYRTES > SYRTIS

SYRTIS *n* area of quicksand

SYRUP *n* solution of sugar in water ▷ *vb* bring to the consistency of syrup

SYRUPED > SYRUP

SYRUPIER > SYRUPY

SYRUPIEST > SYRUPY

SYRUPING > SYRUP

SYRUPLIKE > SYRUP

SYRUPS > SYRUP

SYRUPY *adj* thick and sweet

SYSADMIN *n* computer system administrator

SYSADMINS > SYSADMIN

SYSOP *n* person who runs a system or network

SYSOPS > SYSOP

SYSSITIA *n* ancient Spartan communal meal

SYSSITIAS > SYSSITIA

SYSTALTIC *adj* (esp of the action of the heart) characterized by alternate contractions and dilations

SYSTEM *n* method or set of methods

SYSTEMED *adj* having system

SYSTEMIC *adj* affecting the entire animal or body ▷ *n* systemic pesticide, fungicide, etc

SYSTEMICS > SYSTEMIC

SYSTEMISE *same as* > SYSTEMIZE

SYSTEMIZE *vb* give a system to

SYSTEMS > SYSTEM

SYSTOLE *n* regular contraction of the heart as it pumps blood

SYSTOLES > SYSTOLE

SYSTOLIC > SYSTOLE

SYSTYLE *n* building with different types of columns

SYSTYLES > SYSTYLE

SYTHE *same as* > SITH

SYTHES > SYTHE

SYVER *n* street drain or the grating over it

SYVERS > SYVER

SYZYGAL > SYZYGY

SYZYGETIC > SYZYGY

SYZYGIAL > SYZYGY

SYZYGIES > SYZYGY

SYZYGY *n* position of a celestial body when sun, earth, and the body are in line

S

Tt

TA interj thank you ▷ n thank you

TAAL n language: usually, by implication, Afrikaans

TAALS > TAAL

TAATA child's word for > FATHER

TAATAS > TAATA

TAB n small flap or projecting label ▷ vb supply with a tab

TABANID n stout-bodied fly

TABANIDS > TABANID

TABARD n short sleeveless tunic decorated with a coat of arms, worn in medieval times

TABARDED adj wearing a tabard

TABARDS > TABARD

TABARET n hard-wearing fabric of silk or similar cloth with stripes of satin or moire

TABARETS > TABARET

TABASHEER n dried bamboo sap, used medicinally

TABASHIR same as > TABASHEER

TABASHIRS > TABASHIR

TABBED > TAB

TABBIED > TABBY

TABBIES > TABBY

TABBINET same as > TABINET

TABBINETS > TABBINET

TABBING n act of supplying with tabs

TABBINGS > TABBING

TABBIS n silken cloth

TABBISES > TABBIS

TABBOULEH n kind of Middle Eastern salad made with cracked wheat, mint, parsley, and usually cucumber

TABBOULI same as > TABBOULEH

TABBOULIS > TABBOULI

TABBY vb make (eg a material) appear wavy ▷ n female domestic cat

TABBYHOOD n spinsterhood

TABBYING > TABBY

TABEFIED > TABEFY

TABEFIES > TABEFY

TABEFY vb emaciate or become emaciated

TABEFYING > TABEFY

TABELLION n scribe or notary authorized by the Roman Empire

TABER old variant of > TABOR

TABERD same as > TABARD

TABERDAR n holder of a scholarship at Queen's College, Oxford

TABERDARS > TABERDAR

TABERDS > TABERD

TABERED > TABER

TABERING > TABER

TABERS > TABER

TABES n wasting of a bodily organ or part

TABESCENT adj progressively emaciating

TABETIC > TABES

TABETICS > TABES

TABI n thick-soled Japanese sock, worn with sandals

TABID adj emaciated

TABINET n type of tabbied fabric

TABINETS > TABINET

TABIS > TABI

TABLA n one of a pair of Indian drums played with the hands

TABLAS > TABLA

TABLATURE n any of a number of forms of musical notation, esp for playing the lute, consisting of letters and signs indicating rhythm and fingering

TABLE n piece of furniture with a flat top supported by legs ▷ vb submit (a motion) for discussion by a meeting

TABLEAU n silent motionless group arranged to represent some scene

TABLEAUS > TABLEAU

TABLEAUX > TABLEAU

TABLED > TABLE

TABLEFUL > TABLE

TABLEFULS > TABLE

TABLELAND n high plateau

TABLELESS > TABLE

TABLEMAT n small mat used for protecting the surface of a table from hot dishes

TABLEMATE n someone with whom one shares a table

TABLEMATS > TABLEMAT

TABLES > TABLE

TABLESFUL > TABLE

TABLET n medicinal pill ▷ vb make (something) into a tablet

TABLETED > TABLET

TABLETING > TABLET

TABLETOP n upper surface of a table

TABLETOPS > TABLETOP

TABLETS > TABLET

TABLETTED > TABLET

TABLEWARE n articles such as dishes, plates, knives, forks, etc, used at meals

TABLEWISE adv in the form of a table

TABLIER n (formerly) part of a dress resembling an apron

TABLIERS > TABLIER

TABLING > TABLE

TABLINGS > TABLE

TABLOID n small-sized newspaper with many photographs

TABLOIDS > TABLOID

TABLOIDY adj characteristic of a tabloid newspaper; trashy

TABOGGAN same as > TOBOGGAN

TABOGGANS > TABOGGAN

TABOO n prohibition resulting from religious or social conventions ▷ adj forbidden by a taboo ▷ vb place under a taboo

TABOOED > TABOO

TABOOING > TABOO

TABOOLEY variant of > TABBOULEH

TABOOLEYS > TABOOLEY

TABOOS > TABOO

TABOR vb play the tabor

TABORED > TABOR

TABORER > TABOR

TABORERS > TABOR

TABORET n low stool, originally in the shape of a drum

TABORETS > TABORET

TABORIN same as > TABORET

TABORINE same as > TABOURIN

TABORINES > TABORINE

TABORING > TABOR

TABORINS > TABORIN

TABORS > TABOR

TABOULEH variant of > TABBOULEH

TABOULEHS > TABOULEH

TABOULI same as > TABBOULEH

TABOULIS > TABOULI

TABOUR same as > TABOR

TABOURED > TABOUR

TABOURER > TABOUR

TABOURERS > TABOUR

TABOURET same as > TABORET

TABOURETS > TABOURET

TABOURIN same as > TABOURIN

TABOURING > TABOUR

TABOURINS > TABOURIN

TABOURS > TABOUR

TABRERE same as > TABOR

TABRERES > TABRERE

TABRET n smaller version of a tabor

TABRETS > TABRET

TABS > TAB

TABU same as > TABOO

TABUED > TABU

TABUING > TABU

TABULA n tablet for writing on

TABULABLE > TABULATE

TABULAE > TABULA

TABULAR adj arranged in a table

TABULARLY > TABULAR

TABULATE vb arrange (information) in a table ▷ adj having a flat surface

TABULATED > TABULATE

TABULATES > TABULATE

TABULATOR n key on a typewriter or word processor that sets stops so that data can be arranged and presented in columns

TABULI variant of > TABBOULEH

TABULIS > TABULI

TABUN n organic compound used as a lethal nerve gas

TABUNS > TABUN

TABUS > TABU

TACAHOUT *n* abnormal outgrowth on the tamarisk plant

TACAHOUTS > TACAHOUT

TACAMAHAC *n* any of several strong-smelling resinous gums obtained from certain trees, used in making ointments, incense, etc

TACAN *n* electronic ultrahigh-frequency navigation system for aircraft

TACANS > TACAN

TACE *same as* **>** TASSET

TACES > TACE

TACET *n* musical direction indicating that an instrument or singer does not take part

TACH *n* device for measuring speed

TACHE *n* buckle, clasp, or hook

TACHES > TACHE

TACHINA *n* as in *tachina fly* bristly fly

TACHINID *n* type of fly

TACHINIDS > TACHINID

TACHISM *same as* **>** TACHISME

TACHISME *n* type of action painting evolved in France in which haphazard dabs and blots of colour are treated as a means of instinctive or unconscious expression

TACHISMES > TACHISME

TACHISMS > TACHISM

TACHIST > TACHISM

TACHISTE > TACHISME

TACHISTES > TACHISME

TACHISTS > TACHIST

TACHO *same as* **>** TACHOGRAM

TACHOGRAM *n* graphical record of readings

TACHOS > TACHO

TACHS > TACH

TACHYLITE *same as* **>** TACHYLYTE

TACHYLYTE *n* black basaltic glass often found on the edges of intrusions of basalt

TACHYON *n* hypothetical elementary particle

TACHYONIC > TACHYON

TACHYONS > TACHYON

TACHYPNEA *n* abnormally rapid breathing

TACIT *adj* implied but not spoken

TACITLY > TACIT

TACITNESS > TACIT

TACITURN *adj* habitually uncommunicative

TACK *n* short nail with a large head ▷ *vb* fasten with tacks

TACKBOARD *n* noticeboard

TACKED > TACK

TACKER > TACK

TACKERS > TACK

TACKET *n* nail, esp a hobnail

TACKETS > TACKET

TACKETY > TACKET

TACKEY *same as* **>** TACKY

TACKIER > TACKY

TACKIES *pl n* tennis shoes or plimsolls

TACKIEST > TACKY

TACKIFIED > TACKIFY

TACKIFIER > TACKIFY

TACKIFIES > TACKIFY

TACKIFY *vb* give (eg rubber) a sticky feel

TACKILY > TACKY

TACKINESS > TACKY

TACKING > TACK

TACKINGS > TACK

TACKLE *vb* deal with (a task) ▷ *n* act of tackling an opposing player

TACKLED > TACKLE

TACKLER > TACKLE

TACKLERS > TACKLE

TACKLES > TACKLE

TACKLESS > TACK

TACKLING > TACKLE

TACKLINGS > TACKLE

TACKS > TACK

TACKSMAN *n* leaseholder, esp a tenant in the Highlands who sublets

TACKSMEN > TACKSMAN

TACKY *adj* slightly sticky

TACMAHACK *same as* **>** TACAMAHAC

TACNODE *n* point at which two branches of a curve have a common tangent

TACNODES > TACNODE

TACO *n* tortilla fried until crisp, served with a filling

TACONITE *n* fine-grained sedimentary rock containing magnetite, haematite, and silica, which occurs in the Lake Superior region: a low-grade iron ore

TACONITES > TACONITE

TACOS > TACO

TACRINE *n* drug used to treat Alzheimer's disease

TACRINES > TACRINE

TACT *n* skill in avoiding giving offence

TACTFUL > TACT

TACTFULLY > TACT

TACTIC *n* method or plan to achieve an end

TACTICAL *adj* of or employing tactics

TACTICIAN > TACTICS

TACTICITY *n* quality of regularity in the arrangement of repeated units within a polymer chain

TACTICS *n* art of directing military actions in battle

TACTILE *adj* of or having the sense of touch

TACTILELY > TACTILE

TACTILIST *n* artist whose work strives to appeal to the sense of touch

TACTILITY > TACTILE

TACTION *n* act of touching

TACTIONS > TACTION

TACTISM *another word for* **>** TAXIS

TACTISMS > TACTISM

TACTLESS > TACT

TACTS > TACT

TACTUAL *adj* caused by touch

TACTUALLY > TACTUAL

TAD *n* small bit or piece

TADDIE *short for* **>** TADPOLE

TADDIES > TADDIE

TADPOLE *n* limbless tailed larva of a frog or toad

TADPOLES > TADPOLE

TADS > TAD

TAE *Scots form of the verb* **>** TOE

TAED > TAE

TAEDIUM *archaic spelling of* **>** TEDIUM

TAEDIUMS > TAEDIUM

TAEING > TAE

TAEKWONDO *n* Korean martial art

TAEL *n* unit of weight, used in the Far East

TAELS > TAEL

TAENIA *n* (in ancient Greece) a narrow fillet or headband for the hair

TAENIAE > TAENIA

TAENIAS > TAENIA

TAENIASES **>** TAENIASIS

TAENIASIS *n* infestation with tapeworms

TAENIATE *adj* ribbon-like

TAENIOID *adj* ribbon-like

TAENITE *n* nickel-iron alloy found in meteorites

TAENITES > TAENITE

TAES > TAE

TAFFAREL *same as* **>** TAFFRAIL

TAFFARELS > TAFFAREL

TAFFEREL *same as* **>** TAFFRAIL

TAFFERELS > TAFFEREL

TAFFETA *n* shiny silk or rayon fabric

TAFFETAS *same as* **>** TAFFETA

TAFFETY *same as* **>** TAFFETA

TAFFIA *same as* **>** TAFIA

TAFFIAS > TAFFIA

TAFFIES > TAFFY

TAFFRAIL *n* rail at the back of a ship or boat

TAFFRAILS > TAFFRAIL

TAFFY *same as* **>** TOFFEE

TAFIA *n* type of rum, esp from Guyana or the Caribbean

TAFIAS > TAFIA

TAG *n* label bearing information ▷ *vb* attach a tag to

TAGALONG *n* one who trails behind, esp uninvited; a hanger-on

TAGALONGS > TAGALONG

TAGAREEN *n* junk shop

TAGAREENS > TAGAREEN

TAGBOARD *n* sturdy form of cardboard

TAGBOARDS > TAGBOARD

TAGETES *n* any of a genus of plants with yellow or orange flowers

TAGGANT *n* microscopic material added to substance to identify it

TAGGANTS > TAGGANT

TAGGED > TAG

TAGGEE *n* one who has been made to wear a tag

TAGGEES > TAGGEE

TAGGER *n* one who marks with a tag

TAGGERS > TAGGER

TAGGIER > TAGGY

TAGGIEST > TAGGY

TAGGING > TAG

TAGGINGS > TAG

TAGGY *adj* (of wool, hair, etc) matted

TAGHAIRM *n* form of divination once practised in the Highlands of Scotland

TAGHAIRMS > TAGHAIRM

TAGINE *n* large, heavy N African cooking pot with a conical lid

TAGINES > TAGINE

TAGLESS *adj* having no tag

TAGLIKE *adj* resembling a tag

TAGLINE *n* funny line of joke

TAGLINES > TAGLINE

TAGLIONI *n* type of coat

TAGLIONIS > TAGLIONI

TAGMA *n* distinct region of the body of an arthropod

TAGMATA > TAGMA

TAGMEME *n* class of speech elements all of which may fulfil the same grammatical role

TAGMEMES > TAGMEME

TAGMEMIC > TAGMEME

TAGMEMICS > TAGMEME

TAGRAG *same as* **>** RAGTAG

TAGRAGS > TAGRAG

TAGS > TAG

TAGUAN *n* nocturnal flying squirrel of the East Indies

TAGUANS > TAGUAN

TAHA *n* type of South African bird

TAHAS > TAHA

TAHINA *same as* **>** TAHINI

TAHINAS > TAHINA

TAHINI *n* paste made from ground sesame seeds

TAHINIS > TAHINI

TAHR *n* goatlike mammal of mountainous regions of S and SW Asia

TAHRS > TAHR

TAHSIL *n* administrative division of a zila in certain states in India

TAHSILDAR *n* officer in charge of the collection of revenues, etc, in a tahsil

TAHSILS > TAHSIL

TAI *n* type of sea bream

TAIAHA *n* carved weapon in the form of a staff, now used in Māori ceremonial oratory

TAIAHAS > TAIAHA

TAIG *n* often derogatory term for Roman Catholic

TAIGA *n* belt of coniferous forest

TAIGAS > TAIGA

TAIGLACH *same as* **>** TEIGLACH

TAIGLE *vb* entangle or impede

TAIGLED > TAIGLE

TAIGLES > TAIGLE

TAIGLING > TAIGLE

TAIGS > TAIG

TAIHOA *interj* hold on! no hurry!

TAIKO *n* large Japanese drum

TAIKONAUT *n* astronaut from the People's Republic of China

TAIKOS > TAIKO

TAIL *n* rear part of an animal's body, usu forming a flexible appendage ▷ *adj* at the rear ▷ *vb* follow (someone) secretly

TAILARD *n* one having a tail

TAILARDS > TAILARD

TAILBACK *n* queue of traffic stretching back from an obstruction

TAILBACKS > TAILBACK

TAILBOARD *n* removable or hinged rear board on a truck etc

TAILBONE *nontechnical name for* **>** COCCYX

TAILBONES > TAILBONE

TAILCOAT *n* man's black coat having a horizontal cut over the hips and a tapering tail with a vertical slit up to the waist

TAILCOATS > TAILCOAT

TAILED > TAIL

TAILENDER *n* (in cricket) the batter last in the batting order

TAILER *n* one that tails

TAILERON *n* aileron located on the tailplane of an aircraft

TAILERONS > TAILERON

TAILERS > TAILER

TAILFAN *n* fanned structure at the hind end of a lobster

TAILFANS > TAILFAN

TAILFIN *n* decorative projection at back of car

TAILFINS > TAILFIN

TAILFLIES > TAILFLY

TAILFLY *n* in angling, the lowest fly on a wet-fly cast

TAILGATE *n* door at the rear of a hatchback vehicle ▷ *vb* drive very close behind (a vehicle)

TAILGATED > TAILGATE

TAILGATER > TAILGATE

TAILGATES > TAILGATE

TAILHOOK *n* hook on an aircraft that catches a braking cable

TAILHOOKS > TAILHOOK

TAILING *n* part of a beam, rafter, projecting brick or stone, etc, embedded in a wall

TAILINGS *pl n* waste left over after certain processes, such as from an ore-crushing plant or in milling grain

TAILLAMP *n* rear light

TAILLAMPS > TAILLAMP

TAILLE *n* (in France before 1789) a tax levied by a king or overlord on his subjects

TAILLES > TAILLE

TAILLESS > TAIL

TAILLEUR *n* woman's suit

TAILLEURS > TAILLEUR

TAILLIE *n* (in law) the limitation of an estate or interest to a person and the heirs of his body

TAILLIES > TAILLIE

TAILLIGHT *same as* **>** TAILLAMP

TAILLIKE *adj* resembling a tail

TAILOR *n* person who makes men's clothes ▷ *vb* cut or style (a garment) to specific requirements

TAILORED > TAILOR

TAILORESS *n* female tailor

TAILORING > TAILOR

TAILORS > TAILOR

TAILPIECE *n* piece added at the end of something, for example a report

TAILPIPE *vb* attach an object, esp a tin can, to the tail of an animal

TAILPIPED > TAILPIPE

TAILPIPES > TAILPIPE

TAILPLANE *n* small stabilizing wing at the rear of an aircraft

TAILRACE *n* channel that carries water away from a water wheel, turbine, etc

TAILRACES > TAILRACE

TAILS *adv* with the side of a coin that does not have a portrait of a head on it uppermost

TAILSKID *n* runner under the tail of an aircraft

TAILSKIDS > TAILSKID

TAILSLIDE *n* backwards descent of an aeroplane after stalling while in an upward trajectory

TAILSPIN *n* uncontrolled spinning dive of an aircraft ▷ *vb* go into a tailspin

TAILSPINS > TAILSPIN

TAILSPUN > TAILSPIN

TAILSTOCK *n* casting that slides on the bed of a lathe in alignment with the headstock and is locked in position to support the free end of a workpiece

TAILWATER *n* water flowing in a tailrace

TAILWHEEL *n* wheel fitted to the rear of a vehicle, esp the landing wheel under the tail of an aircraft

TAILWIND *n* wind coming from the rear

TAILWINDS > TAILWIND

TAILYE *same as* **>** TAILLIE

TAILYES > TAILYE

TAILZIE *same as* **>** TAILLIE

TAILZIES > TAILZIE

TAIN *n* tinfoil used in backing mirrors

TAINS > TAIN

TAINT *vb* spoil with a small amount of decay or other bad quality ▷ *n* something that taints

TAINTED > TAINT

TAINTING > TAINT

TAINTLESS > TAINT

TAINTS > TAINT

TAINTURE *n* contamination; staining

TAINTURES > TAINTURE

TAIPAN *n* large poisonous Australian snake

TAIPANS > TAIPAN

TAIRA *same as* **>** TAYRA

TAIRAS > TAIRA

TAIS > TAI

TAISCH *n* (in Scotland) apparition of a person whose death is imminent

TAISCHES > TAISCH

TAISH *same as* **>** TAISCH

TAISHES > TAISH

TAIT *same as* **>** TATE

TAITS > TAIT

TAIVER *same as* **>** TAVER

TAIVERED > TAIVER

TAIVERING > TAIVER

TAIVERS > TAIVER

TAIVERT *adj* Scots word meaning confused or bewildered

TAJ *n* tall conical cap worn as a mark of distinction by Muslims

TAJES > TAJ

TAJINE *same as* **>** TAGINE

TAJINES > TAJINE

TAK *Scots variant spelling of* **>** TAKE

TAKA *n* standard monetary unit of Bangladesh, divided into 100 paise

TAKABLE > TAKE

TAKAHE *n* very rare flightless New Zealand bird

TAKAHES > TAKAHE

TAKAMAKA *same as* **>** TACAMAHAC

TAKAMAKAS > TAKAMAKA

TAKAS > TAKA

TAKE *vb* remove from a place ▷ *n* one of a series of recordings from which the best will be used

TAKEABLE > TAKE

TAKEAWAY *adj* (of food) sold for consumption away from the premises ▷ *n* shop or restaurant selling meals for eating elsewhere

TAKEAWAYS > TAKEAWAY

TAKEDOWN *n* disassembly

TAKEDOWNS > TAKEDOWN

TAKEN > TAKE

TAKEOFF *n* act or process of making an aircraft airborne

TAKEOFFS > TAKEOFF

TAKEOUT *n* shop or restaurant that sells such food

TAKEOUTS > TAKEOUT

TAKEOVER *n* act of taking control of a company by buying a large number of its shares

TAKEOVERS > TAKEOVER

TAKER *n* person who agrees to take something that is offered

TAKERS > TAKER

TAKES > TAKE

TAKEUP *n* claiming or acceptance of something that is due or available

TAKEUPS > TAKEUP

TAKHI *n* type of wild Mongolian horse

TAKHIS > TAKHI

TAKI *same as* **>** TAKHI

TAKIER > TAKY

TAKIEST > TAKY

TAKIN *n* bovid mammal of mountainous regions of S Asia

TAKING > TAKE

TAKINGLY > TAKE

TAKINGS > TAKE

TAKINS > TAKIN

TAKIS > TAKI

TAKKIES > TAKKY

TAKKY n (S Afr) plimsoll

TAKS > TAK

TAKY adj appealing

TALA n standard monetary unit of Samoa, divided into 100 sene

TALAK same as > TALAQ

TALAKS > TALAK

TALANT old variant of > TALON

TALANTS > TALANT

TALAPOIN n smallest of the guenon monkeys of swampy central W African forests, having olive-green fur and slightly webbed digits

TALAPOINS > TALAPOIN

TALAQ n Muslim form of divorce

TALAQS > TALAQ

TALAR n ankle-length robe

TALARIA pl n winged sandals, such as those worn by Hermes

TALARS > TALAR

TALAS > TALA

TALAUNT old variant of > TALON

TALAUNTS > TALAUNT

TALAYOT n ancient Balearic stone tower

TALAYOTS > TALAYOT

TALBOT n ancient breed of large hound

TALBOTS > TALBOT

TALBOTYPE n early type of photographic process (invented by W H Fox Talbot) or a photograph produced using it

TALC n talcum powder ▷ vb apply talc to ▷ adj of, or relating to, talc

TALCED > TALC

TALCIER > TALCY

TALCIEST > TALCY

TALCING > TALC

TALCKED > TALCKY

TALCKIER > TALCKY

TALCKIEST > TALCKY

TALCKING > TALCKY

TALCKY same as > TALCY

TALCOSE > TALC

TALCOUS > TALC

TALCS > TALC

TALCUM n white, grey, brown, or pale green mineral ▷ vb apply talcum to

TALCUMED > TALCUM

TALCUMING > TALCUM

TALCUMS > TALCUM

TALCY adj like, containing, or covered in talc

TALE n story

TALEA n rhythmic pattern in certain mediaeval choral compositions

TALEAE > TALEA

TALEFUL adj having many tales

TALEGALLA n brush turkey, of New Guinea and Australia

TALEGGIO n Italian cheese

TALEGGIOS > TALEGGIO

TALENT n natural ability

TALENTED > TALENT

TALENTS > TALENT

TALER same as > THALER

TALERS > TALER

TALES n group of persons summoned to fill vacancies on a jury panel

TALESMAN > TALES

TALESMEN > TALES

TALEYSIM > TALLITH

TALI > TALUS

TALIGRADE adj (of mammals) walking on the outer side of the foot

TALION n principle of making punishment correspond to the crime

TALIONIC adj of or relating to talion

TALIONS > TALION

TALIPAT same as > TALIPOT

TALIPATS > TALIPAT

TALIPED adj having a club foot ▷ n club-footed person

TALIPEDS > TALIPED

TALIPES n congenital deformity of the foot by which it is twisted in any of various positions

TALIPOT n palm tree of the East Indies

TALIPOTS > TALIPOT

TALISMAN n object believed to have magic power

TALISMANS > TALISMAN

TALK vb express ideas or feelings by means of speech ▷ n speech or lecture

TALKABLE > TALK

TALKATHON n epic bout of discussion or speechifying

TALKATIVE adj fond of talking

TALKBACK n broadcast in which telephone comments or questions from the public are transmitted live

TALKBACKS > TALKBACK

TALKBOX n voice box

TALKBOXES > TALKBOX

TALKED > TALK

TALKER > TALK

TALKERS > TALK

TALKFEST n lengthy discussion

TALKFESTS > TALKFEST

TALKIE n early film with a soundtrack

TALKIER > TALKY

TALKIES > TALKIE

TALKIEST > TALKY

TALKINESS n quality or condition of being talky

TALKING n speech; the act of speaking

TALKINGS > TALKING

TALKS > TALK

TALKTIME n length of time a mobile phone can be used before its battery runs out

TALKTIMES > TALKTIME

TALKY adj containing too much dialogue or inconsequential talk

TALL adj higher than average

TALLAGE n tax levied on Crown lands and royal towns ▷ vb levy a tax (upon)

TALLAGED > TALLAGE

TALLAGES > TALLAGE

TALLAGING > TALLAGE

TALLAISIM > TALLITH

TALLAT same as > TALLET

TALLATS > TALLAT

TALLBOY n high chest of drawers

TALLBOYS > TALLBOY

TALLENT n plenty

TALLENTS > TALLENT

TALLER > TALL

TALLEST > TALL

TALLET n loft

TALLETS > TALLET

TALLGRASS n long grass in North American prairie

TALLIABLE adj taxable

TALLIATE vb levy a tax

TALLIATED > TALLIATE

TALLIATES > TALLIATE

TALLIED > TALLY

TALLIER > TALLY

TALLIERS > TALLY

TALLIES > TALLY

TALLIS variant of > TALLITH

TALLISES > TALLIS

TALLISH adj quite tall

TALLISIM > TALLITH

TALLIT variant of > TALLITH

TALLITES > TALLIT

TALLITH n shawl worn by Jewish males during religious services

TALLITHES > TALLITH

TALLITHIM > TALLITH

TALLITHS > TALLITH

TALLITIM > TALLIT

TALLITOT > TALLIT

TALLITOTH > TALLITH

TALLITS > TALLIT

TALLNESS > TALL

TALLOL n oily liquid used for making soaps, lubricants, etc

TALLOLS > TALLOL

TALLOT same as > TALLET

TALLOTS > TALLOT

TALLOW n hard animal fat used to make candles ▷ vb cover or smear with tallow

TALLOWED > TALLOW

TALLOWING > TALLOW

TALLOWISH > TALLOW

TALLOWS > TALLOW

TALLOWY > TALLOW

TALLS > TALL

TALLY vb (of two things) correspond ▷ n record of a debt or score

TALLYHO n cry to encourage hounds when the quarry is sighted ▷ vb make the cry of tallyho

TALLYHOED > TALLYHO

TALLYHOES > TALLYHO

TALLYHOS > TALLYHO

TALLYING > TALLY

TALLYMAN n scorekeeper or recorder

TALLYMEN > TALLYMAN

TALLYSHOP n shop that allows customers to pay in instalments

TALMA n short cloak

TALMAS > TALMA

TALMUD n primary source of Jewish religious law, consisting of the Mishnah and the Gemara

TALMUDIC > TALMUD

TALMUDISM > TALMUD

TALMUDS > TALMUD

TALON n bird's hooked claw

TALONED > TALON

TALONS > TALON

TALOOKA same as > TALUK

TALOOKAS > TALOOKA

TALPA n sebaceous cyst

TALPAE > TALPA

TALPAS > TALPA

TALUK n subdivision of a district

TALUKA same as > TALUK

TALUKAS > TALUKA

TALUKDAR n person in charge of a taluk

TALUKDARS > TALUKDAR

TALUKS > TALUK

TALUS n bone of the ankle that articulates with the leg bones to form the ankle joint

TALUSES > TALUS

TALWEG same as > THALWEG

TALWEGS > TALWEG

TAM n type of hat

TAMABLE > TAME

TAMAL same as > TAMALE

TAMALE n Mexican dish of minced meat wrapped in maize husks and steamed

TAMALES > TAMALE

TAMALS > TAMAL

TAMANDU same as > TAMANDUA

TAMANDUA n small arboreal edentate mammal

TAMANDUAS > TAMANDUA

TAMANDUS > TAMANDU

t

TAMANOIR n anteater

TAMANOIRS > TAMANOIR

TAMANU n poon tree

TAMANUS > TAMANU

TAMARA n powder consisting of cloves, cinnamon, fennel, coriander, etc

TAMARACK n North American larch, with reddish-brown bark, bluish-green needle-like leaves, and shiny oval cones

TAMARACKS > TAMARACK

TAMARAO same as > TAMARAU

TAMARAOS > TAMARAO

TAMARAS > TAMARA

TAMARAU n small rare member of a cattle tribe in the Philippines

TAMARAUS > TAMARAU

TAMARI n Japanese variety of soy sauce

TAMARILLO n shrub with a red oval edible fruit

TAMARIN n small monkey of South and Central America

TAMARIND n tropical tree

TAMARINDS > TAMARIND

TAMARINS > TAMARIN

TAMARIS > TAMARI

TAMARISK n evergreen shrub with slender branches and feathery flower clusters

TAMARISKS > TAMARISK

TAMASHA n (in India) a show

TAMASHAS > TAMASHA

TAMBAC same as > TOMBAC

TAMBACS > TAMBAC

TAMBAK same as > TOMBAC

TAMBAKS > TAMBAK

TAMBALA n unit of Malawian currency

TAMBALAS > TAMBALA

TAMBER same as > TIMBRE

TAMBERS > TAMBER

TAMBOUR n embroidery frame consisting of two hoops ▷ vb embroider (fabric or a design) on a tambour

TAMBOURA n instrument with a long neck, four strings, and no frets, used in Indian music to provide a drone

TAMBOURAS > TAMBOURA

TAMBOURED > TAMBOUR

TAMBOURER n one who embroiders on a tambour

TAMBOURIN n 18th-century Provençal folk dance

TAMBOURS > TAMBOUR

TAMBUR n old Turkish stringed instrument

TAMBURA n Middle-Eastern stringed

instrument with a long neck

TAMBURAS > TAMBURA

TAMBURIN same as > TAMBURIN

TAMBURINS > TAMBURIN

TAMBURS > TAMBUR

TAME adj (of animals) brought under human control ▷ vb make tame

TAMEABLE > TAME

TAMED > TAME

TAMEIN n Burmese skirt

TAMEINS > TAMEIN

TAMELESS > TAME

TAMELY > TAME

TAMENESS > TAME

TAMER > TAME

TAMERS > TAME

TAMES > TAME

TAMEST > TAME

TAMIN n thin woollen fabric

TAMINE same as > TAMIN

TAMINES > TAMINE

TAMING n act of making (something) tame

TAMINGS > TAMING

TAMINS > TAMIN

TAMIS same as > TAMMY

TAMISE n type of thin cloth

TAMISES > TAMIS

TAMMAR n small scrub wallaby

TAMMARS > TAMMAR

TAMMIE n short for tam-o'-shanter, a traditional Scottish hat

TAMMIED > TAMMY

TAMMIES > TAMMY

TAMMY n glazed woollen or mixed fabric ▷ vb strain (sauce, soup, etc) through a tammy

TAMMYING > TAMMY

TAMOXIFEN n drug that antagonizes the action of oestrogen and is used to treat breast cancer and some types of infertility in women

TAMP vb pack down by repeated taps

TAMPALA n Asian plant, eaten as food

TAMPALAS > TAMPALA

TAMPAN n biting mite

TAMPANS > TAMPAN

TAMPED > TAMP

TAMPER vb interfere ▷ n person or thing that tamps

TAMPERED > TAMPER

TAMPERER > TAMPER

TAMPERERS > TAMPER

TAMPERING > TAMPER

TAMPERS > TAMPER

TAMPING adj very angry ▷ n act or instance of tamping

TAMPINGS > TAMPING

TAMPION n plug placed in a gun's muzzle to keep out moisture and dust

TAMPIONS > TAMPION

TAMPON n absorbent plug of cotton wool inserted into the vagina during menstruation ▷ vb use a tampon

TAMPONADE > TAMPON

TAMPONAGE > TAMPON

TAMPONED > TAMPON

TAMPONING > TAMPON

TAMPONS > TAMPON

TAMPS > TAMP

TAMS > TAM

TAMWORTH n any of a hardy rare breed of long-bodied reddish pigs

TAMWORTHS > TAMWORTH

TAN n brown coloration of the skin from exposure to sunlight ▷ vb (of skin) go brown from exposure to sunlight ▷ adj yellowish-brown

TANA n small Madagascan lemur

TANADAR n commanding officer of an Indian police station

TANADARS > TANADAR

TANAGER n American songbird with a short thick bill

TANAGERS > TANAGER

TANAGRA n type of tanager

TANAGRAS > TANAGRA

TANAGRINE adj of or relating to the tanager

TANAISTE n in Irish politics, the vice-Taoiseach or deputy prime minister of the Republic of Ireland

TANAISTES > TANAISTE

TANALISED adj having been treated with the trademarked timber preservative Tanalith

TANALIZED same as > TANALISED

TANAS > TANA

TANBARK n bark of certain trees, esp the oak and hemlock, used as a source of tannin

TANBARKS > TANBARK

TANDEM n bicycle for two riders, one behind the other

TANDEMS > TANDEM

TANDOOR n type of Indian clay oven

TANDOORI adj (of food) cooked in an Indian clay oven ▷ n Indian method of cooking meat or vegetables on a spit in a clay oven

TANDOORIS > TANDOORI

TANDOORS > TANDOOR

TANE old Scottish variant of > TAKEN

TANG n strong taste or smell ▷ vb cause to ring

TANGA n triangular loincloth worn by indigenous peoples in tropical America

TANGAS > TANGA

TANGED > TANG

TANGELO n hybrid produced by crossing a tangerine tree with a grapefruit tree

TANGELOS > TANGELO

TANGENCE n touching

TANGENCES > TANGENCE

TANGENCY > TANGENT

TANGENT n line that touches a curve without intersecting it

TANGENTAL > TANGENT

TANGENTS > TANGENT

TANGERINE n small orange-like fruit of an Asian citrus tree ▷ adj reddish-orange

TANGHIN n poison formerly used in Madagascar to determine the guilt of crime suspects

TANGHININ n active ingredient in tanghin

TANGHINS > TANGHIN

TANGI n Māori funeral ceremony

TANGIBLE adj able to be touched ▷ n tangible thing or asset

TANGIBLES > TANGIBLE

TANGIBLY > TANGIBLE

TANGIE n water spirit of Orkney, appearing as a figure draped in seaweed, or as a seahorse

TANGIER > TANGY

TANGIES > TANGIE

TANGIEST > TANGY

TANGINESS > TANGY

TANGING > TANG

TANGIS > TANGI

TANGLE n confused mass or situation ▷ vb twist together in a tangle

TANGLED > TANGLE

TANGLER > TANGLE

TANGLERS > TANGLE

TANGLES > TANGLE

TANGLIER > TANGLE

TANGLIEST > TANGLE

TANGLING n act or condition of tangling

TANGLINGS > TANGLING

TANGLY > TANGLE

TANGO n S American dance ▷ vb dance a tango

TANGOED > TANGO

TANGOES > TANGO

TANGOING > TANGO

TANGOIST > TANGO

TANGOISTS > TANGO

TANGOLIKE > TANGO

TANGOS > TANGO

TANGRAM n type of Chinese puzzle

TANGRAMS > TANGRAM

TANGS > TANG

TANGUN n small and sturdy Tibetan pony

TANGUNS > TANGUN

TANGY adj having a pungent, fresh, or briny flavour or aroma

TANH n hyperbolic tangent

TANHS > TANH

TANIST n heir apparent of a Celtic chieftain

TANISTRY > TANIST

TANISTS > TANIST

TANIWHA n mythical Māori monster that lives in water

TANIWHAS > TANIWHA

TANK n container for liquids or gases ▷ vb put or keep in a tank

TANKA n Japanese verse form consisting of five lines

TANKAGE n capacity or contents of a tank or tanks

TANKAGES > TANKAGE

TANKARD n large beer-mug, often with a hinged lid

TANKARDS > TANKARD

TANKAS > TANKA

TANKED > TANK

TANKER n ship or truck for carrying liquid in bulk ▷ vb transport by means of a tanker

TANKERED > TANKER

TANKERING > TANKER

TANKERS > TANKER

TANKFUL n quantity contained in a tank

TANKFULS > TANKFUL

TANKIA n type of boat used in Canton

TANKIAS > TANKIA

TANKIES > TANKY

TANKING n heavy defeat

TANKINGS > TANKING

TANKINI n swimming costume consisting of a camisole top and bikini briefs

TANKINIS > TANKINI

TANKLESS > TANK

TANKLIKE > TANK

TANKS > TANK

TANKSHIP same as > TANKER

TANKSHIPS > TANKSHIP

TANKY n die-hard communist

TANLING n suntanned person

TANLINGS > TANLING

TANNA n Indian police station or army base

TANNABLE > TAN

TANNAGE n act or process of tanning

TANNAGES > TANNAGE

TANNAH same as > TANNA

TANNAHS > TANNAH

TANNAS > TANNA

TANNATE n any salt or ester of tannic acid

TANNATES > TANNATE

TANNED > TAN

TANNER > TAN

TANNERIES > TANNERY

TANNERS > TAN

TANNERY n place where hides are tanned

TANNEST > TAN

TANNIC adj of, containing, or produced from tannin or tannic acid

TANNIE n in S Africa, title of respect used to refer to an elderly woman

TANNIES > TANNIE

TANNIN n vegetable substance used in tanning

TANNING > TAN

TANNINGS > TAN

TANNINS > TANNIN

TANNISH > TAN

TANNOY n sound-amplifying apparatus used as a public-address system ▷ vb announce (something) using a Tannoy system

TANNOYED > TANNOY

TANNOYING > TANNOY

TANNOYS > TANNOY

TANOREXIC n person obsessed with maintaining a tan

TANREC same as > TENREC

TANRECS > TANREC

TANS > TAN

TANSIES > TANSY

TANSY n yellow-flowered plant

TANTALATE n any of various salts of tantalic acid formed when the pentoxide of tantalum dissolves in an alkali

TANTALIC adj of or containing tantalum, esp in the pentavalent state

TANTALISE same as > TANTALIZE

TANTALISM > TANTALISE

TANTALITE n heavy brownish mineral consisting of a tantalum oxide of iron and manganese in orthorhombic crystalline form

TANTALIZE vb torment by showing but withholding something desired

TANTALOUS adj of or containing tantalum in the trivalent state

TANTALUM n hard greyish-white metallic element

TANTALUMS > TANTALUM

TANTALUS n case in which bottles of wine and spirits may be locked with their contents tantalizingly visible

TANTARA n blast, as on a trumpet or horn

TANTARARA same as > TANTARA

TANTARAS > TANTARA

TANTI adj old word for worthwhile

TANTIVIES > TANTIVY

TANTIVY adv at full speed ▷ interj hunting cry, esp at full gallop

TANTO adv too much ▷ n type of Japanese sword

TANTONIES > TANTONY

TANTONY n runt

TANTOS > TANTO

TANTRA n sacred books of Tantrism

TANTRAS > TANTRA

TANTRIC > TANTRA

TANTRISM n teaching of tantra

TANTRISMS > TANTRISM

TANTRIST n person who practises or teaches tantrism

TANTRISTS > TANTRIST

TANTRUM n childish outburst of temper

TANTRUMS > TANTRUM

TANUKI n animal similar to a raccoon, found in Japan

TANUKIS > TANUKI

TANYARD n part of a tannery

TANYARDS > TANYARD

TANZANITE n blue gemstone

TAO n (in Confucian philosophy) the correct course of action

TAONGA n treasure

TAONGAS > TAONGA

TAOS > TAO

TAP vb knock lightly and usu repeatedly ▷ n light knock

TAPA n inner bark of the paper mulberry

TAPACOLO n small bird of Chile and Argentina

TAPACOLOS > TAPACOLO

TAPACULO same as > TAPACOLO

TAPACULOS > TAPACULO

TAPADERA n leather covering for the stirrup on an American saddle

TAPADERAS > TAPADERA

TAPADERO same as > TAPADERA

TAPADEROS > TAPADERO

TAPALO n Latin American scarf, often patterned and brightly coloured

TAPALOS > TAPALO

TAPAS pl n (in Spanish cookery) light snacks or appetizers

TAPE n narrow long strip of material ▷ vb record on magnetic tape

TAPEABLE > TAPE

TAPED > TAPE

TAPELESS > TAPE

TAPELIKE > TAPE

TAPELINE n tape or length of metal marked off in inches, centimetres, etc, used principally for measuring and fitting garments

TAPELINES > TAPELINE

TAPEN adj made of tape

TAPENADE n savoury paste made from capers, olives, and anchovies, with olive oil and lemon juice

TAPENADES > TAPENADE

TAPER > TAPE

TAPERED > TAPE

TAPERER > TAPE

TAPERERS > TAPE

TAPERING > TAPE

TAPERINGS > TAPE

TAPERNESS n state or quality of being tapered

TAPERS > TAPE

TAPERWISE adv in the manner of a taper

TAPES > TAPE

TAPESTRY n fabric decorated with coloured woven designs ▷ vb portray in tapestry

TAPET n example of tapestry ▷ vb decorate with tapestries

TAPETA > TAPETUM

TAPETAL > TAPETUM

TAPETED > TAPET

TAPETI n forest rabbit of Brazil

TAPETING > TAPET

TAPETIS > TAPETI

TAPETS > TAPET

TAPETUM n layer of nutritive cells that surrounds developing spore cells

TAPETUMS > TAPETUM

TAPEWORM n long flat parasitic worm living in the intestines of vertebrates

TAPEWORMS > TAPEWORM

TAPHOLE n hole in a furnace for running off molten metal or slag

TAPHOLES > TAPHOLE

TAPHONOMY n study of the processes affecting an organism after death that result in its fossilization

TAPHOUSE n inn or bar

TAPHOUSES > TAPHOUSE

TAPING n act of taping

TAPINGS > TAPING

TAPIOCA n beadlike starch made from cassava root

TAPIOCAS > TAPIOCA

t

TAPIR n piglike mammal of tropical America and SE Asia, with a long snout

TAPIROID > TAPIR

TAPIROIDS > TAPIROID

TAPIRS > TAPIR

TAPIS n tapestry or carpeting

TAPISES > TAPIS

TAPIST n person who records read out printed matter in an audio format

TAPISTS > TAPIST

TAPLASH n dregs of beer

TAPLASHES > TAPLASH

TAPLESS adj without a tap

TAPPA same as > TAPA

TAPPABLE > TAP

TAPPAS > TAPPA

TAPPED > TAP

TAPPER n person who taps

TAPPERS > TAPPER

TAPPET n short steel rod in an engine, transferring motion from one part to another

TAPPETS > TAPPET

TAPPICE vb hide

TAPPICED > TAPPICE

TAPPICES > TAPPICE

TAPPICING > TAPPICE

TAPPING > TAP

TAPPINGS > TAP

TAPPIT adj crested; topped

TAPROOM n public bar in a hotel or pub

TAPROOMS > TAPROOM

TAPROOT n main root of a plant, growing straight down

TAPROOTED > TAPROOT

TAPROOTS > TAPROOT

TAPS > TAP

TAPSMAN n old word for a barman

TAPSMEN > TAPSMAN

TAPSTER n barman

TAPSTERS > TAPSTER

TAPSTRESS > TAPSTER

TAPSTRIES > TAPSTRY

TAPSTRY adj relating to tapestry ▷ n taproom in a public house

TAPU adj sacred ▷ n Māori religious or superstitious restriction on something ▷ vb put a tapu on something

TAPUED > TAPU

TAPUING > TAPU

TAPUS > TAPU

TAQUERIA n restaurant specializing in tacos

TAQUERIAS > TAQUERIA

TAR n thick black liquid distilled from coal etc ▷ vb coat with tar

TARA same as > TARO

TARABISH n type of card game

TARAIRE n type of New Zealand tree

TARAIRES > TARAIRE

TARAKIHI n common edible sea fish of New Zealand waters

TARAKIHIS > TARAKIHI

TARAMA n cod roe

TARAMAS > TARAMA

TARAMEA n variety of New Zealand speargrass

TARAMEAS > TARAMEA

TARAND n northern animal of legend, now supposed to have been the reindeer

TARANDS > TARAND

TARANTARA same as > TANTARA

TARANTAS same as > TARANTASS

TARANTASS n large horse-drawn four-wheeled Russian carriage without springs

TARANTISM n nervous disorder marked by uncontrollable bodily movement, widespread in S Italy during the 15th to 17th centuries: popularly thought to be caused by the bite of a tarantula

TARANTIST > TARANTISM

TARANTULA n large hairy spider with a poisonous bite

TARAS > TARA

TARAXACUM n perennial plant with dense heads of small yellow flowers and seeds with a feathery attachment

TARBOGGIN same as > TOBOGGAN

TARBOOSH n felt or cloth brimless cap, usually red and often with a silk tassel, formerly worn by Muslim men

TARBOUCHE same as > TARBOOSH

TARBOUSH same as > TARBOOSH

TARBOY n boy who applies tar to the skin of sheep cut during shearing

TARBOYS > TARBOY

TARBUSH same as > TARBOOSH

TARBUSHES > TARBUSH

TARCEL same as > TARCEL

TARCELS > TARCEL

TARDIED > TARDY

TARDIER > TARDY

TARDIES > TARDY

TARDIEST > TARDY

TARDILY > TARDY

TARDINESS > TARDY

TARDIVE adj tending to develop late

TARDO adj (of music) slow; to be played slowly

TARDY adj slow or late ▷ vb delay or impede (something or someone)

TARDYING > TARDY

TARDYON n particle travelling slower than the speed of light

TARDYONS > TARDYON

TARE n weight of the wrapping or container of goods ▷ vb weigh (a package, etc) in order to calculate the amount of tare

TARED > TARE

TARES > TARE

TARGA n as in targa top denotes removable hard roof on a car

TARGAS > TARGA

TARGE vb interrogate

TARGED > TARGE

TARGES > TARGE

TARGET n object or person a missile is aimed at ▷ vb aim or direct

TARGETED > TARGET

TARGETEER n soldier armed with a small round shield

TARGETING n act of targeting

TARGETS > TARGET

TARGING > TARGE

TARIFF n tax levied on imports ▷ vb impose punishment for a criminal offence

TARIFFED > TARIFF

TARIFFING > TARIFF

TARIFFS > TARIFF

TARING > TARE

TARINGS > TARE

TARLATAN n open-weave cotton fabric, used for stiffening garments

TARLATANS > TARLATAN

TARLETAN same as > TARLATAN

TARLETANS > TARLETAN

TARMAC See also > MACADAM

TARMACKED > TARMAC

TARMACS > TARMAC

TARN n small mountain lake

TARNAL adj damned ▷ adv extremely

TARNALLY > TARNAL

TARNATION euphemism for > DAMNATION

TARNISH vb make or become stained or less bright ▷ n discoloration or blemish

TARNISHED > TARNISH

TARNISHER > TARNISH

TARNISHES > TARNISH

TARNS > TARN

TARO n plant with a large edible rootstock

TAROC old variant of > TAROT

TAROCS > TAROC

TAROK old variant of > TAROT

TAROKS > TAROK

TAROS > TARO

TAROT n special pack of cards used mainly in fortune-telling ▷ adj relating to tarot cards

TAROTS > TAROT

TARP informal word for > TARPAULIN

TARPAN n European wild horse common in prehistoric times

TARPANS > TARPAN

TARPAPER n paper coated or impregnated with tar

TARPAPERS > TARPAPER

TARPAULIN n (sheet of) heavy waterproof fabric

TARPON n large silvery clupeoid game fish found in warm Atlantic waters

TARPONS > TARPON

TARPS > TARP

TARRAGON n aromatic herb

TARRAGONS > TARRAGON

TARRAS same as > TRASS

TARRASES > TARRAS

TARRE vb old word meaning to provoke or goad

TARRED > TAR

TARRES > TARRE

TARRIANCE archaic word for > DELAY

TARRIED > TARRY

TARRIER > TARRY

TARRIERS > TARRY

TARRIES > TARRY

TARRIEST > TARRY

TARRINESS > TARRY

TARRING > TAR

TARRINGS > TAR

TARROCK n seabird

TARROCKS > TARROCK

TARROW vb exhibit reluctance

TARROWED > TARROW

TARROWING > TARROW

TARROWS > TARROW

TARRY vb linger or delay ▷ n stay ▷ adj covered in or resembling tar

TARRYING > TAR

TARS > TAR

TARSAL adj of the tarsus or tarsi ▷ n tarsal bone

TARSALGIA n pain in the tarsus

TARSALS > TARSAL

TARSEAL n bitumen surface of a road

TARSEALS > TARSEAL

TARSEL same as > TERCEL

TARSELS > TARSEL

TARSI > TARSUS

TARSIA another term for > INTARSIA

TARSIAS > TARSIA

TARSIER *n* small nocturnal primate of the E Indies, which has very large eyes

TARSIERS > TARSIER

TARSIOID *adj* resembling a tarsier ▷ *n* type of fossil

TARSIOIDS > TARSIOID

TARSIPED *n* generic term for a number of marsupials

TARSIPEDS > TARSIPED

TARSUS *n* bones of the heel and ankle collectively

TART *n* pie or flan with a sweet filling ▷ *adj* sharp or bitter ▷ *adj* (of a flavour, food, etc) sour, acid, or astringent ▷ *vb* (of food, drink, etc) become tart (sour)

TARTAN *n* design of straight lines crossing at right angles

TARTANA *n* small Mediterranean sailing boat

TARTANAS > TARTANA

TARTANE *same as* > TARTANA

TARTANED > TARTAN

TARTANES > TARTANE

TARTANRY *n* derogatory term for excessive use of tartan and other Scottish imagery to produce a distorted sentimental view of Scotland and its history

TARTANS > TARTAN

TARTAR *n* hard deposit on the teeth

TARTARE *n* mayonnaise sauce mixed with hard-boiled egg yolks, herbs, etc

TARTARES > TARTARE

TARTARIC *adj* of or derived from tartar or tartaric acid

TARTARISE *same as* > TARTARIZE

TARTARIZE *vb* impregnate or treat with tartar or tartar emetic

TARTARLY *adj* resembling a tartar

TARTAROUS *adj* consisting of, containing, or resembling tartar

TARTARS > TARTAR

TARTED > TART

TARTER > TART

TARTEST > TART

TARTIER > TARTY

TARTIEST > TARTY

TARTILY > TARTY

TARTINE *n* slice of bread with butter or jam spread on it

TARTINES > TARTINE

TARTINESS > TARTY

TARTING > TART

TARTISH > TART

TARTISHLY > TART

TARTLET *n* individual pastry case with a filling of fruit or other sweet or savoury mixture

TARTLETS > TARTLET

TARTLY > TART

TARTNESS > TART

TARTRATE *n* any salt or ester of tartaric acid

TARTRATED *adj* being in the form of a tartrate

TARTRATES > TARTRATE

TARTS > TART

TARTUFE *same as* > TARTUFFE

TARTUFES > TARTUFE

TARTUFFE *n* person who hypocritically pretends to be deeply pious

TARTUFFES > TARTUFFE

TARTUFI > TARTUFO

TARTUFO *n* Italian mousse-like chocolate dessert

TARTUFOS > TARTUFO

TARTY *adj* provocative in a cheap and bawdy way

TARWEED *n* resinous Californian plant

TARWEEDS > TARWEED

TARWHINE *n* bream of E Australia, silver in colour with gold streaks

TARWHINES > TARWHINE

TARZAN *n* man with great physical strength

TARZANS > TARZAN

TAS > TASS

TASAR *same as* > TUSSORE

TASARS > TASAR

TASBIH *n* form of Islamic prayer

TASBIHS > TASBIH

TASE *vb* stun with a taser gun

TASED > TASE

TASER *vb* use a Taser stun gun on (someone)

TASERED > TASER

TASERING > TASER

TASERS > TASER

TASES > TASE

TASH *vb* stain or besmirch

TASHED > TASH

TASHES > TASH

TASHING > TASH

TASIMETER *n* device for measuring small temperature changes. It depends on the changes of pressure resulting from expanding or contracting solids

TASIMETRY > TASIMETER

TASING > TASE

TASK *n* piece of work to be done ▷ *vb* give someone a task to do

TASKBAR *n* area of computer screen showing what programs are running

TASKBARS > TASKBAR

TASKED > TASK

TASKER > TASK

TASKERS > TASK

TASKING > TASK

TASKINGS > TASK

TASKLESS > TASK

TASKS > TASK

TASKWORK *n* hard or unpleasant work

TASKWORKS > TASKWORK

TASLET *same as* > TASSET

TASLETS > TASLET

TASS *n* cup, goblet, or glass

TASSA *n* type of Indian kettledrum

TASSAS > TASSA

TASSE *same as* > TASSET

TASSEL *n* decorative fringed knot of threads ▷ *vb* adorn with a tassel or tassels

TASSELED > TASSEL

TASSELING > TASSEL

TASSELL *same as* > TASSEL

TASSELLED > TASSEL

TASSELLS > TASSELL

TASSELLY > TASSEL

TASSELS > TASSEL

TASSES > TASSE

TASSET *n* piece of armour to protect the thigh

TASSETS > TASSET

TASSIE *same as* > TASS

TASSIES > TASSIE

TASSO *n* spicy cured pork cut into strips

TASSOS > TASSO

TASSWAGE *vb* to assuage

TASTABLE > TASTE

TASTE *n* sense by which the flavour of a substance is distinguished ▷ *vb* distinguish the taste of (a substance)

TASTEABLE > TASTE

TASTED > TASTE

TASTEFUL *adj* having or showing good taste

TASTELESS *adj* bland or insipid

TASTER *n* person employed to test the quality of food or drink by tasting it

TASTERS > TASTER

TASTES > TASTE

TASTEVIN *n* small shallow cup for wine tasting

TASTEVINS > TASTEVIN

TASTIER > TASTY

TASTIEST > TASTY

TASTILY > TASTY

TASTINESS > TASTY

TASTING > TASTE

TASTINGS > TASTE

TASTY *adj* pleasantly flavoured

TAT *n* tatty or tasteless article(s) ▷ *vb* make (something) by tatting

TATAHASH *n* stew containing potatoes and cheap cuts of meat

TATAMI *n* thick rectangular mat of woven straw

TATAMIS > TATAMI

TATAR *n* brutal person

TATARS > TATAR

TATE *n* small tuft of fibre

TATER *n* potato

TATERS > TATER

TATES > TATE

TATH *vb* (of cattle) to defecate

TATHATA *n* (in Buddhism) ultimate nature of things

TATHATAS > TATHATA

TATHED > TATH

TATHING > TATH

TATHS > TATH

TATIE *same as* > TATTIE

TATIES > TATIE

TATLER *old variant of* > TATTLER

TATLERS > TATLER

TATOU *n* armadillo

TATOUAY *n* large armadillo of South America

TATOUAYS > TATOUAY

TATOUS > TATOU

TATS > TAT

TATSOI *n* variety of Chinese cabbage

TATSOIS > TATSOI

TATT *same as* > TAT

TATTED > TAT

TATTER *vb* make or become torn

TATTERED > TATTER

TATTERING > TATTER

TATTERS > TATTER

TATTERY *same as* > TATTERED

TATTIE *Scot or dialect word for* > POTATO

TATTIER > TATTY

TATTIES > TATTIE

TATTIEST > TATTY

TATTILY > TATTY

TATTINESS > TATTY

TATTING > TAT

TATTINGS > TAT

TATTLE *n* gossip or chatter ▷ *vb* gossip or chatter

TATTLED > TATTLE

TATTLER *n* person who tattles

TATTLERS > TATTLER

TATTLES > TATTLE

TATTLING > TATTLE

TATTLINGS > TATTLE

TATTOO *n* pattern made on the body by pricking the skin and staining it with indelible inks ▷ *vb* make such a pattern on the skin

TATTOOED > TATTOO

TATTOOER > TATTOO

TATTOOERS > TATTOO

TATTOOING > TATTOO
TATTOOIST > TATTOO
TATTOOS > TATTOO
TATTOW *old variant of* > TATTOO
TATTOWED > TATTOW
TATTOWING > TATTOW
TATTOWS > TATTOW
TATTS > TATT
TATTY *adj* worn out, shabby, tawdry, or unkempt
TATU *old variant of* > TATTOO
TATUED > TATU
TATUING > TATU
TATUS > TATU
TAU *n* 19th letter in the Greek alphabet
TAUBE *n* type of German aeroplane
TAUBES > TAUBE
TAUGHT > TEACH
TAUHINU *New Zealand name for* > POPLAR
TAUHINUS > TAUHINU
TAUHOU *same as* > SILVEREYE
TAUHOUS > TAUHOU
TAUIWI *n* Māori term for the non-Māori people of New Zealand
TAUIWIS > TAUIWI
TAULD *vb* old Scots variant of told
TAUNT *vb* tease with jeers ▷ *n* jeering remark ▷ *adj* (of the mast or masts of a sailing vessel) unusually tall
TAUNTED > TAUNT
TAUNTER > TAUNT
TAUNTERS > TAUNT
TAUNTING > TAUNT
TAUNTINGS > TAUNT
TAUNTS > TAUNT
TAUON *n* negatively charged elementary particle
TAUONS > TAUON
TAUPATA *n* New Zealand shrub or tree
TAUPATAS > TAUPATA
TAUPE *adj* brownish-grey ▷ *n* brownish-grey colour
TAUPES > TAUPE
TAUPIE *same as* > TAWPIE
TAUPIES > TAUPIE
TAUREAN *adj* born under or characteristic of Taurus
TAURIC *same as* > TAUREAN
TAURIFORM *adj* in the form of a bull
TAURINE *adj* of, relating to, or resembling a bull ▷ *n* substance obtained from the bile of animals
TAURINES > TAURINE
TAUS > TAU
TAUT *adj* drawn tight ▷ *vb* Scots word meaning to tangle
TAUTAUG *same as* > TAUTOG

TAUTAUGS > TAUTAUG
TAUTED > TAUT
TAUTEN *vb* make or become taut
TAUTENED > TAUTEN
TAUTENING > TAUTEN
TAUTENS > TAUTEN
TAUTER > TAUT
TAUTEST > TAUT
TAUTING > TAUT
TAUTIT *adj* Scots word meaning tangled
TAUTLY > TAUT
TAUTNESS > TAUT
TAUTOG *n* large dark-coloured wrasse, used as a food fish
TAUTOGS > TAUTOG
TAUTOLOGY *n* use of words which merely repeat something already stated
TAUTOMER *n* either of the two forms of a chemical compound that exhibits tautomerism
TAUTOMERS > TAUTOMER
TAUTONYM *n* taxonomic name in which the generic and specific components are the same
TAUTONYMS > TAUTONYM
TAUTONYMY > TAUTONYM
TAUTS > TAUT
TAV *n* 23rd and last letter in the Hebrew alphabet
TAVA *n* thick Indian frying pan
TAVAH *variant of* > TAVA
TAVAHS > TAVAH
TAVAS > TAVA
TAVER *vb* wander about
TAVERED > TAVER
TAVERING > TAVER
TAVERN *n* pub
TAVERNA *n* (in Greece) a guesthouse that has its own bar
TAVERNAS > TAVERNA
TAVERNER *n* keeper of a tavern
TAVERNERS > TAVERNER
TAVERNS > TAVERN
TAVERS > TAVER
TAVERT *adj* bewildered or confused
TAVS > TAV
TAW *vb* convert skins into leather
TAWA *n* tall timber tree from New Zealand
TAWAI *n* New Zealand beech
TAWAIS > TAWAI
TAWAS > TAWA
TAWDRIER > TAWDRY
TAWDRIES > TAWDRY
TAWDRIEST > TAWDRY
TAWDRILY > TAWDRY
TAWDRY *adj* cheap, showy, and of poor quality ▷ *n* gaudy finery of poor quality

TAWED > TAW
TAWER > TAW
TAWERIES > TAWERY
TAWERS > TAW
TAWERY *n* place where tawing is carried out
TAWHAI *same as* > TAWAI
TAWHAIS > TAWHAI
TAWHIRI *n* small New Zealand tree with wavy green glossy leaves
TAWHIRIS > TAWHIRI
TAWIE *adj* easily persuaded or managed
TAWIER > TAWIE
TAWIEST > TAWIE
TAWING > TAW
TAWINGS > TAW
TAWNEY *same as* > TAWNY
TAWNEYS > TAWNEY
TAWNIER > TAWNY
TAWNIES > TAWNY
TAWNIEST > TAWNY
TAWNILY > TAWNY
TAWNINESS > TAWNY
TAWNY *adj* yellowish-brown ▷ *n* light brown to brownish-orange colour
TAWPIE *n* foolish or maladroit girl
TAWPIES > TAWPIE
TAWS *same as* > TAWSE
TAWSE *n* leather strap with one end cut into thongs ▷ *vb* punish (someone) with or as if with a tawse
TAWSED > TAWSE
TAWSES > TAWSE
TAWSING > TAWSE
TAWT *same as* > TAUT
TAWTED > TAWT
TAWTIE > TAWT
TAWTIER > TAWT
TAWTIEST > TAWT
TAWTING > TAWT
TAWTS > TAWT
TAX *n* compulsory payment levied by a government on income, property, etc to raise revenue ▷ *vb* levy a tax on
TAXA > TAXON
TAXABLE *adj* capable of being taxed ▷ *n* person, income, property, etc, that is subject to tax
TAXABLES > TAXABLE
TAXABLY > TAXABLE
TAXACEOUS *adj* relating to a family of coniferous trees that includes the yews
TAXAMETER *old variant of* > TAXIMETER
TAXATION *n* levying of taxes
TAXATIONS > TAXATION
TAXATIVE > TAXATION
TAXED > TAX
TAXEME *n* any element of speech that may differentiate meaning
TAXEMES > TAXEME

TAXEMIC > TAXEME
TAXER > TAX
TAXERS > TAX
TAXES > TAX
TAXI *n* car with a driver that may be hired ▷ *vb* (of an aircraft) run along the ground
TAXIARCH *n* soldier in charge of a Greek taxis
TAXIARCHS > TAXIARCH
TAXICAB *same as* > TAXI
TAXICABS > TAXICAB
TAXIDERMY *n* art of stuffing and mounting animal skins to give them a lifelike appearance
TAXIED > TAXI
TAXIES > TAXIS
TAXIING > TAXI
TAXIMAN *n* taxi driver
TAXIMEN > TAXIMAN
TAXIMETER *n* meter fitted to a taxi to register the fare, based on the length of the journey
TAXING *adj* demanding, onerous
TAXINGLY > TAXING
TAXINGS > TAX
TAXIPLANE *n* aircraft that is available for hire
TAXIS *n* movement of a cell or organism in response to an external stimulus ▷ *n* ancient Greek army unit
TAXISES > TAXIS
TAXITE *n* type of volcanic rock
TAXITES > TAXITE
TAXITIC > TAXITE
TAXIWAY *n* marked path along which aircraft taxi to or from a runway, parking area, etc
TAXIWAYS > TAXIWAY
TAXLESS > TAX
TAXMAN *n* collector of taxes
TAXMEN > TAXMAN
TAXOL *n* trademarked anti-cancer drug
TAXOLS > TAXOL
TAXON *n* any taxonomic group or rank
TAXONOMER > TAXONOMY
TAXONOMIC > TAXONOMY
TAXONOMY *n* classification of plants and animals into groups
TAXONS > TAXON
TAXOR > TAX
TAXORS > TAX
TAXPAID *adj* (of taxable products, esp wine) having had the applicable tax paid already
TAXPAYER *n* person or organization that pays taxes
TAXPAYERS > TAXPAYER
TAXPAYING > TAXPAYER
TAXUS *n* genus of conifers

TAXWISE adv regarding tax

TAXYING > TAXI

TAY Irish dialect word for > TEA

TAYASSUID n peccary

TAYBERRY n hybrid shrub produced by crossing a blackberry, raspberry, and loganberry

TAYRA n large arboreal mammal of Central and South America

TAYRAS > TAYRA

TAYS > TAY

TAZZA n wine cup with a shallow bowl and a circular foot

TAZZAS > TAZZA

TAZZE > TAZZA

TCHICK vb make a clicking noise with the tongue

TCHICKED > TCHICK

TCHICKING > TCHICK

TCHICKS > TCHICK

TCHOTCHKE n trinket

TE n (in tonic sol-fa) seventh degree of any major scale

TEA n drink made from infusing the dried leaves of an Asian bush in boiling water ▷ vb take tea

TEABAG n porous bag of tea leaves for infusion

TEABAGS > TEABAG

TEABERRY n berry of the wintergreen

TEABOARD n tea tray

TEABOARDS > TEABOARD

TEABOWL n small bowl used (instead of a teacup) for serving tea

TEABOWLS > TEABOWL

TEABOX n box for storing tea

TEABOXES > TEABOX

TEABREAD n loaf-shaped cake that contains dried fruit which has been steeped in cold tea before baking: served sliced and buttered

TEABREADS > TEABREAD

TEACAKE n flat bun, usually eaten toasted and buttered

TEACAKES > TEACAKE

TEACART n trolley from which tea is served

TEACARTS > TEACART

TEACH vb tell or show (someone) how to do something

TEACHABLE > TEACH

TEACHABLY > TEACH

TEACHER n person who teaches, esp in a school

TEACHERLY > TEACHER

TEACHERS > TEACHER

TEACHES > TEACH

TEACHIE old form of > TETCHY

TEACHING > TEACH

TEACHINGS > TEACH

TEACHLESS adj unable to be taught

TEACUP n cup out of which tea may be drunk

TEACUPFUL n amount a teacup will hold, about four fluid ounces

TEACUPS > TEACUP

TEAD old word for > TORCH

TEADE same as > TEAD

TEADES > TEADE

TEADS > TEAD

TEAED > TEA

TEAGLE vb raise or hoist using a tackle

TEAGLED > TEAGLE

TEAGLES > TEAGLE

TEAGLING > TEAGLE

TEAHOUSE n restaurant, esp in Japan or China, where tea and light refreshments are served

TEAHOUSES > TEAHOUSE

TEAING > TEA

TEAK n very hard wood of an E Indian tree

TEAKETTLE n kettle for boiling water to make tea

TEAKS > TEAK

TEAKWOOD another word for > TEAK

TEAKWOODS > TEAKWOOD

TEAL n kind of small duck

TEALIGHT n small candle

TEALIGHTS > TEALIGHT

TEALIKE adj resembling tea

TEALS > TEAL

TEAM n group of people forming one side in a game ▷ vb make or cause to make a team

TEAMAKER n person or thing that makes tea

TEAMAKERS > TEAMAKER

TEAMED > TEAM

TEAMER > TEAM

TEAMERS > TEAM

TEAMING > TEAM

TEAMINGS > TEAM

TEAMMATE n fellow member of a team

TEAMMATES > TEAMMATE

TEAMS > TEAM

TEAMSTER n commercial vehicle driver

TEAMSTERS > TEAMSTER

TEAMWISE adv in respect of a team; in the manner of a team

TEAMWORK n cooperative work by a team

TEAMWORKS > TEAMWORK

TEAPOT n container for making and serving tea

TEAPOTS > TEAPOT

TEAPOY n small table or stand with a tripod base

TEAPOYS > TEAPOY

TEAR n drop of fluid appearing in and falling from the eye ▷ vb rip a hole in ▷ vb shed tears

TEARABLE > TEAR

TEARAWAY n wild or unruly person

TEARAWAYS > TEARAWAY

TEARDOWN n demolition; disassembly

TEARDOWNS > TEARDOWN

TEARDROP same as > TEAR

TEARDROPS > TEARDROP

TEARED > TEAR

TEARER > TEAR

TEARERS > TEAR

TEARFUL adj weeping or about to weep

TEARFULLY > TEARFUL

TEARGAS n gas or vapour that makes the eyes smart and water ▷ vb deploy teargas against

TEARGASES > TEARGAS

TEARIER > TEARY

TEARIEST > TEARY

TEARILY > TEARY

TEARINESS > TEARY

TEARING > TEAR

TEARLESS > TEAR

TEARLIKE adj like a tear

TEAROOM same as > TEASHOP

TEAROOMS > TEAROOM

TEARS > TEAR

TEARSHEET n page in a newspaper or periodical that is cut or perforated so that it can be easily torn out

TEARSTAIN n stain or streak left by tears

TEARSTRIP n part of packaging torn to open it

TEARY adj characterized by, covered with, or secreting tears

TEAS > TEA

TEASABLE > TEASE

TEASE vb make fun of (someone) in a provoking or playful way ▷ n person who teases

TEASED > TEASE

TEASEL n plant with prickly leaves and flowers ▷ vb tease (a fabric)

TEASELED > TEASEL

TEASELER > TEASEL

TEASELERS > TEASEL

TEASELING > TEASEL

TEASELLED > TEASEL

TEASELLER > TEASEL

TEASELS > TEASEL

TEASER n annoying or difficult problem

TEASERS > TEASER

TEASES > TEASE

TEASHOP n restaurant where tea and light refreshments are served

TEASHOPS > TEASHOP

TEASING > TEASE

TEASINGLY > TEASE

TEASINGS > TEASE

TEASPOON n small spoon for stirring tea

TEASPOONS > TEASPOON

TEAT n nipple of a breast or udder

TEATASTER n person assessing teas by tasting them

TEATED > TEAT

TEATIME n late afternoon

TEATIMES > TEATIME

TEATS > TEAT

TEAWARE n implements for brewing and serving tea

TEAWARES > TEAWARE

TEAZE old variant of > TEASE

TEAZED > TEAZE

TEAZEL same as > TEASEL

TEAZELED > TEAZEL

TEAZELING > TEAZEL

TEAZELLED > TEAZEL

TEAZELS > TEAZEL

TEAZES > TEAZE

TEAZING > TEAZE

TEAZLE same as > TEASEL

TEAZLED > TEAZLE

TEAZLES > TEAZLE

TEAZLING > TEAZLE

TEBBAD n sandstorm

TEBBADS > TEBBAD

TEC short for > DETECTIVE

TECH n technical college

TECHED adj showing slight insanity

TECHIE n person who is skilled in the use of technology ▷ adj relating to or skilled in the use of technology

TECHIER > TECHY

TECHIES > TECHIE

TECHIEST > TECHY

TECHILY > TECHY

TECHINESS > TECHY

TECHNIC another word for > TECHNIQUE

TECHNICAL adj of or specializing in industrial, practical, or mechanical arts and applied sciences ▷ n small armed military truck

TECHNICS n study or theory of industry and industrial arts

TECHNIKON n technical college

TECHNIQUE n method or skill used for a particular task

TECHNO n type of electronic dance music with a very fast beat

TECHNOID n technician

TECHNOIDS > TECHNOID

TECHNOPOP n pop music sharing certain features with techno

TECHNOS > TECHNO

TECHS > TECH

TECHY same as > TECHIE

TECKEL n dachshund

TECKELS > TECKEL

TECS > TEC

TECTA > TECTUM

TECTAL > TECTUM

TECTIFORM adj in the form of a roof

TECTITE same as > TEKTITE

TECTITES > TECTITE

TECTONIC adj denoting or relating to construction or building

TECTONICS n study of the earth's crust and the forces affecting it

TECTONISM > TECTONIC

TECTORIAL adj as in tectorial membrane membrane in the inner ear that covers the organ of Corti

TECTRICES > TECTRIX

TECTRIX another name for > COVERT

TECTUM n any roof-like structure in the body

TECTUMS > TECTUM

TED vb shake out (hay), so as to dry it

TEDDED > TED

TEDDER n machine equipped with a series of small rotating forks for tedding hay

TEDDERED > TEDDER

TEDDERING > TEDDER

TEDDERS > TEDDER

TEDDIE same as > TEDDY

TEDDIES > TEDDY

TEDDING > TED

TEDDY n teddy bear

TEDIER > TEDY

TEDIEST > TEDY

TEDIOSITY > TEDIOUS

TEDIOUS adj causing fatigue or boredom

TEDIOUSLY > TEDIOUS

TEDISOME old Scottish variant of > TEDIOUS

TEDIUM n monotony

TEDIUMS > TEDIUM

TEDS > TED

TEDY same as > TEDIOUS

TEE n small peg from which a golf ball can be played at the start of each hole ▷ vb position (the ball) ready for striking, on or as if on a tee

TEED > TEE

TEEING > TEE

TEEK adj in Indian English, well

TEEL same as > SESAME

TEELS > TEEL

TEEM vb be full of

TEEMED > TEEM

TEEMER > TEEM

TEEMERS > TEEM

TEEMFUL > TEEM

TEEMING > TEEM

TEEMINGLY > TEEM

TEEMLESS > TEEM

TEEMS > TEEM

TEEN n affliction or woe ▷ n teenager ▷ vb set alight

TEENAGE adj (of a person) aged between 13 and 19 ▷ n this period of time

TEENAGED adj (of a person) aged between 13 and 19

TEENAGER n person aged between 13 and 19

TEENAGERS > TEENAGER

TEENAGES > TEENAGE

TEEND same as > TIND

TEENDED > TEEND

TEENDING > TEEND

TEENDOM n state of being a teenager

TEENDOMS > TEENDOM

TEENDS > TEEND

TEENE same as > TEEN

TEENED > TEEN

TEENER > TEEN

TEENERS > TEEN

TEENES > TEENE

TEENFUL > TEEN

TEENIER > TEENY

TEENIEST > TEENY

TEENING > TEEN

TEENS > TEEN

TEENSIER > TEENSY

TEENSIEST > TEENSY

TEENSY same as > TEENY

TEENTIER > TEENTY

TEENTIEST > TEENTY

TEENTSIER > TEENTSY

TEENTSY same as > TEENY

TEENTY same as > TEENY

TEENY adj extremely small

TEENYBOP adj of, or relating to, a young teenager who avidly follows fashions in music and clothes

TEEPEE same as > TEPEE

TEEPEES > TEEPEE

TEER vb smear; daub

TEERED > TEER

TEERING > TEER

TEERS > TEER

TEES > TEE

TEETER vb wobble or move unsteadily

TEETERED > TEETER

TEETERING > TEETER

TEETERS > TEETER

TEETH > TOOTH

TEETHE vb (of a baby) grow his or her first teeth

TEETHED > TEETHE

TEETHER n object for an infant to bite on during teething

TEETHERS > TEETHER

TEETHES > TEETHE

TEETHING > TEETHE

TEETHINGS > TEETHING

TEETHLESS > TEETH

TEETOTAL adj drinking no alcohol ▷ vb advocate total abstinence from alcohol

TEETOTALS > TEETOTAL

TEETOTUM n spinning top bearing letters of the alphabet on its four sides

TEETOTUMS > TEETOTUM

TEEVEE n television

TEEVEES > TEEVEE

TEF n annual grass, of NE Africa, grown for its grain

TEFF same as > TEF

TEFFS > TEFF

TEFILLAH n either of the pair of blackened square cases containing parchments inscribed with biblical passages, bound by leather thongs to the head and left arm, and worn by Jewish men during weekday morning prayers

TEFILLIN > TEFILLAH

TEFLON n substance used in nonstick cooking vessels

TEFLONS > TEFLON

TEFS > TEF

TEG n two-year-old sheep

TEGG same as > TEG

TEGGS > TEGG

TEGMEN n either of the leathery forewings of the cockroach and related insects

TEGMENTA > TEGMENTUM

TEGMENTAL > TEGMENTUM

TEGMENTUM n one of the hard protective sometimes hairy or resinous specialized leaves surrounding the buds of certain plants

TEGMINA > TEGMEN

TEGMINAL > TEGMEN

TEGS > TEG

TEGU n large South American lizard

TEGUA n type of moccasin

TEGUAS > TEGUA

TEGUEXIN same as > TEGU

TEGUEXINS > TEGUEXIN

TEGULA n one of a pair of coverings of the forewings of certain insects

TEGULAE > TEGULA

TEGULAR adj of, relating to, or resembling a tile or tiles

TEGULARLY > TEGULAR

TEGULATED adj overlapping in the manner of roof tiles

TEGUMEN same as > TEGMEN

TEGUMENT n protective layer around an ovule

TEGUMENTS > TEGUMENT

TEGUMINA > TEGUMEN

TEGUS > TEGU

TEHR same as > TAHR

TEHRS > TEHR

TEHSIL n administrative region in some S Asian countries

TEHSILDAR n person who administrates a tehsil

TEHSILS > TEHSIL

TEIGLACH pl n morsels of dough boiled in honey, eaten as a dessert

TEIID n member of the Teiidae family of lizards

TEIIDS > TEIID

TEIL n lime tree

TEILS > TEIL

TEIN n monetary unit of Kazakhstan

TEIND Scot and northern English word for > TITHE

TEINDED > TEIND

TEINDING > TEIND

TEINDS > TEIND

TEINS > TEIN

TEKKIE variant of > TECHIE

TEKKIES > TEKKIE

TEKNONYMY n practice of naming a child after his or her parent

TEKTITE n small dark glassy object found in several areas around the world

TEKTITES > TEKTITE

TEKTITIC > TEKTITE

TEL same as > TELL

TELA n any delicate tissue or weblike structure

TELAE > TELA

TELAMON n column in the form of a male figure

TELAMONES > TELAMON

TELAMONS > TELAMON

TELARY adj capable of spinning a web

TELCO n telecommunications company

TELCOS > TELCO

TELD same as > TAULD

TELE same as > TELLY

TELECAST vb broadcast by television ▷ n television broadcast

TELECASTS > TELECAST

TELECHIR n robot arm controlled by a human operator

TELECHIRS > TELECHIR

TELECINE n apparatus for producing a television signal from cinematograph film

TELECINES > TELECINE

TELECOM n telecommunications

TELECOMM n telecommunication

TELECOMMS > TELECOMM

TELECOMS same as > TELECOM

TELECON n (short for) teleconference

TELECONS > TELECON

TELECOPY n message or document sent by fax

TELEDU n badger of SE Asia and Indonesia

TELEDUS > TELEDU

TELEFAX another word for > FAX

TELEFAXED > TELEFAX

TELEFAXES > TELEFAX

TELEFILM n TV movie

TELEFILMS > TELEFILM

TELEGA n rough four-wheeled cart used in Russia

TELEGAS > TELEGA

TELEGENIC adj having or showing a pleasant television image

TELEGONIC > TELEGONY

TELEGONY n supposed influence of a previous sire on offspring borne by a female to other sires

TELEGRAM n formerly, a message sent by telegraph ▷ vb send a telegram

TELEGRAMS > TELEGRAM

TELEGRAPH n formerly, a system for sending messages over a distance along a cable ▷ vb communicate by telegraph

TELEMAN n noncommissioned officer in the US navy

TELEMARK n turn in which one ski is placed far forward of the other and turned gradually inwards ▷ vb perform a telemark turn

TELEMARKS > TELEMARK

TELEMATIC adj of, or relating to, the branch of science concerned with the use of technological devices to transmit information over long distances

TELEMEN > TELEMAN

TELEMETER n any device for recording or measuring a distant event and transmitting the data to a receiver or observer ▷ vb obtain and transmit (data) from a distant source, esp from a spacecraft

TELEMETRY n use of electronic devices to record or measure a distant event and transmit the data to a receiver

TELEOLOGY n belief that all things have a predetermined purpose

TELEONOMY n condition of having a fundamental purpose

TELEOSAUR n type of crocodile from the Jurassic period

TELEOST n bony fish with rayed fins and a swim bladder ▷ adj of, relating to, or belonging to this type of fish

TELEOSTS > TELEOST

TELEPATH n person who is telepathic ▷ vb practise telepathy

TELEPATHS > TELEPATH

TELEPATHY n direct communication between minds

TELEPHEME n any message sent by telephone

TELEPHONE n device for transmitting sound over a distance along wires ▷ vb call or talk to (a person) by telephone ▷ adj of or using a telephone

TELEPHONY n system of telecommunications for the transmission of speech or other sounds

TELEPHOTO n short for telephoto lens: a compound camera lens that produces a magnified image of distant objects

TELEPIC n feature-length film made for television

TELEPICS > TELEPIC

TELEPLAY n play written for television

TELEPLAYS > TELEPLAY

TELEPOINT n system providing a place where a cordless telephone can be connected to a telephone network

TELEPORT vb (in science fiction) to transport (a person or object) across a distance instantaneously

TELEPORTS > TELEPORT

TELEPRINT vb print (a message) with a teleprinter

TELERAN n electronic navigational aid

TELERANS > TELERAN

TELERGIC > TELERGY

TELERGIES > TELERGY

TELERGY n name for the form of energy supposedly transferred during telepathy

TELES > TELE

TELESALE > TELESALES

TELESALES n selling of a product or service by telephone

TELESCOPE n optical instrument for magnifying distant objects ▷ vb shorten

TELESCOPY n branch of astronomy concerned with the use and design of telescopes

TELESEME n old-fashioned electric signalling system

TELESEMES > TELESEME

TELESES > TELESIS

TELESHOP vb buy goods by telephone or Internet

TELESHOPS > TELESHOP

TELESIS n purposeful use of natural and social processes to obtain specific social goals

TELESM n talisman

TELESMS > TELESM

TELESTIC adj relating to a hierophant

TELESTICH n short poem in which the last letters of each successive line form a word

TELESTICS n ancient pseudoscientific art of animating statues, idols, etc, or causing them to be inhabited by a deity

TELETEX n international means of communicating text between a variety of terminals

TELETEXES > TELETEX

TELETEXT n system which shows information and news on television screens

TELETEXTS > TELETEXT

TELETHON n lengthy television programme to raise charity funds, etc

TELETHONS > TELETHON

TELETRON n system for showing enlarged televisual images in eg sports stadiums

TELETRONS > TELETRON

TELETYPE vb send typed message by telegraph

TELETYPED > TELETYPE

TELETYPES > TELETYPE

TELEVIEW vb watch television

TELEVIEWS > TELEVIEW

TELEVISE vb broadcast on television

TELEVISED > TELEVISE

TELEVISER > TELEVISE

TELEVISES > TELEVISE

TELEVISOR n apparatus through which one transmits or receives televisual images

TELEWORK vb work from home, communicating by computer, telephone etc

TELEWORKS > TELEWORK

TELEX n international communication service using teleprinters ▷ vb transmit by telex

TELEXED > TELEX

TELEXES > TELEX

TELEXING > TELEX

TELFER n overhead transport system

TELFERAGE n overhead transport system in which an electrically driven truck runs along a single rail or

cable, the lo... suspended in... car beneath ...

TELFERED > TE...

TELFERIC > TEL...

TELFERING > TEL...

TELFERS > TELFER

TELFORD n road built... using a method favour... by Thomas Telford

TELFORDS > TELFORD

TELIA > TELIUM

TELIAL > TELIUM

TELIC adj directed or moving towards some goal

TELICALLY > TELIC

TELICITY n quality of being telic

TELIUM n spore-producing body of some rust fungi in which the teliospores are formed

TELL vb make known in words ▷ n large mound resulting from the accumulation of rubbish

TELLABLE > TELL

TELLAR same as > TILLER

TELLARED > TELLAR

TELLARING > TELLAR

TELLARS > TELLAR

TELLEN same as > TELLIN

TELLENS > TELLEN

TELLER n narrator ▷ vb (of a plant) to produce tillers

TELLERED > TELLER

TELLERING > TELLER

TELLERS > TELLER

TELLIES > TELLY

TELLIN n slim marine bivalve molluscs that live in intertidal sand

TELLING > TELL

TELLINGLY > TELL

TELLINGS > TELL

TELLINOID > TELLIN

TELLINS > TELLIN

TELLS > TELL

TELLTALE n person who reveals secrets ▷ adj revealing

TELLTALES > TELLTALE

TELLURAL adj tellurial; of or relating to the earth

TELLURATE n any salt or ester of telluric acid

TELLURIAN same as > TELLURION

TELLURIC adj of, relating to, or originating on or in the earth or soil

TELLURIDE n any compound of tellurium, esp one formed between tellurium and a more electropositive element or group

TELLURION n instrument that shows how day and night and the seasons result from the tilt of the earth, its rotation on its axis, and its revolution around the sun

TELLURISE same as > TELLURIZE

TELLURITE n any salt or of tellurous acid

TELLURIUM n brittle silvery-white nonmetallic element

TELLURIZE vb mix or combine with tellurium

TELLUROUS adj of or containing tellurium, esp in a low valence state

TELLUS n earth

TELLUSES > TELLUS

TELLY n television

TELLYS > TELLY

TELNET n system allowing remote access to other computers on the same network ▷ vb use a telnet system

TELNETED > TELNET

TELNETING > TELNET

TELNETS > TELNET

TELNETTED > TELNET

TELOI > TELOS

TELOME n fundamental unit of a plant's structure

TELOMERE n either of the ends of a chromosome

TELOMERES > TELOMERE

TELOMES > TELOME

TELOMIC > TELOME

TELOPHASE n final stage of mitosis, during which a set of chromosomes is present at each end of the cell and a nuclear membrane forms around each, producing two new nuclei

TELOS n objective; ultimate purpose

TELOTAXES > TELOTAXIS

TELOTAXIS n movement of an organism in response to one particular stimulus, overriding any response to other stimuli present

TELPHER same as > TELFERAGE

TELPHERED > TELPHER

TELPHERIC > TELPHER

TELPHERS > TELPHER

TELS > TEL

TELSON n segment of the body of crustaceans and arachnids

TELSONIC > TELSON

TELSONS > TELSON

TELT same as > TAULD

TEMAZEPAM n sedative in the form of a gel-like capsule, which is taken orally or melted and injected by drug users

TEMBLOR n earthquake or earth tremor

TEMBLORES > TEMBLOR

TEMBLORS > TEMBLOR

TEME old variant of > TEAM

TEMED > TEME

TEMENE > TEMENOS

TEMENOS n sacred area, esp one surrounding a temple

TEMERITY n boldness or audacity

TEMEROUS > TEMERITY

TEMES > TEME

TEMP same as > TEMPORARY

TEMPED > TEMP

TEMPEH n fermented soya beans

TEMPEHS > TEMPEH

TEMPER n outburst of anger ▷ vb make less extreme

TEMPERA n painting medium for powdered pigments

TEMPERAS > TEMPERA

TEMPERATE adj (of climate) not extreme ▷ vb temper

TEMPERED adj (of a scale) having the frequency differences between notes adjusted in accordance with the system of equal temperament

TEMPERER > TEMPER

TEMPERERS > TEMPER

TEMPERING > TEMPER

TEMPERS > TEMPER

TEMPEST n violent storm ▷ vb agitate or disturb violently

TEMPESTED > TEMPEST

TEMPESTS > TEMPEST

TEMPI > TEMPO

TEMPING n act of temping

TEMPINGS > TEMPING

TEMPLAR n lawyer who has chambers in the Inner or Middle Temple in London

TEMPLARS > TEMPLAR

TEMPLATE n pattern used to cut out shapes accurately

TEMPLATES > TEMPLATE

TEMPLE n building for worship

TEMPLED > TEMPLE

TEMPLES > TEMPLE

TEMPLET same as > TEMPLATE

TEMPLETS > TEMPLET

TEMPO n rate or pace

TEMPORAL adj of time ▷ n any body part relating to or near the temple or temples

TEMPORALS > TEMPORAL

TEMPORARY adj lasting only for a short time ▷ n person, esp a secretary or other office worker, employed on a temporary basis

TEMPORE adv in the time of

TEMPORISE same as > TEMPORIZE

TEMPORIZE vb gain time by negotiation or evasiveness

TEMPOS > TEMPO

TEMPS > TEMP

TEMPT vb entice (a person) to do something wrong

TEMPTABLE > TEMPT

TEMPTED > TEMPT

TEMPTER > TEMPT

TEMPTERS > TEMPT

TEMPTING adj attractive or inviting

TEMPTINGS > TEMPTING

TEMPTRESS n woman who sets out to allure or seduce a man or men

TEMPTS > TEMPT

TEMPURA n Japanese dish of seafood or vegetables dipped in batter and deep-fried

TEMPURAS > TEMPURA

TEMS same as > TEMSE

TEMSE vb sieve

TEMSED > TEMSE

TEMSES > TEMSE

TEMSING > TEMSE

TEMULENCE n drunkenness

TEMULENCE same as > TEMULENCE

TEMULENT > TEMULENCE

TEN n one more than nine ▷ adj amounting to ten

TENABLE adj able to be upheld or maintained

TENABLY > TENABLE

TENACE n holding of two nonconsecutive high cards of a suit, such as the ace and queen

TENACES > TENACE

TENACIOUS adj holding fast

TENACITY > TENACIOUS

TENACULA > TENACULUM

TENACULUM n surgical or dissecting instrument for grasping and holding parts, consisting of a slender hook mounted in a handle

TENAIL same as > TENAILLE

TENAILLE n low outwork in the main ditch between two bastions

TENAILLES > TENAILLE

TENAILLON n outwork shoring up a ravelin

TENAILS > TENAIL

TENANCIES > TENANCY

TENANCY n temporary possession of property owned by somebody else

TENANT n person who rents land or a building ▷ vb hold (land or property) as a tenant

TENANTED > TENANT

TENANTING > TENANT

TENANTRY n tenants collectively

TENANTS > TENANT

TENCH n freshwater game fish of the carp family

TENCHES > TENCH

TEND vb be inclined

TENDANCE n care and attention

TENDANCES > TENDANCE

TENDED > TEND

TENDENCE same as > TENDENCY

TENDENCES > TENDENCE

TENDENCY n inclination to act in a certain way

TENDENZ same as > TENDENCY

TENDENZEN > TENDENZ

TENDER adj not tough ▷ vb offer ▷ n such an offer

TENDERED > TENDER

TENDERER > TENDER

TENDERERS > TENDER

TENDEREST > TENDER

TENDERING > TENDER

TENDERISE same as > TENDERIZE

TENDERIZE vb soften (meat) by pounding or treatment with a special substance

TENDERLY > TENDER

TENDERS > TENDER

TENDING > TEND

TENDINOUS adj of, relating to, possessing, or resembling tendons

TENDON n strong tissue attaching a muscle to a bone

TENDONS > TENDON

TENDRE n care

TENDRES > TENDRE

TENDRESSE n feeling of love; tenderness

TENDRIL n slender stem by which a climbing plant clings

TENDRILED > TENDRIL

TENDRILLY adj of or similar to a tendril

TENDRILS > TENDRIL

TENDRON n shoot

TENDRONS > TENDRON

TENDS > TEND

TENDU n position in ballet

TENDUS > TENDU

TENE same as > TEEN

TENEBRAE n darkness

TENEBRIO n type of small mealworm

TENEBRIOS > TENEBRIO

TENEBRISM n school, style, or method of painting, adopted chiefly by 17th-century Spanish and Neapolitan painters, esp Caravaggio, characterized by large areas of dark colours, usually relieved with a shaft of light

TENEBRIST > TENEBRISM

t

TENEBRITY n darkness; gloominess

TENEBROSE same as > TENEBROUS

TENEBROUS adj gloomy, shadowy, or dark

TENEMENT n (esp in Scotland or the US) building divided into several flats

TENEMENTS > TENEMENT

TENENDUM n part of a deed that specifies the terms of tenure

TENENDUMS > TENENDUM

TENES > TENE

TENESI n monetary unit of Turkmenistan

TENESMIC > TENESMUS

TENESMUS n bowel disorder

TENET n doctrine or belief

TENETS > TENET

TENFOLD n one tenth

TENFOLDS > TENFOLD

TENGE n standard monetary unit of Kazakhstan

TENGES > TENGE

TENIA same as > TAENIA

TENIACIDE n substance, esp a drug, that kills tapeworms

TENIAE > TENIA

TENIAFUGE same as > TENIACIDE

TENIAS > TENIA

TENIASES > TENIASIS

TENIASIS same as > TAENIASIS

TENIOID > TENIA

TENNE n tawny colour

TENNER n ten-pound note

TENNERS > TENNER

TENNES > TENNE

TENNESI same as > TENESI

TENNIES > TENNY

TENNIS n game in which players use rackets to hit a ball back and forth over a net

TENNISES > TENNIS

TENNIST n tennis player

TENNISTS > TENNIST

TENNO n formal title of the Japanese emperor

TENNOS > TENNO

TENNY same as > TENNE

TENON n projecting end on a piece of wood fitting into a slot in another ▷ vb form a tenon on (a piece of wood)

TENONED > TENON

TENONER > TENON

TENONERS > TENON

TENONING > TENON

TENONS > TENON

TENOR n (singer with) the second highest male voice ▷ adj (of a voice or instrument) between alto and baritone

TENORINI > TENORINO

TENORINO n high tenor

TENORIST n musician playing any tenor instrument

TENORISTS > TENORIST

TENORITE n black mineral found in copper deposits and consisting of copper oxide in the form of either metallic scales or earthy masses. Formula: CuO

TENORITES > TENORITE

TENORLESS > TENOR

TENORMAN n person who plays tenor saxophone

TENORMEN > TENORMAN

TENOROON n tenor bassoon

TENOROONS > TENOROON

TENORS > TENOR

TENOTOMY n surgical division of a tendon

TENOUR old variant of > TENOR

TENOURS > TENOUR

TENPENCE n sum of money equivalent to ten pennies

TENPENCES > TENPENCE

TENPENNY adj (of a nail) three inches in length

TENPIN n one of the pins used in tenpin bowling

TENPINS > TENPIN

TENREC n small mammal resembling hedgehogs or shrews

TENRECS > TENREC

TENS > TEN

TENSE adj emotionally strained ▷ vb make or become tense ▷ n form of a verb showing the time of action

TENSED > TENSE

TENSELESS > TENSE

TENSELY > TENSE

TENSENESS > TENSE

TENSER > TENSE

TENSES > TENSE

TENSEST > TENSE

TENSIBLE adj capable of being stretched

TENSIBLY > TENSIBLE

TENSILE adj of tension

TENSILELY > TENSILE

TENSILITY > TENSILE

TENSING > TENSE

TENSION n hostility or suspense ▷ vb tighten

TENSIONAL > TENSION

TENSIONED > TENSION

TENSIONER > TENSION

TENSIONS > TENSION

TENSITIES > TENSITY

TENSITY rare word for > TENSION

TENSIVE adj of or causing tension or strain

TENSON n type of French lyric poem

TENSONS > TENSON

TENSOR n any muscle that can cause a part to become firm or tense

TENSORIAL > TENSOR

TENSORS > TENSOR

TENT n portable canvas shelter ▷ vb camp in a tent

TENTACLE n flexible organ of many invertebrates, used for grasping, feeding, etc

TENTACLED > TENTACLE

TENTACLES > TENTACLE

TENTACULA > TENTACLE

TENTAGE n tents collectively

TENTAGES > TENTAGE

TENTATION n method of achieving the correct adjustment of a mechanical device by a series of trials

TENTATIVE adj provisional or experimental ▷ n investigative attempt

TENTED > TENT

TENTER > TENT

TENTERED > TENT

TENTERING > TENT

TENTERS > TENT

TENTFUL n number of people or objects that can fit in a tent

TENTFULS > TENTFUL

TENTH n (of) number ten in a series ▷ adj coming after the ninth in numbering or counting order, position, time, etc ▷ adv after the ninth person, position, event, etc

TENTHLY same as > TENTH

TENTHS > TENTH

TENTIE adj wary

TENTIER > TENTIE

TENTIEST > TENTIE

TENTIGO n morbid preoccupation with sex

TENTIGOS > TENTIGO

TENTING > TENT

TENTINGS > TENT

TENTLESS > TENT

TENTLIKE > TENT

TENTMAKER n maker of tents

TENTORIA > TENTORIUM

TENTORIAL > TENTORIUM

TENTORIUM n tough membrane covering the upper part of the cerebellum

TENTPOLE n movie whose high earnings offset the cost of less profitable ones

TENTPOLES > TENTPOLE

TENTS > TENT

TENTWISE adv in the manner of a tent

TENTY same as > TENTIE

TENUE n deportment

TENUES > TENUIS

TENUIOUS same as > TENUOUS

TENUIS n (in grammar of classical Greek) the voiceless sto... of

TENUITIES > TE...

TENUITY > TENUO...

TENUOUS adj slight or flimsy

TENUOUSLY > TENUOUS

TENURABLE > TENURE

TENURE n (period of) the holding of an office or position ▷ vb assign a tenured position to

TENURED adj having tenure of office

TENURES > TENURE

TENURIAL > TENURE

TENURING > TENURE

TENUTI > TENUTO

TENUTO adv (of a note) to be held for or beyond its full time value ▷ vb note sustained thus

TENUTOS > TENUTO

TENZON same as > TENSON

TENZONS > TENZON

TEOCALLI n any of various truncated pyramids built by the Aztecs as bases for their temples

TEOCALLIS > TEOCALLI

TEOPAN n enclosure surrounding a teocalli

TEOPANS > TEOPAN

TEOSINTE n tall Central American annual grass, related to maize and grown for forage in the southern US

TEOSINTES > TEOSINTE

TEPA n type of tree native to South America

TEPACHE n type of Mexican soft drink

TEPACHES > TEPACHE

TEPAL n subdivisions of a perianth

TEPALS > TEPAL

TEPAS > TEPA

TEPEE n cone-shaped tent, formerly used by Native Americans

TEPEES > TEPEE

TEPEFIED > TEPEFY

TEPEFIES > TEPEFY

TEPEFY vb make or become tepid

TEPEFYING > TEPEFY

TEPHIGRAM n chart depicting variations in atmospheric conditions relative to altitude

TEPHILLAH same as > TEFILLAH

TEPHILLIN > TEPHILLAH

TEPHRA n solid matter ejected during a volcanic eruption

TEPHRAS > TEPHRA

TEPHRITE n variety of basalt

TEPHRITES > TEPHRITE

t

TEPHRITIC > TEPHRITE

TEPHRITE n manganese ite

TEPID adj slightly warm

TEPIDARIA pl n in Ancient Rome, the warm rooms of the baths

TEPIDER > TEPID

TEPIDEST > TEPID

TEPIDITY > TEPID

TEPIDLY > TEPID

TEPIDNESS > TEPID

TEPOY same as > TEAPOY

TEPOYS > TEPOY

TEQUILA n Mexican alcoholic drink

TEQUILAS > TEQUILA

TEQUILLA same as > TEQUILA

TEQUILLAS > TEQUILLA

TERABYTE n large unit of computer memory

TERABYTES > TERABYTE

TERAFLOP n measure of processing speed, consisting of a thousand billion floating-point operations a second

TERAFLOPS > TERAFLOP

TERAGLIN n edible marine fish of Australia which has fine scales and is blue in colour

TERAGLINS > TERAGLIN

TERAHERTZ n large unit of electrical frequency

TERAI n felt hat with a wide brim worn in subtropical regions

TERAIS > TERAI

TERAKIHI same as > TARAKIHI

TERAKIHIS > TERAKIHI

TERAOHM n unit of resistance equal to 10^{12} ohms

TERAOHMS > TERAOHM

TERAPH n household god or image venerated by ancient Semitic peoples

TERAPHIM > TERAPH

TERAPHIMS > TERAPH

TERAS n monstrosity; teratism

TERATA > TERAS

TERATISM n malformed animal or human, esp in the fetal stage

TERATISMS > TERATISM

TERATOGEN n any substance, organism, or process that causes malformations in a fetus

TERATOID adj resembling a monster

TERATOMA n tumour or group of tumours composed of tissue foreign to the site of growth

TERATOMAS > TERATOMA

TERAWATT n unit of power equal to one million megawatts

TERAWATTS > TERAWATT

TERBIA n amorphous white insoluble powder

TERBIAS > TERBIA

TERBIC > TERBIUM

TERBIUM n rare metallic element

TERBIUMS > TERBIUM

TERCE n third of the seven canonical hours of the divine office

TERCEL n male falcon or hawk, esp as used in falconry

TERCELET same as > TERCEL

TERCELETS > TERCELET

TERCELS > TERCEL

TERCES > TERCE

TERCET n group of three lines of verse that rhyme together

TERCETS > TERCET

TERCIO n regiment of Spanish or Italian infantry

TERCIOS > TERCIO

TEREBENE n mixture of hydrocarbons prepared from oil of turpentine and sulphuric acid, used to make paints and varnishes and medicinally as an expectorant and antiseptic

TEREBENES > TEREBENE

TEREBIC adj as in terebic acid white crystalline carboxylic acid produced by the action of nitric acid on turpentin

TEREBINTH n small anacardiaceous tree with winged leafstalks and clusters of small flowers, and yielding a turpentine

TEREBRA n ancient Roman device used for boring holes in defensive walls

TEREBRAE > TEREBRA

TEREBRANT n type of hymenopterous insect

TEREBRAS > TEREBRA

TEREBRATE adj (of animals, esp insects) having a boring or penetrating organ, such as a sting ▷ vb bore

TEREDINES > TEREDO

TEREDO n marine mollusc that bores into and destroys submerged timber

TEREDOS > TEREDO

TEREFA same as > TREF

TEREFAH same as > TREF

TEREK n type of sandpiper

TEREKS > TEREK

TERES n shoulder muscle

TERESES > TERES

TERETE adj (esp of plant parts) smooth and usually cylindrical and tapering

TERETES > TERETE

TERF old variant of > TURF

TERFE old variant of > TURF

TERFES > TERFE

TERFS > TERF

TERGA > TERGUM

TERGAL > TERGUM

TERGITE n constituent part of a tergum

TERGITES > TERGITE

TERGUM n cuticular plate covering the dorsal surface of a body segment of an arthropod

TERIYAKI adj basted with soy sauce and rice wine and broiled over an open fire ▷ n dish prepared in this way

TERIYAKIS > TERIYAKI

TERM n word or expression ▷ vb name or designate

TERMAGANT n unpleasant and bad-tempered woman

TERMED > TERM

TERMER same as > TERMOR

TERMERS > TERMER

TERMINAL adj (of an illness) ending in death ▷ n place where people or vehicles begin or end a journey

TERMINALS > TERMINAL

TERMINATE vb bring or come to an end

TERMINER n person or thing that limits or determines

TERMINERS > TERMINER

TERMING > TERM

TERMINI > TERMINUS

TERMINISM n philosophical theory

TERMINIST > TERMINIST

TERMINUS n railway or bus station at the end of a line

TERMITARY n termite nest

TERMITE n white antlike insect that destroys timber

TERMITES > TERMITE

TERMITIC > TERMITE

TERMLESS adj without limit or boundary

TERMLIES > TERMLY

TERMLY n publication issued once a term

TERMOR n person who holds an estate for a term of years or until he dies

TERMORS > TERMOR

TERMS > TERM

TERMTIME n time during a term, esp a school or university term

TERMTIMES > TERMTIME

TERN n gull-like sea bird with a forked tail and pointed wings

TERNAL > TERN

TERNARIES > TERNARY

TERNARY adj consisting of three parts ▷ n group of three

TERNATE adj (esp of a leaf) consisting of three leaflets or other parts

TERNATELY > TERNATE

TERNE n alloy of lead containing tin and antimony ▷ vb coat with this alloy

TERNED > TERNE

TERNES > TERNE

TERNING > TERNE

TERNION n group of three

TERNIONS > TERNION

TERNS > TERN

TERPENE n unsaturated hydrocarbon found in the essential oils of many plants

TERPENES > TERPENE

TERPENIC > TERPENE

TERPENOID > TERPENE

TERPINEOL n terpene alcohol with an odour of lilac, present in several essential oils

TERPINOL same as > TERPINEOL

TERPINOLS > TERPINOL

TERRA n (in legal contexts) earth or land

TERRACE n row of houses built as one block ▷ vb form into or provide with a terrace

TERRACED > TERRACE

TERRACES > TERRACE

TERRACING n series of terraces, esp one dividing a slope into a steplike system of flat narrow fields

TERRAE > TERRA

TERRAFORM vb engage in planetary engineering to enhance the capacity of an extraterrestrial planetary environment to sustain life

TERRAIN same as > TERRANE

TERRAINS > TERRAIN

TERRAMARA n neolithic Italian pile-dwelling

TERRAMARE > TERRAMARA

TERRANE n series of rock formations

TERRANES > TERRANE

TERRAPIN n small turtle-like reptile

TERRAPINS > TERRAPIN

TERRARIA > TERRARIUM

TERRARIUM n enclosed container for small plants or animals

TERRAS same as > TRASS

TERRASES > TERRAS

TERRASSE n paved area alongside a café

TERRAZZO n floor of marble chips set in mortar and polished

TERRAZZOS > TERRAZZO
TERREEN old variant of > TUREEN
TERREENS > TERREEN
TERRELLA n magnetic globe designed to simulate and demonstrate the earth's magnetic fields
TERRELLAS > TERRELLA
TERRENE adj of or relating to the earth ⊳ n land
TERRENELY > TERRENE
TERRENES > TERRENE
TERRET n ring on a harness saddle through which the reins are passed
TERRETS > TERRET
TERRIBLE adj very serious ⊳ n something terrible
TERRIBLES > TERRIBLE
TERRIBLY adv in a terrible manner
TERRICOLE n plant or animal living on land
TERRIER n any of various breeds of small active dog
TERRIERS > TERRIER
TERRIES > TERRY
TERRIFIC adj great or intense
TERRIFIED > TERRIFY
TERRIFIER > TERRIFY
TERRIFIES > TERRIFY
TERRIFY vb fill with fear
TERRINE n earthenware dish with a lid
TERRINES > TERRINE
TERRIT same as > TERRET
TERRITORY n district
TERRITS > TERRIT
TERROIR n combination of factors that gives a wine its distinctive character
TERROIRS > TERROIR
TERROR n great fear
TERRORFUL > TERROR
TERRORISE same as > TERRORIZE
TERRORISM n use of violence and intimidation to achieve political ends
TERRORIST n person who employs terror or terrorism, esp as a political weapon
TERRORIZE vb force or oppress by fear or violence
TERRORS > TERROR
TERRY n fabric with small loops covering both sides
TERSE adj neat and concise
TERSELY > TERSE
TERSENESS > TERSE
TERSER > TERSE
TERSEST > TERSE
TERSION n action of rubbing off or wiping
TERSIONS > TERSION
TERTIA same as > TERCIO
TERTIAL same as > TERTIARY
TERTIALS > TERTIAL

TERTIAN adj (of a fever or the symptoms of a disease) occurring every other day ⊳ n tertian fever or symptoms
TERTIANS > TERTIAN
TERTIARY adj third in degree, order, etc ⊳ n any of the tertiary feathers
TERTIAS > TERTIA
TERTIUM adj as in tertium quid unknown or indefinite thing related in some way to two known or definite things, but distinct from both
TERTIUS n third (in a group)
TERTIUSES > TERTIUS
TERTS n card game using 32 cards
TERVALENT same as > TRIVALENT
TERYLENE n tradename for a synthetic polyester fibre or fabric based on terephthalic acid, characterized by lightness and crease resistance and used for clothing, sheets, ropes, sails, etc
TERYLENES > TERYLENE
TERZETTA n tercet
TERZETTAS > TERZETTA
TERZETTI > TERZETTO
TERZETTO n trio, esp a vocal one
TERZETTOS > TERZETTO
TES > TE
TESLA n derived SI unit of magnetic flux density
TESLAS > TESLA
TESSELATE vb cover with small tiles
TESSELLA n little tessera
TESSELLAE > TESSELLA
TESSELLAR adj of or relating to tessellae
TESSERA n small square tile used in mosaics
TESSERACT n cube inside another cube
TESSERAE > TESSERA
TESSERAL > TESSERA
TESSITURA n general pitch level of a piece of vocal music
TESSITURE > TESSITURA
TEST vb try out to ascertain the worth, capability, or endurance of ⊳ n critical examination
TESTA n hard outer layer of a seed
TESTABLE > TEST
TESTACEAN n microscopic animal with hard shell
TESTACIES > TESTATE
TESTACY > TESTATE
TESTAE > TESTA
TESTAMENT n proof or tribute

TESTAMUR n certificate proving an examination has been passed
TESTAMURS > TESTAMUR
TESTATE adj having left a valid will ⊳ n person who dies and leaves a legally valid will
TESTATES > TESTATE
TESTATION > TESTATOR
TESTATOR n maker of a will
TESTATORS > TESTATOR
TESTATRIX same as > TESTATOR
TESTATUM n part of a purchase deed
TESTATUMS > TESTATUM
TESTCROSS vb subject to a testcross, a genetic test for ascertaining whether an individual is homozygous or heterozygous
TESTE n witness
TESTED > TEST
TESTEE n person subjected to a test
TESTEES > TESTEE
TESTER n person or thing that tests or is used for testing
TESTERN vb give (someone) a teston
TESTERNED > TESTERN
TESTERNS > TESTERN
TESTERS > TESTER
TESTES > TESTIS
TESTICLE n either of the two male reproductive glands
TESTICLES > TESTICLE
TESTIER > TESTY
TESTIEST > TESTY
TESTIFIED > TESTIFY
TESTIFIER > TESTIFY
TESTIFIES > TESTIFY
TESTIFY vb give evidence under oath
TESTILY > TESTY
TESTIMONY n declaration of truth or fact ⊳ vb testify
TESTINESS > TESTY
TESTING > TEST
TESTINGS > TEST
TESTIS same as > TESTICLE
TESTON n French silver coin of the 16th century
TESTONS > TESTON
TESTOON same as > TESTON
TESTOONS > TESTOON
TESTRIL same as > TESTRILL
TESTRILL n sixpence
TESTRILLS > TESTRILL
TESTRILS > TESTRIL
TESTS > TEST
TESTUDO n protective cover used by the ancient Roman army
TESTUDOS > TESTUDO

TESTY adj irrit[...] touchy
TET same as > TET[...]
TETANAL > TETAN[...]
TETANIC adj of, relat[...] to, or producing tetan[...] the spasms of tetanus ⊳ n tetanic drug or agent
TETANICAL > TETANUS
TETANICS > TETANIC
TETANIES > TETANY
TETANISE same as > TETANIZE
TETANISED > TETANISE
TETANISES > TETANISE
TETANIZE vb induce tetanus in (a muscle)
TETANIZED > TETANIZE
TETANIZES > TETANIZE
TETANOID > TETANUS
TETANUS n acute infectious disease producing muscular spasms and convulsions
TETANUSES > TETANUS
TETANY n abnormal increase in the excitability of nerves and muscles
TETCHED same as > TECHED
TETCHIER > TETCHY
TETCHIEST > TETCHY
TETCHILY > TETCHY
TETCHY adj cross and irritable
TETE n elaborate hairstyle
TETES > TETE
TETH n ninth letter of the Hebrew alphabet
TETHER n rope or chain for tying an animal to a spot ⊳ vb tie up with rope
TETHERED > TETHER
TETHERING > TETHER
TETHERS > TETHER
TETHS > TETH
TETOTUM same as > TEETOTUM
TETOTUMS > TETOTUM
TETRA n brightly coloured tropical freshwater fish
TETRACID adj (of a base) capable of reacting with four molecules of a monobasic acid
TETRACIDS > TETRACID
TETRACT n sponge spicule with four rays
TETRACTS > TETRACT
TETRAD n group or series of four
TETRADIC > TETRAD
TETRADITE n person who believes that the number four has supernatural significance
TETRADS > TETRAD
TETRAGON n figure with four angles and four sides
TETRAGONS > TETRAGON
TETRAGRAM n any word of four letters
TETRALOGY n series of four related works

TETRA... ...R n four-...lepolymer

T...AMERS > TETRAMER

...TRAPLA n book containing versions of the same text in four languages

TETRAPLAS > TETRAPLA

TETRAPOD n any vertebrate that has four limbs

TETRAPODS > TETRAPOD

TETRAPODY n metrical unit consisting of four feet

TETRARCH n ruler of one fourth of a country

TETRARCHS > TETRARCH

TETRARCHY > TETRARCH

TETRAS > TETRA

TETRAXON n four-pointed spicule

TETRAXONS > TETRAXON

TETRI n currency unit of Georgia

TETRIS > TETRI

TETRODE n electronic valve having four electrodes

TETRODES > TETRODE

TETRONAL n sedative drug

TETRONALS > TETRONAL

TETROSE n type of sugar

TETROSES > TETROSE

TETROXID same as > TETROXIDE

TETROXIDE n any oxide that contains four oxygen atoms per molecule

TETROXIDS > TETROXID

TETRYL n yellow crystalline explosive solid used in detonators

TETRYLS > TETRYL

TETS > TET

TETTER n blister or pimple ▷ vb cause a tetter to erupt (on)

TETTERED > TETTER

TETTERING > TETTER

TETTEROUS > TETTER

TETTERS > TETTER

TETTIX n cicada

TETTIXES > TETTIX

TEUCH Scots variant of > TOUGH

TEUCHAT Scots variant of > TEWIT

TEUCHATS > TEUCHAT

TEUCHER > TEUCH

TEUCHEST > TEUCH

TEUCHTER n in Scotland, derogatory word used by Lowlanders for a Highlander

TEUCHTERS > TEUCHTER

TEUGH same as > TEUCH

TEUGHER > TEUGH

TEUGHEST > TEUGH

TEUGHLY > TEUGH

TEUTONISE same as > TEUTONIZE

TEUTONIZE vb make or become German or Germanic

TEVATRON n machine used in nuclear research

TEVATRONS > TEVATRON

TEW vb work hard

TEWART same as > TUART

TEWARTS > TEWART

TEWED > TEW

TEWEL n horse's rectum

TEWELS > TEWEL

TEWHIT same as > TEWIT

TEWHITS > TEWHIT

TEWING > TEW

TEWIT n lapwing

TEWITS > TEWIT

TEWS > TEW

TEX n unit of weight used to measure yarn density

TEXAS n structure on the upper deck of a paddle-steamer

TEXASES > TEXAS

TEXES > TEX

TEXT n main body of a book as distinct from illustrations etc ▷ vb send a text message to (someone)

TEXTBOOK n standard book on a particular subject ▷ adj perfect

TEXTBOOKS > TEXTBOOK

TEXTED > TEXT

TEXTER n person who communicates by text messaging

TEXTERS > TEXTER

TEXTILE n fabric or cloth, esp woven ▷ adj of (the making of) fabrics

TEXTILES > TEXTILE

TEXTING > TEXT

TEXTINGS > TEXTING

TEXTISM n word typically used in a text message

TEXTISMS > TEXTISM

TEXTLESS > TEXT

TEXTONYM n one of two or more words that can be created by pressing the same combination of numbers on a mobile phone

TEXTONYMS > TEXTONYM

TEXTORIAL adj of or relating to weaving or weavers

TEXTPHONE n phone designed to translate speech into text and vice versa

TEXTS > TEXT

TEXTSPEAK n jargon and abbreviations typically used by frequent senders of text messages

TEXTUAL adj of, based on, or relating to, a text or texts

TEXTUALLY > TEXTUAL

TEXTUARY adj of, relating to, or contained in a text ▷ n textual critic

TEXTURAL > TEXTURE

TEXTURE n structure, feel, or consistency ▷ vb give a distinctive texture to (something)

TEXTURED > TEXTURE

TEXTURES > TEXTURE

TEXTURING > TEXTURE

TEXTURISE same as > TEXTURIZE

TEXTURIZE vb texture

THACK Scots word for > THATCH

THACKED > THACK

THACKING > THACK

THACKS > THACK

THAE Scots word for > THOSE

THAGI same as > THUGGEE

THAGIS > THAGI

THAIM Scots variant of > THEM

THAIRM n catgut

THAIRMS > THAIRM

THALAMI > THALAMUS

THALAMIC > THALAMUS

THALAMUS n either of the two contiguous egg-shaped masses of grey matter at the base of the brain

THALASSIC adj of or relating to the sea

THALE n as in thale cress cruciferous wall plant

THALER n former German, Austrian, or Swiss silver coin

THALERS > THALER

THALI n meal consisting of several small dishes accompanied by rice, bread, etc

THALIAN adj of or relating to comedy

THALIS > THALI

THALLI > THALLUS

THALLIC adj of or containing thallium

THALLINE > THALLUS

THALLIOUS > THALLIUM

THALLIUM n highly toxic metallic element

THALLIUMS > THALLIUM

THALLOID > THALLUS

THALLOUS adj of or containing thallium, esp in the monovalent state

THALLUS n undifferentiated vegetative body of algae, fungi, and lichens

THALLUSES > THALLUS

THALWEG n longitudinal outline of a riverbed from source to mouth

THALWEGS > THALWEG

THAN prep used to introduce the second element of a comparison ▷ n old variant of "then" (that time)

THANA same as > TANA

THANADAR same as > TANADAR

THANADARS > THANADAR

THANAGE n state of being a thane

THANAGES > THANAGE

THANAH same as > TANA

THANAHS > THANAH

THANAS > THANA

THANATISM n belief that the soul ceases to exist when the body dies

THANATIST > THANATISM

THANATOID adj like death

THANATOS n Greek personification of death

THANE n Anglo-Saxon or medieval Scottish nobleman

THANEDOM > THANE

THANEDOMS > THANE

THANEHOOD > THANE

THANES > THANE

THANESHIP > THANE

THANG n thing

THANGKA n (in Tibetan Buddhism) a religious painting on a scroll

THANGKAS > THANGKA

THANGS > THANG

THANK vb express gratitude to

THANKED > THANK

THANKEE interj thank you

THANKER > THANK

THANKERS > THANK

THANKFUL adj grateful

THANKING > THANK

THANKINGS > THANK

THANKIT adj as in be thankit thank God

THANKLESS adj unrewarding or unappreciated

THANKS pl n words of gratitude ▷ interj polite expression of gratitude

THANKYOU n conventional expression of gratitude

THANKYOUS > THANKYOU

THANNA same as > TANA

THANNAH same as > TANA

THANNAHS > THANNAH

THANNAS > THANNA

THANS > THAN

THANX interj (coll.) thank you

THAR same as > TAHR

THARM n stomach

THARMS > THARM

THARS > THAR

THAT pron used to refer to something already mentioned or familiar, or further away

THATAWAY adv that way

THATCH n roofing material of reeds or straw ▷ vb roof (a house) with reeds or straw

THATCHED > THATCH

THATCHER > THATCH

THATCHERS > THATCH

THATCHES > THATCH

THATCHIER > THATCH
THATCHING > THATCH
THATCHT old variant of > THATCHED
THATCHY > THATCH
THATNESS n state or quality of being 'that'
THAUMATIN n type of natural sweetener
THAW vb make or become unfrozen ▷ n thawing
THAWED > THAW
THAWER > THAW
THAWERS > THAW
THAWIER > THAWY
THAWIEST > THAWY
THAWING > THAW
THAWINGS > THAW
THAWLESS > THAW
THAWS > THAW
THAWY adj tending to thaw
THE determiner definite article, used before a noun
THEACEOUS adj relating to a family of evergreen trees and shrubs of tropical and warm regions, which includes the tea plant
THEANDRIC adj both divine and human
THEARCHIC > THEARCHY
THEARCHY n rule or government by God or gods
THEATER same as > THEATRE
THEATERS > THEATER
THEATRAL adj of or relating to the theatre
THEATRE n place where plays etc are performed
THEATRES > THEATRE
THEATRIC adj of or relating to the theatre
THEATRICS n art of staging plays
THEAVE n young ewe
THEAVES > THEAVE
THEBAINE n poisonous white crystalline alkaloid, found in opium but without opioid actions
THEBAINES > THEBAINE
THEBE n monetary unit of Botswana
THEBES > THEBE
THECA n enclosing organ, cell, or spore case
THECAE > THECA
THECAL > THECA
THECATE > THECA
THECODONT adj (of mammals and certain reptiles) having teeth that grow in sockets ▷ n extinct reptile
THEE pron refers to the person addressed: used mainly by Quakers ▷ vb use the word "thee"
THEED > THEE
THEEING > THEE

THEEK Scots variant of > THATCH
THEEKED > THEEK
THEEKING > THEEK
THEEKS > THEEK
THEELIN trade name for > ESTRONE
THEELINS > THEELIN
THEELOL n estriol
THEELOLS > THEELOL
THEES > THEE
THEFT n act or an instance of stealing
THEFTLESS > THEFT
THEFTS > THEFT
THEFTUOUS adj tending to commit theft
THEGITHER Scots variant of > TOGETHER
THEGN same as > THANE
THEGNLY > THEGN
THEGNS > THEGN
THEIC n person who drinks excessive amounts of tea
THEICS > THEIC
THEIN old variant of > THANE
THEINE another name for > CAFFEINE
THEINES > THEINE
THEINS > THEIN
THEIR determiner of, belonging to, or associated in some way with them
THEIRS pron (thing or person) belonging to them
THEIRSELF pron dialect form of themselves: reflexive form of they or them
THEISM n belief in a God or gods
THEISMS > THEISM
THEIST > THEISM
THEISTIC > THEISM
THEISTS > THEISM
THELEMENT n old contraction of "the element"
THELF n old contraction of "the element"
THELITIS n inflammation of the nipple
THELVES > THELF
THELYTOKY n type of reproduction resulting in female offspring only
THEM pron refers to people or things other than the speaker or those addressed
THEMA n theme
THEMATA > THEMA
THEMATIC adj of, relating to, or consisting of a theme or themes ▷ n thematic vowel
THEMATICS > THEMATIC
THEME n main idea or subject being discussed ▷ vb design, decorate,

arrange, etc, in accordance with a theme
THEMED > THEME
THEMELESS > THEME
THEMES > THEME
THEMING > THEME
THEMSELF pron reflexive form of one, whoever, anybody
THEN adv at that time ▷ pron that time ▷ adj existing or functioning at that time ▷ n that time
THENABOUT adv around then
THENAGE old variant of > THANAGE
THENAGES > THENAGE
THENAL adj of or relating to the thenar
THENAR n palm of the hand ▷ adj of or relating to the palm or the region at the base of the thumb
THENARS > THENAR
THENCE adv from that place or time
THENS > THEN
THEOCON n person who believes that religion should play a greater role in politics
THEOCONS > THEOCON
THEOCRACY n government by a god or priests
THEOCRASY n mingling into one of deities or divine attributes previously regarded as distinct
THEOCRAT > THEOCRACY
THEOCRATS > THEOCRACY
THEODICY n branch of theology concerned with defending the attributes of God against objections resulting from physical and moral evil
THEOGONIC > THEOGONY
THEOGONY n origin and descent of the gods
THEOLOG same as > THEOLOGUE
THEOLOGER n theologian
THEOLOGIC > THEOLOGY
THEOLOGS > THEOLOG
THEOLOGUE n theologian
THEOLOGY n study of religions and religious beliefs
THEOMACHY n battle among the gods or against them
THEOMANCY n divination or prophecy by an oracle or by people directly inspired by a god
THEOMANIA n religious madness, esp when it takes the form of believing oneself to be a god
THEONOMY n state of

being governed b...
THEOPATHY n relig... emotion engendere... the contemplation of... meditation upon God
THEOPHAGY n sacramental eating of a god
THEOPHANY n manifestation of a deity to man in a form that, though visible, is not necessarily material
THEORBIST > THEORBO
THEORBO n obsolete form of the lute, having two necks
THEORBOS > THEORBO
THEOREM n proposition that can be proved by reasoning
THEOREMIC > THEOREM
THEOREMS > THEOREM
THEORETIC adj of, or based on, a theory
THEORIC n theory; conjecture
THEORICS > THEORIC
THEORIES > THEORY
THEORIQUE same as > THEORIC
THEORISE same as > THEORIZE
THEORISED > THEORISE
THEORISER > THEORISE
THEORISES > THEORISE
THEORIST n originator of a theory
THEORISTS > THEORIST
THEORIZE vb form theories, speculate
THEORIZED > THEORIZE
THEORIZER > THEORIZE
THEORIZES > THEORIZE
THEORY n set of ideas to explain something
THEOSOPH n proponent of theosophy
THEOSOPHS > THEOSOPH
THEOSOPHY n religious or philosophical system claiming to be based on intuitive insight into the divine nature
THEOTOKOI > THEOTOKOS
THEOTOKOS n mother of God
THEOW n slave in Anglo-Saxon Britain
THEOWS > THEOW
THERALITE n type of igneous rock
THERAPIES > THERAPY
THERAPIST n person skilled in a particular type of therapy
THERAPSID n extinct reptile: considered to be the ancestors of mammals
THERAPY n curing treatment
THERBLIG n basic unit of work in an industrial process

THERBLIGS > THERBLIG

THEREAT adv at that point or time

THEREAWAY adv in that direction

THEREBY adv by that means

THEREFOR adv for this, that, or it

THEREFORE adv consequently, that being so

THEREFROM adv from that or there

THEREIN adv in or into that place or thing

THEREINTO adv into that place, circumstance, etc

THEREMIN n electronic musical instrument, played by moving the hands through electromagnetic fields created by two metal rods

THEREMINS > THEREMIN

THERENESS n quality of having existence

THEREOF adv of or concerning that or it

THEREON archaic word for **>** THEREUPON

THEREOUT another word for **>** THEREFROM

THERES > THERE

THERETO adv that or it

THEREUNTO adv to that

THEREUPON adv immediately after that

THEREWITH adv with or in addition to that

THERIAC n ointment or potion used as an antidote to a poison

THERIACA same as **>** THERIAC

THERIACAL > THERIAC

THERIACAS > THERIACA

THERIACS > THERIAC

THERIAN n animal of the class Theria, a subclass of mammals

THERIANS > THERIAN

THERM n unit of measurement of heat **▷** n public bath

THERMAE pl n public baths or hot springs, esp in ancient Greece or Rome

THERMAL adj of heat **▷** n rising current of warm air

THERMALLY > THERMAL

THERMALS > THERMAL

THERME old variant of **>** THERM

THERMEL n type of thermometer using thermoelectric current

THERMELS > THERMEL

THERMES > THERME

THERMETTE n device, used outdoors, for boiling water rapidly

THERMIC same as **>** THERMAL

THERMICAL same as **>** THERMAL

THERMIDOR adj as in lobster thermidor dish of cooked lobster

THERMION n electron or ion emitted by a body at high temperature

THERMIONS > THERMION

THERMIT variant of **>** THERMITE

THERMITE adj as in thermite process process for reducing metallic oxides

THERMITES > THERMITE

THERMITS > THERMIT

THERMOS n trademark for a stoppered vacuum flask

THERMOSES > THERMOS

THERMOSET n material (esp a synthetic plastic or resin) that hardens permanently after one application of heat and pressure

THERMOTIC adj of or because of heat

THERMS > THERM

THEROID adj of, relating to, or resembling a beast

THEROLOGY n study of mammals

THEROPOD n bipedal carnivorous saurischian dinosaur with strong hind legs and grasping hands

THEROPODS > THEROPOD

THESAURAL > THESAURUS

THESAURI > THESAURUS

THESAURUS n book containing lists of synonyms and related words

THESE determiner form of this used before a plural noun

THESES > THESIS

THESIS n written work submitted for a degree

THESP short for **>** THESPIAN

THESPIAN adj of or relating to drama and the theatre **▷** n actor or actress

THESPIANS > THESPIAN

THESPS > THESP

THETA n eighth letter of the Greek alphabet

THETAS > THETA

THETCH old variant spelling of **>** THATCH

THETCHED > THETCH

THETCHES > THETCH

THETCHING > THETCH

THETE n member of the lowest order of freeman in ancient Athens

THETES > THETE

THETHER old variant of **>** THITHER

THETIC adj (in classical prosody) of, bearing, or relating to a metrical stress

THETICAL another word for **>** THETIC

THEURGIC > THEURGY

THEURGIES > THEURGY

THEURGIST > THEURGY

THEURGY n intervention of a divine or supernatural agency in the affairs of man

THEW n muscle, esp if strong or well-developed

THEWED adj strong; muscular

THEWES > THEW

THEWIER > THEW

THEWIEST > THEW

THEWLESS > THEW

THEWS > THEW

THEWY > THEW

THEY pron people or things other than the speaker or people addressed

THIAMIN same as **>** THIAMINE

THIAMINE n vitamin found in the outer coat of rice and other grains

THIAMINES > THIAMINE

THIAMINS > THIAMIN

THIASUS n people gathered to sing and dance in honour of a god

THIASUSES > THIASUS

THIAZIDE n diuretic drug

THIAZIDES > THIAZIDE

THIAZIN same as **>** THIAZINE

THIAZINE n any of a group of organic compounds containing a ring system composed of four carbon atoms, a sulphur atom, and a nitrogen atom

THIAZINES > THIAZINE

THIAZINS > THIAZIN

THIAZOL same as **>** THIAZOLE

THIAZOLE n colourless liquid with a pungent smell that contains a ring system composed of three carbon atoms, a sulphur atom, and a nitrogen atom

THIAZOLES > THIAZOLE

THIAZOLS > THIAZOL

THIBET n coloured woollen cloth

THIBETS > THIBET

THIBLE n stick for stirring porridge

THIBLES > THIBLE

THICK adj of great or specified extent from one side to the other **▷** vb thicken

THICKED > THICK

THICKEN vb make or become thick or thicker

THICKENED > THICKEN

THICKENER > THICKEN

THICKENS > THICKEN

THICKER > THICK

THICKEST > THICK

THICKET n dense growth of small trees

THICKETED adj covered in thicket

THICKETS > THICKET

THICKETY > THICKET

THICKHEAD n stupid or ignorant person

THICKIE same as **>** THICKO

THICKIES > THICKY

THICKING > THICK

THICKISH > THICK

THICKLEAF n succulent plant with sessile or short-stalked fleshy leaves

THICKLY > THICK

THICKNESS n state of being thick

THICKO n slow-witted unintelligent person

THICKOES > THICKO

THICKOS > THICKO

THICKS > THICK

THICKSET adj stocky in build

THICKSETS > THICKSET

THICKSKIN n insensitive person

THICKY same as **>** THICKO

THIEF n person who steals

THIEFLIKE adj like a thief

THIEVE vb steal

THIEVED > THIEVE

THIEVERY > THIEVE

THIEVES > THIEVE

THIEVING adj given to stealing other people's possessions

THIEVINGS > THIEVING

THIEVISH > THIEF

THIG vb beg

THIGGER > THIG

THIGGERS > THIG

THIGGING > THIG

THIGGINGS > THIG

THIGGIT Scots inflection of **>** THIG

THIGH n upper part of the human leg

THIGHBONE same as **>** FEMUR

THIGHED adj having thighs

THIGHS > THIGH

THIGS > THIG

THILK pron that same

THILL another word for **>** SHAFT

THILLER n horse that goes between the thills of a cart

THILLERS > THILLER

THILLS > THILL

THIMBLE n cap protecting the end of the finger

(when sewing ▷ *vb* use a thimble
THIMBLED > THIMBLE
THIMBLES > THIMBLE
THIMBLING > THIMBLE
THIN *adj* not thick ▷ *vb* make or become thin ▷ *adv* in order to produce something thin
THINCLAD *n* track-and-field athlete
THINCLADS > THINCLAD
THINDOWN *n* reduction in the amount of particles, esp protons, of very high energy reaching and penetrating the earth's atmosphere from outer space
THINDOWNS > THINDOWN
THINE *adj* (something) of or associated with you (thou) ▷ *pron* something belonging to you (thou) ▷ *determiner* of, belonging to, or associated in some way with you (thou)
THING *n* material object
THINGAMY *n* person or thing the name of which is unknown
THINGHOOD *n* existence; state or condition of being a thing
THINGIER > THINGY
THINGIES > THINGY
THINGIEST > THINGY
THINGNESS *n* state of being a thing
THINGS > THING
THINGUMMY *n* person or thing the name of which is unknown, temporarily forgotten, or deliberately overlooked
THINGY *adj* existing in reality; actual
THINK *vb* consider, judge, or believe
THINKABLE *adj* able to be conceived or considered
THINKABLY > THINKABLE
THINKER > THINK
THINKERS > THINK
THINKING > THINK
THINKINGS > THINK
THINKS > THINK
THINLY > THIN
THINNED > THIN
THINNER > THIN
THINNERS > THIN
THINNESS > THIN
THINNEST > THIN
THINNING > THIN
THINNINGS > THIN
THINNISH > THIN
THINS > THIN
THIO *adj* of, or relating to, sulphur
THIOFURAN another name for > THIOPHEN

THIOL *n* any of a class of sulphur-containing organic compounds
THIOLIC > THIOL
THIOLS > THIOL
THIONATE *n* any salt or ester of thionic acid
THIONATES > THIONATE
THIONIC *adj* of, relating to, or containing sulphur
THIONIN same as > THIONINE
THIONINE *n* crystalline derivative of thiazine used as a violet dye to stain microscope specimens
THIONINES > THIONINE
THIONINS > THIONIN
THIONYL *n* of, consisting of, or containing the divalent group SO
THIONYLS > THIONYL
THIOPHEN *n* colourless liquid heterocyclic compound found in the benzene fraction of coal tar and manufactured from butane and sulphur
THIOPHENE same as > THIOPHEN
THIOPHENS > THIOPHEN
THIOPHIL *adj* having an attraction to sulphur
THIOTEPA *n* drug used in chemotherapy
THIOTEPAS > THIOTEPA
THIOUREA *n* white water-soluble crystalline substance with a bitter taste
THIOUREAS > THIOUREA
THIR Scots word for > THESE
THIRAM *n* antifungal agent
THIRAMS > THIRAM
THIRD *adj* of number three in a series ▷ *n* one of three equal parts ▷ *adv* in the third place ▷ *vb* divide (something) by three
THIRDED > THIRD
THIRDHAND *adv* from the second of two intermediaries
THIRDING > THIRD
THIRDINGS > THIRD
THIRDLY > THIRD
THIRDS > THIRD
THIRDSMAN *n* intermediary
THIRDSMEN > THIRDSMAN
THIRL *vb* bore or drill
THIRLAGE *n* obligation imposed upon tenants of certain lands requiring them to have their grain ground at a specified mill
THIRLAGES > THIRLAGE
THIRLED > THIRL
THIRLING > THIRL
THIRLS > THIRL

THIRST *n* desire to drink ▷ *vb* feel thirst
THIRSTED > THIRST
THIRSTER > THIRST
THIRSTERS > THIRSTER
THIRSTFUL > THIRST
THIRSTIER > THIRSTY
THIRSTILY > THIRSTY
THIRSTING > THIRST
THIRSTS > THIRST
THIRSTY *adj* feeling a desire to drink
THIRTEEN *n* three plus ten ▷ *adj* amounting to thirteen ▷ *determiner* amounting to thirteen
THIRTEENS > THIRTEEN
THIRTIES > THIRTY
THIRTIETH *adj* being the ordinal number of thirty in counting order, position, time, etc: often written 30th ▷ *n* one of 30 approximately equal parts of something
THIRTY *n* three times ten ▷ *adj* amounting to thirty ▷ *determiner* amounting to thirty
THIRTYISH *adj* around thirty years of age
THIS *pron* used to refer to a thing or person nearby, just mentioned, or about to be mentioned ▷ *adj* used to refer to the present time
THISAWAY *adv* this way
THISNESS *n* state or quality of being *this*
THISTLE *n* prickly plant with dense flower heads
THISTLES > THISTLE
THISTLIER > THISTLE
THISTLY > THISTLE
THITHER *adv* or towards that place
THITHERTO *adv* until that time
THIVEL same as > THIBLE
THIVELS > THIVEL
THLIPSES > THLIPSIS
THLIPSIS *n* compression, esp of part of the body
THO short for > THOUGH
THOFT *n* bench (in a boat) upon which a rower sits
THOFTS > THOFT
THOLE *n* wooden pin set in the side of a rowing boat to serve as a fulcrum for rowing ▷ *vb* bear or put up with
THOLED > THOLE
THOLEIITE *n* type of volcanic rock
THOLEPIN same as > THOLE
THOLEPINS > THOLEPIN
THOLES > THOLE
THOLI > THOLUS
THOLING > THOLE
THOLOBATE *n* structure supporting a dome

THOLOI > THO...
THOLOS *n* beehi... tomb associated... Mycenaean Greece
THOLUS *n* domed to...
THON Scot word for > YO...
THONDER Scot word for > YONDER
THONG *n* thin strip of leather etc ▷ *vb* decorate with a thong or thongs
THONGED *adj* fastened with a thong
THONGIER > THONGY
THONGIEST > THONGY
THONGING > THONG
THONGS > THONG
THONGY *adj* resembling a thong
THORACAL another word for > THORACIC
THORACES > THORAX
THORACIC *adj* of, near, or relating to the thorax
THORAX *n* part of the body between the neck and the abdomen
THORAXES > THORAX
THORIA > THORIUM
THORIAS > THORIUM
THORIC > THORIUM
THORITE *n* yellow, brownish, or black radioactive mineral
THORITES > THORITE
THORIUM *n* radioactive metallic element
THORIUMS > THORIUM
THORN *n* prickle on a plant ▷ *vb* jag or prick (something) as if with a thorn
THORNBACK *n* European ray with a row of spines along the back and tail
THORNBILL *n* South American hummingbird
THORNBIRD *n* small S American bird
THORNBUSH *n* tree, shrub, or bush with thorns
THORNED > THORN
THORNIER > THORNY
THORNIEST > THORNY
THORNILY > THORNY
THORNING > THORN
THORNLESS > THORN
THORNLIKE > THORN
THORNS > THORN
THORNSET *adj* set with thorns
THORNTREE *n* tree with thorns
THORNY *adj* covered with thorns
THORO (nonstandard) variant spelling of > THOROUGH
THORON *n* radioisotope of radon that is a decay product of thorium
THORONS > THORON
THOROUGH *adj* complete ▷ *n* passage

THOUGHS > THOROUGH
THORP *n small village*
THORPE *same as* > THORP
THORPES > THORPE
THORPS > THORP
THOSE *determiner form of* that *used before a plural noun*
THOTHER *pron old contraction of the other*
THOU *pron used when talking to one person* ▷ *n one thousandth of an inch* ▷ *vb use the word* thou
THOUED > THOU
THOUGH *adv nevertheless*
THOUGHT > THINK
THOUGHTED *adj with thoughts*
THOUGHTEN *adj convinced*
THOUGHTS > THINK
THOUING > THOU
THOUS > THOU
THOUSAND *n ten hundred* ▷ *adj amounting to a thousand* ▷ *determiner amounting to a thousand*
THOUSANDS > THOUSAND
THOWEL *old variant of* > THOLE
THOWELS > THOWEL
THOWL *old variant of* > THOLE
THOWLESS *adj lacking in vigour*
THOWLS > THOWEL
THRAE *same as* > FRAE
THRAIPING *n thrashing*
THRALDOM *same as* > THRALL
THRALDOMS > THRALDOM
THRALL *n state of being in the power of another person* ▷ *vb enslave or dominate*
THRALLDOM *same as* > THRALL
THRALLED > THRALL
THRALLING > THRALL
THRALLS > THRALL
THRANG *n throng* ▷ *vb throng* ▷ *adj crowded*
THRANGED > THRANG
THRANGING > THRANG
THRANGS > THRANG
THRAPPLE *n throat or windpipe* ▷ *vb throttle*
THRAPPLED > THRAPPLE
THRAPPLES > THRAPPLE
THRASH *vb beat, esp with a stick or whip* ▷ *n party*
THRASHED > THRASH
THRASHER *same as* > THRESHER
THRASHERS > THRASHER
THRASHES > THRASH
THRASHIER > THRASHY
THRASHING *n severe beating*
THRASHY *adj relating to thrash punk*

THRASONIC *adj bragging or boastful*
THRAVE *n twenty-four sheaves of corn*
THRAVES > THRAVE
THRAW *vb twist (something); make something thrawn*
THRAWARD *adj contrary or stubborn*
THRAWART *same as* > THRAWARD
THRAWED > THRAW
THRAWING > THRAW
THRAWN *adj crooked or twisted*
THRAWNLY > THRAWN
THRAWS > THRAW
THREAD *n fine strand or yarn* ▷ *vb pass thread through*
THREADED > THREAD
THREADEN *adj made of thread*
THREADER > THREAD
THREADERS > THREAD
THREADFIN *n spiny-finned tropical marine fish*
THREADIER > THREADY
THREADING > THREAD
THREADS *slang word for* > CLOTHES
THREADY *adj of, relating to, or resembling a thread or threads*
THREAP *vb scold*
THREAPED > THREAP
THREAPER > THREAP
THREAPERS > THREAP
THREAPING > THREAP
THREAPIT *variant past participle of* > THREAP
THREAPS > THREAP
THREAT *n declaration of intent to harm*
THREATED > THREAT
THREATEN *vb make or be a threat to*
THREATENS > THREATEN
THREATFUL > THREAT
THREATING > THREAT
THREATS > THREAT
THREAVE *same as* > THRAVE
THREAVES > THREAVE
THREE *n one more than two* ▷ *adj amounting to three* ▷ *determiner amounting to three*
THREEFOLD *adv (having) three times as many or as much* ▷ *adj having three times as many or as much*
THREENESS *n state or quality of being three*
THREEP *same as* > THREAP
THREEPEAT *n third consecutive win of a particular sporting championship* ▷ *vb win a sporting championship for the third consecutive time*
THREEPED > THREEP

THREEPER > THREAP
THREEPERS > THREAP
THREEPING > THREEP
THREEPIT *variant past participle of* > THREEP
THREEPS > THREEP
THREEQUEL *n third instalment in a series of films, books, plays, etc*
THREES > THREE
THREESOME *n group of three*
THRENE *n dirge; threnody*
THRENES > THRENE
THRENETIC > THRENE
THRENODE *same as* > THRENODY
THRENODES > THRENODE
THRENODIC > THRENODY
THRENODY *n lament for the dead*
THRENOS *n threnody; lamentation*
THRENOSES > THRENOS
THREONINE *n essential amino acid that occurs in certain proteins*
THRESH *vb beat (wheat etc) to separate the grain from the husks and straw* ▷ *n act of threshing*
THRESHED > THRESH
THRESHEL *n flail*
THRESHELS > THRESHEL
THRESHER *n any of a genus of large sharks occurring in tropical and temperate seas. They have a very long whiplike tail*
THRESHERS > THRESHER
THRESHES > THRESH
THRESHING > THRESH
THRESHOLD *n bar forming the bottom of a doorway*
THRETTIES > THRETTY
THRETTY *nonstandard variant of* > THIRTY
THREW > THROW
THRICE *adv three times*
THRID *old variant of* > THREAD
THRIDACE *n sedative made from lettuce juice*
THRIDACES > THRIDACE
THRIDDED > THRID
THRIDDING > THRID
THRIDS > THRID
THRIFT *n wisdom and caution with money*
THRIFTIER > THRIFTY
THRIFTILY > THRIFTY
THRIFTS > THRIFT
THRIFTY *adj not wasteful with money*
THRILL *n sudden feeling of excitement* ▷ *vb (cause to) feel a thrill*
THRILLANT *another word for* > THRILLING
THRILLED > THRILL
THRILLER *n book, film, etc with an atmosphere of mystery or suspense*

THRILLERS > THRILLER
THRILLIER > THRILLY
THRILLING *adj very exciting or stimulating*
THRILLS > THRILL
THRILLY *adj causing thrills*
THRIMSA *same as* > THRYMSA
THRIMSAS > THRIMSA
THRIP *same as* > THRIPS
THRIPS *n small slender-bodied insect with piercing mouthparts that feeds on plant sap*
THRIPSES > THRIPS
THRISSEL *Scots variant of* > THISTLE
THRISSELS > THRISSEL
THRIST *old variant of* > THIRST
THRISTED > THRIST
THRISTING > THRIST
THRISTLE *Scots variant of* > THISTLE
THRISTLES > THRISTLE
THRISTS > THRIST
THRISTY > THRIST
THRIVE *vb flourish or prosper*
THRIVED > THRIVE
THRIVEN > THRIVE
THRIVER > THRIVE
THRIVERS > THRIVE
THRIVES > THRIVE
THRIVING > THRIVE
THRIVINGS > THRIVE
THRO *same as* > THROUGH
THROAT *n passage from the mouth and nose to the stomach and lungs* ▷ *vb vocalize in the throat*
THROATED > THROAT
THROATIER > THROATY
THROATILY > THROATY
THROATING > THROAT
THROATS > THROAT
THROATY *adj (of the voice) hoarse*
THROB *vb pulsate repeatedly* ▷ *n throbbing*
THROBBED > THROB
THROBBER > THROB
THROBBERS > THROB
THROBBING > THROB
THROBLESS > THROB
THROBS > THROB
THROE *n pang or pain* ▷ *vb endure throes*
THROED > THROE
THROEING > THROE
THROES *pl n violent pangs or pains*
THROMBI > THROMBUS
THROMBIN *n enzyme that acts on fibrinogen in blood causing it to clot*
THROMBINS > THROMBIN
THROMBOSE *vb become or affect with a thrombus*
THROMBUS *n clot of coagulated blood that forms within a blood*

TIERCERON n (in Gothic architecture) a type of rib on a vault

TIERCES > TIERCE

TIERCET same as > TERCET

TIERCETS > TIERCET

TIERED > TIER

TIERING > TIER

TIERS > TIER

TIES > TIE

TIETAC n fastener for holding a tie in place

TIETACK same as > TIETAC

TIETACKS > TIETACK

TIETACS > TIETAC

TIFF n petty quarrel ▷ vb have or be in a tiff

TIFFANIES > TIFFANY

TIFFANY n sheer fine gauzy fabric

TIFFED > TIFF

TIFFIN n (in India) a light meal, esp at midday ▷ vb take tiffin

TIFFINED > TIFFIN

TIFFING > TIFF

TIFFINGS > TIFF

TIFFINING > TIFFIN

TIFFINS > TIFFIN

TIFFS > TIFF

TIFOSI > TIFOSO

TIFOSO n fanatical fan (esp an Italian F1 fan)

TIFOSOS > TIFOSO

TIFT Scots variant of > TIFF

TIFTED > TIFT

TIFTING > TIFT

TIFTS > TIFT

TIG n child's game

TIGE n trunk of an architectural column

TIGER n large yellow-and-black striped Asian cat

TIGEREYE n golden brown silicified variety of crocidolite, used as an ornamental stone

TIGEREYES > TIGEREYE

TIGERISH > TIGER

TIGERISM n arrogant and showy manner

TIGERISMS > TIGERISM

TIGERLIKE adj resembling a tiger

TIGERLY adj of or like a tiger

TIGERS > TIGER

TIGERWOOD n striped wood used in cabinetmaking

TIGERY > TIGER

TIGES > TIGE

TIGGED > TIG

TIGGER vb damage beyond repair by tinkering

TIGGERED > TIGGER

TIGGERING > TIGGER

TIGGERS > TIGGER

TIGGING > TIG

TIGHT adj stretched or drawn taut ▷ adv in a close, firm, or secure way

TIGHTASS n inhibited or excessively self-controlled person

TIGHTEN vb make or become tight or tighter

TIGHTENED > TIGHTEN

TIGHTENER > TIGHTEN

TIGHTENS > TIGHTEN

TIGHTER > TIGHT

TIGHTEST > TIGHT

TIGHTISH > TIGHT

TIGHTKNIT adj closely integrated

TIGHTLY > TIGHT

TIGHTNESS > TIGHT

TIGHTROPE n rope stretched taut on which acrobats perform

TIGHTS pl n one-piece clinging garment covering the body from the waist to the feet

TIGHTWAD n stingy person

TIGHTWADS > TIGHTWAD

TIGHTWIRE n wire tightrope

TIGLIC adj as in tiglic acid syrupy liquid or crystalline colourless unsaturated carboxylic acid

TIGLON same as > TIGON

TIGLONS > TIGLON

TIGNON n type of cloth headdress

TIGNONS > TIGNON

TIGON n hybrid offspring of a male tiger and a female lion

TIGONS > TIGON

TIGRESS n female tiger

TIGRESSES > TIGRESS

TIGRIDIA n type of tropical American plant

TIGRIDIAS > TIGRIDIA

TIGRINE adj of, characteristic of, or resembling a tiger

TIGRISH > TIGER

TIGRISHLY > TIGER

TIGROID adj resembling a tiger

TIGS > TIG

TIK n South African slang term for crystal meth

TIKA same as > TIKKA

TIKANGA n Māori ways or customs

TIKANGAS > TIKANGA

TIKAS > TIKA

TIKE same as > TYKE

TIKES > TIKE

TIKI n small carving of a grotesque person worn as a pendant ▷ vb take a scenic tour around an area

TIKIED > TIKI

TIKIING > TIKI

TIKIS > TIKI

TIKKA adj marinated in spices and dry-roasted

▷ n act of marking a tikka on the forehead

TIKKAS > TIKKA

TIKOLOSHE same as > TOKOLOSHE

TIKS > TIK

TIKTAALIK n extinct species thought to be a missing link between water and land animals

TIL another name for > SESAME

TILAK n coloured spot or mark worn by Hindus

TILAKS > TILAK

TILAPIA n type of fish

TILAPIAS > TILAPIA

TILBURIES > TILBURY

TILBURY n light two-wheeled horse-drawn open carriage

TILDE n mark used in Spanish to indicate pronunciation

TILDES > TILDE

TILE n flat piece of ceramic, plastic, etc used to cover a roof, floor, or wall ▷ vb cover with tiles

TILED > TILE

TILEFISH n large brightly coloured deep-sea percoid food fish

TILELIKE adj like a tile

TILER > TILE

TILERIES > TILERY

TILERS > TILE

TILERY n place where tiles are produced

TILES > TILE

TILING n tiles collectively

TILINGS > TILING

TILL prep until ▷ vb cultivate (land) ▷ n drawer for money, usu in a cash register

TILLABLE > TILL

TILLAGE n act, process, or art of tilling

TILLAGES > TILLAGE

TILLED > TILL

TILLER n on boats, a handle fixed to the top of a rudderpost to serve as a lever in steering ▷ vb use a tiller

TILLERED > TILLER

TILLERING > TILLER

TILLERMAN n one working a tiller

TILLERMEN > TILLERMAN

TILLERS > TILL

TILLICUM n (in the Pacific Northwest) a friend

TILLICUMS > TILLICUM

TILLIER > TILL

TILLIEST > TILL

TILLING > TILL

TILLINGS > TILL

TILLITE n rock formed from hardened till

TILLITES > TILLITE

TILLS > TILL

TILLY > TILL

TILS > TIL

TILT vb slant at an angle ▷ n slope

TILTABLE > TILT

TILTED > TILT

TILTER > TILT

TILTERS > TILT

TILTH n (condition of) land that has been tilled

TILTHS > TILTH

TILTING > TILT

TILTINGS > TILT

TILTMETER n instrument for measuring the tilt of the earth's surface

TILTROTOR n aircraft with rotors that can be tilted

TILTS > TILT

TILTYARD n (formerly) an enclosed area for tilting

TILTYARDS > TILTYARD

TIMARAU same as > TAMARAU

TIMARAUS > TIMARAU

TIMARIOT n one holding a fief in feudal Turkey

TIMARIOTS > TIMARIOT

TIMBAL n type of kettledrum

TIMBALE n mixture of meat, fish, etc, in a rich sauce

TIMBALES > TIMBALE

TIMBALS > TIMBAL

TIMBER n wood as a building material ▷ adj made out of timber ▷ vb provide with timbers ▷ interj lumberjack's shouted warning when a tree is about to fall

TIMBERED adj made of or containing timber or timbers

TIMBERING n timbers collectively

TIMBERMAN n any of various longicorn beetles that have destructive wood-eating larvae

TIMBERMEN > TIMBERMAN

TIMBERS > TIMBER

TIMBERY > TIMBER

TIMBO n Amazonian vine from which a useful insecticide can be derived

TIMBOS > TIMBO

TIMBRAL adj relating to timbre

TIMBRE n distinctive quality of sound of a voice or instrument

TIMBREL n tambourine

TIMBRELS > TIMBREL

TIMBRES > TIMBRE

TIME n past, present, and future as a continuous whole ▷ vb note the time taken by

TIMEBOMB n bomb containing a timing mechanism that

t

determines the time it will detonate

TIMEBOMBS > TIMEBOMB

TIMECARD n card used with a time clock

TIMECARDS > TIMECARD

TIMED > TIME

TIMEFRAME n period of time within which certain events are scheduled to occur

TIMELESS adj unaffected by time

TIMELIER > TIMELY

TIMELIEST > TIMELY

TIMELINE n graphic representation showing the passage of time as a line

TIMELINES > TIMELINE

TIMELY adj at the appropriate time ▷ adv at the right or an appropriate time

TIMENOGUY n taut rope on a ship

TIMEOUS adj in good time

TIMEOUSLY > TIMEOUS

TIMEOUT n in sport, interruption in play during which players rest, etc

TIMEOUTS > TIMEOUT

TIMEPASS n way of passing the time ▷ vb pass the time

TIMEPIECE n watch or clock

TIMER n device for measuring time

TIMERS > TIMER

TIMES > TIME

TIMESAVER n something that saves time

TIMESCALE n period of time within which events occur or are due to occur

TIMESHARE n time-shared property

TIMESTAMP vb (of a computer) add a record of the date and time of an event to (data)

TIMETABLE n plan showing the times when something takes place, the departure and arrival times of trains or buses, etc ▷ vb set a time when a particular thing should be done

TIMEWORK n work paid for by the length of time taken, esp by the hour or the day

TIMEWORKS > TIMEWORK

TIMEWORN adj showing the adverse effects of overlong use or of old age

TIMID adj easily frightened

TIMIDER > TIMID

TIMIDEST > TIMID

TIMIDITY > TIMID

TIMIDLY > TIMID

TIMIDNESS > TIMID

TIMING n ability to judge when to do or say something so as to make the best effect

TIMINGS > TIMING

TIMIST n one concerned with time

TIMISTS > TIMIST

TIMOCRACY n political unit or system in which possession of property serves as the first requirement for participation in government

TIMOLOL n relaxant medicine used (for example) to reduce blood pressure

TIMOLOLS > TIMOLOL

TIMON n apparatus by which a vessel is steered

TIMONEER n helmsman; tillerman

TIMONEERS > TIMONEER

TIMONS > TIMON

TIMOROUS adj timid

TIMORSOME adj timorous; timid

TIMOTHIES > TIMOTHY

TIMOTHY n as in timothy grass perennial grass of temperate regions

TIMOUS same as > TIMEOUS

TIMOUSLY > TIMOUS

TIMPANA n traditional Maltese baked pasta and pastry dish

TIMPANAS > TIMPANA

TIMPANI pl n set of kettledrums

TIMPANIST > TIMPANI

TIMPANO n kettledrum

TIMPANUM same as > TYMPANUM

TIMPANUMS > TIMPANUM

TIMPS same as > TIMPANI

TIN n soft metallic element ▷ vb (food) into tins

TINA n (slang) crystal meth

TINAJA n large jar for cooling water

TINAJAS > TINAJA

TINAMOU n type of bird of Central and S America

TINAMOUS > TINAMOU

TINAS > TINA

TINCAL another name for > BORAX

TINCALS > TINCAL

TINCHEL n in Scotland, a circle of deer hunters who gradually close in on their quarry

TINCHELS > TINCHEL

TINCT vb tint ▷ adj tinted or coloured

TINCTED > TINCT

TINCTING > TINCT

TINCTS > TINCT

TINCTURE n medicinal extract in a solution of alcohol ▷ vb give a tint or colour to

TINCTURED > TINCTURE

TINCTURES > TINCTURE

TIND vb set alight

TINDAL n petty officer

TINDALS > TINDAL

TINDED > TIND

TINDER n dry easily-burning material used to start a fire

TINDERBOX n formerly, small box for tinder, esp one fitted with a flint and steel

TINDERS > TINDER

TINDERY > TINDER

TINDING > TIND

TINDS > TIND

TINE n prong of a fork or antler ▷ vb lose

TINEA n any fungal skin disease, esp ringworm

TINEAL > TINEA

TINEAS > TINEA

TINED > TINE

TINEID n type of moth of the family which includes the clothes moths

TINEIDS > TINEID

TINES > TINE

TINFOIL n paper-thin sheet of metal, used for wrapping foodstuffs

TINFOILS > TINFOIL

TINFUL n contents of a tin or the amount a tin will hold

TINFULS > TINFUL

TING same as > THING

TINGE n slight tint ▷ vb give a slight tint or trace to

TINGED > TINGE

TINGEING > TINGE

TINGES > TINGE

TINGING > TINGE

TINGLE n (feel) a prickling or stinging sensation ▷ vb feel a mild prickling or stinging sensation, as from cold or excitement

TINGLED > TINGLE

TINGLER > TINGLE

TINGLERS > TINGLE

TINGLES > TINGLE

TINGLIER > TINGLE

TINGLIEST > TINGLE

TINGLING > TINGLE

TINGLINGS > TINGLE

TINGLISH adj exciting

TINGLY > TINGLE

TINGS > TING

TINGUAITE n type of igneous rock

TINHORN n cheap pretentious person, esp a gambler with extravagant claims ▷ adj cheap and showy

TINHORNS > TINHORN

TINIER > TINY

TINIES pl n small children

TINIEST > TINY

TINILY > TINY

TININESS > TINY

TINING > TINE

TINK shortened form of > TINKER

TINKED > TINK

TINKER n derogatory term for travelling mender of pots and pans ▷ vb fiddle with (an engine etc) in an attempt to repair it

TINKERED > TINKER

TINKERER > TINKER

TINKERERS > TINKER

TINKERING > TINKER

TINKERMAN n football coach who continually changes the team line-up or formation between games

TINKERMEN > TINKERMAN

TINKERS > TINKER

TINKERTOY n children's construction set

TINKING > TINK

TINKLE vb ring with a high tinny sound like a small bell ▷ n this sound or action

TINKLED > TINKLE

TINKLER same as > TINKLER

TINKLERS > TINKLER

TINKLES > TINKLE

TINKLIER > TINKLE

TINKLIEST > TINKLE

TINKLING > TINKLE

TINKLINGS > TINKLE

TINKLY > TINKLE

TINKS > TINK

TINLIKE > TIN

TINMAN n one who works with tin or tin plate

TINMEN > TINMAN

TINNED > TIN

TINNER n tin miner

TINNERS > TINNER

TINNIE same as > TINNY

TINNIER > TINNY

TINNIES > TINNY

TINNIEST > TINNY

TINNILY > TINNY

TINNINESS > TINNY

TINNING > TIN

TINNINGS > TIN

TINNITUS n ringing, hissing, or booming sensation in one or both ears, caused by infection of the middle or inner ear, a side effect of certain drugs, etc

TINNY adj (of sound) thin and metallic ▷ n can of beer

TINPLATE n thin steel sheet coated with a layer of tin that protects the steel from corrosion ▷ vb coat (a metal or object) with a layer of tin, usually either by electroplating or by dipping in a bath of molten tin

TINPLATED > TINPLATE

TINPLATES > TINPLATE

TINPOT *adj* worthless or unimportant ▷ *n* pot made of tin

TINPOTS > TINPOT

TINS > TIN

TINSEL *n* decorative metallic strips or threads ▷ *adj* made of or decorated with tinsel ▷ *vb* decorate with or as if with tinsel

TINSELED > TINSEL

TINSELING > TINSEL

TINSELLED > TINSEL

TINSELLY > TINSEL

TINSELRY *n* tinsel-like material

TINSELS > TINSEL

TINSELY *adj* (US) like tinsel

TINSEY old variant of > TINSEL

TINSEYS > TINSEY

TINSMITH *n* person who works with tin or tin plate

TINSMITHS > TINSMITH

TINSNIPS *n* metal cutters

TINSTONE *n* black or brown stone

TINSTONES > TINSTONE

TINT *n* (pale) shade of a colour ▷ *vb* give a tint to

TINTACK *n* tin-plated tack

TINTACKS > TINTACK

TINTED > TINT

TINTER > TINT

TINTERS > TINT

TINTIER > TINTY

TINTIEST > TINTY

TINTINESS > TINTY

TINTING > TINT

TINTINGS > TINT

TINTLESS > TINT

TINTOOKIE *n* in informal Australian English, fawning or servile person

TINTS > TINT

TINTY *adj* having many tints

TINTYPE another name for > FERROTYPE

TINTYPES > TINTYPE

TINWARE *n* objects made of tin plate

TINWARES > TINWARE

TINWORK *n* objects made of tin

TINWORKS *n* place where tin is mined, smelted, or rolled

TINY *adj* very small

TIP *n* narrow or pointed end of anything ▷ *vb* put a tip on

TIPCART *n* cart that can be tipped to empty out its contents

TIPCARTS > TIPCART

TIPCAT *n* game in which a piece of wood is tipped in the air with a stick

TIPCATS > TIPCAT

TIPI variant spelling of > TEPEE

TIPIS > TIPI

TIPLESS > TIP

TIPOFF *n* warning or hint, esp given confidentially

TIPOFFS > TIPOFF

TIPPABLE > TIP

TIPPED > TIP

TIPPEE *n* person who receives a tip, esp regarding share prices

TIPPEES > TIPPEE

TIPPER *n* person who gives or leaves a tip

TIPPERS > TIPPER

TIPPET *n* scarflike piece of fur

TIPPETS > TIPPET

TIPPIER > TIPPY

TIPPIEST > TIPPY

TIPPING > TIP

TIPPINGS > TIP

TIPPLE *vb* drink alcohol habitually, esp in small quantities ▷ *n* alcoholic drink

TIPPLED > TIPPLE

TIPPLER > TIPPLE

TIPPLERS > TIPPLE

TIPPLES > TIPPLE

TIPPLING > TIPPLE

TIPPY *adj* extremely fashionable or stylish

TIPPYTOE same as > TIPTOE

TIPPYTOED > TIPPYTOE

TIPPYTOES > TIPPYTOE

TIPS > TIP

TIPSHEET *n* list of advice or instructions

TIPSHEETS > TIPSHEET

TIPSIER > TIPSY

TIPSIEST > TIPSY

TIPSIFIED > TIPSIFY

TIPSIFIES > TIPSIFY

TIPSIFY *vb* make tipsy

TIPSILY > TIPSY

TIPSINESS > TIPSY

TIPSTAFF *n* court official

TIPSTAFFS > TIPSTAFF

TIPSTAVES > TIPSTAFF

TIPSTER *n* person who sells tips about races

TIPSTERS > TIPSTER

TIPSTOCK *n* detachable section of a gunstock, usually gripped by the left hand of the user

TIPSTOCKS > TIPSTOCK

TIPSY *adj* slightly drunk

TIPT > TIP

TIPTOE *vb* walk quietly with the heels off the ground

TIPTOED > TIPTOE

TIPTOEING > TIPTOE

TIPTOES > TIPTOE

TIPTOP *adj* of the highest quality or condition ▷ *adv* of the highest quality or condition ▷ *n* best in quality

TIPTOPS > TIPTOP

TIPTRONIC *n* type of gearbox that has both automatic and manual options

TIPULA *n* crane fly

TIPULAS > TIPULA

TIPUNA *n* ancestor

TIPUNAS > TIPUNA

TIRADE *n* long angry speech

TIRADES > TIRADE

TIRAGE *n* drawing of wine from a barrel prior to bottling

TIRAGES > TIRAGE

TIRAMISU *n* Italian dessert made with sponge soaked in coffee and Marsala, topped with soft cheese and powdered chocolate

TIRAMISUS > TIRAMISU

TIRASSE *n* mechanism in an organ connecting two pedals

TIRASSES > TIRASSE

TIRE *vb* reduce the energy of, as by exertion

TIRED *adj* exhausted

TIREDER > TIRED

TIREDEST > TIRED

TIREDLY > TIRED

TIREDNESS > TIRED

TIRELESS *adj* energetic and determined

TIRELING *n* fatigued person or animal

TIRELINGS > TIRELING

TIREMAKER same as > TYREMAKER

TIRES > TIRE

TIRESOME *adj* boring and irritating

TIREWOMAN *n* an obsolete term for lady's maid

TIREWOMEN > TIREWOMAN

TIRING > TIRE

TIRINGS > TIRE

TIRITI *n* another name for the Treaty of Waitangi

TIRITIS > TIRITI

TIRL *vb* turn

TIRLED > TIRL

TIRLING > TIRL

TIRLS > TIRL

TIRO same as > TYRO

TIROES > TIRO

TIRONIC variant of > TYRONIC

TIROS > TIRO

TIRR *vb* strip or denude

TIRRED > TIRR

TIRRING > TIRR

TIRRIT *n* panic; scare

TIRRITS > TIRRIT

TIRRIVEE *n* outburst of bad temper; rumpus

TIRRIVEES > TIRRIVEE

TIRRIVIE same as > TIRRIVEE

TIRRIVIES > TIRRIVIE

TIRRS > TIRR

TIS > TI

TISANE *n* infusion of dried or fresh leaves or flowers

TISANES > TISANE

TISICK *n* splutter; cough

TISICKS > TISICK

TISSUAL *adj* relating to tissue

TISSUE *n* substance of an animal body or plant ▷ *vb* weave into tissue

TISSUED > TISSUE

TISSUES > TISSUE

TISSUEY > TISSUE

TISSUING > TISSUE

TISSULAR *adj* relating to tissue

TISWAS *n* state of anxiety or excitement

TISWASES > TISWAS

TIT *n* any of various small songbirds; informal term for a female breast ▷ *vb* jerk or tug

TITAN *n* person who is huge, strong, or very important

TITANATE *n* any salt or ester of titanic acid

TITANATES > TITANATE

TITANESS *n* person who is huge, strong, or very important

TITANIA > TITANIUM

TITANIAS > TITANIA

TITANIC *adj* huge or very important

TITANIS *n* large predatory flightless prehistoric bird

TITANISES > TITANIS

TITANISM *n* titanic power

TITANISMS > TITANISM

TITANITE another name for > SPHENE

TITANITES > TITANITE

TITANIUM *n* strong light metallic element used to make alloys

TITANIUMS > TITANIUM

TITANOUS *adj* of or containing titanium, esp in the trivalent state

TITANS > TITAN

TITBIT *n* tasty piece of food

TITBITS > TITBIT

TITCH *n* small person

TITCHES > TITCH

TITCHIE *adj* very small

TITCHIER > TITCHY

TITCHIEST > TITCHY

TITCHY *adj* very small

TITE *adj* immediately

TITELY *adv* immediately

TITER same as > TITRE

TITERS > TITER

TITFER n hat
TITFERS > TITFER
TITHABLE adj (until 1936) liable to pay tithes
TITHE n esp formerly, one tenth of one's income or produce paid to the church as a tax ▷ vb charge or pay a tithe
TITHED > TITHE
TITHER > TITHE
TITHERS > TITHE
TITHES > TITHE
TITHING > TITHE
TITHINGS > TITHING
TITHONIA n Central American herb with flowers resembling sunflowers
TITHONIAS > TITHONIA
TITI n small omnivorous monkey
TITIAN n reddish gold colour
TITIANS > TITIAN
TITILLATE vb excite or stimulate pleasurably
TITIS > TITI
TITIVATE vb smarten up
TITIVATED > TITIVATE
TITIVATES > TITIVATE
TITIVATOR > TITIVATE
TITLARK another name for > PIPIT
TITLARKS > TITLARK
TITLE n name of a book, film, etc ▷ vb give a title to
TITLED adj aristocratic
TITLELESS > TITLE
TITLER n one who writes titles
TITLERS > TITLE
TITLES > TITLE
TITLING > TITLE
TITLINGS > TITLE
TITLIST n titleholder
TITLISTS > TITLIST
TITMAN n (of pigs) the runt of a litter
TITMEN > TITMAN
TITMICE > TITMOUSE
TITMOSE old spelling of > TITMOUSE
TITMOUSE n any small active songbird
TITOKI n New Zealand evergreen tree with a spreading crown and glossy green leaves
TITOKIS > TITOKI
TITRABLE > TITRATE
TITRANT n solution in a titration that is added to a measured quantity of another solution
TITRANTS > TITRANT
TITRATE vb measure the volume or concentration of (a solution) by titration
TITRATED > TITRATE
TITRATES > TITRATE
TITRATING > TITRATE
TITRATION n operation in which a measured

amount of one solution is added to a known quantity of another solution until the reaction between the two is complete
TITRATOR n device used to perform titration
TITRATORS > TITRATOR
TITRE n concentration of a solution as determined by titration
TITRES > TITRE
TITS > TIT
TITTED > TIT
TITTER vb laugh in a suppressed way ▷ n suppressed laugh
TITTERED > TITTER
TITTERER > TITTER
TITTERERS > TITTER
TITTERING > TITTER
TITTERS > TITTER
TITTIE n sister; young woman
TITTIES > TITTIE
TITTING > TIT
TITTISH adj testy
TITTIVATE same as > TITTIVATE
TITTLE n very small amount ▷ vb chatter; tattle
TITTLEBAT n child's name for the stickleback fish
TITTLED > TITTLE
TITTLES > TITTLE
TITTLING > TITTLE
TITTUP vb prance or frolic ▷ n caper
TITTUPED > TITTUP
TITTUPING > TITTUP
TITTUPPED > TITTUP
TITTUPPY same as > TITTUPY
TITTUPS > TITTUP
TITTUPY adj spritely; lively
TITTY same as > TITTIE
TITUBANCY n staggering or stumbling
TITUBANT adj staggering
TITUBATE vb stagger
TITUBATED > TITUBATE
TITUBATES > TITUBATE
TITULAR adj in name only ▷ n bearer of a title
TITULARLY > TITULAR
TITULARS > TITULAR
TITULARY same as > TITULAR
TITULE same as > TITLE
TITULED > TITULE
TITULES > TITULE
TITULI > TITULUS
TITULING > TITULE
TITULUS n sign attached to the top of the cross during crucifixion
TITUP same as > TITTUP
TITUPED > TITUP
TITUPING > TITUP

TITUPPED > TITUP
TITUPPING > TITUP
TITUPS > TITUP
TITUPY same as > TITTUPY
TIVY same as > TANTIVY
TIX pl n tickets
TIYIN n monetary unit of Uzbekistan and Kyrgyzstan
TIYINS > TIYIN
TIYN same as > TIYIN
TIYNS > TIYN
TIZ n state of confusion
TIZES > TIZ
TIZWAS same as > TISWAS
TIZWASES > TIZWAS
TIZZ same as > TIZZY
TIZZES > TIZZ
TIZZIES > TIZZY
TIZZY n confused or agitated state
TJANTING n pen-like tool used in batik for applying molten wax to fabric
TJANTINGS > TJANTING
TMESES > TMESIS
TMESIS n interpolation of a word between the parts of a compound word
TO prep indicating movement towards, equality or comparison, etc ▷ adv a closed position
TOAD n animal like a large frog
TOADEATER rare word for > TOADY
TOADFISH n spiny-finned bottom-dwelling marine fish of tropical and temperate seas, with a flattened tapering body and a wide mouth
TOADFLAX n plant with narrow leaves and yellow-orange flowers
TOADGRASS another name for > TOADRUSH
TOADIED > TOADY
TOADIES > TOADY
TOADISH > TOAD
TOADLESS adj having no toads
TOADLET n small toad
TOADLETS > TOADLET
TOADLIKE > TOAD
TOADRUSH n annual rush growing in damp lowlands
TOADS > TOAD
TOADSTONE n amygdaloidal basalt occurring in the limestone regions of Derbyshire
TOADSTOOL n poisonous fungus like a mushroom
TOADY n ingratiating person ▷ vb be ingratiating
TOADYING n act of toadying
TOADYINGS > TOADYING
TOADYISH > TOADY
TOADYISM > TOADY

TOADYISMS > TOADY
TOAST n sliced bread browned by heat ▷ vb brown (bread) by heat
TOASTED > TOAST
TOASTER > TOAST
TOASTERS > TOAST
TOASTIE same as > TOASTY
TOASTIER > TOASTY
TOASTIES > TOASTY
TOASTIEST > TOASTY
TOASTING > TOAST
TOASTINGS > TOAST
TOASTS > TOAST
TOASTY n toasted sandwich ▷ adj tasting or smelling like toast
TOAZE variant spelling of > TOZE
TOAZED > TOAZE
TOAZES > TOAZE
TOAZING > TOAZE
TOBACCO n plant with large leaves dried for smoking
TOBACCOES > TOBACCO
TOBACCOS > TOBACCO
TOBIES > TOBY
TOBOGGAN n narrow sledge for sliding over snow ▷ vb ride a toboggan
TOBOGGANS > TOBOGGAN
TOBOGGIN variant spelling of > TOBOGGAN
TOBOGGINS > TOBOGGIN
TOBY n water stopcock at the boundary of a street and house section
TOC n in communications code, signal for letter t
TOCCATA n rapid piece of music for a keyboard instrument
TOCCATAS > TOCCATA
TOCCATE > TOCCATA
TOCCATINA n short toccata
TOCHER n dowry ▷ vb give a dowry to
TOCHERED > TOCHER
TOCHERING > TOCHER
TOCHERS > TOCHER
TOCK n sound made by a clock ▷ vb (of a clock) make such a sound
TOCKED > TOCK
TOCKIER > TOCKY
TOCKIEST > TOCKY
TOCKING > TOCK
TOCKLEY slang word for > PENIS
TOCKLEYS > TOCKLEY
TOCKS > TOCK
TOCKY adj muddy
TOCO n punishment
TOCOLOGY n branch of medicine concerned with childbirth
TOCOS > TOCO
TOCS > TOC
TOCSIN n warning signal
TOCSINS > TOCSIN

TOD n unit of weight, used for wool, etc ⊳ vb produce a tod

TODAY n this day ⊳ adv on this day

TODAYS > TODAY

TODDE same as > TOD

TODDED > TOD

TODDES > TODDE

TODDIES > TODDY

TODDING > TOD

TODDLE vb walk with short unsteady steps ⊳ n act or an instance of toddling

TODDLED > TODDLE

TODDLER n child beginning to walk

TODDLERS > TODDLER

TODDLES > TODDLE

TODDLING > TODDLE

TODDY n sweetened drink of spirits and hot water

TODGER n penis

TODGERS > TODGER

TODIES > TODY

TODS > TOD

TODY n small bird of the Caribbean

TOE n digit of the foot ⊳ vb touch or kick with the toe

TOEA n monetary unit of Papua New Guinea

TOEAS > TOEA

TOEBIE n South African slang for sandwich

TOEBIES > TOEBIE

TOECAP n strengthened covering for the toe of a shoe

TOECAPS > TOECAP

TOECLIP n clip on a bicycle pedal into which the toes are inserted to prevent the foot from slipping

TOECLIPS > TOECLIP

TOED > TOE

TOEHOLD n small space on a mountain for supporting the toe of the foot in climbing

TOEHOLDS > TOEHOLD

TOEIER > TOEY

TOEIEST > TOEY

TOEING > TOE

TOELESS adj not having toes

TOELIKE > TOE

TOENAIL n thin hard clear plate covering part of the upper surface of the end of each toe ⊳ vb join (beams) by driving nails obliquely

TOENAILED > TOENAIL

TOENAILS > TOENAIL

TOEPIECE n part of a shoe that covers the toes

TOEPIECES > TOEPIECE

TOEPLATE n metal reinforcement of the part of the sole of a shoe or boot underneath the toes

TOEPLATES > TOEPLATE

TOERAG n contemptible person

TOERAGGER same as > TOERAG

TOERAGS > TOERAG

TOES > TOE

TOESHOE n ballet pump with padded toes

TOESHOES > TOESHOE

TOETOE same as > TOITOI

TOETOES > TOETOE

TOEY adj (of a person) nervous or anxious

TOFF n well-dressed or upper-class person

TOFFEE n chewy sweet made of boiled sugar

TOFFEES > TOFFEE

TOFFIER > TOFFY

TOFFIES > TOFFY

TOFFIEST > TOFFY

TOFFISH adj belonging to or characteristic of the upper class

TOFFS adj like a toff

TOFFY same as > TOFFEE

TOFORE prep before

TOFT n homestead

TOFTS > TOFT

TOFU n soft food made from soya-bean curd

TOFUS > TOFU

TOFUTTI n tradename for nondairy, soya-based food products

TOFUTTIS > TOFUTTI

TOG n unit for measuring the insulating power of duvets ⊳ vb dress oneself

TOGA n garment worn by citizens of ancient Rome ⊳ vb wear a toga

TOGAE > TOGA

TOGAED > TOGA

TOGAS > TOGA

TOGATE adj clad in a toga

TOGATED same as > TOGATE

TOGAVIRUS n one of family of viruses

TOGE old variant of > TOGA

TOGED > TOGE

TOGES > TOGE

TOGETHER adv in company ⊳ adj organized

TOGGED > TOG

TOGGER vb play football ⊳ n football player

TOGGERED > TOGGER

TOGGERIES > TOGGERY

TOGGERING > TOGGER

TOGGERS > TOGGER

TOGGERY n clothes

TOGGING > TOG

TOGGLE n small bar-shaped button inserted through a loop for fastening ⊳ vb supply or fasten with a toggle or toggles

TOGGLED > TOGGLE

TOGGLER > TOGGLE

TOGGLERS > TOGGLE

TOGGLES > TOGGLE

TOGGLING > TOGGLE

TOGS > TOG

TOGUE n large North American freshwater game fish

TOGUES > TOGUE

TOHEROA n large edible mollusc of New Zealand

TOHEROAS > TOHEROA

TOHO n (to a hunting dog) an instruction to stop

TOHUNGA n Māori priest

TOHUNGAS > TOHUNGA

TOIL n hard work ⊳ vb work hard

TOILE n transparent linen or cotton fabric

TOILED > TOIL

TOILER > TOIL

TOILERS > TOIL

TOILES > TOILE

TOILET n bowl connected to a drain for receiving and disposing of urine and faeces ⊳ vb go to the toilet

TOILETED > TOILET

TOILETING n act of using a toilet for defecation or urination

TOILETRY n object or cosmetic used to clean or groom oneself

TOILETS > TOILET

TOILETTE same as > TOILET

TOILETTES > TOILETTE

TOILFUL same as > TOILSOME

TOILFULLY > TOILFUL

TOILINET n type of fabric with a woollen weft and a cotton or silk warp

TOILINETS > TOILINET

TOILING > TOIL

TOILINGS > TOIL

TOILLESS > TOIL

TOILS > TOIL

TOILSOME adj requiring hard work

TOILWORN adj fatigued, wearied by work

TOING n as in toing and froing state of going back and forth

TOINGS > TOING

TOISE n obsolete French unit of length roughly equal to 2m

TOISEACH n ancient Celtic nobleman

TOISEACHS > TOISEACH

TOISECH same as > TOISEACH

TOISECHS > TOISECH

TOISES > TOISE

TOISON n fleece

TOISONS > TOISON

TOIT vb walk or move in an unsteady manner, as from old age

TOITED > TOIT

TOITING > TOIT

TOITOI n tall grasses with feathery fronds

TOITOIS > TOITOI

TOITS > TOIT

TOKAMAK n reactor used in thermonuclear experiments

TOKAMAKS > TOKAMAK

TOKAY n small gecko of S and SE Asia, having a retractile claw at the tip of each digit

TOKAYS > TOKAY

TOKE n draw on a cannabis cigarette ⊳ vb take a draw on a cannabis cigarette

TOKED > TOKE

TOKEN n sign or symbol ⊳ adj nominal or slight

TOKENED > TOKEN

TOKENING > TOKEN

TOKENISM n policy of making only a token effort, esp to comply with a law

TOKENISMS > TOKENISM

TOKENS > TOKEN

TOKER > TOKE

TOKERS > TOKE

TOKES > TOKE

TOKING > TOKE

TOKO same as > TOCO

TOKOLOGY same as > TOCOLOGY

TOKOLOSHE n (in Bantu folklore) a malevolent mythical manlike animal of short stature

TOKOLOSHI variant of > TOKOLOSHE

TOKOMAK variant spelling of > TOKAMAK

TOKOMAKS > TOKOMAK

TOKONOMA n recess off a living room

TOKONOMAS > TOKONOMA

TOKOS > TOKO

TOKOTOKO n ceremonial carved Māori walking stick

TOKOTOKOS > TOKOTOKO

TOKTOKKIE n large South African beetle

TOLA n unit of weight, used in India

TOLAN n white crystalline derivative of acetylene

TOLANE same as > TOLAN

TOLANES > TOLANE

TOLANS > TOLAN

TOLAR n standard monetary unit of Slovenia

TOLARJEV > TOLAR

TOLARJI > TOLAR

TOLARS > TOLAR

TOLAS > TOLA

TOLBOOTH same as > TOLLBOOTH

TOLBOOTHS > TOLBOOTH

TOLD > TELL

TOLE same as > TOLL

TOLED > TOLE

TOLEDO n type of sword originally made in Toledo

TOLEDOS > TOLEDO

TOLERABLE adj bearable
TOLERABLY
> TOLERABLE
TOLERANCE n acceptance of other people's rights to their own opinions or actions
TOLERANT adj able to tolerate the beliefs, actions, opinions, etc, of others
TOLERATE vb allow to exist or happen
TOLERATED > TOLERATE
TOLERATES > TOLERATE
TOLERATOR > TOLERATE
TOLES > TOLE
TOLEWARE n enamelled or lacquered metal ware, usually gilded
TOLEWARES > TOLEWARE
TOLIDIN same as > TOLIDINE
TOLIDINE n compound used in dyeing and in chemical analysis, esp as an indicator of the presence of free chlorine in water
TOLIDINES > TOLIDINE
TOLIDINS > TOLIDIN
TOLING > TOLE
TOLINGS > TOLE
TOLL vb ring (a bell) slowly and regularly ▷ n tolling
TOLLABLE > TOLL
TOLLAGE same as > TOLL
TOLLAGES > TOLLAGE
TOLLBAR n bar blocking passage of a thoroughfare, raised on payment of a toll
TOLLBARS > TOLLBAR
TOLLBOOTH n booth or kiosk at which a toll is collected
TOLLDISH n dish used to measure out the portion of grain given to a miller as payment for his or her work
TOLLED > TOLL
TOLLER > TOLL
TOLLERS > TOLLER
TOLLEY n large shooting marble used in a game of marbles
TOLLEYS > TOLLEY
TOLLGATE n gate across a toll road or bridge at which travellers must pay
TOLLGATED > TOLLGATE
TOLLGATES > TOLLGATE
TOLLHOUSE n small house at a tollgate occupied by a toll collector
TOLLIE same as > TOLLY
TOLLIES > TOLLY
TOLLING > TOLL
TOLLINGS > TOLL
TOLLMAN n man who collects tolls
TOLLMEN > TOLLMAN
TOLLS > TOLL

TOLLWAY n road on which users must pay tolls to travel
TOLLWAYS > TOLLWAY
TOLLY n castrated calf
TOLSEL n tolbooth
TOLSELS > TOLSEL
TOLSEY n tolbooth
TOLSEYS > TOLBOOTH
TOLT n type of obsolete English writ
TOLTER vb struggle or move with difficulty, as in mud
TOLTERED > TOLTER
TOLTERING > TOLTER
TOLTERS > TOLTER
TOLTS > TOLT
TOLU n sweet-smelling balsam obtained from a South American tree
TOLUATE n any salt or ester of any of the three isomeric forms of toluic acid
TOLUATES > TOLUATE
TOLUENE n colourless volatile flammable liquid obtained from petroleum and coal tar
TOLUENES > TOLUENE
TOLUIC adj as in toluic acid white crystalline derivative of toluene
TOLUID n white crystalline derivative of glycocoll
TOLUIDE variant of > TOLUID
TOLUIDES > TOLUIDE
TOLUIDIDE n chemical deriving from toluene
TOLUIDIN n type of dye
TOLUIDINE n compound used in dye production
TOLUIDINS > TOLUIDIN
TOLUIDS > TOLUID
TOLUOL another name for > TOLUENE
TOLUOLE another name for > TOLUENE
TOLUOLES > TOLUOLE
TOLUOLS > TOLUOL
TOLUS > TOLU
TOLUYL n of, consisting of, or containing any of three groups derived from a toluic acid
TOLUYLS > TOLUYL
TOLYL n of, consisting of, or containing any of three isomeric groups, $CH_3C_6H_4-$, derived from toluene
TOLYLS > TOLYL
TOLZEY n tolbooth
TOLZEYS > TOLZEY
TOM n male cat ▷ adj (of an animal) male ▷ vb prostitute oneself
TOMAHAWK n fighting axe of the Native Americans
TOMAHAWKS > TOMAHAWK

TOMALLEY n fat from a lobster, eaten as a delicacy
TOMALLEYS > TOMALLEY
TOMAN n gold coin formerly issued in Persia
TOMANS > TOMAN
TOMATILLO n Mexican plant bearing edible berries of the same name
TOMATO n red fruit used in salads and as a vegetable
TOMATOES > TOMATO
TOMATOEY > TOMATO
TOMB n grave
TOMBAC n any of various brittle alloys containing copper and zinc
TOMBACK variant spelling of > TOMBAC
TOMBACKS > TOMBAC
TOMBACS > TOMBAC
TOMBAK same as > TOMBAC
TOMBAKS > TOMBAK
TOMBAL adj like or relating to a tomb
TOMBED > TOMB
TOMBIC adj of or relating to tombs
TOMBING > TOMB
TOMBLESS > TOMB
TOMBLIKE > TOMB
TOMBOC n weapon
TOMBOCS > TOMBOC
TOMBOLA n lottery with tickets drawn from a revolving drum
TOMBOLAS > TOMBOLA
TOMBOLO n narrow bar linking a small island with another island or the mainland
TOMBOLOS > TOMBOLO
TOMBOY n girl who acts or dresses like a boy
TOMBOYISH > TOMBOY
TOMBOYS > TOMBOY
TOMBS > TOMB
TOMBSTONE n gravestone
TOMCAT vb (of a man) to be promiscuous
TOMCATS > TOMCAT
TOMCATTED > TOMCAT
TOMCOD n small fish resembling the cod
TOMCODS > TOMCOD
TOME n large heavy book
TOMENTA > TOMENTUM
TOMENTOSE > TOMENTUM
TOMENTOUS > TOMENTUM
TOMENTUM n feltlike covering of downy hairs on leaves and other plant parts
TOMES > TOME
TOMFOOL n fool ▷ vb act the fool
TOMFOOLED > TOMFOOL
TOMFOOLS > TOMFOOL
TOMIA > TOMIUM
TOMIAL > TOMIUM
TOMIUM n sharp edge of a bird's beak
TOMMED > TOM

TOMMIED > TOMMY
TOMMIES > TOMMY
TOMMING > TOM
TOMMY n private in the British Army ▷ vb (formerly) to exploit workers by paying them in goods rather than in money
TOMMYCOD n type of cod
TOMMYCODS > TOMMYCOD
TOMMYING > TOMMY
TOMMYROT n utter nonsense
TOMMYROTS > TOMMYROT
TOMO n shaft formed by the action of water on limestone or volcanic rock
TOMOGRAM n x-ray photograph of a selected plane section of the human body or some other solid object
TOMOGRAMS > TOMOGRAM
TOMOGRAPH n device for making tomograms
TOMORROW n (on) the day after today ▷ adv on the day after today
TOMORROWS > TOMORROW
TOMOS > TOMO
TOMPION same as > TAMPION
TOMPIONS > TOMPION
TOMPON same as > TAMPON
TOMPONED > TOMPON
TOMPONING > TOMPON
TOMPONS > TOMPON
TOMPOT adj as in tompot blenny variety of blenny with tentacles over its eyes
TOMS > TOM
TOMTIT n small European bird that eats insects and seeds
TOMTITS > TOMTIT
TON n unit of weight
TONAL adj written in a key
TONALITE n igneous rock found in the Italian Alps
TONALITES > TONALITE
TONALITIC adj relating to or consisting of tonalite
TONALITY n presence of a musical key in a composition
TONALLY > TONAL
TONANT adj very loud
TONDI > TONDO
TONDINI > TONDINO
TONDINO n small tondo
TONDINOS > TONDINO
TONDO n circular easel painting or relief carving
TONDOS > TONDO
TONE n sound with reference to its pitch, volume, etc ▷ vb harmonize (with)
TONEARM same as > PICKUP
TONEARMS > TONEARM
TONED > TONE

TONELESS adj having no tone

TONEME n phoneme that is distinguished from another phoneme only by its tone

TONEMES > TONEME

TONEMIC > TONEME

TONEPAD n keypad used to transmit information

TONEPADS > TONEPAD

TONER n cosmetic applied to the skin to reduce oiliness

TONERS > TONER

TONES > TONE

TONETIC adj (of a language) distinguishing words by tone as well as by other sounds

TONETICS pl n area of linguistics concentrating on the use of tone to distinguish words semantically

TONETTE n small musical instrument resembling a recorder

TONETTES > TONETTE

TONEY variant spelling of > TONY

TONG vb gather or seize with tongs ▷ n (formerly) a Chinese secret society

TONGA n light two-wheeled vehicle used in rural areas of India

TONGAS > TONGA

TONGED > TONG

TONGER n one who uses tongs to gather oysters

TONGERS > TONGER

TONGING > TONG

TONGMAN another word for > TONGER

TONGMEN > TONGMAN

TONGS pl n large pincers for grasping and lifting

TONGSTER n tong member

TONGSTERS > TONGSTER

TONGUE n muscular organ in the mouth, used in speaking and tasting ▷ vb use the tongue

TONGUED > TONGUE

TONGUELET n small tongue

TONGUES > TONGUE

TONGUING > TONGUE

TONGUINGS > TONGUE

TONIC n medicine to improve body tone ▷ adj invigorating

TONICALLY > TONIC

TONICITY n state, condition, or quality of being tonic

TONICS > TONIC

TONIER > TONY

TONIES > TONY

TONIEST > TONY

TONIFIED > TONIFY

TONIFIES > TONIFY

TONIFY vb give tone to

TONIFYING > TONIFY

TONIGHT n (in or during) the night or evening of this day ▷ adv in or during the night or evening of this day

TONIGHTS > TONIGHT

TONING > TONE

TONINGS > TONE

TONISH > TON

TONISHLY > TON

TONITE n explosive used in quarrying

TONITES > TONITE

TONK vb strike with a heavy blow ▷ n effete or effeminate man

TONKA n as in tonka bean tall leguminous tree of tropical America

TONKED > TONK

TONKER > TONK

TONKERS > TONK

TONKING > TONK

TONKS > TONK

TONLET n skirt of a suit of armour, consisting of overlapping metal bands

TONLETS > TONLET

TONNAG n type of (usually tartan) shawl

TONNAGE n weight capacity of a ship

TONNAGES > TONNAGE

TONNAGS > TONNAG

TONNE same as > TON

TONNEAU n detachable cover to protect the rear part of an open car

TONNEAUS > TONNEAU

TONNEAUX > TONNEAU

TONNELL old spelling of > TUNNEL

TONNELLS > TONNELL

TONNER n something that weighs one ton

TONNERS > TONNE

TONNES > TONNE

TONNISH > TON

TONNISHLY > TON

TONOMETER n instrument for measuring the pitch of a sound, esp one consisting of a set of tuning forks

TONOMETRY > TONOMETER

TONOPLAST n membrane enclosing a vacuole in a plant cell

TONS > TON

TONSIL n small gland in the throat

TONSILAR > TONSIL

TONSILLAR > TONSIL

TONSILS > TONSIL

TONSOR n barber

TONSORIAL adj of a barber or his trade

TONSORS > TONSOR

TONSURE n shaving of all or the top of the head as a religious or monastic

practice ▷ vb shave the head of

TONSURED > TONSURE

TONSURES > TONSURE

TONSURING > TONSURE

TONTINE n type of annuity scheme

TONTINER n subscriber to a tontine

TONTINERS > TONTINER

TONTINES > TONTINER

TONUS n normal tension of a muscle at rest

TONUSES > TONUS

TONY adj stylish or distinctive ▷ n stylish or distinctive person

TOO adv also, as well

TOOART variant spelling of > TUART

TOOARTS > TOOART

TOODLE vb tootle

TOODLED > TOODLE

TOODLES > TOODLE

TOODLING > TOODLE

TOOK > TAKE

TOOL n implement used by hand ▷ vb work on with a tool

TOOLBAG n bag for storing or carrying tools

TOOLBAGS > TOOLBAG

TOOLBAR n row or column of selectable buttons displayed on a computer screen

TOOLBARS > TOOLBAR

TOOLBOX n box for storing or carrying tools

TOOLBOXES > TOOLBOX

TOOLCASE n case for tools

TOOLCASES > TOOLCASE

TOOLCHEST n chest for tools

TOOLED > TOOL

TOOLER > TOOL

TOOLERS > TOOL

TOOLHEAD n adjustable attachment for a machine tool that holds the tool in position

TOOLHEADS > TOOLHEAD

TOOLHOUSE another word for > TOOLSHED

TOOLIE n adult who gatecrashes schools to make advances to the students

TOOLIES > TOOLIE

TOOLING n any decorative work done with a tool

TOOLINGS > TOOLING

TOOLKIT n set of tools designed to be used together or for a particular purpose

TOOLKITS > TOOLKIT

TOOLLESS adj having no tools

TOOLMAKER n person who makes tools

TOOLMAN n person who works with tools

TOOLMEN > TOOLMAN

TOOLPUSH n worker who directs the drilling on an oil rig

TOOLROOM n room, as in a machine shop, where tools are made or stored

TOOLROOMS > TOOLROOM

TOOLS > TOOL

TOOLSET n set of tools associated with a computer application

TOOLSETS > TOOLSET

TOOLSHED n small shed in the garden or yard of a house used for storing tools, esp those for gardening

TOOLSHEDS > TOOLSHED

TOOLTIP n temporary window containing information about a tool, feature, or option on a computer application, website, etc

TOOLTIPS > TOOLTIP

TOOM vb empty (something) ▷ adj empty

TOOMED > TOOM

TOOMER > TOOM

TOOMEST > TOOM

TOOMING > TOOM

TOOMS > TOOM

TOON n large tree of the East Indies and Australia

TOONIE n Canadian two-dollar coin

TOONIES > TOONIE

TOONS > TOON

TOORIE n tassel or bobble on a bonnet

TOORIES > TOORIE

TOOSHIE adj angry

TOOSHIER > TOOSHIE

TOOSHIEST > TOOSHIE

TOOT n short hooting sound ▷ vb (cause to) make such a sound

TOOTED > TOOT

TOOTER > TOOT

TOOTERS > TOOT

TOOTH n bonelike projection in the jaws of most vertebrates for biting and chewing

TOOTHACHE n pain in or near a tooth

TOOTHCOMB n comb with fine teeth set closely together

TOOTHED adj having a tooth or teeth

TOOTHFISH n as in Patagonian toothfish Chilean sea bass

TOOTHFUL n little (esp alcoholic) drink

TOOTHFULS > TOOTHFUL

TOOTHIER > TOOTHY

TOOTHIEST > TOOTHY

TOOTHILY > TOOTHY

TOOTHING > TOOTH

TOOTHINGS > TOOTH

TOOTHLESS > TOOTH

TOOTHLIKE > TOOTH

t

TOOTHPICK n small stick for removing scraps of food from between the teeth

TOOTHS > TOOTH

TOOTHSOME adj delicious or appetizing in appearance, flavour, or smell

TOOTHWASH n tooth-cleaning liquid

TOOTHWORT n parasitic plant

TOOTHY adj having or showing numerous, large, or prominent teeth

TOOTING > TOOT

TOOTLE vb hoot softly or repeatedly ▷ n soft hoot or series of hoots

TOOTLED > TOOTLE

TOOTLER > TOOTLE

TOOTLERS > TOOTLE

TOOTLES > TOOTLE

TOOTLING > TOOTLE

TOOTS Scots version of > TUT

TOOTSED > TOOTS

TOOTSES > TOOTS

TOOTSIE same as > TOOTSY

TOOTSIES > TOOTSY

TOOTSING > TOOTS

TOOTSY same as > TOOTS

TOP n highest point or part ▷ adj at or of the top ▷ vb form a top on

TOPALGIA n pain restricted to a particular spot: a neurotic or hysterical symptom

TOPALGIAS > TOPALGIA

TOPARCH n ruler of a small state or realm

TOPARCHS > TOPARCH

TOPARCHY > TOPARCH

TOPAZ n semiprecious stone in various colours

TOPAZES > TOPAZ

TOPAZINE adj like topaz

TOPCOAT n overcoat

TOPCOATS > TOPCOAT

TOPCROSS n class of hybrid

TOPE vb drink alcohol regularly ▷ n small European shark

TOPECTOMY n (formerly) the surgical removal of part of the cerebral cortex to relieve certain psychiatric disorders

TOPED > TOPE

TOPEE n lightweight hat worn in tropical countries

TOPEES > TOPEE

TOPEK same as > TUPIK

TOPEKS > TOPEK

TOPER > TOPE

TOPERS > TOPE

TOPES > TOPE

TOPFLIGHT adj superior or excellent quality; outstanding

TOPFUL variant spelling of > TOPFULL

TOPFULL adj full to the top

TOPH n variety of sandstone

TOPHE variant spelling of > TOPH

TOPHES > TOPHE

TOPHI > TOPHUS

TOPHS > TOPH

TOPHUS n deposit of sodium urate in the helix of the ear or surrounding a joint

TOPI same as > TOPEE

TOPIARIAN > TOPIARY

TOPIARIES > TOPIARY

TOPIARIST > TOPIARY

TOPIARY n art of trimming trees and bushes into decorative shapes ▷ adj of or relating to topiary

TOPIC n subject of a conversation, book, etc

TOPICAL adj relating to current events ▷ n type of anaesthetic

TOPICALLY > TOPICAL

TOPICALS > TOPICAL

TOPICS > TOPIC

TOPING > TOPE

TOPIS > TOPI

TOPKICK n (formerly) sergeant

TOPKICKS > TOPKICK

TOPKNOT n crest, tuft, decorative bow, etc, on the top of the head

TOPKNOTS > TOPKNOT

TOPLESS adj (of a costume or woman) with no covering for the breasts

TOPLINE vb headline; be the main focus of a newspaper story

TOPLINED > TOPLINE

TOPLINER > TOPLINE

TOPLINERS > TOPLINE

TOPLINES > TOPLINE

TOPLINING > TOPLINE

TOPLOFTY adj haughty or pretentious

TOPMAKER n wool dealer

TOPMAKERS > TOPMAKER

TOPMAKING > TOPMAKER

TOPMAN n sailor positioned in the rigging of the topsail

TOPMAST n mast next above a lower mast on a sailing vessel

TOPMASTS > TOPMAST

TOPMEN > TOPMAN

TOPMINNOW n small American freshwater cyprinodont fish

TOPMOST adj highest or best

TOPNOTCH adj excellent

TOPO n picture of a mountain with details of climbing routes

superimposed on it

TOPOGRAPH n type of x-ray photograph

TOPOI > TOPO

TOPOLOGIC > TOPOLOGY

TOPOLOGY n geometry of the properties of a shape which are unaffected by continuous distortion

TOPOMETRY n measurement of the surface features of a region

TOPONYM n name of a place

TOPONYMAL > TOPONYMY

TOPONYMIC > TOPONYMY

TOPONYMS > TOPONYM

TOPONYMY n study of place names

TOPOS > TOPO

TOPOTYPE n specimen plant or animal taken from an area regarded as the typical habitat

TOPOTYPES > TOPOTYPE

TOPPED > TOP

TOPPER n top hat

TOPPERS > TOPPER

TOPPIER > TOPPY

TOPPIEST > TOPPY

TOPPING > TOP

TOPPINGLY > TOP

TOPPINGS > TOP

TOPPLE vb (cause to) fall over

TOPPLED > TOPPLE

TOPPLES > TOPPLE

TOPPLING > TOPPLE

TOPPY adj (of audio reproduction) having too many high-frequency sounds

TOPS > TOP

TOPSAIL n square sail carried on a yard set on a topmast

TOPSAILS > TOPSAIL

TOPSCORE vb score the highest in a sports match or competition

TOPSCORED > TOPSCORE

TOPSCORES > TOPSCORE

TOPSIDE n lean cut of beef from the thigh containing no bone

TOPSIDER n person in charge

TOPSIDERS > TOPSIDER

TOPSIDES > TOPSIDE

TOPSMAN n chief drover

TOPSMEN > TOPSMAN

TOPSOIL n surface layer of soil ▷ vb spread topsoil on (land)

TOPSOILED > TOPSOIL

TOPSOILS > TOPSOIL

TOPSPIN n spin imparted to make a ball bounce or travel exceptionally far, high, or quickly

TOPSPINS > TOPSPIN

TOPSTITCH vb stitch a line the outside of a

garment, running close to a seam

TOPSTONE n stone forming the top of something

TOPSTONES > TOPSTONE

TOPWATER adj floating on the top of the water

TOPWORK vb graft shoots or twigs onto the main branches of (a tree)

TOPWORKED > TOPWORK

TOPWORKS > TOPWORK

TOQUE same as > TUQUE

TOQUES > TOQUE

TOQUET same as > TOQUE

TOQUETS > TOQUET

TOQUILLA another name for > JIPIJAPA

TOQUILLAS > TOQUILLA

TOR n high rocky hill

TORA variant spelling of > TORAH

TORAH n whole body of traditional Jewish teaching

TORAHS > TORAH

TORAN n (in Indian architecture) an archway

TORANA same as > TORAN

TORANAS > TORANA

TORANS > TORAN

TORAS > TORA

TORBANITE n type of oil shale

TORC same as > TORQUE

TORCH n small portable battery-powered lamp ▷ vb deliberately set (a building) on fire

TORCHABLE > TORCH

TORCHED > TORCH

TORCHER > TORCH

TORCHERE n tall narrow stand for holding a candelabrum

TORCHERES > TORCHERE

TORCHERS > TORCH

TORCHES > TORCH

TORCHIER n standing lamp with a bowl for casting light upwards and so giving all-round indirect illumination

TORCHIERE same as > TORCHIER

TORCHIERS > TORCHIER

TORCHIEST > TORCHY

TORCHING > TORCH

TORCHINGS > TORCH

TORCHLIKE > TORCH

TORCHLIT adj lit by torches

TORCHON n as in torchon lace coarse linen or cotton lace with a simple openwork pattern

TORCHONS > TORCHON

TORCHWOOD n rutaceous tree or shrub of Florida and the Caribbean, with hard resinous wood used for torches

TORCHY adj sentimental; maudlin; characteristic of a torch song
TORCS > TORC
TORCULAR n tourniquet
TORCULARS > TORCULAR
TORDION n old triple-time dance for two people
TORDIONS > TORDION
TORE same as > TORUS
TOREADOR n bullfighter
TOREADORS > TOREADOR
TORERO n bullfighter, esp one on foot
TOREROS > TORERO
TORES > TORE
TOREUTIC > TOREUTICS
TOREUTICS n art of making detailed ornamental reliefs, esp in metal, by embossing and chasing
TORGOCH n type of char
TORGOCHS > TORGOCH
TORI > TORUS
TORIC adj of, relating to, or having the form of a torus
TORICS > TORIC
TORIES > TORY
TORII n gateway, esp one at the entrance to a Japanese Shinto temple
TORMENT vb cause (someone) great suffering ▷ n great suffering
TORMENTA > TORMENTUM
TORMENTED > TORMENT
TORMENTER same as > TORMENTOR
TORMENTIL n creeping plant with yellow four-petalled flowers
TORMENTOR n person or thing that torments
TORMENTS > TORMENT
TORMENTUM n type of Roman catapult
TORMINA n complaints
TORMINAL > TORMINA
TORMINOUS > TORMINA
TORN > TEAR
TORNADE same as > TORNADO
TORNADES > TORNADE
TORNADIC > TORNADO
TORNADO n violent whirlwind
TORNADOES > TORNADO
TORNADOS > TORNADO
TORNILLO n shrub found in Mexico and some southwestern states of the US
TORNILLOS > TORNILLO
TORO n bull
TOROID n surface generated by rotating a closed plane curve about a coplanar line that does not intersect it
TOROIDAL > TOROID
TOROIDS > TOROID
TOROS > TORO

TOROSE adj (of a cylindrical part) having irregular swellings
TOROSITY > TOROSE
TOROT > TORAH
TOROTH > TORAH
TOROUS same as > TOROSE
TORPEDO n self-propelled underwater missile ▷ vb attack or destroy with or as if with torpedoes
TORPEDOED > TORPEDO
TORPEDOER > TORPEDO
TORPEDOES > TORPEDO
TORPEDOS > TORPEDO
TORPEFIED > TORPEFY
TORPEFIES > TORPEFY
TORPEFY n make torpid
TORPID adj sluggish and inactive
TORPIDITY > TORPID
TORPIDLY > TORPID
TORPIDS n series of boat races held at Oxford University
TORPITUDE another word for > TORPOR
TORPOR n torpid state
TORPORS > TORPOR
TORQUATE > TORQUES
TORQUATED > TORQUES
TORQUE n force causing rotation ▷ vb apply torque to (something)
TORQUED > TORQUE
TORQUER > TORQUE
TORQUERS > TORQUE
TORQUES n distinctive band of hair, feathers, skin, or colour around the neck of an animal
TORQUESES > TORQUES
TORQUEY adj providing torque
TORQUIER > TORQUEY
TORQUIEST > TORQUEY
TORQUING > TORQUE
TORR n unit of pressure
TORREFIED > TORREFY
TORREFIES > TORREFY
TORREFY vb dry (drugs, ores, etc) by subjection to intense heat
TORRENT n rushing stream ▷ adj like or relating to a torrent
TORRENTS > TORRENT
TORRET same as > TERRET
TORRETS > TORRET
TORRID adj very hot and dry
TORRIDER > TORRID
TORRIDEST > TORRID
TORRIDITY > TORRID
TORRIDLY > TORRID
TORRIFIED > TORRIFY
TORRIFIES > TORRIFY
TORRIFY same as > TORREFY
TORRS > TORR
TORS > TOR

TORSADE n ornamental twist or twisted cord, as on hats
TORSADES > TORSADE
TORSE same as > TORSO
TORSEL n wooden beam along the top of a wall
TORSELS > TORSEL
TORSES > TORSE
TORSI > TORSO
TORSION n twisting of a part by equal forces being applied at both ends but in opposite directions
TORSIONAL > TORSION
TORSIONS > TORSION
TORSIVE adj twisted
TORSK n fish with a single long dorsal fin
TORSKS > TORSK
TORSO n trunk of the human body
TORSOS > TORSO
TORT n civil wrong or injury for which damages may be claimed
TORTA n (in mining) a flat circular pile of silver ore
TORTAS > TORTA
TORTE n rich cake, originating in Austria
TORTELLI pl n type of stuffed pasta
TORTELLIS > TORTELLI
TORTEN > TORTE
TORTES > TORTE
TORTIE n tortoiseshell cat
TORTIES > TORTIE
TORTILE adj twisted or coiled
TORTILITY > TORTILE
TORTILLA n thin Mexican pancake
TORTILLAS > TORTILLA
TORTILLON another word for > STUMP
TORTIOUS adj having the nature of or involving a tort
TORTIVE adj twisted
TORTOISE n slow-moving land reptile with a dome-shaped shell
TORTOISES > TORTOISE
TORTONI n rich ice cream often flavoured with sherry
TORTONIS > TORTONI
TORTRICES > TORTRIX
TORTRICID n type of small moth of the family which includes the codling moth
TORTRIX n type of moth
TORTRIXES > TORTRIX
TORTS > TORT
TORTUOUS adj winding or twisting
TORTURE vb cause (someone) severe pain or mental anguish ▷ n severe physical or mental pain
TORTURED > TORTURE
TORTURER > TORTURE

TORTURERS > TORTURE
TORTURES > TORTURE
TORTURING > TORTURE
TORTUROUS > TORTURE
TORULA n species of fungal microorganisms
TORULAE > TORULA
TORULAS > TORULA
TORULI > TORULUS
TORULIN n vitamin found in yeast
TORULINS > TORULIN
TORULOSE adj (of something cylindrical) alternately swollen and pinched along its length
TORULOSES > TORULOSIS
TORULOSIS n infection by one of the torula
TORULUS n socket in an insect's head in which its antenna is attached
TORUS n large convex moulding approximately semicircular in cross section, esp one used on the base of a classical column
TORUSES > TORUS
TORY n conservative or reactionary person ▷ adj conservative or reactionary
TOSA n large reddish dog, originally bred for fighting
TOSAS > TOSA
TOSE same as > TOZE
TOSED > TOSE
TOSES > TOSE
TOSH n nonsense ▷ vb tidy or trim
TOSHACH n military leader of a clan
TOSHACHS > TOSHACH
TOSHED > TOSH
TOSHER > TOSH
TOSHERS > TOSH
TOSHES > TOSH
TOSHIER > TOSHY
TOSHIEST > TOSHY
TOSHING > TOSH
TOSHY adj neat; trim
TOSING > TOSE
TOSS vb throw lightly ▷ n tossing
TOSSED > TOSS
TOSSEN old past participle of > TOSS
TOSSER n stupid or despicable person
TOSSERS > TOSSER
TOSSES > TOSS
TOSSIER > TOSSY
TOSSIEST > TOSSY
TOSSILY > TOSSY
TOSSING > TOSS
TOSSINGS > TOSS
TOSSPOT n habitual drinker
TOSSPOTS > TOSSPOT
TOSSUP n instance of tossing up a coin

TOSSUPS > TOSSUP

TOSSY *adj* impudent

TOST *old past participle of* > TOSS

TOSTADA *n* crispy deep-fried tortilla topped with meat, cheese, and refried beans

TOSTADAS > TOSTADA

TOSTADO *same as* > TOSTADA

TOSTADOS > TOSTADO

TOSTONE *n* Mexican dish of fried plantains

TOSTONES > TOSTONE

TOT *n* small child ▷ *vb* total

TOTABLE > TOTE

TOTAL *n* whole, esp a sum of parts ▷ *adj* complete ▷ *vb* amount to

TOTALED > TOTAL

TOTALING > TOTAL

TOTALISE *same as* > TOTALIZE

TOTALISED > TOTALISE

TOTALISER > TOTALISE

TOTALISES > TOTALISE

TOTALISM *n* practice of a dictatorial one party state that regulates every form of life

TOTALISMS > TOTALISM

TOTALIST > TOTALISM

TOTALISTS > TOTALISM

TOTALITY *n* whole amount

TOTALIZE *vb* combine or make into a total

TOTALIZED > TOTALIZE

TOTALIZER > TOTALIZE

TOTALIZES > TOTALIZE

TOTALLED > TOTAL

TOTALLING > TOTAL

TOTALLY > TOTAL

TOTALS > TOTAL

TOTANUS *another name for* > REDSHANK

TOTANUSES > TOTANUS

TOTAQUINE *n* mixture of quinine and other alkaloids derived from cinchona bark, used as a substitute for quinine in treating malaria

TOTARA *n* tall coniferous forest tree of New Zealand

TOTARAS > TOTARA

TOTE *vb* carry (a gun etc) ▷ *n* act of or an instance of toting

TOTEABLE > TOTE

TOTED > TOTE

TOTEM *n* tribal badge or emblem

TOTEMIC > TOTEM

TOTEMISM *n* belief in kinship of groups or individuals having a common totem

TOTEMISMS > TOTEMISM

TOTEMIST > TOTEMISM

TOTEMISTS > TOTEMISM

TOTEMITE > TOTEMISM

TOTEMITES > TOTEMISM

TOTEMS > TOTEM

TOTER > TOTE

TOTERS > TOTE

TOTES > TOTE

TOTHER *n* other ▷ *adj* the other

TOTHERS > TOTHER

TOTIENT *n* quantity of numbers less than, and sharing no common factors with, a number

TOTIENTS > TOTIENT

TOTING > TOTE

TOTITIVE *n* number less than, and having no common factors with, a given number

TOTITIVES > TOTITIVE

TOTS > TOT

TOTTED > TOT

TOTTER *vb* move unsteadily ▷ *n* act or an instance of tottering

TOTTERED > TOTTER

TOTTERER > TOTTER

TOTTERERS > TOTTER

TOTTERING > TOTTER

TOTTERS > TOTTER

TOTTERY > TOTTER

TOTTIE *adj* very small

TOTTIER > TOTTY

TOTTIES > TOTTY

TOTTIEST > TOTTY

TOTTING > TOT

TOTTINGS > TOT

TOTTRING *adj* Shakespearian word referring to ragged cloth or clothing

TOTTY *n* people, esp women, collectively considered as sexual objects ▷ *adj* very small

TOUCAN *n* tropical American bird with a large bill

TOUCANET *n* type of small toucan

TOUCANETS > TOUCANET

TOUCANS > TOUCAN

TOUCH *vb* come into contact with ▷ *n* sense by which an object's qualities are perceived when they come into contact with part of the body ▷ *adj* of a non-contact version of particular sport

TOUCHABLE > TOUCH

TOUCHBACK *n* play in which the ball is put down by a player behind his own goal line when the ball has been put across the goal line by an opponent

TOUCHDOWN *n* moment at which a landing aircraft or spacecraft comes into contact with the landing surface ▷ *vb* (of an aircraft or spacecraft) to land

TOUCHE *interj* acknowledgment a remark or witty reply

TOUCHED *adj* emotionally moved

TOUCHER > TOUCH

TOUCHERS > TOUCH

TOUCHES > TOUCH

TOUCHHOLE *n* hole in the breech of early cannon and firearms through which the charge was ignited

TOUCHIER > TOUCHY

TOUCHIEST > TOUCHY

TOUCHILY > TOUCHY

TOUCHING *adj* emotionally moving ▷ *prep* relating to or concerning

TOUCHINGS > TOUCH

TOUCHLESS > TOUCH

TOUCHLINE *n* side line of the pitch in some games

TOUCHMARK *n* maker's mark stamped on pewter objects

TOUCHPAD *n* part of laptop computer functioning like mouse

TOUCHPADS > TOUCHPAD

TOUCHTONE *adj* of or relating to a telephone dialling system in which each of the buttons pressed generates a tone of a different pitch, which is transmitted to the exchange

TOUCHUP *n* renovation or retouching, as of a painting

TOUCHUPS > TOUCHUP

TOUCHWOOD *n* something, esp dry wood, used as tinder

TOUCHY *adj* easily offended

TOUGH *adj* strong or resilient ▷ *n* rough violent person

TOUGHED > TOUGH

TOUGHEN *vb* make or become tough or tougher

TOUGHENED > TOUGHEN

TOUGHENER > TOUGHEN

TOUGHENS > TOUGHEN

TOUGHER > TOUGH

TOUGHEST > TOUGH

TOUGHIE *n* person who is tough

TOUGHIES > TOUGHIE

TOUGHING > TOUGH

TOUGHISH > TOUGH

TOUGHLY > TOUGH

TOUGHNESS *n* quality or an instance of being tough

TOUGHS > TOUGH

TOUGHY *same as* > TOUGHIE

TOUK *same as* > TUCK

TOUKED > TOUK

TOUKING > TOUK

TOUKS > TOUK

TOULADI *same as* > TULADI

TOULADIS > TOULADI

TOUN *n* town

TOUNS > TOUN

TOUPEE *n* small wig

TOUPEED *adj* wearing a toupee

TOUPEES > TOUPEE

TOUPET *same as* > TOUPEE

TOUPETS > TOUPET

TOUPIE *n* round boneless smoked ham

TOUPIES > TOUPIE

TOUR *n* journey visiting places of interest along the way ▷ *vb* make a tour (of)

TOURACO *n* brightly coloured crested arboreal African bird

TOURACOS > TOURACO

TOURED > TOUR

TOURER *n* large open car with a folding top

TOURERS > TOURER

TOURIE *same as* > TOORIE

TOURIES > TOURIE

TOURING > TOUR

TOURINGS > TOUR

TOURISM *n* tourist travel as an industry

TOURISMS > TOURISM

TOURIST *n* person travelling for pleasure ▷ *adj* of or relating to tourists or tourism

TOURISTA *variant of* > TOURIST

TOURISTAS > TOURISTA

TOURISTED *adj* busy with tourists

TOURISTIC > TOURIST

TOURISTS > TOURIST

TOURISTY *adj* informal term for full of tourists or tourist attractions

TOURNEDOS *n* thick round steak of beef

TOURNEY *n* knightly tournament ▷ *vb* engage in a tourney

TOURNEYED > TOURNEY

TOURNEYER > TOURNEY

TOURNEYS > TOURNEY

TOURNURE *n* outline or contour

TOURNURES > TOURNURE

TOURS > TOUR

TOURTIERE *n* type of meat pie

TOUSE *vb* tangle, ruffle, or disarrange; treat roughly

TOUSED > TOUSE

TOUSER > TOUSE

TOUSERS > TOUSE

TOUSES > TOUSE

TOUSIER > TOUSY

TOUSIEST > TOUSY

TOUSING > TOUSE

TOUSINGS > TOUSE

TOUSLE *vb* make (hair or clothes) ruffled and untidy ▷ *n* disorderly, tangled, or rumpled state

TOUSLED > TOUSLE

TOUSLES > TOUSLE

TOUSLING > TOUSLE
TOUSTIE adj irritable; testy
TOUSTIER > TOUSTIE
TOUSTIEST > TOUSTIE
TOUSY adj tousled
TOUT vb seek business in a persistent manner ▷ n person who sells tickets for a popular event at inflated prices
TOUTED > TOUT
TOUTER > TOUT
TOUTERS > TOUT
TOUTIE adj childishly irritable or sullen
TOUTIER > TOUTIE
TOUTIEST > TOUTIE
TOUTING > TOUT
TOUTON n deep-fried round of bread dough
TOUTONS > TOUTON
TOUTS > TOUT
TOUZE variant spelling of > TOUSE
TOUZED > TOUZE
TOUZES > TOUZE
TOUZIER > TOUZY
TOUZIEST > TOUZY
TOUZING > TOUZE
TOUZLE rare spelling of > TOUSLE
TOUZLED > TOUZLE
TOUZLES > TOUZLE
TOUZLING > TOUZLE
TOUZY variant spelling of > TOUSY
TOVARICH same as > TOVARISCH
TOVARISCH n comrade: a term of address
TOVARISH same as > TOVARISCH
TOW vb drag, esp by means of a rope ▷ n towing
TOWABLE > TOW
TOWAGE n charge made for towing
TOWAGES > TOWAGE
TOWARD same as > TOWARDS
TOWARDLY adj compliant
TOWARDS prep in the direction of
TOWAWAY n vehicle which has been towed away
TOWAWAYS > TOWAWAY
TOWBAR n metal bar on a car for towing vehicles
TOWBARS > TOWBAR
TOWBOAT n another word for tug (the boat)
TOWBOATS > TOWBOAT
TOWED > TOW
TOWEL n cloth for drying things ▷ vb dry or wipe with a towel
TOWELED > TOWEL
TOWELETTE n paper towel
TOWELHEAD n offensive term for someone who wears a turban

TOWELING > TOWEL
TOWELINGS > TOWEL
TOWELLED > TOWEL
TOWELLING n material used for making towels
TOWELS > TOWEL
TOWER n tall structure, often forming part of a larger building ▷ vb rise like a tower
TOWERED adj having a tower or towers
TOWERIER > TOWERY
TOWERIEST > TOWERY
TOWERING adj very tall or impressive
TOWERLESS adj not having a tower
TOWERLIKE adj like a tower
TOWERS > TOWER
TOWERY adj with towers
TOWHEAD n often disparaging term for a person with blond or yellowish hair
TOWHEADED adj having blonde or yellowish hair
TOWHEADS > TOWHEAD
TOWHEE n N American brownish-coloured sparrow
TOWHEES > TOWHEE
TOWIE n truck used for towing
TOWIER > TOW
TOWIES > TOWIE
TOWIEST > TOW
TOWING > TOW
TOWINGS > TOW
TOWKAY n sir
TOWKAYS > TOWKAY
TOWLINE same as > TOWROPE
TOWLINES > TOWLINE
TOWMON same as > TOWMOND
TOWMOND n old word for year
TOWMONDS > TOWMOND
TOWMONS > TOWMON
TOWMONT same as > TOWMOND
TOWMONTS > TOWMONT
TOWN n group of buildings larger than a village
TOWNEE same as > TOWNIE
TOWNEES > TOWNEE
TOWNFOLK same as > TOWNSFOLK
TOWNHALL adj of a variety of the Asian plant moschatel
TOWNHOME another word for > TOWNHOUSE
TOWNHOMES > TOWNHOME
TOWNHOUSE n terraced house in an urban area, esp a fashionable one, often having the main living room on the first floor with an integral garage on the ground floor

TOWNIE n often disparaging term for a resident in a town
TOWNIER > TOWNY
TOWNIES > TOWNY
TOWNIEST > TOWNY
TOWNISH > TOWN
TOWNLAND n division of land of various sizes
TOWNLANDS > TOWNLAND
TOWNLESS > TOWN
TOWNLET n small town
TOWNLETS > TOWNLET
TOWNLIER > TOWNLY
TOWNLIEST > TOWNLY
TOWNLING n person who lives in a town
TOWNLINGS > TOWNLING
TOWNLY adj characteristic of a town
TOWNS > TOWN
TOWNSCAPE n view of an urban scene
TOWNSFOLK n people of a town
TOWNSHIP n small town
TOWNSHIPS > TOWNSHIP
TOWNSITE n site of a town
TOWNSITES > TOWNSITE
TOWNSKIP n old term for a mischievous and roguish child who frequents city streets
TOWNSKIPS > TOWNSKIP
TOWNSMAN n inhabitant of a town
TOWNSMEN > TOWNSMAN
TOWNWARD adv in the direction of the town
TOWNWEAR n clothes suitable for wearing while pursuing activities usually associated with towns
TOWNWEARS > TOWNWEAR
TOWNY adj characteristic of a town
TOWPATH n path beside a canal or river
TOWPATHS > TOWPATH
TOWPLANE n aeroplane that tows gliders
TOWPLANES > TOWPLANE
TOWROPE n rope or cable used for towing a vehicle or vessel
TOWROPES > TOWROPE
TOWS > TOW
TOWSACK n sack made from tow
TOWSACKS > TOWSACK
TOWSE same as > TOUSE
TOWSED > TOWSE
TOWSER > TOWSE
TOWSERS > TOWSE
TOWSES > TOWSE
TOWSIER > TOWSY
TOWSIEST > TOWSY
TOWSING > TOWSE
TOWSY same as > TOUSY
TOWT vb sulk
TOWTED > TOWT
TOWTING > TOWT

TOWTS > TOWT
TOWY > TOW
TOWZE same as > TOUSE
TOWZED > TOWZE
TOWZES > TOWZE
TOWZIER > TOWZY
TOWZIEST > TOWZY
TOWZING > TOWZE
TOWZY same as > TOUSY
TOXAEMIA n blood poisoning
TOXAEMIAS > TOXAEMIA
TOXAEMIC > TOXAEMIA
TOXAPHENE n amber waxy solid with a pleasant pine odour, consisting of chlorinated terpenes, esp chlorinated camphene: used as an insecticide
TOXEMIA same as > TOXAEMIA
TOXEMIAS > TOXAEMIA
TOXEMIC > TOXAEMIA
TOXIC adj poisonous ▷ n toxic substance
TOXICAL adj toxic
TOXICALLY > TOXIC
TOXICANT n toxic substance ▷ adj poisonous
TOXICANTS > TOXICANT
TOXICITY n degree of strength of a poison
TOXICOSES > TOXICOSIS
TOXICOSIS n any disease or condition caused by poisoning
TOXICS > TOXIC
TOXIGENIC adj producing poison
TOXIN n poison of bacterial origin
TOXINE nonstandard variant spelling of > TOXIN
TOXINES > TOXINE
TOXINS > TOXIN
TOXOCARA n parasitic worm infesting the intestines of cats and dogs
TOXOCARAL adj relating to toxocara
TOXOCARAS > TOXOCARA
TOXOID n toxin that has been treated to reduce its toxicity
TOXOIDS > TOXOID
TOXOPHILY n archer
TOY n something designed to be played with ▷ adj designed to be played with ▷ vb play, fiddle, or flirt
TOYBOX n box for toys
TOYBOXES > TOYBOX
TOYCHEST n chest for toys
TOYCHESTS > TOYCHEST
TOYED > TOY
TOYER > TOY
TOYERS > TOY
TOYETIC adj (of a film or television franchise) able to generate revenue via spin-off toys
TOYING > TOY

TOYINGS > TOY
TOYISH *adj* resembling a toy
TOYISHLY > TOYISH
TOYLAND *n* toy industry
TOYLANDS > TOYLAND
TOYLESOME *old spelling of* > TOILSOME
TOYLESS > TOY
TOYLIKE > TOY
TOYLSOM *old spelling of* > TOILSOME
TOYMAN *n* man who sells toys
TOYMEN > TOYMAN
TOYO *n* Japanese straw-like material made out of rice paper and used to make hats
TOYON *n* shrub related to the rose
TOYONS > TOYON
TOYOS > TOYO
TOYS > TOY
TOYSHOP *n* shop selling toys
TOYSHOPS > TOYSHOP
TOYSOME *adj* playful
TOYTOWN *adj* having an unreal and picturesque appearance ▷ *n* place with an unreal and picturesque appearance
TOYTOWNS > TOYTOWN
TOYWOMAN *n* woman who sells toys
TOYWOMEN > TOYWOMAN
TOZE *vb* tease out; (of wool, etc) card
TOZED > TOZE
TOZES > TOZE
TOZIE *n* type of shawl
TOZIES > TOZIE
TOZING > TOZE
TRABEATE *same as* > TRABEATED
TRABEATED *adj* constructed with horizontal beams as opposed to arches
TRABECULA *n* any of various rod-shaped structures that divide organs into separate chambers
TRABS *pl n* training shoes
TRACE *vb* locate or work out (the cause of something) ▷ *n* track left by something
TRACEABLE > TRACE
TRACEABLY > TRACE
TRACED > TRACE
TRACELESS > TRACE
TRACER *n* projectile which leaves a visible trail
TRACERIED > TRACERY
TRACERIES > TRACERY
TRACERS > TRACER
TRACERY *n* pattern of interlacing lines
TRACES > TRACE
TRACEUR *n* parkour participant

TRACEURS > TRACEUR
TRACHEA *n* windpipe
TRACHEAE > TRACHEA
TRACHEAL > TRACHEA
TRACHEARY *adj* using tracheae to breathe
TRACHEAS > TRACHEA
TRACHEATE > TRACHEA
TRACHEID *n* element of xylem tissue consisting of an elongated lignified cell with tapering ends and large pits
TRACHEIDE *same as* > TRACHEID
TRACHEIDS > TRACHEID
TRACHEOLE *n* small trachea found in some insects
TRACHINUS *n* weever fish
TRACHITIS *n* another spelling of tracheitis (inflammation of the trachea)
TRACHLE *vb* (of hair, clothing, etc) make untidy
TRACHLED > TRACHLE
TRACHLES > TRACHLE
TRACHLING > TRACHLE
TRACHOMA *n* chronic contagious disease of the eye characterized by inflammation of the inner surface of the lids and the formation of scar tissue
TRACHOMAS > TRACHOMA
TRACHYTE *n* light-coloured fine-grained volcanic rock
TRACHYTES > TRACHYTE
TRACHYTIC *adj* (of the texture of certain igneous rocks) characterized by a parallel arrangement of crystals, which mark the flow of the lava when still molten
TRACING *n* traced copy
TRACINGS > TRACING
TRACK *n* rough road or path ▷ *vb* follow the trail or path of
TRACKABLE > TRACK
TRACKAGE *n* collective term for the railway tracks in general, or those in a given area or belonging to a particular company, etc
TRACKAGES > TRACKAGE
TRACKBALL *n* device consisting of a small ball, mounted in a cup, which can be rotated to move the cursor around the screen
TRACKBED *n* foundation on which railway tracks are laid
TRACKBEDS > TRACKBED
TRACKED > TRACK
TRACKER > TRACK
TRACKERS > TRACK
TRACKIE *adj* resembling or forming part of a tracksuit

TRACKIES *pl n* loose-fitting trousers with elasticated cuffs
TRACKING *n* act or process of following something or someone
TRACKINGS > TRACKING
TRACKLESS *adj* having or leaving no trace or trail
TRACKMAN *n* workman who lays and maintains railway track
TRACKMEN > TRACKMAN
TRACKPAD *same as* > TOUCHPAD
TRACKPADS > TRACKPAD
TRACKROAD *another word for* > TOWPATH
TRACKS > TRACK
TRACKSIDE *n* area alongside a track
TRACKSUIT *n* warm loose-fitting suit worn by athletes etc, esp during training
TRACKWAY *n* path or track
TRACKWAYS > TRACKWAY
TRACT *n* wide area ▷ *vb* track
TRACTABLE *adj* easy to manage or control
TRACTABLY > TRACTABLE
TRACTATE *n* short tract
TRACTATES > TRACTATE
TRACTATOR *n* person who writes tracts
TRACTED > TRACT
TRACTILE *adj* capable of being drawn out
TRACTING > TRACT
TRACTION *n* pulling, esp by engine power
TRACTIONS > TRACTION
TRACTIVE > TRACTION
TRACTOR *n* motor vehicle with large rear wheels for pulling farm machinery
TRACTORS > TRACTOR
TRACTRIX *n* (in geometry) type of curve
TRACTS > TRACT
TRACTUS *n* anthem sung in some RC masses
TRACTUSES > TRACTUS
TRAD *n* traditional jazz, as revived in the 1950s
TRADABLE > TRADE
TRADE *n* buying, selling, or exchange of goods ▷ *vb* buy and sell ▷ *adj* intended for or available only to people in industry or business
TRADEABLE > TRADE
TRADED > TRADE
TRADEFUL *adj* (of shops, for example) full of trade
TRADELESS > TRADE
TRADEMARK *n* (legally registered) name or symbol used by a firm to distinguish its goods ▷ *vb* label with a trademark

TRADENAME *n* name used by a trade to refer to a commodity, service, etc
TRADEOFF *n* exchange, esp as a compromise
TRADEOFFS > TRADEOFF
TRADER *n* person who engages in trade
TRADERS > TRADER
TRADES > TRADE
TRADESMAN *n* skilled worker
TRADESMEN > TRADESMAN
TRADING > TRADE
TRADINGS > TRADE
TRADITION *n* handing down from generation to generation of customs and beliefs
TRADITIVE *adj* traditional
TRADITOR *n* Christian who betrayed his fellow Christians at the time of the Roman persecutions
TRADITORS > TRADITOR
TRADS > TRAD
TRADUCE *vb* slander
TRADUCED > TRADUCE
TRADUCER > TRADUCE
TRADUCERS > TRADUCE
TRADUCES > TRADUCE
TRADUCIAN > TRADUCE
TRADUCING > TRADUCE
TRAFFIC *n* vehicles coming and going on a road ▷ *vb* trade
TRAFFICKY *adj* (of a street, area, town, etc) busy with motor vehicles
TRAFFICS > TRAFFIC
TRAGAL > TRAGUS
TRAGEDIAN *n* person who acts in or writes tragedies
TRAGEDIES > TRAGEDY
TRAGEDY *n* shocking or sad event
TRAGELAPH *n* mythical animal: a cross between a goat and a stag
TRAGI > TRAGUS
TRAGIC *adj* of or like a tragedy ▷ *n* tragedian
TRAGICAL *same as* > TRAGIC
TRAGICS > TRAGIC
TRAGOPAN *n* pheasant of S and SE Asia, with a brilliant plumage and brightly coloured fleshy processes on the head
TRAGOPANS > TRAGOPAN
TRAGULE *n* mouse deer
TRAGULES > TRAGULE
TRAGULINE *adj* like or characteristic of a tragule
TRAGUS *n* fleshy projection that partially covers the entrance to the external ear
TRAHISON *n* treason
TRAHISONS > TRAHISON

TRAIK vb trudge; trek with difficulty

TRAIKED > TRAIK

TRAIKING > TRAIK

TRAIKIT > TRAIK

TRAIKS > TRAIK

TRAIL n path, track, or road ▷ vb drag along the ground

TRAILABLE adj capable of being trailed

TRAILED > TRAIL

TRAILER n vehicle designed to be towed by another vehicle ▷ vb use a trailer to advertise (something)

TRAILERED > TRAILER

TRAILERS > TRAILER

TRAILHEAD n place where a trail begins

TRAILING adj (of a plant) having a long stem which spreads over the ground or hangs loosely

TRAILLESS adj without trail

TRAILS > TRAIL

TRAILSIDE adj beside a trail

TRAIN vb instruct in a skill ▷ n line of railway coaches or wagons drawn by an engine

TRAINABLE > TRAIN

TRAINBAND n company of English militia from the 16th to the 18th century

TRAINED > TRAIN

TRAINEE n person being trained ▷ adj (of a person) undergoing training

TRAINEES > TRAINEE

TRAINER n person who trains an athlete or sportsman

TRAINERS pl n shoes in the style of those used for sports training

TRAINFUL n quantity of people or cargo that would be capable of filling a train

TRAINFULS > TRAINFUL

TRAINING n process of bringing a person to an agreed standard of proficiency by practice and instruction

TRAININGS > TRAINING

TRAINLESS > TRAIN

TRAINLOAD n quantity of people or cargo sufficient to fill a train

TRAINMAN n man who works on a train

TRAINMEN > TRAINMAN

TRAINS > TRAIN

TRAINWAY n railway track; channel in a built-up area through which a train passes

TRAINWAYS > TRAINWAY

TRAIPSE vb walk wearily

▷ n long or tiring walk

TRAIPSED > TRAIPSE

TRAIPSES > TRAIPSE

TRAIPSING > TRAIPSE

TRAIT n characteristic feature

TRAITOR n person guilty of treason or treachery

TRAITORLY adj of or characteristic of a traitor

TRAITORS > TRAITOR

TRAITRESS > TRAITOR

TRAITS > TRAIT

TRAJECT vb transport or transmit

TRAJECTED > TRAJECT

TRAJECTS > TRAJECT

TRAM same as > TRAMMEL

TRAMCAR same as > TRAMMEL

TRAMCARS > TRAMCAR

TRAMEL variant spelling of > TRAMMEL

TRAMELED > TRAMEL

TRAMELING > TRAMEL

TRAMELL variant spelling of > TRAMMEL

TRAMELLED > TRAMELL

TRAMELLS > TRAMELL

TRAMELS > TRAMEL

TRAMLESS > TRAM

TRAMLINE n tracks on which a tram runs

TRAMLINED adj having tramlines

TRAMLINES > TRAMLINE

TRAMMED > TRAM

TRAMMEL n hindrance to free action or movement ▷ vb hinder or restrain

TRAMMELED > TRAMMEL

TRAMMELER > TRAMMEL

TRAMMELS > TRAMMEL

TRAMMIE n conductor or driver of a tram

TRAMMIES > TRAMMIE

TRAMMING > TRAM

TRAMP vb travel on foot, hike ▷ n homeless person who travels on foot

TRAMPED > TRAMP

TRAMPER n person who tramps

TRAMPERS > TRAMPER

TRAMPET variant spelling of > TRAMPETTE

TRAMPETS > TRAMPET

TRAMPETTE n small trampoline

TRAMPIER > TRAMPY

TRAMPIEST > TRAMPY

TRAMPING > TRAMP

TRAMPINGS > TRAMP

TRAMPISH > TRAMP

TRAMPLE vb tread on and crush ▷ n action or sound of trampling

TRAMPLED > TRAMPLE

TRAMPLER > TRAMPLE

TRAMPLERS > TRAMPLE

TRAMPLES > TRAMPLE

TRAMPLING > TRAMPLE

TRAMPOLIN n variant of trampoline: a tough

canvass sheet suspended by springs from a frame, used by acrobats, gymnasts, etc

TRAMPS > TRAMP

TRAMPY adj (of woman) disreputable

TRAMROAD same as > TRAMWAY

TRAMROADS > TRAMROAD

TRAMS > TRAM

TRAMWAY same as > TRAMLINE

TRAMWAYS > TRAMWAY

TRANCE n unconscious or dazed state ▷ vb put into or as into a trance

TRANCED > TRANCE

TRANCEDLY > TRANCE

TRANCES > TRANCE

TRANCEY adj (of music) characteristic of the trance sub-genre

TRANCHE n portion of something large

TRANCHES > TRANCHE

TRANCHET n stone age cutting tool

TRANCHETS > TRANCHET

TRANCIER > TRANCEY

TRANCIEST > TRANCEY

TRANCING > TRANCE

TRANECT n ferry

TRANECTS > TRANECT

TRANGAM n bauble or trinket

TRANGAMS > TRANGAM

TRANGLE n (in heraldry) a small fesse

TRANGLES > TRANGLE

TRANK n tranquillizer ▷ vb administer a tranquillizer

TRANKED > TRANK

TRANKING > TRANK

TRANKS > TRANK

TRANKUM same as > TRANGAM

TRANKUMS > TRANKUM

TRANNIE n transistor radio

TRANNIES > TRANNY

TRANNY same as > TRANNIE

TRANQ same as > TRANK

TRANQS > TRANQ

TRANQUIL adj calm and quiet

TRANS n short from of translation

TRANSACT vb conduct or negotiate (a business deal)

TRANSACTS > TRANSACT

TRANSAXLE n combined axle and gearbox

TRANSCEND vb rise above

TRANSCODE vb convert (digital computer data) from one format to another

TRANSDUCE vb change one form of energy to another

TRANSE n way through; passage

TRANSECT n sample strip of land used to monitor plant distribution and animal populations within a given area ▷ vb cut or divide crossways

TRANSECTS > TRANSECT

TRANSENNA n screen around a shrine

TRANSEPT n either of the two shorter wings of a cross-shaped church

TRANSEPTS > TRANSEPT

TRANSES > TRANSE

TRANSEUNT adj (of a mental act) causing effects outside the mind

TRANSFARD old past participle of > TRANSFER

TRANSFECT vb transfer genetic material isolated from a cell or virus into another cell

TRANSFER vb move or send from one person or place to another ▷ n transferring

TRANSFERS > TRANSFER

TRANSFIX vb astound or stun

TRANSFIXT > TRANSFIX

TRANSFORM vb change the shape or character of ▷ n result of a mathematical transformation

TRANSFUSE vb give a transfusion to

TRANSGENE n gene that is transferred from an organism of one species to an organism of another species by genetic engineering

TRANSHIP same as > TRANSSHIP

TRANSHIPS > TRANSHIP

TRANSHUME vb (of livestock) move to suitable grazing grounds according to the season

TRANSIENT same as > TRANSEUNT

TRANSIRE n document allowing goods to pass through customs

TRANSIRES > TRANSIRE

TRANSIT n passage or conveyance of goods or people ▷ vb make transit

TRANSITED > TRANSIT

TRANSITS > TRANSIT

TRANSLATE vb turn from one language into another

TRANSMEW old variant of > TRANSMUTE

TRANSMEWS > TRANSMEW

TRANSMIT vb pass (something) from one person or place to another

TRANSMITS > TRANSMIT

TRANSMOVE *vb* change the form, character, or substance of
TRANSMUTE *vb* change the form or nature of
TRANSOM *n* horizontal bar across a window
TRANSOMED > TRANSOM
TRANSOMS > TRANSOM
TRANSONIC *adj* of or relating to conditions when travelling at or near the speed of sound
TRANSPIRE *vb* become known
TRANSPORT *vb* convey from one place to another ▷ *n* business or system of transporting
TRANSPOSE *vb* interchange two things ▷ *n* matrix resulting from interchanging the rows and columns of a given matrix
TRANSSHIP *vb* transfer or be transferred from one ship or vehicle to another
TRANSUDE *vb* (of a fluid) ooze or pass through interstices, pores, or small holes
TRANSUDED > TRANSUDE
TRANSUDES > TRANSUDE
TRANSUME *vb* make an official transcription of
TRANSUMED > TRANSUME
TRANSUMES > TRANSUME
TRANSUMPT *n* official transcription
TRANSVEST *vb* wear clothes traditionally associated with the opposite sex
TRANT *vb* travel from place to place selling goods
TRANTED > TRANT
TRANTER > TRANT
TRANTERS > TRANT
TRANTING > TRANT
TRANTS > TRANT
TRAP *n* device for catching animals ▷ *vb* catch
TRAPAN *same as* > TREPAN
TRAPANNED > TRAPAN
TRAPANNER > TRAPAN
TRAPANS > TRAPAN
TRAPBALL *n* old ball game in which a ball is placed in a see-saw device called a trap, flicked up by a batsman hitting one end of the trap, and then hit with a bat
TRAPBALLS > TRAPBALL
TRAPDOOR *n* door in floor or roof
TRAPDOORS > TRAPDOOR
TRAPE *same as* > TRAIPSE
TRAPED > TRAPE
TRAPES *same as* > TRAIPSE
TRAPESED > TRAPES
TRAPESES > TRAPES

TRAPESING > TRAPES
TRAPEZE *n* horizontal bar suspended from two ropes, used by circus acrobats ▷ *vb* swing on a trapeze
TRAPEZED > TRAPEZE
TRAPEZES > TRAPEZE
TRAPEZIA > TRAPEZIUM
TRAPEZIAL > TRAPEZIUM
TRAPEZII > TRAPEZIUS
TRAPEZING > TRAPEZE
TRAPEZIST *n* trapeze artist
TRAPEZIUM *same as* > TRAPEZOID
TRAPEZIUS *n* either of two flat triangular muscles, one covering each side of the back and shoulders, that rotate the shoulder blades
TRAPEZOID *same as* > TRAPEZIUM
TRAPFALL *n* trapdoor that opens under the feet
TRAPFALLS > TRAPFALL
TRAPING > TRAPE
TRAPLIKE > TRAP
TRAPLINE *n* line of traps
TRAPLINES > TRAPLINE
TRAPNEST *n* nest that holds a hen in place so that the number of eggs it alone produces can be counted
TRAPNESTS > TRAPNEST
TRAPPEAN *adj* of, relating to, or consisting of igneous rock, esp a basalt
TRAPPED > TRAP
TRAPPER *n* person who traps animals for their fur
TRAPPERS > TRAPPER
TRAPPIER > TRAPPY
TRAPPIEST > TRAPPY
TRAPPING > TRAP
TRAPPINGS *pl n* accessories that symbolize an office or position
TRAPPOSE *adj* of or relating to traprock
TRAPPOUS *same as* > TRAPPOSE
TRAPPY *adj* having many traps
TRAPROCK *another name for* > TRAP
TRAPROCKS > TRAPROCK
TRAPS > TRAP
TRAPSE *vb* traipse
TRAPSED > TRAPSE
TRAPSES > TRAPSE
TRAPSING > TRAPSE
TRAPT *old past participle of* > TRAP
TRAPUNTO *n* type of quilting that is only partly padded in a design
TRAPUNTOS > TRAPUNTO
TRASH *n* anything worthless ▷ *vb* attack or destroy maliciously

TRASHCAN *n* dustbin
TRASHCANS > TRASHCAN
TRASHED *adj* drunk
TRASHER > TRASH
TRASHERS > TRASH
TRASHERY > TRASH
TRASHES > TRASH
TRASHIER > TRASHY
TRASHIEST > TRASHY
TRASHILY > TRASHY
TRASHING > TRASH
TRASHMAN *another name for* > BINMAN
TRASHMEN > TRASHMAN
TRASHTRIE *n* trash
TRASHY *adj* cheap, worthless, or badly made
TRASS *n* variety of the volcanic rock tuff
TRASSES > TRASS
TRAT *n* type of fishing line holding a series of baited hooks
TRATS > TRAT
TRATT *short for* > TRATTORIA
TRATTORIA *n* Italian restaurant
TRATTORIE > TRATTORIA
TRATTS > TRATT
TRAUCHLE *n* work or a task that is tiring, monotonous, and lengthy ▷ *vb* walk or work slowly and wearily
TRAUCHLED *adj* exhausted by long hard work or concern
TRAUCHLES > TRAUCHLE
TRAUMA *n* emotional shock
TRAUMAS > TRAUMA
TRAUMATA > TRAUMA
TRAUMATIC > TRAUMA
TRAVAIL *n* labour or toil ▷ *vb* suffer or labour painfully
TRAVAILED > TRAVAIL
TRAVAILS > TRAVAIL
TRAVE *n* stout wooden cage in which difficult horses are shod
TRAVEL *vb* go from one place to another, through an area, or for a specified distance ▷ *n* travelling, esp as a tourist
TRAVELED *same as* > TRAVELLED
TRAVELER *same as* > TRAVELLER
TRAVELERS > TRAVELER
TRAVELING > TRAVEL
TRAVELLED *adj* having experienced or undergone much travelling
TRAVELLER *n* person who makes a journey or travels a lot
TRAVELOG *n* film, lecture, or brochure on travel
TRAVELOGS > TRAVELOG
TRAVELS > TRAVEL

TRAVERSAL > TRAVERSE
TRAVERSE *vb* pass or go over
TRAVERSED > TRAVERSE
TRAVERSER > TRAVERSE
TRAVERSES > TRAVERSE
TRAVERTIN *n* porous rock
TRAVES > TRAVE
TRAVESTY *n* grotesque imitation or mockery ▷ *vb* make or be a travesty of
TRAVIS *same as* > TREVISS
TRAVISES > TRAVIS
TRAVOIS *n* sled used for dragging logs
TRAVOISE *same as* > TRAVOIS
TRAVOISES > TRAVOISE
TRAWL *n* net dragged at deep levels behind a fishing boat ▷ *vb* fish with such a net
TRAWLED > TRAWL
TRAWLER *n* trawling boat
TRAWLERS > TRAWLER
TRAWLEY *same as* > TROLLEY
TRAWLEYS > TRAWLEY
TRAWLING > TRAWL
TRAWLINGS > TRAWL
TRAWLNET *n* large net, usually in the shape of a sock or bag, drawn at deep levels behind special boats (trawlers)
TRAWLNETS > TRAWLNET
TRAWLS > TRAWL
TRAY *n* flat board, usu with a rim, for carrying things
TRAYBAKE *n* flat cake which is baked in a tray and cut into small squares
TRAYBAKES > TRAYBAKE
TRAYBIT *n* threepenny bit
TRAYBITS > TRAYBIT
TRAYCLOTH *n* cloth for covering a tray
TRAYF *adj* not prepared according to Jewish law
TRAYFUL *n* as many or as much as will fit on a tray
TRAYFULS > TRAYFUL
TRAYNE *old spelling of* > TRAIN
TRAYNED > TRAIN
TRAYNES > TRAYNE
TRAYNING > TRAYNE
TRAYS > TRAY
TRAZODONE *n* drug used to treat depression
TREACHER *n* traitor; treacherous person
TREACHERS > TREACHER
TREACHERY *n* wilful betrayal
TREACHOUR *same as* > TREACHER
TREACLE *n* thick dark syrup produced when sugar is refined ▷ *vb* add treacle to
TREACLED > TREACLE
TREACLES > TREACLE

TREACLIER > TREACLE
TREACLING > TREACLE
TREACLY > TREACLE
TREAD vb set one's foot on ▷ n way of walking or dancing
TREADED > TREAD
TREADER > TREAD
TREADERS > TREAD
TREADING > TREAD
TREADINGS > TREAD
TREADLE n lever worked by the foot to turn a wheel ▷ vb work (a machine) with a treadle
TREADLED > TREADLE
TREADLER > TREADLE
TREADLERS > TREADLE
TREADLES > TREADLE
TREADLESS adj (of a tyre, for example) having no tread
TREADLING > TREADLE
TREADMILL n cylinder turned by treading on steps projecting from it
TREADS > TREAD
TREAGUE n agreement to stop fighting
TREAGUES > TREAGUE
TREASON n betrayal of one's sovereign or country
TREASONS > TREASON
TREASURE n collection of wealth, esp gold or jewels ▷ vb prize or cherish
TREASURED > TREASURE
TREASURER n official in charge of funds
TREASURES > TREASURE
TREASURY n storage place for treasure
TREAT vb deal with or regard in a certain manner ▷ n pleasure, entertainment, etc given or paid for by someone else
TREATABLE > TREAT
TREATED > TREAT
TREATER > TREAT
TREATERS > TREAT
TREATIES > TREATY
TREATING > TREAT
TREATINGS > TREAT
TREATISE n formal piece of writing on a particular subject
TREATISES > TREATISE
TREATMENT n medical care
TREATS > TREAT
TREATY n signed contract between states
TREBBIANO n grape used to make wine
TREBLE adj triple ▷ n (singer with or part for) a soprano voice ▷ vb increase three times
TREBLED > TREBLE
TREBLES > TREBLE
TREBLING n act of trebling

TREBLINGS > TREBLING
TREBLY > TREBLE
TREBUCHET n large medieval siege engine for hurling missiles consisting of a sling on a pivoted wooden arm set in motion by the fall of a weight
TREBUCKET same as > TREBUCHET
TRECENTO n 14th century, esp with reference to Italian art and literature
TRECENTOS > TRECENTO
TRECK same as > TREK
TRECKED > TRECK
TRECKING > TRECK
TRECKS > TRECK
TREDDLE variant spelling of > TREADLE
TREDDLED > TREDDLE
TREDDLES > TREDDLE
TREDDLING > TREDDLE
TREDILLE same as > TREDRILLE
TREDILLES > TREDILLE
TREDRILLE n card game for three players
TREE n large perennial plant with a woody trunk
TREED > TREE
TREEHOUSE n house built in tree
TREEING > TREE
TREELAWN n narrow band of grass between a road and a pavement, usually planted with trees
TREELAWNS > TREELAWN
TREELESS > TREE
TREELIKE > TREE
TREELINE n line marking the altitude above which trees will not grow
TREELINES > TREELINE
TREEN adj made of wood ▷ n art of making treenware
TREENAIL n dowel used for pinning planks or timbers together
TREENAILS > TREENAIL
TREENS > TREEN
TREENWARE n dishes and other household utensils made of wood, as by pioneers in North America
TREES > TREE
TREESHIP n state of being a tree
TREESHIPS > TREESHIP
TREETOP n top of a tree
TREETOPS > TREETOP
TREEWARE n books, magazines, or other reading materials that are printed on paper made from wood pulp as opposed to texts in the form of computer software, CD-ROM, audio books, etc
TREEWARES > TREEWARE

TREEWAX n yellowish wax secreted by an oriental scale insect
TREEWAXES > TREEWAX
TREF adj in Judaism, ritually unfit to be eaten
TREFA same as > TREF
TREFAH same as > TREF
TREFOIL n plant, such as clover, with a three-lobed leaf
TREFOILED > TREFOIL
TREFOILS > TREFOIL
TREGETOUR n juggler
TREGGINGS pl n thick close-fitting leggings
TREHALA n edible sugary substance from the cocoon of an Asian weevil
TREHALAS > TREHALA
TREHALOSE n white crystalline disaccharide that occurs in yeast and certain fungi
TREIF same as > TREF
TREIFA same as > TREF
TREILLAGE n latticework
TREILLE another word for > TRELLIS
TREILLES > TREILLE
TREK n long difficult journey, esp on foot ▷ vb make such a journey
TREKKED > TREK
TREKKER > TREK
TREKKERS > TREK
TREKKING n as in pony trekking the act of riding ponies cross-country
TREKKINGS > TREKKING
TREKS > TREK
TRELLIS n framework of horizontal and vertical strips of wood ▷ vb interweave (strips of wood, etc) to make a trellis
TRELLISED > TRELLIS
TRELLISES > TRELLIS
TREM n lever for producing a tremolo on a guitar
TREMA n mark placed over vowel to indicate it is to be pronounced separately
TREMAS > TREMA
TREMATIC adj relating to the gills
TREMATODE n parasitic flatworm
TREMATOID > TREMATODE
TREMBLANT adj (of jewels) set in such a way that they shake when the wearer moves
TREMBLE vb shake or quiver ▷ n trembling
TREMBLED > TREMBLE
TREMBLER n device that vibrates to make or break an electrical circuit
TREMBLERS > TREMBLER
TREMBLES n disease of cattle and sheep characterized by muscular

incoordination and tremor, caused by ingestion of white snakeroot or rayless goldenrod
TREMBLIER > TREMBLE
TREMBLING > TREMBLE
TREMBLOR n earth tremor
TREMBLORS > TREMBLOR
TREMBLY > TREMBLE
TREMIE n metal hopper and pipe used to distribute freshly mixed concrete underwater
TREMIES > TREMIE
TREMOLANT another word for > TREMOLO
TREMOLITE n white or pale green mineral of the amphibole group consisting of calcium magnesium silicate
TREMOLO n quivering effect in singing or playing
TREMOLOS > TREMOLO
TREMOR n involuntary shaking ▷ vb tremble
TREMORED > TREMOR
TREMORING > TREMOR
TREMOROUS > TREMOR
TREMORS > TREMOR
TREMS > TREM
TREMULANT n device on an organ by which the wind stream is made to fluctuate in intensity producing a tremolo effect
TREMULATE vb produce a tremulous sound
TREMULOUS adj trembling, as from fear or excitement
TRENAIL same as > TREENAIL
TRENAILS > TRENAIL
TRENCH n long narrow ditch, esp one used as a shelter in war ▷ adj of or involving military trenches ▷ vb make a trench in (a place)
TRENCHAND old variant of > TRENCHANT
TRENCHANT adj incisive
TRENCHARD same as > TRENCHER
TRENCHED > TRENCH
TRENCHER n wooden plate for serving food
TRENCHERS > TRENCHER
TRENCHES > TRENCH
TRENCHING > TRENCH
TREND n general tendency or direction ▷ vb take a certain trend
TRENDED > TREND
TRENDIER > TRENDY
TRENDIES > TRENDY
TRENDIEST > TRENDY
TRENDIFY vb render fashionable
TRENDILY > TRENDY
TRENDING > TREND

t

TRENDOID n follower of trends

TRENDOIDS > TRENDOID

TRENDS > TREND

TRENDY n consciously fashionable (person) ▷ adj consciously fashionable

TRENDYISM > TRENDY

TRENISE n one of the figures in a quadrille

TRENISES > TRENISE

TRENTAL n mass said in remembrance of a person 30 days after his or her death

TRENTALS > TRENTAL

TREPAN same as > TREPHINE

TREPANG n any of various large sea cucumbers

TREPANGS > TREPANG

TREPANNED > TREPAN

TREPANNER > TREPAN

TREPANS > TREPAN

TREPHINE n surgical sawlike instrument for removing circular sections of bone, esp from the skull ▷ vb remove a circular section of bone from (esp the skull)

TREPHINED > TREPHINE

TREPHINER > TREPHINE

TREPHINES > TREPHINE

TREPID adj trembling

TREPIDANT adj trembling

TREPONEMA n anaerobic spirochaete bacterium that causes syphilis

TREPONEME same as > TREPONEMA

TRES adj very

TRESPASS vb go onto another's property without permission ▷ n trespassing

TRESS n lock of hair, esp a long lock of woman's hair ▷ vb arrange in tresses

TRESSED adj having a tress or tresses as specified

TRESSEL variant spelling of > TRESTLE

TRESSELS > TRESSEL

TRESSES > TRESS

TRESSIER > TRESS

TRESSIEST > TRESS

TRESSING > TRESS

TRESSOUR same as > TRESSURE

TRESSOURS > TRESSOUR

TRESSURE n narrow inner border on a shield, usually decorated with fleurs-de-lys

TRESSURED > TRESSURE

TRESSURES > TRESSURE

TRESSY > TRESS

TREST old variant of > TRESTLE

TRESTLE n board fixed on pairs of spreading legs, used as a support

TRESTLES > TRESTLE

TRESTS > TREST

TRET n (formerly) allowance granted for waste due to transportation

TRETINOIN n retinoid drug used to treat certain skin conditions

TRETS > TRET

TREVALLY n any of various food and game fishes

TREVALLYS > TREVALLY

TREVET same as > TRIVET

TREVETS > TREVET

TREVIS variant spelling of > TREVISS

TREVISES > TREVIS

TREVISS n partition in a stable for keeping animals apart

TREVISSES > TREVISS

TREW old variant spelling of > TRUE

TREWS pl n close-fitting tartan trousers

TREWSMAN n Highlander

TREWSMEN > TREWSMAN

TREY n any card or dice throw with three spots

TREYBIT same as > TRAYBIT

TREYBITS > TREYBIT

TREYF adj not prepared according to Jewish law

TREYFA same as > TREYF

TREYS > TREY

TREZ same as > TREY

TREZES > TREZ

TRIABLE adj liable to be tried judicially

TRIAC n device for regulating the amount of electric current allowed to reach a circuit

TRIACID adj (of a base) capable of reacting with three molecules of a monobasic acid

TRIACIDS > TRIACID

TRIACS > TRIAC

TRIACT adj having three rays ▷ n sponge spicule with three rays

TRIACTINE same as > TRIACT

TRIACTOR n type of bet

TRIACTORS > TRIACTOR

TRIACTS > TRIACT

TRIAD n group of three

TRIADIC n something that has the characteristics of a triad

TRIADICS > TRIADIC

TRIADISM > TRIAD

TRIADISMS > TRIAD

TRIADIST > TRIAD

TRIADISTS > TRIAD

TRIADS > TRIAD

TRIAGE n sorting emergency patients into categories of priority

▷ vb sort (patients) into categories of priority

TRIAGED > TRIAGE

TRIAGES > TRIAGE

TRIAGING > TRIAGE

TRIAL n investigation of a case before a judge ▷ vb test or try out

TRIALED > TRIAL

TRIALING > TRIAL

TRIALISM n belief that man consists of body, soul, and spirit

TRIALISMS > TRIALISM

TRIALIST same as > TRIALLIST

TRIALISTS > TRIALIST

TRIALITY > TRIALISM

TRIALLED > TRIAL

TRIALLING > TRIAL

TRIALLIST n person who takes part in a competition

TRIALOGUE n dialogue between three people

TRIALS > TRIAL

TRIALWARE n computer software that can be used without charge for a limited evaluation period

TRIANGLE n geometric figure with three sides

TRIANGLED > TRIANGLE

TRIANGLES > TRIANGLE

TRIAPSAL adj (of a church) having three apses

TRIARCH n one of three rulers of a triarchy

TRIARCHS > TRIARCH

TRIARCHY n government by three people

TRIASSIC adj of, denoting, or formed in the first period of the Mesozoic era

TRIATHLON n athletic contest in which each athlete competes in three different events: swimming, cycling, and running

TRIATIC n rope between a ship's mastheads

TRIATICS > TRIATIC

TRIATOMIC adj a molecule having three atoms

TRIAXIAL adj having three axes ▷ n sponge spicule with three axes

TRIAXIALS > TRIAXIAL

TRIAXON another name for > TRIAXIAL

TRIAXONS > TRIAXON

TRIAZIN same as > TRIAZINE

TRIAZINE n any of three azines that contain three nitrogen atoms in their molecules

TRIAZINES > TRIAZINE

TRIAZINS > TRIAZIN

TRIAZOLE n heterocyclic compound

TRIAZOLES > TRIAZOLE

TRIAZOLIC > TRIAZOLE

TRIBADE n lesbian, esp one who practises tribadism

TRIBADES > TRIBADE

TRIBADIC > TRIBADE

TRIBADIES > TRIBADY

TRIBADISM n lesbian practice in which one partner lies on top of the other and simulates the male role in heterosexual intercourse

TRIBADY another word for > TRIBADISM

TRIBAL adj of or denoting a tribe or tribes ▷ n member of a tribal community

TRIBALISM n loyalty to a tribe

TRIBALIST > TRIBALISM

TRIBALLY > TRIBAL

TRIBALS > TRIBAL

TRIBASIC adj (of an acid) containing three replaceable hydrogen atoms in the molecule

TRIBBLE n frame for drying paper

TRIBBLES > TRIBBLE

TRIBE n group of clans or families believed to have a common ancestor

TRIBELESS > TRIBE

TRIBES > TRIBE

TRIBESMAN n member of a tribe

TRIBESMEN > TRIBESMAN

TRIBLET n spindle or mandrel used in making rings, tubes, etc

TRIBLETS > TRIBLET

TRIBOLOGY n study of friction, lubrication, and wear between moving surfaces

TRIBRACH n metrical foot of three short syllables

TRIBRACHS > TRIBRACH

TRIBULATE vb trouble

TRIBUNAL n board appointed to inquire into a specific matter

TRIBUNALS > TRIBUNAL

TRIBUNARY > TRIBUNE

TRIBUNATE n office or rank of a tribune

TRIBUNE n people's representative, esp in ancient Rome

TRIBUNES > TRIBUNE

TRIBUTARY n stream or river flowing into a larger one ▷ adj (of a stream or river) flowing into a larger one

TRIBUTE n sign of respect or admiration

TRIBUTER n miner

TRIBUTERS > TRIBUTER

TRIBUTES > TRIBUTE
TRICAR n car with three wheels
TRICARS > TRICAR
TRICE n moment ▷ vb haul up or secure
TRICED > TRICE
TRICEP same as > TRICEPS
TRICEPS n muscle at the back of the upper arm
TRICEPSES > TRICEPS
TRICERION n candlestick with three arms
TRICES > TRICE
TRICHINA n parasitic nematode worm, occurring in the intestines of pigs, rats, and man and producing larvae that form cysts in skeletal muscle
TRICHINAE > TRICHINA
TRICHINAL > TRICHINA
TRICHINAS > TRICHINA
TRICHITE n any of various needle-shaped crystals that occur in some glassy volcanic rocks
TRICHITES > TRICHITE
TRICHITIC > TRICHITE
TRICHOID adj resembling a hair
TRICHOME n any hairlike outgrowth from the surface of a plant
TRICHOMES > TRICHOME
TRICHOMIC > TRICHOME
TRICHORD n musical instrument with three strings
TRICHORDS > TRICHORD
TRICHOSES > TRICHOSIS
TRICHOSIS n any abnormal condition or disease of the hair
TRICHROIC n state of having three colours
TRICHROME adj three-coloured
TRICING > TRICE
TRICITIES > TRICITY
TRICITY n area that comprises three adjoining cities
TRICK n deceitful or cunning action or plan ▷ vb cheat or deceive
TRICKED > TRICK
TRICKER > TRICK
TRICKERS > TRICK
TRICKERY n practice or an instance of using tricks
TRICKIE Scots form of > TRICKY
TRICKIER > TRICKY
TRICKIEST > TRICKY
TRICKILY > TRICKY
TRICKING > TRICK
TRICKINGS > TRICK
TRICKISH same as > TRICKY

TRICKLE vb (cause to) flow in a thin stream or drops ▷ n gradual flow
TRICKLED > TRICKLE
TRICKLES > TRICKLE
TRICKLESS > TRICK
TRICKLET n tiny trickle
TRICKLETS > TRICKLET
TRICKLIER > TRICKLE
TRICKLING > TRICKLE
TRICKLY > TRICKLE
TRICKS > TRICK
TRICKSIER > TRICKSY
TRICKSILY > TRICKSY
TRICKSOME adj full of tricks
TRICKSTER n person who deceives or plays tricks
TRICKSY adj playing tricks habitually
TRICKY adj difficult, needing careful handling
TRICLAD n type of worm having a tripartite intestine
TRICLADS > TRICLAD
TRICLINIA n plural of triclinium: in Ancient Rome, reclining couch
TRICLINIC adj relating to or belonging to the crystal system characterized by three unequal axes, no pair of which are perpendicular
TRICLOSAN n drug used to treat skin infections
TRICOLOR same as > TRICOLOUR
TRICOLORS > TRICOLOR
TRICOLOUR n three-coloured striped flag ▷ adj having or involving three colours
TRICORN n cocked hat with opposing brims turned back and caught in three places ▷ adj having three horns or corners
TRICORNE same as > TRICORN
TRICORNES > TRICORNE
TRICORNS > TRICORN
TRICOT n thin rayon or nylon fabric knitted or resembling knitting, used for dresses, etc
TRICOTINE n twill-weave woollen fabric resembling gabardine
TRICOTS > TRICOT
TRICROTIC adj (of the pulse) having a tracing characterized by three elevations with each beat
TRICTRAC n game similar to backgammon
TRICTRACS > TRICTRAC
TRICUSPID adj having three points, cusps, or segments ▷ n tooth having three cusps

TRICYCLE n three-wheeled cycle ▷ vb ride a tricycle
TRICYCLED > TRICYCLE
TRICYCLER > TRICYCLE
TRICYCLES > TRICYCLE
TRICYCLIC adj (of a chemical compound) containing three rings in the molecular structure ▷ n antidepressant drug having a tricyclic molecular structure
TRIDACNA n giant clam
TRIDACNAS > TRIDACNA
TRIDACTYL adj having three digits on one hand or foot
TRIDARN n sideboard with three levels
TRIDARNS > TRIDARN
TRIDE old spelling of the past tense of > TRY
TRIDENT n three-pronged spear ▷ adj having three prongs
TRIDENTAL adj having three prongs, teeth, etc
TRIDENTED adj having three prongs
TRIDENTS > TRIDENT
TRIDUAN adj three days long
TRIDUUM n period of three days for prayer before a feast
TRIDUUMS > TRIDUUM
TRIDYMITE n form of silica
TRIE old spelling of > TRY
TRIECIOUS adj (of a plant) having male, female, and hermaphroditic flowers
TRIED > TRY
TRIELLA n bet on the winners of three nominated horse races
TRIELLAS > TRIELLA
TRIENE n chemical compound containing three double bonds
TRIENES > TRIENE
TRIENNIA > TRIENNIUM
TRIENNIAL adj happening every three years ▷ n relating to, lasting for, or occurring every three years
TRIENNIUM n period or cycle of three years
TRIENS n Byzantine gold coin worth one third of a solidus
TRIENTES > TRIENS
TRIER n person or thing that tries
TRIERARCH n citizen responsible for fitting out a state trireme, esp in Athens
TRIERS > TRIER
TRIES > TRY

TRIETERIC adj occurring once every two years
TRIETHYL adj consisting of three groups of ethyls
TRIFACIAL adj relating to the trigeminal nerve
TRIFECTA n form of betting in which the punter selects the first three place-winners in a horse race in the correct order
TRIFECTAS > TRIFECTA
TRIFF adj terrific; very good indeed
TRIFFER > TRIFF
TRIFFEST > TRIFF
TRIFFIC adj terrific; very good indeed
TRIFFID n fictional plant that could kill humans
TRIFFIDS > TRIFFID
TRIFFIDY adj resembling a triffid
TRIFID adj divided or split into three parts or lobes
TRIFLE n insignificant thing or amount ▷ vb deal (with) as if worthless
TRIFLED > TRIFLE
TRIFLER > TRIFLE
TRIFLERS > TRIFLE
TRIFLES > TRIFLE
TRIFLING adj insignificant
TRIFLINGS > TRIFLE
TRIFOCAL adj having three focuses ▷ n glasses that have trifocal lenses
TRIFOCALS > TRIFOCAL
TRIFOLD less common word for > TRIPLE
TRIFOLIES > TRIFOLY
TRIFOLIUM n leguminous plant with leaves divided into three leaflets and dense heads of small white, yellow, red, or purple flowers
TRIFOLY same as > TREFOIL
TRIFORIA > TRIFORIUM
TRIFORIAL > TRIFORIUM
TRIFORIUM n arcade above the arches of the nave, choir, or transept of a church
TRIFORM adj having three parts
TRIFORMED same as > TRIFORM
TRIG adj neat or spruce ▷ vb make or become spruce
TRIGAMIES > TRIGAMY
TRIGAMIST > TRIGAMY
TRIGAMOUS > TRIGAMY
TRIGAMY n condition of having three spouses
TRIGEMINI pl n facial nerves
TRIGGED > TRIG

TRIGGER n small lever releasing a catch on a gun or machine ▷ vb set (an action or process) in motion

TRIGGERED > TRIGGER

TRIGGERS > TRIGGER

TRIGGEST > TRIG

TRIGGING > TRIG

TRIGLOT n person who can speak three languages

TRIGLOTS > TRIGLOT

TRIGLY > TRIG

TRIGLYPH n stone block in a Doric frieze, having three vertical channels

TRIGLYPHS > TRIGLYPH

TRIGNESS > TRIG

TRIGO n wheat field

TRIGON n (in classical Greece or Rome) a triangular harp or lyre

TRIGONAL adj triangular

TRIGONIC > TRIGON

TRIGONOUS adj (of stems, seeds, and similar parts) having a triangular cross section

TRIGONS > TRIGON

TRIGOS > TRIGO

TRIGRAM n three-letter inscription

TRIGRAMS > TRIGRAM

TRIGRAPH n combination of three letters used to represent a single speech sound or phoneme, such as *eau* in French *beau*

TRIGRAPHS > TRIGRAPH

TRIGS > TRIG

TRIGYNIAN adj relating to the Trigynia order of plants

TRIGYNOUS adj (of a plant) having three pistils

TRIHEDRA > TRIHEDRON

TRIHEDRAL adj having or formed by three plane faces meeting at a point ▷ n figure formed by the intersection of three lines in different planes

TRIHEDRON n figure determined by the intersection of three planes

TRIHYBRID n hybrid that differs from its parents in three genetic traits

TRIHYDRIC adj (of an alcohol or similar compound) containing three hydroxyl groups

TRIJET n jet with three engines

TRIJETS > TRIJET

TRIJUGATE adj in three pairs

TRIJUGOUS same as > TRIJUGATE

TRIKE n tricycle

TRIKES > TRIKE

TRILBIED adj wearing a trilby

TRILBIES > TRILBY

TRILBY n man's soft felt hat

TRILBYS > TRILBY

TRILD old past tense of > TRILL

TRILEMMA n quandary posed by three alternative courses of action

TRILEMMAS > TRILEMMA

TRILINEAR adj consisting of, bounded by, or relating to three lines

TRILITH same as > TRILITHON

TRILITHIC > TRILITHON

TRILITHON n structure consisting of two upright stones with a third placed across the top, such as those of Stonehenge

TRILITHS > TRILITH

TRILL n rapid alternation between two notes ▷ vb play or sing a trill

TRILLED > TRILL

TRILLER > TRILL

TRILLERS > TRILL

TRILLING > TRILL

TRILLINGS > TRILL

TRILLION n one million million ▷ adj amounting to a trillion

TRILLIONS > TRILLION

TRILLIUM n plant of Asia and North America that has three leaves at the top of the stem with a single white, pink, or purple three-petalled flower

TRILLIUMS > TRILLIUM

TRILLO n (in music) a trill

TRILLOES > TRILL

TRILLS > TRILL

TRILOBAL > TRILOBE

TRILOBATE adj (esp of a leaf) consisting of or having three lobes or parts

TRILOBE n three-lobed thing

TRILOBED adj having three lobes

TRILOBES > TRILOBE

TRILOBITE n small prehistoric sea animal

TRILOGIES > TRILOGY

TRILOGY n series of three related books, plays, etc

TRIM adj neat and smart ▷ vb cut or prune into good shape ▷ n decoration

TRIMARAN n three-hulled boat

TRIMARANS > TRIMARAN

TRIMER n polymer or a molecule of a polymer consisting of three identical monomers

TRIMERIC > TRIMER

TRIMERISM > TRIMER

TRIMEROUS adj (of plants) having parts arranged in groups of three

TRIMERS > TRIMER

TRIMESTER n period of three months

TRIMETER n verse line consisting of three metrical feet ▷ adj designating such a line

TRIMETERS > TRIMETER

TRIMETHYL adj having three methyl groups

TRIMETRIC adj of, relating to, or consisting of a trimeter or trimeters

TRIMIX n gas mixture of nitrogen, helium and oxygen used by deep-sea divers

TRIMIXES > TRIMIX

TRIMLY > TRIM

TRIMMED > TRIM

TRIMMER > TRIM

TRIMMERS > TRIM

TRIMMEST > TRIM

TRIMMING > TRIM

TRIMMINGS > TRIM

TRIMNESS > TRIM

TRIMORPH n substance, esp a mineral, that exists in three distinct forms

TRIMORPHS > TRIMORPH

TRIMOTOR n vehicle with three motors

TRIMOTORS > TRIMOTOR

TRIMPHONE n type of phone designed in the 1960s

TRIMPOT n small instrument for adjusting resistance or voltage

TRIMPOTS > TRIMPOT

TRIMS > TRIM

TRIMTAB n small control surface to enable the pilot to balance an aircraft

TRIMTABS > TRIMTAB

TRIN n triplet

TRINAL > TRINE

TRINARY adj made up of three parts

TRINDLE vb move heavily on (or as if on) wheels

TRINDLED > TRINDLE

TRINDLES > TRINDLE

TRINDLING > TRINDLE

TRINE n aspect of 120° between two planets, an orb of 8° being allowed ▷ adj of or relating to a trine ▷ vb put in a trine aspect

TRINED > TRINE

TRINES > TRINE

TRINGLE n slim rod

TRINGLES > TRINGLE

TRINING > TRINE

TRINITIES > TRINITY

TRINITRIN n pale yellow viscous explosive liquid substance made from glycerol and nitric and sulphuric acids

TRINITY n group of three

TRINKET n small or worthless ornament or piece of jewellery ▷ vb ornament with trinkets

TRINKETED > TRINKET

TRINKETER > TRINKET

TRINKETRY > TRINKET

TRINKETS > TRINKET

TRINKUM n trinket or bauble

TRINKUMS > TRINKUM

TRINODAL adj having three nodes

TRINOMIAL adj consisting of or relating to three terms ▷ n polynomial consisting of three terms

TRINS > TRIN

TRIO n group of three

TRIODE n electronic valve having three electrodes, a cathode, an anode, and a grid

TRIODES > TRIODE

TRIOL n any of a class of alcohols that have three hydroxyl groups per molecule

TRIOLEIN n naturally occurring glyceride of oleic acid, found in fats and oils

TRIOLEINS > TRIOLEIN

TRIOLET n verse form of eight lines

TRIOLETS > TRIOLET

TRIOLS > TRIOL

TRIONES n seven stars of the constellation Ursa Major

TRIONYM another name for > TRINOMIAL

TRIONYMAL > TRIONYM

TRIONYMS > TRIONYM

TRIOR old form of > TRIER

TRIORS > TRIOR

TRIOS > TRIO

TRIOSE n simple monosaccharide produced by the oxidation of glycerol

TRIOSES > TRIOSE

TRIOXID same as > TRIOXIDE

TRIOXIDE n any oxide that contains three oxygen atoms per molecule

TRIOXIDES > TRIOXIDE

TRIOXIDS > TRIOXIDE

TRIOXYGEN technical name for > OXYGEN

TRIP n journey to a place and back, esp for pleasure ▷ vb (cause to) stumble

TRIPACK n pack of three

TRIPACKS > TRIPACK

TRIPART adj composed of three parts

TRIPE n stomach of a cow used as food

TRIPEDAL adj having three feet

TRIPERIES > TRIPERY
TRIPERY n place where tripe is prepared
TRIPES > TRIPE
TRIPEY > TRIPE
TRIPHASE adj having three phases
TRIPHONE n group of three phonemes
TRIPHONES > TRIPHONE
TRIPIER > TRIPE
TRIPIEST > TRIPE
TRIPITAKA n three collections of books making up the Buddhist canon of scriptures
TRIPLANE n aeroplane having three wings arranged one above the other
TRIPLANES > TRIPLANE
TRIPLE adj having three parts ▷ vb increase three times ▷ n something that is, or contains, three times as much as normal
TRIPLED > TRIPLE
TRIPLES > TRIPLE
TRIPLET n one of three babies born at one birth
TRIPLETS > TRIPLET
TRIPLEX n building divided into three separate dwellings ▷ vb separate into three parts
TRIPLEXED > TRIPLEX
TRIPLEXES > TRIPLEX
TRIPLIED > TRIPLY
TRIPLIES > TRIPLY
TRIPLING > TRIPLE
TRIPLINGS > TRIPLE
TRIPLITE n brownish-red phosphate
TRIPLITES > TRIPLITE
TRIPLOID adj having or relating to three times the haploid number of chromosomes ▷ n triploid organism
TRIPLOIDS > TRIPLOID
TRIPLOIDY n triploid state
TRIPLY vb give a reply to a duply
TRIPLYING > TRIPLY
TRIPMAN n man working on a trip
TRIPMEN > TRIPMAN
TRIPOD n three-legged stand, stool, etc
TRIPODAL > TRIPOD
TRIPODIC > TRIPOD
TRIPODIES > TRIPODY
TRIPODS > TRIPOD
TRIPODY n metrical unit consisting of three feet
TRIPOLI n lightweight porous siliceous rock
TRIPOLIS > TRIPOLI
TRIPOS n final examinations for an honours degree at Cambridge University
TRIPOSES > TRIPOS

TRIPPANT adj (in heraldry) in the process of tripping
TRIPPED > TRIP
TRIPPER n tourist
TRIPPERS > TRIPPER
TRIPPERY adj like a tripper
TRIPPET n any mechanism that strikes or is struck at regular intervals, as by a cam
TRIPPETS > TRIPPET
TRIPPIER > TRIPPY
TRIPPIEST > TRIPPY
TRIPPING > TRIP
TRIPPINGS > TRIP
TRIPPLE vb canter
TRIPPLED > TRIPPLE
TRIPPLER > TRIPPLE
TRIPPLERS > TRIPPLE
TRIPPLES > TRIPPLE
TRIPPLING > TRIPPLE
TRIPPY adj suggestive of or resembling the effect produced by a hallucinogenic drug
TRIPS > TRIP
TRIPSES > TRIPSIS
TRIPSIS n act of kneading the body to promote circulation, suppleness, etc
TRIPTAN n drug used to treat migraine
TRIPTANE n colourless highly flammable liquid
TRIPTANES > TRIPTANE
TRIPTANS > TRIPTAN
TRIPTOTE n word that has only three cases
TRIPTOTES > TRIPTOTE
TRIPTYCA variant of > TRIPTYCH
TRIPTYCAS > TRIPTYCA
TRIPTYCH n painting or carving on three hinged panels, often forming an altarpiece
TRIPTYCHS > TRIPTYCH
TRIPTYQUE n customs permit for the temporary importation of a motor vehicle
TRIPUDIA > TRIPUDIUM
TRIPUDIUM n ancient religious dance
TRIPWIRE n wire that activates a trap, mine, etc, when tripped over
TRIPWIRES > TRIPWIRE
TRIPY > TRIPE
TRIQUETRA n ornament in the shape of three intersecting ellipses roughly forming a triangle
TRIRADIAL adj having or consisting of three rays or radiating branches
TRIREME n ancient Greek warship with three rows of oars on each side
TRIREMES > TRIREME
TRISAGION n old hymn

TRISCELE variant spelling of > TRISKELE
TRISCELES > TRISCELE
TRISECT vb divide into three parts, esp three equal parts
TRISECTED > TRISECT
TRISECTOR > TRISECT
TRISECTS > TRISECT
TRISEME n metrical foot of a length equal to three short syllables
TRISEMES > TRISEME
TRISEMIC > TRISEME
TRISERIAL adj arranged in three rows or series
TRISHAW another name for > RICKSHAW
TRISHAWS > TRISHAW
TRISKELE n three-limbed symbol
TRISKELES > TRISKELE
TRISKELIA n plural of singular triskelion: three-limbed symbol
TRISMIC > TRISMUS
TRISMUS n state of being unable to open the mouth
TRISMUSES > TRISMUS
TRISODIUM adj containing three sodium atoms
TRISOME n chromosome occurring three times (rather than twice) in a cell
TRISOMES > TRISOME
TRISOMIC > TRISOMY
TRISOMICS n study of trisomy
TRISOMIES > TRISOMY
TRISOMY n condition of having one chromosome represented three times
TRIST variant spelling of > TRISTE
TRISTATE adj (of a digital computer chip) having high, low, and floating output states
TRISTE adj sad
TRISTESSE n sadness
TRISTEZA n disease affecting citrus trees
TRISTEZAS > TRISTEZA
TRISTFUL same as > TRISTE
TRISTICH n poem, stanza, or strophe that consists of three lines
TRISTICHS > TRISTICH
TRISUL n trident symbol of Siva
TRISULA same as > TRISUL
TRISULAS > TRISULA
TRISULS > TRISUL
TRITANOPE n person who cannot distinguish the colour blue
TRITE adj (of a remark or idea) commonplace and unoriginal ▷ n (on a lyre) the third string from the highest in pitch

TRITELY > TRITE
TRITENESS > TRITE
TRITER > TRITE
TRITES > TRITE
TRITEST > TRITE
TRITHEISM n belief in three gods, esp in the Trinity as consisting of three distinct gods
TRITHEIST > TRITHEISM
TRITHING n tripartition
TRITHINGS > TRITHING
TRITIATE vb replace normal hydrogen atoms in (a compound) by those of tritium
TRITIATED > TRITIATE
TRITIATES > TRITIATE
TRITICAL n trite; hackneyed
TRITICALE n fertile hybrid cereal
TRITICISM n something trite
TRITICUM n type of cereal grass of the genus which includes the wheats
TRITICUMS > TRITICUM
TRITIDE n tritium compound
TRITIDES > TRITIDE
TRITIUM n radioactive isotope of hydrogen
TRITIUMS > TRITIUM
TRITOMA another name for > KNIPHOFIA
TRITOMAS > TRITOMA
TRITON n any of various chiefly tropical marine gastropod molluscs
TRITONE n musical interval consisting of three whole tones
TRITONES > TRITONE
TRITONIA n type of plant with typically scarlet or orange flowers
TRITONIAS > TRITONIA
TRITONS > TRITON
TRITURATE vb grind or rub into a fine powder or pulp ▷ n powder or pulp resulting from this grinding
TRIUMPH n (happiness caused by) victory or success ▷ vb be victorious or successful
TRIUMPHAL adj celebrating a triumph
TRIUMPHED > TRIUMPH
TRIUMPHER > TRIUMPH
TRIUMPHS > TRIUMPH
TRIUMVIR n (esp in ancient Rome) a member of a triumvirate
TRIUMVIRI > TRIUMVIR
TRIUMVIRS > TRIUMVIR
TRIUMVIRY n triumvirate
TRIUNE adj constituting three things in one ▷ n group of three
TRIUNES > TRIUNE

TRIUNITY > TRIUNE
TRIVALENT adj having a valency of three
TRIVALVE n animal having three valves
TRIVALVED adj having three valves
TRIVALVES > TRIVALVE
TRIVET n metal stand for a pot or kettle
TRIVETS > TRIVET
TRIVIA pl n trivial things or details
TRIVIAL adj of little importance
TRIVIALLY > TRIVIAL
TRIVIUM n (in medieval learning) the lower division of the seven liberal arts
TRIVIUMS > TRIVIUM
TRIWEEKLY adv every three weeks ▷ n triweekly publication
TRIZONAL > TRIZONE
TRIZONE n area comprising three zones
TRIZONES > TRIZONE
TROAD same as **>** TROD
TROADE same as **>** TROD
TROADES > TROADE
TROADS > TROAD
TROAK old form of **>** TRUCK
TROAKED > TROAK
TROAKING > TROAK
TROAKS > TROAK
TROAT vb (of a rutting buck) to call or bellow
TROATED > TROAT
TROATING > TROAT
TROATS > TROAT
TROCAR n surgical instrument for removing fluid from bodily cavities
TROCARS > TROCAR
TROCHAIC adj of, relating to, or consisting of trochees ▷ n verse composed of trochees
TROCHAICS > TROCHAIC
TROCHAL adj shaped like a wheel
TROCHAR old variant spelling of **>** TROCAR
TROCHARS > TROCHAR
TROCHE another name for **>** LOZENGE
TROCHEE n metrical foot of one long and one short syllable
TROCHEES > TROCHEE
TROCHES > TROCHE
TROCHI > TROCHUS
TROCHIL same as **>** TROCHILUS
TROCHILI > TROCHILUS
TROCHILIC adj relating to the movement of a hummingbird's wings
TROCHILS > TROCHIL
TROCHILUS n any of several Old World warblers
TROCHISK another word for **>** TROCHE

TROCHISKS > TROCHISK
TROCHITE n joint of a crinoid
TROCHITES > TROCHITE
TROCHLEA n any bony or cartilaginous part with a grooved surface over which a bone, tendon, etc, may slide or articulate
TROCHLEAE > TROCHLEA
TROCHLEAR n as in *trochlear nerve* either one of the fourth pair of cranial nerves, which supply the superior oblique muscle of the eye
TROCHLEAS > TROCHLEA
TROCHOID n curve described by a fixed point on the radius or extended radius of a circle as the circle rolls along a straight line ▷ adj rotating or capable of rotating about a central axis
TROCHOIDS > TROCHOID
TROCHUS n hoop (used in exercise)
TROCHUSES > TROCHUS
TROCK same as **>** TRUCK
TROCKED > TROCK
TROCKEN adj dry (used of wine)
TROCKING > TROCK
TROCKS > TROCK
TROD vb past participle of tread ▷ n path
TRODDEN > TREAD
TRODE same as **>** TROD
TRODES > TRODE
TRODS > TROD
TROELIE same as **>** TROOLIE
TROELIES > TROELIE
TROELY same as **>** TROOLIE
TROFFER n fixture for holding and reflecting light from a fluorescent tube
TROFFERS > TROFFER
TROG vb walk, esp aimlessly or heavily
TROGGED > TROG
TROGGING > TROG
TROGGS n loyalty; fidelity
TROGON n bird of tropical and subtropical America, Africa, and Asia
TROGONS > TROGON
TROGS > TROG
TROIKA n Russian vehicle drawn by three horses abreast
TROIKAS > TROIKA
TROILISM n sexual activity involving three people
TROILISMS > TROILISM
TROILIST > TROILISM
TROILISTS > TROILISM
TROILITE n iron sulphide present in most meteorites

TROILITES > TROILITE
TROILUS n type of large butterfly
TROILUSES > TROILUS
TROIS Scots form of **>** TROY
TROKE same as **>** TRUCK
TROKED > TROKE
TROKES > TROKE
TROKING > TROKE
TROLAND n unit of light intensity in the eye
TROLANDS > TROLAND
TROLL n giant or dwarf in Scandinavian folklore ▷ vb fish by dragging a lure through the water
TROLLED > TROLL
TROLLER > TROLL
TROLLERS > TROLL
TROLLEY n small wheeled table for food and drink ▷ vb transport on a trolley
TROLLEYED > TROLLEY
TROLLEYS pl n men's underpants
TROLLIED > TROLLY
TROLLIES > TROLLY
TROLLING > TROLL
TROLLINGS > TROLL
TROLLISH adj like a troll
TROLLIUS n plant with globe-shaped flowers
TROLLOP n promiscuous or slovenly woman ▷ vb behave like a trollop
TROLLOPED > TROLLOP
TROLLOPEE n loose dress or gown
TROLLOPS > TROLLOP
TROLLOPY > TROLLOP
TROLLS > TROLL
TROLLY same as **>** TROLLEY
TROLLYING > TROLLY
TROMBONE n brass musical instrument with a sliding tube
TROMBONES > TROMBONE
TROMINO n shape made from three squares, each joined to the next along one full side
TROMINOES > TROMINO
TROMINOS > TROMINO
TROMMEL n revolving cylindrical sieve used to screen crushed ore
TROMMELS > TROMMEL
TROMP vb trample
TROMPE n apparatus for supplying the blast of air in a forge
TROMPED > TROMP
TROMPES > TROMPE
TROMPING > TROMP
TROMPS > TROMP
TRON n public weighing machine
TRONA n greyish mineral that occurs in salt deposits
TRONAS > TRONA
TRONC n pool into which waiters, waitresses, hotel workers, etc, pay their tips

TRONCS > TRONC
TRONE same as **>** TRON
TRONES > TRONE
TRONK n jail
TRONKS > TRONK
TRONS > TRON
TROOLIE n large palm leaf
TROOLIES > TROOLIE
TROOP n large group ▷ vb move in a crowd
TROOPED > TROOP
TROOPER n cavalry soldier
TROOPERS > TROOPER
TROOPIAL same as **>** TROUPIAL
TROOPIALS > TROOPIAL
TROOPING > TROOP
TROOPS > TROOP
TROOPSHIP n ship used to transport military personnel
TROOSTITE n reddish or greyish mineral that is a variety of willemite in which some of the zinc is replaced by manganese
TROOZ same as **>** TREWS
TROP adv too, too much
TROPAEOLA n plural of singular tropaeolum (a garden plant)
TROPARIA > TROPARION
TROPARION n short hymn
TROPE n figure of speech ▷ vb use tropes (in speech or writing)
TROPED > TROPE
TROPEOLIN n type of dye
TROPES > TROPE
TROPHESY n disorder of the nerves relating to nutrition
TROPHI pl n collective term for the mandibles and other parts of an insect's mouth
TROPHIC adj of or relating to nutrition
TROPHIED > TROPHY
TROPHIES > TROPHY
TROPHY n cup, shield, etc given as a prize ▷ adj regarded as a highly desirable symbol of wealth or success ▷ vb award a trophy to (someone)
TROPHYING > TROPHY
TROPIC n either of two lines of latitude at 23½°N (tropic of Cancer) or 23½°S (tropic of Capricorn)
TROPICAL adj of or in the tropics ▷ n tropical thing or place
TROPICALS > TROPICAL
TROPICS > TROPIC
TROPIN n adrenal androgen
TROPINE n white crystalline poisonous alkaloid
TROPINES > TROPINE
TROPING > TROPE
TROPINS > TROPIN

TROPISM n tendency of a plant or animal to turn in response to an external stimulus

TROPISMS > TROPISM

TROPIST > TROPISM

TROPISTIC > TROPISM

TROPISTS > TROPISM

TROPOLOGY n use of figurative language in speech or writing

TROPONIN n muscle-tissue protein involved in the controlling of muscle contraction

TROPONINS > TROPONIN

TROPPO adv too much ▷ adj mentally affected by a tropical climate

TROSSERS old form of > TROUSERS

TROT vb (of a horse) move at a medium pace, lifting the feet in diagonal pairs ▷ n trotting

TROTH n pledge of devotion, esp a betrothal ▷ vb promise to marry (someone)

TROTHED > TROTH

TROTHFUL > TROTH

TROTHING > TROTH

TROTHLESS > TROTH

TROTHS > TROTH

TROTLINE n long line suspended across a stream, river, etc, to which shorter hooked and baited lines are attached

TROTLINES > TROTLINE

TROTS > TROT

TROTTED > TROT

TROTTER n pig's foot

TROTTERS > TROTTER

TROTTING > TROT

TROTTINGS > TROT

TROTTOIR n pavement

TROTTOIRS > TROTTOIR

TROTYL n yellow solid used chiefly as a high explosive

TROTYLS > TROTYL

TROU pl n trousers

TROUBLE n (cause of) distress or anxiety ▷ vb (cause to) worry

TROUBLED > TROUBLE

TROUBLER > TROUBLE

TROUBLERS > TROUBLE

TROUBLES > TROUBLE

TROUBLING > TROUBLE

TROUBLOUS adj unsettled or agitated

TROUCH n rubbish

TROUCHES > TROUCH

TROUGH n long open container, esp for animals' food or water ▷ vb eat, consume, or drink greedily

TROUGHED > TROUGH

TROUGHING n as in troughing and peaking reaching the lowest and highest levels in a range

TROUGHS > TROUGH

TROULE old variant of > TROLL

TROULED > TROULE

TROULES > TROULE

TROULING > TROULE

TROUNCE vb defeat utterly

TROUNCED > TROUNCE

TROUNCER > TROUNCE

TROUNCERS > TROUNCE

TROUNCES > TROUNCE

TROUNCING > TROUNCE

TROUPE n company of performers ▷ vb (esp of actors) to move or travel in a group

TROUPED > TROUPE

TROUPER n member of a troupe

TROUPERS > TROUPER

TROUPES > TROUPE

TROUPIAL n any of various American orioles

TROUPIALS > TROUPIAL

TROUPING > TROUPE

TROUSE pl n close-fitting breeches worn in Ireland

TROUSER adj of trousers ▷ vb take (something, esp money), often surreptitiously or unlawfully ▷ n of or relating to trousers

TROUSERED > TROUSERS

TROUSERS pl n two-legged outer garment with legs reaching usu to the ankles

TROUSES > TROUSE

TROUSSEAU n bride's collection of clothing etc for her marriage

TROUT n game fish related to the salmon ▷ vb fish for trout

TROUTER > TROUT

TROUTERS > TROUT

TROUTFUL adj (of a body of water) full of trout

TROUTIER > TROUT

TROUTIEST > TROUT

TROUTING > TROUT

TROUTINGS > TROUT

TROUTLESS > TROUT

TROUTLET n small trout

TROUTLETS > TROUTLET

TROUTLING n small trout

TROUTS > TROUT

TROUTY > TROUT

TROUVERE n any of a group of poets of N France during the 12th and 13th centuries who composed chiefly narrative works

TROUVERES > TROUVERE

TROUVEUR same as > TROUVERE

TROUVEURS > TROUVEUR

TROVE n as in treasure-trove valuable articles found hidden in the earth

TROVER n act of assuming proprietary rights over

goods or property belonging to another

TROVERS > TROVER

TROVES > TROVE

TROW vb think, believe, or trust

TROWED > TROW

TROWEL n hand tool with a wide blade ▷ vb use a trowel on (plaster, soil, etc)

TROWELED > TROWEL

TROWELER > TROWEL

TROWELERS > TROWEL

TROWELING > TROWEL

TROWELLED > TROWEL

TROWELLER > TROWEL

TROWELS > TROWEL

TROWING > TROW

TROWS > TROW

TROWSERS old spelling of > TROUSERS

TROWTH variant spelling of > TROTH

TROWTHS > TROWTH

TROY n as in troy weight system of weights used for precious metals and gemstones, based on the grain, which is identical to the avoirdupois grain

TROYS > TROY

TRUANCIES > TRUANT

TRUANCY > TRUANT

TRUANT n pupil who stays away from school without permission ▷ adj being or relating to a truant ▷ vb play truant

TRUANTED > TRUANT

TRUANTING > TRUANT

TRUANTLY > TRUANT

TRUANTRY > TRUANT

TRUANTS > TRUANT

TRUCAGE n art forgery

TRUCAGES > TRUCAGE

TRUCE n temporary agreement to stop fighting ▷ vb make a truce

TRUCED > TRUCE

TRUCELESS > TRUCE

TRUCES > TRUCE

TRUCHMAN n interpreter; translator

TRUCHMANS > TRUCHMAN

TRUCHMEN > TRUCHMAN

TRUCIAL > TRUCE

TRUCING > TRUCE

TRUCK n railway goods wagon ▷ vb exchange (goods); barter

TRUCKABLE > TRUCK

TRUCKAGE n conveyance of cargo by truck

TRUCKAGES > TRUCKAGE

TRUCKED > TRUCK

TRUCKER n truck driver

TRUCKERS > TRUCKER

TRUCKFUL n amount of something that can be conveyed in a truck

TRUCKFULS > TRUCKFUL

TRUCKIE n truck driver

TRUCKIES > TRUCKIE

TRUCKING n transportation of goods by lorry

TRUCKINGS > TRUCKING

TRUCKLE vb yield weakly or give in ▷ n small wheel

TRUCKLED > TRUCKLE

TRUCKLER > TRUCKLE

TRUCKLERS > TRUCKLE

TRUCKLES > TRUCKLE

TRUCKLINE n organisation that conveys freight by truck

TRUCKLING > TRUCKLE

TRUCKLOAD n amount carried by a truck

TRUCKMAN n truck driver

TRUCKMEN > TRUCKMAN

TRUCKS > TRUCK

TRUCKSTOP n place providing fuel, oil, and often service facilities for truck drivers

TRUCULENT adj aggressively defiant

TRUDGE vb walk heavily or wearily ▷ n long tiring walk

TRUDGED > TRUDGE

TRUDGEN n type of swimming stroke

TRUDGENS > TRUDGEN

TRUDGEON nonstandard variant of > TRUDGEN

TRUDGEONS > TRUDGEON

TRUDGER > TRUDGE

TRUDGERS > TRUDGE

TRUDGES > TRUDGE

TRUDGING > TRUDGE

TRUDGINGS > TRUDGE

TRUE adj in accordance with facts

TRUEBLUE n staunch royalist or Conservative

TRUEBLUES > TRUEBLUE

TRUEBORN adj being such by birth

TRUEBRED adj thoroughbred

TRUED > TRUE

TRUEING > TRUE

TRUELOVE n person that one loves

TRUELOVES > TRUELOVE

TRUEMAN n honest person

TRUEMEN > TRUEMAN

TRUENESS > TRUE

TRUEPENNY n truthful person

TRUER > TRUE

TRUES > TRUE

TRUEST > TRUE

TRUFFE rare word for > TRUFFLE

TRUFFES > TRUFFE

TRUFFLE n edible underground fungus ▷ vb hunt for truffles

TRUFFLED > TRUFFLE

TRUFFLES > TRUFFLE

TRUFFLING > TRUFFLE

TRUG n long shallow basket used by gardeners

TRUGO n game similar to croquet
TRUGOS > TRUGO
TRUGS > TRUG
TRUING > TRUE
TRUISM n self-evident truth
TRUISMS > TRUISM
TRUISTIC > TRUISM
TRULL n prostitute
TRULLS > TRULL
TRULY adv in a true manner
TRUMEAU n section of a wall or pillar between two openings
TRUMEAUX > TRUMEAU
TRUMP adj (card) of the suit outranking the others ▷ vb play a trump card on (another card) ▷ pl n suit outranking the others
TRUMPED > TRUMP
TRUMPERY n something useless or worthless ▷ adj useless or worthless
TRUMPET n valved brass instrument with a flared tube ▷ vb proclaim loudly
TRUMPETED > TRUMPET
TRUMPETER n person who plays the trumpet, esp one whose duty it is to play fanfares, signals, etc
TRUMPETS > TRUMPET
TRUMPING > TRUMP
TRUMPINGS > TRUMP
TRUMPLESS > TRUMP
TRUMPS > TRUMP
TRUNCAL adj of or relating to the trunk
TRUNCATE vb cut short ▷ adj cut short
TRUNCATED adj (of a cone, pyramid, prism, etc) having an apex or end removed by a plane intersection that is usually nonparallel to the base
TRUNCATES > TRUNCATE
TRUNCHEON n club formerly carried by a policeman ▷ vb beat with a truncheon
TRUNDLE vb move heavily on wheels ▷ n act or an instance of trundling
TRUNDLED > TRUNDLE
TRUNDLER n golf or shopping trolley
TRUNDLERS > TRUNDLER
TRUNDLES > TRUNDLE
TRUNDLING > TRUNDLE
TRUNK n main stem of a tree ▷ vb lop or truncate
TRUNKED > TRUNK
TRUNKFISH n tropical fish, having the body encased in bony plates with openings for the fins, eyes, mouth, etc
TRUNKFUL > TRUNK
TRUNKFULS > TRUNK

TRUNKING n cables that take a common route through an exchange building linking ranks of selectors
TRUNKINGS > TRUNKING
TRUNKLESS > TRUNK
TRUNKS pl n shorts worn by a man for swimming
TRUNKWORK n visiting someone secretly in a trunk
TRUNNEL same as > TREENAIL
TRUNNELS > TRUNNEL
TRUNNION n one of a pair of coaxial projections attached to opposite sides of a container, cannon, etc, to provide a support about which it can turn in a vertical
TRUNNIONS > TRUNNION
TRUQUAGE variant of > TRUCAGE
TRUQUAGES > TRUQUAGE
TRUQUEUR n art forger
TRUQUEURS > TRUQUEUR
TRUSS vb tie or bind up ▷ n device for holding a hernia, etc in place
TRUSSED > TRUSS
TRUSSER > TRUSS
TRUSSERS > TRUSS
TRUSSES > TRUSS
TRUSSING n system of trusses, esp for strengthening or reinforcing a structure
TRUSSINGS > TRUSSING
TRUST vb believe in and rely on ▷ n confidence in the truth, reliability, etc of a person or thing ▷ adj of or relating to a trust or trusts
TRUSTABLE > TRUST
TRUSTED > TRUST
TRUSTEE n person holding property on another's behalf ▷ vb act as a trustee
TRUSTEED > TRUSTEE
TRUSTEES > TRUSTEE
TRUSTER > TRUST
TRUSTERS > TRUST
TRUSTFUL adj inclined to trust others
TRUSTIER > TRUSTY
TRUSTIES > TRUSTY
TRUSTIEST > TRUSTY
TRUSTILY > TRUSTY
TRUSTING same as > TRUSTFUL
TRUSTLESS adj untrustworthy
TRUSTOR n person who sets up a trust
TRUSTORS > TRUSTOR
TRUSTS > TRUST
TRUSTY adj faithful or reliable ▷ n trustworthy convict to whom special privileges are granted

TRUTH n state of being true
TRUTHER n person who does not believe official accounts of the 9/11 attacks on the US
TRUTHERS > TRUTHER
TRUTHFUL adj honest
TRUTHIER > TRUTHY
TRUTHIEST > TRUTHY
TRUTHLESS > TRUTH
TRUTHLIKE n truthful
TRUTHS > TRUTH
TRUTHY adj truthful
TRY vb make an effort or attempt ▷ n attempt or effort
TRYE adj very good; select
TRYER variant of > TRIER
TRYERS > TRYER
TRYING > TRY
TRYINGLY > TRY
TRYINGS > TRY
TRYKE variant spelling of > TRIKE
TRYKES > TRYKE
TRYMA n drupe produced by the walnut and similar plants
TRYMATA > TRYMA
TRYOUT n trial or test, as of an athlete or actor
TRYOUTS > TRYOUT
TRYP n parasitic protozoan
TRYPAN modifier as in trypan blue used for staining cells in biological research
TRYPS > TRYP
TRYPSIN n enzyme occurring in pancreatic juice
TRYPSINS > TRYPSIN
TRYPTIC > TRYPSIN
TRYSAIL n small fore-and-aft sail on a sailing vessel
TRYSAILS > TRYSAIL
TRYST n arrangement to meet ▷ vb meet at or arrange a tryst
TRYSTE variant spelling of > TRYST
TRYSTED > TRYST
TRYSTER > TRYST
TRYSTERS > TRYST
TRYSTES > TRYSTE
TRYSTING > TRYST
TRYSTS > TRYST
TRYWORKS n furnace for rendering blubber
TSADDIK variant of > ZADDIK
TSADDIKIM > TSADDIK
TSADDIKS > TSADDIK
TSADDIQ variant of > ZADDIK
TSADDIQIM > TSADDIQ
TSADDIQS > TSADDIQ
TSADE variant spelling of > SADHE
TSADES > TSADE
TSADI variant of > SADHE

TSADIK same as > ZADDIK
TSADIKS > TSADIK
TSADIS > TSADI
TSAMBA n Tibetan dish made from roasted barley and tea
TSAMBAS > TSAMBA
TSANTSA n shrunken head of an enemy kept as a trophy
TSANTSAS > TSANTSA
TSAR n Russian emperor
TSARDOM > TSAR
TSARDOMS > TSAR
TSAREVICH n tsar's son
TSAREVNA n daughter of a Russian tsar
TSAREVNAS > TSAREVNA
TSARINA n wife of a Russian tsar
TSARINAS > TSARINA
TSARISM n system of government by a tsar
TSARISMS > TSARISM
TSARIST > TSARISM
TSARISTS > TSARISM
TSARITSA same as > TSARINA
TSARITSAS > TSARITSA
TSARITZA variant spelling of > TSARITSA
TSARITZAS > TSARITZA
TSARS > TSAR
TSATSKE variant of > TCHOTCHKE
TSATSKES > TSATSKE
TSESSEBE South African variant of > SASSABY
TSESSEBES > TSESSEBE
TSETSE n any of various bloodsucking African flies
TSETSES > TSETSE
TSIGANE variant of > TZIGANE
TSIGANES > TSIGANE
TSIMMES variant spelling of > TZIMMES
TSITSITH n tassels or fringes of thread attached to the four corners of the tallith
TSK vb utter the sound "tsk", usu in disapproval
TSKED > TSK
TSKING > TSK
TSKS > TSK
TSKTSK same as > TSK
TSKTSKED > TSKTSK
TSKTSKING > TSKTSK
TSKTSKS > TSKTSK
TSOORIS variant of > TSURIS
TSORES variant of > TSURIS
TSORIS variant of > TSURIS
TSORRISS variant of > TSURIS
TSOTSI n Black street thug or gang member
TSOTSIS > TSOTSI
TSOURIS variant of > TSURIS

TSOURISES > TSOURIS
TSUBA *n* sword guard of a Japanese sword
TSUBAS > TSUBA
TSUBO *n* unit of area
TSUBOS > TSUBO
TSUNAMI *n* tidal wave, usu caused by an earthquake under the sea
TSUNAMIC > TSUNAMI
TSUNAMIS > TSUNAMI
TSURIS *n* grief or strife
TSURISES > TSURIS
TSUTSUMU *n* Japanese art of wrapping gifts
TSUTSUMUS > TSUTSUMU
TUAN *n* lord
TUANS > TUAN
TUART *n* eucalyptus tree of Australia
TUARTS > TUART
TUATARA *n* large lizard-like New Zealand reptile
TUATARAS > TUATARA
TUATERA *variant spelling of* > TUATARA
TUATERAS > TUATERA
TUATH *n* territory of an ancient Irish tribe
TUATHS > TUATH
TUATUA *n* edible marine bivalve of New Zealand waters
TUATUAS > TUATUA
TUB *n* open, usu round container ▷ *vb* wash (oneself or another) in a tub
TUBA *n* valved low-pitched brass instrument
TUBAE > TUBA
TUBAGE *n* insertion of a tube
TUBAGES > TUBAGE
TUBAIST > TUBA
TUBAISTS > TUBA
TUBAL *adj* of or relating to a tube
TUBAR *another word for* > TUBULAR
TUBAS > TUBA
TUBATE *less common word for* > TUBULAR
TUBBABLE > TUB
TUBBED > TUB
TUBBER > TUB
TUBBERS > TUB
TUBBIER > TUBBY
TUBBIEST > TUBBY
TUBBINESS > TUBBY
TUBBING > TUB
TUBBINGS > TUB
TUBBISH *adj* fat
TUBBY *adj* (of a person) short and fat
TUBE *n* hollow cylinder
TUBECTOMY *n* excision of the Fallopian tubes
TUBED > TUBE
TUBEFUL *n* quantity (of something) that a tube can hold

TUBEFULS > TUBEFUL
TUBELESS *adj* without a tube
TUBELIKE *adj* resembling a tube
TUBENOSE *n* seabird with tubular nostrils on its beak
TUBENOSES > TUBENOSE
TUBER *n* fleshy underground root of a plant such as a potato
TUBERCLE *n* small rounded swelling
TUBERCLED *adj* having tubercles
TUBERCLES > TUBERCLE
TUBERCULA *n* plural of tuberculum (another name for "tubercle")
TUBERCULE *variant of* > TUBERCLE
TUBEROID *adj* resembling a tuber ▷ *n* fleshy root resembling a tuber
TUBEROIDS > TUBEROID
TUBEROSE *same as* > TUBEROUS
TUBEROSES > TUBEROSE
TUBEROUS *adj* (of plants) forming, bearing, or resembling a tuber or tubers
TUBERS > TUBER
TUBES > TUBE
TUBEWELL *n* type of water well
TUBEWELLS > TUBEWELL
TUBEWORK *n* collective term for tubes or tubing
TUBEWORKS > TUBEWORK
TUBEWORM *n* undersea worm
TUBEWORMS > TUBEWORM
TUBFAST *n* period of fasting and sweating in a tub, intended as a cure for disease
TUBFASTS > TUBFAST
TUBFISH *another name for* > GURNARD
TUBFISHES > TUBFISH
TUBFUL *n* amount a tub will hold
TUBFULS > TUBFUL
TUBICOLAR *adj* tube-dwelling
TUBICOLE *n* tube-dwelling creature
TUBICOLES > TUBICOLE
TUBIFEX *n* type of small reddish freshwater worm
TUBIFEXES > TUBIFEX
TUBIFICID *n* type of threadlike annelid worm
TUBIFORM *same as* > TUBULAR
TUBING *n* length of tube
TUBINGS > TUBING
TUBIST > TUBA
TUBISTS > TUBA
TUBLIKE > TUB
TUBS > TUB
TUBULAR *adj* of or shaped like a tube ▷ *n* type of tyre

TUBULARLY > TUBULAR
TUBULARS > TUBULAR
TUBULATE *vb* form or shape into a tube
TUBULATED > TUBULATE
TUBULATES > TUBULATE
TUBULATOR > TUBULATE
TUBULE *n* any small tubular structure
TUBULES > TUBULE
TUBULIN *n* protein forming the basis of microtubules
TUBULINS > TUBULIN
TUBULOSE *adj* tube-shaped; consisting of tubes
TUBULOUS *adj* tube-shaped
TUBULURE *n* tube leading into a retort or other receptacle
TUBULURES > TUBULURE
TUCHIS *n* buttocks
TUCHISES > TUCHIS
TUCHUN *n* (formerly) a Chinese military governor or warlord
TUCHUNS > TUCHUN
TUCHUS *same as* > TUCHIS
TUCHUSES > TUCHUS
TUCK *vb* push or fold into a small space ▷ *n* stitched fold
TUCKAHOE *n* type of edible root
TUCKAHOES > TUCKAHOE
TUCKBOX *n* box used for carrying food to school
TUCKBOXES > TUCKBOX
TUCKED > TUCK
TUCKER *n* food ▷ *vb* weary or tire completely
TUCKERBAG *n* in Australia, bag or box used for carrying food
TUCKERBOX *same as* > TUCKERBAG
TUCKERED > TUCKER
TUCKERING > TUCKER
TUCKERS > TUCKER
TUCKET *n* flourish on a trumpet
TUCKETS > TUCKET
TUCKING *n* act of tucking
TUCKINGS > TUCKING
TUCKS > TUCK
TUCKSHOP *n* shop, esp one in or near a school, where food such as cakes and sweets are sold
TUCKSHOPS > TUCKSHOP
TUCOTUCO *n* colonial burrowing South American rodent
TUCOTUCOS > TUCOTUCO
TUCUTUCO *variant spelling of* > TUCOTUCO
TUCUTUCOS > TUCUTUCO
TUCUTUCU *same as* > TUCOTUCO
TUCUTUCUS > TUCUTUCU
TUFA *n* porous rock formed as a deposit from springs

TUFACEOUS > TUFA
TUFAS > TUFA
TUFF *n* porous rock formed from volcanic dust or ash
TUFFE *old form of* > TUFT
TUFFES > TUFFE
TUFFET *n* small mound or seat
TUFFETS > TUFFET
TUFFS > TUFF
TUFOLI *n* type of tubular pasta
TUFT *n* bunch of feathers, grass, hair, etc held or growing together at the base ▷ *vb* provide or decorate with a tuft or tufts
TUFTED *adj* having a tuft or tufts
TUFTER > TUFT
TUFTERS > TUFT
TUFTIER > TUFT
TUFTIEST > TUFT
TUFTILY > TUFT
TUFTING > TUFT
TUFTINGS > TUFT
TUFTS > TUFT
TUFTY > TUFT
TUG *vb* pull hard ▷ *n* hard pull
TUGBOAT *same as* > TUG
TUGBOATS > TUGBOAT
TUGGED > TUG
TUGGER > TUG
TUGGERS > TUG
TUGGING > TUG
TUGGINGLY > TUG
TUGGINGS > TUG
TUGHRA *n* Turkish Sultan's official emblem
TUGHRAS > TUGHRA
TUGHRIK *same as* > TUGRIK
TUGHRIKS > TUGHRIK
TUGLESS > TUG
TUGRA *variant of* > TUGHRA
TUGRAS > TUGRA
TUGRIK *n* standard monetary unit of Mongolia
TUGRIKS > TUGRIK
TUGS > TUG
TUI *n* New Zealand honeyeater that mimics human speech and the songs of other birds
TUILE *n* type of almond-flavoured dessert biscuit
TUILES > TUILE
TUILLE *n* (in a suit of armour) hanging plate protecting the thighs
TUILLES > TUILLE
TUILLETTE *n* little tuille
TUILYIE *vb* fight
TUILYIED > TUILYIE
TUILYIES > TUILYIE
TUILZIE *variant form of* > TUILYIE
TUILZIED > TUILZIE
TUILZIES > TUILZIE

t

TUINA n form of massage originating in China
TUINAS > TUINA
TUIS > TUI
TUISM n practice of putting the interests of another before one's own
TUISMS > TUISM
TUITION n instruction, esp received individually or in a small group
TUITIONAL > TUITION
TUITIONS > TUITION
TUKTOO same as **>** TUKTU
TUKTOOS > TUKTOO
TUKTU (in Canada) another name for **>** CARIBOU
TUKTUS > TUKTU
TULADI n large trout found in Canada and northern US
TULADIS > TULADI
TULAREMIA n infectious disease of rodents
TULAREMIC > TULAREMIA
TULBAN old form of **>** TURBAN
TULBANS > TULBAN
TULCHAN n skin of a calf placed next to a cow to induce it to give milk
TULCHANS > TULCHAN
TULE n type of bulrush found in California
TULES > TULE
TULIP n plant with bright cup-shaped flowers
TULIPANT n turban
TULIPANTS > TULIPANT
TULIPLIKE > TULIP
TULIPS > TULIP
TULIPWOOD n light soft wood of the tulip tree, used in making furniture and veneer
TULLE n fine net fabric of silk etc
TULLES > TULLE
TULLIBEE n cisco of the Great Lakes of Canada
TULLIBEES > TULLIBEE
TULPA n being or object created through willpower and visualization techniques
TULPAS > TULPA
TULSI n type of basil
TULSIS > TULSI
TULWAR n Indian sabre
TULWARS > TULWAR
TUM informal or childish word for **>** STOMACH
TUMBLE vb (cause to) fall, esp awkwardly or violently **>** n fall
TUMBLEBUG n type of dung beetle
TUMBLED > TUMBLE
TUMBLER n stemless drinking glass
TUMBLERS > TUMBLER
TUMBLES > TUMBLE
TUMBLESET n somersault

TUMBLING > TUMBLE
TUMBLINGS > TUMBLING
TUMBREL n farm cart for carrying dung
TUMBRELS > TUMBREL
TUMBRIL same as **>** TUMBREL
TUMBRILS > TUMBRIL
TUMEFIED > TUMEFY
TUMEFIES > TUMEFY
TUMEFY vb make or become tumid
TUMEFYING > TUMEFY
TUMESCE vb swell
TUMESCED > TUMESCE
TUMESCENT adj swollen or becoming swollen
TUMESCES > TUMESCE
TUMESCING > TUMESCE
TUMID adj (of an organ or part of the body) enlarged or swollen
TUMIDITY > TUMID
TUMIDLY > TUMID
TUMIDNESS > TUMID
TUMMIES > TUMMY
TUMMLER n entertainer employed to encourage audience participation
TUMMLERS > TUMMLER
TUMMY n stomach
TUMOR same as **>** TUMOUR
TUMORAL > TUMOUR
TUMORLIKE > TUMOUR
TUMOROUS > TUMOUR
TUMORS > TUMOR
TUMOUR n abnormal growth in or on the body
TUMOURS > TUMOUR
TUMP n small mound or clump **>** vb make a tump around
TUMPED > TUMP
TUMPHIES > TUMPHY
TUMPHY n dolt; fool
TUMPIER > TUMP
TUMPIEST > TUMP
TUMPING > TUMP
TUMPLINE n (in the US and Canada, esp formerly) leather or cloth band strung across the forehead or chest and attached to a pack or load in order to support it
TUMPLINES > TUMPLINE
TUMPS > TUMP
TUMPY > TUMP
TUMS > TUM
TUMSHIE n turnip
TUMSHIES > TUMSHIE
TUMULAR adj of, relating to, or like a mound
TUMULARY same as **>** TUMULAR
TUMULI > TUMULUS
TUMULOSE adj abounding in small hills or mounds
TUMULOUS same as **>** TUMULOSE
TUMULT n uproar or commotion **>** vb stir up a commotion

TUMULTED > TUMULT
TUMULTING > TUMULT
TUMULTS > TUMULT
TUMULUS n burial mound
TUMULUSES > TUMULUS
TUN n large beer cask **>** vb put into or keep in tuns
TUNA n large marine food fish
TUNABLE adj able to be tuned
TUNABLY > TUNABLE
TUNAS > TUNA
TUNBELLY n large round belly
TUND vb beat; strike
TUNDED > TUND
TUNDING > TUND
TUNDISH n type of funnel
TUNDISHES > TUNDISH
TUNDRA n vast treeless Arctic region with permanently frozen subsoil
TUNDRAS > TUNDRA
TUNDS > TUND
TUNDUN n wooden instrument used by Native Australians in religious rites
TUNDUNS > TUNDUN
TUNE n (pleasing) sequence of musical notes **>** vb adjust (a musical instrument) so that it is in tune
TUNEABLE same as **>** TUNABLE
TUNEABLY > TUNEABLE
TUNEAGE n music
TUNEAGES > TUNEAGE
TUNED > TUNE
TUNEFUL adj having a pleasant tune
TUNEFULLY > TUNEFUL
TUNELESS adj having no melody or tune
TUNER n part of a radio or television receiver for selecting channels
TUNERS > TUNER
TUNES > TUNE
TUNESMITH n composer of light or popular music and songs
TUNEUP n adjustments made to an engine to improve its performance
TUNEUPS > TUNEUP
TUNG n as in tung oil fast-drying oil obtained from the seeds of a central Asian tree
TUNGS > TUNG
TUNGSTATE n salt of tungstic acid
TUNGSTEN n greyish-white metal
TUNGSTENS > TUNGSTEN
TUNGSTIC adj of or containing tungsten, esp in a high valence state

TUNGSTITE n yellow earthy rare secondary mineral that consists of tungsten oxide and occurs with tungsten ores
TUNGSTOUS adj of or containing tungsten in a low valence state
TUNIC n close-fitting jacket forming part of some uniforms
TUNICA n tissue forming a layer or covering of an organ or part
TUNICAE > TUNICA
TUNICATE n minute primitive marine chordate animal **>** adj of, relating to this animal **>** vb wear a tunic
TUNICATED > TUNICATE
TUNICATES > TUNICATE
TUNICIN n cellulose-like substance found in tunicates
TUNICINS > TUNICIN
TUNICKED adj wearing a tunic
TUNICLE n vestment worn at High Mass and other religious ceremonies
TUNICLES > TUNICLE
TUNICS > TUNIC
TUNIER > TUNY
TUNIEST > TUNY
TUNING n set of pitches to which the open strings of a guitar, violin, etc, are tuned
TUNINGS > TUNING
TUNKET n hell
TUNKETS > TUNKET
TUNNAGE same as **>** TONNAGE
TUNNAGES > TUNNAGE
TUNNED > TUN
TUNNEL n underground passage **>** vb make a tunnel (through)
TUNNELED > TUNNEL
TUNNELER > TUNNEL
TUNNELERS > TUNNEL
TUNNELING > TUNNEL
TUNNELLED > TUNNEL
TUNNELLER > TUNNEL
TUNNELS > TUNNEL
TUNNIES > TUNNY
TUNNING > TUN
TUNNINGS > TUN
TUNNY same as **>** TUNA
TUNS > TUN
TUNY adj having an easily discernable melody
TUP n male sheep **>** vb cause (a ram) to mate with a ewe
TUPEK same as **>** TUPIK
TUPEKS > TUPEK
TUPELO n large tree of deep swamps and rivers of the southern US
TUPELOS > TUPELO
TUPIK n tent of seal or caribou skin used for

shelter by the Inuit in summer

TUPIKS > TUPIK

TUPLE n row of values in a relational database

TUPLES > TUPLE

TUPPED > TUP

TUPPENCE same as > TWOPENCE

TUPPENCES > TUPPENCE

TUPPENNY same as > TWOPENNY

TUPPING n act of tupping

TUPPINGS > TUPPING

TUPS > TUP

TUPTOWING n study of Greek grammar

TUPUNA same as > TIPUNA

TUPUNAS > TUPUNA

TUQUE n knitted cap with a long tapering end

TUQUES > TUQUE

TURACIN n red pigment found in touraco feathers

TURACINS > TURACIN

TURACO same as > TOURACO

TURACOS > TURACO

TURACOU variant of > TOURACO

TURACOUS > TURACOU

TURBAN n Muslim, Hindu, or Sikh man's head covering

TURBAND old variant of > TURBAN

TURBANDS > TURBAND

TURBANED > TURBAN

TURBANNED > TURBAN

TURBANS > TURBAN

TURBANT old variant of > TURBAN

TURBANTS > TURBANT

TURBARIES > TURBARY

TURBARY n land where peat or turf is cut or has been cut

TURBETH variant of > TURPETH

TURBETHS > TURBETH

TURBID adj muddy, not clear

TURBIDITE n sediment deposited by a turbidity current

TURBIDITY > TURBID

TURBIDLY > TURBID

TURBINAL same as > TURBINATE

TURBINALS > TURBINAL

TURBINATE adj of or relating to any of the thin scroll-shaped bones situated on the walls of the nasal passages ▷ n turbinate bone

TURBINE n machine or generator driven by gas, water, etc turning blades

TURBINED adj having a turbine

TURBINES > TURBINE

TURBIT n crested breed of domestic pigeon

TURBITH variant of > TURPETH

TURBITHS > TURBITH

TURBITS > TURBIT

TURBO n compressor in an engine

TURBOCAR n car driven by a gas turbine

TURBOCARS > TURBOCAR

TURBOFAN n engine in which a large fan driven by a turbine forces air rearwards to increase thrust

TURBOFANS > TURBOFAN

TURBOJET n gas turbine in which the exhaust gases provide the propulsive thrust to drive an aircraft

TURBOJETS > TURBOJET

TURBOND old variant of > TURBAN

TURBONDS > TURBOND

TURBOPROP n gas turbine for driving an aircraft propeller

TURBOS > TURBO

TURBOT n large European edible flatfish

TURBOTS > TURBOT

TURBULENT adj involving a lot of sudden changes and conflicting elements

TURCOPOLE n lightly armed and highly mobile class of Crusader

TURD n piece of excrement

TURDINE adj of, relating to, or characteristic of thrushes

TURDION variant of > TORDION

TURDIONS > TURDION

TURDOID same as > TURDINE

TURDS > TURD

TURDUCKEN n turkey stuffed with duck stuffed with chicken

TUREEN n serving dish for soup

TUREENS > TUREEN

TURF n short thick even grass ▷ vb cover with turf

TURFED > TURF

TURFEN adj made of turf

TURFGRASS n grass grown for lawns

TURFIER > TURFY

TURFIEST > TURFY

TURFINESS > TURFY

TURFING > TURF

TURFINGS > TURF

TURFITE same as > TURFMAN

TURFITES > TURFITE

TURFLESS > TURF

TURFLIKE > TURF

TURFMAN n person devoted to horse racing

TURFMEN > TURFMAN

TURFS > TURF

TURFSKI n ski down a grassy hill on skis modified with integral wheels

TURFSKIS > TURFSKI

TURFY adj of, covered with, or resembling turf

TURGENCY > TURGENT

TURGENT obsolete word for > TURGID

TURGENTLY > TURGENT

TURGID adj (of language) pompous

TURGIDER > TURGID

TURGIDEST > TURGID

TURGIDITY > TURGID

TURGIDLY > TURGID

TURGITE n red or black mineral consisting of hydrated ferric oxide

TURGITES > TURGITE

TURGOR n normal rigid state of a cell

TURGORS > TURGOR

TURION n perennating bud produced by many aquatic plants

TURIONS > TURION

TURISTA n traveller's diarrhoea

TURISTAS > TURISTA

TURK n obsolete derogatory term for a violent, brutal, or domineering person

TURKEY n large bird bred for food

TURKEYS > TURKEY

TURKIES old form of > TURQUOISE

TURKIESES > TURKIES

TURKIS old form of > TURQUOISE

TURKISES > TURKIS

TURKOIS old form of > TURQUOISE

TURKOISES > TURKOIS

TURKS > TURK

TURLOUGH n seasonal lake or pond

TURLOUGHS > TURLOUGH

TURM n troop of horsemen

TURME variant of > TURM

TURMERIC n yellow spice obtained from the root of an Asian plant

TURMERICS > TURMERIC

TURMES > TURME

TURMOIL n agitation or confusion ▷ vb make or become turbulent

TURMOILED > TURMOIL

TURMOILS > TURMOIL

TURMS > TURM

TURN vb change the position or direction (of) ▷ n turning

TURNABLE > TURN

TURNABOUT n act of turning so as to face a different direction

TURNAGAIN n revolution

TURNBACK n one who turns back (from a challenge, for example)

TURNBACKS > TURNBACK

TURNCOAT n person who deserts one party or cause to join another

TURNCOATS > TURNCOAT

TURNCOCK n (formerly) official employed to turn on the water for the mains supply

TURNCOCKS > TURNCOCK

TURNDOWN adj capable of being or designed to be folded or doubled down ▷ n instance of turning down

TURNDOWNS > TURNDOWN

TURNDUN another name for > TUNDUN

TURNDUNS > TURNDUN

TURNED > TURN

TURNER n person or thing that turns

TURNERIES > TURNERY

TURNERS > TURNER

TURNERY n objects made on a lathe

TURNHALL n building in which gymnastics is taught and practised

TURNHALLS > TURNHALL

TURNING n road or path leading off a main route

TURNINGS > TURNING

TURNIP n root vegetable with orange or white flesh ▷ vb sow (a field) with turnips

TURNIPED > TURNIP

TURNIPING > TURNIP

TURNIPS > TURNIP

TURNIPY adj like a turnip

TURNKEY n jailer ▷ adj denoting a project in which a single contractor has responsibility for the complete job

TURNKEYS > TURNKEY

TURNOFF n road or other way branching off from the main

TURNOFFS > TURNOFF

TURNON n something sexually exciting

TURNONS > TURNON

TURNOUT n number of people appearing at a gathering

TURNOUTS > TURNOUT

TURNOVER n total sales made by a business over a certain period

TURNOVERS > TURNOVER

TURNPIKE n road where a toll is collected at barriers

TURNPIKES > TURNPIKE

TURNROUND n act or process in which a ship, aircraft, etc, unloads passengers and freight at end of a trip and reloads for next trip

TURNS > TURN

TURNSKIN n old name for a werewolf

t

TURNSKINS > TURNSKIN

TURNSOLE n any of various plants having flowers that are said to turn towards the sun

TURNSOLES > TURNSOLE

TURNSPIT n (formerly) a servant or small dog whose job was to turn the spit on which meat, poultry, etc, was roasting

TURNSPITS > TURNSPIT

TURNSTILE n revolving gate for admitting one person at a time

TURNSTONE n shore bird

TURNTABLE n revolving platform

TURNUP n the turned-up fold at the bottom of some trouser legs

TURNUPS > TURNUP

TUROPHILE n person who loves cheese

TURPETH n convolvulaceous plant of the East Indies, having roots with purgative properties

TURPETHS > TURPETH

TURPITUDE n wickedness

TURPS n colourless, flammable liquid

TURPSES > TURPS

TURQUOIS variant of > TURQUOISE

TURQUOISE adj blue-green ▷ n blue-green precious stone

TURR n Newfoundland name for the guillemot

TURRET n small tower

TURRETED adj having or resembling a turret or turrets

TURRETS > TURRET

TURRIBANT old variant of > TURBAN

TURRICAL adj of, relating to, or resembling a turret

TURRS > TURR

TURTLE n sea tortoise

TURTLED > TURTLE

TURTLER > TURTLE

TURTLERS > TURTLE

TURTLES > TURTLE

TURTLING > TURTLE

TURTLINGS > TURTLE

TURVES > TURF

TUSCHE n substance used in lithography for drawing the design

TUSCHES > TUSCHE

TUSH interj exclamation of disapproval or contempt ▷ n small tusk ▷ vb utter the interjection "tush"

TUSHED > TUSH

TUSHERIES > TUSHERY

TUSHERY n use of affectedly archaic language in novels, etc

TUSHES > TUSH

TUSHIE n pair of buttocks

TUSHIES > TUSHIE

TUSHING > TUSH

TUSHKAR variant of > TUSKAR

TUSHKARS > TUSHKAR

TUSHKER variant of > TUSKAR

TUSHKERS > TUSHKER

TUSHY variant of > TUSHIE

TUSK n long pointed tooth of an elephant, walrus, etc ▷ vb stab, tear, or gore with the tusks

TUSKAR n peat-cutting spade

TUSKARS > TUSKAR

TUSKED > TUSK

TUSKER n any animal with prominent tusks, esp a wild boar or elephant

TUSKERS > TUSKER

TUSKIER > TUSK

TUSKIEST > TUSK

TUSKING > TUSK

TUSKINGS > TUSK

TUSKLESS > TUSK

TUSKLIKE > TUSK

TUSKS > TUSK

TUSKY > TUSK

TUSSAC modifier as in tussac grass kind of grass

TUSSAH same as > TUSSORE

TUSSAHS > TUSSAH

TUSSAL > TUSSIS

TUSSAR variant of > TUSSORE

TUSSARS > TUSSAR

TUSSEH variant of > TUSSORE

TUSSEHS > TUSSEH

TUSSER same as > TUSSORE

TUSSERS > TUSSER

TUSSES > TUSSIS

TUSSIS technical name for a > COUGH

TUSSISES > TUSSIS

TUSSIVE > TUSSIS

TUSSLE vb fight or scuffle ▷ n energetic fight, struggle, or argument

TUSSLED > TUSSLE

TUSSLES > TUSSLE

TUSSLING > TUSSLE

TUSSOCK n tuft of grass

TUSSOCKED adj having tussocks

TUSSOCKS > TUSSOCK

TUSSOCKY > TUSSOCK

TUSSOR variant of > TUSSORE

TUSSORE n strong coarse brownish Indian silk obtained from the cocoons of an Oriental saturniid silkworm

TUSSORES > TUSSORE

TUSSORS > TUSSOR

TUSSUCK variant of > TUSSOCK

TUSSUCKS > TUSSUCK

TUSSUR variant of > TUSSORE

TUSSURS > TUSSUR

TUT interj an exclamation of mild disapproval, or surprise ▷ vb express disapproval by the exclamation of "tut-tut." ▷ n payment system based on measurable work done

TUTANIA n alloy of low melting point used mostly for decorative purposes

TUTANIAS > TUTANIA

TUTEE n one who is tutored, esp in a university

TUTEES > TUTEE

TUTELAGE n instruction or guidance, esp by a tutor

TUTELAGES > TUTELAGE

TUTELAR same as > TUTELARY

TUTELARS > TUTELAR

TUTELARY adj having the role of guardian or protector ▷ n tutelary person, deity, or saint

TUTENAG n zinc alloy

TUTENAGS > TUTENAG

TUTIORISM n (in Roman Catholic moral theology) the doctrine that in cases of moral doubt it is best to follow the safer course or that in agreement with the law

TUTIORIST > TUTIORISM

TUTMAN n one who does tutwork

TUTMEN > TUTMAN

TUTOR n person teaching individuals or small groups ▷ vb act as a tutor to

TUTORAGE > TUTOR

TUTORAGES > TUTOR

TUTORED > TUTOR

TUTORESS n female tutor

TUTORIAL n period of instruction with a tutor ▷ adj of or relating to a tutor

TUTORIALS > TUTORIAL

TUTORING > TUTOR

TUTORINGS > TUTOR

TUTORISE variant spelling of > TUTORIZE

TUTORISED > TUTORISE

TUTORISES > TUTORISE

TUTORISM > TUTOR

TUTORISMS > TUTOR

TUTORIZE vb tutor

TUTORIZED > TUTOR

TUTORIZES > TUTORIZE

TUTORS > TUTOR

TUTORSHIP > TUTOR

TUTOYED adj addressed in a familiar way

TUTOYER vb speak to someone on familiar terms

TUTOYERED > TUTOYER

TUTOYERS > TUTOYER

TUTRESS same as > TUTORESS

TUTRESSES > TUTRESS

TUTRICES > TUTRIX

TUTRIX n female tutor; tutoress

TUTRIXES > TUTRIX

TUTS Scots version of > TUT

TUTSAN n woodland shrub of Europe and W Asia

TUTSANS > TUTSAN

TUTSED > TUTS

TUTSES > TUTS

TUTSING > TUTS

TUTTED > TUT

TUTTI adv be performed by the whole orchestra or choir ▷ n piece of tutti music

TUTTIES > TUTTY

TUTTING > TUT

TUTTINGS > TUT

TUTTIS > TUTTI

TUTTY n finely powdered impure zinc oxide

TUTU n short stiff skirt worn by ballerinas

TUTUED adj wearing tutu

TUTUS > TUTU

TUTWORK n work paid using a tut system

TUTWORKER > TUTWORK

TUTWORKS > TUTWORK

TUX short for > TUXEDO

TUXEDO n dinner jacket

TUXEDOED adj wearing a tuxedo

TUXEDOES > TUXEDO

TUXEDOS > TUXEDO

TUXES > TUX

TUYER variant of > TUYERE

TUYERE n water-cooled nozzle through which air is blown into a cupola, blast furnace, or forge

TUYERES > TUYERE

TUYERS > TUYER

TUZZ n tuft or clump of hair

TUZZES > TUZZ

TWA Scots word for > TWO

TWADDLE n silly or pretentious talk or writing ▷ vb talk or write in a silly or pretentious way

TWADDLED > TWADDLE

TWADDLER > TWADDLE

TWADDLERS > TWADDLE

TWADDLES > TWADDLE

TWADDLIER > TWADDLE

TWADDLING > TWADDLE

TWADDLY > TWADDLE

TWAE same as > TWA

TWAES > TWAE

TWAFALD Scots variant of > TWOFOLD

TWAIN n two

TWAINS > TWAIN

TWAITE n herring-like food fish

TWAITES > TWAITE

TWAL n twelve

TWALPENNY n shilling

TWALS > TWAL

TWANG n sharp ringing sound ▷ vb (cause to) make a twang

TWANGED > TWANG

TWANGER > TWANG

TWANGERS > TWANG

TWANGIER > TWANG

TWANGIEST > TWANG

TWANGING > TWANG

TWANGINGS > TWANG

TWANGLE vb make a continuous loose twanging sound

TWANGLED > TWANGLE

TWANGLER > TWANGLE

TWANGLERS > TWANGLE

TWANGLES > TWANGLE

TWANGLING > TWANGLE

TWANGS > TWANG

TWANGY > TWANG

TWANK vb make a sharply curtailed twang

TWANKAY n variety of Chinese green tea

TWANKAYS > TWANKAY

TWANKIES > TWANKY

TWANKS > TWANK

TWANKY same as > TWANKAY

TWAS > TWA

TWASOME same as > TWOSOME

TWASOMES > TWASOME

TWAT n taboo term for female genitals ▷ vb hit or strike violently

TWATS > TWAT

TWATTED > TWAT

TWATTING > TWAT

TWATTLE rare word for > TWADDLE

TWATTLED > TWATTLE

TWATTLER > TWATTLE

TWATTLERS > TWATTLE

TWATTLES > TWATTLE

TWATTLING > TWATTLE

TWAY old variant of > TWAIN

TWAYBLADE n type of orchid

TWAYS > TWAY

TWEAK vb pinch or twist sharply ▷ n tweaking

TWEAKED > TWEAK

TWEAKER n engineer's small screwdriver

TWEAKERS > TWEAKER

TWEAKIER > TWEAK

TWEAKIEST > TWEAK

TWEAKING > TWEAK

TWEAKINGS > TWEAK

TWEAKS > TWEAK

TWEAKY > TWEAK

TWEE adj too sentimental, sweet, or pretty

TWEED n thick woollen cloth

TWEEDIER > TWEEDY

TWEEDIEST > TWEEDY

TWEEDILY adv in a manner characteristic of upper-class people who live in the country

TWEEDLE vb improvise aimlessly on a musical instrument

TWEEDLED > TWEEDLE

TWEEDLER > TWEEDLE

TWEEDLERS > TWEEDLE

TWEEDLES > TWEEDLE

TWEEDLING > TWEEDLE

TWEEDS > TWEED

TWEEDY adj of or made of tweed

TWEEL variant of > TWILL

TWEELED > TWEEL

TWEELING > TWEEL

TWEELS > TWEEL

TWEELY > TWEEL

TWEEN same as > BETWEEN

TWEENAGE adj (of a child) between about eight and fourteen years old

TWEENAGER n child of approximately eight to fourteen years of age

TWEENER same as > TWEENAGER

TWEENERS > TWEENER

TWEENESS > TWEE

TWEENIE same as > TWEENY

TWEENIES > TWEENY

TWEENS > TWEEN

TWEENY n maid who assists both cook and housemaid

TWEEP n person who uses Twitter

TWEEPLE pl n people who communicate via the Twitter website

TWEEPS > TWEEP

TWEER variant of > TWIRE

TWEERED > TWEER

TWEERING > TWEER

TWEERS > TWEER

TWEEST > TWEE

TWEET vb chirp ▷ interj imitation of the thin chirping sound made by small birds

TWEETABLE adj (of a message) short enough to be posted on Twitter

TWEETED > TWEET

TWEETER n loudspeaker reproducing high-frequency sounds

TWEETERS > TWEETER

TWEETING > TWEET

TWEETS > TWEET

TWEETUP n an online meeting of individuals arranged on the social networking website Twitter

TWEETUPS > TWEETUP

TWEEZE vb take hold of or pluck (hair, small objects, etc) with or as if with tweezers

TWEEZED > TWEEZE

TWEEZER same as > TWEEZERS

TWEEZERS pl n small pincer-like tool

TWEEZES > TWEEZE

TWEEZING > TWEEZE

TWELFTH n (of) number twelve in a series ▷ adj of or being number twelve in a series

TWELFTHLY adv after the eleventh person, position, event, etc

TWELFTHS > TWELFTH

TWELVE n two more than ten ▷ adj amounting to twelve ▷ determiner amounting to twelve

TWELVEMO another word for > DUODECIMO

TWELVEMOS > TWELVEMO

TWELVES > TWELVE

TWENTIES > TWENTY

TWENTIETH adj coming after the nineteenth in numbering or counting order, position, time, etc ▷ n one of 20 approximately equal parts of something

TWENTY n two times ten ▷ adj amounting to twenty ▷ determiner amounting to twenty

TWENTYISH adj around 20

TWERK vb dance provocatively by moving the hips rapidly back and forth while raising and lowering the body in a squatting motion

TWERKED > TWERK

TWERKING n type of dance involving rapid hip movement

TWERKINGS > TWERKING

TWERKS > TWERK

TWERP n silly person

TWERPIER > TWERP

TWERPIEST > TWERP

TWERPS > TWERP

TWERPY > TWERP

TWIBIL same as > TWIBILL

TWIBILL n mattock with a blade shaped like an adze at one end and like an axe at the other

TWIBILLS > TWIBILL

TWIBILS > TWIBIL

TWICE adv two times

TWICER n someone who does something twice

TWICERS > TWICER

TWICHILD n person in his or her dotage

TWIDDLE vb fiddle or twirl in an idle way ▷ n act or instance of twiddling

TWIDDLED > TWIDDLE

TWIDDLER > TWIDDLE

TWIDDLERS > TWIDDLE

TWIDDLES > TWIDDLE

TWIDDLIER > TWIDDLE

TWIDDLING > TWIDDLE

TWIDDLY > TWIDDLE

TWIER variant of > TUYERE

TWIERS > TWIER

TWIFOLD variant of > TWOFOLD

TWIFORKED adj having two forks; bifurcate

TWIFORMED adj having two forms

TWIG n small branch or shoot ▷ vb realize or understand

TWIGGED > TWIG

TWIGGEN adj made of twigs

TWIGGER > TWIG

TWIGGERS > TWIG

TWIGGIER > TWIGGY

TWIGGIEST > TWIGGY

TWIGGING > TWIG

TWIGGY adj of or relating to a twig or twigs

TWIGHT old variant of > TWIT

TWIGHTED > TWIGHT

TWIGHTING > TWIGHT

TWIGHTS > TWIGHT

TWIGLESS > TWIG

TWIGLET n small twig

TWIGLETS > TWIGLET

TWIGLIKE > TWIG

TWIGLOO n temporary shelter made from twigs, branches, leaves, etc

TWIGLOOS > TWIGLOO

TWIGS > TWIG

TWIGSOME adj covered with twigs; twiggy

TWILIGHT n soft dim light just after sunset ▷ adj of or relating to the period towards the end of the day

TWILIGHTS > TWILIGHT

TWILIT > TWILIGHT

TWILL n fabric woven to produce parallel ridges ▷ adj of or designating a weave in which the weft yarns are worked around two or more warp yarns ▷ vb weave in this fashion

TWILLED > TWILL

TWILLIES > TWILLY

TWILLING > TWILL

TWILLINGS > TWILL

TWILLS > TWILL

TWILLY n machine having revolving spikes for opening and cleaning raw textile fibres

TWILT variant of > QUILT

TWILTED > TWILT

TWILTING > TWILT

TWILTS > TWILT

TWIN n one of a pair, esp of two children born at one birth ▷ vb pair or be paired

TWINBERRY n creeping wooden plant

TWINBORN adj born as a twin

TWINE n string or cord ▷ vb twist or coil round

TWINED > TWINE

TWINER > TWINE

TWINERS > TWINE

TWINES > TWINE

TWINGE n sudden sharp pain or emotional pang ▷ vb have or cause to have a twinge

TWINGED > TWINGE

TWINGEING > TWINGE

TWINGES > TWINGE

TWINGING > TWINGE

TWINIER > TWINE

TWINIEST > TWINE

TWINIGHT adj (of a baseball double-header) held in the late afternoon and evening

TWINING > TWINE

TWININGLY > TWINE

TWININGS > TWINE

TWINJET n jet aircraft with two engines

TWINJETS > TWINJET

TWINK n white correction fluid for deleting written text ▷ vb twinkle

TWINKED > TWINK

TWINKIE n stupid person

TWINKIES > TWINKIE

TWINKING > TWINK

TWINKLE vb shine brightly but intermittently ▷ n flickering brightness

TWINKLED > TWINKLE

TWINKLER > TWINKLE

TWINKLERS > TWINKLE

TWINKLIER > TWINKLY

TWINKLING n very short time

TWINKLY adj sparkling

TWINKS > TWINK

TWINKY n stereotypically brainless person

TWINLING old name for > TWIN

TWINLINGS > TWINLING

TWINNED > TWIN

TWINNING > TWIN

TWINNINGS > TWIN

TWINS > TWIN

TWINSET n matching jumper and cardigan

TWINSETS > TWINSET

TWINSHIP n condition of being a twin or twins

TWINSHIPS > TWIN

TWINTER n animal that is 2 years old

TWINTERS > TWINTER

TWINY > TWINE

TWIRE vb look intently at with (or as if with) difficulty

TWIRED > TWIRE

TWIRES > TWIRE

TWIRING > TWIRE

TWIRL vb turn or spin around quickly ▷ n whirl or twist

TWIRLED > TWIRL

TWIRLER > TWIRL

TWIRLERS > TWIRL

TWIRLIER > TWIRL

TWIRLIEST > TWIRL

TWIRLING > TWIRL

TWIRLS > TWIRL

TWIRLY > TWIRL

TWIRP same as > TWERP

TWIRPIER > TWIRP

TWIRPIEST > TWIRP

TWIRPS > TWIRP

TWIRPY > TWIRP

TWISCAR variant of > TUSKAR

TWISCARS > TWISCAR

TWIST vb turn out of the natural position ▷ n twisting

TWISTABLE > TWIST

TWISTED > TWIST

TWISTER n swindler

TWISTERS > TWISTER

TWISTIER > TWIST

TWISTIEST > TWIST

TWISTING > TWIST

TWISTINGS > TWIST

TWISTOR n variable corresponding to the coordinates of a point in space and time

TWISTORS > TWISTOR

TWISTS > TWIST

TWISTY > TWIST

TWIT vb poke fun at (someone) ▷ n foolish person

TWITCH vb move spasmodically ▷ n nervous muscular spasm

TWITCHED > TWITCH

TWITCHER n bird-watcher who tries to spot as many rare varieties as possible

TWITCHERS > TWITCHER

TWITCHIER > TWITCHY

TWITCHILY > TWITCHY

TWITCHING > TWITCH

TWITCHY adj nervous, worried, and ill-at-ease

TWITE n N European finch with a brown streaked plumage

TWITES > TWITE

TWITS > TWIT

TWITTED > TWIT

TWITTEN n narrow alleyway

TWITTENS > TWITTEN

TWITTER vb (of birds) utter chirping sounds ▷ n act or sound of twittering

TWITTERED > TWITTER

TWITTERER > TWITTER

TWITTERS > TWITTER

TWITTERY > TWITTER

TWITTING > TWIT

TWITTINGS > TWIT

TWITTISH adj silly; foolish

TWIXT same as > BETWIXT

TWIZZLE vb spin around

TWIZZLED > TWIZZLE

TWIZZLES > TWIZZLE

TWIZZLING > TWIZZLE

TWO n one more than one

TWOCCER > TWOCCING

TWOCCERS > TWOCCING

TWOCCING n act of breaking into a motor vehicle and driving it away

TWOCCINGS > TWOCCING

TWOCKER > TWOCCING

TWOCKERS > TWOCCING

TWOCKING same as > TWOCCING

TWOCKINGS > TWOCKING

TWOER n (in a game) something that scores two

TWOERS > TWOER

TWOFER n single ticket allowing the buyer entrance to two events

TWOFERS > TWOFER

TWOFOLD adj having twice as many or as much ▷ adv by twice as many or as much ▷ n folding piece of theatrical scenery

TWOFOLDS > TWOFOLD

TWONESS n state or condition of being two

TWONESSES > TWONESS

TWONIE same as > TOONIE

TWONIES > TWONIE

TWOONIE variant of > TOONIE

TWOONIES > TWOONIE

TWOPENCE n sum of two pennies

TWOPENCES > TWOPENCE

TWOPENNY adj cheap or tawdry

TWOS > TWO

TWOSEATER n vehicle providing seats for two people

TWOSOME n group of two people

TWOSOMES > TWOSOME

TWOSTROKE adj relating to or designating an internal-combustion engine whose piston makes two strokes for every explosion

TWP adj stupid

TWYER same as > TUYERE

TWYERE variant of > TUYERE

TWYERES > TWYERE

TWYERS > TWYER

TWYFOLD adj twofold

TYCHISM n theory that chance is an objective reality at work in the universe

TYCHISMS > TYCHISM

TYCOON n powerful wealthy businessman; shogun

TYCOONATE n office or rule of a tycoon

TYCOONERY > TYCOON

TYCOONS > TYCOON

TYDE old variant of the past participle of > TIE

TYE n trough used in mining to separate valuable material from dross ▷ vb (in mining) isolate valuable material from dross using a tye

TYED > TYE

TYEE n large northern Pacific salmon

TYEES > TYEE

TYEING > TYE

TYER > TYE

TYERS > TYE

TYES > TYE

TYG n mug with two handles

TYGS > TYG

TYIN variant of > TYIYN

TYING > TIE

TYIYN n money unit of Kyrgyzstan

TYIYNS > TYIYN

TYKE n often offensive term for small cheeky child

TYKES > TYKE

TYKISH > TYKE

TYLECTOMY n excision of a breast tumour

TYLER variant of > TILER

TYLERS > TYLER

TYLOPOD n mammal with padded feet, such as a camel or llama

TYLOPODS > TYLOPOD

TYLOSES > TYLOSIS

TYLOSIN n broad spectrum antibiotic

TYLOSINS > TYLOSIN

TYLOSIS n bladder-like outgrowth from certain cells in woody tissue

TYLOTE n knobbed sponge spicule

TYLOTES > TYLOTE

TYMBAL same as > TIMBAL

TYMBALS > TYMBAL

TYMP n blast furnace outlet through which molten metal flows

TYMPAN same as > TYMPANUM

TYMPANA > TYMPANUM

TYMPANAL adj relating to the tympanum

TYMPANI same as > TIMPANI

TYMPANIC adj of, relating to, or having a tympanum ▷ n part of the temporal bone in the mammalian skull that surrounds the auditory canal

TYMPANICS > TYMPANIC

TYMPANIES > TYMPANY

TYMPANIST > TIMPANI

TYMPANO > TYMPANI

TYMPANS > TYMPAN

TYMPANUM n cavity of the middle ear

TYMPANUMS > TYMPANUM

TYMPANY n distention of the abdomen

TYMPS > TYMP

TYND variant of > TIND

TYNDE variant of > TIND

TYNE variant of > TINE

TYNED variant of > TYNE
TYNES > TYNE
TYNING > TYNE
TYPABLE > TYPE
TYPAL rare word for > TYPICAL
TYPE n class or category ▷ vb print with a typewriter or word processor
TYPEABLE > TYPE
TYPEBAR n one of the bars in a typewriter that carry the type and are operated by keys
TYPEBARS > TYPEBAR
TYPECASE n compartmental tray for storing printer's type
TYPECASES > TYPECASE
TYPECAST vb continually cast (an actor or actress) in similar roles
TYPECASTS > TYPECAST
TYPED > TYPE
TYPEFACE n style of the type
TYPEFACES > TYPEFACE
TYPES > TYPE
TYPESET vb set (text for printing) in type
TYPESETS > TYPESET
TYPESTYLE another word for > TYPEFACE
TYPEWRITE vb write by means of a typewriter
TYPEWROTE > TYPEWRITE
TYPEY variant of > TYPY
TYPHLITIC > TYPHLITIS
TYPHLITIS n inflammation of the caecum
TYPHOID adj of or relating to typhoid fever
TYPHOIDAL > TYPHOID
TYPHOIDIN n culture of dead typhoid bacillus for injection into the skin to test for typhoid fever
TYPHOIDS > TYPHOID
TYPHON n whirlwind
TYPHONIAN > TYPHOON
TYPHONIC > TYPHOON
TYPHONS > TYPHON
TYPHOON n violent tropical storm
TYPHOONS > TYPHOON

TYPHOSE adj relating to typhoid
TYPHOUS > TYPHUS
TYPHUS n infectious feverish disease
TYPHUSES > TYPHUS
TYPIC same as > TYPICAL
TYPICAL adj true to type, characteristic
TYPICALLY > TYPICAL
TYPIER > TYPY
TYPIEST > TYPY
TYPIFIED > TYPIFY
TYPIFIER > TYPIFY
TYPIFIERS > TYPIFY
TYPIFIES > TYPIFY
TYPIFY vb be typical of
TYPIFYING > TYPIFY
TYPING n work or activity of using a typewriter or word processor
TYPINGS > TYPING
TYPIST n person who types with a typewriter or word processor
TYPISTS > TYPIST
TYPO n typographical error
TYPOGRAPH n person skilled in the art of composing type and printing from it
TYPOLOGIC > TYPOLOGY
TYPOLOGY n doctrine or study of types or of the correspondence between them and the realities which they typify
TYPOMANIA n obsession with typology
TYPOS > TYPO
TYPP n unit of thickness of yarn
TYPPS > TYPP
TYPTO vb learn Greek conjugations
TYPTOED > TYPTO
TYPTOING > TYPTO
TYPTOS > TYPTO
TYPY adj (of an animal) typifying the breed
TYRAMINE n colourless crystalline amine derived from phenol
TYRAMINES > TYRAMINE
TYRAN vb act as a tyrant
TYRANED > TYRAN
TYRANING > TYRAN
TYRANNE variant of > TYRAN

TYRANNED > TYRANNE
TYRANNES > TYRANNE
TYRANNESS n female tyrant
TYRANNIC > TYRANNY
TYRANNIES > TYRANNY
TYRANNING > TYRANNE
TYRANNIS n tyrannical government
TYRANNISE same as > TYRANNIZE
TYRANNIZE vb exert power (over) oppressively or cruelly
TYRANNOUS > TYRANNY
TYRANNY n tyrannical rule
TYRANS > TYRAN
TYRANT n oppressive or cruel ruler ▷ vb act the tyrant
TYRANTED > TYRANT
TYRANTING > TYRANT
TYRANTS > TYRANT
TYRE n rubber ring, usu inflated, over the rim of a vehicle's wheel to grip the road ▷ vb fit a tyre or tyres to (a wheel, vehicle, etc)
TYRED > TYRE
TYRELESS > TYRE
TYREMAKER n one who makes tyres
TYRES > TYRE
TYRING > TYRE
TYRO n novice or beginner
TYROCIDIN n antibiotic
TYROES > TYRO
TYRONES > TYRO
TYRONIC > TYRO
TYROPITA n Greek cheese pie
TYROPITAS > TYROPITA
TYROPITTA n Greek cheese pie
TYROS > TYRO
TYROSINE n aromatic nonessential amino acid
TYROSINES > TYROSINE
TYSTIE n black guillemot
TYSTIES > TYSTIE
TYTE variant spelling of > TITE
TYTHE variant of > TITHE
TYTHED > TYTHE
TYTHES > TYTHE
TYTHING > TYTHE
TZADDI same as > SADHE
TZADDIK variant of > ZADDIK

TZADDIKIM > TZADDIK
TZADDIKS > TZADDIK
TZADDIQ variant of > ZADDIK
TZADDIQIM > TZADDIQ
TZADDIQS > TZADDIQ
TZADDIS > TZADDI
TZADIK same as > ZADDIK
TZADIKS > TZADIK
TZAR same as > TSAR
TZARDOM > TZAR
TZARDOMS > TZAR
TZAREVNA variant of > TSAREVNA
TZAREVNAS > TZAREVNA
TZARINA variant of > TSARINA
TZARINAS > TZARINA
TZARISM variant of > TSARISM
TZARISMS > TZARISM
TZARIST > TZARISM
TZARISTS > TZARISM
TZARITZA variant of > TSARITSA
TZARITZAS > TZARITZA
TZARS > TZAR
TZATZIKI n Greek dip made from yogurt, chopped cucumber, and mint
TZATZIKIS > TZATZIKI
TZEDAKAH n charitable donations as a Jewish moral obligation
TZEDAKAHS > TZEDAKAH
TZETSE variant of > TSETSE
TZETSES > TZETSE
TZETZE variant of > TSETSE
TZETZES > TZETZE
TZIGANE n type of Gypsy music
TZIGANES > TZIGANE
TZIGANIES > TZIGANY
TZIGANY variant of > TZIGANE
TZIMMES n traditional Jewish stew
TZITZIS variant of > TSITSITH
TZITZIT variant of > TZITZIT
TZITZITH variant of > TSITSITH
TZURIS variant of > TSURIS
TZURISES > TZURIS

Uu

UAKARI n type of monkey
UAKARIS > UAKARI
UBEROUS adj abundant
UBERTIES > UBERTY
UBERTY n abundance
UBIETIES > UBIETY
UBIETY n condition of being in a particular place
UBIQUE adv everywhere
UBIQUITIN n type of polypeptide
UBIQUITY n state of apparently being everywhere at once; omnipresence
UBUNTU n quality of compassion and humanity
UBUNTUS > UBUNTU
UCKERS n type of naval game
UDAL n form of freehold possession of land used in Orkney and Shetland
UDALLER n person possessing a udal
UDALLERS > UDALLER
UDALS > UDAL
UDDER n large baglike milk-producing gland of cows, sheep, or goats
UDDERED > UDDER
UDDERFUL > UDDER
UDDERLESS > UDDER
UDDERS > UDDER
UDO n stout perennial plant of Japan and China
UDOMETER n archaic term for an instrument for measuring rainfall or snowfall
UDOMETERS > UDOMETER
UDOMETRIC > UDOMETER
UDOMETRY > UDOMETER
UDON n (in Japanese cookery) large noodles made of wheat flour
UDONS > UDON
UDOS > UDO
UDS interj God's or God save
UEY n u-turn
UEYS > UEY
UFO n flying saucer
UFOLOGIES > UFOLOGY
UFOLOGIST > UFOLOGY
UFOLOGY n study of UFOs
UFOS > UFO
UG vb hate
UGALI n type of stiff porridge
UGALIS > UGALI

UGGED > UG
UGGING > UG
UGH interj exclamation of disgust ▷ n sound made to indicate disgust
UGHS > UGH
UGLIED > UGLY
UGLIER > UGLY
UGLIES > UGLY
UGLIEST > UGLY
UGLIFIED > UGLIFY
UGLIFIER > UGLIFY
UGLIFIERS > UGLIFY
UGLIFIES > UGLIFY
UGLIFY vb make or become ugly or more ugly
UGLIFYING > UGLIFY
UGLILY > UGLY
UGLINESS > UGLY
UGLY adj of unpleasant appearance ▷ vb make ugly
UGLYING > UGLY
UGS > UG
UGSOME adj loathsome
UH interj used to express hesitation
UHLAN n member of a body of lancers first employed in the Polish army
UHLANS > UHLAN
UHURU n national independence
UHURUS > UHURU
UILLEAN adj as in uillean pipes bagpipes developed in Ireland
UILLEANN same as > UILLEAN
UINTAHITE same as > UINTAITE
UINTAITE n variety of asphalt
UINTAITES > UINTAITE
UITLANDER n foreigner
UJAMAA n as in ujamaa village communally organized village in Tanzania
UJAMAAS > UJAMAA
UKASE n (in imperial Russia) a decree from the tsar
UKASES > UKASE
UKE short form of > UKULELE
UKELELE same as > UKULELE
UKELELES > UKELELE
UKES > UKE

UKULELE n small guitar with four strings
UKULELES > UKULELE
ULAMA n body of Muslim scholars or religious leaders
ULAMAS > ULAMA
ULAN same as > UHLAN
ULANS > ULAN
ULCER n open sore on the surface of the skin or mucous membrane. ▷ vb make or become ulcerous
ULCERATE vb make or become ulcerous
ULCERATED > ULCERATE
ULCERATES > ULCERATE
ULCERED > ULCER
ULCERING > ULCER
ULCEROUS adj of, like, or characterized by ulcers
ULCERS > ULCER
ULE n rubber tree
ULEMA same as > ULAMA
ULEMAS > ULEMA
ULES > ULE
ULEX n variety of shrub
ULEXES > ULEX
ULEXITE n type of mineral
ULEXITES > ULEXITE
ULICES > ULEX
ULICON same as > EULACHON
ULICONS > ULICON
ULIGINOSE same as > ULIGINOUS
ULIGINOUS adj marshy
ULIKON same as > EULACHON
ULIKONS > ULIKON
ULITIS n gingivitis
ULITISES > ULITIS
ULLAGE n volume by which a liquid container falls short of being full ▷ vb create ullage in
ULLAGED > ULLAGE
ULLAGES > ULLAGE
ULLAGING > ULLAGE
ULLING n process of filling
ULLINGS > ULLING
ULMACEOUS adj relating to the family of deciduous trees and shrubs which includes the elms
ULMIN n substance found in decaying vegetation
ULMINS > ULMIN

ULNA n inner and longer of the two bones of the human forearm
ULNAD adv towards the ulna
ULNAE > ULNA
ULNAR > ULNA
ULNARE n bone in the wrist
ULNARIA > ULNARE
ULNAS > ULNA
ULOSES > ULOSIS
ULOSIS n formation of a scar
ULOTRICHY n state of having woolly or curly hair
ULPAN n Israeli study centre
ULPANIM > ULPAN
ULSTER n man's heavy double-breasted overcoat
ULSTERED adj wearing an ulster
ULSTERS > ULSTER
ULTERIOR adj (of an aim, reason, etc) concealed or hidden
ULTIMA n final syllable of a word
ULTIMACY > ULTIMATE
ULTIMAS > ULTIMA
ULTIMATA > ULTIMATUM
ULTIMATE adj final in a series or process ▷ n most significant, highest, furthest, or greatest thing ▷ vb end
ULTIMATED > ULTIMATE
ULTIMATES > ULTIMATE
ULTIMATUM n final warning stating that action will be taken unless certain conditions are met
ULTIMO adv in or during the previous month
ULTION n vengeance
ULTIONS > ULTION
ULTISOL n reddish-yellow acid soil
ULTISOLS > ULTISOL
ULTRA n person who has extreme or immoderate beliefs or opinions ▷ adj extreme or immoderate, esp in beliefs or opinions
ULTRACHIC adj extremely chic
ULTRACOLD adj extremely cold

ULTRACOOL *adj* extremely cool

ULTRADRY *adj* extremely dry

ULTRAFAST *adj* extremely fast

ULTRAFINE *adj* extremely fine

ULTRAHEAT *vb* sterilize through extreme heat treatment

ULTRAHIGH *adj* as in *ultrahigh frequency* radio-frequency band or radio frequency lying between 3000 and 300 megahertz

ULTRAHIP *adj* extremely trendy

ULTRAHOT *adj* extremely hot

ULTRAISM *n* extreme philosophy, belief, or action

ULTRAISMS > ULTRAISM

ULTRAIST > ULTRAISM

ULTRAISTS > ULTRAISM

ULTRALEFT *adj* of the extreme political Left or extremely radical

ULTRALOW *adj* extremely low

ULTRAPOSH *adj* extremely posh

ULTRAPURE *adj* extremely pure

ULTRARARE *adj* extremely rare

ULTRARED *obsolete word for >* INFRARED

ULTRAREDS > ULTRARED

ULTRARICH *adj* extremely rich

ULTRAS > ULTRA

ULTRASAFE *adj* extremely safe

ULTRASLOW *adj* extremely slow

ULTRASOFT *adj* extremely soft

ULTRATHIN *adj* extremely thin

ULTRATINY *adj* extremely small

ULTRAWIDE *adj* extremely wide

ULU *n* type of knife

ULULANT > ULULATE

ULULATE *vb* howl or wail

ULULATED > ULULATE

ULULATES > ULULATE

ULULATING > ULULATE

ULULATION > ULULATE

ULUS > ULU

ULVA *n* genus of seaweed

ULVAS > ULVA

ULYIE *Scots variant of >* OIL

ULYIES > ULYIE

ULZIE *Scots variant of >* OIL

ULZIES > ULZIE

UM *interj* representation of a common sound made when hesitating in speech ▷ *vb* hesitate while speaking

UMAMI *n* savoury flavour

UMAMIS > UMAMI

UMANGITE *n* type of mineral

UMANGITES > UMANGITE

UMBEL *n* umbrella-like flower cluster

UMBELED *same as >* UMBELLED

UMBELLAR > UMBEL

UMBELLATE > UMBEL

UMBELLED *adj* having umbels

UMBELLET *same as >* UMBELLULE

UMBELLETS > UMBELLET

UMBELLULE *n* any of the small secondary umbels that make up a compound umbel

UMBELS > UMBEL

UMBELULE *n* secondary umbel

UMBELULES > UMBELLULE

UMBER *adj* dark brown to reddish-brown ▷ *n* type of dark brown earth containing ferric oxide (rust) ▷ *vb* stain with umber

UMBERED > UMBER

UMBERING > UMBER

UMBERS > UMBER

UMBERY > UMBER

UMBILICAL *adj* of the navel

UMBILICI > UMBILICUS

UMBILICUS *n* navel

UMBLE *adj* as in *umble pie* (formerly) a pie made from the heart, entrails, etc, of a deer

UMBLES *another term for >* NUMBLES

UMBO *n* small hump projecting from the centre of the cap in certain mushrooms

UMBONAL > UMBO

UMBONATE > UMBO

UMBONES > UMBO

UMBONIC > UMBO

UMBOS > UMBO

UMBRA *n* shadow, esp the shadow cast by the moon onto the earth during a solar eclipse

UMBRACULA *pl n* umbrella-like structures

UMBRAE > UMBRA

UMBRAGE *n* displeasure or resentment ▷ *vb* shade

UMBRAGED > UMBRAGE

UMBRAGES > UMBRAGE

UMBRAGING > UMBRAGE

UMBRAL > UMBRA

UMBRAS > UMBRA

UMBRATED *adj* shown in a faint manner

UMBRATIC > UMBRA

UMBRATILE *adj* shadowy ▷ *n* person who spends their time in the shade or shadows

UMBRE *same as >* UMBRETTE

UMBREL *n* umbrella

UMBRELLA *n* portable device used for protection against rain, consisting of a folding frame covered in material attached to a central rod ▷ *adj* containing or covering many different organizations, ideas, etc

UMBRELLAS > UMBRELLA

UMBRELLO *same as >* UMBRELLA

UMBRELLOS > UMBRELLO

UMBRELS > UMBREL

UMBRERE *n* helmet visor

UMBRERES > UMBRERE

UMBRES > UMBRE

UMBRETTE *n* African wading bird

UMBRETTES > UMBRETTE

UMBRIERE *same as >* UMBRERE

UMBRIERES > UMBRIERE

UMBRIL *same as >* UMBRERE

UMBRILS > UMBRIL

UMBROSE *same as >* UMBROUS

UMBROUS *adj* shady

UMFAZI *n* African married woman

UMFAZIS > UMFAZI

UMIAC *variant of >* UMIAK

UMIACK *variant of >* UMIAK

UMIACKS > UMIACK

UMIACS > UMIAC

UMIAK *n* Inuit boat made of skins

UMIAKS > UMIAK

UMIAQ *same as >* UMIAK

UMIAQS > UMIAQ

UMLAUT *n* mark (¨) placed over a vowel, esp in German, to indicate a change in its sound ▷ *vb* modify by umlaut

UMLAUTED > UMLAUT

UMLAUTING > UMLAUT

UMLAUTS > UMLAUT

UMLUNGU *n* White man: used esp as a term of address

UMLUNGUS > UMLUNGU

UMM *same as >* UM

UMMA *n* Muslim community

UMMAH *same as >* UMMA

UMMAHS > UMMAH

UMMAS > UMMA

UMMED > UM

UMMING > UM

UMP *short for >* UMPIRE

UMPED > UMP

UMPH *same as >* HUMPH

UMPHS > UMPH

UMPIE *informal word for >* UMPIRE

UMPIES > UMPY

UMPING > UMP

UMPIRAGE > UMPIRE

UMPIRAGES > UMPIRE

UMPIRE *n* official who rules on the playing of a game ▷ *vb* act as umpire in (a game)

UMPIRED > UMPIRE

UMPIRES > UMPIRE

UMPIRING > UMPIRE

UMPS > UMP

UMPTEEN *adj* very many ▷ *determiner* very many

UMPTEENTH *n* latest in a tediously long series

UMPTIETH *same as >* UMPTEENTH

UMPTY *same as >* UMPTEEN

UMPY *same as >* UMPIE

UMQUHILE *adv* formerly

UMRA *n* pilgrimage to Mecca that can be made at any time of the year

UMRAH *same as >* UMRA

UMRAHS > UMRAH

UMRAS > UMRA

UMS > UM

UMTEENTH *same as >* UMPTEENTH

UMU *n* type of oven

UMUS > UMU

UMWELT *n* environmental factors affect the behaviour of an animal or individual

UMWELTS > UMWELT

UMWHILE *same as >* UMQUHILE

UN *pron* spelling of 'one' intended to reflect a dialectal or informal pronunciation

UNABASHED *adj* not ashamed or embarrassed

UNABATED *adv* without any reduction in force ▷ *adj* without losing any original force or violence

UNABATING *adj* not growing less in strength

UNABETTED *adj* without assistance

UNABIDING *adj* not lasting

UNABJURED *adj* not denied

UNABLE *adj* lacking the necessary power, ability, or authority (to do something)

UNABORTED *adj* not aborted

UNABRADED *adj* not eroded

UNABUSED *adj* not abused

UNABUSIVE *adj* not abusive

UNACCRUED *adj* not accrued

UNACCUSED *adj* not charged with wrongdoing

UNACERBIC *adj* not acerbic

UNACHING *adj* not aching

u

UNACIDIC *adj* not acidic
UNACTABLE *adj* unable to be acted
UNACTED *adj* not acted or performed
UNACTIVE *adj* inactive ▷ *vb* make (a person) inactive
UNACTIVED > UNACTIVE
UNACTIVES > UNACTIVE
UNADAPTED *adj* not adapted
UNADDED *adj* not added
UNADEPT *adj* not adept ▷ *n* person who is not adept
UNADEPTLY > UNADEPT
UNADEPTS > UNADEPT
UNADMIRED *adj* not admired
UNADOPTED *adj* (of a road) not maintained by a local authority
UNADORED *adj* not adored
UNADORNED *adj* not decorated
UNADULT *adj* not mature
UNADVISED *adj* rash or unwise
UNAFRAID *adj* not frightened or nervous
UNAGED *adj* not old
UNAGEING *adj* not ageing
UNAGILE *adj* not agile
UNAGING *same as* > UNAGEING
UNAGREED *adj* not agreed
UNAI *same as* > UNAU
UNAIDABLE *adj* unable to be helped
UNAIDED *adv* without any help or assistance ▷ *adj* without having received any help
UNAIDEDLY > UNAIDED
UNAIMED *adj* not aimed or specifically targeted
UNAIRED *adj* not aired
UNAIS > UNAI
UNAKIN *adj* not related
UNAKING *Shakespearean form of* > UNACHING
UNAKITE *n* type of mineral
UNAKITES > UNAKITE
UNALARMED *adj* not alarmed
UNALERTED *adj* not alerted
UNALIGNED *adj* not aligned
UNALIKE *adj* not similar
UNALIST *n* priest holding only one benefice
UNALISTS > UNALIST
UNALIVE *adj* unaware
UNALLAYED *adj* not allayed
UNALLEGED *adj* not alleged
UNALLIED *adj* not allied
UNALLOWED *adj* not allowed

UNALLOYED *adj* not spoiled by being mixed with anything else
UNALTERED *adj* not altered
UNAMASSED *adj* not amassed
UNAMAZED *adj* not greatly surprised
UNAMENDED *adj* not amended
UNAMERCED *adj* not amerced
UNAMIABLE *adj* not amiable
UNAMUSED *adj* not entertained, diverted, or laughing
UNAMUSING *adj* not entertaining
UNANCHOR *vb* remove anchor
UNANCHORS > UNANCHOR
UNANELED *adj* not having received extreme unction
UNANIMITY > UNANIMOUS
UNANIMOUS *adj* in complete agreement
UNANNEXED *adj* not annexed
UNANNOYED *adj* not annoyed
UNANXIOUS *adj* not anxious
UNAPPAREL *vb* undress
UNAPPLIED *adj* not applied
UNAPT *adj* not suitable or qualified
UNAPTLY > UNAPT
UNAPTNESS > UNAPT
UNARCHED *adj* not arched
UNARGUED *adj* not debated
UNARISEN *adj* not having risen
UNARM *less common word for* > DISARM
UNARMED *adj* without weapons
UNARMING > UNARM
UNARMORED *adj* without armour
UNARMS > UNARM
UNAROUSED *adj* not aroused
UNARRAYED *adj* not arrayed
UNARTFUL *adj* not artful
UNARY *adj* consisting of, or affecting, a single element or component
UNASHAMED *adj* not embarrassed, esp when doing something some people might find offensive
UNASKED *adv* without being asked to do something ▷ *adj* (of a question) not asked, although sometimes implied

UNASSAYED *adj* untried
UNASSUMED *adj* not assumed
UNASSURED *adj* insecure
UNATONED *adj* not atoned for
UNATTIRED *adj* unclothed
UNATTUNED *adj* unaccustomed
UNAU *n* two-toed sloth
UNAUDITED *adj* not having been audited
UNAUS > UNAU
UNAVENGED *adj* not avenged
UNAVERAGE *adj* not average
UNAVERTED *adj* not averted
UNAVOIDED *adj* not avoided
UNAVOWED *adj* not openly admitted
UNAWAKE *adj* not awake
UNAWAKED *adj* not aroused
UNAWARDED *adj* not awarded
UNAWARE *adj* not aware or conscious ▷ *adv* by surprise
UNAWARELY > UNAWARE
UNAWARES *adv* by surprise
UNAWED *adj* not awed
UNAWESOME *adj* not awesome
UNAXED *adj* not axed
UNBACKED *adj* (of a book, chair, etc) not having a back
UNBAFFLED *adj* not baffled
UNBAG *vb* take out of a bag
UNBAGGED > UNBAG
UNBAGGING > UNBAG
UNBAGS > UNBAG
UNBAITED *adj* not baited
UNBAKED *adj* not having been baked
UNBALANCE *vb* upset the equilibrium or balance of ▷ *n* imbalance or instability
UNBALE *vb* remove from bale
UNBALED > UNBALE
UNBALES > UNBALE
UNBALING > UNBALE
UNBAN *vb* stop banning or permit again
UNBANDAGE *vb* remove bandage from
UNBANDED *adj* not fastened with a band
UNBANKED *adj* not having been banked
UNBANNED > UNBAN
UNBANNING > UNBAN
UNBANS > UNBAN
UNBAPTISE *same as* > UNBAPTIZE
UNBAPTIZE *vb* remove the effect of baptism

UNBAR *vb* take away a bar or bars from
UNBARBED *adj* without barbs
UNBARE *vb* expose
UNBARED > UNBARE
UNBARES > UNBARE
UNBARING > UNBARE
UNBARK *vb* strip bark from
UNBARKED > UNBARK
UNBARKING > UNBARK
UNBARKS > UNBARK
UNBARRED > UNBAR
UNBARRING > UNBAR
UNBARS > UNBAR
UNBASED *adj* not having a base
UNBASHFUL *adj* not shy
UNBASTED *adj* not basted
UNBATED *adj* (of a sword, lance, etc) not covered with a protective button
UNBATHED *adj* unwashed
UNBE *vb* make non-existent
UNBEAR *vb* release (horse) from the bearing rein
UNBEARDED *adj* not having a beard
UNBEARED > UNBEAR
UNBEARING > UNBEAR
UNBEARS > UNBEAR
UNBEATEN *adj* having suffered no defeat
UNBED *vb* remove from bed
UNBEDDED > UNBED
UNBEDDING > UNBED
UNBEDS > UNBED
UNBEEN > UNBE
UNBEGET *vb* deprive of existence
UNBEGETS > UNBEGET
UNBEGGED *adj* not obtained by begging
UNBEGOT *adj* unbegotten
UNBEGUILE *vb* undeceive
UNBEGUN *adj* not commenced
UNBEING *n* non-existence
UNBEINGS > UNBEING
UNBEKNOWN *adv* without the knowledge (of a person) ▷ *adj* not known (to)
UNBELIEF *n* disbelief or rejection of belief
UNBELIEFS > UNBELIEF
UNBELIEVE *vb* disbelieve
UNBELOVED *adj* unhappy in love
UNBELT *vb* unbuckle the belt of (a garment)
UNBELTED > UNBELT
UNBELTING > UNBELT
UNBELTS > UNBELT
UNBEMUSED *adj* not bemused
UNBEND *vb* become less strict or more informal in one's attitudes or behaviour
UNBENDED > UNBEND

UNBENDING *adj* rigid or inflexible
UNBENDS > UNBEND
UNBENIGN *adj* not benign
UNBENT *adj* not bent or bowed
UNBEREFT *adj* not bereft
UNBERUFEN *adj* not called for
UNBESEEM *vb* be unbefitting to
UNBESEEMS > UNBESEEM
UNBESPEAK *vb* annul
UNBESPOKE *adj* not bespoken
UNBIAS *vb* free from prejudice
UNBIASED *adj* not having or showing prejudice or favouritism
UNBIASES > UNBIAS
UNBIASING > UNBIAS
UNBIASSED *same as* > UNBIASED
UNBIASSES > UNBIAS
UNBID *same as* > UNBIDDEN
UNBIDDEN *adj* not ordered or asked
UNBIGOTED *adj* not bigoted
UNBILLED *adj* not having been billed
UNBIND *vb* set free from bonds or chains
UNBINDING > UNBIND
UNBINDS > UNBIND
UNBISHOP *vb* remove from the position of bishop
UNBISHOPS > UNBISHOP
UNBITT *vb* remove (cable) from the bitts
UNBITTED > UNBITT
UNBITTEN *adj* not having been bitten
UNBITTER *adj* not bitter
UNBITTING > UNBITT
UNBITTS > UNBITT
UNBLAMED *vb* not blamed
UNBLENDED *adj* not blended
UNBLENT *same as* > UNBLENDED
UNBLESS *vb* deprive of a blessing
UNBLESSED *adj* deprived of blessing
UNBLESSES > UNBLESS
UNBLEST *same as* > UNBLESSED
UNBLIND *vb* rid of blindness
UNBLINDED > UNBLIND
UNBLINDS > UNBLIND
UNBLOCK *vb* remove a blockage from
UNBLOCKED > UNBLOCK
UNBLOCKS > UNBLOCK
UNBLOODED *adj* not bloodied
UNBLOODY *adj* not covered with blood

UNBLOTTED *adj* not blotted
UNBLOWED *same as* > UNBLOWN
UNBLOWN *adj* (of a flower) still in the bud
UNBLUNTED *adj* not blunted
UNBLURRED *adj* not blurred
UNBOARDED *adj* not boarded
UNBOBBED *adj* not bobbed
UNBODIED *adj* having no body
UNBODING *adj* having no presentiment
UNBOILED *adj* not boiled
UNBOLT *vb* unfasten a bolt of (a door)
UNBOLTED *adj* (of grain, meal, or flour) not sifted
UNBOLTING > UNBOLT
UNBOLTS > UNBOLT
UNBONDED *adj* not bonded
UNBONE *vb* remove bone from
UNBONED *adj* (of meat, fish, etc) not having had the bones removed
UNBONES > UNBONE
UNBONING > UNBONE
UNBONNET *vb* remove the bonnet from
UNBONNETS > UNBONNET
UNBOOKED *adj* not reserved
UNBOOKISH *adj* not studious
UNBOOT *vb* remove boots from
UNBOOTED > UNBOOT
UNBOOTING > UNBOOT
UNBOOTS > UNBOOT
UNBORE *adj* unborn
UNBORN *adj* not yet born
UNBORNE *adj* not borne
UNBOSOM *vb* relieve (oneself) of (secrets or feelings) by telling someone
UNBOSOMED > UNBOSOM
UNBOSOMER > UNBOSOM
UNBOSOMS > UNBOSOM
UNBOTTLE *vb* allow out of bottle
UNBOTTLED > UNBOTTLE
UNBOTTLES > UNBOTTLE
UNBOUGHT *adj* not purchased
UNBOUNCY *adj* not bouncy
UNBOUND *adj* (of a book) not bound within a cover
UNBOUNDED *adj* having no boundaries or limits
UNBOWED *adj* not giving in or submitting
UNBOWING *adj* not bowing
UNBOX *vb* empty a box
UNBOXED > UNBOX
UNBOXES > UNBOX
UNBOXING > UNBOX
UNBRACE *vb* remove tension or strain from

UNBRACED > UNBRACE
UNBRACES > UNBRACE
UNBRACING > UNBRACE
UNBRAID *vb* remove braids from
UNBRAIDED > UNBRAID
UNBRAIDS > UNBRAID
UNBRAKE *vb* stop reducing speed by releasing brake
UNBRAKED > UNBRAKE
UNBRAKES > UNBRAKE
UNBRAKING > UNBRAKE
UNBRANDED *adj* not having a brand name
UNBRASTE *archaic past form of* > UNBRACE
UNBRED *adj* not taught or instructed
UNBREECH *vb* remove breech from
UNBRIDGED *adj* not spanned by a bridge
UNBRIDLE *vb* remove the bridle from (a horse)
UNBRIDLED *adj* (of feelings or behaviour) not controlled in any way
UNBRIDLES > UNBRIDLE
UNBRIEFED *adj* not instructed
UNBRIGHT *adj* not bright
UNBRIZZED *same as* > UNBRUISED
UNBROILED *adj* not broiled
UNBROKE *same as* > UNBROKEN
UNBROKEN *adj* complete or whole
UNBROWNED *adj* not browned
UNBRUISED *adj* not bruised
UNBRUSED *same as* > UNBRUISED
UNBRUSHED *adj* not brushed
UNBUCKLE *vb* undo the buckle or buckles of
UNBUCKLED > UNBUCKLE
UNBUCKLES > UNBUCKLE
UNBUDDED *adj* not having buds
UNBUDGING *adj* not moving
UNBUILD *vb* destroy
UNBUILDS > UNBUILD
UNBUILT > UNBUILD
UNBULKIER > UNBULKY
UNBULKY *adj* not bulky
UNBUNDLE *vb* separate (hardware from software) for sales purposes
UNBUNDLED > UNBUNDLE
UNBUNDLER > UNBUNDLE
UNBUNDLES > UNBUNDLE
UNBURDEN *vb* relieve (one's mind or oneself) of a worry by confiding in someone
UNBURDENS > UNBURDEN
UNBURIED > UNBURY
UNBURIES > UNBURY

UNBURNED *same as* > UNBURNT
UNBURNT *adj* not burnt
UNBURROW *vb* remove from a burrow
UNBURROWS > UNBURROW
UNBURTHEN *same as* > UNBURDEN
UNBURY *vb* unearth
UNBURYING > UNBURY
UNBUSIED > UNBUSY
UNBUSIER > UNBUSY
UNBUSIES > UNBUSY
UNBUSIEST > UNBUSY
UNBUSTED *adj* unbroken
UNBUSY *adj* not busy ▷ *vb* make less busy
UNBUSYING > UNBUSY
UNBUTTON *vb* undo by unfastening the buttons of (a garment)
UNBUTTONS > UNBUTTON
UNCAGE *vb* release from a cage
UNCAGED *adj* at liberty
UNCAGES > UNCAGE
UNCAGING > UNCAGE
UNCAKE *vb* remove compacted matter from
UNCAKED > UNCAKE
UNCAKES > UNCAKE
UNCAKING > UNCAKE
UNCALLED *adj* not called
UNCANDID *adj* not frank
UNCANDLED *adj* not illuminated by candle
UNCANDOUR *n* lack of candour
UNCANNED *adj* not canned
UNCANNIER > UNCANNY
UNCANNILY > UNCANNY
UNCANNY *adj* weird or mysterious
UNCANONIC *adj* unclerical
UNCAP *vb* remove a cap or top from (a container)
UNCAPABLE *same as* > INCAPABLE
UNCAPE *vb* remove the cape from
UNCAPED > UNCAPE
UNCAPES > UNCAPE
UNCAPING > UNCAPE
UNCAPPED > UNCAP
UNCAPPING > UNCAP
UNCAPS > UNCAP
UNCARDED *adj* not carded
UNCARED *adj* as in *uncared for* not cared (for)
UNCAREFUL *adj* careless
UNCARING *adj* thoughtless
UNCART *vb* remove from a cart
UNCARTED > UNCART
UNCARTING > UNCART
UNCARTS > UNCART
UNCARVED *adj* not carved
UNCASE *vb* display
UNCASED > UNCASE
UNCASES > UNCASE
UNCASHED *adj* not cashed
UNCASING > UNCASE

UNCASKED *adj* removed from a cask

UNCAST *adj* not cast ▷ *vb* undo the process of casting

UNCASTED > UNCAST

UNCASTING > UNCAST

UNCASTS > UNCAST

UNCATCHY *adj* not catchy

UNCATE *same as* > UNCINATE

UNCATERED *adj* not catered

UNCAUGHT *adj* not caught

UNCAUSED *adj* not brought into existence by any cause

UNCE *same as* > OUNCE

UNCEASING *adj* continuing without a break

UNCEDED *adj* not ceded

UNCERTAIN *adj* not able to be accurately known or predicted

UNCES > UNCE

UNCESSANT *same as* > INCESSANT

UNCHAIN *vb* remove a chain or chains from

UNCHAINED > UNCHAIN

UNCHAINS > UNCHAIN

UNCHAIR *vb* unseat from chair

UNCHAIRED > UNCHAIR

UNCHAIRS > UNCHAIR

UNCHANCY *adj* unlucky, ill-omened, or dangerous

UNCHANGED *adj* remaining the same

UNCHARGE *vb* unload

UNCHARGED *adj* (of land or other property) not subject to a charge

UNCHARGES > UNCHARGE

UNCHARIER > UNCHARY

UNCHARITY *n* lack of charity

UNCHARM *vb* disenchant

UNCHARMED > UNCHARM

UNCHARMS > UNCHARM

UNCHARNEL *vb* exhume

UNCHARRED *adj* not charred

UNCHARTED *adj* (of an area of sea or land) not having had a map made of it, esp because it is unexplored

UNCHARY *adj* not cautious

UNCHASTE *adj* not chaste

UNCHASTER > UNCHASTE

UNCHECK *vb* remove check mark from

UNCHECKED *adj* not prevented from continuing or growing ▷ *adv* without being stopped or hindered

UNCHECKS > UNCHECK

UNCHEERED *adj* miserable

UNCHEWED *adj* not chewed

UNCHIC *adj* not chic

UNCHICLY > UNCHIC

UNCHILD *vb* deprive of children

UNCHILDED > UNCHILD

UNCHILDS > UNCHILD

UNCHILLED *adj* not chilled

UNCHOKE *vb* unblock

UNCHOKED > UNCHOKE

UNCHOKES > UNCHOKE

UNCHOKING > UNCHOKE

UNCHOSEN *adj* not chosen

UNCHRISOM *adj* unchristened

UNCHURCH *vb* excommunicate

UNCI > UNCUS

UNCIA *n* twelfth part

UNCIAE > UNCIA

UNCIAL *adj* of a writing style used in manuscripts of the third to ninth centuries ▷ *n* uncial letter or manuscript

UNCIALLY > UNCIAL

UNCIALS > UNCIAL

UNCIFORM *adj* having the shape of a hook ▷ *n* any hook-shaped structure or part, esp a small bone of the wrist

UNCIFORMS > UNCIFORM

UNCINAL *same as* > UNCINATE

UNCINARIA *same as* > HOOKWORM

UNCINATE *adj* shaped like a hook

UNCINATED > UNCINATE

UNCINI > UNCINUS

UNCINUS *n* small hooked structure

UNCIPHER *vb* decode

UNCIPHERS > UNCIPHER

UNCITED *adj* not quoted

UNCIVIL *adj* impolite, rude or bad-mannered

UNCIVILLY > UNCIVIL

UNCLAD *adj* having no clothes on

UNCLAIMED *adj* not having been claimed

UNCLAMP *vb* remove clamp from

UNCLAMPED > UNCLAMP

UNCLAMPS > UNCLAMP

UNCLARITY *n* lack of clarity

UNCLASP *vb* unfasten the clasp of (something)

UNCLASPED > UNCLASP

UNCLASPS > UNCLASP

UNCLASSED *adj* not divided into classes

UNCLASSY *adj* not classy

UNCLAWED *adj* not clawed

UNCLE *n* brother of one's father or mother ▷ *vb* refer to as uncle

UNCLEAN *adj* lacking moral, spiritual, or physical cleanliness

UNCLEANED *adj* not cleaned

UNCLEANER > UNCLEAN

UNCLEANLY *adv* in an unclean manner ▷ *adj* characterized by an absence of cleanliness

UNCLEAR *adj* confusing or hard to understand

UNCLEARED *adj* not cleared

UNCLEARER > UNCLEAR

UNCLEARLY > UNCLEAR

UNCLED > UNCLE

UNCLEFT *adj* not cleft

UNCLENCH *vb* relax from a clenched position

UNCLES > UNCLE

UNCLESHIP *n* position of an uncle

UNCLEW *vb* undo

UNCLEWED > UNCLEW

UNCLEWING > UNCLEW

UNCLEWS > UNCLEW

UNCLICHED *adj* not cliched

UNCLIMBED *adj* not climbed

UNCLINCH *same as* > UNCLENCH

UNCLING > UNCLE

UNCLIP *vb* remove clip from

UNCLIPPED > UNCLIP

UNCLIPS > UNCLIP

UNCLIPT *archaic past form of* > UNCLIP

UNCLOAK *vb* remove cloak from

UNCLOAKED > UNCLOAK

UNCLOAKS > UNCLOAK

UNCLOG *vb* remove an obstruction from (a drain, etc)

UNCLOGGED > UNCLOG

UNCLOGS > UNCLOG

UNCLOSE *vb* open or cause to open

UNCLOSED > UNCLOSE

UNCLOSES > UNCLOSE

UNCLOSING > UNCLOSE

UNCLOTHE *vb* take off garments from

UNCLOTHED > UNCLOTHE

UNCLOTHES > UNCLOTHE

UNCLOUD *vb* clear clouds from

UNCLOUDED > UNCLOUD

UNCLOUDS > UNCLOUD

UNCLOUDY *adj* not cloudy

UNCLOVEN *adj* not cleaved

UNCLOYED *adj* not cloyed

UNCLOYING *adj* not cloying

UNCLUTCH *vb* open from tight grip

UNCLUTTER *vb* tidy and straighten up

UNCO *adj* awkward ▷ *n* awkward or clumsy person

UNCOATED *adj* not covered with a layer

UNCOATING *n* process whereby a virus exposes its genome in order to replicate

UNCOBBLED *adj* not cobbled

UNCOCK *vb* remove from a cocked position

UNCOCKED > UNCOCK

UNCOCKING > UNCOCK

UNCOCKS > UNCOCK

UNCODED *adj* not coded

UNCOER > UNCO

UNCOERCED *adj* unforced

UNCOES > UNCO

UNCOEST > UNCO

UNCOFFIN *vb* take out of a coffin

UNCOFFINS > UNCOFFIN

UNCOIL *vb* unwind or untwist

UNCOILED > UNCOIL

UNCOILING > UNCOIL

UNCOILS > UNCOIL

UNCOINED *adj* (of a metal) not made into coin

UNCOLORED *adj* not coloured

UNCOLT *vb* divest of a horse

UNCOLTED > UNCOLT

UNCOLTING > UNCOLT

UNCOLTS > UNCOLT

UNCOMBED *adj* not combed

UNCOMBINE *vb* break apart

UNCOMELY *adj* not attractive

UNCOMFIER > UNCOMFY

UNCOMFY *adj* not comfortable

UNCOMIC *adj* not comical

UNCOMMON *adj* not happening or encountered often

UNCONCERN *n* apathy or indifference

UNCONFINE *vb* remove restrictions from

UNCONFORM *adj* dissimilar

UNCONFUSE *vb* remove confusion from

UNCONGEAL *vb* become liquid again

UNCOOKED *adj* raw

UNCOOL *adj* unsophisticated

UNCOOLED *adj* not cooled

UNCOPE *vb* unmuzzle

UNCOPED > UNCOPE

UNCOPES > UNCOPE

UNCOPING > UNCOPE

UNCORD *vb* release from cords

UNCORDED > UNCORD

UNCORDIAL *adj* unfriendly

UNCORDING > UNCORD

UNCORDS > UNCORD

UNCORK *vb* remove the cork from (a bottle)

UNCORKED > UNCORK

UNCORKING > UNCORK

UNCORKS > UNCORK

UNCORRUPT *adj* not corrupt
UNCOS > UNCO
UNCOSTLY *adj* inexpensive
UNCOUNTED *adj* unable to be counted
UNCOUPLE *vb* disconnect or become disconnected
UNCOUPLED > UNCOUPLE
UNCOUPLER > UNCOUPLE
UNCOUPLES > UNCOUPLE
UNCOURTLY *adj* not courtly
UNCOUTH *adj* lacking in good manners, refinement, or grace
UNCOUTHER > UNCOUTH
UNCOUTHLY > UNCOUTH
UNCOVER *vb* reveal or disclose
UNCOVERED *adj* not covered
UNCOVERS > UNCOVER
UNCOWL *vb* remove hood from
UNCOWLED > UNCOWL
UNCOWLING > UNCOWL
UNCOWLS > UNCOWL
UNCOY *adj* not modest
UNCOYNED *same as* > UNCOINED
UNCRACKED *adj* not cracked
UNCRATE *vb* remove from a crate
UNCRATED > UNCRATE
UNCRATES > UNCRATE
UNCRATING > UNCRATE
UNCRAZY *adj* not crazy
UNCREATE *vb* unmake
UNCREATED > UNCREATE
UNCREATES > UNCREATE
UNCREWED *adj* not crewed
UNCROPPED *adj* not cropped
UNCROSS *vb* cease to cross
UNCROSSED > UNCROSS
UNCROSSES > UNCROSS
UNCROWDED *adj* (of a confined space, area, etc) not containing too many people or things
UNCROWN *vb* take the crown from
UNCROWNED *adj* having the powers, but not the title, of royalty
UNCROWNS > UNCROWN
UNCRUDDED *adj* uncurdled
UNCRUMPLE *vb* remove creases from
UNCRUSHED *adj* not crushed
UNCTION *n* act of anointing with oil in sacramental ceremonies
UNCTIONS > UNCTION
UNCTUOUS *adj* pretending to be kind and concerned
UNCUFF *vb* remove handcuffs from
UNCUFFED > UNCUFF
UNCUFFING > UNCUFF

UNCUFFS > UNCUFF
UNCULLED *adj* not culled
UNCURABLE *same as* > INCURABLE
UNCURABLY > UNCURABLE
UNCURB *vb* remove curbs from (a horse)
UNCURBED > UNCURB
UNCURBING > UNCURB
UNCURBS > UNCURB
UNCURDLED *adj* not curdled
UNCURED *adj* not cured
UNCURIOUS *adj* not curious
UNCURL *vb* move or cause to move out of a curled or rolled up position
UNCURLED > UNCURL
UNCURLING > UNCURL
UNCURLS > UNCURL
UNCURRENT *adj* not current
UNCURSE *vb* remove curse from
UNCURSED > UNCURSE
UNCURSES > UNCURSE
UNCURSING > UNCURSE
UNCURTAIN *vb* reveal
UNCURVED *adj* not curved
UNCUS *n* hooked part or process, as in the human cerebrum
UNCUT *adj* not shortened or censored
UNCUTE *adj* not cute
UNCYNICAL *adj* not cynical
UNDAM *vb* free from a dam
UNDAMAGED *adj* not spoilt or damaged
UNDAMMED > UNDAM
UNDAMMING > UNDAM
UNDAMNED *adj* not damned
UNDAMPED *adj* (of an oscillating system) having unrestricted motion
UNDAMS > UNDAM
UNDARING *adj* not daring
UNDASHED *adj* not dashed
UNDATABLE *adj* not able to be dated
UNDATE *vb* remove date from
UNDATED *adj* (of a manuscript, letter, etc) not having an identifying date
UNDAUNTED *adj* not put off, discouraged, or beaten
UNDAWNING *adj* not dawning
UNDAZZLE *vb* recover from a daze
UNDAZZLED > UNDAZZLE
UNDAZZLES > UNDAZZLE
UNDE *same as* > UNDEE
UNDEAD *adj* alive
UNDEAF *vb* restore hearing to
UNDEAFED > UNDEAF
UNDEAFING > UNDEAF

UNDEAFS > UNDEAF
UNDEALT *adj* not dealt (with)
UNDEAR *adj* not dear
UNDEBASED *adj* not debased
UNDEBATED *adj* not debated
UNDECAGON *n* polygon having eleven sides
UNDECAYED *adj* not rotten
UNDECEIVE *vb* reveal the truth to (someone previously misled or deceived)
UNDECENT *same as* > INDECENT
UNDECIDED *adj* not having made up one's mind
UNDECIMAL *adj* based on the number 11
UNDECK *vb* remove decorations from
UNDECKED > UNDECK
UNDECKING > UNDECK
UNDECKS > UNDECK
UNDEE *adj* wavy
UNDEEDED *adj* not transferred by deed
UNDEFACED *adj* not spoilt
UNDEFIDE *same as* > UNDEFIED
UNDEFIED *adj* not challenged
UNDEFILED *adj* not defiled
UNDEFINED *adj* not defined or made clear
UNDEIFIED > UNDEIFY
UNDEIFIES > UNDEIFY
UNDEIFY *vb* strip of the status of a deity
UNDELAYED *adj* not delayed
UNDELETE *vb* restore (a deleted computer file or text)
UNDELETED *adj* not deleted, or restored after being deleted
UNDELETES > UNDELETE
UNDELIGHT *n* absence of delight
UNDELUDED *adj* not deluded
UNDENIED *adj* not denied
UNDENTED *adj* not dented
UNDER *adv* indicating movement to or position beneath the underside or base ▷ *prep* less than
UNDERACT *vb* play (a role) without adequate emphasis
UNDERACTS > UNDERACT
UNDERAGE *adj* below the required or standard age ▷ *n* shortfall
UNDERAGED *adj* not old enough
UNDERAGES > UNDERAGE

UNDERARM *adj* denoting a style of throwing, bowling, or serving in which the hand is swung below shoulder level ▷ *adv* in an underarm style ▷ *n* armpit
UNDERARMS > UNDERARM
UNDERATE > UNDEREAT
UNDERBAKE *vb* bake insufficiently
UNDERBEAR *vb* endure
UNDERBID *vb* submit a bid lower than that of (others)
UNDERBIDS > UNDERBID
UNDERBIT > UNDERBITE
UNDERBITE *vb* use insufficient acid in etching
UNDERBODY *n* underpart of a body, as of an animal or motor vehicle
UNDERBORE > UNDERBEAR
UNDERBOSS *n* person who is second in command
UNDERBRED *adj* of impure stock
UNDERBRIM *n* part of a hat
UNDERBUD *vb* produce fewer buds than expected
UNDERBUDS > UNDERBUD
UNDERBUSH *n* undergrowth or underbrush
UNDERBUY *vb* buy (stock in trade) in amounts lower than required
UNDERBUYS > UNDERBUY
UNDERCARD *n* event supporting a main event
UNDERCART *n* aircraft undercarriage
UNDERCAST *vb* cast beneath
UNDERCLAD *adj* not wearing enough clothes
UNDERCLAY *n* grey or whitish clay rock containing fossilized plant roots and occurring beneath coal seams. When used as a refractory, it is known as fireclay
UNDERCLUB *vb* use a golf club that will not hit the ball as far as required
UNDERCOAT *n* coat of paint applied before the final coat ▷ *vb* apply an undercoat to a surface
UNDERCOOK *vb* cook for too short a time or at too low a temperature
UNDERCOOL *vb* cool insufficiently
UNDERCUT *vb* charge less than (a competitor) to obtain trade ▷ *n* act or an instance of cutting underneath
UNDERCUTS > UNDERCUT
UNDERDAKS *pl n* underpants

u

UNDERDECK n lower deck of a vessel

UNDERDID > UNDERDO

UNDERDO vb do (something) inadequately

UNDERDOER > UNDERDO

UNDERDOES > UNDERDO

UNDERDOG n person or team in a weak or underprivileged position

UNDERDOGS > UNDERDOG

UNDERDONE adj not cooked enough

UNDERDOSE vb give insufficient dose

UNDERDRAW vb sketch the subject before painting it on the same surface

UNDERDREW > UNDERDRAW

UNDEREAT vb not eat enough

UNDEREATS > UNDEREAT

UNDERFED > UNDERFEED

UNDERFEED vb give too little food to ▷ n apparatus by which fuel, etc, is supplied from below

UNDERFELT n thick felt laid under a carpet to increase insulation

UNDERFIRE vb bake insufficiently

UNDERFISH vb catch fewer fish than the permitted maximum amount

UNDERFLOW n undercurrent

UNDERFONG vb receive

UNDERFOOT adv under the feet

UNDERFUND vb provide insufficient funding

UNDERFUR n layer of dense soft fur occurring beneath the outer coarser fur in certain mammals, such as the otter and seal

UNDERFURS > UNDERFUR

UNDERGIRD vb strengthen or reinforce by passing a rope, cable, or chain around the underside of (an object, load, etc)

UNDERGIRT > UNDERGIRD

UNDERGO vb experience, endure, or sustain

UNDERGOD n subordinate god

UNDERGODS > UNDERGOD

UNDERGOER > UNDERGO

UNDERGOES > UNDERGO

UNDERGONE > UNDERGO

UNDERGOWN n gown worn under another article of clothing

UNDERGRAD n person studying for a first degree; undergraduate

UNDERHAIR n lower layer of animal's hair

UNDERHAND adj sly, deceitful, and secretive ▷ adv in an underhand manner or style

UNDERHEAT vb heat insufficiently

UNDERHUNG adj (of the lower jaw) projecting beyond the upper jaw

UNDERIVED adj not derived

UNDERJAW n lower jaw

UNDERJAWS > UNDERJAW

UNDERKEEP vb suppress

UNDERKEPT > UNDERKEEP

UNDERKILL n less force than is needed to defeat enemy

UNDERKING n ruler subordinate to a king

UNDERLAID adj laid underneath

UNDERLAIN > UNDERLIE

UNDERLAP vb project under the edge of

UNDERLAPS > UNDERLAP

UNDERLAY n felt or rubber laid beneath a carpet to increase insulation and resilience ▷ vb place (something) under or beneath

UNDERLAYS > UNDERLAY

UNDERLEAF n (in liverworts) any of the leaves forming a row on the underside of the stem: usually smaller than the two rows of lateral leaves and sometimes absent

UNDERLET vb let for a price lower than expected or justified

UNDERLETS > UNDERLET

UNDERLIE vb lie or be placed under

UNDERLIER > UNDERLIE

UNDERLIES > UNDERLIE

UNDERLINE vb draw a line under ▷ n line underneath, esp under written matter

UNDERLING n subordinate

UNDERLIP n lower lip

UNDERLIPS > UNDERLIP

UNDERLIT adj lit from beneath

UNDERLOAD vb load incompletely

UNDERMAN vb supply with insufficient staff ▷ n subordinate man

UNDERMANS > UNDERMAN

UNDERMEN > UNDERMAN

UNDERMINE vb weaken gradually

UNDERMOST adj being the furthest under ▷ adv in the lowest place

UNDERN n time between sunrise and noon

UNDERNOTE n undertone

UNDERNS > UNDERN

UNDERPAD n layer of soft foam laid under carpeting

UNDERPADS > UNDERPAD

UNDERPAID adj not paid as much as the job deserves

UNDERPART n lower part or underside of something such as an animal

UNDERPASS n section of a road that passes under another road or a railway line

UNDERPAY vb pay someone insufficiently

UNDERPAYS > UNDERPAY

UNDERPEEP vb peep under

UNDERPIN vb give strength or support to

UNDERPINS > UNDERPIN

UNDERPLAY vb achieve (an effect) by deliberate lack of emphasis

UNDERPLOT n subsidiary plot in a literary or dramatic work

UNDERPROP vb prop up from beneath

UNDERRAN > UNDERRUN

UNDERRATE vb underestimate

UNDERRIPE adj not quite ripe

UNDERRUN vb run beneath

UNDERRUNS > UNDERRUN

UNDERSAID > UNDERSAY

UNDERSAY vb say by way of response

UNDERSAYS > UNDERSAY

UNDERSEA adv below the surface of the sea

UNDERSEAL n coating of tar etc applied to the underside of a motor vehicle to prevent corrosion ▷ vb apply such a coating to a motor vehicle

UNDERSEAS same as > UNDERSEA

UNDERSELF n subconscious or person within

UNDERSELL vb sell at a price lower than that of another seller

UNDERSET n ocean undercurrent ▷ vb support from underneath

UNDERSETS > UNDERSET

UNDERSHOT adj (of the lower jaw) projecting beyond the upper jaw

UNDERSIDE n bottom or lower surface

UNDERSIGN vb sign the bottom (of a document)

UNDERSIZE adj smaller than normal

UNDERSKY n lower sky

UNDERSOIL another word for > SUBSOIL

UNDERSOLD > UNDERSELL

UNDERSONG n accompanying secondary melody

UNDERSOW vb sow a later-growing crop on already-seeded land

UNDERSOWN > UNDERSOW

UNDERSOWS > UNDERSOW

UNDERSPIN n backspin

UNDERTAKE vb agree or commit oneself to (something) or to do (something)

UNDERTANE Shakespearean past participle of > UNDERTAKE

UNDERTAX vb tax insufficiently

UNDERTIME n time spent by an employee at work in non-work-related activities like socializing, surfing the internet, making personal telephone calls, etc

UNDERTINT n slight, subdued, or delicate tint

UNDERTONE n quiet tone of voice

UNDERTOOK past tense of > UNDERTAKE

UNDERTOW n strong undercurrent flowing in a different direction from the surface current

UNDERTOWS > UNDERTOW

UNDERUSE vb use less than normal

UNDERUSED > UNDERUSE

UNDERUSES > UNDERUSE

UNDERVEST another name for > VEST

UNDERVOTE n vote cast but invalid

UNDERWAY adj in progress ▷ adv in progress

UNDERWEAR n clothing worn under the outer garments and next to the skin

UNDERWENT past tense of > UNDERGO

UNDERWING n hind wing of an insect, esp when covered by the forewing

UNDERWIRE vb support with wire underneath

UNDERWIT n half-wit

UNDERWITS > UNDERWIT

UNDERWOOD n small trees, bushes, ferns, etc growing beneath taller trees in a wood or forest

UNDERWOOL n lower layer of an animal's coat

UNDERWORK vb do less work than expected

UNDESERT n lack of worth

UNDESERTS > UNDESERT

UNDESERVE vb fail to deserve

UNDESIRED adj not desired

UNDEVOUT adj not devout

UNDID > UNDO

UNDIES pl n underwear, esp women's

UNDIGHT vb remove

UNDIGHTS > UNDIGHT

UNDIGNIFY vb divest of dignity

UNDILUTED adj (of a liquid) not having any water added to it

UNDIMMED adj (of eyes, light, etc) still bright or shining

UNDINE n female water spirit

UNDINES > UNDINE

UNDINISM n obsession with water

UNDINISMS > UNDINISM

UNDINTED adj not dinted

UNDIPPED adj not dipped

UNDIVIDED adj total and whole-hearted

UNDIVINE adj not divine

UNDO vb open, unwrap ▷ n instance of undoing something

UNDOABLE adj impossible

UNDOCILE adj not docile

UNDOCK vb take out of a dock

UNDOCKED > UNDOCK

UNDOCKING > UNDOCK

UNDOCKS > UNDOCK

UNDOER > UNDO

UNDOERS > UNDO

UNDOES > UNDO

UNDOING n cause of someone's downfall

UNDOINGS > UNDOING

UNDONE adj not done or completed

UNDOOMED adj not doomed

UNDOS > UNDO

UNDOTTED adj not dotted

UNDOUBLE vb stretch out

UNDOUBLED > UNDOUBLE

UNDOUBLES > UNDOUBLE

UNDOUBTED adj certain or indisputable

UNDRAINED adj not drained

UNDRAPE vb remove drapery from

UNDRAPED > UNDRAPE

UNDRAPES > UNDRAPE

UNDRAPING > UNDRAPE

UNDRAW vb open (curtains)

UNDRAWING > UNDRAW

UNDRAWN > UNDRAW

UNDRAWS > UNDRAW

UNDREADED adj not feared

UNDREAMED adj not thought of or imagined

UNDREAMT same as > UNDREAMED

UNDRESS vb take off clothes from (oneself or another) ▷ n partial or complete nakedness ▷ adj characterized by or requiring informal or normal working dress or uniform

UNDRESSED adj partially or completely naked

UNDRESSES > UNDRESS

UNDREST same as > UNDRESSED

UNDREW > UNDRAW

UNDRIED adj not dried

UNDRILLED adj not drilled

UNDRIVEN adj not driven

UNDROSSY adj pure

UNDROWNED adj not drowned

UNDRUNK adj not drunk

UNDUBBED adj (of a film, etc) not dubbed

UNDUE adj greater than is reasonable; excessive

UNDUG adj not having been dug

UNDULANCE > UNDULANT

UNDULANCY > UNDULANT

UNDULANT adj resembling waves

UNDULAR > UNDULATE

UNDULATE vb move in waves ▷ adj having a wavy or rippled appearance, margin, or form

UNDULATED > UNDULATE

UNDULATES > UNDULATE

UNDULATOR > UNDULATE

UNDULLED adj not dulled

UNDULOSE same as > UNDULOUS

UNDULOUS adj undulate

UNDULY adv excessively

UNDUTEOUS same as > UNDUTIFUL

UNDUTIFUL adj not dutiful

UNDY same as > UNDEE

UNDYED adj not dyed

UNDYING adj never ending, eternal

UNDYINGLY > UNDYING

UNDYNAMIC adj not dynamic

UNEAGER adj nonchalant

UNEAGERLY > UNEAGER

UNEARED adj not ploughed

UNEARNED adj not deserved

UNEARTH vb reveal or discover by searching

UNEARTHED > UNEARTH

UNEARTHLY adj ghostly or eerie

UNEARTHS > UNEARTH

UNEASE > UNEASY

UNEASES > UNEASY

UNEASIER > UNEASY

UNEASIEST > UNEASY

UNEASILY > UNEASY

UNEASY adj (of a person) anxious or apprehensive

UNEATABLE adj (of food) so rotten or unattractive as to be unfit to eat

UNEATEN adj (of food) not having been consumed

UNEATH adv not easily

UNEATHES > UNEATH

UNEDGE vb take the edge off

UNEDGED > UNEDGE

UNEDGES > UNEDGE

UNEDGING > UNEDGE

UNEDIBLE variant of > INEDIBLE

UNEDITED adj not edited

UNEFFACED adj not destroyed

UNELATED adj not elated

UNELECTED adj not elected

UNEMPTIED adj not emptied

UNENDED adj without end

UNENDING adj not showing any signs of ever stopping

UNENDOWED adj not endowed

UNENGAGED adj not engaged

UNENJOYED adj not enjoyed

UNENSURED adj not ensured

UNENTERED adj not having been entered previously

UNENVIED adj not envied

UNENVIOUS adj not envious

UNENVYING adj not envying

UNEQUABLE adj unstable

UNEQUAL adj not equal in quantity, size, rank, value, etc ▷ n person who is not equal

UNEQUALED adj (in US English) not equalled

UNEQUALLY > UNEQUAL

UNEQUALS > UNEQUAL

UNERASED adj not rubbed out

UNEROTIC adj not erotic

UNERRING adj never mistaken, consistently accurate

UNESPIED adj unnoticed

UNESSAYED adj untried

UNESSENCE vb deprive of being

UNETH same as > UNEATH

UNETHICAL adj morally wrong

UNEVADED adj not evaded

UNEVEN adj not level or flat

UNEVENER > UNEVEN

UNEVENEST > UNEVEN

UNEVENLY > UNEVEN

UNEVOLVED adj not evolved

UNEXALTED adj not exalted

UNEXCITED adj not aroused to pleasure, interest, agitation, etc

UNEXCUSED adj not excused

UNEXOTIC adj not exotic

UNEXPERT same as > INEXPERT

UNEXPIRED adj not having expired

UNEXPOSED adj not having been exhibited or brought to public notice

UNEXTINCT adj not extinct

UNEXTREME adj not extreme

UNEYED adj unseen

UNFABLED adj not fictitious

UNFACT n event or thing not provable

UNFACTS > UNFACT

UNFADABLE adj incapable of fading

UNFADED adj not faded

UNFADING adj not fading

UNFAILING adj continuous or reliable

UNFAIR adj not right, fair, or just ▷ vb disfigure

UNFAIRED > UNFAIR

UNFAIRER > UNFAIR

UNFAIREST > UNFAIR

UNFAIRING > UNFAIR

UNFAIRLY > UNFAIR

UNFAIRS > UNFAIR

UNFAITH n lack of faith

UNFAITHS > UNFAITH

UNFAKED adj not faked

UNFALLEN adj not fallen

UNFAMED adj not famous

UNFAMOUS adj not famous

UNFANCIED > UNFANCY

UNFANCIER > UNFANCY

UNFANCY vb consider (a sportsperson or team) unlikely to win or succeed ▷ adj not fancy

UNFANNED adj not fanned

UNFASTEN vb undo, untie, or open or become undone, untied, or opened

UNFASTENS > UNFASTEN

UNFAULTY adj not faulty

UNFAVORED adj (in US English) not favoured

UNFAZED adj not disconcerted

UNFEARED adj unafraid

UNFEARFUL adj not scared

UNFEARING adj having no fear

UNFED adj not fed

UNFEED adj unpaid

UNFEELING adj without sympathy

UNFEIGNED adj not feigned

UNFELLED adj not cut down

UNFELT adj not felt

UNFELTED adj not felted

UNFENCE vb remove a fence from

UNFENCED adj not enclosed by a fence

UNFENCES > UNFENCE

UNFENCING > UNFENCE

UNFERTILE same as > INFERTILE

UNFETTER vb release from fetters, bonds, etc

UNFETTERS > UNFETTER

UNFEUDAL adj not feudal

UNFEUED adj not feued

UNFIGURED adj not numbered

UNFILDE archaic form of > UNFILED

UNFILED adj not filed

UNFILIAL adj not filial

UNFILLED adj (of a container, receptacle, etc) not having become or been made full

UNFILMED adj not filmed

UNFINE adj not fine

UNFIRED adj not fired

UNFIRM adj soft or unsteady

UNFISHED adj not used for fishing

UNFIT adj unqualified or unsuitable ▷ vb make unfit

UNFITLY adv in an unfit way

UNFITNESS > UNFIT

UNFITS > UNFIT

UNFITTED adj unsuitable

UNFITTER > UNFIT

UNFITTEST > UNFIT

UNFITTING adj not fitting

UNFIX vb unfasten, detach, or loosen

UNFIXED adj not fixed

UNFIXES > UNFIX

UNFIXING > UNFIX

UNFIXITY n instability

UNFIXT variant of > UNFIXED

UNFLAPPED adj not agitated or excited

UNFLASHY adj not flashy

UNFLAWED adj perfect

UNFLEDGED adj (of a young bird) not having developed adult feathers

UNFLESH vb remove flesh from

UNFLESHED > UNFLESH

UNFLESHES > UNFLESH

UNFLESHLY adj immaterial

UNFLEXED adj unbent

UNFLOORED adj without flooring

UNFLUSH vb lose the colour caused by flushing

UNFLUSHED > UNFLUSH

UNFLUSHES > UNFLUSH

UNFLUTED adj not fluted

UNFLYABLE adj unable to be flown

UNFOCUSED adj blurry

UNFOILED adj not thwarted

UNFOLD vb open or spread out from a folded state

UNFOLDED > UNFOLD

UNFOLDER > UNFOLD

UNFOLDERS > UNFOLD

UNFOLDING > UNFOLD

UNFOLDS > UNFOLD

UNFOLLOW vb stop following a person on a social networking site

UNFOLLOWS > UNFOLLOW

UNFOND adj not fond

UNFOOL vb undeceive

UNFOOLED > UNFOOL

UNFOOLING > UNFOOL

UNFOOLS > UNFOOL

UNFOOTED adj untrodden

UNFORBID adj archaic word meaning unforbidden

UNFORCED adj not forced or having been forced

UNFORGED adj genuine

UNFORGOT adj archaic word meaning unforgotten

UNFORKED adj not forked

UNFORM vb make formless

UNFORMAL same as > INFORMAL

UNFORMED adj in an early stage of development

UNFORMING > UNFORM

UNFORMS > UNFORM

UNFORTUNE n misfortune

UNFOUGHT adj not fought

UNFOUND adj not found

UNFOUNDED adj not based on facts or evidence

UNFRAMED adj not framed

UNFRANKED adj not franked

UNFRAUGHT adj not fraught

UNFREE vb remove freedom from

UNFREED > UNFREE

UNFREEDOM n lack of freedom

UNFREEING > UNFREE

UNFREEMAN n person who is not a freeman

UNFREEMEN > UNFREEMAN

UNFREES > UNFREE

UNFREEZE vb thaw or cause to thaw

UNFREEZES > UNFREEZE

UNFRETTED adj not worried

UNFRIEND vb remove someone from one's list of friends on a social networking site

UNFRIENDS > UNFRIEND

UNFROCK vb deprive (a priest in holy orders) of his or her priesthood

UNFROCKED > UNFROCK

UNFROCKS > UNFROCK

UNFROZE > UNFREEZE

UNFROZEN > UNFREEZE

UNFUELLED adj not fuelled

UNFUMED adj not fumigated

UNFUNDED adj not funded

UNFUNNIER > UNFUNNY

UNFUNNY adj not funny

UNFURL vb unroll or unfold

UNFURLED > UNFURL

UNFURLING > UNFURL

UNFURLS > UNFURL

UNFURNISH vb clear

UNFURRED adj not adorned with fur

UNFUSED adj not fused

UNFUSSIER > UNFUSSY

UNFUSSILY > UNFUSSY

UNFUSSY adj characterized by overelaborate detail

UNGAG vb restore freedom of speech to

UNGAGGED > UNGAG

UNGAGGING > UNGAG

UNGAGS > UNGAG

UNGAIN adj inconvenient

UNGAINFUL > UNGAIN

UNGAINLY adj lacking grace when moving ▷ adv clumsily

UNGALLANT adj not gallant

UNGALLED adj not annoyed

UNGARBED adj undressed

UNGARBLED adj clear

UNGATED adj without gate

UNGAUGED adj not measured

UNGAZED adj as in ungazed at/ungazed upon not gazed (at or upon)

UNGAZING adj not gazing

UNGEAR vb disengage

UNGEARED > UNGEAR

UNGEARING > UNGEAR

UNGEARS > UNGEAR

UNGELDED adj not gelded

UNGENIAL adj unfriendly

UNGENTEEL adj impolite

UNGENTLE adj not gentle

UNGENTLY > UNGENTLE

UNGENUINE adj false

UNGERMANE adj inappropriate

UNGET vb get rid of

UNGETS > UNGET

UNGETTING > UNGET

UNGHOSTLY adj not ghostly

UNGIFTED adj not talented

UNGILD vb remove gilding from

UNGILDED > UNGILD

UNGILDING > UNGILD

UNGILDS > UNGILD

UNGILT > UNGILD

UNGIRD vb remove belt from

UNGIRDED > UNGIRD

UNGIRDING > UNGIRD

UNGIRDS > UNGIRD

UNGIRT adj not belted

UNGIRTH vb release from a girth

UNGIRTHED > UNGIRTH

UNGIRTHS > UNGIRTH

UNGIVING adj inflexible

UNGLAD adj not glad

UNGLAZED adj not glazed

UNGLOSSED adj not glossed

UNGLOVE vb remove glove(s)

UNGLOVED > UNGLOVE

UNGLOVES > UNGLOVE

UNGLOVING > UNGLOVE

UNGLUE vb remove adhesive from

UNGLUED > UNGLUE

UNGLUES > UNGLUE

UNGLUING > UNGLUE

UNGOD vb remove status of being a god from

UNGODDED > UNGOD

UNGODDING > UNGOD

UNGODLIER > UNGODLY

UNGODLIKE adj not godlike

UNGODLILY > UNGODLY

UNGODLY adj unreasonable or outrageous

UNGODS > UNGOD

UNGORD same as > UNGORED

UNGORED adj not gored

UNGORGED same as > UNGORED

UNGOT same as > UNGOTTEN

UNGOTTEN adj not obtained or won

UNGOWN vb remove gown (from)

UNGOWNED > UNGOWN

UNGOWNING > UNGOWN

UNGOWNS > UNGOWN

UNGRACED adj not graced

UNGRADED adj not graded

UNGRASSED adj not covered with grass

UNGRAVELY adv Shakespearian word meaning not in a serious or solemn manner

UNGRAVLY same as > UNGRAVELY

UNGRAZED adj not grazed

UNGREASED adj not greased

UNGREEDY adj not greedy

UNGREEN adj not environmentally friendly

UNGREENER > UNGREEN

UNGROOMED adj not groomed

UNGROUND adj not crushed

UNGROUP vb separate from a group

UNGROUPED adj not placed in a group

UNGROUPS > UNGROUP
UNGROWN *adj* not fully developed
UNGRUDGED *adj* not grudged
UNGUAL *adj* of, relating to, or affecting the fingernails or toenails
UNGUARD *vb* expose (to attack)
UNGUARDED *adj* not protected
UNGUARDS > UNGUARD
UNGUENT *n* ointment
UNGUENTA > UNGUENTUM
UNGUENTS > UNGUENT
UNGUENTUM *same as* **>** UNGUENT
UNGUES > UNGUIS
UNGUESSED *adj* unexpected
UNGUIDED *adj* (of a missile, bomb, etc) not having a flight path controlled either by radio signals or internal preset or self-actuating homing devices
UNGUIFORM *adj* shaped like a nail or claw
UNGUILTY *adj* innocent
UNGUINOUS *adj* fatty
UNGUIS *n* nail, claw, or hoof, or the part of the digit giving rise to it
UNGULA *n* truncated cone, cylinder, etc
UNGULAE > UNGULA
UNGULAR > UNGULA
UNGULATE *n* hoofed mammal
UNGULATES > UNGULATE
UNGULED *adj* hoofed
UNGUM *vb* remove adhesive from
UNGUMMED > UNGUM
UNGUMMING > UNGUM
UNGUMS > UNGUM
UNGYVE *vb* release from shackles
UNGYVED > UNGYVE
UNGYVES > UNGYVE
UNGYVING > UNGYVE
UNHABLE *same as* **>** UNABLE
UNHACKED *adj* not hacked
UNHAILED *adj* not hailed
UNHAIR *vb* remove the hair from (a hide)
UNHAIRED > UNHAIR
UNHAIRER > UNHAIR
UNHAIRERS > UNHAIR
UNHAIRING > UNHAIR
UNHAIRS > UNHAIR
UNHALLOW *vb* desecrate
UNHALLOWS > UNHALLOW
UNHALSED *adj* not hailed
UNHALVED *adj* not divided in half
UNHAND *vb* release from one's grasp
UNHANDED > UNHAND
UNHANDIER > UNHANDY

UNHANDILY > UNHANDY
UNHANDING > UNHAND
UNHANDLED *adj* not handled
UNHANDS > UNHAND
UNHANDY *adj* not skilful with one's hands
UNHANG *vb* take down from hanging position
UNHANGED *adj* not executed by hanging
UNHANGING > UNHANG
UNHANGS > UNHANG
UNHAPPEN *vb* become as though never having happened
UNHAPPENS > UNHAPPEN
UNHAPPIED > UNHAPPY
UNHAPPIER > UNHAPPY
UNHAPPIES > UNHAPPY
UNHAPPILY > UNHAPPY
UNHAPPY *adj* sad or depressed ▷ *vb* make unhappy
UNHARBOUR *vb* force out of shelter
UNHARDIER > UNHARDY
UNHARDY *adj* fragile
UNHARMED *adj* not hurt or damaged in any way
UNHARMFUL *adj* not harmful
UNHARMING *adj* not capable of harming
UNHARNESS *vb* remove the harness from (a horse, etc)
UNHARRIED *adj* not harried
UNHASP *vb* unfasten
UNHASPED > UNHASP
UNHASPING > UNHASP
UNHASPS > UNHASP
UNHASTIER > UNHASTY
UNHASTING *adj* not rushing
UNHASTY *adj* not speedy
UNHAT *vb* doff one's hat
UNHATCHED *adj* (of an egg) not having broken to release the fully developed young
UNHATS > UNHAT
UNHATTED > UNHAT
UNHATTING > UNHAT
UNHAUNTED *adj* not haunted
UNHEAD *vb* remove the head from
UNHEADED *adj* not having a heading
UNHEADING > UNHEAD
UNHEADS > UNHEAD
UNHEAL *vb* expose
UNHEALED *adj* not having healed physically, mentally, or emotionally
UNHEALING *adj* not healing
UNHEALS > UNHEAL
UNHEALTH *n* illness
UNHEALTHS > UNHEALTH
UNHEALTHY *adj* likely to cause poor health

UNHEARD *adj* not listened to
UNHEARSE *vb* remove from a hearse
UNHEARSED > UNHEARSE
UNHEARSES > UNHEARSE
UNHEART *vb* discourage
UNHEARTED > UNHEART
UNHEARTS > UNHEART
UNHEATED *adj* not having been warmed up
UNHEDGED *adj* unprotected
UNHEEDED *adj* noticed but ignored
UNHEEDFUL *adj* not heedful
UNHEEDIER > UNHEEDY
UNHEEDILY *adv* carelessly
UNHEEDING *adj* not heeding
UNHEEDY *adj* not heedful
UNHELE *same as* **>** UNHEAL
UNHELED > UNHELE
UNHELES > UNHELE
UNHELING > UNHELE
UNHELM *vb* remove the helmet of (oneself or another)
UNHELMED > UNHELM
UNHELMING > UNHELM
UNHELMS > UNHELM
UNHELPED *adj* without help
UNHELPFUL *adj* doing nothing to improve a situation
UNHEPPEN *adj* awkward
UNHEROIC *adj* not heroic
UNHERST *archaic past form of* **>** UNHEARSE
UNHEWN *adj* not hewn
UNHIDDEN *adj* not hidden
UNHINGE *vb* derange or unbalance (a person or his or her mind)
UNHINGED > UNHINGE
UNHINGES > UNHINGE
UNHINGING > UNHINGE
UNHIP *adj* not at all fashionable or up to date
UNHIPPER > UNHIP
UNHIPPEST > UNHIP
UNHIRABLE *adj* not fit to be hired
UNHIRED *adj* not hired
UNHITCH *vb* unfasten or detach
UNHITCHED > UNHITCH
UNHITCHES > UNHITCH
UNHIVE *vb* remove from a hive
UNHIVED > UNHIVE
UNHIVES > UNHIVE
UNHIVING > UNHIVE
UNHOARD *vb* remove from a hoard
UNHOARDED > UNHOARD
UNHOARDS > UNHOARD
UNHOLIER > UNHOLY
UNHOLIEST > UNHOLY
UNHOLILY > UNHOLY

UNHOLPEN *same as* **>** UNHELPED
UNHOLY *adj* immoral or wicked
UNHOMELY *adj* not homely
UNHONEST *same as* **>** DISHONEST
UNHONORED *adj* not honoured
UNHOOD *vb* remove hood from
UNHOODED > UNHOOD
UNHOODING > UNHOOD
UNHOODS > UNHOOD
UNHOOK *vb* unfasten the hooks of (a garment)
UNHOOKED > UNHOOK
UNHOOKING > UNHOOK
UNHOOKS > UNHOOK
UNHOOP *vb* remove hoop(s) from
UNHOOPED > UNHOOP
UNHOOPING > UNHOOP
UNHOOPS > UNHOOP
UNHOPED *adj* unhoped-for
UNHOPEFUL *adj* not hopeful
UNHORSE *vb* knock or throw from a horse
UNHORSED > UNHORSE
UNHORSES > UNHORSE
UNHORSING > UNHORSE
UNHOSTILE *adj* not hostile
UNHOUSE *vb* remove from a house
UNHOUSED > UNHOUSE
UNHOUSES > UNHOUSE
UNHOUSING > UNHOUSE
UNHUMAN *adj* inhuman or not human
UNHUMANLY > UNHUMAN
UNHUMBLED *adj* not humbled
UNHUNG > UNHANG
UNHUNTED *adj* not hunted
UNHURRIED *adj* done at a leisurely pace, without any rush or anxiety
UNHURT *adj* not injured in an accident, attack, etc
UNHURTFUL *adj* not hurtful
UNHUSK *vb* remove the husk from
UNHUSKED > UNHUSK
UNHUSKING > UNHUSK
UNHUSKS > UNHUSK
UNI *n* (in informal English) university
UNIALGAL *adj* microbiological term
UNIAXIAL *adj* (esp of plants) having an unbranched main axis
UNIBODIES > UNIBODY
UNIBODY *adj* of a vehicle in which the frame and body are one unit ▷ *n* vehicle in which the frame and body are one unit
UNIBROW *n* informal word for eyebrows that meet above the nose

u

UNIBROWS > UNIBROW
UNICA > UNICUM
UNICED *adj* not iced
UNICITIES > UNICITY
UNICITY *n* oneness
UNICOLOR *same as*
> UNICOLOUR
UNICOLOUR *adj* of one colour
UNICOM *n* designated radio frequency at some airports
UNICOMS > UNICOM
UNICORN *n* imaginary horselike creature with one horn growing from its forehead
UNICORNS > UNICORN
UNICUM *n* unique example or specimen
UNICYCLE *n* one-wheeled vehicle driven by pedals, used in a circus ▷ *vb* ride a unicycle
UNICYCLED > UNICYCLE
UNICYCLES > UNICYCLE
UNIDEAED *adj* not having ideas
UNIDEAL *adj* not ideal
UNIFACE *n* type of tool
UNIFACES > UNIFACE
UNIFIABLE > UNIFY
UNIFIC *adj* unifying
UNIFIED > UNIFY
UNIFIER > UNIFY
UNIFIERS > UNIFY
UNIFIES > UNIFY
UNIFILAR *adj* composed of, having, or using only one wire, thread, filament, etc
UNIFORM *n* special set of clothes for the members of an organization ▷ *adj* regular and even throughout, unvarying ▷ *vb* fit out (a body of soldiers, etc) with uniforms
UNIFORMED > UNIFORM
UNIFORMER > UNIFORM
UNIFORMLY > UNIFORM
UNIFORMS > UNIFORM
UNIFY *vb* make or become one
UNIFYING > UNIFY
UNIFYINGS > UNIFY
UNIJUGATE *adj* (of a compound leaf) having only one pair of leaflets
UNILINEAL *same as*
> UNILINEAR
UNILINEAR *adj* developing in a progressive sequence
UNILLUMED *adj* not illuminated
UNILOBAR *adj* having one lobe
UNILOBED *same as*
> UNILOBAR
UNIMBUED *adj* not imbued
UNIMODAL *adj* having or involving one mode

UNIMPEDED *adj* not stopped or disrupted by anything
UNIMPOSED *adj* not imposed
UNINCITED *adj* unprovoked
UNINDEXED *adj* not indexed
UNINJURED *adj* not having sustained any injury
UNINSTAL *same as*
> UNINSTALL
UNINSTALL *vb* remove from a computer system
UNINSTALS > UNINSTAL
UNINSURED *adj* not covered by insurance
UNINURED *adj* unaccustomed
UNINVITED *adj* not having been asked ▷ *adv* without having been asked
UNINVOKED *adj* not invoked
UNION *n* uniting or being united ▷ *adj* of a trade union
UNIONISE *same as*
> UNIONIZE
UNIONISED > UNIONISE
UNIONISER > UNIONISE
UNIONISES > UNIONISE
UNIONISM *n* principles of trade unions
UNIONISMS > UNIONISM
UNIONIST *n* member or supporter of a trade union ▷ *adj* of or relating to union or unionism, esp trade unionism
UNIONISTS > UNIONIST
UNIONIZE *vb* organize (workers) into a trade union
UNIONIZED > UNIONIZE
UNIONIZER > UNIONIZE
UNIONIZES > UNIONIZE
UNIONS > UNION
UNIPAROUS *adj* (of certain animals) producing a single offspring at each birth
UNIPED *n* person or thing with one foot
UNIPEDS > UNIPED
UNIPLANAR *adj* situated in one plane
UNIPOD *n* one-legged support, as for a camera
UNIPODS > UNIPOD
UNIPOLAR *adj* of, concerned with, or having a single magnetic or electric pole
UNIPOTENT *adj* able to form only one type of cell
UNIQUE *n* person or thing that is unique
UNIQUELY > UNIQUE
UNIQUER > UNIQUE
UNIQUES > UNIQUE

UNIQUEST > UNIQUE
UNIRAMOSE *same as*
> UNIRAMOUS
UNIRAMOUS *adj* (esp of the appendages of crustaceans) consisting of a single branch
UNIRONED *adj* not ironed
UNIRONIC *adj* not ironic
UNIS > UNI
UNISERIAL *adj* in or relating to a single series
UNISEX *adj* designed for use by both sexes ▷ *n* condition of seeming not to belong obviously either to one sex or the other
UNISEXES > UNISEX
UNISEXUAL *adj* of one sex only
UNISIZE *adj* in one size only
UNISON *n* complete agreement
UNISONAL > UNISON
UNISONANT > UNISON
UNISONOUS > UNISON
UNISONS > UNISON
UNISSUED *adj* not issued
UNIT *n* single undivided entity or whole
UNITAGE > UNIT
UNITAGES > UNIT
UNITAL > UNIT
UNITARD *n* all-in-one skintight suit
UNITARDS > UNITARD
UNITARIAN *n* supporter of unity or centralization ▷ *adj* of or relating to unity or centralization
UNITARILY > UNITARY
UNITARY *adj* consisting of a single undivided whole
UNITE *vb* make or become an integrated whole ▷ *n* English gold coin minted in the Stuart period
UNITED *adj* produced by two or more people or things in combination
UNITEDLY > UNITED
UNITER > UNITE
UNITERS > UNITE
UNITES > UNITE
UNITIES > UNITY
UNITING > UNITE
UNITINGS > UNITE
UNITION *n* joining
UNITIONS > UNITION
UNITISE *same as*
> UNITIZE
UNITISED > UNITISE
UNITISER *same as*
> UNITIZER
UNITISERS > UNITISER
UNITISES > UNITISE
UNITISING > UNITISE
UNITIVE *adj* tending to unite or capable of uniting
UNITIVELY > UNITIVE

UNITIZE *vb* convert (an investment trust) into a unit trust
UNITIZED > UNITIZE
UNITIZER *n* person or thing that arranges units into batches
UNITIZERS > UNITIZER
UNITIZES > UNITIZE
UNITIZING > UNITIZE
UNITRUST *n* type of income-producing trust fund
UNITRUSTS > UNITRUST
UNITS > UNIT
UNITY *n* state of being one
UNIVALENT *adj* (of a chromosome during meiosis) not paired with its homologue
UNIVALVE *adj* relating to, designating, or possessing a mollusc shell that consists of a single piece (valve) ▷ *n* gastropod mollusc or its shell
UNIVALVED > UNIVALVE
UNIVALVES > UNIVALVE
UNIVERSAL *adj* of or typical of the whole of mankind or of nature ▷ *n* something which exists or is true in all places and all situations
UNIVERSE *n* whole of all existing matter, energy, and space
UNIVERSES > UNIVERSE
UNIVOCAL *adj* unambiguous or unmistakable ▷ *n* word or term that has only one meaning
UNIVOCALS > UNIVOCAL
UNJADED *adj* not jaded
UNJAM *vb* remove blockage from
UNJAMMED > UNJAM
UNJAMMING > UNJAM
UNJAMS > UNJAM
UNJEALOUS *adj* not jealous
UNJOINED *adj* not joined
UNJOINT *vb* disjoint
UNJOINTED > UNJOINT
UNJOINTS > UNJOINT
UNJOYFUL *adj* not joyful
UNJOYOUS *adj* not joyous
UNJUDGED *adj* not judged
UNJUST *adj* not fair or just
UNJUSTER > UNJUST
UNJUSTEST > UNJUST
UNJUSTLY > UNJUST
UNKED *adj* alien
UNKEELED *adj* without a keel
UNKEMPT *adj* (of the hair) not combed
UNKEMPTLY > UNKEMPT
UNKEND *same as*
> UNKENNED
UNKENNED *adj* unknown
UNKENNEL *vb* release from a kennel

UNKENNELS > UNKENNEL
UNKENT *same as*
> UNKENNED
UNKEPT *adj* not kept
UNKET *same as* > UNKED
UNKID *same as* > UNKED
UNKIND *adj*
unsympathetic or cruel
UNKINDER > UNKIND
UNKINDEST > UNKIND
UNKINDLED *adj* not
kindled
UNKINDLY > UNKIND
UNKING *vb* strip of
sovereignty
UNKINGED > UNKING
UNKINGING > UNKING
UNKINGLY *adj* not kingly
UNKINGS > UNKING
UNKINK *vb* straighten out
UNKINKED > UNKINK
UNKINKING > UNKINK
UNKINKS > UNKINK
UNKISS *vb* cancel (a
previous action) with a
kiss
UNKISSED *adj* not kissed
UNKISSES > UNKISS
UNKISSING > UNKISS
UNKNELLED *adj* not tolled
UNKNIGHT *vb* strip of
knighthood
UNKNIGHTS > UNKNIGHT
UNKNIT *vb* make or
become undone, untied,
or unravelled
UNKNITS > UNKNIT
UNKNITTED > UNKNIT
UNKNOT *vb* disentangle or
undo a knot or knots in
UNKNOTS > UNKNOT
UNKNOTTED > UNKNOT
UNKNOWING *adj* unaware
or ignorant
UNKNOWN *adj* not known
▷ *n* unknown person,
quantity, or thing
UNKNOWNS > UNKNOWN
UNKOSHER *adj* not
conforming to Jewish
religious law
UNLABELED *adj* not
labelled
UNLABORED *adj* not
laboured
UNLACE *vb* loosen or undo
the lacing of (shoes,
garments, etc)
UNLACED *adj* not laced
UNLACES > UNLACE
UNLACING > UNLACE
UNLADE *less common word
for* > UNLOAD
UNLADED > UNLADE
UNLADEN *adj* not laden
UNLADES > UNLADE
UNLADING > UNLADE
UNLADINGS > UNLADE
UNLAID > UNLAY
UNLASH *vb* untie or
unfasten
UNLASHED > UNLASH
UNLASHES > UNLASH

UNLASHING > UNLASH
UNLAST *archaic variant of*
> UNLACED
UNLASTE *archaic variant of*
> UNLACED
UNLATCH *vb* open or
unfasten or come open or
unfastened by the lifting
or release of a latch
UNLATCHED > UNLATCH
UNLATCHES > UNLATCH
UNLAW *vb* penalize
UNLAWED > UNLAW
UNLAWFUL *adj* not
permitted by law
UNLAWING > UNLAW
UNLAWS > UNLAW
UNLAY *vb* untwist (a rope
or cable) to separate its
strands
UNLAYING > UNLAY
UNLAYS > UNLAY
UNLEAD *vb* strip off lead
UNLEADED *adj* (of petrol)
containing less tetraethyl
lead, in order to reduce
environmental pollution
▷ *n* petrol containing a
reduced amount of
tetraethyl lead
UNLEADEDS > UNLEADED
UNLEADING > UNLEAD
UNLEADS > UNLEAD
UNLEAL *adj* treacherous
UNLEARN *vb* try to forget
something learnt or to
discard accumulated
knowledge
UNLEARNED *same as*
> UNLEARNT
UNLEARNS > UNLEARN
UNLEARNT *adj* denoting
knowledge or skills
innately present rather
than learnt
UNLEASED *adj* not leased
UNLEASH *vb* set loose or
cause (something bad)
UNLEASHED > UNLEASH
UNLEASHES > UNLEASH
UNLED *adj* not led
UNLESS *conj* except under
the circumstances that
▷ *prep* except
UNLET *adj* not rented
UNLETHAL *adj* not deadly
UNLETTED *adj* unimpeded
UNLEVEL *adj* not level
▷ *vb* make unbalanced
UNLEVELED > UNLEVEL
UNLEVELS > UNLEVEL
UNLEVIED *adj* not levied
UNLICH *Spenserian form of*
> UNLIKE
UNLICKED *adj* not licked
UNLID *vb* remove lid from
UNLIDDED > UNLID
UNLIDDING > UNLID
UNLIDS > UNLID
UNLIGHTED *adj* not lit
UNLIKABLE *adj* not
likable
UNLIKE *adj* dissimilar or
different ▷ *prep* not like or

typical of ▷ *n* person or
thing that is unlike
another
UNLIKED *adj* not liked
UNLIKELY *adj*
improbable
UNLIKES > UNLIKE
UNLIMBER *vb* disengage
(a gun) from its limber
UNLIMBERS > UNLIMBER
UNLIME *vb* detach
UNLIMED > UNLIME
UNLIMES > UNLIME
UNLIMING > UNLIME
UNLIMITED *adj*
apparently endless
UNLINE *vb* remove the
lining from
UNLINEAL *adj* not lineal
UNLINED *adj* not having
any lining
UNLINES > UNLINE
UNLINING > UNLINE
UNLINK *vb* undo the link
or links between
UNLINKED > UNLINK
UNLINKING > UNLINK
UNLINKS > UNLINK
UNLISTED *adj* not
entered on a list
UNLIT *adj* (of a fire,
cigarette, etc) not lit and
therefore not burning
UNLIVABLE *adj* not fit for
living in
UNLIVE *vb* live so as to
nullify, undo, or live down
(past events or times)
UNLIVED > UNLIVE
UNLIVELY *adj* lifeless
UNLIVES > UNLIVE
UNLIVING > UNLIVE
UNLOAD *vb* remove (cargo)
from (a ship, truck, or
plane)
UNLOADED > UNLOAD
UNLOADER > UNLOAD
UNLOADERS > UNLOAD
UNLOADING > UNLOAD
UNLOADS > UNLOAD
UNLOBED *adj* without
lobes
UNLOCATED *adj* not
located
UNLOCK *vb* unfasten (a
lock or door)
UNLOCKED *adj* not locked
UNLOCKING > UNLOCK
UNLOCKS > UNLOCK
UNLOGICAL *same as*
> ILLOGICAL
UNLOOKED *adj* not looked
(at)
UNLOOSE *vb* set free or
release
UNLOOSED > UNLOOSE
UNLOOSEN *same as*
> UNLOOSE
UNLOOSENS > UNLOOSEN
UNLOOSES > UNLOOSE
UNLOOSING > UNLOOSE
UNLOPPED *adj* not
chopped off

UNLORD *vb* remove from
position of being lord
UNLORDED > UNLORD
UNLORDING > UNLORD
UNLORDLY *adv* not in a
lordlike manner
UNLORDS > UNLORD
UNLOSABLE *adj* unable to
be lost
UNLOST *adj* not lost
UNLOVABLE *adj* too
unpleasant or
unattractive to be loved
UNLOVE *vb* stop loving
UNLOVED *adj* not loved by
anyone
UNLOVELY *adj* unpleasant
in appearance or character
UNLOVES > UNLOVE
UNLOVING *adj* not feeling
or showing love and
affection
UNLUCKIER > UNLUCKY
UNLUCKILY > UNLUCKY
UNLUCKY *adj* having bad
luck, unfortunate
UNLYRICAL *adj* not lyrical
UNMACHO *adj* not macho
UNMADE *adj* (of a bed) with
the bedclothes not
smoothed and tidied
UNMAILED *adj* not sent by
post
UNMAIMED *adj* not injured
UNMAKABLE *adj* unable to
be made
UNMAKE *vb* undo or
destroy
UNMAKER > UNMAKE
UNMAKERS > UNMAKE
UNMAKES > UNMAKE
UNMAKING > UNMAKE
UNMAKINGS > UNMAKE
UNMAN *vb* cause to lose
courage or nerve
UNMANACLE *vb* release
from manacles
UNMANAGED *adj* not
managed
UNMANFUL *adj* unmanly
UNMANLIER > UNMANLY
UNMANLIKE *adj* not
worthy of a man
UNMANLY *adj* not
masculine or virile
UNMANNED *adj* having no
personnel or crew
UNMANNING > UNMAN
UNMANNISH *adj* not
mannish
UNMANS > UNMAN
UNMANTLE *vb* remove
mantle from
UNMANTLED > UNMANTLE
UNMANTLES > UNMANTLE
UNMANURED *adj* not
treated with manure
UNMAPPED *adj* not
charted
UNMARD *same as*
> UNMARRED
UNMARKED *adj* having no
signs of damage or injury
UNMARRED *adj* not marred

u

UNMARRIED adj not married

UNMARRIES > UNMARRY

UNMARRY vb divorce

UNMASK vb remove the mask or disguise from

UNMASKED > UNMASK

UNMASKER > UNMASK

UNMASKERS > UNMASK

UNMASKING > UNMASK

UNMASKS > UNMASK

UNMATCHED adj not equalled or surpassed

UNMATED adj not mated

UNMATTED adj not matted

UNMATURED adj not matured

UNMEANING adj having no meaning

UNMEANT adj unintentional

UNMEEK adj not submissive

UNMEET adj not meet

UNMEETLY > UNMEET

UNMELLOW adj not mellow

UNMELTED adj not melted

UNMENDED adj not mended

UNMERITED adj not merited or deserved

UNMERRIER > UNMERRY

UNMERRY adj not merry

UNMESH vb release from mesh

UNMESHED > UNMESH

UNMESHES > UNMESH

UNMESHING > UNMESH

UNMET adj unfulfilled

UNMETED adj unmeasured

UNMETERED adj not metered

UNMEW vb release from confinement

UNMEWED > UNMEW

UNMEWING > UNMEW

UNMEWS > UNMEW

UNMILKED adj not milked

UNMILLED adj not milled

UNMINDED adj disregarded

UNMINDFUL adj careless, heedless, or forgetful

UNMINED adj not mined

UNMINGLE vb separate

UNMINGLED > UNMINGLE

UNMINGLES > UNMINGLE

UNMIRIER > UNMIRY

UNMIRIEST > UNMIRY

UNMIRY adj not swampy

UNMISSED adj unnoticed

UNMITER same as > UNMITRE

UNMITERED > UNMITER

UNMITERS > UNMITER

UNMITRE vb divest of a mitre

UNMITRED > UNMITRE

UNMITRES > UNMITRE

UNMITRING > UNMITRE

UNMIX vb separate

UNMIXABLE adj incapable of being mixed

UNMIXED > UNMIX

UNMIXEDLY > UNMIXED

UNMIXES > UNMIX

UNMIXING > UNMIX

UNMIXT same as > UNMIX

UNMOANED adj unmourned

UNMODISH adj passé

UNMOLD same as > UNMOULD

UNMOLDED > UNMOLD

UNMOLDING > UNMOLD

UNMOLDS > UNMOLD

UNMOLTEN adj not molten

UNMONEYED adj poor

UNMONIED same as > UNMONEYED

UNMOOR vb weigh the anchor or drop the mooring of (a vessel)

UNMOORED > UNMOOR

UNMOORING > UNMOOR

UNMOORS > UNMOOR

UNMORAL adj outside morality

UNMORALLY > UNMORAL

UNMORTISE vb release from mortise

UNMOTIVED adj without motive

UNMOULD vb change shape of

UNMOULDED > UNMOULD

UNMOULDS > UNMOULD

UNMOUNT vb dismount

UNMOUNTED > UNMOUNT

UNMOUNTS > UNMOUNT

UNMOURNED adj not mourned

UNMOVABLE adj not movable

UNMOVABLY > UNMOVABLE

UNMOVED adj not affected by emotion, indifferent

UNMOVEDLY > UNMOVED

UNMOVING adj still and motionless

UNMOWN adj not mown

UNMUFFLE vb remove a muffle or muffles from

UNMUFFLED > UNMUFFLE

UNMUFFLES > UNMUFFLE

UNMUSICAL adj (of a person) unable to appreciate or play music

UNMUZZLE vb take the muzzle off (a dog, etc)

UNMUZZLED > UNMUZZLE

UNMUZZLES > UNMUZZLE

UNNAIL vb unfasten by removing nails

UNNAILED > UNNAIL

UNNAILING > UNNAIL

UNNAILS > UNNAIL

UNNAMABLE adj that cannot or must not be named

UNNAMED adj not mentioned by name

UNNANELD same as > UNANELED

UNNATIVE adj not native ▷ vb no longer be a native of a place

UNNATIVED > UNNATIVE

UNNATIVES > UNNATIVE

UNNATURAL adj strange and frightening because not usual

UNNEATH adj archaic word for underneath

UNNEEDED adj not needed

UNNEEDFUL adj not needful

UNNERVE vb cause to lose courage, confidence, or self-control

UNNERVED > UNNERVE

UNNERVES > UNNERVE

UNNERVING > UNNERVE

UNNEST vb remove from a nest

UNNESTED > UNNEST

UNNESTING > UNNEST

UNNESTS > UNNEST

UNNETHES same as > UNNEATH

UNNETTED adj not having or not enclosed in a net

UNNOBLE vb strip of nobility

UNNOBLED > UNNOBLE

UNNOBLES > UNNOBLE

UNNOBLING > UNNOBLE

UNNOISIER > UNNOISY

UNNOISY adj quiet

UNNOTED adj not noted

UNNOTICED adj without being seen or noticed

UNNUANCED adj without nuances

UNOAKED adj (of wine) not matured in an oak barrel

UNOBEYED adj not obeyed

UNOBVIOUS adj unapparent

UNOFFERED adj not offered

UNOFTEN adv infrequently

UNOILED adj not lubricated with oil

UNOPEN adj not open

UNOPENED adj closed, barred, or sealed

UNOPPOSED adj not opposed

UNORDER vb cancel an order

UNORDERED adj not ordered

UNORDERLY adj not orderly or disorderly

UNORDERS > UNORDER

UNORNATE same as > INORNATE

UNOWED same as > UNOWNED

UNOWNED adj not owned

UNPACED adj without the aid of a pacemaker

UNPACK vb remove the contents of (a suitcase, trunk, etc)

UNPACKED > UNPACK

UNPACKER > UNPACK

UNPACKERS > UNPACK

UNPACKING > UNPACK

UNPACKS > UNPACK

UNPADDED adj not padded

UNPAGED adj (of a book) having no page numbers

UNPAID adj without a salary or wage

UNPAINED adj not suffering pain

UNPAINFUL adj painless

UNPAINT vb remove paint from

UNPAINTED > UNPAINT

UNPAINTS > UNPAINT

UNPAIRED adj not paired up

UNPALSIED adj not affected with palsy

UNPANEL vb unsaddle

UNPANELS > UNPANEL

UNPANGED adj without pain or sadness

UNPANNEL same as > UNPANEL

UNPANNELS > UNPANNEL

UNPAPER vb remove paper from

UNPAPERED > UNPAPER

UNPAPERS > UNPAPER

UNPARED adj not pared

UNPARTED adj not parted

UNPARTIAL same as > IMPARTIAL

UNPATCHED adj not patched

UNPATHED adj not having a path

UNPAVED adj not covered in paving

UNPAY vb undo

UNPAYABLE adj incapable of being paid

UNPAYING > UNPAY

UNPAYS > UNPAY

UNPEELED adj not peeled

UNPEERED adj unparalleled

UNPEG vb remove the peg or pegs from, esp to unfasten

UNPEGGED > UNPEG

UNPEGGING > UNPEG

UNPEGS > UNPEG

UNPEN vb release from a pen

UNPENNED > UNPEN

UNPENNIED adj not having pennies

UNPENNING > UNPEN

UNPENS > UNPEN

UNPENT archaic past form of > UNPEN

UNPEOPLE vb empty of people

UNPEOPLED > UNPEOPLE

UNPEOPLES > UNPEOPLE

UNPERCH vb remove from a perch

UNPERCHED > UNPERCH

UNPERCHES > UNPERCH

UNPERFECT same as > IMPERFECT

UNPERPLEX vb remove confusion from

UNPERSON n person whose existence is officially denied or ignored

UNPERSONS > UNPERSON

UNPERVERT vb free (someone) from perversion

UNPICK vb undo (the stitches) of (a piece of sewing)

UNPICKED adj (of knitting, sewing, etc) having been unravelled or picked out

UNPICKING > UNPICK

UNPICKS > UNPICK

UNPIERCED adj not pierced

UNPILE vb remove from a pile

UNPILED > UNPILE

UNPILES > UNPILE

UNPILING > UNPILE

UNPILOTED adj unguided

UNPIN vb remove a pin or pins from

UNPINKED adj not decorated with a perforated pattern

UNPINKT same as > UNPINKED

UNPINNED > UNPIN

UNPINNING > UNPIN

UNPINS > UNPIN

UNPITIED adj not pitied

UNPITIFUL adj pitiless

UNPITTED adj not having had pits removed

UNPITYING adj not pitying

UNPLACE same as > DISPLACE

UNPLACED adj not given or put in a particular place

UNPLACES > UNPLACE

UNPLACING > UNPLACE

UNPLAGUED adj not plagued

UNPLAINED adj unmourned

UNPLAIT vb remove plaits from

UNPLAITED > UNPLAIT

UNPLAITS > UNPLAIT

UNPLANKED adj not planked

UNPLANNED adj not intentional or deliberate

UNPLANTED adj not planted

UNPLAYED adj not played

UNPLEASED adj not pleased or displeased

UNPLEATED adj not pleated

UNPLEDGED adj not pledged

UNPLIABLE adj not easily bent

UNPLIABLY > UNPLIABLE

UNPLIANT adj not pliant

UNPLOWED adj not ploughed

UNPLUCKED adj not plucked

UNPLUG vb disconnect (a piece of electrical equipment)

UNPLUGGED adj using acoustic rather than electric instruments

UNPLUGS > UNPLUG

UNPLUMB vb remove lead from

UNPLUMBED adj not measured

UNPLUMBS > UNPLUMB

UNPLUME vb remove feathers from

UNPLUMED > UNPLUME

UNPLUMES > UNPLUME

UNPLUMING > UNPLUME

UNPOETIC adj not poetic

UNPOINTED adj not pointed

UNPOISED adj not poised

UNPOISON vb extract poison from

UNPOISONS > UNPOISON

UNPOLICED adj without police control

UNPOLISH vb remove polish from

UNPOLITE same as > IMPOLITE

UNPOLITIC another word for > IMPOLITIC

UNPOLLED adj not included in an opinion poll

UNPOPE vb strip of popedom

UNPOPED > UNPOPE

UNPOPES > UNPOPE

UNPOPING > UNPOPE

UNPOPULAR adj generally disliked or disapproved of

UNPOSED adj not posed

UNPOSTED adj not sent by post

UNPOTABLE adj undrinkable

UNPOTTED adj not planted in a pot

UNPRAISE vb withhold praise from

UNPRAISED > UNPRAISE

UNPRAISES > UNPRAISE

UNPRAY vb withdraw (a prayer)

UNPRAYED > UNPRAY

UNPRAYING > UNPRAY

UNPRAYS > UNPRAY

UNPREACH vb retract (a sermon)

UNPRECISE same as > IMPRECISE

UNPREDICT vb retract (a previous prediction)

UNPREPARE vb make unprepared

UNPRESSED adj not pressed

UNPRETTY adj unattractive

UNPRICED adj having no fixed or marked price

UNPRIEST vb strip of priesthood

UNPRIESTS > UNPRIEST

UNPRIMED adj not primed

UNPRINTED adj not printed

UNPRISON vb release from prison

UNPRISONS > UNPRISON

UNPRIZED adj not treasured

UNPROBED adj not examined

UNPROP vb remove support from

UNPROPER same as > IMPROPER

UNPROPPED > UNPROP

UNPROPS > UNPROP

UNPROVED adj not having been established as true, valid, or possible

UNPROVEN adj not established as true by evidence or demonstration

UNPROVIDE vb fail to supply requirements for

UNPROVOKE vb remove provocation from

UNPRUNED adj not pruned

UNPUCKER vb remove wrinkles from

UNPUCKERS > UNPUCKER

UNPULLED adj not pulled

UNPURE same as > IMPURE

UNPURELY > UNPURE

UNPURGED adj not purged

UNPURSE vb relax (lips) from pursed position

UNPURSED > UNPURSE

UNPURSES > UNPURSE

UNPURSING > UNPURSE

UNPURSUED adj not followed

UNPUZZLE vb figure out

UNPUZZLED > UNPUZZLE

UNPUZZLES > UNPUZZLE

UNQUAKING adj not quaking

UNQUALIFY vb disqualify

UNQUEEN vb depose from the position of queen

UNQUEENED > UNQUEEN

UNQUEENLY adv not in a queenlike manner

UNQUEENS > UNQUEEN

UNQUELLED adj not quelled

UNQUIET adj anxious or uneasy ▷ n state of unrest ▷ vb disquiet

UNQUIETED > UNQUIET

UNQUIETER > UNQUIET

UNQUIETLY > UNQUIET

UNQUIETS > UNQUIET

UNQUOTE interj expression used to indicate the end of a quotation ▷ vb close (a quotation), esp in printing

UNQUOTED > UNQUOTE

UNQUOTES > UNQUOTE

UNQUOTING > UNQUOTE

UNRACED adj not raced

UNRACKED adj not stretched

UNRAISED adj not raised

UNRAKE vb unearth through raking

UNRAKED adj not raked

UNRAKES > UNRAKE

UNRAKING > UNRAKE

UNRANKED adj not ranked

UNRATED adj not rated

UNRAVAGED adj not ravaged

UNRAVEL vb reduce (something knitted or woven) to separate strands

UNRAVELED > UNRAVEL

UNRAVELS > UNRAVEL

UNRAZED adj not razed

UNRAZORED adj unshaven

UNREACHED adj not reached

UNREAD adj (of a book or article) not yet read

UNREADIER > UNREADY

UNREADILY > UNREADY

UNREADY adj not ready or prepared

UNREAL adj (as if) existing only in the imagination

UNREALISE same as > UNREALIZE

UNREALISM n abstractionism

UNREALITY n quality or state of being unreal, fanciful, or impractical

UNREALIZE vb make unreal

UNREALLY > UNREAL

UNREAPED adj not reaped

UNREASON n irrationality or madness ▷ vb deprive of reason

UNREASONS > UNREASON

UNREAVE vb unwind

UNREAVED > UNREAVE

UNREAVES > UNREAVE

UNREAVING > UNREAVE

UNREBATED adj not refunded

UNREBUKED adj not rebuked

UNRECKED adj disregarded

UNRED same as > UNREAD

UNREDREST adj not redressed

UNREDUCED adj not reduced

UNREDY same as > UNREADY

UNREEL vb unwind from a reel

UNREELED > UNREEL

UNREELER n machine that unwinds something from a reel

UNREELERS > UNREELER

UNREELING > UNREEL

UNREELS > UNREEL

u

UNREEVE vb withdraw (a rope) from a block, thimble, etc
UNREEVED > UNREEVE
UNREEVES > UNREEVE
UNREEVING > UNREEVE
UNREFINED adj (of substances such as petroleum, ores, and sugar) not processed into a pure or usable form
UNREFUTED adj not refuted
UNREIN vb free from reins
UNREINED > UNREIN
UNREINING > UNREIN
UNREINS > UNREIN
UNRELATED adj not connected with each other
UNRELAXED adj not relaxed
UNREMOVED adj not removed
UNRENEWED adj not renewed
UNRENT adj not torn
UNRENTED adj not rented
UNREPAID adj not repaid
UNREPAIR less common word for > DISREPAIR
UNREPAIRS > UNREPAIR
UNRESERVE n candour
UNREST n rebellious state of discontent
UNRESTED adj not rested
UNRESTFUL adj restless
UNRESTING adj not resting
UNRESTS > UNREST
UNRETIRE vb resume work after retiring
UNRETIRED > UNRETIRE
UNRETIRES > UNRETIRE
UNREVISED adj not revised
UNREVOKED adj not revoked
UNRHYMED adj not rhymed
UNRIBBED adj not ribbed
UNRID adj unridden
UNRIDABLE adj not capable of being ridden
UNRIDDEN adj not or never ridden
UNRIDDLE vb solve or puzzle out
UNRIDDLED > UNRIDDLE
UNRIDDLER > UNRIDDLE
UNRIDDLES > UNRIDDLE
UNRIFLED adj (of a firearm or its bore) not rifled
UNRIG vb strip (a vessel) of standing and running rigging
UNRIGGED > UNRIG
UNRIGGING > UNRIG
UNRIGHT n wrong
▷ adj not right or fair
▷ vb make wrong
UNRIGHTED > UNRIGHT
UNRIGHTS > UNRIGHT
UNRIGS > UNRIG

UNRIMED same as > UNRHYMED
UNRINGED adj not having or wearing a ring
UNRINSED adj not rinsed
UNRIP vb rip open
UNRIPE adj not fully matured
UNRIPELY > UNRIPE
UNRIPENED same as > UNRIPE
UNRIPER > UNRIPE
UNRIPEST > UNRIPE
UNRIPPED > UNRIP
UNRIPPING > UNRIP
UNRIPS > UNRIP
UNRISEN adj not risen
UNRIVALED adj (in US English) matchless or unrivalled
UNRIVEN adj not torn apart
UNRIVET vb remove rivets from
UNRIVETED > UNRIVET
UNRIVETS > UNRIVET
UNROASTED adj not roasted
UNROBE same as > DISROBE
UNROBED > UNROBE
UNROBES > UNROBE
UNROBING > UNROBE
UNROLL vb open out or unwind (something rolled or coiled)
UNROLLED > UNROLL
UNROLLING > UNROLL
UNROLLS > UNROLL
UNROOF vb remove the roof from
UNROOFED > UNROOF
UNROOFING > UNROOF
UNROOFS > UNROOF
UNROOST vb remove from a perch
UNROOSTED > UNROOST
UNROOSTS > UNROOST
UNROOT less common word for > UPROOT
UNROOTED > UNROOT
UNROOTING > UNROOT
UNROOTS > UNROOT
UNROPE vb release from a rope
UNROPED > UNROPE
UNROPES > UNROPE
UNROPING > UNROPE
UNROSINED adj not coated with rosin
UNROTTED adj not rotted
UNROTTEN adj not rotten
UNROUGED adj not coloured with rouge
UNROUGH adj not rough
UNROUND vb release (lips) from a rounded position
UNROUNDED adj articulated with the lips spread
UNROUNDS > UNROUND
UNROUSED adj not roused
UNROVE > UNREEVE

UNROVEN > UNREEVE
UNROYAL adj not royal
UNROYALLY > UNROYAL
UNRUBBED adj not rubbed
UNRUDE adj not rude
UNRUFFE same as > UNROUGH
UNRUFFLE vb calm
UNRUFFLED adj calm and unperturbed
UNRUFFLES > UNRUFFLE
UNRULE n lack of authority
UNRULED adj not ruled
UNRULES > UNRULE
UNRULIER > UNRULY
UNRULIEST > UNRULY
UNRULY adj difficult to control or organize
UNRUMPLED adj neat
UNRUSHED adj unhurried
UNRUSTED adj not rusted
UNS > UN
UNSADDLE vb remove the saddle from (a horse)
UNSADDLED > UNSADDLE
UNSADDLES > UNSADDLE
UNSAFE adj dangerous
UNSAFELY > UNSAFE
UNSAFER > UNSAFE
UNSAFEST > UNSAFE
UNSAFETY n lack of safety
UNSAID adj not said or expressed
UNSAILED adj not sailed
UNSAINED adj not blessed
UNSAINT vb remove status of being a saint from
UNSAINTED > UNSAINT
UNSAINTLY adj not saintly
UNSAINTS > UNSAINT
UNSALABLE adj not capable of being sold
UNSALABLY > UNSALABLE
UNSALTED adj not seasoned, preserved, or treated with salt
UNSALUTED adj not saluted
UNSAMPLED adj not sampled
UNSAPPED adj not undermined
UNSASHED adj not furnished with a sash
UNSATABLE adj not able to be sated; insatiable
UNSATED adj not sated
UNSATIATE adj insatiable
UNSATING adj not satisfying
UNSAVED adj not saved
UNSAVORY same as > UNSAVOURY
UNSAVOURY adj distasteful or objectionable
UNSAWED same as > UNSAWN
UNSAWN adj not cut with a saw

UNSAY vb retract or withdraw (something said or written)
UNSAYABLE adj that cannot be said
UNSAYING > UNSAY
UNSAYS > UNSAY
UNSCALE same as > DESCALE
UNSCALED > UNSCALE
UNSCALES > UNSCALE
UNSCALING > UNSCALE
UNSCANNED adj not scanned
UNSCARIER > UNSCARY
UNSCARRED adj not scarred
UNSCARY adj not scary
UNSCATHED adj not harmed or injured
UNSCENTED adj not filled or impregnated with odour or fragrance
UNSCOURED adj not scoured
UNSCREW vb loosen (a screw or lid) by turning it
UNSCREWED > UNSCREW
UNSCREWS > UNSCREW
UNSCYTHED adj not cut with a scythe
UNSEAL vb remove or break the seal of
UNSEALED > UNSEAL
UNSEALING > UNSEAL
UNSEALS > UNSEAL
UNSEAM vb open or undo the seam of
UNSEAMED > UNSEAM
UNSEAMING > UNSEAM
UNSEAMS > UNSEAM
UNSEARED adj not seared
UNSEASON vb affect unfavourably
UNSEASONS > UNSEASON
UNSEAT vb throw or displace from a seat or saddle
UNSEATED > UNSEAT
UNSEATING > UNSEAT
UNSEATS > UNSEAT
UNSECRET adj not secret
▷ vb inform or make aware
UNSECRETS > UNSECRET
UNSECULAR adj not secular
UNSECURED adj (of a loan, etc) secured only against general assets and not against a specific asset
UNSEDUCED adj not seduced
UNSEEABLE adj not able to be seen
UNSEEDED adj (of a player in a sport) not given a top player's position in the opening rounds of a tournament
UNSEEING adj not noticing or looking at anything
UNSEEL vb undo seeling
UNSEELED > UNSEEL

UNSEELIE pl n evil malevolent fairies ▷ adj of or belonging to the unseelie
UNSEELING > UNSEEL
UNSEELS > UNSEEL
UNSEEMING adj unseemly
UNSEEMLY adj not according to expected standards of behaviour ▷ adv in an unseemly manner
UNSEEN adj hidden or invisible ▷ adv without being seen ▷ n passage given to students for translation without them having seen it in advance
UNSEENS > UNSEEN
UNSEIZED adj not seized
UNSELDOM adv frequently
UNSELF vb remove self-centredness from ▷ n lack of self
UNSELFED > UNSELF
UNSELFING > UNSELF
UNSELFISH adj concerned about other people's wishes and needs rather than one's own
UNSELFS > UNSELF
UNSELL vb speak unfavourably and off-puttingly of (something or someone)
UNSELLING > UNSELL
UNSELLS > UNSELL
UNSELVES > UNSELF
UNSENSE vb remove sense from
UNSENSED > UNSENSE
UNSENSES > UNSENSE
UNSENSING > UNSENSE
UNSENT adj not sent
UNSERIOUS adj not serious
UNSERVED adj not served
UNSET adj not yet solidified or firm ▷ vb displace
UNSETS > UNSET
UNSETTING > UNSET
UNSETTLE vb change or become changed from a fixed or settled condition
UNSETTLED adj lacking order or stability
UNSETTLES > UNSETTLE
UNSEVERED adj not severed
UNSEW vb undo stitching of
UNSEWED > UNSEW
UNSEWING > UNSEW
UNSEWN > UNSEW
UNSEWS > UNSEW
UNSEX vb deprive (a person) of the attributes of his or her sex
UNSEXED > UNSEX
UNSEXES > UNSEX
UNSEXIER > UNSEXY
UNSEXIEST > UNSEXY
UNSEXING > UNSEX
UNSEXIST adj not sexist
UNSEXUAL adj not sexual

UNSEXY adj not sexually attractive
UNSHACKLE vb release from shackles
UNSHADED adj not shaded
UNSHADOW vb remove shadow from
UNSHADOWS > UNSHADOW
UNSHAKED same as > UNSHAKEN
UNSHAKEN adj (of faith or feelings) not having been weakened
UNSHALE vb expose
UNSHALED > UNSHALE
UNSHALES > UNSHALE
UNSHALING > UNSHALE
UNSHAMED same as > UNASHAMED
UNSHAPE vb make shapeless
UNSHAPED > UNSHAPE
UNSHAPELY adj not shapely
UNSHAPEN adj having no definite shape
UNSHAPES > UNSHAPE
UNSHAPING > UNSHAPE
UNSHARED adj not shared
UNSHARP adj not sharp
UNSHAVED adj not shaved
UNSHAVEN adj (of a man who does not have a beard) having stubble on his chin because he has not shaved recently
UNSHEATHE vb pull (a weapon) from a sheath
UNSHED adj not shed
UNSHELL vb remove from a shell
UNSHELLED > UNSHELL
UNSHELLS > UNSHELL
UNSHENT adj undamaged
UNSHEWN adj unshown
UNSHIFT vb release the shift key on a keyboard
UNSHIFTED > UNSHIFT
UNSHIFTS > UNSHIFT
UNSHIP vb be or cause to be unloaded, discharged, or disembarked from a ship
UNSHIPPED > UNSHIP
UNSHIPS > UNSHIP
UNSHIRTED adj not wearing a shirt
UNSHOCKED adj not shocked
UNSHOD adj not wearing shoes
UNSHOE vb remove shoes from
UNSHOED same as > UNSHOD
UNSHOEING > UNSHOE
UNSHOES > UNSHOE
UNSHOOT Shakespearean variant of > UNSHOUT
UNSHOOTED > UNSHOOT
UNSHOOTS > UNSHOOT
UNSHORN adj not cut
UNSHOT adj not shot ▷ vb remove shot from

UNSHOTS > UNSHOT
UNSHOTTED > UNSHOT
UNSHOUT vb revoke (an earlier statement) by shouting a contrary one
UNSHOUTED > UNSHOUT
UNSHOUTS > UNSHOUT
UNSHOWIER > UNSHOWY
UNSHOWN adj not shown
UNSHOWY adj not showy
UNSHRIVED same as > UNSHRIVEN
UNSHRIVEN adj not shriven
UNSHROUD vb uncover
UNSHROUDS > UNSHROUD
UNSHRUBD adj not having shrubs
UNSHRUNK adj not shrunk
UNSHUNNED adj not shunned
UNSHUT vb open
UNSHUTS > UNSHUT
UNSHUTTER vb remove shutters from
UNSICKER adj unsettled
UNSICKLED adj not cut with a sickle
UNSIFTED adj not strained
UNSIGHING adj not lamented
UNSIGHT vb obstruct vision of
UNSIGHTED adj not sighted
UNSIGHTLY adj unpleasant to look at
UNSIGHTS > UNSIGHT
UNSIGNED adj (of a letter etc) anonymous
UNSILENT adj not silent
UNSIMILAR adj not similar
UNSINEW vb weaken
UNSINEWED > UNSINEW
UNSINEWS > UNSINEW
UNSINFUL adj without sin
UNSISTING adj Shakespearean term, possibly meaning insisting
UNSIZABLE adj of inadequate size
UNSIZED adj not made or sorted according to size
UNSKILFUL adj lacking dexterity or proficiency
UNSKILLED adj not having or requiring any special skill or training
UNSKIMMED adj not skimmed
UNSKINNED adj not skinned
UNSLAIN adj not killed
UNSLAKED adj not slaked
UNSLICED adj not sliced
UNSLICK adj not slick
UNSLING vb remove or release from a slung position
UNSLINGS > UNSLING
UNSLUICE vb let flow
UNSLUICED > UNSLUICE

UNSLUICES > UNSLUICE
UNSLUNG > UNSLING
UNSMART adj not smart
UNSMILING adj not wearing or assuming a smile
UNSMITTEN adj not smitten
UNSMOKED adj not smoked
UNSMOOTH vb roughen
UNSMOOTHS > UNSMOOTH
UNSMOTE same as > UNSMITTEN
UNSNAG vb remove snags from
UNSNAGGED > UNSNAG
UNSNAGS > UNSNAG
UNSNAP vb unfasten (the snap or catch) of (something)
UNSNAPPED > UNSNAP
UNSNAPS > UNSNAP
UNSNARL vb free from a snarl or tangle
UNSNARLED > UNSNARL
UNSNARLS > UNSNARL
UNSNECK vb unlatch
UNSNECKED > UNSNECK
UNSNECKS > UNSNECK
UNSNUFFED adj not snuffed
UNSOAKED adj not soaked
UNSOAPED adj not rubbed with soap
UNSOBER adj not sober ▷ vb make unrefined in manners
UNSOBERED > UNSOBER
UNSOBERLY > UNSOBER
UNSOBERS > UNSOBER
UNSOCIAL adj avoiding the company of other people
UNSOCKET vb remove from a socket
UNSOCKETS > UNSOCKET
UNSOD same as > UNSODDEN
UNSODDEN adj not soaked
UNSOFT adj hard
UNSOILED adj not soiled
UNSOLACED adj not comforted
UNSOLD adj not sold
UNSOLDER vb remove soldering from
UNSOLDERS > UNSOLDER
UNSOLEMN adj unceremonious
UNSOLID adj not solid
UNSOLIDLY > UNSOLID
UNSOLVED adj not having been solved or explained
UNSONCY same as > UNSONSY
UNSONSIE same as > UNSONSY
UNSONSIER > UNSONSY
UNSONSY adj unfortunate
UNSOOTE adj not sweet
UNSOOTHED adj not soothed

u

UNSORTED adj not sorted
UNSOUGHT adj not sought after
UNSOUL vb cause to be soulless
UNSOULED > UNSOUL
UNSOULING > UNSOUL
UNSOULS > UNSOUL
UNSOUND adj unhealthy or unstable
UNSOUNDED adj not sounded
UNSOUNDER > UNSOUND
UNSOUNDLY > UNSOUND
UNSOURCED adj without a source
UNSOURED adj not soured
UNSOWED same as > UNSOWN
UNSOWN adj not sown
UNSPAR vb open
UNSPARED adj not spared
UNSPARING adj very generous
UNSPARRED > UNSPAR
UNSPARS > UNSPAR
UNSPEAK obsolete word for > UNSAY
UNSPEAKS > UNSPEAK
UNSPED adj not achieved
UNSPELL vb release from a spell
UNSPELLED > UNSPELL
UNSPELLS > UNSPELL
UNSPENT adj not spent
UNSPHERE vb remove from its, one's, etc, sphere or place
UNSPHERED > UNSPHERE
UNSPHERES > UNSPHERE
UNSPIDE same as > UNSPIED
UNSPIED adj unnoticed
UNSPILLED same as > UNSPILT
UNSPILT adj not spilt
UNSPLIT adj not split
UNSPOILED adj not damaged or harmed
UNSPOILT same as > UNSPOILED
UNSPOKE > UNSPEAK
UNSPOKEN adj not openly expressed
UNSPOOL vb unwind from spool
UNSPOOLED > UNSPOOL
UNSPOOLS > UNSPOOL
UNSPOTTED adj without spots or stains
UNSPRAYED adj not sprayed
UNSPRUNG adj without springs
UNSPUN adj not spun
UNSQUARED adj not made into a square shape
UNSTABLE adj lacking stability or firmness
UNSTABLER > UNSTABLE
UNSTABLY > UNSTABLE
UNSTACK vb remove from a stack

UNSTACKED > UNSTACK
UNSTACKS > UNSTACK
UNSTAID adj not staid
UNSTAINED adj not stained
UNSTALKED adj without a stalk
UNSTAMPED adj not stamped
UNSTARCH vb remove starch from
UNSTARRED adj not marked with a star
UNSTARRY adj not resembling or characteristic of a star from the entertainment world
UNSTATE vb deprive of state
UNSTATED adj not having been articulated or uttered
UNSTATES > UNSTATE
UNSTATING > UNSTATE
UNSTAYED adj unhindered
UNSTAYING adj nonstop
UNSTEADY adj not securely fixed ▷ vb make unsteady
UNSTEEL vb make (the heart, feelings, etc) more gentle or compassionate
UNSTEELED > UNSTEEL
UNSTEELS > UNSTEEL
UNSTEMMED adj without a stem
UNSTEP vb remove (a mast) from its step
UNSTEPPED > UNSTEP
UNSTEPS > UNSTEP
UNSTERILE adj not free from living, esp pathogenic, microorganisms
UNSTICK vb free or loosen (something stuck)
UNSTICKS > UNSTICK
UNSTIFLED adj not suppressed
UNSTILLED adj not reduced
UNSTINTED adj not stinted
UNSTIRRED adj not stirred
UNSTITCH vb remove stitching from
UNSTOCK vb remove stock from
UNSTOCKED adj without stock
UNSTOCKS > UNSTOCK
UNSTONED adj not stoned
UNSTOP vb remove the stop or stopper from
UNSTOPPED adj not obstructed or stopped up
UNSTOPPER vb unplug
UNSTOPS > UNSTOP
UNSTOW vb remove from storage
UNSTOWED > UNSTOW
UNSTOWING > UNSTOW

UNSTOWS > UNSTOW
UNSTRAP vb undo the straps fastening (something) in position
UNSTRAPS > UNSTRAP
UNSTRESS n weak syllable ▷ vb become less stressed
UNSTRING vb remove the strings of
UNSTRINGS > UNSTRING
UNSTRIP vb strip
UNSTRIPED adj (esp of smooth muscle) not having stripes
UNSTRIPS > UNSTRIP
UNSTRUCK adj not struck
UNSTRUNG adj emotionally distressed
UNSTUCK adj freed from being stuck, glued, fastened, etc
UNSTUDIED adj natural or spontaneous
UNSTUFFED adj not stuffed
UNSTUFFY adj well-ventilated
UNSTUFT same as > UNSTUFFED
UNSTUNG adj not stung
UNSTYLISH adj unfashionable
UNSUBDUED adj not subdued
UNSUBJECT adj not subject ▷ vb remove from subjugation
UNSUBTLE adj not subtle
UNSUBTLY > UNSUBTLE
UNSUCCESS n failure
UNSUCKED adj not sucked
UNSUIT vb make unsuitable
UNSUITED adj not appropriate for a particular task or situation
UNSUITING > UNSUIT
UNSUITS > UNSUIT
UNSULLIED adj (of a reputation, etc) not stained or tarnished
UNSUMMED adj not calculated
UNSUNG adj not acclaimed or honoured
UNSUNK adj not sunken
UNSUNNED adj not subjected to sunlight
UNSUNNIER > UNSUNNY
UNSUNNY adj not sunny
UNSUPPLE adj rigid
UNSURE adj lacking assurance or self-confidence
UNSURED adj not assured
UNSURELY > UNSURE
UNSURER > UNSURE
UNSUREST > UNSURE
UNSUSPECT adj not open to suspicion
UNSWADDLE same as > UNSWATHE
UNSWATHE vb unwrap
UNSWATHED > UNSWATHE

UNSWATHES > UNSWATHE
UNSWAYED adj not swayed
UNSWEAR vb retract or revoke (a sworn oath)
UNSWEARS > UNSWEAR
UNSWEET adj not sweet
UNSWEPT adj not swept
UNSWOLLEN adj not swollen
UNSWORE > UNSWEAR
UNSWORN > UNSWEAR
UNTACK vb remove saddle and harness, etc, from
UNTACKED > UNTACK
UNTACKING > UNTACK
UNTACKLE vb remove tackle from
UNTACKLED > UNTACKLE
UNTACKLES > UNTACKLE
UNTACKS > UNTACK
UNTACTFUL adj not tactful
UNTAGGED adj without a label
UNTAILED adj tailless
UNTAINTED adj not tarnished, contaminated, or polluted
UNTAKEN adj not taken
UNTAMABLE adj (of an animal or person) not capable of being tamed, subdued, or made obedient
UNTAMABLY > UNTAMABLE
UNTAME vb undo the taming of
UNTAMED adj not brought under human control
UNTAMES > UNTAME
UNTAMING > UNTAME
UNTANGLE vb free from tangles or confusion
UNTANGLED > UNTANGLE
UNTANGLES > UNTANGLE
UNTANNED adj not tanned
UNTAPPED adj not yet used
UNTARRED adj not coated with tar
UNTASTED adj not tasted
UNTAUGHT adj without training or education
UNTAX vb stop taxing
UNTAXABLE adj not taxable
UNTAXED adj not subject to taxation
UNTAXES > UNTAX
UNTAXING > UNTAX
UNTEACH vb cause to disbelieve (teaching)
UNTEACHES > UNTEACH
UNTEAM vb disband a team
UNTEAMED > UNTEAM
UNTEAMING > UNTEAM
UNTEAMS > UNTEAM
UNTEMPER vb soften
UNTEMPERS > UNTEMPER
UNTEMPTED adj not tempted

UNTENABLE *adj* (of a theory, idea, etc) incapable of being defended
UNTENABLY > UNTENABLE
UNTENANT *vb* remove (a tenant)
UNTENANTS > UNTENANT
UNTENDED *adj* not cared for or attended to
UNTENDER *adj* not tender
UNTENT *vb* remove from a tent
UNTENTED > UNTENT
UNTENTIER > UNTENTY
UNTENTING > UNTENT
UNTENTS > UNTENT
UNTENTY *adj* inattentive
UNTENURED *adj* not having tenure
UNTESTED *adj* not having been tested or examined
UNTETHER *vb* untie
UNTETHERS > UNTETHER
UNTHANKED *adj* not thanked
UNTHATCH *vb* remove the thatch from
UNTHAW *same as* > THAW
UNTHAWED *adj* not thawed
UNTHAWING > UNTHAW
UNTHAWS > UNTHAW
UNTHINK *vb* reverse one's opinion about
UNTHINKS > UNTHINK
UNTHOUGHT > UNTHINK
UNTHREAD *vb* draw out the thread or threads from (a needle, etc)
UNTHREADS > UNTHREAD
UNTHRIFT *n* unthrifty person
UNTHRIFTS > UNTHRIFT
UNTHRIFTY *adj* careless with money
UNTHRONE *less common word for* > DETHRONE
UNTHRONED > UNTHRONE
UNTHRONES > UNTHRONE
UNTIDIED > UNTIDY
UNTIDIER > UNTIDY
UNTIDIES > UNTIDY
UNTIDIEST > UNTIDY
UNTIDILY > UNTIDY
UNTIDY *adj* messy and disordered ▷ *vb* make untidy
UNTIDYING > UNTIDY
UNTIE *vb* open or free (something that is tied)
UNTIED > UNTIE
UNTIEING > UNTIE
UNTIES > UNTIE
UNTIL *prep* in or throughout the period before
UNTILE *vb* strip tiles from
UNTILED > UNTILE
UNTILES > UNTILE
UNTILING > UNTILE
UNTILLED *adj* not tilled
UNTILTED *adj* not tilted

UNTIMED *adj* not timed
UNTIMELY *adj* occurring before the expected or normal time ▷ *adv* prematurely or inopportunely
UNTIMEOUS *same as* > UNTIMELY
UNTIN *vb* remove tin from
UNTINGED *adj* not tinged
UNTINNED > UNTIN
UNTINNING > UNTIN
UNTINS > UNTIN
UNTIPPED *adj* not tipped
UNTIRABLE *adj* not able to be fatigued
UNTIRED *adj* not tired
UNTIRING *adj* (of a person or their actions) continuing or persisting without declining in strength or vigour
UNTITLED *adj* without a title
UNTO *prep* to
UNTOILING *adj* not labouring
UNTOLD *adj* incapable of description
UNTOMB *vb* exhume
UNTOMBED > UNTOMB
UNTOMBING > UNTOMB
UNTOMBS > UNTOMB
UNTONED *adj* not toned
UNTORN *adj* not torn
UNTOUCHED *adj* not changed, moved, or affected
UNTOWARD *adj* causing misfortune or annoyance
UNTRACE *vb* remove traces from
UNTRACED *adj* not traced
UNTRACES > UNTRACE
UNTRACING > UNTRACE
UNTRACK *vb* remove from track
UNTRACKED *adj* not tracked
UNTRACKS > UNTRACK
UNTRADED *adj* not traded
UNTRAINED *adj* without formal or adequate training or education
UNTRAPPED *adj* not trapped
UNTREAD *vb* retrace (a course, path, etc)
UNTREADED > UNTREAD
UNTREADS > UNTREAD
UNTREATED *adj* (of an illness, etc) not having been dealt with
UNTRENDY *adj* not trendy
UNTRESSED *adj* not having a tress
UNTRIDE *same as* > UNTRIED
UNTRIED *adj* not yet used, done, or tested
UNTRIM *vb* deprive of elegance or adornment
UNTRIMMED > UNTRIM
UNTRIMS > UNTRIM

UNTROD > UNTREAD
UNTRODDEN > UNTREAD
UNTRUE *adj* incorrect or false
UNTRUER > UNTRUE
UNTRUEST > UNTRUE
UNTRUISM *n* something that is false
UNTRUISMS > UNTRUISM
UNTRULY > UNTRUE
UNTRUSS *vb* release from or as if from a truss
UNTRUSSED > UNTRUSS
UNTRUSSER *n* person who untrusses
UNTRUSSES > UNTRUSS
UNTRUST *n* mistrust
UNTRUSTED *adj* not trusted
UNTRUSTS > UNTRUST
UNTRUSTY *adj* not trusty
UNTRUTH *n* statement that is not true, lie
UNTRUTHS > UNTRUTH
UNTUCK *vb* become or cause to become loose or not tucked in
UNTUCKED > UNTUCK
UNTUCKING > UNTUCK
UNTUCKS > UNTUCK
UNTUFTED *adj* not having tufts
UNTUMBLED *adj* not tumbled
UNTUNABLE *adj* not tuneful
UNTUNABLY > UNTUNABLE
UNTUNE *vb* make out of tune
UNTUNED > UNTUNE
UNTUNEFUL *adj* not tuneful
UNTUNES > UNTUNE
UNTUNING > UNTUNE
UNTURBID *adj* clear
UNTURF *vb* remove turf from
UNTURFED > UNTURF
UNTURFING > UNTURF
UNTURFS > UNTURF
UNTURN *vb* turn in a reverse direction
UNTURNED *adj* not turned
UNTURNING > UNTURN
UNTURNS > UNTURN
UNTUTORED *adj* without formal education
UNTWILLED *adj* not twilled
UNTWINE *vb* untwist, unravel, and separate
UNTWINES > UNTWINE
UNTWINING > UNTWINE
UNTWIST *vb* twist apart and loosen
UNTWISTED > UNTWIST
UNTWISTS > UNTWIST
UNTYING > UNTIE
UNTYINGS > UNTIE
UNTYPABLE *adj* incapable of being typed

UNTYPICAL *adj* not representative or characteristic of a particular type, person, etc
UNUNBIUM *n* chemical element
UNUNBIUMS > UNUNBIUM
UNUNITED *adj* separated
UNUNUNIUM *n* chemical element
UNURGED *adj* not urged
UNUSABLE *adj* not in good enough condition to be used
UNUSABLY > UNUSABLE
UNUSED *adj* not being or never having been used
UNUSEFUL *adj* useless
UNUSHERED *adj* not escorted
UNUSUAL *adj* uncommon or extraordinary
UNUSUALLY > UNUSUAL
UNUTTERED *adj* not uttered
UNVAIL *same as* > UNVEIL
UNVAILE *same as* > UNVEIL
UNVAILED > UNVAIL
UNVAILES > UNVAIL
UNVAILING > UNVAIL
UNVAILS > UNVAIL
UNVALUED *adj* not appreciated or valued
UNVARIED *adj* not varied
UNVARYING *adj* always staying the same
UNVEIL *vb* ceremonially remove the cover from (a new picture, plaque, etc)
UNVEILED > UNVEIL
UNVEILER *n* person who removes a veil
UNVEILERS > UNVEILER
UNVEILING *n* ceremony involving the removal of a veil covering a statue
UNVEILS > UNVEIL
UNVEINED *adj* without veins
UNVENTED *adj* not vented
UNVERSED *adj* not versed
UNVESTED *adj* not vested
UNVETTED *adj* not thoroughly examined
UNVEXED *adj* not annoyed
UNVEXT *same as* > UNVEXED
UNVIABLE *adj* not capable of succeeding, esp financially
UNVIEWED *adj* not viewed
UNVIRTUE *n* state of having no virtue
UNVIRTUES > UNVIRTUE
UNVISITED *adj* not visited
UNVISOR *vb* remove visor from
UNVISORED > UNVISOR
UNVISORS > UNVISOR
UNVITAL *adj* not vital

u

UNVIZARD *same as*
> UNVISOR
UNVIZARDS > UNVIZARD
UNVOCAL *adj* not vocal
UNVOICE *vb* pronounce
without vibration of the
vocal cords
UNVOICED *adj* not
expressed or spoken
UNVOICES > UNVOICE
UNVOICING > UNVOICE
UNVULGAR *adj* not vulgar
UNWAGED *adj* (of a person)
not having a paid job
UNWAKED *same as*
> UNWAKENED
UNWAKENED *adj* not
roused from sleep
UNWALLED *adj* not
surrounded by walls
UNWANING *adj* not waning
UNWANTED *adj* not wanted
or welcome
UNWARDED *adj* not warded
UNWARE *same as*
> UNAWARE
UNWARELY > UNWARE
UNWARES *same as*
> UNAWARES
UNWARIE *same as*
> UNWARY
UNWARIER > UNWARY
UNWARIEST > UNWARY
UNWARILY > UNWARY
UNWARLIKE *adj* not
warlike
UNWARMED *adj* not
warmed
UNWARNED *adj* not warned
UNWARPED *adj* not warped
UNWARY *adj* not careful or
cautious and therefore
likely to be harmed
UNWASHED *adj* as in *the
great unwashed* the masses
UNWASHEDS > UNWASHED
UNWASHEN *same as*
> UNWASHED
UNWASTED *adj* not wasted
UNWASTING *adj* not
wasting
UNWATCHED *adj* (of an
automatic device, such as
a beacon) not manned
UNWATER *vb* dry out
UNWATERED > UNWATER
UNWATERS > UNWATER
UNWATERY *adj* not watery
UNWAXED *adj* not treated
with wax
UNWAYED *adj* having no
routes
UNWEAL *n* ill or sorrow
UNWEALS > UNWEAL
UNWEANED *adj* not
weaned
UNWEAPON *vb* disarm
UNWEAPONS > UNWEAPON
UNWEARIED *adj* not
abating or tiring
UNWEARIER > UNWEARY
UNWEARIES > UNWEARY
UNWEARY *adj* not weary
▷ *vb* refresh or energize

UNWEAVE *vb* undo
(weaving)
UNWEAVES > UNWEAVE
UNWEAVING > UNWEAVE
UNWEBBED *adj* not
webbed
UNWED *adj* not wed
UNWEDDED *adj* not
wedded
UNWEEDED *adj* not
weeded
UNWEENED *adj* unknown
UNWEETING *same as*
> UNWITTING
UNWEIGHED *adj* (of
quantities purchased, etc)
not measured for weight
UNWEIGHT *vb* remove
weight from
UNWEIGHTS
> UNWEIGHT
UNWELCOME *adj*
unpleasant and unwanted
UNWELDED *adj* not welded
UNWELDY *same as*
> UNWIELDY
UNWELL *adj* not healthy, ill
UNWEPT *adj* not wept for or
lamented
UNWET *adj* not wet
UNWETTED *same as*
> UNWET
UNWHIPPED *adj* not
whipped
UNWHIPT *same as*
> UNWHIPPED
UNWHITE *adj* not white
UNWIELDLY *same as*
> UNWIELDY
UNWIELDY *adj* too heavy,
large, or awkward to be
easily handled
UNWIFELY *adj* not like a
wife
UNWIGGED *adj* without a
wig
UNWILFUL *adj*
complaisant
UNWILL *vb* will the
reversal of (something
that has already occurred)
UNWILLED *adj* not
intentional
UNWILLING *adj* reluctant
UNWILLS > UNWILL
UNWIND *vb* relax after a
busy or tense time
UNWINDER > UNWIND
UNWINDERS > UNWIND
UNWINDING > UNWIND
UNWINDS > UNWIND
UNWINGED *adj* without
wings
UNWINKING *adj* vigilant
UNWIPED *adj* not wiped
UNWIRE *vb* remove wiring
from
UNWIRED > UNWIRE
UNWIRES > UNWIRE
UNWIRING > UNWIRE
UNWISDOM *n* imprudence
UNWISDOMS > UNWISDOM
UNWISE *adj* foolish
UNWISELY > UNWISE

UNWISER > UNWISE
UNWISEST > UNWISE
UNWISH *vb* retract or
revoke (a wish)
UNWISHED *adj* not desired
UNWISHES > UNWISH
UNWISHFUL *adj* not
wishful
UNWISHING > UNWISH
UNWIST *adj* unknown
UNWIT *vb* divest of wit
UNWITCH *vb* release from
witchcraft
UNWITCHED > UNWITCH
UNWITCHES > UNWITCH
UNWITS > UNWIT
UNWITTED > UNWIT
UNWITTIER > UNWITTY
UNWITTILY > UNWITTY
UNWITTING *adj* not
intentional
UNWITTY *adj* not clever
and amusing
UNWIVE *vb* remove a wife
from
UNWIVED > UNWIVE
UNWIVES > UNWIVE
UNWIVING > UNWIVE
UNWOMAN *vb* remove
womanly qualities from
UNWOMANED > UNWOMAN
UNWOMANLY *adj* not
womanly
UNWOMANS > UNWOMAN
UNWON *adj* not won
UNWONT *adj*
unaccustomed
UNWONTED *adj* out of the
ordinary
UNWOODED *adj* not
wooded
UNWOOED *adj* not wooed
UNWORDED *adj* not
expressed in words
UNWORK *vb* destroy (work
previously done)
UNWORKED *adj* not worked
UNWORKING > UNWORK
UNWORKS > UNWORK
UNWORLDLY *adj* not
concerned with material
values or pursuits
UNWORMED *adj* not rid of
worms
UNWORN *adj* not having
deteriorated through use
or age
UNWORRIED *adj* not
bothered or perturbed
UNWORTH *n* lack of value
UNWORTHS > UNWORTH
UNWORTHY *adj* not
deserving or worthy
UNWOUND *past tense and
past participle of* > UNWIND
UNWOUNDED *adj* not
wounded
UNWOVE > UNWEAVE
UNWOVEN > UNWEAVE
UNWRAP *vb* remove the
wrapping from
(something)
UNWRAPPED > UNWRAP

UNWRAPS > UNWRAP
UNWREAKED *adj*
unavenged
UNWREATHE *vb* untwist
from a wreathed shape
UNWRINKLE *vb* remove
wrinkles from
UNWRITE *vb* cancel (what
has been written)
UNWRITES > UNWRITE
UNWRITING > UNWRITE
UNWRITTEN *adj* not
printed or in writing
UNWROTE > UNWRITE
UNWROUGHT *adj* not
worked
UNWRUNG *adj* not twisted
UNYEANED *adj* not having
given birth
UNYOKE *vb* release (an
animal, etc) from a yoke
UNYOKED > UNYOKE
UNYOKES > UNYOKE
UNYOKING > UNYOKE
UNYOUNG *adj* not young
UNZEALOUS *adj*
unenthusiastic
UNZIP *vb* unfasten the zip
of (a garment)
UNZIPPED > UNZIP
UNZIPPING > UNZIP
UNZIPS > UNZIP
UNZONED *adj* not divided
into zones
UP *adv* indicating
movement to or position
at a higher place ▷ *adj* of a
high or higher position
▷ *vb* increase or raise
UPADAISY *same as*
> UPSADAISY
UPAITHRIC *adj* without a
roof
UPALONG *n* location away
from a place
UPALONGS > UPALONG
UPAS *n* large Javan tree
with whitish bark and
poisonous milky sap
UPASES > UPAS
UPBEAR *vb* sustain
UPBEARER > UPBEAR
UPBEARERS > UPBEAR
UPBEARING > UPBEAR
UPBEARS > UPBEAR
UPBEAT *adj* cheerful and
optimistic ▷ *n* unaccented
beat
UPBEATS > UPBEAT
UPBIND *vb* bind up
UPBINDING > UPBIND
UPBINDS > UPBIND
UPBLEW > UPBLOW
UPBLOW *vb* inflate
UPBLOWING > UPBLOW
UPBLOWN > UPBLOW
UPBLOWS > UPBLOW
UPBOIL *vb* boil up
UPBOILED > UPBOIL
UPBOILING > UPBOIL
UPBOILS > UPBOIL
UPBORE > UPBEAR
UPBORNE *adj* held up

u

UPBOUND *adj* travelling upwards

UPBOUNDEN *same as* > UPBOUND

UPBOW *n* stroke of the bow from its tip to its nut on a stringed instrument

UPBOWS > UPBOW

UPBRAID *vb* scold or reproach

UPBRAIDED > UPBRAID

UPBRAIDER > UPBRAID

UPBRAIDS > UPBRAID

UPBRAST *same as* > UPBURST

UPBRAY *vb* shame

UPBRAYED > UPBRAY

UPBRAYING > UPBRAY

UPBRAYS > UPBRAY

UPBREAK *vb* escape upwards

UPBREAKS > UPBREAK

UPBRING *vb* rear

UPBRINGS > UPBRING

UPBROKE > UPBREAK

UPBROKEN > UPBREAK

UPBROUGHT > UPBRING

UPBUILD *vb* build up

UPBUILDER > UPBUILD

UPBUILDS > UPBUILD

UPBUILT > UPBUILD

UPBURNING *adj* burning upwards

UPBURST *vb* burst upwards

UPBURSTS > UPBURST

UPBY *same as* > UPBYE

UPBYE *adv* yonder

UPCAST *n* material cast or thrown up ▷ *adj* directed or thrown upwards ▷ *vb* throw or cast up

UPCASTING > UPCAST

UPCASTS > UPCAST

UPCATCH *vb* catch up

UPCATCHES > UPCATCH

UPCAUGHT > UPCATCH

UPCHEER *vb* cheer up

UPCHEERED > UPCHEER

UPCHEERS > UPCHEER

UPCHUCK *vb* vomit

UPCHUCKED > UPCHUCK

UPCHUCKS > UPCHUCK

UPCLIMB *vb* ascend

UPCLIMBED > UPCLIMB

UPCLIMBS > UPCLIMB

UPCLOSE *vb* close up

UPCLOSED > UPCLOSE

UPCLOSES > UPCLOSE

UPCLOSING > UPCLOSE

UPCOAST *adv* up the coast

UPCOIL *vb* make into a coil

UPCOILED > UPCOIL

UPCOILING > UPCOIL

UPCOILS > UPCOIL

UPCOME *vb* come up

UPCOMES > UPCOME

UPCOMING *adj* coming soon

UPCOUNTRY *adj* of or from the interior of a country ▷ *adv* towards or in the interior of a country ▷ *n* interior part of a region or country

UPCOURT *adv* up basketball court

UPCURL *vb* curl up

UPCURLED > UPCURL

UPCURLING > UPCURL

UPCURLS > UPCURL

UPCURVE *vb* curve upwards

UPCURVED > UPCURVE

UPCURVES > UPCURVE

UPCURVING > UPCURVE

UPCYCLE *vb* recycle a disposable product into an object of greater value

UPCYCLED > UPCYCLE

UPCYCLES > UPCYCLE

UPCYCLING > UPCYCLE

UPDART *vb* dart upwards

UPDARTED > UPDART

UPDARTING > UPDART

UPDARTS > UPDART

UPDATE *vb* bring up to date ▷ *n* act of updating or something that is updated

UPDATED > UPDATE

UPDATER > UPDATE

UPDATERS > UPDATE

UPDATES > UPDATE

UPDATING > UPDATE

UPDIVE *vb* leap upwards

UPDIVED > UPDIVE

UPDIVES > UPDIVE

UPDIVING > UPDIVE

UPDO *n* type of hairstyle

UPDOMING *n* expansion of a rock upwards into a dome shape

UPDOMINGS > UPDOMING

UPDOS > UPDO

UPDOVE > UPDIVE

UPDRAFT *n* upwards air current

UPDRAFTS > UPDRAFT

UPDRAG *vb* drag up

UPDRAGGED > UPDRAG

UPDRAGS > UPDRAG

UPDRAUGHT *n* upward movement of air or other gas

UPDRAW *vb* draw up

UPDRAWING > UPDRAW

UPDRAWN > UPDRAW

UPDRAWS > UPDRAW

UPDREW > UPDRAW

UPDRIED > UPDRY

UPDRIES > UPDRY

UPDRY *vb* dry up

UPDRYING > UPDRY

UPEND *vb* turn or set (something) on its end

UPENDED > UPEND

UPENDING > UPEND

UPENDS > UPEND

UPFIELD *adj* in sport, away from the defending team's goal

UPFILL *vb* fill up

UPFILLED > UPFILL

UPFILLING > UPFILL

UPFILLS > UPFILL

UPFLING *vb* throw upwards

UPFLINGS > UPFLING

UPFLOW *vb* flow upwards

UPFLOWED > UPFLOW

UPFLOWING > UPFLOW

UPFLOWS > UPFLOW

UPFLUNG > UPFLING

UPFOLD *vb* fold up

UPFOLDED > UPFOLD

UPFOLDING > UPFOLD

UPFOLDS > UPFOLD

UPFOLLOW *vb* follow

UPFOLLOWS > UPFOLLOW

UPFRONT *adj* open and frank ▷ *adv* (of money) paid out at the beginning of a business arrangement

UPFURL *vb* roll up

UPFURLED > UPFURL

UPFURLING > UPFURL

UPFURLS > UPFURL

UPGANG *n* climb

UPGANGS > UPGANG

UPGATHER *vb* draw together

UPGATHERS > UPGATHER

UPGAZE *vb* gaze upwards

UPGAZED > UPGAZE

UPGAZES > UPGAZE

UPGAZING > UPGAZE

UPGIRD *vb* belt up

UPGIRDED > UPGIRD

UPGIRDING > UPGIRD

UPGIRDS > UPGIRD

UPGIRT *same as* > UPGIRD

UPGO *vb* ascend

UPGOES > UPGO

UPGOING > UPGO

UPGOINGS > UPGO

UPGONE > UPGO

UPGRADE *vb* promote (a person or job) to a higher rank

UPGRADED > UPGRADE

UPGRADER > UPGRADE

UPGRADERS > UPGRADE

UPGRADES > UPGRADE

UPGRADING > UPGRADE

UPGREW > UPGROW

UPGROW *vb* grow up

UPGROWING > UPGROW

UPGROWN > UPGROW

UPGROWS > UPGROW

UPGROWTH *n* process of developing or growing upwards

UPGROWTHS > UPGROWTH

UPGUSH *vb* flow upwards

UPGUSHED > UPGUSH

UPGUSHES > UPGUSH

UPGUSHING > UPGUSH

UPHAND *adj* lifted by hand

UPHANG *vb* hang up

UPHANGING > UPHANG

UPHANGS > UPHANG

UPHAUD *Scots variant of* > UPHOLD

UPHAUDING > UPHAUD

UPHAUDS > UPHAUD

UPHEAP *vb* computing term

UPHEAPED > UPHEAP

UPHEAPING > UPHEAP

UPHEAPS > UPHEAP

UPHEAVAL *n* strong, sudden, or violent disturbance

UPHEAVALS > UPHEAVAL

UPHEAVE *vb* heave or rise upwards

UPHEAVED > UPHEAVE

UPHEAVER > UPHEAVE

UPHEAVERS > UPHEAVE

UPHEAVES > UPHEAVE

UPHEAVING > UPHEAVE

UPHELD > UPHOLD

UPHILD *archaic past form of* > UPHOLD

UPHILL *adj* sloping or leading upwards ▷ *adv* up a slope ▷ *n* difficulty

UPHILLS > UPHILL

UPHOARD *vb* hoard up

UPHOARDED > UPHOARD

UPHOARDS > UPHOARD

UPHOIST *vb* raise

UPHOISTED > UPHOIST

UPHOISTS > UPHOIST

UPHOLD *vb* maintain or defend against opposition

UPHOLDER > UPHOLD

UPHOLDERS > UPHOLD

UPHOLDING > UPHOLD

UPHOLDS > UPHOLD

UPHOLSTER *vb* fit (a chair or sofa) with padding, springs, and covering

UPHOORD *vb* heap up

UPHOORDED > UPHOORD

UPHOORDS > UPHOORD

UPHOVE > UPHEAVE

UPHROE *variant spelling of* > EUPHROE

UPHROES > UPHROE

UPHUDDEN > UPHAUD

UPHUNG > UPHANG

UPHURL *vb* throw upwards

UPHURLED > UPHURL

UPHURLING > UPHURL

UPHURLS > UPHURL

UPJET *vb* stream upwards

UPJETS > UPJET

UPJETTED > UPJET

UPJETTING > UPJET

UPKEEP *n* act, process, or cost of keeping something in good repair

UPKEEPS > UPKEEP

UPKNIT *vb* bind

UPKNITS > UPKNIT

UPKNITTED > UPKNIT

UPLAID > UPLAY

UPLAND *adj* of or in an area of high or relatively high ground ▷ *n* area of high or relatively high ground

UPLANDER *n* person hailing from the uplands

UPLANDERS > UPLANDER

UPLANDISH > UPLAND

UPLANDS > UPLAND

UPLAY *vb* stash

UPLAYING > UPLAY

UPLAYS > UPLAY

UPLEAD *vb* lead upwards

u

UPLEADING > UPLEAD
UPLEADS > UPLEAD
UPLEAN vb lean on something
UPLEANED > UPLEAN
UPLEANING > UPLEAN
UPLEANS > UPLEAN
UPLEANT > UPLEAN
UPLEAP vb jump upwards
UPLEAPED > UPLEAP
UPLEAPING > UPLEAP
UPLEAPS > UPLEAP
UPLEAPT > UPLEAP
UPLED > UPLEAD
UPLIFT vb raise or lift up ▷ n act or process of improving moral, social, or cultural conditions ▷ adj (of a bra) designed to lift and support the breasts
UPLIFTED > UPLIFT
UPLIFTER > UPLIFT
UPLIFTERS > UPLIFT
UPLIFTING adj acting to raise moral, spiritual, cultural, etc, levels
UPLIFTS > UPLIFT
UPLIGHT n lamp or wall light designed or positioned to cast its light upwards ▷ vb light in an upward direction
UPLIGHTED > UPLIGHT
UPLIGHTER n lamp or wall light designed or positioned to cast its light upwards
UPLIGHTS > UPLIGHT
UPLINK n transmitter that sends signals up to a communications satellite ▷ vb send (data) to a communications satellite
UPLINKED > UPLINK
UPLINKING > UPLINK
UPLINKS > UPLINK
UPLIT > UPLIGHT
UPLOAD vb transfer (data or a program) into the memory of another computer
UPLOADED > UPLOAD
UPLOADING > UPLOAD
UPLOADS > UPLOAD
UPLOCK vb lock up
UPLOCKED > UPLOCK
UPLOCKING > UPLOCK
UPLOCKS > UPLOCK
UPLOOK vb look up
UPLOOKED > UPLOOK
UPLOOKING > UPLOOK
UPLOOKS > UPLOOK
UPLYING adj raised
UPMAKE vb make up
UPMAKER > UPMAKE
UPMAKERS > UPMAKE
UPMAKES > UPMAKE
UPMAKING > UPMAKE
UPMAKINGS > UPMAKE
UPMANSHIP n one-upmanship

UPMARKET adj expensive and of superior quality ▷ vb make something upmarket
UPMARKETS > UPMARKET
UPMOST another word for > UPPERMOST
UPO prep upon
UPON prep on
UPPED > UP
UPPER adj higher or highest in physical position, wealth, rank, or status ▷ n part of a shoe above the sole
UPPERCASE adj capitalized ▷ vb capitalize or print in capitals
UPPERCUT n short swinging upward punch delivered to the chin ▷ vb hit (an opponent) with an uppercut
UPPERCUTS > UPPERCUT
UPPERMOST adj highest in position, power, or importance ▷ adv in or into the highest place or position
UPPERPART n highest part
UPPERS > UPPER
UPPILE vb pile up
UPPILED > UPPILE
UPPILES > UPPILE
UPPILING > UPPILE
UPPING > UP
UPPINGS > UP
UPPISH adj snobbish, arrogant, or presumptuous
UPPISHLY > UPPISH
UPPITY adj snobbish, arrogant, or presumptuous
UPPROP vb support
UPPROPPED > UPPROP
UPPROPS > UPPROP
UPRAISE vb lift up
UPRAISED > UPRAISE
UPRAISER > UPRAISE
UPRAISERS > UPRAISE
UPRAISES > UPRAISE
UPRAISING > UPRAISE
UPRAN > UPRUN
UPRATE vb raise the value, rate, or size of, upgrade
UPRATED > UPRATE
UPRATES > UPRATE
UPRATING > UPRATE
UPREACH vb reach up
UPREACHED > UPREACH
UPREACHES > UPREACH
UPREAR vb lift up
UPREARED > UPREAR
UPREARING > UPREAR
UPREARS > UPREAR
UPREST n uprising
UPRESTS > UPREST
UPRIGHT adj vertical or erect ▷ adv vertically or in an erect position ▷ n vertical support, such as a post ▷ vb make upright

UPRIGHTED > UPRIGHT
UPRIGHTLY > UPRIGHT
UPRIGHTS > UPRIGHT
UPRISAL > UPRISE
UPRISALS > UPRISE
UPRISE vb rise up
UPRISEN > UPRISE
UPRISER > UPRISE
UPRISERS > UPRISE
UPRISES > UPRISE
UPRISING n rebellion or revolt
UPRISINGS > UPRISING
UPRIST same as > UPREST
UPRISTS > UPRIST
UPRIVER adv towards or near the source of a river ▷ n area located upstream
UPRIVERS > UPRIVER
UPROAR n disturbance characterized by loud noise and confusion ▷ vb cause an uproar
UPROARED > UPROAR
UPROARING > UPROAR
UPROARS > UPROAR
UPROLL vb roll up
UPROLLED > UPROLL
UPROLLING > UPROLL
UPROLLS > UPROLL
UPROOT vb pull up by or as if by the roots
UPROOTAL > UPROOT
UPROOTALS > UPROOT
UPROOTED > UPROOT
UPROOTER > UPROOT
UPROOTERS > UPROOT
UPROOTING > UPROOT
UPROOTS > UPROOT
UPROSE > UPRISE
UPROUSE vb rouse or stir up
UPROUSED > UPROUSE
UPROUSES > UPROUSE
UPROUSING > UPROUSE
UPRUN vb run up
UPRUNNING > UPRUN
UPRUNS > UPRUN
UPRUSH n upward rush, as of consciousness ▷ vb rush upwards
UPRUSHED > UPRUSH
UPRUSHES > UPRUSH
UPRUSHING > UPRUSH
UPRYST same as > UPREST
UPS > UP
UPSADAISY interj expression of reassurance often uttered when someone stumbles or is lifted up
UPSCALE adj of or for the upper end of an economic or social scale ▷ vb upgrade
UPSCALED > UPSCALE
UPSCALES > UPSCALE
UPSCALING > UPSCALE
UPSEE n drunken revel
UPSEES > UPSEE
UPSELL vb persuade a customer to buy a more expensive or additional item

UPSELLING > UPSELL
UPSELLS > UPSELL
UPSEND vb send up
UPSENDING > UPSEND
UPSENDS > UPSEND
UPSENT > UPSEND
UPSET adj emotionally or physically disturbed or distressed ▷ vb tip over ▷ n unexpected defeat or reversal
UPSETS > UPSET
UPSETTER > UPSET
UPSETTERS > UPSET
UPSETTING > UPSET
UPSEY same as > UPSEE
UPSEYS > UPSEY
UPSHIFT vb move up (a gear)
UPSHIFTED > UPSHIFT
UPSHIFTS > UPSHIFT
UPSHOOT vb shoot upwards
UPSHOOTS > UPSHOOT
UPSHOT n final result or conclusion
UPSHOTS > UPSHOT
UPSIDE n upper surface or part
UPSIDES > UPSIDE
UPSIES > UPSY
UPSILON n 20th letter in the Greek alphabet
UPSILONS > UPSILON
UPSITTING n sitting up of a woman after childbirth
UPSIZE vb increase in size
UPSIZED > UPSIZE
UPSIZES > UPSIZE
UPSIZING > UPSIZE
UPSKILL vb improve the aptitude for work of (a person)
UPSKILLED > UPSKILL
UPSKILLS > UPSKILL
UPSKIRT adj indicating a photograph taken of a woman's exposed underwear without her knowledge or consent
UPSLOPE adv up a or the slope ▷ n upward slope
UPSLOPES > UPSLOPE
UPSOAR vb soar up
UPSOARED > UPSOAR
UPSOARING > UPSOAR
UPSOARS > UPSOAR
UPSOLD > UPSELL
UPSPAKE > UPSPEAK
UPSPEAK vb speak with rising intonation
UPSPEAKS > UPSPEAK
UPSPEAR vb grow upwards in a spear-like manner
UPSPEARED > UPSPEAR
UPSPEARS > UPSPEAR
UPSPOKE > UPSPEAK
UPSPOKEN > UPSPEAK
UPSPRANG > UPSPRING
UPSPRING vb spring up or come into existence

▷ *n* leap forwards or upwards

UPSPRINGS > UPSPRING

UPSPRUNG > UPSPRING

UPSTAGE *adj* at the back half of the stage ▷ *vb* draw attention to oneself from (someone else) ▷ *adv* on, at, or to the rear of the stage ▷ *n* back half of the stage

UPSTAGED > UPSTAGE

UPSTAGER > UPSTAGE

UPSTAGERS > UPSTAGE

UPSTAGES > UPSTAGE

UPSTAGING > UPSTAGE

UPSTAIR *same as* > UPSTAIRS

UPSTAIRS *adv* to or on an upper floor of a building ▷ *n* upper floor ▷ *adj* situated on an upper floor

UPSTAND *vb* rise

UPSTANDS > UPSTAND

UPSTARE *vb* stare upwards

UPSTARED > UPSTARE

UPSTARES > UPSTARE

UPSTARING > UPSTARE

UPSTART *n* person who has risen suddenly to a position of power and behaves arrogantly ▷ *vb* start up, as in surprise, etc

UPSTARTED > UPSTART

UPSTARTS > UPSTART

UPSTATE *adv* towards, in, from, or relating to the outlying or northern sections of a state ▷ *n* outlying, esp northern, sections of a state

UPSTATER > UPSTATE

UPSTATERS > UPSTATE

UPSTATES > UPSTATE

UPSTAY *vb* support

UPSTAYED > UPSTAY

UPSTAYING > UPSTAY

UPSTAYS > UPSTAY

UPSTEP *n* type of vocal intonation

UPSTEPPED > UPSTEP

UPSTEPS > UPSTEP

UPSTIR *vb* stir up ▷ *n* commotion

UPSTIRRED > UPSTIR

UPSTIRS > UPSTIR

UPSTOOD > UPSTAND

UPSTREAM *adj* in or towards the higher part of a stream ▷ *vb* stream upwards

UPSTREAMS > UPSTREAM

UPSTROKE *n* upward stroke or movement, as of a pen or brush

UPSTROKES > UPSTROKE

UPSURGE *n* rapid rise or swell ▷ *vb* surge up

UPSURGED > UPSURGE

UPSURGES > UPSURGE

UPSURGING > UPSURGE

UPSWARM *vb* rise or send upwards in a swarm

UPSWARMED > UPSWARM

UPSWARMS > UPSWARM

UPSWAY *vb* swing in the air

UPSWAYED > UPSWAY

UPSWAYING > UPSWAY

UPSWAYS > UPSWAY

UPSWEEP *n* curve or sweep upwards ▷ *vb* sweep, curve, or brush or be swept, curved, or brushed upwards

UPSWEEPS > UPSWEEP

UPSWELL *vb* swell up or cause to swell up

UPSWELLED > UPSWELL

UPSWELLS > UPSWELL

UPSWEPT > UPSWEEP

UPSWING *n* recovery period in the trade cycle ▷ *vb* swing or move up

UPSWINGS > UPSWING

UPSWOLLEN > UPSWELL

UPSWUNG > UPSWING

UPSY *same as* > UPSEE

UPTA *same as* > UPTER

UPTAK *same as* > UPTAKE

UPTAKE *n* numbers taking up something such as an offer or the act of taking it up ▷ *vb* take up

UPTAKEN > UPTAKE

UPTAKES > UPTAKE

UPTAKING > UPTAKE

UPTAKS > UPTAK

UPTALK *n* style of speech in which every sentence ends with a rising tone ▷ *vb* talk in this manner

UPTALKED > UPTALK

UPTALKING > UPTALK

UPTALKS > UPTALK

UPTEAR *vb* tear up

UPTEARING > UPTEAR

UPTEARS > UPTEAR

UPTEMPO *adj* fast ▷ *n* uptempo piece

UPTEMPOS > UPTEMPO

UPTER *adj* of poor quality

UPTHREW > UPTHROW

UPTHROW *n* upward movement of rocks on one side of a fault plane relative to rocks on the other side ▷ *vb* throw upwards

UPTHROWN > UPTHROW

UPTHROWS > UPTHROW

UPTHRUST *n* upward push

UPTHRUSTS > UPTHRUST

UPTHUNDER *vb* make a noise like thunder

UPTICK *n* rise or increase

UPTICKS > UPTICK

UPTIE *vb* tie up

UPTIED > UPTIE

UPTIES > UPTIE

UPTIGHT *adj* nervously tense, irritable, or angry

UPTIGHTER > UPTIGHT

UPTILT *vb* tilt up

UPTILTED > UPTILT

UPTILTING > UPTILT

UPTILTS > UPTILT

UPTIME *n* time during which a machine, such as a computer, actually operates

UPTIMES > UPTIME

UPTITLING *n* practice of conferring grandiose job titles to employees performing relatively menial jobs

UPTOOK > UPTAKE

UPTORE > UPTEAR

UPTORN > UPTEAR

UPTOSS *vb* throw upwards

UPTOSSED > UPTOSS

UPTOSSES > UPTOSS

UPTOSSING > UPTOSS

UPTOWN *adv* towards, in, or relating to some part of a town that is away from the centre ▷ *n* such a part of town, esp a residential part

UPTOWNER > UPTOWN

UPTOWNERS > UPTOWN

UPTOWNS > UPTOWN

UPTRAIN *vb* train up

UPTRAINED > UPTRAIN

UPTRAINS > UPTRAIN

UPTREND *n* upward trend

UPTRENDS > UPTREND

UPTRILLED *adj* trilled high

UPTURN *n* upward trend or improvement ▷ *vb* turn or cause to turn over or upside down

UPTURNED > UPTURN

UPTURNING > UPTURN

UPTURNS > UPTURN

UPTYING > UPTIE

UPVALUE *vb* raise the value of

UPVALUED > UPVALUE

UPVALUES > UPVALUE

UPVALUING > UPVALUE

UPWAFT *vb* waft upwards

UPWAFTED > UPWAFT

UPWAFTING > UPWAFT

UPWAFTS > UPWAFT

UPWARD *same as* > UPWARDS

UPWARDLY > UPWARD

UPWARDS *adv* from a lower to a higher place, level, condition, etc

UPWELL *vb* well up

UPWELLED > UPWELL

UPWELLING > UPWELL

UPWELLS > UPWELL

UPWENT > UPGO

UPWHIRL *vb* spin upwards

UPWHIRLED > UPWHIRL

UPWHIRLS > UPWHIRL

UPWIND *adv* into or against the wind ▷ *adj* going against the wind ▷ *vb* wind up

UPWINDING > UPWIND

UPWINDS > UPWIND

UPWOUND > UPWIND

UPWRAP *vb* wrap up

UPWRAPS > UPWRAP

UPWROUGHT *adj* wrought up

UR *interj* hesitant utterance used to fill gaps in talking

URACHI > URACHUS

URACHUS *n* cord of tissue connected to the bladder

URACHUSES > URACHUS

URACIL *n* pyrimidine present in all living cells

URACILS > URACIL

URAEI > URAEUS

URAEMIA *n* accumulation of waste products in the blood

URAEMIAS > URAEMIA

URAEMIC > URAEMIA

URAEUS *n* sacred serpent of ancient Egypt

URAEUSES > URAEUS

URALI *n* type of plant

URALIS > URALI

URALITE *n* mineral that replaces pyroxene in some rocks

URALITES > URALITE

URALITIC > URALITE

URALITISE *same as* > URALITIZE

URALITIZE *vb* turn into uralite

URANIA *n* uranium dioxide

URANIAN *adj* heavenly

URANIAS > URANIA

URANIC *adj* of or containing uranium, esp in a high valence state

URANIDE *n* any element having an atomic number greater than that of protactinium

URANIDES > URANIDE

URANIN *n* type of alkaline substance

URANINITE *n* blackish heavy radioactive mineral consisting of uranium oxide in cubic crystalline form together with radium, lead, helium, etc: occurs in coarse granite

URANINS > URANIN

URANISCI > URANISCUS

URANISCUS *n* palate

URANISM *n* homosexuality

URANISMS > URANISM

URANITE *n* any of various minerals containing uranium, esp torbernite or autunite

URANITES > URANITE

URANITIC > URANITE

URANIUM *n* radioactive silvery-white metallic element

URANIUMS > URANIUM

URANOLOGY *n* study of the universe and planets

URANOUS *adj* of or containing uranium, esp in a low valence state

URANYL *n* of, consisting of, or containing the divalent ion UO_2^{2+} or the group $-UO_2$

u

URANYLIC > URANYL
URANYLS > URANYL
URAO *n* type of mineral
URAOS > URAO
URARE *same as* > URALI
URARES > URARE
URARI *same as* > URALI
URARIS > URARI
URASE *same as* > UREASE
URASES > URASE
URATE *n* any salt or ester of uric acid
URATES > URATE
URATIC > URATE
URB *n* urban area
URBAN *adj* of or living in a city or town
URBANE *adj* characterized by courtesy, elegance, and sophistication
URBANELY > URBANE
URBANER > URBANE
URBANEST > URBANE
URBANISE *same as* > URBANIZE
URBANISED > URBANISE
URBANISES > URBANISE
URBANISM *n* character of city life
URBANISMS > URBANISM
URBANIST *n* person who studies towns and cities
URBANISTS > URBANIST
URBANITE *n* resident of an urban community
URBANITES > URBANITE
URBANITY *n* quality of being urbane
URBANIZE *vb* make (a rural area) more industrialized and urban
URBANIZED > URBANIZE
URBANIZES > URBANIZE
URBEX *n* short for urban exploration, the hobby of exploring derelict urban structures
URBEXES > URBEX
URBIA *n* urban area
URBIAS > URBIA
URBS > URB
URCEOLATE *adj* shaped like an urn or pitcher
URCEOLI > URCEOLUS
URCEOLUS *n* organ of a plant
URCHIN *n* mischievous child
URCHINS > URCHIN
URD *n* type of plant with edible seeds
URDE *adj* (in heraldry) having points
URDEE *same as* > URDE
URDS > URD
URDY *n* heraldic line pattern
URE *same as* > AUROCHS
UREA *n* white soluble crystalline compound found in urine
UREAL > UREA
UREAS > UREA

UREASE *n* enzyme that converts urea to ammonium carbonate
UREASES > UREASE
UREDIA > UREDIUM
UREDIAL > UREDIUM
UREDINE > UREDO
UREDINES > UREDO
UREDINIA > UREDINIUM
UREDINIAL > UREDINIUM
UREDINIUM *same as* > UREDIUM
UREDINOUS > UREDO
UREDIUM *n* spore-producing body of some rust fungi in which uredospores are formed
UREDO *less common name for* > URTICARIA
UREDOS > UREDO
UREDOSORI *pl n* spore-producing bodies of some rust fungi in which uredospores are formed; uredia
UREIC > UREA
UREIDE *n* any of a class of organic compounds derived from urea
UREIDES > UREIDE
UREMIA *same as* > URAEMIA
UREMIAS > UREMIA
UREMIC > UREMIA
URENA *n* plant genus
URENAS > URENA
URENT *adj* burning
UREOTELIC *adj* excreting urea
URES > URE
URESES > URESIS
URESIS *n* urination
URETER *n* tube that conveys urine from the kidney to the bladder
URETERAL > URETER
URETERIC > URETER
URETERS > URETER
URETHAN *same as* > URETHANE
URETHANE *n* short for the synthetic material polyurethane ▷ *vb* treat with urethane
URETHANED > URETHANE
URETHANES > URETHANE
URETHANS > URETHAN
URETHRA *n* canal that carries urine from the bladder out of the body
URETHRAE > URETHRA
URETHRAL > URETHRA
URETHRAS > URETHRA
URETIC *adj* of or relating to the urine
URGE *n* strong impulse, inner drive, or yearning ▷ *vb* plead with or press (a person to do something)
URGED > URGE
URGENCE > URGENT
URGENCES > URGENT

URGENCIES > URGENT
URGENCY > URGENT
URGENT *adj* requiring speedy action or attention
URGENTLY > URGENT
URGER > URGE
URGERS > URGE
URGES > URGE
URGING > URGE
URGINGLY > URGE
URGINGS > URGE
URIAL *n* type of sheep
URIALS > URIAL
URIC *adj* of or derived from urine
URICASE *n* type of enzyme
URICASES > URICASE
URIDINE *n* nucleoside present in all living cells in a combined form, esp in RNA
URIDINES > URIDINE
URIDYLIC *adj* as in *uridylic acid* nucleotide consisting of uracil, ribose, and a phosphate group. It is a constituent of RNA
URINAL *n* sanitary fitting used by men for urination
URINALS > URINAL
URINANT *adj* having the head downwards
URINARIES > URINARY
URINARY *adj* of urine or the organs that secrete and pass urine ▷ *n* reservoir for urine
URINATE *vb* discharge urine
URINATED > URINATE
URINATES > URINATE
URINATING > URINATE
URINATION > URINATE
URINATIVE > URINATE
URINATOR > URINATE
URINATORS > URINATE
URINE *n* pale yellow fluid passed as waste from the body ▷ *vb* urinate
URINED > URINE
URINEMIA *same as* > UREMIA
URINEMIAS > URINEMIA
URINEMIC > URINEMIA
URINES > URINE
URINING > URINE
URINOLOGY *same as* > UROLOGY
URINOSE *same as* > URINOUS
URINOUS *adj* of, resembling, or containing urine
URITE *n* part of the abdomen
URITES > URITE
URMAN *n* forest
URMANS > URMAN
URN *n* vase used as a container for the ashes of the dead ▷ *vb* put in an urn
URNAL > URN
URNED > URN

URNFIELD *n* cemetery full of individual cremation urns ▷ *adj* characterized by cremation in urns
URNFIELDS > URNFIELD
URNFUL *n* capacity of an urn
URNFULS > URNFUL
URNING *n* homosexual man
URNINGS > URNING
URNLIKE > URN
URNS > URN
UROBILIN *n* brownish pigment found in faeces and sometimes in urine
UROBILINS > UROBILIN
UROBORIC *n* of or like a uroboros
UROBOROS *same as* > OUROBOROS
UROCHORD *n* notochord of a larval tunicate, typically confined to the tail region
UROCHORDS > UROCHORD
UROCHROME *n* yellowish pigment that colours urine
URODELAN > URODELE
URODELANS > URODELAN
URODELE *n* amphibian of the order which includes the salamanders and newts
URODELES > URODELE
URODELOUS > URODELE
UROGENOUS *adj* producing or derived from urine
UROGRAM *n* X-ray of the urinary tract
UROGRAMS > UROGRAM
UROGRAPHY *n* branch of radiology concerned with X-ray examination of the kidney and associated structures
UROKINASE *n* biochemical catalyst
UROLAGNIA *n* sexual arousal involving urination
UROLITH *n* calculus in the urinary tract
UROLITHIC > UROLITH
UROLITHS > UROLITH
UROLOGIC > UROLOGY
UROLOGIES > UROLOGY
UROLOGIST > UROLOGY
UROLOGY *n* branch of medicine concerned with the urinary system and its diseases
UROMERE *n* part of the abdomen
UROMERES > UROMERE
UROPOD *n* paired appendage forms part of the tailfan in lobsters
UROPODAL > UROPOD
UROPODOUS > UROPOD
UROPODS > UROPOD
UROPYGIA > UROPYGIUM
UROPYGIAL > UROPYGIUM

u

UROPYGIUM n hindmost part of a bird's body, from which the tail feathers grow
UROSCOPIC > UROSCOPY
UROSCOPY n examination of the urine
UROSES > UROSIS
UROSIS n urinary disease
UROSOME n abdomen of arthropods
UROSOMES > UROSOME
UROSTEGE n part of a serpent's tail
UROSTEGES > UROSTEGE
UROSTOMY n type of urinary surgery
UROSTYLE n bony rod forming the last segment of the vertebral column of frogs, toads, and related amphibians
UROSTYLES > UROSTYLE
URP dialect word for > VOMIT
URPED > URP
URPING > URP
URPS > URP
URSA n she-bear
URSAE > URSA
URSID n meteor
URSIDS > URSID
URSIFORM adj bear-shaped or bearlike in form
URSINE adj of or like a bear
URSON n type of porcupine
URSONS > URSON
URTEXT n earliest form of a text
URTEXTE same as > URTEXTS
URTEXTS > URTEXT
URTICA n type of nettle
URTICANT n something that causes itchiness and irritation
URTICANTS > URTICANT
URTICARIA n skin condition characterized by the formation of itchy red or whitish raised patches, usually caused by an allergy
URTICAS > URTICA
URTICATE adj characterized by the presence of weals ▷ vb sting
URTICATED > URTICATE
URTICATES > URTICATE
URUBU n type of bird
URUBUS > URUBU
URUS another name for the > AUROCHS
URUSES > URUS
URUSHIOL n poisonous pale yellow liquid occurring in poison ivy and the lacquer tree
URUSHIOLS > URUSHIOL
URVA n Indian mongoose
URVAS > URVA
US pron refers to the speaker or writer and

another person or other people
USABILITY > USABLE
USABLE adj able to be used
USABLY > USABLE
USAGE n regular or constant use
USAGER n person who has the use of something in trust
USAGERS > USAGER
USAGES > USAGE
USANCE n period of time permitted for the redemption of foreign bills of exchange
USANCES > USANCE
USAUNCE same as > USANCE
USAUNCES > USAUNCE
USE vb put into service or action ▷ n using or being used
USEABLE same as > USABLE
USEABLY > USABLE
USED adj second-hand
USEFUL adj able to be used advantageously or for several different purposes ▷ n odd-jobman or general factotum
USEFULLY > USEFUL
USEFULS > USEFUL
USELESS adj having no practical use
USELESSLY > USELESS
USER n continued exercise, use, or enjoyment of a right, esp in property
USERNAME n name given by computer user to gain access
USERNAMES > USERNAME
USERS > USER
USES > USE
USHER n official who shows people to their seats, as in a church ▷ vb conduct or escort
USHERED > USHER
USHERESS n female usher
USHERETTE n female assistant in a cinema who shows people to their seats
USHERING > USHER
USHERINGS > USHER
USHERS > USHER
USHERSHIP > USHER
USING > USE
USNEA n type of lichen
USNEAS > USNEA
USQUABAE n whisky
USQUABAES > USQUABAE
USQUE n whisky
USQUEBAE same as > USQUABAE
USQUEBAES > USQUABAE
USQUES > USQUE
USTION n burning
USTIONS > USTION
USTULATE adj charred ▷ vb give a charred appearance to

USTULATED > USTULATE
USTULATES > USTULATE
USUAL adj of the most normal, frequent, or regular type ▷ n ordinary or commonplace events
USUALLY adv most often, in most cases
USUALNESS > USUAL
USUALS > USUAL
USUCAPION n method of acquiring property
USUCAPT > USUCAPION
USUCAPTED > USUCAPION
USUCAPTS > USUCAPION
USUFRUCT n right to use and derive profit from a piece of property belonging to another, provided the property itself remains undiminished and uninjured in any way
USUFRUCTS > USUFRUCT
USURE vb be involved in usury
USURED > USURE
USURER n person who lends funds at an exorbitant rate of interest
USURERS > USURER
USURES > USURE
USURESS n female usurer
USURESSES > USURESS
USURIES > USURY
USURING > USURE
USURIOUS > USURY
USUROUS > USURY
USURP vb seize (a position or power) without authority
USURPED > USURP
USURPEDLY > USURP
USURPER > USURP
USURPERS > USURP
USURPING > USURP
USURPINGS > USURP
USURPS > USURP
USURY n practice of lending money at an extremely high rate of interest
USWARD adv towards us
USWARDS same as > USWARD
UT n syllable used in the fixed system of solmization for the note C
UTA n side-blotched lizard
UTAS n eighth day of a festival
UTASES > UTAS
UTE same as > UTILITY
UTENSIL n tool or container for practical use
UTENSILS > UTENSIL
UTERI > UTERUS
UTERINE adj of or affecting the womb
UTERITIS n inflammation of the womb
UTEROTOMY n surgery on the uterus

UTERUS n womb
UTERUSES > UTERUS
UTES > UTE
UTILE n W African tree
UTILES > UTILE
UTILIDOR n above-ground insulated casing for pipes carrying water, sewerage and electricity in permafrost regions
UTILIDORS > UTILIDOR
UTILISE same as > UTILIZE
UTILISED > UTILISE
UTILISER > UTILISE
UTILISERS > UTILISE
UTILISES > UTILISE
UTILISING > UTILISE
UTILITIES > UTILITY
UTILITY n usefulness ▷ adj designed for use rather than beauty
UTILIZE vb make practical use of
UTILIZED > UTILIZE
UTILIZER > UTILIZE
UTILIZERS > UTILIZE
UTILIZES > UTILIZE
UTILIZING > UTILIZE
UTIS n uproar
UTISES > UTIS
UTMOST n the greatest possible degree or amount ▷ adj of the greatest possible degree or amount
UTMOSTS > UTMOST
UTOPIA n real or imaginary society, place, state, etc, considered to be perfect or ideal
UTOPIAN adj of or relating to a perfect or ideal existence ▷ n idealistic social reformer
UTOPIANS > UTOPIAN
UTOPIAS > UTOPIA
UTOPIAST > UTOPIA
UTOPIASTS > UTOPIA
UTOPISM > UTOPIA
UTOPISMS > UTOPIA
UTOPIST > UTOPIA
UTOPISTIC > UTOPIA
UTOPISTS > UTOPIA
UTRICLE n larger of the two parts of the membranous labyrinth of the internal ear
UTRICLES > UTRICLE
UTRICULAR > UTRICLE
UTRICULI > UTRICULUS
UTRICULUS same as > UTRICLE
UTS > UT
UTTER vb express (something) in sounds or words ▷ adj total or absolute
UTTERABLE > UTTER
UTTERANCE n something uttered
UTTERED > UTTER
UTTERER > UTTER
UTTERERS > UTTER

u

UTTEREST > UTTER
UTTERING > UTTER
UTTERINGS > UTTER
UTTERLESS > UTTER
UTTERLY adv extremely
UTTERMOST same as > UTMOST
UTTERNESS > UTTER
UTTERS > UTTER
UTU n reward
UTUS > UTU
UVA n grape or fruit resembling this

UVAE > UVA
UVAROVITE n emerald-green garnet found in chromium deposits: consists of calcium chromium silicate
UVAS > UVA
UVEA n part of the eyeball consisting of the iris, ciliary body, and choroid
UVEAL > UVEA
UVEAS > UVEA
UVEITIC > UVEITIS

UVEITIS n inflammation of the uvea
UVEITISES > UVEITIS
UVEOUS > UVEA
UVULA n small fleshy part of the soft palate that hangs in the back of the throat
UVULAE > UVULA
UVULAR adj of or relating to the uvula ▷ n uvular consonant
UVULARLY > UVULAR

UVULARS > UVULAR
UVULAS > UVULA
UVULITIS n inflammation of the uvula
UXORIAL adj of or relating to a wife
UXORIALLY > UXORIAL
UXORICIDE n act of killing one's wife
UXORIOUS adj excessively fond of or dependent on one's wife

u

Vv

VAC *vb* clean with a vacuum cleaner
VACANCE *n* vacant period
VACANCES > VACANCE
VACANCIES > VACANCY
VACANCY *n* unfilled job
VACANT *adj* (of a toilet, room, etc) unoccupied
VACANTLY > VACANT
VACATABLE > VACATE
VACATE *vb* cause (something) to be empty by leaving
VACATED > VACATE
VACATES > VACATE
VACATING > VACATE
VACATION *n* time when universities and law courts are closed ▷ *vb* take a vacation
VACATIONS > VACATION
VACATUR *n* annulment
VACATURS > VACATUR
VACCINA *same as* > VACCINIA
VACCINAL *adj* of or relating to vaccine or vaccination
VACCINAS > VACCINA
VACCINATE *vb* inject with a vaccine
VACCINE *n* substance designed to make a person immune to a disease
VACCINEE *n* person who has been vaccinated
VACCINEES > VACCINEE
VACCINES > VACCINE
VACCINIA *technical name for* > COWPOX
VACCINIAL > VACCINIA
VACCINIAS > VACCINIA
VACCINIUM *n* shrub genus
VACHERIN *n* soft cheese made from cows' milk
VACHERINS > VACHERIN
VACILLANT *adj* indecisive
VACILLATE *vb* keep changing one's mind or opinions
VACKED > VAC
VACKING > VAC
VACS > VAC
VACUA > VACUUM
VACUATE *vb* empty
VACUATED > VACUATE
VACUATES > VACUATE
VACUATING > VACUATE
VACUATION > VACUATE

VACUIST *n* person believing in the existence of vacuums in nature
VACUISTS > VACUIST
VACUITIES > VACUITY
VACUITY *n* absence of intelligent thought or ideas
VACUOLAR > VACUOLE
VACUOLATE > VACUOLE
VACUOLE *n* fluid-filled cavity in the cytoplasm of a cell
VACUOLES > VACUOLE
VACUOUS *adj* not expressing intelligent thought
VACUOUSLY > VACUOUS
VACUUM *n* empty space from which all or most air or gas has been removed ▷ *vb* clean with a vacuum cleaner
VACUUMED > VACUUM
VACUUMING > VACUUM
VACUUMS > VACUUM
VADE *vb* fade
VADED > VADE
VADES > VADE
VADING > VADE
VADOSE *adj* of or derived from water occurring above the water table
VAE *same as* > VOE
VAES > VAE
VAG *n* vagrant ▷ *vb* arrest someone for vagrancy
VAGABOND *n* person with no fixed home, esp a beggar
VAGABONDS > VAGABOND
VAGAL *adj* of, relating to, or affecting the vagus nerve
VAGALLY > VAGAL
VAGARIES > VAGARY
VAGARIOUS *adj* characterized or caused by vagaries
VAGARISH > VAGARY
VAGARY *n* unpredictable change
VAGGED > VAG
VAGGING > VAG
VAGI > VAGUS
VAGILE *adj* able to move freely
VAGILITY > VAGILE
VAGINA *n* (in female mammals) passage from the womb to the external genitals

VAGINAE > VAGINA
VAGINAL > VAGINA
VAGINALLY > VAGINA
VAGINANT *adj* sheathing
VAGINAS > VAGINA
VAGINATE *adj* (esp of plant parts) having a sheath
VAGINATED > VAGINATE
VAGINITIS *n* inflammation of the vagina
VAGINOSES > VAGINOSIS
VAGINOSIS *n* bacterial vaginal infection
VAGINULA *n* little sheath
VAGINULAE > VAGINULA
VAGINULE *same as* > VAGINULA
VAGINULES > VAGINULE
VAGITUS *n* new-born baby's cry
VAGITUSES > VAGITUS
VAGOTOMY *n* surgical division of the vagus nerve
VAGOTONIA *n* pathological overactivity of the vagus nerve
VAGOTONIC > VAGOTONIA
VAGRANCY *n* state or condition of being a vagrant
VAGRANT *n* person with no settled home ▷ *adj* wandering
VAGRANTLY > VAGRANT
VAGRANTS > VAGRANT
VAGROM *same as* > VAGRANT
VAGS > VAG
VAGUE *adj* not clearly explained ▷ *vb* wander
VAGUED > VAGUE
VAGUELY > VAGUE
VAGUENESS > VAGUE
VAGUER > VAGUE
VAGUES > VAGUE
VAGUEST > VAGUE
VAGUING > VAGUE
VAGUISH *adj* rather vague
VAGUS *n* tenth cranial nerve, which supplies the heart, lungs, and viscera
VAHANA *n* vehicle
VAHANAS > VAHANA
VAHINE *n* Polynesian woman
VAHINES > VAHINE

VAIL *vb* lower (something, such as a weapon), esp as a sign of deference or submission
VAILED > VAIL
VAILING > VAIL
VAILS > VAIL
VAIN *adj* excessively proud, esp of one's appearance
VAINER > VAIN
VAINESSE *n* vainness
VAINESSES > VAINESSE
VAINEST > VAIN
VAINGLORY *n* boastfulness or vanity
VAINLY > VAIN
VAINNESS > VAIN
VAIR *n* fur used to trim robes in the Middle Ages
VAIRE *adj* of Russian squirrel fur
VAIRIER > VAIR
VAIRIEST > VAIR
VAIRS > VAIR
VAIRY > VAIR
VAIVODE *n* European ruler
VAIVODES > VAIVODE
VAJAZZLE *vb* decorate the female genitals with jewellery
VAJAZZLED > VAJAZZLE
VAJAZZLES > VAJAZZLE
VAKAS *n* Armenian priestly garment
VAKASES > VAKAS
VAKASS *n* priest's cloak with a metal breastplate
VAKASSES > VAKASS
VAKEEL *n* ambassador
VAKEELS > VAKEEL
VAKIL *same as* > VAKEEL
VAKILS > VAKIL
VALANCE *n* piece of drapery round the edge of a bed ▷ *vb* provide with a valance
VALANCED > VALANCE
VALANCES > VALANCE
VALANCING > VALANCE
VALE *n* valley ▷ *sentence substitute* farewell
VALENCE *same as* > VALENCY
VALENCES > VALENCE
VALENCIA *n* type of fabric
VALENCIAS > VALENCIA
VALENCIES > VALENCY
VALENCY *n* power of an atom to make molecular bonds

VALENTINE n (person to whom one sends) a romantic card on Saint Valentine's Day, 14th February

VALERATE n salt of valeric acid

VALERATES > VALERATE

VALERIAN n herb used as a sedative

VALERIANS > VALERIAN

VALERIC adj of, relating to, or derived from valerian

VALES > VALE

VALET n man's personal male servant ▷ vb act as a valet (for)

VALETA n old-time dance in triple time

VALETAS > VALETA

VALETE n farewell

VALETED > VALET

VALETES > VALETE

VALETING > VALET

VALETINGS > VALET

VALETS > VALET

VALGOID > VALGUS

VALGOUS same as > VALGUS

VALGUS adj denoting a deformity of a limb ▷ n abnormal position of a limb

VALGUSES > VALGUS

VALI n Turkish civil governor

VALIANCE > VALIANT

VALIANCES > VALIANT

VALIANCY > VALIANT

VALIANT adj brave or courageous ▷ n brave person

VALIANTLY > VALIANT

VALIANTS > VALIANT

VALID adj soundly reasoned

VALIDATE vb make valid

VALIDATED > VALIDATE

VALIDATES > VALIDATE

VALIDER > VALID

VALIDEST > VALID

VALIDITY > VALID

VALIDLY > VALID

VALIDNESS > VALID

VALINE n essential amino acid

VALINES > VALINE

VALIS > VALI

VALISE n small suitcase

VALISES > VALISE

VALIUM n as in valium picnic refers to a day on the New York Stock Exchange when business is slow

VALKYR variant of > VALKYRIE

VALKYRIE n (in Norse mythology) beautiful maiden who collects dead heroes on the battlefield to take to Valhalla

VALKYRIES > VALKYRIE

VALKYRS > VALKYR

VALLAR adj pertaining to a rampart ▷ n gold Roman crown awarded to the first soldier who broke into the enemy's camp

VALLARIES > VALLARY

VALLARS > VALLAR

VALLARY n Roman circular gold crown

VALLATE adj surrounded with a wall

VALLATION n act or process of building fortifications

VALLECULA n any of various natural depressions or crevices

VALLEY n low area between hills, often with a river running through it

VALLEYED adj having a valley

VALLEYS > VALLEY

VALLHUND n as in Swedish vallhund breed of dog

VALLHUNDS > VALLHUND

VALLONIA same as > VALONIA

VALLONIAS > VALLONIA

VALLUM n Roman rampart or earthwork

VALLUMS > VALLUM

VALONEA same as > VALONIA

VALONEAS > VALONEA

VALONIA n acorn cups and unripe acorns of a particular oak

VALONIAS > VALONIA

VALOR same as > VALOUR

VALORISE same as > VALORIZE

VALORISED > VALORISE

VALORISES > VALORISE

VALORIZE vb fix and maintain an artificial price for (a commodity) by governmental action

VALORIZED > VALORIZE

VALORIZES > VALORIZE

VALOROUS > VALOUR

VALORS > VALOR

VALOUR n bravery ▷ n courageous person

VALOURS > VALOUR

VALPROATE n medicament derived from valproic acid

VALPROIC adj as in valproic acid synthetic crystalline compound, used as an anticonvulsive

VALSE another word for > WALTZ

VALSED > VALSE

VALSES > VALSE

VALSING > VALSE

VALUABLE adj having great worth ▷ n valuable article of personal property, esp jewellery

VALUABLES > VALUABLE

VALUABLY > VALUABLE

VALUATE vb value or evaluate

VALUATED > VALUATE

VALUATES > VALUATE

VALUATING > VALUATE

VALUATION n assessment of worth

VALUATOR n person who estimates the value of objects, paintings, etc

VALUATORS > VALUATOR

VALUE n importance, usefulness ▷ vb assess the worth or desirability of

VALUED > VALUE

VALUELESS adj having or possessing no value

VALUER > VALUE

VALUERS > VALUE

VALUES > VALUE

VALUING > VALUE

VALUTA n value of one currency in terms of its exchange rate with another

VALUTAS > VALUTA

VALVAL same as > VALVULAR

VALVAR same as > VALVULAR

VALVASSOR same as > VAVASOR

VALVATE adj furnished with a valve or valves

VALVE n device to control the movement of fluid through a pipe ▷ vb provide with a valve

VALVED > VALVE

VALVELESS > VALVE

VALVELET same as > VALVULE

VALVELETS > VALVELET

VALVELIKE > VALVE

VALVES > VALVE

VALVING > VALVE

VALVULA same as > VALVULE

VALVULAE > VALVULA

VALVULAR adj of or having valves

VALVULE n small valve or a part resembling one

VALVULES > VALVULE

VAMBRACE n piece of armour used to protect the arm

VAMBRACED > VAMBRACE

VAMBRACES > VAMBRACE

VAMOOSE vb leave a place hurriedly

VAMOOSED > VAMOOSE

VAMOOSES > VAMOOSE

VAMOOSING > VAMOOSE

VAMOSE same as > VAMOOSE

VAMOSED > VAMOSE

VAMOSES > VAMOSE

VAMOSING > VAMOSE

VAMP n sexually attractive woman who seduces men ▷ vb (of a woman) to seduce (a man)

VAMPED > VAMP

VAMPER > VAMP

VAMPERS > VAMP

VAMPIER > VAMP

VAMPIEST > VAMP

VAMPING > VAMP

VAMPINGS > VAMP

VAMPIRE n (in folklore) corpse that rises at night to drink the blood of the living ▷ vb assail

VAMPIRED > VAMPIRE

VAMPIRES > VAMPIRE

VAMPIRIC > VAMPIRE

VAMPIRING > VAMPIRE

VAMPIRISE same as > VAMPIRIZE

VAMPIRISH > VAMPIRE

VAMPIRISM n belief in the existence of vampires

VAMPIRIZE vb suck blood from

VAMPISH > VAMP

VAMPISHLY > VAMP

VAMPLATE n piece of metal mounted on a lance to protect the hand

VAMPLATES > VAMPLATE

VAMPS > VAMP

VAMPY > VAMP

VAN n motor vehicle for transporting goods ▷ vb send in a van

VANADATE n any salt or ester of a vanadic acid

VANADATES > VANADATE

VANADIATE same as > VANADATE

VANADIC adj of or containing vanadium, esp in a trivalent or pentavalent state

VANADIUM n metallic element, used in steel

VANADIUMS > VANADIUM

VANADOUS adj of or containing vanadium

VANASPATI n hydrogenated vegetable fat commonly used in India as a substitute for butter

VANDA n type of orchid

VANDAL n person who deliberately damages property

VANDALIC > VANDAL

VANDALISE same as > VANDALIZE

VANDALISH > VANDAL

VANDALISM n wanton or deliberate destruction caused by a vandal or an instance of such destruction

VANDALIZE vb cause damage to (personal or public property) deliberately

VANDALS > VANDAL

VANDAS > VANDA

VANDYKE n short pointed beard ▷ vb cut with deep zigzag indentations

VANDYKED > VANDYKE

VANDYKES > VANDYKE
VANDYKING > VANDYKE
VANE n flat blade on a rotary device such as a weathercock or propeller
VANED > VANE
VANELESS > VANE
VANES > VANE
VANESSA n type of butterfly
VANESSAS > VANESSA
VANESSID n type of butterfly ▷ adj relating to this butterfly
VANESSIDS > VANESSID
VANG n type of rope or tackle on a sailing ship
VANGS > VANG
VANGUARD n unit of soldiers leading an army
VANGUARDS > VANGUARD
VANILLA n seed pod of a tropical climbing orchid, used for flavouring ▷ adj flavoured with vanilla
VANILLAS > VANILLA
VANILLIC adj of, resembling, containing, or derived from vanilla or vanillin
VANILLIN n white crystalline aldehyde found in vanilla
VANILLINS > VANILLIN
VANISH vb disappear suddenly or mysteriously ▷ n second and weaker of the two vowels in a falling diphthong
VANISHED > VANISH
VANISHER > VANISH
VANISHERS > VANISH
VANISHES > VANISH
VANISHING > VANISH
VANITAS n type of Dutch painting
VANITASES > VANITAS
VANITIED adj with vanity units or mirrors
VANITIES > VANITY
VANITORY n vanity unit
VANITY n (display of) excessive pride
VANLOAD n amount van will carry
VANLOADS > VANLOAD
VANMAN n man in control of a van
VANMEN > VANMAN
VANNED > VAN
VANNER n horse used to pull delivery vehicles
VANNERS > VANNER
VANNING > VAN
VANNINGS > VAN
VANPOOL n van-sharing group
VANPOOLS > VANPOOL
VANQUISH vb defeat (someone) utterly
VANS > VAN
VANT archaic word for > VANGUARD

VANTAGE n state, position, or opportunity offering advantage ▷ vb benefit
VANTAGED > VANTAGE
VANTAGES > VANTAGE
VANTAGING > VANTAGE
VANTBRACE n armour for the arm
VANTBRASS > VAMBRACE
VANTS > VANT
VANWARD adv in or towards the front
VAPE vb inhale nicotine vapour (from an electronic cigarette)
VAPED > VAPE
VAPER n one who vapes, inhales nicotine vapour from an electronic cigarette
VAPERS > VAPER
VAPES > VAPE
VAPID adj lacking character, dull
VAPIDER > VAPID
VAPIDEST > VAPID
VAPIDITY > VAPID
VAPIDLY > VAPID
VAPIDNESS > VAPID
VAPING n the practice of inhaling nicotine vapour (from an electronic cigarette)
VAPINGS > VAPING
VAPOR same as > VAPOUR
VAPORABLE > VAPOR
VAPORED > VAPOR
VAPORER > VAPOR
VAPORETTI > VAPORETTO
VAPORETTO n steam-powered passenger boat, as used on the canals in Venice
VAPORIFIC adj producing, causing, or tending to produce vapour
VAPORING > VAPOR
VAPORINGS > VAPOR
VAPORISE same as > VAPORIZE
VAPORISED > VAPORISE
VAPORISER same as > VAPORIZER
VAPORISES > VAPORISE
VAPORISH > VAPOR
VAPORIZE vb change into a vapour
VAPORIZED > VAPORIZE
VAPORIZER n substance that vaporizes or a device that causes vaporization
VAPORIZES > VAPORIZE
VAPORLESS > VAPOR
VAPORLIKE > VAPOR
VAPOROUS same as > VAPORIFIC
VAPORS > VAPOR
VAPORWARE n new software that has not yet been produced
VAPORY > VAPOUR

VAPOUR n moisture suspended in air as steam or mist ▷ vb evaporate
VAPOURED > VAPOUR
VAPOURER > VAPOUR
VAPOURERS > VAPOUR
VAPOURING > VAPOUR
VAPOURISH > VAPOUR
VAPOURS > VAPOUR
VAPOURY > VAPOUR
VAPULATE vb strike
VAPULATED > VAPULATE
VAPULATES > VAPULATE
VAQUERO n cattle-hand
VAQUEROS > VAQUERO
VAR n unit of reactive power of an alternating current
VARA n unit of length used in Spain, Portugal, and South America
VARACTOR n semiconductor diode that acts as a voltage-dependent capacitor
VARACTORS > VARACTOR
VARAN n type of lizard
VARANS > VARAN
VARAS > VARA
VARDIES > VARDY
VARDY n verdict
VARE n rod
VAREC n ash obtained from kelp
VARECH same as > VAREC
VARECHS > VARECH
VARECS > VAREC
VARENYKY pl n Ukrainian stuffed dumplings
VARES > VARE
VAREUSE n type of coat
VAREUSES > VAREUSE
VARGUENO n type of Spanish cabinet
VARGUENOS > VARGUENO
VARIA n collection or miscellany, esp of literary works
VARIABLE adj not always the same, changeable ▷ n something that is subject to variation
VARIABLES > VARIABLE
VARIABLY > VARIABLE
VARIANCE n act of varying
VARIANCES > VARIANCE
VARIANT adj differing from a standard or type ▷ n something that differs from a standard or type
VARIANTS > VARIANT
VARIAS > VARIA
VARIATE n random variable or a numerical value taken by it ▷ vb vary
VARIATED > VARIATE
VARIATES > VARIATE
VARIATING > VARIATE
VARIATION n something presented in a slightly different form
VARIATIVE > VARIATE

VARICEAL adj relating to a varix
VARICELLA n chickenpox
VARICES > VARIX
VARICOID same as > CIRSOID
VARICOSE adj of or resulting from varicose veins
VARICOSED same as > VARICOSE
VARICOSES > VARICOSIS
VARICOSIS n any condition characterized by distension of the veins
VARIED > VARY
VARIEDLY > VARY
VARIEGATE vb alter the appearance of, esp by adding different colours
VARIER n person who varies
VARIERS > VARIER
VARIES > VARY
VARIETAL adj of or forming a variety, esp a biological variety ▷ n wine labelled with the name of the grape from which it is pressed
VARIETALS > VARIETAL
VARIETIES > VARIETY
VARIETY n state of being diverse or various
VARIFOCAL adj gradated to permit any length of vision between near and distant ▷ n lens of this type
VARIFORM adj varying in form or shape
VARIOLA n smallpox
VARIOLAR > VARIOLA
VARIOLAS > VARIOLA
VARIOLATE vb inoculate with the smallpox virus ▷ adj marked or pitted with or as if with the scars of smallpox
VARIOLE n any of the rounded masses that make up the rock variolite
VARIOLES > VARIOLE
VARIOLITE n type of basic igneous rock
VARIOLOID adj resembling smallpox ▷ n mild form of smallpox occurring in persons with partial immunity
VARIOLOUS adj relating to or resembling smallpox
VARIORUM adj containing notes by various scholars or critics or various versions of the text ▷ n edition or text of this kind
VARIORUMS > VARIORUM
VARIOUS adj of several kinds
VARIOUSLY > VARIOUS

V

VARISCITE n green secondary mineral
VARISIZED adj of different sizes
VARISTOR n type of semiconductor device
VARISTORS > VARISTOR
VARITYPE vb produce (copy) on a Varityper ▷ n copy produced on a Varityper
VARITYPED > VARITYPE
VARITYPES > VARITYPE
VARIX n tortuous dilated vein
VARLET n menial servant
VARLETESS n female varlet
VARLETRY n the rabble
VARLETS > VARLET
VARLETTO same as > VARLET
VARLETTOS > VARLETTO
VARMENT same as > VARMINT
VARMENTS > VARMENT
VARMINT n irritating or obnoxious person or animal
VARMINTS > VARMINT
VARNA n any of the four Hindu castes
VARNAS > VARNA
VARNISH n solution of oil and resin, put on a surface to make it hard and glossy ▷ vb apply varnish to
VARNISHED > VARNISH
VARNISHER > VARNISH
VARNISHES > VARNISH
VARNISHY > VARNISH
VAROOM same as > VROOM
VAROOMED same as > VAROOM
VAROOMING same as > VAROOM
VAROOMS same as > VAROOM
VARROA n small parasite
VARROAS > VARROA
VARS > VAR
VARSAL adj universal
VARSITIES > VARSITY
VARSITY n university
VARTABED n position in the Armenian church
VARTABEDS > VARTABED
VARUS adj denoting a deformity of a limb ▷ n abnormal position of a limb
VARUSES > VARUS
VARVE n typically thin band of sediment deposited annually in glacial lakes
VARVED adj having layers of sedimentary deposit
VARVEL n piece of falconry equipment
VARVELLED adj having varvels
VARVELS > VARVEL
VARVES > VARVE

VARY vb change
VARYING > VARY
VARYINGLY > VARY
VARYINGS > VARY
VAS n vessel or tube that carries a fluid
VASA > VAS
VASAL > VAS
VASCULA > VASCULUM
VASCULAR adj relating to vessels
VASCULUM n metal box used by botanists in the field for carrying botanical specimens
VASCULUMS > VASCULUM
VASE n ornamental jar, esp for flowers
VASECTOMY n surgical removal of part of the vas deferens, as a contraceptive method
VASEFUL n contents of a vase
VASEFULS > VASEFUL
VASELIKE > VASE
VASELINE n translucent gelatinous substance obtained from petroleum ▷ vb apply vaseline to
VASELINED > VASELINE
VASELINES > VASELINE
VASES > VASE
VASIFORM > VAS
VASOMOTOR adj (of a drug, agent, nerve, etc) affecting the diameter of blood vessels
VASOSPASM n sudden contraction of a blood vessel
VASOTOCIN n chemical found in birds, reptiles, and some amphibians
VASOTOMY n surgery on the vas deferens
VASOVAGAL adj relating to blood vessels and the vagus nerve
VASSAIL archaic variant of > VASSAL
VASSAILS > VASSAIL
VASSAL n man given land by a lord in return for military service ▷ adj of or relating to a vassal ▷ vb vassalize
VASSALAGE n condition of being a vassal or the obligations to which a vassal was liable
VASSALESS > VASSAL
VASSALISE same as > VASSALIZE
VASSALIZE vb make a vassal of
VASSALLED > VASSAL
VASSALRY n vassalage
VASSALS > VASSAL
VAST adj extremely large ▷ n immense or boundless space
VASTER > VAST
VASTEST > VAST

VASTIDITY n vastness
VASTIER > VASTY
VASTIEST > VASTY
VASTITIES > VAST
VASTITUDE n condition or quality of being vast
VASTITY > VAST
VASTLY > VAST
VASTNESS > VAST
VASTS > VAST
VASTY archaic or poetic word for > VAST
VAT n large container for liquids ▷ vb place, store, or treat in a vat
VATABLE adj subject to VAT
VATFUL n amount enough to fill a vat
VATFULS > VATFUL
VATIC adj of, relating to, or characteristic of a prophet
VATICAL same as > VATIC
VATICIDE n murder of a prophet
VATICIDES > VATICIDE
VATICINAL adj foretelling or prophesying
VATMAN n Customs and Excise employee
VATMEN > VATMAN
VATS > VAT
VATTED > VAT
VATTER n person who works with vats; blender
VATTERS > VATTER
VATTING > VAT
VATU n standard monetary unit of Vanuatu
VATUS > VATU
VAU same as > VAV
VAUCH vb move fast
VAUCHED > VAUCH
VAUCHES > VAUCH
VAUCHING > VAUCH
VAUDOO same as > VOODOO
VAUDOOS > VAUDOO
VAUDOUX same as > VOODOO
VAULT n secure room for storing valuables ▷ vb jump over (something) by resting one's hand(s) on it
VAULTAGE n group of vaults
VAULTAGES > VAULTAGE
VAULTED > VAULT
VAULTER > VAULT
VAULTERS > VAULT
VAULTIER > VAULTY
VAULTIEST > VAULTY
VAULTING n arrangement of ceiling vaults in a building ▷ adj excessively confident
VAULTINGS > VAULTING
VAULTLIKE > VAULT
VAULTS > VAULT
VAULTY adj arched

VAUNCE same as > ADVANCE
VAUNCED > VAUNCE
VAUNCES > VAUNCE
VAUNCING > VAUNCE
VAUNT vb describe or display (success or possessions) boastfully ▷ n boast
VAUNTAGE archaic variant of > VANTAGE
VAUNTAGES > VAUNTAGE
VAUNTED > VAUNT
VAUNTER > VAUNT
VAUNTERS > VAUNT
VAUNTERY n bravado
VAUNTFUL > VAUNT
VAUNTIE same as > VAUNTY
VAUNTIER > VAUNT
VAUNTIEST > VAUNT
VAUNTING > VAUNT
VAUNTINGS > VAUNT
VAUNTS > VAUNT
VAUNTY adj proud
VAURIEN n rascal
VAURIENS > VAURIEN
VAUS > VAU
VAUT same as > VAULT
VAUTE same as > VAULT
VAUTED > VAUTE
VAUTES > VAUTE
VAUTING > VAUT
VAUTS > VAUT
VAV n sixth letter of the Hebrew alphabet
VAVASOR n (in feudal society) vassal who also has vassals himself
VAVASORS > VAVASOR
VAVASORY n lands held by a vavasor
VAVASOUR same as > VAVASOR
VAVASOURS > VAVASOUR
VAVASSOR same as > VAVASOR
VAVASSORS > VAVASSOR
VAVS > VAV
VAW n Hebrew letter
VAWARD n vanguard
VAWARDS > VAWARD
VAWNTIE > VAUNT
VAWNTIER > VAWNTIE
VAWNTIEST > VAWNTIE
VAWS > VAW
VAWTE same as > VAULT
VAWTED > VAWTE
VAWTES > VAWTE
VAWTING > VAWTE
VEAL n calf meat ▷ vb cover with a veil
VEALE same as > VEIL
VEALED > VEAL
VEALER n young bovine animal of up to 14 months old grown for veal
VEALERS > VEALER
VEALES > VEALE
VEALIER > VEAL
VEALIEST > VEAL
VEALING > VEAL
VEALS > VEAL

V

VEALY > VEAL

VECTOR n quantity that has size and direction, such as force ▷ vb direct or guide (a pilot) by directions transmitted by radio

VECTORED > VECTOR

VECTORIAL > VECTOR

VECTORING > VECTOR

VECTORISE same as > VECTORIZE

VECTORIZE vb computing term

VECTORS > VECTOR

VEDALIA n Australian ladybird which is a pest of citrus fruits

VEDALIAS > VEDALIA

VEDETTE n small patrol vessel

VEDETTES > VEDETTE

VEDUTA n painting of a town or city

VEDUTE > VEDUTA

VEDUTISTA n artist who creates vedutas

VEDUTISTI > VEDUTISTA

VEE n letter 'v'

VEEJAY n video jockey

VEEJAYS > VEEJAY

VEENA same as > VINA

VEENAS > VEENA

VEEP n vice president

VEEPEE n vice president

VEEPEES > VEEPEE

VEEPS > VEEP

VEER vb change direction suddenly ▷ n change of course or direction

VEERED > VEER

VEERIES > VEERY

VEERING > VEER

VEERINGLY > VEER

VEERINGS > VEER

VEERS > VEER

VEERY n tawny brown North American thrush

VEES > VEE

VEG n vegetable or vegetables ▷ vb relax

VEGA n tobacco plantation

VEGAN n person who eats no meat, fish, eggs, or dairy products ▷ adj suitable for a vegan

VEGANIC adj farmed without the use of animal products or byproducts

VEGANISM > VEGAN

VEGANISMS > VEGAN

VEGANS > VEGAN

VEGAS > VEGA

VEGELATE n type of chocolate

VEGELATES > VEGELATE

VEGEMITE n informal word for a child

VEGEMITES > VEGEMITE

VEGES > VEG

VEGETABLE n edible plant ▷ adj of or like plants or vegetables

VEGETABLY > VEGETABLE

VEGETAL adj of or relating to plant life ▷ n vegetable

VEGETALLY > VEGETAL

VEGETALS > VEGETAL

VEGETANT adj causing growth or vegetation-like

VEGETATE vb live a dull boring life with no mental stimulation

VEGETATED > VEGETATE

VEGETATES > VEGETATE

VEGETE adj lively

VEGETIST n vegetable cultivator or enthusiast

VEGETISTS > VEGETIST

VEGETIVE adj dull or passive ▷ n vegetable

VEGETIVES > VEGETIVE

VEGGED > VEG

VEGGES > VEG

VEGGIE n vegetable ▷ adj vegetarian

VEGGIES > VEGGIE

VEGGING > VEG

VEGIE variant of > VEGGIE

VEGIES > VEGIE

VEGO adj vegetarian ▷ n vegetarian

VEGOS > VEGO

VEHEMENCE > VEHEMENT

VEHEMENCY > VEHEMENT

VEHEMENT adj expressing strong feelings

VEHICLE n machine for carrying people or objects

VEHICLES > VEHICLE

VEHICULAR > VEHICLE

VEHM n type of medieval German court

VEHME > VEHM

VEHMIC > VEHM

VEHMIQUE > VEHM

VEIL n piece of thin cloth covering the head or face ▷ vb cover with or as if with a veil

VEILED adj disguised

VEILEDLY > VEILED

VEILER > VEIL

VEILERS > VEIL

VEILIER > VEIL

VEILIEST > VEIL

VEILING n veil or the fabric used for veils

VEILINGS > VEILING

VEILLESS > VEIL

VEILLEUSE n small night-light

VEILLIKE > VEIL

VEILS > VEIL

VEILY > VEIL

VEIN n tube that takes blood to the heart ▷ vb diffuse over or cause to diffuse over in streaked patterns

VEINAL > VEIN

VEINED > VEIN

VEINER n wood-carving tool

VEINERS > VEINER

VEINIER > VEIN

VEINIEST > VEIN

VEINING n pattern or network of veins or streaks

VEININGS > VEINING

VEINLESS > VEIN

VEINLET n any small vein or venule

VEINLETS > VEINLET

VEINLIKE > VEIN

VEINOUS > VEIN

VEINS > VEIN

VEINSTONE another word for > GANGUE

VEINSTUFF another word for > GANGUE

VEINULE less common spelling of > VENULE

VEINULES > VEINULE

VEINULET same as > VEINLET

VEINULETS > VEINULET

VEINY > VEIN

VELA > VELUM

VELAMEN n thick layer of dead cells that covers the aerial roots of certain orchids

VELAMINA > VELAMEN

VELAR adj of, relating to, or attached to a velum ▷ n velar sound

VELARIA > VELARIUM

VELARIC > VELAR

VELARISE same as > VELARIZE

VELARISED > VELARISE

VELARISES > VELARISE

VELARIUM n awning used to protect the audience in ancient Roman theatres and amphitheatres

VELARIZE vb pronounce or supplement the pronunciation of (a speech sound) with articulation at the soft palate

VELARIZED > VELARIZE

VELARIZES > VELARIZE

VELARS > VELAR

VELATE adj having or covered with velum

VELATED same as > VELATE

VELATURA n overglaze

VELATURAS > VELATURA

VELCRO n tradename for a fastening consisting of two strips of nylon fabric that are pressed together

VELCROS > VELCRO

VELD n high grassland in southern Africa

VELDS > VELD

VELDSKOEN n leather ankle boot

VELDT same as > VELD

VELDTS > VELDT

VELE same as > VEIL

VELES > VELE

VELETA same as > VALETA

VELETAS > VELETA

VELIGER n free-swimming larva of many molluscs

VELIGERS > VELIGER

VELITES pl n light-armed troops in ancient Rome, drawn from the poorer classes

VELL vb cut turf

VELLEITY n weakest level of desire or volition

VELLENAGE n (in Medieval Europe) status of being a villein

VELLET n velvet

VELLETS > VELLET

VELLICATE vb twitch, pluck, or pinch

VELLON n silver and copper alloy used in old Spanish coins

VELLONS > VELLON

VELLS > VELL

VELLUM n fine calfskin parchment ▷ adj made of or resembling vellum

VELLUMS > VELLUM

VELLUS n as in vellus hair short fine unpigmented hair covering the human body

VELOCE adv be played rapidly

VELOCITY n speed of movement in a given direction

VELODROME n arena with a banked track for cycle racing

VELOUR n fabric similar to velvet

VELOURS same as > VELOUR

VELOUTE n rich white sauce or soup made from stock, egg yolks, and cream

VELOUTES > VELOUTE

VELOUTINE n type of velvety fabric

VELSKOEN n type of shoe

VELSKOENS > VELSKOEN

VELUM n any of various membranous structures

VELURE n velvet or a similar fabric ▷ vb cover with velure

VELURED > VELURE

VELURES > VELURE

VELURING > VELURE

VELVERET n type of velvet-like fabric

VELVERETS > VELVERET

VELVET n fabric with a thick soft pile ▷ vb cover with velvet

VELVETED > VELVET

VELVETEEN n cotton velvet

VELVETIER > VELVET

VELVETING > VELVET

VELVETS > VELVET

VELVETY > VELVET

VENA n vein in the body

VENAE > VENA

VENAL adj easily bribed

VENALITY > VENAL

VENALLY > VENAL
VENATIC adj of, relating to, or used in hunting
VENATICAL same as > VENATIC
VENATION n arrangement of the veins in a leaf or in the wing of an insect
VENATIONS > VENATION
VENATOR n hunter
VENATORS > VENATOR
VEND vb sell
VENDABLE > VEND
VENDABLES > VEND
VENDACE n either of two small whitefish occurring in lakes in Scotland and NW England
VENDACES > VENDACE
VENDAGE n vintage
VENDAGES > VENDAGE
VENDANGE same as > VENDAGE
VENDANGES > VENDANGE
VENDED > VEND
VENDEE n person to whom something, esp real property, is sold
VENDEES > VENDEE
VENDER same as > VENDOR
VENDERS > VENDER
VENDETTA n long-lasting quarrel between people in which they attempt to harm each other
VENDETTAS > VENDETTA
VENDEUSE n female salesperson
VENDEUSES > VENDEUSE
VENDIBLE adj saleable or marketable ▷ n saleable object
VENDIBLES > VENDIBLE
VENDIBLY > VENDIBLE
VENDING > VEND
VENDINGS > VEND
VENDIS same as > VENDACE
VENDISES > VENDIS
VENDISS same as > VENDACE
VENDISSES > VENDIS
VENDITION > VEND
VENDOR n person who sells goods such as newspapers or hamburgers from a stall or cart
VENDORS > VENDOR
VENDS > VEND
VENDU n derogatory name for an anglified Quebecois
VENDUE n public sale
VENDUES > VENDUE
VENDUS > VENDU
VENEER n thin layer of wood etc covering a cheaper material ▷ vb cover (a surface) with a veneer
VENEERED > VENEER
VENEERER > VENEER
VENEERERS > VENEER

VENEERING n material used as veneer or a veneered surface
VENEERS > VENEER
VENEFIC adj having poisonous effects
VENEFICAL same as > VENEFIC
VENENATE vb poison
VENENATED > VENENATE
VENENATES > VENENATE
VENENE n medicine from snake venom
VENENES > VENENE
VENENOSE adj poisonous
VENERABLE adj worthy of deep respect
VENERABLY > VENERABLE
VENERATE vb hold (a person) in deep respect
VENERATED > VENERATE
VENERATES > VENERATE
VENERATOR > VENERATE
VENEREAL adj transmitted by sexual intercourse
VENEREAN n sex addict
VENEREANS > VENEREAN
VENEREOUS adj libidinous
VENERER n hunter
VENERERS > VENERER
VENERIES > VENERY
VENERY n pursuit of sexual gratification
VENETIAN n Venetian blind
VENETIANS > VENETIAN
VENEWE same as > VENUE
VENEWES > VENEWE
VENEY n thrust
VENEYS > VENEY
VENGE vb avenge
VENGEABLE > VENGE
VENGEABLY > VENGE
VENGEANCE n revenge
VENGED > VENGE
VENGEFUL adj wanting revenge
VENGEMENT > VENGE
VENGER > VENGE
VENGERS > VENGE
VENGES > VENGE
VENGING > VENGE
VENIAL adj (of a sin or fault) easily forgiven
VENIALITY > VENIAL
VENIALLY > VENIAL
VENIDIUM n genus of flowering plants
VENIDIUMS > VENIDIUM
VENIN n any of the poisonous constituents of animal venoms
VENINE same as > VENIN
VENINES > VENINE
VENINS > VENIN
VENIRE n list from which jurors are selected
VENIREMAN n person summoned for jury service
VENIREMEN > VENIREMAN

VENIRES > VENIRE
VENISON n deer meat
VENISONS > VENISON
VENITE n musical setting for the 95th psalm
VENITES > VENITE
VENNEL n lane
VENNELS > VENNEL
VENOGRAM n X-ray of a vein
VENOGRAMS > VENOGRAM
VENOLOGY n study of veins
VENOM n malice or spite ▷ vb poison
VENOMED > VENOM
VENOMER > VENOM
VENOMERS > VENOM
VENOMING > VENOM
VENOMLESS > VENOM
VENOMOUS > VENOM
VENOMS > VENOM
VENOSE adj having veins
VENOSITY n excessive quantity of blood in the venous system or in an organ or part
VENOUS adj of veins
VENOUSLY > VENOUS
VENT n outlet releasing fumes or fluid ▷ vb express (an emotion) freely
VENTAGE n small opening
VENTAGES > VENTAGE
VENTAIL n (in medieval armour) a covering for the lower part of the face
VENTAILE same as > VENTAIL
VENTAILES > VENTAILE
VENTAILS > VENTAIL
VENTANA n window
VENTANAS > VENTANA
VENTAYLE same as > VENTAIL
VENTAYLES > VENTAYLE
VENTED > VENT
VENTER > VENT
VENTERS > VENT
VENTIDUCT n air pipe
VENTIFACT n pebble that has been shaped by wind-blown sand
VENTIGE same as > VENTAGE
VENTIGES > VENTIGE
VENTIL n valve on a musical instrument
VENTILATE vb let fresh air into
VENTILS > VENTIL
VENTING > VENT
VENTINGS > VENT
VENTLESS > VENT
VENTOSE adj full of wind ▷ n apparatus sometimes used to assist the delivery of a baby
VENTOSES > VENTOSE
VENTOSITY n flatulence
VENTOUSE n apparatus sometimes used to assist the delivery of a baby
VENTOUSES > VENTOUSE

VENTRAL adj relating to the front of the body ▷ n ventral fin
VENTRALLY > VENTRAL
VENTRALS > VENTRAL
VENTRE same as > VENTURE
VENTRED > VENTRE
VENTRES > VENTRE
VENTRICLE n cavity in an organ such as the heart
VENTRING > VENTRE
VENTRINGS > VENTRE
VENTROUS > VENTRE
VENTS > VENT
VENTURE n risky undertaking, esp in business ▷ vb do something risky
VENTURED > VENTURE
VENTURER > VENTURE
VENTURERS > VENTURE
VENTURES > VENTURE
VENTURI n tube used to control the flow of fluid
VENTURING > VENTURE
VENTURIS > VENTURI
VENTUROUS adj adventurous
VENUE n place where an organized gathering is held
VENUES > VENUE
VENULAR > VENULE
VENULE n any of the small branches of a vein
VENULES > VENULE
VENULOSE > VENULE
VENULOUS > VENULE
VENUS n type of marine bivalve mollusc
VENUSES > VENUS
VENVILLE n type of parish tenure
VENVILLES > VENVILLE
VERA adj as in aloe vera plant substance used in skin and hair preparations
VERACIOUS adj habitually truthful
VERACITY n truthfulness
VERANDA n porch or portico along the outside of a building
VERANDAED > VERANDA
VERANDAH same as > VERANDA
VERANDAHS > VERANDAH
VERANDAS > VERANDA
VERAPAMIL n calcium-channel blocker used in the treatment of some types of irregular heart rhythm
VERATRIA same as > VERATRINE
VERATRIAS > VERATRIA
VERATRIN same as > VERATRINE
VERATRINE n white poisonous mixture obtained from the seeds of sabadilla
VERATRINS > VERATRIN

VERATRUM n genus of herbs
VERATRUMS > VERATRUM
VERB n word that expresses the idea of action, happening, or being
VERBAL adj spoken ▷ n abuse or invective ▷ vb implicate (someone) in a crime by quoting alleged admission of guilt in court
VERBALISE same as > VERBALIZE
VERBALISM n exaggerated emphasis on the importance of words
VERBALIST n person who deals with words alone, rather than facts, ideas, feeling, etc
VERBALITY > VERBAL
VERBALIZE vb express (something) in words
VERBALLED > VERBAL
VERBALLY > VERBAL
VERBALS > VERBAL
VERBARIAN n inventor of words
VERBASCUM See > MULLEIN
VERBATIM adj word for word ▷ adv using exactly the same words
VERBENA n plant with sweet-smelling flowers
VERBENAS > VERBENA
VERBERATE vb lash
VERBIAGE n excessive use of words
VERBIAGES > VERBIAGE
VERBICIDE n person who destroys a word
VERBID n any nonfinite form of a verb or any nonverbal word derived from a verb
VERBIDS > VERBID
VERBIFIED > VERBIFY
VERBIFIES > VERBIFY
VERBIFY another word for > VERBALIZE
VERBILE n person who is best stimulated by words
VERBILES > VERBILE
VERBING n use of nouns as verbs
VERBINGS > VERBING
VERBLESS > VERB
VERBOSE adj speaking at tedious length
VERBOSELY > VERBOSE
VERBOSER > VERBOSE
VERBOSEST > VERBOSE
VERBOSITY > VERBOSE
VERBOTEN adj forbidden
VERBS > VERB
VERD adj as in verd antique dark green mottled impure variety of serpentine marble
VERDANCY > VERDANT
VERDANT adj covered in green vegetation

VERDANTLY > VERDANT
VERDELHO n type of grape
VERDELHOS > VERDELHO
VERDERER n judicial officer responsible for the maintenance of law and order in the royal forests
VERDERERS > VERDERER
VERDEROR same as > VERDERER
VERDERORS > VERDEROR
VERDET n type of verdigris
VERDETS > VERDET
VERDICT n decision of a jury
VERDICTS > VERDICT
VERDIGRIS n green film on copper, brass, or bronze
VERDIN n small W North American tit having grey plumage with a yellow head
VERDINS > VERDIN
VERDIT same as > VERDICT
VERDITE n type of rock used in jewellery
VERDITER n blue-green pigment made from copper
VERDITERS > VERDITER
VERDITES > VERDITE
VERDITS > VERDIT
VERDOY n floral or leafy shield decoration
VERDOYS > VERDOY
VERDURE n flourishing green vegetation
VERDURED > VERDURE
VERDURES > VERDURE
VERDUROUS > VERDURE
VERECUND adj shy or modest
VERGE n grass border along a road ▷ vb move in a specified direction
VERGED > VERGE
VERGENCE n inward or outward turning movement of the eyes in convergence or divergence
VERGENCES > VERGENCE
VERGENCY adj inclination
VERGER n church caretaker
VERGERS > VERGER
VERGES > VERGE
VERGING > VERGE
VERGLAS n thin film of ice on rock
VERGLASES > VERGLAS
VERIDIC same as > VERIDICAL
VERIDICAL adj truthful
VERIER > VERY
VERIEST > VERY
VERIFIED > VERIFY
VERIFIER > VERIFY
VERIFIERS > VERIFY
VERIFIES > VERIFY
VERIFY vb check the truth or accuracy of
VERIFYING > VERIFY

VERILY adv in truth
VERISM n extreme naturalism in art or literature
VERISMO n school of composition that originated in Italian opera
VERISMOS > VERISMO
VERISMS > VERISM
VERIST > VERISM
VERISTIC > VERISM
VERISTS > VERISM
VERITABLE adj rightly called, without exaggeration
VERITABLY > VERITABLE
VERITAS n truth
VERITATES > VERITAS
VERITE adj involving a high degree of realism or naturalism ▷ n this kind of realism in film
VERITES > VERITE
VERITIES > VERITY
VERITY n true statement or principle
VERJUICE n acid juice of unripe grapes, apples, or crab apples ▷ vb make sour
VERJUICED > VERJUICE
VERJUICES > VERJUICE
VERJUS n acid juice of unripe grapes, apples, or crab apples
VERJUSES > VERJUS
VERKRAMP adj bigoted or illiberal
VERLAN n variety of French slang in which the syllables are inverted
VERLANS > VERLAN
VERLIG adj enlightened
VERLIGTE n (during apartheid) a White political liberal
VERLIGTES > VERLIGTE
VERMAL > VERMIS
VERMEIL n gilded silver, bronze, or other metal, used esp in the 19th century ▷ vb decorate with vermeil ▷ adj vermilion
VERMEILED > VERMEIL
VERMEILLE variant of > VERMEIL
VERMEILS > VERMEIL
VERMELL same as > VERMEIL
VERMELLS > VERMELL
VERMES > VERMIS
VERMIAN > VERMIS
VERMICIDE n any substance used to kill worms
VERMICULE n small worm
VERMIFORM adj shaped like a worm
VERMIFUGE n any drug or agent able to destroy or expel intestinal worms

VERMIL same as > VERMEIL
VERMILIES > VERMILY
VERMILION adj orange-red ▷ n mercuric sulphide, used as an orange-red pigment
VERMILLED > VERMIL
VERMILS > VERMIL
VERMILY > VERMEIL
VERMIN pl n animals, esp insects and rodents, that spread disease or cause damage
VERMINATE vb breed vermin
VERMINED adj plagued with vermin
VERMINOUS adj relating to, infested with, or suggestive of vermin
VERMINS > VERMIN
VERMINY > VERMIN
VERMIS n middle lobe connecting the two halves of the cerebellum
VERMOULU adj worm-eaten
VERMOUTH n wine flavoured with herbs
VERMOUTHS > VERMOUTH
VERMUTH same as > VERMOUTH
VERMUTHS > VERMUTH
VERNACLE same as > VERNICLE
VERNACLES > VERNACLE
VERNAL adj occurring in spring
VERNALISE same as > VERNALIZE
VERNALITY > VERNAL
VERNALIZE vb subject (ungerminated or germinating seeds) to low temperatures
VERNALLY > VERNAL
VERNANT > VERNAL
VERNATION n way in which leaves are arranged in the bud
VERNICLE n veronica
VERNICLES > VERNICLE
VERNIER n movable scale on a measuring instrument for taking readings in fractions
VERNIERS > VERNIER
VERNIX n white substance covering the skin of a foetus
VERNIXES > VERNIX
VERONAL n long-acting barbiturate used medicinally
VERONALS > VERONAL
VERONICA n plant with small blue, pink, or white flowers
VERONICAS > VERONICA
VERONIQUE adj (of a dish) garnished with seedless white grapes

V

VERQUERE n type of backgammon game
VERQUERES > VERQUERE
VERQUIRE variant of > VERQUERE
VERQUIRES > VERQUIRE
VERRA Scot word for > VERY
VERREL n ferrule
VERRELS > VERREL
VERREY same as > VAIR
VERRINE n starter, dessert, or other dish served in a glass
VERRINES > VERRINE
VERRUCA n wart, usu on the foot
VERRUCAE > VERRUCA
VERRUCAS > VERRUCA
VERRUCOSE adj covered with warts
VERRUCOUS same as > VERRUCOSE
VERRUGA same as > VERRUCA
VERRUGAS > VERRUGA
VERRY same as > VAIR
VERS n verse
VERSAL n embellished letter
VERSALS > VERSAL
VERSANT n side or slope of a mountain or mountain range
VERSANTS > VERSANT
VERSATILE adj having many skills or uses
VERSE n group of lines forming part of a song or poem ▷ vb write verse
VERSED adj thoroughly knowledgeable (about)
VERSELET n small verse
VERSELETS > VERSELET
VERSEMAN n man who writes verse
VERSEMEN > VERSEMAN
VERSER n versifier
VERSERS > VERSER
VERSES > VERSE
VERSET n short, often sacred, verse
VERSETS > VERSET
VERSICLE n short verse
VERSICLES > VERSICLE
VERSIFIED > VERSIFY
VERSIFIER > VERSIFY
VERSIFIES > VERSIFY
VERSIFORM adj changing in form
VERSIFY vb write in verse
VERSIN same as > VERSINE
VERSINE n mathematical term
VERSINES > VERSINE
VERSING > VERSE
VERSINGS > VERSE
VERSINS > VERSIN
VERSION n form of something, with some differences from other forms ▷ vb keep track of

the changes made to a computer file at different stages
VERSIONAL > VERSION
VERSIONED > VERSION
VERSIONER n translator
VERSIONS > VERSION
VERSO n left-hand page of a book
VERSOS > VERSO
VERST n unit of length used in Russia
VERSTE same as > VERST
VERSTES > VERSTE
VERSTS > VERST
VERSUS prep in opposition to or in contrast with
VERSUTE adj cunning
VERT n right to cut green wood in a forest ▷ vb turn
VERTEBRA n one of the bones that form the spine
VERTEBRAE > VERTEBRA
VERTEBRAL > VERTEBRA
VERTEBRAS > VERTEBRA
VERTED > VERT
VERTEX n point on a geometric figure where the sides form an angle
VERTEXES > VERTEX
VERTICAL adj straight up and down ▷ n vertical direction
VERTICALS > VERTICAL
VERTICES > VERTEX
VERTICIL n circular arrangement of parts about an axis, esp leaves around a stem
VERTICILS > VERTICIL
VERTICITY n ability to turn
VERTIGO n dizziness, usu when looking down from a high place
VERTIGOES > VERTIGO
VERTIGOS > VERTIGO
VERTING > VERT
VERTIPORT n type of airport
VERTISOL n type of clayey soil
VERTISOLS > VERTISOL
VERTS > VERT
VERTU same as > VIRTU
VERTUE same as > VIRTU
VERTUES > VERTUE
VERTUOUS > VERTU
VERTUS > VERTU
VERVAIN n plant with spikes of blue, purple, or white flowers
VERVAINS > VERVAIN
VERVE n enthusiasm or liveliness
VERVEL same as > VARVEL
VERVELLED > VERVEL
VERVELS > VERVEL
VERVEN same as > VERVAIN
VERVENS > VERVEN
VERVES > VERVE

VERVET n variety of a South African guenon monkey
VERVETS > VERVET
VERY adv more than usually, extremely ▷ adj absolute, exact
VESICA n bladder
VESICAE > VESICA
VESICAL adj of or relating to a vesica, esp the urinary bladder
VESICANT n any substance that causes blisters ▷ adj acting as a vesicant
VESICANTS > VESICANT
VESICAS > VESICA
VESICATE vb blister
VESICATED > VESICATE
VESICATES > VESICATE
VESICLE n sac or small cavity, esp one containing fluid
VESICLES > VESICLE
VESICULA n vesicle
VESICULAE > VESICULA
VESICULAR > VESICLE
VESPA n type of wasp
VESPAS > VESPA
VESPER n evening prayer, service, or hymn
VESPERAL n liturgical book containing the prayers, psalms, and hymns used at vespers
VESPERALS > VESPERAL
VESPERS pl n service of evening prayer
VESPIARY n nest or colony of social wasps or hornets
VESPID n insect of the family that includes the common wasp and hornet ▷ adj of or belonging to this family
VESPIDS > VESPID
VESPINE adj of, relating to, or resembling a wasp or wasps
VESPOID adj like a wasp
VESSAIL archaic variant of > VESSEL
VESSAILS > VESSAIL
VESSEL n container or ship ▷ adj contained in a vessel
VESSELED > VESSEL
VESSELS > VESSEL
VEST n undergarment worn on the top half of the body ▷ vb give (authority) to (someone)
VESTA n short friction match, usually of wood
VESTAL adj pure, chaste ▷ n chaste woman
VESTALLY > VESTAL
VESTALS > VESTAL
VESTAS > VESTA
VESTED adj having an existing right to the immediate or future

possession of property
VESTEE n person having a vested interest in something
VESTEES > VESTEE
VESTIARY n room for storing clothes or dressing in, such as a vestry ▷ adj of or relating to clothes
VESTIBULA > VESTIBULE
VESTIBULE n small entrance hall
VESTIGE n small amount or trace
VESTIGES > VESTIGE
VESTIGIA > VESTIGIUM
VESTIGIAL adj remaining after a larger or more important thing has gone
VESTIGIUM n trace
VESTMENT same as > VESTMENT
VESTING > VEST
VESTINGS > VEST
VESTITURE n investiture
VESTLESS > VEST
VESTLIKE > VEST
VESTMENT n garment or robe, esp one denoting office, authority, or rank
VESTMENTS > VESTMENT
VESTRAL > VESTRY
VESTRIES > VESTRY
VESTRY n room in a church used as an office by the priest or minister
VESTRYMAN n member of a church vestry
VESTRYMEN > VESTRYMAN
VESTS > VEST
VESTURAL > VESTURE
VESTURE n garment or something that seems like a garment ▷ vb clothe
VESTURED > VESTURE
VESTURER n person in charge of church vestments
VESTURERS > VESTURER
VESTURES > VESTURE
VESTURING > VESTURE
VESUVIAN n match for lighting cigars
VESUVIANS > VESUVIAN
VET vb check the suitability of ▷ n military veteran
VETCH n climbing plant with a beanlike fruit used as fodder
VETCHES > VETCH
VETCHIER > VETCHY
VETCHIEST > VETCHY
VETCHLING n type of climbing plant
VETCHY adj consisting of vetches
VETERAN n person with long experience in a particular activity ▷ adj long-serving
VETERANS > VETERAN

VETIVER n tall hairless grass of tropical and subtropical Asia
VETIVERS > VETIVER
VETIVERT n oil from the vetiver
VETIVERTS > VETIVERT
VETKOEK n South African cake
VETKOEKS > VETKOEK
VETO n official power to cancel a proposal ▷ vb enforce a veto against
VETOED > VETO
VETOER > VETO
VETOERS > VETO
VETOES > VETO
VETOING > VETO
VETOLESS > VETO
VETS > VET
VETTED > VET
VETTER > VET
VETTERS > VET
VETTING n as in *positive vetting* checking a person's background to assess their suitability of an important post
VETTINGS > VETTING
VETTURA n Italian mode of transport
VETTURAS > VETTURA
VETTURINI > VETTURINO
VETTURINO n person who drives a vettura
VEX vb frustrate, annoy
VEXATION n something annoying
VEXATIONS > VEXATION
VEXATIOUS adj vexing
VEXATORY > VEX
VEXED adj annoyed and puzzled
VEXEDLY > VEXED
VEXEDNESS > VEXED
VEXER > VEX
VEXERS > VEX
VEXES > VEX
VEXIL same as > VEXILLUM
VEXILLA > VEXILLUM
VEXILLAR > VEXILLUM
VEXILLARY > VEXILLUM
VEXILLATE > VEXILLUM
VEXILLUM n vane of a feather
VEXILS > VEXIL
VEXING > VEX
VEXINGLY > VEX
VEXINGS > VEX
VEXT same as > VEXED
VEZIR same as > VIZIER
VEZIRS > VEZIR
VIA prep by way of ▷ n road
VIABILITY > VIABLE
VIABLE adj able to be put into practice
VIABLY > VIABLE
VIADUCT n bridge over a valley
VIADUCTS > VIADUCT
VIAE > VIA

VIAL n small bottle for liquids ▷ vb put into a vial
VIALED > VIAL
VIALFUL > VIAL
VIALFULS > VIAL
VIALING > VIAL
VIALLED > VIAL
VIALLING > VIAL
VIALS > VIAL
VIAMETER n device to measure distance travelled
VIAMETERS > VIAMETER
VIAND n type of food, esp a delicacy
VIANDS > VIAND
VIAS > VIA
VIATIC same as > VIATICAL
VIATICA > VIATICUM
VIATICAL adj of or denoting a road or a journey ▷ n purchase of a terminal patient's life assurance policy so that he or she may make use of the proceeds
VIATICALS > VIATICAL
VIATICUM n Holy Communion given to a person who is dying or in danger of death
VIATICUMS > VIATICUM
VIATOR n traveller
VIATORES > VIATOR
VIATORIAL adj pertaining to travelling
VIATORS > VIATOR
VIBE n feeling or flavour of the kind specified
VIBES pl n vibrations
VIBEX n mark under the skin
VIBEY adj lively and vibrant
VIBICES > VIBEX
VIBIER > VIBEY
VIBIEST > VIBEY
VIBIST n person who plays a vibraphone in a jazz band or group
VIBISTS > VIBIST
VIBRACULA pl n bristle-like polyps in certain bryozoans
VIBRAHARP n type of percussion instrument
VIBRANCE n vibrancy
VIBRANCES > VIBRANCE
VIBRANCY > VIBRANT
VIBRANT adj vigorous in appearance, energetic ▷ n trilled or rolled speech sound
VIBRANTLY > VIBRANT
VIBRANTS > VIBRANT
VIBRATE vb move back and forth rapidly
VIBRATED > VIBRATE
VIBRATES > VIBRATE
VIBRATILE > VIBRATE
VIBRATING > VIBRATE
VIBRATION n vibrating
VIBRATIVE > VIBRATE

VIBRATO n rapid fluctuation in the pitch of a note
VIBRATOR n device that produces vibratory motion
VIBRATORS > VIBRATOR
VIBRATORY > VIBRATE
VIBRATOS > VIBRATO
VIBRIO n curved or spiral rodlike bacterium
VIBRIOID > VIBRIO
VIBRION same as > VIBRIO
VIBRIONIC > VIBRIO
VIBRIONS > VIBRION
VIBRIOS > VIBRIO
VIBRIOSES > VIBRIOSIS
VIBRIOSIS n bacterial disease
VIBRISSA n any of the bristle-like sensitive hairs on the face of many mammals
VIBRISSAE > VIBRISSA
VIBRISSAL > VIBRISSA
VIBRONIC adj of, concerned with, or involving both electronic and vibrational energy levels of a molecule
VIBS pl n type of climbing shoes
VIBURNUM n subtropical shrub with white flowers and berry-like fruits
VIBURNUMS > VIBURNUM
VICAR n member of the clergy in charge of a parish
VICARAGE n vicar's house
VICARAGES > VICARAGE
VICARATE same as > VICARIATE
VICARATES > VICARATE
VICARESS n rank of nun
VICARIAL adj of or relating to a vicar, vicars, or a vicariate
VICARIANT n any of several closely related species, etc, each of which exists in a separate geographical area
VICARIATE n office, rank, or authority of a vicar
VICARIES > VICARY
VICARIOUS adj felt indirectly by imagining what another person experiences
VICARLY > VICAR
VICARS > VICAR
VICARSHIP same as > VICARIATE
VICARY n office of a vicar
VICE n immoral or evil habit or action ▷ adj serving in place of ▷ vb grip (something) with or as if with a vice ▷ prep instead of
VICED > VICE

VICEGERAL adj of or relating to a person who deputizes for another
VICELESS > VICE
VICELIKE > VICE
VICENARY adj relating to or consisting of 20
VICENNIAL adj occurring every 20 years
VICEREGAL adj of a viceroy
VICEREINE n wife of a viceroy
VICEROY n governor of a colony who represents the monarch
VICEROYS > VICEROY
VICES > VICE
VICESIMAL same as > VIGESIMAL
VICHIES > VICHY
VICHY n French mineral water
VICIATE same as > VITIATE
VICIATED > VICIATE
VICIATES > VICIATE
VICIATING > VICIATE
VICINAGE n residents of a particular neighbourhood
VICINAGES > VICINAGE
VICINAL adj neighbouring
VICING > VICE
VICINITY n surrounding area
VICIOSITY same as > VITIOSITY
VICIOUS adj cruel and violent
VICIOUSLY > VICIOUS
VICOMTE n French nobleman
VICOMTES > VICOMTE
VICTIM n person or thing harmed or killed
VICTIMISE same as > VICTIMIZE
VICTIMIZE vb punish unfairly
VICTIMS > VICTIM
VICTOR n person who has defeated an opponent, esp in war or in sport
VICTORESS same as > VICTRESS
VICTORIA n large sweet plum, red and yellow in colour
VICTORIAS > VICTORIA
VICTORIES > VICTORY
VICTORINE n woman's article of clothing
VICTORS > VICTOR
VICTORY n winning of a battle or contest
VICTRESS n female victor
VICTRIX same as > VICTRESS
VICTRIXES > VICTRIX
VICTROLA n gramophone
VICTROLAS > VICTROLA
VICTUAL vb supply with or obtain victuals

V

VICTUALED > VICTUAL
VICTUALER > VICTUAL
VICTUALS pl n food and drink
VICUGNA same as > VICUNA
VICUGNAS > VICUGNA
VICUNA n S American animal like the llama
VICUNAS > VICUNA
VID same as > VIDEO
VIDALIA n type of sweet onion
VIDALIAS > VIDALIA
VIDAME n French nobleman
VIDAMES > VIDAME
VIDE interj look
VIDELICET adv namely: used to specify items
VIDENDA > VIDENDUM
VIDENDUM n that which is to be seen
VIDEO vb record (a TV programme or event) on video ▷ adj relating to or used in producing television images ▷ n recording and showing of films and events
VIDEOCAM n camera for shooting video footage
VIDEOCAMS > VIDEOCAM
VIDEODISC variant of > VIDEODISK
VIDEODISK n disk on which information is stored in digital form
VIDEOED > VIDEO
VIDEOFIT n computer-generated picture of a person sought by the police
VIDEOFITS > VIDEOFIT
VIDEOGRAM n audiovisual recording
VIDEOING > VIDEO
VIDEOLAND n world of television and televised images
VIDEOS > VIDEO
VIDEOTAPE vb record (a TV programme) on video tape
VIDEOTEX n information system that displays data from a distant computer on a screen
VIDEOTEXT n means of representing on a TV screen information that is held in a computer
VIDETTE same as > VEDETTE
VIDETTES > VIDETTE
VIDICON n small television camera tube used in closed-circuit television
VIDICONS > VIDICON
VIDIMUS n inspection
VIDIMUSES > VIDIMUS

VIDIOT n person who watches a lot of low-quality television
VIDIOTS > VIDIOT
VIDS > VID
VIDUAGE n widows collectively
VIDUAGES > VIDUAGE
VIDUAL adj widowed
VIDUITIES > VIDUITY
VIDUITY n widowhood
VIDUOUS adj empty
VIE vb compete (with someone)
VIED > VIE
VIELLE n stringed musical instrument
VIELLES > VIELLE
VIENNA n as in vienna loaf, vienna steak associated with Vienna
VIER > VIE
VIERS > VIE
VIES > VIE
VIEW n opinion or belief ▷ vb think of (something) in a particular way
VIEWABLE > VIEW
VIEWBOOK n promotional booklet for a college or university
VIEWBOOKS > VIEWBOOK
VIEWDATA n interactive form of videotext
VIEWDATAS > VIEWDATA
VIEWED > VIEW
VIEWER n person who watches television
VIEWERS > VIEWER
VIEWIER > VIEWY
VIEWIEST > VIEWY
VIEWINESS > VIEWY
VIEWING n act of watching television
VIEWINGS > VIEWING
VIEWLESS adj (of windows, etc) not affording a view
VIEWLY adj pleasant on the eye
VIEWPHONE n videophone
VIEWPOINT n person's attitude towards something
VIEWPORT n viewable area on a computer display
VIEWPORTS > VIEWPORT
VIEWS > VIEW
VIEWSHED n natural environment visible from a specific point
VIEWSHEDS > VIEWSHED
VIEWY adj having fanciful opinions or ideas
VIFDA same as > VIVDA
VIFDAS > VIFDA
VIFF vb (of an aircraft) change direction abruptly
VIFFED > VIFF
VIFFING > VIFF
VIFFS > VIFF

VIG n interest on a loan that is paid to a moneylender
VIGA n rafter
VIGAS > VIGA
VIGESIMAL adj relating to or based on the number 20
VIGIA n navigational hazard whose existence has not been confirmed
VIGIAS > VIGIA
VIGIL n night-time period of staying awake to look after a sick person, pray, etc
VIGILANCE n careful attention
VIGILANT adj watchful in case of danger
VIGILANTE n person who takes it upon himself or herself to enforce the law
VIGILS > VIGIL
VIGNERON n person who grows grapes for winemaking
VIGNERONS > VIGNERON
VIGNETTE n small illustration placed at the beginning or end of a chapter or book ▷ vb portray in a vignette
VIGNETTED > VIGNETTE
VIGNETTER n device used in printing vignettes
VIGNETTES > VIGNETTE
VIGOR same as > VIGOUR
VIGORISH n type of commission
VIGORO n women's game similar to cricket
VIGOROS > VIGORO
VIGOROSO adv in music, emphatically
VIGOROUS adj having physical or mental energy
VIGORS > VIGOR
VIGOUR n physical or mental energy
VIGOURS > VIGOUR
VIGS > VIG
VIHARA n type of Buddhist temple
VIHARAS > VIHARA
VIHUELA n obsolete plucked stringed instrument of Spain
VIHUELAS > VIHUELA
VIKING n Dane, Norwegian, or Swede who raided by sea between the 8th and 11th centuries
VIKINGISM > VIKING
VIKINGS > VIKING
VILAYET n major administrative division of Turkey
VILAYETS > VILAYET
VILD same as > VILE
VILDE same as > VILE
VILDLY > VILD
VILDNESS > VILD
VILE adj very wicked

VILELY > VILE
VILENESS > VILE
VILER > VILE
VILEST > VILE
VILIACO n scoundrel
VILIACOES > VILIACO
VILIACOS > VILIACO
VILIAGO same as > VILIACO
VILIAGOES > VILIAGO
VILIAGOS > VILIAGO
VILIFIED > VILIFY
VILIFIER > VILIFY
VILIFIERS > VILIFY
VILIFIES > VILIFY
VILIFY vb attack the character of
VILIFYING > VILIFY
VILIPEND vb treat or regard with contempt
VILIPENDS > VILIPEND
VILL n township
VILLA n large house with gardens
VILLADOM > VILLA
VILLADOMS > VILLA
VILLAE > VILLA
VILLAGE n small group of houses in a country area
VILLAGER n inhabitant of a village ▷ adj backward, unsophisticated, or illiterate
VILLAGERS > VILLAGER
VILLAGERY n villages
VILLAGES > VILLAGE
VILLAGEY adj of or like a village
VILLAGIO same as > VILIACO
VILLAGIOS > VILLAGIO
VILLAGREE variant of > VILLAGERY
VILLAIN n wicked person
VILLAINS > VILLAIN
VILLAINY n evil or vicious behaviour
VILLAN same as > VILLEIN
VILLANAGE > VILLAN
VILLANIES > VILLANY
VILLANOUS > VILLAIN
VILLANS > VILLAN
VILLANY same as > VILLAINY
VILLAR > VILL
VILLAS > VILLA
VILLATIC adj of or relating to a villa, village, or farm
VILLEIN n peasant bound in service to his lord
VILLEINS > VILLEIN
VILLENAGE n villein's status
VILLI > VILLUS
VILLIACO n coward
VILLIACOS > VILLIACO
VILLIAGO same as > VILIACO
VILLIAGOS > VILLIAGO

VILLIFORM adj having the form of a villus or a series of villi

VILLOSE same as > VILLOUS

VILLOSITY n state of being villous

VILLOUS adj (of plant parts) covered with long hairs

VILLOUSLY > VILLOUS

VILLS > VILL

VILLUS n one of the finger-like projections in the small intestine of many vertebrates

VIM n force, energy

VIMANA n Indian mythological chariot of the gods

VIMANAS > VIMANA

VIMEN n long flexible shoot that occurs in certain plants

VIMINA > VIMEN

VIMINAL > VIMEN

VIMINEOUS adj having, producing, or resembling long flexible shoots

VIMS > VIM

VIN n French wine

VINA n stringed musical instrument related to the sitar

VINACEOUS adj of, relating to, or containing wine

VINAL n type of manmade fibre

VINALS > VINAL

VINAS > VINA

VINASSE n residue left in a still after distilling spirits, esp brandy

VINASSES > VINASSE

VINCA n type of trailing plant with blue flowers

VINCAS > VINCA

VINCIBLE adj capable of being defeated or overcome

VINCIBLY > VINCIBLE

VINCULA > VINCULUM

VINCULAR adj of or like a vinculum

VINCULUM n horizontal line drawn above a group of mathematical terms

VINCULUMS > VINCULUM

VINDALOO n type of very hot Indian curry

VINDALOOS > VINDALOO

VINDEMIAL adj relating to a grape harvest

VINDICATE vb clear (someone) of guilt

VINE n climbing plant, esp one producing grapes ▷ vb form like a vine

VINEAL adj relating to wines

VINED > VINE

VINEGAR n acid liquid made from wine, beer, or cider ▷ vb apply vinegar to

VINEGARED > VINEGAR

VINEGARS > VINEGAR

VINEGARY adj containing vinegar

VINELESS > VINE

VINELIKE > VINE

VINER n vinedresser

VINERIES > VINERY

VINERS > VINER

VINERY n hothouse for growing grapes

VINES > VINE

VINEW vb become mouldy

VINEWED > VINEW

VINEWING > VINEW

VINEWS > VINEW

VINEYARD n plantation of grape vines, esp for making wine

VINEYARDS > VINEYARD

VINIC adj of, relating to, or contained in wine

VINIER > VINE

VINIEST > VINE

VINIFERA n species of vine

VINIFERAS > VINIFERA

VINIFIED > VINIFY

VINIFIES > VINIFY

VINIFY vb convert into wine

VINIFYING > VINIFY

VINING > VINE

VINO n wine

VINOLENT adj drunken

VINOLOGY n scientific study of vines

VINOS > VINO

VINOSITY n distinctive and essential quality and flavour of wine

VINOUS adj of or characteristic of wine

VINOUSLY > VINOUS

VINS > VIN

VINT vb sell (wine)

VINTAGE n wine from a particular harvest of grapes ▷ adj best and most typical ▷ vb gather (grapes) or make (wine)

VINTAGED > VINTAGE

VINTAGER n grape harvester

VINTAGERS > VINTAGER

VINTAGES > VINTAGE

VINTAGING > VINTAGE

VINTED > VINT

VINTING > VINT

VINTNER n dealer in wine

VINTNERS > VINTNER

VINTRIES > VINTRY

VINTRY n place where wine is sold

VINTS > VINT

VINY > VINE

VINYL n type of plastic, used in mock leather and records ▷ adj of or containing a particular group of atoms

VINYLIC > VINYL

VINYLS > VINYL

VIOL n early stringed instrument preceding the violin

VIOLA n stringed instrument lower in pitch than a violin

VIOLABLE > VIOLATE

VIOLABLY > VIOLATE

VIOLAS > VIOLA

VIOLATE vb break (a law or agreement) ▷ adj violated or dishonoured

VIOLATED > VIOLATE

VIOLATER > VIOLATE

VIOLATERS > VIOLATE

VIOLATES > VIOLATE

VIOLATING > VIOLATE

VIOLATION > VIOLATE

VIOLATIVE > VIOLATE

VIOLATOR > VIOLATE

VIOLATORS > VIOLATE

VIOLD archaic or poetic past form of > VIAL

VIOLENCE n use of physical force, usu intended to cause injury or destruction

VIOLENCES > VIOLENCE

VIOLENT adj using physical force with the intention of causing injury ▷ vb coerce

VIOLENTED > VIOLENT

VIOLENTLY > VIOLENT

VIOLENTS > VIOLENT

VIOLER n person who plays the viol

VIOLERS > VIOLER

VIOLET n plant with bluish-purple flowers ▷ adj bluish-purple

VIOLETS > VIOLET

VIOLIN n small four-stringed musical instrument played with a bow

VIOLINIST n person who plays the violin

VIOLINS > VIOLIN

VIOLIST n person who plays the viola

VIOLISTS > VIOLIST

VIOLONE n double-bass member of the viol family

VIOLONES > VIOLONE

VIOLS > VIOL

VIOMYCIN n type of antibiotic

VIOMYCINS > VIOMYCIN

VIOSTEROL n type of vitamin

VIPER n poisonous snake

VIPERFISH n predatory deep-sea fish

VIPERINE same as > VIPEROUS

VIPERISH same as > VIPEROUS

VIPEROUS adj of, relating to, or resembling a viper

VIPERS > VIPER

VIRAEMIA n condition in which virus particles circulate and reproduce in the bloodstream

VIRAEMIAS > VIRAEMIA

VIRAEMIC > VIRAEMIA

VIRAGO n aggressive woman

VIRAGOES > VIRAGO

VIRAGOISH > VIRAGO

VIRAGOS > VIRAGO

VIRAL adj of or caused by a virus ▷ n video, image, etc that spreads quickly on the internet

VIRALITY n the state of being viral

VIRALLY > VIRAL

VIRALS > VIRAL

VIRANDA same as > VERANDA

VIRANDAS > VIRANDA

VIRANDO same as > VERANDA

VIRANDOS > VIRANDO

VIRE vb turn

VIRED > VIRE

VIRELAI same as > VIRELAY

VIRELAIS > VIRELAI

VIRELAY n old French verse form

VIRELAYS > VIRELAY

VIREMENT n administrative transfer of funds from one part of a budget to another

VIREMENTS > VIREMENT

VIREMIA same as > VIRAEMIA

VIREMIAS > VIREMIA

VIREMIC > VIREMIA

VIRENT adj green

VIREO n American songbird

VIREONINE > VIREO

VIREOS > VIREO

VIRES > VIRE

VIRESCENT adj greenish or becoming green

VIRETOT n as in on the viretot in a rush

VIRETOTS > VIRETOT

VIRGA n wisps of rain or snow that evaporate before reaching the earth

VIRGAE > VIRGA

VIRGAS > VIRGA

VIRGATE adj long, straight, and thin ▷ n obsolete measure of land area

VIRGATES > VIRGATE

VIRGE n rod

VIRGER n rod-bearer

VIRGERS > VIRGER

VIRGES > VIRGE

VIRGIN n person, esp a woman, who has not had sexual intercourse ▷ adj not having had sexual intercourse ▷ vb behave like a virgin

VIRGINAL adj like a virgin ▷ n early keyboard

instrument like a small harpsichord

VIRGINALS > VIRGINAL

VIRGINED > VIRGIN

VIRGINIA n type of flue-cured tobacco grown originally in Virginia

VIRGINIAS > VIRGINIA

VIRGINING > VIRGIN

VIRGINITY n condition or fact of being a virgin

VIRGINIUM former name for > FRANCIUM

VIRGINLY > VIRGIN

VIRGINS > VIRGIN

VIRGULATE adj rod-shaped or rodlike

VIRGULE another name for > SLASH

VIRGULES > VIRGULE

VIRICIDAL > VIRICIDE

VIRICIDE n substance that destroys viruses

VIRICIDES > VIRICIDE

VIRID adj verdant

VIRIDIAN n green pigment consisting of a hydrated form of chromic oxide

VIRIDIANS > VIRIDIAN

VIRIDITE n greenish mineral

VIRIDITES > VIRIDITE

VIRIDITY n quality or state of being green

VIRILE adj having the traditional male characteristics of physical strength and a high sex drive

VIRILELY > VIRILE

VIRILISE same as > VIRILIZE

VIRILISED > VIRILISE

VIRILISES > VIRILISE

VIRILISM n abnormal development in a woman of male secondary sex characteristics

VIRILISMS > VIRILISM

VIRILITY > VIRILE

VIRILIZE vb cause male characteristics to appear in female

VIRILIZED > VIRILIZE

VIRILIZES > VIRILIZE

VIRILOCAL adj living with husband's family

VIRING > VIRE

VIRINO n entity postulated to be the causative agent of BSE

VIRINOS > VIRINO

VIRION n virus in infective form, consisting of an RNA particle within a protein covering

VIRIONS > VIRION

VIRL same as > FERRULE

VIRLS > VIRL

VIROGENE n type of viral gene

VIROGENES > VIROGENE

VIROID n any of various infective RNA particles

VIROIDS > VIROID

VIROLOGIC > VIROLOGY

VIROLOGY n study of viruses

VIROSE adj poisonous

VIROSES > VIROSIS

VIROSIS n viral disease

VIROUS same as > VIROSE

VIRTU n taste or love for curios or works of fine art

VIRTUAL adj having the effect but not the form of

VIRTUALLY adv practically, almost

VIRTUE n moral goodness

VIRTUES > VIRTUE

VIRTUOSA n female virtuoso

VIRTUOSAS > VIRTUOSA

VIRTUOSE > VIRTUOSA

VIRTUOSI > VIRTUOSO

VIRTUOSIC > VIRTUOSO

VIRTUOSO n person with impressive esp musical skill ▷ adj showing exceptional skill or brilliance

VIRTUOSOS > VIRTUOSO

VIRTUOUS adj morally good

VIRTUS > VIRTU

VIRUCIDAL > VIRUCIDE

VIRUCIDE same as > VIRICIDE

VIRUCIDES > VIRUCIDE

VIRULENCE n quality of being virulent

VIRULENCY same as > VIRULENCE

VIRULENT adj extremely bitter or hostile

VIRUS n microorganism that causes disease in humans, animals, and plants

VIRUSES > VIRUS

VIRUSLIKE > VIRUS

VIRUSOID n small plant virus

VIRUSOIDS > VIRUSOID

VIS n power, force, or strength

VISA n permission to enter a country, shown by a stamp on the passport ▷ vb enter a visa into (a passport)

VISAED > VISA

VISAGE n face

VISAGED > VISAGE

VISAGES > VISAGE

VISAGIST same as > VISAGISTE

VISAGISTE n person who designs and applies face make-up

VISAGISTS > VISAGIST

VISAING > VISA

VISARD same as > VIZARD

VISARDS > VISARD

VISAS > VISA

VISCACHA n South American rodent

VISCACHAS > VISCACHA

VISCARIA n type of perennial plant

VISCARIAS > VISCARIA

VISCERA pl n large abdominal organs

VISCERAL adj instinctive

VISCERATE vb disembowel

VISCID adj sticky

VISCIDITY > VISCID

VISCIDLY > VISCID

VISCIN n sticky substance found on plants

VISCINS > VISCIN

VISCOID adj (of a fluid) somewhat viscous

VISCOIDAL same as > VISCOID

VISCOSE same as > VISCOUS

VISCOSES > VISCOSE

VISCOSITY n state of being viscous

VISCOUNT n British nobleman ranking between an earl and a baron

VISCOUNTS > VISCOUNT

VISCOUNTY > VISCOUNT

VISCOUS adj thick and sticky

VISCOUSLY > VISCOUS

VISCUM n shrub genus

VISCUMS > VISCUM

VISCUS n internal organ

VISE vb advise or award a visa to ▷ n (in US English) vice

VISED > VISE

VISEED > VISE

VISEING > VISE

VISELIKE > VICE

VISES > VISE

VISHING n telephone scam used to gain access to credit card numbers or bank details

VISHINGS > VISHING

VISIBLE adj able to be seen ▷ n visible item of trade

VISIBLES > VISIBLE

VISIBLY > VISIBLE

VISIE same as > VIZY

VISIED > VISIE

VISIEING > VISIE

VISIER > VISIE

VISIERS > VISIE

VISIES > VISIE

VISILE n person best stimulated by vision

VISILES > VISILE

VISING > VISE

VISION n ability to see ▷ vb see or show in or as if in a vision

VISIONAL adj of, relating to, or seen in a vision, apparition, etc

VISIONARY adj showing foresight ▷ n visionary person

VISIONED > VISION

VISIONER n visionary

VISIONERS > VISIONER

VISIONING > VISION

VISIONIST n type of visionary

VISIONS > VISION

VISIT vb go or come to see ▷ n instance of visiting

VISITABLE > VISIT

VISITANT n ghost or apparition ▷ adj paying a visit

VISITANTS > VISITANT

VISITATOR n official visitor

VISITE n type of cape

VISITED > VISIT

VISITEE n person who is visited

VISITEES > VISITEE

VISITER variant of > VISITOR

VISITERS > VISITER

VISITES > VISITE

VISITING > VISIT

VISITINGS > VISIT

VISITOR n person who visits a person or place

VISITORS > VISITOR

VISITRESS n female visitor

VISITS > VISIT

VISIVE adj visual

VISNE n neighbourhood

VISNES > VISNE

VISNOMIE same as > VISNOMY

VISNOMIES > VISNOMY

VISNOMY n method of judging character from facial features

VISON n type of mink

VISONS > VISON

VISOR n transparent part of a helmet that pulls down over the face ▷ vb cover, provide, or protect with a visor

VISORED > VISOR

VISORING > VISOR

VISORLESS > VISOR

VISORS > VISOR

VISTA n (beautiful) extensive view ▷ vb make into vistas

VISTAED > VISTA

VISTAING > VISTA

VISTAL > VISTA

VISTALESS > VISTA

VISTAS > VISTA

VISTO same as > VISTA

VISTOS > VISTO

VISUAL adj done by or used in seeing ▷ n sketch to show the proposed layout of an advertisement

VISUALISE same as > VISUALIZE

VISUALIST n visualiser

VISUALITY > VISUAL

VISUALIZE vb form a mental image of
VISUALLY > VISUAL
VISUALS > VISUAL
VITA n curriculum vitae
VITACEOUS adj of a family of flowering plants that includes the grapevine
VITAE > VITA
VITAL adj essential or highly important ▷ n bodily organs that are necessary to maintain life
VITALISE same as > VITALIZE
VITALISED > VITALISE
VITALISER > VITALISE
VITALISES > VITALISE
VITALISM n philosophical doctrine that the phenomena of life cannot be explained in purely mechanical terms
VITALISMS > VITALISM
VITALIST > VITALISM
VITALISTS > VITALISM
VITALITY n physical or mental energy
VITALIZE vb fill with life or vitality
VITALIZED > VITALIZE
VITALIZER > VITALIZE
VITALIZES > VITALIZE
VITALLY > VITAL
VITALNESS > VITAL
VITALS > VITAL
VITAMER n type of chemical
VITAMERS > VITAMER
VITAMIN n one of a group of substances that are essential in the diet
VITAMINE same as > VITAMIN
VITAMINES > VITAMINE
VITAMINIC > VITAMIN
VITAMINS > VITAMIN
VITAS > VITA
VITASCOPE n early type of film projector
VITATIVE adj fond of life
VITE adv musical direction
VITELLARY n location within an egg where the yolk is formed
VITELLI > VITELLUS
VITELLIN n phosphoprotein that is the major protein in egg yolk
VITELLINE adj of or relating to the yolk of an egg
VITELLINS > VITELLIN
VITELLUS n yolk of an egg
VITESSE n speed
VITESSES > VITESSE
VITEX n type of herb
VITEXES > VITEX
VITIABLE > VITIATE
VITIATE vb spoil the effectiveness of

VITIATED > VITIATE
VITIATES > VITIATE
VITIATING > VITIATE
VITIATION > VITIATE
VITIATOR > VITIATE
VITIATORS > VITIATE
VITICETA > VITICETUM
VITICETUM n place where vines are cultivated
VITICIDE n vine killer
VITICIDES > VITICIDE
VITILIGO n area of skin that is white from albinism or loss of melanin pigmentation
VITILIGOS > VITILIGO
VITIOSITY n viciousness
VITIOUS adj mistaken
VITRAGE n light fabric
VITRAGES > VITRAGE
VITRAIL n stained glass
VITRAIN n type of coal
VITRAINS > VITRAIN
VITRAUX > VITRAIL
VITREOUS adj like or made from glass
VITREUM n vitreous body
VITREUMS > VITREUM
VITRIC adj of, relating to, resembling, or having the nature of glass
VITRICS n glassware
VITRIFIED > VITRIFY
VITRIFIES > VITRIFY
VITRIFORM adj having the form or appearance of glass
VITRIFY vb change or be changed into glass or a glassy substance
VITRINE n glass display case or cabinet for works of art, curios, etc
VITRINES > VITRINE
VITRIOL n language expressing bitterness and hatred ▷ vb attack or injure with or as if with vitriol
VITRIOLED > VITRIOL
VITRIOLIC adj (of language) severely bitter or harsh
VITRIOLS > VITRIOL
VITTA n tubelike cavity containing oil that occurs in the fruits of certain plants
VITTAE > VITTA
VITTATE > VITTA
VITTLE obsolete or dialect spelling of > VICTUAL
VITTLED > VITTLE
VITTLES obsolete or dialect spelling of > VICTUALS
VITTLING > VITTLE
VITULAR same as > VITULINE
VITULINE adj of or resembling a calf or veal
VIVA interj long live (a person or thing) ▷ n examination in the form of an interview ▷ vb examine

(a candidate) in a spoken interview
VIVACE adj, adv (to be performed) in a lively manner ▷ n piece of music to be performed in this way
VIVACES > VIVACE
VIVACIOUS adj full of energy and enthusiasm
VIVACITY n quality of being vivacious
VIVAED > VIVA
VIVAING > VIVA
VIVAMENTE adv in a lively manner
VIVANDIER n sutler
VIVARIA > VIVARIUM
VIVARIES > VIVARY
VIVARIUM n place where animals are kept in natural conditions
VIVARIUMS > VIVARIUM
VIVARY same as > VIVARIUM
VIVAS > VIVA
VIVAT interj long live ▷ n expression of acclamation
VIVATS > VIVAT
VIVDA n method of drying meat
VIVDAS > VIVDA
VIVE interj long live
VIVELY adv in a lively manner
VIVENCIES > VIVENCY
VIVENCY n physical or mental energy
VIVER n fish pond
VIVERRA n civet genus
VIVERRAS > VIVERRA
VIVERRID > VIVERRINE
VIVERRIDS > VIVERRINE
VIVERRINE n type of mammal of Eurasia and Africa ▷ adj of this family of mammals
VIVERS > VIVER
VIVES n disease found in horses
VIVIANITE n type of mineral
VIVID adj very bright
VIVIDER > VIVID
VIVIDEST > VIVID
VIVIDITY > VIVID
VIVIDLY > VIVID
VIVIDNESS > VIVID
VIVIFIC adj giving life
VIVIFIED > VIVIFY
VIVIFIER > VIVIFY
VIVIFIERS > VIVIFY
VIVIFIES > VIVIFY
VIVIFY vb animate, inspire
VIVIFYING > VIVIFY
VIVIPARA n animals that produce offspring that develop as embryos within the female parent
VIVIPARY n act of giving birth producing offspring

that have developed as embryos
VIVISECT vb subject (an animal) to vivisection
VIVISECTS > VIVISECT
VIVO adv with life and vigour
VIVRES n provisions
VIXEN n female fox
VIXENISH > VIXEN
VIXENLY > VIXEN
VIXENS > VIXEN
VIZAMENT n consultation
VIZAMENTS > VIZAMENT
VIZARD n means of disguise ▷ vb conceal by means of a disguise
VIZARDED > VIZARD
VIZARDING > VIZARD
VIZARDS > VIZARD
VIZCACHA same as > VISCACHA
VIZCACHAS > VIZCACHA
VIZIED > VIZY
VIZIER n high official in certain Muslim countries
VIZIERATE n position, rank, or authority of a vizier
VIZIERIAL > VIZIER
VIZIERS > VIZIER
VIZIES > VIZY
VIZIR same as > VIZIER
VIZIRATE > VIZIR
VIZIRATES > VIZIR
VIZIRIAL > VIZIR
VIZIRS > VIZIR
VIZIRSHIP > VIZIR
VIZOR same as > VISOR
VIZORED > VIZOR
VIZORING > VIZOR
VIZORLESS > VIZOR
VIZORS > VIZOR
VIZSLA n breed of Hungarian hunting dog
VIZSLAS > VIZSLA
VIZY vb look
VIZYING > VIZY
VIZZIE same as > VIZY
VIZZIED > VIZZIE
VIZZIEING > VIZZIE
VIZZIES > VIZZIE
VLEI n area of low marshy ground
VLEIS > VLEI
VLIES > VLY
VLOG n video weblog ▷ vb make and upload a vlog
VLOGGED > VLOG
VLOGGER n person who keeps a video blog
VLOGGERS > VLOGGER
VLOGGING n action of keeping a video blog
VLOGGINGS > VLOGGING
VLOGS > VLOG
VLY same as > VLEI
VOAR n spring
VOARS > VOAR
VOCAB n vocabulary
VOCABLE n word regarded simply as a sequence of letters or spoken sounds

▷ *adj* capable of being uttered

VOCABLES > VOCABLE
VOCABLY > VOCABLE
VOCABS > VOCAB
VOCABULAR > VOCABLE
VOCAL *adj* relating to the voice ▷ *n* piece of jazz or pop music that is sung
VOCALESE *n* style of jazz singing
VOCALESES > VOCALESE
VOCALIC *adj* of, relating to, or containing a vowel or vowels
VOCALICS *n* non-verbal aspects of voice
VOCALION *n* type of musical instrument
VOCALIONS > VOCALION
VOCALISE *same as* > VOCALIZE
VOCALISED > VOCALISE
VOCALISER > VOCALISE
VOCALISES > VOCALISE
VOCALISM *n* exercise of the voice, as in singing or speaking
VOCALISMS > VOCALISM
VOCALIST *n* singer
VOCALISTS > VOCALIST
VOCALITY > VOCAL
VOCALIZE *vb* express with the voice
VOCALIZED > VOCALIZE
VOCALIZER > VOCALIZE
VOCALIZES > VOCALIZE
VOCALLY > VOCAL
VOCALNESS > VOCAL
VOCALS > VOCAL
VOCATION *n* profession or trade
VOCATIONS > VOCATION
VOCATIVE *n* (in some languages) case of nouns used when addressing a person ▷ *adj* relating to, used in, or characterized by calling
VOCATIVES > VOCATIVE
VOCES > VOX
VOCODER *n* type of synthesizer that uses the human voice as an oscillator
VOCODERS > VOCODER
VOCULAR > VOCULE
VOCULE *n* faint noise made when articulating certain sounds
VOCULES > VOCULE
VODCAST *vb* podcast with video
VODCASTED > VODCAST
VODCASTER > VODCAST
VODCASTS > VODCAST
VODDIES > VODDY
VODDY *n* vodka
VODKA *n* (Russian) spirit distilled from potatoes or grain
VODKAS > VODKA
VODOU *variant of* > VOODOO
VODOUN *same as* > VODUN

VODOUNS > VODOUN
VODOUS > VODOU
VODUN *n* voodoo
VODUNS > VODUN
VOE *n* (in Orkney and Shetland) a small bay or narrow creek
VOEMA *n* vigour or energy
VOEMAS > VOEMA
VOERTSAK *variant of* > VOETSEK
VOERTSEK *variant of* > VOETSEK
VOES > VOE
VOETSAK *same as* > VOETSEK
VOETSEK *interj* S African offensive expression of rejection
VOG *n* air pollution caused by volcanic dust
VOGIE *adj* conceited
VOGIER > VOGIE
VOGIEST > VOGIE
VOGS > VOG
VOGUE *n* popular style ▷ *adj* popular or fashionable ▷ *vb* bring into vogue
VOGUED > VOGUE
VOGUEING *n* dance style of the late 1980s
VOGUEINGS > VOGUEING
VOGUER > VOGUE
VOGUERS > VOGUE
VOGUES > VOGUE
VOGUEY > VOGUE
VOGUIER > VOGUE
VOGUIEST > VOGUE
VOGUING *same as* > VOGUEING
VOGUINGS > VOGUING
VOGUISH > VOGUE
VOGUISHLY > VOGUE
VOICE *n* (quality of) sound made when speaking or singing ▷ *vb* express verbally
VOICED *adj* articulated with accompanying vibration of the vocal cords
VOICEFUL > VOICE
VOICELESS *adj* without a voice
VOICEMAIL *n* facility of leaving recorded message by telephone
VOICEOVER *n* spoken commentary by unseen narrator on film
VOICER > VOICE
VOICERS > VOICE
VOICES > VOICE
VOICING > VOICE
VOICINGS > VOICE
VOID *adj* not legally binding ▷ *n* feeling of deprivation ▷ *vb* make invalid
VOIDABLE *adj* capable of being voided
VOIDANCE *n* annulment, as of a contract
VOIDANCES > VOIDANCE

VOIDED *adj* (of a design) with a hole in the centre of the same shape as the design
VOIDEE *n* light meal eaten before bed
VOIDEES > VOIDEE
VOIDER > VOID
VOIDERS > VOID
VOIDING > VOID
VOIDINGS > VOID
VOIDNESS > VOID
VOIDS > VOID
VOILA *interj* word used to express satisfaction
VOILE *n* light semitransparent fabric
VOILES > VOILE
VOIP *n* voice-over internet protocol
VOIPS > VOIP
VOISINAGE *n* district or neighbourhood
VOITURE *n* type of vehicle
VOITURES > VOITURE
VOITURIER *n* driver of a voiture
VOIVODE *n* type of military leader
VOIVODES > VOIVODE
VOL *n* heraldic wings
VOLA *n* palm of hand or sole of foot
VOLABLE *adj* quick-witted
VOLAE > VOLA
VOLAGE *adj* changeable
VOLANT *adj* in a flying position
VOLANTE *n* Spanish horse carriage
VOLANTES > VOLANTE
VOLAR *adj* of or relating to the palm of the hand or the sole of the foot
VOLARIES > VOLARY
VOLARY *n* large bird enclosure
VOLATIC *adj* flying ▷ *n* creature with wings
VOLATICS > VOLATIC
VOLATILE *adj* liable to sudden change, esp in behaviour ▷ *n* volatile substance
VOLATILES > VOLATILE
VOLCANIAN *same as* > VOLCANIC
VOLCANIC *adj* of or relating to volcanoes
VOLCANICS *n* types of rock
VOLCANISE *same as* > VOLCANIZE
VOLCANISM *n* processes that result in the formation of volcanoes
VOLCANIST *n* person who studies volcanoes
VOLCANIZE *vb* subject to the effects of or change by volcanic heat
VOLCANO *n* mountain with a vent through which lava is ejected

VOLCANOES > VOLCANO
VOLCANOS > VOLCANO
VOLE *n* small rodent ▷ *vb* win by taking all the tricks in a deal
VOLED > VOLE
VOLENS *adj* as in *nolens volens* whether willing or unwilling
VOLERIES > VOLERY
VOLERY *same as* > VOLARY
VOLES > VOLE
VOLET *n* type of veil
VOLETS > VOLET
VOLING > VOLE
VOLITANT *adj* flying or moving about rapidly
VOLITATE *vb* flutter
VOLITATED > VOLITATE
VOLITATES > VOLITATE
VOLITIENT > VOLITION
VOLITION *n* ability to decide things for oneself
VOLITIONS > VOLITION
VOLITIVE *adj* of, relating to, or emanating from the will ▷ *n* (in some languages) a verb form or mood used to express a wish or desire
VOLITIVES > VOLITIVE
VOLK *n* people or nation, esp the nation of Afrikaners
VOLKS > VOLK
VOLKSLIED *n* German folk song
VOLKSRAAD *n* Boer assembly in South Africa in the 19th century
VOLLEY *n* simultaneous discharge of ammunition ▷ *vb* discharge (ammunition) in a volley
VOLLEYED > VOLLEY
VOLLEYER > VOLLEY
VOLLEYERS > VOLLEY
VOLLEYING > VOLLEY
VOLLEYS > VOLLEY
VOLOST *n* (in the former Soviet Union) a rural soviet
VOLOSTS > VOLOST
VOLPINO *n* Italian breed of dog
VOLPINOS > VOLPINO
VOLPLANE *vb* glide in an aeroplane
VOLPLANED > VOLPLANE
VOLPLANES > VOLPLANE
VOLS > VOL
VOLT *n* unit of electric potential ▷ *vb* (in fencing) make a quick movement to avoid a thrust
VOLTA *n* quick-moving Italian dance
VOLTAGE *n* electric potential difference expressed in volts
VOLTAGES > VOLTAGE
VOLTAIC *adj* producing an electric current
VOLTAISM *another name for* > GALVANISM

VOLTAISMS > VOLTAISM
VOLTE same as > VOLT
VOLTED > VOLT
VOLTES > VOLTE
VOLTI adv musical direction
VOLTIGEUR n French infantry member
VOLTING > VOLT
VOLTINISM n number of annual broods of an animal
VOLTMETER n instrument for measuring voltage
VOLTS > VOLT
VOLUBIL same as > VOLUBLE
VOLUBLE adj talking easily and at length
VOLUBLY > VOLUBLE
VOLUCRINE adj relating to birds
VOLUME n size of the space occupied by something ▷ vb billow or surge in volume
VOLUMED > VOLUME
VOLUMES > VOLUME
VOLUMETER n any instrument for measuring the volume of a solid, liquid, or gas
VOLUMETRY n act of measuring by volume
VOLUMINAL > VOLUME
VOLUMING > VOLUME
VOLUMISE same as > VOLUMIZE
VOLUMISED > VOLUMISE
VOLUMISER same as > VOLUMIZER
VOLUMISES > VOLUMISE
VOLUMIST n author
VOLUMISTS > VOLUMIST
VOLUMIZE vb create volume in something
VOLUMIZED > VOLUMIZE
VOLUMIZER n product used to give extra body to hair
VOLUMIZES > VOLUMIZE
VOLUNTARY adj done by choice ▷ n organ solo in a church service
VOLUNTEER n person who offers voluntarily to do something ▷ vb offer one's services
VOLUSPA n Icelandic mythological poem
VOLUSPAS > VOLUSPA
VOLUTE n spiral or twisting turn, form, or object ▷ adj having the form of a volute
VOLUTED > VOLUTE
VOLUTES > VOLUTE
VOLUTIN n granular substance found in cells
VOLUTINS > VOLUTIN
VOLUTION n rolling, revolving, or spiral form or motion
VOLUTIONS > VOLUTION

VOLUTOID > VOLUTE
VOLVA n cup-shaped structure that sheathes the base of the stalk of certain mushrooms
VOLVAE > VOLVA
VOLVAS > VOLVA
VOLVATE > VOLVA
VOLVE vb turn over
VOLVED > VOLVE
VOLVES > VOLVE
VOLVING > VOLVE
VOLVOX n freshwater protozoan
VOLVOXES > VOLVOX
VOLVULI > VOLVULUS
VOLVULUS n abnormal twisting of the intestines causing obstruction
VOM vb vomit
VOMER n thin flat bone separating the nasal passages in mammals
VOMERINE > VOMER
VOMERS > VOMER
VOMICA n pus-containing cavity
VOMICAE > VOMICA
VOMICAS > VOMICA
VOMIT vb eject (the contents of the stomach) through the mouth ▷ n matter vomited
VOMITED > VOMIT
VOMITER > VOMIT
VOMITERS > VOMIT
VOMITING > VOMIT
VOMITINGS > VOMIT
VOMITIVE same as > VOMITORY
VOMITIVES > VOMITIVE
VOMITO n form of yellow fever
VOMITORIA n entrances in an amphitheatre
VOMITORY adj causing vomiting ▷ n vomitory agent
VOMITOS > VOMITO
VOMITOUS adj arousing feelings of disgust
VOMITS > VOMIT
VOMITUS n matter that has been vomited
VOMITUSES > VOMITUS
VOMITY adj resembling or smelling of vomit
VOMMED > VOM
VOMMING > VOM
VOMS > VOM
VONGOLE pl n (in Italian cookery) clams
VOODOO n religion involving ancestor worship and witchcraft ▷ adj of or relating to voodoo ▷ vb affect by or as if by the power of voodoo
VOODOOED > VOODOO
VOODOOING > VOODOO
VOODOOISM same as > VOODOO
VOODOOIST > VOODOO
VOODOOS > VOODOO

VOORKAMER n front room of a house
VOORSKOT n advance payment made to a farmer for crops
VOORSKOTS > VOORSKOT
VOR vb (in dialect) warn
VORACIOUS adj craving great quantities of food
VORACITY > VORACIOUS
VORAGO n chasm
VORAGOES > VORAGO
VORAGOS > VORAGO
VORANT adj devouring
VORLAGE n skiing position
VORLAGES > VORLAGE
VORPAL adj sharp
VORRED > VOR
VORRING > VOR
VORS > VOR
VORTEX n whirlpool
VORTEXES > VORTEX
VORTICAL > VORTEX
VORTICES > VORTEX
VORTICISM n art movement in 20th-century England
VORTICIST > VORTICISM
VORTICITY n rotational spin in a fluid
VORTICOSE adj rotating quickly
VOSTRO adj as in vostro account bank account held by a foreign bank with a British bank
VOTABLE > VOTE
VOTARESS n female votary
VOTARIES > VOTARY
VOTARIST variant of > VOTARY
VOTARISTS > VOTARIST
VOTARY n person dedicated to religion or to a cause ▷ adj ardently devoted to the services or worship of God
VOTE n choice made by a participant in a shared decision ▷ vb make a choice by a vote
VOTEABLE > VOTE
VOTED > VOTE
VOTEEN n devotee
VOTEENS > VOTEEN
VOTELESS > VOTE
VOTER n person who can or does vote
VOTERS > VOTER
VOTES > VOTE
VOTING > VOTE
VOTINGS > VOTE
VOTIVE adj done or given to fulfil a vow ▷ n votive offering
VOTIVELY > VOTIVE
VOTIVES > VOTIVE
VOTRESS > VOTARESS
VOTRESSES > VOTRESS
VOUCH vb give personal assurance ▷ n act of vouching

VOUCHED > VOUCH
VOUCHEE n person summoned to court to defend a title
VOUCHEES > VOUCHEE
VOUCHER n ticket used instead of money to buy specified goods ▷ vb summon someone to court as a vouchee
VOUCHERED > VOUCHER
VOUCHERS > VOUCHER
VOUCHES > VOUCH
VOUCHING > VOUCH
VOUCHSAFE vb give, entrust
VOUDON variant of > VOODOO
VOUDONS > VOUDON
VOUDOU same as > VOODOO
VOUDOUED > VOUDOU
VOUDOUING > VOUDOU
VOUDOUN variant of > VOODOO
VOUDOUNS > VOUDOUN
VOUDOUS > VOUDOU
VOUGE n form of pike used by foot soldiers in the 14th century and later
VOUGES > VOUGE
VOULGE n type of medieval weapon
VOULGES > VOULGE
VOULU adj deliberate
VOUSSOIR n wedge-shaped stone or brick that is used with others to construct an arch
VOUSSOIRS > VOUSSOIR
VOUTSAFE same as > VOUCHSAFE
VOUTSAFED > VOUTSAFE
VOUTSAFES > VOUTSAFE
VOUVRAY n dry white French wine
VOUVRAYS > VOUVRAY
VOW n solemn and binding promise ▷ vb promise solemnly
VOWED > VOW
VOWEL n speech sound made without obstructing the flow of breath ▷ vb say as a vowel
VOWELED adj having vowels
VOWELISE same as > VOWELIZE
VOWELISED > VOWELISE
VOWELISES > VOWELISE
VOWELIZE vb mark the vowel points in (a Hebrew word or text)
VOWELIZED > VOWELIZE
VOWELIZES > VOWELIZE
VOWELLED > VOWEL
VOWELLESS > VOWEL
VOWELLING > VOWEL
VOWELLY > VOWEL
VOWELS > VOWEL
VOWER > VOW
VOWERS > VOW
VOWESS n nun
VOWESSES > VOWESS

V

VOWING > VOW
VOWLESS > VOW
VOWS > VOW
VOX *n* voice or sound
VOXEL *n* term used in computing imaging
VOXELS > VOXEL
VOYAGE *n* long journey by sea or in space ▷ *vb* make a voyage
VOYAGED > VOYAGE
VOYAGER > VOYAGE
VOYAGERS > VOYAGE
VOYAGES > VOYAGE
VOYAGEUR *n* French canoeman who transported furs from trading posts in the North American interior
VOYAGEURS > VOYAGEUR
VOYAGING *n* act of voyaging
VOYAGINGS > VOYAGING
VOYEUR *n* person who obtains pleasure from watching people undressing or having sex
VOYEURISM > VOYEUR
VOYEURS > VOYEUR
VOZHD *n* Russian leader
VOZHDS > VOZHD
VRAIC *n* type of seaweed
VRAICKER *n* person who gathers vraic
VRAICKERS > VRAICKER
VRAICKING *n* act of gathering vraic
VRAICS > VRAIC
VRIL *n* life force
VRILS > VRIL
VROOM *interj* exclamation imitative of a car engine revving up ▷ *vb* move noisily and at high speed

VROOMED > VROOM
VROOMING > VROOM
VROOMS > VROOM
VROT *adj* South African slang for rotten
VROU *n* Afrikaner woman, esp a married woman
VROUS > VROU
VROUW *n* woman
VROUWS > VROUW
VROW *same as* > VROUW
VROWS > VROW
VRYSTATER *n* (in S Africa) inhabitant of the Free State, esp one who is White
VUG *n* small cavity in a rock or vein, usually lined with crystals
VUGG *same as* > VUG
VUGGIER > VUG
VUGGIEST > VUG
VUGGS > VUGG
VUGGY > VUG
VUGH *same as* > VUG
VUGHIER > VUGH
VUGHIEST > VUGH
VUGHS > VUGH
VUGHY > VUG
VUGS > VUG
VUGULAR *adj* relating to vugs
VULCAN *n* blacksmith
VULCANIAN *adj* of or relating to a volcanic eruption
VULCANIC *same as* > VOLCANIC
VULCANISE *same as* > VULCANIZE
VULCANISM *same as* > VOLCANISM
VULCANIST *same as* > VOLCANIST

VULCANITE *n* vulcanized rubber
VULCANIZE *vb* strengthen (rubber) by treating it with sulphur
VULCANS > VULCAN
VULGAR *adj* showing lack of good taste, decency, or refinement ▷ *n* common and ignorant person
VULGARER > VULGAR
VULGAREST > VULGAR
VULGARIAN *n* vulgar (rich) person
VULGARISE *same as* > VULGARIZE
VULGARISM *n* coarse word or phrase
VULGARITY *n* condition of being vulgar
VULGARIZE *vb* make vulgar or too common
VULGARLY > VULGAR
VULGARS > VULGAR
VULGATE *n* commonly recognized text or version ▷ *adj* generally accepted
VULGATES > VULGATE
VULGO *adv* generally
VULGUS *n* the common people
VULGUSES > VULGUS
VULN *vb* wound
VULNED > VULN
VULNERARY *adj* of, relating to, or used to heal a wound ▷ *n* vulnerary drug or agent
VULNERATE *vb* wound
VULNING > VULN
VULNS > VULN
VULPICIDE *n* person who kills foxes
VULPINE *adj* of or like a fox

VULPINISM > VULPINE
VULPINITE *n* type of granular anhydrite
VULSELLA *n* forceps
VULSELLAE > VULSELLA
VULSELLUM *variant of* > VULSELLA
VULTURE *n* large bird that feeds on the flesh of dead animals
VULTURES > VULTURE
VULTURINE *adj* of, relating to, or resembling a vulture
VULTURISH > VULTURE
VULTURISM *n* greed
VULTURN *n* type of turkey
VULTURNS > VULTURN
VULTUROUS *same as* > VULTURINE
VULVA *n* woman's external genitals
VULVAE > VULVA
VULVAL > VULVA
VULVAR > VULVA
VULVAS > VULVA
VULVATE > VULVA
VULVIFORM > VULVA
VULVITIS *n* inflammation of the vulva
VUM *vb* swear
VUMMED > VUM
VUMMING > VUM
VUMS > VUM
VUTTIER > VUTTY
VUTTIEST > VUTTY
VUTTY *adj* dirty
VUVUZELA *n* South African instrument blown by football fans
VUVUZELAS > VUVUZELA
VYING > VIE
VYINGLY > VIE
VYINGS > VIE

V

Ww

WAAC n (formerly) member of the Women's Auxiliary Army Corps

WAACS > WAAC

WAAH interj interjection used to express wailing

WAB same as > WEB

WABAIN same as > OUABAIN

WABAINS > WABAIN

WABBIT adj weary

WABBLE same as > WOBBLE

WABBLED > WABBLE

WABBLER > WABBLE

WABBLERS > WABBLE

WABBLES > WABBLE

WABBLIER > WABBLE

WABBLIEST > WABBLE

WABBLING > WABBLE

WABBLY > WABBLE

WABOOM another word for > WAGENBOOM

WABOOMS > WABOOM

WABS > WAB

WABSTER Scots form of > WEBSTER

WABSTERS > WABSTER

WACK n friend ▷ adj bad or inferior

WACKE n any of various soft earthy rocks that resemble or are derived from basaltic rocks

WACKED adj intoxicated or exhausted

WACKER same as > WACK

WACKERS > WACKER

WACKES > WACKE

WACKEST > WACK

WACKIER > WACKY

WACKIEST > WACKY

WACKILY > WACKY

WACKINESS > WACKY

WACKO adj mad or eccentric ▷ n mad or eccentric person

WACKOES > WACKO

WACKOS > WACKO

WACKS > WACK

WACKY adj eccentric or funny

WACONDA n supernatural force in Sioux belief

WACONDAS > WACONDA

WAD n black earthy ore of manganese ▷ n small mass of soft material ▷ vb form (something) into a wad

WADABLE > WADE

WADD same as > WAD

WADDED > WAD

WADDER > WAD

WADDERS > WAD

WADDIE same as > WADDY

WADDIED > WADDY

WADDIES > WADDY

WADDING > WAD

WADDINGS > WAD

WADDLE vb walk with short swaying steps ▷ n swaying walk

WADDLED > WADDLE

WADDLER > WADDLE

WADDLERS > WADDLE

WADDLES > WADDLE

WADDLIER > WADDLE

WADDLIEST > WADDLE

WADDLING > WADDLE

WADDLY > WADDLE

WADDS > WADD

WADDY n heavy wooden club used by Australian Aborigines ▷ vb hit with a waddy

WADDYING > WADDY

WADE vb walk with difficulty through water or mud ▷ n act or an instance of wading

WADEABLE > WADE

WADED > WADE

WADER n long-legged water bird

WADERS pl n long waterproof boots which completely cover the legs

WADES > WADE

WADGE n large or roughly-cut portion

WADGES > WADGE

WADI n (in N Africa and Arabia) river which is dry except in the wet season

WADIES > WADY

WADING > WADE

WADINGS > WADE

WADIS > WADI

WADMAAL same as > WADMAL

WADMAALS > WADMAAL

WADMAL n coarse thick woollen fabric, formerly woven for outer garments

WADMALS > WADMAL

WADMEL same as > WADMAL

WADMELS > WADMEL

WADMOL same as > WADMAL

WADMOLL same as > WADMAL

WADMOLLS > WADMOLL

WADMOLS > WADMOL

WADS > WAD

WADSET vb pledge or mortgage

WADSETS > WADSET

WADSETT same as > WADSET

WADSETTED > WADSET

WADSETTER > WADSET

WADSETTS > WADSETT

WADT same as > WAD

WADTS > WADT

WADY same as > WADI

WAE old form of > WOE

WAEFUL old form of > WOEFUL

WAENESS n sorrow

WAENESSES > WAENESS

WAES > WAE

WAESOME adj sorrowful

WAESUCK interj alas

WAESUCKS interj alas

WAFER n thin crisp biscuit ▷ vb seal, fasten, or attach with a wafer

WAFERED > WAFER

WAFERING > WAFER

WAFERS > WAFER

WAFERY > WAFER

WAFF n gust or puff of air ▷ vb flutter or cause to flutter

WAFFED > WAFF

WAFFIE n person regarded as having little worth to society

WAFFIES > WAFFIE

WAFFING > WAFF

WAFFLE vb speak or write in a vague wordy way ▷ n vague wordy talk or writing

WAFFLED > WAFFLE

WAFFLER > WAFFLE

WAFFLERS > WAFFLE

WAFFLES > WAFFLE

WAFFLIER > WAFFLE

WAFFLIEST > WAFFLE

WAFFLING > WAFFLE

WAFFLINGS > WAFFLE

WAFFLY > WAFFLE

WAFFS > WAFF

WAFT vb drift or carry gently through the air ▷ n something wafted

WAFTAGE > WAFT

WAFTAGES > WAFT

WAFTED > WAFT

WAFTER n device that causes a draught

WAFTERS > WAFTER

WAFTING > WAFT

WAFTINGS > WAFT

WAFTS > WAFT

WAFTURE n act of wafting or waving

WAFTURES > WAFTURE

WAG vb move rapidly from side to side ▷ n wagging movement

WAGE n payment for work done, esp when paid weekly ▷ vb engage in (an activity)

WAGED > WAGE

WAGELESS > WAGE

WAGENBOOM n S African tree

WAGER vb bet on the outcome of something ▷ n bet on the outcome of an event or activity

WAGERED > WAGER

WAGERER > WAGER

WAGERERS > WAGER

WAGERING n act of wagering

WAGERINGS > WAGERING

WAGERS > WAGER

WAGES > WAGE

WAGGA n blanket or bed covering made out of sacks stitched together

WAGGAS > WAGGA

WAGGED > WAG

WAGGER > WAG

WAGGERIES > WAGGERY

WAGGERS > WAG

WAGGERY n quality of being humorous

WAGGING > WAG

WAGGISH adj jocular or humorous

WAGGISHLY > WAGGISH

WAGGLE vb move with a rapid shaking or wobbling motion ▷ n rapid shaking or wobbling motion

WAGGLED > WAGGLE

WAGGLER n float only the bottom of which is attached to the fishing line

WAGGLERS > WAGGLER

WAGGLES > WAGGLE

WAGGLIER > WAGGLE

WAGGLIEST > WAGGLE

WAGGLING > WAGGLE

WAGGLY > WAGGLE

WAGGON same as > WAGON

WAGGONED > WAGGON

WAGGONER *same as*
> WAGONER
WAGGONERS > WAGGONER
WAGGONING > WAGGON
WAGGONS > WAGGON
WAGHALTER *n* person
likely to be hanged
WAGING > WAGE
WAGMOIRE *obsolete word*
for > QUAGMIRE
WAGMOIRES > WAGMOIRE
WAGON *n* four-wheeled
vehicle for heavy loads
▷ *vb* transport by wagon
WAGONAGE *n* money paid
for transport by wagon
WAGONAGES > WAGONAGE
WAGONED > WAGON
WAGONER *n* person who
drives a wagon
WAGONERS > WAGONER
WAGONETTE *n* light
four-wheeled
horse-drawn vehicle with
two lengthwise seats
facing each other behind a
crosswise driver's seat
WAGONFUL > WAGON
WAGONFULS > WAGON
WAGONING > WAGON
WAGONLESS > WAGON
WAGONLOAD *n* load that is
or can be carried by a
wagon
WAGONS > WAGON
WAGS > WAG
WAGSOME *another word for*
> WAGGISH
WAGTAIL *n* small
long-tailed bird
WAGTAILS > WAGTAIL
WAGYU *n* Japanese breed of
beef cattle
WAGYUS > WAGYU
WAHCONDA *n* supreme
being
WAHCONDAS > WAHCONDA
WAHINE *n* Māori woman,
esp a wife
WAHINES > WAHINE
WAHOO *n* food and game
fish of tropical seas
WAHOOS > WAHOO
WAI *n* in New Zealand, water
WAIATA *n* Māori song
WAIATAS > WAIATA
WAID > WEIGH
WAIDE > WEIGH
WAIF *n* young person who
is, or seems, homeless or
neglected ▷ *vb* treat as a
waif
WAIFED > WAIF
WAIFING > WAIF
WAIFISH > WAIF
WAIFLIKE > WAIF
WAIFS > WAIF
WAIFT *n* piece of lost
property found by
someone other than the
owner
WAIFTS > WAIFT
WAIL *vb* cry out in pain or
misery ▷ *n* mournful cry

WAILED > WAIL
WAILER > WAIL
WAILERS > WAIL
WAILFUL > WAIL
WAILFULLY > WAIL
WAILING > WAIL
WAILINGLY > WAIL
WAILINGS > WAIL
WAILS > WAIL
WAILSOME > WAIL
WAIN *vb* transport ▷ *n*
farm wagon
WAINAGE *n* carriages, etc,
for transportation of
goods
WAINAGES > WAINAGE
WAINED > WAIN
WAINING > WAIN
WAINS > WAIN
WAINSCOT *n* wooden
lining of the lower part of
the walls of a room
▷ *vb* line (a wall of a room)
with a wainscot
WAINSCOTS > WAINSCOT
WAIR *vb* spend
WAIRED > WAIR
WAIRING > WAIR
WAIRS > WAIR
WAIRSH *variant spelling of*
> WERSH
WAIRSHER > WAIRSH
WAIRSHEST > WAIRSH
WAIRUA *n* in New Zealand,
spirit or soul
WAIRUAS > WAIRUA
WAIS > WAI
WAIST *n* part of the trunk
between the ribs and the
hips
WAISTBAND *n* band of
material sewn on to the
waist of a garment to
strengthen it
WAISTBELT *n* belt
WAISTCOAT *n* sleeveless
garment which buttons
up the front, also worn
over a shirt and under a
jacket
WAISTED *adj* having a
waist or waistlike part
WAISTER *n* sailor
performing menial duties
WAISTERS > WAISTER
WAISTING *n* act of
wasting
WAISTINGS > WAISTING
WAISTLESS > WAIST
WAISTLINE *n* (size of) the
waist of a person or
garment
WAISTS > WAIST
WAIT *vb* remain inactive in
expectation (of
something) ▷ *n* act or
period of waiting
WAITE *old form of* > WAIT
WAITED > WAIT
WAITER *n* man who serves
in a restaurant etc ▷ *vb*
serve at table
WAITERAGE *n* service
WAITERED > WAITER

WAITERING *n* act of
serving at table
WAITERS > WAITER
WAITES > WAITE
WAITING > WAIT
WAITINGLY > WAIT
WAITINGS > WAIT
WAITLIST *n* waiting list
WAITLISTS > WAITLIST
WAITRESS *n* woman who
serves people with food
and drink in a restaurant
▷ *vb* work as a waitress
WAITRON *n* waiter or
waitress
WAITRONS > WAITRON
WAITS > WAIT
WAITSTAFF *n* waiters
and waitresses collectively
WAIVE *vb* refrain from
enforcing (a law, right, etc)
WAIVED > WAIVE
WAIVER *n* act or instance
of voluntarily giving up a
claim, right, etc
WAIVERS > WAIVER
WAIVES > WAIVE
WAIVING > WAIVE
WAIVODE *same as*
> VOIVODE
WAIVODES > WAIVODE
WAIWODE *same as*
> VOIVODE
WAIWODES > WAIWODE
WAKA *n* Māori canoe
WAKAME *n* edible seaweed
WAKAMES > WAKAME
WAKANDA *n* supernatural
quality in Native American
belief system
WAKANDAS > WAKANDA
WAKANE *n* type of seaweed
WAKANES > WAKANE
WAKAS > WAKA
WAKE *vb* rouse from sleep
or inactivity ▷ *n* vigil
beside a corpse the night
before the funeral
WAKEBOARD *n* short
surfboard for a rider towed
behind a motorboat ▷ *vb*
ride a wakeboard
WAKED > WAKE
WAKEFUL *adj* unable to
sleep
WAKEFULLY > WAKEFUL
WAKELESS *adj* (of sleep)
deep or unbroken
WAKEMAN *n* watchman
WAKEMEN > WAKEMAN
WAKEN *vb* wake
WAKENED > WAKEN
WAKENER > WAKEN
WAKENERS > WAKEN
WAKENING > WAKEN
WAKENINGS > WAKEN
WAKENS > WAKEN
WAKER > WAKE
WAKERIFE *adj* watchful
WAKERS > WAKE
WAKES > WAKE
WAKF *same as* > WAQF
WAKFS > WAKF

WAKIKI *n* Melanesian
shell currency
WAKIKIS > WAKIKI
WAKING > WAKE
WAKINGS > WAKE
WALD *Scots form of* > WELD
WALDFLUTE *n* organ flute
stop
WALDGRAVE *n* (in
medieval Germany) an
officer with jurisdiction
over a royal forest
WALDHORN *n* organ reed
stop
WALDHORNS > WALDHORN
WALDO *n* gadget for
manipulating objects by
remote control
WALDOES > WALDO
WALDOS > WALDO
WALDRAPP *n* type of ibis
WALDRAPPS > WALDRAPP
WALDS > WALD
WALE *same as* > WEAL
WALED > WALE
WALER > WALE
WALERS > WALE
WALES > WALE
WALI *same as* > VALI
WALIER > WALY
WALIES > WALY
WALIEST > WALY
WALING > WALE
WALIS > WALI
WALISE *same as* > VALISE
WALISES > WALISE
WALK *vb* move on foot with
at least one foot always on
the ground ▷ *n* short
journey on foot, usu for
pleasure
WALKABLE > WALK
WALKABOUT *n* informal
walk among the public by
royalty etc
WALKATHON *n* long walk
done, esp for charity
WALKAWAY *n* easily
achieved victory
WALKAWAYS > WALKAWAY
WALKED > WALK
WALKER *n* person who
walks
WALKERS > WALKER
WALKIES *pl n* as in *go
walkies* a walk
WALKING *adj* (of a person)
considered to possess the
qualities of something
inanimate as specified
▷ *n* act of walking
WALKINGS > WALKING
WALKMILL *same as*
> WAULKMILL
WALKMILLS > WALKMILL
WALKOUT *n* strike
WALKOUTS > WALKOUT
WALKOVER *n* easy victory
WALKOVERS > WALKOVER
WALKS > WALK
WALKUP *n* building with
stairs to upper floors
WALKUPS > WALKUP

w

WALKWAY n path designed for use by pedestrians
WALKWAYS > WALKWAY
WALKYRIE variant of > VALKYRIE
WALKYRIES > WALKYRIE
WALL n structure of brick, stone, etc used to enclose, divide, or support ▷ vb enclose or seal with a wall or walls
WALLA same as > WALLAH
WALLABA n type of S American tree
WALLABAS > WALLABA
WALLABIES > WALLABY
WALLABY n marsupial like a small kangaroo
WALLAH n person involved with or in charge of a specified thing
WALLAHS > WALLAH
WALLAROO n large stocky Australian kangaroo of rocky regions
WALLAROOS > WALLAROO
WALLAS > WALLA
WALLBOARD n thin board made of materials, such as compressed wood fibres or gypsum plaster, between stiff paper, and used to cover walls, partitions, etc
WALLCHART n chart on wall
WALLED > WALL
WALLER > WALL
WALLERS > WALL
WALLET n small folding case for paper money, documents, etc
WALLETS > WALLET
WALLEY n type of jump in figure skating
WALLEYE n fish with large staring eyes
WALLEYED > WALLEYE
WALLEYES > WALLEYE
WALLEYS > WALLEY
WALLFISH n snail
WALLIE same as > WALLY
WALLIER > WALLY
WALLIES > WALLY
WALLIEST > WALLY
WALLING > WALL
WALLINGS > WALL
WALLOP vb hit hard ▷ n hard blow
WALLOPED > WALLOP
WALLOPER n person or thing that wallops
WALLOPERS > WALLOPER
WALLOPING n thrashing ▷ adj large or great
WALLOPS > WALLOP
WALLOW vb revel in an emotion ▷ n act or instance of wallowing
WALLOWED > WALLOW
WALLOWER > WALLOW
WALLOWERS > WALLOW
WALLOWING > WALLOW
WALLOWS > WALLOW

WALLPAPER n decorative paper to cover interior walls ▷ vb cover (walls) with wallpaper
WALLS > WALL
WALLSEND n type of coal
WALLSENDS > WALLSEND
WALLWORT n type of plant
WALLWORTS > WALLWORT
WALLY n stupid person ▷ adj fine, pleasing, or splendid
WALLYBALL n ball game played on court
WALLYDRAG n worthless person or animal
WALNUT n edible nut with a wrinkled shell ▷ adj made from the wood of a walnut tree
WALNUTS > WALNUT
WALRUS n large sea mammal with long tusks
WALRUSES > WALRUS
WALTIER > WALTY
WALTIEST > WALTY
WALTY adj (of a ship) likely to roll over
WALTZ n ballroom dance ▷ vb dance a waltz
WALTZED > WALTZ
WALTZER n person who waltzes
WALTZERS > WALTZER
WALTZES > WALTZ
WALTZING > WALTZ
WALTZINGS > WALTZ
WALTZLIKE > WALTZ
WALY same as > WALLY
WAMBENGER another name for > TUAN
WAMBLE vb move unsteadily ▷ n unsteady movement
WAMBLED > WAMBLE
WAMBLES > WAMBLE
WAMBLIER > WAMBLE
WAMBLIEST > WAMBLE
WAMBLING > WAMBLE
WAMBLINGS > WAMBLE
WAMBLY > WAMBLE
WAME n belly, abdomen, or womb
WAMED > WAME
WAMEFOU Scots variant of > WAMEFUL
WAMEFOUS > WAMEFOU
WAMEFUL n bellyful
WAMEFULS > WAMEFUL
WAMES > WAME
WAMMUL n dog
WAMMULS > WAMMUL
WAMMUS same as > WAMUS
WAMMUSES > WAMMUS
WAMPEE n type of Asian fruit tree
WAMPEES > WAMPEE
WAMPISH vb wave
WAMPISHED > WAMPISH
WAMPISHES > WAMPISH
WAMPUM n shells woven together, formerly used by Native Americans for money

WAMPUMS > WAMPUM
WAMPUS same as > WAMUS
WAMPUSES > WAMPUS
WAMUS n type of cardigan or jacket
WAMUSES > WAMUS
WAN adj pale and sickly looking ▷ vb make or become wan
WANCHANCY adj infelicitous
WAND n thin rod, esp one used in performing magic tricks
WANDER vb move about without a definite destination or aim ▷ n act or instance of wandering
WANDERED > WANDER
WANDERER > WANDER
WANDERERS > WANDER
WANDERING > WANDER
WANDEROO n macaque monkey of India and Sri Lanka, having black fur with a ruff of long greyish fur on each side of the face
WANDEROOS > WANDEROO
WANDERS > WANDER
WANDLE adj supple ▷ vb walk haltingly
WANDLED > WANDLE
WANDLES > WANDLE
WANDLIKE > WAND
WANDLING > WANDLE
WANDOO n eucalyptus tree of W Australia, having white bark and durable wood
WANDOOS > WANDOO
WANDS > WAND
WANE vb decrease gradually in size or strength
WANED > WANE
WANES > WANE
WANEY > WANE
WANG n cheekbone
WANGAN same as > WANIGAN
WANGANS > WANGAN
WANGLE vb get by devious methods ▷ n act or an instance of wangling
WANGLED > WANGLE
WANGLER > WANGLE
WANGLERS > WANGLE
WANGLES > WANGLE
WANGLING > WANGLE
WANGLINGS > WANGLE
WANGS > WANG
WANGUN same as > WANIGAN
WANGUNS > WANGUN
WANHOPE n delusion
WANHOPES > WANHOPE
WANIER > WANY
WANIEST > WANY
WANIGAN n provisions for camp
WANIGANS > WANIGAN
WANING > WANE
WANINGS > WANE

WANION n vehemence
WANIONS > WANION
WANK vb slang word for masturbate ▷ n instance of masturbating ▷ adj bad, useless, or worthless
WANKED > WANK
WANKER n slang word for worthless or stupid person
WANKERS > WANKER
WANKIER > WANKY
WANKIEST > WANKY
WANKING > WANK
WANKLE adj unstable
WANKS > WANK
WANKSTA n derogatory slang word for a person who acts or dresses like a gangster but who is not involved in crime
WANKSTAS > WANKSTA
WANKY adj slang word for pretentious
WANLE same as > WANDLE
WANLY > WAN
WANNA vb spelling of **want to** intended to reflect a dialectal or informal pronunciation
WANNABE adj wanting to be, or be like, a particular person or thing ▷ n person who wants to be, or be like, a particular person or thing
WANNABEE same as > WANNABE
WANNABEES > WANNABEE
WANNABES > WANNABE
WANNED > WAN
WANNEL same as > WANDLE
WANNER > WAN
WANNESS > WAN
WANNESSES > WAN
WANNEST > WAN
WANNIGAN same as > WANIGAN
WANNIGANS > WANNIGAN
WANNING > WAN
WANNION same as > WANION
WANNIONS > WANNION
WANNISH adj rather wan
WANS > WAN
WANT vb need or long for ▷ n act or instance of wanting
WANTAGE n shortage
WANTAGES > WANTAGE
WANTAWAY n footballer who wants to transfer to another club
WANTAWAYS > WANTAWAY
WANTED > WANT
WANTER > WANT
WANTERS > WANT
WANTHILL n molehill
WANTHILLS > WANTHILL
WANTIES > WANTY
WANTING adj lacking ▷ prep without
WANTON adj without motive, provocation, or justification ▷ n sexually

unrestrained or immodest woman ▷ *vb* behave in a wanton manner

WANTONED > WANTON

WANTONER > WANTON

WANTONERS > WANTON

WANTONEST > WANTON

WANTONING > WANTON

WANTONISE *same as* > WANTONIZE

WANTONIZE *vb* behave wantonly

WANTONLY > WANTON

WANTONS > WANTON

WANTS > WANT

WANTY *adj* belt

WANWORDY *adj* without merit

WANWORTH *n* inexpensive purchase

WANWORTHS > WANWORTH

WANY > WANE

WANZE *vb* wane

WANZED > WANZE

WANZES > WANZE

WANZING > WANZE

WAP *vb* strike

WAPENSHAW *n* showing of weapons

WAPENTAKE *n* subdivision of certain shires or counties, esp in the Midlands and North of England

WAPINSHAW *same as* > WAPENSHAW

WAPITI *n* large N American deer

WAPITIS > WAPITI

WAPPED > WAP

WAPPEND *adj* tired

WAPPER *vb* blink

WAPPERED > WAPPER

WAPPERING > WAPPER

WAPPERS > WAPPER

WAPPING > WAP

WAPS > WAP

WAQF *n* endowment in Muslim law

WAQFS > WAQF

WAR *n* fighting between nations ▷ *adj* of, like, or caused by war ▷ *vb* conduct a war

WARAGI *n* Ugandan alcoholic drink made from bananas

WARAGIS > WARAGI

WARATAH *n* Australian shrub with crimson flowers

WARATAHS > WARATAH

WARB *n* dirty or insignificant person

WARBIER > WARB

WARBIEST > WARB

WARBIRD *n* vintage military aeroplane

WARBIRDS > WARBIRD

WARBLE *vb* sing in a trilling voice ▷ *n* act or an instance of warbling

WARBLED > WARBLE

WARBLER *n* any of various small songbirds

WARBLERS > WARBLER

WARBLES > WARBLE

WARBLIER > WARBLY

WARBLIEST > WARBLY

WARBLING > WARBLE

WARBLINGS > WARBLE

WARBLY *adj* said in a quavering manner

WARBONNET *n* headband with trailing feathers worn by certain North American Indian warriors

WARBOT *n* any robot or unmanned vehicle or device designed for and used in warfare

WARBOTS > WARBOT

WARBS > WARB

WARBY > WARB

WARCRAFT *n* skill in warfare

WARCRAFTS > WARCRAFT

WARD *n* room in a hospital for patients needing a similar kind of care ▷ *vb* guard or protect

WARDCORN *n* payment of corn

WARDCORNS > WARDCORN

WARDED > WARD

WARDEN *n* person in charge of a building and its occupants ▷ *vb* act as a warden

WARDENED > WARDEN

WARDENING > WARDEN

WARDENRY > WARDEN

WARDENS > WARDEN

WARDER *vb* guard ▷ *n* prison officer

WARDERED > WARDER

WARDERING > WARDER

WARDERS > WARDER

WARDIAN *n* as in *wardian case* type of glass container for housing delicate plants

WARDING > WARD

WARDINGS > WARD

WARDLESS > WARD

WARDMOTE *n* assembly of the citizens or liverymen of an area

WARDMOTES > WARDMOTE

WARDOG *n* veteran warrior

WARDOGS > WARDOG

WARDRESS *n* female officer in charge of prisoners in a jail

WARDROBE *n* cupboard for hanging clothes in

WARDROBED > WARDROBE

WARDROBER *n* person in charge of someone's wardrobe

WARDROBES > WARDROBE

WARDROOM *n* officers' quarters on a warship

WARDROOMS > WARDROOM

WARDROP *obsolete form of* > WARDROBE

WARDROPS > WARDROP

WARDS > WARD

WARDSHIP *n* state of being a ward

WARDSHIPS > WARDSHIP

WARE *n* articles of a specified type or material ▷ *vb* spend or squander

WARED > WARE

WAREHOU *n* any of several edible saltwater New Zealand fish

WAREHOUS > WAREHOU

WAREHOUSE *n* building for storing goods prior to sale or distribution ▷ *vb* store or place in a warehouse, esp a bonded warehouse

WARELESS *adj* careless

WAREROOM *n* store-room

WAREROOMS > WAREROOM

WARES *pl n* goods for sale

WAREZ *pl n* illegally copied computer software

WARFARE *vb* engage in war ▷ *n* fighting or hostilities

WARFARED > WARFARE

WARFARER > WARFARE

WARFARERS > WARFARE

WARFARES > WARFARE

WARFARIN *n* crystalline compound, used as a medical anticoagulant

WARFARING > WARFARE

WARFARINS > WARFARIN

WARGAME *vb* engage in simulated military conflicts

WARGAMED > WARGAME

WARGAMER *n* person who takes part in wargames

WARGAMERS > WARGAMER

WARGAMES > WARGAME

WARGAMING *n* activity of playing war games

WARHABLE *adj* able to fight in war

WARHEAD *n* explosive front part of a missile

WARHEADS > WARHEAD

WARHORSE *n* (formerly) a horse used in battle

WARHORSES > WARHORSE

WARIBASHI *n* pair of disposable chopsticks

WARIER > WARY

WARIEST > WARY

WARILY > WARY

WARIMENT *n* caution

WARIMENTS > WARIMENT

WARINESS > WARY

WARING > WARE

WARISON *n* (esp formerly) a bugle note used as an order to a military force to attack

WARISONS > WARISON

WARK *Scots form of* > WORK

WARKED > WARK

WARKING > WARK

WARKS > WARK

WARLESS > WAR

WARLIKE *adj* of or relating to war

WARLING *n* one who is not liked

WARLINGS > WARLING

WARLOCK *n* man who practises black magic

WARLOCKRY *n* witchcraft

WARLOCKS > WARLOCK

WARLORD *n* military leader of a nation or part of a nation

WARLORDS > WARLORD

WARM *adj* moderately hot ▷ *vb* make or become warm ▷ *n* warm place or area

WARMAKER *n* one who wages war

WARMAKERS > WARMAKER

WARMAN *n* one experienced in warfare

WARMBLOOD *n* type of horse

WARMED > WARM

WARMEN > WARMAN

WARMER > WARM

WARMERS > WARM

WARMEST > WARM

WARMING > WARM

WARMINGS > WARM

WARMISH > WARM

WARMIST *n* person who believes global warming results from human activity

WARMISTS > WARMIST

WARMLY > WARM

WARMNESS > WARM

WARMONGER *n* person who encourages war

WARMOUTH *n* type of fish

WARMOUTHS > WARMOUTH

WARMS > WARM

WARMTH *n* mild heat

WARMTHS > WARMTH

WARMUP *n* preparatory exercise routine

WARMUPS > WARMUP

WARN *vb* make aware of possible danger or harm

WARNED > WARN

WARNER > WARN

WARNERS > WARN

WARNING *n* something that warns ▷ *adj* giving or serving as a warning

WARNINGLY > WARNING

WARNINGS > WARNING

WARNS > WARN

WARP *vb* twist out of shape ▷ *n* state of being warped

WARPAGE > WARP

WARPAGES > WARP

WARPAINT *n* paint used to decorate the face and body before battle

WARPAINTS > WARPAINT

WARPATH *n* route taken by Native Americans on a warlike expedition

WARPATHS > WARPATH

WARPED > WARP

WARPER > WARP

WARPERS > WARP

WARPING > WARP
WARPINGS > WARP
WARPLANE n any aircraft designed for and used in warfare
WARPLANES > WARPLANE
WARPOWER n ability to wage war
WARPOWERS > WARPOWER
WARPS > WARP
WARPWISE adv (weaving) in the direction of the warp
WARRAGAL same as > WARRIGAL
WARRAGALS > WARRAGAL
WARRAGLE same as > WARRIGAL
WARRAGLES > WARRAGLE
WARRAGUL same as > WARRIGAL
WARRAGULS > WARRAGUL
WARRAN same as > WARRANT
WARRAND same as > WARRANT
WARRANDED > WARRAND
WARRANDS > WARRAND
WARRANED > WARRAN
WARRANING > WARRAN
WARRANS > WARRAN
WARRANT n (document giving) official authorization ▷ vb make necessary
WARRANTED > WARRANT
WARRANTEE n person to whom a warranty is given
WARRANTER > WARRANT
WARRANTOR n person or company that provides a warranty
WARRANTS > WARRANT
WARRANTY n (document giving) a guarantee
WARRAY vb wage war on
WARRAYED > WARRAY
WARRAYING > WARRAY
WARRAYS > WARRAY
WARRE same as > WAR
WARRED > WAR
WARREN n series of burrows in which rabbits live
WARRENER n gamekeeper or keeper of a warren
WARRENERS > WARRENER
WARRENS > WARREN
WARREY same as > WARRAY
WARREYED > WARREY
WARREYING > WARREY
WARREYS > WARREY
WARRIGAL n dingo ▷ adj wild
WARRIGALS > WARRIGAL
WARRING > WAR
WARRIOR n person who fights in a war
WARRIORS > WARRIOR
WARRISON same as > WARISON
WARRISONS > WARRISON
WARS > WAR

WARSAW n type of grouper fish
WARSAWS > WARSAW
WARSHIP n ship designed and equipped for naval combat
WARSHIPS > WARSHIP
WARSLE dialect word for > WRESTLE
WARSLED > WARSLE
WARSLER > WARSLE
WARSLERS > WARSLE
WARSLES > WARSLE
WARSLING > WARSLE
WARST obsolete form of > WORST
WARSTLE dialect form of > WRESTLE
WARSTLED > WARSTLE
WARSTLER > WARSTLE
WARSTLERS > WARSTLE
WARSTLES > WARSTLE
WARSTLING > WARSTLE
WART n small hard growth on the skin
WARTED > WART
WARTHOG n wild African pig with wartlike lumps on the face
WARTHOGS > WARTHOG
WARTIER > WART
WARTIEST > WART
WARTIME n time of war ▷ adj of or in a time of war
WARTIMES > WARTIME
WARTLESS > WART
WARTLIKE > WART
WARTS > WART
WARTWEED n type of plant
WARTWEEDS > WARTWEED
WARTWORT another word for > WARTWEED
WARTWORTS > WARTWORT
WARTY > WART
WARWOLF n Roman engine of war
WARWOLVES > WARWOLF
WARWORK n work contributing to war effort
WARWORKS > WARWORK
WARWORN adj worn down by war
WARY adj watchful or cautious
WARZONE n area where a war is taking place or there is some other violent conflict
WARZONES > WARZONE
WAS > BE
WASABI n Japanese cruciferous plant cultivated for its thick green pungent root
WASABIS > WASABI
WASE n pad to relieve pressure of load carried on head
WASES > WASE
WASH vb clean (oneself, clothes, etc) with water and usu soap ▷ n act or process of washing

WASHABLE n thing that can be washed ▷ adj (esp of fabrics or clothes) capable of being washed without deteriorating
WASHABLES > WASHABLE
WASHAWAY another word for > WASHOUT
WASHAWAYS > WASHAWAY
WASHBAG n small bag for carrying toiletries when travelling
WASHBAGS > WASHBAG
WASHBALL n ball of soap
WASHBALLS > WASHBALL
WASHBASIN n basin for washing the face and hands
WASHBOARD n board having a surface, usually of corrugated metal, on which esp formerly, clothes were scrubbed
WASHBOWL same as > WASHBASIN
WASHBOWLS > WASHBOWL
WASHCLOTH n small piece of cloth used to wash the face and hands
WASHDAY n day on which clothes and linen are washed, often the same day each week
WASHDAYS > WASHDAY
WASHDOWN n the act of washing (oneself or something) down
WASHDOWNS > WASHDOWN
WASHED > WASH
WASHEN > WASH
WASHER n ring put under a nut or bolt or in a tap as a seal ▷ vb fit with a washer
WASHERED > WASHER
WASHERIES > WASHERY
WASHERING > WASHER
WASHERMAN n man who washes clothes for a living
WASHERMEN > WASHERMAN
WASHERS > WASHER
WASHERY n plant at a mine where water or other liquid is used to remove dirt from a mineral, esp coal
WASHES > WASH
WASHHAND n as in washhand basin, washhand stand for the washing of hands
WASHHOUSE n (formerly) building in which laundry was done
WASHIER > WASHY
WASHIEST > WASHY
WASHILY > WASHY
WASHIN n increase in the angle of attack of an aircraft wing towards the wing tip
WASHINESS > WASHY
WASHING n clothes to be washed

WASHINGS > WASHING
WASHINS > WASHIN
WASHLAND n frequently-flooded plain
WASHLANDS > WASHLAND
WASHOUT n complete failure
WASHOUTS > WASHOUT
WASHPOT n pot for washing things in
WASHPOTS > WASHPOT
WASHRAG same as > WASHCLOTH
WASHRAGS > WASHRAG
WASHROOM n toilet
WASHROOMS > WASHROOM
WASHSTAND n piece of furniture designed to hold a basin for washing the face and hands in
WASHTUB n tub or large container used for washing anything, esp clothes
WASHTUBS > WASHTUB
WASHUP n outcome of a process
WASHUPS > WASHUP
WASHWIPE n windscreen spray-cleaning mechanism
WASHWIPES > WASHWIPE
WASHWOMAN n woman who washes clothes for a living
WASHWOMEN > WASHWOMAN
WASHY adj overdiluted or weak
WASM n an obsolete belief; an out-of-fashion 'ism'
WASMS > WASM
WASP n stinging insect with a slender black-and-yellow striped body
WASPIE n tight-waisted corset
WASPIER > WASP
WASPIES > WASPIE
WASPIEST > WASP
WASPILY > WASP
WASPINESS > WASP
WASPISH adj bad-tempered
WASPISHLY > WASPISH
WASPLIKE > WASP
WASPNEST n nest of wasp
WASPNESTS > WASPNEST
WASPS > WASP
WASPY > WASP
WASSAIL n formerly, festivity when much drinking took place ▷ vb drink health of (a person) at a wassail
WASSAILED > WASSAIL
WASSAILER > WASSAIL
WASSAILRY > WASSAIL
WASSAILS > WASSAIL
WASSERMAN n man-shaped sea monster
WASSERMEN > WASSERMAN

W

WASSUP *sentence substitute* what is happening?

WAST *singular form of the past tense of* > BE

WASTABLE > WASTE

WASTAGE *n* loss by wear or waste

WASTAGES > WASTAGE

WASTE *vb* use pointlessly or thoughtlessly ▷ *n* act of wasting or state of being wasted ▷ *adj* rejected as worthless or surplus to requirements

WASTEBIN *n* bin for rubbish

WASTEBINS > WASTEBIN

WASTED > WASTE

WASTEFUL *adj* extravagant

WASTEL *n* fine bread or cake

WASTELAND *n* barren or desolate area of land

WASTELOT *n* piece of waste ground in a city

WASTELOTS > WASTELOT

WASTELS > WASTEL

WASTENESS > WASTE

WASTER *vb* waste ▷ *n* layabout

WASTERED > WASTER

WASTERFUL *Scots variant of* > WASTEFUL

WASTERIE *same as* > WASTERY

WASTERIES > WASTERIE

WASTERING > WASTER

WASTERS > WASTER

WASTERY *n* extravagance

WASTES > WASTE

WASTEWAY *n* open ditch

WASTEWAYS > WASTEWAY

WASTEWEIR *another name for* > SPILLWAY

WASTFULL *obsolete form of* > WASTEFUL

WASTING *adj* reducing the vitality and strength of the body

WASTINGLY > WASTING

WASTINGS > WASTE

WASTNESS *same as* > WASTENESS

WASTREL *n* lazy or worthless person

WASTRELS > WASTREL

WASTRIE *same as* > WASTERY

WASTRIES > WASTRIE

WASTRIFE *n* wastefulness

WASTRIFES > WASTRIFE

WASTRY *n* wastefulness

WASTS > WAST

WAT *adj* wet; drunken

WATAP *n* stringy thread made by Native Americans from the roots of conifers

WATAPE *same as* > WATAP

WATAPES > WATAPE

WATAPS > WATAP

WATCH *vb* look at closely ▷ *n* portable timepiece for the wrist or pocket

WATCHA *interj* greeting meaning 'what are you?'

WATCHABLE *adj* interesting, enjoyable, or entertaining

WATCHBAND *n* watch strap

WATCHBOX *n* sentry's box

WATCHCASE *n* protective case for a watch, generally of metal such as gold, silver, brass, or gunmetal

WATCHCRY *n* slogan used to rally support

WATCHDOG *n* dog kept to guard property

WATCHDOGS > WATCHDOG

WATCHED > WATCH

WATCHER *n* person who watches

WATCHERS > WATCHER

WATCHES > WATCH

WATCHET *n* shade of blue

WATCHETS > WATCHET

WATCHEYE *n* eye with a light-coloured iris

WATCHEYES > WATCHEYE

WATCHFUL *adj* vigilant or alert

WATCHING > WATCH

WATCHLIST *n* list of things to be monitored

WATCHMAN *n* man employed to guard a building or property

WATCHMEN > WATCHMAN

WATCHOUT *n* lookout

WATCHOUTS > WATCHOUT

WATCHWORD *n* word or phrase that sums up the attitude of a particular group

WATE > WIT

WATER *n* clear colourless tasteless liquid that falls as rain and forms rivers etc ▷ *vb* put water on or into

WATERAGE *n* transportation of cargo by means of ships, or the charges for such transportation

WATERAGES > WATERAGE

WATERBED *n* watertight mattress filled with water

WATERBEDS > WATERBED

WATERBIRD *n* any aquatic bird

WATERBUCK *n* any of various antelopes of the swampy areas of Africa, having long curved ridged horns

WATERBUS *n* boat offering regular transport service

WATERDOG *n* dog trained to hunt in water

WATERDOGS > WATERDOG

WATERED > WATER

WATERER > WATER

WATERERS > WATER

WATERFALL *n* place where the waters of a river drop vertically

WATERFOWL *n* bird that swims on water, such as a duck or swan

WATERHEAD *n* source of river

WATERHEN *another name for* > GALLINULE

WATERHENS > WATERHEN

WATERIER > WATERY

WATERIEST > WATERY

WATERILY > WATERY

WATERING > WATER

WATERINGS > WATER

WATERISH > WATER

WATERJET *n* jet of water

WATERJETS > WATERJET

WATERLEAF *n* carved column design

WATERLESS > WATER

WATERLILY *n* any of various aquatic plants having large leaves and showy flowers that float on the surface of the water

WATERLINE *n* level to which a ship's hull will be immersed when afloat

WATERLOG *vb* flood with water

WATERLOGS > WATERLOG

WATERLOO *n* total defeat

WATERLOOS > WATERLOO

WATERMAN *n* skilled boatman

WATERMARK *n* faint translucent design in a sheet of paper ▷ *vb* mark (paper) with a watermark

WATERMEN > WATERMAN

WATERMILL *n* mill driven by water

WATERPOX *n* chickenpox

WATERS > WATER

WATERSHED *n* important period or factor serving as a dividing line

WATERSIDE *n* area of land beside a river or lake

WATERSKI *vb* ski on water towed behind motorboat

WATERSKIS > WATERSKI

WATERWAY *n* river, canal, or other navigable channel used as a means of travel or transport

WATERWAYS > WATERWAY

WATERWEED *n* any of various weedy aquatic plants

WATERWORK *n* machinery, etc for storing, purifying, and distributing water

WATERWORN *adj* worn smooth by the action or passage of water

WATERY *adj* of, like, or containing water

WATERZOOI *n* type of Flemish stew

WATS > WAT

WATT *n* unit of power

WATTAGE *n* electrical power expressed in watts

WATTAGES > WATTAGE

WATTAPE *same as* > WATAP

WATTAPES > WATTAPE

WATTER > WAT

WATTEST > WAT

WATTHOUR *n* unit of energy equal to the power of one watt operating for an hour

WATTHOURS > WATTHOUR

WATTLE *n* branches woven over sticks to make a fence ▷ *adj* made of, formed by, or covered with wattle ▷ *vb* construct from wattle

WATTLED > WATTLE

WATTLES > WATTLE

WATTLESS > WATT

WATTLING > WATTLE

WATTLINGS > WATTLE

WATTMETER *n* meter for measuring electric power in watts

WATTS > WATT

WAUCHT *same as* > WAUGHT

WAUCHTED > WAUCHT

WAUCHTING > WAUCHT

WAUCHTS > WAUCHT

WAUFF *same as* > WAFF

WAUFFED > WAUFF

WAUFFING > WAUFF

WAUFFS > WAUFF

WAUGH *vb* bark

WAUGHED > WAUGH

WAUGHING > WAUGH

WAUGHS > WAUGH

WAUGHT *vb* drink in large amounts

WAUGHTED > WAUGHT

WAUGHTING > WAUGHT

WAUGHTS > WAUGHT

WAUK *vb* full (cloth)

WAUKED > WAUK

WAUKER > WAUK

WAUKERS > WAUK

WAUKING > WAUK

WAUKMILL *same as* > WAULKMILL

WAUKMILLS > WAULKMILL

WAUKRIFE *variant of* > WAKERIFE

WAUKS > WAUK

WAUL *vb* cry or wail plaintively like a cat

WAULED > WAUL

WAULING > WAUL

WAULINGS > WAUL

WAULK *same as* > WAUK

WAULKED > WAULK

WAULKER > WAULK

WAULKERS > WAULK

WAULKING > WAULK

WAULKMILL *n* cloth-fulling mill

WAULKS > WAULK

WAULS > WAUL

WAUR *obsolete form of* > WAR

WAURED > WAUR

WAURING > WAUR

WAURS > WAUR

WAURST > WAUR

WAVE *vb* move the hand to and fro as a greeting or

signal ▷ n moving ridge on water

WAVEBAND n range of wavelengths or frequencies used for a particular type of radio transmission

WAVEBANDS > WAVEBAND

WAVED > WAVE

WAVEFORM n shape of the graph of a wave or oscillation obtained by plotting the value of some changing quantity against time

WAVEFORMS > WAVEFORM

WAVEFRONT n surface associated with a propagating wave and passing through all points in the wave that have the same phase

WAVEGUIDE n solid rod of dielectric or a hollow metal tube, usually of rectangular cross section, used as a path to guide microwaves

WAVELESS > WAVE

WAVELET n small wave

WAVELETS > WAVELET

WAVELIKE > WAVE

WAVELLITE n greyish-white, yellow, or brown mineral

WAVEMETER n instrument for measuring the frequency or wavelength of radio waves

WAVEOFF n signal or instruction to an aircraft not to land

WAVEOFFS > WAVEOFF

WAVER vb hesitate or be irresolute ▷ n act or an instance of wavering

WAVERED > WAVER

WAVERER > WAVER

WAVERERS > WAVER

WAVERIER > WAVERY

WAVERIEST > WAVERY

WAVERING > WAVER

WAVERINGS > WAVER

WAVEROUS same as > WAVERY

WAVERS > WAVER

WAVERY adj lacking firmness

WAVES > WAVE

WAVESHAPE another word for > WAVEFORM

WAVESON n goods floating on waves after shipwreck

WAVESONS > WAVESON

WAVETABLE n table of recorded sound waves used in certain types of synthesizers

WAVEY n snow goose or other wild goose

WAVEYS > WAVEY

WAVICLE n origin of wave

WAVICLES > WAVICLE

WAVIER > WAVY

WAVIES > WAVY

WAVIEST > WAVY

WAVILY > WAVY

WAVINESS > WAVY

WAVING > WAVE

WAVINGS > WAVE

WAVY adj having curves ▷ n snow goose or other wild goose

WAW another name for > VAV

WAWA n speech ▷ vb speak

WAWAED > WAWA

WAWAING > WAWA

WAWAS > WAWA

WAWE same as > WAW

WAWES > WAWE

WAWL same as > WAUL

WAWLED > WAWL

WAWLING > WAWL

WAWLINGS > WAWL

WAWLS > WAWL

WAWS > WAW

WAX n solid shiny fatty or oily substance used for sealing, making candles, etc ▷ vb coat or polish with wax

WAXABLE > WAX

WAXBERRY n waxy fruit of the wax myrtle or the snowberry

WAXBILL n any of various chiefly African finchlike weaverbirds

WAXBILLS > WAXBILL

WAXCLOTH another name for > OILCLOTH

WAXCLOTHS > WAXCLOTH

WAXED > WAX

WAXEN adj made of or like wax

WAXER > WAX

WAXERS > WAX

WAXES > WAX

WAXEYE n small New Zealand bird

WAXEYES > WAXEYE

WAXFLOWER n any of various plants with waxy flowers

WAXIER > WAXY

WAXIEST > WAXY

WAXILY > WAXY

WAXINESS > WAXY

WAXING > WAX

WAXINGS > WAX

WAXLIKE > WAX

WAXPLANT n climbing shrub of E Asia and Australia

WAXPLANTS > WAXPLANT

WAXWEED n type of wild flower

WAXWEEDS > WAXWEED

WAXWING n type of songbird

WAXWINGS > WAXWING

WAXWORK n lifelike wax model of a (famous) person

WAXWORKER > WAXWORK

WAXWORKS > WAXWORK

WAXWORM n waxmoth larva

WAXWORMS > WAXWORM

WAXY adj resembling wax in colour, appearance, or texture

WAY n manner or method ▷ vb travel

WAYANG n type of Indonesian performance with dancers or puppets

WAYANGS > WAYANG

WAYBILL n document stating the nature, origin, and destination of goods being transported

WAYBILLS > WAYBILL

WAYBOARD n thin geological seam separating larger strata

WAYBOARDS > WAYBOARD

WAYBREAD n plantain

WAYBREADS > WAYBREAD

WAYED > WAY

WAYFARE vb travel

WAYFARED > WAYFARE

WAYFARER n traveller

WAYFARERS > WAYFARER

WAYFARES > WAYFARE

WAYFARING > WAYFARE

WAYGOING n leaving

WAYGOINGS > WAYGOING

WAYGONE adj travel-weary

WAYGOOSE same as > WAYZGOOSE

WAYGOOSES > WAYGOOSE

WAYING > WAY

WAYLAID > WAYLAY

WAYLAY vb lie in wait for and accost or attack

WAYLAYER > WAYLAY

WAYLAYERS > WAYLAY

WAYLAYING > WAYLAY

WAYLAYS > WAYLAY

WAYLEAVE n access to property granted by a landowner for payment

WAYLEAVES > WAYLEAVE

WAYLEGGO interj away here! let go!

WAYLESS > WAY

WAYMARK n symbol or signpost marking the route of a footpath ▷ vb mark out with waymarks

WAYMARKED > WAYMARK

WAYMARKS > WAYMARK

WAYMENT vb express grief

WAYMENTED > WAYMENT

WAYMENTS > WAYMENT

WAYPOINT n stopping point on route

WAYPOINTS > WAYPOINT

WAYPOST n signpost

WAYPOSTS > WAYPOST

WAYS > WAY

WAYSIDE n side of a road

WAYSIDES > WAYSIDE

WAYWARD adj erratic, selfish, or stubborn

WAYWARDLY > WAYWARD

WAYWISER n device for measuring distance

WAYWISERS > WAYWISER

WAYWODE n Slavonic governor

WAYWODES > WAYWODE

WAYWORN adj worn or tired by travel

WAYZGOOSE n works outing made annually by a printing house

WAZ same as > WAZZ

WAZIR another word for > VIZIER

WAZIRS > WAZIR

WAZOO n slang word for person's bottom

WAZOOS > WAZOO

WAZZ vb urinate ▷ n act of urinating

WAZZED > WAZZ

WAZZES > WAZZ

WAZZING > WAZZ

WAZZOCK n foolish or annoying person

WAZZOCKS > WAZZOCK

WE pron speaker or writer and one or more others

WEAK adj lacking strength

WEAKEN vb make or become weak

WEAKENED > WEAKEN

WEAKENER > WEAKEN

WEAKENERS > WEAKEN

WEAKENING n act of weakening

WEAKENS > WEAKEN

WEAKER > WEAK

WEAKEST > WEAK

WEAKFISH n any of several sea trouts

WEAKISH > WEAK

WEAKISHLY > WEAK

WEAKLIER > WEAKLY

WEAKLIEST > WEAKLY

WEAKLING n feeble person or animal

WEAKLINGS > WEAKLING

WEAKLY adv feebly ▷ adj weak or sickly

WEAKNESS n being weak

WEAKON n subatomic particle

WEAKONS > WEAKON

WEAKSIDE n (in basketball) side of court away from ball

WEAKSIDES > WEAKSIDE

WEAL n raised mark left on the skin by a blow

WEALD n open or forested country

WEALDS > WEALD

WEALS > WEAL

WEALSMAN n statesman

WEALSMEN > WEALSMAN

WEALTH n state of being rich

WEALTHIER > WEALTHY

WEALTHILY > WEALTHY

WEALTHS > WEALTH

WEALTHY adj possessing wealth

WEAMB same as > WAME

WEAMBS > WEAMB

WEAN vb accustom (a baby or young mammal) to food other than mother's milk
WEANED > WEAN
WEANEL n recently-weaned child or animal
WEANELS > WEANEL
WEANER n person or thing that weans
WEANERS > WEANER
WEANING > WEAN
WEANINGS > WEAN
WEANLING n child or young animal recently weaned
WEANLINGS > WEANLING
WEANS > WEAN
WEAPON vb arm ▷ n object used in fighting
WEAPONED > WEAPON
WEAPONEER n person associated with the use or maintenance of weapons, esp nuclear weapons ▷ vb supply with weapons
WEAPONING > WEAPON
WEAPONISE same as > WEAPONIZE
WEAPONIZE vb adapt (a chemical, bacillus, etc) in such a way that it can be used as a weapon
WEAPONRY n weapons collectively
WEAPONS > WEAPON
WEAR vb have on the body as clothing or ornament ▷ n clothes suitable for a particular time or purpose
WEARABLE adj suitable for wear or able to be worn ▷ n any garment that can be worn
WEARABLES > WEARABLE
WEARED > WEAR
WEARER > WEAR
WEARERS > WEAR
WEARIED > WEARY
WEARIER > WEARY
WEARIES > WEARY
WEARIEST > WEARY
WEARIFUL same as > WEARISOME
WEARILESS adj not wearied or able to be wearied
WEARILY > WEARY
WEARINESS > WEARY
WEARING adj tiring ▷ n act of wearing
WEARINGLY > WEARING
WEARINGS > WEAR
WEARISH adj withered
WEARISOME adj tedious
WEARPROOF adj resistant to damage from normal wear or usage
WEARS > WEAR
WEARY adj tired or exhausted ▷ vb make or become weary
WEARYING > WEARY
WEASAND former name for the > TRACHEA

WEASANDS > WEASAND
WEASEL n small carnivorous mammal with a long body and short legs ▷ vb use ambiguous language to avoid speaking directly or honestly
WEASELED > WEASEL
WEASELER > WEASEL
WEASELERS > WEASEL
WEASELING > WEASEL
WEASELLED > WEASEL
WEASELLER > WEASEL
WEASELLY > WEASEL
WEASELS > WEASEL
WEASELY > WEASEL
WEASON Scots form of > WEASAND
WEASONS > WEASON
WEATHER n day-to-day atmospheric conditions of a place ▷ vb (cause to) be affected by the weather
WEATHERED adj affected by exposure to the action of the weather
WEATHERER > WEATHER
WEATHERLY adj (of a sailing vessel) making very little leeway when close-hauled, even in a stiff breeze
WEATHERS > WEATHER
WEAVE vb make (fabric) by interlacing (yarn) on a loom
WEAVED > WEAVE
WEAVER n person who weaves, esp as a means of livelihood
WEAVERS > WEAVER
WEAVES > WEAVE
WEAVING > WEAVE
WEAVINGS > WEAVE
WEAZAND same as > WEASAND
WEAZANDS > WEAZAND
WEAZEN same as > WIZEN
WEAZENED > WEAZEN
WEAZENING > WEAZEN
WEAZENS > WEAZEN
WEB n net spun by a spider ▷ vb cover with or as if with a web
WEBAPP n application program that is accessed on the internet
WEBAPPS > WEBAPP
WEBBED > WEB
WEBBIE n person who is well versed in the use of the World Wide Web
WEBBIER > WEBBY
WEBBIES > WEBBIE
WEBBIEST > WEBBY
WEBBING n anything that forms a web
WEBBINGS > WEBBING
WEBBY adj of, relating to, resembling, or consisting of a web
WEBCAM n camera that transmits images over the internet

WEBCAMS > WEBCAM
WEBCAST n broadcast of an event over the internet ▷ vb make such a broadcast
WEBCASTED > WEBCAST
WEBCASTER > WEBCAST
WEBCASTS > WEBCAST
WEBCHAT n real time conversation over the internet
WEBCHATS > WEBCHAT
WEBER n SI unit of magnetic flux
WEBERS > WEBER
WEBFED adj (of printing press) printing from rolls of paper
WEBFEET > WEBFOOT
WEBFOOT n foot having the toes connected by folds of skin
WEBFOOTED > WEBFOOT
WEBHEAD n person who uses the Internet a lot
WEBHEADS > WEBHEAD
WEBIFIED > WEBIFY
WEBIFIES > WEBIFY
WEBIFY vb convert (information) for display on the internet
WEBIFYING > WEBIFY
WEBINAR n interactive seminar conducted over the World Wide Web
WEBINARS > WEBINAR
WEBISODE n episode (of a television series) intended for on-line viewing
WEBISODES > WEBISODE
WEBLESS > WEB
WEBLIKE > WEB
WEBLISH n shorthand form of English that is used in text messaging, chat rooms, etc
WEBLISHES > WEBLISH
WEBLOG n person's online journal
WEBLOGGER > WEBLOG
WEBLOGS > WEBLOG
WEBMAIL n system of electronic mail accessed mail via the internet
WEBMAILS > WEBMAIL
WEBMASTER n person responsible for the administration of a website on the World Wide Web
WEBPAGE n page on website
WEBPAGES > WEBPAGE
WEBRING n group of websites organized in a circular structure
WEBRINGS > WEBRING
WEBS > WEB
WEBSITE n group of connected pages on the World Wide Web
WEBSITES > WEBSITE
WEBSPACE n storage space on a web server

WEBSPACES > WEBSPACE
WEBSTER archaic word for > WEAVER
WEBSTERS > WEBSTER
WEBWHEEL n wheel containing a plate or web instead of spokes
WEBWHEELS > WEBWHEEL
WEBWORK n work done using the World Wide Web
WEBWORKS > WEBWORK
WEBWORM n type of caterpillar
WEBWORMS > WEBWORM
WEBZINE n magazine published on the Internet
WEBZINES > WEBZINE
WECHT n agricultural tool ▷ vb winnow (corn)
WECHTED > WECHT
WECHTING > WECHT
WECHTS > WECHT
WED vb marry
WEDDED > WED
WEDDER dialect form of > WEATHER
WEDDERED > WEDDER
WEDDERING > WEDDER
WEDDERS > WEDDER
WEDDING > WED
WEDDINGS > WEDDING
WEDEL variant of > WEDELN
WEDELED > WEDEL
WEDELING > WEDEL
WEDELN n succession of high-speed turns performed in skiing ▷ vb perform a wedeln
WEDELNED > WEDELN
WEDELNING > WEDELN
WEDELNS > WEDELN
WEDELS > WEDEL
WEDGE n piece of material thick at one end and thin at the other ▷ vb fasten or split with a wedge
WEDGED > WEDGE
WEDGELIKE > WEDGE
WEDGES > WEDGE
WEDGEWISE adv in manner of a wedge
WEDGIE n wedge-heeled shoe
WEDGIER > WEDGE
WEDGIES > WEDGIE
WEDGIEST > WEDGE
WEDGING > WEDGE
WEDGINGS > WEDGE
WEDGY > WEDGE
WEDLOCK n marriage
WEDLOCKS > WEDLOCK
WEDS > WED
WEE adj small or short ▷ n instance of urinating ▷ vb urinate
WEED n plant growing where undesired ▷ vb clear of weeds
WEEDBED n body of water having lots of weeds
WEEDBEDS > WEEDBED
WEEDED > WEED
WEEDER > WEED

WEEDERIES > WEEDERY
WEEDERS > WEED
WEEDERY n weed-ridden area
WEEDHEAD n habitual user of marijuana
WEEDHEADS > WEEDHEAD
WEEDICIDE n weed-killer
WEEDIER > WEEDY
WEEDIEST > WEEDY
WEEDILY > WEEDY
WEEDINESS > WEEDY
WEEDING > WEED
WEEDINGS > WEED
WEEDLESS > WEED
WEEDLIKE > WEED
WEEDLINE n edge of a weedbed
WEEDLINES > WEEDLINE
WEEDS pl n widow's mourning clothes
WEEDY adj (of a person) thin and weak
WEEING > WEE
WEEJUNS pl n moccasin-style shoes for casual wear
WEEK n period of seven days, esp one beginning on a Sunday ⊳ adv seven days before or after a specified day
WEEKDAY n any day of the week except Saturday or Sunday
WEEKDAYS > WEEKDAY
WEEKE same as > WICK
WEEKEND n Saturday and Sunday ⊳ vb spend or pass a weekend
WEEKENDED > WEEKEND
WEEKENDER n person spending a weekend holiday in a place, esp habitually
WEEKENDS adv at the weekend, esp regularly or during every weekend
WEEKES > WEEKE
WEEKLIES > WEEKLY
WEEKLONG adj lasting a week
WEEKLY adv happening, done, etc once a week ⊳ n newspaper or magazine published once a week ⊳ adj happening once a week or every week
WEEKNIGHT n evening or night of a weekday
WEEKS > WEEK
WEEL Scot word for > WELL
WEELS > WEEL
WEEM n underground home
WEEMS > WEEM
WEEN vb think or imagine (something)
WEENED > WEEN
WEENIE adj very small ⊳ n wiener
WEENIER > WEENIE
WEENIES > WEENIE
WEENIEST > WEENY
WEENING > WEEN
WEENS > WEEN

WEENSIER > WEENSY
WEENSIEST > WEENSY
WEENSY same as > WEENY
WEENY adj very small
WEEP vb shed tears ⊳ n spell of weeping
WEEPER n person who weeps, esp a hired mourner
WEEPERS > WEEPER
WEEPHOLE n small drain hole in wall
WEEPHOLES > WEEPHOLE
WEEPIE same as > WEEPY
WEEPIER > WEEPY
WEEPIES > WEEPY
WEEPIEST > WEEPY
WEEPILY > WEEPY
WEEPINESS > WEEPY
WEEPING adj (of plants) having slender hanging branches
WEEPINGLY > WEEPING
WEEPINGS > WEEPING
WEEPS > WEEP
WEEPY adj liable to cry ⊳ n sentimental film or book
WEER > WEE
WEES > WEE
WEEST > WEE
WEET dialect form of > WET
WEETE same as > WIT
WEETED > WEETE
WEETEN same as > WIT
WEETER > WEET
WEETEST > WEET
WEETING > WEET
WEETINGLY > WEET
WEETLESS obsolete variant of > WITLESS
WEETS > WEET
WEEVER n type of small fish
WEEVERS > WEEVER
WEEVIL n small beetle that eats grain etc
WEEVILED same as > WEEVILLED
WEEVILLED adj weevil-ridden
WEEVILLY another word for > WEEVILLED
WEEVILS > WEEVIL
WEEVILY another word for > WEEVILLED
WEEWEE vb urinate
WEEWEED > WEEWEE
WEEWEEING > WEEWEE
WEEWEES > WEEWEE
WEFT n cross threads in weaving ⊳ vb form weft
WEFTAGE n texture
WEFTAGES > WEFTAGE
WEFTE n forsaken child
WEFTED > WEFT
WEFTES > WEFTE
WEFTING > WEFT
WEFTS > WEFT
WEFTWISE adv in the direction of the weft
WEID n sudden illness
WEIDS > WEID

WEIGELA n type of shrub
WEIGELAS > WEIGELA
WEIGELIA same as > WEIGELA
WEIGELIAS > WEIGELIA
WEIGH vb have a specified weight
WEIGHABLE > WEIGH
WEIGHAGE n duty paid for weighing goods
WEIGHAGES > WEIGHAGE
WEIGHED > WEIGH
WEIGHER > WEIGH
WEIGHERS > WEIGH
WEIGHING > WEIGH
WEIGHINGS > WEIGH
WEIGHMAN n person responsible for weighing goods
WEIGHMEN > WEIGHMAN
WEIGHS > WEIGH
WEIGHT n heaviness of an object ⊳ vb add weight to
WEIGHTAGE same as > WEIGHTING
WEIGHTED > WEIGHT
WEIGHTER > WEIGHT
WEIGHTERS > WEIGHT
WEIGHTIER > WEIGHTY
WEIGHTILY > WEIGHTY
WEIGHTING n extra allowance paid in special circumstances
WEIGHTS > WEIGHT
WEIGHTY adj important or serious
WEIL n whirlpool
WEILS > WEIL
WEINER same as > WIENER
WEINERS > WEINER
WEIR vb ward off ⊳ n river dam
WEIRD adj strange or bizarre ⊳ vb warn beforehand
WEIRDED > WEIRD
WEIRDER > WEIRD
WEIRDEST > WEIRD
WEIRDIE same as > WEIRDO
WEIRDIES > WEIRDIE
WEIRDING > WEIRD
WEIRDLY > WEIRD
WEIRDNESS > WEIRD
WEIRDO n peculiar person
WEIRDOES > WEIRDO
WEIRDOS > WEIRDO
WEIRDS > WEIRD
WEIRDY n weird person
WEIRED > WEIR
WEIRING > WEIR
WEIRS > WEIR
WEISE same as > WISE
WEISED > WEISE
WEISES > WEISE
WEISING > WEISE
WEIZE same as > WISE
WEIZED > WEIZE
WEIZES > WEIZE
WEIZING > WEIZE
WEKA n flightless New Zealand rail
WEKAS > WEKA

WELAWAY same as > WELLAWAY
WELCH same as > WELSH
WELCHED > WELCH
WELCHER > WELCH
WELCHERS > WELCH
WELCHES > WELCH
WELCHING > WELCH
WELCOME vb greet with pleasure ⊳ n kindly greeting ⊳ adj received gladly
WELCOMED > WELCOME
WELCOMELY > WELCOME
WELCOMER > WELCOME
WELCOMERS > WELCOME
WELCOMES > WELCOME
WELCOMING > WELCOME
WELD vb join (pieces of metal or plastic) by softening with heat ⊳ n welded joint
WELDABLE > WELD
WELDED > WELD
WELDER > WELD
WELDERS > WELD
WELDING > WELD
WELDINGS > WELD
WELDLESS > WELD
WELDMENT n unit composed of welded pieces
WELDMENTS > WELDMENT
WELDMESH n type of fencing consisting of wire mesh reinforced by welding
WELDOR > WELD
WELDORS > WELDOR
WELDS > WELD
WELFARE n wellbeing
WELFARES > WELFARE
WELFARISM n policies or attitudes associated with a welfare state
WELFARIST > WELFARISM
WELFARITE n (US) person who is on welfare
WELK vb wither; dry up
WELKE obsolete form of > WELK
WELKED > WELK
WELKES > WELKE
WELKIN n sky, heavens, or upper air
WELKING > WELK
WELKINS > WELKIN
WELKS > WELK
WELKT adj twisted
WELL adv satisfactorily ⊳ adj in good health ⊳ interj exclamation of surprise, interrogation, etc ⊳ n hole sunk into the earth to reach water, oil, or gas ⊳ vb flow upwards or outwards
WELLADAY interj alas
WELLADAYS interj alas
WELLANEAR interj alas
WELLAWAY interj alas!
WELLAWAYS interj alas

W

WELLBEING n state of being well, happy, or prosperous
WELLBORN adj having been born into a wealthy family
WELLCURB n stone surround at top of well
WELLCURBS > WELLCURB
WELLDOER n moral person
WELLDOERS > WELLDOER
WELLED > WELL
WELLHEAD n source of a well or stream
WELLHEADS > WELLHEAD
WELLHOLE n well shaft
WELLHOLES > WELLHOLE
WELLHOUSE n housing for well
WELLIE n wellington boot
WELLIES > WELLY
WELLING > WELL
WELLINGS > WELL
WELLNESS n state of being in good physical and mental health
WELLS > WELL
WELLSITE n site of well
WELLSITES > WELLSITE
WELLY n energy or commitment
WELS n type of catfish
WELSH vb fail to pay a debt or fulfil an obligation
WELSHED > WELSH
WELSHER > WELSH
WELSHERS > WELSH
WELSHES > WELSH
WELSHING > WELSH
WELT same as > WEAL
WELTED > WELT
WELTER n jumbled mass ▷ vb roll about, writhe, or wallow
WELTERED > WELTER
WELTERING > WELTER
WELTERS > WELTER
WELTING > WELT
WELTINGS > WELT
WELTS > WELT
WEM same as > WAME
WEMB same as > WAME
WEMBS > WEMB
WEMS > WEM
WEN n cyst on the scalp
WENA pron South African word for you
WENCH n young woman ▷ vb frequent the company of prostitutes
WENCHED > WENCH
WENCHER > WENCH
WENCHERS > WENCH
WENCHES > WENCH
WENCHING > WENCH
WEND vb go or travel
WENDED > WEND
WENDIGO n evil spirit or cannibal
WENDIGOES > WENDIGO
WENDIGOS > WENDIGO
WENDING > WEND
WENDS > WEND

WENGE n type of tree found in central and West Africa
WENGES > WENGE
WENNIER > WEN
WENNIEST > WEN
WENNISH > WEN
WENNY > WEN
WENS > WEN
WENT n path
WENTS > WENT
WEPT > WEEP
WERE vb form of the past tense of **be** used after we, you, they, or a plural noun
WEREGILD same as > WERGILD
WEREGILDS > WEREGILD
WEREWOLF n (in folklore) person who can turn into a wolf
WERGELD same as > WERGILD
WERGELDS > WERGELD
WERGELT same as > WERGELD
WERGELTS > WERGELT
WERGILD n price set on a man's life, to be paid as compensation by his slayer
WERGILDS > WERGILD
WERNERITE another name for > SCAPOLITE
WERO n challenge made by an armed Māori warrior to a visitor to a marae
WEROS > WERO
WERRIS slang word for > URINATION
WERRISES > WERRIS
WERSH adj tasteless
WERSHER > WERSH
WERSHEST > WERSH
WERT singular form of the past tense of > BE
WERWOLF same as > WEREWOLF
WERWOLVES > WERWOLF
WESAND same as > WEASAND
WESANDS > WESAND
WESKIT informal word for > WAISTCOAT
WESKITS > WESKIT
WESSAND same as > WEASAND
WESSANDS > WESSAND
WEST n part of the horizon where the sun sets ▷ adj or in the west ▷ adv in, to, or towards the west ▷ vb move in westerly direction
WESTABOUT adv in, to, or towards the west
WESTBOUND adj going towards the west
WESTED > WEST
WESTER vb move or appear to move towards the west ▷ n strong wind or storm from the west
WESTERED > WESTER
WESTERING > WESTER

WESTERLY adj of or in the west ▷ adv towards the west ▷ n wind blowing from the west
WESTERN adj of or in the west ▷ n film or story about cowboys in the western US
WESTERNER n person from the west of a country or area
WESTERNS > WESTERN
WESTERS > WESTER
WESTIE n informal word for a young working-class person from the western suburbs of Sydney
WESTIES > WESTIE
WESTING n movement, deviation, or distance covered in a westerly direction
WESTINGS > WESTING
WESTLIN Scots word for > WESTERN
WESTLINS adv to or in west
WESTMOST adj most western
WESTS > WEST
WESTWARD adv towards the west ▷ n westward part or direction ▷ adj moving, facing, or situated in the west
WESTWARDS same as > WESTWARD
WET adj covered or soaked with water or another liquid ▷ n moisture or rain ▷ vb make wet
WETA n type of wingless insect
WETAS > WETA
WETBACK n Mexican labourer who enters the US illegally
WETBACKS > WETBACK
WETHER n male sheep, esp a castrated one
WETHERS > WETHER
WETLAND n area of marshy land
WETLANDS > WETLAND
WETLY > WET
WETNESS n the state of being wet
WETNESSES > WET
WETPROOF adj waterproof
WETS > WET
WETSUIT n body suit for diving
WETSUITS > WETSUIT
WETTABLE > WET
WETTED > WET
WETTER > WET
WETTERS > WET
WETTEST > WET
WETTIE n wetsuit
WETTIES > WETTIE
WETTING > WET
WETTINGS > WET
WETTISH > WET
WETWARE n humorous term for the brain

WETWARES > WETWARE
WEX obsolete form of > WAX
WEXE obsolete form of > WAX
WEXED > WEX
WEXES > WEX
WEXING > WEX
WEY n measurement of weight
WEYARD obsolete form of > WEIRD
WEYS > WEY
WEYWARD obsolete form of > WEIRD
WEZAND obsolete form of > WEASAND
WEZANDS > WEZAND
WHA Scot word for > WHO
WHACK vb strike with a resounding blow ▷ n such a blow
WHACKED > WHACK
WHACKER > WHACK
WHACKERS > WHACK
WHACKIER > WHACKY
WHACKIEST > WHACKY
WHACKING adj huge ▷ n severe beating ▷ adv extremely
WHACKINGS > WHACKING
WHACKO n mad person
WHACKOES > WHACKO
WHACKOS > WHACKO
WHACKS > WHACK
WHACKY variant spelling of > WACKY
WHAE same as > WHA
WHAISLE Scots form of > WHEEZE
WHAISLED > WHAISLE
WHAISLES > WHAISLE
WHAISLING > WHAISLE
WHAIZLE same as > WHAISLE
WHAIZLED > WHAIZLE
WHAIZLES > WHAIZLE
WHAIZLING > WHAIZLE
WHAKAIRO n art of carving
WHAKAIROS > WHAKAIRO
WHAKAPAPA n genealogy
WHALE n large fish-shaped sea mammal ▷ vb hunt for whales
WHALEBACK n something shaped like the back of a whale
WHALEBOAT n narrow boat from 20 to 30 feet long having a sharp prow and stern, formerly used in whaling
WHALEBONE n horny substance hanging from the upper jaw of toothless whales
WHALED > WHALE
WHALELIKE > WHALE
WHALEMAN n person employed in whaling
WHALEMEN > WHALEMAN
WHALER n ship or person involved in whaling
WHALERIES > WHALERY
WHALERS > WHALER

WHALERY n whaling
WHALES > WHALE
WHALING n hunting of whales for food and oil ▷ adv extremely
WHALINGS > WHALING
WHALLY adj (of eyes) with light-coloured irises
WHAM interj expression indicating suddenness or forcefulness ▷ n forceful blow or impact or the sound produced by such a blow or impact ▷ vb strike or cause to strike with great force
WHAMMED > WHAM
WHAMMIES > WHAMMY
WHAMMING > WHAM
WHAMMO n sound of a sudden collision
WHAMMOS > WHAMMO
WHAMMY n devastating setback
WHAMO same as > WHAMMO
WHAMPLE n strike
WHAMPLES > WHAMPLE
WHAMS > WHAM
WHANAU n (in Māori societies) a family, esp an extended family
WHANAUS > WHANAU
WHANG vb strike or be struck so as to cause a resounding noise ▷ n resounding noise produced by a heavy blow
WHANGAM n imaginary creature
WHANGAMS > WHANGAM
WHANGED > WHANG
WHANGEE n tall woody grass grown for its stems, which are used for bamboo canes
WHANGEES > WHANGEE
WHANGING > WHANG
WHANGS > WHANG
WHAP same as > WHOP
WHAPPED > WHAP
WHAPPER same as > WHOPPER
WHAPPERS > WHAPPER
WHAPPING > WHAP
WHAPS > WHAP
WHARE n Māori hut or dwelling place
WHARENUI n (in New Zealand) meeting house
WHARENUIS > WHARENUI
WHAREPUNI n (in a Māori community) a tall carved building used as a guesthouse
WHARES > WHARE
WHARF n platform at a harbour for loading and unloading ships ▷ vb put (goods, etc) on a wharf
WHARFAGE n accommodation for ships at wharves
WHARFAGES > WHARFAGE
WHARFED > WHARF

WHARFIE n person employed to load and unload ships
WHARFIES > WHARFIE
WHARFING > WHARF
WHARFINGS > WHARF
WHARFS > WHARF
WHARVE n wooden disc or wheel on a shaft serving as a flywheel or pulley
WHARVES > WHARVE
WHAT pron which thing ▷ interj exclamation of anger, surprise, etc ▷ adv in which way, how much ▷ n part; portion
WHATA n building on stilts or a raised platform for storing provisions
WHATAS > WHATA
WHATCHA interj greeting meaning 'what are you?'
WHATEN adj what; what kind of
WHATEVER pron everything or anything that ▷ adj intensive form of what ▷ determiner intensive form of what ▷ interj expression used to show indifference or dismissal
WHATEVS interj whatever
WHATNA another word for > WHATEN
WHATNESS n what something is
WHATNOT n similar unspecified thing
WHATNOTS > WHATNOT
WHATS > WHAT
WHATSIS US form of > WHATSIT
WHATSISES > WHATSIS
WHATSIT n person or thing the name of which is temporarily forgotten
WHATSITS > WHATSIT
WHATSO n of whatever kind
WHATTEN same as > WHATEN
WHAUP n curlew
WHAUPS > WHAUP
WHAUR Scot word for > WHERE
WHAURS > WHAUR
WHEAL same as > WEAL
WHEALS > WHEAL
WHEAR obsolete variant of > WHERE
WHEARE obsolete variant of > WHERE
WHEAT n grain used in making flour, bread, and pasta
WHEATEAR n small songbird
WHEATEARS > WHEATEAR
WHEATEN n type of dog ▷ adj made of the grain or flour of wheat
WHEATENS > WHEATEN

WHEATGERM n vitamin-rich embryo of the wheat kernel
WHEATIER > WHEATY
WHEATIEST > WHEATY
WHEATLAND n region where wheat is grown
WHEATLESS > WHEAT
WHEATMEAL n brown, but not wholemeal, flour
WHEATS > WHEAT
WHEATWORM n parasitic nematode worm that forms galls in the seeds of wheat
WHEATY adj having a wheat-like taste
WHEE interj exclamation of joy, thrill, etc
WHEECH vb move quickly
WHEECHED > WHEECH
WHEECHING > WHEECH
WHEECHS > WHEECH
WHEEDLE vb coax or cajole
WHEEDLED > WHEEDLE
WHEEDLER > WHEEDLE
WHEEDLERS > WHEEDLE
WHEEDLES > WHEEDLE
WHEEDLING > WHEEDLE
WHEEL n disc that revolves on an axle ▷ vb push or pull (something with wheels)
WHEELBASE n distance between a vehicle's front and back axles
WHEELED adj having or equipped with a wheel or wheels
WHEELER n horse or other draught animal nearest the wheel
WHEELERS > WHEELER
WHEELIE n manoeuvre on a bike in which the front wheel is raised off the ground
WHEELIER > WHEELY
WHEELIES > WHEELIE
WHEELIEST > WHEELY
WHEELING > WHEEL
WHEELINGS > WHEEL
WHEELLESS adj having no wheels
WHEELMAN n helmsman
WHEELMEN > WHEELMAN
WHEELS > WHEEL
WHEELSMAN same as > WHEELMAN
WHEELSMEN > WHEELSMAN
WHEELSPIN n rotation of a wheel when it is not achieving any grip on a surface
WHEELWORK n arrangement of wheels in a machine, esp a train of gears
WHEELY adj resembling a wheel
WHEEN n few
WHEENGE Scots form of > WHINGE
WHEENGED > WHEENGE

WHEENGES > WHEENGE
WHEENGING > WHEENGE
WHEENS > WHEEN
WHEEP vb fly quickly and lightly
WHEEPED > WHEEP
WHEEPING > WHEEP
WHEEPLE vb whistle weakly
WHEEPLED > WHEEPLE
WHEEPLES > WHEEPLE
WHEEPLING > WHEEPLE
WHEEPS > WHEEP
WHEESH vb silence (a person, noise, etc) or be silenced
WHEESHED > WHEESH
WHEESHES > WHEESH
WHEESHING > WHEESH
WHEESHT same as > WHEESH
WHEESHTED > WHEESHT
WHEESHTS > WHEESHT
WHEEZE vb breathe with a hoarse whistling noise ▷ n wheezing sound
WHEEZED > WHEEZE
WHEEZER > WHEEZE
WHEEZERS > WHEEZE
WHEEZES > WHEEZE
WHEEZIER > WHEEZE
WHEEZIEST > WHEEZE
WHEEZILY > WHEEZE
WHEEZING > WHEEZE
WHEEZINGS > WHEEZE
WHEEZLE vb make hoarse breathing sound
WHEEZLED > WHEEZLE
WHEEZLES > WHEEZLE
WHEEZLING > WHEEZLE
WHEEZY > WHEEZE
WHEFT same as > WAFT
WHEFTS > WHEFT
WHELK n edible snail-like shellfish
WHELKED adj having or covered with whelks
WHELKIER > WHELK
WHELKIEST > WHELK
WHELKS > WHELK
WHELKY > WHELK
WHELM vb engulf entirely with or as if with water
WHELMED > WHELM
WHELMING > WHELM
WHELMS > WHELM
WHELP n pup or cub ▷ vb (of an animal) give birth
WHELPED > WHELP
WHELPING > WHELP
WHELPLESS > WHELP
WHELPS > WHELP
WHEMMLE vb overturn
WHEMMLED > WHEMMLE
WHEMMLES > WHEMMLE
WHEMMLING > WHEMMLE
WHEN adv at what time? ▷ pron at which time ▷ n question of when
WHENAS conj while; inasmuch as
WHENCE n point of origin ▷ adv from what place or

w

source ▷ *pron* from what place, cause, or origin
WHENCES > WHENCE
WHENCEVER *adv* out of whatsoever place, cause or origin
WHENEVER *adv* at whatever time
WHENS > WHEN
WHENUA *n* land
WHENUAS > WHENUA
WHENWE *n* White immigrant to South Africa from Zimbabwe
WHENWES > WHENWE
WHERE *adv* in, at, or to what place? ▷ *pron* in, at, or to which place ▷ *n* question as to the position, direction, or destination of something
WHEREAS *n* testimonial introduced by whereas
WHEREASES > WHEREAS
WHEREAT *adv* at or to which place
WHEREBY *pron* by which ▷ *adv* how? by what means?
WHEREFOR *adv* for which ▷ *n* explanation or reason
WHEREFORE *adv* why ▷ *n* explanation or reason
WHEREFORS > WHEREFOR
WHEREFROM *adv* from what or where? whence? ▷ *pron* from which place
WHEREIN *adv* in what place or respect? ▷ *pron* in which place or thing
WHEREINTO *adv* into what place? ▷ *pron* into which place
WHERENESS *n* state of having a place
WHEREOF *adv* of what or which person or thing? ▷ *pron* of which person or thing
WHEREON *adv* on what thing or place? ▷ *pron* on which thing, place, etc
WHEREOUT *adv* out of which
WHERES > WHERE
WHERESO *adv* in or to unspecified place
WHERETO *adv* towards what (place, end, etc)? ▷ *pron* which
WHEREUNTO *same as* > WHERETO
WHEREUPON *adv* upon what?
WHEREVER *adv* at whatever place ▷ *pron* at, in, or to every place or point which
WHEREWITH *pron* with or by which ▷ *adv* with what?
WHERRET *vb* strike (someone) ▷ *n* blow, esp a slap on the face
WHERRETED > WHERRET

WHERRETS > WHERRET
WHERRIED > WHERRY
WHERRIES > WHERRY
WHERRIT *vb* worry or cause to worry
WHERRITED > WHERRIT
WHERRITS > WHERRIT
WHERRY *n* any of certain kinds of half-decked commercial boats ▷ *vb* travel in a wherry
WHERRYING > WHERRY
WHERRYMAN > WHERRY
WHERRYMEN > WHERRY
WHERVE *same as* > WHARVE
WHERVES > WHERVE
WHET *vb* sharpen (a tool) ▷ *n* act of whetting
WHETHER *conj* used to introduce any indirect question
WHETS > WHET
WHETSTONE *n* stone for sharpening tools
WHETTED > WHET
WHETTER > WHET
WHETTERS > WHET
WHETTING > WHET
WHEUGH *same as* > WHEW
WHEUGHED > WHEUGH
WHEUGHING > WHEUGH
WHEUGHS > WHEUGH
WHEW *interj* exclamation expressing relief, delight, etc ▷ *vb* express relief
WHEWED > WHEW
WHEWING > WHEW
WHEWS > WHEW
WHEY *n* watery liquid that separates from the curd when milk is clotted
WHEYEY > WHEY
WHEYFACE *n* pale bloodless face
WHEYFACED > WHEYFACE
WHEYFACES > WHEYFACE
WHEYIER > WHEY
WHEYIEST > WHEY
WHEYISH > WHEY
WHEYLIKE > WHEY
WHEYS > WHEY
WHICH *pron* used to request or refer to a choice from different possibilities ▷ *adj* used with a noun in requesting that a particular thing is further identified or distinguished
WHICHEVER *pron* any out of several ▷ *adj* any out of several ▷ *determiner* any (one, two, etc, out of several)
WHICKER *vb* (of a horse) to whinny or neigh
WHICKERED > WHICKER
WHICKERS > WHICKER
WHID *vb* move quickly
WHIDAH *same as* > WHYDAH
WHIDAHS > WHIDAH
WHIDDED > WHID
WHIDDER *vb* move with force

WHIDDERED > WHIDDER
WHIDDERS > WHIDDER
WHIDDING > WHID
WHIDS > WHID
WHIFF *n* puff of air or odour ▷ *vb* come, convey, or go in whiffs
WHIFFED > WHIFF
WHIFFER > WHIFF
WHIFFERS > WHIFF
WHIFFET *n* insignificant person
WHIFFETS > WHIFFET
WHIFFIER > WHIFFY
WHIFFIEST > WHIFFY
WHIFFING > WHIFF
WHIFFINGS > WHIFF
WHIFFLE *vb* think or behave in an erratic or unpredictable way
WHIFFLED > WHIFFLE
WHIFFLER *n* person who whiffles
WHIFFLERS > WHIFFLER
WHIFFLERY *n* frivolity
WHIFFLES > WHIFFLE
WHIFFLING > WHIFFLE
WHIFFS > WHIFF
WHIFFY *adj* smelly
WHIFT *n* brief emission of air
WHIFTS > WHIFT
WHIG *vb* go quickly
WHIGGED > WHIG
WHIGGING > WHIG
WHIGS > WHIG
WHILE *n* period of time
WHILED > WHILE
WHILERE *adv* a while ago
WHILES *adv* at times
WHILEVER *conj* as long as
WHILING > WHILE
WHILK *archaic and dialect word for* > WHICH
WHILLIED > WHILLY
WHILLIES > WHILLY
WHILLY *vb* influence by flattery
WHILLYING > WHILLY
WHILLYWHA *variant of* > WHILLY
WHILOM *adv* formerly ▷ *adj* one-time
WHILST *same as* > WHILE
WHIM *n* sudden fancy ▷ *vb* have a whim
WHIMBERRY *n* whortleberry
WHIMBREL *n* small European curlew with a striped head
WHIMBRELS > WHIMBREL
WHIMMED > WHIM
WHIMMIER > WHIMMY
WHIMMIEST > WHIMMY
WHIMMING > WHIM
WHIMMY *adj* having whims
WHIMPER *vb* cry in a soft whining way ▷ *n* soft plaintive whine
WHIMPERED > WHIMPER
WHIMPERER > WHIMPER
WHIMPERS > WHIMPER

WHIMPLE *same as* > WIMPLE
WHIMPLED > WHIMPLE
WHIMPLES > WHIMPLE
WHIMPLING > WHIMPLE
WHIMS > WHIM
WHIMSEY *same as* > WHIMSY
WHIMSEYS > WHIMSEY
WHIMSICAL *adj* unusual, playful, and fanciful
WHIMSIED > WHIMSY
WHIMSIER > WHIMSY
WHIMSIES > WHIMSY
WHIMSIEST > WHIMSY
WHIMSILY > WHIMSY
WHIMSY *n* capricious idea ▷ *adj* quaint, comical, or unusual
WHIN *n* gorse
WHINBERRY *same as* > WHIMBERRY
WHINCHAT *n* type of songbird
WHINCHATS > WHINCHAT
WHINE *n* high-pitched plaintive cry ▷ *vb* make such a sound
WHINED > WHINE
WHINER > WHINE
WHINERS > WHINE
WHINES > WHINE
WHINEY *same as* > WHINY
WHINGDING *same as* > WINGDING
WHINGE *vb* complain ▷ *n* complaint
WHINGED > WHINGE
WHINGEING > WHINGE
WHINGER > WHINGE
WHINGERS > WHINGE
WHINGES > WHINGE
WHINGIER > WHINGY
WHINGIEST > WHINGY
WHINGING > WHINGE
WHINGY *adj* complaining peevishly, whining
WHINIARD *same as* > WHINYARD
WHINIARDS > WHINIARD
WHINIER > WHINY
WHINIEST > WHINY
WHININESS > WHINY
WHINING > WHINE
WHININGLY > WHINE
WHININGS > WHINE
WHINNIED > WHINNY
WHINNIER > WHINNY
WHINNIES > WHINNY
WHINNIEST > WHINNY
WHINNY *vb* neigh softly ▷ *n* soft neigh ▷ *adj* covered in whin
WHINNYING > WHINNY
WHINS > WHIN
WHINSTONE *n* any dark hard fine-grained rock, such as basalt
WHINY *adj* high-pitched and plaintive
WHINYARD *n* sword
WHINYARDS > WHINYARD

WHIO n New Zealand mountain duck with blue plumage

WHIOS > WHIO

WHIP n cord attached to a handle, used for beating animals or people ▷ vb strike with a whip, strap, or cane

WHIPBIRD n any of several birds having a whistle ending in a whipcrack note

WHIPBIRDS > WHIPBIRD

WHIPCAT n tailor

WHIPCATS > WHIPCAT

WHIPCORD n strong worsted or cotton fabric with a diagonally ribbed surface

WHIPCORDS > WHIPCORD

WHIPCORDY adj whipcord-like

WHIPJACK n beggar imitating a sailor

WHIPJACKS > WHIPJACK

WHIPLASH n quick lash of a whip

WHIPLESS adj without a whip

WHIPLIKE > WHIP

WHIPPED > WHIP

WHIPPER > WHIP

WHIPPERS > WHIP

WHIPPET n racing dog like a small greyhound

WHIPPETS > WHIPPET

WHIPPIER > WHIPPY

WHIPPIEST > WHIPPY

WHIPPING > WHIP

WHIPPINGS > WHIP

WHIPPIT n small canister of nitrous oxide

WHIPPITS > WHIPPIT

WHIPPY adj springy

WHIPRAY n stingray

WHIPRAYS > WHIPRAY

WHIPS > WHIP

WHIPSAW n any saw with a flexible blade, such as a bandsaw ▷ vb saw with a whipsaw

WHIPSAWED > WHIPSAW

WHIPSAWN > WHIPSAW

WHIPSAWS > WHIPSAW

WHIPSNAKE n thin snake like leather whip

WHIPSTAFF n ship's steering bar

WHIPSTALL n stall in which an aircraft goes into a nearly vertical climb, pauses, slips backwards momentarily, and drops suddenly with its nose down

WHIPSTER n insignificant but pretentious or cheeky person, esp a young one

WHIPSTERS > WHIPSTER

WHIPSTOCK n handle of a whip

WHIPT old past tense of > WHIP

WHIPTAIL n type of lizard

WHIPTAILS > WHIPTAIL

WHIPWORM n parasitic worm living in the intestines of mammals

WHIPWORMS > WHIPWORM

WHIR n prolonged soft swish or buzz ▷ vb make or cause to make a whir

WHIRL vb spin or revolve ▷ n whirling movement

WHIRLBAT n thing moved with a whirl

WHIRLBATS > WHIRLBAT

WHIRLED > WHIRL

WHIRLER > WHIRL

WHIRLERS > WHIRL

WHIRLIER > WHIRLY

WHIRLIES n illness induced by excessive use of alcohol or drugs

WHIRLIEST > WHIRLY

WHIRLIGIG same as > WINDMILL

WHIRLING > WHIRL

WHIRLINGS > WHIRL

WHIRLPOOL n strong circular current of water

WHIRLS > WHIRL

WHIRLWIND n column of air whirling violently upwards in a spiral ▷ adj much quicker than normal

WHIRLY adj characterized by whirling

WHIRR same as > WHIR

WHIRRED > WHIR

WHIRRET vb strike with sharp blow

WHIRRETED > WHIRRET

WHIRRETS > WHIRRET

WHIRRIED > WHIRRY

WHIRRIER > WHIRRY

WHIRRIES > WHIRRY

WHIRRIEST > WHIRRY

WHIRRING > WHIR

WHIRRINGS > WHIR

WHIRRS > WHIRR

WHIRRY vb move quickly ▷ adj characteristic of a whir

WHIRRYING > WHIRRY

WHIRS > WHIR

WHIRTLE same as > WORTLE

WHIRTLES > WHIRTLE

WHISH less common word for > SWISH

WHISHED > WHISH

WHISHES > WHISH

WHISHING > WHISH

WHISHT interj hush! be quiet! ▷ adj silent or still ▷ vb make or become silent

WHISHTED > WHISHT

WHISHTING > WHISHT

WHISHTS > WHISHT

WHISK vb move or remove quickly ▷ n quick movement

WHISKED > WHISK

WHISKER n any of the long stiff hairs on the face of a cat or other mammal

WHISKERED adj having whiskers

WHISKERS > WHISKER

WHISKERY adj having whiskers

WHISKET same as > WISKET

WHISKETS > WHISKET

WHISKEY n Irish or American whisky

WHISKEYS > WHISKEY

WHISKIES > WHISKY

WHISKING > WHISK

WHISKS > WHISK

WHISKY n spirit distilled from fermented cereals

WHISPER vb speak softly, without vibration of the vocal cords ▷ n soft voice

WHISPERED > WHISPER

WHISPERER n person or thing that whispers

WHISPERS > WHISPER

WHISPERY > WHISPER

WHISS vb hiss

WHISSED > WHISS

WHISSES > WHISS

WHISSING > WHISS

WHIST same as > WHISHT

WHISTED > WHIST

WHISTING > WHIST

WHISTLE vb produce a shrill sound ▷ n whistling sound

WHISTLED > WHISTLE

WHISTLER n person or thing that whistles

WHISTLERS > WHISTLER

WHISTLES > WHISTLE

WHISTLING > WHISTLE

WHISTS > WHIST

WHIT n smallest particle

WHITE adj of the colour of snow ▷ n colour of snow

WHITEBAIT n small edible fish

WHITEBASS n type of fish

WHITEBEAM n type of tree

WHITECAP n wave with a white broken crest

WHITECAPS > WHITECAP

WHITECOAT n person who wears a white coat

WHITECOMB n fungal disease infecting the combs of certain fowls

WHITED adj as in whited sepulchre hypocrite

WHITEDAMP n mixture of poisonous gases, mainly carbon monoxide, occurring in coal mines

WHITEFACE n white stage make-up

WHITEFISH n type of fish

WHITEFLY n tiny whitish insect that is harmful to greenhouse plants

WHITEHEAD n type of pimple with a white head

WHITELIST n list of e-mail contacts from whom messages are regarded as acceptable by the user ▷ vb put (an email contact) on a whitelist

WHITELY > WHITE

WHITEN vb make or become white or whiter

WHITENED > WHITEN

WHITENER n substance that makes something white or whiter

WHITENERS > WHITENER

WHITENESS > WHITE

WHITENING > WHITEN

WHITENS > WHITEN

WHITEOUT n atmospheric condition in which blizzards or low clouds make it very difficult to see

WHITEOUTS > WHITEOUT

WHITEPOT n custard or milk pudding

WHITEPOTS > WHITEPOT

WHITER > WHITE

WHITES pl n white clothes, as worn for playing cricket

WHITEST > WHITE

WHITETAIL n type of deer

WHITEWALL n pneumatic tyre having white sidewalls

WHITEWARE n white ceramics

WHITEWASH n substance for whitening walls ▷ vb cover with whitewash

WHITEWING n type of bird

WHITEWOOD n light-coloured wood often prepared for staining

WHITEY same as > WHITY

WHITEYS > WHITEY

WHITHER same as > WUTHER

WHITHERED > WHITHER

WHITHERS > WHITHER

WHITIER > WHITY

WHITIES > WHITY

WHITIEST > WHITY

WHITING n edible sea fish

WHITINGS > WHITING

WHITISH > WHITE

WHITLING n type of trout

WHITLINGS > WHITLING

WHITLOW n inflamed sore on a finger or toe, esp round a nail

WHITLOWS > WHITLOW

WHITRACK n weasel or stoat

WHITRACKS > WHITRACK

WHITRET same as > WHITTRET

WHITRETS > WHITRET

WHITRICK n dialect word for a male weasel

WHITRICKS > WHITRICK

WHITS > WHIT

WHITSTER n person who whitens clothes

WHITSTERS > WHITSTER

WHITTAW same as > WHITTAWER
WHITTAWER n person who treats leather
WHITTAWS > WHITTAW
WHITTER variant spelling of > WITTER
WHITTERED > WHITTER
WHITTERS > WHITTER
WHITTLE vb cut or carve (wood) with a knife ▷ n knife, esp a large one
WHITTLED > WHITTLE
WHITTLER > WHITTLE
WHITTLERS > WHITTLE
WHITTLES > WHITTLE
WHITTLING > WHITTLE
WHITTRET n male weasel
WHITTRETS > WHITTRET
WHITY adj of a white colour ▷ n derogatory term for a White person
WHIZ same as > WHIZZ
WHIZBANG n small-calibre shell
WHIZBANGS > WHIZBANG
WHIZZ vb make a loud buzzing sound ▷ n loud buzzing sound
WHIZZBANG same as > WHIZBANG
WHIZZED > WHIZZ
WHIZZER > WHIZZ
WHIZZERS > WHIZZ
WHIZZES > WHIZZ
WHIZZIER > WHIZZY
WHIZZIEST > WHIZZY
WHIZZING > WHIZZ
WHIZZINGS > WHIZZ
WHIZZO same as > WHIZZY
WHIZZY adj using sophisticated technology
WHO pron which person
WHOA interj command used to stop or slow down
WHODUNIT same as > WHODUNNIT
WHODUNITS > WHODUNIT
WHODUNNIT n detective story, play, or film
WHOEVER pron any person who
WHOLE adj containing all the elements or parts ▷ n complete thing or system
WHOLEFOOD n food that has been processed as little as possible ▷ adj of or relating to wholefood
WHOLEMEAL adj (of flour) made from the whole wheat grain
WHOLENESS > WHOLE
WHOLES > WHOLE
WHOLESALE adv dealing by selling goods in large quantities to retailers ▷ n business of selling goods in large quantities and at lower prices to retailers for resale
WHOLESOME adj physically or morally beneficial

WHOLISM same as > HOLISM
WHOLISMS > WHOLISM
WHOLIST same as > HOLIST
WHOLISTIC same as > HOLISTIC
WHOLISTS > WHOLIST
WHOLLY adv completely or totally
WHOLPHIN n whale-dolphin hybrid
WHOLPHINS > WHOLPHIN
WHOM pron objective form of who
WHOMBLE same as > WHEMMLE
WHOMBLED > WHOMBLE
WHOMBLES > WHOMBLE
WHOMBLING > WHOMBLE
WHOMEVER pron objective form of whoever
WHOMMLE same as > WHEMMLE
WHOMMLED > WHOMMLE
WHOMMLES > WHOMMLE
WHOMMLING > WHOMMLE
WHOMP vb strike; thump
WHOMPED > WHOMP
WHOMPING > WHOMP
WHOMPS > WHOMP
WHOMSO pron whom; whomever
WHOOBUB same as > HUBBUB
WHOOBUBS > WHOOBUB
WHOOF same as > WOOF
WHOOFED > WHOOF
WHOOFING > WHOOF
WHOOFS > WHOOF
WHOOMP n sudden loud sound
WHOOMPH same as > WHOOMP
WHOOMPHS > WHOOMPH
WHOOMPS > WHOOMP
WHOONGA n narcotic smoked as a recreational drug in S Africa
WHOONGAS > WHOONGA
WHOOP n shout or cry to express excitement ▷ vb emit a whoop
WHOOPED > WHOOP
WHOOPEE n cry of joy
WHOOPEES > WHOOPEE
WHOOPER n type of swan
WHOOPERS > WHOOPER
WHOOPIE same as > WHOOPEE
WHOOPIES > WHOOPIE
WHOOPING > WHOOP
WHOOPINGS > WHOOPING
WHOOPLA n commotion; fuss
WHOOPLAS > WHOOPLA
WHOOPS interj exclamation of surprise or of apology
WHOOPSIE n animal excrement
WHOOPSIES > WHOOPSIE
WHOOSH n hissing or rushing sound ▷ vb make

or move with a hissing or rushing sound
WHOOSHED > WHOOSH
WHOOSHES > WHOOSH
WHOOSHING > WHOOSH
WHOOSIS n thingamajig
WHOOSISES > WHOOSIS
WHOOT obsolete variant of > HOOT
WHOOTED > WHOOT
WHOOTING > WHOOT
WHOOTS > WHOOT
WHOP vb strike, beat, or thrash ▷ n heavy blow or the sound made by such a blow
WHOPPED > WHOP
WHOPPER n anything unusually large
WHOPPERS > WHOPPER
WHOPPING n beating as punishment ▷ adj unusually large ▷ adv extremely
WHOPPINGS > WHOPPING
WHOPS > WHOP
WHORE n prostitute ▷ vb be or act as a prostitute
WHORED > WHORE
WHOREDOM n activity of whoring or state of being a whore
WHOREDOMS > WHOREDOM
WHORES > WHORE
WHORESON n bastard ▷ adj vile or hateful
WHORESONS > WHORESON
WHORING n act of whoring
WHORINGS > WHORING
WHORISH > WHORE
WHORISHLY > WHORE
WHORL n ring of leaves or petals ▷ vb form a whorl or whorls
WHORLBAT same as > WHIRLBAT
WHORLBATS > WHORLBAT
WHORLED > WHORL
WHORLING > WHORL
WHORLS > WHORL
WHORT n small shrub bearing blackish edible sweet berries
WHORTLE n whortleberry
WHORTLES > WHORTLE
WHORTS > WHORT
WHOSE pron of whom or of which ▷ determiner of whom? belonging to whom?
WHOSESO adj possessive form of whoso
WHOSEVER pron belonging to whoever
WHOSIS n thingamajig
WHOSISES > WHOSIS
WHOSIT n object or person whose name is not known
WHOSITS > WHOSIT
WHOSO archaic word for > WHOEVER
WHOSOEVER same as > WHOEVER

WHOT obsolete variant of > HOT
WHOW interj wow ▷ vb to wow
WHOWED > WHOW
WHOWING > WHOW
WHOWS > WHOW
WHUMMLE same as > WHEMMLE
WHUMMLED > WHUMMLE
WHUMMLES > WHUMMLE
WHUMMLING > WHUMMLE
WHUMP vb make a dull thud ▷ n dull thud
WHUMPED > WHUMP
WHUMPING > WHUMP
WHUMPS > WHUMP
WHUNSTANE Scots variant of > WHINSTONE
WHUP vb defeat totally
WHUPPED > WHUP
WHUPPING > WHUP
WHUPPINGS > WHUPPING
WHUPS > WHUP
WHY adv for what reason ▷ pron because of which ▷ n reason, purpose, or cause of something
WHYDA n type of African bird
WHYDAH n type of black African bird
WHYDAHS > WHYDAH
WHYDAS > WHYDA
WHYDUNIT same as > WHYDUNNIT
WHYDUNITS > WHYDUNIT
WHYDUNNIT n novel, film, etc, concerned with the motives of the criminal rather than his or her identity
WHYEVER adv for whatever reason
WHYS > WHY
WIBBLE vb wobble
WIBBLED > WIBBLE
WIBBLES > WIBBLE
WIBBLING > WIBBLE
WICCA n cult or practice of witchcraft
WICCAN n member of wicca
WICCANS > WICCAN
WICCAS > WICCA
WICE Scots form of > WISE
WICH n variant of wych
WICHES > WICH
WICK n cord through a lamp or candle which carries fuel to the flame ▷ adj lively or active ▷ vb (of a material) draw in (water, fuel, etc)
WICKAPE same as > WICOPY
WICKAPES > WICKAPE
WICKED adj morally bad ▷ n wicked person
WICKEDER > WICKED
WICKEDEST > WICKED
WICKEDLY > WICKED
WICKEDS > WICKED

WICKEN same as > QUICKEN

WICKENS > WICKEN

WICKER adj made of woven cane ▷ n slender flexible twig or shoot, esp of willow

WICKERED > WICKER

WICKERS > WICKER

WICKET n set of three cricket stumps and two bails

WICKETS > WICKET

WICKIES > WICKY

WICKING > WICK

WICKINGS > WICK

WICKIUP n crude shelter made of brushwood, mats, or grass and having an oval frame

WICKIUPS > WICKIUP

WICKLESS > WICK

WICKS > WICK

WICKTHING n creeping animal, such as a woodlouse

WICKY same as > QUICKEN

WICKYUP same as > WICKIUP

WICKYUPS > WICKYUP

WICOPIES > WICOPY

WICOPY n any of various North American trees, shrubs, or herbaceous plants

WIDDER same as > WIDOW

WIDDERS > WIDDER

WIDDIE same as > WIDDY

WIDDIES > WIDDY

WIDDLE vb urinate ▷ n urine

WIDDLED > WIDDLE

WIDDLES > WIDDLE

WIDDLING > WIDDLE

WIDDY vb rope made of twigs

WIDE adj large from side to side ▷ adv the full extent ▷ n (in cricket) a ball outside a batsman's reach

WIDEAWAKE n hat with a low crown and a very wide brim

WIDEBAND n wide bandwidth transmission medium ▷ adj capable of transmitting on a wide bandwidth

WIDEBANDS > WIDEBAND

WIDEBODY n aircraft with a wide fuselage

WIDELY > WIDE

WIDEN vb make or become wider

WIDENED > WIDEN

WIDENER > WIDEN

WIDENERS > WIDEN

WIDENESS > WIDE

WIDENING n act of widening

WIDENINGS > WIDENING

WIDENS > WIDEN

WIDEOUT n footballer who catches passes from the quarterback

WIDEOUTS > WIDEOUT

WIDER > WIDE

WIDES > WIDE

WIDEST > WIDE

WIDGEON same as > WIGEON

WIDGEONS > WIDGEON

WIDGET n any small device, the name of which is unknown or forgotten

WIDGETS > WIDGET

WIDGIE n female larrikin or bodgie

WIDGIES > WIDGIE

WIDISH > WIDE

WIDOW n woman whose husband is dead and who has not remarried ▷ vb cause to become a widow

WIDOWBIRD n whydah

WIDOWED > WIDOW

WIDOWER n man whose wife is dead and who has not remarried

WIDOWERED > WIDOWER

WIDOWERS > WIDOWER

WIDOWHOOD > WIDOW

WIDOWING > WIDOW

WIDOWMAN n widower

WIDOWMEN > WIDOWMAN

WIDOWS > WIDOW

WIDTH n distance from side to side

WIDTHS > WIDTH

WIDTHWAY adj across the width

WIDTHWAYS same as > WIDTHWISE

WIDTHWISE adv in the direction of the width

WIEL same as > WEEL

WIELD vb hold and use (a weapon)

WIELDABLE > WIELD

WIELDED > WIELD

WIELDER > WIELD

WIELDERS > WIELD

WIELDIER > WIELDY

WIELDIEST > WIELDY

WIELDING > WIELD

WIELDLESS adj unwieldy

WIELDS > WIELD

WIELDY adj easily handled, used, or managed

WIELS > WIEL

WIENER n kind of smoked beef or pork sausage, similar to a frankfurter

WIENERS > WIENER

WIENIE same as > WIENER

WIENIES > WIENIE

WIFE n woman to whom a man is married ▷ vb marry

WIFED > WIFE

WIFEDOM n state of being a wife

WIFEDOMS > WIFEDOM

WIFEHOOD > WIFE

WIFEHOODS > WIFE

WIFELESS > WIFE

WIFELIER > WIFE

WIFELIEST > WIFE

WIFELIKE > WIFE

WIFELY > WIFE

WIFES > WIFE

WIFEY n wife

WIFEYS > WIFEY

WIFIE n woman

WIFIES > WIFIE

WIFING > WIFE

WIFTIER > WIFTY

WIFTIEST > WIFTY

WIFTY adj scatterbrained

WIG n artificial head of hair ▷ vb furnish with a wig

WIGAN n stiff fabric

WIGANS > WIGAN

WIGEON n duck found in marshland

WIGEONS > WIGEON

WIGGA same as > WIGGER

WIGGAS > WIGGA

WIGGED > WIG

WIGGER n white youth who adopts Black youth culture

WIGGERIES > WIGGERY

WIGGERS > WIGGER

WIGGERY n wigs

WIGGIER > WIGGY

WIGGIEST > WIGGY

WIGGING > WIG

WIGGINGS > WIG

WIGGLE vb move jerkily from side to side ▷ n wiggling movement

WIGGLED > WIGGLE

WIGGLER > WIGGLE

WIGGLERS > WIGGLE

WIGGLES > WIGGLE

WIGGLIER > WIGGLE

WIGGLIEST > WIGGLE

WIGGLING > WIGGLE

WIGGLY > WIGGLE

WIGGY adj eccentric

WIGHT vb blame ▷ n human being ▷ adj strong and brave

WIGHTED > WIGHT

WIGHTING > WIGHT

WIGHTLY adv swiftly

WIGHTS > WIGHT

WIGLESS > WIG

WIGLET n small wig

WIGLETS > WIGLET

WIGLIKE > WIG

WIGMAKER n person who makes wigs

WIGMAKERS > WIGMAKER

WIGS > WIG

WIGWAG vb move (something) back and forth ▷ n system of communication by flag semaphore

WIGWAGGED > WIGWAG

WIGWAGGER > WIGWAG

WIGWAGS > WIGWAG

WIGWAM n Native American's tent

WIGWAMS > WIGWAM

WIKI n website consisting mainly of user-generated content

WIKIALITY n version of facts which is agreed to be true, but which may not actually be true

WIKIS > WIKI

WIKIUP same as > WICKIUP

WIKIUPS > WIKIUP

WILCO interj expression indicating that the message just received will be complied with

WILD same as > WIELD

WILDCARD n person given entry to competition without qualifying

WILDCARDS > WILDCARD

WILDCAT n European wild animal like a large domestic cat ▷ adj risky and financially unsound ▷ vb drill for petroleum or natural gas in an area having no known reserves

WILDCATS > WILDCAT

WILDED > WILD

WILDER vb lead or be led astray

WILDERED > WILDER

WILDERING > WILDER

WILDERS > WILDER

WILDEST > WILD

WILDFIRE n highly flammable material, such as Greek fire, formerly used in warfare

WILDFIRES > WILDFIRE

WILDFOWL n wild bird that is hunted for sport or food

WILDFOWLS > WILDFOWL

WILDGRAVE same as > WALDGRAVE

WILDING n uncultivated plant

WILDINGS > WILDING

WILDISH > WILD

WILDLAND n land which has not been cultivated

WILDLANDS > WILDLAND

WILDLIFE n wild animals and plants collectively

WILDLIFES > WILDLIFE

WILDLING same as > WILDING

WILDLINGS > WILDLING

WILDLY > WILD

WILDNESS > WILD

WILDS > WILD

WILDWOOD n wood or forest growing in a natural uncultivated state

WILDWOODS > WILDWOOD

WILE n trickery, cunning, or craftiness ▷ vb lure, beguile, or entice

WILED > WILE

WILEFUL adj deceitful

WILES > WILE

WILFUL adj headstrong or obstinate

WILFULLY > WILFUL

WILGA n small drought-resistant tree of Australia

W

WILGAS > WILGA
WILI *n* spirit
WILIER > WILY
WILIEST > WILY
WILILY > WILY
WILINESS > WILY
WILING > WILE
WILIS > WILI
WILJA *same as* **>** WILTJA
WILJAS > WILJA
WILL *vb* used as an auxiliary to form the future tense or to indicate intention, ability, or expectation ▷ *n* strong determination
WILLABLE *adj* able to be wished or determined by the will
WILLED *adj* having a will as specified
WILLEMITE *n* secondary mineral consisting of zinc silicate
WILLER > WILL
WILLERS > WILL
WILLEST > WILL
WILLET *n* large American shore bird
WILLETS > WILLET
WILLEY *same as* **>** WILLY
WILLEYED > WILLEY
WILLEYING > WILLEY
WILLEYS > WILLEY
WILLFUL *same as* **>** WILFUL
WILLFULLY > WILLFUL
WILLIAM *n* as in *sweet william* flowering plant
WILLIAMS > WILLIAM
WILLIE *n* informal word for a penis
WILLIED > WILLY
WILLIES > WILLY
WILLING *adj* ready or inclined (to do something)
WILLINGER > WILLING
WILLINGLY > WILLING
WILLIWAU *same as* **>** WILLIWAW
WILLIWAUS > WILLIWAU
WILLIWAW *n* sudden strong gust of cold wind blowing offshore from a mountainous coast
WILLIWAWS > WILLIWAW
WILLOW *n* tree with thin flexible branches ▷ *vb* open and clean (fibres) with rotating spikes
WILLOWED > WILLOW
WILLOWER *n* willow
WILLOWERS > WILLOWER
WILLOWIER > WILLOWY
WILLOWING > WILLOW
WILLOWISH > WILLOW
WILLOWS > WILLOW
WILLOWY *adj* slender and graceful
WILLPOWER *n* ability to control oneself and one's actions
WILLS > WILL

WILLY *vb* clean in willowing-machine
WILLYARD *adj* timid
WILLYART *same as* **>** WILLYARD
WILLYING > WILLY
WILLYWAW *same as* **>** WILLIWAW
WILLYWAWS > WILLYWAW
WILT *vb* (cause to) become limp or lose strength ▷ *n* act of wilting or state of becoming wilted
WILTED > WILT
WILTING > WILT
WILTJA *n* Aboriginal shelter
WILTJAS > WILTJA
WILTS > WILT
WILY *adj* crafty or sly
WIMBLE *n* any of a number of hand tools used for boring holes ▷ *vb* bore (a hole) with or as if with a wimble
WIMBLED > WIMBLE
WIMBLES > WIMBLE
WIMBLING > WIMBLE
WIMBREL *same as* **>** WHIMBREL
WIMBRELS > WIMBREL
WIMMIN *n* common intentional literary misspelling of 'women'
WIMP *n* feeble ineffectual person ▷ *vb* as in *wimp out* fail to complete something through fear
WIMPED > WIMP
WIMPIER > WIMP
WIMPIEST > WIMP
WIMPINESS > WIMP
WIMPING > WIMP
WIMPISH > WIMP
WIMPISHLY > WIMP
WIMPLE *n* garment framing the face, worn by medieval women and now by nuns ▷ *vb* ripple or cause to ripple or undulate
WIMPLED > WIMPLE
WIMPLES > WIMPLE
WIMPLING > WIMPLE
WIMPS > WIMP
WIMPY > WIMP
WIN *vb* come first in (a competition, fight, etc) ▷ *n* victory, esp in a game
WINCE *vb* draw back, as if in pain ▷ *n* wincing
WINCED > WINCE
WINCER > WINCE
WINCERS > WINCE
WINCES > WINCE
WINCEY *n* plain- or twill-weave cloth
WINCEYS > WINCEY
WINCH *n* machine for lifting or hauling using a cable or chain wound round a drum ▷ *vb* lift or haul using a winch
WINCHED > WINCH

WINCHER > WINCH
WINCHERS > WINCH
WINCHES > WINCH
WINCHING > WINCH
WINCHMAN *n* man who operates winch
WINCHMEN > WINCHMAN
WINCING > WINCE
WINCINGLY *adv* while wincing or in a wincing manner
WINCINGS > WINCE
WINCOPIPE *n* type of plant
WIND *n* current of air ▷ *vb* render short of breath
WINDABLE *n* able to be wound
WINDAC *same as* **>** WINDAS
WINDACS > WINDAC
WINDAGE *n* deflection of a projectile as a result of the effect of the wind
WINDAGES > WINDAGE
WINDAS *n* windlass
WINDASES > WINDAS
WINDBAG *n* person who talks much but uninterestingly
WINDBAGS > WINDBAG
WINDBELL *n* light bell made to be sounded by wind
WINDBELLS > WINDBELL
WINDBILL *n* bill of exchange cosigned by a guarantor
WINDBILLS > WINDBILL
WINDBLAST *n* strong gust of wind
WINDBLOW *n* trees uprooted by wind
WINDBLOWN *adj* blown about by the wind
WINDBLOWS > WINDBLOW
WINDBORNE *adj* (of plant seeds, etc) borne on the wind
WINDBOUND *adj* (of a sailing vessel) prevented from sailing by an unfavourable wind
WINDBREAK *n* fence or line of trees providing shelter from the wind
WINDBURN *n* irritation and redness of the skin caused by prolonged exposure to winds of high velocity
WINDBURNS > WINDBURN
WINDBURNT > WINDBURN
WINDCHILL *n* chilling effect of wind and low temperature
WINDED > WIND
WINDER *n* person or device that winds, as an engine for hoisting the cages in a mine shaft
WINDERS > WINDER
WINDFALL *n* unexpected good luck
WINDFALLS > WINDFALL
WINDFLAW *n* squall

WINDFLAWS > WINDFLAW
WINDGALL *n* soft swelling in the area of the fetlock joint of a horse
WINDGALLS > WINDGALL
WINDGUN *n* air gun
WINDGUNS > WINDGUN
WINDHOVER *dialect name for* **>** KESTREL
WINDIER > WINDY
WINDIEST > WINDY
WINDIGO *same as* **>** WENDIGO
WINDIGOES > WINDIGO
WINDIGOS > WINDIGO
WINDILY > WINDY
WINDINESS > WINDY
WINDING > WIND
WINDINGLY > WINDING
WINDINGS > WIND
WINDLASS *n* winch worked by a crank ▷ *vb* raise or haul (a weight, etc) by means of a windlass
WINDLE *vb* wind something round continuously
WINDLED > WINDLE
WINDLES > WINDLE
WINDLESS > WIND
WINDLING > WINDLE
WINDLINGS > WINDLE
WINDLOAD *n* force on a structure from wind
WINDLOADS > WINDLOAD
WINDMILL *n* machine for grinding or pumping driven by sails turned by the wind ▷ *vb* move or cause to move like the arms of a windmill
WINDMILLS > WINDMILL
WINDOCK *same as* **>** WINNOCK
WINDOCKS > WINDOCK
WINDORE *n* window
WINDORES > WINDORE
WINDOW *n* opening in a wall to let in light or air ▷ *vb* furnish with windows
WINDOWED > WINDOW
WINDOWING > WINDOW
WINDOWS > WINDOW
WINDOWY > WINDOW
WINDPACK *n* snow that has been compacted by the wind
WINDPACKS > WINDPACK
WINDPIPE *n* tube linking the throat and the lungs
WINDPIPES > WINDPIPE
WINDPROOF *adj* not penetrable by wind ▷ *vb* make windproof
WINDRING *adj* winding
WINDROW *n* long low ridge or line of hay or a similar crop ▷ *vb* put (hay or a similar crop) into windrows
WINDROWED > WINDROW
WINDROWER > WINDROW
WINDROWS > WINDROW**

w

WINDS > WIND
WINDSAIL n sail rigged as an air scoop over a hatch or companionway to catch breezes and divert them below
WINDSAILS > WINDSAIL
WINDSES pl n ventilation shafts within mines
WINDSHAKE n crack between the annual rings in wood
WINDSHIP n ship propelled by wind
WINDSHIPS > WINDSHIP
WINDSLAB n crust formed on soft snow by the wind
WINDSLABS > WINDSLAB
WINDSOCK n cloth cone on a mast at an airfield to indicate wind direction
WINDSOCKS > WINDSOCK
WINDSTORM n storm consisting of violent winds
WINDSURF vb sail standing on a board equipped with a mast, sail, and boom
WINDSURFS > WINDSURF
WINDSWEPT adj exposed to the wind
WINDTHROW n uprooting of trees by wind
WINDTIGHT adj impenetrable by wind
WINDUP n prank or hoax
WINDUPS > WINDUP
WINDWARD n direction from which the wind is blowing ▷ adj of or in the direction from which the wind blows ▷ adv towards the wind
WINDWARDS adv in the direction of the wind
WINDWAY n part of wind instrument
WINDWAYS > WINDWAY
WINDY adj denoting a time or conditions in which there is a strong wind
WINE n alcoholic drink made from fermented grapes ▷ adj of a dark purplish-red colour ▷ vb give wine to
WINEBERRY another name for > MAKO
WINED > WINE
WINEGLASS n glass for wine, usually with a small bowl on a stem with a flared base
WINELESS > WINE
WINEMAKER n maker of wine
WINEPRESS n any equipment used for squeezing the juice from grapes in order to make wine
WINERIES > WINERY
WINERY n place where wine is made

WINES > WINE
WINESAP n variety of apple
WINESAPS > WINESAP
WINESHOP n shop where wine is sold
WINESHOPS > WINESHOP
WINESKIN n skin of a sheep or goat sewn up and used as a holder for wine
WINESKINS > WINESKIN
WINESOP n old word for an alcoholic
WINESOPS > WINESOP
WINEY adj having the taste or qualities of wine
WING n one of the limbs or organs of a bird, insect, or bat that are used for flying ▷ vb fly
WINGBACK n football position
WINGBACKS > WINGBACK
WINGBEAT n complete cycle of moving the wing by a bird in flight
WINGBEATS > WINGBEAT
WINGBOW n distinctive band of colour marking the wing of a bird
WINGBOWS > WINGBOW
WINGCHAIR n chair with forward projections from back
WINGDING n noisy lively party or festivity
WINGDINGS > WINGDING
WINGE same as > WHINGE
WINGED adj furnished with wings
WINGEDLY > WINGED
WINGEING > WINGE
WINGER n player positioned on a wing
WINGERS > WINGER
WINGES > WINGE
WINGIER > WINGY
WINGIEST > WINGY
WINGING > WING
WINGLESS adj having no wings or vestigial wings
WINGLET n small wing
WINGLETS > WINGLET
WINGLIKE > WING
WINGMAN n player in the wing position in Australian Rules
WINGMEN > WINGMAN
WINGNUT n nut with projections for gripping with the thumb and finger
WINGNUTS > WINGNUT
WINGOVER n manoeuvre in which the direction of flight of an aircraft is reversed by putting it into a climbing turn until nearly stalled, the nose then being allowed to fall while continuing the turn
WINGOVERS > WINGOVER
WINGS > WING

WINGSPAN n distance between the wing tips of an aircraft, bird, or insect
WINGSPANS > WINGSPAN
WINGSUIT n type of skydiving suit
WINGSUITS > WINGSUIT
WINGTIP n outermost edge of a wing
WINGTIPS > WINGTIP
WINGY adj having wings
WINIER > WINY
WINIEST > WINY
WINING > WINE
WINISH > WINE
WINK vb close and open (an eye) quickly as a signal ▷ n winking
WINKED > WINK
WINKER n person or thing that winks
WINKERS > WINKER
WINKING > WINK
WINKINGLY > WINK
WINKINGS > WINK
WINKLE n shellfish with a spiral shell ▷ vb extract or prise out
WINKLED > WINKLE
WINKLER n one who forces person or thing out
WINKLERS > WINKLER
WINKLES > WINKLE
WINKLING > WINKLE
WINKS > WINK
WINLESS adj not having won anything
WINN n penny
WINNA vb will not
WINNABLE > WIN
WINNARD n heron
WINNARDS > WINNARD
WINNED > WIN
WINNER n person or thing that wins
WINNERS > WINNER
WINNING adj (of a person) charming, attractive, etc
WINNINGLY > WINNING
WINNINGS > WIN
WINNLE same as > WINNLE
WINNLES > WINNLE
WINNOCK n window
WINNOCKS > WINNOCK
WINNOW vb separate (chaff) from (grain) ▷ n device for winnowing
WINNOWED > WINNOW
WINNOWER > WINNOW
WINNOWERS > WINNOW
WINNOWING > WINNOW
WINNOWS > WINNOW
WINNS > WINN
WINO n destitute person who habitually drinks cheap wine
WINOES > WINO
WINOS > WINO
WINS > WIN
WINSEY same as > WINCEY
WINSEYS > WINSEY
WINSOME adj charming or winning

WINSOMELY > WINSOME
WINSOMER > WINSOME
WINSOMEST > WINSOME
WINTER n coldest season ▷ vb spend the winter
WINTERED > WINTER
WINTERER > WINTER
WINTERERS > WINTER
WINTERFED vb past tense of 'winterfeed' (to feed (livestock) in winter when the grazing is not rich enough)
WINTERIER > WINTERY
WINTERING > WINTER
WINTERISE same as > WINTERIZE
WINTERISH > WINTER
WINTERIZE vb prepare (a house, car, etc) to withstand winter conditions
WINTERLY same as > WINTRY
WINTERS > WINTER
WINTERY same as > WINTRY
WINTLE vb reel; stagger
WINTLED > WINTLE
WINTLES > WINTLE
WINTLING > WINTLE
WINTRIER > WINTRY
WINTRIEST > WINTRY
WINTRILY > WINTRY
WINTRY adj of or like winter
WINY same as > WINEY
WINZE n steeply inclined shaft, as for ventilation between levels
WINZES > WINZE
WIPE vb clean or dry by rubbing ▷ n wiping
WIPEABLE adj able to be wiped
WIPED > WIPE
WIPEOUT n instance of wiping out
WIPEOUTS > WIPEOUT
WIPER n any piece of cloth, such as a handkerchief, towel, etc, used for wiping
WIPERS > WIPER
WIPES > WIPE
WIPING > WIPE
WIPINGS > WIPE
WIPPEN n part of hammer action in piano
WIPPENS > WIPPEN
WIRABLE adj that can be wired
WIRE n thin flexible strand of metal ▷ vb fasten with wire
WIRED adj excited or nervous
WIREDRAW vb convert (metal) into wire by drawing through successively smaller dies
WIREDRAWN > WIREDRAW
WIREDRAWS > WIREDRAW
WIREDREW > WIREDRAW

WIREFRAME n visual representation of the structure of a web page

WIREGRASS n fine variety of grass

WIREHAIR n type of terrier

WIREHAIRS > WIREHAIR

WIRELESS adj (of a computer network) connected by radio rather than by cables or fibre optics ⊳ n old-fashioned name for radio ⊳ vb send by wireless

WIRELIKE > WIRE

WIRELINE n telegraph or telephone line

WIRELINES > WIRELINE

WIREMAN n person who installs and maintains electric wiring, cables, etc

WIREMEN > WIREMAN

WIREPHOTO n facsimile of a photograph transmitted electronically via a telephone system

WIRER n person who sets or uses wires to snare rabbits and similar animals

WIRERS > WIRER

WIRES > WIRE

WIRETAP vb obtain information secretly via telegraph or telephone

WIRETAPS > WIRETAP

WIREWAY n tube for electric wires

WIREWAYS > WIREWAY

WIREWORK n functional or decorative work made of wire

WIREWORKS n factory where wire or articles of wire are made

WIREWORM n destructive wormlike beetle larva

WIREWORMS > WIREWORM

WIREWOVE adj woven out of wire

WIRIER > WIRY

WIRIEST > WIRY

WIRILDA n SE Australian acacia tree with edible seeds

WIRILDAS > WIRILDA

WIRILY > WIRY

WIRINESS > WIRY

WIRING n system of wires ⊳ adj used in wiring

WIRINGS > WIRING

WIRRA interj exclamation of sorrow or deep concern

WIRRAH n Australian saltwater fish with bright blue spots

WIRRAHS > WIRRAH

WIRRICOW same as > WORRICOW

WIRRICOWS > WIRRICOW

WIRY adj lean and tough

WIS vb know or suppose (something)

WISARD obsolete spelling of > WIZARD

WISARDS > WISARD

WISDOM n good sense and judgment

WISDOMS > WISDOM

WISE vb guide ⊳ adj having wisdom ⊳ n manner

WISEACRE n person who wishes to seem wise

WISEACRES > WISEACRE

WISEASS n person who thinks he or she is being witty or clever

WISEASSES > WISEASS

WISECRACK n clever, sometimes unkind, remark ⊳ vb make a wisecrack

WISED > WISE

WISEGUY n person who wants to seem clever

WISEGUYS > WISEGUY

WISELIER > WISE

WISELIEST > WISE

WISELING n one who claims to be wise

WISELINGS > WISELING

WISELY > WISE

WISENESS > WISE

WISENT n European bison

WISENTS > WISENT

WISER > WISE

WISES > WISE

WISEST > WISE

WISEWOMAN n witch

WISEWOMEN > WISEWOMAN

WISH vb want or desire ⊳ n expression of a desire

WISHA interj expression of surprise

WISHBONE n V-shaped bone above the breastbone of a fowl

WISHBONES > WISHBONE

WISHED > WISH

WISHER > WISH

WISHERS > WISH

WISHES > WISH

WISHFUL adj too optimistic

WISHFULLY > WISHFUL

WISHING > WISH

WISHINGS > WISH

WISHLESS > WISH

WISHT variant of > WHISHT

WISING > WISE

WISKET n basket

WISKETS > WISKET

WISP n light delicate streak ⊳ vb move or act like a wisp

WISPED > WISP

WISPIER > WISPY

WISPIEST > WISPY

WISPILY > WISPY

WISPINESS > WISPY

WISPING > WISP

WISPISH > WISP

WISPLIKE > WISP

WISPS > WISP

WISPY adj thin, fine, or delicate

WISS vb urinate

WISSED > WIS

WISSES > WIS

WISSING > WIS

WIST vb know

WISTARIA same as > WISTERIA

WISTARIAS > WISTARIA

WISTED > WIST

WISTERIA n climbing shrub with blue or purple flowers

WISTERIAS > WISTERIA

WISTFUL adj sadly longing

WISTFULLY > WISTFUL

WISTING > WIST

WISTITI n marmoset

WISTITIS > WISTITI

WISTLY adv intently

WISTS > WIST

WIT vb detect ⊳ n ability to use words or ideas in a clever and amusing way

WITAN n Anglo-Saxon assembly that met to counsel the king

WITANS > WITAN

WITBLITS n illegally distilled strong alcoholic drink

WITCH n person, usu female, who practises (black) magic ⊳ vb cause or change by or as if by witchcraft

WITCHED > WITCH

WITCHEN n rowan tree

WITCHENS > WITCHEN

WITCHERY n practice of witchcraft

WITCHES > WITCH

WITCHETTY n edible larva of certain Australian moths and beetles

WITCHHOOD > WITCH

WITCHIER > WITCHY

WITCHIEST > WITCHY

WITCHING adj relating to or appropriate for witchcraft ⊳ n witchcraft

WITCHINGS > WITCHING

WITCHKNOT n knot in hair

WITCHLIKE > WITCH

WITCHWEED n type of plant that is a serious pest of grain crops in parts of Africa and Asia

WITCHY adj like a witch

WITE vb blame

WITED > WITE

WITELESS adj witless

WITES > WITE

WITGAT n type of S African tree

WITGATS > WITGAT

WITH prep indicating presence alongside, possession, means of performance, characteristic manner, etc ⊳ n division between flues in chimney

WITHAL adv as well

WITHDRAW vb take or move out or away

WITHDRAWN adj unsociable

WITHDRAWS > WITHDRAW

WITHDREW past tense of > WITHDRAW

WITHE n strong flexible twig suitable for binding things together ⊳ vb bind with withes

WITHED > WITHE

WITHER vb wilt or dry up

WITHERED > WITHER

WITHERER > WITHER

WITHERERS > WITHER

WITHERING > WITHER

WITHERITE n white, grey, or yellowish mineral

WITHEROD n American shrub

WITHERODS > WITHEROD

WITHERS pl n ridge between a horse's shoulder blades

WITHES > WITHE

WITHHAULT > WITHHOLD

WITHHELD > WITHHOLD

WITHHOLD vb refrain from giving

WITHHOLDS > WITHHOLD

WITHIER > WITHY

WITHIES > WITHY

WITHIEST > WITHY

WITHIN adv in or inside ⊳ prep in or inside ⊳ n something that is within

WITHING > WITHE

WITHINS > WITHIN

WITHOUT prep not accompanied by, using, or having ⊳ adv outside ⊳ n person who is without

WITHOUTEN obsolete form of > WITHOUT

WITHOUTS > WITHOUT

WITHS > WITH

WITHSTAND vb oppose or resist successfully

WITHSTOOD > WITHSTAND

WITHWIND n bindweed

WITHWINDS > WITHWIND

WITHY n willow tree, esp an osier ⊳ adj (of people) tough and agile

WITHYWIND same as > WITHWIND

WITING > WITE

WITLESS adj foolish

WITLESSLY > WITLESS

WITLING n person who thinks himself witty

WITLINGS > WITLING

WITLOOF n chicory

WITLOOFS > WITLOOF

WITNESS n person who has seen something happen ⊳ vb see at first hand

WITNESSED > WITNESS

WITNESSER > WITNESS

WITNESSES > WITNESS

WITNEY n type of blanket; heavy cloth

WITNEYS > WITNEY

WITS > WIT

WITTED adj having wit

WITTER vb chatter pointlessly or at unnecessary length ▷ n pointless chat

WITTERED > WITTER

WITTERING > WITTER

WITTERS > WITTER

WITTICISM n witty remark

WITTIER > WITTY

WITTIEST > WITTY

WITTILY > WITTY

WITTINESS > WITTY

WITTING adj deliberate

WITTINGLY > WITTING

WITTINGS > WIT

WITTOL n man who tolerates his wife's unfaithfulness

WITTOLLY > WITTOL

WITTOLS > WITTOL

WITTY adj clever and amusing

WITWALL n golden oriole

WITWALLS > WITWALL

WITWANTON vb be disrespectfully witty

WIVE vb marry (a woman)

WIVED > WIVE

WIVEHOOD obsolete variant of > WIFEHOOD

WIVEHOODS > WIVEHOOD

WIVER another word for > WIVERN

WIVERN same as > WYVERN

WIVERNS > WIVERN

WIVERS > WIVER

WIVES > WIFE

WIVING > WIVE

WIZ shortened form of > WIZARD

WIZARD n magician ▷ adj superb

WIZARDLY > WIZARD

WIZARDRY n magic or sorcery

WIZARDS > WIZARD

WIZEN vb make or become shrivelled ▷ n archaic word for 'weasand' (the gullet)

WIZENED adj shrivelled or wrinkled

WIZENING > WIZEN

WIZENS > WIZEN

WIZES > WIZ

WIZIER same as > VIZIER

WIZIERS > WIZIER

WIZZEN same as > WIZEN

WIZZENS > WIZEN

WIZZES > WIZ

WO archaic spelling of > WOE

WOAD n blue dye obtained from a plant

WOADED adj coloured blue with woad

WOADS > WOAD

WOADWAX n small Eurasian leguminous shrub

WOADWAXEN n small leguminous shrub with yellow flowers producing a yellow dye

WOADWAXES > WOADWAX

WOAH same as > WHOA

WOALD same as > WELD

WOALDS > WOALD

WOBBEGONG n Australian shark with brown-and-white skin

WOBBLE vb move unsteadily ▷ n wobbling movement or sound

WOBBLED > WOBBLE

WOBBLER > WOBBLE

WOBBLERS > WOBBLE

WOBBLES > WOBBLE

WOBBLIER > WOBBLY

WOBBLIES > WOBBLY

WOBBLIEST > WOBBLY

WOBBLING > WOBBLE

WOBBLINGS > WOBBLE

WOBBLY adj unsteady ▷ n temper tantrum

WOBEGONE same as > WOEBEGONE

WOCK same as > WOK

WOCKS > WOCK

WODGE n thick lump or chunk

WODGES > WODGE

WOE n grief

WOEBEGONE adj looking miserable

WOEFUL adj extremely sad

WOEFULLER > WOEFUL

WOEFULLY > WOEFUL

WOENESS > WOE

WOENESSES > WOE

WOES > WOE

WOESOME adj woeful

WOF n fool

WOFS > WOF

WOFUL same as > WOEFUL

WOFULLER > WOFUL

WOFULLEST > WOFUL

WOFULLY > WOFUL

WOFULNESS > WOFUL

WOG n derogatory word for a foreigner, esp one who is not White

WOGGISH > WOG

WOGGLE n ring of leather through which a Scout neckerchief is threaded

WOGGLES > WOGGLE

WOGS > WOG

WOIWODE same as > VOIVODE

WOIWODES > WOIWODE

WOJUS adj (Irish) of a poor quality

WOK n bowl-shaped Chinese cooking pan, used for stir-frying

WOKE > WAKE

WOKEN > WAKE

WOKKA modifier as in wokka board a piece of

fibreboard used as a musical instrument

WOKS > WOK

WOLD same as > WELD

WOLDS > WOLD

WOLF n wild predatory canine mammal ▷ vb eat ravenously

WOLFBERRY n type of shrub

WOLFED > WOLF

WOLFER same as > WOLVER

WOLFERS > WOLFER

WOLFFISH n type of large northern deep-sea fish with large sharp teeth

WOLFHOUND n very large breed of dog

WOLFING > WOLF

WOLFINGS > WOLF

WOLFISH > WOLF

WOLFISHLY > WOLF

WOLFKIN n young wolf

WOLFKINS > WOLFKIN

WOLFLIKE > WOLF

WOLFLING n young wolf

WOLFLINGS > WOLFLING

WOLFRAM another name for > TUNGSTEN

WOLFRAMS > WOLFRAM

WOLFS > WOLF

WOLFSBANE n type of poisonous N temperate plant with yellow hoodlike flowers

WOLFSKIN n skin of wolf used for clothing, etc

WOLFSKINS > WOLFSKIN

WOLLIES > WOLLY

WOLLY n pickled cucumber or olive

WOLVE vb hunt for wolves

WOLVED > WOLVE

WOLVER n person who hunts wolves

WOLVERENE same as > WOLVERINE

WOLVERINE n carnivorous mammal of Arctic regions

WOLVERS > WOLVER

WOLVES > WOLF

WOLVING > WOLVE

WOLVINGS > WOLVE

WOLVISH same as > WOLFISH

WOLVISHLY > WOLVISH

WOMAN n adult human female ▷ adj female ▷ vb provide with a woman or women

WOMANED > WOMAN

WOMANHOOD n state of being a woman

WOMANING > WOMAN

WOMANISE same as > WOMANIZE

WOMANISED > WOMANISE

WOMANISER > WOMANISE

WOMANISES > WOMANISE

WOMANISH adj effeminate

WOMANISM n feminism among black women

WOMANISMS > WOMANISM

WOMANIST > WOMANISM

WOMANISTS > WOMANISM

WOMANIZE vb (of a man) to indulge in many casual affairs with women

WOMANIZED > WOMANIZE

WOMANIZER > WOMANIZE

WOMANIZES > WOMANIZE

WOMANKIND n all women considered as a group

WOMANLESS > WOMAN

WOMANLIER > WOMANLY

WOMANLIKE adj like a woman

WOMANLY adj having qualities traditionally associated with a woman

WOMANNED > WOMAN

WOMANNESS > WOMAN

WOMANNING > WOMAN

WOMANS > WOMAN

WOMB vb enclose ▷ n hollow organ in female mammals where babies develop

WOMBAT n small heavily-built burrowing Australian marsupial

WOMBATS > WOMBAT

WOMBED > WOMB

WOMBIER > WOMBY

WOMBIEST > WOMBY

WOMBING > WOMB

WOMBLIKE > WOMB

WOMBS > WOMB

WOMBY adj hollow; spacious

WOMEN > WOMAN

WOMENFOLK pl n women collectively

WOMENKIND same as > WOMANKIND

WOMERA same as > WOOMERA

WOMERAS > WOMERA

WOMMERA same as > WOOMERA

WOMMERAS > WOMMERA

WOMMIT n foolish person

WOMMITS > WOMMIT

WOMYN same as > WOMAN

WON n standard monetary unit of North Korea ▷ vb live or dwell

WONDER vb be curious about ▷ n wonderful thing ▷ adj spectacularly successful

WONDERED > WONDER

WONDERER > WONDER

WONDERERS > WONDER

WONDERFUL adj very fine

WONDERING > WONDER

WONDERKID n informal word for an exceptionally successful young person

WONDEROUS obsolete variant of > WONDROUS

WONDERS > WONDER

WONDRED adj splendid

WONDROUS adj wonderful ▷ adv (intensifier)

WONGA n money

W

WONGAS > WONGA
WONGI *vb* talk informally
WONGIED > WONGI
WONGIING > WONGI
WONGIS > WONGI
WONING > WON
WONINGS > WON
WONK *n* person who is obsessively interested in a specified subject
WONKERIES > WONKERY
WONKERY *n* activities of a wonk
WONKIER > WONKY
WONKIEST > WONKY
WONKILY *adv* in a wonky manner
WONKISH *adj* like a wonk
WONKS > WONK
WONKY *adj* shaky or unsteady
WONNED > WON
WONNER > WON
WONNERS > WON
WONNING > WON
WONNINGS > WON
WONS > WON
WONT *adj* accustomed ▷ *n* custom ▷ *vb* become or cause to become accustomed
WONTED *adj* accustomed or habituated (to doing something)
WONTEDLY > WONTED
WONTING > WONT
WONTLESS > WONT
WONTON *n* dumpling filled with spiced minced pork
WONTONS > WONTON
WONTS > WONT
WOO *vb* seek the love or affection of (a woman)
WOOABLE *adj* able to be wooed
WOOBUT *same as* > WOOBIT
WOOBUTS > WOOBUT
WOOD *n* substance trees are made of, used in carpentry and as fuel ▷ *adj* made of or using wood ▷ *vb* (of land) plant with trees
WOODBIN *n* box for firewood
WOODBIND *same as* > WOODBINE
WOODBINDS > WOODBIND
WOODBINE *n* honeysuckle
WOODBINES > WOODBINE
WOODBINS > WOODBIN
WOODBLOCK *n* hollow block of wood used as a percussion instrument
WOODBORER *n* type of beetle whose larvae bore into and damage wood
WOODBOX *n* box for firewood
WOODBOXES > WOODBOX
WOODCHAT *n* European and N African songbird with a black-and-white plumage, a reddish-brown crown and a hooked bill

WOODCHATS > WOODCHAT
WOODCHIP *n* textured wallpaper
WOODCHIPS > WOODCHIP
WOODCHOP *n* wood-chopping competition, esp at a show
WOODCHOPS > WOODCHOP
WOODCHUCK *n* N American marmot with coarse reddish-brown fur
WOODCOCK *n* game bird
WOODCOCKS > WOODCOCK
WOODCRAFT *n* ability and experience in matters concerned with living in a wood or forest
WOODCUT *n* (print made from) an engraved block of wood
WOODCUTS > WOODCUT
WOODED *adj* covered with trees
WOODEN *adj* made of wood ▷ *vb* fell or kill (a person or animal)
WOODENED > WOODEN
WOODENER > WOODEN
WOODENEST > WOODEN
WOODENING > WOODEN
WOODENLY > WOODEN
WOODENS > WOODEN
WOODENTOP *n* dull, foolish, or unintelligent person
WOODFERN *n* type of evergreen fern
WOODFERNS > WOODFERN
WOODFREE *adj* (of high-quality paper) made from pulp that has been treated chemically, removing impurities
WOODGRAIN *n* grain in wood
WOODHEN *another name for* > WEKA
WOODHENS > WOODHEN
WOODHOLE *n* store area for wood
WOODHOLES > WOODHOLE
WOODHORSE *n* frame for holding wood being sawn
WOODHOUSE *n* shed for firewood
WOODIE *n* gallows rope
WOODIER > WOODY
WOODIES > WOODIE
WOODIEST > WOODY
WOODINESS > WOODY
WOODING > WOOD
WOODLAND *n* forest ▷ *adj* living in woods
WOODLANDS > WOODLAND
WOODLARK *n* type of Old World lark
WOODLARKS > WOODLARK
WOODLESS > WOOD
WOODLICE > WOODLOUSE
WOODLORE *n* woodcraft skills
WOODLORES > WOODLORE
WOODLOT *n* area restricted to the growing of trees

WOODLOTS > WOODLOT
WOODLOUSE *n* small insect-like creature with many legs
WOODMAN *same as* > WOODSMAN
WOODMEAL *n* sawdust powder
WOODMEALS > WOODMEAL
WOODMEN > WOODMAN
WOODMICE > WOODMOUSE
WOODMOUSE *n* field mouse
WOODNESS > WOOD
WOODNOTE *n* natural musical note or song, like that of a wild bird
WOODNOTES > WOODNOTE
WOODPILE *n* heap of firewood
WOODPILES > WOODPILE
WOODPRINT *another name for* > WOODCUT
WOODRAT *n* pack-rat
WOODRATS > WOODRAT
WOODREEVE *n* steward responsible for wood
WOODROOF *same as* > WOODRUFF
WOODROOFS > WOODROOF
WOODRUFF *n* plant with small sweet-smelling white flowers and sweet-smelling leaves
WOODRUFFS > WOODRUFF
WOODRUSH *n* type of plant, chiefly of the N hemisphere, with grasslike leaves and small brown flowers
WOODS *pl n* closely packed trees forming a forest or wood
WOODSCREW *n* metal screw that tapers to a point so that it can be driven into wood by a screwdriver
WOODSHED *n* small outbuilding where firewood, garden tools, etc, are stored
WOODSHEDS > WOODSHED
WOODSHOCK *n* type of bird
WOODSIA *n* type of small fern with tufted rhizomes and wiry fronds
WOODSIAS > WOODSIA
WOODSIER > WOODSY
WOODSIEST > WOODSY
WOODSKIN *n* canoe made of bark
WOODSKINS > WOODSKIN
WOODSMAN *n* person who lives in a wood or who is skilled at woodwork or carving
WOODSMEN > WOODSMAN
WOODSPITE *n* green woodpecker
WOODSTONE *n* type of stone resembling wood
WOODSTOVE *n* wood-burning stove

WOODSY *adj* of, reminiscent of, or connected with woods
WOODTONE *n* colour matching that of wood
WOODTONES > WOODTONE
WOODWALE *n* green woodpecker
WOODWALES > WOODWALE
WOODWARD *n* person in charge of a forest or wood
WOODWARDS > WOODWARD
WOODWASP *n* large wasplike insect
WOODWASPS > WOODWASP
WOODWAX *same as* > WOODWAXEN
WOODWAXEN *same as* > WOADWAXEN
WOODWAXES > WOODWAX
WOODWIND *n* (of) a type of wind instrument made of wood ▷ *adj* of or denoting a type of wind instrument, such as the oboe
WOODWINDS > WOODWIND
WOODWORK *n* parts of a room or building made of wood
WOODWORKS > WOODWORK
WOODWORM *n* insect larva that bores into wood
WOODWORMS > WOODWORM
WOODWOSE *n* hairy wildman of the woods
WOODWOSES > WOODWOSE
WOODY *adj* (of a plant) having a very hard stem
WOODYARD *n* place where timber is cut and stored
WOODYARDS > WOODYARD
WOOED > WOO
WOOER > WOO
WOOERS > WOO
WOOF *vb* (of dogs) bark or growl
WOOFED > WOOF
WOOFER *n* loudspeaker reproducing low-frequency sounds
WOOFERS > WOOFER
WOOFIER > WOOFY
WOOFIEST > WOOFY
WOOFING > WOOF
WOOFS > WOOF
WOOFTAH *same as* > WOOFTER
WOOFTAHS > WOOFTAH
WOOFTER *n* derogatory term for a male homosexual
WOOFTERS > WOOFTER
WOOFY *adj* with close, dense texture
WOOHOO *interj* expression of joy, approval, etc
WOOING > WOO
WOOINGLY > WOO
WOOINGS > WOO
WOOL *n* soft hair of sheep, goats, etc
WOOLD *vb* wind (rope)
WOOLDED > WOOLD

WOOLDER n stick for winding rope

WOOLDERS > WOOLDER

WOOLDING > WOOLD

WOOLDINGS > WOOLD

WOOLDS > WOOLD

WOOLED same as > WOOLLED

WOOLEN same as > WOOLLEN

WOOLENS > WOOLEN

WOOLER same as > WOOLDER

WOOLERS > WOOLER

WOOLFAT same as > LANOLIN

WOOLFATS > WOOLFAT

WOOLFELL n skin of a sheep or similar animal with the fleece still attached

WOOLFELLS > WOOLFELL

WOOLHAT n poor white person in S States

WOOLHATS > WOOLHAT

WOOLIE n wool garment

WOOLIER > WOOLY

WOOLIES > WOOLY

WOOLIEST > WOOLY

WOOLINESS > WOOLY

WOOLLED adj (of animals) having wool

WOOLLEN adj relating to or consisting partly or wholly of wool ▷ n garment or piece of cloth made of wool

WOOLLENS > WOOLLEN

WOOLLIER > WOOLLY

WOOLLIES > WOOLLY

WOOLLIEST > WOOLLY

WOOLLIKE > WOOL

WOOLLILY > WOOLLY

WOOLLY adj of or like wool ▷ n knitted woollen garment

WOOLMAN n wool trader

WOOLMEN > WOOLMAN

WOOLPACK n cloth or canvas wrapping used to pack a bale of wool

WOOLPACKS > WOOLPACK

WOOLS > WOOL

WOOLSACK n sack containing or intended to contain wool

WOOLSACKS > WOOLSACK

WOOLSEY n cotton and wool blend

WOOLSEYS > WOOLSEY

WOOLSHED n large building in which sheep shearing takes place

WOOLSHEDS > WOOLSHED

WOOLSKIN n sheepskin with wool still on

WOOLSKINS > WOOLSKIN

WOOLWARD adv with woollen side touching the skin

WOOLWORK n embroidery with wool

WOOLWORKS > WOOLWORK

WOOLY same as > WOOLLY

WOOMERA n notched stick used by Australian Aborigines to aid the propulsion of a spear

WOOMERANG same as > WOOMERA

WOOMERAS > WOOMERA

WOON same as > WON

WOONED > WOON

WOONERF n (in the Netherlands) road primarily for cyclists and pedestrians

WOONERFS > WOONERF

WOONING > WOON

WOONS > WOON

WOOPIE n well-off older person

WOOPIES > WOOPIE

WOOPS vb (esp of small child) vomit

WOOPSED > WOOPS

WOOPSES > WOOPS

WOOPSING > WOOPS

WOOPY n well-off older person

WOORALI less common name for > CURARE

WOORALIS > WOORALI

WOORARA same as > WOURALI

WOORARAS > WOORARA

WOORARI same as > WOURALI

WOORARIS > WOORARI

WOOS > WOO

WOOSE same as > WUSS

WOOSEL same as > OUZEL

WOOSELL same as > OUZEL

WOOSELLS > WOOSELL

WOOSELS > WOOSEL

WOOSES > WOOSE

WOOSH same as > WHOOSH

WOOSHED > WOOSH

WOOSHES > WOOSH

WOOSHING > WOOSH

WOOT vb wilt thou?

WOOTZ n Middle-Eastern steel

WOOTZES > WOOTZ

WOOZIER > WOOZY

WOOZIEST > WOOZY

WOOZILY > WOOZY

WOOZINESS > WOOZY

WOOZY adj weak, dizzy, and confused

WOP same as > WHOP

WOPPED > WOP

WOPPING > WOP

WOPS > WOP

WORCESTER n type of woollen fabric

WORD n smallest single meaningful unit of speech or writing ▷ vb express in words

WORDAGE n words considered collectively, esp a quantity of words

WORDAGES > WORDAGE

WORDBOOK n book containing words, usually with their meanings

WORDBOOKS > WORDBOOK

WORDBOUND adj unable to find words to express something

WORDBREAK n point at which a word is divided when it runs over from one line of print to the next

WORDCOUNT n count of words in a document

WORDED > WORD

WORDGAME n any game involving the formation, discovery, or alteration of a word or words

WORDGAMES > WORDGAME

WORDIER > WORDY

WORDIEST > WORDY

WORDILY > WORDY

WORDINESS > WORDY

WORDING n choice and arrangement of words

WORDINGS > WORDING

WORDISH adj talkative

WORDLESS adj inarticulate or silent

WORDLORE n knowledge about words

WORDLORES > WORDLORE

WORDPLAY n verbal wit based on the meanings and ambiguities of words

WORDPLAYS > WORDPLAY

WORDS > WORD

WORDSMITH n person skilled in using words

WORDWRAP n word-processing function that shifts a word at the end of a line to a new line to keep within preset margins

WORDWRAPS > WORDWRAP

WORDY adj using too many words

WORE > WEAR

WORK n physical or mental effort directed to making or doing something ▷ adj of or for work ▷ vb (cause to) do work

WORKABLE adj able to operate efficiently

WORKABLY > WORKABLE

WORKADAY n working day ▷ adj ordinary

WORKADAYS > WORKADAY

WORKBAG n container for implements, tools, or materials

WORKBAGS > WORKBAG

WORKBENCH n heavy table at which a craftsman or mechanic works

WORKBOAT n boat used for tasks

WORKBOATS > WORKBOAT

WORKBOOK n exercise book or textbook used for study, esp a textbook with spaces for answers

WORKBOOKS > WORKBOOK

WORKBOOT n type of sturdy leather boot

WORKBOOTS > WORKBOOT

WORKBOX same as > WORKBAG

WORKBOXES > WORKBOX

WORKDAY another word for > WORKADAY

WORKDAYS > WORKDAY

WORKED adj made or decorated with evidence of workmanship

WORKER n person who works in a specified way

WORKERIST n supporter of working-class politics

WORKERS > WORKER

WORKFARE n scheme under which the government of a country requires unemployed people to do community work or undergo job training in return for social-security payments

WORKFARES > WORKFARE

WORKFLOW n rate of progress of work

WORKFLOWS > WORKFLOW

WORKFOLK pl n working people, esp labourers on a farm

WORKFOLKS same as > WORKFOLK

WORKFORCE n total number of workers

WORKFUL adj hardworking

WORKGIRL n young female manual worker

WORKGIRLS > WORKGIRL

WORKGROUP n collection of networked computers

WORKHORSE n person or thing that does a lot of dull or routine work

WORKHOUR n time set aside for work

WORKHOURS > WORKHOUR

WORKHOUSE n (in England, formerly) institution where the poor were given food and lodgings in return for work

WORKING n operation or mode of operation of something ▷ adj relating to or concerned with a person or thing that works

WORKINGS > WORKING

WORKLESS > WORK

WORKLOAD n amount of work to be done, esp in a specified period

WORKLOADS > WORKLOAD

WORKMAN n manual worker

WORKMANLY adj appropriate to or befitting a good workman

WORKMATE n person who works with another person

WORKMATES > WORKMATE

WORKMEN > WORKMAN

WORKOUT n session of physical exercise for training or fitness

WORKOUTS > WORKOUT

WORKPIECE n piece of metal or other material that is in the process of being worked on or made or has actually been cut or shaped by a hand tool or machine

WORKPLACE n place, such as a factory or office, where people work

WORKPRINT n unfinished print of cinema film

WORKROOM n room in which work, usually manual labour, is done

WORKROOMS
> WORKROOM

WORKS > WORK

WORKSAFE adj (of an internet link) suitable for viewing in the workplace

WORKSHEET n sheet of paper containing exercises to be completed by a student

WORKSHOP n room or building for a manufacturing process ▷ vb perform (a play) with no costumes, set, or musical accompaniment

WORKSHOPS
> WORKSHOP

WORKSHY adj not inclined to work

WORKSITE n area where work is done

WORKSITES > WORKSITE

WORKSOME adj hardworking

WORKSONG n song sung while doing physical work

WORKSONGS > WORKSONG

WORKSPACE n area set aside for work

WORKTABLE n table at which writing, sewing, or other work may be done

WORKTOP n surface used for food preparation

WORKTOPS > WORKTOP

WORKUP n medical examination

WORKUPS > WORKUP

WORKWEAR n clothes, such as overalls, as worn for work in a factory, shop, etc

WORKWEARS > WORKWEAR

WORKWEEK n number of hours or days in a week actually or officially allocated to work

WORKWEEKS > WORKWEEK

WORKWOMAN n female manual worker

WORKWOMEN
> WORKWOMAN

WORLD n planet earth ▷ adj of the whole world

WORLDBEAT n popular music from outside western mainstream

WORLDED adj incorporating worlds

WORLDER n person who belongs to a specified class or domain

WORLDERS > WORLDER

WORLDIE n world-class performance, achievement, person, etc

WORLDIES > WORLDIE

WORLDLIER > WORLDLY

WORLDLING n person who is primarily concerned with worldly matters or material things

WORLDLY adj not spiritual ▷ adv in a worldly manner

WORLDS > WORLD

WORLDVIEW n comprehensive view of human life and the universe

WORLDWIDE adj applying or extending throughout the world

WORM n small limbless invertebrate animal ▷ vb rid of worms

WORMCAST n coil of earth excreted by a burrowing worm

WORMCASTS > WORMCAST

WORMED > WORM

WORMER > WORM

WORMERIES > WORMERY

WORMERS > WORM

WORMERY n piece of apparatus in which worms are kept for study

WORMFLIES > WORMFLY

WORMFLY n type of lure dressed on a double hook

WORMGEAR n gear with screw thread

WORMGEARS > WORMGEAR

WORMHOLE n hole made by a worm in timber, plants, or fruit

WORMHOLED > WORMHOLE

WORMHOLES > WORMHOLE

WORMIER > WORMY

WORMIEST > WORMY

WORMIL n burrowing larva of type of fly

WORMILS > WORMIL

WORMINESS > WORMY

WORMING > WORM

WORMISH > WORM

WORMLIKE > WORM

WORMROOT n plant used to cure worms

WORMROOTS > WORMROOT

WORMS n disease caused by parasitic worms living in the intestines

WORMSEED n any of various plants having seeds or other parts used in medicine to treat worm infestation

WORMSEEDS > WORMSEED

WORMWOOD n bitter plant

WORMWOODS > WORMWOOD

WORMY adj infested with or eaten by worms

WORN > WEAR

WORNNESS n quality or condition of being worn

WORRAL n type of lizard

WORRALS > WORRAL

WORREL same as > WORRAL

WORRELS > WORREL

WORRICOW n frightening creature

WORRICOWS > WORRICOW

WORRIED > WORRY

WORRIEDLY > WORRY

WORRIER > WORRY

WORRIERS > WORRY

WORRIES > WORRY

WORRIMENT n anxiety or the trouble that causes it

WORRISOME adj causing worry

WORRIT vb tease or worry

WORRITED > WORRIT

WORRITING > WORRIT

WORRITS > WORRIT

WORRY vb (cause to) be anxious or uneasy ▷ n (cause of) anxiety or concern

WORRYCOW same as > WORRICOW

WORRYCOWS > WORRYCOW

WORRYGUTS n person who tends to worry, esp about insignificant matters

WORRYING > WORRY

WORRYINGS > WORRY

WORRYWART same as > WORRYGUTS

WORSE vb defeat

WORSED > WORSE

WORSEN vb make or grow worse

WORSENED > WORSEN

WORSENESS n state or condition of being worse

WORSENING n act of worsening

WORSENS > WORSEN

WORSER archaic or nonstandard word for > WORSE

WORSES > WORSE

WORSET n worsted fabric

WORSETS > WORSET

WORSHIP vb show religious devotion to ▷ n act or instance of worshipping

WORSHIPED > WORSHIP

WORSHIPER n worshipper

WORSHIPS > WORSHIP

WORSING > WORSE

WORST n worst thing ▷ vb defeat

WORSTED n type of woollen yarn or fabric

WORSTEDS > WORSTED

WORSTING > WORST

WORSTS > WORST

WORT n any of various plants formerly used to cure diseases

WORTH prep having a value of ▷ n value or price ▷ vb happen or betide

WORTHED > WORTH

WORTHFUL adj worthy

WORTHIED > WORTHY

WORTHIER > WORTHY

WORTHIES > WORTHY

WORTHIEST > WORTHY

WORTHILY > WORTHY

WORTHING > WORTH

WORTHLESS adj without value or usefulness

WORTHS > WORTH

WORTHY adj deserving admiration or respect ▷ n notable person ▷ vb make worthy

WORTHYING > WORTHY

WORTLE n plate with holes for drawing wire through

WORTLES > WORTLE

WORTS > WORT

WOS > WO

WOSBIRD n illegitimate child

WOSBIRDS > WOSBIRD

WOST vb wit, to know

WOT vb wit, to know

WOTCHA same as > WOTCHER

WOTCHER sentence substitute slang term of greeting

WOTS > WOT

WOTTED > WOT

WOTTEST > WOT

WOTTETH > WOT

WOTTING > WOT

WOUBIT n type of caterpillar

WOUBITS > WOUBIT

WOULD > WILL

WOULDEST same as > WOULDST

WOULDS same as > WOULDST

WOULDST singular form of the past tense of > WILL

WOUND vb injure ▷ n injury

WOUNDABLE > WOUND

WOUNDED adj suffering from wounds

WOUNDEDLY > WOUNDED

WOUNDER > WOUND

WOUNDERS > WOUND

WOUNDIER > WOUNDY

WOUNDIEST > WOUNDY

WOUNDILY > WOUNDY

WOUNDING > WOUND

WOUNDINGS > WOUND

WOUNDLESS > WOUND

WOUNDS > WOUND

WOUNDWORT n type of plant formerly used for dressing wounds

WOUNDY adj extreme

WOURALI n plant from which curare is obtained

WOURALIS > WOURALI

WOVE > WEAVE

WOVEN n article made from woven cloth

WOVENS > WOVEN

WOW interj exclamation of astonishment ▷ n

astonishing person or thing ▷ vb be a great success with

WOWED > WOW

WOWEE *stronger form of* > WOW

WOWF *adj* mad

WOWFER > WOWF

WOWFEST > WOWF

WOWING > WOW

WOWS > WOW

WOWSER *n* puritanical person

WOWSERS > WOWSER

WOX > WAX

WOXEN > WAX

WRACK *n* seaweed ▷ *vb* strain or shake (something) violently

WRACKED > WRACK

WRACKFUL *n* ruinous

WRACKING > WRACK

WRACKS > WRACK

WRAITH *n* ghost

WRAITHS > WRAITH

WRANG *Scot word for* > WRONG

WRANGED > WRANG

WRANGING > WRANG

WRANGLE *vb* argue noisily ▷ *n* noisy argument

WRANGLED > WRANGLE

WRANGLER *n* one who wrangles

WRANGLERS > WRANGLER

WRANGLES > WRANGLE

WRANGLING > WRANGLE

WRANGS > WRANG

WRAP *vb* fold (something) round (a person or thing) so as to cover ▷ *n* garment wrapped round the shoulders

WRAPOVER *adj* (of a garment, esp a skirt) not sewn up at one side, but worn wrapped round the body and fastened so that the open edges overlap ▷ *n* such a garment

WRAPOVERS > WRAPOVER

WRAPPAGE *n* material for wrapping

WRAPPAGES > WRAPPAGE

WRAPPED > WRAP

WRAPPER *vb* cover with wrapping ▷ *n* cover for a product

WRAPPERED > WRAPPER

WRAPPERS > WRAPPER

WRAPPING > WRAP

WRAPPINGS > WRAP

WRAPROUND *same as* > WRAPOVER

WRAPS > WRAP

WRAPT *same as* > RAPT

WRASSE *n* colourful sea fish

WRASSES > WRASSE

WRASSLE *same as* > WRESTLE

WRASSLED > WRASSLE

WRASSLES > WRASSLE

WRASSLING > WRASSLE

WRAST *same as* > WREST

WRASTED > WRAST

WRASTING > WRAST

WRASTLE *same as* > WRESTLE

WRASTLED > WRASTLE

WRASTLES > WRASTLE

WRASTLING > WRASTLE

WRASTS > WRAST

WRATE > WRITE

WRATH *n* intense anger ▷ *adj* incensed ▷ *vb* make angry

WRATHED > WRATH

WRATHFUL *adj* full of wrath

WRATHIER > WRATHY

WRATHIEST > WRATHY

WRATHILY > WRATHY

WRATHING > WRATH

WRATHLESS > WRATH

WRATHS > WRATH

WRATHY *same as* > WRATHFUL

WRAWL *vb* howl

WRAWLED > WRAWL

WRAWLING > WRAWL

WRAWLS > WRAWL

WRAXLE *vb* wrestle

WRAXLED > WRAXLE

WRAXLES > WRAXLE

WRAXLING > WRAXLE

WRAXLINGS > WRAXLE

WREAK *vb* inflict (vengeance, etc) or to cause (chaos, etc)

WREAKED > WREAK

WREAKER > WREAK

WREAKERS > WREAK

WREAKFUL *adj* seeking revenge

WREAKING > WREAK

WREAKLESS *adj* unrevengeful

WREAKS > WREAK

WREATH *n* twisted ring or band of flowers or leaves used as a memorial or tribute

WREATHE *vb* form into or take the form of a wreath by twisting together

WREATHED > WREATHE

WREATHEN *adj* twisted into wreath

WREATHER > WREATHE

WREATHERS > WREATHE

WREATHES > WREATHE

WREATHIER > WREATHY

WREATHING > WREATHE

WREATHS > WREATH

WREATHY *adj* twisted into wreath

WRECK *vb* destroy ▷ *n* remains of something that has been destroyed or badly damaged

WRECKAGE *n* wrecked remains

WRECKAGES > WRECKAGE

WRECKED *adj* in a state of intoxication induced by drugs or alcohol

WRECKER *n* formerly, person who lured ships onto the rocks in order to plunder them

WRECKERS > WRECKER

WRECKFISH *n* large sea perch

WRECKFUL *adj* causing wreckage

WRECKING > WRECK

WRECKINGS > WRECK

WRECKS > WRECK

WREN *n* small brown songbird

WRENCH *vb* twist or pull violently ▷ *n* violent twist or pull

WRENCHED > WRENCH

WRENCHER > WRENCH

WRENCHERS > WRENCH

WRENCHES > WRENCH

WRENCHING > WRENCH

WRENS > WREN

WRENTIT *n* type of long-tailed North American bird

WRENTITS > WRENTIT

WREST *vb* twist violently ▷ *n* act or an instance of wresting

WRESTED > WREST

WRESTER > WREST

WRESTERS > WREST

WRESTING > WREST

WRESTLE *vb* fight by grappling with an opponent ▷ *n* act of wrestling

WRESTLED > WRESTLE

WRESTLER > WRESTLE

WRESTLERS > WRESTLE

WRESTLES > WRESTLE

WRESTLING *n* sport in which each contestant tries to overcome the other either by throwing or pinning him or her to the ground or by forcing a submission

WRESTS > WREST

WRETCH *n* despicable person

WRETCHED *adj* miserable or unhappy

WRETCHES > WRETCH

WRETHE *same as* > WREATHE

WRETHED > WRETHE

WRETHES > WRETHE

WRETHING > WRETHE

WRICK *variant spelling (chiefly Brit) of* > RICK

WRICKED > WRICK

WRICKING > WRICK

WRICKS > WRICK

WRIED > WRY

WRIER > WRY

WRIES > WRY

WRIEST > WRY

WRIGGLE *vb* move with a twisting action ▷ *n* wriggling movement

WRIGGLED > WRIGGLE

WRIGGLER > WRIGGLE

WRIGGLERS > WRIGGLE

WRIGGLES > WRIGGLE

WRIGGLIER > WRIGGLE

WRIGGLING > WRIGGLE

WRIGGLY > WRIGGLE

WRIGHT *n* maker

WRIGHTS > WRIGHT

WRING *vb* twist, esp to squeeze liquid out of

WRINGED > WRING

WRINGER *same as* > MANGLE

WRINGERS > WRINGER

WRINGING > WRING

WRINGS > WRING

WRINKLE *n* slight crease, esp one in the skin due to age ▷ *vb* make or become slightly creased

WRINKLED > WRINKLE

WRINKLES > WRINKLE

WRINKLIE *n* old person

WRINKLIER > WRINKLE

WRINKLIES *pl n* derogatory word for old people

WRINKLING > WRINKLE

WRINKLY > WRINKLE

WRIST *n* joint between the hand and the arm ▷ *vb* hit an object with a twist of the wrist

WRISTBAND *n* band around the wrist, esp one attached to a watch or forming part of a long sleeve

WRISTED > WRIST

WRISTER *n* type of shot in hockey

WRISTERS > WRISTER

WRISTIER > WRISTY

WRISTIEST > WRISTY

WRISTING > WRIST

WRISTLET *n* band or bracelet worn around the wrist

WRISTLETS > WRISTLET

WRISTLOCK *n* wrestling hold in which a wrestler seizes his opponent's wrist and exerts pressure against the joints of his hand, arm, or shoulder

WRISTS > WRIST

WRISTY *adj* characterized by considerable movement of the wrist

WRIT *n* written legal command

WRITABLE > WRITE

WRITATIVE *adj* inclined to write a lot

WRITE *vb* mark paper etc with symbols or words

WRITEABLE > WRITE

WRITEOFF *n* uncollectible debt that is cancelled

WRITEOFFS > WRITEOFF

WRITER *n* author

WRITERESS *n* female writer

WRITERLY *adj* of or characteristic of a writer

WRITERS > WRITER

WRITES > WRITE

WRITHE *vb* twist or squirm in or as if in pain ▷ *n* act or an instance of writhing

WRITHED > WRITHE

WRITHEN *adj* twisted

WRITHER > WRITHE

WRITHERS > WRITHE

WRITHES > WRITHE

WRITHING > WRITHE

WRITHINGS > WRITHE

WRITHLED *adj* wrinkled

WRITING > WRITE

WRITINGS > WRITE

WRITS > WRIT

WRITTEN > WRITE

WRIZLED *adj* wrinkled

WROATH *n* unforeseen trouble

WROATHS > WROATH

WROKE > WREAK

WROKEN > WREAK

WRONG *adj* incorrect or mistaken ▷ *adv* in a wrong manner ▷ *n* something immoral or unjust ▷ *vb* treat unjustly

WRONGDOER *n* person who acts immorally or illegally

WRONGED > WRONG

WRONGER > WRONG

WRONGERS > WRONG

WRONGEST > WRONG

WRONGFUL *adj* unjust or illegal

WRONGING > WRONG

WRONGLY > WRONG

WRONGNESS > WRONG

WRONGOUS *adj* unfair

WRONGS > WRONG

WROOT *obsolete form of*

> ROOT

WROOTED > WROOT

WROOTING > WROOT

WROOTS > WROOT

WROTE > WRITE

WROTH *adj* angry

WROTHFUL *same as*

> WRATHFUL

WROUGHT *adj* (of metals) shaped by hammering or beating

WRUNG > WRING

WRY *adj* drily humorous ▷ *vb* twist or contort

WRYBILL *n* New Zealand plover whose bill is bent to one side

WRYBILLS > WRYBILL

WRYER > WRY

WRYEST > WRY

WRYING > WRY

WRYLY > WRY

WRYNECK *n* woodpecker that has a habit of twisting its neck round

WRYNECKS > WRYNECK

WRYNESS > WRY

WRYNESSES > WRY

WRYTHEN *adj* twisted

WUD *Scots form of* **>** WOOD

WUDDED > WUD

WUDDING > WUD

WUDJULA *n* Australian word for a non-Aboriginal person

WUDJULAS > WUDJULA

WUDS > WUD

WUDU *n* practice of ritual washing before daily prayer

WUDUS > WUDU

WUKKAS *pl n* Australian taboo slang expression for no problems

WULFENITE *n* yellow, orange, red, or grey lustrous secondary mineral

WULL *obsolete form of*

> WILL

WULLED > WILL

WULLING > WILL

WULLS > WILL

WUNNER *same as* **>** ONER

WUNNERS > WUNNER

WURLEY *n* Aboriginal hut

WURLEYS > WURLEY

WURLIE *same as* **>** WURLEY

WURLIES > WURLIE

WURST *n* large sausage, esp of a type made in Germany, Austria, etc

WURSTS > WURST

WURTZITE *n* zinc sulphide

WURTZITES > WURTZITE

WURZEL *n* root

WURZELS > WURZEL

WUS *n* casual term of address

WUSES > WUS

WUSHU *n* Chinese martial arts

WUSHUS > WUSHU

WUSS *n* feeble or effeminate person

WUSSES > WUSS

WUSSIER > WUSSY

WUSSIES > WUSSY

WUSSIEST > WUSSY

WUSSY *adj* feeble or effeminate ▷ *n* feeble person

WUTHER *vb* (of wind) blow and roar

WUTHERED > WUTHER

WUTHERING *adj* (of a wind) blowing strongly with a roaring sound

WUTHERS > WUTHER

WUXIA *n* Chinese fiction concerning the adventures of sword-wielding heroes

WUXIAS > WUXIA

WUZ *vb* nonstandard spelling of was

WUZZLE *vb* mix up

WUZZLED > WUZZLE

WUZZLES > WUZZLE

WUZZLING > WUZZLE

WYANDOTTE *n* heavy American breed of domestic fowl

WYCH *n* type of tree having flexible branches

WYCHES > WYCH

WYE *n* y-shaped pipe

WYES > WYE

WYLE *vb* entice

WYLED > WYLE

WYLES > WYLE

WYLIECOAT *n* petticoat

WYLING > WYLE

WYN *n* rune equivalent to English 'w'

WYND *n* narrow lane or alley

WYNDS > WYND

WYNN *same as* **>** WYN

WYNNS > WYNN

WYNS > WYN

WYSIWYG *adj* denoting a computer screen display showing exactly what will print out

WYTE *vb* blame

WYTED > WYTE

WYTES > WYTE

WYTING > WYTE

WYVERN *n* heraldic beast

WYVERNS > WYVERN

W

Xx

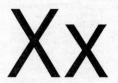

XANTHAM n acacia gum
XANTHAMS > XANTHAM
XANTHAN same as > XANTHAM
XANTHANS > XANTHAN
XANTHATE n any salt or ester of xanthic acid
XANTHATES > XANTHATE
XANTHEIN n soluble part of the yellow pigment that is found in the cell sap of some flowers
XANTHEINS > XANTHEIN
XANTHENE n yellowish crystalline heterocyclic compound used as a fungicide
XANTHENES > XANTHENE
XANTHIC adj of, containing, or derived from xanthic acid
XANTHIN n any of a group of yellow or orange carotene derivatives
XANTHINE n crystalline compound related in structure to uric acid and found in urine, blood, certain plants, and certain animal tissues
XANTHINES > XANTHINE
XANTHINS > XANTHIN
XANTHISM n condition of skin, fur, or feathers in which yellow coloration predominates
XANTHISMS > XANTHISM
XANTHOMA n presence in the skin of fatty yellow or brownish plaques or nodules, esp on the eyelids, caused by a disorder of lipid metabolism
XANTHOMAS > XANTHOMA
XANTHONE n crystalline compound
XANTHONES > XANTHONE
XANTHOUS adj of, relating to, or designating races with yellowish hair and a light complexion
XANTHOXYL n South American plant
XEBEC n small three-masted Mediterranean vessel with both square and lateen sails, formerly used by Algerian pirates and later used for commerce

XEBECS > XEBEC
XED vb marked a cross against
XENIA n influence of pollen upon the form of the fruit developing after pollination
XENIAL > XENIA
XENIAS > XENIA
XENIC adj denoting the presence of bacteria
XENIUM n diplomatic gift
XENOBLAST n type of mineral deposit
XENOCRYST n crystal included within an igneous rock as the magma cooled but not formed from it
XENOGAMY n fertilization by the fusion of male and female gametes from different individuals of the same species
XENOGENIC adj relating to the supposed production of offspring completely unlike either parent
XENOGENY n offspring unlike either parent
XENOGRAFT n tissue graft obtained from a donor of a different species from the recipient
XENOLITH n fragment of rock differing in origin, composition, structure, etc, from the igneous rock enclosing it
XENOLITHS > XENOLITH
XENOMANIA n passion for foreign things
XENOMENIA n menstruation from unusual orifices
XENON n colourless odourless gas found in very small quantities in the air
XENONS > XENON
XENOPHILE n person who likes foreigners or things foreign
XENOPHOBE n person who hates or fears foreigners or strangers
XENOPHOBY n hatred or fear of foreigners or strangers

XENOPHYA n parts of shell or skeleton formed by foreign bodies
XENOPUS n African frog
XENOPUSES > XENOPUS
XENOTIME n yellow-brown mineral
XENOTIMES > XENOTIME
XENURINE adj relating to a type of armadillo ▷ n type of armadillo
XENURINES > XENURINE
XERAFIN n Indian coin
XERAFINS > XERAFIN
XERANSES > XERANSIS
XERANSIS n gradual loss of tissue moisture
XERANTIC > XERANSIS
XERAPHIN same as > XERAFIN
XERAPHINS > XERAPHIN
XERARCH adj (of a sere) having its origin in a dry habitat
XERASIA n dryness of the hair
XERASIAS > XERASIA
XERIC adj of, relating to, or growing in dry conditions
XERICALLY > XERIC
XERISCAPE n landscape designed to conserve water ▷ vb landscape (an area) so that it needs little water
XEROCHASY n release of seeds or pollen on drying
XERODERMA n any abnormal dryness of the skin as the result of diminished secretions from the sweat or sebaceous glands
XEROMA n excessive dryness of the cornea
XEROMAS > XEROMA
XEROMATA > XEROMA
XEROMORPH n xerophilous plant
XEROPHAGY n fasting by eating only dry food
XEROPHILE n plant or animal who likes living in dry surroundings
XEROPHILY > XEROPHILE
XEROPHYTE n xerophilous plant, such as a cactus

XEROSERE n sere that originates in dry surroundings
XEROSERES > XEROSERE
XEROSES > XEROSIS
XEROSIS n abnormal dryness of bodily tissues, esp the skin, eyes, or mucous membranes
XEROSTOMA n abnormal lack of saliva; dryness of the mouth
XEROTES same as > XEROSIS
XEROTIC > XEROSIS
XEROX n trade name for a machine employing a xerographic copying process ▷ vb produce a copy (of a document, etc) using such a machine
XEROXED > XEROX
XEROXES > XEROX
XEROXING > XEROX
XERUS n ground squirrel
XERUSES > XERUS
XI n 14th letter in the Greek alphabet
XIPHOID adj shaped like a sword ▷ n part of the sternum
XIPHOIDAL > XIPHOID
XIPHOIDS > XIPHOID
XIPHOPAGI n Siamese twins joined at the lower sternum
XIS > XI
XOANA > XOANON
XOANON n primitive image of a god supposed to have fallen from heaven
XRAY n code word for the letter X
XRAYS > XRAY
XU n Vietnamese currency unit
XYLAN n yellow polysaccharide consisting of xylose units
XYLANS > XYLAN
XYLEM n plant tissue that conducts water and minerals from the roots to all other parts
XYLEMS > XYLEM
XYLENE n type of hydrocarbon
XYLENES > XYLENE
XYLENOL n synthetic resin made from xylene

XYLENOLS > XYLENOL
XYLIC > XYLEM
XYLIDIN *same as*
 > XYLIDINE
XYLIDINE *n* mixture of
 six isomeric amines
 derived from xylene and
 used in dyes
XYLIDINES > XYLIDINE
XYLIDINS > XYLIDIN
XYLITOL *n* crystalline
 alcohol used as sweetener
XYLITOLS > XYLITOL
XYLOCARP *n* fruit, such as
 a coconut, having a hard
 woody pericarp
XYLOCARPS > XYLOCARP
XYLOGEN *same as* > XYLEM
XYLOGENS > XYLOGEN
XYLOGRAPH *n* engraving

in wood ▷ *vb* print (a
 design, illustration, etc)
 from a wood engraving
XYLOID *adj* of, relating to,
 or resembling wood
XYLOIDIN *n* type of
 explosive
XYLOIDINE *same as*
 > XYLOIDIN
XYLOIDINS > XYLOIDIN
XYLOL *another name (not in
 technical usage) for*
 > XYLENE
XYLOLOGY *n* study of the
 composition of wood
XYLOLS > XYLOL
XYLOMA *n* hard growth in
 fungi
XYLOMAS > XYLOMA
XYLOMATA > XYLOMA

XYLOMETER *n* device for
 measuring the specific
 gravity of wood
XYLONIC *adj* denoting an
 acid formed from xylose
XYLONITE *n* type of
 plastic
XYLONITES
 > XYLONITE
XYLOPHAGE *n* creature
 that eats wood
XYLOPHONE *n* musical
 instrument made of a row
 of wooden bars played
 with hammers
XYLORIMBA *n* large
 xylophone with an
 extended range of five
 octaves
XYLOSE *n* white

crystalline sugar found in
 wood and straw
XYLOSES > XYLOSE
XYLOTOMY *n* preparation
 of sections of wood for
 examination by microscope
XYLYL *n* group of atoms
XYLYLS > XYLYL
XYST *n* long portico, esp
 one used in ancient Greece
 for athletics
XYSTER *n* surgical
 instrument for scraping
 bone
XYSTERS > XYSTER
XYSTI > XYSTUS
XYSTOI > XYSTOS
XYSTOS *same as* > XYST
XYSTS > XYST
XYSTUS *same as* > XYST

X

Yy

YA *n* type of Asian pear

YAAR *n* in informal Indian English, a friend

YAARS > YAAR

YABA *n* informal word for 'yet another bloody acronym'

YABAS > YABA

YABBA *n* form of methamphetamine

YABBAS > YABBA

YABBER *vb* talk or jabber ▷ *n* talk or jabber

YABBERED > YABBER

YABBERING > YABBER

YABBERS > YABBER

YABBIE *same as* > YABBY

YABBIED > YABBY

YABBIES > YABBY

YABBY *n* small freshwater crayfish ▷ *vb* go out to catch yabbies

YABBYING > YABBY

YACCA *n* Australian plant with a woody stem

YACCAS > YACCA

YACHT *n* large boat with sails or an engine ▷ *vb* sail in a yacht

YACHTED > YACHT

YACHTER > YACHT

YACHTERS > YACHT

YACHTIE *n* yachtsman

YACHTIES > YACHTIE

YACHTING *n* sport or practice of navigating a yacht

YACHTINGS > YACHTING

YACHTMAN *same as* > YACHTSMAN

YACHTMEN > YACHTMAN

YACHTS > YACHT

YACHTSMAN *n* person who sails a yacht

YACHTSMEN > YACHTSMAN

YACK *same as* > YAK

YACKA *same as* > YACCA

YACKAS > YACKA

YACKED > YACK

YACKER *same as* > YAKKA

YACKERS > YACKER

YACKING > YACK

YACKS > YACK

YAD *n* hand-held pointer used for reading the sefer torah

YADS > YAD

YAE *same as* > AE

YAFF *vb* bark

YAFFED > YAFF

YAFFING > YAFF

YAFFLE *n* woodpecker with a green back and wings

YAFFLES > YAFFLE

YAFFS > YAFF

YAG *n* artificial crystal

YAGE *n* tropical vine of the Amazon region

YAGER *same as* > JAEGER

YAGERS > YAGER

YAGES > YAGE

YAGGER *n* pedlar

YAGGERS > YAGGER

YAGI *n* type of highly directional aerial

YAGIS > YAGI

YAGS > YAG

YAH *interj* exclamation of derision or disgust ▷ *n* affected upper-class person

YAHOO *n* crude coarse person

YAHOOISM > YAHOO

YAHOOISMS > YAHOO

YAHOOS > YAHOO

YAHRZEIT *n* (in Judaism) the anniversary of the death of a close relative, on which it is customary to kindle a light and recite the Kaddish

YAHRZEITS > YAHRZEIT

YAHS > YAH

YAIRD *Scots form of* > YARD

YAIRDS > YAIRD

YAK *n* Tibetan ox with long shaggy hair ▷ *vb* talk continuously about unimportant matters

YAKHDAN *n* box for carrying ice on a pack animal

YAKHDANS > YAKHDAN

YAKIMONO *n* grilled food

YAKIMONOS > YAKIMONO

YAKITORI *n* Japanese dish consisting of small pieces of chicken skewered and grilled

YAKITORIS > YAKITORI

YAKKA *n* work

YAKKAS > YAKKA

YAKKED > YAK

YAKKER *same as* > YAKKA

YAKKERS > YAKKER

YAKKING > YAK

YAKOW *n* animal bred from a male yak and a domestic cow

YAKOWS > YAKOW

YAKS > YAK

YAKUZA *n* Japanese criminal organization

YALD *adj* vigorous

YALE *n* mythical beast with the body of an antelope (or similar animal) and swivelling horns

YALES > YALE

YAM *n* tropical root vegetable

YAMALKA *same as* > YARMULKE

YAMALKAS > YAMALKA

YAMEN *n* (in imperial China) the office or residence of a public official

YAMENS > YAMEN

YAMMER *vb* whine in a complaining manner ▷ *n* yammering sound

YAMMERED > YAMMER

YAMMERER > YAMMER

YAMMERERS > YAMMER

YAMMERING > YAMMER

YAMMERS > YAMMER

YAMPIES > YAMPY

YAMPY *n* foolish person

YAMS > YAM

YAMULKA *same as* > YARMULKE

YAMULKAS > YAMULKA

YAMUN *same as* > YAMEN

YAMUNS > YAMUN

YANG *n* (in Chinese philosophy) one of two complementary principles maintaining harmony in the universe

YANGS > YANG

YANK *vb* pull or jerk suddenly ▷ *n* sudden pull or jerk

YANKED > YANK

YANKEE *n* code word for the letter Y

YANKEES > YANKEE

YANKER > YANK

YANKERS > YANK

YANKIE *n* shrewish woman

YANKIES > YANKIE

YANKING > YANK

YANKS > YANK

YANQUI *n* slang word for American

YANQUIS > YANQUI

YANTRA *n* diagram used in meditation

YANTRAS > YANTRA

YAOURT *n* yoghurt

YAOURTS > YAOURT

YAP *vb* bark with a high-pitched sound ▷ *n* high-pitched bark ▷ *interj* imitation or representation of the sound of a dog yapping

YAPOCK *same as* > YAPOK

YAPOCKS > YAPOCK

YAPOK *n* type of opossum

YAPOKS > YAPOK

YAPON *same as* > YAUPON

YAPONS > YAPON

YAPP *n* type of book binding

YAPPED > YAP

YAPPER > YAP

YAPPERS > YAP

YAPPIE *n* young aspiring professional

YAPPIER > YAP

YAPPIES > YAPPIE

YAPPIEST > YAP

YAPPING *n* act of yapping

YAPPINGLY > YAP

YAPPINGS > YAPPING

YAPPS > YAPP

YAPPY > YAP

YAPS > YAP

YAPSTER > YAP

YAPSTERS > YAP

YAQONA *n* Polynesian shrub

YAQONAS > YAQONA

YAR *adj* nimble

YARAK *n* fit condition for hunting

YARAKS > YARAK

YARCO *n* derogatory dialect word for a young working-class person who wears casual sports clothes

YARCOS > YARCO

YARD *n* unit of length ▷ *vb* draft (animals), esp to a saleyard

YARDAGE *n* length measured in yards

YARDAGES > YARDAGE

YARDANG *n* ridge formed by wind erosion

YARDANGS > YARDANG

YARDARM n outer end of a ship's yard

YARDARMS > YARDARM

YARDBIRD n inexperienced, untrained, or clumsy soldier, esp one employed on menial duties

YARDBIRDS > YARDBIRD

YARDED > YARD

YARDER n one who drafts animals to a sale yard

YARDERS > YARD

YARDING n group of animals displayed for sale

YARDINGS > YARDING

YARDLAND n archaic unit of land

YARDLANDS > YARDLAND

YARDMAN n farm overseer

YARDMEN > YARDMAN

YARDS > YARD

YARDSTICK n standard against which to judge other people or things

YARDWAND same as > YARDSTICK

YARDWANDS > YARDWAND

YARDWORK n garden work

YARDWORKS > YARDWORK

YARE adj ready, brisk, or eager ▷ adv readily or eagerly

YARELY > YARE

YARER > YARE

YAREST > YARE

YARFA n peat

YARFAS > YARFA

YARK vb make ready

YARKED > YARK

YARKING > YARK

YARKS > YARK

YARMELKE same as > YARMULKE

YARMELKES > YARMELKE

YARMULKA same as > YARMULKE

YARMULKAS > YARMULKA

YARMULKE n skullcap worn by Jewish men

YARMULKES > YARMULKE

YARN n thread used for knitting or making cloth ▷ vb thread with yarn

YARNED > YARN

YARNER > YARN

YARNERS > YARN

YARNING > YARN

YARNS > YARN

YARPHA n peat

YARPHAS > YARPHA

YARR n wild white flower ▷ vb growl or snarl

YARRAMAN n horse

YARRAMANS > YARRAMAN

YARRAMEN > YARRAMAN

YARRAN n type of small hardy tree of inland Australia

YARRANS > YARRAN

YARRED > YARR

YARRING > YARR

YARROW n wild plant with flat clusters of white flowers

YARROWS > YARROW

YARRS > YARR

YARTA Shetland word for > HEART

YARTAS > YARTA

YARTO same as > YARTA

YARTOS > YARTO

YAS > YA

YASHMAC same as > YASHMAK

YASHMACS > YASHMAC

YASHMAK n veil worn by a Muslim woman in public

YASHMAKS > YASHMAK

YASMAK same as > YASHMAK

YASMAKS > YASHMAK

YATAGAN same as > YATAGHAN

YATAGANS > YATAGAN

YATAGHAN n Turkish sword with a curved single-edged blade

YATAGHANS > YATAGHAN

YATE n type of small eucalyptus tree yielding a very hard timber

YATES > YATE

YATTER vb talk at length ▷ n continuous chatter

YATTERED > YATTER

YATTERING > YATTER

YATTERS > YATTER

YAUD Scots word for > MARE

YAUDS > YAUD

YAULD adj alert, spritely, or nimble

YAUP variant spelling of > YAWP

YAUPED > YAUP

YAUPER > YAUP

YAUPERS > YAUP

YAUPING > YAUP

YAUPON n southern US evergreen holly shrub

YAUPONS > YAUPON

YAUPS > YAUP

YAUTIA n Caribbean plant cultivated for its edible leaves and underground stems

YAUTIAS > YAUTIA

YAW vb (of an aircraft or ship) turn to one side or from side to side while moving ▷ n act or movement of yawing

YAWED > YAW

YAWEY > YAWS

YAWIER > YAWY

YAWIEST > YAWY

YAWING > YAW

YAWL n two-masted sailing boat ▷ vb howl, weep, or scream harshly

YAWLED > YAWL

YAWLING > YAWL

YAWLS > YAWL

YAWMETER n instrument for measuring an aircraft's yaw

YAWMETERS > YAWMETER

YAWN vb open the mouth wide and take in air deeply, often when sleepy or bored ▷ n act of yawning

YAWNED > YAWN

YAWNER > YAWN

YAWNERS > YAWN

YAWNIER > YAWN

YAWNIEST > YAWN

YAWNING > YAWN

YAWNINGLY > YAWN

YAWNINGS > YAWN

YAWNS > YAWN

YAWNSOME adj boring

YAWNY > YAWN

YAWP vb gape or yawn, esp audibly ▷ n shout, bark, yelp, or cry

YAWPED > YAWP

YAWPER > YAWP

YAWPERS > YAWP

YAWPING > YAWP

YAWPINGS > YAWP

YAWPS > YAWP

YAWS n infectious tropical skin disease

YAWY adj having or resembling yaws

YAY interj exclamation indicating approval or triumph ▷ n cry of approval

YAYS > YAY

YBET archaic past participle of > BEAT

YBLENT archaic past participle of > BLEND

YBORE archaic past participle of > BEAR

YBOUND archaic past participle of > BIND

YBOUNDEN archaic past participle of > BIND

YBRENT archaic past participle of > BURN

YCLAD archaic past participle of > CLOTHE

YCLED archaic past participle of > CLOTHE

YCLEEPE archaic form of > CLEPE

YCLEEPED > YCLEEPE

YCLEEPES > YCLEEPE

YCLEEPING > YCLEEPE

YCLEPED same as > YCLEPT

YCLEPT adj having the name of

YCOND archaic past participle of > CON

YDRAD archaic past participle of > DREAD

YDRED archaic past participle of > DREAD

YE pron you ▷ adj the

YEA interj yes ▷ adv indeed or truly ▷ sentence substitute aye ▷ n cry of agreement

YEAD vb proceed

YEADING > YEAD

YEADS > YEAD

YEAH n positive affirmation

YEAHS > YEAH

YEALDON n fuel

YEALDONS > YEALDON

YEALING n person of the same age as oneself

YEALINGS > YEALING

YEALM vb prepare for thatching

YEALMED > YEALM

YEALMING > YEALM

YEALMS > YEALM

YEAN vb (of a sheep or goat) to give birth to (offspring)

YEANED > YEAN

YEANING > YEAN

YEANLING n young of a goat or sheep

YEANLINGS > YEANLING

YEANS > YEAN

YEAR n time taken for the earth to make one revolution around the sun, about 365 days

YEARBOOK n reference book published annually containing details of the previous year's events

YEARBOOKS > YEARBOOK

YEARD vb bury

YEARDED > YEARD

YEARDING > YEARD

YEARDS > YEARD

YEAREND n end of the year

YEARENDS > YEAREND

YEARLIES > YEARLY

YEARLING n animal between one and two years old ▷ adj being a year old

YEARLINGS > YEARLING

YEARLONG adj throughout a whole year

YEARLY adv (happening) every year or once a year ▷ adj occurring, done, or appearing once a year or every year ▷ n publication, event, etc, that occurs once a year

YEARN vb want (something) very much

YEARNED > YEARN

YEARNER > YEARN

YEARNERS > YEARN

YEARNING n intense or overpowering longing, desire, or need

YEARNINGS > YEARNING

YEARNS > YEARN

YEARS > YEAR

YEAS > YEA

YEASAYER n person who usually agrees with proposals

YEASAYERS > YEASAYER

YEAST n fungus used to make bread rise and to ferment alcoholic drinks ▷ vb froth or foam

YEASTED > YEAST

YEASTIER > YEASTY
YEASTIEST > YEASTY
YEASTILY > YEASTY
YEASTING > YEAST
YEASTLESS > YEAST
YEASTLIKE > YEAST
YEASTS > YEAST
YEASTY *adj* of, resembling, or containing yeast
YEBO *interj* yes ▷ *sentence substitute* expression of affirmation
YECCH *same as* > YECH
YECCHS > YECCH
YECH *n* expression of disgust
YECHIER > YECHY
YECHIEST > YECHY
YECHS > YECH
YECHY > YECH
YEDE *same as* > YEAD
YEDES > YEDE
YEDING > YEDE
YEED *same as* > YEAD
YEEDING > YEED
YEEDS > YEED
YEELIN *n* person of the same age as oneself
YEELINS > YEELIN
YEESH *interj* interjection used to express frustration
YEGG *n* burglar or safe-breaker
YEGGMAN *same as* > YEGG
YEGGMEN > YEGGMAN
YEGGS > YEGG
YEH *same as* > YEAH
YELD *adj* (of an animal) barren or too young to bear young
YELDRING *n* yellowhammer (bird)
YELDRINGS > YELDRING
YELDROCK *same as* > YELDRING
YELDROCKS > YELDROCK
YELK *n* yolk of an egg
YELKS > YELK
YELL *vb* shout or scream in a loud or piercing way ▷ *n* loud cry of pain, anger, or fear
YELLED > YELL
YELLER > YELL
YELLERS > YELL
YELLING > YELL
YELLINGS > YELL
YELLOCH *vb* yell
YELLOCHED > YELLOCH
YELLOCHS > YELLOCH
YELLOW *n* colour of gold, a lemon, etc ▷ *adj* of this colour ▷ *vb* make or become yellow
YELLOWED > YELLOW
YELLOWER > YELLOW
YELLOWEST > YELLOW
YELLOWFIN *n* type of tuna
YELLOWIER > YELLOW
YELLOWING > YELLOW
YELLOWISH > YELLOW
YELLOWLY > YELLOW

YELLOWS *n* any of various fungal or viral diseases of plants
YELLOWY > YELLOW
YELLS > YELL
YELM *same as* > YEALM
YELMED > YELM
YELMING > YELM
YELMS > YELM
YELP *n* short sudden cry ▷ *vb* utter a sharp or high-pitched cry of pain
YELPED > YELP
YELPER > YELP
YELPERS > YELP
YELPING > YELP
YELPINGS > YELP
YELPS > YELP
YELT *n* young sow
YELTS > YELT
YEMMER *southwest English form of* > EMBER
YEMMERS > YEMMER
YEN *n* monetary unit of Japan ▷ *vb* have a longing
YENNED > YEN
YENNING > YEN
YENS > YEN
YENTA *n* meddlesome woman
YENTAS > YENTA
YENTE *same as* > YENTA
YENTES > YENTE
YEOMAN *n* farmer owning and farming his own land
YEOMANLY *adj* of, relating to, or like a yeoman ▷ *adv* in a yeomanly manner, as in being brave, staunch, or loyal
YEOMANRY *n* yeomen
YEOMEN > YEOMAN
YEOW *interj* interjection used to express pain
YEP *n* affirmative statement
YEPS > YEP
YER *adj* (coll.) your; you
YERBA *n* stimulating South American drink made from dried leaves
YERBAS > YERBA
YERD *vb* bury
YERDED > YERD
YERDING > YERD
YERDS > YERD
YERK *vb* tighten stitches
YERKED > YERK
YERKING > YERK
YERKS > YERK
YERSINIA *n* plague bacterium
YERSINIAE > YERSINIA
YERSINIAS > YERSINIA
YES *interj* expresses consent, agreement, or approval ▷ *n* answer or vote of yes ▷ *sentence substitute* used to express acknowledgment, affirmation, consent, etc ▷ *vb* reply in the affirmative

YESES > YES
YESHIVA *n* traditional Jewish school
YESHIVAH *same as* > YESHIVA
YESHIVAHS > YESHIVAH
YESHIVAS > YESHIVA
YESHIVOT > YESHIVA
YESHIVOTH > YESHIVA
YESK *vb* hiccup
YESKED > YESK
YESKING > YESK
YESKS > YESK
YESSED > YES
YESSES > YES
YESSING > YES
YESSIR *interj* expression of assent to a man
YESSIREE *interj* expression of assent
YESSUM *interj* expression of assent to a woman
YEST *archaic form of* > YEAST
YESTER *adj* of or relating to yesterday
YESTERDAY *n* the day before today ▷ *adv* on or during the day before today
YESTEREVE *n* yesterday evening
YESTERN *same as* > YESTER
YESTREEN *n* yesterday evening
YESTREENS > YESTREEN
YESTS > YEST
YESTY *archaic form of* > YEASTY
YET *adv* up until then or now
YETI *n* large legendary manlike creature alleged to inhabit the Himalayan Mountains
YETIS > YETI
YETT *n* gate or door
YETTIE *n* young, entrepreneurial, and technology-based (person)
YETTIES > YETTIE
YETTS > YETT
YEUK *vb* itch
YEUKED > YEUK
YEUKIER > YEUK
YEUKIEST > YEUKY
YEUKING > YEUK
YEUKS > YEUK
YEUKY > YEUK
YEVE *vb* give
YEVEN > YEVE
YEVES > YEVE
YEVING > YEVE
YEW *n* evergreen tree with needle-like leaves and red berries
YEWEN *adj* made of yew
YEWS > YEW
YEX *vb* hiccup
YEXED > YEX
YEXES > YEX

YEXING > YEX
YEZ *interj* yes
YFERE *adv* together ▷ *n* friend or associate
YFERES > YFERE
YGLAUNST *archaic past participle of* > GLANCE
YGO *archaic past participle of* > GO
YGOE *archaic past participle of* > GO
YIBBLES *adv* perhaps
YICKER *vb* squeal or squeak
YICKERED > YICKER
YICKERING > YICKER
YICKERS > YICKER
YID *n* offensive word for a Jew
YIDAKI *n* long wooden wind instrument played by the Aboriginal peoples of Arnhem Land
YIDAKIS > YIDAKI
YIDS > YID
YIELD *vb* produce or bear ▷ *n* amount produced
YIELDABLE > YIELD
YIELDED > YIELD
YIELDER > YIELD
YIELDERS > YIELD
YIELDING *adj* submissive
YIELDINGS > YIELD
YIELDS > YIELD
YIKE *n* argument, squabble, or fight ▷ *vb* argue, squabble, or fight
YIKED > YIKE
YIKES *interj* expression of surprise, fear, or alarm
YIKING > YIKE
YIKKER *vb* squeal or squeak
YIKKERED > YIKKER
YIKKERING > YIKKER
YIKKERS > YIKKER
YILL *n* ale ▷ *vb* entertain with ale
YILLED > YILL
YILLING > YILL
YILLS > YILL
YIN *Scots word for* > ONE
YINCE *Scots form of* > ONCE
YINDIE *n* person who combines a lucrative career with non-mainstream tastes
YINDIES > YINDIE
YINGYANG *n* two opposing but complementary principles in Chinese philosophy
YINGYANGS > YINGYANG
YINS > YIN
YIP *vb* emit a high-pitched bark
YIPE *same as* > YIPES
YIPES *interj* expression of surprise, fear, or alarm
YIPPED > YIP
YIPPEE *interj* exclamation of joy or pleasure

YIPPER n golfer who suffers from a failure of nerve
YIPPERS > YIPPER
YIPPIE n young person sharing hippy ideals
YIPPIES > YIPPIE
YIPPING > YIP
YIPPY same as > YIPPIE
YIPS > YIP
YIRD vb bury
YIRDED > YIRD
YIRDING > YIRD
YIRDS > YIRD
YIRK same as > YERK
YIRKED > YIRK
YIRKING > YIRK
YIRKS > YIRK
YIRR vb snarl, growl, or yell
YIRRED > YIRR
YIRRING > YIRR
YIRRS > YIRR
YIRTH n earth
YIRTHS > YIRTH
YITE n European bunting with a yellowish head and body and brown streaked wings and tail
YITES > YITE
YITIE same as > YITE
YITIES > YITIE
YITTEN adj frightened
YLEM n original matter from which the basic elements are said to have been formed
YLEMS > YLEM
YLIKE Spenserian form of > ALIKE
YLKE archaic spelling of > ILK
YLKES > YLKE
YMOLT Spenserian past participle of > MELT
YMOLTEN Spenserian past participle of > MELT
YMPE Spenserian form of > IMP
YMPES > YMPE
YMPING > YMPE
YMPT > YMPE
YNAMBU n South American bird
YNAMBUS > YNAMBU
YO interj expression used as a greeting ▷ sentence substitute expression used as a greeting
YOB n bad-mannered aggressive youth
YOBBERIES > YOBBERY
YOBBERY n behaviour typical of aggressive surly youths
YOBBIER > YOBBY
YOBBIEST > YOBBY
YOBBISH adj typical of aggressive surly youths
YOBBISHLY > YOBBISH
YOBBISM > YOB
YOBBISMS > YOB
YOBBO same as > YOB

YOBBOES > YOBBO
YOBBOS > YOBBO
YOBBY adj like a yob
YOBS > YOB
YOCK vb chuckle
YOCKED > YOCK
YOCKING > YOCK
YOCKS > YOCK
YOD n tenth letter in the Hebrew alphabet
YODE > YEAD
YODEL vb sing with abrupt changes between a normal and a falsetto voice ▷ n act or sound of yodelling
YODELED > YODEL
YODELER > YODEL
YODELERS > YODEL
YODELING > YODEL
YODELLED > YODEL
YODELLER > YODEL
YODELLERS > YODEL
YODELLING > YODEL
YODELS > YODEL
YODH same as > YOD
YODHS > YODH
YODLE variant spelling of > YODEL
YODLED > YODLE
YODLER > YODLE
YODLERS > YODLE
YODLES > YODLE
YODLING > YODLE
YODS > YOD
YOGA n Hindu method of exercise and discipline
YOGAS > YOGA
YOGEE same as > YOGI
YOGEES > YOGEE
YOGH n character used in Old and Middle English to represent a palatal fricative
YOGHOURT variant form of > YOGURT
YOGHOURTS > YOGHOURT
YOGHS > YOGH
YOGHURT same as > YOGURT
YOGHURTS > YOGHURT
YOGI n person who practises yoga
YOGIC > YOGA
YOGIN same as > YOGI
YOGINI > YOGI
YOGINIS > YOGI
YOGINS > YOGIN
YOGIS > YOGI
YOGISM > YOGI
YOGISMS > YOGI
YOGOURT same as > YOGURT
YOGOURTS > YOGOURT
YOGURT n slightly sour custard-like food made from milk that has had bacteria added
YOGURTS > YOGURT
YOHIMBE n bark used in herbal medicine
YOHIMBES > YOHIMBE

YOHIMBINE n alkaloid found in the bark of a tropical African tree
YOICK vb urge on foxhounds
YOICKED > YOICK
YOICKING > YOICK
YOICKS interj cry used by huntsmen to urge on the hounds ▷ vb urge on foxhounds
YOICKSED > YOICKS
YOICKSES > YOICKS
YOICKSING > YOICKS
YOJAN n Indian unit of distance
YOJANA same as > YOJAN
YOJANAS > YOJANA
YOJANS > YOJAN
YOK vb chuckle
YOKE n wooden bar put across the necks of two animals to hold them together ▷ vb put a yoke on
YOKED > YOKE
YOKEL n derogatory term for a person who lives in the country and is usu simple and old-fashioned
YOKELESS > YOKE
YOKELISH > YOKEL
YOKELS > YOKEL
YOKEMATE n colleague
YOKEMATES > YOKEMATE
YOKER vb spit
YOKERED > YOKER
YOKERING > YOKER
YOKERS > YOKE
YOKES > YOKE
YOKING > YOKE
YOKINGS > YOKE
YOKKED > YOK
YOKKING > YOK
YOKOZUNA n grand champion sumo wrestler
YOKOZUNAS > YOKOZUNA
YOKS > YOK
YOKUL Shetland word for > YES
YOLD archaic past participle of > YIELD
YOLDRING n yellowhammer (bird)
YOLDRINGS > YOLDRING
YOLK n yellow part of an egg that provides food for the developing embryo
YOLKED > YOLK
YOLKIER > YOLK
YOLKIEST > YOLK
YOLKLESS > YOLK
YOLKS > YOLK
YOLKY > YOLK
YOM n day
YOMIM > YOM
YOMP vb walk or trek laboriously
YOMPED > YOMP
YOMPING > YOMP
YOMPS > YOMP
YON adj that or those over there ▷ adv yonder ▷ pron that person or thing

YOND same as > YON
YONDER adv over there ▷ adj situated over there ▷ determiner being at a distance, either within view or as if within view ▷ n person
YONDERLY > YONDER
YONDERS > YONDER
YONI n female genitalia, regarded as a divine symbol of sexual pleasure
YONIC adj resembling a vulva
YONIS > YONI
YONKER same as > YOUNKER
YONKERS > YONKER
YONKS pl n very long time
YONNIE n stone
YONNIES > YONNIE
YONT same as > YON
YOOF n non-standard spelling of youth
YOOFS > YOOF
YOOP n sob
YOOPS > YOOP
YOPPER n young person employed on a former UK government training programme
YOPPERS > YOPPER
YORE n time long past ▷ adv in the past
YORES > YORE
YORK vb bowl or try to bowl (a batsman) by pitching the ball under or just beyond the bat
YORKED > YORK
YORKER n ball that pitches just under the bat
YORKERS > YORKER
YORKIE n Yorkshire terrier
YORKIES > YORKIE
YORKING > YORK
YORKS > YORK
YORLING n as in yellow yorling yellowhammer
YORLINGS > YORLING
YORP vb shout
YORPED > YORP
YORPING > YORP
YORPS > YORP
YOTTABYTE n very large unit of computer memory
YOU pron person or people addressed ▷ n personality of the person being addressed
YOUK vb itch
YOUKED > YOUK
YOUKING > YOUK
YOUKS > YOUK
YOUNG adj in an early stage of life or growth ▷ n young people in general; offspring
YOUNGER > YOUNG
YOUNGERS n young people
YOUNGEST > YOUNG
YOUNGISH > YOUNG
YOUNGLING n young person, animal, or plant

YOUNGLY adv youthfully
YOUNGNESS > YOUNG
YOUNGS > YOUNG
YOUNGSTER n young person
YOUNGTH n youth
YOUNGTHLY adj youthful
YOUNGTHS > YOUNGTH
YOUNKER n young man
YOUNKERS > YOUNKER
YOUPON same as > YAUPON
YOUPONS > YOUPON
YOUR adj of, belonging to, or associated with you
YOURN dialect form of > YOURS
YOURS pron something belonging to you
YOURSELF pron reflexive form of you
YOURT same as > YURT
YOURTS > YOURT
YOUS pron refers to more than one person including the person or persons addressed but not the speaker
YOUSE same as > YOUS
YOUTH n time of being young
YOUTHEN vb render more youthful-seeming
YOUTHENED > YOUTHEN
YOUTHENS > YOUTHEN
YOUTHFUL adj vigorous or active
YOUTHHEAD same as > YOUTHHOOD
YOUTHHOOD n youth
YOUTHIER > YOUTHY
YOUTHIEST > YOUTHY
YOUTHLESS > YOUTH
YOUTHLY adv young
YOUTHS > YOUTH
YOUTHSOME archaic variant of > YOUTHFUL
YOUTHY Scots word for > YOUNG
YOW vb howl
YOWE Scot word for > EWE
YOWED > YOW
YOWES > YOWE
YOWIE n legendary Australian apelike creature
YOWIES > YOWIE
YOWING > YOW
YOWL n loud mournful cry ▷ vb produce a loud mournful wail or cry
YOWLED > YOWL
YOWLER > YOWL
YOWLERS > YOWL
YOWLEY n yellowhammer (bird)

YOWLEYS > YOWLEY
YOWLING > YOWL
YOWLINGS > YOWL
YOWLS > YOWL
YOWS > YOW
YPERITE n mustard gas
YPERITES > YPERITE
YPIGHT archaic past participle of > PITCH
YPLAST archaic past participle of > PLACE
YPLIGHT archaic past participle of > PLIGHT
YPSILOID > YPSILON
YPSILON same as > UPSILON
YPSILONS > YPSILON
YRAPT Spenserian form of > RAPT
YRAVISHED archaic past participle of > RAVISH
YRENT archaic past participle of > REND
YRIVD archaic past participle of > RIVE
YRNEH n unit of reciprocal inductance
YRNEHS > YRNEH
YSAME Spenserian word for > TOGETHER
YSHEND Spenserian form of > SHEND
YSHENDING > YSHEND
YSHENDS > YSHEND
YSHENT > YSHEND
YSLAKED archaic past participle of > SLAKE
YTOST archaic past participle of > TOSS
YTTERBIA n colourless hygroscopic substance used in certain alloys and ceramics
YTTERBIAS > YTTERBIA
YTTERBIC > YTTERBIUM
YTTERBITE n rare mineral
YTTERBIUM n soft silvery element
YTTERBOUS > YTTERBIUM
YTTRIA n insoluble solid used mainly in incandescent mantles
YTTRIAS > YTTRIA
YTTRIC > YTTRIUM
YTTRIOUS > YTTRIUM
YTTRIUM n silvery metallic element used in various alloys
YTTRIUMS > YTTRIUM
YU n jade
YUAN n standard monetary unit of the People's Republic of China
YUANS > YUAN

YUCA same as > YUCCA
YUCAS > YUCA
YUCCA n tropical plant with spikes of white leaves
YUCCAS > YUCCA
YUCCH interj expression of disgust
YUCH interj expression of disgust
YUCK interj exclamation indicating contempt, dislike, or disgust ▷ vb chuckle
YUCKED > YUCK
YUCKER > YUCK
YUCKERS > YUCK
YUCKIER > YUCKY
YUCKIEST > YUCKY
YUCKINESS > YUCKY
YUCKING > YUCK
YUCKO adj disgusting ▷ interj exclamation of disgust
YUCKS > YUCK
YUCKY adj disgusting, nasty
YUFT n Russia leather
YUFTS > YUFT
YUG same as > YUGA
YUGA n (in Hindu cosmology) one of the four ages of mankind
YUGARIE variant spelling of > EUGARIE
YUGARIES > YUGARIE
YUGAS > YUGA
YUGS > YUG
YUK same as > YUCK
YUKATA n light kimono
YUKATAS > YUKATA
YUKE vb itch
YUKED > YUKE
YUKES > YUKE
YUKIER > YUKY
YUKIEST > YUKY
YUKING > YUKE
YUKKED > YUK
YUKKIER > YUKKY
YUKKIEST > YUKKY
YUKKING > YUK
YUKKY same as > YUCKY
YUKO n score of five points in judo
YUKOS > YUKO
YUKS > YUK
YUKY adj itchy
YULAN n Chinese magnolia with white flowers
YULANS > YULAN
YULE n Christmas
YULES > YULE
YULETIDE n Christmas season
YULETIDES > YULETIDE
YUM interj expression of delight

YUMBERRY n purple-red edible fruit of an E Asian tree
YUMMIER > YUMMY
YUMMIES > YUMMY
YUMMIEST > YUMMY
YUMMINESS > YUMMY
YUMMO adj tasty ▷ interj exclamation of delight or approval
YUMMY adj delicious ▷ interj exclamation indicating pleasure or delight ▷ n delicious food item
YUMP vb leave the ground when driving over a ridge
YUMPED > YUMP
YUMPIE n young upwardly mobile person
YUMPIES > YUMPIE
YUMPING > YUMP
YUMPS > YUMP
YUNX n wryneck
YUNXES > YUNX
YUP n informal affirmative statement
YUPON same as > YAUPON
YUPONS > YUPON
YUPPIE n young highly-paid professional person ▷ adj typical of or reflecting the values of yuppies
YUPPIEDOM > YUPPIE
YUPPIEISH > YUPPIE
YUPPIES > YUPPY
YUPPIFIED > YUPPIFY
YUPPIFIES > YUPPIFY
YUPPIFY vb make yuppie in nature
YUPPY same as > YUPPIE
YUPPYDOM n state of being a yuppie
YUPPYDOMS > YUPPYDOM
YUPS > YUP
YUPSTER same as > YINDIE
YUPSTERS > YUPSTER
YURT n circular tent consisting of a framework of poles covered with felt or skins
YURTA same as > YURT
YURTAS > YURT
YURTS > YURT
YUS > YU
YUTZ n Yiddish word meaning fool
YUTZES > YUTZ
YUZU n type of citrus fruit
YUZUS > YUZU
YWIS adv certainly
YWROKE archaic past participle of > WREAK

y

Zz

ZA n pizza
ZABAIONE n light foamy dessert
ZABAIONES > ZABAIONE
ZABAJONE same as **> ZABAIONE**
ZABAJONES > ZABAIONE
ZABETA n tariff
ZABETAS > ZABETA
ZABRA n small sailing vessel
ZABRAS > ZABRA
ZABTIEH n Turkish police officer
ZABTIEHS > ZABTIEH
ZACATON n coarse grass
ZACATONS > ZACATON
ZACK n Australian five-cent piece
ZACKS > ZACK
ZADDICK adj righteous ▷ n Hasidic Jewish spiritual leader
ZADDICKS > ZADDICK
ZADDIK n Hasidic Jewish leader
ZADDIKIM > ZADDIK
ZADDIKS > ZADDIK
ZAFFAR same as **> ZAFFER**
ZAFFARS > ZAFFAR
ZAFFER n impure cobalt oxide, used to impart a blue colour to enamels
ZAFFERS > ZAFFER
ZAFFIR same as **> ZAFFER**
ZAFFIRS > ZAFFIR
ZAFFRE same as **> ZAFFER**
ZAFFRES > ZAFFRE
ZAFTIG adj ripe or curvaceous
ZAG vb change direction sharply
ZAGGED > ZAG
ZAGGING > ZAG
ZAGS > ZAG
ZAIBATSU n group or combine comprising a few wealthy families that controls industry, business, and finance in Japan
ZAIDA n grandfather
ZAIDAS > ZAIDA
ZAIDEH same as **> ZAIDA**
ZAIDEHS > ZAIDEH
ZAIDIES > ZAIDY
ZAIDY same as **> ZAIDA**
ZAIKAI n Japanese business community
ZAIKAIS > ZAIKAI

ZAIRE n currency used in the former Zaïre
ZAIRES > ZAIRE
ZAITECH n investment in financial markets by a company to supplement its main income
ZAITECHS > ZAITECH
ZAKAT n annual tax on Muslims to aid the poor in the Muslim community
ZAKATS > ZAKAT
ZAKOUSKA > ZAKOUSKI
ZAKOUSKI same as **> ZAKUSKI**
ZAKUSKA > ZAKUSKI
ZAKUSKI pl n hors d'oeuvres, consisting of tiny open sandwiches
ZAMAN n tropical tree
ZAMANG same as **> ZAMAN**
ZAMANGS > ZAMANG
ZAMANS > ZAMAN
ZAMARRA n sheepskin coat
ZAMARRAS > ZAMARRA
ZAMARRO same as **> ZAMARRA**
ZAMARROS > ZAMARRO
ZAMBO n offensive word for a Black person
ZAMBOMBA n drum-like musical instrument
ZAMBOMBAS > ZAMBOMBA
ZAMBOORAK n small swivel-mounted cannon
ZAMBOS > ZAMBO
ZAMBUCK n St John ambulance attendant
ZAMBUCKS > ZAMBUCK
ZAMBUK same as **> ZAMBUCK**
ZAMBUKS > ZAMBUK
ZAMIA n type of plant of tropical and subtropical America
ZAMIAS > ZAMIA
ZAMINDAR n (in India) the owner of an agricultural estate
ZAMINDARI n (in India) a large agricultural estate
ZAMINDARS > ZAMINDAR
ZAMINDARY same as **> ZAMINDARI**
ZAMOUSE n West African buffalo
ZAMOUSES > ZAMOUSE
ZAMPOGNA n Italian bagpipes

ZAMPOGNAS > ZAMPOGNA
ZAMPONE n sausage made from pig's trotters
ZAMPONI > ZAMPONE
ZAMZAWED adj (of tea) having been left in the pot to stew
ZANAMIVIR n drug used to treat influenza
ZANANA same as **> ZENANA**
ZANANAS > ZANANA
ZANDER n European freshwater pikeperch, valued as a food fish
ZANDERS > ZANDER
ZANELLA n twill fabric
ZANELLAS > ZANELLA
ZANIED > ZANY
ZANIER > ZANY
ZANIES > ZANY
ZANIEST > ZANY
ZANILY > ZANY
ZANINESS > ZANY
ZANJA n irrigation canal
ZANJAS > ZANJA
ZANJERO n irrigation supervisor
ZANJEROS > ZANJERO
ZANTE n type of wood
ZANTES > ZANTE
ZANTEWOOD n wood of the zante tree
ZANTHOXYL variant spelling of **> XANTHOXYL**
ZANY adj comical in an endearing way ▷ n clown or buffoon who imitated other performers ▷ vb clown
ZANYING > ZANY
ZANYISH > ZANY
ZANYISM > ZANY
ZANYISMS > ZANY
ZANZA same as **> ZANZE**
ZANZAS > ZANZA
ZANZE n African musical instrument
ZANZES > ZANZE
ZAP vb kill (by shooting) ▷ n energy, vigour, or pep ▷ interj exclamation used to express sudden or swift action
ZAPATA adj (of a moustache) drooping
ZAPATEADO n Spanish dance with stamping and very fast footwork
ZAPATEO n Cuban folk dance

ZAPATEOS > ZAPATEO
ZAPOTILLA n shoe
ZAPPED > ZAP
ZAPPER n remote control for a television etc
ZAPPERS > ZAPPER
ZAPPIER > ZAPPY
ZAPPIEST > ZAPPY
ZAPPING > ZAP
ZAPPY adj energetic
ZAPS > ZAP
ZAPTIAH same as **> ZAPTIEH**
ZAPTIAHS > ZAPTIAH
ZAPTIEH n Turkish police officer
ZAPTIEHS > ZAPTIEH
ZARAPE n blanket-like shawl
ZARAPES > ZARAPE
ZARATITE n green amorphous mineral
ZARATITES > ZARATITE
ZAREBA n stockade or enclosure of thorn bushes around a village or campsite
ZAREBAS > ZAREBA
ZAREEBA same as **> ZAREBA**
ZAREEBAS > ZAREEBA
ZARF n (esp in the Middle East) a holder, usually ornamental, for a hot coffee cup
ZARFS > ZARF
ZARI n thread made from fine gold or silver wire
ZARIBA same as **> ZAREBA**
ZARIBAS > ZARIBA
ZARIS > ZARI
ZARNEC n sulphide of arsenic
ZARNECS > ZARNEC
ZARNICH same as **> ZARNEC**
ZARNICHS > ZARNICH
ZARZUELA n type of Spanish vaudeville or operetta, usually satirical in nature
ZARZUELAS > ZARZUELA
ZAS > ZA
ZASTRUGA variant spelling of **> SASTRUGA**
ZASTRUGI > ZASTRUGA
ZATI n type of macaque
ZATIS > ZATI
ZAX n tool for cutting roofing slate

ZAXES > ZAX

ZAYIN n seventh letter of the Hebrew alphabet

ZAYINS > ZAYIN

ZAZEN n deep meditation undertaken whilst sitting upright with legs crossed

ZAZENS > ZAZEN

ZEA n corn silk

ZEAL n great enthusiasm or eagerness

ZEALANT archaic variant of > ZEALOT

ZEALANTS > ZEALANT

ZEALFUL > ZEAL

ZEALLESS > ZEAL

ZEALOT n fanatic or extreme enthusiast

ZEALOTISM > ZEALOT

ZEALOTRY n extreme or excessive zeal or devotion

ZEALOTS > ZEALOT

ZEALOUS adj extremely eager or enthusiastic

ZEALOUSLY > ZEALOUS

ZEALS > ZEAL

ZEAS > ZEAL

ZEATIN n cytokinin derived from corn

ZEATINS > ZEATIN

ZEBEC variant spelling of > XEBEC

ZEBECK same as > ZEBEC

ZEBECKS > ZEBECK

ZEBECS > ZEBEC

ZEBRA n black-and-white striped African animal of the horse family

ZEBRAFISH n striped tropical fish

ZEBRAIC adj like a zebra

ZEBRANO n type of striped wood

ZEBRANOS > ZEBRANO

ZEBRAS > ZEBRA

ZEBRASS n offspring of a male zebra and a female ass

ZEBRASSES > ZEBRASS

ZEBRAWOOD n tree yielding striped hardwood used in cabinetwork

ZEBRINA n trailing herbaceous plant

ZEBRINAS > ZEBRINA

ZEBRINE > ZEBRA

ZEBRINES > ZEBRA

ZEBRINNY n offspring of a male horse and a female zebra

ZEBROID > ZEBRA

ZEBRULA n offspring of a male zebra and a female horse

ZEBRULAS > ZEBRULA

ZEBRULE same as > ZEBRULA

ZEBRULES > ZEBRULE

ZEBU n Asian ox with a humped back and long horns

ZEBUB n large African fly

ZEBUBS > ZEBUB

ZEBUS > ZEBU

ZECCHIN same as > ZECCHINO

ZECCHINE same as > ZECCHINO

ZECCHINES > ZECCHINE

ZECCHINI > ZECCHINO

ZECCHINO n former gold coin

ZECCHINOS > ZECCHINO

ZECCHINS > ZECCHIN

ZECHIN same as > ZECCHINO

ZECHINS > ZECHIN

ZED n British and New Zealand spoken form of the letter z

ZEDA n grandfather

ZEDAS > ZEDA

ZEDOARIES > ZEDOARY

ZEDOARY n dried rhizome of a tropical Asian plant

ZEDS > ZED

ZEE the US word for > ZED

ZEES > ZEE

ZEIN n protein occurring in maize

ZEINS > ZEIN

ZEITGEBER n agent or event that sets or resets the biological clock

ZEITGEIST n spirit or attitude of a specific time or period

ZEK n Soviet prisoner

ZEKS > ZEK

ZEL n Turkish cymbal

ZELANT alternative form of > ZEALANT

ZELANTS > ZELANT

ZELATOR same as > ZELATRIX

ZELATORS > ZELATOR

ZELATRICE same as > ZELATRIX

ZELATRIX n nun who monitors the behaviour of younger nuns

ZELKOVA n type of elm tree

ZELKOVAS > ZELKOVA

ZELOSO adv with zeal

ZELOTYPIA n morbid zeal

ZELS > ZEL

ZEMINDAR same as > ZAMINDAR

ZEMINDARI > ZEMINDAR

ZEMINDARS > ZEMINDAR

ZEMINDARY n jurisdiction of a zemindar

ZEMSTVA > ZEMSTVO

ZEMSTVO n council in Tsarist Russia

ZEMSTVOS > ZEMSTVO

ZENAIDA n dove

ZENAIDAS > ZENAIDA

ZENANA n part of Muslim or Hindu home reserved for women and girls

ZENANAS > ZENANA

ZENDIK n unbeliever or heretic

ZENDIKS > ZENDIK

ZENDO n place where Zen Buddhists study

ZENDOS > ZENDO

ZENITH n highest point of success or power

ZENITHAL > ZENITH

ZENITHS > ZENITH

ZEOLITE n any of a large group of glassy secondary minerals

ZEOLITES > ZEOLITE

ZEOLITIC > ZEOLITE

ZEP n type of long sandwich

ZEPHYR n soft gentle breeze

ZEPHYRS > ZEPHYR

ZEPPELIN n large cylindrical airship

ZEPPELINS > ZEPPELIN

ZEPPOLE n Italian fritter

ZEPPOLES > ZEPPOLE

ZEPPOLI > ZEPPOLE

ZEPS > ZEP

ZERDA n fennec

ZERDAS > ZERDA

ZEREBA same as > ZAREBA

ZEREBAS > ZEREBA

ZERIBA same as > ZAREBA

ZERIBAS > ZERIBA

ZERK n grease fitting

ZERKS > ZERK

ZERO n (symbol representing) the number o ▷ adj having no measurable quantity or size ▷ vb adjust (an instrument or scale) so as to read zero ▷ determiner no (thing) at all

ZEROED > ZERO

ZEROES > ZERO

ZEROING > ZERO

ZEROS > ZERO

ZEROTH adj denoting a term in a series that precedes the term otherwise regarded as the first term

ZERUMBET n plant stem used as stimulant and condiment

ZERUMBETS > ZERUMBET

ZEST n enjoyment or excitement ▷ vb give flavour, interest, or piquancy to

ZESTED > ZEST

ZESTER n kitchen utensil used to scrape fine shreds of peel from citrus fruits

ZESTERS > ZESTER

ZESTFUL > ZEST

ZESTFULLY > ZEST

ZESTIER > ZEST

ZESTIEST > ZEST

ZESTILY > ZEST

ZESTINESS n quality of being zesty

ZESTING > ZEST

ZESTLESS > ZEST

ZESTS > ZEST

ZESTY > ZEST

ZETA n sixth letter in the Greek alphabet

ZETAS > ZETA

ZETETIC adj proceeding by inquiry ▷ n investigation

ZETETICS > ZETETIC

ZETTABYTE n 10^{21} or 2^{70} bytes

ZEUGMA n figure of speech in which a word is used with two words although appropriate to only one of them

ZEUGMAS > ZEUGMA

ZEUGMATIC > ZEUGMA

ZEUXITE n ferriferous mineral

ZEUXITES > ZEUXITE

ZEX n tool for cutting roofing slate

ZEXES > ZEX

ZEZE n stringed musical instrument

ZEZES > ZEZE

ZHO same as > ZO

ZHOMO n female zho

ZHOMOS > ZHOMO

ZHOOSH vb make more exciting or attractive

ZHOOSHED > ZHOOSH

ZHOOSHES > ZHOOSH

ZHOOSHING > ZHOOSH

ZHOS > ZHO

ZIBELINE n sable or the fur of this animal ▷ adj of, relating to, or resembling a sable

ZIBELINES > ZIBELINE

ZIBELLINE same as > ZIBELINE

ZIBET n large civet of S and SE Asia

ZIBETH same as > ZIBET

ZIBETHS > ZIBETH

ZIBETS > ZIBET

ZIFF n beard

ZIFFIUS n sea monster

ZIFFIUSES > ZIFFIUS

ZIFFS > ZIFF

ZIG same as > ZAG

ZIGAN n gypsy

ZIGANKA n Russian dance

ZIGANKAS > ZIGANKA

ZIGANS > ZIGAN

ZIGGED > ZIG

ZIGGING > ZIG

ZIGGURAT n (in ancient Mesopotamia) a temple in the shape of a pyramid

ZIGGURATS > ZIGGURAT

ZIGS > ZIG

ZIGZAG n line or course having sharp turns in alternating directions ▷ vb move in a zigzag ▷ adj formed in or proceeding in a zigzag ▷ adv in a zigzag manner

ZIGZAGGED > ZIGZAG

ZIGZAGGER > ZIGZAG

ZIGZAGGY adj having sharp turns

ZIGZAGS > ZIGZAG

ZIKKURAT same as > ZIGGURAT

Z

ZIKKURATS > ZIKKURAT
ZIKURAT *same as* > ZIGGURAT
ZIKURATS > ZIKURAT
ZILA *n* administrative district in India
ZILAS > ZILA
ZILCH *n* nothing
ZILCHES > ZILCH
ZILL *n* finger cymbal
ZILLA *same as* > ZILA
ZILLAH *same as* > ZILA
ZILLAHS > ZILLAH
ZILLAS > ZILLA
ZILLION *n* extremely large but unspecified number
ZILLIONS > ZILLION
ZILLIONTH > ZILLION
ZILLS > ZILL
ZIMB *same as* > ZEBUB
ZIMBI *n* cowrie shell used as money
ZIMBIS > ZIMBI
ZIMBS > ZIMB
ZIMOCCA *n* bath sponge
ZIMOCCAS > ZIMOCCA
ZIN *short form of* > ZINFANDEL
ZINC *n* bluish-white metallic element ▷ *vb* coat with zinc
ZINCATE *n* any of a class of salts derived from the amphoteric hydroxide of zinc
ZINCATES > ZINCATE
ZINCED > ZINC
ZINCIC > ZINC
ZINCIER > ZINC
ZINCIEST > ZINC
ZINCIFIED > ZINCIFY
ZINCIFIES > ZINCIFY
ZINCIFY *vb* coat with zinc
ZINCING > ZINC
ZINCITE *n* red or yellow mineral
ZINCITES > ZINCITE
ZINCKED > ZINC
ZINCKIER > ZINC
ZINCKIEST > ZINC
ZINCKIFY *same as* > ZINCIFY
ZINCKING > ZINC
ZINCKY > ZINC
ZINCO *n* printing plate made from zincography
ZINCODE *n* positive electrode
ZINCODES > ZINCODE
ZINCOID > ZINC
ZINCOS > ZINCO
ZINCOUS > ZINC
ZINCS > ZINC
ZINCY > ZINC
ZINDABAD *interj* long live: used as part of a slogan in India, Pakistan, etc
ZINE *n* magazine or fanzine
ZINEB *n* organic insecticide
ZINEBS > ZINEB
ZINES > ZINE
ZINFANDEL *n* type of Californian wine
ZING *n* quality in something that makes it lively or interesting ▷ *vb* make or move with or as if with a high-pitched buzzing sound
ZINGANI > ZINGANO
ZINGANO *n* gypsy
ZINGARA *same as* > ZINGARO
ZINGARE > ZINGARA
ZINGARI > ZINGARO
ZINGARO *n* Italian Gypsy
ZINGED > ZING
ZINGEL *n* small freshwater perch
ZINGELS > ZINGEL
ZINGER > ZING
ZINGERS > ZING
ZINGIBER *n* ginger plant
ZINGIBERS > ZINGIBER
ZINGIER > ZINGY
ZINGIEST > ZINGY
ZINGING > ZING
ZINGS > ZING
ZINGY *adj* vibrant
ZINKE *n* cornett
ZINKED > ZINC
ZINKENITE *n* steel-grey metallic mineral consisting of a sulphide of lead and antimony
ZINKES > ZINKE
ZINKIER > ZINC
ZINKIEST > ZINC
ZINKIFIED > ZINCIFY
ZINKIFIES > ZINKIFY
ZINKIFY *vb* coat with zinc
ZINKING > ZINC
ZINKY > ZINC
ZINNIA *n* plant of tropical and subtropical America
ZINNIAS > ZINNIA
ZINS > ZIN
ZIP *same as* > ZIPPER
ZIPLESS > ZIP
ZIPLINE *n* cable used for transportation across a river, gorge, etc
ZIPLINES > ZIPLINE
ZIPLOCK *adj* fastened with interlocking plastic strips ▷ *vb* seal (a ziplock storage bag)
ZIPLOCKED > ZIPLOCK
ZIPLOCKS > ZIPLOCK
ZIPOLA *n* nothing
ZIPOLAS > ZIPOLA
ZIPPED > ZIP
ZIPPER *n* fastening device operating by means of two rows of metal or plastic teeth ▷ *vb* fasten with a zipper
ZIPPERED *adj* provided or fastened with a zip
ZIPPERING > ZIPPER
ZIPPERS > ZIPPER
ZIPPIER > ZIPPY
ZIPPIEST > ZIPPY
ZIPPILY *adv* in a zippy manner
ZIPPING > ZIP
ZIPPO *n* nothing
ZIPPOS > ZIPPO
ZIPPY *adj* full of energy
ZIPS > ZIP
ZIPTOP *adj* (of a bag) closed with a zipper
ZIPWIRE *same as* > ZIPLINE
ZIPWIRES > ZIPWIRE
ZIRAM *n* industrial fungicide
ZIRAMS > ZIRAM
ZIRCALLOY *n* alloy of zirconium containing small amounts of tin, chromium, and nickel. It is used in pressurized-water reactors
ZIRCALOY *same as* > ZIRCALLOY
ZIRCALOYS > ZIRCALOY
ZIRCON *n* mineral used as a gemstone and in industry
ZIRCONIA *n* white oxide of zirconium, used as a pigment for paints, a catalyst, and an abrasive
ZIRCONIAS > ZIRCONIA
ZIRCONIC > ZIRCONIUM
ZIRCONIUM *n* greyish-white metallic element that is resistant to corrosion
ZIRCONS > ZIRCON
ZIT *n* spot or pimple
ZITE *same as* > ZITI
ZITHER *n* musical instrument consisting of strings stretched over a flat box
ZITHERIST > ZITHER
ZITHERN *same as* > ZITHER
ZITHERNS > ZITHERN
ZITHERS > ZITHER
ZITI *n* type of pasta
ZITIS > ZITI
ZITS > ZIT
ZIZ *same as* > ZIZZ
ZIZANIA *n* aquatic grass
ZIZANIAS > ZIZANIA
ZIZEL *n* chipmunk
ZIZELS > ZIZEL
ZIZIT *same as* > ZIZITH
ZIZITH *variant spelling of* > TSITSITH
ZIZYPHUS *n* jujube tree
ZIZZ *n* short sleep ▷ *vb* take a short sleep, snooze
ZIZZED > ZIZZ
ZIZZES > ZIZZ
ZIZZING > ZIZZ
ZIZZLE *vb* sizzle
ZIZZLED > ZIZZLE
ZIZZLES > ZIZZLE
ZIZZLING > ZIZZLE
ZLOTE > ZLOTY
ZLOTIES > ZLOTY
ZLOTY *n* monetary unit of Poland
ZLOTYCH *same as* > ZLOTY
ZLOTYS > ZLOTY
ZO *n* Tibetan breed of cattle
ZOA > ZOON
ZOAEA *same as* > ZOEA
ZOAEAE > ZOAEA
ZOAEAS > ZOAEA
ZOARIA > ZOARIUM
ZOARIAL > ZOARIUM
ZOARIUM *n* colony of zooids
ZOBO *same as* > ZO
ZOBOS > ZOBO
ZOBU *same as* > ZO
ZOBUS > ZOBU
ZOCALO *n* plaza in Mexico
ZOCALOS > ZOCALO
ZOCCO *n* plinth
ZOCCOLO *same as* > ZOCCO
ZOCCOLOS > ZOCCOLO
ZOCCOS > ZOCCO
ZODIAC *n* imaginary belt in the sky within which the sun, moon, and planets appear to move
ZODIACAL > ZODIAC
ZODIACS > ZODIAC
ZOEA *n* free-swimming larva of a crab or related crustacean
ZOEAE > ZOEA
ZOEAL > ZOEA
ZOEAS > ZOEA
ZOECHROME *same as* > ZOETROPE
ZOECIA > ZOECIUM
ZOECIUM *same as* > ZOOECIUM
ZOEFORM > ZOEA
ZOETIC *adj* pertaining to life
ZOETROPE *n* cylinder-shaped toy with a sequence of pictures on its inner surface which, when viewed through the vertical slits spaced regularly around it while the toy is rotated, produce an illusion of animation
ZOETROPES > ZOETROPE
ZOETROPIC > ZOETROPE
ZOFTIG *adj* ripe or curvaceous
ZOIATRIA *n* veterinary surgery
ZOIATRIAS > ZOIATRIA
ZOIATRICS *n* veterinary surgery
ZOIC *adj* relating to or having animal life
ZOISITE *n* grey, brown, or pink mineral
ZOISITES > ZOISITE
ZOISM *n* belief in magical animal powers
ZOISMS > ZOISM
ZOIST > ZOISM
ZOISTS > ZOISM

ZOL n South African slang for a cannabis cigarette
ZOLPIDEM n drug used to treat insomnia
ZOLPIDEMS > ZOLPIDEM
ZOLS > ZOL
ZOMBI same as > ZOMBIE
ZOMBIE n person who appears to be lifeless or apathetic
ZOMBIES > ZOMBIE
ZOMBIFIED > ZOMBIFY
ZOMBIFIES > ZOMBIFY
ZOMBIFY vb turn into a zombie
ZOMBIISM > ZOMBIE
ZOMBIISMS > ZOMBIE
ZOMBIS > ZOMBI
ZOMBORUK n small swivel-mounted cannon
ZOMBORUKS > ZOMBORUK
ZONA n zone or belt
ZONAE > ZONA
ZONAL adj of, relating to, or of the nature of a zone
ZONALLY > ZONAL
ZONARY same as > ZONAL
ZONATE adj marked with, divided into, or arranged in zones
ZONATED same as > ZONATE
ZONATION n arrangement in zones
ZONATIONS > ZONATION
ZONDA n South American wind
ZONDAS > ZONDA
ZONE n area with particular features or properties ▷ vb divide into zones
ZONED > ZONE
ZONELESS > ZONE
ZONER n something which divides other things into zones
ZONERS > ZONER
ZONES > ZONE
ZONETIME n standard time of the time zone in which a ship is located at sea, each zone extending 7½° to each side of a meridian
ZONETIMES > ZONETIME
ZONING > ZONE
ZONINGS > ZONE
ZONK vb strike resoundingly
ZONKED adj highly intoxicated with drugs or alcohol
ZONKING > ZONK
ZONKS > ZONK
ZONOID adj resembling a zone ▷ n finite vector sum of line segments
ZONOIDS > ZONOID
ZONULA n small zone or belt
ZONULAE > ZONULA
ZONULAR > ZONULE
ZONULAS > ZONULA

ZONULE n small zone, band, or area
ZONULES > ZONULE
ZONULET n small belt
ZONULETS > ZONULET
ZONURE n lizard with ringed tail
ZONURES > ZONURE
ZOO n place where live animals are kept for show
ZOOBIOTIC adj parasitic on or living in association with an animal
ZOOBLAST n animal cell
ZOOBLASTS > ZOOBLAST
ZOOCHORE n plant with the spores or seeds dispersed by animals
ZOOCHORES > ZOOCHORE
ZOOCHORY > ZOOCHORE
ZOOCYTIA > ZOOCYTIUM
ZOOCYTIUM n outer sheath of some social infusorians
ZOOEA same as > ZOEA
ZOOEAE > ZOOEA
ZOOEAL > ZOOEA
ZOOEAS > ZOOEA
ZOOECIA > ZOOECIUM
ZOOECIUM n part of a polyzoan colony that houses the feeding zooids
ZOOEY > ZOO
ZOOGAMETE n gamete that can move independently
ZOOGAMIES > ZOOGAMY
ZOOGAMOUS > ZOOGAMY
ZOOGAMY n sexual reproduction in animals
ZOOGENIC adj produced from animals
ZOOGENIES > ZOOGENY
ZOOGENOUS same as > ZOOGENIC
ZOOGENY n doctrine of formation of animals
ZOOGLEA same as > ZOOGLOEA
ZOOGLEAE > ZOOGLEA
ZOOGLEAL > ZOOGLEA
ZOOGLEAS > ZOOGLEA
ZOOGLOEA n mass of bacteria adhering together by a jelly-like substance derived from their cell walls
ZOOGLOEAE > ZOOGLOEA
ZOOGLOEAL > ZOOGLOEA
ZOOGLOEAS > ZOOGLOEA
ZOOGLOEIC > ZOOGLOEA
ZOOGONIES > ZOOGONY
ZOOGONOUS > ZOOGONY
ZOOGONY same as > ZOOGENY
ZOOGRAFT n animal tissue grafted onto a human body
ZOOGRAFTS > ZOOGRAFT
ZOOGRAPHY n branch of zoology concerned with the description of animals
ZOOID n any independent animal body, such as an individual of a coral colony

ZOOIDAL > ZOOID
ZOOIDS > ZOOID
ZOOIER > ZOO
ZOOIEST > ZOO
ZOOKEEPER n person who cares for animals in a zoo
ZOOKS short form of > GADZOOKS
ZOOLATER > ZOOLATRY
ZOOLATERS > ZOOLATRY
ZOOLATRIA same as > ZOOLATRY
ZOOLATRY n (esp in ancient or primitive religions) the worship of animals as the incarnations of certain deities, symbols of particular qualities or natural forces, etc
ZOOLITE n fossilized animal
ZOOLITES > ZOOLITE
ZOOLITH n fossilized animal
ZOOLITHIC > ZOOLITH
ZOOLITHS > ZOOLITH
ZOOLITIC > ZOOLITE
ZOOLOGIC > ZOOLOGY
ZOOLOGIES > ZOOLOGY
ZOOLOGIST > ZOOLOGY
ZOOLOGY n study of animals
ZOOM vb move or rise very rapidly ▷ n sound or act of zooming
ZOOMABLE adj capable of being viewed at various levels of magnification
ZOOMANCY n divination through observing the actions of animals
ZOOMANIA n extreme or excessive devotion to animals
ZOOMANIAS > ZOOMANIA
ZOOMANTIC > ZOOMANCY
ZOOMED > ZOOM
ZOOMETRIC > ZOOMETRY
ZOOMETRY n branch of zoology concerned with the relative length or size of the different parts of an animal or animals
ZOOMING > ZOOM
ZOOMORPH n representation of an animal form
ZOOMORPHS > ZOOMORPH
ZOOMORPHY > ZOOMORPH
ZOOMS > ZOOM
ZOON same as > ZOOM
ZOONAL > ZOON
ZOONED > ZOON
ZOONIC adj concerning animals
ZOONING > ZOON
ZOONITE n segment of an articulated animal
ZOONITES > ZOONITE
ZOONITIC > ZOONITE
ZOONOMIA same as > ZOONOMY

ZOONOMIAS > ZOONOMIA
ZOONOMIC > ZOONOMY
ZOONOMIES > ZOONOMY
ZOONOMIST > ZOONOMY
ZOONOMY n science of animal life
ZOONOSES > ZOONOSIS
ZOONOSIS n any infection or disease that is transmitted to man from lower vertebrates
ZOONOTIC > ZOONOSIS
ZOONS > ZOON
ZOOPATHY n science of animal diseases
ZOOPERAL > ZOOPERY
ZOOPERIES > ZOOPERY
ZOOPERIST > ZOOPERY
ZOOPERY n experimentation on animals
ZOOPHAGAN n carnivore
ZOOPHAGY n eating other animals
ZOOPHILE n person who is devoted to animals and their protection from practices such as vivisection
ZOOPHILES > ZOOPHILE
ZOOPHILIA n morbid condition in which a person has a sexual attraction to animals
ZOOPHILIC > ZOOPHILE
ZOOPHILY same as > ZOOPHILIA
ZOOPHOBE > ZOOPHOBIA
ZOOPHOBES > ZOOPHOBIA
ZOOPHOBIA n unusual or morbid dread of animals
ZOOPHORI > ZOOPHORUS
ZOOPHORIC > ZOOPHORUS
ZOOPHORUS n frieze with animal figures
ZOOPHYTE n any animal resembling a plant, such as a sea anemone
ZOOPHYTES > ZOOPHYTE
ZOOPHYTIC > ZOOPHYTE
ZOOPLASTY n surgical transplantation to man of animal tissues
ZOOS > ZOO
ZOOSCOPIC > ZOOSCOPY
ZOOSCOPY n condition causing hallucinations of animals
ZOOSPERM n any of the male reproductive cells released in the semen during ejaculation
ZOOSPERMS > ZOOSPERM
ZOOSPORE n asexual spore of some algae and fungi that moves by means of flagella
ZOOSPORES > ZOOSPORE
ZOOSPORIC > ZOOSPORE
ZOOSTEROL n any of a group of animal sterols, such as cholesterol

ZOOT n as in zoot suit man's suit consisting of baggy trousers and a long jacket

ZOOTAXIES > ZOOTAXY

ZOOTAXY n science of the classification of animals

ZOOTECHNY n science of breeding animals

ZOOTHECIA n outer layers of certain protozoans

ZOOTHEISM n treatment of an animal as a god

ZOOTHOME n group of zooids

ZOOTHOMES > ZOOTHOME

ZOOTIER > ZOOTY

ZOOTIEST > ZOOTY

ZOOTOMIC > ZOOTOMY

ZOOTOMIES > ZOOTOMY

ZOOTOMIST > ZOOTOMY

ZOOTOMY n branch of zoology concerned with the dissection and anatomy of animals

ZOOTOXIC > ZOOTOXIN

ZOOTOXIN n toxin, such as snake venom, that is produced by an animal

ZOOTOXINS > ZOOTOXIN

ZOOTROPE same as > ZOETROPE

ZOOTROPES > ZOOTROPE

ZOOTROPHY n nourishment of animals

ZOOTY adj showy

ZOOTYPE n animal figure used as a symbol

ZOOTYPES > ZOOTYPE

ZOOTYPIC > ZOOTYPE

ZOOZOO n wood pigeon

ZOOZOOS > ZOOZOO

ZOPILOTE n small American vulture

ZOPILOTES > ZOPILOTE

ZOPPA adj syncopated

ZOPPO same as > ZOPPA

ZORBING n activity of travelling downhill inside a large air-cushioned hollow ball

ZORBINGS > ZORBING

ZORBONAUT n person who engages in the activity of zorbing

ZORGITE n copper-lead selenide

ZORGITES > ZORGITE

ZORI n Japanese sandal

ZORIL same as > ZORILLA

ZORILLA n skunk-like African musteline mammal having a long black-and-white coat

ZORILLAS > ZORILLA

ZORILLE same as > ZORILLA

ZORILLES > ZORILLE

ZORILLO same as > ZORILLE

ZORILLOS > ZORILLO

ZORILS > ZORIL

ZORINO n skunk fur

ZORINOS > ZORINO

ZORIS > ZORI

ZORRO n hoary fox

ZORROS > ZORRO

ZOS > ZO

ZOSTER n shingles; herpes zoster

ZOSTERS > ZOSTER

ZOUAVE n (formerly) member of a body of French infantry composed of Algerian recruits

ZOUAVES > ZOUAVE

ZOUK n style of dance music that combines African and Latin American rhythms

ZOUKS > ZOUK

ZOUNDS interj mild oath indicating surprise or indignation

ZOWEE same as > ZOWIE

ZOWIE interj expression of pleasurable surprise

ZOYSIA n type of grass with short stiffly pointed leaves, often used for lawns

ZOYSIAS > ZOYSIA

ZUCCHETTI > ZUCCHETTO

ZUCCHETTO n small round skullcap worn by clergymen and varying in colour according to the rank of the wearer

ZUCCHINI n courgette

ZUCCHINIS > ZUCCHINI

ZUCHETTA same as > ZUCCHETTO

ZUCHETTAS > ZUCHETTA

ZUCHETTO same as > ZUCCHETTO

ZUCHETTOS > ZUCHETTO

ZUFFOLI > ZUFFOLO

ZUFFOLO same as > ZUFOLO

ZUFOLI > ZUFOLO

ZUFOLO n small flute

ZUFOLOS > ZUFOLO

ZUGZWANG n (in chess) position in which one player can move only with loss or severe disadvantage ▷ vb manoeuvre (one's opponent) into a zugzwang

ZUGZWANGS > ZUGZWANG

ZULU n (in the NATO phonetic alphabet) used to represent z

ZULUS > ZULU

ZUMBOORUK n small swivel-mounted cannon

ZUPA n confederation of Serbian villages

ZUPAN n head of a zupa

ZUPANS > ZUPAN

ZUPAS > ZUPA

ZUPPA n Italian soup

ZUPPAS > ZUPPA

ZURF same as > ZARF

ZURFS > ZURF

ZUZ n ancient Hebrew silver coin

ZUZIM > ZUZ

ZUZZIM > ZUZ

ZWANZIGER n silver coin formerly used in Southern Germany and Austria until the end of the 19th century

ZWIEBACK n small type of rusk, which has been baked first as a loaf, then sliced and toasted, usually bought ready-made

ZWIEBACKS > ZWIEBACK

ZYDECO n type of Black Cajun music

ZYDECOS > ZYDECO

ZYGA > ZYGON

ZYGAENID adj of the burnet moth genus

ZYGAENOID same as > ZYGAENID

ZYGAL > ZYGON

ZYGANTRA > ZYGANTRUM

ZYGANTRUM n vertebral articulation in snakes and some lizards

ZYGOCACTI n branching cactuses

ZYGODONT adj possessing paired molar cusps

ZYGOID same as > DIPLOID

ZYGOMA n slender arch of bone on each side of the skull of mammals

ZYGOMAS > ZYGOMA

ZYGOMATA > ZYGOMA

ZYGOMATIC adj of or relating to the zygoma

ZYGON n brain fissure

ZYGOPHYTE n plant that reproduces by means of zygospores

ZYGOSE > ZYGOSIS

ZYGOSES > ZYGOSIS

ZYGOSIS n direct transfer of DNA between two cells that are temporarily joined

ZYGOSITY > ZYGOSIS

ZYGOSPERM same as > ZYGOSPORE

ZYGOSPORE n thick-walled sexual spore formed from the zygote of some fungi and algae

ZYGOTE n fertilized egg cell

ZYGOTENE n second stage of the prophase of meiosis, during which homologous chromosomes become associated in pairs (bivalents)

ZYGOTENES > ZYGOTENE

ZYGOTES > ZYGOTE

ZYGOTIC > ZYGOTE

ZYLONITE variant spelling of > XYLONITE

ZYLONITES > ZYLONITE

ZYMASE n mixture of enzymes that is obtained as an extract from yeast and ferments sugars

ZYMASES > ZYMASE

ZYME n ferment

ZYMES > ZYME

ZYMIC > ZYME

ZYMITE n priest who uses leavened bread during communion

ZYMITES > ZYMITE

ZYMOGEN n any of various inactive precursors of enzymes activated by a kinase

ZYMOGENE same as > ZYMOGEN

ZYMOGENES > ZYMOGENE

ZYMOGENIC adj of, or relating to a zymogen

ZYMOGENS > ZYMOGEN

ZYMOGRAM n band of electrophoretic medium showing a pattern of enzymes following electrophoresis

ZYMOGRAMS > ZYMOGRAM

ZYMOID adj relating to a ferment

ZYMOLOGIC > ZYMOLOGY

ZYMOLOGY n chemistry of fermentation

ZYMOLYSES > ZYMOLYSIS

ZYMOLYSIS n process of fermentation

ZYMOLYTIC > ZYMOLYSIS

ZYMOME n glutinous substance that is insoluble in alcohol

ZYMOMES > ZYMOME

ZYMOMETER n instrument for estimating the degree of fermentation

ZYMOSAN n insoluble carbohydrate found in yeast

ZYMOSANS > ZYMOSAN

ZYMOSES > ZYMOSIS

ZYMOSIS same as > ZYMOLYSIS

ZYMOTIC adj of, relating to, or causing fermentation ▷ n disease

ZYMOTICS > ZYMOTIC

ZYMURGIES > ZYMURGY

ZYMURGY n study of fermentation processes

ZYTHUM n Ancient Egyptian beer

ZYTHUMS > ZYTHUM

ZYZZYVA n American weevil

ZYZZYVAS > ZYZZYVA

ZZZ n informal word for sleep

ZZZS > ZZZ